CONSUMERS' GUIDE TO

Top Doctors

BY THE EDITORS OF *CONSUMERS' CHECKBOOK* MAGAZINE

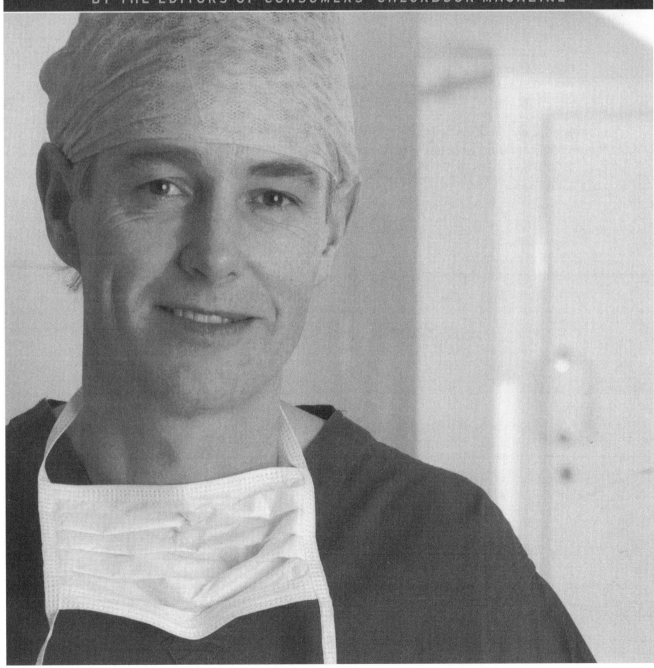

This book is a publication of *Consumers' CHECKBOOK*, which is a program of the Center for the Study of Services, a nonprofit organization dedicated to helping consumers find high-quality, reasonably priced service providers and retailers. Founded in 1974, *CHECKBOOK* is supported by sales of its publications and other research and information products and services, in print and on the Web at *www.checkbook.org*, and by tax-deductible donations from consumers. None of *CHECKBOOK*'s publications or websites accept any advertising.

Consumers' CHECKBOOK magazines, published by the Center in the Boston, Chicago, Philadelphia, San Francisco, Seattle, Twin Cities, and Washington, DC, metropolitan areas, rate the quality and prices of local service firms of various kinds, ranging from auto repair shops to banks to hospitals. *CHECKBOOK* also does survey, research, and analysis activities under contract with government agencies, employer coalitions, nonprofit public sector organizations, and health plans.

More information on *CHECKBOOK* is available at *www.checkbook.org* or by contacting us at:

Consumers' CHECKBOOK
1625 K Street, NW, 8th Floor
Washington, DC 20006
202-347-7283

Notes on board certification information listed in this book:

Contents

Why You Need This Book 7

How to Use This Book 8

How the Lists of Doctors Were Put Together 9

Choosing a Doctor 11

What to Expect From Your Doctor and When to Switch 14

Getting the Best Care Your Doctor Can Give 15

Map 18

Top-Rated Physicians by Area:

Alabama
　　Birmingham Area (Including Jefferson and Shelby Counties) 20

Arizona
　　Phoenix Area (Including Maricopa County). 26

Arkansas
　　See Tennessee–Memphis Area, page 430

California
　　Los Angeles and Orange Counties. 38
　　Riverside and San Bernardino Counties 56
　　Sacramento Area (Including Sacramento County) 61
　　San Diego Area (Including San Diego County) 66
　　San Francisco Bay Area (Including Alameda, Contra Costa, Marin, Napa,
　　　San Francisco, San Mateo, Santa Clara, Santa Cruz, Solano, and Sonoma Counties). . . . 76

Colorado
　　Denver Area (Including Adams, Arapahoe, Denver, and Jefferson Counties). 89

Connecticut
　　Fairfield and New Haven Counties 98
　　Hartford Area (Including Hartford County). 110
　　See also New York–New York Metropolitan Area, page 309

District of Columbia

Washington, DC, Area (Including the District of Columbia, Alexandria,
and Anne Arundel, Arlington, Fairfax, Howard, Loudoun,
Montgomery, Prince George's, and Prince William Counties)......................117

Delaware

See Pennsylvania–Delaware Valley Area, page 401

Florida

Charlotte, Lee, and Collier Counties..135
Jacksonville-St. Augustine Area (Including Clay, Duvall, Nassau, and St. Johns Counties)..139
Pinellas, Hillsborough, Polk, Manatee, and Sarasota Counties 144
South Florida (Including Broward, Miami-Dade, Monroe, and Palm Beach Counties)....153
Volusia, Seminole, Orange, and Brevard Counties 169

Georgia

Atlanta Area (Including Cherokee, Clayton, Cobb, DeKalb, Douglas,
Fayette, Fulton, Gwinnett, Henry, and Rockdale Counties).......................176

Illinois

Chicago Area (Cook, DuPage, Kane, Kendall, Lake, McHenry, and Will Counties) 188
See also Missouri–St. Louis Area, page 267

Indiana

Indianapolis Area (Including Boone, Hamilton, Hancock, Hendricks,
Johnson, Madison, Marion, Morgan, and Shelby Counties) 203
See also Illinois–Chicago Area, page 188
See also Kentucky–Louisville Area, page 208

Kentucky

Louisville Area (Including Bullitt, Clark, Floyd, Jefferson, and Oldham Counties).......208
See also Ohio–Cincinnati Area, page 363

Kansas

See Missouri–Kansas City Area, page 260

Maryland

Baltimore Area (Including Baltimore City and Baltimore County) 214
See also District of Columbia–Washington, DC, Area, page 117

Massachusetts

Boston Area (Including Bristol, Essex, Middlesex,
Norfolk, Plymouth, and Suffolk Counties)....................................223

Michigan

Greater Detroit and Washtenaw County Area (Including Macomb,
Oakland, Washtenaw, and Wayne Counties) 235

Minnesota

Twin Cities Area (Including Anoka, Carver, Dakota, Hennepin,
Ramsey, Scott, Washington, and Wright Counties) 250

Mississippi

See Tennessee–Memphis Area, page 430

Missouri

Kansas City Area (Including Cass, Clay, Jackson,
Johnson, Platte, and Wyandotte Counties) 260
St. Louis Area (Including City of St. Louis and Jefferson,
Madison, St. Charles, St. Clair, and St. Louis Counties) 267

Nevada

Las Vegas Area (Including Clark County) 278

New Jersey

Northern and Central New Jersey (Including Bergen, Essex,
Hudson, Hunterdon, Middlesex, Monmouth, Morris,
Passaic, Somerset, Sussex, Union, and Warren Counties) 283
See also New York–New York Metropolitan Area, page 309
See also Pennsylvania–Delaware Valley Area, page 401

New York

Buffalo Area (Including Erie and Niagara Counties) 305
New York Metropolitan Area (Including New York City,
Long Island, and Westchester County) 309
Rochester Area (Including Monroe County) 339
See also New Jersey–Northern and Central New Jersey, page 283

North Carolina

Forsyth and Guilford Counties 343
Mecklenburg County 349
Triangle Area (Including Durham, Orange, and Wake Counties) 356

Ohio

Cincinnati Area (Including Hamilton County) 363
Cleveland Area (Including Cuyahoga, Lake, and Lorain Counties) 371
Columbus Area (Including Franklin County) 382

Oklahoma

Oklahoma City Area (Including Canadian, Cleveland, and Oklahoma Counties) 388

Oregon

Portland Area (Including Clackamas, Clark, Multnomah, and Washington Counties) . . . 393

Pennsylvania

Delaware Valley Area (Including Bucks, Chester, Delaware, Montgomery,
   and Philadelphia Counties in Pennsylvania; Burlington, Camden,
   and Gloucester Counties in New Jersey; and New Castle County, Delaware) 401
Pittsburgh Area (Including Allegheny County) 414

Rhode Island 423

Tennessee

Memphis Area (Including Crittendon, DeSoto, and Shelby Counties) 430
Nashville Area (Including Davidson County) 435

Texas

Dallas-Fort Worth Area (Including Dallas and Tarrant Counties) 440
Houston Area (Including Harris County) 450
San Antonio Area (Including Bexar County) 460
Travis County 467

Utah

Salt Lake City Area (Including Salt Lake County) 472

Virginia

Norfolk Area (Including City of Norfolk) 477
Richmond-Petersburg Area (Including Cities of Richmond,
   Colonial Heights, Dinwiddie, Hopewell, and Petersburg; and
   Chesterfield, Hanover, Henrico, and Prince George Counties) 481
See also District of Columbia—Washington, DC, Area, page 117

Washington

Puget Sound Area (Including King, Kitsap, Mason, Pierce,
   Skagit, Snohomish, and Thurston Counties) 486
See also Oregon—Portland Area, page 393

Wisconsin

Milwaukee Area (Including Milwaukee County) 496

Appendix A: Is Your Doctor Board Certified? Does It Matter? 503

Appendix B: Where to Complain and
   Get Information on Disciplinary Actions 506

Why You Need This Book

All doctors are not the same. A New York State Department of Health study of heart-bypass and valve-surgery death rates between 2003 and 2005 revealed that, among the state's doctors who performed at least 150 bypass surgeries in the period, nine lost seven percent or more of their patients; six lost fewer than two percent. Those were the differences even after allowing for variation in how sick the patients were.

A 2003 article in the *New England Journal of Medicine* found that thousands of study participants in various parts of the U.S. received less than 55 percent of guideline-recommended care from their providers. For example, 76 percent of diabetics had not received the recommended blood-sugar testing, 35 percent of patients with high-blood pressure had not received the recommended care, and 55 percent of heart-attack patients had not received recommended beta-blocker therapy. Doctors who don't ensure that their patients get the recommended treatments put their patients at substantially increased risk of serious complications or death.

A 1998 study by Dartmouth Medical School researchers looked at several surgical procedures that are frequently over-prescribed. The study found big differences, not just from doctor to doctor, but across regions, in the percent of patients treated with these procedures. Patients were at least six times more likely to be subjected to back surgery, for instance, in one of the studied regions than in another.

A 1998 article in the *American Journal of Medical Quality* reported that the doctors in one-fifth of surveyed hospitals were routinely performing right-heart catheterizations on more than 70 percent of their Medicare heart disease patients although the procedure was judged of relatively little value—and unnecessarily risky for these patients. In contrast, doctors at many other hospitals rarely, if ever, made inappropriate use of this procedure.

Doctor-to-doctor quality differences mean that choosing the wrong doctor might expose you to surgery, powerful drugs, or other treatments that will do you no good, might do you lasting harm, and will certainly contribute to discomfort and inconvenience. By choosing the wrong doctor, you might also miss out on therapy that could cure a disease or repair an injury, or you might get the treatment you need but have it performed so badly that it does you no good. In short, choice of the wrong doctor can result in needless suffering, or even death.

Education in American medical schools and post-medical school training programs is the best in the world. Very few individuals get into the practice of medicine in this country without brains, discipline, and a lot of knowledge. But caring for the human organism is an exceedingly complex business, and not all doctors are equally prepared for the challenge. What's more, practicing medicine requires continual learning. Not all doctors have the same time, commitment, or ability to grow in the profession.

This book will help you find a top doctor. There are other resources, some of which are described in the pages that follow. Some focus on whether doctors have desirable training and certifications. Some report on whether doctors adhere to minimum practice guidelines with regard to consistently giving appropriate tests and treatments. A few, like the New York State study of heart-surgery death rates mentioned above, compare physicians on critical outcomes. And some focus on how well doctors communicate with their patients (*Consumers' CHECKBOOK*, the publisher of this book, has developed some of the leading resources for assessing how well doctors do this). But by asking doctors—as we did for this book—for their assessments of their peers, we can find doctors who really stand out on diagnostic skills, on the ability to work with their colleagues within the system to coordinate care, and on other aspects of care where there is room to excel.

This book lets you do what doctors themselves do when they are looking for care for themselves or for loved ones in a community or specialty field with which they are not completely familiar. They ask other doctors for recommendations. This book has collected recommendations from many thousands of doctors. It draws on what doctors learn about other doctors by reputation and by working with each other on individual cases, in carrying out hospital staff responsibilities, and in other professional activities. It lists more than 23,000 doctors who have received multiple favorable mentions from their peers.

More information on how the lists in this book were created, how to use the lists, and other resources to help you find high-quality doctors is given in the following pages.

How to Use This Book

You can use the lists of top-rated doctors in this book in several ways—

- If you have a doctor and want an independent second opinion, this book will help you find a second-opinion doctor.
- If you are choosing a health plan (health maintenance organization or preferred provider organization), you can use this book to size up the quality of physicians in each of the competing plans' provider directories. You will want a plan that offers you a choice of a substantial number of this book's listed physicians in your area.
- If you don't have a primary care (personal general-care) doctor you trust, you should get one, and this book might help you to identify a few candidates (but note the limits discussed in the box on page 9). Alternatively, you might be able to find a good specialist of a type you know you need (an allergist or dermatologist, for example) from the lists in this book and ask the specialist to recommend a primary care doctor.
- If you have a primary care doctor you trust, you will want to rely heavily on that doctor for referrals to other doctors, but it makes sense to discuss your doctor's referral recommendations. You can ask the doctor about specialists in this book. The doctor might not have thought about some of the options you can suggest or might not shoot quite so high on the quality scale without your prodding.
- Even if you have a good primary care doctor, you might find it saves you time to make your own referrals to specialists of types you know you need—an orthopedist for a broken bone or a plastic surgeon, for example— assuming your health plan allows you to self-refer.
- If your primary care doctor is guided by health plan rules or by the rules of his or her group practice to refer only to a specific specialist of each type, you can check whether the designated specialist is listed in this book. If

not, and if you feel your health problem is more than just a routine case, you might want to discuss with your doctor going outside the rules to use one of the doctors listed in this book.
- If you are not satisfied with a doctor your health plan insists you use, you might choose a doctor from this book and be armed with this book as you argue for a special referral decision.

To use this book effectively, you need to know how it is organized.

Our lists include doctors in more than fifty of the nation's largest Metropolitan Statistical Areas (MSAs). (In some cases, what we have referred to as a single area includes several MSAs—for example, the Miami, Ft. Lauderdale, and West Palm Beach MSAs are all included in what we refer to as "South Florida.")

The doctors are listed within geographic areas. The areas are generally defined by one or more counties, though some of the doctors listed in an area might practice outside county boundaries. The areas are organized within the book by state.

The map on pages 18 and 19 shows the various areas in which the listed doctors are concentrated. It gives the page number at which each area's listing begins. The Table of Contents also lists all the areas and the starting page number for each area.

Within each area, doctors are listed under the specialty for which they were recommended. Within that specialty, they are listed in alphabetical order.

Each doctor's listing gives a few background facts on the doctor and indicates *how many times the doctor was mentioned* by other doctors in his or her community. You might have greatest confidence in the quality of the doctors who received the most mentions (recommendations) from their peers.

How the Lists of Doctors Were Put Together

To identify the "top doctors" listed in this book, we surveyed roughly 340,000 physicians. We surveyed physicians in the areas listed in the Table of Contents. This included more than 50 of the largest Metropolitan Statistical Areas in the U.S. and some additional areas. Within these areas, we surveyed all active, office-based doctors on the American Medical Association (AMA) mailing list. The AMA list is a comprehensive list, which includes both AMA members and doctors who are not AMA members.

We asked each surveyed doctor to tell us which one or two specialists, in each of 35 different specialty fields, he or she "would consider most desirable for care of a loved one."

Our list of doctors in each area contains the names of physicians who were mentioned multiple times by other physicians in their communities. Names appear in the specialty category chosen by the surveyed physicians.

Immediately following each physician's name, we report the number of mentions the physician received in our survey. Because of the nature of the survey, physicians in some specialties with large numbers of practitioners are unlikely to be mentioned more than a few times, while physicians in specialties with only a few practitioners may get a large number of mentions. Also, we received more responses to our survey in some areas of the country than in others. Accordingly, in some specialties and in some areas, we have listed specialists mentioned as few as three times; in other specialties and other areas, the cutoff was 10 mentions or more.

On the list, we indicate the medical school from which each physician graduated and his or her year of graduation. The list also shows what "board certifications," if any, each doctor holds. Board certification means that a physician has taken several years of practical training in a field after graduating from medical school and has passed a difficult exam in that field. Information on board certification comes from the American Board of Medical Specialties (ABMS). We used an ABMS list from April 1, 2009; keep in mind that this list could not include certification information on doctors who were certified after the list was compiled. In May 2009, we asked the American Osteopathic Association (AOA) to tell us about certifications by osteopathic physician specialty boards for the doctors on our list who we identified as having graduated from schools of osteopathic medicine.

Unfortunately, the AOA declined to work with us to provide this information.

We have made great efforts to compile accurate information on addresses, phone numbers, and credentials for each physician, but these facts may have changed by the time you read this book, and no doubt in a book of this size there are some facts that are reported in error.

Keep in mind that our survey didn't ask about all specialties, so some physicians did not have an opportunity to be included on our lists.

Obviously, there are some possible biases in lists of the kind you will find in this book. For example, doctors could recommend close colleagues or other doctors with whom they have financially beneficial back-and-forth referral arrangements. Since we asked for recommendations in 35 specialty fields and invited doctors to recommend two doctors in each field, however, it is likely that most doctors were mentioning many specialists with whom they had no financial connections. It is also possible that some doctors

Lists of Primary Care Physicians Are Limited

We have included on the lists of physicians in this book three large primary care fields—family practice, internal medicine, and pediatrics. Because recommendations in each community were spread across many hundreds of physicians in these fields, very few received even three mentions. So our listings of physicians in any community in these primary care fields don't begin to include the many top-quality primary care doctors in that community. Even in other specialty fields, the likelihood that a doctor will get a substantial number of mentions is affected by the number of other doctors in the same community in the same field. For example, obstetricians/gynecologists and psychiatrists are generally less likely to get a large number of mentions than are cardiac surgeons, since there are relatively few cardiac surgeons who could be mentioned in any community.

who got favorable mentions did so just because they are well-known. They might have gotten negative mentions from other doctors if we had asked for negatives. Nonetheless, favorable mentions by a number of doctors—the more the better—are likely to be a good sign. In fact, our research has found that doctors mentioned by enough other doctors to be included on our list—

- Did not get there by chance alone. Even the small number of mentions some of the listed physicians received from their peers would have been, for most listed specialties, very unlikely to have occurred if the physicians responding to the survey had just been randomly naming other doctors.

- Get much higher ratings than other doctors when we survey patients.
- Are much more likely than other doctors to be board certified.
- Are less likely than other doctors to have disciplinary actions filed against them with state medical boards.
- In the one specialty for which we have good data on outcomes (death rates in cardiac bypass surgery) have better results.

Our list should steer you to some very good candidates.

Choosing a Doctor

Probably the most important single thing you can do to assure yourself high-quality medical care is to form a strong relationship with a good primary care physician. You need a doctor you can trust and talk openly with if a serious medical problem arises. This doctor should be familiar with your medical history, your family relationships, and other factors that can help in diagnosing the physical and emotional causes of health problems. You will rely on this doctor to guide and coordinate your care through the rest of the health care system—to refer you to specialists, for instance, or to coordinate your care during a hospital stay.

Your primary care doctor should be a family practitioner, internist, or pediatrician (for children), or perhaps an obstetrician/gynecologist (for women). If you are in an HMO, you won't be allowed to get your primary care from any other specialty. But even if you have traditional insurance, you are better off not to rely on a more narrow specialist—say, a surgeon—for primary care because a specialist may see the cures for your health problems in the tasks he or she is skilled to perform—surgery, perhaps, where drug therapy would suffice.

Until you have a primary care doctor you fully trust, you will have to take lead responsibility for selecting any specialist you need. This book will be especially valuable to you in that situation. It will also have special value any time you need to select a specialist for a second opinion or any time you become dissatisfied with a specialist to whom your primary care doctor has referred you.

Even if you have a primary care doctor you feel you can rely on for referrals, you will still want to have an active role in choosing specialists. You will get better choices if you discuss a few candidates with your doctor, including candidates you identify in this book. That is especially important if your primary care doctor has reason to select only from a limited set of candidates because of health plan or medical group referral procedures. In addition, only you can judge whether any specialist you use relates well to you personally and is convenient.

When looking for a good primary care doctor, one approach is to ask friends and associates for recommendations. Other options are to get recommendations from a doctor you have known in some other part of the country or from a local specialist you have used.

This book includes listings of a small number of primary care doctors in each community. You can select one of the listed doctors. Alternatively, if you know that you need a specific type of specialist, you can select a specialist of that type using this book (assuming your health plan allows you to go to a specialist of your choice) and you can ask that specialist to recommend primary care doctors.

There are various online directories of physicians. The American Medical Association's (AMA's) online directory is at *www.ama-assn.org*. It lets you locate a doctor by specialty within a local area and gives you basic address and contact information. For doctors who are AMA members—only about 20 percent of all doctors—the site also gives you background on the doctor's medical school and year of graduation, specialty board certifications, and hospital admitting privileges. The American Board of Medical Specialties (ABMS) has a directory at *www.abms.org*. It also allows you to locate a certified doctor by specialty within a local area, and gives you the doctor's city and state.

If you are a member of a health plan, or if you are considering becoming a member and want to know in advance about the doctors you might choose in a plan, you can cross-reference the list of prospects you compile from other sources with the health plan's provider directory. In fact, you also may be able to use the provider directory or the plan's administrative staff as a source of information on prospects. The directories often give background information on doctors so you can find, for example, doctors who use a specific hospital or who are in a certain age range.

Some health plan provider directories also provide information related to quality and cost. For example, Aetna, CIGNA, and UnitedHealthcare all identify doctors who achieve certain quality and efficiency levels in the provider directories they make available to members.

A key consideration for most consumers is how physicians are rated by other patients. *Consumers' CHECKBOOK* (see *www.checkbook.org*) has been publishing ratings of physicians by patients since 1980—based on surveys of *CHECKBOOK* magazine and *Consumer Reports* magazine subscribers. These reports now cover the seven major metropolitan areas where *CHECKBOOK* magazine is published—Boston, Chicago, Philadelphia, San Francisco-Oakland-San-Jose, Seattle-Tacoma, Twin Cities, and Washington, DC. In addition, July 2009 marks the beginning of a program *CHECKBOOK* is sponsoring with the intention of expanding reliable patient ratings of physicians throughout the U.S. The first communities in which results from this new survey program can be found are Denver, Kansas City, and Memphis. Visit *www.checkbook.org* to find out the areas to which this program has been expanded.

There are various websites where patient comments and reports on doctors are collected and reported. The information on such websites is much less reliable than what *CHECKBOOK* provides. For example, these other websites are in many cases subject to manipulation; physicians or their staffs or friends can "stuff the ballot box" with favorable ratings—or unfavorable ratings of competitors they have never visited. The number of raters is in most cases far too small to be reliable. And there is no adjustment made for the fact that some types of patient raters (older patients, for example) tend to give higher ratings and other types (those with many health problems, for example) tend to give lower ratings.

In our own research with consumers we have found that the type of information consumers give the highest priority when selecting a physician is recommendations from other physicians. Physician recommendations are the focus of this book.

When you have identified a few potential candidates to be your primary care doctor, you will want to ask some questions about each. A few can be answered from available lists and directories; others will require a call to the doctor's office; and still others can be answered only by checking with other patients or by meeting—or using—the doctor. The following are a few of the more important questions. Many of these questions will also apply when you are checking out specialists.

- *Does the doctor work as a personal, or family, doctor on a primary care basis? For children, adults, or both?*
- *Is the doctor taking new patients?*
- *If you are a health plan member, is the doctor affiliated with your plan and currently accepting new patients from your plan?*
- *How convenient is the doctor's office? Is there public transportation? Parking? Access for the handicapped?*

Patients and Doctors Tend to Give High Ratings to the Same Doctors

We have found that the doctors recommended by other doctors also tend to get high ratings from patients. We surveyed Washington, DC, area consumers for their ratings of their primary care doctors. Primary care doctors who were recommended by at least five physician peers in our survey of doctors and who got at least 10 ratings in our survey of patients were rated "very good" or "excellent" for "overall quality" by 93 percent of their patients; on average, all other doctors got such favorable ratings from an average of fewer than 85 percent of their surveyed patients.

- *Is the doctor board certified in his or her specialty?* Although a well-recommended doctor who is not board certified may serve you admirably, there is good reason to seek out certification, which means that the doctor has taken at least three to seven years of post-medical school training and has passed a difficult exam. (See Appendix A for further discussion.)
- *Where did the doctor take his or her residency?* If the hospital where the doctor took advanced post-medical-school training—called a "residency"—has a recognizable university tie, this almost assures that the doctor received good instruction—for instance, University of California San Francisco Medical Center or Johns Hopkins Hospital. But just because you can't recognize a university connection in the name of the hospital does not mean there is none. Harvard University uses Massachusetts General, for example.
- *What medical school did the doctor attend?* Virtually all medical schools in the United States are acknowledged to be of relatively high quality. A few other countries, such as Canada, Great Britain, Switzerland, and Belgium, have schools of comparable quality. But remember that most experts think the location of a physician's residency is more revealing than the medical school attended.
- *When did the doctor graduate from medical school?* This tells you roughly how old the doctor is and how fresh his or her training is. You may prefer a doctor who has years of practical experience, who has seen firsthand a vast range of medical problems. But unless this doctor is actively involved in teaching or continuing education programs, he or she may not be aware of many recent medical care developments.
- *At what hospitals can the doctor admit patients?* You do well to have a doctor who can admit patients both at a major teaching hospital, if there is one in your area, and at a well-run community hospital, which might be more pleasant for uncomplicated, low-risk procedures. The *Consumers' Guide to Hospitals*, published by *Consumers' CHECKBOOK*, with ratings of over 4,000 acute care hospitals in the U.S., can help you identify good hospitals. This guide is available in print by calling 800-213-7283 or can be accessed and used online at *www.checkbook.org*. The price for our *Consumers' Guide to Hospitals* is $22.
- *Does the doctor have teaching responsibilities at a hospital?* The answer is important because a teaching position reflects respect from colleagues and also assures that the doctor is regularly exposed to new developments and to questions from medical students and residents.
- *Does the doctor use an electronic health record system?* You can ask the doctor what the system does and how he or she uses it. Will the doctor use the system to record the health history information collected from you and to recall this health history at the time of each encounter with you? Will the doctor use the system to enter lab service orders, x-ray orders, and/or prescription orders; will these orders be communicated directly to labs and

pharmacies for you; and will the results of tests be communicated back to the physician and entered into your personal record electronically? Does the health record system automatically ask the doctor questions; check for possible drug interaction problems; and suggest tests, diagnoses, or treatments? Does the system automatically issue alerts about abnormal tests, the need to follow up on referrals, and other actions the doctor should take? Will it issue reminders to patients?

There is reason to believe that the greatest opportunities for improvements in medical care are in the implementation and use of electronic health record systems. But at this time only about 15 to 20 percent of physicians report using such systems, the systems vary greatly in features and capabilities, many are becoming outdated, and many doctors who have them use only a fraction of the features the systems offer.

- *Does the doctor practice in a group or alone?* Doctors who share an office may share ideas and maintain informal standards of quality. They may also be able to operate more efficiently by sharing costly equipment and specialized staff. Finally, if the group includes doctors with different specialties, referrals are convenient and your medical record can be comprehensive, incorporating all the specialists' comments. On the other hand, doctors who practice in a group with other specialists may be less inclined to refer you to the very top specialist for your condition if there is another doctor within the doctor's group practicing in the specialty for which you need a referral.
- *What are the doctor's hours?* Many doctors schedule weekend or evening hours to accommodate patients' work schedules.
- *How does the doctor cover emergencies on nights and weekends?* If a doctor does not have an arrangement with at least one other doctor to share "on call" duties, be wary. Where will you turn when the doctor is out of town, ill, or at a meeting?
- *Does the doctor give advice over the phone to regular patients? Is there a charge for such advice?* Telephone advice can be a great convenience—a partial substitute for the house call most doctors are reluctant to make. With malpractice liability looking them in the eyes, doctors will be careful about phone advice in questionable cases, but most doctors give some advice over the phone. Very few charge to give phone advice as long as patients come in for office visits occasionally and do not call every few days.

- *What lab, x-ray, and machine diagnostic tests can be done without your having to go to another office?* Having the capability for such tests in your doctor's office is convenient. On the other hand, this close connection might create conflicts of interest leading to more tests or higher costs than you might otherwise incur.
- *What is the usual wait for an appointment for a non-emergency illness or injury? For a routine physical exam?*
- *What is the charge to you for a routine follow-up office visit? For a routine follow-up hospital visit? For a typical general physical exam?* These answers will give you a sense of what the doctor's charges might be for other services also, and of how the doctor's charges relate to the payment rules of your health plan.
- *Will the doctor deal with your insurance carrier?* You save time if your doctor will bill your insurance company directly. If you are on Medicare, it is important to know whether the doctor will accept the Medicare payment as payment in full.
- *Does the doctor prescribe generic drugs when appropriate?* Generic, or non-branded, drugs are usually cheaper and just as good as their brand-name equivalents.

Before making a final decision about a physician, it's a good idea to check whether the physician has been the subject of disciplinary actions. Unfortunately, the information currently available to consumers is limited, but residents of most states can get some information on disciplinary actions from state-run websites. Appendix B lists links to state medical board websites that have information on disciplinary actions.

When you have gathered all the information you can from calls to physicians' offices, talks with friends, this book, and other sources, you may want to visit the physician who looks best to you. This is not uncommon for patients choosing a new primary care doctor, but would be unusual for a specialist. A visit just to meet a doctor should be inexpensive or free. But some consumers will find a meeting of this kind awkward, and some of the doctors we have interviewed share this feeling. As a considerably more expensive alternative, you can schedule a physical exam.

If you do not feel a relationship with a doctor is immediately necessary, keep your notes on the doctors you have checked and simply call your first choice when a medical problem occurs.

What to Expect from Your Doctor and When to Switch

After your first encounter or any subsequent encounter with a doctor, you should feel free to look for a new one if you are not satisfied, and you have a right to your medical records to pass along to your new doctor. But you will be wise not to shop continually from doctor to doctor. An established relationship with a doctor you like and trust is a real asset.

The following are a few performance standards you should expect any doctor to meet—

- Offers reasonably convenient hours.
- Calls you back the same day if you call with a medical question—within a few minutes if you have left a message that there is an emergency—so long as you don't call much more often than you go in for visits.
- Gives helpful medical advice by phone.
- Generally arranges to see you within a day or two if you call with a new (non-emergency) sickness or injury.
- Generally does not keep you waiting more than 15 minutes past your appointment time before serving you.
- Refers you for specialty care when you think you need it.
- Is thorough and careful and seems to be competent.
- Remembers, or consults records about, your medical history and relevant information you have given before.
- Takes a thorough medical history.
- Listens to you, doesn't interrupt you, and makes you feel comfortable about asking questions.
- Checks your progress, tells you about test results, and follows up with other providers you're referred to.
- Explains clearly what is wrong, what is being done, what you need to do, and what you can expect.
- Tells you about your choices and gets you involved in making decisions about your care.
- Seems personally to care about you and your medical problems.
- Spends enough time with you.
- Gives you helpful advice about ways to stay healthy.
- Gets results as good as you believe you can reasonably expect.

Being able to communicate and work well with your doctor is critical. Much research has shown that patients who have a good relationship with a doctor tend to get more accurate diagnoses, respond better to treatment, and recover more quickly. Certainly, you're more likely to do your part in care—taking medicine and making lifestyle changes—if you understand what is expected of you, why it's important, and what effects you can expect to observe.

There are no absolute standards in terms of the waits you should expect and the time you should get with a doctor. You will have to decide what level of service you are comfortable with, given your own reasonable judgment of the urgency of your condition, the time needed for effective communication, and other factors. For example, a doctor who spends a lot of time with you but doesn't ask pertinent questions or devotes the time to talking about himself isn't serving you well.

In a traditional health insurance plan or preferred provider organization plan and in some HMOs, switching doctors is as easy as making an appointment with a new doctor. In many HMOs, you have to inform the customer service department of your intent to switch and you may have to wait until the first of the next month or even the next open enrollment period. In some HMOs that contract with doctors' groups, it's easier to switch to another doctor within the same physician group than to switch to a doctor in another of the HMO's groups.

Even if a plan's standard procedures require you to wait for a period before making a switch, you're likely to be able to move more quickly if you feel a switch is urgent and you ask the plan to make an exception to its rules.

Be sure your new doctor gets your medical records from your old doctor. Remember, in many cases, your history is the most useful aid in diagnosis—more useful than all the tests and x-rays that can be done. If your new doctor isn't interested in getting your old medical records, ask why (it's true that the records may not be easy to read or understand). You may want to get the records to store on your own—or at least be sure the former doctor will save them for many years.

Getting the Best Care Your Doctor Can Give

Whichever doctor you select, how you interact with the doctor will have a big effect on the success of your care. Here are a few suggestions.

Be Sure Your Doctor Takes a Thorough Medical History

If you feel your doctor has not asked about matters that might be important in diagnosing or treating you, volunteer the information. For example, if both of your parents had colon cancer, if your dad had a heart attack at age 40, if you recently had a bout with kidney stones, or if you periodically feel very depressed, let the doctor know.

Find Out About Tests Your Doctor Proposes to Do

Ask your doctor what tests he or she will do during routine visits—mammogram, hemocult to check for blood in your stool, PSA test for prostate cancer, electrocardiogram, sigmoidoscopy to check your rectum and lower colon, cholesterol test, HIV test, test for chlamydia? Ask why specific tests and not others are given. If there are particular medical problems you're concerned about, ask if there are relevant tests and why they do or don't make sense for you.

There's a lot of debate in the medical field about which routine tests are worth doing for which population groups and how often. There are reasons not to give tests: some are unpleasant, some are costly, some pose risks of complications, and all have the possibility of indicating that you have a problem you really don't have—leading to costly, unpleasant, and possibly dangerous treatment. You should be given an opportunity to express your preferences regarding tests, based on information about each test's pros and cons.

You should learn not only about routine tests given during preventive exams but also about any tests prescribed to check out a specific symptom or medical problem. Ask what each test will tell you that you don't already know, how reliable it is, what the risks and costs are, and whether the results might really make any difference in treatment plans.

Be Sure You Are Told the Results of Exams and Treatment

At the time of a doctor visit, ask when the results will be available and how you'll be told of them. Some doctors tell you nothing unless there is a problem. That approach may leave you wondering long after your doctor has the answers. There's also the risk that phone messages will be lost and you won't realize that a doctor called to give you results. If you know that a doctor is supposed to call and when, you'll be able to check back if the time for your report passes.

Discuss the Results of Exams

When you get test results, ask the doctor to compare them to results from previous tests and ask whether there are changes that might be worth making in your life to improve results. Even if your cholesterol count or your weight is within an acceptable range, for example, is it worse than it was? Enough worse to do something about?

Prepare for Appointments

Before a doctor visit—either a visit to a doctor's office or a visit by the doctor when you are in the hospital—get ready. Think what questions you want answered, what symptoms you've had, what treatments you've been giving yourself or that other providers have been giving you.

Write down your questions and other information to be sure you don't forget to mention something. It is a good idea even to bring the medications you've been using with you to the doctor's office.

If the doctor seems to be rushing you through your list of items, explain that discussing these matters is important to you and that you think the doctor should give you enough time. You might want to arrange to have a friend with you for the doctor visit to help you push to get through your questions and to help you remember the doctor's responses. You might even take a tape recorder.

Describe Symptoms in Detail

Does the problem occur only after you've just eaten, after you've exercised heavily, when you've been standing for a long time, only when you urinate? What does it feel like? When did you first notice the problem? Your description is a window on what's going on inside—often a better window than all the examining and testing the doctor can do.

If you have fears that you might have a particular medical condition, tell the doctor. This will give the doctor a chance to investigate those concerns or to assure you that they are unfounded.

Find Out About Getting Answers by Phone

Many questions require a visit to the doctor or tests. But some can be resolved based on what you can communicate by phone. Also, a phone call can often help you determine whether a doctor visit is needed—and how soon.

Ask your doctor if there is a nurse you can talk with about questions you may have. And ask what is the best time to reach the doctor by phone.

Ask for a Full Explanation of Your Diagnosis, Treatment Options, and Outlook for Recovery

When your doctor has had a chance to evaluate your case, be sure you get a full explanation of what he or she has discovered, the choices you have, and what you can expect.

What isn't working right? What caused it? What can be done about it now? If it's curable, what can you do differently to avoid a recurrence—for example, eat differently, exercise differently, sleep differently, sit differently, change jobs, wear a brace?

How sure is the doctor of the diagnosis? What are the other possibilities? What more can be done to confirm the diagnosis? At what cost and what risk?

What are the treatment options? What are the risks and costs? What are the possible benefits in terms of your lifestyle and ability to function? How will you know if the treatment is working? What will you need to report to the doctor?

One of your fundamental rights as a patient is the right to informed consent. If you agree to a treatment—to allow a doctor to act on you with drugs, knives, or other instruments—and it is a treatment you would not have chosen had you better understood your options, the doctor's actions really amount to an assault. That's why responsible doctors understand the importance of trying to answer all your questions.

Ask About Referrals to Specialists

If your doctor refers you to a specialist, ask why a specialist is needed and why that particular specialist was chosen. What is known about his or her expertise and experience with your type of case? Is this the only specialist of this type that your primary doctor is able to refer you to under his or her arrangements with your health plan? Ask the doctor to compare the specialist to whom you are referred versus other specialists listed in this book.

What should you expect the specialist to do? How will the referring doctor remain involved in your care?

If you are not referred to a specialist, ask why not. What extra expertise might a specialist bring to the case?

Remember that some health plans have physician compensation schemes that penalize—or reward—a doctor for making referrals to specialists.

Ask About Medication

If medication is recommended, ask why that particular medication. What benefits is it expected to have? How soon? What are the possible side effects and what should you do if you experience them? How should you take the medication—for example, with meals, at bedtime? Can you take it even though you're taking other medications? What should you do if you forget to take a dose? Will the medication limit your capacity to drive, work, or do other activities?

You may find it useful to have on hand a drug reference book. The *Consumer Drug Reference*, published by Consumer Reports, covers more than 12,000 brandname, generic, and over-the-counter drugs. It costs $44.95.

There are also free Web sites that provide extensive information on drugs—what they are for, possible side effects, interactions, etc. A useful site is *www.nlm.nih.gov*.

Ask About Hospitalization

If hospitalization is not recommended, ask why not. Hospitals are expensive and health plans are interested in cutting costs. If a plan pays its doctors by an arrangement that gives less income when patients are hospitalized, you want to be sure the financial incentives are not causing you to get too little care.

On the other hand, if hospitalization is recommended, ask why. Could the case be handled on an outpatient basis?

Hospitals are dangerous places. In an important report, the Institute of Medicine of the National Academy of Sciences summarized evidence from two major studies indicating just how dangerous: "the results of these two studies imply that at least 44,000 and perhaps as many as 98,000 Americans die in hospitals each year as a result of medical errors." And there are many additional cases where hospital or doctor negligence slows recovery or leads to short-term or long-term disability. What's more, even where there are no errors, infections and other problems can occur.

Also, be sure to ask why a particular hospital was chosen. Is it the only hospital to which your doctor is allowed to refer under arrangements with your health plan?

How complicated is your case? Does it require sophisticated hospital staff or advanced equipment? What are the risks of complications? Will it be important to have close monitoring and quick access to medical staff and equipment at all times? If the case is complicated, a major teaching hospital might be best.

Is your required treatment one for which special training or frequent experience is important? Are there certain hospitals where the staffs have more skill, more experience, or higher success rates than others with this treatment? In many types of cases—such as open heart surgery—research has shown that hospitals that treat a greater number of patients generally have better results.

Get a Second Opinion

If your doctor recommends hospitalization or other treatment that will be expensive, risky, or burdensome, get a second opinion. In such cases, most doctors will encourage second opinions. Most plans will be glad to pay, since the second opinion may lead to a recommendation of less care—and less cost.

If your doctor recommends against certain types of care that you know are available or if you are not confident in your doctor's conclusions or satisfied with the progress of your case, you might want a second opinion to consider more or different care. In a traditional insurance plan or preferred provider organization, you can arrange for a second opinion on your own and the plan will generally pay for it. In some HMO plans, your doctor will have to refer you for the second opinion in order for the plan to pay. Since the second opinion might lead to more care, there may be some resistance to authorizing it. If you think a second opinion is justified, insist on one. If the first and second opinions are in conflict or for some other reason you're still not confident in the conclusions, insist on a third opinion.

If possible, get your second opinion from an entirely independent doctor. If a surgeon who has recommended surgery refers you to another surgeon for a second opinion, it will be difficult for the second doctor to recommend against the advice (and the economic interests) of the first. This book should be useful to you in identifying a doctor to consult for a second opinion. If you read up on your type of case—especially if it is of a type that is being actively researched at certain medical centers—you may come upon names of leading specialists who might be available for advice.

To keep down the cost and time required for a second opinion, have your first doctor send copies of your medical records, x-rays, and lab results to the second opinion doctor. This is standard procedure.

Don't assume that because yours is a straightforward, uncomplicated case there is nothing to learn and there are no decisions to be made. In most cases, there are choices.

This point is brought home by studies done by Dartmouth Medical School researchers and others, looking at variations in medical practice in common types of cases across similar geographic areas. One of these studies found, for example, that about 75 percent of the elderly men in one Maine town had undergone prostate surgery, compared with fewer than 25 percent of men the same age in an adjacent town. Similar variations have been found in rates of hysterectomies, caesarean sections, and other common procedures. Significantly, studies generally find no evidence that such medical practice differences result in differences in the health status of the affected populations.

The implication is that big differences in the ways patients are treated result from differences in the beliefs and customs of different physicians in different communities—possibly influenced by the need to generate fees and not necessarily based on sound evidence of likely benefits to the patient. Even in a common type of case, you can't assume that a physician's standard recommendation is the best option for you.

Do Your Own Medical Research

Asking doctors questions is one way to learn. But you'll learn more—and have a better opportunity to grasp the information at your own pace—if you also seek out online or printed information. There are many sources of this kind of information, including the following online resources—

Healthfinder–*www.healthfinder.gove*
A free gateway to reliable consumer health and human services information developed by the U.S. Department of Health and Human Services.

Mayo Clinic–*www.mayoclinic.com*
General-information website with Mayo's advice and information, including such features as "Diseases and Conditions A-Z," "Condition Centers," "Healthy Living," and "Health Tools."

MedlinePlus–*http://medlineplus.gov*
A consumer-oriented website that brings together authoritative information from the U.S. National Library of Medicine, the National Institutes of Health, and other government agencies and health-related organizations. Includes extensive information about drugs, an illustrated medical encyclopedia, interactive patient tutorials, and recent health news.

PubMed–*www.pubmed.gov*
A service of the U.S. National Library of Medicine that includes over 17 million citations from academic journals for biomedical articles dating back to the 1950s. Includes links to many abstracts, full text articles, and other related resources.

National Guideline Clearinghouse–*www.guideline.gov*
A resource sponsored by the Agency for Healthcare Research and Quality that gives information on current guidelines for the diagnosis and treatment of diseases.

Merck Manual Online Medical Library
www.merckmanuals.com and *www.mercksource.com*
Includes the "Merck Manual—Home Edition," which explains disorders, who is likely to get them, their symptoms, how they're diagnosed, how they might be prevented, how they can be treated, and prognoses. Also includes the "Merck Manual of Health and Aging" and other resources.

University of Pittsburgh Medical Center
www.upmc.com/healthatoz
Consumer-oriented website with information on conditions and diseases, procedures, and drugs. Includes an "anatomy navigator," health tools and calculators, a medical dictionary, and other resources.

As an alternative to these online resources, patients can use available libraries. At any major public library, you can ask for general consumer-oriented medical literature or for medical texts. For more in-depth information, you can use a medical school library. These libraries may also be able to help patients find support groups and organizations that regularly provide information on the patient's type of medical problem.

Puget Sound Area—page 486

Portland Area—page 393

Sacramento Area—page 61

San Francisco Bay Area—page 76

Salt Lake City Area—page 472

Denver Area—page 89

Las Vegas Area—page 278

Los Angeles and Orange Counties—page 38

Riverside and San Bernardino Counties—page 56

Oklahoma City Area—page 388 →

San Diego Area—page 66

Phoenix Area—page 26

Dallas-Fort Worth Area—page 440 →

Travis County—page 467 →

Houston Area—page 450 →

San Antonio Area—page 460 →

Map   19

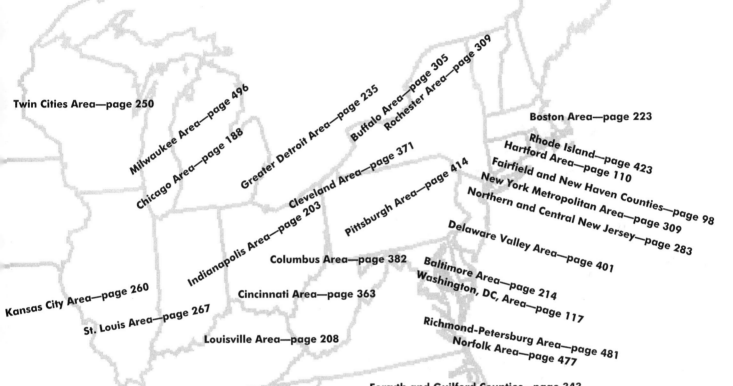

Twin Cities Area—page 250

Milwaukee Area—page 496

Chicago Area—page 188

Greater Detroit Area—page 235

Buffalo Area—page 305

Rochester Area—page 309

Boston Area—page 223

Rhode Island—page 423

Hartford Area—page 110

Fairfield and New Haven Counties—page 98

New York Metropolitan Area—page 309

Northern and Central New Jersey—page 283

Cleveland Area—page 371

Pittsburgh Area—page 414

Delaware Valley Area—page 401

Indianapolis Area—page 203

Columbus Area—page 382

Baltimore Area—page 214

Washington, DC, Area—page 117

Kansas City Area—page 260

Cincinnati Area—page 363

St. Louis Area—page 267

Richmond-Petersburg Area—page 481

Norfolk Area—page 477

Louisville Area—page 208

Forsyth and Guilford Counties—page 343

Triangle Area—page 356

Nashville Area—page 435

Mecklenburg County—page 349

Memphis Area—page 430

Atlanta Area—page 176

Birmingham Area—page 20

Jacksonville-St. Augustine Area—page 139

Volusia, Seminole, Orange, and Brevard Counties—page 169

Pinellas, Hillsborough, Polk, Manatee, and Sarasota Counties—page 144

Charlotte, Lee, and Collier Counties—page 135

South Florida—page 153

Alabama

Birmingham Area

Birmingham Area
Including Jefferson and Shelby Counties

Allergy/Immunology

Bonner, James Ryan (24 mentions)
U of Michigan, 1971 *Certification:* Allergy & Immunology, Infectious Disease, Internal Medicine
2000 6th Ave S, Birmingham, 205-801-8100

Butler, Joseph Landrum (7 mentions)
U of Tennessee, 1976
Certification: Allergy & Immunology, Pediatrics
2010 Patton Chapel Rd #200, Birmingham, 205-979-9537

Larussa, Joseph Bruno (11 mentions)
U of Alabama, 1990 *Certification:* Allergy & Immunology
2700 10th Ave S #401, Birmingham, 205-933-5599

Anesthesiology

Bloomston, Marc Evan (6 mentions)
U of Alabama, 1990 *Certification:* Anesthesiology
52 Medical Park Dr E #321, Birmingham, 205-838-3055

Bullington, John Clifford (3 mentions)
U of Alabama, 1983 *Certification:* Anesthesiology
2010 Brookwood Medical Center Dr, Birmingham, 205-989-1080

Gutierrez, Juan Francisco (3 mentions)
West Virginia U, 1969 *Certification:* Anesthesiology
1600 7th Ave S #420, Birmingham, 205-939-9235

Kentros, Jon (5 mentions)
U of Alabama, 1983 *Certification:* Anesthesiology
800 Montclair Rd, Birmingham, 205-783-3144

Lewis, Richard Joseph (3 mentions)
U of Alabama, 1986
701 Princeton Ave SW, Birmingham, 205-783-3144
3104 Blue Lake Dr #110, Birmingham, 205-783-3144
800 Montclair Rd, Birmingham, 205-592-1785

Martin, Barry William (6 mentions)
FMS-United Kingdom, 1979 *Certification:* Anesthesiology
52 Medical Park Dr E #321, Birmingham, 205-838-3055

Routman, Michael Howard (6 mentions)
Emory U, 1980 *Certification:* Anesthesiology
2010 Brookwood Medical Center Dr, Birmingham, 205-989-1091
2151 Old Rocky Ridge Rd #106, Birmingham, 205-989-1080

Schuster, Abraham (5 mentions)
Emory U, 1984 *Certification:* Anesthesiology
2010 Brookwood Medical Center Dr, Birmingham, 205-989-1091

Spivak, John Charles (6 mentions)
U of Alabama, 1983 *Certification:* Anesthesiology
800 Montclair Rd, Birmingham, 205-592-1785

Varner, Pamela D. (4 mentions)
U of Alabama, 1977 *Certification:* Anesthesiology
619 19th St S, Birmingham, 205-934-9999

Williams, Mark Sloan (4 mentions)
U of South Alabama, 1980 *Certification:* Anesthesiology
1600 Carraway Blvd, Birmingham, 205-502-6817

Cardiac Surgery

Kirklin, James Karl (16 mentions)
Harvard U, 1973 *Certification:* Thoracic Surgery
2000 6th Ave S, Birmingham, 205-934-3368

McGiffin, David Charles (20 mentions)
FMS-Australia, 1975
1530 3rd Ave S #760 THT, Birmingham, 205-934-6580

Richardson, John Burnie (21 mentions)
U of South Alabama, 1982 *Certification:* Thoracic Surgery
2660 10th Ave S #632, Birmingham, 205-939-0023

Riggins, Lee Shefton (9 mentions)
U of Alabama, 1975 *Certification:* Thoracic Surgery
817 Princeton Ave SW #300, Birmingham, 205-780-8980
1022 1st St N #300, Alabaster, 205-664-4842

Cardiology

Arciniegas, Joaquin G. (9 mentions)
FMS-Colombia, 1973 *Certification:* Cardiovascular Disease, Internal Medicine, Interventional Cardiology
2700 10th Ave S #305, Birmingham, 205-939-0139

Bakir, Stephen Espy (5 mentions)
Emory U, 1994
Certification: Cardiovascular Disease, Interventional Cardiology
880 Montclair Rd #170, Birmingham, 205-599-3500

Barnard, Dianne (4 mentions)
U of Massachusetts, 1982
Certification: Cardiovascular Disease, Internal Medicine
2022 Brookwood Medical Center Dr #402, Birmingham, 205-868-4650

Bourge, Robert Charles (7 mentions)
Louisiana State U, 1979 *Certification:* Cardiovascular Disease, Internal Medicine, Nuclear Medicine
1900 University Blvd #THT-311, Birmingham, 205-934-3624

Cavender, James Bradley (5 mentions)
U of Alabama, 1984 *Certification:* Cardiovascular Disease, Internal Medicine, Interventional Cardiology
2022 Brookwood Medical Center Dr #510, Birmingham, 205-877-9290

Cox, Richard Lewis, Jr. (5 mentions)
Wake Forest U, 1974
Certification: Cardiovascular Disease, Internal Medicine
833 St Vincents Dr #500, Birmingham, 205-933-4640

Eagan, John Thomas, Jr. (4 mentions)
U of Alabama, 1986 *Certification:* Cardiovascular Disease, Internal Medicine, Interventional Cardiology
880 Montclair Rd #170, Birmingham, 205-599-3500

Epstein, Andrew Ernest (4 mentions)
U of Rochester, 1977 *Certification:* Cardiovascular Disease, Clinical Cardiac Electrophysiology, Internal Medicine
1530 3rd Ave S #THT-321, Birmingham, 205-731-9365

Honan, Michael Benjamin (6 mentions)
U of Alabama, 1983
Certification: Cardiovascular Disease, Internal Medicine
2022 Brookwood Medical Center Dr #510, Birmingham, 205-877-9290

Jones, Steven Ernest (8 mentions)
U of Alabama, 1986 *Certification:* Cardiovascular Disease, Internal Medicine, Interventional Cardiology
2022 Brookwood Medical Center Dr #510, Birmingham, 205-877-9290

Kay, George Neal (4 mentions)
U of Michigan, 1979 *Certification:* Cardiovascular Disease, Clinical Cardiac Electrophysiology, Internal Medicine
2000 6th Ave S, Birmingham, 205-801-8000

Parks, James Michael (14 mentions)
U of Alabama, 1985 *Certification:* Cardiovascular Disease, Internal Medicine, Interventional Cardiology
833 St Vincents Dr #500, Birmingham, 205-933-4640

Plumb, Vance John (4 mentions)
Duke U, 1973
Certification: Cardiovascular Disease, Internal Medicine
1530 3rd Ave S #321-K, Birmingham, 205-934-2510

Stanley, Alfred W. H., Jr. (7 mentions)
U of Florida, 1966
Certification: Cardiovascular Disease, Internal Medicine
1532 Carraway Blvd #310, Birmingham, 205-250-6964

Dermatology

Abele, Matthew Karl (8 mentions)
Med Coll of Georgia, 1989 *Certification:* Dermatology
2700 10th Ave S #501, Birmingham, 205-939-6890

Herzog, Jo Lynne (7 mentions)
Albert Einstein Coll of Med, 1984 *Certification:* Dermatology
521 Montgomery Hwy, Birmingham, 205-824-4441

Krell, James Michael (11 mentions)
Harvard U, 1989 *Certification:* Dermatology
2100 16th Ave S #202, Birmingham, 205-933-0987

Mercado, Patricia J. (8 mentions)
New Jersey Med Sch, 1980
Certification: Dermatology, Internal Medicine
2000 6th Ave S, Birmingham, 205-996-7546

Monheit, Gary David (15 mentions)
U of Colorado, 1970 *Certification:* Dermatology
2100 16th Ave S #202, Birmingham, 205-933-0987

Soong, Vera Yen (13 mentions)
Louisiana State U, 1985 *Certification:* Dermatology
817 Princeton Ave SW #302, Birmingham, 205-781-6995

Emergency Medicine

Allen, Andrew Mark (5 mentions)
U of Alabama, 1988 *Certification:* Internal Medicine
5778 Willow Lake Dr, Hoover, 800-508-0014

Croushorn, John Marshall (7 mentions)
U of South Alabama, 2000 *Certification:* Emergency Medicine
800 Montclair Rd, Birmingham, 205-592-1404

Frost, Kent Steven (3 mentions)
U of Alabama, 1987 *Certification:* Emergency Medicine
2010 Brookwood Medical Center Dr, Birmingham, 205-877-1138

Glaeser, Peter William (3 mentions)
Med Coll of Wisconsin, 1981
Certification: Pediatric Emergency Medicine, Pediatrics
1600 7th Ave S, Birmingham, 202-939-9587

Gore, Albert Marshall (10 mentions)
U of South Alabama, 1986 *Certification:* Internal Medicine
810 St Vincents Dr, Birmingham, 205-939-7100

Johnson, Carol Mitchell (3 mentions)
U of Alabama, 1983
1022 1st St N #400, Alabaster, 205-664-7570

Lewis, Bobby Rea (3 mentions)
U of Alabama, 1977 *Certification:* Emergency Medicine
1528 Carraway Blvd, Birmingham, 205-250-6064

Phillips, Ricky Lawton (8 mentions)
U of South Alabama, 1979 *Certification:* Emergency Medicine
2010 Brookwood Medical Center Dr, Birmingham, 205-877-1930

Pigott, David (4 mentions)
Columbia U, 1995 *Certification:* Emergency Medicine
619 19th St S #JTN-266, Birmingham, 205-975-7387

Rosko, Christopher Joseph (3 mentions)
Jefferson Med Coll, 1981 *Certification:* Emergency Medicine
2252 Old Tyler Rd, Birmingham, 205-585-7420

Sanford, Janyce Marie (3 mentions)
U of South Alabama, 1986 *Certification:* Emergency Medicine
1802 6th Ave S, Irondale, 205-934-5100

Thomson, Thomas Owen (4 mentions)
U of Alabama, 1993 *Certification:* Emergency Medicine
810 St Vincents Dr, Birmingham, 205-939-7100

Endocrinology

Ennis, Elizabeth D. (14 mentions)
U of South Alabama, 1989 *Certification:* Endocrinology, Diabetes, and Metabolism, Internal Medicine
840 Montclair Rd #317, Birmingham, 205-592-5135

Goncalves, Edison (12 mentions)
FMS-Brazil, 1982 *Certification:* Endocrinology, Diabetes, and Metabolism, Internal Medicine
2022 Brookwood Medical Center Dr #408, Birmingham, 205-870-8198

Prelipcean, Maria (7 mentions)
FMS-Romania, 1993
Certification: Endocrinology, Diabetes, and Metabolism
833 St Vincents Dr #500, Birmingham, 205-933-4640

Teague, Ralph Joe (7 mentions)
U of Alabama, 1975 *Certification:* Internal Medicine
1600 Carraway Blvd, Birmingham, 205-502-6600

Vargas, Rodolfo A. (7 mentions)
FMS-Bolivia, 1970 *Certification:* Internal Medicine
2022 Brookwood Medical Center Dr #307, Birmingham, 205-877-2960
700 18th St S #410, Birmingham, 205-930-9152

Family Practice *(see note on page 9)*

Brewer, Michael Eric (4 mentions)
U of Alabama, 1980
4902 Valleydale Rd, Birmingham, 205-980-8099

Gewin, James Richard (3 mentions)
U of Alabama, 1980 *Certification:* Internal Medicine
3140 Cahaba Heights Rd #A, Birmingham, 205-967-9248

Harrington, Tracy Michael (5 mentions)
U of Virginia, 1976 *Certification:* Family Medicine
930 20th St S #317-B, Birmingham, 205-975-9114

McInnis, Cecil Rush, Jr. (3 mentions)
U of Alabama, 1968 *Certification:* Family Medicine
1 W Lakeshore Pkwy #100, Birmingham, 205-930-2973

Solomon, Eric Stephen (4 mentions)
FMS-Canada, 1977
120 Cahaba Valley Pkwy #201, Pelham, 205-733-1130

Walker, Herbert P., Jr. (5 mentions)
U of Alabama, 1981 *Certification:* Family Medicine
3140 Cahaba Heights Rd, Birmingham, 205-967-7302

Gastroenterology

Champion, Gregory Lynn (8 mentions)
U of South Alabama, 1988
Certification: Gastroenterology, Internal Medicine
513 Brookwood Blvd #401, Birmingham, 205-870-0256

Cochran, Joseph Lynn (5 mentions)
U of Tennessee, 1981
Certification: Gastroenterology, Internal Medicine
1 Independence Plaza #900, Birmingham, 205-271-8000

Denton, William Timothy (13 mentions)
U of Mississippi, 1979
Certification: Gastroenterology, Internal Medicine
513 Brookwood Blvd #401, Birmingham, 205-870-0256

Helman, Colin Alexander (5 mentions)
FMS-South Africa, 1969
Certification: Gastroenterology, Internal Medicine
801 Princeton Ave SW #328, Birmingham, 205-786-5527
840 Montclair Rd #500, Birmingham, 205-595-5504

Lyerly, Ralph Thomas, Jr. (5 mentions)
U of Alabama, 1970
Certification: Gastroenterology, Internal Medicine
1600 Carraway Blvd, Birmingham, 205-502-6000

Mauldin, Jack Lemuel (5 mentions)
U of Florida, 1972
Certification: Gastroenterology, Internal Medicine
801 Princeton Ave SW #328, Birmingham, 205-786-5527
840 Montclair Rd #500, Birmingham, 205-595-5504

Mestre, Jose Ramon (5 mentions)
U of Florida, 1977
Certification: Pediatric Gastroenterology, Pediatrics
1023 22nd St S, Birmingham, 205-714-7760

Newman, Joseph Randall (5 mentions)
U of Alabama, 1987 *Certification:* Gastroenterology
2700 10th Ave S #406, Birmingham, 205-933-0960

Shaffer, Robert Alexander (5 mentions)
U of Alabama, 1999
Certification: Gastroenterology, Internal Medicine
100 Pilot Medical Dr #250, Birmingham, 205-838-3034

Shallcross, John Cotton (5 mentions)
U of Louisville, 1985
Certification: Gastroenterology, Internal Medicine
1 Independence Plaza #900, Birmingham, 205-271-8000

Tobias, Raymond (6 mentions)
FMS-South Africa, 1973
Certification: Gastroenterology, Internal Medicine
1 Independence Plaza #900, Birmingham, 205-271-8000

Truss, Christopher D. (11 mentions)
U of Alabama, 1976
Certification: Gastroenterology, Internal Medicine
2000 6th Ave S, Birmingham, 205-801-8863

General Surgery

Bishop, George Blaine, Jr. (7 mentions)
Vanderbilt U, 1985 *Certification:* Colon & Rectal Surgery, Surgery
860 Montclair Rd #600, Birmingham, 205-595-8985

Blalock, John B., Jr. (4 mentions)
U of Alabama, 1975 *Certification:* Surgery
2660 10th Ave S #238, Birmingham, 205-933-7301

Buck, Gray Carroll, III (5 mentions)
U of Alabama, 1981 *Certification:* Surgery
2700 10th Ave S #209, Birmingham, 205-933-7946

Fischer, Philip J., II (7 mentions)
U of Alabama, 1997 *Certification:* Surgery
800 St Vincents Dr #630, Birmingham, 205-939-6888

Hawn, Mary (6 mentions)
U of Michigan, 1991 *Certification:* Surgery
2000 6th Ave S, Birmingham, 205-975-1932

Kirkland, Richard Ira (6 mentions)
U of Alabama, 1986 *Certification:* Surgery
513 Brookwood Blvd #501, Birmingham, 205-930-8010

Kitchens, Jerry Lester (7 mentions)
U of Alabama, 1987 *Certification:* Surgery
860 Montclair Rd #758, Birmingham, 205-930-8020

Lytle, Richard Allen (5 mentions)
U of Alabama, 1969 *Certification:* Surgery
52 Medical Park Dr E #308, Birmingham, 205-838-3025

Mirelman, Daniel (11 mentions)
FMS-Chile, 1971 *Certification:* Colon & Rectal Surgery, Surgery
2022 Brookwood Medical Center Dr #313, Birmingham, 205-877-2910

Pennington, William Scott, Jr. (8 mentions)
U of Alabama, 1976 *Certification:* Surgery
860 Montclair Rd #600, Birmingham, 205-595-8985

Rader, David Lee (6 mentions)
U of Alabama, 1980 *Certification:* Surgery
833 St Vincents Dr #202, Birmingham, 205-558-4062

Salter-Blackwell, Sally (4 mentions)
U of Alabama, 1996 *Certification:* Surgery
800 St Vincents Dr #510, Birmingham, 205-933-6440

Shumate, Charles Raymond (16 mentions)
U of Alabama, 1984 *Certification:* Surgery
513 Brookwood Blvd #501, Birmingham, 205-930-8010

Tapscott, William James (5 mentions)
U of Alabama, 1993 *Certification:* Surgery
840 Montclair Rd #310, Birmingham, 205-592-5135

Geriatrics

Allman, Richard Mark (5 mentions)
West Virginia U, 1980
Certification: Geriatric Medicine, Internal Medicine
2000 6th Ave S, Birmingham, 205-934-9261

Hematology/Oncology

Atkinson, Ruth C. (6 mentions)
Louisiana State U-Shreveport, 1980
Certification: Hematology, Internal Medicine, Medical Oncology
2022 Brookwood Medical Center Dr #628, Birmingham,
  205-592-7571

Barton, James Clyde (5 mentions)
U of Tennessee, 1971
Certification: Hematology, Internal Medicine, Medical Oncology
2022 Brookwood Medical Center Dr #G105, Birmingham,
  205-877-2888

Cantrell, James E., Jr. (9 mentions)
Emory U, 1977
Certification: Hematology, Internal Medicine, Medical Oncology
810 St Vincents Dr, Birmingham, 205-939-7880

Gore, Ira, Jr. (12 mentions)
Duke U, 1982
Certification: Hematology, Internal Medicine, Medical Oncology
810 St Vincents Dr, Birmingham, 205-939-7880

Harvey, Jimmie H. (16 mentions)
Emory U, 1977
Certification: Internal Medicine, Medical Oncology
880 Montclair Rd #675, Birmingham, 205-592-5077

Larson, Lisa Christine (7 mentions)
SUNY-Upstate Med U, 1983
Certification: Hematology, Internal Medicine, Medical Oncology
2022 Brookwood Medical Center Dr #628, Birmingham,
  205-592-7571

Nabell, Lisle Marie (10 mentions)
U of North Carolina, 1987
Certification: Internal Medicine, Medical Oncology
1513 3rd Ave S WTI #237, Birmingham, 205-934-3061

Windsor, Kevin Stanford (10 mentions)
U of Alabama, 1983
Certification: Internal Medicine, Medical Oncology
880 Montclair Rd #675, Birmingham, 205-592-5077

Infectious Disease

Barnes, David Waddell (22 mentions)
Emory U, 1981
Certification: Infectious Disease, Internal Medicine
833 St Vincents Dr #500, Birmingham, 205-933-4640

Coghlan, Michael Edward (11 mentions)
Johns Hopkins U, 1991 *Certification:* Infectious Disease
2022 Brookwood Medical Center Dr #403, Birmingham,
  205-870-9740

Ennis, David Marion (11 mentions)
U of South Alabama, 1989
Certification: Infectious Disease, Internal Medicine
840 Montclair Rd #606, Birmingham, 205-592-5917

Lapidus, William Ivan (11 mentions)
U of Alabama, 1986
Certification: Infectious Disease, Internal Medicine
840 Montclair Rd #606, Birmingham, 205-592-5917

Pappas, Peter George (7 mentions)
U of Alabama, 1978
Certification: Infectious Disease, Internal Medicine
1900 University Blvd #229, Birmingham, 205-934-5191

Reymann, Michael Thomas (18 mentions)
U of Alabama, 1973
Certification: Infectious Disease, Internal Medicine
2022 Brookwood Medical Center Dr #403, Birmingham,
  205-870-9740

Tucker, Bruce Alan (7 mentions)
U of Miami, 1974
Certification: Infectious Disease, Internal Medicine
833 Princeton Ave SW, Birmingham, 205-206-8220
832 Princeton Ave SW, Birmingham, 205-780-7053

Infertility

Honea, Kathryn Lynne (18 mentions)
U of Alabama, 1979 *Certification:* Obstetrics & Gynecology,
  Reproductive Endocrinology/Infertility
2006 Brookwood Medical Center Dr #508, Birmingham,
  205-870-9784

Houserman, Virginia L. (7 mentions)
U of Missouri, 1978 *Certification:* Obstetrics & Gynecology,
  Reproductive Endocrinology/Infertility
2006 Brookwood Medical Center Dr #508, Birmingham,
  205-870-9784

Steinkampf, Michael Paul (9 mentions)
Louisiana State U, 1981 *Certification:* Obstetrics &
  Gynecology, Reproductive Endocrinology/Infertility
2700 Hwy 280 S #370, Birmingham, 205-874-0000

Internal Medicine *(see note on page 9)*

Browne, Raymond James (5 mentions)
George Washington U, 1985 *Certification:* Internal Medicine
3106 Independence Dr, Birmingham, 205-871-7007

Eisa, Osama Shawky (6 mentions)
Louisiana State U, 1993
832 Princeton Ave SW, Birmingham, 205-206-8461

Farley, John William (3 mentions)
Med Coll of Georgia, 1991
Certification: Hospice and Palliative Medicine, Internal Medicine
2700 10th Ave S #207, Birmingham, 205-930-2060

Frederickson, Robert Morris (3 mentions)
U of Alabama, 1987 *Certification:* Internal Medicine
513 Brookwood Blvd #50, Birmingham, 205-877-2761

Gettinger, David Samuel (5 mentions)
U of California-San Francisco, 1983
Certification: Internal Medicine
2000 6th Ave S, Birmingham, 205-801-7500

Gruman, Alan Lester (3 mentions)
U of Alabama, 1989 *Certification:* Internal Medicine
2000 6th Ave S, Birmingham, 205-801-7500

O'Shields, Hugh P., Jr. (5 mentions)
U of Alabama, 1985 *Certification:* Internal Medicine
1600 Carraway Blvd #801, Birmingham, 205-802-4100

Patterson, William (8 mentions)
U of South Alabama, 1986 *Certification:* Internal Medicine
3106 Independence Dr, Birmingham, 205-871-7007

Riser, Margaret Dick (6 mentions)
U of Alabama, 1979 *Certification:* Internal Medicine
513 Brookwood Blvd #50, Birmingham, 205-877-2761

Riser, Thomas Glover (5 mentions)
U of Alabama, 1982 *Certification:* Internal Medicine
513 Brookwood Blvd #50, Birmingham, 205-877-2761

Rutsky, Edwin Arthur (5 mentions)
Case Western Reserve U, 1965
Certification: Internal Medicine, Nephrology
1530 3rd Ave S #260, Birmingham, 205-934-5642

Stafford, Mark Alan (6 mentions)
U of Alabama, 1978 *Certification:* Internal Medicine
2000 6th Ave S, Birmingham, 205-801-8831

Travelute, Roxanne Renee (5 mentions)
U of Kansas, 1985 *Certification:* Internal Medicine
1817 Oxmoor Rd, Birmingham, 205-879-2002

Welden, Joseph Edward, Jr. (8 mentions)
U of Alabama, 1979 *Certification:* Internal Medicine
833 St Vincents Dr #500, Birmingham, 205-933-4640

Wynne, David Frank (3 mentions)
U of Alabama, 1996 *Certification:* Internal Medicine
860 Montclair Rd #764, Birmingham, 205-595-9222

Nephrology

Giles, Harold Eugene, Jr. (6 mentions)
U of Alabama, 1997 *Certification:* Internal Medicine, Nephrology
817 Princeton Ave SW #206, Birmingham, 205-788-7572
2018 Medical Center Dr #304, Birmingham, 205-879-5111

Old, Christopher Wingate (18 mentions)
U of Alabama, 1974 *Certification:* Internal Medicine, Nephrology
817 Princeton Ave SW #206, Birmingham, 205-788-7572
2018 Medical Center Dr #304, Birmingham, 205-879-5111

Ozbirn, Thomas Washburn (13 mentions)
A T Still U, 1981 *Certification:* Internal Medicine, Nephrology
817 Princeton Ave SW #206, Birmingham, 205-788-7572
2018 Medical Center Dr #304, Birmingham, 205-879-5111

Tharpe, David Lawrence (9 mentions)
Vanderbilt U, 1972 *Certification:* Internal Medicine
817 Princeton Ave SW #206, Birmingham, 205-788-7572
2018 Medical Center Dr #304, Birmingham, 205-879-5111

Neurological Surgery

Harsh, Carter Sibley (8 mentions)
U of Alabama, 1985 *Certification:* Neurological Surgery
800 St Vincents Dr #700, Birmingham, 205-933-8981

Markert, James Macdowell (8 mentions)
Columbia U, 1988 *Certification:* Neurological Surgery
2000 6th Ave S, Birmingham, 205-934-9999

Morris, Enoch C., III (11 mentions)
U of Alabama, 1982
3125 Independence Dr #200, Birmingham, 205-986-5200

Swaid, Swaid Nofal (14 mentions)
U of Alabama, 1976 *Certification:* Neurological Surgery
513 Brookwood Blvd #372, Birmingham, 205-802-6844

Wilson, Thomas A. S., Jr. (13 mentions)
Vanderbilt U, 1987 *Certification:* Neurological Surgery
800 St Vincents Dr #700, Birmingham, 205-933-8981

Zeiger, Herbert Evan, Jr. (13 mentions)
U of Alabama, 1974 *Certification:* Neurological Surgery
1528 Carraway Blvd, Birmingham, 205-250-6805

Neurology

Barr, Clarence William (7 mentions)
U of Tennessee, 1988 *Certification:* Neurology
832 Princeton Ave SW, Birmingham, 205-786-6709

Hudgens, Kyle Randall (8 mentions)
U of Alabama, 1983 *Certification:* Neurology
790 Montclair Rd #210, Birmingham, 205-595-3600

James, Gregory Lamar (12 mentions)
U of Alabama, 1989 *Certification:* Neurology
833 St Vincents Dr #501, Birmingham, 205-918-0507

O'Neal, David Baker (5 mentions)
Med Coll of Georgia, 1980
2660 10th Ave S, Birmingham, 205-939-0203

Pearlman, Robert Lawrence (9 mentions)
Pennsylvania State U, 1984 *Certification:* Neurology
513 Brookwood Blvd #360, Birmingham, 205-877-2876

Pearson, Jane (9 mentions)
U of Alabama, 1974 *Certification:* Neurology
2660 10th Ave S #520, Birmingham, 205-939-0196

Riser, Emily Sherrill (5 mentions)
U of Alabama, 1984
Certification: Neurology, Spinal Cord Injury Medicine
509 Brookwood Blvd #101, Birmingham, 205-877-2255

Riser, John Byron (11 mentions)
U of Alabama, 1984
Certification: Neurology, Spinal Cord Injury Medicine
509 Brookwood Blvd #101, Birmingham, 205-877-2255

Swillie, Rodney Kent (5 mentions)
U of Alabama, 1983 *Certification:* Neurology
790 Montclair Rd #210, Birmingham, 205-595-3600

Obstetrics/Gynecology

Banks, Charles Gregory (4 mentions)
Vanderbilt U, 1987 *Certification:* Obstetrics & Gynecology
2006 Brookwood Medical Center Dr #310, Birmingham,
    205-877-2121

Brock, James Carl (3 mentions)
U of Alabama, 1981 *Certification:* Obstetrics & Gynecology
860 Montclair Rd #625, Birmingham, 205-599-3477

Brown, Cynthia (4 mentions)
Certification: Obstetrics & Gynecology
2006 Brookwood Med Ctr Dr #700, Birmingham, 205-877-5444

Dubois, Lee Burnette (3 mentions)
U of Alabama, 1979 *Certification:* Obstetrics & Gynecology
48 Medical Park Dr E #355, Birmingham, 205-838-3036

Duke, Ashley Jean (3 mentions)
U of Alabama, 2001 *Certification:* Obstetrics & Gynecology
1010 1st St N #350, Alabaster, 205-664-9995

Edwards, John Lee (6 mentions)
U of Alabama, 1988 *Certification:* Obstetrics & Gynecology
806 St Vincents Dr #500, Birmingham, 205-930-1800

Gleason, Brian Patrick (3 mentions)
U of Alabama, 1984 *Certification:* Obstetrics & Gynecology
2000 6th Ave S, Birmingham, 205-801-8000
720 20th St S, Birmingham, 205-934-2051

Goolsby, Rupa Desai (4 mentions)
U of North Carolina, 1990 *Certification:* Obstetrics & Gynecology
880 Montclair Rd #473, Birmingham, 205-271-1600
800 St Vincents Dr #600, Birmingham, 205-271-1600

Gray, Samuel Eugene (3 mentions)
U of Alabama, 1987 *Certification:* Obstetrics & Gynecology
2006 Brookwood Medical Center Dr #310, Birmingham,
    205-877-2121

Kennedy, Karla Grow (3 mentions)
U of South Alabama, 1988 *Certification:* Obstetrics & Gynecology
2006 Brookwood Medical Center Dr #600, Birmingham,
    205-877-2971

McKee, David Smyth, Jr. (4 mentions)
U of Virginia, 1979 *Certification:* Obstetrics & Gynecology
800 St Vincents Dr #500, Birmingham, 205-933-8334

Robinett, Charles Willis, Jr. (7 mentions)
U of Alabama, 1971 *Certification:* Obstetrics & Gynecology
2006 Brookwood Medical Center Dr #310, Birmingham,
    205-877-2802

Smith, Lori Apffel (3 mentions)
Baylor U, 1991 *Certification:* Obstetrics & Gynecology
800 St Vincents Dr #500, Birmingham, 205-933-8334

Snowden, Anne Elizabeth (4 mentions)
Virginia Commonwealth U, 1987
Certification: Obstetrics & Gynecology
806 St Vincents Dr #500, Birmingham, 205-930-1800

Stone, Timothy Lynn (4 mentions)
U of Alabama, 1991 *Certification:* Obstetrics & Gynecology
2700 10th Ave S #306, Birmingham, 205-933-4020

Stradtman, Cecilia M. (3 mentions)
U of Alabama, 1984 *Certification:* Obstetrics & Gynecology
2006 Brookwood Medical Center Dr #700, Birmingham,
    205-877-5444

Straughn, Heidi Jo (3 mentions)
U of Alabama, 1997 *Certification:* Obstetrics & Gynecology
2006 Brookwood Medical Center Dr #300, Birmingham,
    205-397-8850

Walton, Philip Dean (6 mentions)
U of Alabama, 1970 *Certification:* Obstetrics & Gynecology
806 St Vincents Dr #500, Birmingham, 205-930-1800

Ophthalmology

Allison, Thomas McWane (4 mentions)
U of Alabama, 1974 *Certification:* Ophthalmology
2700 10th Ave S #206, Birmingham, 205-933-0439

Callahan, Michael Alston (4 mentions)
U of Alabama, 1971 *Certification:* Ophthalmology
700 18th St S #711, Birmingham, 205-933-6888

Eiland, Susan Horton (4 mentions)
U of Alabama, 1976 *Certification:* Ophthalmology
2700 10th Ave S #404, Birmingham, 205-933-2340

Elsas, Frederick John (4 mentions)
Duke U, 1968 *Certification:* Ophthalmology
1000 19th St S, Birmingham, 205-930-0700

Feagin, Rayder Wyatt, II (6 mentions)
U of Alabama, 1987 *Certification:* Ophthalmology
1009 Montgomery Hwy #200, Birmingham, 205-397-9400

Hays, Sarah Jablecki (6 mentions)
U of Alabama, 1979 *Certification:* Ophthalmology
1 W Lakeshore Dr #220, Birmingham, 205-941-2020

Kline, Lanning Bernard (12 mentions)
Duke U, 1973 *Certification:* Ophthalmology
700 18th St S #601, Birmingham, 205-325-8620

Kloess, Price Mentzel (6 mentions)
U of Alabama, 1984 *Certification:* Ophthalmology
790 Montclair Rd #150, Birmingham, 205-592-3911

McKinnon, Thomas D. (8 mentions)
U of Alabama, 1966 *Certification:* Ophthalmology
1009 Montgomery Hwy #200, Birmingham, 205-397-9400

Morris, Robert Edward (6 mentions)
U of Alabama, 1973 *Certification:* Ophthalmology
1201 11th Ave S #300, Birmingham, 205-933-2625

Owen, John S. (5 mentions)
U of Alabama, 1981 *Certification:* Ophthalmology
1528 Carraway Blvd, Birmingham, 205-250-6000

Orthopedics

Andrews, James Rheuben (7 mentions)
Louisiana State U, 1967 *Certification:* Orthopaedic Surgery
806 St Vincents Dr #415, Birmingham, 205-939-3699

Blum, Michael Francis (4 mentions)
U of Alabama, 1989 *Certification:* Orthopaedic Surgery
4517 Southlake Pkwy #202, Birmingham, 205-985-4111

Bonatz, Ekkehard (3 mentions)
FMS-Germany, 1982
Certification: Orthopaedic Surgery, Surgery of the Hand
4517 Southlake Pkwy #202, Birmingham, 205-985-4111
513 Brookwood Blvd #402, Birmingham, 205-802-6898

Buggay, David Shane (3 mentions)
Emory U, 1993 *Certification:* Orthopaedic Surgery
833 St Vincents Dr #403, Birmingham, 205-939-0447

Buggs, Theodis, Jr. (4 mentions)
U of Alabama, 1980 *Certification:* Orthopaedic Surgery
817 Princeton Ave SW POB2 #108, Birmingham, 205-783-7830

Cain, Edward Lyle, Jr. (9 mentions)
U of Alabama, 1994
Certification: Orthopaedic Sports Medicine, Orthopaedic Surgery
806 St Vincents Dr #415, Birmingham, 205-939-3699

Cuckler, John M. (5 mentions)
New York U, 1975 *Certification:* Orthopaedic Surgery
513 Brookwood Blvd #375, Birmingham, 205-802-4577

Doyle, John Scott (4 mentions)
U of Virginia, 1989 *Certification:* Orthopaedic Surgery
1600 7th Ave S, Birmingham, 205-939-9146

Dugas, Jeffrey Raymond (3 mentions)
Duke U, 1994
Certification: Orthopaedic Sports Medicine, Orthopaedic Surgery
806 St Vincents Dr #415, Birmingham, 205-939-3699

Garth, William Price, Jr. (4 mentions)
Tulane U, 1973
Certification: Orthopaedic Sports Medicine, Orthopaedic Surgery
1600 7th Ave S #402, Birmingham, 205-934-1041

Goldstein, Samuel R. (5 mentions)
U of South Alabama, 1983
Certification: Orthopaedic Sports Medicine, Orthopaedic Surgery
880 Montclair Rd #577, Birmingham, 205-595-6757

Johnson, Thomas Leonard (5 mentions)
U of Alabama, 1982 *Certification:* Orthopaedic Surgery
2700 10th Ave S #200, Birmingham, 205-933-7838

Killian, John Thomas (3 mentions)
U of Alabama, 1979 *Certification:* Orthopaedic Surgery
2660 10th Ave S #107, Birmingham, 205-933-8588

Kissel, Edward U., III (11 mentions)
U of Alabama, 1983 *Certification:* Orthopaedic Surgery
2700 10th Ave S #200, Birmingham, 205-933-7838

Powell, Thomas Edward (4 mentions)
U of Alabama, 1991 *Certification:* Orthopaedic Surgery
513 Brookwood Blvd #200, Birmingham, 205-397-2663

Sherrill, Joseph Madden (6 mentions)
U of Alabama, 1975
Certification: Orthopaedic Surgery, Surgery of the Hand
200 Montgomery Hwy #200, Vestavia Hills, 205-822-9595

Sorrell, Robert Gordon (4 mentions)
U of Alabama, 1986 *Certification:* Orthopaedic Surgery
3525 Independence Dr, Birmingham, 205-802-6700

Wade, Jeffrey Darrell (8 mentions)
U of Alabama, 1990 *Certification:* Orthopaedic Surgery
3525 Independence Dr, Birmingham, 205-802-6700

Wolf, Robert Scott (3 mentions)
U of Pennsylvania, 1993 *Certification:* Orthopaedic Surgery
3525 Independence Dr, Birmingham, 205-802-6700

Otorhinolaryngology

Black, Sheldon Jay (7 mentions)
Emory U, 1988 *Certification:* Otolaryngology
833 St Vincents Dr #402, Birmingham, 205-933-9236

Bragg, Lev Hunter (6 mentions)
U of Alabama, 1982 *Certification:* Otolaryngology
2700 10th Ave S #502, Birmingham, 205-933-2951

Davis, John Christopher (5 mentions)
U of Alabama, 1999 *Certification:* Otolaryngology
4515 Southlake Pkwy #300, Birmingham, 205-985-7393

Favrot, Stephen Reeves (6 mentions)
Tulane U, 1989 *Certification:* Otolaryngology
840 Montclair Rd #218, Birmingham, 205-591-6570
644 2nd St NE #107, Alabaster, 205-621-2020
13 Western Ave, Sylacauga, 256-249-7044

Goodson, Max Alan (10 mentions)
U of Alabama, 1977 *Certification:* Otolaryngology
2018 Brookwood Medical Center Dr #205, Birmingham,
  205-877-2827

Handley, Guy H., III (6 mentions)
U of Alabama, 1984 *Certification:* Otolaryngology
2018 Brookwood Medical Center Dr #205, Birmingham,
  205-877-2827

Peters, Glenn Eidson (9 mentions)
Louisiana State U, 1980 *Certification:* Otolaryngology
2000 6th Ave S, Birmingham, 205-934-9777

Real, Randall Lee (8 mentions)
U of Alabama, 1986 *Certification:* Otolaryngology
832 Princeton Ave SW, Birmingham, 205-780-7053

Sillers, Michael Jay (12 mentions)
U of Alabama, 1988 *Certification:* Otolaryngology
7191 Cahaba Valley Rd #301, Birmingham, 205-980-2091

Waguespack, Richard Wayne (5 mentions)
Louisiana State U, 1975 *Certification:* Otolaryngology
2660 10th Ave S #201, Birmingham, 205-933-9036
2217 Decatur Hwy, Gardendale, 205-933-9036

Pain Medicine

Beretta, James Paul (6 mentions)
Nova Southeastern Coll of Osteopathic Med, 1988
500 Cahaba Park Cir, Birmingham, 205-981-0006

Downey, Mark James (3 mentions)
U of South Alabama, 2002
Certification: Physical Medicine & Rehabilitation
3525 Independence Dr, Birmingham, 205-802-6700

Ness, Timothy John (3 mentions)
U of Iowa, 1988 *Certification:* Anesthesiology, Pain Medicine
1201 11th Ave S, Birmingham, 205-934-6501

Pathology

Alford, Thomas Joseph (6 mentions)
U of Alabama, 1974
Certification: Anatomic Pathology & Clinical Pathology
924 Montclair Rd #200, Birmingham, 205-591-7999

Biggs, Paul Joseph (3 mentions)
Indiana U, 1977 *Certification:* Anatomic Pathology &
  Clinical Pathology, Neuropathology
701 Princeton Ave SW, Birmingham, 205-783-3240

Guerry, Mary Louise (3 mentions)
Med U of South Carolina, 1980
Certification: Anatomic Pathology & Clinical Pathology
800 Montclair Rd, Birmingham, 205-592-5336

Hackney, James R. (6 mentions)
U of South Alabama, 1979 *Certification:* Anatomic
  Pathology & Clinical Pathology, Hematology
924 Montclair Rd #200, Birmingham, 205-591-7999

Kelly, David Reid (3 mentions)
U of Tennessee, 1974 *Certification:* Anatomic Pathology &
  Clinical Pathology, Pediatric Pathology
1600 7th Ave S, Birmingham, 205-939-9634

Klein, Michael Jeffrey (3 mentions)
Temple U, 1973
Certification: Anatomic Pathology & Clinical Pathology
619 19th St S #NP-3545, Birmingham, 205-975-8323

McCall, Caroline P. (3 mentions)
U of Arizona, 1993 *Certification:* Anatomic Pathology &
  Clinical Pathology, Dermatopathology
924 Montclair Rd #200, Birmingham, 205-591-7999

Reddy, Vishnu Vardhan (4 mentions)
FMS-India, 1971 *Certification:* Anatomic Pathology &
  Clinical Pathology, Hematology
619 19th St S, Birmingham, 205-934-6421

Siegal, Gene Philip (7 mentions)
U of Louisville, 1974 *Certification:* Anatomic Pathology
1802 6th Ave S, Birmingham, 205-934-9999

Smith, John Alexander (3 mentions)
U of Missouri, 1974 *Certification:* Clinical Pathology
618 18th St S #230, Birmingham, 205-934-6421

Wilson, Edward Robert, Jr. (4 mentions)
U of Mississippi, 1973 *Certification:* Anatomic Pathology,
  Clinical Pathology, Neuropathology
924 Montclair Rd #200, Birmingham, 205-591-7999

Pediatrics *(see note on page 9)*

Cortopassi, Caesar John (7 mentions)
U of South Alabama, 1977 *Certification:* Pediatrics
1809 Data Dr, Birmingham, 205-987-4444

Elmer, Kenneth Lee (3 mentions)
U of Alabama, 1983 *Certification:* Pediatrics
833 Princeton Ave SW, Birmingham, 205-206-8220
832 Princeton Ave SW, Birmingham, 205-780-7053

Habeeb, Judith Tanquary (4 mentions)
U of Alabama, 1990 *Certification:* Pediatrics
3401 Independence Dr, Birmingham, 205-870-1273

Hamm, Joseph Lyndon (3 mentions)
U of Alabama, 1983 *Certification:* Pediatrics
1936 Old Orchard Rd, Birmingham, 205-978-3200

Israel, Lillian Cordts L. (3 mentions)
Vanderbilt U, 1978 *Certification:* Pediatrics
2409 Acton Rd #171, Birmingham, 205-978-8245

Johnston, William Henry, Jr. (10 mentions)
U of Alabama, 1974 *Certification:* Pediatrics
806 St Vincents Dr #615, Birmingham, 205-933-2750

Levin, Robert Aland (8 mentions)
U of South Alabama, 1976 *Certification:* Pediatrics
2815 Independence Dr, Birmingham, 205-879-7888

Smith, Richard Felix (4 mentions)
U of Alabama, 1971 *Certification:* Pediatrics
1936 Old Orchard Rd, Birmingham, 205-978-3200

Stagno, Sergio B. (4 mentions)
FMS-Chile, 1967 *Certification:* Pediatrics
1600 7th Ave S ACC #600, Birmingham, 205-939-9100

Stone, Linda Johnson (4 mentions)
U of Alabama, 1983 *Certification:* Pediatrics
3300 Cahaba Rd #102, Birmingham, 205-870-7292

Stone, Richard Douglas (4 mentions)
East Carolina U, 1996 *Certification:* Pediatrics
1936 Old Orchard Rd, Birmingham, 205-978-3200

Whitaker, William Vernon (3 mentions)
Vanderbilt U, 1978 *Certification:* Pediatrics
101 Eagle Ridge Dr, Birmingham, 205-995-1004

Plastic Surgery

Duquette, George Robert (8 mentions)
Vanderbilt U, 1976 *Certification:* Plastic Surgery
2022 Brookwood Medical Center Dr #511, Birmingham,
  205-877-2918

O'Brien, Kevin Mark (8 mentions)
U of Texas-Dallas, 1984 *Certification:* Plastic Surgery
2022 Brookwood Medical Center Dr #210, Birmingham,
  205-879-2160

Steinmetz, Stephen R. (14 mentions)
U of Alabama, 1984 *Certification:* Plastic Surgery
2700 10th Ave S #510, Birmingham, 205-930-0980

Vasconez, Luis Oswaldo (12 mentions)
Washington U, 1962 *Certification:* Plastic Surgery, Surgery
510 20th St S #1102, Birmingham, 205-934-3245

Psychiatry

Ascherman, Lee Ian (4 mentions)
Case Western Reserve U, 1982 *Certification:* Child &
  Adolescent Psychiatry, Forensic Psychiatry, Psychiatry
1700 17th Ave S, Birmingham, 205-934-5156

Echols, Kyle Young (3 mentions)
Louisiana State U, 1987 *Certification:* Psychiatry
1031 S Arrington Blvd #A, Birmingham, 205-879-2700

Grayson, Garry Sandlin (4 mentions)
U of Alabama, 1976 *Certification:* Psychiatry
2200 Lakeshore Dr #150, Birmingham, 205-871-6926

Kinney, Francis Cleveland (5 mentions)
U of Alabama, 1985 *Certification:* Geriatric Psychiatry, Psychiatry
1713 6th Ave S, Birmingham, 205-934-6054

Kowalski, Stephen F. (3 mentions)
U of Oklahoma, 1981
Certification: Child & Adolescent Psychiatry, Psychiatry
3300 Cahaba Rd #310, Birmingham, 205-423-9440

Logue, Harry Edward (6 mentions)
Med Coll of Georgia, 1963
100 Century Park S #206, Birmingham, 205-978-7800

Lucas, Joseph Patrick (4 mentions)
U of Alabama, 1990 *Certification:* Psychiatry
3504 Vann Rd #100, Birmingham, 205-655-0585

Patton, Rita Faye W. (3 mentions)
U of Alabama, 1974
Certification: Psychiatry, Psychosomatic Medicine
619 19th St S, Birmingham, 205-934-4011

Tieszen, Stuart Carl (4 mentions)
U of Alabama, 1985 *Certification:* Psychiatry
2018 Brookwood Medical Center Dr #311, Birmingham,
  205-329-7805

Pulmonary Disease

Beaty, Russell Glynn (7 mentions)
U of Alabama, 1987
Certification: Internal Medicine, Pulmonary Disease
880 Montclair Rd #270, Birmingham, 205-802-2000

Carcelen, Manuel Felipe (5 mentions)
FMS-Peru, 1983 *Certification:* Critical Care Medicine, Internal Medicine, Pulmonary Disease
2018 Brookwood Medical Center Dr #115, Birmingham, 205-802-7676

Crain, Michael Ray (11 mentions)
U of South Alabama, 1982 *Certification:* Critical Care Medicine, Internal Medicine, Pulmonary Disease
817 Princeton Ave SW #115, Birmingham, 205-780-1963

Dubois, Gustavo A. (9 mentions)
FMS-Guatemala, 1976 *Certification:* Internal Medicine
2018 Brookwood Medical Center Dr #115, Birmingham, 205-802-7676

Hasson, Jack Harold (5 mentions)
U of Alabama, 1970 *Certification:* Critical Care Medicine, Internal Medicine, Pulmonary Disease
817 Princeton Ave SW #115, Birmingham, 205-780-1963

Hays, William Clarence, III (10 mentions)
Virginia Commonwealth U, 1981 *Certification:* Critical Care Medicine, Internal Medicine, Pulmonary Disease
2660 10th Ave S #528, Birmingham, 205-933-9258

Key, Bruce Maurice (9 mentions)
U of Alabama, 1972
Certification: Internal Medicine, Pulmonary Disease
2660 10th Ave S #528, Birmingham, 205-933-9258

Pappas, Louis Steve (7 mentions)
U of Alabama, 1975
Certification: Internal Medicine, Pulmonary Disease
880 Montclair Rd #270, Birmingham, 205-802-2000

Roney, Christopher Walton (5 mentions)
U of Mississippi, 1997
Certification: Internal Medicine, Pulmonary Disease
2022 Brookwood Medical Center Dr #310, Birmingham, 205-871-9112

Young, Keith Randall, Jr. (6 mentions)
Jefferson Med Coll, 1978 *Certification:* Internal Medicine
1900 University Blvd, Birmingham, 205-934-5400

Radiology—Diagnostic

Bernreuter, Wanda Kay (3 mentions)
Louisiana State U-Shreveport, 1981
Certification: Diagnostic Radiology
2000 6th Ave S, Birmingham, 205-801-8000

Brightbill, Todd Carlin (3 mentions)
Emory U, 1988
Certification: Diagnostic Radiology, Neuroradiology
800 Montclair Rd, Birmingham, 205-592-1257

Cure, Joel Kent (3 mentions)
U of Massachusetts, 1984
Certification: Diagnostic Radiology, Neuroradiology
619 19th St S, Birmingham, 205-975-7848

Koehler, Robert E. (4 mentions)
Cornell U, 1968 *Certification:* Diagnostic Radiology
2000 6th Ave S, Birmingham, 205-934-9999

Lopez, Roberto Ramon (3 mentions)
Columbia U, 1989 *Certification:* Diagnostic Radiology
619 19th St S, Birmingham, 205-934-0711

Marsch, Jeffrey Troy (3 mentions)
U of Cincinnati, 1982 *Certification:* Diagnostic Radiology
2010 Brookwood Medical Center Dr, Birmingham, 205-877-1990
2090 Columbiana Rd #4400, Birmingham, 205-871-7849
3485 Independence Dr, Birmingham, 205-930-0920

Mussleman, John Paul (7 mentions)
U of Alabama, 1971 *Certification:* Diagnostic Radiology
2090 Columbiana Rd #4400, Birmingham, 205-824-8000

Royal, Stuart Alan (6 mentions)
U of Alabama, 1974
Certification: Diagnostic Radiology, Pediatric Radiology
1600 7th Ave S ACC #306, Birmingham, 205-939-9730

Sekar, Balasundaram C. (4 mentions)
2010 Brookwood Medical Center Dr, Birmingham, 205-877-1990
2090 Columbiana Rd #4400, Birmingham, 206-824-8000

Williams, Donald Bryant (4 mentions)
U of Alabama, 1969 *Certification:* Diagnostic Radiology
2010 Brookwood Medical Center Dr, Birmingham, 205-877-1990
2090 Columbiana Rd #4400, Birmingham, 205-871-7849
3485 Independence Dr, Birmingham, 205-930-0920

Radiology—Therapeutic

Dumas, R. Fred, Jr. (10 mentions)
U of Alabama, 1982 *Certification:* Therapeutic Radiology
2010 Brookwood Medical Center Dr, Birmingham, 205-877-2273

Martin, Terry Keith (4 mentions)
U of Alabama, 1980 *Certification:* Diagnostic Radiology
2090 Columbiana Rd #4400, Birmingham, 205-824-8000

Salter, Susan Paula (7 mentions)
U of Alabama, 1991 *Certification:* Radiation Oncology
810 St Vincents Dr, Birmingham, 205-939-7884

Rehabilitation

Denver, Jack David (4 mentions)
U of Mississippi, 1989 *Certification:* Pain Medicine, Physical Medicine & Rehabilitation, Spinal Cord Injury Medicine
3800 Ridgeway Dr, Birmingham, 205-868-2096

Jackson, Amie B. (4 mentions)
Certification: Physical Medicine & Rehabilitation
1717 6th Ave S #190, Birmingham, 205-934-5858

Kezar, Laura Brooks (4 mentions)
Emory U, 1985 *Certification:* Physical Medicine & Rehabilitation
1717 6th Ave S #383, Birmingham, 205-934-6934

Law, Charles Raymond (4 mentions)
East Tennessee State U, 1992 *Certification:* Pediatric Rehabilitation Medicine, Physical Medicine & Rehabilitation
1600 7th Ave S, Birmingham, 205-939-9790

Rheumatology

Abbott, Joel Douglas (7 mentions)
U of South Alabama, 2000
Certification: Internal Medicine, Rheumatology
2145 Highland Ave S #200, Birmingham, 205-933-0320

McLain, David Andrew (12 mentions)
Tulane U, 1974 *Certification:* Internal Medicine, Rheumatology
2229 Cahaba Valley Dr, Birmingham, 205-991-8996
2022 Brookwood Medical Center Dr #211, Birmingham, 205-877-2555

Paul, William Alan (7 mentions)
Med Coll of Georgia, 1980
Certification: Internal Medicine, Rheumatology
2145 Highland Ave S #200, Birmingham, 205-933-0320

Saway, Peter Anthony (15 mentions)
U of Mississippi, 1980
Certification: Internal Medicine, Pain Medicine, Rheumatology
2145 Highland Ave S #200, Birmingham, 205-933-0320

Thoracic Surgery

Cerfolio, Robert (20 mentions)
U of Rochester, 1988 *Certification:* Surgery, Thoracic Surgery
703 19th St S #739, Birmingham, 205-934-5937

Richardson, John Burnie (9 mentions)
U of South Alabama, 1982 *Certification:* Thoracic Surgery
2660 10th Ave S #632, Birmingham, 205-939-0023

Ronson, Russell Scott (5 mentions)
Dartmouth Coll, 1994 *Certification:* Surgery, Thoracic Surgery
2022 Brookwood Medical Center Dr #403, Birmingham, 205-877-2627

Urology

Bragg, Donald Taylor (6 mentions)
U of Alabama, 1988 *Certification:* Urology
48 Medical Park Dr E #350, Birmingham, 205-838-3040

Hamrick, Leon C., Jr. (6 mentions)
U of Alabama, 1981 *Certification:* Urology
2700 10th Ave S #505, Birmingham, 205-933-1573

Joseph, David Barry (6 mentions)
U of Wisconsin, 1980 *Certification:* Pediatric Urology, Urology
1600 7th Ave S, Birmingham, 205-939-9840

Lloyd, Lewis Keith, Jr. (10 mentions)
Tulane U, 1966 *Certification:* Urology
510 20th St S, Birmingham, 205-975-0088
2001 6th Ave S, Birmingham, 205-975-0088

Moody, Thomas Edwin (6 mentions)
U of Alabama, 1973 *Certification:* Urology
3485 Independence Dr, Birmingham, 205-930-0920

Sanfelippo, Carl John (6 mentions)
Med Coll of Wisconsin, 1968 *Certification:* Urology
3485 Independence Dr, Birmingham, 205-930-0920
880 Montclair Rd #377, Birmingham, 205-930-0920

Tully, Albert Scott (13 mentions)
U of Alabama, 1983 *Certification:* Urology
3485 Independence Dr, Birmingham, 205-930-0920

Wells, W. Glen, Jr. (6 mentions)
Louisiana State U, 1972 *Certification:* Urology
2022 Brookwood Medical Center Dr #305, Birmingham, 205-877-2860

Vascular Surgery

Jordan, William D., Jr. (11 mentions)
Emory U, 1988 *Certification:* Vascular Surgery
2000 6th Ave S, Birmingham, 205-934-2003

Whitley, William David (12 mentions)
East Carolina U, 1987 *Certification:* Surgery, Vascular Surgery
2660 10th Ave S #608, Birmingham, 205-939-3495

Arizona

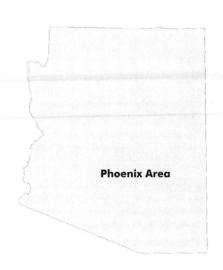

Phoenix Area

Phoenix Area

Including Maricopa County

Allergy/Immunology

Lewis, John Christopher (11 mentions)
Loyola U Chicago, 1982
Certification: Allergy & Immunology, Internal Medicine
13400 E Shea Blvd, Scottsdale, 480-301-8227

Manning, Michael Everett (20 mentions)
U of Texas-Houston, 1986
Certification: Allergy & Immunology, Internal Medicine
7514 E Monterey Way #1, Scottsdale, 480-949-7377
3800 N Central Ave #404, Phoenix, 602-248-9129
10200 N 92nd St #130, Scottsdale, 480-614-8011

Morgan, William Freer, Jr. (24 mentions)
Indiana U, 1970 *Certification:* Allergy & Immunology, Pediatrics
9220 E Mountain View Rd #200, Scottsdale, 480-451-6756
5605 W Eugie Ave #200, Glendale, 602-843-2991
4001 E Baseline Rd #201, Gilbert, 480-545-4000

Schubert, Mark Samuel (30 mentions)
U of Arizona, 1983
Certification: Allergy & Immunology, Internal Medicine
31 W Camelback Rd, Phoenix, 602-277-3337
2525 W Greenway Rd #224, Phoenix, 602-993-7540
941 S Dobson Rd #103, Mesa, 480-834-1352
14420 W Meeker Blvd #209, Sun City West, 602-277-3337
300 W Clarendon Ave #120, Phoenix, 602-277-3337
2905 W Warner Rd #24, Chandler, 480-834-1352

Wong, Darrell Wayne (11 mentions)
Rosalind Franklin U, 1995 *Certification:* Allergy & Immunology
348 E Virginia Ave, Phoenix, 602-266-4114
2601 E Roosevelt St, Phoenix, 602-344-5011
705 S Dobson Rd, Chandler, 480-897-6992

Wong, Duane W. (33 mentions)
Northwestern U, 1984
Certification: Allergy & Immunology, Pediatrics
348 E Virginia Ave, Phoenix, 602-266-4114
2501 E Southern Ave #18, Mesa, 480-897-6992

Anesthesiology

Cavanagh, Harry Joseph, Jr. (8 mentions)
U of Colorado, 1974 *Certification:* Anesthesiology
222 W Thomas Rd #102, Phoenix, 602-234-1803
5847 S 16th St, Phoenix, 602-249-0212

Cole, Daniel John (3 mentions)
Loma Linda U, 1982 *Certification:* Anesthesiology
5777 E Mayo Blvd, Phoenix, 480-342-1800

Couche, Roland M. (3 mentions)
FMS-United Kingdom, 1971 *Certification:* Anesthesiology
1850 N Central Ave #1600, Phoenix, 602-262-8900

Eckhardt, William Francis (3 mentions)
Temple U, 1983 *Certification:* Anesthesiology
1850 N Central Ave #1600, Phoenix, 602-262-8900

Fujihara, Steven W. (3 mentions)
Kansas U Coll of Osteopathic Med, 1979
4441 E McDowell Rd, Phoenix, 602-273-6770

Gieszl, George Scott, Jr. (7 mentions)
U of Cincinnati, 1970 *Certification:* Anesthesiology
2000 E Southern Ave #102, Tempe, 480-820-9141

Johnson, William Thurston (3 mentions)
George Washington U, 1982 *Certification:* Anesthesiology
3255 E Elwood St #110, Phoenix, 602-470-5000
2320 N 3rd St, Phoenix, 602-470-5000

Levin, Joseph Mark (3 mentions)
U of Kansas, 1986 *Certification:* Anesthesiology
1850 N Central Ave #1600, Phoenix, 602-262-8900

Matiski, Thomas John (4 mentions)
U of Pennsylvania, 1985 *Certification:* Anesthesiology
350 W Thomas Rd, Phoenix, 602-200-9021

Matson, Jeffrey Alan (4 mentions)
U of Kansas, 1982 *Certification:* Anesthesiology
13951 N Scottsdale Rd #211, Scottsdale, 602-273-9333

Maze, Aubrey (21 mentions)
FMS-South Africa, 1970 *Certification:* Anesthesiology, Pediatrics
1850 N Central Ave #1600, Phoenix, 602-262-8900

McFadden, Harriet Wade (4 mentions)
U of Colorado, 1982 *Certification:* Anesthesiology
4820 E McDowell Rd #101, Phoenix, 480-421-1014

Reitzel, Keith Eric (3 mentions)
U of Tennessee, 1992 *Certification:* Anesthesiology
2000 E Southern Ave #102, Tempe, 480-820-9141

Sandor, Joseph James (5 mentions)
U of Arizona, 1977 *Certification:* Anesthesiology
1850 N Central Ave #1600, Phoenix, 602-262-8900

Seamans, David Prescott (3 mentions)
Wayne State U, 1994 *Certification:* Anesthesiology, Pain Medicine
13400 E Shea Blvd, Scottsdale, 480-301-8000

Serlin, Steven Peter (5 mentions)
U of Michigan, 1972 *Certification:* Anesthesiology, Pediatrics
1850 N Central Ave #1600, Phoenix, 602-262-8900

Shedd, Steve Alan (3 mentions)
U of Arizona, 1982 *Certification:* Anesthesiology
1850 N Central Ave #1600, Phoenix, 602-262-8900

Smith, Dean Francis, III (13 mentions)
U of Arizona, 1977 *Certification:* Anesthesiology, Pediatrics
1850 N Central Ave #1600, Phoenix, 602-262-8900

Thomas, Richard David (4 mentions)
U of New Mexico, 1989 *Certification:* Anesthesiology
4002 E Main St #1, Mesa, 480-981-9151

Trentman, Terrence Lee (3 mentions)
Tulane U, 1990 *Certification:* Anesthesiology, Pain Medicine
13400 E Shea Blvd, Scottsdale, 480-301-8000

Wicklund, Steven Walter (7 mentions)
Med Coll of Wisconsin, 1992 *Certification:* Anesthesiology
1850 N Central Ave #1600, Phoenix, 602-262-8900

Williams, Mark Lee (6 mentions)
Jefferson Med Coll, 1986 *Certification:* Anesthesiology
13951 N Scottsdale Rd #211, Scottsdale, 480-609-9300

Cardiac Surgery

Arabia, Francisco A. (11 mentions)
Certification: Thoracic Surgery
5777 E Mayo Blvd, Phoenix, 480-342-2270

Ashton, Kenneth Anthony (15 mentions)
St Louis U, 1991 *Certification:* Thoracic Surgery
10930 N Tatum Blvd #103, Phoenix, 602-263-7600

Brady, Kevin Michael (12 mentions)
Emory U, 1995 *Certification:* Surgery, Thoracic Surgery
10930 N Tatum Blvd #103, Phoenix, 602-263-7600

Caskey, Michael P. (21 mentions)
U of Texas-Galveston, 1983 *Certification:* Thoracic Surgery
10930 N Tatum Blvd #103, Phoenix, 602-263-7600

De Valeria, Patrick A. (10 mentions)
Stanford U, 1987 *Certification:* Thoracic Surgery
5777 E Mayo Blvd, Phoenix, 480-515-6296

Dreicer, Victor Stephan (9 mentions)
U of Southern California, 1981 *Certification:* Thoracic Surgery
655 S Dobson Rd #A108, Chandler, 480-835-2250

Fang, Hao (13 mentions)
U of Illinois, 1991 *Certification:* Surgery, Thoracic Surgery
3131 E Clarendon Ave #102, Phoenix, 602-253-9168

Goldstein, Andrew (9 mentions)
Columbia U, 1989 *Certification:* Surgery, Thoracic Surgery
10930 N Tatum Blvd #103, Phoenix, 602-263-7600

Kirshner, Merick Shawn (15 mentions)
Temple U, 1990 *Certification:* Thoracic Surgery
10930 N Tatum Blvd #103, Phoenix, 602-263-7600

Lanza, Louis Angel (13 mentions)
Loyola U Chicago, 1981 *Certification:* Thoracic Surgery
5777 E Mayo Blvd, Phoenix, 480-342-2270

Teodori, Michael Felix (18 mentions)
U of Pennsylvania, 1981 *Certification:* Thoracic Surgery
1920 E Cambridge Ave #304, Phoenix, 602-546-0200

Cardiology

Allison, Rebecca Anne (6 mentions)
U of Mississippi, 1971
Certification: Cardiovascular Disease, Internal Medicine
755 E McDowell Rd, Phoenix, 602-271-5450

Ambrosia, Alphonse M. (5 mentions)
Western U, 1991 *Certification:* Interventional Cardiology
6116 E Arbor Ave #112, Mesa, 480-641-5400

Appleton, Christopher P. (5 mentions)
U of Washington, 1979
Certification: Cardiovascular Disease, Internal Medicine
13400 E Shea Blvd, Scottsdale, 480-301-8000

Byrne, Timothy John (9 mentions)
A T Still U, 1989
Certification: Cardiovascular Disease, Interventional Cardiology
1331 N 7th St #400, Phoenix, 602-277-6181
4444 N 32nd St #175, Phoenix, 602-952-0002

Damian, Andrei (4 mentions)
Certification: Cardiovascular Disease, Internal Medicine
16601 N 40th St #204, Phoenix, 602-867-8644
10210 N 92nd St #301, Scottsdale, 480-391-0555
3805 E Bell Rd #3100, Phoenix, 480-391-0555

Ehrlich, Ira Bert (7 mentions)
Harvard U, 1964
Certification: Cardiovascular Disease, Internal Medicine
500 W Thomas Rd #900, Phoenix, 602-406-8000
13555 W McDowell Rd #206, Goodyear, 623-935-6452
350 W Thomas Rd, Phoenix, 602-406-4708
340 E Palm Ln #175, Phoenix, 602-386-1100

Fitzgerald, John William (10 mentions)
Stanford U, 1971
Certification: Cardiovascular Disease, Internal Medicine
500 W Thomas Rd #500, Phoenix, 602-406-8000
13555 W McDowell Rd #206, Goodyear, 623-935-6452
340 E Palm Ln #175, Phoenix, 602-348-1100

Hines, James Jordan, Jr. (12 mentions)
Northwestern U, 1978 *Certification:* Cardiovascular
Disease, Internal Medicine, Interventional Cardiology
500 W Thomas Rd #500, Phoenix, 602-406-8000
13575 W Indian School Rd, Litchfield Park, 623-935-6452
13555 W McDowell Rd #206, Goodyear, 623-935-6452
340 E Palm Ln #175, Phoenix, 602-386-1100

Jedeikin, Roy (11 mentions)
FMS-South Africa, 1975 *Certification:* Pediatric Cardiology,
    Pediatrics
5847 S 16th St, Phoenix, 602-249-0212
1920 E Cambridge Ave #301, Phoenix, 602-253-6000

Kassel, David Murray (5 mentions)
U of Rochester, 1981
Certification: Cardiovascular Disease, Internal Medicine
6750 E Baywood Ave #301, Mesa, 480-835-6100
1520 S Dobson Rd #209, Mesa, 480-835-6100
10238 E Hampton Ave #104, Mesa, 480-835-6100

Kates, Marc (6 mentions)
U of New England Coll of Osteopathic Med, 1990
Certification: Cardiovascular Disease
3805 E Bell Rd, Phoenix, 602-867-8644

Klag, Joseph V. (10 mentions)
Philadelphia Coll of Osteopathic Med, 1978
Certification: Cardiovascular Disease, Internal Medicine
3805 E Bell Rd #3100, Phoenix, 602-867-8644
19636 N 27th Ave #201, Phoenix, 602-867-8644
10210 N 92nd St #301, Scottsdale, 480-391-0555
50 E Dunlap Ave #101, Phoenix, 602-852-0911

Klassen, Kevin John (4 mentions)
U of California-Los Angeles, 1988
Certification: Cardiovascular Disease
10101 N 92nd St #101, Scottsdale, 480-860-1919

Klee, Daniel Francis (7 mentions)
U of Buffalo, 1990
Certification: Cardiovascular Disease, Interventional Cardiology
595 N Dobson Rd #C-48, Chandler, 480-899-9430

Klein, Neal Alan (4 mentions)
U of Illinois, 1976 *Certification:* Cardiovascular Disease,
    Internal Medicine, Interventional Cardiology
4444 N 32nd St #175, Phoenix, 602-952-0002

Laufer, Nathan (15 mentions)
FMS-Canada, 1977 *Certification:* Cardiovascular Disease,
    Internal Medicine, Interventional Cardiology
1331 N 7th St #375, Phoenix, 602-307-0070

Lynch, John J. (7 mentions)
Creighton U, 1978
Certification: Cardiovascular Disease, Internal Medicine
13400 E Shea Blvd, Scottsdale, 480-301-4100

Maki, Peter Charles (9 mentions)
U of Arizona, 1976 *Certification:* Cardiovascular Disease,
    Internal Medicine, Interventional Cardiology
4444 N 32nd St #175, Phoenix, 602-952-0002

Morgan, John M. (5 mentions)
U of Texas-Galveston, 1992
Certification: Cardiovascular Disease, Interventional Cardiology
4444 N 32nd St #175, Phoenix, 602-952-0002

Nguyen, Tri Minh (5 mentions)
Tulane U, 1997
Certification: Cardiovascular Disease, Internal Medicine
19636 N 27th Ave #408, Phoenix, 623-879-6000

O'Meara, Michael Edward (5 mentions)
U of Cincinnati, 1976
Certification: Cardiovascular Disease, Internal Medicine
6750 E Baywood Ave #301, Mesa, 480-835-6100
1520 S Dobson Rd #209, Mesa, 480-835-6100

Oswood, Bradley Owen (6 mentions)
U of Arizona, 1989
Certification: Cardiovascular Disease, Interventional Cardiology
3099 N Civic Center Plaza, Scottsdale, 480-945-3535
7285 E Earll Dr, Scottsdale, 480-945-3535

Perlstein, Edward (9 mentions)
New Jersey Med Sch, 1969 *Certification:* Cardiovascular
    Disease, Internal Medicine, Interventional Cardiology
6750 E Baywood Ave #301, Mesa, 480-835-6100
1520 S Dobson Rd #209, Mesa, 480-835-6100
10238 E Hampton Ave #104, Mesa, 480-835-6100

Raniolo, John Salvatore (7 mentions)
Philadelphia Coll of Osteopathic Med, 1977
19636 N 27th Ave #408, Phoenix, 623-879-6000

Reinfeld, Allan Robert (6 mentions)
FMS-Philippines, 1982
Certification: Cardiovascular Disease, Internal Medicine
9755 N 90th St #A205, Scottsdale, 480-860-4040

Ritchie, Thomas A. (6 mentions)
Emory U, 1991
Certification: Cardiovascular Disease, Internal Medicine
6750 E Baywood Ave #301, Mesa, 480-835-6100
1520 S Dobson Rd #209, Mesa, 480-835-6100
10238 E Hampton Ave #104, Mesa, 480-835-6100

Rizik, David Gerard (10 mentions)
St Louis U, 1986 *Certification:* Cardiovascular Disease
10101 N 92nd St #101, Scottsdale, 480-860-1919

Robertson, William Scott, II (11 mentions)
U of Colorado, 1975
Certification: Cardiovascular Disease, Internal Medicine
3099 N Civic Center Plaza, Scottsdale, 480-945-3535
7285 E Earll Dr, Scottsdale, 480-945-3535

Sanders, Gregory Philip (4 mentions)
FMS-Canada, 1995
Certification: Cardiovascular Disease, Internal Medicine
500 W Thomas Rd #500, Phoenix, 602-406-8000
13555 W McDowell Rd #206, Goodyear, 623-935-6452
340 E Palm Ln #175, Phoenix, 602-386-1100

Sease, David Ray (5 mentions)
U of Texas-Houston, 1984 *Certification:* Cardiovascular Disease
3805 E Bell Rd #3100, Phoenix, 602-867-8644
19636 N 27th Ave #201, Phoenix, 602-852-0911
10210 N 92nd St #301, Scottsdale, 480-391-0555
50 E Dunlap Ave #101, Phoenix, 602-852-0911

Shah, Mehul (4 mentions)
FMS-India, 1990
Certification: Cardiovascular Disease, Interventional Cardiology
2149 E Baseline Rd #103, Tempe, 480-345-0034

Siegel, Marvin Sanford (6 mentions)
A T Still U, 1975
9100 N 2nd St #321, Phoenix, 602-861-1168
6206 W Bell Rd #5, Glendale, 602-978-1121

Simonie, Frederick Samuel (10 mentions)
Wayne State U, 1976
10210 N 92nd St Medical Bldg 3 #205, Scottsdale, 480-314-1189

Steidley, David Eric (5 mentions)
Robert W Johnson Med Sch, 1995
Certification: Cardiovascular Disease
13400 E Shea Blvd, Scottsdale, 480-301-8000

Stern, Mark Steven (5 mentions)
New York Med Coll, 1971 *Certification:* Cardiovascular
    Disease, Internal Medicine, Interventional Cardiology
1520 S Dobson Rd #209, Mesa, 480-835-6100
6750 E Baywood Ave #301, Mesa, 480-835-6100
10238 E Hampton Ave #104, Mesa, 480-835-6100

Stevenson, Jon Evan (4 mentions)
U of Arizona, 1996 *Certification:* Cardiovascular Disease,
    Internal Medicine, Interventional Cardiology
595 N Dobson Rd #C48, Chandler, 480-899-9430

Stock, John H. (15 mentions)
SUNY-Upstate Med U, 1990 *Certification:* Pediatric Cardiology
1920 E Cambridge Ave #301, Phoenix, 602-253-6000
1432 S Dobson Rd #512, Mesa, 480-969-0052

Surdakowski, Francis Paul (6 mentions)
FMS-Italy, 1975
Certification: Cardiovascular Disease, Internal Medicine
9100 N 2nd St #321, Phoenix, 602-861-1168
18404 N Tatum Blvd #201, Phoenix, 602-867-7217

Dermatology

Connolly, Suzanne Marie (13 mentions)
U of California-San Francisco, 1975
Certification: Dermatological Immunology/Diagnostic and
   Laboratory Immunology, Dermatology
13400 E Shea Blvd, Scottsdale, 480-301-6479

Giancola, Joseph Michael (7 mentions)
U of Missouri, 1990 *Certification:* Dermatology
11130 N Tatum Blvd #100, Phoenix, 602-494-1817

Glick, Ronald M. (15 mentions)
Des Moines U, 1983
3940 E University Dr #1, Mesa, 480-924-9235

Hansen, Ronald Cecil (23 mentions)
U of Iowa, 1968 *Certification:* Dermatology, Pediatrics
1605 N Campbell Ave, Tucson, 520-694-2100
1919 E Thomas Rd, Phoenix, 602-546-0835
2320 N 3rd St, Phoenix, 602-470-5000

Ko, William T. (13 mentions)
Northeastern Ohio U, 1994 *Certification:* Dermatology
2121 W Indian School Rd, Phoenix, 602-277-1449

Luber, Howard Jay (16 mentions)
U of Wisconsin, 1982
Certification: Dermatology, Internal Medicine
11130 N Tatum Blvd #100, Phoenix, 602-494-1817

McCracken, Gary Anthony (11 mentions)
Creighton U, 1992 *Certification:* Dermatology
14275 N 87th St #110, Scottsdale, 480-905-8485

Mendelson, Deborah E. S. (9 mentions)
Ohio State U, 1973
Certification: Dermatology, Dermatopathology
50 E Dunlap Ave #105, Phoenix, 602-944-4626

Powers, Jerold Lynn (7 mentions)
U of Iowa, 1977 *Certification:* Dermatology, Pediatrics
10752 N 89th Pl, Scottsdale, 480-661-0030

Romine, Kristine Ann (15 mentions)
Med Coll of Wisconsin, 1991 *Certification:* Dermatology
4350 E Camelback Rd #A200, Phoenix, 602-954-7546

Stockton, Toni Cyd (6 mentions)
Howard U, 1983 *Certification:* Dermatology
16611 S 40th St #100, Phoenix, 480-610-6366

Waddington, Gary Lee (10 mentions)
U of Nebraska, 1972 *Certification:* Dermatology
4400 N 32nd Ave #250, Phoenix, 602-277-7686
6320 W Union Hills Dr #100, Glendale, 623-376-7600

Yiannias, James A. (12 mentions)
Baylor U, 1988 *Certification:* Dermatology
13400 E Shea Blvd #2-B, Scottsdale, 480-301-8000

Emergency Medicine

Bank, David Ethan (3 mentions)
Columbia U, 1988
Certification: Pediatric Emergency Medicine, Pediatrics
1919 E Thomas Rd, Phoenix, 602-546-1905

Bobrow, Bentley J. (7 mentions)
Certification: Emergency Medicine
5777 E Mayo Blvd, Phoenix, 480-515-6296

Cardall, Taylor Young (3 mentions)
U of California-San Diego, 1999
Certification: Emergency Medicine
7400 E Osborn Rd, Scottsdale, 480-882-4000

Christopher, Michael Carl (5 mentions)
U of Arizona, 1986 *Certification:* Emergency Medicine
350 W Thomas Rd, Phoenix, 602-406-3189

Faux, Neal Nelson (10 mentions)
Tulane U, 1976 *Certification:* Emergency Medicine
511 W Lawrence Rd, Phoenix, 602-870-6316

Finch, Charles Atlee (7 mentions)
Des Moines U, 1994 *Certification:* Emergency Medicine
7400 E Osborn Rd, Scottsdale, 480-882-4000

Goldstein, Charles (3 mentions)
U of Buffalo, 1971 *Certification:* Emergency Medicine
4478 E Mockingbird Ln, Scottsdale, 602-870-6316

Green, John Randolph (6 mentions)
U of Oklahoma, 1981 *Certification:* Emergency Medicine
7400 E Osborn Rd, Scottsdale, 480-882-4000

Hay-Roe, Neil Maddison (3 mentions)
FMS-Canada, 1984 *Certification:* Emergency Medicine
5777 E Mayo Blvd, Phoenix, 480-342-1744

Kelley, James Matthew (3 mentions)
U of Arizona, 1991 *Certification:* Emergency Medicine
5777 E Mayo Blvd, Phoenix, 480-342-1744

Kozak, Paul A. (4 mentions)
George Washington U, 1990 *Certification:* Emergency Medicine
5777 E Mayo Blvd, Phoenix, 480-342-1744

Lum Lung, Michael Patrick (3 mentions)
U of California-San Francisco, 2000
Certification: Emergency Medicine
1400 S Dobson Rd, Mesa, 480-512-3000

Maitem, Jonathan A. (4 mentions)
Kansas U Coll of Osteopathic Med, 1994
19829 N 27th Ave, Phoenix, 623-879-5353

Mann, Eric David (3 mentions)
Kansas U Coll of Osteopathic Med, 1988
3929 E Bell Rd, Phoenix, 602-923-5622

Petri, Roland Wolfgang (4 mentions)
Northwestern U, 1985 *Certification:* Emergency Medicine
5777 E Mayo Blvd, Phoenix, 480-342-1744

Price, Tommy Chris (5 mentions)
Certification: Emergency Medicine
1900 N Higley Rd, Gilbert, 480-543-2600

Richman, Peter B. (3 mentions)
SUNY-Upstate Med U, 1993 *Certification:* Emergency Medicine
13400 E Shea Blvd, Scottsdale, 480-301-8000

Roga, Alan Cigg (8 mentions)
Stony Brook U, 1992 *Certification:* Emergency Medicine
7400 E Osborn Rd, Scottsdale, 480-882-4000

Silides, Paula Jean (3 mentions)
U of Arizona, 1994 *Certification:* Emergency Medicine
1400 S Dobson Rd, Mesa, 480-456-9500

Sokol, Larry Alan (3 mentions)
Rosalind Franklin U, 1980 *Certification:* Emergency Medicine
7400 E Osborn Rd, Scottsdale, 480-882-4000

Stizza, Denis Michael (3 mentions)
U of Arizona, 1982 *Certification:* Emergency Medicine
7400 E Osborn Rd, Scottsdale, 480-882-4000

Streitwieser, David Roy (17 mentions)
U of California-San Diego, 1979
Certification: Emergency Medicine
1300 N 12th St #301, Phoenix, 602-239-6968
23610 N 20th Dr #10, Phoenix, 602-239-6968

Suarez, Joseph Michael (5 mentions)
U of Southern California, 1974
Certification: Emergency Medicine
350 W Thomas Rd, Phoenix, 602-406-3600

Thibeault, Claude Raymond (4 mentions)
FMS-Canada, 1981
1400 S Dobson Rd, Mesa, 480-512-3700

Tukan, Lester Douglas (3 mentions)
U of Illinois, 1982 *Certification:* Emergency Medicine
1300 N 12th St #301, Phoenix, 602-239-6968

Veale, Kevin S. (6 mentions)
Kansas U Coll of Osteopathic Med, 1988
Certification: Emergency Medicine
4722 E Rancho Caliente Dr, Cave Creek, 602-870-6316

York, Clark D. (3 mentions)
Western U, 1989 *Certification:* Emergency Medicine
19829 N 27th Ave, Phoenix, 623-879-5353

Endocrinology

Argueta, Rodolfo (7 mentions)
FMS-Guatemala, 1967
Certification: Endocrinology and Metabolism, Internal Medicine
13400 E Shea Blvd, Scottsdale, 480-301-8000

Bailey, Joan Frances (17 mentions)
Tulane U, 1988 *Certification:* Endocrinology, Diabetes, and
   Metabolism, Internal Medicine
333 E Virginia Ave #220, Phoenix, 602-258-9955

Biesbroeck, Robert C. (11 mentions)
St Louis U, 1976 *Certification:* Endocrinology and
   Metabolism, Internal Medicine
217 S 63rd St #105, Mesa, 480-981-8088

Block, Marshall Burton (10 mentions)
New York Med Coll, 1968
Certification: Endocrinology and Metabolism, Internal Medicine
3522 N 3rd Ave, Phoenix, 602-266-8463
9745 N 90th Pl #B, Scottsdale, 602-266-8463

Brard, Gyan Singhsidhu (12 mentions)
Washington U, 1990 *Certification:* Endocrinology, Diabetes,
   and Metabolism, Internal Medicine
217 S 63rd St #105, Mesa, 480-981-8088

Duick, Daniel Stephen (28 mentions)
Northwestern U, 1967
Certification: Endocrinology and Metabolism, Internal Medicine
3522 N 3rd Ave, Phoenix, 602-266-8463

Hasan, Khalid S. (12 mentions)
FMS-Dominican Republic, 1985
Certification: Pediatric Endocrinology
1919 E Thomas Rd, Phoenix, 602-546-1000

Levy, Philip (19 mentions)
U of Pittsburgh, 1956 *Certification:* Endocrinology and
   Metabolism, Internal Medicine, Nuclear Medicine
1300 N 12th St #600, Phoenix, 602-252-3699

Perelman, Alvin Howard (10 mentions)
FMS-Canada, 1976
Certification: Pediatric Endocrinology, Pediatrics
10900 N Scottsdale Rd #504, Scottsdale, 480-991-2230
9700 N 91st St #B220, Scottsdale, 480-991-2230

Roust, Lori Rae (8 mentions)
Mayo Med Sch, 1986 *Certification:* Endocrinology,
   Diabetes, and Metabolism, Internal Medicine
13400 E Shea Blvd, Scottsdale, 480-301-8000

Rudgear, Kristina Blohm (7 mentions)
U of Nevada, 1999 *Certification:* Endocrinology, Diabetes,
   and Metabolism, Geriatric Medicine, Internal Medicine
7344 E Deer Valley Rd #100, Scottsdale, 480-513-1042

Whitaker, Michael David (9 mentions)
FMS-Canada, 1976
13400 E Shea Blvd, Scottsdale, 480-301-8291

Family Practice *(see note on page 9)*

Austin, Linda Lee (3 mentions)
U of Missouri, 1990
1300 N 12th St #611, Phoenix, 602-254-2200

Borg, Ronald Edward (3 mentions)
U of Nebraska, 1979 *Certification:* Family Medicine
4950 E Elliot Rd, Phoenix, 480-893-2900

Burns, Steven Carl (3 mentions)
U of Oklahoma, 1983 *Certification:* Family Medicine
2034 E Southern Ave #0, Tempe, 480-777-0077

Carrington, Edward Arthur (6 mentions)
FMS-Canada, 1968 *Certification:* Family Medicine
2600 E Southern Ave #F4, Tempe, 480-838-3035

Collins, Roseanne Kelton (4 mentions)
U of Arizona, 1990 *Certification:* Family Medicine
4250 E Camelback Rd #K100, Phoenix, 602-224-9218

Darby-Stewart, Andrea L. (4 mentions)
U of California-Los Angeles, 1997 *Certification:* Family Medicine
13737 N 92nd St, Scottsdale, 480-860-4800

Dearing, James Joseph (5 mentions)
Western U, 1984
750 E Thunderbird Rd #1, Phoenix, 602-942-8512

Dobrusin, Richard Seth (4 mentions)
New York Coll of Osteopathic Med, 1984
1345 E McKellips Rd #106, Mesa, 480-833-1800

Eckert, Ruth Louise (4 mentions)
Indiana U, 1976 *Certification:* Family Medicine
6501 E Greenway Pkwy #160 Bldg 6, Scottsdale, 480-948-9903

Edwards, Frederick David (3 mentions)
U of Arizona, 1979 *Certification:* Family Medicine
13737 N 92nd St, Scottsdale, 480-860-4800

Fauer, Robert Jay (3 mentions)
U of California-Davis, 1982 *Certification:* Family Medicine
4045 E Bell Rd #105, Phoenix, 602-923-6666

Feldman, Martin Alan (3 mentions)
Des Moines U, 1984
3229 E Greenway Rd #101, Phoenix, 602-942-3750

Hopkins, John James, Jr. (3 mentions)
FMS-Mexico, 1983 *Certification:* Family Medicine
13555 W McDowell Rd #101, Goodyear, 623-935-4700

Hoshiwara, Steven Tatsuo (7 mentions)
U of Arizona, 1988 *Certification:* Family Medicine
11209 N Tatum Blvd #180, Phoenix, 602-494-5155

Hovan, Michael John (5 mentions)
U of Colorado, 1990 *Certification:* Family Medicine
13737 N 92nd St, Scottsdale, 480-860-4800

Johnson, Kim David (3 mentions)
FMS-Canada, 1984
4840 E Indian School Rd #101, Phoenix, 602-224-1900

Martin, Dean Thomas (3 mentions)
SUNY-Upstate Med U, 1979 *Certification:* Family Medicine
755 E McDowell Rd, Phoenix, 602-271-3700

McHenry, Lawrence M. (4 mentions)
Des Moines U, 1995
9821 N 95th St #101, Scottsdale, 480-391-5004
2111 E Highland Ave #300, Phoenix, 480-391-5004
1257 W Warner Rd #A4, Chandler, 480-963-6144
725 W Elliot Rd #105, Gilbert, 480-963-6144

Mullins, Janet Lee (3 mentions)
U of New Mexico, 1985 *Certification:* Family Medicine
16611 S 40th St #120, Phoenix, 480-706-4100

Onofrei, Alex J. (3 mentions)
Med Coll of Wisconsin, 1995 *Certification:* Family Medicine
6130 E Brown Rd, Mesa, 480-807-3554

Rada, Gary Alan (6 mentions)
U of Nebraska, 1966 *Certification:* Family Medicine
18404 N Tatum Blvd #101, Phoenix, 602-992-1900

Sieckmann, Paul Wade (3 mentions)
U of Nebraska, 1989 *Certification:* Family Medicine
10210 N 92nd St #106, Scottsdale, 480-661-1755

Stolzberg, Ned Darrel (4 mentions)
U of Massachusetts, 1993 *Certification:* Family Medicine
18700 N 64th Dr #205, Glendale, 623-362-8866

Whitely, Susan Mary (7 mentions)
Ohio State U, 1994 *Certification:* Family Medicine
333 W Thomas Rd #208, Phoenix, 602-230-0777

Wickes, Susan Lee (4 mentions)
U of California-Irvine, 1981 *Certification:* Family Medicine
13737 N 92nd St, Scottsdale, 480-860-4800

Wilder, Susan Shern (3 mentions)
George Washington U, 1988 *Certification:* Family Medicine
13737 N 92nd St, Scottsdale, 480-301-8000
8757 E Bell Rd, Scottsdale, 480-860-5500

Williams, John James (3 mentions)
U of Arizona, 1984 *Certification:* Family Medicine
9327 N 3rd St #100, Phoenix, 602-371-3100

Wolfrey, Jeffrey Douglas (3 mentions)
U of Virginia, 1983 *Certification:* Family Medicine
1300 N 12th St #605, Phoenix, 602-239-4567

Gastroenterology

Altman, Michael Scott (8 mentions)
Tulane U, 1969 *Certification:* Gastroenterology, Internal Medicine
340 E Palm Ln #260, Phoenix, 602-266-1718
10290 N 92nd St #101, Scottsdale, 480-767-3100

Bal, Daljit S. (5 mentions)
Certification: Gastroenterology
14155 N 83rd Ave #122, Peoria, 602-993-3600

Decker, G. Anton (5 mentions)
FMS-South Africa, 1993
Certification: Gastroenterology, Internal Medicine
13400 E Shea Blvd, Scottsdale, 480-301-8000

Foutch, Philip Gregory (6 mentions)
Midwestern U Chicago Coll of Osteopathic Med, 1978
Certification: Gastroenterology, Internal Medicine
1520 S Dobson Rd #302, Mesa, 480-461-1088

Grade, Andrew Justman (5 mentions)
Med Coll of Wisconsin, 1991
1520 S Dobson Rd #302, Mesa, 480-461-1088

Heigh, Russell Irwin (5 mentions)
SUNY-Upstate Med U, 1983
Certification: Gastroenterology, Internal Medicine
13400 E Shea Blvd, Scottsdale, 480-301-8000

Honan, Vincent J. (11 mentions)
Albany Med Coll, 1987 *Certification:* Gastroenterology
1300 N 12th St #603, Phoenix, 602-254-6686

Kenny, Fredrick Ivan (12 mentions)
U of Oklahoma, 1973
Certification: Gastroenterology, Internal Medicine
349 E Coronado Rd, Phoenix, 602-266-5678

Kogan, Frederick J. (5 mentions)
U of Utah, 1979
Certification: Gastroenterology, Internal Medicine
13640 N Plaza Del Rio Blvd, Peoria, 623-876-3840

Leighton, Jonathan Andrew (5 mentions)
U of Arizona, 1981
Certification: Gastroenterology, Internal Medicine
13400 E Shea Blvd, Scottsdale, 480-301-8000

Mellen, Jay Robert (5 mentions)
FMS-Mexico, 1977 *Certification:* Internal Medicine
3501 N Scottsdale Rd #320, Scottsdale, 480-424-7228

Mills, Michael Robert (8 mentions)
Tulane U, 1991 *Certification:* Gastroenterology
349 E Coronado Rd, Phoenix, 602-266-5678

Montes, Ramon G. (10 mentions)
U of Puerto Rico, 1978
Certification: Pediatric Gastroenterology, Pediatrics
9755 N 90th St #C200, Scottsdale, 480-391-8989

Pass, Larry Fred (16 mentions)
Mount Sinai Sch of Med, 1978
Certification: Gastroenterology, Internal Medicine
10290 N 92nd St #200, Scottsdale, 480-391-9400

Ramzan, Nizar Nooruddin (5 mentions)
FMS-Pakistan, 1988
Certification: Gastroenterology, Internal Medicine
8761 E Bell Rd #105, Scottsdale, 480-219-6662

Rock, Michael Vincent (9 mentions)
Hahnemann U, 1971
Certification: Gastroenterology, Internal Medicine
1520 S Dobson Rd #302, Mesa, 480-461-1088

Schenkein, Jacqueline P. (7 mentions)
Mount Sinai Sch of Med, 1977
Certification: Pediatric Gastroenterology, Pediatrics
1520 S Dobson Rd #212, Mesa, 602-546-0940

Schwimmer, Michael T. (8 mentions)
Mount Sinai Sch of Med, 1978
1520 S Dobson Rd #303, Mesa, 480-835-9697

Shapiro, Michael S. (9 mentions)
New York U, 1979
Certification: Gastroenterology, Internal Medicine
10181 N 92nd St #101, Scottsdale, 480-657-3400

Shields, Linda Irene (6 mentions)
Oral Roberts U, 1983
Certification: Gastroenterology, Internal Medicine
10290 N 92nd St #101, Scottsdale, 480-767-3100

Silber, Gary Howard (7 mentions)
U of Maryland, 1981
Certification: Pediatric Gastroenterology, Pediatrics
1919 E Thomas Rd, Phoenix, 602-546-0940
10210 N 92nd St #101, Scottsdale, 602-239-5780
909 E Brill St, Phoenix, 602-239-5780

Wadas, Darrell Duane (13 mentions)
U of Colorado, 1981
Certification: Gastroenterology, Internal Medicine
1300 N 12th St #603, Phoenix, 602-254-6686

Wells, John Joseph (12 mentions)
George Washington U, 1978
Certification: Gastroenterology, Internal Medicine
9327 N 3rd St #306, Phoenix, 602-279-3575
3811 E Bell Rd #304, Phoenix, 602-493-3030

Wiss, Barry R. (5 mentions)
Des Moines U, 1979
19636 N 27th Ave #301, Phoenix, 623-587-0580

Yokois, Nancy Uebler (5 mentions)
Rosalind Franklin U, 1987
Certification: Pediatric Gastroenterology
9755 N 90th St #C200, Scottsdale, 480-391-8989

Zitomer, Norman (11 mentions)
Certification: Gastroenterology, Internal Medicine
8573 E Princess Dr #215B, Scottsdale, 480-563-5757

General Surgery

Austin, James Leslie (5 mentions)
U of Kentucky, 1976 *Certification:* Surgery
755 E McDowell Rd, Phoenix, 602-271-5150
925 E McDowell Rd, Phoenix, 602-239-6800

Brothwell, John James (7 mentions)
Oral Roberts U, 1983 *Certification:* Surgery
5757 W Thunderbird Rd #E265, Glendale, 602-843-8317

Castillo, Charles Edward (11 mentions)
U of New Mexico, 1986 *Certification:* Surgery
1300 N 12th St #505, Phoenix, 602-340-0201
2320 N 3rd St, Phoenix, 602-340-0201

Charles, Edward Hurley (7 mentions)
Med U of South Carolina, 1994 *Certification:* Surgery
5757 W Thunderbird Rd #E265, Glendale, 602-843-8317

Cooper, Richard Edward (6 mentions)
U of Southern California, 1988 *Certification:* Surgery
1500 S Dobson Rd #313, Mesa, 480-969-4138
1520 S Dobson Rd #305, Mesa, 480-969-4138

Davis, Bruce Carlyle (7 mentions)
U of Illinois, 1978 *Certification:* Surgery
6641 E Baywood Ave #B3, Mesa, 480-985-9184
6242 E Arbor Ave #101, Mesa, 480-985-9184

Detlefs, Corey Lane (5 mentions)
U of Arizona, 1986 *Certification:* Surgery, Surgical Critical Care
925 E McDowell Rd, Phoenix, 602-239-2391

Deyden, William (7 mentions)
FMS-Mexico, 1971 *Certification:* Surgery
1520 S Dobson Rd #214, Mesa, 480-833-7441

Donahue, Edward Joseph (6 mentions)
Temple U, 1979 *Certification:* Surgery
333 W Thomas Rd #203, Phoenix, 602-274-6088

Eden, Gary W. (8 mentions)
Philadelphia Coll of Osteopathic Med, 1980
5440 E Southern Ave #105, Mesa, 480-644-0424

Elsner, Heinz Juergen (5 mentions)
Indiana U, 1969 *Certification:* Surgery
1450 S Dobson Rd #A300, Mesa, 480-964-3884

Evani, Venkatarama (5 mentions)
U of Michigan, 1986 *Certification:* Surgery
4250 E Camelback Rd #K-200, Phoenix, 602-977-0136

Freedman, Bruce Edward (11 mentions)
U of Arizona, 1982 *Certification:* Surgery
10290 N 92nd St #305, Scottsdale, 480-941-0866

Gilles, Pierre Claude (8 mentions)
Northwestern U, 1977 *Certification:* Surgery
10210 N 92nd St #207, Scottsdale, 480-860-4466

Gladding, Sandy Burns (4 mentions)
U of Missouri-Kansas City, 1988 *Certification:* Surgery
9305 W Thomas Rd #250, Phoenix, 623-936-5406

Gray, Richard John (7 mentions)
Michigan State U, 1995 *Certification:* Surgery
13400 E Shea Blvd, Scottsdale, 480-301-8000

Grisoni, Enrique (4 mentions)
FMS-Argentina, 1970 *Certification:* Pediatric Surgery
1432 S Dobson Rd #301, Mesa, 480-464-9400

Hernandez, Edgar H. (4 mentions)
U of Utah, 1978 *Certification:* Surgery
1727 W Frye Rd #140, Chandler, 480-821-3632

Matlin, Charles (4 mentions)
Rosalind Franklin U, 1980 *Certification:* Surgery
1728 W Glendale Ave #100, Phoenix, 602-249-0839

McGill, Leigh Craig (7 mentions)
U of Colorado, 1975 *Certification:* Pediatric Surgery
1920 E Cambridge Ave #201, Phoenix, 602-254-5561
5757 W Thunderbird Rd #E-353, Glendale, 602-254-5561

Muddaraj, Rama K. (4 mentions)
FMS-India, 1972 *Certification:* Surgery
13555 W McDowell Rd #204, Goodyear, 623-512-4260

Notrica, David Morris (8 mentions)
Emory U, 1992 *Certification:* Pediatric Surgery, Surgery
1920 E Cambridge Ave #201, Phoenix, 602-254-5561

Perry, Richard Taylor (17 mentions)
U of Arizona, 1976 *Certification:* Surgery
1300 N 12th St #512, Phoenix, 602-258-1519

Petelin, Paul Michael (12 mentions)
Creighton U, 1969 *Certification:* Surgery
500 W Thomas Rd #980, Phoenix, 602-406-8750

Pockaj, Barbara Anamarie (8 mentions)
Vanderbilt U, 1987 *Certification:* Surgery
13400 E Shea Blvd, Scottsdale, 480-301-8000

Rodriguez, Francisco N. (7 mentions)
FMS-Chile, 1984 *Certification:* Surgery
3805 E Bell Rd #4800, Scottsdale, 602-996-4747
10210 N 92nd St #302, Scottsdale, 602-996-4747

Rosenthal, Stephen R. (7 mentions)
U of Toledo, 1981 *Certification:* Surgery
10210 N 92nd St #103, Scottsdale, 480-661-4200

Rula, James Gregory (19 mentions)
U of Mississippi, 1984 *Certification:* Surgery
1500 S Dobson Rd #313, Mesa, 480-969-4138
1520 S Dobson Rd #305, Mesa, 480-969-4138

Runfola, Mark Anthony (6 mentions)
U of Buffalo, 1993 *Certification:* Surgery
1520 S Dobson Rd #305, Mesa, 480-969-4138

Russell, James Craig (4 mentions)
FMS-Canada, 1979 *Certification:* Surgery, Surgical Critical Care
500 W Thomas Rd #750, Phoenix, 602-266-4388
5847 S 16th St, Phoenix, 602-249-0212

Schlinkert, Richard T. (7 mentions)
U of Toledo, 1981 *Certification:* Surgery
13400 E Shea Blvd, Scottsdale, 480-301-8000

Sibley, Elena (5 mentions)
FMS-Canada, 1988 *Certification:* Surgery
3604 N Wells Fargo Ave #L, Scottsdale, 480-947-7401

Singer, Jeffrey Alan (6 mentions)
New York Med Coll, 1976 *Certification:* Surgery
3805 E Bell Rd #4800, Phoenix, 602-996-4747

Van Lier Ribbink, Jeffrey (19 mentions)
Tulane U, 1983 *Certification:* Surgery
10290 N 92nd St #305, Scottsdale, 480-941-0866

Wang, Ping Yeu (7 mentions)
Yale U, 1992 *Certification:* Surgery
13640 N Plaza Del Rio Blvd, Peoria, 623-876-3910

Zacher, Keith Gregory (4 mentions)
Creighton U, 1996 *Certification:* Surgery
3501 N Scottsdale Rd #110, Scottsdale, 480-945-0663

Zannis, Victor John (5 mentions)
U of California-Los Angeles, 1976 *Certification:* Surgery
2525 W Greenway Rd #130, Phoenix, 602-942-8000

Geriatrics

Bernstein, Scott Leland (3 mentions)
U of Illinois, 1992 *Certification:* Internal Medicine
9458 E Ironwood Square Dr #102, Scottsdale, 480-767-7699

Hamilton, Gillian Lowes (3 mentions)
U of Arizona, 1981 *Certification:* Geriatric Medicine,
Hospice and Palliative Medicine, Internal Medicine
1300 N 12th St #605, Phoenix, 602-287-7055

Levy, Kenneth Irwin (8 mentions)
Tufts U, 1986 *Certification:* Geriatric Medicine, Internal Medicine
6838 N 23rd Ave, Phoenix, 602-864-8800

Paull, Dana Michael (3 mentions)
George Washington U, 1981 *Certification:* Internal Medicine
7301 E 2nd St #300, Scottsdale, 480-949-9047

Rollingher, Irving M. (12 mentions)
FMS-Canada, 1984 *Certification:* Internal Medicine
7301 E 2nd St #300, Scottsdale, 480-949-9047

Sampson, Ronald Clifford (4 mentions)
U of Vermont, 1979 *Certification:* Internal Medicine
7525 E Broadway Rd #2, Mesa, 480-981-9800

Hematology/Oncology

Bachrach, Harrison J. (10 mentions)
U of Buffalo, 1981
Certification: Hematology, Internal Medicine, Medical Oncology
6424 E Broadway Rd #104, Mesa, 480-985-5331
1432 S Dobson Rd #106, Mesa, 480-969-3637

Cavalcant, Jack R. (17 mentions)
U of Buffalo, 1973
Certification: Hematology, Internal Medicine, Medical Oncology
1432 S Dobson Rd #106, Mesa, 480-969-3637

Etzl, Michael Matthew, Jr. (6 mentions)
Georgetown U, 1974
Certification: Pediatric Hematology-Oncology, Pediatrics
1919 E Thomas Rd, Phoenix, 602-546-0920

Fitch, Tom Robert (14 mentions)
U of Kansas, 1982 *Certification:* Hematology, Hospice and
Palliative Medicine, Internal Medicine, Medical Oncology
13400 E Shea Blvd, Scottsdale, 480-301-8000

Franks, David Hood, Jr. (6 mentions)
Baylor U, 1968
Certification: Internal Medicine, Medical Oncology
3411 N 5th Ave #400, Phoenix, 602-248-0311

Halepota, Maqbool Alam S. (7 mentions)
FMS-Pakistan, 1985 *Certification:* Medical Oncology
5601 W Eugie Ave #106, Glendale, 480-941-1211

Hecker, Lanny Ian (6 mentions)
U of Miami, 1985
Certification: Hematology, Internal Medicine, Medical Oncology
3330 N 2nd St #400, Phoenix, 602-277-4868
10460 N 92nd St #400, Scottsdale, 480-860-2540
2927 N 7th Ave, Phoenix, 602-406-3153

Isaacs, Jeffrey Dorian (51 mentions)
FMS-South Africa, 1971
Certification: Hematology, Internal Medicine, Medical Oncology
3330 N 2nd St #400, Phoenix, 602-277-4868
11209 N Tatum Blvd #260, Phoenix, 602-494-6800
10460 N 92nd St #400, Scottsdale, 480-860-2540

Kellogg, Christopher M. (6 mentions)
Wayne State U, 1986
Certification: Hematology, Internal Medicine, Medical Oncology
695 S Dobson Rd, Chandler, 480-821-2838

Khanuja, Parvinder Jit S. (8 mentions)
FMS-India, 1983 *Certification:* Hematology, Medical Oncology
695 S Dobson Rd, Chandler, 480-821-2838
6111 E Arbor Ave, Mesa, 480-981-1326

Mendelson, David Strauss (6 mentions)
Ohio State U, 1973
Certification: Hematology, Internal Medicine, Medical Oncology
9023 E Desert Cove Dr #101, Scottsdale, 480-860-5000

Ondreyco, Sharon Marie (6 mentions)
Ohio State U, 1975
Certification: Internal Medicine, Medical Oncology
5601 W Eugie Ave #106, Glendale, 602-978-6255

Paul, David M. (22 mentions)
U of Kansas, 1989 *Certification:* Hematology, Medical Oncology
1300 N 12th St #612, Phoenix, 602-258-4875

Rakkar, Amolnanak S. (7 mentions)
FMS-India, 1989
Certification: Internal Medicine, Medical Oncology
5601 W Eugie Ave #106, Glendale, 602-978-6255

Roberts, Michael S. (15 mentions)
Tufts U, 1979
Certification: Hematology, Internal Medicine, Medical Oncology
3330 N 2nd St, Phoenix, 602-277-4868
10460 N 92nd St #400, Scottsdale, 480-860-2540

Wendt, Albert Guy (11 mentions)
U of Arizona, 1974
Certification: Internal Medicine, Medical Oncology
3411 N 5th Ave #400, Phoenix, 602-248-0448

Zafar, Haider (7 mentions)
FMS-Pakistan, 1989 *Certification:* Hematology, Medical Oncology
5601 W Eugie Ave #106, Glendale, 602-978-6255

Infectious Disease

Blair, Janis E. (10 mentions)
U of Southern California, 1987
Certification: Infectious Disease, Internal Medicine
5777 E Mayo Blvd, Phoenix, 480-342-0161
13400 E Shea Blvd, Scottsdale, 480-301-8000

Burge, John Robert (13 mentions)
Jefferson Med Coll, 1988
10460 N 92nd St #304, Scottsdale, 480-767-7337
3501 N Scottsdale Rd #300, Scottsdale, 480-949-2080

Crowe, Christopher Charles (30 mentions)
Des Moines U, 1987
3501 N Scottsdale Rd #300, Scottsdale, 480-949-7808

Goldberg, John Michael (13 mentions)
U of Pittsburgh, 1995
Certification: Infectious Disease, Internal Medicine
2501 E Southern Ave #22, Tempe, 480-838-1111

Kuberski, Timothy Thomas (20 mentions)
U of Missouri, 1969
Certification: Infectious Disease, Internal Medicine
5757 W Thunderbird Rd #W205, Glendale, 602-439-0274
2423 W Dunlap Ave #100, Phoenix, 602-439-0274

Oscherwitz, Steven Lee (9 mentions)
U of Texas-Dallas, 1986
Certification: Infectious Disease, Internal Medicine
2501 E Southern Ave #22, Tempe, 480-838-1111

Rai, Mandeep K. (12 mentions)
FMS-India, 1989 *Certification:* Infectious Disease
13236 N 7th St, Phoenix, 602-220-2316
13640 N Plaza Del Rio Blvd, Peoria, 623-876-3710

Rudinsky, Mark Francis (23 mentions)
Loyola U Chicago, 1975
Certification: Pediatric Infectious Diseases, Pediatrics
1111 E McDowell Rd #WT5, Phoenix, 602-239-4392
4542 E Mescal St, Phoenix, 602-239-4390

Salas, Steven Dalbert (9 mentions)
U of California-San Diego, 1989
3501 N Scottsdale Rd #300, Scottsdale, 480-949-7808

Infertility

Craig, Harry Randall (12 mentions)
Washington U, 1982 *Certification:* Obstetrics & Gynecology,
    Reproductive Endocrinology/Infertility
2155 E Conference Dr #115, Tempe, 480-831-2445
14861 N Scottsdale Rd #115, Scottsdale, 480-998-9876
6320-B W Union Hills Dr #2700, Glendale, 623-385-7350

Mattox, John Howland (8 mentions)
U of Colorado, 1962 *Certification:* Obstetrics & Gynecology,
    Reproductive Endocrinology/Infertility
1300 N 12th St, Phoenix, 602-343-2767
925 E McDowell Rd, Phoenix, 602-239-4915
1701 E Thomas Rd #101, Phoenix, 602-343-2767

Internal Medicine *(see note on page 9)*

Agnone, Frank Anthony, Jr. (4 mentions)
Georgetown U, 1988
1515 N 9th St #A, Phoenix, 602-258-5545

Asin, Gerald Scott (3 mentions)
U of Oklahoma, 1987 *Certification:* Internal Medicine
11209 N Tatum Blvd #175, Phoenix, 602-652-8900

Bethancourt, Bruce A., Jr. (8 mentions)
U of Arizona, 1980 *Certification:* Internal Medicine
1010 E McDowell Rd #103, Phoenix, 602-254-4424
4400 N 32nd St #140, Phoenix, 602-254-4424

Bloomberg, Robert Joseph (5 mentions)
FMS-Canada, 1976 *Certification:* Internal Medicine
25237 S Sun Lakes Blvd #3, Sun Lakes, 480-895-1090
6301 S McClintock Dr #201, Tempe, 480-838-3100

Borovansky, Jill A. (3 mentions)
13400 E Shea Blvd, Scottsdale, 480-301-8000

Daley, Timothy Michael (4 mentions)
U of Nebraska, 1974 *Certification:* Internal Medicine
13400 E Shea Blvd, Scottsdale, 480-301-8087

De Guzman, John Victor (4 mentions)
Rush U, 1991
4400 N 32nd St #140, Phoenix, 602-258-4018

Elisco, Alvin Bruce (4 mentions)
FMS-Mexico, 1981 *Certification:* Internal Medicine
10900 N Scottsdale Rd #603, Scottsdale, 602-553-8400
2020 N Central Ave #1010, Phoenix, 602-553-8400

Elliott, David Lawrence (3 mentions)
Indiana U, 1975 *Certification:* Internal Medicine
18404 N Tatum Blvd #205, Phoenix, 602-971-5500

Files, Julia Anne (3 mentions)
U of Arizona, 1983 *Certification:* Internal Medicine
13737 N 92nd St, Scottsdale, 480-614-6099

Friedman, Jay Scott (15 mentions)
U of Texas-Dallas, 1983 *Certification:* Internal Medicine
10290 N 92nd St #203, Scottsdale, 480-391-0707

Gassner, Lawrence Phillip (4 mentions)
Washington U, 1988 *Certification:* Internal Medicine
18404 N Tatum Blvd #205, Phoenix, 602-971-5500

Gullen, David John (4 mentions)
U of Arizona, 1975
Certification: Geriatric Medicine, Internal Medicine
3600 N 3rd Ave, Phoenix, 602-277-1458
13400 E Shea Blvd, Scottsdale, 480-301-8087

Ingraham, Paul Rodney (6 mentions)
Louisiana State U, 1985 *Certification:* Internal Medicine
7287 E Earl Dr Bldg D, Scottsdale, 480-840-0800

Johns, Gregory Jacob (3 mentions)
U of Nevada, 1991 *Certification:* Internal Medicine
4400 N 32nd St 3200, Phoenix, 602-522-1900

Kelly, Richard Lee (4 mentions)
U of Texas-San Antonio, 1988 *Certification:* Internal Medicine
3811 E Bell Rd #309, Phoenix, 602-494-5040
3815 E Bell Rd #4100, Phoenix, 602-494-5040

Kimbel, Bruce Keirce, Jr. (3 mentions)
U of Illinois, 1985 *Certification:* Internal Medicine
13400 E Shea Blvd, Scottsdale, 480-301-8000

Kuhl, Wayne Elliott (7 mentions)
U of Iowa, 1972 *Certification:* Internal Medicine
4400 N 32nd St #200, Phoenix, 602-522-1900

Lakin, Douglas Maynard (8 mentions)
Johns Hopkins U, 1987
10250 N 92nd St #216, Scottsdale, 480-614-5800

Leber, Karen Lynn (3 mentions)
Hahnemann U, 1990 *Certification:* Internal Medicine
2600 E Southern Ave #G, Tempe, 480-897-2900

Lee, Marc Lionel (3 mentions)
Wayne State U, 1974
1515 N 9th St #D, Phoenix, 602-252-6855

Levitt, Sandy Lynn (3 mentions)
U of Arizona, 1986 *Certification:* Internal Medicine
2915 E Baseline Rd #101, Gilbert, 480-776-0622

Mayer, Anita Pitot (3 mentions)
Tulane U, 1982
13400 E Shea Blvd, Scottsdale, 480-301-8000

Mengesha, Nolawi Melak (15 mentions)
Albany Med Coll, 1995 *Certification:* Internal Medicine
4400 N 32nd St #140, Phoenix, 602-254-4424

Metzger, Frank J. (3 mentions)
Kansas U Coll of Osteopathic Med, 1978
455 E 4th Pl, Mesa, 480-964-0080

Morgan, Jeffrey William (3 mentions)
Michigan State U Coll of Osteopathic Med, 1992
5757 W Thunderbird Rd #W-310, Glendale, 602-548-7800

Paull, Dana Michael (10 mentions)
George Washington U, 1981 *Certification:* Internal Medicine
7301 E 2nd St #300, Scottsdale, 480-949-9047

Paxton, Donald Eugene (3 mentions)
U of Arizona, 1976 *Certification:* Internal Medicine
500 W Thomas Rd #460, Phoenix, 602-241-9500
202 E Earll Dr #450, Phoenix, 602-241-9500

Poles, Jack Nathan (3 mentions)
Temple U, 1970 *Certification:* Internal Medicine
9100 N 2nd St #121, Phoenix, 602-997-7331

Raju, Jayashree R. (3 mentions)
Midwestern U Chicago Coll of Osteopathic Med, 1992
5757 W Thunderbird Rd #E-155, Glendale, 602-978-4040

Safarian, Raffy Aram (4 mentions)
FMS-Belgium, 1982 *Certification:* Internal Medicine
215 S Power Rd #220, Mesa, 480-981-2700

Sapin, Neil J. (4 mentions)
U of Buffalo, 1971 *Certification:* Internal Medicine
6320 W Union Hills Dr #A-170, Glendale, 623-537-2280

Soriano, Maria Divina F. (3 mentions)
FMS-Philippines, 1990 *Certification:* Internal Medicine
3655 W Anthem Way #A-109, Anthem, 623-505-4479

Staman, Marc Joel (4 mentions)
U of Arizona, 1978 *Certification:* Internal Medicine
350 W Thomas Rd, Phoenix, 602-406-3000

Tingey, Michael Jay (5 mentions)
U of Arizona, 1994 *Certification:* Internal Medicine
2600 E Southern Ave #B2, Tempe, 480-730-5100

Wallace, Mark Randall (8 mentions)
Indiana U, 1988 *Certification:* Internal Medicine
1515 N 9th St #D, Phoenix, 602-252-6855

Young, Peter Si-Hai (4 mentions)
U of Arkansas, 1983 *Certification:* Internal Medicine
3811 E Bell Rd #309, Phoenix, 602-494-5040
3815 E Bell Rd #4100, Phoenix, 602-494-5040

Zipperer, William Paul (4 mentions)
Philadelphia Coll of Osteopathic Med, 1981
455 E 4th Pl, Mesa, 480-964-0080

Nephrology

Boren, Kenneth Ray (6 mentions)
Indiana U, 1972 *Certification:* Endocrinology and
    Metabolism, Internal Medicine, Nephrology
560 W Brown Rd #3006, Mesa, 480-969-8714
135 S Power Rd #110, Mesa, 480-325-7535
2141 E Warner Rd #101, Tempe, 480-969-8714

Chang, Douglas (8 mentions)
U of Kansas, 1985 *Certification:* Internal Medicine, Nephrology
337 E Coronado Rd #201, Phoenix, 602-252-8081

Cherrill, David Alan (7 mentions)
U of Pennsylvania, 1969
Certification: Internal Medicine, Nephrology
7331 E Osborn Dr #150, Scottsdale, 480-994-1238

Cohen, Irvin M. (6 mentions)
U of Maryland, 1972 *Certification:* Internal Medicine, Nephrology
13400 E Shea Blvd, Scottsdale, 480-301-8262

Go, Melissa Michelle (7 mentions)
FMS-Philippines, 1993 *Certification:* Nephrology
337 E Coronado Rd #201, Phoenix, 602-252-8081

Heilman, Raymond L. (10 mentions)
U of Illinois, 1980 *Certification:* Internal Medicine, Nephrology
5777 E Mayo Blvd, Phoenix, 480-342-0161
13400 E Shea Blvd, Scottsdale, 480-301-8000

Joseph, Mark William (12 mentions)
U of Arizona, 1991 *Certification:* Pediatric Nephrology
1919 E Thomas Rd, Phoenix, 602-546-0965

Petrides, Savas (6 mentions)
Hahnemann U, 1989
Certification: Internal Medicine, Nephrology
10200 N 92nd St #240, Scottsdale, 480-551-1057

Rai, Anup (7 mentions)
FMS-India, 1993 *Certification:* Internal Medicine, Nephrology
13943 N 91st Ave #101, Peoria, 623-977-1331
14674 W Mountainview Blvd #204, Surprise, 623-977-1331

Sacks, Paul (15 mentions)
Northwestern U, 1982
Certification: Internal Medicine, Nephrology
15255 N 40th St #135, Phoenix, 602-943-1231

Sturgeon, Georgia Delaney (10 mentions)
West Virginia U, 1985
Certification: Geriatric Medicine, Internal Medicine, Nephrology
7331 E Osborn Dr #150, Scottsdale, 480-994-1238

Swaminathan, Arivazhahan (7 mentions)
FMS-India, 1986 *Certification:* Internal Medicine, Nephrology
5750 W Thunderbird Rd #G-790, Glendale, 602-843-7171

Thomas, Ann (7 mentions)
FMS-India, 1989 *Certification:* Nephrology
10200 N 92nd St #240, Scottsdale, 480-551-1057

Wochos, Daniel Norbert (9 mentions)
U of Wisconsin, 1970
Certification: Internal Medicine, Nephrology
13400 E Shea Blvd, Scottsdale, 480-301-8262

Yee, Berne (14 mentions)
U of Arizona, 1981 *Certification:* Internal Medicine, Nephrology
337 E Coronado Rd #210, Phoenix, 602-252-8081

Neurological Surgery

Barranco, Frank David (22 mentions)
U of Southern California, 1983 *Certification:* Neurological Surgery
2910 N 3rd Ave, Phoenix, 602-406-4760
5757 W Thunderbird Ave #212, Glendale, 602-863-1442
925 E McDowell Rd, Phoenix, 602-254-3151

Dickman, Curtis Alan (11 mentions)
U of Arizona, 1985 *Certification:* Neurological Surgery
2910 N 3rd Ave, Phoenix, 602-406-3932

Ercius, Mark Steven (14 mentions)
U of Illinois, 1978 *Certification:* Neurological Surgery
1520 S Dobson Rd #318, Mesa, 480-833-5209

Fitzpatrick, Brian C. (12 mentions)
U of Buffalo, 1986 *Certification:* Neurological Surgery
7301 E 2nd St #106, Scottsdale, 480-425-8004

Manwaring, Kim Herbert (19 mentions)
U of Washington, 1979 *Certification:* Neurological Surgery
2601 E Roosevelt St, Phoenix, 602-344-5371
1919 E Thomas Rd, Phoenix, 602-344-5371

Marciano, Frederick F. (18 mentions)
Albany Med Coll, 1990 *Certification:* Neurological Surgery
2910 N 3rd Ave, Phoenix, 602-406-4760
7301 E 2nd St #106, Scottsdale, 480-425-8004

Moss, S. David (11 mentions)
U of Utah, 1981 *Certification:* Neurological Surgery
1919 E Thomas Rd, Phoenix, 602-546-0441

Spetzler, Robert F. (44 mentions)
Northwestern U, 1971 *Certification:* Neurological Surgery
2910 N 3rd Ave, Phoenix, 602-406-3489

Theodore, Nicholas (11 mentions)
Georgetown U, 1991 *Certification:* Neurological Surgery
2910 N 3rd Ave, Phoenix, 602-406-3621

Neurology

Adler, Charles Howard (5 mentions)
New York U, 1986 *Certification:* Neurology
13400 E Shea Blvd, Scottsdale, 480-301-8000

Bernes, Saunder Maurice (12 mentions)
Northwestern U, 1977 *Certification:* Neurology with Special Qualifications in Child Neurology, Pediatrics
1919 E Thomas Rd, Phoenix, 602-546-0970

Block, Allan Michael (11 mentions)
Creighton U, 1993 *Certification:* Neurology
10210 N 92nd St #202, Scottsdale, 480-314-5460

Bosch, Erich Peter (6 mentions)
FMS-Austria, 1969 *Certification:* Neurology
13400 E Shea Blvd, Scottsdale, 480-301-8100

Caselli, Richard John (6 mentions)
Columbia U, 1983 *Certification:* Neurology
13400 E Shea Blvd, Scottsdale, 480-301-7162

Dodick, David William (7 mentions)
FMS-Canada, 1990 *Certification:* Neurology, Vascular Neurology
5777 E Mayo Blvd, Phoenix, 480-301-8100

Fineman, Sanford Mark (7 mentions)
U of Texas-Galveston, 1985 *Certification:* Neurology
755 E McDowell Rd, Phoenix, 602-271-3790

Gitt, Jeffrey Scott (6 mentions)
Western U, 1983 *Certification:* Neurology
4921 E Bell Rd #204, Scottsdale, 602-482-2116

Grainger, William Douglas (7 mentions)
U of Arizona, 1981 *Certification:* Neurology
726 N Greenfield Rd #110, Gilbert, 480-834-8885

Hendin, Barry Allen (21 mentions)
Washington U, 1968 *Certification:* Neurology
1331 N 7th St #350, Phoenix, 602-258-3354

Johnson, Darry Scott (6 mentions)
U of Kansas, 1991 *Certification:* Neurology
13760 N 93rd Ave #101, Peoria, 623-876-3940

Kaplan, Allen Mitchell (8 mentions)
Loyola U Chicago, 1966 *Certification:* Neurology with Special Qualifications in Child Neurology, Pediatrics
1919 E Thomas Rd, Phoenix, 602-546-0970

Kaufman, Seth Michael (5 mentions)
Tulane U, 1999
Certification: Neurology, Neuromuscular Medicine
9755 N 90th St #A200, Scottsdale, 480-621-3313

Kumar, Vikram Anand (5 mentions)
New Jersey Med Sch, 2000
1331 N 7th St #275, Phoenix, 602-254-3151

Levine, Todd Dylan (10 mentions)
Duke U, 1993 *Certification:* Neurology
1331 N 7th St #350, Phoenix, 480-860-4800

Moschonas, Constantine (13 mentions)
FMS-Grenada, 1987
9746 N 90th Pl #203, Scottsdale, 480-614-0707

Powers, J. Michael (12 mentions)
U of Iowa, 1971 *Certification:* Neurology
525 N 18th St #602, Phoenix, 602-271-0950
6036 N 19th Ave #506, Phoenix, 602-271-0950

Reese, Gary Norman (13 mentions)
U of Illinois, 1975 *Certification:* Internal Medicine, Neurology
7331 E Osborn Dr #110, Scottsdale, 480-947-7671

Reiser, Jody Beth (7 mentions)
U of Arizona, 1989 *Certification:* Neurology
2702 N 3rd St #2007, Phoenix, 602-200-6999

Schultz, Dale R. (9 mentions)
Midwestern U Chicago Coll of Osteopathic Med, 1970
Certification: Neurology
19841 N 27th Ave #403, Phoenix, 623-780-8838

Steier, Jeffrey D. (5 mentions)
U of Buffalo, 1978 *Certification:* Clinical Neurophysiology, Neurology, Neuromuscular Medicine
9458 E Ironwood Square Dr #101, Scottsdale, 480-314-2099

Suber, David Alan (10 mentions)
Baylor U, 1974 *Certification:* Neurology
2501 E Southern Ave #17, Tempe, 480-838-1000

Travis, Lori Hendin (5 mentions)
U of Arizona, 1998 *Certification:* Neurology
1331 N 7th St #350, Phoenix, 602-258-3354

Winograd, Mark (6 mentions)
Albert Einstein Coll of Med, 1969
Certification: Internal Medicine, Neurology
5757 W Thunderbird Rd #E151, Glendale, 602-843-3811

Obstetrics/Gynecology

Apigo, Maria J. (3 mentions)
Robert W Johnson Med Sch, 1995
Certification: Obstetrics & Gynecology
50 E Dunlap Ave #200, Phoenix, 602-678-1111

Bullaro-Anderer, Deanna L. (3 mentions)
Midwestern U Chicago Coll of Osteopathic Med, 1996
6239 E Brown Rd #112, Mesa, 480-854-2676

Castilla, Julie Anne (4 mentions)
U of Michigan, 1993 *Certification:* Obstetrics & Gynecology
9823 N 95th St #101, Scottsdale, 480-451-8454

Culbertson, Bruce Alan (6 mentions)
Virginia Commonwealth U, 1990
Certification: Obstetrics & Gynecology
530 e tHOMAS rD, Phoenix, 602-351-2229

Damore, Tiersa H. W. (3 mentions)
St Louis U, 1994 *Certification:* Obstetrics & Gynecology
6301 S McClintock Dr #215, Tempe, 480-820-6657

Eckel, Dennis Charles (3 mentions)
Indiana U, 1982 *Certification:* Obstetrics & Gynecology
3501 N Scottsdale Rd #280, Scottsdale, 480-945-6583

Francois, Karrie E. (7 mentions)
Med Coll of Wisconsin, 1995
Certification: Maternal-Fetal Medicine, Obstetrics & Gynecology
6950 Chauncey Ln #150, Phoenix, 480-970-7664

Gomez, Ernesto Morales (4 mentions)
U of Colorado, 1977 *Certification:* Obstetrics & Gynecology
1039 N Country Club Dr, Mesa, 480-834-3784
6644 E Baywood Ave, Mesa, 480-985-8151

Hahn, Carol Ann (3 mentions)
Creighton U, 1989 *Certification:* Obstetrics & Gynecology
333 E Osborn Rd #340, Phoenix, 602-265-9161

Harris, Nancy Bedrick (3 mentions)
Case Western Reserve U, 1986
Certification: Obstetrics & Gynecology
3815 E Bell Rd #4500, Phoenix, 602-992-3162

Holemon, Matthew Lance (3 mentions)
U of Louisville, 1979 *Certification:* Obstetrics & Gynecology
15255 N 40th St #105, Phoenix, 602-867-2690

Huff, Terry Arthur (3 mentions)
Tufts U, 1988 *Certification:* Obstetrics & Gynecology
6242 E Arbor Ave #107, Mesa, 480-897-8000

Ivchenko, Michael W. (3 mentions)
Northeastern Ohio U, 1982 *Certification:* Obstetrics & Gynecology
2501 E Southern Ave #14, Tempe, 480-730-3331

Kaufman, David J. (3 mentions)
New York Coll of Osteopathic Med, 1982
50 E Dunlap Ave #200, Phoenix, 602-678-1111

Kimbro, Laura Therese (3 mentions)
Nova Southeastern Coll of Osteopathic Med, 1990
Certification: Obstetrics & Gynecology
16611 S 40th St #180, Phoenix, 480-785-2100

Kwatra, Julie Baskin (7 mentions)
Ohio State U, 1995 *Certification:* Obstetrics & Gynecology
9823 N 95th St, Scottsdale, 480-451-8454

Kyman, Jack Darryl (3 mentions)
Ohio State U, 1973 *Certification:* Obstetrics & Gynecology
50 E Dunlap Ave #200, Phoenix, 602-678-1111

Laband, Steven J. (4 mentions)
Mount Sinai Sch of Med, 1983
Certification: Obstetrics & Gynecology
3102 E Indian School Rd #130, Phoenix, 602-252-0202

Laughead, Marilyn K. (4 mentions)
U of Arizona, 1971 *Certification:* Obstetrics & Gynecology
9500 E Ironwood Square Dr #124, Scottsdale, 480-860-0550

Lavy, Rebecca Jo (3 mentions)
U of Iowa, 1992 *Certification:* Obstetrics & Gynecology
9377 E Bell Rd #319, Scottsdale, 480-538-5440

Linnerson, Steven Mark (3 mentions)
U of Colorado, 1977 *Certification:* Obstetrics & Gynecology
6301 S McClintock Dr, Tempe, 480-820-6657

Magrina, Javier Francisco (5 mentions)
FMS-Spain, 1972
Certification: Gynecologic Oncology, Obstetrics & Gynecology
13400 E Shea Blvd, Scottsdale, 480-301-8000

Marotz, Robert Jeffrey (4 mentions)
A T Still U, 1979 *Certification:* Obstetrics & Gynecology
4545 E Chandler Blvd #208, Phoenix, 480-961-2330
1950 W Frye Rd, Chandler, 480-895-9555

Marzolf, Susan Marie (3 mentions)
U of Wisconsin, 1992 *Certification:* Obstetrics & Gynecology
13400 E Shea Blvd, Scottsdale, 480-301-8000

Mayer, Staci Ann (3 mentions)
U of Pittsburgh, 1997 *Certification:* Obstetrics & Gynecology
2702 N 3rd St #1000, Phoenix, 602-241-1671

McKernan, Paul Duane (5 mentions)
U of Arizona, 1984 *Certification:* Obstetrics & Gynecology
18699 N 67th Ave #320, Glendale, 623-561-7250

Mechelke, Craig Loren (3 mentions)
Midwestern U Chicago Coll of Osteopathic Med, 1975
815 E University Dr, Mesa, 480-969-3096
4915 E Baseline Rd #126, Gilbert, 480-969-3096

Moon, Jean Marie (3 mentions)
U of Nebraska, 1989 *Certification:* Obstetrics & Gynecology
3501 N Scottsdale Rd #280, Scottsdale, 480-945-6583
10117 N 92nd St #101, Scottsdale, 480-945-6583

Mouer, James Raber (5 mentions)
U of Nebraska, 1964 *Certification:* Obstetrics & Gynecology
500 W Thomas Rd #800, Phoenix, 602-406-3715
222 W Thomas Rd #213, Phoenix, 602-406-3715

Mourad, Jamal (7 mentions)
New York Coll of Osteopathic Med, 1995
Certification: Obstetrics & Gynecology
16611 S 40th St #180, Phoenix, 480-785-2100
2204 S Dobson Rd #202, Mesa, 480-222-0699

Newman, Robert V. (5 mentions)
U of Utah, 1979 *Certification:* Obstetrics & Gynecology
10261 N 92nd St, Scottsdale, 480-443-4437

Saretsky, Robert A. (3 mentions)
Des Moines U, 1977
6525 W Sack Dr #208, Glendale, 623-566-2004

Schwartz, Kathleen Anne (3 mentions)
Vanderbilt U, 1987
Certification: Anatomic Pathology, Obstetrics & Gynecology
11209 N Tatum Blvd #255, Phoenix, 602-494-5050
4530 N 32nd St #100, Phoenix, 602-468-3912

Semrad, Sidney Eugene (3 mentions)
A T Still U, 1982
6944 E Broadway Rd, Mesa, 480-464-2101

Snell, Sarah J. (14 mentions)
Certification: Obstetrics & Gynecology
9500 E Ironwood Square Dr #124, Scottsdale, 480-860-0550

Sorkin-Wells, Valerie (8 mentions)
U of Toledo, 1982 *Certification:* Obstetrics & Gynecology
3815 E Bell Rd #4500, Phoenix, 602-992-3162

Swarup, Monte Rajul (3 mentions)
U of Pittsburgh, 1994 *Certification:* Obstetrics & Gynecology
1950 W Frye Rd, Chandler, 480-895-9555

Szmuc, Edward Dale (4 mentions)
U of Toledo, 1979 *Certification:* Obstetrics & Gynecology
2034 E Southern Ave #T, Tempe, 480-820-9722

Tom, Judy Wonkuen (6 mentions)
Oregon Health Sciences U, 1991
Certification: Obstetrics & Gynecology
5601 W Eugie Ave #100, Glendale, 602-978-1500

Urig, Michael Anthony (6 mentions)
U of Colorado, 1985 *Certification:* Obstetrics & Gynecology
2702 N 3rd St #1000, Phoenix, 602-241-1671
4350 E Ray Rd #117, Phoenix, 480-759-9191
1661 E Camelback Rd #160, Phoenix, 602-241-1674
4530 E Ray Rd #172, Phoenix, 480-759-9191

Villa, Andrew Charles, Jr. (3 mentions)
U of South Florida, 1987 *Certification:* Obstetrics & Gynecology
1951 W Frye Rd, Chandler, 480-895-9555

Webb, George Herbert, III (9 mentions)
Tulane U, 1980 *Certification:* Obstetrics & Gynecology
8752 E Via De Commercio #2, Scottsdale, 480-425-8700

Wilson, Deborah D. (6 mentions)
George Washington U, 1979
Certification: Obstetrics & Gynecology
8997 E Desert Cove Ave 1st Fl, Scottsdale, 480-860-4791

Ophthalmology

Aiello, Joseph Peter (5 mentions)
Tulane U, 1983 *Certification:* Ophthalmology
7245 E Osborn Rd #4, Scottsdale, 480-994-5012
300 E Osborn Rd #201, Phoenix, 602-254-7255
4800 N 22nd St, Phoenix, 602-955-1000

Bullington, Ann (11 mentions)
U of Arizona, 1984 *Certification:* Ophthalmology
3330 N 2nd St #501, Phoenix, 602-266-6888
4400 N 32nd St #280, Phoenix, 602-266-6888

Bullington, Robert H., Jr. (14 mentions)
U of Arizona, 1985 *Certification:* Ophthalmology
3330 N 2nd St #501, Phoenix, 602-266-6888
4400 N 32nd St #280, Phoenix, 602-266-6888

Cassidy, Brendan Patrick (6 mentions)
Albany Med Coll, 1989
1836 N 35th Ave, Phoenix, 602-222-2234
1331 N 7th St #100, Phoenix, 602-222-2234

Cassidy, Craig R. (9 mentions)
Kansas U Coll of Osteopathic Med, 1977
2125 W Indian School Rd, Phoenix, 602-274-4992

Cooper, Dennis Charles (7 mentions)
Washington U, 1971 *Certification:* Ophthalmology
1402 N Miller Rd #C2, Scottsdale, 480-949-1960
7331 E Osborn Dr #130, Scottsdale, 480-949-1960

Hill, Warren Edward (7 mentions)
U of Arizona, 1980 *Certification:* Ophthalmology
5620 E Broadway Rd, Mesa, 480-981-6111

Kahn, Lawrence Stephen (7 mentions)
Indiana U, 1981 *Certification:* Ophthalmology
2450 E Guadalupe Rd #107, Gilbert, 480-507-0600

Kanda, Leslie Akemi (5 mentions)
Northwestern U, 1993 *Certification:* Ophthalmology
300 E Osborn Rd #100, Phoenix, 602-263-8098
2320 N 3rd St, Phoenix, 602-470-5000

Kilpatrick, Dennis Lee (5 mentions)
U of Arizona, 1981 *Certification:* Ophthalmology
7550 E 2nd St, Scottsdale, 480-994-1872
3320 N Miller Rd, Scottsdale, 480-949-1208

Matsumoto, Bertram T. (7 mentions)
Washington U, 1991 *Certification:* Ophthalmology
3200 S Country Club Way, Tempe, 480-839-0206
5110 E Warner Rd #150, Phoenix, 480-783-6893

Moretsky, Sanford L. (13 mentions)
Kansas U Coll of Osteopathic Med, 1974
Certification: Ophthalmology
2125 W Indian School Rd, Phoenix, 602-274-4992
160 W University Dr #1, Mesa, 480-833-0014

O'Neil, James William (9 mentions)
Creighton U, 1987 *Certification:* Ophthalmology
4648 E Shea Blvd #A-100, Phoenix, 480-835-0709
13838 S 46th Pl #105, Phoenix, 480-835-0709
1520 S Dobson Rd #202, Mesa, 480-835-0709
1920 E Cambridge Ave #203, Phoenix, 602-252-9663

Pachtman, Michael Arthur (6 mentions)
U of Kentucky, 1978 *Certification:* Ophthalmology
1520 S Dobson Rd #202, Mesa, 480-835-0709
4648 E Shea Blvd #A-100, Phoenix, 480-835-0709
1220 S Higley Rd #106, Mesa, 480-835-0709

Petelin, Paul Michael, Jr. (5 mentions)
U of Arizona, 1997 *Certification:* Ophthalmology
14275 N 87th St, Scottsdale, 480-483-8882

Plotnik, James Lewis (6 mentions)
U of Michigan, 1989 *Certification:* Ophthalmology
1920 E Cambridge Ave #203, Phoenix, 602-252-9663
20201 N Scottsdale Health Care Dr, Scottsdale, 480-513-6920

Shorb, Stanley Roy (6 mentions)
Jefferson Med Coll, 1966 *Certification:* Ophthalmology
500 W Thomas Rd #250, Phoenix, 602-263-9345
3201 W Peoria Ave #C603, Phoenix, 602-863-2936
7125 E Lincoln Dr #B215, Scottsdale, 480-998-3398

Tozer, Randall Keith (5 mentions)
Southern Illinois U, 1978
Certification: Internal Medicine, Ophthalmology
9811 N 95th St #101, Scottsdale, 480-947-4493

Orthopedics

Beauchamp, Christopher P. (13 mentions)
FMS-Canada, 1978 *Certification:* Orthopaedic Surgery
5779 E Mayo Blvd, Phoenix, 480-342-2762

Bradway, John Kent (4 mentions)
U of Arizona, 1983 *Certification:* Orthopaedic Surgery
10213 N 92nd St #101, Scottsdale, 480-860-6005

Brennan, Michael Joseph (5 mentions)
Med Coll of Wisconsin, 1979 *Certification:* Orthopaedic Surgery
2222 E Highland Ave #425, Phoenix, 602-667-6640

Bruns, Brad Roy (7 mentions)
U of Arizona, 1984 *Certification:* Orthopaedic Surgery
5620 E Bell Rd, Scottsdale, 602-493-9361
13640 N 7th St, Phoenix, 602-863-2040

Crothers, John Howey (9 mentions)
Vanderbilt U, 1970 *Certification:* Orthopaedic Surgery
2940 E Banner Gateway Dr, Gilbert, 480-512-8880

Fox, Jonathan Richard (4 mentions)
U of Nebraska, 1979 *Certification:* Orthopaedic Surgery
4450 S Rural Rd #C-100, Tempe, 480-345-2031

Hedley, Anthony Keith (4 mentions)
FMS-South Africa, 1968
2222 E Highland Ave #400, Phoenix, 602-553-3113
5757 W Thunderbird Rd #W404, Glendale, 602-843-8054
2122 E Highland Ave #300, Phoenix, 602-553-3113

Hrasky, Gregory Michael (7 mentions)
Rush U, 1987 *Certification:* Orthopaedic Surgery
1450 S Dobson Rd, Mesa, 480-551-0300
9003 E Shey Blvd, Scottsdale, 480-551-0300

Kassman, Steven Richard (4 mentions)
U of Buffalo, 1987 *Certification:* Orthopaedic Surgery
444 W Osborn Rd #200, Phoenix, 602-230-1400
20325 51st Ave #124 Bldg 4, Glendale, 602-230-1400

Kozinn, Stuart C. (7 mentions)
U of California-Los Angeles, 1982
Certification: Orthopaedic Surgery
7301 E 2nd St #102, Scottsdale, 480-994-1149
3501 N Scottsdale Rd, Scottsdale, 480-994-1149

Lee, Michael Thomas (10 mentions)
U of Arizona, 1988 *Certification:* Orthopaedic Surgery
2222 E Highland Ave #425, Phoenix, 602-667-6640

Longo, Joseph A., III (5 mentions)
U of Arizona, 1982 *Certification:* Orthopaedic Surgery
3300 N 75th St, Scottsdale, 480-941-5656

Lucero, Edward Michael (6 mentions)
U of California-Los Angeles, 1987
Certification: Orthopaedic Surgery
2222 E Highland Ave #425, Phoenix, 602-667-6640

Martin, Richard Charles (4 mentions)
U of Illinois, 1984 *Certification:* Orthopaedic Surgery
5620 E Bell Rd, Scottsdale, 602-493-9361

Ott, David M. (8 mentions)
U of California-Los Angeles, 1982
Certification: Orthopaedic Surgery
690 N Cofco Center Ct #290, Phoenix, 602-631-1400

Rockowitz, Neal L. (4 mentions)
FMS-Canada, 1982 *Certification:* Orthopaedic Surgery
3104 E Indian School Rd #100, Phoenix, 602-957-1233

Rosen, Marc Jeffrey (5 mentions)
U of Cincinnati, 1976 *Certification:* Orthopaedic Surgery
5605 W Eugie Ave #111, Glendale, 602-298-8888
18699 N 67th Ave #120, Glendale, 623-583-9800

Russo, Vincent J. (10 mentions)
Certification: Orthopaedic Surgery
10290 N 92nd St #103, Scottsdale, 480-860-1322

Salyer, William Allan (4 mentions)
U of Arizona, 1980 *Certification:* Orthopaedic Surgery
690 N Cofco Center Ct #290, Phoenix, 602-258-8029

Sanders, Larry J. (11 mentions)
U of Oklahoma, 1974 *Certification:* Orthopaedic Surgery
1520 S Dobson Rd #312, Mesa, 480-962-8485

Seltzer, Dana Georges (5 mentions)
U of Southern California, 1986 *Certification:* Orthopaedic Surgery
500 W Thomas Rd #850, Phoenix, 602-406-2663
1800 E Van Buren St, Phoenix, 602-267-5373

Shindell, Richard Larry (12 mentions)
Med Coll of Wisconsin, 1982 *Certification:* Orthopaedic Surgery
333 E Osborn Rd #255, Phoenix, 602-604-8941
10210 N 92nd St Plaza 2 #101, Phoenix, 602-604-8941
1500 S Dobson Rd Bldg 2 #200, Mesa, 602-604-8941

Spangehl, Mark Joseph (6 mentions)
FMS-Canada, 1989 *Certification:* Orthopaedic Surgery
5710 E Mayo Blvd, Phoenix, 480-342-2377

Van De Wyngaerde, David G. (5 mentions)
U of Arizona, 1986
444 W Osborn Rd #200, Phoenix, 602-230-1400
690 N Cofco Center Ct #290, Phoenix, 602-631-3161

Whirlow, Janet E. (5 mentions)
Hahnemann U, 1986 *Certification:* Orthopaedic Surgery
10200 N 92nd St #110, Scottsdale, 480-767-0711

White, Gregory Richard (12 mentions)
Vanderbilt U, 1991 *Certification:* Orthopaedic Surgery
1641 E Osborn Rd #6, Phoenix, 602-241-0276

Zeman, David Charles (5 mentions)
U of Arizona, 1981 *Certification:* Orthopaedic Surgery
2222 E Highland Ave #425, Phoenix, 602-667-6640

Otorhinolaryngology

Baldree, Mark Edward (15 mentions)
Loyola U Chicago, 1977 *Certification:* Otolaryngology
4250 E Camelback Rd #K-250, Phoenix, 602-254-9398

Bridge, Robert Stuart (9 mentions)
U of Nebraska, 1984 *Certification:* Otolaryngology
3811 E Bell Rd #3200, Phoenix, 602-788-0088

Chapel, Dan Michael (7 mentions)
U of Missouri, 1984 *Certification:* Otolaryngology
333 E Virginia Ave #101, Phoenix, 602-264-4834
5750 W Thunderbird Rd Bldg A #100, Glendale, 602-938-3205

Dyer, Jeffrey James (7 mentions)
Wake Forest U, 1992 *Certification:* Otolaryngology
11209 N Tatum Blvd, Phoenix, 602-494-5090

Fucci, Michael John (7 mentions)
Hahnemann U, 1987 *Certification:* Neurotology, Otolaryngology
225 S Dobson Rd, Chandler, 480-558-5306

Heiland, Kurt Edward (13 mentions)
U of Arizona, 1992 *Certification:* Otolaryngology
8752 E Via De Commercio #1, Scottsdale, 480-423-3150

Hinni, Michael Lee (8 mentions)
U of Missouri-Kansas City, 1988 *Certification:* Otolaryngology
13400 E Shea Blvd, Scottsdale, 480-301-7144
5777 E Mayo Blvd, Phoenix, 480-342-2928

Macias, John David (8 mentions)
Stanford U, 1988 *Certification:* Neurotology, Otolaryngology
1515 N 9th St #B, Phoenix, 602-257-4228

McKenna, Jeffrey Alan (8 mentions)
U of Arizona, 1986 *Certification:* Otolaryngology
5110 E Warner Rd #100, Phoenix, 480-753-1459

Milligan, John Maurice (16 mentions)
Indiana U, 1979 *Certification:* Otolaryngology
333 E Virginia Ave #101, Phoenix, 602-264-4834
6565 E Greenway Pkwy #101, Scottsdale, 480-948-2056

Orozco, Charles Richard (9 mentions)
U of Washington, 1984 *Certification:* Otolaryngology
4250 E Camelback Rd, Phoenix, 602-253-9026

Raines, John Michael (22 mentions)
U of California-San Francisco, 1974 *Certification:* Otolaryngology
6565 E Greenway Pkwy #101, Scottsdale, 480-948-2056
333 E Virginia Ave #101, Phoenix, 602-264-4834

Simms, David Leslie (9 mentions)
U of Oklahoma, 1984 *Certification:* Otolaryngology
333 E Virginia Ave #101, Phoenix, 602-264-4834
6565 E Greenway Pkwy #101, Scottsdale, 480-948-3959
5750 W Thunderbird Rd #A100, Glendale, 602-938-3205
13260 N 94th Dr #101, Peoria, 623-933-2732

Weiner, Jordan S. (9 mentions)
Albany Med Coll, 1994 *Certification:* Otolaryngology
8752 E Via De Commercio #1, Scottsdale, 480-423-3150

Pain Medicine

Borowsky, Stephen Michael (7 mentions)
Temple U, 1970 *Certification:* Anesthesiology, Pain Medicine
1030 E McDowell Rd, Phoenix, 602-254-1159
5847 S 16th St, Phoenix, 602-249-0212

Rubin, Mark Jonathan (7 mentions)
U of South Florida, 1991 *Certification:* Anesthesiology
20950 N Tatum Blvd #300, Phoenix, 480-222-7246

Spiro, Mark Charles (7 mentions)
U of Cincinnati, 1986
Certification: Anesthesiology, Pain Medicine
2901 N Central Ave #500, Phoenix, 602-277-5222

Stearns, Lisa Jo (7 mentions)
U of Nebraska, 1991 *Certification:* Anesthesiology
1046 N 92nd St #300, Scottsdale, 480-889-0780

Trentman, Terrence Lee (7 mentions)
Tulane U, 1990 *Certification:* Anesthesiology, Pain Medicine
13400 E Shea Blvd, Scottsdale, 480-301-8000

Pathology

Allred, Ted R. (3 mentions)
U of Utah, 1987
Certification: Anatomic Pathology & Clinical Pathology
9003 E Shea Blvd, Scottsdale, 480-860-3100
400 E Osborn Rd, Scottsdale, 480-882-4000
7400 E Pinnacle Peak Rd, Scottsdale, 480-324-7032

Bernert, Richard Alan (3 mentions)
U of Arizona, 1993 *Certification:* Anatomic Pathology &
Clinical Pathology, Dermatopathology
1255 W Washington St, Tempe, 602-685-5211

Burgan, Anthony Ray (3 mentions)
Johns Hopkins U, 1985 *Certification:* Anatomic Pathology &
Clinical Pathology, Cytopathology
1255 W Washington St, Tempe, 602-685-5211

Colby, Thomas Vail (13 mentions)
U of Michigan, 1974 *Certification:* Anatomic Pathology
13400 E Shea Blvd, Scottsdale, 602-301-8000

Davis, Roy I. (3 mentions)
FMS-South Africa, 1970
Certification: Anatomic Pathology & Clinical Pathology
49 E Thomas Rd #101, Phoenix, 602-406-3402
350 W Thomas Rd, Phoenix, 602-406-3000

Devine, Dana Sue (4 mentions)
Kansas U Coll of Osteopathic Med, 1970
19829 N 27th Ave, Phoenix, 623-879-5500

Horne, Donna Gaye (4 mentions)
U of Minnesota, 1973 *Certification:* Anatomic Pathology &
Clinical Pathology, Cytopathology, Hematology
9003 E Shea Blvd, Scottsdale, 480-323-3383

Lambe, Clarke David K. (5 mentions)
U of Arizona, 1975
Certification: Anatomic Pathology & Clinical Pathology
8900 N Central Ave #103, Phoenix, 602-861-3456

Leslie, Kevin Orr (6 mentions)
Albert Einstein Coll of Med, 1978
Certification: Anatomic Pathology & Clinical Pathology
13400 E Shea Blvd, Scottsdale, 480-301-8000

Molloy, Peter (4 mentions)
U of Colorado, 1983
Certification: Anatomic Pathology & Clinical Pathology
1111 E McDowell Rd, Phoenix, 602-239-4580

Pettit, Carolyn Kay (3 mentions)
U of Arizona, 1986
Certification: Anatomic Pathology & Clinical Pathology
1111 E McDowell Rd, Phoenix, 602-239-4580
1255 W Washington St, Tempe, 602-685-5211

Williams, James Winston (3 mentions)
Stanford U, 1972 *Certification:* Anatomic Pathology
13400 E Shea Blvd, Scottsdale, 480-301-7881

Zimmerman, Kent George (6 mentions)
U of Iowa, 1978 *Certification:* Anatomic Pathology &
  Clinical Pathology, Cytopathology
1255 W Washington St, Tempe, 602-685-5211

Pediatrics *(see note on page 9)*

Alexander, David Ralph (5 mentions)
Ohio State U, 1975 *Certification:* Pediatrics
4350 E Camelback Rd #100-G, Phoenix, 602-840-3120

Burke, Susan Kunesh (3 mentions)
U of Arizona, 1987 *Certification:* Pediatrics
7425 E Shea Blvd #101, Scottsdale, 480-609-8100

Campbell, Lindsay Anne (7 mentions)
Rosalind Franklin U, 1991 *Certification:* Pediatrics
4350 E Camelback Rd #G-100, Phoenix, 602-840-3120

Chiles, John G. (3 mentions)
U of Tennessee, 1976 *Certification:* Pediatrics
2152 S Vineyard #129, Mesa, 480-732-0044

Fischler, Ronald Sigmar (7 mentions)
Harvard U, 1973 *Certification:* Pediatrics
10200 N 92nd St #150, Scottsdale, 480-860-8488

Golner, Gerald Howard (4 mentions)
Indiana U, 1969 *Certification:* Pediatrics
6702 N 19th Ave, Phoenix, 602-242-5121

James, Larry Loren (4 mentions)
Baylor U, 1971 *Certification:* Pediatrics
120 S Val Vista Dr, Gilbert, 480-733-6500

Lersch, David Ralph (5 mentions)
U of Arizona, 1978 *Certification:* Pediatrics
7600 N 15th St #130, Phoenix, 602-861-1611

Magalnick, Harold (11 mentions)
SUNY-Downstate Med Coll, 1971 *Certification:* Pediatrics
15650 N Black Canyon Hwy #100, Phoenix, 602-866-0550
2316 W Bethany Home Rd #109, Phoenix, 602-242-7190

Morales, Mark (3 mentions)
U of Southern California, 1981 *Certification:* Pediatrics
7236 S Central Ave, Phoenix, 602-276-5565

Padrez, James Henry, Jr. (8 mentions)
U of Arizona, 1979 *Certification:* Pediatrics
7600 N 15th St #130, Phoenix, 602-861-1611

Saba, Norman Morris (8 mentions)
Johns Hopkins U, 1980 *Certification:* Pediatrics
1520 S Dobson Rd #203, Mesa, 480-839-4848
4824 E Baseline Rd Bldg 3 #125, Mesa, 480-839-4848

Scharff, Milton Kenneth (8 mentions)
U of Texas-Galveston, 1979 *Certification:* Pediatrics
4350 E Camelback Rd #100G, Phoenix, 602-840-3120

Siegel, Jeffrey Earl (4 mentions)
U of Missouri, 1995 *Certification:* Pediatrics
10200 N 92nd St #150, Scottsdale, 480-860-8488

Sotelo, Sergio (4 mentions)
Wright State U, 1983 *Certification:* Pediatrics
8573 E San Alberto Dr #E-100, Scottsdale, 480-778-1732

Stamps, Michael Ray (3 mentions)
Texas Tech U, 1982 *Certification:* Pediatrics
4626 E Shea Blvd #C100, Phoenix, 602-996-0190

Ziltzer, Vivian Gee (7 mentions)
U of Arizona, 1988 *Certification:* Pediatrics
10200 N 92nd St #150, Scottsdale, 480-860-8488

Plastic Surgery

Acharya, Govind G. (6 mentions)
FMS-India, 1969 *Certification:* Plastic Surgery
5121 N Central Ave, Phoenix, 602-266-2772

Bash, Deborah Sue (6 mentions)
Southern Illinois U, 1986 *Certification:* Plastic Surgery
13400 E Shea Blvd, Scottsdale, 480-301-8565

Bass, John Wesley (6 mentions)
U of Missouri-Kansas City, 1982 *Certification:* Plastic Surgery
2398 E Camelback Rd #980, Phoenix, 602-485-1010

Beals, Stephen Paul (8 mentions)
Wayne State U, 1978 *Certification:* Plastic Surgery
500 W Thomas Rd #960, Phoenix, 602-266-9066
7101 E Jackrabbit Rd, Paradise Valley, 602-266-9066

Bunchman, Herbert H., II (8 mentions)
U of Tennessee, 1967 *Certification:* Plastic Surgery, Surgery
1520 S Dobson Rd #314, Mesa, 480-833-5200

Friedland, Jack Arthur (6 mentions)
Northwestern U, 1965 *Certification:* Plastic Surgery, Surgery
7425 E Shea Blvd #103, Scottsdale, 480-905-1700

Hiatt, Karl Brinton (6 mentions)
Duke U, 1983 *Certification:* Plastic Surgery
4540 E Baseline Rd #117, Mesa, 480-844-1410

Holcombe, Travis Case (6 mentions)
Johns Hopkins U, 1986 *Certification:* Plastic Surgery
500 W Thomas Rd #960, Phoenix, 602-266-9066

Jacobsen, William Martin (7 mentions)
U of Illinois, 1986 *Certification:* Plastic Surgery
500 W Thomas Rd #830, Phoenix, 602-212-0100
2400 E Arizona Biltmore Cir #2450, Phoenix, 602-212-0100

Joganic, Edward Francis (8 mentions)
U of Arizona, 1975 *Certification:* Plastic Surgery
500 W Thomas Rd #960, Phoenix, 602-266-9066
124 W Thomas Rd, Phoenix, 602-406-3223

Johnson, Martin Lloyd (8 mentions)
Baylor U, 1975 *Certification:* Plastic Surgery
7101 E Jackrabbit Rd #C, Paradise Valley, 480-994-3996
5410 N Scottsdale Rd #E200, Paradise Valley, 480-994-3996

Mosharrafa, Ali Mostafa (9 mentions)
Baylor U, 1991 *Certification:* Plastic Surgery
3301 N 2nd St, Phoenix, 602-277-7860

Rhee, Paul Hyung (6 mentions)
U of Colorado, 1995 *Certification:* Plastic Surgery
6642 E Baseline Rd #103, Mesa, 480-641-7720

Rowley, John Marshall (7 mentions)
U of Iowa, 1995 *Certification:* Plastic Surgery, Surgery
15810 S 45th St #140, Phoenix, 480-759-3001

Smith, Anthony Albert (7 mentions)
U of Illinois, 1979
Certification: Plastic Surgery, Surgery of the Hand
5777 E Mayo Blvd, Phoenix, 480-342-1379

Spies, Robert James, Jr. (9 mentions)
Ohio State U, 1979 *Certification:* Plastic Surgery
5410 N Scottsdale Rd #C-100, Paradise Valley, 480-890-0600

Psychiatry

Boyer, David Norman (10 mentions)
Wayne State U, 1970 *Certification:* Psychiatry
7520 E 2nd St #1-2, Scottsdale, 480-947-2615

Burstein, Alvin Craig (7 mentions)
Wayne State U, 1976 *Certification:* Psychiatry
5070 N 40th St #220, Phoenix, 480-905-8755

Fulton, William Alexander (5 mentions)
Vanderbilt U, 1979 *Certification:* Child & Adolescent
  Psychiatry, Psychiatry, Psychosomatic Medicine
10188 E Cochise Dr, Scottsdale, 602-329-3727

Kalivas, Linda Lee (6 mentions)
U of Kansas, 1988
Certification: Child & Adolescent Psychiatry, Psychiatry
7510 E 1st St, Scottsdale, 480-429-8222

Krahn, Lois Elaine (11 mentions)
Mayo Med Sch, 1989 *Certification:* Geriatric Psychiatry,
  Psychiatry, Psychosomatic Medicine, Sleep Medicine
13400 E Shea Blvd, Scottsdale, 480-301-8297

McLoone, James Brian (10 mentions)
George Washington U, 1976
Certification: Geriatric Psychiatry, Psychiatry
925 E McDowell Rd, Phoenix, 602-239-6880

Oppenheim, Tracey Sue (4 mentions)
U of Michigan, 1999
Certification: Child & Adolescent Psychiatry, Psychiatry
1440 S Dobson Rd, Mesa, 480-512-4000

Purewal, Satinder Singh (3 mentions)
FMS-India, 1991
6677 W Thunderbird Ave Bldg I #164, Glendale, 623-878-2100

Ricardi, Randall (4 mentions)
Midwestern U Chicago Coll of Osteopathic Med, 1984
Certification: Child & Adolescent Psychiatry, Psychiatry
909 E Brill St, Phoenix, 602-239-6751
1919 E Thomas Rd, Phoenix, 602-546-0990

Schulte, Henry John, III (3 mentions)
U of Michigan, 1970 *Certification:* Psychiatry
7101 E Indian School Rd, Scottsdale, 480-941-9004

Sisley, Suzanne Arlene (4 mentions)
U of Arizona, 1995 *Certification:* Psychiatry
4530 N 32nd Ave #102, Phoenix, 602-218-6872

Spiegel, Richard M. (4 mentions)
Columbia U, 1970 *Certification:* Child & Adolescent
  Psychiatry, Diagnostic Radiology, Psychiatry
7510 E 1st St, Scottsdale, 480-941-4841

Tafur, Mario H. (3 mentions)
FMS-Colombia, 1968 *Certification:* Psychiatry
300 W Clarendon Ave #S215, Phoenix, 602-280-1020
10645 N Tatum Blvd #200, Phoenix, 602-280-1020

Pulmonary Disease

Barnard, Paul Robert (9 mentions)
Creighton U, 1982
Certification: Internal Medicine, Pulmonary Disease
3303 E Baseline Rd #208, Gilbert, 480-962-1650

Beechler, Cash Ralph (14 mentions)
Ohio State U, 1971
Certification: Internal Medicine, Pulmonary Disease
10250 N 92nd St #102, Scottsdale, 480-614-2000

Comp, Robert Allen (11 mentions)
Michigan State U, 1978 *Certification:* Critical Care
  Medicine, Internal Medicine, Pulmonary Disease
9225 N 3rd St #200-B, Phoenix, 602-997-7263

Dick, Cameron Robert (7 mentions)
U of Kansas, 1989
Certification: Critical Care Medicine, Pulmonary Disease
2910 N 3rd St, Phoenix, 602-264-5685

Dishner, William Samuel (7 mentions)
U of North Texas, 1977
334 W 10th Pl #100, Mesa, 480-834-0771
6553 E Bayward #207, Mesa, 480-324-0999
19841 N 27th Ave #203, Phoenix, 602-279-9848

Drachler, David Harold (5 mentions)
U of Michigan, 1968
Certification: Internal Medicine, Pulmonary Disease
9100 N 2nd St #221, Phoenix, 602-943-9494

Farber, Steven Seth (8 mentions)
Des Moines U, 1979
3155 E Southern Pl #201, Mesa, 480-655-8040

Forseth, James Richard (6 mentions)
U of North Dakota, 1980 *Certification:* Critical Care
    Medicine, Internal Medicine, Pulmonary Disease
500 W Thomas Rd #950, Phoenix, 602-274-7195

Gill, Harmeet Singh (5 mentions)
FMS-India, 1986
Certification: Pulmonary Disease, Sleep Medicine
3303 E Baseline Rd #208, Gilbert, 480-962-1650

Helmers, Richard Alan (11 mentions)
U of Iowa, 1980 *Certification:* Critical Care Medicine,
    Internal Medicine, Pulmonary Disease
13400 E Shea Blvd, Scottsdale, 480-301-7149

Loreman, Lorie (5 mentions)
Philadelphia Coll of Osteopathic Med, 1987
Certification: Internal Medicine, Pulmonary Disease
334 W 10th Pl #100, Mesa, 602-279-9848

Nathan, Stephen Perry (9 mentions)
U of Arizona, 1974
Certification: Internal Medicine, Pulmonary Disease
9100 N 2nd St #221, Phoenix, 602-943-9494

Panesar, Kelvin S. (9 mentions)
Baylor U, 1992 *Certification:* Pediatric Pulmonology, Pediatrics
10250 N 92nd St #308, Scottsdale, 480-614-6655
1452 N Higley Rd, Gilbert, 480-614-6655

Parides, George Christopher (11 mentions)
New Jersey Sch of Osteopathic Med, 1982
334 W 10th Pl #100, Mesa, 480-834-0771
6553 E Baywood #207, Mesa, 480-324-0999
19841 N 27th Ave #203, Phoenix, 602-279-9848

Premkumar, Arcot S. (9 mentions)
FMS-India, 1972
Certification: Internal Medicine, Pulmonary Disease
2910 N 3rd St, Phoenix, 602-264-5685

Ronn, Jeffrey Gene (6 mentions)
Michigan State U, 1977 *Certification:* Internal Medicine
18731 N Reems Rd, Surprise, 623-975-0592

Ruzi, Jonathan David (7 mentions)
Cornell U, 1988
Certification: Critical Care Medicine, Pulmonary Disease
10250 N 92nd St #102, Scottsdale, 480-614-2000

Siever, John Richard (8 mentions)
U of Chicago, 1976
Certification: Internal Medicine, Pulmonary Disease
500 W Thomas Rd #950, Phoenix, 602-274-7195

Silverthorn, Amy Anderson (15 mentions)
Baylor U, 1977
Certification: Internal Medicine, Pulmonary Disease
500 W Thomas Rd #950, Phoenix, 602-274-7195
2927 N 7th Ave, Phoenix, 602-406-5864

Slobig, Thomas Joseph (9 mentions)
Med Coll of Wisconsin, 1985 *Certification:* Internal Medicine
3303 E Baseline Rd #208, Gilbert, 480-962-1650

Tillinghast, A. Judson (14 mentions)
Louisiana State U, 1971
Certification: Internal Medicine, Pulmonary Disease
10250 N 92nd St #102, Scottsdale, 480-614-2000

Radiology—Diagnostic

Barclay-White, Belinda M. (3 mentions)
FMS-United Kingdom, 1974 *Certification:* Diagnostic Radiology
8994 E Desert Cove Dr, Scottsdale, 480-314-7600

Bellapravalu, Meenakshi (3 mentions)
FMS-India, 1975
10401 W Thunderbird Blvd, Sun City, 623-876-5360

Collins, Joseph Michael (8 mentions)
U of Illinois, 1980 *Certification:* Diagnostic Radiology
13400 E Shea Blvd, Scottsdale, 480-301-8000

Crowe, John Kenyon (4 mentions)
Duke U, 1969 *Certification:* Diagnostic Radiology
3501 N Scottsdale Rd #130, Scottsdale, 480-425-5000

Green, Barry (3 mentions)
SUNY-Downstate Med Coll, 1968
Certification: Diagnostic Radiology
3501 N Scottsdale Rd #130, Scottsdale, 480-425-5000

Keiper, Mark Douglas (5 mentions)
U of Pennsylvania, 1990
Certification: Diagnostic Radiology, Neuroradiology
3501 N Scottsdale Rd #130, Scottsdale, 480-425-5000

Korn, Ronald Lee (7 mentions)
Stanford U, 1990
Certification: Diagnostic Radiology, Nuclear Medicine
3501 N Scottsdale Rd #130, Scottsdale, 480-425-5000

Kornreich, Michael (5 mentions)
George Washington U, 1976 *Certification:* Diagnostic Radiology
1125 E Southern Ave #300, Mesa, 480-545-9779

Martin, Janet Rose (3 mentions)
U of Arizona, 1996 *Certification:* Diagnostic Radiology
350 W Thomas Rd, Phoenix, 602-406-3430
3501 N Scottsdale Rd #130, Scottsdale, 480-425-5000

Moeser, Phillip Mark (6 mentions)
Med Coll of Wisconsin, 1980 *Certification:* Diagnostic Radiology
250 E Dunlap Ave, Phoenix, 602-943-2381

Muhm, John Robert (5 mentions)
U of Colorado, 1968 *Certification:* Diagnostic Radiology
13400 E Shea Blvd, Scottsdale, 480-301-4707

Shinar, Ron Zohar (3 mentions)
U of California-San Diego, 1999
Certification: Diagnostic Radiology
1111 E McDowell Rd, Phoenix, 602-239-4601

Simon, Howard John (4 mentions)
U of Chicago, 1987 *Certification:* Diagnostic Radiology,
    Vascular & Interventional Radiology
9201 E Mountain View Rd #137, Scottsdale, 480-614-8555

Sterrett, Robert Eugene (3 mentions)
U of Illinois, 1972 *Certification:* Diagnostic Radiology
3707 N 7th St #300, Phoenix, 602-604-7300
1111 E McDowell Rd, Phoenix, 602-239-4601

Radiology—Therapeutic

Chong, Brian Wayne (6 mentions)
FMS-Canada, 1986
Certification: Diagnostic Radiology, Neuroradiology
5777 E Mayo Blvd, Phoenix, 480-515-6296

Gurley, Melissa B. (6 mentions)
U of Missouri-Kansas City, 1992 *Certification:* Diagnostic
    Radiology, Vascular & Interventional Radiology
11209 N Tatum Blvd #140, Phoenix, 602-248-8002
18701 N 67th Ave, Glendale, 623-561-7170

Hirsch, Kevin S. (6 mentions)
Certification: Diagnostic Radiology
2323 W Rose Garden Ln, Phoenix, 623-931-7999

Huettl, Eric A. (4 mentions)
Albert Einstein Coll of Med, 1988 *Certification:* Diagnostic
    Radiology, Vascular & Interventional Radiology
13400 E Shea Blvd, Scottsdale, 480-301-4707
5777 E Mayo Blvd, Phoenix, 480-342-1650

Kasper, David Michael (4 mentions)
FMS-Canada, 1980 *Certification:* Diagnostic Radiology,
    Vascular & Interventional Radiology
5777 E Mayo Blvd, Phoenix, 480-301-8000

Quiet, Coral Ann (4 mentions)
U of Massachusetts, 1985 *Certification:* Radiation Oncology
300 W Clarendon Ave #350, Phoenix, 602-274-4484
16620 N 40th St #C1, Phoenix, 602-274-4484

Rainwater, Joel (4 mentions)
U of Texas-Dallas, 1991 *Certification:* Diagnostic Radiology
1125 E Southern Ave #300, Mesa, 480-545-8119
1400 S Dobson Rd, Mesa, 480-545-8119

Spencer, E. Brooke (5 mentions)
U of Vermont, 1995 *Certification:* Diagnostic Radiology
1125 E Southern Ave #300, Mesa, 480-545-8119

Taylor, Thomas Jackson (4 mentions)
Oregon Health Sciences U, 1968
Certification: Therapeutic Radiology
1400 S Dobson Rd, Mesa, 480-835-3808

Rehabilitation

Blake, Paul Anthony (4 mentions)
Med U of South Carolina, 1979
Certification: Pain Medicine, Physical Medicine & Rehabilitation
1400 S Dobson Ave, Mesa, 480-834-8802

Butters, Matthew Alan (9 mentions)
Mayo Med Sch, 1986
Certification: Physical Medicine & Rehabilitation
13400 E Shea Blvd, Scottsdale, 480-301-7146

Ganter, Bryan Keith (4 mentions)
Oregon Health Sciences U, 1993
Certification: Physical Medicine & Rehabilitation
13400 E Shea Blvd, Scottsdale, 480-301-8000

Geimer, Paul Charles (5 mentions)
Midwestern U Chicago Coll of Osteopathic Med, 1975
Certification: Physical Medicine & Rehabilitation
2400 N Central Ave #306, Phoenix, 602-254-6515

Jackson, J. Carvel (5 mentions)
Western U, 1988
Certification: Physical Medicine & Rehabilitation
303 N Centennial Way, Mesa, 480-649-3111

Kelley, John Paul (6 mentions)
Ohio State U, 1971
Certification: Physical Medicine & Rehabilitation
7301 E 2nd St #315, Scottsdale, 480-947-7711

Kinney, Carolyn Louise (4 mentions)
Boston U, 1981 *Certification:* Physical Medicine & Rehabilitation
9630 E Shea Blvd, Scottsdale, 480-551-5467

Kravetz, Michael Louis (4 mentions)
U of Arizona, 1987
Certification: Pain Medicine, Physical Medicine & Rehabilitation
13460 N 67th Ave, Glendale, 623-878-8800

Kreiner, Daniel Scott (3 mentions)
U of Arizona, 1995
Certification: Physical Medicine & Rehabilitation
4530 E Muirwood Dr #110, Phoenix, 480-763-5808

Kwasnica, Christina Marie (7 mentions)
Northwestern U, 1995 *Certification:* Pediatric Rehabilitation
    Medicine, Physical Medicine & Rehabilitation
222 W Thomas Rd #212, Phoenix, 602-406-6304

Ladin, Kevin Scott (3 mentions)
Med Coll of Pennsylvania, 1988
Certification: Pain Medicine, Physical Medicine & Rehabilitation
1331 N 7th St #360, Phoenix, 602-246-9002

Lockman, Steven David (4 mentions)
U of California-San Diego, 1993
Certification: Physical Medicine & Rehabilitation
9165 W Thunderbird Blvd #100, Peoria, 623-523-6560
14416 W Meeker Blvd #300, Sun City West, 623-523-6560

Noll, Stephen Francis (11 mentions)
U of Nebraska, 1973 *Certification:* Family Medicine,
  Geriatric Medicine, Pain Medicine, Pediatric Rehabilitation
  Medicine, Physical Medicine & Rehabilitation
13400 E Shea Blvd, Scottsdale, 480-301-4050

Quang, Ronald Stephen (3 mentions)
Northeastern Ohio U, 1998
Certification: Physical Medicine & Rehabilitation
9377 E Bell Rd, Scottsdale, 480-563-7648

Singh, Raj Mohan (11 mentions)
FMS-India, 1972
Certification: Physical Medicine & Rehabilitation
10245 N 92nd St #101, Scottsdale, 480-767-0555

Sucher, Benjamin M. (3 mentions)
Michigan State U Coll of Osteopathic Med, 1976
  Certification: Physical Medicine & Rehabilitation
10599 N Tatum Blvd #F-150, Paradise Valley, 480-443-8400

Williams, Candyce Dietra (3 mentions)
Tufts U, 1981 *Certification:* Internal Medicine, Physical
  Medicine & Rehabilitation, Spinal Cord Injury Medicine
1331 N 7th St #190, Phoenix, 602-256-2525

Rheumatology

Caldron, Paul H. (11 mentions)
Oklahoma State U Coll of Osteopathic Med, 1979
Certification: Internal Medicine, Rheumatology
10599 N Tatum Blvd #F-150, Paradise Valley, 480-443-8400
9305 W Thomas Rd #505, Phoenix, 480-834-5200

Harris, Benjamin Keith (8 mentions)
Yale U, 1963 *Certification:* Internal Medicine, Rheumatology
926 E McDowell Rd #206, Phoenix, 602-253-9223

Howard, Paul Frederic (32 mentions)
Georgetown U, 1979
Certification: Internal Medicine, Rheumatology
9097 E Desert Cove #100, Scottsdale, 480-609-4200

Mertz, Lester Ervin (11 mentions)
Med Coll of Wisconsin, 1981
Certification: Internal Medicine, Rheumatology
13400 E Shea Blvd, Scottsdale, 480-301-8318

Nardella, Francis Anthony (11 mentions)
West Virginia U, 1968
Certification: Internal Medicine, Rheumatology
10210 N 92nd St #202, Scottsdale, 480-451-6860

Peters, Eric Alan (9 mentions)
U of Kansas, 1988
Certification: Internal Medicine, Rheumatology
5601 W Eugie Ave #204, Glendale, 602-439-2800
10599 N Tatum Blvd #F150, Scottsdale, 480-443-8400

Schechtman, Joy (14 mentions)
Ohio U Coll of Osteopathic Med, 1980
6818 W Thunderbird Rd, Peoria, 623-566-3550

Tesser, John Robert Paul (15 mentions)
U of Rochester, 1977
Certification: Internal Medicine, Rheumatology
10599 N Tatum Blvd #F-150, Paradise Valley, 480-443-8400
9305 W Thomas Rd #505, Phoenix, 480-443-8400

Thoracic Surgery

Ashton, Kenneth Anthony (5 mentions)
St Louis U, 1991 *Certification:* Thoracic Surgery
10930 N Tatum Blvd #103, Phoenix, 602-263-7600

Bremner, Ross M. (6 mentions)
FMS-South Africa, 1988 *Certification:* Surgery, Thoracic Surgery
500 W Thomas Rd #680, Phoenix, 602-406-4000

Caskey, Michael P. (6 mentions)
U of Texas-Galveston, 1983 *Certification:* Thoracic Surgery
222 W Thomas Rd #311, Phoenix, 602-263-7600
10930 N Tatum Blvd #103, Phoenix, 602-263-7600
5847 S 16th St, Phoenix, 602-249-0212

Fang, Hao (8 mentions)
U of Illinois, 1991 *Certification:* Surgery, Thoracic Surgery
3131 E Clarendon Ave #102, Phoenix, 602-253-9168

Goldstein, Andrew (6 mentions)
Columbia U, 1989 *Certification:* Surgery, Thoracic Surgery
10930 N Tatum Blvd #103, Phoenix, 602-263-7600

Jaroszewski, Dawn E. (6 mentions)
U of Texas-San Antonio, 1998
Certification: Surgery, Thoracic Surgery
5777 E Mayo Blvd, Phoenix, 480-301-8000

Lanza, Louis Angel (5 mentions)
Loyola U Chicago, 1981 *Certification:* Thoracic Surgery
5777 E Mayo Blvd, Phoenix, 480-342-2270

Mican, Camilla Ann (13 mentions)
Rosalind Franklin U, 1978 *Certification:* Thoracic Surgery
13634 N 93rd Ave #100, Peoria, 623-875-6001

Standerfer, Robert Jay, Jr. (7 mentions)
Oregon Health Sciences U, 1976 *Certification:* Thoracic Surgery
1144 E McDowell Rd #406, Phoenix, 602-253-9009

Urology

Alexander, Erik Edwin (8 mentions)
U of Wisconsin, 1993 *Certification:* Urology
9590 E Ironwood Square Dr #125, Scottsdale, 480-272-6400

Andrews, Paul Ernest (15 mentions)
Texas Tech U, 1987 *Certification:* Urology
5777 E Mayo Blvd, Phoenix, 480-342-2951

Argueso-Munoz, Luis (11 mentions)
U of Puerto Rico, 1983 *Certification:* Pediatric Urology, Urology
1920 E Cambridge Ave #302, Phoenix, 620-279-1697

Bailey, Robert Behrens, Jr. (16 mentions)
Yale U, 1981 *Certification:* Urology
1920 E Cambridge Ave #302, Phoenix, 602-279-1697

Bans, Larry Louis (29 mentions)
Cornell U, 1978 *Certification:* Urology
202 E Earl Dr #360, Phoenix, 602-264-4431
10200 N 92nd St #110, Scottsdale, 480-661-2662
2525 E Arizona Biltmore Cir, Phoenix, 602-426-9772

Blick, Shawn David (9 mentions)
Mount Sinai Sch of Med, 1994 *Certification:* Urology
3815 E Bell Rd #3600, Phoenix, 623-935-5522

Bohnert, William Wilbur (7 mentions)
Indiana U, 1965 *Certification:* Urology
202 E Earll Dr #306, Phoenix, 602-264-4431
10200 N 92nd St #110, Scottsdale, 602-264-4431
10117 N 92nd St #103, Scottsdale, 480-661-2662

Brenner, Mark (16 mentions)
A T Still U, 1978
19841 N 27th Ave #201, Phoenix, 623-582-6420

Brito, Cesar Gilberto (22 mentions)
U of Kansas, 1985 *Certification:* Urology
202 E Earll Dr #360, Phoenix, 602-264-4431
10200 N 92nd St #110, Scottsdale, 480-661-2662
10117 N 92nd St #103, Scottsdale, 480-661-2662

Ferrigni, Robert George (11 mentions)
Emory U, 1979 *Certification:* Urology
13400 E Shea Blvd, Scottsdale, 480-301-8000

Fishman, James Richard (8 mentions)
U of Arizona, 1987 *Certification:* Urology
1728 W Glendale Ave #204, Phoenix, 602-242-1556
3805 E Bell Rd #4100, Phoenix, 602-258-2748

Grossklaus, David Jon (14 mentions)
U of Arizona, 1996 *Certification:* Urology
875 N Greenfield Rd #105, Gilbert, 480-897-2727

Harmon, Taz Joseph (9 mentions)
U of Missouri-Kansas City, 1993 *Certification:* Urology
500 W Thomas Rd #600, Phoenix, 602-264-0608

Kletscher, Bruce Alan (14 mentions)
U of Minnesota, 1991 *Certification:* Urology
202 E Earll Dr #360, Phoenix, 602-264-4431
10117 N 92nd St #103, Scottsdale, 480-661-2662

Shahon, Robert Scott (9 mentions)
Tufts U, 1983 *Certification:* Urology
1520 S Dobson Rd #206, Mesa, 480-833-7000

Shapiro, Robert Harris (11 mentions)
U of Michigan, 1991 *Certification:* Urology
9590 E Ironwood Square Dr #125, Scottsdale, 480-272-6400

Vascular Surgery

Brink, Jeromy Scott (17 mentions)
U of Arizona, 1997 *Certification:* Surgery, Vascular Surgery
2601 N 3rd St #203, Phoenix, 602-277-7430

Smith, David Michael (15 mentions)
60818 W Thunderbird Dr, Glendale, 602-263-7600

Stone, William Martin (17 mentions)
Emory U, 1983 *Certification:* Surgery, Vascular Surgery
13400 E Shea Blvd, Scottsdale, 480-301-8254

Vaughn, Cecil C., III (14 mentions)
Louisiana State U, 1988 *Certification:* Surgery, Vascular Surgery
2000 W Bethany Home Rd, Phoenix, 602-249-0212
6771 Thunderbird Ln Bldg 6 #116, Glendale, 623-435-1954

California

Sacramento Area—page 61

San Francisco Bay Area—page 76

Los Angeles and Orange Counties—page 38
Riverside and San Bernardino Counties—page 56
San Diego Area—page 66

Los Angeles and Orange Counties

Allergy/Immunology

Berger, William Ezial (5 mentions)
U of Cincinnati, 1973
Certification: Allergy & Immunology, Pediatrics
27800 Medical Center Rd #244, Mission Viejo, 949-364-2900

Church, Joseph August (7 mentions)
New Jersey Med Sch, 1972
Certification: Allergy & Immunology, Pediatrics
4650 Sunset Blvd, Los Angeles, 323-361-2501

Eitches, Robert William (14 mentions)
SUNY-Upstate Med U, 1978
Certification: Allergy & Immunology, Pediatrics
8631 W 3rd St #925-E, Los Angeles, 310-657-4600

Ellis, Mark Howard (5 mentions)
Tulane U, 1981 *Certification:* Allergy & Immunology, Pediatrics
725 W La Veta Ave #100, Orange, 714-633-6363
455 S Main St, Orange, 714-633-6363

Ferdman, Ronald Maurice (5 mentions)
Hahnemann U, 1987
Certification: Allergy & Immunology, Pediatrics
4650 W Sunset Blvd 3rd Fl, Los Angeles, 323-361-2501

Geller, Bernard David (9 mentions)
SUNY-Downstate Med Coll, 1968
Certification: Allergy & Immunology, Pediatrics
1301 20th St #220, Santa Monica, 310-828-8534

Kaplan, Michael Stuart (6 mentions)
U of Illinois, 1967 *Certification:* Allergy & Immunology, Pediatrics
1515 N Vermont Ave Bldg A 5th Fl, Los Angeles, 800-954-8000

Kim, Kenneth Tongchul (7 mentions)
Harvard U, 1986
Certification: Allergy & Immunology, Internal Medicine
2600 Redondo Ave #400, Long Beach, 562-997-7888

Liao, Otto Younn (4 mentions)
U of Southern California, 1997
Certification: Allergy & Immunology, Internal Medicine
1101 E Bryan Ave #B, Tustin, 714-838-2617

Meltzer, Steven Mark (5 mentions)
U of Southern California, 1981
Certification: Allergy & Immunology
3816 Woodruff Ave #209, Long Beach, 562-496-4749

Rachelefsky, Gary Stuart (4 mentions)
Washington U, 1967
Certification: Allergy & Immunology, Pediatrics
200 UCLA Medical Plaza, Los Angeles, 310-794-6884

Roth, Richard Michael (5 mentions)
St Louis U, 1971 *Certification:* Allergy & Immunology, Pediatrics
12100 Euclid St, Garden Grove, 714-741-3580

Schanker, Howard M. Jay (4 mentions)
SUNY-Downstate Med Coll, 1977
Certification: Allergy & Immunology, Internal Medicine
11620 Wilshire Blvd #200, Los Angeles, 310-312-5050

Sokol, William Nicholas, Jr. (4 mentions)
Ohio State U, 1968
Certification: Allergy & Immunology, Internal Medicine
2011 Westcliff Dr #7, Newport Beach, 949-645-3374
4950 Barranca Pkwy #200, Irvine, 949-651-1427

Spector, Sheldon Laurence (5 mentions)
Wayne State U, 1964
Certification: Allergy & Immunology, Internal Medicine
11645 Wilshire Blvd #1155, Los Angeles, 310-966-9022

Anesthesiology

Ackerman, Stuart Ellis (3 mentions)
Baylor U, 1979 *Certification:* Anesthesiology
16237 Ventura Blvd, Encino, 818-995-5281

Arakaki, Roger (3 mentions)
U of Texas-Galveston, 1981 *Certification:* Anesthesiology
1100 W Stewart Dr, Orange, 714-633-9111
455 S Main St, Orange, 714-997-3000

Berkus, Dean Bruce (3 mentions)
FMS-Mexico, 1977 *Certification:* Anesthesiology
225 S Lake Ave #535, Pasadena, 626-795-6596

Cadogan, Evon Stclaver (6 mentions)
U of Southern California, 1985 *Certification:* Anesthesiology
225 S Lake Ave #535, Pasadena, 626-795-6596

Carpenter, Timothy Harry (3 mentions)
St Louis U, 1989 *Certification:* Anesthesiology
1 Hoag Dr, Newport Beach, 949-764-6954

De Castro, Maria Angelica (3 mentions)
U of Missouri-Kansas City, 1987 *Certification:* Anesthesiology
8700 Beverly Blvd #211, West Hollywood, 213-637-3703

DelloRusso, James K. (3 mentions)
FMS-Mexico, 1981 *Certification:* Anesthesiology
18685 Main St, Huntington Beach, 714-847-6961

Friedman, Arnold S. (3 mentions)
U of Louisville, 1967
Certification: Anesthesiology, Internal Medicine
8700 Beverly Blvd #8211, Los Angeles, 310-423-5841

Friedman, Mitchell Scott (3 mentions)
Hahnemann U, 1988 *Certification:* Anesthesiology
6041 Cadillac Ave, Los Angeles, 323-857-4281

Gittler, Mark Jay (3 mentions)
3330 Lomita Blvd, Torrance, 310-325-9110

Gold, Julian Alan (3 mentions)
New York U, 1974 *Certification:* Anesthesiology
8700 Beverly Blvd, Los Angeles, 310-423-5841

Huang, David H. (3 mentions)
FMS-Canada, 1975
275 Victoria St #2-B, Costa Mesa, 919-722-6178

Kapur, Patricia Ann (3 mentions)
U of Pennsylvania, 1976 *Certification:* Anesthesiology
10833 Le Conte Ave, Los Angeles, 310-825-6761

Kleinman, Wayne Michael (6 mentions)
Virginia Commonwealth U, 1984
Certification: Anesthesiology, Internal Medicine
11999 San Vicente Blvd #440, Los Angeles, 310-440-3131

Maister, Anthony Hugh (3 mentions)
FMS-South Africa, 1973 *Certification:* Anesthesiology
11999 San Vincente Blvd #440, Los Angeles, 310-440-3131

Maskin, Jonathan David (3 mentions)
FMS-South Africa, 1980 *Certification:* Anesthesiology
225 S Lake Ave #535, Pasadena, 626-795-6596

O'Brien, Aidan Patrick (3 mentions)
FMS-Ireland, 1972 *Certification:* Anesthesiology
12401 Washington Blvd, Whittier, 562-698-0811

Strachan, Rodney (3 mentions)
U of Southern California, 1981 *Certification:* Anesthesiology
725 W La Veta Ave #270, Orange, 714-744-0900

Wender, Ronald Howard (3 mentions)
Tulane U, 1973 *Certification:* Anesthesiology
8700 Beverly Blvd #8211, Los Angeles, 310-423-5841

Yost, Paul Bennett (5 mentions)
Baylor U, 1986 *Certification:* Anesthesiology
1100 W Stewart Dr, Orange, 714-633-9111

Cardiac Surgery

Bethencourt, Daniel Miguel (8 mentions)
Yale U, 1979 *Certification:* Thoracic Surgery
2865 Atlantic Ave #205, Long Beach, 562-988-9333

Cohen, Robbin Gerald (13 mentions)
U of Colorado, 1980 *Certification:* Thoracic Surgery
50 Bellefontaine St #403, Pasadena, 626-683-9000
1520 San Pablo St #4300, Los Angeles, 323-442-5849

Gharavi, Mohammad Ali (7 mentions)
Certification: Thoracic Surgery
16255 Ventura Blvd #910, Encino, 818-990-4600

Gheissari, Ali (6 mentions)
U of Michigan, 1983 *Certification:* Thoracic Surgery
1245 Wilshire Blvd #606, Los Angeles, 213-483-1055

Hall, James David (6 mentions)
U of Chicago, 1986 *Certification:* Thoracic Surgery
23451 Madison St #300, Torrance, 310-378-7373

Joyo, Colin Isao (6 mentions)
U of Hawaii, 1977 *Certification:* Thoracic Surgery
447 Old Newport Blvd #200, Newport Beach, 949-650-3350

Laks, Hillel (19 mentions)
FMS-South Africa, 1965 *Certification:* Surgery, Thoracic Surgery
10833 Le Conte Ave, Los Angeles, 310-206-8232

Palafox, Brian Avecilla (8 mentions)
U of California-Irvine, 1975
Certification: Surgery, Thoracic Surgery
1310 W Stewart Dr #503, Orange, 714-997-2224

Perkowski, David J. (11 mentions)
Indiana U, 1973 *Certification:* Thoracic Surgery
1310 W Stewart Dr #503, Orange, 714-997-2224

Robertson, John Marshall (14 mentions)
St Louis U, 1977 *Certification:* Thoracic Surgery
1328 22nd St, Santa Monica, 310-829-8618

Starnes, Vaughn A. (35 mentions)
U of North Carolina, 1977 *Certification:* Thoracic Surgery
1520 San Pablo St #4300, Los Angeles, 323-442-5849
50 Bellefontaine St #403, Pasadena, 626-683-9000
4650 W Sunset Blvd, Los Angeles, 323-660-2450

Trento, Alfredo (16 mentions)
FMS-Italy, 1975 *Certification:* Thoracic Surgery
8701 Gracie Allen Dr #6215, Los Angeles, 310-423-3851

Yokoyama, Taro (9 mentions)
FMS-Japan, 1960 *Certification:* Surgery, Thoracic Surgery
2200 W 3rd St #300, Los Angeles, 213-639-2200

Zusman, Douglas Richard (10 mentions)
Yale U, 1975 *Certification:* Internal Medicine, Thoracic Surgery
447 Old Newport Blvd #200, Newport Beach, 949-650-3350

Cardiology

Allen, Byron John (8 mentions)
U of California-Los Angeles, 1980
Certification: Cardiovascular Disease, Internal Medicine
101 The City Dr S #100, Orange, 714-456-6699

Berdjis, Farhouch (6 mentions)
FMS-Germany, 1983 *Certification:* Pediatric Cardiology
455 S Main St, Orange, 714-547-0900
1120 W La Veta Ave #100, Orange, 714-547-0900
3909 Waring Rd #A, Oceanside, 714-547-0900

Berens, Stephen Clark (3 mentions)
U of California-Los Angeles, 1966
Certification: Cardiovascular Disease, Internal Medicine
2001 Santa Monica Blvd #268-W, Santa Monica, 310-828-4633

Bruss, Jeffrey (5 mentions)
FMS-South Africa, 1982 *Certification:* Cardiovascular
Disease, Internal Medicine, Interventional Cardiology
415 Old Newport Blvd #200, Newport Beach, 949-548-9611

Buchbinder, Neil Alan (7 mentions)
U of Miami, 1968
Certification: Cardiovascular Disease, Internal Medicine
8635 W 3rd St #1190-W, Los Angeles, 310-652-4600

Cannom, David S. (6 mentions)
U of Minnesota, 1967
Certification: Cardiovascular Disease, Internal Medicine
1245 Wilshire Blvd #703, Los Angeles, 213-977-0419

Cobb, Tyson Charles (5 mentions)
U of Cincinnati, 1964
Certification: Cardiovascular Disease, Internal Medicine
1140 W LaVeta Ave #640, Orange, 714-564-3305

Conrad, Gary Loris (7 mentions)
Johns Hopkins U, 1974
Certification: Cardiovascular Disease, Internal Medicine
50 Alessandro Pl #200, Pasadena, 626-793-4139
416 W Las Tunas Dr #205, San Gabriel, 626-308-9225

Corday, Stephen Richard (5 mentions)
Stanford U, 1974
Certification: Cardiovascular Disease, Internal Medicine
8635 W 3rd St #790, Los Angeles, 310-855-8081

De Oliveira, Elizabeth R. (3 mentions)
FMS-Brazil, 1982 *Certification:* Pediatric Cardiology, Pediatrics
1700 E Cesar Chavez Ave #1300, Los Angeles, 323-526-2583
1135 S Sunset Ave, West Covina, 626-337-8900
2001 Santa Monica Blvd, Santa Monica, 310-998-1181
50 Bellafonte St, Pasadena, 626-796-9259

Del Vicario, Michele (7 mentions)
FMS-Canada, 1970 *Certification:* Cardiovascular Disease,
Internal Medicine, Interventional Cardiology
3475 Torrance Blvd, Torrance, 310-784-3705

Durairaj, Azhil (3 mentions)
U of Southern California, 1994
Certification: Cardiovascular Disease, Interventional Cardiology
50 Alessandro Pl #200, Pasadena, 626-254-0074

Fallon, Sandra Philomena (3 mentions)
FMS-Ireland, 1982 *Certification:* Internal Medicine
2020 Santa Monica Blvd #580, Santa Monica, 310-453-4455

Ferry, David Arthur (4 mentions)
Washington U, 1980 *Certification:* Pediatric Cardiology, Pediatrics
5400 Balboa Blvd #202, Encino, 818-784-6269
1359 W Ave #J, Lancaster, 661-726-5000
26357 McBean Pkwy #200, Valencia, 661-284-1311

Fonarow, Gregg Curtis (3 mentions)
U of California-Los Angeles, 1987
Certification: Cardiovascular Disease
200 UCLA Medical Plaza #224, Los Angeles, 310-825-8816

Forman, Steven Todd (5 mentions)
Albany Med Coll, 1991 *Certification:* Cardiovascular
Disease, Internal Medicine, Interventional Cardiology
3771 Katella Ave #300, Los Alamitos, 562-430-7533

Gault, Michael James (3 mentions)
Rosalind Franklin U, 1990
Certification: Cardiovascular Disease, Interventional Cardiology
24411 Health Center Dr #500, Laguna Hills, 949-770-6252

Geft, Ivor Leon (3 mentions)
FMS-South Africa, 1970
8631 W 3rd St #445-E, Los Angeles, 310-659-7537

Guzy, Peter Michael (4 mentions)
U of Toledo, 1973
Certification: Cardiovascular Disease, Internal Medicine
100 UCLA Medical Plaza #535, Los Angeles, 310-209-7450

Harold, John Gordon (4 mentions)
Stony Brook U, 1979 *Certification:* Cardiovascular Disease,
Critical Care Medicine, Geriatric Medicine, Internal Medicine
8635 W 3rd St #WT-750, Los Angeles, 310-659-2030

Haskell, Richard Joseph (8 mentions)
U of California-Los Angeles, 1979 *Certification:* Cardiovascular
Disease, Internal Medicine, Interventional Cardiology
415 Old Newport Blvd #200, Newport Beach, 949-548-9611

Herman, L. Scott (3 mentions)
New York Med Coll, 1974
Certification: Cardiovascular Disease, Internal Medicine
51 N 5th Ave #201, Arcadia, 626-357-1305

Itchhaporia, Dipti (7 mentions)
St Louis U, 1988 *Certification:* Interventional Cardiology
355 Placentia Ave #207B, Newport Beach, 949-548-6634

Kobashigawa, Jon Akira (4 mentions)
Mount Sinai Sch of Med, 1980
Certification: Cardiovascular Disease, Internal Medicine
100 UCLA Medical Plaza #630, Los Angeles, 310-794-1200

Lee, Eric Thomas (4 mentions)
U of Southern California, 1982
Certification: Cardiovascular Disease, Internal Medicine
1808 Verdugo Blvd #414, Glendale, 818-952-1426

Lee, Faye (5 mentions)
Boston U, 1976
Certification: Cardiovascular Disease, Internal Medicine
1245 Wilshire Blvd #812, Los Angeles, 213-481-2222

Lurie, Mark I. (5 mentions)
Rush U, 1973
Certification: Cardiovascular Disease, Internal Medicine
3475 Torrance Blvd #A, Torrance, 310-370-3568

Mahon, Donald John (3 mentions)
Baylor U, 1982 *Certification:* Cardiovascular Disease,
Internal Medicine, Interventional Cardiology
1140 W La Veta Ave #845, Orange, 714-543-5555

Manzanilla, Rainier A. (3 mentions)
U of California-Irvine, 1986
Certification: Interventional Cardiology
1701 E Cesar E Chavez Ave #560, Los Angeles, 323-441-1122

Marwah, Onkarjit Singh (3 mentions)
FMS-India, 1986
Certification: Cardiovascular Disease, Interventional Cardiology
660 W Broadway, Glendale, 818-243-9600

McAveney, Timothy James (3 mentions)
U of Maryland, 1998
Certification: Cardiovascular Disease, Internal Medicine
441 N Lakeview Ave, Anaheim, 888-988-2800

Nakano, Frank Hiroshi (3 mentions)
U of California-Los Angeles, 1962
Certification: Cardiovascular Disease, Internal Medicine
3831 Hughes Ave #702, Culver City, 310-204-1146
414 N Camden Dr #1100, Beverly Hills, 310-278-3400

Narula, Jagat Prakash S. (3 mentions)
FMS-India, 1978
101 The City Dr S, Orange, 888-456-6699

Natterson, Paul David (5 mentions)
U of California-San Diego, 1989
Certification: Cardiovascular Disease
2001 Santa Monica Blvd #280-W, Santa Monica, 310-829-7678

O'Bryan, Carey Law, IV (4 mentions)
Georgetown U, 1995 *Certification:* Cardiovascular Disease
415 Old Newport Blvd, Newport Beach, 949-548-9611

Pelikan, Peter David (9 mentions)
Harvard U, 1979 *Certification:* Cardiovascular Disease,
Internal Medicine, Interventional Cardiology
2001 Santa Monica Blvd #280-W, Santa Monica, 310-829-7678

Rizi, H. Roger (3 mentions)
FMS-Iran, 1973
Certification: Cardiovascular Disease, Internal Medicine
320 E 27th St, Long Beach, 562-490-2133

Rosin, Benjamin Lee (6 mentions)
U of Southern California, 1966
Certification: Cardiovascular Disease, Internal Medicine
3330 Lomita Blvd, Torrance, 310-325-9110

Roth, Raul Fernando (8 mentions)
U of California-Irvine, 1983
Certification: Cardiovascular Disease, Internal Medicine
50 Alessandro Pl #200, Pasadena, 626-254-0074

Santora, Lawrence Joseph (3 mentions)
New York Med Coll, 1976
Certification: Cardiovascular Disease, Internal Medicine
1140 W La Veta Ave #640, Orange, 714-564-3300

Sato, David Alan (4 mentions)
U of Southern California, 1979
Certification: Cardiovascular Disease, Internal Medicine
201 S Buena Vista St #100, Burbank, 818-848-6404

Selvan, Arthur (3 mentions)
Mount Sinai Sch of Med, 1973
Certification: Cardiovascular Disease, Internal Medicine
1200 N Tustin Ave #260, Santa Ana, 714-543-9855

Shah, Prediman Krishan (4 mentions)
FMS-India, 1970
Certification: Cardiovascular Disease, Internal Medicine
8700 Beverly Blvd #5531, Los Angeles, 310-423-3884

Shamji, Munaf Abdul (3 mentions)
U of Kansas, 1992
Certification: Cardiovascular Disease, Interventional Cardiology
16119 Vanowen St, Van Nuys, 818-904-6782

Shiener, Alan (3 mentions)
U of Michigan, 1972
Certification: Cardiovascular Disease, Internal Medicine
4955 Van Nuys Blvd #704, Sherman Oaks, 818-501-5686

Stewart, Cydney Clare (4 mentions)
U of New Mexico, 1985
Certification: Cardiovascular Disease, Internal Medicine
5601 De Soto Ave, Woodland Hills, 818-719-3560

Thumati, Rama (8 mentions)
Certification: Cardiovascular Disease, Internal Medicine, Interventional Cardiology
1866 N Orange Grove Ave #202, Pomona, 909-623-8796

Togioka, Thomas Takashi (4 mentions)
U of California-Irvine, 1985
Certification: Cardiovascular Disease, Internal Medicine
4644 Lincoln Blvd, Marina Del Rey, 310-821-8087

Vahdat, Omid (3 mentions)
U of California-Irvine, 1996 *Certification:* Cardiovascular Disease, Internal Medicine, Interventional Cardiology
3801 Katella Ave #310, Los Alamitos, 562-598-0604

Waider, Winfried (3 mentions)
FMS-Germany, 1966
Certification: Cardiovascular Disease, Internal Medicine
2898 Linden Ave, Long Beach, 562-595-8671

Work, Jeffrey William (4 mentions)
Yale U, 1979
Certification: Cardiovascular Disease, Internal Medicine
18370 Burbank Blvd #707, Tarzana, 818-345-5580

Wright, Richard Forrest (5 mentions)
Harvard U, 1977
Certification: Cardiovascular Disease, Internal Medicine
2001 Santa Monica Blvd #280-W, Santa Monica, 310-829-7678

Wu, George Changho (3 mentions)
New York U, 1995 *Certification:* Cardiovascular Disease
2001 Santa Monica Blvd #280-W, Santa Monica, 310-829-7678

Yeatman, Lawrence A., Jr. (3 mentions)
Yale U, 1970 *Certification:* Cardiovascular Disease, Internal Medicine, Interventional Cardiology
200 Medical Plaza #365, Los Angeles, 310-899-7400

Dermatology

Alai, Nili Niloofar (3 mentions)
U of South Alabama, 1994 *Certification:* Dermatology
26081 Merit Cir #109, Laguna Hills, 949-582-7699

Alfred, Stanley (3 mentions)
Wayne State U, 1967 *Certification:* Dermatology
2001 Santa Monica Blvd #990-W, Santa Monica, 310-829-4484

Ashley, Jeff (3 mentions)
U of Southern California, 1974 *Certification:* Dermatology
2625 W Alameda Ave #517, Burbank, 818-845-8538

Babapour, Reza (3 mentions)
New York Med Coll, 1992 *Certification:* Dermatology
436 N Bedford Dr #212, Beverly Hills, 310-247-0337
1000 W Carson St, Torrance, 310-222-5101

Ball, Marina Aurora (3 mentions)
U of California-Irvine, 1978 *Certification:* Dermatology
1900 E Lambert Rd, Brea, 888-988-2800

Bennett, Richard Gary (6 mentions)
Case Western Reserve U, 1970 *Certification:* Dermatology
1301 20th St #570, Santa Monica, 310-315-0171
200 UCLA Medical Plaza #450, Los Angeles, 310-825-6911
50 Alessandro Pl #130, Pasadena, 626-564-4262

Danesh, Sid Abraham (3 mentions)
FMS-Iran, 1979
316 E Las Tunas Dr #103, San Gabriel, 626-287-9949
240 S La Cienega Blvd #400, Beverly Hills, 310-550-0666

Drayton, Gail (3 mentions)
U of Texas-San Antonio, 1975 *Certification:* Dermatology
11600 Wilshire Blvd #516, Los Angeles, 310-473-6536

Feibleman, Cary Edward (5 mentions)
Oregon Health Sciences U, 1975
Certification: Dermatology, Dermatopathology
701 E 28th St #311, Long Beach, 562-595-4777
1360 W 6th St North Bldg #370, San Pedro, 310-519-8890

Gilbert, Dore J. (3 mentions)
1441 Avocado Ave #806, Newport Beach, 949-718-1222

Goodman, Matthew M. (3 mentions)
U of Arizona, 1983 *Certification:* Dermatology
1125 E 17th St #W248, Santa Ana, 714-547-5151

Hartman, Robert Michael D. (6 mentions)
U of California-Los Angeles, 1982
Certification: Dermatology, Pediatric Dermatology
5400 Balboa Blvd #329, Encino, 818-907-7076

Heller, Alan William (3 mentions)
U of Arizona, 1974 *Certification:* Dermatology, Dermatopathology
1760 Termino Ave #114, Long Beach, 562-498-2459

Kane, Bryna (14 mentions)
U of California-Davis, 1980
3918 Long Beach Blvd #200, Long Beach, 562-989-5512

Kelly, Kristen Marie (3 mentions)
U of California-Los Angeles, 1993 *Certification:* Dermatology
1002 Health Sciences Rd, Irvine, 949-824-7980

Kim, Leonard Hubert (3 mentions)
U of Pennsylvania, 1997 *Certification:* Dermatology
150 N Robertson Blvd #304, Beverly Hills, 310-289-0009

Lao, Irene O. (4 mentions)
Certification: Dermatology
931 Buena Vista St #201, Duarte, 626-303-4626

Lener, Elizabeth Veronika (4 mentions)
U of California-Los Angeles, 1997 *Certification:* Dermatology
600 Corporate Dr #240, Ladera Ranch, 949-364-8411

Liem, Wieke Hoeygiok (3 mentions)
U of California-Irvine, 1989 *Certification:* Dermatology
1506 E Chapman Ave, Orange, 714-538-8556
1401 Avocado Ave #703, Newport Beach, 949-760-0190

Linden, Kenneth George (6 mentions)
U of California-Irvine, 1994 *Certification:* Dermatology
101 The City Dr S, Orange, 714-456-8000

Martinez, John Jesus (3 mentions)
Stanford U, 1985 *Certification:* Dermatology
6 Willard, Irvine, 888-988-2800

McKenzie, Daniel Kenneth (3 mentions)
U of Southern California, 1997 *Certification:* Dermatology
23961 Calle De La Magdalena #500, Laguna Hills, 949-465-8154

Mehlmauer, Marilyn Ann (3 mentions)
U of Southern California, 1976
Certification: Dermatology, Dermatopathology
10 Congress St #320, Pasadena, 626-585-9474

Mekelburg, Brian (3 mentions)
Tufts U, 1977 *Certification:* Dermatology
8631 W 3rd St #ET-1035, Los Angeles, 310-659-9075

Metz, Brandie Jean (3 mentions)
Northwestern U, 2000
15374 Alton Pkwy, Irvine, 714-456-7070

Ong, Hung Van (3 mentions)
U of California-Irvine, 1990 *Certification:* Dermatology
307 Placentia Ave #205, Newport Beach, 949-646-7546

Phelps, Billie Madelyn (5 mentions)
U of California-Los Angeles, 1972
Certification: Dermatology, Dermatopathology
2001 Santa Monica Blvd #855, Santa Monica, 310-829-7728

Pickus, Kurt Fredric (6 mentions)
U of California-Los Angeles, 1965
Certification: Dermatology, Dermatopathology
3440 Lomita Blvd #442, Torrance, 310-530-5451

Quinn, Marion Hope Apter (3 mentions)
U of Chicago, 1972 *Certification:* Dermatology, Internal Medicine
960 E Green St #164, Pasadena, 626-793-7790

Reager, Lauren Lee (5 mentions)
U of California-Los Angeles, 1964
Certification: Dermatology, Dermatopathology
2001 Santa Monica Blvd #990-W, Santa Monica, 310-829-4484

Rosenberg, Robert Michael (3 mentions)
U of California-Davis, 1982 *Certification:* Dermatology
2720 N Harbor Blvd #210, Fullerton, 714-449-6900

Saperstein, Harry W. (8 mentions)
U of Southern California, 1977 *Certification:* Dermatology
8920 Wilshire Blvd #545, Beverly Hills, 310-854-3003

Sherwood, Karen Anne (4 mentions)
Baylor U, 1983 *Certification:* Dermatology
4650 W Sunset Blvd, Los Angeles, 323-361-5488
1346 Foothill Blvd #203, La Canada, 818-790-6726

Silverberg, Nancy Lee (4 mentions)
St Louis U, 1978 *Certification:* Dermatology
1401 Avocado Ave #703, Newport Beach, 949-760-0190

Stevens, Gloria (4 mentions)
Wayne State U, 1985 *Certification:* Dermatology
886 W Foothill Blvd #G, Upland, 909-949-7500

Takahashi, Stefani Reiko (3 mentions)
U of Southern California, 1994
Certification: Dermatology, Pediatric Dermatology
55 E California Blvd #204, Pasadena, 626-397-8323

Vaccaro, Seth Anthony (3 mentions)
U of Southern California, 1983 *Certification:* Dermatology
800 Fairmount Ave #425, Pasadena, 626-449-9992

Weiss, Steven Robert (4 mentions)
George Washington U, 1979
Certification: Dermatology, Internal Medicine
465 N Roxbury Dr #803, Beverly Hills, 310-274-9954

Woodley, David T. (3 mentions)
U of Missouri, 1972 *Certification:* Clinical & Laboratory Dermatology, Dermatology, Internal Medicine
1520 San Pablo St #1000, Los Angeles, 323-442-6200

Emergency Medicine

Anderson, Peter Gregory (4 mentions)
U of Wisconsin, 1973 *Certification:* Emergency Medicine
17100 Euclid St, Fountain Valley, 714-966-7200

Antelyes, Roy Stephen (3 mentions)
U of Southern California, 1977
Certification: Emergency Medicine
3370 Wrightwood Dr, North Hollywood, 626-397-5112
100 W California Blvd, Pasadena, 626-397-5111

Burns, Michael James (3 mentions)
U of California-Irvine, 1975 *Certification:* Emergency Medicine,
Geriatric Medicine, Infectious Disease, Internal Medicine
101 The City Dr S, Orange, 714-456-5239

Candioty, Victor Albert (6 mentions)
U of California-Los Angeles, 1986
Certification: Emergency Medicine, Internal Medicine
1328 22nd St, Santa Monica, 310-582-7089

Carruthers, Gail (4 mentions)
FMS-Canada, 1977 *Certification:* Emergency Medicine,
Pediatric Emergency Medicine
2801 Atlantic Ave, Long Beach, 562-933-2000

Geiderman, Joel Martin (5 mentions)
U of Illinois, 1976 *Certification:* Emergency Medicine
8700 Beverly Blvd, Los Angeles, 310-423-8780

Goldweber, Robert Thomas (3 mentions)
U of California-Los Angeles, 1978
Certification: Emergency Medicine
100 W California Blvd, Pasadena, 626-397-5112

Johnston, Brian Dean (3 mentions)
U of California-San Francisco, 1969
1720 E Cesar Chavez Ave, Los Angeles, 323-268-5000
1700 E Walnut Ave #250, El Segundo, 310-301-2030

Kalter, Stanley M. (3 mentions)
U of Southern California, 1974
Certification: Emergency Medicine, Internal Medicine
100 W California Blvd, Pasadena, 626-397-5112

Kino, Russell Joseph (8 mentions)
FMS-Australia, 1982 *Certification:* Emergency Medicine
1328 22nd St, Santa Monica, 310-582-7089

Langdorf, Mark Ira (5 mentions)
U of California-San Diego, 1984
Certification: Emergency Medicine
101 The City Dr, Orange, 714-456-5239

Loftus, James John (3 mentions)
U of Tennessee, 1970
Certification: Emergency Medicine, Internal Medicine
8700 Beverly Blvd, Los Angeles, 310-423-8780

Lopez, Raul (4 mentions)
U of California-Los Angeles, 1990
Certification: Emergency Medicine
309 W Beverly Blvd, Montebello, 818-340-9988

Lotfipour, Shahram (3 mentions)
Certification: Emergency Medicine
101 The City Dr S, Orange, 714-456-5239

Moreau, Gary Paul (3 mentions)
U of Iowa, 1973 *Certification:* Emergency Medicine,
Pediatric Emergency Medicine
2801 Atlantic Ave, Long Beach, 562-933-2000

Morgan, Marshall Tad (5 mentions)
U of Chicago, 1968 *Certification:* Cardiovascular Disease,
Emergency Medicine, Internal Medicine
10833 Le Conte Ave, Los Angeles, 310-825-2111

Nakashioya, Howard Ken (4 mentions)
U of Southern California, 1983
Certification: Emergency Medicine
1 Hoag Dr, Newport Beach, 949-764-8372

Pratt, Franklin Daniel (3 mentions)
Rosalind Franklin U, 1981
Certification: Emergency Medicine, Internal Medicine
1320 N Eastern Ave, Los Angeles, 323-881-2471

Reich, Gerald Harvey (4 mentions)
U of Tennessee, 1972 *Certification:* Emergency Medicine
3330 Lomita Blvd, Torrance, 310-325-9110

Rudd, Steven Michael (3 mentions)
U of Southern California, 1991
Certification: Emergency Medicine
8700 Beverly Blvd, Los Angeles, 310-423-8780

Shoji, Kent Tadatoshi (8 mentions)
Med Coll of Wisconsin, 1972 *Certification:* Emergency
Medicine, Internal Medicine, Rheumatology
4101 Torrance Blvd, Torrance, 310-303-5600
4650 Lincoln Blvd, Marina Del Rey, 310-823-8911

Silka, Paul Andrew (13 mentions)
Rosalind Franklin U, 1988 *Certification:* Emergency
Medicine
8700 Beverly Blvd, Los Angeles, 310-423-8780

Simsarian, Gregory G. (5 mentions)
U of Southern California, 1986
Certification: Emergency Medicine
24451 Health Center Dr, Laguna Hills, 949-452-3564

Winokur, Robert Henry (3 mentions)
Tufts U, 1981 *Certification:* Emergency Medicine, Pediatric
Emergency Medicine
27700 Medical Center Rd, Mission Viejo, 949-365-2115

Endocrinology

Aftergood, David E. (6 mentions)
New York U, 1977
Certification: Endocrinology and Metabolism, Internal Medicine
99 N La Cienega Blvd #107, Beverly Hills, 310-659-8824

Banskota, Nirmal Kumar (5 mentions)
FMS-India, 1978 *Certification:* Endocrinology and
Metabolism, Internal Medicine, Pediatrics
301 W Huntington Dr #317, Arcadia, 626-446-0559

Barnett, Philip Sol (3 mentions)
FMS-South Africa, 1977
8723 Alden Dr #SSB-290, Los Angeles, 310-423-3870

Beredo, Angelita Santos (3 mentions)
FMS-Philippines, 1974
Certification: Endocrinology and Metabolism, Internal Medicine
301 N Prairie Ave #301, Inglewood, 310-671-2699

Brakin, Mario Ignacio (3 mentions)
FMS-Argentina, 1973
Certification: Pediatric Endocrinology, Pediatrics
2650 Elm Ave #210, Long Beach, 562-595-0166
2801 Atlantic Ave, Long Beach, 562-933-8562

Braunstein, Glenn David (7 mentions)
U of California-San Francisco, 1968
Certification: Endocrinology and Metabolism, Internal Medicine
8700 Beverly Blvd #2119-N, Los Angeles, 310-423-5140

Bush, Michael Alan (5 mentions)
U of Southern California, 1972
Certification: Endocrinology and Metabolism, Internal Medicine
8920 Wilshire Blvd #635, Beverly Hills, 310-652-3870

Chavez, Brian Escala (3 mentions)
Med Coll of Wisconsin, 2000 *Certification:* Endocrinology,
Diabetes, and Metabolism, Internal Medicine
23331 El Toro Rd #102, Lake Forest, 949-916-9100
655 Camino de los Mares #122, San Clemente, 949-916-9100

Choi, H. Helen (5 mentions)
Certification: Endocrinology, Diabetes, and Metabolism,
Internal Medicine
3771 Katella Ave #300, Los Alamitos, 562-430-7533

Chopra, Inder Jit (3 mentions)
FMS-India, 1962
Certification: Endocrinology and Metabolism, Internal Medicine
200 Medical Plaza #530, Los Angeles, 310-825-7922

Cohan, Pejman Eliaszadeh (6 mentions)
U of California-Los Angeles, 1995
Certification: Endocrinology, Diabetes, and Metabolism
150 N Robertson Blvd #210, Beverly Hills, 310-657-3030

Daniels, Mark William (4 mentions)
Stanford U, 1996
Certification: Pediatric Endocrinology, Pediatrics
455 S Main St 1st Fl, Orange, 714-532-8634

Dhillon, Kimvir Singh (4 mentions)
U of Vermont, 1998 *Certification:* Endocrinology, Diabetes,
and Metabolism, Internal Medicine
23961 Calle De La Magdalena #232, Laguna Hills, 949-588-8700

Fisher, Lynda Karen (4 mentions)
SUNY-Downstate Med Coll, 1970
Certification: Pediatric Endocrinology, Pediatrics
4650 Sunset Blvd, Los Angeles, 323-361-4606

Geffner, Mitchell Eugene (3 mentions)
Albert Einstein Coll of Med, 1975
Certification: Pediatric Endocrinology, Pediatrics
4650 W Sunset Blvd, Los Angeles, 323-361-4606

Geller, Jordan Leif (4 mentions)
U of Southern California, 2001 *Certification:* Endocrinology,
Diabetes, and Metabolism, Internal Medicine
8920 Wilshire Blvd #635, Beverly Hills, 310-652-3870

Goldberg, Neil James (4 mentions)
Rosalind Franklin U, 1972 *Certification:* Internal Medicine
9808 Venice Blvd #603, Culver City, 310-558-1836

Kaufman, Francine Ratner (3 mentions)
Rosalind Franklin U, 1976
Certification: Pediatric Endocrinology, Pediatrics
4650 W Sunset Blvd, Los Angeles, 323-361-4606

Kutas, Alex (11 mentions)
Oregon Health Sciences U, 1974
Certification: Endocrinology and Metabolism, Internal Medicine
3300 E South St #103, Lakewood, 562-634-9803

Levine, Gerald Allen (10 mentions)
U of Pittsburgh, 1969
Certification: Endocrinology and Metabolism, Internal Medicine
2001 Santa Monica Blvd #390-W, Santa Monica, 310-453-0559

Manoogian, Cary Michael (4 mentions)
U of Southern California, 1982 *Certification:* Internal Medicine
65 N Madison Ave #800, Pasadena, 626-792-3141

Mayeda, Samuel (3 mentions)
Med Coll of Wisconsin, 1970
Certification: Endocrinology and Metabolism, Internal Medicine
1140 W La Veta Ave #420, Orange, 714-285-1904

O'Connor, Gabrielle (3 mentions)
FMS-Ireland, 1978 *Certification:* Endocrinology, Diabetes,
and Metabolism, Internal Medicine
31852 S Coast Hwy #202, Laguna Beach, 949-499-5338

Prasad, Jeereddi A. (3 mentions)
FMS-India, 1971
Certification: Endocrinology and Metabolism, Internal Medicine
1904 N Orange Grove Ave, Pomona, 909-469-1823
10837 Laurel St #104, Rancho Cucamonga, 909-581-6732

Reddy, Radha (4 mentions)
FMS-India, 1989
Certification: Endocrinology, Diabetes, and Metabolism
10837 Laurel Ave #104, Rancho Cucamonga, 909-581-6732

Reikes, Andrew Reed (6 mentions)
U of California-San Diego, 1989 *Certification:* Endocrinology,
Diabetes, and Metabolism, Internal Medicine
101 The City Dr S, Orange, 888-456-7002
1 Medical Plaza Dr, Irvine, 949-824-2020

Rettinger, Herbert I. (3 mentions)
St Louis U, 1972
Certification: Endocrinology and Metabolism, Internal Medicine
2617 E Chapman Ave #105, Orange, 714-771-5700

Rokaw, Joshua Alan (3 mentions)
Washington U, 1985 *Certification:* Internal Medicine
15211 Vanowen St #100, Van Nuys, 818-778-1920

Rosenblit, Paul David (4 mentions)
FMS-Mexico, 1981
Certification: Endocrinology and Metabolism, Internal Medicine
18821 Delaware St #202, Huntington Beach, 714-375-5572

Sharp, Charles Frederick, Jr. (8 mentions)
U of Miami, 1970 *Certification:* Endocrinology and
Metabolism, Geriatric Medicine, Internal Medicine
10 Congress St #512, Pasadena, 626-449-9013

Singer, Peter Albert (5 mentions)
U of California-San Francisco, 1965
Certification: Endocrinology and Metabolism, Internal Medicine
1520 San Pablo St, Los Angeles, 323-442-5100

Sogol, Paul Barry (4 mentions)
U of California-San Francisco, 1977
Certification: Internal Medicine
18370 Burbank Blvd #211, Tarzana, 818-776-9805

Spamblg, Dorothea E. (3 mentions)
U of California-Los Angeles, 1990 *Certification:*
Endocrinology, Diabetes, and Metabolism, Internal Medicine
221 E Walnut St #115, Pasadena, 626-577-0505

Teresi, Amy Lutz (8 mentions)
Ohio State U, 1986 *Certification:* Endocrinology, Diabetes,
and Metabolism, Internal Medicine
400 Newport Center Dr #502, Newport Beach, 949-644-3568

Truong, Michael P. Minh (3 mentions)
U of California-San Francisco, 1985 *Certification:*
Endocrinology, Diabetes, and Metabolism, Internal Medicine
26800 Crown Valley Pkwy #125, Mission Viejo, 949-364-6000

Tseng, Conrad Jay (4 mentions)
U of Maryland, 1999 *Certification:* Endocrinology, Diabetes,
and Metabolism, Internal Medicine
99 N La Cienega Blvd #107, Beverly Hills, 310-652-3000

Wanski, Zdzislaus Joseph (3 mentions)
U of Pittsburgh, 1973
Certification: Endocrinology and Metabolism, Internal Medicine
1414 S Grand Ave #456, Los Angeles, 213-745-6047

Ziel, Frederick Harold (3 mentions)
U of Southern California, 1981
Certification: Endocrinology and Metabolism, Internal Medicine
5601 De Soto Ave, Woodland Hills, 818-719-4420

Family Practice *(see note on page 9)*

Abbott, Allan Victor (3 mentions)
Indiana U, 1969 *Certification:* Family Medicine, Sports Medicine
1520 San Pablo St #1300, Los Angeles, 323-442-5900

Barke, Jeffrey Ian (3 mentions)
U of California-Irvine, 1990 *Certification:* Family Medicine
17 Corporate Plaza Dr #110, Newport Beach, 949-706-3300

Braunstein, Mark Benjamin (4 mentions)
U of Southern California, 1987 *Certification:* Family Medicine
4955 Van Nuys Blvd #308, Sherman Oaks, 818-907-5088

Brunner, Lance Charles (5 mentions)
U of California-Irvine, 1995 *Certification:* Family Medicine
1900 E 4th St, Santa Ana, 888-988-2800
1900 E Lambert Rd, Brea, 888-988-2800

Honsberger, Pamela Erin (3 mentions)
U of California-Irvine, 1999 *Certification:* Family Medicine
1900 E 4th St, Santa Ana, 714-967-4670

Larsen, Kathryn Marie (3 mentions)
U of Washington, 1981 *Certification:* Family Medicine
1 Medical Plaza Dr, Irvine, 949-824-8600

Matsuura, Stacey Kent (3 mentions)
U of California-Davis, 1977 *Certification:* Family Medicine
21311 Madrona Ave, Torrance, 310-371-1010

Mogannam, Joanne Helen (3 mentions)
U of California-Los Angeles, 1983 *Certification:* Family Medicine
4700 W Sunset Blvd, Los Angeles, 323-783-4011
4760 Sunset Blvd, Los Angeles, 323-783-4011
4950 Sunset Blvd, Los Angeles, 323-783-4011

Quan, Martin Alan (4 mentions)
U of California-Los Angeles, 1977 *Certification:* Family Medicine
10833 Le Conte Ave, Los Angeles, 310-794-9956

Seizer, Steven Philip (5 mentions)
U of California-San Francisco, 1983
Certification: Family Medicine
2001 Santa Monica Blvd #380-W, Santa Monica, 310-586-9002

Gastroenterology

Abrahm, Donald Robert (6 mentions)
U of California-San Francisco, 1980
Certification: Gastroenterology, Internal Medicine
1525 Superior Ave #104, Newport Beach, 949-631-2670

Albers, C. Gregory (6 mentions)
U of California-Los Angeles, 1987
101 The City Dr S, Orange, 888-456-7002

Ashby, Kevin Howard (5 mentions)
U of Michigan, 1987
Certification: Gastroenterology, Internal Medicine
23961 Calle De La Magdalena #500, Laguna Hills, 949-588-8700

Austin, Fernando Herschel (3 mentions)
Hahnemann U, 1975
19066 Monolia Ave, Huntington Beach, 714-378-6750

Bain, Norman Harold (4 mentions)
Indiana U, 1965
Certification: Gastroenterology, Internal Medicine
400 Newport Center Dr, Newport Beach, 949-760-0398

Bedford, Rudolph Albert (3 mentions)
Case Western Reserve U, 1987 *Certification:* Internal Medicine
1301 20th St #280, Santa Monica, 310-829-6789
2336 Santa Monica Blvd #204, Santa Monica, 310-453-4477

Chang, Kenneth J. (5 mentions)
Brown U, 1985 *Certification:* Gastroenterology, Internal Medicine
101 The City Dr S Bldg 23, Orange, 714-456-8440

Chen, Jaime (3 mentions)
U of Pennsylvania, 1999
Certification: Gastroenterology, Internal Medicine
6041 Cadillac Ave, Los Angeles, 323-857-2000

Chen, Joe Meannan (4 mentions)
U of Tennessee, 1989
Certification: Gastroenterology, Internal Medicine
10861 Cherry St #302, Los Alamitos, 562-493-1011

Codini, Rose T. (4 mentions)
Loyola U Chicago, 1975
Certification: Gastroenterology, Internal Medicine
24411 Health Center Dr #430, Laguna Hills, 949-452-3933

Conklin, Jeffrey Lynn (3 mentions)
U of Iowa, 1978 *Certification:* Internal Medicine
8730 Alden Dr, Los Angeles, 310-423-6143

Derezin, Marvin (3 mentions)
Hahnemann U, 1962
Certification: Gastroenterology, Internal Medicine
100 UCLA Medical Plaza #700, Los Angeles, 310-208-5400

Dwyer, Richard Michael (3 mentions)
St Louis U, 1968 *Certification:* Internal Medicine
201 S Alvarado St #407, Los Angeles, 213-483-2470

Edelman, Kalman Jacob (5 mentions)
U of Illinois, 1977
Certification: Gastroenterology, Internal Medicine
55 E California Blvd, Pasadena, 626-440-7201

Edelstein, Marc Andrew (3 mentions)
Boston U, 1995
Certification: Gastroenterology, Internal Medicine
150 N Robertson Blvd #204, Beverly Hills, 310-659-1300

Elson, Nathan Robert (5 mentions)
Tulane U, 1979 *Certification:* Internal Medicine
2001 Santa Monica Blvd #1170-W, Santa Monica, 310-828-9495

Fagen, Neil D. (3 mentions)
Certification: Gastroenterology, Internal Medicine
18546 Roscoe Blvd #300, Northridge, 818-341-4796

Feldman, Edward Jon (6 mentions)
Indiana U, 1969
Certification: Gastroenterology, Internal Medicine
8635 W 3rd St #960, Los Angeles, 310-652-8031

Frankel, Charles Joseph (12 mentions)
U of California-Los Angeles, 1983
Certification: Gastroenterology, Internal Medicine
2001 Santa Monica Blvd #360W, Santa Monica, 310-453-1871

Fullman, Howard Jay (3 mentions)
Northwestern U, 1979
Certification: Gastroenterology, Internal Medicine
6041 Cadillac Ave, Los Angeles, 323-857-2218

Getzug, Sheldon Joel (3 mentions)
U of Southern California, 1959
Certification: Gastroenterology, Internal Medicine
18425 Burbank Blvd #500, Tarzana, 818-708-6000

Giap, Andrew Quocanh (3 mentions)
U of California-Irvine, 1994 *Certification:* Gastroenterology
411 N Lakeview Ave, Anaheim, 714-279-5317

Goldman, Gerald Donald (3 mentions)
Boston U, 1977
Certification: Gastroenterology, Internal Medicine
1866 N Orange Grove Ave #104, Pomona, 909-623-8628

Grant, Kenneth Edward (4 mentions)
Albany Med Coll, 1981 *Certification:* Pediatric Gastroenterology
455 S Main St, Orange, 714-289-4099

Gross, Robert Alan (4 mentions)
U of Pennsylvania, 1970
Certification: Gastroenterology, Internal Medicine
3831 Hughes Ave #706, Culver City, 310-204-4044

Hertz, Danice (8 mentions)
U of California-Los Angeles, 1982
Certification: Gastroenterology, Internal Medicine
2001 Santa Monica Blvd #360W, Santa Monica, 310-453-1871

Hierro, Martha Elva (4 mentions)
U of California-Los Angeles, 1987
1301 20th St #280, Santa Monica, 310-829-6789
2336 Santa Monica Blvd #204, Santa Monica, 310-453-4477

Ibarra, Fernando (3 mentions)
FMS-Mexico, 1979
Certification: Gastroenterology, Internal Medicine
850 S Atlantic Blvd #101, Monterey Park, 626-284-1350

Katz, Mitchell Haven (5 mentions)
SUNY-Downstate Med Coll, 1977
Certification: Pediatric Gastroenterology, Pediatrics
455 S Main St, Orange, 714-289-4099

Kaufman, David J. (3 mentions)
Des Moines U, 1998
Certification: Gastroenterology, Internal Medicine
18 Endeavor #204, Irvine, 949-727-2035

Kun, Thomas Louis (9 mentions)
U of California-Los Angeles, 1968
Certification: Gastroenterology, Internal Medicine
1301 20th St #280, Santa Monica, 310-829-6789
2336 Santa Monica Blvd #204, Santa Monica, 310-453-4477

Kuritzkes, Richard A. (3 mentions)
Certification: Gastroenterology, Internal Medicine
2701 W Alameda Ave #206, Burbank, 818-845-3773
26357 McBean Pkwy, Valencia, 661-284-6217

Littenberg, Glenn David (3 mentions)
U of Southern California, 1973
Certification: Gastroenterology, Internal Medicine
630 S Raymond Ave #240, Pasadena, 626-449-9920

Lo, Simon K. (4 mentions)
New York U, 1982
Certification: Gastroenterology, Internal Medicine
8700 Beverly Blvd, West Hollywood, 310-423-6082

Loewy, Joseph (3 mentions)
FMS-Germany, 1979
8631 W 3rd St #825, Los Angeles, 310-854-0527

Madokoro, Glenn Douglas (5 mentions)
U of California-Los Angeles, 1974
Certification: Gastroenterology, Internal Medicine
351 Hospital Rd #210, Newport Beach, 949-548-8800

Mathews, Sajen J. (4 mentions)
FMS-India, 1986
Certification: Gastroenterology, Internal Medicine
1847 Sunnycrest Dr, Fullerton, 714-446-5831

Mathis, Richard Kaye (5 mentions)
U of California-Los Angeles, 1969
Certification: Pediatric Gastroenterology, Pediatrics
1760 Terminal Ave #300, Long Beach, 562-933-3009
2801 Atlantic Ave, Long Beach, 562-933-3009
3640 La Mita Blvd #102, Torrance, 562-933-3009

Mourani, Samuel (3 mentions)
FMS-Syria, 1988
Certification: Gastroenterology, Internal Medicine
1330 W Covina Blvd #203, San Dimas, 909-592-6157
488 E Santa Clara St #102, Arcadia, 909-592-6157

Nickowitz, Richard Emery (5 mentions)
Cornell U, 1987
Certification: Gastroenterology, Internal Medicine
50 Alessandro Pl #410, Pasadena, 626-793-7114
55 E California Blvd #204, Pasadena, 626-397-8335

Petit, Steven Justin (3 mentions)
U of Southern California, 1974
Certification: Gastroenterology, Internal Medicine
630 S Raymond Ave #240, Pasadena, 626-449-9920

Rosenberg, Peter Morris (3 mentions)
Harvard U, 1993
Certification: Gastroenterology, Internal Medicine
50 Alessandro Pl #410, Pasadena, 626-793-7114

Roth, Bennett Elliot (3 mentions)
Hahnemann U, 1968
Certification: Gastroenterology, Internal Medicine
200 UCLA Medical Plaza #365-A, Los Angeles, 310-825-1597

Severance, Stephen Robert (4 mentions)
Cornell U, 1967
Certification: Gastroenterology, Internal Medicine
2880 Atlantic Ave #100, Long Beach, 562-595-5421

Share, Edward Jonathan (4 mentions)
Jefferson Med Coll, 1974
Certification: Gastroenterology, Internal Medicine
8635 W 3rd St #970, Los Angeles, 310-652-4472

Sherman, James Harold (3 mentions)
U of Southern California, 1967 *Certification:* Internal Medicine
8631 W 3rd St #540, Los Angeles, 310-659-9600

Shiffman, Michael Isaac (4 mentions)
SUNY-Downstate Med Coll, 1973
Certification: Gastroenterology, Internal Medicine
15211 Vanowen St #207, Van Nuys, 818-989-1917

Shindel, Neal Michael (3 mentions)
SUNY-Upstate Med U, 1980
Certification: Gastroenterology, Internal Medicine
15141 Whittier Blvd #260, Whittier, 562-698-0306

Simmons, Timothy C. (4 mentions)
U of Florida, 1974
Certification: Gastroenterology, Internal Medicine
8110 Airport Blvd, Los Angeles, 310-674-0144

Sinatra, Frank Raymond (3 mentions)
U of Southern California, 1971
Certification: Pediatric Gastroenterology, Pediatrics
1242 Mission Rd #10, Los Angeles, 323-226-3691

Singh, Hardeep Marwah (3 mentions)
U of Southern California, 2001
Certification: Gastroenterology, Internal Medicine
1201 W La Veta #211, Orange, 714-639-3363

Stanton, David Brian (3 mentions)
Tufts U, 1981 *Certification:* Gastroenterology, Internal Medicine
1140 W La Veta Ave #555, Orange, 714-835-5100
16300 Sand Canyon Ave #105, Irvine, 949-727-4485

Stein, Theodore Nerber (3 mentions)
Albany Med Coll, 1984
Certification: Gastroenterology, Internal Medicine
99 N La Cienega Blvd #307, Beverly Hills, 310-385-3506

Strom, Carey Bennett (3 mentions)
Rosalind Franklin U, 1980
Certification: Gastroenterology, Internal Medicine
9090 Wilshire Blvd #101, Beverly Hills, 310-550-0400

Thomas, George P. (4 mentions)
FMS-India, 1974
Certification: Gastroenterology, Internal Medicine
622 W Duarte Rd #302, Arcadia, 626-447-0782

Trenbeath, James Michael (4 mentions)
George Washington U, 1974
Certification: Gastroenterology, Internal Medicine
23961 Calle De La Magdalena #130, Laguna Hills, 949-588-8700

Villa, Vincente L., Jr. (3 mentions)
FMS-Philippines, 1968
1510 S Central Ave #300, Glendale, 818-254-1500

Weinstock, Steven (4 mentions)
New York Med Coll, 1974
Certification: Gastroenterology, Internal Medicine
20911 Earl St #280, Torrance, 310-214-7236

Wishingrad, Marc David (3 mentions)
U of California-Los Angeles, 1989 *Certification:* Gastroenterology
2001 Santa Monica Blvd #360W, Santa Monica, 310-453-1871

Yang, Russell David (5 mentions)
Baylor U, 1984 *Certification:* Gastroenterology, Internal Medicine
1520 San Pablo St #1000, Los Angeles, 323-442-5100

Yao, Diana Kelly (6 mentions)
George Washington U, 1990
Certification: Gastroenterology, Internal Medicine
2880 Atlantic Ave #100, Long Beach, 562-595-5421

Zamost, Barry Jay (4 mentions)
Boston U, 1976
Certification: Gastroenterology, Internal Medicine
2880 Atlantic Ave #100, Long Beach, 562-595-5421
3771 Katella Ave #110, Los Alamitos, 562-431-9306

General Surgery

Adashek, Kenneth Wayne (10 mentions)
U of California-Los Angeles, 1970 *Certification:* Surgery
8631 W 3rd St #710-E, Los Angeles, 310-854-0815

Asch, Lester (5 mentions)
Albert Einstein Coll of Med, 1971 *Certification:* Surgery
3801 Katella Ave #212, Los Alamitos, 562-431-6000

Azaren, Kent H. (4 mentions)
U of Rochester, 1978 *Certification:* Surgery
2865 Atlantic Ave #223, Long Beach, 562-424-0421

Baghai, Mercedeh (3 mentions)
U of California-San Francisco, 1997
23451 Madison St #340, Torrance, 310-373-6864

Barragan, Alfonso L. (3 mentions)
FMS-Mexico, 1972 *Certification:* Surgery
850 S Atlantic Blvd #305, Monterey Park, 626-570-6920

Butler, John Albert (5 mentions)
Loyola U Chicago, 1976 *Certification:* Surgery
101 The City Dr S, Orange, 714-456-8030

Carroll, Brendan J. (7 mentions)
Cornell U, 1982 *Certification:* Surgery
8670 Wilshire Blvd #203, Beverly Hills, 310-854-0151

Carvajal, Samuel Humberto (5 mentions)
U of California-San Francisco, 1989 *Certification:* Surgery
1560 E Chevy Chase Dr #430, Glendale, 818-243-1135

Chandler, Charles Francis (3 mentions)
Washington U, 1988 *Certification:* Surgery
10833 Le Conte Ave, Los Angeles, 310-451-8751
1260 15th St #1200, Santa Monica, 310-451-8751

Childs, Tracey Rochelle (3 mentions)
U of California-Los Angeles, 1986
Certification: Colon & Rectal Surgery, Surgery
2021 Santa Monica Blvd #625, Santa Monica, 310-453-8838

Cole, Robert Eli (7 mentions)
Albert Einstein Coll of Med, 1982 *Certification:* Surgery
2121 Wilshire Blvd #302, Santa Monica, 310-264-7300

Coleman, Colleen Linda (3 mentions)
U of Southern California, 1993 *Certification:* Surgery
1441 Avocado Ave #503, Newport Beach, 949-706-2607

Crain, Steven Robert (5 mentions)
Certification: Surgery
5601 De Soto Ave, Woodland Hills, 818-719-2000

Deck, Kenneth Bernard (4 mentions)
Ohio State U, 1973
24411 Health Center Dr #350, Laguna Hills, 949-457-7900

Desantis, Stephen Anthony (3 mentions)
U of California-Los Angeles, 1978 *Certification:* Surgery
26732 Crown Valley Pkwy #351, Mission Viejo, 949-364-1007

DiNome, Maggie L. (5 mentions)
Duke U, 1994 *Certification:* Surgery
2001 Santa Monica Blvd #1170W, Santa Monica, 310-828-8399

Dolich, Matthew Owen (3 mentions)
Stony Brook U, 1992 *Certification:* Surgery, Surgical Critical Care
333 City Blvd W #705, Orange, 714-456-5890

Edrich, Leslie Howard (3 mentions)
New York U, 1980 *Certification:* Surgery
701 E 28th St #400, Long Beach, 562-427-9929

El-Bayar, Hisham Mahmoud (3 mentions)
Georgetown U, 1986 *Certification:* Surgery
1310 W Stewart Dr #307, Orange, 714-538-0342

Fine, Marjorie Blank (4 mentions)
U of California-Los Angeles, 1975 *Certification:* Surgery
2021 Santa Monica Blvd #625E, Santa Monica, 310-453-8838

Ford, Henri Ronald (3 mentions)
Harvard U, 1984 *Certification:* Pediatric Surgery, Surgery
4650 W Sunset Blvd, Los Angeles, 323-361-2322

Friedlander, Melanie Hope (8 mentions)
New Jersey Med Sch, 1993 *Certification:* Surgery
23451 Madison St #340, Torrance, 310-373-6864
1294 W 6th St #106, San Pedro, 310-373-6864

Gilani, Abdollah (3 mentions)
FMS-Germany, 1962 *Certification:* Surgery
11704 Wilshire Blvd #224, Los Angeles, 310-477-2236

Giuliano, Armando Elario (3 mentions)
U of Chicago, 1973 *Certification:* Surgery
2200 Santa Monica Blvd #113, Santa Monica, 310-829-8089

Hines, Oscar Joe (3 mentions)
U of Oklahoma, 1990 *Certification:* Surgery
200 Medical Plaza #214, Los Angeles, 310-794-7788

Hoffman, Allen Lee (5 mentions)
U of Pittsburgh, 1984
Certification: Surgery, Surgical Critical Care
201 S Alvarado St #321, Tarzana, 818-345-9600

Hurwitz, Michael Bruce (4 mentions)
Louisiana State U, 1988 *Certification:* Surgery
1901 Westcliff Dr #2, Newport Beach, 949-631-4890

Hutchinson, William Burke, Jr. (6 mentions)
FMS-Canada, 1971
2001 Santa Monica Blvd #W-790, Santa Monica, 310-453-1786

Kinzinger, Kevin (3 mentions)
U of Southern California, 1984
Certification: Colon & Rectal Surgery, Surgery
100 E Valencia Mesa Dr #101, Fullerton, 714-446-5511

Kuchenbecker, Stephen L. (6 mentions)
U of California-Los Angeles, 1974 *Certification:* Surgery
2001 Santa Monica Blvd #460, Santa Monica, 310-829-9400

Lam, Vinh Thuy (5 mentions)
Harvard U, 1991 *Certification:* Pediatric Surgery, Surgery
1120 W La Veta Ave #100, Orange, 714-289-4704
27800 Medical Center Dr #138, Mission Viejo, 714-361-4480

Lomis, Thomas John (3 mentions)
U of Pittsburgh, 1992 *Certification:* Surgery
15211 Vanowen St #208, Van Nuys, 714-782-3255

Lourie, David Joseph (5 mentions)
Indiana U, 1988 *Certification:* Surgery
50 Bellefontaine St #404, Pasadena, 626-449-0694

McCoy, Robert Emmett (6 mentions)
FMS-Mexico, 1985 *Certification:* Surgery
1950 Sunnycrest Dr, Fullerton, 714-447-3144

McNamara, John Patrick (3 mentions)
Louisiana State U, 1974 *Certification:* Surgery
1294 W 6th St #106, San Pedro, 310-373-6864
23451 Madison St #340, Torrance, 310-373-6864

Minkes, Mark Stanley (4 mentions)
Washington U, 1973 *Certification:* Surgery, Vascular Surgery
11480 Brookshire Ave #111, Downey, 562-904-1651

Morrow, Douglas (9 mentions)
SUNY-Upstate Med U, 1969
18370 Burbank Blvd #607, Tarzana, 818-708-1004

Muenchow, Sharon Kay (3 mentions)
U of Texas-San Antonio, 1972
Certification: Pediatric Surgery, Surgery
800 S Fairmount Ave #325, Pasadena, 626-577-7432

Mule, Joseph Michael (4 mentions)
SUNY-Downstate Med Coll, 1972 *Certification:* Surgery
1211 W La Palma Ave #705, Anaheim, 714-772-6701

O'Connell, Theodore X. (4 mentions)
U of California-Los Angeles, 1969 *Certification:* Surgery
4760 W Sunset Blvd, Los Angeles, 323-783-4924

Pehrsson, Bengt Florian (4 mentions)
FMS-Germany, 1975
Certification: Colon & Rectal Surgery, Surgery
622 W Duarte Rd #301, Arcadia, 626-445-0600

Phillips, Edward H. (12 mentions)
U of Southern California, 1973 *Certification:* Surgery
310 N San Vincente Blvd, West Hollywood, 310-423-9331
8635 W 3rd St #795-W, Los Angeles, 310-423-6967

Powell, Wes Joe (5 mentions)
U of Texas-San Antonio, 1986 *Certification:* Surgery
50 Bellefontaine St #404, Pasadena, 626-449-0694

Quilici, Philippe Jean (5 mentions)
FMS-France, 1979 *Certification:* Surgery
201 S Buena Vista St #425, Burbank, 818-845-1701
8600 Beverly Blvd, Los Angeles, 323-849-2670

Rangel, Decio De Moura (5 mentions)
FMS-Brazil, 1963 *Certification:* Surgery
2001 Santa Monica Blvd #780-W, Santa Monica, 310-828-7454

Sachs, Todd Morgan (3 mentions)
Rosalind Franklin U, 1986 *Certification:* Surgery
6041 Cadillac Ave, Los Angeles, 323-857-2218

Schreier, David Zane (3 mentions)
U of California-Davis, 1991 *Certification:* Surgery
7320 Woodlake Ave #380, West Hills, 818-226-9030

Shofler, Raymond Allen (3 mentions)
Cornell U, 1979 *Certification:* Surgery
2601 W Alameda Ave #314, Burbank, 818-842-9125

Snyder, Lincoln Mackey (3 mentions)
Jefferson Med Coll, 1984 *Certification:* Surgery
351 Hospital Rd #218, Newport Beach, 949-645-8600

Steele, Barry Dennis (7 mentions)
U of California-Los Angeles, 1967 *Certification:* Surgery
320 Superior Ave #190, Newport Beach, 949-631-4353

Stein, James Eric (3 mentions)
Tufts U, 1986 *Certification:* Pediatric Surgery, Surgery
4650 Sunset Blvd, Los Angeles, 323-361-2438

Takahashi, Aileen Miyoko (3 mentions)
New York Med Coll, 1996
Certification: Surgery, Surgical Critical Care
23451 Madison St #340, Torrance, 310-373-6864
1294 W 6th St #106, San Pedro, 310-373-6864

Takasugi, Jan Kinu (6 mentions)
U of California-Los Angeles, 1983 *Certification:* Surgery
6041 Cadillac Ave, Los Angeles, 323-857-2171

Tan, Larissa Rosario (3 mentions)
U of California-Irvine, 1989 *Certification:* Surgery
441 N Lakeview Ave, Anaheim, 888-988-2800

Thompson, Kennith Oliver (3 mentions)
Jefferson Med Coll, 1975 *Certification:* Surgery
7957 Painter Ave #102, Whittier, 562-945-1396

Tyrell, Jon Sands (3 mentions)
U of Southern California, 1987 *Certification:* Surgery
612 W Duarte Rd #602, Arcadia, 626-446-4645

Vanyo, Lori Lee (3 mentions)
Loma Linda U, 1994 *Certification:* Surgery
138 Harvard Ave, Claremont, 909-624-4503

Wallace, William Campbell (6 mentions)
U of Vermont, 1996 *Certification:* Surgery
24411 Health Center Dr #350, Laguna Hills, 949-457-7900

Zablan, Augusto Afable (5 mentions)
FMS-Philippines, 1968 *Certification:* Surgery
2105 Beverly Blvd #213, Los Angeles, 213-413-1752

Geriatrics

Chien, Norman T. (4 mentions)
375 Huntington Dr #G, San Marino, 626-441-4231

Davis, James William, Jr. (6 mentions)
Med U of South Carolina, 1975
Certification: Geriatric Medicine, Internal Medicine
200 UCLA Medical Plaza #420, Los Angeles, 310-206-8272

Eslami, Michelle Saghatol (4 mentions)
FMS-Grenada, 1986
Certification: Geriatric Medicine, Internal Medicine
200 UCLA Medical Plaza #420, Los Angeles, 310-206-8272

Kim, Dohwa (3 mentions)
FMS-South Korea, 1992
Certification: Geriatric Medicine, Internal Medicine
1520 San Pablo St #1000, Los Angeles, 323-442-5100

Mosqueda, Laura A. (5 mentions)
U of Southern California, 1987
Certification: Family Medicine, Geriatric Medicine
101 The City Dr S Pavillion 4, Orange, 714-456-7007

Osterweil, Dan (3 mentions)
FMS-Israel, 1975
4929 Van Nuys Blvd, Sherman Oaks, 818-341-7243

Reuben, David B. (3 mentions)
Emory U, 1977
Certification: Geriatric Medicine, Internal Medicine
10945 Le Conte Ave #2339, Los Angeles, 310-825-8253
200 UCLA Medical Plaza #420, Los Angeles, 310-206-8272

Wang, Robert T. (3 mentions)
U of Miami, 1978 *Certification:* Internal Medicine
5901 W Olympic Blvd, Los Angeles, 310-551-1200

Hematology/Oncology

Agajanian, Richy (4 mentions)
U of California-Irvine, 1998
Certification: Hematology, Internal Medicine, Medical Oncology
12291 Washington Blvd #201, Whittier, 562-698-6888
11480 Brookshire Ave #309, Downey, 562-869-1201
111 W Beverly Blvd #105, Montebello, 323-278-4400

Applebaum, Steven Hersch (7 mentions)
U of Southern California, 1990
Certification: Hematology, Medical Oncology
55 E California Blvd #100, Pasadena, 626-396-2999

Barth, Neil Michael (8 mentions)
U of Toledo, 1977
Certification: Hematology, Internal Medicine, Medical Oncology
4000 W Pacific Coast Hwy #3-C, Newport Beach, 949-631-9000
20162 SW Birch St #200, Newport Beach, 949-631-9000

Blitzer, Jonathan Ben (3 mentions)
SUNY-Upstate Med U, 1980
Certification: Internal Medicine, Medical Oncology
2653 Elm Ave #300, Long Beach, 562-595-7335
5882 Bolsa Ave #100, Huntington Beach, 714-890-1002

Bluming, Avrum Zvi (7 mentions)
Columbia U, 1965
Certification: Hematology, Internal Medicine, Medical Oncology
16133 Ventura Blvd #470, Encino, 818-981-3818

Boasberg, Peter David (3 mentions)
U of California-Irvine, 1970
Certification: Internal Medicine, Medical Oncology
2001 Santa Monica Blvd #560, Santa Monica, 310-582-7927

Bosserman, Linda Diana (4 mentions)
Stanford U, 1981
Certification: Internal Medicine, Medical Oncology
1910 Royalty Dr, Pomona, 909-865-9960
8283 Grove Ave #207, Rancho Cucamonga, 909-949-2242

Carroll, Robert Matthew (3 mentions)
Hahnemann U, 1998
Certification: Hematology, Internal Medicine, Medical Oncology
20162 SW Birch St #200, Newport Beach, 949-553-3330
4000 W Pacific Coast Hwy #3-C, Newport Beach, 949-553-3330

Casciato, Dennis Albert (4 mentions)
U of California-San Francisco, 1964
Certification: Hematology, Internal Medicine, Medical Oncology
5525 Etiwanda Ave #215, Tarzana, 818-705-3900

Chan, David (6 mentions)
U of California-Los Angeles, 1979
Certification: Internal Medicine, Medical Oncology
514 N Prospect Ave #4, Redondo Beach, 310-750-3300

Chang, Johnny Kuofeng (4 mentions)
U of California-Los Angeles, 1998
Certification: Hematology, Internal Medicine, Medical Oncology
16133 Ventura Blvd #470, Encino, 818-981-3818

Cheng, Howard Howing (4 mentions)
Yale U, 1992 *Certification:* Hematology, Medical Oncology
24953 Paseo De Valencia #25-B, Laguna Hills, 949-770-8168

Chou, Jia-Ling (3 mentions)
FMS-China, 1982 *Certification:* Medical Oncology
5601 De Soto Ave, Woodland Hills, 818-719-2000

Curti, Mario (5 mentions)
U of Connecticut, 1993
Certification: Hematology, Internal Medicine, Medical Oncology
3801 Katella Ave #207, Los Alamitos, 562-598-9745

Decker, Robert Wayne (5 mentions)
U of California-Davis, 1981
Certification: Internal Medicine, Medical Oncology
9090 Wilshire Blvd #200, Beverly Hills, 310-888-8680

Dosik, Gary Michael (6 mentions)
U of Illinois, 1971
Certification: Hematology, Internal Medicine, Medical Oncology
16133 Ventura Blvd #470, Encino, 818-981-3818

Drazin, Noam Zvi (4 mentions)
Albert Einstein Coll of Med, 1997
Certification: Internal Medicine, Medical Oncology
200 N Robertson Blvd, Beverly Hills, 310-385-3343

Feinstein, Donald Ivan (4 mentions)
Stanford U, 1958 *Certification:* Hematology, Internal Medicine
1441 Eastlake Ave #3436, Los Angeles, 323-865-3964

Finklestein, Jerry Z. (8 mentions)
FMS-Canada, 1963
Certification: Pediatric Hematology-Oncology, Pediatrics
2653 Elm Ave #200, Long Beach, 562-492-1062
23550 Hawthorne Blvd, Torrance, 562-492-1062

Fong, Minch (7 mentions)
U of California-San Diego, 1992 *Certification:* Medical Oncology
27800 Medical Center Rd #304, Mission Viejo, 949-347-0600

Hamburg, Solomon I. (3 mentions)
New York U, 1981
Certification: Hematology, Internal Medicine, Medical Oncology
9090 Wilshire Blvd #200, Beverly Hills, 310-888-8680

Janis, Mark G. (3 mentions)
U of North Carolina, 1970
Certification: Hematology, Internal Medicine, Medical Oncology
3801 Katella Ave #207, Los Alamitos, 562-598-9745

Koehler, Stephen Charles (4 mentions)
U of California-Irvine, 1974
Certification: Hematology, Internal Medicine, Medical Oncology
50 Bellefontaine St #104, Pasadena, 626-396-2900

Lieber, Daniel Joel (10 mentions)
U of California-Los Angeles, 1976
Certification: Internal Medicine, Medical Oncology
2001 Santa Monica Blvd #560, Santa Monica, 310-582-7911

Lim, Eduardo O. (3 mentions)
FMS-Philippines, 1982
Certification: Hematology, Internal Medicine, Medical Oncology
201 S Alvarado St #505, Los Angeles, 213-484-0146
6200 Wilshire Blvd #1510, Los Angeles, 323-964-1440

Link, John S. (3 mentions)
U of Southern California, 1972
Certification: Internal Medicine, Medical Oncology
701 E 28th St #201, Long Beach, 562-933-7820
14650 Aviation Blvd #200, Hawthorne, 310-539-2300

Lyons, William John (4 mentions)
Med Coll of Wisconsin, 1966
Certification: Hematology, Internal Medicine, Medical Oncology
4301 Atlantic Ave, Long Beach, 562-426-7006
2653 Elm Ave #300, Long Beach, 562-595-7335

McAndrew, Philomena F. (9 mentions)
U of Pennsylvania, 1978
Certification: Hematology, Internal Medicine, Medical Oncology
9090 Wilshire Blvd #200, Beverly Hills, 310-888-8680

Mena, Raul (7 mentions)
U of New Mexico, 1975
Certification: Hematology, Internal Medicine, Medical Oncology
2601 W Alameda Ave #210, Burbank, 818-840-0921

Nagasawa, Lloyd Stuart (6 mentions)
U of Hawaii, 1982
Certification: Internal Medicine, Medical Oncology
27800 Medical Center Rd #304, Mission Viejo, 949-347-0600

Nagourney, Robert Alan (5 mentions)
FMS-Canada, 1979
Certification: Hematology, Internal Medicine, Medical Oncology
750 E 29th St, Long Beach, 562-989-6455

Nishikubo, Carol Yukiko (6 mentions)
U of Southern California, 1990
Certification: Hematology, Internal Medicine, Medical Oncology
2021 Santa Monica Blvd #400-E, Santa Monica, 310-453-5654

Nugent, Diane Jean (5 mentions)
U of California-Los Angeles, 1977
Certification: Pediatric Hematology-Oncology, Pediatrics
455 S Main St, Orange, 714-532-8459

O'Day, Steven John (4 mentions)
Johns Hopkins U, 1988
11818 Wilshire Blvd #200, Los Angeles, 310-231-2121
2001 Santa Monica Blvd #560-W, Santa Monica, 310-582-7900

Orenstein, Allan A. (3 mentions)
U of Rochester, 1973
Certification: Internal Medicine, Medical Oncology
6801 Park Terr #130, Los Angeles, 310-649-7222

Orr, Leo Earsel, Jr. (4 mentions)
Baylor U, 1969
Certification: Internal Medicine, Medical Oncology
1245 Wilshire Blvd #801, Los Angeles, 213-481-3948
1338 S Hope St, Los Angeles, 213-742-5760

Rosenbloom, Barry Eugene (11 mentions)
SUNY-Downstate Med Coll, 1971
Certification: Internal Medicine, Medical Oncology
9090 Wilshire Blvd #200, Beverly Hills, 310-888-8680

Rosenfelt, Fred Paul (3 mentions)
Yale U, 1975 *Certification:* Internal Medicine, Medical Oncology
9090 Wilshire Blvd #200, Beverly Hills, 310-888-8680

Rosove, Michael Harry (4 mentions)
U of California-Los Angeles, 1973
Certification: Hematology, Internal Medicine, Medical Oncology
100 UCLA Medical Plaza #550, Los Angeles, 310-794-4955

Shapiro, Richard Alan (3 mentions)
U of California-Los Angeles, 1968
Certification: Hematology, Internal Medicine, Medical Oncology
612 W Duarte Rd #304, Arcadia, 626-446-4461

Sharma, Sanjay (3 mentions)
Virginia Commonwealth U, 1999
Certification: Hematology, Internal Medicine, Medical Oncology
2151 N Harbor Blvd #2200, Fullerton, 714-446-5900

Shaum, Melani P. (6 mentions)
Northwestern U, 1980
Certification: Hematology, Internal Medicine, Medical Oncology
2001 Santa Monica Blvd #560, Santa Monica, 310-582-7928

Stafford, Benjamin Thomas (4 mentions)
Tulane U, 1969
Certification: Hematology, Internal Medicine, Medical Oncology
612 W Duarte Rd #304, Arcadia, 626-446-4461

Terpenning, Marilou (11 mentions)
Washington U, 1976
Certification: Internal Medicine, Medical Oncology
2021 Santa Monica Blvd #400E, Santa Monica, 310-453-5654

Tetef, Merry Lynn (8 mentions)
Harvard U, 1987 *Certification:* Medical Oncology
4746 Barranca Pkwy, Irvine, 949-652-2959

Vandermolen, Louis A. (11 mentions)
Loyola U Chicago, 1980
Certification: Internal Medicine, Medical Oncology
4000 W Pacific Coast Hwy #3A, Newport Beach, 949-646-6441
1 Hoag Dr, Newport Beach, 949-646-6441

Infectious Disease

Antaki, Jean Edmond (5 mentions)
FMS-Egypt, 1982
801 S Chevy Chase Dr #105, Glendale, 818-242-5299

Armen, Robert Charles (6 mentions)
U of Southern California, 1980
Certification: Infectious Disease, Internal Medicine
845 W La Veta Ave #107, Orange, 714-289-7171

Arrieta, Antonio (7 mentions)
FMS-Peru, 1985 *Certification:* Pediatric Infectious Diseases
455 S Main St 1st Fl, Orange, 714-532-8403

Bailey, Charles Christopher (4 mentions)
U of California-Los Angeles, 1977
Certification: Infectious Disease, Internal Medicine
15 Mareblu #310, Aliso Viejo, 949-448-8861

Bock, Bonnie Virginia (4 mentions)
SUNY-Upstate Med U, 1974 *Certification:* Internal Medicine
1501 Superior Ave #300, Newport Beach, 949-645-9010

Cable, Douglas Charles (4 mentions)
Wayne State U, 1977
Certification: Infectious Disease, Internal Medicine
351 Hospital Rd #604, Newport Beach, 949-574-2628

Cesario, Thomas Charles (4 mentions)
U of Wisconsin, 1965
Certification: Infectious Disease, Internal Medicine
101 The City Dr S, Orange, 714-456-8395

Chia, John Kaisheng (12 mentions)
U of California-Los Angeles, 1979
Certification: Infectious Disease, Internal Medicine
23560 Crenshaw Blvd #101, Torrance, 310-784-5880

Fee, Martin Joseph (5 mentions)
U of Chicago, 1988
Certification: Infectious Disease, Internal Medicine
320 Superior Ave #290, Newport Beach, 949-650-2630

Gluckstein, Daniel Peter (4 mentions)
Washington U, 1981
Certification: Infectious Disease, Internal Medicine
255 E Bonita Ave, Pomona, 909-450-0390

Goldstein, Ellie Julius C. (24 mentions)
SUNY-Downstate Med Coll, 1971
2021 Santa Monica Blvd #740E, Santa Monica, 310-315-1511

Hernandez, Salvador (5 mentions)
Certification: Internal Medicine, Infectious Disease
411 N Lakeview Ave, Anaheim, 888-988-2800

Khaw, Melvin (9 mentions)
16101 Ventura Blvd #340, Encino, 818-788-7500

Lauermann, Michael W. (5 mentions)
U of Southern California, 1974 *Certification:* Internal Medicine
2865 Atlantic Ave #221, Long Beach, 562-427-6368

Lehman, Deborah (4 mentions)
U of California-Los Angeles, 1988
Certification: Pediatric Infectious Diseases, Pediatrics
8700 Beverly Blvd, West Hollywood, 310-423-4471
8723 W Alden Dr #240, West Hollywood, 310-423-4471

Leibowitz, Matthew R. (4 mentions)
Washington U, 1992
Certification: Infectious Disease, Internal Medicine
1245 16th St #309, Santa Monica, 310-319-4371

Litwack, Kenneth David (8 mentions)
U of California-Los Angeles, 1964
Certification: Infectious Disease, Internal Medicine
320 Superior Ave #280, Newport Beach, 949-645-9111

Man, David Gee (7 mentions)
U of California-San Francisco, 1994
Certification: Infectious Disease
50 Bellefontaine St #303, Pasadena, 626-793-6133

Mason, Wilbert Henry (4 mentions)
U of California-Irvine, 1970
Certification: Pediatric Infectious Diseases, Pediatrics
4650 W Sunset Blvd, Los Angeles, 323-361-2509

McCarthy, John David, Jr. (6 mentions)
U of California-Los Angeles, 1981
Certification: Infectious Disease, Internal Medicine
1850 S Azusa Ave #200, Hacienda Heights, 626-912-5767

Milefchik, Eric Niles (10 mentions)
U of Toledo, 1987
Certification: Infectious Disease, Internal Medicine
3400 Lomita Blvd #104, Torrance, 310-326-5648

Mortara, Laurie Ann (7 mentions)
U of Hawaii, 1987
Certification: Infectious Disease, Internal Medicine
2880 Atlantic Ave #170, Long Beach, 562-595-7164

Morton, Linda (5 mentions)
SUNY-Downstate Med Coll, 1980
2021 Santa Monica Blvd #530-E, Santa Monica, 310-315-5499

Nussbaum, Joseph Matthew (4 mentions)
FMS-Mexico, 1981
Certification: Infectious Disease, Internal Medicine
201 S Alvarado St #820, Los Angeles, 213-483-0901

Pegues, David Alexander (5 mentions)
U of Chicago, 1986
Certification: Infectious Disease, Internal Medicine
200 UCLA Medical Plaza #365-B, Los Angeles, 310-825-8061

Perez, Ramon Emilio (5 mentions)
U of California-Los Angeles, 1976
Certification: Infectious Disease, Internal Medicine
17602 17th St, Tustin, 714-491-2871

Petreccia, David Carl (4 mentions)
St Louis U, 1981
Certification: Infectious Disease, Internal Medicine
1275 N Rose Dr #134, Placentia, 714-996-6500

Posalski, Irving (8 mentions)
U of California-Los Angeles, 1973
Certification: Infectious Disease, Internal Medicine
8635 W 3rd St #1185, Los Angeles, 310-855-1960

Rand, David Douglas (5 mentions)
U of Southern California, 1989 *Certification:* Internal Medicine
3400 Lomita Blvd #104, Torrance, 310-326-5648

Ray, Sayan Deb (4 mentions)
U of Toledo, 1997
Certification: Infectious Disease, Internal Medicine
845 W La Veta Ave #107-A, Orange, 714-289-7171

Scheer, Melvin Ira (5 mentions)
Certification: Internal Medicine
1260 15th St #1501, Santa Monica, 310-656-1701

Shriner, Kimberly Anne (7 mentions)
Case Western Reserve U, 1986
Certification: Infectious Disease, Internal Medicine
50 Bellefontaine St #303, Pasadena, 626-793-6133

Sokolov, Richard T., Jr. (9 mentions)
Rosalind Franklin U, 1984
Certification: Infectious Disease, Internal Medicine
8631 W 3rd St #1020-E, Los Angeles, 310-358-5530

Strayer, Gregory Lind (9 mentions)
U of California-Los Angeles, 1975
Certification: Infectious Disease, Internal Medicine
2699 Atlantic Ave, Long Beach, 562-426-3333

Streng, Joel Alden (4 mentions)
U of Cincinnati, 1971
Certification: Pediatric Infectious Diseases, Pediatrics
1135 S Sunset Ave #208, West Covina, 626-851-8880

Uman, Stephen Jonas (6 mentions)
Tulane U, 1969
Certification: Infectious Disease, Internal Medicine
8635 W 3rd St #1180-W, Los Angeles, 310-358-2300

Wallace, Sandra Louise (8 mentions)
U of California-Los Angeles, 1978
Certification: Infectious Disease, Internal Medicine
50 Bellefontaine St #203, Pasadena, 626-793-6133

White, Alan Fraser (5 mentions)
Wake Forest U, 1989 *Certification:* Infectious Disease
23961 Calle De La Magdalena #130, Laguna Hills, 949-588-8700

Zakowski, Phillip Charles (14 mentions)
U of California-Davis, 1977
8635 W 3rd St #1180-W, Los Angeles, 310-358-2300

Infertility

Danzer, Hal Conrad (4 mentions)
St Louis U, 1971 *Certification:* Obstetrics & Gynecology
450 N Roxbury Dr #5, Beverly Hills, 310-277-2393

Marrs, Richard Preston (7 mentions)
U of Texas-Galveston, 1974 *Certification:* Obstetrics &
Gynecology, Reproductive Endocrinology/Infertility
11818 Wilshire Blvd #300, Los Angeles, 310-828-4008

Paulson, Richard John (7 mentions)
U of California-Los Angeles, 1980 *Certification:* Obstetrics &
Gynecology, Reproductive Endocrinology/Infertility
1127 Wilshire Blvd #1400, Los Angeles, 213-975-9990

Rodi, Ingrid Anne (4 mentions)
Brown U, 1979 *Certification:* Obstetrics & Gynecology,
Reproductive Endocrinology/Infertility
1450 10th St #404, Santa Monica, 310-451-8144

Surrey, Mark Wayne (10 mentions)
George Washington U, 1972
Certification: Obstetrics & Gynecology
450 N Roxbury Dr #500, Beverly Hills, 310-277-2393
2403 Castillo St #205, Santa Barbara, 805-569-1950
4080 Loma Vista Rd, Ventura, 805-658-9112

Werlin, Lawrence Bruce (9 mentions)
Mount Sinai Sch of Med, 1976
Certification: Obstetrics & Gynecology
4900 Barranca Pkwy #103, Irvine, 949-726-0600

Internal Medicine *(see note on page 9)*

Berman, James Jonathan (6 mentions)
Temple U, 1974 *Certification:* Internal Medicine
361 Hospital Rd #322, Newport Beach, 949-574-0777

Biscow, Mark Howard (3 mentions)
U of California-Los Angeles, 1981 *Certification:* Internal Medicine
2121 Wilshire Blvd #305, Santa Monica, 310-264-0065

Brettler, Jeffrey William (3 mentions)
U of Chicago, 1986 *Certification:* Internal Medicine
6041 Cadillac Ave, Los Angeles, 323-857-2000

Brousseau, Michael P. (3 mentions)
U of Virginia, 1992 *Certification:* Internal Medicine
150 N Robertson Blvd #115, Beverly Hills, 310-657-9200

Brown, Kenneth Spiers (3 mentions)
Stanford U, 1974 *Certification:* Internal Medicine
1866 N Orange Grove Ave #102-A, Pomona, 909-620-4373

Elihu, Nadia (3 mentions)
Albert Einstein Coll of Med, 1997 *Certification:* Internal Medicine
1310 W Stewart Dr #401, Orange, 714-639-9401

Fuchs, Albert Carol (3 mentions)
U of California-Los Angeles, 1994 *Certification:* Internal Medicine
8500 Wilshire Blvd #605, Beverly Hills, 310-652-1900

Galier, Peter Charles (3 mentions)
U of California-Los Angeles, 1991 *Certification:* Internal Medicine
1131 Wilshire Blvd #100, Santa Monica, 310-458-2381

Gindi, Elie Moe (3 mentions)
U of California-San Francisco, 1979
Certification: Internal Medicine
2080 E Century Park #1605, Los Angeles, 310-553-5535

Gordon, Earl Mark (5 mentions)
U of Miami, 1976 *Certification:* Internal Medicine, Nephrology
2001 Santa Monica Blvd #765W, Santa Monica, 310-453-4599

Hatfield, Glenn E. (3 mentions)
Ohio State U, 1974
Certification: Gastroenterology, Internal Medicine
1245 Wilshire Blvd #903, Los Angeles, 213-977-1144

Herndon, Roy Lee, II (3 mentions)
U of California-Los Angeles, 1960 *Certification:* Internal Medicine
1140 W La Veta Ave #480, Orange, 714-835-6042

Inadomi, Donald Warren (4 mentions)
U of California-Los Angeles, 1979
Certification: Internal Medicine, Nephrology
20911 Earl St #320, Torrance, 310-542-7997

Karubian, Frederick Jalal (3 mentions)
FMS-Mexico, 1983 *Certification:* Internal Medicine
2001 Santa Monica Blvd #761-W, Santa Monica, 310-829-7584

Kuniyoshi, Julie Miye (3 mentions)
U of Hawaii, 1992 *Certification:* Internal Medicine
4870 Barranca Pkwy #250, Irvine, 949-272-3800

Law, Malena S. C. (3 mentions)
Northwestern U, 1999 *Certification:* Internal Medicine
1131 Wilshire Blvd #100, Santa Monica, 310-458-2381

Nachman, Mark (4 mentions)
New York Med Coll, 1973
Certification: Internal Medicine, Nephrology
1301 20th St #290, Santa Monica, 310-315-0111

Prudente, Ernest Louis (6 mentions)
Hahnemann U, 1998 *Certification:* Internal Medicine
2121 Wilshire Blvd #304, Santa Monica, 310-829-7762

Reikes, Andrew Reed (3 mentions)
U of California-San Diego, 1989 *Certification:* Endocrinology,
Diabetes, and Metabolism, Internal Medicine
101 The City Dr S, Orange, 888-456-7002

Scarcella, Louis S. (3 mentions)
U of Southern California, 1978 *Certification:* Internal Medicine
23961 Calle De La Magdalena #130, Laguna Hills, 949-770-7691

Singh, Baldeep (3 mentions)
Northwestern U, 1990 *Certification:* Internal Medicine
100 UCLA Medical Plaza #455, Los Angeles, 310-794-7350

Stefan, Michael Robert (3 mentions)
U of Southern California, 1978 *Certification:* Internal Medicine
2100 W 3rd St #260, Los Angeles, 213-484-2957

Storch, John Christopher (3 mentions)
U of Southern California, 1982 *Certification:* Internal Medicine
350 Old Newport Blvd, Newport Beach, 949-650-2887

Sue, Ronald (4 mentions)
Tufts U, 1981 *Certification:* Internal Medicine
2080 Century Park E #1605, Los Angeles, 310-556-2244

Van, Catherine Thucchan (3 mentions)
U of California-Los Angeles, 1993 *Certification:* Internal Medicine
441 N Lakeview Ave, Anaheim, 888-988-2800
1188 N Euclid St, Anaheim, 888-988-2800

Walter, Richard Louis (3 mentions)
Rosalind Franklin U, 1974 *Certification:* Internal Medicine
5525 Etiwanda Ave #318, Tarzana, 818-528-1270

Wexler, Richard Jay (4 mentions)
U of Oklahoma, 1977 *Certification:* Internal Medicine
10861 Cherry St #301, Los Alamitos, 562-431-3535

Wynstock, Lori Jo (5 mentions)
U of Southern California, 1996 *Certification:* Internal Medicine
50 Bellefontaine St #203, Pasadena, 626-793-6113

Younis, Samy Ahmed (3 mentions)
FMS-Egypt, 1969 *Certification:* Internal Medicine
4050 Barranca Pkwy #240, Irvine, 949-451-9292

Nephrology

Boroujerdi-Rad, Hassan (3 mentions)
Certification: Internal Medicine
9209 Colima Rd #4600, Whittier, 562-907-7616

Chen, May Shu (3 mentions)
U of Chicago, 1992 *Certification:* Internal Medicine, Nephrology
27800 Medical Center Rd #220, Mission Viejo, 949-364-0644

Chiang, Glenn (5 mentions)
St Louis U, 1993
1310 W Stewart Dr #607, Orange, 714-639-4901

Farahmandian, Danny Faraz (3 mentions)
U of California-Los Angeles, 1998
Certification: Internal Medicine, Nephrology
16133 Ventura Blvd #360, Encino, 818-986-6009

Fischmann, George Eugene (7 mentions)
Johns Hopkins U, 1980
Certification: Internal Medicine, Nephrology
5525 Etiwanda Ave #305, Tarzana, 818-705-8787

Friedman, Stuart (3 mentions)
New York Med Coll, 1976
Certification: Internal Medicine, Nephrology
8635 W 3rd St, Los Angeles, 310-652-9162

Froch, Larry (5 mentions)
U of Illinois, 1990 *Certification:* Nephrology
100 UCLA Medical Plaza #690, Los Angeles, 310-824-3664

Gordon, Earl Mark (18 mentions)
U of Miami, 1976 *Certification:* Internal Medicine, Nephrology
2001 Santa Monica Blvd #765W, Santa Monica, 310-453-4599

Grabie, Morris T. (3 mentions)
Albert Einstein Coll of Med, 1972
Certification: Internal Medicine, Nephrology
1301 20th St #200, Santa Monica, 310-829-3639

Graham, Stephen Lawrence (4 mentions)
U of California-Los Angeles, 1975
Certification: Internal Medicine, Nephrology
8635 W 3rd St #485, Los Angeles, 310-652-9162

Grushkin, Carl Mayer (6 mentions)
U of Southern California, 1966
Certification: Pediatric Nephrology, Pediatrics
4650 W Sunset Blvd, Los Angeles, 323-361-2102

Inadomi, Donald Warren (5 mentions)
U of California-Los Angeles, 1979
Certification: Internal Medicine, Nephrology
20911 Earl St #320, Torrance, 310-542-7997

Jabara, Amer Emile (6 mentions)
U of Southern California, 1989
Certification: Internal Medicine, Nephrology
1310 W Stewart Dr #607, Orange, 714-639-4901

Jordan, Stanley Clark (3 mentions)
U of North Carolina, 1973 *Certification:* Diagnostic
Laboratory Immunology, Pediatric Nephrology, Pediatrics
8700 Beverly Blvd, West Hollywood, 310-423-2641

Kleinman, Kenneth Scott (6 mentions)
U of Southern California, 1982
Certification: Internal Medicine, Nephrology
5525 Etiwanda Ave #305, Tarzana, 818-705-8787

Kumar, Nirmal (3 mentions)
FMS-India, 1970 *Certification:* Internal Medicine
1350 N Altadena Dr #100, Pasadena, 626-798-8400

Lashkari, Saman (6 mentions)
U of California-Los Angeles, 1994
Certification: Geriatric Medicine, Nephrology
5525 Etiwanda Ave #211, Tarzana, 818-757-1212

Levine, Michael Marvin (3 mentions)
Baylor U, 1978 *Certification:* Internal Medicine, Nephrology
8635 W 3rd St #865, Los Angeles, 310-652-9162

Levitan, Daniel (4 mentions)
Rush U, 1975 *Certification:* Internal Medicine, Nephrology
255 E Orange Grove Ave #D, Burbank, 818-848-5595
435 Arden Ave #380, Glendale, 818-244-9575
5525 Etiwanda Ave #222, Tarzana, 818-344-0200

Linsey, Michael Scott (10 mentions)
U of California-Davis, 1977
Certification: Internal Medicine, Nephrology
808 S Fair Oaks Ave, Pasadena, 626-577-1675

Makoff, Dwight Lester (6 mentions)
U of California-Los Angeles, 1960
Certification: Internal Medicine, Nephrology
8635 W 3rd St, Los Angeles, 310-652-9162

Movahedi, Hassan (3 mentions)
U of California-Irvine, 1996
Certification: Internal Medicine, Nephrology
411 N Lakeview Ave, Anaheim, 888-988-2800

Nguyen, Minhtri K. (3 mentions)
Certification: Nephrology
200 Medical Plaza #365, Los Angeles, 310-206-7662

Nortman, Donald Franklin (4 mentions)
Harvard U, 1972 *Certification:* Internal Medicine, Nephrology
8635 W 3rd St #865, Los Angeles, 310-659-1668

Opas, Lawrence Marshall (3 mentions)
U of Cincinnati, 1971
Certification: Pediatric Nephrology, Pediatrics
4650 W Sunset Blvd, Los Angeles, 323-361-2102

Pahl, Madeleine Valdes (4 mentions)
U of California-Irvine, 1978
Certification: Internal Medicine, Nephrology
101 The City Dr S Bldg 53 #125, Orange, 714-456-7002

Patak, Ramachandra V. (3 mentions)
FMS-India, 1966 *Certification:* Internal Medicine, Nephrology
18350 Roscoe Blvd #208, Northridge, 818-993-5600

Raj, Ashok Sunder (6 mentions)
FMS-India, 1975
2750 E Washington Blvd #270, Pasadena, 626-794-7075

Rodriguez, Hector Jairo (3 mentions)
FMS-Colombia, 1968
Certification: Internal Medicine, Nephrology
8920 Wilshire Blvd #420, Beverly Hills, 310-276-7058

Sawhney, Ajit Singh (3 mentions)
FMS-India, 1970 *Certification:* Internal Medicine, Nephrology
11190 Warner Ave #407, Fountain Valley, 714-641-9696

Sigala, Jerald Fredrick (8 mentions)
Med Coll of Wisconsin, 1974
Certification: Internal Medicine, Nephrology
307 Placentia Ave #103, Newport Beach, 949-631-9215
1310 W Stewart Dr #607, Orange, 714-639-4901

Tse, Kalok Edmund (4 mentions)
Jefferson Med Coll, 1990
Certification: Internal Medicine, Nephrology
808 S Fair Oaks Ave, Pasadena, 626-577-1675
55 E California Blvd 3rd Fl, Pasadena, 626-577-1675
55 S Raymond Ave #200, Alhambra, 626-570-8005

Veiga, Patricia Ann (3 mentions)
St Louis U, 1985 *Certification:* Pediatric Nephrology, Pediatrics
455 S Main St, Orange, 714-532-8324

Warner, Allen Sheridan (6 mentions)
Dartmouth Coll, 1976
Certification: Internal Medicine, Nephrology
2699 Atlantic Ave, Long Beach, 562-426-3333

Zoller, Karen A. (5 mentions)
U of California-Los Angeles, 1977
Certification: Internal Medicine, Nephrology
3780 Kilroy Airport Way #115, Long Beach, 562-595-7426

Neurological Surgery

Black, Keith Lanier (22 mentions)
U of Michigan, 1981 *Certification:* Neurological Surgery
8631 W 3rd St #800, Los Angeles, 310-423-7900

Brara, Harsimran Singh (5 mentions)
Loyola U Chicago, 1992 *Certification:* Neurological Surgery
1505 N Edgemont St, Los Angeles, 323-783-4704

Caton, William Le Roy, III (9 mentions)
U of Southern California, 1971 *Certification:* Neurological Surgery
630 S Raymond Ave #330, Pasadena, 626-793-8194

Ceverha, Barry Brooke (12 mentions)
U of Southern California, 1974 *Certification:* Neurological Surgery
2865 Atlantic Ave #202, Long Beach, 562-427-5388

Cooper, Martin (6 mentions)
Rosalind Franklin U, 1970 *Certification:* Neurological Surgery
120 S Spalding Dr #400, Beverly Hills, 310-659-6628

Duma, Christopher Michael (12 mentions)
Stony Brook U, 1986 *Certification:* Neurological Surgery
351 Hospital Rd #401, Newport Beach, 949-642-6787

Fineman, Igor (6 mentions)
U of California-Los Angeles, 1994
Certification: Neurological Surgery
630 S Raymond Ave #301, Pasadena, 818-242-5339

Giannotta, Steven Louis (10 mentions)
U of Michigan, 1972 *Certification:* Neurological Surgery
1520 San Pablo St #3800, Los Angeles, 323-442-5720

Kelly, Daniel F. (5 mentions)
Georgetown U, 1986 *Certification:* Neurological Surgery
1328 22nd St, Santa Monica, 310-829-8456

Lawner, Pablo Manuel (6 mentions)
Albany Med Coll, 1973 *Certification:* Neurological Surgery
13320 Riverside Dr #208, Sherman Oaks, 818-783-4949

Linskey, Mark Elwood (8 mentions)
Columbia U, 1986 *Certification:* Neurological Surgery
101 The City Dr S, Orange, 714-456-6966

Martin, Neil Alfred (9 mentions)
Virginia Commonwealth U, 1978
Certification: Neurological Surgery
300 UCLA Medical Plaza #B-200, Los Angeles, 310-825-5482

McComb, James Gordon (7 mentions)
U of Miami, 1965 *Certification:* Neurological Surgery
1300 N Vermont Ave #1006, Los Angeles, 323-361-2169

Muhonen, Michael Gordon (7 mentions)
Oral Roberts U, 1987 *Certification:* Neurological Surgery
1010 W La Veta #710, Orange, 714-633-0942

Noblett, Bradley Deane (7 mentions)
Vanderbilt U, 1988 *Certification:* Neurological Surgery
455 S Main St, Orange, 714-289-4151
1010 W La Veta Ave #710, Orange, 714-633-0942

Palmer, Sylvain (5 mentions)
Johns Hopkins U, 1977 *Certification:* Neurological Surgery
26732 Crown Valley Pkwy #561, Mission Viejo, 949-364-1060

Rayhaun, Abraham B. (5 mentions)
Columbia U, 1990 *Certification:* Neurological Surgery
2888 Long Beach Blvd #240, Long Beach, 562-595-7696

Rich, J. Ronald (9 mentions)
U of Utah, 1964 *Certification:* Neurological Surgery
2811 Wilshire Blvd #840, Santa Monica, 310-315-3404

Ro, Kyoo Sang (6 mentions)
FMS-South Korea, 1966 *Certification:* Neurological Surgery
435 Arden Ave #380, Glendale, 818-240-5241

Rodriguez, Jose Luis (5 mentions)
U of California-Irvine, 1981 *Certification:* Neurological Surgery
255 E Bonita Ave, Pomona, 909-450-0369

Snyder, Melvin (7 mentions)
Tufts U, 1971 *Certification:* Neurological Surgery
21350 Hawthorne Blvd #176, Torrance, 310-540-0965

Taban, Asher H. (6 mentions)
FMS-Iran, 1968 *Certification:* Neurological Surgery
18350 Roscoe Blvd #304, Northridge, 818-993-6063

Weiss, Martin Harvey (5 mentions)
Cornell U, 1963 *Certification:* Neurological Surgery
1520 San Pablo St #3800, Los Angeles, 323-442-5720

Neurology

Amos, Edwin C., III (6 mentions)
U of California-San Francisco, 1983 *Certification:* Neurology
2021 Santa Monica Blvd #525E, Santa Monica, 310-829-2126

Andersson, Peter B. (8 mentions)
FMS-South Africa, 1986
Certification: Clinical Neurophysiology, Neurology
18370 Burbank Blvd #107, Tarzana, 818-996-3880

Andiman, Ronald Marshall (3 mentions)
Albert Einstein Coll of Med, 1967 *Certification:* Neurology
8631 W 3rd St #531-E, Los Angeles, 310-855-7161

Banerji, Sanjay (4 mentions)
Temple U, 1992 *Certification:* Neurology
1245 Wilshire Blvd #804, Los Angeles, 213-977-0844

Belafsky, Melvin A. (4 mentions)
Rosalind Franklin U, 1973 *Certification:* Neurology
2701 W Alameda Ave #202, Burbank, 818-843-8184

Chance, Janet Mary (7 mentions)
FMS-Ireland, 1972 *Certification:* Neurology
307 Placentia Ave #204, Newport Beach, 949-645-0121

Chow, George (5 mentions)
U of California-San Diego, 1985 *Certification:* Neurology
18370 Burbank Blvd #107, Tarzana, 818-996-3880

Chow, William W. (3 mentions)
Certification: Neurology
8635 W 3rd St #450-W, Los Angeles, 310-659-4986

Cohen, Alan Howard (3 mentions)
New York U, 1965 *Certification:* Neurology
3791 Katella Ave #106, Los Alamitos, 562-430-4513

Cohen, Hart C. M. (5 mentions)
FMS-Canada, 1983 *Certification:* Neurology
8635 W 3rd St #450-W, Los Angeles, 310-652-5954

Cramer, Steven Craig (3 mentions)
U of Southern California, 1988
Certification: Internal Medicine, Neurology, Vascular Neurology
101 The City Dr S, Orange, 888-456-7002

Dietz, John Ritter (4 mentions)
Jefferson Med Coll, 1977 *Certification:* Neurology
4910 Van Nuys Blvd #206, Sherman Oaks, 818-995-1174

Edelman, David Lewis (3 mentions)
Northwestern U, 1980 *Certification:* Neurology
23441 Madison St #280, Torrance, 310-373-0391

Espy, Clarke David (4 mentions)
U of Colorado, 1969 *Certification:* Internal Medicine, Neurology
8631 W 3rd St #620, Los Angeles, 310-657-0942

Florin, Jack Hugh (3 mentions)
Albert Einstein Coll of Med, 1970
Certification: Clinical Neurophysiology, Neurology
100 Laguna Rd #208, Fullerton, 714-738-0800

Fortanasce, Vincent M. (4 mentions)
FMS-Italy, 1970 *Certification:* Neurology
665 W Naomi Ave #201, Arcadia, 626-445-8481

Gabriel, Ronald Samuel (3 mentions)
Boston U, 1963 *Certification:* Neurology with Special
   Qualifications in Child Neurology, Pediatrics
2080 Century Park E #203, Los Angeles, 310-277-9533

Gehret, David Allan (6 mentions)
U of Florida, 1981 *Certification:* Neurology
361 Hospital Rd #527, Newport Beach, 949-548-4111

Girard, Philip Marius, Jr. (3 mentions)
Med Coll of Wisconsin, 1975 *Certification:* Neurology
50 Alessandro Pl #120, Pasadena, 626-449-1814

Gold, Michael Edward (9 mentions)
U of Illinois, 1981 *Certification:* Neurology
2021 Santa Monica Blvd #525-E, Santa Monica, 310-829-2126

Gurbani, Suresh Govindram (3 mentions)
FMS-India, 1980 *Certification:* Neurology with Special
   Qualifications in Child Neurology
1135 S Sunset Ave #406, West Covina, 626-813-7850
4811 N Lakeview Ave, Anaheim, 888-988-2800

Helfgott, Paul Conrad (3 mentions)
Boston U, 1978 *Certification:* Neurology
101 E Beverly Blvd #206, Montebello, 323-725-7297

Hermanowicz, Neal Scott (4 mentions)
Temple U, 1985 *Certification:* Neurology
101 The City Dr S, Orange, 714-456-7890
100 Irvine Hall, Irvine, 714-456-8322

Imbus, Charles Eugene (5 mentions)
Ohio State U, 1971 *Certification:* Neurology with Special
   Qualifications in Child Neurology, Pediatrics, Sleep Medicine
665 W Naomi Ave #202, Arcadia, 626-445-6275

Jordan, Sheldon Emanuel (5 mentions)
U of California-Los Angeles, 1977
Certification: Neurology, Pain Medicine
2811 Wilshire Blvd #790, Santa Monica, 310-829-5968

Kazimiroff, Paul Boris (6 mentions)
U of New Mexico, 1975 *Certification:* Neurology with Special
   Qualifications in Child Neurology, Pediatrics
6041 Cadillac Ave, Los Angeles, 323-857-2443

Lake, Jean Louise (4 mentions)
U of California-San Francisco, 1978 *Certification:* Neurology
   with Special Qualifications in Child Neurology, Pediatrics
2880 Atlantic Ave #260, Long Beach, 562-490-3580

Lee, Lance (4 mentions)
Hahnemann U, 1995 *Certification:* Neurology
435 Arden Ave #560, Glendale, 818-243-1501

Martinez, Kenneth Patrick (3 mentions)
U of Southern California, 1997 *Certification:* Neurology
5 Journey #210, Aliso Viejo, 949-305-7122

Minazad, Yafa (3 mentions)
Western U, 2000
630 S Raymond Ave #310, Pasadena, 626-535-9344

Mitchell, Wendy Gayle (3 mentions)
U of California-San Francisco, 1973 *Certification:* Neurology
   with Special Qualifications in Child Neurology, Pediatrics
4650 W Sunset Blvd, Los Angeles, 323-361-2498

O'Carroll, Christopher P. (3 mentions)
FMS-Ireland, 1974
Certification: Internal Medicine, Neurology, Pain Medicine
400 Newport Center Dr #701, Newport Beach, 949-759-8001

O'Connor, Edward Joseph (4 mentions)
U of California-Los Angeles, 1970 *Certification:* Neurology
2811 Wilshire Blvd #790, Santa Monica, 310-829-5968

Omidvar, Omid (5 mentions)
FMS-France, 1993 *Certification:* Neurology
3791 Katella Ave #106, Los Alamitos, 562-430-0094

Preston, William George (3 mentions)
U of Southern California, 1971 *Certification:* Neurology
23961 Calle De La Magdalena #317, Laguna Hills, 949-837-1133

Sadrieh, Kiarash (3 mentions)
Rosalind Franklin U, 2001 *Certification:* Neurology with
   Special Qualifications in Child Neurology
1700 E Cesar Chavez Ave #3000, Los Angeles, 323-978-1200

Scharf, David (3 mentions)
Albert Einstein Coll of Med, 1985 *Certification:* Neurology
4910 Van Nuys Blvd #302, Sherman Oaks, 818-783-0036

Shey, Randolph Barry (3 mentions)
Boston U, 1976 *Certification:* Neurology
701 E 28th St #319, Long Beach, 562-426-3656

Simon, Robert Elliot (5 mentions)
U of California-Irvine, 1973 *Certification:* Neurology
27800 Medical Center Rd #226, Mission Viejo, 949-364-9054

Spitzer, Richard Alan (8 mentions)
Albert Einstein Coll of Med, 1969 *Certification:* Neurology
50 Alessandro Pl #120, Pasadena, 626-449-1814

Stokol, Colin Wilfred (12 mentions)
FMS-South Africa, 1975 *Certification:* Neurology
8631 W 3rd St #531, Los Angeles, 310-855-7161

Trice, Jill Ellen (3 mentions)
Washington U, 1976
725 W La Veta Ave #100, Orange, 714-532-7601
455 S Main St, Orange, 714-532-7601
1120 W La Veta Ave #125, Orange, 714-532-7601

Ullman, Bernard L. (6 mentions)
Jefferson Med Coll, 1978 *Certification:* Neurology
520 N Prospect Ave #309, Redondo Beach, 310-376-9492

Van Houten, Mark Steven (4 mentions)
FMS-Canada, 1984 *Certification:* Neurology
361 Hospital Rd #527, Newport Beach, 949-548-4111

Verghese, Jacob Peter (8 mentions)
FMS-India, 1973 *Certification:* Neurology
307 Placentia Ave #204, Newport Beach, 949-645-0703

Weiner, Leslie Philip (4 mentions)
U of Cincinnati, 1961 *Certification:* Neurology
1520 San Pablo St #3000, Los Angeles, 323-442-5710

Woo, Andrew Han-Tse (8 mentions)
Brown U, 1992 *Certification:* Neurology
2021 Santa Monica Blvd #525-E, Santa Monica, 310-829-2126

Zardouz, Bijan (3 mentions)
FMS-Iran, 1978 *Certification:* Neurology
1220 Hemlock Way #108, Santa Ana, 714-540-2272

Obstetrics/Gynecology

Abusleme-Abedrapo, V. (3 mentions)
FMS-Chile, 1975 *Certification:* Obstetrics & Gynecology
14621 Nordhoff St #2A, Panorama City, 818-891-0678

Chien, Connie S. (3 mentions)
9242 W Olympic Blvd, Beverly Hills, 310-274-8310

Clayton, Weatherford T. (3 mentions)
U of Utah, 1981 *Certification:* Obstetrics & Gynecology
351 Hospital Rd #504, Newport Beach, 949-646-2800

Cropper, Stephanie Janel (4 mentions)
Ohio State U, 1998 *Certification:* Obstetrics & Gynecology
160 E Artesia St #330, Pomona, 909-622-5654

Di Saia, Philip John (5 mentions)
Tufts U, 1963
Certification: Gynecologic Oncology, Obstetrics & Gynecology
101 The City Dr S Bldg 56 #260, Orange, 714-456-5220

Dwight, Mark Alan (3 mentions)
St Louis U, 1988 *Certification:* Obstetrics & Gynecology
637 Lucas Ave, Los Angeles, 213-977-4190

Feldman, Bernard Michael (3 mentions)
Hahnemann U, 1973 *Certification:* Obstetrics & Gynecology
351 Hospital Rd #316, Newport Beach, 949-642-5775

Hakakha, Michele (4 mentions)
U of Hawaii, 1998 *Certification:* Obstetrics & Gynecology
9242 W Olympic Blvd, Beverly Hills, 310-274-8310

Henneberg, Wilbert James (4 mentions)
Rosalind Franklin U, 1973 *Certification:* Obstetrics & Gynecology
10 Congress St #400, Pasadena, 626-449-6223

Jick, Bryan Scott (3 mentions)
U of California-San Diego, 1984
Certification: Obstetrics & Gynecology
800 S Fairmount Ave #101, Pasadena, 626-304-2626

Karlan, Beth Young (3 mentions)
Harvard U, 1982
Certification: Gynecologic Oncology, Obstetrics & Gynecology
8700 Beverly Blvd, West Hollywood, 310-423-0701

Kent, Anne Marie (4 mentions)
U of California-Davis, 1984 *Certification:* Obstetrics & Gynecology
361 Hospital Rd #533, Newport Beach, 949-650-7100

Kivnick, Seth (4 mentions)
U of Michigan, 1980 *Certification:* Obstetrics & Gynecology
1000 W Carson St, Torrance, 310-222-3561

Linzey, E. Michael (3 mentions)
U of California-Irvine, 1972 *Certification:* Obstetrics & Gynecology
1140 W La Veta Ave #770, Orange, 714-835-8715

Liu, Edward Yung (3 mentions)
Wayne State U, 1971 *Certification:* Obstetrics & Gynecology
8631 W 3rd St #1040E, Los Angeles, 310-855-0711

Macer, James Armen (3 mentions)
U of Southern California, 1979
Certification: Obstetrics & Gynecology
10 Congress St #400, Pasadena, 626-449-6223

Mirhashemi, Ramin (3 mentions)
U of Southern California, 1993
Certification: Gynecologic Oncology, Obstetrics & Gynecology
23600 Telo Ave #250, Torrance, 310-375-8446

Moran, James J. M. (3 mentions)
U of Buffalo, 1966 *Certification:* Obstetrics & Gynecology
1301 20th St #270, Santa Monica, 310-828-5511

Naghi, Beni (5 mentions)
FMS-Mexico, 1982 *Certification:* Obstetrics & Gynecology
3400 Lomita Blvd #602, Torrance, 310-326-5150
855 Manhattan Beach Blvd #209, Manhattan Beach,
   310-939-1881

O'Toole, Mary Catherine (4 mentions)
Rosalind Franklin U, 1985 *Certification:* Obstetrics & Gynecology
24411 Health Center Dr #200, Laguna Hills, 949-829-5500
1300 Avenida Vista Hermosa #150, San Clemente, 949-829-5500

Parker, William Howard (4 mentions)
SUNY-Downstate Med Coll, 1974
Certification: Obstetrics & Gynecology
1450 10th St #404, Santa Monica, 310-451-8144

Sadri, Hilla Homi (4 mentions)
FMS-India, 1971 *Certification:* Obstetrics & Gynecology
600 Corporate Dr #210, Ladera Ranch, 949-364-2481

Scharffenberger, James N. (4 mentions)
Georgetown U, 1981 *Certification:* Obstetrics & Gynecology
20911 Earl St #480, Torrance, 310-370-7277

Serden, Scott Peck (6 mentions)
New York Med Coll, 1979 *Certification:* Obstetrics & Gynecology
8631 W 3rd St #510-E, Los Angeles, 310-278-1490

Templeman, Claire Lesley (3 mentions)
FMS-Australia, 1989
1640 Marengo St #505, Los Angeles, 323-226-3416
4650 W Sunset Blvd, Los Angeles, 323-361-2322
1441 Eastlake Ave #7419, Los Angeles, 323-865-3979

To, William C. (3 mentions)
Loma Linda U, 1979 *Certification:* Obstetrics & Gynecology
8635 W 3rd St #W-265, Los Angeles, 310-659-9625

Winter, Marc Lawrence (3 mentions)
U of California-Irvine, 1984 *Certification:* Obstetrics & Gynecology
24411 Health Center Dr #200, Laguna Hills, 949-829-5500
1300 Avenida Vista Hermosa, San Clemente, 949-829-5500

Ophthalmology

Aizuss, David Harlan (4 mentions)
Northwestern U, 1980 *Certification:* Ophthalmology
16311 Ventura Blvd #750, Encino, 818-990-3623
7230 Medical Center Dr #404, West Hills, 818-346-8118

Berg, Alan Mitchel (3 mentions)
Wake Forest U, 1976 *Certification:* Ophthalmology
2625 W Alameda Ave #208, Burbank, 818-845-3557
13320 Riverside Dr #114, Sherman Oaks, 818-501-3937
1437 San Marino Ave, San Marino, 626-795-9793

Borchert, Mark Stephen (4 mentions)
Baylor U, 1983 *Certification:* Ophthalmology
4650 W Sunset Blvd, Los Angeles, 323-361-2347

Boyer, David Stuart (11 mentions)
Rosalind Franklin U, 1972 *Certification:* Ophthalmology
1127 Wilshire Blvd #1620, Los Angeles, 213-483-8810
8641 Wilshire Blvd #210, Beverly Hills, 310-854-6201
12840 Riverside Dr #402, North Hollywood, 818-754-2090

Brame, Cory L. (4 mentions)
U of Texas-San Antonio, 1997 *Certification:* Ophthalmology
360 San Miguel Dr #307, Newport Beach, 949-721-0800

Choi, Thomas Boohun (4 mentions)
U of California-Los Angeles, 1989 *Certification:* Ophthalmology
11480 Brookshire Ave #205, Downey, 562-622-3937

Chuck, Dennis Alvin (3 mentions)
Brown U, 1979 *Certification:* Ophthalmology
1774 Alameda St, Pomona, 909-622-1188

Coleman, Anne Louise (3 mentions)
Virginia Commonwealth U, 1984 *Certification:* Ophthalmology
100 Stein Plaza #2-118, Los Angeles, 310-825-5298

Colvard, D. Michael (3 mentions)
Emory U, 1973 *Certification:* Ophthalmology
5363 Balboa Blvd #545, Encino, 818-906-2929

Cornell, Peter J. (6 mentions)
U of California-Los Angeles, 1984 *Certification:* Ophthalmology
450 N Bedford Dr #101, Beverly Hills, 310-274-9205

Dinsmore, Stephen C. (3 mentions)
Georgetown U, 1975 *Certification:* Ophthalmology
19000 Hawthorne Blvd #110, Torrance, 310-370-3628
927 Deep Valley Dr #290, Rolling Hills Estates, 310-377-4934

Elander, Troy Robert (4 mentions)
Cornell U, 1985 *Certification:* Ophthalmology
242 26th St, Santa Monica, 310-393-0634

Feinfield, Robert Evan (3 mentions)
U of California-San Francisco, 1981 *Certification:* Ophthalmology
2625 W Alameda Ave #208, Burbank, 818-845-3557
13320 Riverside Dr #114, Sherman Oaks, 818-501-3937
1437 San Marino Ave, San Marino, 626-795-9793

Fierson, Walter Miles (3 mentions)
Albert Einstein Coll of Med, 1971 *Certification:* Ophthalmology
1245 W Huntington Dr #109, Arcadia, 626-304-7081

Garwood, John Lawrence (4 mentions)
FMS-Canada, 1979 *Certification:* Ophthalmology
1301 20th St #250, Santa Monica, 310-828-7494

Geisse, Lawrence John (3 mentions)
U of Missouri, 1979 *Certification:* Ophthalmology
4130 Viking Way, Long Beach, 562-496-2020
10861 Cherry St #204, Los Alamitos, 562-598-3160

Hakim, Melinda Ashraf (4 mentions)
Johns Hopkins U, 2001 *Certification:* Ophthalmology
8635 W 3rd St #390, Los Angeles, 310-652-1133

Hartman, Carl Trevor (4 mentions)
Rosalind Franklin U, 1986 *Certification:* Ophthalmology
3300 E South St #105, Lakewood, 562-531-2020
3801 Katella Ave #130, Los Alamitos, 562-598-7738

Hofbauer, John David (3 mentions)
Columbia U, 1975 *Certification:* Ophthalmology
416 N Bedford Dr #300, Beverly Hills, 310-273-2333

Irvine, John Alexander (4 mentions)
U of Southern California, 1982 *Certification:* Ophthalmology
1450 San Pablo St, Los Angeles, 323-442-6335
2617 E Chapman Ave #301, Orange, 714-628-2966

Jones, Robert Leonard (3 mentions)
U of California-Irvine, 1982 *Certification:* Ophthalmology
1401 Avocado Ave #505, Newport Beach, 949-644-0239

Katzin, David Shimon Dov (3 mentions)
U of California-Los Angeles, 1975 *Certification:* Ophthalmology
8631 W 3rd St #610E, Los Angeles, 310-659-9470

Krauss, Howard Ronald (6 mentions)
New York Med Coll, 1977 *Certification:* Ophthalmology
11645 Wilshire Blvd #600, Los Angeles, 310-477-5558

Kuppermann, Baruch (6 mentions)
U of Miami, 1985 *Certification:* Ophthalmology
101 The City Dr S, Orange, 949-824-2020
1 Medical Plaza Dr, Irvine, 949-824-2020

Marrone, Alfred Carl (4 mentions)
SUNY-Downstate Med Coll, 1971 *Certification:* Ophthalmology
3440 Lomita Blvd #451, Torrance, 310-530-0300

Nilles, Jeffrey John (3 mentions)
Northwestern U, 1976 *Certification:* Ophthalmology
1808 Verdugo Blvd #102, Glendale, 818-952-1136

Opatowsky, Ira Elliot (3 mentions)
U of California-San Diego, 1990 *Certification:* Ophthalmology
42543 8th St W #101, Lancaster, 661-948-4373

Patel, Jayantkumar (3 mentions)
2001 Santa Monica Blvd #985, Santa Monica, 310-828-5888

Sacks, David Bernard (4 mentions)
FMS-South Africa, 1968 *Certification:* Ophthalmology
999 N Tustin Ave #122, Santa Ana, 714-542-3961

Schwartz, Donald Norman (5 mentions)
FMS-Mexico, 1977 *Certification:* Ophthalmology
2650 Elm Ave #108, Long Beach, 562-427-5409

Shivaram, Sunil M. (5 mentions)
Harvard U, 1995 *Certification:* Ophthalmology
655 E Foothill Blvd, Claremont, 909-624-8077

Siegel, Eliot Bruce (4 mentions)
U of Pennsylvania, 1978 *Certification:* Ophthalmology
1301 20th St #260, Santa Monica, 310-829-1224

Simjee, Aisha (4 mentions)
FMS-Myanmar, 1968 *Certification:* Ophthalmology
1310 W Stewart Dr #501, Orange, 714-771-2020

Urrea, Paul T. (5 mentions)
U of California-Los Angeles, 1982 *Certification:* Ophthalmology
850 S Atlantic Blvd #301, Monterey Park, 626-289-7699
1700 Cesae Chavez Ave #L-300, Los Angeles, 323-980-9900

Wolstan, Barry James (3 mentions)
U of Minnesota, 1972 *Certification:* Ophthalmology
23600 Telo Ave #100, Torrance, 310-543-2611
21320 Hawthorne Blvd #104, Torrance, 310-543-2611

Wright, Kenneth Weston (4 mentions)
Boston U, 1977 *Certification:* Ophthalmology
520 S San Vincente Blvd, Los Angeles, 310-652-6420

Yu, David Deok (3 mentions)
Wake Forest U, 1987 *Certification:* Ophthalmology
10 Congress St #340, Pasadena, 626-796-5325

Orthopedics

Adamson, Gregory John (3 mentions)
U of Southern California, 1985 *Certification:* Orthopaedic Surgery
39 Congress St #201, Pasadena, 626-795-8051

Bernstein, Robert Matthew (5 mentions)
U of Southern California, 1988 *Certification:* Orthopaedic Surgery
444 S San Vicente Blvd #603, Los Angeles, 310-423-5224

Bernstein, Saul Maurice (3 mentions)
U of California-San Francisco, 1963
Certification: Orthopaedic Surgery
6815 Noble Ave, Van Nuys, 818-901-6690

Bhatia, Nitin Narain (5 mentions)
Baylor U, 1998 *Certification:* Orthopaedic Surgery
101 The City Dr S, Orange, 714-456-8978

Borden, Peter Scott (4 mentions)
George Washington U, 1995 *Certification:* Orthopaedic Surgery
23456 Hawthorne Blvd #200, Torrance, 310-375-8700

Braiker, Barry Michael (3 mentions)
U of California-San Francisco, 1967
Certification: Orthopaedic Surgery
8670 Wilshire Blvd #206, Los Angeles, 310-855-0752

Brien, William W. (3 mentions)
U of California-Los Angeles, 1983
Certification: Orthopaedic Surgery
444 S San Vincente Blvd #603, Los Angeles, 310-423-9955

Caillouette, James T. (4 mentions)
U of Southern California, 1983 *Certification:* Orthopaedic Surgery
22 Corporate Plaza Dr #150, Newport Beach, 949-722-7038

Carlson, Gregory Dean (3 mentions)
Loma Linda U, 1987 *Certification:* Orthopaedic Surgery
280 S Main St #200, Orange, 714-634-4567

Chalian, Christopher A. (5 mentions)
U of Iowa, 1984 *Certification:* Orthopaedic Surgery
2776 N Garey Ave, Pomona, 909-593-7437
7777 Miliken Ave #101A, Rancho Cucamonga, 909-987-7696

Chen, Vincent Wingshun (3 mentions)
New York Med Coll, 1998 *Certification:* Orthopaedic Surgery
707 S Garfield Ave #201, Alhambra, 626-282-1600

Diehl, Richard C., Jr. (5 mentions)
U of Pittsburgh, 1967 *Certification:* Orthopaedic Surgery
39 Congress St #201, Pasadena, 626-795-8051

Dillin, William Hugo (3 mentions)
U of Texas-San Antonio, 1978 *Certification:* Orthopaedic Surgery
6801 Park Ter, Los Angeles, 310-665-7200
2400 E Katella Ave #400, Anaheim, 714-937-1338

Ding, Jean (3 mentions)
Temple U, 1989
301 W Huntington Dr #617, Arcadia, 626-821-0707
723 S Garfield Ave #301, Alhambra, 626-248-9318

Ehrhart, Kevin Michael (7 mentions)
St Louis U, 1974 *Certification:* Orthopaedic Surgery
2020 Santa Monica Blvd, Santa Monica, 310-829-2663

Fox, James Michael (3 mentions)
U of Wisconsin, 1968 *Certification:* Orthopaedic Surgery
7230 Medical Center Dr #503, West Hills, 818-884-2585

Funahashi, Tadashi Ted (4 mentions)
U of California-Los Angeles, 1986
Certification: Orthopaedic Surgery
6670 Alton Pkwy, Irvine, 949-932-5300

Garland, Douglas Edward (3 mentions)
Creighton U, 1969 *Certification:* Orthopaedic Surgery
2760 Atlantic Ave, Long Beach, 562-424-6666

Gilbert, Paul Keith (7 mentions)
U of Southern California, 1983 *Certification:* Orthopaedic Surgery
39 Congress St #201, Pasadena, 626-795-8051

Gupta, Ranjan (7 mentions)
Albany Med Coll, 1992
Certification: Orthopaedic Surgery, Surgery of the Hand
101 The City Dr S, Orange, 714-456-7012

Jackson, Douglas Wayne (5 mentions)
U of Washington, 1966 *Certification:* Orthopaedic Surgery
2760 Atlantic Ave, Long Beach, 562-424-6666

Klapper, Robert C. (5 mentions)
Columbia U, 1983 *Certification:* Orthopaedic Surgery
8737 Beverly Blvd #303, Los Angeles, 310-659-6889

Knapp, Thomas Phillips (4 mentions)
U of Southern California, 1989 *Certification:* Orthopaedic Surgery
2020 Santa Monica Blvd, Santa Monica, 310-829-2663

Kurzweil, Peter Richard (6 mentions)
U of Rochester, 1984 *Certification:* Orthopaedic Surgery
2760 Atlantic Ave, Long Beach, 562-424-6666

Mandelbaum, Bert Roland (11 mentions)
Washington U, 1980 *Certification:* Orthopaedic Surgery
2020 Santa Monica Blvd, Santa Monica, 310-829-2663

Matta, Joel Michael (4 mentions)
Oregon Health Sciences U, 1973
Certification: Orthopaedic Surgery
2001 Santa Monica Blvd #1090, Santa Monica, 310-582-7475

Menendez, Lawrence R. (3 mentions)
New York U, 1979 *Certification:* Orthopaedic Surgery
1520 San Pablo St #2000, Los Angeles, 323-442-5830

Moreland, John Robert (5 mentions)
Baylor U, 1972 *Certification:* Orthopaedic Surgery
2001 Santa Monica Blvd #1280W, Santa Monica, 310-453-1911

Motamedi, Ali Reza (3 mentions)
Tulane U, 1993 *Certification:* Orthopaedic Surgery
1250 16th St, Santa Monica, 310-319-3811

Newman, Mark Alan (4 mentions)
Rosalind Franklin U, 1984 *Certification:* Orthopaedic Surgery
351 Hospital Rd #309, Newport Beach, 949-642-5600

Nottage, Wesley Merrill (3 mentions)
U of California-Irvine, 1974 *Certification:* Orthopaedic Surgery
23961 Calle De La Magdalena #229, Laguna Hills, 949-581-7001

Osterkamp, John Anthony (4 mentions)
U of Southern California, 1979 *Certification:* Orthopaedic Surgery
1818 Verdugo Blvd #402, Glendale, 818-952-0670

Owens, Stephen Gerald (5 mentions)
Loyola U Chicago, 1994 *Certification:* Orthopaedic Surgery
1818 Verdugo Blvd #402, Glendale, 818-952-0670

Penenberg, Brad (7 mentions)
George Washington U, 1978 *Certification:* Orthopaedic Surgery
120 S Spalding Dr #400, Beverly Hills, 310-860-3470

Petrie, Russell Sean (4 mentions)
Mayo Med Sch, 1993 *Certification:* Orthopaedic Surgery
22 Corporate Plaza Dr, Newport Beach, 949-722-7038

Pradhan, Bhupendra (3 mentions)
U of California-Los Angeles, 1998
Certification: Orthopaedic Surgery
2627 E Washington Blvd, Pasadena, 626-797-2002

Quigley, John Thomas (5 mentions)
St Louis U, 1971 *Certification:* Orthopaedic Surgery
301 W Huntington Dr #408, Arcadia, 626-821-0707

Reddy, Krishna V. (3 mentions)
FMS-India, 1980
350 Vinton Ave, Pomona, 909-620-5502

Rosenfeld, Samuel Raymond (4 mentions)
Pennsylvania State U, 1977 *Certification:* Orthopaedic Surgery
1310 W Stewart Dr #508, Orange, 714-633-2111

Sanders, Don Paul (3 mentions)
U of California-Los Angeles, 1979
Certification: Orthopaedic Surgery
23560 Crenshaw Blvd #102, Torrance, 310-784-2355

Savage, Kathleen Rose (3 mentions)
U of Southern California, 1999 *Certification:* Orthopaedic Surgery
3144 Santa Anita Ave, El Monte, 626-444-0333
1700 Caesar Chavez Ave #2200, Los Angeles, 323-264-7600

Secor, Perry Robert (3 mentions)
U of California-Los Angeles, 1981
Certification: Orthopaedic Surgery
3771 Katella Ave #209, Los Alamitos, 562-314-1400

Shanfield, Stewart Lloyd (3 mentions)
U of Texas-San Antonio, 1980 *Certification:* Orthopaedic Surgery
101 Laguna Rd #A, Fullerton, 714-879-0050
17021 Yorba Linda Blvd #100, Yorba Linda, 714-996-6440

Shankwiler, James Alan (4 mentions)
U of Southern California, 1987 *Certification:* Orthopaedic Surgery
39 Congress St #201, Pasadena, 626-795-8051

Shrader, Todd Alan (3 mentions)
U of California-Irvine, 1990 *Certification:* Orthopaedic Surgery
23456 Hawthorne Blvd #300, Torrance, 310-316-6190

Skaggs, David Lee (5 mentions)
Columbia U, 1989 *Certification:* Orthopaedic Surgery
120 S Spalding Dr #401, Beverly Hills, 310-659-2910
4650 W Sunset Blvd, Los Angeles, 323-669-2534

Stevenson, Donald Vincent (3 mentions)
U of Southern California, 1981 *Certification:* Orthopaedic Surgery
575 E Hardy St #105, Inglewood, 310-674-1211

Thomas, Tom Duane (4 mentions)
U of California-Los Angeles, 1987
Certification: Orthopaedic Surgery
26401 Crown Valley Pkwy #101, Mission Viejo, 949-348-4000

Tischler, Alexander H. (3 mentions)
Wayne State U, 1974 *Certification:* Orthopaedic Surgery
22 Corporate Plaza Dr #150, Newport Beach, 949-722-7038

Tolo, Vernon Thorpe (6 mentions)
Johns Hopkins U, 1968 *Certification:* Orthopaedic Surgery
4650 W Sunset Blvd, Los Angeles, 323-361-2142

Weinert, Carl R., Jr. (4 mentions)
U of Pittsburgh, 1971 *Certification:* Orthopaedic Surgery
1310 W Stewart Dr #508, Orange, 714-633-2111
15825 Laguna Canyon Rd #103, Irvine, 714-633-2111

Zapanta, Richard (3 mentions)
U of Southern California, 1973 *Certification:* Orthopaedic Surgery
880 S Atlantic Blvd #205, Monterey Park, 626-289-0178

Zeegen, Erik N. (4 mentions)
U of California-Los Angeles, 1996
Certification: Orthopaedic Surgery
5525 Etiwanda Ave #324, Tarzana, 818-708-9090

Otorhinolaryngology

Adair, Robert John (5 mentions)
U of Southern California, 1973 *Certification:* Otolaryngology
1301 20th St #300, Santa Monica, 310-829-7792

Ahuja, Gurpreet Singh (4 mentions)
FMS-India, 1983 *Certification:* Otolaryngology
101 The City Dr S, Orange, 714-456-7017
455 S Main St, Orange, 714-633-4020
1201 W La Veta Ave #604, Orange, 714-633-4020

Alessi, David Michael (6 mentions)
Wayne State U, 1983 *Certification:* Otolaryngology
8670 Wilshire Blvd #200, Beverly Hills, 310-657-2253

Andrews, Robert Joseph (5 mentions)
U of Florida, 1991 *Certification:* Otolaryngology
1301 20th St #300, Santa Monica, 310-829-7792

Armstrong, William Byron (5 mentions)
U of Washington, 1988 *Certification:* Otolaryngology
101 The City Dr S, Orange, 714-456-7017

Ayoub, Elias Ishaya (3 mentions)
Creighton U, 1974 *Certification:* Otolaryngology
3654 E Imperial Hwy, Lynwood, 310-638-4125
11480 Brookshire Ave #303, Downey, 562-862-5160
15651 Imperial Hwy #105, La Mirada, 562-943-0711
3650 E South St #202, Lakewood, 562-630-3340

Azizzadeh, Babak (3 mentions)
U of California-Los Angeles, 1996 *Certification:* Otolaryngology
8670 Wilshire Blvd #200, Beverly Hills, 310-657-2253

Babajanian, Michel (5 mentions)
U of California-Los Angeles, 1988 *Certification:* Otolaryngology
2080 Century Park E #1700, Los Angeles, 310-201-0717

Bain, Leslie Arnold (5 mentions)
Indiana U, 1970 *Certification:* Otolaryngology
1441 Avocado Ave #706, Newport Beach, 949-720-9170

Battaglia, Steven Andrew (3 mentions)
U of Vermont, 1997 *Certification:* Otolaryngology
65 N Madison Ave #709, Pasadena, 626-796-6164

Bui, Tam Minh (3 mentions)
U of Kentucky, 1984 *Certification:* Otolaryngology
11180 Warner Ave #459, Fountain Valley, 714-545-1133

Butler, David Michael (7 mentions)
New York Med Coll, 1979 *Certification:* Otolaryngology
1301 20th St #300, Santa Monica, 310-829-7792

Colman, Marc F. (4 mentions)
U of Buffalo, 1975 *Certification:* Otolaryngology
3640 Lomita Blvd #104, Torrance, 310-373-6039

Crumley, Roger Lee (4 mentions)
U of Iowa, 1967 *Certification:* Otolaryngology
101 The City Dr S, Orange, 714-456-7017

Economou, Tasia (4 mentions)
Rush U, 1981 *Certification:* Otolaryngology
6041 Cadillac Ave, Los Angeles, 323-857-5505

Geller, Kenneth Allen (5 mentions)
U of Southern California, 1972 *Certification:* Otolaryngology
435 Arden Ave, Glendale, 818-545-7711
4650 Sunset Blvd #58, Los Angeles, 323-361-2145

Griffiths, Chester Frank (7 mentions)
FMS-Dominican Republic, 1982 *Certification:* Otolaryngology
11645 Wilshire Blvd #600, Los Angeles, 310-477-5558
4644 Lincoln Blvd #400, Marina Del Rey, 310-574-1116

Kaufman, Avrum A. (3 mentions)
Des Moines U, 1996
800 Corporate Dr #290, Ladera Ranch, 949-218-5200

Kedeshian, Paul Aram (3 mentions)
New York U, 1992 *Certification:* Otolaryngology
1260 15th St #1200, Santa Monica, 213-385-0105
200 UCLA Medical Plaza #550, Los Angeles, 310-206-6688

Kelley, Timothy Francis (3 mentions)
Wake Forest U, 1989 *Certification:* Otolaryngology
446 Old Newport Blvd #201, Newport Beach, 949-645-3223
2600 Redondo Ave, Long Beach, 562-988-7000

Keschner, David Brian (5 mentions)
U of California-Irvine, 1994 *Certification:* Otolaryngology
441 N Lakeview Ave, Anaheim, 888-988-2800
6670 Alton Pkwy, Irvine, 714-279-4000

Koutnouyan, Hrair Aram (3 mentions)
U of California-San Diego, 1992 *Certification:* Otolaryngology
1505 Wilson Ter #270, Glendale, 818-241-2101
50 Alessandro Pl #230, Pasadena, 626-577-5550

Landman, Michael Dennis (6 mentions)
U of California-Los Angeles, 1967 *Certification:* Otolaryngology
5525 Etiwanda Ave #312, Tarzana, 818-609-0600

Larian, Babak (3 mentions)
U of California-Irvine, 1996 *Certification:* Otolaryngology
8670 Wilshire Blvd #200, Beverly Hills, 310-657-2253

Low, Nelman Chock (3 mentions)
U of California-San Diego, 1982 *Certification:* Otolaryngology
20911 Earl St #260, Torrance, 310-543-5990

Mesrobian, Raffi-Jean (3 mentions)
FMS-Lebanon, 1980 *Certification:* Otolaryngology
2701 W Alameda Ave #307, Burbank, 818-848-7345

Miller, Chipp St. Kevin (5 mentions)
U of California-Los Angeles, 1975 *Certification:* Otolaryngology
1301 20th St #300, Santa Monica, 310-829-7792

Namazie, Ali Reza (5 mentions)
U of California-Los Angeles, 1994 *Certification:* Otolaryngology
4955 Van Nuys Blvd #505, Sherman Oaks, 818-986-5500

Nasseri, Shawn S. (4 mentions)
Harvard U, 1995 *Certification:* Otolaryngology
435 N Bedford Dr #308, Beverly Hills, 310-289-8200

Osborne, Ryan Fredrick (4 mentions)
U of California-Los Angeles, 1996 *Certification:* Otolaryngology
8631 W 3rd St #945-E, Los Angeles, 310-657-0123
160 E Artesia St #360, Pomona, 908-868-7166

Owens, Othella Theresa (3 mentions)
Virginia Commonwealth U, 1978 *Certification:* Otolaryngology
1127 Wilshire Blvd #1604, Los Angeles, 213-250-5470

Reder, Michael Stephen (5 mentions)
U of Wisconsin, 1971 *Certification:* Otolaryngology
16500 Ventura Blvd #320, Encino, 818-986-1200

Roth, Ronald Carl (6 mentions)
U of Southern California, 1973 *Certification:* Otolaryngology
1301 20th St #300, Santa Monica, 310-829-7792

Shih, Tyson (5 mentions)
U of Southern California, 1981 *Certification:* Otolaryngology
151 W Willow St, Pomona, 909-469-1888

Sinha, Uttam Kumar (3 mentions)
FMS-India, 1980 *Certification:* Otolaryngology
1520 San Pablo St #4600, Los Angeles, 323-442-5790

Tan, Jesse William (6 mentions)
Albany Med Coll, 1997 *Certification:* Otolaryngology
2865 Atlantic Ave #225, Long Beach, 562-988-8818

Wells, Phillip Rus (4 mentions)
St Louis U, 1990 *Certification:* Otolaryngology
675 Camino De Los Mares #420, San Clemente, 949-496-2307

Williams, Everard Horton (3 mentions)
Loma Linda U, 1966 *Certification:* Otolaryngology
65 N Madison Ave #709, Pasadena, 626-577-7792

Willner, Ayal (3 mentions)
Albert Einstein Coll of Med, 1988 *Certification:* Otolaryngology
433 E Wardow Rd, Long Beach, 562-427-0550
1441 Avocado Ave #710, Newport Beach, 949-719-9132
2601 Airport Dr #210, Torrance, 310-530-1681

Wohlgemuth, Mark Andrew (6 mentions)
Tufts U, 1978 *Certification:* Otolaryngology
26726 Crown Valley Pkwy #200, Mission Viejo, 949-364-4361
675 Camino De Los Mares #420, San Clemente, 949-364-4361
24411 Health Center Pkwy #370, Laguna Hills, 949-364-4361

Yoshpe, Nina Sarah (10 mentions)
Albert Einstein Coll of Med, 1978 *Certification:* Otolaryngology
433 E Wardow Rd, Long Beach, 562-427-0550
2601 Airport Dr #210, Torrance, 310-530-1681
1401 Avocado Ave #710, Newport Beach, 949-719-9132

Zadeh, Mani Hossein (5 mentions)
U of California-San Diego, 1998 *Certification:* Otolaryngology
2080 Century Park E #1700, Los Angeles, 310-201-0717

Zuckerman, Kenneth P. (5 mentions)
New York U, 1981 *Certification:* Otolaryngology
16300 Sand Canyon Ave #704, Irvine, 949-753-0112

Pain Medicine

Charbonnet, Christopher J. (6 mentions)
U of Southern California, 1992
Certification: Anesthesiology, Pain Medicine
1505 Wilson Ter, Glendale, 818-241-7246
1509 Wilson Terr, Glendale, 818-550-0900

Dimowo, John O. (3 mentions)
FMS-Nigeria, 1983 *Certification:* Anesthesiology, Pain Medicine
1111 W La Palma Ave, Anaheim, 714-999-6105
2101 N Waterman Ave, San Bernardino, 909-883-8711

El-Khoury, George Farid (3 mentions)
FMS-Lebanon, 1978 *Certification:* Anesthesiology, Pain Medicine
2650 Elm Ave #218, Long Beach, 562-424-2900

Fausett, Hilary J. (4 mentions)
U of California-San Francisco, 1991
Certification: Anesthesiology, Pain Medicine
1505 Wilson Terr, Glendale, 818-241-7246

Ferrante, F. Michael (3 mentions)
New York Med Coll, 1980
Certification: Anesthesiology, Internal Medicine, Pain Medicine
10833 Le Conte Ave, Los Angeles, 310-825-6761

Fuller, Nicholas Scott (3 mentions)
U of Buffalo, 1991 *Certification:* Anesthesiology
8700 Beverly Blvd, West Hollywood, 323-866-8600

Kennedy, Richard Leroy (5 mentions)
U of Southern California, 1986
Certification: Anesthesiology, Pain Medicine
1250 S Sunset Ave #100, West Covina, 626-472-0132
255 E Santa Clara St #230, Arcadia, 626-447-7144

Le, Daniel Quoc (4 mentions)
Jefferson Med Coll, 1989
Certification: Anesthesiology, Pain Medicine
351 Hospital Rd #202, Newport Beach, 949-574-5100

Minor, Jorge Damian (3 mentions)
U of Illinois, 1984
Certification: Pain Medicine, Physical Medicine & Rehabilitation
1245 Wilshire Blvd #403, Los Angeles, 213-482-1046

Paicius, Richard Markus (3 mentions)
U of Arizona, 1983 *Certification:* Anesthesiology, Pain Medicine
450 Newport Center Dr #650, Newport Beach, 949-644-5800

Richeimer, Steven Harry (7 mentions)
U of California-San Francisco, 1982
Certification: Anesthesiology, Pain Medicine, Psychiatry
1520 San Pablo St #3420, Los Angeles, 323-442-6202
1441 Eastlake Ave, Los Angeles, 323-865-3761
1500 San Pablo St, Los Angeles, 323-442-6202

Rosner, Howard Lazar (6 mentions)
U of Miami, 1980 *Certification:* Anesthesiology, Pain Medicine
444 S San Vincente Blvd #1101, Los Angeles, 310-423-9600

Shwachman, Benjamin (4 mentions)
U of Illinois, 1964 *Certification:* Anesthesiology, Pain Medicine
315 N 3rd Ave #200, Covina, 626-967-3176

Pathology

Barasch, Sheldon (3 mentions)
U of California-Irvine, 1962 *Certification:* Anatomic Pathology
17150 Newhope St #117, Fountain Valley, 714-433-1330

Craig, John Redfernd (3 mentions)
U of Southern California, 1969
Certification: Anatomic Pathology & Clinical Pathology
101 E Valencia Mesa Dr, Fullerton, 714-992-3907

Esteban, Jose M. (3 mentions)
FMS-Spain, 1976 *Certification:* Anatomic Pathology
501 S Buena Vista St, Burbank, 818-847-6022

Hoshiko, Melvin Glen (6 mentions)
U of California-Irvine, 1973 *Certification:* Anatomic Pathology
& Clinical Pathology, Cytopathology, Medical Microbiology
2801 Atlantic Ave, Long Beach, 562-933-0719

Ibarra, Julio Alberto (3 mentions)
FMS-Mexico, 1978 *Certification:* Anatomic Pathology &
Clinical Pathology, Cytopathology
9920 Talbert Ave, Fountain Valley, 714-378-7081

Kasimian, Dennis (4 mentions)
Tulane U, 1975
Certification: Anatomic Pathology & Clinical Pathology
15107 Vanowen St, Van Nuys, 818-902-2961
15211 Vanowen St #303, Van Nuys, 818-902-2961

Krasne, David Lowell (6 mentions)
U of California-Irvine, 1985
Certification: Anatomic Pathology & Clinical Pathology
1328 22nd St, Santa Monica, 310-829-8101

McLaren, Steven R. (4 mentions)
Midwestern U Chicago Coll of Osteopathic Med, 1991
Certification: Anatomic Pathology & Clinical Pathology
6041 Cadillac Ave, Los Angeles, 323-857-2000

Mendoza, Vivian M. (3 mentions)
U of California-San Francisco, 1986 *Certification:* Anatomic Pathology & Clinical Pathology, Cytopathology
24451 Health Center Dr, Laguna Hills, 949-837-4500

Murakami, Susan Sayeko (3 mentions)
U of Michigan, 1979 *Certification:* Anatomic Pathology & Clinical Pathology, Immunopathology
100 W California Blvd, Pasadena, 626-397-5230

Orlando, Robert Anthony (4 mentions)
New Jersey Med Sch, 1965
Certification: Anatomic Pathology, Clinical Pathology
309 W Beverly Blvd, Montebello, 323-726-1222

Strassle, Philip Otto (3 mentions)
U of Southern California, 1988
Certification: Anatomic Pathology & Clinical Pathology
1798 N Garey Ave, Pomona, 909-865-9824

Turner, Roderick Randolph (5 mentions)
U of California-Los Angeles, 1979 *Certification:* Anatomic Pathology & Clinical Pathology, Hematology
1328 22nd St, Santa Monica, 310-829-8101

Pediatrics *(see note on page 9)*

Abelowitz, Steven (4 mentions)
Certification: Pediatrics
1401 Avocado Ave, Newport Beach, 949-759-1720
25500 Rancho Niguel Rd #110, Laguna Niguel, 949-448-8821

Adler, Robert (3 mentions)
U of California-Los Angeles, 1973 *Certification:* Pediatrics
4650 W Sunset Blvd, Los Angeles, 323-669-2534

Barrow, Ivan Lonsdale (3 mentions)
U of California-Los Angeles, 1995 *Certification:* Pediatrics
6041 Cadillac Ave, Los Angeles, 323-857-2000

Biederman, Aviva D. (5 mentions)
FMS-Argentina, 1970 *Certification:* Pediatrics
8635 W 3rd St #260-W, Los Angeles, 310-652-3324

Downes, Maureen C. (3 mentions)
Georgetown U, 1976 *Certification:* Pediatrics
16300 Sand Canyon Ave St #811, Irvine, 949-753-9000

Friend, Gwen Klyman (4 mentions)
SUNY-Downstate Med Coll, 1966 *Certification:* Pediatrics
3440 Lomita Blvd #240, Torrance, 310-539-2445

Goldberg, Marshall Gary (3 mentions)
U of Iowa, 1962 *Certification:* Allergy & Immunology, Pediatrics
5353 Balboa Blvd #104, Encino, 818-789-7181

Goldin, Alice L. Gentsch (6 mentions)
Jefferson Med Coll, 1967 *Certification:* Pediatrics
20911 Earl St #100, Torrance, 310-370-7759

Gurfield, William Baruch (3 mentions)
New York U, 1968 *Certification:* Pediatrics
1450 10th St #304, Santa Monica, 310-458-1714

Lerner, Marc Alan (4 mentions)
Mount Sinai Sch of Med, 1977
Certification: Developmental-Behavioral Pediatrics, Pediatrics
1 Medical Plaza Dr, Irvine, 949-824-8600

Malphus, Edward Wilson (4 mentions)
U of South Florida, 1975 *Certification:* Pediatrics
2021 Santa Monica Blvd #612, Santa Monica, 310-829-4403

McCormick, Janet Leslie (3 mentions)
U of California-Irvine, 1976 *Certification:* Pediatrics
2840 Long Beach Blvd #315, Long Beach, 562-595-5479

Penso, Jeffrey Steven (3 mentions)
SUNY-Downstate Med Coll, 1969
Certification: Pediatric Nephrology, Pediatrics
9696 Culver Blvd #108, Culver City, 310-204-6897

Sachs, Marshall Harold (3 mentions)
U of Washington, 1962 *Certification:* Pediatrics
2825 Santa Monica Blvd, Santa Monica, 310-829-9935

Samson, John Harry (3 mentions)
Creighton U, 1961 *Certification:* Pediatrics
2921 Redondo Ave, Long Beach, 562-426-5551

Sanford, Margaret C. (3 mentions)
8631 W 3rd St #725-E, Los Angeles, 310-854-3043

Shoji, Elaine Carole (4 mentions)
Columbia U, 1976 *Certification:* Pediatrics
827 Deep Valley Dr #102, Rolling Hills Estates, 310-541-8801

Sloninsky, Liliana Perla (8 mentions)
FMS-Argentina, 1969 *Certification:* Pediatrics
8631 W 3rd St #725-E, Los Angeles, 310-854-3043

Weiss, Michael Alan (5 mentions)
Western U, 1985 *Certification:* Pediatrics
29941 Aventura #F, Rancho Santa Margarita, 949-858-1100

Whitman, Gerald Bruce (4 mentions)
U of Illinois, 1969 *Certification:* Pediatrics
250 N Robertson Blvd #404, Beverly Hills, 310-273-9533

Woo, Dennis Barry (3 mentions)
U of California-Los Angeles, 1975 *Certification:* Pediatrics
2825 Santa Monica Blvd, Santa Monica, 310-829-9935

Woo, Heide (3 mentions)
U of Chicago, 1990 *Certification:* Pediatrics
11318 National Blvd, Los Angeles, 310-231-9150

Plastic Surgery

Ambe, Milind Kishore (3 mentions)
U of California-Irvine, 1988 *Certification:* Plastic Surgery
1441 Avocado Ave #801, Newport Beach, 949-759-5539

Amonic, Robert Stephan (3 mentions)
U of California-Los Angeles, 1963 *Certification:* Plastic Surgery
2001 Santa Monica Blvd #790W, Santa Monica, 310-829-7821

Andersen, James Spackman (3 mentions)
Jefferson Med Coll, 1983 *Certification:* Plastic Surgery
1500 Duarte Rd, Duarte, 626-359-8111

Aronowitz, Joel Alan (4 mentions)
Baylor U, 1982 *Certification:* Plastic Surgery
8635 W 3rd St #1090, Los Angeles, 310-659-0705

Black, James Jens (4 mentions)
Rosalind Franklin U, 1988 *Certification:* Plastic Surgery
22930 Crenshaw Blvd #D, Torrance, 310-530-4200

Bogossian, Norick (3 mentions)
FMS-Iran, 1981
1560 E Chevy Chase Dr #255, Glendale, 818-241-9611

Brenner, Kevin Alan (3 mentions)
Loyola U Chicago, 1997 *Certification:* Plastic Surgery, Surgery
465 N Roxbury Dr #1001, Beverly Hills, 310-777-5400

Carr, Ruth Margaret (7 mentions)
U of Oklahoma, 1977 *Certification:* Plastic Surgery
1301 20th #470, Santa Monica, 310-315-0222

Cox, Brian Allen (4 mentions)
U of Missouri-Kansas City, 1993
Certification: Plastic Surgery, Surgery
1044 S Fair Oaks Ave, Pasadena, 626-449-4859

Elliott, Eugene Douglas (4 mentions)
U of Rochester, 1977 *Certification:* Plastic Surgery
9900 Talbert Ave #101, Fountain Valley, 714-241-0646
1441 Ovacado Ave #710, Newport Beach, 714-241-0646

Evans, Gregory Randolph (6 mentions)
U of Southern California, 1985
Certification: Plastic Surgery, Surgery
200 S Manchester Ave #650, Orange, 714-456-5755

Falvey, Michael Paul (5 mentions)
U of Arizona, 1972 *Certification:* Plastic Surgery
3440 Lomita Blvd #150, Torrance, 310-530-7950

Feinstein, Felix Ronald (3 mentions)
New Jersey Med Sch, 1974 *Certification:* Plastic Surgery
6041 Cadillac Ave, Los Angeles, 323-857-2000

Gross, John Edward (4 mentions)
U of Missouri, 1984 *Certification:* Plastic Surgery
1808 Verdugo Blvd #116, Glendale, 818-790-2280

Grossman, Peter Hylan (4 mentions)
Rosalind Franklin U, 1988 *Certification:* Plastic Surgery
4910 Van Nuys Blvd #306, Sherman Oaks, 818-981-2050

Handel, Neal (3 mentions)
Certification: Plastic Surgery
13400 Riverside Dr #101, Sherman Oaks, 818-788-3973

Kobayashi, Mark Robert (10 mentions)
Tulane U, 1984 *Certification:* Plastic Surgery
200 S Manchester Ave #650, Orange, 714-456-5253

Labowe, Mark L. (4 mentions)
U of California-Los Angeles, 1979 *Certification:* Plastic Surgery
100 UCLA Medical Plaza #747, Los Angeles, 310-824-2550

Miller, Timothy Alden (4 mentions)
U of California-Los Angeles, 1963
Certification: Plastic Surgery, Surgery
200 UCLA Medical Plaza 3465, Los Angeles, 310-206-8134

Mowlavi, Arian S. (3 mentions)
U of California-San Diego, 1998 *Certification:* Plastic Surgery
31542 Coast Hwy #3, Laguna Beach, 949-499-4147

Nichter, Larry Steven (3 mentions)
Boston U, 1978 *Certification:* Plastic Surgery
7677 Center Ave #401, Huntington Beach, 714-902-1100

Orringer, Jay Stewart (8 mentions)
U of Miami, 1980 *Certification:* Plastic Surgery, Surgery
9675 Brighton Way, Beverly Hills, 310-273-1663

Sanders, George Hughy (3 mentions)
Harvard U, 1978 *Certification:* Plastic Surgery
16633 Ventura Blvd #110, Encino, 818-981-3333

Sasaki, Gordon Hiroshi (3 mentions)
Yale U, 1968 *Certification:* Plastic Surgery
800 Fairmount Ave #319, Pasadena, 626-796-3373

Sherman, Randolph (5 mentions)
U of Missouri, 1977
Certification: Plastic Surgery, Surgery, Surgery of the Hand
8635 W 3rd St #770, Los Angeles, 310-423-8350

Slate, Richard Kendrick (3 mentions)
Duke U, 1979 *Certification:* Plastic Surgery
8700 Beverly Blvd, West Hollywood, 310-423-1155

Smith, Andrew Donald (3 mentions)
George Washington U, 1995 *Certification:* Plastic Surgery, Surgery
16300 Sand Canyon Ave #911, Irvine, 949-450-2755

Tiner, Christopher Keoni (3 mentions)
Virginia Commonwealth U, 2001 *Certification:* Plastic Surgery
1044 S Fair Oaks Ave #101, Pasadena, 626-449-4859

Urata, Mark Masaru (3 mentions)
U of Southern California, 1996 *Certification:* Plastic Surgery
4650 W Sunset Blvd, Los Angeles, 323-361-2154

Wali, Devdas (3 mentions)
SUNY-Downstate Med Coll, 1996
Certification: Plastic Surgery, Surgery
155 W Willow St, Pomona, 909-865-2626

Wells, James H. (4 mentions)
U of Texas-Galveston, 1966 *Certification:* Plastic Surgery
2880 Atlantic Ave #290, Long Beach, 562-595-6543

Psychiatry

Borenstein, Daniel Bernard (4 mentions)
U of Colorado, 1962 *Certification:* Psychiatry
151 N Canyon View Dr, Los Angeles, 310-472-7386

Caine, Edwin George (3 mentions)
U of Miami, 1964
3250 Lomita Blvd #205, Torrance, 310-326-5102

Castner, Edward John (3 mentions)
Loma Linda U, 1965 *Certification:* Geriatric Psychiatry, Psychiatry
2810 E Del Mar Blvd #7, Pasadena, 626-577-2855

Chaitin, Barry Frederick (6 mentions)
New York U, 1969 *Certification:* Psychiatry
400 Newport Center Dr #309, Newport Beach, 714-456-5951
101 The City Dr S Bldg 3, Orange, 714-456-5951

Franz, Bettina Eva (3 mentions)
Certification: Psychiatry
6-B Liberty Plaza #110, Aliso Viejo, 949-680-2700

Gitlin, Michael Jay (5 mentions)
U of Pennsylvania, 1975 *Certification:* Psychiatry
10920 Wilshire Blvd #1070, Los Angeles, 310-206-3654

Hanna, Ehab Gamil (3 mentions)
FMS-Egypt, 1989
23961 Calle De La Magdalena #424, Laguna Hills, 949-600-6430

Hayes, Timothy Joseph (5 mentions)
U of Michigan, 1977
Certification: Addiction Psychiatry, Geriatric Psychiatry, Psychiatry
1301 20th St #210, Santa Monica, 310-315-0303

Sternbach, Harvey Allen (7 mentions)
Robert W Johnson Med Sch, 1977 *Certification:* Psychiatry
12300 Wilshire Blvd #330, Los Angeles, 310-979-7774

Pulmonary Disease

Arroyo, Joel E. (3 mentions)
FMS-Peru, 1969
Certification: Internal Medicine, Pulmonary Disease
5305 E Beverly Blvd, Los Angeles, 323-726-3571

Brenner, Matthew (4 mentions)
U of California-San Diego, 1981 *Certification:* Critical Care Medicine, Internal Medicine, Pulmonary Disease
101 The City Dr S, Orange, 714-456-5150

Burrows, James Emory (4 mentions)
U of Cincinnati, 1993
1301 20th St #360, Santa Monica, 310-828-3465

Chang, Robert S. Y. (3 mentions)
Case Western Reserve U, 1972
Certification: Internal Medicine, Pulmonary Disease
3701 Skypark Dr #200, Torrance, 310-378-8900

Ence, Thomas Jenkins (6 mentions)
U of Utah, 1974
Certification: Internal Medicine, Pulmonary Disease
18399 Ventura Blvd #245, Tarzana, 818-609-7536

Fox, Michael Eliot (5 mentions)
U of California-Irvine, 1976 *Certification:* Critical Care Medicine, Internal Medicine, Pulmonary Disease
1310 W Stewart Dr #410, Orange, 714-639-9401
1211 W La Palma Ave #709, Anaheim, 714-778-1943

Gitlin, Steven Mark (3 mentions)
New York Med Coll, 1973
Certification: Internal Medicine, Pulmonary Disease
9735 Wilshire Blvd #245, Beverly Hills, 310-276-5298
2010 Wilshire Blvd #506, Los Angeles, 213-413-5444
18607 Ventura Blvd #101, Tarzana, 818-758-8282

Gurevitch, Michael Joel (16 mentions)
Loyola U Chicago, 1982 *Certification:* Critical Care Medicine, Internal Medicine, Pulmonary Disease
39 Congress St #301, Pasadena, 626-486-0181

Hewlett, Robert I. (5 mentions)
FMS-Australia, 1968
Certification: Internal Medicine, Pulmonary Disease
320 Superior Ave #200, Newport Beach, 949-642-6200

Jasper, Alan C. (3 mentions)
Georgetown U, 1976 *Certification:* Critical Care Medicine, Internal Medicine, Pulmonary Disease
201 S Alvarado St #825, Los Angeles, 213-484-2044

Kasnitz, Paul Stephen (3 mentions)
New York U, 1965
Certification: Internal Medicine, Pulmonary Disease
18399 Ventura Blvd #245, Tarzana, 818-609-7536

Ko, Young-Jae (3 mentions)
FMS-South Korea, 1973
Certification: Internal Medicine, Pulmonary Disease
44215 15th St W #303, Lancaster, 661-945-0723

Krishna, Doddanna (3 mentions)
FMS-India, 1979 *Certification:* Internal Medicine
44215 15th St W #211, Lancaster, 661-726-6600

Kuhn, Gilbert Joseph, Jr. (16 mentions)
Cornell U, 1974 *Certification:* Allergy & Immunology, Critical Care Medicine, Internal Medicine, Pulmonary Disease
1301 20th St #360, Santa Monica, 310-828-3465

Law, James H. (3 mentions)
St Louis U, 1975
Certification: Internal Medicine, Pulmonary Disease
1310 W Stewart Dr #410, Orange, 714-639-9401

Lynch, Joseph Patrick (3 mentions)
Harvard U, 1973
Certification: Internal Medicine, Pulmonary Disease
200 UCLA Medical Plaza #365-B, Los Angeles, 310-825-8061

Madani, Mir Mahmoud (3 mentions)
FMS-Turkey, 1990
Certification: Critical Care Medicine, Internal Medicine
3801 Katella Ave #310, Los Alamitos, 562-598-2141

Makabali, Carlos Garcia (3 mentions)
FMS-Philippines, 1973 *Certification:* Critical Care Medicine, Internal Medicine, Pulmonary Disease
101 E Beverly Blvd #307, Montebello, 323-888-2548

Moricca, Robert Bruce (3 mentions)
U of California-Los Angeles, 1981
Certification: Internal Medicine, Pulmonary Disease
320 Superior Ave #200, Newport Beach, 949-642-6200

Novak, Dennis Ronald (3 mentions)
SUNY-Upstate Med U, 1974
Certification: Internal Medicine, Pulmonary Disease
320 Superior Ave #200, Newport Beach, 949-642-6200

Parke, Robert Edward (3 mentions)
U of Wisconsin, 1973
Certification: Internal Medicine, Pulmonary Disease
1310 W Stewart Dr #410, Orange, 714-639-9401

Patel, Shailesh S. (3 mentions)
FMS-India, 1980
2625 W Alameda Ave #506, Burbank, 818-843-5864

Ramakrishnan, Chitra (3 mentions)
FMS-Grenada, 1998
Certification: Internal Medicine, Pulmonary Disease
959 E Walnut St #120, Pasadena, 626-795-5118
1818 Verdugo Blvd #207, Glendale, 626-304-0782

Ross, Marlowe David (4 mentions)
Johns Hopkins U, 1979
Certification: Internal Medicine, Pulmonary Disease
19582 Beach Blvd #314, Huntington Beach, 714-378-2421

Roston, Warren Lance (4 mentions)
U of California-San Francisco, 1977
Certification: Internal Medicine, Pulmonary Disease
2080 Century Park E #1006, Los Angeles, 310-556-0515

Rovzar, Michael Anthony (5 mentions)
U of California-Irvine, 1981 *Certification:* Critical Care Medicine, Internal Medicine, Pulmonary Disease
30250 Rancho Viejo Rd, San Juan Capistrano, 949-443-4114

Sadana, Gurbinder Singh (3 mentions)
FMS-India, 1968 *Certification:* Critical Care Medicine, Internal Medicine, Pulmonary Disease
1866 N Orange Grove Ave #202, Pomona, 909-623-8796

Schroeder, C. Andrew (3 mentions)
New York Med Coll, 1999
Certification: Internal Medicine, Pulmonary Disease
9401 Wilshire Blvd #515, Beverly Hills, 310-432-4260

Scott, David Jerome (4 mentions)
U of Kentucky, 1974
Certification: Internal Medicine, Pulmonary Disease
3701 Skypark Dr #200, Torrance, 310-378-8900

Sinkowitz, Deren Mark (3 mentions)
New York Med Coll, 1983 *Certification:* Critical Care Medicine, Internal Medicine, Pulmonary Disease
3701 Skypark Dr #200, Torrance, 310-378-8900

Stafford, Jerald Robert (7 mentions)
U of Iowa, 1971
Certification: Critical Care Medicine, Internal Medicine
24411 Health Center Dr #560, Laguna Hills, 949-458-1223

Stricke, Leslie Malvin (5 mentions)
FMS-South Africa, 1970
Certification: Internal Medicine, Pulmonary Disease
8631 W 3rd St #735E, Los Angeles, 310-657-4170

Suh, David Emanuel (3 mentions)
U of California-Los Angeles, 1983 *Certification:* Critical Care Medicine, Internal Medicine, Pulmonary Disease
6041 Cadillac Ave, Los Angeles, 323-857-2000

Wachtel, Andrew Stuart (10 mentions)
Albany Med Coll, 1981 *Certification:* Critical Care Medicine, Internal Medicine, Pulmonary Disease
8635 W 3rd St #965W, Los Angeles, 310-657-3792

Walsh, Patrick Joseph (3 mentions)
U of Washington, 1973
Certification: Internal Medicine, Pulmonary Disease
15243 Vanowen St #411, Van Nuys, 818-787-1050

Weintraub, Bernard S. (3 mentions)
U of California-San Francisco, 1976 *Certification:* Critical Care Medicine, Internal Medicine, Pulmonary Disease
2021 Santa Monica Blvd #335-E, Santa Monica, 310-453-8584

Wolfe, Robert Norton (6 mentions)
U of California-Los Angeles, 1975 *Certification:* Critical Care Medicine, Internal Medicine, Pulmonary Disease
8635 W 3rd St #965W, Los Angeles, 310-657-3792

Yadegar, Shahryar Thomas (4 mentions)
Certification: Critical Care Medicine, Pulmonary Disease
1200 N State St, Los Angeles, 323-226-2345
18399 Ventura Blvd #245, Tarzana, 818-758-0020

Yu, Austin Haw (5 mentions)
Albert Einstein Coll of Med, 1995
Certification: Critical Care Medicine, Pulmonary Disease
3801 Katella Ave #223, Los Alamitos, 562-626-8016

Radiology—Diagnostic

Boswell, William Douglas, Jr. (3 mentions)
Jefferson Med Coll, 1972 *Certification:* Diagnostic Radiology
1441 Eastlake Ave, Los Angeles, 323-865-3203

Brant-Zawadzki, Michael N. (4 mentions)
U of Cincinnati, 1975
Certification: Diagnostic Radiology, Neuroradiology
1 Hoag Dr, Newport Beach, 949-764-5942

Deutsch, Andrew L. (3 mentions)
Columbia U *Certification:* Diagnostic Radiology
44105 15th St W, Lancaster, 661-949-5700

Gee, Carol Sheau-Huei (3 mentions)
U of Iowa, 1980 *Certification:* Diagnostic Radiology
6041 Cadillac Ave, Los Angeles, 323-857-2421

Goldberg, Ross T. (3 mentions)
Tufts U, 1976 *Certification:* Diagnostic Radiology
1450 10th St #206, Santa Monica, 310-394-2761
9675 Brighton Way #240, Beverly Hills, 310-859-8104

Hasso, Anton N. (3 mentions)
Certification: Diagnostic Radiology, Neuroradiology
200 S Manchester Ave, Orange, 714-456-7412

Hedley, Christopher G. (4 mentions)
Baylor U, 1984 *Certification:* Diagnostic Radiology, Vascular
& Interventional Radiology
100 W California Blvd, Pasadena, 626-397-5185

Hoffman, Richard B. (3 mentions)
U of Minnesota, 1961 *Certification:* Nuclear Medicine, Radiology
3330 Lomita Blvd, Torrance, 310-517-4709
3 Hillside Ln, Rolling Hills, 310-541-9659

Joyce, Peter Watson (5 mentions)
U of California-Los Angeles, 1973
Certification: Diagnostic Radiology, Neuroradiology
5455 Wilshire Blvd #1120, Los Angeles, 323-549-3030

Julien, Peter Jay (5 mentions)
U of Miami, 1969 *Certification:* Diagnostic Radiology
8705 Gracie Allen Dr #M-335, Los Angeles, 310-423-8000

Kadell-Wootton, Barbara (3 mentions)
George Washington U, 1963
10833 Le Conte Ave, Los Angeles, 310-825-7130

Kallman, Cindy E. (3 mentions)
Albany Med Coll, 1984 *Certification:* Diagnostic Radiology
8705 Gracie Allen Dr #M-335, Los Angeles, 310-423-8000

Kelly, Kevin Michael (3 mentions)
St Louis U, 1968 *Certification:* Diagnostic Radiology
50 Alessandro Pl #A30, Pasadena, 626-793-6141

Kolanz, Robert Alan (3 mentions)
U of Louisville, 1984 *Certification:* Diagnostic Radiology,
Vascular & Interventional Radiology
100 Oceangate #1000, Long Beach, 310-316-2424
4101 Torrance Blvd, Torrance, 310-303-5703

Lebovic, Joseph (3 mentions)
U of California-Los Angeles, 1973
Certification: Diagnostic Radiology
9675 Brighton Way #240, Beverly Hills, 310-394-2761
1450 10th St #206, Santa Monica, 310-394-2761

Mink, Jerrold Howard (5 mentions)
U of Illinois, 1971 *Certification:* Diagnostic Radiology
8670 Wilshire Blvd #101, Beverly Hills, 310-358-2100

Rowen, Scott Jeffrey (4 mentions)
U of California-Irvine, 1982
Certification: Diagnostic Radiology, Pediatric Radiology
1100 W Stewart Dr, Orange, 714-771-8171

Rubenstein, David Jay (4 mentions)
FMS-Grenada, 1981 *Certification:* Diagnostic Radiology
8227 Reseda Blvd, Reseda, 818-773-6500

Schatz, Charles Joel (4 mentions)
U of Illinois, 1967 *Certification:* Diagnostic Radiology
8750 Wilshire Blvd #100, Beverly Hills, 310-975-1500

Radiology—Therapeutic

Burnison, Christiane Michelle (4 mentions)
Certification: Therapeutic Radiology
8700 Beverly Blvd, Los Angeles, 310-423-8030

Chin, Kenneth Waikiu (3 mentions)
Harvard U, 1974 *Certification:* Diagnostic Radiology,
Vascular & Interventional Radiology
16311 Ventura Blvd #120, Encino, 818-817-7707

Friedman, Marc Louis (4 mentions)
New York U, 1982 *Certification:* Diagnostic Radiology,
Vascular & Interventional Radiology
8705 Gracie Allen Dr #1446, Los Angeles, 310-423-8000

Gorty, Sri Ganesh (3 mentions)
Northeastern Ohio U, 1996 *Certification:* Radiation Oncology
1910 Royalty Dr, Pomona, 909-865-9890

Moorhead, Francis Joseph (3 mentions)
FMS-United Kingdom, 1962 *Certification:* Nuclear
Medicine, Radiology, Therapeutic Radiology
301 W Huntington Dr #120, Arcadia, 626-574-3657

Mowji, Pankaj J. (5 mentions)
FMS-India, 1981 *Certification:* Diagnostic Radiology
441 N Lakeview Ave, Anaheim, 714-279-4000

Rose, Christopher M. (7 mentions)
Harvard U, 1974
Certification: Radiation Oncology, Therapeutic Radiology
9229 Wilsher Blvd, Beverly Hills, 310-205-5700

So, George J. (3 mentions)
U of Chicago, 1991 *Certification:* Diagnostic Radiology,
Vascular & Interventional Radiology
3330 Lomita Blvd, Torrance, 310-325-9110

Steinberg, Michael Lee (4 mentions)
U of Southern California, 1976
Certification: Therapeutic Radiology
200 Medical Plaza #B-265, Los Angeles, 310-828-9771

Stevens, Gerald Frederick (3 mentions)
FMS-Canada, 1972 *Certification:* Diagnostic Radiology
24451 Health Center Dr, Laguna Hills, 949-452-3573
9920 Talbert Ave, Fountain Valley, 714-378-7571
654 Camino de los Mares, San Clemente, 949-489-4507

Wollman, Robert Charles (4 mentions)
New York U, 1989 *Certification:* Radiation Oncology
1328 22nd St, Santa Monica, 310-829-8913

Rehabilitation

Adams, Hugh Richard (4 mentions)
FMS-Mexico, 1975
Certification: Physical Medicine & Rehabilitation
2840 Long Beach Blvd #130, Long Beach, 562-424-8111

Francini, Alexander O. (3 mentions)
U of California-Irvine, 1990 *Certification:* Pain Medicine,
Physical Medicine & Rehabilitation
22 Corporate Plaza Dr, Newport Beach, 949-722-7038

Hegde, Sunil Kumar (12 mentions)
FMS-India, 1982
Certification: Physical Medicine & Rehabilitation
630 S Raymond Ave #120, Pasadena, 626-403-1444

Lynn, Kenneth Robert (3 mentions)
U of California-Irvine, 1985
Certification: Physical Medicine & Rehabilitation
24411 Health Center Dr #690, Laguna Hills, 949-452-7034

Minor, Jorge Damian (4 mentions)
U of Illinois, 1984
Certification: Pain Medicine, Physical Medicine & Rehabilitation
1245 Wilshire Blvd #403, Los Angeles, 213-482-1046

Riggs, Richard Vincent (3 mentions)
Med Coll of Georgia, 1988
Certification: Physical Medicine & Rehabilitation
8631 W 3rd St, Los Angeles, 310-423-2182

Sonka-Maarek, Sherry Ellen (5 mentions)
U of Southern California, 1990 *Certification:* Physical
Medicine & Rehabilitation, Spinal Cord Injury Medicine
1300 W 7th St, San Pedro, 310-514-5377

Rheumatology

Andrews, Brian Sydney (8 mentions)
FMS-Australia, 1969 *Certification:* Allergy & Immunology,
Internal Medicine, Rheumatology
101 The City Dr S Bldg 1 2nd Fl, Orange, 714-456-7101

Bluestone, Rodney H. (4 mentions)
FMS-United Kingdom, 1960
Certification: Internal Medicine, Rheumatology
436 N Bedford Dr #303, Beverly Hills, 310-657-2222

Dore, Robin Kathleen (11 mentions)
U of California-Irvine, 1974
Certification: Internal Medicine, Rheumatology
18102 Irvine Blvd #104, Tustin, 714-505-5500
1120 W La Palma Ave #7, Anaheim, 714-505-5500

Ehresmann, Glenn Richard (7 mentions)
U of California-Irvine, 1973
Certification: Internal Medicine, Rheumatology
1520 San Pablo St, Los Angeles, 323-442-5100

Eng, Bett J. (5 mentions)
U of California-Los Angeles, 1986
Certification: Internal Medicine, Rheumatology
23441 Madison St #340, Torrance, 310-373-0340

Fan, Peng Thim (9 mentions)
FMS-Canada, 1971
Certification: Internal Medicine, Rheumatology
12660 Riverside Dr #200, North Hollywood, 818-980-7010

Forouzesh, Solomon N. (4 mentions)
FMS-Iran, 1973 *Certification:* Internal Medicine
9808 Venice Blvd #604, Culver City, 310-204-6811

Godfrey, Nancy Fujimura (7 mentions)
U of California-Irvine, 1977
Certification: Internal Medicine, Rheumatology
6226 E Spring St #275, Long Beach, 562-496-0546

Goldin, Richard Henry (5 mentions)
U of California-San Francisco, 1967
Certification: Internal Medicine, Rheumatology
23441 Madison St #340, Torrance, 310-373-0340

Horizon, Arash (4 mentions)
U of California-San Diego, 1998
Certification: Internal Medicine, Rheumatology
9001 Wilshire Blvd #200, Beverly Hills, 310-659-7878

Karamlou, Kathy (6 mentions)
George Washington U, 1998
Certification: Internal Medicine, Rheumatology
332 Old Newport Ave, Newport Beach, 949-631-6500

Lehmer, Randy Richard (5 mentions)
U of California-Los Angeles, 1982
Certification: Internal Medicine, Rheumatology
4902 Irvine Center Dr #105, Irvine, 949-262-5740
411 N Lakeview Ave, Anaheim, 888-988-2800

McCurdy, Deborah Kerr (6 mentions)
Hahnemann U, 1976
Certification: Pediatric Rheumatology, Pediatrics
200 Medical Plaza #265, Los Angeles, 310-825-0867
10833 Le Conte Ave, Los Angeles, 310-206-1826

Minna, David Anthony (5 mentions)
St Louis U, 1973 *Certification:* Internal Medicine, Rheumatology
4772 Katella Ave #200, Los Alamitos, 562-596-3365

Noritake, Dean Toshiyuki (10 mentions)
Yale U, 1981 *Certification:* Internal Medicine, Rheumatology
2750 E Washington Blvd #120, Pasadena, 626-296-2910

O'Connor, Brian (5 mentions)
U of California-Davis, 1977 *Certification:* Internal Medicine
675 S Arroyo Pkwy #400, Pasadena, 626-795-4116

Ramer, Sandra Jean (4 mentions)
U of California-Los Angeles, 1972
Certification: Internal Medicine, Rheumatology
1301 20th St #390, Santa Monica, 310-453-3568

Rinaldi, Renee Zaira (5 mentions)
New York Med Coll, 1976
Certification: Internal Medicine, Rheumatology
150 N Robertson Blvd #224, Beverly Hills, 310-860-3409

Shiel, William Chapin, Jr. (5 mentions)
St Louis U, 1979 *Certification:* Internal Medicine, Rheumatology
27871 Medical Center Rd #200, Mission Viejo, 949-364-7246

Susko, Thomas Michael (9 mentions)
FMS-Germany, 1986 *Certification:* Rheumatology
2001 Santa Monica Blvd #783, Santa Monica, 310-829-5557

Thai, Christine Thailan (5 mentions)
U of California-Irvine, 1987 *Certification:* Rheumatology
19582 Beach Blvd #302, Huntington Beach, 714-378-2440

Troum, Orrin Marshall (10 mentions)
FMS-Mexico, 1979
Certification: Internal Medicine, Rheumatology
2336 Santa Monica Blvd #207, Santa Monica, 310-449-1999

Wallace, James Davis (4 mentions)
U of Southern California, 1972
Certification: Internal Medicine, Rheumatology
2699 Atlantic Ave, Long Beach, 562-426-3333

Weinberger, Alan Walter (4 mentions)
U of California-Los Angeles, 1975
Certification: Internal Medicine, Rheumatology
8631 W 3rd St #540, Los Angeles, 310-854-7224

Thoracic Surgery

Bethencourt, Daniel Miguel (5 mentions)
Yale U, 1979 *Certification:* Thoracic Surgery
2865 Atlantic Ave #205, Long Beach, 562-988-9333

Cameron, Robert Brian (5 mentions)
U of California-Los Angeles, 1984
Certification: Surgery, Thoracic Surgery
10833 Le Conte Ave, Los Angeles, 310-267-4612

Chino, Shigeru (8 mentions)
U of California-San Francisco, 1964 *Certification:* Surgery
27601 Forbes Rd #58, Laguna Niguel, 949-348-0459

Cohen, Robbin Gerald (9 mentions)
U of Colorado, 1980 *Certification:* Thoracic Surgery
50 Bellefontaine St #403, Pasadena, 626-683-9000
1520 San Pablo St #4300, Los Angeles, 323-442-5849

Fuller, Clark Beeman (6 mentions)
Creighton U, 1987
8635 W 3rd St #975, Los Angeles, 310-652-0530

McKenna, Robert Joseph, Jr. (15 mentions)
U of Southern California, 1977 *Certification:* Thoracic Surgery
8635 W 3rd St #975-W, Los Angeles, 310-652-0530

Palafox, Brian Avecilla (8 mentions)
U of California-Irvine, 1975
Certification: Surgery, Thoracic Surgery
1310 W Stewart Dr #503, Orange, 714-997-2224

Schaerf, Raymond Harris (7 mentions)
New York Med Coll, 1972 *Certification:* Thoracic Surgery
2601 W Alameda Ave #404, Burbank, 818-843-2334

Starnes, Vaughn A. (6 mentions)
U of North Carolina, 1977 *Certification:* Thoracic Surgery
4650 W Sunset Blvd, Los Angeles, 323-660-2450
50 Bellefontaine St #403, Pasadena, 626-683-9000
1520 San Pablo St #4300, Los Angeles, 323-442-5849

Tse, David Gunnmond (10 mentions)
Wayne State U, 1992 *Certification:* Thoracic Surgery
13652 Cantara St, Panorama City, 818-375-2000
5601 De Soto Ave, Woodland Hills, 818-719-2000
6041 Cadillac Ave, Los Angeles, 323-857-2000
1526 N Edgemont St, Los Angeles, 323-783-4011
25825 S Vermont Ave, Harbor City, 310-325-5111

Urology

Andrews, Roger Norman (4 mentions)
U of Southern California, 1975 *Certification:* Urology
624 W Duarte Rd #203, Arcadia, 626-446-8595

Baghdassarian, Ruben (5 mentions)
FMS-Iran, 1978 *Certification:* Urology
3791 Katella Ave #200, Los Alamitos, 562-598-6166
2888 Long Beach Blvd #265, Long Beach, 562-598-6166

Bishai, Michael B. (4 mentions)
FMS-Egypt, 1973 *Certification:* Urology
112 N Madison Ave, Pasadena, 626-796-8102

Brosman, Stanley Allan (5 mentions)
Indiana U, 1959 *Certification:* Urology
2021 Santa Monica Blvd #510-E, Santa Monica, 310-828-8531

Clayman, Ralph Victor (10 mentions)
U of California-San Diego, 1973 *Certification:* Urology
101 The City Dr S, Orange, 888-456-7002

Cosgrove, Daniel Jeremy (4 mentions)
Med Coll of Pennsylvania, 1996 *Certification:* Urology
16311 Ventura Blvd #1000, Encino, 818-906-0635

De Concini, Dino T. (6 mentions)
Columbia U, 1992 *Certification:* Urology
2021 Santa Monica Blvd #510, Santa Monica, 310-828-8531
8635 W 3rd St #1060, Los Angeles, 310-657-6430

Dekernion, Jean Bayhi (5 mentions)
Louisiana State U, 1965 *Certification:* Surgery, Urology
10833 Le Conte Ave, Los Angeles, 310-206-6453

Duel, Barry Philip (7 mentions)
Harvard U, 1990 *Certification:* Pediatric Urology, Urology
8635 W 3rd St #1070, Los Angeles, 310-423-4700

Freedman, Andrew Laurence (8 mentions)
Northwestern U, 1988 *Certification:* Pediatric Urology, Urology
8635 W 3rd St #1070, Los Angeles, 310-423-4700

Gruenenfelder, Jennifer L. (5 mentions)
Columbia U, 1995 *Certification:* Urology
25200 La Paz Rd #200, Laguna Hills, 949-855-1101
26800 Crown Valley Pkwy #120, Mission Viejo, 949-855-1101

Hardy, Brian William (5 mentions)
FMS-Canada, 1983 *Certification:* Urology
4650 Sunset Blvd #114, Los Angeles, 323-361-2247

Helmbrecht, Leon James (4 mentions)
U of Wisconsin, 1967 *Certification:* Urology
160 E Artesia St #220, Pomona, 909-623-3428

Holden, Stuart (4 mentions)
Cornell U, 1968 *Certification:* Urology
8635 W 3rd St #1-W, Los Angeles, 310-854-9898

Holevas, Richard Eric (4 mentions)
Loma Linda U, 1988 *Certification:* Urology
17742 Beach Blvd #200, Huntington Beach, 714-848-4155
400 Newport Center Dr #411, Newport Beach, 949-760-1131

Ingram, John Edson (5 mentions)
U of California-Los Angeles, 1972 *Certification:* Urology
2888 Long Beach Blvd #346, Long Beach, 562-595-6891
3791 Katella Ave #106, Los Alamitos, 562-430-0581
3771 Katella Ave #210, Los Alamitos, 562-595-6891

Kaplan, Leslie Martin (10 mentions)
Northwestern U, 1981 *Certification:* Urology
2021 Santa Monica Blvd #510-E, Santa Monica, 310-828-8531

Kelly, Mark Joseph (5 mentions)
Albert Einstein Coll of Med, 1984 *Certification:* Urology
2001 Santa Monica Blvd #590W, Santa Monica, 310-829-0039

Khalili, Ramin (4 mentions)
U of California-Los Angeles, 1991 *Certification:* Urology
39 Congress St, Pasadena, 626-486-0184

Loisides, Peter Michael (5 mentions)
U of Pittsburgh, 1990 *Certification:* Urology
2001 Santa Monica Blvd #590W, Santa Monica, 310-829-0039

Michel, Kiarash (7 mentions)
U of Washington, 1993 *Certification:* Urology
8631 W 3rd St #715, Los Angeles, 310-278-8330

Mollenkamp, James S. (4 mentions)
Ohio State U, 1967 *Certification:* Urology
23600 Telo Ave #220, Torrance, 310-534-8400

Navon, Joseph David (4 mentions)
SUNY-Downstate Med Coll, 1991 *Certification:* Urology
18370 Burbank Blvd #514, Tarzana, 818-344-3592

Paul, Joy G. (7 mentions)
FMS-India, 1964 *Certification:* Urology
20911 Earl St #140, Torrance, 301-542-0199

Shapiro, Richard Alan (4 mentions)
Rush U, 1977 *Certification:* Urology
18370 Burbank Blvd #407, Tarzana, 818-996-4242
7345 Medical Center Sr #300, West Hills, 818-346-8736

Skaist, Leonard Bernard (4 mentions)
Tufts U, 1957 *Certification:* Urology
18370 Burbank Blvd #407, Tarzana, 818-996-4242
7345 Medical Center Dr #300, West Hills, 818-346-8736

Skinner, Donald George (4 mentions)
Yale U, 1964 *Certification:* Urology
1441 Eastlake Ave #7416, Los Angeles, 323-865-3707
1510 San Pablo St, Los Angeles, 323-865-3707

Skinner, Eila Curlee (4 mentions)
U of Southern California, 1983 *Certification:* Urology
1441 Eastlake Ave #7416, Los Angeles, 323-865-3705

Solomon, Ronald Samuel (4 mentions)
Albert Einstein Coll of Med, 1980 *Certification:* Urology
1401 Avocado Ave #608, Newport Beach, 949-640-2081

Spitz, Aaron (5 mentions)
Cornell U, 1992 *Certification:* Urology
25200 La Paz Rd #200, Laguna Hills, 949-855-1101

Tanenbaum, Barton (4 mentions)
U of Pittsburgh, 1967 *Certification:* Urology
9400 Brighton Way #404, Beverly Hills, 310-278-2970
201 S Alvarado St #215, Los Angeles, 213-484-9900

Wilson, Timothy Gene (4 mentions)
Oregon Health Sciences U, 1984 *Certification:* Urology
1500 Duarte Rd, Duarte, 626-359-8111

Wu, Henry Horngyih (4 mentions)
New York U, 1992 *Certification:* Urology
3801 Katella Ave #320, Los Alamitos, 562-598-0200

Yun, Scott Kiwun (5 mentions)
U of Virginia, 1987 *Certification:* Urology
8135 Painter Ave #304, Whittier, 562-907-7600

Vascular Surgery

Cossman, David Van (8 mentions)
Yale U, 1971 *Certification:* Surgery, Vascular Surgery
8631 W 3rd St #615, Los Angeles, 310-652-8132
1301 20th St #390, Santa Monica, 310-315-5765

Kohl, Roy Douglass, Jr. (17 mentions)
George Washington U, 1968
Certification: Surgery, Vascular Surgery
10 Congress St #504, Pasadena, 626-792-1211

Puckett, John W. (9 mentions)
Certification: Vascular Surgery
447 Old Newport Blvd #210, Newport Beach, 949-574-7176

Rayhanabad, Simon Baba (7 mentions)
FMS-Iran, 1973 *Certification:* Surgery
3791 Katella Ave #201, Los Alamitos, 562-596-6736
3300 E South St #203, Long Beach, 562-630-8821
9940 Talbert Ave #202, Fountain Valley, 714-378-5547

Vardayo, Joseph Famil (8 mentions)
FMS-Iran, 1975 *Certification:* Surgery
701 E 28th St #314, Long Beach, 562-981-9308

Wagner, Willis Harcourt (17 mentions)
U of Southern California, 1981
Certification: Surgery, Vascular Surgery
8631 W 3rd St #615E, Los Angeles, 310-652-8132
1301 20th St #390, Santa Monica, 310-315-5765

Weaver, Fred Arthur (7 mentions)
U of Southern California, 1979
Certification: Surgery, Surgical Critical Care, Vascular Surgery
1520 San Pablo St #4300, Los Angeles, 323-442-5988

Riverside and San Bernardino Counties

Allergy/Immunology

Munson, James Lee (7 mentions)
Loma Linda U, 1977
Certification: Allergy & Immunology, Pediatrics
245 Terracina Blvd #209-C, Redlands, 909-793-2999

Patel, Amit Ishwarbhai (12 mentions)
FMS-India, 1979
Certification: Allergy & Immunology, Internal Medicine
440 N Mountain Ave #301, Upland, 909-931-4034

Weiss, Sam Jay (11 mentions)
Creighton U, 1980
Certification: Allergy & Immunology, Internal Medicine
39000 Bob Hope Dr #K-303, Rancho Mirage, 760-346-2070

Anesthesiology

Applegate, Richard L., II (3 mentions)
Loma Linda U, 1982 *Certification:* Anesthesiology
11234 Anderson St, Loma Linda, 909-558-4475

Bradshaw, Richard Robert (3 mentions)
U of California-Los Angeles, 1975 *Certification:* Anesthesiology
39000 Bob Hope Dr, Rancho Mirage, 760-340-3911

Brockmann, Douglas Carl (4 mentions)
Loma Linda U, 1978 *Certification:* Anesthesiology, Critical
  Care Medicine, Internal Medicine
350 Terracina Blvd, Redlands, 909-335-5500

Cheng, George Joohock (3 mentions)
Loma Linda U, 1987 *Certification:* Anesthesiology
999 San Bernardino Rd, Upland, 909-920-4848

Chiu, Han-Min (6 mentions)
FMS-Taiwan, 1971 *Certification:* Anesthesiology
1117 E Devonshire Ave, Hemet, 951-652-2811

Digiamarino, Edward D. (3 mentions)
Certification: Anesthesiology
999 San Bernardino Rd, Upland, 909-985-2112

Holmblad, Bruce Ronald (5 mentions)
Med Coll of Wisconsin, 1984 *Certification:* Anesthesiology
6969 Brockton Ave #B, Riverside, 951-686-3575

Korpman, Thelma Z. (3 mentions)
Hahnemann U, 1974 *Certification:* Anesthesiology
2295 S Vineyard St, Ontario, 909-427-7162

Robinson, Lawrence Milton (7 mentions)
Loma Linda U, 1986 *Certification:* Anesthesiology
6969 Brockton Ave #B, Riverside, 951-686-3575

Saunders, Reed Michael (3 mentions)
New York U, 1984 *Certification:* Anesthesiology
39000 Bob Hope Dr, Rancho Mirage, 760-340-3911

Cardiac Surgery

Bailey, Leonard Lee (9 mentions)
Loma Linda U, 1969 *Certification:* Surgery, Thoracic Surgery
11175 Campus St, Loma Linda, 909-558-4354

Gibson, Christopher F. (8 mentions)
U of California-Los Angeles, 1979 *Certification:* Thoracic Surgery
401 E Highland Ave #251, San Bernardino, 909-881-1614
16051 Kasota Rd #900, Apple Valley, 760-946-8181

Razzouk, Anees Jacob (17 mentions)
Loma Linda U, 1982
Certification: Surgical Critical Care, Thoracic Surgery
11234 Anderson St, Loma Linda, 909-558-4200

Wang, Nan (6 mentions)
Loma Linda U, 1983 *Certification:* Surgery, Thoracic Surgery
11234 Anderson St #1617, Loma Linda, 909-558-2822

Wilson, Joseph W. (13 mentions)
U of Arkansas, 1985 *Certification:* Thoracic Surgery
39000 Bob Hope Dr #K108, Rancho Mirage, 760-568-4330

Wood, Michael Neall (9 mentions)
Loma Linda U, 1981 *Certification:* Surgery, Thoracic Surgery
1060 E Foothill Blvd #201, Upland, 909-949-6360

Cardiology

Chen, Chiayu (4 mentions)
Albert Einstein Coll of Med, 1983
Certification: Cardiovascular Disease, Internal Medicine
4500 Brockton Ave #203, Riverside, 951-686-3600

Chou, Eric Cameron (5 mentions)
Med Coll of Georgia, 1997
9611 Sierra Ave, Fontana, 909-609-2042

Hackshaw, Barry Thomas (8 mentions)
Wake Forest U, 1974 *Certification:* Cardiovascular Disease,
  Internal Medicine, Interventional Cardiology
39000 Bob Hope Dr, Rancho Mirage, 760-346-0642

Jutzy, Kenneth Roy (9 mentions)
Loma Linda U, 1977 *Certification:* Cardiovascular Disease,
  Internal Medicine, Interventional Cardiology
11234 Anderson St #1617, Loma Linda, 909-558-4200

Marais, Gary Ernest (8 mentions)
FMS-South Africa, 1973
Certification: Cardiovascular Disease, Internal Medicine
2 W Fern Ave, Redlands, 909-793-3311
33758 Yucaipa Blvd, Yucaipa, 909-795-9747

Quan, Joseph (7 mentions)
U of Vermont, 1977
Certification: Cardiovascular Disease, Internal Medicine
7117 Brockton Ave, Riverside, 951-683-6370

Dermatology

Eremia, Sorin (4 mentions)
U of California-Davis, 1979 *Certification:* Dermatology
4440 Brockton Ave #200, Riverside, 951-275-0988

Kramer, Lewis Loren (6 mentions)
New Jersey Med Sch, 1971 *Certification:* Dermatology
9985 Sierra Ave Bldg 1 6th Fl, Fontana, 909-427-5432

Lee, Sandra Siewpin (7 mentions)
Hahnemann U, 1998 *Certification:* Dermatology
639 N 13th Ave, Upland, 909-981-8929

Torres, Abel (5 mentions)
Mount Sinai Sch of Med, 1979
Certification: Dermatology, Internal Medicine
11370 Anderson St, Loma Linda, 909-558-2890

Emergency Medicine

Guth, Richard Harland (7 mentions)
Loma Linda U, 1973
Certification: Emergency Medicine, Internal Medicine
4445 Magnolia Ave, Riverside, 951-788-3200

Kontaxis, Euthym Nicholas (4 mentions)
Oregon Health Sciences U, 1982 *Certification:* Pediatrics
39000 Bob Hope Dr, Rancho Mirage, 760-340-3911
6 Normandy Way, Rancho Mirage, 602-867-8948

Potts, Larry Ralph (3 mentions)
Loma Linda U, 1973 *Certification:* Emergency Medicine
999 San Bernardino Rd, Upland, 909-985-2811

Endocrinology

Alnabelsi, Mohammad K. (6 mentions)
FMS-Syria, 1982
39000 Bob Hope Dr #K-208, Rancho Mirage, 760-773-5350

Chandiok, Suvesh (5 mentions)
FMS-India, 1975
Certification: Endocrinology and Metabolism, Internal Medicine
7117 Brockton Ave, Riverside, 951-683-6370

Guleria, Pushpinder S. (7 mentions)
FMS-India, 1989
555 E Tachevah Dr #1-W-201, Palm Springs, 760-969-4100
40055 Bob Hope Dr #J, Rancho Mirage, 760-969-4100

Murdoch, John Lamont (10 mentions)
Loma Linda U, 1963
Certification: Endocrinology and Metabolism, Internal Medicine
11370 Anderson St, Loma Linda, 909-558-2870
400 N Pepper Ave, Colton, 909-580-6275

Family Practice *(see note on page 9)*

Benson, Mark L. (4 mentions)
Des Moines U, 1979
41555 Cook St #130, Palm Desert, 760-340-2682

Branch, John D. (3 mentions)
Western U, 1985 *Certification:* Family Medicine
4646 Brockton Ave #202-3, Riverside, 951-774-2952

Fagan, John Andrew (6 mentions)
Loyola U Chicago, 1986
Certification: Family Medicine, Geriatric Medicine
8263 Grove Ave #203, Rancho Cucamonga, 909-982-7741

Lee, James Michael (5 mentions)
U of Oklahoma, 1980 *Certification:* Family Medicine
7777 Milliken Ave #220, Rancho Cucamonga, 909-484-4234

Mohr, Gina Marie (3 mentions)
Loma Linda U, 1996 *Certification:* Family Medicine
25455 Barton Rd #204B, Loma Linda, 909-558-6600

Schneider, Joseph A., Jr. (5 mentions)
Georgetown U, 1983 *Certification:* Family Medicine
6848 Magnolia Ave #130, Riverside, 951-683-1174

Gastroenterology

Annunziata, Gary M. (8 mentions)
Midwestern U Chicago Coll of Osteopathic Med, 1989
Certification: Gastroenterology, Internal Medicine
3900 Bob Hope Dr #275, Rancho Mirage, 760-321-2500

Huang, Galen Chung-Liang (7 mentions)
U of Miami, 1975
Certification: Gastroenterology, Internal Medicine
6958 Brockton Ave #202, Riverside, 951-788-1450

Hung, Chuang Ti (5 mentions)
FMS-Taiwan, 1977
Certification: Gastroenterology, Internal Medicine
629 N 13th Ave, Upland, 909-985-2709

Mishra, Vinod (9 mentions)
FMS-India, 1974
Certification: Gastroenterology, Internal Medicine
6958 Brockton Ave #201, Riverside, 951-784-6790

Tornay, Anthony S., Jr. (7 mentions)
Jefferson Med Coll, 1969
Certification: Gastroenterology, Internal Medicine
39000 Bob Hope Dr #P-203, Rancho Mirage, 760-776-4280

Walter, Michael Harry (7 mentions)
Loma Linda U, 1973
Certification: Gastroenterology, Internal Medicine
11370 Anderson St #3625, Loma Linda, 909-558-2850

General Surgery

Basinger, Bradley Bruce (4 mentions)
U of Kansas, 1985 *Certification:* Surgery
2 W Fern Ave, Redlands, 909-793-3311

Beseth, Bryce Douglass (7 mentions)
Certification: Surgery, Vascular Surgery
591 N 13th Ave, Upland, 909-946-5320

Cacdac, Ricardo Gonzalez (4 mentions)
FMS-Philippines, 1982 *Certification:* Surgery
72780 Country Club Dr #C-306, Rancho Mirage, 760-779-1828

Catalano, Richard Daniel (7 mentions)
Loma Linda U, 1976 *Certification:* Surgery, Surgical Critical Care
11370 Anderson St #2100, Loma Linda, 909-558-2822

Gosney, Wallace George (7 mentions)
Loma Linda U, 1960 *Certification:* Surgery, Thoracic Surgery
591 N 13th Ave #6, Upland, 909-946-6221

Harms, Lawrence Arthur (6 mentions)
Loma Linda U, 1983 *Certification:* Surgery, Surgical Critical Care
9985 Sierra Ave, Fontana, 909-427-3909

Ihde, Janet Kay (3 mentions)
Loma Linda U, 1977 *Certification:* Surgery
35800 Bob Hope Dr #225, Rancho Mirage, 760-324-4466

Keenan, Robert Nicolas (3 mentions)
U of Texas-Dallas, 2001 *Certification:* Surgery
521 E Elder St #205, Fallbrook, 760-728-6106
25405 Hancock Ave 202, Murrieta, 951-698-4650

Michaelian, Melvyn J. (4 mentions)
Certification: Surgery
25405 Hancock Ave #100, Murrieta, 951-698-4650
521 E Elder St #205, Fallbrook, 760-728-6106

Nagappan, Subbu (3 mentions)
U of Illinois, 1983 *Certification:* Surgery
3660 Arlington Ave, Riverside, 951-683-6370

Nurick, Harvey (9 mentions)
Baylor U, 1979 *Certification:* Surgery
7111 Indiana Ave #100, Riverside, 951-276-9012

Schulz, Karl A. (5 mentions)
Loyola U Chicago, 1979
39000 Bob Hope Dr #P212, Rancho Mirage, 760-346-8771

Schulz, Peter Robert (9 mentions)
Loyola U Chicago, 1982 *Certification:* Surgery
39000 Bob Hope Dr #212, Rancho Mirage, 760-346-8771

Sharma, Surendra Kumar (5 mentions)
FMS-India, 1973 *Certification:* Surgery
4020 W Florida Ave, Hemet, 951-652-3300

Spivack, Brian Lee (3 mentions)
Med Coll of Pennsylvania, 1988 *Certification:* Surgery
591 N 13th Ave #1, Upland, 909-946-5320

Zekos, Nicholas Valerios (3 mentions)
FMS-Greece, 1968
7117 Brockton Ave, Riverside, 951-683-6370

Geriatrics

Cohen, Harvey Donald (4 mentions)
FMS-Belgium, 1976
Certification: Geriatric Medicine, Internal Medicine
8330 Red Oak St #201, Rancho Cucamonga, 909-987-2528

Corr, Andrew Philip (3 mentions)
Washington U, 1994 *Certification:* Internal Medicine
3660 Arlington Ave, Riverside, 951-683-6370

Cuyegkeng, Thomas Xaviercasas (4 mentions)
Certification: Family Medicine, Hospice and Palliative Medicine
9961 Sierra Ave, Fontana, 888-750-0036

Larsen, James Peter (3 mentions)
Loma Linda U, 1982
Certification: Geriatric Medicine, Internal Medicine
11370 Anderson St #3200, Loma Linda, 909-558-2896

Hematology/Oncology

Bosserman, Linda D. (8 mentions)
Certification: Internal Medicine, Medical Oncology
8283 Grove Ave #207, Rancho Cucamonga, 909-949-2242
1910 Royalty Dr, Pomona, 909-865-9960
1502 Arrow Hwy, La Verne, 909-593-4333

Chen, Chien-Shing S. (5 mentions)
Certification: Internal Medicine, Medical Oncology
11370 Anderson St, Loma Linda, 909-558-2884

Dreisbach, Luke Philip (10 mentions)
U of Texas-Houston, 1994
Certification: Hematology, Internal Medicine, Medical Oncology
39800 Bob Hope Dr #C, Rancho Mirage, 760-568-3613
205 N 1st St #B, Blythe, 760-365-0107

Dreisbach, Philip Brien (8 mentions)
New Jersey Med Sch, 1969
Certification: Internal Medicine, Medical Oncology
39800 Bob Hope Dr #C, Rancho Mirage, 760-568-3613
264 N Highland Springs Ave #C, Banning, 909-845-3575
205 N 1st St #B, Blythe, 760-921-3377
57475 29 Palms Hwy #101, Yucca Valley, 760-365-0107

Gupta, Naveen (5 mentions)
FMS-India, 1975
Certification: Hematology, Internal Medicine, Medical Oncology
360 E 7th St #B, Upland, 909-946-6792

Hilliard, Dennis Alan (5 mentions)
Loma Linda U, 1975
Certification: Internal Medicine, Medical Oncology
7000 Boulder Ave, Highland, 909-862-1191
6109 W Ramsey St, Banning, 909-862-1191
401 E Highland Ave #C, San Bernardino, 909-886-6806

Mendoza, Evelyn Fidellaga (4 mentions)
FMS-Philippines, 1984
Certification: Hematology, Internal Medicine, Medical Oncology
301 N San Jacinto St, Hemet, 951-696-0498

Saab, Ghaleb Aadel (5 mentions)
FMS-Lebanon, 1974
Certification: Hematology, Internal Medicine, Medical Oncology
7117 Brockton Ave 3rd Fl, Riverside, 951-321-6350

Vafai, Davood (8 mentions)
FMS-Iran, 1981 *Certification:* Internal Medicine
40075 Bob Hope Dr #A, Rancho Mirage, 760-341-3688

Infectious Disease

Bassi, Sohanjeet S. (13 mentions)
Certification: Infectious Disease, Internal Medicine
1135 S Sunset Ave #208, West Covina, 626-851-8880

Beutler, Steven Merrill (9 mentions)
U of Chicago, 1977
Certification: Infectious Disease, Internal Medicine
350 Terracina Blvd, Redlands, 909-882-3966

Blomquist, Ingrid K. (7 mentions)
Loma Linda U, 1981
Certification: Infectious Disease, Internal Medicine
11370 Anderson St #3300, Loma Linda, 909-558-2624

Cone, Lawrence Arthur (7 mentions)
FMS-Switzerland, 1954 *Certification:* Allergy & Immunology, Infectious Disease, Internal Medicine, Medical Oncology
39000 Bob Hope Dr #P-308, Rancho Mirage, 760-346-5688

Kerkar, Shubha J. (8 mentions)
FMS-India, 1983
Certification: Infectious Disease, Internal Medicine
1180 N Indian Canyon Dr #E-218, Palm Springs, 760-416-4921

Larson, Steven Edwin (9 mentions)
Med Coll of Wisconsin, 1975
Certification: Infectious Disease, Internal Medicine
3660 Arlington Ave, Riverside, 951-683-6370

Liquete, Johnny Ang (8 mentions)
FMS-Philippines, 1982
14114 Business Center Dr #D, Moreno Valley, 951-697-1150

Infertility

Jacobson, John Douglas (3 mentions)
Loma Linda U, 1970 *Certification:* Obstetrics & Gynecology
11370 Anderson St #3950, Loma Linda, 909-558-2851

Patton, William Carleton (4 mentions)
Loma Linda U, 1969 *Certification:* Obstetrics & Gynecology, Reproductive Endocrinology/Infertility
11370 Anderson St #3950, Loma Linda, 909-558-2851

Internal Medicine *(see note on page 9)*

Chai, Michael (6 mentions)
Eastern Virginia Med Sch, 1993 *Certification:* Internal Medicine
1113 Alta Ave #106, Upland, 909-920-6672

Chang, Peter Yeong-Jen (3 mentions)
U of Miami, 1979 *Certification:* Internal Medicine
3975 Jackson St #102, Riverside, 951-359-0660

Hay, Douglas John (3 mentions)
Loma Linda U, 1980 *Certification:* Internal Medicine
1300 E Cooley Dr, Colton, 909-370-4100

Lipton, Peter Jay (3 mentions)
U of California-San Diego, 1976 *Certification:* Internal Medicine
73733 Fred Waring Dr #204, Palm Desert, 760-776-9511

Mikhail, Mina N. (5 mentions)
FMS-Egypt, 1978 *Certification:* Internal Medicine
4000 14th St #209, Riverside, 951-788-8332

Riewe, G. Michael (3 mentions)
Mayo Med Sch, 1976 *Certification:* Internal Medicine
3660 Arlington Ave, Riverside, 951-683-6370

Stottlemyer, Debra L. (3 mentions)
Loma Linda U, 1986
Certification: Geriatric Medicine, Internal Medicine
11370 Anderson St, Loma Linda, 909-558-2870

Thio, Shelly Chenchen (3 mentions)
Loma Linda U, 1995 *Certification:* Internal Medicine
10800 Magnolia Ave, Riverside, 951-353-2000

Nephrology

Erlanger, Howard N. (5 mentions)
Des Moines U, 1985 *Certification:* Internal Medicine, Nephrology
1100 N Palm Canyon Dr #211, Palm Springs, 760-323-1155

Gebreselassie, W. (6 mentions)
FMS-Hungary, 1981
Certification: Geriatric Medicine, Internal Medicine, Nephrology
9961 Sierra Ave, Fontana, 888-750-0036

Herrman, Jan Michael (5 mentions)
Louisiana State U-Shreveport, 1980
Certification: Internal Medicine, Nephrology
3361 Sierra Ave, Fontana, 888-750-0036

Lee, Joseph Jyh-Chung (11 mentions)
FMS-Taiwan, 1971 *Certification:* Internal Medicine, Nephrology
3660 Park Sierra Dr, Riverside, 951-687-2800

Serros, Edward Refugio (5 mentions)
Stanford U, 1974 *Certification:* Internal Medicine, Nephrology
399 E Highland Ave #100, San Bernardino, 909-882-0702

Stone, Bryan Lawrence (5 mentions)
Boston U, 1993 *Certification:* Internal Medicine, Nephrology
1180 N Indian Canyon Dr #W-308, Palm Springs, 760-416-4819

Stone, Richard Alan (6 mentions)
Tufts U, 1970 *Certification:* Internal Medicine, Nephrology
39000 Bob Hope Dr #P316, Rancho Mirage, 760-568-0383

Sun, Chao-Huang (5 mentions)
FMS-Taiwan, 1979 *Certification:* Internal Medicine, Nephrology
3660 Park Sierra Dr #208, Riverside, 951-687-2800

Neurological Surgery

Clark, Lawrence Erwin (8 mentions)
Loma Linda U, 1979
4000 14th St #302, Riverside, 951-682-3583

Etebar, Shahin (9 mentions)
U of California-Irvine, 1990 *Certification:* Neurological Surgery
39000 Bob Hope Dr #410, Rancho Mirage, 760-346-8058

Lederhaus, Scott C. (7 mentions)
Certification: Neurological Surgery
255 E Bonita Ave Bldg 9, Pomona, 909-450-0369

Limonadi, Farhad Mohammad (6 mentions)
Dartmouth Coll, 1998
39000 Bob Hope Dr #410, Rancho Mirage, 760-346-8058

Rodriguez, Jose Luis (10 mentions)
U of California-Irvine, 1981 *Certification:* Neurological Surgery
255 E Bonita Ave Bldg 9, Pomona, 909-450-0369

Neurology

Ibrahim, Waseem Nicola (7 mentions)
FMS-Egypt, 1982 *Certification:* Neurology
4000 14th St #408, Riverside, 951-788-2224

Jordan, Kenneth George (5 mentions)
Columbia U, 1971 *Certification:* Internal Medicine, Neurology
399 E Highland Ave #316, San Bernardino, 909-881-1031

Klein, Robert Allen (5 mentions)
West Virginia U, 1972 *Certification:* Neurology
7000 Boulder Ave, Highland, 909-862-1191

Lipiz, Jorge Progreso (4 mentions)
FMS-Mexico, 1979 *Certification:* Neurology
10800 Magnolia Ave, Riverside, 951-353-4747

Nazareth, Ivor Joseph (5 mentions)
FMS-India, 1963 *Certification:* Neurology
39000 Bob Hope Dr #W309, Rancho Mirage, 760-568-3563

Nazemi, Reza (8 mentions)
FMS-Iran, 1973 *Certification:* Neurology
39000 Bob Hope Dr #K308, Rancho Mirage, 760-341-3400

Rai, Baldev Singh (4 mentions)
FMS-India, 1978
Certification: Clinical Neurophysiology, Neurology
4500 Brockton Ave #205, Riverside, 951-784-7190

Ries, Jeffrey Dean (7 mentions)
Western U, 1984
1175 E Arrow Hwy #J, Upland, 909-579-0779

Obstetrics/Gynecology

Adams, Berneva Joy (5 mentions)
Loma Linda U, 1975 *Certification:* Obstetrics & Gynecology
9961 Sierra Ave, Fontana, 888-750-0036

Armada, Robert (4 mentions)
Michigan State U Coll of Osteopathic Med, 1979
901 San Bernardino Rd #301, Upland, 909-931-3365

Carden, Dennis Matthew (3 mentions)
Certification: Obstetrics & Gynecology
400 N Pepper Ave, Colton, 909-580-1000

De Mersseman, John Arthur (3 mentions)
U of Colorado, 1970 *Certification:* Obstetrics & Gynecology
555 Tachevah Dr #201-W, Palm Springs, 760-323-9309

Easter, Thomas Terence (3 mentions)
FMS-Mexico, 1980
600 N Mountain Ave #A-104, Upland, 909-931-1033

Elfelt, Timothy James (4 mentions)
FMS-Mexico, 1982 *Certification:* Obstetrics & Gynecology
25460 Medical Center Dr #100, Murrieta, 951-677-4748

Gaio, Karen Lynn (5 mentions)
Loma Linda U, 1991
25455 Barton Rd #208-A, Loma Linda, 909-799-7900

Glaser, Joseph Edward (3 mentions)
Indiana U, 1980 *Certification:* Obstetrics & Gynecology
25460 Medical Center Dr #100, Murrieta, 951-677-4748

Munson, Laurel Jones (7 mentions)
Loma Linda U, 1978 *Certification:* Obstetrics & Gynecology
25455 Barton Rd #208-A, Loma Linda, 909-799-7900

Murray, Rick D. (3 mentions)
Loma Linda U, 1975
Certification: Maternal-Fetal Medicine, Obstetrics & Gynecology
9961 Sierra Ave, Fontana, 909-427-5000

Ojeda, Alonso Rafael (3 mentions)
Loma Linda U, 1979 *Certification:* Obstetrics & Gynecology
9041 Magnolia Ave 3rd Fl #303, Riverside, 951-688-4100

Srivastava, Shanta (3 mentions)
FMS-India, 1964 *Certification:* Obstetrics & Gynecology
811 E 11th St #104, Upland, 909-985-0793

Ophthalmology

Fabricant, Robert Neal (8 mentions)
U of California-San Diego, 1974 *Certification:* Ophthalmology
555 N 13th Ave, Upland, 909-982-8846
12550 Amargosa Rd #B, Victorville, 760-241-6366

Glendrange, Ray Rogers (3 mentions)
Loma Linda U, 1986 *Certification:* Ophthalmology
4605 Brockton Ave #100, Riverside, 951-686-4911

Kreter, James Karl (4 mentions)
Virginia Commonwealth U, 1980 *Certification:* Ophthalmology
7117 Brockton Ave, Riverside, 951-782-3091

Pabalan, Francisco Javier (3 mentions)
Albany Med Coll, 1981 *Certification:* Ophthalmology
4440 Brockton Ave #130, Riverside, 951-243-2266

Rimmer, Steven Owen (7 mentions)
U of California-San Diego, 1989 *Certification:* Ophthalmology
2 W Fern Ave, Redlands, 909-793-3311

Roeske, Richmond Emmerson (5 mentions)
Loma Linda U, 1996 *Certification:* Ophthalmology
555 N 13th Ave, Upland, 909-982-8846
12550 Amargosa Rd #B, Victorville, 760-241-6366

Rosenquist, Robert Charles, Jr. (4 mentions)
Loma Linda U, 1977 *Certification:* Ophthalmology
9961 Sierra Ave, Fontana, 888-750-0036

Schultz, Gerald Raymond (3 mentions)
New York Med Coll, 1963 *Certification:* Ophthalmology
81893 Doctor Carreon Blvd #2, Indio, 760-342-9991
58471 29 Palms Hwy #302, Yucca Valley, 760-228-1766

Schwartz, Leonard (6 mentions)
SUNY-Upstate Med U, 1974 *Certification:* Ophthalmology
39000 Bob Hope Dr #W-105, Rancho Mirage, 760-340-4700

Siegel, Lance Mitchell (4 mentions)
Virginia Commonwealth U, 1990
Certification: Ophthalmology, Pediatrics
1246 E Arrow Hwy, Upland, 909-931-9675
14075 Hesperia Rd, Victorville, 760-843-9333
8822-B Limonite Ave, Riverside, 909-931-9675

Smith, William Berwyn (3 mentions)
Loma Linda U, 1973
Certification: Internal Medicine, Ophthalmology
41877 Enterprise Cir N #110, Temecula, 951-296-2244

Williams, Erik Jan (4 mentions)
U of California-Los Angeles, 1969 *Certification:* Ophthalmology
36921 Cook St #103, Palm Desert, 760-568-3111

Orthopedics

Chalian, Christopher A. (9 mentions)
Certification: Orthopaedic Surgery
2776 N Garey Ave, Pomona, 909-593-7437

Graff-Radford, Adrian S. (5 mentions)
FMS-South Africa, 1971 *Certification:* Orthopaedic Surgery
39000 Bob Hope Dr, Rancho Mirage, 760-568-2684

Gustafson, George Allen (3 mentions)
Loma Linda U, 1970 *Certification:* Orthopaedic Surgery
10459 Mountain View Ave #B, Loma Linda, 909-478-5600

Heinen, Gregory Thomas (3 mentions)
Yale U, 1993
Certification: Orthopaedic Sports Medicine, Orthopaedic Surgery
4444 Magnolia Ave, Riverside, 951-682-5661

Husain, Asghar (7 mentions)
U of Miami, 1992 *Certification:* Orthopaedic Surgery
7777 Milliken Ave #330, Rancho Cucamonga, 909-989-4400

Liu, Paul C. (3 mentions)
Certification: Orthopaedic Sports Medicine, Orthopaedic Surgery
9961 Sierra Ave, Fontana, 909-609-2008

Murphy, Robert Ward (5 mentions)
U of Kansas, 1969 *Certification:* Orthopaedic Surgery
39000 Bob Hope Dr, Rancho Mirage, 760-568-2684

Stanton, Paul Andrew (3 mentions)
Wayne State U, 1989 *Certification:* Orthopaedic Surgery
15990 Tuscola Rd, Apple Valley, 760-242-4808

Ward, Michelle D. (6 mentions)
Certification: Orthopaedic Surgery
2776 N Garey Ave, Pomona, 909-593-7437

Otorhinolaryngology

Arasoghli, Sam (4 mentions)
Certification: Otolaryngology
297 W Artesia St #A, Pomona, 909-623-1503

Barton, Stuart Martin (7 mentions)
U of Southern California, 1963 *Certification:* Otolaryngology
39000 Bob Hope Dr #W301, Rancho Mirage, 760-340-4566

Church, Christopher Alan (10 mentions)
Loma Linda U, 1996 *Certification:* Otolaryngology
11370 Anderson St #2100, Loma Linda, 909-558-2822

Feinberg, Gary Mitchell (5 mentions)
Tufts U, 1982 *Certification:* Otolaryngology
6950 Brockton Ave #3, Riverside, 951-788-1447

Gebhart, Robert Norman (7 mentions)
U of Cincinnati, 1967 *Certification:* Otolaryngology
39000 Bob Hope Dr #W301, Rancho Mirage, 760-340-4566

Hwang, Allen Lee (4 mentions)
Loma Linda U, 1986 *Certification:* Otolaryngology
9961 Sierra Ave, Fontana, 888-750-0036

Jung, Timothy Tae Kun (8 mentions)
Loma Linda U, 1974 *Certification:* Otolaryngology
3975 Jackson St #202, Riverside, 951-352-7920

Kaplan, Robert I. (5 mentions)
FMS-Mexico, 1974
4646 Brockton Ave #302, Riverside, 951-774-2770

McCarthy, Stuart Andress (7 mentions)
U of Cincinnati, 1977 *Certification:* Otolaryngology
1330 San Bernardino Rd #J, Upland, 909-981-5406

Pain Medicine

Erlendson, Lee Wayne (8 mentions)
Vanderbilt U, 1980 *Certification:* Anesthesiology, Pain Medicine
39300 Bob Hope Dr #B-1203, Rancho Mirage, 760-773-3075

Maddox, Jan Paul (5 mentions)
FMS-Mexico, 1975 *Certification:* Anesthesiology, Pain Medicine
4500 Brockton Ave #305, Riverside, 951-715-3963

Pathology

Bearman, Robert Marshal (3 mentions)
Tufts U, 1972 *Certification:* Anatomic Pathology
16850 Bear Valley Rd, Victorville, 760-241-8000

De Castro, Dulce Ramos (3 mentions)
FMS-Philippines, 1977
Certification: Anatomic Pathology & Clinical Pathology
999 San Bernardino Rd, Upland, 909-985-2811

Kaminsky, David Barry (3 mentions)
New York Med Coll, 1970
Certification: Anatomic Pathology & Clinical Pathology
74-785 Hwy 111 #101, Indian Wells, 760-776-8989
81-719 Dr Carreon Blvd #D, Indio, 760-863-4085

Pediatrics *(see note on page 9)*

Ambrose, Peter David (4 mentions)
SUNY-Upstate Med U, 1966 *Certification:* Pediatrics
7777 Milliken Ave #130, Rancho Cucamonga, 909-941-7008

Aquino, Jesusa T. (3 mentions)
FMS-Philippines, 1990 *Certification:* Pediatrics
742 W Highland Ave, San Bernardino, 909-881-7320

Coit, Alan Samuel (4 mentions)
George Washington U, 1973 *Certification:* Pediatrics
39300 Bob Hope Dr #B-1108, Rancho Mirage, 760-340-4621

Curtis, Donald D. (4 mentions)
U of Utah, 1960 *Certification:* Pediatrics
7777 Milliken Ave #130, Rancho Cucamonga, 909-941-7008

Du, Leticia (3 mentions)
FMS-Philippines, 1979
41238 Margarita Rd #106, Temecula, 951-506-9392

Loh, Michelle Harumi Leinaala (6 mentions)
Loma Linda U *Certification:* Pediatrics
11401 Heacock St #330, Moreno Valley, 951-247-8697

Mackey, Timothy Walton (4 mentions)
U of Texas-Galveston, 1986 *Certification:* Pediatrics
6950 Brockton Ave #5, Riverside, 951-686-8223

Mailander, Mary Monica (4 mentions)
Georgetown U, 1978 *Certification:* Pediatrics
1300 E Cooley Dr, Colton, 909-370-4100
245 Terracina Blvd #202, Redlands, 909-335-0200

Rao, Ravindra (3 mentions)
FMS-India, 1974 *Certification:* Pediatrics
11370 Anderson St #B-100, Loma Linda, 909-558-2848

Sharpe, Lawrence Donald (5 mentions)
Med Coll of Wisconsin, 1970 *Certification:* Pediatrics
7117 Brockton Ave, Riverside, 951-683-6370

Plastic Surgery

Aaronson, Scott Michael (5 mentions)
U of Miami, 1978 *Certification:* Plastic Surgery
1221 N Indian Canyon Dr, Palm Springs, 760-325-5255

Childers, Ben Jason (8 mentions)
U of Louisville, 1989 *Certification:* Plastic Surgery
4605 Brockton Ave #200, Riverside, 951-781-4339

Elias, Grace Salim (4 mentions)
Loma Linda U, 1979 *Certification:* Plastic Surgery
7117 Brockton Ave, Riverside, 951-782-3796

Hardesty, Robert Alan (7 mentions)
Loma Linda U, 1978 *Certification:* Plastic Surgery
4646 Brockton Ave #302-3, Riverside, 951-686-7600

Sogioka, Norman Yasuo (5 mentions)
Loma Linda U, 1973 *Certification:* Plastic Surgery
9985 Sierra Ave, Fontana, 909-609-2008

Psychiatry

Chundu, Sai B. (3 mentions)
FMS-India, 1981
770 Magnolia Ave #1F, Corona, 951-737-1917
36243 Inland Valley Dr #50, Wildomar, 951-696-5220

Edelmuth, Evelyn R. (3 mentions)
FMS-Argentina, 1980
44530 San Pablo Ave #202, Palm Desert, 760-341-6026

Johnson, Cameron Jay (4 mentions)
Loma Linda U, 1989
11374 Mountain View Ave, Loma Linda, 909-558-4505
1710 Barton Rd, Redlands, 909-558-9200

Summerour, Robert Brooke (4 mentions)
Loma Linda U, 1971 *Certification:* Psychiatry
5887 Brockton Ave #A, Riverside, 951-275-8500

Pulmonary Disease

Arakaki, Craig Kiyoshi (6 mentions)
U of California-Irvine, 1985 *Certification:* Critical Care
  Medicine, Internal Medicine, Pulmonary Disease
9961 Sierra Ave, Fontana, 866-454-3485

Gold, Philip Michael (4 mentions)
U of California-Los Angeles, 1962
Certification: Internal Medicine, Pulmonary Disease
11370 Anderson St #3300, Loma Linda, 909-558-2896

Lau, Kam-Yung (5 mentions)
FMS-Taiwan, 1973
Certification: Internal Medicine, Pediatrics, Pulmonary Disease
7117 Brockton Ave, Riverside, 951-683-6370

Lu, Chong-Ping (4 mentions)
FMS-Taiwan, 1970
Certification: Internal Medicine, Pulmonary Disease
1000 E Latham Ave #E, Hemet, 951-925-7653

Mojarad, Mohammad (5 mentions)
FMS-Iran, 1971
Certification: Internal Medicine, Pulmonary Disease
3900 Bob Hope Dr Probes Bldg #317, Rancho Mirage,
  760-568-6333

Sandhu, Rohinder Kaur (4 mentions)
FMS-India, 1982
Certification: Internal Medicine, Pulmonary Disease
9655 Monte Vista Ave #402, Montclair, 909-626-7205
160 E Artesia St #350, Pomona, 909-622-7692
255 E Bonita Ave, Pomona, 909-450-0158

Shankel, Theodore Lee (5 mentions)
Loma Linda U, 1988 *Certification:* Critical Care Medicine,
  Internal Medicine, Pulmonary Disease
2 W Fern Ave, Redlands, 909-793-3311

Simons, Jeffrey Richard (5 mentions)
U of Vermont, 1966
Certification: Internal Medicine, Pulmonary Disease
5887 Brockton Ave #B, Riverside, 909-781-3672

Sneider, Ronald Edward (5 mentions)
U of Illinois, 1970
Certification: Internal Medicine, Pulmonary Disease
39000 Bob Hope Dr #K214, Rancho Mirage, 760-346-7336

Tavakoli, Shahriyar (8 mentions)
U Central del Caribe, 1988 *Certification:* Critical Care
  Medicine, Internal Medicine, Pulmonary Disease
39000 Bob Hope Dr #K307, Rancho Mirage, 760-674-4846

Utzurrum, Frankie D. (7 mentions)
FMS-Philippines, 1967
Certification: Internal Medicine, Pulmonary Disease
99 N San Antonio Ave #370, Upland, 909-946-6342

Radiology—Diagnostic

Bryan, Patrick Joseph (4 mentions)
FMS-Ireland, 1967
999 San Bernardino Rd, Upland, 909-466-4231

Cohn, Morton James (3 mentions)
Harvard U, 1989 *Certification:* Diagnostic Radiology
39000 Bob Hope Dr, Rancho Mirage, 760-773-1251

Elly, Mehran Kadkhodaei (3 mentions)
U of California-Irvine, 1995 *Certification:* Diagnostic Radiology
39000 Bob Hope Dr, Rancho Mirage, 760-773-1251

Feller, John Francis (3 mentions)
Ohio State U, 1987 *Certification:* Diagnostic Radiology
74785 US Hwy 111 #101, Indian Wells, 760-776-8989

Fisher, Kendra L. (3 mentions)
Certification: Diagnostic Radiology
11234 Anderson St #2605, Loma Linda, 909-558-4370

Herman, Brian Keith (3 mentions)
U of California-Los Angeles, 1991
Certification: Diagnostic Radiology
39000 Bob Hope Dr, Rancho Mirage, 760-773-1251

Kelly, William M. (3 mentions)
Tulane U, 1978 *Certification:* Diagnostic Radiology
72980 Fred Waring Dr #A, Palm Desert, 760-776-8001

Kirk, Shannon Richard (3 mentions)
Loma Linda U, 1994 *Certification:* Diagnostic Radiology
11234 Anderson St #2605, Loma Linda, 909-558-4370

Massee, Donald R. (5 mentions)
Certification: Diagnostic Radiology
2020 Iowa Ave #103, Riverside, 951-781-2270
18300 US Hwy 18, Apple Valley, 760-242-2311

Wallman, James K. (4 mentions)
U of Vermont, 1974 *Certification:* Diagnostic Radiology
2 Fern Ave, Redlands, 909-793-3311

Radiology—Therapeutic

Chang, Chan Nam (4 mentions)
FMS-Taiwan, 1976 *Certification:* Diagnostic Radiology
10800 Magnolia Ave, Riverside, 951-353-2000

Cherne, Mel (3 mentions)
Loma Linda U, 1983 *Certification:* Diagnostic Radiology, Vascular & Interventional Radiology
2020 Iowa Ave #103, Riverside, 951-788-3000

Elly, Mehran Kadkhodaei (5 mentions)
U of California-Irvine, 1995 *Certification:* Diagnostic Radiology
39000 Bob Hope Dr, Rancho Mirage, 760-773-1251

Greenberg, Peter (6 mentions)
U of California-Los Angeles, 1981
Certification: Therapeutic Radiology
77840 Flora Dr, Palm Desert, 760-200-8777
40055 Bob Hope Dr, Rancho Mirage, 760-200-8777

Herman, Brian Keith (7 mentions)
U of California-Los Angeles, 1991
Certification: Diagnostic Radiology
39000 Bob Hope Dr, Rancho Mirage, 760-773-1251

Pierantoni, Vincente (3 mentions)
Certification: Diagnostic Radiology
9985 Sierra Ave, Fontana, 909-427-5000

Rehabilitation

Brandstater, Cherry Lynn (3 mentions)
Loma Linda U, 1975
2 W Fern Ave, Redlands, 909-793-3311

Goodlow, Gerald Ross (5 mentions)
Wayne State U, 1984
Certification: Physical Medicine & Rehabilitation
9985 Sierra Ave, Fontana, 909-427-6463
9961 Sierra Ave, Fontana, 909-427-6463

Johnson, Vance Zachary (4 mentions)
Loma Linda U, 1995
Certification: Pain Medicine, Physical Medicine & Rehabilitation
900 E Washington St #100, Colton, 909-433-3272
900 S Main St #105, Corona, 951-278-4740

Strum, Scott Russell (5 mentions)
Loma Linda U, 1990
Certification: Pain Medicine, Physical Medicine & Rehabilitation
11406 Loma Linda Dr #300, Loma Linda, 909-558-6277

White, Joy Michele (3 mentions)
Virginia Commonwealth U, 1997
Certification: Physical Medicine & Rehabilitation
78822 Hwy 111, La Quinta, 760-564-7000

Rheumatology

Hirschberg, Joel Mark (12 mentions)
George Washington U, 1976
Certification: Internal Medicine, Rheumatology
39000 Bob Hope Dr #P-102, Rancho Mirage, 760-340-6660

Putnoky, Gilbert John (9 mentions)
St Louis U, 1973 *Certification:* Internal Medicine, Rheumatology
2 W Fern Ave, Redlands, 909-793-3311

Thakker, Suman P. (10 mentions)
FMS-India, 1973 *Certification:* Internal Medicine, Rheumatology
16850 Bear Valley Rd, Victorville, 760-241-8000

Thoracic Surgery

Gosney, Wallace George (6 mentions)
Loma Linda U, 1960 *Certification:* Surgery, Thoracic Surgery
591 N 13th Ave #6, Upland, 909-946-6221

Wilson, Joseph W. (8 mentions)
U of Arkansas, 1985 *Certification:* Thoracic Surgery
39000 Bob Hope Dr #K108, Rancho Mirage, 760-568-4330

Urology

Ching, Victor Choy (12 mentions)
Loma Linda U, 1977 *Certification:* Urology
1175 E Arrow Hwy #E, Upland, 909-985-9737

Lander, Elliot Barton (5 mentions)
U of California-Irvine, 1986 *Certification:* Urology
72780 Country Club Dr #C-301, Rancho Mirage, 760-776-0040

Page, William Robert (9 mentions)
U of Miami, 1974 *Certification:* Urology
39000 Bob Hope Dr #W-412, Rancho Mirage, 760-346-8555

Pietro, Timothy John (8 mentions)
Baylor U, 1982 *Certification:* Urology
4500 Brockton Ave #204, Riverside, 951-693-7620

Tsai, Christopher K. (9 mentions)
Loma Linda U, 1994 *Certification:* Urology
1175 E Arrow Hwy #E, Upland, 909-985-9737

Vascular Surgery

Gosney, Wallace George (11 mentions)
Loma Linda U, 1960 *Certification:* Surgery, Thoracic Surgery
591 N 13th Ave #6, Upland, 909-946-6221

Sacramento Area
Including Sacramento County

Allergy/Immunology

Chipps, Bradley Elliott (32 mentions)
U of Texas-Galveston, 1972 *Certification:* Allergy &
Immunology, Pediatric Pulmonology, Pediatrics
5609 J St, Sacramento, 916-453-8696
3100 Douglas Blvd, Roseville, 916-453-8696

Jakle, Christopher (14 mentions)
U of California-Los Angeles, 1976 *Certification:* Allergy &
Immunology, Internal Medicine, Rheumatology
6600 Bruceville Rd, Sacramento, 916-688-2106

Nagy, Stephen Mears, Jr. (12 mentions)
Tufts U, 1964
Certification: Allergy & Immunology, Internal Medicine
4801 J St #A, Sacramento, 916-456-4782
3250 Fortune Ct, Auburn, 530-889-8501
729 Sunrise Ave #603, Roseville, 916-789-7996
6600 Bruceville Rd, Sacramento, 916-525-6040
8110 Timberlake Way, Sacramento, 916-688-1139

Anesthesiology

Anderson, Jeffrey Lee (6 mentions)
Loma Linda U, 1985 *Certification:* Anesthesiology
1650 Creekside Dr, Folsom, 916-983-7490

Bell, Michael David (5 mentions)
Med Coll of Georgia, 1979 *Certification:* Anesthesiology
6600 Bruceville Rd, Sacramento, 916-688-2573

Clayton, Jeffrey Paul (4 mentions)
Med Coll of Wisconsin, 1990 *Certification:* Anesthesiology
3315 Watt Ave, Sacramento, 916-481-6800

Dasen, Kevin Robert (3 mentions)
Certification: Anesthesiology
2025 Morse Ave, Sacramento, 916-973-5000

De Voe, Robert Patrick (3 mentions)
Creighton U, 1982 *Certification:* Anesthesiology
3939 J St #310, Sacramento, 916-733-6990

Estep, David Loring (4 mentions)
U of California-San Diego, 1980 *Certification:* Anesthesiology
3315 Watt Ave, Sacramento, 916-481-6800

Glenesk, Gary Andrew (3 mentions)
Loma Linda U, 1983 *Certification:* Anesthesiology
1650 Creekside Dr, Folsom, 916-983-7490

Humphreys, Harold Keith (3 mentions)
U of Nevada, 1987 *Certification:* Anesthesiology
3315 Watt Ave, Sacramento, 916-481-6800

Kumata, Dennis Shuso (4 mentions)
U of Southern California, 1985 *Certification:* Anesthesiology
6600 Bruceville Rd, Sacramento, 916-525-6040

Moore, Patrick Arthur (5 mentions)
U of Louisville, 1979 *Certification:* Anesthesiology
3939 J St #310, Sacramento, 916-733-6990

Niswander, David Gwynne (3 mentions)
Med Coll of Pennsylvania, 1982
2025 Morse Ave, Sacramento, 916-973-5243

Weber, Joel Bradley (9 mentions)
Robert W Johnson Med Sch, 1987 *Certification:* Anesthesiology
6600 Bruceville Rd, Sacramento, 916-688-2000

Wolf, David Lewis (7 mentions)
U of California-Davis, 1987 *Certification:* Anesthesiology
6409 Lincoln Ave, Carmichael, 209-956-7725

Cardiac Surgery

Ingram, Michael Thomas (21 mentions)
U of Southern California, 1979 *Certification:* Thoracic Surgery
5301 F St #111, Sacramento, 916-452-8291

Morris, Allen Scott (13 mentions)
Wayne State U, 1981 *Certification:* Thoracic Surgery
3941 J St #270, Sacramento, 916-733-6850
6401 Coyle Ave #316, Carmichael, 916-733-6850

Shankar, Kuppe G. (7 mentions)
FMS-India, 1961 *Certification:* Surgery, Thoracic Surgery
5301 F St #111, Sacramento, 916-452-8291
3811 Winding Creek Rd, Sacramento, 916-773-3077
2221 Stockton Blvd, Sacramento, 916-734-2680

Cardiology

Arthur, Arvin (6 mentions)
Indiana U, 1966 *Certification:* Cardiovascular Disease,
Internal Medicine, Interventional Cardiology
5301 F St #207, Sacramento, 916-452-2011
3939 J St #300, Sacramento, 916-452-2011

Baron, Scott Bernard (13 mentions)
New Jersey Med Sch, 1979 *Certification:* Cardiovascular
Disease, Internal Medicine, Interventional Cardiology
6347 Coyle Ave, Carmichael, 916-967-4278

Hemphill, Jonathan A. (5 mentions)
FMS-Grenada, 1982 *Certification:* Cardiovascular Disease,
Internal Medicine, Interventional Cardiology
6347 Coyle Ave, Carmichael, 916-967-4278

Joye, James Anthony (10 mentions)
U of California-Davis, 1972
Certification: Cardiovascular Disease, Internal Medicine
2025 Morse Ave, Sacramento, 916-973-5243

Low, Reginald Inman (14 mentions)
U of California-Davis, 1975 *Certification:* Cardiovascular
Disease, Internal Medicine, Interventional Cardiology
3941 J St #260, Sacramento, 916-736-2323
4860 Y St, Sacramento, 916-734-3761
1010 Hurley Way #500, Sacramento, 916-734-3764
6401 Coyle Ave #416, Carmichael, 916-734-3764
2315 Stockton Blvd, Sacramento, 916-734-3764
8120 Timberlake Way #108, Sacramento, 916-734-3764

Matlof, Harvey Jay (5 mentions)
Washington U, 1966
Certification: Cardiovascular Disease, Internal Medicine
5301 F St #117, Sacramento, 916-733-1788

Rose, Steven Douglas (15 mentions)
U of California-San Francisco, 1974
Certification: Cardiovascular Disease, Internal Medicine
6600 Bruceville Rd, Sacramento, 916-688-4000

Rozema, Raymond Jay (14 mentions)
Wayne State U, 1981
Certification: Cardiovascular Disease, Internal Medicine
6600 Bruceville Rd, Sacramento, 916-688-2106

Schott, Robert James (6 mentions)
U of Michigan, 1981
Certification: Cardiovascular Disease, Internal Medicine
5301 F St #117, Sacramento, 916-733-1788

Takeda, Patricia Ann (9 mentions)
Johns Hopkins U, 1976
Certification: Cardiovascular Disease, Internal Medicine
3941 J St #260, Sacramento, 916-736-2323
1111 Exposition Blvd #700, Sacramento, 916-736-2323
8120 Timberlake Way #108, Sacramento, 916-688-5551

Woodruff, David E., Jr. (5 mentions)
Emory U, 1968
Certification: Cardiovascular Disease, Internal Medicine
5301 F St #117, Sacramento, 916-733-1788

Dermatology

Bass, Lawrence James (8 mentions)
U of Michigan, 1967
Certification: Dermatology, Dermatopathology
5340 Elvas Ave #600, Sacramento, 916-739-1505

Giustina, Thomas Anthony (15 mentions)
Oregon Health Sciences U, 1982 *Certification:* Dermatology
6600 Bruceville Rd, Sacramento, 916-688-2410

Goetz, Carl Stephen (8 mentions)
U of Nebraska, 1972 *Certification:* Dermatology
6401 Coyle Ave #315, Carmichael, 916-966-6444

Haas, Ann F. (6 mentions)
Certification: Dermatology
1020 29th St #570-A, Sacramento, 916-733-3792

Huber, Paula Wendy (11 mentions)
U of California-Davis, 1983
Certification: Dermatology, Internal Medicine
6600 Bruceville Rd, Sacramento, 916-688-2045

Okimoto, Jan Akemi (6 mentions)
Harvard U, 1982 *Certification:* Dermatology, Internal Medicine
10725 International Dr, Rancho Cordova, 916-631-3010
2025 Morse Ave, Sacramento, 916-978-1475

Silverstein, Marc Aron (6 mentions)
U of California-Los Angeles, 1985 *Certification:* Dermatology
1 Scripps Dr #300, Sacramento, 916-920-0871

Tanghetti, Emil Anthony (13 mentions)
U of California-Los Angeles, 1976 *Certification:* Dermatology
5601 J St, Sacramento, 916-454-5922

Emergency Medicine

Berman, David A. (5 mentions)
Des Moines U, 1979
Certification: Emergency Medicine, Pediatrics
2025 Morse Ave, Sacramento, 916-973-6633

Carl, Michael Leon (3 mentions)
U of California-Davis, 1992 *Certification:* Emergency Medicine
6600 Bruceville Rd, Sacramento, 916-525-6040

Gordon, Bruce L. (9 mentions)
Louisiana State U, 1971 *Certification:* Emergency Medicine
8350 Auburn Blvd #100, Citrus Heights, 310-451-4442

Hollingshead, Kossuth F., Jr. (3 mentions)
U of Mississippi, 1976 *Certification:* Emergency Medicine
8230 Post Rd, Fair Oaks, 916-863-5727

Kuppermann, Nathan (6 mentions)
U of California-San Francisco, 1985
Certification: Pediatric Emergency Medicine
2315 Stockton Blvd, Sacramento, 916-734-3624
4150 V St, Sacramento, 916-734-5010

Label, Norman (3 mentions)
Certification: Emergency Medicine, Family Medicine
3300 Douglas Blvd #405, Roseville, 916-782-5705

Loeffler, Rodney Alan (3 mentions)
U of California-Los Angeles, 1981
Certification: Emergency Medicine, Internal Medicine
6600 Bruceville Rd, Sacramento, 916-688-2535

Nations, John Kelly (9 mentions)
Louisiana State U, 1978 *Certification:* Emergency Medicine
2801 L St, Sacramento, 916-733-3003

Oliver, Robert (4 mentions)
Certification: Emergency Medicine
4001 J St, Sacramento, 916-453-4545

Patel, Pankaj Bhanu (5 mentions)
U of Cincinnati, 1982 *Certification:* Emergency Medicine
2025 Morse Ave, Sacramento, 916-973-5000

Rodgerson, Jeff Daniel (3 mentions)
U of Utah, 1996 *Certification:* Emergency Medicine
6600 Bruceville Rd, Sacramento, 916-525-6040

Schorer, Steven (4 mentions)
Certification: Emergency Medicine
3300 Douglass Blvd #405, Rosedale, 916-960-2000
6501 Coyle Ave, Carmichael, 916-537-5000

Turnipseed, Samuel Dean (4 mentions)
East Carolina U, 1987
Certification: Emergency Medicine, Internal Medicine
2315 Stockton Blvd, Sacramento, 916-734-3624

Wiesenfarth, John Michael (7 mentions)
Rosalind Franklin U, 1994 *Certification:* Emergency Medicine
2025 Morse Ave, Sacramento, 916-973-5000

Williams, Terry Martin (6 mentions)
U of California-San Diego, 1980
Certification: Emergency Medicine
6600 Bruceville Rd, Sacramento, 916-688-2410

Wood, John Dwight (12 mentions)
Des Moines U, 1976 *Certification:* Emergency Medicine
3300 Douglas St #405, Roseville, 916-782-5705

Endocrinology

Adams, Sallie O. (24 mentions)
Dartmouth Coll, 1976
Certification: Endocrinology and Metabolism, Internal Medicine
1020 29th St #270, Sacramento, 916-733-8233

Cushard, William Green, Jr. (15 mentions)
U of Maryland, 1964 *Certification:* Endocrinology and
Metabolism, Internal Medicine, Nuclear Medicine
77 Scripps Dr #200, Sacramento, 916-929-3381

Ostrander, Patricia L. (9 mentions)
U of California-Davis, 1987 *Certification:* Endocrinology,
Diabetes, and Metabolism, Internal Medicine
3160 Folsom Blvd, Sacramento, 916-733-3333
6555 Coyle Ave, Carmichael, 916-536-3600

Smith, Craig Scott (19 mentions)
U of California-Los Angeles, 1977
Certification: Endocrinology and Metabolism, Internal Medicine
6600 Bruceville Rd, Sacramento, 916-688-4644

Family Practice *(see note on page 9)*

Chinn, Rebecca G. (3 mentions)
Jefferson Med Coll, 1993 *Certification:* Family Medicine
3939 J St #210, Sacramento, 916-451-5678

Fujikawa, Kevin Del (3 mentions)
Loma Linda U, 1985 *Certification:* Family Medicine
4944 Sunrise Blvd #H, Fair Oaks, 916-966-8158

Johnson, Willie Clenzo (5 mentions)
U of Minnesota, 1983 *Certification:* Family Medicine
6600 Bruceville Rd, Sacramento, 916-688-2106

Leff, Marion (7 mentions)
Virginia Commonwealth U, 1976 *Certification:* Family Medicine
1201 Alhambra Blvd #300, Sacramento, 916-451-4400

Price, Christopher Alan (3 mentions)
U of California-San Francisco, 1994
Certification: Family Medicine
5030 J St #201, Sacramento, 916-455-1155
2000 O St #210, Sacramento, 916-442-1011

Sockolov, Ronald (4 mentions)
U of California-Los Angeles, 1981 *Certification:* Family Medicine
1 Scripps Dr #202, Sacramento, 916-927-1114

Tepper, Eric Glen (4 mentions)
Drexel U, 2000 *Certification:* Family Medicine
5030 J St #201, Sacramento, 916-455-1155

Gastroenterology

Arenson, David M. (18 mentions)
FMS-South Africa, 1977
Certification: Gastroenterology, Internal Medicine
3941 J St #450, Sacramento, 916-454-0655

Gandhi, Gautam Navin (11 mentions)
FMS-India, 1973
Certification: Gastroenterology, Internal Medicine
3941 J St #450, Sacramento, 916-454-0655

Goldstein, Jeffrey A. (6 mentions)
Northwestern U, 1972
Certification: Gastroenterology, Internal Medicine
3941 J St #450, Sacramento, 916-454-0655

Koldinger, Ralph Eddye (6 mentions)
George Washington U, 1963
Certification: Gastroenterology, Internal Medicine
3941 J St #450, Sacramento, 916-454-0655

Lawson, Michael James (16 mentions)
FMS-Australia, 1974
Certification: Gastroenterology, Internal Medicine
2025 Morse Ave, Sacramento, 916-973-5000

Pauly-Petrich, Mary P. (11 mentions)
U of Chicago, 1975 *Certification:* Gastroenterology, Internal
Medicine, Transplant Hepatology
2025 Morse Ave, Sacramento, 916-973-5243

General Surgery

Aguilar, Michael Murillo (5 mentions)
U of Washington, 1992
800 Howe Ave #300, Sacramento, 916-568-5564
79 Scripps Dr #202, Sacramento, 916-923-3100
6501 Coyle Ave, Carmichael, 916-537-5000

Beneke, Michael Alan (9 mentions)
U of Minnesota, 1995 *Certification:* Surgery
2800 L St, Sacramento, 916-454-6868

Cox, Ryan Joseph (10 mentions)
U of California-Irvine, 1973 *Certification:* Surgery
6600 Bruceville Rd, Sacramento, 916-688-2014

Eaker, Joyce Mewhinney (5 mentions)
U of California-San Francisco, 1987 *Certification:* Surgery
2800 L St, Sacramento, 916-454-6868

Graves, Gregory Murray (8 mentions)
Rush U, 1974 *Certification:* Surgery
2800 L St #200, Sacramento, 916-454-6900

Gylling, Scott Fredric (4 mentions)
U of Wisconsin, 1981 *Certification:* Surgery
2025 Morse Ave, Sacramento, 916-973-6119

La Rue, Scarlet Lisa (6 mentions)
U of California-Irvine, 1978 *Certification:* Surgery
6600 Bruceville Rd, Sacramento, 916-688-2014

Morse, Eric Donald (8 mentions)
U of California-Los Angeles, 1985 *Certification:* Surgery
6555 Coyle Ave #285, Carmichael, 916-536-3500

Neuhaus, Ann Corbett (8 mentions)
U of California-San Francisco, 1994 *Certification:* Surgery
6600 Bruceville Rd, Sacramento, 916-688-2000

Owens, Leon Joseph (5 mentions)
U of Michigan, 1976 *Certification:* Surgery, Surgical Critical Care
6555 Coyle Ave #340, Carmichael, 916-965-3311

Owens, Mark Parr (9 mentions)
U of Michigan, 1963 *Certification:* Surgery
6555 Coyle Ave #341, Carmichael, 916-961-2311
4717 Saca Ln, Carmichael, 916-961-2311

Patching, Steven Craig (9 mentions)
U of California-Davis, 1979 *Certification:* Surgery
300 University Ave #221, Sacramento, 916-568-5564
800 Howe Ave #300, Sacramento, 916-568-5564

Rayner, Anthony Allen (5 mentions)
Stanford U, 1975 *Certification:* Surgery
6600 Bruceville Rd, Sacramento, 916-688-2014

Roberts, Mark William (5 mentions)
Loma Linda U, 1990 *Certification:* Surgery
1580 Creekside Dr #130, Folsom, 916-983-6400

Roe, John Patrick (5 mentions)
U of Toledo, 1975 *Certification:* Colon & Rectal Surgery, Surgery
6600 Bruceville Rd, Sacramento, 916-688-2014

Smith, George Jeffrey (7 mentions)
George Washington U, 1980 *Certification:* Surgery
1600 Eureka Rd, Roseville, 916-973-5000

Swanson, Christian Alan (20 mentions)
St Louis U, 1990 *Certification:* Surgery
3160 Folsom Blvd, Sacramento, 916-733-3314
8120 Timberlake Way #107, Sacramento, 916-681-6000

Young, John William (5 mentions)
U of California-San Francisco, 1969
3160 Folsom Blvd, Sacramento, 916-733-3333

Geriatrics

Gunther Maher, Michael G. (5 mentions)
U of California-Davis, 1986
Certification: Geriatric Medicine, Internal Medicine
6600 Bruceville Rd, Sacramento, 916-688-2106
2025 Morse Ave, Sacramento, 916-973-5000

Rogers, Janice Granzella (5 mentions)
6600 Bruceville Rd, Sacramento, 916-688-2410

Hematology/Oncology

Bobolis, Kristie A. (6 mentions)
Certification: Hematology, Internal Medicine, Medical Oncology
2 Medical Plaza #200, Roseville, 916-782-5106

Ferronato, Steven Ray (6 mentions)
U of Arizona, 1979
Certification: Hematology, Internal Medicine, Medical Oncology
6600 Bruceville Rd, Sacramento, 916-688-2086

Jolly, Kent Wayne (6 mentions)
U of California-San Francisco, 1985
Certification: Pediatric Hematology-Oncology
2025 Morse Ave, Sacramento, 916-973-7342

Lalchandani, Ram (9 mentions)
U of Connecticut, 1979
Certification: Hematology, Internal Medicine, Medical Oncology
6555 Coyle Ave #301, Carmichael, 916-962-1550
3939 J St #360, Sacramento, 916-736-1536

Mandell, Gilbert Lewis (7 mentions)
U of Connecticut, 1973
Certification: Internal Medicine, Medical Oncology
6600 Bruceville Rd, Sacramento, 916-688-2086

Miller, Robert Stephen (13 mentions)
Virginia Commonwealth U, 1985
Certification: Internal Medicine, Medical Oncology
2800 L St #300, Sacramento, 916-454-6700

Ong, Delphine Wong (10 mentions)
FMS-Philippines, 1982
Certification: Internal Medicine, Medical Oncology
2800 L St, Sacramento, 916-454-6700

Wang, Stephen Eugene (11 mentions)
Jefferson Med Coll, 1995
Certification: Hematology, Medical Oncology
6600 Bruceville Rd, Sacramento, 916-688-2000

Infectious Disease

Belko, John (11 mentions)
SUNY-Downstate Med Coll, 1995
Certification: Pediatric Infectious Diseases, Pediatrics
6600 Bruceville Rd, Sacramento, 916-688-2000

Cohen, Stuart Harvey (11 mentions)
Rosalind Franklin U, 1978
Certification: Infectious Disease, Internal Medicine
2221 Stockton Blvd, Sacramento, 916-734-2737
4150 V St, Sacramento, 916-734-3741

De Felice, Richard David (21 mentions)
Loyola U Chicago, 1974 *Certification:* Critical Care Medicine,
  Infectious Disease, Internal Medicine, Pulmonary Disease
77 Cadillac Dr #210, Sacramento, 916-325-1040

Stack, Richard Robert (17 mentions)
U of Southern California, 1979 *Certification:* Infectious
  Disease, Internal Medicine, Pulmonary Disease
6660 Coyle Ave #350, Carmichael, 916-482-7621
6555 Coyle Ave, Carmichael, 916-536-3560
77 Cadillac Dr #210, Sacramento, 916-325-1040

Velji, Anvarali (11 mentions)
FMS-Ireland, 1972
Certification: Infectious Disease, Internal Medicine
6600 Bruceville Rd, Sacramento, 916-688-2000

Wong, Gordon Alvin (14 mentions)
U of California-Los Angeles, 1965 *Certification:* Infectious
  Disease, Internal Medicine, Pulmonary Disease
3941 J St #354, Sacramento, 916-733-6870

Infertility

Andreyko, Janice (4 mentions)
Certification: Obstetrics & Gynecology, Reproductive
  Endocrinology/Infertility
1130 Conroy Ln #100, Roseville, 916-773-2229

Boyers, Stephen P. (4 mentions)
Certification: Obstetrics & Gynecology, Reproductive
  Endocrinology/Infertility
2521 Stockton Blvd #4200, Sacramento, 916-734-6106

Klooster, Curt H. (4 mentions)
Certification: Obstetrics & Gynecology
1600 Eureka Rd, Roseville, 916-784-4148

Internal Medicine *(see note on page 9)*

Abate, Michael Jon (4 mentions)
U of Vermont, 1992
500 University Ave #200, Sacramento, 916-733-3777
2801 K St #520, Sacramento, 916-733-5091

Catapano, Michael Lewis (3 mentions)
FMS-Mexico, 1976 *Certification:* Internal Medicine
801 Alhambra Blvd #4, Sacramento, 916-444-6060

Chang, Bayard Won (8 mentions)
Georgetown U, 1987 *Certification:* Internal Medicine
3939 J St #340, Sacramento, 916-733-6858
500 University Ave #111, Sacramento, 916-929-2526

Chew, Stanley Hong (3 mentions)
U of California-San Francisco, 1976
Certification: Internal Medicine
5025 J St #309, Sacramento, 916-453-1946

De Bruin, Robert Jay (3 mentions)
U of Florida, 1979 *Certification:* Internal Medicine
1600 Creekside Dr #3800, Folsom, 916-984-7830

Fitzgerald, Faith Thayer (5 mentions)
U of California-San Francisco, 1969
Certification: Internal Medicine
2025 Morse Ave, Sacramento, 916-973-5235
2221 Stockton Blvd, Sacramento, 916-734-2737
2315 Stockton Blvd, Sacramento, 916-734-2177
2825 J St #400, Sacramento, 916-734-2177

Flaningam, Michael Andrew (3 mentions)
Rosalind Franklin U, 1997 *Certification:* Internal Medicine
2801 K St #520, Sacramento, 916-733-5090

Homler, Howard Jack (5 mentions)
U of California-Irvine, 1978 *Certification:* Internal Medicine
6660 Coyle Ave #250, Carmichael, 916-962-2035

Kelly-Reif, Steven M. (5 mentions)
SUNY-Upstate Med U, 1982 *Certification:* Internal Medicine
2025 Morse Ave, Sacramento, 916-973-5000

Kwok, Monice Jane (6 mentions)
U of California-Davis, 1979
500 University Ave #220, Sacramento, 916-679-3693

Lehman, David Howard (5 mentions)
U of California-San Francisco, 1970
Certification: Internal Medicine, Rheumatology
5025 J St #315, Sacramento, 916-452-1294
5025 J St #206, Sacramento, 916-733-5090

Link, Joseph Leonard (3 mentions)
U of California-San Diego, 1979 *Certification:* Internal Medicine
6600 Bruceville Rd, Sacramento, 916-688-2000

Oide, Jon Sunao (5 mentions)
U of California-Davis, 1997 *Certification:* Internal Medicine
9201 Big Horn Blvd, Elk Grove, 916-478-5000

Padilla, David Allen (3 mentions)
U of Illinois, 1990 *Certification:* Internal Medicine
8680 Greenback Ln, Orangevale, 916-987-2700

Tak, Andrew Jungwon (3 mentions)
Wayne State U, 1992
500 University Ave, Sacramento, 916-646-4583

Ullery, Michael Chris (3 mentions)
U of California-Los Angeles, 1987 *Certification:* Internal Medicine
500 University Ave #200, Sacramento, 916-920-1200

Wigginton, Scott Michael (8 mentions)
U of California-San Diego, 1979 *Certification:* Internal Medicine
5340 Elvas Ave #300, Sacramento, 916-457-7424

Nephrology

Ballenger, John Ray (11 mentions)
U of Oklahoma, 1974
Certification: Internal Medicine, Nephrology
77 Cadillac Dr #130, Sacramento, 916-929-8564
300 University Ave, Sacramento, 916-929-8564

Hu, Kai-Ting (11 mentions)
Med Coll of Pennsylvania, 1995 *Certification:* Nephrology
6600 Bruceville Rd, Sacramento, 916-688-2000

Mezger, Matthew Sullivan (15 mentions)
U of California-Davis, 1980
Certification: Internal Medicine, Nephrology
77 Cadillac Dr #130, Sacramento, 916-929-8564
300 University Ave, Sacramento, 916-929-8564

Rathore, Vijay S. (7 mentions)
FMS-India, 1987 *Certification:* Nephrology
6600 Bruceville Rd, Sacramento, 916-688-2106
2221 Stockton Blvd, Sacramento, 916-734-2737

Ruggles, Stanley William (8 mentions)
U of California-San Francisco, 1963
Certification: Internal Medicine, Nephrology
7919 Pebble Beach Dr #201, Citrus Heights, 916-961-7391
77 Cadillac Dr #130, Sacramento, 916-929-8564
300 University Ave, Sacramento, 916-929-8564

Neurological Surgery

Ciricillo, Samuel F. (19 mentions)
Emory U, 1986 *Certification:* Neurological Surgery
2800 L St, Sacramento, 916-454-6850

Cobb, Cully Alton (26 mentions)
Vanderbilt U, 1969 *Certification:* Neurological Surgery
2801 K St #300, Sacramento, 916-733-5028
3939 J St #380, Sacramento, 916-733-5028

French, Barry Norman (11 mentions)
FMS-Canada, 1968 *Certification:* Neurological Surgery
2801 K St #300, Sacramento, 916-733-5028
3939 J St #380, Sacramento, 916-733-5028

Hawk, Mark Wade (9 mentions)
U of California-Davis, 1994 *Certification:* Neurological Surgery
2025 Morse Ave, Sacramento, 916-973-5000
4860 Y St, Sacramento, 916-734-3588

Yen, John K. H., Jr. (10 mentions)
Albany Med Coll, 1969 *Certification:* Neurological Surgery
3939 J St #380, Sacramento, 916-682-7938
200 B St #F, Davis, 530-756-8859

Neurology

Akins, Paul Taylor (7 mentions)
U of Tennessee, 1991
Certification: Neurology, Vascular Neurology
500 University Ave #110, Sacramento, 916-641-8205
2800 L St, Sacramento, 916-641-8205

Atkinson, Richard Presley (9 mentions)
Certification: Neurology, Vascular Neurology
2800 L St #500, Sacramento, 916-454-6850

Au, William Joong Why (18 mentions)
U of California-Irvine, 1975 *Certification:* Neurology
500 University Ave #110, Sacramento, 916-641-8205
2315 Stockton Blvd, Sacramento, 916-454-6850
4860 Y St, Sacramento, 916-454-6850
2800 L St, Sacramento, 916-454-6850

Bissell, John Albert (10 mentions)
Harvard U, 1969 *Certification:* Neurology
6600 Bruceville Rd, Sacramento, 916-688-2410

Knox, Stephen Fredrich (5 mentions)
U of Texas-Dallas, 1985
Certification: Internal Medicine, Neurology
500 University Ave #110, Sacramento, 916-641-8205
2800 L St #500, Sacramento, 916-454-6850

Lui, For Shing (6 mentions)
FMS-China, 1978 *Certification:* Neurology, Vascular Neurology
2025 Morse Ave, Sacramento, 916-973-5175
4537 Valmonte Dr, Sacramento, 916-973-5175

Schafer, John Arthur (13 mentions)
U of Chicago, 1971 *Certification:* Internal Medicine, Neurology
3160 Folsom Blvd, Sacramento, 916-733-3333
6555 Coyle Ave, Carmichael, 916-536-3670

Shatzel, Alan J. (6 mentions)
Certification: Clinical Neurophysiology, Neurology, Sleep Medicine
3000 Q St, Sacramento, 916-733-3372

Skaff, Peter T. (6 mentions)
Albany Med Coll, 1997 *Certification:* Neurology
6555 Coyle Ave, Carmichael, 916-536-3670

Obstetrics/Gynecology

Cragun, Jeffrey Richard (7 mentions)
U of California-Los Angeles, 1982
Certification: Obstetrics & Gynecology
1600 Creekside Dr #2500, Folsom, 916-983-3500
1735 Creekside Dr, Folsom, 916-983-3500
3160 Folsom Blvd, Sacramento, 916-733-3350

Fox, Gary Michael (3 mentions)
U of Miami, 1976 *Certification:* Obstetrics & Gynecology
6600 Bruceville Rd, Sacramento, 916-688-2106

Fritz-Zavacki, Susan (3 mentions)
Southern Illinois U, 1979 *Certification:* Obstetrics & Gynecology
5030 J St #200, Sacramento, 916-451-8001

Gregg, Laurie C. (5 mentions)
U of California-Los Angeles, 1991
Certification: Obstetrics & Gynecology
2277 Fair Oaks Blvd #355, Sacramento, 916-927-3178

Hays, Barbara June (6 mentions)
U of California-Davis, 1980 *Certification:* Obstetrics & Gynecology
5030 J St #200, Sacramento, 916-451-8001

Ketchum, Darcy Carroll (3 mentions)
Cornell U, 1985 *Certification:* Obstetrics & Gynecology
1201 Alhambra Blvd #320, Sacramento, 916-455-2229

Knight, Orel Harvey (10 mentions)
U of California-Davis, 1977 *Certification:* Obstetrics & Gynecology
5301 F St #318, Sacramento, 916-733-1740

Locke, Alexander, III (7 mentions)
Vanderbilt U, 1986 *Certification:* Obstetrics & Gynecology
6600 Bruceville Rd, Sacramento, 916-688-2055

McClure, Elizabeth Mary (9 mentions)
U of California-Los Angeles, 1989
1201 Alhambra Blvd #320, Sacramento, 916-455-2229

Polansky, Steven (3 mentions)
SUNY-Downstate Med Coll, 1971
Certification: Obstetrics & Gynecology
5821 Jameson Ct, Carmichael, 916-486-0411
2288 Auburn Blvd #101, Sacramento, 916-920-0848

Rosellini, Therese Eyre (3 mentions)
Western U, 1995 *Certification:* Obstetrics & Gynecology
8170 Laguna Blvd #105, Elk Grove, 916-684-6996

Smith, Lloyd Herbert (3 mentions)
U of California-Davis, 1981
Certification: Gynecologic Oncology, Obstetrics & Gynecology
4860 Y St #2500, Sacramento, 916-734-6941
2315 Stockton Blvd, Sacramento, 916-734-6946
4501 X St, Sacramento, 916-734-6946

Ophthalmology

Bliss, Lewis S. (5 mentions)
U of Texas-Galveston, 1982 *Certification:* Ophthalmology
6620 Coyle Ave #200, Carmichael, 916-863-3143
5773 Greenback Ln, Sacramento, 916-863-3143

Grutzmacher, Richard Don (6 mentions)
Northwestern U, 1976
Certification: Internal Medicine, Ophthalmology
1515 River Park Dr #100, Sacramento, 916-649-1515

Hine, James Ernest (4 mentions)
Med Coll of Wisconsin, 1974 *Certification:* Ophthalmology
2025 Morse Ave, Sacramento, 916-973-5000
1650 Response Rd, Sacramento, 916-784-4185

Jones, Richard Arnold (10 mentions)
U of Texas-Galveston, 1983 *Certification:* Ophthalmology
4925 J St, Sacramento, 916-452-8105

Kidwell, Thomas Paul (5 mentions)
U of Texas-Dallas, 1979 *Certification:* Ophthalmology
10725 International Dr, Rancho Cordova, 916-631-3000

Lewis, Richard Alan (5 mentions)
Northwestern U, 1978 *Certification:* Ophthalmology
3939 J St #102, Sacramento, 916-455-9938
1515 River Park Dr #100, Sacramento, 916-649-1515

Martel, Joseph Ruben (9 mentions)
U of Wisconsin, 1978 *Certification:* Ophthalmology
1020 29th St #140, Sacramento, 916-635-6161
3701 J St #104, Sacramento, 916-451-3990
11216 Trinity River Dr #H, Rancho Cordova, 916-635-6161

Peabody, Robert Ross, Jr. (5 mentions)
George Washington U, 1987 *Certification:* Ophthalmology
1700 Alhambra Blvd #202, Sacramento, 916-731-8040

Serdahl, Christian Lee (5 mentions)
U of Southern California, 1987 *Certification:* Ophthalmology
4925 J St, Sacramento, 916-452-8105
2620 Hurley Way #A, Sacramento, 916-453-1111

Wendel, Robert Thomas (9 mentions)
U of Michigan, 1979 *Certification:* Ophthalmology
3939 J St #106, Sacramento, 916-454-4861
6660 Coyle Ave #330, Carmichael, 916-967-1110
1805 N California #406, Stockton, 209-461-5291
1400 Florida Ave #212, Modesto, 209-549-8444
460 W East Ave #110, Chico, 530-899-2251

Orthopedics

Blumenfeld, Thomas J. (4 mentions)
Certification: Orthopaedic Surgery
1020 29th St #450, Sacramento, 916-733-5066

Coward, David Byron (4 mentions)
U of Southern California, 1978 *Certification:* Orthopaedic Surgery
2801 K St #310, Sacramento, 916-454-6677

Howell, Stephen Miller (8 mentions)
Northwestern U, 1981
8100 Timberlake Way #F, Sacramento, 916-689-7370
3939 J St #100, Sacramento, 916-733-6819

Leathers, Michael Worth (5 mentions)
U of California-Davis, 1977 *Certification:* Orthopaedic Surgery
2801 K St #330, Sacramento, 916-733-5049

Manske, David John (5 mentions)
U of California-Davis, 1981 *Certification:* Orthopaedic Surgery
6600 Bruceville Rd, Sacramento, 916-688-2106

Mar, Timothy Paul (5 mentions)
U of California-Los Angeles, 1983
Certification: Orthopaedic Surgery
2801 K St #330, Sacramento, 916-733-5049

Nagy, Stephen Mears, III (7 mentions)
U of California-Los Angeles, 1994
Certification: Orthopaedic Surgery
6600 Bruceville Rd, Sacramento, 916-688-2000

Nielsen, Michael William (5 mentions)
U of California-Los Angeles, 1973
Certification: Orthopaedic Surgery
1201 Alhambra Blvd #400, Sacramento, 916-731-7800
1020 29th St #680, Sacramento, 916-733-5057

Ryle, Garrett Patrick (5 mentions)
U of California-Davis, 1975 *Certification:* Orthopaedic Surgery
1201 Alhambra Blvd #400, Sacramento, 916-731-7800

Tai, David Wenkiang (8 mentions)
Michigan State U, 1983 *Certification:* Orthopaedic Surgery
2801 K St #325, Sacramento, 916-733-8710

Otorhinolaryngology

Appelblatt, Nancy Haley (10 mentions)
U of Michigan, 1977 *Certification:* Otolaryngology
3810 J St, Sacramento, 916-736-3399

Bernstein, Philip (9 mentions)
FMS-South Africa, 1970 *Certification:* Otolaryngology
3810 J St, Sacramento, 916-736-3399

Blazun, Judith Marie (7 mentions)
U of California-Los Angeles, 1986 *Certification:* Otolaryngology
1201 Alhambra Blvd #420, Sacramento, 916-731-7707

Fenton, Wayne Huxley, Jr. (7 mentions)
U of California-Los Angeles, 1981 *Certification:* Otolaryngology
6600 Bruceville Rd, Sacramento, 916-688-2045

Isaacs, Richard Scott (8 mentions)
Wayne State U, 1988 *Certification:* Otolaryngology
6600 Bruceville Rd, Sacramento, 916-688-2106
7300 Wyndham Dr, Sacramento, 916-525-6371

Kearns, Michael Joseph (7 mentions)
U of California-Irvine, 1980 *Certification:* Otolaryngology
3810 J St, Sacramento, 916-966-2700
6555 Coyle Ave #340, Carmichael, 916-966-2700

Lue, Allen Jungchen (7 mentions)
Baylor U, 1996 *Certification:* Otolaryngology
6600 Bruceville Rd, Sacramento, 916-688-2082

McKennan, Kevin Xavier (9 mentions)
Albany Med Coll, 1978 *Certification:* Otolaryngology
3810 J St, Sacramento, 916-736-3399
1111 Exposition Blvd, Sacramento, 916-736-3408

Pain Medicine

Bicocca, Michael (9 mentions)
Northeastern Ohio U, 1993
Certification: Anesthesiology, Pain Medicine
6600 Bruceville Rd, Sacramento, 916-525-6040
2801 K St #410, Sacramento, 916-733-8277

Snook, Lee Thomas, Jr. (8 mentions)
U of Nevada, 1980
Certification: Anesthesiology, Internal Medicine, Pain Medicine
2288 Auburn Blvd #106, Sacramento, 916-568-8338

Pathology

Abele, John Stephen (7 mentions)
U of California-San Francisco, 1973 *Certification:* Anatomic
Pathology & Clinical Pathology, Cytopathology
3301 C St #103C, Sacramento, 916-444-0889

Amott, Thomas Russell (4 mentions)
U of California-San Francisco, 1971 *Certification:* Anatomic
Pathology & Clinical Pathology, Forensic Pathology
2420 J St, Sacramento, 916-447-6267

Caccamo, Dario (3 mentions)
FMS-Argentina, 1978
Certification: Anatomic Pathology, Cytopathology, Neuropathology
2420 J St, Sacramento, 916-446-0424
3301 C St #200-E, Sacramento, 916-446-0424

Hess, Eva Goldschmidt (10 mentions)
U of California-Davis, 1989
Certification: Anatomic Pathology & Clinical Pathology
6600 Bruceville Rd, Sacramento, 916-688-2303

Mazoujian, Gwen (3 mentions)
Duke U, 1979
Certification: Anatomic Pathology & Clinical Pathology
2420 J St, Sacramento, 916-446-0424

Musicant, Jonathan Edward (3 mentions)
U of Michigan, 1987 *Certification:* Anatomic Pathology &
Clinical Pathology, Cytopathology
6501 Coyle Ave, Carmichael, 916-537-5275

Thornberry, Donald Scott (3 mentions)
Tulane U, 1981 *Certification:* Anatomic Pathology &
Clinical Pathology, Cytopathology
2025 Morse Ave, Sacramento, 916-973-5243

Yu, Ruby Shuen Ngok (5 mentions)
FMS-China, 1975
Certification: Anatomic Pathology & Clinical Pathology
6600 Bruceville Rd, Sacramento, 916-525-6040

Pediatrics *(see note on page 9)*

Bagge, Lynn Ann (3 mentions)
George Washington U, 1997 *Certification:* Pediatrics
1650 Response Rd, Sacramento, 916-733-5090

Bloom, Evan David (5 mentions)
U of California-San Francisco, 1982 *Certification:* Pediatrics
6600 Bruceville Rd, Sacramento, 916-525-6040

Cohen, Gregrey Seth (3 mentions)
U of Arizona, 1987 *Certification:* Pediatrics
6555 Coyle Ave #190, Carmichael, 916-536-3520

Farrell, Robert Edward (4 mentions)
U of Cincinnati, 1968 *Certification:* Pediatrics
5301 F St #220, Sacramento, 916-455-8000
77 Cadillac Dr #130, Sacramento, 916-929-3100

Goore, Zoey Jayne (3 mentions)
Certification: Pediatrics
2521 Stockton Blvd, Sacramento, 916-734-3112

Gould, Richard Alan (8 mentions)
U of New Mexico, 1983 *Certification:* Pediatrics
425 University Ave #200, Sacramento, 916-924-9337

McCrimons, Daniel Everett (5 mentions)
Columbia U, 1979 *Certification:* Pediatrics
5030 J St #301, Sacramento, 916-451-8430

Takemoto, Fern Sumi (3 mentions)
U of Hawaii, 1987 *Certification:* Pediatrics
6555 Coyle Ave #190, Carmichael, 916-536-3500

Van Schenck, Don R. (11 mentions)
U of California-Davis, 1978
2 Scripps Dr #310, Sacramento, 916-924-8754

Volpe, Silvana Maria (3 mentions)
U of California-Los Angeles, 1981 *Certification:* Pediatrics
6600 Bruceville Rd, Sacramento, 916-688-2106

Plastic Surgery

Johnson, Debra Jolyn (10 mentions)
Stanford U, 1981 *Certification:* Plastic Surgery
95 Scripps Dr, Sacramento, 916-929-1833

Kaufman, David Lawrence (4 mentions)
Harvard U, 1996 *Certification:* Plastic Surgery
2220 E Bidwell St, Folsom, 916-983-9895

Lim, Alan Young (4 mentions)
U of California-San Diego, 1979 *Certification:* Plastic Surgery
6600 Bruceville Rd, Sacramento, 916-688-2014

Longo, Charles T. (4 mentions)
Certification: Plastic Surgery
4250 H St #3, Sacramento, 916-456-8756

Wandel, Amy G. (5 mentions)
Rosalind Franklin U, 1983 *Certification:* Plastic Surgery, Surgery
6555 Coyle Ave #210, Carmichael, 800-887-8982
3000 Q St 5th Fl, Sacramento, 916-733-3314

Yamahata, Wayne Ichiro (9 mentions)
U of California-Davis, 1978 *Certification:* Plastic Surgery
95 Scripps Dr, Sacramento, 916-929-1833

Psychiatry

Green, William Howard, Jr. (4 mentions)
U of Louisville, 1974 *Certification:* Psychiatry
6600 Bruceville Rd, Sacramento, 916-688-2000

Kaufman, Benjamin (7 mentions)
U of California-San Francisco, 1962 *Certification:* Psychiatry
2801 K St #215, Sacramento, 916-733-5055

Mehtani, Janak (4 mentions)
FMS-India, 1973 *Certification:* Psychiatry
2951 Fulton Ave, Sacramento, 916-486-7555
6501 Coyle Ave, Carmichael, 916-537-5000

Pulmonary Disease

Arai, Randy Chester (5 mentions)
Tufts U, 1979
Certification: Internal Medicine, Pulmonary Disease
3941 J St #354, Sacramento, 916-733-6870
3160 Folsom Blvd, Sacramento, 916-733-3346

Chow, Norman Synlai (5 mentions)
Cornell U, 1984 *Certification:* Critical Care Medicine,
Internal Medicine, Pulmonary Disease
6600 Bruceville Rd, Sacramento, 916-688-2410

De Felice, Richard David (5 mentions)
Loyola U Chicago, 1974 *Certification:* Critical Care Medicine,
Infectious Disease, Internal Medicine, Pulmonary Disease
77 Cadillac Dr #210, Sacramento, 916-325-1040

Jones, Jeffry Howard (9 mentions)
St Louis U, 1993
Certification: Internal Medicine, Pulmonary Disease
500 University Ave #260, Sacramento, 916-925-2096

Lutch, John Stuart (6 mentions)
Tufts U, 1966 *Certification:* Critical Care Medicine, Internal
Medicine, Pulmonary Disease
2025 Morse Ave, Sacramento, 916-973-5243
2055 Morse Ave, Sacramento, 916-973-5858

Marelich, Gregory Paul (8 mentions)
St Louis U, 1989 *Certification:* Critical Care Medicine,
Internal Medicine, Pulmonary Disease
6600 Bruceville Rd, Sacramento, 916-688-2410

Murphy, Peter Joseph (10 mentions)
FMS-Ireland, 1970 *Certification:* Critical Care Medicine,
Internal Medicine, Pulmonary Disease
3637 Mission Ave #6, Carmichael, 916-482-7621
6660 Coyle Ave #350, Carmichael, 916-482-7621
6501 Coyle Ave, Carmichael, 916-537-5000
77 Cadillac Dr #210, Sacramento, 916-325-1040

Shragg, Thomas Andrew (6 mentions)
U of California-Davis, 1975 *Certification:* Critical Care
Medicine, Internal Medicine, Pulmonary Disease
77 Cadillac Dr #210, Sacramento, 916-325-1040
2801 K St #500, Sacramento, 916-325-1050

Yee, Alan Russell (9 mentions)
Loma Linda U, 1975
Certification: Internal Medicine, Pulmonary Disease
77 Cadillac Dr #210, Sacramento, 916-325-1040

Yee, Ngaiming (7 mentions)
Columbia U, 1974 *Certification:* Critical Care Medicine,
Internal Medicine, Pulmonary Disease
6600 Bruceville Rd, Sacramento, 916-688-2410

Radiology—Diagnostic

Brown, Paul Richard (4 mentions)
U of Rochester, 1978 *Certification:* Diagnostic Radiology,
Internal Medicine, Vascular & Interventional Radiology
3291 Ramos Cir, Sacramento, 916-363-4040
6305 Coyle Ave, Carmichael, 916-363-4040
4001 J St, Sacramento, 916-453-4414

Demarco, Roland D. (3 mentions)
Certification: Diagnostic Radiology
1500 Expo Pkwy, Sacramento, 916-646-8300

Dirkx, Cynthia Ann (3 mentions)
Certification: Diagnostic Radiology
2025 Morse Ave, Sacramento, 916-973-5000

Fellmeth, Brian David (5 mentions)
U of Hawaii, 1983 *Certification:* Diagnostic Radiology,
Vascular & Interventional Radiology
3291 Ramos Cir, Sacramento, 916-983-7476
6305 Coyle Ave, Carmichael, 916-363-4040
7601 Hospital Dr #100, Sacramento, 916-423-2027

Gorges, Sandra W. (4 mentions)
Certification: Diagnostic Radiology, Pediatric Radiology
4860 Y St, Sacramento, 916-734-3606
2315 Stockton Blvd, Sacramento, 800-482-3284

Gunter, Brian Andrew (6 mentions)
Loyola U Chicago, 1990
6600 Bruceville Rd, Sacramento, 916-525-6040

Moitoza, David John (3 mentions)
Washington U, 1983 *Certification:* Diagnostic Radiology
6600 Bruceville Rd, Sacramento, 916-688-2785

Nieves, Miguel Angel (7 mentions)
U of Puerto Rico, 1984
Certification: Diagnostic Radiology, Neuroradiology
3291 Ramos Cir, Sacramento, 916-983-7476
6305 Coyle Ave, Carmichael, 916-363-4040

Seidenwurm, David Jay (3 mentions)
Harvard U, 1982
Certification: Diagnostic Radiology, Neuroradiology
1500 Expo Pkwy, Sacramento, 916-498-8391
2801 L St, Sacramento, 916-733-3061

Tran, Long (3 mentions)
Ohio U Coll of Osteopathic Med, 1999
Certification: Diagnostic Radiology
6600 Bruceville Rd, Sacramento, 916-688-2000

Vogel, Patrick Michael (5 mentions)
Duke U, 1981 *Certification:* Diagnostic Radiology, Vascular
& Interventional Radiology
1500 Expo Pkwy, Sacramento, 916-646-8300
2801 L St, Sacramento, 916-733-3061

Radiology—Therapeutic

Brown, Paul Richard (7 mentions)
U of Rochester, 1978 *Certification:* Diagnostic Radiology,
  Internal Medicine, Vascular & Interventional Radiology
3291 Ramos Cir, Sacramento, 916-363-4040
6305 Coyle Ave, Carmichael, 916-363-4040
4001 J St, Sacramento, 916-453-4414

Davis, Lawrence Geoffrey (8 mentions)
Howard U, 1991 *Certification:* Diagnostic Radiology,
  Vascular & Interventional Radiology
3160 Folsom Blvd, Sacramento, 916-733-3377
6600 Bruceville Rd, Sacramento, 916-525-6040

Fellmeth, Brian David (7 mentions)
U of Hawaii, 1983 *Certification:* Diagnostic Radiology,
  Vascular & Interventional Radiology
3291 Ramos Cir, Sacramento, 916-983-7476
6305 Coyle Ave, Carmichael, 916-363-4040
7601 Hospital Dr #100, Sacramento, 916-423-2027

Vogel, Patrick Michael (6 mentions)
Duke U, 1981 *Certification:* Diagnostic Radiology, Vascular
  & Interventional Radiology
1500 Expo Pkwy, Sacramento, 916-646-8300
2801 L St, Sacramento, 916-733-3061

Rehabilitation

Abels, Alicia Marie (5 mentions)
U of Southern California, 1982
Certification: Physical Medicine & Rehabilitation
1600 Creekside Dr #2400, Folsom, 916-984-3430
3908 J St #4, Sacramento, 916-737-8441

Davis, Brian Adam (3 mentions)
Meharry Med Coll, 1992
Certification: Physical Medicine & Rehabilitation, Sports Medicine
4860 Y St, Sacramento, 916-734-7041

Felix, Michael Salutillo (6 mentions)
Creighton U, 1985
Certification: Physical Medicine & Rehabilitation
6600 Bruceville Rd, Sacramento, 916-688-2410

Kilmer, David Daniel (3 mentions)
U of California-Davis, 1985 *Certification:* Neuromuscular
  Medicine, Physical Medicine & Rehabilitation
4860 Y St, Sacramento, 916-734-7041
2315 Stockton Blvd, Sacramento, 916-734-2925

Mann, Stephen Irving (7 mentions)
U of Wisconsin, 1980
Certification: Physical Medicine & Rehabilitation
2801 K St #410, Sacramento, 916-733-5024

Portwood, Margaret Mary (6 mentions)
Oregon Health Sciences U, 1977
Certification: Physical Medicine & Rehabilitation
3701 J St #105, Sacramento, 916-453-0292
2825 J St #435, Sacramento, 916-440-8001

Reddy, Vinaykumar Moola (3 mentions)
U of Nevada, 1996
Certification: Physical Medicine & Rehabilitation
5340 Elvas Ave #200, Sacramento, 775-747-6434
4420 Duckhorn Dr #200, Sacramento, 916-419-9900

Rinzler, Gary S. (3 mentions)
Certification: Physical Medicine & Rehabilitation
6600 Bruceville Rd, Sacramento, 916-688-2410

TeSelle, Marian (5 mentions)
Certification: Physical Medicine & Rehabilitation
2025 Morse Ave, Sacramento, 916-973-5000

Rheumatology

Miller-Blair, Dana J. (8 mentions)
St Louis U, 1983 *Certification:* Internal Medicine, Rheumatology
6600 Bruceville Rd #D, Sacramento, 916-688-2330

Scalapino, Ja Nahn Carol (11 mentions)
U of California-San Francisco, 1979
Certification: Internal Medicine, Rheumatology
1020 29th St #270, Sacramento, 916-733-8233
2801 K St #505, Sacramento, 916-454-7500

Wiesner, Kenneth Billings (23 mentions)
FMS-Canada, 1969
Certification: Internal Medicine, Rheumatology
107 Scripps Dr #100, Sacramento, 916-922-7021

Thoracic Surgery

Graves, Gregory Murray (8 mentions)
Rush U, 1974 *Certification:* Surgery
2800 L St #200, Sacramento, 916-454-6900

Maxwell, Stephen Daniel (9 mentions)
Certification: Surgery, Thoracic Surgery
6600 Coyle Ave #3, Carmichael, 916-965-0282

Moore, Jeffrey Scranton (9 mentions)
Loma Linda U, 1983 *Certification:* Surgery
1600 Eureka Rd, Roseville, 916-784-5433

Urology

Generao, Suzanne Eileen (6 mentions)
Georgetown U, 1999 *Certification:* Urology
2801 K St #205, Sacramento, 916-733-5005

Hekmat, Kiumars (7 mentions)
FMS-Iran, 1971 *Certification:* Urology
6600 Mercy Ct #150, Fair Oaks, 916-961-9696
500 University Ave #200, Sacramento, 916-921-1615

Little, James Martin (9 mentions)
U of California-Davis, 1977 *Certification:* Urology
6600 Bruceville Rd, Sacramento, 916-525-6040

Naftulin, Brian Neil (27 mentions)
U of Southern California, 1985 *Certification:* Urology
1561 Creekside Dr #170, Folsom, 916-983-5557
500 University Ave #200, Sacramento, 916-921-1615

Vascular Surgery

Park, Thomas Chin (22 mentions)
Certification: Surgery, Vascular Surgery
500 University Ave #260, Sacramento, 916-929-6705

Rodriguez, Victor Manuel (21 mentions)
U of California-Davis, 1996
Certification: Surgery, Vascular Surgery
6600 Bruceville Rd, Sacramento, 916-688-2014

San Diego Area

Including San Diego County

Allergy/Immunology

Friedman, Noah Joshua (6 mentions)
Columbia U, 1986 *Certification:* Allergy & Immunology
7060 Clairemont Mesa Blvd Fl 5, San Diego, 858-573-0299

Jaffer, Adrian M. (7 mentions)
FMS-South Africa, 1966 *Certification:* Allergy &
  Immunology, Internal Medicine, Rheumatology
9850 Genesee Ave #810, La Jolla, 858-457-3270

Mellon, Michael Harvey (7 mentions)
Temple U, 1972 *Certification:* Allergy & Immunology, Pediatrics
7060 Clairemont Mesa Blvd, San Diego, 619-528-5000

Ostrom, Nancy Kay (7 mentions)
Mayo Med Sch, 1980
Certification: Allergy & Immunology, Pediatrics
9610 Granite Ridge Dr #B, San Diego, 858-292-1144
477 N El Camino Real #D-302, Encinitas, 858-292-1144

Pauls, John David (10 mentions)
FMS-Canada, 1993
Certification: Allergy & Immunology, Internal Medicine
2001 4th Ave, San Diego, 619-446-1549

Prenner, Bruce M. (10 mentions)
U of Buffalo, 1970
Certification: Allergy & Immunology, Pediatrics
6386 Alvarado Ct #210, San Diego, 619-286-6687

Schatz, Michael (8 mentions)
Northwestern U, 1970
Certification: Allergy & Immunology, Internal Medicine
7060 Clairemont Mesa Blvd 5th Fl, San Diego, 858-573-5397

Simon, Ronald Alan (12 mentions)
Rosalind Franklin U, 1974
Certification: Allergy & Immunology, Internal Medicine
10666 N Torrey Pines Rd, La Jolla, 858-554-8614
15025 Innovation Dr, San Diego, 858-487-1800

Welch, Michael Joseph (12 mentions)
U of California-Los Angeles, 1976
Certification: Allergy & Immunology, Pediatrics
9610 Granite Ridge Dr #B, San Diego, 858-292-1144
625 W Citracado Pkwy #206, Escondido, 858-292-1144

Woessner, Katharine M. (8 mentions)
U of Miami, 1991 *Certification:* Allergy & Immunology
10666 N Torrey Pines Rd, La Jolla, 858-554-8614
15025 Innovation Dr, San Diego, 858-487-1800

Anesthesiology

Arnold, John Edward (4 mentions)
Mayo Med Sch, 1980 *Certification:* Anesthesiology
3626 Ruffin Rd, San Diego, 858-565-9666

Cary, Christopher William (3 mentions)
U of California-Los Angeles, 1984 *Certification:* Anesthesiology
3626 Ruffin Rd, San Diego, 858-565-9666

Corey, Paul William (3 mentions)
U of Colorado, 1975 *Certification:* Anesthesiology
3626 Ruffin Rd, San Diego, 858-565-9666

Diveley, Kent (4 mentions)
Baylor U, 1982 *Certification:* Anesthesiology
3626 Ruffin Rd, San Diego, 858-565-9666

Dockweiler, David Wayne (3 mentions)
Albert Einstein Coll of Med, 1980 *Certification:*
  Anesthesiology, Internal Medicine, Pulmonary Disease
3626 Ruffin Rd, San Diego, 858-565-9666

Farrell, Thomas R. (3 mentions)
Tulane U, 1969 *Certification:* Anesthesiology, Internal Medicine
3626 Ruffin Rd, San Diego, 858-565-9666

Foltz, Bradley Davis (3 mentions)
U of Washington, 1983 *Certification:* Anesthesiology
3626 Ruffin Rd, San Diego, 858-565-9666

Giap, Brandon Cuongquoc (3 mentions)
U of Texas-Galveston, 1988 *Certification:* Anesthesiology
3626 Ruffin Rd, San Diego, 858-565-9666

Glazener, Christopher H. (5 mentions)
FMS-Mexico, 1979 *Certification:* Anesthesiology, Pain Medicine
770 Washington St #101, San Diego, 619-299-9530

Heinle, Andrew Thomas (3 mentions)
U of Southern California, 1988 *Certification:* Anesthesiology
3626 Ruffin Rd, San Diego, 858-565-9666

Hendricks, P. Lance (3 mentions)
U of Southern California, 1966 *Certification:* Anesthesiology
3626 Ruffin Rd, San Diego, 858-565-9666

Mariano, Edward Rivera (3 mentions)
Georgetown U, 1999 *Certification:* Anesthesiology
200 W Arbor Dr, San Diego, 619-543-5720

Perkins, Stanley Wanlass (3 mentions)
Harvard U, 1980 *Certification:* Anesthesiology
2929 Health Center Dr, San Diego, 619-446-1530

Rodarte, Alexander (3 mentions)
Stanford U, 1975
Certification: Anesthesiology, Critical Care Medicine, Pediatrics
3626 Ruffin Rd, San Diego, 858-565-9666

Sonthalia, Deepak Kumar (3 mentions)
U of California-San Diego, 1998 *Certification:* Anesthesiology
4647 Zion Ave, San Diego, 619-528-5000

Wardrip, Eric Allen (3 mentions)
U of Iowa, 1981 *Certification:* Anesthesiology
320 Santa Fe Dr #100, Encinitas, 760-632-6662

Cardiac Surgery

Baradarian, Sam (7 mentions)
Stony Brook U, 1992 *Certification:* Surgery, Thoracic Surgery
7910 Frost St #330, San Diego, 858-939-6830

Dembitsky, Walter Powell (12 mentions)
U of Missouri, 1968 *Certification:* Surgery, Thoracic Surgery
7910 Frost St #330, San Diego, 858-300-4747
8008 Frost St #104, San Diego, 858-541-6830

Folkerth, Theodore L. (8 mentions)
Indiana U, 1965 *Certification:* Surgery, Thoracic Surgery
3998 Vista Way #C-204, Oceanside, 760-726-2500

Hemp, James Robert (7 mentions)
Uniformed Services U of Health Sciences, 1983
Certification: Surgery, Thoracic Surgery, Vascular Surgery
10666 N Torrey Pines Rd, La Jolla, 619-297-5600
4033 3rd Ave #210, San Diego, 619-297-5600

Lin, Yuan H. (8 mentions)
Certification: Thoracic Surgery
765 Medical Center Ct #216, Chula Vista, 619-421-1111
8851 Center Dr #200, La Mesa, 619-644-1154

Tyner, John Jeffrey (16 mentions)
Emory U, 1979
Certification: Surgery, Surgical Critical Care, Thoracic Surgery
4033 3rd Ave #210, San Diego, 619-297-5600
10666 N Torrey Pines Rd, La Jolla, 858-554-8122

Cardiology

Athill, Charles Anselmo (6 mentions)
Harvard U, 1991 *Certification:* Cardiovascular Disease,
  Clinical Cardiac Electrophysiology
3131 Berger Ave #200, San Diego, 858-244-6800

Bier, Alan Jay (5 mentions)
Albert Einstein Coll of Med, 1979
Certification: Cardiovascular Disease, Internal Medicine
2929 Health Center Dr, San Diego, 858-499-2777

Blanchard, Daniel G. (6 mentions)
U of California-San Diego, 1985
Certification: Cardiovascular Disease, Internal Medicine
200 W Arbor Dr, San Diego, 858-657-8530
9350 Campus Point Dr #D, La Jolla, 858-657-8530

Buchbinder, Maurice (4 mentions)
FMS-Canada, 1978
Certification: Cardiovascular Disease, Internal Medicine
9834 Genesee Ave #310, La Jolla, 858-625-4488

Carr, Kenneth Warren (7 mentions)
U of California-San Diego, 1978
Certification: Cardiovascular Disease, Internal Medicine
3231 Waring Ct #O, Oceanside, 760-941-9440

Ceretto, William Joe (4 mentions)
U of Colorado, 1973
Certification: Cardiovascular Disease, Internal Medicine
6386 Alvarado Ct #310, San Diego, 619-229-5050

Charlat, Martin Lorne (16 mentions)
FMS-Canada, 1981 *Certification:* Cardiovascular Disease,
  Internal Medicine, Interventional Cardiology
9834 Genesee #300, La Jolla, 858-824-2900
320 Santa Fe Dr #204, Encinitas, 760-944-7300

Effron, Marc Kersten (6 mentions)
Stanford U, 1978
Certification: Cardiovascular Disease, Internal Medicine
9834 Genesee Ave #300, La Jolla, 858-824-2900

Hoagland, Peter M. (10 mentions)
Columbia U, 1978
Certification: Cardiovascular Disease, Internal Medicine
3131 Berger Ave, San Diego, 858-244-6800

Jaski, Brian Ernest (6 mentions)
Harvard U, 1979 *Certification:* Cardiovascular Disease,
  Internal Medicine, Interventional Cardiology
3131 Berger Ave #200, San Diego, 858-244-6800

Johnson, Allen Dress (6 mentions)
Johns Hopkins U, 1965
Certification: Cardiovascular Disease, Internal Medicine
10666 N Torrey Pines Rd, La Jolla, 858-455-9100

Katz, Richard Alan (4 mentions)
Cornell U, 1970
Certification: Cardiovascular Disease, Internal Medicine
5555 Reservoir Dr #112, San Diego, 619-287-7060

Keen, William Daniel, Jr. (4 mentions)
New Jersey Med Sch, 1986
Certification: Cardiovascular Disease, Internal Medicine
4647 Zion Ave, San Diego, 877-236-0333

Kimura, Bruce John (6 mentions)
U of California-San Diego, 1989
Certification: Cardiovascular Disease, Internal Medicine
4060 4th Ave #205, San Diego, 619-435-1660
230 Prospect Pl #250, Coronado, 619-435-1660

Leahy, Dennis Robert (7 mentions)
Columbia U, 1973 *Certification:* Cardiovascular Disease,
  Internal Medicine, Interventional Cardiology
488 E Valley Pkwy #201, Escondido, 760-743-0546

Noll, H. Elizabeth (5 mentions)
U of California-Los Angeles, 1981 *Certification:* Cardiovascular
  Disease, Clinical Cardiac Electrophysiology, Internal Medicine
2929 Health Center Dr, San Diego, 858-499-2777

Ostrander, David Ross (5 mentions)
New York U, 1975 *Certification:* Cardiovascular Disease,
  Internal Medicine, Interventional Cardiology
2929 Health Center Dr, San Diego, 858-499-2777

Phillips, Paul Sydney (6 mentions)
U of Rochester, 1980 *Certification:* Cardiovascular Disease,
  Internal Medicine, Interventional Cardiology
4060 4th Ave #206, San Diego, 619-297-0014

Rapeport, Kevin Barnard (5 mentions)
FMS-South Africa, 1980 *Certification:* Cardiovascular
  Disease, Internal Medicine, Interventional Cardiology
8851 Center Dr #612, La Mesa, 619-265-4020

Rogers, John David (4 mentions)
Rosalind Franklin U, 1990 *Certification:* Cardiovascular Disease
10666 N Torrey Pines Rd, La Jolla, 858-455-9100

Rubenson, David Samuel (5 mentions)
U of California-Los Angeles, 1973
Certification: Cardiovascular Disease, Internal Medicine
10666 N Torrey Pines Rd, La Jolla, 858-554-8186

Spiegel, David Anton (7 mentions)
U of Colorado, 1978 *Certification:* Cardiovascular Disease,
  Internal Medicine, Interventional Cardiology
3909 Waring Rd #A, Oceanside, 760-630-2550

Zamudio, Fernando A. (4 mentions)
Creighton U, 1963
Certification: Cardiovascular Disease, Internal Medicine
6655 Alvarado Rd, San Diego, 619-583-0511

Dermatology

Boiko, Susan (4 mentions)
U of Michigan, 1978
Certification: Dermatology, Pediatric Dermatology, Pediatrics
400 Craven Rd, San Marcus, 619-528-5000

Burrows, William Mead, Jr. (6 mentions)
U of Vermont, 1967 *Certification:* Dermatology
15025 Innovation Dr, San Diego, 858-487-1800

Eichenfield, Lawrence F. (6 mentions)
Mount Sinai Sch of Med, 1984
Certification: Dermatology, Pediatric Dermatology
8010 Frost St #602, San Diego, 858-966-6795

Friedlander, Shelia F. (6 mentions)
U of Chicago, 1979
Certification: Dermatology, Pediatric Dermatology, Pediatrics
8010 Frost St #602, San Diego, 858-874-6795

Gilbertson, Erik Olaf (10 mentions)
Northwestern U, 1992 *Certification:* Dermatology
10862 Calle Verde #A, La Mesa, 619-670-5400

Harpster, Elaine F. (4 mentions)
U of California-San Diego, 1985 *Certification:* Dermatology
8933 Activity Rd, San Diego, 858-499-2600

Kaplan, Lee Allan (8 mentions)
U of California-San Diego, 1977 *Certification:* Dermatology
9850 Genesee Ave, La Jolla, 858-362-8800

Mafong, Erick Alfonso (4 mentions)
U of California-San Diego, 1997 *Certification:* Dermatology
319 F St #102, Chula Vista, 619-476-1200
4060 4th Ave #209, San Diego, 619-298-9535

O'Grady, Terence C. (4 mentions)
Uniformed Services U of Health Sciences, 1980
Certification: Dermatology, Dermatopathology
200 W Arbor Dr, San Diego, 619-543-5764
4168 Front St, San Diego, 619-543-5580

Pelle, Michelle Terez (4 mentions)
Jefferson Med Coll, 1997 *Certification:* Dermatology
4065 3rd Ave #102, San Diego, 619-542-0013

Scheinberg, Robert Stanley (7 mentions)
New York U, 1972 *Certification:* Dermatology
9850 Genesee Ave #530, La Jolla, 858-558-0677
499 N El Camino Real #B-101, Encinitas, 760-942-1311
3613 Vista Way, Oceanside, 760-758-5340

Emergency Medicine

Accardi, Andrew Jason (3 mentions)
New York Med Coll, 1997 *Certification:* Emergency Medicine
354 Santa Fe Dr, Encinitas, 760-633-7686

Clark, Richard Franklin (3 mentions)
Virginia Commonwealth U, 1986
Certification: Emergency Medicine, Medical Toxicology
9300 Campus Point Dr, La Jolla, 619-543-6463

Colaprete, Peter (6 mentions)
FMS-Belgium, 1978 *Certification:* Emergency Medicine,
  Undersea & Hyperbaric Medicine
5555 Grossmont Center Dr, La Mesa, 619-740-4401

Engevik, Russell Wayne (3 mentions)
George Washington U, 1983 *Certification:* Emergency Medicine
555 E Valley Pkwy, Escondido, 760-739-3300

Evans, Shawn Devin (7 mentions)
U of California-Irvine, 1993 *Certification:* Emergency Medicine
9888 Genesee Ave, La Jolla, 858-626-6902

Fox, Dale A. (4 mentions)
FMS-Canada, 1979 *Certification:* Emergency Medicine
5500 Grossmont Center Dr, La Mesa, 619-740-4401

Fredericks, John Charles, Jr. (3 mentions)
U of California-Irvine, 1975
Certification: Emergency Medicine, Internal Medicine
555 E Valley Pkwy, Escondido, 760-739-3300

Guss, David Alan (7 mentions)
Med Coll of Wisconsin, 1976
Certification: Emergency Medicine, Internal Medicine
9300 Campus Point Dr, La Jolla, 619-543-6400
200 W Arbor Dr Frnt, San Diego, 619-543-6463

Kakehashi, Robert Kevin (3 mentions)
U of California-Los Angeles, 1981 *Certification:* Internal Medicine
10666 N Torrey Pines Rd, La Jolla, 858-554-8638

Kanegaye, John Terry (3 mentions)
New York U, 1988
Certification: Pediatric Emergency Medicine, Pediatrics
3020 Childrens Way, San Diego, 858-966-8036

Kobernick, Marc Evan (4 mentions)
U of California-Davis, 1978
Certification: Emergency Medicine, Internal Medicine
5555 Grossmont Center Dr, La Mesa, 619-740-4401

Mathis, Philip Craig (3 mentions)
U of Southern California, 1976
Certification: Emergency Medicine, Internal Medicine
555 E Valley Pkwy, Escondido, 760-739-3300

Ochs, Melvin Anthony (3 mentions)
U of Iowa, 1967 *Certification:* Emergency Medicine
435 H St, Chula Vista, 619-691-7290

Tamsen, Mark Jeffrey (3 mentions)
U of Arizona, 1979 *Certification:* Emergency Medicine
250 Prospect Pl, Coronado, 619-225-6200
3434 Midway Dr #1002, San Diego, 619-972-0600

Watt, Timothy Scott (4 mentions)
Certification: Emergency Medicine
2133 Merida Ct, La Jolla, 858-456-1533

Endocrinology

Argoud, Georges Maxime (6 mentions)
Loyola U Chicago, 1980
Certification: Endocrinology and Metabolism, Internal Medicine
2120 Thibodo Rd #202, Vista, 760-806-5890
865 3rd Ave #101, Chula Vista, 619-426-7910

Christiansen, Louis G. (6 mentions)
U of California-San Diego, 1999 *Certification:* Endocrinology,
  Diabetes, and Metabolism, Internal Medicine
2001 4th Ave, San Diego, 858-499-2777
2929 Health Center Dr, San Diego, 858-499-2777

Dailey, George Eugene, III (5 mentions)
U of Alabama, 1971
Certification: Endocrinology and Metabolism, Internal Medicine
10666 N Torrey Pines Rd, La Jolla, 858-455-9100

Einhorn, Daniel (30 mentions)
Tufts U, 1977
Certification: Endocrinology and Metabolism, Internal Medicine
9850 Genesee Ave #415, La Jolla, 858-622-7200

Fink, Raymond Irwin (9 mentions)
FMS-Canada, 1977
Certification: Endocrinology and Metabolism, Internal Medicine
8851 Center Dr #404, La Mesa, 619-463-1293
9850 Genesee Ave #415, La Jolla, 858-622-7004
1594A S Imperial Ave, El Centro, 760-337-8803

Guerin, Chris Kenneth (8 mentions)
Loyola U Chicago, 1978
Certification: Endocrinology and Metabolism, Internal Medicine
3927 Waring Rd #C, Oceanside, 760-941-9850

Marx, Christopher Walter (5 mentions)
U of California-San Diego, 1983
Certification: Endocrinology and Metabolism, Internal Medicine
15025 Innovation Dr, San Diego, 858-487-1800

McCallum, James David O. (9 mentions)
FMS-Ireland, 1990
Certification: Endocrinology, Diabetes, and Metabolism
10666 N Torrey Pines Rd #MS-212-A, La Jolla, 858-554-7876

Sandler, Jeffrey Allan (7 mentions)
U of Illinois, 1971
Certification: Endocrinology and Metabolism, Internal Medicine
4060 4th Ave #508, San Diego, 619-497-6188

Wu, Patricia Shen Chi (6 mentions)
FMS-United Kingdom, 1984
3033 Bunker Hill St, San Diego, 619-528-5000

Family Practice *(see note on page 9)*

Anderson, Wayne Roy (3 mentions)
U of California-Los Angeles, 1979 *Certification:* Family Medicine
10862 Calle Verde #A, La Mesa, 619-670-5400

Barron, Robert Henry, Jr. (4 mentions)
U of California-Los Angeles, 1980 *Certification:* Family Medicine
2095 W Vista Way 3218, Vista, 760-630-3562

Beeson, Stephen Charles (3 mentions)
U of California-San Diego, 1991 *Certification:* Family Medicine
16950 Via Tazon, San Diego, 858-499-2600

Chuan, Julie Jeouling (3 mentions)
U of California-Los Angeles, 2001
Certification: Family Medicine, Sports Medicine
9909 Mira Mesa Blvd #200, San Diego, 858-657-7750

Dale, Tracy (3 mentions)
U of California-San Diego, 1989 *Certification:* Family Medicine
6860 Avenida Encinas, Carlsbad, 619-528-5000

Green, Steven Aaron (8 mentions)
U of California-San Diego, 1985 *Certification:* Family Medicine
8901 Activity Rd, San Diego, 858-499-2600

Hodsman, Hugh Kenneth (3 mentions)
FMS-Canada, 1979 *Certification:* Family Medicine
145 Thunder Dr, Vista, 760-941-9002

Johnson, Roy Robert (4 mentions)
U of California-Los Angeles, 1976 *Certification:* Family Medicine
28743 Valley Center Rd #B, Valley Center, 760-749-0824

Kesling, Bradham Hanks (3 mentions)
Wayne State U, 1971
5525 Grossmont Center Dr #200, La Mesa, 619-644-6500

Light, Cyril Stanley B. (5 mentions)
Albert Einstein Coll of Med, 1980 *Certification:* Family Medicine
8901 Activity Rd, San Diego, 858-499-2704

Peters, Robert Edwin (4 mentions)
Loma Linda U, 1995
7920 Frost St #304-B, San Diego, 858-874-0248

Soppe, Glenn George (5 mentions)
U of California-Davis, 1987 *Certification:* Family Medicine
345 Saxony Rd #204, Encinitas, 760-944-8402

Van Buskirk, Michael Lee (4 mentions)
FMS-Mexico, 1978 *Certification:* Family Medicine
310 Santa Fe Dr #212, Encinitas, 760-753-5594

Gastroenterology

Brozinsky, Steven (4 mentions)
SUNY-Downstate Med Coll, 1972
Certification: Gastroenterology, Internal Medicine
752 Medical Center Ct #301, Chula Vista, 619-421-1155
610 Euclid Ave #301, National City, 619-421-1155

Diamant, Caroline T. (4 mentions)
U of Missouri-Kansas City, 1988
Certification: Gastroenterology, Internal Medicine
3811 Valley Centre Dr, San Diego, 858-453-9200

Epsten, Robert M., Jr. (4 mentions)
Jefferson Med Coll, 1980
Certification: Gastroenterology, Internal Medicine
4060 4th Ave #240, San Diego, 619-291-6064

Goldklang, Robert Henry (13 mentions)
U of Buffalo, 1987
Certification: Gastroenterology, Internal Medicine
700 Gardenview Ct #102, Encinitas, 760-783-0441
9850 Genesee Ave #810, La Jolla, 858-453-5200

Haynes, Kevin Scott (5 mentions)
Creighton U, 1981 *Certification:* Internal Medicine
4060 4th Ave #240, San Diego, 619-291-6064

Kamyar, Rokay Ghulam A. (6 mentions)
FMS-Japan, 1970
Certification: Gastroenterology, Internal Medicine
5119 Garfield St, La Mesa, 619-460-4055

Krol, Thomas Casimir (5 mentions)
Loyola U Chicago, 1978
Certification: Gastroenterology, Internal Medicine
3923 Waring Rd #A, Oceanside, 760-724-8782

Kumar, Piyush (8 mentions)
FMS-Zambia, 1982
Certification: Gastroenterology, Internal Medicine
700 Garden View Ct #102, Encinitas, 760-436-8881

Lipkis, Donald Charles (9 mentions)
U of Southern California, 1973
Certification: Gastroenterology, Internal Medicine
6719 Alvarado Rd #206, San Diego, 619-287-9100

Person, John Lester (8 mentions)
U of Iowa, 1979
Certification: Gastroenterology, Internal Medicine
2929 Health Center Dr, San Diego, 858-499-2702

Pockros, Paul Joseph (5 mentions)
U of Southern California, 1978
Certification: Gastroenterology, Internal Medicine
10666 N Torrey Pines Rd, La Jolla, 858-554-8879

Rothman, Jeffery Bruce (5 mentions)
Certification: Gastroenterology, Internal Medicine
3923 Waring Rd #A, Oceanside, 760-724-8782

Savides, Thomas John (8 mentions)
U of California-San Diego, 1987
Certification: Gastroenterology, Internal Medicine
9350 Campus Point Dr, La Jolla, 619-543-2347

Weinman, David Steven (5 mentions)
Jefferson Med Coll, 1986
Certification: Gastroenterology, Internal Medicine
2929 Health Center Dr, San Diego, 858-499-2777

Wolosin, James David (4 mentions)
U of California-Davis, 1982
Certification: Gastroenterology, Internal Medicine
2929 Health Center Dr, San Diego, 858-499-2777

General Surgery

Barrera, Hugo Hernan (4 mentions)
U of Maryland, 1992 *Certification:* Surgery
855 3rd Ave #3340, Chula Vista, 619-425-0797

Bhoyrul, Sunil (5 mentions)
FMS-United Kingdom, 1989 *Certification:* Surgery
15025 Innovation Dr, San Diego, 858-487-1800

Bouvet, Michael (8 mentions)
U of Washington, 1989 *Certification:* Surgery
3855 Health Sciences Dr #1102, La Jolla, 858-822-6100

Cloyd, David Wickham (4 mentions)
U of Nebraska, 1980 *Certification:* Surgery
215 S Hickory St #216, Escondido, 760-489-5955

Day, Amy Lightner (3 mentions)
U of California-Los Angeles, 1997 *Certification:* Surgery
10666 N Torrey Pines Rd, La Jolla, 858-455-9100

Deemer, Andrew R. (3 mentions)
U of California-San Diego, 1984 *Certification:* Surgery
3998 Vista Way #C200, Oceanside, 760-724-5352

Easter, David Wayne (5 mentions)
Yale U, 1983 *Certification:* Surgery
9350 Campus Point Dr, La Jolla, 858-657-7000
200 W Arbor Dr, San Diego, 619-543-6222

Exume, Amilcar Anthony (3 mentions)
U of California-San Diego, 1983 *Certification:* Surgery
400 Craven Rd, San Marcos, 619-528-5000

Fierer, Adam Samuel (8 mentions)
U of California-San Diego, 1989 *Certification:* Surgery
3998 Vista Way #C-200, Oceanside, 760-724-5352

Flint, Frank Bryce (7 mentions)
U of Michigan, 1962 *Certification:* Surgery
860 Jamacha Rd #205, El Cajon, 619-440-2427

Galloway, Gillian Que (3 mentions)
U of California-Irvine, 1990 *Certification:* Surgery
9850 Genesee #560, La Jolla, 858-452-0306

Greer, Edward Gerard (3 mentions)
U of California-Irvine, 1965 *Certification:* Surgery
225 E 2nd Ave #350, Escondido, 760-745-2273

Hardin, Chelsea S. (4 mentions)
Certification: Surgery
5565 Grossmont Center Dr Bldg 1 #221, La Mesa, 619-462-8100

Hilfiker, Mary Lenora (3 mentions)
Wright State U, 1988 *Certification:* Pediatric Surgery, Surgery
8010 Frost St #414, San Diego, 858-966-7711

Hyde, Paul Vincent B. (16 mentions)
FMS-South Africa, 1966 *Certification:* Surgery
9850 Genesee Ave #660, La Jolla, 858-452-5054

Imler, Gregory Phillip (7 mentions)
U of Cincinnati, 1983 *Certification:* Surgery
2020 Genesee Ave, San Diego, 858-541-6531

Krishnamoorthy, Mohan (3 mentions)
FMS-Canada, 1992 *Certification:* Surgery
7910 Frost St #450, San Diego, 858-565-0104

Kroener, John Mitchell (8 mentions)
U of California-San Diego, 1976 *Certification:* Surgery
3998 Vista Way #C200, Oceanside, 760-724-5352

Kurtzhals, Pamela L. (3 mentions)
Certification: Surgery
15004 Innovation Dr, San Diego, 858-487-1800
10666 N Torrey Pines Rd, La Jolla, 858-455-9100
3811 Valley Center Dr, San Diego, 858-764-3000

Levine, Ira David (4 mentions)
SUNY-Upstate Med U, 1967
4060 4th Ave #440, San Diego, 619-298-8891

Lin, Hong-Der (3 mentions)
FMS-Taiwan, 1976 *Certification:* Surgery
5565 Grossmont Center Dr #221, La Mesa, 619-462-8100

Manly, Robert James (3 mentions)
U of Nebraska, 1975 *Certification:* Surgery
2020 Genesee Ave, San Diego, 858-541-6531

Moossa, Abdool Rahim (3 mentions)
FMS-United Kingdom, 1965
9300 Campus Point Dr, La Jolla, 858-657-6113

Mueller, George A. (6 mentions)
Certification: Surgery
7930 Frost St #101, San Diego, 858-565-0104

Olson, Cheryl Lorraine (3 mentions)
U of Colorado, 1989 *Certification:* Surgery
9850 Genesee Ave #660, La Jolla, 858-452-5054

Orr, Carl Eric (3 mentions)
U of Colorado, 1985 *Certification:* Surgery
5565 Grossmont Center Dr #221, La Mesa, 619-462-8100

Paluch, Thomas Allen (3 mentions)
Loyola U Chicago, 1982 *Certification:* Surgery
4405 Vandever Ave, San Diego, 619-662-1222

Rajgopal, Ujwala (4 mentions)
FMS-India, 1989 *Certification:* Surgery
320 Santa Fe Dr #300, Encinitas, 760-753-5667

Rumsey, Eugene William, Jr. (4 mentions)
George Washington U, 1973 *Certification:* Surgery
4060 4th Ave #330, San Diego, 619-298-9931

Sanford, Arthur Hendrick (6 mentions)
Georgetown U, 1980 *Certification:* Surgery
10666 N Torrey Pines Rd, La Jolla, 858-455-9100

Sherman, Mark Jason (6 mentions)
U of California-San Diego, 1989 *Certification:* Surgery
9850 Genesee Ave #660, La Jolla, 858-452-5054

Steele, John Thomas (5 mentions)
Med U of South Carolina, 1987
Certification: Surgery, Surgical Critical Care
215 S Hickory St #112, Escondido, 760-489-5955

Stiles, Geoffrey Martin (4 mentions)
U of Southern California, 1985 *Certification:* Surgery
7910 Frost St #430, San Diego, 858-279-5599

Takata, Mark Christopher (6 mentions)
FMS-St Maarten, 2001 *Certification:* Surgery
10666 N Torrey Pines Rd, La Jolla, 858-455-9100

Tanaka, Elaine Galearmon (3 mentions)
U of California-San Diego, 1997 *Certification:* Surgery
10666 N Torrey Pines Rd, La Jolla, 858-455-9100

Tremblay, Laurier J., Jr. (15 mentions)
U of South Florida, 1980 *Certification:* Surgery
6699 Alvarado Rd #2210, San Diego, 619-286-0242

Zorn, George Griffith, III (8 mentions)
Loyola U Chicago, 1974 *Certification:* Surgery
4060 4th Ave #330, San Diego, 619-681-1933

Geriatrics

Bulow, Kwi Young Byun (4 mentions)
U of Chicago, 1984
Certification: Geriatric Medicine, Internal Medicine
3350 La Jolla Village Dr, San Diego, 858-552-8585

De Monte, Robert William (6 mentions)
Emory U, 1982
Certification: Geriatric Medicine, Internal Medicine
10666 N Torrey Pines Rd, La Jolla, 858-554-6158

Israel, Andrew Glenn (4 mentions)
Columbia U, 1976 *Certification:* Internal Medicine
4060 4th Ave #505, San Diego, 619-298-1318

Norcross, William Arthur (4 mentions)
Duke U, 1974 *Certification:* Family Medicine, Geriatric Medicine
330 Lewis St, San Diego, 619-543-6737

Hematology/Oncology

Andrey, Jeffrey William (6 mentions)
Loyola U Chicago, 1991
Certification: Hematology, Internal Medicine, Medical Oncology
15025 Innovation Dr, San Diego, 858-487-1800

Bemiller, Lynn S. (6 mentions)
Certification: Hematology, Internal Medicine, Medical Oncology
2929 Health Center Dr, San Diego, 858-499-2777

Bessudo, Alberto (4 mentions)
FMS-Mexico, 1989 *Certification:* Medical Oncology
477 N El Camino Real #C206, Encinitas, 760-452-3340

Bodkin, David James (4 mentions)
Georgetown U, 1984
Certification: Internal Medicine, Medical Oncology
5555 Grossmont Center Dr, La Mesa, 619-644-3030

Devitt, Jenny J. (5 mentions)
FMS-Canada, 1988 *Certification:* Medical Oncology
4647 Zion Ave, San Diego, 619-528-5000

Frakes, Laurie Ann (6 mentions)
FMS-Canada, 1991 *Certification:* Medical Oncology
477 N El Camino Real #C-204, Encinitas, 760-452-3340
161 Thunder Dr #106, Vista, 760-452-3340

Hampshire, Andrew Philip (4 mentions)
Ohio State U, 1997
Certification: Hematology, Internal Medicine, Medical Oncology
2929 Health Center Dr, San Diego, 800-827-4277

Just, Richard Gerald (7 mentions)
Rosalind Franklin U, 1967
Certification: Hematology, Internal Medicine, Medical Oncology
625 W Citracado Pkwy #110, Escondido, 760-747-8935

Kossman, Charles Richard (15 mentions)
U of Colorado, 1973
Certification: Internal Medicine, Medical Oncology
5555 Reservoir Dr #306, San Diego, 619-287-9910

Kossman, Steven Edward (7 mentions)
Tulane U, 1993 *Certification:* Hematology, Medical Oncology
5555 Reservoir Dr #306, San Diego, 619-287-9910

Kosty, Michael Paul (5 mentions)
George Washington U, 1979
Certification: Hematology, Internal Medicine, Medical Oncology
10666 N Torrey Pines Rd, La Jolla, 858-554-9559
15025 Innovation Dr, San Diego, 858-592-1312

Kroener, Joan Scheublein (4 mentions)
U of California-San Diego, 1976
Certification: Hematology, Internal Medicine, Medical Oncology
10666 N Torrey Pines Rd #MS-312, La Jolla, 858-554-8629

Lamon, Joel (10 mentions)
U of Southern California, 1973
Certification: Hematology, Internal Medicine, Medical Oncology
701 E Grand Ave #100, Escondido, 760-737-2666

Mason, James R. (5 mentions)
Certification: Internal Medicine, Medical Oncology
10666 N Torrey Pines Rd #MF-312, La Jolla, 858-455-9100

Parker, Barbara Ann (7 mentions)
Stanford U, 1981
Certification: Internal Medicine, Medical Oncology
3855 Health Sciences Dr #0987, La Jolla, 858-822-6100

Paroly, Warren Steven (4 mentions)
U of Cincinnati, 1972
Certification: Internal Medicine, Medical Oncology
3925 Waring Rd #C, Oceanside, 760-758-5770

Polikoff, Jonathan A. (4 mentions)
Albany Med Coll, 1977
Certification: Hematology, Internal Medicine, Medical Oncology
4647 Zion Ave, San Diego, 877-236-0333

Saleh, Alfred (5 mentions)
Albany Med Coll, 1975
Certification: Internal Medicine, Medical Oncology
3075 Health Center Dr #102, San Diego, 858-637-7888

Saven, Alan (5 mentions)
FMS-South Africa, 1982
Certification: Internal Medicine, Medical Oncology
10666 N Torrey Pines Rd, La Jolla, 858-455-9100

Shiftan, Thomas A. (6 mentions)
Certification: Hematology, Internal Medicine, Medical Oncology
3075 Health Center Dr #102, San Diego, 858-637-7888

Stanton, William, III (10 mentions)
Washington U, 1970
4033 3rd Ave #300, San Diego, 619-299-2570

Wilkinson, John R. (4 mentions)
U of Southern California, 1982
Certification: Hematology, Internal Medicine, Medical Oncology
5555 Reservoir Dr #306, San Diego, 619-287-9910

Infectious Disease

Ballon-Landa, Gonzalo R. (11 mentions)
Northwestern U, 1977
Certification: Infectious Disease, Internal Medicine
4136 Bachman Pl, San Diego, 619-298-1443

Bradley, John Scott (15 mentions)
U of California-Davis, 1976
Certification: Pediatric Infectious Diseases, Pediatrics
3020 Children's Way, San Diego, 858-495-7785

Butera, Michael Lawrence (16 mentions)
SUNY-Downstate Med Coll, 1983
Certification: Infectious Disease, Internal Medicine
6699 Alvarado Rd #2308, San Diego, 619-462-9010

Cabinian, Antonio E. (7 mentions)
FMS-Philippines, 1980
Certification: Infectious Disease, Internal Medicine
3400 E 8th St #107, National City, 619-267-0200

Chinn, Raymond Yau Wong (11 mentions)
U of Texas-Houston, 1973
Certification: Infectious Disease, Internal Medicine
7910 Frost St #320, San Diego, 858-292-4211

Higginbottom, Philip A. (13 mentions)
Columbia U, 1974
Certification: Infectious Disease, Internal Medicine
10666 N Torrey Pines Rd, La Jolla, 858-554-8096
200 W Arbor Dr #8201, San Diego, 858-554-8096
15025 Innovation Dr, San Diego, 858-554-8096

Kollisch, Nancy Ruth (7 mentions)
Johns Hopkins U, 1976
Certification: Infectious Disease, Internal Medicine
8008 Frost St #200, San Diego, 619-296-9883

Kuriyama, Steve Michael (13 mentions)
U of California-San Diego, 1980
Certification: Infectious Disease, Internal Medicine
122 Escondido Ave #101, Vista, 760-806-9263

Miller, Herman Howard, II (11 mentions)
9834 Genesee Ave #412, La Jolla, 858-457-8600

Miradi, Mohammed (8 mentions)
FMS-Iran, 1981
Certification: Infectious Disease, Internal Medicine
8851 Center Dr #310, La Mesa, 619-644-1483
5565 Grossmont Center Dr #3, La Mesa, 619-644-1483

Redfield, David Charles (21 mentions)
New York U, 1974 *Certification:* Internal Medicine
10666 N Torrey Pines Rd, La Jolla, 858-455-9100
15025 Innovation Dr, San Diego, 858-554-8005

Sawyer, Mark Harrison (7 mentions)
U of Chicago, 1980
Certification: Pediatric Infectious Diseases, Pediatrics
3020 Childrens Way, San Diego, 858-495-7785

Infertility

Hummel, William P. (13 mentions)
Tufts U, 1979 *Certification:* Obstetrics & Gynecology
11515 El Camino Real #100, San Diego, 858-794-6363

Kettel, L. Michael (9 mentions)
U of Arizona, 1983 *Certification:* Obstetrics & Gynecology,
 Reproductive Endocrinology/Infertility
11515 El Camino Real #100, San Diego, 858-794-6363

Morales, Arlene Joan (9 mentions)
Johns Hopkins U, 1986 *Certification:* Obstetrics &
 Gynecology, Reproductive Endocrinology/Infertility
8010 Frost St, San Diego, 858-505-5500

Rakoff, Jeffrey Steven (9 mentions)
Jefferson Med Coll, 1971 *Certification:* Obstetrics & Gynecology
10666 N Torrey Pines Rd, La Jolla, 858-554-8630

Internal Medicine *(see note on page 9)*

Abou, Paul Yousif (6 mentions)
FMS-Iraq, 1988
Certification: Clinical Pathology, Internal Medicine
5525 Grossmont Center Dr #609, La Mesa, 619-465-0711

Arnstein, Dayna Gene (5 mentions)
U of California-San Diego, 1989 *Certification:* Internal Medicine
3811 Valley Centre Dr, San Diego, 858-764-3000

Babikian, Gregory Phillip (3 mentions)
U of Kansas, 1992 *Certification:* Internal Medicine
3811 Valley Centre Dr, San Diego, 858-453-9200

Diamant, Joel Charles (3 mentions)
U of Illinois, 1990 *Certification:* Internal Medicine
10666 N Torrey Pines Rd, La Jolla, 858-554-7809

Ehlers, Rolf (4 mentions)
Case Western Reserve U, 1982 *Certification:* Internal Medicine
8765 Aero Dr #130, San Diego, 858-541-0181

Israel, Andrew Glenn (7 mentions)
Columbia U, 1976 *Certification:* Internal Medicine
4060 4th Ave #505, San Diego, 619-298-1318

Kobayashi, Gary Louis (3 mentions)
U of California-Los Angeles, 1985 *Certification:* Internal Medicine
145 Thunder Dr, Vista, 760-630-5464

Kornblit, Murray Jack (3 mentions)
FMS-Belgium, 1975
6386 Alvarado Ct #310, San Diego, 619-229-5050

Le Levier, Jon Anton (3 mentions)
U of California-Los Angeles, 1977 *Certification:* Internal Medicine
2067 W Vista Way #200, Vista, 760-726-2180

Marino, John Benjamin, III (6 mentions)
SUNY-Downstate Med Coll, 1971 *Certification:* Internal Medicine
6386 Alvarado Ct #310, San Diego, 619-229-5050

Pasha, Sabiha (3 mentions)
FMS-Pakistan, 1991
Certification: Hospice and Palliative Medicine, Internal Medicine
555 E Valley Pkwy, Escondido, 760-739-2371
15721 Pomerado Rd, Poway, 858-485-6644

Phillips, William Blaine, Jr. (3 mentions)
U of Pennsylvania, 1981
Certification: Endocrinology and Metabolism, Internal Medicine
310 Santa Fe Dr #111, Encinitas, 760-943-1923

Rathbun, Brent Eugene (3 mentions)
U of California-San Diego, 1994
Certification: Internal Medicine, Pediatrics
12710 Carmel Country Rd, San Diego, 858-794-3838

Sani, Armelia (4 mentions)
Dartmouth Coll, 1992 *Certification:* Internal Medicine
330 Lewis St, San Diego, 619-471-9250

Speckart, Paul Fredrick (5 mentions)
Tulane U, 1968
Certification: Endocrinology and Metabolism, Internal Medicine
3260 3rd Ave, San Diego, 619-297-3737

Tecca, Donald Phillip (3 mentions)
U of California-Irvine, 1980 *Certification:* Internal Medicine
7830 Clairemont Mesa Blvd, San Diego, 858-268-1111

Williams, Howard V. (5 mentions)
U of Southern California, 1982 *Certification:* Internal Medicine
4060 4th Ave #505, San Diego, 619-298-1318

Nephrology

Barager, Richard Russell (8 mentions)
U of Minnesota, 1981
Certification: Internal Medicine, Nephrology
3300 Vista Way #B, Oceanside, 760-967-9900

Baranski, Joel Justin (6 mentions)
Med Coll of Wisconsin, 1988
Certification: Internal Medicine, Nephrology
4060 4th Ave #220, San Diego, 619-299-2350

Boiskin, Mark Maurice (7 mentions)
FMS-South Africa, 1986
Certification: Internal Medicine, Nephrology
9834 Genesee Ave #112, La Jolla, 858-558-8150

Fadda, George Z. (12 mentions)
FMS-Lebanon, 1983 *Certification:* Internal Medicine, Nephrology
8851 Center Dr #304, La Mesa, 619-461-3880
5555 Reservoir Dr #207, San Diego, 619-287-0732

Friend, Peter Sayre (6 mentions)
U of Pennsylvania, 1969
Certification: Internal Medicine, Nephrology
9850 Genesee Ave #810, La Jolla, 858-453-9460

King, Andrew James (16 mentions)
Northwestern U, 1983
Certification: Internal Medicine, Nephrology
15025 Innovation Dr, San Diego, 858-487-1800

Lilley, John Joseph (7 mentions)
U of California-Los Angeles, 1970
Certification: Internal Medicine, Nephrology
625 E Grand Ave, Escondido, 760-745-1551
635 E Grand Ave, Escondido, 760-745-1551

Miller, Lucy M. (5 mentions)
FMS-Brazil, 1982 *Certification:* Nephrology
5555 Reservoir Dr #207, San Diego, 619-287-0732

Ramenofsky, James Alan (5 mentions)
Harvard U, 1976 *Certification:* Internal Medicine, Nephrology
3300 Vista Way #B, Oceanside, 760-967-9900

Shapiro, Mark Harry (6 mentions)
U of Pittsburgh, 1987
Certification: Internal Medicine, Nephrology
625 E Grand Ave, Escondido, 760-745-1551
635 E Grand Ave, Escondido, 760-745-1551

Steer, Dylan Lior (5 mentions)
Duke U, 1995 *Certification:* Nephrology
9850 Genesee Ave #810, La Jolla, 619-299-2350

Steinberg, Steven Marc (6 mentions)
New York Med Coll, 1968
Certification: Internal Medicine, Nephrology
4060 4th Ave #220, San Diego, 619-461-3880
7910 Frost St #220, La Mesa, 619-461-3880
8851 Center Dr #304, La Mesa, 619-461-3880

Stella, Frank Joseph (7 mentions)
Creighton U, 1969 *Certification:* Internal Medicine
5555 Reservoir Dr #207, San Diego, 619-287-0732

Neurological Surgery

Alksne, John Fergus (8 mentions)
U of Washington, 1958 *Certification:* Neurological Surgery
200 W Arbor Dr, San Diego, 619-543-5540

Altenau, Lance Luke (10 mentions)
U of Cincinnati, 1970 *Certification:* Neurological Surgery
752 Medical Center Ct #206, Chula Vista, 619-297-4481
2100 5th Ave #200, San Diego, 619-297-4481

Barba, David (7 mentions)
U of Southern California, 1979 *Certification:* Neurological Surgery
200 W Arbor Dr, San Diego, 619-543-5540
6645 Alvarado Rd, San Diego, 619-287-7661

Ghosh, Sanjay (10 mentions)
U of Michigan, 1995 *Certification:* Neurological Surgery
6645 Alvarado Rd, San Diego, 619-229-3105

Ostrup, Richard Cyrus (20 mentions)
U of California-Davis, 1979 *Certification:* Neurological Surgery
9850 Genesee Ave #770, La Jolla, 619-297-4481
2100 5th Ave #200, San Diego, 619-297-4481

Ott, Kenneth H. (11 mentions)
Certification: Neurological Surgery
2100 5th Ave #200, San Diego, 619-297-4481

Soumekh, Massoud Hertzel (8 mentions)
Certification: Neurological Surgery
8008 Frost St #401, San Diego, 858-560-8544

Uchiyama, Christopher M. (17 mentions)
U of Southern California, 1992 *Certification:* Neurological Surgery
15025 Innovation Dr, San Diego, 858-487-1800

Neurology

Braheny, Sherry Lee (7 mentions)
Tulane U, 1974 *Certification:* Neurology
8851 Center Dr #600, La Mesa, 619-589-6106

Chippendale, Thomas John (14 mentions)
U of California-Irvine, 1980 *Certification:* Neurology
320 Santa Fe Dr #108, Encinitas, 760-631-3000
3907 Waring Rd #2, Oceanside, 760-631-3000
6501 Coyle Ave, Carmichael, 916-537-5000

Delaney, Patrick Anthony (4 mentions)
St Louis U, 1987 *Certification:* Neurology
6645 Alvarado Rd #229, San Diego, 619-287-0147

Devor, William Nicholas (5 mentions)
U of California-San Francisco, 1980 *Certification:* Neurology
4405 Vandever Ave, San Diego, 619-528-5000

Evans, Sean Jeffrey (4 mentions)
U of California-San Diego, 2001 *Certification:* Neurology
200 W Arbor Dr, San Diego, 619-543-3500
6645 Alvarado Rd #229, San Diego, 619-287-0147

Gao, Er-Kai (5 mentions)
FMS-China, 1983 *Certification:* Neurology
8851 Center Dr #603, La Mesa, 619-667-4545

Gratianne, Roberto (4 mentions)
FMS-Mexico, 1980 *Certification:* Neurology
360 H St, Chula Vista, 619-585-7227

Hawkins, Randall Searle (5 mentions)
Yale U, 1976 *Certification:* Neurology
2001 4th Ave, San Diego, 858-499-2777
16950 Via Tazon, San Diego, 858-499-2600

Jablecki, Charles K. (12 mentions)
Harvard U, 1969
Certification: Clinical Neurophysiology, Neurology
550 Washington St #221, San Diego, 619-296-1234

Jackson, Christy M. (6 mentions)
U of Texas-Galveston, 1989 *Certification:* Neurology
10666 Torrey Pines Rd, La Jolla, 858-544-8896

Kalafut, Mary Ann (4 mentions)
Wayne State U, 1993 *Certification:* Neurology
15025 Innovation Dr, San Diego, 858-487-1800

Lobatz, Michael Allan (13 mentions)
U of Illinois, 1977 *Certification:* Neurology
320 Santa Fe Dr #205, Encinitas, 760-942-1390

Martin, Frederic Rene (4 mentions)
Yale U, 1983 *Certification:* Neurology
4060 4th Ave #208, San Diego, 619-298-0752

Nespeca, Mark Peter (9 mentions)
Case Western Reserve U, 1978 *Certification:* Neurology with Special Qualifications in Child Neurology, Pediatrics
625 W Kino Pkwy, Escondido, 960-737-0197

Otis, Shirley M. (4 mentions)
Tufts U, 1962
10666 N Torrey Pines Rd, La Jolla, 858-554-8892

Raffer, Paul Kenneth (5 mentions)
New Jersey Med Sch, 1972 *Certification:* Neurology
750 Medical Center Ct #13, Chula Vista, 619-421-6741

Romine, John Stanley (7 mentions)
U of Arkansas, 1969 *Certification:* Neurology
10666 N Torrey Pines Rd, La Jolla, 858-554-8799

Schim, Jack D. (4 mentions)
U of California-San Diego, 1981 *Certification:* Neurology
3907 Waring Rd #2, Oceanside, 760-631-3000
9850 Genesee Ave #220, La Jolla, 858-452-0996
320 Santa Fe Dr #108, Encinitas, 760-942-1390

Obstetrics/Gynecology

Barile, Vera Ann (3 mentions)
FMS-Mexico, 1983 *Certification:* Obstetrics & Gynecology
9333 Genesee Ave #170, San Diego, 858-882-8350

Barmeyer, Robert Allan (7 mentions)
U of California-San Diego, 1978
Certification: Obstetrics & Gynecology
2929 Health Center Dr, San Diego, 858-499-2702

Brody, Christine Z. (4 mentions)
U of California-Los Angeles, 1991
Certification: Obstetrics & Gynecology
2067 W Vista Way #225, Vista, 760-758-3000
477 N El Camino Real #A208, Encinitas, 760-758-3000

Deak, Pamela W. (4 mentions)
Virginia Commonwealth U, 1994
Certification: Obstetrics & Gynecology
200 W Arbor Dr Mail Code 8433, San Diego, 619-543-6777

Fenton, Douglas Kent (7 mentions)
U of Colorado, 1982 *Certification:* Obstetrics & Gynecology
2067 W Vista Way #225, Vista, 760-758-3000
477 N El Camino Real #A208, Encinitas, 760-758-3000

Goicoechea, Frank Javier (3 mentions)
U of California-San Francisco, 1978
Certification: Obstetrics & Gynecology
8851 Center Dr #408, La Mesa, 619-698-2212

Ho, Mylien Vu (5 mentions)
U of Nebraska, 1986 *Certification:* Obstetrics & Gynecology
5555 Reservoir Dr #205, San Diego, 619-286-5858

Hoppe, Diana Elizabeth (4 mentions)
U of California-San Diego, 1989
Certification: Obstetrics & Gynecology
317 N El Camino Real #306, Encinitas, 760-944-1000

Lee, Kirstin Anderson (5 mentions)
U of California-Los Angeles, 1988
Certification: Obstetrics & Gynecology
9850 Genesee Ave #600, La Jolla, 858-453-0753

McHugh, John Paul (3 mentions)
Harvard U, 1995 *Certification:* Obstetrics & Gynecology
1809 National Ave, San Diego, 619-515-2300

McNally, Colleen P. (6 mentions)
Northwestern U, 1988 *Certification:* Obstetrics & Gynecology
8010 Frost St #301, San Diego, 858-292-7200

Melin, June Dae (3 mentions)
U of Southern California, 1984
Certification: Obstetrics & Gynecology
3023 Bunker Hill St #205, San Diego, 858-581-0081

Miller, Christine B. (3 mentions)
U of Pittsburgh, 1992 *Certification:* Obstetrics & Gynecology
200 W Arbor Dr, San Diego, 619-543-6222

Mitchell, Dale Robert (4 mentions)
Georgetown U, 1982 *Certification:* Obstetrics & Gynecology
9333 Genesee Ave #170, San Diego, 858-882-8350

Moore, Thomas Richard (7 mentions)
Yale U, 1979
Certification: Maternal-Fetal Medicine, Obstetrics & Gynecology
9350 Campus Point Dr, La Jolla, 858-657-8745

Naponic, Mearl Aaron (3 mentions)
Temple U, 1966 *Certification:* Obstetrics & Gynecology
8851 Center Dr #500, La Mesa, 619-461-2660

O'Hara, Gary C. (4 mentions)
Certification: Obstetrics & Gynecology
2929 Health Center Dr, San Diego, 858-499-2702

Pattengill, Catherine (3 mentions)
U of Nevada, 1997 *Certification:* Obstetrics & Gynecology
4405 Vandever Ave, San Diego, 619-528-5000

Petersen, Sandra Rose (4 mentions)
U of Wisconsin, 1979 *Certification:* Obstetrics & Gynecology
4060 4th Ave #610, San Diego, 619-497-2430

Rodriguez, Madeline (3 mentions)
Boston U, 1984 *Certification:* Obstetrics & Gynecology
3998 Vista Way #C202, Oceanside, 760-758-1220

Saffer, Craig Sean (5 mentions)
FMS-South Africa, 1989 *Certification:* Obstetrics & Gynecology
7920 Frost St #401, San Diego, 858-277-9378

Willems, John Joseph (3 mentions)
New York Med Coll, 1973 *Certification:* Obstetrics & Gynecology
10666 N Torrey Pines Rd, La Jolla, 858-455-9100
3811 Valley Centre Dr, San Diego, 858-764-9080

Williams, Alisa Lynn (3 mentions)
U of Tennessee, 1985 *Certification:* Obstetrics & Gynecology
4060 4th Ave #640, San Diego, 619-299-3111

Ophthalmology

Brown, Stuart Irwin (3 mentions)
U of Illinois, 1957 *Certification:* Ophthalmology
200 W Arbor Dr, San Diego, 858-534-6290
9415 Campus Point Dr, La Jolla, 858-534-6290

Campbell, David Crawford (4 mentions)
U of Rochester, 1972
Certification: Internal Medicine, Ophthalmology
4060 4th Ave #405, San Diego, 619-297-9131

Chen, Paul Hongdze (4 mentions)
Harvard U, 1996 *Certification:* Ophthalmology
1905 Calle Barcelona #208, Carlsbad, 760-930-9696

Cook, Glenn Bradley (3 mentions)
U of California-Davis, 1987 *Certification:* Ophthalmology
5555 Reservoir Dr #300, San Diego, 619-286-9077
6501 Coyle Ave, Carmichael, 916-537-5000

Couris, Michael Theodore (3 mentions)
Georgetown U, 1992 *Certification:* Ophthalmology
3969 4th Ave #301, San Diego, 619-291-6191

Feldman, Sandy Tina (3 mentions)
Rush U, 1982 *Certification:* Ophthalmology
6255 Lusk Blvd #100, San Diego, 838-452-3937

Friedlaender, Mitchell H. (7 mentions)
U of Michigan, 1969 *Certification:* Ophthalmology
10666 N Torrey Pines Rd, La Jolla, 858-554-7996

Granet, David Bruce (3 mentions)
Yale U, 1987 *Certification:* Ophthalmology
9415 Campus Point Dr, La Jolla, 858-534-2020
200 W Arbor Dr, San Diego, 619-543-6244

Greider, Bradley William (5 mentions)
Stanford U, 1980 *Certification:* Ophthalmology
2067 W Vista Way #120, Vista, 760-758-2020

Groesbeck, Gary Dickson (3 mentions)
U of California-San Diego, 1982 *Certification:* Ophthalmology
780 Shadowridge Dr, Vista, 760-599-6466

Kikkawa, Don Osami (4 mentions)
St Louis U, 1987 *Certification:* Ophthalmology
9415 Campus Point Dr, La Jolla, 858-534-6290
200 W Arbor Dr, San Diego, 858-534-6290

Leung, Richard J. (3 mentions)
U of Maryland, 1981 *Certification:* Ophthalmology
8008 Frost St #407, San Diego, 858-278-9900
3075 Health Center Dr #403, San Diego, 858-278-9900

Linebarger, Eric John (3 mentions)
U of Utah, 1994 *Certification:* Ophthalmology
3075 Health Center Dr #401, San Diego, 858-939-5400

Lipson, Barry Kenneth (5 mentions)
U of Michigan, 1984 *Certification:* Ophthalmology
3075 Health Center Dr #401, San Diego, 619-699-1566
16950 Via Tazon, San Diego, 858-499-2600

Mannor, Geva (6 mentions)
Northwestern U, 1986 *Certification:* Ophthalmology
15025 Innovation Dr, San Diego, 858-487-1800

Morris, Jeffrey Bruce (3 mentions)
U of Texas-Houston, 1983 *Certification:* Ophthalmology
477 N El Camino Real #C202, Encinitas, 760-631-3500
3909 Waring Rd #B, Oceanside, 760-631-3500

Nanduri, Padma (3 mentions)
U of Rochester, 1994 *Certification:* Ophthalmology
9834 Genesee Ave #406, La Jolla, 858-450-1010

O'Halloran, Henry Swift (3 mentions)
FMS-Ireland, 1991 *Certification:* Ophthalmology
3030 Childrens Way #109, San Diego, 858-309-7702
625 W Citracado Pkwy #206, Escondido, 760-755-7600
477 NE Camino Real #302, Encinitas, 760-944-5545

Quiceno, Jose Ivan (3 mentions)
FMS-Colombia, 1983
10666 N Torrey Pines Rd, La Jolla, 858-554-7996
310 Santa Fe Dr, Ancinitas, 760-633-7020

Scotti, Frank Anthony (4 mentions)
New Jersey Med Sch, 1978 *Certification:* Ophthalmology
320 Santa Fe Dr #104, Encinitas, 760-943-7141

Smith, Mark David (3 mentions)
U of Southern California, 1984 *Certification:* Ophthalmology
550 Washington St #723, San Diego, 619-299-1554
3231 Waring Ct #S, Oceanside, 760-631-6144

Tornambe, Paul Edward (4 mentions)
Creighton U, 1972 *Certification:* Ophthalmology
12630 Monte Vista Rd #104, Poway, 858-451-1911

Treger, Paul Leslie (5 mentions)
SUNY-Upstate Med U, 1972 *Certification:* Ophthalmology
5555 Reservoir Dr #300, San Diego, 619-286-9077
6501 Coyle Ave, Carmichael, 916-537-5000

Yoo, Reuben Taekyu (3 mentions)
Tufts U, 1995 *Certification:* Ophthalmology
15025 Innovation Dr, San Diego, 858-487-1800

Zablit, K. Victor (3 mentions)
FMS-Lebanon, 1979 *Certification:* Ophthalmology
15004 Innovation Dr, San Diego, 858-487-1800

Zubyk, Nicholas Anton (5 mentions)
Georgetown U, 1974 *Certification:* Ophthalmology
3405 Kenyon St #513, San Diego, 619-226-1877

Orthopedics

Alleyne, Neville (5 mentions)
Mount Sinai Sch of Med, 1983
3905 Waring Rd, Oceanside, 760-724-9000

Amory, David William, Jr. (3 mentions)
Tulane U, 1991 *Certification:* Orthopaedic Surgery
3998 Vista Way #B, Oceanside, 760-724-5173

Averill, Robert McMath, Jr. (4 mentions)
Cornell U, 1970 *Certification:* Orthopaedic Surgery
4060 4th Ave #700, San Diego, 619-299-8500

Bentley, Christian Derek (3 mentions)
Rush U, 1994 *Certification:* Orthopaedic Surgery
3998 Vista Way #B, Oceanside, 760-724-5173

Brown, Richard Alan (3 mentions)
Duke U, 1985
Certification: Orthopaedic Surgery, Surgery of the Hand
9850 Genesee Ave #210, La Jolla, 858-535-1075

Bruffey, James Douglas (5 mentions)
Ohio State U, 1994 *Certification:* Orthopaedic Surgery
10666 N Torrey Pines Rd, La Jolla, 858-554-5330
310 Santa Fe Dr, Encinitas, 760-753-5594

Bugbee, William Dick (3 mentions)
U of California-San Diego, 1988
Certification: Orthopaedic Surgery
10666 N Torrey Pines Rd, La Jolla, 858-554-7993
3811 Valley Centre Dr, San Diego, 858-764-3331

Cooperman, Andrew Martin (3 mentions)
U of California-San Diego, 1984
Certification: Orthopaedic Sports Medicine, Orthopaedic Surgery
2023 W Vista Way #B, Vista, 760-726-5800

Copp, Steven Norris (6 mentions)
U of California-San Diego, 1983
Certification: Orthopaedic Surgery
10666 N Torrey Pines Rd, La Jolla, 858-554-8519
7425 Mission Valley Rd #200, San Diego, 858-268-9500

Davidson, William Howard (4 mentions)
Cornell U, 1969 *Certification:* Orthopaedic Surgery
4060 4th Ave #700, San Diego, 619-299-8500

Fait, James Michael (3 mentions)
U of California-Davis, 1996 *Certification:* Orthopaedic Surgery
4405 Vandever Ave, San Diego, 619-528-5000

Finkenberg, John Glenn (3 mentions)
U of California-Los Angeles, 1984
Certification: Orthopaedic Surgery
5555 Reservoir Dr #104, San Diego, 619-286-9480
6501 Coyle Ave, Carmichael, 916-537-5000

Freeman, Roger Arnold, Jr. (4 mentions)
U of Kentucky, 1972 *Certification:* Orthopaedic Surgery
7485 Mission Valley Rd #103, San Diego, 858-277-9000

Fronek, Jan (8 mentions)
U of Rochester, 1978 *Certification:* Orthopaedic Surgery
10666 N Torrey Pines Rd, La Jolla, 858-554-9753

Garfin, Steven Robert (6 mentions)
U of Minnesota, 1972 *Certification:* Orthopaedic Surgery
9350 Campus Point Dr, La Jolla, 858-657-8200
200 W Arbor Dr, San Diego, 619-543-6312

Gelb, Robert Ira (3 mentions)
New York Med Coll, 1980 *Certification:* Orthopaedic Surgery
320 Santa Fe Dr #110, Encinitas, 760-943-6700

Hacker, Scott Alan (4 mentions)
U of California-Irvine, 1997 *Certification:* Orthopaedic Surgery
5555 Reservoir Dr #104, San Diego, 619-286-9480
6501 Coyle Ave, Carmichael, 916-537-5000

Hanson, Peter Bagley (7 mentions)
U of California-Irvine, 1986 *Certification:* Orthopaedic Surgery
5565 Grossmont Center Dr Bldg 3 #256, La Mesa, 619-462-3131

Heiser, Joel Martin (4 mentions)
U of California-Los Angeles, 1975
Certification: Orthopaedic Surgery
2023 W Vista Way #B, Vista, 760-726-5800

Jacobson, Mark David (3 mentions)
U of Southern California, 1989 *Certification:* Orthopaedic Surgery
5555 Reservoir Dr #104, San Diego, 619-286-9480
6501 Coyle Ave, Carmichael, 916-537-5000

Jankiewicz, Joseph John (4 mentions)
Georgetown U, 1985 *Certification:* Orthopaedic Surgery
2929 Health Center Dr, San Diego, 858-939-6504
525 3rd Ave, Chula Vista, 649-585-4320

Kaska, Serge Charles (3 mentions)
Dartmouth Coll, 1999 *Certification:* Orthopaedic Surgery
488 E Valley Pkwy, Escondido, 760-432-6311

Knutson, Thomas Ronald (9 mentions)
Loma Linda U, 1982 *Certification:* Orthopaedic Surgery
161 N Date St, Escondido, 760-743-4789

Lenihan, Michael Ryan (3 mentions)
U of Southern California, 1986 *Certification:* Orthopaedic Surgery
752 Medical Center Ct #201, Chula Vista, 619-421-3400
955 Lane Ave #200, Chula Vista, 619-421-3400

Miles, John William, II (3 mentions)
U of California-Davis, 1983 *Certification:* Orthopaedic Surgery
5525 Grossmont Center Dr, La Mesa, 619-644-6609

Newton, Peter Owen (3 mentions)
U of Texas-Dallas, 1987 *Certification:* Orthopaedic Surgery
3030 Children's Way #410, San Diego, 858-966-6789
3020 Childrens Way, San Diego, 858-966-6789

Sachs, Raymond Alan (3 mentions)
Loyola U Chicago, 1972 *Certification:* Orthopaedic Surgery
4647 Zion Ave, San Diego, 619-441-0067

Santore, Richard Felice (4 mentions)
U of Pennsylvania, 1975 *Certification:* Orthopaedic Surgery
7910 Frost St #200, San Diego, 858-278-8300

Sanzone, Anthony Gerard (3 mentions)
Loyola U Chicago, 1991 *Certification:* Orthopaedic Surgery
955 Lane Ave #200, Chula Vista, 619-421-4200
3760 Convoy St #114, San Diego, 619-421-4200

Schwartz, Alexandra K. (3 mentions)
U of California-Los Angeles, 1994
Certification: Orthopaedic Surgery
200 W Arbor Dr, San Diego, 619-543-5555

Selecky, Mark Thomas (3 mentions)
U of Pennsylvania, 1992 *Certification:* Orthopaedic Surgery
752 Medical Center Ct #201, Chula Vista, 619-421-3400
955 Lane Ave #200, Chula Vista, 619-421-3400

Skyhar, Michael John (5 mentions)
Oregon Health Sciences U, 1981
Certification: Orthopaedic Surgery
320 Santa Fe Dr #110, Encinitas, 760-943-6700

Swenson, F. Craig (3 mentions)
Georgetown U, 1980 *Certification:* Orthopaedic Surgery
9850 Genesee Ave #210, La Jolla, 858-535-1075

Tonks, Robert Dean (3 mentions)
U of Texas-Houston, 1984 *Certification:* Orthopaedic Surgery
8010 Frost St #604, San Diego, 858-576-9901

Walker, Richard Hugh (4 mentions)
U of Chicago, 1977 *Certification:* Orthopaedic Surgery
10666 N Torrey Pines Rd, La Jolla, 858-455-9100

Wallace, Charles Douglas (3 mentions)
U of Michigan, 1988 *Certification:* Orthopaedic Surgery
3030 Childrens Way #410, San Diego, 858-966-6789

Wile, Peter Bartholomew (7 mentions)
U of Michigan, 1976 *Certification:* Orthopaedic Surgery
4060 4th Ave #700, San Diego, 619-299-8500

Otorhinolaryngology

Berry, Julie Ann (5 mentions)
U of California-San Diego, 1997 *Certification:* Otolaryngology
2023 W Vista Way, Vista, 760-726-2440

Fitzgerald, Patrick J. (6 mentions)
Georgetown U, 1993 *Certification:* Otolaryngology
15525 Pomerado Rd #C-1, Poway, 858-485-7870

Jimenez, Carlos Federico (6 mentions)
U of Puerto Rico, 1978 *Certification:* Otolaryngology
577 3rd Ave, Chula Vista, 619-426-5181

Keefe, Michael Arthur (6 mentions)
Case Western Reserve U, 1984 *Certification:* Otolaryngology
10670 Wexford St, San Diego, 858-499-2600

Lebovits, Marc Jeffry (10 mentions)
U of California-San Francisco, 1974 *Certification:* Otolaryngology
2023 W Vista Way #J, Vista, 760-726-2440

Magit, Anthony Edmund (8 mentions)
U of California-San Diego, 1985 *Certification:* Otolaryngology
317 N El Camino Real #501, Encinitas, 760-944-6377
3030 Children's Way #402, San Diego, 858-974-6700
625 W Citracado Pkwy #206, Escondido, 760-737-0197

Mahdavi, Mahmood (8 mentions)
FMS-Iran, 1967 *Certification:* Otolaryngology
9850 Genesee Ave #710, La Jolla, 858-458-9955

Mansfield, Perry Thomas (8 mentions)
FMS-Canada, 1987 *Certification:* Otolaryngology
6645 Alvarado Rd, San Diego, 619-229-4901

Miya, Gary Yuhei (7 mentions)
Creighton U, 1992 *Certification:* Otolaryngology
4060 4th Ave #410, San Diego, 619-298-7109

Pransky, Seth Marc (6 mentions)
Washington U, 1980 *Certification:* Otolaryngology
3030 Children's Way #420, San Diego, 858-966-4085
317 N El Camino Real #501, Encinitas, 858-966-4085
625 W Citracado Pkwy #206, Escondido, 858-966-4085
25485 Medical Center Dr #100, Murrieta, 951-600-1640

Saad, John Joseph (6 mentions)
FMS-Lebanon, 1979 *Certification:* Otolaryngology
10666 N Torrey Pines Rd, La Jolla, 858-455-9100

Tesar, Charles Berry (6 mentions)
U of New Mexico, 1978 *Certification:* Otolaryngology
2929 Health Center Dr, San Diego, 858-499-2702

Weeks, Brian Hunter (6 mentions)
U of Michigan, 1996 *Certification:* Otolaryngology
6645 Alvarado Rd #4000, San Diego, 619-229-4900

Weisman, Robert Alan (5 mentions)
Washington U, 1973 *Certification:* Otolaryngology
3855 Health Sciences Dr, La Jolla, 858-822-6100

Pain Medicine

Smith, Kevin Sanford (6 mentions)
Marshall U, 1986 *Certification:* Anesthesiology
7910 Frost St #280, San Diego, 619-398-2988

Wagner, Robert Lee, Jr. (6 mentions)
U of Southern California, 1978 *Certification:* Anesthesiology, Critical Care Medicine, Internal Medicine, Pain Medicine
9834 Genesee Ave #312, La Jolla, 858-453-7128

Wailes, Robert E. (10 mentions)
Wake Forest U, 1981 *Certification:* Anesthesiology, Pain Medicine
320 Santa Fe Dr #309, Encinitas, 760-753-1104
3998 Vista Way #C106, Oceanside, 760-941-7336

Wallace, Mark Steven (12 mentions)
Creighton U, 1987 *Certification:* Anesthesiology, Pain Medicine
9350 Campus Point Dr #C, La Jolla, 858-657-6082

Wilson, William Leroy (10 mentions)
Certification: Anesthesiology, Pain Medicine
8881 Fletcher Pkwy #360, La Mesa, 619-460-2700

Pathology

Bylund, David John (4 mentions)
Vanderbilt U, 1980 *Certification:* Anatomic Pathology & Clinical Pathology, Immunopathology
4077 5th Ave, San Diego, 619-260-7032

Kane, Edward (3 mentions)
Uniformed Services U of Health Sciences, 1985
Certification: Anatomic Pathology & Clinical Pathology, Cytopathology
10666 N Torrey Pines Rd MC 211C, La Jolla, 858-554-8605

Robin, Howard S. (3 mentions)
Certification: Anatomic Pathology & Clinical Pathology, Immunopathology
7901 Frost St, San Diego, 858-939-3660

Safrin, Richard Edward (6 mentions)
U of California-San Diego, 1980 *Certification:* Anatomic Pathology & Clinical Pathology, Medical Microbiology
6655 Alvarado Rd, San Diego, 619-229-3135

Sakas, Edward Lawrence (4 mentions)
U of Florida, 1975
10666 N Torrey Pines Rd, La Jolla, 858-455-9100

Spinosa, John Christopher (3 mentions)
U of California-San Diego, 1987
Certification: Anatomic Pathology & Clinical Pathology
9888 Genesee Ave, La Jolla, 858-626-6006

Steele, Julie Bridges (3 mentions)
St Louis U, 1995
Certification: Anatomic Pathology & Clinical Pathology
34800 Bob Wilson Dr, San Diego, 858-554-8605

Tench, William David (5 mentions)
Vanderbilt U, 1975 *Certification:* Anatomic Pathology & Clinical Pathology, Cytopathology
555 E Valley Pkwy, Escondido, 760-739-3037
15615 Pomerado Rd, Poway, 858-613-4000

Walker, Frederick Douglas (5 mentions)
Loyola U Chicago, 1974
Certification: Anatomic Pathology & Clinical Pathology
4647 Zion Ave, San Diego, 619-528-5393

Wilcox, Gary James (3 mentions)
U of Buffalo, 1973 *Certification:* Anatomic Pathology & Clinical Pathology, Blood Banking
4002 Vista Way, Oceanside, 760-940-3358

Pediatrics *(see note on page 9)*

Battey, Janet Maude (3 mentions)
U of California-San Diego, 1980 *Certification:* Pediatrics
15004 Innovation Dr, San Diego, 858-487-1800

Boies, Eyla Glee (4 mentions)
Washington U, 1978 *Certification:* Pediatrics
17824 Highlands Ranch Cir, Poway, 858-496-4800

Buchta, Richard Michael (6 mentions)
Loyola U Chicago, 1967 *Certification:* Pediatrics
3811 Valley Centre Dr, San Diego, 858-764-3000

Dalforno, Victor Michael (3 mentions)
Creighton U, 1969 *Certification:* Pediatrics
3230 Waring Ct #J, Oceanside, 760-941-4498

Feghali, Rita Jamil (3 mentions)
U of California-San Diego, 1998 *Certification:* Pediatrics
4405 Vandever Ave 2nd Fl, San Diego, 619-516-6170

Jacobson, Eugenia J. (3 mentions)
Certification: Pediatrics
7910 Frost St #335, San Diego, 858-576-8010

Kafka, John Abraham (4 mentions)
U of California-San Diego, 1977 *Certification:* Pediatrics
5525 Grossmont Center Dr, La Mesa, 619-644-6900
200 W Arbor Dr Frnt, San Diego, 619-644-6900

Karp, Michael William (3 mentions)
Northwestern U, 1987 *Certification:* Pediatrics
2067 W Vista Way #280, Vista, 760-941-3630

Mills, Suzanne (3 mentions)
U of Pittsburgh, 1982 *Certification:* Pediatrics
12395 El Camino Real #217, San Diego, 858-481-1151

Sanford, Michelle Marie (3 mentions)
Michigan State U, 1983 *Certification:* Pediatrics
3811 Valley Centre Dr, San Diego, 858-764-3000

Snyder, Joel Myron (3 mentions)
U of Maryland, 1973 *Certification:* Pediatrics
6475 Alvarado Rd #120, San Diego, 619-583-6133

Spiegel, Ben Jeffrey (10 mentions)
U of California-San Diego, 1982 *Certification:* Pediatrics
3811 Valley Centre Dr, San Diego, 858-764-3000

Vu, Myloan Thi (3 mentions)
U of Nebraska, 1987 *Certification:* Pediatrics
5555 Reservoir Dr, San Diego, 619-582-9072

Walls, Richard Parker (4 mentions)
U of Southern California, 1979 *Certification:* Pediatrics
7300 Girard Ave #106, La Jolla, 858-459-4351

Weintraub, Gerald David (3 mentions)
Virginia Commonwealth U, 1970 *Certification:* Pediatrics
3230 Waring Ct #P, Oceanside, 760-806-5720

Wright, Wendy Kay (3 mentions)
Oregon Health Sciences U, 1987 *Certification:* Pediatrics
3020 Childrens Way, San Diego, 858-966-5841

Plastic Surgery

Arya, Jyoti (4 mentions)
Tulane U, 1994 *Certification:* Surgery
10666 N Torrey Pines Rd MS 115, La Jolla, 858-554-9940

Barttelbort, Scott Walter (4 mentions)
Southern Illinois U, 1979 *Certification:* Plastic Surgery
8929 University Center Ln #210, San Diego, 858-623-9394

Bolitho, Douglas Glynn (9 mentions)
FMS-South Africa, 1986
9834 Genesee Ave #311, La Jolla, 858-458-5100

Brahme, Johan Erik (5 mentions)
U of California-San Diego, 1981 *Certification:* Plastic Surgery
9850 Genesee Ave #130, La Jolla, 858-452-1981

Halls, Michael J. (9 mentions)
FMS-Canada, 1977
Certification: Plastic Surgery, Surgery of the Hand
6386 Alvarado Ct #330, San Diego, 619-286-6446

McCarthy, Lawrence Joseph (5 mentions)
Tufts U, 1967 *Certification:* Plastic Surgery
3927 Waring Rd #A, Oceanside, 760-758-1525

Rudolph, Ross (5 mentions)
Columbia U, 1966 *Certification:* Plastic Surgery, Surgery
10666 N Torrey Pines Rd, La Jolla, 858-455-9100
3811 Valley Center Dr, San Diego, 858-764-9040

Schneider, Gerald Lane (5 mentions)
U of Arizona, 1973 *Certification:* Plastic Surgery
10666 N Torrey Pines Rd, La Jolla, 858-554-9606

Psychiatry

Arnicar, Dolph J. (3 mentions)
George Washington U, 1982 *Certification:* Psychiatry
8899 University Center Ln, San Diego, 858-455-5040

Dupont, Renee Marie (6 mentions)
Tulane U, 1982 *Certification:* Psychiatry
1011 Devonshire Dr #D, Encinitas, 760-635-5631

Ettari, Charles Vincent (3 mentions)
U of Southern California, 1968 *Certification:* Psychiatry
9834 Genessee Ave #427, La Jolla, 858-552-8928

Nicolas, Fadi Joseph (3 mentions)
FMS-Syria, 1994 *Certification:* Psychiatry
7850 Vista Hill Ave, San Diego, 858-278-4110
765 3rd Ave #301, Chula Vista, 619-528-4600
7901 Frost St, San Diego, 619-528-4600

Pulmonary Disease

Bagheri, Kaveh (8 mentions)
FMS-Grenada, 1987 *Certification:* Critical Care Medicine,
Internal Medicine, Pulmonary Disease
8851 Center Dr #405, La Mesa, 619-589-2535

Brazinsky, Shari Anne (4 mentions)
Stony Brook U, 1988 *Certification:* Critical Care Medicine,
Internal Medicine, Pulmonary Disease
6699 Alvarado Rd #2308, San Diego, 619-462-9010

Burrows, Craig Mitchell (4 mentions)
SUNY-Upstate Med U, 1993 *Certification:* Critical Care
Medicine, Internal Medicine, Pulmonary Disease
488 E Valley Pkwy #314, Escondido, 760-489-1458
15611 Pomerado Rd #580, Poway, 760-489-1458

Chang, Jacqueline Anne (5 mentions)
Stanford U, 1993
Certification: Critical Care Medicine, Pulmonary Disease
10666 N Torrey Pines Rd, La Jolla, 858-455-9100

Corona, Frank Edward (7 mentions)
FMS-Mexico, 1971
Certification: Internal Medicine, Pulmonary Disease
3231 Waring Ct #D, Oceanside, 760-758-7402

Eisman, Scott A. (8 mentions)
U of Kansas, 1982 *Certification:* Critical Care Medicine,
Internal Medicine, Pulmonary Disease
6501 Coyle Ave, Carmichael, 916-537-5000

Elias, Darlene Joan (4 mentions)
U of California-San Francisco, 1980
Certification: Internal Medicine, Pulmonary Disease
15004 Innovation Dr, San Diego, 858-487-1800

Federman, Edward Charles (5 mentions)
SUNY-Upstate Med U, 1982 *Certification:* Critical Care
Medicine, Internal Medicine, Pulmonary Disease
6699 Alvarado Rd #2308, San Diego, 619-287-7991

Harrell, James Hatley, II (4 mentions)
U of California-Irvine, 1966 *Certification:* Internal Medicine
200 W Arbor Dr, San Diego, 619-543-6222

Hoffman, Deborah A. (4 mentions)
U of Miami, 1994 *Certification:* Critical Care Medicine,
Internal Medicine, Pulmonary Disease
2929 Health Center Dr, San Diego, 858-499-2777
16950 Via Tazon, San Diego, 858-499-2600
5525 Grossmont Center Dr, La Mesa, 619-644-6600

Lichter, Julian Phillip (5 mentions)
FMS-South Africa, 1973 *Certification:* Critical Care
Medicine, Internal Medicine, Pulmonary Disease
4033 3rd Ave #300, San Diego, 619-299-2570

McCaul, David Scott (8 mentions)
Baylor U, 1980
Certification: Internal Medicine, Pulmonary Disease
9850 Genesee Ave #780, La Jolla, 858-625-7200

Nielsen, Martin Moran (6 mentions)
U of California-Los Angeles, 1972 *Certification:* Critical Care
Medicine, Internal Medicine, Pulmonary Disease
3231 Waring Ct #L, Oceanside, 760-758-7474

Sarnoff, Robert Benjamin (17 mentions)
New York U, 1974
Certification: Internal Medicine, Pulmonary Disease
10666 N Torrey Pines Rd, La Jolla, 858-554-8862

Weiss, Marvin Cecil (6 mentions)
U of Chicago, 1979
Certification: Internal Medicine, Pulmonary Disease
4647 Zion Ave, San Diego, 877-236-0333

Ziolo, Karen M. (4 mentions)
New York Coll of Osteopathic Med, 1996 *Certification:* Critical
Care Medicine, Internal Medicine, Pulmonary Disease
4647 Zion Ave, San Diego, 619-528-5000

Radiology—Diagnostic

Ellison, Harry Peter (3 mentions)
Albert Einstein Coll of Med, 1974
Certification: Diagnostic Radiology
5565 Grossmont Center Dr #1, La Mesa, 619-460-4920

Lizerbram, Eric Keith (5 mentions)
U of Southern California, 1991 *Certification:* Diagnostic Radiology
477 N El Camino Real #A-102, Encinitas, 619-849-9729
3366 5th Ave, San Diego, 619-849-9729
2466 1st Ave, San Diego, 619-849-9729

Moreland, Stephen I., III (3 mentions)
Oregon Health Sciences U, 1984
Certification: Diagnostic Radiology
9850 Genesee Ave #110, La Jolla, 858-626-4270

O'Shaughnessy, Louise S. (5 mentions)
U of California-Los Angeles, 1981
Certification: Diagnostic Radiology
6386 Alvarado Ct #121, San Diego, 800-948-1998

Press, Gary Allen (5 mentions)
Washington U, 1980
Certification: Diagnostic Radiology, Neuroradiology
4647 Zion Ave, San Diego, 619-528-5000

Resnick, Donald Laurence (3 mentions)
Cornell U, 1966 *Certification:* Diagnostic Radiology
3350 La Jolla Village Dr, San Diego, 858-552-8585
10666 N Torrey Pines Rd, La Jolla, 858-552-8585

Rickards, Paul Jeffrey (3 mentions)
U of Southern California, 1993 *Certification:* Diagnostic
Radiology, Vascular & Interventional Radiology
488 E Valley Pkwy #100, Escondido, 760-739-5400
355 E Grand Ave, Escondido, 760-480-6519
15725 Pomerado Rd, Poway, 858-485-6500

Senac, Melvin Orian, Jr. (4 mentions)
Loma Linda U, 1977
Certification: Diagnostic Radiology, Pediatric Radiology
3020 Childrens Way, San Diego, 858-966-5861

Sobel, David Felix (3 mentions)
New York Med Coll, 1975
Certification: Diagnostic Radiology, Neuroradiology
10666 N Torrey Pines Rd, La Jolla, 858-455-9100

Taggart, Steven James (3 mentions)
U of New Mexico, 1982 *Certification:* Diagnostic Radiology
488 E Valley Pkwy #100, Escondido, 760-520-8500
321 W Mission Ave, Escondido, 760-739-3350
555 E Valley Pkwy, Escondido, 760-739-3350

Tartar, V. Marie (3 mentions)
U of Arizona, 1986 *Certification:* Diagnostic Radiology
10666 N Torrey Pines Rd, La Jolla, 858-455-9100

Varney, Robert Ralph (3 mentions)
Duke U, 1979 *Certification:* Diagnostic Radiology, Internal
Medicine, Neuroradiology, Vascular & Interventional Radiology
320 Santa Fe Dr #LL8, Encinitas, 760-633-7770
7301 Girard Ave #B, La Jolla, 848-454-4235
4150 Regents Park Row #195, La Jolla, 858-622-6464
9888 Genesee Ave, La Jolla, 858-626-4270
10150 Sorrento Valley Rd #320, San Diego, 858-454-4235

Yang, Peter J. (6 mentions)
U of Buffalo, 1980 *Certification:* Diagnostic Radiology
5565 Grossmont Center Dr #2-1, La Mesa, 619-460-4920
5555 Grossmont Center Dr, La Mesa, 619-465-0711
8881 Fletcher Pkwy #102, La Mesa, 619-465-0711

Radiology—Therapeutic

Gooding, Justin Mathias (3 mentions)
Georgetown U, 1992 *Certification:* Diagnostic Radiology,
Vascular & Interventional Radiology
3156 Vista Way #100, Oceanside, 760-547-8000

Hodgens, David Wayne (3 mentions)
Loma Linda U, 1976 *Certification:* Therapeutic Radiology
9888 Genesee Ave, La Jolla, 858-626-6864
916 Sycamore Ave, Vista, 858-616-6864

Knowles, Harry Joseph, Jr. (5 mentions)
Jefferson Med Coll, 1977 *Certification:* Diagnostic Radiology
10666 N Torrey Pines Rd, La Jolla, 858-455-9100

Moore, Brian Scott (3 mentions)
U of California-San Diego, 1988 *Certification:* Diagnostic
Radiology, Vascular & Interventional Radiology
5565 Grossmont Center Dr #1, La Mesa, 619-460-4920

Ponec, Donald J., Jr. (6 mentions)
U of California-San Diego, 1983 *Certification:* Diagnostic
Radiology, Vascular & Interventional Radiology
4002 Vista Way, Oceanside, 760-940-7470

Roberts, Anne Christine (3 mentions)
U of California-San Diego, 1982 *Certification:* Diagnostic
  Radiology, Vascular & Interventional Radiology
200 W Arbor Dr, San Diego, 619-543-3405
9300 Campus Point Dr, La Jolla, 858-657-6650

Schechter, Mark Steven (3 mentions)
Pennsylvania State U, 1979 *Certification:* Diagnostic
  Radiology, Vascular & Interventional Radiology
2466 1st Ave, San Diego, 619-849-9729
501 Washington St #510, San Diego, 619-849-9729
675 Camino De Los mares #101, San Clemente, 949-499-5344
12620 Monte Vista Rd #A, Poway, 858-487-9729

Tripuraneni, Prabhakar (7 mentions)
FMS-India, 1976 *Certification:* Therapeutic Radiology
10666 N Torrey Pines Rd #MSB-1, La Jolla, 858-554-2000

Zentner, Phillip Gregory (3 mentions)
Vanderbilt U, 1990 *Certification:* Radiation Oncology
751 Medical Center Ct, Chula Vista, 619-482-5851
5555 Grossmont Center Dr, La Mesa, 619-644-4500

Rehabilitation

Arcilla, Gerard Castro (3 mentions)
FMS-Philippines, 1979
Certification: Physical Medicine & Rehabilitation
6645 Alvarado Rd, San Diego, 619-326-0128

Esmaeili, Keyvan (4 mentions)
FMS-St Maarten, 1997
Certification: Physical Medicine & Rehabilitation
215 S Hickey #118, Escondido, 760-432-6644

Guzman, Oscar F. (3 mentions)
FMS-Bolivia, 1978
Certification: Physical Medicine & Rehabilitation
555 Washington St, San Diego, 619-684-4300

Hon, Roxanne (12 mentions)
FMS-Ireland, 1991
Certification: Physical Medicine & Rehabilitation
8851 Center Dr #6200, La Mesa, 619-697-7900

Rheumatology

Brion, Paul Harold (7 mentions)
New Jersey Med Sch, 1994 *Certification:* Rheumatology
2023 W Vista Way #H, Vista, 760-724-5800

Fox, Robert I. (6 mentions)
Certification: Internal Medicine
9850 Genesee Ave #810, La Jolla, 858-457-2023

Fronek, Zdenka (5 mentions)
U of Rochester, 1980
Certification: Internal Medicine, Rheumatology
8933 Activity Rd, San Diego, 858-653-6175

Kaplan, Roy Alan (12 mentions)
Yale U, 1972 *Certification:* Internal Medicine, Rheumatology
345 Saxony Rd #105, Encinitas, 760-753-7374

Nguyen, Katherine H. (6 mentions)
Certification: Internal Medicine, Rheumatology
202 Lewis St, San Diego, 619-293-0351
200 W Arbor Dr, San Diego, 619-543-5764

Nolan, Frank Joseph (8 mentions)
U of California-Los Angeles, 1973
Certification: Internal Medicine, Rheumatology
2023 W Vista Way #H, Vista, 760-724-5800

Pischel, Ken Donald (10 mentions)
Washington U, 1979
Certification: Internal Medicine, Rheumatology
10666 N Torrey Pines Rd, La Jolla, 858-554-8819

Sheets, Robert Miller (5 mentions)
Baylor U, 1974 *Certification:* Pediatric Rheumatology, Pediatrics
8110 Birmingham Way, San Diego, 858-966-8082
3020 Children's Way, San Diego, 858-966-8082

Skol, Edward Vanhuysen (5 mentions)
New York Med Coll, 1999
Certification: Internal Medicine, Rheumatology
10666 N Torrey Pines Rd, La Jolla, 858-554-5637

Williams, Gary William (5 mentions)
U of Iowa, 1973 *Certification:* Internal Medicine, Rheumatology
10666 N Torrey Pines Rd, La Jolla, 858-455-9100

Thoracic Surgery

Dilley, Ralph Brown (7 mentions)
Stanford U, 1959
Certification: Surgery, Thoracic Surgery, Vascular Surgery
10666 N Torrey Pines Rd, La Jolla, 858-554-8988

Lin, Yuan H. (8 mentions)
Certification: Thoracic Surgery
765 Medical Center Ct #216, Chula Vista, 619-421-1111
8851 Center Dr #200, La Mesa, 619-644-1154

Urology

Bridge, Stephen Stewart (8 mentions)
U of Texas-Houston, 1982 *Certification:* Urology
4060 4th Ave #310, San Diego, 619-297-4707

Brown, Scott Logan (6 mentions)
Rosalind Franklin U, 1993 *Certification:* Urology
8851 Center Dr #502, La Mesa, 619-828-1000

Cohen, Edward Steven (7 mentions)
U of California-Davis, 1984 *Certification:* Urology
9850 Genesee Ave #440, La Jolla, 858-453-5944
320 Santa Fe Dr #305, Encinitas, 760-436-4558

Friedel, William E. (5 mentions)
Albert Einstein Coll of Med, 1966 *Certification:* Urology
8851 Center Dr #502, La Mesa, 619-828-1000

Gaylis, Franklin David (8 mentions)
FMS-South Africa, 1980 *Certification:* Urology
8851 Center Dr #501, La Mesa, 619-697-2456

Hathorn, Robert Wesley (5 mentions)
U of Texas-Dallas, 1989 *Certification:* Urology
9834 Genesee Ave #421, La Jolla, 858-458-0099

Kane, Christopher Joseph (5 mentions)
Uniformed Services U of Health Sciences, 1989
Certification: Urology
200 W Arbor Dr, San Diego, 858-822-6187

MacIntyre, Ronald Charles (7 mentions)
Wayne State U, 1981 *Certification:* Urology
2929 Health Center Dr, San Diego, 619-939-6621

Masters, Robert Harrison (6 mentions)
U of Utah, 1962 *Certification:* Urology
3405 Kenyon St #504, San Diego, 619-226-8200

Naitoh, John (5 mentions)
U of California-San Diego, 1990 *Certification:* Urology
9850 Genesee Ave #440, La Jolla, 858-453-5944
320 Santa Fe Dr #305, Encinitas, 760-436-4558

Salem, Carol Elizabeth (5 mentions)
U of Southern California, 1991 *Certification:* Urology
4060 Fourth Ave #310, San Diego, 619-297-4707

Tran, Michael Quikhoa (5 mentions)
U of California-Los Angeles, 1993 *Certification:* Urology
15004 Innovation Dr, San Diego, 858-487-1800

Vapnek, Evan Michael (5 mentions)
SUNY-Downstate Med Coll, 1991 *Certification:* Urology
4033 3rd Ave #400, San Diego, 619-299-0670

Vascular Surgery

Dilley, Ralph Brown (11 mentions)
Stanford U, 1959
Certification: Surgery, Thoracic Surgery, Vascular Surgery
10666 N Torrey Pines Rd, La Jolla, 858-554-8988

Guzzetta, Vincent Joseph (10 mentions)
Med Coll of Wisconsin, 1970 *Certification:* Vascular Surgery
6719 Alvarado Rd #303, San Diego, 619-286-9311
6501 Coyle Ave, Carmichael, 916-537-5000

Sedwitz, Marc Maltaire (9 mentions)
Boston U, 1978 *Certification:* Surgery, Vascular Surgery
9850 Genesee Ave #560, La Jolla, 858-452-0306

San Francisco Bay Area

Including Alameda, Contra Costa, Marin, Napa, San Francisco, San Mateo, Santa Clara, Santa Cruz, Solano, and Sonoma Counties

Allergy/Immunology

Blessing-Moore, Joann (6 mentions)
SUNY-Upstate Med U, 1972 *Certification:* Allergy & Immunology, Pediatric Pulmonology, Pediatrics
780 Welch Rd #204, Palo Alto, 650-688-8480
101 S San Mateo Dr #311, San Mateo, 650-696-8236

Bocian, Robert Charles (6 mentions)
U of Illinois, 1987 *Certification:* Allergy & Immunology
795 El Camino Real, Palo Alto, 650-853-2981

Choy, Anita Carmen (7 mentions)
FMS-Australia, 1987 *Certification:* Allergy & Immunology
1101 Welch Rd #A2, Palo Alto, 650-322-3847

Cook, David Allen (13 mentions)
Tufts U, 1975 *Certification:* Allergy & Immunology, Pediatrics
130 La Casa Via #209, Walnut Creek, 925-935-6252

Davidson, Jeffrey Mitchell (4 mentions)
FMS-Canada, 1980
Certification: Allergy & Immunology, Internal Medicine
180 Montgomery St #2370, San Francisco, 415-433-6673
2100 Webster St #202, San Francisco, 415-433-6673

Giannini, Avraham V. (4 mentions)
FMS-Italy, 1968 *Certification:* Allergy & Immunology, Pediatrics
909 Hyde St #633, San Francisco, 415-346-8022

Kishiyama, Jeffrey Lee (4 mentions)
Creighton U, 1988 *Certification:* Allergy & Immunology
3329 Mission Dr, Santa Cruz, 831-479-6933
285 South Dr #1, Mountain View, 650-210-9292
2287 Mowry Ave #E, Fremont, 510-797-5555
4050 Moorpark Ave, San Jose, 408-243-2700

Leong, Russell Evan (6 mentions)
U of California-San Francisco, 1978 *Certification:* Pediatrics
3838 California St #108, San Francisco, 415-221-0320

Levenson, Toby (4 mentions)
Northwestern U, 1990 *Certification:* Allergy & Immunology
2287 Mowry Ave #E, Fremont, 510-797-5555
9360 No Name Uno #140, Gilroy, 408-848-1800
285 South Dr #1, Mountain View, 650-210-9292
4050 Moorpark Ave, San Jose, 408-243-2700

Mulligan, Michael Joseph (4 mentions)
U of California-San Diego, 1986
Certification: Allergy & Immunology
701 E El Camino Real, Mountain View, 650-934-7888

Orlowski, James Joseph (19 mentions)
New York Med Coll, 1977 *Certification:* Allergy & Immunology
270 International Cir Bldg 2N, San Jose, 408-972-3380

Reid, Michael John (4 mentions)
Oregon Health Sciences U, 1966
1100 Pear Tree Ln, Napa, 707-254-9337
369 Pine St #422, San Francisco, 415-788-4128

Rubinstein, Steven Wayne (9 mentions)
Case Western Reserve U, 1980
Certification: Allergy & Immunology, Pediatrics
701 E El Camino Real, Mountain View, 650-934-7888

Schultz, Nathan David (5 mentions)
Ohio State U, 1969
Certification: Allergy & Immunology, Pediatrics
130 La Casa Via Bldg 2 #209, Walnut Creek, 925-935-6252

Singh, Priti Gupta (11 mentions)
FMS-Zambia, 1978
Certification: Allergy & Immunology, Pediatrics
611 S Milpitas Blvd, Milpitas, 408-945-2650

Tam, Schuman (10 mentions)
Med Coll of Wisconsin, 1987
Certification: Allergy & Immunology, Internal Medicine
6850 Geary Blvd, San Francisco, 415-751-6800
1030 Sir Francis Drake Blvd, Kentfield, 415-460-6686

Wolfe, James Dennis (15 mentions)
U of California-San Francisco, 1972 *Certification:* Allergy & Immunology, Internal Medicine, Pulmonary Disease
4050 Moorpark Ave, San Jose, 408-243-2700
393 Blossom Hill Rd #315, San Jose, 408-281-7400
3329 Mission Dr, Santa Cruz, 831-479-6933

Anesthesiology

Andris, Joseph J. (3 mentions)
Philadelphia Coll of Osteopathic Med, 1976
Certification: Anesthesiology
99 Montecillo Rd, San Rafael, 415-444-2000

Bane, Brian Joseph (3 mentions)
Loyola U Chicago, 1985 *Certification:* Anesthesiology
99 Montecillo Rd, San Rafael, 415-444-2186

Chamberlin, Keith John (3 mentions)
Georgetown U, 1979 *Certification:* Anesthesiology
1537 4th St #136, San Rafael, 415-927-4070

Chassy, Joel Raymond (6 mentions)
FMS-Mexico, 1979 *Certification:* Anesthesiology
250 Hospital Pkwy, San Jose, 408-972-7000

Chen, Lily Heidi (4 mentions)
FMS-Canada, 1974 *Certification:* Anesthesiology
2450 Ashby Ave, Berkeley, 510-204-1526

Daly, Martha Yacoe (6 mentions)
U of Michigan, 1982 *Certification:* Anesthesiology
710 Lawrence Expy, Santa Clara, 408-236-6400

Eisler, Edward Allen (3 mentions)
Northwestern U, 1981 *Certification:* Anesthesiology
2333 Buchanan St 3rd Fl, San Francisco, 415-600-6325

Feld, Lawrence H. (3 mentions)
SUNY-Downstate Med Coll, 1980
Certification: Anesthesiology, Pediatrics
3700 California St 3rd Fl, San Francisco, 415-600-2059

Guglielmino, Gary Thomas (3 mentions)
Creighton U, 1978
Certification: Anesthesiology, Internal Medicine
2420 Camino Ramon #270, San Ramon, 925-543-0140

Holtzapple, Thomas P. (10 mentions)
U of Washington, 1986 *Certification:* Anesthesiology
700 Lawrence Expy, Santa Clara, 408-851-1000

Horn, Allan Jan (3 mentions)
U of California-San Francisco, 1980 *Certification:* Anesthesiology
3875 Telegraph Ave, Oakland, 510-547-2244

Hunter, Richard John (4 mentions)
U of California-San Francisco, 1976 *Certification:* Anesthesiology
795 El Camino Real, Palo Alto, 650-321-4121

Jaffe, Richard Andrew (3 mentions)
U of Miami, 1985 *Certification:* Anesthesiology
300 Pasteur Dr #H3580, Palo Alto, 650-723-6411

Lampe, George Henry (5 mentions)
Indiana U, 1980 *Certification:* Anesthesiology
718 University Ave #211, Los Gatos, 408-354-2114

Loftus, John Richard (7 mentions)
George Washington U, 1983 *Certification:* Anesthesiology
280 W MacArthur Blvd, Oakland, 510-752-1000

Morton, David Paul (6 mentions)
Stanford U, 1981 *Certification:* Anesthesiology
250 Hospital Pkwy, San Jose, 408-972-6164

Newswanger, David Warren (9 mentions)
U of California-Irvine, 1982 *Certification:* Anesthesiology
710 Lawrence Expy 2nd Fl #200, Santa Clara, 408-851-6020

Patel, Divyesh M. (5 mentions)
FMS-Canada, 1991 *Certification:* Anesthesiology
250 Hospital Pkwy, San Jose, 408-972-6164

Pearl, Ronald Gary (5 mentions)
U of Chicago, 1977 *Certification:* Anesthesiology, Critical Care Medicine, Internal Medicine
300 Pasteur Dr, Palo Alto, 650-723-5024

Rama, Arun Natesan (3 mentions)
Loyola U Chicago, 1992 *Certification:* Anesthesiology
700 Lawrence Expy #200, Santa Clara, 408-851-6020

Rummell, David Reese (5 mentions)
Oregon Health Sciences U, 1976 *Certification:* Anesthesiology
250 Hospital Pkwy, San Jose, 408-972-7188

Sorensen, Karl Marius (3 mentions)
Med Coll of Wisconsin, 1980 *Certification:* Anesthesiology
701 E El Camino Real, Mountain View, 650-404-8444

Yamaguchi, Lorna Yoshi (3 mentions)
Stanford U, 1977 *Certification:* Anesthesiology, Critical Care Medicine, Internal Medicine, Pulmonary Disease
250 Hospital Pkwy, San Jose, 408-972-7000

Yuan, San Shing (4 mentions)
SUNY-Buffalo, 1984 *Certification:* Anesthesiology
2440 Camino Ramon #260, San Ramon, 925-210-4599

Cardiac Surgery

Dharan, Murai (7 mentions)
Certification: Surgery, Thoracic Surgery
5401 Norris Canyon Rd #202, San Ramon, 925-973-9000

Flachsbart, Keith David (12 mentions)
U of Nebraska, 1971 *Certification:* Thoracic Surgery
2350 Geary Blvd 1st Fl, San Francisco, 415-833-3800

Hanley, Frank Louis, Jr. (10 mentions)
Tufts U, 1978 *Certification:* Thoracic Surgery
300 Pasteur Dr, Palo Alto, 650-724-2925

Morales, Rodolfo A. (7 mentions)
FMS-Mexico, 1968 *Certification:* Surgery, Thoracic Surgery
3803 S Bascom Ave #102, Campbell, 408-559-1018

Robbins, Robert Clayton (6 mentions)
U of Mississippi, 1983 *Certification:* Surgery, Thoracic Surgery
300 Pasteur Dr Faulk Bldg 2nd Fl, Palo Alto, 650-725-3828

Schwartz, Steven Michael (6 mentions)
U of California-Irvine, 1981 *Certification:* Thoracic Surgery
3803 S Bascom Ave #102, Campbell, 408-559-1018

Cardiology

Anderson, Edward Temple (4 mentions)
U of Pennsylvania, 1969
Certification: Cardiovascular Disease, Internal Medicine
1950 University Ave, East Palo Alto, 650-617-8100
2900 Whipple Ave #205, Redwood City, 650-363-5262

Ansari, Maria Niloofar (3 mentions)
U of Michigan, 1994 *Certification:* Cardiovascular Disease
2350 Geary Blvd, San Francisco, 415-833-2616

Argenal, Agustin John (7 mentions)
U of California-Davis, 1975
Certification: Cardiovascular Disease, Internal Medicine
2485 High School Ave #100, Concord, 925-671-0610

Bails, Richard Phipps (4 mentions)
U of California-San Francisco, 1971
Certification: Cardiovascular Disease, Internal Medicine
2450 Ashby Ave 2nd Fl, Berkeley, 510-204-1691

Bausback, Kurt Neil (4 mentions)
Stanford U, 1982
Certification: Cardiovascular Disease, Internal Medicine
2581 Samaritan Dr #202, San Jose, 408-358-3939

Benedick, Bruce Allan (3 mentions)
U of Utah, 1986
Certification: Cardiovascular Disease, Internal Medicine
1950 University Ave, East Palo Alto, 650-617-8100
2900 Whipple Ave #205, Redwood City, 650-363-5262

Berke, David Kenneth (3 mentions)
Columbia U, 1969 *Certification:* Cardiovascular Disease,
Internal Medicine, Interventional Cardiology
2287 Mowry Ave #D, Fremont, 510-797-9924

Bernstein, Daniel (3 mentions)
New York U, 1978 *Certification:* Pediatric Cardiology, Pediatrics
725 Welch Rd #B, Palo Alto, 650-497-8000

Blumberg, Robert Stephen (8 mentions)
U of California-San Francisco, 1971
Certification: Cardiovascular Disease, Internal Medicine
1150 Veterans Blvd, Redwood City, 650-299-2045

Brindis, Ralph G. (4 mentions)
Emory U, 1977 *Certification:* Cardiovascular Disease,
Internal Medicine, Interventional Cardiology
280 W MacArthur Blvd, Oakland, 510-752-6474

Brown, Michael Andrew (4 mentions)
Yale U, 1993
Certification: Cardiovascular Disease, Internal Medicine
1399 Ygnacio Valley Rd #11, Walnut Creek, 925-937-1770

Carlton, Timothy Alan (4 mentions)
U of California-San Francisco, 1976 *Certification:* Cardiovascular
Disease, Internal Medicine, Interventional Cardiology
365 Lennon Ln #210, Walnut Creek, 925-944-1100

Casey, Joseph M. (3 mentions)
Tufts U, 1972 *Certification:* Cardiovascular Disease,
Internal Medicine, Interventional Cardiology
2400 Samaritan Dr #200, San Jose, 408-369-7500

Chatterjee, Kamalendu K. (6 mentions)
FMS-India, 1956
Certification: Cardiovascular Disease, Internal Medicine
350 Parnassus Ave #300, San Francisco, 415-353-2873
505 Parnassus Ave, San Francisco, 415-353-2873

Daniels, Ethan Howard (4 mentions)
Rush U, 1981 *Certification:* Cardiovascular Disease,
Internal Medicine, Interventional Cardiology
710 Lawrence Expy 3rd Fl, Santa Clara, 408-851-3355

Edelen, John S. (5 mentions)
Columbia U, 1969 *Certification:* Cardiovascular Disease,
Internal Medicine, Interventional Cardiology
2450 Ashby Ave 2nd Fl, Berkeley, 510-204-1691

Gee, David Sam (4 mentions)
U of California-San Francisco, 1980
Certification: Cardiovascular Disease, Internal Medicine
1425 S Main St, Walnut Creek, 925-295-4000

Gee, Garwood (3 mentions)
U of California-San Diego, 1981 *Certification:* Cardiovascular
Disease, Internal Medicine, Interventional Cardiology
280 W MacArthur Blvd 2nd Fl, Oakland, 510-752-6474

Gershengorn, Kent N. (3 mentions)
SUNY-Buffalo, 1965
Certification: Cardiovascular Disease, Internal Medicine
2 Bon Air Rd #100, Larkspur, 415-927-0666
165 Rowland Way #103, Novato, 415-878-2910

Go, Mateo, Jr. (11 mentions)
Tulane U, 1977 *Certification:* Cardiovascular Disease,
Internal Medicine, Interventional Cardiology
270 International Cir Bldg 2N, San Jose, 408-972-6380
2425 Samaritan Dr, San Jose, 408-972-7107

Goldschlager, Nora B. Fox (4 mentions)
New York U, 1965
Certification: Cardiovascular Disease, Internal Medicine
1001 Potrero Ave #5G1, San Francisco, 415-206-8315

Hirschfeld, David Seth (4 mentions)
Harvard U, 1967
Certification: Cardiovascular Disease, Internal Medicine
2585 Samaritan Dr #303, San Jose, 408-358-3458

Hopkins, Greg (3 mentions)
3536 Mendocino Ave #200, Santa Rosa, 707-573-6166

Hu, Bob (3 mentions)
Stanford U, 1984
Certification: Cardiovascular Disease, Internal Medicine
87 Encina Ave, Palo Alto, 650-853-2975

Hu, Charlotte (5 mentions)
U of California-Los Angeles, 1978 *Certification:*
Cardiovascular Disease, Internal Medicine
270 International Cir Bldg 2N, San Jose, 408-972-6380

Hui, Peter Yeeman (10 mentions)
U of California-Los Angeles, 1982 *Certification:* Cardiovascular
Disease, Internal Medicine, Interventional Cardiology
2100 Webster St #516, San Francisco, 415-923-3006

Hunt, Sharon Ann (3 mentions)
Stanford U, 1972
Certification: Cardiovascular Disease, Internal Medicine
300 Pasteur Dr, Palo Alto, 650-498-6605

Jacobson, Lester Barry (6 mentions)
U of Chicago, 1967
Certification: Cardiovascular Disease, Internal Medicine
2340 Clay St #226, San Francisco, 415-923-3565

Karmarkar, Sushil Vasudeo (4 mentions)
Rush U, 1984 *Certification:* Cardiovascular Disease,
Internal Medicine, Interventional Cardiology
1425 S Main St, Walnut Creek, 925-295-4050

Kavanaugh, Patrick Eugene (10 mentions)
U of New Mexico, 1977
Certification: Cardiovascular Disease, Internal Medicine
2485 High School Ave #100, Concord, 925-671-0610

Kennedy, John Martin (3 mentions)
Brown U, 1992 *Certification:* Cardiovascular Disease
99 Montecillo Rd, San Rafael, 415-444-2000

Killebrew, Ellen Jane (3 mentions)
New Jersey Med Sch, 1965
Certification: Cardiovascular Disease, Internal Medicine
901 Nevin Ave, Richmond, 510-307-1585

Krishnaswami, Ashok (4 mentions)
FMS-India, 1990 *Certification:* Cardiovascular Disease
270 International Cir, San Jose, 408-972-6380

Lee, Albert Pok Hoy (4 mentions)
U of California-San Francisco, 1974 *Certification:* Cardiovascular
Disease, Internal Medicine, Interventional Cardiology
2250 Hayes St #204, San Francisco, 415-933-9100

Lee, Arthur Chin (3 mentions)
U of California-Davis, 1978 *Certification:* Cardiovascular
Disease, Internal Medicine, Interventional Cardiology
2425 Samaritan Dr, San Jose, 408-972-7107
710 Lawrence Expy, Santa Clara, 408-851-6727

Levin, Eleanor Gwen (7 mentions)
U of California-San Francisco, 1979
Certification: Cardiovascular Disease, Internal Medicine
710 Lawrence Expy, Santa Clara, 408-851-3355

Ludmer, Paul Louis (4 mentions)
U of California-San Francisco, 1980
Certification: Cardiovascular Disease, Internal Medicine
365 Hawthorne Ave #201, Oakland, 510-452-1345
106 La Casa Via #140, Walnut Creek, 925-274-2860

Mailhot, James (4 mentions)
Georgetown U, 1964
Certification: Cardiovascular Disease, Internal Medicine
2340 Clay St #525, San Francisco, 415-600-1099

Master, Robert Coleman (4 mentions)
Northwestern U, 1974
Certification: Cardiovascular Disease, Internal Medicine
701 E El Camino Real, Mountain View, 650-404-3300

Mead, R. Hardwin (5 mentions)
Stanford U, 1979 *Certification:* Cardiovascular Disease,
Clinical Cardiac Electrophysiology, Internal Medicine
1950 University Ave, East Palo Alto, 650-617-8100
2900 Whipple Ave #205, Redwood City, 650-363-5262

Morelli, Remo Lucio (5 mentions)
U of California-San Francisco, 1976
Certification: Cardiovascular Disease, Internal Medicine
1 Shrader St #600, San Francisco, 415-666-3220

Nathan, Mark David (5 mentions)
Brown U, 1976
Certification: Cardiovascular Disease, Internal Medicine
106 La Casa Via #140, Walnut Creek, 925-274-2860
5201 Norris Canyon Rd #220, San Ramon, 925-277-1900

Pathak, Anjali Sharma (3 mentions)
FMS-India, 1989
Certification: Cardiovascular Disease, Internal Medicine
39400 Paseo Padre Pkwy, Fremont, 510-248-3363

Podolin, Richard Alan (7 mentions)
Stanford U, 1979 *Certification:* Cardiovascular Disease,
Internal Medicine, Interventional Cardiology
1 Shrader St #600, San Francisco, 415-666-3220

Raskoff, William Jay (3 mentions)
Stanford U, 1970
Certification: Cardiovascular Disease, Internal Medicine
2350 Geary Blvd, San Francisco, 415-833-2616

Ricks, William Bassett (9 mentions)
Northwestern U, 1970
Certification: Cardiovascular Disease, Internal Medicine
2581 Samaritan Dr #202, San Jose, 408-358-3939

Roge, Claude Lucien-Louis (5 mentions)
FMS-France, 1973 *Certification:* Pediatric Cardiology, Pediatrics
710 Lawrence Expy 1st Fl #190, Santa Clara, 408-851-9894

Rosenfeld, Howard Michael (3 mentions)
Harvard U, 1988 *Certification:* Pediatric Cardiology, Pediatrics
747 52nd St, Oakland, 510-428-3380

Saba, Ziad S. (4 mentions)
FMS-Lebanon, 1987 *Certification:* Pediatric Cardiology, Pediatrics
747 52nd St, Oakland, 510-428-3380

Singh, Rajinder (3 mentions)
FMS-India, 1974 *Certification:* Cardiovascular Disease,
Internal Medicine, Interventional Cardiology
1667 Dominican Way #230, Santa Cruz, 831-464-3801

Sperling, David Charles (4 mentions)
Case Western Reserve U, 1970
Certification: Cardiovascular Disease, Internal Medicine
2 Bon Air Rd #100, Larkspur, 415-927-0666

St. Goar, Frederick Godley (4 mentions)
Harvard U, 1984 *Certification:* Cardiovascular Disease,
Internal Medicine, Interventional Cardiology
2660 Grant Rd, Mountain View, 650-969-8600

Stanger, Paul (3 mentions)
SUNY-Buffalo, 1961 *Certification:* Pediatric Cardiology, Pediatrics
400 Parnassus Ave 2nd Fl, San Francisco, 415-353-2008

Steimle, Anthony Edward (15 mentions)
U of California-San Francisco, 1989
Certification: Cardiovascular Disease, Internal Medicine
710 Lawrence Expy, Santa Clara, 408-851-3355

Tede, Nikola Hella (4 mentions)
George Washington U, 1990 *Certification:* Pediatric Cardiology
3700 California St #B-55, San Francisco, 415-600-0718

Vagelos, Randall H. (6 mentions)
Columbia U, 1983 *Certification:* Cardiovascular Disease,
Internal Medicine, Interventional Cardiology
300 Pasteur Dr #279, Palo Alto, 650-723-6406

Yee, Rupsa (3 mentions)
U of Pittsburgh, 1990 *Certification:* Cardiovascular Disease
2100 Webster St #516, San Francisco, 415-923-3006

Yeung, Alan Ching-Yuen (3 mentions)
Harvard U, 1984 *Certification:* Cardiovascular Disease,
Internal Medicine, Interventional Cardiology
300 Pasteur Dr #H2103, Palo Alto, 650-723-0180

Zaroff, Jonathan Gordon (3 mentions)
U of Chicago, 1992
Certification: Cardiovascular Disease, Internal Medicine
2350 Geary Blvd, San Francisco, 415-833-2616

Dermatology

Abuabara, Fuad (5 mentions)
Stanford U, 1979 *Certification:* Dermatology
701 E El Camino Real, Mountain View, 650-934-7676

Becker, Brad Alan (4 mentions)
U of California-San Francisco, 1989 *Certification:* Dermatology
3801 Howe St, Oakland, 510-752-1145

Becker, Edward V. (6 mentions)
Boston U, 1975 *Certification:* Dermatology
2255 Ygnacio Valley Rd #B1, Walnut Creek, 925-945-7005

Berger, Timothy George (3 mentions)
U of Texas-Southwestern, 1975
Certification: Dermatology, Dermatopathology
1707 Divisadero St 3rd Fl, San Francisco, 415-353-7800

Blumenkranz, Recia Kott (4 mentions)
U of Miami, 1981 *Certification:* Dermatology
1225 Crane St #102, Menlo Park, 650-323-0276

Bortz, Jeffrey Thomas (9 mentions)
U of Iowa, 1989 *Certification:* Dermatology
106 La Casa Via #240, Walnut Creek, 925-932-7704

Chan, Jennifer Marie (5 mentions)
Stanford U, 1996 *Certification:* Dermatology
701 E El Camino Real, Mountain View, 650-934-7676

Colby, Sara Louise (3 mentions)
Case Western Reserve U, 1978 *Certification:* Dermatology
2400 Samaritan Dr #203, San Jose, 408-369-5600

Crawford, Peggy Sue (3 mentions)
Northwestern U, 1973 *Certification:* Dermatology
450 6th Ave 3rd Fl, San Francisco, 415-833-2202

Cruciger, Quita Virginia (4 mentions)
U of Texas-Houston, 1979 *Certification:* Dermatology
2100 Webster St #428, San Francisco, 415-923-3115

Deneau, David G. (6 mentions)
Stanford U, 1970 *Certification:* Dermatology, Dermatopathology
795 El Camino Real, Palo Alto, 650-853-2982

Fiore, Michelle M. (3 mentions)
FMS-Canada, 1982 *Certification:* Internal Medicine
1010 Laurel St, San Carlos, 650-591-8501

Frieden, Ilona Josephine (9 mentions)
U of California-San Francisco, 1977
Certification: Dermatology, Pediatric Dermatology, Pediatrics
1701 Divisadero St 3rd Fl, San Francisco, 415-353-7800

Gellin, Gerald Alan (5 mentions)
New York U, 1958 *Certification:* Dermatology
3838 California St #805, San Francisco, 415-668-2400

Gorsulowsky, David C. (5 mentions)
Louisiana State U, 1980 *Certification:* Dermatology
39210 State St #218, Fremont, 510-790-0477

Greenberg, Joseph Harold (3 mentions)
U of Minnesota, 1967
Certification: Dermatology, Internal Medicine
500 Professional Center Dr #511, Novato, 415-897-9624
750 Las Gallinas Ave #205, San Rafael, 415-472-3903

Ho, Diana Quynhdao (3 mentions)
Tufts U, 1999 *Certification:* Dermatology
276 International Cir, San Jose, 408-972-3590

Howard, Renee Marie (10 mentions)
U of California-San Francisco, 1984
Certification: Dermatology, Pediatric Dermatology
5000 Civic Center Dr, San Rafael, 415-499-0100

Kaymen, Amelia Hewitt (3 mentions)
Rush U, 1981 *Certification:* Dermatology, Internal Medicine
3905 Sacramento St #303, San Francisco, 415-933-8490

Kim, Youn-Hee (4 mentions)
Stanford U, 1984 *Certification:* Dermatology
900 Blake Wilbur Dr #W0001, Palo Alto, 650-723-6316

Kwan, William Warren (3 mentions)
U of Southern California, 1990 *Certification:* Dermatology
360 Post St #1005, San Francisco, 415-217-3880

Lane, Alfred T. (10 mentions)
Ohio State U, 1973 *Certification:* Dermatology, Pediatrics
770 Welch Rd #300, Palo Alto, 650-723-6105

Magid, Morgan Lawrence (4 mentions)
Vanderbilt U, 1984 *Certification:* Dermatology
1661 Soquel Dr #E, Santa Cruz, 831-476-2444

Maurer, Toby Annette (3 mentions)
FMS-Canada, 1987 *Certification:* Dermatology
1569 Sloat Blvd #314, San Francisco, 415-353-9339

Melnikoff, Robert Michael (3 mentions)
FMS-Canada, 1958 *Certification:* Dermatology
2016 Forest Ave #5, San Jose, 408-286-4600

Menkes, Andrew Bernard (6 mentions)
FMS-Canada, 1974 *Certification:* Dermatology, Internal Medicine
2490 Hospital Dr #201, Mountain View, 650-962-4600

Morganroth, Greg Scot (3 mentions)
U of Michigan, 1990 *Certification:* Dermatology
525 South Dr #115, Mountain View, 650-969-5600

Parke, Pamela J. (7 mentions)
Northwestern U, 1975 *Certification:* Dermatology
710 Lawrence Expy #472, Santa Clara, 408-851-4650

Potozkin, Jerome Robert (3 mentions)
New York U, 1988 *Certification:* Dermatology
110 Tampico, Walnut Creek, 925-838-4900
911 San Ramon Valley Blvd #100, Danville, 925-838-4900

Rodan, Kathryn P. (3 mentions)
U of Southern California, 1983 *Certification:* Dermatology
3300 Webster St #1106, Oakland, 510-763-2662

Schmidt, Christopher Paul (3 mentions)
Georgetown U, 1984 *Certification:* Dermatology
15215 National Ave #204, Los Gatos, 408-356-2147

Schneider, Jeffrey S. (3 mentions)
New York U, 1977 *Certification:* Dermatology, Internal Medicine
99 Montecillo Rd, San Rafael, 415-444-2939

Shpall, Steven Neil (4 mentions)
U of Colorado, 1980 *Certification:* Dermatology
555 Castro St, Mountain View, 650-903-3000

Swengel, Steven Lloyd (14 mentions)
U of Illinois, 1976 *Certification:* Dermatology
276 International Cir 3rd Fl, San Jose, 408-972-3275
2440 Samaritan Dr #2, San Jose, 408-369-7100

Tuffanelli, Lucia R. (3 mentions)
Med Coll of Wisconsin, 1982 *Certification:* Dermatology
450 Sutter St #1306, San Francisco, 415-781-4083

Tun, Tin Tin (3 mentions)
Jefferson Med Coll, 1991 *Certification:* Dermatology
701 E El Camino Real, Mountain View, 650-934-7676

Yadav, Sandhya Eileen (9 mentions)
Northwestern U, 1987 *Certification:* Dermatology
710 Lawrence Expy 4th Fl #472, Santa Clara, 408-851-4650

Zipperstein, Kory James (3 mentions)
U of Kansas, 1987 *Certification:* Dermatology
450 6th Ave 3rd Fl, San Francisco, 415-833-2202

Emergency Medicine

Auerbach, Paul Stuart (4 mentions)
Duke U, 1977 *Certification:* Emergency Medicine
701 Welch Rd #C, Palo Alto, 650-723-6576

Birdsall, David Andrew (4 mentions)
Tulane U, 1994 *Certification:* Emergency Medicine
2540 East St, Concord, 925-674-2333

Bulloch, George Cook (6 mentions)
U of Illinois, 1972 *Certification:* Emergency Medicine
1150 Veterans Blvd, Redwood City, 650-299-2200

Koscove, Eric Milton (3 mentions)
Cornell U, 1979
Certification: Emergency Medicine, Internal Medicine
710 Lawrence Expy, Santa Clara, 408-857-1000

Kutner, Charles Jay (3 mentions)
SUNY-Buffalo, 1983 *Certification:* Internal Medicine
250 Hospital Pkwy, San Jose, 408-972-6140

McLean, James Eugene (3 mentions)
U of Louisville, 1977 *Certification:* Emergency Medicine
280 W MacArthur Blvd, Oakland, 510-752-1190

Meharg, John Joseph (5 mentions)
Albany Med Coll, 1977
Certification: Emergency Medicine, Internal Medicine
170 Alameda De Las Pulgas, Redwood City, 650-367-5541

Ng, David Thien Saik (3 mentions)
Howard U, 1983
280 W MacArthur Blvd, Oakland, 510-752-1000

Peitz, Thomas John (4 mentions)
U of California-Los Angeles, 1990
Certification: Emergency Medicine
2333 Buchanan St, San Francisco, 415-600-3333

Rokeach, Michael Harvey (3 mentions)
U of Miami, 1973 *Certification:* Internal Medicine
2333 Buchanan St, San Francisco, 415-600-3333

Rooke, Christopher Thomas (3 mentions)
Eastern Virginia Med Sch, 1991
Certification: Emergency Medicine
2333 Buchanan St, San Francisco, 415-600-3333

Shikora, Stuart B. (3 mentions)
Hahnemann U, 1973
Certification: Emergency Medicine, Internal Medicine
2540 East St, Concord, 925-674-2333

Singh, Ramavtar (4 mentions)
FMS-India, 1976
Certification: Emergency Medicine, Internal Medicine
250 Hospital Pkwy, San Jose, 408-972-7000

Stuart, Pamela J. (3 mentions)
SUNY-Upstate Med U, 1986 *Certification:* Emergency Medicine
15585 Monterey St #B, Morgan Hill, 408-778-4684

Yellin, Marc Ben (3 mentions)
U of Southern California, 1983
Certification: Emergency Medicine
1555 Soquel Dr, Santa Cruz, 831-462-7710

Endocrinology

Alloo, Robert Gibson (6 mentions)
St Louis U, 1975 *Certification:* Internal Medicine
710 Lawrence Expy, Santa Clara, 408-851-1000

Ammon, Randall Allen (7 mentions)
Johns Hopkins U, 1976
Certification: Endocrinology and Metabolism, Internal Medicine
1 Country Club Plaza, Orinda, 925-254-3805

Basina, Marina (5 mentions)
FMS-Russia, 1987 *Certification:* Endocrinology, Diabetes,
and Metabolism, Internal Medicine
280 W MacArthur Blvd, Oakland, 510-752-1000

Buckingham, Bruce Alder (5 mentions)
U of California-San Diego, 1972
Certification: Pediatric Endocrinology, Pediatrics
14777 Los Gatos Blvd #200, Los Gatos, 408-356-0911

Cherlin, Richard S. (9 mentions)
Albert Einstein Coll of Med, 1972 *Certification:*
Endocrinology and Metabolism, Internal Medicine
15899 Los Gatos Almaden Rd #12, Los Gatos, 408-358-2663

Dowdell, Lynn Anne (14 mentions)
FMS-Canada, 1985 *Certification:* Endocrinology, Diabetes,
and Metabolism, Internal Medicine
260 International Cir Bldg 1N 2nd Fl, San Jose, 408-972-7000

Eng, Grace Siwah (5 mentions)
U of Michigan, 1999 *Certification:* Endocrinology, Diabetes,
and Metabolism, Internal Medicine
350 30th St #320, Oakland, 510-465-6700

Gaudiani, Linda Marie (5 mentions)
Boston U, 1976
Certification: Endocrinology and Metabolism, Internal Medicine
900 S Eliseo Dr #201, Greenbrae, 415-461-1780

Hsu, Frank Siu-Fung (5 mentions)
Baylor U, 1976
Certification: Endocrinology and Metabolism, Internal Medicine
21297 Foothill Blvd #102, Hayward, 510-538-4870

Jaffe, Marc Gregory (5 mentions)
Baylor U, 1988 *Certification:* Endocrinology, Diabetes, and
Metabolism, Internal Medicine
1200 El Camino Real, South San Francisco, 650-742-2100

Kan, Patricia Belle (15 mentions)
Albert Einstein Coll of Med, 1979
Certification: Endocrinology and Metabolism, Internal Medicine
260 International Cir Bldg 1N 2nd Fl, San Jose, 408-972-7000

Kaye, Todd Bradley (5 mentions)
U of California-San Francisco, 1986 *Certification:*
Endocrinology, Diabetes, and Metabolism, Internal Medicine
701 E El Camino Real, Mountain View, 650-934-7500

Kimmerling, George (8 mentions)
U of Illinois, 1970
Certification: Endocrinology and Metabolism, Internal Medicine
3838 California St #108, San Francisco, 415-221-7273

Misra, Pratima (5 mentions)
FMS-India, 1977
Certification: Pediatric Endocrinology, Pediatrics
276 International Cir, San Jose, 408-972-6137
710 Lawrence Expy, Santa Clara, 408-972-6137

Myers, E. Ann (6 mentions)
2250 Hayes St, San Francisco, 415-668-6767

Tyrell, James Blakely (5 mentions)
FMS-Canada, 1966
400 Parnassus Ave 5th Fl, San Francisco, 415-353-2350

Woeber, Kenneth Alois (5 mentions)
FMS-South Africa, 1957
Certification: Endocrinology and Metabolism, Internal Medicine
1600 Divisadero St #C-427, San Francisco, 415-885-7574
400 Parnassus Ave 5th Fl, San Francisco, 415-353-2350

Zlock, Douglas William (5 mentions)
Temple U, 1986 *Certification:* Endocrinology, Diabetes, and
Metabolism, Internal Medicine
2255 Ygnacio Valley Rd #A, Walnut Creek, 925-937-9984

Family Practice *(see note on page 9)*

Bishop, Barbara Muriel (4 mentions)
Northwestern U, 1973 *Certification:* Family Medicine,
Geriatric Medicine, Hospice and Palliative Medicine
1580 Valencia St #201, San Francisco, 415-550-0811

Hopkins, Joseph Richard (3 mentions)
Stanford U, 1973
Certification: Family Medicine, Geriatric Medicine
211 Quarry Rd 3rd Fl, Palo Alto, 650-723-6963

Kenessey, Bela Steven (3 mentions)
U of Southern California, 1989 *Certification:* Family Medicine
5601 Norris Canyon Rd #230, San Ramon, 925-277-1600

Lake, Roger Floyd (8 mentions)
Harvard U, 1976 *Certification:* Family Medicine
260 International Cir Bldg 1N, San Jose, 408-362-4791

Lim, Jocelyn G. (3 mentions)
Western U, 1988 *Certification:* Family Medicine
9460 No Name Uno #230, Gilroy, 408-842-1544

Mar, John Chune (6 mentions)
U of California-Davis, 1977
Certification: Family Medicine, Geriatric Medicine
280 Hospital Pkwy Bldg D, San Jose, 408-362-4791

O'Hanrahan, Tighe R. (4 mentions)
U of California-San Francisco, 1971
Certification: Family Medicine
120 La Casa Via #106, Walnut Creek, 925-934-5380

Pellegrin, James (3 mentions)
Case Western Reserve U, 1977 *Certification:* Family Medicine
143 E Main St, Los Gatos, 408-354-3920

Roth, Daniel Eli (6 mentions)
U of Southern California, 1982 *Certification:* Family Medicine
1 Shrader St #578, San Francisco, 415-876-5762

Shore, Lawrence Gleason (9 mentions)
Mount Sinai Sch of Med, 1978 *Certification:* Family Medicine
3838 California St #806, San Francisco, 415-386-5388

Suard, Thomas E. (3 mentions)
U of California-Los Angeles, 1982 *Certification:* Family Medicine
1155 Trancas St, Napa, 707-252-4781

Topkis, Brian F. (4 mentions)
Philadelphia Coll of Osteopathic Med, 1977
2021 Mt Diablo Blvd #100, Walnut Creek, 925-930-9978

Whitgob, Stephen John (4 mentions)
U of California-Davis, 1972 *Certification:* Family Medicine
2850 Telegraph Ave #130, Berkeley, 510-883-9883

Yu, Edward Mancheung (3 mentions)
U of California-Los Angeles, 1992 *Certification:* Family Medicine
701 E El Camino Real, Mountain View, 650-404-8370

Zimmer, James Kirk (4 mentions)
FMS-Canada, 1973
15066 Los Gatos Almaden Rd, Los Gatos, 408-377-9180

Gastroenterology

Ahn, Michael Sangwook (5 mentions)
U of Chicago, 1993 *Certification:* Gastroenterology
710 Lawrence Expy #248, Santa Clara, 408-236-6400

Augustyn, Damian Henry (4 mentions)
Harvard U, 1978
Certification: Gastroenterology, Internal Medicine
2100 Webster St #423, San Francisco, 415-923-3059

Balaa, Marwan (6 mentions)
FMS-Lebanon, 1979
Certification: Gastroenterology, Internal Medicine
2520 Samaritan Dr #201, San Jose, 408-402-9990

Berquist, William Eric (6 mentions)
Northwestern U, 1975 *Certification:* Pediatric
Gastroenterology, Pediatric Transplant Hepatology, Pediatrics
730 Welch Rd, Palo Alto, 650-736-7642

Burbige, Eugene John (9 mentions)
SUNY-Upstate Med U, 1970
Certification: Gastroenterology, Internal Medicine
2485 High School Ave #115, Concord, 925-686-1302

Fox, Jeffrey Mark (4 mentions)
U of California-San Diego, 1997
Certification: Gastroenterology, Internal Medicine
99 Montecillo Rd, San Rafael, 415-444-2000

Fung, Spencer T. (6 mentions)
U of California-San Diego, 1994 *Certification:* Gastroenterology
710 Lawrence Expy, Santa Clara, 408-851-2750

Gleghorn, Elizabeth Ellen (5 mentions)
Stony Brook U, 1980
Certification: Pediatric Gastroenterology, Pediatrics
747 52nd St, Oakland, 510-428-3058

Hargrave, Thomas B., III (5 mentions)
U of California-Los Angeles, 1979
Certification: Gastroenterology, Internal Medicine
3300 Webster St #312, Oakland, 510-444-3297

Heyman, Melvin Bernard (4 mentions)
U of California-Los Angeles, 1976
Certification: Pediatric Gastroenterology, Pediatrics
400 Parnassus Ave 2nd Fl, San Francisco, 415-476-5892

Hurwitz, Alfred Lewis (8 mentions)
Harvard U, 1967
Certification: Gastroenterology, Internal Medicine
455 O'Connor Dr #350, San Jose, 408-294-4272

Keledjian, Varujan Arek (4 mentions)
FMS-Armenia, 1981
Certification: Gastroenterology, Internal Medicine
2222 East St #300, Concord, 925-682-7730
3903 Lone Tree Way #205, Antioch, 925-754-8710

Kung, Henry I-Tsai (6 mentions)
SUNY-Downstate Med Coll, 1976 *Certification:*
Gastroenterology, Internal Medicine
120 La Casa Via #107, Walnut Creek, 925-945-6070

Man, Kevin Michael (6 mentions)
Med Coll of Wisconsin, 1988
Certification: Gastroenterology, Internal Medicine
450 Sutter St #1203, San Francisco, 415-362-3336

Marcus, Samuel Neal (4 mentions)
FMS-United Kingdom, 1977 *Certification:* Gastroenterology
2490 Hospital Dr #211, Mountain View, 650-988-7488

Melnick, Jane Susan (11 mentions)
U of California-San Francisco, 1977
Certification: Gastroenterology, Internal Medicine
2100 Webster St #423, San Francisco, 415-923-3577

Morton, Cynthia Jane (11 mentions)
U of Texas-Southwestern, 1983
Certification: Gastroenterology, Internal Medicine
280 W MacArthur Blvd, Oakland, 510-752-1282
901 Nevin Ave, Richmond, 510-307-3027

Nano, David John (9 mentions)
U of Southern California, 1981
Certification: Gastroenterology, Internal Medicine
701 E El Camino Real, Mountain View, 650-934-7575

Ready, Joanna Bernedette (19 mentions)
Med Coll of Wisconsin, 1984 *Certification:* Gastroenterology,
   Internal Medicine, Transplant Hepatology
710 Lawrence Expy 2nd Fl, Santa Clara, 408-851-2750

Shlager, Lyle Mark (7 mentions)
Tufts U, 1982 *Certification:* Gastroenterology, Internal Medicine
2238 Geary Blvd, San Francisco, 415-833-3514

Stein, David Emil (5 mentions)
Wayne State U, 1975
Certification: Gastroenterology, Internal Medicine
2440 Samaritan Dr #1, San Jose, 408-626-7375

Sundberg, Richard Alan (4 mentions)
Creighton U, 1974
Certification: Gastroenterology, Internal Medicine
3838 California St #416, San Francisco, 415-387-8800

Thenemann, Gordon James (10 mentions)
U of Minnesota, 1970
Certification: Gastroenterology, Internal Medicine
270 International Cir Bldg 2N, San Jose, 408-972-6530

Thurston, William Benjamin (4 mentions)
U of California-Los Angeles, 1972
Certification: Gastroenterology, Internal Medicine
270 International Cir Bldg 2N, San Jose, 408-972-6599

Verhille, Michael Scott (6 mentions)
U of Illinois, 1984
Certification: Gastroenterology, Internal Medicine
3838 California St #416, San Francisco, 415-387-8800

Young, Harvey S. (4 mentions)
Northwestern U, 1979
Certification: Gastroenterology, Internal Medicine
900 Welch Rd #103, Palo Alto, 650-324-8881

Zamani, Saeed (5 mentions)
FMS-Iran, 1983
Certification: Gastroenterology, Internal Medicine
112 La Casa Via #320, Walnut Creek, 925-939-5599

General Surgery

Abel, Michael Endre (6 mentions)
Case Western Reserve U, 1977
Certification: Colon & Rectal Surgery, Surgery
3838 California St #616, San Francisco, 415-668-0411
2100 Webster St #520, San Francisco, 415-923-3020

Badger, James T. (5 mentions)
U of California-Davis, 1985 *Certification:* Surgery
1101 Welch Rd #C9, Palo Alto, 650-321-8200

Banks, Edward Wallace (5 mentions)
Indiana U, 1975 *Certification:* Surgery
99 Montecillo Rd, San Rafael, 415-444-2950

Bertelsen, Carl Andrew (6 mentions)
U of Cincinnati, 1979 *Certification:* Surgery
2450 Samaritan Dr #1, San Jose, 408-358-1855

Bitar-Godfrey, Nancy A. (5 mentions)
U of Pennsylvania, 1983 *Certification:* Surgery
710 Lawrence Expy 2nd Fl, Santa Clara, 408-851-2000

Cassani, Carla Maria (6 mentions)
Stanford U, 1983 *Certification:* Surgery
701 E El Camino Real, Mountain View, 650-404-8400

Chavez, Annette (5 mentions)
Stanford U, 1984 *Certification:* Surgery
710 Lawrence Expy 2nd Fl, Santa Clara, 408-851-2000

De Boisblanc, Michael W. (5 mentions)
Tulane U, 1995 *Certification:* Surgery
365 Lennon Ln #250, Walnut Creek, 925-932-6330

Groeger, Eugene Carroll (5 mentions)
Creighton U, 1974 *Certification:* Surgery
2645 Ocean Ave #307, San Francisco, 415-239-2300

Gutman, Jeffrey John (8 mentions)
U of Nevada, 1982 *Certification:* Surgery
14850 Los Gatos Blvd, Los Gatos, 408-358-2868

Hiler, Kevin Richard (7 mentions)
U of Texas-Galveston, 1979 *Certification:* Surgery
1700 California St #550, San Francisco, 415-292-8999

Keny, Hemant Vasant (6 mentions)
U of Illinois, 1995 *Certification:* Surgery
280 Hospital Pkwy Bldg A, San Jose, 408-972-3100

Kerlin, Deborah Lynn (4 mentions)
U of California-Davis, 1983 *Certification:* Surgery
112 La Casa Via #340, Walnut Creek, 925-945-7600

Kutner, Susan Etta (15 mentions)
Stony Brook U, 1978 *Certification:* Surgery
280 Hospital Pkwy Bldg A, San Jose, 408-972-6010

Marks, Shelley Astrid (6 mentions)
Rosalind Franklin U, 1993 *Certification:* Surgery
795 El Camino Real #3E, Palo Alto, 650-853-2985

Moorstein, Bruce David (4 mentions)
Wayne State U, 1974 *Certification:* Surgery
350 30th St #430, Oakland, 925-284-3510
911 Moraga Rd #201, Lafayette, 925-284-3510

O'Neal, Kelly Careen (8 mentions)
U of California-Irvine, 1982 *Certification:* Surgery
280 W MacArthur Blvd, Oakland, 510-752-6405

Otero, Fernando Ruan (5 mentions)
U of California-San Diego, 1983 *Certification:* Surgery
365 Lennon Ln #250, Walnut Creek, 925-798-4606

Richards, Peter Cromwell (4 mentions)
George Washington U, 1975 *Certification:* Surgery
3838 California St #612-A, San Francisco, 415-221-0735

Roan, Ralph Roman (8 mentions)
Ohio State U, 1967 *Certification:* Surgery
3838 California St #610, San Francisco, 415-752-1001

Rolle, Thomas Mark (6 mentions)
U of California-Davis, 1980 *Certification:* Surgery
1425 S Main St, Walnut Creek, 925-295-4110

Rosas, Efren Escalante (21 mentions)
Stanford U, 1987 *Certification:* Surgery
280 Hospital Pkwy Bldg A, San Jose, 408-972-6010

Selivanov, Valerij (4 mentions)
Case Western Reserve U, 1973
280 Hospital Pkwy Bldg A, San Jose, 408-972-3100

Stanten, Steven Albert (11 mentions)
Georgetown U, 1982 *Certification:* Surgery
365 Hawthorne Ave #101, Oakland, 510-465-5523

Stevenson, John Michael (14 mentions)
U of California-Los Angeles, 1989 *Certification:* Surgery
710 Lawrence Expy 2nd Fl #286, Santa Clara, 408-851-2000

Strichartz, Seth Douglas (6 mentions)
U of California-Los Angeles, 1984 *Certification:* Surgery
701 E El Camino Real, Mountain View, 650-404-8400

Stricker, James William (4 mentions)
U of California-San Francisco, 1981
Certification: Colon & Rectal Surgery, Surgery
2238 Geary Blvd #2E, San Francisco, 415-833-3385

Walsh, Hugh Glynn (5 mentions)
U of Southern California, 1968 *Certification:* Surgery
455 O'Connor Dr #370, San Jose, 408-297-5775

Welton, Mark Lane (4 mentions)
U of California-Los Angeles, 1984
Certification: Colon & Rectal Surgery, Surgery
875 Blake Wilbur Dr #F, Palo Alto, 650-723-5461

Whang, Karen (4 mentions)
Temple U, 1994 *Certification:* Surgery
795 El Camino Real #3-E, Palo Alto, 650-853-2985

Yee, Laurence Franklin (5 mentions)
U of Pittsburgh, 1990
Certification: Colon & Rectal Surgery, Surgery
2100 Webster St #520, San Francisco, 415-923-3020
3838 California St #616, San Francisco, 415-668-0411

Geriatrics

Clark-Sayles, Catharine T. (3 mentions)
U of Colorado, 1979 *Certification:* Internal Medicine
1341S Eliseo Dr #100, Greenbrae, 415-464-8169

King-Angell, Joan L. (5 mentions)
U of California-San Francisco, 1985
Certification: Geriatric Medicine, Internal Medicine
3801 Howe St #4B, Oakland, 510-752-1000

Plonka, Edward Anthony (8 mentions)
U of California-Los Angeles, 1982 *Certification:* Internal Medicine
851 Fremont Rd #103, Los Altos, 650-941-8313

Pompei, Peter (4 mentions)
U of Chicago, 1977
Certification: Geriatric Medicine, Internal Medicine
300 Pasteur Dr #A175, Palo Alto, 650-723-6961

Sandoval-Perry, Julie L. (5 mentions)
U of California-San Diego, 1994
Certification: Geriatric Medicine, Internal Medicine
280 W MacArthur Blvd, Oakland, 510-675-5500

Teresi, Marci Jo (6 mentions)
Loyola U Chicago, 1987
Certification: Geriatric Medicine, Internal Medicine
710 Lawrence Expy, Santa Clara, 408-554-9800

Hematology/Oncology

Ayyar, Rajeshwari (8 mentions)
FMS-India, 1972
Certification: Hematology, Internal Medicine, Medical Oncology
710 Lawrence Expy 4th Fl, Santa Clara, 408-851-4323

Baer, David Matthew (6 mentions)
U of California-San Francisco, 1975
Certification: Internal Medicine, Medical Oncology
280 W MacArthur Blvd, Oakland, 510-752-6487
901 Nevin Ave, Richmond, 510-752-2325

Baron, Ari David (4 mentions)
Tufts U, 1990 *Certification:* Medical Oncology
2100 Webster St #225, San Francisco, 415-923-3012

Canales, Sandra (5 mentions)
Howard U, 1986 *Certification:* Medical Oncology
1150 Veterans Blvd, Redwood City, 650-299-4840

Cassidy, Michael J. (8 mentions)
Boston U, 1973
Certification: Internal Medicine, Medical Oncology
2001 Dwight Way, Berkeley, 510-204-1591

Cecchi, Gary R. (4 mentions)
Tufts U, 1979
Certification: Hematology, Internal Medicine, Medical Oncology
2001 Dwight Way, Berkeley, 510-204-6402

Cheng, David Shao Kong (4 mentions)
FMS-Canada, 1972
Certification: Internal Medicine, Medical Oncology
39275 Mission Blvd #203, Fremont, 510-791-1115

Feiner, Robert Howard (14 mentions)
New York Med Coll, 1975
Certification: Hematology, Internal Medicine
710 Lawrence Expy 4th Fl, Santa Clara, 408-851-4323

Fischetti, Michael Russel (4 mentions)
Albany Med Coll, 1970
Certification: Internal Medicine, Medical Oncology
710 Lawrence Expy, Santa Clara, 408-851-4323

Ganey, John T. (4 mentions)
Uniformed Services U of Health Sciences, 1982
Certification: Hematology, Internal Medicine, Medical Oncology
2700 Grant St #106, Concord, 925-687-2570
3220 Lone Tree Way #100, Antioch, 925-778-0679

Gordon, Peter W. (8 mentions)
Northwestern U, 1979
Certification: Internal Medicine, Medical Oncology
235 W MacArthur Blvd, Oakland, 510-752-1295
901 Nevin Ave, Richmond, 510-307-2325

Grant, Kathleen Marjorie (4 mentions)
U of Minnesota, 1970
Certification: Internal Medicine, Hematology, Medical Oncology
2100 Webster St #225, San Francisco, 415-923-3012

Hufford, Stephen Thomas (8 mentions)
U of Southern California, 1983
Certification: Hematology, Internal Medicine, Medical Oncology
3838 California St #707, San Francisco, 415-668-0160

Hung, Shaun S. J. (6 mentions)
FMS-Taiwan, 1978
Certification: Hematology, Internal Medicine, Medical Oncology
710 Lawrence Expy 4th Fl, Santa Clara, 408-851-4323

Kral, Juliet Marie (5 mentions)
U of Southern California, 1990 *Certification:* Internal Medicine
888 Oak Grove Ave #12, Menlo Park, 650-324-4400

Lewis, Bradley H. (7 mentions)
U of California-Los Angeles, 1979
Certification: Hematology, Internal Medicine
2001 Dwight Way, Berkeley, 510-204-1591

Mason, Joseph Edward (12 mentions)
U of Oklahoma, 1974
Certification: Internal Medicine, Medical Oncology
270 International Cir Bldg 2N, San Jose, 408-972-6560

Quock, Justin Poy (4 mentions)
Rosalind Franklin U, 1994
Certification: Internal Medicine, Medical Oncology
909 Hyde St #501, San Francisco, 415-398-5100
929 Clay St #207, San Francisco, 415-398-5100

Rubenstein, Martin Donald (7 mentions)
Stanford U, 1976 *Certification:* Hematology, Internal Medicine
50 E Hamilton Ave #200, Campbell, 408-376-2300

Rugo, Hope S. (4 mentions)
U of Pennsylvania, 1984
Certification: Internal Medicine, Medical Oncology
1600 Divisadero St #2, San Francisco, 415-353-7070

Sirott, Matthew Nelson (4 mentions)
Med Coll of Pennsylvania, 1986
Certification: Internal Medicine, Medical Oncology
400 Taylor Blvd #202, Pleasant Hill, 925-932-4567

Tai, Edmund Wing-To (6 mentions)
Albert Einstein Coll of Med, 1982
Certification: Internal Medicine, Medical Oncology
701 E El Camino Real, Mountain View, 650-934-7600

Venook, Alan Paul (5 mentions)
U of California-San Francisco, 1980
Certification: Hematology, Internal Medicine, Medical Oncology
1600 Divisadero St, San Francisco, 415-353-9888

Weisberg, Laurie Jane (5 mentions)
Stanford U, 1979
Certification: Hematology, Internal Medicine, Medical Oncology
1200 El Camino Real, South San Francisco, 650-742-2908

Wilson, Byron Eric (6 mentions)
Harvard U, 1990
20055 Lake Chabot Rd #130, Castro Valley, 510-888-0657
1999 Mowry Ave #H, Fremont, 510-794-5320

Yavorkovsky, Leonid Lazar (9 mentions)
FMS-Latvia, 1978
Certification: Hematology, Internal Medicine, Medical Oncology
270 International Cir, San Jose, 408-972-6560

Yu, Peter (6 mentions)
Brown U, 1980
Certification: Hematology, Internal Medicine, Medical Oncology
701 E El Camino Real, Mountain View, 650-934-7600

Infectious Disease

Armstrong, Robert Werner (16 mentions)
Stanford U, 1965
Certification: Infectious Disease, Internal Medicine
340 Dardanelli Ln #26, Los Gatos, 408-374-5340

Baxter, Roger Paul (13 mentions)
U of California-Los Angeles, 1984
Certification: Infectious Disease, Internal Medicine
3801 Howe St 3rd Fl, Oakland, 510-752-1275

Binstock, Peter David (7 mentions)
U of Oklahoma, 1980
Certification: Infectious Disease, Internal Medicine
365 Lennon Ln #200, Walnut Creek, 925-947-2334

Boggs, John Michael (7 mentions)
U of California-San Diego, 1984
Certification: Infectious Disease, Internal Medicine
795 El Camino Real, Palo Alto, 650-853-2977

Gordon, Shelley Merle (13 mentions)
Cornell U, 1979
Certification: Infectious Disease, Internal Medicine
2100 Webster St #400, San Francisco, 415-923-3883

Kemper, Carol Ann (9 mentions)
U of Minnesota, 1985
Certification: Infectious Disease, Internal Medicine
701 E El Camino Real, Mountain View, 650-934-7599

Lillo, Mark Robert (10 mentions)
Baylor U, 1983
Certification: Infectious Disease, Internal Medicine
710 Lawrence Expy 4th Fl, Santa Clara, 408-554-9800

Majumder, Sumit Kumar (10 mentions)
FMS-India, 1983
Certification: Infectious Disease, Internal Medicine
340 Dardanelli Ln #26, Los Gatos, 408-374-5340

Morozumi, Pius Anthony (8 mentions)
U of California-Irvine, 1974 *Certification:* Pediatrics
276 International Cir 1st Fl #C1, San Jose, 408-362-4740

Petru, Ann Margaret (7 mentions)
U of California-San Francisco, 1978
Certification: Pediatric Infectious Diseases, Pediatrics
747 52nd St, Oakland, 510-428-3336

Slome, Sally Bryna (7 mentions)
U of North Carolina, 1983
Certification: Infectious Disease, Internal Medicine
280 W MacArthur Blvd, Oakland, 510-752-1000

Stiller, Robert Lee (25 mentions)
U of Wisconsin, 1976
Certification: Infectious Disease, Internal Medicine
270 International Cir Bldg 2N, San Jose, 408-972-6530

Wasserman, Ronald Bret (10 mentions)
U of California-San Diego, 1984
Certification: Infectious Disease, Internal Medicine
365 Lennon Ln #200, Walnut Creek, 925-947-2334

Wiviott, Lory David (10 mentions)
Albert Einstein Coll of Med, 1982
Certification: Infectious Disease, Internal Medicine
2100 Webster St #400, San Francisco, 415-923-3883

Infertility

Adamson, G. David (6 mentions)
FMS-Canada, 1973 *Certification:* Obstetrics & Gynecology,
Reproductive Endocrinology/Infertility
540 University Ave #200, Palo Alto, 650-322-1900
2581 Samaritan Dr #302, San Jose, 408-356-5000

Chenette, Philip E. (5 mentions)
Indiana U, 1983 *Certification:* Obstetrics & Gynecology,
Reproductive Endocrinology/Infertility
55 Francisco St #500, San Francisco, 415-834-3000

Feigenbaum, Seth L. (4 mentions)
Northwestern U, 1983 *Certification:* Obstetrics &
Gynecology, Reproductive Endocrinology/Infertility
2238 Geary Blvd, San Francisco, 415-833-2000

Galen, Donald Issac (4 mentions)
U of Southern California, 1968
Certification: Obstetrics & Gynecology
1999 Mowry Ave #1, Fremont, 925-867-1800
3160 Crow Canyon Rd #150, San Ramon, 925-867-1800

Herbert, Carl Morse (4 mentions)
U of Florida, 1978 *Certification:* Obstetrics & Gynecology,
Reproductive Endocrinology/Infertility
55 Francisco St #500, San Francisco, 415-834-3000

Weckstein, Louis Norman (4 mentions)
U of Michigan, 1980 *Certification:* Obstetrics & Gynecology
3160 Crow Canyon Rd #150, San Ramon, 925-867-1800
1999 Mowry Ave #1, Fremont, 925-867-1800

Westphal, Lynn Marie (4 mentions)
Stanford U, 1987 *Certification:* Obstetrics & Gynecology,
Reproductive Endocrinology/Infertility
900 Welch Rd #350, Palo Alto, 650-498-7911

Internal Medicine *(see note on page 9)*

Bressler, David Ian (6 mentions)
U of California-Davis, 1980 *Certification:* Internal Medicine
2700 Grant St #200, Concord, 925-677-0500

Chase, Randolph Hugh (7 mentions)
Stanford U, 1973 *Certification:* Internal Medicine
3838 California St #608, San Francisco, 415-668-2851

Chaudhary, Rakesh Singh (3 mentions)
U of California-San Francisco, 1994
Certification: Internal Medicine
710 Lawrence Expy, Santa Clara, 408-554-9800

Clement, Michael John (3 mentions)
Oregon Health Sciences U, 1979 *Certification:* Internal Medicine
280 W MacArthur Blvd, Oakland, 510-752-1000

Endo, Paul Takeshi (4 mentions)
U of California-San Diego, 1976 *Certification:* Internal Medicine
106 La Casa Via #100, Walnut Creek, 925-280-8777

Frambach, Bruce Holbrook (3 mentions)
U of Southern California, 1982 *Certification:* Internal Medicine
260 International Cir Bldg 1N, San Jose, 408-972-7000

Gordon, Malcolm (8 mentions)
U of Southern California, 1978 *Certification:* Internal Medicine
280 Hospital Pkwy Bldg C, San Jose, 408-972-7000

Hom, Barbara Mah (3 mentions)
U of Michigan, 1981 *Certification:* Internal Medicine
320 Dardanelli Ln #25-B, Los Gatos, 408-370-7801

Lemon, F. Calvin (4 mentions)
Washington U, 1959 *Certification:* Internal Medicine
5601 Norris Canyon Rd #200, San Ramon, 925-277-3070

Maclean, Susan D. (3 mentions)
Stanford U, 1985 *Certification:* Internal Medicine
710 Lawrence Expy #272, Santa Clara, 408-236-4921

McPhee, Stephen Joseph (3 mentions)
Johns Hopkins U, 1977 *Certification:* Internal Medicine
400 Parnassus Ave 4th Fl, San Francisco, 415-353-4624

Naughton, James Lee (3 mentions)
Harvard U, 1972 *Certification:* Internal Medicine
2160 Appian Way #200, Pinole, 510-724-9110

Nguyen, Bien Dinh (3 mentions)
U of California-Davis, 1985 *Certification:* Internal Medicine
260 International Cir, San Jose, 408-972-7000

O'Keefe, Philip Joseph (4 mentions)
Loyola U Chicago, 1972 *Certification:* Internal Medicine
45 Castro St #138, San Francisco, 415-558-8200

Ogden, David Lanier (3 mentions)
Rosalind Franklin U, 1993
1341 S Eliseo Dr #100, Greenbrae, 415-464-8169

Parmer, William Brent (3 mentions)
Columbia U, 1972 *Certification:* Internal Medicine
3838 California St #305, San Francisco, 415-387-8805

Patton, Mary Gray (4 mentions)
U of California-San Francisco, 1983
Certification: Internal Medicine
280 W MacArthur Blvd, Oakland, 510-752-6497

Point, Cynthia Anne (3 mentions)
West Virginia U, 1985 *Certification:* Internal Medicine
3801 Sacramento St #100, San Francisco, 415-750-6510

Quinn, Geoffrey Cornelius (3 mentions)
Cornell U, 1992 *Certification:* Internal Medicine
3838 California St #600, San Francisco, 415-668-1147

Sinnott, James Scott (4 mentions)
U of Southern California, 1980
Certification: Critical Care Medicine, Internal Medicine
1033 3rd St, San Rafael, 415-444-2940

Souvignier, Douglas Louis (4 mentions)
U of California-Los Angeles, 1988 *Certification:* Internal Medicine
701 E El Camino Real, Mountain View, 650-934-7808

Strauss, William Larry (4 mentions)
U of Kansas, 1977 *Certification:* Geriatric Medicine,
  Hospice and Palliative Medicine, Internal Medicine
346 Rheem Blvd #105, Moraga, 925-376-5161

Sun, Sheryl Lamb (8 mentions)
U of California-San Francisco, 1985
Certification: Internal Medicine
710 Lawrence Expy 2nd Fl, Santa Clara, 408-554-9800

Tim, Leslie Susanchan (3 mentions)
U of California-San Diego, 1982 *Certification:* Internal Medicine
350 30th St #320, Oakland, 510-465-6700

Urman, Jeffrey David (3 mentions)
Cornell U, 1972 *Certification:* Internal Medicine, Rheumatology
555 Castro St, Mountain View, 650-903-3000

Wood, Scott Herring (4 mentions)
U of Florida, 1978 *Certification:* Internal Medicine
401 Burgess Dr, Menlo Park, 650-325-9955

Yamashita, Dale Tetsuo (5 mentions)
Northwestern U, 1981 *Certification:* Internal Medicine
710 Lawrence Expy 3rd Fl, Santa Clara, 408-554-9800

Yokoyama, Suzanne Emi (3 mentions)
U of Hawaii, 1986
260 International Cir Bldg 1N, San Jose, 408-362-4791

Nephrology

Curzi, Mario Paul (6 mentions)
Vanderbilt U, 1979 *Certification:* Internal Medicine, Nephrology
112 La Casa Via #210, Walnut Creek, 925-944-0351

Di Raimondo, Carol Rogers (5 mentions)
Vanderbilt U, 1980 *Certification:* Internal Medicine, Nephrology
112 La Casa Via #210, Walnut Creek, 925-944-0351

Feldman, Charles Alan (6 mentions)
Washington U, 1972 *Certification:* Internal Medicine, Nephrology
1190 Veterans Blvd Cypress Bldg #B, Redwood City,
  650-299-2015

Goldberg, David Arthur (4 mentions)
U of Wisconsin, 1970
Certification: Internal Medicine, Nephrology
3838 California St #305, San Francisco, 415-221-2112

Gottheiner, Toby I. (9 mentions)
FMS-South Africa, 1969
Certification: Internal Medicine, Nephrology
750 Welch Rd #214, Palo Alto, 650-328-8385

Haut, Lewis Lee (5 mentions)
Harvard U, 1973 *Certification:* Internal Medicine, Nephrology
2039 Forest Ave #301, San Jose, 408-998-8800

Karlinsky, Malcolm Lyle (7 mentions)
U of Illinois, 1973 *Certification:* Internal Medicine, Nephrology
2905 Telegraph Ave, Berkeley, 510-841-4525

Kasselik, Mark Juergen (4 mentions)
George Washington U, 1984
Certification: Internal Medicine, Nephrology
1580 Valencia St #806, San Francisco, 415-647-6660
2100 Webster St #405, San Francisco, 415-923-3456

Lambert, Mark Clawson (4 mentions)
Columbia U, 1969 *Certification:* Internal Medicine, Nephrology
1300 S Eliseo Dr #100, Greenbrae, 415-925-3075

Law, David (7 mentions)
FMS-Taiwan, 1984 *Certification:* Internal Medicine, Nephrology
280 W MacArthur Blvd, Oakland, 510-752-1000

Levy, Lawrence Allen (4 mentions)
Albert Einstein Coll of Med, 1970
Certification: Internal Medicine, Nephrology
1300 S Eliseo Dr #100, Greenbrae, 415-925-3075

Mazbar, Sami Albert (22 mentions)
FMS-Egypt, 1980 *Certification:* Internal Medicine, Nephrology
710 Lawrence Expy, Santa Clara, 408-851-4600

Oliver, Richard Eugene (4 mentions)
Baylor U, 1974 *Certification:* Internal Medicine
5720 Stoneridge Mall Rd #250, Pleasanton, 925-463-1680

Peters, William Allison (8 mentions)
U of California-San Francisco, 1976
Certification: Internal Medicine, Nephrology
275 Hospital Pkwy #600, San Jose, 408-972-6069

Ramaswamy, Deepa (16 mentions)
FMS-India, 1993 *Certification:* Internal Medicine, Nephrology
275 Hospital Pkwy #600, San Jose, 408-972-6069

Riordan, John W. (6 mentions)
U of Texas-Galveston, 1987 *Certification:* Nephrology
2100 Webster St #412, San Francisco, 415-923-3815

Tilles, Steven Mark (9 mentions)
U of California-Los Angeles, 1978
Certification: Internal Medicine, Nephrology
2505 Samaritan Dr #405, San Jose, 408-356-8133

Yao, Andrea Lee (4 mentions)
New Jersey Med Sch, 1996
Certification: Internal Medicine, Nephrology
27303 Sleepy Hollow Ave, Hayward, 510-784-2769

Zarghamee, Shahrzad S. (4 mentions)
Med Coll of Wisconsin, 1991 *Certification:* Nephrology
74 E El Camino Real 2nd Fl, Mountain View, 650-934-7400

Neurological Surgery

Adey, Geoffrey Robert (8 mentions)
U of Colorado, 1989 *Certification:* Neurological Surgery
1455 Montego Dr #200, Walnut Creek, 925-937-0404

Andrews, Brian Thomas (24 mentions)
U of California-San Francisco, 1981
Certification: Neurological Surgery
45 Castro St #421, San Francisco, 415-600-7760

Berger, Mitchell (8 mentions)
U of Miami, 1979 *Certification:* Neurological Surgery
400 Parnassus Ave #A808, San Francisco, 415-353-7500

Chen, Terence Ling (13 mentions)
Yale U, 1984 *Certification:* Neurological Surgery
1455 Montego Dr #200, Walnut Creek, 925-937-0404

Edwards, Michael Steven (8 mentions)
Tulane U, 1970 *Certification:* Neurological Surgery
730 Welch Rd, Palo Alto, 650-497-8775

Randall, Jeffrey Blaine (6 mentions)
U of Michigan, 1984 *Certification:* Neurological Surgery
20055 Lake Chabot Rd #110, Castro Valley, 510-886-3138

Rosario, Marshal Del (6 mentions)
U of Hawaii, 1975 *Certification:* Neurological Surgery
50 E Hamilton Ave #120, Campbell, 408-374-0401

Sheridan, William Francis (8 mentions)
U of California-Los Angeles, 1985
Certification: Neurological Surgery
1150 Veterans Blvd, Redwood City, 650-299-2290

Steinberg, Gary Kenneth (9 mentions)
Stanford U, 1980 *Certification:* Neurological Surgery
300 Pasteur Dr #R281, Palo Alto, 650-723-5575

Sun, Peter Peiyuan (6 mentions)
Columbia U, 1991 *Certification:* Neurological Surgery
744 52nd St #5203, Oakland, 510-428-3319

Tang, Gordon (6 mentions)
U of Southern California, 1993 *Certification:* Neurological Surgery
2510 Webster St #300, Berkeley, 510-841-8700

Weber, Peter Broun (11 mentions)
Emory U, 1986 *Certification:* Neurological Surgery
2100 Webster St #115, San Francisco, 415-885-8628

Weinstein, Philip Ralph (6 mentions)
New York U, 1965 *Certification:* Neurological Surgery
400 Parnassus Ave #A311, San Francisco, 415-353-2739

Welsh, Joseph E. (8 mentions)
Stanford U, 1975 *Certification:* Neurological Surgery
701 E El Camino Real, Mountain View, 650-404-8222

Neurology

Amgott-Kwan, Garrick P. (8 mentions)
Albert Einstein Coll of Med, 1986 *Certification:* Neurology
280 W MacArthur Blvd, Oakland, 510-752-6509

Andrews, Bret D. (5 mentions)
Michigan State U, 1996 *Certification:* Neurology
280 W MacArthur Blvd, Oakland, 510-752-1000

Bhandari, Rajan (11 mentions)
FMS-India, 1977 *Certification:* Neurology
275 Hospital Pkwy #800, San Jose, 408-972-6700

Cassini, Peter Craig (4 mentions)
Med Coll of Ohio, 1993 *Certification:* Neurology
1101 Welch Rd #C5, Palo Alto, 650-324-4300

Collins, Eric (4 mentions)
Certification: Addiction Psychiatry, Psychiatry,
  Psychosomatic Medicine
5401 Norris Canyon Rd #306, San Ramon, 925-277-0101
365 Hawthorne Ave #203, Oakland, 510-834-5778

Cooper, Joanna Anat (5 mentions)
FMS-Israel, 1975 *Certification:* Neurology
2850 Telegraph Ave #110, Berkeley, 510-849-0499

Culberson, Charles Gregory (7 mentions)
U of Illinois, 1974 *Certification:* Neurology
275 Hospital Pkwy #800, San Jose, 408-972-6700

Douville, Arthur W. (6 mentions)
U of Kansas, 1971 *Certification:* Neurology
14901 National Ave #202, Los Gatos, 408-356-7147

Greenwald, Leland Mark (6 mentions)
U of Southern California, 1986 *Certification:* Neurology
701 E El Camino Real, Mountain View, 650-934-7300

Hansen, Susan Ruth (7 mentions)
George Washington U, 1979 *Certification:* Neurology
2500 Hospital Dr Bldg 10, Mountain View, 650-691-1171

Hayward, Jean Constance (4 mentions)
U of North Carolina, 1982 *Certification:* Neurology with
  Special Qualifications in Child Neurology, Pediatrics
3505 Broadway Blvd Mosswood Bldg, Oakland, 510-752-7813

Hess, Jay Ronald (4 mentions)
U of Pennsylvania, 1972 *Certification:* Neurology, Neuropathology
701 E El Camino Real, Mountain View, 650-934-7300

Holtz, Steven J. (11 mentions)
Boston U, 1974 *Certification:* Neurology
108 La Casa Via #105, Walnut Creek, 925-939-9400

Kitt, Donald Conrad (10 mentions)
U of Southern California, 1982
Certification: Internal Medicine, Neurology
3838 California St #114, San Francisco, 415-751-7753

Lin, Janet Fraida (7 mentions)
New Jersey Med Sch, 1977 *Certification:* Neurology
108 La Casa Via #105, Walnut Creek, 925-939-9400

Lowenstein, Daniel Henry (4 mentions)
Harvard U, 1983 *Certification:* Neurology
400 Parnassus Ave 8th Fl, San Francisco, 415-353-2437

McCarthy, Richard John (5 mentions)
Johns Hopkins U, 1991
Certification: Clinical Neurophysiology, Neurology
99 Montecillo Rd, San Rafael, 415-444-2905

Miller, Robert Gordon (6 mentions)
Cornell U, 1970 *Certification:* Neurology
2324 Sacramento St #150, San Francisco, 415-600-3604

North, Will Adlai (4 mentions)
Ohio State U, 1991 *Certification:* Neurology
27303 Sleepy Hollow Ave, Hayward, 510-784-4607

Sachdev, Harmeet Singh (6 mentions)
FMS-India, 1973 *Certification:* Neurology
2577 Samaritan Dr #710, San Jose, 408-356-2164

Sankar, D. Philip (4 mentions)
Albany Med Coll, 1993 *Certification:* Neurology with Special
  Qualifications in Child Neurology
710 Lawrence Expy, Santa Clara, 408-851-1160

Smith, Wade Stafne (4 mentions)
U of Washington, 1989
Certification: Neurology, Vascular Neurology
400 Parnassus Ave 8th Fl, San Francisco, 415-353-1489

So, Yuen Tat (4 mentions)
Yale U, 1982 *Certification:* Neurology
300 Pasteur Dr #A-343, Palo Alto, 650-723-5184

Starkey, Randall Robert (5 mentions)
Mayo Med Sch, 1979 *Certification:* Neurology
5401 Norris Canyon Rd #306, San Ramon, 925-277-0101
365 Hawthorne Ave #203, Oakland, 510-834-5778

Stephens, Raymond Martin (7 mentions)
U of California-San Diego, 1978
Certification: Neurology, Vascular Neurology
108 La Casa Via #105, Walnut Creek, 925-939-9400

Tasch, Edwin Simeon (10 mentions)
U of Chicago, 1993 *Certification:* Neurology, Vascular Neurology
710 Lawrence Expy, Santa Clara, 408-851-4435

Telfer, Robert Baldwin (5 mentions)
Washington U, 1965 *Certification:* Clinical Neurophysiology,
  Neurology, Vascular Neurology
1750 El Camino Real #106, Burlingame, 650-697-6632

Volpi, Brad Allen (7 mentions)
U of Connecticut, 1978 *Certification:* Neurology
108 La Casa Via #105, Walnut Creek, 925-939-9400

Wrubel, Bradley Thomas (7 mentions)
U of Illinois, 1989
Certification: Clinical Neurophysiology, Neurology
2850 Telegraph Ave #110, Berkeley, 510-849-0499

Obstetrics/Gynecology

Ahsan, Arzou Diane (4 mentions)
U of California-San Francisco, 1998
Certification: Obstetrics & Gynecology
2915 Telegraph Ave #200, Berkeley, 510-845-8047

Albertson, Patti Kim (7 mentions)
U of Iowa, 1981 *Certification:* Obstetrics & Gynecology
276 International Cir 2nd Fl, San Jose, 408-362-4740

Altman, Sondra Joyce (3 mentions)
Boston U, 1979 *Certification:* Obstetrics & Gynecology
120 La Casa Via #104, Walnut Creek, 925-947-5945

Blumenstock, Edward M. (3 mentions)
U of California-San Francisco, 1971
Certification: Obstetrics & Gynecology
365 Hawthorne Ave #301, Oakland, 510-893-1700

Callen, Karen Richter (4 mentions)
Tulane U, 1984 *Certification:* Obstetrics & Gynecology
3838 California St #812, San Francisco, 415-666-1250

Eastman, Ann Krovoza (5 mentions)
U of Southern California, 1987
Certification: Obstetrics & Gynecology
3779 Piedmont Ave 2nd Fl, Oakland, 510-752-1100

Forgy, Andrea P. (3 mentions)
Loyola U Chicago, 1993 *Certification:* Obstetrics & Gynecology
555 Castro St, Mountain View, 650-903-3000

Francisco, David Lee (3 mentions)
Oregon Health Sciences U, 1983
Certification: Obstetrics & Gynecology
2485 Hospital Dr #321, Mountain View, 650-988-7660

Galland, David Bernard (3 mentions)
U of Rochester, 1978 *Certification:* Obstetrics & Gynecology
5 Bon Air Rd #117, Larkspur, 415-924-4870

Garcia, Karen Belinda (5 mentions)
U of California-Davis, 1991 *Certification:* Obstetrics & Gynecology
276 International Cir, San Jose, 408-362-4791

Green, Laurie Rae (8 mentions)
Harvard U, 1976 *Certification:* Obstetrics & Gynecology
3838 California St #316, San Francisco, 415-379-9600

Honegger, Marilyn M. (3 mentions)
U of California-Los Angeles, 1976
Certification: Obstetrics & Gynecology
12 Camino Encinas #15, Orinda, 925-254-9000
2999 Regent St #701, Berkeley, 925-254-9000

Horowitz, Jordan Jay (3 mentions)
U of Chicago, 1975 *Certification:* Obstetrics & Gynecology
3625 California St, San Francisco, 415-668-1010

Imig, Mary L. (4 mentions)
Howard U, 1986 *Certification:* Obstetrics & Gynecology
15151 National Ave, Los Gatos, 408-356-0431

Inouye, Takeshi (3 mentions)
Tufts U, 1989 *Certification:* Obstetrics & Gynecology
515 South Dr #21, Mountain View, 650-934-7956

Katz, Michael (4 mentions)
FMS-Israel, 1972
Certification: Maternal-Fetal Medicine, Obstetrics & Gynecology
1 Daniel Burnham Ct, San Francisco, 415-202-1200

Lam, Fung H. (4 mentions)
Tufts U, 1981 *Certification:* Obstetrics & Gynecology
3838 California St #812, San Francisco, 415-666-1250

Lanner-Cusin, Katarina E. (3 mentions)
U of California-San Francisco, 1981
Certification: Obstetrics & Gynecology
2915 Telegraph Ave #200, Berkeley, 510-845-8047

Levin, David Keith (3 mentions)
Georgetown U, 1977 *Certification:* Obstetrics & Gynecology
710 Lawrence Expy 3rd Fl, Santa Clara, 408-554-9820

Mason, Nancy Elizabeth (3 mentions)
Stanford U, 1977 *Certification:* Obstetrics & Gynecology
1101 Welch Rd #A8, Palo Alto, 650-329-1293

Miller, Philip Daniel (3 mentions)
Oregon Health Sciences U, 1972
Certification: Obstetrics & Gynecology
710 Lawrence Expy 3rd Fl, Santa Clara, 408-554-9820

Nicholson, Martina (3 mentions)
FMS-Mexico, 1981 *Certification:* Obstetrics & Gynecology
1661 Soquel Dr #A, Santa Cruz, 831-476-7676

Nishimine, Jimmy Hisao (3 mentions)
U of California-Irvine, 1969 *Certification:* Obstetrics & Gynecology
2507 Ashby Ave, Berkeley, 510-644-3000

Olander, Heidi Poncetta (7 mentions)
Dartmouth Coll, 1991 *Certification:* Obstetrics & Gynecology
276 International Cir 2nd Fl, San Jose, 408-362-4740

Polito, John Francis (3 mentions)
U of Virginia, 1976 *Certification:* Obstetrics & Gynecology
1300 Bancroft Ave #G4, San Leandro, 510-483-1234

Robertson, Patricia Anne (3 mentions)
U of Texas-San Antonio, 1976
Certification: Maternal-Fetal Medicine, Obstetrics & Gynecology
2356 Sutter St, San Francisco, 415-353-2566
400 Parnassus Ave, San Francisco, 415-353-2566

Schaaf, Mary E. (10 mentions)
Johns Hopkins U, 1978 *Certification:* Obstetrics & Gynecology
276 International Cir 2nd Fl, San Jose, 408-362-4740

Smarr, Susan Christine (11 mentions)
U of North Carolina, 1983 *Certification:* Obstetrics & Gynecology
710 Lawrence Expy 3rd Fl, Santa Clara, 408-554-9820

Wells, Stephen Robert (3 mentions)
Louisiana State U, 1990 *Certification:* Obstetrics & Gynecology
110 Tampico #220, Walnut Creek, 925-935-5356

Wharton, Kurt Rodney (5 mentions)
Boston U, 1984 *Certification:* Obstetrics & Gynecology
970 Dewing Ave #201, Lafayette, 925-962-0002

Wiggins, Donna Ann (6 mentions)
U of Alabama, 1985 *Certification:* Obstetrics & Gynecology
3838 California St #812, San Francisco, 415-666-1250

Wilner, Gerald P. (3 mentions)
SUNY-Buffalo, 1965 *Certification:* Obstetrics & Gynecology
5 Bon Air Rd #117, Larkspur, 415-924-9770

Yee, Pearl J. (3 mentions)
U of California-Irvine, 1983 *Certification:* Obstetrics & Gynecology
2340 Irving St, San Francisco, 415-753-2929

Young, Michelle Lynn (4 mentions)
U of Southern California, 1987
Certification: Obstetrics & Gynecology
710 Lawrence Expy #390, Santa Clara, 408-554-9820

Ophthalmology

Aguilar, Gabriel Linton (4 mentions)
U of California-Los Angeles, 1974 *Certification:* Ophthalmology
909 Hyde St #530, San Francisco, 415-775-3392

Barsoumian, Krikor L. (4 mentions)
FMS-Lebanon, 1974
2440 Samaritan Dr #3, San Jose, 408-226-4141

Basham, Arthur Alden (6 mentions)
U of California-Irvine, 1977 *Certification:* Ophthalmology
212 Oak Meadow Dr, Los Gatos, 408-354-4740

Blumenkranz, Mark Scott (8 mentions)
Brown U, 1975 *Certification:* Ophthalmology
1225 Crane St #202, Menlo Park, 650-323-0231

Campbell, John Roy (4 mentions)
U of Washington, 1975 *Certification:* Ophthalmology
901 E St #285, San Rafael, 415-454-5565
165 Rowland Way #307, Novato, 415-454-5565

Chang, William Jerry (4 mentions)
Stanford U, 1982 *Certification:* Ophthalmology
1150 Veterans Blvd, Redwood City, 650-299-2000

Chou, Tina Marie (3 mentions)
U of California-Los Angeles, 1993 *Certification:* Ophthalmology
1299 Newell Hill Pl #103, Walnut Creek, 925-947-0505
5275 Clairmont Ave, Oakland, 510-428-3226

Cruciger, Marc Petty (3 mentions)
U of Texas-Houston, 1973 *Certification:* Ophthalmology
3838 California St #501, San Francisco, 415-668-2118

Day, Susan H. (4 mentions)
Louisiana State U, 1975 *Certification:* Ophthalmology
2340 Clay St #100, San Francisco, 415-202-1500

Del Carmen, Jocelynlou F. (3 mentions)
Harvard U, 1993 *Certification:* Ophthalmology
795 El Camino Real, Palo Alto, 650-853-2974

Denny, Kevin (5 mentions)
New York U, 1980 *Certification:* Ophthalmology
2201 Webster St, San Francisco, 415-567-8200

Egbert, Peter Roy (4 mentions)
Yale U, 1967 *Certification:* Ophthalmology
900 Blake Wilbur Dr #W3002, Palo Alto, 650-723-6995

Erny, Barbara (3 mentions)
Stanford U, 1988 *Certification:* Ophthalmology
323 N Matilda Ave, Sunnyvale, 408-524-5900

Fishman, Martin Lee (3 mentions)
U of California-San Francisco, 1970 *Certification:* Ophthalmology
431 Monterey Ave #3, Los Gatos, 408-354-9510

Friedman, Neil J. (3 mentions)
Harvard U, 1992 *Certification:* Ophthalmology
900 Welch Rd #402, Palo Alto, 650-324-0056

Good, William Vance (4 mentions)
U of Cincinnati, 1977 *Certification:* Ophthalmology, Psychiatry
2340 Clay St #100, San Francisco, 415-202-1500
5 Bon Air Rd #127, Greenbrae, 415-202-1500

Graham, Karen T. (3 mentions)
Baylor U, 1992 *Certification:* Ophthalmology
2222 East St #365, Concord, 925-687-8280

Greene, Stuart (8 mentions)
SUNY-Buffalo, 1972 *Certification:* Ophthalmology
710 Lawrence Expy 4th Fl, Santa Clara, 408-851-1000

Hwang, David Genpai (3 mentions)
U of California-San Francisco, 1984 *Certification:* Ophthalmology
8 Koret Way #U-545, San Francisco, 415-476-3705
533 Parnassus Ave, San Francisco, 415-476-3705

Ip, Kenneth C. (4 mentions)
U of California-Irvine, 1994 *Certification:* Ophthalmology
1635 Divisadero St, San Francisco, 415-833-3907

Karlen, Kris Martin (9 mentions)
Albert Einstein Coll of Med, 1986 *Certification:* Ophthalmology
611 S Milpitas Blvd, Milpitas, 408-851-4100

Kramer, David Mathias (14 mentions)
Rosalind Franklin U, 1985 *Certification:* Ophthalmology
5755 Cottle Rd Bldg 2, San Jose, 408-972-3100

Lewis, John Michael (7 mentions)
U of California-Davis, 1991 *Certification:* Ophthalmology
710 Lawrence Expy, Santa Clara, 408-851-4100

Manche, Edward Emanuel (3 mentions)
Albert Einstein Coll of Med, 1990 *Certification:* Ophthalmology
900 Blake Wilbur Dr #W3002, Palo Alto, 650-498-7020

Nevitt, Judith Brooke (4 mentions)
Stanford U, 1986 *Certification:* Ophthalmology
900 Welch Rd #402, Palo Alto, 650-324-0056

Prusiner, Paul Edward (3 mentions)
U of California-San Francisco, 1978 *Certification:* Ophthalmology
1033 3rd St, San Rafael, 415-444-2990

Rombakis, Andrew Socrates (3 mentions)
U of Iowa, 1980 *Certification:* Ophthalmology
395 Hickey Blvd, Daly City, 650-301-5800

Schwartz, Lee Kenneth (5 mentions)
Tufts U, 1970 *Certification:* Internal Medicine, Ophthalmology
2250 Hayes St, San Francisco, 415-387-8887
2300 California St #300, San Francisco, 415-921-7555

Sorenson, Andrew Lee (4 mentions)
U of California-San Diego, 1993 *Certification:* Ophthalmology
3010 Colby St #114, Berkeley, 510-848-1413

Sorenson, Robert Lynn (7 mentions)
U of California-San Diego, 1980 *Certification:* Ophthalmology
3010 Colby St #114, Berkeley, 510-848-1413

Sudesh, Rattehalli R. (3 mentions)
FMS-India, 1986 *Certification:* Ophthalmology
710 Lawrence Expy, Santa Clara, 408-851-1000

Volpicelli, Mark (5 mentions)
U of California-San Diego, 1985 *Certification:* Ophthalmology
1174 Castro St #100, Mountain View, 650-961-2585

Wisdom, Jerald E. (8 mentions)
Brown U, 1992 *Certification:* Ophthalmology
5755 Cottle Rd Bldg 2, San Jose, 408-972-3100

Orthopedics

Anderson, Jeffrey John (5 mentions)
U of California-San Francisco, 1979
Certification: Orthopaedic Surgery
333 O'Connor Dr, San Jose, 408-297-3484

Belzer, John Pieter (6 mentions)
Yale U, 1988 *Certification:* Orthopaedic Surgery
3838 California St, San Francisco, 415-433-7003
1240 S Eliseo Dr #101, Greenbrae, 415-461-1600

Blatz, Douglas John (3 mentions)
SUNY-Upstate Med U, 1972 *Certification:* Orthopaedic Surgery
10430 S De Anza Blvd #230, Cupertino, 408-374-5700

Casanave, Alden Bernard (3 mentions)
U of California-Los Angeles, 1982
Certification: Orthopaedic Surgery
900 Kiely Blvd, Santa Clara, 408-236-6451
710 Lawrence Expy, Santa Clara, 408-851-1850

Cheng, Joseph C. (3 mentions)
Northwestern U, 1989 *Certification:* Orthopaedic Surgery
15035 E 14th St, San Leandro, 510-481-3400

Cheng, Margaret Susan (4 mentions)
Duke U, 1987 *Certification:* Orthopaedic Surgery
260 International Cir 1st Fl, San Jose, 408-972-6310

Coufal, Christopher J. (3 mentions)
U of Texas-Houston, 1992 *Certification:* Orthopaedic Surgery
2405 Shadelands Dr, Walnut Creek, 925-939-8585
350 John Muir Pkwy #100, Brentwood, 925-939-8585

Cox, Christopher Verploeg (5 mentions)
U of California-San Francisco, 1986
Certification: Orthopaedic Surgery
3838 California St #715, San Francisco, 415-668-8010

Diab, Mohammad (5 mentions)
Stanford U, 1990 *Certification:* Orthopaedic Surgery
400 Parnassus Ave #300, San Francisco, 415-353-2967

Dickinson, Jon Alan (3 mentions)
Tulane U, 1985 *Certification:* Orthopaedic Surgery
3838 California St #715, San Francisco, 415-668-8010
1240 S Eliseo Dr #101, Greenbrae, 415-461-1600

Eppley, Robert Alfred (6 mentions)
Case Western Reserve U, 1983 *Certification:* Orthopaedic Surgery
2999 Regent St #225, Berkeley, 510-704-7760
25 Orinda Way, Orinda, 510-704-7760

Escay, Mari (6 mentions)
FMS-Philippines, 1972 *Certification:* Orthopaedic Surgery
260 International Cir, San Jose, 408-972-3030

Fortune, John Edwin (9 mentions)
Creighton U, 1985 *Certification:* Orthopaedic Surgery
260 International Cir Bldg 1N, San Jose, 408-972-3030

Gilbert, Robert James (9 mentions)
Ohio State U, 1967 *Certification:* Orthopaedic Surgery
3838 California St #715, San Francisco, 415-668-8010

Goodman, Stuart Barry (4 mentions)
FMS-Canada, 1978 *Certification:* Orthopaedic Surgery
900 Brake Wilber, Palo Alto, 650-723-5644

Gorek, Josef Ernst (5 mentions)
U of California-Los Angeles, 1989
Certification: Orthopaedic Surgery
280 W MacArthur Blvd, Oakland, 510-752-1000

Hartford, James Matthew (3 mentions)
Dartmouth Coll, 1989 *Certification:* Orthopaedic Surgery
795 El Camino Real, Palo Alto, 650-853-2951
3200 Kearney St, Fremont, 650-853-2951

Hoffinger, Scott Andrew (9 mentions)
U of Michigan, 1983 *Certification:* Orthopaedic Surgery
106 La Casa Via #220, Walnut Creek, 925-939-8687
747 52nd St, Oakland, 510-428-3238

Hoffman, Robert Paul (4 mentions)
SUNY-Downstate Med Coll, 1973
Certification: Orthopaedic Surgery, Surgery of the Hand
280 W MacArthur Blvd, Oakland, 510-752-1000

Hsu, Ken-Yao (3 mentions)
SUNY-Downstate Med Coll, 1976
Certification: Orthopaedic Surgery
1 Shrader St #450, San Francisco, 415-750-5836

Hu, Serena Shaw (3 mentions)
FMS-Canada, 1984 *Certification:* Orthopaedic Surgery
400 Parnassus Ave Fl3 #A-311, San Francisco, 415-353-2739

Jaureguito, John William (3 mentions)
St Louis U, 1989 *Certification:* Orthopaedic Surgery
3555 Beacon Ave, Fremont, 510-739-6520

Jeter, Grady Lynn (3 mentions)
U of Oklahoma, 1962 *Certification:* Orthopaedic Surgery
2430 Samaritan Dr, San Jose, 408-559-4343

Johnson, James Elbert (6 mentions)
U of Cincinnati, 1970
Certification: Orthopaedic Surgery, Surgery of the Hand
1200 El Camino Real, South San Francisco, 650-742-2191

Knight, John Marshall (3 mentions)
Creighton U, 1978 *Certification:* Orthopaedic Surgery
5201 Norris Canyon Rd #300, San Ramon, 925-939-8585
2405 Shadelands Dr, Walnut Creek, 925-939-8585

Lannin, John V. (6 mentions)
U of Minnesota, 1978 *Certification:* Orthopaedic Surgery
795 El Camino Rd, Palo Alto, 650-853-2951

Lowenberg, David W. (5 mentions)
U of California-Los Angeles, 1985
Certification: Orthopaedic Surgery
2100 Webster St #117, San Francisco, 415-600-3835

Lundy, Gordon Collins (3 mentions)
U of California-San Francisco, 1985
Certification: Orthopaedic Surgery
2100 Webster St #109, San Francisco, 415-923-3015

Maloney, William Joseph (3 mentions)
Columbia U, 1983 *Certification:* Orthopaedic Surgery
900 Blake Wilbur Dr #W1001, Palo Alto, 650-723-5643

Matthews, Joseph George, II (5 mentions)
Jefferson Med Coll, 1978 *Certification:* Orthopaedic Surgery
260 International Cir 1st Fl, San Jose, 408-972-6310

Merson, John Kenneth (3 mentions)
U of California-Los Angeles, 1984
Certification: Orthopaedic Surgery
1800 Sutter St #100, Concord, 925-691-0500

Miranda, Ramiro Acosta (4 mentions)
U of California-San Francisco, 1979
Certification: Orthopaedic Surgery
2405 Shadelands Dr, Walnut Creek, 925-939-8585

Parker, John Neff (3 mentions)
George Washington U, 1979 *Certification:* Orthopaedic Surgery
763 Altos Oaks Dr #1, Los Altos, 650-917-9135

Reidel, Sandra Lee (3 mentions)
Stanford U, 1976
260 International Cir 1st Fl, San Jose, 408-972-6310

Rinsky, Lawrence Allen (8 mentions)
U of Cincinnati, 1971 *Certification:* Orthopaedic Surgery
730 Welch Rd, Palo Alto, 650-723-5243

Rosenblatt, Solon Lee (4 mentions)
Temple U, 1990
99 Montecillo Rd, San Rafael, 415-444-4430

Sanghvi, Rahul Siddharth (16 mentions)
U of Michigan, 1985 *Certification:* Orthopaedic Surgery
710 Lawrence Expy, Santa Clara, 408-851-1850

Test, Eric (3 mentions)
George Washington U, 1979
701 E El Camino Real, Mountain View, 650-934-7111

Wirganowicz, Philip Z. (3 mentions)
U of California-Los Angeles, 1990
Certification: Orthopaedic Surgery
280 W MacArthur Blvd, Oakland, 510-752-1000

Otorhinolaryngology

Agbayani, Romeo Crane, Jr. (5 mentions)
Tufts U, 1993 *Certification:* Otolaryngology
1000 S Eliseo Dr #103, Greenbrae, 415-461-9770

Arnstein, David Paul (5 mentions)
George Washington U, 1984 *Certification:* Otolaryngology
15861 Winchester Blvd, Los Gatos, 408-395-6121

Butt, Fidelia Yuanshin (5 mentions)
George Washington U, 1992 *Certification:* Otolaryngology
710 Lawrence Expy, Santa Clara, 408-851-2950

Dray, Todd Gardner (14 mentions)
U of Utah, 1991 *Certification:* Otolaryngology
710 Lawrence Expy 2nd Fl, Santa Clara, 408-851-2950

Drury, Bernard James (4 mentions)
Columbia U, 1981 *Certification:* Otolaryngology
2961 Summit St #1, Oakland, 510-465-0941

Engel, Thomas L. (8 mentions)
U of Michigan, 1976 *Certification:* Otolaryngology
3838 California St #505, San Francisco, 415-751-4914

Fann, Patrick Chi (4 mentions)
Stanford U, 1987 *Certification:* Otolaryngology
701 E El Camino Real, Mountain View, 650-934-7900

Ford, Lloyd Clark (4 mentions)
Hahnemann U, 1996 *Certification:* Otolaryngology
2121 Ygnacio Valley Rd #G2, Walnut Creek, 925-932-3112
2700 Grant St #104, Concord, 925-685-7400

Friduss, Michael Eric (7 mentions)
U of Illinois, 1983 *Certification:* Otolaryngology
710 Lawrence Expy, Santa Clara, 408-851-2950
2440 Samaritan Dr #2, San Jose, 408-851-8200

Jackler, Robert Keith (6 mentions)
Boston U, 1979 *Certification:* Neurotology, Otolaryngology
801 Welch Rd, Palo Alto, 650-723-5281

Jacobsen, Bruce Edward (18 mentions)
Loma Linda U, 1976 *Certification:* Otolaryngology
280 Hospital Pkwy Bldg B, San Jose, 408-972-6580

Kerbavaz, Richard Joseph (7 mentions)
U of California-San Diego, 1979 *Certification:* Otolaryngology
2316 Dwight Way, Berkeley, 510-845-4500

Lando, Matthew John (4 mentions)
U of California-Davis, 1982 *Certification:* Otolaryngology
3553 Whipple Rd, Union City, 510-675-4241
39400 Paseo Padre Pkwy, Fremont, 510-248-3000

MacLean, William Beck (4 mentions)
Hahnemann U, 1987 *Certification:* Otolaryngology
280 Hospital Pkwy Bldg B, San Jose, 408-972-6580

Messner, Anna Hopeman (4 mentions)
Wake Forest U, 1989 *Certification:* Otolaryngology
730 Welch Rd, Palo Alto, 650-497-8841

Mickel, Robert Allen (7 mentions)
U of Pennsylvania, 1977 *Certification:* Otolaryngology
3838 California St #505, San Francisco, 415-751-4914

Mischer, Carolyn Field (4 mentions)
U of Texas-Southwestern, 1980 *Certification:* Otolaryngology
1300 Crane St, Menlo Park, 650-498-6500

Mizono, Gary Shigeo (4 mentions)
U of California-San Diego, 1979 *Certification:* Otolaryngology
99 Montecillo Rd, San Rafael, 415-444-2919

Murphy, Michael P. (6 mentions)
St Louis U, 1994 *Certification:* Otolaryngology
1776 Ygnacio Valley Rd #210, Walnut Creek, 925-933-8462
5401 Norris Canyon Rd #300, San Ramon, 925-242-0647

Nelson, Lionel Marshall (4 mentions)
Yale U, 1969 *Certification:* Otolaryngology
2505 Samaritan Dr #510, San Jose, 408-358-6163

Obana, Kathryn Kiyomi (4 mentions)
U of California-Davis, 1984 *Certification:* Otolaryngology
701 E El Camino Real, Mountain View, 650-934-7900

Swedenborg, Jon Eric (7 mentions)
Vanderbilt U, 1990 *Certification:* Otolaryngology
280 Hospital Pkwy Bldg B, San Jose, 408-972-6580

Wolf, Linda Weinman (15 mentions)
Albert Einstein Coll of Med, 1977 *Certification:* Otolaryngology
280 Hospital Pkwy Bldg B, San Jose, 408-972-6580

Pain Medicine

Abaci, Peter Aziz (5 mentions)
U of Southern California, 1991
Certification: Anesthesiology, Pain Medicine
15047 Los Gatos Blvd #200, Los Gatos, 408-364-6799

Brose, William George (3 mentions)
U of Kansas, 1984 *Certification:* Anesthesiology, Pain Medicine
1900 O'Farrell St #250, San Mateo, 650-645-1100

Chakerian, Maia Ursula (3 mentions)
U of New Mexico, 1984
Certification: Anesthesiology, Pain Medicine
14601 S Bascom Ave #100, Los Gatos, 408-356-0503

Fisk, Stephen (10 mentions)
U of Miami, 1974
Certification: Anesthesiology, Critical Care Medicine
710 Lawrence Expy, Santa Clara, 408-851-1000

Gaeta, Raymond Richard (4 mentions)
Stanford U, 1985 *Certification:* Anesthesiology, Critical Care
   Medicine, Pain Medicine
300 Pasteur Dr Boswell Bldg #A408, Palo Alto, 650-725-5852

Kandula, Vittal Kumar Rao (3 mentions)
FMS-India, 1986 *Certification:* Anesthesiology, Pain Medicine
275 Hospital Pkwy, San Jose, 408-972-3364

Krane, Elliot Jeffrey (4 mentions)
U of Arizona, 1977 *Certification:* Anesthesiology, Pediatrics
300 Pasteur Dr #H-3582, Palo Alto, 650-725-5848
730 Welch Rd, Palo Alto, 650-725-5848

Mackey, Sean Charles (4 mentions)
U of Arizona, 1994 *Certification:* Anesthesiology, Pain Medicine
300 Pasteur Dr Boswell Bldg #A408, Palo Alto, 650-725-9636

Morley, Brendan Patrick (3 mentions)
U of California-Los Angeles, 1990 *Certification:* Anesthesiology
6699 Telegraph Ave #202, Oakland, 510-647-5101

Movva, Prasad Anjaneya (8 mentions)
FMS-India, 1986 *Certification:* Anesthesiology, Pain Medicine
250 Hospital Pkwy, San Jose, 408-972-7000

Panjabi, Ravi S. (3 mentions)
FMS-India, 1984 *Certification:* Anesthesiology, Pain Medicine
19850 Lake Chabot Rd, Castro Valley, 510-582-8555
1081 Market Pl #100, San Ramon, 510-582-8555

Patel, Darshan (11 mentions)
FMS-India, 1986 *Certification:* Anesthesiology, Pain Medicine
250 Hospital Pkwy, San Jose, 408-972-6630

Savala, Robert Anthony (5 mentions)
U of California-San Francisco, 1992
Certification: Anesthesiology, Pain Medicine
1635 Divisadero St #525, San Francisco, 415-346-8555

Pathology

Engleman, Ephraim Philip (9 mentions)
U of California-San Diego, 1978
Certification: Anatomic Pathology & Clinical Pathology
250 Hospital Pkwy, San Jose, 408-972-7255

Gould, Robert Michael (13 mentions)
Albert Einstein Coll of Med, 1977
Certification: Anatomic Pathology & Clinical Pathology
250 Hospital Pkwy, San Jose, 408-972-7258

Lambert, Joelle Maud (5 mentions)
St Louis U, 1984
Certification: Anatomic Pathology & Clinical Pathology
700 Lawrence Expy #204, Santa Clara, 408-851-6100

Moretto, John C. (5 mentions)
Stanford U, 1990
Certification: Anatomic Pathology, Dermatopathology
3700 California St 4th Fl, San Francisco, 415-600-4495

Ranchod, Mahendra (5 mentions)
FMS-South Africa, 1965 *Certification:* Anatomic Pathology
100 Albright Way #C, Los Gatos, 408-866-5227

Rumore, Gregory Joseph (6 mentions)
New Jersey Med Sch, 1980
Certification: Anatomic Pathology & Clinical Pathology
280 W MacArthur Blvd, Oakland, 510-752-6813

Santamaria-Fries, Monica (9 mentions)
FMS-Colombia, 1981
Certification: Anatomic Pathology & Clinical Pathology
710 Lawrence Expy, Santa Clara, 408-851-1000

Pediatrics *(see note on page 9)*

Abbott, Myles Bruce (7 mentions)
U of Miami, 1972 *Certification:* Pediatrics
2999 Regent St #325, Berkeley, 925-438-1100
96 Davis Rd #2, Orinda, 925-438-1100

Aicardi, Eileen Ziomek (4 mentions)
U of California-San Francisco, 1974 *Certification:* Pediatrics
3641 California St, San Francisco, 415-668-0888
61 Camino Alto #102, Mill Valley, 415-388-6303

Albin, Catherine L. (4 mentions)
Stanford U, 1981
Certification: Pediatric Critical Care Medicine, Pediatrics
710 Lawrence Expy, Santa Clara, 408-851-1160

Anderson, Jane E. (3 mentions)
U of California-Los Angeles, 1975 *Certification:* Pediatrics
2330 Post St #320, San Francisco, 415-885-7478

Bantug, Concepcion (3 mentions)
U of California-Los Angeles, 1994 *Certification:* Pediatrics
276 International Cir, San Jose, 408-362-4740

Bergen, Randy E. (3 mentions)
U of Minnesota, 1982 *Certification:* Pediatrics
1425 S Main St, Walnut Creek, 925-295-4070

Copeland, Elizabeth C. (3 mentions)
Georgetown U, 1999 *Certification:* Pediatrics
7225 Rainbow Dr, San Jose, 408-524-5750

Dow, Richard Jay (4 mentions)
Ohio State U, 1991 *Certification:* Pediatrics
1206 Strawberry Village, Mill Valley, 415-380-2020

Ernster, Martin Frank (3 mentions)
U of California-San Francisco, 1977 *Certification:* Pediatrics
3641 California St, San Francisco, 415-668-0888
61 Camino Alto #103, Mill Valley, 415-388-6303

Garona, Juan Emilio (3 mentions)
FMS-Argentina, 1977 *Certification:* Pediatrics
701 E El Camino Real, Mountain View, 650-934-7956

Gonda, William Stuart (8 mentions)
Case Western Reserve U, 1978 *Certification:* Pediatrics
3641 California St, San Francisco, 415-668-0888
61 Camino Alto #103, Mill Valley, 415-388-6303

Gordon, Calvin Owen (7 mentions)
New York Med Coll, 1977 *Certification:* Pediatrics
276 International Cir 1st Fl, San Jose, 408-362-4740

Kadas, Robert Irwin (3 mentions)
U of Southern California, 1966 *Certification:* Pediatrics
1505 St Alphonsus Ct, Alamo, 925-837-4225

Kohl, Julie Beth (3 mentions)
Stanford U, 1988 *Certification:* Pediatrics
555 Castro St, Mountain View, 650-903-3000

Lewis, Gena Lee (5 mentions)
Temple U, 1995 *Certification:* Pediatrics
5220 Claremont Ave, Oakland, 510-428-3129

Miller, Carol Ann N. (3 mentions)
Stanford U, 1975 *Certification:* Pediatrics
400 Parnassus Ave 2nd Fl, San Francisco, 415-353-2000

Moore, Michael John (3 mentions)
U of Vermont, 1989 *Certification:* Pediatrics
7225 Rainbow Dr, San Jose, 408-524-5750
701 E El Camino Real, Mountain View, 650-934-7911

Ng, Lawrence Ming Loy (3 mentions)
FMS-Hong Kong, 1965 *Certification:* Pediatrics
101 Callan Ave #401, San Leandro, 510-357-7077
345 9th St #204, Oakland, 510-839-1072

Oken, Richard Leslie (3 mentions)
U of California-San Francisco, 1971 *Certification:* Pediatrics
2999 Regent St #325, Berkeley, 925-438-1100
96 Davis Rd #2, Orinda, 925-438-1100

Orloff, Sheldon (3 mentions)
U of Illinois, 1970 *Certification:* Pediatrics
3505 Broadway 12th Fl, Oakland, 510-752-1000

Pai, Meena Prakash (3 mentions)
FMS-India, 1990 *Certification:* Pediatrics
276 International Cir 1st Fl, San Jose, 408-362-4740

Sexton, Kathryn Volk (3 mentions)
U of Iowa, 1973 *Certification:* Pediatrics
1000 S Eliseo Dr #1-A, Greenbrae, 415-461-5436

Tannenbaum, Jesse Allen (3 mentions)
U of Miami, 1981 *Certification:* Pediatrics
710 Lawrence Expy #248, Santa Clara, 408-236-6400

Whyte, Lynne Meador (6 mentions)
Duke U, 1987 *Certification:* Pediatrics
1505 St Alphonsus Way, Alamo, 925-837-4225

Wu, Flora Chieh (4 mentions)
U of California-San Diego, 1977 *Certification:* Pediatrics
276 International Cir, San Jose, 408-972-6136

Yee, Clifford Kuangjui (4 mentions)
Northwestern U, 1994 *Certification:* Pediatrics
710 Lawrence Expy, Santa Clara, 408-554-9810

Yoffee, Hanley Jay (3 mentions)
U of Michigan, 1978 *Certification:* Pediatrics
276 International Cir 1st Fl, San Jose, 408-362-4740

Plastic Surgery

Behmand, Ramin A. (3 mentions)
Case Western Reserve U, 1995 *Certification:* Plastic Surgery
1776 Ygnacio Valley Rd #108, Walnut Creek, 925-939-9200

Berkowitz, R. Laurence (3 mentions)
Ohio State U, 1973 *Certification:* Plastic Surgery
3803 S Bascom Ave #100, Campbell, 408-559-7177

Bindiger, Alan (4 mentions)
Albany Med Coll, 1980 *Certification:* Plastic Surgery
280 Hospital Pkwy Bldg A, San Jose, 408-972-6010

Buncke, Gregory M. (3 mentions)
Georgetown U, 1981
Certification: Plastic Surgery, Surgery of the Hand
101 N El Camino Real #A, San Mateo, 650-342-8989
45 Castro St #121, San Francisco, 415-565-6136

Connolly, John Patrick (7 mentions)
Georgetown U, 1996 *Certification:* Plastic Surgery
1174 Castro #200, Mountain View, 650-404-8240

Daane, Stephen Preble (3 mentions)
Tufts U, 1989 *Certification:* Plastic Surgery
2186 Geary Blvd #212, San Francisco, 415-561-0542

Du Long, Mark Joseph (8 mentions)
Brown U, 1986 *Certification:* Plastic Surgery
710 Lawrence Expy, Santa Clara, 408-851-2000

Friedenthal, Roger Philip (5 mentions)
Yale U, 1962 *Certification:* Plastic Surgery
3838 California St #404, San Francisco, 415-752-2066

Hoffman, Daryl Kristan (3 mentions)
U of New Mexico, 1985 *Certification:* Plastic Surgery
900 Welch Rd #110, Palo Alto, 650-325-1118
2581 Samaritan Dr #102, San Jose, 408-356-4241

Hoffman, William Yanes (4 mentions)
U of Rochester, 1977 *Certification:* Plastic Surgery
350 Parnassus Ave #509, San Francisco, 415-353-4287

Ikeda, Clyde J. (6 mentions)
New York Med Coll, 1979
Certification: Plastic Surgery, Surgery of the Hand
1199 Bush St #640, San Francisco, 415-775-1199

Jacobs, Daniel Irwin (9 mentions)
Case Western Reserve U, 1985 *Certification:* Plastic Surgery
280 Hospital Pkwy Bldg A, San Jose, 408-972-3100

Jellinek, Charles Gregory (3 mentions)
Albany Med Coll, 1972 *Certification:* Plastic Surgery
15251 National Ave #207, Los Gatos, 408-356-0052

Lau, Glen Kee (3 mentions)
Tufts U, 1973 *Certification:* Plastic Surgery
80 Grand Ave #810, Oakland, 510-451-6950
3511 School St, Lafayette, 925-283-4821

Lynd, Melody (4 mentions)
80 E Hamilton Ave, Campbell, 408-871-1000

Mariotti, Eric Robert (4 mentions)
Jefferson Med Coll, 1993 *Certification:* Plastic Surgery
2222 East St #310, Concord, 925-685-4533

Marten, Timothy James (3 mentions)
U of California-Davis, 1982 *Certification:* Plastic Surgery
450 Sutter St #2222, San Francisco, 415-677-9937

Maser, Benjamin Mark (4 mentions)
Jefferson Med Coll, 1991
Certification: Plastic Surgery, Surgery of the Hand
795 El Camino Real, Palo Alto, 650-853-2916

Menard, Robert Michael (4 mentions)
Stanford U, 1992 *Certification:* Plastic Surgery
710 Lawrence Expy, Santa Clara, 408-851-2000
2440 Samaritan Dr #2, San Jose, 408-851-8200

Milliken, Ronald (6 mentions)
FMS-Canada, 1976
710 Lawrence Expy, Santa Clara, 408-851-2349

Minami, Roland Takashi (3 mentions)
U of Southern California, 1970 *Certification:* Plastic Surgery
1240 S Eliseo Dr #102, Greenbrae, 415-461-1240

Prescott, Bradford True (4 mentions)
U of California-San Francisco, 1984 *Certification:* Plastic Surgery
100 N Wiget Ln #100, Walnut Creek, 925-935-9717

Santoro, Timothy Dan (4 mentions)
U of Utah, 1994 *Certification:* Plastic Surgery, Surgery
710 Lawrence Expy, Santa Clara, 408-851-2000

Schendel, Stephen Alfred (3 mentions)
U of Hawaii, 1983 *Certification:* Plastic Surgery
770 Welch Rd #400, Palo Alto, 650-497-8201

Smith, Tina M. (5 mentions)
Jefferson Med Coll, 1982 *Certification:* Plastic Surgery
1425 S Main St, Walnut Creek, 925-295-5885

Weston, Jane (3 mentions)
Stanford U, 1979 *Certification:* Plastic Surgery
3351 El Camino Real #201, Atherton, 650-363-0300

White, David Norman (3 mentions)
Georgetown U, 1977 *Certification:* Plastic Surgery
795 El Camino Real, Palo Alto, 650-853-2916

Wotowic, Paul J. (3 mentions)
Tulane U, 1978 *Certification:* Otolaryngology, Plastic Surgery
5201 Norris Canyon Rd #330, San Ramon, 925-866-6778

Zandi, Iraj (3 mentions)
FMS-Iran, 1965 *Certification:* Plastic Surgery
2557 Mowry Ave #20, Fremont, 510-796-9850

Psychiatry

Gerson-Schreiber, Abram (3 mentions)
Temple U, 1975 *Certification:* Psychiatry
3555 Whipple Rd, Union City, 510-675-3080

Hirsch, Rebecca Leah (3 mentions)
Rosalind Franklin U, 2000 *Certification:* Psychiatry
5755 Cottle Rd Bldg 4, San Jose, 408-972-3095

McCormick, Mark Gerald F. (7 mentions)
Yale U, 1973 *Certification:* Psychiatry
19000 E Homestead Rd, Cupertino, 408-366-4400

McNamara, Denise Ann (6 mentions)
U of California-San Francisco, 1983 *Certification:* Psychiatry
19000 E Homestead Rd Bldg #2, Cupertino, 408-366-4400

Mordecai, Donald James (8 mentions)
Stanford U, 1994 *Certification:* Psychiatry
5755 Cottle Rd Bldg 4, San Jose, 408-972-3095

Prey, William Taylor (3 mentions)
Pennsylvania State U, 1980 *Certification:* Psychiatry
2345 California St, San Francisco, 415-346-8599

Vaschetto, Nestor Luis (3 mentions)
FMS-Argentina, 1975 *Certification:* Psychiatry
190 N Wiget Ln #103, Walnut Creek, 925-930-8865

Pulmonary Disease

Butcher, Laura Lee (14 mentions)
U of Texas-San Antonio, 1980
Certification: Internal Medicine, Pulmonary Disease
270 International Cir Bldg 2N, San Jose, 408-972-6560

Chausow, Alan Martin (6 mentions)
Washington U, 1976
Certification: Internal Medicine, Pulmonary Disease
701 E El Camino Real, Mountain View, 650-934-7144

Dailey, Thomas Matthew (15 mentions)
U of California-Los Angeles, 1984 *Certification:* Critical Care Medicine, Internal Medicine, Pulmonary Disease
710 Lawrence Expy 2nd Fl, Santa Clara, 408-851-2570

Goya, David S. (7 mentions)
Texas Coll of Osteopathic Med, 1982 *Certification:* Critical Care Medicine, Internal Medicine, Pulmonary Disease
710 Lawrence Expy 2nd Fl, Santa Clara, 408-851-2570

Hardy, Karen Ann (5 mentions)
Med Coll of Ohio, 1979
Certification: Pediatric Pulmonology, Pediatrics
1100 Larkspur Landing Cir #150, Larkspur, 415-461-3498
3700 California St #B-554, San Francisco, 510-428-3305
747 52nd St, Oakland, 510-428-3305

Ho, Donald (5 mentions)
U of California-Los Angeles, 1973 *Certification:* Critical Care Medicine, Internal Medicine, Pulmonary Disease
1720 El Camino Real #150, Burlingame, 650-697-5367

Lewis, Nancy Church (6 mentions)
U of California-Los Angeles, 1979
Certification: Pediatric Pulmonology, Pediatrics
5565 W Las Positas Blvd #3208, Pleasanton, 925-280-8131

MacDannald, Harry Joseph (6 mentions)
U of California-Davis, 1972
Certification: Internal Medicine, Pulmonary Disease
130 La Casa Via #2-208, Walnut Creek, 925-944-0166

Marland, Albert MacInnes (5 mentions)
Georgetown U, 1976
Certification: Internal Medicine, Pulmonary Disease
15215 National Ave #200, Los Gatos, 408-358-8112

McQuitty, John Crocker (8 mentions)
U of Michigan, 1970
Certification: Pediatric Pulmonology, Pediatrics
521 Parnassus Ave, San Francisco, 415-476-2072

Miyasaki, Neal Takashi (6 mentions)
U of California-Davis, 1973 *Certification:* Internal Medicine
3838 California St #409, San Francisco, 415-387-7800

Rizk, Norman Wade (11 mentions)
Yale U, 1976 *Certification:* Critical Care Medicine, Internal Medicine, Pulmonary Disease
300 Pasteur Dr Boswell Bldg #A-283, Palo Alto, 650-725-7061

Salfen, S. J. (6 mentions)
U of Missouri, 1974
15215 National Ave #101, Los Gatos, 408-356-2224

Taharka, Ananse Chukwu (6 mentions)
U of Cincinnati, 1979 *Certification:* Critical Care Medicine, Internal Medicine, Pulmonary Disease
280 W MacArthur Blvd, Oakland, 510-752-1000

Radiology—Diagnostic

Baker, Brian Lanier (7 mentions)
Rosalind Franklin U, 1987
900 Kiely Blvd, Santa Clara, 408-851-5071

Baker, Edward L. (5 mentions)
Georgetown U, 1975 *Certification:* Diagnostic Radiology
2333 Buchanan St 2nd Fl, San Francisco, 415-600-3232

Barakos, Jerome Antonio (5 mentions)
U of Southern California, 1986
Certification: Diagnostic Radiology, Neuroradiology
2333 Buchanan St 2nd Fl, San Francisco, 415-600-3232

Baron, Andrea Lynn (4 mentions)
Emory U, 1987 *Certification:* Diagnostic Radiology
250 Hospital Pkwy, San Jose, 408-972-7100

Borofsky, Harriet (3 mentions)
Certification: Diagnostic Radiology
1783 El Camino Real, Burlingame, 650-696-5515
100 S San Mateo Dr, San Mateo, 650-696-4550
222 W 39th Ave, San Mateo, 650-573-2681

Fischbein, Nancy Jane (4 mentions)
Harvard U, 1989
Certification: Diagnostic Radiology, Neuroradiology
300 Pasteur Dr #5047, Palo Alto, 650-723-7426

Futerman, Cheryl Lynn (3 mentions)
U of Cincinnati, 1986 *Certification:* Diagnostic Radiology
400 Channing Ave, Palo Alto, 650-323-1343

Hoddick, William Kevin (4 mentions)
Case Western Reserve U, 1979 *Certification:* Diagnostic Radiology
1601 Ygnacio Valley Rd, Walnut Creek, 925-296-7156

Hoffman, Kenneth Lawrence (6 mentions)
FMS-Canada, 1986 *Certification:* Diagnostic Radiology
250 Hospital Pkwy 1st Fl, San Jose, 408-972-7100

Jeffrey, Robert Brooke, Jr. (4 mentions)
Jefferson Med Coll, 1974 *Certification:* Diagnostic Radiology
300 Pasteur Dr #1307, Palo Alto, 650-723-8463

Kristensen, Torben B. (4 mentions)
U of Chicago, 1991 *Certification:* Diagnostic Radiology
701 E El Camino Real, Mountain View, 650-934-7700

Leung, Ann (4 mentions)
Certification: Diagnostic Radiology
300 Pasteur Dr #5078, Palo Alto, 650-725-0541

Lindan, Camilla Elspeth (3 mentions)
U of Pennsylvania, 1986 *Certification:* Diagnostic Radiology
2425 Geary Blvd 2nd Fl, San Francisco, 415-833-3700

Martin, Kenneth Wade (5 mentions)
U of California-San Diego, 1982
Certification: Diagnostic Radiology
747 52nd St, Oakland, 510-428-3410

Murao, John David (3 mentions)
U of Illinois, 1981
Certification: Diagnostic Radiology, Internal Medicine
795 El Camino Real, Palo Alto, 650-321-4121

O'Donohue, James (14 mentions)
Michigan State U, 1979 *Certification:* Diagnostic Radiology
250 Hospital Pkwy #100, San Jose, 408-972-7100

Rizzo, Michael Joseph (3 mentions)
U of Michigan, 1984 *Certification:* Diagnostic Radiology
280 W MacArthur Blvd, Oakland, 510-752-7455

Van Dalsem, Volney F., III (3 mentions)
Stanford U, 1975 *Certification:* Diagnostic Radiology
451 Sherman Ave, Palo Alto, 650-721-3379

Wollman, David Bruce (7 mentions)
U of California-San Diego, 1997
Certification: Diagnostic Radiology
700 Lawrence Expy, Santa Clara, 408-851-5020

Yacoe, Marshall Edwin (6 mentions)
U of Virginia, 1987 *Certification:* Diagnostic Radiology, Vascular & Interventional Radiology
700 Lawrence Expy 1st Fl, Santa Clara, 408-236-6400

Radiology—Therapeutic

Baker, Edward L. (5 mentions)
Georgetown U, 1975 *Certification:* Diagnostic Radiology
2333 Buchanan St 2nd Fl, San Francisco, 415-600-3232

Donaldson, Sarah Susan (5 mentions)
Harvard U, 1968 *Certification:* Therapeutic Radiology
875 Blake Wilbur Dr #G-225, Palo Alto, 650-723-6195

Finch, Ira John (7 mentions)
Boston U, 1979 *Certification:* Diagnostic Radiology
2540 East St, Concord, 925-295-1500

Hoppe, Richard (5 mentions)
Cornell U, 1971 *Certification:* Therapeutic Radiology
875 Blake Wilbur Dr #G-224, Palo Alto, 650-723-5510

Ostrow, Kenneth Scott (5 mentions)
U of California-San Francisco, 1990 *Certification:* Diagnostic Radiology, Vascular & Interventional Radiology
700 Lawrence Expy, Santa Clara, 408-236-4420

Rhee, John Shik (5 mentions)
Tufts U, 1994 *Certification:* Diagnostic Radiology
2450 Ashby Ave, Berkeley, 925-296-7150

Swift, Patrick Sean (4 mentions)
U of Pennsylvania, 1984 *Certification:* Radiation Oncology
2001 Dwight Way, Berkeley, 510-204-1244

Wack, Jon Philip (4 mentions)
U of California-San Francisco, 1968
Certification: Diagnostic Radiology
2333 Buchanan St 2nd Fl, San Francisco, 415-600-3232

Yacoe, Marshall Edwin (14 mentions)
U of Virginia, 1987 *Certification:* Diagnostic Radiology, Vascular & Interventional Radiology
710 Lawrence Expy 1st Fl, Santa Clara, 408-851-5020

Rehabilitation

Aftonomos, Lefkos B. (4 mentions)
U of Nebraska, 1975
Certification: Physical Medicine & Rehabilitation
100 S San Mateo Dr, San Mateo, 650-696-4300

Aguilar, Christine Mary (3 mentions)
U of California-San Diego, 1985
Certification: Pediatric Rehabilitation Medicine, Pediatrics, Physical Medicine & Rehabilitation
3505 Broadway 6th Fl, Oakland, 510-752-6561

Dana, John Aird, Jr. (4 mentions)
U of California-San Diego, 1991 *Certification:* Physical Medicine & Rehabilitation, Spinal Cord Injury Medicine
1981 N Broadway #180, Walnut Creek, 925-906-0400

Haining, Robert Rahn (4 mentions)
FMS-Mexico, 1980 *Certification:* Pediatric Rehabilitation Medicine, Pediatrics, Physical Medicine & Rehabilitation
747 52nd St 2nd Fl, Oakland, 510-428-3655

Mandac, Benjamin Reyes (3 mentions)
U of California-Davis, 1984 *Certification:* Pediatric Rehabilitation
  Medicine, Pediatrics, Physical Medicine & Rehabilitation
710 Lawrence Expy, Santa Clara, 408-851-9200

Rome, Scott Andrew (4 mentions)
Temple U, 1990 *Certification:* Physical Medicine & Rehabilitation
45 Castro St #200, San Francisco, 415-600-7710

Smith, Wayne (5 mentions)
Certification: Physical Medicine & Rehabilitation
275 Hospital Pkwy 3rd Fl, San Jose, 408-972-7160

Rheumatology

Abel, Thomas (19 mentions)
FMS-Canada, 1971
Certification: Internal Medicine, Rheumatology
260 International Cir Bldg 1N, San Jose, 408-362-4791

Birnbaum, Neal Sheldon (15 mentions)
Ohio State U, 1970
Certification: Internal Medicine, Rheumatology
2100 Webster St #112, San Francisco, 415-923-3060

Burns, Thomas Michael (14 mentions)
SUNY-Downstate Med Coll, 1978
Certification: Internal Medicine, Rheumatology
710 Lawrence Expy, Santa Clara, 405-851-2221

Dixit, Rajiv Kumar (6 mentions)
FMS-Kenya, 1975 *Certification:* Internal Medicine, Rheumatology
5201 Norris Canyon Rd #305, San Ramon, 925-867-9090
120 La Casa Via #204, Walnut Creek, 925-210-1050

Ellman, Jonathan Barney (8 mentions)
Rosalind Franklin U, 1972
Certification: Internal Medicine, Rheumatology
2850 Telegraph Ave #120, Berkeley, 925-254-9641

Fye, Kenneth Hjort (7 mentions)
U of California-San Francisco, 1968
Certification: Internal Medicine, Rheumatology
400 Parnassus Ave Plaza Lvl #587, San Francisco, 415-353-2497

Lambert, Rhonda Elaine (7 mentions)
U of Texas-Southwestern, 1983
Certification: Internal Medicine, Rheumatology
500 Arguello St #100, Redwood City, 650-851-4900

Sack, Kenneth Edward (8 mentions)
Tufts U, 1968 *Certification:* Internal Medicine, Rheumatology
400 Parnassus Ave Plaza #A555, San Francisco, 415-353-2497

Shoor, Stanford Mervyn (15 mentions)
Stanford U, 1979 *Certification:* Internal Medicine, Rheumatology
710 Lawrence Expy 2nd Fl, Santa Clara, 408-851-1000

Thoracic Surgery

Anastassiou, Peter Thomas (4 mentions)
Baylor U, 1983
2100 Webster St #411, San Francisco, 415-600-7860

Granelli, Steven Guy (4 mentions)
U of Virginia, 1978 *Certification:* Surgery
280 W MacArthur Blvd, Oakland, 510-752-1000

Grey, Douglas Peter (4 mentions)
U of California-Irvine, 1975
Certification: Thoracic Surgery, Vascular Surgery
2238 Geary Blvd 2nd Fl, San Francisco, 415-833-3383
99 Monticello Rd 2nd Fl, San Rafael, 415-444-2950

Jablons, David Mark (5 mentions)
Albany Med Coll, 1984 *Certification:* Thoracic Surgery
1600 Divisadero St, San Francisco, 415-885-3882

Katske, Gordon Eric (5 mentions)
Rosalind Franklin U, 1970 *Certification:* Thoracic Surgery
555 Knowles Dr #109, Los Gatos, 408-395-2299

Straznicka, Michaela (6 mentions)
U of Miami, 1994 *Certification:* Surgery, Thoracic Surgery
365 Lennon Ln #250, Walnut Creek, 925-932-6330

Whyte, Richard Ian (7 mentions)
U of Pittsburgh, 1983 *Certification:* Surgery, Thoracic Surgery
300 Pasteur Dr, Palo Alto, 650-723-6649

Urology

Aigen, Arnold Bruce (5 mentions)
Mount Sinai Sch of Med, 1982 *Certification:* Urology
701 E El Camino Real, Mountain View, 650-934-7555

Baskin, Laurence Seth (10 mentions)
U of California-Los Angeles, 1986
Certification: Pediatric Urology, Urology
400 Parnassus Ave #A610, San Francisco, 415-353-2065

Bassett, James Brandon (6 mentions)
Boston U, 1980 *Certification:* Urology
795 El Camino Real 3rd Fl, Palo Alto, 650-853-2988

Bennett, Patrick Mulvey (5 mentions)
U of California-San Francisco, 1989 *Certification:* Urology
1000 S Eliseo Dr #201, Greenbrae, 415-461-4000

Crotty, James Robert (7 mentions)
Boston U, 1979 *Certification:* Urology
280 Hospital Pkwy Bldg B, San Jose, 408-972-7000

Kamarei, Mehdi (8 mentions)
U of Pittsburgh, 1995 *Certification:* Urology
710 Lawrence Expy, Santa Clara, 408-851-4515

Pelavin, Jacqueline (7 mentions)
U of Illinois, 1984 *Certification:* Urology
710 Lawrence Expy, Santa Clara, 408-851-4515

Sharlip, Ira Dorian (5 mentions)
U of Pennsylvania, 1965 *Certification:* Internal Medicine, Urology
2100 Webster St #222, San Francisco, 415-202-0250

Shortliffe, Linda M. D. (5 mentions)
Stanford U, 1975 *Certification:* Pediatric Urology, Urology
300 Pasteur Dr #S287, Palo Alto, 650-724-7608
730 Welch Rd, Palo Alto, 650-497-8201

St. Lezin, Mark Allen (8 mentions)
U of California-Los Angeles, 1987 *Certification:* Urology
280 W MacArthur Blvd, Oakland, 510-752-1000

Taylor, Stephen Paul (9 mentions)
U of California-San Francisco, 1974 *Certification:* Urology
2222 East St #250, Concord, 925-609-7220
1455 Montego #101, Walnut Creek, 925-937-7740

Tsang, Timothy Hay-Chitt (12 mentions)
Stanford U, 1986 *Certification:* Urology
280 Hospital Pkwy Bldg B, San Jose, 408-972-6095

Werboff, Lawrence Henry (6 mentions)
U of Pittsburgh, 1974 *Certification:* Urology
2186 Geary Blvd #214, San Francisco, 415-922-3255

Vascular Surgery

Ceraldi, Christopher M. (9 mentions)
Med U of South Carolina, 1986
Certification: Surgery, Vascular Surgery
280 W MacArthur Blvd, Oakland, 510-752-1105

Grey, Douglas Peter (7 mentions)
U of California-Irvine, 1975
Certification: Thoracic Surgery, Vascular Surgery
2238 Geary Blvd 2nd Fl, San Francisco, 415-833-3383
99 Monticello Rd 2nd Fl, San Rafael, 415-444-2950

Groeger, Eugene Carroll (6 mentions)
Creighton U, 1974 *Certification:* Surgery
2645 Ocean Ave #307, San Francisco, 415-239-2300

Hayashi, Roger Mark (8 mentions)
U of California-Los Angeles, 1975
Certification: Surgery, Vascular Surgery
2512 Samaritan Ct #E, San Jose, 408-358-8272

Lam, Everett Yatwah (8 mentions)
Jefferson Med Coll, 1996 *Certification:* Surgery, Vascular Surgery
280 Hospital Pkwy Bldg A, San Jose, 408-972-3100

Long, John Bradley, Jr. (6 mentions)
U of California-Los Angeles, 1978 *Certification:* Vascular Surgery
3838 California St #612A, San Francisco, 415-221-7056

Olcott, Cornelius, IV (9 mentions)
Columbia U, 1967 *Certification:* Surgery, Vascular Surgery
300 Pasteur Dr #H3600, Palo Alto, 650-725-5227

Pak, Laura Kim (5 mentions)
U of Pennsylvania, 1993 *Certification:* Surgery, Vascular Surgery
2 Bon Air Rd #100, Larkspur, 415-927-0666
165 Rowland Way #103, Novato, 415-878-2910

Webb, Ronald Lee (15 mentions)
U of Texas-Southwestern, 1971 *Certification:* Vascular Surgery
130 La Casa Via Bldg 1 #201, Walnut Creek, 925-932-5313
365 Hawthorne Ave #103, Oakland, 510-832-6131

Colorado

Denver Area

Including Adams, Arapahoe, Denver, and Jefferson Counties

Allergy/Immunology

Adinoff, Allen David (5 mentions)
U of Michigan, 1977
Certification: Allergy & Immunology, Pediatrics
9331 S Colorado Blvd #100, Highlands Ranch, 303-795-8177

Atkins, Fred McDaniel (10 mentions)
U of Texas-Houston, 1975
Certification: Allergy & Immunology, Pediatrics
1400 Jackson St, Denver, 303-398-1148
13123 E 16th Ave, Aurora, 720-777-6181

Avner, Sanford Eldon (6 mentions)
SUNY-Downstate Med Coll, 1966
Certification: Allergy & Immunology, Pediatrics
10099 Ridgegate Pkwy #400, Lone Tree, 303-706-9923
9397 Crown Crest Blvd #400, Parker, 303-840-5677

Dreskin, Stephen Charles (4 mentions)
Emory U, 1977 *Certification:* Allergy & Immunology,
Diagnostic Laboratory Immunology, Internal Medicine
1635 N Ursula St, Aurora, 720-848-1940

Ebadi, Mark Alee (9 mentions)
U of Nebraska, 1997
Certification: Allergy & Immunology, Internal Medicine
125 Rampart Way #100, Denver, 720-858-7600

Greos, Leon Samuel (6 mentions)
U of Southern California, 1984
Certification: Allergy & Immunology
125 Rampart Way #100, Denver, 720-858-7600
14000 E Arapahoe Rd #110, Englewood, 303-632-3694

Liu, Andrew H. (4 mentions)
U of Massachusetts, 1985 *Certification:* Allergy & Immunology
1400 Jackson St, Denver, 303-398-1143

McDermott, Robert Arnold (5 mentions)
U of Colorado, 2000
Certification: Allergy & Immunology, Internal Medicine
2520 S Grand Ave #209, Glenwood Springs, 970-947-0600

Olson, Grant C. (6 mentions)
U of Colorado, 1983
Certification: Allergy & Immunology, Pediatrics
1667 Cole Blvd #200, Lakewood, 720-858-7600

Rumbyrt, Jeffrey Scot (4 mentions)
Loyola U Chicago, 1989 *Certification:* Allergy & Immunology
14142 Denver West Pkwy #345, Lakewood, 303-234-1067
1746 Cole Blvd #320, Lakewood, 303-234-1067

Silvers, William Samuel (11 mentions)
Indiana U, 1974
Certification: Allergy & Immunology, Internal Medicine
7180 E Orchard Rd #208, Englewood, 303-740-0998

Weber, Richard W. (5 mentions)
U of Wisconsin, 1969
Certification: Allergy & Immunology, Internal Medicine
1400 Jackson St, Denver, 303-388-4461

Williams, John Mark (4 mentions)
U of South Dakota, 1986
Certification: Allergy & Immunology, Internal Medicine
280 Exempla Cir, Lafayette, 720-536-7625

Anesthesiology

Baird, Bruce Robert (5 mentions)
U of Colorado, 1987 *Certification:* Anesthesiology
333 W Hampden Ave #600, Englewood, 303-761-5646

Berman, Jonathan Culver (4 mentions)
U of Colorado, 1986 *Certification:* Anesthesiology
9191 Grant St, Thornton, 303-451-7800

Brookens, Bruce Ragsdale (9 mentions)
Northwestern U, 1972 *Certification:* Anesthesiology
333 W Hampden Ave #600, Englewood, 303-761-5646

Clark, Randall Miles (4 mentions)
U of Colorado, 1982 *Certification:* Anesthesiology
13123 E 16th Ave, Aurora, 720-777-6226

Crino, Donald Gerard (3 mentions)
U of Colorado, 1991
333 W Hampden Ave #600, Englewood, 303-761-5646

Ellis, Ronald David (3 mentions)
Loma Linda U, 1980 *Certification:* Anesthesiology
333 W Hampden Ave #600, Englewood, 303-761-5646

Keyes, Thomas John (4 mentions)
U of Colorado, 1991 *Certification:* Anesthesiology
4231 W 16th Ave, Denver, 719-537-0712

Mattison, Roger Alan (3 mentions)
U of Minnesota, 1968 *Certification:* Anesthesiology, Pediatrics
1665 N Ursula St, Aurora, 720-848-4428

Piccone, Anthony David (3 mentions)
U of Colorado, 1985
10099 Ridgegate Pkwy, Lone Tree, 720-225-5000

Sederberg, James H. (3 mentions)
U of Nebraska, 1976 *Certification:* Anesthesiology
455 Sherman St #510, Denver, 303-377-6825

Theil, David Richard (5 mentions)
Indiana U, 1983 *Certification:* Anesthesiology, Internal Medicine
455 Sherman St #510, Denver, 303-377-6825

Veit, Andrew Michael (3 mentions)
Med Coll of Wisconsin, 1992 *Certification:* Anesthesiology
1601 E 19th Ave #5610, Denver, 303-830-8229

Cardiac Surgery

Cleveland, Joseph C., Jr. (9 mentions)
U of Washington, 1991 *Certification:* Surgery, Thoracic Surgery
1055 Clermont St, Denver, 303-399-8020
12631 E 17th Ave, Aurora, 303-724-2799

Guber, Myles Stuart (16 mentions)
Northwestern U, 1980 *Certification:* Thoracic Surgery
950 E Harvard Ave #550, Denver, 303-778-6527

Nene, Shriram Madhav (12 mentions)
Washington U, 1993 *Certification:* Surgery, Thoracic Surgery
1390 S Potomac St #120, Aurora, 303-695-1313

Parker, Richard Keith (27 mentions)
U of Nebraska, 1968 *Certification:* Surgery, Thoracic Surgery
1601 E 19th Ave #5000, Denver, 303-861-8158

Propp, John George (13 mentions)
U of Colorado, 1977
1390 S Potomac St #120, Aurora, 303-695-1313

Walker, Edwin Lance (13 mentions)
U of North Carolina, 1970
Certification: Surgery, Thoracic Surgery
4101 W Conejos Pl #250, Denver, 303-595-2700

Cardiology

Altman, John David (3 mentions)
U of Minnesota, 1992
Certification: Cardiovascular Disease, Interventional Cardiology
4101 W Conejos Pl #100, Denver, 303-595-2600

Bateman, Cinthia (5 mentions)
SUNY-Upstate Med U, 1998 *Certification:* Cardiovascular
   Disease, Internal Medicine, Interventional Cardiology
1000 Southpark Dr, Littleton, 303-744-1065
10103 Ridgegate Pkwy #303, Lone Tree, 303-744-1065

Benedict, Claudia K. (3 mentions)
U of Cincinnati, 1984
Certification: Cardiovascular Disease, Internal Medicine
8300 Alcott St #102, Westminster, 303-595-2600

Carroll, John D. (3 mentions)
U of Chicago, 1976 *Certification:* Cardiovascular Disease,
   Internal Medicine, Interventional Cardiology
12605 E 16th Ave, Aurora, 720-848-5300

Crisman, Thomas Stephen (7 mentions)
Boston U, 1990 *Certification:* Cardiovascular Disease
1601 E 19th Ave #5000, Denver, 303-839-7100

Dauber, Ira Mitchell (4 mentions)
Cornell U, 1977 *Certification:* Cardiovascular Disease,
   Internal Medicine, Interventional Cardiology
1000 Southpark Dr, Littleton, 303-744-1065

Godfrey, Clarke C., II (4 mentions)
Case Western Reserve U, 1966
Certification: Cardiovascular Disease, Internal Medicine
1601 E 19th Ave #5000, Denver, 303-861-4674

Greenberg, Jerry Howard (9 mentions)
New Jersey Med Sch, 1978
Certification: Cardiovascular Disease, Internal Medicine
1421 S Potomac St #40, Aurora, 303-750-0822
1444 S Potomac St #300, Aurora, 303-750-0822

Hergott, Lawrence Joseph (3 mentions)
U of Minnesota, 1971
Certification: Cardiovascular Disease, Internal Medicine
12605 E 16th Ave, Aurora, 720-848-5300

Ivy, David Dunbar (6 mentions)
Tulane U, 1988 *Certification:* Pediatric Cardiology, Pediatrics
13123 E 16th Ave, Aurora, 720-777-6820

Kim, Kelly Y. (3 mentions)
Brown U, 1994 *Certification:* Cardiovascular Disease,
   Clinical Cardiac Electrophysiology
3655 Lutheran Pkwy #201, Wheat Ridge, 720-284-3900

Lang, Christopher Anthony (5 mentions)
U of Cincinnati, 1979 *Certification:* Cardiovascular Disease,
   Internal Medicine, Interventional Cardiology
2045 Franklin 3rd Fl, Denver, 303-861-3610

Levitt, Peter Warren (3 mentions)
U of Pittsburgh, 1971
Certification: Cardiovascular Disease, Internal Medicine
499 E Hampden Ave #250, Englewood, 303-744-1065

Lindenfeld, Joann (8 mentions)
U of Michigan, 1973
Certification: Cardiovascular Disease, Internal Medicine
1645 N Ursula St, Aurora, 720-848-0850

Martel, Douglas Richard (3 mentions)
U of Texas-San Antonio, 1984 *Certification:* Cardiovascular
   Disease, Internal Medicine, Interventional Cardiology
13402 W Coal Mine Ave #240, Littleton, 720-284-3900
3655 Lutheran Pkwy #201, Wheat Ridge, 720-284-3900

Miklin, Jerry Sam (4 mentions)
U of Colorado, 1978 *Certification:* Cardiovascular Disease,
   Internal Medicine, Interventional Cardiology
3655 Lutheran Pkwy #201, Wheat Ridge, 720-284-3900

Molk, Barry Leon Abner (8 mentions)
U of Colorado, 1971
Certification: Cardiovascular Disease, Internal Medicine
10103 Ridgegate Pkwy #103, Lone Tree, 303-645-0090

Nawaz, Dilsher (3 mentions)
FMS-Egypt, 1983
1601 E 19th Ave #5000, Denver, 303-839-7100

Pacheco, Jose (5 mentions)
Harvard U, 1977
Certification: Cardiovascular Disease, Internal Medicine
8407 Bryant St, Westminster, 303-430-3160

Pachelo, George Michael (3 mentions)
U of Colorado, 1975
950 E Harvard Ave #480, Denver, 303-778-6880

Prager, Nelson Arthur (4 mentions)
U of Colorado, 1984
Certification: Cardiovascular Disease, Clinical Cardiac
   Electrophysiology, Internal Medicine, Interventional Cardiology
1421 S Potomac St #40, Aurora, 303-750-0822
1444 S Potomac St #300, Aurora, 303-750-0822

Prevedel, John Arthur (3 mentions)
Creighton U, 1981 *Certification:* Cardiovascular Disease,
   Internal Medicine, Interventional Cardiology
1601 E 19th Ave #5000, Denver, 303-839-7100

Ptasnic, Michael (4 mentions)
Michigan State U, 1975
4101 W Conejos Pl #100, Denver, 303-595-2600
4545 E 9th Ave #610, Denver, 303-595-2600

Rubenstein, Jeffrey Dan (6 mentions)
U of North Carolina, 1980
4101 W Conejos Pl #100, Denver, 303-595-2600
4545 E 9th Ave #610, Denver, 303-595-2600

Schaffer, Michael Stuart (5 mentions)
U of Minnesota, 1976
Certification: Pediatric Cardiology, Pediatrics
13123 E 16th Ave, Aurora, 720-777-6820

Smith, Barry Ray (3 mentions)
U of Wisconsin, 1974
Certification: Cardiovascular Disease, Internal Medicine
950 E Harvard Ave #480, Denver, 303-778-6880

Subbarao, Vijay D. (6 mentions)
FMS-India, 1989 *Certification:* Cardiovascular Disease
4101 W Conejos Pl #100, Denver, 303-595-2600
4545 E 9th Ave #610, Denver, 303-331-9121

Thompson, Donald Charles (4 mentions)
U of Oklahoma, 1990 *Certification:* Cardiovascular Disease
4101 W Conejos Pl #100, Denver, 303-595-2600
4545 E 9th Ave #610, Denver, 303-595-2600

Valent, Scott Richard (4 mentions)
U of Vermont, 1990 *Certification:* Interventional Cardiology
3655 Lutheran Pkwy #201, Wheat Ridge, 780-284-3900

Van Benthuysen, Karyl Max (4 mentions)
Duke U, 1976
Certification: Cardiovascular Disease, Internal Medicine
1000 Southpark Dr, Littleton, 303-744-1065

Wolfel, Eugene Edward (4 mentions)
Jefferson Med Coll, 1976
Certification: Cardiovascular Disease, Internal Medicine
12605 E 16th Ave, Aurora, 720-848-5300

Dermatology

Asarch, Richard Gordon (7 mentions)
U of Iowa, 1969 *Certification:* Dermatology, Dermatopathology
3701 S Clarkson St #400, Englewood, 303-761-7797

Capin, Leslie Rosanne (8 mentions)
U of Colorado, 1982 *Certification:* Dermatology
830 Potomac Cir #355, Aurora, 303-340-3378
19641 E Parker Sq Dr #E, Parker, 303-840-3311
100 Elkrun Dr #202, Basalt, 303-350-4500
9570 Kingston Ct #100, Englewood, 303-350-4500

Cohen, Joel Lee (5 mentions)
Mount Sinai Sch of Med, 1996 *Certification:* Dermatology
10099 Ridge Gate Pkwy #260, Lone Tree, 303-799-4260
499 E Hampden Ave #450, Englewood, 303-756-7546

Hill, Stanley Paul (5 mentions)
U of Cincinnati, 1993 *Certification:* Dermatology
17560 S Golden Rd #100, Golden, 303-526-1117

Huff, James Clark (5 mentions)
U of Texas-Dallas, 1969
Certification: Dermatological Immunology/Diagnostic and
   Laboratory Immunology, Dermatology, Internal Medicine
1665 N Ursula St, Aurora, 720-848-0500

Johnson, Karen Joy (4 mentions)
U of Colorado, 2000 *Certification:* Dermatology
4700 Hale Pkwy #140, Denver, 303-388-8807

Lemon, Meg (11 mentions)
U of Colorado, 1991 *Certification:* Dermatology
7000 E Belleview Ave #209, Greenwood Village, 303-850-9715
2005 Franklin St #175, Denver, 303 831 0400

Morelli, Joseph Gerald (7 mentions)
Harvard U, 1981 *Certification:* Dermatology, Pediatrics
13123 E 16th Ave, Aurora, 720-777-8445

Muldrow, Margaret E. (12 mentions)
Johns Hopkins U, 1990 *Certification:* Dermatology
1411 S Potomac St #170, Aurora, 303-369-4003
1601 E 19th Ave #4450, Denver, 303-830-2900

Norris, David Albert (4 mentions)
Duke U, 1973 *Certification:* Dermatological Immunology/
   Diagnostic and Laboratory Immunology, Dermatology
1665 N Ursula St, Aurora, 720-848-0500

Papadeas, Gregory G. (11 mentions)
Philadelphia Coll of Osteopathic Med, 1988
710 Summit Blvd #102, Frisco, 970-668-9650
1390 S Potomac St #124, Aurora, 303-368-8611
12645 E Euclid Dr, Centennial, 303-493-1910
30960 Stagecoach Blvd #W-14, Evergreen, 303-670-7065

Reed, Barbara Ruth (8 mentions)
U of Colorado, 1968 *Certification:* Dermatology
2200 E 18th Ave, Denver, 303-322-7789

Sawada, Kathleen Yumi (5 mentions)
Wake Forest U, 1981 *Certification:* Dermatology
1536 Cole Blvd Bldg 4, Lakewood, 303-463-9600

Wright, Robert Chase (6 mentions)
Indiana U, 1968 *Certification:* Dermatology, Dermatopathology
1551 Milky Way, Denver, 303-426-4525
8550 W 38th Ave #108, Wheat Ridge, 303-426-4525

Emergency Medicine

Avner, David Bryan (3 mentions)
U of Virginia, 1999 *Certification:* Emergency Medicine
3033 S Parker Rd #800, Aurora, 303-306-7783

Bajaj, Lalit (4 mentions)
U of California-San Francisco, 1996
Certification: Pediatric Emergency Medicine, Pediatrics
13123 E 16th Ave, Aurora, 303-724-5555

Bothner, Joan P. (3 mentions)
U of Texas-Galveston, 1983
Certification: Pediatric Emergency Medicine, Pediatrics
13123 E 16th Ave, Aurora, 720-777-2806

Friedenson, David Gerard (3 mentions)
U of Massachusetts, 1996 *Certification:* Emergency Medicine
3033 S Parker Rd #800, Aurora, 303-306-7783

Heinz, Stephen Michael (5 mentions)
Wayne State U, 1980 *Certification:* Emergency Medicine
3033 S Parker Rd #800, Aurora, 303-306-7783

Lansville, Frank R. (4 mentions)
Western U, 1992 *Certification:* Emergency Medicine
3033 S Parker Rd #800, Aurora, 303-306-7783

Lefkowits, Donald Jay (9 mentions)
Dartmouth Coll, 1978
Certification: Emergency Medicine, Internal Medicine
3033 S Parker Rd #800, Aurora, 303-306-7783

Lowenstein, Steven Ralph (4 mentions)
Mount Sinai Sch of Med, 1976
Certification: Emergency Medicine, Internal Medicine
4200 E 9th Ave, Denver, 303-372-5500

Murphy, Carla Elizabeth (3 mentions)
U of North Texas, 1982 *Certification:* Emergency Medicine
8300 W 38th Ave, Wheat Ridge, 303-425-2089

Rosenberg, David Evan (3 mentions)
George Washington U, 1987 *Certification:* Emergency Medicine
2550 S Parker Rd #206, Aurora, 303-741-3997

Sassu, George P. (3 mentions)
Midwestern U Chicago Coll of Osteopathic Med, 1985
Certification: Emergency Medicine
3033 S Parker Rd #800, Aurora, 303-306-7783

Schmidt, Robert Daniel (3 mentions)
Virginia Commonwealth U, 1987
Certification: Emergency Medicine
4231 W 16th Ave, Denver, 303-629-3982

Shields, Brian Thomas (3 mentions)
U of Toledo, 1991 *Certification:* Emergency Medicine
4231 W 16th Ave, Denver, 303-674-0978

Ziller, Andrew Bernard (4 mentions)
Case Western Reserve U, 1986
Certification: Emergency Medicine, Internal Medicine
3033 S Parker Rd #800, Aurora, 303-306-7783

Endocrinology

Barter, Mark (5 mentions)
U of Colorado, 1972
Certification: Endocrinology and Metabolism, Internal Medicine
4101 W Conejos Pl #300, Denver, 303-629-2091
9141 Grant St #120, Denver, 720-872-2321

Buckley, Linda Lee (4 mentions)
U of Colorado, 2000 *Certification:* Endocrinology, Diabetes, and Metabolism, Internal Medicine
601 E Hampton, Englewood, 303-321-2644

Eagan, Margaret Anne (4 mentions)
Georgetown U, 1990
4500 E 9th Ave #640, Denver, 303-394-9355

Haas, Romana Moezzi (5 mentions)
Case Western Reserve U, 1999 *Certification:* Endocrinology, Diabetes, and Metabolism, Internal Medicine
4600 Hale Pkwy #490, Denver, 303-329-7876

Hone, Jennifer (14 mentions)
George Washington U, 1989
Certification: Endocrinology, Diabetes, and Metabolism
4600 Hale Pkwy #490, Denver, 303-329-7876

Kerstein, Howard Jay (6 mentions)
U of Colorado, 1966
Certification: Endocrinology and Metabolism, Internal Medicine
3865 Cherry Creek North Dr #322, Denver, 303-394-2888

Lifschitz, Mervyn Leon (7 mentions)
FMS-South Africa, 1970
Certification: Endocrinology and Metabolism, Internal Medicine
4545 E 9th Ave #310, Denver, 303-388-4673

McDermott, Michael Thomas (10 mentions)
Tulane U, 1977
Certification: Endocrinology and Metabolism, Internal Medicine
1635 N Ursula St, Aurora, 720-848-2650

Osa, Steven Ray (12 mentions)
Cornell U, 1977
Certification: Endocrinology and Metabolism, Internal Medicine
850 E Harvard Ave #405, Denver, 303-722-4683

Rees-Jones, Robert Winston (21 mentions)
Harvard U, 1979
Certification: Endocrinology and Metabolism, Internal Medicine
1550 S Potomac St #260, Aurora, 303-369-9445

Tong, Kevin T. (4 mentions)
Certification: Endocrinology, Diabetes, and Metabolism, Internal Medicine
3655 Lutheran Pkwy #407, Wheat Ridge, 303-403-3000
1805 Kipling St #100, Lakewood, 303-232-7500

Family Practice *(see note on page 9)*

Cain, Jeffrey James (3 mentions)
Oregon Health Sciences U, 1985 *Certification:* Family Medicine
3055 Roslyn St #100, Denver, 720-848-9000

Lumian, Daniel Rothschild (4 mentions)
U of Kansas, 1978 *Certification:* Family Medicine
1750 Race St, Denver, 303-355-7414

Morrison, John David (4 mentions)
Case Western Reserve U, 1972 *Certification:* Family Medicine
950 E Harvard Ave #110, Denver, 303-777-0577

Pattridge, Mark Frederick (3 mentions)
U of Colorado, 1984 *Certification:* Family Medicine
17601 S Golden Rd, Golden, 303-278-4600

Rail, Carla Jean (3 mentions)
U of Colorado, 1984 *Certification:* Family Medicine
8550 W 38th Ave #206, Wheat Ridge, 303-953-7700

Steiner, Jane Carolyn (3 mentions)
U of Colorado, 1981 *Certification:* Family Medicine
4545 E 9th Ave #245, Denver, 303-320-4414

Zonca, Jonathan Dennis (8 mentions)
Michigan State U, 1999 *Certification:* Family Medicine
4500 E 9th Ave #320, Denver, 303-322-7325

Gastroenterology

Anouna, Sam (4 mentions)
SUNY-Downstate Med Coll, 1974 *Certification:* Internal Medicine
4500 E 9th Ave #560, Denver, 303-252-4442
10001 Washington St #2, Denver, 303-388-6874

Ayres, Steven Jay (8 mentions)
U of Minnesota, 1977
Certification: Gastroenterology, Internal Medicine
2005 Franklin St #280, Denver, 303-321-7018

Dahl, Carl Robert (10 mentions)
U of Colorado, 1971
Certification: Gastroenterology, Internal Medicine
8550 W 38th Ave #300, Wheat Ridge, 303-463-3900

Fieman, Richard Allen (4 mentions)
U of Colorado, 1976
Certification: Gastroenterology, Internal Medicine
1300 S Potomac St #104, Aurora, 303-671-5553
9397 Crown Crest Blvd #311, Parker, 303-766-4516

Fishman, Jonathan Paul (20 mentions)
FMS-South Africa, 1995
Certification: Gastroenterology, Internal Medicine
4500 E 9th Ave #720, Denver, 303-355-3525

Goff, John Sawyer (7 mentions)
U of California-Irvine, 1975
Certification: Gastroenterology, Internal Medicine
7000 W Colfax Ave #B, Lakewood, 303-573-9951

Hanna, Philip Dale (5 mentions)
U of Colorado, 1980
Certification: Gastroenterology, Internal Medicine
10103 Ridgegate Pkwy #312, Lone Tree, 303-790-7334

Kim, Lawrence Sangil (4 mentions)
Johns Hopkins U, 1992 *Certification:* Gastroenterology
10103 Ridgegate Pkwy #312, Lone Tree, 303-790-7334

Levine, Joel Seth (4 mentions)
SUNY-Downstate Med Coll, 1971
Certification: Gastroenterology, Internal Medicine
1635 N ursula St, Aurora, 720-848-2777

Linkow, Mark Allen (7 mentions)
U of Colorado, 1971
Certification: Gastroenterology, Internal Medicine
4500 E 9th Ave #720, Denver, 303-355-3525

Reveille, Robert Matthew (9 mentions)
U of Maryland, 1984
Certification: Gastroenterology, Internal Medicine
7000 W Colfax Ave #B, Lakewood, 303-573-9951

Richman, Lee Kenneth (4 mentions)
New York U, 1971
Certification: Gastroenterology, Internal Medicine
8550 W 38th Ave #300, Wheat Ridge, 303-463-3900

Sabel, John Stephen (5 mentions)
U of Virginia, 1972
Certification: Gastroenterology, Internal Medicine
10103 Ridge Gate Pkwy #312, Lone Tree, 303-790-7334
499 E Hampden Ave #420, Englewood, 303-788-8888

Weiner, Kenneth Jay (12 mentions)
Certification: Gastroenterology
2005 Franklin St #280, Denver, 303-321-7018

General Surgery

Baer, David A. (4 mentions)
U of Colorado, 1986 *Certification:* Surgery
401 W Hampden Pl #23, Englewood, 303-788-8989

Barnes, Stephen Matthew (3 mentions)
Loyola U Chicago, 1988 *Certification:* Surgery
9397 Crown Crest Blvd #210, Parker, 303-805-9802

Bell, Reginald C. W. (4 mentions)
Virginia Commonwealth U, 1985 *Certification:* Surgery
401 W Hampden Pl #230, Englewood, 303-788-8989

Clark, Sallie Brooks (5 mentions)
U of Tennessee, 1984 *Certification:* Surgery
1421 S Potomac St #110, Aurora, 303-337-5600
8200 E Belleview Ave #102, Englewood, 303-224-9722

Cross, Jeffrey Schuyler (12 mentions)
Brown U, 1985 *Certification:* Surgery
2460 W 26th Ave #420C, Denver, 303-480-3565

DeLine, James (4 mentions)
Creighton U, 1984 *Certification:* Surgery
401 W Hampden Pl #230, Englewood, 303-788-8989

Ehrichs, Edward L., Jr. (5 mentions)
U of Colorado, 1968 *Certification:* Surgery
1550 S Potomac St #350, Aurora, 303-369-1066

Georgescu, Doru I. E. (3 mentions)
FMS-Romania, 1980 *Certification:* Surgery
9351 Grant St #400, Denver, 303-452-0059

Kortz, Eric Owen (7 mentions)
U of Colorado, 1982 *Certification:* Surgery
601 E Hampden Ave #470, Englewood, 303-789-1877

Long, David Michael (3 mentions)
U of Colorado, 1973 *Certification:* Surgery, Thoracic Surgery
8300 Alcott St #201, Westminster, 303-428-0004

Macdonald, Robert M. (12 mentions)
George Washington U, 1991 *Certification:* Surgery
4545 E 9th Ave #460, Denver, 303-388-2922
1606 Prairie Center Pkwy #200, Brighton, 303-659-5165

McIntyre, Robert C., Jr. (3 mentions)
Tulane U, 1987 *Certification:* Surgery, Surgical Critical Care
1635 N Ursula St, Aurora, 720-848-2700

Moore, John B. (5 mentions)
Certification: Surgery
777 Bannock St, Denver, 303-436-6558

Moore, Joyce Ann (4 mentions)
U of Colorado, 1989 *Certification:* Surgery
4500 E 9th Ave #710, Denver, 303-320-7826
10103 Ridgegate Pkwy #350, Lone Tree, 303-320-7826

Mozia, Nelson Ike (9 mentions)
Wake Forest U, 1975
Certification: Colon & Rectal Surgery, Surgery
8550 W 38th Ave #205, Wheat Ridge, 303-467-8987

Napierkowski, Michael T. (4 mentions)
U of Chicago, 1994 *Certification:* Surgery
4545 E 9th Ave #460, Denver, 303-388-2922
1606 Prairie Center Pkwy #200, Brighton, 303-659-5165

Pearlman, Nathan William (5 mentions)
U of Illinois, 1966 *Certification:* Surgery
1635 N Ursula St, Aurora, 720-848-0300

Plaus, William Joseph (14 mentions)
Harvard U, 1980 *Certification:* Surgery
4545 E 9th Ave #460, Denver, 303-388-2922
1606 Prairie Center Pkwy #200, Brighton, 303-659-5165

Ridge, Brian Alfred (4 mentions)
U of Utah, 1983 *Certification:* Surgery, Vascular Surgery
7805 W 38th Ave, Wheat Ridge, 303-431-2900

Rosenberger, Alan Bruce (8 mentions)
Ohio State U, 1977 *Certification:* Surgery
9351 Grant St #400, Thornton, 303-452-0059

Rothenberg, Steven (3 mentions)
U of Colorado, 1984 *Certification:* Pediatric Surgery, Surgery
1601 E 19th Ave #5500, Denver, 303-839-6001

Seale, Fred C. (3 mentions)
Baylor U, 1994 *Certification:* Surgery
3455 Lutheran Pkwy #290, Wheat Ridge, 303-467-1400

Smith, Edwin Ray (4 mentions)
U of Texas-Dallas, 1979 *Certification:* Surgery
7750 S Broadway #230, Littleton, 303-798-8811

Stiegmann, Gregory Van (4 mentions)
U of Illinois, 1975 *Certification:* Surgery
12631 E 17th Ave, Aurora, 720-848-2700

Vansickle, David Patrick (3 mentions)
7750 S Broadway #150, Littleton, 303-734-8650
7780 S Broadway #260, Littleton, 303-734-8650

Vaughn, Edward Allen (5 mentions)
U of New Mexico, 1982 *Certification:* Surgery
2045 Franklin St, Denver, 303-338-4545

Vernon, Walter Benson (4 mentions)
Harvard U, 1980 *Certification:* Surgery, Surgical Critical Care
2555 S Downing St #130, Denver, 303-777-7112

Waring, Bruce J. (7 mentions)
U of Colorado, 1987 *Certification:* Surgery
3555 Lutheran Pkwy #380, Wheat Ridge, 303-940-8200

Young, Shawn E. (5 mentions)
U of North Dakota, 1998 *Certification:* Surgery
1601 E 19th Ave #4500, Denver, 303-831-6100

Geriatrics

Morgenstern, Nora Ellerbe (3 mentions)
Stanford U, 1977 *Certification:* Geriatric Medicine, Hospice
and Palliative Medicine, Internal Medicine
2550 S Parker Rd #400, Aurora, 303-636-3308

Murphy, Donald Jerome (4 mentions)
U of Colorado, 1982 *Certification:* Internal Medicine
499 E Hampden Ave #100, Englewood, 303-306-4321
850 E Harvard Ave #305, Denver, 303-306-4321

Wallace, Jeffrey Irving (7 mentions)
U of Michigan, 1984
Certification: Geriatric Medicine, Internal Medicine
1635 N Ursula St, Aurora, 720-848-3400

Wasserman, Michael Ross (3 mentions)
U of Texas-Galveston, 1985
Certification: Geriatric Medicine, Internal Medicine
1400 S Potomac St #150, Aurora, 303-695-2930
499 E Hampden Ave #100, Englewood, 303-869-2269

Hematology/Oncology

Bourg, Wilson Charles, III (4 mentions)
Louisiana State U, 1973
Certification: Hematology, Internal Medicine, Medical Oncology
2045 Franklin St, Denver, 303-861-3302

Brunvand, Mark Wilson (5 mentions)
U of Colorado, 1982
Certification: Internal Medicine, Medical Oncology
1800 Williams St #200, Denver, 303-388-4876

Caskey, Jennifer Hurd (11 mentions)
U of Massachusetts, 1975
Certification: Hematology, Internal Medicine, Medical Oncology
4045 Wadsworth Blvd #210, Wheat Ridge, 303-467-3490

Di Bella, Nicholas Joseph (5 mentions)
U of Southern California, 1965
Certification: Hematology, Internal Medicine, Medical Oncology
1700 S Potomac St, Aurora, 303-418-7600

Diab, Sami (4 mentions)
FMS-Syria, 1988 *Certification:* Medical Oncology
1700 S Potomac St, Aurora, 303-418-7600
22 W Dry Creek Cir, Littleton, 303-730-4700

Feiner, Alan Stuart (9 mentions)
U of Colorado, 1973 *Certification:* Hematology, Internal Medicine
4700 E Hale Pkwy #400, Denver, 303-321-0302

Greffe, Brian Scott (5 mentions)
FMS-Canada, 1983
Certification: Pediatric Hematology-Oncology, Pediatrics
13123 E 16th Ave #115, Aurora, 720-777-6741

Hassell, Kathryn Severson (4 mentions)
U of Minnesota, 1986
Certification: Hematology, Internal Medicine, Medical Oncology
1665 N Ursula St, Aurora, 720-848-0300

Hays, Taru (4 mentions)
FMS-India, 1961
Certification: Pediatric Hematology-Oncology, Pediatrics
13123 E 16th Ave, Aurora, 303-861-6740

Hesky, Richard Brice (8 mentions)
U of Arizona, 1978
Certification: Internal Medicine, Medical Oncology
2005 Franklin St Bldg 2 #170, Denver, 303-860-9100

Hinshaw, Ioana M. (6 mentions)
FMS-Romania, 1988
Certification: Internal Medicine, Medical Oncology
1800 Williams St #200, Denver, 303-388-4876

Kantor, Robert Scott (6 mentions)
Wayne State U, 1986
Certification: Hematology, Internal Medicine, Medical Oncology
8805 W 14th Ave #102, Lakewood, 303-232-0602
34 Van Gordon St #120, Lakewood, 303-232-0602
1700 S Potomac St, Aurora, 303-418-7600
22 W Dry Creek Cir, Littleton, 303-730-4700

Kenney, Thomas James, III (4 mentions)
U of Maryland, 1998
Certification: Hematology, Internal Medicine, Medical Oncology
2555 S Downing St #240, Denver, 303-715-7030

Lee, William Eng (5 mentions)
U of Pittsburgh, 1990
Certification: Internal Medicine, Medical Oncology
9451 Huron St, Denver, 303-650-4042

Matous, Jeffrey Victor (8 mentions)
U of Washington, 1985
Certification: Internal Medicine, Medical Oncology
1800 Williams St, Denver, 303-388-4876

Napoli, Joseph Nicholas (7 mentions)
St Louis U, 1970
Certification: Hematology, Internal Medicine, Medical Oncology
8805 W 14th Ave #102, Lakewood, 303-232-0602

Odom, Lorrie F. (4 mentions)
U of Colorado, 1969
Certification: Pediatric Hematology-Oncology, Pediatrics
1601 E 19th Ave #6600, Denver, 303-832-2344

Parra, Michael Theodore (6 mentions)
Creighton U, 1984 *Certification:* Internal Medicine
401 W Hampden Pl #250, Englewood, 303-733-9971
10103 Ridgegate Pkwy #106, Lone Tree, 303-733-9971

Tolley, Russell Clayton (7 mentions)
U of Virginia, 1985
Certification: Hematology, Internal Medicine, Medical Oncology
8820 Huron St, Thornton, 303-386-7622

Infectious Disease

Blum, Raymond Neil (17 mentions)
U of Colorado, 1983
Certification: Infectious Disease, Internal Medicine
1601 E 19th Ave #3650, Denver, 303-831-4774

Desjardin, Jeffrey Allen (6 mentions)
Vanderbilt U, 1990 *Certification:* Infectious Disease
3885 Upham St #200, Wheat Ridge, 303-425-9245

Fujita, Norman Kazuhisa (25 mentions)
U of Southern California, 1975
Certification: Infectious Disease, Internal Medicine
3885 Upham St #200, Wheat Ridge, 303-425-9245

Glode, Mary Patricia Rose (5 mentions)
Washington U, 1972
Certification: Pediatric Infectious Diseases, Pediatrics
13123 E 16th Ave, Aurora, 720-777-6981

Golub, Burton Phillip (6 mentions)
Boston U, 1965 *Certification:* Internal Medicine
601 E Hampden Ave #340, Englewood, 303-788-5900

Greenberg, Kenneth S. (9 mentions)
Des Moines U, 1986
4545 E 9th Ave #120, Denver, 303-393-8050

Harte, Jonathan Stuart (17 mentions)
Robert W Johnson Med Sch, 1990
Certification: Infectious Disease
1550 S Potomac St #270, Aurora, 303-750-1800

Mason, Susan Ruth (20 mentions)
Tufts U, 1979 *Certification:* Infectious Disease, Internal Medicine
3885 Upham St #200, Wheat Ridge, 303-425-9245

Neid, James Michael, Jr. (5 mentions)
U of Nebraska, 1995 *Certification:* Infectious Disease
1550 S Potomac St #270, Aurora, 303-750-1800

Young, Benjamin (6 mentions)
Certification: Infectious Disease
4545 E 9th Ave #120, Denver, 303-393-8050

Infertility

Albrecht, Bruce Henry (9 mentions)
U of Colorado, 1974 *Certification:* Obstetrics & Gynecology,
   Reproductive Endocrinology/Infertility
271 W County Line Rd, Littleton, 303-794-0045
300 Exempla Cir #370, Lafayette, 303-449-1084

Minjarez, Debra Ann (7 mentions)
Stanford U, 1993 *Certification:* Obstetrics & Gynecology,
   Reproductive Endocrinology/Infertility
4545 E 9th Ave #420, Denver, 303-355-2555
10290 Ridge Gate Cir, Lone Tree, 303-788-8300

Schoolcraft, William Blaine (16 mentions)
U of Kansas, 1979 *Certification:* Obstetrics & Gynecology
10290 Ridgegate Cir, Lone Tree, 303-788-8300

Internal Medicine *(see note on page 9)*

Aboaf, Alan P. (4 mentions)
Albert Einstein Coll of Med, 1989 *Certification:* Internal Medicine
1400 S Potomac St #190, Aurora, 303-369-4932

Aikin, John Douglas, Jr. (4 mentions)
U of Texas-Houston, 1979 *Certification:* Internal Medicine
200 W County Line Rd #310, Highlands Ranch, 303-791-2841

Anderson, Robert James (3 mentions)
U of Nebraska, 1968
Certification: Geriatric Medicine, Internal Medicine, Nephrology
12631 E 17th Ave #B-178, Aurora, 303-724-1785
4200 E 9th Ave, Denver, 303-315-7765

Apke, Richard Joseph (3 mentions)
Creighton U, 1982 *Certification:* Internal Medicine
51 W 84th Ave #300, Denver, 303-428-0533

Brown, Gerald Douglas (3 mentions)
U of Illinois, 1973 *Certification:* Internal Medicine
6169 S Balsam Way #190, Littleton, 303-933-8240

Carson, Robert Ian (3 mentions)
U of Colorado, 1992 *Certification:* Internal Medicine
155 S Madison St #210, Denver, 303-333-5456

Citron, Daniel Craig (4 mentions)
U of Texas-Dallas, 1977 *Certification:* Internal Medicine
4545 E 9th Ave #670, Denver, 303-320-7744

Cohen, Brent Michael (4 mentions)
George Washington U, 1990 *Certification:* Internal Medicine
4525 E 8th Ave, Denver, 303-329-6500

Colson, Ronald Scott (4 mentions)
U of Illinois, 1990 *Certification:* Internal Medicine
4545 E 9th Ave #670, Denver, 303-320-7744

Earnest, Mark Allen (4 mentions)
Vanderbilt U, 1990 *Certification:* Internal Medicine
1635 N Ursula St, Aurora, 720-848-2300
360 S Garfield St #500, Denver, 303-372-3000

Feinberg, Lawrence E. (7 mentions)
U of Rochester, 1972
Certification: Gastroenterology, Internal Medicine
1635 N Ursula 5th Fl, Aurora, 720-848-2300

Ghincea, Tunde (3 mentions)
FMS-Romania, 1985 *Certification:* Internal Medicine
1601 E 19th Ave #3700, Denver, 303-861-7001

Kick, Steven David (3 mentions)
U of Oklahoma, 1987 *Certification:* Internal Medicine
1635 N Ursula St, Aurora, 720-848-2300

Krebs, Steve Richard (4 mentions)
Eastern Virginia Med Sch, 1989 *Certification:* Internal Medicine
7821 W 38th Ave, Wheat Ridge, 303-422-2343

Mangalik, Saurabh (3 mentions)
U of Colorado, 1994 *Certification:* Internal Medicine
4545 E 9th Ave #630, Denver, 303-320-2929

Mellman, David Lewis (7 mentions)
U of Colorado, 1994 *Certification:* Internal Medicine
4545 E 9th Ave #630, Denver, 303-320-2929

Miranda, Charles Henry (3 mentions)
U of California-San Francisco, 1990
Certification: Internal Medicine
1801 High St 2nd Fl, Denver, 303-869-2160

Ricca, Christopher Edward (4 mentions)
Washington U, 1996 *Certification:* Internal Medicine
7310 E Arapahoe Rd #200, Centennial, 303-740-0400

Spies, Carol Susan (6 mentions)
Tulane U, 1983 *Certification:* Internal Medicine
499 E Hampden Ave #400, Englewood, 303-788-1620

Stuebner, Jon Woodford (3 mentions)
Tulane U, 1970 *Certification:* Internal Medicine
14000 E Arapahoe Rd #300, Centennial, 303-617-7786

Tanaka, David Joseph (5 mentions)
U of Washington, 1983 *Certification:* Internal Medicine
360 S Garfield St #500, Denver, 720-848-9500

Winn, David Brian (4 mentions)
Northwestern U, 1993 *Certification:* Internal Medicine
1721 E 19th Ave #510, Denver, 303-863-7377

Nephrology

Anger, Michael Scott (5 mentions)
Hahnemann U, 1981
Certification: Internal Medicine, Nephrology
8410 Decatur St, Westminster, 303-430-7000

Dillingham, Mark Allan (10 mentions)
Yale U, 1977 *Certification:* Internal Medicine
950 E Harvard Ave #240, Denver, 303-871-0977

Esson, Matthew Lingle (6 mentions)
U of Colorado, 1995 *Certification:* Nephrology
8410 Decatur St, Westminster, 303-430-7000

Fisch, Bruce Jeffrey (8 mentions)
U of Colorado, 1990 *Certification:* Nephrology
10099 Ridge Gate Pkwy #310, Lone Tree, 303-799-8760

Gillum, David Michael (5 mentions)
U of Colorado, 1977 *Certification:* Internal Medicine, Nephrology
1750 Pierce St, Lakewood, 303-232-3366
5265 Vance St #2, Arvada, 303-232-3366

Klein, Melvyn Harvey (7 mentions)
SUNY-Downstate Med Coll, 1966
Certification: Internal Medicine, Nephrology
7720 S Broadway #220, Littleton, 303-996-7555

Lum, Gary Michael (4 mentions)
Wake Forest U, 1970
13103 E 16th Ave #B-308, Aurora, 720-777-6263

Pluss, Richard Gary (5 mentions)
U of Colorado, 1971 *Certification:* Internal Medicine, Nephrology
950 E Harvard Ave #240, Denver, 303-871-0977

Rocklin, Michael Alan (4 mentions)
Baylor U, 1995 *Certification:* Nephrology
4545 E 9th Ave #150, Denver, 303-991-0993

Sakiewicz, Paul George (4 mentions)
FMS-Austria, 1991 *Certification:* Internal Medicine, Nephrology
1411 S Potomac St #360, Aurora, 303-755-7681

Senkfor, Stuart Ivan (9 mentions)
Case Western Reserve U, 1985
Certification: Internal Medicine, Nephrology
4545 E 9th Ave #150, Denver, 303-991-0993

Singh, Harmeet (8 mentions)
FMS-India, 1986 *Certification:* Internal Medicine, Nephrology
1750 Pierce St, Lakewood, 303-232-3366

Teitelbaum, Isaac (5 mentions)
SUNY-Downstate Med Coll, 1979
Certification: Internal Medicine, Nephrology
1635 N Ursula St, Aurora, 720-848-0748

Yanover, Melissa J. (11 mentions)
U of Pittsburgh, 1977
Certification: Internal Medicine, Nephrology
1750 Pierce St, Lakewood, 303-232-3366
5265 Vance St #2, Arvada, 303-232-3366

Neurological Surgery

Drewek, Michael James (6 mentions)
U of Wisconsin, 1993 *Certification:* Neurological Surgery
4101 W Conejos Pl #225, Denver, 303-595-6765

Elliott, John Paul (9 mentions)
Columbia U, 1988 *Certification:* Neurological Surgery
499 E Hampden Ave #220, Englewood, 303-783-8844

Johnson, Stephen David (6 mentions)
U of Tennessee, 1974 *Certification:* Neurological Surgery
1601 E 19th Ave #4400, Denver, 303-861-2266

Lillehei, Kevin Owen (18 mentions)
U of Minnesota, 1979 *Certification:* Neurological Surgery
1635 N Ursula St, Aurora, 303-493-8333

Markey, Sean Edward (6 mentions)
U of Colorado, 1997
7750 S Broadway #150, Littleton, 303-734-8650
7780 S Broadway #260, Littleton, 303-734-8650

Nichols, John Stephan (6 mentions)
U of Texas-Dallas, 1984 *Certification:* Neurological Surgery
4101 W Conejos Pl #225, Denver, 303-595-6765

Oro, John James Forteza (6 mentions)
U of Texas-Galveston, 1978 *Certification:* Neurological Surgery
1444 S Potomac St #170, Aurora, 303-481-0035

Shogan, Stephen Harvey (17 mentions)
U of Michigan, 1976 *Certification:* Neurological Surgery
4600 Hale Pkwy #410, Denver, 303-333-8740

Neurology

Alexander, Mihaela G. (4 mentions)
FMS-Romania, 1987 *Certification:* Neurology
7780 S Broadway #360, Littleton, 303-730-2883
10099 Ridgegate Pkwy, Lone Tree, 303-730-2883

Bennett, Jeffrey L. (4 mentions)
Stanford U, 1993 *Certification:* Neurology
1635 N Ursula St, Aurora, 720-848-2080

Bentley, William Howard (7 mentions)
U of Texas-Dallas, 1974 *Certification:* Neurology
1375 E 20th Ave 3rd Fl, Denver, 303-861-3380

Bryniarski, Elizabeth (5 mentions)
FMS-Poland, 1991
1444 S Potomac St #170, Aurora, 303-481-0030

Crosby, James Andrew (4 mentions)
Kansas U Coll of Osteopathic Med, 1976 *Certification:* Neurology
9141 Grant St #237, Denver, 303-452-1292

Feldman, Alexander (5 mentions)
Certification: Neurology
1721 E 19th Ave #468, Denver, 303-863-0501

Ginsburg, Stanley Herbert (5 mentions)
U of Colorado, 1960 *Certification:* Neurology
4545 E 9th Ave #510, Denver, 303-321-0700

London, Scott Franklin (9 mentions)
U of Vermont, 1985 *Certification:* Neurology
8585 W 14th Ave #A, Lakewood, 303-629-5600

McNutt, J. Trevor (7 mentions)
U of Texas-Houston, 1998 *Certification:* Neurology
7720 S Broadway #150, Littleton, 720-283-6573

Parsons, Julie Anne (4 mentions)
U of Colorado, 1989 *Certification:* Neurology with Special
Qualifications in Child Neurology
13123 E 16th Ave #B-155, Aurora, 720-777-6895

Redosh, Douglas John (6 mentions)
Temple U, 1990 *Certification:* Neurology
3550 Lutheran Pkwy #200, Wheat Ridge, 303-425-9900

Ringel, Steven Peter (8 mentions)
U of Michigan, 1968 *Certification:* Neurology
1635 N Ursula St, Aurora, 720-848-2080

Smith, Don Benson (4 mentions)
Emory U, 1974
Certification: Internal Medicine, Neurology, Vascular Neurology
601 E Hampden Ave #500, Englewood, 303-781-4485

Smith, Richard Hunt (9 mentions)
U of Colorado, 1979 *Certification:* Neurology, Vascular Neurology
8585 W 14th Ave #A, Lakewood, 303-629-5600

Treihaft, Marc Mitchell (6 mentions)
Case Western Reserve U, 1974 *Certification:* Neurology
3535 S Lafayette St #204, Englewood, 303-788-1700

Wolff, Adam Jonathen (6 mentions)
Certification: Clinical Neurophysiology, Neurology
950 E Howard Ave #620, Denver, 303-715-9024

Obstetrics/Gynecology

Abman, Carolyn Frank (3 mentions)
Northwestern U, 1980 *Certification:* Obstetrics & Gynecology
7720 S Broadway #440, Littleton, 303-795-0890
601 E Hampden Ave #550, Englewood, 303-795-0890

Davis, Karlotta Margaret (4 mentions)
U of Michigan, 1981 *Certification:* Obstetrics & Gynecology
1635 N Ursula St, Aurora, 720-848-1800

Dix, Corinne Rochelle (4 mentions)
U of Colorado, 1981 *Certification:* Obstetrics & Gynecology
4500 E 9th Ave #200S, Denver, 303-399-0055
10099 Ridgegate Pkwy #280, Lone Tree, 303-708-0055

Forschner, David Carlson (3 mentions)
Johns Hopkins U, 1995 *Certification:* Obstetrics & Gynecology
1601 E 19th Ave #4200, Denver, 303-861-4914

Keeler, F. Brent (3 mentions)
U of Colorado, 1977 *Certification:* Obstetrics & Gynecology
14991 E Hampden Ave #165, Aurora, 303-690-8340

Kitahama-D'Ambrosia, Yuko (4 mentions)
Louisiana State U, 1996 *Certification:* Obstetrics & Gynecology
4500 E 9th Ave #200, Denver, 303-399-0055

Levy, Hal Bruce (5 mentions)
U of Colorado, 1983 *Certification:* Obstetrics & Gynecology
4500 E 9th Ave #200, Denver, 303-399-0055

McCrann, Elizabeth Y. (3 mentions)
U of Iowa, 1984 *Certification:* Obstetrics & Gynecology
2005 Franklin St #440, Denver, 303-866-8260

Moison, Susan Armagast (6 mentions)
U of Colorado, 1984 *Certification:* Obstetrics & Gynecology
4500 E 9th Ave #300, Denver, 303-322-2240

Moore, Kelly Leigh (3 mentions)
Ohio State U, 1998 *Certification:* Obstetrics & Gynecology
4600 E Hole Pkwy #420, Denver, 303-320-8499

Schultze, Peter Michel (3 mentions)
Northwestern U, 1994 *Certification:* Obstetrics & Gynecology
14701 E Exposition Ave, Aurora, 303-614-7461

Sweeney, Thomas Ives (3 mentions)
Creighton U, 1982 *Certification:* Obstetrics & Gynecology
7950 Kipling St #201, Arvada, 303-424-6466
3555 Lutheran Pkwy #210, Wheat Ridge, 303-467-2800

Watson, David Lee (3 mentions)
Tulane U, 1985 *Certification:* Obstetrics & Gynecology
2551 E 84th Ave #100, Westminster, 303-426-2580

Wester, Robert James (7 mentions)
Creighton U, 1978 *Certification:* Obstetrics & Gynecology
2005 Franklin St #630, Denver, 303-866-8186

Zarlengo, Gerald Vincent (3 mentions)
U of Colorado, 1982 *Certification:* Obstetrics & Gynecology
2005 Franklin St #440, Denver, 303-866-8260

Ophthalmology

Brock, Rebecca Jane (3 mentions)
U of Colorado, 1987 *Certification:* Ophthalmology
4999 E Kentucky Ave #102, Denver, 303-691-0777

Campbell, Thomas P. (7 mentions)
Georgetown U, 1981 *Certification:* Ophthalmology
4350 Wadsworth Blvd #350, Wheat Ridge, 303-424-7572

Conahan, James Bernard (3 mentions)
Creighton U, 1987 *Certification:* Ophthalmology
409 S Wilcox St, Castle Rock, 303-660-6535
9330 S University Blvd #220, Highlands Ranch, 303-346-8400

DeSantis, Diana M. (3 mentions)
Baylor U, 1987 *Certification:* Ophthalmology
4875 Ward Rd #600, Wheat Ridge, 303-456-9456
9094 E Mineral Ave #200, Englewood, 303-456-9456

Goldstein, Joel (7 mentions)
U of Colorado, 1966 *Certification:* Ophthalmology
4999 E Kentucky Ave #201, Denver, 303-691-0505

Grin, Jennifer Mia (6 mentions)
U of Connecticut, 1997 *Certification:* Ophthalmology
1411 S Potomac St #140, Aurora, 303-337-3937

Jacobs, Jason Matthew (10 mentions)
Duke U, 1997 *Certification:* Ophthalmology
950 E Harvard Ave #320, Denver, 303-282-5467

Kadler, Karen Mary (3 mentions)
U of Michigan, 1980 *Certification:* Ophthalmology
4999 E Kentucky Ave #200, Denver, 303-758-1611

King, Robert Allen (5 mentions)
U of Colorado, 1981 *Certification:* Ophthalmology
4875 Ward Rd #600, Wheat Ridge, 303-456-9456
9094 E Mineral Ave #200, Englewood, 303-456-9456

Larkin, Thomas Patrick (5 mentions)
U of Minnesota, 1967 *Certification:* Ophthalmology
2480 S Downing St #100, Denver, 303-777-5455

Mandava, Naresh (7 mentions)
Albany Med Coll, 1992 *Certification:* Ophthalmology
1675 N Ursula St, Aurora, 720-848-2020

Maus, Todd Lawrence (3 mentions)
U of Minnesota, 1995 *Certification:* Ophthalmology
13772 Denver West Pkwy #100, Lakewood, 303-279-6600

Miller, Michael Lawrence (3 mentions)
FMS-Canada, 1988 *Certification:* Ophthalmology
2480 S Downing St #100, Denver, 303-777-5455

Podgorski, Steven Francis (3 mentions)
Vanderbilt U, 1978 *Certification:* Ophthalmology
601 E Hampden Ave #490, Englewood, 303-761-9944

Reeves, Diana (3 mentions)
Boston U, 1995 *Certification:* Ophthalmology
7180 E Orchard Rd #200, Centennial, 303-220-0393
10359 Federal Blvd #100, Westminster, 303-220-0393

Repine, Karen Toth (3 mentions)
U of Colorado, 1987 *Certification:* Ophthalmology
8381 Southpark Ln, Littleton, 303-788-8848

Self, William Grady, Jr. (10 mentions)
U of Michigan, 1970 *Certification:* Ophthalmology
8403 Bryant St, Westminster, 303-426-4810

Spivack, Lawrence D. (3 mentions)
Tufts U, 1976 *Certification:* Ophthalmology
6881 S Yosemite St, Centennial, 303-740-9310

Taravella, Michael Joseph (8 mentions)
U of Colorado, 1981 *Certification:* Ophthalmology
1675 Ursula St #731, Aurora, 720-848-2500

Wise, Ronald Eric (5 mentions)
FMS-South Africa, 1986 *Certification:* Ophthalmology
1435 Wazee St #101, Denver, 303-299-9473

Orthopedics

Bazaz, Rajesh (3 mentions)
U of Michigan, 1997 *Certification:* Orthopaedic Surgery
1601 E 19th Ave #6000, Denver, 303-321-1333

Crane, Hal Steven (10 mentions)
U of Tennessee, 1980 *Certification:* Orthopaedic Surgery
4700 E Hale Pkwy #550, Denver, 303-321-6600

Dennis, Douglas Alan (3 mentions)
U of Toledo, 1979 *Certification:* Orthopaedic Surgery
2535 S Downing St #100, Denver, 720-524-1367

Desai, Bharat Mohanlal (3 mentions)
Temple U, 1990
660 Golden Ridge Rd #250, Golden, 303-233-1223

Erickson, Mark Alan (3 mentions)
Wright State U, 1989 *Certification:* Orthopaedic Surgery
13123 E 16th Ave, Aurora, 720-777-6615

Gersoff, Wayne Keith (4 mentions)
SUNY-Upstate Med U, 1981 *Certification:* Orthopaedic Surgery
8101 E Lowry Blvd #230, Denver, 303-344-9090
10103 Ridgegate Pkwy #112, Lone Tree, 720-895-0111

Hsin, Joseph (3 mentions)
Certification: Orthopaedic Surgery
80 Health Parks Dr #230, Louisville, 303-665-2603
3455 Lutheran Pkwy #200, Wheat Ridge, 303-456-6000
3550 Lutheran Pkwy #201, Wheat Ridge, 303-456-6000

Isaacs, Christopher L. (3 mentions)
A T Still U, 1986
9141 Grant St #B10, Thornton, 303-450-6800

Lammens, Peter Nelson (3 mentions)
FMS-Canada, 1990 *Certification:* Orthopaedic Surgery
660 Golden Ridge Rd #250, Golden, 303-233-1223

Loucks, David Craig (4 mentions)
FMS-Canada, 1998 *Certification:* Orthopaedic Surgery
14100 E Apapahoe Rd #B370, Centennial, 303-699-7325
9777 S Yosemite St, Lone Tree, 303-699-7325

McCarty, Eric Cleveland (4 mentions)
U of Colorado, 1993 *Certification:* Orthopaedic Surgery
1635 N Ursula St, Aurora, 303-493-8333

McNair, Patrick Joseph (4 mentions)
St Louis U, 1994 *Certification:* Orthopaedic Surgery
660 Golden Ridge Rd #250, Golden, 303-233-1223

Mills, Mark Fredrick (4 mentions)
Case Western Reserve U, 1983 *Certification:* Orthopaedic Surgery
660 Golden Ridge Rd #250, Golden, 303-233-1223

Muffly, James Trotter (3 mentions)
Jefferson Med Coll, 1978 *Certification:* Orthopaedic Surgery
799 E Hampden Ave #310, Englewood, 303-788-7840

Parker, Andrew William (12 mentions)
Northwestern U, 1986 *Certification:* Orthopaedic Surgery
4700 E Hale Pkwy #550, Denver, 303-321-6600

Parks, Edward Hudson (9 mentions)
Yale U, 1988 *Certification:* Orthopaedic Surgery
1601 E 19th Ave #6000, Denver, 303-321-1333

Seemann, Mitchell Dean (3 mentions)
U of Toledo, 1986 *Certification:* Orthopaedic Surgery
660 Golden Ridge Rd #250, Golden, 303-233-1223

Wilkins, Ross Montgomery (4 mentions)
Wayne State U, 1978 *Certification:* Orthopaedic Surgery
1601 E 19th Ave #3300, Denver, 303-837-0072

Otorhinolaryngology

Barcz, Dennis Victor (4 mentions)
U of Wisconsin, 1978 *Certification:* Otolaryngology
7850 Vance Dr #225, Arvada, 303-431-8881

Barron, James Lee (8 mentions)
U of Colorado, 1974 *Certification:* Otolaryngology
3550 Lutheran Pkwy W #102B, Wheat Ridge, 303-425-0449

Campana, John Patrick (4 mentions)
U of Iowa, 1987 *Certification:* Otolaryngology
360 S Garfield #400, Denver, 303-372-3180
2555 S Downing St #100, Denver, 303-778-5658

Chan, Kenny (5 mentions)
Loma Linda U, 1977
13123 E 16th Ave, Aurora, 720-777-2806

Dart, Douglas Jay (8 mentions)
U of Colorado, 1983 *Certification:* Otolaryngology
8300 N Alcott St #302, Westminster, 303-487-0834
3895 Upham St #201, Wheat Ridge, 303-487-0834

Kingdom, Todd Thorton (6 mentions)
Emory U, 1991 *Certification:* Otolaryngology
1400 Jackson St, Denver, 303-388-4461
1635 N Ursula St, Aurora, 720-848-2820

Reichman, Owen Stanley (8 mentions)
U of Utah, 1986 *Certification:* Otolaryngology
4500 E 9th Ave #610, Denver, 303-316-7048

Pain Medicine

Engen, Phillip Lee (8 mentions)
U of Kansas, 1989 *Certification:* Anesthesiology, Pain Medicine
7809 W 38th Ave #100, Wheat Ridge, 303-463-6000
8300 W 38th Ave, Wheat Ridge, 303-463-6000

Morris, Gary Richard (8 mentions)
U of Kansas, 1979 *Certification:* Anesthesiology
455 Sherman St #510, Denver, 303-744-8644

Schwettmann, Rick S. (5 mentions)
Certification: Anesthesiology, Pain Medicine
499 E Hampden Ave, Englewood, 303-761-8385

Pathology

Achenbach, Greg Alan (4 mentions)
U of Kansas, 1972 *Certification:* Anatomic Pathology &
Clinical Pathology, Medical Microbiology
4567 E 9th Ave, Denver, 303-320-2250

Chu, Henry Donald (5 mentions)
U of California-San Francisco, 1979 *Certification:* Anatomic
Pathology & Clinical Pathology, Dermatopathology
7444 W Alaska Dr #250, Lakewood, 303-592-7284

De Masters, Bette Kay K. (4 mentions)
U of Wisconsin, 1977 *Certification:* Anatomic Pathology &
Clinical Pathology, Neuropathology
12631 E 17th Ave, Aurora, 303-724-2301

Fitzpatrick, James Edward (3 mentions)
U of Arkansas, 1976
Certification: Dermatology, Dermatopathology
1665 Ursula St, Aurora, 720-848-0500

Madsen, Walter Edward (4 mentions)
St Louis U, 1983
Certification: Anatomic Pathology & Clinical Pathology
6116 E Warren Ave, Denver, 303-512-0888
1719 E 19th Ave, Denver, 303-512-0888

Sirgi, Karim Emile (5 mentions)
FMS-Lebanon, 1986 *Certification:* Anatomic Pathology &
Clinical Pathology, Cytopathology
6116 E Warren Ave, Denver, 303-512-0888
1719 E 19th Ave, Denver, 303-839-6851

Spurlock, Richard Glenn (3 mentions)
West Virginia U, 1978 *Certification:* Anatomic Pathology &
Clinical Pathology, Cytopathology
11000 E 45th Ave, Denver, 303-404-4010

Stoffel, Philip Turner (4 mentions)
U of Colorado, 1976
Certification: Anatomic Pathology & Clinical Pathology
6116 E Warren Ave, Denver, 303-512-0888

Truell, John Edward (4 mentions)
U of Nebraska, 1966 *Certification:* Anatomic Pathology &
Clinical Pathology, Medical Microbiology
501 E Hampden Ave, Englewood, 303-788-6130

Pediatrics *(see note on page 9)*

Andrews, Lynn Ann (3 mentions)
Tulane U, 1988 *Certification:* Pediatrics
4900 E Kentucky Ave, Denver, 303-756-0101

Berman, Stephen (3 mentions)
Temple U, 1971 *Certification:* Pediatrics
13123 E 16th Ave, Aurora, 720-777-2740

Dorighi, Matthew Patrick (3 mentions)
St Louis U, 1997 *Certification:* Pediatrics
4900 E Kentucky Ave, Denver, 303-756-0101

Gablehouse, Barbara Lynn (3 mentions)
U of Colorado, 1987 *Certification:* Pediatrics
3555 Lutheran Pkwy #340, Wheat Ridge, 303-996-6005

Makovsky, Noah Jay (5 mentions)
U of Colorado, 1999 *Certification:* Pediatrics
2975 Roslyn St #100, Denver, 303-399-7900

Markson, Jay Arthur (10 mentions)
U of Colorado, 1981 *Certification:* Pediatrics
1625 Marion St, Denver, 303-830-7337

Mathie, Jody Lynne (4 mentions)
U of Cincinnati, 1981 *Certification:* Pediatrics
4900 E Kentucky Ave, Denver, 303-756-0101

Perry, Steven Spencer (4 mentions)
Texas Tech U, 1990 *Certification:* Pediatrics
4900 E Kentucky Ave, Denver, 303-756-0101

Prina, Dean Michael (4 mentions)
U of California-San Diego, 1979
919 Jasmine St #100, Denver, 303-388-4256
9785 Maroon Cir #G-104, Englewood, 305-779-1172

Plastic Surgery

Atagi, Tanya Aya (7 mentions)
Stanford U, 1994 *Certification:* Plastic Surgery
10099 Ridgegate Pkwy #430, Lone Tree, 303-327-7300

Bershof, John Fox (6 mentions)
U of Colorado, 1983 *Certification:* Otolaryngology, Plastic Surgery
4500 E 9th Ave #470, Denver, 303-399-7662

Brown, William C. (10 mentions)
FMS-Canada, 1983 *Certification:* Plastic Surgery, Surgery
1578 Humboldt St, Denver, 303-830-7200

Caparro, Philippe Angelo (4 mentions)
Boston U, 1992 *Certification:* Plastic Surgery
4600 Hale Pkwy #100, Denver, 303-320-5566

Charles, David Michael (5 mentions)
FMS-South Africa, 1966 *Certification:* Plastic Surgery
1578 Humboldt St, Denver, 303-830-7200

Folk, Stacey Nicol (12 mentions)
U of Colorado, 1991 *Certification:* Plastic Surgery
4545 E 9th Ave, Denver, 303-321-6608

Gerow, Royal Kent (5 mentions)
Tulane U, 1982 *Certification:* Plastic Surgery
2045 Franklin St, Denver, 303-861-3368

Grossman, John Alan (6 mentions)
Cornell U, 1967 *Certification:* Plastic Surgery, Surgery
4600 Hale Pkwy #100, Denver, 303-320-5566

Mouchantat, Richard Alan (8 mentions)
Tufts U, 1989 *Certification:* Plastic Surgery
3280 Wadsworth Blvd #100, Wheat Ridge, 303-232-8585

Pav, John Michael (4 mentions)
Boston U, 1976 *Certification:* Plastic Surgery
3280 Wadsworth Blvd #100, Wheat Ridge, 303-232-8585

Psychiatry

Allen, Stephen Michael (3 mentions)
U of Colorado, 1977 *Certification:* Psychiatry
3601 S Clarkson St, Englewood, 303-741-0239

Yancey, Asa Greenwood, Jr. (3 mentions)
Boston U, 1981
Certification: Child & Adolescent Psychiatry, Pediatrics, Psychiatry
8095 E Prentice Ave, Greenwood Village, 303-740-0400
9000 E Nichols Ave #240, Centennial, 303-740-0400
7310 E Arapahoe Rd #200, Englewood, 303-740-0400

Pulmonary Disease

Bost, Thomas Ward (5 mentions)
U of Michigan, 1983 *Certification:* Critical Care Medicine,
Internal Medicine, Pulmonary Disease
4101 W Conejos Pl #200, Denver, 303-629-2100

Buckley, John Edward (3 mentions)
Rush U, 1980
Certification: Internal Medicine, Pulmonary Disease
51 W 84th Ave #210, Denver, 303-427-1601

Clifford, Dennis Patrick (7 mentions)
U of Minnesota, 1978
Certification: Internal Medicine, Pulmonary Disease
8550 W 38th Ave #202, Wheat Ridge, 303-940-1661

Ellis, James Harvey, Jr. (3 mentions)
U of Kansas, 1967
Certification: Internal Medicine, Pulmonary Disease
1400 Jackson St, Denver, 303-398-1703

Emrie, Philip Alan (5 mentions)
U of Colorado, 1981
Certification: Internal Medicine, Pulmonary Disease
8550 W 38th Ave #202, Wheat Ridge, 303-940-1661

Fenton, James Joseph (6 mentions)
Ohio State U, 1990
Certification: Critical Care Medicine, Pulmonary Disease
499 E Hampden Ave #300, Englewood, 303-788-8500

Forrester, Joseph Michael (13 mentions)
Wayne State U, 1982 *Certification:* Critical Care Medicine,
Internal Medicine, Pulmonary Disease
1400 S Potomac St #110, Aurora, 303-745-0000

Good, James Tucker, Jr. (7 mentions)
U of Kansas, 1972
Certification: Internal Medicine, Pulmonary Disease
1400 Jackson St, Denver, 303-788-8500

Kotake, Susan (4 mentions)
U of Pennsylvania, 1995 *Certification:* Critical Care
   Medicine, Internal Medicine, Pulmonary Disease
4500 E 9th Ave #540, Denver, 303-320-1221

Lange, Neale Rayne (3 mentions)
FMS-South Africa, 1989 *Certification:* Critical Care
   Medicine, Internal Medicine, Pulmonary Disease
4101 W Conejos Pl #200, Denver, 303-629-2100

Lapidus, Robert Jay (6 mentions)
U of Buffalo, 1975
Certification: Internal Medicine, Pulmonary Disease
8550 W 38th Ave #202, Wheat Ridge, 303-940-1661

McClellan, Michael D. (7 mentions)
U of Illinois, 1981 *Certification:* Critical Care Medicine,
   Internal Medicine, Pulmonary Disease
51 W 84th Ave #210, Denver, 303-427-1601

Pluss, William Thomas (11 mentions)
U of Colorado, 1978
Certification: Internal Medicine, Pulmonary Disease
4500 E 9th Ave #540, Denver, 303-320-1221

Schwartz, Jeffrey Steven (4 mentions)
U of Michigan, 1975 *Certification:* Critical Care Medicine,
   Internal Medicine, Pulmonary Disease
1721 E 19th Ave #366, Denver, 303-863-0300

Sharma, Surit Kumar (6 mentions)
U of Chicago, 1992 *Certification:* Critical Care Medicine,
   Internal Medicine, Pulmonary Disease
1400 S Potomac St #110, Aurora, 303-745-0000
10103 Ridgegate #313, Lone Tree, 303-745-0000

Stelzner, Thomas Joseph (3 mentions)
SUNY-Upstate Med U, 1978 *Certification:* Critical Care
   Medicine, Internal Medicine, Pulmonary Disease
1375 E 20th Ave, Denver, 303-861-3640

Warner, Mary Laird (6 mentions)
Vanderbilt U, 1990
499 E Hampden Ave #300, Englewood, 303-788-8500

Zamora, Martin Robert (4 mentions)
U of Colorado, 1983 *Certification:* Internal Medicine
1635 N Ursula St, Aurora, 303-493-8333

Radiology—Diagnostic

Fisher, Andrew Joel (6 mentions)
Duke U, 1992 *Certification:* Diagnostic Radiology
10700 E Geddes Ave #200, Englewood, 303-761-9190

Fleishman, Matthew (5 mentions)
Columbia U, 1989
Certification: Diagnostic Radiology, Nuclear Medicine
10700 E Geddes Ave #200, Englewood, 303-761-9190

Friedland, Jeffrey Adam (3 mentions)
U of Florida, 1991
Certification: Diagnostic Radiology, Pediatric Radiology
10700 E Geddes Ave #200, Englewood, 303-761-9190

George, Stephen George (4 mentions)
Pennsylvania State U, 1980 *Certification:* Diagnostic Radiology
938 Bannock St, Denver, 303-914-8800

Gerhold, John Patrick (3 mentions)
Northwestern U, 1977 *Certification:* Diagnostic Radiology
   with Special Competence in Nuclear Radiology
1719 E 19th Ave, Denver, 303-839-6000

Goldstein, Ross Andrew (5 mentions)
U of Wisconsin, 1996
Certification: Diagnostic Radiology, Neuroradiology
8300 W 38th Ave, Wheat Ridge, 303-753-1191

Kemp, Jennifer L. (4 mentions)
U of Kansas, 1994 *Certification:* Diagnostic Radiology
938 Bannock St, Denver, 303-914-8800

Kornbluth, Craig Marc (7 mentions)
Rosalind Franklin U, 1997 *Certification:* Diagnostic Radiology
938 Bannock St, Denver, 303-914-8800

Lynch, David Augustine (3 mentions)
FMS-Ireland, 1979 *Certification:* Diagnostic Radiology
4200 E 9th Ave, Denver, 303-270-8402
1400 Jackson St, Denver, 303-388-4461

Russ, Paul David (3 mentions)
U of Pennsylvania, 1979 *Certification:* Diagnostic Radiology
1635 N Ursula St, Aurora, 720-848-1860
1055 Clermont St, Denver, 303-399-8020

Strain, John Douglas (5 mentions)
U of Colorado, 1977 *Certification:* Diagnostic Radiology,
   Neuroradiology, Pediatric Radiology
13123 E 1th Ave, Aurora, 720-777-8630

Radiology—Therapeutic

Ahn, Samuel Tonghee (3 mentions)
U of Missouri-Kansas City, 1989
Certification: Diagnostic Radiology
8300 W 38th Ave, Wheat Ridge, 303-753-1191

Durham, Janette Denham (3 mentions)
Indiana U, 1983 *Certification:* Diagnostic Radiology,
   Vascular & Interventional Radiology
12401 E 17th Ave #L-954, Aurora, 720-848-6561

Howell, Kathryn Tilden (4 mentions)
U of Colorado, 1984 *Certification:* Radiation Oncology
22 W Dry Creek Cir, Littleton, 303-730-4700
1800 Williams St #100, Denver, 303-839-6530
4700 Hale Pkwy #150, Denver, 303-839-6530

Malden, Eric Stuart (5 mentions)
Washington U, 1992 *Certification:* Diagnostic Radiology,
   Vascular & Interventional Radiology
10700 E Geddes Ave #200, Englewood, 303-761-9190

Podolak, Michael Joseph (3 mentions)
Duke U, 1988 *Certification:* Diagnostic Radiology, Vascular
   & Interventional Radiology
2045 Franklin St, Denver, 303-338-3456

Yakes, Wayne Francis (4 mentions)
Creighton U, 1979
Certification: Diagnostic Radiology, Neuroradiology
501 E Hampden Ave #4600, Englewood, 303-788-4280

Rehabilitation

Draznin, Elena (5 mentions)
FMS-Belarus, 1969
Certification: Physical Medicine & Rehabilitation
701 E Hampden Ave #320, Englewood, 303-788-4106

Goldberg, Sheldon (3 mentions)
FMS-Mexico, 1983 *Certification:* Physical Medicine &
   Rehabilitation, Spinal Cord Injury Medicine
4485 Wadsworth Blvd #105, Wheat Ridge, 303-424-6565

Matthews, Dennis Jerome (4 mentions)
U of Colorado, 1975
Certification: Neuromuscular Medicine, Pediatric
   Rehabilitation Medicine, Physical Medicine & Rehabilitation
13123 E 16th Ave, Aurora, 720-777-2806

Mulica, David Patterson (3 mentions)
FMS-Mexico, 1982 *Certification:* Physical Medicine &
   Rehabilitation, Spinal Cord Injury Medicine
1375 E 20th Ave, Denver, 303-861-3105

Primack, Scott (5 mentions)
Des Moines U, 1988
Certification: Physical Medicine & Rehabilitation
8200 E Belleview Ave #380-E, Greenwood Village, 720-875-0551

Rheumatology

Bray, Vance Jay (6 mentions)
Emory U, 1986 *Certification:* Internal Medicine, Rheumatology
200 Spruce St #100, Denver, 303-394-2828

Charney, Michael (12 mentions)
U of Rochester, 1984
Certification: Internal Medicine, Rheumatology
200 Spruce St #100, Denver, 303-394-2828

Glassman, Kenneth Paul (5 mentions)
U of Cincinnati, 1979
Certification: Internal Medicine, Rheumatology
200 Spruce St #100, Denver, 303-394-2828

Hollister, John Roger (7 mentions)
Case Western Reserve U, 1966
Certification: Pediatric Rheumatology, Pediatrics
13611 E Colfax Ave #B-311, Aurora, 303-493-8333

Kassan, Stuart S. (7 mentions)
George Washington U, 1972
Certification: Internal Medicine, Rheumatology
4200 W Conejos Pl #314, Denver, 303-892-6033

Korman, David Scott (5 mentions)
Hahnemann U, 1993
Certification: Internal Medicine, Rheumatology
4500 E 9th Ave #500, Denver, 303-861-2190

Meehan, Richard Thomas (5 mentions)
U of Texas-Houston, 1974
Certification: Internal Medicine, Rheumatology
1400 Jackson St, Denver, 303-388-4461

Soep, Jennifer Beth (7 mentions)
Tufts U, 1994 *Certification:* Pediatric Rheumatology, Pediatrics
13123 E 16th Ave 3rd Fl, Aurora, 720-777-6132

Spencer, Robert Thornham (5 mentions)
U of Oklahoma, 1986
Certification: Internal Medicine, Rheumatology
701 E Hampden Ave #410, Englewood, 303-788-1312

Weiss, Judith (10 mentions)
U of Pennsylvania, 1977
Certification: Internal Medicine, Rheumatology
5130 W 80th Ave #A-102, Westminster, 303-427-5979

West, Sterling Gaylord (6 mentions)
Emory U, 1976 *Certification:* Internal Medicine, Rheumatology
1635 N Ursula St, Aurora, 303-493-8333

Westerman, Eric Mason (6 mentions)
Western U, 1987
701 E Hampden Ave #410, Englewood, 303-788-1312

Thoracic Surgery

Guber, Myles Stuart (8 mentions)
Northwestern U, 1980 *Certification:* Thoracic Surgery
950 E Harvard Ave #550, Denver, 303-778-6527

Nene, Shriram Madhav (6 mentions)
Washington U, 1993 *Certification:* Surgery, Thoracic Surgery
1390 S Potomac St #120, Aurora, 303-695-1313

Parker, Richard Keith (15 mentions)
U of Nebraska, 1968 *Certification:* Surgery, Thoracic Surgery
1601 E 19th Ave #5000, Denver, 303-861-8158

Propp, John George (6 mentions)
U of Colorado, 1977
1390 S Potomac St #120, Aurora, 303-695-1313

Urology

Abernathy, Brett Bailey (9 mentions)
Northwestern U, 1984 *Certification:* Urology
2777 Mile High Stadium Cir, Denver, 303-421-1203

Cahn, David J. (4 mentions)
Albert Einstein Coll of Med, 1990 *Certification:* Urology
255 Union Blvd #400, Lakewood, 303-985-2550

Eigner, Edward Brandt (5 mentions)
Case Western Reserve U, 1986 *Certification:* Urology
850 E Harvard Ave #525, Denver, 303-733-8848
7720 S Broadway #330, Littleton, 303-733-8848
10103 Ridgegate Pkwy #G-23, Lone Tree, 303-733-8848

Galansky, Stanley Howard (10 mentions)
U of Florida, 1977 *Certification:* Urology
850 E Harvard Ave #525, Denver, 303-733-8848
10103 Ridgegate Pkwy #G-23, Lone Tree, 303-733-8848
7720 S Broadway #330, Littleton, 303-733-8848

Gerig, Nel Elisabeth (9 mentions)
U of California-Los Angeles, 1991 *Certification:* Urology
4545 E 9th Ave #480, Denver, 303-388-9321

Glass, Michael Austin (4 mentions)
U of Oklahoma, 1992 *Certification:* Urology
1411 S Potomac St #250, Aurora, 303-695-6106

Heppe, Richard Keith (4 mentions)
Virginia Commonwealth U, 1986 *Certification:* Urology
2777 Mile High Stadium Cir, Denver, 303-825-8822

Karsh, Lawrence Ivan (4 mentions)
Rosalind Franklin U, 1978 *Certification:* Urology
2777 Mile High Stadium Cir, Denver, 303-421-1203

Maniatis, William Nicholas (4 mentions)
U of Colorado, 1965 *Certification:* Urology
1411 S Potomac St #250, Aurora, 303-695-6106

May, Donald J. (4 mentions)
U of Colorado, 1991 *Certification:* Urology
2777 Mile High Stadium Cir, Denver, 303-421-1203

Philpott, Alexander C. (7 mentions)
U of Colorado, 1986 *Certification:* Urology
2777 Mile High Stadium Cir, Denver, 303-421-1203

Ragan, David C. (5 mentions)
Case Western Reserve U, 1993 *Certification:* Urology
2777 Mile High Stadium Cir, Denver, 303-421-1203

Rosen, Reuven Ernest (4 mentions)
Rosalind Franklin U, 1961 *Certification:* Urology
4545 E 9th Ave #480, Denver, 303-388-9321

Ruyle, Stephen Robert (13 mentions)
Dartmouth Coll, 1984 *Certification:* Urology
2777 Mile High Stadium Cir, Denver, 303-825-8822

Sarram, Ali Mohammad (6 mentions)
U of Washington, 1995 *Certification:* Urology
1411 S Potomac St #250, Aurora, 303-695-6106

Snyder, Jeffrey Alan (4 mentions)
FMS-Mexico, 1980 *Certification:* Urology
4500 E 9th Ave #530, Denver, 303-320-0200

Zukosky, Derick K. (4 mentions)
Michigan State U Coll of Osteopathic Med, 1998
255 Union Blvd #400, Lakewood, 303-985-2550
3550 Lutheran Pkwy #G-20, Wheat Ridge, 303-985-2550

Vascular Surgery

Brantigan, Charles Otto (7 mentions)
Johns Hopkins U, 1968 *Certification:* Surgery, Surgical Critical Care, Thoracic Surgery, Vascular Surgery
2253 Downing St, Denver, 303-830-8822

Carlson, Roy Edwin (12 mentions)
Ohio State U, 1969 *Certification:* Surgery
950 E Harvard Ave #550, Denver, 303-778-6527

Cooper, Michael Allen (12 mentions)
U of Nebraska, 1984 *Certification:* Surgery, Vascular Surgery
4545 E 9th Ave #240, Denver, 303-388-7265
4600 Hale Pkwy #460, Denver, 303-388-7265

Hammond, Sharon Lucille (9 mentions)
Uniformed Services U of Health Sciences, 1982 *Certification:* Surgery, Vascular Surgery
4600 Hale Pkwy #460, Denver, 303-388-7265

Rehring, Thomas F. (8 mentions)
Northwestern U, 1990 *Certification:* Surgery, Vascular Surgery
2045 Franklin St, Denver, 303-338-4545

Ridge, Brian Alfred (6 mentions)
U of Utah, 1983 *Certification:* Surgery, Vascular Surgery
7805 W 38th Ave, Wheat Ridge, 303-431-2900

Weinstein, Eric S. (7 mentions)
U of Buffalo, 1981 *Certification:* Surgery, Vascular Surgery
950 E Harvard Ave #550, Denver, 303-778-6527

Connecticut

Hartford Area—page 110

Fairfield and New Haven Counties—page 98

New York Metropolitan Area—page 309

Fairfield and New Haven Counties

Allergy/Immunology

Backman, Kenneth Scott (12 mentions)
Cornell U, 1991 *Certification:* Allergy & Immunology
55 Walls Dr #405, Fairfield, 203-259-7070
500 Monroe Tpke #205, Monroe, 203-445-1960

Biondi, Robert Michael (8 mentions)
Creighton U, 1964
Certification: Allergy & Immunology, Pediatrics
148 East Ave #3-G, Norwalk, 203-838-4034
2 1/2 Dearfield Dr, Greenwich, 203-869-2080
80 Mill River St #2100, Stamford, 203-357-1511

Kantor, Fred Stuart (7 mentions)
New York U, 1956
Certification: Allergy & Immunology, Internal Medicine
789 Howard Ave, New Haven, 203-785-4629

Lindner, Paul Scott (13 mentions)
U of Buffalo, 1985
Certification: Allergy & Immunology, Internal Medicine
22 5th St, Stamford, 203-978-0072

Randolph, Christopher C. (12 mentions)
U of Rochester, 1980
Certification: Allergy & Immunology, Pediatrics
1389 W Main St #205, Waterbury, 203-755-7080

Rockwell, William James (9 mentions)
Albany Med Coll, 1973
Certification: Allergy & Immunology, Pediatrics
4675 Main St, Bridgeport, 203-374-6103

Santilli, John, Jr. (10 mentions)
Georgetown U, 1968
Certification: Allergy & Immunology, Pediatrics
4675 Main St, Bridgeport, 203-374-6103

Sproviero, Joseph (12 mentions)
Columbia U, 1985
Certification: Allergy & Immunology, Internal Medicine
148 East Ave #3-G, Norwalk, 203-838-4034
2 1/2 Dearfield Dr, Greenwich, 203-869-2080
80 Mill River St #2100, Stamford, 203-357-1511

Anesthesiology

Barash, Paul George (6 mentions)
U of Kentucky, 1967 *Certification:* Anesthesiology
333 Cedar St #TMP3, New Haven, 203-785-2802
867 Robert Treat Ext, Orange, 203-795-0369

Beiles, Paul Russell (5 mentions)
Rosalind Franklin U, 1991 *Certification:* Anesthesiology
24 Stevens St, Norwalk, 203-852-2276

Bernstein, David Bruce (6 mentions)
Mount Sinai Sch of Med, 1996 *Certification:* Anesthesiology
5 Perryridge Rd, Greenwich, 203-661-5330

Bladek, Thomas Robert (6 mentions)
FMS-Grenada, 1982 *Certification:* Anesthesiology
4 Armstrong Rd, Shelton, 203-929-7353
2800 Main St, Bridgeport, 203-576-5436

Buonafede, Dennis S. (4 mentions)
FMS-St Maarten, 1983 *Certification:* Anesthesiology
267 Grant St, Bridgeport, 202-384-3072

Clement, Raymond Leonard (4 mentions)
FMS-Mexico, 1982 *Certification:* Anesthesiology
140 Grandview Ave #103, Waterbury, 203-757-7000

Dalsania, Amrital M. (3 mentions)
FMS-India, 1971 *Certification:* Anesthesiology
391 Broad St, Meriden, 203-439-9393

Freilich, Jay D. (3 mentions)
Northeastern Ohio U, 1986 *Certification:* Anesthesiology
30 Shelburne Rd, Stamford, 203-348-2614
1055 Washington Blvd #440, Stamford, 203-348-2614
32 Strawberry Hill Ct, Stamford, 203-961-1345

Healey, Susan Assenberg (4 mentions)
U of Connecticut, 1993 *Certification:* Anesthesiology
4 Armstrong Rd, Shelton, 203-929-7353

Hughes, Richard Alan (6 mentions)
New York Med Coll, 1989 *Certification:* Anesthesiology
24 Stevens St, Norwalk, 203-852-2276
40 Cross St, Norwalk, 203-852-3104

Jaffe, Merrill Bert (7 mentions)
Rosalind Franklin U, 1981 *Certification:* Anesthesiology
32 Strawberry Hill Ct, Stamford, 203-961-1345
30 Shelburne Rd, Stamford, 203-348-2614
1055 Washington Blvd #440, Stamford, 203-348-2614

Kitain, Eric Martin (6 mentions)
Cornell U, 1980 *Certification:* Anesthesiology
24 Stevens St, Norwalk, 203-852-2276
40 Cross St, Norwalk, 203-852-3104

Lamba, Amarjit Singh (7 mentions)
FMS-India, 1974 *Certification:* Anesthesiology
267 Grant St, Bridgeport, 203-384-3174

Mulla, Adil D. (5 mentions)
Certification: Anesthesiology
24 Hospital Ave, Danbury, 203-739-7118

Petersen, Neil Francis (3 mentions)
FMS-Mexico, 1981 *Certification:* Anesthesiology
140 Grandview Ave #103, Waterbury, 203-757-7000

Rosenblatt, William H. (3 mentions)
Mount Sinai Sch of Med, 1985 *Certification:* Anesthesiology
330 Cedar St #TMP-3, New Haven, 203-785-2802

Rosenblum, Martin (4 mentions)
267 grant St, Bridgeport, 203-384-3072
7365 Main St #310, Stratford, 203-384-3463

Ruskis, Alan F. (3 mentions)
Tufts U, 1975 *Certification:* Anesthesiology
1423 Chapel St, New Haven, 203-865-3852

Schiffmiller, Mark W. (4 mentions)
FMS-Mexico, 1982 *Certification:* Anesthesiology
140 Grandview Ave #103, Waterbury, 203-757-7000

Sharnick, Stephen Vincent (4 mentions)
U of Connecticut, 1984 *Certification:* Anesthesiology
24 Hospital Ave, Danbury, 203-797-7118
95 Locust Ave, Danbury, 203-797-7742

Shelley, Kirk Harry (3 mentions)
Pennsylvania State U, 1981
Certification: Anesthesiology, Internal Medicine
15 York St, New Haven, 203-785-2802

Tagliavia, Alfonso Andrew (5 mentions)
SUNY-Downstate Med Coll, 1993 *Certification:* Anesthesiology
5 Perryridge Rd, Greenwich, 203-863-3364

Vaughn, Douglas (4 mentions)
Hahnemann U, 1991 *Certification:* Anesthesiology
333 Cedar St #TMP3, New Haven, 203-785-2802
40 Buttonwood Cir, Cheshire, 203-785-7998

Vogel, Wolf Alljoscha (3 mentions)
Stony Brook U, 1998 *Certification:* Anesthesiology
2800 Main St, Bridgeport, 203-576-5436
4 Armstrong Rd, Shelton, 203-929-7353

Watson, Charles Barnes (4 mentions)
U of Maryland, 1973
Certification: Anesthesiology, Critical Care Medicine
267 Grant St, Bridgeport, 203-384-3692

Cardiac Surgery

Elefteriades, John Alex (15 mentions)
Yale U, 1976 *Certification:* Thoracic Surgery
333 Cedar St #121FMB, New Haven, 203-785-2705

Hashim, Sabet W. (10 mentions)
FMS-Lebanon, 1975 *Certification:* Thoracic Surgery
800 Howard Ave, New Haven, 203-562-2818

Robinson, Malcolm Clive (11 mentions)
FMS-New Zealand, 1970
267 Grant St, Bridgeport, 203-384-3000

Shaw, Richard K. (8 mentions)
Albert Einstein Coll of Med, 1968 *Certification:* Surgery
330 Orchard St #107, New Haven, 203-562-2257

Squitieri, Rafael Paolo (27 mentions)
Mount Sinai Sch of Med, 1993
Certification: Surgery, Thoracic Surgery
2800 Main St, Bridgeport, 203-576-5708

Cardiology

Alexander, Jonathan (8 mentions)
Albert Einstein Coll of Med, 1973
Certification: Cardiovascular Disease, Internal Medicine
24 Hospital Ave, Danbury, 203-797-7155
150 Danbury Rd #301, Ridgefield, 203-438-1323

Augenbraun, Charles Barry (9 mentions)
U of Pennsylvania, 1978
Certification: Cardiovascular Disease, Internal Medicine
40 Cross St #200, Norwalk, 203-845-2160

Berkwits, Kieve Michael (4 mentions)
FMS-Mexico, 1979 *Certification:* Pediatric Cardiology, Pediatrics
226 Mill Hill Ave #3, Bridgeport, 203-384-3394
267 Grant St, Bridgeport, 203-384-3394

Berman, Jeffrey N. (4 mentions)
Harvard U, 1985 *Certification:* Cardiovascular Disease,
Internal Medicine, Interventional Cardiology
134 Round Hill Rd, Fairfield, 203-254-2452

Borkowski, Henry (5 mentions)
Harvard U, 1972
Certification: Cardiovascular Disease, Internal Medicine
455 Chase Pkwy, Waterbury, 203-573-1435

Cabin, Henry Scott (5 mentions)
Yale U, 1975 *Certification:* Cardiovascular Disease, Internal
Medicine, Interventional Cardiology
11 Harrison Ave, Branford, 203-483-8300

Cleman, Michael William (5 mentions)
Johns Hopkins U, 1977 *Certification:* Cardiovascular
Disease, Internal Medicine, Interventional Cardiology
11 Harrison Ave, Branford, 203-483-8300

Cohen, Lawrence Sorel (5 mentions)
New York U, 1958
Certification: Cardiovascular Disease, Internal Medicine
333 Cedar St, New Haven, 203-785-4128
789 Howard Ave, New Haven, 203-785-4629

Del Vecchio, Alexander (5 mentions)
Albert Einstein Coll of Med, 1996 *Certification:* Cardiovascular
Disease, Clinical Cardiac Electrophysiology, Internal Medicine
55 Holly Hill Ln #240, Greenwich, 203-863-4210

Dobkin, Dennis Lee (4 mentions)
SUNY-Upstate Med U, 1979
Certification: Cardiovascular Disease, Internal Medicine
455 Chase Pkwy, Waterbury, 203-573-1435

Driesman, Mitchell H. (13 mentions)
Brown U, 1977 *Certification:* Cardiovascular Disease,
Internal Medicine, Interventional Cardiology
1305 Post Rd #LL, Fairfield, 203-292-2000
999 Silver Ln #1-A, Trumbull, 203-385-1111

Farrell, William Joseph (5 mentions)
U of Iowa, 1987 *Certification:* Cardiovascular Disease,
Internal Medicine, Interventional Cardiology
1062 Barnes Rd #300, Wallingford, 203-265-9831
22 Masonic Ave, Wallingford, 203-679-5000

Fisher, Lawrence Irwin (5 mentions)
U of Buffalo, 1985
Certification: Cardiovascular Disease, Internal Medicine
7 Germantown Rd #2A, Danbury, 203-794-0090
1305 Post Rd, Fairfield, 203-794-0090
25 Germantown Rd #2-B, Danbury, 203-794-0090

Fishman, Robert Fredric (10 mentions)
Boston U, 1985 *Certification:* Cardiovascular Disease,
Internal Medicine, Interventional Cardiology
1305 Post Rd #105, Fairfield, 203-292-2000
999 Silver Ln #1-A, Trumbull, 203-385-1111

Grauer, Leonard Edwin (6 mentions)
Yale U, 1968
Certification: Cardiovascular Disease, Internal Medicine
60 Temple St #6-C, New Haven, 203-773-3055

Green, Jeffrey Adam (10 mentions)
New York Med Coll, 1998
Certification: Cardiovascular Disease, Internal Medicine
80 Mill River St #1300, Stamford, 203-348-7410

Howes, Christopher J. (5 mentions)
Albert Einstein Coll of Med, 1989 *Certification:* Cardiovascular
Disease, Internal Medicine, Interventional Cardiology
55 Holly Hill Ln #240, Greenwich, 203-863-4210

Jacoby, Steven Scott (7 mentions)
Harvard U, 1979
Certification: Cardiovascular Disease, Internal Medicine
40 Temple St #6A, New Haven, 203-789-2272
1591 Boston Post Rd #202, Guilford, 203-453-7050
339 Boston Post Rd #340, Orange, 203-891-2140
60 Washington Ave #103, Hamden, 203-281-1065

Kett, Kevin Gerard (6 mentions)
Stony Brook U, 1982 *Certification:* Cardiovascular Disease,
Internal Medicine, Interventional Cardiology
455 Chase Pkwy #100, Waterbury, 203-573-1435

Kirmser, Ralph Joseph (5 mentions)
Yale U, 1971
Certification: Cardiovascular Disease, Internal Medicine
40 Cross St #200, Norwalk, 203-845-2160
2800 Main St, Bridgeport, 203-845-2160

Kramer, Harvey Merrill (5 mentions)
U of Virginia, 1978
Certification: Cardiovascular Disease, Internal Medicine
24 Hospital Ave, Danbury, 203-797-7155

Kunkes, Steven Harris (8 mentions)
Mount Sinai Sch of Med, 1973 *Certification:* Cardiovascular
Disease, Geriatric Medicine, Internal Medicine
1305 Post Rd #LL, Fairfield, 203-292-2000

Landesman, Richard Howard (6 mentions)
U of Vermont, 1966
Certification: Cardiovascular Disease, Internal Medicine
80 Mill River St, Stamford, 203-348-7410

Lomnitz, David J. (14 mentions)
Certification: Cardiovascular Disease
40 Cross St #200, Norwalk, 203-845-2160

Marieb, Mark A. (4 mentions)
Boston U, 1984 *Certification:* Cardiovascular Disease,
Clinical Cardiac Electrophysiology, Internal Medicine
330 Orchard St #210, New Haven, 203-867-5400

Meizlish, Jay L. (11 mentions)
New York U, 1977 *Certification:* Cardiovascular Disease, Internal
Medicine, Interventional Cardiology, Nuclear Medicine
1305 Post Rd #105, Fairfield, 203-292-2000
999 Silver Ln, Trumbull, 203-385-1111

Mukherjee, Sandip (13 mentions)
Texas Tech U, 1988 *Certification:* Cardiovascular Disease
1591 Boston Post Rd #202, Guilford, 203-453-7050
325 Boston Post Rd #340, Orange, 203-891-2140
60 Washington Ave #103, Hamden, 203-281-1065

Neeson, Francis John (8 mentions)
New York U, 1985
Certification: Cardiovascular Disease, Internal Medicine
75 Holly Hill Ln, Greenwich, 203-869-6960

Pollack, Brian David (7 mentions)
Mount Sinai Sch of Med, 1987
Certification: Cardiovascular Disease, Internal Medicine
1305 Post Rd, Fairfield, 203-794-0090
25 Germantown Rd #2-B, Danbury, 203-794-0090
24 Hospital Ave, Danbury, 203-797-7000
30 Prospect St #200, Ridgefield, 203-438-9621

Portnay, Edward Lowell (4 mentions)
Tufts U, 1997 *Certification:* Cardiovascular Disease,
Internal Medicine, Interventional Cardiology
1177 Summer St #5, Stamford, 203-353-1133
40 Cross St #200, Norwalk, 203-845-2160

Pun, Manuel Carlos (5 mentions)
FMS-Mexico, 1979
Certification: Cardiovascular Disease, Internal Medicine
2979 Main St, Bridgeport, 203-333-8800

Schussheim, Adam Evan (7 mentions)
Harvard U, 1993 *Certification:* Cardiovascular Disease
1305 Post Rd #105, Fairfield, 203-292-2000
999 Silver Ln #1-A, Trumbull, 203-385-1111

Schuster, Edward Harvey (7 mentions)
Rosalind Franklin U, 1976
Certification: Cardiovascular Disease, Internal Medicine
1177 Summer St, Stamford, 203-353-1133

Werner, Craig Sweetsir (4 mentions)
Med U of South Carolina, 1987 *Certification:* Cardiovascular
Disease, Internal Medicine, Interventional Cardiology
2979 Main St, Bridgeport, 203-333-8800

Wolfson, Steven (4 mentions)
New York U, 1963
Certification: Cardiovascular Disease, Internal Medicine
40 Temple St #6A, New Haven, 203-789-2272

Yap, Jesus Fulay, Jr. (4 mentions)
FMS-Philippines, 1968
Certification: Cardiovascular Disease, Internal Medicine
1177 Summer St, Stamford, 203-353-1133

Young, Lawrence Howard (4 mentions)
Yale U, 1980
Certification: Cardiovascular Disease, Internal Medicine
800 Howard Ave, New Haven, 203-785-4629
333 Cedar St, New Haven, 203-785-4102

Dermatology

Alter, Jeffrey Norman (12 mentions)
New York U, 1976 *Certification:* Dermatology
1078 W Main St, Waterbury, 203-757-1585
2 Pomperaug Office Pk #208, Southbury, 203-264-3990

Antaya, Richard Joseph (10 mentions)
Tufts U, 1989
Certification: Dermatology, Pediatric Dermatology, Pediatrics
800 Howard Ave, New Haven, 203-785-4632
2 S Church St #305, New Haven, 203-789-1249

Bevilacqua, Paula M. (6 mentions)
New York U, 1985 *Certification:* Dermatology
677 S Main St, Cheshire, 203-250-7577

Bolognia, Jean Lynn (8 mentions)
Yale U, 1980 *Certification:* Dermatology
800 Howard Ave, New Haven, 203-785-4632
2 Church St S #305, New Haven, 203-789-1249

Castiglione, Frank M., Jr. (5 mentions)
New York Med Coll, 1979 *Certification:* Dermatology
1844 Whitney Ave #1, Hamden, 203-281-5445

Connors, Richard Charles (5 mentions)
Cornell U, 1967 *Certification:* Dermatology, Dermatopathology
1 Perryridge Rd, Greenwich, 203-622-0808

Dietz, Stephanie Babion (5 mentions)
U of Pennsylvania, 1995 *Certification:* Dermatology
1290 Summer St #3600, Stamford, 203-325-3576

Federman, Grace Liang (5 mentions)
New York U, 1986 *Certification:* Dermatology, Internal Medicine
25 Tamarack Ave, Danbury, 203-797-8990

Feinberg, Dennis Lowell (5 mentions)
SUNY-Upstate Med U, 1976
Certification: Dermatology, Internal Medicine
2875 Main St, Stratford, 203-375-3411

Godwin, Loyd Seth (8 mentions)
New York U, 1998 *Certification:* Dermatology
2890 Main St #C, Stratford, 203-375-8200

Goldberg, Barry S. (6 mentions)
Certification: Dermatology, Pediatrics
25 Tamarack Ave, Danbury, 203-797-8990

Kolenik, Steven A., III (5 mentions)
Yale U, 1990 *Certification:* Dermatology
761 Main Ave, Norwalk, 203-810-4151
1250 Summer St #201, Stamford, 203-975-1112

Leffell, David J. (7 mentions)
FMS-Canada, 1981 *Certification:* Dermatology, Internal Medicine
460 St Ronan St, New Haven, 203-785-6808
40 Temple St #5-A, New Haven, 203-785-3466

Lerner, Seth Perry (10 mentions)
Boston U, 1981 *Certification:* Dermatology
160 Hawley Ln #104, Trumbull, 203-377-0639
162 Kings Hwy N, Westport, 203-222-0198

Maiocco, Kenneth Joseph (10 mentions)
U of Rochester, 1967 *Certification:* Dermatology
4639 Main St, Bridgeport, 203-374-5546

Naidorf, Ellen Sheiman (5 mentions)
Columbia U, 1975 *Certification:* Dermatology, Pediatrics
22 Long Ridge Rd, Stamford, 203-964-1103

Noonan, Michael Patrick (5 mentions)
New York U, 1988
Certification: Dermatology, Pediatric Dermatology
160 Hawley Ln, Trumbull, 203-377-0639

Oestreicher, Mark Ian (11 mentions)
Albany Med Coll, 1974
Certification: Dermatology, Internal Medicine
160 Hawley Ln #104, Trumbull, 203-377-0639
162 Kings Hwy N, Westport, 203-222-0198

Patrignelli, Robert John (7 mentions)
Georgetown U, 1991
965 White Plains Rd, Trumbull, 203-261-0800

Pesce, Katherine Jane (6 mentions)
U of Connecticut, 1996 *Certification:* Dermatology
4699 Main St #212, Bridgeport, 203-372-8949

Pruzan, Debra Lynn (9 mentions)
U of Pennsylvania, 1986 *Certification:* Dermatology
1290 Summer St #3600, Stamford, 203-325-3576

Romano, Salvatore V., Jr. (7 mentions)
Yale U, 1975 *Certification:* Dermatology
171 Grandview Ave #103, Waterbury, 203-757-8919

Watsky, Kalman Lewis (12 mentions)
Boston U, 1983 *Certification:* Dermatology
330 Orchard St #103, New Haven, 203-789-4045

Emergency Medicine

Begg, William V., III (5 mentions)
New York Med Coll, 1989 *Certification:* Emergency Medicine
24 Hospital Ave, Danbury, 203-797-7101

Boris, Gregory L. (3 mentions)
Certification: Emergency Medicine
130 Division Sr, Derby, 203-732-7222

Capodanno, Robert James (6 mentions)
New York Coll of Osteopathic Med, 1993
24 Stevens St, Norwalk, 203-852-2000

Carius, Michael Lee (4 mentions)
U of Colorado, 1973 *Certification:* Emergency Medicine
34 Maple St, Norwalk, 203-852-2281

D'Onofrio, Gail Long (3 mentions)
Boston U, 1987 *Certification:* Emergency Medicine
464 Congress Ave #260, New Haven, 203-688-2222

Doran, Brian John (8 mentions)
Rosalind Franklin U, 1996 *Certification:* Emergency Medicine
5 Perryridge Rd, Greenwich, 203-863-3637

Ferrigno, Rockman Farrell (6 mentions)
Yale U, 2001 *Certification:* Emergency Medicine
267 Grant St, Bridgeport, 203-384-3566

Holland, Stephen Timothy (4 mentions)
FMS-Mexico, 1983 *Certification:* Emergency Medicine
56 Franklin St, Waterbury, 203-709-6004

Illuzzi, Frank Anthony (3 mentions)
Georgetown U, 1998 *Certification:* Emergency Medicine
2800 Main St, Bridgeport, 203-576-5177

Jacoby, Peter J. (4 mentions)
Certification: Emergency Medicine
56 Franklin St, Waterbury, 203-709-3534

Jordan, Bernard Bryan (4 mentions)
Kansas U Coll of Osteopathic Med, 1989
267 Grant St, Bridgeport, 203-384-3923

Maisel, Jonathan Alan (13 mentions)
SUNY-Downstate Med Coll, 1982
Certification: Emergency Medicine, Internal Medicine
267 Grant St, Bridgeport, 203-384-3566

McGovern, Brian Richard (8 mentions)
Columbia U, 1992 *Certification:* Emergency Medicine
Norwalk Hospital, Norwalk, 203-852-2281

Michos, Christopher John (3 mentions)
New Jersey Med Sch, 1990 *Certification:* Emergency Medicine
64 Robbins St, Waterbury, 203-573-6000

Santucci, Karen Ann (3 mentions)
SUNY-Downstate Med Coll, 1989
Certification: Pediatric Emergency Medicine, Pediatrics
20 York St, New Haven, 203-785-7998

Tilden, Fred (4 mentions)
Certification: Emergency Medicine
435 Lewis Ave, Meriden, 203-694-8278

Werdmann, Michael John (5 mentions)
U of Cincinnati, 1977 *Certification:* Emergency Medicine,
  Internal Medicine, Pediatric Emergency Medicine, Pediatrics
267 Grant St, Bridgeport, 203-384-3923

Wright, Kenneth Jordan (6 mentions)
George Washington U, 1973 *Certification:* Emergency Medicine
24 Stevens St, Norwalk, 203-852-2000

Endocrinology

Arden-Cordone, Mary E. (7 mentions)
New York U, 1989 *Certification:* Endocrinology, Diabetes,
  and Metabolism, Internal Medicine
1275 Summer St #A1, Stamford, 203-359-2444

Benaviv-Meskin, Danielle P. (6 mentions)
Jefferson Med Coll, 2000 *Certification:* Endocrinology,
  Diabetes, and Metabolism, Internal Medicine
4699 Main St #105, Bridgeport, 203-374-6162

Gniadek, Thomas Carl (6 mentions)
U of Connecticut, 1976
Certification: Endocrinology and Metabolism, Internal Medicine
1389 W Main St #224, Waterbury, 203-755-7711

Goldberg-Berman, Judith (6 mentions)
Cornell U, 1987 *Certification:* Endocrinology, Diabetes, and
  Metabolism, Internal Medicine
4 Dearfield Dr #102, Greenwich, 203-622-9160
5 Perryridge Rd, Greenwich, 203-863-3000

Guoth, Maria (23 mentions)
FMS-Hungary, 1980
Certification: Endocrinology, Diabetes, and Metabolism
5520 Park Ave #306, Trumbull, 203-373-7388

Inzucchi, Silvio Edward (13 mentions)
Harvard U, 1985 *Certification:* Endocrinology, Diabetes,
  and Metabolism, Internal Medicine
789 Howard Ave, New Haven, 203-785-5564

Kayne, Richard Donald (6 mentions)
Yale U, 1976
Certification: Endocrinology and Metabolism, Internal Medicine
577 S Main St, Cheshire, 203-272-1619

Mayerson, Adam Blake (6 mentions)
Albert Einstein Coll of Med, 1996 *Certification:*
  Endocrinology, Diabetes, and Metabolism, Internal Medicine
200 Orchard St #207, New Haven, 203-777-6730

Olson, Beatriz (13 mentions)
Columbia U, 1984 *Certification:* Endocrinology, Diabetes,
  and Metabolism, Internal Medicine
850 Straits Tpke #204, Middlebury, 203-758-2594

Padilla, Alfred John (8 mentions)
Northwestern U, 1972
Certification: Endocrinology and Metabolism, Internal Medicine
4 Dearfield Dr, Greenwich, 203-622-9160
5 Perryridge Rd, Greenwich, 203-863-3000

Pantaleo, Antonio (7 mentions)
FMS-Italy, 1989 *Certification:* Endocrinology, Diabetes, and
  Metabolism, Internal Medicine
1275 Summer St #A-1, Stamford, 203-359-2444

Rich, Glenn Michael (14 mentions)
Cornell U, 1986 *Certification:* Endocrinology, Diabetes, and
  Metabolism, Internal Medicine
15 Corporate Dr #2-1, Trumbull, 203-459-5100

Robin, Noel Ira (10 mentions)
SUNY-Downstate Med Coll, 1965
Certification: Endocrinology and Metabolism, Internal Medicine
30 Shelburne Rd, Stamford, 203-325-7485

Rosa, Joseph Angelo, Jr. (13 mentions)
FMS-Mexico, 1982
Certification: Endocrinology and Metabolism, Internal Medicine
4699 Main St #105, Bridgeport, 203-374-6162

Savino, Robert R. (8 mentions)
New York Coll of Osteopathic Med, 1988 *Certification:*
  Endocrinology, Diabetes, and Metabolism, Internal Medicine
25 Germantown Rd #A, Danbury, 203-731-2020

Sotsky, Mindy J. (9 mentions)
761 Main Ave #201, Norwalk, 203-838-4000

Werner, Linda S. (10 mentions)
U of Pennsylvania, 1991 *Certification:* Endocrinology, Diabetes, and Metabolism, Internal Medicine
3180 Main St #105, Bridgeport, 203-372-7200

Family Practice *(see note on page 9)*

Acosta, Rodrigo (7 mentions)
U of Texas-Dallas, 1984
Certification: Family Medicine, Geriatric Medicine
32 Strawberry Hill Ct #41096, Stamford, 203-977-2566

Ahern, James Kelly (4 mentions)
U of Cincinnati, 1979 *Certification:* Family Medicine
77 Danbury Rd, Ridgefield, 203-431-6342

Blum, Theodore James (3 mentions)
SUNY-Downstate Med Coll, 1975 *Certification:* Family Medicine
5 School St, Bethel, 203-743-0799

Bookas, Timothy (6 mentions)
New York Coll of Osteopathic Med, 1990
Certification: Family Medicine
520 West Ave, Norwalk, 203-838-4000

Brumberger, Bruce Joel (4 mentions)
U of Connecticut, 1974 *Certification:* Family Medicine
816 Broad St #24, Meriden, 203-634-0086

Cigno, Thomas Vincent (4 mentions)
Tufts U, 1986 *Certification:* Family Medicine
77 Danbury Rd, Ridgefield, 203-431-6342

Filiberto, Cosmo (7 mentions)
FMS-Italy, 1976
Certification: Family Medicine, Geriatric Medicine
3715 Main St #200, Bridgeport, 203-372-4065

Forest, Lee Jon (3 mentions)
New York Coll of Osteopathic Med, 1998
2184 Main St, Stratford, 203-378-9002

Greeley, John Michael (4 mentions)
FMS-Mexico, 1977 *Certification:* Family Medicine
1450 Washington Blvd, Stamford, 203-348-2937

Herbert, Joshua Bryan (4 mentions)
FMS-Grenada, 1996 *Certification:* Family Medicine
30 Buxton Farm Rd #110, Stamford, 203-322-7070

Ju, Jennifer Meheh (3 mentions)
Jefferson Med Coll, 2000 *Certification:* Family Medicine
4699 Main St #201, Bridgeport, 203-372-9002

Jutkowitz, David Michael (3 mentions)
New York Med Coll, 1973
Certification: Internal Medicine, Pediatrics
1950 Main St, Stratford, 203-377-6923

Maki, Wendy (3 mentions)
U of Minnesota, 1991 *Certification:* Family Medicine
96 Danbury Rd, Ridgefield, 203-438-0874

Mascia, Robert Angelo (3 mentions)
Wright State U, 1980 *Certification:* Family Medicine
60 Old New Milford Rd, Brookfield, 203-775-6365

Nurena, Kathleen Rocio (3 mentions)
Albert Einstein Coll of Med, 1999 *Certification:* Family Medicine
90 Morgan St #108, Stamford, 203-359-9997
1351 Washington Blvd, Stamford, 203-621-3700

Ralabate, James Patrick (4 mentions)
Albany Med Coll, 1981 *Certification:* Internal Medicine, Pediatrics
2890 Main St #A, Stratford, 203-378-3646

Robin, Marc (3 mentions)
FMS-Canada, 1997 *Certification:* Family Medicine
32 Strawberry Hill Ct #41096, Stamford, 203-977-2566

Scifo, Francis Raymond (3 mentions)
FMS-Mexico, 1979
2595 Main St, Stratford, 203-386-0366

Svogun, John (3 mentions)
FMS-India, 1982
520 West Ave, Norwalk, 203-838-4000
345 Main Ave, Norwalk, 203-846-8740
761 Main Ave #2, Norwalk, 203-838-4000

Waynik, Myra (6 mentions)
FMS-South Africa, 1967
3715 Main St #200, Bridgeport, 203-372-4065

Gastroenterology

Bedford, Charles Andrew (5 mentions)
Tufts U, 1992 *Certification:* Gastroenterology
2890 Main St, Stratford, 203-375-1200
267 Grant St, Bridgeport, 203-384-3394

Bennick, Michael Charles (8 mentions)
Temple U, 1983
Certification: Gastroenterology, Internal Medicine
40 Temple St #4-A, New Haven, 203-777-0304

Bonheim, Nelson Alfred (11 mentions)
Rosalind Franklin U, 1970
Certification: Gastroenterology, Internal Medicine
500 W Putnam Ave #100, Greenwich, 203-863-2900

Brand, Myron Howard (6 mentions)
U of North Carolina, 1972
Certification: Gastroenterology, Internal Medicine
40 Temple St #4-A, New Haven, 203-562-2556

Dettmer, Robert Michael (12 mentions)
Albert Einstein Coll of Med, 1994 *Certification:* Gastroenterology
32 Strawberry Hill Ct, Stamford, 203-348-5355

Ernstoff, Jon Jeffrey (5 mentions)
FMS-Belgium, 1978
Certification: Gastroenterology, Internal Medicine
455 Lewis Ave #106, Meriden, 203-272-6499

Fiorito, Joseph John (6 mentions)
Columbia U, 1983
Certification: Gastroenterology, Internal Medicine
24 Hospital Ave, Danbury, 203-797-7038
95 Locust Ave, Danbury, 203-797-7742

Gordon, Donald Gary (9 mentions)
Emory U, 1981 *Certification:* Gastroenterology, Internal Medicine
16 Hospital Ave #303, Danbury, 203-794-8020
7 Germantown Rd #1-B, Danbury, 203-794-8020

Grossman, Edward Theodore (5 mentions)
Albert Einstein Coll of Med, 1963
Certification: Gastroenterology, Internal Medicine
425 Post Rd, Fairfield, 203-292-9000

Hale, William Benton (20 mentions)
U of Wisconsin, 1980
Certification: Gastroenterology, Internal Medicine
30 Steven St #D, Norwalk, 203-852-2278

Khaghan, Neda (5 mentions)
Mount Sinai Sch of Med, 1995
Certification: Gastroenterology, Internal Medicine
500 W Putnam Ave #100, Greenwich, 203-863-2900

Lagarde, Suzanne Paula (10 mentions)
Cornell U, 1975
Certification: Gastroenterology, Internal Medicine
40 Temple St #4-A, New Haven, 203-562-2556

Lam, Chunwang (7 mentions)
Certification: Gastroenterology, Internal Medicine
888 White Plains Rd #110, Trumbull, 203-459-4451

Landau, Alan Eric (5 mentions)
Boston U, 1985
Certification: Gastroenterology, Internal Medicine
888 White Plains Rd #110, Trumbull, 203-459-4451

Levine, Edwin Gregg (7 mentions)
SUNY-Downstate Med Coll, 1987
Certification: Gastroenterology, Internal Medicine
888 White Plains Rd, Trumbull, 203-459-4451

Mauer, Kenneth Ray (6 mentions)
New York U, 1983
Certification: Gastroenterology, Internal Medicine
425 Post Rd 1st Fl, Fairfield, 203-292-9000

Meighan, Dennis M. (12 mentions)
U of New England Coll of Osteopathic Med, 1982
Certification: Gastroenterology, Internal Medicine
30 Stevens St, Norwalk, 203-852-3455

Nelson, Alan M. (5 mentions)
Georgetown U, 1974
Certification: Gastroenterology, Internal Medicine
4641 Main St #1, Bridgeport, 203-374-4966

Sammarco, Frank (8 mentions)
FMS-Mexico, 1983
Certification: Gastroenterology, Internal Medicine
520 West Ave #7, Norwalk, 203-838-4000

Sheinbaum, Richard Charles (6 mentions)
Temple U, 1979
Certification: Gastroenterology, Internal Medicine
144 Morgan St, Stamford, 203-348-5355
32 Strawberry Hill Ct #41042, Stamford, 203-348-5355

Soloway, Gregory Noel (13 mentions)
Cornell U, 1986
Certification: Gastroenterology, Internal Medicine
2890 Main St, Stratford, 203-375-1200

Taubin, Howard Leslie (6 mentions)
U of Virginia, 1965
Certification: Gastroenterology, Internal Medicine
2890 Main St, Stratford, 203-574-3007

Waldstreicher, Stuart (11 mentions)
New York Med Coll, 1982
Certification: Gastroenterology, Internal Medicine
166 W Broad St #303, Stamford, 203-967-2100

Woods, Strick Jonathan (6 mentions)
Wake Forest U, 1985 *Certification:* Internal Medicine
425 Post Rd, Fairfield, 203-292-9000
2660 Main St #203, Bridgeport, 203-333-3328

Zlotoff, Ronald Alan (9 mentions)
U of Oklahoma, 1977
Certification: Gastroenterology, Internal Medicine
140 Grandview Ave, Waterbury, 203-755-4515

Zwas, Felice Rosel (5 mentions)
Columbia U, 1980
Certification: Gastroenterology, Internal Medicine
500 W Putnam Ave #100, Greenwich, 203-863-2900

General Surgery

Borruso, John Joseph (4 mentions)
Hahnemann U, 1981 *Certification:* Surgery
111 Osborne St, Danbury, 203-797-7131
385 Main St, Southbury, 203-797-7131

Bull, Sherman Marsh (13 mentions)
Columbia U, 1962 *Certification:* Surgery
1351 Washington Blvd, Stamford, 203-276-5959

Choi, Laura H. (4 mentions)
Certification: Surgery
111 Osborne St 2nd Fl, Danbury, 203-739-7131

Duerr, L. Sean (12 mentions)
U of Vermont, 1973 *Certification:* Surgery
2900 Main St #1-F, Stratford, 203-378-4500

Famiglietti, John Benjamin (7 mentions)
Cornell U, 1974 *Certification:* Surgery
46 Federal Rd, Danbury, 203-743-3877

Floch, Craig Lawrence (7 mentions)
Rosalind Franklin U, 1989 *Certification:* Surgery
2800 Main St, Bridgeport, 203-576-5436
148 East Ave #3-A, Norwalk, 203-899-0744

Floch, Neil Robert (7 mentions)
Boston U, 1992 *Certification:* Surgery
148 East Ave #3-A, Norwalk, 203-899-0744

Fotovat, Ahmad (10 mentions)
FMS-Iran, 1975 *Certification:* Surgery
115 Technology Dr #C-100, Trumbull, 203-268-5212

Garvey, Richard John (8 mentions)
Georgetown U, 1974 *Certification:* Surgery
310 Mill Hill Ave, Bridgeport, 203-366-3211

Gordon, Joseph Robert (4 mentions)
U of Chicago, 1981 *Certification:* Surgery
107 Newtown Rd #2C, Danbury, 203-798-8083

Horowitz, Nina Ruth (10 mentions)
Columbia U, 1979 *Certification:* Surgery
46 Prince St #301, New Haven, 203-562-3577

Kenler, Andrew Scott (16 mentions)
Cornell U, 1988 *Certification:* Surgery
1305 Post Rd #125, Fairfield, 203-373-9015
5520 Park Ave #207, Trumbull, 203-373-9015

Knight, David Clough (10 mentions)
FMS-Ireland, 1981 *Certification:* Surgery
1211 W Main St, Waterbury, 203-757-1587

Leff, Peter David (4 mentions)
New York Med Coll, 1989 *Certification:* Surgery
455 Lewis Ave #216, Meriden, 203-634-0134

Longo, Walter E. (5 mentions)
Certification: Colon & Rectal Surgery, Surgery
800 Howard Ave, New Haven, 203-785-2616
40 Temple St #1-A, New Haven, 203-785-2616

Lovanio, Richard Gabriel (4 mentions)
New Jersey Med Sch, 1966 *Certification:* Surgery
2660 Main St #110, Bridgeport, 203-332-4744

McWhorter, Philip John (11 mentions)
Cornell U, 1973
77 Lafayette Pl #301, Greenwich, 203-863-4300

Meinke, Alan Kurt (14 mentions)
Wayne State U, 1978 *Certification:* Surgery
125 Kings Hwy N, Westport, 203-226-0771

Miller, Kevin D. (8 mentions)
Columbia U, 1994 *Certification:* Surgery
1351 Washington Blvd, Stamford, 203-276-5959

Molinelli, Bruce M. (11 mentions)
Certification: Surgery
77 Lafayette Pl, Greenwich, 203-863-4300

Passeri, Daniel Joseph (7 mentions)
Yale U, 1975 *Certification:* Surgery
888 White Plains Rd, Trumbull, 203-459-2666

Patil, Vijay M. (4 mentions)
FMS-India, 1968
46 Federal Rd, Danbury, 203-743-3877

Petrotos, Athanassios (6 mentions)
FMS-Greece, 1991 *Certification:* Surgery
77 Lafayette Pl, Greenwich, 203-863-4300

Richi, Abdelaziz (4 mentions)
FMS-Syria, 1971 *Certification:* Surgery, Thoracic Surgery
1389 W Main St #322, Waterbury, 203-753-0877

Salem, Ronald R. (5 mentions)
FMS-Zimbabwe, 1978 *Certification:* Surgery
333 Cedar St, New Haven, 203-785-3577
800 Howard Ave, New Haven, 203-785-4079

Shetty, Jayakara (5 mentions)
FMS-India, 1973 *Certification:* Surgery
134 Grandview Ave #209, Waterbury, 203-755-6666

Stein, Stephen Alan (17 mentions)
Harvard U, 1967 *Certification:* Surgery
46 Prince St #301, New Haven, 203-787-2862

Geriatrics

Cooney, Leo Mathias, Jr. (18 mentions)
Yale U, 1969 *Certification:* Geriatric Medicine, Internal Medicine, Rheumatology
874 Howard Ave, New Haven, 203-688-6361

Hoffman, Pamela Beth (8 mentions)
U of Virginia, 1978 *Certification:* Internal Medicine
2800 Main St, Bridgeport, 203-576-5710

Ott, Casey Kevin (4 mentions)
FMS-Israel, 1996 *Certification:* Internal Medicine
22 Old Waterbury Rd, Southbury, 203-262-1200
108 Main St N, Southbury, 203-262-4240

Skudlarska, Beata (12 mentions)
FMS-Poland, 1992
Certification: Geriatric Medicine, Internal Medicine
95 Armory Rd, Stratford, 203-384-3388

Tinetti, Mary Elizabeth (7 mentions)
U of Michigan, 1978 *Certification:* Internal Medicine
789 Howard Ave, New Haven, 203-688-6361

Hematology/Oncology

Abrams, Martin Barry (6 mentions)
Tufts U, 1980 *Certification:* Internal Medicine, Medical Oncology
24 Hospital Ave, Danbury, 203-830-4607

Alfano, Francis D. (6 mentions)
Columbia U, 1978
Certification: Internal Medicine, Medical Oncology
1075 Chase Pkwy #B, Waterbury, 203-755-6311

Bar, Michael Henry (9 mentions)
Columbia U, 1983
Certification: Hematology, Internal Medicine, Medical Oncology
34 Shelburne Rd, Stamford, 203-325-2695

Bowen, Joseph John (8 mentions)
Georgetown U, 1977
Certification: Hematology, Internal Medicine, Medical Oncology
1075 Chase Pkwy #A, Waterbury, 203-591-3077

Boyd, Donald Barry (9 mentions)
Cornell U, 1979
Certification: Internal Medicine, Medical Oncology
15 Valley Dr #2, Greenwich, 203-869-2111

Cooper, Robert Bruce (9 mentions)
U of Pittsburgh, 1971
Certification: Internal Medicine, Medical Oncology
24 Hospital Ave, Danbury, 203-792-5303

Dressler, Kenneth Alex (10 mentions)
Harvard U, 1985
Certification: Hematology, Internal Medicine, Medical Oncology
425 Post Rd, Fairfield, 203-255-4545

Duda, Edward Andrew (7 mentions)
Yale U, 1984
Certification: Hematology, Internal Medicine, Medical Oncology
425 Post Rd, Fairfield, 203-255-4545
4699 Main St, Bridgeport, 203-371-5228

Duffy, Thomas P. M. (10 mentions)
Johns Hopkins U, 1962
Certification: Hematology, Internal Medicine
800 Howard Ave 2nd Fl, New Haven, 203-785-4744

Fischbach, Neal Asher (10 mentions)
Harvard U, 1995 *Certification:* Medical Oncology
15 Corporate Dr, Trumbull, 203-459-0262
111 Beach Rd, Fairfield, 203-255-2766

Folman, Robert Starr (7 mentions)
U of Buffalo, 1972
Certification: Internal Medicine, Medical Oncology
15 Corporate Dr, Trumbull, 203-459-0262
111 Beach Rd, Fairfield, 203-255-2766

Frank, Richard Carlysle (6 mentions)
Stony Brook U, 1989
Certification: Hematology, Medical Oncology
24 Stevens St, Norwalk, 203-845-2128

Hollister, Dickerman, Jr. (9 mentions)
U of Virginia, 1975
Certification: Hematology, Internal Medicine, Medical Oncology
77 Lafayette Pl, Greenwich, 203-863-3737

Katz, Martin Edward (8 mentions)
U of Pennsylvania, 1972
Certification: Internal Medicine, Medical Oncology
2080 Whitney Ave #240, Hamden, 203-407-8002

Lo, Kwokming Steve (18 mentions)
Harvard U, 1985
Certification: Hematology, Internal Medicine, Medical Oncology
34 Shelburne Rd, Stamford, 203-325-2695

McNamara, Joseph Michael (8 mentions)
FMS-Italy, 1982
Certification: Pediatric Hematology-Oncology, Pediatrics
405 Church St, Guilford, 203-453-2013

Nair, Kesav G. (6 mentions)
FMS-India, 1970
Certification: Internal Medicine, Medical Oncology
40 Cross St, Norwalk, 203-845-2000

Sabbath, Kert David (17 mentions)
Boston U, 1979
Certification: Hematology, Internal Medicine, Medical Oncology
1075 Chase Pkwy, Waterbury, 203-755-6311

Tansino, Gary Francis (6 mentions)
SUNY-Downstate Med Coll, 1984
Certification: Internal Medicine, Medical Oncology
455 Lewis Ave, Meriden, 203-238-7747

Weinstein, Paul Leslie (7 mentions)
Rosalind Franklin U, 1970
Certification: Hematology, Internal Medicine, Medical Oncology
34 Shelburne Rd, Stamford, 203-325-2695

Witt, David H. (15 mentions)
New York U, 1978
Certification: Hematology, Internal Medicine, Medical Oncology
5520 Park Ave #203, Trumbull, 203-334-7400

Zelkowitz, Richard Scott (25 mentions)
New York Med Coll, 1983
Certification: Hematology, Internal Medicine, Medical Oncology
24 Stevens St, Norwalk, 203-845-2148
40 Cross St, Norwalk, 203-845-2000

Infectious Disease

Aronin, Steven Isador (10 mentions)
FMS-Dominica, 1991
Certification: Infectious Disease, Internal Medicine
140 Grandview Ave #101, Waterbury, 203-574-4187
64 Robbins St, Waterbury, 203-573-7228

Cipriani, Ralph J. (11 mentions)
Albert Einstein Coll of Med, 1996
Certification: Infectious Disease, Internal Medicine
5 Perryridge Rd, Greenwich, 203-863-3270

Golden, Marjorie Phyllis (6 mentions)
Albany Med Coll, 1986
Certification: Infectious Disease, Internal Medicine
330 Orchard St, New Haven, 203-789-3422
1450 Chapel St, New Haven, 203-789-3566

Herbin, Joseph Thomas (9 mentions)
FMS-Switzerland, 1965 *Certification:* Internal Medicine
2150 Black Rock Tpke, Fairfield, 203-384-0451

Kim, Grace Park (12 mentions)
Northwestern U, 1986
2800 Main St, Bridgeport, 203-659-1599

Klein, Debra Adler (11 mentions)
Albert Einstein Coll of Med, 1984
190 Broad St, Stamford, 203-276-1000
1100 Bedford St, Stamford, 203-323-4458

Levitz, Robert E. (7 mentions)
Certification: Infectious Disease, Internal Medicine
80 Seymour St, Hartford, 860-545-5000

Libertin, Claudia Ruth (4 mentions)
U of Toledo, 1978 *Certification:* Infectious Disease, Internal Medicine, Medical Microbiology
6 Business Parks Dr, Branford, 203-777-9183

Lobo, David John (9 mentions)
FMS-India, 1994
Certification: Infectious Disease, Internal Medicine
2876 Main St, Stratford, 203-383-4466

McLeod, Gavin Xavier (17 mentions)
U of Connecticut, 1985
Certification: Infectious Disease, Internal Medicine
166 W Broad St #202, Stamford, 203-353-1427

Miljkovic, Goran (8 mentions)
FMS-Croatia, 1991
Certification: Infectious Disease, Internal Medicine
2890 Main St #D, Stratford, 203-383-4466

Nee, Paul Francis, Jr. (14 mentions)
New York Med Coll, 1994 *Certification:* Infectious Disease
14 Mountain View Dr, Brookfield, 203-797-7413
95 Locust Ave, Danbury, 203-797-7413

Parry, Michael Frank (17 mentions)
Columbia U, 1970
Certification: Infectious Disease, Internal Medicine
166 W Broad St #202, Stamford, 203-353-1427

Passalacqua, Joanne (10 mentions)
SUNY-Upstate Med U, 1992
Certification: Infectious Disease, Internal Medicine
2150 Black Rock Tpke, Fairfield, 203-384-0451

Pino, Paolo A. (11 mentions)
U of New England Coll of Osteopathic Med, 2001
Certification: Infectious Disease, Internal Medicine
40 Cross St, Norwalk, 203-845-4800

Quagliarello, Vincent J. (5 mentions)
Washington U, 1980
Certification: Infectious Disease, Internal Medicine
789 Howard Ave, New Haven, 203-785-7998

Sabetta, James Robert (17 mentions)
Brown U, 1978
Certification: Infectious Disease, Internal Medicine
5 Perryridge Rd, Greenwich, 203-869-8838

Saul, Zane Kevin (40 mentions)
FMS-Grenada, 1985
Certification: Infectious Disease, Internal Medicine
2890 Main St #D, Stratford, 203-383-4466

Schleiter, Gary Steven (15 mentions)
Wake Forest U, 1980
Certification: Infectious Disease, Internal Medicine
24 Hospital Ave, Danbury, 203-797-7413
70 Main St, Danbury, 203-791-5030

Simms, Michael Francis (9 mentions)
New York Med Coll, 1979
Certification: Infectious Disease, Internal Medicine
56 Franklin St, Waterbury, 203-709-6000
799 New Haven Rd, Naugatuck, 203-709-6000

Stratidis, John (4 mentions)
FMS-Saba, 2000
Certification: Infectious Disease, Internal Medicine
95 Locust Ave 2nd Fl, Danbury, 203-739-7413

Topal, Jeffrey Edward (5 mentions)
Tufts U, 1991
789 Howard Ave, New Haven, 203-688-9361

Urbina-Reyes, Brenda Y. (11 mentions)
U of Puerto Rico, 1997
Certification: Infectious Disease, Internal Medicine
24 Stevens St, Norwalk, 203-845-2128
40 Cross St, Norwalk, 203-845-4837

Villanueva, Merceditas S. (8 mentions)
Washington U, 1985
Certification: Infectious Disease, Internal Medicine
140 Grandview Ave #L-01, Waterbury, 203-574-4187
64 Robbins St, Waterbury, 203-573-7228

Yee, Arthur (20 mentions)
U of Connecticut, 1982
Certification: Infectious Disease, Internal Medicine
40 Cross St 4th Fl, Norwalk, 203-845-2000

Infertility

Doyle, Michael B. (9 mentions)
U of California-San Francisco, 1985
Certification: Obstetrics & Gynecology
4920 Main St #301, Bridgeport, 203-373-1200
148 East Ave #2-C, Norwalk, 203-855-1200
339 Boston Post Rd #380, Orange, 203-799-1200

Lavy, Gad (9 mentions)
FMS-Israel, 1980 *Certification:* Obstetrics & Gynecology, Reproductive Endocrinology/Infertility
1275 Summer St #201, Stamford, 203-325-3200
9 Washington Ave, Hamden, 203-248-2353

Levi, Andrew Joseph (10 mentions)
U of Rochester, 1995 *Certification:* Obstetrics & Gynecology, Reproductive Endocrinology/Infertility
5520 Park Ave #103, Trumbull, 203-372-6700

Internal Medicine *(see note on page 9)*

Altbaum, Robert Alan (13 mentions)
Harvard U, 1975 *Certification:* Internal Medicine
162 Kings Hwy N, Westport, 203-226-0731

Brunetti, James A. (3 mentions)
U of New England Coll of Osteopathic Med, 1993
31 River Rd #200, Cos Cob, 203-661-9433

Coopersmith, Leslie (3 mentions)
Robert W Johnson Med Sch, 1985
Certification: Internal Medicine
80 Phoenix Ave #303, Waterbury, 203-756-2826

Denowitz, Jill Grossman (4 mentions)
Albert Einstein Coll of Med, 1988 *Certification:* Internal Medicine
162 Kings Hwy N, Westport, 203-226-0731

Dorosario, Arnold E. (7 mentions)
FMS-Spain, 1975 *Certification:* Internal Medicine
4699 Main St #105, Bridgeport, 203-374-6162

Dreyer, Neil Paul (8 mentions)
New York U, 1967 *Certification:* Internal Medicine, Nephrology
51 Schuyler Ave #1, Stamford, 203-327-1187

Edelmann, Christopher M. (4 mentions)
Albert Einstein Coll of Med, 1995 *Certification:* Internal Medicine
42 Sherwood Pl, Greenwich, 203-869-0502

Epstein, Serle Mindell (5 mentions)
Mount Sinai Sch of Med, 1979 *Certification:* Internal Medicine
6 Woodland Rd, Madison, 203-245-7959

Fennell, Gail M. (4 mentions)
Certification: Internal Medicine
75 Holly Hill Ln, Greenwich, 203-869-6960

Finnerty, James William (4 mentions)
Georgetown U, 1979 *Certification:* Internal Medicine
2 Elizabeth St, Bethel, 203-791-2221

Fisher, Steven Alan (9 mentions)
Mount Sinai Sch of Med, 1984 *Certification:* Internal Medicine
15 Corporate Dr, Trumbull, 203-459-5100

Kaplan, Fred M. (3 mentions)
George Washington U, 1978 *Certification:* Internal Medicine
162 Kings Hwy N, Westport, 203-226-0731

Kaufman, Richard Enoch (3 mentions)
Yale U, 1971
Certification: Allergy & Immunology, Internal Medicine
960 Main St, Branford, 203-488-6358

Kocinsky, Daniel Thomas (3 mentions)
New Jersey Med Sch, 1998 *Certification:* Internal Medicine
888 White Plains Rd #203, Trumbull, 203-459-0408

Listokin, Ted E. (3 mentions)
New York U, 1991 *Certification:* Internal Medicine
1450 Washington Blvd, Stamford, 203-327-9321

Mann, Marc Eliot (5 mentions)
Johns Hopkins U, 1972 *Certification:* Internal Medicine
2440 Whitney Ave, Hamden, 203-288-9650

Melchinger, David Barry (3 mentions)
Yale U, 1966 *Certification:* Internal Medicine
100 York St #2E, New Haven, 203-787-3588

Miller, Denis John (6 mentions)
FMS-South Africa, 1967
500 E Main St #212, Branford, 203-481-5665

Neuberger, Santi John (3 mentions)
FMS-Mexico, 1982 *Certification:* Internal Medicine
90 Morgan St, Stamford, 203-324-9955

Olin, Craig Howard (6 mentions)
New York U, 1993 *Certification:* Internal Medicine
5 High Ridge Park #104, Stamford, 203-968-9500

Osnoss, Kenneth Lawrence (4 mentions)
Tufts U, 1975
Certification: Internal Medicine, Pulmonary Disease
24 Hospital Ave, Danbury, 203-797-7173
95 Locust Ave, Danbury, 203-797-7742

Pinto, Edward R. (6 mentions)
FMS-India, 1971
Certification: Cardiovascular Disease, Internal Medicine
52 Beach Rd #107, Fairfield, 203-254-1663

Pizzuto, David Joseph (6 mentions)
New York Med Coll, 1984 *Certification:* Internal Medicine
1211 W Main St, Waterbury, 203-756-6148

Rastogi, Amit (5 mentions)
New Jersey Med Sch, 1994 *Certification:* Internal Medicine
4699 Main St #105, Bridgeport, 203-374-6162

Rosenberg, Remi Max (3 mentions)
New York U, 2000 *Certification:* Internal Medicine
51 Schuyler Ave, Stamford, 203-327-1187

Sarfeh, James (6 mentions)
Albany Med Coll, 1978 *Certification:* Internal Medicine
422 Highland Ave, Cheshire, 203-272-7251

Sica, Daniel G. (4 mentions)
U of Toledo, 1982 *Certification:* Internal Medicine
888 White Plains Rd, Trumbull, 203-459-0408

Smerling, Neil Edward (4 mentions)
FMS-Grenada, 1988 *Certification:* Internal Medicine
111 Beach Rd, Fairfield, 203-259-7442

Spano, Frank (13 mentions)
Albert Einstein Coll of Med, 1984 *Certification:* Internal Medicine
15 Corporate Dr #2-1, Trumbull, 203-459-5100

Toksoy, Selami 'John' Can (3 mentions)
Stony Brook U, 1997 *Certification:* Internal Medicine
17 Hillhouse Ave, New Haven, 203-432-0076

Tortora, Peter C. (3 mentions)
FMS-Dominica, 1985 *Certification:* Internal Medicine
1300 Post Rd #202, Fairfield, 203-255-8827

Tortorello, Joseph (3 mentions)
New York Med Coll, 1998 *Certification:* Internal Medicine
4699 Main St #105, Bridgeport, 203-374-6162

Vaid, Chetan (4 mentions)
New Jersey Med Sch, 1995 *Certification:* Internal Medicine
75 Holly Hill Ln, Greenwich, 203-869-6960

Nephrology

Brown, Eric Yale (11 mentions)
Emory U, 1985 *Certification:* Internal Medicine, Nephrology
30 Commerce Rd, Stamford, 203-324-7666

Chan, Brenda Shang (7 mentions)
Certification: Nephrology
30 Commerce Rd, Stamford, 203-324-7666

Feintzeig, Irwin David (12 mentions)
U of Chicago, 1979 *Certification:* Internal Medicine, Nephrology
900 Madison Ave, Bridgeport, 203-335-0195

Fogel, Mitchell Andrew (14 mentions)
U of Pennsylvania, 1982
Certification: Internal Medicine, Nephrology
900 Madison Ave #209, Bridgeport, 203-335-0195

Gavin, James Patrick (8 mentions)
Hahnemann U, 1985
Certification: Internal Medicine, Nephrology
900 Madison Ave, Bridgeport, 203-335-0195

Gervasi, Richard Terry (9 mentions)
Albany Med Coll, 1999
Certification: Internal Medicine, Nephrology
40 Cross St #400, Norwalk, 203-845-4800

Hines, William Harold (7 mentions)
Cornell U, 1981 *Certification:* Internal Medicine, Nephrology
30 Commerce Rd, Stamford, 203-324-7666

Hunt, William Allen (14 mentions)
Certification: Internal Medicine, Nephrology
900 Madison Ave, Bridgeport, 203-335-0195

Pronovost, Paul Henry (6 mentions)
U of Connecticut, 1990
Certification: Internal Medicine, Nephrology
140 Grandview Ave, Waterbury, 203-757-5798

Renda, Joseph Leonard (8 mentions)
Yale U, 1968 *Certification:* Internal Medicine
140 Grandview Ave #104, Waterbury, 203-597-9733

Roer, David Alan (7 mentions)
FMS-Dominica, 1984
Certification: Internal Medicine, Nephrology
850 Straits Tpke, Middlebury, 203-758-1800

Walsh, Francis Xavier (6 mentions)
New York Med Coll, 1967
Certification: Internal Medicine, Nephrology
31 River Rd #200, Cos Cob, 203-661-9433

Wiener, Paul Bennett (14 mentions)
SUNY-Downstate Med Coll, 1971
Certification: Internal Medicine, Nephrology
40 Cross St, Norwalk, 203-845-2000

Neurological Surgery

Batson, Ramon Antonio (17 mentions)
SUNY-Upstate Med U, 1980 *Certification:* Neurological Surgery
67 Sand Pit Rd #208, Danbury, 203-792-2003

Goodrich, Isaac (13 mentions)
Med Coll of Georgia, 1964 *Certification:* Neurological Surgery
330 Orchard St #316, New Haven, 203-781-3400
60 Temple St #5B, New Haven, 203-781-3400

Lipow, Kenneth Irwin (12 mentions)
Albert Einstein Coll of Med, 1978
Certification: Neurological Surgery
267 Grant St, Bridgeport, 203-384-4500

Mintz, Abraham (19 mentions)
FMS-Mexico, 1982 *Certification:* Neurological Surgery
5520 Park Ave #210, Trumbull, 203-372-6460

Piepmeier, Joseph Massa (9 mentions)
U of Tennessee, 1975 *Certification:* Neurological Surgery
333 Cedar St, New Haven, 203-785-2810
800 Howard Ave, New Haven, 203-785-2791

Rosenstein, Cory Charles (15 mentions)
Case Western Reserve U, 1985 *Certification:* Neurological Surgery
70 Mill River St #LL3, Stamford, 203-324-3504

Shahid, Syed Javed (30 mentions)
FMS-Pakistan, 1972 *Certification:* Neurological Surgery
67 Sand Pit Rd #208, Danbury, 203-792-2003

Shear, Perry Alan (16 mentions)
FMS-Canada, 1984 *Certification:* Neurological Surgery
340 Capitol Ave, Bridgeport, 203-337-2600
75 Kings Hwy Cutoff, Fairfield, 203-337-2600
31 Kent Ln, Trumbull, 203-337-2600
2909 Main St, Bridgeport, 203-337-2600

Spencer, Dennis Dee (12 mentions)
Washington U, 1971 *Certification:* Neurological Surgery
333 Cedar St, New Haven, 203-785-2285

Zimmerman, Gary Alan (13 mentions)
SUNY-Downstate Med Coll, 1990
Certification: Neurological Surgery
267 Grant St, Bridgeport, 203-384-4500

Neurology

Barasch, Philip Marc (6 mentions)
SUNY-Downstate Med Coll, 1976 *Certification:* Neurology
2590 Main St, Stratford, 203-377-5988
4 Corporate Dr #192, Shelton, 203-924-8664
52 Beach Rd #202, Fairfield, 203-254-0284

Beck, Lawrence Steven (9 mentions)
FMS-Mexico, 1977 *Certification:* Internal Medicine, Neurology
2590 Main St, Stratford, 203-377-5988
52 Beach Rd #202, Fairfield, 203-254-0284
4 Corporate Dr #192, Shelton, 203-924-8664

Butler, James Bell, Jr. (6 mentions)
FMS-Belgium, 1979 *Certification:* Internal Medicine, Neurology
2590 Main St, Stratford, 203-377-5988
4 Corporate Dr #192, Shelton, 203-924-8664
52 Beach Rd #202, Fairfield, 203-254-0284

Eisen, Steven Leslie (7 mentions)
Albany Med Coll, 1966 *Certification:* Psychiatry
1211 W Main St, Waterbury, 203-753-5700

Kaplove, Kenneth Alan (8 mentions)
Hahnemann U, 1979 *Certification:* Neurology
60 Westwood Ave #320, Waterbury, 203-756-8995
1579 Straits Tpke, Middlebury, 203-756-8995

Knorr, Amy Marie (6 mentions)
Yale U, 1994 *Certification:* Neurology
40 Cross St #330, Norwalk, 203-845-2233

Levy, Susan Ruth (6 mentions)
Wake Forest U, 1978 *Certification:* Neurology with Special
    Qualifications in Child Neurology, Pediatrics
5 Durham Rd #1, Guilford, 203-453-2181

McAllister, Peter Joseph (10 mentions)
U of Connecticut, 1991 *Certification:* Neurology
75 Kings Hwy Cutoff, Fairfield, 203-333-1133
670 Boston Post Rd Apt 11, Milford, 203-877-1414

McVeety, James (6 mentions)
FMS-Italy, 1975 *Certification:* Internal Medicine, Neurology
60 Dogwood Cir, Woodbridge, 203-789-2100
330 Orchard St #216, New Haven, 203-789-6047

Murphy, John Matthew (12 mentions)
Robert W Johnson Med Sch, 1985 *Certification:* Neurology
69 Sand Pit Rd #300, Danbury, 203-748-2551
24 Hospital Ave, Danbury, 203-739-7000

Nahm, Frederick Kiin (6 mentions)
U of Michigan, 1996 *Certification:* Neurology
49 Lake Ave, Greenwich, 203-661-9383

Nallainathan, Sanath-Kumar (5 mentions)
FMS-Sri Lanka, 1964 *Certification:* Neurology with Special
    Qualifications in Child Neurology
2590 Main St, Stratford, 203-377-5988
52 Beach Rd #202, Fairfield, 203-254-0284
4 Corporate Dr #192, Shelton, 203-924-8664

Quan Hong, Anthony (6 mentions)
FMS-Ireland, 1992 *Certification:* Neurology
75 Kings Hwy Cutoff, Fairfield, 203-333-1133
670 Boston Post Rd #11, Milford, 203-877-1414

Resor, Louise D. (13 mentions)
1290 Summer St #3200, Stamford, 203-978-0283

Rusk, Alice Hampton (9 mentions)
U of Connecticut, 1991 *Certification:* Neurology
49 Lake Ave #206, Greenwich, 203-869-6446

Sena, Kanaga N. (15 mentions)
FMS-Sri Lanka, 1969 *Certification:* Neurology
2590 Main St, Stratford, 203-377-5988
4 Corporate Dr #192, Shelton, 203-924-8664
52 Beach Rd #202, Fairfield, 203-254-0284

Siegel, Kenneth Colman (5 mentions)
Meharry Med Coll, 1969 *Certification:* Neurology
75 Kings Hwy Cutoff, Fairfield, 203-333-1133
670 Boston Post Rd #11, Milford, 203-877-1414

Story, Daryl Robert (8 mentions)
New York Med Coll, 1997
Certification: Neurology, Vascular Neurology
40 Cross St #330, Norwalk, 203-845-2233

Werdiger, Norman S. (7 mentions)
Cornell U, 1977 *Certification:* Neurology
2 Church St S #303, New Haven, 203-624-7893

Xistris, Evangelos D. (5 mentions)
U of Buffalo, 1974 *Certification:* Neurology
22 5th St, Stamford, 203-359-1206

Obstetrics/Gynecology

Albini, S. Mark (5 mentions)
FMS-Grenada, 1987 *Certification:* Obstetrics & Gynecology
133 Scovill St #303, Waterbury, 203-575-1811
152 Meadow St, Naugatuck, 203-723-4471
503 Wolcott Rd, Wolcott, 203-575-1811

Asis, Antonio (3 mentions)
U of Rochester, 1993 *Certification:* Obstetrics & Gynecology
1435 Chapel St, New Haven, 203-562-6741
2679 Whitney Ave, Hamden, 203-281-1181
277 Main St, West Haven, 203-937-1900

Ayoub, Thomas Victor (9 mentions)
New York U, 1980 *Certification:* Obstetrics & Gynecology
10 South St, Ridgefield, 203-894-3777

Berman, Michael Richard (3 mentions)
New York Med Coll, 1970 *Certification:* Obstetrics & Gynecology
687 Main St, Branford, 203-488-8306
1062 Barnes Rd #305, Wallingford, 203-949-0450
46 Prince St #403, New Haven, 203-777-6293
8 E Main St, Clinton, 860-669-6522

Besser, Gary S. (5 mentions)
FMS-Mexico, 1981 *Certification:* Obstetrics & Gynecology
190 W Broad St, Stamford, 203-325-4321

Bharucha, Mamata Jitendra (5 mentions)
FMS-India, 1973 *Certification:* Obstetrics & Gynecology
3180 Main St #202, Bridgeport, 203-374-0404
115 Technology Dr #A-300, Trumbull, 203-452-8888

Blair, Emily (9 mentions)
Des Moines U, 1986 *Certification:* Obstetrics & Gynecology
1735 Post Rd, Fairfield, 203-256-3990
1220 Linden Ave, Stratford, 203-380-4666

Brown, Michele Dory (3 mentions)
George Washington U, 1979
Certification: Obstetrics & Gynecology
999 Summer St #302, Stamford, 203-353-1446

Carolan, Stephen F. (3 mentions)
Certification: Obstetrics & Gynecology
14 Rye Ridge Plaza, Rye Brook, NY, 914-253-4912
1 Theall Rd, Rye, NY, 914-253-4912

Chere, Mitchel (3 mentions)
FMS-Mexico, 1978 *Certification:* Obstetrics & Gynecology
133 Scovill St #303, Waterbury, 203-575-1811
152 Meadow St, Naugatuck, 203-723-4471
503 Wolcott Rd, Wolcott, 203-575-1811

Cuteri, Joseph A. (5 mentions)
FMS-Mexico, 1984 *Certification:* Obstetrics & Gynecology
965 White Plains Rd 2nd Fl, Trumbull, 203-261-6600

Darak, Leah Anne (3 mentions)
Boston U, 1991 *Certification:* Obstetrics & Gynecology
3180 Main St #202, Bridgeport, 203-374-0404
2 Daniels Farm Rd, Trumbull, 203-374-0404
115 Technology Dr #A-300, Trumbull, 203-452-8888

Finkelstein, Morris C. (4 mentions)
New York Med Coll, 1985 *Certification:* Obstetrics & Gynecology
500 W Putnam Ave, Greenwich, 203-622-0303
40 Heights Rd #2, Darien, 203-662-0607

Garofalo, John Matthew (3 mentions)
New York Med Coll, 1979 *Certification:* Obstetrics & Gynecology
30 Stevens St #A, Norwalk, 203-855-3535

Goldstone, Leslie Marla (3 mentions)
FMS-Israel, 1987 *Certification:* Obstetrics & Gynecology
5520 Park Ave #302, Trumbull, 203-374-1018

Gottschall, Daniel Scott (3 mentions)
Hahnemann U, 1993 *Certification:* Obstetrics & Gynecology
4749 Main St, Bridgeport, 203-374-5013

Hagberg, Donna Joan (3 mentions)
U of Rochester, 1989 *Certification:* Obstetrics & Gynecology
1 Perryridge Rd, Greenwich, 203-869-8353

Hage, Pierre S. (3 mentions)
FMS-Lebanon, 1988 *Certification:* Obstetrics & Gynecology
3180 Main St #202, Bridgeport, 203-374-0404
115 Technology Dr #A-300, Trumbull, 203-452-8888

Helm, Charles Brian (3 mentions)
St Louis U, 1980 *Certification:* Obstetrics & Gynecology
185 Center St #H, Wallingford, 203-284-1060
435 Lewis Ave #201, Meriden, 203-238-4488
680 S Main St, Cheshire, 203-271-2401

Holden, Richard Capel (3 mentions)
U of Cincinnati, 1978 *Certification:* Obstetrics & Gynecology
140 Grandview Ave #202, Waterbury, 203-755-2344

Komarynsky, Irene I. (4 mentions)
U of Chicago, 1979 *Certification:* Obstetrics & Gynecology
166 W Broad St #301, Stamford, 203-325-9920

Landry, Arthur Bernard, III (3 mentions)
U of Connecticut, 1992 *Certification:* Obstetrics & Gynecology
134 Grandview Ave #210, Waterbury, 203-754-2535

Laser, Mark Robert (4 mentions)
Yale U, 1990 *Certification:* Obstetrics & Gynecology
999 Silver Ln #2A, Trumbull, 203-386-0044
267 Grant St, Bridgeport, 203-384-3394

Lynch, Vincent Arthur (3 mentions)
New York Med Coll, 1967 *Certification:* Obstetrics & Gynecology
46 Prince St #207, New Haven, 203-787-2264
6 Woodland Rd #1, Madison, 203-245-3850

Minkin, Mary Jane (7 mentions)
Yale U, 1975 *Certification:* Obstetrics & Gynecology
135 Goose Ln, Guilford, 203-453-4450
40 Temple St #7-A, New Haven, 203-789-2011
180 Westbrook Rd, Essex, 860-767-0223

Moscarelli, Richard D., Jr. (3 mentions)
Columbia U, 1994 *Certification:* Obstetrics & Gynecology
6 Woodland Rd #1, Madison, 203-245-3850
46 Prince St #207, New Haven, 203-787-2264

Ofer, Adam (3 mentions)
SUNY-Upstate Med U, 1999 *Certification:* Obstetrics & Gynecology
12 Avery Pl, Westport, 203-227-5125
400 Stillson Rd #5, Fairfield, 203-335-9633
40 Cross St #250, Norwalk, 203-840-1507

Ravski, Norman Abram (4 mentions)
New York Med Coll, 1978 *Certification:* Obstetrics & Gynecology
46 Prince St #403, New Haven, 203-777-6293
687 Main St, Branford, 203-488-8306
1062 Barnes Rd #305, Wallingford, 203-949-0450
8 E Main St, Clinton, 860-669-6522

Rosenman, Stephen David (3 mentions)
FMS-Belgium, 1973 *Certification:* Obstetrics & Gynecology
267 Grant St, Bridgeport, 203-384-3000

Ruben, Richard Stanley (3 mentions)
George Washington U, 1971
Certification: Obstetrics & Gynecology
90 Locust Ave, Danbury, 203-792-5005
38-B Grove St, Lynchfield, 203-438-3322

Sauter, Elizabeth Anne (3 mentions)
Cornell U, 1984 *Certification:* Obstetrics & Gynecology
12 Avery Pl, Westport, 203-227-5125
400 Stillson Rd #5, Fairfield, 203-335-9633
40 Cross St #250, Norwalk, 203-840-1507

Schechter, Michael D. (3 mentions)
New York U, 1988 *Certification:* Obstetrics & Gynecology
500 W Putnam Ave, Greenwich, 203-622-0303
40 Heights Rd #2, Darien, 203-662-0607

Simon, Howard (3 mentions)
FMS-Mexico, 1975 *Certification:* Obstetrics & Gynecology
687 Main St, Branford, 203-488-8306
1062 Barnes Rd #305, Wallingford, 203-949-0450
46 Prince St #403, New Haven, 203-777-6293
8 E Main St, Clinton, 860-669-6522

Szeto, Marjorie (7 mentions)
New York U, 1985 *Certification:* Obstetrics & Gynecology
12 Avery Pl, Westport, 203-227-5125
400 Stillson Rd #5, Fairfield, 203-335-9633
40 Cross St #250, Norwalk, 203-840-1507

Tamura, Rose Marie (3 mentions)
U of Pennsylvania, 1978 *Certification:* Obstetrics & Gynecology
90 Locust Ave, Danbury, 203-438-3322
38 Grove St #11-B, Ridgefield, 203-438-3322

Ugol, Jay Harold (3 mentions)
Georgetown U, 1982 *Certification:* Obstetrics & Gynecology
761 Main Ave #100, Norwalk, 203-644-1100
30 Stevens Dr #1, Norwalk, 203-644-1160

Wartel, Lawrence Jay (3 mentions)
Tufts U, 1966 *Certification:* Obstetrics & Gynecology
675 S Main St, Cheshire, 203-272-1811
136 Sherman Ave #502, New Haven, 203-562-5181
420 E Main St #3, Branford, 203-481-7018
326 W Main St #207, Milford, 203-877-6652
7 Meigs Ave #1-A, Madison, 203-250-2125

Weinstein, David Barry (3 mentions)
Rosalind Franklin U, 1969 *Certification:* Obstetrics & Gynecology
190 W Broad St, Stamford, 203-325-4321

Ophthalmology

Bacal, Darron Adam (5 mentions)
Jefferson Med Coll, 1992 *Certification:* Ophthalmology
202 Cherry St, Milford, 203-878-1236
339 Boston Post Rd, Orange, 203-795-0766
2 Trap Falls Rd #104, Shelton, 203-944-0464
1236 Main St, Branford, 203-488-5688

Branden, Peter John (4 mentions)
Columbia U, 1985 *Certification:* Ophthalmology
1201 W Main St #100, Waterbury, 203-597-9100
40 Temple St #5-B, New Haven, 203-777-3937
22 Old Waterbury Rd #202, Southbury, 203-597-9100
6 Business Park Dr, Ranford, 203-488-5411

Falkenstein, Ralph Jay (5 mentions)
Yale U, 1969 *Certification:* Ophthalmology
69 Sand Pit Rd #101, Danbury, 203-791-2020

Hersh, Stanley Blair (4 mentions)
Rosalind Franklin U, 1969 *Certification:* Ophthalmology
1201 W Main St #100, Waterbury, 203-597-9100
22 Old Waterbury Rd #202, Southbury, 203-597-9100

Kaplan, Jeffrey Neal (15 mentions)
Stony Brook U, 1981 *Certification:* Ophthalmology
4699 Main St #106, Bridgeport, 203-374-8182

Lesser, Robert Lewis (11 mentions)
Cornell U, 1967 *Certification:* Ophthalmology
40 Temple St, New Haven, 203-777-3937
1201 W Main St #100, Waterbury, 203-597-9100
22 Old Waterbury Rd #202, Southbury, 203-597-9100

Levada, Andrew Joseph (5 mentions)
Harvard U, 1976 *Certification:* Internal Medicine, Ophthalmology
1201 W Main St #100, Waterbury, 203-597-9100
40 Temple St #5-B, New Haven, 203-777-3937
22 Old Waterbury Rd #202, Southbury, 203-597-9100
6 Business Park Dr, Ranford, 203-488-5411

Mandava, Suresh (9 mentions)
Yale U, 1993 *Certification:* Ophthalmology
4 Dearfield Dr, Greenwich, 203-869-3082
1250 Summer St #301, Stamford, 203-869-3082

Manjoney, Delia Mary (11 mentions)
U of Vermont, 1977 *Certification:* Ophthalmology, Pediatrics
2720 Main St, Bridgeport, 203-576-6500

Ostriker, Glenn E. (4 mentions)
New York U, 1982 *Certification:* Ophthalmology
71 Strawberry Hill Ave, Stamford, 203-348-6300

Paul, Matthew David (5 mentions)
Columbia U, 1980 *Certification:* Ophthalmology
69 Sand Pit Rd #101, Danbury, 203-791-2020

Rose, Aron Dana (5 mentions)
New York Med Coll, 1985 *Certification:* Ophthalmology
40 Temple St #5-B, New Haven, 203-789-2020

Silverstone, David Edward (5 mentions)
New York Med Coll, 1973 *Certification:* Ophthalmology
40 Temple St #5B, New Haven, 203-789-2020

Small, Peter Alan (6 mentions)
Columbia U, 1981 *Certification:* Ophthalmology
2119 Post Rd, Fairfield, 203-259-7400

Soloway, Scott Merrill (8 mentions)
U of Rochester, 1974 *Certification:* Ophthalmology
40 Temple St #7D, New Haven, 203-777-1100

Steckel, Mark Charles (4 mentions)
U of Buffalo, 1984 *Certification:* Ophthalmology
140 Sherman St, Fairfield, 203-256-1320

Tsai, James C. (7 mentions)
Stanford U, 1989 *Certification:* Ophthalmology
40 Temple St #106, New Haven, 203-785-2020

Weber, Richard Barry (4 mentions)
Albert Einstein Coll of Med, 1976
Certification: Internal Medicine, Ophthalmology
1275 Summer St, Stamford, 203-353-1857

Wong, James Jung Yuen (11 mentions)
New York Med Coll, 1976 *Certification:* Ophthalmology
102 East Ave 1st Fl, Norwalk, 203-838-4119

Zimmerman, Neal Jason (4 mentions)
Jefferson Med Coll, 1978 *Certification:* Ophthalmology
166 Waterbury Rd, Prospect, 203-758-5733

Orthopedics

Aversa, John Michael (5 mentions)
SUNY-Downstate Med Coll, 1967
Certification: Orthopaedic Surgery
2408 Whitney Ave, Hamden, 203-407-3500
330 Orchard St #105, New Haven, 203-789-2211
330 Boston Post Rd, Orange, 203-795-4784
1000 Yale Ave #201, Wallingford, 203-265-1800

Backe, Henry Anthony, Jr. (5 mentions)
Temple U, 1986
Certification: Orthopaedic Surgery, Surgery of the Hand
75 Kings Hwy Cutoff, Fairfield, 203-337-2600
2909 Main St, Stratford, 203-337-2600

Bindelglass, David Fred (15 mentions)
Columbia U, 1985 *Certification:* Orthopaedic Surgery
75 Kings Hwy Cutoff, Fairfield, 203-377-5108
555 Bridgeport Ave, Shelton, 203-944-0042
2900 Main St, Stratford, 203-377-5108

Boone, Peter Stuart (12 mentions)
U of Pennsylvania, 1985 *Certification:* Orthopaedic Surgery
888 White Plains Rd, Trumbull, 203-268-2882
1055 Post Rd, Fairfield, 203-254-1055

Brand, Michael Gary (7 mentions)
U of Rochester, 1984 *Certification:* Orthopaedic Surgery
73 Sand Pit Rd #101, Danbury, 203-797-1500
226 White St, Danbury, 203-797-1500
67 Sand Pit Rd, Danbury, 203-797-1770

Brittis, Dante Anthony (9 mentions)
New York Med Coll, 1987 *Certification:* Orthopaedic Surgery
75 Kings Hwy Cutoff, Fairfield, 203-337-2600
555 Bridgeport Ave, Shelton, 203-337-2600

Dawe, Robert Vincent (5 mentions)
New York Med Coll, 1975 *Certification:* Orthopaedic Surgery
75 Kings Hwy, Fairfield, 203-337-2600
2900 Main St, Stratford, 203-337-2600

DeLuca, Peter Anthony (6 mentions)
Duke U, 1981 *Certification:* Orthopaedic Surgery
1000 Yale Ave #201, Wallingford, 203-265-1800
258 Broad St, Milford, 203-882-3373
84 N Main St, Branford, 203-483-2509

Elfenbein, David Henry (5 mentions)
Albert Einstein Coll of Med, 1995
Certification: Orthopaedic Surgery
33 Hospital Ave, Danbury, 203-792-5558
90 Grove St #107, Ridgefield, 203-431-6515

Fish, Daniel Nelson (5 mentions)
U of Rochester, 1987 *Certification:* Orthopaedic Surgery
60 Old New Milford Rd #3G, Brookfield, 203-775-6205

Friedlaender, Gary E. (4 mentions)
U of Michigan, 1969 *Certification:* Orthopaedic Surgery
800 Howard Ave, New Haven, 203-785-2579
20 Commerce Park, Milford, 203-882-8138
281 Seaside Ave, Milford, 203-877-4206

Girasole, Gerald J. (4 mentions)
Certification: Orthopaedic Surgery
888 White Plains Rd, Trumbull, 203-268-2882
1055 Post Rd #1, Fairfield, 203-254-1055

Hughes, Peter William (4 mentions)
New York Med Coll, 1972 *Certification:* Orthopaedic Surgery
90 Morgan St, Stamford, 203-325-4087

Irving, John Francis (4 mentions)
Tulane U, 1982 *Certification:* Orthopaedic Surgery
469 W Main St, Branford, 203-315-6784
199 Whitney Ave, New Haven, 203-315-6784
2200 Whitney Ave #270, Hamden, 203-315-6784
30 Commerce Park #3-B, Milford, 203-315-6784

Kaplan, Michael Jay (4 mentions)
U of Vermont, 1987 *Certification:* Orthopaedic Surgery
1579 Straits Tpke, Middlebury, 203-758-1272

Kaplan, Norman Robert (4 mentions)
New York Med Coll, 1977 *Certification:* Orthopaedic Surgery
450 Boston Post Rd #201, Guilford, 203-453-6340
330 Boston Post Rd, Orange, 203-795-4784
330 Orchard St #101, New Haven, 203-789-2211
2408 Whitney Ave, Hamden, 203-248-6325

Kavanagh, Brian (5 mentions)
U of Connecticut, 1979 *Certification:* Orthopaedic Surgery
6 Greenwich Office Pk, Greenwich, 203-869-1145

Keggi, John Marbury (9 mentions)
U of Wisconsin, 1988 *Certification:* Orthopaedic Surgery
1579 Straits Tpke #E, Middlebury, 203-598-0700

Lynch, Michael Matheke (11 mentions)
Dartmouth Coll, 1984 *Certification:* Orthopaedic Surgery
40 Cross St #300, Norwalk, 203-845-2200

Marks, Michael Robert (5 mentions)
George Washington U, 1982 *Certification:* Orthopaedic Surgery
40 Cross St #300, Norwalk, 203-845-2200

McCallum, John Duncan, III (4 mentions)
U of Pennsylvania, 1989 *Certification:* Orthopaedic Surgery
2408 Whitney Ave, Hamden, 203-407-3545
450 Boston Post Rd #201, Guilford, 203-407-3500
258 Broad St, Milford, 203-882-3373
84 E Main St, Branford, 203-483-2509

Olson, Eric Jon (7 mentions)
Columbia U, 1984 *Certification:* Orthopaedic Surgery
1211 W Main St, Waterbury, 203-755-0163

Polifroni, Nicholas V. (11 mentions)
New York Med Coll, 1977 *Certification:* Orthopaedic Surgery
131 Kings Hwy N, Westport, 203-226-1027
40 Cross St #300, Norwalk, 203-853-1811

Protomastro, Paul D. (4 mentions)
Jefferson Med Coll, 1995
Certification: Orthopaedic Surgery, Surgery of the Hand
40 Cross St #300, Norwalk, 203-853-1811
131 Kings Hwy N, Westport, 203-226-1027

Redler, Michael Ross (5 mentions)
U of Connecticut, 1982 *Certification:* Orthopaedic Surgery
888 White Plains Rd, Trumbull, 203-268-2882
1055 Post Rd, Fairfield, 203-254-1055

Reznik, Alan Mark (6 mentions)
Yale U, 1983 *Certification:* Orthopaedic Surgery
469 W Main St, Branford, 203-315-6784
199 Whitney Ave, New Haven, 203-315-6784
2200 Whitney Ave #270, Hamden, 203-315-6784
30 Commerce Park #3-B, Milford, 203-315-6784

Sethi, Paul Michael (7 mentions)
Certification: Orthopaedic Sports Medicine, Orthopaedic Surgery
6 Greenwich Office Park, Greenwich, 203-869-1145

Wetmore, Robert Satterlee (4 mentions)
Dartmouth Coll, 1978 *Certification:* Orthopaedic Surgery
1579 Straits Tpke, Middlebury, 203-758-1760

Otorhinolaryngology

Astrachan, David Isaac (8 mentions)
Yale U, 1984 *Certification:* Otolaryngology
2200 Whitney Ave #260, Hamden, 203-248-8409
141 Durham Rd #21, Madison, 203-245-5899
40 Commerce Pk, Milford, 203-876-1159

Coffey, Tom Kendall (30 mentions)
Columbia U, 1986 *Certification:* Otolaryngology
15 Corporate Dr #2-8, Trumbull, 203-452-7081

Klarsfeld, Jay H. (7 mentions)
Mount Sinai Sch of Med, 1981 *Certification:* Otolaryngology
107 Newtown Rd #2A, Danbury, 203-830-4700
901 Ethan Allen Hwy, Ridgefield, 203-438-9641

Klenoff, Bruce Howard (14 mentions)
Tufts U, 1969 *Certification:* Otolaryngology
32 Strawberry Hill Ct, Stamford, 203-353-0000

Kveton, John Francis (8 mentions)
St Louis U, 1978 *Certification:* Neurotology, Otolaryngology
46 Prince St #601, New Haven, 203-752-1726

Levin, Richard Alan (9 mentions)
Tufts U, 1987 *Certification:* Otolaryngology
1305 Post Rd #302, Fairfield, 203-259-4700

Parker, Andrew Justin (7 mentions)
Robert W Johnson Med Sch, 1995 *Certification:* Otolaryngology
148 East Ave #2I, Norwalk, 203-866-8121

Pearl, Adam Warren (15 mentions)
Mount Sinai Sch of Med, 1996 *Certification:* Otolaryngology
15 Corporate Dr #2-8, Trumbull, 203-452-7081

Salzer, Stephen Jeffrey (11 mentions)
Johns Hopkins U, 1989 *Certification:* Otolaryngology
49 Lake Ave #5, Greenwich, 203-869-2030
166 W Broad St #304, Stamford, 203-348-7797

Sasaki, Clarence T. (8 mentions)
Yale U, 1966 *Certification:* Otolaryngology
800 Howard Ave 4th Fl, New Haven, 203-785-2593

Schiff, Neil Franklin (10 mentions)
Tufts U, 1991 *Certification:* Otolaryngology
21 W Main St #3, Waterbury, 203-574-3777
1 Pomperaug Office Park #204, Southbury, 203-264-2909

Vining, Eugenia (11 mentions)
Yale U, 1987 *Certification:* Otolaryngology
954 Main St, Branford, 203-481-0003
46 Prince St, New Haven, 203-752-1726

Weiss, Robert Lawrence (11 mentions)
Pennsylvania State U, 1991 *Certification:* Otolaryngology
40 Cross St #230, Norwalk, 203-845-2244

Winicki, Raymond Edward (8 mentions)
New York U, 1993 *Certification:* Otolaryngology
171 Grandview Ave #201, Waterbury, 203-753-8833

Pain Medicine

Kairschenbaum, Lawrence P. (10 mentions)
New York Med Coll, 1982
75 Kings Hwy Cutoff #101, Fairfield, 203-337-2600

Kloth, David (7 mentions)
New York U, 1987 *Certification:* Anesthesiology, Pain Medicine
69 Sand Pit Rd #204, Danbury, 203-792-5118
4920 Main St #308, Bridgeport, 203-372-7197
1389 W Main St Tower 2 #123, Waterbury, 203-596-7302
148 East Ave #3D, Norwalk, 800-461-4383
131 Kent Rd, New Milford, 800-461-4383
109 Newtown Rd, Danbury, 203-792-5118

Levi, David Charles (9 mentions)
New Jersey Med Sch, 1995
Certification: Anesthesiology, Pain Medicine
109 Newtown Rd, Danbury, 203-792-5118
1389 W Main St #123, Waterbury, 203-596-7302

Sood, Pardeep Kumar (15 mentions)
FMS-India, 1979 *Certification:* Anesthesiology
5520 Park Ave #303, Trumbull, 203-373-7330

Pathology

Anderson, Thomas Peter (3 mentions)
U of Connecticut, 1978
Certification: Anatomic Pathology & Clinical Pathology
134 Grandview Ave #108, Waterbury, 203-573-6720
64 Robbins St, Waterbury, 203-573-6000

Babkowski, Robert C. (7 mentions)
U of Rochester, 1990 *Certification:* Anatomic Pathology &
   Clinical Pathology, Cytopathology
30 Shelburne Rd, Stamford, 203-276-7420

Chacho, Mary S. (3 mentions)
Loyola U Chicago, 1981 *Certification:* Anatomic Pathology &
   Clinical Pathology, Cytopathology
24 Hospital Ave, Danbury, 203-739-7453

Costa, Jose Casals (3 mentions)
FMS-Spain, 1967 *Certification:* Anatomic Pathology
20 York St, New Haven, 203-785-5788

Eisen, Richard Neil (8 mentions)
SUNY-Downstate Med Coll, 1984
Certification: Anatomic Pathology
5 Perryridge Rd, Greenwich, 203-863-3061

Frederick, William George (4 mentions)
Wayne State U, 1985
Certification: Anatomic Pathology & Clinical Pathology
56 Franklin St, Waterbury, 203-709-6000

Lowell, David Maurice (4 mentions)
Cornell U, 1958
Certification: Anatomic Pathology & Clinical Pathology
134 Grandview Ave #108, Waterbury, 203-573-7364
64 Robbins St, Waterbury, 203-573-7364

McNiff, Jennifer Madison (5 mentions)
U of Vermont, 1986 *Certification:* Anatomic Pathology &
   Clinical Pathology, Dermatopathology
333 Cedar St, New Haven, 203-785-4094

Nair, Saraswathi (13 mentions)
FMS-Russia, 1975
Certification: Anatomic Pathology & Clinical Pathology
24 Maple St, Norwalk, 203-852-2657
34 Maple St, Norwalk, 203-852-2657

Nash, Irwin (4 mentions)
Columbia U, 1969 *Certification:* Anatomic Pathology &
   Clinical Pathology, Hematology, Internal Medicine
1450 Chapel St, New Haven, 203-789-3088

Pinto, Marguerite M. (19 mentions)
FMS-India, 1970 *Certification:* Anatomic Pathology &
   Clinical Pathology, Cytopathology
267 Grant St, Bridgeport, 203-384-3302

Sieber, Steven Charles (5 mentions)
Yale U, 1987 *Certification:* Anatomic Pathology
24 Hospital Ave, Danbury, 203-797-7000

Wagner-Reiss, Katherine (3 mentions)
Jefferson Med Coll, 1979 *Certification:* Anatomic Pathology
   & Clinical Pathology, Cytopathology
2800 Main St, Bridgeport, 203-576-5032

Pediatrics *(see note on page 9)*

Alonso, Luis (4 mentions)
FMS-Spain, 1969 *Certification:* Pediatrics
1062 Barnes Rd #102, Wallingford, 203-294-6328
288 Highland Ave, Cheshire, 203-271-3610

Angoff, Ronald (6 mentions)
U of Cincinnati, 1973 *Certification:* Pediatrics
325 S Main St, Cheshire, 203-271-1541
200 Orchard St #108, New Haven, 203-865-3737

Canny, Christopher R. (4 mentions)
Washington U, 1976 *Certification:* Pediatrics
9 Washington Ave, Hamden, 203-287-0552

Chessin, Robert David (4 mentions)
Johns Hopkins U, 1973
Certification: Developmental-Behavioral Pediatrics, Pediatrics
4699 Main St #215, Bridgeport, 203-452-8322
4 Corporate Dr #290, Shelton, 203-452-8322
15 Corporate Dr #1-5, Trumbull, 203-452-8322

Cronin, Harold Scott (4 mentions)
FMS-Mexico, 1976 *Certification:* Pediatrics
4637 Main St, Bridgeport, 203-374-3001

Ertl, John Edward (3 mentions)
SUNY-Downstate Med Coll, 1970
Certification: Pediatric Hematology-Oncology, Pediatrics
41 Germantown Rd #201, Danbury, 203-744-1680

Fischbein, Charles A. (6 mentions)
U of Buffalo, 1970 *Certification:* Pediatrics
160 Robbins St, Waterbury, 203-755-2999
1 Pomperaug Office Pk #201, Southbury, 203-755-2999

Fountas, Diane Louise (4 mentions)
Dartmouth Coll, 1981 *Certification:* Pediatrics
1389 W Main St #325, Waterbury, 203-753-6776

Freedman, Richard Michael (8 mentions)
Boston U, 1975
Certification: Neonatal-Perinatal Medicine, Pediatrics
4699 Main St #215, Bridgeport, 203-452-8322
4 Corporate Dr #290, Shelton, 203-452-8322
15 Corporate Dr #I-5, Trumbull, 203-452-8322

Golenbock, Robert Bruce (5 mentions)
Albert Einstein Coll of Med, 1972 *Certification:* Pediatrics
107 Newtown Rd #1D, Danbury, 203-790-0822

Gruskay, Jeffrey Alan (4 mentions)
Yale U, 1981
Certification: Neonatal-Perinatal Medicine, Pediatrics
20 Commerce Park, Milford, 203-882-2066

Hemenway, Charles G., Jr. (6 mentions)
Tufts U, 1969 *Certification:* Pediatrics
111 Beach Rd, Fairfield, 203-256-9249

Hochstadt, Judith Koper (5 mentions)
SUNY-Downstate Med Coll, 1978 *Certification:* Pediatrics
15 Corporate Dr #15, Trumbull, 203-452-8322

Hufnagel, Joseph W. (3 mentions)
Philadelphia Coll of Osteopathic Med, 1993
Certification: Pediatrics
55 Danbury Rd, Wilton, 203-762-3363

Klenk, Rosemary Ellen (3 mentions)
Cornell U, 1980 *Certification:* Pediatrics
183 Cherry St, New Canaan, 203-972-5232
166 W Broad St #103, Stamford, 203-323-1770

Korval, Arnold Barry (9 mentions)
St Louis U, 1974 *Certification:* Pediatrics
8 W End Ave, Old Greenwich, 203-637-3212

Leib, Susan Mezey (3 mentions)
Albert Einstein Coll of Med, 1987 *Certification:* Pediatrics
38B Grove St, Ridgefield, 203-438-9557

Lialios, Minas (3 mentions)
FMS-Greece, 1982 *Certification:* Pediatrics
7 Park St, Norwalk, 203-840-7566

Machado, Anapaula Raposo (4 mentions)
Med Coll of Pennsylvania, 1987 *Certification:* Pediatrics
107 Newtown Rd #1D, Danbury, 203-790-0822

Mann, Cynthia Frances (3 mentions)
Yale U, 1976 *Certification:* Pediatrics
2200 Whitney Ave, Hamden, 203-287-5400

Marconi, Jeanne (3 mentions)
FMS-Mexico, 1985 *Certification:* Pediatrics
61 East Ave, Norwalk, 203-838-8414

Owens, Jeffrey Allen (4 mentions)
Jefferson Med Coll, 1996 *Certification:* Pediatrics
1563 Post Rd E, Westport, 203-319-3939

Ralabate, James Patrick (3 mentions)
Albany Med Coll, 1981
Certification: Internal Medicine, Pediatrics
2890 Main St #A, Stratford, 203-378-3646

Rudolph, Jane Elizabeth (3 mentions)
U of Connecticut, 1978 *Certification:* Pediatrics
179 Roseland Ave, Waterbury, 203-574-4747

Small, Martha Yepes (4 mentions)
Columbia U, 1981 *Certification:* Pediatrics
4699 Main St, Bridgeport, 203-452-8322

Sollinger, Jonathan Eliot (3 mentions)
U of Connecticut, 1999 *Certification:* Pediatrics
1563 Post Rd E, Westport, 203-319-3939

Spiesel, Sydney Zane (5 mentions)
Yale U, 1975
8 Lunar Dr, Woodbridge, 203-397-5211

Swidler, Sanford L. (5 mentions)
New York U, 1980 *Certification:* Pediatrics
126 Morgan St, Stamford, 203-327-1055

Woodward, Janet Caroline (4 mentions)
Columbia U, 1981 *Certification:* Pediatrics
1563 Post Rd E, Westport, 203-319-3939

Zelson, Joseph Harold (4 mentions)
New York U, 1965 *Certification:* Pediatrics
339 Boston Post Rd #250, Orange, 203-795-6025

Plastic Surgery

Chicarilli, Zeno N. (8 mentions)
Tufts U, 1977 *Certification:* Otolaryngology, Plastic Surgery
40 Temple St #7E, New Haven, 203-782-9720
5 Durham Rd, Guilford, 203-453-7766

Gewirtz, Harold Stanley (7 mentions)
Johns Hopkins U, 1975
Certification: Plastic Surgery, Surgery of the Hand
70 Mill River St, Stamford, 203-325-1381

Goldenberg, David Michael (9 mentions)
New York Med Coll, 1982 *Certification:* Plastic Surgery
107 Newtown Rd #2A, Danbury, 203-830-4700

Goldman, Boris Edward (7 mentions)
U of Connecticut, 1990 *Certification:* Plastic Surgery
901 Ethan Allen Hwy #101, Ridgefield, 203-791-9661

Islam, Sohel (6 mentions)
Cornell U, 1991
Certification: Plastic Surgery, Surgery of the Hand
107 Newtown Rd #2C, Danbury, 203-791-9661

O'Connell, Joseph Brady (12 mentions)
Cornell U, 1981 *Certification:* Plastic Surgery
208 Post Rd W, Westport, 203-454-0044

Restifo, Richard Joseph (6 mentions)
Harvard U, 1986 *Certification:* Plastic Surgery
539 Danbury Rd, Wilton, 203-834-7700
59 Elm St #560, New Haven, 203-772-1444

Rosenthal, Jeffrey Steven (6 mentions)
FMS-Mexico, 1977 *Certification:* Plastic Surgery
75 Kings Hwy Cutoff, Fairfield, 203-335-3223

Sureddi, Prasad Sathya (10 mentions)
FMS-India, 1975 *Certification:* Plastic Surgery
714 Chase Pkwy, Waterbury, 203-757-2772

Weinstein, Mark Holcombe (6 mentions)
U of Rochester, 1969 *Certification:* Plastic Surgery, Surgery
136 Sherman Ave #407, New Haven, 203-624-0673

Psychiatry

Abrams, Linus S. (3 mentions)
New York Med Coll, 1988 *Certification:* Psychiatry
4 Dearfield Dr, Greenwich, 203-861-2654

D'Apice, Joseph Patrick (3 mentions)
St Louis U, 1965 *Certification:* Psychiatry
545 Mill Plain Rd, Fairfield, 203-255-6330

Demac, Alex Ralph (3 mentions)
U of California-San Diego, 1989 *Certification:* Psychiatry
4 Midland Rd, Waterbury, 203-757-3299

Fischbein, Ellen Ruth N. (4 mentions)
U of Buffalo, 1970 *Certification:* Pediatrics, Psychiatry
355 Highland Ave #101, Cheshire, 203-272-1208

Glucksman, Myron Lawrence (4 mentions)
U of Washington, 1959 *Certification:* Psychiatry
68 Marchant Rd, Redding, 203-938-1188

Ligorski, Mark William Lloyd (4 mentions)
FMS-Mexico, 1981 *Certification:* Psychiatry
72 North St #201, Danbury, 203-798-0068

Lorefice, Laurence Santo (3 mentions)
U of Pennsylvania, 1975 *Certification:* Psychiatry
1037 E Putnam Ave, Riverside, 203-637-4006

Morgan, Charles J. (3 mentions)
267 Grant St, Bridgeport, 203-384-3897
223 Mill Hill Ave #3, Bridgeport, 203-384-3897

Mueller, F. Carl (3 mentions)
U of Connecticut, 1982
Certification: Geriatric Psychiatry, Psychiatry
999 Summer St #200, Stamford, 203-357-7773

Pomeraniec, Lazaro (5 mentions)
FMS-Argentina, 1974
340-F Main St, Bridgeport, 203-579-9736

Possick, Stanley Gerald (3 mentions)
U of Pennsylvania, 1970 *Certification:* Psychiatry
303 Whitney Ave #5, New Haven, 203-782-1511

Schechter, Justin Owen (4 mentions)
Stony Brook U, 1981
Certification: Forensic Psychiatry, Psychiatry
22 5th St, Stamford, 203-323-7760

Smith, Jo Ann Margaret (4 mentions)
SUNY-Upstate Med U, 1974 *Certification:* Psychiatry
156 Old Studio Rd, New Canaan, 203-966-6611

Waynik, Mark (8 mentions)
FMS-Mexico, 1979 *Certification:* Psychiatry
52 Beach Rd, Fairfield, 203-254-2000
160 Hawley Ln #200, Trumbull, 203-386-0096

Pulmonary Disease

Berman, Lewis (6 mentions)
Albert Einstein Coll of Med, 1987 *Certification:* Critical Care Medicine, Internal Medicine, Pulmonary Disease
24 Stevens St, Norwalk, 203-852-2254

Chupp, Geoffrey Lowell (5 mentions)
George Washington U, 1990
300 Cedar St, New Haven, 203-785-3207

Fine, Jonathan Michael (5 mentions)
Yale U, 1981 *Certification:* Critical Care Medicine, Internal Medicine, Pulmonary Disease
24 Stevens St, Norwalk, 203-855-3543
34 Maple St, Norwalk, 203-852-2392

Fitzgerald, William B. (10 mentions)
Boston U, 1981
Certification: Internal Medicine, Pulmonary Disease
3180 Main St #201, Bridgeport, 203-371-5400

Gerstenhaber, Brett John (6 mentions)
SUNY-Downstate Med Coll, 1971
Certification: Internal Medicine, Pulmonary Disease
60 Temple St, New Haven, 203-789-1338

Giosa, Richard Peter (5 mentions)
Wake Forest U, 1981
Certification: Internal Medicine, Pulmonary Disease
455 Lewis Ave #200, Meriden, 203-238-9446

Greenspan, Philip Ernest (5 mentions)
Ohio State U, 1998 *Certification:* Critical Care Medicine, Internal Medicine, Pulmonary Disease
501 Kings Hwy E #204, Fairfield, 203-372-7715

Hill, David Gary (6 mentions)
Med Coll of Pennsylvania, 1991 *Certification:* Critical Care Medicine, Internal Medicine, Pulmonary Disease
170 Grandview Ave, Waterbury, 203-759-3666

Kurtz, Caroline Paula (6 mentions)
New York U, 1984 *Certification:* Critical Care Medicine, Internal Medicine, Pulmonary Disease
30 Stevens St #C, Norwalk, 203-855-3888

Manfredi, Christopher E. (7 mentions)
U of New England Coll of Osteopathic Med, 1993
Certification: Critical Care Medicine, Pulmonary Disease
30 Stevens St #C, Norwalk, 203-855-3888

Matthay, Richard A. (7 mentions)
Tufts U, 1970 *Certification:* Critical Care Medicine, Internal Medicine, Pulmonary Disease
789 Howard Ave, New Haven, 203-785-4198
333 Cedar St #1, New Haven, 203-785-4196
20 York St, New Haven, 203-785-4198

McCalley, Stuart Wesley (6 mentions)
Case Western Reserve U, 1969
Certification: Internal Medicine, Pulmonary Disease
75 Holly Hill Ln, Greenwich, 203-869-6960

Oelberg, David Alan (6 mentions)
FMS-Canada, 1990 *Certification:* Critical Care Medicine, Internal Medicine, Pulmonary Disease
24 Hospital Ave, Danbury, 203-739-7070

Rudolph, Daniel Jay (18 mentions)
New York U, 1982 *Certification:* Critical Care Medicine, Internal Medicine, Pulmonary Disease
15 Corporate Dr, Trumbull, 203-261-3980

Sachs, Paul (9 mentions)
New York U, 1982 *Certification:* Critical Care Medicine, Internal Medicine, Pulmonary Disease
190 W Broad St, Stamford, 203-348-2437

Sherter, Carl Beryl (9 mentions)
Tufts U, 1967 *Certification:* Critical Care Medicine, Internal Medicine, Pulmonary Disease
170 Grandview Ave, Waterbury, 203-759-3666

Simkovitz, Philip (19 mentions)
Boston U, 1982 *Certification:* Critical Care Medicine, Internal Medicine, Pulmonary Disease
5520 Park Ave #202, Trumbull, 203-365-0577

Tanoue, Lynn Tomie (9 mentions)
Yale U, 1982 *Certification:* Critical Care Medicine, Internal Medicine, Pulmonary Disease
300 York St, New Haven, 203-785-4198

Thau, Steven Averill (6 mentions)
Albert Einstein Coll of Med, 1994
Certification: Critical Care Medicine, Pulmonary Disease
190 W Broad St, Stamford, 203-348-2437

Turetsky, Arthur Saul (6 mentions)
Albert Einstein Coll of Med, 1974
Certification: Internal Medicine, Pulmonary Disease
15 Corporate Dr, Trumbull, 203-261-3980

Twohig, Kevin James (6 mentions)
U of Massachusetts, 1983
Certification: Internal Medicine, Pulmonary Disease
60 Temple St, New Haven, 203-789-1338
1591 Boston Post Rd #201, Guilford, 203-453-2019

Winter, Stephen Michael (8 mentions)
Cornell U, 1981 *Certification:* Critical Care Medicine, Internal Medicine, Pulmonary Disease
24 Stevens St, Norwalk, 203-852-2392

Radiology—Diagnostic

Allen, Kenneth Stuntz (5 mentions)
U of Massachusetts, 1982 *Certification:* Diagnostic Radiology
64 Robbins St, Waterbury, 203-756-8911
134 Grandview Ave #101, Waterbury, 203-756-8911
799 New Haven Rd, Naugatuck, 203-573-6279

Bauman, James Stephan (10 mentions)
Cornell U, 1980 *Certification:* Diagnostic Radiology
148 East Ave, Norwalk, 203-838-4886

Bokhari, Jamal (3 mentions)
FMS-Pakistan, 1985
Certification: Diagnostic Radiology, Neuroradiology
20 York St, New Haven, 203-785-2688

Carter, Anthony Robert (4 mentions)
Med Coll of Wisconsin, 1978 *Certification:* Diagnostic Radiology
134 Grandview Ave, Waterbury, 203-756-8911
64 Robbins St, Waterbury, 203-573-7674
799 New Haven Rd #8, Naugatuck, 203-723-8470

Cohen, Steven C. (7 mentions)
Certification: Diagnostic Radiology
15 Corporate Dr #B-10, Trumbull, 203-337-9729
1315 Washington Blvd, Stamford, 203-356-9729

Durhan, Linda Susan (3 mentions)
St Louis U, 1977 *Certification:* Diagnostic Radiology
101 N Plains Industrial Rd, Wallingford, 203-949-2700
680 S Main St, Cheshire, 203-272-3595
816 Broad St #13, Meriden, 203-235-2577
50 S Main St, Wallingford, 203-269-1485
435 Lewis Ave, Meriden, 203-694-8444

Fey, Christopher Philip (4 mentions)
Yale U, 1993 *Certification:* Diagnostic Radiology, Nuclear Medicine, Nuclear Radiology
49 Lake Ave #1, Greenwich, 203-869-6220
5 Perryridge Rd, Greenwich, 203-863-3084

Gagliardi, Joseph Anthony (3 mentions)
New York Med Coll, 1986 *Certification:* Diagnostic Radiology
2800 Main St, Bridgeport, 203-488-2843

Gahbauer, Helmuth W. (5 mentions)
FMS-Germany, 1972
Certification: Diagnostic Radiology, Neuroradiology
1450 Chapel St, New Haven, 203-789-3124

Gruen, David Richard (7 mentions)
Cornell U, 1991 *Certification:* Diagnostic Radiology
148 East Ave #1-N, Norwalk, 203-838-4886

Hammers, Lynwood William (3 mentions)
Philadelphia Coll of Osteopathic Med, 1979
Certification: Diagnostic Radiology
2 Church St S #110, New Haven, 203-773-8959

Harley, William Dale (3 mentions)
Harvard U, 1972
Certification: Diagnostic Radiology, Neuroradiology
6 Shelburne Rd, Stamford, 203-359-0130

Hodges, Laura J. (3 mentions)
Albert Einstein Coll of Med, 1994 *Certification:* Diagnostic
  Radiology, Vascular & Interventional Radiology
49 Lake Ave, Greenwich, 203-869-6220
5 Perryridge Rd, Greenwich, 203-863-3084

Hyson, Eric Archibald (7 mentions)
U of Pennsylvania, 1975 *Certification:* Diagnostic Radiology,
  Vascular & Interventional Radiology
64 Robbins St, Waterbury, 203-573-7124
134 Grandview Ave, Waterbury, 203-756-8911

Israel, Gary M. (5 mentions)
Certification: Diagnostic Radiology
20 York St, New Haven, 203-737-2362

Karol, Ian Gilbert (7 mentions)
Albert Einstein Coll of Med, 1992
Certification: Diagnostic Radiology
267 Grant St, Bridgeport, 203-337-9729
15 Corporate Dr #B-10, Trumbull, 203-337-9729
1055 Post Rd, Fairfield, 203-337-9729
320 Boston Post Rd, Orange, 203-337-9729
4 Corporate Dr #182, Shelton, 203-337-9729
1315 Washington Blvd, Stamford, 203-337-9729
2876 Main St, Stratford, 203-337-9729

Kaye, Alan (3 mentions)
U of Connecticut, 1979 *Certification:* Diagnostic Radiology
267 Grant St, Bridgeport, 203-337-9729
15 Corporate Dr #B-10, Trumbull, 203-337-9729
2876 Main St, Stratford, 203-337-9729
1055 Post Rd, Fairfield, 203-337-9729
4 Corporate Dr #182, Shelton, 203-337-9729
1315 Washington Blvd, Stamford, 203-337-9729

Kier, Ruben (9 mentions)
Duke U, 1982 *Certification:* Diagnostic Radiology
267 Grant St, Bridgeport, 203-337-9729
15 Corporate Dr #B-10, Trumbull, 203-337-9729
1055 Post Rd, Fairfield, 203-337-9729
320 Boston Post Rd, Orange, 203-337-9729
4 Corporate Dr #182, Shelton, 203-337-9729
1315 Washington Blvd, Stamford, 203-337-9729
2876 Main St, Stratford, 203-337-9726

King, Michael H. (3 mentions)
Rosalind Franklin U, 1995 *Certification:* Diagnostic Radiology
30 Shelburne Rd, Stamford, 203-276-2602

Lee, Ronald P. (10 mentions)
New York U, 1986 *Certification:* Diagnostic Radiology
148 East Ave #1-N, Norwalk, 203-838-4886

Levine, Alan Harris (5 mentions)
SUNY-Downstate Med Coll, 1973
Certification: Diagnostic Radiology, Neuroradiology
148 East Ave #1-N, Norwalk, 203-838-4886

Mullen, David Joshua (3 mentions)
Albert Einstein Coll of Med, 1983
Certification: Diagnostic Radiology
49 Lake Ave #1, Greenwich, 203-869-6220
5 Perryridge Rd, Greenwich, 203-863-3084

Olcese, Paolo Daniel (3 mentions)
U of Vermont, 1994 *Certification:* Diagnostic Radiology
385 Main St S Bldg 2, Southbury, 203-267-5800

Shimkin, Peter Michael (5 mentions)
U of Pennsylvania, 1965 *Certification:* Radiology
15 Corporate Dr #B-10, Trumbull, 203-337-9729
267 Grant St, Bridgeport, 203-337-9729
1055 Post Rd, Fairfield, 203-337-9729
320 Boston Post Rd, Orange, 203-337-9729
4 Corporate Dr #182, Shelton, 203-337-9729
1315 Washington Blvd, Stamford, 203-337-9729
2876 Main St, Stratford, 203-337-9729

Specht, Neil Theodore (6 mentions)
FMS-Philippines, 1983
Certification: Diagnostic Radiology, Internal Medicine
2600 Main St, Bridgeport, 203-331-4500
2800 Main St, Bridgeport, 203-372-2887

Strauss, Edward Bruce (3 mentions)
Yale U, 1979 *Certification:* Diagnostic Radiology, Nuclear
  Radiology, Vascular & Interventional Radiology
34 Maple St, Norwalk, 203-852-2720

Sullivan, Scott James (8 mentions)
Georgetown U, 1991
Certification: Diagnostic Radiology, Neuroradiology
49 Lake Ave #1, Greenwich, 203-869-6220
5 Perryridge Rd, Greenwich, 203-863-3084

Thakur, Ravi K. (8 mentions)
Certification: Diagnostic Radiology
W Broad St & Shelburn Rd, Stamford, 203-276-7860

Torstenson, Guy Edward (6 mentions)
Albany Med Coll, 1966 *Certification:* Radiology
2800 Main St, Bridgeport, 203-576-6000

Williams, Scott Charles (3 mentions)
George Washington U, 1987
Certification: Diagnostic Radiology, Nuclear Medicine
267 Grant St, Bridgeport, 203-337-9729
15 Corporate Dr #B-10, Trumbull, 203-337-9729
1055 Post Rd, Fairfield, 203-337-9729
320 Boston Post Rd, Orange, 203-337-9729
4 Corporate Dr #182, Shelton, 203-337-9729
1315 Washington Blvd, Stamford, 203-337-9729
2876 Main St, Stratford, 203-337-9729

Radiology—Therapeutic

Berger, Paul Steven (7 mentions)
New York U, 1969 *Certification:* Radiology, Therapeutic Radiology
15 Corporate Dr, Trumbull, 203-384-3168
267 Grant St, Bridgeport, 203-384-3168

Bitterman, Jeffrey Alan (7 mentions)
New York U, 1975 *Certification:* Therapeutic Radiology
25 Newell Rd #C-11, Bristol, 860-582-9800

Cardinale, Francis S. (5 mentions)
New York Med Coll, 1971 *Certification:* Therapeutic Radiology
670 George St, New Haven, 203-777-6209
1450 Chapel St, New Haven, 203-789-3124

Cardinale, Joseph Guy (8 mentions)
New York Med Coll, 1980 *Certification:* Therapeutic Radiology
1450 Chapel St, New Haven, 203-789-3131

Dowling, Sean William (6 mentions)
Yale U, 1983 *Certification:* Internal Medicine, Radiation Oncology
34 Shelburne Rd, Stamford, 203-325-7885

Masino, Frank Anthony (8 mentions)
Albert Einstein Coll of Med, 1978
Certification: Therapeutic Radiology
34 Shelburne Rd, Stamford, 203-325-7886

Pathare, Pradip Madhukar (9 mentions)
FMS-India, 1973 *Certification:* Radiology, Therapeutic Radiology
34 Maple St, Norwalk, 203-852-2720

Specht, Neil Theodore (5 mentions)
FMS-Philippines, 1983
Certification: Diagnostic Radiology, Internal Medicine
2660 Main St, Bridgeport, 203-331-4500
2800 Main St, Bridgeport, 203-372-2887

Strauss, Edward Bruce (7 mentions)
Yale U, 1979 *Certification:* Diagnostic Radiology, Nuclear
  Radiology, Vascular & Interventional Radiology
34 Maple St, Norwalk, 203-852-2720

Zinn, Kenneth Miles (5 mentions)
SUNY-Downstate Med Coll, 1992 *Certification:* Diagnostic
  Radiology, Vascular & Interventional Radiology
15 Corporate Dr #B-10, Trumbull, 203-337-9729
267 Grant St, Bridgeport, 203-337-9729
1055 Post Rd, Fairfield, 203-337-9729
320 Boston Post Rd, Orange, 203-337-9729
4 Corporate Dr #182, Shelton, 203-337-9729
1315 Washington Blvd, Stamford, 203-337-9729
2876 Main St, Stratford, 203-337-9729

Rehabilitation

Aaronson, Beth Sandy (5 mentions)
Stony Brook U, 1990 *Certification:* Physical Medicine &
  Rehabilitation, Spinal Cord Injury Medicine
24 Hospital Ave #10E, Danbury, 203-797-7440
235 Main St, Danbury, 203-797-7440

Cohen, Isaac (3 mentions)
FMS-Israel, 1996
Certification: Pain Medicine, Physical Medicine & Rehabilitation
888 White Plains Rd, Trumbull, 203-268-2882

Grant, Linda F. (7 mentions)
Certification: Physical Medicine & Rehabilitation
5 Perryridge Rd, Greenwich, 203-863-4290
2015 W Main St, Stamford, 203-863-2880

O'Brien, John William (4 mentions)
FMS-Grenada, 1981
Certification: Physical Medicine & Rehabilitation
50 Gaylord Farm Rd, Wallingford, 203-284-2879
8 Devine St, North Haven, 203-230-9226
175 Sherman Ave, New Haven, 203-789-3439
687 Campbell Ave, West Haven, 203-789-3439
11 Mountaincrest Dr, Cheshire, 203-789-3439

Patel, Bhavesh R. (3 mentions)
Certification: Pain Medicine, Physical Medicine & Rehabilitation
500 Chase Pkwy, Waterbury, 203-573-1167

Petrillo, Claudio (6 mentions)
FMS-Brazil, 1972
Certification: Physical Medicine & Rehabilitation
698 West Ave, Norwalk, 203-523-0100

Prywes, Mitchell (4 mentions)
FMS-Mexico, 1983
Certification: Physical Medicine & Rehabilitation
105 Newtown Rd, Danbury, 203-744-4343

Rosen, Marc Lewis (6 mentions)
Albert Einstein Coll of Med, 1987
Certification: Physical Medicine & Rehabilitation
698 West Ave, Norwalk, 203-523-0100

Trowbridge, Randolph Lee (4 mentions)
New York Med Coll, 1986
Certification: Physical Medicine & Rehabilitation
67 Sand Pit Rd #301, Danbury, 203-778-8326
109 Newtown Rd #2, Danbury, 203-778-8326

Webb, Lisa Blanchette (3 mentions)
U of Connecticut, 1994
Certification: Neurology, Physical Medicine & Rehabilitation
4 Corporate Dr #192, Shelton, 203-924-8664
2590 Main St, Stratford, 203-377-5988

Yuan, Andrew (5 mentions)
Ohio U Coll of Osteopathic Med, 1987
1735 Post Rd #7, Fairfield, 203-256-4733

Rheumatology

Abeles, Aryeh M. (7 mentions)
Emory U, 1999 *Certification:* Internal Medicine, Rheumatology
816 Broad St #14, Meriden, 203-235-6402

Cassetta, Michael A. (14 mentions)
Kansas U Coll of Osteopathic Med, 1999
Certification: Internal Medicine, Rheumatology
15 Corporate Dr #2-1, Trumbull, 203-459-5100

Danehower, Richard Lloyd (9 mentions)
U of Pennsylvania, 1965
Certification: Internal Medicine, Rheumatology
49 Lake Ave #2, Greenwich, 203-869-5715

Di Sabatino, Charles Anthony (14 mentions)
Boston U, 1972 *Certification:* Internal Medicine, Rheumatology
60 Temple St #6A, New Haven, 203-789-2255

Guadagnoli, Germano A. (11 mentions)
FMS-Italy, 1986 *Certification:* Rheumatology
3180 Main St, Bridgeport, 203-371-6969

Hutchinson, Gordon John (12 mentions)
FMS-Switzerland, 1976
Certification: Internal Medicine, Rheumatology
136 Sherman Ave, New Haven, 203-785-0885

Karp, Sharon (7 mentions)
Brown U, 1983 *Certification:* Internal Medicine, Rheumatology
1450 Washington Blvd #1, Stamford, 203-327-9321

Nascimento, Joao M. A. (14 mentions)
FMS-Portugal, 1984
Certification: Internal Medicine, Rheumatology
3203 Main St, Bridgeport, 203-371-0009

Novack, Stuart Neil (7 mentions)
SUNY-Upstate Med U, 1966
Certification: Internal Medicine, Rheumatology
40 Cross St, Norwalk, 203-845-4800

Podell, David Neil (18 mentions)
U of Rochester, 1980
Certification: Internal Medicine, Rheumatology
64 Robbins St, Waterbury, 203-573-7281

Rose, Roberta F. (10 mentions)
U of California-San Francisco, 1981
Certification: Internal Medicine, Rheumatology
40 Cross St, Norwalk, 203-845-4800

Trock, David Haris (10 mentions)
New York Med Coll, 1984
Certification: Internal Medicine, Rheumatology
25 Germantown Rd, Danbury, 203-731-2000

Vietorisz, Tomas J. (8 mentions)
Mount Sinai Sch of Med, 1988
Certification: Internal Medicine, Rheumatology
80 Mill River St #2400, Stamford, 203-348-9455

Thoracic Surgery

Detterbeck, Frank C. (7 mentions)
Northwestern U, 1983 *Certification:* Thoracic Surgery
330 Cedar Sr, New Haven, 203-785-4931

Federico, John A. (9 mentions)
Certification: Surgery
330 Orchard St #300, New Haven, 203-787-3488

Hall, Timothy Scott (11 mentions)
Temple U, 1982
Certification: Surgery, Surgical Critical Care, Thoracic Surgery
30 Shelburne Rd, Stamford, 203-276-7470

Lettera, James V. (24 mentions)
Georgetown U, 1977 *Certification:* Thoracic Surgery
501 Kings Hwy E #112, Fairfield, 203-382-1900
9 Cots St #2D, Shelton, 203-922-7870
40 Cross St, Norwalk, 203-845-2035

Squitieri, Rafael Paolo (9 mentions)
Mount Sinai Sch of Med, 1993
Certification: Surgery, Thoracic Surgery
2800 Main St, Bridgeport, 203-576-5708

Walker, Michael James (14 mentions)
Jefferson Med Coll, 1988 *Certification:* Thoracic Surgery
27 Hospital Ave #405, Danbury, 203-797-1811
95 Locust Ave, Danbury, 203-797-1811

Waters, Paul F. (7 mentions)
Certification: Surgery
77 Lafayette Pl, Greenwich, 203-863-4250

Urology

Batter, Stephen J. (9 mentions)
U of Rochester, 1992 *Certification:* Urology
12 Elmcrest Ter, Norwalk, 203-853-4200

Colberg, John Wayne (10 mentions)
Washington U, 1985 *Certification:* Urology
800 Howard Ave, New Haven, 203-785-2815

Dodds, Peter Robert (20 mentions)
Columbia U, 1977 *Certification:* Urology
12 Elmcrest Ter, Norwalk, 203-853-4200

Flanagan, Michael John (8 mentions)
Robert W Johnson Med Sch, 1985 *Certification:* Urology
1579 Straights Tpke, Middleury, 203-757-8361

Gorelick, Jeffrey I. (12 mentions)
Northwestern U, 1983 *Certification:* Urology
51-53 Kenosia Ave, Danbury, 203-748-0330

Muldoon, Lawrence Daniel (13 mentions)
Northwestern U, 1984 *Certification:* Urology
425 Post Rd, Fairfield, 203-254-1576

Paraiso, Edward Biasbas (10 mentions)
Albert Einstein Coll of Med, 1994 *Certification:* Urology
160 Hawley Ln #002, Trumbull, 203-375-3456
52 Bench Rd, Fairfield, 203-315-3456
267 Grant St, Bridgeport, 203-375-3456

Pinto, Arthur C. (10 mentions)
FMS-India, 1977 *Certification:* Urology
52 Bench Rd, Fairfield, 203-255-6825
160 Hawley Ln #2, Trumbull, 203-375-3456

Serels, Scott Reed (8 mentions)
New York U, 1992 *Certification:* Urology
12 Elmcrest Ter, Norwalk, 203-853-4200

Small, Jeffrey Daniel (14 mentions)
New York Med Coll, 1987 *Certification:* Urology
4695 Main St, Bridgeport, 203-372-4419
267 Grant St, Bridgeport, 203-372-4419

Viner, Nicholas Andre (11 mentions)
Vanderbilt U, 1968 *Certification:* Urology
160 Hawley Ln #102, Trumbull, 203-375-3456
1305 Post Rd #212, Fairfield, 203-255-6825
52 Bench Rd, Fairfield, 203-375-3456
267 Grant St, Bridgeport, 203-375-3456

Waxberg, Jonathan A. (13 mentions)
U of Cincinnati, 1980 *Certification:* Urology
35 Hoyt St, Stamford, 203-324-2268

Weinstein, Robert Phillip (8 mentions)
SUNY-Downstate Med Coll, 1995 *Certification:* Urology
160 Hawley Ln #002, Trumbull, 203-375-3456
52 Bench Rd, Fairfield, 203-375-3456
267 Grant St, Bridgeport, 203-375-3456

Weiss, Robert Martin (8 mentions)
SUNY-Downstate Med Coll, 1960 *Certification:* Urology
800 Howard Ave, New Haven, 203-785-2815
333 Cedar St #321, New Haven, 203-785-2140

Vascular Surgery

De Natale, Ralph Wayne (15 mentions)
FMS-Italy, 1979 *Certification:* Vascular Surgery
280 State St, North Haven, 203-288-2886

Huribal, Marsel (20 mentions)
FMS-St Maarten, 1987 *Certification:* Vascular Surgery
999 Silver Ln #2B, Trumbull, 203-375-2861
32 Strawberry Hill Ct #5, Stamford, 203-425-2790
1449 Waterbury Rd #101, Southbury, 203-262-9979

Hartford Area
Including Hartford County

Allergy/Immunology

Bedard, Robert Michael (25 mentions)
U of Cincinnati, 1974
Certification: Allergy & Immunology, Internal Medicine
483 W Middle Tpke #323, Manchester, 860-649-0601
64 Palomba Dr #2, Enfield, 860-232-9911
836 Farmington Ave #207, West Hartford, 860-232-9911

Cohen, Leonard (13 mentions)
New York U, 1977
Certification: Allergy & Immunology, Internal Medicine
928 Farmington Ave, West Hartford, 860-233-6293

Mendelson, Louis Moses (27 mentions)
Virginia Commonwealth U, 1965
Certification: Allergy & Immunology, Pediatrics
836 Farmington Ave #207, West Hartford, 860-649-0601
483 Middle Tpke W #323, Manchester, 860-232-9911
64 Palomba Dr #2, Enfield, 860-741-8152

Rosen, James Paul (12 mentions)
SUNY-Downstate Med Coll, 1974
Certification: Allergy & Immunology, Pediatrics
836 Farmington Ave #207, West Hartford, 860-232-9911
483 Middle Tpke W #323, Manchester, 860-649-0601
64 Palomba Dr #2, Enfield, 860-741-8152
540 Saybrook Rd #220, Middletown, 860-344-0562
40 Dale Rd #203, Avon, 860-677-5249

Anesthesiology

Contois, Leo Mark (4 mentions)
U of Missouri-Kansas City, 1986 *Certification:* Anesthesiology
114 Woodland St, Hartford, 860-714-6654

Hortvet, Laurel Ann (4 mentions)
U of Wisconsin, 1986 *Certification:* Anesthesiology
111 Founders Plaza, East Hartford, 760-545-2117
80 Seymour St, Hartford, 860-545-2117

Loiacono, Michael Anthony (5 mentions)
New York Coll of Osteopathic Med, 1988
Certification: Anesthesiology
100 Grand St, New Britain, 860-563-0700

Martin, Thomas J. (7 mentions)
Georgetown U, 1984 *Certification:* Anesthesiology
111 Founders Plaza #300, East Hartford, 860-282-0833
85 Seymour St, Hartford, 860-545-8177

Miller, Robert Keith (3 mentions)
SUNY-Upstate Med U, 1987 *Certification:* Anesthesiology
111 Founders Plaza #300, East Hartford, 860-282-0833
85 Seymour St, Hartford, 860-545-8127

Moraski, Gwendolyn Martha (7 mentions)
U of Connecticut, 1985
Certification: Anesthesiology, Pain Medicine
114 Woodland St, Hartford, 860-714-6654

Mort, Thomas Craig (4 mentions)
U of Toledo, 1984
Certification: Anesthesiology, Critical Care Medicine
111 Founders Plaza #300, East Hartford, 860-282-0833
85 Seymour St, Hartford, 860-545-8127

Piserchia, Gerald George (4 mentions)
Temple U, 1976
Certification: Anesthesiology, Critical Care Medicine
111 Founders Plaza #300, East Hartford, 860-282-0833
85 Seymour St, Hartford, 860-545-8127

Rosenberg, Franklin Ira (3 mentions)
FMS-Mexico, 1981 *Certification:* Anesthesiology
114 Woodland St, Hartford, 860-714-6654

Satterfield, John Myron (3 mentions)
U of Nebraska, 1984 *Certification:* Anesthesiology
100 Grand St, New Britain, 860-224-5266

Waberski, Witold (5 mentions)
FMS-Poland, 1980
Certification: Anesthesiology, Critical Care Medicine
80 Seymour St, Hartford, 860-545-2117
473 Silver Ln, East Hartford, 860-545-2117

Wells, Kenneth Hubert (4 mentions)
Temple U, 1972 *Certification:* Anesthesiology
111 Founders Plaza #300, East Hartford, 860-282-0833
85 Seymour St, Hartford, 860-545-8127

Wilson, Gary Stephen (3 mentions)
Temple U, 1979 *Certification:* Anesthesiology
114 Woodland St #30301, Hartford, 860-714-6654

Cardiac Surgery

Gallagher, Robert Craig (18 mentions)
Med U of South Carolina, 1980 *Certification:* Thoracic Surgery
85 Seymour St #325, Hartford, 860-522-7181

Hammond, Jonathan Acton (15 mentions)
Harvard U, 1984 *Certification:* Thoracic Surgery
85 Seymour St #725, Hartford, 860-524-5905

Martinez, William Vincent (23 mentions)
Jefferson Med Coll, 1986 *Certification:* Thoracic Surgery
1000 Asylum Ave #3201-A, Hartford, 860-714-1094

Takata, Hiroyoshi (20 mentions)
FMS-Japan, 1965 *Certification:* Surgery, Thoracic Surgery
85 Seymour St #325, Hartford, 860-522-7181

Cardiology

Bloom, Ronald Jeffrey (4 mentions)
FMS-Grenada, 1982
Certification: Cardiovascular Disease, Internal Medicine
711 Cottage Grove Rd, Bloomfield, 860-242-8756

Cardon, James Pratt (11 mentions)
U of Rochester, 1984
Certification: Cardiovascular Disease, Internal Medicine
100 Retreat Ave #811, Hartford, 860-522-5712

Cardone, John Thomas (10 mentions)
U of Buffalo, 1980
Certification: Cardiovascular Disease, Internal Medicine
19 Woodland St #35, Hartford, 860-525-1234
21 Hartford St #211, Hartford, 860-525-8901
7 Elm St #201, Enfield, 860-741-6678

Casey, David Madigan (4 mentions)
Georgetown U, 1998
Certification: Cardiovascular Disease, Internal Medicine
704 Hebron Ave, Glastonbury, 860-249-9175
85 Seymour St #805, Hartford, 860-249-9175
65 Memorial Rd #405, West Hartford, 860-249-9175
100 Simsbury Rd #202, Avon, 860-249-9175

Cohen, Steven Robert (13 mentions)
U of Connecticut, 1979
Certification: Cardiovascular Disease, Internal Medicine
1000 Asylum Ave #4300, Hartford, 860-527-6247

Dahhan, Hazar (4 mentions)
FMS-Syria, 1979
Certification: Cardiovascular Disease, Internal Medicine
26 Haynes St, Manchester, 860-643-5443

Dougherty, James Edward (12 mentions)
Georgetown U, 1974
Certification: Cardiovascular Disease, Internal Medicine
2928 Main St, Glastonbury, 860-522-0604
85 Seymour St #719, Hartford, 860-522-0604

Duncan, Brett Hunter (5 mentions)
Rosalind Franklin U, 1994 *Certification:* Cardiovascular Disease
100 Retreat Ave #811, Hartford, 860-522-5712

Hager, Wesley David (11 mentions)
Columbia U, 1968
Certification: Cardiovascular Disease, Internal Medicine
263 Farmington Ave, Farmington, 860-679-3343

Horowitz, Steven Matthew (8 mentions)
Mount Sinai Sch of Med, 1977
Certification: Cardiovascular Disease, Internal Medicine
85 Seymour St #805, Hartford, 860-249-9175
65 Memorial Rd #405, West Hartford, 860-249-9175
704 Hebron Ave, Glastonbury, 860-249-9175
100 Simsbury Rd #202, Avon, 860-249-9175

Kennedy, Kathleen A. (4 mentions)
Albany Med Coll, 1983
Certification: Cardiovascular Disease, Internal Medicine
1000 Asylum Ave #4310, Hartford, 860-525-8901
21 Woodland St #211, Hartford, 860-525-8901

La Sala, Anthony Francis (7 mentions)
New York Med Coll, 1974
Certification: Cardiovascular Disease, Internal Medicine
85 Seymour St #805, Hartford, 860-249-9175

Leopold, Harris Blake (4 mentions)
SUNY-Upstate Med U, 1982
Certification: Pediatric Cardiology, Pediatrics
282 Washington St, Hartford, 860-545-9400

Owlia, Dariush (4 mentions)
FMS-Iran, 1968
Certification: Cardiovascular Disease, Internal Medicine
100 Retreat Ave #811, Hartford, 860-522-5712

Pareles, Lawrence Miles (5 mentions)
U of Connecticut, 1977
Certification: Cardiovascular Disease, Internal Medicine
85 Seymour St #805, Hartford, 860-249-9175
65 Memorial Rd #405, West Hartford, 860-249-9175
704 Hebron Ave, Glastonbury, 860-249-9175
100 Simsbury Rd #202, Avon, 860-249-9175

Rizvi, Asad Ali (4 mentions)
FMS-Pakistan, 1994
Certification: Cardiovascular Disease, Internal Medicine
100 Retreat Ave #811, Hartford, 860-522-5712

Sappington, Joseph Boyle (4 mentions)
George Washington U, 1970 *Certification:* Cardiovascular
    Disease, Internal Medicine, Interventional Cardiology
1000 Asylum Ave #3211, Hartford, 860-525-7357
300 Hebron Ave #213, Glastonbury, 860-525-7357

Schulman, Peter (9 mentions)
Tufts U, 1974
Certification: Cardiovascular Disease, Internal Medicine
263 Farmington Ave, Farmington, 860-679-3343
381 Hopmeadow St, Simsbury, 860-651-1669
141 Dowd Ave, Canton, 860-693-6951

Walden, Jeffrey Howard (7 mentions)
New York U, 1995
Certification: Cardiovascular Disease, Internal Medicine
85 Seymour St #719, Hartford, 860-522-0604
2928 Main St, Glastonbury, 860-522-0604

White, Peter Paul (4 mentions)
U of Connecticut, 1982 *Certification:* Cardiovascular
    Disease, Internal Medicine, Interventional Cardiology
1000 Asylum Ave #4300, Hartford, 860-527-6247

Dermatology

Gart, Glenn Stanton (9 mentions)
Creighton U, 1990 *Certification:* Dermatology
255 N Main St, Bristol, 860-589-1405

Grant-Kels, Jane Margaret (17 mentions)
Cornell U, 1974 *Certification:* Dermatology, Dermatopathology
263 Farmington Ave #310, Farmington, 860-679-4600

Kugelman, Lisa Catherine (22 mentions)
U of Connecticut, 1987 *Certification:* Dermatology
65 Memorial Rd #450, West Hartford, 860-523-1087

Last, Gary Lee (8 mentions)
U of Oklahoma, 1978 *Certification:* Dermatology
580 Cottage Grove Rd, Bloomfield, 860-242-8644

Nathanson, Robert Bennett (8 mentions)
Albany Med Coll, 1966 *Certification:* Dermatology
61 S Main St #309, West Hartford, 860-561-1350

Pennoyer, Jennifer White (19 mentions)
U of Connecticut, 1996 *Certification:* Dermatology
701 Cottage Grove Rd #E110, Bloomfield, 860-243-3020

Zweig, Elliot Charles (9 mentions)
SUNY-Downstate Med Coll, 1976
Certification: Dermatology, Internal Medicine
41 N Main St #211, West Hartford, 860-561-0580

Emergency Medicine

Dansky, Perry Maxwell (3 mentions)
FMS-Grenada, 1988
114 Woodland St, Hartford, 860-714-4701

Drescher, Michael Joseph (5 mentions)
FMS-Israel, 1992 *Certification:* Emergency Medicine
80 Seymour St, Hartford, 860-545-4377

Fuller, Robert Peter (10 mentions)
Loyola U Chicago, 1992 *Certification:* Emergency Medicine
263 Farmington Ave, Farmington, 860-679-3486

Pito, Louis V. (3 mentions)
100 Grand St, New Britain, 860-224-5675

Regan, Thomas Joseph (3 mentions)
U of Massachusetts, 1989 *Certification:* Emergency Medicine
263 Farmington Ave #MC-1930, Farmington, 860-679-3504

Robinson, Kenneth John (4 mentions)
U of Pittsburgh, 1991 *Certification:* Emergency Medicine
80 Seymour St, Hartford, 860-545-5388

Smally, Alan Jon (19 mentions)
U of Florida, 1974 *Certification:* Emergency Medicine
263 Farmington Ave, Farmington, 860-679-3486

Wagner, Cliff William (3 mentions)
FMS-Grenada, 1987 *Certification:* Emergency Medicine
41 Brewster Rd, Bristol, 860-585-3433

Wolf, Scott A. (3 mentions)
New York Coll of Osteopathic Med, 1991
Certification: Internal Medicine
80 Seymour St, Hartford, 860-985-9152

Endocrinology

Domenichini, David John (10 mentions)
FMS-Italy, 1987
Certification: Endocrinology, Diabetes, and Metabolism
85 Seymour St #1022, Hartford, 860-524-1175

Lassman, Marshall Nathan (13 mentions)
U of Rochester, 1968
Certification: Endocrinology and Metabolism, Internal Medicine
1000 Asylum Ave #4310, Hartford, 860-247-2137
300 Hebron Ave #213, Glastonbury, 860-247-2137

Malchoff, Carl Douglas (8 mentions)
U of Rochester, 1978
Certification: Endocrinology and Metabolism, Internal Medicine
263 Farmington Ave, Farmington, 860-679-2100

McDermott, Patrick Hugh (11 mentions)
SUNY-Downstate Med Coll, 1986 *Certification:*
  Endocrinology, Diabetes, and Metabolism, Internal Medicine
85 Seymour St #1022, Hartford, 860-560-7778

Oberstein, Robert Marc (17 mentions)
Mount Sinai Sch of Med, 1994
Certification: Endocrinology, Diabetes, and Metabolism
100 Retreat Ave #400, Hartford, 860-547-1278

Wettstein, Markus (12 mentions)
FMS-Dominica, 1990
Certification: Endocrinology, Diabetes, and Metabolism
85 Seymour St #1022, Hartford, 860-524-1175

Family Practice *(see note on page 9)*

Belsky, Mark (5 mentions)
SUNY-Upstate Med U, 1978 *Certification:* Family Medicine
675 Tower Ave #401, Hartford, 860-714-2913

Cementina, Alan Michael (3 mentions)
U of Southern California, 1983 *Certification:* Family Medicine
99 Woodland St, Hartford, 860-714-4212

Deshaies, Michael R. (4 mentions)
U of New England Coll of Osteopathic Med, 1997
Certification: Internal Medicine
704 Hebron Ave, Glastonbury, 860-659-1379

Goldberg, Jeffrey Robert (3 mentions)
U of Connecticut, 1994 *Certification:* Family Medicine
25 Collins Rd, Bristol, 860-589-8882

Harrison-Atlas, Richard E. (3 mentions)
U of Connecticut, 1978 *Certification:* Family Medicine
675 Tower Ave #401, Hartford, 860-714-2913

Li, Charlene Ching (3 mentions)
SUNY-Upstate Med U, 1977 *Certification:* Family Medicine
851 Marshall Phelps Rd, Windsor, 860-683-0756

Luger, Steven W. (4 mentions)
U of Rochester, 1979 *Certification:* Family Medicine
1060 Day Hill Rd #203, Windsor, 860-683-2690

O'Brien, Stephen Thomas (3 mentions)
U of Vermont, 1971 *Certification:* Family Medicine
113 Elm St #302, Enfield, 860-741-3069

Orientale, Eugene, Jr. (3 mentions)
Cornell U, 1987
Certification: Family Medicine, Geriatric Medicine
99 Woodland St, Hartford, 860-714-4212

Rodriguez, Alberto J. (3 mentions)
U Central del Caribe, 1980 *Certification:* Family Medicine
345 N Main St #245, West Hartford, 860-236-3000

Gastroenterology

Cappa, Joseph A. (14 mentions)
Mount Sinai Sch of Med, 1987
Certification: Gastroenterology, Internal Medicine
85 Seymour St #700, Hartford, 860-246-2277
2928 Main St, Glastonbury, 860-246-2277

Gelwan, Jeffrey Stuart (15 mentions)
SUNY-Downstate Med Coll, 1981
Certification: Gastroenterology, Internal Medicine
85 Seymour St #700, Hartford, 860-246-2277
2928 Main St, Glastonbury, 860-246-2277

Nestler, Jeffry Laurence (15 mentions)
New York Med Coll, 1985
Certification: Gastroenterology, Internal Medicine
85 Seymour St #1000, Hartford, 860-246-2571

Polio, John (17 mentions)
Boston U, 1979
Certification: Gastroenterology, Internal Medicine
1000 Asylum Ave #3215, Hartford, 860-522-1171

Van Linda, Brian Michael (8 mentions)
Georgetown U, 1977
Certification: Gastroenterology, Internal Medicine
30 Jordan Ln, Wethersfield, 860-674-8830
44 Dale Rd, Avon, 860-674-8830

Weiser, Jeffrey Steven (9 mentions)
Mount Sinai Sch of Med, 1992
Certification: Gastroenterology, Internal Medicine
85 Seymour St #700, Hartford, 860-246-2277
6 Northwestern Dr #302, Bloomfield, 860-246-2277

Zaldonis, Anthony T., Jr. (7 mentions)
Hahnemann U, 1979
Certification: Gastroenterology, Internal Medicine
44 Dale Rd, Avon, 860-674-8830
19 Woodland Dr #43, Hartford, 860-674-8830
146 Hazard Ave, Enfield, 860-674-8830

General Surgery

Banever, Thomas Clark (6 mentions)
Tufts U, 1972 *Certification:* Surgery
100 Retreat Ave #808, Hartford, 860-249-9189

Bloom, George Peter (7 mentions)
Cornell U, 1969 *Certification:* Surgery
85 Seymour St #415, Hartford, 860-246-2071
120 Simsbury Rd, Avon, 860-246-2071

Cohen, Jeffrey Lewis (7 mentions)
Columbia U, 1982 *Certification:* Colon & Rectal Surgery, Surgery
85 Seymour St #425, Hartford, 860-548-7336

Da Silva, John Michael (13 mentions)
U of Connecticut, 1981 *Certification:* Surgery
290 Collins St, Hartford, 860-522-1024
146 Hazard Ave #207, Enfield, 860-522-1024
300 Hebron Ave #207, Glastonbury, 860-522-1024

Daoud, Ibrahim Michel (9 mentions)
FMS-Syria, 1971 *Certification:* Surgery
95 Woodland St, Hartford, 860-714-6871

Kozol, Robert Anthony (5 mentions)
SUNY-Upstate Med U, 1979 *Certification:* Surgery
263 Farmington Ave, Farmington, 860-679-3540

Orlando, Rocco, III (32 mentions)
U of Connecticut, 1978
Certification: Surgery, Surgical Critical Care
80 Seymour St, Hartford, 860-246-2071
85 Seymour St #415, Hartford, 860-246-2071

Oviedo, Alvaro (5 mentions)
FMS-Colombia, 1965 *Certification:* Surgery
1000 Asylum Ave #2106, Hartford, 860-249-8595
150 Hazard Ave, Enfield, 860-249-8595

Piorkowski, Robert J. (6 mentions)
Georgetown U, 2003 *Certification:* Surgery
85 Seymour St #401, Hartford, 860-696-2040
80 Fisher Dr, Avon, 860-696-2040
1260 Silas Deane Hwy, Wethersfield, 860-696-2040
74 Mack St, Windsor, 860-696-2040

Raynor, R. Winfield (5 mentions)
New York Med Coll, 1980 *Certification:* Surgery
116 E Center St #12, Manchester, 860-646-8888

Sardella, William Vincent (5 mentions)
Tufts U, 1983 *Certification:* Colon & Rectal Surgery, Surgery
85 Seymour St #425, Hartford, 860-548-7336

Vignati, Paul Vincent (11 mentions)
Tufts U, 1986 *Certification:* Colon & Rectal Surgery, Surgery
85 Seymour St #425, Hartford, 860-548-7336

Zarfos, Kristen A. (6 mentions)
Certification: Surgery
1000 Asylum Ave, Hartford, 860-714-5237
3 Oaks Plaza, Higganum, 860-714-5237
631 S Quaker Ln, West Hartford, 860-714-5237

Geriatrics

Coll, Patrick Pacelli (17 mentions)
FMS-Ireland, 1981
Certification: Family Medicine, Geriatric Medicine
263 Farmington Ave, Farmington, 860-679-8400

Dicks, Robert Scott (10 mentions)
Wayne State U, 1979
Certification: Geriatric Medicine, Internal Medicine
75 Great Pond Rd, Simsbury, 860-458-3758
40 Loeffler Rd, Bloomfield, 860-380-5150

Rowland, Frederick North (11 mentions)
U of Connecticut, 1987
Certification: Geriatric Medicine, Internal Medicine
114 Woodland St, Hartford, 860-714-4749

Hematology/Oncology

Baker, William Jeffrey (6 mentions)
Tufts U, 1984
Certification: Hematology, Internal Medicine, Medical Oncology
85 Retreat Ave, Hartford, 860-249-6291
112 Mansfield Ave, Willimantic, 860-456-9116
80 Fisher Dr, Avon, 860-674-0088

Bona, Robert D. (19 mentions)
SUNY-Upstate Med U, 1980
Certification: Hematology, Internal Medicine, Medical Oncology
263 Farmington Ave, Farmington, 860-679-2100

Davis, Lynn Keyes (7 mentions)
U of Connecticut, 1972
Certification: Hematology, Internal Medicine, Medical Oncology
43 Woodland St #G-80, Hartford, 860-527-5803
73-A Haynes St, Manchester, 860-646-0670

De Fusco, Patricia A. (11 mentions)
Boston U, 1980
Certification: Internal Medicine, Medical Oncology
100 Retreat Ave #605, Hartford, 860-246-6647
1260 Silas Deane Hwy, Wethersfield, 860-246-6647

Firshein, Stephen Ira (16 mentions)
U of Michigan, 1972
Certification: Hematology, Internal Medicine, Medical Oncology
100 Retreat Ave #605, Hartford, 860-246-6647
704 Hebron Ave #201, Glastonbury, 860-659-1379

Hegde, Upendra Pandurang (7 mentions)
FMS-India, 1984 *Certification:* Hematology, Medical Oncology
263 Farmington Ave, Farmington, 860-679-2100

Nerenstone, Stacy Ruth (6 mentions)
Columbia U, 1981
Certification: Internal Medicine, Medical Oncology
85 Retreat Ave, Hartford, 860-249-6291
80 Fisher Dr, Avon, 860-674-0088

Rabinowe, Susan N. (6 mentions)
New York U, 1981
Certification: Internal Medicine, Medical Oncology
94 Woodland St, Hartford, 860-714-4680

Siegel, Robert David (17 mentions)
Columbia U, 1981
Certification: Hematology, Internal Medicine, Medical Oncology
85 Retreat Ave, Hartford, 860-249-6291
80 Fisher Dr, Avon, 860-674-0088

Silver, Joel Steven (12 mentions)
Jefferson Med Coll, 1984
Certification: Hematology, Internal Medicine, Medical Oncology
43 Woodland St #G-80, Hartford, 860-527-5803

Infectious Disease

Cooper, Brian W. (9 mentions)
Tufts U, 1979 *Certification:* Infectious Disease, Internal Medicine
80 Seymour St, Hartford, 860-545-2878

Feder, Henry Morton, Jr. (11 mentions)
Jefferson Med Coll, 1971 *Certification:* Family Medicine,
Pediatric Infectious Diseases, Pediatrics
282 Washington St, Hartford, 860-545-9490

Lawlor, Michael Timothy (42 mentions)
Georgetown U, 1985
Certification: Infectious Disease, Internal Medicine
100 Retreat Ave #903, Hartford, 860-246-2351

Lyons, Robert William (9 mentions)
Yale U, 1964 *Certification:* Infectious Disease, Internal Medicine
114 Woodland St, Hartford, 860-714-4903

Smith, Cheryl Ann (21 mentions)
U of Connecticut, 1979
Certification: Infectious Disease, Internal Medicine
114 Woodland St, Hartford, 860-714-4903

Tress, Jonathan (15 mentions)
Michigan State U, 1976
Certification: Infectious Disease, Internal Medicine
100 Retreat Ave #200, Hartford, 860-548-9293

Infertility

Luciano, Anthony Adolfo (8 mentions)
U of Connecticut, 1973 *Certification:* Obstetrics &
Gynecology, Reproductive Endocrinology/Infertility
100 Grand St #E3, New Britain, 860-224-5467

Nulsen, John Clement (8 mentions)
Case Western Reserve U, 1980 *Certification:* Obstetrics &
Gynecology, Reproductive Endocrinology/Infertility
263 Farmington Ave, Farmington, 860-679-4580

Olivar, August Chong (13 mentions)
FMS-Peru, 1967 *Certification:* Obstetrics & Gynecology,
Reproductive Endocrinology/Infertility
100 Retreat Ave #900, Hartford, 860-525-8283

Internal Medicine *(see note on page 9)*

Ardolino, Sally Ann (4 mentions)
U of Connecticut, 1982 *Certification:* Internal Medicine
1007 Farmington Ave #9, West Hartford, 860-586-7825

Chung, Kyung Hi (3 mentions)
U of Pennsylvania, 1975 *Certification:* Internal Medicine
85 Seymour St #1000, Hartford, 860-247-1842

Genser, Stuart Scott (4 mentions)
Med Coll of Pennsylvania, 1976 *Certification:* Internal Medicine
45 S Main St #203, West Hartford, 860-233-5133
631 Quaker Ln S, West Hartford, 860-233-5133

Kosowicz, Lynn Yaeger (3 mentions)
U of Connecticut, 1986 *Certification:* Internal Medicine
263 Farmington Ave #200, Farmington, 860-679-4477

Manger, Thomas Mitchel (3 mentions)
U of Connecticut, 1994 *Certification:* Internal Medicine
263 Farmington Ave #200, Farmington, 860-679-4477

Mintell, David F. (3 mentions)
Certification: Internal Medicine
320 Western Blvd Bldg B #104, Glastonbury, 860-633-6832
969 Hebron Ave, Glastonbury, 860-633-6832

Papandrea, John David (12 mentions)
Albany Med Coll, 1984 *Certification:* Internal Medicine
1000 Asylum Ave, Hartford, 860-714-5416

Petronio, Angela Maria (4 mentions)
Certification: Internal Medicine
85 Seymour St #700, Hartford, 860-246-2277

Pinou, Anne Evangela (4 mentions)
Robert W Johnson Med Sch, 1981
Certification: Internal Medicine
1260 Silas Deane Hwy #105, Wethersfield, 860-258-3464

Polatnick, Mark Jason (7 mentions)
George Washington U, 1996 *Certification:* Internal Medicine
1000 Asylum Ave #3207, Hartford, 860-714-5416

Rosenberg, Ralph (3 mentions)
U of Toledo, 1979 *Certification:* Internal Medicine
36 E Main St, Avon, 860-677-5533

Rotenberg, Donald Andrew (3 mentions)
Boston U, 1965 *Certification:* Internal Medicine, Nephrology
85 Seymour St #900, Hartford, 860-241-0700
1260 Silas Deane Hwy #106, Wethersfield, 860-241-0700

Schmetterling, Jack Alan (7 mentions)
Albert Einstein Coll of Med, 1983 *Certification:* Internal Medicine
336 N Main St, West Hartford, 860-232-4891

Tan, Sharon So (4 mentions)
FMS-Philippines, 1995
Certification: Geriatric Medicine, Internal Medicine
1000 Asylum Ave #3207, Hartford, 860-714-5416

Truex, Richard Hall (4 mentions)
Albany Med Coll, 1976 *Certification:* Internal Medicine
1260 Silas Deane Hwy #103, Wethersfield, 860-563-9518

Vella, Paul Michael (3 mentions)
FMS-Grenada, 1988 *Certification:* Internal Medicine
969 Hebron Ave, Glastonbury, 860-633-1131

Nephrology

Carley, Matthew D. (12 mentions)
Albany Med Coll, 1983
Certification: Internal Medicine, Nephrology
85 Seymour St #900, Hartford, 860-241-0700
1260 Silas Deane Hwy #106, Wethersfield, 860-241-0700

D'Avella, John Francis (13 mentions)
Georgetown U, 1972 *Certification:* Internal Medicine, Nephrology
85 Seymour St #900, Hartford, 860-241-0700
1260 Silas Deane Hwy, Wethersfield, 860-241-0700

Kaplan, Andre (8 mentions)
FMS-Belgium, 1978 *Certification:* Internal Medicine, Nephrology
263 Farmington Ave, Farmington, 860-679-4888

Laut, Jeffrey M. (10 mentions)
Albany Med Coll, 1985
Certification: Internal Medicine, Nephrology
85 Seymour St, Hartford, 860-241-0700
1260 Silas Deane Hwy #106, Wethersfield, 860-241-0700

Moustakakis, Michael N. (8 mentions)
U of Texas-Galveston, 1995
Certification: Internal Medicine, Nephrology
701 Cottage Grove Rd #A-210, Bloomfield, 860-769-9866

Post, Jarrod Bret (13 mentions)
Eastern Virginia Med Sch, 1993
Certification: Internal Medicine, Nephrology
85 Seymour St, Hartford, 860-241-0700
1260 Silas Deane Hwy #106, Wethersfield, 860-241-0700

Rasoulpour, Majid (9 mentions)
FMS-Iran, 1970 *Certification:* Pediatric Nephrology, Pediatrics
282 Washington St, Hartford, 860-545-9395

Sankaranarayanan, N. (8 mentions)
FMS-India, 1994 *Certification:* Internal Medicine, Nephrology
701 Cottage Grove Rd #A-210, Bloomfield, 860-769-9866

Tray, Kory (8 mentions)
Certification: Internal Medicine, Nephrology
85 Seymour St #900, Hartford, 860-241-0700

Neurological Surgery

Lange, Stephan Charles (17 mentions)
U of California-Irvine, 1976 *Certification:* Neurological Surgery
1000 Asylum Ave #3208, Hartford, 860-522-7121
704 Hebron Ave #103, Glastonbury, 860-522-7121
73 Cedar St, New Britain, 860-522-7121
7 Elm St #307, Enfield, 860-522-7121

Wakefield, Andrew Ervin (17 mentions)
U of Connecticut, 1992 *Certification:* Neurological Surgery
360 Bloomfield Ave #209, Windsor, 860-698-1311

Neurology

Belt, Gary H. (9 mentions)
Mount Sinai Sch of Med, 1981 *Certification:* Clinical
Neurophysiology, Internal Medicine, Neurology
580 Cottage Grove Rd #106, Bloomfield, 860-243-9709
281 Hartford Tpke #106, Vernon Rockville, 860-872-2762

Conway, Stephen Robert (41 mentions)
Columbia U, 1979 *Certification:* Internal Medicine, Neurology
85 Seymour St #800, Hartford, 860-522-4429
6 Northwestern Dr #302, Bloomfield, 860-522-4429
2928 Main St #302, Glastonbury, 860-522-4429

Macinski, Zachary P. (7 mentions)
SUNY-Downstate Med Coll, 1978
Certification: Neurology, Vascular Neurology
1000 Asylum Ave #4304, Hartford, 860-522-3711

Silverman, Isaac Edward (9 mentions)
U of Pennsylvania, 1995
Certification: Neurology, Vascular Neurology
85 Seymour St #800, Hartford, 860-522-4429
2928 Main St #302, Glastonbury, 860-522-4429
6 Northwestern Dr #302, Bloomfield, 860-522-4429

Silvers, David Steven (14 mentions)
Tufts U, 1990 *Certification:* Neurology
85 Seymour St #800, Hartford, 860-522-4429
6 Northwestern Dr #302, Bloomfield, 860-522-4429
2928 Main St #302, Glastonbury, 860-522-4429

Wade, Peter Barry (17 mentions)
Tufts U, 1982
Certification: Internal Medicine, Neurology, Vascular Neurology
1000 Asylum Ave #4304, Hartford, 860-522-3711

Obstetrics/Gynecology

Beller, Peter James (4 mentions)
Pennsylvania State U, 1981 *Certification:* Obstetrics & Gynecology
80 Seymour St #5037, Hartford, 860-545-2795

Brennan, Tracy E. (7 mentions)
Northwestern U, 1983 *Certification:* Obstetrics & Gynecology
2638 Main St, Glastonbury, 860-547-0306
136 Retreat Ave, Hartford, 860-547-0306
330 Western Blvd, Glastonbury, 860-547-0306

Colliton, Felice Dugas (6 mentions)
Georgetown U, 1986 *Certification:* Obstetrics & Gynecology
19 Woodland St #31, Hartford, 860-728-1212
35 Nod Rd #203, Avon, 860-409-1540
31 Sycamore St #105, Glastonbury, 860-633-8550

Cortland, Renee Mailloux (3 mentions)
U of Connecticut, 1997 *Certification:* Obstetrics & Gynecology
533 Cottage Grove Rd, Bloomfield, 860-769-6820
85 Seymour St #1019, Hartford, 860-246-4029

Doelger, Peter Joseph (8 mentions)
New York U, 1986 *Certification:* Obstetrics & Gynecology
85 Seymour St #1019, Hartford, 860-246-4029
533 Cottage Grove Rd #208, Bloomfield, 860-769-6820
100 Simsbury Rd #206, Avon, 860-676-4825

Dreiss, Richard James (4 mentions)
Robert W Johnson Med Sch, 1982
Certification: Obstetrics & Gynecology
300 Kensington Ave, New Britain, 860-224-6205
100 Grand St, New Britain, 860-224-5011

Ellis, Maria Lynne (4 mentions)
U of Massachusetts, 1990 *Certification:* Obstetrics & Gynecology
19 Woodland St #31, Hartford, 860-728-1212
35 Nod Rd #203, Avon, 860-409-1540
31 Sycamore St #105, Glastonbury, 860-633-8550

Graham, Neville Joseph (3 mentions)
Temple U, 1983 *Certification:* Obstetrics & Gynecology
136 Retreat Ave, Hartford, 860-547-0306
30 W Avon Rd #4, Avon, 860-547-0306
100 Simsbury Rd, Avon, 860-547-0306
330 Western Blvd, Glastonbury, 860-547-0306

Greene, John F., Jr. (4 mentions)
U of Buffalo, 1983 *Certification:* Obstetrics & Gynecology
80 Seymour St, Hartford, 860-545-2780

Karabatsos, Yanna Marisa (5 mentions)
Michigan State U, 1997 *Certification:* Obstetrics & Gynecology
19 Woodland St #31, Hartford, 860-728-1212
31 Sycamore St #105, Glastonbury, 860-633-8550
35 Nod Rd #203, Avon, 860-409-1540

Kates, Richard Joel (7 mentions)
Columbia U, 1970 *Certification:* Obstetrics & Gynecology
100 Retreat Ave #201, Hartford, 860-246-8568
399 Farmington Ave #230, Farmington, 860-246-8568
148 Eastern Blvd, Glastonbury, 860-246-8568
1084 Cromwell Ave #1, Rocky Hill, 860-246-8568

Lazor, Lawrence Zidovsky (9 mentions)
U of Connecticut, 1990 *Certification:* Obstetrics & Gynecology
533 Cottage Grove Rd, Bloomfield, 860-769-6820
85 Seymour St #1019, Hartford, 860-246-4029
1260 Silas Deane Hwy, Wethersfield, 860-246-4029

Levine, Tracy E. (3 mentions)
U of Connecticut, 1994 *Certification:* Obstetrics & Gynecology
533 Cottage Grove Rd, Bloomfield, 860-246-4029
85 Seymour St #1019, Hartford, 860-246-4029
704 Hebron Ave #201, Glastonbury, 860-246-4029
580 Cottage Grove Rd #208, Bloomfield, 860-246-2351
1260 Silas Deane Hwy #105, Wethersfield, 860-246-2351

Massucco, Anne Marie (7 mentions)
U of Vermont, 1983 *Certification:* Obstetrics & Gynecology
35 Nod Rd #203, Avon, 860-409-1540
31 Sycamore St #105, Glastonbury, 860-633-8550
19 Woodland St #31, Hartford, 860-728-1212

Rasoulpour, Mina R. (4 mentions)
FMS-Iran, 1972 *Certification:* Obstetrics & Gynecology
8 Ellsworth Rd, West Hartford, 860-233-8523
40 Center St, Windsor Locks, 860-233-8523
100 Retreat Ave #305, Hartford, 860-233-8523

Rau, Frederick James (4 mentions)
U of Connecticut, 1984 *Certification:* Obstetrics & Gynecology
100 Retreat Ave #201, Hartford, 860-246-8568
399 Farmington Ave #230, Farmington, 860-246-8568
148 Eastern Blvd #102, Glastonbury, 860-246-8568
1084 Cromwell Ave #1, Rocky Hill, 860-246-8568

Robinson, Ellen Judith (8 mentions)
U of Connecticut, 1980 *Certification:* Obstetrics & Gynecology
148 Eastern Blvd, Glastonbury, 860-246-8568
399 Farmington Ave #230, Farmington, 860-246-8568
100 Retreat Ave #201, Hartford, 860-246-8568
1084 Cromwell Ave #1, Rocky Hill, 860-246-8568

Taylor, Linda Temple (4 mentions)
U of Michigan, 1981 *Certification:* Obstetrics & Gynecology
100 Retreat Ave #201, Hartford, 860-246-8568
399 Farmington Ave #230, Farmington, 860-246-8568
148 Eastern Blvd, Glastonbury, 860-246-8568
1084 Cromwell Ave #1, Rocky Hill, 860-246-8568

Wiseman, Valerie Ann (6 mentions)
U of Kansas, 1983 *Certification:* Obstetrics & Gynecology
19 Woodland St #31, Hartford, 860-728-1212
35 Nod Rd #203, Avon, 860-409-1540
31 Sycamore St #105, Glastonbury, 860-633-8550

Ophthalmology

Dolin, Scott Lloyd (6 mentions)
U of Connecticut, 1980 *Certification:* Ophthalmology
55 Nye Rd #104, Glastonbury, 860-633-6634
51 E Main St, Avon, 860-676-0809

Gaudio, Alexander Rudolph (8 mentions)
Yale U, 1963 *Certification:* Ophthalmology
85 Seymour St #522, Hartford, 860-549-2020

Gaudio, Paul Anton (5 mentions)
Albert Einstein Coll of Med, 1997 *Certification:* Ophthalmology
85 Seymour St #522, Hartford, 860-549-2020

Gilbert, C. Mitchell (12 mentions)
Johns Hopkins U, 1981 *Certification:* Ophthalmology
85 Seymour St #522, Hartford, 860-527-6473
704 Hebron Ave #200, Glastonbury, 860-527-6473
499 Farmington Ave #100, Farmington, 860-678-0202

Gingold, Michael Philip (6 mentions)
U of Virginia, 1983 *Certification:* Ophthalmology
499 Farmington Ave #100, Farmington, 860-678-0202
704 Hebron Ave #100, Glastonbury, 860-678-0202

Mitchell, Paul Ralph (5 mentions)
George Washington U, 1970 *Certification:* Ophthalmology
366 Colt Hwy, Farmington, 860-409-0449
131 New London Tpke #200, Glastonbury, 860-657-8400

Ratchford, Mary Gina (5 mentions)
Albany Med Coll, 1990 *Certification:* Ophthalmology
279 New Britain Rd #6, Berlin, 860-829-8939
505 Willard Ave, Newington, 860-829-8939

Suchecki, Jeanine (6 mentions)
SUNY-Downstate Med Coll, 1990 *Certification:* Ophthalmology
263 Farmington Ave, Farmington, 860-679-3540

Suski, Edmund Thaddeus (6 mentions)
Hahnemann U, 1976 *Certification:* Ophthalmology
19 Woodland St #44, Hartford, 860-247-2169
162 Mountain Rd, Suffield, 860-668-6781

Wand, Martin (6 mentions)
Yale U, 1968 *Certification:* Ophthalmology
85 Seymour St #522, Hartford, 860-527-6473
499 Farmington Ave #100, Farmington, 860-678-0202
704 Hebron Ave #200, Glastonbury, 860-527-6473

Orthopedics

Arciero, Robert Alan (8 mentions)
Georgetown U, 1980 *Certification:* Orthopaedic Surgery
263 Farmington Ave, Farmington, 860-679-6645

Carangelo, Robert James (5 mentions)
U of Connecticut, 1988 *Certification:* Orthopaedic Surgery
40 Hart St, New Britain, 860-223-8553
55 Meridian Ave #2-B, Southington, 860-223-8553

Grady-Benson, John C. (15 mentions)
Northwestern U, 1985 *Certification:* Orthopaedic Surgery
85 Seymour St #607, Hartford, 860-549-3210
2928 Main St, Glastonbury, 860-549-3210
499 Farmington Ave #300, Farmington, 860-549-3210
225 Hopmeadow St, Weatogue, 860-549-3210
1060 Day Hill Rd #201, Windsor, 860-549-3210

Joyce, Michael Edward (6 mentions)
Washington U, 1987 *Certification:* Orthopaedic Surgery
84 Glastonbury Blvd #101, Glastonbury, 860-652-8883

Lena, Chris James (5 mentions)
U of Connecticut, 1992 *Certification:* Orthopaedic Surgery
85 Seymour St #607, Hartford, 860-549-3210
499 Farmington Ave #300, Farmington, 860-549-3210

Lewis, Courtland Gillett (9 mentions)
U of Vermont, 1979 *Certification:* Orthopaedic Surgery
499 Farmington Ave #300, Farmington, 860-549-3210

Mara, John Joseph (7 mentions)
St Louis U, 1978 *Certification:* Orthopaedic Surgery
1000 Asylum Ave #2108, Hartford, 860-525-4469
35 Nod Rd, Avon, 860-525-4469

McAllister, Robert W. (10 mentions)
U of Connecticut, 1989
1000 Asylum Ave #2108, Hartford, 860-525-4469
35 Nod Rd #105, Avon, 860-525-4469

Nissen, Carl Wilson (5 mentions)
U of Connecticut, 1990 *Certification:* Orthopaedic Surgery
282 Washington St, Hartford, 860-284-0220
399 Farmington Ave, Farmington, 860-284-0220

Schutzer, Steven Fredric (10 mentions)
U of Virginia, 1978 *Certification:* Orthopaedic Surgery
2928 Main St, Glastonbury, 860-549-3210
499 Farmington Ave #300, Farmington, 860-549-3210

Selden, Steven Edward (5 mentions)
Johns Hopkins U, 1974 *Certification:* Orthopaedic Surgery
510 Cottage Grove Rd, Bloomfield, 860-243-1414
74 Mack St, Windsor, 860-243-1414

Zimmermann, Gordon A. (8 mentions)
Georgetown U, 1974 *Certification:* Orthopaedic Surgery
85 Seymour St #607, Hartford, 860-549-3210
499 Farmington Ave #300, Farmington, 860-549-3210

Otorhinolaryngology

Bonaiuto, Gregory S. (21 mentions)
U of Connecticut, 1992 *Certification:* Otolaryngology
85 Seymour St #318, Hartford, 860-493-1950
676 Hebron St, Glastonbury, 860-493-1950

Lafreniere, Denis Charles (10 mentions)
U of Connecticut, 1987 *Certification:* Otolaryngology
263 Farmington Ave #130, Farmington, 860-679-2804

Lehmann, William B. (7 mentions)
Yale U, 1963 *Certification:* Otolaryngology
85 Seymour St #318, Hartford, 860-493-1950

Newman, Richard Arthur (7 mentions)
FMS-Belgium, 1971 *Certification:* Otolaryngology
85 Seymour St #318, Hartford, 860-493-1950
15 Palomba Dr, Enfield, 860-745-4900

Robertson, Russell Wright (10 mentions)
Albany Med Coll, 1966 *Certification:* Otolaryngology
85 Seymour St #519, Hartford, 860-246-3773

Sawyer, Jeffrey Alan (8 mentions)
Tufts U, 1979 *Certification:* Otolaryngology
300 Hebron Ave #202, Glastonbury, 860-659-2759

Zachs, Todd Adam (14 mentions)
U of Connecticut, 1985 *Certification:* Otolaryngology
901 Farmington Ave, West Hartford, 860-586-2111
893 Main St #103, East Hartford, 860-586-2111

Pain Medicine

Kost, Jonathan Anthony (9 mentions)
FMS-St Maarten, 1985
Certification: Anesthesiology, Pain Medicine
40 Brewster Rd, Bristol, 860-585-3040

Squier, Raymond C. (11 mentions)
U of Connecticut, 1982
Certification: Anesthesiology, Pain Medicine
114 Woodland St, Hartford, 860-714-6654

Pathology

Barrows, George Henry (4 mentions)
U of Louisville, 1972
Certification: Anatomic Pathology & Clinical Pathology,
    Chemical Pathology, Hematology, Radioisotopic Pathology
114 Woodland St, Hartford, 860-714-4050

Conlon, Michele B. (4 mentions)
U of Connecticut, 1979 *Certification:* Anatomic Pathology &
    Clinical Pathology, Hematology
71 Haynes St, Manchester, 860-646-1222

Fiel-Gan, Mary Desiree C. (4 mentions)
FMS-Philippines, 1989 *Certification:* Anatomic Pathology &
    Clinical Pathology, Cytopathology
80 Seymour St, Hartford, 860-545-2117
111 Founders Plaza, East Hartford, 860-282-4137

Ludwig, Mark Edward (8 mentions)
Certification: Anatomic Pathology, Cytopathology
80 Seymour St, Hartford, 860-282-4137

Muller, Richard Charles (4 mentions)
St Louis U, 1980
Certification: Anatomic Pathology & Clinical Pathology
80 Seymour St, Hartford, 860-545-2255
111 Founders Plaza #30, East Hartford, 860-282-4137

Ricci, Andrew, Jr. (10 mentions)
Certification: Anatomic Pathology & Clinical Pathology
80 Seymour St, Hartford, 860-545-2866

Sanders, M. Melinda (4 mentions)
U of Toledo, 1979
Certification: Anatomic Pathology, Cytopathology
263 Farmington Ave, Farmington, 860-679-3386

Pediatrics *(see note on page 9)*

Brown, David Lewis (4 mentions)
SUNY-Downstate Med Coll, 1972
Certification: Neonatal-Perinatal Medicine, Pediatrics
6 Northwestern Dr #101, Bloomfield, 860-242-8330
1086 Elm St, Rocky Hill, 860-529-6124

Corcoran, Della Moore (8 mentions)
U of Connecticut, 1993 *Certification:* Pediatrics
970 Farmington Ave #201, West Hartford, 860-561-4300

De Silva, Hema (3 mentions)
FMS-Sri Lanka, 1965
Certification: Neonatal-Perinatal Medicine, Pediatrics
114 Woodland St, Hartford, 860-714-4455

Distefano, Leo Joseph, III (7 mentions)
U of Rochester, 1990 *Certification:* Pediatrics
970 Farmington Ave #201, West Hartford, 860-561-4300

Fote, John Joseph (3 mentions)
New Jersey Med Sch, 1970 *Certification:* Pediatrics
546 Cromwell Ave, Rocky Hill, 860-721-7561

Freilich, Cecille Rachel (4 mentions)
U of Connecticut, 1980 *Certification:* Pediatrics
379 Naubuc Ave, Glastonbury, 860-652-3325

Harvey, Richard Charles (4 mentions)
U of Connecticut, 1974 *Certification:* Pediatrics
505 Willard Ave #2C, Newington, 860-666-5601

Jannuzzi, Peter Jude (8 mentions)
Georgetown U, 1982 *Certification:* Pediatrics
101 Main St, Unionville, 860-673-6124

MacGilpin, Douglas H. (5 mentions)
Meharry Med Coll, 1974 *Certification:* Pediatrics
505 Willard Ave #2-C, Newington, 860-666-5601
282 Washington St, Hartford, 860-545-9300

O'Neill, Margaret Mary (6 mentions)
U of Connecticut, 1992 *Certification:* Pediatrics
970 Farmington Ave #201, West Hartford, 860-561-4300

Patel, Nima G. (4 mentions)
FMS-India, 1972
81 S Main St #5, West Hartford, 860-521-4044

Ramanan, Chitraleka (4 mentions)
FMS-India, 1964 *Certification:* Pediatrics
1162 New Britain Ave, West Hartford, 860-236-3084

Rubin, Viviann Mattson (3 mentions)
Yale U, 1989 *Certification:* Pediatrics
6 Northwestern Dr #101, Bloomfield, 860-529-6124

Weinerman, Harry C. (6 mentions)
U of Connecticut, 1986 *Certification:* Pediatrics
6 Northwestern Dr #101, Bloomfield, 860-529-6124

Wilion, Felicia Maraline (3 mentions)
U of Connecticut, 1987 *Certification:* Pediatrics
6 Northwestern Dr #101, Bloomfield, 860-529-6124

Ziogas, Barbara Frances (3 mentions)
U of Connecticut, 1991 *Certification:* Pediatrics
1 Forest Park Dr, Farmington, 860-677-1112

Plastic Surgery

Castiglione, Charles Leonard (42 mentions)
Columbia U, 1981 *Certification:* Plastic Surgery, Surgery
85 Seymour St #401, Hartford, 860-548-7338
399 Farmington Ave, Farmington, 860-548-7338
704 Hebron Ave #103, Glastonbury, 860-548-7338
1084 Cromwell Ave, Rocky Hill, 860-548-7338

Schreiber, Jonathan Scot (32 mentions)
New York U, 1986 *Certification:* Plastic Surgery
1 Barnard Ln #102, Bloomfield, 860-243-1889
263 Farmington Ave, Farmington, 860-679-3540

Psychiatry

Blair, C. Lee (5 mentions)
U of Connecticut, 1981 *Certification:* Psychiatry
826 Farmington Ave #221-C, West Hartford, 860-523-1451

Calabrese, Lori (3 mentions)
Johns Hopkins U, 1989
1330 Sullivan Ave, South Windsor, 860-648-9755

Fogg-Waberski, Joanna H. (5 mentions)
FMS-Poland, 1980 *Certification:* Geriatric Psychiatry, Psychiatry
400 Washington St, Hartford, 860-545-7189

Fox, Evan (7 mentions)
Rosalind Franklin U, 1988
25 Concord St, Glastonbury, 860-430-1150
400 Washington St, Hartford, 860-430-1150
300 Hebron Ave #107, Glastonbury, 860-430-1150

Goldstein, Laurence Joseph (4 mentions)
U of Connecticut, 1982
85 Seymour St #1025, Hartford, 860-527-8588

Herzog, Alfred (4 mentions)
U of Pennsylvania, 1967 *Certification:* Psychiatry
200 Retreat Ave, Hartford, 860-545-7103

Namerow, Lisa Beth (7 mentions)
U of Connecticut, 1988
Certification: Child & Adolescent Psychiatry, Pediatrics, Psychiatry
200 Retreat Ave, Hartford, 860-545-7493

Rao, Surita (3 mentions)
FMS-India, 1988 *Certification:* Addiction Psychiatry, Psychiatry
500 Blue Hills Ave, Hartford, 860-714-3506

Rothschild, Bruce Stephen (7 mentions)
U of Vermont, 1985 *Certification:* Psychiatry
40 Dale Rd #201, Avon, 860-676-9350
34 Jerome Ave #110, Bloomfield, 860-243-5024

Schwartz, Harold I. (6 mentions)
Columbia U, 1979 *Certification:* Psychiatry
200 Retreat Ave, Hartford, 860-545-7280

Selzer, Gerard B. (3 mentions)
SUNY-Upstate Med U, 1969 *Certification:* Psychiatry
100 Retreat Ave #901, Hartford, 860-523-1736
333 Bloomfield Ave #A, West Hartford, 860-523-1736

Pulmonary Disease

Conway, Michael Mead (31 mentions)
U of California-San Francisco, 1973
Certification: Internal Medicine, Pulmonary Disease
85 Seymour St #923, Hartford, 860-547-1876
704 Hebron Ave, Glastonbury, 860-547-1876
1260 Silas Deane Hwy, Wethersfield, 860-547-1876

Foley, Raymond John (5 mentions)
New York Coll of Osteopathic Med, 1993 *Certification:* Critical Care Medicine, Internal Medicine, Pulmonary Disease
263 Farmington Ave, Farmington, 860-679-3343

Gerardi, Daniel Anthony (10 mentions)
U of Connecticut, 1988 *Certification:* Critical Care Medicine, Internal Medicine, Pulmonary Disease
114 Woodland St, Hartford, 860-714-4055

Grise, David Patrick (6 mentions)
Robert W Johnson Med Sch, 1974
Certification: Internal Medicine, Pulmonary Disease
27 Sycamore St #100, Glastonbury, 860-659-0581
1000 Asylum Ave #2100, Hartford, 860-247-2530

Knauft, Robert Frederic (11 mentions)
Case Western Reserve U, 1969
Certification: Internal Medicine, Pulmonary Disease
85 Seymour St #923, Hartford, 860-547-1876
710 Hebron Ave #201, Glastonbury, 860-659-6272
701-B Cottage Grove Rd #220, Bloomfield, 860-243-8131
1260 Silas Deane Hwy #106, Wethersfield, 860-258-3460

Lahiri, Bimalin (15 mentions)
FMS-India, 1960
Certification: Internal Medicine, Pulmonary Disease
114 Woodland St, Hartford, 860-714-4055

McNamee, Michael Joseph (7 mentions)
Columbia U, 1975 *Certification:* Critical Care Medicine, Internal Medicine, Pulmonary Disease
100 Grand St, New Britain, 860-224-5242

Metersky, Mark Lewis (5 mentions)
New York U, 1985 *Certification:* Critical Care Medicine, Internal Medicine, Pulmonary Disease
263 Farmington Ave, Farmington, 860-679-3343

Pope, James Samuel (6 mentions)
U of Virginia, 1999 *Certification:* Critical Care Medicine, Internal Medicine, Pulmonary Disease
533 Cottage Grove Rd, Bloomfield, 860-243-8131
85 Seymour St #923, Hartford, 860-547-1876

Rodgers, John William (5 mentions)
U of Connecticut, 1974
Certification: Internal Medicine, Pulmonary Disease
27 Sycamore St #100, Glastonbury, 860-659-0581

Shore, Eric Thomas (14 mentions)
U of Pennsylvania, 1977 *Certification:* Critical Care Medicine, Internal Medicine, Pulmonary Disease
85 Seymour St #923, Hartford, 860-547-1876
701 Cottage Grove Rd #B220, Bloomfield, 860-243-8131
710 Hebron Ave #201, Glastonbury, 860-659-6272
1260 Silas Deane Hwy #106, Wethersfield, 860-258-3460

Radiology—Diagnostic

Brown, Robert Timothy (4 mentions)
FMS-Canada, 1980
Certification: Diagnostic Radiology, Pediatric Radiology
85 Seymour St #200, Hartford, 860-246-6589
1260 Silas Dean Hwy #104, Wethersfield, 860-563-7844
704 Hebron Ave #100, Glastonbury, 860-659-9595
941 Farmington Ave, West Hartford, 860-231-1900

Cronin, Edward Bowen (10 mentions)
U of Vermont, 1979 *Certification:* Diagnostic Radiology, Nuclear Medicine, Nuclear Radiology
85 Seymour St #200, Hartford, 860-246-6589
941 Farmington Ave, West Hartford, 860-231-1900
1260 Silas Dean Hwy #104, Wethersfield, 860-563-7844
100 Simsbury Rd #101, Avon, 860-678-8527
704 Hebron Ave #100, Glastonbury, 860-659-9595

Firestone, Michael I. (4 mentions)
Tulane U, 1997 *Certification:* Diagnostic Radiology
114 Woodland St, Hartford, 860-714-4000

Foxman, Ethan Bradley (5 mentions)
Stanford U, 1997
Certification: Diagnostic Radiology, Neuroradiology
85 Seymour St #200, Hartford, 860-246-6589
80 Seymour St, Hartford, 860-545-5000
100 Simsbury Rd #101, Avon, 860-678-8527
704 Hebron Ave #100, Glastonbury, 860-678-8527
941 Farmington Ave, West Hartford, 860-231-1900
137 Hazard Ave, Enfield, 860-246-6589
399 Farmington Ave, Farmington, 860-246-6589

Markowitz, Stuart Keith (10 mentions)
Rosalind Franklin U, 1981 *Certification:* Diagnostic Radiology
85 Seymour St #200, Hartford, 860-246-6589
80 Seymour St, Hartford, 860-545-5000
100 Simsbury Rd #101, Avon, 860-678-8527
704 Hebron Ave #100, Glastonbury, 860-659-9595
941 Farmington Ave, West Hartford, 860-231-1900
137 Hazard Ave, Enfield, 860-246-6589
399 Farmington Ave, Farmington, 860-246-6589

Opalacz, John Paul (5 mentions)
St Louis U, 1977 *Certification:* Diagnostic Radiology
85 Seymour St #200, Hartford, 860-246-6589
941 Farmington Ave, West Hartford, 860-231-1900
1260 Silas Deane Hwy #104, Wethersfield, 860-563-7844

Straub, Joseph John (4 mentions)
U of Iowa, 1972 *Certification:* Diagnostic Radiology, Vascular & Interventional Radiology
85 Seymour St #200, Hartford, 860-246-6589
80 Seymour St, Hartford, 860-545-5000
100 Simsbury Rd #101, Avon, 860-678-8527
704 Hebron Ave #100, Glastonbury, 860-659-9595
941 Farmington Ave, West Hartford, 860-231-1900
137 Hazard Ave, Enfield, 860-246-6589
399 Farmington Ave, Farmington, 860-246-6589

Twohig, Michael Thomas (14 mentions)
New York Med Coll, 1984 *Certification:* Diagnostic Radiology
1000 Asylum Ave #3201-E, Hartford, 860-525-3322

Volpe, John Paul (7 mentions)
Certification: Diagnostic Radiology
85 Seymour St #200, Hartford, 860-246-6589

Radiology—Therapeutic

Kaplan, Bruce Michael (8 mentions)
U of South Florida, 1979 *Certification:* Therapeutic Radiology
94 Woodland St, Hartford, 860-714-4568

Salner, Andrew L. (10 mentions)
Brown U, 1976 *Certification:* Therapeutic Radiology
80 Seymour St, Hartford, 860-545-2803

Rehabilitation

Krug, Robert James (11 mentions)
Stony Brook U, 1992
Certification: Physical Medicine & Rehabilitation
490 Blue Hills Ave, Hartford, 860-714-2647

Miller, Thomas Bradley, Jr. (10 mentions)
U of Connecticut, 1996 *Certification:* Internal Medicine, Physical Medicine & Rehabilitation
490 Blue Hills Ave, Hartford, 860-714-2647

Pesce, William J. (3 mentions)
Philadelphia Coll of Osteopathic Med, 1989
Certification: Physical Medicine & Rehabilitation
2150 Corbin Ave, New Britain, 860-827-4816
11 Bellevue Ave, Bristol, 860-582-4999

Rosati, Dennis Lee (6 mentions)
Emory U, 1982 *Certification:* Physical Medicine & Rehabilitation
220 Farmington Ave #1, Farmington, 860-677-7246

Seetharama, Subramani (11 mentions)
FMS-India, 1983 *Certification:* Physical Medicine & Rehabilitation, Spinal Cord Injury Medicine, Sports Medicine
2150 Corbin Ave, New Britain, 860-827-4973
85 Seymour St #604, Hartford, 860-545-5107
4455 S Main St, West Hartford, 860-561-1254

Rheumatology

Dixon, Jonathan Allan (29 mentions)
Harvard U, 1970 *Certification:* Internal Medicine, Rheumatology
85 Seymour #1003, Hartford, 860-246-4260
256 N Main St, Manchester, 860-246-4260

Parke, Ann Leslie (9 mentions)
FMS-United Kingdom, 1971
Certification: Internal Medicine, Rheumatology
1000 Asylum Ave #2114, Hartford, 860-714-5816

Stocker, Ralph Peter (10 mentions)
U of Kansas, 1979
Certification: Internal Medicine, Rheumatology
85 Seymour St #1003, Hartford, 860-244-9400
54 W Avon Rd, Avon, 860-675-3688

Thoracic Surgery

Lowe, Robert (27 mentions)
Harvard U, 1972
Certification: Thoracic Surgery, Vascular Surgery
85 Seymour St #911, Hartford, 860-522-4158

Thayer, John O., Jr. (27 mentions)
Brown U, 1977 *Certification:* Thoracic Surgery
1000 Asylum Ave #3201-A, Hartford, 860-714-1094

Urology

Albertsen, Peter C. (13 mentions)
Columbia U, 1978 *Certification:* Urology
263 Farmington Ave, Farmington, 860-679-4100

Bosco, Peter John (14 mentions)
Georgetown U, 1984 *Certification:* Urology
19 Woodland St #23, Hartford, 860-522-2251
146 Hazard Ave #202, Enfield, 860-763-4171

Ely, Matthew Griswold (10 mentions)
New Jersey Med Sch, 1972 *Certification:* Urology
85 Seymour St #416, Hartford, 860-947-8500
6 Northwestern Dr #202, Bloomfield, 860-947-8500
55 Nye Rd #104, Glastonbury, 860-947-8500
399 farmington Ave #200, Farmington, 860-947-8500

Shichman, Steven Jon (20 mentions)
U of Connecticut, 1986 *Certification:* Urology
120 Simsburg Rd, Avon, 860-947-8500
85 Seymour St #416, Hartford, 860-947-8500

Viets, Douglas Hartley (9 mentions)
St Louis U, 1974 *Certification:* Urology
85 Seymour St #416, Hartford, 860-947-8500
74 Mack St, Windsor, 860-947-8500
120 Simsburg Rd, Avon, 860-947-8500

Vascular Surgery

Gallagher, James Joseph (38 mentions)
U of Connecticut, 1977 *Certification:* Vascular Surgery
85 Seymour St #911, Hartford, 860-522-4158

Ruby, Steven Todd (20 mentions)
Columbia U, 1978 *Certification:* Surgery, Vascular Surgery
263 Farmington Ave, Farmington, 860-679-7692

District of Columbia

Washington, DC, Area

Washington, DC, Area

Including the District of Columbia, Alexandria, and Anne Arundel, Arlington, Fairfax, Howard, Loudoun, Montgomery, Prince George's, and Prince William Counties

Allergy/Immunology

Bergman, Kenneth Robert (7 mentions)
U of Rochester, 1967
Certification: Allergy & Immunology, Internal Medicine
13890 Braddock Rd #206, Centreville, VA, 703-263-2333

Boltansky, Howard (41 mentions)
U of Maryland, 1978
Certification: Allergy & Immunology, Internal Medicine
3301 New Mexico Ave NW #223, Washington, DC, 202-966-7100
6410 Rockledge Dr #308, Bethesda, MD, 202-966-7100

Brody, Dan T. (9 mentions)
U of Maryland, 1992 *Certification:* Allergy & Immunology
3301 New Mexico Ave NW #223, Washington, DC, 202-966-7100
6410 Rockledge Dr #308, Bethesda, MD, 301-966-7100

Chang, Betty W. (14 mentions)
New York U, 1978
Certification: Allergy & Immunology, Pediatrics
10810 Connecticut Ave, Kensington, MD, 301-929-7163

Ein, Daniel (26 mentions)
Albert Einstein Coll of Med, 1964
Certification: Allergy & Immunology, Internal Medicine
2150 Pennsylvania Ave NW, Washington, DC, 202-741-2770

Fishman, Henry J. (7 mentions)
U of Rochester, 1979
Certification: Allergy & Immunology, Internal Medicine
2141 K St NW #206, Washington, DC, 202-833-3500
5454 Wisconsin Ave #1420, Chevy Chase, MD, 301-718-7979

Helbing, Claus Karl L. (6 mentions)
FMS-Germany, 1963
Certification: Allergy & Immunology, Pediatrics
4534 John Marr Dr #A, Annandale, VA, 703-750-9450
6210 Old Keene Mill Ct, Springfield, VA, 703-569-7737

Josephs, Shelby Harold (22 mentions)
Duke U, 1975 *Certification:* Allergy & Immunology, Pediatrics
6410 Rockledge Dr #304, Bethesda, MD, 301-530-7907

Kaliner, Michael Aron (33 mentions)
U of Maryland, 1967
Certification: Allergy & Immunology, Internal Medicine
5454 Wisconsin Ave #700, Chevy Chase, MD, 301-986-9262
11002 Veirs Mill Rd #414, Wheaton, MD, 301-962-5800

Latkin, Peter Charles (7 mentions)
New York Med Coll, 1968
Certification: Allergy & Immunology, Pediatrics
6201 Leesburg Pike #300, Falls Church, VA, 703-534-2445

Loria, Richard Claude (13 mentions)
FMS-Spain, 1983
Certification: Allergy & Immunology, Internal Medicine
46400 Benedict Dr #3, Sterling, VA, 703-430-0833
6888 Elm St #301, McLean, VA, 703-356-8290

McNally, Patricia Ann (8 mentions)
Georgetown U, 1987
Certification: Allergy & Immunology, Internal Medicine
6501 Loisdale Ct, Springfield, VA, 703-922-1415

Miller, A. Larry (7 mentions)
FMS-Netherlands, 1968
311 Maple Ave W #H, Vienna, VA, 703-938-5660

Raphael, Gordon David (6 mentions)
Emory U, 1981
Certification: Allergy & Immunology, Internal Medicine
4915 Auburn Ave #202, Bethesda, MD, 301-907-3442

Schuster, Donna L. F. (9 mentions)
U of Miami, 1972 *Certification:* Allergy & Immunology, Pediatrics
100 Elden St #10, Herndon, VA, 703-689-2000

Shier, Jerome Michael (42 mentions)
New Jersey Med Sch, 1982
Certification: Allergy & Immunology, Pediatrics
15201 Shady Grove Rd #201, Rockville, MD, 301-869-7820
10301 Georgia Ave #306, Silver Spring, MD, 301-681-6055

Simpson, John Alva (8 mentions)
U of South Carolina, 1981 *Certification:* Allergy & Immunology
6355 Walker Ln #307, Alexandria, VA, 703-778-8201
6305 Castle Pl #2-D, Falls Church, VA, 703-534-5500

Vaghi, Vincent James (15 mentions)
Georgetown U, 1977 *Certification:* Pediatrics
50 W Edmonston Dr #301, Rockville, MD, 301-251-3704
19519 Doctors Dr, Germantown, MD, 301-972-9433

White, Martha Vetter (7 mentions)
Virginia Commonwealth U, 1978
Certification: Allergy & Immunology, Pediatrics
11102 Veirs Mill Rd #414, Wheaton, MD, 301-962-5800

Anesthesiology

Beauregard, John Francis (5 mentions)
Georgetown U, 1986 *Certification:* Anesthesiology
5255 Loughboro Rd NW 1st Fl, Washington, DC, 202-537-4589

Berrigan, Michael J. (7 mentions)
George Washington U, 1986 *Certification:* Anesthesiology
900 23rd St NW, Washington, DC, 202-715-4560

Chester, William Lamar (12 mentions)
U of Miami, 1982 *Certification:* Anesthesiology
9901 Medical Center Dr, Rockville, MD, 240-826-6000

Clougherty, Patrick W. (6 mentions)
U of Pittsburgh, 1982 *Certification:* Anesthesiology
3300 Gallows Rd, Falls Church, VA, 703-776-3138

Dangerfield, Paul F. (4 mentions)
George Washington U, 1995 *Certification:* Anesthesiology
900 23rd St NW, Washington, DC, 202-715-4750

Enjetti, Pamela Enid (4 mentions)
FMS-India, 1975
2300 Opitz Blvd, Woodbridge, VA, 703-670-1357

Epstein, Todd Adam (7 mentions)
George Washington U, 1979 *Certification:* Anesthesiology
8600 Old Georgetown Rd, Bethesda, MD, 301-896-6711

Escario, Francisco Tan (4 mentions)
FMS-Philippines, 1972
Certification: Anesthesiology, Critical Care Medicine
2300 Opitz Blvd, Woodbridge, VA, 703-670-1357

Hanowell, Susan Jeane T. (4 mentions)
George Washington U, 1973 *Certification:* Anesthesiology
8600 Old Georgetown Rd, Bethesda, MD, 301-896-3100

Healy, Gary Joseph (5 mentions)
SUNY-Downstate Med Coll, 1966 *Certification:* Anesthesiology
3001 Hospital Dr, Cheverly, MD, 301-618-6100

Hetherington, Richard G. (4 mentions)
New York Coll of Osteopathic Med, 1985
Certification: Anesthesiology, Pain Medicine
11341 Sunset Hills Rd, Reston, VA, 703-471-0919

Hopper, Steven Moore (9 mentions)
U of Kentucky, 1975 *Certification:* Anesthesiology
8600 Old Georgetown Rd, Bethesda, MD, 301-896-3874

Kekoler, Lance James (4 mentions)
New York Coll of Osteopathic Med, 1988
Certification: Anesthesiology
5255 Loughboro Rd NW, Washington, DC, 202-243-2280

Konigsberg, James Louis (4 mentions)
George Washington U, 1981
Certification: Anesthesiology, Internal Medicine
3300 Gallows Rd, Falls Church, VA, 703-776-3138

Lee, Chul Jai (5 mentions)
FMS-South Korea, 1972 *Certification:* Anesthesiology
1500 Forest Glen Rd, Silver Spring, MD, 301-942-8799

Martin, Stephen Douglas (4 mentions)
U of Texas-Galveston, 1981
9901 Medical Center Dr, Rockville, MD, 240-826-7324

Mesrobian, Robert Bennett (9 mentions)
Loyola U Chicago, 1976
Certification: Anesthesiology, Pediatrics
3300 Gallows Rd, Falls Church, VA, 703-776-3138

Reynolds, Michael (5 mentions)
FMS-Chile, 1980 *Certification:* Anesthesiology
1500 Forest Glen Rd, Silver Spring, MD, 301-942-8792

Scheinman, Gerald Mark (5 mentions)
Georgetown U, 1984 *Certification:* Anesthesiology
9901 Medical Center Dr, Rockville, MD, 240-826-7324

Snyder, Douglas Scott (5 mentions)
Eastern Virginia Med Sch, 1980 *Certification:*
   Anesthesiology, Critical Care Medicine, Internal Medicine
110 Irving St NW #G-226, Washington, DC, 202-877-7504

Sylvester, Carl L. (16 mentions)
Georgetown U, 1968 *Certification:* Anesthesiology
5255 Loughboro Rd NW, Washington, DC, 202-537-4589

Walsh, M. Scott (7 mentions)
New York U, 1981
Certification: Anesthesiology, Internal Medicine
1701 N George Mason Dr #2D, Arlington, VA, 703-558-6173

Cardiac Surgery

Garcia, Jorge M. (27 mentions)
FMS-Philippines, 1964 *Certification:* Surgery, Thoracic Surgery
110 Irving St NW, Washington, DC, 202-877-5039

Lefrak, Edward Arthur (35 mentions)
Indiana U, 1969 *Certification:* Thoracic Surgery
2921 Telestar Ct, Falls Church, VA, 703-280-5858

Massimiano, Paul Stephen (26 mentions)
Georgetown U, 1978 *Certification:* Thoracic Surgery
1625 N George Mason Dr, Arlington, VA, 703-280-5858
2921 Telestar Ct, Falls Church, VA, 703-280-5858

Cardiology

Akbari, Marjaneh (8 mentions)
Virginia Commonwealth U, 1984 *Certification:* Cardiovascular
   Disease, Internal Medicine, Interventional Cardiology
3020 Hamaker Ct #500, Fairfax, VA, 703-289-1207

Battle, William Enloe (4 mentions)
Emory U, 1964
Certification: Cardiovascular Disease, Internal Medicine
5530 Wisconsin Ave #700, Chevy Chase, MD, 301-654-6442

Benheim, Alan Eric (6 mentions)
Georgetown U, 1987 *Certification:* Pediatric Cardiology, Pediatrics
8316 Arlington Blvd #610, Fairfax, VA, 703-573-0504

Bigham, Harry (7 mentions)
Harvard U, 1982 *Certification:* Cardiovascular Disease,
   Internal Medicine, Interventional Cardiology
6410 Rockledge Dr #200, Bethesda, MD, 301-897-5301

Bodurian, Edward Nubar (17 mentions)
U of Maryland, 1978 *Certification:* Cardiovascular Disease,
   Internal Medicine, Interventional Cardiology
5530 Wisconsin Ave #515, Chevy Chase, MD, 301-656-4064

Bon Tempo, Carl P. (5 mentions)
Georgetown U, 1969 *Certification:* Cardiovascular Disease,
   Internal Medicine, Interventional Cardiology
8505 Arlington Blvd #200, Fairfax, VA, 703-698-8525

Bren, George B. (16 mentions)
Northwestern U, 1975
Certification: Cardiovascular Disease, Internal Medicine
8926 Woodyard Rd #601, Clinton, MD, 202-785-4966
2440 M St NW #314, Washington, DC, 202-785-4966
3600 Leonardtown Rd #103, Waldorf, MD, 301-932-5890

Brill, David M. (6 mentions)
Harvard U, 1980 *Certification:* Cardiovascular Disease,
   Internal Medicine, Interventional Cardiology
7901 Maple Ave, Takoma Park, MD, 301-891-7000

Dao, Tung (4 mentions)
Eastern Virginia Med Sch, 1997
Certification: Cardiovascular Disease, Internal Medicine
6410 Rockledge Dr #200, Bethesda, MD, 301-897-5301

Davenport, Nancy J. (6 mentions)
George Washington U, 1985 *Certification:* Cardiovascular
   Disease, Internal Medicine, Interventional Cardiology
3301 New Mexico Ave NW #202, Washington, DC, 202-686-9801
106 Irving St NW #116, Washington, DC, 202-686-9801

Deychak, Yuri (6 mentions)
Ohio State U, 1984
Certification: Cardiovascular Disease, Interventional Cardiology
6410 Rockledge Dr #200, Bethesda, MD, 301-897-5301

Di Bianco, Robert (5 mentions)
SUNY-Buffalo, 1972
Certification: Cardiovascular Disease, Internal Medicine
15215 Shady Grove Rd #306, Rockville, MD, 301-990-0040
7901 Maple Ave, Takoma Park, MD, 301-891-7000

Dwyer, Sean M. (11 mentions)
Georgetown U, 1976
Certification: Cardiovascular Disease, Internal Medicine
5454 Wisconsin Ave #925, Chevy Chase, MD, 301-656-9070

Esposito, Aldo Richard (4 mentions)
Georgetown U, 1980 *Certification:* Cardiovascular Disease,
   Internal Medicine, Interventional Cardiology
12011 Lee Jackson Hwy, Fairfax, VA, 703-383-5448

Fernicola, Daniel Jerome (4 mentions)
Georgetown U, 1988
Certification: Cardiovascular Disease, Internal Medicine
15215 Shady Grove Rd #306, Rockville, MD, 301-990-0040
7901 Maple Ave, Takoma Park, MD, 301-891-7000

Fisher, Gary Philip (9 mentions)
U of Maryland, 1970
Certification: Cardiovascular Disease, Internal Medicine
5530 Wisconsin Ave #700, Chevy Chase, MD, 301-656-3334

Galioto, Frank Martin, Jr. (7 mentions)
New York Med Coll, 1968
Certification: Pediatric Cardiology, Pediatrics
8318 Arlington Blvd #250, Fairfax, VA, 703-876-8410
9707 Medical Center Dr, Rockville, MD, 301-424-8484

Glick, Brian Neal (4 mentions)
Mount Sinai Sch of Med, 1986
Certification: Cardiovascular Disease, Internal Medicine
611 S Carlin Springs Rd #405, Arlington, VA, 703-671-2490

Goldberg, Daniel Joseph (4 mentions)
New York Med Coll, 1976
Certification: Cardiovascular Disease, Internal Medicine
15225 Shady Grove Rd #201, Rockville, MD, 301-670-3000
18109 Prince Philip Dr #125, Olney, MD, 301-634-4800

Goldberg, Samuel David (12 mentions)
U of Maryland, 1969
Certification: Cardiovascular Disease, Internal Medicine
6410 Rockledge Dr #200, Bethesda, MD, 301-897-5301

Golden, John Seth (15 mentions)
Robert W Johnson Med Sch, 1985 *Certification:* Cardiovascular
   Disease, Internal Medicine, Interventional Cardiology
12011 Lee Jackson Hwy, Fairfax, VA, 703-383-5488

Gravino, Frank N. (9 mentions)
Boston U, 1974
Certification: Cardiovascular Disease, Internal Medicine
10313 Georgia Ave #306, Silver Spring, MD, 301-681-9095

Griffen, Daniel L., III (5 mentions)
U of Iowa, 1982
Certification: Cardiovascular Disease, Internal Medicine
15225 Shady Grove Rd #201, Rockville, MD, 301-670-3000
7350 Van Dusen Rd #410, Laurel, MD, 301-924-0166

Itscoitz, Samuel Burt (6 mentions)
George Washington U, 1964
Certification: Cardiovascular Disease, Internal Medicine
10313 Georgia Ave #306, Silver Spring, MD, 301-681-9095

Katz, Richard Jeffrey (5 mentions)
New York U, 1972
Certification: Cardiovascular Disease, Internal Medicine
2150 Pennsylvania Ave NW #4-414, Washington, DC,
   202-741-2323

Kent, Kenneth Mitchell (11 mentions)
Emory U, 1965
110 Irving St NW #4B1, Washington, DC, 202-877-5975

Kiernan, Joseph Mortimer (10 mentions)
Virginia Commonwealth U, 1982 *Certification:* Cardiovascular
   Disease, Internal Medicine, Interventional Cardiology
8503 Arlington Blvd #120, Fairfax, VA, 703-573-3494

Lee, Benjamin Irving (6 mentions)
Georgetown U, 1977 *Certification:* Cardiovascular Disease,
   Internal Medicine, Interventional Cardiology
106 Irving St NW #2700, Washington, DC, 202-726-5484
2131 K St NW #800, Washington, DC, 202-822-9356

Lieberman, Eric Bruce (5 mentions)
Emory U, 1987
Certification: Cardiovascular Disease, Interventional Cardiology
1400 Forest Glen Rd #200, Silver Spring, MD, 301-681-5700

Lindgren, Keith Merritt (4 mentions)
Harvard U, 1963 *Certification:* Cardiovascular Disease,
   Internal Medicine, Interventional Cardiology
7901 Maple Ave, Takoma Park, MD, 301-891-7000

Magee, P. F. Adrian (7 mentions)
FMS-Ireland, 1981
Certification: Cardiovascular Disease, Internal Medicine
5514 Alma Ln #200, Springfield, VA, 703-813-1242

Martin, Gerard Robert (9 mentions)
SUNY-Upstate Med U, 1981
Certification: Pediatric Cardiology, Pediatrics
111 Michigan Ave NW #200, Washington, DC, 202-476-2020

Matthews, Robert (6 mentions)
U of Michigan, 1968
Certification: Cardiovascular Disease, Internal Medicine
3299 Woodburn Rd #200, Annandale, VA, 703-573-2045

McGrath, Francis John (12 mentions)
Georgetown U, 1975
Certification: Cardiovascular Disease, Internal Medicine
1625 N George Mason Dr #414, Arlington, VA, 703-524-7202

Miller, Lawrence Allan (6 mentions)
SUNY-Buffalo, 1976 *Certification:* Cardiovascular Disease,
Internal Medicine, Interventional Cardiology
4660 Kenmore Ave #1200, Alexandria, VA, 703-751-8111
8503 Arlington Blvd #120, Fairfax, VA, 703-573-3494

Milner, Mark Robert (4 mentions)
U of Rochester, 1981
Certification: Cardiovascular Disease, Internal Medicine
6410 Rockledge Dr #200, Bethesda, MD, 301-897-5301

Mousavi, Morteza (4 mentions)
FMS-Iran, 1968
Certification: Cardiovascular Disease, Internal Medicine
2296 Opitz Blvd #340, Woodbridge, VA, 703-878-0941

Nayak, Pradeep Ramnath (7 mentions)
U of Virginia, 1986
Certification: Cardiovascular Disease, Internal Medicine
44035 Riverside Pkwy #150, Leesburg, VA, 703-858-9538
1860 Town Center Dr #120, Reston, VA, 703-437-5977
3700 Joseph Siewick Dr #102, Fairfax, VA, 703-648-3266
130 Park St SE #100, Vienna, VA, 703-281-1265

O'Brien, John T. (14 mentions)
Georgetown U, 1977 *Certification:* Cardiovascular Disease,
Internal Medicine, Interventional Cardiology
3299 Woodburn Rd #200, Annandale, VA, 703-573-0740

O'Brien, Paul John (7 mentions)
U of Virginia, 1986
Certification: Cardiovascular Disease, Internal Medicine
4660 Kenmore Ave #800, Alexandria, VA, 703-751-6668

Parente, Antonio Rocco (16 mentions)
Georgetown U, 1984
Certification: Cardiovascular Disease, Internal Medicine
1625 N George Mason Dr #414, Arlington, VA, 703-524-7202

Pichard, Augusto D. (5 mentions)
FMS-Chile, 1969 *Certification:* Cardiovascular Disease,
Internal Medicine, Interventional Cardiology
110 Irving St NW #4B1, Washington, DC, 202-877-5975

Reiner, Jonathan Samuel (5 mentions)
Georgetown U, 1986 *Certification:* Cardiovascular Disease,
Internal Medicine, Interventional Cardiology
2150 Pennsylvania Ave NW #414, Washington, DC, 202-741-3333

Rogan, Kevin Michael (5 mentions)
Tufts U, 1981 *Certification:* Cardiovascular Disease,
Internal Medicine, Interventional Cardiology
3299 Woodburn Rd #200, Annandale, VA, 703-698-6255

Rosenberg, Joel (14 mentions)
Tulane U, 1973 *Certification:* Cardiovascular Disease,
Internal Medicine, Interventional Cardiology
2131 K St NW #800, Washington, DC, 202-822-9356

Rosenblatt, Arnold J. (4 mentions)
George Washington U, 1975
Certification: Cardiovascular Disease, Internal Medicine
8101 Hinson Farm Rd #408, Alexandria, VA, 703-780-9014
6355 Walker Ln #406, Alexandria, VA, 703-313-0943
8988 Lorton Station Blvd #200, Lorton, VA, 703-339-5381

Rosenfeld, Stephen Philip (6 mentions)
U of Cincinnati, 1974
Certification: Cardiovascular Disease, Internal Medicine
4660 Kenmore Ave #1200, Alexandria, VA, 703-751-8111

Ross, Elizabeth Meehan (8 mentions)
U of Maryland, 1978
Certification: Cardiovascular Disease, Internal Medicine
2021 K St NW #315, Washington, DC, 202-775-0955

Rubin, Lawrence Richard (4 mentions)
U of Virginia, 1991 *Certification:* Cardiovascular Disease
4660 Kenmore Ave #1200, Alexandria, VA, 703-751-8111

Rubin, Richard Elliott (12 mentions)
Johns Hopkins U, 1977
Certification: Cardiovascular Disease, Internal Medicine
5530 Wisconsin Ave #700, Chevy Chase, MD, 301-654-6442

Sabia, Peter James (5 mentions)
U of Maryland, 1984 *Certification:* Cardiovascular Disease,
Internal Medicine, Interventional Cardiology
1400 Forest Glen Rd, Silver Spring, MD, 301-681-5700

Satler, Lowell Franklin (6 mentions)
Albany Med Coll, 1978 *Certification:* Cardiovascular
Disease, Internal Medicine, Interventional Cardiology
110 Irving St NW #4B1, Washington, DC, 202-877-5975

Schneider, Alan Ira (11 mentions)
U of Maryland, 1989 *Certification:* Cardiovascular Disease,
Clinical Cardiac Electrophysiology, Internal Medicine
10313 Georgia Ave #306, Silver Spring, MD, 301-681-9095

Segal, Herman Benjamin (8 mentions)
Tufts U, 1965
Certification: Cardiovascular Disease, Internal Medicine
10313 Georgia Ave #306, Silver Spring, MD, 301-681-9095

Seides, Stuart Floyd (7 mentions)
Cornell U, 1970 *Certification:* Cardiovascular Disease,
Internal Medicine, Interventional Cardiology
106 Irving St NW #2700, Washington, DC, 202-723-5524

Shapiro, Stephen Robert (7 mentions)
New York U, 1967 *Certification:* Pediatric Cardiology, Pediatrics
8318 Arlington Blvd #250, Fairfax, VA, 703-876-8410
9707 Medical Center Dr #100, Rockville, MD, 301-424-8484

Sherber, Harvey S. (5 mentions)
Tufts U, 1969 *Certification:* Cardiovascular Disease,
Internal Medicine, Interventional Cardiology
8505 Arlington Blvd #200, Fairfax, VA, 703-698-8525

Sofat, Sameer (7 mentions)
FMS-India, 1990 *Certification:* Cardiovascular Disease
10110 Molecular Dr #200, Rockville, MD, 301-610-4000

Sofat, Shubir (4 mentions)
FMS-India, 1992
Certification: Cardiovascular Disease, Internal Medicine
10110 Molecular Dr #200, Rockville, MD, 301-610-4000

Stevenson, Roger, Jr. (7 mentions)
U of Texas-San Antonio, 1972
Certification: Cardiovascular Disease, Internal Medicine
6410 Rockledge Dr #200, Bethesda, MD, 301-897-5301

Summers, Anne Elizabeth (7 mentions)
Med Coll of Pennsylvania, 1980
Certification: Cardiovascular Disease, Internal Medicine
8316 Arlington Blvd #500, Fairfax, VA, 703-641-9161
1830 Town Center Dr #405, Reston, VA, 703-481-9191

Talesnick, Barry Steven (6 mentions)
New York Med Coll, 1980
Certification: Cardiovascular Disease, Internal Medicine
5454 Wisconsin Ave #925, Chevy Chase, MD, 301-656-9070

Watkins, Anthony Evans (6 mentions)
Howard U, 1966 *Certification:* Cardiovascular Disease,
Internal Medicine, Nuclear Medicine
106 Irving St NW #3200N, Washington, DC, 202-726-7474

Weinstein, Richard Ira (4 mentions)
U of Maryland, 1989 *Certification:* Cardiovascular Disease
18109 Prince Philip Dr #125, Olney, MD, 301-634-4800
15225 Shady Grove Rd #201, Rockville, MD, 301-670-3000

Yazdani, Shawn (4 mentions)
New York U, 1991
810 Ashton Ave #200, Manassas, VA, 703-335-8750
559 Frost Ave #102, Warrenton, VA, 540-341-7530

Zinsmeister, Bruce Walter (6 mentions)
SUNY-Downstate Med Coll, 1975 *Certification:* Cardiovascular
Disease, Internal Medicine, Interventional Cardiology
8830 Cameron Ct #601, Silver Spring, MD, 301-587-7040
106 Irving St NW #404, Washington, DC, 202-291-3270

Dermatology

Bajoghli, Amir Ali (6 mentions)
Virginia Commonwealth U, 1994 *Certification:* Dermatology
2200 Opitz Blvd #245, Woodbridge, VA, 703-492-4140
8130 Boone Blvd #340, Vienna, VA, 703-893-1114

Barnett, Jay Mark (17 mentions)
Boston U, 1987 *Certification:* Dermatology
2401 Research Blvd, Rockville, MD, 301-990-6565
5411 W Cedar Ln #102A, Bethesda, MD, 301-530-3396
18109 Prince Philip Dr #370, Olney, MD, 301-774-0613
200 Harry S Truman Pkwy #270, Annapolis, MD, 410-897-0272

Berberian, Brenda Jean (22 mentions)
Georgetown U, 1982 *Certification:* Dermatology
5530 Wisconsin Ave #1443, Chevy Chase, MD, 301-656-7660

Berk, Sanders Harris (8 mentions)
U of Maryland, 1969 *Certification:* Dermatology
19221 Montgomery Village Ave #C12, Montgomery Village, MD,
301-840-2266

Bruckner, Nancy E. V. (6 mentions)
George Washington U, 1976 *Certification:* Dermatology
6731 Whittier Ave #B, McLean, VA, 703-790-5850

Castiello, Richard Joseph (7 mentions)
Cornell U, 1967 *Certification:* Dermatology
5530 Wisconsin Ave #1418, Chevy Chase, MD, 301-986-1880

Fuchs, Glenn H. (10 mentions)
New York U, 1977 *Certification:* Dermatology
611 S Carlin Springs Rd #502, Arlington, VA, 703-578-1770
2021 K St NW #508, Washington, DC, 202-223-6830

Giannelli, Vincenzo (7 mentions)
FMS-Italy, 1985 *Certification:* Dermatology
2440 M St NW #313, Washington, DC, 202-775-1792
110 Irving St NW #2B-44, Washington, DC, 202-877-6227

Giblin, Walter John (10 mentions)
Georgetown U, 1984 *Certification:* Dermatology
15225 Shady Grove Rd #303, Rockville, MD, 301-216-2980

Hartley, Alvanus Howland (6 mentions)
U of Vermont, 1977 *Certification:* Dermatology, Pediatrics
55 Stokely Rd #F, Prince Frederick, MD, 410-535-5855

Henry, Julie P. (10 mentions)
Georgetown U, 1985 *Certification:* Dermatology
9004 Fern Park Dr, Burke, VA, 703-425-5300

Isaac, Melda Ann (7 mentions)
Pennsylvania State U, 1991 *Certification:* Dermatology
2440 M St NW #703, Washington, DC, 202-393-7546

Isaacson, Dale Hilton (12 mentions)
George Washington U, 1977 *Certification:* Dermatology
1828 L St NW #850, Washington, DC, 202-822-9591

Jaffe, Mark Jonathan (24 mentions)
Georgetown U, 1979 *Certification:* Dermatology
6410 Rockledge Dr #402, Bethesda, MD, 301-530-4800

Katz, Robert (8 mentions)
George Washington U, 1961
Certification: Dermatology, Dermatopathology
11510 Old Georgetown Rd, Rockville, MD, 301-881-4124

Kazakis, Alexandra Mary (6 mentions)
U of Virginia, 1983 *Certification:* Dermatology
3022 Williams Dr #101, Fairfax, VA, 703-573-5252

Kim, Ho Jin (9 mentions)
Virginia Commonwealth U, 1994
Certification: Pediatric Dermatology
21165 Whitfield Pl #106, Sterling, VA, 703-433-9460
8371 Greensboro Dr #A, McLean, VA, 703-893-3710

Lindgren, Ann M. (12 mentions)
Harvard U, 1989 *Certification:* Dermatology
6410 Rockledge Dr #402, Bethesda, MD, 301-530-4800

Lockshin, Norman Ansel (23 mentions)
Ohio State U, 1967 *Certification:* Dermatology
10313 Georgia Ave #309, Silver Spring, MD, 301-681-7000

McNeely, Marsha Carol (8 mentions)
U of Texas-Galveston, 1982
Certification: Dermatological Immunology/Diagnostic and
   Laboratory Immunology, Dermatology
1120 19th St NW #250, Washington, DC, 202-955-6995

Norvell, Samuel Strudwick, Jr. (15 mentions)
U of Alabama, 1975 *Certification:* Dermatology
9707 Medical Center Dr #130, Rockville, MD, 301-738-0047

O'Neill, John Francis, Jr. (17 mentions)
Georgetown U, 1982 *Certification:* Dermatology
6410 Rockledge Dr #402, Bethesda, MD, 301-530-4800

O'Neill, Margaret Stevens (10 mentions)
Yale U, 1991 *Certification:* Dermatology
5454 Wisconsin Ave #1225, Chevy Chase, MD, 301-951-7905

Peck, Gary Lawrence (6 mentions)
U of Michigan, 1962 *Certification:* Dermatology
4800 Montgomery Ln #M50, Bethesda, MD, 301-652-3244
110 Irving St NW #C2151, Washington, DC, 202-877-2551

Prussick, Ronald (8 mentions)
FMS-Canada, 1987 *Certification:* Dermatology
7930 Old Georgetown Rd, Bethesda, MD, 301-657-3622
198 Thomas Johnson Dr #5, Frederick, MD, 301-694-9500

Rivera, Michelle Antonia (12 mentions)
Cornell U, 1980 *Certification:* Dermatology
1635 N George Mason Dr #400, Arlington, VA, 703-524-7206

Sawchuk, William Samuel (14 mentions)
U of Michigan, 1981 *Certification:* Dermatology
8320 Old Courthouse Rd #303, Vienna, VA, 703-532-7211

Silverman, Robert Alan (29 mentions)
U of Virginia, 1977
Certification: Dermatology, Pediatric Dermatology, Pediatrics
8316 Arlington Blvd #524, Fairfax, VA, 703-641-0083

Stolar, Edward Harvey (6 mentions)
George Washington U, 1981 *Certification:* Dermatology
1712 I St NW #712, Washington, DC, 202-659-2223

Emergency Medicine

Cope, Gregory Walter (7 mentions)
George Washington U, 1994 *Certification:* Emergency Medicine
4940 Eastern Ave, Baltimore, MD, 410-550-0359

Delvecchio, James Anthony (6 mentions)
Georgetown U, 1989 *Certification:* Emergency Medicine
1500 Forest Glen Rd, Silver Spring, MD, 301-754-7503

Desimone, John V. (7 mentions)
Georgetown U, 1980 *Certification:* Emergency Medicine
3800 Reservoir Rd NW CCC Bldg Fl Ground, Washington, DC,
   202-444-2119

Dubin, Jeffrey Scott (6 mentions)
U of Maryland, 1992 *Certification:* Emergency Medicine
110 Irving St NW, Washington, DC, 202-877-2048

Falcone, Angelo Leonard (6 mentions)
Georgetown U, 1990 *Certification:* Emergency Medicine,
   Pediatric Emergency Medicine
9901 Medical Center Dr, Rockville, MD, 240-826-7550

Fitzgerald, Michael F. B. (9 mentions)
Georgetown U, 1981 *Certification:* Emergency Medicine
5255 Loughboro Rd NW, Washington, DC, 202-537-4080

Leonard, Barton Walker (6 mentions)
George Washington U, 1995 *Certification:* Emergency Medicine
8600 Old Georgetown Rd, Bethesda, MD, 301-896-3880

Lisse, Darren Stuart (9 mentions)
Georgetown U, 1980 *Certification:* Emergency Medicine
20010 Century Blvd #200, Germantown, MD, 301-921-7900

Scott, James Lee (7 mentions)
U of Arizona, 1983 *Certification:* Emergency Medicine
2150 Pennsylvania Ave NW, Washington, DC, 202-741-2911

Endocrinology

Burman, Kenneth Dale (34 mentions)
U of Missouri, 1970
Certification: Endocrinology and Metabolism, Internal Medicine
110 Irving St NW #1A50B, Washington, DC, 202-877-2835

Dempsey, Michael Anthony (31 mentions)
Harvard U, 1983
Certification: Endocrinology and Metabolism, Internal Medicine
3200 Tower Oaks Blvd #250, Rockville, MD, 301-770-7373

Link, Kathleen Mary (12 mentions)
Southern Illinois U, 1976
Certification: Pediatric Endocrinology, Pediatrics
3020 Hamaker Ct #502, Fairfax, VA, 703-849-8440
3650 Joseph Siewick Dr #305, Fairfax, VA, 703-648-1831

Lipson, Ace (44 mentions)
Washington U, 1973
Certification: Endocrinology and Metabolism, Internal Medicine
1120 19th St NW #200, Washington, DC, 202-296-3443

Liu, Linda (13 mentions)
Brown U, 1980
Certification: Endocrinology and Metabolism, Internal Medicine
6001 Montrose Rd #211, Rockville, MD, 301-468-1451

Petrick, Patricia Anne (13 mentions)
U of Pittsburgh, 1978
Certification: Endocrinology and Metabolism, Internal Medicine
6001 Montrose Rd #211, Rockville, MD, 301-468-1451

Ramey, James N. (15 mentions)
Columbia U, 1968
Certification: Endocrinology and Metabolism, Internal Medicine
1120 19th St NW #200, Washington, DC, 202-296-0670

Rodbard, Helena (16 mentions)
FMS-Brazil, 1972
Certification: Endocrinology and Metabolism, Internal Medicine
3200 Tower Oaks Blvd #250, Rockville, MD, 301-770-7373

Rogacz, Suzanne (25 mentions)
U of North Carolina, 1980
Certification: Endocrinology and Metabolism, Internal Medicine
3020 Hamaker Ct #502, Fairfax, VA, 703-648-1831
3650 Joseph Siewick Dr #305, Fairfax, VA, 703-648-1831

Ross, Peter Stephen (26 mentions)
Harvard U, 1973
Certification: Endocrinology and Metabolism, Internal Medicine
3020 Hamaker Ct #502, Fairfax, VA, 703-849-8440
3650 Joseph Siewick Dr #305, Fairfax, VA, 703-648-1831

Santangelo, Robert Paul (12 mentions)
Albert Einstein Coll of Med, 1965 *Certification:* Internal Medicine
1635 N George Mason Dr #350, Arlington, VA, 703-528-6616

Sklar, Mark Mendel (9 mentions)
Boston U, 1984
Certification: Endocrinology and Metabolism, Internal Medicine
3 Washington Cir NW #303, Washington, DC, 202-887-4769

Wartofsky, Leonard (11 mentions)
George Washington U, 1964
Certification: Endocrinology and Metabolism, Internal Medicine
110 Irving St NW #2A62, Washington, DC, 202-877-3109

Family Practice *(see note on page 9)*

Bartram, Scott Fox (4 mentions)
Northwestern U, 1979 *Certification:* Family Medicine
407 N Washington St #104, Falls Church, VA, 703-237-7707

Bowles, Richard B., Jr. (5 mentions)
U of Virginia, 1970 *Certification:* Family Medicine
13890 Braddock Rd #201, Centreville, VA, 703-631-0331

Byer, Barry (6 mentions)
U of Miami, 1969
131 E Broad St #102, Falls Church, VA, 703-532-5436

Cosgrove, Lauren Elise (8 mentions)
U of North Carolina, 1980 *Certification:* Family Medicine
1396 Piccard Dr, Rockville, MD, 301-548-5700

Edgecombe, Glenn Robert (3 mentions)
Med Coll of Ohio, 1977 *Certification:* Family Medicine
7700 Old Branch Ave #B201, Clinton, MD, 301-868-0150

Friedland, Melissa Beth (3 mentions)
Howard U, 1984 *Certification:* Family Medicine
2415 Musgrove Rd #105, Silver Spring, MD, 301-989-0193

Gil, Kevin Michael (10 mentions)
George Washington U, 1980
Certification: Family Medicine, Geriatric Medicine
14816 Physicians Ln #253, Rockville, MD, 301-610-6313

Ginsberg, Robert Jay (3 mentions)
U of Maryland, 1980 *Certification:* Family Medicine
2415 Musgrove Rd #209, Silver Spring, MD, 301-989-8892

Horne, Allen Bernard (6 mentions)
Virginia Commonwealth U, 1972 *Certification:* Family Medicine
6715 Whittier Ave #100, McLean, VA, 703-356-5700

Howard, Monica Jean (3 mentions)
Howard U, 1995 *Certification:* Family Medicine
302 King Farm Blvd #130, Rockville, MD, 301-947-6816
20528 Boland Farm Rd #104, Germantown, MD, 301-972-0400

Hunter, Bradley J. (5 mentions)
Western U, 1999 *Certification:* Family Medicine
10400 Connecticut Ave #606, Kensington, MD, 301-942-2212

Jones, Samuel Moseley (10 mentions)
Virginia Commonwealth U, 1979 *Certification:* Family Medicine
3650 Joseph Siewick Dr #400, Fairfax, VA, 703-391-2020

Katon, Richard Norman (4 mentions)
SUNY-Downstate Med Coll, 1967
20528 Boland Farm Rd #104, Germantown, MD, 301-972-0400
302 King Farm Blvd #130, Rockville, MD, 301-972-0400

Keyes, Janice Lynn (5 mentions)
Virginia Commonwealth U, 1983 *Certification:* Family Medicine
13890 Braddock Rd #201, Centreville, VA, 703-631-0331

Kitchen, Robert Henry, Jr. (3 mentions)
Tulane U, 1976 *Certification:* Family Medicine
6501 Loisdale Ct, Springfield, VA, 703-922-1507

Lynch, G. Michael (3 mentions)
Jefferson Med Coll, 1978 *Certification:* Family Medicine
3914 Centreville Rd #250, Chantilly, VA, 703-620-5601

Mendel, Peter Allan (6 mentions)
U of Miami, 1981 *Certification:* Family Medicine
3401 Commission Ct #201, Lake Ridge, VA, 703-490-6265

Nahin, Barry Robert (8 mentions)
George Washington U, 1990 *Certification:* Family Medicine
20528 Boland Farm Rd #104, Germantown, MD, 301-972-0400

Overton, Eugene Willis (3 mentions)
U of Virginia, 1971 *Certification:* Family Medicine
4001 Fair Ridge Dr #101, Fairfax, VA, 703-385-6789

Rajvanshi, Amit Kumar (3 mentions)
FMS-India, 1984 *Certification:* Family Medicine
121 Congressional Ln #409, Rockville, MD, 301-881-0230
9801 Georgia Ave #118, Silver Spring, MD, 301-593-2440

Shmorhun, Eugene Andrew (5 mentions)
U of Maryland, 1982 *Certification:* Family Medicine
3027 Javier Rd, Fairfax, VA, 703-573-6400

Umosella, Charles Anthony (6 mentions)
Georgetown U, 1982 *Certification:* Family Medicine
7625 Wisconsin Ave #101, Bethesda, MD, 301-951-0420
6188 Oxen Hill Rd #704, Oxon Hill, MD, 301-839-2790

Unger, Christopher Pelham (3 mentions)
U of Pennsylvania, 1969
Certification: Family Medicine, Internal Medicine
8218 Wisconsin Ave #208, Bethesda, MD, 301-986-9495

Wilson, Howard E. (4 mentions)
Howard U, 1979 *Certification:* Family Medicine
2041 Georgia Ave NW #1700-C, Washington, DC, 202-865-3200

Winchell, Cheryl (3 mentions)
Case Western Reserve U, 1970 *Certification:* Family Medicine
19241 Montgomery Village Ave #E10, Montgomery Village, MD,
301-926-4222

Wise, Andrew Edmund (6 mentions)
Duke U, 1986 *Certification:* Family Medicine, Sports Medicine
6160 Fuller Ct, Alexandria, VA, 703-922-0203

Wohler, Brett Alan (4 mentions)
U of Virginia, 1986 *Certification:* Family Medicine
6160 Fuller Ct, Alexandria, VA, 703-922-0234

Gastroenterology

Albert, Michael B. (11 mentions)
Johns Hopkins U, 1982
Certification: Gastroenterology, Internal Medicine
2141 K St NW #208, Washington, DC, 202-223-5544

Axelrad, Andrew Marc (6 mentions)
New York Med Coll, 1989 *Certification:* Gastroenterology
1800 Town Center Dr #220, Reston, VA, 703-435-3366

Bakhshi, Ajay (6 mentions)
FMS-India, 1974 *Certification:* Allergy & Immunology,
Gastroenterology, Internal Medicine, Rheumatology
9406 Old Georgetown Rd, Bethesda, MD, 301-530-5142

Bashir, R. Martin (8 mentions)
George Washington U, 1989
106 Irving St NW #205, Washington, DC, 202-829-0170
5530 Wisconsin Ave #1640, Chevy Chase, MD, 301-718-0600

Blosser, R. Allen (7 mentions)
Eastern Virginia Med Sch, 1988 *Certification:* Gastroenterology
360 Maple Ave W #E, Vienna, VA, 703-281-1023

Christopher, Nicholas L. (8 mentions)
U of Michigan, 1963
Certification: Gastroenterology, Internal Medicine
3301 New Mexico Ave NW #232, Washington, DC, 202-966-3376

Duffy, Lynn Frances (18 mentions)
Georgetown U, 1979
Certification: Pediatric Gastroenterology, Pediatrics
3020 Hamaker Ct #202, Fairfax, VA, 571-226-5600
15020 Shady Grove Rd #315, Rockville, MD, 301-340-1341

Finkel, Robert Gregg (8 mentions)
U of Pittsburgh, 1989 *Certification:* Gastroenterology
10801 Lockwood Dr #200, Silver Spring, MD, 301-593-2002
3410 Olandwood Ct #206, Olney, MD, 301-570-1326
15005 Shady Grove Rd #310, Rockville, MD, 301-279-2255
20528 Boland Farm Rd #201, Germantown, MD, 301-528-8200

Garone, Michael Alan (8 mentions)
Albany Med Coll, 1980
Certification: Gastroenterology, Internal Medicine
3700 Joseph Siewick Dr #308, Fairfax, VA, 703-716-8700
3022 Williams Dr #301, Fairfax, VA, 703-698-8960

Gelfand, Richard Lowell (13 mentions)
Georgetown U, 1979
Certification: Gastroenterology, Internal Medicine
10215 Fernwood Rd #404, Bethesda, MD, 301-493-5210
5550 Friendship Blvd #T-90, Chevy Chase, MD, 301-654-2521

Gloger, Mark Steven (6 mentions)
Georgetown U, 1988
Certification: Gastroenterology, Internal Medicine
9711 Medical Center Dr #308, Rockville, MD, 301-251-1244

Gold, Michael Stephen (8 mentions)
SUNY-Downstate Med Coll, 1963
Certification: Gastroenterology, Internal Medicine
110 Irving St NW #3A3A7, Washington, DC, 202-877-7108

Gupta, Pradeep Kumar (14 mentions)
Howard U, 1988 *Certification:* Gastroenterology
1715 N George Mason Dr #204, Arlington, VA, 703-522-7476
8301 Arlington Blvd #405, Fairfax, VA, 703-560-6106

Harrington, Samuel Parker (10 mentions)
U of Wisconsin, 1977
Certification: Gastroenterology, Internal Medicine
3301 New Mexico Ave NW #232, Washington, DC, 202-966-3376

Herman, Gabriel Bryan (16 mentions)
Georgetown U, 1973
Certification: Gastroenterology, Internal Medicine
8301 Arlington Blvd #405, Fairfax, VA, 703-560-6106
1715 N George Mason Dr #204, Arlington, VA, 703-522-7476

Immel, Walter William (6 mentions)
Dartmouth Coll, 1981
Certification: Gastroenterology, Internal Medicine
5510 Alma Ln, Springfield, VA, 703-642-5990

Kerzner, Benny (8 mentions)
FMS-South Africa, 1967
Certification: Pediatric Gastroenterology, Pediatrics
111 Michigan Ave NW #100, Washington, DC, 202-476-3031

Korman, Louis Yves (16 mentions)
SUNY-Upstate Med U, 1975
Certification: Gastroenterology, Internal Medicine
2021 K St NW #T110, Washington, DC, 202-296-3449
5530 Wisconsin Ave #820, Chevy Chase, MD, 301-654-2521

Laessig, Susan Lamme (7 mentions)
U of Maryland, 1980
Certification: Gastroenterology, Internal Medicine
106 Irving St NW #205, Washington, DC, 202-829-0170
5530 Wisconsin Ave #1640, Chevy Chase, MD, 301-718-0600

Leibowitz, Ian Howard (10 mentions)
FMS-Grenada, 1982 *Certification:* Internal Medicine,
Pediatric Gastroenterology, Pediatrics
3020 Hamaker Ct #202, Fairfax, VA, 571-226-5600
100 Elden St #12, Herndon, VA, 571-226-5600
8650 Sudley Rd #410, Manassas, VA, 571-226-5600

Levy, Arnold Glenn (7 mentions)
George Washington U, 1971
Certification: Gastroenterology, Internal Medicine
10801 Lockwood Dr #200, Silver Spring, MD, 301-593-2002
3410 Olandwood Ct #206, Olney, MD, 301-593-2002

Malhotra, Suresh Kumar (6 mentions)
FMS-India, 1980
Certification: Gastroenterology, Internal Medicine
4660 Kenmore Ave #810, Alexandria, VA, 703-823-0333

Marion, Lester Irwin (8 mentions)
Tulane U, 1972 *Certification:* Gastroenterology, Internal Medicine
5530 Wisconsin Ave #1640, Chevy Chase, MD, 301-718-0600
106 Irving St NW #205, Washington, DC, 202-829-0170

Morton, Robert Edmund (10 mentions)
Duke U, 1968 *Certification:* Gastroenterology, Internal Medicine
1715 N George Mason Dr #204, Arlington, VA, 703-522-7476
8301 Arlington Blvd #405, Fairfax, VA, 703-560-6106

O'Kieffe, Donald Ary, Jr. (14 mentions)
Yale U, 1964 *Certification:* Gastroenterology, Internal Medicine
2021 K St NW #T110, Washington, DC, 202-296-3449
5530 Wisconsin Ave #820, Chevy Chase, MD, 301-654-2521

Pollack, Eric Andrew (6 mentions)
Cornell U, 1992
Certification: Gastroenterology, Internal Medicine
10215 Fernwood Rd #404, Bethesda, MD, 301-493-5210

Procaccino, Frank (6 mentions)
George Washington U, 1987 *Certification:* Gastroenterology
4660 Kenmore Ave #200, Alexandria, VA, 703-823-3750

Prosky, Martin Gary (7 mentions)
SUNY-Downstate Med Coll, 1985
Certification: Gastroenterology, Internal Medicine
3301 Woodburn Rd #107, Annandale, VA, 703-876-0437
1635 N George Mason Dr #485, Arlington, VA, 703-876-0437

Ranard, Richard Craig (13 mentions)
Georgetown U, 1982
Certification: Gastroenterology, Internal Medicine
3020 Hamaker Ct #102, Fairfax, VA, 703-560-3510

Rubin, Barry Michael (7 mentions)
George Washington U, 1988 *Certification:* Gastroenterology
20528 Boland Farm Rd, Germantown, MD, 301-593-2002
15005 Shady Grove Rd #310, Rockville, MD, 301-593-2002

Schindler, Michael Scott (11 mentions)
U of Massachusetts, 1982
Certification: Gastroenterology, Internal Medicine
10801 Lockwood Dr #200, Silver Spring, MD, 301-593-2002
3410 Olandwood Ct #206, Olney, MD, 301-570-1326
20528 Boland Farm Rd #201, Germantown, MD, 301-528-8200

Schulman, Alan Neil (7 mentions)
Harvard U, 1972
Certification: Gastroenterology, Internal Medicine
14955 Shady Grove Rd #150, Rockville, MD, 301-340-3252

Schwartz, Michael Jay (7 mentions)
U of Rochester, 1977
Certification: Gastroenterology, Internal Medicine
2021 K St NW #T110, Washington, DC, 202-296-3449
5530 Wisconsin Ave #820, Chevy Chase, MD, 301-654-2521

Shenk, Ian Marshall (8 mentions)
Johns Hopkins U, 1965
Certification: Gastroenterology, Internal Medicine
6501 Loisdale Ct, Springfield, VA, 703-922-1313

Shoham, Myron Alan (8 mentions)
Boston U, 1971
Certification: Gastroenterology, Internal Medicine
360 Maple Ave W #E, Vienna, VA, 703-281-1023

Weinstein, Michael Lee (7 mentions)
Northwestern U, 1980
Certification: Gastroenterology, Internal Medicine
2021 K St NW #T110, Washington, DC, 202-296-8981
5530 Wisconsin Ave #820, Chevy Chase, MD, 301-654-2521

Wolke, Anita Marsha (7 mentions)
Med U of South Carolina, 1978
Certification: Gastroenterology, Internal Medicine
1800 Town Center Dr #220, Reston, VA, 703-435-3366

General Surgery

Ahmed, Robert Frank (15 mentions)
Georgetown U, 1987 *Certification:* Surgery
4001 Fair Ridge Dr #304, Fairfax, VA, 703-359-8640
3301 Woodburn Rd #306, Annandale, VA, 703-359-8640

Alley, Katherine Louise (5 mentions)
George Washington U, 1974
6410 Rockledge Dr #504, Bethesda, MD, 301-493-8500

Askew, Allyson Ann (14 mentions)
Tulane U, 1982 *Certification:* Pediatric Surgery, Surgery
3301 Woodburn Rd #205, Annandale, VA, 703-560-2236

Boyle, Lisa Marie (5 mentions)
Georgetown U, 1982 *Certification:* Surgery
110 Irving St NW #G247, Washington, DC, 202-877-5611

Brody, Frederick (6 mentions)
Certification: Surgery
2150 Pennsylvania Ave NW, Washington, DC, 202-741-2587

Butler, John Davis, Jr. (8 mentions)
Johns Hopkins U, 1986 *Certification:* Surgery
106 Irving St NW, Washington, DC, 202-877-7000

Ceppa, Pedro Ricardo (5 mentions)
FMS-Argentina, 1969 *Certification:* Surgery
14300 Gallant Fox Ln #224, Bowie, MD, 301-262-7740
1140 Varnum St NW #104, Washington, DC, 202-832-8320

Colliver, Craig Paul (6 mentions)
U of Maryland, 1993 *Certification:* Surgery
9707 Medical Center Dr #200, Rockville, MD, 301-251-4128

Dekker, Jan J. (6 mentions)
FMS-Netherlands, 1971 *Certification:* Surgery
8316 Arlington Blvd #410, Fairfax, VA, 703-573-6985

Finelli, Frederick (13 mentions)
SUNY-Buffalo, 1979 *Certification:* Surgery
106 Irving St NW #3400, Washington, DC, 202-877-7788

Gillian, George Kevin (5 mentions)
U of Missouri, 1992 *Certification:* Surgery
8988 Lorton Station Blvd #202, Lorton, VA, 703-313-8808

Goicochea-Mancilla, J. R. (6 mentions)
FMS-Peru, 1975 *Certification:* Surgery
8218 Wisconsin Ave #212, Bethesda, MD, 301-657-9445
19241 Montgomery Village Ave #23, Gaithersburg, MD,
   301-977-7923

Guzzetta, Philip Conte (5 mentions)
Med Coll of Wisconsin, 1972
Certification: Pediatric Surgery, Surgery
111 Michigan Ave NW #W4200, Washington, DC, 202-476-2151
9850 Key West Ave 2nd Fl, Rockville, MD, 301-424-1755

Hafner, Gordon Harold (10 mentions)
George Washington U, 1983 *Certification:* Surgery
3301 Woodlawn Rd #306, Annandale, VA, 703-359-8640
4001 Fair Ridge Dr #304, Fairfax, VA, 703-359-8640

Hanowell, Ernest Dalton (24 mentions)
George Washington U, 1973 *Certification:* Surgery
6410 Rockledge Dr #403, Bethesda, MD, 301-897-5450

Knoll, Stanley Marc (15 mentions)
Rosalind Franklin U, 1968 *Certification:* Surgery
2440 M St NW #706, Washington, DC, 202-331-1234

Kodama, Teruaki (10 mentions)
Creighton U, 1989 *Certification:* Surgery
8316 Arlington Blvd #410, Fairfax, VA, 703-573-6985

Kreutz, Berny J. (20 mentions)
FMS-Colombia, 1962 *Certification:* Surgery
2420 Rockledge Dr #2500, Bethesda, MD, 301-897-8650

Lin, Paul Pohyen (9 mentions)
Harvard U, 1987 *Certification:* Surgery
2150 Pennsylvania Ave NW, Washington, DC, 202-741-3203

Marmon, Louis Michael (7 mentions)
Temple U, 1981
Certification: Pediatric Surgery, Surgery, Surgical Critical Care
9715 Medical Center Dr #300, Rockville, MD, 301-762-2424

Martin, Mami (6 mentions)
Georgetown U, 1996 *Certification:* Surgery
1715 N George Mason Dr #403, Arlington, VA, 703-528-0768
1830 Town Center Dr #309, Reston, VA, 703-481-8282

Mason, Kenneth Grant (14 mentions)
Howard U, 1977 *Certification:* Surgery
1715 N George Mason Dr #403, Arlington, VA, 703-528-0768
1830 Town Center Dr #309, Reston, VA, 703-481-8282

Moynihan, John Joseph, Jr. (31 mentions)
Georgetown U, 1980 *Certification:* Surgery
3301 Woodburn Rd #306, Annandale, VA, 703-359-8640
4001 Fair Ridge Dr #304, Fairfax, VA, 703-359-8640

Newman, Kurt Douglas (6 mentions)
Duke U, 1978 *Certification:* Pediatric Surgery, Surgery
111 Michigan Ave NW, Washington, DC, 202-476-2151
4900 Massachusetts Ave NW #320, Washington, DC,
   202-895-3860

Omeish, Esam Salem (5 mentions)
Georgetown U, 1993 *Certification:* Surgery
2849 Duke St #14, Alexandria, VA, 703-780-8902

Oristian, Eric Alfred (24 mentions)
Georgetown U, 1978 *Certification:* Surgery
2730 University Blvd W #216, Wheaton, MD, 301-942-4080

Palmer, Michael Lee (6 mentions)
U of Kansas, 1982 *Certification:* Surgery
3301 New Mexico Ave NW #206, Washington, DC, 202-895-1440

Paul, Martin G. (34 mentions)
Northwestern U, 1983 *Certification:* Surgery
3301 New Mexico Ave NW #206, Washington, DC, 202-895-1440

Petrucci, Peter Edward (16 mentions)
Georgetown U, 1969 *Certification:* Surgery
3301 New Mexico Ave NW #206, Washington, DC, 202-895-1440

Purkert, William John (38 mentions)
Georgetown U, 1979 *Certification:* Surgery
8316 Arlington Blvd #410, Fairfax, VA, 703-573-6985

Robey, James W. (8 mentions)
Georgetown U, 1991 *Certification:* Surgery
8218 Wisconsin Ave #407, Bethesda, MD, 301-986-4288

Sandiford, John Alan (17 mentions)
FMS-United Kingdom, 1970 *Certification:* Surgery
1715 N George Mason Dr #403, Arlington, VA, 703-528-0768
1830 Town Center Dr #309, Reston, VA, 703-481-8282

Sandler, Glenn Lewis (29 mentions)
U of Maryland, 1989 *Certification:* Surgery
9707 Medical Center Dr #200, Rockville, MD, 301-251-4128
20528 Boland Farm Rd #202, Germantown, MD, 301-251-4128

Seneca, Russell P. (11 mentions)
Georgetown U, 1967 *Certification:* Surgery
4001 Fair Ridge Dr #304, Fairfax, VA, 703-359-8640

Starin, Lawrence Robert (9 mentions)
Columbia U, 1983 *Certification:* Surgery
3921 Ferrara Dr, Silver Spring, MD, 301-933-4283
15225 Shady Grove Rd #302, Rockville, MD, 301-933-4283

Turgeon, Daniel Gilles (13 mentions)
Georgetown U, 1980 *Certification:* Surgery
1800 Town Center Dr #312, Reston, VA, 703-796-0370

Zorc, Thomas G. (10 mentions)
Georgetown U, 1985 *Certification:* Surgery
5530 Wisconsin Ave #1455, Chevy Chase, MD, 301-656-6700

Geriatrics

Cobbs, Elizabeth Lipton (23 mentions)
George Washington U, 1981 *Certification:* Geriatric Medicine,
   Hospice and Palliative Medicine, Internal Medicine
2150 Pennsylvania Ave NW #2-116, Washington, DC,
   202-741-2222
50 Irving St NW, Washington, DC, 202-745-8240

Crantz, Joanne Gittleson (28 mentions)
George Washington U, 1979 *Certification:* Internal Medicine
8316 Arlington Blvd #310, Fairfax, VA, 703-641-0333

Kaufman, Ava Anita (26 mentions)
Case Western Reserve U, 1979
Certification: Geriatric Medicine, Internal Medicine
8218 Wisconsin Ave #103, Bethesda, MD, 301-215-8480

McConnell, Lila T. (18 mentions)
Georgetown U, 1976 *Certification:* Internal Medicine
5530 Wisconsin Ave #1400, Chevy Chase, MD, 301-656-9170

Roth, Katalin Eve (6 mentions)
Yale U, 1982 *Certification:* Geriatric Medicine, Internal Medicine
2150 Pennsylvania Ave NW, Washington, DC, 202-741-2222

Taler, George Abraham (11 mentions)
U of Maryland, 1975
Certification: Family Medicine, Geriatric Medicine
100 Irving St NW #EB-3114, Washington, DC, 202-877-0218

Turkewitz, Stuart J. (6 mentions)
SUNY-Buffalo, 1981
Certification: Geriatric Medicine, Internal Medicine
7500 Greenway Center Dr #430, Greenbelt, MD, 301-345-5857

Hematology/Oncology

Barr, Frederick Greiner (8 mentions)
Northwestern U, 1975
Certification: Internal Medicine, Medical Oncology
5454 Wisconsin Ave #1300, Chevy Chase, MD, 301-657-8587
2101 Medical Park Dr #200, Silver Spring, MD, 301-933-3216

Beveridge, Roy Ainsworth (8 mentions)
Cornell U, 1983
Certification: Internal Medicine, Medical Oncology
8503 Arlington Blvd #400, Fairfax, VA, 703-280-5390

Boccia, Ralph Vincent (22 mentions)
FMS-Mexico, 1977
Certification: Hematology, Internal Medicine, Medical Oncology
6420 Rockledge Dr #4100, Bethesda, MD, 301-571-0019
20500 Seneca Meadows Pkwy #2500, Germantown, MD,
   301-571-0019

Butler, Thomas Parke (12 mentions)
Case Western Reserve U, 1971
Certification: Internal Medicine, Medical Oncology
1635 N George Mason Dr #170, Arlington, VA, 703-528-7303
8503 Arlington Blvd #400, Fairfax, VA, 703-280-5390

Catlett, Joseph P. (6 mentions)
West Virginia U, 1984
Certification: Hematology, Internal Medicine, Medical Oncology
110 Irving St NW #C2151, Washington, DC, 202-877-2843

Dunning, David Marshall (10 mentions)
Virginia Commonwealth U, 1979
Certification: Hematology, Internal Medicine, Medical Oncology
8503 Arlington Blvd #400, Fairfax, VA, 703-280-5390

Feigert, John Morris (13 mentions)
Cornell U, 1983
Certification: Hematology, Internal Medicine, Medical Oncology
8503 Arlington Blvd #400, Fairfax, VA, 703-208-9200
1635 N George Mason Dr #170, Arlington, VA, 703-528-7303

Felice, Anthony Joseph (7 mentions)
SUNY-Downstate Med Coll, 1985
Certification: Hematology, Internal Medicine, Medical Oncology
1860 Town Center Dr #460, Reston, VA, 703-709-8205

Francis, Peter (7 mentions)
New York U, 1985 *Certification:* Infectious Disease, Internal
   Medicine, Medical Oncology
4660 Kenmore Ave #1018, Alexandria, VA, 703-823-5322

Goldstein, Kenneth (17 mentions)
Case Western Reserve U, 1966
Certification: Hematology, Internal Medicine, Medical Oncology
2141 K St NW #707, Washington, DC, 202-293-5382
5530 Wisconsin Ave #1125, Chevy Chase, MD, 301-951-3366

Greenberg, Jay (22 mentions)
U of Pennsylvania, 1976
Certification: Pediatric Hematology-Oncology, Pediatrics
9850 Key West Ave, Rockville, MD, 301-765-5400

Haggerty, Joseph Michael (14 mentions)
Virginia Commonwealth U, 1982
Certification: Internal Medicine, Medical Oncology
9707 Medical Center Dr #300, Rockville, MD, 301-424-6231
10605 Concord St #300, Kensington, MD, 301-929-0765

Hendricks, Carolyn B. (8 mentions)
Johns Hopkins U, 1985
Certification: Internal Medicine, Medical Oncology
6410 Rockledge Dr #506, Bethesda, MD, 301-897-1503

Heyer, David Michael (6 mentions)
U of Michigan, 1985
Certification: Internal Medicine, Medical Oncology
1860 Town Center Dr #460, Reston, VA, 703-709-8205

Kales, Arthur Norman (8 mentions)
U of Chicago, 1965
Certification: Hematology, Internal Medicine, Medical Oncology
8503 Arlington Blvd #400, Fairfax, VA, 703-280-5390

Katcher, Daniel (9 mentions)
U of Vermont, 1972
Certification: Hematology, Internal Medicine, Medical Oncology
2280 Opitz Blvd #300, Woodbridge, VA, 703-897-5358
7901 Lake Manassas Dr, Gainesville, VA, 571-222-2200

Kressel, Bruce Robert (28 mentions)
Tufts U, 1973
Certification: Hematology, Internal Medicine, Medical Oncology
2141 K St NW #707, Washington, DC, 202-293-5382
5530 Wisconsin Ave #1125, Chevy Chase, MD, 301-951-3366

Malkovska, Vera (6 mentions)
FMS-Czech Republic, 1984
110 Irving St NW #C2151, Washington, DC, 202-877-2159

Meister, Robert Jay (7 mentions)
Ohio State U, 1975
Certification: Hematology, Internal Medicine, Medical Oncology
1635 N George Mason Dr #170, Arlington, VA, 703-528-7303
8503 Arlington Blvd #400, Fairfax, VA, 703-280-5390

Miller, Kenneth David (11 mentions)
Tufts U, 1982 *Certification:* Internal Medicine, Medical Oncology
18111 Prince Philip Dr #327, Olney, MD, 301-774-6136

Orloff, Gregory Joshua (8 mentions)
Yale U, 1986
Certification: Hematology, Internal Medicine, Medical Oncology
8503 Arlington Blvd #400, Fairfax, VA, 703-280-5390

Perdahl-Wallace, Eva B. (8 mentions)
FMS-Sweden, 1981 *Certification:* Pediatric Hematology-Oncology
6565 Arlington Blvd #200, Falls Church, VA, 703-531-3627

Priebat, Dennis Arnold (9 mentions)
Stony Brook U, 1975
Certification: Hematology, Internal Medicine, Medical Oncology
110 Irving St NW #C2151, Washington, DC, 202-877-2842

Priego, Victor Manuel (8 mentions)
FMS-Mexico, 1974 *Certification:* Medical Oncology
6420 Rockledge Dr #4100, Bethesda, MD, 301-571-0019
20500 Seneca Meadows Pkwy #2500, Germantown, MD,
    301-571-0019

Pushkas, Gabriel Peter (8 mentions)
FMS-Hungary, 1968
Certification: Internal Medicine, Medical Oncology
11510 Old Georgetown Rd, Rockville, MD, 301-881-3940

Rajagopal, Chitra Desikan (6 mentions)
FMS-India, 1986 *Certification:* Medical Oncology
18111 Prince Philip Dr #327, Olney, MD, 301-774-6136
9715 Medical Center Dr #221, Rockville, MD, 301-774-6136
6000 Executive Blvd #302, Rockville, MD, 301-774-6136

Rajendra, Rangappa (6 mentions)
FMS-India, 1981
Certification: Internal Medicine, Medical Oncology
44055 Riverside Pkwy #224, Leesburg, VA, 703-858-3110

Robert, Nicholas James (11 mentions)
FMS-Canada, 1974 *Certification:* Anatomic Pathology,
    Hematology, Internal Medicine, Medical Oncology
8503 Arlington Blvd #400, Fairfax, VA, 703-280-5390

Shad, Aziza Tahir (7 mentions)
FMS-Pakistan, 1977
3800 Reservoir Rd NW, Washington, DC, 202-444-7599

Sherer, Peter Bruce (9 mentions)
Albany Med Coll, 1972
Certification: Hematology, Internal Medicine, Medical Oncology
3921 Ferrara Dr, Wheaton, MD, 301-946-6420
3618 Olandwood Ct #111, Olney, MD, 301-946-6420

Smith, Frederick Pearson (23 mentions)
St Louis U, 1973
Certification: Internal Medicine, Medical Oncology
5454 Wisconsin Ave #1300, Chevy Chase, MD, 202-243-0101

Sotos, George Aristides (19 mentions)
Virginia Commonwealth U, 1988
Certification: Internal Medicine, Medical Oncology
9707 Medical Center Dr #300, Rockville, MD, 301-424-6231
10605 Concord St #300, Kensington, MD, 301-929-0765

Spira, Alexander Illya (6 mentions)
New York U, 1997
Certification: Internal Medicine, Medical Oncology
8503 Arlington Blvd #400, Fairfax, VA, 703-280-5390

Staal, Stephen Paul (6 mentions)
U of California-San Diego, 1972
Certification: Internal Medicine, Medical Oncology
1221 Mercantile Ln, Upper Marlboro, MD, 301-618-5500

Tabbara, Imad (9 mentions)
Certification: Hematology, Internal Medicine, Medical Oncology
2150 Pennsylvania Ave NW #3107, Washington, DC,
    202-741-2210

Trehan, Ram Swarup (6 mentions)
FMS-India, 1979
Certification: Internal Medicine, Medical Oncology
50 W Edmonston Dr #303, Rockville, MD, 301-424-1559
1400 Forest Glen Rd #435, Silver Spring, MD, 301-593-9035

Ueno, Winston Mizuo (17 mentions)
Creighton U, 1966
Certification: Internal Medicine, Medical Oncology
4660 Kenmore Ave #1018, Alexandria, VA, 703-823-5322

Wallmark, John Michael (6 mentions)
Hahnemann U, 1992
Certification: Hematology, Medical Oncology
10605 Concord St #300, Kensington, MD, 301-929-0765
9707 Medical Center Dr #300, Rockville, MD, 301-424-6231

Wilkinson, Mary Judith (18 mentions)
Stanford U, 1983
Certification: Hematology, Internal Medicine, Medical Oncology
8501 Arlington Blvd #340, Fairfax, VA, 703-207-0733

Infectious Disease

Abbruzzese, Mark R. (38 mentions)
FMS-Montserrat, 1981
4910 Massachusetts Ave NW #304, Washington, DC,
    202-537-7400

Davis, William Arthur, II (25 mentions)
West Virginia U, 1973
Certification: Infectious Disease, Internal Medicine
4910 Massachusetts Ave NW #304, Washington, DC,
    202-537-7400

Holman, Robert Paul (22 mentions)
Georgetown U, 1982
Certification: Infectious Disease, Internal Medicine
1635 N George Mason Dr #180, Arlington, VA, 703-276-7798

Jacobs, Ruth Marie (12 mentions)
U of Kansas, 1980 *Certification:* Allergy & Immunology,
    Infectious Disease, Internal Medicine
15001 Shady Grove Rd #110, Rockville, MD, 301-315-9515

Kane, James Gregory, Jr. (23 mentions)
U of Maryland, 1968
Certification: Infectious Disease, Internal Medicine
4910 Massachusetts Ave NW, Washington, DC, 202-537-7400

Keim, Daniel Edward (23 mentions)
Yale U, 1968 *Certification:* Pediatrics
2730-C Prosperity Ave, Fairfax, VA, 703-226-2280

Kumar, Princy Nirmal (9 mentions)
FMS-India, 1980
Certification: Infectious Disease, Internal Medicine
3800 Reservoir Rd NW #110, Washington, DC, 202-687-6845

Levy, Charles Steven (10 mentions)
Cornell U, 1973
Certification: Infectious Disease, Internal Medicine
2100 Pennsylvania Ave NW, Washington, DC, 202-872-7196
1221 Mercantile Ln, Largo, MD, 301-618-5859

Morrison, Allan Joseph, Jr. (19 mentions)
U of Virginia, 1980
Certification: Infectious Disease, Internal Medicine
3289 Woodburn Rd #200, Annandale, VA, 703-560-7900

Parenti, David Michael (19 mentions)
Georgetown U, 1977
Certification: Infectious Disease, Internal Medicine
2150 Pennsylvania Ave NW, Washington, DC, 202-741-2234

Poretz, Donald Martin (22 mentions)
Virginia Commonwealth U, 1966
Certification: Infectious Disease, Internal Medicine
3289 Woodburn Rd #200, Annandale, VA, 703-560-7900

Posorske, Lynette H. (31 mentions)
U of Connecticut, 1987
Certification: Infectious Disease, Internal Medicine
8630 Fenton St #230, Silver Spring, MD, 301-588-2525

Rosenthal, Jonathan Harry (9 mentions)
Columbia U, 1983
Certification: Infectious Disease, Internal Medicine
6501 Loisdale Ct, Springfield, VA, 703-922-1313

Sall, Richard Kenneth (12 mentions)
Boston U, 1983
Certification: Infectious Disease, Internal Medicine
3700 Joseph Siewick Dr #209, Fairfax, VA, 703-758-2664

Schmidt, Mary Elizabeth (18 mentions)
Med Coll of Pennsylvania, 1984
Certification: Infectious Disease, Internal Medicine
3289 Woodburn Rd #200, Annandale, VA, 703-560-7900

Soni, Marsha Diane (16 mentions)
Med Coll of Georgia, 1984
Certification: Infectious Disease, Internal Medicine
3700 Joseph Siewick Dr #209, Fairfax, VA, 703-758-2664

Symington, John Sante (11 mentions)
St Louis U, 1986
Certification: Infectious Disease, Internal Medicine
8988 Lorton Station Blvd #204, Lorton, VA, 703-339-3524

Trinh, Phuong D. (49 mentions)
U of Maryland, 1980
Certification: Infectious Disease, Internal Medicine
8630 Fenton St #230, Silver Spring, MD, 301-588-2525

Wiedermann, Bernhard L. (9 mentions)
Baylor U, 1978
Certification: Pediatric Infectious Diseases, Pediatrics
111 Michigan Ave NW, Washington, DC, 202-476-5051

Infertility

Asmar, Pierre (8 mentions)
Certification: Obstetrics & Gynecology
4316 Evergreen Ln, Annandale, VA, 703-658-3100
1830 Town Center Dr #306, Reston, VA, 703-481-1500
14955 Shady Grove Rd #250, Rockville, MD, 240-314-0600

11110 Medical Campus Rd #243, Hagerstown, MD,
    301-665-4608

Chang, Frank Edgar (20 mentions)
Baylor U, 1979 *Certification:* Obstetrics & Gynecology,
    Reproductive Endocrinology/Infertility
15001 Shady Grove Rd #400, Rockville, MD, 301-340-1188

Gindoff, Paul R. (8 mentions)
New York U, 1981 *Certification:* Obstetrics & Gynecology,
    Reproductive Endocrinology/Infertility
2150 Pennsylvania Ave NW 6th Fl #300, Washington, DC,
    202-741-2570
8233 Old Courthouse Rd #150, Vienna, VA, 703-319-1985
1830 Town Center Dr #207, Reston, VA, 703-319-1985

Levy, Michael Jeremy (14 mentions)
FMS-South Africa, 1982 *Certification:* Obstetrics &
Gynecology, Reproductive Endocrinology/Infertility
15001 Shady Grove Rd #400, Rockville, MD, 301-340-1188

Littman, Burt A. (6 mentions)
Georgetown U, 1977 *Certification:* Obstetrics & Gynecology,
Reproductive Endocrinology/Infertility
9711 Medical Center Dr #214, Rockville, MD, 301-424-1904

Muasher, Suheil (8 mentions)
FMS-Lebanon, 1976 *Certification:* Obstetrics & Gynecology,
Reproductive Endocrinology/Infertility
8501 Arlington Blvd #500, Fairfax, VA, 703-876-6311

Rifka, Safa Michel (8 mentions)
FMS-Lebanon, 1972 *Certification:* Obstetrics & Gynecology,
Reproductive Endocrinology/Infertility
10215 Fernwood Rd #301, Bethesda, MD, 301-897-8850
2440 M St NW #401, Washington, DC, 202-293-6567

Sagoskin, Arthur William (6 mentions)
Med Coll of Pennsylvania, 1978
Certification: Obstetrics & Gynecology
15001 Shady Grove Rd #400, Rockville, MD, 301-340-1188

Simon, James Alan (8 mentions)
Rush U, 1978 *Certification:* Obstetrics & Gynecology,
Reproductive Endocrinology/Infertility
1850 M St NW #450, Washington, DC, 202-293-1000

Stillman, Robert Joseph (17 mentions)
Georgetown U, 1973 *Certification:* Obstetrics & Gynecology,
Reproductive Endocrinology/Infertility
15001 Shady Grove Rd #400, Rockville, MD, 301-340-1188

Internal Medicine *(see note on page 9)*

Adams, Michael John (3 mentions)
Georgetown U, 1992 *Certification:* Internal Medicine
3800 Reservoir Rd NW, Washington, DC, 202-444-2000

Amedeo, R. Michael (3 mentions)
Georgetown U, 1979 *Certification:* Internal Medicine
1715 N George Mason Dr #306, Arlington, VA, 703-276-0630

Arling, Bryan Jeremy (12 mentions)
Harvard U, 1969 *Certification:* Internal Medicine
2440 M St NW #817, Washington, DC, 202-833-5707

Assatourians, Linda Jane (4 mentions)
George Washington U, 1999 *Certification:* Internal Medicine
2141 K St NW #600, Washington, DC, 202-223-2283

Bahadori, Lila Mojdeh (4 mentions)
Robert W Johnson Med Sch, 1988
Certification: Critical Care Medicine, Pulmonary Disease
10301 Georgia Ave #304, Silver Spring, MD, 301-681-7200

Berger, Brent Asher (6 mentions)
U of Maryland, 1986 *Certification:* Internal Medicine
10215 Fernwood Rd #100, Bethesda, MD, 301-493-4440

Berkman, Peter Morris (3 mentions)
Columbia U, 1959 *Certification:* Internal Medicine, Nephrology
106 Irving St NW #403, Washington, DC, 202-291-1645

Bisk, Penny L. (4 mentions)
Cornell U, 1977 *Certification:* Internal Medicine
10301 Georgia Ave #301, Silver Spring, MD, 301-754-1950

Blee, Robert H. (8 mentions)
Georgetown U, 1976 *Certification:* Internal Medicine
5530 Wisconsin Ave #1400, Chevy Chase, MD, 301-656-9170

Boland, Brian John (3 mentions)
U of Virginia, 1971 *Certification:* Internal Medicine
1625 N George Mason Dr #434, Arlington, VA, 703-522-1860

Broderick, Dawn (5 mentions)
U of Hawaii, 1990 *Certification:* Internal Medicine
18109 Prince Philip Dr #275, Olney, MD, 301-774-5400

Cary, John Francis (5 mentions)
U of Maryland, 1984 *Certification:* Internal Medicine
9303 Forest Point Cir, Manassas, VA, 703-257-7749

Chretien, Jane S. Henkel (4 mentions)
New Jersey Med Sch, 1966
Certification: Infectious Disease, Internal Medicine
8120 Woodmont Ave #320, Bethesda, MD, 301-656-4010

Cole, Carmella Ann (6 mentions)
Virginia Commonwealth U, 1983 *Certification:* Internal Medicine
110 Irving St NW #1A50, Washington, DC, 202-877-2835

Correnty, Patrick Anthony (6 mentions)
Pennsylvania State U, 1995
1715 N George Mason Dr #201, Arlington, VA, 703-243-0040

Corson, Audrey P. (4 mentions)
U of Colorado, 1982 *Certification:* Internal Medicine
8120 Woodmont Ave #320, Bethesda, MD, 301-656-4010

Crantz, Joanne Gittleson (4 mentions)
George Washington U, 1979 *Certification:* Internal Medicine
8316 Arlington Blvd #310, Fairfax, VA, 703-641-0333

Cullen, Edward T. (3 mentions)
Georgetown U, 1978 *Certification:* Internal Medicine
6188 Oxon Hill Rd #704, Oxon Hill, MD, 301-839-2790
7625 Wisconsin Ave #101, Bethesda, MD, 240-497-1570

Dunford, Christopher C. (4 mentions)
U of California-San Francisco, 1981
Certification: Internal Medicine
615 W Montgomery Ave, Rockville, MD, 301-762-6148

Dunn, Mitchell B. (8 mentions)
Duke U, 1979 *Certification:* Internal Medicine
2021 K St NW #512, Washington, DC, 202-293-3636

Eisenbaum, Marc Allen (5 mentions)
George Washington U, 1981 *Certification:* Internal Medicine
3700 Joseph Siewick Dr #203, Fairfax, VA, 703-758-8200

El-Bayoumi, Jehan (8 mentions)
U of Michigan, 1985 *Certification:* Internal Medicine
2150 Pennsylvania Ave NW, Washington, DC, 202-741-2222

Fecanin, Peter J. (3 mentions)
Georgetown U, 1976 *Certification:* Internal Medicine
3020 Hamaker Ct #403, Fairfax, VA, 703-207-8600

Fields, Robert P. (4 mentions)
Tulane U, 1984 *Certification:* Internal Medicine
18109 Prince Philip Dr #200, Olney, MD, 301-774-7115

Fox, Julie Kramer (3 mentions)
New York U, 1988 *Certification:* Internal Medicine
2101 Medical Park Dr #210, Silver Spring, MD, 301-681-8000

Gavora, Les Hugh (10 mentions)
George Washington U, 1983 *Certification:* Internal Medicine
3020 Hamaker Ct #403, Fairfax, VA, 703-207-8600

Goozh, Joel Lee (3 mentions)
Virginia Commonwealth U, 1967 *Certification:* Internal Medicine
10401 Old Georgetown Rd, Bethesda, MD, 301-897-2757

Graves, George W. (3 mentions)
Georgetown U, 1981 *Certification:* Internal Medicine
5530 Wisconsin Ave #925, Chevy Chase, MD, 301-654-4850

Heinen, Robert J. (4 mentions)
U of Maryland, 1980 *Certification:* Internal Medicine
4660 Kenmore Ave #604, Alexandria, VA, 703-751-6773

Horowitz, Beth Carrie (4 mentions)
U of California-San Francisco, 1984
Certification: Internal Medicine
2021 K St NW #512, Washington, DC, 202-293-3636

Hwang, Erica W. (6 mentions)
U of Michigan, 1994 *Certification:* Internal Medicine
8120 Woodmont Ave #320, Bethesda, MD, 301-656-4010

Kanter, Sue Danziger (4 mentions)
Tufts U, 1994 *Certification:* Internal Medicine
6410 Rockledge Dr #308, Bethesda, MD, 301-530-0400

Kline, Prudence (3 mentions)
Robert W Johnson Med Sch, 1978
Certification: Internal Medicine
2021 K St NW #512, Washington, DC, 202-293-3636

Koritzinsky, Gary Marc (5 mentions)
U of Wisconsin, 1983 *Certification:* Internal Medicine
2141 K St NW #407, Washington, DC, 202-466-4016

Krakower, Brian Mark (3 mentions)
Georgetown U, 1988 *Certification:* Internal Medicine
1515 Chain Bridge Rd #308, McLean, VA, 703-356-6700

Lee, Donna (4 mentions)
Stony Brook U, 1990 *Certification:* Internal Medicine
201 N Washington St, Falls Church, VA, 703-237-4000

Lennon, Frederick F. (3 mentions)
Temple U, 1984 *Certification:* Internal Medicine
6211 Centreville Rd #700, Centreville, VA, 703-222-0002

Li, Theodore Chi-Mei (9 mentions)
Cornell U, 1977 *Certification:* Internal Medicine
3301 New Mexico Ave NW #348, Washington, DC, 202-362-4467

Lipson, Ace (3 mentions)
Washington U, 1973
Certification: Endocrinology and Metabolism, Internal Medicine
1120 19th St NW #200, Washington, DC, 202-296-3443

McBreen, Brian Patrick (3 mentions)
Georgetown U, 1995
3301 New Mexico Ave NW #205, Washington, DC, 202-895-0050

McNamara, Thomas J. (9 mentions)
Georgetown U, 1981 *Certification:* Internal Medicine
10215 Fernwood Rd #100, Bethesda, MD, 301-493-4440
19735 Germantown Rd #100, Germantown, MD, 301-528-9272

Merlino, Robin Beth (9 mentions)
U of Michigan, 1980 *Certification:* Internal Medicine
3020 Hamaker Ct #B-106, Fairfax, VA, 703-208-9944

Meyer, Wayne Lewis (6 mentions)
U of Virginia, 1982 *Certification:* Internal Medicine
9715 Medical Center Dr #214, Rockville, MD, 301-294-2955

Minton, Stephen Mark (4 mentions)
U of Virginia, 1988 *Certification:* Internal Medicine
4660 Kenmore Ave #710, Alexandria, VA, 703-370-9002

Mizus, Irving (7 mentions)
Albany Med Coll, 1978 *Certification:* Critical Care Medicine,
Internal Medicine, Pulmonary Disease
10605 Concord St #500, Kensington, MD, 301-942-2977

Montalbano, Foster R. (3 mentions)
FMS-Montserrat, 1981 *Certification:* Internal Medicine
6355 Walker Ln #310, Alexandria, VA, 703-971-8600

Muir, Timothy David (6 mentions)
Georgetown U, 1997 *Certification:* Internal Medicine
1715 N George Mason Dr #307, Arlington, VA, 703-243-0040

Murphy, Dennis Richard (4 mentions)
Georgetown U, 1983 *Certification:* Internal Medicine
3800 Reservoir Rd NW 6th Fl, Washington, DC, 202-444-8168

Nealon, Kevin G. (4 mentions)
Georgetown U, 1976
5530 Wisconsin Ave #925, Chevy Chase, MD, 301-654-4850

Newman, Michael Arthur (11 mentions)
U of Rochester, 1969 *Certification:* Internal Medicine
2021 K St NW #404, Washington, DC, 202-466-8118

Noel, Roger A. (6 mentions)
Georgetown U, 1968 *Certification:* Internal Medicine
8316 Arlington Blvd #234, Fairfax, VA, 703-560-0300

Oser, Irnest Stephen (3 mentions)
Hahnemann U, 1968
10301 Georgia Ave #304, Silver Spring, MD, 301-681-7200

Patterson, David Wayne (7 mentions)
Vanderbilt U, 1985 *Certification:* Internal Medicine
2440 M St NW #817, Washington, DC, 202-833-5707

Remy, Terri (4 mentions)
George Washington U, 1989 *Certification:* Internal Medicine
6060 Arlington Blvd, Falls Church, VA, 703-533-2222

Restifo, Mary D. (3 mentions)
Case Western Reserve U, 1967
Certification: Cardiovascular Disease, Internal Medicine
3301 New Mexico Ave NW #348, Washington, DC, 202-362-4467

Rogers, David E. (3 mentions)
FMS-United Kingdom, 1988 *Certification:* Internal Medicine
5530 Wisconsin Ave #1400, Chevy Chase, MD, 301-656-9170

Rosenbaum, Barry Norman (13 mentions)
U of Maryland, 1964 *Certification:* Internal Medicine
3720 Farragut Ave 2nd Fl, Kensington, MD, 301-949-4242

Schubert, Richard D. (4 mentions)
SUNY-Downstate Med Coll, 1972
Certification: Internal Medicine, Rheumatology
3301 New Mexico Ave NW #348, Washington, DC, 202-362-4467

Shor, Samuel Mark (6 mentions)
Med U of South Carolina, 1982 *Certification:* Internal Medicine
1860 Town Center Dr #230, Reston, VA, 703-709-1119

Stone, Alan William (9 mentions)
Yale U, 1966 *Certification:* Internal Medicine
2021 K St NW #404, Washington, DC, 202-466-8118

Stone, Theresa Ann (3 mentions)
Georgetown U, 1993 *Certification:* Internal Medicine
1145 19th St NW #700, Washington, DC, 202-223-5333

Suskiewicz, Lewis (5 mentions)
Georgetown U, 1972 *Certification:* Internal Medicine
5510 Alma Ln, Springfield, VA, 703-642-5990

Tauber, Ira (5 mentions)
George Washington U, 1971
Certification: Internal Medicine, Pulmonary Disease
10301 Georgia Ave #304, Silver Spring, MD, 301-681-7200

Taubman, Edward Philip (4 mentions)
New York Med Coll, 1976 *Certification:* Internal Medicine
18109 Prince Philip Dr #275, Olney, MD, 301-774-5400

Taweel, Fred Fadel (5 mentions)
Virginia Commonwealth U, 1988 *Certification:* Internal Medicine
1850 Town Center Pkwy #209, Reston, VA, 703-437-5532

Temme, Joel McGovern (9 mentions)
U of Virginia, 1978 *Certification:* Internal Medicine
4660 Kenmore Ave #604-A, Alexandria, VA, 703-823-8300

Tesoriero, Thomas Anthony (6 mentions)
U of Rochester, 1981 *Certification:* Internal Medicine
2100 Pennsylvania Ave NW, Washington, DC, 202-872-7000

Tyroler, Jay Cary (7 mentions)
Virginia Commonwealth U, 1985 *Certification:* Internal Medicine
3650 Joseph Siewick Dr #204, Fairfax, VA, 703-264-0521

Umhau, Andrew Nufer (6 mentions)
Duke U, 1985 *Certification:* Internal Medicine
3301 New Mexico Ave NW #348, Washington, DC, 202-362-4467

Wittig, Suzanne Herten (5 mentions)
Georgetown U, 1998 *Certification:* Internal Medicine
1715 N George Mason Dr #307, Arlington, VA, 703-243-0040

Yamamoto, Kristin Thomas (5 mentions)
U of Michigan, 1994 *Certification:* Internal Medicine
3301 New Mexico Ave NW #348, Washington, DC, 202-362-4467

Yau, Linda Lee (7 mentions)
Johns Hopkins U, 1994 *Certification:* Internal Medicine
3301 New Mexico Ave NW #348, Washington, DC, 202-362-4467

Zanetti, Christopher John (3 mentions)
Robert W Johnson Med Sch, 1990
Certification: Internal Medicine
1515 Chain Bridge Rd #308, McLean, VA, 703-356-6700

Nephrology

Assefi, Ali Reza (17 mentions)
FMS-United Kingdom, 1984
Certification: Internal Medicine, Nephrology
46396 Benedict Dr #220, Sterling, VA, 703-961-0488
280 Hatcher Ave, Purcellville, VA, 703-961-0488
13135 Lee Jackson Memorial Hwy #135, Fairfax, VA,
   703-961-0488
5695 King Center Dr #105, Alexandria, VA, 703-961-0488

Bass, Raymond Allen (22 mentions)
U of Michigan, 1973 *Certification:* Internal Medicine, Nephrology
3941 Ferrara Dr, Wheaton, MD, 301-942-5355
15225 Shady Grove Rd #302, Rockville, MD, 301-330-0550

Burka, Steven Arthur (23 mentions)
George Washington U, 1976
Certification: Internal Medicine, Nephrology
5530 Wisconsin Ave #914, Chevy Chase, MD, 301-654-3803

Cheriyan, Ranjit K. (11 mentions)
FMS-India, 1979 *Certification:* Internal Medicine, Nephrology
1635 N George Mason Dr #215, Arlington, VA, 703-841-0707
3930 Walnut St #101, Fairfax, VA, 703-246-9246

Dosa, Stefan (8 mentions)
FMS-Czech Republic, 1967
Certification: Internal Medicine, Nephrology
730 24th St NW #17, Washington, DC, 202-337-7660

Fildes, Robert Duane (18 mentions)
FMS-Belgium, 1978
Certification: Pediatric Nephrology, Pediatrics
8505 Arlington Blvd #100, Fairfax, VA, 703-970-2600

Hecht, Barry (9 mentions)
Albert Einstein Coll of Med, 1970
Certification: Internal Medicine, Nephrology
3941 Ferrara Dr, Wheaton, MD, 301-942-5355

Hellman, Stephen M. (27 mentions)
U of Miami, 1976 *Certification:* Internal Medicine
6240 Montrose Rd, Rockville, MD, 301-231-7111

Howard, Andrew David (9 mentions)
Tulane U, 1980 *Certification:* Internal Medicine, Nephrology
7801 Old Branch Ave #202, Clinton, MD, 301-868-9414
2616 Sherwood Hall Ln #209, Alexandria, VA, 703-360-3100

Mackow, Robert Carey (12 mentions)
New Jersey Med Sch, 1979
Certification: Internal Medicine, Nephrology
13135 Lee Jackson Memorial Hwy #135, Fairfax, VA,
   703-961-0488

Mahoney, David Lucas (9 mentions)
Boston U, 1985 *Certification:* Internal Medicine, Nephrology
13135 Lee Jackson Memorial Hwy #135, Fairfax, VA,
   703-961-0488

Nossuli, A. Kaldun (7 mentions)
FMS-Lebanon, 1970 *Certification:* Internal Medicine, Nephrology
4915 Auburn Ave #104, Bethesda, MD, 301-907-6640

Perlmutter, Jeffrey Alan (27 mentions)
Columbia U, 1983 *Certification:* Internal Medicine, Nephrology
6240 Montrose Rd, Rockville, MD, 301-231-7111

Rakowski, Thomas Anthony (13 mentions)
Hahnemann U, 1969
Certification: Internal Medicine, Nephrology
1635 N George Mason Dr #215, Arlington, VA, 703-841-0707

Rosen, Mark Stewart (10 mentions)
U of Pennsylvania, 1972
Certification: Internal Medicine, Nephrology
3941 Ferrara Dr, Wheaton, MD, 301-942-5355

Schwartz, Philip Jay (14 mentions)
Pennsylvania State U, 1978
Certification: Internal Medicine, Nephrology
15225 Shady Grove Rd #302, Rockville, MD, 301-330-0550

Seiken, Gail Leslie (7 mentions)
Uniformed Services U of Health Sciences, 1986
Certification: Internal Medicine, Nephrology
4915 Auburn Ave #104, Bethesda, MD, 301-907-4646

Vaccarezza, Stephen G. (7 mentions)
U of Chicago, 1981 *Certification:* Internal Medicine, Nephrology
6240 Montrose Rd, Rockville, MD, 301-231-7111

Neurological Surgery

Azzam, Charles (11 mentions)
FMS-Lebanon, 1979 *Certification:* Neurological Surgery
3301 Woodburn Rd #105, Annandale, VA, 703-205-6210
1916 Opitz Blvd, Woodbridge, VA, 703-551-4113

Caputy, Anthony James (11 mentions)
U of Virginia, 1980 *Certification:* Neurological Surgery
2150 Pennsylvania Ave NW 7th Fl #420, Washington, DC,
   202-741-2750
8318 Arlington Blvd #305, Fairfax, VA, 703-645-8711

French, Kathleen B. (11 mentions)
Boston U, 1980 *Certification:* Neurological Surgery
3020 Hamaker Ct #B104, Fairfax, VA, 703-641-4877

Hope, Donald Gerard (21 mentions)
U of Maryland, 1982 *Certification:* Neurological Surgery
3016 Williams Dr, Fairfax, VA, 703-560-1146
1830 Town Center Dr #103, Reston, VA, 703-478-2200

Kobrine, Arthur Irwin (24 mentions)
Northwestern U, 1968 *Certification:* Neurological Surgery
2440 M St NW #315, Washington, DC, 202-293-7136

Melisi, James William (13 mentions)
SUNY-Downstate Med Coll, 1986
Certification: Neurological Surgery
1800 Town Center Dr #418, Reston, VA, 703-796-1111
8644 Sudley Rd #308, Manassas, VA, 703-796-1111

Nguyen, Ben Lam (12 mentions)
Harvard U, 1992 *Certification:* Neurological Surgery
8501 Arlington Blvd #330, Fairfax, VA, 703-876-4270
1860 Town Center Dr #335, Reston, VA, 703-876-4270

Riedel, Charles Jess (15 mentions)
U of Cincinnati, 1984 *Certification:* Neurological Surgery
1625 N George Mason Dr #445, Arlington, VA, 703-248-0111

Schwartz, Frederic Tovi (18 mentions)
George Washington U, 1969 *Certification:* Neurological Surgery
5530 Wisconsin Ave #1147, Chevy Chase, MD, 301-652-6621

Neurology

Alexandrova, Natalia (7 mentions)
FMS-Russia, 1991
1635 N George Mason Dr #420, Arlington, VA, 703-536-4000

Anderson, Frank Hughes (11 mentions)
Harvard U, 1970 *Certification:* Neurology
5454 Wisconsin Ave #820, Chevy Chase, MD, 301-652-0881

Avin, Brian Howard (10 mentions)
Rosalind Franklin U, 1972
Certification: Internal Medicine, Neurology
2730 University Blvd W #410, Wheaton, MD, 301-949-6655

Cintron, Ruben (10 mentions)
Wake Forest U, 1990 *Certification:* Neurology
12007 Sunrise Valley Dr #120, Reston, VA, 703-264-1361

Cochran, John (9 mentions)
Jefferson Med Coll, 1973
Certification: Internal Medicine, Neurology
1500 N Beauregard St #300, Alexandria, VA, 703-845-1500
8505 Arlington Blvd #405, Fairfax, VA, 703-280-1234

Einbinder, Larry M. (7 mentions)
U of Maryland, 1978 *Certification:* Neurology
1201 Seven Locks Rd #101, Rockville, MD, 301-562-7200

Emsellem, Helene Audrey (6 mentions)
George Washington U, 1977 *Certification:* Neurology
5454 Wisconsin Ave #1725, Chevy Chase, MD, 301-654-1575

Friedman, Alan Jerry (8 mentions)
Cornell U, 1974 *Certification:* Internal Medicine, Neurology
9715 Medical Center Dr #531, Rockville, MD, 301-251-1771

Hari Hall, Kalpana M. (7 mentions)
Eastern Virginia Med Sch, 1996
Certification: Clinical Neurophysiology, Neurology
5454 Wisconsin Ave #1720, Chevy Chase, MD, 301-562-7200
2141 K St NW #503, Washington, DC, 301-562-7200

Jaitly, Rakesh (8 mentions)
FMS-India, 1977 *Certification:* Neurology
5530 Wisconsin Ave #806, Chevy Chase, MD, 301-949-0607
10400 Connecticut Ave #202, Kensington, MD, 301-949-0607

Katz, David Michael (8 mentions)
SUNY-Buffalo, 1988 *Certification:* Neurology
7830 Old Georgetown Rd #C-20, Bethesda, MD, 301-540-2700

Kelly, John Joseph, Jr. (6 mentions)
Yale U, 1969 *Certification:* Neurology
2150 Pennsylvania Ave NW #7-404, Washington, DC,
    202-741-2700

Kurtzke, Robert Nevin (10 mentions)
Georgetown U, 1985
Certification: Clinical Neurophysiology, Neurology
3020 Hamaker Ct #400, Fairfax, VA, 703-876-0800

Kurzrok, Neal Mark (6 mentions)
Med Coll of Pennsylvania, 1982 *Certification:* Neurology
1160 Varnum St NE #204, Washington, DC, 202-526-4495
106 Irving St NW #412, Washington, DC, 202-526-4495

Laureno, Robert (11 mentions)
Cornell U, 1971 *Certification:* Neurology
110 Irving St NW #2A44, Washington, DC, 202-877-6435

Lavenstein, Bennett Louis (8 mentions)
U of Maryland, 1970 *Certification:* Neurology with Special
    Qualifications in Child Neurology, Pediatrics
111 Michigan Ave NW, Washington, DC, 202-476-2120
8501 Arlington Blvd #200, Fairfax, VA, 571-226-8368

London, Gary Wayne (6 mentions)
Northwestern U, 1968 *Certification:* Neurology
1201 Seven Locks Rd #101, Rockville, MD, 301-562-7200
3801 International Dr #210, Silver Spring, MD, 301-562-7200

Luban, Norman Alan (7 mentions)
Albert Einstein Coll of Med, 1971 *Certification:* Neurology
5530 Wisconsin Ave #806, Chevy Chase, MD, 301-949-0607
10400 Connecticut Ave #202, Kensington, MD, 301-949-0607

McClintock, William Morris (7 mentions)
U of Virginia, 1978 *Certification:* Neurology with Special
    Qualifications in Child Neurology, Pediatrics
8501 Arlington Blvd #200, Fairfax, VA, 571-226-8368

Moore, David Gaither (6 mentions)
Indiana U, 1981 *Certification:* Neurology
1160 Varnum St NE #204, Washington, DC, 202-526-4495
106 Irving St NW #412, Washington, DC, 202-526-4495

Pearl, Phillip Lawrence (13 mentions)
U of Maryland, 1984 *Certification:* Clinical Neurophysiology,
    Neurodevelopmental Disabilities, Neurology with Special
    Qualifications in Child Neurology, Pediatrics
8501 Arlington Blvd #200, Fairfax, VA, 571-226-8368

Peters, Jon David (6 mentions)
Georgetown U, 1980 *Certification:* Neurology
12007 Sunrise Valley Dr #120, Reston, VA, 703-478-0440

Pulaski, Philip David (16 mentions)
Johns Hopkins U, 1977 *Certification:* Neurology
2141 K St NW #503, Washington, DC, 202-223-1450

Richardson, Perry Kimball (12 mentions)
George Washington U, 1984
Certification: Clinical Neurophysiology, Neurology, Pain Medicine
2150 Pennsylvania Ave NW #7-404, Washington, DC,
    202-741-2700

Rosenbaum, Faye R. (12 mentions)
Rush U, 1984 *Certification:* Neurology
1635 N George Mason Dr #420, Arlington, VA, 703-536-4000

Satinsky, David (19 mentions)
U of Pennsylvania, 1964 *Certification:* Neurology
1201 Seven Locks Rd #101, Rockville, MD, 301-424-5630

Schlosberg, Marc F. (7 mentions)
Georgetown U, 1987 *Certification:* Neurology
106 Irving St NW #410, Washington, DC, 202-877-5119

Sigmund, Linda S. (11 mentions)
Georgetown U, 1981 *Certification:* Neurology
3020 Hamaker Ct #400, Fairfax, VA, 703-876-0800

Simsarian, James Parsons (14 mentions)
Columbia U, 1966 *Certification:* Neurology
2030 Hamaker Ct #400, Fairfax, VA, 703-876-0800

Tornatore, Carlo S. (8 mentions)
Georgetown U, 1986 *Certification:* Neurology
3800 Reservoir Rd NW PHC 7th Fl, Washington, DC,
    202-444-8525

Watkin, Terry (8 mentions)
FMS-Belgium, 1976 *Certification:* Neurology with Special
    Qualifications in Child Neurology, Pediatrics
12007 Sunrise Valley Dr #120, Reston, VA, 703-478-0440

Obstetrics/Gynecology

Adler, Alf Karl (7 mentions)
George Washington U, 1980
Certification: Obstetrics & Gynecology
2296 Opitz Blvd #350, Woodbridge, VA, 703-680-5327
385 Garrisonville Rd #204, Stafford, VA, 540-659-3089

Alagia, Damian P., III (3 mentions)
Georgetown U, 1982 *Certification:* Obstetrics & Gynecology
6845 Elm St #600, McLean, VA, 703-748-9880

Andersen, Glenna R. (14 mentions)
U of Virginia, 1981 *Certification:* Obstetrics & Gynecology
8501 Arlington Blvd #300, Fairfax, VA, 703-560-1611

Anderson, Glenn (3 mentions)
Georgetown U, 1977 *Certification:* Family Medicine
9409 Old Burke Lake Rd #B, Burke, VA, 703-978-4200

Band, Darryn Marc (5 mentions)
U of Maryland, 1989 *Certification:* Obstetrics & Gynecology
10313 Georgia Ave #202, Silver Spring, MD, 301-681-9171
15225 Shady Grove Rd #306, Rockville, MD, 301-869-7644

Barter, James Francis (3 mentions)
U of Virginia, 1977
6301 Executive Blvd, Rockville, MD, 301-770-4967

Bathgate, Susanne Lee (3 mentions)
George Washington U, 1986
Certification: Maternal-Fetal Medicine, Obstetrics & Gynecology
2150 Pennsylvania Ave NW, Washington, DC, 202-741-2500

Beckerman, Richard Jay (4 mentions)
Georgetown U, 1986 *Certification:* Obstetrics & Gynecology
4910 Massachusetts Ave NW #112, Washington, DC,
    202-244-3523

Berger-Weiss, Jessica (4 mentions)
New York U, 1989 *Certification:* Obstetrics & Gynecology
10801 Lockwood Dr #320, Silver Spring, MD, 301-681-3400

Bissell, Marion C. (3 mentions)
New York Med Coll, 1984 *Certification:* Obstetrics & Gynecology
6355 Walker Ln #408, Alexandria, VA, 703-719-5901

Blank, Kenneth Alan (6 mentions)
U of Maryland, 1982 *Certification:* Obstetrics & Gynecology
2141 K St NW #808, Washington, DC, 202-331-9293

Bohon, Constance Joan (3 mentions)
George Washington U, 1978
Certification: Obstetrics & Gynecology
2141 K St NW #808, Washington, DC, 202-331-9293

Bonn, Bruce Gary (4 mentions)
Albany Med Coll, 1980 *Certification:* Obstetrics & Gynecology
2311 M St NW #304, Washington, DC, 202-331-0577

Brantz, Arthur Jay (3 mentions)
FMS-Mexico, 1978 *Certification:* Obstetrics & Gynecology
3070 Crain Hwy, Waldorf, MD, 301-893-2326

Bridges, Robert Russell (3 mentions)
U of Alabama, 1982 *Certification:* Obstetrics & Gynecology
2440 M St NW #416, Washington, DC, 202-223-3006

Burke, Brendan F. (17 mentions)
Georgetown U, 1987 *Certification:* Obstetrics & Gynecology
5530 Wisconsin Ave #850, Chevy Chase, MD, 301-652-7623

Busch, Rebecca Joanne (5 mentions)
Louisiana State U, 1985 *Certification:* Obstetrics & Gynecology
1145 19th St NW 410, Washington, DC, 202-331-1740
407 N Washington St, Falls Church, VA, 703-533-9211

Caskie, Sandra (4 mentions)
George Washington U, 1982
Certification: Obstetrics & Gynecology
1715 N George Mason Dr #302, Arlington, VA, 703-816-4152

Cauble, Kathleen (3 mentions)
U of Arizona, 1981 *Certification:* Obstetrics & Gynecology
1800 Town Center Dr #120, Reston, VA, 703-834-6244

Cobbs, Gwendolyn Patterson (3 mentions)
Georgetown U, 1992
1715 N George Mason Dr #302, Arlington, VA, 703-816-4152
19450 Deerfield Ave #150, Landsdowne, VA, 703-816-4152

Colie, Christine Frances (3 mentions)
Georgetown U, 1987 *Certification:* Obstetrics & Gynecology
3800 Reservoir Rd NW PHC#3, Washington, DC, 202-444-8531

Di Paolo, Sanda F. (3 mentions)
Georgetown U, 1989 *Certification:* Obstetrics & Gynecology
3801 N Fairfax Dr #31, Arlington, VA, 703-351-9700
1515 Chain Bridge Rd #204, McLean, VA, 703-356-7868

Dickman, Craig Allen (13 mentions)
U of Maryland, 1980 *Certification:* Obstetrics & Gynecology
15215 Shady Grove Rd #300, Rockville, MD, 301-424-3444
10801 Lockwood Dr #290, Silver Spring, MD, 301-593-5595

Elliott, J. Jeffrey (13 mentions)
Georgetown U, 1977 *Certification:* Obstetrics & Gynecology
1635 N George Mason Dr #300, Arlington, VA, 703-525-8800

Footer, Robert Dennis (3 mentions)
George Washington U, 1975
3301 New Mexico Ave NW #336, Washington, DC, 202-362-0355
6282 Montrose Rd, Rockville, MD, 301-468-3004

Fraga, Vivian M. (10 mentions)
Georgetown U, 1981 *Certification:* Obstetrics & Gynecology
5454 Wisconsin Ave #1005, Chevy Chase, MD, 301-654-2182

Gaba, Nancy D. (5 mentions)
George Washington U, 1993
Certification: Obstetrics & Gynecology
2150 Pennsylvania Ave NW, Washington, DC, 202-741-2500

Gomez Lobo, Veronica (5 mentions)
Georgetown U, 1989 *Certification:* Obstetrics & Gynecology
3020 14th St NW, Washington, DC, 202-745-4300

Gopal, Sarita (5 mentions)
Med Coll of Pennsylvania, 1988
Certification: Obstetrics & Gynecology
4001 Fair Ridge Dr #301, Fairfax, VA, 703-359-5900

Hafizi, Ghazaleh (4 mentions)
Howard U, 1990 *Certification:* Obstetrics & Gynecology
3301 Woodburn Rd #307, Annandale, VA, 703-573-7772
1860 Town Center Dr #260, Reston, VA, 703-787-0199

Heintze, Achim Jurgen (3 mentions)
FMS-Germany, 1967 *Certification:* Obstetrics & Gynecology
4910 Massachusetts Ave NW #112, Washington, DC,
    202-244-3523

Hill, Charles F., Jr. (3 mentions)
Georgetown U, 1975 *Certification:* Obstetrics & Gynecology
5454 Wisconsin Ave #1035, Chevy Chase, MD, 301-654-5700
1145 19th St NW #410, Washington, DC, 202-331-1740
407 N Washington St #101, Falls Church, VA, 703-533-9211

Hodges, Walter James, Jr. (6 mentions)
Georgetown U, 1989 *Certification:* Obstetrics & Gynecology
4001 Fair Ridge Dr #202, Fairfax, VA, 703-591-2223

Imershein, Sara Louise (5 mentions)
Emory U, 1980 *Certification:* Obstetrics & Gynecology
2311 M St NW #304, Washington, DC, 202-466-4800

Jerome, Marilyn Concetta (15 mentions)
U of Cincinnati, 1978 *Certification:* Obstetrics & Gynecology
4910 Massachusetts Ave NW #112, Washington, DC,
202-244-3523

Johnson, Heather Lee (3 mentions)
Yale U, 1979 *Certification:* Obstetrics & Gynecology
1145 19th St NW #410, Washington, DC, 202-331-1740
5454 Wisconsin Ave #1035, Chevy Chase, MD, 301-654-5700
407 N Washington St #105, Falls Church, VA, 703-533-9211

Kaler, Lori Michele (3 mentions)
U of Illinois, 1985 *Certification:* Obstetrics & Gynecology
10401 Old Georgetown Rd #307, Bethesda, MD, 301-897-0945

Kleinman, Bradford Allan (6 mentions)
U of Maryland, 1976 *Certification:* Obstetrics & Gynecology
1400 Forest Glen Rd #500, Silver Spring, MD, 301-681-6772

Ladd, Jill Jayson (3 mentions)
Georgetown U, 1977 *Certification:* Obstetrics & Gynecology
15215 Shady Grove Rd #300, Rockville, MD, 301-424-3444
10801 Lockwood Dr #290, Silver Spring, MD, 301-593-5595

Lin, Jeffrey Y. (4 mentions)
Albany Med Coll, 1984
Certification: Gynecologic Oncology, Obstetrics & Gynecology
5255 Loughboro Rd NW, Washington, DC, 202-243-5295

Ma, Peter Lun Yan (3 mentions)
Howard U, 1978 *Certification:* Obstetrics & Gynecology
10810 Connecticut Ave Bldg 1, Kensington, MD, 301-929-7001

Maanavi, Darya Berta (4 mentions)
Eastern Virginia Med Sch, 1987
Certification: Obstetrics & Gynecology
8501 Arlington Blvd #300, Fairfax, VA, 703-560-1611

Maddox, John Frank, III (5 mentions)
U of California-San Francisco, 1977
Certification: Obstetrics & Gynecology
8316 Arlington Blvd #420, Fairfax, VA, 703-698-8060
3700 Joseph Siewick Dr #302, Fairfax, VA, 703-698-8060

Malone, Sharon Denise (7 mentions)
Columbia U, 1988 *Certification:* Obstetrics & Gynecology
4910 Massachusetts Ave NW #112, Washington, DC,
202-244-3523

Margolis, Richard Sheldon (4 mentions)
George Washington U, 1969
Certification: Obstetrics & Gynecology
10215 Fernwood Rd #101, Bethesda, MD, 301-530-2235
9711 Medical Center Dr #320, Rockville, MD, 301-330-5401

McCue, Raymond Leo, III (3 mentions)
Georgetown U, 1979 *Certification:* Obstetrics & Gynecology
9304 Forest Point Cir, Manassas, VA, 703-368-1969

Mims, Oscar Lugrie, Jr. (4 mentions)
Howard U, 1983
Certification: Maternal-Fetal Medicine, Obstetrics & Gynecology
7620 Carroll Ave #101, Takoma Park, MD, 301-891-6622

Muasher, Lisa (3 mentions)
Certification: Obstetrics & Gynecology
8501 Arlington Blvd #300, Fairfax, VA, 703-560-1611

Mufarrij, Imad Sami (4 mentions)
FMS-Lebanon, 1980 *Certification:* Obstetrics & Gynecology
4000 Mitchellville Rd #308, Bowie, MD, 301-805-0095
2121 Medical Park Dr #6, Silver Spring, MD, 301-592-0899
7301 Hanover Pkwy, Greenbelt, MD, 301-220-2225
11500 Old Georgetown Rd LL, Rockville, MD, 301-881-3260

Newman, Richard S. (3 mentions)
George Washington U, 1978
Certification: Obstetrics & Gynecology
2141 K St NW #808, Washington, DC, 202-331-9293

Norman, Brad Howard (3 mentions)
FMS-Dominican Republic, 1985
Certification: Obstetrics & Gynecology
1400 Forest Glen Rd #525, Silver Spring, MD, 301-593-8101
7350 Van Dusen Rd #470, Laurel, MD, 301-490-8882

O'Regan, Maureen (3 mentions)
Georgetown U, 1972
1625 N George Mason Dr #474, Arlington, VA, 703-528-6300
104 Elden St #16, Herndon, VA, 703-437-8080

Piness, Jane E. (4 mentions)
Georgetown U, 1986 *Certification:* Obstetrics & Gynecology
1635 N George Mason Dr #185, Arlington, VA, 703-717-4093

Powers, David Neil (3 mentions)
U of Pennsylvania, 1977 *Certification:* Obstetrics & Gynecology
2440 M St NW #503, Washington, DC, 202-835-8363
4825 Bethesda Ave #300, Bethesda, MD, 301-652-5111

Reiter, Mark Bruce (6 mentions)
Georgetown U, 1973 *Certification:* Obstetrics & Gynecology
1145 19th St NW #410, Washington, DC, 202-331-1740
5454 Wisconsin Ave #1035, Chevy Chase, MD, 301-654-5700
407 N Washington St #105, Falls Church, VA, 703-533-9211

Renzi, Gerald R. (6 mentions)
Howard U, 1980 *Certification:* Obstetrics & Gynecology
9715 Medical Center Dr #330, Rockville, MD, 301-424-1696

Sanz, Luis E. (3 mentions)
Georgetown U, 1976 *Certification:* Obstetrics & Gynecology
1625 N George Mason Dr #475, Arlington, VA, 703-717-4000

Scott, Thomas Walter (4 mentions)
George Washington U, 1975
Certification: Obstetrics & Gynecology
106 Little Falls St, Falls Church, VA, 703-241-1851

Siegel, Marc Evan (4 mentions)
Georgetown U, 1991 *Certification:* Obstetrics & Gynecology
4660 Kenmore Ave #1100, Alexandria, VA, 703-370-0400

Sine, Mary Heather (5 mentions)
Georgetown U, 1993 *Certification:* Obstetrics & Gynecology
10313 Georgia Ave #202, Silver Spring, MD, 301-681-9101
15225 Shady Grove Rd #306, Rockville, MD, 301-869-7644

Stas, Michelle (4 mentions)
U of Virginia, 1994 *Certification:* Obstetrics & Gynecology
209 Elden St #209, Herndon, VA, 703-435-2574
6355 Walker Ln #508, Alexandria, VA, 703-971-7633
3554 Chain Bridge Rd #302, Fairfax, VA, 703-273-6635

Steren, Albert Joseph (3 mentions)
George Washington U, 1987
Certification: Gynecologic Oncology, Obstetrics & Gynecology
6301 Executive Blvd, Rockville, MD, 301-770-4967

Tchabo, Jean-Gilles (7 mentions)
FMS-Canada, 1972 *Certification:* Obstetrics & Gynecology
1715 N George Mason Dr #404, Arlington, VA, 703-558-6591

Townsend, Lewis Rhodes (3 mentions)
George Washington U, 1981
Certification: Obstetrics & Gynecology
10215 Fernwood Rd #250, Bethesda, MD, 301-897-9817
5255 Loughboro Rd NW Hayes Hall #527, Washington, DC,
301-897-9817

Tran, Thu (3 mentions)
Ohio State U, 1987 *Certification:* Obstetrics & Gynecology
9715 Medical Center Dr, Rockville, MD, 301-424-1696

Travers, Charles Kenneth (5 mentions)
George Washington U, 1973
Certification: Obstetrics & Gynecology
10801 Lockwood Dr #320, Silver Spring, MD, 301-681-3400

Tyau, Laurie Sy (9 mentions)
Med Coll of Pennsylvania, 1989
Certification: Obstetrics & Gynecology
10313 Georgia Ave #202, Silver Spring, MD, 301-681-9101
15225 Shady Grove Rd #306, Rockville, MD, 301-869-7644

Wolf, Kathy Eileen (6 mentions)
Georgetown U, 1993 *Certification:* Obstetrics & Gynecology
10680 Main St #190, Fairfax, VA, 703-691-1188

Wolfgram, Edward Joseph (6 mentions)
Rosalind Franklin U, 1985
Certification: Obstetrics & Gynecology
10215 Fernwood Rd #101, Bethesda, MD, 301-530-2235
9711 Medical Center Dr #320, Rockville, MD, 301-330-5401

Zaita, Jamie L. (4 mentions)
Boston U, 1992 *Certification:* Obstetrics & Gynecology
4001 Fair Ridge Dr #202, Fairfax, VA, 703-591-2223

Ophthalmology

Adelson, Andrew J. (4 mentions)
U of Maryland, 1982 *Certification:* Ophthalmology
1145 19th St NW #607, Washington, DC, 202-496-9181

Ashburn, Frank S. (6 mentions)
Georgetown U, 1973 *Certification:* Ophthalmology
8330 Boone Blvd #160, Vienna, VA, 703-442-8129
4910 Massachusetts Ave NW #21, Washington, DC, 202-686-6700

Bahn, Charles Frederick (4 mentions)
Tulane U, 1977 *Certification:* Ophthalmology
4848 Battery Ln #102, Bethesda, MD, 301-657-3022

Baum, Michael (9 mentions)
Georgetown U, 1973 *Certification:* Ophthalmology
8830 Cameron St #105, Silver Spring, MD, 301-587-1800

Butrus, Salim Iliyya (4 mentions)
FMS-Lebanon, 1979 *Certification:* Ophthalmology
650 Pennsylvania Ave SE #270, Washington, DC, 202-544-1900

Carlson, Mary Susan D. (4 mentions)
Georgetown U, 1985 *Certification:* Ophthalmology
201 N Washington St 2nd Fl, Falls Church, VA, 703-237-4027

Chavis, Richard M. (5 mentions)
U of Missouri, 1971 *Certification:* Ophthalmology
6410 Rockledge Dr #208, Bethesda, MD, 301-493-9600

Deegan, William Francis (4 mentions)
Tufts U, 1988 *Certification:* Ophthalmology
6355 Walker Ln #502, Alexandria, VA, 703-313-8822
5454 Wisconsin Ave #1540, Chevy Chase, MD, 301-656-8100
8505 Arlington Blvd #300, Fairfax, VA, 703-698-9335

Dressler, Linda B. (4 mentions)
Harvard U, 1982 *Certification:* Ophthalmology
12011 Lee Jackson Hwy #305, Fairfax, VA, 703-273-2398

Duplessie, Michael David (9 mentions)
FMS-Ireland, 1989
10215 Fernwood Rd #98, Bethesda, MD, 301-493-6404

Falls, Mark David (10 mentions)
Jefferson Med Coll, 1987 *Certification:* Ophthalmology
3020 Hamaker Ct #503, Fairfax, VA, 703-698-2020
8150 Leesburg Pike #909, Vienna, VA, 703-790-1780

Feldman, Robert Charles (5 mentions)
Boston U, 1982 *Certification:* Ophthalmology
11300 Rockville Pike #708, Rockville, MD, 301-231-6567
15005 Shady Grove Rd #100, Rockville, MD, 301-231-6567

Forster, David John (7 mentions)
SUNY-Buffalo, 1985 *Certification:* Ophthalmology
3650 Joseph Siewick Dr #102, Fairfax, VA, 703-620-2701
6231 Leesburg Pike #608, Falls Church, VA, 703-534-3900
6355 Walker Ln #405, Alexandria, VA, 703-922-0906

Gabry, Jerome Benjamin (4 mentions)
Washington U, 1975 *Certification:* Ophthalmology
9801 Georgia Ave #221, Silver Spring, MD, 301-681-5050

Gaspar, Maurice Leonard (7 mentions)
Albert Einstein Coll of Med, 1977 *Certification:* Ophthalmology
1635 N George Mason Dr #100, Arlington, VA, 703-524-5777

Geist, Craig Erwin (6 mentions)
Virginia Commonwealth U, 1983
Certification: Ophthalmology
2150 Pennsylvania Ave NW #2A, Washington, DC, 202-741-2800

Goodglick, Todd Alan (5 mentions)
U of California-Los Angeles, 1984
Certification: Internal Medicine, Ophthalmology
5454 Wisconsin Ave #950, Chevy Chase, MD, 301-654-5114

Gould, Herbert Bennett (4 mentions)
New York U, 1971 *Certification:* Ophthalmology
16220 S Frederick Ave #204, Gaithersburg, MD, 301-963-9222

Gross, Holly Michele (5 mentions)
U of Michigan, 1991 *Certification:* Ophthalmology
5283 Corporate Dr #201, Frederick, MD, 301-662-4545

Hammerman, Murray F. (4 mentions)
Georgetown U, 1960 *Certification:* Ophthalmology
501 N Frederick Ave #108, Gaithersburg, MD, 301-926-3900
11400 Rockville Pike #301, Rockville, MD, 301-881-5888

Helfgott, Maxwell Alan (11 mentions)
George Washington U, 1972 *Certification:* Ophthalmology
1133 20th St NW #B-150, Washington, DC, 202-296-4900
3200 Tower Oak Blvd #210, Rockville, MD, 301-770-2424

Holzman, Marc J. (4 mentions)
Howard U, 1979 *Certification:* Ophthalmology
2021 K St NW #416, Washington, DC, 202-296-1333

Huang, Harry H. (17 mentions)
U of Maryland, 1983 *Certification:* Ophthalmology
5630 Shields Dr, Bethesda, MD, 301-897-3322

Hutcheon, Marcia Louise (7 mentions)
U of Pennsylvania, 1980 *Certification:* Ophthalmology
1395 Piccard Dr #105, Rockville, MD, 301-977-0167

Jaafar, Mohamad Sami (7 mentions)
FMS-Lebanon, 1978 *Certification:* Ophthalmology
111 Michigan Ave NW #4600, Washington, DC, 202-476-3015
8501 Arlington Blvd #200, Fairfax, VA, 571-226-8380
9850 Key West Ave 2nd Fl, Rockville, MD, 301-424-1755

Jacobson, Howard John (6 mentions)
FMS-South Africa, 1975 *Certification:* Ophthalmology
1145 19th St NW #335, Washington, DC, 202-331-4044

Karlin, Kenneth Michael (4 mentions)
Louisiana State U, 1980 *Certification:* Ophthalmology
6845 Elm St #611, McLean, VA, 703-356-6880
1800 Town Center Dr #317, Reston, VA, 703-437-3900

Kaufman, Robert B. (5 mentions)
SUNY-Buffalo, 1971 *Certification:* Ophthalmology
26135 Ridge Rd, Damascus, MD, 301-253-6565
8218 Wisconsin Ave #316, Bethesda, MD, 301-986-8856

Keys, Marshall P. (9 mentions)
Wayne State U, 1964 *Certification:* Ophthalmology
121 Congressional Ln #601, Rockville, MD, 301-231-7070

Kolsky, Martin Paul (18 mentions)
SUNY-Upstate Med U, 1966 *Certification:* Ophthalmology
106 Irving St NW #321 S, Washington, DC, 202-882-0200

Leto, Carl Joseph (8 mentions)
Tufts U, 1980 *Certification:* Ophthalmology
8150 Leesburg Pike #909, Vienna, VA, 703-790-1780
3020 Hamaker Ct #503, Fairfax, VA, 703-698-2020

Levine, David Jay (8 mentions)
Tufts U, 1973 *Certification:* Ophthalmology
19271 Montgomery Village Ave #H2, Montgomery Village, MD, 301-977-2300

Malouf, Alan Roy (5 mentions)
U of Maryland, 1985 *Certification:* Ophthalmology
17000 Science Dr #106, Bowie, MD, 301-805-9200

Martin, Neil (7 mentions)
Johns Hopkins U, 1976 *Certification:* Ophthalmology
5454 Wisconsin Ave #950, Chevy Chase, MD, 301-654-5114

Martinez, J. Alberto (4 mentions)
Georgetown U, 1987 *Certification:* Ophthalmology
6410 Rockledge Dr #610, Bethesda, MD, 301-896-0890

McAteer, Mary Beth (6 mentions)
Georgetown U, 1982 *Certification:* Ophthalmology
6231 Leesburg Pike #608, Falls Church, VA, 703-534-3900
3650 Joseph Siewick Dr #102, Fairfax, VA, 703-620-2701
6355 Walker Ln #405, Alexandria, VA, 703-922-0906

Nasrallah, Fadi Phillip (4 mentions)
FMS-Lebanon, 1981 *Certification:* Ophthalmology
3289 Woodburn Rd #270, Annandale, VA, 703-849-8601
1145 19th St NW #500, Washington, DC, 202-833-1668
6410 Rockledge Dr #400, Bethesda, MD, 301-530-5200

Nik, Narieman Ahmadi (5 mentions)
FMS-Iran, 1974 *Certification:* Ophthalmology
9801 Georgia Ave #340, Silver Spring, MD, 301-593-0500
6196 Oxon Hill Rd #440, Oxon Hill, MD, 301-839-3000

O'Neill, John Francis (5 mentions)
Georgetown U, 1956 *Certification:* Ophthalmology
2 Wisconsin Cir #200, Chevy Chase, MD, 301-215-7100

Palestine, Alan Gary (4 mentions)
U of Rochester, 1978 *Certification:* Ophthalmology
1145 19th St NW #500, Washington, DC, 202-833-1668
6410 Rockledge Dr #400, Bethesda, MD, 301-530-5200
3289 Woodburn Rd #270, Annandale, VA, 703-849-8601

Parelhoff, Edward (6 mentions)
Johns Hopkins U, 1978 *Certification:* Ophthalmology
2296 Opitz Blvd #120, Woodbridge, VA, 703-670-4700
8134 Old Keene Mill Rd #300, Springfield, VA, 703-451-6111

Rajpal, Rajesh Kumar (4 mentions)
Virginia Commonwealth U, 1987 *Certification:* Ophthalmology
5842 Hubbard Dr, Rockville, MD, 301-770-6888
8180 Greensboro Dr #140, McLean, VA, 703-827-5454

Rich, William L., III (14 mentions)
Georgetown U, 1972 *Certification:* Ophthalmology
6231 Leesburg Pike, Falls Church, VA, 703-534-3900
3650 Joseph Siewick Dr #102, Fairfax, VA, 703-620-2701

Rubinfeld, Roy Scott (8 mentions)
SUNY-Downstate Med Coll, 1982 *Certification:* Ophthalmology
5454 Wisconsin Ave #950, Chevy Chase, MD, 301-654-5114

Schwartz, Arthur Lewis (4 mentions)
Albert Einstein Coll of Med, 1968 *Certification:* Ophthalmology
5454 Wisconsin Ave #950, Chevy Chase, MD, 301-654-5114

Seidman, David Jay (14 mentions)
U of Pennsylvania, 1982 *Certification:* Ophthalmology
6231 Leesburg Pike #608, Falls Church, VA, 703-534-3900
3650 Joseph Siewick Dr #102, Fairfax, VA, 703-620-2701
6355 Walker Ln #405, Alexandria, VA, 703-922-0906

Stopak, Samuel Sheldon (4 mentions)
Emory U, 1984 *Certification:* Ophthalmology
2440 M St NW #516, Washington, DC, 202-659-0066

Thomas, Nancy Eve (4 mentions)
U of Pennsylvania, 1968 *Certification:* Ophthalmology
4301 48th St NW, Washington, DC, 202-363-4300

Tigani, Michael Carmine (6 mentions)
Vanderbilt U, 1983 *Certification:* Ophthalmology
1515 Chain Bridge Rd #G17, McLean, VA, 703-356-5484
5530 Wisconsin Ave #1527, Chevy Chase, MD, 301-657-4171

Von Fricken, Manfred A. (7 mentions)
Washington U, 1975 *Certification:* Ophthalmology
8505 Arlington Blvd #300, Fairfax, VA, 703-698-9335
6355 Walker Ln #502, Alexandria, VA, 703-313-8822

Wanicur, David Murray (5 mentions)
U of Pittsburgh, 1965 *Certification:* Ophthalmology
11400 Rockville Pike #301, Rockville, MD, 301-881-5888
501 N Frederick Ave #108, Gaithersburg, MD, 301-926-3900

Orthopedics

Ackerman, R. Marshall (5 mentions)
U of Pittsburgh, 1962 *Certification:* Orthopaedic Surgery
9715 Medical Center Dr #415, Rockville, MD, 301-340-9200

Annunziata, Christopher C. (6 mentions)
Georgetown U, 1994
Certification: Orthopaedic Sports Medicine, Orthopaedic Surgery
8320 Old Courthouse Rd #100, Vienna, VA, 703-288-7891
1635 N George Mason Dr #310, Arlington, VA, 703-525-6100

Avery, Gordon L. (9 mentions)
SUNY-Buffalo, 1974 *Certification:* Orthopaedic Surgery
1635 N George Mason Dr #310, Arlington, VA, 703-525-6100
8320 Old Courthouse Rd #100, Vienna, VA, 703-288-7891

Barth, Richard Werner (10 mentions)
Northwestern U, 1987
Certification: Orthopaedic Surgery, Surgery of the Hand
2021 K St NW #400, Washington, DC, 202-466-5151
5454 Wisconsin Ave #1000, Chevy Chase, MD, 301-657-1996

Bender, Andrew William (6 mentions)
Tufts U, 1980 *Certification:* Orthopaedic Surgery
9715 Medical Center Dr #415, Rockville, MD, 301-340-9200
19735 Germantown Rd #120, Germantown, MD, 301-528-8090

Bieber, Edward Jonathan (16 mentions)
Georgetown U, 1978
Certification: Orthopaedic Surgery, Surgery of the Hand
10215 Fernwood Rd #506, Bethesda, MD, 301-530-1010

Bobrow, Philip David (5 mentions)
SUNY-Buffalo, 1977 *Certification:* Orthopaedic Surgery
5530 Wisconsin Ave #1660, Chevy Chase, MD, 301-657-9876

Cassidy, Michael Patrick (10 mentions)
Georgetown U, 1979 *Certification:* Orthopaedic Surgery
3301 Woodburn Rd #208, Annandale, VA, 703-560-9495

Caulfield, J. Patrick (7 mentions)
Georgetown U, 1965 *Certification:* Orthopaedic Surgery
10215 Fernwood Rd #506, Bethesda, MD, 301-530-1010

Connell, Marc Donald (11 mentions)
Georgetown U, 1986 *Certification:* Orthopaedic Surgery
2021 K St NW #516, Washington, DC, 202-833-1147
5454 Wisconsin Ave #1000, Chevy Chase, MD, 301-657-1996

Desiderio, Vincent Guy (7 mentions)
Georgetown U, 1974 *Certification:* Orthopaedic Surgery
3301 New Mexico Ave NW #248, Washington, DC, 202-659-9836

Evans, Brian George (8 mentions)
New Jersey Med Sch, 1987 *Certification:* Orthopaedic Surgery
3800 Reservoir Rd NW, Washington, DC, 202-444-8766

Fine, Kenneth Michael (5 mentions)
Northwestern U, 1985
Certification: Orthopaedic Sports Medicine, Orthopaedic Surgery
9711 Medical Center Dr, Rockville, MD, 301-251-1433
3 Washington Cir NW #404, Washington, DC, 301-251-1433
20500 Seneca Meadows Pkwy, Germantown, MD, 301-251-1433

Fleeter, Thomas B. (5 mentions)
Howard U, 1979 *Certification:* Orthopaedic Surgery
1860 Town Center Dr #300, Reston, VA, 703-435-6604
6201 Centreville Rd #600, Centreville, VA, 703-378-4860

Gluck, Gabriel (6 mentions)
FMS-Canada, 1972 *Certification:* Orthopaedic Surgery
8702 Sudley Rd, Manassas, VA, 703-361-3590

Goldsmith, Michael Eric (9 mentions)
New York U, 1994 *Certification:* Orthopaedic Surgery
5530 Wisconsin Ave #1660, Chevy Chase, MD, 301-657-9876

Grossman, Richard Mark (6 mentions)
Georgetown U, 1980 *Certification:* Orthopaedic Surgery
5454 Wisconsin Ave #1000, Chevy Chase, MD, 301-657-1996
2021 K St NW #516, Washington, DC, 202-833-1147

Gunther, Stephen Flack (10 mentions)
Albany Med Coll, 1967 *Certification:* Orthopaedic Surgery
110 Irving St NW #3B28, Washington, DC, 202-877-6664

Hanway, Jeffrey Lynn (5 mentions)
Harvard U, 1988 *Certification:* Orthopaedic Surgery
8501 Arlington Blvd #200, Fairfax, VA, 571-226-8380

Hawken, Samuel McComas (6 mentions)
Georgetown U, 1972 *Certification:* Orthopaedic Surgery
3301 Woodburn Rd #208, Annandale, VA, 703-560-9495

Johnson, David C. (9 mentions)
Yale U, 1973 *Certification:* Orthopaedic Surgery
106 Irving St NW #215, Washington, DC, 202-291-9266

Kittredge, Ben W., IV (7 mentions)
U of Virginia, 1990 *Certification:* Orthopaedic Surgery
6355 Walker Ln #202, Alexandria, VA, 703-921-9130
2805 Duke St, Alexandria, VA, 703-823-2101

Klein, Thomas Joseph (10 mentions)
Georgetown U, 1984 *Certification:* Orthopaedic Surgery
1850 Town Center Pkwy #400, Reston, VA, 703-689-0300

Lewis, Randall Jeffrey (15 mentions)
Harvard U, 1969 *Certification:* Orthopaedic Surgery
2021 K St NW #400, Washington, DC, 202-466-5151
5454 Wisconsin Ave #1000, Chevy Chase, MD, 301-657-1996

Madden, Mark Patrick (10 mentions)
Georgetown U, 1984 *Certification:* Orthopaedic Surgery
1850 Town Center Pkwy #400, Reston, VA, 703-689-0300

Martinelli, Thomas A. (9 mentions)
Georgetown U, 1985 *Certification:* Orthopaedic Surgery
6355 Walker Ln #202, Alexandria, VA, 703-921-9130
2805 Duke St, Alexandria, VA, 703-823-2101

Pereles, Daniel Joseph (11 mentions)
U of Pennsylvania, 1987
Certification: Orthopaedic Sports Medicine, Orthopaedic Surgery
10400 Connecticut Ave #C, Kensington, MD, 301-949-8100

Perim, David Mark (6 mentions)
Georgetown U, 1985 *Certification:* Orthopaedic Surgery
18111 Prince Philip Dr #221, Olney, MD, 301-977-1300
9850 Key West Ave #120, Rockville, MD, 301-762-4800
1400 Forest Glen Rd #400, Silver Spring, MD, 301-589-3324
19532 Doctors Dr, Germantown, MD, 301-515-2607

Rankin, Edward Anthony (5 mentions)
Meharry Med Coll, 1965 *Certification:* Orthopaedic Surgery
1160 Varnum St NE #312, Washington, DC, 202-526-7031

Reing, Michael (11 mentions)
Georgetown U, 1973
3301 Woodburn Rd #309, Annandale, VA, 703-573-2219

Rockower, Stephen (5 mentions)
Temple U, 1975 *Certification:* Orthopaedic Surgery
6000 Executive Blvd #510, Rockville, MD, 301-770-7900

Romness, David William (12 mentions)
Eastern Virginia Med Sch, 1984
Certification: Orthopaedic Surgery
1635 N George Mason Dr #310, Arlington, VA, 703-525-6100
8320 Old Courthouse Rd #100, Vienna, VA, 703-288-7891

Sadlack, William James (5 mentions)
St Louis U, 1971 *Certification:* Orthopaedic Surgery
6410 Rockledge Rd #309, Bethesda, MD, 301-530-3220

Schluntz, Kurt Christian (10 mentions)
Columbia U, 1988 *Certification:* Orthopaedic Surgery
10215 Fernwood Rd #506, Bethesda, MD, 301-530-1010

Schneider, Philip Leon (16 mentions)
Howard U, 1983 *Certification:* Orthopaedic Surgery
10400 Connecticut Ave #C, Kensington, MD, 301-949-8100

Shaffer, Benjamin Scott (9 mentions)
U of Florida, 1984 *Certification:* Orthopaedic Surgery
5454 Wisconsin Ave #1000, Chevy Chase, MD, 301-657-1996
2021 K St NW #516, Washington, DC, 202-833-1147

Stinger, Robert B. (6 mentions)
Georgetown U, 1981 *Certification:* Orthopaedic Surgery
3301 Woodburn Rd #208, Annandale, VA, 703-560-9495

Thal, Raymond (5 mentions)
Loyola U Chicago, 1984 *Certification:* Orthopaedic Surgery
1860 Town Center Dr #300, Reston, VA, 703-435-6604

Thompson, Terry Lamar (5 mentions)
Howard U, 1983 *Certification:* Orthopaedic Surgery
2041 Georgia Ave NW #4300, Washington, DC, 202-865-1183

Tosi, Laura Lowe (8 mentions)
Harvard U, 1977 *Certification:* Orthopaedic Surgery
111 Michigan Ave NW, Washington, DC, 202-476-4063

Tuck, Steven Louis (24 mentions)
U of Chicago, 1975
Certification: Orthopaedic Surgery, Surgery of the Hand
9715 Medical Center Dr #415, Rockville, MD, 301-340-9200
19735 Germantown Rd #120, Germantown, MD, 301-528-8090

Unger, Anthony Steven (6 mentions)
SUNY-Buffalo, 1980 *Certification:* Orthopaedic Surgery
2021 K St NW #400, Washington, DC, 202-466-5151
5454 Wisconsin Ave #1000, Chevy Chase, MD, 301-657-1996

Witte, Jeffrey Francis (5 mentions)
U of Michigan, 1967 *Certification:* Orthopaedic Surgery
9715 Medical Center Dr #415, Rockville, MD, 301-340-9200
19735 Germantown Rd #120, Germantown, MD, 301-528-8090

Otorhinolaryngology

Bahadori, Robert Shahram (25 mentions)
Cornell U, 1989 *Certification:* Otolaryngology
8316 Arlington Blvd #300, Fairfax, VA, 703-573-7600
1850 Town Center Pkwy #305, Reston, VA, 703-834-2900
6201 Centreville Rd #400, Centreville, VA, 703-573-7600

Bianchi, David Alan (15 mentions)
George Washington U, 1984 *Certification:* Otolaryngology
2415 Musgrove Rd #203, Silver Spring, MD, 301-989-2300

Bosworth, John M., Jr. (14 mentions)
Uniformed Services U of Health Sciences, 1987
Certification: Otolaryngology
15235 Shady Grove Rd #100, Rockville, MD, 301-294-6514

Davidson, Bruce John (8 mentions)
West Virginia U, 1987 *Certification:* Otolaryngology
3800 Reservoir Rd NW Gorman Bldg 1st Fl, Washington, DC,
202-444-8186

Deeb, Ziad Elias (16 mentions)
FMS-Israel, 1967 *Certification:* Otolaryngology
110 Irving St NW #GA4, Washington, DC, 202-877-9403

Epstein, Stephen (8 mentions)
Rosalind Franklin U, 1964 *Certification:* Otolaryngology
9715 Medical Center Dr #528, Rockville, MD, 301-340-1355

Feldman, Bruce Allen (34 mentions)
Harvard U, 1965 *Certification:* Otolaryngology
5454 Wisconsin Ave #1535, Chevy Chase, MD, 301-652-8847
6410 Rockledge Dr #305, Bethesda, MD, 301-581-0610
20528 Boland Farm Rd #210, Germantown, MD, 301-515-6314

Feldman, Douglas Edward (11 mentions)
Harvard U, 1973 *Certification:* Otolaryngology
1145 19th St NW #402, Washington, DC, 202-466-7747
5454 Wisconsin Ave #1535, Chevy Chase, MD, 301-652-8847
20528 Boland Farm Rd #210, Germantown, MD, 301-652-8847
6410 Rockledge Dr #305, Bethesda, MD, 301-652-8847

Furst, Eric Jonathan (7 mentions)
Baylor U, 1986 *Certification:* Otolaryngology
5504 Backlick Rd, Springfield, VA, 703-941-9552

Golden, Lindsay (9 mentions)
U of Maryland, 1984 *Certification:* Otolaryngology
19211 Montgomery Village Ave #B23, Gaithersburg, MD,
301-963-6334
10801 Lockwood Dr #360, Silver Spring, MD, 301-593-5200

Lee, Patty (11 mentions)
Washington U, 1989 *Certification:* Otolaryngology
8316 Arlington Blvd #300, Fairfax, VA, 703-573-7600
6201 Centreville Rd #400, Centreville, VA, 703-573-7600
1850 Town Center Pkwy #305, Reston, VA, 703-834-2900

Mahat, V. Patrick (8 mentions)
Georgetown U, 1971 *Certification:* Otorhinolaryngology
3301 New Mexico Ave NW #310, Washington, DC, 202-363-2363

Marion, Edward David (7 mentions)
George Washington U, 1972 *Certification:* Otolaryngology
8314 Traford Ln #C, Springfield, VA, 703-644-7800
6231 Leesburg Pike #500, Falls Church, VA, 703-536-2729

McBride, Timothy Paul (20 mentions)
U of Virginia, 1977 *Certification:* Otolaryngology
8316 Arlington Blvd #300, Fairfax, VA, 703-573-7600
6201 Centreville Rd #400, Centreville, VA, 703-573-7600
1850 Town Center Pkwy #305, Reston, VA, 703-834-2900

Oppenheim, Josh Paul (9 mentions)
Wake Forest U, 1982 *Certification:* Otolaryngology
8314 Traford Ln #C, Springfield, VA, 703-644-7800
6231 Leesburg Pike #500, Falls Church, VA, 703-536-2729

Oringher, Seth Franklin (16 mentions)
George Washington U, 1986 *Certification:* Otolaryngology
20528 Boland Farm Rd #210, Germantown, MD, 301-515-6314
5454 Wisconsin Ave #1535, Chevy Chase, MD, 301-652-8847

Picken, Catherine (19 mentions)
Northwestern U, 1979 *Certification:* Otolaryngology
2021 K St NW #206, Washington, DC, 202-785-5000

Prasad, Sanjay (10 mentions)
U of Maryland, 1985 *Certification:* Otolaryngology
10215 Fernwood Rd #301, Bethesda, MD, 301-493-9409
8505 Arlington Blvd #270, Fairfax, VA, 703-352-3758

Rubinstein, Mark Isaac (25 mentions)
Jefferson Med Coll, 1983 *Certification:* Otolaryngology
8316 Arlington Blvd #300, Fairfax, VA, 703-573-7600
1850 Town Center Pkwy #305, Reston, VA, 703-834-2900
6201 Centreville Rd #400, Centreville, VA, 703-573-7600

Siegel, Michael B. (24 mentions)
U of Pennsylvania, 1986 *Certification:* Otolaryngology
15235 Shady Grove Rd #100, Rockville, MD, 301-942-7905

Spagnoli, Scott David (11 mentions)
U of Michigan, 1979 *Certification:* Otolaryngology
1635 N George Mason Dr #250, Arlington, VA, 703-524-1212

Troost, Thomas Rudolph (11 mentions)
Georgetown U, 1983 *Certification:* Otolaryngology
2150 Pennsylvania Ave NW 6th Fl, Washington, DC, 202-741-3410

Winkler, Thomas Paul (14 mentions)
Georgetown U, 1987 *Certification:* Otolaryngology
5530 Wisconsin Ave #1455, Chevy Chase, MD, 301-656-8630

Pain Medicine

Arvanaghi, Babak (17 mentions)
U of Maryland, 1991 *Certification:* Anesthesiology, Pain Medicine
6410 Rockledge Dr #110, Bethesda, MD, 301-530-7303
2112 F St NW, Washington, DC, 202-775-7246

Cernea, Andrei (6 mentions)
Albert Einstein Coll of Med, 1989
Certification: Anesthesiology, Pain Medicine
5255 Loughboro Rd NW, Washington, DC, 202-537-4589

Cherrick, Abraham Alan (13 mentions)
U of Missouri, 1980
Certification: Physical Medicine & Rehabilitation
2800 Shirlington Rd #102, Arlington, VA, 703-998-8824
6355 Walker Ln #507, Alexandria, VA, 703-971-4604

Chester, William Lamar (4 mentions)
U of Miami, 1982 *Certification:* Anesthesiology
9901 Medical Center Dr, Rockville, MD, 240-826-6000

Denney, Roger Alan (5 mentions)
U of Missouri, 1987 *Certification:* Anesthesiology, Pain Medicine
3289 Woodburn Rd #210, Annandale, VA, 703-208-6600

Dombrowski, John Francis (15 mentions)
Georgetown U, 1989 *Certification:* Anesthesiology
3301 New Mexico Ave NW #346, Washington, DC, 202-362-4787

Fischer, Greg David (7 mentions)
U of Pittsburgh, 1993
Certification: Anesthesiology, Pain Medicine
3289 Woodburn Rd #210, Annandale, VA, 703-208-6600

Freeman, Robert W. (6 mentions)
George Washington U, 1992 *Certification:* Anesthesiology
1500 Forest Glen Rd, Silver Spring, MD, 301-933-8840

Friedlis, Mayo Frederick (6 mentions)
Wayne State U, 1979
Certification: Physical Medicine & Rehabilitation
150 Elden St #240, Herndon, VA, 703-738-4335
3031 Javier Rd #100, Fairfax, VA, 703-560-8280

Gerwin, Robert David (7 mentions)
U of Chicago, 1964 *Certification:* Neurology
7830 Old Georgetown Rd #C15, Bethesda, MD, 301-656-0220

Heit, Howard Allen (11 mentions)
U of Pittsburgh, 1971
Certification: Gastroenterology, Internal Medicine
8316 Arlington Blvd #232, Fairfax, VA, 703-698-6151

Huffman, John M., Jr. (13 mentions)
Wake Forest U, 1989 *Certification:* Anesthesiology, Pain Medicine
1500 Forest Glen Rd, Silver Spring, MD, 301-933-8840

Klaiman, Mark David (7 mentions)
FMS-Israel, 1989
Certification: Physical Medicine & Rehabilitation
6410 Rockledge Dr #210, Bethesda, MD, 301-493-8884
3301 New Mexico Ave NW #302, Washington, DC, 301-493-8884

Rhodes, Leeann (12 mentions)
U of Maryland, 1990 *Certification:* Anesthesiology, Pain Medicine
110 Irving St NW #G012, Washington, DC, 202-877-3442
1145 19th St NW #850, Washington, DC, 202-223-9040

Sylvester, Carl L. (5 mentions)
Georgetown U, 1968 *Certification:* Anesthesiology
5255 Loughboro Rd NW, Washington, DC, 202-243-2280

Zuckerman, Lester Alan (4 mentions)
Mount Sinai Sch of Med, 1989
Certification: Anesthesiology, Pain Medicine
11921 Rockville Pike #505, Rockville, MD, 301-881-7246
75 Thomas Johnson Dr #C, Frederick, MD, 301-620-0012

Pathology

Ahlgren, Alice (9 mentions)
Georgetown U, 1977
Certification: Anatomic Pathology & Clinical Pathology
1850 Town Center Pkwy, Reston, VA, 703-830-3633

Barton, Joel Hinds (6 mentions)
U of Texas-Galveston, 1978
Certification: Anatomic Pathology & Clinical Pathology
113 Driscoll Way, Gaithersburg, MD, 301-279-6094

Brown, Barrett Bolton, Jr. (6 mentions)
George Washington U, 1987
Certification: Anatomic Pathology & Clinical Pathology
3289 Woodburn Rd #110, Annandale, VA, 703-698-1080

Busseniers, Anne E. (6 mentions)
FMS-Belgium, 1983
Certification: Anatomic Pathology, Cytopathology
3 Washington Cir NW #303, Washington, DC, 202-463-5149
6420 Rockledge Dr #1200, Bethesda, MD, 202-463-5149

Fleury, Thomas A. (8 mentions)
Georgetown U, 1976
Certification: Anatomic Pathology & Clinical Pathology
5255 Loughboro Rd NW, Washington, DC, 202-537-4651

Gutman, Pablo Daniel (7 mentions)
FMS-Argentina, 1986 *Certification:* Anatomic Pathology &
Clinical Pathology, Cytopathology, Hematology
1500 Forest Glen Rd, Silver Spring, MD, 301-754-7330

Lack, Ernest E., Jr. (7 mentions)
U of Minnesota, 1971
Certification: Anatomic Pathology, Clinical Pathology
110 Irving St NW, Washington, DC, 202-877-5254

Neumann, Mary Paula (6 mentions)
U of Minnesota, 1982 *Certification:* Anatomic Pathology &
Clinical Pathology, Cytopathology
4320 Seminary Rd, Alexandria, VA, 703-504-3726

Oertel, Yolanda Castillo (7 mentions)
FMS-Peru, 1964 *Certification:* Anatomic Pathology, Cytopathology
110 Irving St NW #C1219, Washington, DC, 202-877-0040

Schwartz, Arnold Melvin (22 mentions)
U of Miami, 1978
Certification: Anatomic Pathology & Clinical Pathology
2300 I St NW #601, Washington, DC, 202-994-8804

Shaffer, Margaret (5 mentions)
George Washington U, 1989
Certification: Anatomic Pathology & Clinical Pathology
5255 Loughboro Rd NW, Washington, DC, 202-537-4651

Sidawy, Mary Khayat (7 mentions)
FMS-Syria, 1978 *Certification:* Anatomic Pathology &
Clinical Pathology, Cytopathology
3800 Reservoir Rd NW, Washington, DC, 202-687-8053

Smith, William Irvin, Jr. (8 mentions)
U of Pittsburgh, 1972
Certification: Anatomic Pathology & Clinical Pathology
8600 Old Georgetown Rd, Bethesda, MD, 301-896-2566

Stay, Ellsworth James (6 mentions)
Michigan State U, 1973
Certification: Anatomic Pathology & Clinical Pathology
1701 N George Mason Dr, Arlington, VA, 703-558-6550

Pediatrics *(see note on page 9)*

Albert, Morris Sheldon (3 mentions)
Boston U, 1960 *Certification:* Pediatrics
18111 Prince Philip Dr #311, Olney, MD, 301-774-4100
423 E Ridgeville Blvd, Mount Airy, MD, 301-831-7511

Anders, Theodore H. (5 mentions)
U of Rochester, 1956 *Certification:* Pediatrics
5225 Connecticut Ave NW #103, Washington, DC, 202-363-0300

Atiyeh, Bassam A. (6 mentions)
FMS-Lebanon, 1985
107 N Virginia Ave, Falls Church, VA, 703-532-4446

Balfour, Guillermo A. (3 mentions)
FMS-Argentina, 1959 *Certification:* Pediatrics
3301 New Mexico Ave NW #238, Washington, DC, 202-537-1180

Barkin, Joan Walls (5 mentions)
Columbia U, 1972
5640 Nicholson Ln #2, Rockville, MD, 301-984-8112

Bennett, Howard Jay (5 mentions)
George Washington U, 1977 *Certification:* Pediatrics
5225 Connecticut Ave NW, Washington, DC, 202-363-0300

Berger, Linda M. (3 mentions)
U of Maryland, 1992 *Certification:* Pediatrics
903 Russell Ave #301, Gaithersburg, MD, 301-869-2292

Bernstein, Jeffrey Paul (6 mentions)
U of Virginia, 1985 *Certification:* Pediatrics
12501 Prosperity Dr #100, Silver Spring, MD, 301-681-6730

Botsford, Thomas Henrich (4 mentions)
SUNY-Buffalo, 1977 *Certification:* Pediatrics
6000 Executive Blvd #310, Rockville, MD, 301-881-7995

Brasch, Leah Florence (6 mentions)
U of Colorado, 1980 *Certification:* Pediatrics
4601 N Park Ave, Chevy Chase, MD, 301-656-2745

Casey, Catherine Sue (11 mentions)
Virginia Commonwealth U, 1974 *Certification:* Pediatrics
1715 N George Mason Dr #205, Arlington, VA, 703-522-7300

Clapp, Deborah Gray (3 mentions)
Virginia Commonwealth U, 1978 *Certification:* Pediatrics
2946 Sleepy Hollow Rd #3-B, Falls Church, VA, 703-534-1000

Coggeshall, Charles P. (12 mentions)
U of Texas-Galveston, 1975 *Certification:* Pediatrics
6000 Executive Blvd #310, Rockville, MD, 301-881-7995

Cohen, Lawrence Franklin (4 mentions)
Duke U, 1972
Certification: Pediatric Hematology-Oncology, Pediatrics
10313 Georgia Ave #303, Silver Spring, MD, 301-681-7020

Coleman, Raymond Hugh (6 mentions)
Tufts U, 1973 *Certification:* Pediatrics
11119 Rockville Pike #310, Rockville, MD, 301-468-9225

Crim, Lisa Margarethe (3 mentions)
U of Cincinnati, 1987 *Certification:* Pediatrics
3700 Joseph Siewick Dr #300, Fairfax, VA, 703-758-7100
8316 Traford Ln, Springfield, VA, 703-569-8400

Crock, Thomas Rankin (8 mentions)
George Washington U, 1973 *Certification:* Pediatrics
2946 Sleepy Hollow Rd #3-B, Falls Church, VA, 703-534-1000

Dubinsky, Diane E. (3 mentions)
George Washington U, 1982 *Certification:* Pediatrics
3650 Joseph Siewick Dr, Fairfax, VA, 703-391-0900
6211 Centreville Rd, Centreville, VA, 703-391-0900

Feroli, Edward Joseph (3 mentions)
George Washington U, 1960 *Certification:* Pediatrics
19251 Montgomery Village Ave #F10, Gaithersburg, MD,
301-926-3633

Fox, Eduardo Raul (3 mentions)
U of Virginia, 1995 *Certification:* Pediatrics
2946 Sleepy Hollow Rd #3-B, Falls Church, VA, 703-534-1000

Gober, Alan Edward (9 mentions)
U of Maryland, 1974 *Certification:* Pediatrics
4 Professional Dr #116, Gaithersburg, MD, 301-977-1103
3949 Ferrara Dr, Wheaton, MD, 301-933-4210

Goldman, William David (4 mentions)
George Washington U, 1975 *Certification:* Pediatrics
1715 N George Mason Dr #205, Arlington, VA, 703-522-7300

Goldstein, Linda Harriet (6 mentions)
New York U, 1980 *Certification:* Pediatrics
4601 N Park Ave, Chevy Chase, MD, 301-656-2745

Hamburger, Ellen Kravis (4 mentions)
U of Pennsylvania, 1981 *Certification:* Pediatrics
2141 K St NW #401, Washington, DC, 202-833-4543

Harrison, Stephen (6 mentions)
U of Michigan, 1975 *Certification:* Pediatrics
1830 Town Center Dr #205, Reston, VA, 703-435-3636

Hellerstein, Ann I. (4 mentions)
U of Missouri-Kansas City, 1985 *Certification:* Pediatrics
501 N Frederick Ave, Gaithersburg, MD, 301-258-7158

Hogan, Martha L. Wyrick (3 mentions)
Georgetown U, 1968 *Certification:* Pediatrics
8316 Traford Ln, Springfield, VA, 703-569-8400
3700 Joseph Siewick Dr #300, Fairfax, VA, 703-569-8400

Jones, Richard Lee (10 mentions)
Virginia Commonwealth U, 1971 *Certification:* Pediatrics
8401 Connecticut Ave #201, Chevy Chase, MD, 301-907-3960

Kaplan, Amy Beth (4 mentions)
George Washington U, 1995 *Certification:* Pediatrics
9715 Medical Center Dr #230, Rockville, MD, 301-279-6750

Karp, Evan Brett (3 mentions)
Wake Forest U, 1989
410 Maple Ave W #5, Vienna, VA, 703-938-2244

Korengold, George Matthew (4 mentions)
George Washington U, 1972 *Certification:* Pediatrics
11325 Seven Locks Rd #238, Potomac, MD, 301-299-8930

Kornfeld, Dana Lee (4 mentions)
U of Pennsylvania, 1990
Certification: Adolescent Medicine, Pediatrics
5612 Spruce Tree Ave, Bethesda, MD, 301-564-5880

Lee, Peggy B. K. (4 mentions)
FMS-United Kingdom, 1988 *Certification:* Pediatrics
6000 Executive Blvd #310, Rockville, MD, 301-881-7995

Libby, Russell Clark (4 mentions)
George Washington U, 1979 *Certification:* Pediatrics
3020 Hamaker Ct #200, Fairfax, VA, 703-573-2432
131 Elden St #312, Herndon, VA, 703-435-5202

Maggid, Mindy J. F. (3 mentions)
Georgetown U, 1992 *Certification:* Pediatrics
15215 Shady Grove Rd #303, Rockville, MD, 301-330-3216

McDowell, Robert L., Jr. (4 mentions)
Harvard U, 1974
Certification: Neonatal-Perinatal Medicine, Pediatrics
4900 Massachusetts Ave NW, Washington, DC, 202-966-5000

Miller, David Richard (7 mentions)
U of Vermont, 1975 *Certification:* Pediatrics
18109 Prince Philip Dr #375, Olney, MD, 301-774-5800
1 N Main St, Mount Airy, MD, 301-831-5333

Palumbo, Francis M. (9 mentions)
Georgetown U, 1972 *Certification:* Pediatrics
4900 Massachusetts Ave NW, Washington, DC, 202-966-5000

Peebles, Paul T. (9 mentions)
Case Western Reserve U, 1967
Certification: Pediatric Hematology-Oncology, Pediatrics
5612 Spruce Tree Ave, Bethesda, MD, 301-564-5880

Pillsbury, L. Harrison (4 mentions)
Georgetown U, 1977 *Certification:* Pediatrics
4900 Massachusetts Ave NW, Washington, DC, 202-966-5000

Plotsky, Carol Ann (5 mentions)
George Washington U, 1986 *Certification:* Pediatrics
15215 Shady Grove Rd #303, Rockville, MD, 301-330-3216

Reitman, David Samuel (3 mentions)
Tufts U, 1997 *Certification:* Adolescent Medicine, Pediatrics
15000 Broschart Rd, Rockville, MD, 301-251-6991

Rossbach, Christopher N. (3 mentions)
Virginia Commonwealth U, 1989 *Certification:* Pediatrics
8316 Traford Ln, Springfield, VA, 703-569-8400
3700 Joseph Siewick Dr #300, Fairfax, VA, 703-569-8400

Schwartz, Richard Harvey (6 mentions)
Georgetown U, 1965 *Certification:* Pediatrics
100 East St SE #301, Vienna, VA, 703-938-5555

Shanahan, Sheila Ann (6 mentions)
Med Coll of Pennsylvania, 1969 *Certification:* Pediatrics
4900 Massachusetts Ave NW, Washington, DC, 202-966-5000

Shearin, Robert B. (3 mentions)
U of North Carolina, 1968 *Certification:* Pediatrics
8401 Connecticut Ave #201, Chevy Chase, MD, 301-907-3960

Solomon, Herbert M. (3 mentions)
Georgetown U, 1963 *Certification:* Pediatrics
10301 Georgia Ave #106, Silver Spring, MD, 301-681-6000
2401 Research Blvd #370, Rockville, MD, 301-990-1664

Sullivan, Thomas J. (3 mentions)
New Jersey Med Sch, 1964 *Certification:* Pediatrics
1990 Old Bridge Rd #101, Woodbridge, VA, 703-491-4131
4660 Kenmore Ave #500, Alexandria, VA, 703-212-6600

Takai, Sandra Anne (5 mentions)
U of Maryland, 1980 *Certification:* Pediatrics
19735 Germantown Rd #200, Germantown, MD, 301-540-0811

Taylor, Stuart Barry (4 mentions)
U of Maryland, 1983 *Certification:* Pediatrics
903 Russell Ave #301, Gaithersburg, MD, 301-869-2292

Weich, Stuart Y. (3 mentions)
George Washington U, 1988 *Certification:* Pediatrics
10301 Georgia Ave #106, Silver Spring, MD, 301-681-6000
2401 Research Blvd #370, Rockville, MD, 301-990-1664

Weiner, Paul Russell (5 mentions)
U of Maryland, 1985 *Certification:* Pediatrics
5612 Spruce Tree Ave, Bethesda, MD, 301-564-5880

Wiedermann, Bernhard L. (3 mentions)
Baylor U, 1978
Certification: Pediatric Infectious Diseases, Pediatrics
111 Michigan Ave NW, Washington, DC, 202-476-5051

Zeh, Debra Anne (3 mentions)
SUNY-Downstate Med Coll, 1979 *Certification:* Pediatrics
8303 Arlington Blvd #201, Fairfax, VA, 703-573-2018
10134 Colvin Run Rd #D, Great Falls, VA, 703-757-7950

Plastic Surgery

Attinger, Christopher E. (6 mentions)
Yale U, 1981 *Certification:* Plastic Surgery
3800 Reservoir Rd NW, Washington, DC, 202-444-9686

Boyajian, Michael John (12 mentions)
New York U, 1976 *Certification:* Plastic Surgery
111 Michigan Ave NW #100, Washington, DC, 202-476-2157
9850 Key West Ave, Rockville, MD, 301-424-1755
8501 Arlington Blvd, Fairfax, VA, 571-226-8380
4900 Massachusetts Ave NW #320, Washington, DC,
    202-895-3860

Colgan, Diane Leslee (9 mentions)
Med Coll of Pennsylvania, 1967
Certification: Plastic Surgery, Surgery
9800 Falls Rd #105, Potomac, MD, 301-299-6644

Dick, Gregory Oskar (28 mentions)
New York Med Coll, 1980 *Certification:* Plastic Surgery
9711 Medical Center Dr #100, Rockville, MD, 301-251-2600

Duda, Gloria (7 mentions)
U of Miami, 1984 *Certification:* Plastic Surgery
6845 Elm St #708, McLean, VA, 703-893-1111

Dufresne, Craig Roger (20 mentions)
Columbia U, 1977 *Certification:* Plastic Surgery
5530 Wisconsin Ave #1235, Chevy Chase, MD, 301-654-9151
8501 Arlington Blvd #420, Fairfax, VA, 703-207-3065

Forman, Douglas Lee (10 mentions)
U of Pennsylvania, 1990 *Certification:* Plastic Surgery
11210 Old Georgetown Rd, North Bethesda, MD, 301-881-7770

Friedman, Roger Jay (29 mentions)
George Washington U, 1978 *Certification:* Plastic Surgery
11210 Old Georgetown Rd, North Bethesda, MD, 301-881-7770

Gartside, Roberta Lee (12 mentions)
Temple U, 1981 *Certification:* Plastic Surgery
1800 Town Center Dr #412, Reston, VA, 703-742-8004
3299 Woodburn Rd #340, Annandale, VA, 703-204-2706

Goldberg, Andrew Gregg (10 mentions)
New Jersey Med Sch, 1984 *Certification:* Plastic Surgery
3700 Joseph Siewick Dr #301, Fairfax, VA, 703-264-0904

Gottlieb, Wendy Ruth (7 mentions)
U of Virginia, 1996 *Certification:* Plastic Surgery
1850 Town Center Pkwy #301, Reston, VA, 703-668-9499
1635 N George Mason Dr #140, Arlington, VA, 703-668-9499

Hopping, Steven Blair (6 mentions)
U of Cincinnati, 1975 *Certification:* Otolaryngology
2440 M St NW #205, Washington, DC, 202-785-3175

Iorianni, Philip (9 mentions)
George Washington U, 1982 *Certification:* Plastic Surgery, Surgery
10810 Connecticut Ave, Kensington, MD, 301-929-7100

Leithauser, Lance Garner (8 mentions)
U of Michigan, 1973 *Certification:* Plastic Surgery
9715 Medical Center Dr #535, Rockville, MD, 301-294-9400

Macht, Steven Danl (6 mentions)
George Washington U, 1972 *Certification:* Plastic Surgery
2021 K St NW #217, Washington, DC, 202-887-8120

Munasifi, Talal Ahmad (22 mentions)
FMS-Iraq, 1971 *Certification:* Plastic Surgery
1635 N George Mason Dr #380, Arlington, VA, 703-841-0399

Oldham, Roger Jay (23 mentions)
Indiana U, 1969 *Certification:* Plastic Surgery
10215 Fernwood Rd #412, Bethesda, MD, 301-530-6100

Olding, Michael Joseph (17 mentions)
U of Kentucky, 1980 *Certification:* Plastic Surgery
2150 Pennsylvania Ave NW 9th Fl, Washington, DC, 202-741-3240

Otero, Susan Early (13 mentions)
George Washington U, 1980 *Certification:* Plastic Surgery
2400 M St NW #200, Washington, DC, 202-785-4187

Price, Gordon Wesley (7 mentions)
Wake Forest U, 1977 *Certification:* Plastic Surgery
5550 Friendship Blvd #130, Chevy Chase, MD, 301-652-7700
3299 Woodburn Rd #490, Annandale, VA, 703-560-2850

Ruff, Paul Gray, IV (8 mentions)
Eastern Virginia Med Sch, 1993
Certification: Plastic Surgery, Surgery
2440 M St NW #200, Washington, DC, 202-785-4187

Sanzaro, Thomas Joseph (10 mentions)
Georgetown U, 1977 *Certification:* Plastic Surgery
4530 Connecticut Ave NW #112, Washington, DC, 202-686-6270
3301 New Mexico Ave NW #206, Washington, DC, 202-895-1440

Shapiro, Carol Sadie (7 mentions)
Med Coll of Pennsylvania, 1965 *Certification:* Plastic Surgery
1940 Opitz Blvd, Woodbridge, VA, 703-494-1163
9001 Digges Rd #205, Manassas, VA, 703-361-2628

Spear, Scott Lawrence (9 mentions)
U of Chicago, 1972 *Certification:* Plastic Surgery
3800 Reservoir Rd NW, Washington, DC, 202-444-8612

Zahir, Khalique Syed (10 mentions)
West Virginia U, 1992 *Certification:* Plastic Surgery, Surgery
6410 Rockledge Dr #201, Bethesda, MD, 301-530-8300
3301 Woodburn Rd #202, Annandale, VA, 703-208-0783

Psychiatry

Akman, Jeffrey Scott (8 mentions)
George Washington U, 1981 *Certification:* Psychiatry
2150 Pennsylvania Ave NW 8th Fl, Washington, DC, 202-741-2880

Amitin, Sigmund Allen (3 mentions)
U of Maryland, 1964
1203 West St #C, Annapolis, MD, 410-269-0670

Brain, Lawrence Alfred (3 mentions)
FMS-Australia, 1967 *Certification:* Child Psychiatry, Psychiatry
7910 Woodmont Ave #1300, Bethesda, MD, 301-654-2255

Buyse, Valerie Josephine (3 mentions)
Boston U, 1972 *Certification:* Psychiatry
2110 Gallows Rd #D, Vienna, VA, 703-893-2429

Diamond, Michael Steven (3 mentions)
U of Pittsburgh, 1987 *Certification:* Psychiatry
4701 Willard Ave #233, Chevy Chase, MD, 301-657-4570

Doyle, Brian Bowles (7 mentions)
FMS-Canada, 1966 *Certification:* Psychiatry
1325 18th St NW #209, Washington, DC, 202-296-5877

Epstein, Steven Alan (7 mentions)
U of Pennsylvania, 1985
Certification: Psychiatry, Psychosomatic Medicine
3800 Reservoir Rd NW Kober-Cogan Bldg #605,
    Washington, DC, 202-687-8869

Fogarty, Thomas Michael (10 mentions)
Georgetown U, 1982 *Certification:* Internal Medicine, Psychiatry
10369-A Democracy Ln, Fairfax, VA, 703-383-6933

Glasser, Michael (5 mentions)
FMS-Philippines, 1978
Certification: Geriatric Psychiatry, Psychiatry
9055 Shady Grove Ct, Gaithersburg, MD, 301-330-0400
4405 East West Hwy #301, Bethesda, MD, 301-330-0440

Irwin, David Stanford (5 mentions)
Case Western Reserve U, 1966 *Certification:* Psychiatry
16220 S Frederick Rd #308, Gaithersburg, MD, 301-840-1077

Johnson, Robert W. (3 mentions)
U of Illinois, 1980 *Certification:* Psychiatry
2251 Pimmit Dr #C3, Falls Church, VA, 703-883-9033

Kehr, Bruce A. (3 mentions)
Georgetown U, 1975 *Certification:* Psychiatry
5920 Hubbard Dr, Rockville, MD, 301-984-9791

Khot, Vikram S. (3 mentions)
FMS-India, 1981 *Certification:* Psychiatry
8680 Hospital Way, Manassas, VA, 703-369-8464

Lockwood, David Walter (3 mentions)
Cornell U, 1960 *Certification:* Psychiatry
8730 Preston Pl, Chevy Chase, MD, 301-656-3119

Lorenz, Patrick C. (8 mentions)
Georgetown U, 1968 *Certification:* Psychiatry
3301 New Mexico Ave NW #344, Washington, DC, 202-363-2662

McMurrer, James P., Jr. (4 mentions)
Georgetown U, 1967 *Certification:* Child Psychiatry, Psychiatry
8316 Arlington Blvd #600, Fairfax, VA, 703-698-5220

Moscarillo, Frank Mark (6 mentions)
Georgetown U, 1961 *Certification:* Psychiatry
5454 Wisconsin Ave #1220, Chevy Chase, MD, 301-951-7220

Moss, Audrey (6 mentions)
Georgetown U, 1980 *Certification:* Geriatric Psychiatry,
    Psychiatry, Psychosomatic Medicine
1715 N George Mason Dr #409, Arlington, VA, 703-243-4373

Palys, Garsutis K. (5 mentions)
SUNY-Buffalo, 1973 *Certification:* Psychiatry
3416 Olandwood Ct #201, Olney, MD, 301-774-9400

Peterson, Stephen William (10 mentions)
U of Tennessee, 1974
Certification: Psychiatry, Psychosomatic Medicine
216 Michigan Ave NE FL 2, Washington, DC, 202-877-6333

Pfeffer, Bruce Paul (8 mentions)
New York U, 1970 *Certification:* Child Psychiatry, Psychiatry
10000 Falls Rd #208, Potomac, MD, 301-983-5103

Polakoff, Steven A. (5 mentions)
Georgetown U, 1981 *Certification:* Geriatric Psychiatry, Psychiatry
5530 Wisconsin Ave #852, Chevy Chase, MD, 301-718-0313

Prasad, C. M. (3 mentions)
FMS-Mexico, 1984
611 S Carlin Springs Rd #301, Arlington, VA, 703-578-0601

Rives, James Vell (3 mentions)
U of Alabama, 1995 *Certification:* Psychiatry
450 W Broad St, Falls Church, VA, 703-533-5899

Robb, Adelaide Sherwood (3 mentions)
Johns Hopkins U, 1987
Certification: Child & Adolescent Psychiatry, Psychiatry
8501 Arlington Blvd #240, Fairfax, VA, 571-226-8380
6191 Executive Blvd, Rockville, MD, 301-231-9010

Smoller, Bruce Melvyn (3 mentions)
Tulane U, 1969 *Certification:* Psychiatry
5530 Wisconsin Ave #806, Chevy Chase, MD, 301-951-4466
1810 Michael Faraday Dr, Reston, VA, 301-951-4466

Vogel, Donald Bruce (4 mentions)
U of Maryland, 1967 *Certification:* Psychiatry
13975 Connecticut Ave, Silver Spring, MD, 301-460-7444

Walsh, Thomas L. (3 mentions)
SUNY-Buffalo, 1974 *Certification:* Child Psychiatry, Psychiatry
6700 Old McLean Village Dr, McLean, VA, 703-442-9784

Wise, Thomas Nathan (19 mentions)
Duke U, 1969 *Certification:* Psychiatry, Psychosomatic Medicine
3300 Gallows Rd, Falls Church, VA, 703-776-3626

Wylie, John V. (9 mentions)
Columbia U, 1969 *Certification:* Psychiatry
12 7th St NE, Washington, DC, 202-544-6658

Pulmonary Disease

Ball, Joseph Austin (13 mentions)
Georgetown U, 1991 *Certification:* Pulmonary Disease
16220 S Frederick Ave #213, Gaithersburg, MD, 301-963-2770

Berger, Ira L. (11 mentions)
SUNY-Downstate Med Coll, 1987
Certification: Internal Medicine, Pulmonary Disease
1201 Seven Locks Rd #111, Rockville, MD, 301-762-5019

Bloom, Robert Leslie (12 mentions)
Tufts U, 1973 *Certification:* Critical Care Medicine, Internal
    Medicine, Pulmonary Disease
3289 Woodburn Rd #350, Annandale, VA, 703-641-8616

Casolaro, Mario Anthony (9 mentions)
Georgetown U, 1980
Certification: Internal Medicine, Pulmonary Disease
1400 S Joyce St #126, Arlington, VA, 703-521-6662

Clayton, James Ernest (20 mentions)
Creighton U, 1976
Certification: Pediatric Pulmonology, Pediatrics
2730-A Prosperity Ave, Fairfax, VA, 703-289-1410

Cleary, John Brian (12 mentions)
George Washington U, 1971
Certification: Internal Medicine, Pulmonary Disease
3650 Joseph Siewck Dr #307, Fairfax, VA, 703-391-8804
8650 Sudley Rd #212, Manassas, VA, 703-369-7788

Clinton, Mark Joseph (8 mentions)
Robert W Johnson Med Sch, 1986 *Certification:* Critical
    Care Medicine, Internal Medicine, Pulmonary Disease
2296 Opitz Blvd #230, Woodbridge, VA, 703-878-0924
385 Garrisonville Rd, Stafford, VA, 540-288-9343

Cohen, D. Scott (16 mentions)
U of Miami, 1983 *Certification:* Critical Care Medicine,
    Internal Medicine, Pulmonary Disease
5530 Wisconsin Ave #930, Chevy Chase, MD, 301-656-7374

Cooper, Byron Stanley (10 mentions)
Washington U, 1973
Certification: Internal Medicine, Pulmonary Disease
2440 M St NW #810, Washington, DC, 202-833-3000

Gross, David Charles (12 mentions)
SUNY-Downstate Med Coll, 1978
Certification: Internal Medicine, Pulmonary Disease
2440 M St NW #810, Washington, DC, 202-833-3000
106 Irving St NW #412S, Washington, DC, 202-833-3000

Hamm, Peter Gerard (17 mentions)
Columbia U, 1980 *Certification:* Critical Care Medicine,
    Internal Medicine, Pulmonary Disease
5530 Wisconsin Ave #930, Chevy Chase, MD, 301-656-7374

Kariya, Steven Toshihiro (22 mentions)
Cornell U, 1980 *Certification:* Critical Care Medicine,
    Internal Medicine, Pulmonary Disease
11501 Georgia Ave #515, Wheaton, MD, 301-942-2977

Lamberti, James Paul (19 mentions)
U of Pennsylvania, 1980 *Certification:* Critical Care
    Medicine, Internal Medicine, Pulmonary Disease
3289 Woodburn Rd #350, Annandale, VA, 703-641-8616

Larsen, Ylene A. (12 mentions)
Georgetown U, 1978 *Certification:* Internal Medicine
5530 Wisconsin Ave #930, Chevy Chase, MD, 301-656-7374

Mayo, Frank Joseph (13 mentions)
Ohio State U, 1973
Certification: Internal Medicine, Pulmonary Disease
16220 S Frederick Ave #213, Gaithersburg, MD, 301-963-2770

Miller, Gary H. (12 mentions)
New York U, 1977
Certification: Internal Medicine, Pulmonary Disease
2440 M St NW #810, Washington, DC, 202-833-3000

Mizus, Irving (12 mentions)
Albany Med Coll, 1978 *Certification:* Critical Care Medicine,
    Internal Medicine, Pulmonary Disease
10605 Concord St #500, Kensington, MD, 301-942-2977

Picone, Carlos (8 mentions)
FMS-Argentina, 1990 *Certification:* Critical Care Medicine,
    Internal Medicine, Pulmonary Disease
5530 Wisconsin Ave #930, Chevy Chase, MD, 301-656-7374

Pollack, Alan R. (9 mentions)
U of Maryland, 1981
Certification: Internal Medicine, Pulmonary Disease
1201 Seven Locks Rd #111, Rockville, MD, 301-762-5020

Robinson, Richard George (9 mentions)
Cornell U, 1975
Certification: Internal Medicine, Pulmonary Disease
2296 Opitz Blvd #230, Woodbridge, VA, 703-878-0924
385 Garrisonville Rd, Stafford, VA, 540-288-9343

Rosenberg, Samuel M. (17 mentions)
U of Maryland, 1984 *Certification:* Internal Medicine,
    Pediatric Pulmonology, Pediatrics
9711 Medical Center Dr #212, Rockville, MD, 301-738-7011
610 Solarex Ct #B, Frederick, MD, 301-738-7011

Schoenberger, Carl I. (30 mentions)
Tufts U, 1976 *Certification:* Critical Care Medicine, Internal
    Medicine, Pulmonary Disease
16220 S Frederick Rd #213, Gaithersburg, MD, 301-963-2770

Weiner, Jay Harlan (12 mentions)
George Washington U, 1975
Certification: Internal Medicine, Pulmonary Disease
11501 Georgia Ave #515, Wheaton, MD, 301-942-2977

Wigton, Roger Bruce (9 mentions)
U of Cincinnati, 1973 *Certification:* Critical Care Medicine,
    Internal Medicine, Pulmonary Disease
5216 Dawes Ave, Alexandria, VA, 703-931-4746

Zimmet, Steven Michael (10 mentions)
U of Virginia, 1968 *Certification:* Internal Medicine
1400 S Joyce St #126, Arlington, VA, 703-521-6662

Radiology—Diagnostic

Artiles, Carlos (4 mentions)
U of Connecticut, 1982
Certification: Diagnostic Radiology, Neuroradiology
4660 Kenmore Ave #608, Alexandria, VA, 703-751-5055
2200 Opitz Blvd #335, Woodbridge, VA, 703-494-3340
4001 Prince William Pkwy #302, Woodbridge, VA, 703-494-3309

Backer, Joseph Anthony (5 mentions)
Indiana U, 1965 *Certification:* Radiology
1701 N George Mason Dr, Arlington, VA, 703-558-6151

Bortnick, Bruce J. (7 mentions)
Howard U, 1979 *Certification:* Diagnostic Radiology
9850 Key West Ave, Rockville, MD, 240-864-1100

Bulas, Dorothy Isabella (5 mentions)
Med Coll of Pennsylvania, 1981 *Certification:* Diagnostic
  Radiology, Pediatric Radiology, Pediatrics
111 Michigan Ave NW, Washington, DC, 202-884-5432

Butch, Rodney James (17 mentions)
Yale U, 1975
Certification: Diagnostic Radiology, Internal Medicine
2722 Merilee Dr #230, Fairfax, VA, 703-698-4444

Clark, Letitia Renee (6 mentions)
SUNY-Buffalo, 1979 *Certification:* Diagnostic Radiology
3301 New Mexico Ave NW #324, Washington, DC, 202-686-1316

Cochrane, William James (4 mentions)
FMS-United Kingdom, 1964
Certification: Obstetrics & Gynecology
3022 Williams Dr #200, Fairfax, VA, 703-698-8800

Cohen, Lawrence Michael (4 mentions)
Georgetown U, 1982 *Certification:* Diagnostic Radiology
5454 Wisconsin Ave, Chevy Chase, MD, 301-652-3410

Curcio, Christopher M. (5 mentions)
Johns Hopkins U, 1978 *Certification:* Diagnostic Radiology
8261 Willow Oak Corporate Dr, Fairfax, VA, 703-205-3600

Di Piazza, Howard Joseph (6 mentions)
Georgetown U, 1980 *Certification:* Diagnostic Radiology
  with Special Competence in Nuclear Radiology
1500 Forest Glen Rd, Silver Spring, MD, 301-754-7350
2121 Medical Park Dr, Silver Spring, MD, 301-681-8242

Eisenberg, Lara Beth (8 mentions)
Med Coll of Wisconsin, 1993 *Certification:* Diagnostic Radiology
8600 Old Georgetown Rd, Bethesda, MD, 301-896-2060

Goodwin, Lyndon Keith (4 mentions)
U of Maryland, 1979 *Certification:* Diagnostic Radiology
2722 Merilee Dr #230, Fairfax, VA, 703-698-4444

Hill, Michael Christopher (8 mentions)
FMS-United Kingdom, 1970 *Certification:* Diagnostic Radiology
900 23rd St NW 1st Fl, Washington, DC, 202-715-5154

Jelinek, James Stephen (6 mentions)
Virginia Commonwealth U, 1983
Certification: Diagnostic Radiology, Neuroradiology
110 Irving St NW, Washington, DC, 202-877-6088

Jerath, Nakul (4 mentions)
U of Chicago, 1993
Certification: Diagnostic Radiology, Pediatric Radiology
2722 Merilee Dr #230, Fairfax, VA, 703-698-4444

Klein, Mark Elliot (9 mentions)
SUNY-Downstate Med Coll, 1978
Certification: Diagnostic Radiology
2141 K St NW #111, Washington, DC, 202-223-9722
10215 Fernwood Rd #50, Bethesda, MD, 301-564-1054

Korsvik, Holly (4 mentions)
Certification: Diagnostic Radiology
9711 Medical Center Dr #310, Rockville, MD, 301-762-2550
9850 Key West Ave, Rockville, MD, 240-864-1100

Lande, Ian M. (4 mentions)
FMS-Canada, 1979
Certification: Diagnostic Radiology, Neuroradiology
4445 Willard Ave #200, Chevy Chase, MD, 703-280-9800
2141 K St NW #900, Washington, DC, 703-280-9800

McWey, Russell Eugene (5 mentions)
Med U of South Carolina, 1983 *Certification:* Diagnostic
  Radiology with Special Competence in Nuclear Radiology,
  Nuclear Medicine, Vascular & Interventional Radiology
1701 N George Mason Dr, Arlington, VA, 703-558-6151

Muskie, Julia J. (6 mentions)
FMS-United Kingdom, 1990
Certification: Diagnostic Radiology, Neuroradiology
5255 Loughboro Rd NW, Washington, DC, 202-537-4791
1145 19th St NW #205, Washington, DC, 202-452-0601

Narang, Anil K. (4 mentions)
Des Moines U, 1980 *Certification:* Diagnostic Radiology,
  Neuroradiology, Vascular & Interventional Radiology
2121 Medical Park Dr, Silver Spring, MD, 301-681-8242

Newman, Richard David (10 mentions)
Yale U, 1975 *Certification:* Diagnostic Radiology
5255 Loughboro Rd NW, Washington, DC, 202-537-4791

Oliverio, Patrick J. (4 mentions)
West Virginia U, 1988
Certification: Diagnostic Radiology, Neuroradiology
2722 Merrilee Dr #230, Fairfax, VA, 703-698-4444

Rubin, Carole Zubicki (6 mentions)
George Washington U, 1988 *Certification:* Diagnostic Radiology
3022 Williams Dr, Fairfax, VA, 703-698-8800
2121 Medical Park Dr #2, Silver Spring, MD, 301-681-8242

Tu, Raymond King (4 mentions)
Uniformed Services U of Health Sciences, 1989
Certification: Diagnostic Radiology
7401 Forbes Blvd #A, Seabrook, MD, 301-464-6400
5454 Wisconsin Ave #1765, Chevy Chase, MD, 301-652-3410
2121 K St NW #100, Washington, DC, 202-223-5211

Vezina, Gilbert Louis (6 mentions)
FMS-Canada, 1983
Certification: Diagnostic Radiology, Neuroradiology
111 Michigan Ave #2400, Washington, DC, 202-476-4700

Volberg, Frank M., Jr. (10 mentions)
Duke U, 1969 *Certification:* Diagnostic Radiology
2722 Merrilee Dr #230, Fairfax, VA, 703-698-4444

Wolfman, Mark Gary (4 mentions)
Case Western Reserve U, 1971 *Certification:* Diagnostic Radiology
8600 Old Georgetown Rd, Bethesda, MD, 301-896-2060

Radiology—Therapeutic

Dick, Bradley Wayne (26 mentions)
Georgetown U, 1983 *Certification:* Diagnostic Radiology,
  Vascular & Interventional Radiology
8600 Old Georgetown Rd, Bethesda, MD, 301-896-2060

Gage, Irene (14 mentions)
Boston U, 1988 *Certification:* Radiation Oncology
5255 Loughboro Rd NW, Washington, DC, 202-537-4787

Karr, Stewart Brian (22 mentions)
New York U, 1986 *Certification:* Diagnostic Radiology,
  Vascular & Interventional Radiology
1500 Forest Glen Rd, Silver Spring, MD, 301-754-7350
2121 Medical Park Dr, Silver Spring, MD, 301-576-1100

Olan, Wayne Jeffrey (11 mentions)
Rosalind Franklin U, 1989 *Certification:* Diagnostic Radiology
8600 Old Georgetown Rd, Bethesda, MD, 301-896-2069

Sibley, Gregory Scott (15 mentions)
U of Michigan, 1990 *Certification:* Radiation Oncology
5255 Loughboro Rd NW, Washington, DC, 202-537-4787

Van Breda, Arina (15 mentions)
Boston U, 1976 *Certification:* Diagnostic Radiology,
  Vascular & Interventional Radiology
4320 Seminary Rd, Alexandria, VA, 703-504-7950

Rehabilitation

Aseff, John Namer (5 mentions)
Ohio State U, 1973
Certification: Physical Medicine & Rehabilitation
102 Irving St NW, Washington, DC, 202-877-1916

Cherrick, Abraham Alan (5 mentions)
U of Missouri, 1980
Certification: Physical Medicine & Rehabilitation
2800 Shirlington Rd #102, Arlington, VA, 703-998-8824
6355 Walker Ln #507, Alexandria, VA, 703-971-4604

Fink, Kathleen (12 mentions)
New Jersey Med Sch, 1992
Certification: Pain Medicine, Physical Medicine & Rehabilitation
6410 Rockledge Dr #600, Bethesda, MD, 301-581-8030

Ganjei, Ali Gholizadeh (5 mentions)
Virginia Commonwealth U, 1986
Certification: Physical Medicine & Rehabilitation
2501 Parkers Ln, Alexandria, VA, 703-664-7285
3600 Joseph Siewick Dr, Fairfax, VA, 703-391-3642

Gisolfi, Roger Vincent (6 mentions)
Georgetown U, 1966 *Certification:* Physical Medicine &
  Rehabilitation, Spinal Cord Injury Medicine
2501 Parkers Ln, Alexandria, VA, 703-664-7285

Grant, Kathryn Eileen (5 mentions)
Virginia Commonwealth U, 1976
Certification: Physical Medicine & Rehabilitation
1625 N George Mason Dr, Arlington, VA, 703-558-6507

Im, Dukjin (5 mentions)
U of Michigan, 1990 *Certification:* Pediatric Rehabilitation
  Medicine, Physical Medicine & Rehabilitation
8505 Arlington Blvd #100, Fairfax, VA, 703-970-2617

Klaiman, Mark David (12 mentions)
FMS-Israel, 1989
Certification: Physical Medicine & Rehabilitation
6410 Rockledge Dr #210, Bethesda, MD, 301-493-8884
3301 New Mexico Ave NW #302, Washington, DC, 301-493-8884

Sheehan, Terrence Patrick (7 mentions)
SUNY-Buffalo, 1990 *Certification:* Physical Medicine &
  Rehabilitation, Spinal Cord Injury Medicine
9909 Medical Center Dr, Rockville, MD, 240-864-6000

Shin, Wan (12 mentions)
FMS-South Korea, 1968
Certification: Physical Medicine & Rehabilitation
3300 Gallows Rd, Falls Church, VA, 703-776-6086

Toerge, John Edward (12 mentions)
Midwestern U, 1974
Certification: Physical Medicine & Rehabilitation
3800 Reservoir Rd NW 4th Fl, Washington, DC, 202-444-1257

Rheumatology

Baraf, Herbert S. B. (20 mentions)
SUNY-Downstate Med Coll, 1973
Certification: Internal Medicine, Rheumatology
2730 University Blvd W #310, Wheaton, MD, 301-942-7600
14955 Shady Grove Rd #230, Rockville, MD, 301-251-5910

Borenstein, David Gilbert (10 mentions)
Johns Hopkins U, 1973
Certification: Internal Medicine, Rheumatology
2021 K St NW #300, Washington, DC, 202-293-1470

Diiorio, Emma G. (15 mentions)
New York U, 1987
Certification: Internal Medicine, Rheumatology
2730 University Blvd W #310, Wheaton, MD, 301-942-7600
14955 Shady Grove Rd #230, Rockville, MD, 301-251-5910

Lacks, Susan (18 mentions)
Duke U, 1979 *Certification:* Internal Medicine, Rheumatology
2141 K St NW #407, Washington, DC, 202-293-8855

Laukaitis, Joseph Peter (12 mentions)
SUNY-Upstate Med U, 1983
Certification: Internal Medicine, Rheumatology
2141 K St NW #407, Washington, DC, 202-293-8855

Litman, Deborah Sharon (9 mentions)
Virginia Commonwealth U, 1978
Certification: Internal Medicine, Rheumatology
5530 Wisconsin Ave #1445, Chevy Chase, MD, 301-215-4167

Mullins, William W., Jr. (12 mentions)
Harvard U, 1978 *Certification:* Internal Medicine, Rheumatology
10215 Fernwood Rd #303, Bethesda, MD, 301-493-2500

Nguyen, Phong Quang (11 mentions)
U of Florida, 1983
Certification: Internal Medicine, Rheumatology
8316 Arlington Blvd #602, Fairfax, VA, 703-573-0130
1860 Town Center Dr #130, Reston, VA, 703-709-9174
44055 Riverside Pkwy #242, Leesburg, VA, 703-858-7222

Schechter, Stephen Leslie (17 mentions)
Georgetown U, 1969
Certification: Internal Medicine, Rheumatology
10215 Fernwood Rd #303, Bethesda, MD, 301-493-2500

Siegel, Evan Lloyd (23 mentions)
Boston U, 1984 *Certification:* Internal Medicine, Rheumatology
14955 Shady Grove Rd #230, Rockville, MD, 301-251-5910
2730 University Blvd W #310, Wheaton, MD, 301-942-7600

White, Patience Haydock (9 mentions)
Harvard U, 1974 *Certification:* Internal Medicine, Rheumatology
2150 Pennsylvania Ave NW, Washington, DC, 202-741-3333

Wilkenfeld, Morris Jack (21 mentions)
George Washington U, 1973
Certification: Internal Medicine, Rheumatology
3022 Williams Dr #100, Fairfax, VA, 703-573-9220

Thoracic Surgery

Corso, Paul Joseph (13 mentions)
George Washington U, 1969 *Certification:* Thoracic Surgery
110 Irving St NW #1E3, Washington, DC, 202-877-7464

Kiernan, Paul Darlington (50 mentions)
Georgetown U, 1974 *Certification:* Thoracic Surgery
2921 Telestar Ct #140, Falls Church, VA, 703-280-5858

Levin, Barry Jay (49 mentions)
Emory U, 1970 *Certification:* Thoracic Surgery
10215 Fernwood Rd #405, Bethesda, MD, 301-897-5620

Margolis, Marc (9 mentions)
FMS-South Africa, 1987 *Certification:* Surgery, Thoracic Surgery
2175 K St NW #300, Washington, DC, 202-775-8600

Markovitz, Lawrence J. (9 mentions)
Mount Sinai Sch of Med, 1980 *Certification:* Thoracic Surgery
2101 Medical Park Dr #304, Silver Spring, MD, 301-270-8111
1201 Seven Locks Rd #111, Rockville, MD, 301-270-8111

Rhee, John Wonyong (14 mentions)
Jefferson Med Coll, 1984 *Certification:* Surgery, Thoracic Surgery
4320 Seminary Rd, Alexandria, VA, 703-504-7880

Soberman, Mark Steven (37 mentions)
Emory U, 1983 *Certification:* Thoracic Surgery
106 Irving St NW #3150N, Washington, DC, 202-723-7391

Urology

Aron, Barry (14 mentions)
New York U, 1968 *Certification:* Urology
9715 Medical Center Dr #404, Rockville, MD, 301-424-0433

Ball, Robert Alan (19 mentions)
Jefferson Med Coll, 1985 *Certification:* Urology
8503 Arlington Blvd #310, Fairfax, VA, 703-876-1791

Basile, John Joseph (12 mentions)
Virginia Commonwealth U, 1981 *Certification:* Urology
3020 Hamaker Ct #B111, Fairfax, VA, 703-876-0288

Belman, A. Barry (11 mentions)
Northwestern U, 1964 *Certification:* Pediatric Urology, Urology
111 Michigan Ave NW #4400, Washington, DC, 202-476-5042
9850 Key West Ave, Rockville, MD, 301-424-1755

Bloom, Leonard Stuart (17 mentions)
U of Maryland, 1984 *Certification:* Urology
2730 University Blvd W #516, Wheaton, MD, 301-933-9660
9707 Medical Center Dr #310, Rockville, MD, 301-309-8850
15225 Shady Grove Rd, Rockville, MD, 301-358-1919

Chung, Simon Sinmin (18 mentions)
Hahnemann U, 1987 *Certification:* Urology
3700 Joseph Siewick Dr #208, Fairfax, VA, 703-208-4200
8503 Arlington Blvd #310, Fairfax, VA, 703-208-4200

Constantinople, Nicholas (16 mentions)
Georgetown U, 1970 *Certification:* Urology
3301 New Mexico Ave NW #311, Washington, DC, 202-364-3434

Dejter, Stephen William, Jr. (27 mentions)
U of Maryland, 1983 *Certification:* Urology
3301 New Mexico Ave NW #311, Washington, DC, 202-364-3434

Dunne, Edward F., Jr. (12 mentions)
Georgetown U, 1984
3301 New Mexico Ave NW #311, Washington, DC, 202-364-3434

Frazier, Harold A., II (8 mentions)
Dartmouth Coll, 1984 *Certification:* Urology
2021 K St NW #408, Washington, DC, 202-223-1024

Friedlander, Gary Scott (15 mentions)
Georgetown U, 1987 *Certification:* Urology
15225 Shady Grove Rd #307, Rockville, MD, 301-258-1919
2730 University Blvd W, Wheaton, MD, 301-258-1919

Gibbons, Myles David (11 mentions)
Virginia Commonwealth U, 1972 *Certification:* Urology
3800 Reservoir Rd NW 4th Fl, Washington, DC, 202-444-4914
8501 Arlington Blvd 2nd Fl, Fairfax, VA, 571-226-8380

Joel, Andrew Burns (9 mentions)
Boston U, 1997 *Certification:* Urology
1625 N George Mason Dr #415, Arlington, VA, 703-717-4200

Lieberman, Murray (12 mentions)
Georgetown U, 1981 *Certification:* Urology
10401 Old Georgetown Rd #306, Bethesda, MD, 301-530-1700
6410 Rockledge Dr #503, Bethesda, MD, 301-530-1700
19504 Doctors Dr, Germantown, MD, 301-530-1700

Litvak, Juan Pablo (12 mentions)
U of Maryland, 1997 *Certification:* Urology
6410 Rockledge Dr #503, Bethesda, MD, 301-530-1700
19504 Doctors Dr, Germantown, MD, 301-530-1700

Lynch, John Hugh (9 mentions)
Georgetown U, 1973 *Certification:* Urology
3800 Reservoir Rd NW #4038, Washington, DC, 202-444-4922

Mordkin, Robert Mark (13 mentions)
U of Southern California, 1992 *Certification:* Urology
1625 N George Mason Dr #415, Arlington, VA, 703-717-4200

Phillips, Michael Howard (26 mentions)
U of Colorado, 1979 *Certification:* Urology
2021 K St NW #408, Washington, DC, 202-223-1024

Rushton, H. Guilford, Jr. (17 mentions)
Med U of South Carolina, 1978 *Certification:* Urology
111 Michigan Ave NW #4400, Washington, DC, 202-476-5042
9850 Key West Ave, Rockville, MD, 301-424-1755
13922 Baltimore Ave, Laurel, MD, 240-568-7000

Sher, Robert Jay (14 mentions)
George Washington U, 1976 *Certification:* Urology
15225 Shady Grove Rd #307, Rockville, MD, 301-258-1919
2730 University Blvd W, Wheaton, MD, 301-258-1919

Stanton, Michael Joseph (10 mentions)
Georgetown U, 1977 *Certification:* Urology
10215 Fernwood Rd #630, Bethesda, MD, 301-493-2505

Verghese, Mohan (9 mentions)
FMS-India, 1976 *Certification:* Urology
110 Irving St NW #2149, Washington, DC, 202-877-3968

White, Jonathan Lee (18 mentions)
Georgetown U, 1987 *Certification:* Urology
15225 Shady Grove Rd #307, Rockville, MD, 301-258-1919
2730 University Blvd W, Wheaton, MD, 301-258-1919

Vascular Surgery

Fox, Robert Louis (27 mentions)
New Jersey Med Sch, 1978 *Certification:* Vascular Surgery
9715 Medical Center Dr #105, Rockville, MD, 301-762-0277
915 Toll House Ave #101, Frederick, MD, 240-529-1414

Kozloff, Louis (25 mentions)
U of Pennsylvania, 1969 *Certification:* Vascular Surgery
8218 Wisconsin Ave #204, Bethesda, MD, 301-652-1208

Mukherjee, Dipankar (35 mentions)
FMS-India, 1976 *Certification:* Surgery, Vascular Surgery
2921 Telestar Ct, Falls Church, VA, 703-876-0580

Neville, Richard (27 mentions)
U of Maryland, 1983 *Certification:* Surgery, Vascular Surgery
3800 Reservoir Rd NW, Washington, DC, 202-444-2255
1830 Town Center Dr #401, Reston, VA, 703-880-9500

Ruben, Garry Dennis (29 mentions)
U of Maryland, 1977 *Certification:* Surgery
11120 New Hampshire Ave #201, Silver Spring, MD,
  301-681-3900

Trout, Hugh Henry, III (49 mentions)
Duke U, 1967 *Certification:* Surgery, Vascular Surgery
8218 Wisconsin Ave #204, Bethesda, MD, 301-652-1208

Florida

Jacksonville-St. Augustine Area—page 139

Volusia, Seminole, Orange, and Brevard Counties—page 169

Pinellas, Hillsborough, Polk, Manatee,
and Sarasota Counties—page 144

Charlotte, Lee, and Collier Counties—page 135

South Florida—page 153

Charlotte, Lee, and Collier Counties

Allergy/Immunology

Rosenbach, Kevin Philip (6 mentions)
New Jersey Med Sch, 1992
15495 Tamiami Trail N #119, Naples, 259-596-5560

Stanaland, Brett Eric (26 mentions)
U of South Florida, 1989
Certification: Allergy & Immunology, Internal Medicine
1000 Goodlette Rd N #200, Naples, 941-434-6200

Anesthesiology

Bisbee, Charles Ayrton (3 mentions)
Med Coll of Georgia, 1983 *Certification:* Anesthesiology
3949 Evans Ave #102, Fort Myers, 239-939-2622

Brooks, Millard Colin, Jr. (3 mentions)
U of Texas-Houston, 1986 *Certification:* Anesthesiology
1336 Creekside Blvd #1, Naples, 239-261-1158

Gezzar, William Walter (3 mentions)
U of Miami, 1982 *Certification:* Anesthesiology
4048 Evans Ave #303, Fort Myers, 239-332-5344

Gregg, Ralph (4 mentions)
U of Maryland, 1987 *Certification:* Anesthesiology
4048 Evans Ave #303, Fort Myers, 239-332-5344

Muppavarapu, Swaroop (4 mentions)
FMS-India, 1977 *Certification:* Anesthesiology
21298 Olean Blvd, Port Charlotte, 941-629-1181

Nolan, John Francis (4 mentions)
U of South Florida, 1990
Certification: Anesthesiology, Critical Care Medicine
1336 Creekside Blvd #1, Naples, 941-261-1158

Shucavage, Bernard Mark (3 mentions)
Loma Linda U, 1983 *Certification:* Anesthesiology
3949 Evans Ave, Fort Myers, 239-939-2622

Statfeld, Robert Alan (3 mentions)
FMS-Mexico, 1982 *Certification:* Anesthesiology
1336 Creekside Blvd #1, Naples, 239-261-1158

Torres, Frederick T. K. (3 mentions)
FMS-Philippines, 1991 *Certification:* Anesthesiology
6101 Pine Ridge Rd, Naples, 239-348-4252

Turner, Robert Madison (3 mentions)
Med Coll of Georgia, 1986 *Certification:* Anesthesiology
3949 Evans Ave #102, Fort Myers, 239-939-2622

Whalley, David Graham (4 mentions)
FMS-United Kingdom, 1968 *Certification:* Anesthesiology
6101 Pine Ridge Rd, Naples, 239-348-4252

Cardiac Surgery

Hummel, Brian Wendell (9 mentions)
U of Iowa, 1977 *Certification:* Thoracic Surgery
2675 Winkler Ave #490, Fort Myers, 239-277-1135
311 9th St N #301, Naples, 239-649-0440
8010 Summerlin Lakes Dr #100, Fort Myers, 239-939-1767

Schultz, Scot Christian (13 mentions)
U of Miami, 1989 *Certification:* Thoracic Surgery
311 Tamiami Trail N #301, Naples, 239-939-1767
8010 Summerlin Lakes Dr #100, Fort Myers, 239-939-1767

Stapleton, Dennis John (14 mentions)
Wayne State U, 1979 *Certification:* Thoracic Surgery
311 Tamiami Trail N #301, Naples, 239-649-0440

Cardiology

Boucek, Francis Charles (5 mentions)
U of Florida, 1972 *Certification:* Cardiovascular Disease,
Internal Medicine, Interventional Cardiology
800 Goodlette Rd N #340, Naples, 239-403-8888

Burton, Michael Erick (6 mentions)
Emory U, 1987 *Certification:* Cardiovascular Disease,
Clinical Cardiac Electrophysiology, Internal Medicine
3501 Healthcenter Blvd, Bonita Springs, 239-992-9335
9800 S Healthpark Dr #320, Fort Myers, 239-433-8888

Chazal, Richard A. (8 mentions)
U of South Florida, 1977
Certification: Cardiovascular Disease, Internal Medicine
9800 S Healthpark Dr #320, Fort Myers, 239-433-8888

Conrad, James A. (3 mentions)
U of Wisconsin, 1981 *Certification:* Cardiovascular Disease,
Internal Medicine, Interventional Cardiology
16261 Bass Rd, Fort Myers, 239-274-8866

Cook, William Rush (3 mentions)
U of Pittsburgh, 1981
Certification: Cardiovascular Disease, Internal Medicine
6101 Pine Ridge Rd, Naples, 239-348-4400

Flynn, Michael Scott (10 mentions)
St Louis U, 1986 *Certification:* Cardiovascular Disease,
Internal Medicine, Interventional Cardiology
606 9th St, Naples, 239-403-9569

Levine, Ronald Lee (4 mentions)
Virginia Commonwealth U, 1989
Certification: Cardiovascular Disease, Interventional Cardiology
680 2nd Ave N #304, Naples, 941-261-7711

Liccini, Raymond P., Jr. (3 mentions)
Harvard U, 1989 *Certification:* Cardiovascular Disease,
Internal Medicine, Interventional Cardiology
12645 New Brittany Blvd Bldg 15, Fort Myers, 239-936-2220

Lopez, Mario Jose (3 mentions)
FMS-Dominican Republic, 1981
Certification: Cardiovascular Disease, Internal Medicine
3340 Tamiami Trail, Port Charlotte, 941-764-5858

Roth, Tracey (3 mentions)
FMS-Israel, 1989
Certification: Cardiovascular Disease, Interventional Cardiology
680 2nd Ave N #304, Naples, 239-261-7711

Schneider, Maurice S. (4 mentions)
FMS-United Kingdom, 1973 *Certification:* Cardiovascular
Disease, Internal Medicine, Interventional Cardiology
6101 Pine Ridge Rd, Naples, 239-348-4000

Talano, James Vincent (3 mentions)
Loyola U Chicago, 1965
Certification: Cardiovascular Disease, Internal Medicine
700 2nd Ave N #301, Naples, 239-261-2000

Towe, Kenneth Michael (3 mentions)
U of Miami, 1992
Certification: Cardiovascular Disease, Interventional Cardiology
708 Del Prado Blvd S #3, Cape Coral, 239-938-2000
1550 Barkley Cir, Fort Myers, 239-938-2000

West, Steven Reynolds (3 mentions)
Indiana U, 1979
Certification: Cardiovascular Disease, Internal Medicine
13411 Parker Commons Blvd #101, Fort Myers, 239-415-4900

Dermatology

Camisa, Charles (6 mentions)
Mount Sinai Sch of Med, 1977
Certification: Dermatological Immunology/Diagnostic and
Laboratory Immunology, Dermatology
6101 Pine Ridge Rd, Naples, 239-348-4000

Eichler, Craig Jeffrey (4 mentions)
U of Florida, 1989 *Certification:* Dermatology
6101 Pine Ridge Rd, Naples, 239-348-4000

Goodman, David Seth (5 mentions)
Mount Sinai Sch of Med, 1983 *Certification:* Dermatology
9125 Corsea Del Fontana Way #100, Naples, 239-598-4004

Lambert, Rebecca Woodruff (5 mentions)
Columbia U, 1998 *Certification:* Dermatology
2235 Venetian Ct #1, Naples, 239-596-9337

Schleider, Nancy (5 mentions)
U of Miami, 1981 *Certification:* Dermatology
13691 Metro Pkwy #420, Fort Myers, 239-768-2057

Spencer, Stephen (8 mentions)
U of South Florida, 1982 *Certification:* Dermatology
1111 Tamiami Trail, Punta Gorda, 941-833-4400
3161 Harbor Blvd #A, Port Charlotte, 941-613-2400

Yag-Howard, Cynthia J. (4 mentions)
U of South Florida, 1993 *Certification:* Dermatology
1000 Goodlette Rd N #100, Naples, 239-649-8384

Emergency Medicine

Abood, Richard George (4 mentions)
U of Michigan, 1993 *Certification:* Emergency Medicine
7955 Airport Pulling Rd N #102, Naples, 239-593-3232

Dalley, Anthony (3 mentions)
FMS-Jamaica, 1976 *Certification:* Emergency Medicine
2776 Cleveland Ave, Fort Myers, 239-334-5329

Hamann, Christopher G. (3 mentions)
Med Coll of Wisconsin, 1997 *Certification:* Emergency Medicine
6101 Pine Ridge Rd, Naples, 239-348-4000

Hobbs, Larry Allen (8 mentions)
U of Miami, 1982 *Certification:* Emergency Medicine
2727 Winkler Ave, Fort Myers, 239-939-8611

James, Raymond A. (5 mentions)
21298 Olean Blvd, Port Charlotte, 941-627-6130

Krembs, Gerhard Anton, II (6 mentions)
George Washington U, 1977 *Certification:* Emergency Medicine
350 7th St N, Naples, 239-436-5000

Lee, Douglas Scott (3 mentions)
New Jersey Med Sch, 1999 *Certification:* Emergency Medicine
2776 Cleveland Ave, Fort Myers, 239-332-1111

Tober, Robert Boyd (6 mentions)
St Louis U, 1975 *Certification:* Emergency Medicine
6400 David Blvd, Naples, 239-403-2600
120 Goodlette Rd N, Naples, 239-261-6600

Endocrinology

Anksh, Vita (9 mentions)
FMS-Lithuania, 1992 *Certification:* Endocrinology,
    Diabetes, and Metabolism, Internal Medicine
9010 Strada Stell Ct #203, Naples, 239-254-1316

Brodie, Todd David (13 mentions)
U of Southern California, 1979 *Certification:* Endocrinology
    and Metabolism, Internal Medicine
730 Goodlette Rd N #205, Naples, 239-436-3666

Cugini, Christy (9 mentions)
FMS-Dominica, 1985 *Certification:* Endocrinology,
    Diabetes, and Metabolism, Internal Medicine
400 8th St N, Naples, 239-649-3322

Family Practice *(see note on page 9)*

Alessi, Albert G. (5 mentions)
Nova Southeastern Coll of Osteopathic Med, 1994
9400 Bonita Beach Rd SE #102, Bonita Springs, 239-992-5444

Boynton, Douglas Lee (4 mentions)
U of Florida, 1984 *Certification:* Family Medicine
400 8th St N, Naples, 239-649-3303

Burdzy, Jon Patrick (3 mentions)
Nova Southeastern Coll of Osteopathic Med, 1998
7780 Cambridge Manor Pl #C, Fort Myers, 239-275-6778

Drew, Daniel Joseph (3 mentions)
Indiana U, 1993 *Certification:* Family Medicine
11121 Health Park Blvd #800, Naples, 941-598-5755
11181 Health Park Blvd #2265, Naples, 239-598-5755

Droffner, Mark Charles (3 mentions)
Des Moines U, 1984
Certification: Family Medicine, Geriatric Medicine
260 Milus St, Punta Gorda, 941-637-0911

Poling, Robert A. (4 mentions)
Northeastern Ohio U, 1994 *Certification:* Family Medicine
1850 San Marco Rd #C, Marco Island, 239-394-8252

Van Dongen, John P. (3 mentions)
FMS-South Africa, 1982 *Certification:* Family Medicine
599 Tamiami Trail N #308, Naples, 239-643-7888

Gastroenterology

Joseph, Sovi (6 mentions)
FMS-India, 1973
Certification: Gastroenterology, Internal Medicine
3440 Tamicami Trail #1, Port Charlotte, 941-258-9500

Liberski, Susan Mary (10 mentions)
Med Coll of Pennsylvania, 1985
Certification: Gastroenterology, Internal Medicine
1064 Goodlette Rd N, Naples, 239-649-1186

Meckstroth, Steven Arthur (5 mentions)
U of Miami, 1987 *Certification:* Gastroenterology
1656 Medical Blvd #301, Naples, 239-593-6201

Phillips, Raymond Wynne (8 mentions)
Washington U, 1981
Certification: Gastroenterology, Internal Medicine
1064 Goodlette Rd N, Naples, 239-649-1186

Weiss, Michael Hugh (6 mentions)
U of South Florida, 1986
Certification: Gastroenterology, Internal Medicine
4790 Barkley Cir, Fort Myers, 239-275-8882

Wiesen, Scott Laurence (5 mentions)
Jefferson Med Coll, 1986
Certification: Gastroenterology, Internal Medicine
150 Tamiami Trail N #2, Naples, 239-434-0009

Yudelman, Paul Lewis (5 mentions)
FMS-United Kingdom, 1984
Certification: Gastroenterology, Internal Medicine
7152 Coca Sabal Ln, Fort Myers, 239-939-9939

General Surgery

Brockman, Jb, Jr. (4 mentions)
Rosalind Franklin U, 1999 *Certification:* Surgery
311 Tamiami Trail N #308, Naples, 239-417-0085

Goldberger, Jacob H. (5 mentions)
Indiana U, 1971 *Certification:* Surgery
13685 Doctors Way #210, Fort Myers, 239-274-7600

Jordan, Jacob Henszey (16 mentions)
Baylor U, 1984 *Certification:* Surgery
2335 Tamiami Trail N #501, Naples, 941-263-0011

Kammerlocher, Thad Conan (5 mentions)
U of Oklahoma, 1992 *Certification:* Surgery, Vascular Surgery
1206 Country Club Blvd, Cape Coral, 239-574-7454

Kowalsky, Thomas Earl (5 mentions)
Temple U, 1980 *Certification:* Surgery
21 Barkley Cir, Fort Myers, 239-939-2616

Lamon, David Jonathan (7 mentions)
U of Cincinnati, 1996 *Certification:* Surgery
311 Tamiami Trail N #308, Naples, 239-417-0085

Liberman, Mark Avery (6 mentions)
Uniformed Services U of Health Sciences, 1985
Certification: Surgery
6101 Pine Ridge Rd, Naples, 239-348-4000

Powell, Kevin Lamar (4 mentions)
U of Cincinnati, 2000 *Certification:* Surgery
311 Tamiami Trail N #308, Naples, 239-417-0085

Geriatrics

Bolla, Leela Reddy (3 mentions)
FMS-India, 1981
Certification: Geriatric Medicine, Internal Medicine
6101 Pine Ridge Rd, Naples, 239-597-0544
1890 SW Health Pkwy #100, Naples, 239-597-0544

Garry, Ronald Thomas (10 mentions)
Stony Brook U, 1996
Certification: Geriatric Medicine, Internal Medicine
2450 Goodlette Rd N #101, Naples, 239-643-8750

Hematology/Oncology

Grossman, Joel Scott (6 mentions)
Wake Forest U, 1994 *Certification:* Medical Oncology
400 8th St N, Naples, 239-261-5511

Hart, Lowell L. (11 mentions)
SUNY-Upstate Med U, 1980
Certification: Hematology, Internal Medicine, Medical Oncology
3840 Broadway, Fort Myers, 239-275-6400
15681 New Hampshire Ct, Fort Myers, 239-437-4444

Harwin, William Neil (12 mentions)
Baylor U, 1978
Certification: Hematology, Internal Medicine, Medical Oncology
15681 New Hampshire Ct, Fort Myers, 941-437-4444

Morris, Daniel J. (6 mentions)
U of Pittsburgh, 1981
Certification: Hematology, Internal Medicine, Medical Oncology
400 8th St N, Naples, 239-649-3335

Rubin, Mark Stephen (10 mentions)
Columbia U, 1988
Certification: Hematology, Internal Medicine, Medical Oncology
9776 Bonita Beach, Bonita Springs, 239-947-3092

Teufel, Thomas Edgar (6 mentions)
U of Cincinnati, 1979
Certification: Hematology, Internal Medicine, Medical Oncology
811 Del Prado Blvd S, Cape Coral, 239-772-3544

Infectious Disease

Brown, Mark Allen, Jr. (12 mentions)
U of South Florida, 1990
Certification: Infectious Disease, Internal Medicine
800 Goodlette Rd N #370, Naples, 239-643-8760

Forszpaniak, Christine (11 mentions)
FMS-Poland, 1980
Certification: Infectious Disease, Internal Medicine
848 1st Ave N #230, Naples, 941-434-7779

Saunders, Mary Beth (12 mentions)
Kansas U Coll of Osteopathic Med, 1992
9981 S Healthpark Dr #279, Fort Myers, 239-343-9710

Infertility

Sweet, Craig Richard (9 mentions)
Southern Illinois U, 1985 *Certification:* Obstetrics &
Gynecology, Reproductive Endocrinology/Infertility
12611 World Plaza Ln, Fort Myers, 239-275-8118

Internal Medicine *(see note on page 9)*

D'Agostino, Anthony M. (3 mentions)
U of South Florida, 1992 *Certification:* Internal Medicine
1350 Tamiami Trail N, Naples, 941-262-6111

Ferguson, George William (10 mentions)
U of Miami, 1985 *Certification:* Internal Medicine
787 4th Ave S, Naples, 239-352-5600

Henricks, Douglas Glenn (4 mentions)
Wayne State U, 1978 *Certification:* Internal Medicine
6311 S Pointe Blvd, Fort Myers, 239-275-0040

Koop, Hermes Onno (4 mentions)
U of Texas-Galveston, 1984 *Certification:* Internal Medicine
800 Goodlette Rd N #200, Naples, 239-643-8710

Kordonowy, Raymond W. (3 mentions)
U of Kansas, 1990 *Certification:* Internal Medicine
6311 S Pointe Blvd, Fort Myers, 941-275-0040

Mantell, Paul Douglas (4 mentions)
Hahnemann U, 1980 *Certification:* Internal Medicine
1569 Matthew Dr, Fort Myers, 239-939-1700

Tovardias, Glenn A. V. (4 mentions)
FMS-India, 1992 *Certification:* Internal Medicine
42 Barkley Cir #2, Fort Myers, 239-275-3036

Wilson, Kathleen Sue W. (3 mentions)
U of Iowa, 1975
Certification: Gastroenterology, Internal Medicine
522 Carlton St, Wauchula, 863-773-2425

Nephrology

Bialkin, Steven Richard (6 mentions)
FMS-St Maarten, 1998
Certification: Internal Medicine, Nephrology
400 8th St N, Naples, 239-649-3334

Gadallah, Merit Fawzi F. (7 mentions)
FMS-Libya, 1979 *Certification:* Internal Medicine, Nephrology
1213 Piper Blvd #101, Naples, 239-254-0099

Mouracade, Mary (10 mentions)
Wake Forest U, 1992
7981 Gladiolus Dr, Fort Myers, 239-939-0999

Russo, Mark Steven (12 mentions)
SUNY-Downstate Med Coll, 1995
Certification: Internal Medicine, Nephrology
878 109th Ave N #2, Naples, 239-513-1002

Sterrett, James Reid (6 mentions)
Virginia Commonwealth U, 1971
Certification: Internal Medicine, Nephrology
6101 Pine Ridge Rd, Naples, 239-348-4000

Neurological Surgery

Colon, Gary Paul (14 mentions)
Cornell U, 1991 *Certification:* Neurological Surgery
730 Goodlette Rd N #100, Naples, 941-262-1721

Correnti, Gary Jay (9 mentions)
U of Pennsylvania, 1988 *Certification:* Neurological Surgery
12700 Creekside Ln #101, Fort Myers, 239-432-0774

Dernbach, Paul David (12 mentions)
Med Coll of Wisconsin, 1981 *Certification:* Neurological Surgery
730 Goodlette Rd N #100, Naples, 239-262-8971

Gerber, Mark Benjamin (10 mentions)
U of Oklahoma, 1994 *Certification:* Neurological Surgery
670 Goodlette Rd N, Naples, 239-649-1662
8380 Riverwalk Park Blvd #320, Fort Myers, 239-437-1121

Neurology

Driscoll, Paul Francis (9 mentions)
U of Florida, 1983 *Certification:* Neurology
12670 Whitehall Dr, Fort Myers, 239-936-3554
1003 Del Prado Blvd S #202, Cape Coral, 239-574-4242
63 Barkley Cir #101, Fort Myers, 239-936-3554

Holt, William Alan (6 mentions)
Nova Southeastern Coll of Osteopathic Med, 1986
Certification: Neurology, Vascular Neurology
4161 Tamiami Trail #201, Fort Myers, 941-764-0800

Justiz, William Andrew (7 mentions)
U of Miami, 1994 *Certification:* Neurology
730 Goodlette Rd N #100, Naples, 941-262-8971

Levy-Reis, Igor (9 mentions)
FMS-Brazil, 1992
Certification: Clinical Neurophysiology, Neurology
877 111th Ave N #1, Naples, 239-594-8306

Schwartz, Eileen J. L. (5 mentions)
New Jersey Med Sch, 1972 *Certification:* Neurology
38 Barkley Cir #2, Fort Myers, 239-936-1700

Obstetrics/Gynecology

Alexander, Jody Lee (3 mentions)
Wayne State U, 1976 *Certification:* Obstetrics & Gynecology
1890 SW Health Pkwy #205, Naples, 239-592-1388

Auld, Heather Vivian (3 mentions)
U of South Dakota, 1982 *Certification:* Obstetrics & Gynecology
9021 Park Royal Dr, Fort Myers, 239-482-6881

Brothers, Betsy (5 mentions)
Certification: Obstetrics & Gynecology
1890 SW Health Pkwy #303, Naples, 239-593-0990

Campbell, Kevin S. (3 mentions)
U of South Florida, 1982 *Certification:* Obstetrics & Gynecology
9981 S Healthpark Dr, Fort Myers, 239-432-3500
19910 S Tamiami Trail #C, Estero, 239-498-5292

Crandall, Blane M. (5 mentions)
Certification: Obstetrics & Gynecology
1660 Medical Blvd #101, Naples, 239-596-2300

Devall, Diana Dillingham (3 mentions)
U of Tennessee, 1986 *Certification:* Obstetrics & Gynecology
9981 S Healthpark Dr, Fort Myers, 239-432-3500
4761 S Cleveland Ave, Fort Myers, 239-432-3500

Heitmann, Jeffrey Alan (9 mentions)
Wake Forest U, 1984 *Certification:* Obstetrics & Gynecology
1660 Medical Blvd #300, Naples, 941-513-0053

Hidlebaugh, Dennis Allen (3 mentions)
U of Colorado, 1980 *Certification:* Obstetrics & Gynecology
6101 Pine Ridge Rd, Naples, 239-348-4000

Humphrey, Wendy Sue (3 mentions)
U of Toledo, 1982 *Certification:* Obstetrics & Gynecology
1890 SW Health Pkwy #303, Naples, 239-593-0990

Kamerman, Max Leopold (4 mentions)
Ponce Sch of Med, 1999 *Certification:* Obstetrics & Gynecology
775 1st Ave N, Naples, 239-262-3399

Kovaz, Blaise Matthew (3 mentions)
U of Florida, 1985 *Certification:* Obstetrics & Gynecology
1265 Viscaya Pkwy, Cape Coral, 239-432-5858
1255 Viscaya Pkwy #200, Cape Coral, 239-574-2229
9021 Park Royal Dr, Fort Myers, 239-574-2229

Morris, Cherrie R. (3 mentions)
New Jersey Med Sch, 1994 *Certification:* Obstetrics & Gynecology
9981 S Healthpark Dr, Fort Myers, 239-432-3500

Saint Paul, Cecile (3 mentions)
Hahnemann U, 1985 *Certification:* Obstetrics & Gynecology
1412 Royal Palm Square Blvd #102, Fort Myers, 239-274-9700

Stubbs, Rex Elliott, Jr. (3 mentions)
Med Coll of Georgia, 1980
Certification: Anesthesiology, Obstetrics & Gynecology
9021 Park Royal Dr, Fort Myers, 239-433-9899

Ophthalmology

Elmquist, Eric Trevor (3 mentions)
Kansas U Coll of Osteopathic Med, 1981
Certification: Ophthalmology
12670 New Brittany Blvd #102, Fort Myers, 239-936-2020

Fisher, George Briton, III (4 mentions)
Michigan State U Coll of Osteopathic Med, 1995
681 Goodlette Rd N #120, Naples, 239-262-4798

Gorovoy, Mark S. (7 mentions)
George Washington U, 1977 *Certification:* Ophthalmology
12381 S Cleveland Ave #300, Fort Myers, 239-939-1444

Klein, David Michael (4 mentions)
SUNY-Downstate Med Coll, 1975 *Certification:* Ophthalmology
1620 Tamiami Trail #101, Port Charlotte, 941-764-0035

Walker, Joseph P. (3 mentions)
New York Med Coll, 1974 *Certification:* Ophthalmology
6901 International Center Blvd, Fort Myers, 239-939-4323
2525 Harbor Blvd #302, Port Charlotte, 941-627-4422

Wing, Glenn L. (3 mentions)
Tufts U, 1975 *Certification:* Ophthalmology
6901 International Center Blvd, Fort Myers, 239-939-4323
2525 Harbor Blvd #302, Port Charlotte, 941-627-4422

Zimm, Jeffrey Luke (4 mentions)
Loyola U Chicago, 1986 *Certification:* Ophthalmology
1435 Immokalee Rd, Naples, 941-592-5511
6900 Daniels Pkwy #23-C, Fort Myers, 239-768-7022

Zusman, Neil Bryan (4 mentions)
Wayne State U, 1984 *Certification:* Ophthalmology
3430 Tamiami Trail #A, Port Charlotte, 941-624-4500

Orthopedics

Bertram, Herbert Morton (8 mentions)
U of Louisville, 1984
1009 Crosspointe Dr #2, Naples, 239-592-0373

Fifer, John Sherwood, Jr. (4 mentions)
U of South Florida, 1976 *Certification:* Orthopaedic Surgery
8350 Riverwalk Park Blvd #1, Fort Myers, 239-482-5399

Goldberg, Steven Scott (4 mentions)
New Jersey, Med Sch, 1999 *Certification:* Orthopaedic Surgery
6101 Pine Ridge Rd, Naples, 239-348-4400

Guerra, James John (7 mentions)
Northwestern U, 1989
Certification: Orthopaedic Sports Medicine, Orthopaedic Surgery
1706 Medical Blvd #201, Naples, 239-593-3500

Humbert, Edward Thomas, Jr. (4 mentions)
2780 Cleveland Ave #709, Fort Myers, 239-337-2003

Kagan, John Curry (4 mentions)
U of South Florida, 1976 *Certification:* Orthopaedic Surgery
2745 Swamp Cabbage Ct #305, Fort Myers, 239-936-6778
2721 Del Prado Blvd S #250, Cape Coral, 239-574-0011

Kapp, Howard Joseph (7 mentions)
Case Western Reserve U, 1982 *Certification:* Orthopaedic Surgery
130 Tamiami Trail N #220, Naples, 941-434-5700

Mead, Leon Paul (5 mentions)
Wayne State U, 1983
Certification: Orthopaedic Sports Medicine, Orthopaedic Surgery
730 Goodlette Rd N #201, Naples, 239-262-1119

Parent, Thomas Eric (5 mentions)
U of Pittsburgh, 1989
Certification: Orthopaedic Surgery, Surgery of the Hand
400 8th St N, Naples, 239-649-3313

Shannon, Frederick Brett (5 mentions)
Midwestern U Chicago Coll of Osteopathic Med, 1980
Certification: Orthopaedic Surgery
15821 Hollyfern Ct, Fort Myers, 239-432-5100
9800 S Healthpark Dr #110, Fort Myers, 239-432-5100

Zehr, Robert Joseph (5 mentions)
St Louis U, 1985 *Certification:* Orthopaedic Surgery
6101 Pine Ridge Rd, Naples, 239-348-4000

Otorhinolaryngology

Andrews, Phillip Edward (9 mentions)
Med Coll of Georgia, 1966 *Certification:* Otolaryngology
39 Barkley Cir, Fort Myers, 239-936-1616

Bello, Steven Louis (10 mentions)
Washington U, 1986 *Certification:* Otolaryngology
1459 Ridge St 2nd Fl, Naples, 239-262-6668

Kane, Patrick M. (8 mentions)
Med Coll of Wisconsin, 1978 *Certification:* Otolaryngology
848 1st Ave N #330, Naples, 941-263-8855

Laskowski, William (7 mentions)
FMS-Canada, 1967 *Certification:* Otolaryngology
400 8th St N, Naples, 239-262-1171

Roberts, Jay Kirk (7 mentions)
Case Western Reserve U, 1983 *Certification:* Otolaryngology
6101 Pine Ridge Rd, Naples, 239-348-4000

Pain Medicine

Friedman, Stephen Lyle (6 mentions)
Rosalind Franklin U, 1988
Certification: Anesthesiology, Pain Medicine
11161 Health Park Blvd, Naples, 941-436-6711

Isaacson, Wayne (4 mentions)
SUNY-Upstate Med U, 1990
Certification: Anesthesiology, Pain Medicine
2721 Del Prado Blvd #100-A, Cape Coral, 239-242-8010
4035 Evans Ave, Fort Myers, 239-939-7375

Paine, Gregory Francis (5 mentions)
U of Virginia, 1992 *Certification:* Anesthesiology, Pain Medicine
1336 Creekside Blvd #1, Naples, 239-261-1158

Worden, James Joseph, Jr. (5 mentions)
U of Miami, 1969 *Certification:* Anesthesiology, Pain Medicine
730 Goodlette Rd N #200, Naples, 239-659-6400

Pathology

Blue, Mary Kathleen (4 mentions)
Indiana U, 1981 *Certification:* Anatomic Pathology &
Clinical Pathology, Cytopathology, Medical Microbiology
3949 Evans Ave #403, Fort Myers, 239-939-2305

Boyd, Peter Raymond (6 mentions)
New York Med Coll, 1975
Certification: Anatomic Pathology, Clinical Pathology
4351 Tamiami Trail N, Naples, 239-263-1777

Dipasquale, Bruno (5 mentions)
FMS-Italy, 1984
Certification: Anatomic Pathology & Clinical Pathology
6101 Pine Ridge Rd, Naples, 239-348-4000

Greider, Harvey David (5 mentions)
U of Illinois, 1969
Certification: Anatomic Pathology & Clinical Pathology
350 7th St N, Naples, 239-436-5000

Seidenstein, Lawrence (7 mentions)
SUNY-Upstate Med U, 1970 *Certification:* Anatomic Pathology
& Clinical Pathology, Hematology, Immunopathology
2727 Winkler Ave, Fort Myers, 239-939-8588

Pediatrics *(see note on page 9)*

Casanova, Ena Carmen (3 mentions)
FMS-Dominican Republic, 1982 *Certification:* Pediatrics
3508 Tamiami Trail #C, Port Charlotte, 941-883-3313

Kash, Irwin Jay (3 mentions)
U of Illinois, 1969 *Certification:* Pediatrics
4751 Mount Cleveland Ave, Fort Myers, 239-343-9888

Lopez, Deborah M. (3 mentions)
FMS-St Maarten, 1990
Certification: Pediatric Critical Care Medicine, Pediatrics
11190 Health Park Blvd, Naples, 239-552-7555

Pietroniro, Anthony G. (3 mentions)
Tulane U, 1989 *Certification:* Pediatrics
4751 Mount Cleveland Ave, Fort Myers, 239-343-9888

Shepard, Debra Jean (6 mentions)
U of Alabama, 1994 *Certification:* Pediatrics
1845 Veterans Park Dr #260, Naples, 239-254-7602
1008 Goodlette Rd N #100, Naples, 239-262-8226

Sherman, Martin Jeffrey (6 mentions)
Tufts U, 1974 *Certification:* Pediatrics
650 Del Prado Blvd S #107, Cape Coral, 239-939-1000
4751 S Cleveland Ave, Fort Myers, 239-939-1000

Wilson, Robert Wilcox (5 mentions)
Nova Southeastern Coll of Osteopathic Med, 1988
Certification: Pediatrics
2940 Immokalee Rd #2, Naples, 239-598-5750

Plastic Surgery

Brueck, Robert John (4 mentions)
U of Illinois, 1973 *Certification:* Plastic Surgery
3700 Central Ave #1, Fort Myers, 239-939-5233
14 Del Prado Blvd N #301, Cape Coral, 239-772-1930

Garramone, Ralph Ronald (4 mentions)
New York Med Coll, 1987 *Certification:* Plastic Surgery
8660 College Pkwy #100, Fort Myers, 941-482-1900

Mazza, Joseph Fedele (4 mentions)
SUNY-Upstate Med U, 1982 *Certification:* Plastic Surgery
12640 Creekside Ln, Fort Myers, 239-482-7676

Ritrosky, John David (4 mentions)
U of Florida, 1989 *Certification:* Plastic Surgery
12640 World Plaza Ln Bldg 71, Fort Myers, 239-275-8898

Turk, Andrew E. (5 mentions)
Tulane U, 1986 *Certification:* Plastic Surgery
6101 Pine Ridge Rd, Naples, 239-348-4000

Psychiatry

Arias, Bernardo De Jesus (3 mentions)
FMS-Dominican Republic, 1985 *Certification:* Psychiatry
3191 Harbor Blvd #A, Port Charlotte, 941-766-9555

Fabacher, Jeffrey E. (3 mentions)
Louisiana State U, 1979 *Certification:* Psychiatry
700 2nd Ave N #302, Naples, 239-261-8188

Rieche, Omar (3 mentions)
U of South Florida, 1991
Certification: Child & Adolescent Psychiatry, Psychiatry
1705 Colonial Blvd #B-1, Fort Myers, 239-278-7788

Schaerf, Frederick Warren (7 mentions)
U of Maryland, 1983 *Certification:* Forensic Psychiatry, Psychiatry
14271 Metropolis Ave #A, Fort Myers, 239-939-7777

Pulmonary Disease

Bookman, Kenneth (5 mentions)
FMS-Israel, 1999 *Certification:* Critical Care Medicine,
Internal Medicine, Pulmonary Disease
3021 Airport Pulling Rd N #103, Naples, 239-430-2929

Cohen, Howard Leonard (12 mentions)
Northwestern U, 1987
Certification: Critical Care Medicine, Pulmonary Disease
3021 Airport Pulling Rd #103, Naples, 239-213-7000

Hannan, Stephen Edward (13 mentions)
U of Florida, 1982 *Certification:* Critical Care Medicine,
Internal Medicine, Pulmonary Disease
9981 S Healthpark Dr #454, Fort Myers, 239-343-6800

Harrington, Douglas William (11 mentions)
Des Moines U, 1986 *Certification:* Critical Care Medicine,
Internal Medicine, Pulmonary Disease
400 8th St N, Naples, 239-649-3347

Maas, Carlos (7 mentions)
FMS-Paraguay, 1980
3161 Harbor Blvd #B, Port Charlotte, 941-613-1777

Sporn, Gary Kevin (7 mentions)
New Jersey Med Sch, 1990 *Certification:* Critical Care
Medicine, Internal Medicine, Pulmonary Disease
1012 Goodlette Rd N #100, Naples, 239-403-1060

Tolep, Kenneth Andrew (10 mentions)
SUNY-Upstate Med U, 1986 *Certification:* Critical Care
Medicine, Internal Medicine, Pulmonary Disease
9981 S Healthpark Dr #454, Fort Myers, 239-343-6800

Radiology—Diagnostic

Bielfelt, Bruce Harvey (4 mentions)
Midwestern U Chicago Coll of Osteopathic Med, 1976
21298 Olean Blvd, Port Charlotte, 941-624-7032

Fueredi, Adam (3 mentions)
Med Coll of Wisconsin, 1961 *Certification:* Radiology
4330 Tamiami Trail E, Naples, 239-793-7717

Kaye, Marc David (3 mentions)
U of Miami, 1976 *Certification:* Diagnostic Radiology,
Vascular & Interventional Radiology
2950 Cleveland Clinic Blvd, Weston, 954-689-5123

Knific, Randolph John (6 mentions)
Case Western Reserve U, 1982 *Certification:* Diagnostic Radiology
3660 Broadway, Fort Myers, 239-458-3368

Krivisky, Brian Allan (4 mentions)
Mount Sinai Sch of Med, 1982 *Certification:* Diagnostic Radiology
3680 Broadway, Fort Myers, 239-936-2316
1110 Lee Blvd, Lehigh Acres, 239-344-1000
805 Del Prado Blvd S, Cape Coral, 239-458-1744
6140 Winkler Rd #A, Fort Myers, 239-489-4426

Meli, Robert Joseph (4 mentions)
Med Coll of Wisconsin, 1967 *Certification:* Diagnostic Radiology
1441 Ridge St, Naples, 239-643-2905

Presbrey, Thomas George (3 mentions)
Rush U, 1984 *Certification:* Diagnostic Radiology
63 Barkley Cir #100, Fort Myers, 239-938-3560

Saif, Mai Frieda (3 mentions)
FMS-Ireland, 1983 *Certification:* Diagnostic Radiology
2726 Swamp Cabbage Ct, Fort Myers, 239-938-3500

Theobald, Michael R. (5 mentions)
Georgetown U, 1991 *Certification:* Diagnostic Radiology
1441 Ridge St, Naples, 239-643-1155

Weiss, Michael Jon (3 mentions)
Med Coll of Pennsylvania, 1988
2776 Cleveland Ave, Fort Myers, 239-334-5326

Radiology—Therapeutic

Mantz, Constantine A. (4 mentions)
U of Chicago, 1995 *Certification:* Radiation Oncology
1419 SE 8th Ter, Cape Coral, 239-772-3202
7341 Gladiolus Dr, Fort Myers, 239-489-3420
3680 Broadway, Fort Myers, 239-936-0380

Rehabilitation

Jen, Lian C. (4 mentions)
New Jersey Sch of Osteopathic Med, 1993
Certification: Physical Medicine & Rehabilitation
3089 Tamiami Trail, Port Charlotte, 941-627-9768

Kanar, Colin Lee (7 mentions)
Wayne State U, 1990
Certification: Pain Medicine, Physical Medicine & Rehabilitation
1855 Veterans Park Dr #101, Naples, 239-261-0926

Kelley, Edward Sean (5 mentions)
U of Pittsburgh, 1988
Certification: Pain Medicine, Physical Medicine & Rehabilitation
730 Goodlette Rd N #203, Naples, 239-643-1070

Rheumatology

Cohen, Harley Joseph (14 mentions)
Jefferson Med Coll, 1999
Certification: Internal Medicine, Rheumatology
400 8th St N, Naples, 239-261-5511

Kowal, Catherine Nina (8 mentions)
FMS-St Maarten, 1985
1855 Veterans Park Dr #103, Naples, 239-596-5220

Thoracic Surgery

Hummel, Brian Wendell (6 mentions)
U of Iowa, 1977 *Certification:* Thoracic Surgery
2675 Winkler Ave #490, Fort Myers, 239-277-1135
311 9th St N #301, Naples, 239-649-0440
8010 Summerlin Lakes Dr #100, Fort Myers, 239-939-1767

Metke, Michael Partlow (7 mentions)
Oregon Health Sciences U, 1974 *Certification:* Thoracic Surgery
2675 Winkler Ave #490, Fort Myers, 239-277-1135
311 9th St N #301, Naples, 239-649-0440
8010 Summerlin Lakes Dr #100, Fort Myers, 239-939-1767

Urology

D'Angelo, Michael Francis (9 mentions)
Creighton U, 1996 *Certification:* Urology
6101 Pine Ridge Rd, Naples, 239-352-6670

Figlesthaler, William M. (7 mentions)
U of North Carolina, 1992 *Certification:* Urology
990 Tamiami Trail N, Naples, 239-434-6300

Jay, Jonathan Keith (5 mentions)
U of Michigan, 1991 *Certification:* Urology
6101 Pine Ridge Rd, Naples, 239-495-3000
28930 Trails Edge Rd, Bonita Springs, 239-495-3000

Paletsky, Steven Harold (7 mentions)
Med U of South Carolina, 1973 *Certification:* Urology
7335 Gladiolus Dr, Fort Myers, 239-689-6677

Spellberg, David Mark (9 mentions)
Rush U, 1986 *Certification:* Urology
1132 Goodlette Rd N, Naples, 239-434-8565
26800 S Tamiami Trail #360, Bonita Springs, 239-495-3000
973 N Collier Blvd, Marco Island, 239-434-8565
990 Tamiami Trail N, Naples, 239-434-6300

Wise, Kendall Lee (5 mentions)
Vanderbilt U, 1982 *Certification:* Urology
1044 Goodlette Rd N, Naples, 239-261-5400

Vascular Surgery

Kowalsky, Thomas Earl (7 mentions)
Temple U, 1980 *Certification:* Surgery
21 Barkley Cir, Fort Myers, 239-939-2616

Rajasinghe, Hiranya A. (8 mentions)
Duke U, 1992 *Certification:* Surgery, Vascular Surgery
800 Goodlette Rd N #230, Naples, 239-436-2800
2450 Goodlette Rd N #102, Naples, 239-643-8794

Sadighi, Abraham (9 mentions)
Med U of South Carolina, 1979 *Certification:* Surgery
2675 Winkler Ave #490, Fort Myers, 239-277-1135

Jacksonville-St. Augustine Area

Including Clay, Duvall, Nassau, and St. Johns Counties

Allergy/Immunology

Guarderas, Juan C. (15 mentions)
FMS-Argentina, 1983
Certification: Allergy & Immunology, Internal Medicine
4500 San Pablo Rd S, Jacksonville, 904-953-2451

Mizrahi, Edward Alan (15 mentions)
U of Florida, 1972
Certification: Allergy & Immunology, Internal Medicine
1895 Kingsley Ave #401, Orange Park, 904-272-5251

Prabhu, Sudhir Laxman (14 mentions)
FMS-India, 1973 *Certification:* Allergy & Immunology, Pediatrics
4123 University Blvd S #B, Jacksonville, 904-636-9100

Anesthesiology

Crum, Paul Miller, Jr. (4 mentions)
U of Virginia, 1993 *Certification:* Anesthesiology
710 Lomax St, Jacksonville, 904-355-6583

Feinglass, Neil Gordon (6 mentions)
Vanderbilt U, 1983
Certification: Anesthesiology, Critical Care Medicine
4500 San Pablo Rd, Jacksonville, 904-956-3328

Koehler, David Craig (4 mentions)
U of California-San Diego, 1991 *Certification:* Anesthesiology
1 Shircliff Way, Jacksonville, 903-308-7300

Miller, Deevid Oscar (3 mentions)
Duke U, 1983 *Certification:* Anesthesiology
2021 Kingsley Ave #105, Orange Park, 904-276-5400

Redfern, Robert Earle (3 mentions)
Med Coll of Georgia, 1979 *Certification:* Anesthesiology
655 W 8th St, Jacksonville, 904-244-4195

Thomas, Susan Jane (3 mentions)
Wayne State U, 1987 *Certification:* Anesthesiology
3316 S 3rd St #200, Jacksonville Beach, 904-247-8181

Cardiac Surgery

Agnew, Richard Clarke (11 mentions)
Vanderbilt U, 1975 *Certification:* Thoracic Surgery
4500 San pablo Rd, Jacksonville, 904-956-3200

Cousar, Charles Donaldson (12 mentions)
Johns Hopkins U, 1981 *Certification:* Surgery, Thoracic Surgery
1824 King St #200, Jacksonville, 904-384-3343
836 Prudential Dr #1804, Jacksonville, 904-398-8147

Lee, Raymond (12 mentions)
Harvard U, 1988 *Certification:* Surgery, Thoracic Surgery
1824 King St #200, Jacksonville, 904-384-3343
836 Prudential Dr #1804, Jacksonville, 904-398-8147

Still, Robert Jay (19 mentions)
Johns Hopkins U, 1984
Certification: Surgery, Thoracic Surgery, Vascular Surgery
836 Prudential Dr #1804, Jacksonville, 904-398-3888
1824 King St #200, Jacksonville, 904-384-3343

Cardiology

Ashchi, Majdi (5 mentions)
Nova Southeastern Coll of Osteopathic Med, 1989
Certification: Cardiovascular Disease, Interventional Cardiology
3900 University Blvd S, Jacksonville, 904-493-3333
1681 Eagle Harbor Pkwy #B, Orange Park, 904-644-0092
9765 San Jose Blvd #5, Jacksonville, 904-493-3333

Blackshear, Joseph Lynnfield (7 mentions)
Mayo Med Sch, 1978
Certification: Cardiovascular Disease, Internal Medicine
4500 San Pablo Rd S, Jacksonville, 904-953-7279

Dillahunt, Paul H., II (3 mentions)
Ohio State U, 1973 *Certification:* Cardiovascular Disease,
   Internal Medicine, Interventional Cardiology
820 Prudential Dr #112, Jacksonville, 904-396-5996
1340 S 18th St #202, Fernandina Beach, 904-261-9786

Ettedgui, Jose Alberto (5 mentions)
FMS-Venezuela, 1982 *Certification:* Pediatric Cardiology
1443 San Marco Blvd, Jacksonville, 904-493-2272

Khatib, Yazan (3 mentions)
FMS-Syria, 1989
Certification: Cardiovascular Disease, Interventional Cardiology
3900 University Blvd S, Jacksonville, 904-493-3333
9765 San Jose Blvd #5, Jacksonville, 904-493-3333
1681 Eagle Harbor Pkwy #B, Orange Park, 904-644-0092

Koren, Michael Jay (4 mentions)
Harvard U, 1985
Certification: Cardiovascular Disease, Internal Medicine
6428 Beach Blvd, Jacksonville, 904-724-1717
4085 University Blvd S #1, Jacksonville, 904-730-0101

Litt, Marc Richard (6 mentions)
U of Cincinnati, 1983 *Certification:* Cardiovascular Disease,
   Internal Medicine, Interventional Cardiology
836 Prudential Dr #1700, Jacksonville, 904-398-0125

Oken, Keith Robinson (4 mentions)
U of Virginia, 1985
Certification: Cardiovascular Disease, Internal Medicine
4500 San Pablo Rd S, Jacksonville, 904-953-7361

Patterson, Jay Richard (3 mentions)
East Tennessee State U, 1986 *Certification:* Cardiovascular
   Disease, Clinical Cardiac Electrophysiology, Internal Medicine
1824 King St #300, Jacksonville, 904-388-1820

Patton, John Norman (5 mentions)
FMS-Ireland, 1974 *Certification:* Cardiovascular Disease,
   Internal Medicine, Interventional Cardiology
4500 San Pablo Rd S, Jacksonville, 904-953-7279

Pilcher, George Stapleton (3 mentions)
Med Coll of Georgia, 1978 *Certification:* Cardiovascular
   Disease, Internal Medicine, Interventional Cardiology
1824 King St #300, Jacksonville, 904-388-1820

Rama, Pamela R. (4 mentions)
FMS-Philippines, 1988
1361 13th Ave S #70, Jacksonville Beach, 904-338-0855

Safford, Robert Eugene (3 mentions)
Mayo Med Sch, 1977
Certification: Cardiovascular Disease, Internal Medicine
4500 San Pablo Rd S, Jacksonville, 904-953-7277

Schrank, Joel Palmer (3 mentions)
Case Western Reserve U, 1964
Certification: Cardiovascular Disease, Internal Medicine
836 Prudential Dr #1700, Jacksonville, 904-398-0125

Stroh, David (6 mentions)
Philadelphia Coll of Osteopathic Med, 1984
Certification: Cardiovascular Disease, Internal Medicine
2021 Kingsley Ave #104, Orange Park, 904-398-0998

Wainwright, William Randolph (3 mentions)
Med Coll of Georgia, 1976
Certification: Cardiovascular Disease, Internal Medicine
1361 13th Ave S #270, Jacksonville Beach, 904-338-0855

Dermatology

Bernhardt, Michael Jay (15 mentions)
Emory U, 1980 *Certification:* Dermatology
2054 Park St, Jacksonville, 904-387-4991

Kwong, Pearl Chu (9 mentions)
FMS-Canada, 1990
Certification: Dermatology, Pediatric Dermatology
10175 Fortune Pkwy #1203, Jacksonville, 904-519-5292

Trimble, James William (5 mentions)
U of Florida, 1977 *Certification:* Dermatology
6890 Belfort Oaks Pl, Jacksonville, 904-296-1313

Emergency Medicine

Gilberstadt, Frank Huson (4 mentions)
Med Coll of Georgia, 1990 *Certification:* Emergency Medicine
1 Shircliff Way, Jacksonville, 904-308-8435

Gilligan, Brian Patrick (3 mentions)
U of Minnesota, 1993
Certification: Pediatric Emergency Medicine
820 Prudential Dr #713, Jacksonville, 904-396-5682

Patel, Rajnikant Ambalal (5 mentions)
FMS-India, 1971 *Certification:* Emergency Medicine
820 Prudential Dr #713, Jacksonville, 904-396-5682

Silvers, Scott Michael (7 mentions)
U of Rochester, 1997 *Certification:* Emergency Medicine
4500 San Pablo Rd, Jacksonville, 904-953-2000

Smowton, Jeffrey Stephen (6 mentions)
U of Florida, 1986
Certification: Emergency Medicine, Internal Medicine
820 Prudential Dr #713, Jacksonville, 904-396-5682

Stromberg, Richard Miles (9 mentions)
FMS-Mexico, 1975 *Certification:* Emergency Medicine
820 Prudential Dr #713, Jacksonville, 904-396-5682

Szymanski, Theodore John, Jr. (3 mentions)
Michigan State U Coll of Osteopathic Med, 1981
Certification: Emergency Medicine
4500 San Pablo Rd S, Jacksonville, 904-953-2000

Vukich, David Jonathan (3 mentions)
U of Colorado, 1976 *Certification:* Emergency Medicine
655 W 8th St, Jacksonville, 904-244-4107

Endocrinology

Dajani, Lorraine H. (6 mentions)
FMS-Argentina, 1982
Certification: Endocrinology, Internal Medicine
915 W Monroe St #200, Jacksonville, 904-384-2240
3550 University Blvd S #301, Jacksonville, 904-384-2240

Smallridge, Robert C. (7 mentions)
Virginia Commonwealth U, 1970
Certification: Endocrinology and Metabolism, Internal Medicine
4500 San Pablo Rd S, Jacksonville, 904-953-2000

Sutton, David Rickenbecke (11 mentions)
Wake Forest U, 1987
Certification: Endocrinology, Diabetes, and Metabolism
915 W Monroe St #200, Jacksonville, 904-384-2240
3550 University Blvd S #301, Jacksonville, 904-384-2240

Family Practice *(see note on page 9)*

Bartilucci, Darlene M. (3 mentions)
FMS-Grenada, 1995 *Certification:* Family Medicine
4085 University Blvd S, Jacksonville, 904-737-1171

Booras, Charles H. (6 mentions)
U of South Florida, 1981 *Certification:* Family Medicine
1922 University Blvd S, Jacksonville, 904-721-7844

Cassidy, Harvey Donald (3 mentions)
Jefferson Med Coll, 1977 *Certification:* Family Medicine
4500 San Pablo Rd S, Jacksonville, 904-953-2000

Presutti, Richard J. (3 mentions)
Nova Southeastern Coll of Osteopathic Med, 1993
Certification: Family Medicine
4500 San Pablo Rd S, Jacksonville, 904-952-6722

Willis, Floyd Banard (5 mentions)
Morehouse Coll, 1986 *Certification:* Family Medicine
4500 San Pablo Rd S, Jacksonville, 904-953-2000

Gastroenterology

Abbassi, Abdi (4 mentions)
FMS-Iran, 1986 *Certification:* Gastroenterology
1820 Barrs St #615, Jacksonville, 904-388-8686

Bass, Robert Terrell, Jr. (4 mentions)
Med Coll of Georgia, 1988 *Certification:* Gastroenterology
570 Jacksonville Dr, Jacksonville Beach, 904-241-8448

Cabi, Mehmet Akin (5 mentions)
U of Toledo, 1991 *Certification:* Gastroenterology
3 Shircliff Way #400, Jacksonville, 904-381-9393

Cangemi, John Richard (4 mentions)
Brown U, 1978 *Certification:* Gastroenterology, Internal Medicine
4500 San Pablo Rd S, Jacksonville, 904-953-2000

Goldberg, Lawrence S. (4 mentions)
New York U, 1973
Certification: Gastroenterology, Internal Medicine
4800 Belfort Rd 2nd Fl, Jacksonville, 904-398-3262

Groover, Jack Richard (4 mentions)
U of Maryland, 1968
Certification: Gastroenterology, Internal Medicine
4800 Belfort Rd 2nd Fl, Jacksonville, 904-398-3262

Hoffman, Jeffrey Stephen (4 mentions)
U of Washington, 1987 *Certification:* Gastroenterology
1375 Roberts Dr #204, Jacksonville Beach, 904-247-0056

Lambiase, Louis Robert (6 mentions)
U of Miami, 1987
Certification: Gastroenterology, Internal Medicine
653-1 W 8th St, Jacksonville, 904-633-0797
280 Dundas Dr, Jacksonville, 904-633-0175

Madhok, Dinesh (5 mentions)
FMS-India, 1984
Certification: Gastroenterology, Internal Medicine
1883 Kingsley Ave #1100, Orange Park, 904-264-9797

Patel, Anand Hasmukhrai (4 mentions)
FMS-United Kingdom, 1996
Certification: Gastroenterology, Internal Medicine
4800 Belfort Rd, Jacksonville, 904-398-7205

Sack, Todd L. (13 mentions)
U of California-San Francisco, 1980
Certification: Gastroenterology, Internal Medicine
3 Shircliff Way #400, Jacksonville, 904-381-9393

Taufiq, Salik (6 mentions)
FMS-Pakistan, 1988
Certification: Pediatric Gastroenterology, Pediatrics
807 Childrens Way, Jacksonville, 904-390-3600

General Surgery

Bowers, Gary John (8 mentions)
U of Miami, 1980 *Certification:* Surgery
836 Prudential Dr #1107, Jacksonville, 904-398-0033

Brinkman, John David (4 mentions)
U of Nebraska, 1985 *Certification:* Surgery, Surgical Critical Care
1555 Kingsley Ave #503, Orange Park, 904-278-5088

Chappano, Paul Joseph (10 mentions)
U of Pittsburgh, 1993 *Certification:* Surgery
2 Shircliff Way #900, Jacksonville, 904-389-8861

Chisholm, George E. (3 mentions)
Med Coll of Georgia, 1981 *Certification:* Surgery
2 Shircliff Way #900, Jacksonville, 904-388-6681

Contarini, Osvaldo (5 mentions)
FMS-Italy, 1970 *Certification:* Surgery
3636 University Blvd S #B, Jacksonville, 904-737-3150

Crump, John (6 mentions)
U of Missouri, 1978 *Certification:* Surgery
836 Prudential Dr #1107, Jacksonville, 904-398-0033

Dokler, Maryanne Louise (3 mentions)
Creighton U, 1978 *Certification:* Pediatric Surgery
807 Childrens Way, Jacksonville, 904-390-3740

Eyyunni, Ramanujam S. (3 mentions)
FMS-India, 1973 *Certification:* Surgery
201 Health Park Blvd #214, St Augustine, 904-824-9164

Fechtel, Douglas James (3 mentions)
Med Coll of Georgia, 1983 *Certification:* Surgery
1370 13th Ave S #116, Jacksonville Beach, 904-247-3858

Felger, Theodore Stevens (11 mentions)
U of Virginia, 1976 *Certification:* Surgery
836 Prudential Dr #1107, Jacksonville, 904-398-0033

Hagan, Kenneth Dale (4 mentions)
Emory U, 1988 *Certification:* Surgery
3599 University Blvd S #909, Jacksonville, 904-399-5678

Hartigan, Joseph Robert (4 mentions)
U of South Florida, 1989 *Certification:* Surgery
4203 Belfort Rd #215, Jacksonville, 904-296-4141

Martin, Joseph Kirk (3 mentions)
U of Alabama, 1974
4500 San Pablo Rd S, Jacksonville, 904-953-2000

McLaughlin, Sarah Ann (3 mentions)
U of Missouri-Kansas City, 2001 *Certification:* Surgery
4500 San Pablo Rd S, Jacksonville, 904-953-2000

Polley, Gordon M. (3 mentions)
U of South Florida, 1986 *Certification:* Surgery
836 Prudential Dr #1107, Jacksonville, 904-398-0033

Smith, C. Daniel (3 mentions)
U of Minnesota, 1986 *Certification:* Surgery
4500 San Pablo Rd S, Jacksonville, 904-953-2000

Webb, George Steven (3 mentions)
U of Louisville, 1978 *Certification:* Surgery
3599 University Blvd S #909, Jacksonville, 904-399-5678
836 Prudential Dr #1107, Jacksonville, 904-398-0033

Geriatrics

Glock, Richard David (4 mentions)
West Virginia U, 1973
Certification: Geriatric Medicine, Internal Medicine
8614 Baymeadows Way #100, Jacksonville, 904-396-0450

Hematology/Oncology

Abubakr, Yousif A. (6 mentions)
FMS-Sudan, 1986
Certification: Internal Medicine, Medical Oncology
5742 Booth Rd, Jacksonville, 904-739-7779

Di Mascio, Jeffrey (5 mentions)
Philadelphia Coll of Osteopathic Med, 1997
14546 Old St Augustine Rd #317, Jacksonville, 904-260-9445

Fox, Leann Lessl (6 mentions)
U of South Alabama, 1988 *Certification:* Medical Oncology
2 Shircliff Way #800, Jacksonville, 904-388-2620

Gaddis, Thomas Gray (5 mentions)
Louisiana State U-Shreveport, 1987
Certification: Medical Oncology
1375 Roberts Dr #103, Jacksonville Beach, 904-997-3800

Hunger, Kevin Kirby (7 mentions)
U of Virginia, 1986
Certification: Internal Medicine, Medical Oncology
2 Shircliff Way #800, Jacksonville, 904-388-2620

Joyce, Michael John (5 mentions)
St Louis U, 1984
Certification: Pediatric Hematology-Oncology, Pediatrics
807 Childrens Way, Jacksonville, 904-390-3789

Joyce, Robert Allyn (5 mentions)
Georgetown U, 1968 *Certification:* Internal Medicine
1235 San Marco Blvd #3, Jacksonville, 904-202-7048

Mahajan, Suneel Laxman (5 mentions)
FMS-India, 1974
Certification: Hematology, Internal Medicine, Medical Oncology
5742 Booth Rd, Jacksonville, 904-739-7779

Maples, William James (8 mentions)
U of Wisconsin, 1982
Certification: Internal Medicine, Medical Oncology
4500 San Pablo Rd S, Jacksonville, 904-953-2000

Marks, Alan Roy (7 mentions)
FMS-Belgium, 1975
Certification: Hematology, Internal Medicine, Medical Oncology
1235 San Marco Blvd #3, Jacksonville, 904-493-5100

Solberg, Lawrence A. (5 mentions)
St Louis U, 1975 *Certification:* Hematology, Internal Medicine
4500 San Pablo Rd S, Jacksonville, 904-953-7290

Stone, Joel Avrum (6 mentions)
U of Virginia, 1974
Certification: Internal Medicine, Medical Oncology
2 Shircliff Way #800, Jacksonville, 904-388-2619

Thomas, Unni C. (8 mentions)
FMS-India, 1989
Certification: Hematology, Internal Medicine, Medical Oncology
841 Prudential Dr #180, Jacksonville, 904-306-9229

Infectious Disease

Alvarez-Elcoro, Salvador (9 mentions)
FMS-Mexico, 1971
Certification: Infectious Disease, Internal Medicine
4500 San Pablo Rd S, Jacksonville, 904-953-2000

Meyer, Kenneth Stephen (15 mentions)
Robert W Johnson Med Sch, 1984
Certification: Infectious Disease, Internal Medicine
820 Prudential Dr #515, Jacksonville, 904-396-4886

Midani, Samir (7 mentions)
FMS-Syria, 1983
Certification: Pediatric Infectious Diseases, Pediatrics
807 Childrens Way, Jacksonville, 904-858-3869

Montoya, Jean-Paul (9 mentions)
U of South Florida, 1996
Certification: Infectious Disease, Internal Medicine
2 Shircliff Way #610, Jacksonville, 904-387-5027

Infertility

Winslow, Kevin Lane (12 mentions)
U of South Florida, 1984 *Certification:* Obstetrics &
Gynecology, Reproductive Endocrinology/Infertility
836 Prudential Dr, Jacksonville, 904-399-5620

Internal Medicine *(see note on page 9)*

Edwards, Linda Robertson (4 mentions)
East Carolina U, 1981 *Certification:* Internal Medicine
653 W 8th St, Jacksonville, 904-244-0411

Garmendia, Jose Manuel (5 mentions)
U of South Florida, 1985
Certification: Geriatric Medicine, Internal Medicine
2636 Oak St, Jacksonville, 904-384-5553

Glock, Richard David (9 mentions)
West Virginia U, 1973
Certification: Geriatric Medicine, Internal Medicine
8614 Baymeadows Way #100, Jacksonville, 904-396-0450

Grochmal, Richard A. (4 mentions)
Georgetown U, 1980 *Certification:* Internal Medicine
8614 Baymeadows Way #100, Jacksonville, 904-396-0450

Hartigan, Daniel Edward (6 mentions)
Creighton U, 1980 *Certification:* Internal Medicine
4500 San Pablo Rd S, Jacksonville, 904-953-6722

Levenson, Ilene Singer (4 mentions)
U of Florida, 1982 *Certification:* Internal Medicine
6144 Gazebo Park Pl S #102, Jacksonville, 904-880-8892

Madaffari, Catherine C. (5 mentions)
U of Miami, 1993 *Certification:* Internal Medicine
4745 Sutton Park Ct #701, Jacksonville, 904-821-0405

Millan, Joseph Marion (4 mentions)
U of Florida, 1982 *Certification:* Internal Medicine
1702 Osceola St, Jacksonville, 904-388-6770

Narvel, Ravish Ismail (3 mentions)
FMS-India, 1987 *Certification:* Internal Medicine
3960 Oak St, Jacksonville, 904-265-3344

Nixon, Kenneth Edmund (4 mentions)
Meharry Med Coll, 1981 *Certification:* Family Medicine
1760 Edgewood Ave W, Jacksonville, 904-610-9109

Reed, Alice (4 mentions)
Med Coll of Georgia, 1988
357 11th Ave S, Jacksonville Beach, 904-249-6556

Nephrology

Brumback, Michael Beirns (5 mentions)
U of North Carolina, 1997
Certification: Internal Medicine, Nephrology
2 Shircliff Way #415, Jacksonville, 904-389-5333

Davis, Robert Glenn (17 mentions)
U of Florida, 1977 *Certification:* Internal Medicine, Nephrology
3129 Hendricks Ave, Jacksonville, 904-398-8266

Smart, James Benny, Jr. (11 mentions)
Med Coll of Georgia, 1990 *Certification:* Nephrology
1801 Barrs St #415, Jacksonville, 904-389-5333
2 Shircliff Way #415, Jacksonville, 904-389-5333

Neurological Surgery

Chandler, Howard C. (8 mentions)
Emory U, 1951 *Certification:* Neurological Surgery
836 Prudential Dr #1001, Jacksonville, 904-388-6518

Garcia Bengochea, Javier (13 mentions)
Tulane U, 1985 *Certification:* Neurological Surgery
836 Prudential Dr #1001, Jacksonville, 904-388-6518

Monteiro, Paulo (7 mentions)
FMS-Brazil, 1974 *Certification:* Neurological Surgery
836 Prudential Dr #1001, Jacksonville, 904-388-6518

Reimer, Ronald (6 mentions)
U of Florida, 1980 *Certification:* Neurological Surgery
4500 San Pablo Rd S, Jacksonville, 904-953-2252

Spatola, Mark Arthur (6 mentions)
New Jersey Med Sch, 1981 *Certification:* Neurological Surgery
2021 Kingsley Ave #101, Orange Park, 904-276-3376

Wharen, Robert Ellsworth (8 mentions)
Pennsylvania State U, 1979 *Certification:* Neurological Surgery
4500 San Pablo Rd, Jacksonville, 904-953-2000

Neurology

Asad, Syed Ali (4 mentions)
FMS-Pakistan, 1995 *Certification:* Neurology, Nuclear Medicine
2736 University Blvd W #3, Jacksonville, 904-367-0574

Block, Harvey Steven (8 mentions)
U of Miami, 1982 *Certification:* Neurology
1820 Barrs St #724, Jacksonville, 904-308-7959

Brott, Thomas Gordon (4 mentions)
U of Chicago, 1974 *Certification:* Neurology, Vascular Neurology
4500 San Pablo Rd S, Jacksonville, 904-953-0556

Emas, Mark Kevin (7 mentions)
Temple U, 1988 *Certification:* Neurology
4085 University Blvd S #3, Jacksonville, 904-448-4180

Maquera, Victor Adalberto (5 mentions)
FMS-Mexico, 1982 *Certification:* Neurology
1895 Kingsley Ave #903, Orange Park, 904-276-1663

Snyder, Thomas Morrison (7 mentions)
Northwestern U, 1977 *Certification:* Neurology
1370 13th Ave S #215, Jacksonville Beach, 904-249-1041

Obstetrics/Gynecology

Andres, Frank James (3 mentions)
Louisiana State U, 1987 *Certification:* Obstetrics & Gynecology
3627 University Blvd S #340, Jacksonville, 904-398-1202

Baird, Tim (7 mentions)
U of Texas-Galveston, 1980 *Certification:* Obstetrics & Gynecology
6879 Southpoint Dr N, Jacksonville, 904-296-2441

Barnes, Harrison Wade, Jr. (4 mentions)
Med Coll of Georgia, 1975 *Certification:* Obstetrics & Gynecology
836 Prudential Dr #1207, Jacksonville, 904-399-4862

Dupree, Robert Edward, Jr. (3 mentions)
FMS-Mexico, 1982 *Certification:* Obstetrics & Gynecology
201 Health Park Blvd #215, St Augustine, 904-825-3629

Garcia, Martin Anthony (4 mentions)
Vanderbilt U, 1979 *Certification:* Obstetrics & Gynecology
836 Prudential Dr #1207, Jacksonville, 904-398-9499

Rodriguez, Lorraine (3 mentions)
U of Illinois, 1991 *Certification:* Obstetrics & Gynecology
6879 Southpoint Dr N, Jacksonville, 904-296-2441

Sekine, Kenneth Michael (3 mentions)
FMS-Mexico, 1975 *Certification:* Obstetrics & Gynecology
11945 San Jose Blvd #400, Jacksonville, 904-262-5333
836 Prudential Dr #802, Jacksonville, 904-399-5787

Ophthalmology

Adams, Charles P., Jr. (4 mentions)
Emory U, 1978 *Certification:* Ophthalmology
1034 Riverside Ave, Jacksonville, 904-354-2114

Bolling, James P., III (5 mentions)
U of Kentucky, 1980 *Certification:* Ophthalmology
4500 San Pablo Rd S, Jacksonville, 904-953-2232
807 Childrens Way, Jacksonville, 904-390-3600

Hossain, Tawhid S. (4 mentions)
Case Western Reserve U, 1992 *Certification:* Ophthalmology
301 Health Park Blvd #215, St Augustine, 904-794-5999

Levenson, Jeffrey H. (10 mentions)
U of Florida, 1984 *Certification:* Ophthalmology
751 Oak St #200, Jacksonville, 904-366-3781

Shmunes, Neil (6 mentions)
Med Coll of Georgia, 1981 *Certification:* Ophthalmology
3316 3rd St S #103, Jacksonville Beach, 904-241-7865

Smithwick, Walter, IV (5 mentions)
Vanderbilt U, 1993 *Certification:* Ophthalmology
2535 Riverside Ave, Jacksonville, 904-388-6548

Wolchok, Eugene B. (4 mentions)
U of Buffalo, 1966 *Certification:* Ophthalmology
3636 University Blvd S #A2, Jacksonville, 904-739-0606

Orthopedics

Bahri, Georges (4 mentions)
FMS-Lebanon, 1973
6100 Kennerly Rd, Jacksonville, 904-739-0050

Berrey, B. Hudson, Jr. (3 mentions)
U of Texas-Galveston, 1977 *Certification:* Orthopaedic Surgery
655 W 8th St, Jacksonville, 904-244-5942
4555 Emerson St #100, Jacksonville, 904-633-0150

Blasser, Kurt Emerick (4 mentions)
Temple U, 1978 *Certification:* Orthopaedic Surgery
4500 San Pablo Rd S, Jacksonville, 904-953-2496

Brodersen, Mark Preston (3 mentions)
U of Iowa, 1975 *Certification:* Orthopaedic Surgery
4500 San Pablo Rd S, Jacksonville, 904-953-2000

Deshmukh, Rahul Vinod (11 mentions)
Harvard U, 1997 *Certification:* Orthopaedic Surgery
1503 Oak St, Jacksonville, 904-634-0640

Hardy, Philip Ronald (4 mentions)
FMS-United Kingdom, 1972 *Certification:* Orthopaedic Surgery
1325 San Marco Blvd #200, Jacksonville, 904-346-3465

Heekin, Richard David (5 mentions)
Uniformed Services U of Health Sciences, 1985
Certification: Orthopaedic Surgery
1503 Oak St, Jacksonville, 904-634-0640

Kitay, Garry (3 mentions)
Columbia U, 1990
Certification: Orthopaedic Surgery, Surgery of the Hand
1325 San Marco Blvd #200, Jacksonville, 904-346-3465

Longenecker, Stanton Lee (3 mentions)
Tulane U, 1976 *Certification:* Orthopaedic Surgery
1801 Barrs St #300, Jacksonville, 904-388-1400

Lucie, Richard Stephen (3 mentions)
Med Coll of Georgia, 1975
Certification: Orthopaedic Sports Medicine, Orthopaedic Surgery
1325 San Marco Blvd #200, Jacksonville, 904-346-3465

Murphy, Kevin P. (3 mentions)
Uniformed Services U of Health Sciences, 1987
10475 Centurion Pkwy #220, Jacksonville, 904-634-0640

Neal, Kevin Michael (4 mentions)
U of Oklahoma, 1998 *Certification:* Orthopaedic Surgery
807 Childrens Way, Jacksonville, 904-390-3731

Norman, Harold Lynn (3 mentions)
U of Arkansas, 1972 *Certification:* Orthopaedic Surgery
2 Shircliff Way #300-A, Jacksonville, 904-388-1400

O'Connor, Mary Irene (4 mentions)
Med Coll of Pennsylvania, 1985
Certification: Orthopaedic Surgery
4500 San Pablo Rd S, Jacksonville, 904-953-2496
807 Childrens Way, Jacksonville, 904-390-3600

Tandron, Carlos Rafael (4 mentions)
Emory U, 1984 *Certification:* Orthopaedic Surgery
1325 San Marco Blvd #200, Jacksonville, 904-346-3465

Whitaker, Dale Alan (6 mentions)
U of South Florida, 1984 *Certification:* Orthopaedic Surgery
410 Jacksonville Dr, Jacksonville Beach, 904-241-1204

Otorhinolaryngology

Brink, Jeffrey Einar (7 mentions)
U of Florida, 1992 *Certification:* Otolaryngology
3316 3rd St S #102, Jacksonville Beach, 904-247-4070
1411 S 14th St #A, Fernandina Beach, 904-321-4341

Josephson, Gary David (6 mentions)
SUNY-Downstate Med Coll, 1990 *Certification:* Otolaryngology
807 Childrens Way, Jacksonville, 904-390-3707

Lisska, Lawrence Albert (14 mentions)
Ohio State U, 1970 *Certification:* Otolaryngology
4130 Salisbury Rd #1900, Jacksonville, 904-281-0234

Loper, Robert Michael (9 mentions)
U of Mississippi, 1977 *Certification:* Otolaryngology
3 Shircliff Way #322, Jacksonville, 904-384-8088

Snowden, Robert Todd (9 mentions)
Vanderbilt U, 1995 *Certification:* Otolaryngology
14546 Old St Augustine Rd #401, Jacksonville, 904-268-5366

Wilkinson, Albert H., III (6 mentions)
Tulane U, 1984 *Certification:* Otolaryngology
14546 Old Saint Augustine Rd #401, Jacksonville, 904-268-5366

Pain Medicine

Florete, Orlando G., Jr. (3 mentions)
FMS-Philippines, 1981 *Certification:* Anesthesiology
1325 San Marco Blvd, Jacksonville, 904-306-9860

Ghazi, Salim Michel (3 mentions)
FMS-Lebanon, 1986 *Certification:* Anesthesiology, Pain Medicine
4500 San Pablo Rd S, Jacksonville, 904-956-3192

Roberts, Christopher (4 mentions)
U of Colorado, 1993 *Certification:* Anesthesiology, Pain Medicine
10475 Centurion Pkwy N #201, Jacksonville, 904-223-3321

Woeste, John Theodore, Jr. (4 mentions)
U of Florida, 1989 *Certification:* Anesthesiology, Pain Medicine
1351 13th Ave S #140, Jacksonville, 904-270-2706

Pathology

Cantrell, Brett Bennett (4 mentions)
Med U of South Carolina, 1975 *Certification:* Anatomic Pathology
1 Shircliff Way, Jacksonville, 904-308-3804

Dundore, Paul Allen (5 mentions)
Eastern Virginia Med Sch, 1990
Certification: Anatomic Pathology & Clinical Pathology
800 Prudential Dr, Jacksonville, 304-202-2829
14550 St Augustine Rd, Jacksonville, 904-821-6818

Goldstein, Jeffrey David (10 mentions)
Emory U, 1976 *Certification:* Anatomic Pathology & Clinical
   Pathology, Pediatric Pathology
800 Prudential Dr, Jacksonville, 904-202-1347
1350 13th Ave S, Jacksonville Beach, 904-202-1347

Jones, Arthur Denton (3 mentions)
U of Tennessee, 1973 *Certification:* Anatomic Pathology &
   Clinical Pathology, Cytopathology, Dermatopathology
4500 San Pablo Rd S, Jacksonville, 904-956-3318

Menke, David McMurtrie (4 mentions)
Indiana U, 1981 *Certification:* Anatomic Pathology &
   Clinical Pathology, Hematology
4500 San Pablo Rd S, Jacksonville, 904-953-2000

Sandler, E. Dayan (4 mentions)
U of California-San Francisco, 1985
Certification: Anatomic Pathology & Clinical Pathology
800 Prudential Dr, Jacksonville, 904-202-8103

Pediatrics *(see note on page 9)*

Arango, Carlos A. (3 mentions)
FMS-Colombia, 1985
Certification: Pediatric Infectious Diseases, Pediatrics
8274 Bayberry Rd, Jacksonville, 904-737-3800

Baker, Julie Elizabeth R. (4 mentions)
Wake Forest U, 1978 *Certification:* Pediatrics
2121 Park St, Jacksonville, 904-387-6200
8750 Perimeter Park Blvd #101, Jacksonville, 904-387-6200

Colyer, Robert Fairlie, Jr. (4 mentions)
Emory U, 1974 *Certification:* Pediatrics
2121 Park St, Jacksonville, 904-387-6200
8750 Perimeter Park Blvd #101, Jacksonville, 904-387-6200

Hardman, Amy Winterbotham (3 mentions)
Vanderbilt U, 1994 *Certification:* Pediatrics
8750 Perimeter Park Blvd #101, Jacksonville, 904-387-6200
2121 Park St, Jacksonville, 904-387-6200

Harris, Jeremy Niles (4 mentions)
Wright State U, 1984 *Certification:* Pediatrics
3636 University Blvd S #B, Jacksonville, 904-448-3387

Mas, Miguel Angel (4 mentions)
FMS-Dominican Republic, 1984 *Certification:* Pediatrics
300 Health Park Blvd #3006, St Augustine, 904-461-1560
1301 Plantation Island Dr S #404, St Augustine, 904-461-1560

O'Reilly, Barbara M. (3 mentions)
FMS-Spain, 1984
1370 13th Ave S #216, Jacksonville Beach, 904-246-0644

Thornton, Randolph Edens (5 mentions)
Virginia Commonwealth U, 1983 *Certification:* Pediatrics
2606 Park St, Jacksonville, 904-388-4646

Threlkel, Robert Hays (3 mentions)
Duke U, 1966 *Certification:* Pediatrics
2121 Park St, Jacksonville, 904-387-6200
8750 Perimeter Park Blvd #101, Jacksonville, 904-387-6200

Walker, Martha K. (3 mentions)
Med Coll of Georgia, 1978 *Certification:* Pediatrics
3945 San Jose Park Dr, Jacksonville, 904-731-3530

Plastic Surgery

Burk, Robert William, III (7 mentions)
Duke U, 1988 *Certification:* Plastic Surgery
209 Ponte Vedra Park Dr, Ponte Vedra Beach, 904-273-6200

Scioscia, Paul J. (5 mentions)
U of Pittsburgh, 1987 *Certification:* Plastic Surgery
209 Ponte Vedra Park Dr, Ponte Vedra Beach, 904-273-6200

Waldorf, James Curtis (7 mentions)
U of Kansas, 1977 *Certification:* Plastic Surgery
4500 San Pablo Rd S, Jacksonville, 904-953-2073

Psychiatry

Burak, Carl Stanton (3 mentions)
Temple U, 1968 *Certification:* Psychiatry
482 Jacksonville Dr, Jacksonville Beach, 904-247-3600

Hunt, William Martin, III (4 mentions)
U of Miami, 1978 *Certification:* Psychiatry
3190 Post St, Jacksonville, 904-384-0668

Larson, James Lionel (3 mentions)
Loyola U Chicago, 1968 *Certification:* Psychiatry
1543 Kingsley Ave #14, Orange Park, 904-264-4998

Lin, Siong-Chi (4 mentions)
FMS-Philippines, 1982 *Certification:* Psychiatry
4500 San Pablo Rd S, Jacksonville, 904-953-7287

Merritt, Thomas Carey (4 mentions)
Med Coll of Georgia, 1982
Certification: Geriatric Psychiatry, Psychiatry
4500 San Pablo Rd S, Jacksonville, 904-953-2000

Olds, Robert Willard (3 mentions)
Ohio State U, 1976 *Certification:* Psychiatry
301 Health Park Blvd #106, St Augustine, 904-824-7884

Sanchez, Eduardo A. (3 mentions)
FMS-Spain, 1964 *Certification:* Psychiatry
1667 Atlantic Blvd, Jacksonville, 904-398-9861

Shah, Atul Mukutbhai (3 mentions)
FMS-India, 1974 *Certification:* Psychiatry
1545 Huffingham Rd, Jacksonville, 904-725-6463

Vijapura, Amit Kanaiyala (3 mentions)
FMS-India, 1983 *Certification:* Psychiatry
9141 Cypress Green Dr #1, Jacksonville, 904-733-7333

Pulmonary Disease

Bagnoli, Stephen (7 mentions)
New Jersey Med Sch, 1976
Certification: Internal Medicine, Pulmonary Disease
3599 University Blvd S #901, Jacksonville, 904-398-6971

Cury, James Davis (9 mentions)
U of Miami, 1981 *Certification:* Critical Care Medicine,
   Internal Medicine, Pulmonary Disease
655 W 8th St, Jacksonville, 904-244-3071

Hudak, Bonnie Boyer (6 mentions)
Johns Hopkins U, 1982 *Certification:* Neonatal-Perinatal
   Medicine, Pediatric Pulmonology, Pediatrics
807 Childrens Way, Jacksonville, 904-390-3788

Johnson, Margaret Mary (5 mentions)
Jefferson Med Coll, 1990 *Certification:* Critical Care
   Medicine, Internal Medicine, Pulmonary Disease
4500 San Pablo Rd S, Jacksonville, 904-953-2000

Mentz, William Marshall (5 mentions)
West Virginia U, 1977
Certification: Internal Medicine, Pulmonary Disease
425 N Lee St #203, Jacksonville, 904-354-8200

Millstone, Stuart Zachary (6 mentions)
Wayne State U, 1977 *Certification:* Critical Care Medicine,
   Internal Medicine, Pulmonary Disease
1893 Kingsley Ave #C, Orange Park, 904-276-2044

Namen, Andrew Michael (9 mentions)
Med Coll of Georgia, 1994
Certification: Critical Care Medicine, Pulmonary Disease
800 Prudential Dr, Jacksonville, 904-202-2353

Reid, Richard Alton (6 mentions)
Indiana U, 1966 *Certification:* Critical Care Medicine,
   Internal Medicine, Pulmonary Disease
800 Prudential Dr, Jacksonville, 904-202-2353

Radiology—Diagnostic

Bancroft, Josiah W., III (3 mentions)
U of Florida, 1989 *Certification:* Diagnostic Radiology,
   Vascular & Interventional Radiology
1800 Barrs St, Jacksonville, 904-308-8049
1 Shircliff Way, Jacksonville, 904-308-8049

Bridges, Mellena Davis (4 mentions)
Med Coll of Georgia, 1992 *Certification:* Diagnostic Radiology
4500 San Pablo Rd S, Jacksonville, 904-953-6696

Merinbaum, Debbie Riddle (6 mentions)
U of South Florida, 1989
Certification: Diagnostic Radiology, Pediatric Radiology
807 Childrens Way, Jacksonville, 904-390-3797

Mori, Kurt Wick (6 mentions)
New York Med Coll, 1976 *Certification:* Diagnostic
   Radiology, Vascular & Interventional Radiology
3599 University Blvd S #300, Jacksonville, 904-399-5550

Sharp, Barbara Lea (4 mentions)
Columbia U, 1982 *Certification:* Diagnostic Radiology
3599 University Blvd S #300, Jacksonville, 904-399-5550

Taliaferro, Robert Blair (4 mentions)
U of South Florida, 1986 *Certification:* Diagnostic Radiology
301 Health Park Blvd #217, St Augustine, 904-824-8813

Williams, Hugh Jones, Jr. (3 mentions)
U of Minnesota, 1978 *Certification:* Diagnostic Radiology,
   Vascular & Interventional Radiology
4500 San Pablo Rd S, Jacksonville, 904-953-6208

Radiology—Therapeutic

Mori, Kurt Wick (7 mentions)
New York Med Coll, 1976 *Certification:* Diagnostic
   Radiology, Vascular & Interventional Radiology
3599 University Blvd S #300, Jacksonville, 904-399-5550

Sanchez, Frank William (7 mentions)
U of Buffalo, 1980 *Certification:* Diagnostic Radiology,
   Vascular & Interventional Radiology
3599 University Blvd S #300, Jacksonville, 904-399-5550

Rehabilitation

Dorsher, Peter Thomas (3 mentions)
Rush U, 1985 *Certification:* Physical Medicine & Rehabilitation
4500 San Pablo Rd S, Jacksonville, 904-953-2823

Rizzo, Thomas Dignan, Jr. (8 mentions)
Georgetown U, 1985
Certification: Physical Medicine & Rehabilitation
4500 San Pablo Rd S, Jacksonville, 904-953-2000

Weiss, Howard B. (7 mentions)
New York Coll of Osteopathic Med, 1988
Certification: Physical Medicine & Rehabilitation
6800 Southpoint Pkwy #101, Jacksonville, 904-296-9939

Rheumatology

Ginsburg, William Wilcher (7 mentions)
Temple U, 1970 *Certification:* Internal Medicine, Rheumatology
4500 San Pablo Rd S, Jacksonville, 904-953-2000

Mathews, Steven Dell (6 mentions)
FMS-Mexico, 1982
6863 Belfort Oaks Pl, Jacksonville, 904-296-8516

Thoracic Surgery

Cousar, Charles Donaldson (12 mentions)
Johns Hopkins U, 1981 *Certification:* Surgery, Thoracic Surgery
1824 King St #200, Jacksonville, 904-384-3343
836 Prudential Dr #1804, Jacksonville, 904-398-8147

Odell, John Andrew (8 mentions)
FMS-South Africa, 1973
4500 San Pablo Rd S, Jacksonville, 904-953-2000

Still, Robert Jay (6 mentions)
Johns Hopkins U, 1984
Certification: Surgery, Thoracic Surgery, Vascular Surgery
836 Prudential Dr #1804, Jacksonville, 904-398-3888
1824 King St #200, Jacksonville, 904-384-3343

Urology

Cobb, Charles Gary (9 mentions)
Vanderbilt U, 1992 *Certification:* Urology
836 Prudential Dr #1502, Jacksonville, 904-886-4820

Mona, Mohammed Noman (5 mentions)
FMS-Syria, 1971 *Certification:* Urology
3599 University Blvd S #905, Jacksonville, 904-396-9096
3599 University Blvd S #103, Jacksonville, 904-359-0841

Swartz, Douglas Allan (11 mentions)
U of Texas-Houston, 1979 *Certification:* Urology
836 Prudential Dr #1502, Jacksonville, 904-396-5540

Vascular Surgery

Still, Robert Jay (7 mentions)
Johns Hopkins U, 1984
Certification: Surgery, Thoracic Surgery, Vascular Surgery
836 Prudential Dr #1804, Jacksonville, 904-398-3888
1824 King St #200, Jacksonville, 904-384-3343

Pinellas, Hillsborough, Polk, Manatee, and Sarasota Counties

Allergy/Immunology

Bloom, Frederick Lawry (15 mentions)
Med Coll of Wisconsin, 1971
2650 Bahia Vista St #304, Sarasota, 941-366-9711

Danziger, Roger Noland (8 mentions)
Boston U, 1986 *Certification:* Allergy & Immunology
5404 Cortez Rd W, Bradenton, 941-761-1911

Fox, Roger Williams (9 mentions)
St Louis U, 1975
Certification: Allergy & Immunology, Internal Medicine
13801 Bruce B Downs Blvd #502, Tampa, 813-971-9743

Jamieson, Donna M. (9 mentions)
U of Buffalo, 1980
Certification: Allergy & Immunology, Internal Medicine
2650 Bahia Vista St #304, Sarasota, 941-366-9711

Klemawesch, Stephen James (10 mentions)
U of Alabama, 1974
Certification: Allergy & Immunology, Internal Medicine
6294 1st Ave N, St Petersburg, 727-345-1900

Ledford, Dennis Keith (18 mentions)
U of Tennessee, 1976
Certification: Allergy & Immunology, Diagnostic Laboratory
  Immunology, Internal Medicine, Rheumatology
13801 Bruce B Downs Blvd #502, Tampa, 813-971-9743
12901 Bruce B Downs Blvd, Tampa, 813-974-2201

Lockey, Richard Funk (15 mentions)
Temple U, 1965
Certification: Allergy & Immunology, Internal Medicine
13801 Bruce B Downs Blvd #502, Tampa, 813-971-9743

Sher, Mandel Reid (20 mentions)
Northwestern U, 1976 *Certification:* Allergy & Immunology,
  Pediatric Rheumatology, Pediatrics
11200 Seminole Blvd #310, Largo, 727-397-8557

Windom, Hugh Harmon (12 mentions)
Duke U, 1985
Certification: Allergy & Immunology, Internal Medicine
4040 Sawyer Rd, Sarasota, 941-927-4888

Anesthesiology

Beckenstein, Charles Robert (4 mentions)
SUNY-Downstate Med Coll, 1984 *Certification:* Anesthesiology
3100 E Fletcher Ave, Tampa, 813-971-6000

Defreitas, Edward Albert (3 mentions)
Certification: Anesthesiology, Internal Medicine
2010 59th St W #5600, Bradenton, 941-798-3524

Elinger, John Howard (3 mentions)
U of Michigan, 1978
Certification: Anesthesiology, Critical Care Medicine
880 6th St S #110, St Petersburg, 727-456-3288

Epstein, Jay Harlan (4 mentions)
Case Western Reserve U, 1992
Certification: Anesthesiology, Critical Care Medicine
300 Jeffords Sr #B, Clearwater, 727-441-1524

Kaufman, Marc Aaron (3 mentions)
U of Maryland, 1985 *Certification:* Anesthesiology
1033 Martin Luther King St, St Petersburg, 727-456-3288

Kramer, Daniel (3 mentions)
Ohio U Coll of Osteopathic Med, 1993
Certification: Anesthesiology
119 Oakfield Dr, Brandon, 813-681-5551

Mangar, Devanand (10 mentions)
SUNY-Upstate Med U, 1985 *Certification:* Anesthesiology
360 Blanca Ave, Tampa, 813-844-4434
2 Columbia Dr, Tampa, 813-870-0176

Moroney, Thomas Roger (3 mentions)
U of Miami, 1992 *Certification:* Anesthesiology
2700 W Dr Martin Luther King Jr Blvd #460, Tampa,
  813-350-7244

Olson, Suzanne Marie (3 mentions)
U of Florida, 1991 *Certification:* Anesthesiology
2010 59th St W #5600, Bradenton, 941-798-3524

Rudolph, Alan Theodore (3 mentions)
Rosalind Franklin U, 1968 *Certification:* Anesthesiology
300 Jeffords St #B, Clearwater, 727-442-1413

Silver, Richard Barry (4 mentions)
U of Maryland, 1977 *Certification:* Anesthesiology
3100 E Fletcher Ave, Tampa, 813-615-7294

Valentine, Dwight Donald (3 mentions)
U of South Florida, 1985 *Certification:* Anesthesiology
1200 7th Ave N, St Petersburg, 727-825-1100

Cardiac Surgery

Beggs, Martin L. (10 mentions)
U of Texas-Houston, 1989 *Certification:* Thoracic Surgery
1435 S Osprey Ave #200, Sarasota, 941-952-1913

Bronleewe, Scott Howarth (7 mentions)
U of South Florida, 1982 *Certification:* Surgery, Thoracic Surgery
3000 E Fletcher Ave #320, Tampa, 813-910-0027

Chapa, Liberato (8 mentions)
FMS-Mexico, 1970 *Certification:* Thoracic Surgery
455 Pinellas St #320, Clearwater, 727-446-2273

Diliberto, Joseph Francis (10 mentions)
Med Coll of Wisconsin, 1986 *Certification:* Thoracic Surgery
8588 Starkey Rd #E, Largo, 727-398-9600

Fong, Jonathan C. (6 mentions)
Certification: Thoracic Surgery
706 The Rialto, Venice, 941-484-8004

Lazzara, Robert Ralph (6 mentions)
Emory U, 1985 *Certification:* Thoracic Surgery
3003 W Dr Martin Luther King Jr Blvd, Tampa, 813-875-8988
3003 W Martin Luther King Dr, Tampa, 813-875-8988

Lewis, Clifton Thomas P. (11 mentions)
U of Alabama, 1983 *Certification:* Surgery, Thoracic Surgery
1435 S Osprey Ave #200, Sarasota, 941-952-1913

Messina, Jack John (6 mentions)
Albany Med Coll, 1968 *Certification:* Thoracic Surgery
1600 Lakeland Hills Blvd, Lakeland, 863-680-7810

Peterson, Richard James (6 mentions)
Mayo Med Sch, 1979 *Certification:* Thoracic Surgery
623 39th St W #2, Bradenton, 941-744-2640

Quintessenza, James A. (6 mentions)
U of Florida, 1981 *Certification:* Thoracic Surgery
3005 W Dr Martin Luther King Blvd, Tampa, 813-554-8343
625 6th Ave S #475, St Petersburg, 727-822-6666

Sheffield, Cedric Dewayne (6 mentions)
Duke U, 1986 *Certification:* Surgery, Thoracic Surgery
4 Columbia Dr #820, Tampa, 813-844-3228

Cardiology

Ballal, Natraj N. (3 mentions)
FMS-India, 1982 *Certification:* Pediatric Cardiology, Pediatrics
2727 W Dr Martin Luther King Jr Blvd #620, Tampa,
  813-874-1662

Canedo, Mario (6 mentions)
FMS-Bolivia, 1970
Certification: Cardiovascular Disease, Internal Medicine
13701 Bruce B Downs Blvd #101, Tampa, 813-971-2600
6101 Webb Rd #206, Tampa, 813-884-0897

Culp, Stephen Crompton (3 mentions)
U of Vermont, 1986 *Certification:* Cardiovascular Disease,
  Internal Medicine, Interventional Cardiology
1852 Hillview St #308, Sarasota, 941-917-4250

Curtis, Anne (3 mentions)
Certification: Cardiovascular Disease, Clinical Cardiac
  Electrophysiology, Internal Medicine
12901 Bruce B Downs Blvd, Tampa, 813-974-2201
2 Tampa General Cir, Tampa, 813-259-0600

Ebersole, Douglas Glenn (3 mentions)
U of Miami, 1986 *Certification:* Cardiovascular Disease,
  Internal Medicine, Interventional Cardiology
1600 Lakeland Hills Blvd, Lakeland, 863-680-7973

Garcia, Juan A. (3 mentions)
FMS-Argentina, 1972
Certification: Cardiovascular Disease, Internal Medicine
13701 Bruce B Downs Blvd #101, Tampa, 813-971-2600
6101 Webb Rd #206, Tampa, 813-884-0897

Glover, Matthew U. (4 mentions)
U of South Florida, 1975 *Certification:* Cardiovascular
    Disease, Internal Medicine, Interventional Cardiology
2814 W Virginia Ave, Tampa, 813-875-9000

Harrison, Eric Edward (3 mentions)
U of Kentucky, 1969
Certification: Cardiovascular Disease, Internal Medicine
602 S Audubon Ave #B, Tampa, 813-348-4885

Henry, James Gifford (3 mentions)
U of Oklahoma, 1965
Certification: Pediatric Cardiology, Pediatrics
880 6th St S #280, St Petersburg, 727-767-4200

Henson, Kenneth Daryl (4 mentions)
U of Mississippi, 1984 *Certification:* Cardiovascular
    Disease, Internal Medicine, Interventional Cardiology
3830 Bee Ridge Rd #201, Sarasota, 941-929-1039

Khant, Ranchhod Naranbhai (3 mentions)
FMS-India, 1979
Certification: Cardiovascular Disease, Internal Medicine
3920 Galen Ct, Sun City Center, 813-634-7200
635 Eichenfeld Dr, Brandon, 813-684-6000

Kohl, David Wolters (3 mentions)
U of North Carolina, 1979 *Certification:* Cardiovascular
    Disease, Internal Medicine, Interventional Cardiology
4805 49th St N, St Petersburg, 727-526-6624

Liebert, Hugh Peter (3 mentions)
Georgetown U, 1981 *Certification:* Cardiovascular Disease,
    Internal Medicine, Interventional Cardiology
1400 59th St W, Bradenton, 941-795-2468

Malek, Javad (3 mentions)
FMS-Iran, 1966
Certification: Cardiovascular Disease, Internal Medicine
11404 N 56th St, Tampa, 813-988-5700

Mester, Stephen Wade (3 mentions)
U of Florida, 1983
Certification: Cardiovascular Disease, Internal Medicine
635 Eichenfeld Dr, Brandon, 813-684-6000
3920 Galen Ct, Sun City Center, 813-634-9274

Montalvo, Alberto E. (3 mentions)
Temple U, 1978 *Certification:* Cardiovascular Disease,
    Internal Medicine, Interventional Cardiology
316 Manatee Ave W, Bradenton, 941-748-2277

Nguyen, Van Quan (3 mentions)
U of Louisville, 1989
1840 Mease Dr #200, Safety Harbor, 727-724-8611

Owen, Philip Selwyn (3 mentions)
FMS-Canada, 1982 *Certification:* Cardiovascular Disease,
    Internal Medicine, Interventional Cardiology
130 Pablo St, Lakeland, 863-284-5020

Post, James Robert (7 mentions)
New York U, 1988 *Certification:* Cardiovascular Disease
1615 Pasadena Ave S #300, South Pasadena, 727-490-3030

Prida, Xavier Enrique (4 mentions)
U of Miami, 1980 *Certification:* Cardiovascular Disease,
    Internal Medicine, Interventional Cardiology
2814 W Virginia Ave, Tampa, 813-875-9000

Rosenthal, Andrew D. (3 mentions)
Mount Sinai Sch of Med, 1984 *Certification:* Cardiovascular
    Disease, Internal Medicine, Interventional Cardiology
560 Jackson St N, St Petersburg, 727-329-1600

Saef, Jerold Lawrence (3 mentions)
U of South Florida, 1981 *Certification:* Cardiovascular
    Disease, Internal Medicine, Nuclear Medicine
3830 Bee Ridge Rd #201, Sarasota, 941-929-1039

Satya, Yemuna (4 mentions)
U of Miami, 1994 *Certification:* Cardiovascular Disease
3231 Gulf Gate Dr #101, Sarasota, 941-924-1193

Schwartz, Hardy Jed (4 mentions)
FMS-Canada, 1997
Certification: Cardiovascular Disease, Internal Medicine
1852 Hillview St #308, Sarasota, 941-917-4250

Sheppard, Robert Charles (4 mentions)
New York Med Coll, 1986 *Certification:* Cardiovascular
    Disease, Clinical Cardiac Electrophysiology
560 Jackson St N #100, St Petersburg, 727-329-1600

Smith, James O., III (3 mentions)
U of South Florida, 1981 *Certification:* Cardiovascular
    Disease, Internal Medicine, Interventional Cardiology
3000 Medical Park Dr #500, Tampa, 813-971-2424

Stromquist, Philip Stan (3 mentions)
FMS-Belgium, 1982 *Certification:* Cardiovascular Disease,
    Internal Medicine, Interventional Cardiology
2 Tampa General Cir, Tampa, 813-974-2201
526 Riviera Dr, Tampa, 813-348-4885
4 Columbia Dr #725, Tampa, 813-259-0600

Sullebarger, John T. (3 mentions)
Johns Hopkins U, 1983 *Certification:* Cardiovascular
    Disease, Internal Medicine, Interventional Cardiology
509 S Armenia Ave #200, Tampa, 813-353-1515

Wassmer, Peter Ramon C. (3 mentions)
FMS-Philippines, 1985 *Certification:* Cardiovascular Disease
1615 Pasadena Ave S #300, South Pasadena, 727-490-3030

Weston, Mark William (3 mentions)
Indiana U, 1981 *Certification:* Cardiovascular Disease,
    Internal Medicine, Interventional Cardiology
409 Bayshore Blvd, Tampa, 813-251-0793

Yamada, David Michael (4 mentions)
Northwestern U, 1995 *Certification:* Cardiovascular Disease
1852 Hillview St #308, Sarasota, 941-917-4250

Yaryura, Ricardo A. (4 mentions)
FMS-Canada, 1990
Certification: Cardiovascular Disease, Interventional Cardiology
2881 Hyde Park St, Sarasota, 941-366-1888

Dermatology

Albergo, Robert Patrick (4 mentions)
U of Rochester, 1978 *Certification:* Dermatology
4132 Woodlands Pkwy, Palm Harbor, 727-786-5100

Beard, Jeffrey Sherman (4 mentions)
U of Kentucky, 1987 *Certification:* Dermatology
1416 59th St W, Bradenton, 941-794-5246

Bedi, Monica Kaur (4 mentions)
U of Florida, 1998 *Certification:* Dermatology
3830 Bee Ridge Rd #200, Sarasota, 941-927-5178
3501 Cortez Rd W #3, Bradenton, 941-752-0066

Demetree, John William (4 mentions)
U of South Florida, 1974 *Certification:* Dermatology
5857 21st Ave W #A, Bradenton, 941-792-8252

Donelan, Peter A. (5 mentions)
U of South Florida, 1978 *Certification:* Dermatology
3000 E Fletcher Ave #200, Tampa, 813-972-1229

Fenske, Neil Alan (6 mentions)
St Louis U, 1973 *Certification:* Dermatology, Dermatopathology
12901 Bruce B Downs Blvd, Tampa, 813-974-2920
12902 Magnolia Dr #3057, Tampa, 813-974-2920
17 Davis Blvd #402, Tampa, 813-974-2920

Hanno, Ruth Harriet (4 mentions)
U of Pennsylvania, 1976
Certification: Dermatology, Dermatopathology
15310 Amberly Dr #150, Tampa, 813-978-8888

Haynes, Melanie Renee (4 mentions)
Louisiana State U, 1985
Certification: Dermatology, Internal Medicine
9005 Belcher Rd, Pinellas Park, 727-545-3372

Hernandez, Alfred D. (4 mentions)
U of Miami, 1973 *Certification:* Dermatology
1849 S Osprey Ave, Sarasota, 941-957-4767

Jawitz, Jack Charles (5 mentions)
SUNY-Downstate Med Coll, 1977
Certification: Dermatology, Internal Medicine
2919 26th St W, Bradenton, 941-755-2255

Kelly, Timothy Francis (6 mentions)
U of South Florida, 1978 *Certification:* Dermatology
32615 US Hwy 19 N #1, Palm Harbor, 727-785-7667

Kirk, John Forrest (6 mentions)
U of Florida, 1991 *Certification:* Dermatology
4444 Central Ave, St Petersburg, 727-328-0900

Menendez, Luis Terry (6 mentions)
U of Miami, 1971 *Certification:* Dermatology
3011 W Swann Ave, Tampa, 813-879-8436

Milam, Cathy Press (6 mentions)
U of South Florida, 1984 *Certification:* Dermatology
7400 S Tamiami Trail, Sarasota, 941-364-8220

Miller, Richard A. (5 mentions)
3657 Madaca Ln, Tampa, 813-264-5447
2525 Pasadena Ave S #U, South Pasadena, 727-363-6688
115 Highland Ave NE, Largo, 727-585-8591

Nelson, Christopher Grant (8 mentions)
U of Iowa, 1971 *Certification:* Dermatology
350 6th St S, St Petersburg, 727-895-8131

Oliva, Stepan (4 mentions)
Med U of South Carolina, 1994 *Certification:* Dermatology
560 Ave K SE, Winter Haven, 863-299-3376

Sultenfuss, Thomas Joseph (4 mentions)
Tulane U, 1977 *Certification:* Dermatology
1022 Main St #R, Dunedin, 727-734-6710

Trunnell, Thomas Newton (4 mentions)
U of Iowa, 1968 *Certification:* Dermatology
13801 Bruce B Downs Blvd #306, Tampa, 813-977-1024

Vasiloudes, Panayiotis E. (5 mentions)
FMS-Germany, 1987 *Certification:* Dermatology
5210 Webb Rd, Tampa, 813-882-9986
1005 E Boyer St, Tarpon Springs, 727-934-7638
4238 W Kennedy Blvd, Tampa, 813-879-6040

Weinkle, Susan Holloway (4 mentions)
U of Florida, 1978 *Certification:* Dermatology
5601 21st Ave W #A, Bradenton, 941-794-5432

Wiley, Henry Ernest, III (5 mentions)
U of Florida, 1974 *Certification:* Dermatology, Dermatopathology
1425 S Howard Ave, Tampa, 813-253-2635

Emergency Medicine

Acosta, Anthony (6 mentions)
U of Miami, 1975
Certification: Emergency Medicine, Family Medicine
701 6th St S, St Petersburg, 727-893-6100

Colgate, William Wayne (3 mentions)
U of Nebraska, 1989 *Certification:* Emergency Medicine
1700 S Tamiami Trail, Sarasota, 941-917-8507

Dooley, Donna Maack (3 mentions)
Kansas U Coll of Osteopathic Med, 1990
701 6th St S, St Petersburg, 727-893-6100

Fell, Scott D. (4 mentions)
Philadelphia Coll of Osteopathic Med, 1993
Certification: Emergency Medicine
540 The Rialto, Venice, 941-483-7000

Garby, Brian Milton (3 mentions)
U of South Florida, 1979
Certification: Emergency Medicine, Internal Medicine
1700 S Tamiami Trail, Sarasota, 941-917-8507

Gerlach, James H. (3 mentions)
200 Ave F NE, Winter Haven, 863-293-1121

Hernandez, Dennis Arnaldo (3 mentions)
Certification: Pediatric Emergency Medicine, Pediatrics
2727 W Dr Martin Luther King Jr Blvd #300, Tampa,
  813-874-5707

Holland, Reuben W., III (4 mentions)
West Virginia U, 1985 *Certification:* Emergency Medicine
1700 S Tamiami Trail, Sarasota, 941-917-8507

Melton, James David, III (3 mentions)
Certification: Emergency Medicine
1324 Lakeland Hills Blvd, Lakeland, 863-687-1100

Newman, Steven Robert (4 mentions)
Rosalind Franklin U, 1978 *Certification:* Emergency Medicine
1700 S Tamiami Trail, Sarasota, 941-917-8507

Pidala, Anthony I., Jr. (3 mentions)
U of Miami, 1980
Certification: Emergency Medicine, Internal Medicine
3001 W Martin Luther King Jr Blvd, Tampa, 813-874-5707

Soler, Joseph Manuel (5 mentions)
U of Miami, 1975 *Certification:* Emergency Medicine
315 75th St W, Bradenton, 941-761-1616

Steele, Paul Keith (4 mentions)
FMS-St Maarten, 1986 *Certification:* Internal Medicine
201 14th St SW, Largo, 727-581-6984

Zika, Blake A. (3 mentions)
Des Moines U, 2000
206 2nd St E, Bradenton, 941-746-5111

Endocrinology

Chandra, Sumesh (8 mentions)
FMS-India, 1967 *Certification:* Endocrinology and Metabolism, Internal Medicine, Nuclear Medicine
3000 E Fletcher Ave #350, Tampa, 813-977-5557

Concepcion, Renato C. (6 mentions)
FMS-Philippines, 1985
Certification: Endocrinology, Diabetes, and Metabolism
3709 W Hamilton Ave #9, Tampa, 813-936-7119

Declue, Terry Joe (11 mentions)
U of South Florida, 1982 *Certification:* Pediatric Endocrinology
3001 W Dr Martin Luther King Jr Blvd, Tampa, 813-554-8420

Lupo, Mark Armin (8 mentions)
U of Florida, 1997 *Certification:* Endocrinology, Diabetes, and Metabolism, Internal Medicine
5741 Bee Ridge Rd #500, Sarasota, 941-342-9750

Morrison, Anthony Douglas (10 mentions)
FMS-Canada, 1963 *Certification:* Endocrinology and Metabolism, Endocrinology, Diabetes, and Metabolism, Internal Medicine
12901 Bruce B Downs Blvd, Tampa, 813-974-2918

Nowakowski, Kevin John (9 mentions)
FMS-Mexico, 1981 *Certification:* Internal Medicine
1609 Pasadena Ave S #4N, South Pasadena, 727-345-5222

O'Malley, Brendan C. (12 mentions)
FMS-United Kingdom, 1970 *Certification:* Internal Medicine
13901 Bruce B Downs Blvd, Tampa, 813-615-7620

Placheril, Lillibet M. (8 mentions)
FMS-India, 1987 *Certification:* Endocrinology, Diabetes, and Metabolism, Internal Medicine
1906 59th St W Bldg B, Bradenton, 941-795-1915

Sainz-De-La-Pena, Manuel (9 mentions)
U of Puerto Rico, 1983 *Certification:* Endocrinology and Metabolism
2727 W Martin Luther King Blvd #450, Tampa, 813-875-8453

Family Practice *(see note on page 9)*

Brownlee, H. James, Jr. (4 mentions)
SUNY-Upstate Med U, 1976 *Certification:* Family Medicine
12901 Bruce B Downs Blvd, Tampa, 813-974-2918

Calzadilla, Rafael J. (3 mentions)
FMS-Venezuela, 1981
1720 Manatee Ave E, Bradenton, 941-747-4661

Diaz, Ivan (3 mentions)
FMS-Dominican Republic, 1997 *Certification:* Family Medicine
4710 S Florida Ave, Lakeland, 863-284-6800

Dunn, Kevin Joseph (3 mentions)
U of Kentucky, 1995 *Certification:* Family Medicine
6128 S Tamiami Trail, Sarasota, 941-923-5882

Evans, Corey Hadley (3 mentions)
St Louis U, 1976 *Certification:* Family Medicine, Geriatric Medicine, Sports Medicine
5101 Brittany Dr S, St Petersburg, 727-867-2151
700 6th St S, St Petersburg, 727-893-6153

Francis, David James (3 mentions)
Ohio State U, 1999 *Certification:* Family Medicine
5405 Park St N, Seminole, 727-547-8425

Fraser, Jeffrey Paul (3 mentions)
Philadelphia Coll of Osteopathic Med, 1995
Certification: Family Medicine
1720 E Venice Ave 2nd Fl, Venice, 941-483-9730

Gross, John Allan (3 mentions)
Ohio State U, 2002
Certification: Family Medicine, Sports Medicine
116 1st St N, St Petersburg, 727-895-5210

Ina, Richard John (3 mentions)
U of South Florida, 1988 *Certification:* Family Medicine
3000 E Fletcher Ave #300, Tampa, 813-975-1727

Price, Martha Ann (5 mentions)
Med U of South Carolina, 1980 *Certification:* Family Medicine
3211 W Azeele St, Tampa, 813-879-3334

Roetzheim, Richard George (4 mentions)
U of Illinois, 1985 *Certification:* Family Medicine
12901 Bruce B Downs Blvd, Tampa, 813-974-2918

Rosequist, Robert B. (3 mentions)
U of South Florida, 1980 *Certification:* Family Medicine
1942 Highland Oaks Blvd #A, Lutz, 813-948-3838
5251 Village Market, Wesley Chapel, 813-991-6000

Smith, Alan Alford (3 mentions)
U of Louisville, 1983 *Certification:* Family Medicine
630 Pasadena Ave S, St Petersburg, 727-345-7100

Tawil, Albert (4 mentions)
Jefferson Med Coll, 1962
Certification: Family Medicine, Geriatric Medicine
508 S Habana Ave #360, Tampa, 813-876-5548

Gastroenterology

Aviles, Louis (5 mentions)
Harvard U, 1987
Certification: Gastroenterology, Internal Medicine
1007 Jeffords St #102, Clearwater, 727-442-7181

Berman, Arthur Lee (6 mentions)
A T Still U, 1981
8250 Bryan Dairy Rd #200, Seminole, 727-544-1600

Berner, Jody Scott (7 mentions)
U of Rochester, 1987
Certification: Gastroenterology, Internal Medicine
401 Corbett St #220, Clearwater, 727-443-0100
1305 S Fort Harrison Ave, Clearwater, 727-631-0915

Brady, Patrick George (5 mentions)
New Jersey Med Sch, 1968
Certification: Gastroenterology, Internal Medicine
12901 Bruce B Downs Blvd, Tampa, 813-974-2201

Caradonna, Joseph Scott (7 mentions)
Indiana U, 1967
Certification: Gastroenterology, Internal Medicine
14547 Bruce B Downs Blvd, Tampa, 813-977-8985

Edgerton, Norman Bruce, Jr. (6 mentions)
U of Florida, 1973
Certification: Gastroenterology, Internal Medicine
2706 W Dr Martin Luther King Jr Blvd #A, Tampa, 813-875-8650

Glamour, Tejinder Singh (5 mentions)
FMS-India, 1985 *Certification:* Gastroenterology
6225 66th St, Pinellas Park, 727-521-0994

Hanan, Morris Rubin (6 mentions)
U of Alabama, 1975
Certification: Gastroenterology, Internal Medicine
508 S Habana Ave #260, Tampa, 813-876-9191

Khazanchi, Arun (7 mentions)
FMS-Grenada, 1996
Certification: Gastroenterology, Internal Medicine
8340 Lakewood Ranch Blvd #101, Bradenton, 941-361-1100

Nord, Heinz Juergen (6 mentions)
FMS-Germany, 1964
12901 Bruce B Downs Blvd, Tampa, 813-974-4115

Roddenberry, John Douglas (4 mentions)
U of Florida, 1984
Certification: Gastroenterology, Internal Medicine
1886 59th St W, Bradenton, 941-794-1980

Rosario, Angel Manuel (4 mentions)
U Central del Caribe, 1981 *Certification:* Gastroenterology
7171 N Dale Mabry Hwy #305, Tampa, 813-930-8816
3633 Little Rd #104, New Port Richey, 727-372-5547

Saco, Louis S. (5 mentions)
Georgetown U, 1976
Certification: Gastroenterology, Internal Medicine
1600 Lakeland Hills Blvd, Lakeland, 863-680-7463

Simmons, David Banks (4 mentions)
U of Florida, 1989 *Certification:* Gastroenterology
320 1st St N, Winter Haven, 863-422-6300

Southerland, John C. (4 mentions)
FMS-Ireland, 1995
Certification: Gastroenterology, Internal Medicine
2089 Hawthorne St #200, Sarasota, 941-365-6556

Sreenath, Belur S. (4 mentions)
FMS-India, 1974
Certification: Gastroenterology, Internal Medicine
3901 66th St N #201, St Petersburg, 727-345-5500
1300 S Fort Harrison Ave #100, Clearwater, 727-447-3100

General Surgery

Albrink, Michael Hunter (6 mentions)
Ohio State U, 1978 *Certification:* Surgery, Surgical Critical Care
2-A Columbia Dr, Tampa, 813-974-2201

Andersen, Philip Howard (4 mentions)
Med Coll of Wisconsin, 1964 *Certification:* Surgery
13801 Bruce B Downs Blvd #506, Tampa, 813-977-2200

Berry, David Griffith (3 mentions)
Jefferson Med Coll, 1976 *Certification:* Surgery
1840 Mease Dr #301, Safety Harbor, 727-712-3233
646 Virginia St #201, Dunedin, 727-712-3233

Brannan, Anthony N. (10 mentions)
Vanderbilt U, 1980 *Certification:* Colon & Rectal Surgery, Surgery
4700 N Habana Ave #403, Tampa, 813-879-5010

Bunch, Gary Milton (3 mentions)
U of Kentucky, 1988 *Certification:* Surgery
200 3rd Ave W #110, Bradenton, 941-744-2700

Campbell, Sylvia L. (4 mentions)
U of South Florida, 1977 *Certification:* Surgery
217 S Matanzas Ave, Tampa, 813-875-2655

Cannella, Xavier F., Jr. (5 mentions)
FMS-Dominica, 1983 *Certification:* Surgery
10549 N Florida Ave #I, Tampa, 813-933-9666

Christensen, James Arlo (4 mentions)
Indiana U, 1968 *Certification:* Surgery
4600 N Habana Ave #21, Tampa, 813-877-8201

Clarke, John Mitchell (3 mentions)
U of Virginia, 1962 *Certification:* Surgery
1615 Pasadena Ave S #4-C, South Pasadena, 727-345-2929

Collins, Paul Steven (5 mentions)
U of South Florida, 1979
Certification: Surgery, Surgical Critical Care, Vascular Surgery
960 7th Ave N, St Petersburg, 727-821-8101

Echevarria, David F. (3 mentions)
U of Miami, 1988 *Certification:* Surgery
4700 N Habana Ave #403, Tampa, 813-879-5010

Erbella, Jose, Jr. (5 mentions)
U of Miami, 1999 *Certification:* Surgery
200 3rd Ave W, Bradenton, 941-744-2700
315 75th St W, Bradenton, 941-761-3405

Erickson, Kurt Victor (3 mentions)
U of South Florida, 1997 *Certification:* Surgery
1106 Druid Rd S #301, Clearwater, 727-446-5681
8839 Bryan Dairy Rd #310, Largo, 727-446-5681

Fansler, Richard F. (5 mentions)
U of Florida, 1988 *Certification:* Surgery
1609 Pasadena Ave S #2-C, South Pasadena, 727-302-9000
12955 Seminole Blvd #3, Largo, 727-584-9500

Feinman, Larry Jay (5 mentions)
Philadelphia Coll of Osteopathic Med, 1981
2401 W Bay Dr #602, Largo, 727-501-1600

Golub, Richard William (3 mentions)
Albert Einstein Coll of Med, 1984
Certification: Colon & Rectal Surgery, Surgery
3333 Cattlemen Rd #206, Sarasota, 941-341-0042

Harmel, Richard Paul, Jr. (3 mentions)
Harvard U, 1972 *Certification:* Pediatric Surgery, Surgery
880 6th St S #210, St Petersburg, 727-767-4170

Hart, Vanessa Marie (4 mentions)
Rush U, 1991 *Certification:* Surgery
960 7th Ave N, St Petersburg, 727-821-8101

Haslup, Forrest Copley (3 mentions)
U of South Florida, 1981 *Certification:* Surgery, Vascular Surgery
4728 N Habana Ave #303, Tampa, 813-870-4064

Holec, Sidney Wayne (3 mentions)
U of Texas-Dallas, 1973 *Certification:* Surgery
436 Nokomis Ave S, Venice, 941-488-7742

Howard, Fred Irving, III (3 mentions)
U of Missouri, 1996 *Certification:* Surgery
635 1st St N, Winter Haven, 863-294-0670

Kulman, Harold Lewis (3 mentions)
U of Buffalo, 1968 *Certification:* Surgery
1921 Waldemere St #504, Sarasota, 941-957-1700

McAllister, Earl Wayne (6 mentions)
Louisiana State U, 1980
Certification: Surgery, Surgical Critical Care
13801 Bruce B Downs Blvd #506, Tampa, 813-977-2200

McRae, Freddie L. (3 mentions)
Certification: Surgery
1099 5th Ave N #210, St Petersburg, 727-820-7756

Murphy, Eugene Anthony (3 mentions)
FMS-Ireland, 1983 *Certification:* Surgery, Vascular Surgery
601 7th St S, St Petersburg, 727-894-1818

Napoliello, David Andrew (4 mentions)
Georgetown U, 1994 *Certification:* Surgery
8340 Lakewood Ranch Blvd #101, Lakewood Ranch,
    941-388-9525
825 Venetian Pkwy, Venice, 941-388-9525
1201 Jacranda Blvd, Bradenton, 941-388-9525

Nora, John Deganaweida (9 mentions)
Northwestern U, 1982 *Certification:* Surgery, Vascular Surgery
1921 Waldemere St #705, Sarasota, 941-365-1400

Novak, Russell Warren (11 mentions)
U of Florida, 1981 *Certification:* Surgery
1921 Waldemere St #705, Sarasota, 941-917-6300

Papachristou, Dimitrios N. (4 mentions)
FMS-Greece, 1965 *Certification:* Surgery
508 S Habana Ave #380, Tampa, 813-875-9739

Patel, Ravindra R. (4 mentions)
FMS-India, 1979
Certification: Surgery, Undersea & Hyperbaric Medicine
7171 N Dale Mabry Hwy #402, Tampa, 813-933-3324

Patel, Sharadchandra I. (3 mentions)
FMS-India, 1975 *Certification:* Surgery
7171 N Dale Mabry Hwy #402, Tampa, 813-933-3324

Rosemurgy, Alexander, II (4 mentions)
U of Michigan, 1979 *Certification:* Surgery
2-A Columbia Dr, Tampa, 813-974-2201

Schmidt, Rick Jeffrey (10 mentions)
Emory U, 1979 *Certification:* Surgery
1840 Mease Dr #301, Safety Harbor, 727-712-3233

Thigpen, Jack B., Jr. (5 mentions)
U of Miami, 1974 *Certification:* Surgery
1600 Lakeland Hills Blvd, Lakeland, 863-680-7486

Tyler, Gilman R., Jr. (5 mentions)
Virginia Commonwealth U, 1981 *Certification:* Surgery
602 S Audubon Ave #A, Tampa, 813-877-1415

Wendel, Nanette Kathleen (3 mentions)
Northwestern U, 1990 *Certification:* Surgery
5601 21st Ave W #D, Bradenton, 941-748-1471

Williams, Larry Ross (4 mentions)
U of Illinois, 1978 *Certification:* Surgery, Vascular Surgery
1201 7th Ave N, St Petersburg, 727-894-4738

Geriatrics

Adriano, Ruben Domingo (3 mentions)
FMS-Philippines, 1982
Certification: Geriatric Medicine, Internal Medicine
2625 S Florida Ave, Lakeland, 863-284-5112

Bonilla, R. Maurice (3 mentions)
Certification: Geriatric Medicine, Internal Medicine
3402 W Gables Ct, Tampa, 813-254-0222
905 W Platt St, Tampa, 813-254-0222

Rafool, Gordon Joseph (4 mentions)
Med Coll of Georgia, 1968
Certification: Family Medicine, Geriatric Medicine
635 1st St N, Winter Haven, 863-294-0670

Robinson, Bruce Eugene (4 mentions)
U of South Florida, 1975
Certification: Geriatric Medicine, Internal Medicine
5880 Rand Blvd #205, Sarasota, 941-917-7197

Hematology/Oncology

Al-Hassani, Yasir Adil (4 mentions)
FMS-Iraq, 1986
3000 E Fletcher Ave #210, Tampa, 813-971-5012

Alemar, Jose (4 mentions)
U of Puerto Rico, 1999
Certification: Hematology, Internal Medicine, Medical Oncology
1840 Mease Dr #309, Safety Harbor, 727-216-1141

Altemose, Rand William (4 mentions)
Med U of South Carolina, 1973
Certification: Internal Medicine, Medical Oncology
4612 N Habana Ave #200, Tampa, 813-875-2341

Auerbach, Lewis Edward (7 mentions)
New York Med Coll, 1981
Certification: Internal Medicine, Medical Oncology
604 Medical Care Dr, Brandon, 813-685-6827

Barbosa, Jerry Levy (5 mentions)
FMS-Spain, 1969
Certification: Pediatric Hematology-Oncology, Pediatrics
12220 Bruce B Downs Blvd, Tampa, 813-631-5001
880 6th St S #140, St Petersburg, 727-767-4167

Berry, Brian Thomas (4 mentions)
U of Southern California, 1991 *Certification:* Medical Oncology
2401 60th St Ct W, Bradenton, 941-792-1881

Blanco, Rafael William (5 mentions)
Tulane U, 1976
Certification: Internal Medicine, Medical Oncology
4301 N Habana Ave #1, Tampa, 813-875-2300

Brown, Richard H. (11 mentions)
U of Vermont, 1984
Certification: Hematology, Internal Medicine, Medical Oncology
1970 Golf St, Sarasota, 941-957-1000

Cassell, Robert Holland (4 mentions)
Duke U, 1979 *Certification:* Internal Medicine, Medical Oncology
3525 Lakeland Hills Blvd, Lakeland, 863-603-6565

Chu, Luis (6 mentions)
U of Florida, 1990 *Certification:* Hematology, Medical Oncology
1970 Golf St, Sarasota, 941-957-1000

Eakle, Janice Evelyn (4 mentions)
U of Louisville, 1997
Certification: Internal Medicine, Medical Oncology
600 N Cattlemen Rd #200, Sarasota, 941-377-9993

George, Christopher B. (10 mentions)
U of South Florida, 1976
Certification: Hematology, Internal Medicine, Medical Oncology
4301 N Habana Ave #5, Tampa, 813-875-2300

Hano, Andrew Edwin (7 mentions)
Des Moines U, 1977
8787 Bryan Dairy Rd #210, Largo, 727-397-9641

Knipe, Richard Alan (9 mentions)
U of Florida, 1989
Certification: Internal Medicine, Medical Oncology
1201 5th Ave N #505, St Petersburg, 727-821-0017

Lane, Frank Benjamin, Jr. (4 mentions)
Temple U, 1965 *Certification:* Hematology, Internal Medicine
2605 W Swann Ave #400, Tampa, 813-872-0702

Lautersztain, Julio (6 mentions)
FMS-Argentina, 1974 *Certification:* Anatomic Pathology &
    Clinical Pathology, Internal Medicine, Medical Oncology
4301 N Habana Ave #1, Tampa, 813-875-2300

Nadiminti, Yallappa (6 mentions)
FMS-India, 1971
Certification: Hematology, Internal Medicine, Medical Oncology
401 Manatee Ave E #B, Bradenton, 941-748-2217
6310 Health Pkwy #200, Bradenton, 941-907-4737

Patel, Hitesh C. (4 mentions)
FMS-India, 1986 *Certification:* Hematology, Medical Oncology
303 Pinellas St #330, Clearwater, 727-447-8100

Rossbach, Hans-Christoph (4 mentions)
FMS-Germany, 1986
Certification: Pediatric Hematology-Oncology
3001 W Dr Martin Luther King Jr Blvd, Tampa, 813-321-6820

Schiff, Ron David (7 mentions)
St Louis U, 1980
Certification: Hematology, Internal Medicine, Medical Oncology
13601 Bruce B Downs Blvd #310, Tampa, 813-632-7547

Schreiber, Fred James (4 mentions)
U of Pennsylvania, 1974
Certification: Internal Medicine, Medical Oncology
1730 Lakeland Hills Blvd, Lakeland, 863-680-7000
1600 Lakeland Hills Blvd, Lakeland, 863-680-7000

Tebbi, Cameron K. (6 mentions)
FMS-Iran, 1967
Certification: Pediatric Hematology-Oncology, Pediatrics
3001 W Dr Martin Luther King Jr Blvd, Tampa, 813-321-6820

Tetreault, Scott A. (9 mentions)
U of Miami, 1991 *Certification:* Medical Oncology
600 N Cattlemen Rd #200, Sarasota, 941-377-9993

Whorf, Robert Charles (6 mentions)
U of Rochester, 1998
Certification: Internal Medicine, Medical Oncology
2401 60th St Ct W, Bradenton, 941-792-1881

Wright, David Donald (5 mentions)
U of South Florida, 1996
Certification: Hematology, Internal Medicine, Medical Oncology
4612 N Habana Ave, Tampa, 813-875-2341

Ziegler, Lane Douglas (7 mentions)
A T Still U, 1985
8787 Bryan Dairy Rd #210, Largo, 727-397-9641

Infectious Disease

Busciglio, Lindell Lee (14 mentions)
U of South Florida, 1993
Certification: Infectious Disease, Internal Medicine
4729 N Habana Ave, Tampa, 813-251-8444

Cancio, Margarita (13 mentions)
U of South Florida, 1982
Certification: Infectious Disease, Internal Medicine
4729 N Habana Ave, Tampa, 813-251-8444

Dumois, Juan Antonio, Jr. (10 mentions)
U of South Florida, 1987
Certification: Pediatric Infectious Diseases
880 6th St S #240, St Petersburg, 727-767-4160

Emmanuel, Patricia J. (6 mentions)
U of Florida, 1986
Certification: Pediatric Infectious Diseases, Pediatrics
17 Davis Blvd #200, Tampa, 813-259-8800

Godofsky, Eliot Warren (14 mentions)
Georgetown U, 1987 *Certification:* Infectious Disease
6010 Pointe West Blvd, Bradenton, 941-746-2711

Gordillo, Manuel E. (6 mentions)
FMS-Peru, 1986
1425 S Osprey Ave #1, Sarasota, 941-366-9060

Holder, Clinton Douglas (9 mentions)
U of South Florida, 1981
Certification: Infectious Disease, Internal Medicine
1955 1st Ave N #101, St Petersburg, 727-898-3464

Lipman, Mark Lee (8 mentions)
Vanderbilt U, 1983
Certification: Infectious Disease, Internal Medicine
1425 S Osprey Ave #1, Sarasota, 941-366-9060

Milam, Michael Walter (9 mentions)
U of South Florida, 1984 *Certification:* Internal Medicine
1425 S Osprey Ave #1, Sarasota, 941-366-9060

Prieto, Jose R. (9 mentions)
Ponce Sch of Med, 1985
605 Medical Care Dr, Brandon, 813-681-6474

Sinnott, John Thomas, IV (6 mentions)
U of South Alabama, 1978
Certification: Infectious Disease, Internal Medicine
2 Columbia Dr, Tampa, 813-844-4174

Suksanong, Ming-Quan (6 mentions)
FMS-Thailand, 1970
Certification: Pediatric Infectious Diseases, Pediatrics
1752 Dr Martin Luther King Jr St N, St Petersburg, 727-823-7224

Infertility

Goodman, Sandra Beth (10 mentions)
Robert W Johnson Med Sch, 1987 *Certification:* Obstetrics
& Gynecology, Reproductive Endocrinology/Infertility
5245 E Fletcher Ave, Tampa, 813-914-7304
3165 N McMullen Booth Rd #F-2, Clearwater, 727-724-0702

Verkauf, Barry Stephen (7 mentions)
Tulane U, 1965 *Certification:* Obstetrics & Gynecology,
Reproductive Endocrinology/Infertility
2919 W Swann Ave #305, Tampa, 813-870-3553

Yeko, Timothy Raymond (5 mentions)
U of Wisconsin, 1982 *Certification:* Obstetrics &
Gynecology, Reproductive Endocrinology/Infertility
2919 W Swann Ave #305, Tampa, 813-870-3553
612 Medical Care Dr, Brandon, 813-661-9114
4 Columbia Dr, Tampa, 813-877-5459

Zbella, Edward Andrew (6 mentions)
U of Illinois, 1980 *Certification:* Obstetrics & Gynecology,
Reproductive Endocrinology/Infertility
2454 N McMullen Booth Rd #601, Clearwater, 727-796-7705
7171 N Dale Mabry Hwy #405, Tampa, 813-933-9166
3268 66th St N, St Petersburg, 727-341-1991

Internal Medicine *(see note on page 9)*

Cohen, Louis Mark (3 mentions)
SUNY-Upstate Med U, 1982 *Certification:* Internal Medicine
1921 Waldemere St #814, Sarasota, 951-953-9080

Cohen, Richard David (3 mentions)
Emory U, 1968 *Certification:* Internal Medicine
4900 N Habana Ave, Tampa, 813-876-6311

Corral, Kent Richardson (4 mentions)
U of South Florida, 1978 *Certification:* Internal Medicine
4700 N Habana Ave #103, Tampa, 813-348-0224

Creevy, Joseph James (3 mentions)
Georgetown U, 1997 *Certification:* Internal Medicine
3333 Cattlemen Rd, Sarasota, 941-371-3337

Di Pietro, Jon George (4 mentions)
Indiana U, 1978 *Certification:* Internal Medicine
2727 W Martin Luther King Jr Blvd #450, Tampa, 813-875-8453

Kahan, Bruce Allan (4 mentions)
Virginia Commonwealth U, 1981 *Certification:* Internal Medicine
3665 Madaca Ln, Tampa, 813-960-7533

Kirkman, Lee Clarke (4 mentions)
U of Alabama, 1974 *Certification:* Critical Care Medicine,
Internal Medicine, Pulmonary Disease
4902 Eisenhower Blvd #300, Tampa, 813-636-2000
4730 N Habana Ave #305, Tampa, 813-872-7737

Mishner, Harvey Stuart (3 mentions)
U of Maryland, 1978 *Certification:* Internal Medicine
8340 Lakewood Ranch Blvd #350, Lakewood Ranch,
941-907-0588

O'Brien, Kevin Edward (4 mentions)
U of Miami, 1993 *Certification:* Internal Medicine
12901 Bruce B Downs Blvd #MDC-80, Tampa, 813-974-2271

Tullis, Charles Stuart (3 mentions)
U of Florida, 1969 *Certification:* Internal Medicine
1600 Lakeland Hills Blvd, Lakeland, 863-680-7000

Wilkinson, Thomas Craig (4 mentions)
U of South Florida, 1982 *Certification:* Internal Medicine
408 Manatee Ave E, Bradenton, 941-748-1331

Zamore, Gary Alan (5 mentions)
Emory U, 1972 *Certification:* Internal Medicine
2919 W Swann Ave #203, Tampa, 813-870-1747

Nephrology

Alveranga, Denise Yvonne (5 mentions)
Robert W Johnson Med Sch, 1977
Certification: Internal Medicine, Nephrology
3450 E Fletcher Ave #310, Tampa, 813-972-1654

Braxtan, Thomas Newby (6 mentions)
U of Minnesota, 1972
Certification: Internal Medicine, Nephrology
508 Manatee Ave E, Bradenton, 941-744-0024

Campos, Alfonso (6 mentions)
FMS-Peru, 1974 *Certification:* Pediatric Nephrology, Pediatrics
13101 Bruce B Downs Blvd, Tampa, 813-259-8760
800 6th St S, St Petersburg, 727-767-4180

Cover, Domenick Enzo (6 mentions)
Tulane U, 1981 *Certification:* Internal Medicine, Nephrology
1921 Waldemere St #413, Sarasota, 941-917-6585

Palomino, Celestino (7 mentions)
FMS-Dominican Republic, 1980 *Certification:* Internal Medicine
3701 Manatee Ave W, Bradenton, 941-746-5840

Perlman, Sharon Adrienne (8 mentions)
Albert Einstein Coll of Med, 1977
Certification: Pediatric Nephrology, Pediatrics
801 6th St S, St Petersburg, 727-892-4181

Sotolongo, Ignacio A. (8 mentions)
FMS-Dominican Republic, 1985 *Certification:* Nephrology
601 7th St S, St Petersburg, 727-824-8274

Weinstein, Samuel Steven (10 mentions)
New Jersey Med Sch, 1972
Certification: Internal Medicine, Nephrology
409 Bayshore Blvd, Tampa, 813-251-8017

Neurological Surgery

Balis, Gene Alan (11 mentions)
Hahnemann U, 1967 *Certification:* Neurological Surgery
3000 E Fletcher Ave #340, Tampa, 813-977-3776

Boyer, Kevin Louis (8 mentions)
Creighton U, 1988 *Certification:* Neurological Surgery
7005 Cortez Rd W 1st Fl, Bradenton, 941-750-0602

Clarke, Henry Bushnell (12 mentions)
U of Michigan, 1985 *Certification:* Neurological Surgery
603 7th St S #540, St Petersburg, 727-553-7550

Colbassani, Harold James (7 mentions)
Georgetown U, 1982 *Certification:* Neurological Surgery
646 Virginia St #600, Dunedin, 727-733-4151

Cutler, Scott Gregory (6 mentions)
FMS-Mexico, 1975 *Certification:* Neurological Surgery
4726 N Habana Ave #201, Tampa, 813-874-9922

Fine, Andrew David (9 mentions)
U of Florida, 1994 *Certification:* Neurological Surgery
5831 Bee Ridge Rd #100, Sarasota, 941-308-5700

Glasser, Ryan Scott (9 mentions)
U of Oklahoma, 1989 *Certification:* Neurological Surgery
5831 Bee Ridge Rd #100, Sarasota, 941-308-5700

Louis, Kenneth Maliq (6 mentions)
Wayne State U, 1977 *Certification:* Neurological Surgery
3000 E Fletcher Ave #340, Tampa, 813-977-3776

Mayer, Peter Lee (11 mentions)
Dartmouth Coll, 1987 *Certification:* Neurological Surgery
5831 Bee Ridge Rd #100, Sarasota, 941-308-5700

Rydell, Ralph Edward (8 mentions)
U of Minnesota, 1965 *Certification:* Neurological Surgery
5106 N Armenia Ave #1, Tampa, 813-879-8080

Vale, Fernando L. (6 mentions)
U of Puerto Rico, 1991 *Certification:* Neurological Surgery
2-A Columbia Dr #300, Tampa, 813-259-0929

Van Loveren, Harry Ronald (9 mentions)
U of Cincinnati, 1979 *Certification:* Neurological Surgery
2-A Columbia Dr 7th Fl, Tampa, 813-974-7618

Neurology

Bass, Edward (5 mentions)
FMS-Canada, 1972 *Certification:* Neurology
4710 N Habana Ave #200, Tampa, 813-878-2800

Cohen, Steven Roger (8 mentions)
Johns Hopkins U, 1982 *Certification:* Neurology with
Special Qualifications in Child Neurology
601 7th St S, St Petersburg, 727-824-7132

Cuervo, Herminio (4 mentions)
FMS-Spain, 1972
3842 S Florida Ave, Lakeland, 863-647-1684

De Sousa, Garcia Jose (4 mentions)
FMS-India, 1974 *Certification:* Neurology
3334 66th St N, St Petersburg, 727-341-1333

Franklin, Michael Arnold (4 mentions)
SUNY-Downstate Med Coll, 1987 *Certification:* Neurology
1099 5th Ave N, St Petersburg, 727-820-7701

Gonzalez, Ralph F. (6 mentions)
U of Miami, 1995 *Certification:* Neurology, Vascular Neurology
3930 8th Ave W, Bradenton, 941-746-3115

Grant, Edmund Guy, Jr. (13 mentions)
U of Florida, 1979 *Certification:* Neurology
13801 Bruce B Downs Blvd #401, Tampa, 813-971-8811

Hanes, Gregory Paul (4 mentions)
Drexel U, 1999 *Certification:* Clinical Neurophysiology, Neurology
1921 Waldemere St #701, Sarasota, 941-487-2160

Khademi, Ardeshir (4 mentions)
Certification: Neurology, Vascular Neurology
1840 Mease Dr #407B, Safety Harbor, 727-712-1567

Loh, Frank Li (5 mentions)
Albany Med Coll, 1986 *Certification:* Neurology
5857B 21st Ave W, Bradenton, 941-761-7699

Negroski, Donald (5 mentions)
U of Toledo, 1981 *Certification:* Neurology
1921 Waldemere St #701, Sarasota, 941-917-6222
1211 Jacaranda Blvd, Venice, 941-917-6222

Pedregal, Arthur John (4 mentions)
U of Miami, 1994 *Certification:* Neurology
4710 N Habana Ave #303, Tampa, 813-879-7940

Sergay, Stephen Michael (10 mentions)
FMS-South Africa, 1970 *Certification:* Neurology
2919 W Swann Ave #401, Tampa, 813-872-1548

Steen, Susan Jane (5 mentions)
U of Florida, 1978 *Certification:* Neurology
2919 W Swann Ave #401, Tampa, 813-872-1578

Stein, Daniel P. (4 mentions)
Certification: Neurology
1921 Waldemere St #701, Sarasota, 941-487-2160
1211 Jacaranda Blvd, Venice, 941-487-2160

Traviesa, Daniel Carlos (5 mentions)
U of Miami, 1971
Certification: Clinical Neurophysiology, Neurology
1600 Lakeland Hills Blvd, Lakeland, 863-680-7000

Wierichs, Frank Joseph, Jr. (4 mentions)
Emory U, 1971 *Certification:* Neurology
420 Tamiami Trail S #302, Venice, 941-484-3234

Winters, Paul Regan (8 mentions)
U of Florida, 1972 *Certification:* Neurology
13801 Bruce B Downs Blvd #401, Tampa, 813-971-8811

Obstetrics/Gynecology

Biss, Kimberly O. (3 mentions)
Tufts U, 1993 *Certification:* Obstetrics & Gynecology
625 6th Ave S #350, St Petersburg, 727-456-0080

Butler, Madelyn Espinosa (3 mentions)
U of Florida, 1990 *Certification:* Obstetrics & Gynecology
15260 Amberly Dr, Tampa, 813-875-8032
2716 W Virginia Ave, Tampa, 813-875-8032

Carlson, Jeffrey (3 mentions)
U of South Florida, 1980 *Certification:* Obstetrics & Gynecology
6450 38th Ave N #200, St Petersburg, 727-344-6060

Easterling, Gary Wade (3 mentions)
Wayne State U, 1987 *Certification:* Obstetrics & Gynecology
5741 Bee Ridge Rd #390, Sarasota, 941-379-6331

Fallieras, Nicholas George (3 mentions)
U of Tennessee, 1972 *Certification:* Obstetrics & Gynecology
2818 W Virginia Ave, Tampa, 813-872-8551
727 W Fletcher Ave, Tampa, 813-908-2229

Finazzo, Michael S. (3 mentions)
U of Miami, 1984 *Certification:* Obstetrics & Gynecology
1921 Waldemere St #307, Sarasota, 941-917-8565
929 S Tamiami Trail, Osprey, 941-917-8565
5350 University Pkwy #101, Sarasota, 941-917-8565

Gilby, Jennifer Russell (3 mentions)
U of Florida, 1996 *Certification:* Obstetrics & Gynecology
1600 Martin Luther King Jr St N, St Petersburg, 727-456-0750

Greenberg, Steven L. (3 mentions)
U of Texas-Dallas, 1986 *Certification:* Obstetrics & Gynecology
3268 Cove Bend Dr, Tampa, 813-971-4555
3743 Mary Weather Ln, Wesley Chapel, 813-973-0398

Igel, Stephen (3 mentions)
FMS-Spain, 1977
600 Lakeview Rd #D, Clearwater, 727-461-7611

Liebert, Karen M. F. (3 mentions)
Georgetown U, 1981 *Certification:* Obstetrics & Gynecology
1850 59th St W #B, Bradenton, 941-792-4993

Mammel, James Bryant (3 mentions)
U of Michigan, 1981 *Certification:* Obstetrics & Gynecology
1600 Lakeland Hills Blvd, Lakeland, 863-680-7000

Matta, Jose R. (4 mentions)
FMS-Mexico, 1976
513 Manatee Ave E, Bradenton, 941-745-1616

Sullivan, John E., Jr. (3 mentions)
U of South Florida, 1982 *Certification:* Obstetrics & Gynecology
2439 Bee Ridge Rd, Sarasota, 941-955-8076

Swor, Gregory Michael (6 mentions)
U of South Florida, 1981 *Certification:* Obstetrics & Gynecology
1617 S Tuttle Ave #1-A, Sarasota, 941-330-8885

Towsley, Greg Andrew (3 mentions)
U of South Florida, 1992 *Certification:* Obstetrics & Gynecology
1921 Waldemere St #802, Sarasota, 941-917-7888

Van Zandt, Stephanie (3 mentions)
U of South Florida, 1986 *Certification:* Obstetrics & Gynecology
401 Corbett St #400, Clearwater, 727-462-2229

Wahba, Irene N. (4 mentions)
Certification: Obstetrics & Gynecology
15260 Amberly Dr, Tampa, 813-769-2778

Yenari, Jon (3 mentions)
Tulane U, 1995 *Certification:* Obstetrics & Gynecology
3333 Cattlemen Rd #200, Sarasota, 941-379-1700

Ophthalmology

Drucker, Mitchell David (4 mentions)
U of Florida, 1981 *Certification:* Ophthalmology
12901 Bruce B Downs Blvd, Tampa, 813-974-3820

Grizzard, William Sanderson (3 mentions)
U of Miami, 1972 *Certification:* Ophthalmology
602 S Macdill Ave, Tampa, 727-443-4225

Gross, Steven A. (3 mentions)
U of Illinois, 1981 *Certification:* Neurology with Special
Qualifications in Child Neurology, Ophthalmology
32615 US Hwy 19 N #6, Palm Harbor, 727-772-7712

Hess, Jeffrey Bruce (7 mentions)
Baylor U, 1971 *Certification:* Ophthalmology
880 6th St S #350, St Petersburg, 727-767-4393

Kolodner, Harry (3 mentions)
Boston U, 1971 *Certification:* Ophthalmology
33920 US Hwy 19 N #275, Palm Harbor, 727-784-1121

Lorenzen, Timothy Robert (3 mentions)
U of Florida, 1986 *Certification:* Ophthalmology
3000 W Martin Luther King Jr Blvd, Tampa, 813-877-2020

Mendelblatt, Frank Irving (7 mentions)
U of Miami, 1960 *Certification:* Ophthalmology
600 6th St S, St Petersburg, 727-822-6763

Pavan, Peter Reed (5 mentions)
Harvard U, 1972 *Certification:* Internal Medicine, Ophthalmology
12901 Bruce B Downs Blvd, Tampa, 813-974-1530
13127 USF Magnolia Dr, Tampa, 813-974-3820

Pope, Daniel Ball, Jr. (4 mentions)
U of Kentucky, 1978 *Certification:* Ophthalmology
426 Manatee Ave W, Bradenton, 941-708-9000

Rothberg, David Stanley (3 mentions)
U of Texas-San Antonio, 1978 *Certification:* Ophthalmology
3820 Tampa Rd #101, Palm Harbor, 727-785-6422

Schwartz, Thomas L. (3 mentions)
U of Texas-Galveston, 1985 *Certification:* Ophthalmology
1219 S East Ave #105, Sarasota, 941-957-4216

Sever, Raymond Joseph (4 mentions)
U of Miami, 1960 *Certification:* Ophthalmology
13602 N 46th St, Tampa, 813-972-4444

Slonim, Charles Bard (3 mentions)
New York Med Coll, 1978 *Certification:* Ophthalmology
4444 E Fletcher Ave #D, Tampa, 813-971-3846

Williams-Wallace, Nancy Elizabeth (4 mentions)
Howard U, 1986 *Certification:* Ophthalmology
3115 W Swann Ave, Tampa, 813-879-7711
10817 Blooming Dale Ave, Riverview, 813-879-7711
407 W Blooming Dale Ave, Brandon, 813-879-7711

Orthopedics

Abdo, Richard Victor (3 mentions)
SUNY-Upstate Med U, 1982 *Certification:* Orthopaedic Surgery
1011 Jeffords St Bldg C, Clearwater, 727-446-5993

Alexander, Vlad Al (5 mentions)
Ohio State U, 1995 *Certification:* Orthopaedic Surgery
12416 66th St N, Largo, 727-547-4700

Askins, Roland Vance, III (5 mentions)
U of Florida, 1991 *Certification:* Orthopaedic Surgery
4937 Clark Rd, Sarasota, 941-342-6404

Bernasek, Thomas Lane (5 mentions)
Creighton U, 1981 *Certification:* Orthopaedic Surgery
13020 N Telecom Pkwy, Tampa, 813-978-9700

Bolhofner, Brett (3 mentions)
U of South Florida, 1980 *Certification:* Orthopaedic Surgery
4600 4th St N, St Petersburg, 727-527-5272

Burke, Brian Daniel (3 mentions)
West Virginia U, 1996 *Certification:* Orthopaedic Surgery
601 7th St S, St Petersburg, 727-894-1818

Castellvi, Antonio E. (3 mentions)
FMS-Spain, 1976 *Certification:* Orthopaedic Surgery
13020 N Telecom Pkwy, Tampa, 813-978-9700
2727 W Martin Luther King Blvd #630, Tampa, 813-978-9700

Craythorne, Charles Barry (3 mentions)
U of Miami, 1988 *Certification:* Orthopaedic Surgery
613 S Magnolia Ave #1, Tampa, 813-254-9586

Eaton, Katulle Koco (13 mentions)
Johns Hopkins U, 1987 *Certification:* Orthopaedic Surgery
900 Carillon Pkwy #311, St Petersburg, 727-573-5626

Horan, Patrick James (3 mentions)
Tufts U, 1991 *Certification:* Orthopaedic Surgery
11603 Sheldon Rd, Tampa, 813-792-9843

Hughes, W. Allen, II (3 mentions)
Northwestern U, 1982 *Certification:* Orthopaedic Surgery
1011 Jeffords St Bldg C, Clearwater, 727-446-5993

Lamar, Daniel Scott, Jr. (3 mentions)
U of South Florida, 1998 *Certification:* Orthopaedic Surgery
6015 Pointe West Blvd, Bradenton, 941-792-1404

Love, Sheila Marie (5 mentions)
Northwestern U, 1981 *Certification:* Orthopaedic Surgery
2727 Dr Martin Luther King Jr Blvd #720, Tampa, 813-879-2663
625 6th Ave S #450, St Petersburg, 727-898-2663

Mehserle, William Lee (3 mentions)
Emory U, 1986 *Certification:* Orthopaedic Surgery
1525 Tamiami Trail S #602, Venice, 941-497-2663

Messieh, Samuel S. (3 mentions)
FMS-Canada, 1983 *Certification:* Orthopaedic Surgery
2231 North Blvd W #A, Davenport, 863-419-9301

Oliver, Brian Charles (3 mentions)
U of Florida, 1985 *Certification:* Orthopaedic Surgery
3251 N McMullen Booth Rd #201, Clearwater, 727-725-6231

Padgett, Larry R., Jr. (3 mentions)
U of North Carolina, 1992 *Certification:* Orthopaedic Surgery
250 3rd St NW #201, Winter Haven, 863-318-9696

Patel, Ashvin Ishvar (3 mentions)
Tufts U, 1988 *Certification:* Orthopaedic Surgery
5741 Bee Ridge Rd #370, Sarasota, 941-365-0655

Sanders, Roy W. (4 mentions)
New York U, 1980 *Certification:* Orthopaedic Surgery
13020 N Telecom Pkwy, Tampa, 813-978-9700

Schulak, David Jay (3 mentions)
Yale U, 1969 *Certification:* Orthopaedic Surgery
21756 State Rd 54 #102, Lutz, 813-977-4767
13701 Bruce B Downs Blvd #115, Tampa, 813-977-4767

Sforzo, Christopher R. (3 mentions)
Loyola U Chicago, 1998 *Certification:* Orthopaedic Surgery
5831 Bee Ridge Rd #200, Sarasota, 941-378-5100
8340 Lakewood Ranch Blvd #320, Lakewood Ranch,
   941-378-5100

Sugar, David Allen (3 mentions)
U of South Florida, 1992 *Certification:* Orthopaedic Surgery
2750 Bahia Vista St #100, Sarasota, 941-951-2663

Valadie, Alan Lee (4 mentions)
U of Florida, 1991 *Certification:* Orthopaedic Surgery
6015 Pointe West Blvd, Bradenton, 941-792-1404

Valadie, Arthur Leon, III (8 mentions)
U of Florida, 1991 *Certification:* Orthopaedic Surgery
6015 Pointe West Blvd, Bradenton, 941-792-1404

Vo, Phuc (3 mentions)
U of Florida, 1986
Certification: Orthopaedic Sports Medicine, Orthopaedic Surgery
1600 Lakeland Hills Blvd, Lakeland, 863-680-7000

Wasylik, Michael Andrew (3 mentions)
Ohio State U, 1968 *Certification:* Orthopaedic Surgery
2919 W Swann Ave #201, Tampa, 813-877-9413

Otorhinolaryngology

Agnello, Peter Fry (5 mentions)
Boston U, 1996 *Certification:* Otolaryngology
3450 E Fletcher Ave #350, Tampa, 813-972-3353

Anthony, Steven L. (6 mentions)
Kansas U Coll of Osteopathic Med, 1988
8787 Bryan Dairy Rd #340, Largo, 727-397-8551
1330 S Fort Harrison Ave, Clearwater, 727-441-3588

Bartels, Loren Jay (4 mentions)
U of South Florida, 1974 *Certification:* Otolaryngology
4 Columbia Dr #610, Tampa, 813-844-4900
4566 Keysville Ave, Spring Hill, 813-844-4900

Blake, George Banister (5 mentions)
U of South Florida, 1988 *Certification:* Otolaryngology
605 S Fremont Ave, Tampa, 813-251-0209

Cressman, Wade Russell (5 mentions)
St Louis U, 1987 *Certification:* Otolaryngology
801 6th St S, St Petersburg, 727-329-5400

Deems, Daniel Anthony (12 mentions)
U of Pennsylvania, 1992 *Certification:* Otolaryngology
8451 Shade Ave #107, Sarasota, 941-355-2767

Espinola, Trina Elena (6 mentions)
Tulane U, 1987 *Certification:* Otolaryngology
625 6th Ave S #385, St Petersburg, 727-553-7100

Goodman, Arnold Lawrence (7 mentions)
U of Miami, 1983 *Certification:* Otolaryngology
3450 E Fletcher Ave #350, Tampa, 813-972-3353

Morrow, John Stephen (5 mentions)
Tulane U, 1989 *Certification:* Otolaryngology
1099 5th Ave N #200, St Petersburg, 727-820-7708

Orobello, Peter W., Jr. (6 mentions)
U of Cincinnati, 1983 *Certification:* Otolaryngology
10080 Balaye Run Dr, Tampa, 727-329-5400

Requena, Ricardo (4 mentions)
Nova Southeastern Coll of Osteopathic Med, 1989
Certification: Otolaryngology
1551 W Bay Dr, Largo, 727-581-8767
3131 N McMullen Booth Rd, Clearwater, 727-581-8767

Seper, Janet Lynn (5 mentions)
Rush U, 1991 *Certification:* Otolaryngology
3450 E Fletcher Ave #350, Tampa, 813-972-3353

Shea, Roger Marks (5 mentions)
Med U of South Carolina, 1990 *Certification:* Otolaryngology
5432 Bee Ridge Rd #140, Sarasota, 941-371-2244

Vincent, Daniel Ashley, Jr. (4 mentions)
U of South Florida, 1990 *Certification:* Otolaryngology
4714 N Armenia Ave #200, Tampa, 813-258-0404
4655 Keysville Ave, Spring Hill, 352-688-0800

Pain Medicine

Brown, Lora Lee (5 mentions)
U of Texas-Galveston, 1997
Certification: Anesthesiology, Pain Medicine
5101 4th Ave Cir E #500, Bradenton, 941-792-2251
6015 Pointe Blvd W, Bradenton, 941-792-1404

Bundschu, Richard Haas (4 mentions)
U of Miami, 1991 *Certification:* Anesthesiology, Pain Medicine
6015 Pointe West Blvd, Bradenton, 941-792-2251

Chowdhari, Shaukat H. (3 mentions)
FMS-Pakistan, 1982 *Certification:* Anesthesiology
14501 Bruce B Downs Blvd, Tampa, 813-977-2222

Columbus, Lynne Carr (4 mentions)
Philadelphia Coll of Osteopathic Med, 1990
Certification: Anesthesiology
3890 Tampa Rd #308, Palm Harbor, 727-789-0891

Dennison, Stanley Robert (4 mentions)
FMS-Dominican Republic, 1987
1921 W Dr Martin Luther King Jr Blvd, Tampa, 813-876-7600

Derasari, Manjul D. (5 mentions)
FMS-India, 1974 *Certification:* Anesthesiology, Pain Medicine
1912 E Busch Blvd, Tampa, 813-933-5900

Erb, Donald Louis (4 mentions)
Philadelphia Coll of Osteopathic Med, 1988
Certification: Anesthesiology, Pain Medicine
5880 Rand Blvd #206, Sarasota, 941-917-4500

Friedman, Charles Kim (4 mentions)
Nova Southeastern Coll of Osteopathic Med, 1986
Certification: Anesthesiology, Pain Medicine
6640 78th Ave #A, Pinellas Park, 727-518-8660

Giraldo, Kenneth A. (3 mentions)
FMS-Colombia, 1984
Certification: Anesthesiology, Pain Medicine
5831 Bee Ridge Rd #100, Sarasota, 941-954-4373
1211 Jacaronda Blvd, Venice, 941-343-1040

Kaiafas, Demetrios N. (4 mentions)
Indiana U, 1993 *Certification:* Anesthesiology
430 Morton Plant St #210, Clearwater, 727-446-4506

Lubin, Edward (4 mentions)
Albert Einstein Coll of Med, 1993
Certification: Anesthesiology, Pain Medicine
601 1st St N, Winter Haven, 863-294-0670

Miguel, Rafael Victor (3 mentions)
FMS-Spain, 1981 *Certification:* Anesthesiology, Pain Medicine
12902 Magnolia Dr #2149, Tampa, 813-972-8486
12901 Bruce B Downs Blvd, Tampa, 813-974-2201

Ramos, Fabian Alonso (4 mentions)
FMS-Ecuador, 1988 *Certification:* Anesthesiology
601 Manatee Ave W, Bradenton, 941-708-9555

Trimble, Gerald Edward (3 mentions)
U of South Florida, 1986
Certification: Anesthesiology, Pain Medicine
603 7th St S #340, St Petersburg, 727-553-7313
1831 N Belcher Rd #AZ, Clearwater, 727-553-7313

Pathology

Browarsky, Irwin (5 mentions)
Rosalind Franklin U, 1968 *Certification:* Anatomic
   Pathology & Clinical Pathology, Cytopathology, Hematology
2 Columbia Dr, Tampa, 813-844-7431
5751 Hoover Blvd, Tampa, 813-886-8334

Davis, Kern M. (3 mentions)
U of South Florida, 1980 *Certification:* Anatomic Pathology
   & Clinical Pathology, Cytopathology
1200 7th Ave N, St Petersburg, 727-825-1014
4563 Central Ave #A, St Petersburg, 727-328-7800

Davis, Larry Joe (3 mentions)
U of Tennessee, 1966 *Certification:* Anatomic Pathology &
   Clinical Pathology, Cytopathology, Hematology
701 6th St S, St Petersburg, 727-893-6182

Duque, Ricardo Ernesto (3 mentions)
FMS-Colombia, 1973 *Certification:* Anatomic Pathology
1125 Bartow Rd #101-A, Lakeland, 863-683-7171

Reed, Thomas Joseph (4 mentions)
U of Virginia, 1980 *Certification:* Anatomic Pathology &
   Clinical Pathology, Hematology
2001 Webber St, Sarasota, 941-362-8900

Stonesifer, Kurt John (4 mentions)
U of Texas-Galveston, 1981 *Certification:* Anatomic Pathology & Clinical Pathology, Cytopathology
3100 E Fletcher Ave, Tampa, 813-615-7278
5751 Hoover Blvd, Tampa, 813-886-8334

Pediatrics *(see note on page 9)*

Adler, Philip (4 mentions)
U of Vermont, 1953 *Certification:* Pediatrics
10909 W Linebaugh Ave #100, Tampa, 813-792-8878

Borkowf, Shirley Phyllis (3 mentions)
FMS-South Africa, 1953 *Certification:* Pediatrics
6550 Gunn Hwy, Tampa, 813-968-2710

Brown, W. Michael (5 mentions)
U of South Florida, 1990 *Certification:* Pediatrics
700 6th St S, St Petersburg, 727-893-6116

Cibran, Mariano Diego S. (3 mentions)
FMS-Spain, 1973
4278 28th St N, St Petersburg, 727-822-1896
4105 49th St N, St Petersburg, 727-528-6900

Featherman, Donald Scott (6 mentions)
U of Florida, 1984 *Certification:* Pediatrics
2020 Cattlemen Rd #600, Sarasota, 941-955-5191

Giangreco, Catherine M. (3 mentions)
Certification: Pediatrics
4861 27th St W, Bradenton, 941-755-0800

Lipschutz, Fred Ian (4 mentions)
U of Pennsylvania, 1976 *Certification:* Pediatrics
4446 E Fletcher Ave #A, Tampa, 813-971-6700
5259 Village Market, Wesley Chapel, 813-973-0333

Nelson, Robert M. (3 mentions)
Certification: Neonatal-Perinatal Medicine, Pediatrics
17 Davis Blvd #200, Tampa, 813-259-8867

Patranella, Pamela M. (3 mentions)
Texas Tech U, 1984 *Certification:* Pediatrics
2855 5th Ave N, St Petersburg, 727-323-2727

Reilly, Elizabeth M. (3 mentions)
FMS-Ireland, 1992 *Certification:* Pediatrics
2137 16th St N, St Petersburg, 727-822-1896

Reiner, Christopher David (4 mentions)
U of South Florida, 1975 *Certification:* Pediatrics
2803 W St Isabel St, Tampa, 813-875-3896
2803 W Saint Isabel St, Tampa, 813-875-3896

Wassenaar, John William (3 mentions)
U of Florida, 1985 *Certification:* Internal Medicine
929 S Tamiami Trail #101, Osprey, 941-917-4700

Yee, Patrick Christopher (3 mentions)
U of South Florida, 1994 *Certification:* Pediatrics
3638 Madaca Ln, Tampa, 813-968-6610

Plastic Surgery

Berger, Lewis Herman (6 mentions)
New York Med Coll, 1968 *Certification:* Plastic Surgery, Surgery
2901St Isabel St #2-C, Tampa, 813-877-7658
2901 St Isabel St #A-3, Tampa, 813-877-7658

Fernandez, Enrique J. (4 mentions)
U of Florida, 1979 *Certification:* Plastic Surgery
2902 59th St W #A, Bradenton, 941-795-2088

Gallant, Michael Charles (6 mentions)
Yale U, 1971 *Certification:* Plastic Surgery
880 6th St S #450, St Petersburg, 727-767-4920

Graham, Braun Howard (4 mentions)
Indiana U, 1977 *Certification:* Plastic Surgery
2255 S Tamiami Trail, Sarasota, 941-366-8897

Halpern, David Eric (6 mentions)
New York U, 1987
Certification: Plastic Surgery, Surgery, Surgery of the Hand
120 S Fremont Ave, Tampa, 813-871-5000

O'Brien, John James, Jr. (4 mentions)
U of Buffalo, 1987 *Certification:* Plastic Surgery
7855 38th Ave N, St Petersburg, 727-341-2408

Radocha, Richard Francis (4 mentions)
Hahnemann U, 1979 *Certification:* Plastic Surgery
635 1st St N, Winter Haven, 863-294-0670

Redmon, Henry Arvil (6 mentions)
U of South Florida, 1978 *Certification:* Plastic Surgery
707 W Fletcher Ave, Tampa, 813-264-2676

Renard, Andre (5 mentions)
FMS-Belgium, 1966 *Certification:* Plastic Surgery
2401 University Pkwy #204, Sarasota, 941-351-6131

Ruas, Ernesto Jose (8 mentions)
Johns Hopkins U, 1980 *Certification:* Plastic Surgery
603 S Boulevard, Tampa, 813-259-1550

Smith, David John, Jr. (4 mentions)
Indiana U, 1973 *Certification:* Plastic Surgery
2 Tampa general Cir, Tampa, 813-259-0929
12902 magnolia Dr, Tampa, 813-979-3980

Psychiatry

Borge, Carlos A. (3 mentions)
FMS-Mexico, 1977
80 S Tuttle Ave #110, Sarasota, 941-330-9080

Cavitt, Mark Allen (3 mentions)
East Tennessee State U, 1989
Certification: Child & Adolescent Psychiatry, Psychiatry
801 6th St S, St Petersburg, 727-767-8477

Devine, Charles Durwood (3 mentions)
U of South Florida, 1995 *Certification:* Psychiatry
336 E Bloomingdale Ave, Brandon, 813-689-2466

Fabisiak, Danuta B. (3 mentions)
2110 58th St W, Bradenton, 941-795-7222

Fernandez, Francisco (3 mentions)
Tufts U, 1979
3515 E Fletcher Ave, Tampa, 813-974-8900

Milian, Nestor Eduardo (4 mentions)
U of Miami, 1982 *Certification:* Psychiatry
3102 W Waters Ave #103, Tampa, 813-636-2000

Panting, David (3 mentions)
FMS-Honduras, 1985 *Certification:* Psychiatry
3645 Cortez Rd W #110, Bradenton, 941-739-0323

Saa, Alfonso H. (4 mentions)
FMS-Colombia, 1973
Certification: Geriatric Psychiatry, Psychiatry
508 S Habana Ave #255, Tampa, 813-875-8550

Walker, Charles Gordon (3 mentions)
U of Florida, 1965
720 W Martin Luther King Blvd, Tampa, 813-223-5434
720 W Dr Martin Luther King Jr Blvd, Tampa, 813-223-5434

Pulmonary Disease

Abel, Warren Russell (5 mentions)
U of South Florida, 1985 *Certification:* Critical Care Medicine, Internal Medicine, Pulmonary Disease
1201 5th Ave N #206, St Petersburg, 727-822-6661

Bonilla, Claudina A. (4 mentions)
FMS-Dominican Republic, 1983 *Certification:* Critical Care Medicine, Internal Medicine, Pulmonary Disease
1840 Mease Dr #405, Safety Harbor, 727-724-9395

Ebel, Theron Arthur (7 mentions)
Indiana U, 1970 *Certification:* Critical Care Medicine, Internal Medicine, Pulmonary Disease
3000 E Fletcher Ave #270, Tampa, 813-977-7794

Fort, Peter Lawrence (4 mentions)
George Washington U, 1991 *Certification:* Internal Medicine, Pulmonary Disease, Sleep Medicine
5955 17th Ave W, Bradenton, 941-794-3900
2415 University Pkwy #217, Sarasota, 941-358-2288

Horiuchi, Todd Ken (9 mentions)
Washington U, 1995
Certification: Critical Care Medicine, Pulmonary Disease
1895 Floyd St, Sarasota, 941-366-5864

Katz, Adam S. (5 mentions)
SUNY-Upstate Med U, 1991
4129 N Armenia Ave, Tampa, 813-879-3699

Kreitzer, Stephen M. (8 mentions)
Albert Einstein Coll of Med, 1971
Certification: Internal Medicine, Pulmonary Disease
2919 W Swann Ave #105, Tampa, 813-877-5337

Kriseman, Anthony David (6 mentions)
FMS-South Africa, 1975
Certification: Pediatric Pulmonology, Pediatrics
12220 Bruce B Downs Blvd, Tampa, 727-767-4146
880 6th St S #390, St Petersburg, 727-767-4146

Law, David Edward (4 mentions)
U of Alabama, 1976 *Certification:* Internal Medicine, Pulmonary Disease, Sleep Medicine
2210 61st St W, Bradenton, 941-792-0611

Mylett, Janine McGlone (6 mentions)
U of Cincinnati, 1988 *Certification:* Critical Care Medicine, Internal Medicine, Pulmonary Disease
2210 61st St W, Bradenton, 941-792-0611

Peters, John T. (5 mentions)
Des Moines U, 1992 *Certification:* Pulmonary Disease
520 8th St W, Bradenton, 941-744-1336

Reina, Domenick Joseph (4 mentions)
U of Florida, 1986
Certification: Critical Care Medicine, Pulmonary Disease
4620 N Habana Ave #101, Tampa, 813-875-9362

Smith, Mark Anthony (5 mentions)
U of Illinois, 1978
Certification: Internal Medicine, Pulmonary Disease
4620 N Habana Ave #101, Tampa, 813-875-9362

Solomon, David Allan (10 mentions)
U of Maryland, 1969
Certification: Internal Medicine, Pulmonary Disease
2 Columbia Dr, Tampa, 813-844-7233
12901 N Bruce B Downs Blvd, Tampa, 813-974-2553
217 S Cedar, Tampa, 813-254-1578

Stein, Robert J. (5 mentions)
U of Miami, 1983
Certification: Internal Medicine, Pulmonary Disease
1840 Mease Dr #400, Safety Harbor, 727-725-6128

Swisher, John W. (5 mentions)
Jefferson Med Coll, 1989
Certification: Internal Medicine, Pulmonary Disease
3920 Bee Ridge Rd Bldg C #C, Sarasota, 941-923-8353

Thacker, Robert Eugene (9 mentions)
U of Illinois, 1976 *Certification:* Critical Care Medicine, Internal Medicine, Pulmonary Disease
601 7th St S, St Petersburg, 727-894-1818

Radiology—Diagnostic

Arrington, John A. (6 mentions)
U of South Florida, 1983
Certification: Diagnostic Radiology, Neuroradiology
3301 Usf Alumni Dr, Tampa, 813-972-3351

Berlet, Matthew Howard (4 mentions)
New Jersey Med Sch, 1986
Certification: Diagnostic Radiology, Neuroradiology
3001 W Martin Luther King Blvd, Tampa, 813-870-4600
4516 N Armenia Ave, Tampa, 813-870-4919

Bonsack, Timothy Alan (3 mentions)
Emory U, 1983
Certification: Diagnostic Radiology, Pediatric Radiology, Pediatrics
3001 W Martin Luther King Blvd, Tampa, 813-870-4600
4516 N Armenia Ave, Tampa, 813-870-4919

Call, Glenn Alan (3 mentions)
U of Chicago, 1987
Certification: Diagnostic Radiology, Neuroradiology
747 6th Ave S, St Petersburg, 727-898-3647

Halme, Tracy Lee (5 mentions)
U of South Florida, 1995
4516 N Armenia Ave, Tampa, 813-870-4919

Martinez, Carlos Rodrigo (6 mentions)
Temple U, 1972
Certification: Diagnostic Radiology, Neuroradiology
2700 University Sq Dr, Tampa, 813-253-2721
4C Columbia Dr #110, Tampa, 813-251-6500
4700 N Habana Ave #105, Tampa, 813-872-2638
4719 N Habana Ave, Tampa, 813-874-7000

Murtagh, Frederick Reed (5 mentions)
Temple U, 1971
Certification: Diagnostic Radiology, Neuroradiology
3301 Usf Alumni Dr, Tampa, 813-972-3351

Price, Brent Coppedge (5 mentions)
U of South Florida, 1978 *Certification:* Diagnostic Radiology
747 6th Ave S, St Petersburg, 727-898-3647

Rozin, Roman (4 mentions)
U of Pittsburgh, 1996 *Certification:* Diagnostic Radiology
1250 S Tamaimi Trail #103, Sarasota, 941-951-2100

Stein, Bernard David (4 mentions)
U of Pittsburgh, 1969 *Certification:* Radiology
508 S Habana Ave #160, Tampa, 813-877-6511
2901 W Swann Ave, Tampa, 813-873-6460

Radiology—Therapeutic

Berlet, Matthew Howard (7 mentions)
New Jersey Med Sch, 1986
Certification: Diagnostic Radiology, Neuroradiology
3001 W Martin Luther King Blvd, Tampa, 813-870-4600
4516 N Armenia Ave, Tampa, 813-870-4919

Calkins, Alison Ruth (3 mentions)
Indiana U, 1981 *Certification:* Therapeutic Radiology
3001 W Dr Martin Luther King Jr Blvd, Tampa, 813-870-4160

Call, Glenn Alan (3 mentions)
U of Chicago, 1987
Certification: Diagnostic Radiology, Neuroradiology
747 6th Ave S, St Petersburg, 727-898-3647

Davis, Andrew George (3 mentions)
Washington U, 1983 *Certification:* Diagnostic Radiology,
   Vascular & Interventional Radiology
1106 Druid Rd S #302, Clearwater, 727-441-3711

Greenberg, Harvey Michael (4 mentions)
U of Pittsburgh, 1972 *Certification:* Internal Medicine,
   Medical Oncology, Therapeutic Radiology
12902 Magnolia Dr, Tampa, 813-979-3980

Miller, Robert Joseph (5 mentions)
Ohio State U, 1974
Certification: Internal Medicine, Therapeutic Radiology
701 6th St S, St Petersburg, 727-893-6103

Niedzwiecki, Gerald A. (3 mentions)
U of Rochester, 1990 *Certification:* Diagnostic Radiology,
   Vascular & Interventional Radiology
2655 State Rd 580 #202, Clearwater, 727-791-7300
2730 N McMullen Booth Rd #100, Clearwater, 727-791-7300

Zwiebel, Bruce Robert (4 mentions)
New York U, 1986 *Certification:* Diagnostic Radiology,
   Vascular & Interventional Radiology
1 Tampa General Cir #J-342, Tampa, 813-844-4570
2700 University Square Dr, Tampa, 813-251-5822

Rehabilitation

Batas, Venerando (5 mentions)
FMS-Philippines, 1977
Certification: Physical Medicine & Rehabilitation
2914 N Boulevard, Tampa, 813-228-7696

Beard, Margita Vrana (4 mentions)
FMS-Germany, 1987
Certification: Physical Medicine & Rehabilitation
1416 59th St W, Bradenton, 941-794-3998

De Jesus, Alexander, Jr. (5 mentions)
Robert W Johnson Med Sch, 1986
Certification: Physical Medicine & Rehabilitation
6400 Edgelake Dr, Sarasota, 941-921-8600

Eichberg, Rodolfo D. (7 mentions)
FMS-Argentina, 1963
Certification: Physical Medicine & Rehabilitation
2914 N Blvd, Tampa, 813-228-7696

Kornberg, Paul Bryan (10 mentions)
U of Miami, 1994
Certification: Physical Medicine & Rehabilitation
2914 North Blvd, Tampa, 813-228-7696

Lopez-Mendez, Ada (3 mentions)
U of Puerto Rico, 1981
Certification: Internal Medicine, Rheumatology
200 Ave F NE, Winter Haven, 863-297-1865

Patterson, James Ray (4 mentions)
U of Tennessee, 1978
Certification: Physical Medicine & Rehabilitation
3102 E 138th Ave #512, Tampa, 813-979-4094

Reiskind, Marc Alan (3 mentions)
Med Coll of Georgia, 1989
Certification: Physical Medicine & Rehabilitation
2191 9th Ave N #115, St Petersburg, 727-327-2600

Tsai, David S. (3 mentions)
U of Michigan, 1991
Certification: Physical Medicine & Rehabilitation
4110 Manatee Ave W, Bradenton, 941-750-0602

Williams, Karen Linda (6 mentions)
U of Missouri-Kansas City, 1984
Certification: Physical Medicine & Rehabilitation
2191 9th Ave N #270, St Petersburg, 727-327-2600

Rheumatology

Drucker, Yoel (7 mentions)
FMS-Israel, 1988 *Certification:* Rheumatology
3500 S Tamiami Trail, Sarasota, 941-365-0770
411 Commercial Ct #D, Venice, 941-484-4409

Fraser, Susan Mary (7 mentions)
Wayne State U, 1978
Certification: Internal Medicine, Rheumatology
601 7th St S, St Petersburg, 727-894-1818

Germain, Bernard F. (6 mentions)
Med Coll of Georgia, 1966
Certification: Internal Medicine, Rheumatology
13801 Bruce B Downs Blvd #101, Tampa, 813-978-1500

McIlwain, Harris Hugh (5 mentions)
Emory U, 1973 *Certification:* Geriatric Medicine, Internal
   Medicine, Rheumatology
4700 N Habana Ave #201, Tampa, 813-879-5485
500 Vonderburg Dr #214, Brandon, 813-685-5555
13801 Bruce B Downs Blvd #406, Tampa, 813-971-5550

Rosen, Adam Michael (5 mentions)
U of Illinois, 1989 *Certification:* Rheumatology
520 D St #C, Clearwater, 727-443-6400

Sebba, Anthony (6 mentions)
FMS-South Africa, 1977
Certification: Internal Medicine, Rheumatology
36338 US Hwy 19 N, Palm Harbor, 727-773-9793

Silverfield, Joel Charles (6 mentions)
Emory U, 1976 *Certification:* Internal Medicine, Rheumatology
4700 N Habana Ave #201, Tampa, 813-879-5485
500 Vonderburg Dr #214, Brandon, 813-685-5555
13801 Bruce B Downs Blvd #406, Tampa, 813-971-5550

Small, Daniel (5 mentions)
Brown U, 1975 *Certification:* Internal Medicine, Rheumatology
3500 S Tamiami Trail, Sarasota, 941-365-0770

Spuza-Milord, Michelle (5 mentions)
FMS-Dominican Republic, 1985
5100 Seminole Blvd, St Petersburg, 727-319-4535

Thoracic Surgery

Alkire, Mark Jefferson (6 mentions)
Louisiana State U, 1984 *Certification:* Surgery, Thoracic Surgery
4 Columbia Dr #860, Tampa, 813-258-4533
4051 Upper Creek Dr #102, Sun City Center, 813-258-4533
6101 Webb Rd #307, Tampa, 813-258-4533

Beggs, Martin L. (5 mentions)
U of Texas-Houston, 1989 *Certification:* Thoracic Surgery
1435 S Osprey Ave #200, Sarasota, 941-952-1913

James, George K. (6 mentions)
FMS-India, 1967
4513 N Armenia Ave, Tampa, 813-879-2277

Rovin, Joshua David (6 mentions)
U of Louisville, 1996 *Certification:* Surgery, Thoracic Surgery
6006 49th St N #310, St Petersburg, 727-490-5040

Urology

Acosta, Rudolph (7 mentions)
U of Florida, 1981 *Certification:* Urology
12408 N 56th St #1, Tampa, 813-980-3104

Bilik, Alfred Joseph, Jr. (6 mentions)
Georgetown U, 1989 *Certification:* Urology
1 S School Ave #200, Sarasota, 941-309-7000
3191 Harbour Blvd #C, Port Charlotte, 941-309-7000

Bryant, Kenneth Rawn (6 mentions)
U of Florida, 1978 *Certification:* Urology
601 7th St S, St Petersburg, 727-824-7146

Bukkapatnam, Raviender (5 mentions)
U of Alabama, 1998 *Certification:* Urology
1 Davis Blvd #604, Tampa, 813-258-9565

Camuzzi, Marco A. (5 mentions)
Nova Southeastern Coll of Osteopathic Med, 1998
Certification: Urology
6450 38th Ave N #110, St Petersburg, 727-345-2274

Curtis, Gerard Anthony (5 mentions)
U of Miami, 1992 *Certification:* Urology
2401 University Pkwy #104, Sarasota, 941-358-6777

Hill, George Austin (5 mentions)
U of Miami, 1987 *Certification:* Urology
200 3rd Ave W #210, Bradenton, 941-752-1553

Hochberg, David A. (6 mentions)
U of Miami, 1995 *Certification:* Urology
4700 N Habana Ave #505, Tampa, 813-877-7434

Klavans, Mitchell Scott (5 mentions)
Eastern Virginia Med Sch, 1984 *Certification:* Urology
430 Morton Plant St #206, Clearwater, 727-446-6345

Lockhart, Jorge L. (5 mentions)
FMS-Uruguay, 1971 *Certification:* Urology
12902 Magnolia Dr, Tampa, 813-972-4673
4 Columbia Dr #730, Tampa, 813-972-8418

Rucker, George Bino (5 mentions)
U of Virginia, 1995 *Certification:* Urology
200 3rd Ave W #210, Bradenton, 941-752-1553

Smith, Matthew Stephen (6 mentions)
Georgetown U, 1975 *Certification:* Urology
3525 Lakeland Hills Blvd, Lakeland, 863-603-6565

Treiman, Alan Richard (5 mentions)
Duke U, 1980 *Certification:* Urology
1921 Waldemere St #310, Sarasota, 941-917-8488

Yadven, Mitchell Wade (5 mentions)
George Washington U, 1991 *Certification:* Urology
200 3rd Ave W #210, Bradenton, 941-792-0340

Vascular Surgery

James, George K. (8 mentions)
FMS-India, 1967
4513 N Armenia Ave, Tampa, 813-879-2277

Samson, Russell Howard (12 mentions)
FMS-South Africa, 1972 *Certification:* Vascular Surgery
600 N Cattlemen Rd #220, Sarasota, 941-371-6565

Showalter, David Paul (8 mentions)
U of Kansas, 1984 *Certification:* Surgery, Vascular Surgery
600 N Cattlemen Rd #220, Sarasota, 941-371-6565

Silverman, Steven Howard (8 mentions)
U of Miami, 1983 *Certification:* Surgery, Vascular Surgery
1921 Waldemere St #504, Sarasota, 941-957-1700

South Florida

Including Broward, Miami-Dade, Monroe, and Palm Beach Counties

Allergy/Immunology

Benenati, Susan Vento (8 mentions)
U of South Florida, 1984
Certification: Allergy & Immunology, Internal Medicine
7000 SW 62nd Ave #510, Miami, 305-665-1623

Carro, Jose (9 mentions)
FMS-Dominican Republic, 1982
3100 SW 62nd Ave, Miami, 305-662-8272
777 E 25th St #311, Hialeah, 305-444-2486
2601 SW 37th Ave #502, Miami, 305-444-2486
7000 SW 97th Ave #116, Miami, 305-444-2486

Cox, Linda S. (10 mentions)
Northwestern U, 1985
Certification: Allergy & Immunology, Internal Medicine
5333 N Dixie Hwy #210, Oakland Park, 954-771-0928

Eisermann-Rogers, Kathryn (6 mentions)
FMS-Germany, 1982
Certification: Allergy & Immunology, Pediatrics
7000 SW 62nd Ave #510, South Miami, 305-665-1623

Faraci, John Patrick (5 mentions)
U of Kentucky, 1980
Certification: Allergy & Immunology, Pediatrics
500 University Blvd #116, Jupiter, 561-627-4767

Friedman, Stuart Andrew (14 mentions)
FMS-Spain, 1976
Certification: Allergy & Immunology, Internal Medicine
5162 Linton Blvd #201, Delray Beach, 561-495-2580
9250 Glades Rd, Boca Raton, 561-391-0005

Gluck, Joan Chernoff (8 mentions)
New York U, 1972
9035 Sunset Dr #202, Miami, 305-279-3366
9000 SW 137th Ave #213, Miami, 305-279-3366

Gonzalez, Gabriel E. (8 mentions)
U of Puerto Rico, 1977
Certification: Allergy & Immunology, Pediatrics
12959 Pamls West Dr #230, Loxahatchee, 561-790-2258
11211 Prosperity Farms Rd #C113, Palm Beach Gardens,
   561-624-2919

Klimas, Nancy Grace (4 mentions)
U of Miami, 1980 *Certification:* Diagnostic Laboratory
   Immunology, Internal Medicine
1120 NW 14th St, Miami, 305-243-3291

Lamas, Ana Maria (12 mentions)
Yale U, 1983
Certification: Allergy & Immunology, Internal Medicine
175 W 49th St, Hialeah, 305-822-3761
2000 SW 27th Ave #301, Miami, 305-461-2010

Lanz, Miguel Jose (4 mentions)
U of Miami, 1992 *Certification:* Allergy & Immunology, Pediatrics
365 Alcazar Ave, Coral Gables, 305-445-0441

Louie, Steven J. (6 mentions)
SUNY-Downstate Med Coll, 1978
Certification: Allergy & Immunology, Internal Medicine
5507 S Congress Ave #140, Atlantis, 561-965-6685

Martell, Frank Jose (4 mentions)
U of South Florida, 1990 *Certification:* Allergy & Immunology
7150 W 20th Ave #106, Hialeah, 305-362-7762
348 Minorca Ave, Coral Gables, 305-445-9422

Mirmelli, Philip Craig (7 mentions)
U of Miami, 1973 *Certification:* Allergy & Immunology, Pediatrics
400 Authur Godfrey Rd #504, Miami Beach, 305-538-8339

Pacin, Michael Paul (4 mentions)
Washington U, 1969
Certification: Allergy & Immunology, Internal Medicine
9035 Sunset Dr #202, Miami, 305-279-3366
11880 SW 40th St #304, Miami, 305-279-3366

Piniella, Carlos Jesus (5 mentions)
U of Miami, 1988 *Certification:* Allergy & Immunology
9275 SW 152nd St #210, Miami, 305-255-9577

Sinclair, Elysee H. (4 mentions)
Med Coll of Pennsylvania, 1974 *Certification:* Pediatrics
10167 NW 31st St #200, Coral Springs, 954-340-8797

Stein, Mark Rodger (20 mentions)
Jefferson Med Coll, 1968
Certification: Allergy & Immunology, Internal Medicine
840 US Hwy 1 #235, North Palm Beach, 561-626-2006
618 E Ocean Blvd #4, Stuart, 561-626-2006
12983 Southern Blvd #204, Loxahatchee, 561-659-5916
1411 N Flagler Dr #4100, West Palm Beach, 561-659-5916

Ubals, Elena Marta (7 mentions)
FMS-Spain, 1979 *Certification:* Allergy & Immunology, Pediatrics
7413 Miami Lakes Dr, Hialeah, 305-823-1369
475 Biltmore Way #204, Coral Gables, 305-444-9177

Wallace, Dana Vonnette (12 mentions)
U of Tennessee, 1972
Certification: Allergy & Immunology, Pediatrics
2699 Stirling Rd #B305, Fort Lauderdale, 954-963-5363

Young, Mark Phillip (5 mentions)
U Central del Caribe, 1982
Certification: Allergy & Immunology, Pediatrics
7800 SW 87th Ave #C-340, Miami, 305-595-0109
30 SE 7th St #C, Boca Raton, 305-595-0109

Anesthesiology

Abraham, Edward C. (10 mentions)
U of Miami, 1983 *Certification:* Anesthesiology
9370 SW 72nd St #A-250, Miami, 305-596-6505

Berlin, Richard Ellis (3 mentions)
Michigan State U, 1988 *Certification:* Anesthesiology
1613 N Harrison Pkwy Bldg C #200, Sunrise, 954-838-2500

Cooney, John Franklin (5 mentions)
Mayo Med Sch, 1977 *Certification:* Anesthesiology, Pain Medicine
1500 N Dixie Hwy #103, West Palm Beach, 561-833-8893

Davila, Jose Jorge (3 mentions)
Columbia U, 1986 *Certification:* Anesthesiology
5000 University Dr, Coral Gables, 305-448-9018

De Young, Robert Arnold (4 mentions)
Northwestern U, 1969 *Certification:* Anesthesiology
1613 N Harrison Pkwy #200, Sunrise, 954-838-2371

Drourr, Nathaniel Robert (3 mentions)
Stony Brook U, 1992 *Certification:* Anesthesiology, Pain Medicine
1210 S Old Dixie Hwy, Jupiter, 561-743-5073

Edbril, Steven David (4 mentions)
Albert Einstein Coll of Med, 1991 *Certification:* Anesthesiology
5352 Linton Blvd, Delray Beach, 561-498-4440

Greenfield, Andrew Jay (5 mentions)
Temple U, 1988 *Certification:* Anesthesiology
1613 NW 136th Ave, Sunrise, 954-838-2371

Hazday, Nelson (4 mentions)
FMS-Dominican Republic, 1981
Certification: Anesthesiology, Internal Medicine
5000 University Dr, Coral Gables, 305-448-9018

Machado, Raphael, Jr. (3 mentions)
Certification: Anesthesiology
8900 N Kendall Dr, Miami, 305-270-3621

McCarthy, Martin Francis (5 mentions)
FMS-Ireland, 1975 *Certification:* Anesthesiology
8900 N Kendall Dr, Miami, 786-596-1960

Meister, Michael Jay (4 mentions)
U of South Florida, 1984 *Certification:* Anesthesiology
6200 SW 73rd St, South Miami, 305-662-8192

Rodman, Richard Harvey (5 mentions)
Yale U, 1981 *Certification:* Anesthesiology
1411 N Flagler Dr #4000, West Palm Beach, 561-833-0882

Wittels, S. Howard (3 mentions)
U of Miami, 1980 *Certification:* Anesthesiology
4300 Alton Rd, Miami Beach, 305-647-2345

Cardiac Surgery

Dorman, Malcolm Joel (10 mentions)
Rosalind Franklin U, 1967
Certification: Surgery, Thoracic Surgery
5301 S Congress Ave, Lake Worth, 561-548-4900

Gieseke, William Donald (7 mentions)
Indiana U, 1969 *Certification:* Surgery, Thoracic Surgery
5130 Linton Blvd #B2, Delray Beach, 561-499-8025

Green, Robert Arthur (8 mentions)
U of Michigan, 1968 *Certification:* Surgery, Thoracic Surgery
350 NW 84th Ave #300, Plantation, 954-475-9535

Katz, Arthur Herman (10 mentions)
New York Med Coll, 1985 *Certification:* Thoracic Surgery
801 Meadows Rd #104, Boca Raton, 561-955-6300

Lamelas, Joseph (33 mentions)
FMS-Dominican Republic, 1982 *Certification:* Thoracic Surgery
8950 N Kendall Dr #607, Miami, 305-598-4446

Lester, Joseph Lancelot, III (10 mentions)
U of Miami, 1968 *Certification:* Surgery, Thoracic Surgery
5511 S Congress Ave #135, Atlantis, 561-548-4900
5301 S Congress Ave, Lake Worth, 561-548-4900

Perryman, Richard Alan (7 mentions)
FMS-United Kingdom, 1967 *Certification:* Thoracic Surgery
1150 N 35th Ave #440, Hollywood, 954-985-6939

Tabry, Imad Fouad (12 mentions)
FMS-Lebanon, 1970 *Certification:* Surgery, Thoracic Surgery
1625 SE 3rd Ave #601, Fort Lauderdale, 954-462-4413

Williams, Donald B. (13 mentions)
Jefferson Med Coll, 1974 *Certification:* Thoracic Surgery
1295 NW 14th St #H, Miami, 305-325-5694

Cardiology

Agatston, Arthur Stephen (4 mentions)
New York U, 1973
Certification: Cardiovascular Disease, Internal Medicine
1691 Michigan Ave #500, Miami Beach, 305-538-3828

Aitken, Percy W. (7 mentions)
FMS-Bolivia, 1985
4685 Ponce De Leon Blvd, Coral Gables, 305-661-2504

Aldousany, Abulwahab (4 mentions)
FMS-Iraq, 1974 *Certification:* Neonatal-Perinatal Medicine, Pediatric Cardiology, Pediatrics
8955 SW 87th Ct #110, Miami, 305-270-1113

Angella, Farahnaz (3 mentions)
U of Florida, 1994 *Certification:* Cardiovascular Disease, Clinical Cardiac Electrophysiology
5511 S Congress Ave, Lake Worth, 561-434-0353

Bartzokis, Thomas C. (4 mentions)
Harvard U, 1983 *Certification:* Cardiovascular Disease, Internal Medicine, Interventional Cardiology
1000 NW 9th Ct #101, Boca Raton, 561-368-4444

Berlin, Howard Frederick (11 mentions)
Jefferson Med Coll, 1975
Certification: Cardiovascular Disease, Internal Medicine
1150 N 35th Ave #605, Hollywood, 954-981-3331

Blacher, Lawrence (7 mentions)
Albert Einstein Coll of Med, 1978
Certification: Cardiovascular Disease, Internal Medicine
8950 N Kendall Dr #601, Miami, 305-279-4500

Braun, Michael Jeffrey (3 mentions)
Temple U, 1991 *Certification:* Cardiovascular Disease
1150 N 35th Ave #605, Hollywood, 954-981-3331

Bush, Howard Seth (4 mentions)
New York Med Coll, 1982 *Certification:* Cardiovascular Disease, Internal Medicine, Interventional Cardiology
2950 Cleveland Clinic Blvd 2nd Fl, Weston, 954-659-5290

Carr, Matthew L. (4 mentions)
Albert Einstein Coll of Med, 1966
3001 NW 49th Ave #100, Lauderdale Lakes, 954-731-1101

Castriz, Jorge Luis (4 mentions)
FMS-Dominican Republic, 1983
Certification: Cardiovascular Disease, Interventional Cardiology
500 university Blvd #208, Jupiter, 561-627-6600

Cohen, Yale Mayer (3 mentions)
U of Pittsburgh, 1992
Certification: Cardiovascular Disease, Internal Medicine
3702 Washington St #401, Hollywood, 954-967-6550

Conde, Cesar Augusto (4 mentions)
FMS-Peru, 1968
Certification: Cardiovascular Disease, Internal Medicine
4302 Alton Rd #100, Miami Beach, 305-534-4564

Coy, Kevin Michael (3 mentions)
U of Florida, 1986 *Certification:* Cardiovascular Disease, Internal Medicine, Interventional Cardiology
3801 Biscayne Blvd #300, Miami, 305-571-0620

Cueto, Juan Carlos (3 mentions)
U of Miami, 1990
1990 SW 27th Ave #2, Miami, 305-442-1159

Cusnir, Henry (5 mentions)
FMS-Colombia, 1993 *Certification:* Cardiovascular Disease, Internal Medicine, Interventional Cardiology
3001 NW 49th Ave #100, Lauderdale Lakes, 954-731-1101

Diaz-Cruz, Candido F. (5 mentions)
FMS-Spain, 1973
Certification: Cardiovascular Disease, Internal Medicine
3661 S Miami Ave #407, Miami, 305-860-8808

Dylewski, John Richard (3 mentions)
U of Miami, 1991 *Certification:* Cardiovascular Disease
7000 SW 62nd Ave #210, South Miami, 305-662-2530

Erenrich, Norman Henry (5 mentions)
FMS-Canada, 1976 *Certification:* Cardiovascular Disease, Critical Care Medicine, Internal Medicine
1401 Forum Way #300, West Palm Beach, 561-478-1104
5507 S Congress Ave #110, Lake Worth, 561-478-1104

Feldman, Theodore (3 mentions)
Albert Einstein Coll of Med, 1980
Certification: Cardiovascular Disease, Internal Medicine
4685 Ponce De Leon Blvd, Coral Gables, 305-661-2534

Fenster, Jeffrey Scott (6 mentions)
FMS-Israel, 1995 *Certification:* Cardiovascular Disease, Internal Medicine, Interventional Cardiology
3355 Burns Rd #201, Palm Beach Gardens, 561-296-5225

Funt, David S. (4 mentions)
New York U, 1979
Certification: Cardiovascular Disease, Internal Medicine
9980 Central Park Blvd N #304, Boca Raton, 561-483-8335
10075 Jog Rd #202, Boynton Beach, 561-731-3541

Gabor, Ronald M. (3 mentions)
Albert Einstein Coll of Med, 1992
Certification: Cardiovascular Disease
9980 Central Park Blvd N #304, Boca Raton, 561-483-8335
10075 Jog Rd #202, Boynton Beach, 561-731-3541

Guerra, Oscar Rafael (6 mentions)
FMS-St Maarten, 1987 *Certification:* Cardiovascular Disease
836 Ponce De Leon Blvd, Coral Gables, 305-446-9658

Guzman, Jose Aogusto (4 mentions)
FMS-Dominican Republic, 1987
Certification: Cardiovascular Disease
1150 N 35th Ave #605, Hollywood, 954-981-3331
603 N Flamingo Rd #255, Penbrook Pines, 954-437-9116

Hamburg, Curtis Andrew (4 mentions)
Albert Einstein Coll of Med, 1978
Certification: Cardiovascular Disease, Internal Medicine
8950 N Kendall Dr #601, Miami, 305-279-4500

Iskowitz, Steven Bruce (5 mentions)
U of Pittsburgh, 1981
Certification: Pediatric Cardiology, Pediatrics
2825 N State Rd 7 #302, Margate, 954-972-1600

Krasner, Stephen Edward (5 mentions)
Albert Einstein Coll of Med, 1980
Certification: Cardiovascular Disease, Internal Medicine
5401 S Congress Ave #102, Atlantis, 561-733-3989

Lakow, Michael Bruce (3 mentions)
Mount Sinai Sch of Med, 1987
Certification: Cardiovascular Disease
5401 S Congress Ave #102, Atlantis, 561-733-3989

Lloret, Ramon Luis (4 mentions)
U of Miami, 1982 *Certification:* Cardiovascular Disease, Internal Medicine, Interventional Cardiology
7400 SW 87th Ave #100, Miami, 305-275-8200

Marquez, Jose Leonardo (3 mentions)
FMS-Dominican Republic, 1980
Certification: Cardiovascular Disease, Internal Medicine
2140 W 68th St #403, Hialeah, 305-285-7282
3659 S Miami Ave #4001, Miami, 305-556-6363

Mas, Madeline Sartick (4 mentions)
Georgetown U, 1984 *Certification:* Pediatric Cardiology
3659 S Miami Ave #3002, Miami, 305-858-7940
8940 N Kendall Dr #603-E, Miami, 305-858-7940

Mayorga-Cortes, Alvaro (3 mentions)
FMS-Mexico, 1968
Certification: Cardiovascular Disease, Internal Medicine
8950 N Kendall Dr #405, Miami, 305-412-7225

Meyer, Keith Douglas (7 mentions)
U of Rochester, 1979
Certification: Cardiovascular Disease, Internal Medicine
1411 N Flagler Dr #9500, West Palm Beach, 561-820-0122

Musaffi, Albert (5 mentions)
New York U, 1980
Certification: Cardiovascular Disease, Internal Medicine
5501 S Congress Ave #102, Atlantis, 561-733-3989

Neff, Edward Michael (4 mentions)
Temple U, 1969
Certification: Cardiovascular Disease, Internal Medicine
495 Biltmore Way #202, Coral Gables, 305-443-5291

Pearl, Frank Jay (3 mentions)
Jefferson Med Coll, 1974
Certification: Cardiovascular Disease, Internal Medicine
1150 N 35th Ave #605, Hollywood, 954-981-3331

Perloff, David Edward (3 mentions)
U of Miami, 1991
Certification: Cardiovascular Disease, Internal Medicine
1625 SE 3rd Ave #721, Fort Lauderdale, 954-523-3422

Quesada-Mendez, Ramon (6 mentions)
FMS-El Salvador, 1980 *Certification:* Cardiovascular Disease, Internal Medicine, Interventional Cardiology
8950 N Kendall Dr #501, Miami, 305-412-3558

Ray, Michael Earl (3 mentions)
SUNY-Downstate Med Coll, 1969
Certification: Cardiovascular Disease, Internal Medicine
1401 Forum Way #300, West Palm Beach, 561-478-1104
5507 S Congress Ave #110, Lake Worth, 561-478-1104

Roberts, Jonathan S. (6 mentions)
U of Miami, 1982 *Certification:* Cardiovascular Disease, Internal Medicine, Interventional Cardiology
8950 N Kendall Dr #601, Miami, 305-279-4500

Rondino, Paul Louis (4 mentions)
U of Miami, 1989
Certification: Cardiovascular Disease, Internal Medicine
1 W Sample Rd #204, Pompano Beach, 954-478-0300

Russo, Charles Damian (10 mentions)
New York Med Coll, 1981
Certification: Cardiovascular Disease, Internal Medicine
4725 N Federal Hwy #401, Fort Lauderdale, 954-772-2136

Sanzobrino, Brenda W. (4 mentions)
FMS-Mexico, 1983 *Certification:* Internal Medicine
2301 N University Dr #112, Pembroke Pines, 954-963-6500

Schneider, Ricky Marc (4 mentions)
Yale U, 1977
Certification: Cardiovascular Disease, Internal Medicine
7421 N University Dr #101, Tamarac, 954-721-6666

Schrager, Bernard Robert (4 mentions)
U of Miami, 1977
Certification: Cardiovascular Disease, Internal Medicine
8950 N Kendall Dr #601, Miami, 305-279-4500

Seckler, Jonathan I. (4 mentions)
Mount Sinai Sch of Med, 1991
Certification: Cardiovascular Disease, Interventional Cardiology
1000 NW 9th Ct #101, Boca Raton, 561-368-4444

Segall, Peter Howard (4 mentions)
FMS-Canada, 1973
Certification: Cardiovascular Disease, Internal Medicine
4308 Alton Rd #870, Miami Beach, 305-538-8504

Steiman, David Mark (3 mentions)
George Washington U, 1985
Certification: Cardiovascular Disease, Internal Medicine
350 NW 84th Ave #211, Plantation, 954-978-5293

Vogt-Lowell, Robert W. (4 mentions)
U of Puerto Rico, 1986 *Certification:* Pediatric Cardiology
7765 SW 87th Ave #110, Miami, 305-595-1833
7735 NW 146th St #302, Miami, 305-595-1833
3501 Health Center Blvd #2145, Bonita Springs, 305-595-1833

Von Sohsten, Roberto L. (3 mentions)
FMS-Brazil, 1990
Certification: Cardiovascular Disease, Interventional Cardiology
5401 S Congress Ave #102, Atlantis, 561-967-5033
1397 Medical Parks Blvd #300, Wellington, 561-798-4900
6056 Boynton Beach Blvd, Boynton Beach, 561-737-9227

Zakheim, Richard Manuel (4 mentions)
Albert Einstein Coll of Med, 1962
Certification: Pediatric Cardiology, Pediatrics
3200 SW 60th Ct #104, Miami, 305-662-8301

Zelcer, Alan A. (9 mentions)
New York U, 1981 *Certification:* Cardiovascular Disease,
Internal Medicine, Interventional Cardiology
5210 Linton Blvd #101, Delray Beach, 561-495-7230

Dermatology

Beer, Kenneth Robert (6 mentions)
U of Pennsylvania, 1989
Certification: Dermatology, Dermatopathology
1500 N Dixie Hwy #305, West Palm Beach, 561-655-9055
641 University Blvd #212, Jupiter, 561-655-9055

Colsky, Arthur Spencer (4 mentions)
U of Miami, 1994 *Certification:* Dermatology
6280 SW 72nd St, South Miami, 305-740-6181

Cosmides, James C. (4 mentions)
West Virginia U, 1967
Certification: Dermatology, Dermatopathology
427 Biltmore Way #107, Coral Gables, 305-443-2983

Duarte, Ana Margarita (9 mentions)
U of Miami, 1988
Certification: Dermatology, Pediatric Dermatology
3100 SW 62nd Ave, Miami, 305-669-6555

Fayne, Scott (5 mentions)
U of Miami, 1983 *Certification:* Dermatology
1002 S Old Dixie Hwy #302, Jupiter, 561-746-9500
4495 Military Trail #204, Jupiter, 561-746-9500

Glick, Brad Peter (6 mentions)
Nova Southeastern Coll of Osteopathic Med, 1989
2960 N State Rd 7 #101, Margate, 954-974-3664

Gonzalez, Ana Isabel (5 mentions)
U of Miami, 1985 *Certification:* Dermatology
401 Miracle Mile #307, Coral Gables, 305-444-7733

Green, Howard Allen (4 mentions)
Boston U, 1985 *Certification:* Dermatology, Internal Medicine
120 Butler St #A, West Palm Beach, 561-659-1510
10335 N Military Trail #A, Palm Beach Gardens, 561-622-6976

Herschthal, David Howard (4 mentions)
New York Med Coll, 1976 *Certification:* Dermatology
7421 N University Dr #301, Tamarac, 954-722-3900
7280 W Palmetto Park #210, Boca Raton, 954-722-3900

Hertz, Kenneth Clark (4 mentions)
Harvard U, 1972 *Certification:* Dermatology
9065 SW 87th Ave #109, Miami, 305-271-7800

Julien, Juana Maria (4 mentions)
Columbia U, 1985 *Certification:* Dermatology
10095 SW 88th St #103, Miami, 305-274-7878

Kerdel, Francisco Armando (8 mentions)
FMS-United Kingdom, 1979
Certification: Dermatological Immunology/Diagnostic and
Laboratory Immunology, Dermatology
1400 NW 12th Ave #4, Miami, 305-324-2110

Perez, Gregory L. (12 mentions)
Mayo Med Sch, 1991 *Certification:* Dermatology
4610 N Federal Hwy, Fort Lauderdale, 954-771-0582

Plotkin, Adam Scott (9 mentions)
U of Pennsylvania, 1992 *Certification:* Dermatology
5210 Linton Blvd #307, Delray Beach, 561-499-0660
30 SE 6th St, Boca Raton, 561-395-6704

Rabinovitz, Harold Steven (5 mentions)
U of Miami, 1977 *Certification:* Dermatology
201 NW 82nd Ave #103, Plantation, 954-693-9648
1600 NW 10th Ave 1st Fl, Miami, 305-243-4472

Rivlin, Dan (4 mentions)
New York U, 1987 *Certification:* Dermapathology, Dermatology
4308 Alton Rd #510, Miami Beach, 305-674-8865

Rodriguez-Valdes, Jose M. (6 mentions)
3661 S Miami Ave #102, Miami, 305-854-7814
7100 W 20th Ave, Hialeah, 305-825-3650

Schachner, Lawrence Alan (9 mentions)
U of Nebraska, 1972 *Certification:* Dermatology, Pediatrics
1444 NW 9th Ave, Miami, 305-243-6704
1295 NW 14th St, Miami, 305-243-6704

Sobel, Stuart Alan (13 mentions)
Tufts U, 1972 *Certification:* Dermatology
4340 Sheridan St, Hollywood, 954-983-5533

Sofman, Michael Sanford (4 mentions)
Robert W Johnson Med Sch, 1985 *Certification:* Dermatology
4340 Sheridan St #101, Hollywood, 305-983-5533

Wiltz, Hector (4 mentions)
Temple U, 1983 *Certification:* Dermatology
5250 SW 59th Ave, Miami, 305-227-9233

Zwecker, Warren Stuart (11 mentions)
Boston U, 1978 *Certification:* Dermatology
4495 Military Trail #204, Jupiter, 561-296-1122

Emergency Medicine

Cohen, Terry Bruce (8 mentions)
Jefferson Med Coll, 1975 *Certification:* Allergy &
Immunology, Emergency Medicine, Internal Medicine
800 Meadows Rd, Boca Raton, 561-395-7100

Fowler, David McMullin (3 mentions)
FMS-United Kingdom, 1978 *Certification:* Emergency Medicine
7016 Spyglass Ave, Parkland, 877-751-1157

Greenberg, Kenneth Jay (5 mentions)
FMS-Mexico, 1982 *Certification:* Internal Medicine
7201 N University Dr, Tamarac, 954-724-6225

Isaacson, Louis H. (10 mentions)
Des Moines U, 1976
5000 W Oakland Park Blvd, Fort Lauderdale, 954-735-6000

Keroff, Frederick Michael (5 mentions)
Rosalind Franklin U, 1975
Certification: Emergency Medicine, Family Medicine
3501 Johnson St, Hollywood, 954-265-6307

Mathen, Santosh K. (7 mentions)
FMS-India, 1971 *Certification:* Emergency Medicine
5352 Linton Blvd, Delray Beach, 561-495-3115

McFarland, R. Scott, III (4 mentions)
U of Alabama, 1980 *Certification:* Emergency Medicine
3360 Burns Rd, Palm Beach Gardens, 561-694-7172

Medina Mejia, Francisco A. (3 mentions)
FMS-El Salvador, 1980
8900 N Kendall Dr, Miami, 305-596-1960

Nichol, Currin McNairy (4 mentions)
U of Arkansas, 1983 *Certification:* Family Medicine
3278 N Federal Hwy #186, Fort Lauderdale, 954-942-3597

Patricoff, Tracey C. (3 mentions)
U of South Florida, 1987 *Certification:* Internal Medicine
6200 SW 73rd St, South Miami, 305-662-8181

Pessah, Aryeh Joseph (5 mentions)
FMS-Israel, 1995 *Certification:* Emergency Medicine
800 Meadows Rd, Boca Raton, 561-395-7100

Portuondo, Jose Enrique (6 mentions)
Tulane U, 1973 *Certification:* Emergency Medicine
7250 W Lago Dr, Coral Gables, 305-669-3469

Rumball, Caswell John (6 mentions)
FMS-Canada, 1980 *Certification:* Emergency Medicine
5301 S Congress Ave, Atlantis, 561-548-3549

Scheppke, Kenneth Andrew (3 mentions)
Stony Brook U, 1992 *Certification:* Emergency Medicine
5301 S Congress Ave, Lake Worth, 561-548-3549

Shroff, Burjis Nariman (6 mentions)
FMS-Pakistan, 1973 *Certification:* Emergency Medicine
5352 Linton Blvd, Delray Beach, 561-498-4440

Soria, David Michael (4 mentions)
Ohio State U, 1993
10101 W Forest Hill Blvd, Wellington, 561-798-8535

Tavarez, Ligio Antonio (5 mentions)
FMS-Dominican Republic, 1981 *Certification:* Pediatrics
8900 N Kendall Dr, Miami, 305-270-3677

Thau, A. Adam (4 mentions)
FMS-St Maarten, 1984
2801 State Rd 7, Margate, 954-978-4003

Endocrinology

Andrade, Agustin A. (4 mentions)
FMS-Ecuador, 1989
Certification: Endocrinology, Diabetes, and Metabolism
4308 Alton Rd #310, Miami Beach, 305-672-7560

Ashkar, Fuad S. (4 mentions)
FMS-Lebanon, 1962 *Certification:* Nuclear Medicine
11760 SW 40th St #535, Miami, 305-553-6744

Baquerizo, Hernan (6 mentions)
FMS-Ecuador, 1979
Certification: Endocrinology and Metabolism, Internal Medicine
3661 S Miami Ave #203, Miami, 305-859-9837

Bendix, Marcelo Vianna (4 mentions)
FMS-Brazil, 1985 *Certification:* Endocrinology, Diabetes,
and Metabolism, Internal Medicine
9740 South West 40th St, Miami, 305-227-5300

Biederman, Edward Barry (5 mentions)
New York U, 1973
Certification: Endocrinology and Metabolism, Internal Medicine
4701 N Federal Hwy #A27, Fort Lauderdale, 954-938-9966

Cohen, Martin S. (11 mentions)
SUNY-Downstate Med Coll, 1968
Certification: Endocrinology and Metabolism, Internal Medicine
7800 SW 87th Ave #130, Miami, 305-270-1571

Fili, Michael Dominick (14 mentions)
U of Miami, 1984 *Certification:* Endocrinology, Diabetes,
and Metabolism, Internal Medicine
8600 SW 92nd St #103, Miami, 305-274-5700

Freedman, Renee Jeanne (4 mentions)
FMS-Canada, 1998 *Certification:* Endocrinology, Diabetes,
and Metabolism, Internal Medicine
5210 Linton Blvd #205, Delray Beach, 561-495-1606
1500 NW 10th Ave #205, Boca Raton, 561-391-1085

Harrell, Richard Mack (7 mentions)
U of North Carolina, 1979
Certification: Endocrinology and Metabolism, Internal Medicine
6405 N Federal Hwy #404, Fort Lauderdale, 954-267-0997

Horowitz, Barry Scot (7 mentions)
Albert Einstein Coll of Med, 1987 *Certification:*
Endocrinology, Diabetes, and Metabolism, Internal Medicine
1515 N Flagler Dr #430, West Palm Beach, 561-659-6336

Jellinger, Paul Stephen (13 mentions)
Wayne State U, 1969
Certification: Endocrinology and Metabolism, Internal Medicine
1150 N 35th Ave #590, Hollywood, 954-963-7100

Jones, Kathryn D. (6 mentions)
U of South Dakota, 1981
Certification: Endocrinology and Metabolism, Internal Medicine
1500 NW 10th Ave #205, Boca Raton, 561-391-1085
5210 Linton Blvd #205, Delray Beach, 561-495-1606

Kaye, William A. (9 mentions)
Brown U, 1976 *Certification:* Endocrinology and
Metabolism, Internal Medicine, Nephrology
1515 N Flagler Dr #430, West Palm Beach, 561-659-6336

Krieger, Diane Rachel (5 mentions)
U of California-San Francisco, 1982
Certification: Endocrinology and Metabolism, Internal Medicine
6141 Sunset Dr #402, South Miami, 305-665-2300

Mata, Cristina B. (7 mentions)
U of Miami, 1985
4701 N Federal Hwy #A27, Fort Lauderdale, 954-938-9966

Mellman, Michael Jay (7 mentions)
U of Michigan, 1987
Certification: Endocrinology, Diabetes, and Metabolism
10075 Jog Rd #207, Boynton Beach, 561-374-8969

Nahmias, Harvan (8 mentions)
Indiana U, 1973
Certification: Endocrinology and Metabolism, Internal Medicine
2929 N University Dr #205, Coral Springs, 954-752-8800

Nemery, Robin Lynne (5 mentions)
SUNY-Upstate Med U, 1980
Certification: Pediatric Endocrinology, Pediatrics
1150 N 35th Ave #520, Hollywood, 954-265-6984

Novak, Stephen Bruce (8 mentions)
Tufts U, 1972
Certification: Endocrinology and Metabolism, Internal Medicine
1150 N 35th Ave #590, Hollywood, 954-963-7100

Nyman, Asa Margareta (8 mentions)
FMS-Sweden, 1978
12300 Hwy A-1-A S #109, Palm Beach Gardens, 561-799-6881

Pita, Julio Cesar (11 mentions)
Washington U, 1972
Certification: Endocrinology and Metabolism, Internal Medicine
6705 Red Rd #714, Coral Gables, 305-662-1160

Pollock, Jeffrey Marshall (5 mentions)
Rosalind Franklin U, 1988
201 NW 82nd Ave #505, Plantation, 954-617-0322

Quintero, Luis Carlos (7 mentions)
FMS-Panama, 1978 *Certification:* Endocrinology, Diabetes,
and Metabolism
420 S Dixie Hwy #4E, Coral Gables, 305-666-9963

Vinik, Bryan Shaun (6 mentions)
U of Michigan, 1990
1500 NW 10th Ave #205, Boca Raton, 561-391-1085
5210 Linton Blvd #205, Delray Beach, 561-495-1606

Weissman, Peter N. (4 mentions)
New York U, 1966
Certification: Endocrinology and Metabolism, Internal Medicine
7867 N Kendall Dr #80, Miami, 305-595-0777

Family Practice *(see note on page 9)*

Apicella, Vincent M. (3 mentions)
Nova Southeastern Coll of Osteopathic Med, 2001
1037 S State Rd 7 #211, Wellington, 561-798-3030

Coronel, Monica Cruz (3 mentions)
Ponce Sch of Med, 1998 *Certification:* Family Medicine
3301 Johnson St, Hollywood, 954-989-6650

Diamond, Michael Alan (3 mentions)
U of Miami, 1982 *Certification:* Family Medicine
9220 SW 72nd St #200, Miami, 305-279-2256

Ermine, Pamela M. (3 mentions)
2015 Ocean Dr, Boynton Beach, 561-737-4777

Granat, Pepi (3 mentions)
U of Miami, 1962 *Certification:* Family Medicine
7800 Red Rd #202, South Miami, 305-661-7609
7800 SW 57th Ave #202, South Miami, 305-444-6408

Hays, Richard Michael (5 mentions)
U of Florida, 1983 *Certification:* Family Medicine
1397 Medical Parks Blvd, Wellington, 561-784-0202

Lazar, Mark Howard (7 mentions)
FMS-South Africa, 1982 *Certification:* Family Medicine
3301 Johnson St, Hollywood, 954-989-6650

Rogovin, Mark J. (3 mentions)
New York Coll of Osteopathic Med, 1989
Certification: Family Medicine
8188 Jog Rd, Boynton Beach, 561-742-4460
8200 Jog Rd #102, Boynton Beach, 561-439-5200
6056 Boynton Beach Blvd #145, Boynton Beach, 561-737-9227

Steiner, Joshua Zvi (3 mentions)
Nova Southeastern Coll of Osteopathic Med, 2000
4430 Sheridan St #A, Hollywood, 954-989-3100

Warshaw, Ira Greg (4 mentions)
Robert W Johnson Med Sch, 1979 *Certification:* Family Medicine
1216 US Hwy 1, North Palm Beach, 561-626-1000

Werbin, Mario (4 mentions)
U of Miami, 1985 *Certification:* Family Medicine
3301 Johnson St, Hollywood, 954-989-6650

Gastroenterology

Baikovitz, Howard Israel (3 mentions)
U of Miami, 1989
Certification: Gastroenterology, Internal Medicine
603 N Flamingo Rd #258, Pembroke Pines, 954-430-2343

Barkin, Jamie Steven (10 mentions)
U of Miami, 1970
Certification: Gastroenterology, Internal Medicine
4300 Alton Rd #2522, Miami Beach, 305-674-2240

Bassan, Isaac (6 mentions)
U of Miami, 1980
Certification: Gastroenterology, Internal Medicine
4302 Alton Rd #850, Miami Beach, 305-532-2999
2601 NE 178th St, North Miami Beach, 305-532-2999

Bloom, John Desmond, Jr. (3 mentions)
FMS-Mexico, 1983
Certification: Gastroenterology, Internal Medicine
2500 E Commercial Blvd #C, Fort Lauderdale, 954-771-9920

Blum, Michael Lloyd (3 mentions)
FMS-Philippines, 1983
Certification: Gastroenterology, Internal Medicine
4675 Linton Blvd #202, Delray Beach, 561-495-5700

Botoman, Vlaicu Alin (10 mentions)
Johns Hopkins U, 1980
2021 E Commercial Blvd #202, Fort Lauderdale, 954-202-7850

Calleja, Gustavo Armando (3 mentions)
U of Miami, 1982
Certification: Gastroenterology, Internal Medicine
7500 SW 87th Ave #200, Miami, 305-913-0666

Cohen, Harvey Michael (3 mentions)
SUNY-Upstate Med U, 1972
Certification: Gastroenterology, Internal Medicine
951 NW 13th St #2-E, Boca Raton, 561-368-3455
5258 Linton Blvd #202, Delray Beach, 561-499-8227

Diamond, Kenneth Laurence (3 mentions)
Rosalind Franklin U, 1982
Certification: Gastroenterology, Internal Medicine
7431 N University Dr #201, Tamarac, 954-724-5900

Estrin, Howard Morris (4 mentions)
FMS-Canada, 1981
Certification: Gastroenterology, Internal Medicine
21110 Biscayne Blvd #200, Miami, 305-937-2307

Feller, Edward Jay (4 mentions)
SUNY-Downstate Med Coll, 1965
Certification: Gastroenterology, Internal Medicine
8353 SW 124th St #203, Miami, 305-259-8720

Fiedler, Lawrence Michael (4 mentions)
Mount Sinai Sch of Med, 1993 *Certification:* Gastroenterology
2902 N University Dr, Coral Springs, 954-344-2522

Fishbein, Paul Gerald (4 mentions)
U of Pennsylvania, 1974
Certification: Gastroenterology, Internal Medicine
8950 N Kendall Dr #506, Miami, 305-595-2710

Fishman, Robert Stephen (6 mentions)
Harvard U, 1971
Certification: Gastroenterology, Internal Medicine
951 NW 13th St #2-E, Boca Raton, 561-368-3455
5258 Linton Blvd #202, Delray Beach, 561-499-8227

Garcia, Nelson (4 mentions)
U of Miami, 1996
Certification: Gastroenterology, Internal Medicine
9085 SW 87th Ave #205, Miami, 305-274-5500

Garelick, Jeffrey H. (4 mentions)
Albert Einstein Coll of Med, 1990
2001 N Flagler Dr, West Palm Beach, 561-691-0320
3370 Burns Rd #104, Palm Beach Gardens, 561-691-0320

Garjian, Pamela Lynn (4 mentions)
FMS-Mexico, 1979
Certification: Gastroenterology, Internal Medicine
6910 N Kendall Dr, Miami, 305-669-1115
6910 SW 88th St, Miami, 305-669-1115

Gluck, Charles Arthur (9 mentions)
Washington U, 1978
Certification: Gastroenterology, Internal Medicine
4700 Sheridan St #M, Hollywood, 305-963-0888

Gonzalez-Vallina, Ruben (4 mentions)
FMS-Dominican Republic, 1982
Certification: Pediatric Gastroenterology, Pediatrics
9260 SW 72nd St #217, Miami, 305-271-7330

Gubbins, Guillermo P. (3 mentions)
FMS-Peru, 1984
Certification: Gastroenterology, Internal Medicine
3661 S Miami Ave #1006, Miami, 305-854-2621

Hellman, David Craig (3 mentions)
Nova Southeastern Coll of Osteopathic Med, 1988
10151 Enterprise Center Blvd #103, Boynton Beach,
  561-733-0379

Hernandez, Richard E. (3 mentions)
FMS-Dominica, 1980
Certification: Gastroenterology, Internal Medicine
7765 SW 87th Ave #105, Miami, 305-274-0808

Jacob, Leslie (3 mentions)
FMS-Nigeria, 1985 *Certification:* Gastroenterology
9910 Sandalfoot Blvd #7, Boca Raton, 561-487-4110

Katz, Nicholas Charles (4 mentions)
Wright State U, 1982
Certification: Gastroenterology, Internal Medicine
7475 N University Dr, Tamarac, 954-721-5400

Kaufman, Norman Max (7 mentions)
U of Tennessee, 1972
Certification: Gastroenterology, Internal Medicine
8399 W Oakland Park Blvd #C, Sunrise, 954-747-1161

Litzenblatt, Ira Marvin (3 mentions)
U of Michigan, 1975
Certification: Gastroenterology, Internal Medicine
4701 N Federal Hwy #A10, Fort Lauderdale, 954-351-1100

Llaneza, Pedro P. (8 mentions)
FMS-Chile, 1982
Certification: Gastroenterology, Internal Medicine
9195 SW 72nd St #120, Miami, 305-598-9090

Migicovsky, Barry L. (3 mentions)
FMS-Canada, 1984 *Certification:* Gastroenterology
4700 Sheridan St #M, Hollywood, 954-961-8400

Murphy, Denis Michael (3 mentions)
New York Med Coll, 1970
Certification: Gastroenterology, Internal Medicine
1411 N Flagler Dr #7800, West Palm Beach, 561-832-1643

Neimark, Sidney (8 mentions)
Hahnemann U, 1977
Certification: Gastroenterology, Internal Medicine
1411 N Flagler Dr #3000, West Palm Beach, 561-820-1441

Palmer, Dean Ellis (4 mentions)
FMS-South Africa, 1995
Certification: Gastroenterology, Internal Medicine
1951 SW 172nd Ave #203, Miramar, 954-499-2505

Peicher, Jack (5 mentions)
U of Miami, 1983
Certification: Gastroenterology, Internal Medicine
4701 N Federal Hwy #A10, Fort Lauderdale, 954-351-1100

Railey, Dean James (5 mentions)
U of Miami, 1985
Certification: Gastroenterology, Internal Medicine
8399 W Oakland Park Blvd #C, Sunrise, 954-747-1161

Rams, Hugo, Jr. (8 mentions)
U of Miami, 1981
Certification: Gastroenterology, Internal Medicine
4685 Ponce De Leon Blvd #101, Coral Gables, 305-666-5534

Rosen, Seth David (8 mentions)
U of Maryland, 1986
Certification: Gastroenterology, Internal Medicine
6140 SW 70th St, South Miami, 305-665-7523

Rothman, S. Lawrence (4 mentions)
U of Kansas, 1969
Certification: Gastroenterology, Internal Medicine
7500 SW 87th Ave #200, Miami, 305-913-0666

Sackel, Stephen Gary (7 mentions)
Tufts U, 1979 *Certification:* Gastroenterology, Internal Medicine
5601 N Dixie Hwy #405, Fort Lauderdale, 954-491-3301
660 Glades rD #200, Boca Raton, 561-393-6800

Schonfeld, Wayne Brent (8 mentions)
U of Miami, 1977
Certification: Gastroenterology, Internal Medicine
4700 Sheridan St #M, Hollywood, 954-961-8400

Senzatimore, Salvatore (4 mentions)
New York Med Coll, 1989
Certification: Gastroenterology, Internal Medicine
1117 N Olive #203, West Palm Beach, 561-659-5466

Serrano-Cancino, Hector (3 mentions)
FMS-Mexico, 1972
Certification: Gastroenterology, Internal Medicine
3659 S Miami Ave #5001, Miami, 305-285-0996

Simon, Todd (6 mentions)
Des Moines U, 1990 *Certification:* Gastroenterology
5401 S Congress Ave #211, Lake Worth, 561-964-8221
1397 Medical Park Blvd #100, Wellington, 561-798-1700

Tano, Mario E. (4 mentions)
FMS-Dominican Republic, 1981 *Certification:* Pediatrics
1150 N 35th Ave #545, Hollywood, 954-967-9400

Taub, Sheldon Jeffrey (8 mentions)
Wayne State U, 1974
Certification: Gastroenterology, Internal Medicine
1002 S Old Dixie Hwy #201, Jupiter, 561-744-2200

Veloso, Angel, Jr. (6 mentions)
FMS-Spain, 1975
Certification: Gastroenterology, Internal Medicine
7500 SW 8th St #309, Miami, 305-262-6060

Watson, John Raymond (3 mentions)
Stony Brook U, 1980
Certification: Gastroenterology, Internal Medicine
2500 E Commercial Blvd #C, Fort Lauderdale, 954-771-9920

Weiss, David Scott (9 mentions)
U of South Florida, 1988 *Certification:* Gastroenterology
11011 Sheridan St #109, Cooper City, 954-431-7724
4700 Sheridan St #M, Hollywood, 954-961-8400

Wenger, Jeffrey Stuart (4 mentions)
Robert W Johnson Med Sch, 1987
Certification: Gastroenterology, Internal Medicine
1411 N Flagler Dr #7200, West Palm Beach, 561-802-9050

Zakko, Wisam Fuad (7 mentions)
FMS-Iraq, 1981
Certification: Gastroenterology, Internal Medicine
2021 E Commercial Blvd #202, Fort Lauderdale, 954-202-7850

General Surgery

Bass, Thomas Lynn (5 mentions)
Virginia Commonwealth U, 1991
Certification: Surgery, Surgical Critical Care
1150 N 35th Ave #540, Hollywood, 954-966-8559

Canning, William Michael (9 mentions)
Harvard U, 1984 *Certification:* Surgery
8950 N Kendall Dr #402, Miami, 305-630-9898

Carrasquilla, Carlos (4 mentions)
FMS-Colombia, 1962 *Certification:* Surgery
4900 W Oakland Park Blvd #306, Fort Lauderdale,
  954-739-5531

Casey, Joseph John (3 mentions)
Northwestern U, 1977 *Certification:* Surgery
4725 N Federal Hwy 2nd Fl, Fort Lauderdale, 954-772-6700

Cohen, Brett (5 mentions)
U of Miami, 1997 *Certification:* Surgery
1150 N 35th Ave #540, Hollywood, 954-966-8559

Colletta, Joseph Anthony (7 mentions)
Jefferson Med Coll, 1977 *Certification:* Surgery
670 Glades Rd #300, Boca Raton, 561-395-2626

Corbitt, John Dewey, Jr. (4 mentions)
Emory U, 1964 *Certification:* Surgery
142 John F Kennedy Dr, Lake Worth, 561-439-1500

Derhagopian, Robert Paul (3 mentions)
Tufts U, 1969 *Certification:* Surgery
7000 SW 62nd Ave #B, Miami, 305-662-2466

Edelman, David Steven (9 mentions)
Wake Forest U, 1982 *Certification:* Surgery
8940 N Kendall Dr #804-E, Miami, 305-271-4080

Garcia, Pete (6 mentions)
Wayne State U, 1986 *Certification:* Surgery
2700 SW 3rd Ave #1B, Miami, 305-856-8445

Goff, Steven Grayson (6 mentions)
Indiana U, 1980 *Certification:* Surgery
1397 Medical Park Blvd #100, Wellington, 561-964-2211

Gomez, Eddie (4 mentions)
FMS-Mexico, 1994 *Certification:* Surgery
3661 S Miami Ave #301, Miami, 305-285-5090

Gonzalez, Anthony M. (3 mentions)
U of Miami, 1994 *Certification:* Surgery
7800 SW 87th Ave #210, Miami, 305-271-9777

Grossman, Martin Barry (4 mentions)
Rosalind Franklin U, 1970 *Certification:* Surgery
21097 NE 27th Ct #210, Aventura, 305-936-2565

Herman, Frederick Neil (8 mentions)
U of Miami, 1977 *Certification:* Colon & Rectal Surgery, Surgery
350 NW 84th Ave #311, Plantation, 954-476-9899

Higgins, Daniel R. (10 mentions)
U of Pennsylvania, 1981 *Certification:* Surgery
1201 N Olive Ave, West Palm Beach, 561-655-4334

Hyland, Paul Frederick (3 mentions)
U of Miami, 1986 *Certification:* Surgery
229 George Bush Blvd, Delray Beach, 561-272-1234

Jacobs, Moises (5 mentions)
U of Miami, 1979 *Certification:* Surgery
3361 S Miami Ave #301, Miami, 305-285-5090

Klein, Matthew Allan (3 mentions)
U of Texas-San Antonio, 1977 *Certification:* Surgery
670 Glades Rd #300, Boca Raton, 561-395-2626

Kurtz, David Irwin (3 mentions)
Temple U, 1984 *Certification:* Colon & Rectal Surgery, Surgery
1411 N Flagler Dr #9400, West Palm Beach, 561-659-7702

Levi, Joe Umberto (5 mentions)
U of Florida, 1967 *Certification:* Surgery
1475 NW 12th Ave, Miami, 305-243-4211

Levine, Jonathan Scott (6 mentions)
U of Miami, 1981 *Certification:* Surgery
4801 N Federal Hwy #101, Fort Lauderdale, 954-202-0242

Livingstone, Alan (3 mentions)
FMS-Canada, 1971 *Certification:* Surgery
1475 NW 12th Ave, Miami, 305-243-4902

Long, Julie Ann (3 mentions)
U of Florida, 1979
Certification: Pediatric Surgery, Surgery, Surgical Critical Care
1150 N 35th Ave #555, Hollywood, 954-981-0072

Lopez-Viego, Miguel Angel (4 mentions)
U of Miami, 1986 *Certification:* Surgery, Vascular Surgery
2800 S Seacrest Blvd #200, Boynton Beach, 561-736-8200
1640 S Congress Ave #101, Palm Springs, 561-965-3923

Mallis, Michael John, Jr. (3 mentions)
Philadelphia Coll of Osteopathic Med, 1997
3467 W Hillsboro Blvd #B, Deerfield Beach, 954-574-0252

Moffat, Frederick L., Jr. (4 mentions)
FMS-Canada, 1977 *Certification:* Surgery
1475 NW 12th Ave #3550, Miami, 305-243-4902

Mostafavi, Armaghan Amy (3 mentions)
Boston U, 1991 *Certification:* Surgery, Vascular Surgery
1640 S Congress Ave #101, Lake Worth, 561-965-3923
2800 S Seacrest Blvd #200, Boynton Beach, 561-736-8200

Mueller, George Lester (3 mentions)
Baylor U, 1976 *Certification:* Surgery
2800 S Seacrest Blvd #200, Boynton Beach, 561-732-8200

Pidhorecky, Ihor (4 mentions)
Mount Sinai Sch of Med, 1993 *Certification:* Surgery
601 N Flamingo Rd #211, Pembroke Pines, 954-447-4480
603 N Flamingo Rd #265, Pembroke Pines, 954-450-1617

Porterfield, Lee Alan (3 mentions)
Wayne State U, 1974 *Certification:* Surgery
875 Meadows Rd, Boca Raton, 561-395-3344

Rimmer, John Anthony P. (4 mentions)
FMS-United Kingdom, 1982 *Certification:* Surgery
210 Jupiter Lakes Blvd Bldg 5000 #202, Jupiter, 561-748-1242

Sader, Camil Nabih (4 mentions)
U of Maryland, 1998 *Certification:* Surgery
3467 W Hillsboro Blvd #B, Deerfield Beach, 954-574-0252

Salazar, Juan A. (6 mentions)
U of South Florida, 1980 *Certification:* Surgery
6705 Red Rd #504, Coral Gables, 305-669-7331

Sereda, Dexter Calvin (3 mentions)
U of Miami, 1983 *Certification:* Surgery
601 N Flamingo Rd #207, Pembroke Pines, 954-447-4480

Shachner, Mark Steven (6 mentions)
Yale U, 1985 *Certification:* Surgery
3100 Coral Hills Dr #207, Coral Springs, 954-755-0111

Shapiro, Andrew Justin (4 mentions)
Wright State U, 1997 *Certification:* Surgery
142 John F Kennedy Dr, Lake Worth, 561-439-1500

Shasha, Itzhak Ike (4 mentions)
FMS-Mexico, 1979 *Certification:* Surgery
1201 N Olive Ave, West Palm Beach, 561-655-4334

Sleeman, Danny (3 mentions)
FMS-Canada, 1981 *Certification:* Surgery, Surgical Critical Care
1475 NW 12th Ave, Miami, 305-243-4211

Snow, Jeffrey Paul (3 mentions)
Johns Hopkins U, 1982
Certification: Colon & Rectal Surgery, Surgery
603 N Flamingo Rd #265, Pembroke Pines, 954-450-1617
3157 N University Dr #102, Pembroke Pines, 954-450-1617

Tershakovec, George Roman (5 mentions)
U of Miami, 1980 *Certification:* Surgery
975 Baptist Way #201, Homestead, 305-247-4555

Verdeja, Juan-Carlos (13 mentions)
U of Miami, 1984 *Certification:* Surgery
7800 SW 87th Ave #B210, Miami, 305-271-9777

Weinberger, Jeremy Saul (4 mentions)
Temple U, 1998 *Certification:* Surgery
7800 SW 87th Ave #200, Miami, 305-279-9210

Wideroff, Jonathan I. (9 mentions)
Med Coll of Pennsylvania, 1977 *Certification:* Surgery
670 Glades Rd #300, Boca Raton, 561-395-2626

Willis, Irvin Howard (6 mentions)
U of Cincinnati, 1964 *Certification:* Surgery
4302 Alton Rd #630, Miami Beach, 305-534-6050

Geriatrics

Colburn, Mary Martha (4 mentions)
Michigan State U, 1989 *Certification:* Geriatric Medicine
400 Executive Center Dr #102, West Palm Beach, 561-683-2220

Groene, Linda Ann (4 mentions)
Louisiana State U, 1981
Certification: Geriatric Medicine, Internal Medicine
6405 N Federal Hwy #102-C, Fort Lauderdale, 954-772-0062

Guida, Vincent Francis (3 mentions)
Albany Med Coll, 1972 *Certification:* Internal Medicine
5601 N Dixie Hwy #412, Oakland Park, 954-491-2140

Levine, Felice (7 mentions)
U of South Florida, 1989
Certification: Geriatric Medicine, Internal Medicine
120 John F Kennedy Dr #120, Lake Worth, 561-641-2926

Hematology/Oncology

Adler, Howard Andrew (4 mentions)
New York U, 1988 *Certification:* Hematology, Medical Oncology
1001 NW 13th St #201, Boca Raton, 561-416-8869
6282 Linton Blvd, Delray Beach, 561-495-8307
7593 Boynton Beach Blvd, Boynton Beach, 561-292-5100

Ahr, David J. (4 mentions)
Georgetown U, 1969
Certification: Hematology, Internal Medicine
1309 N Flagler Dr, West Palm Beach, 561-366-4100

Alves, Ney Ricardo Ferraz (6 mentions)
FMS-Brazil, 1989 *Certification:* Hematology, Medical Oncology
3850 Hollywood Blvd #1-B, Hollywood, 954-961-9200

Antunez-De Mayolo, Jorge (3 mentions)
FMS-Peru, 1983
Certification: Hematology, Internal Medicine, Medical Oncology
3659 S Miami Ave #2001, Miami, 305-854-8801

Begas, Albert (6 mentions)
U of Miami, 1982
Certification: Internal Medicine, Medical Oncology
1001 NW 13th St #201, Boca Raton, 561-495-8307
6282 Linton Blvd, Delray Beach, 561-495-8307

Behrmann, Frances A. (4 mentions)
U Central del Caribe, 1993 *Certification:* Medical Oncology
6200 Sunset Dr #601, South Miami, 305-595-2141

Blaustein, Arnold Saul (4 mentions)
U of Maryland, 1966
Certification: Hematology, Internal Medicine, Medical Oncology
4306 Alton Rd, Miami Beach, 305-535-3300
2845 Aventura Blvd #247, Miami, 305-692-5400

Brito, Rogelio Alberto (5 mentions)
Nova Southeastern Coll of Osteopathic Med, 1992
Certification: Medical Oncology
2623 S Seacrest Blvd #216, Boynton Beach, 561-742-0065

Citron, Peter L. (6 mentions)
U of Buffalo, 1970
Certification: Hematology, Internal Medicine
6200 Sunset Dr #601, South Miami, 305-595-2141

Cusnir, Mike (6 mentions)
FMS-Colombia, 1994
Certification: Hematology, Internal Medicine, Medical Oncology
4306 Alton Rd, Miami Beach, 305-535-3310
2845 Aventura Blvd, Aventura, 305-692-5400

Daghistani, Doured (4 mentions)
Certification: Pediatric Hematology-Oncology, Pediatrics
8940 N Kendall Dr #300, Miami, 305-274-1662
1611 NW 12th Ave, Miami, 305-585-7752

Dennis, David K. (4 mentions)
New York U, 1985
Certification: Hematology, Internal Medicine, Medical Oncology
260 SW 84th Ave #C, Plantation, 954-370-8585

Escalon, Enrique Alberto (4 mentions)
FMS-El Salvador, 1969
Certification: Pediatric Hematology-Oncology, Pediatrics
3100 SW 62nd Ave #121, Miami, 305-663-6812

Faig, Douglas Eric (9 mentions)
New York U, 1976 *Certification:* Blood Banking,
  Hematology, Internal Medicine, Medical Oncology
5700 N Federal Hwy #5, Fort Lauderdale, 954-776-1800

Faria, Rohan Francis (3 mentions)
FMS-India, 1993 *Certification:* Hematology, Medical Oncology
7431 N University Dr #110, Tamarac, 954-726-0036

Garcia, Eduardo A. (4 mentions)
U of Miami, 1988
Certification: Hematology, Internal Medicine, Medical Oncology
4685 S Congress Ave #200, Lake Worth, 561-965-1864
2300 S Congress Ave #103, Boynton Beach, 561-732-2440

Garrido, Sara M. (6 mentions)
FMS-Colombia, 1988
Certification: Hematology, Internal Medicine, Medical Oncology
8940 N Kendall Dr #905-E, Miami, 305-595-2141

Gomez, Eduardo Gustavo (3 mentions)
Ohio State U, 1973
Certification: Internal Medicine, Medical Oncology
7100 W 20th Ave #501, Hialeah, 305-556-7416
11760 SW 40th St #741, Miami, 305-556-7416

Green, Robert Jeffrey (7 mentions)
Duke U, 1993 *Certification:* Internal Medicine, Medical Oncology
1309 N Flagler Dr, West Palm Beach, 561-366-4100

Greenhawt, Michael Henry (3 mentions)
Jefferson Med Coll, 1973
Certification: Internal Medicine, Medical Oncology
20950 NE 27th Ct #203, Miami, 305-935-5960
1150 N 35th Ave #330, Hollywood, 954-364-4370
603 N Flamingo Rd #151, Pembroke Pines, 954-435-8300

Guerra, Manuel Luis (4 mentions)
FMS-Mexico, 1983
3659 S Miami Ave #2007, Miami, 305-856-6753

Guida, Carlos Manuel (3 mentions)
FMS-Costa Rica, 1985 *Certification:* Internal Medicine
351 NW 42nd Ave #409, Miami, 305-643-6500

Hanif, Iftikhar (7 mentions)
FMS-Pakistan, 1984
Certification: Pediatric Hematology-Oncology, Pediatrics
1150 N 35th Ave #520, Hollywood, 954-265-2234

Hussein, Atif Mahmoud (3 mentions)
FMS-Lebanon, 1983
Certification: Hematology, Internal Medicine, Medical Oncology
1150 N 35th Ave #170S, Hollywood, 954-986-6363

Jacobson, Robert Julian (3 mentions)
FMS-South Africa, 1966 *Certification:* Hematology
1309 N Flagler Dr, West Palm Beach, 561-366-4100
1395 State Rd 7 #310, Wellington, 561-366-4100

Kalman, Alfred Martin (3 mentions)
SUNY-Downstate Med Coll, 1978
Certification: Hematology, Internal Medicine, Medical Oncology
7431 N University Dr #110, Tamarac, 954-726-0036

Kaywin, Paul Robert (8 mentions)
Boston U, 1973
Certification: Hematology, Internal Medicine, Medical Oncology
8940 N Kendall Dr #300E, Miami, 305-595-2141

Krill, Elisa Anne (4 mentions)
U of Michigan, 1990 *Certification:* Hematology, Medical Oncology
4306 Alton Rd, Miami Beach, 305-535-3300
2845 Aventura Blvd #247, Miami, 305-692-5401

Larcada, Alberto (3 mentions)
U of Puerto Rico, 1982
Certification: Hematology, Internal Medicine, Medical Oncology
6200 Sunset Dr #601, South Miami, 305-595-2141

Lin, Paul Jiu-Yuan (3 mentions)
U of Rochester, 1997
Certification: Hematology, Internal Medicine, Medical Oncology
3918 Via Poinciana #1, Lake Worth, 561-439-4682

Mckeen, Elisabeth Anne (6 mentions)
Albany Med Coll, 1974
Certification: Internal Medicine, Medical Oncology
1309 N Flagler Dr, West Palm Beach, 561-366-4100
3401 PGA Blvd #200, West Palm Beach, 561-366-4151
1395 State Rd 7 #310, Wellington, 561-366-4151

Niederman, Thomas Mj (6 mentions)
Washington U, 1994
Certification: Internal Medicine, Medical Oncology
2623 S Seacrest Blvd #108, Boynton Beach, 561-737-6556

Noy, Jose Julian (3 mentions)
U of Miami, 1972 *Certification:* Internal Medicine
3659 S Miami Ave #2003, Miami, 305-285-0726

Reddy, Samarth L. (5 mentions)
Wayne State U, 1996
Certification: Hematology, Internal Medicine, Medical Oncology
21020 State Rd 7, Boca Raton, 561-482-6611
9970 Central Park Blvd N #304, Boca Raton, 561-482-6611

Reich, Elizabeth Ann (3 mentions)
Med Coll of Pennsylvania, 1968 *Certification:* Internal Medicine
431 University Blvd, Jupiter, 561-748-2488
1025 Military Trail #209, Jupiter, 561-748-2488

Richter, Harold (8 mentions)
SUNY-Upstate Med U, 1982
Certification: Hematology, Internal Medicine, Medical Oncology
6282 Linton Blvd, Delray Beach, 561-495-8307
1001 NW 13th St #201, Boca Raton, 561-416-8869

Rodriguez-Torres, Ramon (3 mentions)
FMS-Cuba, 1951 *Certification:* Pediatric Cardiology, Pediatrics
11760 SW 40th St #741, Miami, 305-229-9919

Rosenfeld, Calvin Stuart (3 mentions)
FMS-Mexico, 1978
Certification: Internal Medicine, Medical Oncology
3700 Washington St #100, Hollywood, 954-983-6305

Roskos, Rudolph Ralph (3 mentions)
U of Wisconsin, 1977
Certification: Pediatric Hematology-Oncology, Pediatrics
1600 S Andrews Ave, Fort Lauderdale, 954-355-4527

Rothschild, Neal Evan (7 mentions)
New Jersey Med Sch, 1981
Certification: Hematology, Internal Medicine, Medical Oncology
1309 N Flagler Dr, West Palm Beach, 561-366-4100
3401 PGA Blvd #340, West Palm Beach, 561-366-4100

Seigel, Leonard Jonathan (6 mentions)
George Washington U, 1975
Certification: Hematology, Internal Medicine, Medical Oncology
4725 N Federal Hwy 2nd Fl, Fort Lauderdale, 954-267-7700

Skelton, Jane D. (5 mentions)
FMS-Canada, 1980
Certification: Internal Medicine, Medical Oncology
1001 NW 13th St #201, Boca Raton, 561-416-8869
6282 Linton Blvd, Delray Beach, 561-495-8307

Spitz, Daniel Lewis (4 mentions)
Med U of South Carolina, 1980
Certification: Hematology, Internal Medicine, Medical Oncology
1309 N Flagler Dr, West Palm Beach, 561-366-4111
1395 State Rd 7 #310, Wellington, 561-366-4111

Thenappan, Arunachalam (4 mentions)
FMS-India, 1983 *Certification:* Hematology, Medical Oncology
4685 S Congress Ave #200, Lake Worth, 561-965-1864
2300 S Congress Ave #103, Boynton Beach, 561-732-2440

Tolnai, Edit (4 mentions)
FMS-Hungary, 1991 *Certification:* Hematology, Medical Oncology
1240 S Old Dixie Hwy 2nd Fl #200, Jupiter, 561-366-4100
1309 N Flagler Dr, West Palm Beach, 561-366-4100

Troner, Michael B. (9 mentions)
SUNY-Downstate Med Coll, 1968
Certification: Internal Medicine, Medical Oncology
8940 N Kendall Dr #300-E, Miami, 305-595-2141

Villa, Luis (4 mentions)
Harvard U, 1970 *Certification:* Anatomic Pathology & Clinical
   Pathology, Hematology, Internal Medicine, Medical Oncology
3659 S Miami Ave #6002, Miami, 305-854-8080

Vogel, Charles Lewis (3 mentions)
Yale U, 1964 *Certification:* Internal Medicine, Medical Oncology
21020 State Rd 7, Boca Raton, 561-883-7600

Wallach, Howard William (3 mentions)
U of Pennsylvania, 1969
Certification: Hematology, Internal Medicine, Medical Oncology
8940 N Kendall Dr #300E, Miami, 305-595-2141

Wang, Grace (21 mentions)
U of Miami, 1976
Certification: Hematology, Internal Medicine, Medical Oncology
8940 N Kendall Dr #300E, Miami, 305-595-2141

Weiss, Steven (5 mentions)
Albert Einstein Coll of Med, 1984
Certification: Internal Medicine, Medical Oncology
8170 Royal Palm Blvd, Coral Springs, 954-974-0400

Wittlin, Frederick Neal (8 mentions)
St Louis U, 1978
Certification: Internal Medicine, Medical Oncology
1150 N 35th Ave #330, Hollywood, 954-364-4370
20950 NE 27th Ct #203, Miami, 305-935-5960
603 N Flamingo Rd #151, Pembroke Pines, 954-435-8300

Xiques, Sergio Jose (3 mentions)
FMS-Dominican Republic, 1982
Certification: Internal Medicine, Medical Oncology
11760 SW 40th St #420, Miami, 305-225-8804
777 E 25th St #411, Hialeah, 305-836-2711

Infectious Disease

Baker, H. Barry (18 mentions)
Tufts U, 1973 *Certification:* Infectious Disease, Internal Medicine
7800 SW 87th Ave #260, Miami, 305-595-4590

Bush, Larry Marc (19 mentions)
Med Coll of Pennsylvania, 1982
Certification: Infectious Disease, Internal Medicine
5503 S Congress Ave #104, Atlantis, 561-967-0101

Carden, George Alexander, III (5 mentions)
Columbia U, 1975
Certification: Infectious Disease, Internal Medicine
1411 N Flagler Dr #7900, West Palm Beach, 561-655-8448

Cardenas, Julio V. (6 mentions)
FMS-Peru, 1975
Certification: Infectious Disease, Internal Medicine
1050 NW 15th St #205, Boca Raton, 561-393-8224
5210 Linton Blvd #202, Delray Beach, 561-496-1095

Chan, Joseph Cho-Leuk (5 mentions)
U of California-San Francisco, 1977
Certification: Infectious Disease, Internal Medicine
4300 Alton Rd #450, Miami, 305-674-2766

Cohen, Carlos A. (5 mentions)
FMS-Argentina, 1983 *Certification:* Infectious Disease
16244 S Military Triangle #750, Delray, 561-381-3443

Dickinson, Gordon M., Jr. (5 mentions)
U of Utah, 1969
Certification: Infectious Disease, Internal Medicine
1475 NW 12th Ave, Miami, 305-243-7618

Droller, David Gabriel (7 mentions)
New York U, 1974
Certification: Infectious Disease, Internal Medicine
1600 S Andrews Ave, Fort Lauderdale, 954-712-6427

Gorensek, Margaret J. (6 mentions)
Case Western Reserve U, 1981 *Certification:* Infectious Disease,
   Internal Medicine, Pediatric Infectious Diseases, Pediatrics
1930 NE 47th ST #104, Fort Lauderdale, 954-493-9752

Heiman, Donald F. (13 mentions)
Rush U, 1980 *Certification:* Infectious Disease, Internal Medicine
5458 Town Center Rd #2, Boca Raton, 561-395-8699

Jacobson, Nathan Arthur (8 mentions)
Jefferson Med Coll, 1975
Certification: Infectious Disease, Internal Medicine
7800 SW 87th Ave #B260, Miami, 305-595-4590

Komaiha, Hamed A. (5 mentions)
FMS-Egypt, 1981
Certification: Infectious Disease, Internal Medicine
2901 Coral Hills Dr #220, Coral Springs, 954-345-0404

Krisko, Istvan (6 mentions)
Baylor U, 1963 *Certification:* Internal Medicine
1515 N Flagler Dr #800, West Palm Beach, 561-655-0506

Laufer, Pablo Marcelo (8 mentions)
Certification: Pediatric Infectious Diseases, Pediatrics
3200 SW 60th Ct #206, Miami, 305-662-8378

Levine, Richard (20 mentions)
Albany Med Coll, 1976
Certification: Infectious Disease, Internal Medicine
7800 SW 87th Ave #B-260, Miami, 305-595-4590

Mbaga, Ines I. (5 mentions)
FMS-Tanzania, 1989
Certification: Infectious Disease, Internal Medicine
1050 NW 15th St, Boca Raton, 561-393-8224
5210 Linton Blvd #202, Delray Beach, 561-496-1095

Murillo, Jorge (6 mentions)
FMS-Venezuela, 1971
Certification: Infectious Disease, Internal Medicine
8700 N Kendall Dr #100, Miami, 305-595-1594

Perez-Morales, Juan Carlos (6 mentions)
FMS-Dominican Republic, 1983 *Certification:* Infectious Disease
8700 N Kendall Dr #100, Miami, 305-595-1594

Perez-Tirse, Jose Angel (4 mentions)
FMS-Chile, 1985 *Certification:* Internal Medicine
11760 SW 40th St #502, Miami, 305-226-8484

Ramirez, Ramon (5 mentions)
San Juan Bautista Sch of Med, 1981
Certification: Internal Medicine
7421 N University Dr #309, Tamarac, 954-721-9494

Ramos, Otto Marino (9 mentions)
FMS-Spain, 1977
Certification: Pediatric Infectious Diseases, Pediatrics
3200 SW 60th Ct #206, Miami, 305-662-8378

Ratzan, Kenneth Roy (6 mentions)
Harvard U, 1965
Certification: Infectious Disease, Internal Medicine
4300 Alton Rd, Miami Beach, 305-673-5490

Reid, Robert (7 mentions)
FMS-Dominican Republic, 1987
Certification: Pediatric Infectious Diseases, Pediatrics
3427 Johnson St, Hollywood, 954-989-5010

Saxe, Susan Elizabeth (4 mentions)
FMS-Grenada, 1987
Certification: Infectious Disease, Internal Medicine
1050 NW 15th St #205, Boca Raton, 561-393-8224
5210 Linton Blvd #202, Delray Beach, 561-496-1095

Sieracki, Lynette (4 mentions)
Kansas U Coll of Osteopathic Med, 1982
Certification: Internal Medicine
4900 W Oakland Park Blvd #203, Fort Lauderdale, 954-733-5991

Sklaver, Allen Robert (6 mentions)
George Washington U, 1972
Certification: Infectious Disease, Internal Medicine
7353 NW 4th St, Plantation, 954-584-9111

Spitzer, Roger Daniel (9 mentions)
U of Miami, 1985
Certification: Infectious Disease, Internal Medicine
4420 Sheridan St #A, Hollywood, 954-962-0040

Suarez, Andres Benavides (6 mentions)
FMS-Peru, 1972
Certification: Infectious Disease, Internal Medicine
11211 Prosperity Farms Rd #B-105, Palm Beach Gardens, 561-626-2914

Uttamchandani, Raj B. (8 mentions)
FMS-Philippines, 1976
Certification: Infectious Disease, Internal Medicine
7000 SW 62nd Ave #320, South Miami, 305-740-6071

Zide, Nelson Robert (14 mentions)
U of Miami, 1966
Certification: Infectious Disease, Internal Medicine
4420 Sheridan St #A, Hollywood, 954-962-0040

Infertility

Barrionuevo, Marcelo J. (4 mentions)
FMS-Argentina, 1987 *Certification:* Obstetrics & Gynecology, Reproductive Endocrinology/Infertility
400 W Hiatus Rd #205, Pembroke Pines, 954-919-0400

Eisermann, Juergen G. (12 mentions)
FMS-Germany, 1980 *Certification:* Obstetrics & Gynecology
7300 SW 62nd Pl, Miami, 305-662-7901
1 SW 129th Ave #205, Pembroke Pines, 954-433-7060

Gelman, Kenneth Mark (5 mentions)
New York Med Coll, 1982
Certification: Endocrinology and Metabolism, Internal Medicine
9900 Stirling Rd #300, Hollywood, 954-432-2228

Hoffman, David Irwin (4 mentions)
Temple U, 1978 *Certification:* Obstetrics & Gynecology, Reproductive Endocrinology/Infertility
3401 PGA Blvd #400, Palm Beach Gardens, 561-775-8717
2960 N State Rd #300, Margate, 954-247-6200

Jacobs, Michael Harris (10 mentions)
Case Western Reserve U, 1979 *Certification:* Obstetrics & Gynecology, Reproductive Endocrinology/Infertility
8950 N Kendall Dr #103, Miami, 305-596-4013

Manko, Gene Fredric (12 mentions)
U of Pennsylvania, 1972 *Certification:* Obstetrics & Gynecology
600 Heritage Dr #200, Jupiter, 561-354-1525

Ory, Steven Jay (4 mentions)
Baylor U, 1976 *Certification:* Obstetrics & Gynecology, Reproductive Endocrinology/Infertility
2960 N State Rd 7 #300, Margate, 954-247-6200

Internal Medicine *(see note on page 9)*

Caruso, Mark Peter (3 mentions)
U of Miami, 1980 *Certification:* Internal Medicine
7101 SW 99th Ave #108, Miami, 305-630-3300

Cava, Robert Charles (4 mentions)
Brown U, 1979 *Certification:* Critical Care Medicine, Geriatric Medicine, Internal Medicine
4950 S Le Jeune Rd #H, Coral Gables, 305-669-0690

Cepero, Rodolfo Joseph (3 mentions)
New York Med Coll, 1986
6201 SW 70th St #103, South Miami, 305-668-6155

Chie-For, Basil Shiew H. (3 mentions)
FMS-South Africa, 1979 *Certification:* Internal Medicine
1001 NW 13th St #101, Boca Raton, 561-995-7800

Fleites, Jorge (4 mentions)
U of Miami, 1993
9220 SW 72nd St #102, Miami, 305-274-6422

Greenstein, Marc H. (3 mentions)
U of Miami, 1990 *Certification:* Internal Medicine
9850 Stirling Rd #103, Hollywood, 954-437-1500

Heron, James Charles (4 mentions)
Med Coll of Wisconsin, 1993 *Certification:* Internal Medicine
5401 S Congress Ave #218, Lake Worth, 561-968-0307

Lysaker, Earl Cedric (3 mentions)
U of Minnesota, 1979 *Certification:* Internal Medicine
1397 Medical Park Blvd #340, Wellington, 561-795-2008

Mitch, Cindy Kay (3 mentions)
FMS-Canada, 1989
9085 SW 87th Ave #201, Miami, 305-270-2229

Mitrani, Alberto Armando (8 mentions)
U of Miami, 1984 *Certification:* Internal Medicine
283 Catalonia Ave #101, Coral Gables, 305-476-7771

Moskowitz, Bruce Warren (4 mentions)
U of Miami, 1974 *Certification:* Internal Medicine
1411 N Flagler Dr #9300, West Palm Beach, 561-833-6116

Nochimson, Ross David (3 mentions)
New York Med Coll, 1977 *Certification:* Internal Medicine
4994 N University Dr, Lauderhill, 954-748-9300

O'Connor, Gerald James (4 mentions)
U of Illinois, 1973 *Certification:* Internal Medicine, Nephrology
1411 N Flagler Dr #4600, West Palm Beach, 561-659-4004

Rubin, John F. (3 mentions)
U of Maryland, 1986 *Certification:* Internal Medicine
660 Glades Rd #110, Boca Raton, 561-391-7575

Saitowitz, Alan Michael (4 mentions)
FMS-South Africa, 1991 *Certification:* Internal Medicine
3467 W Hillsboro Blvd #A, Deerfield Beach, 954-420-0886

Schlein, Andrew Evan (6 mentions)
New York U, 1987 *Certification:* Internal Medicine
6056 Boynton Beach Blvd #145, Boynton Beach, 561-737-9227

Simons, William Morris (3 mentions)
Hahnemann U, 1975 *Certification:* Internal Medicine
5401 S Congress Ave #218, Lake Worth, 561-968-0307

Singer, Caren Bebchuck (3 mentions)
U of South Florida, 1980 *Certification:* Internal Medicine
255 SE 14th St #1B, Fort Lauderdale, 954-467-8222

Sklaver, Allen Robert (5 mentions)
George Washington U, 1972
Certification: Infectious Disease, Internal Medicine
7353 NW 4th St, Plantation, 954-584-9111

Stern, David J. (3 mentions)
Philadelphia Coll of Osteopathic Med, 1979
4601 Congress Ave, West Palm Beach, 561-840-4699
4601 N Congress Ave, West Palm Beach, 561-840-4699

Stone, Charles B. (3 mentions)
U of Miami, 1995 *Certification:* Internal Medicine
3700 Washington St #305, Hollywood, 954-981-7070

Wacks, Robert Alan (5 mentions)
FMS-Italy, 1978
1501 Presidential Way #1, West Palm Beach, 561-844-8899

Wasserman, Bryan Jay (4 mentions)
SUNY-Downstate Med Coll, 1979 *Certification:* Internal Medicine
5258 Linton Blvd #305, Delray Beach, 561-496-4000

Wellen, Marvin (4 mentions)
FMS-Mexico, 1973
17971 Biscayne Blvd #208, Aventura, 305-931-0555

Yesner, Alan Jay (3 mentions)
U of Miami, 1976 *Certification:* Internal Medicine
4800 NE 20th Ter #101, Fort Lauderdale, 954-493-8666
4801 N Federal Hwy #102, Fort Lauderdale, 954-493-8666

Young, Perri Elizabeth (7 mentions)
U of Miami, 1999 *Certification:* Internal Medicine
6200 Sunset Dr #501, South Miami, 305-663-0609

Nephrology

Almeida, Mario A. (13 mentions)
FMS-Dominican Republic, 1983
1150 Campo Sano Ave #401, Coral Gables, 305-669-3360

Amrose, David Scott (6 mentions)
George Washington U, 1994
Certification: Internal Medicine, Nephrology
1411 N Flagler Dr #4700, West Palm Beach, 561-833-7600

Arrascue, Jose F. (9 mentions)
FMS-Peru, 1973 *Certification:* Critical Care Medicine, Internal Medicine, Nephrology
5503 S Congress Ave #103, Atlantis, 561-965-7228
3925 W Boynton Beach Blvd #110, Boynton Beach, 561-752-9636

Bailin, Joshua Jay (16 mentions)
Emory U, 1980 *Certification:* Internal Medicine, Nephrology
5503 S Congress Ave #103, Lantana, 561-965-7228

Barreto, Gaspar Alejandro (5 mentions)
FMS-Cuba, 1986 *Certification:* Internal Medicine, Nephrology
9193 SW 72nd St #200, Miami, 305-273-9377

Bejar, Carlos (8 mentions)
FMS-Dominican Republic, 1987
Certification: Internal Medicine, Nephrology
2001 NE 48th St #4, Fort Lauderdale, 954-771-3929
300 NW 70th #302, Plantation, 954-771-3929

Busse, Jorge Carlos (13 mentions)
FMS-Dominican Republic, 1981
Certification: Internal Medicine, Nephrology
9193 SW 72nd St #200, Miami, 305-273-9377

Esquenazi, Marcos B. (5 mentions)
Wayne State U, 1993 *Certification:* Nephrology
7900 SW 57th Ave #21, South Miami, 305-662-3984
99 Campbell Dr, Homestead, 305-662-3984

Feinroth, Martin (8 mentions)
FMS-Ireland, 1975 *Certification:* Internal Medicine, Nephrology
1150 N 35th Ave #660, Hollywood, 954-989-9553

Garcia Mayol, Luis (5 mentions)
FMS-Spain, 1975 *Certification:* Internal Medicine
747 Ponce De Leon Blvd #605, Coral Gables, 305-445-4535

Geronemus, Robert Perry (9 mentions)
Albert Einstein Coll of Med, 1974
Certification: Internal Medicine, Nephrology
2951 NW 49th Ave #101, Fort Lauderdale, 954-739-2511

Hoffman, David Samuel (9 mentions)
U of Tennessee, 1971
Certification: Internal Medicine, Nephrology
7900 S Red Rd #21, South Miami, 305-662-3984
99 NE 8th St, Homestead, 305-662-3984
7900 SW 57th Ave #21, South Miami, 305-662-3984

Lazar, Ira L. (7 mentions)
FMS-Mexico, 1976 *Certification:* Internal Medicine, Nephrology
1905 Clint Moore Rd #212, Boca Raton, 561-989-9070
6268 N Federal Hwy, Fort Lauderdale, 954-771-0860

Mullen, James Peter (6 mentions)
U of Miami, 1979 *Certification:* Internal Medicine, Nephrology
4425 Military Trail #212, Jupiter, 561-833-7600
1411 N Flagler Dr #4700, West Palm beach, 561-833-7600

Panos, John (9 mentions)
U of Buffalo, 1997 *Certification:* Internal Medicine, Nephrology
1905 Clint Moore Rd #212, Boca Raton, 954-771-0860

Pellegrini, Edgardo Luis (8 mentions)
FMS-Argentina, 1969
Certification: Internal Medicine, Nephrology
9193 SW 72nd St #200, Miami, 305-273-9377

Ramirez, Felix Ignacio (6 mentions)
FMS-Spain, 1977 *Certification:* Pediatric Nephrology, Pediatrics
3200 SW 60th Ct #304, Miami, 305-662-8352
6125 SW 31st St, Miami, 305-662-8352
1000 Joe Dimaggio Dr, Hollywood, 954-987-2000

Scott, David Adam (6 mentions)
U of Pennsylvania, 1991
Certification: Internal Medicine, Nephrology
5210 Linton Blvd #105, Delray Beach, 561-496-1160

Stemmer, Craig Lawrence (4 mentions)
Med Coll of Wisconsin, 1981
Certification: Internal Medicine, Nephrology
2900 N Military Trail #195, Boca Raton, 561-241-6667

Valle, Gabriel Alonso (13 mentions)
FMS-Peru, 1981 *Certification:* Critical Care Medicine,
  Geriatric Medicine, Internal Medicine, Nephrology
2001 NE 48th Ct #4, Fort Lauderdale, 954-771-3929
300 NW 70th Ave #302, Plantation, 954-771-3929

Vangelder, James Peter (9 mentions)
U of Cincinnati, 1968
Certification: Internal Medicine, Nephrology
3700 Washington St #500, Hollywood, 954-962-0338

Waterman, Jack (11 mentions)
Philadelphia Coll of Osteopathic Med, 1981
2543 Burns Rd, Palm Beach Gardens, 561-627-6454

Neurological Surgery

Gieseke, F. Gary (11 mentions)
1930 NE 47th St #200, Fort Lauderdale, 954-771-4251

Gonzalez-Arias, Sergio M. (16 mentions)
FMS-Spain, 1976 *Certification:* Neurological Surgery
8940 N Kendall Dr #707-E, Miami, 305-271-6159

Grabel, Jordan Carel (8 mentions)
Brown U, 1985 *Certification:* Neurological Surgery
1411 N Flagler Dr #5900, West Palm Beach, 561-833-6388

Green, Barth Armand (12 mentions)
Indiana U, 1969 *Certification:* Neurological Surgery
1095 NW 14th Ter, Miami, 305-243-6946
1475 NW 12th Ave, Miami, 305-243-6946

Heros, Roberto Cosme (9 mentions)
U of Tennessee, 1968 *Certification:* Neurological Surgery
1095 NW 14th Ter, Miami, 305-243-6672

Joy, Jose L. (10 mentions)
U Central del Caribe, 1985 *Certification:* Neurological Surgery
8950 N Kendall Dr #406, Miami, 305-225-1777

Moore, Matthew Raymond (8 mentions)
Yale U, 1986 *Certification:* Neurological Surgery
1930 NE 47th St #200, Fort Lauderdale, 954-771-4251
7171 N University Dr #200, Fort Lauderdale, 954-771-4251

Pasarin, Guillermo A. (7 mentions)
U of Miami, 1986 *Certification:* Neurological Surgery
350 NW 84th Ave #108, Plantation, 954-475-9244
50 E Sample Rd #201, Pompano Beach, 954-781-3545

Rodriguez, Luis A. (10 mentions)
FMS-Colombia, 1976 *Certification:* Neurological Surgery
1150 N 35th Ave #300, Hollywood, 954-985-1490

Traina, Joseph Anthony (14 mentions)
U of Miami, 1977 *Certification:* Neurological Surgery
6200 Sunset Dr #403, South Miami, 305-670-7823

Zorman, Greg (20 mentions)
Cornell U, 1977 *Certification:* Neurological Surgery
1150 N 35th Ave #300, Hollywood, 954-985-1490

Zucker, Lloyd (8 mentions)
Robert W Johnson Med Sch, 1982
Certification: Neurological Surgery
5130 Linton Blvd #E-3, Delray Beach, 561-499-5633
670 Glades Rd #100, Boca Raton, 561-499-5633

Neurology

Albornoz, John L. (3 mentions)
Georgetown U, 1986
3659 S Miami Ave #6003, Miami, 305-857-9996

Alfonso, Israel (3 mentions)
FMS-Spain, 1975
Certification: Clinical Neurophysiology, Neurology with
  Special Qualifications in Child Neurology, Pediatrics
3200 SW 60th Ct #302, Miami, 305-662-8330

Aptman, Michael (4 mentions)
U of Pittsburgh, 1971 *Certification:* Neurology
8940 N Kendall Dr #802E, Miami, 305-595-4041

Boltz, Frederick Joseph (14 mentions)
FMS-Grenada, 1982 *Certification:* Internal Medicine, Neurology
1601 Clint Moore Rd #120, Boca Raton, 561-392-6446

Brown, Stuart Barry (3 mentions)
Jefferson Med Coll, 1959 *Certification:* Neurology,
  Neurology with Special Qualifications in Child Neurology
4440 Sheridan St, Hollywood, 954-961-2423

Chamely, Abraham Anthony (12 mentions)
FMS-Jamaica, 1978 *Certification:* Neurology
7225 N University Dr #102, Tamarac, 954-484-2270

Dickens, Willis Norman (3 mentions)
U of Illinois, 1957 *Certification:* Neurology
1625 SE 3rd Ave #620, Fort Lauderdale, 954-524-6527

Dokson, Joel Steven (4 mentions)
U of Miami, 1967 *Certification:* Neurology
4925 Sheridan St #200, Hollywood, 954-981-3850

Feinberg, Marc Howard (6 mentions)
SUNY-Downstate Med Coll, 1991 *Certification:* Neurology
1601 Clint Moore Rd #120, Boca Raton, 561-392-6446

Ginsberg, Paul Lawrence (4 mentions)
U of Pennsylvania, 1971 *Certification:* Neurology
4925 Sheridan St #200, Hollywood, 954-981-3850

Goldenberg, James Nathan (5 mentions)
U of South Florida, 1989 *Certification:* Neurology
140 John F Kennedy Dr, Lake Worth, 561-968-6767

Goldstein, Mark A. (5 mentions)
Emory U, 1977 *Certification:* Internal Medicine, Neurology
140 John F Kennedy Dr, Atlantis, 561-968-6767

Grant, Timothy Lawrence (3 mentions)
U of Miami, 1976 *Certification:* Neurology
6141 Sunset Dr #301, Miami, 305-665-5552
9090 NW 87 Court #101, Miami, 305-274-1500

Hammond, Thomas Craig (9 mentions)
New York U, 1975 *Certification:* Internal Medicine, Neurology
1841 NE 45th St, Fort Lauderdale, 954-776-5010
50 E Sample Rd #200, Pompano Beach, 954-942-3991

Harris, Jonathan Oren (3 mentions)
U of Pennsylvania, 1982
Certification: Internal Medicine, Neurology
1841 NE 45th St, Fort Lauderdale, 954-776-5010
50 E Sample Rd #200, Pompano Beach, 954-942-3991

Herskowitz, Allan (7 mentions)
U of Miami, 1967 *Certification:* Neurology
9090 SW 87th Ct #200, Miami, 305-596-2080

Herskowitz, Brad J. (7 mentions)
U of Miami, 1996 *Certification:* Neurology
9090 SW 87th Ct #200, Miami, 305-596-2080

Hoche, Jubran A. (5 mentions)
Certification: Neurology
3800 Johnson St #E, Hollywood, 954-983-5631

Kobetz, Steven Allen (4 mentions)
U of Miami, 1975 *Certification:* Neurology
8940 N Kendall Dr #802-E, Miami, 305-595-4041

Kreger, Howard Lawrence (3 mentions)
U of Miami, 1994 *Certification:* Neurology
4300 Alton Rd, Miami Beach, 305-532-2464

Lesser, Martin Allan (7 mentions)
Case Western Reserve U, 1977
Certification: Neurology, Vascular Neurology
7225 N University Dr #102, Tamarac, 954-484-2270
3540 N Pine Island Rd, Sunrise, 954-484-2270

Lopez, Javier Edgardo (3 mentions)
U of Puerto Rico, 1998 *Certification:* Neurology
6200 Sunset Dr #305, South Miami, 305-665-6501

Lopez, Raul Ignacio (10 mentions)
U of Florida, 1963 *Certification:* Neurology
3661 S Miami Ave #209, Miami, 305-856-8942

Maniar, Mayur Chandulal (3 mentions)
FMS-India, 1980 *Certification:* Neurology
3540 Pine Island Rd, Sunrise, 954-475-4811

Norona, Fernando (3 mentions)
New York Med Coll, 1991 *Certification:* Neurology
880 NW 13th St #3B, Boca Raton, 561-394-0005

Pao, Linda M. (8 mentions)
Brown U, 1991 *Certification:* Neurology
601 University Blvd #102, Jupiter, 561-748-2297

Racher, David Andrew (6 mentions)
Rush U, 1978 *Certification:* Internal Medicine, Neurology
8940 N Kendall Dr #802-E, Miami, 305-595-4041

Ramirez-Mejia, Carlos A. (3 mentions)
FMS-Colombia, 1985 *Certification:* Neurology
8940 N Kendall Dr #802E, Miami, 305-595-4041

Sadowsky, Carl Howard (5 mentions)
Cornell U, 1971 *Certification:* Neurology
4631 N Congress Ave #200, West Palm Beach, 561-845-0500

Schwartz, Harvey David (8 mentions)
U of Florida, 1973 *Certification:* Neurology
4925 Sheridan St #200, Hollywood, 954-981-3850

Schwartzbard, Julie Beth (4 mentions)
U of Miami, 1993
21000 NE 28th Ave #205, Miami, 305-933-5993

Stafford, James Mark (7 mentions)
Nova Southeastern Coll of Osteopathic Med, 1986
Certification: Neurology
601 University Blvd, Jupiter, 561-748-2297

Swerdloff, Marc Arthur (4 mentions)
Albany Med Coll, 1982 *Certification:* Neurology
50 E Sample Rd #200, Pompano Beach, 954-942-3991

Teman, Allen J. (3 mentions)
Albany Med Coll, 1986 *Certification:* Neurology
9750 NW 33rd St #207, Coral Springs, 954-346-0500

Wheeler, Steve Dereal (3 mentions)
Dartmouth Coll, 1976 *Certification:* Neurology
5975 Sunset Dr #501, South Miami, 305-595-4041

Zaret, Bruce Stephen (4 mentions)
Jefferson Med Coll, 1974
Certification: Internal Medicine, Neurology
3540 N Pine Island Rd, Sunrise, 954-321-1776

Zuniga, Jose Antonio (5 mentions)
FMS-Peru, 1971 *Certification:* Neurology
4631 N Congress Ave #200, West Palm Beach, 561-845-0500

Obstetrics/Gynecology

Abreu, Jose Jesus (3 mentions)
Jefferson Med Coll, 1988 *Certification:* Obstetrics & Gynecology
7150 W 20th Ave #202, Hialeah, 305-822-8229

Alvarez-Perez, Fernando Julio (4 mentions)
FMS-Spain, 1976
3661 S Miami Ave #106, Miami, 305-854-9966

Baer, Kenneth Allen (3 mentions)
Jefferson Med Coll, 1964 *Certification:* Obstetrics & Gynecology
7330 SW 62nd Pl #330, South Miami, 305-665-1133
7300 SW 62nd Pl 3rd Fl, South Miami, 305-665-1133

Beil, Susan Joy (5 mentions)
Stony Brook U, 1984 *Certification:* Obstetrics & Gynecology
6853 SW 18th St #301, Boca Raton, 561-368-3775
5000 W Boynton Beach Blvd #200, Boynton Beach,
   561-734-5710

Bernick, Brian Anthony (5 mentions)
Rosalind Franklin U, 1995 *Certification:* Obstetrics & Gynecology
1050 NW 15th St #215-A, Boca Raton, 561-392-7704

Bone, Melanie Kaye (4 mentions)
Albany Med Coll, 1985 *Certification:* Obstetrics & Gynecology
550 S Quadrille Blvd #201, West Palm Beach, 561-832-1970

Burigo, John Andrew (3 mentions)
New York Med Coll, 1975 *Certification:* Obstetrics & Gynecology
1515 N Flagler Dr #700, West Palm Beach, 561-655-3331
3401 PGA Blvd #320, Palm Beach Gardens, 561-627-6801

De La Torre, Armando O. (4 mentions)
FMS-Spain, 1977
7200 NW 7th St #150, Miami, 305-264-6270
777 E 25th St #209, Hialeah, 305-691-2311
3900 NW 79th Ave #225, Miami, 305-597-0089

Elkin, Aaron (3 mentions)
U of Miami, 1991 *Certification:* Obstetrics & Gynecology
1130 E Hallandale Beach Blvd #A, Hallandale Beach,
   954-458-0909

Feldman, Robert Allen (4 mentions)
U of Miami, 1984 *Certification:* Obstetrics & Gynecology
6141 Sunset Dr #401, South Miami, 305-667-4511

Gates, E. Jason (3 mentions)
U of South Florida, 1991
Certification: Gynecologic Oncology, Obstetrics & Gynecology
6405 N Federal Hwy #402, Fort Lauderdale, 954-771-8888

Greenspan, Carrie (4 mentions)
Northwestern U, 1982 *Certification:* Obstetrics & Gynecology
7451 Wiles Rd #106, Coral Springs, 954-345-1117

Hirschberg, Karen Robin (3 mentions)
U of Florida, 1983 *Certification:* Obstetrics & Gynecology
1150 N 35th Ave #400, Hollywood, 954-963-6363
601 N Flamingo Rd #205, Pembroke Pines, 954-431-1211

James, Geoffrey Nigel (4 mentions)
Meharry Med Coll, 1971 *Certification:* Obstetrics & Gynecology
7800 SW 87th Ave #120, Miami, 305-412-6004

James, Jason Seth (5 mentions)
U of Miami, 1999 *Certification:* Obstetrics & Gynecology
7800 SW 87th Ave #120, Miami, 305-412-6004

Kalstone, Charles Edward (4 mentions)
U of Michigan, 1964 *Certification:* Obstetrics & Gynecology
6141 Sunset Dr #401, South Miami, 305-667-4511

Kaufman, Samuel (3 mentions)
Temple U, 1982 *Certification:* Obstetrics & Gynecology
6853 SW 18th St #301, Boca Raton, 561-368-3775
5000 W Boynton Beach Blvd #200, Boynton Beach,
   561-734-5710

Kellogg, Spencer Fay (5 mentions)
U of Miami, 1976 *Certification:* Obstetrics & Gynecology
8950 N Kendall Dr #302, Miami, 305-595-4070
91200 Overseas Hwy #17, Tavernier, 305-595-4070

Knowlton, Sarah (4 mentions)
U of Tennessee, 1990 *Certification:* Obstetrics & Gynecology
1395 S State Rd 7 #450, Wellington, 561-798-1233

Lichtinger, Moises W. (4 mentions)
FMS-Mexico, 1976 *Certification:* Obstetrics & Gynecology
4701 N Federal Hwy Bldg B, Fort Lauderdale, 954-229-6000
1625 SE 3rd Ave, Fort Lauderdale, 954-467-1210

Litt, Jeffrey Mark (6 mentions)
Temple U, 1981 *Certification:* Obstetrics & Gynecology
600 Heritage Dr #210, Jupiter, 561-354-1515

Lopez-Beecham, Maria Victoria (4 mentions)
U of Florida, 1990 *Certification:* Obstetrics & Gynecology
9595 N Kendall Dr #103, Miami, 305-279-8222

Marimon, Tomas Ignacio (3 mentions)
FMS-Dominican Republic, 1980
Certification: Obstetrics & Gynecology
11760 SW 40th St #518, Miami, 305-553-2888

Miller, Joyce R. (3 mentions)
Med Coll of Wisconsin, 1988
Certification: Obstetrics & Gynecology
7000 SW 62nd Ave #350, South Miami, 305-665-9644

Morad, Manuel J. (3 mentions)
U of Miami, 1986
8940 N Kendall Dr #804-E, Miami, 305-445-2873

Newman, Stewart Paul (3 mentions)
U of South Florida, 1984 *Certification:* Obstetrics & Gynecology
6853 SW 18th St #301, Boca Raton, 561-368-3775
5000 W Boynton Beach Blvd #200, Boynton Beach,
   561-734-5710

Penalver, Manuel Angel (3 mentions)
U of Miami, 1977
Certification: Gynecologic Oncology, Obstetrics & Gynecology
5000 University Dr, Miami, 305-663-7001
7100 W 20th Ave, Hialeah, 305-828-8688

Phillips, Edward Francis (3 mentions)
Albany Med Coll, 1977 *Certification:* Obstetrics & Gynecology
7000 SW 62nd Ave #350, South Miami, 305-665-9644

Rodriguez, Frank (3 mentions)
SUNY-Upstate Med U, 1986 *Certification:* Obstetrics & Gynecology
560 Village Blvd #200, West Palm Beach, 561-686-3666

Rudolph, Jane E. (3 mentions)
Rosalind Franklin U, 1990 *Certification:* Obstetrics & Gynecology
6853 SW 18th St #301, Boca Raton, 561-368-3775
5000 W Boynton Beach Blvd #200, Boynton Beach,
   561-734-5710

Salkind, Glenn Lawrence (3 mentions)
Rosalind Franklin U, 1971 *Certification:* Obstetrics & Gynecology
8950 N Kendall Dr #507, Miami, 305-279-3773

Sherman, Peter Andrew (3 mentions)
U of Miami, 1969 *Certification:* Obstetrics & Gynecology
1515 N Flagler Dr #700, West Palm Beach, 561-655-3331
3401 PGA Blvd #320, Palm Beach Gardens, 561-627-6801

Tudela, Francisco G. (4 mentions)
FMS-Spain, 1976 *Certification:* Obstetrics & Gynecology
777 E 25th St #106, Hialeah, 305-691-1171

Villa, Letty (6 mentions)
Boston U, 1980
6705 SW 57th Ave #420, Coral Gables, 305-667-8418

Vizoso, Javier (4 mentions)
Yale U, 1985 *Certification:* Obstetrics & Gynecology
7300 SW 62nd Pl 3rd Fl, South Miami, 305-665-1133

Yasin, Salih Yunis (4 mentions)
FMS-Jordan, 1980
1150 NW 14th St, Miami, 305-243-5175

Zann, Geoffrey Joseph (3 mentions)
New York Med Coll, 1982 *Certification:* Obstetrics & Gynecology
660 Glades Rd #240, Boca Raton, 561-368-2005

Ophthalmology

Alfonso, Eduardo (8 mentions)
Yale U, 1980 *Certification:* Ophthalmology
900 NW 17th St, Miami, 305-326-6303

Aran, Alberto J. (6 mentions)
Tulane U, 1981 *Certification:* Ophthalmology
1097 S Le Jeune Rd, Miami, 305-461-1300

Bizer, Wayne F. (3 mentions)
Midwestern U Chicago Coll of Osteopathic Med, 1972
7800 W Oakland Park Blvd #206, Sunrise, 954-749-8000

Buznego, Carlos (11 mentions)
Washington U, 1987 *Certification:* Ophthalmology
8940 N Kendall Dr #400E, Miami, 305-598-2020

Daubert, Jack Steven (6 mentions)
Certification: Ophthalmology
1050 Monterey Rd #104, Stuart, 772-283-2020
1515 N Flagler Dr #500, West Palm Beach, 561-659-9700

Dorfman, Mark S. (3 mentions)
Albany Med Coll, 1989 *Certification:* Ophthalmology
2740 Hollywood Blvd, Hollywood, 954-925-2740
603 N Flamingo Rd #250, Pembroke Pines, 954-431-2777

Duffner, Lee Roy (3 mentions)
Med Coll of Wisconsin, 1962 *Certification:* Ophthalmology
2740 Hollywood Blvd, Hollywood, 954-925-2740
603 N Flamingo Rd #250, Pembroke Pines, 954-431-2777

Eisner, Eugene Mark (4 mentions)
U of Michigan, 1967 *Certification:* Ophthalmology
8940 N Kendall Dr #400E, Miami, 305-598-2020

Epstein, Gil Alan (3 mentions)
Tufts U, 1975 *Certification:* Ophthalmology
7800 W Oakland Park Blvd #206, Sunrise, 954-741-5555

Flynn, Harry Weisiger, Jr. (3 mentions)
U of Virginia, 1971 *Certification:* Ophthalmology
900 NW 17th St, Miami, 305-326-6118

Haft, Brian Ira (4 mentions)
U of Florida, 1984 *Certification:* Ophthalmology
11406 Okeechobee Blvd, Royal Palm Beach, 561-798-2020

Hopen, Gary Robert (5 mentions)
Jefferson Med Coll, 1977 *Certification:* Ophthalmology
3419 Johnson St, Hollywood, 954-989-2800

Katzen, Lawrence B. (4 mentions)
U of Miami, 1974 *Certification:* Ophthalmology
901 N Congress Ave #104, Boynton Beach, 561-732-8005
1601 Forum Pl #101, West Palm Beach, 561-688-1204

Kay, Matthew Dean (3 mentions)
Temple U, 1987 *Certification:* Ophthalmology
9980 Central Park Blvd N #126, Boca Raton, 561-487-6600
2925 Aventura Blvd #102, Aventura, 305-931-2673
2000 Palm Lake Blvd, West Palm Beach, 561-478-2015

Kohn, Alan N. (3 mentions)
Washington U, 1973 *Certification:* Ophthalmology
2505 Metrocentre Blvd #300, West Palm Beach, 561-478-2003

Kronish, Jan Warren (3 mentions)
Harvard U, 1983 *Certification:* Ophthalmology
16201 Military Trail, Delray Beach, 561-498-8100

Litinsky, Steven Malcolm (3 mentions)
Albany Med Coll, 1970 *Certification:* Ophthalmology
16201 S Military Trail, Delray Beach, 561-734-0267

Lopez, Pedro F. (7 mentions)
U of Miami, 1986 *Certification:* Ophthalmology
8940 N Kendall Dr #400-E, Miami, 305-598-2020

Lores, Edward Frank (4 mentions)
Emory U, 1970 *Certification:* Ophthalmology
4950 S Le Jeune Rd #D, Coral Gables, 305-667-1666

Mendelsohn, Alan David (4 mentions)
Northwestern U, 1982 *Certification:* Ophthalmology
4651 Sheridan St #100, Hollywood, 954-894-1500

Miller, Bruce Alan (4 mentions)
U of Miami, 1988 *Certification:* Ophthalmology
220 SW 84th Ave #204, Plantation, 954-424-5959

Murray, Timothy Garrett (3 mentions)
Johns Hopkins U, 1985 *Certification:* Ophthalmology
900 NW 17th St, Miami, 305-326-6166

Neely, Iley Coleman (5 mentions)
U of Mississippi, 1986 *Certification:* Ophthalmology
5601 N Dixie Hwy #115, Oakland Park, 954-771-4271

Perlman, Jeffrey Mark (3 mentions)
New York Med Coll, 1988 *Certification:* Ophthalmology
950 NW 13th St, Boca Raton, 561-391-8300

Rosenfeld, Steven Ira (3 mentions)
Yale U, 1980 *Certification:* Ophthalmology
16201 S Military Trail, Delray Beach, 561-498-8100

Sandberg, Joel Sheldon (4 mentions)
Johns Hopkins U, 1967 *Certification:* Ophthalmology
2740 Hollywood Blvd, Hollywood, 954-925-2740

Schechter, Barry Alan (3 mentions)
SUNY-Downstate Med Coll, 1988 *Certification:* Ophthalmology
1717 W Woolbright Rd, Boynton Beach, 561-737-5500

Shuster, Alan Roger (7 mentions)
U of Miami, 1986 *Certification:* Ophthalmology
2055 Military Trail #307, Jupiter, 561-744-9667

Simon, David Richard (3 mentions)
U of Miami, 1971 *Certification:* Ophthalmology
201 N University Dr #106, Plantation, 954-472-2007

Skolnick, Keith Andrew (5 mentions)
U of South Florida, 1996 *Certification:* Ophthalmology
7800 W Oakland Park Blvd #206, Sunrise, 954-749-8000

Spektor, Frank Edwin (4 mentions)
FMS-South Africa, 1973 *Certification:* Ophthalmology
8940 N Kendall Dr #400E, Miami, 305-598-2020

Trattler, Henry Leonard (8 mentions)
U of Maryland, 1966 *Certification:* Ophthalmology
8940 N Kendall Dr #400E, Miami, 305-598-2020

Trattler, William Bennett (7 mentions)
U of Miami, 1992 *Certification:* Ophthalmology
8940 N Kendall Dr #400E, Miami, 305-598-2020

Warman, Roberto (6 mentions)
FMS-Mexico, 1980 *Certification:* Ophthalmology
3100 SW 62nd Ave #103, Miami, 305-662-8390

Wolfe, Russell Masaru (4 mentions)
New Jersey Med Sch, 1985 *Certification:* Ophthalmology
3419 Johnson St, Hollywood, 954-989-2800

Orthopedics

Barrios, Ivan Jesus (4 mentions)
FMS-Spain, 1964 *Certification:* Orthopaedic Surgery
592 SW 27th Ave, Miami, 305-441-0591

Blythe, Stephen Earl (4 mentions)
Indiana U, 1970 *Certification:* Orthopaedic Surgery
4950 S Le Jeune Rd #G, Coral Gables, 305-667-0660

Bromson, Mark Steven (3 mentions)
U of Pennsylvania, 1987 *Certification:* Orthopaedic Surgery
660 Glades Rd #460, Boca Raton, 561-391-5515

Chalal, Joseph Brad (3 mentions)
U of Pennsylvania, 1982 *Certification:* Orthopaedic Surgery
7593 Boynton Beach Blvd #280, Boynton Beach, 561-733-5888

Cook, Frank Forshee (11 mentions)
U of Florida, 1980 *Certification:* Orthopaedic Surgery
2055 Military Trail #200, Jupiter, 561-694-7776
3401 Pga Blvd #500, West Palm Beach, 561-694-7776

Cooney, Michael (6 mentions)
Emory U, 1981 *Certification:* Orthopaedic Surgery
3401 Pga Blvd #500, West Palm Beach, 561-694-7776

Cooper, Jack Sewell (4 mentions)
U of Virginia, 1965 *Certification:* Orthopaedic Surgery
1150 Campo Sano Ave #301, Coral Gables, 305-666-3310

Eismont, Frank Joseph (4 mentions)
U of Rochester, 1973 *Certification:* Orthopaedic Surgery
1475 NW 12th Ave, Miami, 305-585-7138
1611 NW 12th Ave, Miami, 305-585-7138

Fernandez, Joseph I. (13 mentions)
Tulane U, 1988 *Certification:* Orthopaedic Surgery
8940 SW 88th St #101E, Miami, 305-275-5677
8940 N Kendall Dr #101E, Miami, 305-275-5677
9135 SW 87th Ave, Miami, 305-279-2335

Gerard, Fredric Michael (6 mentions)
SUNY-Downstate Med Coll, 1972
Certification: Orthopaedic Surgery
7225 N University Dr #202, Tamarac, 954-739-9700

Hammerman, Marc Z. (6 mentions)
Georgetown U, 1976 *Certification:* Orthopaedic Surgery
4310 Sheridan St, Hollywood, 954-989-3500

Hechtman, Keith Sheldon (4 mentions)
U of Miami, 1983
Certification: Orthopaedic Sports Medicine, Orthopaedic Surgery
1150 Campo Sano Ave #200, Coral Gables, 305-669-3320

Javech, Nestor Joaquin (4 mentions)
U of Miami, 1981 *Certification:* Orthopaedic Surgery
9165 SW 87th Ave, Miami, 305-279-3784

Kalbac, Daniel Gerard (8 mentions)
U of Miami, 1986 *Certification:* Orthopaedic Surgery
6701 Sunset Dr #201, South Miami, 305-661-7601

Kanell, Daniel Ryan (3 mentions)
U of Pittsburgh, 1965 *Certification:* Orthopaedic Surgery
789 S Federal Hwy #106, Fort Lauderdale, 954-522-3355

Kleinhenz, Dominic James (3 mentions)
Case Western Reserve U, 1972 *Certification:* Orthopaedic Surgery
1821 NE 25th St, Lighthouse Point, 954-942-0321
9970 Central Park Blvd N #400, Boca Raton, 561-483-1600

Kohn, Marvin Alan (5 mentions)
FMS-Mexico, 1978
4801 S Congress Ave, Lake Worth, 561-967-6500
6056 Boynton Beach Blvd #215, Boynton Beach, 561-967-6500

Krant, David Alan (3 mentions)
Harvard U, 1966 *Certification:* Orthopaedic Surgery
3702 Washington St #101, Hollywood, 954-272-2225

Leone, William A., Jr. (4 mentions)
Emory U, 1984 *Certification:* Orthopaedic Surgery
4725 N Federal Hwy, Fort Lauderdale, 954-958-4800

Press, Jeffrey Alan (4 mentions)
New York U, 1988 *Certification:* Orthopaedic Surgery
7593 Boynton Beach Blvd, Boynton Beach, 561-733-5888

Rattey, Theresa Ellen (3 mentions)
FMS-Canada, 1987 *Certification:* Orthopaedic Surgery
4801 S Congress Ave #301, Lake Worth, 561-967-6500
6056 Boynton Beach Blvd #215, Boynton Beach, 561-967-6500

Reilly, Michael Thomas (4 mentions)
U of Miami, 1983
Certification: Orthopaedic Sports Medicine, Orthopaedic Surgery
4875 N Federal Hwy #800, Fort Lauderdale, 954-771-3334

Robla, Julio (5 mentions)
U of Florida, 1988
Certification: Orthopaedic Sports Medicine, Orthopaedic Surgery
9135 SW 87th Ave, Miami, 305-279-2322
8940 N Kendall Dr #101-E, Miami, 305-275-6770

Roche, Martin (4 mentions)
FMS-Ireland, 1990 *Certification:* Orthopaedic Surgery
4725 N Federal Hwy, Fort Lauderdale, 954-958-4800

Swirsky, Stephen M. (3 mentions)
Nova Southeastern Coll of Osteopathic Med, 1998
Certification: Orthopaedic Surgery
3100 SW 62nd Ave 1st Fl, Miami, 305-662-8366
2900 S Commerce Pkwy, Weston, 305-662-8366

Taylor, Kenneth Warren (6 mentions)
Boston U, 1991 *Certification:* Orthopaedic Surgery
4440 Sheridan St, Hollywood, 954-963-3500
601 N Flamingo Rd #101, Hollywood, 954-438-0446

Temple, H. Thomas (3 mentions)
Jefferson Med Coll, 1986 *Certification:* Orthopaedic Surgery
1400 NW 12th Ave #2, Miami, 305-325-4475

Tidwell, Michael Allen (3 mentions)
U of Nebraska, 1978 *Certification:* Orthopaedic Surgery
3100 SW 62nd Ave 1st Fl, Miami, 305-662-8366

Troiano, Christopher J. (3 mentions)
New York Med Coll, 1984 *Certification:* Orthopaedic Surgery
7225 N University Dr #202, Tamarac, 954-739-9700

Umlas, Marc Evan (4 mentions)
Stanford U, 1988 *Certification:* Orthopaedic Surgery
4302 Alton Rd #950, Miami Beach, 305-532-4224

Uribe, John William (8 mentions)
U of North Carolina, 1976
Certification: Orthopaedic Sports Medicine, Orthopaedic Surgery
1150 Campo Sano Ave #200, Coral Gables, 305-669-3320

Zann, Robert Bruce (6 mentions)
Wayne State U, 1975 *Certification:* Orthopaedic Surgery
1401 NW 9th Ave, Boca Raton, 561-395-5733

Zvijac, John Edward (4 mentions)
U of Buffalo, 1986
Certification: Orthopaedic Sports Medicine, Orthopaedic Surgery
1150 Campo Sano Ave #200, Coral Gables, 305-669-3320

Otorhinolaryngology

Agresti, Carolyn Joyce (6 mentions)
Tulane U, 1987
1515 N Flagler Dr #600, West Palm Beach, 561-659-2266

Aronsohn, Michael Scott (4 mentions)
U of Florida, 1999 *Certification:* Otolaryngology
1601 Clint Moore Rd #135, Boca Raton, 561-391-3333

Arrieta, Agustin Javier (7 mentions)
U of Miami, 2000 *Certification:* Otolaryngology
8940 N Kendall Dr #504-E, Miami, 305-595-6200
4675 Ponce De Leon Blvd #204, Coral Gables, 305-666-0203
925 NE 30th Terr #214, Homestead, 305-245-5881

Dattolo, Robert Anthony (4 mentions)
St Louis U, 1986 *Certification:* Otolaryngology
1515 N Flagler Dr #600, West Palm Beach, 561-659-2266

De Cardenas, Gaston (7 mentions)
FMS-Spain, 1965 *Certification:* Otolaryngology
3100 SW 62nd Ave #124, Miami, 305-662-8316

Ditkowsky, William Allen (10 mentions)
U of Miami, 1974 *Certification:* Otolaryngology
9275 SW 152nd St #212, Village of Palmetto Bay, 305-255-5995

Dougherty, Brian Edward (11 mentions)
Mount Sinai Sch of Med, 1981 *Certification:* Otolaryngology
8940 N Kendall Dr #504E, Miami, 305-595-6200
4675 Ponce De Leon Blvd #204, Coral Gables, 305-666-0203

Emmer, Curtis David (5 mentions)
Des Moines U, 1991
927 45th St #101, West Palm Beach, 561-848-5579
10111 W Foresthill Blvd #355, Wellington, 561-790-3329
200 Northpoint Pkwy, West Palm Beach, 561-615-0110

Fletcher, Steven Mark (6 mentions)
U of Miami, 1983 *Certification:* Otolaryngology
8940 N Kendall Dr #504-E, Miami, 305-595-6200
925 NE 30th Terr #214, Homestead, 305-245-5881

Georgakakis, George (5 mentions)
U of Miami, 1995 *Certification:* Otolaryngology
4801 N Federal Hwy #302, Fort Lauderdale, 954-493-8773

Hanft, Kendall Lisa (6 mentions)
U of Miami, 1988 *Certification:* Otolaryngology
2419 E Commercial Blvd #301, Fort Lauderdale, 954-776-0620

Hesse, Sabine Vera (4 mentions)
Ponce Sch of Med, 1996 *Certification:* Otolaryngology
1150 N 35th Ave #205-N, Hollywood, 954-583-7770

Houle, James G. (8 mentions)
Albany Med Coll, 1988 *Certification:* Otolaryngology
660 Glades Rd #400, Boca Raton, 561-750-2100

Johnson, Curtis Drew (5 mentions)
Nova Southeastern Coll of Osteopathic Med, 1986
220 SW 84th Ave #101, Plantation, 954-476-0400

Krieger, Myles Keith (6 mentions)
Jefferson Med Coll, 1972 *Certification:* Otolaryngology
1150 N 35th Ave #205, Hollywood, 954-963-3222

Kronberg, Frank Gary (9 mentions)
Albert Einstein Coll of Med, 1980 *Certification:* Otolaryngology
8940 N Kendall Dr #504E, Miami, 305-595-6200
4675 Ponce Dr Leon Blvd #204, Coral Gables, 305-666-0203

Midgley, Harry C., III (6 mentions)
U of Vermont, 1977 *Certification:* Otolaryngology
2055 Military Trail, Jupiter, 561-748-9898
200 Northpoint Pkwy, West Palm Beach, 561-615-0110

Owens, Michael Howard (10 mentions)
U of South Florida, 1984 *Certification:* Otolaryngology
4675 Ponce De Leon Blvd #204, Coral Gables, 305-666-0203
8940 N Kendall Dr #504-E, Miami, 305-595-6200
9000 SW 137th Ave #115, Miami, 305-666-0203
9915 NW 41st Ave #220, Miami, 305-666-0203

Portela, Rafael Ramon (5 mentions)
Pennsylvania State U, 1981 *Certification:* Otolaryngology
3100 SW 62nd Ave #124, Miami, 305-669-7144

Randhawa, Ravinder Singh (6 mentions)
Nova Southeastern Coll of Osteopathic Med, 1992
16244 S Military Trail #710, Delray Beach, 561-638-8505

Selden, Bruce Stuart (4 mentions)
Rosalind Franklin U, 1967 *Certification:* Otolaryngology
2855 N University Dr #300, Coral Springs, 954-752-4377

Slomka, William Stuart (4 mentions)
Virginia Commonwealth U, 1986 *Certification:* Otolaryngology
3015 S Congress Ave #6, Lake Worth, 561-966-4100

Sukenik, Mark Abraham (4 mentions)
Emory U, 1993 *Certification:* Otolaryngology
4700 Sheridan St #K, Hollywood, 954-966-7000
601 N Flamingo Rd #106, Pembroke Pines, 954-432-6620

Widick, Mark Hayden (4 mentions)
U of Florida, 1987 *Certification:* Otolaryngology
900 NW 13th St #206, Boca Raton, 954-942-6868
1 W Sample Rd #103, Pompano Beach, 954-942-6868

Pain Medicine

Chaitoff, Kevin Alan (5 mentions)
Wright State U, 1984 *Certification:* Anesthesiology, Pain Medicine
1500 N Dixie Hwy #103, West Palm Beach, 561-833-8893

Cooney, John Franklin (5 mentions)
Mayo Med Sch, 1977 *Certification:* Anesthesiology, Pain Medicine
1500 N Dixie Hwy #103, West Palm Beach, 561-833-8893

Drourr, Nathaniel Robert (7 mentions)
Stony Brook U, 1992 *Certification:* Anesthesiology, Pain Medicine
1210 S Old Dixie Hwy, Jupiter, 561-743-5073

Fox, Ira Bobby (4 mentions)
FMS-Mexico, 1984 *Certification:* Anesthesiology, Pain Medicine
4485 N State Rd 7, Lauderdale Lakes, 954-735-0096
7171 N University Dr #316, Tamarac, 954-720-3188

Gorfine, Lawrence Stanley (3 mentions)
FMS-Italy, 1974 *Certification:* Anesthesiology, Pain Medicine
2290 10th Ave N #600, Lake Worth, 561-649-8770

Luck, George Robert (4 mentions)
Tulane U, 1984
Certification: Anesthesiology, Hospice and Palliative Medicine
800 Meadows Rd, Boca Raton, 561-955-7100

Lustgarten, Moises (5 mentions)
FMS-Venezuela, 1993
Certification: Anesthesiology, Pain Medicine
8755 SW 94th St #300, Miami, 305-279-3223

Mesa, Antonio (3 mentions)
Kansas U Coll of Osteopathic Med, 1999
Certification: Neurology, Pain Medicine
7800 SW 87th Ave #B-250, Miami, 305-670-7650

Paglia, Anthony Louis (3 mentions)
New York Med Coll, 1991 *Certification:* Anesthesiology
2500 E Hallandale Beach Blvd #811, Hallandale Beach, 954-458-1199

Regenbaum, Sheldon (3 mentions)
FMS-South Africa, 1982 *Certification:* Anesthesiology
901 45th St, West Palm Beach, 561-833-8893
1500 N Dixie Hwy #103, West Palm Beach, 561-833-8893
1511 Prosperity Farms Rd #400, West Palm Beach, 561-848-3861

Rosenblatt, Melanie (3 mentions)
1 W Sample Rd #104, Pompano Beach, 954-941-5556

Ruiz, Francisco Javier (5 mentions)
Certification: Anesthesiology, Pain Medicine
3659 S Miami Ave #5008, Miami, 305-285-9432

Serpa, John Anthony (3 mentions)
FMS-Dominican Republic, 1988
Certification: Anesthesiology, Pain Medicine
7150 W 20th Ave #209, Hialeah, 305-702-9209

Suarez, Emilio (5 mentions)
New York Coll of Osteopathic Med, 1985
Certification: Anesthesiology, Pain Medicine
5975 Sunset Dr #804, South Miami, 305-740-2336

Szeinfeld, Marcos (6 mentions)
FMS-Uruguay, 1974 *Certification:* Anesthesiology, Pain Medicine
1930 NE 47th St #300, Fort Lauderdale, 954-493-5048

Vega, Andres (4 mentions)
U of Florida, 1981 *Certification:* Anesthesiology
1435 W 49th Pl #500, Hialeah, 305-364-1123
7100 W 20th Ave #601, Hialeah, 305-828-6520

Vilasuso, Francisco X. (3 mentions)
U of Miami, 1980 *Certification:* Anesthesiology, Pain Medicine
6280 Sunset Dr #410, Miami, 305-661-3502

Pathology

Amazon, Kip (3 mentions)
U of Miami, 1977 *Certification:* Anatomic Pathology & Clinical Pathology, Chemical Pathology
20900 Biscayne Blvd, Aventura, 305-682-7360

Cohen, Albert (5 mentions)
FMS-Mexico, 1976
Certification: Anatomic Pathology & Clinical Pathology
5352 Linton Blvd, Delray Beach, 561-495-3185
5150 Linton Blvd #250, Delray Beach, 561-638-7577

Cove, Harvey (6 mentions)
Tulane U, 1968 *Certification:* Anatomic Pathology & Clinical Pathology, Cytopathology, Dermatopathology
300 Butler St, West Palm Beach, 561-659-0770

Ganjei, Parvin (3 mentions)
FMS-Iran, 1973 *Certification:* Anatomic Pathology & Clinical Pathology, Cytopathology
1611 NW 12th Ave, Miami, 305-585-6055

Garen, Paul Douglas (4 mentions)
U of Florida, 1980
Certification: Clinical Pathology, Neuropathology
300 Butler St, West Palm Beach, 561-659-0770

Gould, Edwin Warren (14 mentions)
U of Missouri, 1978 *Certification:* Anatomic Pathology & Clinical Pathology, Dermatopathology
8900 N Kendall Dr, Miami, 305-596-6525

Johnson, Gordon Leslie (8 mentions)
St Louis U, 1975
Certification: Anatomic Pathology & Clinical Pathology
8201 W Broward Blvd, Plantation, 561-798-8559

Kambour, Michael T., Jr. (7 mentions)
U of Miami, 1978
Certification: Anatomic Pathology & Clinical Pathology
4665 Ponce De Leon Blvd, Coral Gables, 786-268-6050

Mark, Thomas X. (7 mentions)
U of Miami, 1978
Certification: Anatomic Pathology & Clinical Pathology
5000 University Dr, Coral Gables, 305-669-3471

Nadji, Mehrdad (3 mentions)
FMS-Iran, 1969 *Certification:* Anatomic Pathology & Clinical Pathology, Cytopathology
1611 NW 12th Ave, Miami, 305-585-6194

Otrakji, Christian Leon (3 mentions)
FMS-Lebanon, 1984 *Certification:* Anatomic Pathology & Clinical Pathology, Cytopathology
6200 SW 73rd St, South Miami, 786-662-8168

Pierce, Alan David (3 mentions)
St Louis U, 1975
Certification: Anatomic Pathology & Clinical Pathology
8201 W Broward Blvd, Plantation, 954-452-2115
10101 W Forest Hill Blvd, West Palm Beach, 561-798-8500

Poppiti, Robert John (4 mentions)
U of Miami, 1980
Certification: Anatomic Pathology & Clinical Pathology
4300 Alton Rd #2400, Miami Beach, 305-674-2277

Reineke, Fred William (5 mentions)
St Louis U, 1977
Certification: Anatomic Pathology & Clinical Pathology
3141 W McNab Rd, Fort Lauderdale, 954-977-6977

Renshaw, Andrew Alexander (3 mentions)
Harvard U, 1989 *Certification:* Anatomic Pathology & Clinical Pathology, Cytopathology
8900 N Kendall Dr Bldg BCVI 5th Fl, Miami, 786-596-6525

Rosen, Leslie Bruce (3 mentions)
SUNY-Downstate Med Coll, 1979 *Certification:* Anatomic Pathology & Clinical Pathology, Dermatopathology
895 SW 30th Ave #101, Pompano Beach, 800-330-6770

Sonkin, Eli David (3 mentions)
U of Kentucky, 1969
Certification: Anatomic Pathology & Clinical Pathology
5000 W Oakland Park Blvd, Lauderdale Lakes, 954-486-5832

Tapia, Raul H. (3 mentions)
FMS-Dominica, 1981
Certification: Anatomic Pathology & Clinical Pathology, Blood Banking/Transfusion Medicine, Cytopathology
4725 N Federal Hwy, Fort Lauderdale, 954-492-5728

Torrent, Jose Rafael (3 mentions)
FMS-Spain, 1974
Certification: Anatomic Pathology & Clinical Pathology
11750 SW 40th St, Miami, 305-227-5579

Williams, William Dale (3 mentions)
Robert W Johnson Med Sch, 1979
Certification: Anatomic Pathology & Clinical Pathology
872 NE 79th St, Boca Raton, 954-786-7370
201 E Sample Rd, Deerfield, 954-786-7370

Pediatrics *(see note on page 9)*

Blanco, Jack J. (4 mentions)
Certification: Pediatrics
951 NW 13th St #5D, Boca Raton, 561-392-7266

Cintas, Maura (3 mentions)
FMS-Dominican Republic, 1986 *Certification:* Pediatrics
9000 SW 137th Ave #204, Miami, 305-383-1902
14704 SW 56th St, Miami, 305-383-0000

Edelstein, Jaime (5 mentions)
FMS-Spain, 1963 *Certification:* Pediatrics
358 San Lorenzo Ave 3rd Fl, Coral Gables, 305-444-6882

Faske, Ivy (5 mentions)
U of South Florida, 1984 *Certification:* Pediatrics
3365 Burns Rd #206, West Palm Beach, 561-626-4677

Finer, Michael Allen (3 mentions)
SUNY-Upstate Med U, 1976 *Certification:* Pediatrics
7001 SW 87th Ave, Miami, 305-271-8222

Gill, Howard S. (3 mentions)
FMS-Mexico, 1984 *Certification:* Pediatrics
1900 E Commercial Blvd #202, Fort Lauderdale, 954-351-5840

Keller, Linda C. (4 mentions)
U of Miami, 1987 *Certification:* Pediatrics
8750 SW 144th St #100, Miami, 305-253-5585

Kramer, Gary Michael (4 mentions)
FMS-Israel, 1998 *Certification:* Pediatrics
4950 S Le Jeune Rd #F, Coral Gables, 305-665-3523

Legorburu-Selem, Sarah G. (5 mentions)
FMS-Spain, 1978 *Certification:* Pediatrics
305 Granello Ave, Coral Gables, 305-446-2546

Lopez, Pedro (3 mentions)
FMS-Spain, 1960 *Certification:* Pediatrics
3311 Ponce De Leon Blvd, Coral Gables, 305-444-4457

Luchtan, Alberto (3 mentions)
FMS-Argentina, 1967 *Certification:* Pediatrics
5458 Town Center Rd, Boca Raton, 561-391-6210

Newcomm, Phillip Gary, Jr. (3 mentions)
Med U of South Carolina, 1987 *Certification:* Pediatrics
305 Granello Ave, Coral Gables, 305-446-2546

Nunez-Martin, Rigoberto M. (3 mentions)
FMS-Spain, 1975
8900 SW 117th Ave #B101, Miami, 305-270-1910

Ocampo, Norina B. (10 mentions)
Georgetown U, 1988 *Certification:* Pediatrics
9970 Central Park Blvd N #204, Boca Raton, 561-487-5437

Patino, Carlos Alberto (3 mentions)
FMS-Colombia, 1989 *Certification:* Pediatrics
17870 NW 2nd St, Pembroke Pines, 954-450-9050

Romear, Ronald Anthony (3 mentions)
Wayne State U, 1986
2141 S Hwy A1-A Alt #230, Jupiter, 561-743-9810
5205 Village Blvd, West Palm Beach, 561-242-0505

Rub, Beny (3 mentions)
FMS-Mexico, 1984 *Certification:* Pediatrics
21110 Biscayne Blvd #308, Miami, 305-932-1007
1190 NW 95th St #409, Miami, 305-696-9490

San Jorge, Maria Carlota (3 mentions)
FMS-Dominican Republic, 1982 *Certification:* Pediatrics
2560 Rca Blvd #113, Palm Beach Gardens, 561-626-5790

Tanis, Arnold L. (3 mentions)
U of Chicago, 1951 *Certification:* Pediatrics
4500 Sheridan St, Hollywood, 954-966-8000

Zuba, Stanley Martin (4 mentions)
FMS-Dominica, 1987 *Certification:* Pediatrics
125 Riviera Dr, Tavernier, 305-853-0558
91550 Overseas Hwy #209, Tavernier, 305-853-0558

Plastic Surgery

Applebaum, David J. (4 mentions)
Baylor U, 1984 *Certification:* Plastic Surgery
1599 NW 9th Ave, Boca Raton, 561-347-7777

Barnavon, Yoav (7 mentions)
FMS-Canada, 1984 *Certification:* Plastic Surgery
1150 N 35th Ave #550, Hollywood, 954-987-8100

Dabbah, Albert (6 mentions)
U of Maryland, 1987 *Certification:* Plastic Surgery
9970 Central Park Blvd N #201, Boca Raton, 561-488-1700

Dardano, Anthony N. (9 mentions)
Nova Southeastern Coll of Osteopathic Med, 1990
Certification: Plastic Surgery, Surgery
1000 NW 9th Ct #202, Boca Raton, 561-361-0065

Herman, Brad Paul (4 mentions)
Rosalind Franklin U, 1984 *Certification:* Plastic Surgery
8940 N Kendall Dr #903-E, Miami, 305-595-2969

Kelly, Michael Edward (7 mentions)
U of Illinois, 1984 *Certification:* Plastic Surgery
8940 N Kendall Dr #903E, Miami, 305-663-1418

Levin, Joel Murray (6 mentions)
U of Miami, 1965 *Certification:* Plastic Surgery, Surgery
8700 N Kendall Dr #206, Miami, 305-665-1017

Lickstein, David Alan (4 mentions)
Northwestern U, 1993 *Certification:* Plastic Surgery, Surgery
11020 RCA Center Dr #2010, Palm Beach Gardens,
  561-881-8800

Marshall, Deirdre M. (5 mentions)
Stanford U, 1987 *Certification:* Plastic Surgery
3100 SW 62nd Ave, Miami, 305-662-8234

Pillersdorf, Alan Barth (8 mentions)
Georgetown U, 1980
Certification: Plastic Surgery, Surgery, Surgery of the Hand
1620 S Congress Ave #100, Palm Springs, 561-968-7111
10115 W Forest Hilll #400, Wellington, 561-790-5554

Schuster, Steven Howard (11 mentions)
New Jersey Med Sch, 1979 *Certification:* Plastic Surgery
1905 Clint Moore Rd #101, Boca Raton, 561-912-9191

Schwartz, Richard Gary (5 mentions)
Indiana U, 1973 *Certification:* Plastic Surgery
1500 N Dixie Hwy #304, West Palm Beach, 561-833-4022

Serure, Alan Scott (6 mentions)
U of Miami, 1979 *Certification:* Plastic Surgery
7300 SW 62nd Pl #200, South Miami, 305-669-0184

Simon, Sean Adam (4 mentions)
U of Miami, 1999 *Certification:* Plastic Surgery, Surgery
6200 Sunset Dr #501, South Miami, 305-668-0496

Storch, Michael David (4 mentions)
Georgetown U, 1969 *Certification:* Plastic Surgery
21110 Biscayne Blvd #103, Miami, 305-932-3200

Stuzin, James Morris (6 mentions)
U of Florida, 1978 *Certification:* Plastic Surgery
3225 Aviation Ave #100, Miami, 305-854-8828

Turner, Vernon Powell (4 mentions)
Emory U, 1969 *Certification:* Plastic Surgery
3536 N Federal Hwy #100, Fort Lauderdale, 954-568-3031

Weiser, Jonathan R. (4 mentions)
U of Miami, 1984 *Certification:* Plastic Surgery
3449 Johnson St, Hollywood, 954-964-4113

Wolf, Carlos Loft (5 mentions)
U of Miami, 1983 *Certification:* Otolaryngology
8940 N Kendall Dr #903E, Miami, 305-270-1418

Wolfe, Stephen Anthony (6 mentions)
Harvard U, 1965 *Certification:* Plastic Surgery, Surgery
6280 Sunset Dr #400, South Miami, 305-662-4111
3200 SW 62nd Ave #2230, Miami, 305-662-4111

Psychiatry

Arison, Zipora (3 mentions)
FMS-Israel, 1975 *Certification:* Psychiatry
2438 E Commercial Blvd, Fort Lauderdale, 954-776-7868

Edison, Neil H. (3 mentions)
New York Med Coll, 1969 *Certification:* Psychiatry
3107 Stirling Rd #103, Fort Lauderdale, 954-986-1179

Epstein, Merrill Hugh (4 mentions)
U of Vermont, 1973 *Certification:* Geriatric Psychiatry, Psychiatry
4800 N Federal Hwy #A205, Boca Raton, 561-368-3388

Extein, Irl Lawrence (12 mentions)
Yale U, 1974 *Certification:* Psychiatry
16244 Military Trail #325, Delray Beach, 561-499-6716

Gonzalez, Carlos Pedro (4 mentions)
Northwestern U, 1978 *Certification:* Psychiatry
1500 San Remo Ave #205, Coral Gables, 305-669-6800

Gross, David Arlen (4 mentions)
U of Florida, 1973 *Certification:* Psychiatry
4800 Linton Blvd Bldg D #503, Delray Beach, 561-496-1281

Jordan, James Allen (3 mentions)
Indiana U, 1959 *Certification:* Psychiatry
2340 NE 53rd St, Fort Lauderdale, 954-491-7835

Levin, Richard Wender (4 mentions)
Emory U, 1974 *Certification:* Psychiatry
3810 Hollywood Blvd, Hollywood, 954-962-3888

Padilla, Americo F. (3 mentions)
FMS-Dominican Republic, 1981
Certification: Child & Adolescent Psychiatry, Psychiatry
3100 SW 62nd Ave, Miami, 305-663-8439

Rejtman, Jaime Svartz (5 mentions)
FMS-Colombia, 1963 *Certification:* Psychiatry
3001 NW 49th Ave #202, Fort Lauderdale, 954-733-7202

Remensone, Leonid A. (3 mentions)
FMS-Russia, 1984
2800 Seacrest Blvd #140, Boynton Beach, 561-742-2260

Rodriguez-Garcia, Manuel (3 mentions)
U of Puerto Rico, 1978 *Certification:* Psychiatry
3661 S Miami Ave #610, Miami, 305-858-4666
6705 Red Rd #306, Coral Gables, 305-666-8300

Rooney, David Bryan (4 mentions)
FMS-St Maarten, 1982
2340 NE 53rd St, Fort Lauderdale, 954-771-3147

Rothe, Eugenio Miguel (3 mentions)
FMS-Chile, 1982 *Certification:* Forensic Psychiatry, Psychiatry
2199 Ponce de Leon Blvd #304, Coral Gables, 305-774-1699

Storper, Henry Michael (3 mentions)
George Washington U, 1969 *Certification:* Psychiatry
9275 SW 152nd St #108B, Village of Palmetto Bay, 305-252-0533

Pulmonary Disease

Adelman, Mark (3 mentions)
Virginia Commonwealth U, 1980
Certification: Internal Medicine, Pulmonary Disease
9980 Central Park Blvd N #322, Boca Raton, 561-488-2988

Azar, George Peter, Jr. (3 mentions)
FMS-Dominica, 1984
Certification: Internal Medicine, Pulmonary Disease
3075 NW 35th Ave, Lauderdale Lakes, 954-739-2235

Baron, Kenneth Michael (6 mentions)
U of Texas-Galveston, 1986
Certification: Internal Medicine, Pulmonary Disease
9980 Central Park Blvd N #322, Boca Raton, 561-488-2988
15340 Jog Rd #203, Delray Beach, 561-498-7332

Barrio, Juan Luis (5 mentions)
Ponce Sch of Med, 1981
Certification: Internal Medicine, Pulmonary Disease
9495 SW 72nd St #B210, Miami, 305-274-3322

Baum, Deborah R. (6 mentions)
FMS-South Africa, 1986 *Certification:* Pulmonary Disease
1601 Clint Moore Rd #100, Boca Raton, 561-939-0200

Benjamin, Rodney Graham (5 mentions)
FMS-South Africa, 1977
Certification: Internal Medicine, Pulmonary Disease
6250 Sunset Dr, South Miami, 786-662-8400
6200 SW 73rd St, South Miami, 786-662-8400

Birriel, Jose A. (4 mentions)
U Central del Caribe, 1980 *Certification:* Pediatrics
9291 Glades Rd #302, Boca Raton, 954-583-1056
4101 NW 3rd Ct #8, Plantation, 954-583-1056

Bolton, Edgar Bryant (3 mentions)
Philadelphia Coll of Osteopathic Med, 1969
7369 Sheridan St #302, Hollywood, 954-981-3700
3200 S University Dr, Davie, 954-262-1000

Brady, Ted Hugh (4 mentions)
Midwestern U Chicago Coll of Osteopathic Med, 1986
9800 W Sample Rd #B, Coral Springs, 954-341-3739

Choy, Rogelio A. (4 mentions)
FMS-Peru, 1969
Certification: Internal Medicine, Pulmonary Disease
3355 Burns Rd #304, West Palm Beach, 561-627-3336

Ciment, Larry M. (3 mentions)
Albert Einstein Coll of Med, 1970 *Certification:* Internal Medicine
4302 Alton Rd #210, Miami Beach, 305-673-2744

Coopersmith, Edward Mark (7 mentions)
FMS-Spain, 1971
Certification: Internal Medicine, Pulmonary Disease
5333 N Dixie Hwy #201, Oakland Park, 954-491-3440

Davis, Barry Leonard (9 mentions)
Tufts U, 1974
Certification: Internal Medicine, Pulmonary Disease
951 NW 13th St #2A, Boca Raton, 561-391-1666

Diaz, Carlos Enrique (4 mentions)
U of Puerto Rico, 1985 *Certification:* Pediatric Pulmonology
8700 N Kendall Dr, Miami, 305-270-2080

Feingold, Ilan Allan (4 mentions)
FMS-Canada, 1975
Certification: Internal Medicine, Pulmonary Disease
6200 SW 73rd St #400, South Miami, 786-662-5229

Franco, Maria E. (3 mentions)
FMS-Colombia, 1987
Certification: Pediatric Pulmonology, Pediatrics
3200 SW 60th Ct, Miami, 305-662-8380

Frankel, Joel (5 mentions)
SUNY-Downstate Med Coll, 1975
Certification: Internal Medicine, Pulmonary Disease
2951 NW 49th Ave #202, Fort Lauderdale, 954-486-1250

Gidel, Louis Thomas (4 mentions)
U of Miami, 1986
Certification: Internal Medicine, Pulmonary Disease
7000 SW 62nd Ave #201, South Miami, 305-661-9404

Gittler, Steven Benjamin (11 mentions)
Mount Sinai Sch of Med, 1985
Certification: Critical Care Medicine, Internal Medicine,
   Pulmonary Disease, Sleep Medicine
7369 Sheridan St #302, Hollywood, 954-981-3700

Gonzalez, Hugo Francisco (5 mentions)
U of Miami, 1978
Certification: Internal Medicine, Pulmonary Disease
3661 S Miami Ave #901, Miami, 305-856-8669

Gotkin, Brian Mitchell (7 mentions)
U of Miami, 1993 *Certification:* Critical Care Medicine,
   Internal Medicine, Pulmonary Disease, Sleep Medicine
7369 Sheridan St #302, Hollywood, 954-981-3700
3700 Washington St #500, Hollywood, 954-981-3700

Gustman, Paul Morton (4 mentions)
Virginia Commonwealth U, 1969
Certification: Internal Medicine, Pulmonary Disease
8780 SW 92nd St #210, Miami, 305-275-7575
9035 SW 72nd St #103, Miami, 305-275-7575

Hoffberger, Darren Seth (3 mentions)
Nova Southeastern Coll of Osteopathic Med, 1998
1 W Sample Rd #304, Pompano Beach, 954-941-1100

Keller, Fernando Angel (4 mentions)
FMS-Peru, 1980
Certification: Internal Medicine, Pulmonary Disease
2623 S Seacrest Blvd #214, Boynton Beach, 561-731-2269

Labi, Marlon Amos (4 mentions)
FMS-Chile, 1981
Certification: Internal Medicine, Pulmonary Disease
9800 W Sample Rd #B, Coral Springs, 954-341-3739

Ludwig, P. William (4 mentions)
New York U, 1961
Certification: Internal Medicine, Pulmonary Disease
5401 S Congress Ave #204, Atlantis, 561-967-4118

Magcalas, Mario M. (4 mentions)
FMS-Philippines, 1986 *Certification:* Critical Care Medicine,
   Internal Medicine, Pulmonary Disease
10794 Pines Blvd #205, Pembroke Pines, 954-538-8543
7100 W 20th Ave #504, Hialeah, 305-820-1555

Mangas, Mario Jose (5 mentions)
FMS-Dominican Republic, 1983
Certification: Internal Medicine, Pulmonary Disease
11880 SW 40th St #416, Miami, 305-227-0604

Moas, Carlos M. (3 mentions)
U of South Florida, 1982 *Certification:* Critical Care
   Medicine, Internal Medicine, Pulmonary Disease
3661 S Miami Ave #1008, Miami, 305-854-2284

Moas, Raul (4 mentions)
U of South Florida, 1979 *Certification:* Critical Care
   Medicine, Internal Medicine, Pulmonary Disease
3659 S Miami Ave #5004, Miami, 305-854-0616

Palumbo, Ralph (7 mentions)
Med Coll of Pennsylvania, 1997 *Certification:* Critical Care
   Medicine, Internal Medicine, Pulmonary Disease
1601 Clint Moore Rd #100, Boca Raton, 561-939-0200

Parker, R. Latanae (4 mentions)
Tulane U, 1971
Certification: Internal Medicine, Pulmonary Disease
7000 SW 62nd Ave #201, South Miami, 305-661-9404

Patel, Vinodrai Muljibhai (3 mentions)
FMS-India, 1970
Certification: Internal Medicine, Pulmonary Disease
7050 NW 4th St #203, Plantation, 954-791-5300

Penaranda, Ruben D. (8 mentions)
U of Miami, 1983 *Certification:* Critical Care Medicine,
   Internal Medicine, Pulmonary Disease
1150 Campo Sano Ave #300, Miami, 305-779-7381

Rosen, Allen E. (9 mentions)
Mount Sinai Sch of Med, 1977 *Certification:* Critical Care
   Medicine, Internal Medicine, Pulmonary Disease
1411 N Flagler Dr #7000, West Palm Beach, 561-659-1000

Salazar, Jose Antonio (3 mentions)
FMS-Spain, 1972
Certification: Internal Medicine, Pulmonary Disease
3661 S Miami Ave #1008, Miami, 305-854-2284

Sallent, Jorge Antonio (3 mentions)
FMS-Dominican Republic, 1979
Certification: Pediatric Pulmonology, Pediatrics
500 US Hwy 1, West Palm Beach, 561-863-0105

Sanchez, Carlos (3 mentions)
FMS-Dominican Republic, 1989
Certification: Critical Care Medicine
5401 S Congress Ave, Atlantis, 561-967-4118
1411 N Flagler Dr #6100, West Palm Beach, 561-651-7005

Schreibman, Noah Brad (5 mentions)
Albert Einstein Coll of Med, 1996 *Certification:* Critical Care
   Medicine, Internal Medicine, Pulmonary Disease
9980 Central Park Blvd N #322, Boca Raton, 561-488-2988
15340 Jog Rd #203, Delray Beach, 561-998-7330

Scott, Ronald Joseph (3 mentions)
Boston U, 1973
Certification: Internal Medicine, Pulmonary Disease
5333 N Dixie Hwy #201, Oakland Park, 954-491-3440

Simpser, Moises D. (5 mentions)
FMS-Mexico, 1969 *Certification:* Pediatrics
3200 SW 60th Ct #203, Miami, 305-662-8380

Singer, Glenn Richard (3 mentions)
U of South Florida, 1978
Certification: Internal Medicine, Pulmonary Disease
1625 SE 3rd Ave, Fort Lauderdale, 954-522-7226

Tabak, Jeremy I. (5 mentions)
New York U, 1978 *Certification:* Critical Care Medicine,
   Internal Medicine, Pulmonary Disease
7000 SW 62nd Ave, South Miami, 305-661-9404

Valor, Raul R. (7 mentions)
FMS-Dominican Republic, 1982
Certification: Pulmonary Disease
11880 Bird Rd #416, Miami, 305-227-0604
242 NW 42nd Ave, Miami, 305-448-0809

Weissberger, David (4 mentions)
Pennsylvania State U, 1974
Certification: Internal Medicine, Pulmonary Disease
5401 S Congress Ave #204, Atlantis, 561-967-4118

Zaltzman, Matthew Louis (5 mentions)
FMS-South Africa, 1974
Certification: Internal Medicine, Pulmonary Disease
1411 N Flagler Dr #6100, West Palm Beach, 561-651-7005
5401 Congress Ave #2001, Lantana, 561-967-4118

Radiology—Diagnostic

Altman, Nolan Roger (3 mentions)
U of Miami, 1979
3100 SW 62nd Ave, Miami, 305-666-6511

Boyle, Thomas Patrick (3 mentions)
Columbia U, 1983 *Certification:* Diagnostic Radiology
101 JFK Dr, Atlantis, 561-968-3310

Braffman, Bruce Howard (3 mentions)
Albert Einstein Coll of Med, 1982
Certification: Diagnostic Radiology, Neuroradiology
3501 Johnson St, Hollywood, 954-985-5892
9050 Pines Blvd #200, Pembroke Pines, 954-437-4800

Burke, Robert David (3 mentions)
U of Louisville, 1981 *Certification:* Diagnostic Radiology
5405 Okeechobee Blvd #101, West Palm Beach, 561-697-4250

Calderon, Roberto J., Jr. (3 mentions)
FMS-Nicaragua, 1976 *Certification:* Diagnostic Radiology
   with Special Competence in Nuclear Radiology
11750 SW 40th St, Miami, 305-227-5563

Esserman, Lisa Ellen (4 mentions)
U of Miami, 1981 *Certification:* Diagnostic Radiology
7500 SW 87th Ave #100, Miami, 305-740-5100

Goodwin, Donald William (5 mentions)
U of Miami, 1973 *Certification:* Diagnostic Radiology
733 US Hwy 1, North Palm Beach, 561-841-8588

Horst, Carrie J. (5 mentions)
Kansas U Coll of Osteopathic Med, 1998
Certification: Diagnostic Radiology
7500 South West 87 Ave #100, Miami, 305-740-5100

Litt, Richard Erwin (4 mentions)
U of Alabama, 1956 *Certification:* Radiology
3100 SW 62nd Ave, Miami, 305-666-6511

Messinger, Neil Howard (4 mentions)
SUNY-Downstate Med Coll, 1963 *Certification:* Radiology
8900 N Kendall Dr, Miami, 786-596-5917

Rosenkrantz, Carl (5 mentions)
U of Miami, 1977 *Certification:* Diagnostic Radiology
5352 Linton Blvd, Delray Beach, 561-495-3170

Rubinson, Howard Alan (3 mentions)
Hahnemann U, 1975 *Certification:* Diagnostic Radiology
2929 E Commercial Blvd #600, Fort Lauderdale, 954-636-2290

Rush, Michael J. (9 mentions)
U of South Florida, 1977 *Certification:* Diagnostic
Radiology, Vascular & Interventional Radiology
4701 N Federal Hwy, Fort Lauderdale, 954-771-8177
2929 E Commercial Blvd, Fort Lauderdale, 954-636-2290
160 NW 170th St, North Miami Beach, 305-654-5028
2001 W 68th St, Hialeah, 305-364-2152
2900 N Military Trail, Boca Raton, 561-314-2505

Stamler, Cliff Edward (3 mentions)
U of Miami, 1977 *Certification:* Diagnostic Radiology
8900 N Kendall Dr, Miami, 305-598-5917

Thorpe, Michael Scott (4 mentions)
U of Florida, 1992 *Certification:* Diagnostic Radiology
5000 University Dr, Miami, 305-669-2324

Williams, Lorna Sohn (3 mentions)
Robert W Johnson Med Sch, 1991
5301 S Congress Ave, Lake Worth, 561-965-7300

Ziffer, Jack Andrew (3 mentions)
U of Miami, 1983 *Certification:* Diagnostic Radiology,
Nuclear Medicine, Nuclear Radiology
8900 N Kendall Dr, Miami, 786-596-5917

Radiology—Therapeutic

Benenati, James Francis (3 mentions)
U of South Florida, 1984 *Certification:* Diagnostic
Radiology, Vascular & Interventional Radiology
8900 N Kendall Dr, Miami, 786-596-7050

Bengoa, Federico G. (3 mentions)
Tufts U, 1996 *Certification:* Diagnostic Radiology
9050 Pines Blvd, Pembroke Pines, 954-442-8346
3501 Johnson St, Hollywood, 954-985-5886

Dass, Kishore Kumar (4 mentions)
Loyola U Chicago, 1989 *Certification:* Radiation Oncology
10141 W Forest Hill Blvd, Wellington, 561-793-6500

Guben, Jon Kopel (3 mentions)
FMS-Dominica, 1980 *Certification:* Diagnostic Radiology,
Vascular & Interventional Radiology
1600 S Andrews Ave, Fort Lauderdale, 954-355-5500

Kaplan, Edward J. (3 mentions)
Albany Med Coll, 1989 *Certification:* Radiation Oncology
4850 W Oakland Park Blvd #C, Lauderdale Lakes, 954-485-7707

Katzen, Barry Theodore (8 mentions)
U of Miami, 1970 *Certification:* Diagnostic Radiology,
Vascular & Interventional Radiology
8900 N Kendall Dr, Miami, 786-596-7050

Lewin, Alan Albert (3 mentions)
George Washington U, 1973 *Certification:* Hematology,
Internal Medicine, Medical Oncology, Therapeutic Radiology
8900 N Kendall Dr, Miami, 786-596-6566

Lewis, Anne Magaret (3 mentions)
Wayne State U, 1991
10335 N Military Trail, Palm Beach Gardens, 561-624-1717

O'Connor, David K. (3 mentions)
U of Miami, 1994 *Certification:* Diagnostic Radiology,
Vascular & Interventional Radiology
2815 S Seacrest Blvd, Boynton Beach, 561-737-7733

Osterman, Floyd A., Jr. (3 mentions)
U of Miami, 1972 *Certification:* Diagnostic Radiology,
Vascular & Interventional Radiology
21000 NE 28th Ave #202, Miami, 305-932-7800

Rush, Michael J. (5 mentions)
U of South Florida, 1977 *Certification:* Diagnostic
Radiology, Vascular & Interventional Radiology
4701 N Federal Hwy, Fort Lauderdale, 954-636-2290
2929 E Commercial Blvd, Fort Lauderdale, 954-636-2290

Sundararaman, Srinath (3 mentions)
Wright State U, 1993 *Certification:* Radiation Oncology
3501 Johnson St, Hollywood, 954-985-5886

Tate, Charles Franklin (4 mentions)
U of Miami, 1973 *Certification:* Diagnostic Radiology,
Vascular & Interventional Radiology
2555 Ponce De leaon Blvd 4th Fl, Miami, 954-351-5999

Williams, Timothy Ransom (3 mentions)
Med Coll of Georgia, 1983 *Certification:* Radiation Oncology
800 Meadows Rd, Boca Raton, 561-393-4111
16313 S Military Trail, Delray Beach, 561-637-7200

Rehabilitation

Aiken, Bradley Milton (6 mentions)
U of Maryland, 1980
Certification: Physical Medicine & Rehabilitation
8900 N Kendall Dr, Miami, 305-596-6520

Alshon, Joseph James (3 mentions)
Philadelphia Coll of Osteopathic Med, 1984
Certification: Pain Medicine, Physical Medicine & Rehabilitation
14000 Military Trail #210, Delray Beach, 561-495-5950

Bell, John E. (3 mentions)
Nova Southeastern Coll of Osteopathic Med, 1990
Certification: Physical Medicine & Rehabilitation
2901 Coral Hills Dr #250, Coral Springs, 954-753-9337

Epstein, Bryce Elliot (4 mentions)
FMS-Mexico, 1984
Certification: Physical Medicine & Rehabilitation
21000 NE 28th Ave #104, Miami, 305-937-1999

Farber, Jeffrey Steven (3 mentions)
New York Med Coll, 1988
Certification: Physical Medicine & Rehabilitation
300 Royal Palm Way, Palm Beach, 561-659-5443

Lerner, Lauren Lipshutz (5 mentions)
Boston U, 1980 *Certification:* Physical Medicine & Rehabilitation
4399 N Nob Hill Rd, Sunrise, 954-746-1505

Lipkin, David Lawrence (3 mentions)
FMS-Belgium, 1963
Certification: Physical Medicine & Rehabilitation
4701 N Meridian Ave, Miami Beach, 305-672-1256

Mansourian, Vartgez K. (3 mentions)
Med Coll of Georgia, 1988 *Certification:* Pain Medicine, Physical
Medicine & Rehabilitation, Spinal Cord Injury Medicine
951 NW 13th St #2-B, Boca Raton, 561-750-7110

Mendelsohn, Jay Sherman (3 mentions)
Jefferson Med Coll, 1977
Certification: Physical Medicine & Rehabilitation
3230 Stirling Rd, Hollywood, 954-963-5000
3800 N Miami Ave, Miami, 305-576-8585

Nevares, Ibiza (3 mentions)
U Central del Caribe, 1991
7100 W Commercial Blvd #105, Lauderhill, 954-578-2292

Novick, Alan Keith (7 mentions)
U of Florida, 1987
Certification: Physical Medicine & Rehabilitation
1150 N 35th Ave #390, Hollywood, 954-981-3341

Penalba, Claudia Elena (8 mentions)
FMS-Mexico, 1981
Certification: Physical Medicine & Rehabilitation
6705 Red Rd #516, Coral Gables, 305-403-2921

Picard, Daniel Adam (3 mentions)
Albany Med Coll, 1988
Certification: Physical Medicine & Rehabilitation
2815 S Seacrest Blvd, Boynton Beach, 561-381-3425

Rolnick, Murray S. (3 mentions)
FMS-Guatemala, 1983
20601 Old Cutler Rd, Miami, 305-259-6476

Rubenstein, Mark Allen (5 mentions)
SUNY-Upstate Med U, 1989
Certification: Pain Medicine, Physical Medicine & Rehabilitation
4495 Military Trail #209, Jupiter, 561-832-5000

Rubin, Stuart Alan (3 mentions)
New York Med Coll, 1988
Certification: Pain Medicine, Physical Medicine & Rehabilitation
10151 Enterprise Center Blvd #107, Boynton Beach,
561-738-2000

Rheumatology

Alboukrek, David (8 mentions)
FMS-Guatemala, 1982
Certification: Internal Medicine, Rheumatology
5162 Linton Blvd #101, Delray Beach, 561-498-1114
1050 NW 15th St #212-A, Boca Raton, 561-368-5611

Baca, Shawn Bonifacio (9 mentions)
U of New Mexico, 1987
Certification: Internal Medicine, Rheumatology
1050 NW 15th St #212A, Boca Raton, 561-368-5611
5162 Linton Blvd #101, Delray Beach, 561-498-1114

Cerejo, Rui P. (5 mentions)
Midwestern U Chicago Coll of Osteopathic Med, 1997
Certification: Internal Medicine, Rheumatology
1515 N Flagler Dr #620, West Palm Beach, 561-659-4242

Chang, Richard L. (5 mentions)
U of Miami, 1986 *Certification:* Internal Medicine, Rheumatology
10820 SW 113th Pl, Miami, 305-270-8083
45 NW 4th St, Homestead, 305-270-8083

De Solo, Santiago Miguel (9 mentions)
FMS-Dominican Republic, 1987
6150 Sunset Dr, Miami, 305-661-2299

Garces, Margarita Rosa (5 mentions)
FMS-Colombia, 1996
Certification: Internal Medicine, Rheumatology
6141 Sunset Dr #501, South Miami, 305-661-6615

Glick, Richard Stephen (5 mentions)
U of Pennsylvania, 1973
Certification: Internal Medicine, Rheumatology
6405 N Federal Hwy #105, Fort Lauderdale, 954-772-3660

Greer, Jonathan Michael (5 mentions)
U of Florida, 1983
Certification: Internal Medicine, Rheumatology
1620 S Congress Ave #201, Palm Springs, 561-439-1800

Kahn, Charles Bader (5 mentions)
Jefferson Med Coll, 1963
Certification: Internal Medicine, Rheumatology
4700 Sheridan St #C, Hollywood, 954-961-3252

Kimmel, Steven Charles (5 mentions)
New York U, 1986
Certification: Internal Medicine, Rheumatology
7431 N University Dr #300, Tamarac, 954-724-5560

Pachon, Jaime A. (5 mentions)
FMS-Colombia, 1988
Certification: Internal Medicine, Rheumatology
6141 Sunset Dr #501, South Miami, 305-661-6615

Riskin, Wayne Gerald (10 mentions)
U of Miami, 1971 *Certification:* Internal Medicine, Rheumatology
4700 Sheridan St #C, Hollywood, 954-961-3252

Ritter, Jeffrey Sanders (6 mentions)
George Washington U, 1980
Certification: Internal Medicine, Rheumatology
6150 Sunset Dr, South Miami, 305-661-2299

Rivas-Chacon, Rafael F. (5 mentions)
FMS-El Salvador, 1980
Certification: Internal Medicine, Rheumatology
3200 SW 60th Ct, Miami, 305-663-8505
3427 Johnson St, Hollywood, 305-663-8505

Ross, Michael David (6 mentions)
Emory U, 1970 *Certification:* Internal Medicine, Rheumatology
1620 S Congress Ave #201, Palm Springs, 561-439-1800

Rovira, Jose Ramon (5 mentions)
U of Miami, 1974 *Certification:* Internal Medicine, Rheumatology
11760 SW 40th St #646, Miami, 305-552-5354

Schweitz, Michael Carl (13 mentions)
George Washington U, 1972
Certification: Internal Medicine, Rheumatology
1515 N Flagler Dr #620, West Palm Beach, 561-659-4242

Vidal, Angel Francisco (5 mentions)
U of Nebraska, 1972
Certification: Internal Medicine, Rheumatology
11880 SW 40th St #202, Miami, 305-552-7020
7100 W 20th Ave #704, Hialeah, 305-821-1110

Virshup, Arthur Matthew (9 mentions)
SUNY-Upstate Med U, 1967
1515 N Flagler Dr #620, West Palm Beach, 561-659-4242

Weitz, Michael Alan (14 mentions)
Cornell U, 1974 *Certification:* Internal Medicine, Rheumatology
6150 Sunset Dr, Miami, 305-661-2299

Thoracic Surgery

Block, Mark Ian (11 mentions)
Yale U, 1987 *Certification:* Surgery, Thoracic Surgery
1150 N 35th Ave #660, Hollywood, 954-983-7113

Dylewski, Mark Richard (9 mentions)
U of Miami, 1993 *Certification:* Surgery, Thoracic Surgery
6201 SW 70th St #104, South Miami, 305-663-5864

Hwang, Ing-Sei (6 mentions)
FMS-Taiwan, 1966 *Certification:* Surgery, Thoracic Surgery
7301 N University Dr #206, Tamarac, 954-722-2788

Lamelas, Joseph (7 mentions)
FMS-Dominican Republic, 1982 *Certification:* Thoracic Surgery
8950 N Kendall Dr #607, Miami, 305-598-4446

Scoma, Robert Steven (12 mentions)
U of Texas-Dallas, 1986 *Certification:* Thoracic Surgery
1411 N Flagler Dr #8300, West Palm Beach, 561-832-1234

Waxman, Jonathan (8 mentions)
FMS-Mexico, 1997 *Certification:* Surgery, Thoracic Surgery
670 Glades Rd #300, Boca Raton, 954-395-2626

Williams, Roy Francis (6 mentions)
SUNY-Downstate Med Coll, 1988 *Certification:* Thoracic Surgery
8950 N Kendall Dr #607W, Miami, 305-598-4446

Urology

Antosek, Richard B. (5 mentions)
Philadelphia Coll of Osteopathic Med, 1981
8890 W Oakland Park Blvd #304, Sunrise, 954-748-4771

Becker, Edward Rene (4 mentions)
FMS-Dominican Republic, 1980
12953 Palms West Dr #201, Loxahatchee, 561-790-2111
530 W Sagamore, Clewiston, 561-790-2111
1630 S Congress Ave #202, Palm Springs, 561-790-2111
1100 S Main St #101, Belle Glade, 561-790-2111

Borland, Raymond Neill (18 mentions)
Johns Hopkins U, 1987 *Certification:* Urology
1411 N Flagler Dr #5300, West Palm Beach, 561-833-5594

Brown, Ruskin Wells (5 mentions)
Vanderbilt U, 1976 *Certification:* Urology
1411 N Flagler Dr #5300, West Palm Beach, 561-833-5594

Cohen, William Malcolm (4 mentions)
U of Miami, 1967 *Certification:* Urology
7400 SW 87th Ave #240, Miami, 305-270-6000
151 NW 11th St #202-B, Homestead, 305-245-1002

Flack, Charles Edward (4 mentions)
U of Toledo, 1985 *Certification:* Pediatric Urology, Urology
10301 Hagen Ranch Rd #720, Boynton Beach, 561-736-7313
5325 Greenwood Ave #203, West Palm Beach, 561-736-7313

Gomez, Cosme A. (26 mentions)
FMS-Dominican Republic, 1983 *Certification:* Urology
7265 SW 93rd Ave #201, Miami, 305-275-5525

Gosalbez Rafel, Rafael (4 mentions)
FMS-Spain, 1983 *Certification:* Pediatric Urology, Urology
3200 SW 60th Ct #104, Miami, 305-669-6448
700 N Hiatus Rd #216, Pembroke Pines, 954-433-5300

Jacobs, Michael Alon (6 mentions)
U of Southern California, 1983 *Certification:* Urology
3370 Burns Rd #101, Palm Beach Gardens, 561-624-9797

Kaplan, Marshall Mayer (5 mentions)
Loyola U Chicago, 1967 *Certification:* Urology
7710 NW 71 Ct, Tamarac, 954-726-6868

Labbie, Andrew Scott (9 mentions)
Northwestern U, 1982 *Certification:* Pediatric Urology, Urology
3200 SW 60th Ct #104, Miami, 305-669-6448
700 N Hiatus Rd #216, Pembroke Pines, 954-433-5300

Licht, Mark Robert (9 mentions)
U of Rochester, 1988 *Certification:* Urology
1601 Clint Moore Rd #182, Boca Raton, 561-955-5025

Masel, Jonathan Lloyd (6 mentions)
U of Miami, 1993 *Certification:* Urology
1150 N 35th Ave 3200, Hollywood, 954-961-7500

Mekras, John Aristedes (8 mentions)
U of Miami, 1986 *Certification:* Urology
7051 SW 62nd Ave, Miami, 305-661-8977

Papir, Dani (4 mentions)
U of Miami, 1985 *Certification:* Urology
8940 N Kendall Dr #602E, Miami, 305-598-3227

Pines, Jack A. (6 mentions)
Tulane U, 1982 *Certification:* Urology
2500 E Hallandale Beach Blvd #PH-2, Hallandale Beach, 954-456-6500

Pinon, Avelino Andres (5 mentions)
U of Miami, 1984 *Certification:* Urology
7400 SW 87th Ave #240, Miami, 305-270-6000
151 NW 11th St #202-B, Homestead, 305-245-1002
8000 W Flagler St, Miami, 305-262-3666

Puig, Robert (6 mentions)
U of Miami, 1993 *Certification:* Urology
7265 SW 93rd Ave #201, Miami, 305-275-5525

Rubinowicz, Diego Martin (6 mentions)
Med Coll of Wisconsin, 1995 *Certification:* Urology
12983 Southern Blvd #206, Loxahatchee, 561-671-4321

Sachedina, Azeem Madatali (4 mentions)
Loyola U Chicago, 1980 *Certification:* Urology
7421 N University Dr #310, Tamarac, 954-722-4950

Soloway, Mark Stephen (4 mentions)
Case Western Reserve U, 1968 *Certification:* Urology
1150 NW 14th St #309, Miami, 305-243-6596
1400 NW 10th Ave #507, Miami, 305-243-6591

Taub, Marc Eric (8 mentions)
Wayne State U, 1971 *Certification:* Urology
670 Glades Rd #200, Boca Raton, 561-391-6470

Tocci, Paul Edward (4 mentions)
U of Florida, 1970 *Certification:* Urology
4800 NE 20th Ter #404, Fort Lauderdale, 954-491-4950

Tripp, Benjamin Mark (4 mentions)
FMS-Canada, 1990 *Certification:* Urology
10075 Jog Rd #306, Boynton Beach, 561-499-8048
5130 Linton Blvd #C-1, Delray Beach, 561-499-8048

Yore, Lawrence M. (6 mentions)
Med Coll of Pennsylvania, 1984 *Certification:* Urology
5130 Linton Blvd #F6, Delray Beach, 561-496-4444

Vascular Surgery

Kang, Steven Sukho (9 mentions)
Harvard U, 1986 *Certification:* Surgery, Vascular Surgery
6200 SW 73rd St, Miami, 305-668-1660

Motta, John Crowley (12 mentions)
U of South Florida, 1987 *Certification:* Surgery, Vascular Surgery
670 Glades Rd #300, Boca Raton, 561-498-8555

Mueller, George Lester (9 mentions)
Baylor U, 1976 *Certification:* Surgery
2800 S Seacrest Blvd #200, Boynton Beach, 561-732-8200

Palamara, Arthur E. (9 mentions)
FMS-Italy, 1971
3850 Hollywood Blvd #302, Hollywood, 954-989-5533

Puente, Orlando Antonio (7 mentions)
FMS-Chile, 1980 *Certification:* Surgery
8955 SW 87th Ct #112, Miami, 305-596-0600

Reiss, Ian Michael (8 mentions)
Columbia U, 1964 *Certification:* Surgery
6200 SW 73rd St, Miami, 305-668-1660

Revilla, Antonio G., Jr. (8 mentions)
Certification: Surgery
1880 E Commercial Blvd #3, Fort Lauderdale, 954-772-0949

Sivina, Manuel (9 mentions)
FMS-Peru, 1969 *Certification:* Surgery
4300 Alton Rd #2240, Miami Beach, 305-674-2760

Zeltzer, Jack (8 mentions)
FMS-Canada, 1970
1397 Medical Park Blvd #100, Wellington, 561-964-2211

Volusia, Seminole, Orange, and Brevard Counties

Allergy/Immunology

Alidina, Laila Walji (12 mentions)
Med Coll of Pennsylvania, 1976
Certification: Allergy & Immunology, Pediatrics
661 E Altamonte Dr #315, Altamonte Springs, 407-339-3002
7758 Wallace Rd #J, Orlando, 407-351-4328

Anderson, Michael Warren (10 mentions)
FMS-Dominica, 1984
Certification: Allergy & Immunology, Internal Medicine
63 W Underwood St, Orlando, 407-872-1110
10000 W Colonial Dr, Orlando, 407-872-1110

Minor, Mark William (10 mentions)
West Virginia U, 1982
Certification: Allergy & Immunology, Internal Medicine
2290 W Eau Gallie Blvd #205, Melbourne, 321-757-5550

Schwartz, Eugene Franklin (12 mentions)
Albert Einstein Coll of Med, 1978
Certification: Allergy & Immunology, Pediatrics
793 Douglas Ave, Altamonte Springs, 407-862-5824
140 Town Loop Blvd #202, Orlando, 407-859-9099
2754 Enterprise Rd, Orange City, 386-774-9022
7560 Red Bug Lake Rd #2064, Oviedo, 407-366-7387
250 N Alafaya Trail #130, Orlando, 407-380-7991

Anesthesiology

Anderson, Mark Daniel (4 mentions)
Dartmouth Coll, 1982
Certification: Anesthesiology, Internal Medicine
291 Southall Ln, Maitland, 407-667-0505

Angert, Kevin Charles (5 mentions)
Northeastern Ohio U, 1981 *Certification:* Anesthesiology
291 Southhall Ln, Maitland, 407-667-0505

Appelblatt, Steven L. (3 mentions)
U of Michigan, 1983 *Certification:* Anesthesiology
400 N Mills Ave, Orlando, 407-872-2244

Espinola, Arturo F. (4 mentions)
FMS-Dominican Republic, 1981
1401 W Seminole Blvd, Sanford, 407-321-4500

House, Jeffrey Thomas (3 mentions)
U of Chicago, 1982 *Certification:* Anesthesiology
291 Southhall Ln, Maitland, 407-667-0505

Mann, Michael Stephan (3 mentions)
U of South Florida, 1991 *Certification:* Anesthesiology
291 Southhall Ln, Maitland, 407-667-0505

Merrell, Walter Jerry (5 mentions)
Vanderbilt U, 1982 *Certification:* Anesthesiology
291 Southhall Ln, Maitland, 407-667-0505

Murbach, Roger Steven (5 mentions)
Rosalind Franklin U, 1984 *Certification:* Anesthesiology
400 N Mills Ave, Orlando, 407-872-2244

Stockton, Edward Alan (6 mentions)
U of Michigan, 1983 *Certification:* Anesthesiology
400 N Mills Ave, Orlando, 407-872-2244

Stoltzfus, Daniel Paul (3 mentions)
U of Texas-Houston, 1983
Certification: Anesthesiology, Critical Care Medicine
291 Southhall Ln, Maitland, 407-667-0505

Cardiac Surgery

Accola, Kevin Donn (16 mentions)
U of Illinois, 1984 *Certification:* Thoracic Surgery
217 Hillcrest St, Orlando, 407-425-1566

Bott, Jeffrey Norman (10 mentions)
U of Florida, 1990 *Certification:* Surgery, Thoracic Surgery
217 Hillcrest St, Orlando, 407-425-1566

Palmer, George Joseph, III (11 mentions)
Creighton U, 1981 *Certification:* Surgery, Thoracic Surgery
217 Hillcrest St, Orlando, 407-425-1566

Sand, Mark Evan (23 mentions)
U of Rochester, 1978 *Certification:* Surgery, Thoracic Surgery
217 Hillcrest St, Orlando, 407-425-1566

Cardiology

Arab, Dinesh (3 mentions)
FMS-India, 1995 *Certification:* Cardiovascular Disease,
Internal Medicine, Interventional Cardiology
873 Sterthaus Ave, Ormond Beach, 386-671-0691

Boswell, Robert Blan (3 mentions)
Vanderbilt U, 1971
Certification: Cardiovascular Disease, Internal Medicine
2320 N Orange Ave, Orlando, 407-896-0054
4150 US 27 S, Sebring, 863-386-0054
3102 Kurt St, Eustis, 352-357-0055

Carson, Thomas P. (3 mentions)
U of South Florida, 1979
Certification: Pediatric Cardiology, Pediatrics
3813 Oakwater Cir, Orlando, 407-902-2866

Chapman, Enrique J. (5 mentions)
FMS-Spain, 1978
Certification: Cardiovascular Disease, Internal Medicine
60 W Gore St, Orlando, 407-650-1300

Dalton, Robert Paul, Jr. (3 mentions)
U of Oklahoma, 1991 *Certification:* Interventional Cardiology
60 W Gore St #210, Orlando, 407-650-1300

Domescek, Ronald Richard (3 mentions)
SUNY-Upstate Med U, 1983 *Certification:* Cardiovascular
Disease, Internal Medicine, Interventional Cardiology
60 W Gore St #210, Orlando, 407-650-1300

Einhorn, Arnold Mark (10 mentions)
FMS-Grenada, 1982
Certification: Cardiovascular Disease, Internal Medicine
10000 W Colonial Dr, Ocoee, 407-351-5384
1717 S Orange Ave #105, Orlando, 407-351-5384

Elsakr, Ashraf Shoukry (5 mentions)
FMS-Egypt, 1984
Certification: Cardiovascular Disease, Interventional Cardiology
840 Dunlawton Ave #A, Port Orange, 386-304-9672

Fahey, Francis Joseph (4 mentions)
New York Med Coll, 1989
Certification: Cardiovascular Disease, Internal Medicine
1613 N Mills Ave, Orlando, 407-894-4474
689 E Altamonte Dr, Altamonte Springs, 407-767-7262
2984 Alfaya Trail #1000, Oviedo, 407-588-1585
4638 Sun 'n Lake Blvd, Sebring, 863-386-0055

Fornace, Donald J. (3 mentions)
Philadelphia Coll of Osteopathic Med, 1983
1184 Ocean Shore Blvd, Ormond Beach, 386-441-6636

Greenwood, Scott Douglas (5 mentions)
Washington U, 1977
Certification: Cardiovascular Disease, Internal Medicine
60 W Gore St, Orlando, 407-650-1300

Grullon, Carlos P. (3 mentions)
Certification: Cardiovascular Disease, Internal Medicine,
Interventional Cardiology
910 Williston Park Point #1000, Lake Mary, 407-833-8028
1565 Saxon Blvd #201, Deltona, 386-532-1232

Henderson, David Alan (6 mentions)
West Virginia U, 1980 *Certification:* Cardiovascular Disease,
Internal Medicine, Interventional Cardiology
873 Sterthaus Ave #302, Ormond Beach, 386-615-1521

Hippalgaonkar, Rajendra (4 mentions)
FMS-India, 1979
Certification: Cardiovascular Disease, Internal Medicine
1403 Medical Plaza Dr #106, Sanford, 407-330-9900
932 Saxon Blvd #A, Orange City, 386-774-2100

Jamidar, Humayun A. (6 mentions)
FMS-Ireland, 1980 *Certification:* Cardiovascular Disease,
Internal Medicine, Interventional Cardiology
311 N Clyde Morris Blvd #320, Daytona Beach, 386-255-5331

Jamnadas, Pradipkumar P. (3 mentions)
FMS-United Kingdom, 1981 *Certification:* Cardiovascular
Disease, Internal Medicine, Interventional Cardiology
1900 N Mills Ave #107, Orlando, 407-896-7899

Karas, Steven Peter (6 mentions)
Duke U, 1983 *Certification:* Cardiovascular Disease,
Internal Medicine, Interventional Cardiology
200 E Sheridan Rd #G, Melbourne, 321-725-4500

Pollak, Scott Jonathan (5 mentions)
Indiana U, 1981
Certification: Cardiovascular Disease, Clinical Cardiac
Electrophysiology, Internal Medicine, Interventional Cardiology
1745 N Mills Ave, Orlando, 407-841-7151

Rao, Ravi (3 mentions)
Northwestern U, 1992
Certification: Cardiovascular Disease, Interventional Cardiology
7075 N US Hwy 1 #200, Port St John, 321-636-6914
1709 Garden St, Titusville, 321-636-6914

Rao, Surya P. (3 mentions)
Certification: Cardiovascular Disease
7075 N US Hwy 1 #200, Port St John, 321-636-6914
1709 Garden St, Titusville, 321-636-6914

Rodriguez, Arsenio Ralph (6 mentions)
U of Florida, 1984 *Certification:* Cardiovascular Disease,
Internal Medicine, Interventional Cardiology
1745 N Mills Ave #100, Orlando, 407-841-7151

Ronaldson, James Michael (3 mentions)
FMS-Grenada, 1983
Certification: Cardiovascular Disease, Internal Medicine
200 E Sheridan Rd, Melbourne, 321-725-4500

Schwartz, Kerry Martin (4 mentions)
Emory U, 1974
Certification: Cardiovascular Disease, Internal Medicine
1613 N Mills Ave, Orlando, 407-894-4474
2984 Alfaya Trail #1000, Oviedo, 407-588-1585
4638 Sun 'n Lake Blvd, Sebring, 863-386-0055

Story, William Emory (3 mentions)
Emory U, 1976
Certification: Cardiovascular Disease, Internal Medicine
1745 N Mills Ave #100, Orlando, 407-841-7151

Swain, Thomas William (3 mentions)
Hahnemann U, 1980
Certification: Cardiovascular Disease, Internal Medicine
200 E Sheridan Rd, Melbourne, 321-725-4500

Tarver, James Henry, III (3 mentions)
Boston U, 1988 *Certification:* Cardiovascular Disease
60 W Gore St #210, Orlando, 407-650-1300

Taussig, Andrew Steven (11 mentions)
Emory U, 1978 *Certification:* Cardiovascular Disease,
Internal Medicine, Interventional Cardiology
1745 N Mills Ave #100, Orlando, 407-841-7151

Vallario, Lawrence Edward (4 mentions)
U of Florida, 1981
Certification: Cardiovascular Disease, Internal Medicine
1565 Saxon Blvd #202, Deltona, 386-532-1232
910 Williston Park Pt #1000, Lake Mary, 407-833-8028

Walker, John Leslie (3 mentions)
U of Iowa, 1973
Certification: Cardiovascular Disease, Internal Medicine
873 Sterthaus Ave #302, Ormond Beach, 386-677-5351

Weinstein, Irwin Ross (4 mentions)
SUNY-Buffalo, 1976 *Certification:* Cardiovascular Disease,
Internal Medicine, Interventional Cardiology
60 W Gore St, Orlando, 407-650-1300

Whitworth, Hall Baker, Jr. (7 mentions)
Emory U, 1978 *Certification:* Cardiovascular Disease,
Internal Medicine, Interventional Cardiology
1745 N Mills Ave, Orlando, 407-841-7151

Dermatology

Johnson, Jerri L. (12 mentions)
U of Florida, 1985 *Certification:* Dermatology
411 Maitland Ave #1001, Altamonte Springs, 407-260-2606

Knight, James Matthew (7 mentions)
Indiana U, 2000 *Certification:* Dermatology
1111 S Orange Ave #4, Orlando, 407-992-0660

Knipe, Ronald Charles (13 mentions)
U of Florida, 1990 *Certification:* Dermatology
1111 S Orange Ave 4th Fl, Orlando, 407-581-2888
70 W Gore St #200A, Orlando, 407-581-2888

Meisenheimer, John Long (7 mentions)
U of Kentucky, 1983 *Certification:* Dermatology
7300 Sandlake Commons Blvd #105, Orlando, 407-352-2444

Parks, Jeffrey Dean (6 mentions)
U of Nebraska, 1993 *Certification:* Dermatology
400 Lakebridge Plaza Dr, Ormond Beach, 904-677-9044

Possick, Sidney (5 mentions)
Tufts U, 1965 *Certification:* Dermatology
655 N Clyde Morris Blvd #B, Daytona Beach, 386-252-5578

Sevigny, Gina Mollis (10 mentions)
U of Florida, 1994 *Certification:* Dermatology
305 Clyde Morris Blvd #150, Ormond Beach, 386-615-1771

Tabas, Maxine (12 mentions)
Washington U, 1980 *Certification:* Dermatology
1901 Lee Rd, Winter Park, 407-647-7300

Emergency Medicine

Bullard, Timothy Bruce (3 mentions)
U of Florida, 1976
Certification: Emergency Medicine, Internal Medicine
1414 Kuhl Ave, Orlando, 407-841-5111

Clark, Mark Christopher (7 mentions)
U of South Florida, 1984 *Certification:* Emergency
Medicine, Pediatric Emergency Medicine
1414 S Orange Ave, Orlando, 407-841-5210

Corbett, Steven Charles (3 mentions)
Wayne State U, 1979 *Certification:* Emergency Medicine
9400 Turkey Lake Rd, Orlando, 407-351-8500

Knight, Stephen Senne (4 mentions)
U of South Florida, 1976 *Certification:* Emergency Medicine
701 W Plymouth Ave, Deland, 386-943-4650

O'Brien, John Francis (7 mentions)
Wayne State U, 1981 *Certification:* Emergency Medicine
1414 S Orange Ave, Orlando, 407-841-5111

Poole, William Randall (4 mentions)
U of Alabama, 1980 *Certification:* Emergency Medicine
601 E Altamonte Dr, Altamonte Springs, 407-767-2314
601 E Rollins St, Orlando, 407-767-2314
201 N Parks Ave, Apopka, 407-767-2314
7727 Lake Underhill Rd, Orlando, 407-767-2314

Springer, Peter Charles (3 mentions)
Tulane U, 1997 *Certification:* Emergency Medicine
303 N Clyde Morris Blvd, Daytona Beach, 386-253-3238

Tesar, James Daniel (3 mentions)
U of Wisconsin, 1982 *Certification:* Emergency Medicine
1512 S Orange Ave, Orlando, 407-841-5236

Weiner, Tracy I. (3 mentions)
Nova Southeastern Coll of Osteopathic Med, 1994
Certification: Emergency Medicine
1055 Saxon Blvd, Orange City, 386-917-5000

Endocrinology

Bourne, Kimberley Ann (11 mentions)
U of South Florida, 1990
Certification: Endocrinology, Diabetes, and Metabolism
6150 Metrowest Blvd #105, Orlando, 407-293-2150

Desrosiers, Paul Michael (10 mentions)
U of North Carolina, 1974
Certification: Pediatric Endocrinology, Pediatrics
32 W Gore St 3rd Fl, Orlando, 321-841-3303

Glickman, Penny Sue (19 mentions)
U of South Florida, 1985 *Certification:* Endocrinology,
Diabetes, and Metabolism, Internal Medicine
635 N Maitland Ave, Maitland, 407-629-4901

Pacheco, Carlos Alberto (18 mentions)
FMS-Dominica, 1985 *Certification:* Endocrinology,
Diabetes, and Metabolism, Internal Medicine
635 N Maitland Ave, Maitland, 407-629-4901

Roberts, Victor Lawrence (10 mentions)
FMS-Mexico, 1979
Certification: Endocrinology and Metabolism, Internal Medicine
1561 W Fairbanks Ave #200, Winter Park, 407-331-1117

Family Practice *(see note on page 9)*

Billmeier, David Walter (4 mentions)
U of Florida, 1995 *Certification:* Family Medicine
790 Dunlawton Ave #E, Port Orange, 386-760-1877

Dana, Gary Carl (3 mentions)
U of Florida, 1992 *Certification:* Family Medicine
7125 Murrell Rd #D, Melbourne, 321-242-8790

Hardy, Philip Todd (3 mentions)
Loma Linda U, 1994 *Certification:* Family Medicine
7800 Lake Underhill Rd, Orlando, 407-282-2244

Janovitz, Richard Henry (4 mentions)
U of Miami, 1975 *Certification:* Family Medicine
2863 Delaney Ave, Orlando, 407-843-1620

Kramer, Lawrence Donald (3 mentions)
Philadelphia Coll of Osteopathic Med, 1972
Certification: Family Medicine
1340 Tuskawilla Rd #101, Winter Springs, 407-699-1160

Krupitsky, Andrew E. (4 mentions)
New York Coll of Osteopathic Med, 1984
249 Maitland Ave #1000, Altamonte Springs, 407-332-6366

Parrillo, Jan Carl (4 mentions)
U of Florida, 1984 *Certification:* Family Medicine
2863 Delaney Ave, Orlando, 407-843-1620

Pursley, Timothy Jay (11 mentions)
Loma Linda U, 1994 *Certification:* Family Medicine
402 Lake Howell Rd, Maitland, 407-628-4312

Taraschi, Peter William (3 mentions)
Philadelphia Coll of Osteopathic Med, 1984
6100 Minton Rd NW #102, Palm Bay, 321-724-1171

Waldheim, Eddie C., Jr. (12 mentions)
U of South Florida, 1982
Certification: Family Medicine, Geriatric Medicine
402 Lake Howell Rd, Maitland, 407-628-4312

Gastroenterology

Bornstein, Jeffrey Arthur (5 mentions)
George Washington U, 1989
Certification: Pediatric Gastroenterology
83 W Columbia St, Orlando, 321-841-3338

Kartsonis, Athan Paul (5 mentions)
U of Miami, 1981
Certification: Gastroenterology, Internal Medicine
1301 Hickory St, Melbourne, 321-984-1981

Lebioda, David Henry (5 mentions)
Indiana U, 1980
Certification: Gastroenterology, Internal Medicine
623 Maitland Ave #2200, Altamonte Springs, 407-830-8661
8000 Red Bug Lake Rd #226, Oviedo, 407-830-8661

Levine, Henry (8 mentions)
Johns Hopkins U, 1976
Certification: Gastroenterology, Internal Medicine
1817 N Mills Ave, Orlando, 407-896-1726
255 Citrus Tower Blvd #207, Clermont, 407-896-1726

Mayoral, William (9 mentions)
FMS-Colombia, 1989
Certification: Gastroenterology, Internal Medicine
1817 N Mills Ave, Orlando, 407-896-1726
4106 W Lake Mary Blvd #201, Lake Mary, 407-896-1726
431 W Oak St, Kissimmee, 407-896-1726

Moulis, Harry (8 mentions)
U of Miami, 1987 *Certification:* Gastroenterology
3635 S Clyde Morris Blvd #100, Port Orange, 386-788-1242
305 Clyde Morris Blvd #270, Ormond Beach, 386-671-6111

Prado, Martin Gino F. (6 mentions)
FMS-Philippines, 1989
1070 N Stone St #D, Deland, 386-822-9410

Ruderman, William Brandon (15 mentions)
Columbia U, 1977
Certification: Gastroenterology, Internal Medicine
1817 N Mills Ave, Orlando, 407-896-1726
4106 W Lake May Blvd, Lake Mary, 407-896-1726
7432 Red Bug Lake Rd, Oviedo, 407-896-1726

Schuman, Elliot Howard (5 mentions)
U of Miami, 1976
Certification: Gastroenterology, Internal Medicine
825 Century Medical Dr #A, Titusville, 321-269-0747

Shafran, Ira (7 mentions)
Ohio State U, 1974
Certification: Gastroenterology, Internal Medicine
701 W Morse Blvd, Winter Park, 407-629-8121

Stella, Gregory John (6 mentions)
Johns Hopkins U, 1979
Certification: Gastroenterology, Internal Medicine
3635 S Clyde Morris Blvd #100, Port Orange, 386-788-1242
305 Clyde Morris Blvd #270, Ormond Beach, 386-671-6111

Straker, Richard J., II (9 mentions)
U of Toledo, 1982
Certification: Gastroenterology, Internal Medicine
623 Maitland Ave #2200, Altamonte Springs, 407-830-8661
8000 Red Bug Lake Rd, Oviedo, 407-830-8661

Styne, Philip Nathan (6 mentions)
U of Miami, 1976
Certification: Gastroenterology, Internal Medicine
1817 N Mills Ave, Orlando, 407-896-1726
4106 W Lake Mary Blvd #201, Lake Mary, 407-896-1726

General Surgery

Barr, Louis H. (9 mentions)
Georgetown U, 1973 *Certification:* Surgery
2501 N Orange Ave #411, Orlando, 407-303-7399

Black, Harry Huntley (4 mentions)
U of Florida, 1984 *Certification:* Surgery
201 N Clyde Morris Blvd #100, Daytona Beach, 386-238-3295

Childers, Timothy Charles (12 mentions)
U of Florida, 1995 *Certification:* Surgery
1181 Orange Ave, Winter Park, 407-647-1331

Davis, Kenley B. (4 mentions)
Howard U, 1980 *Certification:* Surgery
250 N Alafaya Trail #110, Orlando, 407-381-3904

Demers, Marc Lafrance (6 mentions)
Boston U, 1985 *Certification:* Surgery
14 W Gore St, Orlando, 407-423-3815

Donohoe, Michael Joseph (4 mentions)
New Jersey Med Sch, 1982 *Certification:* Surgery
685 Peachwood Dr, Deland, 386-738-1144

Fabian, Michael Anthony (4 mentions)
Duke U, 1986 *Certification:* Surgery
1890 LPGA Blvd #250, Daytona Beach, 386-274-0250

Huether, William Leonard (4 mentions)
U of South Florida, 1994 *Certification:* Surgery
4106 W Lake Mary Blvd #330, Lake Mary, 407-833-9195

Kahky, Michael Paul (5 mentions)
SUNY-Downstate Med Coll, 1982 *Certification:* Surgery
1400 S Orange Ave, Orlando, 407-648-3800
14 W Gore St, Orlando, 407-423-3815

Mahan, Thomas Kepner (5 mentions)
U of Maryland, 1994 *Certification:* Surgery
1181 Orange Ave, Winter Park, 407-647-1331

Morgan, Ross Allan (8 mentions)
U of Michigan, 1982 *Certification:* Pediatric Surgery, Surgery
1814 Lucerne Terr #A, Orlando, 407-540-1000

Olinde, John Garnier (4 mentions)
Louisiana State U, 1995 *Certification:* Surgery
1344 S Apollo Blvd #D, Melbourne, 321-724-1084

Portoghese, Joseph D. (8 mentions)
U of South Florida, 1982 *Certification:* Surgery
2501 N Orange Ave #411, Orlando, 407-303-7399

Posada, Roberto G. (8 mentions)
FMS-Dominican Republic, 1982 *Certification:* Surgery
1181 Orange Ave, Winter Park, 407-647-1331

Ramshaw, David Gorton (9 mentions)
U of Florida, 1991 *Certification:* Surgery
1890 LPGA Blvd #250, Daytona Beach, 386-274-0250

Rasmussen, Ronald Ray (4 mentions)
Michigan State U, 1996 *Certification:* Surgery
873 Sterthaus Ave #212A, Ormond Beach, 386-676-6436

Robertson, John William, Jr. (4 mentions)
U of Florida, 1979 *Certification:* Surgery
4106 W Lake Mary Blvd #330, Lake Mary, 407-833-9195

Smith, Jeffrey Richard (7 mentions)
U of Florida, 1994 *Certification:* Surgery
14 W Gore St, Orlando, 407-423-3815
9430 Turkey Lake Rd #118, Orlando, 407-423-3815
22 W Underwood St, Orlando, 407-423-3815

Steinbaum, Jeremy D. (4 mentions)
U of Miami, 1989 *Certification:* Surgery
1053 Medical Center Dr #242, Orange City, 386-775-0333

Thompson, Clifford Todd (7 mentions)
U of Florida, 1990 *Certification:* Surgery
1130 Hickory St, Melbourne, 321-725-4500

Wiese, Jon Dick (5 mentions)
U of Nebraska, 1983 *Certification:* Surgery
521 W State Rd 434 #308, Longwood, 407-767-5808

Zambos, John Mitchell (6 mentions)
West Virginia U, 1983 *Certification:* Surgery
605 N Washington Ave #200, Titusville, 321-383-2630

Geriatrics

Biggs, Paul Robert (3 mentions)
Uniformed Services U of Health Sciences, 1981
Certification: Family Medicine
1344 S Apollo Blvd #A, Melbourne, 321-956-0122

Cole, Ariel Forrester (3 mentions)
U of South Florida, 1999
Certification: Family Medicine, Geriatric Medicine
2501 N Orange Ave #235, Orlando, 407-303-1967

Mercado, Carlos Eduardo (4 mentions)
FMS-Colombia, 1988
Certification: Family Medicine, Geriatric Medicine
1307 S International Pkwy #2091, Lake Mary, 407-771-0404

Oslos, Neil Robert (3 mentions)
Indiana U, 1978
Certification: Family Medicine, Geriatric Medicine
303 N Clyde Morris Blvd, Daytona Beach, 386-254-4165

Page, Ralph Patrick (3 mentions)
FMS-Italy, 1979
Certification: Geriatric Medicine, Internal Medicine
1026 Florida Ave S, Rockledge, 321-631-1400

Wadsworth, Lyle Edward (3 mentions)
Vanderbilt U, 1975 *Certification:* Geriatric Medicine,
    Hospice and Palliative Medicine, Internal Medicine
890 N Boundary Ave #102, Deland, 386-740-0224

Hematology/Oncology

Dodd, Paul Melton, III (8 mentions)
Baylor U, 1992
Certification: Hematology, Internal Medicine, Medical Oncology
325 Clyde Morris Blvd #450, Ormond Beach, 386-673-2442
1075 Mason Ave, Daytona Beach, 386-441-3033
800 Dunlawton Blvd #101, Port Orange, 386-767-6977

Dunn, Philip Herbert (6 mentions)
Duke U, 1976 *Certification:* Internal Medicine, Medical Oncology
2501 N Orange Ave #381, Orlando, 407-898-5452
255 Moray Ln, Winter Park, 407-628-5594

Durkin, Walter James (5 mentions)
Loyola U Chicago, 1971
Certification: Hematology, Internal Medicine, Medical Oncology
303 N Clyde Morris Blvd, Daytona Beach, 386-254-4212
1688 W Granada Blvd, Ormond Beach, 386-615-4400
401 Palmetto St, New Smyrna Beach, 386-424-5038

Giusti, Vincent F. (5 mentions)
U of Pennsylvania, 1964
Certification: Pediatric Hematology-Oncology, Pediatrics
50 W Sturtevant St, Orlando, 321-841-1851

Grow, William Barron (5 mentions)
U of Florida, 1996
Certification: Hematology, Internal Medicine, Medical Oncology
2501 N Orange Ave #381, Orlando, 407-898-5452
255 Moray Ln, Winter Park, 407-898-5452

Molthrop, David Charles (14 mentions)
Louisiana State U, 1987 *Certification:* Medical Oncology
2501 N Orange Ave #381, Orlando, 407-898-5452
255 Moray Ln, Winter Park, 407-898-5452

Ortega, Gregory Luis (6 mentions)
FMS-Dominican Republic, 1979
Certification: Hematology, Internal Medicine, Medical Oncology
1061 Medical Center Dr Summit Bldg #110, Orange City,
    386-774-1223
2100 W 1st St, Sanford, 407-323-2250

Reynolds, Robert B. (6 mentions)
FMS-Ireland, 1984
Certification: Internal Medicine, Medical Oncology
2501 N Orange Ave, Orlando, 407-898-2343
394 E Altamonte Dr #312, Altamonte Springs, 407-834-5151

Wall, Judith E. (5 mentions)
FMS-Grenada, 1985
Certification: Pediatric Hematology-Oncology, Pediatrics
1717 S Orange Ave #100, Orlando, 407-650-7230

Weiss, Richard Carl (5 mentions)
Hahnemann U, 1979
Certification: Hematology, Internal Medicine, Medical Oncology
1688 W Granada Blvd, Ormond Beach, 386-615-4400
303 N Clyde Morris Blvd, Daytona Beach, 386-254-4212

Zehngebot, Lee M. (23 mentions)
U of Pennsylvania, 1976
Certification: Internal Medicine, Medical Oncology
2501 N Orange Ave #381, Orlando, 407-898-5452
255 Moray Ln, Winter Park, 407-628-5594

Infectious Disease

Barile, Anthony John (9 mentions)
U of Miami, 1993
Certification: Infectious Disease, Internal Medicine
300 Michigan Ave, Melbourne, 321-676-6322

Carrizosa Navarro, Jaime (8 mentions)
FMS-Colombia, 1966
Certification: Infectious Disease, Internal Medicine
685 Palm Springs Dr #2A, Altamonte Springs, 407-830-5577

Crespo, Antonio (7 mentions)
FMS-Venezuela, 1993
Certification: Infectious Disease, Internal Medicine
1012 Lucerne Terr, Orlando, 407-423-1039

Garcia-Dimayuga, Eloisa (9 mentions)
FMS-Philippines, 1986 *Certification:* Infectious Disease
303 N Clyde Morris Blvd, Daytona Beach, 386-238-2235

Licitra, Carmelo Mario (11 mentions)
U of Florida, 1982
Certification: Infectious Disease, Internal Medicine
1012 Lucerne Terr, Orlando, 407-423-1039

McClelland, James Joseph (14 mentions)
U of South Florida, 1979
Certification: Infectious Disease, Internal Medicine
3909 N Orange Ave, Orlando, 407-896-9660

Sieger, Barry Edwin (8 mentions)
Boston U, 1968
Certification: Infectious Disease, Internal Medicine
77 W Underwood St, Orlando, 321-841-7750

Spoto, Vincent M. (8 mentions)
U of South Florida, 1988
Certification: Infectious Disease, Internal Medicine
218 Strathy Ln, Winter Park, 407-629-9400

Infertility

De Vane, Gary Williams (13 mentions)
Baylor U, 1971 *Certification:* Obstetrics & Gynecology,
   Reproductive Endocrinology/Infertility
3435 Pinehurst Ave, Orlando, 407-740-0909

Loy, Randall Alan (6 mentions)
Med Coll of Georgia, 1983 *Certification:* Obstetrics &
   Gynecology, Reproductive Endocrinology/Infertility
3435 Pinehurst Ave, Orlando, 407-740-0909

Internal Medicine *(see note on page 9)*

Anderson, Kyle Raymond (3 mentions)
Vanderbilt U, 1986 *Certification:* Internal Medicine
5305 Babcock St NE, Palm Bay, 321-676-9009

Collins, Donald Michael (9 mentions)
Wake Forest U, 1994 *Certification:* Internal Medicine
1109 Lucerne Terr, Orlando, 407-843-4251

Covelli, Frank Joseph (3 mentions)
FMS-Italy, 1969 *Certification:* Internal Medicine
331 N Maitland Ave #C1, Maitland, 407-644-2218

Davis, Glen Franklin (6 mentions)
U of Miami, 1978 *Certification:* Internal Medicine
4106 W Lake Mary Blvd #301, Lake Mary, 407-333-2503

Kapoor, Rajan (4 mentions)
FMS-India, 1989 *Certification:* Internal Medicine
471 N Semoran Blvd, Winter Park, 407-678-5656

Mancini, John Daniel (4 mentions)
U of South Florida, 1985 *Certification:* Internal Medicine
1855 Hollywood Ave, Winter Park, 407-645-2334

McGrath, Kimberly Neal (3 mentions)
Virginia Commonwealth U, 1976 *Certification:* Internal Medicine
95 Bulldog Blvd #101, Melbourne, 321-722-9731
903 Jordan Blass #101, Melbourne, 321-253-4032

Nashed, Magdy Samuel (4 mentions)
FMS-Egypt, 1972
3953 S Nova Rd, Port Orange, 386-788-9461

Pressley, Kevin (3 mentions)
Kirksville Coll of Osteopathic Med, 1987
4474 Edgewater Dr, Orlando, 407-297-8007

Ryan, John Francis (6 mentions)
SUNY-Downstate Med Coll, 1977 *Certification:* Internal Medicine
4106 W Lake Mary Blvd #301, Lake Mary, 407-333-2503

Seth, Monisha Alpna (4 mentions)
U of Pennsylvania, 1998 *Certification:* Internal Medicine
7975 Lake Underhill Rd #220, Orlando, 407-303-6511

Simmons, David Robert (5 mentions)
Baylor U, 1990 *Certification:* Internal Medicine
5201 Raymond St, Orlando, 407-629-1599

Smuckler, David Todd (6 mentions)
Georgetown U, 1978
Certification: Geriatric Medicine, Internal Medicine
818 S Main Ln, Orlando, 321-841-6600

Nephrology

Abbott, Lionel Charme (8 mentions)
FMS-Chile, 1971 *Certification:* Internal Medicine, Nephrology
3885 Oakwater Cir, Orlando, 407-851-5600
3000 N Orange Ave #D, Orlando, 407-851-5600

Cohen, Jeffrey Mark (8 mentions)
Washington U, 1985 *Certification:* Internal Medicine, Nephrology
3885 Oakwater Cir, Orlando, 407-851-5600
3000 N Orange Ave #D, Orlando, 407-851-5600

Patel, Vinod B. (8 mentions)
FMS-India, 1969 *Certification:* Internal Medicine, Nephrology
544 Health Blvd, Daytona Beach, 386-322-6340

Purandare, Vinayak Vishnu (6 mentions)
FMS-India, 1976 *Certification:* Internal Medicine, Nephrology
401 Lakebridge Plaza Dr, Ormond Beach, 386-672-8595

Ramirez, Jorge (7 mentions)
FMS-Mexico, 1985 *Certification:* Pediatric Nephrology
83 W Columbia St, Orlando, 321-841-7970

Ranjit, Uday Krishnalal (8 mentions)
FMS-India, 1981 *Certification:* Internal Medicine, Nephrology
2501 N Orange Ave #537, Orlando, 407-894-4693

Rodriguez, Alfred (7 mentions)
FMS-Dominican Republic, 1987
Certification: Internal Medicine, Nephrology
766 N Sun Dr #3030, Lake Mary, 407-444-2800

Sackel, Howard Allen (11 mentions)
SUNY-Upstate Med U, 1976
Certification: Internal Medicine, Nephrology
2501 N Orange Ave #537, Orlando, 407-894-4693

Singh, Joscelyn Peter (8 mentions)
FMS-Jamaica, 1984 *Certification:* Internal Medicine, Nephrology
335 Clyde Morris Blvd #260, Ormond Beach, 386-672-4001
385 Palm Coast Pkwy SW #2, Palm Coast, 386-672-4001

Warren, Joseph Woodman (10 mentions)
West Virginia U, 1970
Certification: Internal Medicine, Nephrology
2501 N Orange Ave #537N, Orlando, 407-323-4348

Neurological Surgery

Behrmann, Donald Lee (13 mentions)
Indiana U, 1986 *Certification:* Neurological Surgery
1605 W Fairbanks Ave, Winter Park, 407-975-0200

Field, Melvin (10 mentions)
U of Florida, 1996 *Certification:* Neurological Surgery
1605 W Fairbanks Ave, Winter Park, 407-975-0200

Kuhn, William Brian (10 mentions)
Indiana U, 1983 *Certification:* Neurological Surgery
311 N Clyde Morris Blvd #550, Daytona Beach, 386-255-8582

Paine, Jonathan Treat (9 mentions)
U of Florida, 1981 *Certification:* Neurological Surgery
1305 S Valentine, Melbourne, 321-727-2468

Razack, Nizam Mohamed (10 mentions)
SUNY-Buffalo, 1990 *Certification:* Neurological Surgery
32 W Gore St 5th Fl, Orlando, 407-423-7172
7350 Sandlake Commons Blvd #3305, Orlando, 407-423-7172
1315 S International Pkwy #1111, Lake Mary, 407-206-3755

Sawin, Paul Douglas (19 mentions)
U of Iowa, 1991 *Certification:* Neurological Surgery
1605 W Fairbanks Ave, Winter Park, 407-975-0200

Vinas, Federico C. (9 mentions)
FMS-Argentina, 1987 *Certification:* Neurological Surgery
311 N Clyde Morris Blvd #550, Daytona Beach, 386-253-7644

Neurology

Davis, Ronald Gerard (6 mentions)
East Carolina U, 1990 *Certification:* Neurology with Special
   Qualifications in Child Neurology, Pediatrics
7485 Sandlake Commons Blvd, Orlando, 407-293-1122

Dinkla, Hendrik (9 mentions)
U of Miami, 1984 *Certification:* Neurology
742 W Plymouth Ave, Deland, 386-736-8622

Gold, Scott Larry (5 mentions)
U of Miami, 1979 *Certification:* Neurology
1535 W NASA Blvd #A, Melbourne, 321-984-2133

Goodman, Ira Jay (9 mentions)
Med Coll of Pennsylvania, 1979 *Certification:* Neurology
828 Main Ln, Orlando, 407-841-2452

Honeycutt, William David (10 mentions)
U of Alabama, 1987 *Certification:* Neurology
301 N Maitland Ave, Maitland, 407-647-5996

Isa, Arnaldo (10 mentions)
U of Florida, 1992 *Certification:* Neurology
301 N Maitland Ave, Maitland, 407-647-5996

Klafter, Mark J. (5 mentions)
Midwestern U Coll of Osteopathic Med, 1990
Certification: Neurology
3849 Oakwater Cir, Orlando, 407-240-1762

Menkin, Martin (6 mentions)
Wake Forest U, 1972 *Certification:* Neurology
60 Columbia St #C, Orlando, 407-650-8075

Oppenheim, Ronald Edward (5 mentions)
U of Cincinnati, 1979 *Certification:* Neurology
1400 S Orlando Ave, Winter Park, 407-645-3151

Rosenberg, Stephen Jay (7 mentions)
U of Pennsylvania, 1971 *Certification:* Neurology
6001 Vineland Rd #116, Orlando, 407-352-1112

Scott, James Arthur (10 mentions)
U of Florida, 1986 *Certification:* Neurology
311 N Clyde Morris Blvd #490, Daytona Beach, 386-673-2500
8 Mirror Lake Dr, Ormond Beach, 386-673-2500

Sunter, William Robert, Jr. (5 mentions)
U of Miami, 1985 *Certification:* Neurology
200 E Sheridan Rd, Melbourne, 321-725-4500

Unger, Richard Mahlon, Jr. (6 mentions)
Med U of South Carolina, 1996 *Certification:* Neurology
116 Silver Palm Ave, Melbourne, 321-725-6999

Obstetrics/Gynecology

Carbiener, Pamela Parke (6 mentions)
U of South Dakota, 1988 *Certification:* Obstetrics & Gynecology
1890 LPGA Blvd #160, Daytona Beach, 386-252-4701

Cortez, Stephen James (3 mentions)
Tufts U, 1989 *Certification:* Obstetrics & Gynecology
1890 LPGA Blvd #160, Daytona Beach, 386-252-4701

De Freese, Craig Norman (4 mentions)
SUNY-Upstate Med U, 1981 *Certification:* Obstetrics & Gynecology
661 E Altamonte Dr #224, Altamonte Springs, 407-830-9000

Dukes, Steven Louis (4 mentions)
Med Coll of Georgia, 1991 *Certification:* Obstetrics & Gynecology
100 Perth Ln, Winter Park, 407-645-5565

Gibbs, Thomas Crawford (7 mentions)
FMS-Mexico, 1979 *Certification:* Obstetrics & Gynecology
820 Lucerne Terr, Orlando, 407-648-5101

Haddox, Linda (3 mentions)
Texas A&M U, 1992 *Certification:* Obstetrics & Gynecology
500 Health Blvd, Daytona Beach, 386-252-5858

Hill, D. Ashley (4 mentions)
U of South Florida, 1990 *Certification:* Obstetrics & Gynecology
235 E Princeton St #200, Orlando, 407-303-1444

Lambert, Lori Kathryn (3 mentions)
U of Florida, 1985 *Certification:* Obstetrics & Gynecology
7051 Dr Phillips Blvd #5, Orlando, 407-363-2000

Lazar, Arnold Joseph (5 mentions)
U of Iowa, 1973 *Certification:* Obstetrics & Gynecology
1551 Clay St, Winter Park, 407-644-5371
7200 Stonerock Cir, Orlando, 407-345-1041

Meyers, John William (4 mentions)
Louisiana State U, 1993 *Certification:* Obstetrics & Gynecology
1445 Dunn Ave, Daytona Beach, 386-258-0123

Moore, Melissa Marie (3 mentions)
U of Iowa, 1995 *Certification:* Obstetrics & Gynecology
100 Perth Ln, Winter Park, 407-645-5565

Peppy, Terrence Samuel (4 mentions)
SUNY-Buffalo, 1991 *Certification:* Obstetrics & Gynecology
7472 Doc's Grove Cir, Orlando, 407-381-7366

Sange, Sally Harris (3 mentions)
Virginia Commonwealth U, 1986
Certification: Obstetrics & Gynecology
210 N Grove St, Merritt Island, 321-452-7878

Sweet, Jon Forrest (3 mentions)
Wayne State U, 1989 *Certification:* Obstetrics & Gynecology
661 E Altamonte Dr #318, Altamonte Springs, 407-303-5204
4106 W Lake Mary Blvd #130, Lake Mary, 407-303-5204

Tortorella, Michael James (6 mentions)
U of Florida, 1981 *Certification:* Obstetrics & Gynecology
7300 Sandlake Commons Blvd #320, Orlando, 407-363-1003

Vagovic, Richard John, Jr. (4 mentions)
U of Miami, 1985 *Certification:* Obstetrics & Gynecology
517 Health Blvd, Daytona Beach, 386-274-1005

Van Wert, John West (4 mentions)
Vanderbilt U, 1984 *Certification:* Obstetrics & Gynecology
531 N Maitland Ave, Maitland, 321-397-1212

Wagaman, Rebecca A. (3 mentions)
U of South Florida, 1985 *Certification:* Obstetrics & Gynecology
330 E Hibiscus Blvd, Melbourne, 321-725-1530

Wilstrup, Mark Alan (4 mentions)
Baylor U, 1980 *Certification:* Obstetrics & Gynecology
1551 Clay St, Winter Park, 407-644-5371
7200 Stonerock Cir, Orlando, 407-345-1041

Ophthalmology

Auerbach, David Barry (6 mentions)
New York Coll of Osteopathic Med, 1993
225 W State Rd 434 #111, Longwood, 407-767-6411
249 Moray Ln, Winter Park, 407-767-6411
1781 Park Center Dr #220, Orlando, 407-398-7730

Blumenfeld, Louis C. (6 mentions)
FMS-Canada, 1989 *Certification:* Ophthalmology
225 W State Rd 434 #111, Longwood, 407-398-7730
249 Moray Ln, Winter Park, 407-398-7730
1781 Park Center Dr #220, Orlando, 407-398-7730

Gold, Robert Stuart (12 mentions)
Tulane U, 1982 *Certification:* Ophthalmology
225 W State Rd 434 #111, Longwood, 407-398-7730
249 Moray Ln, Winter Park, 407-398-7730
1781 Park Center Dr #220, Orlando, 407-398-7730

Jablonski, Richard Alan (4 mentions)
Midwestern U Coll of Osteopathic Med, 1974
Certification: Ophthalmology
26 N Beach St #C, Ormond Beach, 386-673-3344

Kropp, Thomas Michael (7 mentions)
U of Florida, 1980 *Certification:* Ophthalmology
305 E New York Ave, Deland, 386-734-2931
1900 N Orange Ave, Orlando, 407-896-1400

Lugo, Miguel (4 mentions)
Temple U, 1981 *Certification:* Ophthalmology
661 E Altamonte Dr #223, Altamonte Springs, 407-260-2255

Sakowitz, Howard Jay (4 mentions)
SUNY-Downstate Med Coll, 1980 *Certification:* Ophthalmology
1061 Medical Center Dr #204, Orange City, 386-574-0700
313 N Mangoustine Ave, Sanford, 386-574-0700

Spertus, Alan David (4 mentions)
Albert Einstein Coll of Med, 1983 *Certification:* Ophthalmology
790 Dunlawton Ave #A, Port Orange, 386-767-0053
345 Clyde Morris Blvd #330, Ormond Beach, 386-672-4244

Orthopedics

Bryan, James McMaster (4 mentions)
Rush U, 1991 *Certification:* Orthopaedic Surgery
1075 Mason Ave, Daytona Beach, 386-673-5525
1890 LPGA Blvd #240, Daytona Beach, 386-673-5525
1185 Dunlawton Blvd #104, Port Orange, 386-673-5525

Cole, J. Dean (7 mentions)
Certification: Orthopaedic Surgery
2501 N Orange Ave #340, Orlando, 407-895-8890

Daouk, Ayman Ahmad (4 mentions)
U of Florida, 1997 *Certification:* Orthopaedic Surgery
661 E Altamonte Dr #325, Altamonte Springs, 407-303-5126

Heard, Charles William (9 mentions)
Med Coll of Georgia, 1976 *Certification:* Orthopaedic Surgery
345 W Michigan St #114, Orlando, 407-843-9083
9430 Turkey Lake Rd #116, Orlando, 407-345-1234

Jablonski, Michael Victor (6 mentions)
U of Florida, 1995 *Certification:* Orthopaedic Surgery
2876 S Osceola Ave, Orlando, 407-236-0404
515 W State Rd 434 #210, Longwood, 407-767-9610
3451 Technological Ave #15, Orlando, 407-380-8705

McCutchen, John W. (10 mentions)
U of Missouri, 1976 *Certification:* Orthopaedic Surgery
1285 Orange Ave, Winter Park, 407-647-2287

Morris, Hugh Bailey (5 mentions)
Duke U, 1981 *Certification:* Orthopaedic Surgery
1285 Orange Ave, Winter Park, 407-647-2287

Murrah, Robert Leland, Jr. (6 mentions)
Duke U, 1983 *Certification:* Orthopaedic Surgery
121 W Underwood St, Orlando, 407-423-7777

Newfield, Jeffrey Todd (4 mentions)
Nova Southeastern Coll of Osteopathic Med, 1991
255 S Yonge St, Ormond Beach, 386-672-8350

Reed, Stephen Mitchell (8 mentions)
U of South Florida, 1981 *Certification:* Orthopaedic Surgery
1053 Medical Center Dr #101, Orange City, 386-774-2500
1337 S International Pkwy #1341, Lake Mary, 407-333-4507

Ryan, James Patrick (4 mentions)
U of Oklahoma, 1978 *Certification:* Orthopaedic Surgery
659 Douglas Ave, Altamonte Springs, 407-869-8879

Tall, Reginald Lamont (4 mentions)
Case Western Reserve U, 1984 *Certification:* Orthopaedic Surgery
1285 Orange Ave #200, Winter Park, 407-647-2287

Topoleski, Tamara Ann (4 mentions)
New York Med Coll, 1990 *Certification:* Orthopaedic Surgery
100 W Gore St #500, Orlando, 407-254-2500
515 W State Rd 434 #310, Longwood, 407-834-1556
7350 Sandlake Commons Blvd #2212, Orlando, 407-425-1556

White, George Malcolm (7 mentions)
Johns Hopkins U, 1981 *Certification:* Orthopaedic Surgery
801 N Orange Ave #600, Orlando, 407-841-2100
652 Palm Springs Dr, Altamonte Springs, 407-841-2100

Williamson, Charles B. (4 mentions)
SUNY-Downstate Med Coll, 1975
Certification: Orthopaedic Surgery
3635 S Clyde Morris Blvd #600, Port Orange, 386-760-2888

Otorhinolaryngology

Bibliowicz, Michael M. (9 mentions)
Ohio U Coll of Osteopathic Med, 1984
5830 Lake Underhill Rd, Orlando, 407-658-0228
8000 Red Bug Lake Rd, Oviedo, 407-658-0228

Kosko, James Regis, Jr. (6 mentions)
U of Pittsburgh, 1989 *Certification:* Otolaryngology
1507 S Hiawassee Rd #103, Orlando, 407-253-1000

Mokris, Michael Scott (9 mentions)
U of Cincinnati, 1980 *Certification:* Otolaryngology
1781 Park Center Dr, Orlando, 407-351-0675

Munier, Michael Anthony (11 mentions)
Columbia U, 1987 *Certification:* Otolaryngology
1050 W Granada Blvd, Ormond Beach, 386-677-8808
1720 Dunlawton Ave, Port Orange, 386-760-6601

Saffran, Alan Jeffrey (7 mentions)
Columbia U, 1986 *Certification:* Otolaryngology
7251 University Blvd #300, Winter Park, 407-677-0066

Seltzer, Howard Michael (7 mentions)
U of Florida, 1976 *Certification:* Otolaryngology
804 Dunlawton Ave, Port Orange, 386-788-4644

Spector, Brian Cory (10 mentions)
U of Florida, 1995 *Certification:* Otolaryngology
201 N Lakemont Ave #100, Winter Park, 407-644-4883
44 W Michigan St, Orlando, 407-422-4921

Pain Medicine

Amune, Evans Ehin (4 mentions)
FMS-Russia, 1990 *Certification:* Anesthesiology, Pain Medicine
2501 N Orange, Orlando, 407-303-9662

Ariani, Kayvan (6 mentions)
Stanford U, 1991 *Certification:* Anesthesiology, Pain Medicine
2501 N Orange, Orlando, 407-303-9662
661 E Altamonte Dr #328, Altamonte Springs, 407-303-9662

Creamer, Michael Joseph (4 mentions)
Midwestern U Coll of Osteopathic Med, 1987
Certification: Pain Medicine, Physical Medicine &
  Rehabilitation, Spinal Cord Injury Medicine
100 W Gore St #203, Orlando, 407-649-8707

Malik, Vinod K. (6 mentions)
FMS-India, 1988 *Certification:* Anesthesiology, Pain Medicine
1671 N Clyde Morris Blvd #100, Daytona Beach, 386-274-2977
790 Dunlawton Blvd #D, Port Orange, 386-274-2977
21 Hospital Dr #170, Palm Coast, 386-586-2280

Mayfield, William Ross (4 mentions)
U of Tennessee, 1972
Certification: Anesthesiology, Pain Medicine
201 N Clyde Morris Blvd #120, Daytona Beach, 386-254-4029

Stern, Ronald Julius (4 mentions)
Rush U, 1978
Certification: Anesthesiology, Pain Medicine, Pediatrics
1696 Hibiscus Blvd #B, Melbourne, 321-723-4723

Yanamadula, Dinash K. (4 mentions)
FMS-Dominica, 1997
Certification: Pain Medicine, Physical Medicine & Rehabilitation
725 W Granda Blvd #22, Ormond Beach, 386-274-0097

Pathology

Green, Thomas J. (4 mentions)
Certification: Anatomic Pathology & Clinical Pathology
569 Health Blvd #A, Daytona Beach, 386-258-7668

Guarda, Luis Alberto (11 mentions)
FMS-Chile, 1972 *Certification:* Anatomic Pathology &
   Clinical Pathology, Cytopathology
601 E Rollins St, Orlando, 407-303-5600

Kilpatrick, Timothy M. (3 mentions)
U of Florida, 1980 *Certification:* Anatomic Pathology &
   Clinical Pathology, Dermatopathology
411 Maitland Ave #1002, Altamonte Springs, 407-260-0158

Pearl, Gary Steven (8 mentions)
Emory U, 1977 *Certification:* Anatomic Pathology, Clinical
   Pathology, Neuropathology
1414 Kuhl Ave, Orlando, 407-841-5111

Radi, Michael (5 mentions)
Vanderbilt U, 1982 *Certification:* Anatomic Pathology &
   Clinical Pathology, Cytopathology
601 E Rollins St, Orlando, 407-303-1932

Wheeler, Ross Charles (3 mentions)
Louisiana State U, 1992 *Certification:* Anatomic Pathology
   & Clinical Pathology, Dermatopathology
601 E Rollins St, Orlando, 407-303-5600

Pediatrics *(see note on page 9)*

Britton, Brooke Coleman (4 mentions)
U of Pittsburgh, 1998 *Certification:* Pediatrics
414 N Mills Ave, Orlando, 407-841-7290
7051 Dr Phillips Blvd, Orlando, 407-351-3315

Chopra, Neena Phull (3 mentions)
FMS-India, 1971 *Certification:* Pediatrics
633 Dunlawton Ave #I, Port Orange, 386-756-1937

Didea, Mark Brian (5 mentions)
U of Florida, 1980 *Certification:* Pediatrics
414 N Mills Ave, Orlando, 407-841-7290
7051 Dr Phillips Blvd, Orlando, 407-351-3315

Guedes, Beny Lester (5 mentions)
U of Florida, 1969 *Certification:* Pediatrics
615 E Princeton St #400, Orlando, 407-894-8556

Holson, Brenda Brown (3 mentions)
Vanderbilt U, 1978 *Certification:* Pediatrics
846 Lake Howell Rd, Maitland, 407-767-2477
1000 W Broadway #214, Oviedo, 407-767-2477

Savona, Joseph Francis (3 mentions)
Ohio State U, 1973 *Certification:* Pediatrics
8000 Red Bug Lake Rd #230, Oviedo, 407-365-4499

Seibel, Matthew A. (3 mentions)
Howard U, 1981 *Certification:* Pediatrics
601 W Michigan St, Orlando, 407-317-7430
92 W Miller St, Orlando, 321-843-7777

Smith, Samuel Norman, III (3 mentions)
Nova Southeastern Coll of Osteopathic Med, 1988
Certification: Pediatrics
846 Lake Howell Rd, Maitland, 407-767-2477
1000 W Broadway St, Oviedo, 407-767-2477

Van Wert, Anne Karen (4 mentions)
U of Texas-Galveston, 1984 *Certification:* Pediatrics
846 Lake Howell Rd, Maitland, 407-767-2477

Weare, John Lawrence, Jr. (4 mentions)
U of Florida, 1986 *Certification:* Pediatrics
233 6th Ave, Indialantic, 321-951-9087

Plastic Surgery

Cicilioni, Orlando Joseph (6 mentions)
Jefferson Med Coll, 1992 *Certification:* Plastic Surgery, Surgery
1000 N Maitland Ave, Maitland, 407-681-3223

Clark, Clifford Pray (10 mentions)
U of Florida, 1986 *Certification:* Plastic Surgery
701 W Morse Blvd #220, Winter Park, 407-629-5555

Pope, George Haynes (7 mentions)
Louisiana State U-Shreveport, 1981
Certification: Otolaryngology, Plastic Surgery
3872 Oakwater Cir, Orlando, 407-857-6261

Rotatori, Donald Scott (12 mentions)
Case Western Reserve U, 1985 *Certification:* Plastic Surgery
800 W Morse Blvd #5, Winter Park, 407-628-5476

Slade, Clement Lawrence (11 mentions)
Duke U, 1973 *Certification:* Plastic Surgery
3635 S Clyde Morris Blvd #400, Port Orange, 386-756-9400

Stieg, Frank Henry, III (7 mentions)
U of Cincinnati, 1980
Certification: Otolaryngology, Plastic Surgery
851 W Morse Blvd, Winter Park, 407-647-4601

Zamora, Sergio Martin (9 mentions)
FMS-Mexico, 1990 *Certification:* Plastic Surgery
1890 LPGA Blvd #150, Daytona Beach, 386-615-0665

Psychiatry

Allen, Luis G. (8 mentions)
FMS-Mexico, 1988 *Certification:* Geriatric Psychiatry, Psychiatry
615 E Princeton St #3A, Orlando, 407-896-8097

Bernal, Ricardo (3 mentions)
FMS-Colombia, 1991 *Certification:* Psychiatry
8751 Commodity Cir, Orlando, 407-226-2777

Blankemeier, John Louis (3 mentions)
Georgetown U, 1980 *Certification:* Child Psychiatry, Psychiatry
2180 N Park Ave #320, Winter Park, 407-629-6440

Cohen, Robert Eric (3 mentions)
Albert Einstein Coll of Med, 1991
Certification: Geriatric Psychiatry, Psychiatry
2123 Franklin Dr NE, Palm Bay, 321-724-1614
1351 Bedford Dr, Melbourne, 321-757-6799

Dunn, Kelly Lynn (3 mentions)
Pennsylvania State U, 1989
Certification: Geriatric Psychiatry, Psychiatry
1696 W Hibiscus Blvd #A, Melbourne, 321-725-0554

Greenblum, David N. (5 mentions)
Certification: Forensic Psychiatry, Geriatric Psychiatry, Psychiatry
805 Century Medical Dr #C, Titusville, 321-269-7659

Kolin, Irving S. (4 mentions)
SUNY-Buffalo, 1965 *Certification:* Geriatric Psychiatry, Psychiatry
1065 W Morse Blvd #202, Winter Park, 407-644-1122

Krotenberg, Jeffrey (3 mentions)
Kansas U Coll of Osteopathic Med, 1984 *Certification:* Psychiatry
305 Waymont Ct #111, Lake Mary, 407-324-0405

Mota-Castillo, Manuel (4 mentions)
FMS-Dominican Republic, 1979 *Certification:* Psychiatry
1061 Medical Center Dr #305, Orange City, 386-917-7610

Oh, Stephen S. (4 mentions)
FMS-South Korea, 1970 *Certification:* Psychiatry
341 N Clyde Morris Blvd, Daytona Beach, 386-258-6455

Quinones, Jose Enrique (4 mentions)
U of Kansas, 1978
Certification: Child & Adolescent Psychiatry, Psychiatry
2248 Winter Woods Blvd, Winter Park, 407-681-6003

Saavedra, Lillian T. (3 mentions)
FMS-Russia, 1969 *Certification:* Psychiatry
1315 S Orange Ave #3E, Orlando, 407-849-0227

Sarkar, Patricia Anne (3 mentions)
FMS-Jamaica, 1977 *Certification:* Psychiatry
1555 Howell Branch Rd #B4, Winter Park, 407-644-2121

Seiler, Earnest E., III (3 mentions)
U of South Florida, 1986 *Certification:* Psychiatry
1696 W Hibiscus Blvd #A, Melbourne, 321-725-0554

Pulmonary Disease

Ailani, Rajesh Kanayalal (6 mentions)
FMS-India, 1993 *Certification:* Critical Care Medicine,
   Internal Medicine, Pulmonary Disease, Sleep Medicine
1055 N Dixie Frwy #2, New Smyrna Beach, 386-423-0505

Ajayi, Akinyemi Olutoye (6 mentions)
FMS-Nigeria, 1992
Certification: Pediatric Pulmonology, Pediatrics, Sleep Medicine
8061 Spyglass Hill Rd #103, Melbourne, 407-898-2767

Aldarondo, Sigfredo (21 mentions)
U of Puerto Rico, 1976
Certification: Internal Medicine, Pulmonary Disease
1110 N Kentucky Ave, Winter Park, 407-539-2766

Feibelman, Richard Young (5 mentions)
U of Mississippi, 1980
Certification: Internal Medicine, Pulmonary Disease
515 W State Rd 434 #201, Longwood, 407-265-7775

Haim, Yitzhak D. (11 mentions)
FMS-Israel, 1985
Certification: Critical Care Medicine, Pulmonary Disease
326 N Mills Ave, Orlando, 407-841-1100

Herran, Juan Jose (5 mentions)
U of Puerto Rico, 1976
Certification: Internal Medicine, Pulmonary Disease
717 E Michigan St, Orlando, 407-515-8585

Layish, Daniel Tzvi (12 mentions)
Boston U, 1990 *Certification:* Critical Care Medicine,
   Internal Medicine, Pulmonary Disease
326 N Mills Ave, Orlando, 407-841-1100

Scanlon, Edward Kevin (7 mentions)
U of Missouri-Kansas City, 1984 *Certification:* Critical Care
   Medicine, Internal Medicine, Pulmonary Disease
1075 Town Center Dr, Orange City, 386-917-0333
749 Sterling Center Pl, Lake Mary, 407-321-8230

Smith, Paul Travis (5 mentions)
U of Utah, 1980 *Certification:* Critical Care Medicine,
   Internal Medicine, Pulmonary Disease
1075 Town Center Dr, Orange City, 386-917-0333
749 Sterling Center Pl, Lake Mary, 407-321-8230

Wahba, W. Wahba (5 mentions)
FMS-Egypt, 1971
Certification: Internal Medicine, Pulmonary Disease
1360 Mason Ave #A, Daytona Beach, 386-258-7100
621 S Nova Rd, Ormond Beach, 386-258-7100
3949 S Nova Rd, Port Orange, 386-258-7100
4869 Palm Coast Pkwy #4, Palm Coast, 386-258-7100

White, R. Steven (5 mentions)
U of Louisville, 1979
Certification: Internal Medicine, Pulmonary Disease
601 N Clyde Morris Blvd, Daytona Beach, 386-252-3985

Radiology—Diagnostic

Bagby, Richard Julian (4 mentions)
Emory U, 1966
Certification: Diagnostic Radiology, Nuclear Medicine
398 E Altamonte Dr, Altamonte Springs, 407-331-9355

Campbell, John Blake (4 mentions)
U of Minnesota, 1959
Certification: Pediatric Radiology, Pediatrics, Radiology
20 W Kaley St, Orlando, 407-423-5511

Clayman, Allan Steven (4 mentions)
U of Cincinnati, 1968 *Certification:* Diagnostic Radiology
20 W Kaley St, Orlando, 407-423-2581

Colvin, Lawrence Joseph (4 mentions)
Indiana U, 1972 *Certification:* Diagnostic Radiology
1414 Kuhl Ave, Orlando, 407-841-5111

Elenberger, Charlotte D. (3 mentions)
Med U of South Carolina, 1989
Certification: Diagnostic Radiology
1640 N Maitland Ave, Maitland, 407-363-2772
9350 Turkey Lake Rd, Orlando, 407-363-2772

Harding, David Ronald (4 mentions)
U of Florida, 1980 *Certification:* Diagnostic Radiology
1414 Kuhl Ave, Orlando, 321-841-5229

Logsdon, Gregory Alan (3 mentions)
SUNY-Buffalo, 1984
Certification: Diagnostic Radiology, Pediatric Radiology
601 E Rollins St, Orlando, 407-200-2355

Smith, Susan Silverman (3 mentions)
U of Texas-Dallas, 1991
Certification: Diagnostic Radiology, Pediatric Radiology
1414 Kuhl Ave, Orlando, 407-841-8122

Radiology—Therapeutic

Andriole, Joseph Gerald (7 mentions)
Howard U, 1980 *Certification:* Diagnostic Radiology
20 W Kaley St, Orlando, 407-423-2581

George, Richard William (4 mentions)
U of Florida, 1994 *Certification:* Diagnostic Radiology,
  Vascular & Interventional Radiology
20 W Kaley St, Orlando, 407-423-2581

Golden, Nanialei Matsu (4 mentions)
Rosalind Franklin U, 1994 *Certification:* Radiation Oncology
1130-A S Hickory St, Melbourne, 321-409-1956

Weppelmann, Burkhard (4 mentions)
FMS-Germany, 1974
Certification: Radiation Oncology, Therapeutic Radiology
601 E Altamonte Dr, Altamonte Springs, 407-303-2271

Rehabilitation

Bagnoli, Nick George (9 mentions)
West Virginia Sch of Osteopathic Med, 1993
Certification: Physical Medicine & Rehabilitation
1220 Sligh Blvd, Orlando, 407-210-4251

Freed, Mitchell Jay (14 mentions)
Vanderbilt U, 1984
Certification: Physical Medicine & Rehabilitation
2501 N Orange Ave #505S, Orlando, 407-898-2924

Geis, Carolyn C. (6 mentions)
U of Texas-Galveston, 1990
Certification: Physical Medicine & Rehabilitation
38 Old Bridge Way, Ormond Beach, 386-947-4641

Haddock, David Gene (3 mentions)
Ohio State U, 1987
Certification: Physical Medicine & Rehabilitation
10345 Orangewood Blvd, Orlando, 407-352-6900
1400 S Orlando Ave #304, Winter Park, 407-352-6900

Imfeld, Matthew Damian (3 mentions)
U of Toledo, 1987
Certification: Physical Medicine & Rehabilitation
10345 Orangewood Blvd, Orlando, 407-352-6900
1400 S Orlando Ave #304, Winter Park, 407-352-6900

Narula, Geeta I. (5 mentions)
FMS-India, 1970
Certification: Physical Medicine & Rehabilitation
2501 N Orange Ave #505, Orlando, 407-898-2924

Portee, David (4 mentions)
U of Michigan, 1982
Certification: Physical Medicine & Rehabilitation
32 W Gore St, Orlando, 407-649-6151

Rheumatology

Freeman, Pamela Gail (20 mentions)
Washington U, 1977
Certification: Internal Medicine, Rheumatology
3160 Southgate Commerce Blvd #30, Orlando, 407-859-4540

Hasselbring, Caryn Grace (11 mentions)
Washington U, 1982
Certification: Internal Medicine, Rheumatology
3160 Southgate Commerce Blvd #30, Orlando, 407-859-4540

Kohen, Michael David (9 mentions)
U of Florida, 1967 *Certification:* Allergy & Immunology,
  Internal Medicine, Rheumatology
709 N Clyde Morris Blvd, Daytona Beach, 386-252-1632

Sladek, Gary Dean (12 mentions)
U of Miami, 1977 *Certification:* Internal Medicine, Rheumatology
2501 N Orange Ave #538, Orlando, 407-894-8696

Tsai, Yong H. (8 mentions)
FMS-China, 1981 *Certification:* Allergy & Immunology,
  Internal Medicine, Rheumatology
1430 Mason Ave, Daytona Beach, 386-676-0307

Thoracic Surgery

Ferrero, Alessandro (13 mentions)
FMS-Italy, 1967 *Certification:* Surgery, Thoracic Surgery
180 S Knowles Ave #1, Winter Park, 407-628-1300

Greene, Michael Art (6 mentions)
U of Missouri, 1986 *Certification:* Surgery, Thoracic Surgery
1355 Hickory St S #202, Melbourne, 321-434-5396

Herrera, Luis Javier (6 mentions)
U of Puerto Rico, 1998 *Certification:* Surgery, Thoracic Surgery
1400 S Orange Ave, Orlando, 407-648-5384

Johnston, Alan Dale (11 mentions)
U of Miami, 1975 *Certification:* Thoracic Surgery
1400 S Orange Ave, Orlando, 407-648-5384

Litke, Bradley S. (6 mentions)
U of Texas-Houston, 1990
Certification: Surgery, Thoracic Surgery
588 Sterthaus Ave, Ormond Beach, 386-672-9501

Urology

Brady, Jeffrey Daniel (5 mentions)
SUNY-Upstate Med U, 1992 *Certification:* Urology
1812 N Mills Ave, Orlando, 407-897-3499

Gundian, Julio C., Jr. (8 mentions)
Tulane U, 1984 *Certification:* Urology
1812 N Mills Ave, Orlando, 407-897-3499

Hermansen, Dane Karsten (5 mentions)
Virginia Commonwealth U, 1981 *Certification:* Urology
300 Clyde Morris Blvd #C, Ormond Beach, 386-673-5100
9 Pine Cone Dr #105, Palm Coast, 386-673-5100
790 Dunlawton Blvd #H, Port Orange, 386-673-5100

Parr, Gregory Alan (6 mentions)
Wayne State U, 1986 *Certification:* Urology
300 Clyde Morris Blvd #C, Ormond Beach, 386-322-8880
790 Dunlawton Ave #H, Port Orange, 386-322-8880

Rich, Mark Alan (6 mentions)
FMS-Mexico, 1981 *Certification:* Pediatric Urology, Urology
1717 S Orange Ave, Orlando, 407-650-7260

Sujka, Stan K. (6 mentions)
FMS-Grenada, 1982 *Certification:* Urology
9430 Turkey Lake Rd #106, Orlando, 407-352-8151
41 W Kaley St, Orlando, 407-843-6645

Thill, Jeffrey Richard (9 mentions)
U of Iowa, 1988 *Certification:* Urology
1812 N Mills Ave, Orlando, 407-897-3499

Traficante, Dale Robert (6 mentions)
Rosalind Franklin U, 1994 *Certification:* Urology
1890 LPGA Blvd #220, Daytona Beach, 386-274-5757

Vaughan, David John (10 mentions)
U of Cincinnati, 1980 *Certification:* Urology
1812 N Mills Ave, Orlando, 407-897-3499

Welch, James Lambertson (5 mentions)
U of Florida, 1982 *Certification:* Urology
41 W Kaley St, Orlando, 407-843-6645
9430 Turkey Lake Rd #106, Orlando, 407-352-8151

Zabinski, Peter Paul (7 mentions)
FMS-Mexico, 1975 *Certification:* Urology
1405 S Pine St, Melbourne, 321-729-6135

Vascular Surgery

Clift, Delos Robert (23 mentions)
Wayne State U, 1978 *Certification:* Surgery
3000 N Orange Ave #A, Orlando, 407-472-0840

Cohen, Michael Jon (11 mentions)
Ohio State U, 1977 *Certification:* Vascular Surgery
1200 Sligh Blvd, Orlando, 407-648-4323

Winter, Robert Peter (12 mentions)
Emory U, 1983 *Certification:* Surgery, Vascular Surgery
400 S Maitland Ave, Maitland, 407-539-2100

Georgia

Atlanta Area

Atlanta Area

Including Cherokee, Clayton, Cobb, DeKalb, Douglas, Fayette, Fulton, Gwinnett, Henry, and Rockdale Counties

Allergy/Immunology

Fineman, Stanley Mark (10 mentions)
Emory U, 1973 *Certification:* Allergy & Immunology, Pediatrics
1519 Johnson Ferry Rd #200, Marietta, 770-973-5578
895 Canton Rd NE #200, Marietta, 770-428-4477

Gottlieb, George Robert (11 mentions)
New York U, 1975
Certification: Allergy & Immunology, Pediatrics
2675 N Decatur Rd #404, Decatur, 404-294-4761
2151 Fountain Dr #103, Snellville, 770-979-3796

Guydon, Linda Denise (13 mentions)
Harvard U, 1980
Certification: Allergy & Immunology, Internal Medicine
4310 Johns Creek Pkwy #130, Swanee, 770-495-6258
2296 Henderson Mill Rd NE #300, Atlanta, 770-953-3384

Segall, Nathan (8 mentions)
U of Alabama, 1973
Certification: Allergy & Immunology, Internal Medicine
980 Johnson Ferry Rd NE #1080, Atlanta, 404-705-9170
175 Country Club Dr #A, Stockbridge, 770-507-0707

Sheerin, Kathleen Ann (10 mentions)
Duke U, 1983 *Certification:* Allergy & Immunology, Pediatrics
2045 Peachtree Rd NE #333, Atlanta, 404-351-5711
1990 Riverside Pkwy, Lawrenceville, 770-995-1537

Silk, Howard Jay (7 mentions)
Boston U, 1982 *Certification:* Allergy & Immunology, Pediatrics
2296 Henderson Mill Rd #300, Atlanta, 770-491-9300
1240 Hwy 54 W Bldg 300 #310, Fayetteville, 770-461-6400

Stahlman, Jon Edward (8 mentions)
Emory U, 1993 *Certification:* Allergy & Immunology
2390 Wall St SE, Conyers, 770-922-5696
565 Old Norcross Rd, Lawrenceville, 770-995-5131
2200 Century Pkwy, Atlanta, 404-417-9333

Tanner, David Duane (10 mentions)
Vanderbilt U, 1974
Certification: Allergy & Immunology, Pediatrics
2045 Peachtree Rd NE #333, Atlanta, 404-351-5711
4310 Johns Creek Pkwy #130, Suwanee, 770-495-6258

Zora, John Alfred (7 mentions)
Pennsylvania State U, 1979
Certification: Allergy & Immunology, Pediatrics
1990 Riverside Pkwy, Lawrenceville, 770-995-1537
401 S Main St #C-1, Alpharetta, 770-475-0807

Anesthesiology

Abdel-Ghani, Ghaleb A. (3 mentions)
FMS-Egypt, 1968 *Certification:* Anesthesiology
1365 Clifton Rd NE, Atlanta, 404-778-4149

Adair, Thomas Marion, Jr. (3 mentions)
U of Alabama, 1997 *Certification:* Anesthesiology
531 Roselane St NW #750, Marietta, 770-794-0477

Bannister, Carolyn F. (4 mentions)
Duke U, 1985
Certification: Anesthesiology, Internal Medicine, Pediatrics
1365 Clifton Rd NE, Atlanta, 404-785-6670
1405 Clifton Rd NE, Atlanta, 404-785-6670

Bonner, William Richard (3 mentions)
U of Alabama, 1983 *Certification:* Anesthesiology, Pediatrics
1001 Johnson Ferry Rd NE, Atlanta, 404-785-2008

Buchwald, Ira Philip (3 mentions)
Emory U, 1981 *Certification:* Anesthesiology
1001 Johnson Ferry Rd NE, Atlanta, 404-785-2008

Carlson, James Lee (4 mentions)
U of Wisconsin, 1980
Certification: Anesthesiology, Pain Medicine
5671 Peachtree Dunwoody Rd NE #530, Atlanta, 404-257-1415

Clayton, Jonathan (4 mentions)
U of South Alabama, 1993 *Certification:* Anesthesiology
1984 Peachtree Rd NW #515, Atlanta, 404-351-1745

Clifton, Charles L., Jr. (12 mentions)
Emory U, 1982 *Certification:* Anesthesiology
2171 W Park Ct #A, Stone Mountain, 404-501-5265

Davis, Lee Swearingen (4 mentions)
Med Coll of Georgia, 1983 *Certification:* Anesthesiology
1000 Johnson Ferry Rd NE, Atlanta, 770-645-9181

Lee, Charles Hyokjae (3 mentions)
Emory U, 1992 *Certification:* Anesthesiology
531 Roselane St NW #750, Marietta, 770-794-0477

Lewis, Thomas Necy (3 mentions)
U of Alabama, 1986 *Certification:* Anesthesiology
1984 Peachtree Rd NW #515, Atlanta, 404-351-1745

Miller, Bruce Earl (3 mentions)
Med Coll of Georgia, 1984
Certification: Anesthesiology, Critical Care Medicine
1365 Clifton Rd NE, Atlanta, 404-785-6670

Mogelnicki, Stanley R. (4 mentions)
Certification: Anesthesiology
145 N Medical Pkwy, Woodstock, 770-592-3000

Neeld, John Bruce, Jr. (4 mentions)
Vanderbilt U, 1966 *Certification:* Anesthesiology
1000 Johnson Ferry Rd NE, Atlanta, 404-851-8917

Palmore, Marvin M., Jr. (3 mentions)
Dartmouth Coll, 1986 *Certification:* Anesthesiology
2171 W Park Ct #A, Stone Mountain, 678-514-1991

West, Thomas Blair (3 mentions)
Wake Forest U, 1981
Certification: Anesthesiology, Internal Medicine
1000 Johnson Ferry Rd NE, Atlanta, 404-851-8917

Zaidan, James Ronald (3 mentions)
West Virginia U, 1971 *Certification:* Anesthesiology
1364 Clifton Rd NE, Atlanta, 404-778-3903

Cardiac Surgery

Brown, W. Morris, III (6 mentions)
Med Coll of Georgia, 1985 *Certification:* Thoracic Surgery
95 Collier Rd NW #2055, Atlanta, 404-355-9515

Cooper, William Arthur (10 mentions)
U of Missouri-Kansas City, 1992
Certification: Surgery, Thoracic Surgery
55 Whitcher St NE #270, Marietta, 404-778-8340

Gott, John Parker (10 mentions)
U of Louisville, 1981 *Certification:* Thoracic Surgery
95 Collier Rd #2055, Atlanta, 404-355-9515

Guyton, Robert Allan (17 mentions)
Harvard U, 1971 *Certification:* Thoracic Surgery
550 Peachtree St NE 6th Fl, Atlanta, 404-686-2513

Kauten, James Richard (15 mentions)
Rosalind Franklin U, 1978 *Certification:* Thoracic Surgery
95 Collier Rd NW #2055, Atlanta, 404-355-9515

Miller, Jeffrey S. (6 mentions)
Baylor U, 1991 *Certification:* Surgery, Thoracic Surgery
5665 Peachtree Dunwoody Rd NE, Atlanta, 404-252-6104

Murphy, Douglas Alfred (21 mentions)
U of Pennsylvania, 1975
Certification: Internal Medicine, Thoracic Surgery
5665 Peachtree Dunwoody Rd NE, Atlanta, 404-252-6104

Puskas, John D. (6 mentions)
Harvard U, 1986 *Certification:* Surgery, Thoracic Surgery
550 Peachtree St NE, Atlanta, 404-686-2513

Cardiology

Balk, Michael Alan (3 mentions)
U of Pennsylvania, 1987 *Certification:* Cardiovascular Disease
1000 Johnson Ferry Rd NE, Atlanta, 404-256-2525
56 Johnson Ferry Rd NW #880, Atlanta, 404-256-2525
5670 Peachtree Dunwoody Rd NE #880, Atlanta, 404-256-2525

Battey, Louis L., Jr. (3 mentions)
Emory U, 1978
Certification: Cardiovascular Disease, Internal Medicine
275 Collier Rd NW #500, Atlanta, 404-355-6562

Brown, Charles Lafayette (8 mentions)
Louisiana State U, 1984 *Certification:* Cardiovascular
Disease, Internal Medicine, Interventional Cardiology
275 Collier Rd NW #500, Atlanta, 404-355-6562

Campbell, Robert M. (6 mentions)
Emory U, 1978 *Certification:* Pediatric Cardiology, Pediatrics
5455 Meridian Mark Rd #530, Atlanta, 404-256-2593

Caras, David Sarandos (4 mentions)
Med Coll of Georgia, 1988
Certification: Cardiovascular Disease, Internal Medicine
55 Whitcher St NE #350, Marietta, 770-424-6893

Chandra, Sandeep (3 mentions)
Meharry Med Coll, 1992
Certification: Cardiovascular Disease, Internal Medicine
4375 Johns Creek Pkwy #350, Sawanee, 770-622-1622
1468 Montreal Rd, Tucker, 770-638-1400
5910 Hillandale Dr #350, Lithonia, 678-578-8900

Chen, Jack Paiyang (5 mentions)
Cornell U, 1988
Certification: Cardiovascular Disease, Interventional Cardiology
5670 Peachtree Dunwoody Rd NE #880, Atlanta, 404-256-2525
56 Johnson Ferry Rd NW #880, Atlanta, 404-256-2525

Clements, Stephen D., Jr. (3 mentions)
Med Coll of Georgia, 1966
Certification: Cardiovascular Disease, Internal Medicine
1365 Clifton Rd NE #2100, Atlanta, 404-778-3468

Cook, Arthur John, Jr. (4 mentions)
Vanderbilt U, 1976
Certification: Cardiovascular Disease, Internal Medicine
275 Collier Rd NW #500, Atlanta, 404-352-3495

Coralli, Richard John (3 mentions)
Emory U, 1974
Certification: Cardiovascular Disease, Internal Medicine
2665 N Decatur Rd #260, Decatur, 404-297-9077

Corrigan, Victor E., II (3 mentions)
Med Coll of Georgia, 1983 *Certification:* Cardiovascular
Disease, Internal Medicine, Interventional Cardiology
1140 Hammond Dr #300, Atlanta, 404-851-5400

Dhruva, Nimish N. (4 mentions)
Certification: Cardiovascular Disease
95 Collier Rd NW #2035, Atlanta, 404-355-9815
101 Yorktown Dr, Fayetteville, 770-460-4062
1267 Hwy 54 W #2200, Fayetteville, 770-716-0051
275 Collier Rd #300, Atlanta, 404-355-9815

Dooley, Kenneth J. (3 mentions)
FMS-Ireland, 1969 *Certification:* Pediatric Cardiology, Pediatrics
1700 Tree Ln #330, Snellville, 404-256-2593
2835 Brandywine Rd #300, Atlanta, 404-256-2593

Dorsey, Anthony Conway (3 mentions)
U of Connecticut, 1997
Certification: Cardiovascular Disease, Internal Medicine
1468 Montreal Rd, Tucker, 770-638-1400
5910 Hillandale Dr #350, Lithonia, 404-501-1000

Douglas, John S., Jr. (3 mentions)
Certification: Cardiovascular Disease, Internal Medicine,
Interventional Cardiology
1365 Clifton Rd NE, Atlanta, 404-727-7040

Douglass, Paul L. (9 mentions)
Meharry Med Coll, 1976 *Certification:* Cardiovascular
Disease, Internal Medicine, Interventional Cardiology
999 Peachtree St NE #850, Atlanta, 404-874-1788

Eisenberg, Steven Jay (4 mentions)
Mount Sinai Sch of Med, 1989
Certification: Cardiovascular Disease
5669 Peachtree Dunwoody Rd NE #170, Atlanta, 404-252-8377

Gangasani, Sreenivasulu R. (3 mentions)
FMS-India, 1993 *Certification:* Cardiovascular Disease
755 Walther Rd, Lawrenceville, 770-962-0399
2850 Hog Mountain Rd #101, Dacula, 770-962-0399

Guest, Thomas Michael (4 mentions)
Case Western Reserve U, 1992
Certification: Cardiovascular Disease
5669 Peachtree Dunwoody Rd NE #170, Atlanta, 404-252-8377

Hershey, Jeffrey A. (3 mentions)
Certification: Cardiovascular Disease
6335 Hospital Pkwy #110, Johns Creek, 404-778-8240

Isakow, Julian Tevya (3 mentions)
FMS-South Africa, 1992 *Certification:* Cardiovascular Disease
1700 Hospital South Dr #409, Austell, 770-424-6893
55 Whitcher St NE #350, Marietta, 770-424-6893

King, Spencer Bidwell, III (3 mentions)
Med Coll of Georgia, 1963 *Certification:* Cardiovascular
Disease, Internal Medicine, Interventional Cardiology
5669 Peachtree Dunwoody Rd #315, Atlanta, 404-250-6400

Kirschbaum, Paul Allan (5 mentions)
Albert Einstein Coll of Med, 1979
Certification: Cardiovascular Disease, Internal Medicine
2665 N Decatur Rd #260, Decatur, 404-297-9077

Knopf, William Douglas (4 mentions)
Emory U, 1979 *Certification:* Cardiovascular Disease,
Internal Medicine, Interventional Cardiology
1140 Hammond Dr #300, Atlanta, 404-851-5400

Lesser, Laurence M. (7 mentions)
U of Buffalo, 1970
Certification: Cardiovascular Disease, Internal Medicine
1700 Tree Ln #170, Snellville, 770-979-1200

Lutz, Jerre Frederick (5 mentions)
Emory U, 1972
Certification: Cardiovascular Disease, Internal Medicine
2675 N Decatur Rd #607, Decatur, 404-778-2165
1365 Clifton Rd NE, Atlanta, 404-778-2165

Miller, Joseph Irvin, III (4 mentions)
Emory U, 1995 *Certification:* Cardiovascular Disease
275 Collier Rd NW #500, Atlanta, 404-355-6562

Morris, Douglas Claude (5 mentions)
Baylor U, 1968 *Certification:* Cardiovascular Disease,
Internal Medicine, Interventional Cardiology
35 Linden Ave NE, Atlanta, 404-778-2253
1365 Clifton Rd NE #A-2205, Atlanta, 404-778-2253
340 Blvd NE #608, Atlanta, 404-778-2253

Padove, Lee Brian (4 mentions)
Med Coll of Georgia, 1984
Certification: Cardiovascular Disease, Internal Medicine
960 Johnson Ferry Rd NE #336, Atlanta, 404-252-7400

Pettus, Charles William (4 mentions)
Mercer U, 1989 *Certification:* Cardiovascular Disease
101 Yorktown Dr #209, Fayetteville, 770-460-4062
20 Francis Pl, Sharpsburg, 770-460-4062
275 Collier Rd NW #300, Atlanta, 404-355-9815

Reitman, Arthur Brian (3 mentions)
Louisiana State U, 1995
Certification: Cardiovascular Disease, Interventional Cardiology
55 Whitcher St NE #350, Marietta, 770-424-6893

Robinson, Sheila Ann (5 mentions)
U of Texas-Galveston, 1983
Certification: Cardiovascular Disease, Internal Medicine
999 Peachtree St NE #850, Atlanta, 404-874-1788

Sacks, Harvey Norton (3 mentions)
Indiana U, 1973
Certification: Cardiovascular Disease, Internal Medicine
148 Bill Carruth Pkwy #100, Hiram, 678-324-4444

Sandler, Manfred Allan (3 mentions)
FMS-South Africa, 1982 *Certification:* Cardiovascular Disease
3540 Duluth Park Ln #200, Duluth, 770-497-1413
755 Walther Rd, Lawrenceville, 770-962-0399
4365 Johns Creek Pkwy #450, Suwanee, 678-417-9873
3855 Pleasant Hill Rd #380, Duluth, 770-962-0399
601 Professional Dr #370, Lawrenceville, 770-962-0399

Sherman, Stanley William (4 mentions)
Emory U, 1973
Certification: Cardiovascular Disease, Internal Medicine
2801 N Decatur Rd #295, Decatur, 404-778-7667

Shirazi, Syed Haider Ali (4 mentions)
FMS-Pakistan, 1969
Certification: Cardiovascular Disease, Internal Medicine
1380 Milstead Ave NE #E, Conyers, 770-483-9330

Silverman, Barry David (8 mentions)
Ohio State U, 1967
Certification: Cardiovascular Disease, Internal Medicine
960 Johnson Ferry Rd NE #500, Atlanta, 404-256-2525
5670 Peachtree Dunwoody Rd NE #880, Atlanta, 404-256-2525

Silverman, Mark Edwin (4 mentions)
U of Chicago, 1963
Certification: Cardiovascular Disease, Internal Medicine
1968 Peachtree Rd NW, Atlanta, 404-605-3368

Song, David Hyosup (3 mentions)
U of North Carolina, 1992
Certification: Cardiovascular Disease, Internal Medicine
1468 Montreal Rd, Tucker, 770-638-1400
4375 Johns Creek Pkwy #350, Sawanee, 770-622-1622
5910 Hillandale Dr #350, Lithonia, 678-578-8900

Sperling, Laurence Steven (8 mentions)
Emory U, 1989 *Certification:* Cardiovascular Disease
1525 Clifton Rd NE #209, Atlanta, 404-778-2898

Videlefsky, Neill (7 mentions)
FMS-South Africa, 1985
Certification: Pediatric Cardiology, Pediatrics
500 Medical Center Blvd #340, Lawrenceville, 770-995-6684
980 Johnson Ferry Rd #560, Atlanta, 770-995-6684

Videlefsky, Searle Warren (3 mentions)
FMS-South Africa, 1987 *Certification:* Cardiovascular Disease
600 Professional Dr #220, Lawrenceville, 770-962-4895
1700 Tree Ln #480, Snellville, 770-979-4990

Wickliffe, Charles Walton (4 mentions)
Emory U, 1967
Certification: Cardiovascular Disease, Internal Medicine
95 Collier Rd NW #2075, Atlanta, 404-355-1440
275 Collier Rd NW #500, Atlanta, 404-355-6562

Williams, Byron R., Jr. (4 mentions)
Certification: Cardiovascular Disease, Internal Medicine
550 Peachtree St, Atlanta, 404-686-2501

Wilson, Joseph S., Jr. (9 mentions)
Emory U, 1977 *Certification:* Cardiovascular Disease,
   Internal Medicine, Interventional Cardiology
755 Mount Vernon Hwy NE #530, Atlanta, 404-252-7970

Dermatology

Caputo, Raymond Vincent (19 mentions)
U of Miami, 1973 *Certification:* Dermatology
960 Johnson Ferry NE #226, Atlanta, 404-255-0787

Casey, Darren Lawrence (4 mentions)
Mount Sinai Sch of Med, 1991 *Certification:* Dermatology
1218 W Paces Ferry Rd NW, Atlanta, 404-525-7409

Chastain, Mark Alan (4 mentions)
Tulane U, 1996 *Certification:* Dermatology
1625 Hwy 34E #A, Newnan, 770-502-0202
175 White St NW #100, Marietta, 770-422-5557

Cooper, Jerry Lee (5 mentions)
Ohio State U, 1962 *Certification:* Dermatology
2171 Northlake Pkwy #100, Tucker, 404-269-8000

Cox, Gregory James (5 mentions)
U of Arkansas, 1982 *Certification:* Dermatology
2719 Felton Dr, East Point, 404-763-4153

Davis-Boutte, Windell C. (5 mentions)
U of California-Los Angeles, 1993 *Certification:* Dermatology
4650 Stone Mountain Hwy, Lilburn, 404-286-3178
4150 Snapfinger Woods Dr #205, Decatur, 404-286-3178

Detlefs, Richard Lyle (4 mentions)
Wake Forest U, 1977 *Certification:* Dermatology, Pediatrics
2045 Peachtree Rd NE #200, Atlanta, 404-351-7546
1519 Johnson Ferry Rd #100, Marietta, 770-971-3376

Ellner, Kenneth Mark (4 mentions)
Baylor U, 1985 *Certification:* Dermatology
5673 Peachtree Dunwoody Rd NE #850, Atlanta, 404-252-4333
3400 Old Milton Pkwy #C-340, Alpharetta, 770-664-5225

Forney, Virginia R. (5 mentions)
Emory U, 1996 *Certification:* Dermatology
3131 Maple Dr NE #102, Atlanta, 404-816-7900
107 W Paces Ferry Rd NW, Atlanta, 404-816-7900

Levin, Jay Alan (6 mentions)
Med Coll of Georgia, 1983 *Certification:* Dermatology
5667 Peachtree Dunwoody Rd NE #200, Atlanta, 404-252-4110

Olansky, David Charles (4 mentions)
Emory U, 1976 *Certification:* Dermatology
3379 Peachtree Rd NE 5th Fl, Atlanta, 404-355-5484
1105 Upper Hembree Rd #A, Roswell, 770-410-7860

Papadopoulos, Diamondis J. (9 mentions)
FMS-Greece, 1982 *Certification:* Dermatology, Pediatrics
875 Johnson Ferry Rd NE #300, Atlanta, 404-248-4891
5667 Peachtree Dunwoody #180, Atlanta, 404-248-4891

Rachal, Mack James (4 mentions)
U of Texas-Houston, 1989 *Certification:* Dermatology
550 Peachtree St NE #1230, Atlanta, 404-870-9871

Spraker, Mary Katherine (13 mentions)
U of Wisconsin, 1974 *Certification:* Dermatology, Pediatrics
1365 Clifton Rd NE #A-1400, Atlanta, 404-778-3336

Stonecipher, Marcus R. (4 mentions)
East Tennessee State U, 1986
Certification: Dermatology, Internal Medicine
1951 Clairmont Rd, Decatur, 404-321-4600

Swerlick, Robert Andrew (4 mentions)
U of Virginia, 1979 *Certification:* Dermatological Immunology/
   Diagnostic and Laboratory Immunology, Dermatology
1365 Clifton Rd NE, Atlanta, 404-778-3333

Warner, Janice Murphy (5 mentions)
Robert W Johnson Med Sch, 1983
Certification: Dermatology, Internal Medicine
1550 Mulkey Rd, Austell, 770-732-1137

Washington, Carl V., Jr. (4 mentions)
U of Michigan, 1984 *Certification:* Dermatology
1365 Clifton Rd NE #A, Atlanta, 404-778-3355

Wiegand, Stewart Earle (5 mentions)
Baylor U, 1965 *Certification:* Dermatology
755 Mount Vernon Hwy NE #110, Atlanta, 404-256-9692

Wilborn, Wesley Samson (5 mentions)
Meharry Med Coll, 1963 *Certification:* Dermatology
285 Blvd NE #320, Atlanta, 404-659-1795

Emergency Medicine

Crosley, Pascal G. (7 mentions)
New York Coll of Osteopathic Med, 2000
Certification: Emergency Medicine
2701 N Decatur Rd, Decatur, 404-501-5350

Goo, David Joseph (3 mentions)
U of Missouri, 1986
Certification: Pediatric Emergency Medicine, Pediatrics
1405 Clifton Rd NE, Atlanta, 404-785-7141

Higgins, Robert George (5 mentions)
Mayo Med Sch, 1980 *Certification:* Emergency Medicine
11180 State Bridge Rd #501, Alpharetta, 770-754-0788
5610 Bethelview Rd, Cumming, 770-205-2804
1121 Johnson Ferry Rd, Marietta, 770-509-1025

Holmes, John Leonard (3 mentions)
Oregon Health Sciences U, 1987
Certification: Emergency Medicine
3360 Westover Way SE, Conyers, 770-918-3040

Meadors, Patricia Herndon (4 mentions)
Emory U, 1977
1968 Peachtree Rd NW, Atlanta, 404-605-3297

Perez, Henry (10 mentions)
Tulane U, 1985 *Certification:* Emergency Medicine
5665 Peachtree Dunwoody Rd NE, Atlanta, 404-851-7294

Redwood, William Thomas (5 mentions)
U of Mississippi, 1987 *Certification:* Emergency Medicine
677 Church St, Marietta, 770-793-5700

Segerman, Stuart Charles (3 mentions)
U of North Carolina, 1978
Certification: Emergency Medicine, Pediatrics
5665 Peachtree Dunwoody Rd NE, Atlanta, 404-851-7294

Sue, Sean Reinald (3 mentions)
Duke U, 1995 *Certification:* Emergency Medicine
1700 Medical Way, Snellville, 707-736-2376

Upshaw, Thomas Stephen (3 mentions)
U of Chicago, 1983 *Certification:* Family Medicine
1968 Peachtree Rd NW, Atlanta, 404-605-3297

Endocrinology

Anderson, Stephen W., II (5 mentions)
U of Virginia, 1978 *Certification:* Pediatrics
5455 Meridian Marks Rd NE #200, Atlanta, 404-255-0015

Arkin, David Barry (7 mentions)
Emory U, 1984
Certification: Endocrinology and Metabolism, Internal Medicine
758 Old Norcross Rd #175, Lawrenceville, 770-339-1387
3655 Howell Ferry Rd #200, Duluth, 770-339-1387

Bode, Bruce Welsh (6 mentions)
Emory U, 1981 *Certification:* Internal Medicine
77 Collier Rd NW #2080, Atlanta, 404-355-4393

Brown, Darwin Lauren (11 mentions)
U of Tennessee, 1994 *Certification:* Endocrinology,
   Diabetes, and Metabolism, Internal Medicine
2665 N Decatur Rd #520, Decatur, 404-299-2223
1380 Milstead Ave #H, Conyers, 770-388-0118

Felner, Eric Ian (5 mentions)
Emory U, 1994 *Certification:* Pediatric Endocrinology, Pediatrics
2015 Uppergate Dr, Atlanta, 404-778-2400

Greenlee, Mary Carol (5 mentions)
Indiana U, 1980
Certification: Endocrinology and Metabolism, Internal Medicine
77 Collier Rd NW #2080, Atlanta, 404-355-4393

Jacobson, David Harvey (11 mentions)
Emory U, 1978
Certification: Endocrinology and Metabolism, Internal Medicine
2665 N Decatur Rd #520, Decatur, 404-299-2223
1380 Milstead Ave #H, Conyers, 770-388-0118

Musey, Victoria C. (7 mentions)
FMS-Canada, 1972
Certification: Endocrinology and Metabolism, Internal Medicine
550 Peachtree St NE #1010, Atlanta, 404-523-1745

Odugbesan, Ola (6 mentions)
FMS-Nigeria, 1977
Certification: Endocrinology, Diabetes, and Metabolism
758 Old Norcross Rd #175, Lawrenceville, 770-339-1387

Parks, John Scott (6 mentions)
U of Pennsylvania, 1966
Certification: Pediatric Endocrinology, Pediatrics
2015 Uppergate Dr NE, Atlanta, 404-778-2400

Reed, J. H. Chip (11 mentions)
Emory U, 1979
Certification: Endocrinology and Metabolism, Internal Medicine
1475 Holcomb Bridge Rd #129, Roswell, 678-325-2250

Rosenbloom, Seymour Joseph (5 mentions)
Albany Med Coll, 1969 *Certification:* Internal Medicine
55 Whitcher St NE #400, Marietta, 770-422-2004

Silverman, Victor Eli (28 mentions)
Med Coll of Georgia, 1973
Certification: Endocrinology and Metabolism, Internal Medicine
5667 Peachtree Dunwoody Rd #150, Atlanta, 404-256-0775

Welch, Norman Spencer, Jr. (8 mentions)
Emory U, 1981
Certification: Endocrinology and Metabolism, Internal Medicine
77 Collier Rd NW #2080, Atlanta, 404-355-4393

Family Practice *(see note on page 9)*

Andrews, Catherine S. (5 mentions)
U of Virginia, 1979 *Certification:* Family Medicine
3825 Cherokee St NW, Kennesaw, 770-422-1400

Bat, Thomas Edward (3 mentions)
U of Mississippi, 1985 *Certification:* Family Medicine
3400 Old Milton Pkwy #C270, Alpharetta, 770-442-1911

Bush, Dwana Marie (4 mentions)
Emory U, 1980
Certification: Family Medicine, Hospice and Palliative Medicine
171 Mount Paran Rd NE, Atlanta, 404-255-5774

Crenshaw, Martha House (3 mentions)
Tulane U, 1978 *Certification:* Family Medicine
1805 Parke Plaza Cir #101, Stone Mountain, 770-469-7000

Epstein, Benjamin Harris (3 mentions)
Tulane U, 1984
Certification: Family Medicine, Geriatric Medicine
2840-A La Vista Rd, Decatur, 404-639-9180

Rogers, Phillip R. (3 mentions)
Certification: Family Medicine
1776 Old Spring House Ln #200, Atlanta, 770-454-0094

Seyfried, Michael Paul (5 mentions)
U of South Alabama, 1983
Certification: Family Medicine, Occupational Medicine
1776 Old Spring House Ln #200, Atlanta, 770-454-0091

Wheeler, James Henson (3 mentions)
U of Alabama, 1971 *Certification:* Family Medicine
993 Johnson Ferry Rd NE #210, Atlanta, 404-256-1727

Gastroenterology

Albert, Clive (7 mentions)
Certification: Gastroenterology, Internal Medicine
1100 Northside Forsyth Dr #330, Cumming, 770-889-9901

Ayinala, Srinivasa Rao (4 mentions)
FMS-India, 1992
Certification: Gastroenterology, Internal Medicine
4375 Johns Creek Pkwy #340, Suwanee, 678-775-0293
301 Phillip Blvd NW #A, Lawrenceville, 770-822-5560
1100 Northside Forsyth Dr #200, Cumming, 770-781-4010

Brandenberg, David Saul (4 mentions)
Georgetown U, 1972
5671 Peachtree Dunwoody #600, Atlanta, 404-257-9000
1700 Tree Ln #190, Snellville, 770-972-4780

Burse, Luther, Jr. (4 mentions)
Morehouse Coll, 1991
Certification: Gastroenterology, Internal Medicine
550 Peachtree St NE #1750, Atlanta, 404-881-8800

Claiborne, Thomas S., Jr. (4 mentions)
Vanderbilt U, 1971
Certification: Gastroenterology, Internal Medicine
95 Collier Rd NW #4055, Atlanta, 404-355-1690

Cohen, Stanley Allen (7 mentions)
Ohio State U, 1972
Certification: Pediatric Gastroenterology, Pediatrics
5455 Meridian Mark Rd NE #440, Atlanta, 404-257-0799

Di Santis, Dennis Ernest (4 mentions)
Loyola U Chicago, 1969
Certification: Gastroenterology, Internal Medicine
2675 N Decatur Rd #506, Decatur, 404-299-1679

Elliott, Norman Lynn (5 mentions)
Yale U, 1979 *Certification:* Gastroenterology, Internal Medicine
550 Peachtree St NE #1600, Atlanta, 404-881-1094
2001 Professional Way #270, Woodstock, 770-926-0771
101 Riverstone Vista #101, Blue Ridge, 706-632-8008

Fixelle, Alan Mark (6 mentions)
New York Med Coll, 1980
Certification: Gastroenterology, Internal Medicine
5669 Peachtree Dunwoody Rd NE #270, Atlanta, 404-255-1000

Fortson, William Camp (4 mentions)
Med Coll of Georgia, 1980
Certification: Gastroenterology, Internal Medicine
61 Whitcher St NE #3100, Marietta, 770-429-0031

Friedman, Richard Jeffrey (7 mentions)
New York Med Coll, 1974
Certification: Gastroenterology, Internal Medicine
5671 Peachtree Dunwoody Rd #600, Atlanta, 404-252-4940

Galambos, Michael Robert (8 mentions)
Emory U, 1984 *Certification:* Gastroenterology, Internal Medicine
95 Collier Rd NW #4085, Atlanta, 404-355-3200

Galvez, Luis Manuel (5 mentions)
FMS-Venezuela, 1980
Certification: Gastroenterology, Internal Medicine
5671 Peachtree Dunwoody Rd NE #600, Atlanta, 404-257-9000
1340 Upper Hembree Rd, Roswell, 678-762-0676

Gold, Benjamin David (10 mentions)
George Washington U, 1987
Certification: Pediatric Gastroenterology
2015 Upper Gate Dr, Atlanta, 404-778-2400

Han, Agnes Hegyone (5 mentions)
Mount Sinai Sch of Med, 1987 *Certification:* Gastroenterology
960 Johnson Ferry Rd NE #515, Atlanta, 404-252-7703

Hirsh, Eugene H. (6 mentions)
U of Buffalo, 1975
Certification: Gastroenterology, Internal Medicine
5669 Peachtree Dunwoody Rd NE #270, Atlanta, 404-255-1000

Kamean, Jeffrie Lloyd (5 mentions)
Mount Sinai Sch of Med, 1992 *Certification:* Gastroenterology
2675 N Decatur Rd #305, Decatur, 404-299-8320

Kanji, Kiran Jagdish (4 mentions)
Emory U, 1997 *Certification:* Gastroenterology, Internal Medicine
1265 Hwy 54 W, Fayetteville, 678-817-6550

Kommor, Ross Alan (4 mentions)
U of Kentucky, 1982
Certification: Gastroenterology, Internal Medicine
120 Stoneridge Pkwy #110, Woodstock, 770-429-0031
61 Whitcher St NE #3100, Marietta, 770-429-0031

McGahan, Thomas Patrick (6 mentions)
Emory U, 1989 *Certification:* Gastroenterology, Internal Medicine
5669 Peachtree Dunwoody Rd NE #210, Atlanta, 404-255-4333

Morris, Steven J. (7 mentions)
U of Buffalo, 1973
Certification: Gastroenterology, Internal Medicine
550 Peachtree St NE #1600, Atlanta, 404-881-1094

Rausher, David Benjamin (6 mentions)
SUNY-Downstate Med Coll, 1977
Certification: Gastroenterology, Internal Medicine
2665 N Decatur Rd #550, Decatur, 404-297-6970

Rudert, Cynthia S. (4 mentions)
U of Louisville, 1979
Certification: Gastroenterology, Internal Medicine
5555 Peachtree Dunwoody Rd NE #312, Atlanta, 404-943-9820

Schorr, Scott W. (4 mentions)
U of Texas-Galveston, 1988
Certification: Gastroenterology, Internal Medicine
763 Old Norcross Rd, Lawrenceville, 678-985-2000
1800 Tree Ln Rd #190, Snellville, 678-985-2000

Shaw, Christopher T. (4 mentions)
Virginia Commonwealth U, 1977
Certification: Gastroenterology, Internal Medicine
5671 Peachtree Dunwoody Rd NE #600, Atlanta, 404-257-9000

Stern, Mark Alan (5 mentions)
Emory U, 1992 *Certification:* Gastroenterology
2675 N Decatur Rd #506, Decatur, 404-299-1679

Tanner, William Gordon, Jr. (4 mentions)
Vanderbilt U, 1993
Certification: Gastroenterology, Internal Medicine
721 Wellness Way #220, Lawrenceville, 770-995-7989

Waring, John Patrick (7 mentions)
Creighton U, 1980
Certification: Gastroenterology, Internal Medicine
95 Collier Rd NW #4075, Atlanta, 404-355-3200

Wisebram, Diane Leigh (7 mentions)
U of Nebraska, 1979
Certification: Gastroenterology, Internal Medicine
980 Johnson Ferry Rd NE #820, Atlanta, 404-252-9307

Wolf, Douglas Charles (5 mentions)
West Virginia U, 1979
Certification: Gastroenterology, Internal Medicine
5671 Peachtree Dunwoody Rd NE #600, Atlanta, 404-257-9000

Yanda, Randy Joseph (6 mentions)
U of Iowa, 1984
Certification: Gastroenterology, Internal Medicine
95 Collier Rd NW #4055, Atlanta, 404-355-1690

General Surgery

Abend, Melvin N. (5 mentions)
Tufts U, 1964 *Certification:* Surgery
4553 N Shallowford Rd #40B, Atlanta, 770-455-3753

Andersen, Chris Steven (9 mentions)
Emory U, 1983 *Certification:* Surgery
55 Whitcher St NE #260, Marietta, 770-423-0395

Barber, William Alan (6 mentions)
Med Coll of Georgia, 1982 *Certification:* Surgery
77 Collier Rd NW #2050, Atlanta, 404-351-1002

Bleacher, John C. (6 mentions)
Wright State U, 1988 *Certification:* Pediatric Surgery, Surgery
1371 Church St #200, Marietta, 404-252-3353
5455 Meridian Marks Rd NE #570, Atlanta, 404-252-3353

Brand, Theodore (3 mentions)
Northwestern U, 1978 *Certification:* Pediatric Surgery
5455 Meridian Marks Rd NE #570, Atlanta, 404-252-3353

Cummings, C. Richard, Jr. (5 mentions)
Certification: Surgery
980 Johnson Ferry Rd NE #760, Atlanta, 404-252-0503

Daneker, George W., Jr. (8 mentions)
U of Maryland, 1983 *Certification:* Surgery
5673 Peachtree Dunwoody Rd NE, Atlanta, 404-252-6118

Dillard, Gayla (3 mentions)
Meharry Med Coll, 1982 *Certification:* Surgery
1364 Wellbrook Cir, Conyers, 770-761-7171

Duncan, Titus Dewayne (4 mentions)
U of Oklahoma, 1978 *Certification:* Surgery
315 Blvd NE #224, Atlanta, 404-881-8020
4200 Northside Pkwy Bldg 8, Atlanta, 404-233-3833

Galloway, John Russell (4 mentions)
Emory U, 1981 *Certification:* Surgery
1365 Clifton Rd NE Bldg #A, Atlanta, 404-778-5986

Garcha, Iqbal Singh (11 mentions)
Med Coll of Georgia, 1991 *Certification:* Surgery
3400 Old Milton Pkwy #C-440, Alpharetta, 678-297-9707

Glasson, Julie Robin (4 mentions)
Harvard U, 1992
Certification: Pediatric Surgery, Surgery, Surgical Critical Care
5455 Meridian Marks Rd NE #570, Atlanta, 404-252-3353

Gorjala, Srinivasa Kumar (3 mentions)
New Jersey Med Sch, 1992 *Certification:* Surgery
4000 Corporate Center Dr, Morrow, 770-474-7287

Goza, John Sams (4 mentions)
U of South Carolina, 1992 *Certification:* Surgery
1265 Hwy 54 W #500, Fayetteville, 770-719-5660

Harper, Andrew Scott (3 mentions)
Emory U, 1985 *Certification:* Surgery
1364 Wellbrook Cir NE, Conyers, 770-922-4024

Hart, Christopher John (4 mentions)
U of Alabama, 1992 *Certification:* Surgery
6920 McGinniss Ferry Rd #340, Suwanee, 770-232-2911

Henry, Waights Gibbs, III (3 mentions)
Med Coll of Georgia, 1967 *Certification:* Surgery
790 Church St NW #570, Marietta, 770-428-0462

Hoadley, Jeffrey Scott (6 mentions)
Emory U, 1989 *Certification:* Surgery
5667 Peachtree Dunwoody Rd NE #380, Atlanta, 404-255-4901

Hoffman, Michael Alan (4 mentions)
Emory U, 1984 *Certification:* Surgery
980 Johnson Ferry Rd NE #760, Atlanta, 404-255-8304
11975 Morris Rd #125, Alpharetta, 404-255-8304

Kennedy, John S. (4 mentions)
Certification: Surgery
2665 N Decatur Rd #730, Decatur, 404-508-4320

Ludi, Gary Allen (17 mentions)
U of Colorado, 1981 *Certification:* Surgery
5673 Peachtree Dunwoody Rd #300, Atlanta, 404-252-6118

Luke, Joseph Patrick (12 mentions)
Med Coll of Georgia, 1982 *Certification:* Surgery
3400 Old Milton Pkwy #C440, Alpharetta, 678-297-9707
5670 Peachtree Dunwoody Rd #920, Atlanta, 404-847-0664

Martin, Wallace Ford (3 mentions)
Emory U, 1979 *Certification:* Surgery
600 Professional Dr #250, Lawrenceville, 770-962-9977

McCarter, Freda Danielle (3 mentions)
U of Cincinnati, 1996 *Certification:* Surgery
1136 Cleveland Ave #519, Atlanta, 404-765-6577
1014 Hospital Dr, Stockbridge, 404-765-6577
550 Peachtree St #1400, Atlanta, 404-765-6577

Mims, Joseph Paul (11 mentions)
Med Coll of Georgia, 1988 *Certification:* Surgery
95 Collier Rd NW #6015, Atlanta, 404-351-5959

Moyo, Mutinhima R. (3 mentions)
Emory U, 2001 *Certification:* Surgery
2500 Hospital Blvd #410, Roswell, 770-667-4991

O'Reilly, Michael Joseph (3 mentions)
U of Texas-Dallas, 1981 *Certification:* Surgery
800 Canton Rd, Marietta, 770-424-4328

Odom, Stephen Joseph (4 mentions)
Virginia Commonwealth U, 1988 *Certification:* Surgery
1810 Mulkey Rd #105, Austell, 770-944-0686

Organ, Brian Christopher (5 mentions)
Washington U, 1981 *Certification:* Surgery
285 Boulevard NE #620, Atlanta, 404-588-1717

Park, David Dongwon (3 mentions)
U of Missouri-Kansas City, 1988 *Certification:* Surgery
5673 Peachtree Dunwoody Rd #300, Atlanta, 404-252-6118

Parker, Paul Mackie (7 mentions)
U of North Carolina, 1981 *Certification:* Pediatric Surgery
1975 Century Blvd NE #6, Atlanta, 404-982-9938

Phillips, Rogsbert F. (3 mentions)
Columbia U, 1977 *Certification:* Surgery
5910 Hillandale Dr #104, Lithonia, 678-418-3990

Quill, Stephen Gerard (3 mentions)
Georgetown U, 1990 *Certification:* Surgery
3540 Duluth Park Ln #290, Duluth, 770-418-1627

Quinones, Michael Anthony (6 mentions)
Harvard U, 1986 *Certification:* Surgery
2675 N Decatur Rd #609, Decatur, 404-501-9170
5900 Hillandale Dr #245, Lithonia, 404-501-9170

Ricketts, Richard Randall (4 mentions)
Northwestern U, 1973 *Certification:* Pediatric Surgery, Surgery
1975 Century Blvd NE #6, Atlanta, 404-982-9938

Ruben, David Mark (7 mentions)
Med Coll of Georgia, 1980 *Certification:* Surgery
3400 Old Milton Pkwy #C-440, Alpharetta, 678-297-9707
5670 Peachtree Dunwoody Dr #920, Atlanta, 404-847-0664

Shaak, George William (5 mentions)
Louisiana State U, 1984 *Certification:* Surgery
980 Johnson Ferry Rd NE #760, Atlanta, 404-255-8304
11975 Morris Rd #125, Alpharetta, 404-255-8304

Stapleton, Sidney L., Jr. (5 mentions)
Emory U, 1966 *Certification:* Surgery
2665 N Decatur Rd #350, Decatur, 404-501-7081

Steinberg, Scott David (8 mentions)
Mount Sinai Sch of Med, 1995 *Certification:* Surgery
2665 N Decatur Rd #350, Decatur, 404-501-7081

Werbel, Gordon Bradley (3 mentions)
Indiana U, 1983 *Certification:* Surgery
1800 Tree Ln #330, Snellville, 770-978-0561
500 Medical Center Blvd #360, Lawrenceville, 770-513-2155

Wilkiemeyer, Mark Boswell (3 mentions)
Tulane U, 1998 *Certification:* Surgery
5667 Peachtree Dunwoody Rd NE #380, Atlanta, 404-255-4901

Wilson, Bryant Whitley (3 mentions)
Med Coll of Georgia, 1983 *Certification:* Surgery
95 Collier Rd NW #6015, Atlanta, 404-351-5959

Wilson, Russell A. (5 mentions)
U of Texas-Dallas, 1991 *Certification:* Surgery
1265 Hwy 54 W #500-B, Fayetteville, 770-719-5660

Wyatt, Mark Steven (3 mentions)
U of Florida, 1986 *Certification:* Surgery
1790 Mulkey Rd #9A, Austell, 770-944-7818

Geriatrics

Flacker, Jonathan M. (3 mentions)
U of Chicago, 1990
Certification: Geriatric Medicine, Internal Medicine
1821 Clifton Rd NE, Atlanta, 404-728-6363

Parker, Monica Willis (5 mentions)
U of Nebraska, 1986 *Certification:* Family Medicine
1821 Clifton Rd NE, Atlanta, 404-728-6363

Tenover, Joyce Sander (4 mentions)
George Washington U, 1980
Certification: Geriatric Medicine, Internal Medicine
1821 Clifton Rd NE, Atlanta, 404-728-6331

Hematology/Oncology

Afshani, Victoria Lynn (4 mentions)
U of Pennsylvania, 1995
Certification: Hematology, Medical Oncology
1501 Milstead Rd NE #110, Conyers, 770-760-9949

Allen, Robert S. (5 mentions)
Certification: Internal Medicine, Medical Oncology
105 Collier Rd NW #3040, Atlanta, 404-355-9243

Andrews, Michael B. (4 mentions)
Certification: Hematology, Internal Medicine, Medical Oncology
340 Kennestone Hospital Blvd #200, Marietta, 770-281-5100

Austin, Colleen Shane (11 mentions)
SUNY-Upstate Med U, 1977
Certification: Internal Medicine, Medical Oncology
5670 Peachtree Dunwoody Rd NE #1100, Atlanta, 404-851-2310

Ballard, Wiley Perry, III (9 mentions)
Emory U, 1978
Certification: Hematology, Internal Medicine, Medical Oncology
275 Collier Rd NW #400, Atlanta, 404-350-9853

Bender, Jonathan C. (5 mentions)
Ohio State U, 1995 *Certification:* Hematology, Medical Oncology
1265 Hwy 54 W #500, Fayetteville, 678-829-1060

Carter, Richard Allan (4 mentions)
New Jersey Med Sch, 1992
Certification: Hematology, Medical Oncology
1506 Klondike Rd SW #205, Conyers, 770-761-7260

Collins, Douglas Caldwell (8 mentions)
U of Washington, 1977 *Certification:* Internal Medicine
320 Parkway Dr NE #232, Atlanta, 404-892-5950

Dubovsky, Daniel William (11 mentions)
FMS-South Africa, 1968
5670 Peachtree Dunwoody Rd NE #1100, Atlanta, 404-851-2330

Feinberg, Bruce Alan (6 mentions)
Philadelphia Coll of Osteopathic Med, 1982
2712 Lawrenceville Hwy, Decatur, 770-496-5555
1501 Milstead Rd #110, Conyers, 770-760-9949

Freedman, Allan (4 mentions)
U of Vermont, 1977
Certification: Internal Medicine, Medical Oncology
1700 Tree Ln #490, Snellville, 770-979-2828

Galleshaw, Janice Ann (9 mentions)
Med Coll of Georgia, 1985 *Certification:* Medical Oncology
3400 Old Milton Pkwy #535, Alpharetta, 678-566-6995
1100 Johnson Ferry Rd NE #600, Atlanta, 678-566-6995

Heffner, Leonard T., Jr. (4 mentions)
Wake Forest U, 1969
1365 Clifton Rd NE Bldg C #A, Atlanta, 404-778-5799

Jolly, Pradeep Chander (6 mentions)
FMS-India, 1977
Certification: Hematology, Internal Medicine, Medical Oncology
1100 Johnson Ferry Rd NE #600, Atlanta, 404-256-4777

Landis, Anthony Mark (4 mentions)
Philadelphia Coll of Osteopathic Med, 1977
Certification: Internal Medicine, Medical Oncology
600 Professional Dr #210, Lawrenceville, 770-963-8030

Lawson, David Hardman (5 mentions)
Emory U, 1974
Certification: Internal Medicine, Medical Oncology
1365 Clifton Rd NE, Atlanta, 404-778-1900

Lesesne, Joseph Bancroft (9 mentions)
Duke U, 1976 *Certification:* Internal Medicine, Medical Oncology
1100 Johnson Ferry Rd NE #600, Atlanta, 404-256-4777
1835 Savoy Dr #300, Atlanta, 770-496-9400

McCoy, Frank P. (4 mentions)
Certification: Hematology, Internal Medicine, Medical Oncology
340 Kennestone Hospital Blvd #200, Marietta, 770-281-5100

Miller, Debra Kay (4 mentions)
Wake Forest U, 1990
1700 Hospital South Dr #300, Austell, 770-944-2830

Moore, Melvin Robert (4 mentions)
Wayne State U, 1968
Certification: Internal Medicine, Medical Oncology
2712 Lawrenceville Hwy, Decatur, 770-496-5555
2675 N Decatur Rd #701, Decatur, 404-294-8750

Reddy, Silpa Cheepuloti (6 mentions)
Virginia Commonwealth U, 1994
Certification: Hematology, Medical Oncology
1357 Hembree Rd #230, Roswell, 770-740-9664
5670 Peachtree Dunwoody Rd NE #1100, Atlanta, 404-851-2300

Saker, Alexander, Jr. (6 mentions)
Med Coll of Georgia, 1986
Certification: Hematology, Internal Medicine, Medical Oncology
600 Professional Dr #210, Lawrenceville, 770-963-8030

Sarma, Ramaseshu P. (6 mentions)
FMS-India, 1976 *Certification:* Pediatrics
75 Piedmont Ave NE #700, Atlanta, 404-756-1480

Srinivasiah, Jayanthi (7 mentions)
FMS-India, 1984 *Certification:* Hematology, Medical Oncology
2675 N Decatur Rd #701, Decatur, 404-294-8750
2712 Lawrenceville Hwy #510, Decatur, 770-496-5555

Steis, Ronald George (6 mentions)
U of Pittsburgh, 1978
Certification: Internal Medicine, Medical Oncology
1357 Hembree Rd #230, Roswell, 770-740-9664

Szabo, Stephen Michael (15 mentions)
Cornell U, 1993
Certification: Hematology, Internal Medicine, Medical Oncology
2712 Lawrenceville Hwy, Decatur, 770-496-5555
6325 W Johns Crossing Bldg 1000 #107, Duluth, 770-623-8965

Tamim, Hiba M. (4 mentions)
FMS-Lebanon, 1989
Certification: Hematology, Internal Medicine, Medical Oncology
2665 N Decatur Rd #740, Decatur, 404-321-1950

Volas-Redd, Gena H. (4 mentions)
Pennsylvania State U, 1994 *Certification:* Medical Oncology
340 Kennestone Hospital Blvd #100, Marietta, 770-590-8311
228 Riverstone Dr, Canton, 770-479-1870

Infectious Disease

Blass, Mitchell Adam (6 mentions)
Emory U, 1992
Certification: Infectious Disease, Internal Medicine
5671 Peachtree Dunwoody Rd NE #300, Atlanta, 404-256-4111

Boden, Milton Derrick (5 mentions)
Med Coll of Georgia, 1990
Certification: Infectious Disease, Internal Medicine
2665 N Decatur Rd #330, Decatur, 404-297-9755

Brachman, Philip S., Jr. (7 mentions)
Emory U, 1987
Certification: Infectious Disease, Internal Medicine
2001 Peachtree Rd NE #640, Atlanta, 404-355-3161

Capparell, Robert (16 mentions)
U of Rochester, 1975
Certification: Infectious Disease, Internal Medicine
5671 Peachtree Dunwoody Rd NE #300, Atlanta, 404-256-4111

Cohen, Howard Joel (25 mentions)
Med Coll of Georgia, 1977
Certification: Infectious Disease, Internal Medicine
1350 Upper Hembree Rd #100-B, Roswell, 770-442-1990
960 Johnson Ferry Rd NE #430, Atlanta, 404-851-0081

Dailey, Michael Parker (8 mentions)
Wayne State U, 1975
Certification: Infectious Disease, Internal Medicine
11660 Alpharetta Hwy #430, Roswell, 770-255-1069

Diamond, Lee Alan (5 mentions)
Mount Sinai Sch of Med, 1978
Certification: Infectious Disease, Internal Medicine
6285 Garden Walk Blvd #A, Riverdale, 770-991-1500

Dickensheets, David L. (5 mentions)
Jefferson Med Coll, 1980
Certification: Infectious Disease, Internal Medicine
11660 Alpharetta Hwy #430, Roswell, 770-255-1069

Dretler, Robin Henry (11 mentions)
Tufts U, 1978 *Certification:* Infectious Disease, Internal Medicine
2665 N Decatur Rd #330, Decatur, 404-297-9755

Drummond, John Andrew (6 mentions)
U of Alabama, 1973 *Certification:* Internal Medicine
35 Collier Rd NW #175, Atlanta, 404-446-0456

Harrison, Harvey Robert (5 mentions)
Harvard U, 1974
Certification: Pediatric Infectious Diseases, Pediatrics
993 Johnson Ferry Rd NE #F-370, Atlanta, 404-252-4611

Havlik, Joseph Anthony, Jr. (5 mentions)
Rosalind Franklin U, 1986
Certification: Infectious Disease, Internal Medicine
1700 Hospital S Dr #402, Austell, 770-739-8282

Keyserling, Harry Leroy (4 mentions)
Georgetown U, 1977
Certification: Pediatric Infectious Diseases, Pediatrics
2015 Upper Gate Dr, Atlanta, 404-727-5642

Lopez, Carlos E. (8 mentions)
U of Puerto Rico, 1969
Certification: Infectious Disease, Internal Medicine
2001 Peachtree Rd NE #640, Atlanta, 404-355-3161

Martin, Paul Dwight (10 mentions)
U of Louisville, 1984
Certification: Infectious Disease, Internal Medicine
575 Professional Dr #370, Lawrenceville, 770-995-0466

Melton, Dennis Mitchell (7 mentions)
U of Tennessee, 1985
Certification: Infectious Disease, Internal Medicine
340 Blvd NE #210, Atlanta, 404-588-4680

Nguyen, Hieu Thi (6 mentions)
U of Oklahoma, 1985
Certification: Infectious Disease, Internal Medicine
2665 N Decatur Rd #340, Decatur, 404-501-7455

Oakley, Lisa Anne (10 mentions)
U of Louisville, 1981
Certification: Infectious Disease, Internal Medicine
1700 Hospital South Dr #402, Austell, 770-739-8282

Raizes, Elliot G. (11 mentions)
Certification: Infectious Disease, Internal Medicine
575 Professional Dr #370, Lawrenceville, 770-995-0466

Shore, Steven Lewis (9 mentions)
Johns Hopkins U, 1967
Certification: Pediatric Infectious Diseases, Pediatrics
993 Johnson Ferry Rd NE #F-370, Atlanta, 404-252-4611

Webster, Samuel Easely (6 mentions)
West Virginia U, 1975
980 Johnson Ferry Rd NE #250, Atlanta, 404-252-9140

Williamson, Margaret (6 mentions)
Emory U, 1993
Certification: Infectious Disease, Internal Medicine
5671 Peachtree Dunwoody Rd NE #300, Atlanta, 404-256-4111

Wurapa, Anson Kwame (5 mentions)
SUNY-Upstate Med U, 1994 *Certification:* Infectious Disease
2665 N Decatur Rd #340, Decatur, 404-501-7455

Infertility

Hasty, Lisa A. (11 mentions)
Emory U, 1985 *Certification:* Obstetrics & Gynecology,
  Reproductive Endocrinology/Infertility
100 Stoneforest Dr #300, Woodstock, 770-928-2276
5909 Peachtree Dunwoody Rd #720, Atlanta, 770-928-2276
35 Collier Rd #M-215, Atlanta, 770-928-2276
6470 E Johns Crossing #200, Duluth, 770-928-2276

Kort, Hilton Isadore (17 mentions)
FMS-South Africa, 1970
1150 Lake Hearn Dr NE #400, Atlanta, 404-257-1900

Mitchell-Leef, Dorothy E. (11 mentions)
U of Louisville, 1975 *Certification:* Obstetrics & Gynecology
1150 Lake Hearn Dr NE #400, Atlanta, 404-250-6852

Shapiro, Daniel Berns (6 mentions)
Emory U, 1988 *Certification:* Obstetrics & Gynecology,
  Reproductive Endocrinology/Infertility
1150 Lake Hearn Dr NE #400, Atlanta, 404-257-1900

Toledo, Andrew Anthony (8 mentions)
U of South Florida, 1979 *Certification:* Obstetrics &
  Gynecology, Reproductive Endocrinology/Infertility
1150 Lake Hearn Dr NE #400, Atlanta, 404-256-6972

Internal Medicine *(see note on page 9)*

Ahn, Kelly Jung (3 mentions)
Emory U, 1993 *Certification:* Internal Medicine
755 Mount Vernon Hwy NE #500, Atlanta, 404-256-9544

Bandukwala, Ibrez Rafiq (3 mentions)
U of North Carolina, 1997 *Certification:* Internal Medicine
550 Peachtree St NE #1550, Atlanta, 404-892-2131
5673 Peachtree Dunwoody Rd NE #775, Atlanta, 404-256-8500

Benson, Samantha Talley (3 mentions)
Emory U, 1998 *Certification:* Internal Medicine
3340 Paddocks Pkwy, Suwanee, 678-474-9633

Biggs, Barbara Conner (3 mentions)
U of Mississippi, 1982 *Certification:* Internal Medicine
1431 White Cir, Marietta, 678-797-6830

Cantwell, Ryan Victor (3 mentions)
Morehouse Coll, 1997 *Certification:* Internal Medicine
320 Kennestone Hospital Blvd #201, Marietta, 770-427-2457

Chervu, Indira (3 mentions)
FMS-India, 1984 *Certification:* Internal Medicine, Nephrology
55 Whitcher St NE #460, Marietta, 770-427-7389

Cucher, Bobb Gary (4 mentions)
Rosalind Franklin U, 1971 *Certification:* Internal Medicine
993 Johnson Ferry Rd NE #130, Atlanta, 404-252-0221

Davis, Donald Crawford (3 mentions)
Emory U, 1976 *Certification:* Internal Medicine
1525 Clifton Rd NE, Atlanta, 404-778-3276

Di Fulco, Thomas John (5 mentions)
Emory U, 1975 *Certification:* Internal Medicine
1462 Montreal Rd #303, Tucker, 770-938-9761

Fowler, Reginald Stephen (3 mentions)
Tufts U, 1978 *Certification:* Internal Medicine
232 19th St #7220, Atlanta, 404-367-3000

Gower, William J., III (3 mentions)
Emory U, 1978 *Certification:* Internal Medicine
755 Mount Vernon Hwy NE #500, Atlanta, 404-256-9544

Hansen, Richard Daniel (4 mentions)
George Washington U, 1981 *Certification:* Internal Medicine
5505 Peachtree Dunwoody Rd NE #650, Atlanta, 404-256-1104

Harsch, John Arthur (5 mentions)
Washington U, 1983 *Certification:* Internal Medicine
105 Carnegie Pl #103, Fayetteville, 770-716-7999
1035 Southwest Dr #200, Stockbridge, 770-716-7999

Herman, Lee Edward (4 mentions)
Med Coll of Georgia, 1994 *Certification:* Internal Medicine
4365 Johns Creek Pkwy #420, Suwanee, 678-957-1910

Herrera, Robert Dennis (3 mentions)
Georgetown U, 1994 *Certification:* Internal Medicine
5505 Peachtree Dunwoody Rd NE #650, Atlanta, 404-256-1104

Herzog, Lonnie (5 mentions)
U of Florida, 1982 *Certification:* Internal Medicine
5670 Peachtree Dunwoody Rd NE #1200, Atlanta, 404-255-9100

Jacobs, Norman F., Jr. (4 mentions)
SUNY-Upstate Med U, 1971 *Certification:* Internal Medicine
2712 N Decatur Rd, Decatur, 404-294-1227

Kaplan, Richard David (3 mentions)
Certification: Internal Medicine
5505 Peachtree Dunwoody Rd NE #650, Atlanta, 404-256-3135

Leaderman, Adam Joseph (3 mentions)
Emory U, 1982 *Certification:* Internal Medicine
5673 Peachtree Dunwoody Rd NE #775, Atlanta, 404-256-8500

Levine, Marshall Richard (3 mentions)
Cornell U, 1974 *Certification:* Internal Medicine
35 Collier Rd NW #M-260, Atlanta, 404-367-3100

Martin, Joseph Henry, Jr. (3 mentions)
Duke U, 1982 *Certification:* Internal Medicine
550 Peachtree St NE #1420, Atlanta, 404-526-9111

Masor, Jonathan Jay (6 mentions)
New Jersey Med Sch, 1983 *Certification:* Internal Medicine
1525 Clifton Rd NE, Atlanta, 404-778-3266

Maxa, Richard Reid (3 mentions)
Vanderbilt U, 1993 *Certification:* Internal Medicine
3505 Duluth Park Ln #400, Duluth, 678-597-3180

Partin, Clyde, Jr. (3 mentions)
Emory U, 1983 *Certification:* Internal Medicine
1525 Clifton Rd NE, Atlanta, 404-778-2700

Reeves, Harrison Walton (3 mentions)
Certification: Internal Medicine
550 Peachtree St NE #1550, Atlanta, 404-892-2131

Rozin, Spencer Ian (6 mentions)
U of Oklahoma, 1987 *Certification:* Internal Medicine
721 Wellness Way #100, Lawrenceville, 770-709-0900

Seltman, Marc Alan (7 mentions)
Tulane U, 1984 *Certification:* Internal Medicine
5505 Peachtree Dunwoody Rd NE #650, Atlanta, 404-256-3135

Shulman, Scott Jeffrey (7 mentions)
Emory U, 1987 *Certification:* Internal Medicine
5673 Peachtree Dunwoody Rd NE #775, Atlanta, 404-256-8500
550 Peachtree St NE #1550, Atlanta, 404-892-2131

Spivey, James David (3 mentions)
Baylor U, 1989 *Certification:* Internal Medicine
1109 W Peachtree St NW, Atlanta, 404-607-1777

Stovall, Raymond Lee (3 mentions)
Med Coll of Georgia, 1982 *Certification:* Internal Medicine
600 Professional Dr #150, Lawrenceville, 678-376-1800

Nephrology

Brathwaite, Michel (5 mentions)
Temple U, 1989 *Certification:* Internal Medicine, Nephrology
1987 Candler Rd, Decatur, 404-534-0183
121 Linden Ave NE #102, Decatur, 404-815-7217
2669 Church St, Atlanta, 404-209-0113
3620 Martin Luther King Jr Dr, Atlanta, 404-534-0183
2485 Park Center Blvd, Decatur, 404-564-4991

Chatoth, Dinesh (9 mentions)
FMS-India, 1991 *Certification:* Internal Medicine, Nephrology
1115 Harrington Rd, Lawrenceville, 678-990-5260

Chervu, Indira (8 mentions)
FMS-India, 1984 *Certification:* Internal Medicine, Nephrology
55 Whitcher St NE #460, Marietta, 770-427-7389

Cleveland, William Howard (8 mentions)
U of Pittsburgh, 1974
Certification: Internal Medicine, Nephrology
1987 Candler Rd, Decatur, 404-534-0183
121 Linden Ave NE #102, Atlanta, 404-815-7217
3620 Martin Luther King Blvd, Atlanta, 404-534-0183
2485 Park Cnter Blvd, Decatur, 404-564-4991
2669 Church St, Atlanta, 404-209-0113

Frederickson, Edward Dent (4 mentions)
Emory U, 1980 *Certification:* Internal Medicine, Nephrology
35 Collier Rd NW #610, Atlanta, 404-355-2023

Handelsman, Stuart (6 mentions)
Albert Einstein Coll of Med, 1975
Certification: Internal Medicine, Nephrology
980 Johnson Ferry Rd NE #410, Atlanta, 404-252-0256

Harish, Dwarakinath (4 mentions)
FMS-India, 1986 *Certification:* Nephrology
601-A Professional Dr, Lawrenceville, 678-377-3305

Hill, Susan C. (20 mentions)
Virginia Commonwealth U, 1977
Certification: Internal Medicine, Nephrology
5671 Peachtree Dunwoody Rd NE #500, Atlanta, 404-255-1030

Howard, Angus Collins, Jr. (10 mentions)
Med Coll of Georgia, 1986
Certification: Internal Medicine, Nephrology
3620 Martin Luther King Jr Dr SW, Atlanta, 404-534-0183
1987 Candler Rd, Decatur, 404-534-0184
2669 Church St, Atlanta, 404-209-0113
2485 Park Center Blvd, Decatur, 404-564-4991
121 Linden Ave NE #102, Atlanta, 404-815-7217

Jansen, Robert David (5 mentions)
Emory U, 1979 *Certification:* Internal Medicine, Nephrology
55 Whitcher St NE #460, Marietta, 770-427-7389
120 Stonebridge Pkwy #330, Woodstock, 770-427-7389

Katz, Michael Stephen (4 mentions)
FMS-South Africa, 1985 *Certification:* Nephrology
35 Collier Rd NW #610, Atlanta, 404-355-2023

Knowlton, Gregory Bates (9 mentions)
West Virginia U, 1973
Certification: Internal Medicine, Nephrology
5671 Peachtree Dunwoody Rd NE #500, Atlanta, 404-255-1030

Muro, Karen (7 mentions)
U of California-Irvine, 1986
Certification: Internal Medicine, Nephrology
497 Winn Way #A-210, Decatur, 404-294-7033
5250 Snapfinger Park Dr, Lithonia, 770-808-6227
1285 Wellbrook Cir, Conyers, 770-922-0209
2096 McGhee Rd, Snellville, 678-990-5260
7215 Industrial Blvd, Covington, 770-788-7464

Sherwinter, Julius (4 mentions)
U of Pennsylvania, 1973 *Certification:* Pediatrics
5501 Chamblee Dunwoody Rd, Dunwoody, 770-394-2358

Warshaw, Barry Louis (9 mentions)
Emory U, 1972 *Certification:* Pediatric Nephrology, Pediatrics
2015 Uppergate Dr NE, Atlanta, 404-727-5750

Neurological Surgery

Barrow, Daniel Louis (14 mentions)
Southern Illinois U, 1979 *Certification:* Neurological Surgery
1365B Clifton Rd NE #2200, Atlanta, 404-778-5770

Boydston, William Roy (12 mentions)
Med Coll of Georgia, 1985 *Certification:* Neurological Surgery
5455 Meridian Mark Rd NE #540, Atlanta, 404-255-6509

Clare, Christopher Edward (8 mentions)
Med U of South Carolina, 1985
Certification: Neurological Surgery
5671 Peachtree Dunwoody Rd NE #340, Atlanta, 404-851-2200
35 Collier Rd NW #115, Atlanta, 404-350-7907

Disch, Steven Paul (11 mentions)
U of Alabama, 1981 *Certification:* Neurological Surgery
2500 Hospital Blvd #310, Roswell, 770-664-9600

Hartman, Michael G. (8 mentions)
U of Toledo, 1984 *Certification:* Neurological Surgery
1700 Tree Ln #430, Snellville, 770-979-8080
2785 Lawrenceville Hwy #100, Decatur, 404-292-4612

Hudgins, Roger James (10 mentions)
U of Alabama, 1979 *Certification:* Neurological Surgery
5455 Meridian Mark Rd NE #540, Atlanta, 404-255-6509

Javed, Tariq (9 mentions)
FMS-United Kingdom, 1980 *Certification:* Neurological Surgery
631 Campbell Hill St NW #100, Marietta, 770-422-0444

Khajavi, Kaveh (8 mentions)
Georgetown U, 1989 *Certification:* Neurological Surgery
2675 N Decatur Rd #710, Decatur, 404-299-3338

Rodts, Gerald Edward, Jr. (9 mentions)
Columbia U, 1987 *Certification:* Neurological Surgery
59 Executive Park South NE, Atlanta, 404-778-7000

Steuer, Max R. (22 mentions)
Baylor U, 1985 *Certification:* Neurological Surgery
1100 Northside Forsythe Dr #345, Cumming, 404-256-2633
5670 Peachtree Dunwoody Rd NE #990, Atlanta, 404-256-2633

Tomaras, Christopher R. (10 mentions)
U of Tennessee, 1992 *Certification:* Neurological Surgery
5670 Peachtree Dunwoody Rd NE #990, Atlanta, 404-256-2633
1100 Northside Forsythe Dr #345, Cumming, 404-256-2633

Neurology

Franco, Richard David (7 mentions)
Emory U, 1963 *Certification:* Internal Medicine, Neurology
993 Johnson Ferry Rd NE Bldg F #120, Atlanta, 404-256-3720

Goldstein, Edward Morris (5 mentions)
Johns Hopkins U, 1985 *Certification:* Neurology with
Special Qualifications in Child Neurology
5505 Peachtree Dunwoody Rd NE #500, Atlanta, 404-256-3535

Gwynn, Matthews Weber (12 mentions)
U of Virginia, 1985 *Certification:* Internal Medicine, Neurology
993 Johnson Ferry Rd NE #F-120, Atlanta, 404-256-3720

Harris, Mark Irwin (7 mentions)
Rosalind Franklin U, 1982 *Certification:* Neurology
4275 Johns Creek Pkwy #C, Suwanee, 770-454-4685

Hedaya, Ellis Victor (11 mentions)
Johns Hopkins U, 1976
Certification: Clinical Neurophysiology, Neurology
550 Peachtree St NE #1200, Atlanta, 404-221-1899
3200 Downwood Cir NW #550, Atlanta, 404-351-0205

Kelman, Leslie (12 mentions)
FMS-South Africa, 1967 *Certification:* Neurology
5671 Peachtree Dunwoody #620, Atlanta, 404-843-9958

Krawiecki, Nicolas S. (5 mentions)
FMS-France, 1974 *Certification:* Neurology with Special
Qualifications in Child Neurology, Pediatrics
2015 Upper Gate Dr NE, Atlanta, 404-778-2400

Lakhanpal, Arun (5 mentions)
FMS-India, 1980 *Certification:* Neurology
1700 Tree Ln #350, Snellville, 770-978-3578
475 Philip Blvd #100, Lawrenceville, 770-985-3300

Lexow, Stephen Stewart (4 mentions)
U of Florida, 1974 *Certification:* Neurology
2665 N Decatur Rd #620, Decatur, 404-501-7526

McCasland, Barry John (8 mentions)
Georgetown U, 1994 *Certification:* Neurology
5671 Peachtree Dunwoody Rd NE #515, Atlanta, 404-531-0334

Olson, David Albert (7 mentions)
Emory U, 1989 *Certification:* Neurology
2665 N Decatur Rd #540, Decatur, 404-508-4008

Penix, LaRoy (5 mentions)
Johns Hopkins U, 1984 *Certification:* Neurology
80 Jesse Hill Jr Dr SE, Atlanta, 404-616-0587

Ranadive, Virendra V. (4 mentions)
FMS-India, 1988 *Certification:* Neurology
1250 Hwy 54 W #201, Fayetteville, 770-716-1562

Re, Peter Keith (4 mentions)
Emory U, 1966 *Certification:* Neurology
780 Canton Rd NE #400, Marietta, 770-422-3602

Sanders, Keith Alan (5 mentions)
Emory U, 1987 *Certification:* Neurology, Vascular Neurology
993 Johnson Ferry Rd NE #F-120, Atlanta, 404-256-3720

Schub, Howard Sheldon (9 mentions)
U of North Carolina, 1976 *Certification:* Neurology with
Special Qualifications in Child Neurology, Pediatrics
5505 Peachtree Dunwoody Rd NE #500, Atlanta, 404-256-3535
5455 Meridian Mark Rd #200, Atlanta, 404-785-2490

Stuart, Douglas Scott (10 mentions)
Emory U, 1988 *Certification:* Neurology
95 Collier Rd NW #4045, Atlanta, 404-351-2270
3200 Downwood Cir #550, Atlanta, 404-351-0205
550 Peachtree St NE #1200, Atlanta, 404-221-1899

Weissman, Joseph Daniel (5 mentions)
Case Western Reserve U, 1982 *Certification:* Neurology
2665 N Decatur Rd #630, Decatur, 404-501-7555

Williamson, Mitchell Todd (7 mentions)
Emory U, 1989 *Certification:* Neurology
601 Professional Dr #160, Lawrenceville, 770-995-0555
385 Pleasant Hill Rd #200, Duluth, 770-495-0332

Obstetrics/Gynecology

Arkin, Eva S. (6 mentions)
Emory U, 1980 *Certification:* Obstetrics & Gynecology
5505 Peachtree Dunwoody Rd NE #200, Atlanta, 404-257-0170

Arluck, Jessica C. (4 mentions)
Ohio State U, 1990 *Certification:* Obstetrics & Gynecology
550 Peachtree St NE 9th Fl, Atlanta, 404-686-8121

Bearman, Dale Mitchell (4 mentions)
Tufts U, 1981 *Certification:* Obstetrics & Gynecology
5780 Peachtree Dunwoody Rd NE #195, Atlanta, 404-256-4667
11459 Johns Creek Pkwy #200, Johns Creek, 770-623-0910

Bonk, Catherine Mary (5 mentions)
Emory U, 1986 *Certification:* Obstetrics & Gynecology
315 Winn Way, Decatur, 404-299-9724
449 Pleasant Hill Rd NW #200, Lilburn, 770-923-5033

Browne, Paul Christopher (3 mentions)
Duke U, 1981
Certification: Maternal-Fetal Medicine, Obstetrics & Gynecology
2665 N Decatur Rd #750, Decatur, 770-279-3838
1383 Manchester Dr #B, Conyers, 770-279-3838
1279 Hwy 54 W #200, Fayetteville, 770-279-3838

Cook, Nancy Hickam (4 mentions)
U of Louisville, 1982 *Certification:* Obstetrics & Gynecology
275 Collier Rd NW #100-B, Atlanta, 404-352-3656

Cook, William T. (3 mentions)
U of Michigan, 1985 *Certification:* Obstetrics & Gynecology
1267 Hwy 54 W #3200, Fayetteville, 770-632-9900

Croft, Barbara Nason (3 mentions)
Emory U, 1978 *Certification:* Obstetrics & Gynecology
275 Collier Rd NW #100-A, Atlanta, 404-352-1235

Davis-Williams, Camille (6 mentions)
Emory U, 1981 *Certification:* Obstetrics & Gynecology
550 Peachtree St NE #1470, Atlanta, 404-589-2670

Espy, Goodman Basil, III (3 mentions)
Tulane U, 1962 *Certification:* Obstetrics & Gynecology
72 Plaza Way NW, Marietta, 770-422-8700

Garcia-Saul, Jose A. (5 mentions)
Duke U, 1977 *Certification:* Obstetrics & Gynecology
11975 Morris Rd #300, Alpharetta, 770-521-2295

Gumer, Arthur (3 mentions)
George Washington U, 1984
Certification: Obstetrics & Gynecology
5780 Peachtree Dunwoody Rd NE #195, Atlanta, 404-256-4667
11459 Johns Creek Pkwy #200, Johns Creek, 770-623-0910

Johnston, Janice W. (4 mentions)
Emory U, 1977 *Certification:* Obstetrics & Gynecology
105 Collier Rd NW #2030, Atlanta, 404-352-1235
275 Collier Rd NW #100-A, Atlanta, 404-352-1235

Levitt, Brian Allen (3 mentions)
Wayne State U, 1983 *Certification:* Obstetrics & Gynecology
1700 tree Ln #200, Decatur, 678-904-7210
2685 Milscott Dr, Decatur, 678-904-7210

Long, George Dalton (3 mentions)
Tulane U, 1982 *Certification:* Obstetrics & Gynecology
980 Johnson Ferry Rd NE #800, Atlanta, 404-256-2871

Ludwig-Arona, Audrey Jean (3 mentions)
U of Cincinnati, 1991 *Certification:* Obstetrics & Gynecology
500 Medical Center Blvd #290, Lawrenceville, 770-962-5100

Marcus, Jeffrey Alan (4 mentions)
George Washington U, 1989
1121 Johnson Ferry Rd #150, Marietta, 770-977-1510
11459 Johns Creek Pkwy #200, Johns Creek, 770-623-0910

McFarling, Harry M., III (3 mentions)
Emory U, 1980 *Certification:* Obstetrics & Gynecology
275 Collier Rd #100-C, Atlanta, 404-355-0320

Ralsten, Matthew Murrill (3 mentions)
Marshall U, 2002
1267 Hwy 54 W #3200, Fayetteville, 770-632-9900

Sharon, Thomas Edward, Jr. (4 mentions)
Emory U, 1990 *Certification:* Obstetrics & Gynecology
975 Johnson Ferry Rd NE #400, Atlanta, 404-252-1137
1519 Johnson Ferry Rd #175, Marietta, 770-565-2233
3890 Johns Creek Pkwy #300, Suwanee, 678-775-2300

Soufi, Winifred Lin (3 mentions)
U of Illinois, 1992 *Certification:* Obstetrics & Gynecology
980 Johnson Ferry Rd NE #720, Atlanta, 404-252-3898

Street, Elizabeth Ann (7 mentions)
Emory U, 1985 *Certification:* Obstetrics & Gynecology
574 Church St NE, Marietta, 770-427-0285

Suarez, Ramon Adolfo (6 mentions)
Emory U, 1978 *Certification:* Obstetrics & Gynecology
275 Collier Rd NW #100-B, Atlanta, 404-352-3656

Taylor, Richard James (3 mentions)
U of Kentucky, 1972 *Certification:* Obstetrics & Gynecology
275 Collier Rd NW #100-B, Atlanta, 404-352-3656

Wiist, Lance Jordan (3 mentions)
U of Louisville, 1979 *Certification:* Obstetrics & Gynecology
761 Old Norcross Rd, Lawrenceville, 770-513-4000

Wiskind, Anne Kessler (4 mentions)
Emory U, 1985 *Certification:* Obstetrics & Gynecology
1800 Peachtree St NW, Atlanta, 678-539-5980

Ophthalmology

Aaron, Maria M. (3 mentions)
Vanderbilt U, 1995 *Certification:* Ophthalmology
550 Peachtree St NE 9th Fl, Atlanta, 404-686-1574
1365 Clifton Rd NE, Atlanta, 404-778-5814

Borger, Howard Edward (4 mentions)
U of Texas-Houston, 1983 *Certification:* Ophthalmology
805 Campbell Hill St NW, Marietta, 770-424-5669

Cobb, John Thurman (3 mentions)
Vanderbilt U, 1978 *Certification:* Ophthalmology
3975 Lawrenceville Hwy NW, Lilburn, 770-923-5000
5671 Peachtree Dunwoody Rd NE #400, Atlanta, 404-256-1507

Crowley, Bruce Patterson (4 mentions)
Med Coll of Georgia, 1987 *Certification:* Ophthalmology
130 Vann St NE #230, Marietta, 770-425-1341
1680-C Mulkey Rd, Austell, 770-426-2000
290 Merchants Sq #1, Dallas, 770-445-8885

Dunbar, Mark Robert (3 mentions)
Emory U, 1980 *Certification:* Ophthalmology
2500 Hospital Blvd #115, Roswell, 770-475-0123
868 Buford Rd, Cumming, 770-475-0123

Frank, James H. (3 mentions)
U of Illinois, 1990 *Certification:* Ophthalmology
95 Collier Rd NW #3000, Atlanta, 404-351-2220

Gabianelli, Eugene B. (4 mentions)
Washington U, 1987 *Certification:* Ophthalmology
550 Peachtree St NE #1500, Atlanta, 404-897-6810
1100 Johnson Ferry Rd NE #1070, Atlanta, 404-531-9988

Gordon, Peter Alfred (3 mentions)
Emory U, 1979 *Certification:* Ophthalmology
1457 Scott Blvd, Decatur, 404-292-2500

Greenberg, Marc Fredrick (5 mentions)
U of Illinois, 1990 *Certification:* Ophthalmology
5445 Meridian Marks Rd NE #220, Atlanta, 404-255-2419

Jacobson, Michael Scott (4 mentions)
U of Connecticut, 1982 *Certification:* Ophthalmology
465 Winn Way #100, Atlanta, 404-299-5209
155 Medical Way #E, Riverdale, 770-907-9400

Kozarsky, Alan Mark (4 mentions)
Albert Einstein Coll of Med, 1978 *Certification:* Ophthalmology
95 Collier Rd NW #3000, Atlanta, 404-350-1425

Lampert, Scott I. (3 mentions)
Jefferson Med Coll, 1974 *Certification:* Ophthalmology
1100 Johnsons Ferry Rd NE #593, Atlanta, 404-255-9096
114 Cherry St NE #F, Marietta, 770-218-1888

Leff-Goldstein, Gayle T. (4 mentions)
Med Coll of Georgia, 1997
465 Winn Way #140, Decatur, 404-298-5557

Levine, Stephen Barry (6 mentions)
SUNY-Downstate Med Coll, 1967 *Certification:* Ophthalmology
5671 Peachtree Dunwoody Rd NE #400, Atlanta, 404-256-9600

Lipsky, Stephen Neil (7 mentions)
U of Buffalo, 1991 *Certification:* Ophthalmology
1233 Eagles Landing Pkwy #C, Stockbridge, 770-506-3931
5671 Peachtree Dunwoody Rd NE #400, Atlanta, 404-256-9600
2700 Hwy 34 E Bldg 100, Newnan, 678-423-7700

Long, Brian Delos (3 mentions)
Med Coll of Georgia, 1993 *Certification:* Ophthalmology
1265 Hwy 54 W, Fayetteville, 770-719-7950

Martin, Daniel Frank (4 mentions)
Johns Hopkins U, 1986 *Certification:* Ophthalmology
1365-B Clifton Rd NE, Atlanta, 404-778-4456

Mohney, Mark William (3 mentions)
Wayne State U, 1981 *Certification:* Ophthalmology
95 Collier Rd NW #3000, Atlanta, 404-351-2220

Palay, David Andrew (3 mentions)
Emory U, 1987 *Certification:* Ophthalmology
993 Johnson Ferry Rd NE #D-250, Atlanta, 404-252-1194

Pare, Richard Elliot (3 mentions)
Emory U, 1990 *Certification:* Ophthalmology
868 Buford Rd, Cumming, 770-889-1211
2500 Hospital Blvd #115, Roswell, 770-475-0123

Pollard, Zane Franklin (6 mentions)
Tulane U, 1966 *Certification:* Ophthalmology
5445 Meridian Mark Rd NE #220, Atlanta, 404-255-2419

Roach, J. Michael (3 mentions)
Med Coll of Georgia, 1995 *Certification:* Ophthalmology
3225 Cumberland Blvd SE, Atlanta, 404-351-2220

Salit, Jeri Sue (10 mentions)
U of Southern California, 1981 *Certification:* Ophthalmology
5671 Peachtree Dunwoody Rd NE #440, Atlanta, 770-923-5000
3975 Lawrenceville Hwy NW, Lilburn, 770-923-5000

Silverman, Stuart Harold (3 mentions)
Albert Einstein Coll of Med, 1966 *Certification:* Ophthalmology
5243 Snapfinger Woods Dr #101, Decatur, 770-981-9010

Stulting, Robert Doyle, Jr. (3 mentions)
Duke U, 1976 *Certification:* Ophthalmology
1365 Clifton Rd NE #B, Atlanta, 404-778-5818
875 Johnson Ferry Rd NE, Atlanta, 404-778-7777

Thomas, William Kevin (5 mentions)
Emory U, 1971 *Certification:* Ophthalmology
5671 Peachtree Dunwoody Rd NE #400, Atlanta, 404-256-1507

Tucker, Charles Howell (4 mentions)
Med Coll of Georgia, 1983 *Certification:* Ophthalmology
101 Yorktown Dr #225, Fayetteville, 770-460-4286

Orthopedics

Bircoll, Lawrence Alan (3 mentions)
U of Michigan, 1988 *Certification:* Orthopaedic Surgery
2680 Lawrenceville Hwy #100, Decatur, 770-491-3003

Branch, Thomas Paul (6 mentions)
Emory U, 1981 *Certification:* Orthopaedic Surgery
1014 Sycamore Dr #B, Decatur, 404-299-1700

Bruce, Robert Wallace, Jr. (4 mentions)
Vanderbilt U, 1988 *Certification:* Orthopaedic Surgery
59 Executive Park South NE, Atlanta, 404-778-3350

Busch, Michael Thomas (3 mentions)
Northwestern U, 1980 *Certification:* Orthopaedic Surgery
5445 Meridian Mark Rd NE #250, Atlanta, 404-255-1933
4850 Sugarloaf Pkwy #501, Lawrenceville, 404-255-1933

Covall, David J. (3 mentions)
Certification: Orthopaedic Surgery
1100 Northside Forsythe Dr #340, Cumming, 770-475-2710

Duralde, Xavier Ampuero (3 mentions)
Columbia U, 1983 *Certification:* Orthopaedic Surgery
2045 Peachtree Rd NE #700, Atlanta, 404-355-0743
1901 Phoenix Blvd #200, College Park, 404-355-0743

Edwards, Christopher R. (3 mentions)
Morehouse Coll, 1988 *Certification:* Orthopaedic Surgery
285 Boulevard NE #110, Atlanta, 404-265-6701
500 Medical Center Blvd #390, Lawrenceville, 770-962-0758
1431 White Cir, Marietta, 404-265-6701

Fowler, David Franklin (4 mentions)
Indiana U, 1980 *Certification:* Orthopaedic Surgery
5555 Peachtree Dunwoody Rd NE #101, Atlanta, 404-303-8665

Gillogly, Scott D. (3 mentions)
Duke U, 1980 *Certification:* Orthopaedic Surgery
3200 Downwood Cir NW #500, Atlanta, 404-352-4500

Karsch, Robert E. (8 mentions)
U of Pennsylvania, 1989 *Certification:* Orthopaedic Surgery
993 C Johnson Ferry Rd, Atlanta, 404-845-0777
1014 Sycamore Dr #B, Decatur, 404-299-1700

Kress, Kenneth James (15 mentions)
Cornell U, 1985 *Certification:* Orthopaedic Surgery
5671 Peachtree Dunwoody Rd #900, Atlanta, 404-847-9999

Martin, Stephanie Sue (5 mentions)
Vanderbilt U, 1994 *Certification:* Orthopaedic Surgery
1605 Chantilly Dr NE #310, Atlanta, 404-321-9900

McCollam, Stephen Mason (5 mentions)
Tulane U, 1982
Certification: Orthopaedic Surgery, Surgery of the Hand
2001 Peachtree Rd NE #705, Atlanta, 404-355-0743
1901 Phoenix Blvd #200, Atlanta, 404-355-0743

McElligott, Thomas Joseph (3 mentions)
New York Med Coll, 1987 *Certification:* Orthopaedic Surgery
2415 Wall St SE #B, Conyers, 770-760-0234

McLeod, Hugh Carroll, III (4 mentions)
U of Mississippi, 1976 *Certification:* Orthopaedic Surgery
1163 Johnson Ferry Rd #200, Marietta, 770-977-7777

Miller, Drew Vincent (3 mentions)
Cornell U, 1984 *Certification:* Orthopaedic Surgery
5671 Peachtree Dunwoody Rd NE #900, Atlanta, 404-847-9999

Monson, David Kevin (3 mentions)
U of Iowa, 1982 *Certification:* Orthopaedic Surgery
59 Executive Park South NE, Atlanta, 404-778-3350

Richin, Paul F. (3 mentions)
Georgetown U, 1972 *Certification:* Orthopaedic Surgery
505 Irvin Ct #200, Decatur, 404-294-4111

Roberson, James Ray (7 mentions)
U of Texas-Dallas, 1977 *Certification:* Orthopaedic Surgery
59 Executive Park South NE, Atlanta, 404-778-3350

Rosenstein, Byron David (6 mentions)
Northwestern U, 1982 *Certification:* Orthopaedic Surgery
5671 Peachtree Dunwoody #850, Atlanta, 404-847-9999

Royster, R. Marvin (6 mentions)
Med Coll of Georgia, 1980 *Certification:* Orthopaedic Surgery
2045 Peachtree Rd NE #700, Atlanta, 404-355-0743
5955 State Bridge Rd #250, Johns Creek, 404-355-0743

Schmidt, Todd Allen (5 mentions)
U of Minnesota, 1983 *Certification:* Orthopaedic Surgery
915 Eagles Landing Pkwy, Stockbridge, 770-506-4350
1265 Hwy 54 W #308, Fayetteville, 770-460-1900

Schmitt, Elbert William, Jr. (4 mentions)
Emory U, 1962 *Certification:* Orthopaedic Surgery
1605 Chantilly Dr NE #310, Atlanta, 404-321-9900
575 Professional Dr #550, Atlanta, 770-237-9055

Schmitz, Michael Lee (3 mentions)
Boston U, 1990 *Certification:* Orthopaedic Surgery
5445 Meridian Marks Rd NE #250, Atlanta, 404-255-1933

Smith, Stephen William (3 mentions)
Vanderbilt U, 1990
2001 Peachtree Rd NE #705, Atlanta, 404-355-0743

Wertheim, Steven Blake (7 mentions)
Case Western Reserve U, 1981
Certification: Orthopaedic Sports Medicine, Orthopaedic Surgery
5671 Peachtree Dunwoody Rd NE #900, Atlanta, 404-847-9999
2550 Windy Hill Rd SE #317, Marietta, 770-933-1900

Xerogeanes, John William (6 mentions)
Emory U, 1992 *Certification:* Orthopaedic Surgery
59 Executive Park South NE, Atlanta, 404-778-7137

Otorhinolaryngology

Abramson, Peter Jay (4 mentions)
Emory U, 1991 *Certification:* Otolaryngology
5673 Peachtree Dunwoody Rd NE #150, Atlanta, 404-297-4230
2665 N Decatur Rd #320, Decatur, 404-297-4230

Browning, Donald Gene, Jr. (7 mentions)
U of Arkansas, 1986 *Certification:* Otolaryngology
748 Old Norcross Rd #100, Lawrenceville, 770-339-1500

Chin, Kingsley Norman (4 mentions)
U of California-San Francisco, 1990 *Certification:* Otolaryngology
1720 Peachtree St #200, Atlanta, 404-351-5045

Dockery, Keith M. (6 mentions)
U of Tennessee, 1982 *Certification:* Otolaryngology
2045 Peachtree Rd NE #500, Atlanta, 404-350-7966

Golde, Andrew Robert (11 mentions)
FMS-Canada, 1988 *Certification:* Otolaryngology
960 Johnson Ferry Rd NE #200, Atlanta, 404-943-0090

Gower, Verlia Cole (4 mentions)
Wake Forest U, 1988 *Certification:* Otolaryngology
5455 Meridian Mark Rd NE #130, Atlanta, 404-255-2033
355 Power Rd #201, Marietta, 404-255-2033
3300 Old Milton Pkwy #275, Alpharetta, 404-255-2033

Griner, Nancy R. (5 mentions)
Indiana U, 1980 *Certification:* Otolaryngology
1700 Tree Lane Rd #320, Snellville, 770-985-6233
3540 Duluth Park Ln #280, Duluth, 678-985-8650

Grist, William James (5 mentions)
Med Coll of Georgia, 1975 *Certification:* Otolaryngology
1365 Clifton Rd NE 2nd Fl #A, Atlanta, 404-778-3216

Hoddeson, Robert B. (8 mentions)
U of Texas-Galveston, 1980 *Certification:* Otolaryngology
2665 N Decatur Rd #320, Decatur, 404-297-4230
1700 Tree Ln #470, Snellville, 404-297-4230

Johns, Michael Marieb, III (4 mentions)
Certification: Otolaryngology
550 Peachtree St NE #9, Atlanta, 404-778-3381

Kim, Jenny Christine (4 mentions)
St Louis U, 1999 *Certification:* Otolaryngology
5673 Peachtree Dunwoody Rd NE #150, Atlanta, 404-297-4230
2665 N Decatur Rd #320, Decatur, 404-279-4230

Leslie, Yvette V. (7 mentions)
1390 Montreal Rd #120, Tucker, 770-939-7707
5900 Hillandale Dr #345, Lithonia, 770-593-3328

Parks, David Leonard (13 mentions)
Med Coll of Georgia, 1984 *Certification:* Otolaryngology
320 Kennestone Hospital Blvd #107, Marietta, 770-793-7613
148 Bill Carruth Pkwy #220, Hiram, 770-505-0023

Robb, Philip Kurt (4 mentions)
U of Missouri, 1985 *Certification:* Otolaryngology
3400 Old Milton Pkwy Bldg C #480, Alpharetta, 770-410-0202

Rollins, Chester Palmour (6 mentions)
Med Coll of Georgia, 1983 *Certification:* Otolaryngology
1720 Peachtree St #200, Atlanta, 404-351-5045

Roth, Jeffrey (7 mentions)
SUNY-Upstate Med U, 1991 *Certification:* Otolaryngology
4385 Johns Creek Pkwy #250, Suwanee, 770-723-1368
1960 Riverside Pkwy #101, Lawrenceville, 770-237-3000

Shaw, Elizabeth Ann (6 mentions)
U of Florida, 1995 *Certification:* Otolaryngology
5670 Peachtree Dunwoody Rd NE #1280, Atlanta, 404-257-1589
980 Johnson Ferry Rd NE #110, Atlanta, 404-256-5428

Stolovitzky, Jose Pablo (7 mentions)
FMS-Argentina, 1983 *Certification:* Otolaryngology
1700 Tree Ln #470, Snellville, 404-297-4230
2665 N Decatur Rd, Decatur, 404-297-4230
5673 Peachtree Dunwoody Ln, Atlanta, 404-297-4230

Thomsen, James Richard (7 mentions)
Wright State U, 1983 *Certification:* Otolaryngology
5455 Meridian Mark Rd NE #130, Atlanta, 404-255-2033
3300 Old Milton Pkwy #275, Alpharetta, 404-255-2033

Todd, Norman Wendell, Jr. (6 mentions)
Tulane U, 1969 *Certification:* Otolaryngology
2015 Uppergate Dr, Atlanta, 404-778-3381
4850 Sugarloaf Pkwy, Lawrenceville, 404-785-8659

Vick, Michael Lamar (7 mentions)
Louisiana State U-Shreveport, 1996 *Certification:* Otolaryngology
320 Kennestone Hospital Blvd #107, Marietta, 770-793-7613
148 Bill Carruth Pkwy #220, Hiram, 770-505-0023

Yanta, Mark J. (6 mentions)
U of Texas-Dallas, 1990 *Certification:* Otolaryngology
2500 Hospital Blvd #450, Roswell, 770-343-8675
980 Johnson Ferry Rd NE #880, Atlanta, 404-255-5565

Zweig, Julie Lyn (5 mentions)
Emory U, 1995 *Certification:* Otolaryngology, Sleep Medicine
4385 Johns Creek Pkwy #250, Suwanee, 770-723-1368
1960 Riverside Pkwy #101, Lawrenceville, 770-237-3000

Pain Medicine

Baumann, Patricia L. (4 mentions)
Emory U, 1988 *Certification:* Anesthesiology, Pain Medicine
550 Peachtree St NE, Atlanta, 404-686-2410

Brownlow, Roy Charles (4 mentions)
Certification: Anesthesiology, Pain Medicine
1755 hwy 34-E #1302, Newnan, 770-252-7557

Doherty, Dennis C. (5 mentions)
Certification: Anesthesiology, Pain Medicine
1150 Hammond Dr NE #B-2120, Atlanta, 770-551-4350

Duralde, Rodrigo Ampuero (6 mentions)
U of Tennessee, 1986
Certification: Anesthesiology, Pain Medicine
2001 Peachtree Rd NE #200, Atlanta, 404-351-7654
1800 Peachtree St NW #400, Atlanta, 404-351-7854

Hord, Allen Henry (4 mentions)
U of Kentucky, 1983 *Certification:* Anesthesiology, Pain Medicine
3200 Downwood Cir, Atlanta, 404-350-0980

Hurd, Thomas Eric (5 mentions)
Northwestern U, 1979
Certification: Anesthesiology, Critical Care Medicine
400 Tower Rd NE #350, Marietta, 770-590-1078
677 Church St NW, Marietta, 770-590-1078
55 Whitcher St NE #130, Marietta, 770-590-1078

Keeton, William Frederick (5 mentions)
U of Mississippi, 1966 *Certification:* Anesthesiology
200 E Ponce De Leon Ave #250, Decatur, 404-351-7654

MacNeill, Charles A., Jr. (4 mentions)
Emory U, 1977 *Certification:* Anesthesiology, Pain Medicine
5730 Glenridge Dr #100, Sandy Springs, 404-816-3000

Porter, John Gilbertson (4 mentions)
U of Cincinnati, 1978
Certification: Anesthesiology, Pain Medicine
790 Church St NE #550, Marietta, 770-419-9902

Reisman, Richard Marc (4 mentions)
New York Med Coll, 1978 *Certification:* Anesthesiology
1000 Medical Center Blvd, Lawrenceville, 770-963-9905

Rizor, Randy Frank (4 mentions)
U of Toledo, 1976 *Certification:* Anesthesiology, Pain Medicine
18 RIverbend Dr #150, Rome, 706-314-1900
790 Church St #550, Marietta, 770-419-9902

Pathology

Abramowsky, Carlos R. (3 mentions)
FMS-Panama, 1968 *Certification:* Anatomic Pathology,
   Clinical Pathology, Pediatric Pathology
1405 Clifton Rd NE, Atlanta, 404-785-6499

Brat, Daniel Jay (3 mentions)
Mayo Med Sch, 1994
Certification: Anatomic Pathology, Neuropathology
1364 Clifton Rd NE, Atlanta, 404-712-1266

Delgado, Richard George (3 mentions)
Med Coll of Georgia, 1991
Certification: Anatomic Pathology & Clinical Pathology
1000 Medical Center Blvd, Lawrenceville, 678-442-4500

Du Puis, Mark Howard (4 mentions)
U of Illinois, 1979 *Certification:* Anatomic Pathology &
   Clinical Pathology, Cytopathology
1968 Peachtree Rd NW, Atlanta, 404-605-3247

Finan, Marian Claire (3 mentions)
Pennsylvania State U, 1980
Certification: Dermatology, Dermatopathology
6095 Barfield Rd NE #200, Atlanta, 404-851-1766

Hargreaves, Hilary Kay (6 mentions)
U of Miami, 1975
Certification: Anatomic Pathology & Clinical Pathology
2701 N Decatur Rd, Decatur, 404-501-5256

Kennedy, Jan Cecelia (4 mentions)
Emory U, 1984
Certification: Anatomic Pathology & Clinical Pathology
2701 N Decatur Rd, Decatur, 404-501-5256

McNeill, William Frank (4 mentions)
Med U of South Carolina, 1983 *Certification:* Anatomic
   Pathology & Clinical Pathology, Cytopathology, Hematology
2701 N Decatur Rd, Decatur, 404-501-5256

O'Neal, Aileen P. (4 mentions)
1412 Milstead Ave NE, Conyers, 770-918-3082

Sewell, Charles Whitaker (3 mentions)
Emory U, 1969
Certification: Anatomic Pathology & Clinical Pathology
1364 Clifton Rd NE #H185C, Atlanta, 404-712-7003

Stargel, Michael Don (3 mentions)
U of Texas-Dallas, 1972
Certification: Anatomic Pathology & Clinical Pathology
5665 Peachtree Dunwoody Rd NE, Atlanta, 404-851-7144

Walker, Bruce Franklin (6 mentions)
Emory U, 1985
Certification: Anatomic Pathology & Clinical Pathology
1968 Peachtree Rd NW, Atlanta, 404-605-3247

Pediatrics *(see note on page 9)*

Harrison, Harvey Robert (4 mentions)
Harvard U, 1974
Certification: Pediatric Infectious Diseases, Pediatrics
993 Johnson Ferry Rd NE #F-370, Atlanta, 404-252-4611

King, Stephen (4 mentions)
SUNY-Downstate Med Coll, 1969 *Certification:* Pediatrics
2155 Post Oak Tritt Rd #100, Marietta, 770-973-4700
755 Mt Vernon Hwy, Atlanta, 404-255-6335

Knox, John Charles (5 mentions)
Emory U, 1978 *Certification:* Pediatrics
1100 Lake Hearn Dr NE #100, Atlanta, 404-256-3178

Koenig, Allison Jill (3 mentions)
Johns Hopkins U, 1998 *Certification:* Pediatrics
105 Collier Rd NW #4060, Atlanta, 404-351-6662

Maxey, Joy Ann (3 mentions)
Med Coll of Georgia, 1984 *Certification:* Pediatrics
3091 Maple Dr NE #315, Atlanta, 404-261-2666

Mekelburg, Kirsten Silverman (3 mentions)
Certification: Pediatrics
755 Mount Vernon Hwy NE #150, Atlanta, 404-303-1314

Papciak, Michael Ralph (3 mentions)
U of Michigan, 1967 *Certification:* Pediatrics
3400-A Old Milton Pkwy #330, Alpharetta, 770-751-6111

Snitzer, Joseph Albert, III (11 mentions)
Med Coll of Georgia, 1963 *Certification:* Pediatrics
1405 Clifton Rd NE, Atlanta, 404-325-6104

Tanenbaum, Marc Alan (4 mentions)
U of Pennsylvania, 1973 *Certification:* Pediatrics
2155 Post Oak Tritt Rd #100, Marietta, 770-973-4700
755 Mount Vernon Hwy NE #420, Atlanta, 404-255-6335
120 Stonebridge Pkwy #410, Woodstock, 770-517-6804

Weil, Richard Lawrence (4 mentions)
Georgetown U, 1980 *Certification:* Pediatrics
105 Collier Rd NW #4060, Atlanta, 404-351-6662

Wilkov, Jane Louise (3 mentions)
Emory U, 1982 *Certification:* Pediatrics
350 Winn Way, Decatur, 404-508-1177

Plastic Surgery

Beegle, Phillip Harold, Jr. (11 mentions)
Med Coll of Georgia, 1975 *Certification:* Plastic Surgery
975-C Johnson Ferry Rd NE #100, Atlanta, 404-256-1311
15 Cavender St, Newnan, 770-253-6616

Bootstaylor, Lisa B. (6 mentions)
Albert Einstein Coll of Med, 1989 *Certification:* Plastic Surgery
550 Peachtree St NE #1480, Atlanta, 404-240-2804
1368 Wellbrook Cir #A, Conyers, 404-240-2804

Burstein, Fernando David (8 mentions)
U of Kansas, 1980 *Certification:* Otolaryngology, Plastic Surgery
975 Johnson Ferry Rd NE #100, Atlanta, 404-256-1311
3300 Old Milton Pkwy Bldg C #125, Alpharetta, 770-663-4644

Elliott, Lester F. (6 mentions)
Vanderbilt U, 1976 *Certification:* Plastic Surgery
975 Johnson Ferry Rd NE #100, Atlanta, 404-256-1311

Hester, Thomas Roderick, Jr. (9 mentions)
Emory U, 1967 *Certification:* Plastic Surgery, Surgery
3200 Downwood Cir NW #640, Atlanta, 404-351-0051

Howard, Brian Keith (6 mentions)
U of Rochester, 1990
Certification: Otolaryngology, Plastic Surgery
1357 Hembree Rd #200, Roswell, 770-619-9566

Mackay, Gregory James (5 mentions)
Med U of South Carolina, 1987 *Certification:* Plastic Surgery
5673 Peachtree Dunwoody Rd NE #870, Atlanta, 404-255-2975

Nahai, Foad (7 mentions)
FMS-United Kingdom, 1969 *Certification:* Plastic Surgery
3200 Downwood Cir #640, Atlanta, 404-351-0051

West, Donald Keith (5 mentions)
Emory U, 1983 *Certification:* Plastic Surgery
823 Campbell Hill St NW, Marietta, 770-425-0118

Williams, Joseph Kerwin (11 mentions)
U of Mississippi, 1990 *Certification:* Plastic Surgery
975 Johnson Ferry Rd NE #100, Atlanta, 404-256-1311

Woods, Joseph Milliken, IV (8 mentions)
Temple U, 1985 *Certification:* Plastic Surgery
275 Collier Rd NW #200, Atlanta, 404-292-4223
2665 N Decatur Rd #650, Decatur, 404-292-4223

Work, Frederick T., Jr. (7 mentions)
Morehouse Coll, 1986 *Certification:* Surgery
1 Baltimore Pl NW #400, Atlanta, 404-885-9675

Psychiatry

Antin, Todd Mitchell (8 mentions)
U of Miami, 1989
Certification: Addiction Psychiatry, Geriatric Psychiatry, Psychiatry
465 Winn Way #221, Decatur, 404-292-3810

Brown, Samuel G. Burnette (4 mentions)
Duke U, 1972 *Certification:* Psychiatry
27 Lenox Pointe NE, Atlanta, 404-237-3210

Firestone, Scott Darryl (4 mentions)
U of Miami, 1987 *Certification:* Psychiatry
550 Peachtree St NE 7th Fl, Atlanta, 404-686-8424

Nemeroff, Charles Barnet (3 mentions)
U of North Carolina, 1981
Certification: Geriatric Psychiatry, Psychiatry
1365 Clifton Rd NE, Atlanta, 404-727-5881

Slayden, Robert McLean (5 mentions)
U of Tennessee, 1969
7000 Peachtree Dunwoody Rd NE, Atlanta, 770-393-1880

Waugh, Lyndon Dale (3 mentions)
Duke U, 1971 *Certification:* Psychiatry
7000 Peachtree Dunwoody Rd NE #100, Atlanta, 770-393-1880

Pulmonary Disease

Albin, Robert Jon (6 mentions)
Emory U, 1980
Certification: Internal Medicine, Pulmonary Disease
5667 Peachtree Dunwoody Rd NE #260, Atlanta, 404-252-7200

Botnick, Warren Clifford (5 mentions)
Med Coll of Georgia, 1986 *Certification:* Critical Care
   Medicine, Internal Medicine, Pulmonary Disease
2665 N Decatur Rd #230, Decatur, 404-499-0533

Callahan, Daniel Francis (5 mentions)
Med Coll of Georgia, 1985
Certification: Internal Medicine, Pulmonary Disease
1357 Hembree Rd #100, Roswell, 770-343-8760

De Marini, Thomas P. (10 mentions)
Northwestern U, 1983
Certification: Internal Medicine, Pulmonary Disease
2665 N Decatur Rd #430, Decatur, 770-922-2217
1380 Milstead Ave #C, Conyers, 770-922-2217
320 Winway #103, Decatur, 770-922-2217

Dowdell, William Thomas (4 mentions)
U of Cincinnati, 1983 *Certification:* Critical Care Medicine,
   Internal Medicine, Pulmonary Disease, Sleep Medicine
55 Whitcher St NE #420, Marietta, 770-422-1372

Eaton, Stephanie (5 mentions)
U of California-Irvine, 1996 *Certification:* Critical Care
   Medicine, Internal Medicine, Pulmonary Disease
5505 Peachtree Dunwoody Rd NE #370, Atlanta, 404-257-0006

Harris, Steven Edward (4 mentions)
Tulane U, 1989
Certification: Internal Medicine, Pulmonary Disease
3820 Medical Park Dr, Austell, 770-948-6041
55 Whitcher St NE #160, Marietta, 770-514-7550

Jackson, Harold Damon (5 mentions)
Med U of South Carolina, 1987 *Certification:* Critical Care
   Medicine, Internal Medicine, Pulmonary Disease
2665 N Decatur Rd #430, Decatur, 404-294-4018

Kaplan, Lawrence David (4 mentions)
Emory U, 1978
Certification: Internal Medicine, Pulmonary Disease
600 Professional Dr #160, Lawrenceville, 770-995-0630
3540 Duluth Park Ln #240, Duluth, 770-995-0630

Leeper, Kenneth Vedious (7 mentions)
Case Western Reserve U, 1979
Certification: Internal Medicine, Pulmonary Disease
550 Peachtree St NE 6th Fl, Atlanta, 404-686-2506

Lesnick, Burton Louis (5 mentions)
Boston U, 1988 *Certification:* Pediatric Pulmonology
1100 Lake Hearn Dr NE #450, Atlanta, 404-252-7339

Mauldin, Gregory Loy (4 mentions)
Med Coll of Georgia, 1987 *Certification:* Critical Care
  Medicine, Internal Medicine, Pulmonary Disease
1800 Tree Ln #200, Snellville, 770-979-0367
1000 Medical Center Blvd, Lawrenceville, 770-979-0367

McGann, William F., Jr. (6 mentions)
St Louis U, 1983 *Certification:* Critical Care Medicine,
  Internal Medicine, Pulmonary Disease
600 Professional Dr #160, Lawrenceville, 770-995-0630

Melby, Kenneth (5 mentions)
U of Minnesota, 1979 *Certification:* Critical Care Medicine,
  Internal Medicine, Pulmonary Disease
5667 Peachtree Dunwoody Rd NE #350, Atlanta, 404-252-7200

Pollock, Mark Taffel (5 mentions)
Vanderbilt U, 1984 *Certification:* Critical Care Medicine,
  Internal Medicine, Pulmonary Disease
2665 N Decatur Rd #230, Decatur, 404-499-0533
5700 Hillandale Dr #190, Lithonia, 678-418-9898

Scott, Peter Hill (5 mentions)
Indiana U, 1975 *Certification:* Pediatric Pulmonology, Pediatrics
1100 Lake Hearn Dr NE #450, Atlanta, 404-252-7339

Silverboard, Howard P. (6 mentions)
U of Alabama, 1997 *Certification:* Critical Care Medicine,
  Internal Medicine, Pulmonary Disease
5505 Peachtree Dunwoody Rd NE #370, Atlanta, 404-257-0006

Staton, Gerald Wayne, Jr. (5 mentions)
Med Coll of Georgia, 1976 *Certification:* Critical Care
  Medicine, Internal Medicine, Pulmonary Disease
550 Peachtree St NE Medical Bldg 6th Fl, Atlanta, 404-686-2505
1365 Clifton Rd NE Bldg A 4th Fl, Atlanta, 404-686-2505

Westerman, David Elliot (5 mentions)
FMS-South Africa, 1971
Certification: Internal Medicine, Pulmonary Disease
5667 Peachtree Dunwoody Rd NE #350, Atlanta, 404-252-7200

Radiology—Diagnostic

Chezmar, Judith Lynn (3 mentions)
U of Cincinnati, 1981 *Certification:* Diagnostic Radiology
1984 Peachtree Rd NW #505, Atlanta, 404-352-1409

Eberhardt, Linton Webster (3 mentions)
Med Coll of Georgia, 1998 *Certification:* Diagnostic Radiology
2701 N Decatur Rd, Decatur, 404-501-5200

Feiner, Clifford M. (3 mentions)
New York Med Coll, 1985 *Certification:* Diagnostic Radiology
1000 Johnson Ferry Rd NE, Atlanta, 404-851-6347

Finley, Joseph Clayton (3 mentions)
Emory U, 1966 *Certification:* Diagnostic Radiology
1000 Medical Center Blvd, Lawrenceville, 678-442-2420

Garrison, Martha H. (3 mentions)
Emory U, 1992 *Certification:* Diagnostic Radiology
4181 Hospital Dr NE, Covington, 770-385-7800

Grattan-Smith, J. Damien (9 mentions)
FMS-Australia, 1983
Certification: Diagnostic Radiology, Pediatric Radiology
1001 Johnson Ferry Rd NE, Atlanta, 404-785-2162
3155 N Point Pkwy Bldg A #150, Alpharetta, 404-785-7226

Hudgins, Patricia A. (4 mentions)
U of California-San Francisco, 1980
1364 Clifton Rd NE, Atlanta, 404-712-4583

McNair, John Rufus, Jr. (4 mentions)
Emory U, 1985
Certification: Diagnostic Radiology, Neuroradiology
1255 Hwy 54 W, Fayetteville, 770-719-7000

Ostrow, Todd David (3 mentions)
U of Maryland, 1987
Certification: Diagnostic Radiology, Neuroradiology
1000 Johnson Ferry Rd NE, Atlanta, 404-851-6347

Phillips, Val M. (6 mentions)
New Jersey Med Sch, 1978 *Certification:* Diagnostic Radiology
1000 Medical Center Blvd, Lawrenceville, 678-442-2420

Pont, Michael Stuart (3 mentions)
New Jersey Med Sch, 1983
Certification: Diagnostic Radiology, Neuroradiology
1000 Johnson Ferry Rd NE, Atlanta, 404-851-8820

Simoneaux, Stephen F. (3 mentions)
U of Miami, 1988
Certification: Diagnostic Radiology, Pediatric Radiology
1405 Clifton Rd NE, Atlanta, 404-785-6532

Radiology—Therapeutic

Belcher, Kelvin Keith (3 mentions)
U of Texas Houston, 1991 *Certification:* Diagnostic
  Radiology, Vascular & Interventional Radiology
2701 N Decatur Rd, Decatur, 404-501-1000
2801 Dekalb Mediccal Pkwy, Lithonia, 404-501-8000

Citron, Steven Joshua (5 mentions)
U of North Carolina, 1984 *Certification:* Diagnostic
  Radiology, Vascular & Interventional Radiology
1984 Peachtree Rd NW #505, Atlanta, 404-352-1409

Holladay, David Adams (3 mentions)
U of Alabama, 1986 *Certification:* Radiation Oncology
2675 N Decatur Rd, Decatur, 404-501-7700

Jacobs, Louis Howard (3 mentions)
Mount Sinai Sch of Med, 1975 *Certification:* Diagnostic Radiology
1984 Peachtree Rd NW #505, Atlanta, 404-352-1409
1968 Peachtree Rd, Atlanta, 404-605-2927

Levy, Jason Redfield (3 mentions)
New York U, 1995 *Certification:* Diagnostic Radiology,
  Vascular & Interventional Radiology
1000 Johnson Ferry Rd NE, Atlanta, 404-851-8820

Lipman, John Crawford (4 mentions)
Georgetown U, 1985 *Certification:* Diagnostic Radiology,
  Vascular & Interventional Radiology
3903 S Cobb Dr #230, Smyrna, 770-953-2600

Randolph, Erich Graham (3 mentions)
Mount Sinai Sch of Med, 1979 *Certification:* Radiation Oncology
1475 Montreal Rd, Tucker, 770-270-5085
1000 Johnson Ferry Rd NE, Atlanta, 404-851-8850
320 Pkwy, Atlanta, 404-265-3521

Rao, Ashutosh Vaddadi (3 mentions)
Emory U, 1996 *Certification:* Diagnostic Radiology,
  Vascular & Interventional Radiology
3950 Austell Rd, Austell, 678-581-3830

Schwaibold, Frederick P. (4 mentions)
Philadelphia Coll of Osteopathic Med, 1984
Certification: Radiation Oncology
1968 Peachtree Rd NW, Atlanta, 404-605-1117

York, James Alan (4 mentions)
Tufts U, 1992 *Certification:* Diagnostic Radiology, Vascular
  & Interventional Radiology
1000 Medical Center Blvd, Lawrenceville, 678-442-2420

Rehabilitation

Bhole, Sunil (6 mentions)
FMS-India, 1980
Certification: Physical Medicine & Rehabilitation
3215 McClure Bridge Rd, Duluth, 678-312-6010

Cotliar, Rochelle (3 mentions)
SUNY-Downstate Med Coll, 1986
Certification: Physical Medicine & Rehabilitation
100 Lacy St NW #150, Marietta, 770-793-7635

Feeman, Mark W. (6 mentions)
Des Moines U, 1985
Certification: Physical Medicine & Rehabilitation
2675 N Decatur Rd #315, Decatur, 404-659-5909
2121 Fountain Dr, Snellville, 404-659-5909

Leslie, Donald Peck (3 mentions)
U of Tennessee, 1972
Certification: Physical Medicine & Rehabilitation
2020 Peachtree Rd NW, Atlanta, 404-350-7779

Rheumatology

Botstein, Gary Robert (12 mentions)
Harvard U, 1975 *Certification:* Internal Medicine, Rheumatology
2712 N Decatur Rd, Decatur, 404-299-0187

Butler, Elizabeth Darsey (6 mentions)
Med Coll of Georgia, 1980
Certification: Internal Medicine, Rheumatology
550 Peachtree St NE #1035, Atlanta, 404-577-1112

Fishman, Alan Bruce (7 mentions)
Tufts U, 1974 *Certification:* Internal Medicine, Rheumatology
5673 Peachtree Dunwoody Rd NE #775, Atlanta, 404-256-8500
3400 Old Milton Rd #500, Alpharetta, 678-775-2284

Goldman, John Abner (10 mentions)
U of Cincinnati, 1966 *Certification:* Allergy & Immunology,
  Internal Medicine, Rheumatology
5555 Peachtree Dunwoody Rd NE #293, Atlanta, 404-252-0230

Lawrence, Theresa Anna B. (7 mentions)
Tufts U, 1978 *Certification:* Rheumatology
600 Professional Dr #260, Lawrenceville, 770-822-1090
3855 Pleasant Hill Rd #350, Duluth, 770-622-5282

Lieberman, Jefrey Dale (13 mentions)
Ohio State U, 1984
Certification: Internal Medicine, Rheumatology
2712 N Decatur Rd, Decatur, 404-296-4911

Myerson, Gary Edward (34 mentions)
FMS-Philippines, 1977
Certification: Internal Medicine, Rheumatology
980 Johnson Ferry Rd NE #220, Atlanta, 404-255-5956

Parris, Glenn R. (7 mentions)
U of Buffalo, 1987 *Certification:* Rheumatology
989 Lawrenceville Hwy, Lawrenceville, 770-962-1616

Vogler, Larry Benard (9 mentions)
Baylor U, 1973 *Certification:* Pediatric Rheumatology, Pediatrics
2015 Uppergate Dr, Atlanta, 404-778-2400

Wilson, William Hayes (11 mentions)
Emory U, 1985 *Certification:* Internal Medicine
2001 Peachtree Rd NE #205, Atlanta, 404-351-2551

Thoracic Surgery

Force, Seth Daniel (7 mentions)
Tulane U, 1994 *Certification:* Surgery, Thoracic Surgery
1365 Clifton Rd NE Bldg A #2100, Atlanta, 404-778-5040

Fritz, Robert C. (7 mentions)
Emory U, 1977 *Certification:* Surgery
3500 McClure Bridge Rd, Duluth, 770-476-7047
601 Professional Dr, Lawrenceville, 770-513-1738

Houck, Ward Vaughn (7 mentions)
Med U of South Carolina, 1994
Certification: Surgery, Thoracic Surgery
61 Whitcher St NE #4120, Marietta, 770-424-9732

Mayfield, William Rodger (21 mentions)
Med Coll of Georgia, 1981 *Certification:* Thoracic Surgery
61 Whitcher St #4120, Marietta, 770-424-9732

Miller, Joseph Irvin, Jr. (16 mentions)
Emory U, 1965 *Certification:* Surgery, Thoracic Surgery
550 Peachtree St NE 6th Fl, Atlanta, 404-321-0111

Moore, John Everett (17 mentions)
U of Louisville, 1975 *Certification:* Thoracic Surgery
5671 Peachtree Dunwoody Rd NE #50, Atlanta, 404-252-9063

Stubbs, Michael Barry (10 mentions)
Emory U, 1974 *Certification:* Thoracic Surgery
465 Winn Way #211, Decatur, 404-292-4348

Urology

Allen, William F., III (5 mentions)
Louisiana State U, 1981 *Certification:* Urology
95 Collier Rd NW #6025, Atlanta, 404-352-9260

Banks, David Wood, Sr. (7 mentions)
Emory U, 1979 *Certification:* Urology
1100 Northside Dr #410, Cumming, 678-947-6199
11685 Alpharetta Hwy #270, Roswell, 678-947-6199
6335 Hospital Pkwy #208, Duluth, 770-814-7884

Bennett, James Kent (7 mentions)
Duke U, 1979 *Certification:* Urology
128 North Ave NE #100, Atlanta, 404-881-0966

Emerson, Thomas E. (7 mentions)
Med Coll of Georgia, 1983 *Certification:* Urology
55 Whitcher St NE #250, Marietta, 770-428-4475
1680 Mulkey Rd, Austell, 770-948-8858
300 Tower Rd NE #150, Marietta, 678-594-0070

Futral, Allen Ashley, III (5 mentions)
U of Virginia, 1991 *Certification:* Urology
1501 Milstead Rd #100, Conyers, 770-760-9900

Goldberg, Howard Craig (7 mentions)
SUNY-Downstate Med Coll, 1983 *Certification:* Urology
600 Professional Dr #120, Lawrenceville, 770-963-8444

Green, Bruce G. (12 mentions)
SUNY-Downstate Med Coll, 1968 *Certification:* Urology
755 Mount Vernon Hwy NE #200, Atlanta, 404-256-2670

Hader, Joan Ellen (7 mentions)
Med Coll of Georgia, 1987 *Certification:* Urology
5673 Peachtree Dunwoody Rd NE #910, Atlanta, 404-255-3822

Kirsch, Andrew Jared (5 mentions)
SUNY-Downstate Med Coll, 1990
Certification: Pediatric Urology, Urology
5445 Meridian Mark Rd NE #420, Atlanta, 404-252-5206

Levinson, Alan Keith (14 mentions)
Med Coll of Pennsylvania, 1984 *Certification:* Urology
2685 Milscott Dr, Decatur, 404-294-3727

Massad, Charlotte Anne (9 mentions)
Eastern Virginia Med Sch, 1983
Certification: Pediatric Urology, Urology
5445 Meridian Mark Rd NE #420, Atlanta, 404-252-5206
500 Medical Center Blvd #220, Lawrenceville, 404-252-5206

Miller, Scott David (9 mentions)
Med Coll of Georgia, 1990 *Certification:* Urology
5670 Peachtree Dunwoody Rd NE #1250, Atlanta, 404-256-1844

Nabors, William Ledford (5 mentions)
Med Coll of Georgia, 1983 *Certification:* Urology
5669 Peachtree Dunwoody Rd NE, Atlanta, 404-255-3822
5673 Peachtree Dunwoody Rd NE #910, Atlanta, 404-255-3822

Sanders, William H., Jr. (5 mentions)
Emory U, 1988 *Certification:* Urology
980 Johnson Ferry Rd NE #490, Atlanta, 404-257-0133

Scaljon, William Michael (6 mentions)
U of Tennessee, 1973 *Certification:* Urology
95 Collier Rd NW #6025, Atlanta, 404-352-9260

Scherz, Hal Craig (5 mentions)
U of Texas-San Antonio, 1981
Certification: Pediatric Urology, Urology
5445 Meridian Marks Plaza #420, Atlanta, 404-252-5206
790 Church St #430, Marietta, 770-429-9100
11975 Moms Rd #330, Alpharetta, 770-772-4427

Schoborg, Thomas William (6 mentions)
Emory U, 1973 *Certification:* Urology
285 Blvd NE #215, Atlanta, 404-524-5082

Shelfo, Scott W. (5 mentions)
Albany Med Coll, 1991 *Certification:* Urology
1260 Hwy 54 W #204, Fayetteville, 770-460-9777

Sherlag, Anthony Paul (5 mentions)
Wayne State U, 1984 *Certification:* Urology
1700 Tree Ln #420, Snellville, 770-979-9427
500 Medical Center Blvd #220, Lawrenceville, 770-979-9427

Shessel, Fred Steven (6 mentions)
Yale U, 1974 *Certification:* Urology
11975 Morris Rd #330, Atlanta, 770-772-4427
5670 Peachtree Dunwoody Rd NE #1250, Atlanta, 770-772-4427

Smith, Edwin Agan (6 mentions)
Emory U, 1988 *Certification:* Pediatric Urology, Urology
5445 Meridian Mark Rd NE #420, Atlanta, 404-252-5206
790 Church St NE #430, Marietta, 770-429-9100

Townsend, Murphy F., III (7 mentions)
U of North Carolina, 1990 *Certification:* Urology
55 Whitcher St NE #250, Marietta, 770-428-4475

White, John Maxwell, Jr. (8 mentions)
Emory U, 1977 *Certification:* Urology
3200 Downwood Cir NW #680, Atlanta, 404-355-7272

Vascular Surgery

Battey, Patrick Mell (16 mentions)
Emory U, 1979 *Certification:* Vascular Surgery
35 Collier Rd NW #185, Atlanta, 404-351-9741

Chervu, Arun (8 mentions)
Cornell U, 1984 *Certification:* Surgery, Vascular Surgery
1700 Hospital South Dr #410, Austell, 770-944-8315
61 Whitcher St NE #2100, Marietta, 770-423-0595
6002 Professional Pkwy #240, Douglasville, 770-874-0572
148 Bill Carruth Pkwy #380, Hiram, 770-874-0703

H'Doubler, Peter B., Jr. (18 mentions)
Harvard U, 1981 *Certification:* Surgery, Vascular Surgery
5669 Peachtree Dunwoody Rd NE #100, Atlanta, 404-256-0404
2500 Hospital Blvd #420, Roswell, 678-242-1193

Hafner, David Howell (11 mentions)
Med Coll of Georgia, 1980 *Certification:* Vascular Surgery
61 Whitcher St NE #2100, Marietta, 770-426-5005
120 Stoneridge Pkwy #320, Woodstock, 770-874-7631
148 Bill Carruth Pkwy #380, Hiram, 770-874-0703

Lewinstein, Charles Jay (7 mentions)
U of Southern California, 1981 *Certification:* Vascular Surgery
5671 Peachtree Dunwoody Rd NE #250, Atlanta, 404-256-0170

Mittenthal, Mark Jay (9 mentions)
Albany Med Coll, 1975 *Certification:* Surgery, Vascular Surgery
5669 Peachtree Dunwoody Rd NE #100, Atlanta, 404-256-0404
2500 Hospital Blvd #420, Roswell, 678-242-1193

Moomey, Charles Bruce, Jr. (7 mentions)
U of Tennessee, 1994 *Certification:* Surgery, Vascular Surgery
600 Professional Dr #250, Lawrenceville, 770-962-9977

Oweida, Steven Wassel (11 mentions)
Emory U, 1983 *Certification:* Surgery, Vascular Surgery
120 Stoneridge Pkwy #320, Woodstock, 770-874-7631
61 Whitcher St NE #2100, Marietta, 770-423-0595
6002 Professional Pkwy #240, Douglasville, 770-874-0572
1700 Hospital South Dr #410, Austell, 770-944-8315
148 Bill Carruth Pkwy #380, Hiram, 770-874-0703

Rheudasil, James Mark (11 mentions)
U of Texas-Dallas, 1983 *Certification:* Surgery, Vascular Surgery
5669 Peachtree Dunwoody Rd NE #100, Atlanta, 404-255-1161
2500 Hospital Blvd #420, Roswell, 678-242-1193

Rose, William Wagner, III (8 mentions)
Michigan State U, 1990 *Certification:* Vascular Surgery
2675 N Decatur Rd #410, Decatur, 404-299-6488

Illinois

Chicago Area—page 188

St. Louis Area—page 267

Chicago Area

Cook, DuPage, Kane, Kendall, Lake, McHenry, and Will Counties

Allergy/Immunology

Beckman, Dawn Brigitte (4 mentions)
Loyola U Chicago, 1995 *Certification:* Allergy & Immunology
454 Pennsylvania Ave #220, Glen Ellyn, 630-545-7833
1801 S Highland Ave #220, Lombard, 630-545-7833
636 Raymond Dr #300, Naperville, 630-545-7833

Corey, Jacquelynne P. (4 mentions)
U of Illinois, 1979 *Certification:* Otolaryngology
5758 S Maryland Ave, Chicago, 773-702-1865

Detjen, Paul Finley (8 mentions)
Washington U, 1984
Certification: Allergy & Immunology, Internal Medicine
534 Green Bay Rd, Kenilworth, 847-256-5505

Gewurz, Anita A. (7 mentions)
Albany Med Coll, 1970
Certification: Allergy & Immunology, Pediatrics
1725 W Harrison St #117, Chicago, 312-942-6296

Grammer, Leslie Carroll (5 mentions)
Northwestern U, 1976
Certification: Allergy & Immunology, Diagnostic Laboratory
　Immunology, Internal Medicine, Occupational Medicine
675 N St Clair St #18-250, Chicago, 312-695-8624

Greenberger, Paul Allen (11 mentions)
Indiana U, 1973 *Certification:* Allergy & Immunology,
　Diagnostic Laboratory Immunology, Internal Medicine
675 N St Clair St #18-250, Chicago, 312-695-8624

Kentor, Paul Martin (10 mentions)
U of Illinois, 1970
Certification: Allergy & Immunology, Internal Medicine
636 Church St #605, Evanston, 847-864-0810
580 Roger Williams Ave, Highland Park, 847-433-5340
1215 Old McHenry Rd #130B, Buffalo Grove, 847-634-1690

McGrath, Kris Graham (10 mentions)
U of Iowa, 1979
Certification: Allergy & Immunology, Internal Medicine
500 N Michigan Ave #1640, Chicago, 312-222-9500

Moran, Jacqueline V. (3 mentions)
Indiana U, 1997
Certification: Allergy & Immunology, Internal Medicine
454 Pennsylvania Ave #220, Glen Ellyn, 630-545-7833
636 Raymond Dr #300, Naperville, 630-545-7833

Moy, James Ngaiman (3 mentions)
U of Illinois, 1984 *Certification:* Allergy & Immunology
1725 W Harrison St #117, Chicago, 312-942-6296

Nimmagadda, Sai R. (7 mentions)
FMS-India, 1987 *Certification:* Allergy & Immunology
2500 W Higgins Rd #220, Hoffman Estates, 847-885-1400
1849 Green Bay Rd #220, Highland Park, 847-433-7660
1460 N Halsted Ave #404, Chicago, 773-883-0274

Ozog, Diane Louise (7 mentions)
Rosalind Franklin U, 1982
Certification: Allergy & Immunology, Pediatrics
130 S Main St #202, Lombard, 630-652-0606
1288 Rickert Dr #100, Naperville, 630-652-0606

Peters, Anju T. (5 mentions)
U of Michigan, 1993
Certification: Allergy & Immunology, Internal Medicine
675 N St Clair St #18-250, Chicago, 312-695-8624

Pongracic, Jacqueline Ann (3 mentions)
Northwestern U, 1985
Certification: Allergy & Immunology, Internal Medicine
2515 N Clark St 7th Fl, Chicago, 773-327-3710

Renold, Frederick K. (6 mentions)
FMS-Switzerland, 1981
Certification: Allergy & Immunology, Internal Medicine
9301 Golf Rd #301, Des Plaines, 847-635-7300
7447 Talcott Ave #422, Chicago, 773-775-2600
800 W Biesterfield Rd, Elk Grove Village, 847-981-7300
1515 W Dundee Rd, Arlington Heights, 847-392-7355
1710 N Randall Rd, Elgin, 847-622-0378

Richmond, G. Wendell (5 mentions)
U of Oklahoma, 1976
Certification: Allergy & Immunology, Internal Medicine
908 N Elm St #205, Hinsdale, 630-455-0456

Robinson, John A. (5 mentions)
Certification: Internal Medicine, Rheumatology
2160 S 1st Ave #54-121, Maywood, 708-216-5335

Sonin, Lee (3 mentions)
U of Illinois, 1979
Certification: Allergy & Immunology, Internal Medicine
241 Golf Mill Ctr #820, Niles, 847-298-5151
800 Biesterfield Rd #4002, Elk Grove Village, 847-364-0028
455 S Roselle Rd #206, Schaumburg, 847-364-0028

Tobin, Mary Catherine (5 mentions)
Rush U, 1977
Certification: Allergy & Immunology, Internal Medicine
1725 W Harrison St #117, Chicago, 312-942-6296
610 S Maple Ave #2700, Oak Park, 312-563-3282

Anesthesiology

Baughman, Verna Lee (3 mentions)
Loyola U Chicago, 1981 *Certification:* Anesthesiology
1740 W Taylor St #3200W, Chicago, 312-996-4020

Belusko, Ronald J. (3 mentions)
Loyola U Chicago, 1978 *Certification:* Anesthesiology
2160 S 1st Ave, Maywood, 708-216-3612

Bissing, Mary Kay (4 mentions)
Midwestern U, 1980 *Certification:* Anesthesiology
1775 Dempster St, Park Ridge, 847-723-5524

Blasco, Thomas Andrew (3 mentions)
Loyola U Chicago, 1977 *Certification:* Anesthesiology
1775 Dempster St, Park Ridge, 847-723-5524

Childers, Sara J. (3 mentions)
U of Kentucky, 1981 *Certification:* Anesthesiology
251 E Huron St #5-704, Chicago, 312-926-5149

Colombo, James Anthony (5 mentions)
U of Cincinnati, 1990
Certification: Anesthesiology, Critical Care Medicine
1775 Dempster St, Park Ridge, 847-723-5524

Edelstein, Steven Brian (4 mentions)
U of Cincinnati, 1989 *Certification:* Anesthesiology
2160 S 1st Ave, Maywood, 708-216-0414

Feld, James Martin (4 mentions)
Wayne State U, 1974 *Certification:* Anesthesiology, Critical
　Care Medicine, Internal Medicine
1740 W Taylor St #3200-W, Chicago, 312-996-4016

Hefner, George G. (4 mentions)
Northwestern U, 1988
Certification: Anesthesiology, Pain Medicine
660 N Westmoreland Rd, Lake Forest, 847-223-5890

Jellish, Walter Scott (3 mentions)
Rush U, 1986 *Certification:* Anesthesiology
2160 S 1st Ave #3114, Maywood, 708-216-6450

Laurito, Charles Edward (3 mentions)
U of Pittsburgh, 1975
Certification: Anesthesiology, Pain Medicine
1801 W Taylor St #4-E, Chicago, 312-355-0510

Martucci, John Patrick (5 mentions)
Ohio State U, 1989 *Certification:* Anesthesiology
3815 Highland Ave, Downers Grove, 630-275-1152

Marymont, Jesse H., III (3 mentions)
St Louis U, 1983 *Certification:* Anesthesiology
2650 Ridge Ave, Evanston, 847-570-2760

Monma, Dean Taylor (4 mentions)
Northwestern U, 1987 *Certification:* Anesthesiology
25 N Winfield Rd, Winfield, 630-933-1600

Rosen, David (3 mentions)
U of Illinois, 1992 *Certification:* Anesthesiology
1775 Dempster St, Park Ridge, 847-723-5524

Schechter, Howard Owen (3 mentions)
U of Illinois, 1964 *Certification:* Anesthesiology
871 Dryden Ln, Highland Park, 847-433-7267
355 Ridge Ave, Evanston, 847-316-4000

Schneider, Karen Lynn (3 mentions)
U of Michigan, 1982 *Certification:* Anesthesiology
1775 Dempster St, Park Ridge, 847-723-5524

Soden, William Gerard (3 mentions)
Ohio State U, 1981 *Certification:* Anesthesiology, Critical
Care Medicine, Internal Medicine
1775 Dempster St, Park Ridge, 847-723-5524

Szokol, Joseph William (5 mentions)
U of Southern California, 1991 *Certification:* Anesthesiology
2650 Ridge Ave, Evanston, 847-570-2760

Tuman, Kenneth James (4 mentions)
U of Chicago, 1980
Certification: Anesthesiology, Critical Care Medicine
1653 W Congress Pkwy, Chicago, 312-942-6450

Vender, Jeffery Stephen (6 mentions)
Northwestern U, 1975
Certification: Anesthesiology, Critical Care Medicine
2650 Ridge Ave, Evanston, 847-570-2760

Young, David E. (4 mentions)
U of Arkansas, 1983
Certification: Anesthesiology, Obstetrics & Gynecology
1775 Dempster St, Park Ridge, 847-723-5524

Cardiac Surgery

Alexander, John C. (9 mentions)
Duke U, 1972
1000 Central St #800 Walgreen Bldg #3507, Evanston,
847-570-2868

Bakhos, Mamdouh (11 mentions)
FMS-Syria, 1971 *Certification:* Thoracic Surgery
2160 S 1st Ave Bldg 110 #6243, Maywood, 708-327-2503

Goldin, Marshall David (15 mentions)
U of Illinois, 1963 *Certification:* Surgery, Thoracic Surgery
1725 W Harrison St #1156, Chicago, 312-563-2762

Grieco, John Gregory (9 mentions)
Loyola U Chicago, 1977 *Certification:* Thoracic Surgery
2650 Warrenville Rd #280, Downers Grove, 630-324-7913

Joob, Axel William (17 mentions)
U of Michigan, 1981 *Certification:* Thoracic Surgery
1600 W Dempster St #103, Park Ridge, 847-635-9006

Pappas, Patroklos Steven (12 mentions)
U of Illinois, 1983 *Certification:* Surgery, Thoracic Surgery
4400 W 95th St #205, Oak Lawn, 708-346-4040

Cardiology

Al-Sadir, Jafar M. (4 mentions)
FMS-Iraq, 1964
Certification: Cardiovascular Disease, Internal Medicine
5758 S Maryland Ave #5-C, Chicago, 773-702-9461

Billhardt, Roger Alan, Jr. (3 mentions)
Loyola U Chicago, 1975
Certification: Cardiovascular Disease, Internal Medicine
1725 W Harrison St #1138, Chicago, 312-243-6800

Bonow, Robert Ogden (8 mentions)
U of Pennsylvania, 1973
Certification: Cardiovascular Disease, Internal Medicine
675 N St Clair St #19-100, Chicago, 312-695-4965

Briller, Joan Ellen (4 mentions)
U of Connecticut, 1981
Certification: Cardiovascular Disease, Internal Medicine
840 S Wood St 9th Fl, Chicago, 312-996-6730

Brookfield, Leslie Anne (4 mentions)
Med Coll of Ohio, 1981
Certification: Cardiovascular Disease, Internal Medicine
1255 N Milwaukee Ave, Glenview, 847-294-5490

Bufalino, Vincent John (3 mentions)
Loyola U Chicago, 1977
Certification: Cardiovascular Disease, Internal Medicine
429 N York St, Elmhurst, 630-782-4050
801 S Washington St, Naperville, 630-527-2730
1 E County Line Rd, Sandwich, 815-786-2722

Cahill, John Michael (4 mentions)
Loyola U Chicago, 1981 *Certification:* Cardiovascular
Disease, Internal Medicine, Interventional Cardiology
429 N York St, Elmhurst, 630-782-4050

Calvin, James Eldon (3 mentions)
FMS-Canada, 1975
Certification: Cardiovascular Disease, Internal Medicine
1725 W Harrison St #1159, Chicago, 312-942-5020

Campbell, David Robert (3 mentions)
Cornell U, 1984
Certification: Cardiovascular Disease, Internal Medicine
2151 Waukegan Rd #100, Bannockburn, 847-444-5300

Chamberlin, Jack Richard (3 mentions)
U of Nebraska, 1991
Certification: Cardiovascular Disease, Interventional Cardiology
701 Biesterfield Rd, Elk Grove Village, 847-981-3680

Chhablani, Ramesh (7 mentions)
FMS-India, 1967 *Certification:* Cardiovascular Disease,
Internal Medicine, Interventional Cardiology
1725 W Harrison St #1138, Chicago, 312-243-6800

Cohen, Ian David (3 mentions)
FMS-South Africa, 1986
Certification: Cardiovascular Disease, Interventional Cardiology
3118 N Ashland Ave, Chicago, 773-880-9722
4646 N Marine Dr, Chicago, 773-564-5900
2740 W Foster Ave, Chicago, 773-880-9723

Davison, Richard (6 mentions)
FMS-Argentina, 1963
Certification: Cardiovascular Disease, Internal Medicine
675 N St Clair St #19-100, Chicago, 312-695-2745

Diamond, Peter (4 mentions)
Loyola U Chicago, 1978
Certification: Cardiovascular Disease, Internal Medicine
5151 W 95th St, Oak Lawn, 708-952-7444

Du Brow, Ira Will (5 mentions)
U of Illinois, 1966 *Certification:* Pediatric Cardiology, Pediatrics
1775 Dempster St, Park Ridge, 847-723-6465
1675 W Dempster St 3rd Fl, Park Ridge, 847-723-6465

Eybel, Carl Eugene (3 mentions)
U of Illinois, 1969
Certification: Cardiovascular Disease, Internal Medicine
1725 W Harrison St #1138, Chicago, 312-243-6800
3825 Highland Ave #3C, Downers Grove, 630-964-4551

Follman, Duane Frederick (6 mentions)
U of Illinois, 1983 *Certification:* Cardiovascular Disease,
Internal Medicine, Interventional Cardiology
11 Saltcreek Ln, Hinsdale, 630-789-3422

Foschi, Alberto Eleodoro (4 mentions)
FMS-Argentina, 1973 *Certification:* Cardiovascular Disease,
Internal Medicine, Interventional Cardiology
800 Austin St #454, Evanston, 847-864-4370

Giardina, John Joseph (3 mentions)
Rosalind Franklin U, 1982 *Certification:* Cardiovascular
Disease, Internal Medicine, Interventional Cardiology
25 N Winfield Rd, Winfield, 630-933-8100

Greenfield, Stuart (3 mentions)
FMS-Canada, 1988 *Certification:* Cardiovascular Disease
211 E Ontario St #510, Chicago, 312-642-9858

Greenspahn, Bruce Robert (6 mentions)
U of Illinois, 1975 *Certification:* Cardiovascular Disease,
Internal Medicine, Interventional Cardiology
1875 Dempster St #555, Park Ridge, 847-698-5500

Hale, David Joseph (3 mentions)
Loyola U Chicago, 1971
Certification: Cardiovascular Disease, Internal Medicine
701 Biesterfield Rd, Elk Grove Village, 847-981-3680

Herstberg, Anna (3 mentions)
FMS-Latvia, 1977
1875 Dempster St #555, Park Ridge, 847-698-5500

Jones, Paul Anthony (6 mentions)
U of Illinois, 1986
Certification: Internal Medicine, Interventional Cardiology
2525 S Michigan Ave, Chicago, 312-567-2380

Kanakis, Charles D., Jr. (3 mentions)
U of Illinois, 1969 *Certification:* Cardiovascular Disease,
Internal Medicine, Interventional Cardiology
1875 Dempster St #555, Park Ridge, 847-698-5500

Kondos, George Theodore (13 mentions)
Rosalind Franklin U, 1978 *Certification:* Internal Medicine
1801 W Taylor St #3C, Chicago, 312-996-6480

Krause, Philip Burton (3 mentions)
Rosalind Franklin U, 1987
Certification: Cardiovascular Disease, Interventional Cardiology
9669 Kenton #206, Skokie, 847-676-1333

Krauss, Daniel Edward (3 mentions)
U of Pennsylvania, 1987
Certification: Cardiovascular Disease, Internal Medicine
11 Salt Creek Ln, Hinsdale, 630-789-3422

Lewis, Bruce Edward (4 mentions)
Rush U, 1984 *Certification:* Cardiovascular Disease,
Internal Medicine, Interventional Cardiology
2160 S 1st Ave Bldg 107 #1855, Maywood, 708-216-9447
2900 N Lake Shore Dr 1st Fl, Chicago, 773-665-3391
1 S 260 Summit Ave, Oakbrook Terrace, 708-216-9447

Leya, Ferdinand (6 mentions)
FMS-Poland, 1977 *Certification:* Cardiovascular Disease,
Internal Medicine, Interventional Cardiology
2160 S 1st Ave #1036, Maywood, 708-216-4225
1030 W Higgins Rd #103, Park Ridge, 708-216-4225

Lichtenberg, Robert C. (4 mentions)
Loyola U Chicago, 1982 *Certification:* Cardiovascular
Disease, Internal Medicine, Pediatrics
3231 S Euclid Ave #201, Berwyn, 708-783-2055

Mayer, Thomas A. (3 mentions)
Rush U, 1983 *Certification:* Cardiovascular Disease,
Internal Medicine, Interventional Cardiology
767 Park Ave W #340, Highland Park, 847-432-1580
2151 Waukegan Rd #101, Bannockburn, 847-444-5319

McKiernan, Thomas Louis (13 mentions)
Loyola U Chicago, 1974
Certification: Cardiovascular Disease, Internal Medicine
2160 S 1st Ave, Maywood, 708-327-2749
1S260 Summit Ave, Oakbrook Terrace, 708-327-2749

Mehlman, David Joel (9 mentions)
Johns Hopkins U, 1973
Certification: Cardiovascular Disease, Internal Medicine
675 N St Clair St #19G-100, Chicago, 312-695-4965

Miller, Scott Martin (5 mentions)
U of Illinois, 1978 *Certification:* Cardiovascular Disease,
   Clinical Cardiac Electrophysiology, Internal Medicine
1875 Dempster St #555, Park Ridge, 847-698-5500

Millman, William Leonard (5 mentions)
U of Illinois, 1972 *Certification:* Cardiovascular Disease,
   Internal Medicine, Interventional Cardiology
7411 Lake St #2110, River Forest, 708-488-1122
2550 Oak Park Ave, Berwyn, 708-795-0383

Neuberger, Stephen Mark (3 mentions)
Emory U, 1991 *Certification:* Pediatric Cardiology
1325 Highland Ave, Aurora, 630-801-2505
1675 W Dempster St 3rd Fl, Park Ridge, 847-723-6465

O'Donoghue, John Kevin (4 mentions)
Georgetown U, 1965 *Certification:* Cardiovascular Disease,
   Internal Medicine, Interventional Cardiology
1 Erie Ct, Oak Park, 708-488-1122
7411 Lake St #2110, River Forest, 708-488-1122
120 Oakbrook Ctr #410, Oakbrook, 708-488-1122

Pacold, Ivan V. (3 mentions)
U of Chicago, 1976
Certification: Cardiovascular Disease, Internal Medicine
2160 S 1st Ave, Maywood, 708-327-2746
1950 S Harlem Ave, North Riverside, 708-354-9250

Patel, Parag V. (4 mentions)
Des Moines U, 1992 *Certification:* Interventional Cardiology
1775 Ballard Rd, Park Ridge, 847-318-2500
1875 Dempster St #525, Park Ridge, 847-698-3600

Quinn, Thomas J. (6 mentions)
Loyola U Chicago, 1979
Certification: Cardiovascular Disease, Internal Medicine
2850 W 95th St #305, Evergreen Park, 708-425-7272
12432 S Harlem Ave, Palos Heights, 708-425-7272

Rigolin, Vera H. (3 mentions)
Northwestern U, 1988 *Certification:* Cardiovascular Disease
675 N St Clair St #19-100, Chicago, 312-695-4965

Rosenbush, Stuart William (3 mentions)
U of Illinois, 1976 *Certification:* Cardiovascular Disease,
   Internal Medicine, Interventional Cardiology
1725 W Harrison St #1138, Chicago, 312-563-3233
9701 Knox Ave, Skokie, 312-563-3233

Rowan, Daniel A. (4 mentions)
Midwestern U Coll of Osteopathic Med, 1986
Certification: Cardiovascular Disease, Internal Medicine,
   Interventional Cardiology
2850 W 95th St #305, Evergreen Park, 708-425-7272
12432 S Harlem Ave, Palos Heights, 708-425-7272

Rowley, Stephen Michael (4 mentions)
SUNY-Upstate Med U, 1982
Certification: Cardiovascular Disease, Critical Care
   Medicine, Internal Medicine, Interventional Cardiology
3825 Highland Ave #400, Downers Grove, 630-719-4799

Ruzumna, Paul Aaron (3 mentions)
Wayne State U, 1992 *Certification:* Cardiovascular Disease
1632 W Central Rd, Arlington Heights, 847-253-8050

Sabri, Moustafa Nagui M. (5 mentions)
FMS-Egypt, 1981 *Certification:* Cardiovascular Disease,
   Internal Medicine, Interventional Cardiology
1875 Dempster St #555, Park Ridge, 847-698-5500

Sidorow, Barry Jay (4 mentions)
Washington U, 1979
Certification: Cardiovascular Disease, Internal Medicine
333 Chestnut St #101, Hinsdale, 630-325-9010
5201 Willow Springs Rd, La Grange, 630-325-9010

Silverman, Irwin M. (3 mentions)
Rosalind Franklin U, 1977
Certification: Cardiovascular Disease, Internal Medicine
1713 Central St, Evanston, 847-869-1499
2501 Compass Dr #100, Glenview, 847-901-5252

Silverman, Paul Richard (3 mentions)
U of Chicago, 1985 *Certification:* Cardiovascular Disease,
   Internal Medicine, Interventional Cardiology
4400 W 95th St #407, Oak Lawn, 708-636-7575
12400 Harlem Ave #110, Palos Heights, 708-636-7575

Sita, Gilbert Anthony (3 mentions)
FMS-Colombia, 1983 *Certification:* Cardiovascular Disease,
   Internal Medicine, Interventional Cardiology
1632 W Central Rd, Arlington Heights, 847-253-8050

Sorrentino, Matthew J. (5 mentions)
U of Chicago, 1984
Certification: Cardiovascular Disease, Internal Medicine
5841 S Maryland Ave, Chicago, 773-702-6924

Stephan, William Joseph (3 mentions)
Tufts U, 1987 *Certification:* Cardiovascular Disease,
   Internal Medicine, Interventional Cardiology
76 W Countryside Pkwy, Yorkville, 630-553-2722
801 S Washington St, Naperville, 630-527-2756

Stone, Neil Joseph (4 mentions)
Northwestern U, 1968
Certification: Cardiovascular Disease, Internal Medicine
211 E Chicago Ave #1050, Chicago, 312-944-6677

Upton, Mark Thornton (6 mentions)
FMS-Canada, 1973
Certification: Cardiovascular Disease, Internal Medicine
233 E Erie St #412, Chicago, 312-573-1322

Waligora, Michael James (4 mentions)
St Louis U, 1992 *Certification:* Cardiovascular Disease
2501 Compass Rd #100, Glenview, 847-901-5252
1713 Central St, Evanston, 847-869-1499

Wallis, Diane E. (3 mentions)
Northwestern U, 1979 *Certification:* Cardiovascular
   Disease, Critical Care Medicine, Internal Medicine
3825 Highland Ave #400, Downers Grove, 630-719-4799

Dermatology

Ackerman, Rollie Sue (4 mentions)
Washington U, 1978 *Certification:* Dermatology
2604 Dempster St #101, Park Ridge, 847-699-0501

Aronson, Iris Klawir (4 mentions)
U of Illinois, 1970
Certification: Dermatological Immunology/Diagnostic and
   Laboratory Immunology, Dermatology
1801 W Taylor St #3E, Chicago, 312-996-6966

Berti, Jeffrey Jerome (3 mentions)
U of Illinois, 1994 *Certification:* Dermatology
6825 Kingery Hwy, Willowbrook, 630-321-0303

Bhatia, Ashish C. (4 mentions)
Northeastern Ohio U, 1999 *Certification:* Dermatology
636 Raymond Dr #304, Naperville, 630-547-5040

Brieva, Joaquin Carlos (12 mentions)
FMS-Colombia, 1983 *Certification:* Dermatology
676 N St Clair St #1600, Chicago, 312-695-8106

Bronson, Darryl Murray (8 mentions)
U of Illinois, 1976 *Certification:* Dermatology, Dermatopathology
767 Park Ave W #310, Highland Park, 847-432-4650

Chao-Lichon, Nancy Shan (4 mentions)
U of Illinois, 1978 *Certification:* Dermatology
2340 S Highland Ave #340, Lombard, 630-932-2099
511 Thornhill Dr, Carol Stream, 630-462-7676

Drabkin, Oliver Hershel (3 mentions)
Ohio State U, 1967
3900 W 95th St #12, Evergreen Park, 708-423-7550

Fretzin, David F. (5 mentions)
U of Iowa, 1960 *Certification:* Dermatology, Dermatopathology
41 S Prospect Ave, Park Ridge, 847-823-1960

Goldin, Harry Mark (3 mentions)
U of Kentucky, 1980
Certification: Dermatology, Internal Medicine
4709 W Golf Rd #1000, Skokie, 847-677-2080

Greenberg, Michael Alan (5 mentions)
U of Illinois, 1974 *Certification:* Dermatology
800 Biesterfield Rd #3002, Elk Grove Village, 847-364-4717

Handler, Raymond Morton (4 mentions)
U of Illinois, 1961 *Certification:* Dermatology
8780 W Golf Rd #303, Niles, 847-299-1044
7447 W Talcott Ave #366, Chicago, 773-774-8877

Herrmann, James J. (4 mentions)
Northwestern U, 1991 *Certification:* Dermatology
199 Town Sq #A, Wheaton, 630-871-6690

Keane, John Thomas (3 mentions)
Loyola U Chicago, 1972
Certification: Dermatology, Dermatopathology
16105 S La Grange Rd, Orland Park, 708-636-3765

Kelleher, Matthew Robert (5 mentions)
U of Illinois, 1988 *Certification:* Dermatology
2400 Glenwood Ave, Joliet, 815-741-4343
1520 Bond St, Naperville, 630-357-7536

Lapinski, Paula Kaye (3 mentions)
Northwestern U, 1997 *Certification:* Dermatology
1051 Essington Rd #280, Joliet, 815-744-8554
20646 S La Grange Rd #104, Frankfort, 815-744-8554

Levine, Lawrence E. (4 mentions)
Loyola U Chicago, 1979 *Certification:* Dermatology
800 Austin St #460, Evanston, 847-864-0370

Lorber, David A. (6 mentions)
U of Illinois, 1981 *Certification:* Dermatology, Internal Medicine
9711 Skokie Blvd, Skokie, 847-675-9711
1220 Meadow Rd #210, Northbrook, 847-559-0090

Maloney, Karen Lynn (3 mentions)
Loyola U Chicago, 1984
Certification: Dermatology, Internal Medicine, Pediatrics
317 W Illinois St #A, St Charles, 630-443-7223

Mancini, Anthony J. (8 mentions)
U of Arizona, 1991
Certification: Dermatology, Pediatric Dermatology
2515 N Clark St #905, Chicago, 773-327-3446
2150 Pfingsten Rd, Glenview, 800-543-7362

Massa, Mary Catherine (5 mentions)
Loyola U Chicago, 1976 *Certification:* Dermatology,
   Dermatopathology, Internal Medicine
6319 S Fairview Ave #102, Westmont, 630-968-4500

Moore, Julie Anne (5 mentions)
Creighton U, 1986 *Certification:* Dermatology
675 W North Ave #506, Melrose Park, 708-450-5086
2340 S Highland Ave #350, Lombard, 630-932-2099

Neubauer, Steven Werner (3 mentions)
Virginia Commonwealth U, 1982
Certification: Dermatology, Pediatrics
2400 Glenwood Ave, Joliet, 815-741-4343
1520 Bond St, Naperville, 630-357-7536

O'Donoghue, Maryanne (5 mentions)
Georgetown U, 1965 *Certification:* Dermatology
120 Oakbrook Mall #410, Oakbrook, 630-574-5860

Paller, Amy Susan (5 mentions)
Stanford U, 1978
Certification: Dermatology, Pediatric Dermatology, Pediatrics
2515 N Clark St #905, Chicago, 773-327-3446

Peters, Neill Torsten, Jr. (4 mentions)
U of Michigan, 1993 *Certification:* Dermatology
200 S Michigan Ave #805, Chicago, 312-922-3815
5525 S Pulaski Rd, Chicago, 773-585-1955

Remlinger, Kathleen Ann (3 mentions)
Loyola U Chicago, 1975 *Certification:* Dermatology,
  Hematology, Internal Medicine, Medical Oncology
2972 Indian Trail Rd, Aurora, 630-236-4257

Schultz, Bryan C. (4 mentions)
Loyola U Chicago, 1974 *Certification:* Dermatology
1050 W Chicago Ave, Oak Park, 708-383-6366

Solomon, Lawrence Marvin (5 mentions)
FMS-Switzerland, 1959 *Certification:* Dermatology
2401 Ravine Way #101, Glenview, 847-724-1995

Soltani, Keyoumars (4 mentions)
FMS-Iran, 1965
Certification: Dermatological Immunology/Diagnostic and
  Laboratory Immunology, Dermatology, Dermatopathology
5758 S Maryland Ave #6C, Chicago, 773-702-6559

Taub, Amy Forman (3 mentions)
Northwestern U, 1985 *Certification:* Dermatology
275 Parkway Dr, Lincolnshire, 847-459-6400

Tharp, Michael Dean (5 mentions)
Ohio State U, 1974 *Certification:* Dermatology, Internal Medicine
1725 W Harrison St #264, Chicago, 312-942-2195

Wagner, Annette (3 mentions)
FMS-Canada, 1988
Certification: Dermatology, Pediatric Dermatology
880 W Central Rd, Arlington Heights, 224-625-2180
2300 N Children's Plaza, Chicago, 773-327-3446
2301 Enterprise Dr, Westchester, 708-836-4800

Wise, Ronald David (5 mentions)
U of Illinois, 1974 *Certification:* Dermatology
30 N Michigan Ave #1301, Chicago, 312-332-7303
9550 W 167th St, Orland Park, 708-873-4500

Zahner, Scott Lawrence (6 mentions)
U of Illinois, 1989 *Certification:* Dermatology
908 N Elm St #309, Hinsdale, 630-455-1756
2435 W Dean St #2E, St Charles, 630-443-7800

Zugerman, Charles (4 mentions)
Temple U, 1972 *Certification:* Dermatology
676 N St Clair St #1840, Chicago, 312-337-4020

Emergency Medicine

Adams, James Gregory (4 mentions)
Georgetown U, 1988 *Certification:* Emergency Medicine
259 E Erie #100, Chicago, 312-694-7000

Cichon, Mark E. (3 mentions)
Midwestern U Coll of Osteopathic Med, 1985
2160 S 1st Ave, Maywood, 708-327-2546

Cooper, Mary Ann (3 mentions)
Michigan State U, 1974 *Certification:* Emergency Medicine
808 S Wood St, Chicago, 312-413-7489

Erickson, Timothy Bruce (4 mentions)
Rosalind Franklin U, 1986 *Certification:* Emergency Medicine
1740 W Taylor St, Chicago, 312-413-7393

Feldman, Richard M. (3 mentions)
Jefferson Med Coll, 1970 *Certification:* Emergency Medicine
836 W Wellington Ave #1725, Chicago, 773-296-7054

Graff, Jeffrey Gilbert (3 mentions)
U of Illinois, 1975 *Certification:* Emergency Medicine
2100 Pfingsten Rd, Glenview, 847-657-5632
2650 Ridge Ave, Evanston, 847-570-2114

Hess, Frederick Charles (4 mentions)
Northwestern U, 1977
Certification: Emergency Medicine, Internal Medicine
2650 Ridge Ave, Evanston, 847-570-2114

Maloney, William Edward (7 mentions)
U of Illinois, 1988 *Certification:* Emergency Medicine
355 Ridge Ave, Evanston, 847-316-2345

Narasimhan, Kris S. (4 mentions)
FMS-India, 1972 *Certification:* Emergency Medicine
1775 Dempster St, Park Ridge, 847-723-5150

Ortinau, John Michael (3 mentions)
Loyola U Chicago, 1976
Certification: Emergency Medicine, Family Medicine
800 Biesterfield Rd, Elk Grove Village, 847-437-5500

Peabody, Joseph Francis (4 mentions)
U of Illinois, 1996
Certification: Emergency Medicine, Internal Medicine
1775 Dempster St, Park Ridge, 847-723-5156

Probst, Beatrice Dorthea (4 mentions)
Indiana U, 1983
Certification: Emergency Medicine, Internal Medicine
2160 S 1st Ave #232, Maywood, 708-327-2554

Rumoro, Dino P. (6 mentions)
Midwestern U, 1990 *Certification:* Emergency Medicine
1653 W Congress Pkwy, Chicago, 312-942-3162

Schaider, Jeffrey J. (4 mentions)
Northwestern U, 1985 *Certification:* Emergency Medicine
1900 W Polk St, Chicago, 312-864-0060

Schurgin, Brian R. (3 mentions)
U of Michigan, 1986 *Certification:* Emergency Medicine
3249 S Oak Park Ave, Berwyn, 703-783-9100

Spanierman, Clifford S. (5 mentions)
FMS-Dominican Republic, 1986
Certification: Pediatric Emergency Medicine
1775 Dempster St, Park Ridge, 847-723-5154

Sutherland, Herbert N. (3 mentions)
U of North Texas Coll of Osteopathic Med, 1978
Certification: Emergency Medicine
25 N Winfield Rd, Winfield, 630-933-1600

Thompson, David Alan (3 mentions)
U of Illinois, 1985
Certification: Emergency Medicine, Internal Medicine
3249 S Oak Park Ave, Berwyn, 708-783-9100

Endocrinology

Bielski, Steven Joseph (6 mentions)
Loyola U Chicago, 1986 *Certification:* Endocrinology,
  Diabetes, and Metabolism, Internal Medicine
302 Randall Rd #304, Geneva, 630-208-6775

Carter, Judy Ann (5 mentions)
Columbia U, 1987 *Certification:* Endocrinology, Diabetes,
  and Metabolism, Internal Medicine
520 S Maple Ave, Oak Park, 708-383-9300

Charnogursky, Gerald A. (8 mentions)
U of Pennsylvania, 1979
Certification: Endocrinology and Metabolism, Internal Medicine
2160 S 1st Ave 3rd Fl, Maywood, 708-216-0160
9608 Roberts Rd, Hickory Hill, 708-233-2488

Domont, Lawrence Alan (8 mentions)
Indiana U, 1974
Certification: Endocrinology and Metabolism, Internal Medicine
1775 Ballard Rd, Park Ridge, 847-318-2400

Emanuele, MaryAnn (15 mentions)
Loyola U Chicago, 1975
Certification: Endocrinology and Metabolism, Internal Medicine
2160 S 1st Ave Bldg 106, Maywood, 708-216-9218

Lieblich, Jeffrey Martin (5 mentions)
U of Pennsylvania, 1972
Certification: Endocrinology and Metabolism, Internal Medicine
1971 2nd St #100, Highland Park, 847-432-5510
890 Garfield Ave #211, Libertyville, 847-680-7717

Mazzone, Theodore (5 mentions)
Northwestern U, 1977
Certification: Endocrinology and Metabolism, Internal Medicine
1801 W Taylor St #1C, Chicago, 312-413-3631

Molitch, Mark Ellis (13 mentions)
U of Pennsylvania, 1969
Certification: Endocrinology and Metabolism, Internal Medicine
675 N St Clair St #14-100, Chicago, 312-695-7970

Philipson, Louis Harry (7 mentions)
U of Chicago, 1986 *Certification:* Endocrinology, Diabetes,
  and Metabolism, Internal Medicine
5758 S Maryland Ave 5th Fl #5A, Chicago, 773-702-6138

Purdy, Lisa P. (6 mentions)
FMS-Canada, 1986
Certification: Endocrinology, Diabetes, and Metabolism
9977 Woods Dr, Skokie, 847-663-8340
225 N Milwaukee Ave, Vernon Hills, 847-663-8340

Sievertsen, Grant D., Jr. (5 mentions)
U of Pennsylvania, 1974
Certification: Endocrinology and Metabolism, Internal Medicine
908 N Elm St #301, Hinsdale, 630-323-3540

Weiss, Roy Emanuel (10 mentions)
FMS-Israel, 1985 *Certification:* Endocrinology, Diabetes,
  and Metabolism, Internal Medicine
5758 S Maryland Ave #5A, Chicago, 773-702-9653
5841 S Maryland Ave #MC-1027, Chicago, 773-702-2373

Zeller, W. Patrick (6 mentions)
Loyola U Chicago, 1977
2001 Geary Ave #240, Wheaton, 630-416-4501
2007 95th St #101, Naperville, 630-416-4501

Family Practice *(see note on page 9)*

Boll, Robert F. (3 mentions)
Midwestern U, 1987 *Certification:* Family Medicine
15300 West Ave #220, Orland Park, 708-403-8400

Brander, William John (4 mentions)
Rush U, 1986 *Certification:* Family Medicine
850 Busse Hwy, Park Ridge, 847-825-0300

Carney, Mary Lang (3 mentions)
Rosalind Franklin U, 1976 *Certification:* Family Medicine
800 Austin St #166, Evanston, 847-316-8700

Daum, Thomas Dillon (3 mentions)
U of Kentucky, 1978 *Certification:* Family Medicine
2850 W 95th St #403, Evergreen Park, 708-423-2662

De Ramos, Dave A. (3 mentions)
Midwestern U, 1988 *Certification:* Family Medicine
303 E Army Trail Rd #300, Bloomingdale, 630-545-8300

Eisenstein, Steven Joseph (3 mentions)
Northwestern U, 1986 *Certification:* Family Medicine
1885 Shermer Rd, Northbrook, 847-272-4600

Feldman, Elizabeth (3 mentions)
Mount Sinai Sch of Med, 1983
Certification: Adolescent Medicine, Family Medicine
4600 N Ravenswood Ave 2nd Fl, Chicago, 773-561-7500

Friedman, Michael Harry (3 mentions)
U of Illinois, 1988 *Certification:* Family Medicine
1431 N Western Ave #406, Chicago, 312-633-5841

Kamen, Marcy (3 mentions)
Loyola U Chicago, 1989 *Certification:* Family Medicine
1885 Shermer Rd, Northbrook, 847-272-4600

Lis, Linda Ann (3 mentions)
Georgetown U, 1988
Certification: Family Medicine, Sports Medicine
11 Salt Creek Ln #125, Hinsdale, 630-655-1177

Peters, Michael Edward (4 mentions)
U of Illinois, 1987 *Certification:* Family Medicine
3360 La Crosse Ln #106, Naperville, 630-696-4404

Robertson, Russell G. (3 mentions)
Wayne State U, 1982
Certification: Family Medicine, Geriatric Medicine
2100 Pfingsten Rd #2020, Glenview, 847-657-1820

Rothschild, Steven K. (5 mentions)
U of Michigan, 1980 *Certification:* Family Medicine
1700 W Van Buren St #470, Chicago, 312-942-0400

Sage, John William (7 mentions)
Loyola U Chicago, 1973
Certification: Family Medicine, Internal Medicine
431 Lakeview Ct #D, Mount Prospect, 847-296-3040

Siebert, Joseph Edward (4 mentions)
U of Illinois, 1975 *Certification:* Family Medicine
4900 Main St, Downers Grove, 630-963-5440

Tranmer, Patrick Anthony (7 mentions)
U of Iowa, 1977 *Certification:* Family Medicine
722 Maxwell St #235, Chicago, 312-996-2901
1919 W Taylor St, Chicago, 312-996-7000

Gastroenterology

Adler, Douglas Roark (4 mentions)
Ohio State U, 1979
Certification: Gastroenterology, Internal Medicine
4711 Golf Rd #500, Skokie, 847-677-1170

Alasadi, Rameez (4 mentions)
FMS-Syria, 1992 *Certification:* Gastroenterology
880 W Central #4500, Arlington Heights, 847-398-2777

Berger, Scott Alan (4 mentions)
Mount Sinai Sch of Med, 1984 *Certification:*
Gastroenterology, Internal Medicine
1243 Rickart Dr, Naperville, 630-527-6450

Gekas, Paul Michael (4 mentions)
Loyola U Chicago, 1972
Certification: Gastroenterology, Internal Medicine
302 Randall Rd #308, Geneva, 630-208-7388

Goldberg, Michael Jerome (7 mentions)
U of Illinois, 1975
Certification: Gastroenterology, Internal Medicine
2450 Ridge Rd, Evanston, 847-657-1900

Goldstein, Jay Lawrence (6 mentions)
U of Illinois, 1978
Certification: Gastroenterology, Internal Medicine
840 S Wood St #1020-N, Chicago, 312-996-1926

Gupta, Harsh Vardhan (5 mentions)
FMS-India, 1976
Certification: Gastroenterology, Internal Medicine
800 Austin St #403, Evanston, 847-491-9020

Hanauer, Stephen Brett (7 mentions)
U of Illinois, 1977
Certification: Gastroenterology, Internal Medicine
5841 S Maryland Ave #4076, Chicago, 773-702-1466
5758 S Maryland Ave #6-B, Chicago, 773-702-1466

Hirano, Ikuo (4 mentions)
U of Pennsylvania, 1990 *Certification:* Gastroenterology
675 N St Clair St #17-250, Chicago, 312-695-5620

Hoscheit, Donald C., II (8 mentions)
Loyola U Chicago, 1982
Certification: Gastroenterology, Internal Medicine
100 Spalding Dr #208, Naperville, 630-717-2600
302 Randall Rd #210, Geneva, 630-377-7096
25 N Winfield Rd #LL01, Winfield, 630-980-2601

Janda, Robert Charles (6 mentions)
U of Illinois, 1983
Certification: Gastroenterology, Internal Medicine
911 N Elm St #128, Hinsdale, 630-789-2260

Keshavarzian, Ali (15 mentions)
FMS-Iran, 1976
Certification: Gastroenterology, Internal Medicine
1725 W Harrison St Bldg 1 #207, Chicago, 312-942-5861
9601 Knoxx St #103, Skokie, 847-933-6040

Layden, Thomas Joseph (5 mentions)
Loyola U Chicago, 1969
Certification: Gastroenterology, Internal Medicine
1801 W Taylor St #1B, Chicago, 312-996-3800

Lee, Douglas Art (6 mentions)
Northwestern U, 1991 *Certification:* Gastroenterology
9921 Southwest Hwy, Oak Lawn, 708-499-5678
1300 Copperfield Ave #4050, Joliet, 815-723-9278

Mahdavian, Mani (4 mentions)
FMS-Iran, 1992 *Certification:* Gastroenterology
2010 S Arlington Heights Rd #215, Arlington Heights,
847-290-3800

McKenna, Michael Emmett (4 mentions)
Loyola U Chicago, 1977
Certification: Gastroenterology, Internal Medicine
360 W Butterfield Rd #280, Elmhurst, 630-833-0653
3825 Highland Ave #307, Downers Grove, 630-833-0653

Meiselman, Mick Scott (12 mentions)
Northwestern U, 1979
Certification: Gastroenterology, Internal Medicine
506 Green Bay Rd, Kenilworth, 847-256-3495

Moller, Neal Alan (4 mentions)
U of Chicago, 1984
Certification: Gastroenterology, Internal Medicine
625 Roger Williams Ave #101, Highland Park, 847-433-3460

Morgan, George Edward (6 mentions)
U of Illinois, 1984
Certification: Gastroenterology, Internal Medicine
1259 Rickert Dr #108, Naperville, 630-416-7006
3825 Highland Ave Tower 2 #307, Downers Grove, 630-852-1009
360 W Butterfield Rd #280, Elmhurst, 630-416-7006

O'Reilly, Daniel Joseph (5 mentions)
Loyola U Chicago, 1977
Certification: Gastroenterology, Internal Medicine
12150 S Harlem Ave, Palos Heights, 708-226-2687

O'Riordan, Kenneth I. (5 mentions)
FMS-Ireland, 1988
Certification: Gastroenterology, Internal Medicine
675 N St Clair St 17th Fl #250, Chicago, 312-695-5620

Parsons, Willis Gilman (6 mentions)
Vanderbilt U, 1989 *Certification:* Gastroenterology
880 W Central Rd #4500, Arlington Heights, 847-398-2777

Shapiro, Alan Brian (5 mentions)
U of Illinois, 1984
Certification: Gastroenterology, Internal Medicine
4711 Golf Rd #500, Skokie, 847-677-1170

Silas, Dean Nicholas (9 mentions)
U of Illinois, 1984
Certification: Gastroenterology, Internal Medicine
7900 N Milwaukee Ave #19, Niles, 847-318-9595

Smith, Matthew Blake (5 mentions)
U of Chicago, 1987 *Certification:* Gastroenterology
360 W Butterfield Rd #280, Elmhurst, 630-833-0653
3825 Highland Ave #307, Downers Grove, 360-833-0653

Sweeney, Philip Patrick (5 mentions)
U of Illinois, 1980
Certification: Gastroenterology, Internal Medicine
950 N York Rd #101, Hinsdale, 630-325-4255

Tsang, Tatkin (4 mentions)
Northwestern U, 1978
Certification: Gastroenterology, Internal Medicine
1824 Wilmette Ave, Wilmette, 847-256-3355

Vanagunas, Arvydas (8 mentions)
U of Illinois, 1973
Certification: Gastroenterology, Internal Medicine
675 N St Clair St #17-250, Chicago, 312-695-5620

General Surgery

Abcarian, Herand (7 mentions)
FMS-Iran, 1965 *Certification:* Colon & Rectal Surgery, Surgery
675 W North Ave #406, Melrose Park, 708-450-5075
1801 W Taylor St #3F, Chicago, 312-355-4300

Altimari, Anthony F. (8 mentions)
Rosalind Franklin U, 1983 *Certification:* Surgery
7 Blanchard Cir #104, Wheaton, 630-668-0833

Andrews, John Robert (4 mentions)
U of Illinois, 1985 *Certification:* Colon & Rectal Surgery, Surgery
800 N Westmoreland Rd #205, Lake Forest, 847-945-3112

Aranha, Gerard Victor (7 mentions)
FMS-India, 1968 *Certification:* Surgery
2160 S 1st Ave Clinic A, Maywood, 708-327-2647

Benedetti, Enrico (4 mentions)
FMS-Italy, 1985 *Certification:* Surgery
1801 W Taylor St #3F, Chicago, 312-355-4300

Bilimoria, Malcolm M. (7 mentions)
Northwestern U, 1991 *Certification:* Surgery
2650 Ridge Ave #103, Evanston, 847-570-1334

Bloom, Allen D. (3 mentions)
Northwestern U, 1982 *Certification:* Surgery
2020 Ogden Ave #210, Aurora, 630-585-0200

Cacioppo, Phillip Leon (8 mentions)
Loyola U Chicago, 1967 *Certification:* Surgery
800 Biesterfield Rd #202, Elk Grove Village, 847-806-0106

Dahlinghaus, Daniel Louis (4 mentions)
Loyola U Chicago, 1974 *Certification:* Surgery
7447 W Talcott Ave #427, Chicago, 773-631-9699

De Haan, David Robert (4 mentions)
U of Michigan, 1993 *Certification:* Surgery
1801 S Highland Ave #220, Lombard, 630-873-8700
100 Spalding Dr #300, Naperville, 630-873-8700

Dehaan, Michael Robert (8 mentions)
U of Illinois, 1985 *Certification:* Surgery
1 Erie Ct #6010, Oak Park, 708-383-4300
7411 Lake St, River Forest, 708-383-4300

Dillon, Bruce Campbell (7 mentions)
Eastern Virginia Med Sch, 1977 *Certification:* Surgery
908 N Elm St #310, Hinsdale, 630-325-3310

Doolas, Alexander (11 mentions)
U of Illinois, 1960 *Certification:* Surgery
1725 W Harrison St #810, Chicago, 312-738-2743

Douglas, Daniel Joseph (6 mentions)
Rosalind Franklin U, 1982
Certification: Surgery, Vascular Surgery
908 N Elm St #310, Hinsdale, 630-325-3310

England, Gale Marie (3 mentions)
Rush U, 1993 *Certification:* Surgery
473 W Army Trail Rd #107, Bloomingdale, 630-307-7799
3815 Highland Ave #107, Downers Grove, 630-307-7799

Geissler, Grant Howard (4 mentions)
U of Illinois, 1985 *Certification:* Pediatric Surgery
901 Biesterfield Rd #213, Elk Grove Village, 847-390-0330
2150 Pfingsten Rd, Glenview, 847-390-0330
25 N Winfield Rd, Winfield, 847-390-0330
880 W Central Rd #6400, Arlington Heights, 847-390-0330

Grabowski, Stephen Tad (4 mentions)
U of Illinois, 1992 *Certification:* Surgery
800 Biesterfield Rd #3004, Elk Grove Village, 847-439-7515
155 N Barrington Rd, Hoffman Estates, 847-439-7515

Greenberg, James Joseph (3 mentions)
U of Missouri-Kansas City, 1991 *Certification:* Surgery
3245 Grove Ave #202, Berwyn, 708-484-0621
40 S Clay #218, Hinsdale, 630-325-5070

Guske, Paul Jeffrey (3 mentions)
Med Coll of Wisconsin, 1991 *Certification:* Surgery
800 Biesterfield Rd #101, Elk Grove Village, 847-290-9200
1614 W Central Rd #105, Arlington Heights, 847-255-9697

Hamby, John Allen (5 mentions)
Rush U, 1981 *Certification:* Surgery
1200 S York Rd #4220, Elmhurst, 630-758-8838

Hann, Sang Erk (5 mentions)
FMS-South Korea, 1964 *Certification:* Surgery
1875 W Dempster #280, Park Ridge, 847-824-7740

Hopkins, William Michael (3 mentions)
Loyola U Chicago, 1976 *Certification:* Surgery
4400 W 95th St #413, Oak Lawn, 708-346-4055
18210 S La Grange Rd, Tinley Park, 708-478-4407

Hyser, Matthew Joseph (4 mentions)
Rush U, 1985 *Certification:* Surgery, Surgical Critical Care
800 Austin St #563, Evanston, 847-869-0522

Joyce, Christopher David (3 mentions)
Loyola U Chicago, 1986 *Certification:* Surgery
1300 Copperfield Ave #1060, Joliet, 815-723-8571

Kacey, Daniel James (4 mentions)
Loyola U Chicago, 1981
Certification: Surgery, Surgical Critical Care
2525 S Michigan Ave 2nd Fl, Chicago, 312-567-2191

Kaplan, Edwin Louis (3 mentions)
U of Pennsylvania, 1961 *Certification:* Surgery
5758 S Maryland Ave #6A, Chicago, 773-702-6155

Kaplan, Gerald (3 mentions)
U of Illinois, 1962 *Certification:* Surgery
3000 N Halsted St #305, Chicago, 773-296-3030

Khorsand, Joubin (7 mentions)
FMS-Iran, 1973 *Certification:* Surgery
8901 Golf Rd #305, Des Plaines, 847-299-8844
431 Lakeview Ct #D, Mount Prospect, 847-296-3040

Krueger, Barbara Lynn (8 mentions)
Emory U, 1988 *Certification:* Surgery
4400 W 95th St #413, Oak Lawn, 708-346-4055
18210 S La Grange Rd, Tinley Park, 708-478-4407

Loris, Barbara Dawn (3 mentions)
Rush U, 1993 *Certification:* Surgery
767 Park Ave W #320, Highland Park, 847-432-2770

Maker, Vijay Kumar (3 mentions)
FMS-India, 1967 *Certification:* Surgery
3000 W Halsted Ave, Chicago, 773-296-5346

Millikan, Keith William (6 mentions)
Rush U, 1984 *Certification:* Surgery
1725 W Harrison St #810, Chicago, 312-738-2743

Montana, Louis Ciaccia (5 mentions)
Rush U, 1987 *Certification:* Surgery
120 Spalding Dr #100, Naperville, 630-961-0423

Mueller, Kyle Henry (3 mentions)
U of Illinois, 1999 *Certification:* Surgery
676 N St Clair St #1525, Chicago, 312-475-9327

Muldoon, Joseph Phillip (4 mentions)
Wayne State U, 1989
Certification: Colon & Rectal Surgery, Surgery
9977 Woods Dr, Skokie, 847-570-1470
2100 Pfingsten Rd #3000, Glenview, 847-570-1470

Otto, Scott Christopher (4 mentions)
Rush U, 1998 *Certification:* Surgery
1641 N Milwaukee Ave #13, Libertyville, 847-816-7495

Peckler, M. Scott (4 mentions)
Loyola U Chicago, 1969 *Certification:* Surgery
7900 N Milwaukee Ave #2-22, Niles, 847-967-9430

Perez-Tamayo, Alejandra M. (3 mentions)
U of Illinois, 1981 *Certification:* Surgery
2525 S Michigan Ave 2nd Fl, Chicago, 312-567-2199

Prachand, Vivek Narayan (3 mentions)
Northwestern U, 1994 *Certification:* Surgery
5841 S Maryland Ave, Chicago, 773-834-8360
5758 S Maryland Ave #6-A, Chicago, 773-834-1155

Prinz, Richard Allen (6 mentions)
Loyola U Chicago, 1972 *Certification:* Surgery
1725 W Harrison St #818, Chicago, 312-942-6511

Prystowsky, Jay Bressler (3 mentions)
Pennsylvania State U, 1983 *Certification:* Surgery
675 N St Clair St #17-250, Chicago, 312-695-8918

Saclarides, Theodore John (5 mentions)
U of Miami, 1982 *Certification:* Colon & Rectal Surgery, Surgery
1725 W Harrison St #810, Chicago, 312-942-6543

Saletta, John Daniel (3 mentions)
Loyola U Chicago, 1962 *Certification:* Surgery
1875 W Dempster St #280, Park Ridge, 847-723-5990

Santaniello, John M. (3 mentions)
Loyola U Chicago, 1995
Certification: Surgery, Surgical Critical Care
2160 S 1st Ave, Maywood, 708-327-2680

Sener, Stephen Francis (4 mentions)
Northwestern U, 1977 *Certification:* Surgery
2650 Ridge Ave #106, Evanston, 847-570-1328
2150 Pfingsten Rd, Glenview, 847-570-1328

Shah, Manoj (3 mentions)
Rush U, 1982 *Certification:* Surgery, Surgical Critical Care
1875 W Dempster St #280, Park Ridge, 847-723-5990

Soper, Nathaniel Jolas (5 mentions)
U of Iowa, 1980 *Certification:* Surgery
675 N St Clair St #17-250, Chicago, 312-695-8918

Spitz, James Stephen (4 mentions)
Rosalind Franklin U, 1989
Certification: Colon & Rectal Surgery, Surgery
2601 Compass Rd, Glenview, 847-901-5263

Stryker, Steven John (5 mentions)
Northwestern U, 1978
Certification: Colon & Rectal Surgery, Surgery
676 N St Clair St #1525A, Chicago, 312-943-5427
680 N Lake Shore Dr #1202, Chicago, 312-274-9898

Sulkowski, Robert James (3 mentions)
Loyola U Chicago, 1986
Certification: Surgery, Surgical Critical Care
7900 N Milwaukee Ave #2-22, Niles, 847-967-9430

Thill, Rodney Howard (3 mentions)
Loyola U Chicago, 1990 *Certification:* Surgery
4400 W 95th St #413, Oak Lawn, 708-346-4055
18210 S La Grange Rd, Tinley Park, 708-478-4407

Ujiki, Gerald Toshimi (6 mentions)
Northwestern U, 1962 *Certification:* Surgery
676 N St Clair St #1525, Chicago, 312-664-8748

Velasco, Jose Manuel (3 mentions)
FMS-Spain, 1970 *Certification:* Surgery, Surgical Critical Care
9669 N Kenton Ave #204, Skokie, 847-982-1095

Witt, Thomas Roy (4 mentions)
Northwestern U, 1975 *Certification:* Surgery
1725 W Harrison St #409, Chicago, 312-942-2302

Yang, Eric Y. T. (3 mentions)
Northwestern U, 1987 *Certification:* Surgery
5201 Willow Springs Rd, La Grange, 708-579-0018

Geriatrics

Braund, Victoria Louise (4 mentions)
U of North Dakota, 1986
Certification: Geriatric Medicine, Internal Medicine
2050 Pfingsten Rd #330, Glenview, 847-998-4100

Goldberg, Barry Richard (5 mentions)
U of California-Los Angeles, 1979 *Certification:* Internal Medicine
625 Roger Williams Ave #101, Highland Park, 847-433-3460

Gorbien, Martin John (8 mentions)
FMS-Mexico, 1983
1725 W Harrison St #955, Chicago, 312-942-7030

Lazar, Aaron Jack (4 mentions)
Rush U, 1982 *Certification:* Family Medicine, Geriatric Medicine
100 Spalding Dr #400, Naperville, 630-717-2646

Moss, Robert Jay (6 mentions)
U of Illinois, 1978
Certification: Family Medicine, Geriatric Medicine
1775 Ballard Rd, Park Ridge, 847-318-2500

Pomerantz, Rhoda Solomon (4 mentions)
Med Coll of Pennsylvania, 1963 *Certification:* Internal Medicine
2900 N Lake Shore Dr 12th Fl, Chicago, 773-665-3606

Sheehan, Myles Nicholas (8 mentions)
Dartmouth Coll, 1981
Certification: Geriatric Medicine, Internal Medicine
2160 S 1st Ave Bldg 120 #310, Maywood, 708-216-8887

Sier, Herbert Charles (7 mentions)
Virginia Commonwealth U, 1980
Certification: Geriatric Medicine, Internal Medicine
345 E Superior St 3rd Fl, Chicago, 312-238-6100

Hematology/Oncology

Barhamand, Fariborze B. (5 mentions)
FMS-India, 1972
Certification: Internal Medicine, Medical Oncology
100 Spalding Dr #110, Naperville, 630-369-1501
2622 83rd St, Darien, 630-985-1345

Baron, Joseph Mandel (6 mentions)
U of Chicago, 1962
Certification: Hematology, Internal Medicine, Medical Oncology
5758 S Maryland Ave, Chicago, 773-702-6149

Bitran, Jacob David (10 mentions)
U of Illinois, 1971
Certification: Hematology, Internal Medicine, Medical Oncology
1700 Luther Ln #2200, Park Ridge, 847-268-8200
7900 N Milwaukee Ave #16, Niles, 847-268-8200

Bonomi, Philip David (9 mentions)
U of Illinois, 1970
Certification: Internal Medicine, Medical Oncology
1725 W Harrison St, Chicago, 312-942-3312

Dragon, Leon H. (9 mentions)
U of Illinois, 1971
Certification: Internal Medicine, Medical Oncology
757 Park Ave W, Highland Park, 847-480-3800

Evrard, Marilyn Louise (4 mentions)
U of Illinois, 1978
Certification: Internal Medicine, Medical Oncology
1200 S York Rd #3280, Elmhurst, 630-941-8280

Gaynor, Ellen (5 mentions)
U of Wisconsin, 1978
Certification: Hematology, Internal Medicine, Medical Oncology
2160 S 1st Ave Bldg 112, Maywood, 708-327-3101
157 Marian Dr, Homer Glen, 708-327-3101

Goodell, William R. (5 mentions)
Wayne State U, 1986
Certification: Pediatric Hematology-Oncology, Pediatrics
1675 W Dempster St Yacktman Childrens Pavillion 2nd Fl,
   Park Ridge, 847-318-9330

Gordon, Leo I. (5 mentions)
U of Cincinnati, 1973
Certification: Hematology, Internal Medicine, Medical Oncology
675 N St Clair St #21-100, Chicago, 312-695-0990

Grad, Gary Irving (6 mentions)
U of Chicago, 1989
Certification: Internal Medicine, Medical Oncology
800 Biesterfield Rd #2, Elk Grove Village, 847-437-3312
3701 Algonquin Rd #900, Rolling Meadows, 847-870-4100

Gradishar, William John (4 mentions)
U of Illinois, 1982
Certification: Internal Medicine, Medical Oncology
676 N St Clair St #21-100, Chicago, 312-695-0990

Gregory, Stephanie Ann (8 mentions)
Med Coll of Pennsylvania, 1965
Certification: Hematology, Internal Medicine
1725 W Harrison St #855, Chicago, 312-563-2320

Hakimian, David (4 mentions)
U of Illinois, 1987
Certification: Hematology, Internal Medicine, Medical Oncology
8915 Golf Rd, Niles, 847-827-9060

Hannigan, James E., Jr. (4 mentions)
U of Chicago, 1981
Certification: Internal Medicine, Medical Oncology
1325 Memorial Dr, La Grange, 708-579-3418
4400 W 95th St #308, Oak Lawn, 708-346-9935

Hantel, Alexander (6 mentions)
U of Illinois, 1981
Certification: Internal Medicine, Medical Oncology
24600 W 127th St Bldg B #100, Plainfield, 630-527-3788
120 Spalding Dr #111, Naperville, 630-527-3788

Hoffman, Philip Charles (7 mentions)
Jefferson Med Coll, 1972
Certification: Hematology, Internal Medicine, Medical Oncology
5841 S Maryland Ave, Chicago, 773-702-6109
2800 W 95th St, Evergreen Park, 708-229-6001

Kaden, Bruce Richard (5 mentions)
U of Illinois, 1972
Certification: Hematology, Internal Medicine, Medical Oncology
8915 Golf Rd, Niles, 847-827-9060

Kaminer, Lynne Susan (12 mentions)
Washington U, 1982
Certification: Hematology, Internal Medicine, Medical Oncology
2650 Ridge Ave #800, Evanston, 847-570-2515
2100 Pfingsten Rd, Glenview, 847-657-5826

Klein, Leonard M. (7 mentions)
SUNY-Buffalo, 1975
Certification: Hematology, Internal Medicine, Medical Oncology
8915 Golf Rd, Niles, 847-827-9060

Kozloff, Mark Farrel (4 mentions)
U of Michigan, 1972 *Certification:* Internal Medicine
6701 159th St #1, Tinley Park, 708-444-2226
71 W 156th St #401, Harvey, 708-339-4800

Lestingi, Timothy Michael (4 mentions)
Ohio State U, 1988
Certification: Internal Medicine, Medical Oncology
1700 Luther Ln, Park Ridge, 847-268-8200
7900 N Milwaukee Ave #16-B, Niles, 847-268-8200

Micetich, Kenneth Craig (6 mentions)
Loyola U Chicago, 1974
Certification: Internal Medicine, Medical Oncology
2160 S 1st Ave Bldg 112, Maywood, 708-327-3144
157 Marian Dr, Homer Glen, 708-327-3144

Nand, Sucha (4 mentions)
FMS-India, 1971
Certification: Hematology, Internal Medicine, Medical Oncology
2160 S 1st Ave Bldg 112, Maywood, 708-327-3182

Patel, Jyoti Dinker (4 mentions)
Indiana U, 1996
Certification: Internal Medicine, Medical Oncology
676 N St Clair St #21-850, Chicago, 312-695-6180

Ramadurai, Jayanthi Raghu (4 mentions)
FMS-India, 1983
Certification: Hematology, Internal Medicine, Medical Oncology
4901 W 79th St #2/3, Burbank, 708-636-1177

Slivnick, David Joel (4 mentions)
U of Illinois, 1983
Certification: Hematology, Internal Medicine, Medical Oncology
1800 Hollister Dr #112, Libertyville, 847-367-6781

Stiff, Patrick Joseph (6 mentions)
Loyola U Chicago, 1975
Certification: Hematology, Internal Medicine, Medical Oncology
2160 S 1st Ave #255, Maywood, 708-327-3148

Tellez, Claudia (6 mentions)
U of Illinois, 1990 *Certification:* Hematology, Medical Oncology
676 N St Clair St #2140, Chicago, 312-664-5400

Tsarwhas, Dean George (4 mentions)
Northeastern Ohio U, 1987
Certification: Internal Medicine, Medical Oncology
1800 Hollister Dr #112, Libertyville, 847-367-6781
27750 W Route 22 #G-80, Barrington, 847-367-6781

Venugopal, Parameswaran (4 mentions)
FMS-India, 1976
1725 W Harrison St #809, Chicago, 312-563-2238

Wong, Alton C. T. (4 mentions)
Med Coll of Wisconsin, 1978
Certification: Hematology, Internal Medicine, Medical Oncology
5525 S Pulaski Rd, Chicago, 773-585-1955
2600 S Michigan Ave, Chicago, 312-567-2000

Infectious Disease

Andreoni, John Michael (7 mentions)
Loyola U Chicago, 1985
Certification: Infectious Disease, Internal Medicine
7804 W College Dr #1-NW, Palos Heights, 708-361-5778

Augustinsky, James Brian (7 mentions)
U of Chicago, 1985
Certification: Infectious Disease, Internal Medicine
636 Raymond Dr #204, Naperville, 630-548-4811

Citronberg, Robert J. (13 mentions)
U of Connecticut, 1989
Certification: Infectious Disease, Internal Medicine
7900 N Milwaukee Ave #231, Niles, 847-663-9400

Kerchberger, Vern H., Jr. (6 mentions)
Emory U, 1979
Certification: Infectious Disease, Internal Medicine
1300 E Central Rd #C, Arlington Heights, 847-255-5029

Semel, Jeffery David (7 mentions)
U of Chicago, 1973
Certification: Infectious Disease, Internal Medicine
185 N Milwaukee Ave #225, Lincolnshire, 847-733-5707
757 Park Ave W #2850, Highland Park, 847-657-5959
1000 Central St #800, Evanston, 847-657-5959

Sherman, Edward Mark (6 mentions)
Rosalind Franklin U, 1980
Certification: Infectious Disease, Internal Medicine
950 N York Rd #108, Hinsdale, 630-941-5265

Sokalski, Stephen J. (9 mentions)
Midwestern U, 1969
4440 W 95th St, Oak Lawn, 708-684-5676

Spear, Joel B. (6 mentions)
Northeastern Ohio U, 1982
Certification: Infectious Disease, Internal Medicine
2900 N Lake Shore Dr, Chicago, 773-665-3261

Trenholme, Gordon Mark (7 mentions)
Med Coll of Wisconsin, 1969
Certification: Infectious Disease, Internal Medicine
600 S Paulina St #140-143, Chicago, 312-942-5865

Waitley, David William (7 mentions)
Rosalind Franklin U, 1984
Certification: Infectious Disease, Internal Medicine
500 E Ogden Ave #C, Hinsdale, 630-654-4201

Weinstein, Robert Alan (8 mentions)
Cornell U, 1972
Certification: Infectious Disease, Internal Medicine
1901 W Harrison St, Chicago, 312-864-4589

Zar, Fred Arthur (7 mentions)
U of Illinois, 1979
Certification: Infectious Disease, Internal Medicine
840 S Wood St #725C, Chicago, 312-413-0312

Infertility

Confino, Edmond (4 mentions)
FMS-Israel, 1975 *Certification:* Obstetrics & Gynecology,
 Reproductive Endocrinology/Infertility
675 N St Clair St #14-200, Chicago, 312-695-7269

Davies, Susan Ann (4 mentions)
Rush U, 1990 *Certification:* Obstetrics & Gynecology,
 Reproductive Endocrinology/Infertility
4250 Dempster St, Skokie, 847-763-8850
999 Plaza Dr #630, Schaumburg, 847-763-8850

Jacobs, Laurence Alan (4 mentions)
Northwestern U, 1975 *Certification:* Obstetrics & Gynecology
135 N Arlington Heights Rd #195, Buffalo Grove, 847-215-8899
3703 W Lake Ave #106, Glenview, 847-998-8200
5911 Northwest Hwy #205, Crystal Lake, 815-356-7034

Kaplan, Brian R. (7 mentions)
FMS-South Africa, 1981 *Certification:* Obstetrics & Gynecology
900 N Kingsbury Rd #RW6, Chicago, 312-222-8230

Miller, Charles E. (12 mentions)
Northwestern U, 1977 *Certification:* Obstetrics & Gynecology
1900 E Golf Rd #L-125, Schaumburg, 847-593-1040
120 Osler Dr, Naperville, 630-428-2229

Molo, Mary Wood (7 mentions)
Southern Illinois U, 1982 *Certification:* Obstetrics &
 Gynecology, Reproductive Endocrinology/Infertility
1725 W Harrison St #408-E, Chicago, 312-997-2229

Niederberger, Craig S. (4 mentions)
U of Pittsburgh, 1986 *Certification:* Urology
900 N Michigan Ave #1420, Chicago, 312-440-5127

Rapisarda, John Joseph (5 mentions)
U of Michigan, 1985 *Certification:* Obstetrics & Gynecology
3703 W Lake St #106, Glenview, 847-998-8200
135 N Arlington Heights Rd #195, Buffalo Grove, 847-215-8899
2592 Grand Ave #208, Lindenhurst, 847-356-0483

Rinehart, John Scott (6 mentions)
St Louis U, 1978 *Certification:* Obstetrics & Gynecology,
 Reproductive Endocrinology/Infertility
2500 Ridge Ave #200, Evanston, 847-869-7777
25 N Winfield Rd #411, Winfield, 630-221-8131
3825 Highland Ave #2M, Downers Grove, 630-960-2570

Uhler, Meike Lian (4 mentions)
Tulane U, 1986 *Certification:* Obstetrics & Gynecology,
 Reproductive Endocrinology/Infertility
2056 Westings Ave #130, Naperville, 630-305-7576
1S224 Summit Ave #302, Oakbrook Terrace, 630-889-7900

Internal Medicine *(see note on page 9)*

Bresnahan, Timothy James (3 mentions)
Loyola U Chicago, 1974 *Certification:* Internal Medicine
183 Addison Ave, Elmhurst, 630-834-8450

Butter, John Earl (3 mentions)
Northwestern U, 1991 *Certification:* Internal Medicine
675 N St Clair St #18-200, Chicago, 312-695-8630

Carbone, Robert Anthony (3 mentions)
Loyola U Chicago, 1976 *Certification:* Internal Medicine
908 N Elm St #301, Hinsdale, 630-323-3540

Costas, Angelo Andy (6 mentions)
Loyola U Chicago, 1993 *Certification:* Internal Medicine
200 S Michigan Ave #805, Chicago, 312-922-3815

Davis, Andrew M. (3 mentions)
U of Chicago, 1980 *Certification:* Internal Medicine, Public
Health & General Preventive Medicine
5758 S Maryland Ave #3051, Chicago, 773-702-0240

De Angeles, Steven James (3 mentions)
Southern Illinois U, 1989 *Certification:* Internal Medicine
200 S Michigan Ave #830, Chicago, 312-922-2500

Delorenzo, Anthony William (3 mentions)
U of North Texas Coll of Osteopathic Med, 1992
6847 Kingery Hwy, Willowbrook, 630-655-9555

Dillon, Charles David (3 mentions)
Georgetown U, 1980 *Certification:* Internal Medicine
680 N Lake Shore Dr #118, Chicago, 312-503-6000

Djordjevic, Dragan (3 mentions)
Rush U, 1991 *Certification:* Internal Medicine
1725 W Harrison St #318, Chicago, 312-738-2966

Gallagher, Thomas Joseph (4 mentions)
U of Chicago, 1989 *Certification:* Internal Medicine
908 N Elm St #301, Hinsdale, 630-323-3540

Gawne, Stephen Ryan (3 mentions)
U of Illinois, 1983 *Certification:* Internal Medicine
2160 S 1st Ave, Maywood, 708-354-9250

Giger, Charles C. (3 mentions)
Loyola U Chicago, 1981 *Certification:* Internal Medicine
1200 S York Rd #3250, Elmhurst, 630-758-8885

Jaffe, Harry J. (3 mentions)
Georgetown U, 1971 *Certification:* Internal Medicine
1713 Central St, Evanston, 847-475-8888

Kanarek, David Allen (3 mentions)
Cornell U, 1977 *Certification:* Internal Medicine
4160 RFD #304, Long Grove, 847-634-2090

Kolbaba, Scott James (4 mentions)
U of Illinois, 1977 *Certification:* Internal Medicine
7 Blanchard Cir #106, Wheaton, 630-668-5985

Lewis, Gerald Howard (4 mentions)
U of Illinois, 1976 *Certification:* Internal Medicine
960 Rand Rd #205, Des Plaines, 847-298-0310

Martin, Gary Joseph (3 mentions)
U of Illinois, 1978
Certification: Cardiovascular Disease, Internal Medicine
675 N St Clair St #18-200, Chicago, 312-695-8630

Newberger, Todd Stuart (3 mentions)
Northwestern U, 1985 *Certification:* Internal Medicine
1713 Central St, Evanston, 847-475-1333

Nugent, Colleen M. (3 mentions)
Georgetown U, 1996 *Certification:* Internal Medicine
2501 Compass Rd #110, Glenview, 847-998-0010

O'Leary, Brian Michael (6 mentions)
Northwestern U, 1985 *Certification:* Internal Medicine
1020 E Ogden Ave #115, Naperville, 630-717-8707

Ringel, Paul Bernard (5 mentions)
Rush U, 1978 *Certification:* Internal Medicine
3000 N Halsted St #509, Chicago, 773-296-5090

Sankary, Edward Charles (3 mentions)
U of Texas-San Antonio, 1993 *Certification:* Internal Medicine
16621 107th Ct, Orland Park, 708-873-7350

Schraufnagel, Mary Ellen (3 mentions)
U of Illinois, 1978 *Certification:* Internal Medicine
7411 Lake St #L120, River Forest, 708-488-1919

Schwartz, Mindy Alyce (3 mentions)
Loyola U Chicago, 1982 *Certification:* Internal Medicine
5758 S Maryland Ave, Chicago, 773-702-6840

Stern, Scott David C. (3 mentions)
U of Chicago, 1984 *Certification:* Internal Medicine
5841 S Maryland Ave #3051, Chicago, 773-702-9460

Tosetti, Patrick Arthur (3 mentions)
U of Chicago, 1982 *Certification:* Internal Medicine
675 N St Clair St #18-200, Chicago, 312-695-8630

Trunsky, Jefferey Andrew (3 mentions)
Wayne State U, 1990 *Certification:* Internal Medicine
675 N St Clair St #18-200, Chicago, 312-695-8630

Tulley, John Edward (3 mentions)
U of Illinois, 1974 *Certification:* Internal Medicine
1801 W Taylor St #3A, Chicago, 312-355-1700

Weschler, Frank Joseph (3 mentions)
Tufts U, 1978 *Certification:* Internal Medicine
2501 Compass Rd #100, Glenview, 847-901-5200

Zimmanck, Robert Donald, Jr. (3 mentions)
U of Illinois, 1981 *Certification:* Internal Medicine
1775 Ballard Rd, Park Ridge, 847-318-9340

Nephrology

Arruda, Jose Antonio L. (7 mentions)
FMS-Brazil, 1967 *Certification:* Internal Medicine, Nephrology
1801 W Taylor St, Chicago, 312-996-6736

Berns, Arnold Steven (8 mentions)
Northwestern U, 1971
Certification: Internal Medicine, Nephrology
2277 W Howard St, Chicago, 773-508-0110

Bregman, Harold (9 mentions)
SUNY-Downstate Med Coll, 1974
Certification: Internal Medicine, Nephrology
8901 Golf Rd #203, Des Plaines, 847-294-5160

Coe, Fredric Lawrence (6 mentions)
U of Chicago, 1961 *Certification:* Internal Medicine
5841 S Maryland Ave #MC-5100, Chicago, 773-702-0125

Ghossein, Cybele (7 mentions)
Albert Einstein Coll of Med, 1990
Certification: Internal Medicine, Nephrology
675 N St Clair St #250, Chicago, 312-695-0596

Guglielmi, Kelly E. (7 mentions)
Med Coll of Wisconsin, 1990
Certification: Internal Medicine, Nephrology
3650 W 95th St, Evergreen Park, 708-422-7715
16605 S 107th Ct, Orland Park, 708-226-9860

Julka, Naresh Kumar (9 mentions)
FMS-India, 1969 *Certification:* Internal Medicine, Nephrology
3825 Highland Ave #4C, Downers Grove, 630-968-1595

Kniaz, Daniel (12 mentions)
Med Coll of Wisconsin, 1981
Certification: Internal Medicine, Nephrology
8901 Golf Rd #203, Des Plaines, 847-294-5160

Korbet, Stephen Michael (7 mentions)
Rush U, 1979 *Certification:* Internal Medicine, Nephrology
1426 W Washington Blvd, Chicago, 312-829-1424

Lash, James Phillip (5 mentions)
U of Chicago, 1981 *Certification:* Internal Medicine, Nephrology
820 S Wood St, Chicago, 312-996-7729

Miller, Kenneth (5 mentions)
Rosalind Franklin U, 1968
Certification: Pediatric Nephrology, Pediatrics
1480 Renaissance Dr #211, Park Ridge, 847-297-6374
1012 95th St #4, Naperville, 847-297-6374
4440 W 95th St, Oak Lawn, 847-297-6374

Nora, Nancy Ann (10 mentions)
FMS-Ireland, 1985 *Certification:* Internal Medicine, Nephrology
767 Park Ave W #260, Highland Park, 847-432-7222

Oyama, Joseph Hikaru (5 mentions)
U of Illinois, 1965 *Certification:* Internal Medicine, Nephrology
3650 W 95th St, Evergreen Park, 708-422-7715
16605 S 107th Ct, Orland Park, 708-226-9860

Paparello, James Joseph (8 mentions)
U of Connecticut, 1996
Certification: Internal Medicine, Nephrology
675 N St Clair St #18-250, Chicago, 312-695-0596

Rodby, Roger Alan (6 mentions)
U of Illinois, 1982 *Certification:* Internal Medicine, Nephrology
1426 W Washington Blvd, Chicago, 312-850-8434

Vertuno, Leonard Louis (5 mentions)
Northwestern U, 1964
Certification: Internal Medicine, Nephrology
2160 S 1st Ave B1-102 #3661, Maywood, 708-216-3306

Zikos, Demetrios H. (6 mentions)
FMS-Greece, 1977 *Certification:* Internal Medicine, Nephrology
3650 W 95th St, Evergreen Park, 708-422-7715
16605 S 107th Ct, Orland Park, 708-226-9860

Neurological Surgery

Batjer, Henry Huntington, III (13 mentions)
U of Texas-Southwestern, 1977
Certification: Neurological Surgery
675 N St Clair St #20-250, Chicago, 312-695-8143

Bauer, Jerry (6 mentions)
U of Illinois, 1974 *Certification:* Neurological Surgery
1875 Dempster St #605, Park Ridge, 847-698-1088

Bovis, George Kostas (8 mentions)
Northwestern U, 1993 *Certification:* Neurological Surgery
1875 Dempster St #605, Park Ridge, 847-698-1088

Cerullo, Leonard John (9 mentions)
Jefferson Med Coll, 1970 *Certification:* Neurological Surgery
4501 N Winchester Ave 2nd Fl, Chicago, 773-250-0400

Charbel, Fady Toufic (7 mentions)
FMS-Lebanon, 1984 *Certification:* Neurological Surgery
912 S Wood St #451N, Chicago, 312-996-4842

Ciric, Ivan S. (9 mentions)
FMS-Yugoslavia, 1958 *Certification:* Neurological Surgery
2650 Ridge Ave #4222, Evanston, 847-570-1440
1000 Central St #800, Evanston, 847-570-1440

Citow, Jonathan Stuart (9 mentions)
U of Illinois, 1992 *Certification:* Neurological Surgery
712 S Milwaukee Ave, Libertyville, 847-362-1848

Cozzens, Jeffrey Warren (7 mentions)
U of Illinois, 1978 *Certification:* Neurological Surgery
1000 Central St #800, Evanston, 847-570-1440
2650 Ridge Ave #4222, Evanston, 847-570-1440

Cybulski, George Raymond (6 mentions)
U of Illinois, 1980 *Certification:* Neurological Surgery
675 N St Clair St #20-25D, Chicago, 312-695-8143

Kazan, Robert Peter (10 mentions)
Loyola U Chicago, 1973 *Certification:* Neurological Surgery
20 E Ogden Ave, Hinsdale, 630-655-1229

Kranzler, Leonard Irwin (8 mentions)
Northwestern U, 1963 *Certification:* Neurological Surgery
3000 N Halsted St #701, Chicago, 773-296-6666

Origitano, Thomas Charles (11 mentions)
Loyola U Chicago, 1984 *Certification:* Neurological Surgery
2160 S 1st Ave Bldg 105 #1900, Maywood, 708-216-8920
140 E Loop Rd, Wheaton, 708-216-8920

Ruge, John Robert (20 mentions)
Northwestern U, 1983 *Certification:* Neurological Surgery
1875 W Dempster St #605, Park Ridge, 847-698-1088

Shea, John Francis (7 mentions)
St Louis U, 1972 *Certification:* Neurological Surgery
2160 S 1st Ave Bldg 150 #1900, Maywood, 708-216-3480

Neurology

Allen, Neil (6 mentions)
U of Illinois, 1965 *Certification:* Internal Medicine, Neurology
3545 Lake Ave #100, Wilmette, 847-251-1800
1535 Lake Cook Rd #601, Northbrook, 847-251-1800
71 Waukegan Rd #300, Lake Bluff, 847-251-1800

Bijari, Armita (4 mentions)
Rush U, 1989 *Certification:* Clinical Neurophysiology, Neurology
333 Chestnut St #102, Hinsdale, 630-986-8770

Biller, Jose (6 mentions)
FMS-Uruguay, 1974 *Certification:* Neurology, Vascular Neurology
2160 S 1st Ave #105-2700, Maywood, 708-216-2438

Burke, Allan Martin (9 mentions)
Columbia U, 1976 *Certification:* Neurology
233 E Erie St #500, Chicago, 312-944-0063

Di Santo, Kerry Therese (5 mentions)
Rush U, 1990 *Certification:* Neurology
333 Chestnut St #102, Hinsdale, 630-986-8770

Echiverri, Henry Zosimo C. (5 mentions)
FMS-Philippines, 1981 *Certification:* Neurology
3S517 Winfield Rd, Warrenville, 630-836-9121

Frank, Helge Gerhard (6 mentions)
Loyola U Chicago, 1972 *Certification:* Neurology
20 E Ogden Ave, Hinsdale, 630-325-8730
800 Biesterfield Rd, Elk Grove Village, 630-325-8730

Gorelick, Philip Benj (6 mentions)
Loyola U Chicago, 1977
Certification: Neurology, Vascular Neurology
912 S Wood St #855, Chicago, 312-996-1757

Heller, Scott Lewis (7 mentions)
U of Illinois, 1980 *Certification:* Neurology
211 E Chicago Ave #740, Chicago, 312-943-1340

Hier, Daniel Barnet (5 mentions)
Harvard U, 1973 *Certification:* Neurology
1801 W Taylor St, Chicago, 312-355-0510

Ho, Sam Ung (5 mentions)
Northwestern U, 1973 *Certification:* Neurology
221 E Huron St #12-202, Chicago, 312-787-9499

Larsen, David Scott (4 mentions)
Rush U, 1992 *Certification:* Neurology
1220 Hobson Rd #244, Naperville, 630-357-9308

Lewis, Steven Lester (5 mentions)
Stanford U, 1983 *Certification:* Neurology, Vascular Neurology
1725 W Harrison St #1118, Chicago, 312-942-5936

Merchut, Michael P. (4 mentions)
Loyola U Chicago, 1979 *Certification:* Clinical
   Neurophysiology, Internal Medicine, Neurology
2160 S 1st Ave Bldg 102 #2700, Maywood, 708-216-4258

Metrick, Scott Alan (6 mentions)
U of Illinois, 1977
Certification: Clinical Neurophysiology, Neurology
900 N Westmoreland Rd #220, Lake Forest, 847-482-0300

Paleologos, Nina Angeline (4 mentions)
Rush U, 1985 *Certification:* Neurology
2650 Ridge Ave #309, Evanston, 847-570-2570

Reiss, Merrell Dee (4 mentions)
U of Oklahoma, 1955
Certification: Neurology, Psychiatry, Vascular Neurology
800 Biesterfield Rd #2009, Elk Grove Village, 847-952-9140

Rubinstein, Wayne Abraham (11 mentions)
U of Chicago, 1986
Certification: Clinical Neurophysiology, Neurology, Sleep Medicine
9301 Golf Rd #303, Des Plaines, 847-298-4088
1875 W Dempster St #B06, Park Ridge, 847-723-7024

Schneck, Michael Joel (4 mentions)
Cornell U, 1987 *Certification:* Neurology, Vascular Neurology
2160 S 1st Ave Bldg 105 #2700, Maywood, 708-216-3407

Schwartz, Michael Robert (6 mentions)
New York Med Coll, 1971 *Certification:* Neurology
11824 Southwest Hwy #100, Palos Heights, 708-361-0222

Shah, Nishant S. (5 mentions)
FMS-India, 1990 *Certification:* Neurology with Special
   Qualifications in Child Neurology, Pediatrics
1675 Dempster St 3rd Fl, Park Ridge, 847-318-9330

Vick, Nicholas Alan (9 mentions)
U of Chicago, 1965 *Certification:* Neurology
2650 Ridge Ave #309, Evanston, 847-570-2570

Wichter, Melvin David (6 mentions)
New York Med Coll, 1971 *Certification:* Neurology
11824 Southwest Hwy #100, Palos Heights, 708-361-0222

Wolf, Steven Bruce (4 mentions)
Rosalind Franklin U, 1977 *Certification:* Neurology
9301 Golf Rd #303, Des Plaines, 847-298-4088

Obstetrics/Gynecology

Axelrod, Joseph Robert (3 mentions)
Rush U, 1995 *Certification:* Obstetrics & Gynecology
4225 W 95th St, Oak Lawn, 708-423-2300
18210 S La Grange Rd #206, Tinley Park, 708-478-4872

Cardone, Joan Therese (4 mentions)
U of Illinois, 1991 *Certification:* Obstetrics & Gynecology
545 Plainfield Rd #C, Willowbrook, 630-654-2229

Cislak, Carol Margaret (6 mentions)
Northwestern U, 1983 *Certification:* Obstetrics & Gynecology
2500 Ridge Ave #311, Evanston, 847-869-5800
135 N Arlington Heights Rd #101, Buffalo Grove, 847-537-5200

Elam, Gloria L. (3 mentions)
Meharry Med Coll, 1986 *Certification:* Obstetrics & Gynecology
1801 W Taylor St, Chicago, 312-413-7500

Flosi, Sam F. (3 mentions)
Midwestern U, 1987 *Certification:* Obstetrics & Gynecology
16609 S 107th Ct, Orland Park, 708-645-8080

Gallo, Martin Robert (3 mentions)
Northwestern U, 1986 *Certification:* Obstetrics & Gynecology
3743 Highland Ave #1002, Downers Grove, 630-435-6107

Gianopoulos, John George (9 mentions)
Loyola U Chicago, 1977
Certification: Maternal-Fetal Medicine, Obstetrics & Gynecology
2160 S 1st Ave, Maywood, 708-216-4033

Hammond, Cassing (3 mentions)
U of Missouri-Kansas City, 1988
Certification: Obstetrics & Gynecology
675 N St Clair St #14-200, Chicago, 312-695-7382
680 N Lakeshore Dr #1317, Chicago, 312-926-7700

Hobbs, John (5 mentions)
U of Minnesota, 1975 *Certification:* Obstetrics & Gynecology
201 E Huron St #11-105, Chicago, 312-266-2229

Holt, Linda Hughey (3 mentions)
U of Chicago, 1977 *Certification:* Obstetrics & Gynecology
4905 Old Orchard Shopping Ctr, Skokie, 847-673-3130

Jenks, James David (3 mentions)
Northwestern U, 1979 *Certification:* Obstetrics & Gynecology
3825 Highland Ave #3-K, Downers Grove, 630-968-2144

Johnson, Janice Lynn (4 mentions)
U of Illinois, 1984 *Certification:* Obstetrics & Gynecology
800 Austin St #354, Evanston, 847-491-6890
64 Old Orchard Ctr, Skokie, 847-673-1011

Kamel, Elena Mara (4 mentions)
Cornell U, 1984 *Certification:* Obstetrics & Gynecology
737 N Michigan Ave #600, Chicago, 312-440-3810
1535 Lake Cook Rd #503, Northbrook, 847-291-3999

Kelly, Virginia (3 mentions)
Certification: Obstetrics & Gynecology
3825 Highland Ave #3-K, Downers Grove, 630-968-2144

Kilpatrick, Sarah Jestin (5 mentions)
Tulane U, 1985
Certification: Maternal-Fetal Medicine, Obstetrics & Gynecology
1801 W Taylor St #4C, Chicago, 312-996-7006

Kooperman, Steven A. (3 mentions)
Rush U, 1981 *Certification:* Obstetrics & Gynecology
880 W Central Rd #6200, Arlington Heights, 847-483-0350
1630 W Central Rd, Arlington Heights, 847-394-3553

Levy, Richard James (3 mentions)
Northwestern U, 1982 *Certification:* Obstetrics & Gynecology
121 S Wilke Rd #515, Arlington Heights, 847-577-2229

McInerney, John V. (3 mentions)
Midwestern U, 1983
11824 Southwest Hwy #200, Palos Heights, 708-923-1919

Moses, Scott David (4 mentions)
U of Illinois, 1993 *Certification:* Obstetrics & Gynecology
680 N Lake Shore Dr #810, Chicago, 312-926-8811

Nye, Elizabeth Robin (4 mentions)
Rush U, 1985 *Certification:* Obstetrics & Gynecology
625 N Michigan Ave #210, Chicago, 312-670-2530
1725 W Harrison St #845, Chicago, 312-942-6477

Potkul, Ronald Keith (4 mentions)
U of Chicago, 1981
Certification: Gynecologic Oncology, Obstetrics & Gynecology
2160 S 1st Ave, Maywood, 708-327-3314

Saleh, Hani Jacob (4 mentions)
FMS-Mexico, 1984 *Certification:* Obstetrics & Gynecology
2550 Compass Rd #J, Glenview, 847-998-9600
2500 Ridge Ave #303, Evanston, 847-475-1224

Strassner, Howard Taft (3 mentions)
U of Chicago, 1974
Certification: Maternal-Fetal Medicine, Obstetrics & Gynecology
1725 W Harrison St, Chicago, 312-997-2229

Streicher, Lauren Francia (3 mentions)
U of Illinois, 1982 *Certification:* Obstetrics & Gynecology
680 N Lake Shore Dr #117, Chicago, 312-654-1166

Tan, Merita R. (3 mentions)
Rosalind Franklin U, 1989 *Certification:* Obstetrics & Gynecology
737 N Michigan Ave #950, Chicago, 312-751-7515

Tong, Yam-Shun (3 mentions)
Midwestern U, 1987
1 Erie Ct #6040, Oak Park, 708-386-1301

Warner, Susan Lynn (3 mentions)
Med Coll of Ohio, 1980 *Certification:* Obstetrics & Gynecology
135 N Arlington Heights, Buffalo Grove, 847-864-1200
1000 Central St #752, Evanston, 847-864-1200

Weeks, Peter John (8 mentions)
Rush U, 1984 *Certification:* Obstetrics & Gynecology
231 S Gary Ave #114, Bloomingdale, 630-893-8585
7 Blanchard Cir #102, Wheaton, 630-893-8585
120 Spalding Dr #309, Naperville, 630-893-8585
2940 Rollingbridge Rd #300, Naperville, 630-893-8585

Ophthalmology

Azar, Demetri (3 mentions)
Certification: Ophthalmology
1855 W Taylor St, Chicago, 312-996-4356
30 N Michigan Ave, Chicago, 312-996-4356

Berman, Andrew Alan (3 mentions)
Loyola U Chicago, 1981 *Certification:* Ophthalmology
9630 Kenton Ave, Skokie, 847-677-1631
1971 2nd St #500, Highland Park, 847-433-5888

Colis, Minou W. (3 mentions)
Boston U, 1981 *Certification:* Ophthalmology
2440 Ravine Way #600, Glenview, 847-724-9400

Cronin, Cathleen Mary (3 mentions)
Loyola U Chicago, 1978 *Certification:* Ophthalmology
1200 S York Rd, Elmhurst, 630-941-2625

Curnyn, Kimberlee Marie (4 mentions)
U of Illinois, 1989 *Certification:* Ophthalmology
800 Biesterfield Rd #710, Elk Grove Village, 847-253-4040
1100 W Central Rd #205, Arlington Heights, 847-253-4040
1855 W Taylor St #278, Chicago, 847-253-4040

Dangles, George John (3 mentions)
U of Illinois, 1978 *Certification:* Ophthalmology
4340 W 95th St #301, Oak Lawn, 708-499-3100

Deutsch, Thomas Alan (8 mentions)
Rush U, 1979 *Certification:* Ophthalmology
1725 W Harrison St #918, Chicago, 312-942-2734

Epstein, Randy Jay (3 mentions)
Rush U, 1980 *Certification:* Ophthalmology
1585 N Barrington Rd #502, Hoffman Estates, 847-882-5900
1725 W Harrison St #928, Chicago, 312-942-5300
806 Central Ave #300, Highland Park, 847-432-6010

Foody, Robert Joseph (3 mentions)
Loyola U Chicago, 1984 *Certification:* Ophthalmology
2020 Ogden Ave #165, Aurora, 630-897-5104
1300 N Highland Ave #1, Aurora, 630-897-5104

Greenberg, Daniel Right (4 mentions)
U of Illinois, 1984 *Certification:* Ophthalmology
5140 N California Ave #565, Chicago, 773-271-3139
800 Austin St #256, Evanston, 847-492-8434
7447 W Talcott Ave #300, Chicago, 773-631-0062

Gupta, Balaji (3 mentions)
Northwestern U, 1988 *Certification:* Ophthalmology
2602 W 83rd St, Darien, 630-495-2220
1200 S York Rd #3100, Elmhurst, 630-782-6222
2500 S Highland Ave #110, Lombard, 630-495-2220

Hanlon, John Patrick, Jr. (4 mentions)
U of Illinois, 1983 *Certification:* Ophthalmology
2850 W 95th St #401, Evergreen Park, 708-499-5500

Herst, Barry S. (3 mentions)
Loyola U Chicago, 1977 *Certification:* Ophthalmology
2800 N Sheridan Rd #103, Chicago, 773-975-4300
4905 Old Orchard Ctr #430, Skokie, 847-674-8400

Hirshman, Marshall (4 mentions)
U of Illinois, 1961 *Certification:* Ophthalmology
8901 Golf Rd #200, Des Plaines, 847-824-3127

Jay, Walter Michael (6 mentions)
U of Chicago, 1976 *Certification:* Ophthalmology
2160 S 1st Ave, Maywood, 708-216-8563
9608 S Roberts Rd, Hickory Hill, 708-233-5333

Kaplan, Bruce Howard (4 mentions)
Loyola U Chicago, 1989 *Certification:* Ophthalmology
444 N Northwest Hwy #360, Park Ridge, 847-823-2140

Kraff, Colman Ross (3 mentions)
Rush U, 1985 *Certification:* Ophthalmology
25 E Washington St #606, Chicago, 312-444-1111

Lissner, William (3 mentions)
Northwestern U, 1969 *Certification:* Ophthalmology
25 E Washington St #606, Chicago, 312-444-1111

Lyon, Alice Thayer (3 mentions)
U of Chicago, 1987 *Certification:* Ophthalmology
675 N St Clair St #15-150, Chicago, 312-695-8150

Macsai-Kaplan, Marian S. (3 mentions)
Rush U, 1984
2050 Pfingsten Rd #220, Glenview, 847-657-1860

McLachlan, Daniel Lawrence (3 mentions)
Northwestern U, 1974 *Certification:* Ophthalmology
1001 Ogden Ave, Downers Grove, 630-963-3937

Mittelman, David (4 mentions)
U of Illinois, 1969 *Certification:* Ophthalmology
1875 W Dempster St #610, Park Ridge, 847-292-2020

Mizen, Thomas Robert (3 mentions)
Rosalind Franklin U, 1980 *Certification:* Ophthalmology
1725 W Harrison St #928, Chicago, 312-942-3500
6187 S Archer Ave, Chicago, 773-581-2000

Mono, Jeffrey Alan (3 mentions)
U of Michigan, 1980 *Certification:* Ophthalmology
8901 Golf Rd #200, Des Plaines, 847-824-3127

Packo, Kirk Henry (5 mentions)
St Louis U, 1979 *Certification:* Ophthalmology
1725 W Harrison St #915, Chicago, 312-942-2117
71 W 156th St #400, Harvey, 708-596-8710

Palmer, David Joshua (3 mentions)
U of Chicago, 1980 *Certification:* Ophthalmology
111 N Wabash Ave #1609, Chicago, 312-855-1550
3633 W Lake Ave #301, Glenview, 847-901-0333

Panton, Peter John (4 mentions)
Brown U, 1982 *Certification:* Ophthalmology
7740 W North Ave, Elmwood Park, 708-452-7200

Rubenstein, Jonathan B. (4 mentions)
Rush U, 1981 *Certification:* Ophthalmology
9711 N Skokie Blvd #C, Skokie, 847-677-8989
1725 W Harrison St #918, Chicago, 312-942-2734

Springer, David Scott (4 mentions)
U of Cincinnati, 1983 *Certification:* Ophthalmology
1 Erie Ct #6140, Oak Park, 708-848-2400
7411 Lake St #1140, River Forest, 708-488-1900

Stein, Robert M. (3 mentions)
Rosalind Franklin U, 1976 *Certification:* Ophthalmology
9711 N Skokie Blvd #C, Skokie, 847-677-8989
1725 W Harrison St #918, Chicago, 312-942-2734

Sugar, Joel (7 mentions)
U of Michigan, 1969 *Certification:* Ophthalmology
1855 W Taylor St #3164, Chicago, 312-996-8937

Ticho, Benjamin Hendrik (4 mentions)
U of Michigan, 1987 *Certification:* Ophthalmology
10436 Southwest Hwy #101, Chicago Ridge, 708-423-4070
600 Ravinia Pl, Orland Park, 708-873-0088

Tsipursky, Svetlana (3 mentions)
FMS-Russia, 1974 *Certification:* Ophthalmology
2640 Golf Rd #120, Glenview, 847-724-0101

Wolin, Lawrence David (4 mentions)
Loyola U Chicago, 1978 *Certification:* Ophthalmology
1602 W Central Rd, Arlington Heights, 847-255-3515

Wyse, Tamara Buchmann (5 mentions)
U of Illinois, 1991 *Certification:* Ophthalmology
4709 Golf Rd, Skokie, 847-328-2020

Orthopedics

Asselmeier, Marc Alan (3 mentions)
U of Illinois, 1986 *Certification:* Orthopaedic Surgery
100 Spalding Dr #300, Naperville, 630-717-2626
430 Pennsylvania Ave #240, Glen Ellyn, 630-790-1872

Bach, Bernard R., Jr. (4 mentions)
U of Cincinnati, 1979 *Certification:* Orthopaedic Surgery
1725 W Harrison St #1063, Chicago, 312-243-4244
800 S Wells St, Chicago, 312-432-2353

Berger, Richard Arlen (4 mentions)
Tufts U, 1989 *Certification:* Orthopaedic Surgery
1725 W Harrison St #1063, Chicago, 312-243-4244
800 S Wells St, Chicago, 312-243-4244

Bowen, Mark Kevin (4 mentions)
Cornell U, 1985 *Certification:* Orthopaedic Surgery
680 N Lake Shore Dr #1028, Chicago, 312-664-6848
2501 Compass Rd #125, Glenview, 847-901-5268

Brackett, E. Boone, III (5 mentions)
Baylor U, 1961 *Certification:* Orthopaedic Surgery
1125 Westgate St, Oak Park, 708-848-7700

Bresch, James Richard (4 mentions)
Loyola U Chicago, 1989 *Certification:* Orthopaedic Surgery
1009 W Hwy 22 #100, Fox River Grove, 847-842-9366
8901 Golf Rd #300, Des Plaines, 847-824-3198

Breslow, Marc Jason (3 mentions)
Rush U, 1995 *Certification:* Orthopaedic Surgery
150 N River Rd #100, Des Plaines, 847-375-3000
9000 Waukegan Rd #200, Morton Grove, 847-375-3000

Bush-Joseph, Charles (10 mentions)
U of Michigan, 1983
Certification: Orthopaedic Sports Medicine, Orthopaedic Surgery
1725 W Harrison St #1063, Chicago, 312-243-4244
800 S Wells St, Chicago, 312-431-3400
2450 S Wolf Rd 2nd Fl, Westchester, 708-236-2750

Daley, Robert Joseph (5 mentions)
Loyola U Chicago, 1982 *Certification:* Orthopaedic Surgery
420 Nelson Rd, New Lenox, 815-462-3474
550 W Ogden Ave, Hinsdale, 630-323-6116
951 Essington Rd, Joliet, 815-744-4551

Firlit, George Stephen (3 mentions)
Loyola U Chicago, 1977 *Certification:* Orthopaedic Surgery
9301 Golf Rd #101, Des Plaines, 847-296-0303

Ghanayem, Alexander John (3 mentions)
Northwestern U, 1989 *Certification:* Orthopaedic Surgery
2160 S 1st Ave, Maywood, 708-216-3475
7511 Lamont Rd, Darien, 708-216-3834

Goldstein, Wayne M. (8 mentions)
U of Illinois, 1978 *Certification:* Orthopaedic Surgery
9000 Waukegan Rd #200, Morton Grove, 847-375-3000

Haskell, Saul Simon (3 mentions)
Vanderbilt U, 1955 *Certification:* Orthopaedic Surgery
205 W Randolph St, Chicago, 312-920-9804
7126 N Lincoln Ave, Lincolnwood, 847-676-5979

Holmes, George B., Jr. (3 mentions)
Yale U, 1980 *Certification:* Orthopaedic Surgery
800 S Wells St #M30, Chicago, 312-431-3400
610 S Maple Ave #1400, Oak Park, 708-383-0770
25 N Winfield Rd, Winfield, 312-431-3400

Kalainov, David Mark (3 mentions)
Johns Hopkins U, 1991
Certification: Orthopaedic Surgery, Surgery of the Hand
737 N Michigan Ave #700, Chicago, 312-337-6960

Kramer, Andrea S. (5 mentions)
Temple U, 1993 *Certification:* Orthopaedic Surgery
9000 Waukegan Rd #200, Morton Grove, 847-375-3000
4400 W 95th St, Oak Lawn, 847-375-3000
1200 Westmoreland Rd, Lake Forest, 847-375-3000
150 N River Rd, Des Plaines, 847-375-3000

Kudrna, James Charles (6 mentions)
Northwestern U, 1976 *Certification:* Orthopaedic Surgery
2401 Ravine Way #200, Glenview, 847-998-5680

Light, Terry Richard (5 mentions)
Rosalind Franklin U, 1973
Certification: Orthopaedic Surgery, Surgery of the Hand
2160 S 1st Ave, Maywood, 708-216-3280
1S260 Summit Ave, Oakbrook Terrace, 630-953-6600

Luke, Kevin Wesley (3 mentions)
Rush U, 1984 *Certification:* Orthopaedic Surgery
7600 W College Dr #3, Palos Heights, 708-361-0600

Mardjetko, Steven Michael (3 mentions)
U of Illinois, 1982 *Certification:* Orthopaedic Surgery
9000 Waukegan Rd #200, Morton Grove, 847-375-3000

Mash, Steven Jay (3 mentions)
Rosalind Franklin U, 1973 *Certification:* Orthopaedic Surgery
4115 Fairview Ave, Downers Grove, 630-968-1881
15900 W 127th St #111, Lemont, 630-243-7385

Nuber, Gordon William (7 mentions)
Wayne State U, 1978 *Certification:* Orthopaedic Surgery
680 N Lake Shore Dr #1028, Chicago, 312-664-6848

Palutsis, Gregory Raymond (5 mentions)
Loyola U Chicago, 1981 *Certification:* Orthopaedic Surgery
1144 Wilmette Ave, Wilmette, 847-998-5680
2401 Ravine Way #200, Glenview, 847-998-5680
2350 Ravine Way #600, Glenview, 847-998-5680

Peabody, Terrance Danl (5 mentions)
U of California-Irvine, 1985 *Certification:* Orthopaedic Surgery
5758 S Maryland Ave #4B, Chicago, 773-702-3442

Prinz, Paul Terry (4 mentions)
U of Chicago, 1988
Certification: Orthopaedic Surgery, Surgery of the Hand
348 Sherwood Ct, La Grange, 708-352-8975
675 W North Ave #607, Melrose Park, 708-681-7809

Raab, David Jerome (4 mentions)
Northwestern U, 1985 *Certification:* Orthopaedic Surgery
9000 Waukegan Rd #200, Morton Grove, 847-375-3000

Rosenberg, Aaron Glen (4 mentions)
Albany Med Coll, 1978 *Certification:* Orthopaedic Surgery
1725 W Harrison St #1063, Chicago, 312-243-4244

Schafer, Michael F. (4 mentions)
U of Iowa, 1967 *Certification:* Orthopaedic Surgery
675 N St Clair St #17-100, Chicago, 312-695-6800

Schiffman, Kenneth Lewis (4 mentions)
U of South Florida, 1981
Certification: Orthopaedic Surgery, Surgery of the Hand
550 W Ogden St, Hinsdale, 630-323-6116
2940 Rollingridge Rd #102, Naperville, 630-579-6500

Simon, Michael A. (4 mentions)
U of Michigan, 1967 *Certification:* Orthopaedic Surgery
5758 S Maryland Ave #4B, Chicago, 773-702-3442

Smith, David Joseph (3 mentions)
U of Chicago, 1974 *Certification:* Orthopaedic Surgery
5540 W 111th St, Oak Lawn, 708-423-8440
19550 Governors Hwy, Flossmoor, 708-794-2900

Sonnenberg, John David (3 mentions)
U of Illinois, 1976 *Certification:* Orthopaedic Surgery
2850 Wabash Ave #100, Chicago, 312-842-4600
8735 S Merrion Ln, Hometown, 708-425-1150
9717 Western Ave, Chicago, 713-239-5495

Stover, Michael David (4 mentions)
U of Iowa, 1990 *Certification:* Orthopaedic Surgery
2160 S 1st Ave #1700, Maywood, 708-216-8563
1 S 260 Summit Ave, Oakbrook, 708-216-8563

Stulberg, S. David (4 mentions)
U of Michigan, 1969 *Certification:* Orthopaedic Surgery
680 N Lake Shore Dr #1028, Chicago, 312-664-6848

Tonino, Pietro M. (4 mentions)
Northwestern U, 1981 *Certification:* Orthopaedic Surgery
2160 S 1st Ave, Maywood, 708-216-8730

Tu, Kevin Chingyun (3 mentions)
Loyola U Chicago, 1998 *Certification:* Orthopaedic Surgery
1200 S York Rd #4190, Elmhurst, 630-782-1174
850 Biesterfield Rd #2011, Elk Grove Village, 847-439-2314

Wardell, Steven Robert (3 mentions)
U of Illinois, 1990 *Certification:* Orthopaedic Surgery
7600 W College Dr #3, Palos Heights, 708-361-0600

Otorhinolaryngology

Bulger, Richard Francis (4 mentions)
U of Illinois, 1967 *Certification:* Otolaryngology
950 N York Rd #109, Hinsdale, 630-654-1391
215 Remington Blvd #L, Bolingbrook, 630-759-0065

Caldarelli, David Donald (8 mentions)
U of Illinois, 1965 *Certification:* Otolaryngology
1725 W Harrison St #308, Chicago, 312-733-4341

Conley, David Bertram, Jr. (5 mentions)
U of Chicago, 1989 *Certification:* Otolaryngology
675 N St Clair St #15-200, Chicago, 312-695-8182

Delicata, Dino Sandro (4 mentions)
Rush U, 1975 *Certification:* Otolaryngology
1034 Warren Ave, Downers Grove, 630-960-5310

Donzelli, Joseph J., III (7 mentions)
Rosalind Franklin U, 1993 *Certification:* Otolaryngology
1247 Rickert Dr #200, Naperville, 630-420-2323

Doshi, Salil Vinod (4 mentions)
U of Pittsburgh, 1991 *Certification:* Otolaryngology
1S450 Summit Ave #390, Oakbrook Terrace, 630-792-9300
1111 Superior St #411, Melrose Park, 708-345-5549

Farrell, Brian Patrick (7 mentions)
Loyola U Chicago, 1981 *Certification:* Otolaryngology
2850 W 95th St #403, Evergreen Park, 708-229-5254
16001 108th Ave, Orland Park, 708-460-0007

Friedman, Michael (5 mentions)
U of Illinois, 1972 *Certification:* Otolaryngology
30 N Michigan Ave #1107, Chicago, 312-236-3642
3000 N Halsted St #401, Chicago, 773-296-7040

Gerber, Mark Evan (6 mentions)
Loyola U Chicago, 1989 *Certification:* Otolaryngology
2150 Pfingsten Rd, Glenview, 847-486-6550
100 Central St, Evanston, 847-570-1360

Leonetti, John Patrick (6 mentions)
Loyola U Chicago, 1982 *Certification:* Otolaryngology
2160 S 1st Ave Bldg 105, Maywood, 708-216-3664
140 E Loop Rd, Wheaton, 708-216-3659

Marra, Silvio (5 mentions)
U of Illinois, 1991 *Certification:* Otolaryngology
16001 S 108th Ave, Orland Park, 708-460-0007
2850 W 95th St #403, Evergreen Park, 708-460-0007

Mhoon, Ernest Edward, Jr. (6 mentions)
U of Chicago, 1973 *Certification:* Otolaryngology
5758 S Maryland Ave #4-H, Chicago, 773-702-6143

Miller, Robert Paul (7 mentions)
Loyola U Chicago, 1974 *Certification:* Otolaryngology
8780 W Golf Rd #200, Niles, 847-674-5585
64 Old Orchard Ctr #630, Skokie, 847-674-5585
767 Park Ave W #B-500, Highland Park, 847-674-5585
1900 Hollister Dr #220, Libertyville, 847-674-5585

Mishell, Joseph Hirsh (4 mentions)
U of Illinois, 1985 *Certification:* Otolaryngology
1160 Park Ave W #4N, Highland Park, 847-433-5555
4160 Robert P Coffin Rd #103, Long Grove, 847-913-0005

Nielsen, Thomas John (6 mentions)
Rush U, 1984 *Certification:* Otolaryngology
1725 W Harrison St #938, Chicago, 312-942-2175
610 S Maple Ave #3700, Oak Park, 708-660-6430

Pelzer, Harold (5 mentions)
Northwestern U, 1979 *Certification:* Otolaryngology
675 N St Clair St #15-200, Chicago, 312-695-8182

Petruzzelli, Guy Joseph (9 mentions)
Rush U, 1987 *Certification:* Otolaryngology
1725 W Harrison St #218, Chicago, 312-942-6100

Pollak, Alan Charles (4 mentions)
Rush U, 1988 *Certification:* Otolaryngology
9150 N Crawford Ave #206, Skokie, 847-679-1605
2900 N Lake Shore Dr, Chicago, 847-679-1605
4640 N Marine Dr, Chicago, 847-679-1605

Pritikin, Jordan Bruce (6 mentions)
Rush U, 1990 *Certification:* Otolaryngology
111 W Washington St #903, Chicago, 312-372-9355

Rejowski, James Edward (6 mentions)
Rush U, 1978 *Certification:* Otolaryngology
950 N York Rd #109, Hinsdale, 630-654-1391
215 Remington Blvd #L, Bolingbrook, 630-759-0065

Schonberg, Jeffrey P. (7 mentions)
U of Cincinnati, 1982 *Certification:* Otolaryngology
3633 W Lake Ave #300, Glenview, 847-328-4141
1000 Central St #741, Evanston, 847-328-4141
9700 Kenton Ave #403, Skokie, 847-328-4141

Soltes, Steven Francis (7 mentions)
Loyola U Chicago, 1977 *Certification:* Otolaryngology
4400 W 95th St #304, Oak Lawn, 708-422-0500

Stankiewicz, James Adam (5 mentions)
U of Chicago, 1974 *Certification:* Otolaryngology
2160 S 1st Ave Bldg 105 #1870, Maywood, 708-216-9637

Stenson, Kerstin Marie (5 mentions)
Rosalind Franklin U, 1988 *Certification:* Otolaryngology
5841 S Maryland Ave, Chicago, 773-702-6690

Tojo, David Paul (14 mentions)
U of Cincinnati, 1987 *Certification:* Otolaryngology
1875 W Dempster St #301, Park Ridge, 847-685-1000

Walker, Regina Paloyan (4 mentions)
Northwestern U, 1986
Certification: Otolaryngology, Sleep Medicine
333 Chestnut St #L-03, Hinsdale, 630-655-0722

Walner, David Linden Jay (6 mentions)
Rosalind Franklin U, 1990 *Certification:* Otolaryngology
8780 W Golf Rd #200, Niles, 847-674-5585
64 Old Orchard Ctr #630, Skokie, 847-674-5585
767 Park Ave W #B-500, Highland Park, 847-674-5585
1900 Hollister Dr #220, Libertyville, 847-674-5585
1675 Dempster St, Park Ridge, 847-674-5585

Yeh, Stephen (4 mentions)
Northwestern U, 1971 *Certification:* Otolaryngology
2150 Pfingsten Rd #2270, Glenview, 847-998-0470
1000 Central St #725, Evanston, 847-492-8800

Pain Medicine

Barkin, Robert (3 mentions)
1725 W Harrison St Bldg 3 #550, Chicago, 312-942-6631

Belavic, Andrew M., Jr. (3 mentions)
FMS-Dominica, 1986 *Certification:* Anesthesiology
1200 S York Rd 1st Fl, Elmhurst, 630-782-7836

Benzon, Honorio T. (3 mentions)
FMS-Philippines, 1971
Certification: Anesthesiology, Pain Medicine
251 E Huron St #F5704, Chicago, 312-926-2000

Buvanendran, Asokumar (3 mentions)
FMS-Nigeria, 1989 *Certification:* Anesthesiology, Pain Medicine
1725 W Harrison St Bldg 3 #550, Chicago, 312-942-6631

Gilbert, Hugh Charles (3 mentions)
Ohio State U, 1969 *Certification:* Anesthesiology, Pain Medicine
2650 Ridge Ave #3905, Evanston, 847-570-2287

Goodman, Ira Jeffrey (3 mentions)
Rush U, 1983 *Certification:* Anesthesiology, Pain Medicine
2350 Ravine Way #600, Glenview, 630-371-9980
7055 Highgrove Blvd #100, Burr Ridge, 630-371-9980

Jain, Neeraj (3 mentions)
Northeastern Ohio U, 1988
Certification: Anesthesiology, Pain Medicine
908 N Elm St #109, Hinsdale, 630-985-7246
9550 W 167th St, Orland Park, 630-985-7246
5540 W 111th St, Oak Lawn, 708-403-4443

Koehn, Gary Lee (4 mentions)
Rush U, 1983 *Certification:* Anesthesiology, Pain Medicine
5201 Willow Springs Rd #120, La Grange, 630-734-1038
1100 E Norris Dr, Ottawa, 630-734-1038
150 W High St, Morris, 630-734-1038

Kurzydlowski, Henry S. (6 mentions)
Rosalind Franklin U, 1982 *Certification:* Anesthesiology
1875 Dempster St, Park Ridge, 847-723-2294
1051 W Rand Rd, Arlington Heights, 847-426-3932
1300 Busch Pkwy, Buffalo Grove, 847-426-3932
9000 Waukegan Rd, Morton Grove, 847-426-3932

Laurito, Charles Edward (4 mentions)
U of Pittsburgh, 1975
Certification: Anesthesiology, Pain Medicine
1801 W Taylor St #4-E, Chicago, 312-355-1101

Lubenow, Timothy Robert (4 mentions)
Med Coll of Wisconsin, 1983
Certification: Anesthesiology, Pain Medicine
1725 W Harrison St #550, Chicago, 312-942-6631
7600 College Dr, Palos Heights, 708-923-9771

Pantle-Fisher, Friedl H. (6 mentions)
FMS-Germany, 1975 *Certification:* Anesthesiology, Pain Medicine
5758 S Maryland Ave #2E, Chicago, 773-834-2130

Stanos, Steven P. (3 mentions)
Nova Southeastern Coll of Osteopathic Med, 1995
Certification: Pain Medicine, Physical Medicine & Rehabilitation
980 N Michigan Ave #300, Chicago, 312-238-7800

Twaddle, Martha L. (3 mentions)
Indiana U, 1985 *Certification:* Internal Medicine
2050 Claire Ct, Glenview, 847-467-7423

Variakojis, Renata Jurate (4 mentions)
U of Chicago, 1992 *Certification:* Anesthesiology, Pain Medicine
7600 W College Dr, Palos Heights, 708-361-5550

Pathology

Almanaseer, Imad Y. (5 mentions)
FMS-Iraq, 1977 *Certification:* Anatomic Pathology & Clinical Pathology, Hematology
1775 Dempster St, Park Ridge, 847-723-6268

Atkinson, Janis Marie (4 mentions)
Rush U, 1986 *Certification:* Anatomic Pathology & Clinical Pathology, Cytopathology
355 Ridge Ave, Evanston, 847-316-4000

Kish, Janet Kay (4 mentions)
U of Illinois, 1982 *Certification:* Anatomic Pathology & Clinical Pathology, Cytopathology
120 N Oak St, Hinsdale, 630-856-7850

Montag, Anthony Gerard (4 mentions)
Med Coll of Wisconsin, 1979
Certification: Anatomic Pathology & Clinical Pathology
5841 S Maryland Ave, Chicago, 773-702-9318

Rao, Sambasiva M. (5 mentions)
FMS-India, 1966 *Certification:* Anatomic Pathology
251 E Huron St #7-220, Chicago, 312-926-2446

Pediatrics *(see note on page 9)*

Beaty, Eileen Marie (3 mentions)
U of Illinois, 1986 *Certification:* Pediatrics
2530 Ridge Ave #201, Evanston, 847-869-0892
1431 McHenry Rd #107, Buffalo Grove, 847-913-9120

Fischer, Ann Brigid (3 mentions)
FMS-Canada, 1982 *Certification:* Pediatrics
6300 W Roosevelt Rd, Oak Park, 708-848-8240

Kaye, Bennett A. (3 mentions)
U of Illinois, 1978 *Certification:* Pediatrics
2835 N Sheffield Ave #501, Chicago, 773-348-8300
1500 Shermer Rd #NW, Northbrook, 847-480-1500

Lechman, Peter Andrew (3 mentions)
U of Illinois, 1995 *Certification:* Pediatrics
201 E Huron St #12-130, Chicago, 312-926-7337

Matray, Mark Chester (4 mentions)
Loyola U Chicago, 1980 *Certification:* Pediatrics
4727 S Willow Springs Rd, La Grange, 708-588-0088

Narayan, Laxmi (3 mentions)
FMS-India, 1966
Certification: Pediatric Endocrinology, Pediatrics
1725 W Harrison St #940, Chicago, 312-563-2340

Nelson, Martine Therese (4 mentions)
Loyola U Chicago, 1982 *Certification:* Pediatrics
2745 Maple Ave #2-A, Lisle, 630-717-9600

Saleh, Nabil (3 mentions)
FMS-Egypt, 1966 *Certification:* Pediatrics
1111 Superior St #412, Melrose Park, 708-450-0112

Schwab, Joel Gerson (4 mentions)
New York Med Coll, 1971 *Certification:* Pediatrics
5841 S Maryland Ave, Chicago, 773-702-3575

Traisman, Edward Samuel (3 mentions)
Northwestern U, 1981 *Certification:* Pediatrics
1325 Howard St #203, Evanston, 847-869-4300

Plastic Surgery

Angelats, Juan (7 mentions)
FMS-Peru, 1967 *Certification:* Plastic Surgery
2160 S 1st Ave Mulcahy Clinic Bldg 2nd Fl, Maywood, 708-216-3581
1S260 Summit Ave, Oakbrook Terrace, 630-953-6600

Cook, John Querin (6 mentions)
Northwestern U, 1980 *Certification:* Plastic Surgery
737 N Michigan Ave #760, Chicago, 312-751-2112
118 Green Bay Rd, Winnetka, 847-446-7562

Dumanian, Gregory A. (7 mentions)
U of Chicago, 1987
Certification: Plastic Surgery, Surgery, Surgery of the Hand
675 N St Clair St #19-250, Chicago, 312-695-6022

Fenner, Geoffrey Craig (8 mentions)
Indiana U, 1988 *Certification:* Plastic Surgery
1000 Central St #840, Evanston, 847-570-1300

Few, Julius Warren, Jr. (7 mentions)
U of Chicago, 1992 *Certification:* Plastic Surgery
875 N Michigan Ave #3850, Chicago, 312-202-0882

Fine, Neil Anthony (5 mentions)
U of California-Los Angeles, 1987 *Certification:* Plastic Surgery
675 N St Clair St #19-250, Chicago, 312-695-6022

Gottlieb, Lawrence Jay (6 mentions)
Pennsylvania State U, 1977 *Certification:* Plastic Surgery
5841 S Maryland Ave, Chicago, 773-702-6302

Kalimuthu, Ramasamy (4 mentions)
FMS-India, 1971
Certification: Plastic Surgery, Surgery of the Hand
5346 W 95th St, Oak Lawn, 708-636-8222

Kraus, Helen (7 mentions)
Northwestern U, 1980 *Certification:* Plastic Surgery
7447 W Talcott Ave #327, Chicago, 773-774-3030

Mustoe, Thomas Anthony (5 mentions)
Harvard U, 1978 *Certification:* Otolaryngology, Plastic Surgery
675 N St Clair St #19-250, Chicago, 312-695-6022

Placik, Otto Joseph (5 mentions)
Northwestern U, 1987 *Certification:* Plastic Surgery
880 W Central Rd #3100, Arlington Heights, 847-398-1660
680 N Lake Shore Dr #830, Chicago, 312-787-5313
845 N Michigan Ave #923-E, Chicago, 312-787-5313

Polley, John W. (9 mentions)
Northwestern U, 1983 *Certification:* Plastic Surgery
1725 W Harrison St #425, Chicago, 312-563-3000

Saulis, Alexandrina S. (5 mentions)
Northwestern U, 1996 *Certification:* Plastic Surgery
120 E Ogden Ave #204, Hinsdale, 630-920-9404

Schechter, Loren Slone (14 mentions)
U of Chicago, 1994 *Certification:* Plastic Surgery
9000 Waukegan Rd 2nd Fl, Morton Grove, 847-967-5122

Sylora, Roxanne Libi (5 mentions)
U of Illinois, 1995 *Certification:* Plastic Surgery
2850 W 95th St, Evergreen Park, 708-952-1030

Thomas, James Regan (4 mentions)
U of Missouri, 1972
60 E Delaware Pl #1460, Chicago, 312-255-8812
1200 S York Rd #4280, Elmhurst, 630-758-8790

Tresley, Gilbert Elliot (4 mentions)
Northwestern U, 1977 *Certification:* Plastic Surgery
120 Oakbrook Ctr #809, Oakbrook, 630-571-7290

Vandevender, Darl Kirk (7 mentions)
U of Illinois, 1986 *Certification:* Plastic Surgery, Surgery
2160 S 1st Ave, Maywood, 708-327-2653
1 S 260 Summit Ave, Oakbrook Terrace, 708-327-2653

Psychiatry

Bagri, Sushil (5 mentions)
FMS-India, 1972 *Certification:* Psychiatry
1725 W Harrison St #744, Chicago, 312-942-0118

Chor, Philip Noble (4 mentions)
U of Cincinnati, 1972 *Certification:* Psychiatry
1725 W Harrison St, Chicago, 312-243-8277

Davis, Gilla Prizant (3 mentions)
Northwestern U, 1975 *Certification:* Psychiatry
310 N Happ Rd #204, Northfield, 847-441-9933

Dresner, Nehama (6 mentions)
Loyola U Chicago, 1986
Certification: Psychiatry, Psychosomatic Medicine
1 E Erie St #355, Chicago, 312-573-0900

Loiterstein, Daniel Aaron (3 mentions)
U of Missouri, 1998
Certification: Geriatric Psychiatry, Internal Medicine, Psychiatry
1725 W Harrison St #955, Chicago, 312-942-7030

McGrath, Harold Francis (4 mentions)
U of Illinois, 1965
14400 S John Humphrey #200, Orland Park, 708-226-1360

Miller, Frederick Eugene (3 mentions)
U of Chicago, 1983 *Certification:* Psychiatry
2650 Ridge Ave, Evanston, 847-570-2540

Renshaw, Domeena Cynthia (3 mentions)
FMS-South Africa, 1960 *Certification:* Psychiatry
2160 S 1st Ave Bldg 54 #222, Maywood, 708-216-3752

Shaw, Geoffrey Sydney (5 mentions)
FMS-United Kingdom, 1988
Certification: Geriatric Psychiatry, Psychiatry
191 Waukegan Rd #120, Northfield, 847-716-1302

Pulmonary Disease

Balk, Robert Allen (8 mentions)
U of Missouri-Kansas City, 1978 *Certification:* Critical Care Medicine, Internal Medicine, Pulmonary Disease
1725 W Harrison St #054, Chicago, 312-942-6744

Barsanti, Carl Michael (8 mentions)
Loyola U Chicago, 1975 *Certification:* Critical Care
   Medicine, Internal Medicine, Pulmonary Disease
2340 S Highland Ave #230, Lombard, 630-932-2040

Corbridge, Thomas Charles (6 mentions)
U of Chicago, 1984 *Certification:* Critical Care Medicine,
   Internal Medicine, Pulmonary Disease
675 N St Clair St #18-250, Chicago, 312-695-1800

Dugan, Guy Michael (4 mentions)
U of Texas-Southwestern, 1984
Certification: Allergy & Immunology, Critical Care Medicine,
   Internal Medicine, Pulmonary Disease
800 Biesterfield Rd #510, Elk Grove Village, 847-981-3660

Freedman, Neil Stuart (6 mentions)
New York U, 1992 *Certification:* Critical Care Medicine,
   Internal Medicine, Pulmonary Disease
2151 Waukegan Rd #110, Bannockburn, 847-236-1300

Garrity, Edward R., Jr. (7 mentions)
Loyola U Chicago, 1976
Certification: Internal Medicine, Pulmonary Disease
5841 S Maryland Ave #L011, Chicago, 773-834-1119

Huml, Jeffrey Paul (7 mentions)
Loyola U Chicago, 1982 *Certification:* Critical Care
   Medicine, Internal Medicine, Pulmonary Disease
25 N Winfield Rd #204, Winfield, 630-690-4993

Kern, Richard Donald (4 mentions)
U of Texas-Southwestern, 1979
Certification: Critical Care Medicine, Internal Medicine,
   Pulmonary Disease, Sleep Medicine
2800 W 95th St, Evergreen Park, 708-424-9288

Klein, Elizabeth Mary (5 mentions)
U of Illinois, 1979 *Certification:* Critical Care Medicine,
   Internal Medicine, Pulmonary Disease
8780 W Golf Rd #102, Niles, 847-759-4770

Marinelli, Anthony M. (9 mentions)
Northwestern U, 1973 *Certification:* Critical Care Medicine,
   Internal Medicine, Pulmonary Disease
3 Erie Ct #3000, Oak Park, 708-383-7899

McLeod, Evan George (6 mentions)
U of California-San Francisco, 1971
Certification: Internal Medicine, Pulmonary Disease
2800 W 95th St, Evergreen Park, 708-424-9288

Moisan, Terrence C. (4 mentions)
Loyola U Chicago, 1974 *Certification:* Internal Medicine,
   Occupational Medicine, Pulmonary Disease
12255 S 80th Ave #203, Palos Heights, 708-448-1400

Ray, Daniel William (9 mentions)
Washington U, 1982 *Certification:* Critical Care Medicine,
   Internal Medicine, Pulmonary Disease
2650 Ridge Ave #5304, Evanston, 847-570-2713
2100 Pfingsten Rd #3000, Glenview, 847-570-2713

Ries, Michael (8 mentions)
Rosalind Franklin U, 1975 *Certification:* Critical Care
   Medicine, Internal Medicine, Pulmonary Disease
9700 N Kenton #306, Skokie, 847-679-8470
2800 N Sheridan Rd #301, Chicago, 773-935-5556

Schraufnagel, Dean E. (4 mentions)
U of Wisconsin, 1974 *Certification:* Critical Care Medicine,
   Internal Medicine, Pulmonary Disease
1801 W Taylor St #3-A, Chicago, 312-355-1700

Stone, Arvey Max (4 mentions)
Washington U, 1981 *Certification:* Critical Care Medicine,
   Internal Medicine, Pulmonary Disease
8780 W Golf Rd #102, Niles, 847-759-4770

Vaishnav, Prakash J. (4 mentions)
FMS-India, 1971
Certification: Internal Medicine, Pulmonary Disease
17495 La Grange Rd, Tinley Park, 708-226-7000
12935 S Gregory St, Blue Island, 708-388-4624
12820 S Ridgeland Ave #B, Palos Heights, 708-371-8006

Walsh, John Martin (4 mentions)
Loyola U Chicago, 1982
Certification: Internal Medicine, Pulmonary Disease
903 Infantry Dr #400, Joliet, 815-725-2653
1300 Copperfield Ave #4060, Joliet, 815-740-1301

Zinn, Mary Elizabeth (6 mentions)
Loyola U Chicago, 1982 *Certification:* Critical Care
   Medicine, Internal Medicine, Pulmonary Disease
100 Spalding Dr #200, Naperville, 630-355-8776

Radiology—Diagnostic

Anastos, John Peter (3 mentions)
Midwestern U Coll of Osteopathic Med, 1989
Certification: Diagnostic Radiology
1775 Dempster St, Park Ridge, 847-723-8236

Connolly, John E., Jr. (3 mentions)
Med Coll of Wisconsin, 1992 *Certification:* Diagnostic Radiology
2233 W Division St, Chicago, 312-770-2000

Demos, Terrence Constant (3 mentions)
U of Illinois, 1963 *Certification:* Diagnostic Radiology
2160 S 1st Ave, Maywood, 708-216-8625

Escamilla, Carlos H. (3 mentions)
FMS-Mexico, 1960 *Certification:* Radiology
355 Ridge Ave, Evanston, 847-316-4000

Gore, Richard Michael (4 mentions)
Northwestern U, 1977 *Certification:* Diagnostic Radiology
2650 Ridge Ave #G507, Evanston, 847-570-2475

Hart, Eric Michael (3 mentions)
Northwestern U, 1988 *Certification:* Diagnostic Radiology
676 N St Clair St #800, Chicago, 312-695-3737

Hoff, Frederick Lawrence (3 mentions)
U of Michigan, 1986 *Certification:* Diagnostic Radiology
201 E Huron St 4th Fl, Chicago, 312-926-6366

Laurent, Elisa A. (3 mentions)
Med Coll of Pennsylvania, 1984
1775 Dempster St, Park Ridge, 847-723-8236

Lomasney, Laurie (3 mentions)
U of Cincinnati, 1986 *Certification:* Diagnostic Radiology
2160 S 1st Ave, Maywood, 708-216-6256

McFadden, John Charles (4 mentions)
Loyola U Chicago, 1971
Certification: Pediatric Radiology, Radiology
1775 Dempster St, Park Ridge, 847-723-6189

Miller, Frank Howard (3 mentions)
Northwestern U, 1988 *Certification:* Diagnostic Radiology
201 E Huron St 4th Fl, Chicago, 312-926-6366

Mintzer, Richard A. (4 mentions)
U of Louisville, 1969 *Certification:* Diagnostic Radiology
1182 Northbrook Ct, Northbrook, 847-509-1818

Newmark, Geraldine M. (3 mentions)
Yale U, 1988 *Certification:* Diagnostic Radiology
2650 Ridge Ave #G507, Evanston, 847-570-2475

Phillips, John Vincent (3 mentions)
U of Illinois, 1976 *Certification:* Diagnostic Radiology
400 W Higgins Rd, Park Ridge, 847-268-8900

Posniak, Harold Victor (4 mentions)
FMS-South Africa, 1974 *Certification:* Diagnostic Radiology
2160 S 1st Ave #0046, Maywood, 708-216-3912

Schultz, Kurt Robert (3 mentions)
Loyola U Chicago, 1981
Certification: Diagnostic Radiology, Internal Medicine
3815 Highland Ave, Downers Grove, 630-275-3684

Silvers, Robert Ira (4 mentions)
Rush U, 1993 *Certification:* Diagnostic Radiology
718 Glenview Ave, Highland Park, 847-480-3744

Turner, David Arthur (4 mentions)
U of Chicago, 1965
Certification: Diagnostic Radiology, Nuclear Medicine
1653 W Congress Pkwy, Chicago, 312-942-5805

Valvassori, Galdino E. (3 mentions)
FMS-Italy, 1952 *Certification:* Radiology
1740 W Taylor St #2483, Chicago, 312-996-0235

Radiology—Therapeutic

Abrams, Ross Allen (4 mentions)
U of Pennsylvania, 1973 *Certification:* Hematology, Internal
   Medicine, Medical Oncology, Radiation Oncology
500 S Paulina St Flr 1, Chicago, 312-942-5751

Borge, Marc Andrew (3 mentions)
U of Chicago, 1989 *Certification:* Diagnostic Radiology,
   Vascular & Interventional Radiology
2160 S 1st Ave, Maywood, 708-216-8932

Burstein, Scott Paul (3 mentions)
U of Illinois, 1981 *Certification:* Diagnostic Radiology,
   Vascular & Interventional Radiology
3815 Highland Ave, Downers Grove, 630-275-3684

Griem, Katherine Leslie (3 mentions)
Harvard U, 1982
Certification: Radiation Oncology, Therapeutic Radiology
500 S Paulina St 1st Fl, Chicago, 312-942-5751

Hirsch, Arica (3 mentions)
Northwestern U, 1991 *Certification:* Radiation Oncology
901 W Wellington Ave, Chicago, 773-296-7089

Messersmith, Richard N. (9 mentions)
Northwestern U, 1981 *Certification:* Diagnostic Radiology,
   Vascular & Interventional Radiology
1775 Dempster St, Park Ridge, 847-723-5032

Owens, Charles Albert (3 mentions)
U of Illinois, 1985 *Certification:* Diagnostic Radiology,
   Vascular & Interventional Radiology
1740 W Taylor St #2483, Chicago, 312-996-0234

Sewall, Luke Edward (5 mentions)
Johns Hopkins U, 1988 *Certification:* Diagnostic Radiology,
   Vascular & Interventional Radiology
5101 Willow Springs Rd, La Grange, 708-245-7474
120 N Oak St, Hinsdale, 708-245-7474

Shirazi, Syed Javed H. (3 mentions)
FMS-Pakistan, 1968 *Certification:* Therapeutic Radiology
2800 W 95th St, Evergreen Park, 708-423-6286
7800 W 122nd St, Palos Heights, 708-448-9393

Shownkeen, Harish N. (3 mentions)
FMS-India, 1978
Certification: Diagnostic Radiology, Neuroradiology
25 N Winfield Rd 3rd Fl, Winfield, 877-792-7246

Small, William, Jr. (3 mentions)
Northwestern U, 1990 *Certification:* Radiation Oncology
251 E Huron St #676-72, Chicago, 312-926-2000

Vogelzang, Robert L. (3 mentions)
Rosalind Franklin U, 1977 *Certification:* Diagnostic
   Radiology, Vascular & Interventional Radiology
251 E Huron St #4-710, Chicago, 312-926-5112

Rehabilitation

Aliga, Norman Asis (4 mentions)
FMS-Philippines, 1976
Certification: Physical Medicine & Rehabilitation
26-W-171 Roosevelt Rd, Wheaton, 630-462-5581

Dugan, Sheila Ann (3 mentions)
U of Illinois, 1994
Certification: Pain Medicine, Physical Medicine & Rehabilitation
1725 W Harrison St #970, Chicago, 312-563-4081

Fitzgerald, Colleen Marie (3 mentions)
Northwestern U, 1996
Certification: Physical Medicine & Rehabilitation
345 E Superior St, Chicago, 312-238-6030

Flanagan, M. Norton (5 mentions)
Loyola U Chicago, 1962 *Certification:* Orthopaedic Surgery,
   Physical Medicine & Rehabilitation
1775 Ballard Rd, Park Ridge, 847-318-2500

Gittler, Michelle Sue (5 mentions)
U of Illinois, 1988 *Certification:* Physical Medicine &
   Rehabilitation, Spinal Cord Injury Medicine
1401 S California Ave, Chicago, 773-522-5823

Keeshin, Susan Silverman (4 mentions)
Rosalind Franklin U, 1991
Certification: Physical Medicine & Rehabilitation
755 Skokie Blvd, Northbrook, 847-272-7426

Kirschner, Kristi Leigh (4 mentions)
U of Chicago, 1986
Certification: Physical Medicine & Rehabilitation
345 E Superior St #1136, Chicago, 312-238-4744

Lis, Susan Dennis (5 mentions)
SUNY-Downstate Med Coll, 1987 *Certification:* Physical
   Medicine & Rehabilitation, Spinal Cord Injury Medicine
1775 Ballard Rd, Park Ridge, 847-318-2500

Oken, Jeffrey Edward (3 mentions)
U of Illinois, 1987 *Certification:* Pain Medicine, Physical
   Medicine & Rehabilitation, Spinal Cord Injury Medicine
17W682 Butterfield Rd #300, Oakbrook Terrace, 630-909-6518
26W171 Roosevelt Rd, Wheaton, 630-462-4070

Press, Joel Murray (5 mentions)
U of Illinois, 1984
Certification: Physical Medicine & Rehabilitation
1030 N Clark St 5th Fl, Chicago, 312-238-7767

Roth, Elliot Jay (3 mentions)
Northwestern U, 1982
Certification: Physical Medicine & Rehabilitation
345 E Superior St #0-821, Chicago, 312-238-4637

Sliwa, James A. (4 mentions)
Midwestern U, 1980
Certification: Physical Medicine & Rehabilitation
345 E Superior St, Chicago, 312-238-4093

Young, James Allen (7 mentions)
Indiana U, 1979
Certification: Neurology, Physical Medicine & Rehabilitation
1725 W Harrison St #1018, Chicago, 312-942-8905

Rheumatology

Adams, Elaine Mary (6 mentions)
Loyola U Chicago, 1978
Certification: Internal Medicine, Rheumatology
2160 S 1st Ave Bldg 102 #7603, Maywood, 708-216-3313

Barr, Walter Gerard (15 mentions)
Loyola U Chicago, 1975
Certification: Internal Medicine, Rheumatology
675 N St Clair St #14-100, Chicago, 312-695-8628

Brown, Calvin R. (6 mentions)
Wayne State U, 1979
Certification: Internal Medicine, Rheumatology
1725 W Harrison St #1017, Chicago, 312-563-2800

Broy, Susan Borre (7 mentions)
U of Illinois, 1981
Certification: Internal Medicine, Rheumatology
150 N River Rd #100, Des Plaines, 847-375-3000
9000 Waukegan Rd #200, Morton Grove, 847-375-3000

Cohen, Lewis Michael (6 mentions)
U of Cincinnati, 1971
Certification: Internal Medicine, Rheumatology
1000 Central St #800, Evanston, 847-570-2503

Curran, James Joseph (5 mentions)
U of Illinois, 1976
Certification: Internal Medicine, Rheumatology
5841 S Maryland Ave, Chicago, 773-702-1232

Drevlow, Barbara Ellen (6 mentions)
U of Minnesota, 1987
Certification: Internal Medicine, Rheumatology
2400 Chestnut Ave #A, Glenview, 847-657-3530

Eisenberg, Gerald Marc (9 mentions)
Rosalind Franklin U, 1976
Certification: Internal Medicine, Rheumatology
150 N River Rd #100, Des Plaines, 847-375-3000
9000 Waukegan Rd #200, Morton Grove, 847-375-3000

Iammartino, Albert John (5 mentions)
U of Illinois, 1975
Certification: Internal Medicine, Rheumatology
1S224 Summit Ave #107, Oakbrook Terrace, 630-268-0200

Katz, Robert Stephen (6 mentions)
U of Maryland, 1970
Certification: Internal Medicine, Rheumatology
1725 W Harrison St #1039, Chicago, 312-226-8228
200 S Michigan Ave #830, Chicago, 312-922-2500

Skosey, John Lyle (5 mentions)
U of Chicago, 1961
Certification: Internal Medicine, Rheumatology
150 N Michigan Ave, Chicago, 847-375-3000
9000 Waukegan Rd, Morton Grove, 847-375-3000

Thoracic Surgery

Blum, Matthew G. (7 mentions)
Johns Hopkins U, 1992 *Certification:* Surgery, Thoracic Surgery
675 N St Clair St #21-700, Chicago, 312-695-3800

Ferguson, Mark Kendric (9 mentions)
U of Chicago, 1977 *Certification:* Thoracic Surgery
5841 S Maryland Ave #E-500, Chicago, 773-702-3551

Joob, Axel William (14 mentions)
U of Michigan, 1981 *Certification:* Thoracic Surgery
1600 W Dempster St #103, Park Ridge, 847-635-9006

Liptay, Michael Justin (18 mentions)
Northwestern U, 1988 *Certification:* Surgery, Thoracic Surgery
1725 W Harrison St #774, Chicago, 312-738-3732
9669 Kenton Ave #604, Skokie, 312-738-3732

Muasher, Issa Elias (7 mentions)
FMS-Lebanon, 1971 *Certification:* Thoracic Surgery
950 N York Rd #104, Hinsdale, 630-920-8501

Snow, Norman Jay (6 mentions)
U of Vermont, 1970 *Certification:* Thoracic Surgery
1801 W Taylor St, Chicago, 312-996-4942

Warren, William Howard (7 mentions)
FMS-Canada, 1976 *Certification:* Thoracic Surgery
1725 W Harrison St #774, Chicago, 312-738-3732

Urology

Bales, Gregory Thomas (5 mentions)
Tufts U, 1990 *Certification:* Urology
5841 S Maryland Ave #2D, Chicago, 773-702-6325
5758 S Maryland Ave #2D, Chicago, 773-702-6325

Blum, Michael David (6 mentions)
Northwestern U, 1979 *Certification:* Urology
750 Green Bay Rd, Winnetka, 847-501-3434

Bockrath, John Michael (4 mentions)
Northwestern U, 1976 *Certification:* Urology
1259 Rickert Dr #200, Naperville, 630-369-1572
251 N Cass St, West Mont, 630-369-1572

Brandt, Mark Thompson (5 mentions)
Wayne State U, 1986 *Certification:* Urology
7447 W Talcott Ave #427, Chicago, 773-775-0800
1875 Dempster St #506, Park Ridge, 847-823-4700
7900 N Milwaukee Ave, Niles, 847-470-1500

Carter, Michael Frank (4 mentions)
Georgetown U, 1966 *Certification:* Urology
201 E Huron St #10-200, Chicago, 312-926-3535

Coogan, Christopher Lee (5 mentions)
Rush U, 1990 *Certification:* Urology
1725 W Harrison St #758, Chicago, 312-666-2410

Dalton, Daniel Patrick (4 mentions)
Northwestern U, 1983 *Certification:* Urology
201 E Huron St #10-200, Chicago, 312-926-3535

Flanigan, Robert Charles (9 mentions)
Case Western Reserve U, 1972 *Certification:* Surgery, Urology
2160 S 1st Ave, Maywood, 708-216-5100

Freedman, Neil R. (4 mentions)
U of Michigan, 1974
767 Park Ave W #180, Highland Park, 847-432-4066
4711 W Golf Rd, Skokie, 847-673-6505

Garnett, John Ewell (4 mentions)
Rush U, 1978 *Certification:* Urology
201 E Huron St #10-200, Chicago, 312-926-3535

Gerber, Glenn Scott (4 mentions)
U of Chicago, 1986 *Certification:* Urology
5758 S Maryland Ave, Chicago, 773-702-6326

Gluckman, Gordon Robert (6 mentions)
Northwestern U, 1989 *Certification:* Urology
1875 W Dempster #365, Park Ridge, 847-823-3185

Gonzalez, Chris Michael (4 mentions)
U of Iowa, 1994 *Certification:* Urology
675 N St Clair St #20-150, Chicago, 312-695-8146

Hoeksema, Jerome (9 mentions)
Wayne State U, 1974 *Certification:* Urology
1725 W Harrison St #352, Chicago, 312-563-5000

Hoyme, Kermit Dan (5 mentions)
U of Illinois, 1968 *Certification:* Urology
10400 Southwest Hwy, Chicago Ridge, 708-423-8706
16632 S 107th Ct, Orland Park, 708-349-6350

Kaplinsky, Robert Scott (8 mentions)
U of Vermont, 1990 *Certification:* Urology
7447 W Talcott Ave #427, Chicago, 773-775-0800
7900 N Milwaukee Ave #17, Niles, 847-470-1500
1875 Dempster St #506, Park Ridge, 847-823-4700

Keeler, Thomas Connare (7 mentions)
Indiana U, 1981 *Certification:* Urology
1000 Central St #720, Evanston, 847-475-8600
2150 Pfingsten Rd #2260, Glenview, 847-657-5730

Kozlowski, James Michael (5 mentions)
Northwestern U, 1975 *Certification:* Surgery, Urology
675 N St Clair St #20-150, Chicago, 312-695-8146

Lee, Ronald David (5 mentions)
Loyola U Chicago, 1977 *Certification:* Urology
1875 Dempster St #365, Park Ridge, 847-823-3185

Levine, Laurence Adan (8 mentions)
U of Colorado, 1980 *Certification:* Urology
1725 W Harrison St #352, Chicago, 312-563-5000

Lyon, Paul Bayard (4 mentions)
U of Chicago, 1989 *Certification:* Urology
1259 Rickert Dr #200, Naperville, 630-369-1572
251 N Cass St, Westmont, 630-369-1572

McGuire, Michael Shane (5 mentions)
U of Chicago, 1990 *Certification:* Urology
9711 Skokie Blvd #H, Skokie, 847-676-2400

McVary, Kevin T. (5 mentions)
Northwestern U, 1983 *Certification:* Urology
675 N St Clair St #20-150, Chicago, 312-695-8146

Moran, George Gaw (4 mentions)
St Louis U, 1977 *Certification:* Urology
5201 Willow Springs Rd #380, La Grange, 708-354-2550

Mutchnik, Steven E. (5 mentions)
U of Chicago, 1992 *Certification:* Urology
757 W Park Ave #3800, Highland Park, 847-480-3993
9669 N Kenton Ave #608, Skokie, 847-677-4111

Pasciak, Robert Marion (4 mentions)
Loyola U Chicago, 1978 *Certification:* Urology
1259 Rickert Dr #200, Naperville, 630-369-1572
251 N Cass St, Westmont, 630-369-1572

Pessis, Dennis Aaron (4 mentions)
Rosalind Franklin U, 1973 *Certification:* Urology
900 N Westmoreland Rd #225, Lake Forest, 847-234-3300
1725 W Harrison St #762, Chicago, 312-563-3447

Ross, Lawrence Steven (4 mentions)
U of Chicago, 1965 *Certification:* Urology
900 N Michigan #1420, Chicago, 312-440-5127

Schacht, Mark (5 mentions)
U of Michigan, 1978 *Certification:* Urology
800 Austin St #569, Evanston, 847-328-8884
111 N Wabash Ave #1210, Chicago, 312-641-6288

Sharifi, Roohollah (4 mentions)
FMS-Iran, 1965 *Certification:* Urology
1801 W Taylor St #3F, Chicago, 312-355-4300

Sylora, James Arthur (6 mentions)
Loyola U Chicago, 1989 *Certification:* Urology
2850 W 95th St #302, Evergreen Park, 708-422-2242
12800 S Ridgeland #F, Palos Heights, 708-923-2400

Totonchi, Emil Fadhil H. (5 mentions)
FMS-Iraq, 1968 *Certification:* Urology
860 N Clark St, Chicago, 312-944-2848
836 W Wellington Ave, Chicago, 773-296-7159

Turk, Thomas Maynard T. (5 mentions)
Virginia Commonwealth U, 1992 *Certification:* Urology
2160 S 1st Ave 54 Bldg 2nd Fl, Maywood, 708-216-4076

Young, Michael Jay (5 mentions)
Rush U, 1985 *Certification:* Urology
836 W Wellington Ave, Chicago, 773-296-7159
711 W North Ave #212, Chicago, 312-867-7430

Vascular Surgery

Golan, John Frederick (12 mentions)
Loyola U Chicago, 1978 *Certification:* Vascular Surgery
495 Central Ave #200, Northfield, 847-441-2700

Matsumura, Jon Steven (7 mentions)
Northwestern U, 1988 *Certification:* Surgery, Vascular Surgery
201 E Huron St #10-105, Chicago, 312-695-4965
675 N St Clair St, Chicago, 312-695-2714

McCarthy, Walter John (13 mentions)
Wayne State U, 1978 *Certification:* Vascular Surgery
1725 W Harrison St #1156, Chicago, 312-942-8272

Painter, Thomas Anderson (9 mentions)
Ohio State U, 1980 *Certification:* Vascular Surgery
15 S Dryden Pl, Arlington Heights, 847-577-5814

Pearce, William Henderson, Jr. (6 mentions)
U of Colorado, 1975
Certification: Surgery, Surgical Critical Care, Vascular Surgery
675 N St Clair St #19-100, Chicago, 312-695-2714

Piano, Giancarlo (7 mentions)
Loyola U Chicago, 1981 *Certification:* Surgery, Vascular Surgery
2525 S Michigan Ave #2, Chicago, 312-567-2013
5758 S Maryland Ave 6th Fl, Chicago, 773-702-6128

Chicago Area—page 188

Indianapolis Area—page 203

Louisville Area—page 208

Indiana

Indianapolis Area

Including Boone, Hamilton, Hancock, Hendricks, Johnson, Madison, Marion, Morgan, and Shelby Counties

Allergy/Immunology

Goldberg, Pinkus (5 mentions)
Med Coll of Pennsylvania, 1975
Certification: Allergy & Immunology, Internal Medicine
3266 N Meridian St #900, Indianapolis, 317-924-8297

Holbreich, Mark (6 mentions)
FMS-Belgium, 1976
Certification: Allergy & Immunology, Pediatrics
8902 N Meridian St #100, Indianapolis, 317-574-0230

Leickly, Frederick E. (6 mentions)
Case Western Reserve U, 1980
Certification: Allergy & Immunology, Pediatrics
702 Barnhill Dr #2750, Indianapolis, 317-274-7205
11725 N Illinois St #450, Carmel, 317-688-5700

Wu, L. Y. Frank (12 mentions)
FMS-Taiwan, 1966
Certification: Allergy & Immunology, Pediatrics
8402 Harcourt Rd #606, Indianapolis, 317-872-4213

Anesthesiology

Burke, Brent Curtis (3 mentions)
Indiana U, 1981 *Certification:* Anesthesiology
5445 E 16th St, Indianapolis, 317-355-7000

Crook, David Edward (3 mentions)
Indiana U, 2000 *Certification:* Anesthesiology
8111 S Emerson Ave, Indianapolis, 317-865-5000

Need, Michael John (3 mentions)
Indiana U, 1988 *Certification:* Anesthesiology
1600 Albany St, Beech Grove, 317-567-2179

Cardiac Surgery

Beckman, Daniel J. (14 mentions)
Indiana U, 1980
Certification: Surgical Critical Care, Thoracic Surgery
1801 N Senate Blvd #755, Indianapolis, 317-923-1787

Brown, John William (11 mentions)
Indiana U, 1970 *Certification:* Thoracic Surgery
545 Barnhill Dr #EH-215, Indianapolis, 317-274-7150
7970 N Illinois St, Indianapolis, 317-259-4045

Fehrenbacher, John Wayne (7 mentions)
Indiana U, 1976 *Certification:* Thoracic Surgery
1801 N Senate Blvd #755, Indianapolis, 317-923-1787

Gerdisch, Marc William (8 mentions)
Loyola U Chicago, 1987 *Certification:* Thoracic Surgery
5255 E Stop 11 Rd #200, Indianapolis, 317-851-2331

Robison, Robert Joseph (7 mentions)
Indiana U, 1979 *Certification:* Thoracic Surgery
8433 Harcourt Rd, Indianapolis, 317-583-7600

Turrentine, Mark William (8 mentions)
U of Kansas, 1983 *Certification:* Thoracic Surgery
545 Barnhill Dr, Indianapolis, 317-274-1121

Cardiology

Berg, William Joseph (8 mentions)
U of Illinois, 1984 *Certification:* Cardiovascular Disease,
Internal Medicine, Interventional Cardiology
5330 E Stop 11 Rd, Indianapolis, 317-893-1900

Caldwell, Randall Lee (3 mentions)
Indiana U, 1971 *Certification:* Pediatric Cardiology, Pediatrics
702 Barnhill Dr #RR-127, Indianapolis, 317-274-8906

Gill, William Joseph (4 mentions)
Indiana U, 1998
Certification: Cardiovascular Disease, Internal Medicine
1800 N Senate Blvd #4000, Indianapolis, 317-962-4800

Hallam, Clifford Charles (3 mentions)
Indiana U, 1973
Certification: Cardiovascular Disease, Internal Medicine
8333 Naab Rd #400, Indianapolis, 317-338-6666

Harlamert, Edward Allen (5 mentions)
Indiana U, 1983
Certification: Cardiovascular Disease, Internal Medicine
8075 N Shadeland Ave #350, Indianapolis, 317-621-9700

Hickman, Horace Omer, Jr. (5 mentions)
Indiana U, 1970 *Certification:* Cardiovascular Disease,
Internal Medicine, Interventional Cardiology
5330 E Stop 11 Rd, Indianapolis, 317-783-8800

MacPhail, Blair S. (3 mentions)
Indiana U, 1985
Certification: Cardiovascular Disease, Internal Medicine
8075 N Shadeland Ave #100, Indianapolis, 317-621-9700

O'Donnell, Jacqueline Ann (3 mentions)
Indiana U, 1975
Certification: Cardiovascular Disease, Internal Medicine
1800 N Capitol Ave #4000, Indianapolis, 317-962-0561
1801 Senate Blvd #300, Indianapolis, 317-924-5444

Parr, Kirk Lenox (3 mentions)
Indiana U, 1980 *Certification:* Cardiovascular Disease,
Internal Medicine, Interventional Cardiology
1801 N Senate Blvd #300, Indianapolis, 317-924-5444
8333 Naab Rd #400, Indianapolis, 317-338-6666

Pitts, Douglas Edmond (7 mentions)
Indiana U, 1978
Certification: Cardiovascular Disease, Internal Medicine
8333 Naab Rd #400, Indianapolis, 317-338-6666
1115 Ronald reagan Pkwy #329, Avon, 317-217-2300

Taliercio, Charles Paul (3 mentions)
Johns Hopkins U, 1979
Certification: Cardiovascular Disease, Internal Medicine
8333 Naab Rd #400, Indianapolis, 317-338-6666

Williams, Eric Stephen (3 mentions)
Indiana U, 1971
Certification: Cardiovascular Disease, Internal Medicine
1801 N Senate Blvd #4000, Indianapolis, 317-962-0551
1800 N Capitol Ave, Indianapolis, 317-274-4391

Dermatology

Greist, Mary A. Coffey (4 mentions)
Indiana U, 1973 *Certification:* Dermatology, Dermatopathology
6820 Parkdale Pl #211, Indianapolis, 317-329-7050

Hanke, C. William (6 mentions)
U of Iowa, 1971 *Certification:* Dermatology, Dermatopathology
5125 Green Braes East Dr, Indianapolis, 317-582-8484
13450 N Meridian Dr #355, Carmel, 317-582-8484

McCallister, Robert Edward (4 mentions)
Indiana U, 1980 *Certification:* Dermatology, Internal Medicine
6920 Parkdale Pl #210, Indianapolis, 317-299-3444

Moores, William Bradley (4 mentions)
Indiana U, 1963 *Certification:* Dermatology, Dermatopathology
1801 N Senate Blvd #745, Indianapolis, 317-926-3739

Rehme, Christopher Gavin (4 mentions)
Indiana U, 1973 *Certification:* Dermatology
1801 N Senate Blvd #745, Indianapolis, 317-926-3739
8180 Clearvista Dr #345, Indianapolis, 317-926-3739
1818 N Riley Hwy, Indianapolis, 317-926-3739

Sechrist, Keeter D. (10 mentions)
Indiana U, 1980 *Certification:* Dermatology
1801 N Senate Blvd #745, Indianapolis, 317-926-3739
11900 N Pennsylvania St, Indianapolis, 317-926-3739

Storm, Richard Mason (4 mentions)
Indiana U, 1979 *Certification:* Dermatology
1350 E County Line Rd #A, Indianapolis, 317-887-7684

Treadwell, Patricia Anne (5 mentions)
Cornell U, 1977 *Certification:* Dermatology, Pediatrics
550 N University Blvd, Indianapolis, 317-278-1469
702 Barnhill Dr #1300, Indianapolis, 317-274-2801
3840 N Sherman Dr, Indianapolis, 317-541-3400

Turchan, Kirsten (6 mentions)
Indiana U, 1988 *Certification:* Pediatric Dermatology
1801 Senate Blvd #745, Indianapolis, 317-926-3739

Emergency Medicine

Bick, Stewart Edward (4 mentions)
Indiana U, 1978 *Certification:* Emergency Medicine
2001 W 86th St, Indianapolis, 317-338-2121

McGoff, John Patrick (7 mentions)
Indiana U, 1984 *Certification:* Emergency Medicine
1500 N Ritter Ave, Indianapolis, 317-355-5040

McGrath, Roland B. (4 mentions)
U of Kansas, 1972
Certification: Emergency Medicine, Internal Medicine
1001 W 10th St, Indianapolis, 317-630-7276

Profeta, Louis Mark (5 mentions)
Indiana U, 1990 *Certification:* Emergency Medicine
2001 W 86th St, Indianapolis, 317-338-8035

Shufflebarger, Charles M. (4 mentions)
Indiana U, 1984 *Certification:* Emergency Medicine
1701 N Senate Blvd, Indianapolis, 317-962-8880

Todd, Randall Marden (9 mentions)
Ohio State U, 1985 *Certification:* Emergency Medicine
8121 S Emerson Ave, Indianapolis, 317-783-8148

Endocrinology

Ayers, Dawn M. (5 mentions)
Indiana U, 1989
Certification: Endocrinology, Diabetes, and Metabolism
395 Westfield Rd #D, Noblesville, 317-776-3520

Bain, Catherine Lang (5 mentions)
Indiana U, 1987
Certification: Endocrinology, Diabetes, and Metabolism
8333 Naab Rd #400, Indianapolis, 317-338-6666

Edmondson, James W. (5 mentions)
Indiana U, 1969 *Certification:* Internal Medicine
100 Hospital Ln #205, Danville, 317-745-7445

Khairi, Rashid A. (4 mentions)
FMS-Pakistan, 1964
Certification: Endocrinology and Metabolism, Internal Medicine
7440 N Shadeland Ave #200, Indianapolis, 317-621-1006

Lee, Domingo Anthony (5 mentions)
Indiana U, 1989
7440 N Shadeland Ave #100, Indianapolis, 317-621-1006

Meacham, James Earl (4 mentions)
U of Louisville, 1981 *Certification:* Internal Medicine, Pediatrics
9240 N Meridian St #200, Indianapolis, 317-843-0000

Pescovitz, Ora Hirsch (3 mentions)
Northwestern U, 1979
Certification: Pediatric Endocrinology, Pediatrics
702 Barnhill Dr #5960, Indianapolis, 317-274-3889

Priscu, Ana (6 mentions)
FMS-Romania, 1984
Certification: Endocrinology, Diabetes, and Metabolism
8051 S Emerson Ave #340, Indianapolis, 317-865-5904

Roudebush, Corbin Proctor (6 mentions)
U of Chicago, 1971 *Certification:* Internal Medicine
9240 N Meridian St #200, Indianapolis, 317-843-0000

Family Practice *(see note on page 9)*

Beardsley, Richard Lee (3 mentions)
Indiana U, 1979
Certification: Family Medicine, Geriatric Medicine
2030 Churchman Ave, Beech Grove, 317-786-9285

Enright, Patrick Joseph (3 mentions)
Indiana U, 1979 *Certification:* Family Medicine
2030 Churchman Ave, Beech Grove, 317-786-9285

Fogle, Norman Lee (4 mentions)
Indiana U, 1974 *Certification:* Family Medicine
7250 Clearvista Dr #350, Indianapolis, 317-841-6545
6910 Hillsdale Ct, Indianapolis, 317-841-6545

Krol, John Edward (4 mentions)
Indiana U, 1978 *Certification:* Family Medicine
6320 Ferguson St, Indianapolis, 317-252-5585

Larosa, Michael Salvatore (3 mentions)
Indiana U, 1988 *Certification:* Family Medicine
6920 Parkdale Pl #110, Indianapolis, 317-328-6820

Gastroenterology

Bishop, Robert Huffman (4 mentions)
Indiana U, 1972 *Certification:* Internal Medicine
8424 Naab Rd #3-J, Indianapolis, 317-872-7396

Ciaccia, Donato (5 mentions)
Med Coll of Wisconsin, 1989 *Certification:* Gastroenterology
7950 N Shadeland Ave #350, Indianapolis, 317-578-2600

Elmore, Michael Francis (5 mentions)
Indiana U, 1972
Certification: Gastroenterology, Internal Medicine
8051 S Emerson Ave #200, Indianapolis, 317-865-2955

Fitzgerald, Joseph Francis (6 mentions)
Indiana U, 1965 *Certification:* Pediatrics
702 Barnhill Dr, Indianapolis, 317-274-3774

Lemmel, Gregory Todd (4 mentions)
U of Cincinnati, 1991 *Certification:* Gastroenterology
8051 S Emerson Ave #200, Indianapolis, 317-865-2955

Molleston, Jean Pappas (6 mentions)
Washington U, 1986 *Certification:* Pediatric
Gastroenterology, Pediatric Transplant Hepatology
702 Barnhill Dr, Indianapolis, 317-274-3774

Patel, Mehul Magan (5 mentions)
FMS-Grenada, 1999
Certification: Gastroenterology, Internal Medicine
1801 Senate Blvd #400, Indianapolis, 317-962-6300

Rex, Douglas Kevin (12 mentions)
Indiana U, 1980
Certification: Gastroenterology, Internal Medicine
550 N University Blvd #4100, Indianapolis, 317-274-0912

General Surgery

Arregui, Maurice Efrain (3 mentions)
U of Texas-Dallas, 1977
8402 Harcourt Rd 3815, Indianapolis, 317-872-1158

Diekhoff, Edward John (7 mentions)
Indiana U, 1986 *Certification:* Surgery
701 E County Line Rd #201, Greenwood, 317-865-8000

Edwards, Mark Alan (7 mentions)
Indiana U, 1984 *Certification:* Surgery
8240 Naab Rd #100, Indianapolis, 317-872-9580

Graffis, Richard Fred (5 mentions)
Indiana U, 1971 *Certification:* Surgery
1801 N Senate Blvd #635, Indianapolis, 317-923-7211

Haag, Brian Willis (4 mentions)
Indiana U, 1978
1801 Senate Blvd #635, Indianapolis, 317-923-7211

Jansen, Jon J. (7 mentions)
Indiana U, 1989 *Certification:* Surgery
8040 Clearvista Pkwy #240, Indianapolis, 317-621-5450

Mandelbaum, Jonathan A. (10 mentions)
Indiana U, 1984 *Certification:* Surgery
5255 E Stop 11 Rd, Indianapolis, 317-865-4800

Micon, Larry Thomas (3 mentions)
Indiana U, 1982 *Certification:* Surgery, Surgical Critical Care
1801 Senate Blvd #635, Indianapolis, 317-923-7211

Nigh, Andrew David (6 mentions)
Indiana U, 1980 *Certification:* Surgery
1801 N Senate Blvd #635, Indianapolis, 317-923-7211

Pavlik, Joseph Jerome (3 mentions)
Indiana U, 1986 *Certification:* Surgery
8040 Clearvista Pkwy #240, Indianapolis, 317-621-5450
1500 N Ritter Ave, Indianapolis, 317-621-5450

Pulawski, Gregory John (3 mentions)
Northwestern U, 1984 *Certification:* Surgery
4880 Century Plaza Rd #200, Indianapolis, 317-293-4113

Rescorla, Frederick John (4 mentions)
U of Wisconsin, 1981
Certification: Pediatric Surgery, Surgery, Surgical Critical Care
702 Barnhill Dr #2500, Indianapolis, 317-274-4681

Stevens, Larry Howard (9 mentions)
Indiana U, 1984 *Certification:* Surgery
1801 Senate Blvd #635, Indianapolis, 317-923-7211

Geriatrics

Healey, Diane Weisman (3 mentions)
Indiana U, 1983
Certification: Geriatric Medicine, Internal Medicine
8220 Naab Rd #101, Indianapolis, 317-338-7780

Healey, Patrick Joseph (4 mentions)
Indiana U, 1983
Certification: Geriatric Medicine, Internal Medicine
82420 Naab Rd #101, Indianapolis, 317-338-7780

Hurley, Daniel Joseph (5 mentions)
Loyola U Chicago, 1977 *Certification:* Internal Medicine
1919 Albany St #100, Beech Grove, 317-859-1090

Lammers, John Eugene (6 mentions)
U of South Alabama, 1982
Certification: Geriatric Medicine, Internal Medicine
1633 N Capitol Ave #322, Indianapolis, 317-962-2929

Hematology/Oncology

Bhatia, Sumeet (8 mentions)
FMS-India, 1992 *Certification:* Hematology, Medical Oncology
7229 Clearvista Dr, Indianapolis, 317-927-0825
1701 Senate Blvd #C, Indianapolis, 317-962-9000

Butler, Fred Oliver (4 mentions)
Indiana U, 1976
Certification: Hematology, Internal Medicine, Medical Oncology
6820 Parkdale Pl #200, Indianapolis, 317-329-7430

Cripe, Larry Dean (3 mentions)
Rush U, 1984 *Certification:* Internal Medicine
535 Barnhill Dr, Indianapolis, 317-274-0920
550 N University Blvd, Indianapolis, 317-274-8660

Einhorn, Lawrence Henry (6 mentions)
U of Iowa, 1967
Certification: Internal Medicine, Medical Oncology
535 Barnhill Dr #473, Indianapolis, 317-274-0920

Greenspan, Andrew Ross (4 mentions)
U of Louisville, 1984
Certification: Internal Medicine, Medical Oncology
6845 Rama Dr, Indianapolis, 317-841-5656

Greist, Anne (4 mentions)
FMS-United Kingdom, 1977
Certification: Hematology, Internal Medicine, Medical Oncology
8402 Harcourt Rd #500, Indianapolis, 317-871-0000

Loehrer, Patrick Joseph (3 mentions)
Rush U, 1978 *Certification:* Internal Medicine, Medical Oncology
535 Barnhill Dr #473, Indianapolis, 317-278-7418

Logie, Keith Woodard (5 mentions)
U of Virginia, 1977
Certification: Internal Medicine, Medical Oncology
10212 Lantern Rd, Fishers, 317-841-5656

Markham, Raymond E., Jr. (4 mentions)
U of Virginia, 1977 *Certification:* Hematology, Internal Medicine
6820 Parkdale Pl #200, Indianapolis, 317-329-7430

Mayer, Mary Louise (11 mentions)
Indiana U, 1987
Certification: Hematology, Internal Medicine, Medical Oncology
8851 Southpointe Dr #A1, Indianapolis, 317-889-5838

Schultz, Stephen Michael (7 mentions)
U of Minnesota, 1982
Certification: Hematology, Internal Medicine, Medical Oncology
3266 N Meridian St, Indianapolis, 317-228-3393
8424 Naab Rd #2-J, Indianapolis, 317-228-3393

Wu, Hillary Hongyun (4 mentions)
FMS-China, 1987
Certification: Hematology, Internal Medicine, Medical Oncology
6845 Rama Dr, Indianapolis, 317-964-5200

Infectious Disease

Baker, Robert L. (11 mentions)
Indiana U, 1978
Certification: Infectious Disease, Internal Medicine
12321 Hancock St, Carmel, 317-587-2300

Belcher, Christopher E. (6 mentions)
U of California-San Diego, 1994
Certification: Pediatric Infectious Diseases, Pediatrics
10610 N Pennsylvania St #A, Carmel, 317-587-2300

Cox, David Timothy (7 mentions)
Indiana U, 1990
5255 E Stop 11 Rd, Indianapolis, 317-215-8976

Fraiz, Joseph (6 mentions)
Indiana U, 1982
Certification: Infectious Disease, Internal Medicine
10610 N Pennsylvania St #A, Carmel, 317-587-2300

Kohler, Richard Bruce (6 mentions)
Temple U, 1971 *Certification:* Internal Medicine
1001 W 10th St, Indianapolis, 317-630-6262
550 University Blvd, Indianapolis, 317-274-8660

Misra, Ravi Kant (11 mentions)
Northeastern Ohio U, 1999
Certification: Infectious Disease, Internal Medicine
10610 N Pennsylvania St #A, Indianapolis, 317-587-2300
12302 Hancock St, Carmel, 317-587-2300
1633 N Capital Ave #750, Indianapolis, 317-962-0958

Norris, Steven Andrew (7 mentions)
Indiana U, 1983
Certification: Infectious Disease, Internal Medicine
7430 N Shadeland Ave #230, Indianapolis, 317-841-6420

Slama, Thomas George (10 mentions)
Indiana U, 1973
Certification: Infectious Disease, Internal Medicine
8240 Naab Rd #300, Indianapolis, 317-870-1970

Wack, Matthew Francis (5 mentions)
U of Toledo, 1986 *Certification:* Internal Medicine
1633 N Capitol Ave #750, Indianapolis, 317-962-0953

Infertility

Bonaventura, Leo Mark (7 mentions)
Indiana U, 1970 *Certification:* Obstetrics & Gynecology,
  Reproductive Endocrinology/Infertility
11725 N Illinois St #345, Carmel, 317-814-4570

Cline, Donald Lee (6 mentions)
Indiana U, 1964 *Certification:* Obstetrics & Gynecology
2020 W 86th St #310, Indianapolis, 317-872-1515

Jarrett, John Crow, II (5 mentions)
Case Western Reserve U, 1977 *Certification:* Obstetrics &
  Gynecology, Reproductive Endocrinology/Infertility
11725 Illinois St #515, Carmel, 317-814-4110
1111 Ronald Reagan Pkwy #C-1100, Avon, 317-217-2525
800 Clearvista Pkwy #450, Indianapolis, 317-621-2348
602 W University Ave, Urbana, IL, 217-383-3191

Internal Medicine *(see note on page 9)*

Abels, Linda Feiwell (3 mentions)
Indiana U, 1989 *Certification:* Internal Medicine
9240 N Meridian St #270, Indianapolis, 317-815-9042

Braverman, Gerald L. (7 mentions)
Jefferson Med Coll, 1972 *Certification:* Internal Medicine
701 E County Line Rd #101, Greenwood, 317-885-2860

Coss, Kevin Charles (9 mentions)
U of Toledo, 1984 *Certification:* Internal Medicine
8101 Clearvista Pkwy #200, Indianapolis, 317-621-5390

Dudley, Todd Martin (3 mentions)
Indiana U, 1988 *Certification:* Internal Medicine
701 E County Line Rd #101, Greenwood, 317-885-2860

Elmes, George A. (6 mentions)
Indiana U, 1984 *Certification:* Internal Medicine
8240 Naab Rd 3220, Indianapolis, 317-338-7902

Horine, Randall Keith (4 mentions)
Indiana U, 1976 *Certification:* Internal Medicine
9240 N Meridian St S#160, Indianapolis, 317-574-2286

Schaefer, John Frederick (4 mentions)
Indiana U, 1981 *Certification:* Internal Medicine
1801 N Senate Blvd #400, Indianapolis, 317-962-5807

Nephrology

Andreoli, Sharon Phillips (4 mentions)
Indiana U, 1978 *Certification:* Pediatric Nephrology, Pediatrics
702 Barnhill Dr #RR-230, Indianapolis, 317-274-2563

Bloom, Ronald Kevin (13 mentions)
U of Toledo, 1984 *Certification:* Internal Medicine, Nephrology
1315 N Arlington Ave #210, Indianapolis, 317-353-8985

Bolander, James Edwin, II (7 mentions)
Indiana U, 1990 *Certification:* Internal Medicine, Nephrology
1801 N Senate Blvd #355, Indianapolis, 317-924-8425
5255 E Stop 11 Rd #440, Indianapolis, 317-882-2857

Bucki, Jennifer J. (3 mentions)
Indiana U, 1992 *Certification:* Internal Medicine, Nephrology
5255 E Stop 11 Rd #440, Indianapolis, 317-882-2857
1801 N Senate Ave #355, Indianapolis, 317-924-8420

Kindig, Wendy Louise (5 mentions)
Indiana U, 1977 *Certification:* Internal Medicine, Nephrology
1801 N Senate Blvd #355, Indianapolis, 317-924-8425

Kraus, Michael Alan (3 mentions)
Indiana U, 1985 *Certification:* Internal Medicine, Nephrology
550 University Blvd #UH-1115, Indianapolis, 317-962-0200

Taber, Tim E. (4 mentions)
Indiana U, 1981 *Certification:* Internal Medicine, Nephrology
550 N University Blvd #4601, Indianapolis, 317-274-4370

Whelan, Joseph Donald (5 mentions)
U of Louisville, 1990 *Certification:* Internal Medicine, Nephrology
8330 Naab Rd #234, Indianapolis, 317-875-0034

Neurological Surgery

Boaz, Joel Christopher (8 mentions)
Indiana U, 1982 *Certification:* Neurological Surgery
702 Barnhill Dr #1134, Indianapolis, 317-278-4940

Hall, David Charles (8 mentions)
FMS-United Kingdom, 1977 *Certification:* Neurological Surgery
1801 N Senate Blvd #610, Indianapolis, 317-396-1300

James, Steven Mutsu (6 mentions)
Indiana U, 1985 *Certification:* Neurological Surgery
1801 Senate Blvd #610, Beech Grove, 317-396-1300

Payner, Troy Denning (8 mentions)
U of Cincinnati, 1988 *Certification:* Neurological Surgery
1801 N Senate Blvd #610, Indianapolis, 317-396-1300
8333 Nabb Rd #250, Indianapolis, 317-396-1300

Sartorius, Carl Joseph (7 mentions)
Indiana U, 1983 *Certification:* Neurological Surgery
8333 Naab Rd #250, Indianapolis, 317-396-1300
1801 Senate Blvd #610, Indianapolis, 317-396-1300

Turner, Michael Stanley (15 mentions)
Med Coll of Wisconsin, 1976 *Certification:* Neurological Surgery
1801 Senate Blvd #610, Indianapolis, 317-396-1275

Neurology

Alonso, Robert Joseph (8 mentions)
Indiana U, 1978 *Certification:* Internal Medicine, Neurology
1801 N Senate Blvd #510, Indianapolis, 317-962-5824

Cooper, William H. (4 mentions)
Certification: Neurology
4880 Century Plaza Rd #200, Indianapolis, 317-293-4113
12425 Old Meridian St #A1, Carmel, 317-848-1402

D'Ambrosio, Leo Thomas (7 mentions)
Indiana U, 1984 *Certification:* Neurology
5136 E Stop 11 Rd #26, Indianapolis, 317-859-1020

Fleck, James Dennis (3 mentions)
Indiana U, 1992 *Certification:* Neurology, Vascular Neurology
1801 Senate Blvd #510, Indianapolis, 317-962-5828

Hale, Bradford Rawson (3 mentions)
Ohio State U, 1964 *Certification:* Neurology with Special
  Qualifications in Child Neurology, Pediatrics
6820 Parkdale Pl #105, Indianapolis, 317-328-6730

Haller, Andrea Leigh (4 mentions)
U of California-San Francisco, 1997 *Certification:* Neurology
7250 Clearvista Dr #330, Indianapolis, 317-863-2095
1400 N Ritter Ave #451, Indianapolis, 317-356-8301

Josephson, David Alan (13 mentions)
Indiana U, 1971 *Certification:* Neurology
8402 Harcourt Rd #615, Indianapolis, 317-338-9191

Pappas, James Christopher (6 mentions)
Indiana U, 1988
1633 N Capitol Ave #200, Indianapolis, 317-962-1600
201 Pennsylvania Pkwy, Indianapolis, 317-817-1010

Pascuzzi, Robert Mark (8 mentions)
Indiana U, 1979 *Certification:* Neurology
1050 Wishard Blvd 6th Fl, Indianapolis, 317-630-6146
545 Barnhill Dr, Indianapolis, 317-274-8800

Scott, John Randolph (7 mentions)
Indiana U, 1971 *Certification:* Neurology
1801 N Senate Blvd #510, Indianapolis, 317-962-5828

Obstetrics/Gynecology

Box, Kristina McKee (5 mentions)
Indiana U, 1983 *Certification:* Obstetrics & Gynecology
7120 Clearvista Dr #4000, Indianapolis, 317-577-7444

Moon, Amy Lynne (3 mentions)
Indiana U, 1997 *Certification:* Obstetrics & Gynecology
11725 Illinois St #350, Carmel, 317-814-4500

Moore, David Harry (3 mentions)
Indiana U, 1982
Certification: Gynecologic Oncology, Obstetrics & Gynecology
5255 E Stop 11 Rd #310, Indianapolis, 317-851-2555

Rothenberg, Jeffrey M. (4 mentions)
FMS-Israel, 1992 *Certification:* Obstetrics & Gynecology
550 University Blvd, Indianapolis, 317-274-8231

Sutton, Gregory P. (3 mentions)
U of Michigan, 1976
Certification: Gynecologic Oncology, Obstetrics & Gynecology
8301 Harcourt Rd #202, Indianapolis, 317-415-6740

Ophthalmology

Abrams, John Howard (6 mentions)
Indiana U, 1984 *Certification:* Ophthalmology
11455 N Meridian St #100, Carmel, 317-846-4223
1801 Senate Blvd #620, Indianapolis, 317-926-6699
6920 Parkdale Pl #206, Indianapolis, 317-293-1420

Alig, Howard Marion (4 mentions)
Vanderbilt U, 1968 *Certification:* Ophthalmology
110 N 17th Ave #100, Beech Grove, 317-783-8700

Box, David Franklin (4 mentions)
Indiana U, 1983 *Certification:* Ophthalmology
6423 S East St, Indianapolis, 317-782-8844

Keener, Gerald Theron (4 mentions)
Indiana U, 1968 *Certification:* Ophthalmology
1400 N Ritter Ave #276, Indianapolis, 317-352-1841

Klapper, Stephen Roth (3 mentions)
Indiana U, 1992 *Certification:* Ophthalmology
11900 N Pennsylvania St #104, Carmel, 317-818-1000
5255 E Stop 11 Rd #410, Indianapolis, 317-818-1000

Lanter, Earl Edward (4 mentions)
Indiana U, 1984 *Certification:* Ophthalmology
1550 E County Line Rd #326, Indianapolis, 317-887-7777

LaTona, John (3 mentions)
Rosalind Franklin U, 1991 *Certification:* Ophthalmology
1400 N Ritter Ave #281, Indianapolis, 317-357-8663
7250 Clearvista Dr #180, Indianapolis, 317-594-9410

Robinson, Daniel John (4 mentions)
Indiana U, 1986 *Certification:* Ophthalmology
2020 W 86th St #200, Indianapolis, 317-871-5900
4880 Century Plaza Rd #140, Indianapolis, 317-328-0901

Sprunger, Derek Todd (5 mentions)
Indiana U, 1985 *Certification:* Ophthalmology
550 University Blvd, Indianapolis, 317-274-8937
702 Rotary Cir, Indianapolis, 317-274-8103

Whitson, William E. (3 mentions)
Med Coll of Wisconsin, 1982 *Certification:* Ophthalmology
901 E 86th St, Indianapolis, 317-844-5500
1115 N Ronald Reagan Pkwy #223, Avon, 317-217-3937

Orthopedics

Earl, Jarvis (3 mentions)
4880 Century Plaza Rd #200, Indianapolis, 317-293-4113

Fisher, David Alan (4 mentions)
Indiana U, 1982 *Certification:* Orthopaedic Surgery
8450 Northwest Blvd, Indianapolis, 317-802-2000

Jackson, Richard Wayne (5 mentions)
Indiana U, 1978 *Certification:* Orthopaedic Surgery
1550 E County Line Rd #200, Indianapolis, 317-497-6497

Kayes, Kosmas John (7 mentions)
Indiana U, 1990 *Certification:* Orthopaedic Surgery
1707 W 86th St, Indianapolis, 317-415-5555

Kolisek, Frank Russell (3 mentions)
U of Illinois, 1986 *Certification:* Orthopaedic Surgery
5255 E Stop 11 Rd #300, Indianapolis, 317-884-5200

Leaming, Eric Stewart (7 mentions)
Indiana U, 1977 *Certification:* Orthopaedic Surgery
1400 N Ritter Ave #351, Indianapolis, 317-588-2663
8040 Clearvista Pkwy #500, Indianapolis, 317-588-2663

Rettig, Lance Arthur (3 mentions)
Indiana U, 1997
Certification: Orthopaedic Surgery, Surgery of the Hand
201 Pennsylvania Pkwy #200, Indianapolis, 317-817-1200

Scheid, Douglas Kevin (4 mentions)
Indiana U, 1984 *Certification:* Orthopaedic Surgery
1801 N Senate Blvd #200, Indianapolis, 317-917-4195
8450 Northwest Blvd, Indianapolis, 317-802-2000

Todderud, Edward Paul (3 mentions)
Indiana U, 1982 *Certification:* Orthopaedic Surgery
7930 N Shadeland Ave, Indianapolis, 317-588-2663
1400 N Ritter Ave #351, Indianapolis, 317-588-2663

Wurtz, Lawrence Daniel (4 mentions)
U of South Alabama, 1984 *Certification:* Orthopaedic Surgery
541 Clinical Dr #600, Indianapolis, 317-274-3227

Otorhinolaryngology

Borrowdale, Richard W. (4 mentions)
Loyola U Chicago, 1984 *Certification:* Otolaryngology
12188-A N Meridian St #375, Carmel, 317-926-1056

Dunniway, Heidi Marie (5 mentions)
U of Illinois, 1994 *Certification:* Otolaryngology
5255 E Stop 11 Rd #400, Indianapolis, 317-882-4288

Fairchild, Thomas Hayes (8 mentions)
Indiana U, 1979 *Certification:* Otolaryngology
5255 E Stop 11 Rd #400, Indianapolis, 317-882-4288
2200 John R Wooden Dr #205, Martinsville, 317-882-4288

Goldenberg, John David (6 mentions)
Indiana U, 1992 *Certification:* Otolaryngology
11725 Illinois St #445, Carmel, 317-844-7059

Hackett, Scott Andrew (4 mentions)
Indiana U, 1986 *Certification:* Otolaryngology
8803 N Meridian St #200, Indianapolis, 317-844-5656
12065 Old Meridian St #205, Carmel, 317-844-5656

Miner, James Darl (7 mentions)
Indiana U, 1983 *Certification:* Otolaryngology
8040 Clearvista Pkwy #350, Indianapolis, 317-844-7059
9002 N Meridian St #222, Indianapolis, 317-844-7059

Miyamoto, Richard C. (8 mentions)
Indiana U, 1996 *Certification:* Otolaryngology
702 Barnhill Dr, Indianapolis, 317-274-3556

Myers, Michael Wade (7 mentions)
U of Michigan, 1988 *Certification:* Otolaryngology
8040 Clearvista Pkwy #350, Indianapolis, 317-844-7059
11725 Illinois St #445, Carmel, 317-844-7059

Pain Medicine

Dunipace, Judith Ann (4 mentions)
Indiana U, 1991 *Certification:* Anesthesiology, Pain Medicine
5110 Commerce Square Dr, Indianapolis, 317-887-9999

Nitu, Alexandru (4 mentions)
FMS-Romania, 1993 *Certification:* Neurology, Pain Medicine
6820 Parkdale Pl #105, Indianapolis, 317-328-6730

Shukla, Chetan R. (3 mentions)
FMS-India, 1988 *Certification:* Anesthesiology, Pain Medicine
1801 N Senate Blvd, Indianapolis, 317-876-5197

Wellington, Joshua Rollin (3 mentions)
U of Toledo, 1999
Certification: Pain Medicine, Physical Medicine & Rehabilitation
550 University Blvd, Indianapolis, 317-274-2891

Pathology

Bonnin, Jose M. (4 mentions)
FMS-Paraguay, 1972 *Certification:* Anatomic Pathology &
  Clinical Pathology, Neuropathology
635 Barnhill Dr, Indianapolis, 317-274-4806

Clark, Steven Allen (10 mentions)
Indiana U, 1979 *Certification:* Anatomic Pathology &
  Clinical Pathology, Cytopathology
8111 S Emerson Ave, Indianapolis, 317-865-5181

Glant, Michael Douglas (3 mentions)
Indiana U, 1976 *Certification:* Anatomic Pathology &
  Clinical Pathology, Cytopathology
9550 Zionsville Rd #200, Indianapolis, 317-872-0116

Pediatrics *(see note on page 9)*

Kidd, Baron Lee (3 mentions)
Indiana U, 1977 *Certification:* Pediatrics
373 Meridian Parke Ln #C-1, Greenwood, 317-882-0136

Mazurek, Jill Suzanne (3 mentions)
Indiana U, 1991 *Certification:* Pediatrics
12065 Old Meridian St #100, Carmel, 317-844-5351

Nanagas, Victor Cruz, III (4 mentions)
Ohio State U, 1998 *Certification:* Pediatrics
8101 Clearvista Pkwy #185, Indianapolis, 317-621-9000

Tetrick, Letha Louise (4 mentions)
Indiana U, 1986 *Certification:* Pediatrics
8101 Clearvista Pkwy #185, Indianapolis, 317-621-9000

Yancy, Eric A. (4 mentions)
Creighton U, 1976 *Certification:* Pediatrics
1815 N Capitol Ave #304, Indianapolis, 317-925-7795

Plastic Surgery

Coleman, John Joseph, III (7 mentions)
Harvard U, 1973 *Certification:* Plastic Surgery, Surgery
545 Barnhill Dr Emerson Hall Bldg, Indianapolis, 317-274-8106

Havlik, Robert John (5 mentions)
Yale U, 1984
Certification: Plastic Surgery, Surgery, Surgery of the Hand
545 Barnhill Dr, Indianapolis, 317-274-2430
702 Barnhill Dr, Indianapolis, 317-274-2430

Hughes, Charles Edgar, III (6 mentions)
Northwestern U, 1969 *Certification:* Plastic Surgery
8051 S Emerson Ave #450, Indianapolis, 317-859-3259

Jones, Christopher Shaw (4 mentions)
U of Texas-Dallas, 1981 *Certification:* Plastic Surgery
11450 N Meridian #225, Carmel, 317-848-5512

Sadove, A. Michael (8 mentions)
Loyola U Chicago, 1974 *Certification:* Plastic Surgery
170 W 106th St, Indianapolis, 317-575-0330

Sando, William Craig (9 mentions)
Washington U, 1979 *Certification:* Plastic Surgery
11450 N Meridian #225, Carmel, 317-848-5512

Southern, Thomas Earl (7 mentions)
Indiana U, 1970 *Certification:* Plastic Surgery
1815 N Capitol Ave #311, Indianapolis, 317-926-1356

Psychiatry

Diaz, David Ray (3 mentions)
Indiana U, 1985
Certification: Psychiatry, Psychosomatic Medicine
2601 Cold Springs Rd, Indianapolis, 317-941-4458

Gilbert, Anne Hluchan (3 mentions)
Indiana U, 1983 *Certification:* Psychiatry
1701 Senate Blvd #3C, Indianapolis, 317-962-2622

Konkle, Amy D. Mc Kay (3 mentions)
Indiana U, 1968
819 E 64th St #220, Indianapolis, 317-254-3800

Tandy, James Bruce (3 mentions)
Indiana U, 1980 *Certification:* Psychiatry
6930 E 71st St, Indianapolis, 317-841-8600

Theobald, Dale Eugene (3 mentions)
Indiana U, 1983 *Certification:* Addiction Psychiatry,
    Hospice and Palliative Medicine, Psychiatry
7229 Clearvista Dr, Indianapolis, 317-621-4300

Pulmonary Disease

Byron, William Andrew (5 mentions)
Indiana U, 1976
Certification: Internal Medicine, Pulmonary Disease
11590 N Meridian St #400, Carmel, 317-566-0104

Daly, Robert Stoke (4 mentions)
Indiana U, 1973
Certification: Internal Medicine, Pulmonary Disease
1250 E County Line Rd #2, Indianapolis, 317-885-3677

Eigen, Howard (3 mentions)
SUNY-Upstate Med U, 1968 *Certification:* Pediatric Critical
    Care Medicine, Pediatric Pulmonology, Pediatrics
702 Barnhill Dr #4270, Indianapolis, 317-274-7208

Kinsella, Charles E. (5 mentions)
St Louis U, 1987 *Certification:* Critical Care Medicine,
    Internal Medicine, Pulmonary Disease
1040 Greenwood Springs Blvd, Greenwood, 317-893-0888

Mueller, Manfred Paul (3 mentions)
Indiana U, 1982
Certification: Internal Medicine, Pulmonary Disease
701 E County Line Rd #101, Greenwood, 317-885-2334

Naum, Chris Carl (5 mentions)
Indiana U, 1983 *Certification:* Critical Care Medicine,
    Internal Medicine, Pulmonary Disease
1801 N Senate Ave #230, Indianapolis, 317-962-5820
6850 Parkdale Pl, Indianapolis, 317-272-8050

Niemeier, Michael Ray (5 mentions)
Indiana U, 1979 *Certification:* Critical Care Medicine,
    Internal Medicine, Pulmonary Disease
1801 N Senate Ave #230, Indianapolis, 317-962-5820
6850 Parkdale Pl, Indianapolis, 317-328-6635

Rhodes, Richard Heywood (6 mentions)
U of Louisville, 1985
Certification: Internal Medicine, Pulmonary Disease
7250 Clearvista Dr #120, Indianapolis, 317-621-5676
1400 N Ritter Ave #375, Indianapolis, 317-357-8371

Rubeiz, George John (3 mentions)
FMS-Lebanon, 1985 *Certification:* Critical Care Medicine,
    Internal Medicine, Pulmonary Disease
1400 N Ritter Ave #375, Indianapolis, 313-562-6000

Tsangaris, Michael Nathan (4 mentions)
Indiana U, 1983 *Certification:* Pediatric Pulmonology
11725 Illinois St #450, Carmel, 317-688-5700

Weller, Robert William (5 mentions)
Indiana U, 1981
Certification: Internal Medicine, Pulmonary Disease
1801 Senate Blvd #230, Indianapolis, 317-962-5820
6850 Parkdale Pl, Indianapolis, 317-272-8050

Radiology—Diagnostic

Clark, Kathy Sands (5 mentions)
Indiana U, 1986
Certification: Diagnostic Radiology, Pediatric Radiology
5901 Technology Center Dr, Indianapolis, 317-328-5050

Scales, Richard L. (4 mentions)
Indiana U, 1980 *Certification:* Diagnostic Radiology
1500 Albany St #906, Beech Grove, 317-787-3296

Sequeira, Franklin W. (3 mentions)
FMS-India, 1973 *Certification:* Diagnostic Radiology
1500 Albany St #906, Beech Grove, 317-787-3296

Radiology—Therapeutic

Garrett, Peter George (3 mentions)
FMS-Canada, 1977 *Certification:* Therapeutic Radiology
8111 S Emerson Ave, Indianapolis, 317-865-5171
950 N Meridian St #920, Indianapolis, 317-865-5171

Gupta, Rajat (3 mentions)
U of Toledo, 1998 *Certification:* Diagnostic Radiology
1500 Albany St #906, Beech Grove, 317-787-3296

Sequeira, Franklin W. (9 mentions)
FMS-India, 1973 *Certification:* Diagnostic Radiology
1500 Albany St #906, Beech Grove, 317-787-3296

Rehabilitation

Lipson, Nancy P. (4 mentions)
Wayne State U, 1984 *Certification:* Physical Medicine &
    Rehabilitation, Spinal Cord Injury Medicine
1801 Senate Blvd #610, Indianapolis, 317-396-1300
8333 Nabb Rd #250, Indianapolis, 317-396-1300

Rheumatology

Batt, David Seth (12 mentions)
Jefferson Med Coll, 1976
Certification: Internal Medicine, Rheumatology
1801 N Senate Blvd #315, Indianapolis, 317-962-3500

Bowyer, Suzanne L. (10 mentions)
Certification: Allergy & Immunology, Pediatric
    Rheumatology, Pediatrics
699 W Dr #307, Indianapolis, 317-274-2172

Lautzenheiser, Richard L. (9 mentions)
Indiana U, 1970 *Certification:* Internal Medicine, Rheumatology
8802 N Meridian St #108, Indianapolis, 317-844-6444

Neucks, Steven H. (5 mentions)
St Louis U, 1975 *Certification:* Internal Medicine, Rheumatology
7155 Shadeland Sta #110, Indianapolis, 317-577-9999

Thoracic Surgery

Beckman, Daniel J. (6 mentions)
Indiana U, 1980
Certification: Surgical Critical Care, Thoracic Surgery
1801 N Senate Blvd #755, Indianapolis, 317-923-1787

Freeman, Richard Kent, II (8 mentions)
Tufts U, 1990 *Certification:* Surgery, Thoracic Surgery
8433 Harcourt Rd #100, Indianapolis, 317-583-7600

Hormuth, David Andrew (8 mentions)
Indiana U, 1983 *Certification:* Surgery, Thoracic Surgery
1801 N Senate Blvd #755, Indianapolis, 317-923-1787

Kesler, Kenneth Allen (6 mentions)
Indiana U, 1979 *Certification:* Thoracic Surgery
545 Barnhill Dr #EH-215, Indianapolis, 317-274-2394

Urology

Brunk, Glen Arthur (5 mentions)
Indiana U, 1975 *Certification:* Urology
679 E County Line Rd, Greenwood, 317-859-7222

Cain, Mark Patrick (7 mentions)
Oregon Health Sciences U, 1987
Certification: Pediatric Urology, Urology
702 Barnhill Dr, Indianapolis, 317-274-7446

Lingeman, James Edward (6 mentions)
Indiana U, 1974 *Certification:* Urology
1801 Senate Blvd #220, Indianapolis, 317-962-3700

Rink, Richard Carlos (6 mentions)
Indiana U, 1978 *Certification:* Pediatric Urology, Urology
702 Barnhill Dr #1739, Indianapolis, 317-274-7472

Steele, Ronald Edward (9 mentions)
Indiana U, 1970 *Certification:* Urology
1801 Senate Blvd #220, Indianapolis, 317-962-3700

Stuhldreher, David B. (6 mentions)
Indiana U, 1987 *Certification:* Urology
1270-A N Post Rd, Indianapolis, 317-895-6095

Vaught, Jeffery Dean (8 mentions)
Indiana U, 1989 *Certification:* Urology
679 E County Line Rd, Greenwood, 317-859-7222

Vascular Surgery

Dalsing, Michael Cletus (9 mentions)
Med Coll of Wisconsin, 1978
Certification: Surgery, Surgical Critical Care, Vascular Surgery
1801 Senate Blvd, Indianapolis, 317-962-0280

Landis, Michael Edward (7 mentions)
Georgetown U, 1993 *Certification:* Surgery, Vascular Surgery
5255 E Stop 11 Rd #200, Indianapolis, 317-851-2323

McCready, Robert Alan (7 mentions)
U of Vermont, 1975 *Certification:* Vascular Surgery
1801 Senate Blvd #755, Indianapolis, 317-923-1787

Kentucky

Cincinnati Area—page 363

Louisville Area—page 208

Louisville Area

Including Bullitt, Clark, Floyd, Jefferson, and Oldham Counties

Allergy/Immunology

Feger, Timothy Alan (9 mentions)
U of Louisville, 1990 *Certification:* Allergy & Immunology
9800 Shelbyville Rd #220, Louisville, 502-429-8585

Garcia, Daniel Paul (23 mentions)
U of Louisville, 1973
Certification: Allergy & Immunology, Pediatrics
9113 Leesgate Rd, Louisville, 502-429-0708
3930 Dupont Cir, Louisville, 502-426-1621
234 E Gray St #464, Louisville, 502-583-1427

Sublett, James Lee (11 mentions)
U of Louisville, 1975
Certification: Allergy & Immunology, Pediatrics
9800 Shelbyville Rd #220, Louisville, 502-429-8585

Anesthesiology

Akaydin, Ahmet Saban (3 mentions)
U of Kentucky, 1986 *Certification:* Anesthesiology
4000 Kresge Way, Louisville, 502-473-2132

Balatbat, Joselito T. (3 mentions)
FMS-Philippines, 1989 *Certification:* Anesthesiology
601 S Floyd St #407, Louisville, 502-629-2880

Behr, Mark Robert (5 mentions)
U of Louisville, 1985 *Certification:* Anesthesiology
3101 Breckenridge Ln #1-A, Louisville, 502-897-1839
3920 Dutchmans Ln, Louisville, 502-897-1839

Bouvette, Michael John (4 mentions)
U of Louisville, 1995 *Certification:* Anesthesiology
200 Abraham Flexnew Way, Louisville, 502-587-4203

Fitzgerald, Marjorie (7 mentions)
U of Louisville, 1982 *Certification:* Anesthesiology
332 W Broadway #810, Louisville, 502-583-0909

Heine, Michael Francis (3 mentions)
U of Louisville, 1977 *Certification:* Anesthesiology
530 S Jackson St, Louisville, 502-852-5851

Heine, Timothy Allen (4 mentions)
U of Louisville, 1988 *Certification:* Anesthesiology
332 W Broadway #810, Louisville, 502-583-0909

Miller, Barry Herbert (3 mentions)
Indiana U, 1989 *Certification:* Anesthesiology
1850 State St, New Albany, IN, 812-945-3916
1919 State St #306, New Albany, IN, 812-948-9215

Morris, Richard Ray (4 mentions)
U of Louisville, 1986 *Certification:* Anesthesiology
332 W Broadway #810, Louisville, 502-583-0909

Raju, Revathy (3 mentions)
FMS-India, 1977 *Certification:* Anesthesiology
231 E Chestnut St, Louisville, 502-629-1234

Savage, Stephen Patrick (9 mentions)
U of Kentucky, 1982 *Certification:* Anesthesiology
4000 Kresge Way, Louisville, 502-773-1300

Cardiac Surgery

Austin, Erle Harris (14 mentions)
Harvard U, 1974 *Certification:* Thoracic Surgery
201 Abraham Flexner Way #1200, Louisville, 502-583-8383

Dowling, Robert Dominick (10 mentions)
U of Pittsburgh, 1985 *Certification:* Thoracic Surgery
201 Abraham Flexner Way #1200, Louisville, 502-583-8383

Etoch, Steven Wayne (13 mentions)
U of Arkansas, 1991 *Certification:* Thoracic Surgery
3 Audubon Plaza Dr #560, Louisville, 502-636-8004

Ganzel, Brian L. (32 mentions)
U of Nebraska, 1978 *Certification:* Thoracic Surgery
201 Abraham Flexner Way #1200, Louisville, 502-561-2180

Pollock, Samuel Baker, Jr. (29 mentions)
U of Kentucky, 1980 *Certification:* Thoracic Surgery
3900 Kresge Way #46, Louisville, 502-899-3858

Cardiology

Arensman, Frederick William (9 mentions)
Indiana U, 1975 *Certification:* Pediatric Cardiology, Pediatrics
916 Dupont Rd, Louisville, 502-454-7107

Beanblossom, Brian Todd (6 mentions)
U of Louisville, 1988 *Certification:* Cardiovascular Disease
6420 Dutchmans Pkwy #200, Louisville, 502-891-8300

Bessen, Matthew (7 mentions)
Rosalind Franklin U, 1982
Certification: Cardiovascular Disease, Internal Medicine
225 Abraham Flexner Way #305, Louisville, 502-585-4321

Boone, James Whitsitt (11 mentions)
U of Louisville, 1984 *Certification:* Pediatric Cardiology
916 Dupont Rd, Louisville, 502-454-7107

Dillon, William Christian (7 mentions)
Indiana U, 1991
Certification: Cardiovascular Disease, Interventional Cardiology
6420 Dutchmans Pkwy #200, Louisville, 502-891-8300

Donovan, James Patrick (5 mentions)
U of Kentucky, 1994 *Certification:* Cardiovascular Disease
6420 Dutchmans Pkwy #200, Louisville, 502-891-8300

Henes, Christopher G. (5 mentions)
Yale U, 1980 *Certification:* Internal Medicine
6420 Dutchmans Pkwy #200, Louisville, 502-891-8300

Licandro, Rudolph F. (6 mentions)
Georgetown U, 1980
Certification: Cardiovascular Disease, Internal Medicine
3900 Kresge Way #60, Louisville, 502-893-7710

Mandrola, John Michael (4 mentions)
U of Connecticut, 1989 *Certification:* Cardiovascular
Disease, Clinical Cardiac Electrophysiology
6420 Dutchmans Pkwy #200, Louisville, 502-891-8300

Raible, Steven Joseph (13 mentions)
Ohio State U, 1976 *Certification:* Cardiovascular Disease,
Internal Medicine, Interventional Cardiology
201 Abraham Flexner Way #1101, Louisville, 502-581-1951

Smith, Janet Lynn (6 mentions)
U of Louisville, 1976
Certification: Cardiovascular Disease, Internal Medicine
6420 Dutchmans Pkwy #200, Louisville, 502-891-8300

Stavens, Chris Todulos S. (4 mentions)
FMS-Greece, 1977
Certification: Cardiovascular Disease, Internal Medicine
250 E Liberty St #1001, Louisville, 502-589-7907

Weiss, Morris Milton, Jr. (4 mentions)
U of Louisville, 1958
Certification: Cardiovascular Disease, Internal Medicine
225 Abraham Flexner Way #305, Louisville, 502-585-4321

Xenopoulos, Nicholas (7 mentions)
FMS-Greece, 1985 *Certification:* Cardiovascular Disease,
Internal Medicine, Interventional Cardiology
250 E Liberty St #1001, Louisville, 502-589-7907

Dermatology

Callen, Jeffrey Phillip (12 mentions)
U of Michigan, 1972
Certification: Dermatology, Internal Medicine
310 E Broadway #200, Louisville, 502-583-1749

Kulp-Shorten, Carol L. (9 mentions)
U of Louisville, 1985 *Certification:* Dermatology
310 E Broadway #200, Louisville, 502-583-1749

Schrodt, Barbara Jo (8 mentions)
U of Louisville, 1995
Certification: Dermatology, Pediatric Dermatology
6400 Dutchmans Pkwy #345, Louisville, 502-896-6355

Smith, Stephen Zalmon (8 mentions)
Johns Hopkins U, 1971
Certification: Dermatology, Dermatopathology
3950 Kresge Way #305, Louisville, 502-896-8803

Yusk, Janice Ann Woods (9 mentions)
U of Tennessee, 1966 *Certification:* Dermatology
4938 Brownsboro Rd #206, Louisville, 502-339-2922

Emergency Medicine

Becht, Shannon Marie (3 mentions)
U of Louisville, 1999 *Certification:* Emergency Medicine
200 E Chestnut St, Louisville, 502-629-7200

Bosse, George Michael (3 mentions)
U of Louisville, 1983 *Certification:* Emergency Medicine,
Internal Medicine, Medical Toxicology
530 S Jackson St, Louisville, 502-852-5689

Daniel, Lisa Michelle (3 mentions)
U of Louisville, 1987 *Certification:* Emergency Medicine
4000 Kresge Way, Louisville, 502-899-7646

Danzl, Daniel Frank (4 mentions)
Ohio State U, 1976 *Certification:* Emergency Medicine
130 Hunters Station Way, Sellersburg, IN, 812-246-4808

Gerughty, Jack Ray (7 mentions)
U of Louisville, 1985 *Certification:* Emergency Medicine
4000 Kresge Way, Louisville, 502-899-7646
6000 Brownsboro Park Blvd #B, Louisville, 502-897-8141

Kinlaw, Dennis Franklin (3 mentions)
U of Louisville, 1975 *Certification:* Emergency Medicine
4000 Kresge Way, Louisville, 502-899-7646

Purvis, Gregory Martin (6 mentions)
U of Louisville, 1995 *Certification:* Emergency Medicine
4000 Kresge Way, Louisville, 502-899-7646

Smock, William Spafford (6 mentions)
U of Louisville, 1990 *Certification:* Emergency Medicine
530 S Jackson St, Louisville, 502-852-5689

Wojda, Robert Z. (7 mentions)
FMS-Poland, 1985 *Certification:* Family Medicine
4000 Kresge Way, Louisville, 502-899-7716

Endocrinology

Bybee, David Earl (22 mentions)
U of Kentucky, 1972
Certification: Endocrinology and Metabolism, Internal Medicine
100 E Liberty St #400, Louisville, 502-587-6010

Foster, Michael Bruce (16 mentions)
U of Tennessee, 1975
Certification: Pediatric Endocrinology, Pediatrics
210 E Gray St, Louisville, 502-629-8821

Morrow, Philip Gilmer (8 mentions)
U of Louisville, 1972 *Certification:* Internal Medicine
4003 Kresge Way #400, Louisville, 502-895-4263

Self, Mary Theresa (21 mentions)
U of Louisville, 1985 *Certification:* Endocrinology, Diabetes,
and Metabolism, Internal Medicine
100 E Liberty St #400, Louisville, 502-587-6010

Williams, Frederick A. (11 mentions)
U of Louisville, 1978
Certification: Endocrinology and Metabolism, Internal Medicine
100 E Liberty St #400, Louisville, 502-587-6010

Family Practice *(see note on page 9)*

Applegate, Steven Carson (5 mentions)
U of Louisville, 1982
11612 Main St, Louisville, 502-245-4174

Beanblossom, Robert Lee (5 mentions)
U of Louisville, 1961
6801 Dixie Hwy #106, Louisville, 502-937-3864

Fisher, Anna Marie (3 mentions)
Indiana U, 1987 *Certification:* Family Medicine
1919 State St #205, New Albany, IN, 812-948-9500

Lalude, A. O'Tayo (3 mentions)
U of Southern California, 1975
2500 W Market St, Louisville, 502-778-8400

Murphy, Patrick Joseph, Jr. (4 mentions)
U of Louisville, 1978
Certification: Family Medicine, Geriatric Medicine
215 Central Ave #102, Louisville, 502-852-7449

Pitcock, Christopher V. (7 mentions)
U of Louisville, 1991
Certification: Family Medicine, Sports Medicine
9420 Brownsboro Rd, Louisville, 502-426-4264

Potts, Gregory Joseph (3 mentions)
U of Louisville, 1991 *Certification:* Family Medicine
9420 Brownsboro Rd, Louisville, 502-426-4264

Reynolds, Jeffrey Leo (8 mentions)
U of Louisville, 1984 *Certification:* Family Medicine
9569 Taylorsville Rd #109, Louisville, 502-240-0315

Wheeler, Patricia Wiley (3 mentions)
U of Louisville, 1991 *Certification:* Family Medicine
9520 Ormsby Station Rd, Louisville, 502-426-0606

Wheeler, Stephen Frank (6 mentions)
U of Louisville, 1980 *Certification:* Family Medicine
215 Central #100, Louisville, 502-852-2822

Gastroenterology

Adler, Edward Charles (10 mentions)
FMS-Belgium, 1980
Certification: Gastroenterology, Internal Medicine
4001 Dutchmans Ln #7B, Louisville, 502-896-4711

Bronner, Mark Howard (9 mentions)
U of Louisville, 1980 *Certification:* Internal Medicine
1169 Eastern Pkwy #G58, Louisville, 502-452-9567

Brown, Paul Eugene (8 mentions)
U of Louisville, 1985
Certification: Gastroenterology, Internal Medicine
1169 Eastern Pkwy #G58, Louisville, 502-452-9567

Dresner, David Michael (7 mentions)
U of Tennessee, 1984
Certification: Gastroenterology, Internal Medicine
825 University Woods Dr #3, New Albany, IN, 812-945-0145

Heine, Kevin James (15 mentions)
U of Louisville, 1985
Certification: Gastroenterology, Internal Medicine
3950 Kresge Way #207, Louisville, 502-893-0034

Horlander, John C. (6 mentions)
U of Louisville, 1995
Certification: Gastroenterology, Internal Medicine
1169 Eastern Pkwy #G58, Louisville, 502-452-9567

Jones, Whitney Fox (15 mentions)
U of Louisville, 1987
Certification: Gastroenterology, Internal Medicine
225 Abraham Flexner Way #402, Louisville, 502-568-6616

Kaikaus, Raja Mohammad (9 mentions)
FMS-Pakistan, 1978
Certification: Gastroenterology, Internal Medicine
225 Abraham Flexner Way #402, Louisville, 502-568-6616

Makk, Laszlo Johnkirtley (11 mentions)
U of Louisville, 1989 *Certification:* Gastroenterology
3950 Kresge Way #207, Louisville, 502-893-0220

Siciliano, Gerard Vincent (6 mentions)
Albert Einstein Coll of Med, 1991
Certification: Gastroenterology, Internal Medicine
4001 Dutchmans Ln #7B, Louisville, 502-896-4711

Stutts, John Thomas (9 mentions)
U of Louisville, 1994 *Certification:* Pediatrics
234 E Gray St #858, Louisville, 502-629-5796

General Surgery

Bond, Sheldon John (4 mentions)
Med Coll of Wisconsin, 1983
Certification: Pediatric Surgery, Surgery, Surgical Critical Care
234 E Gray St #766, Louisville, 502-583-7337

Brown, Carter Matthew (12 mentions)
U of Louisville, 1986 *Certification:* Surgery
4121 Dutchmans Ln Medical Plaza 3 #607, Louisville,
502-899-6470

Chipman, Janet Renee (12 mentions)
U of Louisville, 1990 *Certification:* Surgery
4001 Kresge Way #210, Louisville, 502-895-1995

De Weese, Robert Craig (14 mentions)
U of Louisville, 1989 *Certification:* Surgery
4121 Dutchmans Ln #607, Louisville, 502-899-6470

Fallat, Mary Elizabeth (5 mentions)
SUNY-Upstate Med U, 1979
Certification: Pediatric Surgery, Surgery
234 E Gray St #766, Louisville, 502-583-7337

Foley, David Sommerville (4 mentions)
U of Buffalo, 1994 *Certification:* Pediatric Surgery, Surgery
234 E Gray St #766, Louisville, 502-583-7337

Hoagland, William Pierce (12 mentions)
U of Louisville, 1983 *Certification:* Surgery
3950 Kresge Way #404, Louisville, 502-897-7411

Kelty, Stephen Jerome (8 mentions)
U of Louisville, 1986 *Certification:* Surgery
3 Audubon Plaza Dr #530, Louisville, 502-637-3311
3950 Kresge Way #100, Louisville, 502-897-1488
4121 Dutchmans Ln #607, Louisville, 502-899-6470

Marcum, Marc Alan (5 mentions)
U of Louisville, 1986 *Certification:* Surgery
4001 Kresge Way #210, Louisville, 502-895-1995

McCullough, James Y., Jr. (5 mentions)
U of Louisville, 1973 *Certification:* Surgery
700 E Spring St, New Albany, IN, 812-944-6488

McMasters, Kelly Marc (4 mentions)
Robert W Johnson Med Sch, 1989 *Certification:* Surgery
401 E Chestnut St #710, Louisville, 502-583-8303

Nagaraj, H. S. (4 mentions)
FMS-India, 1964 *Certification:* Pediatric Surgery
234 E Gray St #766, Louisville, 502-583-7337

Pokorny, Richard Michael (13 mentions)
U of Louisville, 1992 *Certification:* Surgery
4001 Kresge Way #210, Louisville, 502-895-1995

Stevens, Gregory Lee (7 mentions)
U of Louisville, 1979 *Certification:* Surgery
4001 Kresge Way #210, Louisville, 502-895-1995

Stewart, Robert Calvert (6 mentions)
U of Louisville, 1988 *Certification:* Surgery
2355 Poplar Level Rd #304, Louisville, 502-366-1090
250 E Liberty St #504, Louisville, 502-366-1090
1903 Hebron Lane #204, Hillview, 502-366-1090
4402 Churchman Ave #302, Louisville, 502-366-1090

Walker, Jon David (4 mentions)
U of Kentucky, 1973 *Certification:* Surgery
3 Audubon Plaza Dr #450, Louisville, 502-636-0800

Williams, Russell Alan (19 mentions)
U of Louisville, 1985 *Certification:* Surgery
201 Abraham Flexner Way #902, Louisville, 502-583-5948

Geriatrics

Furman, Christian Davis (9 mentions)
U of Louisville, 1996
Certification: Geriatric Medicine, Internal Medicine
215 Central Ave, Louisville, 502-562-6810

Morrison, Charles Ross (7 mentions)
U of Kentucky, 1972
Certification: Geriatric Medicine, Internal Medicine
210 E Gray St #700, Louisville, 502-629-5400

Murphy, Patrick Joseph, Jr. (9 mentions)
U of Louisville, 1978
Certification: Family Medicine, Geriatric Medicine
215 Central Ave #102, Louisville, 502-852-7449

O'Brien, James Gerard (10 mentions)
FMS-Ireland, 1968
Certification: Family Medicine, Geriatric Medicine
215 Central Ave #102, Louisville, 502-852-7449

Hematology/Oncology

Bertolone, Salvatore J. (10 mentions)
U of Louisville, 1970
Certification: Pediatric Hematology-Oncology, Pediatrics
601 S Floyd St #403, Louisville, 502-629-7750

Cervera, Alfonso (6 mentions)
FMS-Mexico, 1988
Certification: Hematology, Internal Medicine, Medical Oncology
100 E Liberty St #502, Louisville, 502-561-8200

Hadley, Terence James (9 mentions)
Columbia U, 1974 *Certification:* Hematology, Internal Medicine
1 Audubon Plaza Dr, Louisville, 502-636-7845
2755 Poplar Level Rd #405, Louisville, 502-636-7845

Hargis, Jeffrey Brian (11 mentions)
U of Cincinnati, 1984
Certification: Hematology, Internal Medicine, Medical Oncology
100 E Liberty St #502, Louisville, 502-561-8200
4500 Churchman Ave #300, Louisville, 502-368-0345

Joseph, Udaya Geeth (11 mentions)
FMS-India, 1978
Certification: Hematology, Internal Medicine, Medical Oncology
4003 Kresge Way #500, Louisville, 502-897-1166

Kommor, Michael Devon (15 mentions)
U of Louisville, 1985
Certification: Hematology, Internal Medicine, Medical Oncology
4003 Kresge Way #500, Louisville, 502-897-1166

Kosfeld, Rodney Edward (16 mentions)
U of Louisville, 1977
Certification: Hematology, Internal Medicine
100 E Liberty St #502, Louisville, 502-561-8200

La Rocca, Renato Vincenzo (8 mentions)
Cornell U, 1982
Certification: Internal Medicine, Medical Oncology
100 E Liberty St #500, Louisville, 502-561-8200

Stevens, Don Ambros (6 mentions)
Certification: Internal Medicine, Medical Oncology
3991 Dutchmans Ln #405, Louisville, 502-899-3366

Webb, Charles David (6 mentions)
U of Louisville, 1987
Certification: Hematology, Internal Medicine, Medical Oncology
4003 Kresge Way #500, Louisville, 502-897-1166

Infectious Disease

Bryant, Kristina Angel (10 mentions)
U of Louisville, 1994
Certification: Pediatric Infectious Diseases, Pediatrics
571 S Floyd St #321, Louisville, 502-852-8632

Marshall, Gary Scott (11 mentions)
Vanderbilt U, 1983
Certification: Pediatric Infectious Diseases, Pediatrics
571 S Floyd St #321, Louisville, 502-852-8632

Melo, Julio Cesar (32 mentions)
FMS-Colombia, 1970
Certification: Infectious Disease, Internal Medicine
234 E Gray St #652, Louisville, 502-587-9478
8516 Cheffield Dr, Louisville, 502-587-9478

Ramirez, Julio Alberto (11 mentions)
FMS-Argentina, 1976
Certification: Infectious Disease, Internal Medicine
401 E Chestnut St #310, Louisville, 502-584-8563

Schulz, Paul Samuel (11 mentions)
U of Louisville, 1999
Certification: Infectious Disease, Internal Medicine
716 W Broadway, Louisville, 502-595-7700

Infertility

Cook, Christine Louise (10 mentions)
U of Louisville, 1971 *Certification:* Obstetrics & Gynecology
601 S Floyd St #300, Louisville, 502-271-5999
550 S Jackson St, Louisville, 502-561-8850

Nakajima, Steven T. (11 mentions)
St Louis U, 1982 *Certification:* Obstetrics & Gynecology,
   Reproductive Endocrinology/Infertility
401 E Chestnut St #400, Louisville, 502-271-5999
550 S Jackson St, Louisville, 502-629-2448

Internal Medicine *(see note on page 9)*

Barry, Mary Germaine (13 mentions)
U of Louisville, 1984 *Certification:* Internal Medicine
825 Barret Ave, Louisville, 502-540-7200

Britt, David Brian (3 mentions)
U of Louisville, 1986
225 Abraham Flexner Way #304, Louisville, 502-585-1200

Byrum, Henry Blair, Jr. (3 mentions)
U of Vermont, 1974 *Certification:* Internal Medicine
210 E Gray St #700, Louisville, 502-629-5400

Costel, Esther Elizabeth (3 mentions)
Duke U, 1979 *Certification:* Infectious Disease, Internal Medicine
4002 Kresge Way #100, Louisville, 502-897-1121

Currie, W. Alan (3 mentions)
U of Louisville, 1996
3991 Dutchmans Pkwy #140, Louisville, 502-899-6552

Hornaday, Charles Edwin, Jr. (5 mentions)
Vanderbilt U, 1980 *Certification:* Internal Medicine
4002 Kresge Way #100, Louisville, 502-897-1121

Loehle, Lawrence Douglass (5 mentions)
U of Louisville, 1977 *Certification:* Internal Medicine
210 E Gray St #700, Louisville, 502-629-5400

Loheide, Paul Joseph (3 mentions)
U of Louisville, 1998 *Certification:* Internal Medicine
2425 Lime Kiln Ln, Louisville, 502-899-7163

Overley, David Joseph (5 mentions)
U of Louisville, 1990 *Certification:* Internal Medicine
6400 Dutchmans Pkwy #140, Louisville, 502-259-5284

Rogers, Matthew P. (12 mentions)
U of Louisville, 1991 *Certification:* Internal Medicine
3920 Dutchmans Ln #312, Louisville, 502-896-4246

Schurfranz, Thomas A. (8 mentions)
Certification: Internal Medicine
4002 Kresge Way #100, Louisville, 502-897-1121

Townes, Brenda Igo (5 mentions)
U of Louisville, 1989 *Certification:* Internal Medicine
3900 Kresge Way #54, Louisville, 502-896-6696

Upton, Roy Dale (3 mentions)
U of Louisville, 1976 *Certification:* Internal Medicine
4003 Kresge Way #228, Louisville, 502-893-5100

Nephrology

Aronoff, George Rodger (10 mentions)
Indiana U, 1975 *Certification:* Internal Medicine, Nephrology
615 S Preston St, Louisville, 502-852-5757

Hayden, Patrick Sergio (9 mentions)
U of Louisville, 1997 *Certification:* Internal Medicine, Nephrology
6400 Dutchmans Pkwy #250, Louisville, 502-587-9660

Shoemaker, Lawrence R. (7 mentions)
Vanderbilt U, 1986 *Certification:* Pediatric Nephrology, Pediatrics
210 E Gray St #1000, Louisville, 502-629-3972

Woo, Danny (23 mentions)
U of Louisville, 1978 *Certification:* Internal Medicine, Nephrology
6400 Dutchman Pkwy #250, Louisville, 502-587-9660

Neurological Surgery

Guarnaschelli, John J. (23 mentions)
U of Louisville, 1967 *Certification:* Neurological Surgery
225 Abraham Flexner Way #505, Louisville, 502-584-4121
3920 DUtchmans Ln, Louisville, 502-584-4121

Moriarty, Thomas M. (19 mentions)
Mount Sinai Sch of Med, 1991 *Certification:* Neurological Surgery
210 E Gray St #115, Louisville, 502-583-1697

Reiss, Steven J. (18 mentions)
Tulane U, 1982 *Certification:* Neurological Surgery
3900 Kresge Way #51, Louisville, 502-895-6700
1900 Bluegrass Ave #107, Louisville, 502-363-6010

Villanueva, Wayne G. (30 mentions)
Columbia U, 1989 *Certification:* Neurological Surgery
3900 Kresge Way #51, Louisville, 502-891-8981

Neurology

Alt, Michael Gerard (6 mentions)
Philadelphia Coll of Osteopathic Med, 1982
Certification: Clinical Neurophysiology, Neurology
4002 Kresge Way #124, Louisville, 502-897-5997

Gebel, James Matthew, Jr. (6 mentions)
U of Cincinnati, 1991
Certification: Neurology, Vascular Neurology
250 E Liberty St, Louisville, 502-589-6177

Meckler, Jason Michael (13 mentions)
Certification: Neurology
250 E Liberty St #202, Louisville, 502-589-6177

Meckler, Roy Jeffrey (12 mentions)
Case Western Reserve U, 1968 *Certification:* Neurology
250 E Liberty St #202, Louisville, 502-589-6177

Melton, John Walker (7 mentions)
Tulane U, 1985 *Certification:* Neurology
4000 Kresage Way, Louisville, 502-899-1193
4001 Dutchman Ln, Louisville, 502-899-1193

Puri, Vinay (22 mentions)
FMS-India, 1988 *Certification:* Neurodevelopmental Disabilities,
    Neurology with Special Qualifications in Child Neurology
601 S Floyd St #500, Louisville, 502-589-8033

Remmel, Kerri S. (8 mentions)
Certification: Neurology, Vascular Neurology
601 S Floyd St #503, Louisville, 502-562-8009

Obstetrics/Gynecology

Alumbaugh, Kimberly Ann (6 mentions)
U of Missouri, 1986
4121 Dutchmans Ln #500, Louisville, 502-894-9494

Bell, Angela Lynn (3 mentions)
Indiana U, 1994 *Certification:* Obstetrics & Gynecology
4121 Dutchmans Ln #500, Louisville, 502-894-9494

Booth, Rebecca Jane (5 mentions)
U of Louisville, 1985 *Certification:* Obstetrics & Gynecology
3900 Kresge Way #30, Louisville, 502-891-8700

Buck, James Samuel (4 mentions)
U of Louisville, 1988
4130 Dutchmans Ln #400, Louisville, 502-897-0697

Cartwright, Mary M. (5 mentions)
U of Louisville, 1985 *Certification:* Obstetrics & Gynecology
3900 Kresge Way #30, Louisville, 502-891-8700

Evans, Jennifer Crawford (3 mentions)
Tulane U, 1996 *Certification:* Obstetrics & Gynecology
4121 Dutchmans Ln #300, Louisville, 502-899-6700

Feitelson, Anna Kathleen (3 mentions)
U of Louisville, 1996 *Certification:* Obstetrics & Gynecology
4121 Dutchmans Ln #300, Louisville, 502-899-6700
5129 Dixie Hwy #307, Louisville, 317-875-7333
210 E Gray St #802, Louisville, 502-629-2830

Graham, James Michael (4 mentions)
U of Louisville, 1979 *Certification:* Obstetrics & Gynecology
4130 Dutchmans Ln #400, Louisville, 502-897-0697

Grider, Ann-Regran (3 mentions)
U of Louisville, 1994 *Certification:* Obstetrics & Gynecology
3900 Kresge Way #30, Louisville, 502-891-8700

Hertweck, S. Paige (4 mentions)
U of Louisville, 1986 *Certification:* Obstetrics & Gynecology
401 E Chestnut St, Louisville, 502-271-5999
550 S Jackson St, Louisville, 502-561-8850

Hill, Pamela McQuillen (3 mentions)
U of Tennessee, 1994 *Certification:* Obstetrics & Gynecology
4121 Dutchmans Ln #500, Louisville, 502-894-9494

Lebder, Stephen Patrick (3 mentions)
Ohio State U, 1995 *Certification:* Obstetrics & Gynecology
4001 Dutchmans Ln #3A, Louisville, 502-893-6777
332 W Broadway #216, Louisville, 502-583-8334
6208 Preston Hwy, Louisville, 502-968-6979

Link, James M., Jr. (5 mentions)
U of Louisville, 1986 *Certification:* Obstetrics & Gynecology
3940 Dupont Cir, Louisville, 502-895-1111

Newman, Nancy Jane (5 mentions)
U of Louisville, 1982 *Certification:* Obstetrics & Gynecology
4121 Dutchmans Ln #300, Louisville, 502-899-6700
5129 Dixie Hwy #305, Louisville, 502-447-9288
210 E Gray St #802, Louisville, 502-629-2830

Reinstine, Jonathan H. (8 mentions)
U of Virginia, 1982 *Certification:* Obstetrics & Gynecology
4121 Dutchmans Ln #300, Louisville, 502-899-6700
210 E Gray St #802, Louisville, 502-629-2830
5129 Dixie Hwy #305, Louisville, 502-447-9288

Riely, Jacqueline H. (4 mentions)
Tulane U, 1997 *Certification:* Obstetrics & Gynecology
1919 State St #340, New Albany, IN, 812-945-5233

Stauble, Mary Elaine (3 mentions)
U of Louisville, 1979 *Certification:* Obstetrics & Gynecology
3920 Dutchmans Ln #306, Louisville, 502-425-8866

Wygal, Janet (3 mentions)
U of Louisville, 1976 *Certification:* Obstetrics & Gynecology
4001 Kresge Way #324, Louisville, 502-894-4408

Ophthalmology

Arterberry, Joe Franklin (4 mentions)
Vanderbilt U, 1976 *Certification:* Ophthalmology
224 E Broadway #110, Louisville, 502-561-0412

Berberich, Susan Marie (9 mentions)
U of Louisville, 1984 *Certification:* Ophthalmology
6400 Dutchmans Pkwy #125, Louisville, 502-896-8700

Black, Bradley Charles (4 mentions)
Indiana U, 1977 *Certification:* Ophthalmology
302 W 14th St #100, Jeffersonville, IN, 812-284-0660
1919 State St #140, New Albany, IN, 812-948-4680

Bloom, Steven Mark (5 mentions)
Med Coll of Pennsylvania, 1984 *Certification:* Ophthalmology
4010 Dupont Cir #380, Louisville, 502-895-0040

Burns, Frank Ramsey, Jr. (4 mentions)
U of Missouri, 1986 *Certification:* Ophthalmology
5135 Dixie Hwy #15, Louisville, 502-447-7315
13324 Shelbyville Rd, Louisville, 502-245-0305

Douglas, Craig Hamilton (11 mentions)
U of Louisville, 1973 *Certification:* Ophthalmology
4121 Dutchmans Ln #410, Louisville, 502-897-9881

Eiferman, Richard Andrew (4 mentions)
Med Coll of Wisconsin, 1972 *Certification:* Ophthalmology
6400 Dutchmans Pkwy #220, Louisville, 502-895-4200

Gossman, Melvin Douglas (4 mentions)
U of Buffalo, 1976 *Certification:* Ophthalmology
2302 Hurstbourne Village Dr #700, Louisville, 502-495-2122

Greene, Brennan Patrick (4 mentions)
U of Louisville, 1991 *Certification:* Ophthalmology
1536 Story Ave, Louisville, 502-589-1500

Harmon, Heather Lynn (4 mentions)
U of Louisville, 1996 *Certification:* Ophthalmology
6400 Dutchmans Pkwy #125, Louisville, 502-896-8700

Lee, Julie Summers (6 mentions)
Med Coll of Georgia, 1983 *Certification:* Ophthalmology
3950 Kresge Way #105, Louisville, 502-893-9825

Murphy, Sean Frederick (7 mentions)
Wayne State U, 1985 *Certification:* Ophthalmology
1536 Story Ave, Louisville, 502-589-1500

Rychwalski, Paul Joseph (6 mentions)
Med Coll of Wisconsin, 1993 *Certification:* Ophthalmology
301 E Muhammad Ali Blvd, Louisville, 502-852-5466

Smith, Kenneth Ray, II (4 mentions)
U of Louisville, 1997 *Certification:* Ophthalmology
9700 Park Plaza Ave #103, Louisville, 502-429-3937

Orthopedics

Bloemer, Gary Fred (4 mentions)
U of Louisville, 1982 *Certification:* Orthopaedic Surgery
3 Audubon Plaza Dr #220, Louisville, 502-636-9226

Ellis, R. John, Jr. (6 mentions)
U of Louisville, 1977
100 E Liberty St #600, Louisville, 502-587-1236
5129 Dixie Hwy #301, Louisville, 502-449-0449

George, Kittie (9 mentions)
U of Louisville, 1995 *Certification:* Orthopaedic Surgery
4001 Kresge Way #100, Louisville, 502-897-6579

Goodin, Robert Allan (4 mentions)
U of Louisville, 1996 *Certification:* Orthopaedic Surgery
4130 Dutchmans Ln #300, Louisville, 502-897-1794

Grossfeld, Stacie Lynne (5 mentions)
U of Louisville, 1991 *Certification:* Orthopaedic Surgery
4003 Kresge Way #300, Louisville, 502-212-2663
6106 Crestwood Sta, Crestwood, 502-243-3097

Jacks, Laura Kroening (6 mentions)
Hahnemann U, 1993 *Certification:* Orthopaedic Surgery
4121 Dutchmans Ln #603, Louisville, 502-384-5678

Kuiper, Scott David (4 mentions)
U of Louisville, 1987 *Certification:* Orthopaedic Surgery
4130 Dutchmans Ln #300, Louisville, 502-897-1794

Makk, Stephen Paul (6 mentions)
U of Louisville, 1990 *Certification:* Orthopaedic Surgery
4001 Kresge Way #100, Louisville, 502-897-6579

Malkani, Arthur L. (11 mentions)
Columbia U, 1986 *Certification:* Orthopaedic Surgery
201 Abraham Flexner Way #100, Louisville, 502-587-8222
4950 Norton Healthcare Blvd, Louisville, 502-423-1460

Nawab, Akbar (5 mentions)
U of Louisville, 1996 *Certification:* Orthopaedic Surgery
100 E Liberty St #600, Louisville, 502-587-1236
10216 Taylorsville Rd #600, Louisville, 502-267-0267

Pomeroy, Donald Lloyd (7 mentions)
U of Louisville, 1980 *Certification:* Orthopaedic Surgery
4331 Churchman Ave, Louisville, 502-364-0902
3991 Dutchmans Ln #302, Louisville, 502-364-0902

Renda, William Murat (7 mentions)
U of Louisville, 1978 *Certification:* Orthopaedic Surgery
4001 Kresge Way #100, Louisville, 502-897-6579

Smith, Mark Glendeaux (4 mentions)
U of Louisville, 1987 *Certification:* Orthopaedic Surgery
100 E Liberty St #600, Louisville, 502-587-1236

Sweet, Richard Alexander (7 mentions)
U of Kentucky, 1976 *Certification:* Orthopaedic Surgery
4130 Dutchmans Ln #300, Louisville, 502-897-1794

Otorhinolaryngology

Bumpous, Jeffrey Milton (11 mentions)
U of Louisville, 1988 *Certification:* Otolaryngology
401 E Chestnut St #710, Louisville, 502-583-8303

Chmiel, Stanley Stephen (7 mentions)
Med Coll of Wisconsin, 1969 *Certification:* Otolaryngology
4003 Kresge Way #227, Louisville, 502-893-3342

Hawkins, Brian Louis (7 mentions)
U of Louisville, 1988 *Certification:* Otolaryngology
4950 Norton Healthcare Blvd #209, Louisville, 502-425-5556
1905 W Hebron Ln, Shepardsville, 502-425-5556

Hodge, Kenneth Martin (19 mentions)
U of Louisville, 1981 *Certification:* Otolaryngology
4004 Dupont Cir #220, Louisville, 502-893-0159
118 Patriot Dr #106, Bardstown, 502-893-0159

Murphy, Bryan Douglas (17 mentions)
U of Louisville, 1989 *Certification:* Otolaryngology
4003 Kresge Way #227, Louisville, 502-893-3342

Secor, Chad Philip (9 mentions)
Certification: Otolaryngology
4003 Kresge Way #227, Louisville, 502-893-3342

Silk, Kenneth Lynn (11 mentions)
U of Michigan, 1967 *Certification:* Otolaryngology
6420 Dutchmans Pkwy #380, Louisville, 502-894-8441

Pain Medicine

Collis, Dean Stanley (6 mentions)
U of Louisville, 1995 *Certification:* Anesthesiology
315 E Broadway #250, Louisville, 502-589-4765

Collis, Ricky Stanley (6 mentions)
U of Louisville, 1992 *Certification:* Anesthesiology
315 E Broadway #250, Louisville, 502-589-4765

Dunbar, Elmer Emmett (9 mentions)
U of Louisville, 1978 *Certification:* Anesthesiology
6400 Dutchmans Pkwy #60, Louisville, 502-897-3500

Murphy, James Patrick (8 mentions)
Certification: Anesthesiology, Pain Medicine
3020 Eastpoint Pkwy, Louisville, 502-736-3636

Reasor, Gary Lloyd (10 mentions)
U of Louisville, 1988 *Certification:* Anesthesiology, Pain Medicine
4121 Dutchmans Ln #606, Louisville, 502-896-9877

Pathology

Ackermann, Douglas M. (11 mentions)
U of Louisville, 1981
Certification: Anatomic Pathology & Clinical Pathology
1169 Eastern Pkwy #G71, Louisville, 502-456-6211

Buchino, John Joseph (8 mentions)
U of Louisville, 1974 *Certification:* Anatomic Pathology, Clinical Pathology, Pediatric Pathology, Pediatrics
231 E Chestnut St, Louisville, 502-629-7900

Burns, Carolyn Dee (5 mentions)
U of Missouri, 1986
Certification: Anatomic Pathology & Clinical Pathology
1169 Eastern Pkwy #G-71, Louisville, 502-456-4700
200 Abraham Flexner Way, Louisville, 502-587-4330

Corey, Tracey S. (4 mentions)
U of Louisville, 1987
Certification: Anatomic Pathology, Forensic Pathology
810 Barret Ave, Louisville, 502-852-5587

Jones, Walter David (5 mentions)
U of Louisville, 1972
Certification: Anatomic Pathology & Clinical Pathology
1850 State St, New Albany, IN, 812-948-7408

Martin, Alvin Wayne (4 mentions)
U of Louisville, 1982 *Certification:* Anatomic Pathology & Clinical Pathology, Hematology
530 S Jackson St, Louisville, 502-852-0029

Matthews, Timothy Harold (3 mentions)
U of Louisville, 1983
Certification: Anatomic Pathology & Clinical Pathology
4000 Kresge Way, Louisville, 502-897-8230

O'Connor, Dennis Michael (5 mentions)
U of Virginia, 1974
Certification: Anatomic Pathology, Obstetrics & Gynecology
4001 Dutchmans Ln, Louisville, 502-897-9594
2307 Greene Way, Louisville, 502-897-9594

Richardson, Mark Edward (8 mentions)
U of Louisville, 1980
Certification: Anatomic Pathology & Clinical Pathology
4000 Kresge Way, Louisville, 502-897-8226

Pediatrics *(see note on page 9)*

Abrams, Karen J. (5 mentions)
U of Louisville, 1984 *Certification:* Pediatrics
3333 Bardstown Rd, Louisville, 502-452-6337

Church, Stephen Howard (7 mentions)
U of Louisville, 1977 *Certification:* Pediatrics
4171 Westport Rd, Louisville, 502-896-8868

Cowley, Claire Ellen (3 mentions)
U of Louisville, 1976 *Certification:* Pediatrics
400 Blankenbaker Pkwy #200, Louisville, 502-244-6373

Hinkebein, James Michael (4 mentions)
U of Louisville, 1974 *Certification:* Pediatrics
9905 Shelbyville Rd, Louisville, 502-425-5166

Jones, Lawrence Morel (3 mentions)
U of Louisville, 1979 *Certification:* Pediatrics
4171 Westport Rd, Louisville, 502-896-8868

Katz, David Seth (4 mentions)
Tufts U, 1977 *Certification:* Pediatrics
3333 Bardstown Rd, Louisville, 502-452-6337

Kim, John Won (3 mentions)
U of Louisville, 1998 *Certification:* Pediatrics
6801 Dixie Hwy #113, Louisville, 502-935-5633

Laney, Markus Eric (3 mentions)
East Carolina U, 1999 *Certification:* Pediatrics
231 E Chestnut St, Louisville, 502-896-8868
4171 Westport Rd, Louisville, 502-896-8868

McCormick, Thomas Edward (3 mentions)
U of Louisville, 1987 *Certification:* Pediatrics
9905 Shelbyville Rd, Louisville, 502-425-5166

Meiners, Joseph Francis (3 mentions)
U of Louisville, 1992 *Certification:* Pediatrics
4010 Dupont Cir #283, Louisville, 502-897-1727

Nassim, Cynthia Grinde (4 mentions)
U of Missouri, 1983 *Certification:* Pediatrics
2305 Green Valley Rd, New Albany, IN, 812-949-0405

Purcell, Patricia Marie (8 mentions)
U of Toledo, 1994 *Certification:* Pediatrics
4171 Westport Rd, Louisville, 502-896-8868

Russell, Stephanie M. (3 mentions)
U of Louisville, 1997 *Certification:* Pediatrics
10639 Meeting St #101, Louisville, 502-425-7827

Sepehri, Bahram (3 mentions)
FMS-Iran, 1973 *Certification:* Pediatrics
1425 State St #100, New Albany, IN, 812-945-2229

Sturgeon, Gerald Francis (3 mentions)
U of Kentucky, 1965 *Certification:* Pediatrics
4010 Dupont Cir #283, Louisville, 502-897-1727

Wampler, Jeff Lee (5 mentions)
U of Louisville, 1980 *Certification:* Pediatrics
400 Blankenbaker Pkwy #200, Louisville, 502-244-6373

Plastic Surgery

Banis, Joseph Charles (12 mentions)
George Washington U, 1973 *Certification:* Plastic Surgery
901 Dupont Rd #202, Louisville, 502-589-8000

Calobrace, Michael B. (13 mentions)
Indiana U, 1989 *Certification:* Plastic Surgery
2341 Lime Kiln Ln, Louisville, 502-899-9979

Chariker, Mark E., Jr. (15 mentions)
Med U of South Carolina, 1983
Certification: Plastic Surgery, Surgery of the Hand
444 S 1st St #200, Louisville, 502-568-4800

Noel, Robert Thomas (10 mentions)
U of Louisville, 1985 *Certification:* Plastic Surgery
4001 Kresge Way #220, Louisville, 502-895-5466

O'Daniel, T. Gerald, Jr. (19 mentions)
U of Louisville, 1984 *Certification:* Otolaryngology, Plastic Surgery
444 S 1st St #200, Louisville, 502-584-1109

Psychiatry

Bensenhaver, Charles B. (3 mentions)
U of Louisville, 1986 *Certification:* Psychiatry
3430 Newburg Rd #212, Louisville, 502-454-8800

Casey, David Allan (3 mentions)
U of Louisville, 1981 *Certification:* Geriatric Psychiatry, Psychiatry
401 E Chestnut St #610, Louisville, 502-813-6600

Davis, Mary Helen (3 mentions)
U of Louisville, 1982 *Certification:* Psychiatry
4001 Dutchmans Ln #1-A, Louisville, 502-899-2673

Pellegrini, Adrian Joseph (5 mentions)
U of Louisville, 1983 *Certification:* Psychiatry
4003 Kresge Way #224, Louisville, 502-899-9980

Peters, Christopher K. (5 mentions)
U of Louisville, 1994
Certification: Child & Adolescent Psychiatry, Psychiatry
200 E Chestnut St, Louisville, 502-852-6941

Schrodt, G. Randolph, Jr. (7 mentions)
U of Louisville, 1979 *Certification:* Psychiatry
105 N Lyndon Ln, Louisville, 502-327-7701

Wright, Jesse H., III (3 mentions)
Jefferson Med Coll, 1969 *Certification:* Psychiatry
401 E Chestnut St #610, Louisville, 502-813-6600

Pulmonary Disease

Anderson, Kenneth Charles (20 mentions)
U of Louisville, 1986 *Certification:* Hospice and Palliative Medicine, Pulmonary Disease
4003 Kresge Way #312, Louisville, 502-899-7377

App, Walter Edward (6 mentions)
U of Louisville, 1979 *Certification:* Critical Care Medicine, Internal Medicine, Pulmonary Disease
1169 Eastern Pkwy #3310, Louisville, 502-238-3178
4606 Greenwood Rd, Louisville, 502-937-2209

Eid, Nemr Salem (9 mentions)
FMS-Belgium, 1980
Certification: Pediatric Pulmonology, Pediatrics
234 E Gray St #270, Louisville, 502-852-3772

Haller, Harold Dale, Jr. (8 mentions)
U of Louisville, 1990
Certification: Critical Care Medicine, Pulmonary Disease
4003 Kresge Way #312, Louisville, 502-899-7377

Horowitz, Joel Adam (7 mentions)
Temple U, 1973
4003 Kresge Way #312, Louisville, 502-899-7377

Karman, Robert John (5 mentions)
U of Cincinnati, 1990 *Certification:* Critical Care Medicine, Pulmonary Disease, Sleep Medicine
100 W Market St #2, Louisville, 502-587-8000

McConnell, John Wesley (15 mentions)
Med Coll of Georgia, 1982 *Certification:* Internal Medicine
100 W Market St #2, Louisville, 502-587-8000

Morton, Ronald Lee (7 mentions)
U of Illinois, 1988 *Certification:* Pediatric Pulmonology
234 E Gray St #270, Louisville, 502-852-3772

Wiese, Tanya Ann (5 mentions)
Michigan State U Coll of Osteopathic Med, 1995
100 W Market St #2, Louisville, 502-587-8000

Radiology—Diagnostic

Bagga, Ranjit Singh (3 mentions)
U of Chicago, 1994 *Certification:* Diagnostic Radiology
4000 Kresge Way, Louisville, 502-895-5405

Buse, Robert Otto, Jr. (6 mentions)
U of Cincinnati, 1992
Certification: Diagnostic Radiology, Neuroradiology
702 Executive Park, Louisville, 502-895-5405

Corrigan, Theresa M. (4 mentions)
U of Louisville, 1986
Certification: Diagnostic Radiology, Nuclear Radiology
200 Abraham Flexner Way, Louisville, 502-587-4231

Joyce, Margie (6 mentions)
U of Louisville, 1979
Certification: Diagnostic Radiology, Pediatric Radiology
231 E Chestnut St, Louisville, 502-629-7650

Kline, Mitchell Jay (3 mentions)
New York Med Coll, 1994 *Certification:* Diagnostic Radiology
1214 Spring St #2, Jeffersonville, IN, 812-283-5950

Klink, John Frederick, III (4 mentions)
Indiana U, 1985 *Certification:* Diagnostic Radiology
217 E Chestnut St, Louisville, 502-587-4231
200 Abraham Flexner Way, Louisville, 502-561-3840
222 S 1st St #501, Louisville, 502-583-2731

Kogan, Anna (7 mentions)
Stony Brook U, 1995 *Certification:* Diagnostic Radiology
702 Executive Park, Louisville, 502-895-5405

Moeller, Karen (3 mentions)
U of Cincinnati, 1990
Certification: Diagnostic Radiology, Neuroradiology
231 E Chestnut St, Louisville, 502-629-7661

Steinbock, Robert Ted (7 mentions)
Harvard U, 1977 *Certification:* Diagnostic Radiology
4000 Kresge Way, Louisville, 502-895-5405

Tatum, Clifton Mattingly (5 mentions)
U of Louisville, 1983 *Certification:* Diagnostic Radiology,
Vascular & Interventional Radiology
234 E Gray St #850, Louisville, 502-228-2834

Radiology—Therapeutic

Birkhead, Ben McKenney (10 mentions)
U of Louisville, 1964 *Certification:* Therapeutic Radiology
801 Barret Ave #106, Louisville, 502-589-4421

Paris, Kristie Jones (5 mentions)
U of Louisville, 1982 *Certification:* Therapeutic Radiology
1313 St Anthony Pl, Louisville, 502-625-4401

Rehabilitation

Chou, Rodney Vincent (5 mentions)
U of Louisville, 1992
Certification: Physical Medicine & Rehabilitation
1170 E Broadway #100, Louisville, 502-583-4700

Gleis, Linda Hood (5 mentions)
U of Louisville, 1978
Certification: Physical Medicine & Rehabilitation
800 Zorn Ave, Louisville, 502-287-5105

Gormley, John Michael (11 mentions)
U of Louisville, 1991
Certification: Physical Medicine & Rehabilitation
220 Abraham Flexner Way, Louisville, 502-584-3376

Hargett, Lewis (5 mentions)
Meharry Med Coll, 1987
Certification: Physical Medicine & Rehabilitation
1900 Bluegrass Ave #100, Louisville, 502-366-8021

Mook, Kenneth Allan (6 mentions)
U of Louisville, 1994
Certification: Physical Medicine & Rehabilitation
220 Abraham Flexner Way, Louisville, 502-584-3376

Stevens, Douglas Phillip (9 mentions)
U of Kentucky, 1987 *Certification:* Physical Medicine &
Rehabilitation, Spinal Cord Injury Medicine
220 Abraham Flexner Way, Louisville, 502-584-3376

Thompson, Robert Lee (4 mentions)
U of Louisville, 1987
1170 E Broadway #100, Louisville, 502-583-4700

Williamson, William Piatt (4 mentions)
U of Louisville, 1986
Certification: Physical Medicine & Rehabilitation
220 Abraham Flexner Way, Louisville, 502-584-3376
3104 Blackiston Blvd, New Albany, IN, 812-941-6156

Rheumatology

Crump, Gary Lee (20 mentions)
U of Louisville, 1983
Certification: Internal Medicine, Rheumatology
3430 Newburg Rd #250, Louisville, 502-893-3963

Stern, Steven Harry (18 mentions)
Eastern Virginia Med Sch, 1980
Certification: Internal Medicine, Rheumatology
100 E Liberty St #700, Louisville, 502-583-5836

Thoracic Surgery

Bowling, Roy Glenn (11 mentions)
U of Louisville, 1978 *Certification:* Thoracic Surgery
201 Abraham Flexner Way #1004, Louisville, 502-589-3173
3900 Kresge Way #50, Louisville, 502-897-1776

Kraut, Jonathan David (11 mentions)
FMS-Grenada, 1999
201 Abraham Flexner Way #1004, Louisville, 502-589-3173

Linker, Robert William (17 mentions)
U of Louisville, 1978 *Certification:* Thoracic Surgery
6400 Dutchmans Pkwy #331, Louisville, 502-589-3173

Urology

Casale, Anthony Joseph (13 mentions)
U of Kentucky, 1977 *Certification:* Pediatric Urology, Urology
234 E Gray St #662, Louisville, 502-629-4220

Harty, James Ignatius (8 mentions)
FMS-Ireland, 1969 *Certification:* Urology
250 E Liberty St #602, Louisville, 502-584-0651

Jackson, Morris B., II (10 mentions)
Certification: Urology
3900 Kresge Way #40, Louisville, 502-899-9830

Rao, Ganesh Srinivas (10 mentions)
FMS-India, 1993 *Certification:* Urology
6500 Preston Hwy, Louisville, 502-962-2000
101 Hospital Blvd, Jeffersonville, IN, 812-282-3899

Smith, Christopher E. W. (8 mentions)
U of Louisville, 1992 *Certification:* Urology
3900 Kresge Way #40, Louisville, 502-897-7172

Witten, Frederick Rehm (8 mentions)
U of Louisville, 1979 *Certification:* Urology
912 Dupont Rd, Louisville, 502-897-5147

Vascular Surgery

Bergamini, Thomas Michael (19 mentions)
U of Louisville, 1983
Certification: Surgery, Surgical Critical Care, Vascular Surgery
4003 Kresge Way #100, Louisville, 502-897-5139

Jung, Matthew Thomas (17 mentions)
U of Missouri, 1992 *Certification:* Vascular Surgery
4003 Kresge Way #100, Louisville, 502-897-5139

Self, Stephen Bender (20 mentions)
U of Louisville, 1985 *Certification:* Surgery, Vascular Surgery
201 Abraham Flexner Way #1004, Louisville, 502-589-3173

Maryland

Baltimore Area—page 214

Washington, DC, Area—page 117

Baltimore Area

Including Baltimore City and Baltimore County

Allergy/Immunology

Bacon, John Richard (18 mentions)
George Washington U, 1974
Certification: Allergy & Immunology, Pediatrics
120 Sister Pierre Dr #201, Towson, 410-321-0284

Bochner, Bruce Scott (6 mentions)
U of Illinois, 1982
Certification: Allergy & Immunology, Internal Medicine
5501 Hopkins Bayview Cir, Baltimore, 410-550-2301

Creticos, Peter Socrates (6 mentions)
Med U of South Carolina, 1978
5501 Hopkins Bayview Cir, Baltimore, 410-550-2112

Mardiney, Michael R., Jr. (6 mentions)
New Jersey Med Sch, 1960 *Certification:* Allergy & Immunology
61 E Padonia Rd, Lutherville-Timonium, 410-561-4488

Matz, Jonathan (6 mentions)
Certification: Allergy & Immunology, Internal Medicine
20 Crossroads Dr #16, Owings Mills, 410-363-6144
10 Warren Rd #115, Cockeysville, 410-667-0807
7939 Honeygo Blvd #219, Nottingham, 410-931-0404

Sekhsaria, Sudhir (8 mentions)
Certification: Allergy & Immunology
201 E University Pkwy, Baltimore, 410-554-6516
9106 Philadelphia Rd, White Marsh, 410-391-3404

Anesthesiology

Dominguez, Jose Enrique (3 mentions)
U of Maryland, 1988 *Certification:* Anesthesiology
6701 N Charles St, Towson, 410-296-4616

Dono, Patrick Anthony (3 mentions)
George Washington U, 1987 *Certification:* Anesthesiology
14820 Physicians Ln, Rockville, 301-838-9606
7401 Osler Dr #108, Towson, 301-838-9606

Greenberg, Andrew A. (3 mentions)
Certification: Anesthesiology
9000 Franklin Square Dr, Rosedale, 443-777-7179

Hogge, Lewis Herbert, Jr. (3 mentions)
Eastern Virginia Med Sch, 1986 *Certification:* Anesthesiology
6701 N Charles St, Towson, 410-296-4616

Kuchar, John Joseph, Jr. (4 mentions)
Jefferson Med Coll, 1985 *Certification:* Anesthesiology
1132 Annapolis Rd, Odenton, 410-674-0020

Loeliger, William Neuhard (4 mentions)
Jefferson Med Coll, 1980 *Certification:* Anesthesiology
6701 N Charles St, Towson, 410-296-4616

Malinow, Andrew Mark (6 mentions)
U of Maryland, 1981 *Certification:* Anesthesiology
22 S Greene St #S-11-C, Baltimore, 410-328-6120

Martz, Douglas G., Jr. (3 mentions)
Certification: Anesthesiology
22 S Greene St, Baltimore, 410-328-6120

Nyhan, Daniel (3 mentions)
FMS-Ireland, 1979 *Certification:* Anesthesiology
600 N Wolfe St #711, Baltimore, 410-955-7519

Shapiro, Richard Morris (4 mentions)
Rosalind Franklin U, 1980 *Certification:* Anesthesiology,
   Critical Care Medicine, Internal Medicine
201 E University Pkwy #226, Baltimore, 410-261-8489

Sieber, Frederick Edmund (5 mentions)
U of Pittsburgh, 1981 *Certification:* Anesthesiology
4940 Eastern Ave, Baltimore, 410-955-6353

Tarantino, David P. (4 mentions)
Brown U, 1986 *Certification:* Anesthesiology, Pain Medicine
5401 Old Court Rd, Randallstown, 410-521-2200

Zuckerberg, Aaron Leonard (6 mentions)
U of Massachusetts, 1986 *Certification:* Anesthesiology,
   Pediatric Critical Care Medicine, Pediatrics
2401 W Belvedere Ave, Baltimore, 410-601-9193

Cardiac Surgery

Baumgartner, William Anthony (13 mentions)
U of Kentucky, 1973 *Certification:* Thoracic Surgery
600 N Wolfe St #618, Baltimore, 410-955-5248

Brown, James Morris (7 mentions)
U of Pennsylvania, 1985 *Certification:* Surgery, Thoracic Surgery
22 S Greene St #N4W94, Baltimore, 410-328-5842

Cameron, Duke Edward (26 mentions)
Yale U, 1978 *Certification:* Thoracic Surgery
600 N Wolfe St #618, Baltimore, 410-955-2698

Dibos, Luis Andres (7 mentions)
Ponce Sch of Med, 1988 *Certification:* Thoracic Surgery
201 E University Pkwy #LL-08, Baltimore, 410-554-6550

Finney, R. C. Stewart (14 mentions)
Johns Hopkins U, 1986 *Certification:* Thoracic Surgery
7601 Osler Dr #W-25S, Towson, 410-337-1783

Fiocco, Michael (14 mentions)
Certification: Thoracic Surgery
3333 N Calvert St, Baltimore, 410-554-6550

Griffith, Bartley Perry (6 mentions)
Jefferson Med Coll, 1974 *Certification:* Thoracic Surgery
22 S Greene St #N4-W-94, Baltimore, 410-328-5842

Sequeira, Alejandro (8 mentions)
FMS-Nicaragua, 1968 *Certification:* Surgery, Thoracic Surgery
2435 W Belvedere Ave #35, Baltimore, 410-601-0900

Cardiology

Applefeld, Mark Michael (3 mentions)
U of Maryland, 1969
Certification: Cardiovascular Disease, Internal Medicine
301 St Paul Pl #310, Baltimore, 410-332-9752
7602 Belair Rd, Baltimore, 410-332-9752
301 Saint Paul St, Baltimore, 410-547-1885

Benitez, Robert Michael (6 mentions)
Certification: Cardiovascular Disease, Internal Medicine
22 S Greene St, Baltimore, 410-328-5396

Blumenthal, Roger Scott (7 mentions)
Cornell U, 1985
Certification: Cardiovascular Disease, Internal Medicine
600 N Wolfe St #524, Baltimore, 410-955-7376
110 W Timonium Rd #2-C, Timonium, 410-308-7170

Brenner, Joel Ira (4 mentions)
New York Med Coll, 1970
Certification: Pediatric Cardiology, Pediatrics
601 N Caroline St #7325, Baltimore, 410-955-5987

Cohen, Miriam L. (8 mentions)
U of Maryland, 1964
200 E 33rd St #551, Baltimore, 410-243-4982

Cummings, Charles C. (4 mentions)
Certification: Cardiovascular Disease, Internal Medicine
1838 Greene Tree Rd #535, Pikesville, 410-653-3923
410 Malcolm Dr #A, Westminster, 410-857-1200

Fisher, Stacy (6 mentions)
U of Maryland, 1994 *Certification:* Cardiovascular Disease
1838 Greene Tree Rd #535, Pikesville, 410-653-3923

Gaskin, Peter (3 mentions)
FMS-Jamaica *Certification:* Pediatric Cardiology, Pediatrics
4-C North Ave #423, Bel Air, 410-328-6749
22 S Greene St, Baltimore, 410-328-6749

Gurbel, Paul Alfred (4 mentions)
U of Maryland, 1983 *Certification:* Cardiovascular Disease,
   Internal Medicine, Interventional Cardiology
5051 Greenspring Ave #304, Baltimore, 410-521-5600

Ince, Carlos Sidney, Jr. (4 mentions)
Duke U, 1992 *Certification:* Cardiovascular Disease
3449 Wilkens Ave #300, Baltimore, 410-644-5111

Israel, Warren (4 mentions)
Hahnemann U, 1972
Certification: Cardiovascular Disease, Internal Medicine
2411 W Belvedere Ave #202, Baltimore, 410-367-6939

Kahn, Brian H. (3 mentions)
U of Maryland, 1981
Certification: Cardiovascular Disease, Internal Medicine
7602 Belair Rd, Baltimore, 410-663-6986

Mason, Steven Janney (5 mentions)
Harvard U, 1972
Certification: Cardiovascular Disease, Internal Medicine
9105 Franklin Square Dr #209, Rosedale, 410-574-1330

Meilman, Henry (3 mentions)
New York U, 1977 *Certification:* Cardiovascular Disease,
   Internal Medicine, Interventional Cardiology
3333 N Calvert St #500, Baltimore, 410-366-5600

Midei, Mark Gene (6 mentions)
Northeastern Ohio U, 1981 *Certification:* Cardiovascular
   Disease, Internal Medicine, Interventional Cardiology
7505 Osler Dr #103-A, Towson, 410-427-2580

Morris, Frank Hugh (3 mentions)
U of Maryland, 1975 *Certification:* Cardiovascular Disease,
   Internal Medicine, Interventional Cardiology
7501 Isler Dr 3rd Fl, Towson, 410-583-1170

Mugmon, Marc Alain (3 mentions)
George Washington U, 1973
Certification: Cardiovascular Disease, Internal Medicine
3333 N Calvert St #500, Baltimore, 410-366-5600

Plantholt, Stephen Joseph (5 mentions)
U of Maryland, 1977
Certification: Cardiovascular Disease, Internal Medicine
3449 Wilkens Ave #300, Baltimore, 410-644-5111

Pollock, Stephen Herbert (3 mentions)
U of Maryland, 1975
Certification: Cardiovascular Disease, Internal Medicine
7505 Osler Dr #103-A, Towson, 410-427-2580

Porterfield, James K. (14 mentions)
West Virginia U, 1980
Certification: Cardiovascular Disease, Internal Medicine
6569 N Charles St #600, Towson, 410-825-5150

Pristoop, Allan Sanford (3 mentions)
U of Maryland, 1967
Certification: Cardiovascular Disease, Internal Medicine
1838 Greene Tree Rd #535, Pikesville, 410-653-3923

Quartner, Jeffrey Lee (3 mentions)
U of Maryland, 1975
Certification: Cardiovascular Disease, Internal Medicine
1838 Greene Tree Rd #535, Pikesville, 410-653-3923

Riley, Reed D. (11 mentions)
Johns Hopkins U, 1988 *Certification:* Cardiovascular Disease
600 N Wolfe St, Baltimore, 410-955-3116
6701 N Charles St, Baltimore, 443-849-8989

Russell, Stuart Dean (3 mentions)
U of Washington, 1991
Certification: Cardiovascular Disease, Internal Medicine
601 N Caroline St, Baltimore, 410-955-5708

Schamp, David Julian (3 mentions)
U of Maryland, 1983 *Certification:* Cardiovascular Disease,
   Clinical Cardiac Electrophysiology, Internal Medicine
3333 N Calvert St #500, Baltimore, 410-366-5600

Schechter, Ronald David (5 mentions)
U of Maryland, 1982
Certification: Cardiovascular Disease, Internal Medicine
7501 Osler Dr, Towson, 410-339-7910

Scheel, Janet N. (3 mentions)
Certification: Pediatric Cardiology, Pediatrics
601 N Caroline St, Baltimore, 410-955-5987

Sura, Amish Chandrakant (3 mentions)
U of North Carolina, 2000
Certification: Cardiovascular Disease, Internal Medicine
301 St Paul Pl #310, Baltimore, 410-332-9752

Tanio, Jennifer W. (3 mentions)
Certification: Cardiovascular Disease
10755 Falls Rd #340, Lutherville, 410-583-2740

Traill, Thomas Anthony (6 mentions)
FMS-United Kingdom, 1971
601 N Caroline St #7213, Baltimore, 410-614-3140

Zawodny, Robert Vincent (3 mentions)
U of Maryland, 1983 *Certification:* Cardiovascular Disease,
   Internal Medicine, Interventional Cardiology
301 St Paul Place #310, Baltimore, 410-547-1885
7672 Belair Rd, Baltimore, 410-663-8100

Ziegelstein, Roy Charles (5 mentions)
Boston U, 1986
Certification: Cardiovascular Disease, Internal Medicine
4940 Eastern Ave, Baltimore, 410-550-0536

Dermatology

Anderson, Regina Helen (13 mentions)
U of Oklahoma, 1977
Certification: Dermatology, Internal Medicine
4100 N Charles St #114, Baltimore, 410-889-7600

Beacham, Bruce Edmund (6 mentions)
U of Maryland, 1975
Certification: Dermatology, Internal Medicine
1205 York Rd #20, Lutherville, 410-583-2328

Cohen, Bernard Alan (15 mentions)
Johns Hopkins U, 1977
Certification: Dermatology, Pediatric Dermatology, Pediatrics
601 N Caroline St, Baltimore, 410-955-2049
10755 Falls Rd #360, Lutherville, 410-583-2727

Epstein, Bonnie S. (7 mentions)
Boston U, 1981 *Certification:* Dermatology
2360 W Joppa Rd #208, Lutherville, 410-823-0350

Esterson, Faith Debra (5 mentions)
U of California-San Diego, 1989 *Certification:* Dermatology
1838 Greene Tree Rd #121, Pikesville, 410-486-3990

Jampel, Risa Maura (6 mentions)
Yale U, 1982 *Certification:* Dermatology
21 Crossroads Dr #325, Owings Mills, 410-356-0171

Lowitt, Mark Harris (11 mentions)
Tulane U, 1987 *Certification:* Dermatology
6565 N Charles St #315, Towson, 410-321-1195

Simmons-O'Brien, Eva F. (5 mentions)
Yale U, 1988 *Certification:* Dermatology
8320 Bellona Ave #20, Towson, 410-821-7546
601 N Caroline St, Baltimore, 410-933-1272

Sweren, Ronald Jay (6 mentions)
U of Maryland, 1976 *Certification:* Dermatology, Pediatrics
601 N Caroline St, Baltimore, 410-955-5933
10755 Falls Rd #350, Lutherville, 410-847-3767

Wolfe, Irving Darryl (8 mentions)
U of Maryland, 1968 *Certification:* Dermatology
21 Crossroads Dr #255, Owings Mills, 410-363-2320

Emergency Medicine

Barish, Robert Alan (3 mentions)
New York Med Coll, 1979
Certification: Emergency Medicine, Internal Medicine
22 S Hreen St, Baltimore, 410-706-3100

Bessent, Carl Timothy (3 mentions)
U of Maryland, 1973
Certification: Emergency Medicine, Internal Medicine
7601 Osler Dr #200, Towson, 410-821-7471

Bessman, Edward S. (3 mentions)
Certification: Emergency Medicine
4940 Eastern Ave, Baltimore, 410-550-0497

Browne, Brian Joseph (4 mentions)
SUNY-Downstate Med Coll, 1979
Certification: Emergency Medicine
110 S Pace St #200 6th Fl, Baltimore, 410-328-8025

Cunningham, Gail Patricia (4 mentions)
Georgetown U, 1987 *Certification:* Emergency Medicine
7601 Osler Dr #200, Towson, 410-821-7471

Faber, Clifford Stephen (4 mentions)
U of Maryland, 1977
Certification: Emergency Medicine, Internal Medicine
5401 Old Court Rd, Randallstown, 410-496-8715

Frankel, Dov (3 mentions)
FMS-Israel, 2003 *Certification:* Emergency Medicine
2401 W Belvedere Ave, Baltimore, 410-601-9000

Kelen, Gabor D. (5 mentions)
Certification: Emergency Medicine
600 N Wolfe St, Baltimore, 410-955-2280

Rothkin, Michael B. (9 mentions)
FMS-Dominica, 1988
5401 Old Court Rd, Randallstown, 410-521-5950

Scruggs, Kevin (5 mentions)
Certification: Emergency Medicine
5601 Loch Raven Blvd, Baltimore, 443-444-8000

Sternlicht, Jeffrey Paul (5 mentions)
SUNY-Downstate Med Coll, 1994
Certification: Emergency Medicine
6701 N Charles St, Towson, 443-849-2226

Strauss, David Lloyd (3 mentions)
U of Maryland, 1978 *Certification:* Emergency Medicine
6701 N Charles St, Baltimore, 443-849-2225

Wogan, John McLain (8 mentions)
Georgetown U, 1980
Certification: Emergency Medicine, Internal Medicine
6701 N Charles St, Towson, 443-849-2225

Endocrinology

Cheikh, Issam E. (7 mentions)
FMS-Syria, 1968
Certification: Endocrinology and Metabolism, Internal Medicine
201 E University Pkwy #501, Baltimore, 410-554-4511

Cooper, David Stephen (13 mentions)
Tufts U, 1973 *Certification:* Endocrinology and Metabolism,
   Endocrinology, Diabetes, and Metabolism, Internal Medicine
601 N Caroline St 7th Fl, Baltimore, 410-502-4926

Dicke, James A. (6 mentions)
Certification: Endocrinology, Diabetes, and Metabolism,
Internal Medicine
6701 N Charles St, Towson, 410-296-5484
826 Washington Rd, Westminster, 410-751-2510

Donner, Thomas Walter (11 mentions)
U of Virginia, 1986 *Certification:* Endocrinology, Diabetes,
and Metabolism, Internal Medicine
22 S Greene St #N-6-W-100, Baltimore, 410-328-6584
419 W Redwood St 600, Baltimore, 410-328-6542

Ladenson, Paul William (10 mentions)
Harvard U, 1975
Certification: Endocrinology and Metabolism, Internal Medicine
1830 E Monument St #333, Baltimore, 410-955-3663

Mersey, James Harris (10 mentions)
Johns Hopkins U, 1972
Certification: Endocrinology and Metabolism, Internal Medicine
6535 N Charles St #400, Baltimore, 410-828-7417

Shomali, Mansur Elias (5 mentions)
FMS-Canada, 1994 *Certification:* Endocrinology, Diabetes,
and Metabolism, Internal Medicine
201 E University Pkwy #501, Baltimore, 410-554-4511

Valente, William Albert (12 mentions)
U of Maryland, 1974
Certification: Endocrinology and Metabolism, Internal Medicine
900 Caton Ave, Baltimore, 410-368-3120

Family Practice *(see note on page 9)*

Ferentz, Kevin Scott (4 mentions)
U of Buffalo, 1983 *Certification:* Family Medicine
29 S Paca St, Baltimore, 410-328-8792

Hamidi, Cyrus (4 mentions)
U of Maryland, 1994 *Certification:* Family Medicine
913 Ridgebrook Rd #312, Sparks Glencoe, 410-472-6560

King, Joyce Ellen (4 mentions)
U of Michigan, 1989 *Certification:* Family Medicine
9101 Franklin Square Dr #205, Rosedale, 443-777-2000

Niehoff, John Michael (3 mentions)
Pennsylvania State U, 1981
Certification: Family Medicine, Sports Medicine
9101 Franklin Square Dr #205, Rosedale, 443-777-2000

Stewart, Donald Wallace (3 mentions)
U of Maryland, 1955
711 W 40th St #212-A, Baltimore, 410-366-1838

Valle, Paul Anthony, Jr. (3 mentions)
U of Maryland, 1981
Certification: Family Medicine, Geriatric Medicine
6565 N Charles St #313, Towson, 443-849-3680

Whiteford, Sarah D. (3 mentions)
U of Maryland, 1998 *Certification:* Family Medicine
6565 N Charles St #411, Towson, 443-849-2707

Zebley, Joseph Wildman (3 mentions)
U of Maryland, 1976 *Certification:* Family Medicine
2 Hamill Rd #222, Baltimore, 443-524-4481

Gastroenterology

Bedine, Marshall Stephen (10 mentions)
Boston U, 1967
Certification: Gastroenterology, Internal Medicine
10751 Fall Rd #301, Lutherville, 410-583-2633

Darwin, Peter Edwin (5 mentions)
U of Maryland, 1990
Certification: Gastroenterology, Internal Medicine
22 S Greene St, Baltimore, 410-328-8729

Goldberg, Neil David (7 mentions)
U of Maryland, 1977
Certification: Gastroenterology, Internal Medicine
7505 Osler Dr #307, Towson, 410-296-4210

Greenwald, Bruce David (6 mentions)
U of Maryland, 1987
Certification: Gastroenterology, Internal Medicine
419 W Redwood St #600, Baltimore, 410-328-5196
22 S Greene St, Baltimore, 410-328-8731

Hansen, F. Christian, III (5 mentions)
Johns Hopkins U, 1982
Certification: Gastroenterology, Internal Medicine
10751 Falls Rd #303, Lutherville-Timonium, 410-583-2630

Hutcheon, David Forbes (8 mentions)
Columbia U, 1973
Certification: Gastroenterology, Internal Medicine
10751 Falls Rd #303, Lutherville, 410-583-2630

Posner, David Browne (5 mentions)
U of Maryland, 1970
Certification: Gastroenterology, Internal Medicine
301 Saint Paul St #718, Baltimore, 410-332-9592

Tuchman, David N. (7 mentions)
Albert Einstein Coll of Med, 1976
Certification: Pediatric Gastroenterology, Pediatrics
2411 W Belvedere Ave #407, Baltimore, 410-601-8663

Tucker, Harold Jeffrey (5 mentions)
U of Maryland, 1973
Certification: Gastroenterology, Internal Medicine
10751 Falls Rd #303, Lutherville, 410-583-2630

Wolf, Edward Jay (11 mentions)
SUNY-Downstate Med Coll, 1980
Certification: Gastroenterology, Internal Medicine
7704 Quarterfield Rd #A, Glen Burnie, 410-863-4899

General Surgery

Buck, James Russell (5 mentions)
Johns Hopkins U, 1974 *Certification:* Pediatric Surgery
5900 Cedar Ln, Columbia, 443-849-6201
6565 N Charles St #305, Towson, 443-849-6201
520 Upper Chesapeake Dr, Bel Air, 443-849-6201

Cameron, John Lemuel (6 mentions)
Johns Hopkins U, 1962 *Certification:* Surgery, Thoracic Surgery
600 N Wolfe St #679, Baltimore, 410-955-5166

Choti, Michael Andrew (3 mentions)
Yale U, 1983 *Certification:* Surgery
600 N Wolfe St #665, Baltimore, 410-955-7113

Colombani, Paul Michael (3 mentions)
U of Kentucky, 1976 *Certification:* Pediatric Surgery, Surgery
600 N Wolfe St, Baltimore, 410-955-5000

Davis, Alan Steven (5 mentions)
U of Maryland, 1977 *Certification:* Surgery
21 Crossroads Dr #360, Owings Mills, 410-356-0410

Del Corro, Alberto (5 mentions)
FMS-Philippines, 1972 *Certification:* Surgery
9101 Franklin Square Dr #212, Rosedale, 410-391-3637

Duncan, Mona (10 mentions)
Cornell U, 1998 *Certification:* Surgery
716 Maiden Choice Ln #202, Catonsville, 410-719-0090
11055 Little Patuxent Pkwy #211, Columbia, 410-719-0090

Farha, Maen Jamal (6 mentions)
FMS-Lebanon, 1982 *Certification:* Surgery
7505 Osler Dr #310, Towson, 410-321-8720

Ferris, P. Jeffrey (5 mentions)
U of Maryland, 1984
Certification: Colon & Rectal Surgery, Surgery
9103 Franklin Square Dr #307, Baltimore, 443-777-6225

Fitzpatrick, James L. (8 mentions)
U of Maryland, 1982 *Certification:* Surgery
301 St Paul Pl #304, Baltimore, 410-332-9265
301 Saint Paul St, Baltimore, 410-332-9265

Gertner, Marc Howard (13 mentions)
Ohio State U, 1973 *Certification:* Surgery
23 Crossroads Dr #410, Owings Mills, 410-581-0700

Gurfinchel, Gregory (3 mentions)
Certification: Surgery
7310 Ritchie Hwy #515, Glen Burnie, 410-760-4344

Hamamoto, Gary (4 mentions)
Rosalind Franklin U, 1979 *Certification:* Surgery
23 Crossroads Dr #410, Owings Mills, 410-581-0700

Lidor, Anne O. (3 mentions)
New York Med Coll, 1996 *Certification:* Surgery
4940 Eastern Ave, Baltimore, 410-550-1226

Ross, Laurence Hirsch (5 mentions)
Case Western Reserve U, 1979 *Certification:* Surgery
1205 York Rd #22, Lutherville, 410-821-6260

Rotolo, Francis Steven (21 mentions)
U of Michigan, 1981 *Certification:* Surgery
1205 York Rd #22, Lutherville, 410-821-6260

Schultz, Michael Jonathan (4 mentions)
U of Maryland, 1971 *Certification:* Surgery
7501 Osler Dr #205, Towson, 410-427-5510

Turner, Joel Ari (7 mentions)
U of Maryland, 1992 *Certification:* Surgery
6569 N Charles St #506, Towson, 443-849-2395

Geriatrics

Black, Jason Wesley (3 mentions)
U of California-Davis, 1996
Certification: Family Medicine, Geriatric Medicine
6565 N Charles St #209, Towson, 443-849-3184

Burton, John Russell (10 mentions)
FMS-Canada, 1965
Certification: Geriatric Medicine, Internal Medicine, Nephrology
5505 Hopkins Bayview Cir, Baltimore, 410-550-0925

Christmas, Colleen (3 mentions)
U of Connecticut, 1993
Certification: Geriatric Medicine, Internal Medicine
5505 Hopkins Bayview Cir, Baltimore, 410-550-0925

Daly, Mel Patrick (3 mentions)
FMS-Ireland, 1981
Certification: Family Medicine, Geriatric Medicine
6565 N Charles St #209, Towson, 443-849-3184

Finucane, Thomas Emmett (14 mentions)
Emory U, 1978
Certification: Geriatric Medicine, Internal Medicine
5505 Hopkins Bayview Cir, Baltimore, 410-550-0925

Gloth, F. Michael, III (3 mentions)
Certification: Internal Medicine
5505 Hopkins Bayview Cir, Baltimore, 410-550-3420

Richardson, James Paul (3 mentions)
U of Maryland, 1980 *Certification:* Family Medicine,
Geriatric Medicine, Hospice and Palliative Medicine, Public
Health & General Preventive Medicine
700 Geipe Rd #200, Catonsville, 410-368-6000

Riley, W. Anthony (4 mentions)
6565 N Charles St #209, Towson, 443-849-3184

Hematology/Oncology

Aung, Sein (5 mentions)
FMS-Myanmar, 1983
Certification: Hematology, Internal Medicine, Medical Oncology
9103 Franklin Square Dr #2200, Baltimore, 443-777-7147

Bahrami, Hossein (3 mentions)
FMS-Iran, 2001
550 N Broadway, Baltimore, 410-955-8841

Bell, William Robert (3 mentions)
Georgetown U, 1963 *Certification:* Internal Medicine
306 Northfield Pl, Baltimore, 410-235-4686

Celano, Paul (6 mentions)
Mount Sinai Sch of Med, 1981
Certification: Internal Medicine, Medical Oncology
6701 N Charles St #205, Towson, 410-828-3051

Cohen, Gary Irvin (14 mentions)
U of Maryland, 1975
Certification: Hematology, Internal Medicine, Medical Oncology
6569 N Charles St #205, Towson, 410-828-3051

Donegan, Robert Brendan (4 mentions)
U of Maryland, 1991 *Certification:* Hematology, Medical Oncology
6569 N Charles St #205, Towson, 443-849-3051

Donehower, Ross Carl (4 mentions)
U of Minnesota, 1974
Certification: Internal Medicine, Medical Oncology
10755 Falls Rd, Lutherville-Timonium, 410-583-2970

Downs, John Christopher (3 mentions)
SUNY-Upstate Med U, 1981
Certification: Internal Medicine, Medical Oncology
7505 Osler Dr #302, Towson, 410-494-9099

Erlich, Rodrigo B. (8 mentions)
FMS-Brazil, 1987
Certification: Internal Medicine, Medical Oncology
2401 W Belvedere Ave, Baltimore, 410-601-4710

Feldman, Marvin Jack (7 mentions)
George Washington U, 1968
Certification: Hematology, Internal Medicine, Medical Oncology
227 St Paul Pl, Baltimore, 410-783-5858

Fetting, John Howard, III (9 mentions)
Johns Hopkins U, 1975
Certification: Internal Medicine, Medical Oncology, Psychiatry
10753 Falls Rd #415, Lutherville, 410-583-2970

Grossman, Neil J. (4 mentions)
Boston U, 1976
Certification: Pediatric Hematology-Oncology, Pediatrics
22 S Greene St #N-5E, Baltimore, 410-328-6749

Hahn, Davis Milford (5 mentions)
U of Virginia, 1971
Certification: Internal Medicine, Medical Oncology
5601 Loch Raven Blvd #103, Baltimore, 443-444-3991

Heyman, Meyer Reuben (3 mentions)
U of Maryland, 1970
Certification: Hematology, Internal Medicine, Medical Oncology
900 Caton Ave, Baltimore, 410-368-2917

Huslig, Richard Lawrence (4 mentions)
U of Miami, 1985 *Certification:* Medical Oncology
7505 Osler Dr #302, Towson, 410-494-9099

Ledakis, Panayotis (3 mentions)
FMS-Greece, 1987 *Certification:* Hematology, Medical Oncology
227 St Paul Pl, Baltimore, 410-783-5858

Miller, Carole Brennan (5 mentions)
U of Maryland, 1984
Certification: Internal Medicine, Medical Oncology
900 Caton Ave, Baltimore, 410-368-2909

Nesbitt, John Allison, III (5 mentions)
Johns Hopkins U, 1971
Certification: Hematology, Internal Medicine
200 E 33rd St #351, Baltimore, 410-235-4777

Padgett, Charles Allen (4 mentions)
Johns Hopkins U, 1973
Certification: Internal Medicine, Medical Oncology
5601 Loch Raven Blvd #103, Baltimore, 443-444-3996

Silva, Hector R. (4 mentions)
U Central del Caribe, 1980
Certification: Internal Medicine, Medical Oncology
7505 Osler Dr #302, Towson, 410-494-9099

Streiff, Michael Blake (6 mentions)
Johns Hopkins U, 1988
Certification: Hematology, Internal Medicine, Medical Oncology
600 N Wolfe St, Baltimore, 410-502-8642

Wiley, Joseph Michael (4 mentions)
U of Maryland, 1982
Certification: Pediatric Hematology-Oncology, Pediatrics
2401 W Belvedere Ave, Baltimore, 410-601-5303

Infectious Disease

Auwaerter, Paul Gisbert (9 mentions)
Columbia U, 1988
Certification: Infectious Disease, Internal Medicine
10753 Falls Rd #325, Lutherville-Timonium, 410-583-2774

Bahrain, Michelle L. (4 mentions)
Certification: Infectious Disease, Internal Medicine
9000 Franklin Sq Dr, Rosedale, 443-777-7138

Banerjee, Chandralekha (9 mentions)
U of Maryland, 1982
Certification: Infectious Disease, Internal Medicine
827 Linden Ave #3-F, Baltimore, 410-225-8404
5601 Lochraven Blvd, Baltimore, 443-444-4723

Bartlett, John Gill (10 mentions)
SUNY-Upstate Med U, 1963 *Certification:* Internal Medicine
1830 E Monument St #447, Baltimore, 410-955-7634

Berg, Richard Albert (14 mentions)
Cornell U, 1975
Certification: Infectious Disease, Internal Medicine
10755 Falls Rd #450, Lutherville, 410-583-2711

Campbell, Wayne N. (8 mentions)
Certification: Infectious Disease, Internal Medicine
200 E 33rd St 3rd Fl, Baltimore, 410-554-2284

Eder, Paul Arle (4 mentions)
Med Coll of Wisconsin, 1984 *Certification:* Infectious Disease
200 E 33rd St #640, Baltimore, 410-366-4441

Geckler, Ronald W. (4 mentions)
U of Florida, 1969
Certification: Infectious Disease, Internal Medicine
301 Saint Paul St, Baltimore, 301-332-9692

Haile, Charles A. (25 mentions)
U of Maryland, 1974
Certification: Infectious Disease, Internal Medicine
7505 Osler Dr #404, Towson, 410-337-7097

Levin, Michael Lee (5 mentions)
U of Maryland, 1963 *Certification:* Internal Medicine
2835 Smith Ave #207, Baltimore, 410-484-0102

Levy, Daniel Benjamin (4 mentions)
Johns Hopkins U, 1995
Certification: Infectious Disease, Internal Medicine
6701 N Charles St #5105, Towson, 443-849-3594

Salahuddin, Daliah K. (4 mentions)
FMS-Bangladesh, 1973
Certification: Infectious Disease, Internal Medicine
20 Crossroads Dr #101, Owings Mills, 410-902-1144

Wolff, Marcos Aurelio (4 mentions)
FMS-Brazil, 1986
Certification: Infectious Disease, Internal Medicine
9000 Franklin Square Dr, Rosedale, 443-777-7138

Zenilman, Jonathan Mark (6 mentions)
SUNY-Downstate Med Coll, 1981
Certification: Infectious Disease, Internal Medicine
4940 Eastern Ave Bldg B 3rd Fl, Baltimore, 410-550-0501

Infertility

Garcia, Jairo E. (5 mentions)
FMS-Colombia, 1969
10753 Falls Rd #335, Lutherville, 410-616-7140

Katz, Eugene (8 mentions)
FMS-Chile, 1978 *Certification:* Obstetrics & Gynecology, Reproductive Endocrinology/Infertility
6569 N Charles St #406, Baltimore, 410-512-8300

Padilla, Santiago Luis (6 mentions)
U of Puerto Rico, 1978 *Certification:* Obstetrics & Gynecology, Reproductive Endocrinology/Infertility
110 West Rd #102, Towson, 410-296-6400
2014 S Tollgate Rd #107, Bel Air, 410-569-1984

Internal Medicine *(see note on page 9)*

Akkad, Ayman Fathi (3 mentions)
FMS-Egypt, 1983 *Certification:* Internal Medicine
7600 Osler Dr #411, Towson, 410-832-5525

Alexander, Jeffrey S. (6 mentions)
Tulane U, 1990 *Certification:* Internal Medicine
120 Sister Pierre Dr #101, Towson, 443-901-0301

Angell, Charles Samuel (7 mentions)
Yale U, 1969 *Certification:* Internal Medicine
10755 Falls Rd #200, Lutherville, 410-583-7114

Bell, Stuart Bruce (4 mentions)
U of Maryland, 1977 *Certification:* Internal Medicine
200 E 33rd St #650, Baltimore, 410-889-8388

Domenici, Louis Joseph (3 mentions)
U of Maryland, 1978 *Certification:* Internal Medicine
22 S Greene St, Baltimore, 410-328-5196

Fairchild, Emily Stewart (3 mentions)
SUNY-Downstate Med Coll, 1977
Certification: Endocrinology and Metabolism, Internal Medicine
22 S Greene St, Baltimore, 410-328-5196

Fine, Ira Ted (3 mentions)
U of Maryland, 1975
Certification: Internal Medicine, Rheumatology
10753 Falls Rd #225, Lutherville, 410-583-2828

Frank, Dana Hunt (7 mentions)
George Washington U, 1978 *Certification:* Internal Medicine
10755 Falls Rd #200, Lutherville, 410-583-7112

Iglehart, Iredell W., III (3 mentions)
Johns Hopkins U, 1983
Certification: Internal Medicine, Rheumatology
6301 N Charles St #5, Baltimore, 410-372-0300

Josephs, Barry (3 mentions)
U of Maryland, 1978 *Certification:* Internal Medicine
7600 Osler Dr #311, Towson, 410-296-1467

Kaplan, Harry William (3 mentions)
New York U, 1989 *Certification:* Internal Medicine
4000 Old Court Rd #301, Baltimore, 410-653-0000

Krohe, Timothy Lee (9 mentions)
Johns Hopkins U, 1990 *Certification:* Internal Medicine
10755 Falls Rd #200, Lutherville, 410-583-7108

Lamos, Mark Allan (3 mentions)
Wayne State U, 1982 *Certification:* Internal Medicine
9 Schilling Rd, Hunt Valley, 410-771-9220

Lansdale, Thomas F., III (3 mentions)
Case Western Reserve U, 1982 *Certification:* Internal Medicine
6535 N Charles St #500, Baltimore, 410-296-4181

Magaziner, Jeffrey Lance (4 mentions)
U of Maryland, 1993 *Certification:* Internal Medicine
10755 Falls Rd, Lutherville, 410-583-2888

Malinow, Louis Barry (6 mentions)
U of Maryland, 1994 *Certification:* Internal Medicine
2700 Quarry Lake Dr #290, Baltimore, 410-484-4000

Malinow, Stanford Howard (3 mentions)
U of Maryland, 1968 *Certification:* Internal Medicine
2700 Quarry Lake Dr #290, Baltimore, 410-484-4000

Miller, Redonda Gail (3 mentions)
Johns Hopkins U, 1992 *Certification:* Internal Medicine
601 N Caroline St, Baltimore, 410-955-0670

Molavi, Rameen James (3 mentions)
Johns Hopkins U, 1996 *Certification:* Internal Medicine
10755 Falls Rd #470, Lutherville, 410-583-2790

Poulton, Scott Craig (5 mentions)
U of Maryland, 1986 *Certification:* Internal Medicine
405 Frederick Rd #204, Catonsville, 410-747-8773

Savadel, Patricia Ann (3 mentions)
Johns Hopkins U, 1981 *Certification:* Internal Medicine
10755 Falls Rd #200, Lutherville, 410-583-7177

Weglein, Donald Thomas (3 mentions)
U of Maryland, 1978 *Certification:* Internal Medicine
6535 N Charles St #450, Towson, 410-828-9828

Zolet, David Isaac (3 mentions)
Virginia Commonwealth U, 1979 *Certification:* Internal Medicine
9105 Franklin Square Dr #309, Rosedale, 443-777-8300

Nephrology

Al-Talib, Khalid Khalil (6 mentions)
FMS-Iraq, 1981 *Certification:* Internal Medicine, Nephrology
827 Linden Ave, Baltimore, 410-225-8480
9103 Franklin Square Dr #301, Baltimore, 443-777-6540

Amin, Akshay Narendra (4 mentions)
New York U, 1984 *Certification:* Internal Medicine, Nephrology
2 Hamill Rd #344, Baltimore, 410-323-3500

Choi, Michael J. (6 mentions)
Certification: Nephrology
1830 E Monument St, Baltimore, 410-955-5268

Fine, Derek Michael (4 mentions)
Johns Hopkins U, 1994 *Certification:* Nephrology
601 N Caroline St, Baltimore, 410-955-0670

Ghandour, Elias C. (8 mentions)
FMS-Lebanon, 1985 *Certification:* Internal Medicine, Nephrology
5601 Loch Raven Blvd #3-N, Baltimore, 443-444-3775

Greenwell, Robert C., Jr. (5 mentions)
U of Maryland, 1985 *Certification:* Internal Medicine, Nephrology
301 St Paul Pl #605, Baltimore, 410-332-1111
516 N Rolling Rd #107, Baltimore, 410-332-1111

Mandell, Ira Norman (10 mentions)
SUNY-Downstate Med Coll, 1972
Certification: Internal Medicine, Nephrology
1838 Greene Tree Rd #245, Pikesville, 410-602-7792

Philipson, Jonathan David (4 mentions)
FMS-Italy, 1979 *Certification:* Internal Medicine, Nephrology
2 Hamill Rd #344, Baltimore, 410-323-3500

Posner, Jeffrey N. (14 mentions)
Certification: Internal Medicine, Nephrology
1838 Greene Tree Rd #245, Pikesville, 410-602-7792
2405 York Rd #103, Lutherville, 410-308-3040

Rossiter, Kevin Allan (12 mentions)
Robert W Johnson Med Sch, 1983
Certification: Internal Medicine, Nephrology
9103 Franklin Square Dr #301, Rosedale, 443-777-6540

Weir, Matthew Ryan (4 mentions)
U of Virginia, 1978 *Certification:* Internal Medicine, Nephrology
22 S Greene St #N-3-W-143, Baltimore, 410-328-5720

Yen, Michael Chih-Wai (5 mentions)
FMS-China, 1965 *Certification:* Internal Medicine, Nephrology
821 N Eutaw St #401, Baltimore, 410-225-8947

Neurological Surgery

Bethel, Amiel Wren (10 mentions)
U of Pennsylvania, 1991 *Certification:* Neurological Surgery
6535 N Charles St #600, Towson, 443-849-4270
295 Stoner Ave #301, Westminster, 443-849-4270

Brem, Henry (7 mentions)
Harvard U, 1978 *Certification:* Neurological Surgery
600 N Wolfe St #133, Baltimore, 410-955-2248
601 N Caroline St, Baltimore, 410-955-2248

Carson, Benjamin Solomon (16 mentions)
U of Michigan, 1977 *Certification:* Neurological Surgery
600 N Wolfe St Harvey Bldg #811, Baltimore, 410-955-7888

Davis, Reginald James (8 mentions)
Johns Hopkins U, 1980 *Certification:* Neurological Surgery
6535 N Charles St #600, Baltimore, 443-849-4270

Eisenberg, Howard Michael (7 mentions)
SUNY-Downstate Med Coll, 1964
Certification: Neurological Surgery
22 S Greene St #S-12-D, Baltimore, 410-328-6034

Garonzik, Ira Martin (9 mentions)
Emory U, 1997 *Certification:* Neurological Surgery
10751 Falls Rd #420, Lutherville, 410-616-7900

Naff, Neal Jamison (17 mentions)
Johns Hopkins U, 1991 *Certification:* Neurological Surgery
10751 Falls Rd #301, Lutherville-Timonium, 410-616-7600

Olivi, Alessandro (7 mentions)
FMS-Italy, 1979 *Certification:* Neurological Surgery
600 N Wolfe St, Baltimore, 410-955-0703

Simard, J. Marc (7 mentions)
Creighton U, 1980 *Certification:* Neurological Surgery
22 S Greene St #12-D, Baltimore, 410-328-0850

Tamargo, Rafael Jesus (6 mentions)
Columbia U, 1984 *Certification:* Neurological Surgery
600 N Wolfe St Meye Bldg #8-181, Baltimore, 410-614-1533
601 N Caroline St, Baltimore, 410-614-1533

Neurology

Fleishman, Jerold Howard (10 mentions)
FMS-Grenada, 1983 *Certification:* Neurology
9000 Franklin Sq Dr, Rosedale, 443-777-7320

Genut, Abraham Allan (6 mentions)
U of Maryland, 1971 *Certification:* Neurology
7600 Osler Dr #105, Towson, 410-821-1377

Goldszmidt, Adrian Javier (3 mentions)
Harvard U, 1992 *Certification:* Neurology
5051 Greenspring Ave #300, Baltimore, 410-601-9515

Hillis, Argye Elizabeth (3 mentions)
Johns Hopkins U, 1995 *Certification:* Neurology
600 N Wolfe St Meye Bldg #6-113, Baltimore, 410-614-2381

Llinas, Rafael H. (4 mentions)
New York U, 1994 *Certification:* Neurology, Vascular Neurology
4940 Eastern Ave, Baltimore, 410-550-5624

McArthur, Justin Charles (5 mentions)
FMS-United Kingdom, 1979
Certification: Internal Medicine, Neurology
600 N Wolfe St Meyer Bldg #109, Baltimore, 410-955-3730

Moses, Howard (21 mentions)
U of Illinois, 1954 *Certification:* Neurology
1205 York Rd #39B, Lutherville, 410-494-0191

Mwaisela, Francis J. (8 mentions)
FMS-Tanzania, 1976 *Certification:* Clinical Neurophysiology
7401 Osler Dr #213, Towson, 410-321-6055

Pula, Thaddeus Peter (3 mentions)
U of Maryland, 1976 *Certification:* Neurology
827 Linden Ave, Baltimore, 410-225-8290

Rabin, Bruce Arlan (7 mentions)
U of Miami, 1989
Certification: Clinical Neurophysiology, Neurology
10755 Falls Rd #460, Lutherville, 410-616-7188
2411 W Belvedere Ave #202, Baltimore, 410-616-7188

Rosenberg, Jason David (4 mentions)
Harvard U, 1998 *Certification:* Neurology
4940 Eastern Ave, Baltimore, 410-550-5624

Shafrir, Yuval (3 mentions)
FMS-Israel, 1983 *Certification:* Neurology with Special
    Qualifications in Child Neurology
2435 W Belvedere Ave #32, Baltimore, 410-601-8300

Strauss, Steven L. (3 mentions)
Certification: Neurology
9000 Franklin Square Dr, Rosedale, 443-777-7320

Taylor, Richard Leslie (3 mentions)
U of Maryland, 1975
Certification: Clinical Neurophysiology, Neurology
22 West Rd #101, Towson, 410-823-3600

Weiss, Howard David (10 mentions)
Northwestern U, 1971 *Certification:* Neurology
2411 W Belvedere Ave #202, Baltimore, 410-367-7600

Wolf, James Sipos (6 mentions)
Indiana U, 1974 *Certification:* Neurology
6565 N Charles St #415, Towson, 410-821-7939

Obstetrics/Gynecology

Adashek, Steven Jeffrey (4 mentions)
U of Florida, 1983 *Certification:* Obstetrics & Gynecology
1205 York Rd #12, Lutherville, 410-296-8001

Anderson, Jean Rene (3 mentions)
Vanderbilt U, 1979 *Certification:* Obstetrics & Gynecology
10755 Falls Rd #420, Lutherville, 410-583-2749
600 N Wolfe St #247, Baltimore, 410-614-4496

Aziz, Basharat Jabeen (3 mentions)
FMS-Pakistan, 1969 *Certification:* Obstetrics & Gynecology
7505 Osler Dr #203, Towson, 410-823-1150

Genadry, Rene (3 mentions)
FMS-Lebanon, 1971 *Certification:* Obstetrics & Gynecology
10755 Falls Rd #330, Lutherville, 410-583-2991

Harman, Christopher R. (4 mentions)
22 S Greene St #N-6-E-16, Baltimore, 410-328-3865

Kates, Margery Ann (5 mentions)
U of Miami, 1985 *Certification:* Obstetrics & Gynecology
23 Crossroads Dr #220, Owings Mills, 410-581-9200

Khouzami, Victor Antonios (7 mentions)
FMS-Lebanon, 1974
Certification: Maternal-Fetal Medicine, Obstetrics & Gynecology
6565 N Charles St #406, Towson, 443-849-2568

Merryman, Ginny (3 mentions)
Vanderbilt U, 1986 *Certification:* Obstetrics & Gynecology
6569 N Charles St #501, Towson, 410-938-8960

Ottenritter, Robert Edgar (4 mentions)
FMS-Mexico, 1982
6565 N Charles St #212, Towson, 410-823-1120

Pleeter, Joel Franklin (3 mentions)
SUNY-Downstate Med Coll, 1990
Certification: Obstetrics & Gynecology
37 Walker Ave #100, Baltimore, 410-653-6500

Ritter, Carol Ann (3 mentions)
Med Coll of Wisconsin, 1983
Certification: Obstetrics & Gynecology
8415 Bellona Ln #213, Towson, 410-296-2557

Rosenshein, Neil Bruce (5 mentions)
U of Florida, 1969
Certification: Gynecologic Oncology, Obstetrics & Gynecology
301 St Paul Pl, Baltimore, 410-332-9205
11110 Medical Campus Rd #243-A, Hagerstown, 301-665-4640

Weitz, Claire Marie (7 mentions)
Albany Med Coll, 1979
Certification: Maternal-Fetal Medicine, Obstetrics & Gynecology
6565 N Charles St #406, Towson, 443-849-2568

Zern, Ruthann Theresa (8 mentions)
Duke U, 1979 *Certification:* Obstetrics & Gynecology
7505 Osler Dr #402, Baltimore, 410-339-7447
2103 Laurel Bush Rd, Bel Air, 410-515-7600

Ophthalmology

Abrams, Donald Andrew (3 mentions)
Med Coll of Pennsylvania, 1984 *Certification:* Ophthalmology
2411 W Belvedere Ave #6, Baltimore, 410-601-6480
2700 Quarry Lake Dr #180, Baltimore, 410-601-2020

Dankner, Stuart Roy (4 mentions)
SUNY-Upstate Med U, 1970 *Certification:* Ophthalmology
2 Hamill Rd #345, Baltimore, 410-433-8488
6100 Daylong Ln #207, Clarksville, 443-535-8755
1380 Progress Way #108, Eldersburg, 710-795-9590

Doxanas, Marcos Thomas (4 mentions)
U of Virginia, 1976 *Certification:* Ophthalmology
6231 N Charles St, Baltimore, 410-377-2044

Elman, Michael Joel (5 mentions)
Wayne State U, 1979 *Certification:* Ophthalmology
9114 Philadelphia Rd #310, Rosedale, 410-686-3000
1838 Greene Tree Rd #170, Pikesville, 410-653-0084

Fiergang, Dean L. (3 mentions)
Med Coll of Pennsylvania, 1991 *Certification:* Ophthalmology
2 Hamill Rd #345, Baltimore, 410-433-8488
6100 Daylong Ln #207, Clarksville, 443-535-8755
1380 Progress Way #108, Eldersburg, 410-795-9590

Honig, Marc Adam (3 mentions)
Johns Hopkins U, 1990 *Certification:* Ophthalmology
23 Crossroads Dr #310, Owings Mills, 410-581-1500

Jensen, Allan David (8 mentions)
Johns Hopkins U, 1968 *Certification:* Ophthalmology
200 E 33rd St #426, Baltimore, 410-235-1133
86 State Cir, Annapolis, 410-263-3492

Jun, Albert S. (3 mentions)
Emory U, 1997 *Certification:* Ophthalmology
600 N Wolfe St, Baltimore, 410-955-5490

Loeb, Robert Andrew (4 mentions)
U of Maryland, 1977 *Certification:* Ophthalmology
1105 N Point Blvd #323, Baltimore, 410-282-5544
6830 Hospital Dr #100, Baltimore, 410-574-1991

Miller, Neil Richard (4 mentions)
Johns Hopkins U, 1971 *Certification:* Ophthalmology
600 N Wolfe St #B-109, Baltimore, 410-955-5080

Rismondo, Vivian (4 mentions)
FMS-Croatia, 1973 *Certification:* Neurology
6569 N Charles St #505, Towson, 443-849-8082

Seitzman, Gerami Donyel (3 mentions)
U of Michigan, 1999 *Certification:* Ophthalmology
2411 W Belvedere Ave #6, Baltimore, 410-601-5991

Stark, Walter Jackson (4 mentions)
U of Oklahoma, 1967 *Certification:* Ophthalmology
10755 Falls Rd, Lutherville-Timonium, 410-955-5490

Strauss, Leon (3 mentions)
U of Maryland, 1982 *Certification:* Ophthalmology
1777 Reisterstown Rd #380, Pikesville, 410-484-5550

Waeltermann, Joanne M. (3 mentions)
Certification: Ophthalmology
1011 Frederick Rd, Catonsville, 410-744-0400
419 W Redmond St #420, Baltimore, 410-328-6533

Weinberg, Robert Stephen (4 mentions)
Johns Hopkins U, 1969 *Certification:* Ophthalmology
4940 Eastern Ave, Baltimore, 410-550-2362

Wilkinson, Charles Patton (4 mentions)
Johns Hopkins U, 1966 *Certification:* Ophthalmology
6569 N Charles St #505, Towson, 443-849-2644

Zimmerman, Amy (5 mentions)
U of Maryland, 1990 *Certification:* Ophthalmology
8556 Fort Smallwood Rd, Pasadena, 410-437-4440
1105 N Point Blvd #323, Baltimore, 410-282-5954
6830 Hospital Dr, Baltimore, 410-282-5544

Orthopedics

Dalury, David Francis (6 mentions)
Dartmouth Coll, 1984 *Certification:* Orthopaedic Surgery
8322 Bellona Ave #100, Baltimore, 410-337-7900

Delanois, Ronald (3 mentions)
Uniformed Services U of Health Sciences, 1991
Certification: Orthopaedic Surgery
2401 W Belvedere Ave, Baltimore, 410-601-8500

Dvorkin, Michael L. (3 mentions)
Certification: Orthopaedic Surgery
1050 S North Point Rd #101, Baltimore, 410-282-7600

Ebert, Frank Ross (3 mentions)
Temple U, 1979 *Certification:* Orthopaedic Surgery
3333 N Calvert St #400, Baltimore, 410-554-2850
1407 York Rd #100-A, Lutherville, 410-821-8894

Frassica, Frank J. (5 mentions)
Certification: Orthopaedic Surgery
600 N Wolfe St, Baltimore, 410-502-2698

Jacobs, Michael Aaron (4 mentions)
Columbia U, 1979 *Certification:* Orthopaedic Surgery
5601 Loch Raven Blvd #405, Baltimore, 443-444-4764

Johnson, Carl Alvin (3 mentions)
Johns Hopkins U, 1977 *Certification:* Orthopaedic Surgery
4940 Eastern Ave, Baltimore, 410-550-0453

Khanna, Akhil Jay (3 mentions)
Georgetown U, 1995 *Certification:* Orthopaedic Surgery
5601 Loch Raven Blvd #G-1, Baltimore, 410-444-4730

Koehler, Stewart L., Jr. (4 mentions)
U of Maryland, 1978 *Certification:* Orthopaedic Surgery
6565 N Charles St 606, Towson, 410-583-0160

Koman, Jon David (3 mentions)
Rosalind Franklin U, 1994 *Certification:* Orthopaedic Surgery
2700 Quarry Lake Dr #300, Baltimore, 410-377-8900
4 Park Center Ct #102, Owings Mills, 410-377-8900

Ludwig, Steven Craig (4 mentions)
Robert W Johnson Med Sch, 1993
Certification: Orthopaedic Surgery
1 Texas Station Ct #300, Lutherville, 410-683-2120

Matthews, Leslie Scott (15 mentions)
Baylor U, 1976 *Certification:* Orthopaedic Surgery
3333 N Calvert St #400, Baltimore, 410-554-2865

Mears, Simon Cavendish (3 mentions)
U of Pittsburgh, 1996 *Certification:* Orthopaedic Surgery
4924 Campbell Blvd #130, Baltimore, 443-442-2080

O'Donnell, John Brendan (4 mentions)
U of North Carolina, 1980 *Certification:* Orthopaedic Surgery
3333 N Calvert St #400, Baltimore, 410-554-2270

Riley, Lee Hunter, III (5 mentions)
Johns Hopkins U, 1986 *Certification:* Orthopaedic Surgery
601 N Caroline St #5231, Baltimore, 410-955-6930

Scheerer, Michael Thomas (3 mentions)
U of Maryland, 1977 *Certification:* Orthopaedic Surgery
2700 Quarry Lake Dr #300, Baltimore, 410-581-6799
6565 N Charles St #504, Towson, 410-377-8900

Schmidt, Leroy Michael (5 mentions)
U of Maryland, 1984 *Certification:* Orthopaedic Surgery
6565 N Charles St #606, Towson, 410-583-0160

Silverstein, Scott Lee (3 mentions)
U of Pittsburgh, 1995 *Certification:* Orthopaedic Surgery
3421 benson Ave #100, Baltimore, 410-644-1880
5999 Harpers Farm Rd #250, Columbia, 410-644-1880

Sponseller, Paul David (4 mentions)
U of Michigan, 1980 *Certification:* Orthopaedic Surgery
601 N Caroline St #5260, Baltimore, 410-955-3870

Tortolani, Paul Justin (6 mentions)
Cornell U, 1997 *Certification:* Orthopaedic Surgery
8322 Bellona Ave #100, Towson, 410-337-7900
7505 Osler Dr #104, Towson, 410-337-8888

Waldman, Barry Jay (3 mentions)
Johns Hopkins U, 1992 *Certification:* Orthopaedic Surgery
2700 Quarry Lake Dr #300, Baltimore, 410-377-8900
4 Park Center Ct #102, Owings Mills, 410-377-8900

Wilckens, John H. (5 mentions)
Certification: Orthopaedic Surgery
4940 Eastern Ave, Baltimore, 410-550-0453

Otorhinolaryngology

Clayton, Robert Andrew (6 mentions)
U of Maryland, 1986 *Certification:* Otolaryngology
120 Sister Pierre Dr #202, Towson, 410-825-3900
2014 Tollgate Rd #101, Bel Air, 410-569-7200

Diehn, Karl William (13 mentions)
U of Maryland, 1975 *Certification:* Otolaryngology
6565 N Charles #601, Baltimore, 410-821-5151

Flint, Paul Warren (5 mentions)
Baylor U, 1982 *Certification:* Otolaryngology
601 N Caroline St, Baltimore, 410-955-6240

Goldstone, Andrew Curt (12 mentions)
Jefferson Med Coll, 1985 *Certification:* Otolaryngology
6565 N Charles St #601, Baltimore, 410-821-5151

Kaplan, Brian Andrew (6 mentions)
U of Virginia, 1998 *Certification:* Otolaryngology
6535 N Charles St #200-A, Towson, 410-821-5151
6565 N Charles St #601, Towson, 410-821-5151

Kashima, Matthew L. (6 mentions)
Certification: Otolaryngology
4940 Eastern Ave, Baltimore, 410-550-2368

Kunar, Dario Rajendra (13 mentions)
Johns Hopkins U, 1993 *Certification:* Otolaryngology
6565 N Charles St #601, Baltimore, 410-821-5151

Weiss, Michael David (6 mentions)
Johns Hopkins U, 1976 *Certification:* Otolaryngology
23 Crossroads Dr #400, Owings Mills, 410-356-2626

Pain Medicine

Block, Brian Michael (4 mentions)
Case Western Reserve U, 1998
Certification: Anesthesiology, Pain Medicine
8322 Bellona Ave #330, Towson, 410-825-6945

Brokaw, Jason Phipps (4 mentions)
Virginia Commonwealth U, 1999
Certification: Pain Medicine, Physical Medicine & Rehabilitation
2700 Quarry Lake Dr #300, Baltimore, 410-377-8900
4 Park Center Ct #102, Owings Mills, 410-377-8900

Christo, Paul Jordan (5 mentions)
U of Louisville, 1995 *Certification:* Anesthesiology, Pain Medicine
550 N Broadway #301, Baltimore, 410-955-1818

Elsamanoudi, Ibrahim Ahmed (5 mentions)
Certification: Anesthesiology, Pain Medicine
201 E University Pkwy, Baltimore, 410-554-2000

Maine, David (4 mentions)
U of Rochester, 2002 *Certification:* Anesthesiology, Pain Medicine
301 St Paul Pl #321, Baltimore, 410-322-9036

Sugar, Ross Carl (4 mentions)
Virginia Commonwealth U, 1998
Certification: Pain Medicine, Physical Medicine & Rehabilitation
2401 W Belvedere Ave, Baltimore, 410-601-5597

Pathology

Argani, Pedram A. (3 mentions)
Certification: Anatomic Pathology
401 N BBroadway #2242, Baltimore, 410-955-8117

Askin, Frederic Barton (7 mentions)
U of Virginia, 1964 *Certification:* Anatomic Pathology
600 N Wolfe St #600, Baltimore, 410-550-0671

Burger, Peter C. (4 mentions)
Northwestern U, 1966
Certification: Anatomic Pathology, Neuropathology
600 N Wolfe St #710, Baltimore, 410-955-8378

Epstein, Jonathan Ira (6 mentions)
Boston U, 1981 *Certification:* Anatomic Pathology
600 N Wolfe St, Baltimore, 410-614-6330
401 N Broadway #2242, Baltimore, 410-614-6330

Larsen, Moira Potash (4 mentions)
Johns Hopkins U, 1986
Certification: Anatomic Pathology, Clinical Pathology
5601 Loch Raven Blvd, Baltimore, 443-444-4178

McTighe, Arthur Henry (3 mentions)
U of Pittsburgh, 1969
Certification: Anatomic Pathology & Clinical Pathology,
  Cytopathology, Dermatopathology, Medical Microbiology
201 E University Pkwy, Baltimore, 410-554-2750

Palermo, Robert Allen (3 mentions)
Mount Sinai Sch of Med, 1978
Certification: Anatomic Pathology & Clinical Pathology
6701 N Charles St, Towson, 443-849-2257

Siegel, Howard Leonard (11 mentions)
U of Maryland, 1981
Certification: Anatomic Pathology & Clinical Pathology
6701 N Charles St, Towson, 410-849-2247

Pediatrics *(see note on page 9)*

Ancona, Robert John (4 mentions)
Johns Hopkins U, 1972
Certification: Pediatric Infectious Diseases, Pediatrics
2 Hamill Rd #405, Baltimore, 410-323-1144

Bhagtani, Harsha R. (4 mentions)
Pennsylvania State U, 1998 *Certification:* Pediatrics
9101 Franklin Square Dr #205, Rosedale, 443-777-2000

Brown, Ralph Stuart (3 mentions)
Johns Hopkins U, 1971 *Certification:* Pediatrics
2435 W Belvedere Ave #52, Baltimore, 410-601-8301

Caplan, Steven Elliot (3 mentions)
U of Rochester, 1975 *Certification:* Pediatrics
2411 W Belvedere Ave #308, Baltimore, 410-601-8383

Doran, Timothy Francis (14 mentions)
Tufts U, 1977 *Certification:* Pediatrics
6565 N Charles St #306, Towson, 410-512-6444

Feldman, Stephen Ross (3 mentions)
Virginia Commonwealth U, 1979 *Certification:* Pediatrics
8600 Lasalle Rd #105, Towson, 410-823-5232
4C North Ave #400, Bel Air, 410-638-0239

Fragetta, James Edward (8 mentions)
U of Tennessee, 1990 *Certification:* Pediatrics
10807 Falls Rd #200, Lutherville-Timonium, 410-321-9393

Ganunis, Travis (5 mentions)
Certification: Pediatrics
10755 Falls Rd #260, Lutherville-Timonium, 410-583-2955

Gisriel Bittar, Deborah (4 mentions)
Johns Hopkins U, 1983 *Certification:* Pediatrics
515 Fairmount Ave #200, Towson, 410-828-8938

Goldstein, Jason Neil (4 mentions)
Johns Hopkins U, 2001 *Certification:* Pediatrics
10755 Falls Rd #260, Lutherville-Timonium, 410-583-2955

Krugman, Scott Daniel (3 mentions)
Dartmouth Coll, 1995 *Certification:* Pediatrics
9101 Franklin Square Dr #205, Baltimore, 443-777-2000
9000 Franklin Square Dr, Rosedale, 443-777-7128
5009 Honeygo Center Dr #225, Perry Hall, 443-725-2100

Lake, Alan Mason (10 mentions)
U of Cincinnati, 1973 *Certification:* Pediatrics
10807 Falls Rd #200, Lutherville, 410-321-9393

Roskes, Saul David (3 mentions)
Johns Hopkins U, 1963
Certification: Pediatric Nephrology, Pediatrics
10807 Falls Rd #200, Lutherville-Timonium, 410-321-9393

Schuberth, Kenneth Charles (3 mentions)
Johns Hopkins U, 1973
Certification: Allergy & Immunology, Pediatrics
10807 Falls Rd #200, Lutherville, 410-321-9393

Starr, Barnaby Frederick (3 mentions)
Cornell U, 1982 *Certification:* Pediatrics
2 Hamill Rd #405, Baltimore, 410-323-1144

Winkelstein, Amy Link (3 mentions)
Yale U, 2000 *Certification:* Pediatrics
10807 Falls Rd #200, Lutherville-Timonium, 410-321-9393

Plastic Surgery

Basner, Adam Lawrence (6 mentions)
Columbia U, 1989 *Certification:* Plastic Surgery
1304 Bellona Ave, Lutherville, 410-616-3000

Chang, Bernard Won (6 mentions)
U of California-Los Angeles, 1984 *Certification:* Plastic Surgery
227 St Paul Pl, Baltimore, 410-332-9700

Cohen, Michael David (7 mentions)
Tulane U, 1986 *Certification:* Plastic Surgery
8322 Bellona Ave #300, Towson, 410-296-0414

Crawley, William Allen (6 mentions)
Johns Hopkins U, 1979 *Certification:* Plastic Surgery
6565 N Charles St #401, Baltimore, 410-494-1450

Manson, Paul Nellis (13 mentions)
Northwestern U, 1968 *Certification:* Plastic Surgery
601 N Caroline St #8152-F, Baltimore, 410-955-9469

Ringelman, Paul Robert (9 mentions)
U of Maryland, 1984 *Certification:* Plastic Surgery
7401 Osler Dr #208, Baltimore, 410-823-3885

Psychiatry

Adler, Samuel Elliot (4 mentions)
Virginia Commonwealth U, 1973 *Certification:* Psychiatry
2401 W Belvedere Ave, Baltimore, 410-601-5461

Brandt, Harry Andrew (3 mentions)
U of Maryland, 1983 *Certification:* Psychiatry
7601 Osler Dr, Towson, 410-337-1090
6535 N Charles St #300, Towson, 410-938-5252

De Paulo, J. Raymond, Jr. (4 mentions)
Johns Hopkins U, 1972 *Certification:* Psychiatry
600 N Wolfe St St Meyer Bldg #4-113, Baltimore, 410-955-3266

Feinberg, Andrew Gary (3 mentions)
New Jersey Med Sch, 1981 *Certification:* Psychiatry
1104 Kenilworth Dr #209, Towson, 410-825-6666

Ferrans, Victor (4 mentions)
Tulane U, 1989 *Certification:* Psychiatry
2324 W Joppa Rd #220, Lutherville-Timonium, 410-583-2623

Haerian, Mohammad (3 mentions)
FMS-Iran, 1968 *Certification:* Child Psychiatry, Psychiatry
120 Sister Pierre Dr #407, Towson, 443-279-2000

Hagaman, Scott Dennis (4 mentions)
25 Dutton Ave, Catonsville, 410-455-0366

Lion, John Rene (4 mentions)
Albany Med Coll, 1965 *Certification:* Psychiatry
2 Village Sq #217, Baltimore, 410-433-6333

Lipsey, John Richard (3 mentions)
Johns Hopkins U, 1978 *Certification:* Psychiatry
600 N Wolfe St #3-181, Baltimore, 410-955-7162

McHugh, Paul Rodney (3 mentions)
Harvard U, 1956 *Certification:* Neurology, Psychiatry
600 N Wolfe St #119, Baltimore, 410-502-3150

Shaya, Elias Karim (7 mentions)
FMS-Lebanon, 1984 *Certification:* Geriatric Psychiatry, Psychiatry
5601 Loch Raven Blvd #406, Baltimore, 443-444-4540

Solberg, Kim Kilkowski (4 mentions)
U of Maryland, 1989 *Certification:* Psychiatry
6701 N Charles St #211, Towson, 443-849-2368

Treisman, Glenn Jordan (4 mentions)
U of Michigan, 1987 *Certification:* Psychiatry
600 N Wolfe St #113, Baltimore, 410-955-6328

Pulmonary Disease

Barr, Linda Freda (7 mentions)
U of Maryland, 1984 *Certification:* Critical Care Medicine,
  Internal Medicine, Pulmonary Disease
7505 Osler Dr #409, Towson, 410-321-5651

Britt, Edward James (4 mentions)
Tufts U, 1972
Certification: Internal Medicine, Pulmonary Disease
419 Redwood St #600, Baltimore, 410-706-2171

Buescher, Philip C. (5 mentions)
Certification: Critical Care Medicine, Internal Medicine,
  Pulmonary Disease
3333 N Calvert St #650, Baltimore, 410-467-4470

Eppler, John Henry, Jr. (5 mentions)
U of Cincinnati, 1979 *Certification:* Critical Care Medicine,
  Internal Medicine, Pulmonary Disease
7505 Osler Dr #409, Towson, 410-321-5651

Jacobs, Howard Terry (7 mentions)
U of Maryland, 1981 *Certification:* Critical Care Medicine,
  Internal Medicine, Pulmonary Disease
20 Crossroads Dr #210, Owings Mills, 410-363-7500

Nissim, Jack Edward (4 mentions)
Johns Hopkins U, 1971
Certification: Internal Medicine, Pulmonary Disease
7505 Osler Dr #410, Towson, 410-321-5651

Polito, Albert John (4 mentions)
New York U, 1989
Certification: Internal Medicine, Pulmonary Disease
301 St Paul Pl, Baltimore, 410-332-9145

Rizk, Salim (5 mentions)
FMS-Lebanon, 1987
Certification: Critical Care Medicine, Pulmonary Disease
3333 N Calvert St #650, Baltimore, 410-467-4470

Schwartz, Mitchell Lonny (7 mentions)
New Jersey Med Sch, 1987
Certification: Critical Care Medicine, Pulmonary Disease
6535 N Charles St #550, Towson, 410-494-1662

Scott, Penelope Pate (6 mentions)
Johns Hopkins U, 1971
Certification: Internal Medicine, Pulmonary Disease
5601 Loch Raven Blvd #512, Baltimore, 443-444-4835

Selinger, Stephen Robert (6 mentions)
Johns Hopkins U, 1979 *Certification:* Critical Care
Medicine, Internal Medicine, Pulmonary Disease
9103 Franklin Square Dr, Rosedale, 410-682-5282

Sloane, Peter Jeffrey (8 mentions)
Cornell U, 1985 *Certification:* Critical Care Medicine,
Internal Medicine, Pulmonary Disease
3333 N Calvert St #650, Baltimore, 410-467-4470

Steiner, Howard (8 mentions)
U of Maryland, 1983 *Certification:* Critical Care Medicine,
Internal Medicine, Pulmonary Disease, Sleep Medicine
5601 Loch Raven Blvd #512, Baltimore, 443-444-4835

Terry, Peter Browne (6 mentions)
St Louis U, 1968
Certification: Internal Medicine, Pulmonary Disease
1830 E Monument St 5th Fl, Baltimore, 410-614-0157

Radiology—Diagnostic

Ahn, Hyo Seung (3 mentions)
FMS-South Korea, 1971
Certification: Diagnostic Radiology, Neuroradiology
21 Crossroads Dr #100, Owings Mills, 410-363-6677

Andrew, Blair Jameson (5 mentions)
Dartmouth Coll, 1982 *Certification:* Diagnostic Radiology
9000 Franklin Sq Dr, Baltimore, 443-777-7150

Fishman, Elliot Keith (7 mentions)
U of Maryland, 1977 *Certification:* Diagnostic Radiology
601 N Caroline St #3254, Baltimore, 410-955-5173

Garfinkel, Darryl Jay (3 mentions)
U of Maryland, 1972 *Certification:* Diagnostic Radiology
21 Crossroads Dr #100, Owings Mills, 410-356-8186
200 Hospital Dr #Ll-20, Glen Burnie, 410-582-9729
2080 York Rd #160, Lutherville, 443-436-4700

Goodman, Lee Allan (3 mentions)
U of Maryland, 1973 *Certification:* Diagnostic Radiology
6701 N Charles St, Towson, 443-849-2320

Kraut, Michael Alan (3 mentions)
Albert Einstein Coll of Med, 1986
Certification: Diagnostic Radiology, Neuroradiology
600 N Wolfe St, Baltimore, 410-955-6500

Ma, Loralie Dawn (3 mentions)
U of Illinois, 1991
Certification: Diagnostic Radiology, Nuclear Radiology
7253 Ambassador Rd, Baltimore, 443-436-1116
6715 N Charles St, Baltimore, 410-296-5610

Munitz, Henry Alexander (6 mentions)
FMS-South Africa, 1975
6701 N Charles St, Towson, 410-580-2325

Sexton, Carlton Clark (8 mentions)
Duke U, 1978 *Certification:* Diagnostic Radiology, Neuroradiology
3333 N Calvert St, Baltimore, 410-554-2585
7 W Ridgely Rd, Timonium, 410-561-4674
21 Crossroads Dr #100, Owings Mills, 410-363-6677

Sill, David Carroll (3 mentions)
U of Pittsburgh, 1991 *Certification:* Diagnostic Radiology
301 Saint Paul Pl 1st Fl, Baltimore, 410-332-9268

White, Charles Stephen (4 mentions)
U of Buffalo, 1984
Certification: Diagnostic Radiology, Internal Medicine
22 S Greene St, Baltimore, 410-328-3477

Radiology—Therapeutic

Blumberg, Albert Leopold (5 mentions)
Jefferson Med Coll, 1974
Certification: Radiation Oncology, Therapeutic Radiology
6701 N Charles St, Towson, 410-828-2540

Brijbasi, Troy Andre (3 mentions)
U of Maryland, 1997 *Certification:* Diagnostic Radiology
7253 Ambassador Rd, Baltimore, 443-436-1151
9000 Franklin Sqr Dr, Baltimore, 443-777-7150

Gailloud, Philippe Edmond (3 mentions)
FMS-Switzerland, 1991
600 N Wolfe St, Baltimore, 410-955-8525

Kinnison, Malonnie Lee (4 mentions)
U of Michigan, 1976 *Certification:* Diagnostic Radiology,
Internal Medicine, Vascular & Interventional Radiology
7253 Ambassador Rd, Baltimore, 443-436-1100
6701 N Charles St, Towson, 410-281-9100

Regine, William Frank (3 mentions)
SUNY-Upstate Med U, 1987 *Certification:* Radiation Oncology
22 S Greene St, Baltimore, 410-328-7237

Wharam, Moody De Witt, Jr. (3 mentions)
U of Virginia, 1969 *Certification:* Therapeutic Radiology
600 N Wolfe St, Baltimore, 410-955-8964

Widlus, David Michael (4 mentions)
Albany Med Coll, 1981 *Certification:* Diagnostic Radiology,
Vascular & Interventional Radiology
22 S Greene St, Baltimore, 410-328-3477

Zinreich, Eva Sara (4 mentions)
FMS-Romania, 1970
Certification: Radiology, Therapeutic Radiology
6701 N Charles St, Towson, 443-849-2540

Rehabilitation

Brown, Scott E. (4 mentions)
Certification: Pain Medicine, Physical Medicine & Rehabilitation
2401 W Belvedere Ave, Baltimore, 410-601-5597

Hoffberg, Howard Joel (4 mentions)
Mount Sinai Sch of Med, 1980
Certification: Pain Medicine, Physical Medicine & Rehabilitation
10085 Red Run Blvd #404, Owings Mills, 410-363-7246

Reinstein, Leon (3 mentions)
U of Maryland, 1969
Certification: Physical Medicine & Rehabilitation
2401 W Belvedere Ave, Baltimore, 410-601-5923

Shear, Michael Stephen (3 mentions)
U of Maryland, 1982
Certification: Physical Medicine & Rehabilitation
1920 Greenspring Dr #125, Lutherville-Timonium,
 410-308-4900
3333 N Calvert St #350, Baltimore, 410-554-2253

Silver, Kenneth H. C. (4 mentions)
U of Maryland, 1980
Certification: Physical Medicine & Rehabilitation
5601 Loch Raven Blvd #403, Baltimore, 443-444-4700

Zorowitz, Richard David (4 mentions)
Tulane U, 1985 *Certification:* Physical Medicine &
Rehabilitation, Spinal Cord Injury Medicine
4940 Eastern Ave, Baltimore, 410-550-0438

Rheumatology

Bathon, Joan Marie (5 mentions)
U of Maryland, 1978
Certification: Internal Medicine, Rheumatology
5501 Hopkins Bayview Cir #1-B7, Baltimore, 410-550-8089

Fine, Ira Ted (17 mentions)
U of Maryland, 1975
Certification: Internal Medicine, Rheumatology
10753 Falls Rd #225, Lutherville, 410-583-2828

George, Stephen W. (5 mentions)
Certification: Internal Medicine, Pediatric Rheumatology,
Rheumatology
4801 Dorsey Hall Dr #226, Ellicott City, 410-992-7440

Hauptman, Howard Warren (14 mentions)
FMS-Grenada, 1982
Certification: Internal Medicine, Rheumatology
1220-B E Joppa Rd #310, Towson, 410-494-1888

Hellmann, David Bruce (10 mentions)
Johns Hopkins U, 1977
Certification: Internal Medicine, Rheumatology
4940 Eastern Ave #B-1N, Baltimore, 410-550-0516

Holt, Peter Anthony (7 mentions)
Johns Hopkins U, 1978
Certification: Internal Medicine, Rheumatology
5601 Loch Raven Blvd #509, Baltimore, 443-444-4840

Nasseri, Nasser (6 mentions)
FMS-Dominica *Certification:* Internal Medicine, Rheumatology
2900 S Hanover St, Baltimore, 410-350-8280
4 E Rolling Rd #110, Catonsville, 410-744-0661

Wigley, Fredrick Martin (5 mentions)
U of Florida, 1972
Certification: Internal Medicine, Rheumatology
5501 Hopkins Bayview Cir #1-B7, Baltimore, 410-550-2400

Ziminski, Carol Mary (5 mentions)
Yale U, 1976 *Certification:* Internal Medicine, Rheumatology
5601 Loch Raven Blvd #508, Baltimore, 443-444-4646

Thoracic Surgery

Battafarano, Richard J. (7 mentions)
Hahnemann U, 1988 *Certification:* Surgery, Thoracic Surgery
22 S Greene St, Baltimore, 410-328-6366

Cohen, Neri M. (12 mentions)
U of Maryland, 1989 *Certification:* Surgery, Thoracic Surgery
6569 N Charles St #701, Towson, 443-849-3470

Harley, Daniel Peter (7 mentions)
New York Med Coll, 1971 *Certification:* Thoracic Surgery
9103 Franklin Square Dr #309, Rosedale, 410-686-5887

Heitmiller, Richard F., II (20 mentions)
Johns Hopkins U, 1979 *Certification:* Surgery, Thoracic Surgery
3333 N Calvert St #610, Baltimore, 410-554-2063

Krasna, Mark Jonathan (8 mentions)
FMS-Israel, 1982 *Certification:* Thoracic Surgery
7505 Osler Dr #303, Baltimore, 410-427-2220

Skaryak, Lynne Ann (6 mentions)
Duke U, 1989 *Certification:* Surgery, Thoracic Surgery
2435 W Belvedere Ave, Baltimore, 410-601-6491

Yang, Stephen Clyde (17 mentions)
Virginia Commonwealth U, 1984
Certification: Surgery, Thoracic Surgery
600 N Wolf St, Baltimore, 410-614-3891

Urology

Boyle, Karen Elizabeth (5 mentions)
Albany Med Coll, 1998 *Certification:* Urology
600 N Wolfe St, Baltimore, 410-955-6100
6535 N Charles St #625, Baltimore, 410-825-5454

Dietrick, Daniel Dean (6 mentions)
Johns Hopkins U, 1987 *Certification:* Urology
8322 Bellona Ave #202, Towson, 410-825-6310

Dowling, William Thomas (6 mentions)
Virginia Commonwealth U, 1992 *Certification:* Urology
6830 Hospital Dr #204, Rosedale, 410-391-6131

Gearhart, John Phillip (8 mentions)
U of Louisville, 1975 *Certification:* Urology
200 N Wolfe St #LL, Baltimore, 410-955-6108

Lerner, Brad Douglas (14 mentions)
U of Maryland, 1984 *Certification:* Urology
3333 N Calvert St #545, Baltimore, 410-467-7665

Murphy, Joseph Brian (6 mentions)
FMS-Ireland, 1973 *Certification:* Urology
615 W McPhail Dr #207, Bel Air, 410-803-4653
7505 Osler Dr #508, Towson, 410-296-5333

Partin, Alan Wayne (7 mentions)
Johns Hopkins U, 1989 *Certification:* Urology
601 N Caroline St 4th Fl, Baltimore, 410-955-6108

Redwood, Stanley Mark (9 mentions)
Brown U, 1986 *Certification:* Urology
5051 Greenspring Ave #302, Baltimore, 410-542-4700
21 Crossroads Dr #450, Owings Mills, 410-581-1602
2 Park Center Ct #1, Owings Mills, 410-356-0884

Smyth, Thomas Burk (7 mentions)
Johns Hopkins U, 1986 *Certification:* Urology
8322 Bellona Ave #202, Towson, 410-825-6310

Tutrone, Ronald Francis (15 mentions)
Robert W Johnson Med Sch, 1987 *Certification:* Urology
6535 N Charles St #625, Baltimore, 410-825-5454

Walsh, Patrick Craig (11 mentions)
Case Western Reserve U, 1964 *Certification:* Urology
601 N Caroline St #4235, Baltimore, 410-955-6100
600 N Wolfe St, Baltimore, 410-955-6100

Vascular Surgery

Golueke, Peter J. (15 mentions)
Certification: Vascular Surgery
6565 N Charles St #605, Towson, 410-825-4928

Perler, Bruce Alan (11 mentions)
Duke U, 1976 *Certification:* Vascular Surgery
600 N Wolfe St Harvey Bldg #611, Baltimore, 410-955-2618

Massachusetts

Boston Area

Boston Area

Including Bristol, Essex, Middlesex, Norfolk, Plymouth, and Suffolk Counties

Allergy/Immunology

Arm, Jonathan Peter (8 mentions)
FMS-United Kingdom, 1977 *Certification:* Allergy & Immunology
850 Boylston St #540, Chestnut Hill, 617-278-0300

Bleier, Joel George (7 mentions)
U of Michigan, 1973
Certification: Allergy & Immunology, Internal Medicine
1 City Hall Mall, Medford, 781-395-2922

Castells, Mariana (8 mentions)
FMS-Spain, 1979
Certification: Allergy & Immunology, Internal Medicine
1 Jimmy Fund Way Smith Bldg #626, Boston, 617-732-9850
850 Boylston St, Boston, 617-732-9850
75 Francis St, Boston, 617-732-9850

Gurka, Gary Philip (8 mentions)
Tufts U, 1981 *Certification:* Internal Medicine
63 Massachusetts Ave, Arlington, 781-648-2540

Long, Aidan Angelo (7 mentions)
FMS-Ireland, 1980 *Certification:* Allergy & Immunology
55 Fruit St, Boston, 617-726-3850

MacLean, James A. (6 mentions)
FMS-Canada, 1985
Certification: Allergy & Immunology, Internal Medicine
114 Highland Ave, Salem, 978-745-3711
55 Fruit St, Boston, 617-726-3850
80 Lindall St, Danvers, 978-777-0970

Ohman, John Levi (5 mentions)
U of Vermont, 1965
Certification: Allergy & Immunology, Internal Medicine
25 Boylston St #215, Chestnut Hill, 617-232-1690
800 Washington St, Boston, 617-636-5333

Saryan, John Armen (15 mentions)
Johns Hopkins U, 1977
Certification: Allergy & Immunology, Pediatrics
31 Mall Rd, Burlington, 781-744-8442

Sheffer, Albert L. (7 mentions)
George Washington U, 1956
Certification: Allergy & Immunology, Internal Medicine
850 Boylston St #540, Chestnut Hill, 617-278-0300
40 2nd Ave, Waltham, 781-522-9000

Steinberg, Daniel Gary (6 mentions)
Boston U, 1987
Certification: Allergy & Immunology, Internal Medicine
25 Boylston St #215, Chestnut Hill, 617-232-1690

Wang-Dohlman, Ann (7 mentions)
U of Massachusetts, 1979
Certification: Allergy & Immunology, Pediatrics
2000 Washington St #205, Newton, 617-527-3440

Wong, Johnson Tai (5 mentions)
U of California-San Francisco, 1980
Certification: Allergy & Immunology, Internal Medicine
8 Hawthorne Pl #104, Boston, 617-742-5730
200 Washington St, Newton, 617-969-2957

Young, Michael Chung-En (9 mentions)
Yale U, 1979 *Certification:* Allergy & Immunology, Pediatrics
851 Main St #21, South Weymouth, 781-331-1060

Anesthesiology

Azocar, Ruben Jose (3 mentions)
FMS-Venezuela, 1993
Certification: Anesthesiology, Critical Care Medicine
690 Canton St #325, Westwood, 781-407-7771

Berde, Charles Benjamin (3 mentions)
Stanford U, 1980
Certification: Anesthesiology, Pain Medicine, Pediatrics
300 Longwood Ave, Boston, 617-355-6995

Bode, Robert Harry, Jr. (5 mentions)
Case Western Reserve U, 1978 *Certification:* Anesthesiology
125 Parker Hill Ave, Boston, 617-754-5111

Borromeo, Carl J. (3 mentions)
U of Rochester, 1992 *Certification:* Anesthesiology
41 Mall Rd, Burlington, 781-744-8132

Davies-Lepie, Sara Ruth (3 mentions)
FMS-United Kingdom, 1973
41 Mall Rd, Burlington, 781-744-8132

Donahue, Patrick Joseph (3 mentions)
Tufts U, 1983 *Certification:* Anesthesiology
690 Canton St #325, Westwood, 781-407-7771

Fox, John Alan (3 mentions)
Yale U, 1979 *Certification:* Anesthesiology
75 Francis St, Boston, 617-732-8280

Gessner, James Stanton (4 mentions)
Harvard U, 1972 *Certification:* Anesthesiology, Pediatrics
1153 Centre St, Jamaica Plain, 617-983-7181

Hannenberg, Alexander A. (5 mentions)
Tufts U, 1979 *Certification:* Anesthesiology
2014 Washington St, Newton, 617-243-6298

Joffe, Jacob Milton (3 mentions)
Harvard U, 1980 *Certification:* Anesthesiology
2014 Washington St, Newton, 617-243-6298

Lisbon, Alan (4 mentions)
New York U, 1976
Certification: Anesthesiology, Critical Care Medicine
1 Deaconess Rd, Boston, 617-754-2702

Long, Keith Linton (3 mentions)
U of Arizona, 1987 *Certification:* Anesthesiology
41 Highland Ave, Winchester, 781-756-7243

Ortega, Elindio Rafael (4 mentions)
FMS-Dominican Republic, 1980 *Certification:* Anesthesiology
690 Canton St #325, Westwood, 781-407-7771

Panzica, Peter Joseph (3 mentions)
Stony Brook U, 1991 *Certification:* Anesthesiology
330 Brookline Ave #Cc539, Boston, 617-754-2675

Ricciardone, Marguerite M. (3 mentions)
Tufts U, 1982 *Certification:* Anesthesiology, Internal Medicine
41 Mall Rd, Burlington, 781-744-8132

Satwicz, Paul R. (7 mentions)
U of California-San Francisco, 1978
Certification: Anesthesiology, Pain Medicine
2014 Washington St, Newton, 617-243-6298

Teague, Paul David (5 mentions)
Tufts U, 1985 *Certification:* Anesthesiology
41 Mall Rd, Burlington, 781-744-8132

Wurm, W. Heinrich (8 mentions)
FMS-Russia, 1967 *Certification:* Anesthesiology, Pain Medicine
800 Washington St, Boston, 617-636-6044

Cardiac Surgery

Akins, Cary Willard (10 mentions)
Harvard U, 1970   *Certification:* Thoracic Surgery
55 Fruit St #COX-648, Boston, 617-726-8218

Cohn, Lawrence Harvey (21 mentions)
Stanford U, 1962   *Certification:* Surgery, Thoracic Surgery
15 Francis St, Boston, 617-732-6569

Vlahakes, Gus John (12 mentions)
Harvard U, 1975
Certification: Surgery, Surgical Critical Care, Thoracic Surgery
55 Fruit St, Boston, 617-726-1861

Cardiology

Alexander, Sidney (3 mentions)
Harvard U, 1957
Certification: Cardiovascular Disease, Internal Medicine
41 Mall Rd, Burlington, 781-744-8461

Antman, Elliott Marshall (4 mentions)
Columbia U, 1974
Certification: Cardiovascular Disease, Internal Medicine
75 Francis St, Boston, 617-732-7149

Baughman, Kenneth Lee (4 mentions)
U of Missouri, 1972
Certification: Cardiovascular Disease, Internal Medicine
70 Francis St Shapiro Bldg, Boston, 857-307-4000

Birkhead, Richard Gartner (4 mentions)
SUNY-Upstate Med U, 1983
Certification: Cardiovascular Disease, Internal Medicine
27 Village Sq, Chelmsford, 978-256-6607

Boucher, Charles Allen (5 mentions)
Columbia U, 1972
Certification: Cardiovascular Disease, Internal Medicine
8 Hawthorne Pl #110, Boston, 617-726-8511

Conway, Laurence A. (6 mentions)
FMS-Ireland, 1989   *Certification:* Cardiovascular Disease,
   Internal Medicine, Interventional Cardiology
170 Governors Ave, Medford, 781-395-4909

Davidoff, Ravin (8 mentions)
FMS-South Africa, 1977
Certification: Cardiovascular Disease, Internal Medicine
85 E Concord St 5th Fl, Boston, 617-638-9557
732 Harrison Ave Preston Bldg 4th Fl, Boston, 617-638-7490

De Sanctis, Roman William (10 mentions)
Harvard U, 1955
Certification: Cardiovascular Disease, Internal Medicine
55 Fruit St, Boston, 617-726-2889

Estes, Nathan Anthony, III (6 mentions)
U of Cincinnati, 1977   *Certification:* Cardiovascular Disease,
   Clinical Cardiac Electrophysiology, Internal Medicine
800 Washington St, Boston, 617-636-6156

Fifer, Michael A. (5 mentions)
Harvard U, 1978
Certification: Cardiovascular Disease, Internal Medicine
55 Fruit St Bigelow Bldg 8th Fl, Boston, 617-726-1832

Fulton, David Roger (6 mentions)
Cornell U, 1974   *Certification:* Pediatric Cardiology, Pediatrics
300 Longwood Ave, Boston, 617-355-2079

Goldhaber, Samuel Zachary (6 mentions)
Harvard U, 1976
Certification: Cardiovascular Disease, Internal Medicine
70 Francis St Shapiro Bldg, Boston, 857-307-4000

Goldman, Mark Robert (4 mentions)
Harvard U, 1971
Certification: Cardiovascular Disease, Internal Medicine
2000 Washington St #562, Newton, 617-527-1335

Hoshino, Peter Kenji (3 mentions)
Boston U, 1979
Certification: Cardiovascular Disease, Internal Medicine
541 Main St #400, South Weymouth, 781-952-1200

Jacobs, Alice Rochelle (3 mentions)
St Louis U, 1975
Certification: Cardiovascular Disease, Endocrinology and
   Metabolism, Internal Medicine, Interventional Cardiology
732 Harrison Ave 4th Fl, Boston, 617-638-7490
88 E Newton St #C818, Boston, 617-638-8700

Januzzi, James Louis, Jr. (3 mentions)
New York Med Coll, 1994   *Certification:* Cardiovascular Disease
55 Fruit St, Boston, 617-726-3443

Jiang, Joseph Ping (3 mentions)
Yale U, 1990
Certification: Cardiovascular Disease, Interventional Cardiology
70 Pleasant St, South Weymouth, 781-331-2000

Josephson, Mark Eric (3 mentions)
Columbia U, 1969   *Certification:* Cardiovascular Disease,
   Clinical Cardiac Electrophysiology, Internal Medicine
330 Brookline Ave, Boston, 617-667-8800

Kannam, Joseph Peter (7 mentions)
Boston U, 1989   *Certification:* Cardiovascular Disease
535 Boylston St, Boston, 617-667-8800

Kinnunen, Paula Marie (4 mentions)
Johns Hopkins U, 1979
Certification: Cardiovascular Disease, Internal Medicine
41 Mall Rd, Burlington, 781-744-8019

Kirshenbaum, James M. (5 mentions)
Harvard U, 1979   *Certification:* Cardiovascular Disease,
   Internal Medicine, Interventional Cardiology
75 Francis St, Boston, 857-307-1967

Konstam, Marvin Amnon (5 mentions)
Columbia U, 1975   *Certification:* Cardiovascular Disease,
   Diagnostic Radiology, Internal Medicine
800 Washington St, Boston, 617-636-6293

Kosowsky, Bernard David (3 mentions)
Harvard U, 1962
Certification: Cardiovascular Disease, Internal Medicine
736 Cambridge St, Brighton, 617-789-3149

Lampert, Steven (3 mentions)
U of Vermont, 1976
Certification: Cardiovascular Disease, Internal Medicine
133 Brookline Ave 2nd Fl, Boston, 617-421-6050
26 City Hall Mall, Medford, 781-306-5300

Levinson, John Raphael (5 mentions)
Stanford U, 1983
Certification: Cardiovascular Disease, Internal Medicine
535 Boylston St #7, Boston, 617-247-3444

Lewis, Stanley Mark (3 mentions)
Albany Med Coll, 1975
Certification: Cardiovascular Disease, Internal Medicine
330 Brookline Ave, Boston, 617-667-4786

Lilly, Leonard Stuart (5 mentions)
Albany Med Coll, 1977
Certification: Cardiovascular Disease, Internal Medicine
1153 Centre St 4th Fl, Boston, 617-983-7420

Lindsey, Harold E., Jr. (5 mentions)
Harvard U, 1971
Certification: Cardiovascular Disease, Internal Medicine
133 Brookline Ave #2, Boston, 617-421-6050

Manning, Warren J. (4 mentions)
Harvard U, 1983
Certification: Cardiovascular Disease, Internal Medicine
330 Brookline Ave, Boston, 617-667-2192

Marks, Anthony Dana (4 mentions)
Yale U, 1985   *Certification:* Cardiovascular Disease, Internal
   Medicine, Interventional Cardiology
541 Main St #400, South Weymouth, 781-952-1200

McFarland, James Curtis (4 mentions)
Emory U, 1964
Certification: Cardiovascular Disease, Internal Medicine
55 Fruit St #5-B, Boston, 617-726-3453

Mirbach, Bruce Edward (7 mentions)
U of Cincinnati, 1974
Certification: Cardiovascular Disease, Internal Medicine
41 Mall Rd, Burlington, 781-744-8019

Mudge, Gilbert Horton (5 mentions)
Columbia U, 1970
Certification: Cardiovascular Disease, Internal Medicine
70 Francis St Shapiro Bldg, Boston, 857-307-4000

Nesto, Richard William (7 mentions)
Tufts U, 1976
Certification: Cardiovascular Disease, Internal Medicine
41 Mall Rd, Burlington, 781-744-8962

Newburger, Jane W. (3 mentions)
Harvard U, 1974   *Certification:* Pediatric Cardiology, Pediatrics
300 Longwood Ave Farley Bldg #217, Boston, 617-355-5427

O'Gara, Patrick T. (9 mentions)
Northwestern U, 1978
Certification: Cardiovascular Disease, Internal Medicine
75 Francis St, Boston, 857-307-1990

Pastore, John O. (6 mentions)
Yale U, 1967
Certification: Cardiovascular Disease, Internal Medicine
736 Cambridge St, Boston, 617-789-5173

Philippides, George John (6 mentions)
Albert Einstein Coll of Med, 1985   *Certification:* Internal Medicine
732 Harrison Ave #402, Boston, 617-638-7490

Ramirez, Alberto (3 mentions)
FMS-Colombia, 1962
Certification: Cardiovascular Disease, Internal Medicine
1153 Centre St, Boston, 617-983-7441

Roberts, David Joseph (4 mentions)
U of Vermont, 1979   *Certification:* Cardiovascular Disease,
   Internal Medicine, Interventional Cardiology
81 Highland Ave 5th Fl, Salem, 978-744-5900

Rubenstein, Joel Jay (4 mentions)
Harvard U, 1964
Certification: Cardiovascular Disease, Internal Medicine
2000 Washington St #562, Newton, 617-527-1335

Salem, Deeb (3 mentions)
Boston U, 1968
Certification: Cardiovascular Disease, Internal Medicine
860 Washington St 6th Fl, Boston, 617-636-5604

Stevenson, William Gregory (4 mentions)
Tulane U, 1979   *Certification:* Cardiovascular Disease,
   Clinical Cardiac Electrophysiology, Internal Medicine
75 Francis St, Boston, 617-732-7535

Udelson, James Eric (3 mentions)
New York Med Coll, 1981
Certification: Cardiovascular Disease, Internal Medicine
800 Washington St, Boston, 617-636-8066

Waldman, Howard Mark (6 mentions)
SUNY-Buffalo, 1981   *Certification:* Internal Medicine
81 Highland Ave 5th Fl, Salem, 978-744-5900

Zimetbaum, Peter Jeremy (7 mentions)
Albert Einstein Coll of Med, 1990   *Certification:*
   Cardiovascular Disease, Clinical Cardiac Electrophysiology
330 Brookline Ave, Boston, 617-667-8800

Dermatology

Amster, Mark Stewart (4 mentions)
SUNY-Downstate Med Coll, 1987   *Certification:* Dermatology
280 Washington St #212, Brighton, 617-783-7100

Arndt, Kenneth A. (5 mentions)
Yale U, 1961 *Certification:* Dermatology
1244 Boylston St #302, Chestnut Hill, 617-731-1600

Cohen, Jay Leslie (4 mentions)
New Jersey Med Sch, 1987 *Certification:* Dermatology
464 Hillside Ave #303, Needham, 781-449-3588

Dover, Jeffrey S. (7 mentions)
FMS-Canada, 1981 *Certification:* Dermatology
1244 Boylston St #302, Chestnut Hill, 617-731-1600

Gellis, Stephen Elias (11 mentions)
Harvard U, 1973
Certification: Dermatology, Pediatric Dermatology, Pediatrics
300 Longwood Ave, Boston, 617-355-6126
482 Bedford St, Lexington, 781-672-2100

Gilchrest, Barbara Ann D. (4 mentions)
Harvard U, 1971 *Certification:* Dermatology, Internal Medicine
720 Harrison Ave #915, Boston, 617-638-7420
609 Albany St #J507, Boston, 617-638-5500

Grande, Donald J. (6 mentions)
Boston U, 1973 *Certification:* Dermatology
92 High St #T21, Medford, 781-391-0778
92 Montvale Ave, Stoneham, 781-391-0778

Grevelink, Suzanne (5 mentions)
Duke U, 1989 *Certification:* Dermatology, Pediatric Dermatology
955 Main St #G6, Winchester, 781-729-4878

Haynes, Harley Anderson (13 mentions)
Harvard U, 1963 *Certification:* Dermatology
221 Longwood Ave, Boston, 617-732-4918

Johnson, Richard Allen (4 mentions)
FMS-Canada, 1966 *Certification:* Dermatology, Internal Medicine
50 Staniford St #200, Boston, 617-726-2914

Mackool, Bonnie Teresa (8 mentions)
Boston U, 1989 *Certification:* Dermatology
50 Staniford St #200, Boston, 617-726-2914

Moschella, Samuel Leonard (6 mentions)
Tufts U, 1946 *Certification:* Dermatology, Dermatopathology
41 Mall Rd, Burlington, 781-273-8445

O'Brien, Robert Joseph, Jr. (5 mentions)
Tufts U, 1986
955 Main St #G6, Winchester, 781-729-4878

Olbricht, Suzanne M. (4 mentions)
Baylor U, 1976 *Certification:* Dermatology, Internal Medicine
41 Mall Rd, Burlington, 781-744-8348

Renna, Francis Scott (4 mentions)
Tufts U, 1970 *Certification:* Dermatology
2000 Washington St #120, Newton, 617-969-0210

Reynolds, Rachel Victoria (4 mentions)
U of Pennsylvania, 1996 *Certification:* Dermatology
25 Boylston St #104, Chestnut Hill, 617-754-0350

Sober, Arthur Joel (5 mentions)
George Washington U, 1968
Certification: Dermatology, Internal Medicine
50 Staniford St #200, Boston, 617-726-2914

Stern, Robert (5 mentions)
Yale U, 1970 *Certification:* Dermatology
330 Brookline Ave 2nd Fl, Boston, 617-667-3753
25 Boylston St, Chestnut Hill, 617-754-0350

Werth, Stephen Gregory (5 mentions)
Vanderbilt U, 1985 *Certification:* Dermatology, Internal Medicine
500 Congress St #2-H, Quincy, 617-773-7431
100 Highland St #226, Milton, 617-696-5300
2110 Dorchester Ave #206, Dorchester Center, 617-698-0954

Emergency Medicine

Barnewolt, Brien Alfred (4 mentions)
Northwestern U, 1987 *Certification:* Emergency Medicine
800 Washington St, Boston, 617-636-4720

Bechtel, David John (4 mentions)
Tufts U, 1978 *Certification:* Internal Medicine
41 Mall Rd, Burlington, 781-273-8100

Brown, David (3 mentions)
Columbia U, 1989
Certification: Emergency Medicine, Internal Medicine
55 Fruit St, Boston, 617-726-5273

Creighton, Malcolm Adam (4 mentions)
Dartmouth Coll, 1981 *Certification:* Emergency Medicine
41 Mall Rd, Burlington, 781-273-5100

Edlow, Jonathan A. (7 mentions)
U of Maryland, 1978
Certification: Emergency Medicine, Internal Medicine
1 Deaconess Rd, Boston, 617-754-2329

Fleisher, Gary Robert (5 mentions)
Jefferson Med Coll, 1973 *Certification:* Emergency
   Medicine, Pediatric Emergency Medicine, Pediatrics
300 Longwood Ave, Boston, 617-355-5022

Herman, Richard Scott (4 mentions)
Tufts U, 1977
Certification: Emergency Medicine, Internal Medicine
235 N Pearl St, Brockton, 508-427-3075

Howard, Kristin Lynes (3 mentions)
Boston U, 1992 *Certification:* Emergency Medicine
2014 Washington St, Newton, 617-243-6000

Larson, Richard Eric (4 mentions)
FMS-Philippines, 1981 *Certification:* Emergency Medicine
1153 Centre St, Jamaica Plain, 617-983-7192

Lemons, Mark Francis (8 mentions)
Med Coll of Wisconsin, 1984 *Certification:* Emergency Medicine
2014 Washington St, Newton, 617-243-6040

McGinn, Cynthia G. (3 mentions)
Georgetown U, 1976
Certification: Emergency Medicine, Internal Medicine
330 Mount Auburn St, Cambridge, 617-499-5025

Noble, Vicki Elizabeth (3 mentions)
U of Pennsylvania, 1999 *Certification:* Emergency Medicine
55 Fruit St, Boston, 617-726-5655

O'Neil, Edward Thomas (3 mentions)
Albert Einstein Coll of Med, 1978
70 East St, Methuen, 978-687-0151

Olshaker, Jonathan S. (4 mentions)
George Washington U, 1982 *Certification:* Emergency Medicine
1 Boston Medical Center Pl, Boston, 617-414-4930

Pearlmutter, Mark David (8 mentions)
Tufts U, 1984
Certification: Emergency Medicine, Internal Medicine
736 Cambridge St, Brighton, 617-789-2639

Reisman, Jerald Lewis (4 mentions)
George Washington U, 1971
Certification: Emergency Medicine, Internal Medicine
170 Governors Ave, Medford, 781-306-6300

Walls, Ron M. (7 mentions)
FMS-Canada, 1979 *Certification:* Emergency Medicine
75 Francis St, Boston, 617-732-5989

Wolfe, Richard E. (7 mentions)
FMS-France, 1983 *Certification:* Emergency Medicine
1 Deaconess Rd, Boston, 617-754-2347

Endocrinology

Cushing, Gary W. (9 mentions)
U of Massachusetts, 1980
Certification: Endocrinology and Metabolism, Internal Medicine
41 Mall Rd Fl 4E, Burlington, 781-273-8492

Daniels, Gilbert Harlan (18 mentions)
Harvard U, 1966
Certification: Endocrinology and Metabolism, Internal Medicine
15 Parkman St #730-S, Boston, 617-726-8430

Dluhy, Robert George (9 mentions)
Harvard U, 1962
Certification: Endocrinology and Metabolism, Internal Medicine
221 Longwood Ave, Boston, 617-732-5666

Garber, Jeffrey Richard (8 mentions)
Stony Brook U, 1974
Certification: Endocrinology and Metabolism, Internal Medicine
133 Brookline Ave, Boston, 617-421-1380
3 Fenway Plaza, Boston, 617-421-1380

Godine, John Elliott (8 mentions)
Harvard U, 1976
Certification: Endocrinology and Metabolism, Internal Medicine
50 Staniford St #340, Boston, 617-726-8722

Hodge, Mary Beth (5 mentions)
Tufts U, 1981
Certification: Endocrinology and Metabolism, Internal Medicine
41 Mall Rd, Burlington, 781-273-8493

Kerouz, Nada (4 mentions)
FMS-Lebanon, 1988 *Certification:* Endocrinology, Diabetes,
   and Metabolism, Internal Medicine
11 Shore Rd, Winchester, 781-729-1810

Le Boff, Meryl Susan (5 mentions)
New Jersey Med Sch, 1975
Certification: Endocrinology and Metabolism, Internal Medicine
221 Longwood Ave #2, Boston, 617-732-5666

Marglin, Arnold (4 mentions)
Columbia U, 1961 *Certification:* Internal Medicine
851 Main St #18, South Weymouth, 781-335-7113

Pallotta, Johanna A. (4 mentions)
New York Med Coll, 1962
Certification: Endocrinology and Metabolism, Internal Medicine
330 Brookline Ave, Boston, 617-667-4016

Sadeghi-Nejad, Abdollah (4 mentions)
U of Chicago, 1964
Certification: Pediatric Endocrinology, Pediatrics
800 Washington St #346, Boston, 617-636-5335

Spack, Norman Paul (5 mentions)
U of Rochester, 1969
Certification: Pediatric Endocrinology, Pediatrics
300 Longwood Ave, Boston, 617-355-7476

Family Practice *(see note on page 9)*

D'Angelo, Henry A., Jr. (3 mentions)
U of Massachusetts, 1992 *Certification:* Family Medicine
111 Norfolk St, Walpole, 508-660-1200

Golden, Steven Terry (5 mentions)
SUNY-Upstate Med U, 1978 *Certification:* Family Medicine
223 Chief Justice Cushing Hwy #301, Cohasset, 781-383-6261

Jack, Brian William (3 mentions)
U of Massachusetts, 1981 *Certification:* Family Medicine
1 Boston Medical Center Pl, Boston, 617-414-2080

Labarge, Harlow Francis (3 mentions)
FMS-Mexico, 1982 *Certification:* Family Medicine
195 School St, Manchester, 978-526-7507

Markovitz, Dennis I. (5 mentions)
Loyola U Chicago, 1978 *Certification:* Family Medicine
259 Swanton St #A, Winchester, 781-721-4616

Martin, Maurice Joseph (3 mentions)
New York U, 1976 *Certification:* Family Medicine
1020 Broadway, Somerville, 617-628-2160

Rockett, Ronda Appelbaum (5 mentions)
Boston U, 1998 *Certification:* Family Medicine
173 Worcester St, Wellesley, 781-235-7900

Sagov, Stanley E. (4 mentions)
FMS-South Africa, 1967 *Certification:* Family Medicine
11 Water St #1A, Arlington, 781-648-9700

Wertheimer, Randy Fair (3 mentions)
Boston U, 1977 *Certification:* Family Medicine
1493 Cambridge St, Cambridge, 617-665-1117
195 Canal St, Malden, 781-338-0500

Gastroenterology

Anastopoulos, Harry T. (4 mentions)
Boston U, 1983
Certification: Gastroenterology, Internal Medicine
110 Francis St #8-E, Boston, 617-667-2135

Aserkoff, Bernard Ralph (4 mentions)
Georgetown U, 1965
Certification: Gastroenterology, Internal Medicine
55 Fruit St, Boston, 617-724-5995

Bailen, Laurence Scott (6 mentions)
Tufts U, 1993 *Certification:* Gastroenterology, Internal Medicine
2000 Washington St #368, Newton, 617-969-1227

Banks, Peter Alan (8 mentions)
Columbia U, 1961
Certification: Gastroenterology, Internal Medicine
75 Francis St, Boston, 617-732-6747

Carr-Locke, David L. (7 mentions)
FMS-United Kingdom, 1972
75 Francis St, Boston, 617-732-7414

Chuttani, Ram (12 mentions)
FMS-India, 1984
330 Brookline Ave, Boston, 617-667-0162
175 Worcester St, Wellesley Hills, 617-754-0800

Curtis, Richard Lee (9 mentions)
Cornell U, 1975
Certification: Gastroenterology, Internal Medicine
2000 Washington St #368, Newton, 617-969-1227

Falchuk, Zalman Myron (4 mentions)
Harvard U, 1967
Certification: Gastroenterology, Internal Medicine
110 Francis St #8E, Boston, 617-632-8623

Farraye, Francis Anthony (4 mentions)
Albert Einstein Coll of Med, 1982
Certification: Gastroenterology, Internal Medicine
88 E Newton St, Boston, 617-414-7539

Fawaz, Karim Adib (5 mentions)
FMS-Lebanon, 1967
230 Highland Ave, Somerville, 617-591-4422

Janowski, Douglas Albert (5 mentions)
U of Miami, 1997
Certification: Gastroenterology, Internal Medicine
800 Washington St #233, Boston, 617-636-5623

Kelsey, Peter Baker (5 mentions)
Columbia U, 1979
Certification: Gastroenterology, Internal Medicine
55 Fruit St Blake Bldg 4th Fl, Boston, 617-724-6044

Lee, Dennis Elliott (4 mentions)
Columbia U, 1980
Certification: Gastroenterology, Internal Medicine
2000 Washington St #368, Newton, 617-969-1227

Libby, Eric David (7 mentions)
Harvard U, 1987 *Certification:* Gastroenterology
955 Main St #206, Winchester, 781-729-5855

Lichtenstein, David Roth (5 mentions)
U of Pennsylvania, 1985
Certification: Gastroenterology, Internal Medicine
830 Harrison Ave, Boston, 617-638-6525
85 E Concord St #700, Boston, 617-638-6525

Mitty, Roger D. (8 mentions)
New York U, 1988 *Certification:* Gastroenterology
11 Nevins St #402, Brighton, 617-562-5432

Nunes, David Patrick (5 mentions)
FMS-Ireland, 1984
Certification: Gastroenterology, Internal Medicine
830 Harrison Ave, Boston, 617-638-6525
85 E Concord St #700, Boston, 617-638-6525

Pleskow, Douglas Keith (4 mentions)
SUNY-Buffalo, 1982
Certification: Gastroenterology, Internal Medicine
110 Francis St 8th Fl #8E, Boston, 617-632-8623

Smith, Bernard F. (4 mentions)
New York U, 1977
Certification: Gastroenterology, Internal Medicine
1085 Main St, South Weymouth, 781-331-2922

Vermeulen, John Paul (4 mentions)
Case Western Reserve U, 1979
Certification: Gastroenterology, Internal Medicine
1085 Main St, South Weymouth, 781-331-2922

Warner, Andrew Simon (6 mentions)
Rosalind Franklin U, 1987 *Certification:* Gastroenterology
41 Mall Rd, Burlington, 781-744-8494

General Surgery

Ashley, Stanley Waite (8 mentions)
Cornell U, 1981 *Certification:* Surgery, Surgical Critical Care
75 Francis St, Boston, 617-732-6730

Becker, James Murdoch (7 mentions)
Case Western Reserve U, 1975 *Certification:* Surgery
88 E Newton St, Boston, 617-638-8600

Begos, Dennis Gerard (4 mentions)
New York Med Coll, 1990
Certification: Colon & Rectal Surgery, Surgery
91 Montvale Ave #208, Stoneham, 781-395-7304

Berger, David L. (6 mentions)
U of Pennsylvania, 1990 *Certification:* Surgery, Vascular Surgery
15 Parkman St, Boston, 617-724-6980

Birkett, Desmond (3 mentions)
FMS-United Kingdom, 1963 *Certification:* Surgery
41 Mall Rd, Burlington, 781-744-8576

Brams, David Mendel (3 mentions)
Cornell U, 1987 *Certification:* Surgery
41 Mall Rd, Burlington, 781-744-8831
1 Essex Center Dr, Peabody, 781-744-8831

Brooks, David Church (6 mentions)
Brown U, 1976 *Certification:* Surgery
75 Francis St, Boston, 617-732-6337

Callery, Mark Philip (4 mentions)
Albany Med Coll, 1985 *Certification:* Surgery
330 Brookline Ave, Boston, 617-667-3798

Camer, Stephen Joseph (3 mentions)
Tufts U, 1965 *Certification:* Surgery
125 Parker Hill Ave, Roxbury Crossing, 617-277-9700

Critchlow, Jonathan Francis (7 mentions)
U of California-San Diego, 1978
Certification: Surgery, Surgical Critical Care
110 Francis St #3-A, Boston, 617-632-8132

Cronin, Claire Tine (3 mentions)
Tufts U, 1995 *Certification:* Surgery
2000 Washington St #365, Newton, 617-244-5355

Driscoll, Robert Patrick (3 mentions)
New York Med Coll, 1981 *Certification:* Surgery
780 Main St #2-A, Weymouth, 781-335-4815

Fernandez-Del-Castillo, C. (3 mentions)
FMS-Mexico, 1983
15 Parkman St Wang Bldg #460, Boston, 617-726-5644

Ferrante, Giovanni A. (3 mentions)
Stanford U, 1981 *Certification:* Surgery, Vascular Surgery
780 Main St #2A, Weymouth, 781-335-4815

Hodin, Richard Aaron (4 mentions)
Tulane U, 1984 *Certification:* Surgery
15 Parkman St Wang #460, Boston, 617-724-2570

Jenkins, Roger Lewin (3 mentions)
U of Vermont, 1977 *Certification:* Surgery
41 Mall Rd, Burlington, 781-744-2500

Kahan, Morton Gerald (5 mentions)
Harvard U, 1969 *Certification:* Surgery
2000 Washington St #365, Newton, 617-244-5355

Kenney, Pardon Robert (5 mentions)
Brown U, 1975 *Certification:* Surgery, Surgical Critical Care
1153 Centre St, Jamaica Plain, 617-983-7212

Lillehei, Craig Walton (4 mentions)
Harvard U, 1976
Certification: Pediatric Surgery, Surgery, Surgical Critical Care
300 Longwood Ave Fegan 3, Boston, 617-355-7800

Lopez, Marvin Jose (6 mentions)
FMS-Mexico, 1970 *Certification:* Surgery
11 Nevins St #201, Brighton, 617-789-2442

McAneny, David (10 mentions)
Georgetown U, 1983 *Certification:* Surgery
830 Harrison Ave #3400, Boston, 617-638-8446

Mowschenson, Peter M. (6 mentions)
FMS-United Kingdom, 1973 *Certification:* Surgery
1180 Beacon St 6th Fl #6B, Brookline, 617-735-8868

Munson, John Lawrence (15 mentions)
U of Massachusetts, 1979 *Certification:* Surgery
41 Mall Rd, Burlington, 781-273-8377

Nixon, Robert E. (3 mentions)
Albany Med Coll, 1989 *Certification:* Surgery
535 Faunce Corner Rd, North Dartmouth, 508-996-3991

O'Donnell, Kevin Francis (3 mentions)
Tufts U, 1972 *Certification:* Surgery
11 Nevins St, Boston, 617-789-2442

Rattner, David William (5 mentions)
Johns Hopkins U, 1978 *Certification:* Surgery
15 Parkman St Wang Bldg #460, Boston, 617-726-1893

Shoji, Brent Tadayoshi (7 mentions)
U of California-Los Angeles, 1982 *Certification:* Surgery
75 Francis St, Boston, 617-732-6319

Von Ryll Gryska, Paul (7 mentions)
New York Med Coll, 1980
2000 Washington St #365, Newton, 617-244-5355

Warshaw, Andrew Louis (7 mentions)
Harvard U, 1963 *Certification:* Surgery
55 Fruit St 5th Fl WHT 506, Boston, 617-726-8254

Wei, John Pin (3 mentions)
Boston U, 1982 *Certification:* Surgery
41 Mall Rd, Burlington, 781-744-8972
1 Essex Center Dr, Peabody, 781-744-8972

Williams, Martin James (4 mentions)
Harvard U, 1982 *Certification:* Internal Medicine, Surgery
2110 Dorchester Ave #207, Dorchester, 617-296-4709

Zinner, Michael Jeffrey (3 mentions)
U of Florida, 1971 *Certification:* Surgery
75 Francis St, Boston, 617-732-8181

Geriatrics

Arslanian, Armen H. (5 mentions)
FMS-Lebanon, 1992
Certification: Geriatric Medicine, Internal Medicine
88 Montvale Ave, Stoneham, 781-481-9255

Auerbach, Heidi P. (3 mentions)
Brown U, 1988
Certification: Geriatric Medicine, Internal Medicine
850 Harrison Ave 2nd Fl, Boston, 617-414-4639

Dupee, Richard Mayo (4 mentions)
Tufts U, 1971 *Certification:* Geriatric Medicine, Internal Medicine
65 Walnut St #440, Wellesley, 781-235-9089

Fabiny, Anne Rebecca (3 mentions)
U of Wisconsin, 1992
Certification: Family Medicine, Geriatric Medicine
103 Garland St, Everett, 617-665-1029

Kennedy, Arthur R. (3 mentions)
Boston U, 1973
Certification: Geriatric Medicine, Internal Medicine
2014 Washington St, Newton, 617-243-6433

Lipsitz, Lewis Arnold (5 mentions)
U of Pennsylvania, 1977
Certification: Geriatric Medicine, Internal Medicine
1200 Centre St, Roslindale, 617-325-8000

Marcantonio, Edward Ralph (4 mentions)
Harvard U, 1987
Certification: Geriatric Medicine, Internal Medicine
110 Francis St #1B, Boston, 617-632-8696

Minaker, Kenneth Lloyd (3 mentions)
FMS-Canada, 1972
165 Cambridge St 5th Fl, Boston, 617-726-4600
10 Longwood Dr, Westwood, 781-493-6813

Saltsman, Wayne Stuart (9 mentions)
Boston U, 1997
Certification: Geriatric Medicine, Internal Medicine
41 Mall Rd, Burlington, 781-744-8399

Hematology/Oncology

Anamur, Murat A. (6 mentions)
FMS-Turkey, 1981
Certification: Hematology, Internal Medicine, Medical Oncology
295 Varnum Ave, Lowell, 978-937-6653

Anderson, Michael Jon (4 mentions)
Yale U, 1978
Certification: Hematology, Internal Medicine, Medical Oncology
51 Performance Dr, South Weymouth, 781-337-9091

Ardman, Blair (4 mentions)
Jefferson Med Coll, 1977
Certification: Hematology, Internal Medicine, Medical Oncology
295 Varnum Ave, Lowell, 978-937-6800

Bern, Murray Morris (3 mentions)
Tulane U, 1970
Certification: Hematology, Internal Medicine, Medical Oncology
99 Lincoln St, Framingham, 508-383-8510
15 Caswell Ln, Plymouth, 508-383-8510
830 Boylston St #209, Chestnut Hill, 508-383-8510

Bjornson, Barbara H. (5 mentions)
Boston U, 1975
Certification: Hematology, Internal Medicine, Medical Oncology
620 Washington St, Winchester, 781-756-8388

Block, Caroline Cole (9 mentions)
U of Michigan, 1985
Certification: Hematology, Internal Medicine, Medical Oncology
65 Walnut St #420, Wellesley, 781-237-0700

Bowker, Beverly Louise (4 mentions)
Jefferson Med Coll, 1986 *Certification:* Medical Oncology
7 Alfred St #230, Woburn, 781-756-2301

Drews, Reed Edward (4 mentions)
Harvard U, 1983
Certification: Hematology, Internal Medicine, Medical Oncology
330 Brookline Ave Rabb Bldg #430, Boston, 617-667-2131

Erban, John Kalil, III (4 mentions)
Tufts U, 1981
Certification: Hematology, Internal Medicine, Medical Oncology
55 Fruit St #9-A, Boston, 617-724-4800

Ernst, Timothy (3 mentions)
U of Nebraska, 1980
Certification: Internal Medicine, Medical Oncology
67 Union St #206, Natick, 508-655-0065

Everett, James R., II (3 mentions)
Tufts U, 1970 *Certification:* Internal Medicine, Medical Oncology
51 Performance Dr, Weymouth, 781-337-9091

Goldberg, Joan Helpern (3 mentions)
Harvard U, 1970 *Certification:* Hematology, Internal Medicine
133 Brookline Ave #4, Boston, 617-421-5950

Gore, Stacey Monica (5 mentions)
U of Michigan, 1981
Certification: Hematology, Internal Medicine, Medical Oncology
133 Brookline Ave 4th Fl, Boston, 617-421-8726

Hesketh, Paul Joseph (8 mentions)
U of Connecticut, 1978
Certification: Hematology, Internal Medicine, Medical Oncology
736 Cambridge St, Brighton, 617-789-2318
70 Walnut St, Foxboro, 508-543-6371

Jacobson, Joseph O. (4 mentions)
Boston U, 1979
Certification: Hematology, Internal Medicine, Medical Oncology
17 Centennial Dr, Peabody, 978-977-3434

Kuter, David John (4 mentions)
Harvard U, 1978
Certification: Hematology, Internal Medicine, Medical Oncology
55 Fruit St Yawkey #7, Boston, 617-726-8743

Kuter, Irene (3 mentions)
Harvard U, 1978
Certification: Hematology, Internal Medicine, Medical Oncology
55 Fruit St Yawkey #9, Boston, 617-724-4800

Lange, Roger Frederick (3 mentions)
Harvard U, 1969 *Certification:* Internal Medicine
330 Brookline Ave 9th Fl, Boston, 617-667-2127
330 Mount Auburn St Wyman Bldg, Cambridge, 617-499-5166

Lynch, Thomas James, Jr. (4 mentions)
Yale U, 1986 *Certification:* Internal Medicine, Medical Oncology
55 Fruit St 7th Fl #7B, Boston, 617-724-1136

Musto, Paul C. (4 mentions)
Michigan State U, 1977
Certification: Hematology, Internal Medicine, Medical Oncology
10 Willard St, Quincy, 617-479-3550

Sanz-Altamira, Pedro M. (3 mentions)
FMS-Spain, 1988
Certification: Hematology, Internal Medicine, Medical Oncology
70 East St, Methuen, 978-685-7811
1 General St Lamprey Bldg 4th Fl, Lawrence, 978-946-8230

Schnipper, Lowell E. (6 mentions)
SUNY-Downstate Med Coll, 1968
Certification: Internal Medicine, Medical Oncology
330 Brookline Ave Rabb Bldg #430, Boston, 617-667-3666

Schwartz, Joel Howard (4 mentions)
Harvard U, 1971
Certification: Internal Medicine, Medical Oncology
17 Centennial Dr, Peabody, 978-977-3434

Shulman, Lawrence Nathan (10 mentions)
Harvard U, 1975
Certification: Hematology, Internal Medicine, Medical Oncology
44 Binney St, Boston, 617-632-2277

Shuster, Todd David (3 mentions)
U of Rochester, 1989 *Certification:* Medical Oncology
41 Mall Rd, Burlington, 781-744-8410

Spieler, Paul Jeffrey (3 mentions)
New York U, 1971
Certification: Hematology, Internal Medicine, Medical Oncology
62 Brown St, Haverhill, 978-521-8590
25 Highland Ave, Newburyport, 978-463-1049

Steinberg, David (4 mentions)
Harvard U, 1964
Certification: Hematology, Internal Medicine, Medical Oncology
41 Mall Rd, Burlington, 781-273-8400

Weiner, Neil Joseph (7 mentions)
George Washington U, 1969
Certification: Hematology, Internal Medicine
41 Mall Rd, Burlington, 781-273-8400

Weintraub, Lewis Robert (5 mentions)
Harvard U, 1958 *Certification:* Hematology, Internal Medicine
830 Harrison Ave 3rd Fl, Boston, 617-638-6428

Weissmann, Lisa B. (3 mentions)
New York U, 1981
Certification: Hematology, Internal Medicine, Medical Oncology
300 Mount Auburn St, Cambridge, 617-497-9646

Wisch, Jeffrey Stewart (5 mentions)
Mount Sinai Sch of Med, 1977
Certification: Hematology, Internal Medicine, Medical Oncology
65 Walnut St 4th Fl #420, Wellesley, 781-237-0700

Wolfe, Lawrence Chas (8 mentions)
Harvard U, 1976
Certification: Pediatric Hematology-Oncology, Pediatrics
800 Washington St, Boston, 617-636-5535

Infectious Disease

Adler, Jonathan Loewy (6 mentions)
Cornell U, 1965
Certification: Infectious Disease, Internal Medicine
15 Dix St, Winchester, 781-729-0788

Basgoz, Nesli Ozden (6 mentions)
Northwestern U, 1983
Certification: Infectious Disease, Internal Medicine
55 Fruit St, Boston, 617-726-3906

Butler, Edward P. (7 mentions)
Tufts U, 1975 *Certification:* Infectious Disease, Internal Medicine
170 Governors Ave, Medford, 781-306-6265

Carling, Philip C., Jr. (7 mentions)
Cornell U, 1969
Certification: Infectious Disease, Internal Medicine
2100 Dorchester Ave, Dorchester, 617-296-4000

Drapkin, Mark S. (14 mentions)
SUNY-Downstate Med Coll, 1969
Certification: Infectious Disease, Internal Medicine
2014 Washington St, Newton, 617-243-5436

Duncan, Robert Atwater (6 mentions)
U of Connecticut, 1987
Certification: Infectious Disease, Internal Medicine
41 Mall Rd, Burlington, 781-744-8608

Ellerin, Todd Bradley (8 mentions)
Tufts U, 1998 *Certification:* Infectious Disease, Internal Medicine
55 Fogg Rd, Weymouth, 781-340-8571

Karchmer, Adolf Waller (13 mentions)
Harvard U, 1964 *Certification:* Internal Medicine
110 Francis St #GB, Boston, 617-632-0760

McGowan, Katherine (5 mentions)
Tufts U, 1975 *Certification:* Infectious Disease, Internal Medicine
1153 Centre St, Jamaica Plain, 617-522-4943
170 Morton St, Jamaica Plain, 617-522-4943

Meissner, Herman Cody (10 mentions)
Tufts U, 1973
Certification: Pediatric Infectious Diseases, Pediatrics
800 Washington St #321, Boston, 617-636-8100

Pasternack, Mark Steven (6 mentions)
Harvard U, 1975
Certification: Infectious Disease, Internal Medicine
15 Parkman St, Boston, 617-726-2374
275 Cambridge St #530, Boston, 617-643-2582

Ross, John James (5 mentions)
FMS-Canada, 1992
Certification: Infectious Disease, Internal Medicine
75 Francis St, Boston, 617-278-0607

Sax, Paul Edward (15 mentions)
Harvard U, 1987
Certification: Infectious Disease, Internal Medicine
75 Francis St, Boston, 617-732-8881

Snydman, David Richard (7 mentions)
U of Pennsylvania, 1972
Certification: Infectious Disease, Internal Medicine
750 Washington St #238, Boston, 617-636-5788

Sulis, Carol Ann (8 mentions)
Columbia U, 1979
Certification: Infectious Disease, Internal Medicine
1 Boston Medical Center Pl Dowling 3N, Boston, 617-414-4958

Treadwell, Thomas Leigh (5 mentions)
Dartmouth Coll, 1977
Certification: Infectious Disease, Internal Medicine
115 Lincoln St, Framingham, 508-383-1563

Worthington, Michael G. (11 mentions)
Johns Hopkins U, 1965 *Certification:* Internal Medicine
736 Cambridge St, Brighton, 617-789-2372

Infertility

Alper, Michael M. (5 mentions)
FMS-Canada, 1978 *Certification:* Obstetrics & Gynecology, Reproductive Endocrinology/Infertility
130 2nd Ave, Waltham, 781-434-6500

Ginsburg, Elizabeth Sarah (4 mentions)
New York U, 1985 *Certification:* Obstetrics & Gynecology, Reproductive Endocrinology/Infertility
75 Francis St, Boston, 617-732-4455

Hornstein, Mark Donald (5 mentions)
U of Cincinnati, 1982 *Certification:* Obstetrics & Gynecology, Reproductive Endocrinology/Infertility
75 Francis St, Boston, 617-732-4648
2014 Washington St, Newton, 617-243-5200

Oskowitz, Selwyn Phillip (6 mentions)
FMS-South Africa, 1970 *Certification:* Obstetrics & Gynecology
1 Brookline Pl #602, Brookline, 617-735-9000

Penzias, Alan Stewart (5 mentions)
SUNY-Downstate Med Coll, 1986 *Certification:* Obstetrics & Gynecology, Reproductive Endocrinology/Infertility
2300 Crown Colony Dr, Quincy, 617-793-1100
130 2nd Ave, Waltham, 781-434-6500

Toth, Thomas Louis (4 mentions)
U of Missouri-Kansas City, 1986 *Certification:* Obstetrics & Gynecology, Reproductive Endocrinology/Infertility
55 Fruit St Yawkey Bldg #10-A, Boston, 617-724-3513

Weiss, Robert Martin (5 mentions)
Robert W Johnson Med Sch, 1984 *Certification:* Obstetrics & Gynecology, Reproductive Endocrinology/Infertility
10 Hospital Dr, Holyoke, 413-534-1124

Internal Medicine *(see note on page 9)*

Adler, Jonathan Loewy (5 mentions)
Cornell U, 1965
Certification: Infectious Disease, Internal Medicine
15 Dix St, Winchester, 781-729-0788

Angiolillo, Dea Francesca (3 mentions)
Harvard U, 1979 *Certification:* Internal Medicine
230 Worcester St, Wellesley, 781-431-5205

Aronson, Mark David (4 mentions)
SUNY-Upstate Med U, 1966 *Certification:* Internal Medicine
330 Brookline Ave, Boston, 617-667-2422

Barber, Thomas Ward (3 mentions)
U of Connecticut, 1984 *Certification:* Internal Medicine
114 Whitwell St, Quincy, 617-376-5637
720 Harrison Ave #508, Boston, 617-638-7999

Bass, Jeffrey (3 mentions)
U of Pennsylvania, 1982 *Certification:* Internal Medicine
25 Boylston St, Chestnut Hill, 617-739-7061

Bush, Booker T., Jr. (4 mentions)
Yale U, 1978 *Certification:* Internal Medicine
330 Brookline Ave, Boston, 617-667-2422

Cohen, Brian Jeffrey (4 mentions)
U of North Carolina, 1978
Certification: Internal Medicine, Nephrology
800 Washington St, Boston, 617-636-7386

Criscitiello, Ronald P. (3 mentions)
SUNY-Upstate Med U, 1977 *Certification:* Internal Medicine
267 Boston Rd #20, North Billerica, 978-663-6666
37 Broadway, Arlington, 781-641-0100

Dodson, David C. (3 mentions)
FMS-Canada, 1979 *Certification:* Internal Medicine
2000 Washington St, Newton, 781-235-5200
372 Washington St, Wellesley, 781-235-5200

Dowling, John Joseph (5 mentions)
Tufts U, 1972 *Certification:* Internal Medicine
29 Crafts St #400, Newton, 617-964-7530

Flier, Steven Ross (4 mentions)
Albert Einstein Coll of Med, 1975
Certification: Internal Medicine, Nephrology
1244 Boylston St #306, Chestnut Hill, 617-731-0058

Gogjian, Michael Alan (3 mentions)
Tufts U, 1979
575 Turnpike St #22, North Andover, 978-689-9488

Goodson, John David (3 mentions)
Stanford U, 1975 *Certification:* Internal Medicine
15 Parkman St #Wacc625, Boston, 617-726-7939

Jen, Phyllis (5 mentions)
SUNY-Downstate Med Coll, 1975 *Certification:* Internal Medicine
75 Francis St #E, Boston, 617-732-6315

Johnson, Erica Ellen (3 mentions)
U of Massachusetts, 1975
Certification: Hematology, Internal Medicine
2000 Washington St #423, Newton, 617-332-3011

Kopelman, Richard Ira (4 mentions)
Duke U, 1974 *Certification:* Internal Medicine
800 Washington St, Boston, 617-636-4349

Krasinski, Ronald (3 mentions)
Georgetown U, 1972
29 Crafts St #400, Newton, 617-964-7530

Levin, Michael Simon (3 mentions)
Wayne State U, 1976
Certification: Critical Care Medicine, Internal Medicine
2000 Washington St #445, Newton, 617-965-1118

Mushlin, Stuart Bruce (6 mentions)
Cornell U, 1973 *Certification:* Internal Medicine
75 Francis St, Boston, 857-307-4100

Napolitana, Guy (8 mentions)
Stony Brook U, 1984 *Certification:* Internal Medicine
41 Mall Rd, Burlington, 781-744-8697

Solomon, Martin Phillip (3 mentions)
Tufts U, 1974 *Certification:* Internal Medicine
1180 Beacon St #1B, Brookline, 617-278-1700

Weinreb, Wayne Howard (3 mentions)
New York U, 1979
Certification: Gastroenterology, Internal Medicine
203 Main St, North Reading, 978-664-1990

Wolf, Marshall Alan (11 mentions)
Harvard U, 1963 *Certification:* Internal Medicine
75 Francis St, Boston, 857-307-4100

Woo, Beverly (7 mentions)
Stanford U, 1974 *Certification:* Internal Medicine
75 Francis St #F, Boston, 617-732-6043

Nephrology

Bazari, Hasan (9 mentions)
Albert Einstein Coll of Med, 1983
Certification: Internal Medicine, Nephrology
55 Fruit St Bigelow #1003, Boston, 617-726-5050

Chawla, Rajinder Singh (5 mentions)
FMS-India, 1972 *Certification:* Internal Medicine, Nephrology
851 Main St #1, South Weymouth, 781-337-6500

Dash, Anthony Zeiger (7 mentions)
U of Washington, 1986
Certification: Internal Medicine, Nephrology
736 Cambridge St, Brighton, 617-789-2588

Gilligan, Hannah M. (4 mentions)
FMS-France, 1990 *Certification:* Internal Medicine, Nephrology
41 Mall Rd, Burlington, 781-744-8430

Haddad, Eduardo Da Silva (7 mentions)
FMS-Brazil, 1975 *Certification:* Internal Medicine, Nephrology
50 Prospect St #301, Lawrence, 978-686-4343

Hazar, Derya Bora (4 mentions)
FMS-Turkey, 1988 *Certification:* Internal Medicine, Nephrology
2100 Dorchester Ave, Dorchester, 617-739-2100

Herrin, John Thomas (4 mentions)
FMS-Australia, 1961
Certification: Pediatric Nephrology, Pediatrics
300 Longwood Ave, Boston, 617-355-6129

Levey, Andrew S. (5 mentions)
Boston U, 1976 *Certification:* Internal Medicine, Nephrology
35 Kneeland St 4th Fl, Boston, 617-636-5866

Milner, Lawrence Selwyn (5 mentions)
FMS-South Africa, 1974
Certification: Pediatric Nephrology, Pediatrics
800 Washington St #201, Boston, 617-636-7295

Neuringer, Julia Rose (5 mentions)
Brown U, 1985 *Certification:* Internal Medicine, Nephrology
2104 Washington St, Newton, 617-244-6940

Segall, Franklin Dorian (4 mentions)
Albert Einstein Coll of Med, 1975
Certification: Internal Medicine, Nephrology
300 Mount Auburn St #515, Cambridge, 617-864-1571

Seifter, Julian Lawrence (9 mentions)
Albert Einstein Coll of Med, 1975
Certification: Internal Medicine, Nephrology
75 Francis St, Boston, 617-732-7482

Singh, Ajay K. (4 mentions)
FMS-United Kingdom, 1984
75 Francis St, Boston, 617-732-5951

Steinman, Theodore I. (8 mentions)
Georgetown U, 1964 *Certification:* Internal Medicine, Nephrology
330 Brookline Ave #Da517, Boston, 617-667-2147

Strom, James Alan (9 mentions)
Yale U, 1974 *Certification:* Internal Medicine, Nephrology
736 Cambridge St, Brighton, 617-783-3995

Yager, Henry Martin (11 mentions)
Boston U, 1966 *Certification:* Internal Medicine, Nephrology
2104 Washington St, Newton, 617-244-6940

Ying, Christopher Y. (6 mentions)
Columbia U, 1977 *Certification:* Internal Medicine, Nephrology
41 Mall Rd, Burlington, 781-273-8430

Neurological Surgery

Chin, Lawrence S. (8 mentions)
U of Michigan, 1987 *Certification:* Neurological Surgery
88 E Newton St, Boston, 617-638-8992

Cook, Bruce Richard (7 mentions)
George Washington U, 1981 *Certification:* Neurological Surgery
354 Merrimack St, Lawrence, 978-687-2321
10 George St #300, Lowell, 978-458-1463

Cosgrove, Rees (16 mentions)
FMS-Canada, 1980 *Certification:* Neurological Surgery
41 Mall Rd, Burlington, 781-744-1990

Day, Arthur Linwood (7 mentions)
Louisiana State U, 1972 *Certification:* Neurological Surgery
75 Francis St, Boston, 617-525-7777

Heilman, Carl Barnes (17 mentions)
U of Pennsylvania, 1986 *Certification:* Neurological Surgery
800 Washington St, Boston, 617-636-5860

Scott, R. Michael (14 mentions)
Temple U, 1966 *Certification:* Neurological Surgery
300 Longwood Ave, Boston, 617-355-6011

Woodard, Eric John (11 mentions)
Pennsylvania State U, 1985 *Certification:* Neurological Surgery
125 Parker Hill Ave, Boston, 617-754-6576

Wu, Julian K. (8 mentions)
U of Connecticut, 1981 *Certification:* Neurological Surgery
800 Washington St, Boston, 617-636-4500

Neurology

Almozlino, Avraham (3 mentions)
FMS-Israel, 1983 *Certification:* Neurology, Sleep Medicine
2000 Washington St Green Bldg #567, Newton, 617-928-1500

Apetauerova, Diana (3 mentions)
FMS-Czech Republic, 1989 *Certification:* Neurology
41 Mall Rd, Burlington, 781-744-8632

Caplan, Louis Robert (8 mentions)
U of Maryland, 1962
Certification: Internal Medicine, Neurology, Vascular Neurology
330 Brookline Ave, Boston, 617-632-8911

Chaves, Claudia J. (3 mentions)
FMS-Brazil, 1986 *Certification:* Neurology, Vascular Neurology
16 Hayden Ave, Lexington, 781-372-7194

Chavin, Jeffrey Michael (3 mentions)
Temple U, 1990 *Certification:* Neurology
800 Washington St, Boston, 617-636-7581

Chervin, Paul Niesen (3 mentions)
Duke U, 1967 *Certification:* Neurology with Special
   Qualifications in Child Neurology, Pediatrics
604 Main St, Woburn, 781-935-3710
800 W Cummings Park Washington St, Woburn, 781-935-3710

Fullerton, Albert L., III (3 mentions)
Tufts U, 1973 *Certification:* Neurology
604 Main St, Woburn, 781-935-3710
800 W Cummings Park Washington St, Woburn, 781-935-3710

Greer, David Matthew (3 mentions)
U of Florida, 1995 *Certification:* Neurology, Vascular Neurology
55 Fruit St #WACC-733, Boston, 617-726-8459

Gross, Paul Thomas (5 mentions)
Hahnemann U, 1976 *Certification:* Neurology
41 Mall Rd #7W, Burlington, 781-744-8955
1 Essex Center Dr, Peabody, 978-538-4690

Jones, H. Royden, Jr. (6 mentions)
Northwestern U, 1962 *Certification:* Clinical
   Neurophysiology, Neurology, Neuromuscular Medicine
41 Mall Rd, Burlington, 781-273-8630

Kase, Carlos S. (5 mentions)
FMS-Chile, 1967 *Certification:* Neurology, Vascular Neurology
720 Harrison Ave #707, Boston, 617-638-8456

Khoshbin, Shahram (5 mentions)
Johns Hopkins U, 1972 *Certification:* Neurology
75 Francis St, Boston, 617-732-7432

Lehrich, James (3 mentions)
Harvard U, 1962 *Certification:* Neurology
15 Parkman St #828, Boston, 617-726-3783

Levy, Sanford Maurice (3 mentions)
Rosalind Franklin U, 1968 *Certification:* Neurology
6 Essex Center Dr, Peabody, 978-532-8010

Libenson, Mark H. (3 mentions)
FMS-Canada, 1985
Certification: Clinical Neurophysiology, Neurology with
   Special Qualifications in Child Neurology, Pediatrics
300 Longwood Ave, Boston, 617-355-8071
482 Bedford St, Lexington, 781-672-2100
500 Salem St, Wilmington, 617-355-8071

Markowitz, Larry (5 mentions)
Yale U, 1976 *Certification:* Neurology
90 Libbey Pkwy #102, Weymouth, 781-335-3900

Moray, Jonathan Scott (4 mentions)
Mount Sinai Sch of Med, 1985 *Certification:* Neurology
10 George St #300, Lowell, 978-458-1463

O'Neal, Mary Angela (4 mentions)
Oregon Health Sciences U, 1984 *Certification:* Neurology
851 Main St, South Weymouth, 781-331-4923

Otis, James Andrew (3 mentions)
New York Med Coll, 1985 *Certification:* Neurology, Pain Medicine
720 Harrison Ave #707, Boston, 617-638-8456

Ronthal, Michael (5 mentions)
FMS-South Africa, 1961 *Certification:* Neurology
330 Brookline Ave, Boston, 617-667-3176

Ropper, Allan Howard (19 mentions)
Cornell U, 1974 *Certification:* Internal Medicine, Neurology
75 Francis St #BB-204, Boston, 617-732-8047

Rosman, Norman Paul (3 mentions)
FMS-Canada, 1959 *Certification:* Neurodevelopmental
   Disabilities, Neurology, Neurology with Special
   Qualifications in Child Neurology, Pediatrics
800 Washington St #213, Boston, 617-414-4501

Ross, Marjorie Helen (6 mentions)
Georgetown U, 1988
Certification: Clinical Neurophysiology, Neurology
2000 Washington St #567, Newton, 617-969-1723

Russell, James Adams (8 mentions)
Philadelphia Coll of Osteopathic Med, 1980 *Certification:*
   Clinical Neurophysiology, Neurology, Neuromuscular Medicine
41 Mall Rd, Burlington, 781-744-8632

Samuels, Martin Allen (33 mentions)
U of Cincinnati, 1971 *Certification:* Internal Medicine, Neurology
75 Francis St, Boston, 617-732-7432

Selbst, Richard Glen (3 mentions)
Temple U, 1977 *Certification:* Neurology
354 Merrimack St Bldg 1, Lawrence, 978-687-2321

Sudarsky, Lewis Richard (3 mentions)
Harvard U, 1974 *Certification:* Neurology
75 Francis St, Boston, 617-525-5504

Tandon, Deepak Sham (3 mentions)
FMS-India, 1973 *Certification:* Neurology
125 Parker Hill Ave #F300, Roxbury Crossing, 617-731-0016

Tarsy, Daniel (3 mentions)
New York U, 1966 *Certification:* Neurology
330 Brookline Ave #KS 228, Boston, 617-667-0519

Thaler, David Emile (6 mentions)
FMS-United Kingdom, 1992
Certification: Neurology, Vascular Neurology
800 Washington St, Boston, 617-636-5848

Toran, Marybeth E. (3 mentions)
Tufts U, 1998 *Certification:* Neurology
2000 Washington St #567, Newton, 617-969-1723

Venna, Nagagopal (4 mentions)
FMS-India, 1968 *Certification:* Neurology
15 Parkman St Wang Bldg #835, Boston, 617-726-7643

Weinberg, David Henry (5 mentions)
U of Pennsylvania, 1980 *Certification:* Neurology
736 Cambridge St, Boston, 617-789-2375

Young, Anne Buckingham (3 mentions)
Johns Hopkins U, 1973 *Certification:* Neurology
15 Parkman St #WAC835, Boston, 617-724-9234

Obstetrics/Gynecology

Barbieri, Robert (3 mentions)
Harvard U, 1977 *Certification:* Endocrinology and
   Metabolism, Internal Medicine, Obstetrics & Gynecology,
   Reproductive Endocrinology/Infertility
75 Francis St #ASBI-3-073, Boston, 617-732-4265

Beatty, Thomas Leary, Jr. (7 mentions)
East Carolina U, 1981 *Certification:* Obstetrics & Gynecology
2000 Washington St Green Bldg #764, Newton, 617-965-7800

Becker, Warren Jay (3 mentions)
New York Med Coll, 1962 *Certification:* Obstetrics & Gynecology
40 Centre St, Brookline, 617-566-0121

Bunnell, Marikim Wolter (7 mentions)
U of Connecticut, 1988 *Certification:* Obstetrics & Gynecology
1 Brookline Pl #522, Brookline, 617-731-3400

Coffey, Christopher John (3 mentions)
Med Coll of Wisconsin, 1988
Certification: Obstetrics & Gynecology
383 Paradise Rd, Swampscott, 781-599-2600

Cohen, Bruce Frederick (4 mentions)
U of Pennsylvania, 1990
Certification: Maternal-Fetal Medicine, Obstetrics & Gynecology
1 Brookline Pl #123, Brookline, 617-754-5550

Federschneider, Jerome M. (3 mentions)
U of Arizona, 1973 *Certification:* Obstetrics & Gynecology
1 Brookline Pl #322, Brookline, 617-735-8910

Frigoletto, Fredric D., Jr. (3 mentions)
Boston U, 1962
Certification: Maternal-Fetal Medicine, Obstetrics & Gynecology
32 Fruit St #416, Boston, 617-724-3775

Fuller, Arlan Frank, Jr. (3 mentions)
Harvard U, 1971
Certification: Gynecologic Oncology, Obstetrics & Gynecology
88 Montvale Ave, Winchester, 781-279-4064

Greenberg, James A. (3 mentions)
New York U, 1988 *Certification:* Obstetrics & Gynecology
1153 Centre St #36, Jamaica Plain, 617-983-7003

Kennison, Robert David (3 mentions)
Tufts U, 1960 *Certification:* Obstetrics & Gynecology
800 Washington St, Boston, 617-636-5000

Klapholz, Henry (5 mentions)
Albert Einstein Coll of Med, 1971
Certification: Obstetrics & Gynecology
115 Lincoln St, Framingham, 508-383-8727

Lichter, Eric Douglas (3 mentions)
SUNY-Downstate Med Coll, 1977
Certification: Obstetrics & Gynecology
1180 Beacon St #6-D, Brookline, 617-879-0393

McLellan, Robert (4 mentions)
U of Maryland, 1980
Certification: Gynecologic Oncology, Obstetrics & Gynecology
41 Mall Rd, Burlington, 781-744-8563

Reilly, Raymond J. (10 mentions)
FMS-United Kingdom, 1958
Certification: Obstetrics & Gynecology
1 Brookline Pl #522, Brookline, 617-731-3400

Ricciotti, Hope Anne (4 mentions)
Dartmouth Coll, 1990 *Certification:* Obstetrics & Gynecology
55 Dimock St, Roxbury, 617-442-8800

Riley, Laura Elizabeth (6 mentions)
U of Pittsburgh, 1985
Certification: Maternal-Fetal Medicine, Obstetrics & Gynecology
55 Fruit St, Boston, 617-724-2229

Shakr, Christo John (3 mentions)
FMS-Lebanon, 1981 *Certification:* Obstetrics & Gynecology
49 Pearl St, Brockton, 508-584-3505
300 Congress St #102, Quincy, 617-479-6636

Shapter, Anne Patricia (6 mentions)
U of Connecticut, 1990
Certification: Gynecologic Oncology, Obstetrics & Gynecology
41 Mall Rd, Burlington, 781-744-2933

Shaw, Jennifer Lynn (3 mentions)
Albany Med Coll, 1989 *Certification:* Obstetrics & Gynecology
720 Harrison Ave, Boston, 617-638-8000

Waddell, Franklin Bernard (4 mentions)
U of North Carolina, 1976 *Certification:* Obstetrics & Gynecology
3 Woodlawn Rd #314, Stoneham, 781-979-9233

Yum, Mimi Ryung (3 mentions)
U of Pennsylvania, 1993 *Certification:* Obstetrics & Gynecology
1 Brookline Pl #423, Brookline, 617-566-1535

Zuckerman, Andrea Lynn (3 mentions)
Tufts U, 1989 *Certification:* Obstetrics & Gynecology
860 Washington St, Boston, 617-636-5289

Ophthalmology

Berson, Frank Gerald (4 mentions)
Harvard U, 1971 *Certification:* Ophthalmology
330 Brookline Ave Shapiro Bldg 5th Fl, Boston, 617-667-3391

Bhatt, Amita K. (4 mentions)
Yale U, 1987 *Certification:* Ophthalmology
2000 Washington St Green Bldg #462, Newton, 617-964-1050

Bienfang, Don Carl (3 mentions)
Harvard U, 1965 *Certification:* Ophthalmology
75 Francis St, Boston, 617-732-7432
330 Brookline Ave, Boston, 617-667-3391

Chang, Romeo Kwan (4 mentions)
FMS-Philippines, 1973 *Certification:* Ophthalmology
464 Hillside Ave #205, Needham, 781-726-7333

Cotter, Paul B., Jr. (3 mentions)
SUNY-Buffalo, 1976 *Certification:* Ophthalmology
179 Quincy St, Brockton, 508-586-0256

Duker, Jay Selig (4 mentions)
Jefferson Med Coll, 1984 *Certification:* Ophthalmology
260 Tremont St 9th Fl, Boston, 617-636-4358
1 Washington St #212, Wellesley, 781-237-6770

Eagle, Janine Rauch (4 mentions)
Dartmouth Coll, 1994 *Certification:* Ophthalmology
50 Prospect St, Lawrence, 978-688-6182
451 Andover St, North Andover, 978-794-8118
62 Brown St, Haverhill, 978-521-5653

Fine, Laura C. (3 mentions)
U of Pennsylvania, 1997 *Certification:* Ophthalmology
50 Staniford St #600, Boston, 617-367-4800
52 2nd Ave 2nd Fl, Waltham, 781-487-2200

Finkelstein, Elliot M. (4 mentions)
Washington U, 1961 *Certification:* Ophthalmology
1371 Beacon St #100, Brookline, 617-734-8090

Foster, Charles Stephen (3 mentions)
Duke U, 1969 *Certification:* Ophthalmology
5 Cambridge Ctr 8th Fl, Cambridge, 617-577-0369
1440 Main St 8th Fl, Waltham, 781-891-9300

Hedges, Thomas Reed (6 mentions)
Tufts U, 1975 *Certification:* Ophthalmology
800 Washington St #450, Boston, 617-636-5488

Hutchinson, B. Thomas (6 mentions)
Harvard U, 1958 *Certification:* Ophthalmology
50 Staniford St #6, Boston, 617-367-4800

Jacobs, Deborah Sue (3 mentions)
Harvard U, 1987 *Certification:* Ophthalmology
464 Hillside Ave #205, Needham, 781-726-7333

Kaufman, Jay Henry (9 mentions)
Harvard U, 1966 *Certification:* Ophthalmology
2000 Washington St #462, Newton, 617-964-1050

Lacy, Robert Tulloch (4 mentions)
Cornell U, 1967 *Certification:* Ophthalmology
100 Highland St #202, Milton, 617-696-0750
696 Main St, South Weymouth, 781-331-3300
1900 Crown Colony Dr #301, Quincy, 617-770-4400
146 Church St, Pembroke, 781-826-2308

Marx, Jeffrey Lewis (5 mentions)
Stony Brook U, 1990 *Certification:* Ophthalmology
41 Mall Rd, Burlington, 781-744-8555
1 Essex Center Dr, Peabody, 978-538-4400

Patten, James Thomas (3 mentions)
Med Coll of Wisconsin, 1970 *Certification:* Ophthalmology
1155 Centre St #35, Jamaica Plain, 617-524-7055
825 Washington St #230, Norwood, 781-769-8880

Richter, Claudia (3 mentions)
U of Texas-Southwestern, 1977 *Certification:* Ophthalmology
50 Staniford St #600, Boston, 617-367-4800
52 2nd Ave 2nd Fl, Waltham, 781-487-2200

Sang, Delia Nai-Yueh (5 mentions)
Columbia U, 1975 *Certification:* Ophthalmology
50 Staniford St #6, Boston, 617-367-4800
1101 Beacon St #3-E, Brookline, 617-731-1760

Shingleton, Bradford John (8 mentions)
U of Michigan, 1977 *Certification:* Ophthalmology
50 Staniford St #600, Boston, 617-367-4800
282 Route 130 & Cotuit Rd, Sandwich, 617-367-4800
88 Ansel Hallet Rd, West Yarmouth, 617-367-4800

Smith, Jill Ann (6 mentions)
Duke U, 1992 *Certification:* Ophthalmology
2000 Washington St Green Bldg #462, Newton, 617-964-1050

Soukiasian, Sarkis Haig (6 mentions)
Tufts U, 1983 *Certification:* Internal Medicine, Ophthalmology
41 Mall Rd, Burlington, 978-538-4430
1 Essex Center Dr, Peabody, 978-538-4430

Stampfer, Kenneth (5 mentions)
Albert Einstein Coll of Med, 1968 *Certification:* Ophthalmology
300 Mount Auburn St #417, Cambridge, 617-354-0909

Umlas, James Warren (3 mentions)
Harvard U, 1991 *Certification:* Ophthalmology
131 ORNAC, Concord, 978-369-1310
21 Worthen Rd, Lexington, 781-862-1620
281 Massachusetts Ave, Arlington, 781-648-1620

Wasson, Paul Joseph (3 mentions)
Case Western Reserve U, 1981 *Certification:* Ophthalmology
1900 Crown Colony Dr #301, Quincy, 617-472-5242
10 N Pearl St, Brockton, 617-472-5242

Weissman, Irving Louis (3 mentions)
New York U, 1966 *Certification:* Ophthalmology
280 Washington St #308, Brighton, 617-787-5503

Wu, Helen Kuomei (5 mentions)
Ohio State U, 1986 *Certification:* Ophthalmology
260 Tremont St 9th Fl, Boston, 617-636-4358

Orthopedics

Bono, James Vincent (3 mentions)
Albany Med Coll, 1987 *Certification:* Orthopaedic Surgery
125 Parker Hill Ave #573, Roxbury Crossing, 617-731-6337

Brick, Gregory William (10 mentions)
FMS-New Zealand, 1977
45 Francis St 1st Fl, Boston, 617-732-5322

Burke, Dennis William (8 mentions)
Loyola U Chicago, 1978 *Certification:* Orthopaedic Surgery
55 Fruit St Yawkey #3-B, Boston, 617-726-3411

Cassidy, Charles (5 mentions)
Northwestern U, 1987
Certification: Orthopaedic Surgery, Surgery of the Hand
800 Washington St, Boston, 617-636-5150

Curtis, Alan Steven (3 mentions)
U of Massachusetts, 1985 *Certification:* Orthopaedic Surgery
830 Boylston St #107, Chestnut Hill, 617-264-1100
840 Winter St, Waltham, 781-890-2133

Emans, John Barker, II (4 mentions)
Harvard U, 1970 *Certification:* Orthopaedic Surgery
300 Longwood Ave Hunnewell Bldg 2nd Fl, Boston, 617-355-6021
482 Bedford St, Lexington, 781-672-2100
9 Hope Ave, Waltham, 781-216-2100

English, Diane M. (3 mentions)
Tufts U, 1972 *Certification:* Orthopaedic Surgery
11 Nevins St #403, Brighton, 617-254-1247

Evans, Ira Kenneth, Jr. (3 mentions)
Vanderbilt U, 1983 *Certification:* Orthopaedic Surgery
1 Orthopedic Dr, Peabody, 978-818-6350
195 School St, Manchester, 978-818-6350

Feiler, Helene Eve (5 mentions)
Tufts U, 1989 *Certification:* Orthopaedic Surgery
150 Presidential Way #110, Woburn, 781-782-1300

Foster, Timothy Earle (3 mentions)
Boston U, 1986 *Certification:* Orthopaedic Surgery
720 Harrison Ave #805, Boston, 617-638-5633
915 Commonwealth Ave 2nd Fl, Boston, 617-638-5633

Gebhardt, Mark Clyde (4 mentions)
U of Cincinnati, 1975 *Certification:* Orthopaedic Surgery
330 Brookline Ave, Boston, 617-667-2140

Gill, Thomas James, IV (7 mentions)
Harvard U, 1990 *Certification:* Orthopaedic Surgery
175 Cambridge St #400, Boston, 617-726-7797

Hanmer, Alfred W. (4 mentions)
Tufts U, 1983 *Certification:* Orthopaedic Surgery
2000 Washington St #341, Newton, 617-964-0024

Healy, William L. (5 mentions)
SUNY-Downstate Med Coll, 1978
Certification: Orthopaedic Surgery
41 Mall Rd, Burlington, 781-744-7700

Hoerner, Thomas Earl (3 mentions)
Cornell U, 1978 *Certification:* Orthopaedic Surgery
16 Palham Rd, Salem, NH, 603-898-2244

Karlson, James A. (3 mentions)
Brown U, 1988 *Certification:* Orthopaedic Surgery
235 Cypress St, Brookline, 617-738-8642
300 Mount Auburn St #505, Cambridge, 617-491-6766

Kasparyan, Nurhan George (4 mentions)
Boston U, 1991
Certification: Orthopaedic Surgery, Surgery of the Hand
41 Mall Rd, Burlington, 781-744-3023

Kornack, Fulton C. (3 mentions)
U of Massachusetts, 1980 *Certification:* Orthopaedic Surgery
1 Lyons St, Dedham, 781-329-1400

Lemos, Mark Jason (3 mentions)
U of Pennsylvania, 1986 *Certification:* Orthopaedic Surgery
41 Mall Rd, Burlington, 781-744-8692
1 Essex Center Dr, Peabody, 781-744-8692

Leslie, Bruce Maynard (4 mentions)
SUNY-Upstate Med U, 1978
Certification: Orthopaedic Surgery, Surgery of the Hand
2000 Washington St #341, Newton, 617-332-5150

McConville, Owen Robert (4 mentions)
Tufts U, 1986 *Certification:* Orthopaedic Surgery
51 Performance Dr #300, Weymouth, 781-331-4450

Micheli, Lyle Joseph (6 mentions)
Harvard U, 1966 *Certification:* Orthopaedic Surgery
319 Longwood Ave, Boston, 617-355-6028

Pierce, Ralph Wendell (5 mentions)
Harvard U, 1970 *Certification:* Orthopaedic Surgery
955 Main St #305, Winchester, 781-729-9577

Ready, John E. (5 mentions)
FMS-Canada, 1982 *Certification:* Orthopaedic Surgery
75 Francis St, Boston, 617-732-5368

Richmond, John C. (4 mentions)
Tufts U, 1976 *Certification:* Orthopaedic Surgery
830 Boylston St, Chestnut Hill, 617-264-1100

Rockett, Sean Edward (3 mentions)
Tufts U, 1993 *Certification:* Orthopaedic Surgery
2000 Washington St #322, Newton, 617-527-5040
67 Union St #407, Natick, 508-655-0471

Scott, Richard David (5 mentions)
Temple U, 1968 *Certification:* Orthopaedic Surgery
125 Parker Hill Ave, Roxbury Crossing, 617-738-9151

Sheehan, Lester John (7 mentions)
Tufts U, 1975 *Certification:* Orthopaedic Surgery
11 Nevins St #303, Brighton, 617-787-2308

Siliski, John Michael (4 mentions)
Harvard U, 1977 *Certification:* Orthopaedic Surgery
1 Hawthorne Pl #105, Boston, 617-726-8441
125 Parker Hill Ave, Boston, 617-726-8441

Simmons, Barry Putnam (3 mentions)
Columbia U, 1965
Certification: Orthopaedic Surgery, Surgery of the Hand
75 Francis St, Boston, 617-732-5378

Thornhill, Thomas Stone (8 mentions)
Cornell U, 1970
Certification: Internal Medicine, Orthopaedic Surgery
75 Francis St, Boston, 617-732-5383

Tornetta, Paul, III (3 mentions)
SUNY-Downstate Med Coll, 1987
Certification: Orthopaedic Surgery
850 Harrison Ave, Boston, 617-414-4865

Wilk, Richard Michael (4 mentions)
Jefferson Med Coll, 1985 *Certification:* Orthopaedic Surgery
41 Mall Rd, Burlington, 781-273-8227

Wright, Robert John (5 mentions)
FMS-New Zealand, 1983 *Certification:* Orthopaedic Surgery
291 Independence Dr, West Roxbury, 617-541-6350
75 Francis St, Boston, 617-732-5322

Zahner, Evan John (3 mentions)
Columbia U, 1992 *Certification:* Orthopaedic Surgery
11 Nevins St #303, Brighton, 617-787-2308

Otorhinolaryngology

Bhattacharyya, Neil (12 mentions)
U of Illinois, 1992 *Certification:* Otolaryngology
45 Francis St, Boston, 617-525-6500

Brown, Jeffrey Stuart (5 mentions)
U of Pittsburgh, 1986 *Certification:* Otolaryngology
15 Dix St, Winchester, 781-729-8845
7 Alfred St, Woburn, 781-937-3001

Catalano, Peter Joseph (4 mentions)
Mount Sinai Sch of Med, 1985 *Certification:* Otolaryngology
41 Mall Rd, Burlington, 781-744-8450

Dolan, Robert William (5 mentions)
St Louis U, 1988 *Certification:* Otolaryngology
41 Mall Rd, Burlington, 781-744-8450
1 Essex Center Dr, Peabody, 978-538-4320

Gallivan, Kathleen Holly (4 mentions)
Tufts U, 1995 *Certification:* Otolaryngology
7 Alfred St, Woburn, 781-937-3001
15 Dix St #D, Winchester, 781-729-8845

Grillone, Gregory Angelo (10 mentions)
Mount Sinai Sch of Med, 1983 *Certification:* Otolaryngology
830 Harrison Ave #1400, Boston, 617-638-8124

Grundfast, Kenneth Martin (7 mentions)
SUNY-Upstate Med U, 1969 *Certification:* Otolaryngology
830 Harrison Ave #1400, Boston, 617-638-8124

Lauretano, Arthur Michael (4 mentions)
Boston U, 1988 *Certification:* Otolaryngology
3 Meeting House Rd #24, Chelmsford, 978-256-5557

McGill, Trevor J. (5 mentions)
FMS-Ireland, 1967 *Certification:* Otolaryngology
300 Longwood Ave, Boston, 617-355-8859
9 Hope Ave, Waltham, 781-672-2201

Nuss, Roger Charles (4 mentions)
Harvard U, 1988 *Certification:* Otolaryngology
300 Longwood Ave, Boston, 617-355-6460
482 Bedford St, Lexington, 781-672-2100
9 Hope Ave, Waltham, 781-216-2100

Ota, Harold Gregory (5 mentions)
U of Massachusetts, 1981 *Certification:* Otolaryngology
1493 Cambridge St #781, Cambridge, 617-665-2555
103 Garland St, Everett, 617-389-2727

Rebeiz, Elie Edmond (8 mentions)
FMS-Lebanon, 1984 *Certification:* Otolaryngology
439 S Union St #101, Lawrence, 978-686-2983
750 Washington St #850, Boston, 617-636-1664

Rounds, Mark Filios (8 mentions)
U of Rochester, 1991 *Certification:* Otolaryngology
2000 Washington St #668, Newton, 617-573-4117

Shapiro, Jo (7 mentions)
George Washington U, 1980 *Certification:* Otolaryngology
45 Francis St, Boston, 617-525-6500

Stern, Robert Alan (7 mentions)
Hahnemann U, 1982 *Certification:* Otolaryngology
736 Cambridge St, Brighton, 617-789-3064
11 Nevins St #504, Brighton, 617-787-9877

Vernick, David Murray (4 mentions)
Johns Hopkins U, 1977 *Certification:* Neurotology, Otolaryngology
1244 Boylston St #303, Chestnut Hill, 617-383-6800

Pain Medicine

Bajwa, Zahid Hussain (3 mentions)
FMS-Pakistan, 1986 *Certification:* Neurology, Pain Medicine
330 Brookline Ave, Boston, 617-667-5558

Berde, Charles Benjamin (9 mentions)
Stanford U, 1980
Certification: Anesthesiology, Pain Medicine, Pediatrics
300 Longwood Ave, Boston, 617-355-6995

Dwarakanath, Gopala K. (3 mentions)
FMS-India, 1973 *Certification:* Anesthesiology, Pain Medicine
295 Varnum Ave, Lowell, 978-937-6460

Hutcheson, John James (4 mentions)
Rosalind Franklin U, 1989
Certification: Anesthesiology, Pain Medicine
444 Washington St, Woburn, 781-756-7246
41 Highland Ave, Winchester, 781-756-7246

Jackel, Jeffrey Stuart (3 mentions)
Hahnemann U, 1982
Certification: Anesthesiology, Pain Medicine
2100 Dorchester Ave, Dorchester, 617-296-7246

Kowal, Andrew G. (7 mentions)
Albany Med Coll, 1992
Certification: Anesthesiology, Pain Medicine
41 Mall Rd, Burlington, 781-744-5090

Novak, Gordon Marc (5 mentions)
Med Coll of Wisconsin, 1993
Certification: Anesthesiology, Pain Medicine
736 Cambridge St, Brighton, 617-789-5144

Otis, James Andrew (4 mentions)
New York Med Coll, 1985
Certification: Neurology, Pain Medicine
720 Harrison Ave #707, Boston, 617-638-8456

Ross, Edgar Larry (7 mentions)
Wayne State U, 1980 *Certification:* Anesthesiology, Pain Medicine
850 Boylston St #320, Chestnut Hill, 617-732-9060

Satwicz, Paul R. (10 mentions)
U of California-San Francisco, 1978
Certification: Anesthesiology, Pain Medicine
2014 Washington St, Newton, 617-243-6142

Sukiennik, Andrew (3 mentions)
FMS-Poland, 1986 *Certification:* Anesthesiology, Pain Medicine
444 Washington St, Woburn, 781-756-7246

Pathology

De Las-Morenas, Antonio (4 mentions)
FMS-Spain, 1978
Certification: Anatomic Pathology, Cytopathology
670 Albany St 3rd Fl, Boston, 617-414-5059

Feen, Dennis Joseph (8 mentions)
George Washington U, 1967
Certification: Anatomic Pathology & Clinical Pathology
2014 Washington St, Newton, 617-243-6140

Fletcher, Christopher (5 mentions)
FMS-United Kingdom, 1981
75 Francis St, Boston, 617-732-8558

Schnitt, Stuart Jay (5 mentions)
Albany Med Coll, 1979
Certification: Anatomic Pathology & Clinical Pathology
330 Brookline Ave #E112, Boston, 617-667-4344

Silverman, Mark Lawrence (4 mentions)
U of Connecticut, 1975 *Certification:* Anatomic Pathology
41 Mall Rd, Burlington, 781-744-8046

Pediatrics *(see note on page 9)*

Bernstein, Shelly C. (4 mentions)
U of Chicago, 1980 *Certification:* Pediatrics
486 Boston Post Rd, Weston, 781-899-4456

Brown, Charles Stanley (5 mentions)
Tufts U, 1979 *Certification:* Pediatrics
2000 Washington St #468, Newton, 617-965-6700

Brown, Jane Audry (4 mentions)
Harvard U, 1983 *Certification:* Pediatrics
111 Lincoln St, Needham, 781-444-7186

Bunnell, Bruce Willard (7 mentions)
U of Connecticut, 1987 *Certification:* Pediatrics
1 Brookline Pl #327, Brookline, 617-735-8585

Cloherty, John Patrick (5 mentions)
Boston U, 1962
Certification: Neonatal-Perinatal Medicine, Pediatrics
319 Longwood Ave #4, Boston, 617-277-7320

Curran, Marjorie A. (3 mentions)
Albany Med Coll, 1989 *Certification:* Pediatrics
55 Fruit St #6600, Boston, 617-726-2728

Goldston, James Ira (3 mentions)
Tufts U, 1987
258 Washington St, Wellesley Hills, 781-431-2360

Higgins, James T. (3 mentions)
Harvard U, 1974 *Certification:* Pediatrics
72 Highland Ave, Salem, 978-745-3050
84 Highland Ave, Salem, 978-745-3050

Karlson, Lynne Karen (5 mentions)
Tufts U, 1981 *Certification:* Pediatrics
800 Washington St, Boston, 617-636-5255

Link, David Armand (4 mentions)
Albert Einstein Coll of Med, 1971
Certification: Pediatric Nephrology, Pediatrics
1493 Cambridge St, Cambridge, 617-665-1497

Mandell, Frederick (5 mentions)
U of Vermont, 1964 *Certification:* Pediatrics
850 Boylston St #400, Chestnut Hill, 617-731-0200

Michaels, Robert Steven (6 mentions)
Harvard U, 1977 *Certification:* Pediatrics
319 Longwood Ave 4th Fl, Boston, 617-277-7320

Petit, Kevin P. (3 mentions)
Brown U, 1980
Certification: Neonatal-Perinatal Medicine, Pediatrics
750 Washington St, Boston, 617-636-5322

Roth, Sally S. (5 mentions)
Case Western Reserve U, 1968 *Certification:* Pediatrics
637 Washington St #202, Brookline, 617-232-2811

Spingarn, Roger Weil (4 mentions)
Hahnemann U, 1990
Certification: Adolescent Medicine, Pediatrics
1400 Centre St #203, Newton, 617-244-9929

Vogler, Michael Alan (4 mentions)
U of Michigan, 1982 *Certification:* Pediatrics
7 Alfred St, Woburn, 781-933-6236
820 Turnpike St #A, North Andover, 978-557-5712

Vonnegut, Mark (3 mentions)
Harvard U, 1979 *Certification:* Pediatrics
21 Totman St #2, Quincy, 617-745-0050

Wilson, Claire Marie (4 mentions)
Harvard U, 1977 *Certification:* Pediatrics
20 Wall St, Burlington, 781-221-2800

Young, Gregory John (6 mentions)
Columbia U, 1987 *Certification:* Pediatrics
319 Longwood Ave #4, Boston, 617-277-7320

Plastic Surgery

Bartlett, Richard Alan (5 mentions)
Jefferson Med Coll, 1982 *Certification:* Plastic Surgery
1 Brookline Pl #620, Brookline, 617-735-1800

Breuing, Karl H. (4 mentions)
FMS-Germany, 1980 *Certification:* Plastic Surgery
75 Francis St, Boston, 617-732-6725

Bryan, David James (6 mentions)
Harvard U, 1981 *Certification:* Plastic Surgery
41 Mall Rd, Burlington, 781-273-8584

Chatson, George Peter (4 mentions)
New York U, 1987 *Certification:* Plastic Surgery
555 Turnpike St #52, North Andover, 978-687-1151

Di Edwardo, Christine A. (4 mentions)
Boston U, 1992 *Certification:* Plastic Surgery, Surgery
16 Hayden Ave, Lexington, 781-372-7070
1 Essex Center Dr, Peabody, 781-372-7070

Eriksson, Elof K. O. (4 mentions)
FMS-Sweden, 1969 *Certification:* Plastic Surgery
75 Francis St, Boston, 617-732-5093

Feldman, Joel Joseph (4 mentions)
Harvard U, 1969 *Certification:* Plastic Surgery, Surgery
300 Mount Auburn St #304, Cambridge, 617-661-5998

Hall, Jonathan Daniel (5 mentions)
Washington U, 1983
Certification: Plastic Surgery, Surgery of the Hand
92 Montvale Ave, Stoneham, 781-245-7930

Harlow, Courtland L., Jr. (5 mentions)
Boston U, 1971 *Certification:* Plastic Surgery
851 Main St #17, South Weymouth, 781-337-2552

Hergrueter, Charles Arthur (6 mentions)
Harvard U, 1981 *Certification:* Plastic Surgery
75 Francis St, Brookline, 617-732-6634
850 Boylston St, Chestnut Hill, 617-732-6634

Lenehan, Joseph Matthew (5 mentions)
U of Vermont, 1969
Certification: Plastic Surgery, Surgery, Surgery of the Hand
55 Fogg Rd, South Weymouth, 781-340-4100

May, James Warren, Jr. (4 mentions)
Northwestern U, 1969 *Certification:* Plastic Surgery, Surgery
15 Parkman St #WACC-453, Boston, 617-726-8220

Morris, Donald Jay (4 mentions)
U of Rochester, 1982
Certification: Plastic Surgery, Surgery of the Hand
235 Cypress St #210, Brookline, 617-383-6250

Mulliken, John Butler (5 mentions)
Columbia U, 1964 *Certification:* Plastic Surgery, Surgery
300 Longwood Ave, Boston, 617-355-7686

Orgill, Dennis P. (8 mentions)
Harvard U, 1985 *Certification:* Plastic Surgery, Surgery
45 Francis St, Boston, 617-732-5456

Pribaz, Julian J. (10 mentions)
FMS-Australia, 1972 *Certification:* Plastic Surgery
75 Francis St, Boston, 617-732-6390

Rogers, Gary F. (4 mentions)
Tulane U, 1991 *Certification:* Orthopaedic Surgery, Plastic Surgery, Surgery of the Hand
300 Longwood Ave, Boston, 617-355-8509

Sampson, Christian Edward (4 mentions)
Boston U, 1986
Certification: Plastic Surgery, Surgery of the Hand
75 Francis St, Boston, 617-732-6297

Slavin, Sumner Andrew (4 mentions)
U of Vermont, 1973 *Certification:* Plastic Surgery
1101 Beacon St #7E, Brookline, 617-277-7010

Volpe, A. George (6 mentions)
FMS-Canada, 1985 *Certification:* Plastic Surgery
29 Crafts St #370, Newton, 617-244-2600
11 Nevins St #502, Boston, 617-244-2600

Psychiatry

Badaracco, Mary Anne D. (8 mentions)
Harvard U, 1975 *Certification:* Child Psychiatry, Psychiatry
185 Pilgrim Rd Deaconess 1, Boston, 617-632-0907

Berenbaum, Isidore L. (3 mentions)
Georgetown U, 1975 *Certification:* Geriatric Psychiatry, Psychiatry, Psychosomatic Medicine
88 E Newton St Robinson Bldg #B410, Boston, 617-638-8670

Bloomingdale, Kerry (4 mentions)
Certification: Psychiatry
330 Brookline Ave 2nd Fl, Boston, 617-667-4735

Greenberg, William Ephraim (3 mentions)
U of Pennsylvania, 1976 *Certification:* Psychiatry
330 Brookline Ave #205, Boston, 617-667-2740

Harnett, David S. (3 mentions)
New York U, 1977 *Certification:* Geriatric Psychiatry, Psychiatry
170 Governors Ave, Medford, 781-306-6000

Prince, Jefferson Bruce (3 mentions)
Emory U, 1991
Certification: Child & Adolescent Psychiatry, Psychiatry
57 Highland Ave, Salem, 978-745-2100

Sullivan, Mary Anna (7 mentions)
Columbia U, 1980 *Certification:* Psychiatry
41 Mall Rd, Burlington, 781-744-8869

Pulmonary Disease

Beamis, John Francis, Jr. (11 mentions)
U of Vermont, 1970 *Certification:* Critical Care Medicine, Internal Medicine, Pulmonary Disease
41 Mall Rd, Burlington, 781-744-8480

Celli, Bartolome (12 mentions)
FMS-Venezuela, 1970
Certification: Internal Medicine, Pulmonary Disease
736 Cambridge St, Brighton, 617-789-2545

Dorkin, Henry Lawrence (6 mentions)
Johns Hopkins U, 1974
Certification: Pediatric Pulmonology, Pediatrics
55 Fruit St #101, Boston, 617-726-8707

Fanta, Christopher Glen (25 mentions)
Harvard U, 1975
Certification: Internal Medicine, Pulmonary Disease
15 Francis St, Boston, 617-732-6770
850 Boylston St #437, Chestnut Hill, 617-278-0540

Gray, Anthony W., Jr. (4 mentions)
U of Pittsburgh, 1985 *Certification:* Critical Care Medicine, Internal Medicine, Pulmonary Disease
41 Mall Rd, Burlington, 781-273-8480

Hayes, Gerard (4 mentions)
Tufts U, 1983 *Certification:* Internal Medicine
11 Nevins St #202, Brighton, 617-779-6700
231 Moody St, Waltham, 781-899-6226

Kanarek, David John (4 mentions)
FMS-South Africa, 1962
Certification: Internal Medicine, Pulmonary Disease
15 Parkman St Wang Bldg #ACC-536, Boston, 617-726-5198

Mazzotta, John Francis (4 mentions)
Tufts U, 1974
Certification: Internal Medicine, Pulmonary Disease
16 Central St, South Weymouth, 781-331-6570

Schiffman, Robert L. (4 mentions)
Columbia U, 1976
Certification: Internal Medicine, Pulmonary Disease
330 Mount Auburn St #419, Cambridge, 617-354-8771

Silvestri, Ronald Chiko (4 mentions)
Harvard U, 1974
Certification: Internal Medicine, Pulmonary Disease
330 Brookline Ave #KB23, Boston, 617-667-5864

Tarpy, Robert Edward (4 mentions)
U of Massachusetts, 1988
Certification: Critical Care Medicine, Pulmonary Disease
1153 Centre St #4990, Jamaica Plain, 617-983-7224

Vernovsky, Inna (4 mentions)
FMS-Lithuania, 1990
Certification: Critical Care Medicine, Pulmonary Disease
2014 Washington St, Newton, 617-243-6000

Villanueva, Andrew Garcia (11 mentions)
U of California-San Diego, 1980 *Certification:* Critical Care Medicine, Internal Medicine, Pulmonary Disease
41 Mall Rd, Burlington, 781-744-8480

Radiology—Diagnostic

Barest, Glenn David (3 mentions)
U of Cincinnati, 1991
Certification: Diagnostic Radiology, Neuroradiology
88 E Newton St, Boston, 617-414-7476

Davidoff, Ashley (3 mentions)
FMS-South Africa, 1975 *Certification:* Diagnostic Radiology
736 Cambridge St, Brighton, 617-789-2762

Duva-Frissora, Audrey D. (3 mentions)
Tufts U, 1987 *Certification:* Diagnostic Radiology
85 Herrick St, Beverly, 978-927-6385

Fortunato, Robert Paul (3 mentions)
U of Virginia, 1978 *Certification:* Diagnostic Radiology
41 Highland Ave, Winchester, 781-756-7178

Hannon, Robert Christopher (3 mentions)
U of Vermont, 1968
Certification: Radiology, Vascular & Interventional Radiology
70 East St, Methuen, 978-687-0151

Hill, James R. (3 mentions)
Tufts U, 1989 *Certification:* Diagnostic Radiology
125 Parker Hill Ave, Boston, 617-754-6695

Homer, Marc Jared (3 mentions)
New York U, 1971 *Certification:* Diagnostic Radiology
800 Washington St, Boston, 617-636-0045

Kelley, Russell Alden (3 mentions)
U of Cincinnati, 1977
Certification: Diagnostic Radiology, Internal Medicine
55 Fogg Rd, South Weymouth, 781-340-8846

McCauley, Roy G. Kerr (3 mentions)
FMS-Ireland, 1964
Certification: Diagnostic Radiology, Pediatric Radiology
800 Washington St #213, Boston, 617-636-7940

Mueller, Peter Raff (5 mentions)
U of Cincinnati, 1973 *Certification:* Diagnostic Radiology
55 Fruit St, Boston, 617-726-8396

Rastegar, Joan (3 mentions)
Harvard U, 1989 *Certification:* Diagnostic Radiology
2014 Washington St, Newton, 617-243-6000

Sarno, Robert Charles (3 mentions)
Tufts U, 1970
Certification: Diagnostic Radiology, Nuclear Radiology
800 Washington St, Boston, 617-636-0040

Scholz, Francis Joseph (4 mentions)
Georgetown U, 1969 *Certification:* Diagnostic Radiology
41 Mall Rd, Burlington, 781-744-8170

Zamani, Amir Arsalan (4 mentions)
FMS-Iran, 1973
Certification: Diagnostic Radiology, Neuroradiology
75 Francis St, Boston, 617-732-7260

Radiology—Therapeutic

Choi, In Sup (5 mentions)
FMS-South Korea, 1972
Certification: Diagnostic Radiology, Neuroradiology
41 Mall Rd, Burlington, 781-744-8170

D'Amico, Anthony Victor (3 mentions)
U of Pennsylvania, 1990 *Certification:* Radiation Oncology
480 Hawthorn St, North Dartmouth, 508-979-5858
75 Francis St #ASB1-L2, Boston, 617-732-7936

Girard, Mark J. (3 mentions)
Harvard U, 1986 *Certification:* Diagnostic Radiology, Vascular & Interventional Radiology
81 Highland Ave, Salem, 978-354-4421

Heidbreder, Richard Charles (3 mentions)
U of Illinois, 1981 *Certification:* Therapeutic Radiology
7 Alfred St, Woburn, 781-756-2308
620 Washington St, Winchester, 781-756-8300

Kaplan, Irving David (3 mentions)
Stanford U, 1985 *Certification:* Radiation Oncology
330 Brookline Ave, Boston, 617-667-2345

Lo, Theodore C. M. (6 mentions)
Jefferson Med Coll, 1970 *Certification:* Therapeutic Radiology
41 Mall Rd, Burlington, 781-744-8780
1 Essex Center Dr, Peabody, 781-744-8780

Loeffler, Jay Steven (5 mentions)
Brown U, 1982 *Certification:* Therapeutic Radiology
55 Fruit St, Boston, 617-724-1548

Molgaard, Christopher P. (8 mentions)
Baylor U, 1984 *Certification:* Diagnostic Radiology, Vascular & Interventional Radiology
41 Mall Rd, Burlington, 781-744-8170

Norbash, Alexander M. (3 mentions)
U of Missouri-Kansas City, 1986
Certification: Diagnostic Radiology, Neuroradiology
720 Harrison Ave 7th Fl, Boston, 617-638-6610

Wazer, David Edward (3 mentions)
New York U, 1982 *Certification:* Radiation Oncology
800 Washington St, Boston, 617-636-7673

Zietman, Anthony Laurence (4 mentions)
FMS-United Kingdom, 1983 *Certification:* Radiation Oncology
55 Fruit St, Boston, 617-726-2000

Rehabilitation

Bloch, Rina (5 mentions)
U of Louisville, 1983 *Certification:* Physical Medicine & Rehabilitation, Spinal Cord Injury Medicine
800 Washington St #400, Boston, 617-636-3003

Hartigan, Carol (3 mentions)
U of Virginia, 1987
Certification: Physical Medicine & Rehabilitation
125 Parker Hill Ave, Roxbury Crossing, 617-754-5246

Ozel, Ayca Deniz (4 mentions)
U of Minnesota, 1986
Certification: Physical Medicine & Rehabilitation
2 Rehabilitation Way, Woburn, 781-935-5050

Rainville, James (5 mentions)
U of Massachusetts, 1978
Certification: Physical Medicine & Rehabilitation
125 Parker Hill Ave, Roxbury Crossing, 617-754-5246
830 Boylston St, Brookline, 617-754-6826

Webster, Harry Clark (10 mentions)
U of California-San Francisco, 1977
Certification: Pediatrics, Physical Medicine & Rehabilitation
78 Boston Rd N, Billerica, 978-667-5123

Williams, Steve Ray (4 mentions)
Eastern Virginia Med Sch, 1994 *Certification:* Physical Medicine & Rehabilitation, Spinal Cord Injury Medicine
732 Harrison Ave, Boston, 617-638-7911

Rheumatology

Anderson, Ronald James (9 mentions)
Albany Med Coll, 1963
Certification: Internal Medicine, Rheumatology
75 Francis St, Boston, 617-732-5345

Coblyn, Jonathan Scott (11 mentions)
Johns Hopkins U, 1974
Certification: Internal Medicine, Rheumatology
45 Francis St, Boston, 617-732-5347

Dellaripa, Paul Francis (5 mentions)
U of Connecticut, 1989
Certification: Internal Medicine, Rheumatology
75 Francis St, Boston, 617-732-5325
850 Boylston St, Boston, 617-732-9500

Docken, William Peter (5 mentions)
U of Chicago, 1971
Certification: Internal Medicine, Rheumatology
850 Boylston St #130, Chestnut Hill, 617-732-9500

Fitzgerald, Lisa Mary (5 mentions)
Tufts U, 1981 *Certification:* Internal Medicine, Rheumatology
110 Francis St #4B, Boston, 617-632-8658
300 Mount Auburn St #410, Cambridge, 617-576-1102

Goldenberg, Don Lee (5 mentions)
U of Wisconsin, 1969
Certification: Internal Medicine, Rheumatology
2000 Washington St #304, Newton, 617-527-7485

Kay, Jonathan (5 mentions)
U of California-San Francisco, 1983
Certification: Internal Medicine, Rheumatology
55 Fruit St Yawkey #2-C, Boston, 617-726-7938
40 2nd Ave #300, Waltham, 781-487-4300

Massarotti, Elena Maria (21 mentions)
Tufts U, 1984 *Certification:* Internal Medicine, Rheumatology
260 Tremont St, Boston, 617-636-5990

Merkel, Peter Alexander (5 mentions)
Yale U, 1988 *Certification:* Internal Medicine, Rheumatology
720 Harrison Ave 4th Fl, Boston, 617-638-7460

Pastan, Robert Stephen (5 mentions)
Boston U, 1973 *Certification:* Internal Medicine, Rheumatology
3 Woodland Rd #413, Stoneham, 781-322-7304

Schneller, Stuart Joel (5 mentions)
Med Coll of Wisconsin, 1975
Certification: Internal Medicine, Rheumatology
11 Nevins St #303, Brighton, 617-787-5111
725 Concord Ave, Cambridge, 617-787-5111

Shmerling, Robert H. (7 mentions)
Harvard U, 1983 *Certification:* Internal Medicine, Rheumatology
110 Francis St #4B, Boston, 617-632-8658

Simms, Robert William (6 mentions)
U of Rochester, 1980
Certification: Internal Medicine, Rheumatology
720 Harrison Ave #401, Boston, 617-638-4310

Sundel, Robert Picard (9 mentions)
Boston U, 1982 *Certification:* Allergy & Immunology, Pediatric Rheumatology, Pediatrics
300 Longwood Ave Fegan Bldg 6th Fl, Boston, 617-355-6493
9 Hope Ave, Waltham, 781-216-2100

Weinblatt, Michael E. (5 mentions)
U of Maryland, 1975
Certification: Internal Medicine, Rheumatology
45 Francis St, Boston, 617-732-5325
2 Blackburn Park, Gloucester, 978-281-1500

Thoracic Surgery

Bueno, Raphael (7 mentions)
Harvard U, 1985
Certification: Surgery, Surgical Critical Care, Thoracic Surgery
75 Francis St, Boston, 617-732-6824

Daly, Benedict Dudley T. (7 mentions)
Boston U, 1965 *Certification:* Surgery, Thoracic Surgery
88 E Newton St #B402, Boston, 617-638-7350

Gaissert, Henning Arthur (7 mentions)
FMS-Germany, 1984 *Certification:* Surgery, Thoracic Surgery
55 Fruit St, Boston, 617-726-5341
2014 Washington St, Newton, 617-243-6447

Mathisen, Douglas James (9 mentions)
U of Illinois, 1974 *Certification:* Thoracic Surgery
55 Fruit St Blake Bldg #1570, Boston, 617-726-6826

Mentzer, Steven James (7 mentions)
U of Minnesota, 1981
Certification: Surgery, Surgical Critical Care, Thoracic Surgery
75 Francis St, Boston, 617-732-6824

Sugarbaker, David John (26 mentions)
Cornell U, 1979 *Certification:* Thoracic Surgery
75 Francis St, Boston, 617-732-6824

Wain, John Charles, Jr. (8 mentions)
Jefferson Med Coll, 1980 *Certification:* Thoracic Surgery
55 Fruit St Blake Bldg #1570, Boston, 617-726-5200

Williamson, Christina (13 mentions)
U of Wisconsin, 1976 *Certification:* Thoracic Surgery
41 Mall Rd 5th Fl, Burlington, 781-744-8340

Wright, Cameron Dorrans (9 mentions)
U of Michigan, 1980 *Certification:* Surgery, Thoracic Surgery
55 Fruit St, Boston, 617-726-5801

Urology

Babayan, Richard Khosrov (4 mentions)
Indiana U, 1975 *Certification:* Urology
720 Harrison Ave #606, Boston, 617-638-8485

De Wolf, William Charles (4 mentions)
Northwestern U, 1967 *Certification:* Urology
330 Brookline Ave #440, Boston, 617-667-3739

Doyle, Christopher Joseph (8 mentions)
Harvard U, 1979 *Certification:* Urology
45 Francis St, Boston, 617-732-6325

Edelstein, Robert Alex (4 mentions)
Oregon Health Sciences U, 1988 *Certification:* Urology
151 Warren St #205, Lowell, 978-458-1409
31 Village Sq, Chelmsford, 978-256-9507

Eyre, Robert Carnes (10 mentions)
U of Virginia, 1976 *Certification:* Urology
1153 Centre St, Boston, 617-732-9806
319 Longwood Ave 1st Fl, Boston, 617-975-2321

Kearney, Gary Paul (5 mentions)
U of California-San Francisco, 1965 *Certification:* Urology
319 Longwood Ave, Boston, 617-277-0100

Klauber, George Thomas (6 mentions)
FMS-United Kingdom, 1964 *Certification:* Urology
800 Washington St #92, Boston, 617-636-5360

Lamont, Jeffrey Scott (8 mentions)
Boston U, 1985 *Certification:* Urology
2000 Washington St #443, Newton, 617-527-1716

Libertino, John Andrew (8 mentions)
Georgetown U, 1965 *Certification:* Urology
41 Mall Rd, Burlington, 781-273-8420

Long, John Pershing (8 mentions)
Harvard U, 1983 *Certification:* Urology
2000 Washington St #443, Boston, 617-527-1716

McGovern, Francis James (10 mentions)
Case Western Reserve U, 1983 *Certification:* Urology
1 Hawthorne Pl #109, Boston, 617-726-3560

Morgentaler, Abraham (5 mentions)
Harvard U, 1982 *Certification:* Urology
1 Brookline Pl #624, Brookline, 617-277-5000

O'Leary, Michael Philip (4 mentions)
George Washington U, 1980 *Certification:* Urology
45 Francis St, Boston, 617-732-6325

Retik, Alan Burton (5 mentions)
Cornell U, 1957 *Certification:* Urology
300 Longwood Ave Hunnewell Bldg 3rd Fl, Boston, 617-355-3339

Richie, Jerome Paul (8 mentions)
U of Texas-Galveston, 1969 *Certification:* Urology
45 Francis St, Boston, 617-732-6325

Tiffany, Peter Nelson (8 mentions)
U of Virginia, 1980 *Certification:* Urology
3 Woodland Rd #216, Stoneham, 781-979-0661

Tuerk, Ingolf A. (9 mentions)
FMS-Germany, 1989
736 Cambridge St, Boston, 617-787-8181

Vascular Surgery

Cambria, Richard Paul (11 mentions)
Columbia U, 1977 *Certification:* Vascular Surgery
15 Parkman St Wang Bldg #440, Boston, 617-726-8278

Campbell, David Robert (9 mentions)
FMS-United Kingdom, 1974
Certification: Surgery, Vascular Surgery
110 Francis St #5-C, Boston, 617-632-9848

Gibbons, Gary William (6 mentions)
U of Cincinnati, 1971
732 Harrison Ave, Boston, 617-414-6840

Goodenough, Richard Duane (6 mentions)
U of Michigan, 1978 *Certification:* Surgery, Vascular Surgery
55 Highland Ave #202, Salem, 978-744-1458

Jewell, Edward Ryan (14 mentions)
U of Vermont, 1975 *Certification:* Vascular Surgery
41 Mall Rd, Burlington, 781-744-8577

La Muraglia, Glenn M. (6 mentions)
Harvard U, 1979 *Certification:* Surgery, Vascular Surgery
15 Parkman St #440, Boston, 617-726-6997

Mackey, William Charles (6 mentions)
Duke U, 1977
Certification: Surgery, Surgical Critical Care, Vascular Surgery
800 Washington St, Boston, 617-636-5927

Pomposelli, Frank Bernard (13 mentions)
Boston U, 1979 *Certification:* Vascular Surgery
110 Francis St, Boston, 617-632-9847

Woodson, Jonathan (6 mentions)
New York U, 1979 *Certification:* Internal Medicine, Surgery,
  Surgical Critical Care, Vascular Surgery
88 E Newton St #D506, Boston, 617-638-8488

Michigan

Greater Detroit Area

Greater Detroit and Washtenaw County Area

Including Macomb, Oakland, Washtenaw, and Wayne Counties

Allergy/Immunology

Appleyard, Jennifer Kay (8 mentions)
Wayne State U, 1989
Certification: Allergy & Immunology, Internal Medicine
17770 Mack Ave, Grosse Pointe, 313-885-6367

Fordyce, James George (8 mentions)
Wayne State U, 1974
Certification: Allergy & Immunology, Pediatrics
20200 Outer Dr, Dearborn, 313-565-3565

Hurwitz, Martin Elliot (17 mentions)
U of Cincinnati, 1974 *Certification:* Allergy & Immunology,
Pediatric Pulmonology, Pediatrics
1500 E Medical Center Dr, Ann Arbor, 248-349-5752
26850 Providence Pkwy #503, Novi, 248-349-5752

Lauter, Carl Burton (24 mentions)
Wayne State U, 1965 *Certification:* Allergy & Immunology,
Infectious Disease, Internal Medicine
3601 W 13 Mile Rd, Royal Oak, 248-551-7330
3535 W 13 Mile Rd #305, Royal Oak, 248-551-0495

Leflein, Jeffrey Glenn (10 mentions)
FMS-Dominica, 1987
Certification: Allergy & Immunology, Pediatrics
1500 E Medical Center Dr #R-1018, Ann Arbor, 248-349-5752
26850 Providence Pkwy #503, Novi, 248-349-5752

Magdea, Ilie (8 mentions)
FMS-Romania, 1961 *Certification:* Allergy & Immunology
20200 Outer Dr, Dearborn, 313-565-3565

Nageotte, Christian G. (7 mentions)
FMS-St Maarten, 1998
Certification: Allergy & Immunology, Pediatrics
2799 W Grand Blvd, Detroit, 313-916-2600
39450 W 12 Mile Rd, Novi, 248-344-2490

Oberdoerster, Deborah A. T. (9 mentions)
U of Toledo, 1982 *Certification:* Internal Medicine
5333 McAuley Dr #5011, Ypsilanti, 734-572-8834

Ringwald, Ulrich Otto (10 mentions)
FMS-Germany, 1966
Certification: Allergy & Immunology, Internal Medicine
1135 W University Dr #135, Rochester Hills, 248-651-0606

Savliwala, Mohammedi N. (6 mentions)
FMS-India, 1981 *Certification:* Allergy & Immunology, Pediatrics
10 W Square Lake Rd #301, Bloomfield Hills, 248-335-0200

Sweet, Lawrence Collins (6 mentions)
U of Michigan, 1956
Certification: Allergy & Immunology, Internal Medicine
18161 W 13 Mile Rd #C, Southfield, 248-646-3131

Tawila, Mohamad Yahia (7 mentions)
Wayne State U, 1986
Certification: Allergy & Immunology, Internal Medicine
3600 W 13 Mile Rd, Royal Oak, 248-549-0777
43200 Dequindre Rd #101, Sterling Heights, 586-323-2600

Tulin-Silver, Jeffrey (8 mentions)
Boston U, 1972
Certification: Allergy & Immunology, Internal Medicine
6330 Orchard Lake Rd #110, West Bloomfield, 248-932-0082

Vinuya, Ricardo Z. (9 mentions)
FMS-Philippines, 1985
Certification: Allergy & Immunology, Pediatrics
32270 Telegraph Rd #175, Bingham Farms, 248-723-0817

Anesthesiology

Arbit, Philip Jerome (3 mentions)
Wayne State U, 1992 *Certification:* Anesthesiology
28050 Grand River Ave, Farmington Hills, 248-471-8720

Balakrishnan, Guruswamy (3 mentions)
FMS-India, 1975 *Certification:* Anesthesiology
2799 W Grand Blvd, Detroit, 313-916-2545

Beer, Roderick Walter (6 mentions)
U of Michigan, 1978 *Certification:* Anesthesiology, Pain Medicine
5301 McAuley Dr #210, Ypsilanti, 734-712-1313

Bernard, Michael Lawrence (3 mentions)
Wayne State U, 1999 *Certification:* Anesthesiology
16001 W 9 Mile Rd, Southfield, 248-849-8138

Betel, Aaron Paul (3 mentions)
U of Michigan, 1988 *Certification:* Anesthesiology
6071 W Outer Dr, Detroit, 313-966-3300

Borrego, Ricardo David (5 mentions)
FMS-Mexico, 1983 *Certification:* Anesthesiology
18100 Oakwood Blvd #100, Dearborn, 313-240-7668

Brown, Morris (7 mentions)
Wayne State U, 1976 *Certification:* Anesthesiology, Critical
Care Medicine, Internal Medicine
2799 W Grand Blvd, Detroit, 313-916-7648

Grant, James David (9 mentions)
Wayne State U, 1987 *Certification:* Anesthesiology
3601 W 13 Mile Rd, Royal Oak, 248-898-1905

Guslits, Benjamin Gerald (4 mentions)
FMS-Canada, 1983
Certification: Anesthesiology, Critical Care Medicine
2006 Hogback Rd #5, Detroit, 734-786-4931

Hartrick, Craig Timothy (3 mentions)
Wayne State U, 1980 *Certification:* Anesthesiology, Pain Medicine
3601 W 13 Mile Rd, Royal Oak, 248-828-5100

Huraibi, Hussein A., III (3 mentions)
Wayne State U, 1995 *Certification:* Anesthesiology, Pain Medicine
2040 Monroe St #206, Dearborn, 313-565-6782

Nakhleh, Tawfiq E. (3 mentions)
Michigan State U Coll of Osteopathic Med, 1986
18101 Oakwood Blvd #206, Dearborn, 313-982-5159

Padilla, Robert C. (5 mentions)
Wayne State U, 1982
Certification: Anesthesiology, Internal Medicine
44405 Woodward Ave, Pontiac, 248-858-3023

Pappas, John Louis (3 mentions)
Michigan State U, 1991
Certification: Anesthesiology, Pain Medicine
3601 W 13 Mile Rd, Royal Oak, 248-828-5100

Peleman, Robert Raymond (4 mentions)
Wayne State U, 1984 *Certification:* Anesthesiology
15855 19 Mile Rd, Clinton Township, 586-263-2371

Proud Foot, Matthew J. (3 mentions)
Michigan State U Coll of Osteopathic Med, 1993
18181 Oakwood Blvd #206, Dearborn, 313-982-5159

Reddy, Kallam Subba (3 mentions)
FMS-India, 1970 *Certification:* Anesthesiology
2799 W Grand Blvd, Detroit, 313-916-7306

Reynolds, Paul Irvin (3 mentions)
Wayne State U, 1981 *Certification:* Anesthesiology, Pediatrics
1500 E Medical Center Dr, Ann Arbor, 734-936-6983

Rotter, Steven Jay (3 mentions)
Wayne State U, 1988 *Certification:* Anesthesiology
11800 E 12 Mile Rd, Warren, 586-573-5260

Shankle, Matthew Marvin (5 mentions)
Wayne State U, 1988 *Certification:* Anesthesiology
441 S Livernois Rd #190, Rochester Hills, 248-656-9696

Silvasi, Daniel Louis (4 mentions)
Wayne State U, 1985 *Certification:* Anesthesiology
3601 W 13 Mile Rd, Royal Oak, 248-898-1905

Smith, Peter Christian (4 mentions)
Wayne State U, 1982 *Certification:* Anesthesiology
18181 Oakwood Blvd #206, Dearborn, 313-593-7000

Stoyanovich, Christ S. (3 mentions)
Michigan State U Coll of Osteopathic Med, 1980
13355 E 10 Mile Rd, Warren, 586-759-7963

Talsma, Samuel Eugene (4 mentions)
U of Michigan, 1985 *Certification:* Anesthesiology
2006 Hogback Rd #5, Ann Arbor, 734-786-4931

Terner, Sandor Robert (3 mentions)
Michigan State U Coll of Osteopathic Med, 1995
Certification: Anesthesiology
28050 Grand River Ave, Farmington, 248-471-8720

Tocco-Bradley, Rosalia (9 mentions)
Harvard U, 1988 *Certification:* Anesthesiology, Pain Medicine
5301 McAuley Dr #210, Ypsilanti, 734-712-1313

Tremper, Kevin Keefe (6 mentions)
U of California-Irvine, 1978 *Certification:* Anesthesiology
1500 E Medical Center Dr, Ann Arbor, 734-936-4280

Wang, Chung Y. (3 mentions)
Certification: Anesthesiology
441 S Livernois Rd #190, Rochester Hills, 248-656-9696

Zaremba, Daniel Edward (3 mentions)
Wayne State U, 1989 *Certification:* Anesthesiology
37389 Fiore Trail, Clinton Township, 313-343-1000
33080 Utica Rd, Fraser, 586-296-7250

Cardiac Surgery

Altshuler, Jeffrey Marc (7 mentions)
Wayne State U, 1980 *Certification:* Surgery, Thoracic Surgery
1663 W Big Beaver Rd, Troy, 248-643-8633

Bassett, Joseph Samuel (10 mentions)
Wayne State U, 1961 *Certification:* Surgery, Thoracic Surgery
1663 W Big Beaver Rd, Troy, 248-643-8633

Deeb, George Michael (13 mentions)
U of Pittsburgh, 1975 *Certification:* Thoracic Surgery
1500 E Medical Center Dr #212, Ann Arbor, 734-936-4984

Fazzalari, Franco Larry (8 mentions)
U of Michigan, 1990 *Certification:* Thoracic Surgery
1135 W University Dr #205, Rochester Hills, 248-601-6190
1101 W University Dr, Rochester Hills, 248-652-5000

Harrington, Steven Dale (12 mentions)
Wayne State U, 1980 *Certification:* Surgery, Thoracic Surgery
38800 Garfield Rd #100, Clinton Township, 586-286-6900

Hoffberger, Jonathan D. (7 mentions)
Nova Southeastern Coll of Osteopathic Med, 1996
1818 Oakwood Blvd #400, Dearborn, 313-436-2422

Kong, Bobby Kipak (17 mentions)
St Louis U, 1983 *Certification:* Thoracic Surgery
5325 Elliott Dr #102, Ypsilanti, 734-712-5500

Prager, Richard Laurence (9 mentions)
SUNY-Downstate Med Coll, 1971 *Certification:* Thoracic Surgery
1500 E Medical Center Dr #2120, Ann Arbor, 734-936-4974

Pruitt, Andy Lee (14 mentions)
U of Kentucky, 1990 *Certification:* Thoracic Surgery
5325 Elliott Dr #102, Ypsilanti, 734-712-5500

Robinson, Phillip Lorane (8 mentions)
Wayne State U, 1983 *Certification:* Surgery, Thoracic Surgery
1663 W Big Beaver Rd, Troy, 248-643-8633

Sakwa, Marc Peter (22 mentions)
Columbia U, 1980 *Certification:* Thoracic Surgery
1663 W Big Beaver Rd, Troy, 248-643-8633

Sell, Timothy Lynn (10 mentions)
Duke U, 1987 *Certification:* Surgery, Thoracic Surgery
17000 Hubbard Dr #100, Dearborn, 313-441-1440

Shannon, Francis Louis (12 mentions)
Mount Sinai Sch of Med, 1978
Certification: Surgery, Thoracic Surgery
1663 W Big Beaver Rd, Troy, 248-643-8633

Washington, Bruce C. (11 mentions)
Wayne State U, 1977 *Certification:* Thoracic Surgery
18181 Oakwood Blvd #102, Dearborn, 313-982-5533

Cardiology

Ajluni, Steven Cameel (5 mentions)
Wayne State U, 1986
Certification: Cardiovascular Disease, Internal Medicine
4600 Investment Dr #200, Troy, 248-267-5050

Almany, Steven Lee (4 mentions)
Michigan State U, 1984 *Certification:* Cardiovascular Disease, Internal Medicine, Interventional Cardiology
4600 Investment Dr #200, Troy, 248-267-5050

Bagnasco, Frank Anthony (4 mentions)
Wayne State U, 1973
Certification: Cardiovascular Disease, Internal Medicine
44555 Woodward Ave #507, Pontiac, 248-335-8170

Berman, Aaron David (5 mentions)
Mount Sinai Sch of Med, 1982 *Certification:* Cardiovascular Disease, Internal Medicine, Interventional Cardiology
27901 Woodward Ave, Berkley, 248-837-2505

Bowers, Terry Richard (3 mentions)
U of Michigan, 1990
Certification: Cardiovascular Disease, Interventional Cardiology
4600 Investment Dr #200, Troy, 248-267-5050

Brodsky, Marc Steven (3 mentions)
U of Michigan, 1983
Certification: Cardiovascular Disease, Internal Medicine
6900 Orchard Lake Rd #106, West Bloomfield, 248-788-4278

Choksi, Nishit Arvind (11 mentions)
FMS-India, 1982 *Certification:* Cardiovascular Disease, Internal Medicine, Interventional Cardiology
1695 12 Mile Rd #220, Berkley, 248-582-1480

Cutler, Nancy (5 mentions)
Certification: Pediatric Cardiology, Pediatrics
3535 W 13 Mile Rd #707, Royal Oak, 248-551-0487

Dabbous, Samir (6 mentions)
FMS-Lebanon, 1976 *Certification:* Cardiovascular Disease, Internal Medicine, Interventional Cardiology
22060 Beech St, Dearborn, 313-563-3640
19725 Allen Rd Bldg 2, Brownstown Township, 734-479-4250

Dangovian, Michael I. (5 mentions)
Des Moines U, 1984
555 Barclay Cir #150, Rochester Hills, 734-459-7444

David, Shukri Wadi (6 mentions)
FMS-St Maarten, 1983 *Certification:* Cardiovascular Disease, Internal Medicine, Interventional Cardiology
22250 Providence Dr #705, Southfield, 248-552-9858

Devlin, William (3 mentions)
FMS-Canada, 1988 *Certification:* Cardiovascular Disease
4600 Investment Dr #200, Troy, 248-267-5050

Dixon, Simon Richard (3 mentions)
FMS-New Zealand, 1991
3601 W 13 Mile Rd, Royal Oak, 248-898-4163

Eagle, Kim Allen (9 mentions)
Tufts U, 1979
Certification: Cardiovascular Disease, Internal Medicine
1500 E Medical Center Dr #3910, Ann Arbor, 734-936-5275
24 Frank Lloyd Wright Dr, Ann Arbor, 734-998-7400

Friedman, Harold Zalman (3 mentions)
U of Michigan, 1979 *Certification:* Cardiovascular Disease, Internal Medicine, Interventional Cardiology
44038 Woodward Ave #200, Bloomfield Hills, 248-335-1064

Girard, Steven Eugene (3 mentions)
Mayo Med Sch, 1994 *Certification:* Cardiovascular Disease
5325 Elliott Dr, Ypsilanti, 734-712-8000

Gowman, David P. (4 mentions)
Des Moines U, 1990
28080 Grand River Ave #300, Farmington Hills, 248-615-7300

Greenbaum, Adam Brett (4 mentions)
New York U, 1992
Certification: Cardiovascular Disease, Interventional Cardiology
2799 W Grand Blvd, Detroit, 313-916-2600

Grines, Cindy Lee (3 mentions)
Ohio State U, 1980 *Certification:* Cardiovascular Disease, Internal Medicine, Interventional Cardiology
3601 W 13 Mile Rd, Royal Oak, 248-898-4163

Harber, Daniel Robert (6 mentions)
Michigan State U Coll of Osteopathic Med, 1988
23822 Ford Rd, Dearborn Heights, 313-359-0200

Hubbard, Bradley Loren (3 mentions)
Rush U, 1985
Certification: Cardiovascular Disease, Internal Medicine
5325 Elliott Dr, Ypsilanti, 734-712-8000
14555 Levan Rd #203, Livonia, 734-462-3233

Kahn, Joel Kaufman (6 mentions)
U of Michigan, 1983 *Certification:* Cardiovascular Disease, Internal Medicine, Interventional Cardiology
4600 Investment Dr #200, Troy, 248-267-5050

Kassab, Elias Habib (5 mentions)
FMS-Belgium, 1982 *Certification:* Cardiovascular Disease, Internal Medicine, Interventional Cardiology
22060 Beech St, Dearborn, 313-563-3640
19725 Allen Rd Bldg #2, Brownstown Township, 734-479-4250

Kazmierski, John Florian (5 mentions)
Des Moines U, 1976
1030 Harrington St #101, Mount Clemens, 586-468-8500

Kerner, Nathan Jeffrey (3 mentions)
Wayne State U, 1981
Certification: Cardiovascular Disease, Internal Medicine
26400 W 12 Mile Rd #120, Southfield, 248-304-3200

Kozlowski, Jay Henry (3 mentions)
Wayne State U, 1978
Certification: Cardiovascular Disease, Internal Medicine
1 William Carls Dr, Commerce Township, 248-937-4764

La Londe, Thomas A. (8 mentions)
Wayne State U, 1983 *Certification:* Cardiovascular Disease, Internal Medicine, Interventional Cardiology
24211 Little Mack Ave, St Clair Shores, 586-498-0440

Lee, Cheng-Chong (4 mentions)
FMS-Taiwan, 1966 *Certification:* Cardiovascular Disease, Internal Medicine, Interventional Cardiology
6742 Park Ave, Allen Park, 313-928-2333

Lewis, Barry Kent (5 mentions)
A T Still U, 1976
30055 Northwestern Hwy, Farmington Hills, 248-865-9898
47601 Grand River Ave, Novi, 248-380-6624

Marsalese, Dominic L. (4 mentions)
Wayne State U, 1981 *Certification:* Cardiovascular Disease, Internal Medicine, Interventional Cardiology
27901 Woodward Ave #300, Berkley, 248-551-5000

McCallister, Ben D. (5 mentions)
Vanderbilt U, 1984
Certification: Cardiovascular Disease, Internal Medicine
5325 Elliott Dr #201, Ypsilanti, 734-712-8000
1600 S Canton Rd #345, Canton, 734-398-7515
14650 E Old US 12 3rd Floor #1, Chelsea, 734-712-8000

Miller, Lynn Keith (5 mentions)
Wayne State U, 1976
Certification: Cardiovascular Disease, Internal Medicine
29645 W 14 Mile Rd #200, Farmington Hills, 248-932-3700

Naoum, Joseph Basim (4 mentions)
Wayne State U, 1979
Certification: Cardiovascular Disease, Internal Medicine
133 S Main St, Mount Clemens, 586-465-1326

O'Donnell, Michael Joseph (4 mentions)
Loyola U Chicago, 1982 *Certification:* Cardiovascular
Disease, Internal Medicine, Interventional Cardiology
5325 Elliott Dr #203-A, Ypsilanti, 734-712-8000

Patel, Kirit Chhotabhai (6 mentions)
FMS-India, 1978 *Certification:* Cardiovascular Disease,
Internal Medicine, Interventional Cardiology
43344 Woodward Ave #111, Bloomfield Hills, 248-333-1170

Rasak, Mark Allan (4 mentions)
Des Moines U, 1988
28080 Grand River Ave #300, Farmington Hills, 248-615-7300

Riba, Arthur Lee (7 mentions)
Albert Einstein Coll of Med, 1973
Certification: Cardiovascular Disease, Internal Medicine
18181 Oakwood Blvd #101, Dearborn, 313-996-7280

Rubenfire, Melvyn (3 mentions)
Wayne State U, 1965
Certification: Cardiovascular Disease, Internal Medicine
24 Frank Lloyd Wright Dr, Ann Arbor, 734-998-7400
1500 E Medical Center Dr, Ann Arbor, 734-763-7718

Salka, Muhammad-Samer (3 mentions)
FMS-Lebanon, 1985
Certification: Cardiovascular Disease, Interventional Cardiology
15120 Michigan Ave, Dearborn, 313-624-8417
4020 Venoy Rd #200, Wayne, 734-729-6710

Shea, Michael James (9 mentions)
U of Michigan, 1975
Certification: Cardiovascular Disease, Internal Medicine
1500 E Medical Center Dr #SPC-5853, Ann Arbor, 734-936-5260
24 Frank Lloyd Wright Dr, Ann Arbor, 734-647-7321

Smith, Frank Alfred (3 mentions)
Wayne State U, 1972
Certification: Cardiovascular Disease, Internal Medicine
5325 Elliott Dr #203, Ann Arbor, 734-712-8000
1600 S Canton Rd #345, Canton, 734-398-7515
128 Van Buren St, Chelsea, 734-712-8000
14650 E Old US 12 3rd Floor #1, Chelsea, 734-712-8000

Smith, Stephen Timothy (7 mentions)
Michigan State U, 1980
Certification: Cardiovascular Disease, Internal Medicine
2799 W Grand Blvd, Detroit, 313-916-2600

Timmis, Steven B. (5 mentions)
Wayne State U, 1991
Certification: Cardiovascular Disease, Interventional Cardiology
16800 W 12 Mile Rd, Southfield, 248-569-9797

Truccone, Nestor Jose (3 mentions)
FMS-Argentina, 1965
Certification: Pediatric Cardiology, Pediatrics
43380 Woodward Ave #105, Bloomfield Hills, 248-335-8500
18181 Oakwood Blvd #205, Dearborn, 313-271-3566

Vedala, Giridhar (3 mentions)
Jefferson Med Coll, 1993 *Certification:* Cardiovascular Disease
5325 Elliott Dr, Ypsilanti, 734-712-8000
7575 Grand River Ave #206, Brighton, 810-844-7750

Weaver, Wayne Douglas (6 mentions)
Tufts U, 1971
Certification: Cardiovascular Disease, Internal Medicine
2799 W Grand Blvd, Detroit, 313-916-2600

Winston, Stuart A. (10 mentions)
Michigan State U Coll of Osteopathic Med, 1978
5325 Elliott Dr #203, Ypsilanti, 734-712-8000

Zainea, Mark Anthony (7 mentions)
Wayne State U, 1987
Certification: Cardiovascular Disease, Interventional Cardiology
21250 Hall Rd #200, Clinton Township, 586-783-1111
25910 Kelly Rd #B, Roseville, 586-772-3366

Dermatology

Altman, David Andrew (7 mentions)
U of Michigan, 1989 *Certification:* Dermatology
11900 E 12 Mile Rd #201, Warren, 586-574-2800

Auster, Barry Isaac (6 mentions)
U of Michigan, 1974 *Certification:* Dermatology
31420 Northwestern Hwy #150, Farmington Hills, 248-538-0109

Berry, Ali (5 mentions)
Wayne State U, 2002 *Certification:* Dermatology
49650 Cherry Hill Rd #230, Canton, 734-495-1506

Byrd, Roger C. (7 mentions)
Midwestern U Chicago Coll of Osteopathic Med, 1967
405 Barclay Cir #104, Rochester Hills, 248-853-3131

Cardellio, Anthony (4 mentions)
Midwestern U Chicago Coll of Osteopathic Med, 1967
30950 Campbell St, Warren, 586-573-3500

Chapel, Thomas Austin (5 mentions)
Wayne State U, 1967
Certification: Dermatology, Dermatopathology
2814 Monroe St, Dearborn, 313-561-5311
7300 N Canton Center Rd, Canton, 734-454-8001

Cohen, Carl Jerome (4 mentions)
FMS-Canada, 1960 *Certification:* Dermatology
44555 Woodward Ave #504, Pontiac, 248-335-6725

Dombrowski, Helene Claire (4 mentions)
Wayne State U, 1985 *Certification:* Dermatology
23100 Cherry Hill St #10, Dearborn, 313-563-6655

Dorman, Michael Andrew (9 mentions)
Columbia U, 1987 *Certification:* Dermatology
6330 Orchard Lake Rd #120, West Bloomfield, 248-855-3366
9640 Commerce Rd, Commerce Township, 248-855-3366

Ellis, Charles Norman (6 mentions)
U of Michigan, 1977 *Certification:* Dermatology
1500 E Medical Center Dr, Ann Arbor, 734-936-4054

Field, Stephen Ira (4 mentions)
U of Michigan, 1975 *Certification:* Dermatology
28333 Harper Ave, St Clair Shores, 586-776-9770

Fivenson, David Paul (7 mentions)
U of Michigan, 1984 *Certification:* Dermatological Immunology/
Diagnostic and Laboratory Immunology, Dermatology
2799 W Grand Blvd, Detroit, 313-916-2972
3001 Miller Rd, Ann Arbor, 734-222-9630

Gildenberg, Stuart Roger (5 mentions)
Wayne State U, 1986 *Certification:* Dermatology
11900 E 12 Mile Rd #201, Warren, 586-574-2800

Goldfarb, Michael Thomas (9 mentions)
U of Michigan, 1981 *Certification:* Dermatology
2051 Monroe St, Dearborn, 313-563-1212

Hamzavi, Iltefat H. (14 mentions)
Certification: Dermatology
43151 Dalcoma Dr #1, Clinton Township, 586-286-8720
2950 Keewahdin Rd, Fort Gratiot, 734-495-1506

Johnson, Timothy M. (5 mentions)
U of Texas-Houston, 1984 *Certification:* Dermatology
1500 E Medical Center Dr, Ann Arbor, 734-936-4068

Kleinsmith, D'Anne Marie (4 mentions)
Wayne State U, 1976 *Certification:* Dermatology
6900 Orchard Lake Rd #209, West Bloomfield, 248-855-7500

La Fond, Ann Ammond (5 mentions)
U of Michigan, 1980 *Certification:* Dermatology
8584 Canton Center Rd, Canton, 734-455-8180

Laing, Kathrin Freitag (5 mentions)
U of Michigan, 1980 *Certification:* Dermatology
2433 Oak Valley Dr #400, Ann Arbor, 734-477-0200

Lim, Henry Wan Peng (10 mentions)
SUNY-Downstate Med Coll, 1975
Certification: Dermatological Immunology/Diagnostic and
Laboratory Immunology, Dermatology
3031 W Grand Blvd #800, Detroit, 313-916-4060

Manz-Dulac, Lisa Allyn (6 mentions)
SUNY-Upstate Med U, 1987 *Certification:* Dermatology
20030 Mack Ave, Grosse Pointe Woods, 313-884-3380

Moiin, Ali (6 mentions)
U of California-Davis, 1991 *Certification:* Dermatology
1575 W Big Beaver Rd #C-12, Troy, 248-643-7677
14555 Livan Rd, Livonia, 734-591-2000
4160 John R St #507, Detroit, 313-966-7585

Ramos, Daisy Pelayo (7 mentions)
FMS-Philippines, 1962 *Certification:* Dermatology
1559 W Big Beaver Rd #E-20, Troy, 248-649-2330

Shwayder, Tor Adam (14 mentions)
U of Michigan, 1980
Certification: Dermatology, Pediatric Dermatology, Pediatrics
3031 W Grand Blvd #800, Detroit, 313-916-2161

Singer, Robert Steven (6 mentions)
U of Michigan, 1992 *Certification:* Dermatology
29255 Northwestern Hwy #200, Southfield, 248-353-0880

Spurlin, David Vincent (6 mentions)
Howard U, 1993 *Certification:* Dermatology
33301 Woodward Ave, Birmingham, 248-642-9111

Stone, Richard Alan (4 mentions)
Wayne State U, 1977 *Certification:* Dermatology
16100 19 Mile Rd #200, Clinton Township, 586-226-7200

Watnick, Kay Elizabeth (5 mentions)
U of Michigan, 1983 *Certification:* Dermatology
6900 Orchard Lake Rd #209, West Bloomfield, 244-855-7500

Youshock, Eva (4 mentions)
Northwestern U, 1981 *Certification:* Dermatology
6700 N Rochester Rd #212, Rochester Hills, 248-650-1510

Emergency Medicine

Barsan, William George (6 mentions)
Ohio State U, 1975 *Certification:* Emergency Medicine
1500 E Medical Center Dr, Ann Arbor, 734-763-4964

Bauer, David Bruce (4 mentions)
Wayne State U, 1984 *Certification:* Emergency Medicine
1101 W University Dr, Rochester, 248-652-5311

Christopher, Gary Dennis (5 mentions)
Wayne State U, 1979
Certification: Emergency Medicine, Family Medicine
18101 Oakwood Blvd, Dearborn, 313-593-7000

Desmond, Jeffrey Skutt (8 mentions)
U of Texas-Houston, 1987 *Certification:* Emergency Medicine
1500 E Medical Center Dr, Ann Arbor, 734-763-9849

Filips, Kurt W. (4 mentions)
Des Moines U, 1985 *Certification:* Emergency Medicine,
Pediatric Emergency Medicine, Pediatrics
3601 W 13 Mile Rd, Royal Oak, 248-551-5000

Garfield, Mitchell (3 mentions)
A T Still U, 1987
18101 Oakwood Blvd, Dearborn, 313-593-7000

Gibb, Kenneth Alan (3 mentions)
Wayne State U, 1980 *Certification:* Emergency Medicine
3601 W 13 Mile Rd, Royal Oak, 248-898-2015

Hutchinson, Christopher (3 mentions)
U of Michigan, 1997 *Certification:* Emergency Medicine
3601 W 13 Mile Rd, Royal Oak, 248-898-2015

Irvin, Charlene Babcock (3 mentions)
U of Michigan, 1986 *Certification:* Emergency Medicine
22101 Moross Rd, Grosse Pointe, 313-343-8797

Khoury, Nabil (3 mentions)
U of Michigan, 1989
Certification: Emergency Medicine, Internal Medicine
6777 W Maple Rd, West Bloomfield, 248-661-4100

Knazik, Stephen Robert (6 mentions)
Michigan State U Coll of Osteopathic Med, 1979
Certification: Emergency Medicine, Pediatric Emergency
   Medicine
3901 Beaubien St, Detroit, 313-745-0115

Koltonow, Sanford H. (7 mentions)
Wayne State U, 1980 *Certification:* Emergency Medicine
3601 W 13 Mile Rd, Royal Oak, 248-898-2015

Lewandowski, Christopher (4 mentions)
Med Coll of Wisconsin, 1982
Certification: Emergency Medicine, Internal Medicine
2799 W Grand Blvd, Detroit, 313-916-2811

McCurren, Robert H., IV (4 mentions)
Baylor U, 1997 *Certification:* Emergency Medicine
2333 Biddle St, Wyandotte, 734-246-6995

McGraw, Steve (6 mentions)
Michigan State U Coll of Osteopathic Med, 1992
Certification: Emergency Medicine
16001 W 9 Mile Rd, Southfield, 248-849-3015

Mikhail, Michael George (6 mentions)
U of Michigan, 1987 *Certification:* Emergency Medicine
2000 Green Rd #300, Ann Arbor, 734-712-3456

Mitchiner, James C. (5 mentions)
U of Illinois, 1979 *Certification:* Emergency Medicine
5301 McAuley Dr, Ipsilanti, 734-712-3000

Pearl, Steven Mark (9 mentions)
Wayne State U, 1989 *Certification:* Emergency Medicine
1101 W University Dr, Rochester Hills, 248-652-5000

Rivers, Emanuel Phillip (3 mentions)
U of Michigan, 1981 *Certification:* Critical Care Medicine,
   Emergency Medicine, Internal Medicine
2799 W Grand Blvd, Detroit, 313-916-1801

Sendi, Jeffrey Alan (6 mentions)
Michigan State U Coll of Osteopathic Med, 1992
18101 Oakwood Blvd, Dearborn, 313-593-7000
15855 19th Mile Rd, Citizen Township, 586-263-2601

Swor, Robert Albert (3 mentions)
Michigan State U Coll of Osteopathic Med, 1979
Certification: Emergency Medicine
3601 W 13 Mile Rd, Royal Oak, 248-898-2015

Vieder, Sanford J. (3 mentions)
Michigan State U Coll of Osteopathic Med, 1988
28050 Grand River Ave, Farmington Hills, 248-471-8562

Walters, Bradford L. (6 mentions)
Wayne State U, 1978 *Certification:* Emergency Medicine
3601 W 13 Mile Rd, Royal Oak, 248-898-2015

Weaver, David Russell (3 mentions)
West Virginia Sch of Osteopathic Med, 1981
5450 Fort St, Trenton, 734-671-3800

Endocrinology

Al-Kassab, Abdulsalam K. (16 mentions)
FMS-Iraq, 1977 *Certification:* Endocrinology, Diabetes, and
   Metabolism, Internal Medicine
2970 Crooks Rd #A, Rochester Hills, 248-844-1873

Alzohaili, Opada (7 mentions)
FMS-Syria, 1990
Certification: Endocrinology, Diabetes, and Metabolism
4700 Greenfield Rd, Dearborn, 313-945-6100

Bone, Henry Grady, III (6 mentions)
U of Washington, 1972
Certification: Endocrinology and Metabolism, Internal Medicine
22201 Moross Rd #260, Detroit, 313-640-7700

Edelson, Gary William (13 mentions)
George Washington U, 1986 *Certification:* Endocrinology,
   Diabetes, and Metabolism, Internal Medicine
6900 Orchard Lake Rd #204, West Bloomfield, 248-855-5620

Estigarribia, Juan Angel (6 mentions)
FMS-Paraguay, 1972 *Certification:* Endocrinology, Diabetes,
   and Metabolism, Internal Medicine
23550 Park St #201, Dearborn, 313-277-0075

Garcia, Michael (7 mentions)
U of Michigan, 1969
Certification: Endocrinology and Metabolism, Internal Medicine
6900 Orchard Lake Rd #204, West Bloomfield, 248-855-5620
44199 Dequindre Rd #103, Troy, 248-855-5620

Khoury, Sleman Albert (13 mentions)
FMS-Syria, 1976
Certification: Endocrinology and Metabolism, Internal Medicine
15125 Northline Rd, Southgate, 734-282-3138

Langer, Eric Scott (7 mentions)
New York Coll of Osteopathic Med, 1985
14049 E 13 Mile Rd #7, Warren, 810-294-4820

Ospina Ovalle, Luis F. (25 mentions)
FMS-Colombia, 1968
Certification: Endocrinology and Metabolism, Internal Medicine
17412 W 13 Mile Rd, Beverly Hills, 248-258-8740
44199 Dequindre Rd #304, Troy, 248-964-6064

Paul, Sander J. (5 mentions)
U of Michigan, 1983
Certification: Endocrinology and Metabolism, Internal Medicine
1949 12 Mile Rd #200, Berkley, 248-543-3700

Rosenblatt, Solomon (9 mentions)
U of Connecticut, 1974
Certification: Endocrinology and Metabolism, Internal Medicine
1949 12 Mile Rd #200, Berkley, 248-543-3700

Sanfield, Jeffrey Alan (26 mentions)
Wayne State U, 1981
Certification: Endocrinology and Metabolism, Internal Medicine
5333 McAuley Dr #6014, Ypsilanti, 734-434-4430

Taylor, Charles Irwin (9 mentions)
Wayne State U, 1969
Certification: Endocrinology and Metabolism, Internal Medicine
6900 Orchard Lake Rd #204, West Bloomfield, 248-855-5620

Thomas, Abraham (5 mentions)
Columbia U, 1989 *Certification:* Endocrinology, Diabetes,
   and Metabolism, Internal Medicine
2799 W Grand Blvd, Detroit, 313-916-2092
6777 W Maple Rd, West Bloomfield, 248-661-4100

Whitehouse, Fred W. (8 mentions)
U of Illinois, 1949
Certification: Endocrinology and Metabolism, Internal Medicine
3031 W Grand Blvd #800, Detroit, 313-916-2131

Family Practice *(see note on page 9)*

Askar, Maan Adel Yakoub (3 mentions)
FMS-Iraq, 1984 *Certification:* Family Medicine
26000 Hoover Rd #102, Warren, 586-427-1351

Bowman, William Pepper (5 mentions)
Wayne State U, 1982 *Certification:* Family Medicine
595 Barclay Cir #D, Rochester Hills, 248-852-5355

Breakey, Robert Andrew (3 mentions)
U of Michigan, 1981 *Certification:* Family Medicine
2004 Hogback Rd #14, Ann Arbor, 734-971-1188

Burtka, James Andrew (3 mentions)
Michigan State U Coll of Osteopathic Med, 1994
36040 Dequindre Rd, Sterling Heights, 586-939-9160

Chen, Roger Huan (3 mentions)
U of Maryland, 1998 *Certification:* Family Medicine
2004 Hogback Rd #14, Ann Arbor, 734-971-1188

Costea, George Charles (3 mentions)
Des Moines U, 1976 *Certification:* Family Medicine
30695 Little Mack Ave #200, Roseville, 586-294-9600

Fisher, Cynthia Lou (4 mentions)
U of Michigan, 1978 *Certification:* Family Medicine
44300 Dequindre Rd, Sterling Heights, 248-964-0400

Karle, Christine L. (3 mentions)
Michigan State U Coll of Osteopathic Med, 1983
455 Barclay Cir #D, Rochester Hills, 248-852-9596

Merrelli, Bradford James (5 mentions)
Wayne State U, 1983 *Certification:* Family Medicine
595 Barclay Cir #D, Rochester Hills, 248-852-5355

Misch, Paul Walter (5 mentions)
Michigan State U, 1981 *Certification:* Family Medicine
44300 Dequindre Rd, Sterling Heights, 248-964-0400

O'Connor, Thomas Patrick (3 mentions)
U of Michigan, 1981 *Certification:* Internal Medicine
375 Briarwood Cir Bldg 3, Ann Arbor, 734-998-7207

Peters, David Wayne (4 mentions)
Wayne State U, 1980 *Certification:* Family Medicine
23870 Michigan Ave, Dearborn, 313-565-6800

Przybylski, Albert A. (3 mentions)
Des Moines U, 1992
36549 Harper Ave #B, Clinton Township, 586-791-3150

Schenk, Maryjean (3 mentions)
Wayne State U, 1983
Certification: Family Medicine, Occupational Medicine
1135 University Dr, Rochester Hills, 248-650-6301

Schooley, Susan (5 mentions)
U of Massachusetts, 1980 *Certification:* Family Medicine
4401 Conner Ave, Detroit, 313-823-9800

Tangalos, Theodore Louis (5 mentions)
Wayne State U, 1994 *Certification:* Family Medicine
43455 Schoenherr Rd #2, Sterling Heights, 586-726-4823

Thiry, Steven James (12 mentions)
U of Michigan, 1980 *Certification:* Family Medicine
3200 W Liberty Rd #C, Ann Arbor, 734-761-2581

Welker, Donald Bernard (7 mentions)
Wayne State U, 1984 *Certification:* Family Medicine
23870 Michigan Ave, Dearborn, 313-565-6800

Gastroenterology

Adler, Larry A. (5 mentions)
Wayne State U, 1984
Certification: Gastroenterology, Internal Medicine
5300 Elliott Dr, Ypsilanti, 734-434-6262

Alexander, Thomas J. (4 mentions)
Michigan State U, 1979
Certification: Gastroenterology, Internal Medicine
264 W Maple Rd #200, Troy, 248-273-9930

Arman, Mohammed A. (7 mentions)
FMS-Iraq, 1985 *Certification:* Gastroenterology
2040 Monroe St #207, Dearborn, 313-724-9170

Belknap, William Michael (5 mentions)
Wayne State U, 1978
Certification: Pediatric Gastroenterology, Pediatrics
1701 South Blvd E #300, Rochester Hills, 248-844-9710
4600 Investment Dr #380, Troy, 248-267-6222

Bologna, Sante Dominic (5 mentions)
Wayne State U, 1985
Certification: Gastroenterology, Internal Medicine
4600 Investment Dr #380, Troy, 248-267-6222
1701 South Blvd E #300, Rochester Hills, 248-844-9710
44199 Dequindre Rd, Troy, 248-828-6032

Bral, Kambiz (5 mentions)
FMS-Grenada, 1987
Certification: Gastroenterology, Internal Medicine
2700 S Rochester Rd, Rochester Hills, 248-844-2700

Brown, Kimberly Ann (6 mentions)
Wayne State U, 1985 *Certification:* Gastroenterology,
Internal Medicine, Transplant Hepatology
2799 W Grand Blvd, Detroit, 313-916-8632

Cannon, Michael Edward (5 mentions)
Wayne State U, 1992 *Certification:* Gastroenterology
264 W Maple Rd #200, Troy, 248-273-9930

Cascio, Richard A., Jr. (5 mentions)
FMS-Grenada, 1989 *Certification:* Gastroenterology
28963 Little Mack Ave #101, St Clair Shores, 586-447-0700

Dahlstedt, Dennis Arthur (4 mentions)
Wayne State U, 1977
Certification: Gastroenterology, Internal Medicine
44199 Dequindre Rd, Troy, 248-879-2111

De Vore, Mark Samuel (5 mentions)
U of Cincinnati, 1984
Certification: Gastroenterology, Internal Medicine
22250 Providence Dr #703, Southfield, 248-569-1770
26850 Providence Pkwy #350, Novi, 248-569-1770

Donat, Mehmet Emin (6 mentions)
FMS-Canada, 1993 *Certification:* Gastroenterology
1701 South Blvd E #300, Rochester Hills, 248-844-9710

Duffy, Michael Charles (13 mentions)
Louisiana State U, 1974
Certification: Gastroenterology, Internal Medicine
264 W Maple Rd, Troy, 248-273-9930

Gebara, Souheil (4 mentions)
FMS-Syria, 1980 *Certification:* Pediatric Gastroenterology
3535 W 13 Mile Rd #707, Royal Oak, 248-551-0487

Gun, Samuel H. (4 mentions)
Des Moines U, 1989
37399 Garfield Rd #104, Clinton Township, 586-286-5400

Gunaratnam, Naresh Thomas (4 mentions)
U of Virginia, 1991 *Certification:* Gastroenterology
5300 Elliott Dr, Ypsilanti, 734-434-6262

Ibrahim, Ghaith M. (4 mentions)
FMS-Syria, 1990 *Certification:* Gastroenterology
27560 Hoover Rd, Warren, 586-757-6400

Klein, Steven Robert (4 mentions)
Western U, 1982
28080 Grand River Ave #306, Farmington Hills, 248-471-8982
2300 Haggerty Rd #1010, Novi, 248-553-2200

Krasman, Manus Leon (4 mentions)
U of Michigan, 1975
Certification: Gastroenterology, Internal Medicine
5300 Elliott Dr, Ypsilanti, 734-434-6262

Levinson, Jay Raphael (5 mentions)
Wayne State U, 1980
Certification: Gastroenterology, Internal Medicine
30055 Northwestern Hwy #250, Farmington Hills, 248-985-5000

Maas, Luis Carlos (4 mentions)
FMS-Paraguay, 1967
Certification: Gastroenterology, Internal Medicine
30055 Northwestern Hwy #250, Farmington Hills, 248-985-5000

Nostrant, Timothy Thomas (8 mentions)
U of Buffalo, 1973
Certification: Gastroenterology, Internal Medicine
1500 E Medical Center Dr #3912-K, Ann Arbor, 734-936-4775

Patel, Atulkumar S. (8 mentions)
FMS-United Kingdom, 1980
Certification: Gastroenterology, Internal Medicine
264 W Maple Rd #200, Troy, 248-273-9930

Peleman, Rene Richard (5 mentions)
Wayne State U, 1981
Certification: Gastroenterology, Internal Medicine
37555 Garfield Rd #125, Clinton Township, 586-263-7150

Piper, Michael Howard (6 mentions)
Wayne State U, 1981
Certification: Gastroenterology, Internal Medicine
11900 E 12 Mile Rd #307, Warren, 586-573-8380
30055 Northwestern Hwy #250, Farmington Hills, 248-985-5000

Polidori, Gregg (7 mentions)
Wayne State U, 1986
Certification: Gastroenterology, Internal Medicine
27209 Lahser Rd #124, Southfield, 248-353-3026

Puccio, Jeff Eugene (11 mentions)
Wayne State U, 1988 *Certification:* Gastroenterology
2021 Monroe St #101, Dearborn, 313-277-4177

Scheinfeld, Ben A. (4 mentions)
FMS-Canada, 1989
19020 Fort St, Riverview, 734-362-5100

Shehab, Thomas Michael (11 mentions)
Wayne State U, 1995 *Certification:* Gastroenterology
5300 Elliott Dr, Ypsilanti, 734-434-6262

Silverman, Ann Lynne (4 mentions)
Albert Einstein Coll of Med, 1982
Certification: Gastroenterology, Internal Medicine
6777 W Maple Rd, West Bloomfield, 248-661-7889

Slone, Charles Raymond (4 mentions)
Wayne State U, 1971 *Certification:* Internal Medicine
2021 Monroe St #201, Dearborn, 313-565-9390

Stawick, Laurence E. (6 mentions)
Wayne State U, 1974
Certification: Gastroenterology, Internal Medicine
22250 Providence Dr #604, Southfield, 248-380-6625
26850 Providence Pkwy #350, Novi, 248-569-1770

Stoler, Robert Leslie (6 mentions)
U of Michigan, 1985
Certification: Gastroenterology, Internal Medicine
5300 Elliott Dr, Ypsilanti, 734-434-6262

Strasius, Stanley R. (7 mentions)
Loyola U Chicago, 1968
Certification: Gastroenterology, Internal Medicine
5325 Elliott Dr, Ypsilanti, 734-434-6262

Takriti, Mones (10 mentions)
FMS-Syria, 1979
Certification: Gastroenterology, Internal Medicine
44555 Woodward Ave #304, Pontiac, 248-858-3878

Veneri, Robert Joseph (10 mentions)
Wayne State U, 1983
Certification: Gastroenterology, Internal Medicine
28963 Little Mack Ave #101, St Clair Shores, 586-447-0700

Weber, John Raymond, Jr. (4 mentions)
U of Michigan, 1986
Certification: Gastroenterology, Internal Medicine
1701 South Blvd E #300, Rochester Hills, 248-844-9710

Wille, Richard Thomas (6 mentions)
U of Michigan, 1990
Certification: Gastroenterology, Internal Medicine
1701 South Blvd E #300, Rochester Hills, 248-844-9710
44199 Dequindre Rd, Troy, 248-828-6032

General Surgery

Albaran, Renato Galido (6 mentions)
U of Maryland, 1991 *Certification:* Surgery
245 Barclay Cir #400, Rochester Hills, 248-853-9177
42370 Van Dyke Ave #105, Sterling Heights, 586-731-5700

Arneson, Wallace A., Jr. (10 mentions)
Harvard U, 1974 *Certification:* Surgery
5325 Elliott Dr #104, Ypsilanti, 734-712-8150

Atwal, Mandip Singh (3 mentions)
Des Moines U, 1995
26164 Van Dyke Ave, Center Line, 586-759-2005

Audet, Isabelle (5 mentions)
809 W Dryden Rd, Metamora, 810-678-8150

Barnwell, John Maclin (3 mentions)
Howard U, 1989 *Certification:* Surgery
18709 Meyers Rd, Detroit, 313-864-8456
461 W Huron Ave 6th Fl #608, Pontiac, 248-857-6889

Baumann, John Conrad (3 mentions)
Michigan State U Coll of Osteopathic Med, 1973
3231 West Rd, Trenton, 734-675-1200

Bierema, Timothy Alan (7 mentions)
Michigan State U, 1984 *Certification:* Surgery
4550 Investment Dr #270, Troy, 248-267-5015

Bolton, Steven (3 mentions)
Wayne State U, 1976 *Certification:* Surgery
44555 Woodward Ave #201, Pontiac, 248-335-9449

Browning, Daniel Patrick (7 mentions)
Michigan State U, 1982 *Certification:* Surgery
4550 Investment Dr #270, Troy, 248-267-5015

Burney, Richard E., Jr. (4 mentions)
Harvard U, 1969 *Certification:* Surgery
1500 E Medical Center Dr, Ann Arbor, 734-936-5738

Chan, Winston K. (3 mentions)
FMS-Canada, 1988
3535 W 13 Mile Rd #748, Royal Oak, 248-551-2400

Cleary, Robert Kevin (5 mentions)
Wayne State U, 1984
Certification: Colon & Rectal Surgery, Surgery
5325 Elliott Dr #104, Ypsilanti, 734-712-8150

Courtney, James Thomas (9 mentions)
Wayne State U, 1982 *Certification:* Surgery
3535 W 13 Mile Rd #209, Royal Oak, 248-288-1660

Czako, Peter Ferencz (9 mentions)
Wayne State U, 1987 *Certification:* Surgery
3535 W 13 Mile Rd #645, Royal Oak, 248-551-8180

Dekhne, Nayana S. (4 mentions)
FMS-India, 1988 *Certification:* Surgery
3601 W 13 Mile Rd, Royal Oak, 248-551-3300

Desrochers, Randal Philip (3 mentions)
U of Michigan, 1981 *Certification:* Surgery
5325 Elliott Dr #104, Ypsilanti, 734-712-8150

Dulchavsky, Scott A. (5 mentions)
Wayne State U, 1983 *Certification:* Surgery, Surgical Critical Care
2799 W Grand Blvd, Detroit, 313-916-2600

Elkus, Robert Michael (4 mentions)
U of Michigan, 1983 *Certification:* Surgery
6777 W Maple Rd, West Bloomfield, 248-661-4100

Ferguson, Lorenzo (3 mentions)
Meharry Med Coll, 1977 *Certification:* Surgery
22250 Providence Dr #201, Southfield, 248-569-4228

Friedman, Paul Bruce (3 mentions)
U of Michigan, 1985 *Certification:* Surgery
18181 Oakwood Blvd #209, Dearborn, 734-462-1525
14555 Levan Rd #307, Livonia, 734-462-1525

Hawasli, Abdelkader Al (6 mentions)
FMS-Syria, 1978 *Certification:* Surgery
24911 Little Mack Ave #B, St Clair Shores, 586-774-8811

Hinshaw, Keith Alan (6 mentions)
Wayne State U, 1982 *Certification:* Surgery
245 Barclay Cir #400, Rochester Hills, 248-853-9177
42370 Van Dyke Ave #105, Sterling Heights, 586-731-5700

Howells, Greg Alan (4 mentions)
U of Michigan, 1974 *Certification:* Surgery
3535 W 13 Mile Rd #204, Royal Oak, 248-551-9090

Jacobs, Michael John (3 mentions)
FMS-Grenada, 1996 *Certification:* Surgery
22250 Providence Dr #700, Southfield, 248-559-5115

Janczyk, Randy James (3 mentions)
U of Texas-San Antonio, 1995
Certification: Surgery, Surgical Critical Care
3535 W 13 Mile Rd #204, Royal Oak, 248-551-9090

Jury, Robert Paul (14 mentions)
Wayne State U, 1979 *Certification:* Surgery
3535 W 13 Mile Rd #645, Royal Oak, 248-551-8180

Kestenberg, William Lee (4 mentions)
U of Michigan, 1984 *Certification:* Surgery
7001 Orchard Lake Rd #120, West Bloomfield, 248-539-3027

Kimball, Beth Camille (5 mentions)
U of Chicago, 1990 *Certification:* Surgery
5325 Elliott Dr #104, Ypsilanti, 734-712-8150

Klein, Michael David (3 mentions)
Case Western Reserve U, 1971
Certification: Pediatric Surgery, Surgery
3901 Beaubien Blvd, Detroit, 313-831-3220

Korda, Peter Joseph (6 mentions)
FMS-Romania, 1974 *Certification:* Surgery
1135 W University Dr #240, Rochester Hills, 248-651-0200

Krause, Kevin Robert (3 mentions)
Wayne State U, 1994 *Certification:* Surgery
3535 W 13 Mile Rd #645, Royal Oak, 248-551-8180

Kreske, Edward David (8 mentions)
Michigan State U, 1995 *Certification:* Surgery
5325 Elliott Dr #104, Ypsilanti, 734-712-8150

Langenburg, Scott Edward (3 mentions)
U of Michigan, 1990 *Certification:* Pediatric Surgery, Surgery
3901 Beaubien St, Detroit, 313-831-3220

Lewis, Zachary H. (4 mentions)
Michigan State U Coll of Osteopathic Med, 1985
3231 West Rd, Trenton, 734-675-6885

Lulek, James Randolph (15 mentions)
U of Michigan, 1974 *Certification:* Surgery
18181 Oakwood Blvd #209, Dearborn, 313-271-8560
7300 N Canton Center Rd, Canton, 734-454-8001

Mazzeo, Robert Joseph (5 mentions)
Certification: Surgery
5325 Elliott Dr #104, Ypsilanti, 734-712-8150

McIntosh, Bruce Burr (4 mentions)
Wayne State U, 1989 *Certification:* Surgery
1701 South Blvd E #270, Rochester Hills, 248-853-3100

McKany, Malik E. (4 mentions)
FMS-Iraq, 1979 *Certification:* Surgery
44555 Woodward Ave #101, Pontiac, 248-858-3800
6770 Dixie Hwy #311, Clarkston, 248-625-3231

Mulholland, Michael William (3 mentions)
Northwestern U, 1978
Certification: Surgery, Surgical Critical Care
1500 E Medical Center DrTaubman Ctr #2920, Ann Arbor, 734-936-5738

Nathanson, Saul David (3 mentions)
FMS-South Africa, 1966 *Certification:* Surgery
2799 W Grand Blvd, Detroit, 313-916-2600

Phillips, Eduardo (3 mentions)
FMS-Mexico, 1965 *Certification:* Surgery
6900 Orchard Lake Rd #203, West Bloomfield, 248-865-2575

Rebock, Michael David (4 mentions)
Philadelphia Coll of Osteopathic Med, 1991
28080 Grand River Ave #208N, Farmington Hills, 248-478-7733

Reddy, Prabhaker N. (4 mentions)
Certification: Surgery
43331 Commons Dr, Clinton Township, 586-263-5410

Robbins, James Michael (10 mentions)
Tulane U, 1988 *Certification:* Surgery, Surgical Critical Care
3535 W 13 Mile Rd, Royal Oak, 248-551-3000

Sheth, Akash Rushikumar (4 mentions)
Wayne State U, 1991 *Certification:* Surgery
21000 E 12 Mile Rd #112, St Clair Shores, 586-771-8900

Sheth, Dharti Rushikumar (4 mentions)
Wayne State U, 1994 *Certification:* Surgery
21000 E 12 Mile Rd #112, St Clair Shores, 586-771-8900

Siegel, Thomas Samuel (3 mentions)
Wayne State U, 1977 *Certification:* Surgery
18181 Oakwood Blvd #307, Dearborn, 313-593-0810

Silapasvang, Sumet (7 mentions)
FMS-Thailand, 1968
22250 Providence Dr #700, Southfield, 248-559-5115

Talpos, Gary Brian (5 mentions)
U of Michigan, 1974 *Certification:* Surgery
2799 W Grand Blvd, Detroit, 313-916-3033

Taylor, Michael George (5 mentions)
Wayne State U, 1984 *Certification:* Surgery
22646 E 9 Mile Rd #C, St Clair Shores, 586-443-5400

Turfah, Fuad (7 mentions)
FMS-Lebanon, 1987
Certification: Colon & Rectal Surgery, Surgery
1811 Monroe St, Dearborn, 313-565-4010

Velanovich, Vic (6 mentions)
Wayne State U, 1987 *Certification:* Surgery
2799 W Grand Blvd #K-8, Detroit, 313-556-8984

Wahl, Wendy Lynn (4 mentions)
Stony Brook U, 1988
Certification: Surgery, Surgical Critical Care
1500 E Medical Center Dr, Ann Arbor, 734-936-5738

Weaver, Donald Willard (10 mentions)
Loma Linda U, 1974 *Certification:* Surgery
4160 John R St #615, Detroit, 313-745-4195

Webber, John Daniel (3 mentions)
Wayne State U, 1992 *Certification:* Surgery
4160 John R St #615, Detroit, 313-745-4195

Wesen, Cheryl (3 mentions)
Temple U, 1980 *Certification:* Surgery
19229 Mack Ave #34, Grosse Pointe, 313-647-3900

Geriatrics

Allen, Susan J. (6 mentions)
FMS-Ireland, 1994 *Certification:* Geriatric Medicine
3535 W 13 Mile Rd #108, Royal Oak, 248-551-8305

Craig, Darrell Wayne (4 mentions)
U of Texas-Galveston, 1978
Certification: Geriatric Medicine, Internal Medicine
5361 McAuley Dr, Ypsilanti, 734-712-5189

Dengiz, Alan Nahit (14 mentions)
U of Michigan, 1974
Certification: Geriatric Medicine, Internal Medicine
5361 McAuley Dr, Ann Arbor, 734-712-5189

Hyde, Kristina Lynn (5 mentions)
Wayne State U, 1984
Certification: Geriatric Medicine, Internal Medicine
3535 W 13 Mile Rd #108, Royal Oak, 248-551-8305

Imam, Khaled (4 mentions)
FMS-Syria, 1978 *Certification:* Endocrinology and Metabolism, Geriatric Medicine, Internal Medicine
3601 W 13 Mile Rd #108, Royal Oak, 248-551-8305
3535 W 13 Mile Rd #108, Royal Oak, 248-551-1756

Kamath, Satish N. (5 mentions)
FMS-India, 1972
Certification: Geriatric Medicine, Internal Medicine
24100 Oxford St, Dearborn, 313-274-2500

Krol, Gregory Donald (3 mentions)
Michigan State U, 1977
Certification: Geriatric Medicine, Internal Medicine
3500 15 Mile Rd, Sterling Heights, 586-977-9300
3635 Forest Hill Dr, Bloomfield Hills, 586-977-9300

Morrison, Evan Seth (5 mentions)
Hahnemann U, 1985
Certification: Geriatric Medicine, Internal Medicine
3145 W Clark Rd #201, Ypsilanti, 734-528-5700

Upton, Cathy A. (4 mentions)
Wayne State U, 1980 *Certification:* Internal Medicine
5361 McAuley Dr #201, Ypsilanti, 734-528-5700

Hematology/Oncology

Agnone, Eugene John, Jr. (5 mentions)
Wayne State U, 1975
Certification: Internal Medicine, Medical Oncology
18223 E 10 Mile Rd #100, Roseville, 810-778-5880

Akhtar, Adil (5 mentions)
FMS-Pakistan, 1986 *Certification:* Hospice and Palliative Medicine, Internal Medicine, Medical Oncology
44199 Dequindre Rd #315, Troy, 248-813-9677

Balaraman, Savitha (5 mentions)
FMS-India, 1995
Certification: Internal Medicine, Medical Oncology
27301 Dequindre Rd #314, Madison Heights, 248-399-4400

Berkovic, Michael (5 mentions)
Des Moines U, 1973
27301 Dequindre Rd #314, Madison Heights, 248-399-4400

Bloom, Robert Eric (6 mentions)
Wayne State U, 1978
Certification: Hematology, Internal Medicine, Medical Oncology
22301 Foster Winter Dr #200, Southfield, 248-552-0620
47601 Grand River Ave #B-229, Novi, 248-344-2000

Boxwala, Iqbal Gulamabbas (4 mentions)
FMS-India, 1982
Certification: Internal Medicine, Medical Oncology
3577 W 13 Mile Rd #103, Royal Oak, 248-288-4500
4550 Investment Dr #220, Troy, 248-267-6569

Chottiner, Elaine Gayle (17 mentions)
U of Michigan, 1980
Certification: Hematology, Internal Medicine, Medical Oncology
5301 Huron River Dr #C-139, Ypsilanti, 734-712-1000

Decker, David Arnold (11 mentions)
Wayne State U, 1974
Certification: Internal Medicine, Medical Oncology
3577 W 13 Mile Rd #404, Royal Oak, 248-551-6900

Doyle, Thomas Joseph (6 mentions)
Michigan State U, 1976
Certification: Internal Medicine, Medical Oncology
2799 W Grand Blvd, Detroit, 313-916-2778

Eisenberg, Leopoldo (8 mentions)
FMS-Mexico, 1967
28455 Haggerty Rd #203, Novi, 248-324-4444

Fata, Farid T. (7 mentions)
FMS-Lebanon, 1991
Certification: Hematology, Internal Medicine, Medical Oncology
543 N Main St #223, Rochester, 248-650-1090
2520 S Telegraph Rd, Bloomfield Hills, 248-650-1090
1295 Barry Rd, LaPeer, 810-667-6141

Flaherty, Lawrence Edgar (4 mentions)
St Louis U, 1978
Certification: Hematology, Internal Medicine, Medical Oncology
4100 John R St, Detroit, 800-527-6266

Folbe, Mitchell Howard (5 mentions)
Wayne State U, 1992 *Certification:* Medical Oncology
115 E Long Lake Rd, Troy, 248-879-2500

Franklin, Roman (5 mentions)
Wayne State U, 1973
Certification: Hematology, Internal Medicine, Medical Oncology
6770 Dixie Hwy #106-A, Clarkston, 248-625-2071

Goldman, Lyle Steven (10 mentions)
Albany Med Coll, 1981
Certification: Hematology, Internal Medicine, Medical Oncology
22301 Foster Winter Dr #200, Southfield, 248-552-0620
47601 Grand River Ave #2-S, Novi, 248-344-2000

Goodman, Judie (5 mentions)
Des Moines U, 1980
22301 Foster Winter Dr #200, Southfield, 248-552-0620

Gordon, Craig J. (5 mentions)
Des Moines U, 1983
30160 Orchard Lake Rd #100, Farmington Hills, 248-538-1000

Jaiyesimi, Ishmael (9 mentions)
Western U, 1986
Certification: Hematology, Internal Medicine, Medical Oncology
3577 W 13 Mile Rd #404, Royal Oak, 248-551-6900

Krishnan, Rajan Seshadri (4 mentions)
FMS-India, 1966
Certification: Hematology, Internal Medicine, Medical Oncology
44405 Woodward Ave #202, Pontiac, 248-858-2270

Leonard, Robert Jay (6 mentions)
Wayne State U, 1981
Certification: Hematology, Internal Medicine, Medical Oncology
19229 Mack Ave #24, Grosse Pointe Woods, 313-884-5522
11885 E 12 Mile Rd #110-A, Warren, 313-884-5522

Main, Charles Alexander, Jr. (6 mentions)
Wayne State U, 1964
Certification: Pediatric Hematology-Oncology, Pediatrics
3601 W 13 Mile Rd #101, Royal Oak, 248-551-0360
3577 W 13 Mile Rd #101, Royal Oak, 248-551-0360

Margolis, Harold (10 mentions)
Kansas U Coll of Osteopathic Med, 1967
27301 Dequindre Rd #314, Madison Heights, 248-399-4400

Margolis, Jeffrey H. (19 mentions)
Case Western Reserve U, 1993
Certification: Internal Medicine, Medical Oncology
27301 Dequindre Rd #314, Madison Heights, 248-399-4400
3577 W 13 Mile Rd, Royal Oak, 248-399-4400

McKenzie, Michael (4 mentions)
Midwestern U Chicago Coll of Osteopathic Med, 1971
42815 Garfield Rd #201, Clinton Township, 586-286-0902
21100 Allen Rd, Woodhaven, 734-365-5154

Parikh, Rajul Bachubhai (7 mentions)
FMS-India, 1983
Certification: Hematology, Internal Medicine, Medical Oncology
3577 W 13 Mile Rd #103, Royal Oak, 248-288-4500
4550 Investment Dr #220, Troy, 248-288-4500

Shah, Mukesh Shantilal (4 mentions)
FMS-India, 1979
Certification: Internal Medicine, Medical Oncology
1135 W University Dr #220, Rochester Hills, 248-656-4900

Signori, Oscar Raul (8 mentions)
FMS-Argentina, 1974
Certification: Internal Medicine, Medical Oncology
4900 Mercury Dr #100, Dearborn, 313-271-5577

Stella, Philip Jeffery (9 mentions)
Michigan State U, 1978
Certification: Internal Medicine, Medical Oncology
5301 E Huron River Dr #C-139, Ypsilanti, 734-712-1000

Tapazoglou, Efstathios (5 mentions)
FMS-Greece, 1976
Certification: Internal Medicine, Medical Oncology
11900 E 12 Mile Rd #210, Warren, 586-558-4700

Thomas, Shanti (4 mentions)
FMS-India, 1982 *Certification:* Medical Oncology
15750 Northline Rd, Southgate, 734-283-7511
18100 Oakwood Blvd #205, Deerwood, 313-441-1569

Wollner, Ira Steven (4 mentions)
New Jersey Med Sch, 1979
Certification: Internal Medicine, Medical Oncology
2799 W Grand Blvd, Detroit, 313-916-2600

Zakalik, Dana (4 mentions)
U of Michigan, 1983
Certification: Hematology, Internal Medicine, Medical Oncology
3577 W 13 Mile Rd #404, Royal Oak, 248-551-6900

Infectious Disease

Band, Jeffrey David (5 mentions)
U of Michigan, 1973
Certification: Infectious Disease, Internal Medicine
3601 W 13 Mile Rd, Royal Oak, 248-551-4041
3535 W 13 Mile Rd #305, Royal Oak, 248-551-0495

Blackburn, Gerald W. (7 mentions)
Midwestern U Chicago Coll of Osteopathic Med, 1973
28050 Grand River Ave, Farmington Hills, 248-471-8314

Bohra, Mustafa Siraj (5 mentions)
Wayne State U, 1996
Certification: Infectious Disease, Internal Medicine
15120 Michigan Ave, Dearborn, 313-582-2142

Brooks, Alison Kay (7 mentions)
Northeastern Ohio U, 1995 *Certification:* Infectious Disease
22301 Foster Winter Dr, Southfield, 248-552-0620

Cox, Donald (5 mentions)
Michigan State U Coll of Osteopathic Med, 1981
35600 Central City Pkwy #101, Westland, 734-762-4850

Craig, Charles Poe (8 mentions)
U of Pittsburgh, 1961 *Certification:* Internal Medicine
4870 W Clark Rd #204, Ypsilanti, 734-528-9111
620 Byron Rd #1100, Howell, 734-528-9111

Drelichman, Vilma S. (5 mentions)
FMS-Paraguay, 1971
Certification: Infectious Disease, Internal Medicine
22301 Foster Winter Dr #200, Southfield, 248-552-0620
47601 Grand River Ave #2-S, Novi, 248-344-9200

Fan, Wiley (7 mentions)
Michigan State U Coll of Osteopathic Med, 1979
28080 Grand River Ave, Farmington Hills, 248-471-8314

Freij, Bishara Joudeh (12 mentions)
FMS-Lebanon, 1980
Certification: Pediatric Infectious Diseases, Pediatrics
3535 W 13 Mile Rd #707, Royal Oak, 248-551-0487

Gowda, Sachi (22 mentions)
FMS-India, 1980
Certification: Infectious Disease, Internal Medicine
1854 W Auburn Rd #200, Rochester Hills, 248-853-2323

Healy, Shaun Patrick (14 mentions)
Wayne State U, 1988
Certification: Infectious Disease, Internal Medicine
24350 Orchard Lake Rd #111, Farmington Hills, 248-615-0889

Johnson, Leonard Blaise (10 mentions)
Michigan State U, 1993
Certification: Infectious Disease, Internal Medicine
19251 Mack Ave #333, Grosse Pointe, 313-343-7280
22201 Moross Rd, Detroit, 313-343-7774

Lauter, Carl Burton (23 mentions)
Wayne State U, 1965 *Certification:* Allergy & Immunology,
Infectious Disease, Internal Medicine
3601 W 13 Mile Rd, Royal Oak, 248-551-7330
3535 W 13 Mile Rd #305, Royal Oak, 248-551-0495

Ognjan, Anthony Fabian (5 mentions)
Michigan State U Coll of Osteopathic Med, 1983
Certification: Infectious Disease, Internal Medicine
1000 Harrington St, Mount Clemens, 586-493-8139
43900 Garfield Rd #201, Clinton Township, 586-412-5139

Otto, Michael Henry (21 mentions)
U of Michigan, 1981
Certification: Infectious Disease, Internal Medicine
5333 McAuley Dr #3106, Ypsilanti, 734-712-8600

Sobel, Jack David (6 mentions)
FMS-South Africa, 1965
Certification: Infectious Disease, Internal Medicine
3990 John R St, Detroit, 313-745-7105
3750 Woodward Ave, Detroit, 313-745-4525

Sunstrum, James Cameron (17 mentions)
FMS-Canada, 1977
Certification: Infectious Disease, Internal Medicine
1934 Monroe St, Dearborn, 313-565-7464

Vaclav, Joyce Kilborn (5 mentions)
New York Coll of Osteopathic Med, 1985
2333 Biddle Ave, Wyandotte, 734-246-6000

Zervos, Marcus John (16 mentions)
Wayne State U, 1979
Certification: Infectious Disease, Internal Medicine
2799 W Gaurd Blvd, Detroit, 313-916-2556

Infertility

Ayers, Jonathan William T. (9 mentions)
U of Michigan, 1975 *Certification:* Obstetrics & Gynecology,
Reproductive Endocrinology/Infertility
3145 W Clark Rd #301, Ypsilanti, 734-434-4766

Brinton, David A. (7 mentions)
U of Utah, 1976 *Certification:* Obstetrics & Gynecology
3535 W 13 Mile Rd, Royal Oak, 248-898-5000
4190 Telegraph Rd #1500, Bloomfield Hills, 248-203-0900

Hayes, Maria Ferraro (9 mentions)
Indiana U, 1977 *Certification:* Obstetrics & Gynecology,
Reproductive Endocrinology/Infertility
18180 Oakwood Blvd #109, Dearborn, 313-299-6650
43900 Garfield Rd #228, Clinton Township, 586-416-1800

Mersol-Barg, Michael S. (7 mentions)
Ohio State U, 1984 *Certification:* Obstetrics & Gynecology,
Reproductive Endocrinology/Infertility
300 Park St #460, Birmingham, 248-593-6990

Randolph, John Francis (5 mentions)
U of Cincinnati, 1980 *Certification:* Obstetrics &
Gynecology, Reproductive Endocrinology/Infertility
475 Market Pl, Ann Arbor, 734-763-7323

Strickler, Ronald Clayton (5 mentions)
FMS-Canada, 1967 *Certification:* Obstetrics & Gynecology,
Reproductive Endocrinology/Infertility
3031 W Grand Blvd, Detroit, 313-916-2454

Internal Medicine *(see note on page 9)*

Bonema, John Douglas (3 mentions)
Wayne State U, 1987 *Certification:* Internal Medicine
4600 Investment Dr #300, Troy, 248-267-5000

Carion, William Robert (3 mentions)
Wayne State U, 1980 *Certification:* Internal Medicine
15959 Paul Rd #410, Macomb, 586-776-4200
27550 Schoenherr Rd #200, Warren, 586-776-4200

Carman, Jack Howard (3 mentions)
SUNY-Downstate Med Coll, 1970 *Certification:* Internal Medicine
3145 W Clark Rd #401, Ypsilanti, 734-528-5700

Doig, Christopher T. (4 mentions)
Michigan State U Coll of Osteopathic Med, 1984
18306 Middlebelt Rd, Livonia, 734-462-2360

Fine, Paul Leonard (4 mentions)
U of Michigan, 1989 *Certification:* Internal Medicine
1500 E Medical Center Dr Taubman Ctr #3116, Ann Arbor,
734-936-5582

Hardwicke, Mary Beth (4 mentions)
Wayne State U, 1984 *Certification:* Internal Medicine
23411 E Jefferson Ave #100, St Clair Shores, 586-778-4080

Hayner, James B. (3 mentions)
Certification: Internal Medicine
10020 Prof Center Dr, Hamburg, 810-231-0252

Housel, Cynthia A. (3 mentions)
Des Moines U, 1988
37399 Garfield Rd #106, Clinton Township, 586-226-3500

Johannessen, Lynne Carol (3 mentions)
Wayne State U, 1980 *Certification:* Internal Medicine
6777 W Maple Rd, West Bloomfield, 248-661-4100

Keimig, William Charles, Jr. (6 mentions)
Michigan State U, 1974 *Certification:* Internal Medicine
2799 W Grand Blvd, Detroit, 313-916-9100

Kolbe, Karl Francis (3 mentions)
Wayne State U, 1977 *Certification:* Internal Medicine
38865 Dequindre Rd #106, Troy, 248-720-2626

Korkigian, Armen Ara (3 mentions)
Kansas U Coll of Osteopathic Med, 1978
2635 Coolidge Hwy, Berkley, 248-541-2512

Krol, Gregory Donald (3 mentions)
Michigan State U, 1977
Certification: Geriatric Medicine, Internal Medicine
3500 15 Mile Rd, Sterling Heights, 586-977-9300

Lewis, Scott Gilbert (3 mentions)
Wayne State U, 1982 *Certification:* Internal Medicine
29201 Telegraph Rd #404, Southfield, 248-355-0880

Lipson, Peter Arthur (3 mentions)
Rush U, 1998 *Certification:* Internal Medicine
16800 W 12 Mile Rd #100, Southfield, 248-483-5300

McClelland, Steven Craig (3 mentions)
Wayne State U, 1992 *Certification:* Internal Medicine
555 W 14 Mile Rd #100, Clawson, 248-655-1400

Meri, Abdelwahab Ismael (3 mentions)
Wayne State U, 2000 *Certification:* Internal Medicine
135 Barclay Cir #100, Rochester Hills, 248-852-2277

Najor, Lanore Patricia (3 mentions)
A T Still U, 1988 *Certification:* Internal Medicine
31815 Southfield Rd #12, Beverly Hills, 248-646-8166

Norton, Kathleen M. (5 mentions)
U of Cincinnati, 1986 *Certification:* Internal Medicine
3290 W Big Beaver Rd #420, Troy, 248-649-9700

Oberdoerster, Mark C. (7 mentions)
U of Toledo, 1982 *Certification:* Internal Medicine
2200 Green Rd #B, Ann Arbor, 734-994-7446
255 N Lilly Rd, Canton, 734-981-3300

Rosenbaum, Lewis Herman (4 mentions)
U of Michigan, 1975 *Certification:* Geriatric Medicine,
   Internal Medicine, Rheumatology
3535 W 13 Mile Rd #635, Royal Oak, 248-551-7009

Rottman, Michael (4 mentions)
FMS-Grenada, 1981 *Certification:* Internal Medicine
11900 E 12 Mile Rd #300, Warren, 586-751-7515

Sabin, Bradley Howard (5 mentions)
Northwestern U, 1992 *Certification:* Internal Medicine
3290 W Big Beaver Rd #420, Troy, 248-649-9700

Samarian, Bruce (3 mentions)
Wayne State U, 1976 *Certification:* Internal Medicine
1695 W 12 Mile Rd #200, Berkley, 248-548-9090

Sanson, Michael Stanley (4 mentions)
Michigan State U, 1993 *Certification:* Internal Medicine
3145 W Clark Rd #401, Ypsilanti, 734-528-5700

Skoney, Joseph Anthony (6 mentions)
Wayne State U, 1985 *Certification:* Internal Medicine
4600 Investment Dr #300, Troy, 248-267-5000

Small, Jami Michele (3 mentions)
Cornell U, 1991 *Certification:* Internal Medicine
4600 Investment Dr #300, Troy, 248-267-5000

Tai, Arthur Wenyuan (3 mentions)
Michigan State U, 1982 *Certification:* Internal Medicine
1915 Pauline Blvd, Ann Arbor, 734-995-2259

White, Daniel Britton (3 mentions)
George Washington U, 1961
135 Barclay Cir, Rochester Hills, 248-852-2277

Winston, David Murray (5 mentions)
U of Michigan, 1971 *Certification:* Internal Medicine
2090 Commonwealth Blvd, Ann Arbor, 734-995-0303

Wissman, Sheryl Ann (5 mentions)
Wayne State U, 1987 *Certification:* Internal Medicine, Pediatrics
72 S Washington St #204, Oxford, 248-628-2233
425 N Park Blvd #201, Lake Orion, 248-628-2233

Nephrology

Akbar, Syed Shah Ali (4 mentions)
FMS-India, 1970 *Certification:* Internal Medicine, Nephrology
14752 Northline Rd, Southgate, 734-285-5030

Al-Saghir, Fahd (6 mentions)
FMS-Syria, 1989 *Certification:* Internal Medicine, Nephrology
44200 Woodward Ave #209, Pontiac, 248-253-0330

Berkowitz, Paul Alan (4 mentions)
U of Buffalo, 1985 *Certification:* Internal Medicine, Nephrology
5333 McAuley Dr #4003, Ypsilanti, 734-712-3470

Biederman, Jason Isaac (4 mentions)
Michigan State U Coll of Osteopathic Med, 1998
18302 Middlebelt Rd, Livonia, 248-478-1500

Dancey, Eric Andrew (5 mentions)
Wayne State U, 1993 *Certification:* Internal Medicine, Nephrology
5333 McAuley Dr #4003, Ypsilanti, 734-712-3470

Dancik, Jerry Allen (19 mentions)
Wayne State U, 1972 *Certification:* Internal Medicine, Nephrology
3535 W 13 Mile Rd #247, Royal Oak, 248-288-9340
4600 Investment Dr #290, Troy, 248-267-5010

Dhillon, Sundeep Singh (4 mentions)
Northeastern Ohio U, 1992
Certification: Internal Medicine, Nephrology
4600 Investment Dr #290, Troy, 248-288-9340

Dumler, Francis (8 mentions)
FMS-Peru, 1971 *Certification:* Internal Medicine, Nephrology
3535 W 13 Mile Rd #644, Royal Oak, 248-551-1010

Faber, Mark Douglas (4 mentions)
Wayne State U, 1982 *Certification:* Internal Medicine, Nephrology
2799 W Grand Blvd, Detroit, 313-916-2600

Hillyer, Robert Edward (4 mentions)
U of Oklahoma, 1980
Certification: Internal Medicine, Nephrology
27209 Lahser Rd #222, Southfield, 586-558-9033

Kroneman, Olaf Coron, III (7 mentions)
Michigan State U, 1977
Certification: Internal Medicine, Nephrology
1695 W 12 Mile Rd #250, Berkley, 248-414-3874
44199 Dequindre Rd, Troy, 248-414-3874

Margolis, Kim (4 mentions)
U of Cincinnati, 1981 *Certification:* Internal Medicine
11900 E 12 Mile Rd #200, Warren, 586-558-9033
27209 Lasher Rd #222, Southfield, 248-799-0434

Marrone, Mark G. (7 mentions)
FMS-St Maarten, 1990
Certification: Internal Medicine, Nephrology
18302 Middlebelt Rd, Livonia, 248-478-1500

Master, Usman Ghani H. A. (4 mentions)
FMS-St Maarten, 1983
Certification: Internal Medicine, Nephrology
44200 Woodward Ave #209, Pontiac, 248-253-0330

Mattoo, Tej K. (5 mentions)
FMS-India, 1975 *Certification:* Pediatric Nephrology, Pediatrics
3901 Beaubien St, Detroit, 313-745-5604

Michaels, Robert Stuart (6 mentions)
Northwestern U, 1969
Certification: Internal Medicine, Nephrology
29877 Telegraph Rd #301, Southfield, 248-359-2370

Migdal, Stephen Donald (5 mentions)
Wayne State U, 1969 *Certification:* Internal Medicine, Nephrology
4160 John R St #917, Detroit, 313-745-7145

Prada, Arturo (9 mentions)
FMS-Colombia, 1970
Certification: Internal Medicine, Nephrology
6700 N Rochester Rd #110, Rochester Hills, 248-652-1202

Provenzano, Robert (5 mentions)
Wayne State U, 1983 *Certification:* Internal Medicine, Nephrology
22201 Moross Rd #150, Detroit, 810-886-8787

Rehan, Ahmed (9 mentions)
FMS-Pakistan, 1976 *Certification:* Internal Medicine, Nephrology
5333 McAuley Dr #4003, Ypsilanti, 734-712-3470

Smith, Paul Gordon (7 mentions)
U of Michigan, 1977 *Certification:* Internal Medicine, Nephrology
5333 McAuley Dr #4003, Ypsilanti, 734-712-3470

Speck, John Peyton (20 mentions)
Wayne State U, 1977 *Certification:* Internal Medicine, Nephrology
27901 Woodward Ave #210, Berkley, 248-414-5377

Steigerwalt, Susan P. (4 mentions)
U of Michigan, 1977 *Certification:* Internal Medicine, Nephrology
18000 E Warren St, Detroit, 313-884-4686

Valentini, Rudolph Peter (8 mentions)
Wayne State U, 1989
Certification: Pediatric Nephrology, Pediatrics
3901 Beaubien St, Detroit, 313-745-5604

Yee, Jerry (5 mentions)
Jefferson Med Coll, 1982
Certification: Internal Medicine, Nephrology
2799 W Grand Blvd, Detroit, 313-916-2600

Neurological Surgery

Brodkey, Jason Adler (8 mentions)
Case Western Reserve U, 1990 *Certification:* Neurological Surgery
5315 Elliott Dr #102, Ypsilanti, 734-434-4110

Chandler, William Frederick (9 mentions)
U of Michigan, 1971 *Certification:* Neurological Surgery
1500 E Medical Center Dr #3552, Ann Arbor, 734-936-5020

Croissant, Paul Dennis (8 mentions)
Hahnemann U, 1964 *Certification:* Neurological Surgery
799 Denison Ct, Bloomfield Hills, 248-751-7246

Junn, Frederick S. C. (13 mentions)
FMS-Canada, 1986 *Certification:* Neurological Surgery
18181 Oakwood Blvd #411, Dearborn, 313-982-5290

Malik, Ghaus Muhammad (30 mentions)
FMS-Pakistan, 1968 *Certification:* Neurological Surgery
2799 W Grand Blvd #K-11, Detroit, 313-916-1093
6777 W Maple Rd, West Bloomfield, 248-661-6417

Nida, Todd Young (8 mentions)
U of Minnesota, 1988 *Certification:* Neurological Surgery
44555 Woodward Ave #506, Pontiac, 248-334-2568

Rock, Jack P. (11 mentions)
U of Miami, 1979 *Certification:* Neurological Surgery
2799 W Grand Blvd, Detroit, 313-916-1094

Rosenblum, Mark Lester (10 mentions)
New York Med Coll, 1969 *Certification:* Neurological Surgery
2799 W Grand Blvd, Detroit, 313-916-2241
6777 W Maple Rd, West Bloomfield, 248-661-6417

Soo, Teck Mun (13 mentions)
FMS-Ireland, 1987 *Certification:* Neurological Surgery
22250 Providence Dr #601, Southfield, 248-569-7745

Thomas, Geoffrey Michael (11 mentions)
U of Michigan, 1980 *Certification:* Neurological Surgery
5315 Elliott Dr #102, Ypsilanti, 734-434-4110

Zakalik, Karol (17 mentions)
U of Michigan, 1980 *Certification:* Neurological Surgery
3535 W 13 Mile Rd #504, Royal Oak, 248-551-3020

Neurology

Aboukasm, Amer G. (4 mentions)
FMS-Lebanon, 1984 *Certification:* Neurology
25100 Kelly Rd, Roseville, 586-771-7440

Al-Hakim, M. Mazen (5 mentions)
3535 W 13 Mile Rd #240, Royal Oak, 248-551-5566

Alexiou, Anastasios (4 mentions)
FMS-Belgium, 1985 *Certification:* Neurology
5333 McAuley Dr Rm 3003, Ypsilanti, 734-712-1400

Angus, Elizabeth Jean (4 mentions)
FMS-Canada, 1979
Certification: Clinical Neurophysiology, Neurology
2799 W Grand Blvd, Detroit, 313-916-2600

Boudouris, William Dean (6 mentions)
Michigan State U Coll of Osteopathic Med, 1993
28595 Orchard Lake Rd #200, Farmington Hills, 248-553-0010

Cullis, Paul Anthony (4 mentions)
FMS-United Kingdom, 1979 *Certification:* Neurology
25100 Kelly Rd, Roseville, 586-771-7440

Elias, Stanton Bernard (11 mentions)
U of Pittsburgh, 1972 *Certification:* Neurology
2799 W Grand Blvd #K-11, Detroit, 313-916-2600

Ernstoff, Raina M. (4 mentions)
Wayne State U, 1970 *Certification:* Neurology
3535 W 13 Mile Rd, Royal Oak, 248-551-3000

Fellows, Jonathan (12 mentions)
Michigan State U Coll of Osteopathic Med, 1996
28595 Orchard Lake Rd #200, Farmington Hills, 248-553-0010

Glass, Lionel (6 mentions)
FMS-Netherlands, 1966
43494 Woodward Ave #103, Bloomfield Hills, 248-338-8400

Gramprie, James Robert (4 mentions)
Wayne State U, 1979 *Certification:* Neurology
905 W Eisenhower Cir #108, Ann Arbor, 734-665-6638

Hickenbottom, Susan Lynn (4 mentions)
U of Iowa, 1993 *Certification:* Neurology
5333 McAuley Dr #3003, Ypsilanti, 734-712-1400

Hidalgo, Cesar D. (11 mentions)
FMS-Philippines, 1974
Certification: Clinical Neurophysiology, Neurology
595 Barclay Cir #C, Rochester Hills, 248-852-1777

Khan, Muhammad Alamgir (4 mentions)
FMS-Pakistan, 1980
940 W Avon Rd #8, Rochester Hills, 248-651-5600

Leuchter, William Michael (19 mentions)
FMS-Canada, 1970 *Certification:* Neurology
26400 W 12 Mile Rd #170, Southfield, 248-208-8787

Levy, Robert J. (17 mentions)
U of Pittsburgh, 1978 *Certification:* Neurology
5333 McAuley Dr #R-3003, Ypsilanti, 734-572-1400

Lisak, Robert Philip (4 mentions)
Columbia U, 1965 *Certification:* Neurology
4201 St Antoine St #8-D, Detroit, 313-577-1242

Marcus, Andrew Leonard (4 mentions)
Wayne State U, 1979 *Certification:* Neurology, Vascular Neurology
3815 Pelham St #14, Dearborn, 313-730-9100

Mounayer, Sami H. (20 mentions)
FMS-Syria, 1970 *Certification:* Neurology
3535 W 13 Mile Rd #240, Royal Oak, 248-551-5566
44199 Dequindre Rd #112, Troy, 248-879-5775

Newman, Daniel Seth (4 mentions)
U of Michigan, 1983
Certification: Neurology, Neuromuscular Medicine
2799 W Grand Blvd, Detroit, 313-916-2594

Nigro, Michael A. (7 mentions)
Philadelphia Coll of Osteopathic Med, 1966
Certification: Neurology
28595 Orchard Lake Rd #200, Farmington Hills, 248-553-0010

Pawlak, Anne M. (6 mentions)
Michigan State U Coll of Osteopathic Med, 1979
28595 Orchard Lake Rd #200, Farmington Hills, 248-553-0010

Rossman, Howard S. (5 mentions)
Michigan State U Coll of Osteopathic Med, 1974
28595 Orchard Lake Rd #200, Farmington Hills, 248-553-0010

Segall, John David (10 mentions)
U of Michigan, 1973 *Certification:* Internal Medicine, Neurology
5333 McAuley Dr #R-3003, Ypsilanti, 734-712-1400

Selwa, Linda M. (4 mentions)
U of Michigan, 1986
Certification: Clinical Neurophysiology, Neurology
1500 E Medical Center Dr Taubman Ctr #1324, Ann Arbor,
734-936-9010

Silverman, Bruce M. (8 mentions)
Des Moines U, 1983
22250 Providence Dr #602, Southfield, 248-443-1666
414 Union St #101, Milford, 248-685-8435
27555 Middlebelt Rd, Farmington Hills, 248-478-5512

Singer, Daniel Paul (9 mentions)
Michigan State U Coll of Osteopathic Med, 1997
Certification: Diagnostic Radiology, Neuroradiology, Nuclear
   Medicine, Nuclear Radiology, Pediatric Radiology
6255 Inkster Rd #304, Garden City, 734-525-4466
28595 Orchard Lake Rd #200, Farmington Hills, 248-553-0010

Voci, James Matthew (7 mentions)
U of Pennsylvania, 1987 *Certification:* Neurology
19699 E 8 Mile Rd, St Clair Shores, 586-445-9900
35025 Harper Ave, Clinton Township, 486-445-9900

Woodruff, Brian Eric (4 mentions)
Michigan State U, 1999 *Certification:* Neurology with
   Special Qualifications in Child Neurology
24 Frank Lloyd Wright Dr Lobby L #2300, Ann Arbor,
734-930-5300

Young, Esther Laura (4 mentions)
Midwestern U Arizona Coll of Osteopathic Med, 2001
3950 S Rochester Rd #1300, Rochester Hills, 248-844-6000

Obstetrics/Gynecology

Beals, Joseph Anthony (4 mentions)
Wayne State U, 1980 *Certification:* Obstetrics & Gynecology
390 Park St #109, Birmingham, 248-647-5660

Beemer, Wesley H., III (5 mentions)
U of Michigan, 1983 *Certification:* Obstetrics & Gynecology
4936 W Clark Rd #100, Ypsilanti, 734-434-6200
7575 Grand River Rd #208, Brighton, 810-844-7741

Bernal, Humberto G. (5 mentions)
FMS-El Salvador, 1973 *Certification:* Obstetrics & Gynecology
18100 Oakwood Blvd #203, Dearborn, 313-336-7400

Cash, Charles Terrell, Jr. (6 mentions)
Wayne State U, 1977 *Certification:* Obstetrics & Gynecology
18101 Oakwood Blvd #410, Dearborn, 313-982-5430

Chu, Betty Shuwein (4 mentions)
U of Michigan, 1995 *Certification:* Obstetrics & Gynecology
6483 Citation Dr #A, Clarkston, 248-922-0856
11051 Hall Rd #110, Utica, 586-726-6556

Davidson, Brent Norman (10 mentions)
U of Louisville, 1981 *Certification:* Obstetrics & Gynecology
6777 W Maple Rd, West Bloomfield, 248-661-7018

De Grood, Rossana Motiu (4 mentions)
U of Michigan, 1982 *Certification:* Obstetrics & Gynecology
4940 W Clark Rd #100, Ypsilanti, 734-434-0477
990 W Ann Arbor Trail #302, Plymouth, 313-995-1442

Deenadayalu, Rajiv Joseph (5 mentions)
U of Cincinnati, 1995 *Certification:* Obstetrics & Gynecology
4936 W Clark Rd #100, Ypsilanti, 734-434-6200

Goldfarb, Robert Steven (3 mentions)
Wayne State U, 1983 *Certification:* Obstetrics & Gynecology
6777 W Maple Rd, West Bloomfield, 248-661-6425

Greene, Daniel James (3 mentions)
Michigan State U, 1991 *Certification:* Obstetrics & Gynecology
1000 W University Dr #207, Rochester Hills, 248-656-2022
58851 Van Dyke Rd #106, Washington, 586-992-9567

Hartmann, Deborah Irma (3 mentions)
Wayne State U, 1988
11300 E 13 Mile Rd, Warren, 586-574-1313

Hutton, Lenny Jay (3 mentions)
Wayne State U, 1980 *Certification:* Obstetrics & Gynecology
6900 Orchard Lake Rd #306, West Bloomfield, 248-855-6663
909 W Maple Rd #110, Clawson, 248-288-1237

Jones, Theodore Benjamin (6 mentions)
Temple U, 1982
Certification: Maternal-Fetal Medicine, Obstetrics & Gynecology
3750 Woodward Ave #200, Detroit, 313-993-4645

Knapp, John Anthony (5 mentions)
Wayne State U, 1987 *Certification:* Obstetrics & Gynecology
29751 Little Mack Ave, Roseville, 586-415-6200

Kwaiser, Ty Maurice (4 mentions)
Wayne State U, 1993 *Certification:* Obstetrics & Gynecology
44199 Dequindre Rd #415, Troy, 248-964-6061

Leach, Harold Robert (3 mentions)
Wayne State U, 1974 *Certification:* Obstetrics & Gynecology
6900 Orchard Lake Rd #306, West Bloomfield, 248-855-6663
909 W Maple Rd #110, Clawson, 248-855-6663

McCloskey, Jacalyn Ann (4 mentions)
Wayne State U, 1987 *Certification:* Obstetrics & Gynecology
555 S Old Woodward Ave #500, Birmingham, 248-647-9860

McMurtrie, Daniel George (4 mentions)
U of Michigan, 1978 *Certification:* Obstetrics & Gynecology
4936 W Clark Rd #100D, Ypsilanti, 734-434-6200

Meyer, Thomas Louis (3 mentions)
U of Toledo, 1984 *Certification:* Obstetrics & Gynecology
25080 Michigan Ave, Dearborn, 313-730-8880

Nehra, Anthony John (5 mentions)
Wayne State U, 1973 *Certification:* Obstetrics & Gynecology
1135 W University Dr #305, Rochester Hills, 248-656-2600

Perry, Stephen Paul (3 mentions)
Wayne State U, 1993 *Certification:* Obstetrics & Gynecology
11051 Hall Rd #110, Utica, 586-726-6556

Prysak, Michael Francis (3 mentions)
U of Michigan, 1973 *Certification:* Obstetrics & Gynecology
22151 Moross Rd #313, Detroit, 313-343-3494

Sanborn, John Robert (4 mentions)
U of Michigan, 1975 *Certification:* Obstetrics & Gynecology
555 S Old Woodward Ave #500, Birmingham, 248-647-9860

Smith, Joann Marie (3 mentions)
U of Michigan, 1984 *Certification:* Obstetrics & Gynecology
6405 Telegraph Rd #K-1, Bloomfield Township, 248-642-7710

Treadwell, Marjorie C. (4 mentions)
U of Michigan, 1984
Certification: Maternal-Fetal Medicine, Obstetrics & Gynecology
3750 Woodward Ave #200, Detroit, 313-993-4645
1500 E Medical Center Dr, Andover, 734-763-4264

Van De Ven, Cosmas J. M. (8 mentions)
FMS-Netherlands, 1986
Certification: Maternal-Fetal Medicine, Obstetrics & Gynecology
1500 E Medical Center Dr #F4835, Ann Arbor, 734-936-7573

Voutsos, Lester James (3 mentions)
Michigan State U, 1982 *Certification:* Obstetrics & Gynecology
46325 W 12 Mile mRd #250, Novi, 248-465-1200

Williams, Rebecca J. (4 mentions)
Boston U, 1975 *Certification:* Obstetrics & Gynecology
29201 Telegraph Rd #605, Southfield, 248-784-0600

Ophthalmology

Abrams, Gary Wayne (3 mentions)
U of Oklahoma, 1968 *Certification:* Ophthalmology
4717 St Antoine St, Detroit, 313-577-1355
4717 Saint Antoine St, Detroit, 313-577-8900

Apple, Martin Ira (3 mentions)
Wayne State U, 1981 *Certification:* Ophthalmology
28905 Northwestern Hwy, Southfield, 248-358-3937
2300 Haggerty Rd #1050, West Bloomfield, 248-669-9866
20500 Eureka Rd #200, Taylor, 734-283-0500

Bachynski, Brian Nicholas (5 mentions)
FMS-Canada, 1979 *Certification:* Ophthalmology
2799 W Grand Blvd #K-10, Detroit, 313-916-3270

Baker, Delores Faye (3 mentions)
U of Colorado, 1976
6071 W Outer Dr, Detroit, 313-966-9333
26400 W 12 Mile Rd #140, Southfield, 248-352-6884

Baker, John Douglas (5 mentions)
Wayne State U, 1967 *Certification:* Ophthalmology
3901 Beaubien St, Detroit, 313-745-3937
2355 Monroe St, Dearborn, 313-561-1777
6900 Orchard Lake Rd #105, West Bloomfield, 248-538-7400

Barletta, John Peter (6 mentions)
Wayne State U, 1990 *Certification:* Ophthalmology
5333 McAuley Dr Rm 6109, Ypsilanti, 734-434-6000

Bergman, Ronald Howard (4 mentions)
U of Michigan, 1989 *Certification:* Ophthalmology
29990 Northwestern Hwy, Farmington Hills, 248-538-6463

Christianson, Murray Dale (3 mentions)
FMS-Canada, 1974 *Certification:* Ophthalmology
2799 W Grand Blvd, Detroit, 313-916-2600

Clune, Michael Joseph (4 mentions)
Georgetown U, 1989 *Certification:* Ophthalmology
47100 Schoenherr Rd #F, Shelby Township, 586-247-2020
25511 Little Mack Ave #A, St Clair Shores, 586-774-2020

Colombo, Charles George (5 mentions)
FMS-Canada, 1972 *Certification:* Ophthalmology
1701 South Blvd E #180, Rochester Hills, 248-293-5166
1455 S Lapeer Rd #110, Lake Orion, 248-814-7139

Derr, Frank Nelson (4 mentions)
Wayne State U, 1969 *Certification:* Ophthalmology
375 Barclay Cir, Rochester Hills, 248-852-3636

Di Lorenzo, A. Luisa (6 mentions)
FMS-Ireland, 1988
Certification: Internal Medicine, Ophthalmology
2877 Crooks Rd #B, Troy, 248-822-7003

Edwards, Paul Andrew (6 mentions)
FMS-Jamaica, 1979 *Certification:* Ophthalmology
2799 W Grand Blvd, Detroit, 313-916-2600

Farjo, Ayad A. (3 mentions)
Certification: Ophthalmology
7949 N Canton Center Rd, Canton, 734-913-8884

Fuller, Barry Roger (3 mentions)
Jefferson Med Coll, 1994 *Certification:* Ophthalmology
5333 McAuley Dr #6109, Ypsilanti, 734-434-6000

Greenberg, Dana Jennifer (4 mentions)
Tufts U, 1996 *Certification:* Ophthalmology
3001 W Big Beaver Rd #105, Troy, 248-649-2820

Gupta, Kamal (3 mentions)
FMS-United Kingdom, 1980 *Certification:* Ophthalmology
23832 Southfield Rd, Southfield, 248-552-8700
19335 Allen Rd, Brownstown Township, 734-479-5580

Hart, John Charles, Jr. (10 mentions)
Wayne State U, 1991 *Certification:* Ophthalmology
6900 Orchard Lake Rd #307, West Bloomfield, 248-855-1020

Imami, Nauman Riaz (4 mentions)
U of Florida, 1992 *Certification:* Ophthalmology
2799 W Grand Blvd, Detroit, 313-916-2600

Katz, Gregory Joseph (3 mentions)
U of Illinois, 1989 *Certification:* Ophthalmology
5333 McAuley Dr Rm 6109, Ypsilanti, 734-434-6000

Klein, James William (3 mentions)
U of Illinois, 1971 *Certification:* Ophthalmology
21711 Greater Mack Ave, St Clair Shores, 586-774-6820

Kobet, Keith Andrew (3 mentions)
U of Michigan, 1976 *Certification:* Ophthalmology
7949 N Canton Center Rd, Canton, 734-459-7850

Lichter, Paul Richard (6 mentions)
U of Michigan, 1964 *Certification:* Ophthalmology
1000 Wall St, Ann Arbor, 734-764-6468

Neff, Howard Mark (5 mentions)
U of Michigan, 1986 *Certification:* Ophthalmology
6777 W Maple Rd, West Bloomfield, 248-661-6469

Porretta, Anthony Charles (3 mentions)
Med Coll of Wisconsin, 1965 *Certification:* Ophthalmology
29990 Northwestern Hwy, Farmington Hills, 248-538-6463

Ramocki, John Martin (3 mentions)
Wayne State U, 1981 *Certification:* Ophthalmology
4717 Saint Antoine St, Detroit, 313-577-8900
4717 St Antoine St, Detroit, 313-577-1356
15055 S Plaza Dr, Taylor, 734-287-8000

Rao, Rajesh Chalichama (4 mentions)
U of Michigan, 1992 *Certification:* Ophthalmology
6900 Orchard Lake Rd #105, West Bloomfield, 248-538-7400

Raphtis, Efthemios Sam (7 mentions)
Certification: Ophthalmology
432 W University Dr, Rochester, 248-651-6122

Roarty, John Denis (9 mentions)
Wayne State U, 1983 *Certification:* Ophthalmology, Pediatrics
427000 Garfield Rd #200, Clinton Township, 586-532-3380
2355 Monroe St, Dearborn, 313-561-4466

Rolain, Mark Allen (3 mentions)
Wayne State U, 1989 *Certification:* Ophthalmology
2251 N Squirrel Rd #206, Auburn Hills, 248-475-2230

Sensoli, Anthony Michael (4 mentions)
U of Michigan, 1986 *Certification:* Ophthalmology
1600 Commerce Park Dr #100, Chelsea, 734-475-5970
2350 E Stadium Blvd #10, Ann Arbor, 734-971-3879

Simonian, Sidney Kay (3 mentions)
Michigan State U Coll of Osteopathic Med, 1977
Certification: Ophthalmology
27483 Dequindre Rd #303-B, Madison Heights, 248-547-6656

Spigelman, Alan Victor (4 mentions)
U of Illinois, 1981 *Certification:* Ophthalmology
1750 S Telegraph Rd #205, Bloomfield Hills, 248-333-2900

Spoor, Thomas C. (3 mentions)
Certification: Ophthalmology
27450 Schoenherr Rd #200, Warren, 810-582-7860

Sugar, Alan (4 mentions)
U of Michigan, 1969 *Certification:* Ophthalmology
1000 Wall St, Ann Arbor, 734-763-8122

Tisch, Rebecca (5 mentions)
Albany Med Coll, 1985 *Certification:* Ophthalmology
7949 N Canton Center Rd, Canton, 734-459-7850

Weingarten, Mark David (3 mentions)
Wayne State U, 1989 *Certification:* Ophthalmology
1135 W University Dr #346, Rochester, 248-650-2255

Wilkinson, W. Scott (6 mentions)
Wayne State U, 1985 *Certification:* Ophthalmology
44555 Woodward Ave #203, Pontiac, 248-334-4931

Williams, George Arthur (3 mentions)
Northwestern U, 1978 *Certification:* Ophthalmology
3535 W 13 Mile Rd #555, Royal Oak, 248-551-2020

Yu, Vincent Chiwhan (6 mentions)
Wayne State U, 1987 *Certification:* Ophthalmology
23550 Park St #200, Dearborn, 313-724-2273

Orthopedics

Carpenter, James Ely (5 mentions)
U of Michigan, 1984
Certification: Orthopaedic Sports Medicine, Orthopaedic Surgery
24 Frank Llotd Wright Dr, Ann Arbor, 735-930-7400

Chrissos, Michael George (4 mentions)
U of Toledo, 1993 *Certification:* Orthopaedic Surgery
5315 Elliott Dr #201, Ypsilanti, 734-712-2230

Colen, Robert Paul (5 mentions)
Western U, 1994
25500 Meadow Brook Rd #275, Livonia, 248-381-5777

Demers, Michael Rene (6 mentions)
Wayne State U, 1983 *Certification:* Orthopaedic Surgery
24715 Little Mack Ave #100, St Clair Shores, 586-779-7970

Ditkoff, Thomas Joseph (4 mentions)
Wayne State U, 1971 *Certification:* Orthopaedic Surgery
6900 Orchard Lake Rd #103, West Bloomfield, 248-855-7400
3535 W 13 Mile Rd, Royal Oak, 248-551-9100
27207 Lahser Rd #200B, Southfield, 248-663-1900

Easton, Richard William (4 mentions)
Michigan State U, 1987 *Certification:* Orthopaedic Surgery
44199 Dequindre Rd #250, Troy, 248-879-8441

Greene, Perry William, III (19 mentions)
Wayne State U, 1985 *Certification:* Orthopaedic Surgery
30575 Woodward Ave #100, Royal Oak, 248-280-8550
3535 W 13 Mile Rd #605, Royal Oak, 248-551-9100

Haynes, Michael Bernard (6 mentions)
U of California-Davis, 1976 *Certification:* Orthopaedic Surgery
22250 Providence Dr #401, Southfield, 248-349-7015
26750 Providence Pkwy #200, Novi, 248-349-7015

Henderson, Bruce Thomas (4 mentions)
U of Michigan, 1972 *Certification:* Orthopaedic Surgery
44555 Woodward Ave #407, Pontiac, 248-334-0524

Herkowitz, Harry Norman (4 mentions)
Wayne State U, 1974 *Certification:* Orthopaedic Surgery
26025 Lahser Rd #200-B, Southfield, 248-663-1900

Housner, Gregory William (8 mentions)
Wayne State U, 1989 *Certification:* Orthopaedic Surgery
23550 Park St #100, Dearborn, 313-730-0500

Kassab, Safa Salim (6 mentions)
Wayne State U, 1991 *Certification:* Orthopaedic Surgery
44555 Woodward Ave #105, Pontiac, 248-335-2977

Lock, Terrence Ralph (4 mentions)
Wayne State U, 1983
Certification: Orthopaedic Sports Medicine, Orthopaedic Surgery
131 Kercheval Ave, Grosse Pointe, 313-882-7900
6525 2nd Ave, Detroit, 313-972-4060

Masini, Michael Alipio (8 mentions)
U of Michigan, 1986 *Certification:* Orthopaedic Surgery
5315 Elliott Dr #201, Ypsilanti, 734-712-2230

Meisel, Ronald L. (4 mentions)
Michigan State U Coll of Osteopathic Med, 1989
21550 Harrington St #A, Clinton Township, 586-627-1100
8180 26 Mile Rd, Shelby Township, 586-627-1100

Mendelson, Jeffrey D. (5 mentions)
Certification: Orthopaedic Surgery
14555 Levan Rd #215, Livonia, 734-542-0200

Milia, Marc Joseph (4 mentions)
U of Michigan, 1998 *Certification:* Orthopaedic Surgery
21031 Michigan Ave, Dearborn, 313-277-6700

O'Keefe, Thomas Joseph (11 mentions)
Northwestern U, 1972 *Certification:* Orthopaedic Surgery
5315 Elliott Dr #304, Ypsilanti, 734-712-0655

Parsons, Theodore W. (4 mentions)
Uniformed Services U of Health Sciences, 1986
Certification: Orthopaedic Surgery
2799 W Grand Blvd, Detroit, 800-436-7936

Pellerito, Benedict Peter (4 mentions)
Michigan State U, 1993 *Certification:* Orthopaedic Surgery
15420 19 Mile Rd #300, Clinton Township, 586-412-1411

Plagens, Douglas Gerard (7 mentions)
Wayne State U, 1991 *Certification:* Orthopaedic Surgery
23550 Park St #100, Dearborn, 313-730-0500

Prince, Allen Renald (4 mentions)
Kansas U Coll of Osteopathic Med, 1982
3100 Cross Creek Pkwy #200, Auburn Hills, 248-377-8000

Roodbeen, Craig William (5 mentions)
Wayne State U, 1990 *Certification:* Orthopaedic Surgery
1350 Kirts Blvd #160, Troy, 248-244-9426

Silberg, Eric T. (6 mentions)
U of Michigan, 1993 *Certification:* Orthopaedic Surgery
21031 Michigan Ave, Dearborn, 313-277-6700

Suleiman, Jiab Hasan (7 mentions)
A T Still U, 1997
23500 Park St #3, Dearborn, 313-565-4948

Verner, James J., Jr. (4 mentions)
Rosalind Franklin U, 1983 *Certification:* Orthopaedic Surgery
27207 Lahser Rd #200-B, Southfield, 248-663-1900
6900 Orchard Lake Rd #103, West Bloomfield, 248-855-7400

Wiater, Jerome Patrick (8 mentions)
Wayne State U, 1967 *Certification:* Orthopaedic Surgery
17877 W 14 Mile Rd, Beverly Hills, 248-644-3921

Zaltz, Ira (5 mentions)
U of Pennsylvania, 1990 *Certification:* Orthopaedic Surgery
30575 Woodward Ave #100, Royal Oak, 248-280-8550
2799 W Grand Blvd, Detroit, 313-916-2600

Otorhinolaryngology

Akervall, Jan Anders (6 mentions)
FMS-Sweden, 1990
28300 Orchard Lake Rd #100, Farmington Hills, 248-737-4030

Bahu, Samer John (7 mentions)
Wayne State U, 1996 *Certification:* Otolaryngology
6770 Dixie Hwy #306, Clarkston, 248-625-8450
44200 Woodward Ave #201, Pontiac, 248-334-9490

Bogdasarian, Ronald Spahr (7 mentions)
SUNY-Upstate Med U, 1972 *Certification:* Otolaryngology
5333 McAuley Dr #2017, Ypsilanti, 734-434-3200

Boucher, Rudrick Edward (5 mentions)
Wayne State U, 1965 *Certification:* Otolaryngology
32000 Woodward Ave, Royal Oak, 248-549-6060

Brooks, James Steven (5 mentions)
U of Michigan, 1983 *Certification:* Otolaryngology
29275 Northwestern Hwy #208, Southfield, 248-356-7772
115 E Long Lake Rd, Troy, 248-828-7500

Davis, David Mervyn (9 mentions)
FMS-South Africa, 1965
22250 Providence Dr #301, Southfield, 248-569-5985

Ho, Laurence (11 mentions)
U of Michigan, 1983 *Certification:* Otolaryngology
5333 McAuley Dr #2017, Ypsilanti, 734-434-3200

Hoff, Paul Theodore (13 mentions)
U of Michigan, 1993 *Certification:* Otolaryngology
5333 McAuley Dr Rm 2017, Ypsilanti, 734-434-3200

Jacobs, John Robert (5 mentions)
Northwestern U, 1975 *Certification:* Otolaryngology
43494 Woodward Ave #210, Bloomfield Hills, 248-335-9800
27177 Lahser Rd #203, Southfield, 248-357-4151

Kewson, Danny Tobias (8 mentions)
Wayne State U, 1999 *Certification:* Otolaryngology
2421 Monroe St #201, Dearborn, 313-562-4100
7300 Canton Center Rd, Canton, 734-454-2710

Leider, Jeffrey Scott (9 mentions)
U of Michigan, 1988 *Certification:* Otolaryngology
23700 Orchard Lake Rd #A, Farmington Hills, 248-615-4368
24001 Orchard Lake Rd #170, Farmington, 248-615-4368

Lopatin, Fred (6 mentions)
Michigan State U Coll of Osteopathic Med, 1991
15212 Michigan Ave, Dearborn, 313-582-8853

Madgy, David N. (5 mentions)
Des Moines U, 1984
27207 Lahser Rd, Southfield, 248-357-2060
37555 Garfield Rd #105, Clinton Township, 810-286-8377
3901 Beaubien St, Detroit, 313-745-9048
42700 Garfield Rd #230, Clinton Township, 586-532-3444

Megler, Daniel Djuraskovic (8 mentions)
FMS-Serbia, 1966 *Certification:* Otolaryngology
21000 E 12 Mile Rd #111, St Clair Shores, 586-779-7610
43750 Garfield Rd #101, Clinton Township, 586-263-7400

Nowak, Peggyann (8 mentions)
U of Toledo, 1982 *Certification:* Otolaryngology
6900 Orchard Lake Rd #314, West Bloomfield, 248-855-7530
4600 Investment Dr #360, Troy, 248-267-5004

Pinnock, Lascelles (5 mentions)
Wayne State U, 1976 *Certification:* Otolaryngology
14575 Southfield Rd, Allen Park, 313-381-8787

Scapini, David Alexander (15 mentions)
Wayne State U, 1986 *Certification:* Otolaryngology
543 N Main St #122, Rochester, 248-652-0044
11080 Hall Rd #A, Sterling Heights, 586-254-7200

Seidman, Michael David (10 mentions)
U of Michigan, 1986 *Certification:* Otolaryngology
6777 W Maple Rd, West Bloomfield, 248-661-7211

Succar, Bashar (6 mentions)
FMS-Egypt, 1971 *Certification:* Otolaryngology
6770 Dixie Hwy #306, Clarkston, 248-625-8450
44200 Woodward Ave #201, Pontiac, 248-334-9490

Waitzman, Ariel Andre (6 mentions)
FMS-Canada, 1992 *Certification:* Otolaryngology
15212 Michigan Ave, Dearborn, 313-582-8853

Weimert, Thomas Anthony (8 mentions)
U of Michigan, 1973 *Certification:* Otolaryngology
5333 McAuley Dr #2017 Reichert Health Bldg, Ypsilanti, 734-434-3200

Pain Medicine

Beer, Roderick Walter (4 mentions)
U of Michigan, 1978 *Certification:* Anesthesiology, Pain Medicine
5301 McAuley Dr #210, Ypsilanti, 734-712-1313

Chatas, John William (4 mentions)
U of Michigan, 1987 *Certification:* Anesthesiology, Pain Medicine
3520 Green Ct #100, Ann Arbor, 734-995-7246

Dobritt, Dennis W. (8 mentions)
Philadelphia Coll of Osteopathic Med, 1981
Certification: Anesthesiology, Pain Medicine
36650 5 Mile Rd #101, Livonia, 734-953-7110
30575 N Woodward S #200, Royal Oak, 248-435-4328
26850 Providence Pkwy #260, Novi, 248-735-8272

Huraibi, Hussein A., III (7 mentions)
Wayne State U, 1995 *Certification:* Anesthesiology, Pain Medicine
2040 Monroe St #206, Dearborn, 313-565-6782

Kerkar, Pramod Datta (5 mentions)
FMS-India, 1976 *Certification:* Anesthesiology
3990 John R St, Detroit, 313-745-8521
5456 15 Mile Rd #101, Sterling Heights, 313-745-8521

Richter, Kenneth John (4 mentions)
Michigan State U Coll of Osteopathic Med, 1978
Certification: Hospice and Palliative Medicine, Physical Medicine & Rehabilitation
44555 Woodward Ave #302, Pontiac, 248-858-3949

Sikorsky, Michael Hughes (4 mentions)
Michigan State U Coll of Osteopathic Med, 1997
Certification: Anesthesiology, Pain Medicine
3601 W 13 Mile Rd, Royal Oak, 248-828-5100

Washabaugh, Edward Peter (6 mentions)
U of Michigan, 1989 *Certification:* Anesthesiology, Pain Medicine
3520 Green Ct #100, Ann Arbor, 734-995-7246

Pathology

Abrams, Gerald David (3 mentions)
U of Michigan, 1955 *Certification:* Anatomic Pathology
1500 E Medical Center Dr, Ann Arbor, 734-936-6776

Bernacki, Edward G., Jr. (5 mentions)
Wayne State U, 1969 *Certification:* Anatomic Pathology & Clinical Pathology, Cytopathology
3601 W 13 Mile Rd, Royal Oak, 248-898-5000

Cotton, Jenny Pearl (3 mentions)
U of Kentucky, 1990 *Certification:* Anatomic Pathology & Clinical Pathology, Dermatopathology
5301 E Huron River Dr, Ann Arbor, 734-712-3165

Furlong, James Walter, Jr. (5 mentions)
U of Michigan, 1981 *Certification:* Anatomic Pathology & Clinical Pathology, Cytopathology
44405 Woodward Ave 2nd Fl, Pontiac, 248-858-3190

Gehani, Suresh Kumar (3 mentions)
FMS-India, 1970
Certification: Anatomic Pathology & Clinical Pathology
468 Cadieux Rd, Grosse Pointe, 313-343-1615

Goldstein, Neal Stewart (6 mentions)
U of Wisconsin, 1987
Certification: Anatomic Pathology & Clinical Pathology
3601 W 13 Mile Rd, Royal Oak, 248-551-5000

Herman, Gilbert Eugene (6 mentions)
Wayne State U, 1981
Certification: Anatomic Pathology & Clinical Pathology
28050 Grand River Ave, Farmington Hills, 248-471-8255

Hirsch, Samuel David (9 mentions)
St Louis U, 1978
Certification: Anatomic Pathology & Clinical Pathology
5301 E Huron River Dr, Ann Arbor, 734-712-3184

Klionsky, David Lee (5 mentions)
Northwestern U, 1981
Certification: Anatomic Pathology & Clinical Pathology
1101 W University Dr, Rochester Hills, 248-652-5000

Kolins, Mark Douglas (6 mentions)
Wayne State U, 1977 *Certification:* Anatomic Pathology &
  Clinical Pathology, Blood Banking, Hematology
3601 W 13 Mile Rd, Royal Oak, 248-898-5000
44201 Dequindre Rd, Troy, 248-964-4102

Kupsky, William Joseph (3 mentions)
Harvard U, 1978
Certification: Anatomic Pathology, Neuropathology
3990 John R St, Detroit, 313-745-8555

Mervak, Timothy (3 mentions)
Wayne State U, 1982 *Certification:* Anatomic Pathology &
  Clinical Pathology, Blood Banking/Transfusion Medicine
16001 W 9 Mile Rd, Southfield, 248-849-3270

Myers, Jeffrey L. (3 mentions)
Washington U, 1981 *Certification:* Anatomic Pathology
1500 E Medical Center Dr, Ann Arbor, 800-862-7284

Peeples, Thomas Carmichael (4 mentions)
FMS-France, 1979 *Certification:* Anatomic Pathology &
  Clinical Pathology, Cytopathology, Hematology
44405 Woodward Ave, Pontiac, 248-858-3190
15855 19 Mile Rd, Clinton Township, 586-263-2300

Sakr, Wael (4 mentions)
FMS-Syria, 1980 *Certification:* Anatomic Pathology
3990 John R St, Detroit, 313-745-2526

Schaldenbrand, John David (3 mentions)
Wayne State U, 1980 *Certification:* Anatomic Pathology &
  Clinical Pathology, Cytopathology, Hematology
5301 E Huron River Dr, Ypsilanti, 734-712-5989

Schaldenbrand, Michael F. (5 mentions)
Wayne State U, 1978 *Certification:* Anatomic Pathology &
  Clinical Pathology, Hematology
18101 Oakwood Blvd, Dearborn, 313-593-7965

Silveira, Scott Goodwin (3 mentions)
U of Kansas, 1991
Certification: Anatomic Pathology & Clinical Pathology
18101 Oakwood Blvd, Dearborn, 313-593-7965

Watts, John Collins (4 mentions)
Case Western Reserve U, 1971
Certification: Anatomic Pathology & Clinical Pathology
3601 W 13 Mile Rd, Royal Oak, 248-898-9060

Zarbo, Richard John (5 mentions)
U of Connecticut, 1981
Certification: Anatomic Pathology & Clinical Pathology
2799 W Grand Blvd, Detroit, 313-916-2326

Pediatrics *(see note on page 9)*

Anderberg, Roger Brian (3 mentions)
Baylor U, 1972 *Certification:* Pediatrics
3100 E Eisenhower Pkwy #100, Ann Arbor, 734-971-9344

Barone, Charles James (3 mentions)
George Washington U, 1977 *Certification:* Pediatrics
2799 W Grand Blvd, Detroit, 313-916-2657
1 Ford Pl, Detroit, 313-874-9591

Burrows, Heather Lee (3 mentions)
U of Michigan, 2000 *Certification:* Pediatrics
4260 Plymouth Rd, Ann Arbor, 734-647-5680

Chung, William J. (3 mentions)
FMS-South Korea, 1968 *Certification:* Pediatrics
930 W Avon Rd #17, Rochester Hills, 248-651-5454

Coleman, Kimberlee Recchia (3 mentions)
U of Michigan, 1988 *Certification:* Pediatrics
43097 Woodward Ave #201, Bloomfield Hills, 248-454-9000

Dumont, Allen Dale (5 mentions)
U of Michigan, 1966 *Certification:* Pediatrics
911 Brown St, Ann Arbor, 734-769-3702

Eastman, Jay Ward (3 mentions)
Wayne State U, 1972 *Certification:* Pediatrics
2055 E 14 Mile Rd #120, Birmingham, 248-645-1740

Faber, Seth Adam (3 mentions)
Wayne State U, 1999 *Certification:* Pediatrics
6900 Orchard Lake Rd #206, West Bloomfield, 248-855-7510

Green-Lee, Carmen Patrice (3 mentions)
U of Michigan, 1990 *Certification:* Pediatrics
3100 E Eisenhower Pkwy #100, Ann Arbor, 734-971-9344

Guthikonda, Rao N. (3 mentions)
Certification: Pediatrics
30260 Cherry Hill Rd #A, Garden City, 734-466-9000

Levinson, Martin P. (6 mentions)
Wayne State U, 1977 *Certification:* Pediatrics
31600 Telegraph Rd #100, Bingham Farms, 248-642-5437

Levy, Robert Stuart (3 mentions)
U of Michigan, 1978 *Certification:* Pediatrics
2845 Monroe St, Dearborn, 313-730-0070

Mali, Vikram Vishwanath (5 mentions)
Michigan State U, 1996 *Certification:* Pediatrics
44199 Dequindre Rd, Troy, 248-828-3888

O'Shea, Mary Doherty (4 mentions)
U of Michigan, 1990 *Certification:* Pediatrics
31815 Southfield Rd #32, Beverly Hills, 248-644-1221
5555 Metropolitan Pkwy #300, Sterling Heights, 586-268-7110
32100 Telegraph Rd #110, Franklin, 248-644-1221

Schnur, Thomas James (9 mentions)
Wayne State U, 1977 *Certification:* Pediatrics
1349 S Rochester Rd #215, Rochester Hills, 248-652-3300

Soler, Mirta Travieso (4 mentions)
FMS-Dominican Republic, 1982 *Certification:* Pediatrics
23133 Orchard Lake Rd #100, Farmington, 248-477-0100

Soskolne, Errol Israel (6 mentions)
FMS-South Africa, 1973 *Certification:* Pediatrics
5301 McAuley Dr, Ypsilanti, 734-712-3325

Swartz, Beth Robinson (3 mentions)
Boston U, 1985 *Certification:* Pediatrics
6777 W Maple Rd, West Bloomfield, 248-661-6420

Weinberg, Neal Roger (5 mentions)
Wayne State U, 1976 *Certification:* Pediatrics
4936 W Clark Rd #101, Ypsilanti, 734-434-3000

Williams, Michael James (3 mentions)
Wayne State U, 1991 *Certification:* Internal Medicine, Pediatrics
1701 South Blvd E #250, Rochester Hills, 248-293-1002

Wozniak, Maria M. (5 mentions)
FMS-Poland, 1982 *Certification:* Pediatrics
2055 E 14 Mile Rd #120, Birmingham, 248-645-1740

Youn, Amy Elizabeth (3 mentions)
Michigan State U, 1999 *Certification:* Pediatrics
44199 Dequindre Rd, Troy, 248-828-3888

Plastic Surgery

Beil, Richard Jacob, Jr. (13 mentions)
Ohio State U, 1986 *Certification:* Plastic Surgery
5333 McAuley Dr #R-501, Ypsilanti, 734-712-2323

Busuito, Michael Joseph (11 mentions)
Wayne State U, 1981 *Certification:* Plastic Surgery
1080 Kirts Blvd #700, Troy, 248-362-2300

Darian, Vigen (6 mentions)
U of Michigan, 1978
Certification: Otolaryngology, Plastic Surgery, Surgery of the Hand
39450 12 Mile Rd, Novi, 248-661-6478

Gellis, Michael Barry (7 mentions)
Wayne State U, 1971 *Certification:* Plastic Surgery
3601 W 13 Mile Rd, Royal Oak, 248-642-4846
36800 Woodward Ave #109, Bloomfield Township, 248-642-4846

Hajjar, Raymond Thomas, Jr. (7 mentions)
Midwestern U Chicago Coll of Osteopathic Med, 1989
31100 Telegraph Rd #280, Bingham Farms, 248-208-8844

Hing, David Ng (7 mentions)
U of Michigan, 1975
Certification: Plastic Surgery, Surgery of the Hand
5333 McAuley Dr #R-5001, Ypsilanti, 734-712-2323

Izenberg, Paul Herbert (11 mentions)
Wake Forest U, 1969 *Certification:* Plastic Surgery
5333 McAuley Dr #R-5001, Ypsilanti, 734-712-2323

Jackson, Ian Thomas (8 mentions)
FMS-United Kingdom, 1959 *Certification:* Plastic Surgery
16001 W 9 Mile Rd, Southfield, 248-849-5800

Mucci, Samuel John (8 mentions)
Temple U, 1988 *Certification:* Plastic Surgery, Surgery
2585 Crooks Rd, Troy, 248-283-1115

Shaheen, Kenneth William (6 mentions)
Wayne State U, 1983 *Certification:* Plastic Surgery, Surgery
2585 Crooks Rd, Troy, 248-283-1110

Sherbert, Daniel Dennis (10 mentions)
Michigan State U, 1987 *Certification:* Plastic Surgery
5807 W Maple Rd #177, West Bloomfield, 248-865-6400

Vasileff, William James (8 mentions)
U of Michigan, 1974 *Certification:* Otolaryngology, Plastic Surgery
525 Southfield Rd, Birmingham, 248-644-0670

Vyas, Satish Chandra (7 mentions)
FMS-India, 1968 *Certification:* Plastic Surgery
22190 Garrison St #301, Dearborn, 313-277-0500

Psychiatry

Browne, Malachy Francis P. (4 mentions)
FMS-Ireland, 1974 *Certification:* Psychiatry
43171 Dalcoma Dr #5, Clinton Township, 586-226-0682

Coffey, Charles Edward (7 mentions)
Duke U, 1979 *Certification:* Neurology, Psychiatry
1 Ford Pl, Detroit, 313-874-6887

Connolly, Brian Andrew (5 mentions)
FMS-Ireland, 1969 *Certification:* Psychiatry
189 Townsend St #300, Birmingham, 248-642-3737

Dean, Randy (4 mentions)
Wayne State U, 1986 *Certification:* Child & Adolescent
  Psychiatry, Forensic Psychiatry, Psychiatry
E-4111 Andover Rd #220, Bloomfield Hills, 248-290-5400

Guerrero, Raul Jaime (4 mentions)
FMS-Mexico, 1972 *Certification:* Psychiatry
131 Kercheval Ave #390, Grosse Pointe Farms, 313-885-6400

Gurevich, David (5 mentions)
FMS-Israel, 1968
32270 Telegraph Rd #240, Bingham Farms, 248-593-1717

Jackson, Richard Steven (4 mentions)
Wayne State U, 1986 *Certification:* Child & Adolescent
  Psychiatry, Forensic Psychiatry, Psychiatry
E-4111 Andover Rd #220, Bloomfield, 248-290-5400

Kezlarian, Jeffrey Avedis (5 mentions)
Wayne State U, 1979 *Certification:* Psychiatry
3290 W Big Beaver Rd #509, Troy, 248-290-2220

Kole, Bernard Elliott (3 mentions)
Wayne State U, 1985 *Certification:* Forensic Psychiatry,
  Geriatric Psychiatry, Psychiatry, Psychosomatic Medicine
6016 W Maple Rd #700, West Bloomfield, 248-626-1700

Maclean, Lisa Marie (5 mentions)
Michigan State U, 1993 *Certification:* Psychiatry
1 Ford Pl, Detroit, 800-653-6568

Mehta, Haresh S. (7 mentions)
FMS-India, 1975
Certification: Child Psychiatry, Geriatric Psychiatry, Psychiatry
25869 Kelly Rd #A, Roseville, 586-773-6020

Newell, Audrey Riker (3 mentions)
Harvard U, 1986 *Certification:* Child & Adolescent
  Psychiatry, Psychiatry, Psychosomatic Medicine
201 3rd St #300, Belleville, 734-467-2482
2001 Merriman Rd, Westland, 734-727-1000
33155 Annapolis St, Wayne, 734-467-2482

Patel, Hiten Chandrakant (4 mentions)
FMS-India, 1979 *Certification:* Geriatric Psychiatry, Psychiatry
40000 Grand River Ave #306, Novi, 248-426-9900

Piccinini, Robert G. (3 mentions)
Michigan State U Coll of Osteopathic Med, 1992
43157 Schoenherr Rd, Sterling Heights, 586-997-9619

Reddy, Juvvala M. (4 mentions)
FMS-India, 1972 *Certification:* Psychiatry
950 W Avon Rd #3, Rochester Hills, 248-652-3310

Sackeyfio, Alexander H. (3 mentions)
FMS-United Kingdom, 1972 *Certification:* Psychiatry
23800 Orchard Lake Rd #104, Farmington Hills, 248-471-0785

Tancer, Manuel Ellis (3 mentions)
U of Arizona, 1984 *Certification:* Psychiatry
4201 Saint Antoine St, Detroit, 888-362-7792
2751 E Jefferson, Detroit, 313-577-1396

Trunsky, Ronald Edwin (4 mentions)
U of Michigan, 1956 *Certification:* Psychiatry
28800 Orchard Lake Rd #250, Farmington Hills, 248-932-2500

Vaziri, Habib (3 mentions)
FMS-Iran, 1960 *Certification:* Psychiatry
44555 Woodward Ave #405, Pontiac, 248-335-4010

Zelnik, Thomas Charles (5 mentions)
U of Michigan, 1978 *Certification:* Psychiatry
2008 Hogback Rd #7, Ann Arbor, 734-712-3456

Pulmonary Disease

Ahmad, Fazal (4 mentions)
FMS-Pakistan, 1968
Certification: Internal Medicine, Pulmonary Disease
44555 Woodward Ave #402, Pontiac, 248-335-1110

Allen, Samuel Abraham (5 mentions)
Midwestern U Chicago Coll of Osteopathic Med, 1996
Certification: Critical Care Medicine, Internal Medicine,
  Pulmonary Disease
44199 Dequindre Rd #618, Troy, 248-879-5620

Belen, Jack Elliott (5 mentions)
Midwestern U Chicago Coll of Osteopathic Med, 1972
31410 Northwestern Hwy #G, Farmington Hills, 248-538-1350
1 William Carls Dr, Commerce Township, 248-937-3395

Dunn, Marc Mitchell (15 mentions)
U of Michigan, 1977
Certification: Internal Medicine, Pulmonary Disease
26657 Woodward Ave #202, Huntington Woods, 248-548-2114

Eichenhorn, Michael Serle (7 mentions)
U of Michigan, 1975 *Certification:* Critical Care Medicine,
  Internal Medicine, Pulmonary Disease
2799 W Grand Blvd, Detroit, 313-916-2436

Galens, Stephen Andrew (6 mentions)
U of Michigan, 1990 *Certification:* Critical Care Medicine,
  Internal Medicine, Pulmonary Disease
44199 Dequindre Rd #618, Troy, 248-879-5620

Go, Robert O. (5 mentions)
Certification: Critical Care Medicine, Internal Medicine,
  Pulmonary Disease
1083 Suncrest Dr #B, LaPeer, 810-667-3111
950 W Avon Rd #A-2, Rochester Hills, 248-651-6430

Greenberger, Marc Joel (4 mentions)
U of Michigan, 1989
Certification: Pulmonary Disease, Sleep Medicine
26657 Woodward Ave #202, Huntington Woods, 248-548-2114

Harkaway, Paul Stephen (9 mentions)
Wayne State U, 1980 *Certification:* Critical Care Medicine,
  Internal Medicine, Pulmonary Disease
5333 McAuley Dr #3111, Ypsilanti, 734-712-7688

Jamal, Maan A. (4 mentions)
FMS-Syria, 1987
Certification: Internal Medicine, Pulmonary Disease
30117 Schoener Rd #100-D, Warren, 586-751-8844

Kaplan, Philip (6 mentions)
A T Still U, 1989
39650 Orchard Hill Pl #100, Novi, 248-449-7010

Martinez, Fernando Jose (4 mentions)
U of Florida, 1983 *Certification:* Critical Care Medicine,
  Internal Medicine, Pulmonary Disease
1500 E Medical Center Dr Taubman Ctr #3916, Ann Arbor,
  734-936-5201

O'Neill, Alfonso Victor (12 mentions)
Wayne State U, 1980
Certification: Internal Medicine, Pulmonary Disease
25631 Little Mack Dr #202, St Clair Shores, 586-774-3090

Patton, William Fulmer (12 mentions)
Wayne State U, 1976 *Certification:* Critical Care Medicine,
  Internal Medicine, Pulmonary Disease
5333 McAuley Dr #3111, Ypsilanti, 734-712-7688

Pensler, Mark Irwin (6 mentions)
U of Michigan, 1974 *Certification:* Critical Care Medicine,
  Internal Medicine, Pulmonary Disease, Sleep Medicine
2333 Biddle Ave, Wyandotte, 734-324-3528

Ravi Krishnan, Korembeth (11 mentions)
FMS-India, 1969 *Certification:* Critical Care Medicine,
  Internal Medicine, Pulmonary Disease
3535 W 13 Mile Rd #507, Royal Oak, 248-551-0497

Reagle, Robert Raymond (4 mentions)
Philadelphia Coll of Osteopathic Med, 1979
Certification: Internal Medicine, Pulmonary Disease
441 S Livernois Rd #180, Rochester Hills, 248-652-2708

Sak, Daniel James (5 mentions)
Michigan State U Coll of Osteopathic Med, 1978
44555 Woodward Ave #402, Pontiac, 248-335-1110

Seidman, Joel Cary (8 mentions)
U of Michigan, 1973
Certification: Internal Medicine, Pulmonary Disease
3535 W 13 Mile Rd #507, Royal Oak, 248-551-0497

Simoff, Michael James (7 mentions)
Wayne State U, 1990 *Certification:* Critical Care Medicine,
  Internal Medicine, Pulmonary Disease
2799 W Grand Blvd, Detroit, 313-916-2421

Stevens, Keith Michael (9 mentions)
Michigan State U Coll of Osteopathic Med, 1985
44199 Dequindre Rd #618, Troy, 248-879-5620

Ventimiglia, William Anthony (6 mentions)
St Louis U, 1983 *Certification:* Critical Care Medicine,
  Internal Medicine, Pulmonary Disease
21000 E 12 Mile Rd #100, St Clair Shores, 586-772-5550

Victor, Lyle Dorn (6 mentions)
Mount Sinai Sch of Med, 1971
Certification: Internal Medicine, Pulmonary Disease
18101 Oakwood Blvd, Dearborn, 313-593-8844

Radiology—Diagnostic

Bloom, David Adam (3 mentions)
Certification: Diagnostic Radiology, Pediatric Radiology
3601 W 13 Mile Rd, Royal Oak, 248-898-1961

Brown, Manuel Lawrence (3 mentions)
Wayne State U, 1972
Certification: Diagnostic Radiology, Nuclear Medicine
2799 W Grand Blvd, Detroit, 313-916-3344

Dunnick, Nicholas Reed (3 mentions)
Cornell U, 1969 *Certification:* Diagnostic Radiology
1500 E Medical Center Dr, Ann Arbor, 734-998-9664

Ferguson, Eric Clifton (4 mentions)
U of Michigan, 1997 *Certification:* Diagnostic Radiology
5301 E Huron River Dr, Ypsilanti, 734-712-3456
5333 Mcauley Dr, Ypsilanti, 734-712-8350
5301 Mcauley Dr, Ypsilanti, 734-434-9770

Garver, Kimberly Ann (3 mentions)
U of Michigan, 1989 *Certification:* Diagnostic Radiology
5301 E Huron River Dr, Ann Arbor, 734-712-3052

Gibson, Donald P. (3 mentions)
Certification: Diagnostic Radiology, Pediatric Radiology
3601 W 13 Mile Rd, Royal Oak, 248-898-6064

Gonda, Roger Linwood, Sr. (4 mentions)
U of Michigan, 1960 *Certification:* Radiology
6245 Inkster Rd, Garden City, 734-458-3412
27285 W Warren St, Dearborn Heights, 313-563-0650
23100 Providence Dr#420, Southfield, 248-569-4353
16001 W Nine Mile Rd, Southfield, 248-849-3043

Gross, Barry Howard (4 mentions)
U of Michigan, 1977 *Certification:* Diagnostic Radiology
1500 E Medical Center Dr, Ann Arbor, 734-936-4358

Kellam, David A. (3 mentions)
Philadelphia Coll of Osteopathic Med, 1956
355 Barclay Cir, Rochester Hills, 248-299-8000
50 N Perry St, Pontiac, 248-338-5604

Maldonado, Victor (4 mentions)
FMS-Guatemala, 1976
Certification: Diagnostic Radiology, Pediatric Radiology
44405 Woodward Ave #205, Bloomfield Hills, 248-858-3266
22101 Moross Rd, Detroit, 800-801-8882

Mezwa, Duane Gary (4 mentions)
Wayne State U, 1979 *Certification:* Diagnostic Radiology
3601 W 13 Mile Rd, Royal Oak, 248-828-5100
100 E Big Beaver Rd, Troy, 248-457-7663

Patel, Sureshchandra C. (6 mentions)
FMS-India, 1969 *Certification:* Neuroradiology, Radiology
2799 W Grand Blvd, Detroit, 313-916-1374

Roumanis, Sophia Millis (4 mentions)
U of Michigan, 1979 *Certification:* Diagnostic Radiology
840 Oakwood Blvd, Dearborn, 313-359-7650

Sanders, William Paul (3 mentions)
U of Michigan, 1981
Certification: Diagnostic Radiology, Neuroradiology
2799 W Grand Blvd, Detroit, 313-916-2600

Scharer, Katherine Ann (3 mentions)
Wayne State U, 1986 *Certification:* Diagnostic Radiology
1101 W University Dr, Rochester, 248-652-5000

Segel, Mark Calvin (3 mentions)
U of Texas-Dallas, 1981 *Certification:* Diagnostic Radiology
15855 19 Mile Rd, Clinton Township, 586-263-2400

Varde, Kanak Arun (3 mentions)
FMS-India, 1972 *Certification:* Diagnostic Radiology
1101 W University Dr, Rochester Hills, 248-652-5325

Vollman, Dennis Paul (3 mentions)
Michigan State U Coll of Osteopathic Med, 1979
15300 Trenton Rd, Southgate, 248-642-6449

Wang, Ay-Ming (4 mentions)
FMS-Taiwan, 1966
Certification: Diagnostic Radiology, Neuroradiology
3601 W 13 Mile Rd, Royal Oak, 248-551-1005

Yates, David Scott (3 mentions)
Wayne State U, 1979 *Certification:* Diagnostic Radiology
18101 Oakwood Blvd, Dearborn, 313-593-7301

Radiology—Therapeutic

Arterbery, Elayne (3 mentions)
U of Michigan, 1988 *Certification:* Radiation Oncology
1101 W University Dr, Rochester Hills, 248-650-4580

Chuba, Paul Joseph (5 mentions)
Wayne State U, 1992 *Certification:* Radiation Oncology
11800 E 12 Mile Rd, Warren, 586-573-5186
22101 Moross Rd, Grosse Pointe, 313-343-4000

McLaughlin, Patrick William (3 mentions)
Wayne State U, 1981 *Certification:* Internal Medicine,
Medical Oncology, Radiation Oncology
22301 Foster Winter Dr, Southfield, 248-849-3321
47601 W Grand River, Novi, 248-449-4300

Movsas, Benjamin (3 mentions)
Washington U, 1990 *Certification:* Radiation Oncology
2799 W Grand Blvd, Detroit, 313-916-1021

Sanders, William Paul (6 mentions)
U of Michigan, 1981
Certification: Diagnostic Radiology, Neuroradiology
2799 W Grand Blvd, Detroit, 313-916-2600

Sarosi, Michael George (3 mentions)
U of Michigan, 1986 *Certification:* Diagnostic Radiology,
Vascular & Interventional Radiology
5333 McAuley Dr #6016, Ypsilanti, 734-434-9770

Thompson, Brent Craig (4 mentions)
Washington U, 1989 *Certification:* Diagnostic Radiology,
Neuroradiology, Vascular & Interventional Radiology
18101 Oakwood BLvd, Dearborn, 313-593-7292

Vicini, Frank Andrea (5 mentions)
Wayne State U, 1985 *Certification:* Radiation Oncology
3601 W 13 Mile Rd, Royal Oak, 248-551-1219

Rehabilitation

Alpiner, Neal Marc (3 mentions)
Wayne State U, 1988
Certification: Pediatrics, Physical Medicine & Rehabilitation
43555 Dalcoma Dr #4, Clinton Township, 586-228-2882
4949 Coolidge Hwy, Royal Oak, 586-228-2882

Arbit, Steven Mark (3 mentions)
Wayne State U, 1988
Certification: Physical Medicine & Rehabilitation
8391 Commerce Rd #107, Commerce Township, 248-360-8660
10 W Square Lake Rd #110, Bloomfield Hills, 248-335-9099
1135 W University Dr #425, Rochester, 248-650-5861

Bauer, Raymond Thomas (4 mentions)
Wayne State U, 1993
Certification: Physical Medicine & Rehabilitation
25311 Little Mack Ave #B, St Clair Shores, 586-498-2400

Chodoroff, Gary (8 mentions)
Wayne State U, 1981
Certification: Physical Medicine & Rehabilitation
30100 Telegraph Rd #177, Bingham Farms, 248-647-1470

Colwell, Miles Owen, Jr. (3 mentions)
Texas Tech U, 1986
Certification: Physical Medicine & Rehabilitation
325 E Eisenhower Pkwy #100, Ann Arbor, 734-998-6644

Dabrowski, Edward Ralph (3 mentions)
Wayne State U, 1980
Certification: Physical Medicine & Rehabilitation
28595 Orchard Lake Rd #200, Farmington Hills, 313-993-2757
3901 Beaubien St, Detroit, 313-745-5481

Ellenberg, Maury Ruben (4 mentions)
Wayne State U, 1973 *Certification:* Internal Medicine, Pain
Medicine, Physical Medicine & Rehabilitation
28455 Haggerty Rd #200, Novi, 248-893-3200

Grant, Lisa B. (3 mentions)
Wayne State U, 1993 *Certification:* Physical Medicine &
Rehabilitation, Spinal Cord Injury Medicine
3535 W 13 Mile Rd #437, Royal Oak, 248-288-2210

Gross, Steven (5 mentions)
Michigan State U Coll of Osteopathic Med, 1983
Certification: Physical Medicine & Rehabilitation
5333 McAuley Dr, Ypsilanti, 734-712-0050

Harwood, Steven Charles (6 mentions)
U of Michigan, 1984
Certification: Physical Medicine & Rehabilitation
5333 McAuley Dr, Ypsilanti, 734-712-0050

Kovan, Eric Allen (6 mentions)
Michigan State U Coll of Osteopathic Med, 1994
Certification: Physical Medicine & Rehabilitation
28455 Haggerty Rd #200, Novi, 248-893-3200

Leonard, James Arthur (3 mentions)
U of Michigan, 1972
Certification: Physical Medicine & Rehabilitation
325 E Eisenhower Pkwy, Ann Arbor, 734-647-6594
2850 S Industrial Hwy #400, Ann Arbor, 734-647-6594

Long, Randi Jo (4 mentions)
U of Tennessee, 1990
Certification: Physical Medicine & Rehabilitation
1777 Axtell Dr #107, Troy, 248-649-0450

Maltese, John Thomas, Jr. (5 mentions)
U of Toledo, 1986
Certification: Physical Medicine & Rehabilitation
3535 W 13 Mile Rd #437, Royal Oak, 248-288-2210

Mishack, Krisztina (3 mentions)
FMS-Syria, 1988
Certification: Physical Medicine & Rehabilitation
1135 W University Dr #425, Rochester Hills, 248-650-5861

Papalekas, Pano Lee (4 mentions)
U of Toledo, 1987
Certification: Physical Medicine & Rehabilitation
46591 Romeo Plank Rd #100, Macomb, 586-226-6070
25311 Little Mack Ave #B, St Clair Shores, 586-498-2400

Perlman, Owen Zachary (4 mentions)
U of Michigan, 1978
Certification: Physical Medicine & Rehabilitation
5333 McAuley Dr, Ypsilanti, 734-712-0050

Richter, Kenneth John (6 mentions)
Michigan State U Coll of Osteopathic Med, 1978
Certification: Hospice and Palliative Medicine, Physical
Medicine & Rehabilitation
44555 Woodward Ave #302, Pontiac, 248-858-3949

Roth, Brian Michael (7 mentions)
Wayne State U, 1990
Certification: Physical Medicine & Rehabilitation
1135 W University Dr #425, Rochester Hills, 248-650-5861
10 W Square Lake Rd #110, Bloomfield Hills, 248-335-9099

Sesi, Timothy Peter (4 mentions)
Wayne State U, 1989
Certification: Physical Medicine & Rehabilitation
44555 Woodward Ave #302, Pontiac, 248-858-3949

Sessa, Gino Renato (6 mentions)
Wayne State U, 1994 *Certification:* Physical Medicine &
Rehabilitation, Spinal Cord Injury Medicine
3535 W 13 Mile Rd #437, Royal Oak, 248-288-2210

Shapiro, Paul (6 mentions)
Michigan State U, 1978
Certification: Physical Medicine & Rehabilitation
5333 McAuley Dr #5106, Ypsilanti, 734-712-0050

Spires, Mary Catherine (4 mentions)
Michigan State U, 1988 *Certification:* Physical Medicine &
Rehabilitation, Spinal Cord Injury Medicine
2850 S Industrial Hwy #400, Ann Arbor, 734-936-7185
325 E Eisenhower Pkwy #100, Ann Arbor, 734-936-7185

Steinberg, David Paul (6 mentions)
U of Chicago, 1991
Certification: Pain Medicine, Physical Medicine & Rehabilitation
5333 McAuley Dr #5106, Ypsilanti, 734-434-6660

Tamler, Martin Scott (5 mentions)
Indiana U, 1988
Certification: Physical Medicine & Rehabilitation
3535 W 13 Mile Rd #437, Royal Oak, 248-288-2210

Taylor, Ronald Steven (12 mentions)
Wayne State U, 1973 *Certification:* Physical Medicine &
Rehabilitation
3535 W 13 Mile Rd #437, Royal Oak, 248-288-2210

Wilson, Stephen (4 mentions)
Wayne State U, 1993
Certification: Pain Medicine, Physical Medicine & Rehabilitation
24345 Harper Ave, St Clair Shores, 586-563-3300

Yoon, In Kwang (5 mentions)
FMS-South Korea, 1968
Certification: Physical Medicine & Rehabilitation
17000 Hubbard Dr #800, Dearborn, 313-240-7595

Rheumatology

Bateman, Judith Lee (9 mentions)
Stony Brook U, 1988
Certification: Internal Medicine, Rheumatology
32270 Telegraph Rd #120, Bingham Farms, 248-646-1965

Brennan, Timothy Andrew (7 mentions)
Wayne State U, 1976 *Certification:* Internal Medicine
24100 Little Mack Ave, St Clair Shores, 586-777-7577
29200 Harper Ave, St Clair Shores, 586-777-7577

Garber, Martin E. (6 mentions)
Des Moines U, 1986
Certification: Internal Medicine, Rheumatology
2004 Hogback Rd, Ann Arbor, 734-477-0211

McCune, William Joseph (9 mentions)
U of Cincinnati, 1975
Certification: Internal Medicine, Rheumatology
1500 E Medical Center Dr, Ann Arbor, 734-936-4000

Menerey, Kathleen Ann (10 mentions)
U of Michigan, 1980
Certification: Internal Medicine, Rheumatology
2004 Hogback Rd #1, Ann Arbor, 734-477-0211

Pevzner, Martin Mitchell (26 mentions)
Wayne State U, 1970
Certification: Internal Medicine, Rheumatology
7192 N Main St, Clarkston, 810-646-1965
32270 Telegraph Rd #120, Bingham Farms, 248-646-1965

Santos, Delfin (9 mentions)
FMS-Chile, 1985 *Certification:* Internal Medicine, Rheumatology
135 Barclay Cir #100, Rochester, 248-852-2277

Silverman, Larry Jay (11 mentions)
Wayne State U, 1982
Certification: Internal Medicine, Rheumatology
28625 Northwestern Hwy #223, Southfield, 248-350-3190

Skender, Joseph George (8 mentions)
Wayne State U, 1985
Certification: Internal Medicine, Rheumatology
32270 Telegraph Rd #120, Bingham Farms, 248-646-1965

Tower, John (8 mentions)
Michigan State U Coll of Osteopathic Med, 1985
1701 South Blvd E #140, Rochester Hills, 248-853-0803

Thoracic Surgery

Camero, Luis Gabriel (11 mentions)
FMS-Colombia, 1969 *Certification:* Thoracic Surgery
25810 Kelly Rd #1, Roseville, 810-777-8440

Chmielewski, Gary William (30 mentions)
Loyola U Chicago, 1988 *Certification:* Surgery, Thoracic Surgery
3577 W 13 Mile Rd #301, Royal Oak, 248-551-0669

Hilu, John Massoud (8 mentions)
Wayne State U, 1986 *Certification:* Surgery, Thoracic Surgery
18181 Oakwood Blvd #102, Dearborn, 313-436-2422

Orringer, Mark Burton (16 mentions)
U of Pittsburgh, 1967 *Certification:* Surgery, Thoracic Surgery
1500 E Medical Center Dr Taubman Ctr #2120, Ann Arbor, 734-936-4973

Sullivan, Vita Veronika (18 mentions)
U of Chicago, 1997 *Certification:* Surgery, Thoracic Surgery
5325 Elliott Dr #102, Ypsilanti, 734-712-5500

Welsh, Robert James (30 mentions)
Wayne State U, 1984
Certification: Surgery, Surgical Critical Care, Thoracic Surgery
3577 W 13 Mile Rd #301, Royal Oak, 248-551-0669

Urology

Ahmed, Muzammil (8 mentions)
U of Michigan, 1993 *Certification:* Urology
4700 Greenfield Rd, Dearborn, 313-945-6100

Badalament, Robert Anthony (10 mentions)
Emory U, 1980 *Certification:* Urology
1135 W University Dr #420, Rochester Hills, 248-650-4699

Cotant, Michael Gerard (5 mentions)
Wayne State U, 1987 *Certification:* Urology
4405 Woodward Ave #201, Pontiac, 248-322-6103
20952 E 12 Mile Rd #200, St Clair Shores, 586-771-4820

Diokno, Ananias Cornejo (7 mentions)
FMS-Philippines, 1965 *Certification:* Urology
3535 W 13 Mile Rd #407, Royal Oak, 248-551-0640

Gudziak, Marko Roman (7 mentions)
New York U, 1987 *Certification:* Urology
130 Town Center Blvd #101, Troy, 248-740-0670
44405 Woodward Ave, Pontiac, 248-322-6103

Guz, Brian Vaughn (5 mentions)
U of Michigan, 1985 *Certification:* Urology
20952 E 12 Mile Rd #200, St Clair Shores, 586-771-4820

Kass, Evan J. (8 mentions)
SUNY-Downstate Med Coll, 1968 *Certification:* Urology
2221 Livernois Rd #103, Troy, 248-519-0305

Kernen, Kenneth Moderato (5 mentions)
Wayne State U, 1993 *Certification:* Urology
130 Town Center Blvd #101, Troy, 248-740-0670
6900 Orchard Lake Rd, Bloomfield, 248-539-9036

Kleer, Eduardo (5 mentions)
Wayne State U, 1989 *Certification:* Urology
5333 McAuley Dr #3001, Ypsilanti, 734-712-8100
1600 S Canton Center Rd #350, Canton, 734-712-8100
7575 Grand River Ave #202, Brighton, 734-712-8100

Kumar, Anil B. (6 mentions)
FMS-India, 1976 *Certification:* Urology
2450 Walton Blvd, Rochester Hills, 248-650-0096
4000 Highland Rd #109, Waterford, 248-682-9480

Lutz, Michael David (6 mentions)
Rosalind Franklin U, 1981 *Certification:* Urology
29201 Telegraph Rd #460, Southfield, 248-353-3060

McHugh, Timothy Alan (5 mentions)
U of Pittsburgh, 1971 *Certification:* Urology
5333 McAuley Dr #3001, Ypsilanti, 734-712-8100

Menon, Mani (8 mentions)
FMS-India, 1969 *Certification:* Urology
2799 W Grand Blvd, Detroit, 313-916-2062

Peabody, James Ogden (7 mentions)
U of Michigan, 1985 *Certification:* Urology
2799 W Grand Blvd, Detroit, 313-916-2062

Peters, Kenneth Michael (5 mentions)
Case Western Reserve U, 1991 *Certification:* Urology
31157 Woodward Ave, Birmingham, 248-336-0123

Relle, James David (7 mentions)
FMS-Canada, 1988 *Certification:* Urology
29201 Telegraph Rd #460, Southfield, 248-353-3060

Sarle, Richard Charles (5 mentions)
U of Vermont, 1999 *Certification:* Urology
18100 Oakwood Blvd #315, Dearborn, 313-271-0066

Schervish, Edward William (5 mentions)
Loyola U Chicago, 1984 *Certification:* Urology
11051 Hall Rd #200, Utica, 586-771-4820
20952 E 12 Mile Rd #200, St Clair Shores, 586-771-4820
44199 Dequindre Rd #615, Troy, 248-828-8066
6900 Orchard Lake Rd #211, West Bloomfield, 248-539-9036
22201 Moross Rd #275, Detroit, 313-886-4910
4707 St Antoine St, Detroit, 313-745-6957
28800 Ryan Rd #220, Warren, 248-737-1970

Schock, Jeffrey (6 mentions)
New Jersey Sch of Osteopathic Med, 1994
17405 Hall Rd, Macomb, 734-261-7401
14800 Farmington Rd #103, Livonia, 734-261-7401
25500 Meadow Brook Rd #225, Novi, 248-426-1300
13251 E 10 Mile Rd #200, Warren, 586-758-0123

Sirls, Larry T., II (6 mentions)
U of Michigan, 1987 *Certification:* Urology
31157 Woodward Ave, Royal Oak, 248-336-0123

Smith, James Bernard (5 mentions)
Case Western Reserve U, 1977 *Certification:* Urology
22250 Providence Dr #203, Southfield, 248-569-4897

Solomon, Michael Hugh (34 mentions)
FMS-South Africa, 1970 *Certification:* Urology
533 McCauley Dr #3001, Ypsilanti, 734-712-8100
9900 W Ann Arbor Trail #201, Plymouth, 734-712-8100
7575 Grand River Rd #202, Brighton, 734-712-8100

Spencer, William Flanders (5 mentions)
U of Michigan, 1983 *Certification:* Urology
31157 Woodward Ave, Royal Oak, 248-336-0123

Telang, Dinesh John (5 mentions)
U of Michigan, 1988 *Certification:* Urology
18325 E 10 Mile Rd #200, Roseville, 586-773-6300

Torriglia, Jorge Rene (7 mentions)
FMS-Argentina, 1971 *Certification:* Urology
18100 Oakwood Blvd #315, Dearborn, 313-271-0066

Winfield, Raymond Joseph, Jr. (6 mentions)
U Central del Caribe, 1981 *Certification:* Urology
22250 Providence Dr #203, Southfield, 248-569-4897

Vascular Surgery

Bove, Paul Guy (13 mentions)
U of Michigan, 1988
Certification: Surgery, Surgical Critical Care, Vascular Surgery
3601 W 13 Mile Rd, Royal Oak, 248-551-1465

Brown, Otto William (12 mentions)
Wayne State U, 1975 *Certification:* Surgery, Vascular Surgery
31700 Telegraph Rd #140, Bingham Farms, 248-433-0881

Hans, Sachinder Singh (9 mentions)
FMS-India, 1969
Certification: Surgery, Surgical Critical Care, Vascular Surgery
28411 Hoover Rd, Warren, 586-573-8030

Long, Graham William (15 mentions)
Wayne State U, 1987 *Certification:* Surgery, Vascular Surgery
3601 W 13 Mile Rd, Royal Oak, 248-551-1465

Rimar, Steven Daniel (27 mentions)
U of Michigan, 1980 *Certification:* Surgery, Vascular Surgery
4600 Investment Dr #250, Troy, 248-267-5005

Whitehouse, Walter M., Jr. (23 mentions)
U of Michigan, 1973 *Certification:* Surgery, Vascular Surgery
5325 Elliott Dr #104, Ypsilanti, 734-712-8150

Wolk, Seth William (12 mentions)
Harvard U, 1983 *Certification:* Surgery, Vascular Surgery
5325 Elliott Dr #104, Ypsilanti, 734-712-8150

Minnesota

Twin Cities Area

Twin Cities Area

Including Anoka, Carver, Dakota, Hennepin, Ramsey, Scott, Washington, and Wright Counties

Allergy/Immunology

Blumenthal, Malcolm Nolan (12 mentions)
U of Minnesota, 1958
Certification: Allergy & Immunology, Internal Medicine
420 Delaware St SE #5A, Minneapolis, 612-626-6804

Geller, Gary Richard (10 mentions)
Rosalind Franklin U, 1969
Certification: Allergy & Immunology, Pediatrics
565 S Snelling Ave, St Paul, 651-698-0386

Lind, Timothy Howard (9 mentions)
U of Rochester, 1979
Certification: Allergy & Immunology, Internal Medicine
2220 Riverside Ave, Minneapolis, 612-371-1600

Morris, Richard John (17 mentions)
U of Rochester, 1972
Certification: Allergy & Immunology, Internal Medicine
12000 Elm Creek Blvd #200, Maple Grove, 763-420-1010

Ott, Nancy Lorene (9 mentions)
U of Minnesota, 1984
Certification: Allergy & Immunology, Pediatrics
18315 Cascade Dr #170, Eden Prairie, 952-949-0399
3955 Parklawn Ave, Edina, 952-831-4454

Sveum, Richard James (12 mentions)
U of Minnesota, 1979
Certification: Allergy & Immunology, Pediatrics
3800 Park Nicollet Blvd #2N, St Louis Park, 952-993-3090

Wexler, Michael Ross (8 mentions)
U of Minnesota, 1982
Certification: Allergy & Immunology, Pediatrics
12450 Wayzata Blvd #215, Minnetonka, 952-546-6866

Anesthesiology

Belani, Kumar Girdharidas (4 mentions)
FMS-India, 1974
Certification: Anesthesiology, Critical Care Medicine
420 Delaware St SE #M-515, Minneapolis, 612-624-9990

Bertram, Lawrence John (6 mentions)
U of Wisconsin, 1987 *Certification:* Anesthesiology
14700 28th Ave N #20, Plymouth, 763-559-3779
6500 Excelsior Blvd, Minneapolis, 763-559-3779

Bryan, Roy Gordon (4 mentions)
U of Minnesota, 1982 *Certification:* Anesthesiology
6401 France Ave S, Minneapolis, 952-924-5187

Burke, Mitchell Sim (5 mentions)
U of Minnesota, 1984 *Certification:* Anesthesiology
2545 Chicago Ave S #311, Minneapolis, 612-871-7639

Dassenko, David Alan (4 mentions)
Loma Linda U, 1979 *Certification:* Anesthesiology, Pediatric
  Critical Care Medicine, Pediatrics
14700 28th Ave N #20, Plymouth, 763-559-3779
2525 Chicago Ave S, Minneapolis, 612-813-6000

Hong, Back Ki (6 mentions)
FMS-South Korea, 1971 *Certification:* Anesthesiology
120 S 6th St #155, Minneapolis, 612-347-7226

Layman, Matthew Douglas (7 mentions)
U of New Mexico, 1985 *Certification:* Anesthesiology
640 Jackson St, St Paul, 800-495-0127
2450 Riverside Ave, Minneapolis, 800-495-0127

McCormick, Paul Charles (4 mentions)
Ohio State U, 1983 *Certification:* Anesthesiology
2525 Chicago Ave S #1522, Minneapolis, 612-813-6260

Nissen, Mark Davis (4 mentions)
U of Illinois, 1979 *Certification:* Anesthesiology
2545 Chicago Ave S #311, Minneapolis, 612-871-7639

Sweeney, Michael Francis (6 mentions)
U of Wisconsin, 1976 *Certification:* Anesthesiology,
  Pediatric Critical Care Medicine, Pediatrics
420 Delaware St SE #M-515, Minneapolis, 612-624-9990

Turner, James Merrill (4 mentions)
U of Minnesota, 1977
Certification: Anesthesiology, Internal Medicine
500 S Maple St, Waconia, 952-442-2191

Violante, Edward Vincent (4 mentions)
U of Illinois, 1985 *Certification:* Anesthesiology
3800 Park Nicollet Blvd, St Louis Park, 952-993-5150

Cardiac Surgery

Eales, Frazier (16 mentions)
U of Minnesota, 1976 *Certification:* Thoracic Surgery
920 E 28th St #610, Minneapolis, 612-863-6900

Joyce, Lyle Damon (26 mentions)
Baylor U, 1973 *Certification:* Thoracic Surgery
420 Delaware St SE, Minneapolis, 612-624-8130

Kshettry, Vibhu R. (16 mentions)
FMS-India, 1973 *Certification:* Thoracic Surgery
920 E 28th St 6th Fl #610, Minneapolis, 612-863-6900

Spooner, Ted H. (20 mentions)
SUNY-Buffalo, 1979 *Certification:* Thoracic Surgery
6400 Excelsior Blvd, St Louis Park, 952-993-3246

Cardiology

Asinger, Richard William (9 mentions)
U of Iowa, 1969
Certification: Cardiovascular Disease, Internal Medicine
701 Park Ave #O-5, Minneapolis, 612-873-2875

Baran, Kenneth, Jr. (4 mentions)
George Washington U, 1982 *Certification:* Cardiovascular
  Disease, Internal Medicine, Interventional Cardiology
225 Smith Ave N #500, St Paul, 651-292-0616
1600 St Johns Blvd #200, St Paul, 651-779-9449

Battista, Stephen C. (7 mentions)
U of Texas-Houston, 1985 *Certification:* Cardiovascular
  Disease, Internal Medicine, Interventional Cardiology
6405 France Ave S #W200, Edina, 952-924-9005

Benton, Steven (4 mentions)
U of Iowa, 1981
Certification: Cardiovascular Disease, Internal Medicine
225 Smith Ave N #500, St Paul, 651-292-0616
1600 St Johns Blvd #200, St Paul, 651-779-9449

Burns, Durand Ernest (5 mentions)
U of Minnesota, 1991 *Certification:* Cardiovascular Disease
920 E 28th St #300, Minneapolis, 612-863-3900

Burton, David (4 mentions)
FMS-Israel, 1981 *Certification:* Pediatric Cardiology, Pediatrics
1515 St Francis Ave #250, Shakopee, 612-813-8800
347 Smith Ave N #603, St Paul, 651-221-0900
2545 Chicago Ave #106, Minneapolis, 612-813-8800

Chambers, Jeffrey (6 mentions)
Wayne State U, 1989
Certification: Cardiovascular Disease, Interventional Cardiology
4040 Coon Rapids Blvd NW #120, Minneapolis, 763-427-9980

Chapel, Norman Phillip (4 mentions)
U of Pennsylvania, 1977
Certification: Cardiovascular Disease, Internal Medicine
6405 France Ave S #W200, Edina, 952-924-9005

Collins, Vincent Ross (4 mentions)
Stanford U, 1974
Certification: Cardiovascular Disease, Internal Medicine
6500 Excelsior Blvd, St Louis Park, 952-993-3246
1415 St Francis Ave, Shakopee, 952-993-7750

Erhard, Mark Wayne (5 mentions)
U of South Florida, 1986 *Certification:* Cardiovascular
Disease, Interventional Cardiology
17 Exchange St W #750, St Paul, 651-232-4340
1675 Beam Ave #210, St Paul, 651-232-4340
1875 Woodwinds Dr #240, Woodbury, 651-232-4340

Fine, David Gregory (4 mentions)
Johns Hopkins U, 1982
Certification: Cardiovascular Disease, Internal Medicine
825 S 8th St #1116, Minneapolis, 612-338-0952

Graham, Kevin J. (11 mentions)
U of Minnesota, 1981
Certification: Cardiovascular Disease, Internal Medicine
920 E 28th St #300, Minneapolis, 612-863-3900

Gremmels, David Bryan (4 mentions)
U of Chicago, 1995 *Certification:* Pediatric Cardiology, Pediatrics
2545 Chicago Ave S #106, Minneapolis, 612-813-8800
347 Smith Ave N #603, St Paul, 651-221-0900
1515 St Francis Ave #250, Shakopee, 612-813-8800

Harris, Kevin Michael (4 mentions)
U of Minnesota, 1988
Certification: Cardiovascular Disease, Internal Medicine
920 E 28th St #300, Minneapolis, 612-863-3900

Haugland, John Mark (4 mentions)
U of Minnesota, 1976 *Certification:* Cardiovascular Disease,
Internal Medicine, Interventional Cardiology
6490 Excelsior Blvd, St Louis Park, 952-993-3246

Hedberg, Priscilla Ann (5 mentions)
U of Minnesota, 1983
Certification: Cardiovascular Disease, Internal Medicine
1600 St Johns Blvd #200, St Paul, 651-779-9449
225 Smith Ave N #100, St Paul, 651-292-0616

Heifetz, Steven Mark (8 mentions)
Med Coll of Wisconsin, 1983 *Certification:* Cardiovascular
Disease, Internal Medicine, Interventional Cardiology
6405 France Ave S #W200, Edina, 952-924-9005

Henry, Timothy Darrell (8 mentions)
U of California-San Francisco, 1982 *Certification:* Cardiovascular
Disease, Internal Medicine, Interventional Cardiology
920 E 28th St #40, Minneapolis, 612-863-7372

Homans, David C. (10 mentions)
Tufts U, 1976
Certification: Cardiovascular Disease, Internal Medicine
6400 Excelsior Blvd, St Louis Park, 952-993-3246

Johnson, Randall Karl (4 mentions)
George Washington U, 1973
Certification: Cardiovascular Disease, Internal Medicine
920 E 28th St #300, Minneapolis, 612-863-3900

Ketroser, Robert Alan (6 mentions)
U of Minnesota, 1980
Certification: Cardiovascular Disease, Internal Medicine
6405 France Ave S #W200-W300, Edina, 952-924-9005

Kottke, Thomas E. (8 mentions)
U of Minnesota, 1974
Certification: Cardiovascular Disease, Internal Medicine
640 Jackson St #3, St Paul, 651-254-4887

Lesser, John Raymond (6 mentions)
U of Florida, 1981 *Certification:* Cardiovascular Disease,
Internal Medicine, Interventional Cardiology
920 E 28th St 2nd Fl, Minneapolis, 612-863-3900
800 E 28th St 2nd Fl, Minneapolis, 612-863-3900

Longe, Terrence Frederick (4 mentions)
Wayne State U, 1981
Certification: Cardiovascular Disease, Internal Medicine
920 E 28th St #300, Minneapolis, 612-863-3900

McGinn, Andrew Lamb (10 mentions)
St Louis U, 1982
Certification: Cardiovascular Disease, Internal Medicine
3300 Oakdale Ave N #200, Minneapolis, 763-520-2000

Moller, James Herman (4 mentions)
Stanford U, 1958 *Certification:* Pediatric Cardiology, Pediatrics
420 Delaware St SE, Minneapolis, 612-626-2790

Morrison, James Paul (5 mentions)
U of Wisconsin, 1978 *Certification:* Cardiovascular Disease,
Internal Medicine, Interventional Cardiology
2220 Riverside Ave, Minneapolis, 612-349-8322
640 Jackson St, St Paul, 651-254-4785

Nelson, William Bert (6 mentions)
U of Minnesota, 1993 *Certification:* Cardiovascular Disease
640 Jackson St #3, St Paul, 651-254-4887

Panetta, Carmelo James (4 mentions)
U of Texas-Galveston, 1991
Certification: Cardiovascular Disease, Interventional Cardiology
6500 Excelsior Blvd, St Louis Park, 952-993-3246

Paulsen, Pamela R. (4 mentions)
Med Coll of Wisconsin, 1987
Certification: Cardiovascular Disease
3300 Oakdale Ave N #200, Robbinsdale, 763-520-2000
2855 Campus Dr #550, Plymouth, 763-520-4949

Pritzker, Marc Richard (5 mentions)
U of Minnesota, 1976
Certification: Cardiovascular Disease, Internal Medicine
516 Delaware St SE #3B, Minneapolis, 612-625-3600

Pyles, Lee (4 mentions)
West Virginia U, 1983
Certification: Pediatric Cardiology, Pediatrics
225 Smith Ave N #504, St Paul, 651-265-7575
420 Delaware St SE #MMC-94, Minneapolis, 612-626-2755

Sharkey, Scott W. (6 mentions)
Tufts U, 1977
Certification: Cardiovascular Disease, Internal Medicine
500 S Maple St, Waconia, 952-442-7843

Simonson, Jay Scott (4 mentions)
U of Minnesota, 1982 *Certification:* Cardiovascular Disease,
Clinical Cardiac Electrophysiology, Internal Medicine
6490 Excelsior Blvd, St Louis Park, 952-993-3246

Singh, Amarjit (13 mentions)
FMS-India, 1965 *Certification:* Pediatric Cardiology, Pediatrics
2545 Chicago Ave S #106, Minneapolis, 612-813-8800
347 Smith Ave N #603, St Paul, 651-221-0900

Thatcher, Jackson L., Jr. (5 mentions)
U of South Florida, 1982 *Certification:* Cardiovascular
Disease, Internal Medicine, Interventional Cardiology
6400 Excelsior Blvd, St Louis Park, 952-993-3246

Tschida, Victor Henry (5 mentions)
U of Minnesota, 1967
Certification: Cardiovascular Disease, Internal Medicine
225 Smith Ave N #506, St Paul, 651-292-0616
1600 St Johns Blvd #200, Maplewood, 651-779-9449

Vatterott, Pierce (4 mentions)
U of Missouri-Kansas City, 1980 *Certification:* Cardiovascular
Disease, Clinical Cardiac Electrophysiology, Internal Medicine
225 Smith Ave N #500, St Paul, 651-292-0616
1600 St Johns Blvd #200, St Paul, 651-779-9449

Dermatology

Bart, Bruce Joseph (6 mentions)
U of Minnesota, 1961
Certification: Dermatology, Dermatopathology
825 S 8th St #M50, Minneapolis, 612-347-6450
701 Park Ave, Minneapolis, 612-873-2300

Bender, Mitchell Elliott (22 mentions)
U of Kentucky, 1974 *Certification:* Dermatology
3316 W 66th St #200, Edina, 952-920-3808
775 Prairie Center Dr #370, Eden Prairie, 952-920-3808

Bohjanen, Kimberly (7 mentions)
U of Michigan, 1993 *Certification:* Dermatology
516 Delaware St SE #5, Minneapolis, 612-625-5656

Fenyk, John Raymond, Jr. (9 mentions)
U of Virginia, 1975 *Certification:* Dermatology
516 Delaware St SE, Minneapolis, 612-625-5656

Holmes, H. Spencer (17 mentions)
U of Rochester, 1966 *Certification:* Dermatology
3800 Park Nicollet Blvd, St Louis Park, 952-993-3260

Lee, Jennifer Marie (7 mentions)
U of Minnesota, 1997 *Certification:* Dermatology
3316 W 66th St #200, Minneapolis, 952-920-3808
775 Prairie Center Dr #370, Eden Prairie, 952-920-3808

Leitch, Nancy Ann (6 mentions)
U of Minnesota, 1991 *Certification:* Dermatology
2765 Kelley Pkwy #100, Orono, 952-345-4222

Long, Sherri A. (7 mentions)
U of Iowa, 1984 *Certification:* Dermatology
2220 Riverside Ave, Minneapolis, 952-967-7616
401 Phalen Blvd, St Paul, 651-254-7400

Madhok, Rajneesh (13 mentions)
U of North Dakota, 1984 *Certification:* Dermatology
3316 W 66th St #200, Edina, 952-920-3808
775 Prairie Center Dr #370, Eden Prairie, 952-920-3808

Prawer, Steven Earl (8 mentions)
U of Minnesota, 1967 *Certification:* Dermatology
7205 University Ave NE, Fridley, 763-571-4000
500 Osborne Rd NE #330, Fridley, 763-571-4000
18315 Cascade Dr #150, Eden Prairie, 763-571-4000

Schlick, Cynthia Anne (7 mentions)
U of Minnesota, 1986
Certification: Dermatology, Internal Medicine
1120 Wayzata Blvd E #100, Wayzata, 952-476-6733

Soutor, Carol Ann (15 mentions)
U of Minnesota, 1973 *Certification:* Dermatology
2220 Riverside Ave, Minneapolis, 612-371-1600

Zelickson, Brian David (10 mentions)
Mayo Med Sch, 1986 *Certification:* Dermatology
250 Central Ave N #128, Wayzata, 952-473-1286
825 Nicollet Mall #1002, Minneapolis, 612-338-0711
4100 W 50th St, Edina, 952-929-8888

Emergency Medicine

Abelson, Samuel Eli (8 mentions)
U of Minnesota, 1983 *Certification:* Internal Medicine
800 E 28th St, Minneapolis, 612-863-4233

Asplin, Brent Roger (7 mentions)
Mayo Med Sch, 1995 *Certification:* Emergency Medicine
640 Jackson St, St Paul, 651-254-3044

Carolan, Patrick L. (8 mentions)
Med Coll of Wisconsin, 1982
Certification: Pediatric Emergency Medicine, Pediatrics
2525 Chicago Ave S, Minneapolis, 612-813-6843

Coon, Gary Allyn (8 mentions)
U of Michigan, 1977 *Certification:* Emergency Medicine
6500 Excelsior Blvd, St Louis Park, 952-993-5353

Dvorak, David (6 mentions)
U of Illinois, 1990 *Certification:* Emergency Medicine
7301 Ohms Ln #650, Edina, 952-835-9880

Kapsner, Christopher E. (5 mentions)
U of Minnesota, 1991 *Certification:* Emergency Medicine
800 E 28th St, Minneapolis, 612-863-4233

Kocken, Paula Fink (5 mentions)
Indiana U, 1983
Certification: Pediatric Emergency Medicine, Pediatrics
2525 Chicago Ave S, Minneapolis, 612-813-6843

Peterson, David Roy (6 mentions)
Loyola U Chicago, 1984 *Certification:* Internal Medicine
800 E 28th St, Minneapolis, 612-863-4233

Plouff, Robert (9 mentions)
Med Coll of Wisconsin, 1985
Certification: Pediatric Emergency Medicine, Pediatrics
2525 Chicago Ave S, Minneapolis, 612-813-6117

Quaday, Karen A. (6 mentions)
Wayne State U, 1984
Certification: Emergency Medicine, Internal Medicine
640 Jackson St, St Paul, 651-254-1809

Schwitzer, Kent William (5 mentions)
U of Iowa, 1978 *Certification:* Emergency Medicine
6500 Excelsior Blvd, St Louis Park, 952-993-5353

Endocrinology

Bantle, John Peter (14 mentions)
U of Minnesota, 1972
Certification: Endocrinology and Metabolism, Internal Medicine
516 Delaware St SE Clinic 6A, Minneapolis, 612-625-5165

Corbett, Victor Alan (11 mentions)
U of Minnesota, 1969
Certification: Endocrinology and Metabolism, Internal Medicine
255 Smith Ave N #100, St Paul, 651-241-5000

Fish, Lisa Humphrey (12 mentions)
Brown U, 1981
Certification: Endocrinology and Metabolism, Internal Medicine
3800 Park Nicollet Blvd #5N, St Louis Park, 952-993-3708

Leebaw, Wayne Frederick (19 mentions)
Case Western Reserve U, 1969
Certification: Endocrinology and Metabolism, Internal Medicine
7701 York Ave S #180, Edina, 952-927-7810

Mulmed, Lawrence Neil (19 mentions)
U of Iowa, 1969
Certification: Endocrinology and Metabolism, Internal Medicine
710 E 24th St #405, Minneapolis, 612-336-5000

Stesin, Mark Phillip (28 mentions)
U of Minnesota, 1980 *Certification:* Internal Medicine
3366 Oakdale Ave N #408, Robbinsdale, 763-520-5876
2855 Campus Dr #650, Minneapolis, 763-520-5876
920 E 28th St #540, Minneapolis, 763-520-5876

Family Practice *(see note on page 9)*

Bixby, Mark Rollins (4 mentions)
U of Illinois, 1978 *Certification:* Family Medicine
1020 W Broadway, Minneapolis, 612-302-8200

Buck, Christopher G., II (4 mentions)
U of Minnesota, 1985 *Certification:* Family Medicine
3850 Park Nicollet Blvd, St Louis Park, 952-993-3123

Burns, Sheldon Robert (4 mentions)
U of Minnesota, 1974 *Certification:* Emergency Medicine, Family Medicine, Sports Medicine
5301 Vernon Ave S, Edina, 952-925-2200

Canfield, John Lee (5 mentions)
U of Minnesota, 1972 *Certification:* Family Medicine
7250 France Ave S #410, Edina, 952-831-1551

Feist, Richard (3 mentions)
U of Minnesota, 1979 *Certification:* Family Medicine
410 Church St SE #4, Minneapolis, 612-625-3222

Flint, Melissa P. (3 mentions)
U of Minnesota, 1995
Certification: Family Medicine, Geriatric Medicine
407 W 66th St, Richfield, 612-798-8800

Gamradt, Barbara Rae (3 mentions)
U of Minnesota, 1977 *Certification:* Family Medicine
5301 Vernon Ave S, Edina, 952-925-2200

Garske, Peter G. (3 mentions)
U of Minnesota, 1975 *Certification:* Family Medicine
3800 Park Nicollet Blvd, St Louis Park, 952-993-3123

Hallberg, Jon Scott (4 mentions)
U of Minnesota, 1992 *Certification:* Family Medicine
516 Delaware St SE #3A, Minneapolis, 612-624-9499

Kazim, Mumtaz A. (6 mentions)
FMS-India, 1980 *Certification:* Family Medicine
5301 Vernon Ave S, Edina, 952-925-2200

Kelly, Kevin Michael (3 mentions)
U of Minnesota, 1981 *Certification:* Family Medicine
606 24th Ave S #813, Minneapolis, 612-332-1534

Kline, Sally Ann (3 mentions)
U of Minnesota, 1986 *Certification:* Family Medicine
8455 Flying Cloud Dr #200, Eden Prairie, 952-993-7400

Knopp, William David (3 mentions)
U of Cincinnati, 1988
Certification: Family Medicine, Sports Medicine
300 Lake Dr E, Chanhassen, 952-993-4300

Laroy, James Paul (3 mentions)
Northwestern U, 1986 *Certification:* Family Medicine
6440 Nicollet Ave S, Richfield, 612-861-1622

Nelson, Bryan Allen (4 mentions)
U of Minnesota, 1998 *Certification:* Family Medicine
11475 Robinson Dr NW, Coon Rapids, 763-754-4600

Nelson, Kevin Craig (3 mentions)
Rush U, 1988 *Certification:* Family Medicine
6440 Nicollet Ave S, Richfield, 612-861-1622

Price, Phillip James (3 mentions)
U of North Dakota, 1976 *Certification:* Family Medicine
2855 Campus Dr #400, Plymouth, 763-577-7400

Springer, Jeremy Scott (3 mentions)
U of Minnesota, 1987
Certification: Adolescent Medicine, Family Medicine
6600 Excelsior Blvd #160, St Louis Park, 952-993-7700

Taube, Rochelle Ramseier (3 mentions)
U of Minnesota, 1987
Certification: Family Medicine, Sports Medicine
6363 France Ave S #525, Edina, 952-926-6489

Thul, Thomas Leonard (4 mentions)
U of Minnesota, 1985 *Certification:* Family Medicine
2500 Como Ave, St Paul, 952-967-7955

Trehus, Eric Todd (4 mentions)
U of Minnesota, 1981 *Certification:* Family Medicine
205 S Wabasha St, St Paul, 952-967-5584

Gastroenterology

Conroy, Lucinda (8 mentions)
U of Minnesota, 1982
Certification: Gastroenterology, Internal Medicine
1973 Sloan Pl #200, St Paul, 651-772-5700

Ferenci, David Alan (15 mentions)
U of Pennsylvania, 1984 *Certification:* Pediatric Gastroenterology
2200 University Ave W #120, St Paul, 612-871-1145

Ganz, Robert Alan (10 mentions)
U of Illinois, 1980
Certification: Gastroenterology, Internal Medicine
15700 37th Ave N #300, Plymouth, 612-871-1145
5705 W Old Shakopee Rd #150, Bloomington, 612-871-1145

Jafri, Irshad Hasan (11 mentions)
FMS-Pakistan, 1985 *Certification:* Gastroenterology
435 Phalen Blvd, St Paul, 651-254-8686

Kennedy, Michelle Samaha (11 mentions)
U of Cincinnati, 1988 *Certification:* Pediatric Gastroenterology
2200 University Ave W #120, St Paul, 612-871-1145

Leon, Samuel Howard (16 mentions)
U of Illinois, 1980
Certification: Gastroenterology, Internal Medicine
15700 37th Ave N #300, Plymouth, 612-871-1145
5705 W Old Shakopee Rd #150, Bloomington, 612-871-1145

Mackie, Robert Dale (8 mentions)
U of Minnesota, 1976
Certification: Gastroenterology, Internal Medicine
15700 37th Ave N #300, Plymouth, 612-871-1145
5705 W Old Shakopee Rd #150, Bloomington, 612-871-1145

Purdy, Bryce Herbert (16 mentions)
U of Minnesota, 1977
Certification: Gastroenterology, Internal Medicine
3366 Oakdale Ave N #200, Robbinsdale, 763-287-5000

Shaw, Michael James (9 mentions)
U of Michigan, 1979
Certification: Gastroenterology, Internal Medicine
6500 Excelsior Blvd #4820, St Louis Park, 952-993-3240

Stafford, Richard James (15 mentions)
U of Iowa, 1975
Certification: Pediatric Gastroenterology, Pediatrics
2200 University Ave W #120, St Paul, 612-871-1145

Tombers, Joseph Mathew (16 mentions)
Med Coll of Wisconsin, 1964
Certification: Gastroenterology, Internal Medicine
15700 37th Ave N #300, Plymouth, 612-871-1145
5705 W Old Shakopee Rd #150, Bloomington, 612-871-1145

General Surgery

Benn, Paul Luhman (9 mentions)
U of Chicago, 1981 *Certification:* Surgery
6405 France Ave S #W440, Edina, 952-927-7004

Bretzke, Margit Lynn (8 mentions)
U of Minnesota, 1979 *Certification:* Surgery
2545 Chicago Ave S #500, Minneapolis, 612-863-7770

Croston, James Kevin (7 mentions)
U of South Dakota, 1984 *Certification:* Surgery
3300 Oakdale Ave, Robbinsdale, 763-780-6699
9825 Hospital Dr #105, Maple Grove, 763-780-6699

Dries, David James (6 mentions)
U of Chicago, 1980 *Certification:* Surgery, Surgical Critical Care
401 Phalen Blvd, St Paul, 651-254-7400

England, Michael David (6 mentions)
Mayo Med Sch, 1986 *Certification:* Surgery
1973 Sloan Pl #225, Maplewood, 651-224-1347

Graber, John N. (9 mentions)
St Louis U, 1977 *Certification:* Surgery
920 E 28th St #300, Minneapolis, 612-863-6800

Granja, Jorge A. (6 mentions)
U of California-Los Angeles, 1986 *Certification:* Surgery
606 24th Ave S #119, Minneapolis, 612-672-2992

Hope, Roy Elder (6 mentions)
Indiana U, 1980 *Certification:* Surgery
1973 Sloan Pl #225, St Paul, 651-224-1347

Johnson, Dawn (7 mentions)
U of Iowa, 1992 *Certification:* Surgery
3366 Oakdale Ave N #506, Robbinsdale, 763-520-1230

Kelly, Peter Hoyt (6 mentions)
U of Minnesota, 1984 *Certification:* Surgery
310 Smith Ave N #330, St Paul, 651-227-6351
1655 Beam Ave #302, Maplewood, 651-227-6351

Maurer, David John (8 mentions)
U of Wisconsin, 1982 *Certification:* Surgery
303 E Nicollet Blvd, Burnsville, 952-435-4140

Mestitz, Steven (7 mentions)
U of Minnesota, 1981 *Certification:* Surgery
5100 Gamble Dr #100, St Louis Park, 952-967-7977
3366 Oakdale Ave N #200, Robbinsdale, 952-967-7977

Miller, John Braun (8 mentions)
U of Tennessee, 1978 *Certification:* Surgery
280 Smith Ave N #311, St Paul, 651-224-1347
1655 Beam Ave #204, Maplewood, 651-224-1347

Morris, Todd John (7 mentions)
U of Minnesota, 1987 *Certification:* Surgery
401 Phalen Blvd, St Paul, 651-254-7400

Ney, Arthur Leland (11 mentions)
U of Minnesota, 1977
Certification: Surgery, Surgical Critical Care
701 Park Ave, Minneapolis, 612-873-8701

O'Leary, John Francis (5 mentions)
U of Minnesota, 1977 *Certification:* Surgery
2545 Chicago Ave S #510, Minneapolis, 952-285-6879
800 E 28th St, Minneapolis, 612-863-3150

Odland, Mark Douglas (8 mentions)
U of North Dakota, 1978 *Certification:* Surgery
701 Park Ave, Minneapolis, 612-873-8701

Omlie, William Richard (5 mentions)
U of Minnesota, 1981 *Certification:* Surgery, Vascular Surgery
6405 France Ave S #W440, Edina, 952-929-6994
6525 France Ave S #275, Edina, 952-831-8346

Ose, Kevin John (12 mentions)
U of Kansas, 1989 *Certification:* Surgery
3800 Park Nicollet Blvd, St Louis Park, 952-993-3180

Pierce, Bradley Robert (6 mentions)
U of Minnesota, 1996 *Certification:* Surgery
6405 France Ave S #W440, Edina, 952-927-7004

Roland, Christopher F. (6 mentions)
U of Minnesota, 1985 *Certification:* Surgery, Vascular Surgery
6405 France Ave S #W440, Edina, 952-927-7004

Rustad, David Gordon (6 mentions)
Johns Hopkins U, 1979 *Certification:* Pediatric Surgery
2545 Chicago Ave S #104, Minneapolis, 612-813-8000
303 E Nicollet Blvd #220, Burnsville, 612-813-8000
6060 Clearwater Dr #110, Minnetonka, 612-813-8000

Saltzman, Daniel Alan (5 mentions)
U of Minnesota, 1990 *Certification:* Pediatric Surgery, Surgery
420 Delaware St SE #MMC-195, Minneapolis, 612-626-4214

Saylor, Howard L., III (5 mentions)
U of South Dakota, 1977 *Certification:* Surgery
6405 France Ave S #W440, Edina, 952-927-7004

Schlaefer, James Gerard (5 mentions)
U of Wisconsin, 1981 *Certification:* Surgery
11475 Robinson Dr NW, Coon Rapids, 763-754-4600
3366 Oakdale Ave N #200, Robbinsdale, 763-287-5000

Schmeling, David John (8 mentions)
U of Minnesota, 1984 *Certification:* Pediatric Surgery
347 Smith Ave N #502, St Paul, 612-813-8000
2545 Chicago Ave #104, Minneapolis, 612-813-8000

Shearen, John Gregory (12 mentions)
U of Minnesota, 1979 *Certification:* Surgery
1690 University Ave W #270, St Paul, 651-224-1347
1973 Sloan Pl #225, Maplewood, 561-224-1347

Steadland, Kevin (5 mentions)
U of Minnesota, 1988 *Certification:* Surgery
3960 Coon Rapids Blvd NW #104, Coon Rapids, 763-236-9000

Stoltenberg, John Jerome (7 mentions)
U of Iowa, 1971 *Certification:* Surgery
500 Osborne Rd NE #125, Fridley, 763-780-6699

Svendsen, Charles Allen (7 mentions)
U of Minnesota, 1992 *Certification:* Surgery
6490 Excelsior Blvd, St Louis Park, 952-993-3180
1415 St Francis Ave, Shakopee, 952-993-3180

Tuttle, Todd Michael (5 mentions)
Johns Hopkins U, 1988 *Certification:* Surgery
424 Harvard St SE, Minneapolis, 612-273-9670

Wetherille, Robert E., III (5 mentions)
U of Minnesota, 1976 *Certification:* Surgery
3800 Park Nicollet Blvd, St Louis Park, 952-993-3180
14000 Fairview Dr, Burnsville, 952-993-3180

Wilton, Peter Bernard (5 mentions)
FMS-South Africa, 1980 *Certification:* Surgery
310 Smith Ave N #330, St Paul, 651-227-6351
1655 Beam Ave #302, Maplewood, 651-227-6351

Zera, Richard Thomas (5 mentions)
U of Minnesota, 1980 *Certification:* Surgery
701 Park Ave S, Minneapolis, 612-873-2810

Geriatrics

Holm, Alvin Clark (9 mentions)
U of Iowa, 1984
Certification: Geriatric Medicine, Internal Medicine
559 Capitol Blvd, St Paul, 651-326-2150

Olson, Jennifer (16 mentions)
U of Minnesota, 1979
Certification: Geriatric Medicine, Internal Medicine
3850 Park Nicollet Blvd, St Louis Park, 952-993-5041

Sandler, Victor Michael (9 mentions)
U of Minnesota, 1976
Certification: Hospice and Palliative Medicine, Internal Medicine
701 25th Ave S #505, Minneapolis, 612-455-2040

Stein, Daniel Joshua (6 mentions)
Virginia Commonwealth U, 1983 *Certification:* Internal Medicine
701 25th Ave S #505, Minneapolis, 612-455-2040

Von Sternberg, Thomas L. (13 mentions)
Ohio State U, 1980
Certification: Family Medicine, Geriatric Medicine
2220 Riverside Ave, Minneapolis, 612-371-1600

Hematology/Oncology

Amatruda, Thomas T., III (6 mentions)
Yale U, 1978
Certification: Hematology, Internal Medicine, Medical Oncology
3435 W Broadway Ave, Robbinsdale, 763-520-7887
3300 Oakdale Ave N #100, Robbinsdale, 763-520-7887
500 Osborne Rd NE #215, Fridley, 763-786-1620

Bendel, Anne (8 mentions)
U of Minnesota, 1987
Certification: Pediatric Hematology-Oncology
2525 Chicago Ave S #4150, Minneapolis, 612-813-5940

Bender, Gail Papermaster (5 mentions)
U of Minnesota, 1975
Certification: Internal Medicine, Medical Oncology
6363 France Ave S #610, Edina, 952-836-3645
500 S Maple St, Waconia, 952-442-2191

Cardamone, Joseph M., Jr. (6 mentions)
U of Pennsylvania, 1963
Certification: Hematology, Internal Medicine, Medical Oncology
3960 Coon Rapids Blvd NW #311, Coon Rapids, 763-236-9090

Carlson, Jon Paul (16 mentions)
U of Minnesota, 1970 *Certification:* Internal Medicine
3800 Park Nicollet Blvd, St Louis Park, 952-993-3248

Dien, Philip Y. (7 mentions)
Dartmouth Coll, 1981
Certification: Hematology, Internal Medicine, Medical Oncology
675 Nicollet Blvd #200, Burnsville, 952-892-7190

Duane, Stephen (8 mentions)
U of Minnesota, 1979
Certification: Internal Medicine, Medical Oncology
3800 Park Nicollet Blvd, St Louis Park, 952-993-3248

Flynn, Patrick James (10 mentions)
U of Minnesota, 1975
Certification: Hematology, Internal Medicine, Medical Oncology
800 E 28th St #405, Minneapolis, 612-863-8585

Flynn, Thomas Patrick (11 mentions)
U of Minnesota, 1975
Certification: Hematology, Internal Medicine, Medical Oncology
800 E 28th St Piper Bldg #405, Minneapolis, 612-872-8600

Howe, Craig Walter S. (5 mentions)
Cornell U, 1978
Certification: Internal Medicine, Medical Oncology
310 Smith Ave N #460, St Paul, 651-602-5200

Hurley, Randolph William (15 mentions)
U of Wisconsin, 1987
Certification: Hematology, Medical Oncology
640 Jackson St, St Paul, 651-254-3572
1210 1st St W, Hastings, 651-438-1800
2220 Riverside Ave S, Minneapolis, 612-349-8374

Londer, Harold Norris (9 mentions)
U of Minnesota, 1973
Certification: Internal Medicine, Medical Oncology
3435 W Broadway #1135, Robbinsdale, 763-520-7887

MacRae, Margaret Ann (5 mentions)
U of Minnesota, 1974
Certification: Internal Medicine, Medical Oncology
800 E 28th St #405, Minneapolis, 612-863-8585

Messinger, Yoav H. (5 mentions)
FMS-Israel, 1987
Certification: Pediatric Hematology-Oncology, Pediatrics
345 Smith Ave N, St Paul, 651-220-6732

Moertel, Christopher L. (9 mentions)
U of Minnesota, 1984
Certification: Pediatric Hematology-Oncology
347 Smith Ave N #301, St Paul, 651-220-6732

Morton, Colleen Tracy (7 mentions)
FMS-South Africa, 1992
Certification: Hematology, Internal Medicine, Medical Oncology
2220 Riverside Ave, Minneapolis, 952-967-7616
640 Jackson St, St Paul, 651-254-3456

Neglia, Joseph Philip (6 mentions)
Loma Linda U, 1981
Certification: Pediatric Hematology-Oncology, Pediatrics
420 Delaware St SE, Minneapolis, 612-626-2778

Nwaneri, Matthew Obinna (7 mentions)
FMS-Nigeria, 1989 *Certification:* Hematology, Medical Oncology
800 E 28th St #405, Minneapolis, 612-863-8585

Rank, Brian Harvey (8 mentions)
U of Minnesota, 1979
Certification: Hematology, Internal Medicine, Medical Oncology
2220 Riverside Ave, Minneapolis, 612-371-1600

Rausch, Douglas John (7 mentions)
Wayne State U, 1980
Certification: Hematology, Internal Medicine, Medical Oncology
701 Park Ave, Minneapolis, 612-873-6369

Reding, Mark (5 mentions)
U of Minnesota, 1992
Certification: Hematology, Medical Oncology
424 Harvard St SE #M-100, Minneapolis, 612-625-5411

Rousey, Steven Ross (6 mentions)
U of Kansas, 1985
Certification: Hematology, Internal Medicine, Medical Oncology
6363 France Ave S #300, Edina, 952-928-2900
560 Maple St S #100, Waconia, 952-442-6006

Sborov, Mark Douglas (10 mentions)
U of Minnesota, 1975
Certification: Internal Medicine, Medical Oncology
6363 France Ave S #300, Edina, 952-928-2900

Schwartz, Burton Stewart (8 mentions)
Meharry Med Coll, 1968
Certification: Hematology, Internal Medicine, Medical Oncology
800 E 28th St #405, Minneapolis, 612-863-8585

Schwerkoske, John F. (5 mentions)
Ohio State U, 1978
Certification: Hematology, Internal Medicine, Medical Oncology
6025 Lake Rd #110, Woodbury, 651-602-5200

Seng, John Edward (15 mentions)
U of Minnesota, 1992
Certification: Hematology, Medical Oncology
800 E 28th St #405, Minneapolis, 612-863-8585

Weigel, Brenda (6 mentions)
FMS-Canada, 1993 *Certification:* Pediatrics
420 Delaware St SE, Minneapolis, 612-626-1926

Weinshel, Eric Lewis (9 mentions)
Tufts U, 1985 *Certification:* Internal Medicine, Medical Oncology
6363 France Ave S #300, Edina, 952-928-2900
675 Nicollet Blvd #200, Burnsville, 952-892-7190

Zander, Paul Joseph (9 mentions)
U of Minnesota, 1989
Certification: Hematology, Internal Medicine, Medical Oncology
800 E 28th St #405, Minneapolis, 612-863-8585

Infectious Disease

Belani, Kiran Kumar (17 mentions)
FMS-India, 1976
Certification: Pediatric Infectious Diseases, Pediatrics
2525 Chicago Ave S, Minneapolis, 612-813-6105

Dittes, Steven Mark (16 mentions)
U of South Dakota, 1982
Certification: Infectious Disease, Internal Medicine
6363 France Ave S #400, Edina, 952-920-2070

Kish, Mary Ann Elizabeth (19 mentions)
Ohio State U, 1977
Certification: Infectious Disease, Internal Medicine
3366 Oakdale Ave N #200, Robbinsdale, 763-287-5000
401 Phalen Blvd, St Paul, 651-254-7400

Kravitz, Gary Robert (22 mentions)
Northwestern U, 1977
Certification: Infectious Disease, Internal Medicine
1959 Sloan Pl #200, St Paul, 651-772-6235

Martin, Harold Luther, Jr. (17 mentions)
U of North Carolina, 1988
Certification: Infectious Disease, Internal Medicine
3800 Park Nicollet Blvd, St Louis Park, 952-993-3131

Obaid, Stephen Robert (19 mentions)
Mayo Med Sch, 1978
Certification: Infectious Disease, Internal Medicine
6363 France Ave S #400, Edina, 952-920-2070

Schrock, Christian Gerald (16 mentions)
U of Iowa, 1972
Certification: Infectious Disease, Internal Medicine
3366 Oakdale Ave N #520, Robbinsdale, 763-520-4320

Sonnesyn, Steven William (17 mentions)
U of Colorado, 1987 *Certification:* Infectious Disease
11676 Wayzata Blvd, Minnetonka, 952-746-8360

Infertility

Campbell, Bruce Franklin (14 mentions)
U of Minnesota, 1972 *Certification:* Obstetrics & Gynecology
2800 Chicago Ave S #300, Minneapolis, 612-863-5390

Malo, John William (11 mentions)
Albany Med Coll, 1974 *Certification:* Obstetrics & Gynecology
991 Sibley Memorial Hwy #100, Lilydale, 651-379-3110

Nagel, Theodore Christian (13 mentions)
Cornell U, 1963
Certification: Endocrinology and Metabolism, Internal Medicine,
   Obstetrics & Gynecology, Reproductive Endocrinology/Infertility
606 24th Ave S #500, Minneapolis, 612-627-4564

Internal Medicine *(see note on page 9)*

Arnason, Frederick Ray (4 mentions)
U of North Dakota, 1988 *Certification:* Internal Medicine
2001 Blaisdell Ave S, Minneapolis, 952-993-8006

Bache-Wiig, Ben (16 mentions)
U of Wisconsin, 1983 *Certification:* Internal Medicine
3366 Oakdale Ave N #315, Robbinsdale, 763-587-7900
50 Central Ave, Osseo, 763-587-7900
9825 Hospital Dr #300, Maple Grove, 763-587-7900

Balke, Jeffrey (3 mentions)
U of Minnesota, 1989 *Certification:* Internal Medicine
1515 St Frances Ave #100, Shakopee, 952-403-3535

Beck, Richard Lee (3 mentions)
U of Minnesota, 1970 *Certification:* Internal Medicine
8240 Golden Valley Dr, Golden Valley, 952-993-8300

Benson, Bradley John (5 mentions)
Vanderbilt U, 1994 *Certification:* Internal Medicine, Pediatrics
516 Delaware St SE #3A, Minneapolis, 612-624-9499

Butler, John C. (4 mentions)
Washington U, 1980
Certification: Geriatric Medicine, Internal Medicine
3930 Northwoods Dr, Arden Hills, 651-490-6700

Callaghan, Charles Leo (3 mentions)
Loyola U Chicago, 1993 *Certification:* Internal Medicine
17 Exchange St W #420, St Paul, 651-232-4125

Conroy, William Everett (3 mentions)
U of Minnesota, 1986 *Certification:* Internal Medicine
3800 Park Nicollet Blvd, St Louis Park, 952-993-1500

Cummings, Michael Kevin (7 mentions)
U of Minnesota, 1986 *Certification:* Internal Medicine
8100 W 78th St #100, Edina, 952-914-8100

Finell, James Joseph (4 mentions)
U of Minnesota, 1979 *Certification:* Internal Medicine
17 Exchange St W #420, St Paul, 651-232-4125

Gantzer, Heather (7 mentions)
Washington U, 1985 *Certification:* Internal Medicine
3850 Park Nicollet Blvd 3rd Fl, St Louis Park, 952-993-3333

Gehrig, Donald Eugene (3 mentions)
Indiana U, 1976 *Certification:* Internal Medicine
393 Dunlap St N #834, St Paul, 651-644-5610

Gotlieb, Paul Steven (9 mentions)
U of Minnesota, 1989 *Certification:* Internal Medicine
3400 W 66th St #385, Edina, 952-920-2761

Ivins, Gary Martin (8 mentions)
U of Illinois, 1982 *Certification:* Internal Medicine
6545 France Ave S #225, Edina, 952-927-7079

Klevan, David Henry (3 mentions)
U of Minnesota, 1974
Certification: Geriatric Medicine, Internal Medicine
2500 Como Ave, St Paul, 651-641-6200

Krieger, Darrell Anthony (5 mentions)
U of Texas-Southwestern, 1983 *Certification:* Internal Medicine
3366 Oakdale Ave N #215, Robbinsdale, 763-587-7900
50 Central Ave, Osseo, 763-587-7900
9825 Hospital Dr #300, Maple Grove, 763-587-7900

Lehman, Gregory (7 mentions)
U of Wisconsin, 1981 *Certification:* Internal Medicine
3850 Park Nicollet Blvd, St Louis Park, 952-993-3123

Macomber, David Wright (3 mentions)
U of Minnesota, 1996 *Certification:* Internal Medicine
516 Delaware St SE #3A, Minneapolis, 612-624-9499

Meyer, Charles Robert (5 mentions)
Northwestern U, 1974 *Certification:* Internal Medicine
3400 W 66th St #385, Edina, 952-920-2761

Miley, Mary Ann Zitur (4 mentions)
U of Minnesota, 1987 *Certification:* Internal Medicine
3007 Harbor Ln N, Plymouth, 952-993-8900

Morrison, George H., III (9 mentions)
Creighton U, 1977 *Certification:* Internal Medicine
407 W 66th St, Richfield, 612-798-8800

Nelson, Averial E. (3 mentions)
U of Minnesota, 1977
2004 Ford Pkwy, St Paul, 651-696-8800

Nerenberg, Lex Aaron (4 mentions)
U of Minnesota, 1982 *Certification:* Internal Medicine
2805 Campus Dr #345, Plymouth, 763-520-2980

Ogden, William Barlow (8 mentions)
Northwestern U, 1970 *Certification:* Internal Medicine
255 Smith Ave N #100, St Paul, 651-241-5000
1560 Beam Ave, Maplewood, 651-241-5000

Quebral, Bernard Racho (5 mentions)
FMS-Philippines, 1990 *Certification:* Internal Medicine
8450 Seasons Pkwy, Woodbury, 651-702-5300

Radosevich, Steven Gerard (3 mentions)
U of Minnesota, 1977 *Certification:* Internal Medicine
2500 Como Ave, St Paul, 952-967-7955

Reed, Jason Jerome (4 mentions)
U of Iowa, 1994
920 E 28th St #740, Minneapolis, 612-870-7711

Rodel, Donna Marie (6 mentions)
U of Minnesota, 1986 *Certification:* Internal Medicine
8100 W 78th St #100, Edina, 952-914-8100

Schmidt, Mark Joseph (3 mentions)
U of Minnesota, 1973
Certification: Gastroenterology, Internal Medicine
825 S 8th St #600, Minneapolis, 612-332-3517

Skarda, Paula Kay (3 mentions)
U of Minnesota, 1993 *Certification:* Internal Medicine, Pediatrics
401 Phalen Blvd, St Paul, 651-967-7875

Smiley, David Charles (3 mentions)
U of Wisconsin, 1986 *Certification:* Internal Medicine
3366 Oakdale Ave N #215, Robbinsdale, 763-587-7900
50 Central Ave, Osseo, 763-587-7900
9825 Hospital Dr #300, Maple Grove, 763-587-7900

Spears, Samuel William (3 mentions)
Med Coll of Wisconsin, 1998 *Certification:* Internal Medicine
3400 W 66th St #385, Edina, 952-920-2761

Sutter, Paul M. (6 mentions)
Northwestern U, 1982 *Certification:* Internal Medicine
8100 W 78th St #100, Edina, 952-914-8100

Tsai, Steve Yuanchung (3 mentions)
U of Minnesota, 1975 *Certification:* Internal Medicine
303 E Nicollet Blvd #200, Burnsville, 952-460-4000

Vaurio, C. Edward (4 mentions)
U of Minnesota, 1968 *Certification:* Internal Medicine
825 S 8th St #600, Minneapolis, 612-332-3517

Walcher, David J. (3 mentions)
U of Minnesota, 1976 *Certification:* Internal Medicine
6545 France Ave S #225, Edina, 952-927-7079

Warren, James Bryan (3 mentions)
U of Minnesota, 1978 *Certification:* Internal Medicine
401 Phalen Blvd, St Paul, 651-254-3456

Weisz, Cynthia Lee (8 mentions)
U of Minnesota, 1994 *Certification:* Internal Medicine
3366 Oakdale Ave N #215, Robbinsdale, 763-587-7900
50 Central Ave, Osseo, 763-587-7900
9825 Hospital Dr #300, Maple Grove, 763-587-7900

Woolley, Anthony Coburn (4 mentions)
U of Minnesota, 1981
Certification: Internal Medicine, Nephrology
3850 Park Nicollet Blvd, St Louis Park, 952-993-3333

Worner, Tod Jared (4 mentions)
U of Minnesota, 2000 *Certification:* Internal Medicine
8100 W 78th St #100, Edina, 952-914-8100

Nephrology

Abraham, Paul Allan (21 mentions)
U of Minnesota, 1974
Certification: Internal Medicine, Nephrology
401 Phalen Blvd, St Paul, 651-254-7850

Davin, Thomas Dennis (32 mentions)
Johns Hopkins U, 1972
Certification: Internal Medicine, Nephrology
4310 Nicollet Ave S, Minneapolis, 612-823-8001

Gray, John R. (12 mentions)
U of North Dakota, 1987
Certification: Internal Medicine, Nephrology
4080 W Broadway Ave #132, Robbinsdale, 763-544-0696

Opsahl, John Alfred (7 mentions)
U of Minnesota, 1979
Certification: Internal Medicine, Nephrology
6490 Excelsior Blvd #W300, St Louis Park, 952-993-3265

Sinaiko, Alan Robert (7 mentions)
U of Minnesota, 1965
Certification: Pediatric Nephrology, Pediatrics
516 Delaware St SE, Minneapolis, 612-626-6777

Somermeyer, Michael Grant (9 mentions)
U of Iowa, 1977 *Certification:* Critical Care Medicine,
Internal Medicine, Nephrology
4080 W Broadway Ave #132, Robbinsdale, 763-544-0696

Somerville, James H. (21 mentions)
U of Maryland, 1975 *Certification:* Internal Medicine, Nephrology
6363 France Ave S #400, Edina, 952-920-2070

Stuart, William Scott, Jr. (7 mentions)
U of Nebraska, 1996 *Certification:* Internal Medicine, Nephrology
6490 Excelsior Blvd #300W, St Louis Park, 952-993-3242

Synhavsky, Arkady (15 mentions)
U of Minnesota, 1979
Certification: Internal Medicine, Nephrology
2085 Rice St, Roseville, 651-489-9035

Thielen, Kimberlee Ann (9 mentions)
U of Minnesota, 1990 *Certification:* Critical Care Medicine,
Internal Medicine, Nephrology
4310 Nicollet Ave S, Minneapolis, 612-823-8001

Neurological Surgery

Bergman, Thomas Alan (18 mentions)
U of Minnesota, 1982 *Certification:* Neurological Surgery
913 E 26th St #305, Minneapolis, 612-871-7278

Dyste, Gregg Norman (17 mentions)
U of Minnesota, 1983 *Certification:* Neurological Surgery
9145 Springbrook Dr #202, Coon Rapids, 763-427-1137
800 E 28th St #304, Minneapolis, 763-427-1137

Nagib, Mahmoud Gamal (36 mentions)
FMS-Egypt, 1973 *Certification:* Neurological Surgery
913 E 26th St #305, Minneapolis, 612-871-7278

Neurology

Altafullah, Irfan M. (9 mentions)
FMS-India, 1981 *Certification:* Neurology, Vascular Neurology
4225 Golden Valley Rd, Golden Valley, 763-588-0661

Anderson, David Clifford (7 mentions)
U of Minnesota, 1969
Certification: Internal Medicine, Neurology, Vascular Neurology
516 Delaware St SE, Minneapolis, 612-624-1903
701 Park Ave #200, Minneapolis, 612-873-2595

Breningstall, Galen (8 mentions)
U of Texas-Galveston, 1979 *Certification:* Neurology with
Special Qualifications in Child Neurology, Pediatrics
200 University Ave E, St Paul, 651-291-2840
305 E Nicollet Blvd, Burnsville, 952-223-3400

Burstein, Lawrence (8 mentions)
U of Arizona, 1979 *Certification:* Neurology with Special
Qualifications in Child Neurology, Pediatrics
910 E 26th St #210, Minneapolis, 612-879-1000

Charnas, Lawrence Richard (5 mentions)
U of Pennsylvania, 1981 *Certification:* Clinical Biochemical/
Molecular Genetics, Clinical Genetics, Neurology, Neurology
with Special Qualifications in Child Neurology
516 Delaware St SE, Minneapolis, 612-626-6777

Hanson, Sandra Kay (12 mentions)
U of Minnesota, 1987 *Certification:* Neurology
6490 Excelsior Blvd #E500, St Louis Park, 952-993-3200

Horowitz, Charles Harold (14 mentions)
U of Minnesota, 1984 *Certification:* Neurology
4225 Golden Valley Rd, Golden Valley, 763-588-0661

Janousek, Steven Timothy (14 mentions)
U of Minnesota, 1984 *Certification:* Neurology with Special
Qualifications in Child Neurology
910 E 26th St #210, Minneapolis, 612-879-1000

Langer, Sara (7 mentions)
U of Minnesota, 1985 *Certification:* Neurology
910 E 26th St #210, Minneapolis, 612-879-1500

Norback, Bruce Allan (8 mentions)
U of Minnesota, 1969 *Certification:* Neurology
4225 Golden Valley Rd, Golden Valley, 763-588-0661

Ormiston, Charles Foster (7 mentions)
U of North Dakota, 1979 *Certification:* Neurology
1650 Beam Ave, Maplewood, 651-221-9051

Randa, Daniel Craig (6 mentions)
U of Iowa, 1972 *Certification:* Neurology
3833 Coon Rapids Blvd NW #100, Coon Rapids, 763-427-8320
919 Northland Blvd, Princeton, 763-389-6353
150 10th St, Mailaca, 320-983-7400

Rogin, Joanne Belle (5 mentions)
U of Minnesota, 1977 *Certification:* Neurology
4225 Golden Valley Rd, Golden Valley, 763-588-0661

Schanfield, Paul Morris (7 mentions)
U of Minnesota, 1972 *Certification:* Neurology
1650 Beam Ave, Maplewood, 651-221-9051

Shronts, Richard Foster (10 mentions)
U of Minnesota, 1973 *Certification:* Internal Medicine, Neurology
910 E 26th St #210, Minneapolis, 612-879-1000

Taylor, Frederick Robert (5 mentions)
U of New Mexico, 1977 *Certification:* Neurology with Special
Qualifications in Child Neurology, Pediatrics
6490 Excelsior Blvd #E500, Minneapolis, 952-993-3200

Trusheim, John Edwin (9 mentions)
U of Missouri, 1980 *Certification:* Neurology
3400 W 66th St #150, Edina, 952-920-7200

Obstetrics/Gynecology

Beadle, Edward Michael (7 mentions)
U of Minnesota, 1978 *Certification:* Obstetrics & Gynecology
7450 France Ave S #240, Edina, 952-893-9100

Curran, David Lee (5 mentions)
Dartmouth Coll, 1984 *Certification:* Obstetrics & Gynecology
305 E Nicollet Blvd #393, Burnsville, 952-435-9505
3625 W 65th St #100, Edina, 952-920-7001

Elfstrand, Elizabeth P. (3 mentions)
U of Minnesota, 1989 *Certification:* Obstetrics & Gynecology
801 Nicollet Mall #400, Minneapolis, 612-333-2503
3250 W 66th St #200, Edina, 952-927-6561
2805 Campus Dr #245, Plymouth, 763-577-7460

Flom, Andrea Jeanne (4 mentions)
U of Minnesota, 1986 *Certification:* Obstetrics & Gynecology
3250 W 66th St #200, Edina, 952-927-6561
801 Nicollet Mall #400, Minneapolis, 612-333-2503

Gibeau, Lynne Marie (3 mentions)
U of Minnesota, 1994 *Certification:* Obstetrics & Gynecology
121 S 8th St #600, Minneapolis, 612-333-4822
2800 Chicago Ave S, Minneapolis, 612-333-4822

Kilburg, Elizabeth Alma (3 mentions)
U of Minnesota, 1982 *Certification:* Obstetrics & Gynecology
121 S 8th St #600, Minneapolis, 612-333-4822
2800 Chicago Ave S #101, Minneapolis, 612-333-4822

Kreider, Joan Elizabeth (3 mentions)
Med Coll of Ohio, 1978 *Certification:* Obstetrics & Gynecology
2635 University Ave W #160, St Paul, 651-254-3500

La Valleur, June (4 mentions)
U of Minnesota, 1987 *Certification:* Obstetrics & Gynecology
420 Delaware St SE #1C, Minneapolis, 612-626-3444
606 24th Ave S #300, Minneapolis, 612-273-7111

Larose, Mark Robert (3 mentions)
St Louis U, 1988 *Certification:* Obstetrics & Gynecology
424 W Hwy 5, Waconia, 952-442-4461

Lawson, Lex Coulter (3 mentions)
U of Minnesota, 1978 *Certification:* Obstetrics & Gynecology
500 Osborne Rd NE #255, Fridley, 763-786-6011

Less, Ronald (4 mentions)
Rush U, 1992 *Certification:* Obstetrics & Gynecology
1655 Beam Ave #102, Maplewood, 651-770-1385
17 Exchange St W #622, St Paul, 651-227-9141

Levitan, Judith Amy (3 mentions)
U of Minnesota, 1990 *Certification:* Obstetrics & Gynecology
121 S 8th St #600, Minneapolis, 612-333-4822
2800 Chicago Ave S #101, Minneapolis, 612-333-4822

Lupo, Virginia Ruth (9 mentions)
U of Minnesota, 1976
Certification: Maternal-Fetal Medicine, Obstetrics & Gynecology
825 S 8th St #M50, Minneapolis, 612-347-6450

Maag, Linda Jean (3 mentions)
Northwestern U, 1991 *Certification:* Obstetrics & Gynecology
801 Nicollet Mall #400, Minneapolis, 612-333-2503
3250 W 66th St #200, Edina, 952-927-6561
2805 Campus Dr #245, Plymouth, 763-577-7460

Messina, Andrea (4 mentions)
SUNY-Buffalo, 1989 *Certification:* Obstetrics & Gynecology
5320 Hyland Greens Dr, Bloomington, 952-993-3282

Mies, Annette N. (4 mentions)
U of Minnesota, 1983 *Certification:* Obstetrics & Gynecology
8650 Hudson Blvd #325, Lake Elmo, 651-227-9141
14655 Galaxy Ave, Apple Valley, 952-953-9259

Nielsen, Jon Scott (3 mentions)
U of Minnesota, 1976 *Certification:* Obstetrics & Gynecology
3366 Oakdale Ave N #450, Robbinsdale, 763-587-7000
2855 Campus Dr #600, Minneapolis, 763-587-7025

Petersen, Diane E. B. (10 mentions)
U of Minnesota, 1985 *Certification:* Obstetrics & Gynecology
121 S 8th St #600, Minneapolis, 612-333-4822
2800 Chicago Ave S, Minneapolis, 612-333-4822

Peterson, Ronald John (3 mentions)
Northwestern U, 1973 *Certification:* Obstetrics & Gynecology
801 Nicollet Mall #400, Minneapolis, 612-333-2503
3250 W 66th St #200, Edina, 952-927-6561
2805 Campus Dr #245, Plymouth, 763-577-7460

Schaffer, Janet (5 mentions)
U of Minnesota, 1990 *Certification:* Obstetrics & Gynecology
3800 Park Nicollet Blvd, St Louis Park, 952-993-3282

Strathy, Janette H. (6 mentions)
Mayo Med Sch, 1981 *Certification:* Obstetrics & Gynecology
3800 Park Nicollet Blvd, St Louis Park, 952-993-3123

Teigen, Gregg Allan (3 mentions)
St Louis U, 1993 *Certification:* Obstetrics & Gynecology
14001 Ridgedale Dr #200, Minnetonka, 952-249-2000
800 Prairie Center Dr #130, Eden Prairie, 952-249-2000

Thorp, Deborah Ann (5 mentions)
U of Minnesota, 1984 *Certification:* Obstetrics & Gynecology
2001 Blaisdell Ave S, Minneapolis, 952-993-3282

Toppin, Barbara Carnett (3 mentions)
U of Cincinnati, 1982 *Certification:* Obstetrics & Gynecology
1875 Woodwinds Dr #110, Woodbury, 651-686-6400

Trygstad, Eric William (3 mentions)
U of Minnesota, 1978 *Certification:* Obstetrics & Gynecology
2220 Riverside Ave, Minneapolis, 952-967-7619

Votel, Joanne B. (4 mentions)
U of Minnesota, 1984 *Certification:* Obstetrics & Gynecology
1737 Beam Ave, Maplewood, 651-770-3320

Wilbrand-Conley, Ingrid E. (3 mentions)
Creighton U, 1978 *Certification:* Obstetrics & Gynecology
1737 Beam Ave, St Paul, 651-770-3320

Ophthalmology

Benegas, Nancy Mayer (9 mentions)
U of Minnesota, 1993 *Certification:* Ophthalmology
8600 Nicollet Ave S, Minneapolis, 952-887-6600
8325 Seasons Pkwy, Woodbury, 651-702-5873

Cantrill, Herbert Lee (4 mentions)
Harvard U, 1972 *Certification:* Ophthalmology
7760 France Ave S #310, Edina, 952-929-1131
2855 Campus Dr #510, Plymouth, 763-550-1002
393 Dunlap St N #231, St Paul, 651-644-8993
3701 12th St N #102, St Cloud, 320-654-8353
4815 W Arrowhead Rd #210, Hermantown, 218-625-5020

Carpel, Emmett Franklin (7 mentions)
Hahnemann U, 1968 *Certification:* Ophthalmology
8600 Nicollet Ave S, Bloomington, 952-887-6600
5100 Gamble Dr #100, St Louis Park, 952-595-6498

Day, Daniel Kilgore (10 mentions)
U of Iowa, 1977 *Certification:* Internal Medicine, Ophthalmology
3366 Oakdale Ave N #402, Robbinsdale, 763-416-7600
2805 Campus Dr #105, Plymouth, 763-416-7600

Diegel, John Timothy (7 mentions)
U of Minnesota, 1972 *Certification:* Ophthalmology
3900 Park Nicollet Blvd, St Louis Park, 952-993-3150

Engel, Kevin Charles (5 mentions)
U of Minnesota, 2003
825 S 8th St, Minneapolis, 612-347-5278
701 Parks Ave #P-7, Minneapolis, 612-873-5577

Everson, Marshall H., Jr. (4 mentions)
U of Minnesota, 1985 *Certification:* Ophthalmology
14050 Nicollet Ave #101, Burnsville, 952-435-4170
7450 France Ave S #100, Edina, 952-832-8100

Freeman, Richard Scott (7 mentions)
U of Minnesota, 1982 *Certification:* Ophthalmology
6060 Clearwater Dr #150, Minnetonka, 763-416-7600
12000 Elm Creek Blvd #100, Maple Grove, 763-416-7600

Hardten, David Ronald (4 mentions)
U of Kansas, 1987 *Certification:* Ophthalmology
710 E 24th St #100, Minneapolis, 612-813-3600
9801 Dupont Ave S, Bloomington, 952-888-5800

Harrison, Andrew Richard (4 mentions)
U of Missouri, 1993 *Certification:* Ophthalmology
6405 France Ave S #W460, Edina, 952-925-4161
420 Delaware St SE, Minneapolis, 612-625-4400

Janda, Alvina Marie (4 mentions)
U of Wisconsin, 1980 *Certification:* Ophthalmology
8600 Nicollet Ave S, Bloomington, 952-886-7050

Kobrin, Jerry L. (9 mentions)
Rosalind Franklin U, 1973 *Certification:* Ophthalmology
401 Phalen Blvd, St Paul, 651-967-7611

Mitchell, James Murray (4 mentions)
Duke U, 1975 *Certification:* Ophthalmology
3100 W 70th St, Edina, 952-848-8300

Nathenson, Aaron Louis (4 mentions)
U of Minnesota, 1965 *Certification:* Ophthalmology
825 S 8th St #M16, Minneapolis, 612-347-6450

Nelson, J. Daniel (5 mentions)
U of Minnesota, 1975 *Certification:* Ophthalmology
401 Phalen Blvd, St Paul, 651-254-7400

Ostrow, Robert David (4 mentions)
U of Minnesota, 1966 *Certification:* Ophthalmology
5851 Duluth St #215, Golden Valley, 763-546-8422
2855 Campus Dr #520, Plymouth, 763-553-0288

Rakes, Steven Michael (8 mentions)
U of Nebraska, 1982 *Certification:* Ophthalmology
3900 Park Nicollet Blvd, St Louis Park, 952-993-3150

Ramsay, Robert Carlson (7 mentions)
FMS-Canada, 1968 *Certification:* Ophthalmology
7760 France Ave S #310, Edina, 952-929-1131
2855 Campus Dr #510, Minneapolis, 763-550-1002

Sadowsky, Alan Eugene (4 mentions)
U of Minnesota, 1981 *Certification:* Ophthalmology
6341 University Ave NE, Fridley, 763-572-5705

Sher, Neal A. (7 mentions)
Boston U, 1971 *Certification:* Ophthalmology
825 Nicollet Mall, Minneapolis, 612-338-4861

Summers, Carole Gail (7 mentions)
U of Minnesota, 1979 *Certification:* Ophthalmology
516 Delaware St SE #9-100, Minneapolis, 612-625-4400
3900 Park Nicollet Blvd, St Louis Park, 612-625-4400

Terry, Joseph Matthew (4 mentions)
Tufts U, 1971 *Certification:* Ophthalmology
420 Delaware St SE, Minneapolis, 612-625-9600
1 Veterans Dr, Minneapolis, 612-725-2000

Zwickey, Todd Alan (4 mentions)
U of Minnesota, 1981 *Certification:* Ophthalmology
3100 W 70th St, Edina, 952-848-8300

Orthopedics

Buss, Daniel Dufva (13 mentions)
U of Minnesota, 1983 *Certification:* Orthopaedic Surgery
2800 Chicago Ave S #400, Minneapolis, 612-339-2300
8100 W 78th St #230, Edina, 612-339-2300
2000 Abbott NW Ct #320, Sartell, 612-339-2300

Cheng, Edward Y. (8 mentions)
Northwestern U, 1983 *Certification:* Orthopaedic Surgery
2512 S 7th St #R102, Minneapolis, 612-273-9400

Cole, Peter Alexander (6 mentions)
U of Miami, 1990 *Certification:* Orthopaedic Surgery
640 Jackson St, St Paul, 651-254-8300
435 Phalen Blvd, St Paul, 651-254-8300

Daly, Peter John (8 mentions)
Mayo Med Sch, 1986 *Certification:* Orthopaedic Surgery
17 Exchange St W #307, St Paul, 651-842-5430
1875 Woodwinds Dr #150, Woodbury, 651-842-5430

Damrow, Paul Richard (8 mentions)
U of Minnesota, 1986 *Certification:* Orthopaedic Surgery
2001 Blaisdell Ave S, Minneapolis, 952-993-8000
6490 Excelsior Blvd, St Louis Park, 952-993-3230

Drake, Douglas Albert (5 mentions)
U of Minnesota, 1972
Certification: Orthopaedic Surgery, Surgery of the Hand
3250 W 66th St #100, Edina, 952-920-0970
920 E 28th St #440, Minneapolis, 952-920-0970

Gannon, James Mark (9 mentions)
U of Minnesota, 1986 *Certification:* Orthopaedic Surgery
1600 St Johns Blvd #101, Maplewood, 651-842-5430
8675 Valley Creek Rd, Woodbury, 651-842-5430

Hauck, Rolf Severin (7 mentions)
U of Colorado, 1983 *Certification:* Orthopaedic Surgery
3366 Oakdale Ave N #103, Robbinsdale, 763-520-7870
2855 Campus Dr #660, Plymouth, 763-520-7870

Heller, Mark Albert (4 mentions)
U of Minnesota, 1991 *Certification:* Orthopaedic Surgery
701 25th Ave S #505, Minneapolis, 612-455-2008

Hunt, Allan Fai (6 mentions)
U of Minnesota, 1994 *Certification:* Orthopaedic Surgery
15800 95th Ave N, St Louis Park, 952-993-3230
5320 Hyand Greens Dr, Bloomington, 952-993-2400

La Prade, Robert Francis (4 mentions)
U of Illinois, 1987 *Certification:* Orthopaedic Surgery
2512 S 7th St #102, Minneapolis, 612-273-9400

Larson, Christopher M. (7 mentions)
U of Minnesota, 1995
Certification: Orthopaedic Sports Medicine, Orthopaedic Surgery
775 Prairie Center Dr #250, Eden Prairie, 952-944-2519
701 25th Ave S #304, Minneapolis, 952-944-2519

Larson, James Richard (6 mentions)
U of Minnesota, 1973 *Certification:* Orthopaedic Surgery
2800 Chicago Ave S #400, Minneapolis, 612-879-6623
2000 Abbott Northwestern Dr #320, St Cloud, 612-879-6623
8100 W 78th St #225, Edina, 612-879-6623

Nelson, Thomas E. (9 mentions)
U of Minnesota, 1986 *Certification:* Orthopaedic Surgery
7373 France Ave S #312, Edina, 952-832-0076

O'Neill, Brian T. (4 mentions)
Mayo Med Sch, 1988
Certification: Orthopaedic Sports Medicine, Orthopaedic Surgery
3366 Oakdale Ave N #103, Robbinsdale, 763-520-7870
2855 Campus Dr #660, Minneapolis, 763-520-7870

Riggi, Kayvon Scott (6 mentions)
Mayo Med Sch, 1988 *Certification:* Orthopaedic Surgery
2855 Campus Dr #660, Plymouth, 952-920-0970
3250 W 66th St #100, Edina, 952-920-0970

Schmidt, Andrew Howard (4 mentions)
U of California-San Diego, 1988
Certification: Orthopaedic Surgery
825 S 8th St, Minneapolis, 612-347-2233
913 S 7th St, Minneapolis, 612-873-4301

Steubs, John Arthur (6 mentions)
U of Minnesota, 1979
8100 N Land Dr, Bloomington, 952-831-8742

Strathy, Greg (5 mentions)
Mayo Med Sch, 1980 *Certification:* Orthopaedic Surgery
6490 Excelsior Blvd #E400, St Louis Park, 952-993-3230

Sundberg, Stephen Bruce (13 mentions)
U of Minnesota, 1979 *Certification:* Orthopaedic Surgery
200 University Ave E, St Paul, 651-291-2848
6060 Clearwater Dr #100, Minnetonka, 952-936-0977

Switzer, Julie (4 mentions)
Stanford U, 1994 *Certification:* Orthopaedic Surgery
640 Jackson St, St Paul, 651-254-8300
435 Phalen Blvd, Minneapolis, 651-254-8300

Szalapski, Edward William (4 mentions)
U of Minnesota, 1984 *Certification:* Orthopaedic Surgery
600 W 98th St #150, Bloomington, 952-927-7565
6363 France Ave S #404, Edina, 952-927-4525

Templeman, David Clyde (4 mentions)
U of Iowa, 1981 *Certification:* Orthopaedic Surgery
913-S 7th St, Minneapolis, 612-873-4301

Teynor, Joseph Thomas (7 mentions)
U of Minnesota, 1981 *Certification:* Orthopaedic Surgery
6363 France Ave S #404, Edina, 952-927-4525
600 W 98th St, Bloomington, 952-881-3112

Varecka, Thomas Francis (4 mentions)
SUNY-Buffalo, 1974 *Certification:* Orthopaedic Surgery
2805 Campus Dr #425, Plymouth, 763-383-0770

Walker, Kevin Richard (6 mentions)
U of Minnesota, 1991 *Certification:* Orthopaedic Surgery
200 University Ave E, St Paul, 651-291-2848
6060 Clearwater Dr #100, Minnetonka, 952-936-0977

Otorhinolaryngology

Biel, Merrill A. (19 mentions)
U of Illinois, 1981 *Certification:* Otolaryngology
2211 Park Ave S, Minneapolis, 612-871-1144
5851 Duluth St #204, Golden Valley, 763-513-9513
6545 France Ave S #650, Edina, 952-925-3905

Brown, Carl Allen (16 mentions)
U of Minnesota, 1973 *Certification:* Otolaryngology
2211 Park Ave S, Minneapolis, 612-871-1144
347 Smith Ave N, St Paul, 612-871-1144

Griebie, Matthew Scott (10 mentions)
U of Minnesota, 1982 *Certification:* Otolaryngology
6545 France Ave S #650, Edina, 952-925-3905
303 E Nicollet Blvd #333, Burnsville, 952-435-3050

Lander, Timothy Alan (6 mentions)
U of Minnesota, 1996 *Certification:* Otolaryngology
910 E 26th St #323, Minneapolis, 612-874-1292

Malone, Barbara Newman (13 mentions)
U of Michigan, 1982 *Certification:* Otolaryngology
2080 Woodwinds Dr #240, Woodbury, 651-702-0750
1675 Beam Ave #200, Maplewood, 651-770-1105
225 N Smith Ave #502, Woodbury, 651-645-0691
3440 O'Leary Ln #102, Eagan, 651-452-1509

Rimell, Franklin Lipman (9 mentions)
Rosalind Franklin U, 1988 *Certification:* Otolaryngology
516 Delaware St SE 8th Fl, Minneapolis, 612-626-0486

Rosario, Inell Coeseta (6 mentions)
U of Minnesota, 1992 *Certification:* Otolaryngology
2080 Woodwinds Dr #120, Woodbury, 651-702-0750
3440 Oleary Ln #102, Eagan, 651-452-1509
225 N Smith Ave #502, St Paul, 651-645-0691
1675 Beam Ave #200, Maplewood, 651-770-1105

Schmidt, Derek Joseph (6 mentions)
U of Minnesota, 1999 *Certification:* Otolaryngology
640 Jackson St, St Paul, 651-254-3456

Sidman, James David (17 mentions)
Dartmouth Coll, 1982 *Certification:* Otolaryngology
910 E 26th St #323, Minneapolis, 612-874-1292

Tansek, Karin M. (6 mentions)
Michigan State U, 1976 *Certification:* Otolaryngology
2855 Campus Dr #630, Plymouth, 763-520-2950
3366 Oakdale Ave N #150, Robbinsdale, 763-520-7840
9825 Hospital Dr, Maple Grove, 763-520-7840

Pain Medicine

Belgrade, Miles J. (16 mentions)
U of Illinois, 1982 *Certification:* Neurology, Pain Medicine
2450 Riverside Ave, Minneapolis, 612-273-5400

Hess, Todd Michael (12 mentions)
U of Minnesota, 1986 *Certification:* Anesthesiology
280 N Smith Ave #600, St Paul, 651-241-7246

Lutz, Lon J. (4 mentions)
U of North Dakota, 1985 *Certification:* Anesthesiology
1700 University Ave W, St Paul, 651-232-5348
17 Exchange St W #310, St Paul, 651-842-5465

Monsein, Matthew Robert (19 mentions)
Albert Einstein Coll of Med, 1975
3915 Golden Valley Rd, Minneapolis, 763-520-0412

Schultz, David Matthew (13 mentions)
U of Minnesota, 1981
Certification: Anesthesiology, Pain Medicine
7400 France Ave S #100, Edina, 763-537-6000
2104 Northdale Blvd NW, Coon Rapids, 763-537-6000

Pathology

Dale, Virginia (9 mentions)
U of Minnesota, 1983
Certification: Anatomic Pathology & Clinical Pathology
3300 Oakdale Ave N, Robbinsdale, 763-520-5525

Lillemoe, Tamera Jensen (6 mentions)
U of Minnesota, 1985
Certification: Anatomic Pathology & Clinical Pathology
800 E 28th St, Minneapolis, 612-863-4670

Snover, Dale Craig (8 mentions)
Pennsylvania State U, 1977 *Certification:* Anatomic Pathology
6401 France Ave S, Minneapolis, 952-924-5152

Weatherby, Richard P., Jr. (9 mentions)
Mayo Med Sch, 1978
Certification: Anatomic Pathology & Clinical Pathology
500 S Maple St, Waconia, 952-442-2191

Pediatrics *(see note on page 9)*

Anderson, Renner Stephen (5 mentions)
U of Minnesota, 1975 *Certification:* Pediatrics
15111 Twelve Oaks Center Dr, Minnetonka, 952-993-4570

Anderson, Timothy John (8 mentions)
U of Minnesota, 1983 *Certification:* Pediatrics
501 E Nicollet Blvd #200, Burnsville, 952-898-5900

Chawla, Pamela (3 mentions)
Certification: Pediatrics
345 Smith Ave N, St Paul, 651-220-6000

Estrin, David Lee (3 mentions)
U of Minnesota, 1974 *Certification:* Pediatrics
2805 Campus Dr #235, Plymouth, 952-401-8222

Hogan, Marjorie Joan (5 mentions)
Stanford U, 1977 *Certification:* Adolescent Medicine, Pediatrics
701 Park Ave, Minneapolis, 612-873-2435

Inman, Steven Verne (10 mentions)
U of Minnesota, 1982 *Certification:* Pediatrics
5111 Minnetonka Blvd, St Louis Park, 952-922-4200

Jacob, Abraham K. (3 mentions)
Med Coll of Ohio, 1994 *Certification:* Pediatrics
2535 University Ave SE, Minneapolis, 612-672-2350

Kovarik, Teresa Frances (4 mentions)
U of Virginia, 1983 *Certification:* Pediatrics
2500 Como Ave, St Paul, 651-641-6200

Kuperman, Allen Phillip (6 mentions)
U of Minnesota, 1975 *Certification:* Pediatrics
12720 Bass Lake Rd, Maple Grove, 763-559-2861

Le Fevere, Thomas Vernon (3 mentions)
U of Minnesota, 1975 *Certification:* Pediatrics
3955 Parklawn Ave #200, Edina, 952-831-4454
18315 Cascade Dr #170, Eden Prairie, 952-949-0399

Marker, Stephen Clarence (3 mentions)
U of Minnesota, 1967
Certification: Pediatric Infectious Diseases, Pediatrics
2001 Blaisdell Ave S, Minneapolis, 952-993-8000

Martin, Douglas M. (6 mentions)
Mayo Med Sch, 1976 *Certification:* Pediatrics
300 Lake Dr E, Chanhassen, 952-993-4300

McCord, James (6 mentions)
Indiana U, 1982 *Certification:* Pediatrics
347 Smith Ave N #302, St Paul, 651-220-6700

Rzepka, Andrew Austin (8 mentions)
Med Coll of Ohio, 1987 *Certification:* Pediatrics
6000 Earle Brown Dr, Brooklyn Center, 952-993-4900

Segal, Robert Mayer (5 mentions)
U of Minnesota, 1984 *Certification:* Pediatrics
2525 Chicago Ave S, Minneapolis, 612-813-6107

Snellman, Leonard W., III (7 mentions)
Northwestern U, 1979 *Certification:* Pediatrics
1430 Hwy 96 E, White Bear Lake, 651-426-1980

Stang, Howard J. (4 mentions)
U of North Carolina, 1977 *Certification:* Pediatrics
1430 Hwy 96 E, White Bear Lake, 952-967-6614

Stealey, Thomas Ray (4 mentions)
West Virginia U, 1976 *Certification:* Pediatrics
6545 France Ave S #400, Edina, 952-920-9191

Thompson, Theodore Robert (4 mentions)
U of Pennsylvania, 1969
Certification: Neonatal-Perinatal Medicine, Pediatrics
420 Delaware St SE #MMC-39, Minneapolis, 612-626-2841

Wegmann, Kent Wayne (3 mentions)
Indiana U, 1981 *Certification:* Pediatrics
347 Smith Ave N #302, St Paul, 651-220-6700

Plastic Surgery

Christensen, Marie (12 mentions)
Georgetown U, 1975 *Certification:* Plastic Surgery
3900 Park Nicollet Blvd, St Louis Park, 952-993-3504

Fasching, Michael Cloud (10 mentions)
Mayo Med Sch, 1980 *Certification:* Plastic Surgery
2805 Campus Dr #335, Plymouth, 763-577-7500

Harrington, Jennifer Lynn (6 mentions)
Loma Linda U, 1994 *Certification:* Plastic Surgery
7373 France Ave S #510, Edina, 651-290-7600

Hilger, Peter Andrew (6 mentions)
U of Minnesota, 1974 *Certification:* Otolaryngology
7373 France Ave S #410, Edina, 952-844-0404
401 Phalen Blvd, St Paul, 651-254-8550
500 Osborne Rd NE #330, Fridley, 763-786-9024

Kallianien, Loree K. (8 mentions)
U of Michigan, 1991
401 Phalen Blvd, St Paul, 651-254-8290

Landis, George Harold (6 mentions)
U of Arizona, 1988 *Certification:* Plastic Surgery
2855 Campus Dr #500, Plymouth, 763-551-8985

Migliori, Mark R. (13 mentions)
Brown U, 1987 *Certification:* Plastic Surgery
7450 France Ave S #220, Edina, 952-925-1111

Muldowney, J. Bart (13 mentions)
Northwestern U, 1976 *Certification:* Plastic Surgery
7450 France Ave S #220, Edina, 952-925-1111

Nemecek, Jane R. (8 mentions)
U of Missouri, 1985 *Certification:* Plastic Surgery
3900 Park Nicollet Blvd, St Louis Park, 952-993-3504

Schubert, Warren Vincent (10 mentions)
U of North Dakota, 1978 *Certification:* Plastic Surgery
640 Jackson St, St Paul, 651-254-3792

Van Beek, Allen Lester (6 mentions)
U of Minnesota, 1968
Certification: Plastic Surgery, Surgery of the Hand
7373 France Ave S #510, Edina, 952-830-1028

Wood, Robert Jon (7 mentions)
U of Minnesota, 1984 *Certification:* Plastic Surgery
200 University Ave E, St Paul, 651-602-3277
6060 Clearwater Dr #100, Minnetonka, 952-936-0977

Psychiatry

Bebchuk, Joseph M. (4 mentions)
FMS-Canada, 1988 *Certification:* Psychiatry
3800 Park Nicollet Blvd, St Louis Park, 952-993-3123

Colon, Eduardo Anibal (6 mentions)
U of Puerto Rico, 1979
Certification: Psychiatry, Psychosomatic Medicine
914 S 8th St #D110, Minneapolis, 612-347-2218

Crow, Scott John (3 mentions)
U of Minnesota, 1988 *Certification:* Psychiatry
2450 Riverside Ave, Minneapolis, 612-273-9807

Feldman, Michael Julian (3 mentions)
U of North Carolina, 1971 *Certification:* Psychiatry
3800 Park Nicollet Blvd, St Louis Park, 952-993-3307

Gibbs, Timothy P. (4 mentions)
U of Minnesota, 1983
Certification: Child & Adolescent Psychiatry, Psychiatry
800 E 28th St, Minneapolis, 612-863-5327

Goering, Paul Francis (4 mentions)
U of Minnesota, 1988 *Certification:* Psychiatry
333 N Smith Ave, St Paul, 651-241-8565

Groat, Ronald Douglas (8 mentions)
U of Minnesota, 1976 *Certification:* Psychiatry
6525 Drew Ave S, Edina, 952-920-6748

Heinrich, Richard Lester (3 mentions)
U of Chicago, 1971 *Certification:* Psychiatry
8101 34th Ave S 6th Fl, Bloomington, 952-883-7118

Hermansen, Bruce Allen (3 mentions)
U of Minnesota, 1982 *Certification:* Psychiatry
640 Jackson St, St Paul, 651-254-4786
5625 Cenex Dr, Inver Grove Heights, 651-552-1720

Joos, Heidi Louise (3 mentions)
U of Michigan, 1971 *Certification:* Psychiatry
6500 Excelsior Blvd, St Louis Park, 952-993-3307

Knudson, Dean Kevin (4 mentions)
George Washington U, 1984
Certification: Geriatric Psychiatry, Psychiatry
1900 Silverlake Rd #110, New Brighton, 651-628-9566

Larson, Eric Whitesell (3 mentions)
Mayo Med Sch, 1983
Certification: Addiction Psychiatry, Psychiatry
6525 Drew Ave S, Edina, 952-920-6748

Lentz, Richard David (5 mentions)
U of Rochester, 1969
Certification: Pediatric Nephrology, Pediatrics, Psychiatry
2001 Blaisdell Ave S, Minneapolis, 952-993-8011

Main, Bart (3 mentions)
Indiana U, 1977 *Certification:* Child Psychiatry, Psychiatry
1185 Town Center Dr, Eagan, 651-681-1600
327 S Marshall Rd, Shakopee, 651-769-6500
7616 Currell Blvd #290, Woodbury, 651-769-6550

Philander, Dennis Alan (5 mentions)
FMS-South Africa, 1967
Certification: Forensic Psychiatry, Psychiatry
5851 Duluth St #115, Golden Valley, 763-543-6971

Simon, John Ernest (3 mentions)
U of Nebraska, 1976 *Certification:* Psychiatry
701 25th Ave S #S-303, Minneapolis, 612-333-9954

Tranglc, Michael Arno (3 mentions)
U of Minnesota, 1980 *Certification:* Psychiatry
5100 Gamble Dr #100, St Louis Park, 952-593-8777

Zander, Janet Adele (3 mentions)
U of Minnesota, 1976 *Certification:* Psychiatry
640 Jackson St, St Paul, 651-254-4786

Pulmonary Disease

Bonham, David (7 mentions)
Tulane U, 1971 *Certification:* Critical Care Medicine,
  Internal Medicine, Pulmonary Disease
225 Smith Ave N #300, St Paul, 651-224-5895

Colbert, Robert Lee (10 mentions)
U of Minnesota, 1980 *Certification:* Critical Care Medicine,
  Internal Medicine, Pulmonary Disease
3366 Oakdale Ave N #605, Robbinsdale, 763-520-2940

Flink, James (7 mentions)
U of Minnesota, 1974 *Certification:* Critical Care Medicine,
  Internal Medicine, Pulmonary Disease
225 Smith Ave N #300, St Paul, 651-224-5895

Harmon, Keith Robert (11 mentions)
Vanderbilt U, 1982 *Certification:* Critical Care Medicine,
  Internal Medicine, Pulmonary Disease, Sleep Medicine
6490 Excelsior Blvd #300, St Louis Park, 952-993-1240

Hertz, Marshall (8 mentions)
U of Michigan, 1978
Certification: Internal Medicine, Pulmonary Disease
516 Delaware St SE #2A, Minneapolis, 612-626-6100

Iber, Conrad (10 mentions)
U of Illinois, 1974 *Certification:* Internal Medicine,
  Pulmonary Disease, Sleep Medicine
701 S Park Ave #G5, Minneapolis, 612-873-2625

Kaye, Mitchell G. (21 mentions)
U of Minnesota, 1984 *Certification:* Critical Care Medicine,
  Internal Medicine, Pulmonary Disease
920 E 28th St #700, Minneapolis, 612-863-3750

Komadina, Kevin Harris (7 mentions)
Loyola U Chicago, 1981 *Certification:* Critical Care
  Medicine, Internal Medicine, Pulmonary Disease
6490 Excelsior Blvd #300W, St Louis Park, 952-993-3242

Kubic, Paul T. (8 mentions)
U of Minnesota, 1974
Certification: Pediatric Pulmonology, Pediatrics
347 Smith Ave N #601, St Paul, 651-220-7000

Kurachek, Stephen Charles (9 mentions)
U of Miami, 1978 *Certification:* Pediatric Critical Care
  Medicine, Pediatric Pulmonology, Pediatrics
2545 Chicago Ave S #617, Minneapolis, 612-863-3226

McEvoy, Charlene E. (8 mentions)
U of Minnesota, 1986 *Certification:* Internal Medicine,
  Pulmonary Disease, Sleep Medicine
401 Phalen Blvd, St Paul, 651-254-7400

McNamara, John J. (11 mentions)
U of Florida, 1980
Certification: Pediatric Pulmonology, Pediatrics
2545 Chicago Ave S #617, Minneapolis, 612-863-3226

Nahum, Avi (14 mentions)
U of Chicago, 1985 *Certification:* Critical Care Medicine,
  Internal Medicine, Pulmonary Disease
640 Jackson St, St Paul, 651-254-5529
401 Phalen Blvd, St Paul, 651-254-7670

Radiology—Diagnostic

Bauer, Nellie G. (4 mentions)
Creighton U, 1991 *Certification:* Diagnostic Radiology
9855 Hospital Dr, Maple Grove, 763-398-4400
3366 Oakdale Ave N #604, Robbinsdale, 763-398-6600

Fritts, Hollis M., Jr. (5 mentions)
U of Texas-Galveston, 1981 *Certification:* Diagnostic Radiology
5775 Wayzata Blvd #190, Minneapolis, 952-541-1840
910 Sibley Memorial Hwy, Mendota Heights, 651-455-5500

Gross, David Allen (4 mentions)
U of North Dakota, 1987 *Certification:* Diagnostic Radiology
500 S Mable St, Waconia, 952-442-2191

Inampudi, Subba Rao (12 mentions)
FMS-India, 1972 *Certification:* Diagnostic Radiology,
  Vascular & Interventional Radiology
800 E 28th St, Minneapolis, 612-863-4808

Johnson, Randall David (5 mentions)
Harvard U, 1976
Certification: Diagnostic Radiology, Internal Medicine
6500 Excelsior Blvd, St Louis Park, 952-993-5391

Knutzen, Anders Mark (5 mentions)
Harvard U, 1990 *Certification:* Diagnostic Radiology
250 Thompson St, St Paul, 651-297-6505

Larkin, Brian Thomas (4 mentions)
U of Minnesota, 1983
Certification: Diagnostic Radiology, Neuroradiology
9855 Hospital Dr, Maple Grove, 763-398-4400
3366 Oakdale Ave N #604, Robbinsdale, 763-398-6600

Lukens, Jeffrey Arthur (4 mentions)
U of Michigan, 1979 *Certification:* Diagnostic Radiology
7373 France Ave S #204, Edina, 952-345-4178
6405 France Ave S #W440, Edina, 952-345-4178
5203 Vernon Ave S, Minneapolis, 952-848-0104

Mize, William Alan (9 mentions)
U of Cincinnati, 1988
Certification: Diagnostic Radiology, Pediatric Radiology
2525 Chicago Ave S, Minneapolis, 612-813-6248

Murray-Carpenter, Becky L. (5 mentions)
U of Minnesota, 1980
Certification: Diagnostic Radiology, Pediatric Radiology
345 Smith Ave N, St Paul, 651-220-6147

Patterson, Richard John (10 mentions)
Ohio State U, 1982
Certification: Diagnostic Radiology, Pediatric Radiology
2525 Chicago Ave S, Minneapolis, 612-813-6248

Peltola, Thomas William (4 mentions)
Albany Med Coll, 1984 *Certification:* Diagnostic Radiology
9855 Hospital Dr, Maple Grove, 763-398-4400
3366 Oakdale Ave N #604, Robbinsdale, 763-398-6600

Plunkett, Michael Bonner (5 mentions)
Mayo Med Sch, 1984 *Certification:* Diagnostic Radiology
800 E 28th St, Minneapolis, 612-863-4261

Tashjian, Joseph Harry (13 mentions)
Mayo Med Sch, 1976 *Certification:* Diagnostic Radiology
640 Jackson St, St Paul, 651-254-3766

Truwit, Charles L. (4 mentions)
Georgetown U, 1982 *Certification:* Diagnostic Radiology with
  Special Competence in Nuclear Radiology, Neuroradiology
701 Park Ave, Minneapolis, 612-873-2718

Yock, Douglas Harold, Jr. (6 mentions)
Harvard U, 1973
Certification: Diagnostic Radiology, Neuroradiology
800 E 28th St, Minneapolis, 612-863-5446

Radiology—Therapeutic

Grabowski, Carol (6 mentions)
U of Minnesota, 1988
Certification: Hospice and Palliative Medicine, Radiation Oncology
800 E 28th St, Minneapolis, 612-863-4060

Inampudi, Subba Rao (12 mentions)
FMS-India, 1972 *Certification:* Diagnostic Radiology,
  Vascular & Interventional Radiology
800 E 28th St, Minneapolis, 612-863-4808

Tubman, David Edward (6 mentions)
FMS-Canada, 1972 *Certification:* Diagnostic Radiology
800 E 28th St, Minneapolis, 612-863-4000

Rehabilitation

Boyle, Stephanie Iverson (6 mentions)
Michigan State U, 1986
Certification: Physical Medicine & Rehabilitation
6490 Excelsior Blvd, St Louis Park, 952-993-6770

Dykstra, Dennis Dale (5 mentions)
U of Cincinnati, 1976
Certification: Pediatrics, Physical Medicine & Rehabilitation
516 Delaware St SE #1-A, Minneapolis, 612-626-6688

Hutchison, Nancy Ash (6 mentions)
Wake Forest U, 1979
800 E 28th St #1750, Minneapolis, 612-863-4495
800 E 20th St, Minneapolis, 612-863-4495

Koerner, Rebecca Mae (6 mentions)
U of North Dakota, 1978
Certification: Physical Medicine & Rehabilitation
401 Phalen Blvd 4th Fl, St Paul, 651-254-7760

Seizert, Barbara Pittner (5 mentions)
Jefferson Med Coll, 1979
Certification: Physical Medicine & Rehabilitation
800 E 28th St #1750, Minneapolis, 612-863-4495

Speier, Jennine Latorre (10 mentions)
U of Minnesota, 1981
Certification: Physical Medicine & Rehabilitation
800 E 28th St #1750, Minneapolis, 612-863-4495

Taniguchi, Marshall (12 mentions)
U of Michigan, 1985 *Certification:* Pediatric Rehabilitation
  Medicine, Physical Medicine & Rehabilitation
200 University Ave E, St Paul, 651-291-2848

Thompson, Marilyn Adele (7 mentions)
U of Minnesota, 1983 *Certification:* Physical Medicine &
  Rehabilitation, Spinal Cord Injury Medicine
800 E 28th St #1750, Minneapolis, 612-863-4495

Wei, Frank Yishen (8 mentions)
Ohio State U, 1986
Certification: Pain Medicine, Physical Medicine & Rehabilitation
6600 France Ave S #615, Edina, 952-926-8747
301 2nd St NE, New Prague, 952-758-4431

Rheumatology

Dorman, Walter H. (16 mentions)
U of Maryland, 1972
Certification: Internal Medicine, Rheumatology
7250 France Ave S #215, Edina, 952-893-1959

Hargrove, Jody Kay (17 mentions)
U of Minnesota, 1983
Certification: Internal Medicine, Rheumatology
7250 France Ave S #215, Edina, 952-893-1959

Harkcom, Thomas Michael (16 mentions)
Mayo Med Sch, 1977
Certification: Internal Medicine, Rheumatology
401 Phalen Blvd, St Paul, 651-254-7800
2220 Riverside Ave #2, Minneapolis, 612-371-1715

Schned, Eric Steven (16 mentions)
Columbia U, 1975
Certification: Internal Medicine, Rheumatology
3800 Park Nicollet Blvd, St Louis Park, 952-993-3280

Vehe, Richard Karl (15 mentions)
Washington U, 1985 *Certification:* Pediatric Rheumatology
420 Delaware St SE, Minneapolis, 612-626-4873
200 University Ave E, St Paul, 651-229-3892

Waytz, Paul Harvey (22 mentions)
U of Illinois, 1973
Certification: Internal Medicine, Rheumatology
7250 France Ave S #215, Edina, 952-893-1959

Thoracic Surgery

Maddaus, Michael Anthony (14 mentions)
U of Minnesota, 1982 *Certification:* Surgery, Thoracic Surgery
516 Delaware St SE, Minneapolis, 612-624-9122
424 Harvard St #M100, Minneapolis, 612-624-9122

Solfelt, Mark (9 mentions)
U of Minnesota, 1986 *Certification:* Surgery, Thoracic Surgery
4040 Coon Rapids Blvd NW #100, Coon Rapids, 763-236-9500

Spooner, Ted H. (9 mentions)
SUNY-Buffalo, 1979 *Certification:* Thoracic Surgery
6400 Excelsior Blvd, St Louis Park, 952-993-3246

Urology

Aliabadi, Hossein Ali (14 mentions)
FMS-India, 1980 *Certification:* Urology
3850 Parks Nicollet Blvd 4th Fl, St Louis Park, 952-993-3333

Hulbert, John C. (8 mentions)
FMS-United Kingdom, 1975 *Certification:* Urology
6363 France Ave S #500, Edina, 952-920-7660
303 E Nicollet Blvd #310, Burnsville, 952-920-7668

Kaylor, William M., Jr. (14 mentions)
Ohio State U, 1984 *Certification:* Urology
6363 France Ave S #500, Edina, 952-920-7660
303 E Nicollet Blvd #310, Burnsville, 952-920-7668

Kern, Abraham (11 mentions)
Northwestern U, 1974 *Certification:* Urology
920 E 28th St #720, Minneapolis, 612-870-9569
7450 France Ave #250, Edina, 952-920-6577

Knoedler, Christopher J. (14 mentions)
U of Minnesota, 1984 *Certification:* Urology
1655 Beam Ave #206, Maplewood, 651-999-6896

Pergament, Michael Lee (10 mentions)
Emory U, 1968 *Certification:* Urology
6025 Lake Run #200, Woodbury, 651-999-6938
360 Sherman St #400, St Paul, 651-999-6800

Reinberg, Yuri (11 mentions)
FMS-Israel, 1980 *Certification:* Pediatric Urology, Urology
2545 Chicago Ave S #104, Minneapolis, 612-813-8000
500 Osborne Rd NE #125, Fridley, 612-813-8000

Stormont, Thomas James (8 mentions)
Med Coll of Wisconsin, 1987 *Certification:* Urology
1500 Curve Crest Blvd, Stillwater, 651-439-1234
700 Rivard St, Somerset, WI, 651-439-1234

Utz, William Joseph (13 mentions)
Tulane U, 1985 *Certification:* Urology
6525 France Ave S #200, Edina, 952-927-6501

Vascular Surgery

Alden, Peter Brown (14 mentions)
U of Wisconsin, 1981 *Certification:* Surgery, Vascular Surgery
920 E 28th St #300, Minneapolis, 612-863-6800

Miller, John Braun (15 mentions)
U of Tennessee, 1978 *Certification:* Surgery
280 Smith Ave N #311, St Paul, 651-224-1347
1655 Beam Ave #204, Maplewood, 651-224-1347

Omlie, William Richard (22 mentions)
U of Minnesota, 1981 *Certification:* Surgery, Vascular Surgery
6525 France Ave S #275, Edina, 952-831-8346
6405 France Ave S #W440, Edina, 952-927-7004

Roland, Christopher F. (16 mentions)
U of Minnesota, 1985 *Certification:* Surgery, Vascular Surgery
6405 France Ave S #W440, Edina, 952-927-7004

Missouri

Kansas City Area—page 260

St. Louis Area—page 267

Kansas City Area

Including Cass, Clay, Jackson, Johnson, Platte, and Wyandotte Counties

Allergy/Immunology

Abdou, Nabih I. (13 mentions)
FMS-Egypt, 1957 *Certification:* Allergy & Immunology,
Diagnostic Laboratory Immunology
4330 Wornall Rd 4th Fl #40, Kansas City, MO, 816-531-0930

Frankel, Scott Jay (12 mentions)
Washington U, 1979
Certification: Allergy & Immunology, Internal Medicine
8675 College Blvd #200, Overland Park, KS, 913-491-5501

Levine, H. Terry (9 mentions)
Tulane U, 1985
Certification: Allergy & Immunology, Internal Medicine
10787 Nall Ave #200, Overland Park, KS, 913-491-3300

Stechschulte, Daniel J. (12 mentions)
St Louis U, 1962 *Certification:* Allergy & Immunology, Diagnostic
Laboratory Immunology, Internal Medicine, Rheumatology
3901 Rainbow Blvd, Kansas City, KS, 913-588-6008

Wald, Jeffrey Allen (8 mentions)
U of Missouri, 1980
Certification: Allergy & Immunology, Internal Medicine
8675 College Blvd #200, Overland Park, KS, 913-491-5501

Anesthesiology

Armstrong, Andrew Egan (4 mentions)
U of Kansas, 2000 *Certification:* Anesthesiology
2316 E Meyer Blvd, Kansas City, MO, 816-276-4000

Chaffee, Terry Lee (3 mentions)
U of Kansas, 1979 *Certification:* Anesthesiology
3901 Rainbow Blvd, Kansas City, KS, 913-588-6670

Davis, Dirk Bennett (3 mentions)
U of Kansas, 1989 *Certification:* Anesthesiology, Pain Medicine
2316 E Meyer Blvd, Kansas City, MO, 816-276-4000

Kelly, James B., Jr. (7 mentions)
Certification: Anesthesiology
4401 Wornall Rd, Kansas City, MO, 816-932-3679

Kindscher, James David (3 mentions)
U of Kansas, 1982 *Certification:* Anesthesiology
3901 Rainbow Blvd, Kansas City, KS, 913-588-6670

LaSalle, Anthony David (4 mentions)
5001 College Blvd #103, Leawood, KS, 913-339-9437

Matthews, Jeffrey Mark (5 mentions)
Wake Forest U, 1983 *Certification:* Anesthesiology
4401 Wornall Rd, Kansas City, MO, 816-529-4253

McNitt, Jay Dean (5 mentions)
U of Kansas, 1984 *Certification:* Anesthesiology
4401 Wornall Rd, Kansas City, MO, 816-389-6030

Mestad, Peter Harold (4 mentions)
U of California-Los Angeles, 1973
Certification: Anesthesiology, Pediatrics
2401 Gillham Rd, Kansas City, MO, 816-234-3000

Morgan, Richard Lloyd (6 mentions)
U of Kansas, 1980 *Certification:* Anesthesiology, Hospice
and Palliative Medicine, Pain Medicine
1000 Carondelet Dr, Kansas City, MO, 816-943-3926

Robinson, John David (6 mentions)
U of Kansas, 1974 *Certification:* Anesthesiology, Pain Medicine
10540 Barkley St #70, Shawnee Mission, KS, 913-676-2679
9100 W 74th St, Shawnee Mission, KS, 913-676-2679
10950 Grandview St #200, Overland Park, KS, 913-642-4900

Trempy, Gregory Alden (3 mentions)
U of Kansas, 1986 *Certification:* Anesthesiology, Pain Medicine
9100 W 74th St, Overland Park, KS, 913-676-2679
10950 Grandview St #200, Overland Park, KS, 913-642-4900

Venneman, Charles R., II (5 mentions)
U of Kansas, 1986 *Certification:* Anesthesiology, Pain Medicine
1000 Carondelet Dr, Kansas City, MO, 816-943-2251

Wendelburg, Blake Eugene (3 mentions)
U of Kansas, 1992 *Certification:* Anesthesiology
9100 W 74th St, Overland Park, KS, 913-642-4900

Cardiac Surgery

Borkon, Alan Michael (27 mentions)
Johns Hopkins U, 1975
Certification: Surgical Critical Care, Thoracic Surgery
4320 Wornall Rd #50, Kansas City, MO, 816-931-3312

Gorton, Michael Earl (12 mentions)
U of Kansas, 1986 *Certification:* Surgery, Thoracic Surgery
3901 Rainbow Blvd #1232, Kansas City, KS, 913-588-5000
8000 NW Mace Rd, Kansas City, MO, 816-746-8175

Hannah, Hamner, III (12 mentions)
U of Virginia, 1964 *Certification:* Surgery, Thoracic Surgery
6400 Prospect Ave #382, Kansas City, MO, 816-523-7088

Muehlebach, Gregory F. (21 mentions)
St Louis U, 1989 *Certification:* Thoracic Surgery
3901 Rainbow Blvd, Kansas City, KS, 913-588-7743

Seligson, Frederic Lee (19 mentions)
U of Pittsburgh, 1982 *Certification:* Surgery, Thoracic Surgery
6400 Prospect Ave #382, Kansas City, MO, 816-523-7088

Cardiology

Akin, Carl David (4 mentions)
U of Kansas, 1973
Certification: Cardiovascular Disease, Internal Medicine
19550 E 39th St #220, Independence, MO, 816-461-6837

Bogart, Douglas Barry (14 mentions)
U of Kansas, 1971 *Certification:* Cardiovascular Disease,
Internal Medicine, Interventional Cardiology
2301 Holmes St 5th Fl, Kansas City, MO, 816-404-1225

Green, Bob Ed (4 mentions)
U of Iowa, 1991 *Certification:* Cardiovascular Disease
9119 W 74th St #350, Shawnee Mission, KS, 913-789-3290
19550 E 39th St #225, Independence, KS, 816-795-5595

Hockstad, Eric Scott (8 mentions)
U of Michigan, 1989
Certification: Cardiovascular Disease, Interventional Cardiology
6420 Prospect #T509, Kansas City, MO, 816-523-4525
3200 NE Ralph Powell Rd, Lee's Summit, MO, 816-525-1600

Jackson, Jay Allen (7 mentions)
U of Missouri-Kansas City, 1978
Certification: Cardiovascular Disease, Internal Medicine
9119 W 74th St #350, Overland Park, KS, 913-789-3290

Mancuso, Gerald Michael (6 mentions)
Creighton U, 1986
930 Carondelet Dr #200, Kansas City, MO, 816-941-7727

Montgomery, Michael Allen (6 mentions)
U of Kansas, 1971 *Certification:* Cardiovascular Disease,
Internal Medicine, Interventional Cardiology
2790 Clay Edwards Dr #520, Kansas City, MO, 816-221-6750
9411 N Oak Trfy #266, Kansas City, MO, 816-468-1919

O'Keefe, James H., Jr. (9 mentions)
Baylor U, 1982
Certification: Cardiovascular Disease, Internal Medicine
4330 Wornall Rd #2000, Kansas City, MO, 816-931-1883

Pierson, George Burdette (8 mentions)
U of Kansas, 1981
Certification: Cardiovascular Disease, Internal Medicine
12200 W 106th St #320, Lenexa, KS, 913-227-0506

Porter, Charles Boyd (10 mentions)
U of Kansas, 1977
Certification: Cardiovascular Disease, Internal Medicine
10787 Nall Ave #300, Overland Park, KS, 913-588-9400
3901 Rainbow Blvd #G600, Kansas City, KS, 913-588-9697

Stevens, Tracy Leigh (15 mentions)
U of Missouri-Kansas City, 1990
Certification: Cardiovascular Disease
4330 Wornall Rd #2000, Kansas City, MO, 816-931-1883
5844 NW Barry Rd #230, Kansas City, MO, 816-587-2500

Dermatology

Goldstein, Glenn David (13 mentions)
U of Kansas, 1981 *Certification:* Dermatology
11550 Granada Ln, Leawood, KS, 913-451-7546

Hall, John Charles (20 mentions)
U of Nebraska, 1972 *Certification:* Dermatology
4400 Broadway St #416, Kansas City, MO, 816-561-7783

Kaplan, David Louis (20 mentions)
Wake Forest U, 1981
Certification: Dermatology, Internal Medicine
4601 W 109th St #116, Shawnee Mission, KS, 913-469-1115

Kirby, Holly Fritch (6 mentions)
Yale U, 1978
11201 Nall Ave #100, Leawood, KS, 913-451-3030

McCune, Mark Alan (8 mentions)
U of Kansas, 1977 *Certification:* Dermatology
10600 Quivira Rd #450, Lenexa, KS, 913-541-3230

Reisz, Colleen Marie (16 mentions)
U of Kansas, 1988 *Certification:* Dermatology
5330 N Oak Trfy #201, Kansas City, MO, 816-454-0666
8800 W 75th St #140, Shawnee Mission, KS, 913-722-5551

Rupp, John Francis (6 mentions)
Creighton U, 1989 *Certification:* Dermatology
1010 Carondelet Dr #A-125, Kansas City, MO, 816-942-1150

Sabin, Shawn Renee (7 mentions)
U of Iowa, 1988 *Certification:* Dermatology
11550 Granada Ln, Leawood, KS, 913-451-7546

Emergency Medicine

Allin, Dennis Michael (3 mentions)
U of Kansas, 1983 *Certification:* Emergency Medicine,
   Undersea & Hyperbaric Medicine
3901 Rainbow Blvd, Kansas City, KS, 913-588-6504

Beamon, Richard Frederick (4 mentions)
U of Missouri, 1973 *Certification:* Emergency Medicine
10500 Quivira Rd, Lenexa, KS, 913-541-5340

Block, Dennis William (4 mentions)
Des Moines U, 1983 *Certification:* Emergency Medicine
201 NW R D Mize Rd, Blue Springs, MO, 816-655-5450
19600 E 39th St, Independence, MO, 816-698-7000

Bonness, Robert Kent (6 mentions)
U of Nebraska, 1983 *Certification:* Emergency Medicine
4401 Wornall Rd, Kansas City, MO, 816-932-2000

Carter, Gary Lee (5 mentions)
U of Missouri-Kansas City, 1984
Certification: Emergency Medicine
2800 Clay Edwards Dr, Kansas City, MO, 816-346-7220

Dill, Laura Lynn (3 mentions)
U of Missouri-Kansas City, 1989
Certification: Emergency Medicine
5721 W 119th St, Overland Park, KS, 913-498-6533

Greenwood, Patrick Joseph (4 mentions)
U of Missouri, 1991 *Certification:* Emergency Medicine
1000 Carondelet Dr, Kansas City, MO, 816-943-2711

Holcomb, Mark Stephen (5 mentions)
U of Iowa, 1975 *Certification:* Emergency Medicine
10500 Quivira Rd, Lenexa, KS, 913-541-5340

Koch, Kevin Joseph (8 mentions)
U of Missouri-Kansas City, 1980
Certification: Emergency Medicine
12300 Metcalf Ave, Overland Park, KS, 913-676-2000
9100 W 74th St, Overland Park, KS, 913-676-2214

Lisbon, David P., Jr. (3 mentions)
Georgetown U, 1991 *Certification:* Emergency Medicine
3901 Rainbow Blvd, Kansas City, KS, 913-588-6504

Lorei, John Michael (5 mentions)
U of Iowa, 1987 *Certification:* Emergency Medicine
4401 Wornall Rd, Kansas City, MO, 816-932-2171

Miller, Denise Kendall (3 mentions)
U of Nebraska, 1992
6601 Rockhill Rd, Kansas City, MO, 913-469-1411
1509 W Truman Rd, Independence, MO, 816-836-8100

Robb, Brian Jon (3 mentions)
Kansas U Coll of Osteopathic Med, 1984
2525 Glenn Hendren Dr, Liberty, MO, 816-792-7000

Rosenthal, Richard Hyman (6 mentions)
U of Missouri-Kansas City, 1976
Certification: Emergency Medicine
10500 Quivira Rd, Lenexa, KS, 913-541-5340

Russell, Steven L. (4 mentions)
U of Missouri-Kansas City, 1981
Certification: Emergency Medicine
2800 Clay Edwards Dr, Kansas City, MO, 816-346-7220

Saber, Arman (3 mentions)
U of Kansas, 1996 *Certification:* Emergency Medicine
12300 Metcalf Ave, Overland Park, KS, 913-676-2000
9100 W 74th St, Overland Park, KS, 913-676-2214

Scholes, Alison Maria (6 mentions)
U of Missouri, 1997 *Certification:* Emergency Medicine
4401 Wornall Rd, Kansas City, MO, 816-932-2171

Stephens, Thad Alan (3 mentions)
U of Kansas, 1991 *Certification:* Emergency Medicine
1000 Carondelet Dr, Kansas City, MO, 816-943-2711

Vodonick, David Smith (5 mentions)
U of Kansas, 1980 *Certification:* Emergency Medicine
12300 Metcalf Ave, Overland Park, KS, 913-676-2000
9100 W 47th St, Overland Park, KS, 913-676-2214

Weaver, Michael Lawayne (5 mentions)
U of Missouri-Kansas City, 1977
Certification: Emergency Medicine
4401 Wornall Rd, Kansas City, MO, 816-932-2171

Endocrinology

Andrews, William Vincent (6 mentions)
Creighton U, 1983 *Certification:* Internal Medicine
19550 E 39th St S #245, Independence, MO, 816-373-0655

Graves, Leland, III (9 mentions)
U of Missouri-Kansas City, 1983
Certification: Endocrinology and Metabolism, Internal Medicine
3901 Rainbow Blvd #MS-2024, Kansas City, KS, 913-588-1227

Green, Andrew Judah (14 mentions)
U of Michigan, 1981
Certification: Endocrinology and Metabolism, Internal Medicine
5701 W 119th St #345, Overland Park, KS, 913-894-1595
5520 College Blvd #330, Leawood, KS, 913-451-9888

Griffin, Marie L. (6 mentions)
12330 Metcalf Ave #400, Overland Park, KS, 913-317-7990

Hamburg, Mitchell Stephen (24 mentions)
U of Kansas, 1979
Certification: Endocrinology and Metabolism, Internal Medicine
4321 Washington St #3000, Kansas City, MO, 816-932-3100

Hellman, Richard (7 mentions)
Rosalind Franklin U, 1966
Certification: Endocrinology and Metabolism, Internal Medicine
2790 Clay Edwards Dr #1250, Kansas City, MO, 816-421-3700

Kallsen, Jeffrey David (10 mentions)
U of Iowa, 1993
Certification: Endocrinology, Diabetes, and Metabolism
12330 Metcalf Ave #400, Overland Park, KS, 913-317-7990

Rosen, Howard Mark (10 mentions)
Pennsylvania State U, 1983
Certification: Endocrinology and Metabolism, Internal Medicine
2790 Clay Edwards Dr #1250, Kansas City, MO, 816-421-3700

Silver, Bradd Joel (17 mentions)
Emory U, 1976
Certification: Endocrinology and Metabolism, Internal Medicine
8901 W 74th St #30, Shawnee Mission, KS, 913-676-7585

Family Practice *(see note on page 9)*

Bollier, Rene Philippe (10 mentions)
U of Kansas, 1984 *Certification:* Family Medicine
1004 Carondelet Dr #300A, Kansas City, MO, 816-941-9030

Bradley, Douglas La Monte (3 mentions)
U of Missouri, 1980 *Certification:* Family Medicine
206 E North Ave, Belton, MO, 816-331-7900

Burns, Bryan Wayne (3 mentions)
U of Kansas, 1995 *Certification:* Family Medicine
15435 W 134th Pl, Olathe, KS, 913-782-7515

Feder, Joel Maurice (7 mentions)
Kansas U Coll of Osteopathic Med, 1975
6740 W 121st St, Overland Park, KS, 913-894-6500

Graham, David Evans (4 mentions)
U of Kansas, 1974 *Certification:* Family Medicine
20375 W 151st St #105, Olathe, KS, 913-782-8487

Kamel, Sahar R. (4 mentions)
FMS-Egypt, 1982 *Certification:* Family Medicine
7301 E Frontage Rd #100, Shawnee Mission, KS, 913-384-4040

Nelson, Darryl Kent (3 mentions)
U of Missouri-Kansas City, 1986 *Certification:* Family Medicine
2000 SE Blue Pkwy #270-B, Lee's Summit, MO, 816-524-8488

Nolker, Stephen Glen (3 mentions)
U of Kansas, 1994 *Certification:* Family Medicine
4620 J C Nichols Pkwy #405, Kansas City, MO, 816-932-6100

Sly, Anne Kathleen (4 mentions)
U of Missouri-Kansas City, 1978 *Certification:* Family
   Medicine, Geriatric Medicine, Internal Medicine
6650 Troost Ave #201, Kansas City, MO, 816-276-7600

Stastny, Todd Alan (3 mentions)
U of Nebraska, 1987 *Certification:* Family Medicine
1700 NW Mock Ave, Blue Springs, MO, 816-228-1500

Thompson, Gary Alan (6 mentions)
U of Kansas, 1984 *Certification:* Family Medicine
4620 J C Nichols Pkwy #405, Kansas City, MO, 816-932-6100

Gastroenterology

Allen, Mark James (11 mentions)
U of Kansas, 1978
Certification: Gastroenterology, Internal Medicine
4321 Washington St #5600, Kansas City, MO, 816-561-2000

Brock, Arthur Lee (6 mentions)
U of Kansas, 1973
Certification: Gastroenterology, Internal Medicine
3800 S Whitney Ave #200, Independence, MO, 816-478-4887
19600 E 39th St, Independence, MO, 816-478-4887

Buser, William Dwight (11 mentions)
U of Kansas, 1980
Certification: Gastroenterology, Internal Medicine
10200 W 105th St #200, Overland Park, KS, 913-495-9600

Connor, Michael John (8 mentions)
U of Kansas, 1996
Certification: Gastroenterology, Internal Medicine
6420 Prospect Ave #T407, Kansas City, MO, 816-333-5424

Ginsberg, Brent William (11 mentions)
Columbia U, 1976
Certification: Gastroenterology, Internal Medicine
6420 Prospect Ave #T407, Kansas City, MO, 816-333-5424

Hartong, William Allen (7 mentions)
U of Kansas, 1971
Certification: Gastroenterology, Internal Medicine
10200 W 105th St #200, Overland Park, KS, 913-495-9600

Helzberg, John Henry (24 mentions)
U of Rochester, 1980
Certification: Gastroenterology, Internal Medicine
4321 Washington St #5600, Kansas City, MO, 816-561-2000

Olyaee, Seyed Mojtaba (5 mentions)
FMS-Iran, 1985
Certification: Gastroenterology, Transplant Hepatology
3901 Rainbow Rd, Kansas City, KS, 913-588-8400

Vardakis, Gregory M. (5 mentions)
Kansas U Coll of Osteopathic Med, 1990
206 NW Mock Ave, Blue Springs, MO, 816-229-1191

Walden, James Madison (5 mentions)
Baylor U, 1981 *Certification:* Gastroenterology, Internal Medicine
2790 Clay Edwards Dr #1210, Kansas City, MO, 816-527-0031

General Surgery

Anderson, Craig Allen (5 mentions)
U of Kansas, 1985 *Certification:* Surgery
20375 W 151st St #463, Olathe, KS, 913-782-8577

Cates, Joe (7 mentions)
U of Missouri-Kansas City, 1987
Certification: Surgery, Vascular Surgery
10730 Nall Ave #101, Overland Park, KS, 913-754-2800

Drahota, Lawrence James (6 mentions)
U of Nebraska, 1982 *Certification:* Surgery
10600 Quivira Rd #410, Lenexa, KS, 913-541-3240

Evans, Joseph Cedric, Jr. (5 mentions)
U of Missouri, 1970 *Certification:* Surgery
1901 E Valley View Pkwy #B, Independence, MO, 816-254-9292

Higgins, Edward F., Jr. (4 mentions)
SUNY-Upstate Med U, 1978
Certification: Surgery, Vascular Surgery
10730 Nall Ave #101, Overland Park, KS, 913-754-2800

Hitchcock, Charles Thomas (4 mentions)
U of Kansas, 1973 *Certification:* Surgery
8901 W 74th St #356, Overland Park, KS, 913-677-2508

Hoehn, Stanley David (8 mentions)
Loma Linda U, 1994 *Certification:* Surgery
8901 W 74th St #356, Overland Park, KS, 913-677-2508

James, Kelly Michael (5 mentions)
Albert Einstein Coll of Med, 1987 *Certification:* Surgery
1901 E Valley View Pkwy #B, Independence, MO, 816-254-9292

Joyce, Rex Marion (8 mentions)
U of Kansas, 1982 *Certification:* Surgery
373 W 101st Terr #210, Kansas City, MO, 816-333-9500

Lowe, Bettina (4 mentions)
U of Kansas, 1993 *Certification:* Surgery
8901 W 74th St #356, Overland Park, KS, 913-677-2508

Ludwig, Lee Vetter (4 mentions)
U of Kansas, 1981 *Certification:* Surgery
8919 Parallel Pkwy #206, Kansas City, KS, 913-334-6800

McCroskey, Lon Charles (15 mentions)
U of Kansas, 1976 *Certification:* Surgery
5701 W 119th St #331, Overland Park, KS, 913-696-1146

Moore, B. Todd (9 mentions)
Northwestern U, 1996 *Certification:* Surgery
4323 Wornall Rd 1st Fl, Kansas City, MO, 816-932-2836

Nelson, Paul William (4 mentions)
U of Kansas, 1977 *Certification:* Surgery
4320 Wornall Rd #240, Kansas City, MO, 816-932-7900

Oza, Mangesh Dhruv (4 mentions)
U of Missouri-Kansas City, 1996 *Certification:* Surgery
5400 N Oak Trfy #1-101, Kansas City, MO, 816-455-3990

Petelin, Joseph Bernard (15 mentions)
U of Kansas, 1976 *Certification:* Surgery
9119 W 74th St #255, Shawnee Mission, KS, 913-432-5420

Roh, Joseph Jerome (5 mentions)
U of Nebraska, 1981 *Certification:* Surgery
373 W 101st Terr #210, Kansas City, MO, 816-333-6681

Sclar, William Charles (6 mentions)
U of Michigan, 1972 *Certification:* Surgery
10600 Quivira Rd #410, Lenexa, KS, 913-541-3240

Sharp, Ronald John (4 mentions)
Certification: Pediatric Surgery, Surgery, Surgical Critical Care
2401 Gillham Rd, Kansas City, MO, 816-234-3575
5808 W 110th St, Overland Park, KS, 913-696-8000

Shook, John William (11 mentions)
U of Missouri-Kansas City, 1984 *Certification:* Surgery
4323 Wornall Rd #308, Kansas City, MO, 816-932-7900

Spehar, Pascal Edward (6 mentions)
U of Kansas, 1989 *Certification:* Surgery
19550 E 39th St #325, Independence, MO, 816-373-4646

Werner, F. Scott (5 mentions)
U of Missouri, 1980 *Certification:* Surgery
2750 Clay Edwards Dr #312, Kansas City, MO, 816-453-4000
2521 Glen Hendren Dr, Liberty, MO, 816-781-8311

Geriatrics

Farrell, Kevin Eugene (3 mentions)
Kansas U Coll of Osteopathic Med, 1997
3014 Oak St, Kansas City, MO, 816-931-1278

Holt, Peter Scott (24 mentions)
U of Kansas, 1984 *Certification:* Internal Medicine
4440 Broadway St, Kansas City, MO, 816-561-9200

Hematology/Oncology

Belt, Robert Julian (16 mentions)
U of Colorado, 1971
Certification: Internal Medicine, Medical Oncology
4320 Wornall Rd #212, Kansas City, MO, 816-531-2740

Corum, Larry Ray (5 mentions)
U of Kansas, 1998
Certification: Hematology, Internal Medicine, Medical Oncology
20375 W 151st St #208, Olathe, KS, 913-780-4000

Custer, Galen Milton (5 mentions)
U of Kansas, 1975
Certification: Internal Medicine, Medical Oncology
12200 W 110th St, Overland Park, KS, 913-234-0400

De Wolfe, Mark Herbert (5 mentions)
U of Minnesota, 1977
Certification: Internal Medicine, Medical Oncology
2000 NE Vivion Rd, Kansas City, MO, 816-454-1658

Fleming, Allan Roger (5 mentions)
U of Kansas, 1969
Certification: Internal Medicine, Medical Oncology
3901 Rainbow Blvd, Kansas City, KS, 913-588-6029

Hinton, Stuart W. (8 mentions)
U of Missouri-Kansas City, 1995
Certification: Hematology, Internal Medicine, Medical Oncology
4320 Wornall Rd #212, Kansas City, MO, 816-531-2740

McKittrick, Richard J. (5 mentions)
U of Kansas, 1986
Certification: Internal Medicine, Medical Oncology
1000 E 101st Ter, Kansas City, MO, 816-333-1326

Neubauer, Marcus Alan (9 mentions)
U of Kansas, 1988
Certification: Internal Medicine, Medical Oncology
12200 W 110th St, Overland Park, KS, 913-234-0400

Pendergrass, Kelly Bruce (7 mentions)
U of Kansas, 1975
Certification: Internal Medicine, Medical Oncology
1000 E 101st Terr, Kansas City, MO, 816-333-1326

Rosen, Larry Alan (8 mentions)
U of Kansas, 1976 *Certification:* Internal Medicine
4881 NE Goodview Cir, Lee's Summit, MO, 816-478-2050

Sheehan, Maureen (7 mentions)
U of Kansas, 1987
Certification: Hematology, Internal Medicine, Medical Oncology
8700 N Greenhills Rd, Kansas City, MO, 816-746-4570

Sirridge, Christopher F. (6 mentions)
U of Missouri-Kansas City, 1978
Certification: Hematology, Internal Medicine, Medical Oncology
8700 N Green Hills Rd, Kansas City, MO, 816-746-4570

Skikne, Barry Sim (10 mentions)
FMS-South Africa, 1969
Certification: Hematology, Internal Medicine
2330 Shawnee Mission Pkwy, Westwood, KS, 913-588-6029

Stephenson, William T. (6 mentions)
U of Kansas, 1990 *Certification:* Medical Oncology
2316 E Meyer Blvd, Kansas City, MO, 816-276-4700

Talley, Robert Louis (7 mentions)
U of Texas-Galveston, 1974
Certification: Hematology, Internal Medicine, Medical Oncology
4881 NE Goodview Cir, Lee's Summit, MO, 816-478-2050

Infectious Disease

Brewer, Joseph Hampton (16 mentions)
U of Kansas, 1976 *Certification:* Internal Medicine
4320 Wornall Rd #440, Kansas City, MO, 816-531-1550

Driks, Michael Robert (12 mentions)
U of Miami, 1981
Certification: Infectious Disease, Internal Medicine
6400 Prospect Ave #392, Kansas City, MO, 816-822-8486

Geha, Daniel Joseph (12 mentions)
Creighton U, 1988
Certification: Infectious Disease, Internal Medicine
8800 State Line Rd, Leawood, KS, 913-383-9099

Hinthorn, Daniel Robert (17 mentions)
U of Kansas, 1967
Certification: Infectious Disease, Internal Medicine
3901 Rainbow Blvd, Kansas City, KS, 913-588-6035

McKinsey, David Stephen (16 mentions)
U of Missouri, 1981
Certification: Infectious Disease, Internal Medicine
6400 Prospect Ave #392, Kansas City, MO, 816-822-8486

McKinsey, Joel Perry (9 mentions)
U of Missouri, 1994 *Certification:* Infectious Disease
6400 Prospect Ave #392, Kansas City, MO, 816-822-8486

O'Connor, Mary Cecelia (10 mentions)
Med Coll of Wisconsin, 1985
Certification: Infectious Disease, Internal Medicine
6400 Prospect Ave #392, Kansas City, MO, 816-822-8486

Wekullo, Verra Lorraine Namulanda (8 mentions)
FMS-Kenya, 1995
Certification: Infectious Disease, Internal Medicine
19550 E 39th St, Independence, MO, 816-254-2552

Infertility

Brabec, Celeste Johnson (8 mentions)
U of Texas-Houston, 1991 *Certification:* Obstetrics &
Gynecology, Reproductive Endocrinology/Infertility
12200 W 106th St #120, Overland Park, KS, 913-894-2323

Gehlbach, Dan Lee (7 mentions)
U of Kansas, 1983 *Certification:* Obstetrics & Gynecology,
Reproductive Endocrinology/Infertility
20375 W 151st St #403, Olathe, KS, 913-780-4300

Lyles, Rodney (16 mentions)
U of Oklahoma, 1974 *Certification:* Obstetrics &
Gynecology, Reproductive Endocrinology/Infertility
12200 W 106th St #120, Overland Park, KS, 913-894-2323

Starks, Gregory Charles (9 mentions)
Jefferson Med Coll, 1973 *Certification:* Obstetrics & Gynecology
2790 Clay Edwards Dr #625, Kansas City, MO, 816-421-3115
6400 Prospect Ave #598, Kansas City, MO, 816-444-6888

Stewart, Daniel Louis (8 mentions)
U of Kansas, 1987 *Certification:* Obstetrics & Gynecology
8800 W 75th St #101, Overland Park, KS, 913-432-7161

Internal Medicine *(see note on page 9)*

Bautz, James Bonanno (3 mentions)
Harvard U, 1985 *Certification:* Internal Medicine
4321 Washington St #3000, Kansas City, MO, 816-932-3100

Carothers, Karmel Lynn (3 mentions)
U of Kansas, 1989 *Certification:* Internal Medicine
19550 E 39th St #245, Independence, MO, 816-373-0655

Diederich, Paul Gregory (10 mentions)
U of Kansas, 1976 *Certification:* Internal Medicine
4320 Wornall Rd #530, Kansas City, MO, 816-753-4312

Dunlap, John Lewis (12 mentions)
U of Kansas, 1976 *Certification:* Internal Medicine
5701 W 119th St #145, Overland Park, KS, 913-491-6633

Gillbanks, Marjon M. (3 mentions)
Loyola U Chicago, 1986 *Certification:* Internal Medicine
19550 E 39th St S #245, Independence, MO, 816-373-0655

Goldberg, John Miles (4 mentions)
U of Kansas, 1987 *Certification:* Internal Medicine
5701 W 119th St #240, Overland Park, KS, 913-345-8500

Gordon, Mark Ernest (3 mentions)
Michigan State U, 1978
2700 Clay Edwards Dr #400, Kansas City, MO, 816-421-4240

Hoeper, Samuel Dietrich, Jr. (4 mentions)
Creighton U, 1973 *Certification:* Internal Medicine
6420 Prospect Ave #T101, Kansas City, MO, 816-363-4100

Ling, Sally (4 mentions)
U of California-San Francisco, 1982
Certification: Internal Medicine
4401 Wornall Rd, Kansas City, MO, 816-932-0340

Mann, Kenneth Ross (3 mentions)
U of Kansas, 1979 *Certification:* Internal Medicine
2700 Clay Edwards Dr #400, Kansas City, MO, 816-421-4240

Nulton, Carnie Clements (3 mentions)
U of Kansas, 1985 *Certification:* Internal Medicine
2330 Shawnee Mission Pkwy #2201, Westwood, KS,
913-588-9800

Oxler, John Edward, Jr. (3 mentions)
U of Kansas, 1972 *Certification:* Internal Medicine
21 N 12th St #110, Kansas City, KS, 913-722-4240
8800 W 75th St #300, Shawnee Mission, KS, 913-722-4240

Perryman, John C. (8 mentions)
U of Kansas, 1976 *Certification:* Internal Medicine
4321 Washington St #3000, Kansas City, MO, 816-932-3100

Salvaggio, Bruce Hughes (3 mentions)
U of Kansas, 1978 *Certification:* Internal Medicine
4320 Wornall Rd #530, Kansas City, MO, 816-753-4312

Schermoly, Martin Joseph (5 mentions)
U of Kansas, 1984 *Certification:* Internal Medicine
20375 W 151st St #301, Olathe, KS, 913-782-8300

Short, Bruce Herschel (7 mentions)
U of Kansas, 1977 *Certification:* Internal Medicine
10601 Quivira Rd #200, Lenexa, KS, 913-541-3340

Stamos, George Earl (4 mentions)
U of Iowa, 1972 *Certification:* Internal Medicine
10601 Quivira Rd #200, Lenexa, KS, 913-541-3340

Sutton, Matthew Botkin (4 mentions)
U of Missouri-Kansas City, 1992 *Certification:* Internal Medicine
4321 Washington St #3000, Kansas City, MO, 816-932-3100

Wendland, Robert James (3 mentions)
St Louis U, 1987 *Certification:* Internal Medicine
1010 Carondelet Dr #224A, Kansas City, MO, 816-943-0706

Wilt, David Alan (5 mentions)
U of Kansas, 1983 *Certification:* Internal Medicine
6420 Prospect Ave #T101, Kansas City, MO, 816-363-4100

Nephrology

Bender, Walter Louis, Jr. (11 mentions)
Johns Hopkins U, 1979
Certification: Internal Medicine, Nephrology
6530 Troost Ave #A, Kansas City, MO, 816-361-0670
650 Carondelet Dr #A, Kansas City, MO, 816-361-0670

Benson, Larry Edward (7 mentions)
U of Kansas, 1966 *Certification:* Internal Medicine
2790 Clay Edwards Dr #410, Kansas City, MO, 816-474-9353

Birenboim, Nancy (9 mentions)
U of Kansas, 1981 *Certification:* Internal Medicine, Nephrology
6400 Prospect Ave #480, Kansas City, MO, 816-444-4806

Duncan, Kirk Alan (14 mentions)
U of Kansas, 1978 *Certification:* Internal Medicine, Nephrology
8901 W 74th St #2, Shawnee Mission, KS, 913-381-0622
1295 E 151st St #7, Olathe, KS, 913-381-0622

Golder, Robert Edward (10 mentions)
U of Missouri-Kansas City, 1991
Certification: Internal Medicine, Nephrology
6400 Prospect Ave #480, Kansas City, MO, 816-444-4806

Lambert, Michael Brent (12 mentions)
U of Oklahoma, 1985 *Certification:* Internal Medicine
3550 S 4th St #282, Shawnee Mission, KS, 913-441-5757
6850 Hillyop Rd #100, Shawnee, KS, 913-441-5757
8901 W 74th St #120, Overland Park, KS, 913-441-5757

Mertz, Jim Ivan (9 mentions)
U of Kansas, 1973 *Certification:* Internal Medicine, Nephrology
4320 Wornall Rd #208, Kansas City, MO, 816-531-0552

Muther, Richard Scurlock (18 mentions)
U of Kansas, 1975 *Certification:* Critical Care Medicine,
Internal Medicine, Nephrology
6530 Troost Ave #A, Kansas City, MO, 816-361-0670
650 Carondelet Dr #A, Kansas City, MO, 816-361-0670

Wood, Barry Craig (11 mentions)
U of Kansas, 1973 *Certification:* Internal Medicine, Nephrology
4320 Wornall Rd #208, Kansas City, MO, 816-531-0552

Neurological Surgery

Camarata, Paul Joseph (32 mentions)
U of Kansas, 1986 *Certification:* Neurological Surgery
4440 Broadway St #510, Kansas City, MO, 816-561-4655

Chilton, Jonathan David (17 mentions)
U of Rochester, 1981 *Certification:* Neurological Surgery
6420 Prospect Ave #T411, Kansas City, MO, 816-363-2500

Clough, John Arthur (9 mentions)
U of Kansas, 1994 *Certification:* Neurological Surgery
1010 Carondelet Dr #105, Kansas City, MO, 816-942-0200

Hess, Steven Joe (15 mentions)
U of Kansas, 1986 *Certification:* Neurological Surgery
9119 W 74th St #260, Shawnee Mission, KS, 913-432-1100
20375 W 151st St #205, Olathe, KS, 913-829-3311

O'Boynick, Paul Leonard (18 mentions)
U of Kansas, 1973 *Certification:* Neurological Surgery
9119 W 74th St, Merriam, KS, 913-588-6117
20375 W 151st St, Olathe, KS, 913-829-3311

Reintjes, Stephen Lewis (19 mentions)
U of Kansas, 1983 *Certification:* Neurological Surgery
2750 Clay Edwards Dr #410, North Kansas City, MO,
816-471-8114
4400 Broadway St #510, Kansas City, MO, 816-561-4655

Neurology

Allen, Arthur Austin, II (19 mentions)
U of Kansas, 1968 *Certification:* Neurology
8800 W 75th St #100, Shawnee Mission, KS, 913-384-4200

Arkin, Karen M. (4 mentions)
U of Texas-Houston, 1988 *Certification:* Neurology
4400 Broadway St #520, Kansas City, MO, 816-531-4080

Arkin, Steven Michael (6 mentions)
Rush U, 1989 *Certification:* Neurology
4400 Broadway St #520, Kansas City, MO, 816-531-4080

Bettinger, Irene E. (13 mentions)
U of Pennsylvania, 1966
4400 Broadway St #520, Kansas City, MO, 816-531-4080

Boutwell, Christine M. (7 mentions)
U of Missouri-Kansas City, 1993 *Certification:* Neurology
4400 Broadway St #520, Kansas City, MO, 816-531-4080

Harlan, John Woody (7 mentions)
Duke U, 1978 *Certification:* Neurology
2000 SE Blue Pkwy #270-A, Kansas City, MO, 816-524-1700

Hedges, Kathryn Ann (5 mentions)
U of Nebraska, 1988 *Certification:* Neurology
2000 SE Blue Pkwy #270-A, Kansas City, MO, 816-524-1700

Hollenbeck, Larry Clayton (10 mentions)
U of Kansas, 1982 *Certification:* Neurology
2790 Clay Edwards Dr #500, Kansas City, MO, 816-472-5157

Hon, Sarah J. (6 mentions)
Kansas U Coll of Osteopathic Med, 1993 *Certification:* Neurology
2790 Clay Edwards Dr #500, Kansas City, MO, 816-472-5157

Kelley, Gordon Richard (8 mentions)
FMS-Canada, 1977
Certification: Internal Medicine, Neurology, Vascular Neurology
8800 W 75th St #100, Shawnee Mission, KS, 913-384-4200

Riley, Terrence Lee (5 mentions)
U of Missouri, 1974 *Certification:* Aerospace Medicine,
Neurology, Occupational Medicine, Vascular Neurology
2000 SE Blue Pkwy #270-A, Kansas City, MO, 816-524-1700

Ryan, Michael Edwin (7 mentions)
U of Kansas, 1972 *Certification:* Neurology
8800 W 75th St #100, Shawnee Mission, KS, 913-384-4200

Sand, John Joseph (4 mentions)
U of Iowa, 1982 *Certification:* Neurology
6420 Prospect Ave #503, Kansas City, MO, 816-361-8684

Weinstein, Charles Lynn (8 mentions)
U of Kansas, 1971 *Certification:* Neurology
4400 Broadway St #520, Kansas City, MO, 816-531-4080

Zwibelman, Jay Scott (4 mentions)
U of Missouri-Kansas City, 1986 *Certification:* Neurology
601 N Mur Len Rd #8, Olathe, KS, 913-642-8941

Obstetrics/Gynecology

Adams, Kenneth Allen (5 mentions)
Washington U, 1989 *Certification:* Obstetrics & Gynecology
19550 E 39th St S #310, Independence, MO, 816-350-1200

Calkins, John William (3 mentions)
U of Kansas, 1976 *Certification:* Obstetrics & Gynecology
3901 Rainbow Blvd #2028, Kansas City, KS, 913-588-6268
10777 Nall Ave #200, Overland Park, KS, 913-588-8580

Cederlind, Cranston Jay (3 mentions)
U of Kansas, 1971 *Certification:* Obstetrics & Gynecology
7440 Frontage Rd, Shawnee, KS, 913-236-6455

Estrada, Analuina (5 mentions)
U of Kansas, 1993 *Certification:* Obstetrics & Gynecology
20375 W 151st St #250, Olathe, KS, 913-764-6262

Galvin, Mara Celeste (3 mentions)
Southern Illinois U, 1981 *Certification:* Obstetrics & Gynecology
20 NE St Lukes Blvd #310, Lee's Summit, MO, 816-282-7809
1004 Carondelet Dr #315, Kansas City, MO, 816-942-3339

Gordon, Stephen Moss (3 mentions)
Kansas U Coll of Osteopathic Med, 1979
Certification: Obstetrics & Gynecology
1004 Carondelet Dr #407, Kansas City, MO, 816-942-3060

Johnson, Rebecca Sue (3 mentions)
U of Iowa, 1980 *Certification:* Obstetrics & Gynecology
2790 Clay Edwards Dr #625, Kansas City, MO, 816-421-3115
6400 Prospect Ave #598, Kansas City, MO, 816-444-6888

Lintecum, Frederick Bruce (8 mentions)
U of Kansas, 1979 *Certification:* Obstetrics & Gynecology
4320 Wornall Rd #720, Kansas City, MO, 816-531-2111

Lofton, Brenda Joyce (3 mentions)
Baylor U, 1981 *Certification:* Obstetrics & Gynecology
5525 W 119th St #200, Overland Park, KS, 913-491-4020
7315 Frontage Rd #100, Shawnee Mission, KS, 913-491-4020

Martin, Melanie Anne (4 mentions)
U of Kansas, 1985 *Certification:* Obstetrics & Gynecology
7440 Frontage Rd, Shawnee, KS, 913-236-6455

Matile, Gerald Ulysses (8 mentions)
U of Kansas, 1982 *Certification:* Obstetrics & Gynecology
4400 Broadway St #302, Kansas City, MO, 816-931-9344
11401 Nall Ave #205, Leawood, KS, 816-931-9344

Miller, Gerald Lee, Jr. (3 mentions)
Northwestern U, 1968 *Certification:* Obstetrics & Gynecology
6400 Prospect Ave #598, Kansas City, MO, 816-444-6888
600 NW Murray Rd, Lee's Summit, MO, 816-524-8575
17053 S 71 Hwy #204, Belton, MO, 816-331-6920

Moore, Julie Minton (3 mentions)
U of Missouri-Kansas City, 1986
Certification: Obstetrics & Gynecology
4400 Broadway St #302, Kansas City, MO, 816-931-9344
11401 Nall Ave #205, Leawood, KS, 816-931-9344

Morris, Terry Vaughn (4 mentions)
U of Texas-Galveston, 1975 *Certification:* Obstetrics & Gynecology
19550 E 39th St S #310, Independence, MO, 816-350-1200

Saleh, George Atiya (3 mentions)
Kansas U Coll of Osteopathic Med, 1977
200 NE 54th St #111, Kansas City, MO, 816-455-7400

Snider, Bruce Benjamin (4 mentions)
U of Kansas, 1986 *Certification:* Obstetrics & Gynecology
20375 W 151st St #250, Olathe, KS, 913-764-6262

Strickland, Julie Lubker (3 mentions)
U of Missouri, 1984 *Certification:* Obstetrics & Gynecology
2301 Holmes St, Kansas City, MO, 816-404-5150
2401 Gillham Rd, Kansas City, MO, 816-234-3000

Sullivan, Bradley Huse (5 mentions)
U of Kansas, 1979 *Certification:* Obstetrics & Gynecology
6400 Prospect Ave #598, Kansas City, MO, 816-444-6888
2790 Clay Edwards Dr #625, Kansas City, MO, 816-421-3115
600 NW Murray Rd #206, Lee's Summit, MO, 816-524-8575

Thomas, Marty Hollister (3 mentions)
U of Kansas, 1979 *Certification:* Obstetrics & Gynecology
10600 Quivira Rd #320, Overland Park, KS, 913-894-8700
12330 Metcalf Ave #420, Overland Park, KS, 913-696-1900

Ophthalmology

Donnelly, William Patrick (5 mentions)
U of Kansas, 1976 *Certification:* Ophthalmology
1004 Carondelet Dr #400, Kansas City, MO, 816-942-8333

Fox, Gregory Mark (5 mentions)
U of Michigan, 1987 *Certification:* Ophthalmology
9119 W 74th St #268, Shawnee Mission, KS, 913-831-7400
8350 N St Clair Ave #220, Kansas City, MO, 816-505-3400

Hembree, Kathryn Ann (4 mentions)
U of Missouri-Kansas City, 1986 *Certification:* Ophthalmology
1200 Landmark Ave, Liberty, MO, 816-792-1900

Hettinger, Michael Eugene (7 mentions)
U of Tennessee, 1975 *Certification:* Ophthalmology
7504 Antioch Rd, Overland Park, KS, 913-341-3100

Lyon, David Baker (5 mentions)
SUNY-Upstate Med U, 1984 *Certification:* Ophthalmology
5811 NW Barry Rd, Kansas City, MO, 913-261-2020
4741 S Arrowhead Dr, Independence, MO, 913-261-2020
4321 Washington St #2100, Kansas City, MO, 913-261-2020
2401 Gillham Rd, Kansas City, MO, 913-261-2020
11213 Nall Ave #100, Leawood, KS, 913-261-2020
151 W 151st St #100, Olathe, KS, 913-261-2020
601 E Russell Ave #A, Warrensburg, MO, 913-261-2020

Migliazzo, Carl V. (4 mentions)
U of Missouri, 1979 *Certification:* Ophthalmology
7504 Antioch Rd, Overland Park, KS, 913-341-3100

O'Connell, Sara Seacat (5 mentions)
U of Kansas, 1984 *Certification:* Ophthalmology
7504 Antioch Rd, Overland Park, KS, 913-341-3100

Place, Kenneth Craig (4 mentions)
U of Kansas, 1973 *Certification:* Ophthalmology
9009 Roe Ave, Prairie Village, KS, 913-385-9009

Sabates, Nelson Raymond (7 mentions)
U of Missouri-Kansas City, 1986 *Certification:* Ophthalmology
4321 Washington St #2100, Kansas City, MO, 913-261-2020
3500 W 75th St #100, Prairie Village, KS, 913-261-2020
3800 W 75th St, Shawnee Mission, KS, 913-261-2020
11213 Nall Ave #100, Shawnee Mission, KS, 913-261-2020
2300 Holmes St, Kansas City, MO, 913-261-2020

Stiles, Michael Craig (4 mentions)
U of Kansas, 1985 *Certification:* Ophthalmology
7200 W 129th St, Overland Park, KS, 913-897-9299
7400 Stateline Rd, Prairie Village, KS, 913-588-6600

Whittaker, Thomas Joseph (4 mentions)
U of Kansas, 1990 *Certification:* Ophthalmology
3901 Rainbow Blvd, Kansas City, KS, 913-588-6600

Orthopedics

Barnthouse, Cris David (5 mentions)
U of Kansas, 1981 *Certification:* Orthopaedic Surgery
3651 College Blvd #100-A, Leawood, KS, 913-319-7500

Bernhardt, Mark (6 mentions)
U of Kansas, 1983 *Certification:* Orthopaedic Surgery
4320 Wornall Rd #610, Kansas City, MO, 913-319-7600
3657 College Blvd, Leawood, KS, 913-319-7600

Bohn, William Worthington (4 mentions)
U of Kansas, 1981 *Certification:* Orthopaedic Surgery
20920 W 151st St #100, Olathe, KS, 913-782-1148

Bruce, Robert Paul (7 mentions)
U of Kansas, 1982 *Certification:* Orthopaedic Surgery
10701 Nall Ave #200, Leawood, KS, 913-381-5225

Cook, Scott Michael (4 mentions)
U of Kansas, 1997 *Certification:* Orthopaedic Surgery
3651 College Blvd #100-B, Leawood, KS, 913-362-0031

Gaddy, Burrel C., Jr. (4 mentions)
U of Texas-Dallas, 1990 *Certification:* Orthopaedic Surgery
8800 W 75th St #350, Shawnee Mission, KS, 913-362-8317

Gardiner, Robert Charles (9 mentions)
U of Kansas, 1986 *Certification:* Orthopaedic Surgery
4320 Wornall Rd #610, Kansas City, MO, 913-531-5757
3651 College Blvd #100-A, Leawood, KS, 913-319-7500

Gurba, Danny Michael (5 mentions)
U of Kansas, 1979 *Certification:* Orthopaedic Surgery
4320 Wornall Rd #610, Kansas City, MO, 913-531-5757
3651 College Blvd, Leawood, KS, 913-319-7500

Hummel, Gregory Lane (5 mentions)
U of Missouri, 1979 *Certification:* Orthopaedic Surgery
19550 E 39th St S #205, Independence, MO, 816-252-7300

Humphrey, Mark Steven (5 mentions)
U of Kansas, 1984 *Certification:* Orthopaedic Surgery
12200 W 106th St #400, Lenexa, KS, 913-541-8897

Joyce, Steven Thomas (9 mentions)
U of Kansas, 1973 *Certification:* Orthopaedic Surgery
4320 Wornall Rd #610, Kansas City, MO, 816-531-5757
3651 College Blvd #100-A, Leawood, KS, 913-319-7500

Kindred, Brian Charles (5 mentions)
U of Kansas, 1990 *Certification:* Orthopaedic Surgery
20920 W 151st St #100, Olathe, KS, 913-782-1148

Luallin, Scott Raymond (8 mentions)
U of Kansas, 1988 *Certification:* Orthopaedic Surgery
10777 Nall Ave #300, Leawood, KS, 913-642-0200

McCormack, Thomas Joseph (4 mentions)
U of Missouri, 1991 *Certification:* Orthopaedic Surgery
7900 Lees Summit Rd, Kansas City, MO, 816-404-7650

Rasmussen, Mark Richard (4 mentions)
U of Kansas, 1988 *Certification:* Orthopaedic Surgery
3651 College Blvd #100-B, Leawood, KS, 913-362-0031

Rasmussen, Thomas Joseph (6 mentions)
U of Kansas, 1986 *Certification:* Orthopaedic Surgery
3651 College Blvd #100-B, Leawood, KS, 913-362-0031

Rhoades, Charles Edward (6 mentions)
U of Kansas, 1978 *Certification:* Orthopaedic Surgery
3651 College Blvd, Leawood, KS, 913-319-7600
4320 Wornall Rd #610, Kansas City, MO, 913-319-7600

Romito, John Anthony (6 mentions)
U of Kansas, 1973
12200 W 106th St #400, Lenexa, KS, 913-541-8897

Rosenthal, Howard Glenn (5 mentions)
U of Arizona, 1985 *Certification:* Orthopaedic Surgery
5701 W 119th St #308, Leawood, KS, 913-498-6840

Samuelson, Thomas Scott (7 mentions)
U of Iowa, 1988 *Certification:* Orthopaedic Surgery
10701 Nall Ave #200, Leawood, KS, 913-381-5225

Toby, Edward Bruce (5 mentions)
Indiana U, 1981
Certification: Orthopaedic Surgery, Surgery of the Hand
3901 Rainbow Blvd #3017, Kansas City, KS, 913-588-6131

Otorhinolaryngology

Girod, Douglas Allen (13 mentions)
U of California-San Francisco, 1985 *Certification:* Otolaryngology
3901 Rainbow Blvd #3010, Kansas City, KS, 913-588-6700

Katz, Fred S. (10 mentions)
U of Kansas, 1979 *Certification:* Otolaryngology
8901 W 74th St #145, Shawnee Mission, KS, 913-722-0020

Maslan, Mark Jeffrey (9 mentions)
U of Missouri-Kansas City, 1980 *Certification:* Otolaryngology
6400 Prospect Ave #346, Kansas City, MO, 816-333-6996
5701 W 119th St #425, Leawood, KS, 913-663-5100

Rudman, David Todd (7 mentions)
U of Missouri, 1995 *Certification:* Otolaryngology
5701 W 119th St #425, Leawood, KS, 913-663-5100

Spake, Robert Vanneman (12 mentions)
U of Kansas, 1977 *Certification:* Otolaryngology
4320 Wornall Rd #512, Kansas City, MO, 816-753-5663

Thompson, Robert Freeman (12 mentions)
U of Missouri, 1985 *Certification:* Otolaryngology
12200 W 106th St #310, Overland Park, KS, 913-599-4800
930 Carondelet Dr #305, Kansas City, MO, 816-941-9200

Tsue, Terance Ted (6 mentions)
Johns Hopkins U, 1989 *Certification:* Otolaryngology
3901 Rainbow Blvd #3010, Kansas City, KS, 913-588-6700

Walton, Mark Stephen (8 mentions)
Creighton U, 1985 *Certification:* Otolaryngology
12200 W 106th St #310, Overland Park, KS, 913-599-4800

Pain Medicine

Griffith, Patrick David (7 mentions)
U of Missouri-Kansas City, 1989 *Certification:* Anesthesiology
2970 Clay Edwards Dr, Kansas City, MO, 816-221-4114

Morgan, Richard Lloyd (8 mentions)
U of Kansas, 1980 *Certification:* Anesthesiology, Hospice and Palliative Medicine, Pain Medicine
1000 Carondelet Dr, Kansas City, MO, 816-943-3926

Opper, Susan Simmons (8 mentions)
U of Kansas, 1983
4401 Wornall Rd, Kansas City, MO, 816-932-2932

Pathology

Borek, Deborah Ann (4 mentions)
U of Colorado, 1978 *Certification:* Anatomic Pathology & Clinical Pathology, Blood Banking
2750 Clay Edwards Dr #420, Kansas City, MO, 816-241-3338

Breckenridge, Robert L. (3 mentions)
Jefferson Med Coll, 1974 *Certification:* Anatomic Pathology & Clinical Pathology, Blood Banking, Medical Microbiology
2750 Clay Edwards Dr #420, Kansas City, MO, 816-241-3338

Dobson, John Robert, III (4 mentions)
U of Nebraska, 1990 *Certification:* Anatomic Pathology & Clinical Pathology, Cytopathology
10330 Hickman Mills Dr, Kansas City, MO, 816-412-7004

Elson, Craig Ellsworth (5 mentions)
U of Michigan, 1983 *Certification:* Anatomic Pathology & Clinical Pathology, Cytopathology
10730 Nall Ave #102, Leawood, KS, 913-341-6297

Fraga, Garth Robert (4 mentions)
U of Chicago, 1994 *Certification:* Anatomic Pathology & Clinical Pathology, Dermatopathology
2750 Clay Edwards Dr #420, Kansas City, MO, 816-241-3338

Kerley, Spencer Wells (5 mentions)
U of Kansas, 1986
Certification: Anatomic Pathology & Clinical Pathology
7800 W 110th St, Overland Park, KS, 913-338-4070

Pena, Francisco L. (4 mentions)
FMS-Philippines, 1982
Certification: Anatomic Pathology & Clinical Pathology
2316 E Meyer Blvd, Kansas City, MO, 913-541-5596

Plapp, Frederick Vaughn (6 mentions)
U of Kansas, 1975 *Certification:* Clinical Pathology
4401 Wornall Rd, Kansas City, MO, 816-932-3335

Tawfik, Ossama William (8 mentions)
FMS-Egypt, 1978 *Certification:* Anatomic Pathology & Clinical Pathology, Cytopathology
3901 Rainbow Blvd, Kansas City, KS, 913-588-7070

Woodroof, Janet Marie (3 mentions)
U of Kansas, 1987 *Certification:* Anatomic Pathology & Clinical Pathology, Hematology
1000 Carondelet Dr, Kansas City, MO, 816-943-2642

Zucker, Marjorie Lynette (4 mentions)
FMS-South Africa, 1969
Certification: Anatomic Pathology & Clinical Pathology
4401 Wornall Rd, Kansas City, MO, 816-932-2411

Pediatrics *(see note on page 9)*

Davis, Carolyn Thornton (4 mentions)
U of Kansas, 1986 *Certification:* Pediatrics
12541 Foster St #260, Overland Park, KS, 913-906-0900

Holleman, David Norman (3 mentions)
U of Missouri, 1986 *Certification:* Pediatrics
4400 Broadway St #206, Kansas City, MO, 816-561-8100
701 NW Commerce Dr #102, Lee's Summit, MO, 816-554-3646

Jackson, Robert Vincent (6 mentions)
U of Missouri, 1977 *Certification:* Pediatrics
8901 W 74th St #10, Shawnee Mission, KS, 913-362-1660

Maxwell, Robert Arnold (4 mentions)
U of Kansas, 1973 *Certification:* Pediatrics
8901 W 74th St #10, Shawnee Mission, KS, 913-362-1660

McIntosh, Michele C. (3 mentions)
Baylor U, 1973 *Certification:* Pediatrics
11200 E Winner Rd, Independence, MO, 816-836-4300

Metzl, Kurt (3 mentions)
U of Kansas, 1960 *Certification:* Pediatrics
1004 Carondelet Dr #310, Kansas City, MO, 816-942-5437

Monzon, Carlos Manuel (3 mentions)
FMS-Guatemala, 1976
Certification: Pediatric Hematology-Oncology, Pediatrics
20375 W 151st St #251, Olathe, KS, 913-782-2525

Moylan, Charles Vincent (8 mentions)
U of Missouri, 1984 *Certification:* Pediatrics
4400 Broadway St #206, Kansas City, MO, 816-561-8100
701 NW Commerce Dr #102, Lee's Summit, MO, 816-554-3646

Nelson, Bryan Claude (3 mentions)
U of Kansas, 1975 *Certification:* Pediatrics
8800 W 75th St #220, Shawnee Mission, KS, 913-384-5500

Powell, Alan Edward (4 mentions)
U of Texas-Dallas, 1964 *Certification:* Pediatrics
3151 NE Carnegie Dr #B, Lee's Summit, MO, 816-373-4001

Waters, Jeffrey Arthur (13 mentions)
U of Missouri, 1973 *Certification:* Pediatrics
4400 Broadway St #206, Kansas City, MO, 816-561-8100

Plastic Surgery

Bene, Richard John, Jr. (6 mentions)
U of Kansas, 1987
Certification: Plastic Surgery, Surgery of the Hand
5401 College Blvd #203, Leawood, KS, 913-663-3838
9401 N Oak Traffic Light #100, Kansas City, MO, 816-436-3262

Cannova, Joseph V. (6 mentions)
U of Missouri-Kansas City, 1991 *Certification:* Plastic Surgery
11501 Granada Ln, Leawood, KS, 913-451-3722

Geraghty, Thomas Edmund (6 mentions)
U of Kansas, 1972 *Certification:* Plastic Surgery
4444 N Belleview Ave #204, Kansas City, MO, 816-455-3062
4620 J C Nichols Pkwy #503, Kansas City, MO, 816-455-3772

Gutek, Edward Philip (14 mentions)
FMS-Canada, 1967 *Certification:* Plastic Surgery
11501 Granada Ln, Leawood, KS, 913-451-3722

Korentager, Richard A. (9 mentions)
FMS-Canada, 1983 *Certification:* Plastic Surgery
9119 W 74th St #306, Overland Park, KS, 913-432-0001

McClung, Mark Wallace (7 mentions)
U of Texas-Dallas, 1986 *Certification:* Plastic Surgery
11501 Granada Ln, Leawood, KS, 913-451-3722

Nouhan, Regina Marie (8 mentions)
Washington U, 1987
Certification: Plastic Surgery, Surgery of the Hand
5401 College Blvd #203, Leawood, KS, 913-663-3838
9401 N Oak Traffic Light #100, Kansas City, MO, 816-436-3262

Quinn, John Michael (9 mentions)
U of Missouri-Kansas City, 1981 *Certification:* Plastic Surgery
6920 W 121st St #102, Overland Park, KS, 913-492-3443

Psychiatry

Burd, Jeremy Alexander (5 mentions)
Pennsylvania State U, 1996
Certification: Geriatric Psychiatry, Psychiatry
4400 Broadway St #407, Kansas City, MO, 816-932-1711

Hill, Todd P. (4 mentions)
Kansas U Coll of Osteopathic Med, 2000 *Certification:* Psychiatry
200 NE 54th St #101 Bldg 2, Kansas City, MO, 816-453-6777

Huk, Stephen George (6 mentions)
St Louis U, 1981
Certification: Child & Adolescent Psychiatry, Psychiatry
4500 College Blvd #304, Leawood, KS, 913-338-0400
4470 Belleview Ave #207, Gladstone, MO, 913-338-0400

Pro, John Dennis (11 mentions)
U of Kansas, 1973 *Certification:* Geriatric Psychiatry, Psychiatry
200 NE Missouri Rd #302, Lee's Summit, MO, 816-523-0103

Samuelson, Stephen Daryl (6 mentions)
U of Kansas, 1986 *Certification:* Psychiatry
4500 College Blvd #304, Leawood, KS, 913-338-0400
4470 Belleview Ave #207, Gladstone, MO, 913-338-0400

Segraves, Steven Deane (3 mentions)
U of Kansas, 1986 *Certification:* Geriatric Psychiatry, Psychiatry
8900 State Line Rd #380, Leawood, KS, 913-385-7252

Warner, Richard Ballweg (6 mentions)
U of Kansas, 1972 *Certification:* Psychiatry
7011 W 121st St #105, Overland Park, KS, 913-345-1191

Wisner, John Henry (4 mentions)
U of Kansas, 1976 *Certification:* Psychiatry
3901 Rainbow Blvd #4015, Kansas City, KS, 913-588-6400

Pulmonary Disease

Bradley, James K. (8 mentions)
Emory U, 1977 *Certification:* Critical Care Medicine,
  Internal Medicine, Pulmonary Disease
20375 W 151st St #451, Olathe, KS, 913-829-0446

Brook, Charles Jeffrey (9 mentions)
U of Chicago, 1969
Certification: Internal Medicine, Pulmonary Disease
6420 Prospect Ave #T303, Kansas City, MO, 816-333-1919

Caruso, Alfred Cosmo (5 mentions)
FMS-Mexico, 1983
Certification: Critical Care Medicine, Internal Medicine
1004 Carondelet Dr #410, Kansas City, MO, 816-389-6100

Henry, Joseph Eric (7 mentions)
U of Kansas, 1968
Certification: Internal Medicine, Pulmonary Disease
8901 W 74th St #348, Overland Park, KS, 913-432-8000
2790 Clay Edwards Dr #620, Kansas City, MO, 816-474-3700

Hill, Rodney W. (15 mentions)
U of Kansas, 1974 *Certification:* Critical Care Medicine,
  Internal Medicine, Pulmonary Disease
8901 W 74th St #390, Shawnee Mission, KS, 913-362-0300

Lem, Vincent M. (26 mentions)
U of Kansas, 1978 *Certification:* Critical Care Medicine,
  Internal Medicine, Pulmonary Disease
4321 Washington St #6000, Kansas City, MO, 816-756-2255

Migliazzo, Anthony G. (9 mentions)
U of Missouri-Kansas City, 1980 *Certification:* Internal
  Medicine, Pulmonary Disease
4911 S Arrowhead Dr #201, Independence, MO, 816-478-8113
4721 S Cliff Ave #203, Independence, MO, 816-478-8113

Nelson, John Beckwith (15 mentions)
U of Missouri-Kansas City, 1975
Certification: Internal Medicine, Pulmonary Disease
8919 Parallel Pkwy #203, Kansas City, KS, 913-599-3800
10550 Quivira Rd #335, Overland Park, KS, 913-599-3800

Nelson, Michael Eugene (13 mentions)
U of Kansas, 1985 *Certification:* Critical Care Medicine,
  Internal Medicine, Pulmonary Disease
8901 W 74th St #390, Shawnee Mission, KS, 913-362-0300

Schwartz, Bruce Allen (13 mentions)
Ohio State U, 1976 *Certification:* Critical Care Medicine,
  Internal Medicine, Pulmonary Disease
4321 Washington St #6000, Kansas City, MO, 816-756-2255

Smith, Timothy William (5 mentions)
U of Kansas, 1974 *Certification:* Critical Care Medicine,
  Internal Medicine, Pulmonary Disease
1004 Carondelet Dr #410, Kansas City, MO, 816-389-6100

Stites, Steven William (5 mentions)
U of Missouri, 1986 *Certification:* Critical Care Medicine,
  Internal Medicine, Pulmonary Disease
3901 Rainbow Blvd, Kansas City, KS, 913-588-6046

Waxman, Michael James (6 mentions)
U of Kansas, 1976 *Certification:* Critical Care Medicine,
  Internal Medicine, Pulmonary Disease
6420 Prospect Ave #T303, Kansas City, MO, 816-333-1919

Williams, Wade Luther (8 mentions)
U of Kansas, 1990
Certification: Critical Care Medicine, Pulmonary Disease
10550 Quivira Rd #335, Overland Park, KS, 913-599-3800

Wurtz, Mary Margaret (8 mentions)
U of Nebraska, 1984
Certification: Internal Medicine, Pulmonary Disease
4911 S Arrowhead Dr #201, Independence, MO, 816-478-8113

Yagan, Mark Brian (5 mentions)
U of Missouri-Kansas City, 1989
Certification: Critical Care Medicine, Pulmonary Disease
4321 Washington St #6000, Kansas City, MO, 816-756-2255

Radiology—Diagnostic

Bergh, James Robert (4 mentions)
U of Kansas, 1984
Certification: Diagnostic Radiology, Internal Medicine,
  Nuclear Medicine, Vascular & Interventional Radiology
10500 Quivira Rd, Overland Park, KS, 913-541-5000

Gubin, Barry (5 mentions)
U of Missouri-Kansas City, 1984
Certification: Diagnostic Radiology
2316 E Meyer Blvd, Kansas City, MO, 816-276-4141

Kunin, Jeffrey Russell (3 mentions)
U of Texas-Galveston, 1987 *Certification:* Diagnostic Radiology
6320 Manchester Ave #46, Kansas City, MO, 816-358-0333
4401 Wornall Rd, Kansas City, MO, 816-932-2550

Moffat, Robert Edward (3 mentions)
U of Kansas, 1968 *Certification:* Diagnostic Radiology
9212 Nieman Rd, Overland Park, KS, 913-599-6777
9100 W 74th St, Overland Park, KS, 913-676-2310

Nelson, Douglas Leroy (5 mentions)
U of Kansas, 1984 *Certification:* Diagnostic Radiology
9212 Neiman Rd, Overland Park, KS, 913-599-6777

O'Toole, Patrick Michael (3 mentions)
U of Missouri-Kansas City, 1986
Certification: Diagnostic Radiology, Neuroradiology
1000 Carondelet Dr, Kansas City, MO, 816-943-2270

Perry, Mark Alan (4 mentions)
Washington U, 1987 *Certification:* Diagnostic Radiology
9100 W 74th St, Overland Park, KS, 913-676-2310
9212 Nieman Rd, Overland Park, KS, 913-599-6777

Smith, William Payne (5 mentions)
U of Kansas, 1977 *Certification:* Diagnostic Radiology
3901 Rainbow Blvd, Kansas City, KS, 913-588-6804

Wetzel, Louis Herman (3 mentions)
U of Kansas, 1982 *Certification:* Diagnostic Radiology
3901 Rainbow Blvd #4032, Kansas City, KS, 913-588-6805

Radiology—Therapeutic

Coster, James Richard (5 mentions)
U of Illinois, 1988 *Certification:* Radiation Oncology
12000 W 110th St #100, Overland Park, KS, 913-469-0002

Cozad, Scott Cameron (5 mentions)
U of Kansas, 1988 *Certification:* Radiation Oncology
6601 Winchester Ave #230, Kansas City, MO, 816-313-2677
2529 Glenn Hendren Dr #G-40, Liberty, MO, 816-415-2147

Johnson, Philip Lee (7 mentions)
U of Kansas, 1990
Certification: Diagnostic Radiology, Neuroradiology
3901 Rainbow Blvd, Kansas City, KS, 913-588-3901

Lee, Graham (5 mentions)
FMS-Zimbabwe, 1978 *Certification:* Diagnostic Radiology,
  Neuroradiology, Vascular & Interventional Radiology
2316 E Meyer Blvd, Kansas City, MO, 816-276-4000

Smalley, Stephen Rhoads (5 mentions)
U of Missouri-Kansas City, 1979 *Certification:* Internal
  Medicine, Medical Oncology, Radiation Oncology
20375 W 151st St #180, Olathe, KS, 913-768-7200
6601 Winchester Ave #230, Kansas City, MO, 816-313-2677
2750 Clay Edwards Dr #L-12, North Kansas City, MO,
  816-691-5216
2316 E Meyer Blvd, Kansas City, MO, 816-276-4161
5721 W 119th St, Overland Park, KS, 913-498-6270

Yetter, Ellen Marie (10 mentions)
U of Kansas, 1993 *Certification:* Diagnostic Radiology,
  Vascular & Interventional Radiology
12300 Metcalf Ave, Overland Park, KS, 913-317-7678

Rehabilitation

Berger, Gary Geoffrey (9 mentions)
Philadelphia Coll of Osteopathic Med, 1983
Certification: Physical Medicine & Rehabilitation
5701 W 119th St #116, Overland Park, KS, 913-339-9550

Kelly, Charles Roland (8 mentions)
U of Kansas, 1964
Certification: Physical Medicine & Rehabilitation
4320 Wornall Rd #440, Kansas City, MO, 816-931-3013
4400 Broadway St #540, Kansas City, MO, 816-931-3013

Navato-Dehning, Cielo (3 mentions)
U of Missouri-Kansas City, 1984 *Certification:* Physical
  Medicine & Rehabilitation, Spinal Cord Injury Medicine
5701 W 110th St #100, Overland Park, KS, 919-642-7400

Patel, Atul Thakorbhai (9 mentions)
Baylor U, 1988 *Certification:* Physical Medicine &
  Rehabilitation, Spinal Cord Injury Medicine
10701 Nall Ave #200, Leawood, KS, 913-381-5225

Rosenberg, Stephen N. (3 mentions)
Kansas U Coll of Osteopathic Med, 1998
Certification: Physical Medicine & Rehabilitation
9100 W 74th St, Shawnee Mission, KS, 913-424-9670

Smithson, David Gerard (4 mentions)
U of Minnesota, 1985
Certification: Physical Medicine & Rehabilitation
1010 Carondelet Dr #329, Kansas City, MO, 816-943-4554

Steinle, Brad Taylor (11 mentions)
U of Kansas, 1997
Certification: Physical Medicine & Rehabilitation
4400 Broadway St #520, Kansas City, MO, 816-932-2020

Zarr, James Schuyler (7 mentions)
U of Missouri, 1981
Certification: Physical Medicine & Rehabilitation
2700 Clay Edwards Dr #320, Kansas City, MO, 816-472-8005

Rheumatology

Box, Mark Stephens (10 mentions)
U of Missouri, 1987
Certification: Internal Medicine, Rheumatology
1010 Carondelet Dr #224-A, Kansas City, MO, 816-943-0706

Huston, Kent K. (12 mentions)
Certification: Internal Medicine, Rheumatology
4330 Wornall Rd #40, Kansas City, MO, 816-531-0930

Jones, Cameron Bruce (12 mentions)
U of Kansas, 1976
Certification: Internal Medicine, Rheumatology
450 E 4th St #200, Kansas City, MO, 816-753-5736

Warner, Ann E. (23 mentions)
U of Kansas, 1983 *Certification:* Allergy & Immunology,
  Internal Medicine, Rheumatology
4330 Wornall Rd #40, Kansas City, MO, 816-531-0930

Thoracic Surgery

Borkon, Alan Michael (11 mentions)
Johns Hopkins U, 1975
Certification: Surgical Critical Care, Thoracic Surgery
4320 Wornall Rd #50, Kansas City, MO, 816-931-3312

Gorton, Michael Earl (9 mentions)
U of Kansas, 1986 *Certification:* Surgery, Thoracic Surgery
3901 Rainbow Blvd #1232, Kansas City, KS, 913-588-7743
8000 NW Mace Rd, Kansas City, MO, 816-746-8175

Hannah, Hamner, III (8 mentions)
U of Virginia, 1964 *Certification:* Surgery, Thoracic Surgery
6400 Prospect Ave #382, Kansas City, MO, 816-523-7088

Muehlebach, Gregory F. (11 mentions)
St Louis U, 1989 *Certification:* Thoracic Surgery
3901 Rainbow Blvd, Kansas City, KS, 913-588-7743

Seligson, Frederic Lee (11 mentions)
U of Pittsburgh, 1982 *Certification:* Surgery, Thoracic Surgery
6400 Prospect Ave #382, Kansas City, MO, 816-523-7088

Urology

Austenfeld, Mark Steven (12 mentions)
U of Kansas, 1983 *Certification:* Urology
4321 Washington St #5300, Kansas City, MO, 816-531-1234
12330 Metcalf Ave #200, Overland Park, KS, 913-317-7560
1301 S Main St, Ottawa, KS, 785-229-8200

Bock, David Bruce (8 mentions)
U of Oklahoma, 1985 *Certification:* Urology
5525 W 119th St #220, Overland Park, KS, 913-338-5585

Davis, Bradley Edward (19 mentions)
U of Kansas, 1986 *Certification:* Urology
10550 Quivira Rd #105, Overland Park, KS, 913-438-3833
4321 Washington St #4100, Kansas City, MO, 913-438-3833
20375 W 151st St #201, Olathe, KS, 913-782-2020

Emmott, David Fielding (9 mentions)
U of Oklahoma, 1979 *Certification:* Urology
8901 W 74th St #380, Shawnee Mission, KS, 913-831-1003

Holzbeierlein, Jeffrey M. (7 mentions)
U of Oklahoma, 1994 *Certification:* Urology
3901 Rainbow Blvd #3016, Kansas City, KS, 913-588-7564

Leifer, Gary (7 mentions)
Johns Hopkins U, 1979 *Certification:* Urology
5525 W 119th St #220, Overland Park, KS, 913-338-5585

Strickland, John Taylor (19 mentions)
U of Missouri, 1984 *Certification:* Urology
8901 W 74th St #380, Shawnee Mission, KS, 913-831-1003
10701 Nall Ave #100, Overland Park, KS, 913-831-1003

Tackett, Russell Edward (10 mentions)
U of Missouri, 1980 *Certification:* Urology
6400 Prospect Ave #440, Kansas City, MO, 816-361-0277
373 W 101st Terr #218, Kansas City, MO, 816-361-0277

Thrasher, James Brantley (10 mentions)
Med U of South Carolina, 1986 *Certification:* Urology
3901 Rainbow Blvd #3045, Kansas City, KS, 913-588-6152

Vascular Surgery

Arnspiger, Richard C., II (14 mentions)
U of Kansas, 1982 *Certification:* Vascular Surgery
7420 Switzer St, Shawnee, KS, 913-262-9201

Beezley, Michael Janssen (20 mentions)
U of Kansas, 1973 *Certification:* Surgery, Vascular Surgery
7420 Switzer St, Shawnee, KS, 913-262-9201
20375 W 151st St #350, Olathe, KS, 913-262-9201

Cates, Joe (16 mentions)
U of Missouri-Kansas City, 1987
Certification: Surgery, Vascular Surgery
10730 Nall Ave #101, Overland Park, KS, 913-754-2800

St. Louis Area

Including City of St. Louis and Jefferson, Madison, St. Charles, St. Clair, and St. Louis Counties

Allergy/Immunology

Dykewicz, Mark Steven (10 mentions)
St Louis U, 1981
Certification: Allergy & Immunology, Internal Medicine
3660 Vista Ave, St Louis, 314-977-6070

Korenblat, Phillip Erwin (32 mentions)
U of Arkansas, 1960
Certification: Allergy & Immunology, Internal Medicine
1040 N Mason Rd #115, St Louis, 314-542-0606

Schneider, Susan Bromberg (15 mentions)
Yale U, 1977
Certification: Allergy & Immunology, Internal Medicine
222 S Woods Mill Rd #750-N, Chesterfield, 314-205-6060

Slavin, Raymond Granam (29 mentions)
St Louis U, 1956
Certification: Allergy & Immunology, Internal Medicine
3660 Vista Ave #203, St Louis, 314-977-6070

Thiel, John Allen (15 mentions)
St Louis U, 1960 *Certification:* Allergy & Immunology
621 S New Ballas Rd #368A, St Louis, 314-872-7958

Tillinghast, Jeffrey Paul (17 mentions)
Washington U, 1980
Certification: Allergy & Immunology, Internal Medicine
1040 N Mason Rd #115, St Louis, 314-542-0606

Anesthesiology

Androphy, Jay Bennett (4 mentions)
Rosalind Franklin U, 1992 *Certification:* Anesthesiology
615 S New Ballas Rd, St Louis, 636-386-9224

Arnold, Donald Edward (6 mentions)
U of Wisconsin, 1984 *Certification:* Anesthesiology
615 S New Ballas Rd, St Louis, 314-251-6988

Avidan, Michael S. (3 mentions)
660 S Euclid St #8054, St Louis, 314-286-1045

Bashiti, Mohammad F. (4 mentions)
FMS-Egypt, 1971 *Certification:* Anesthesiology
232 S Woods Mill Rd, St Louis, 314-205-6199

Bell, Stephen N. (3 mentions)
New York U, 1966 *Certification:* Anesthesiology
450 N New Ballas Rd, St Louis, 314-991-0776

Bucol, Kevin Donovan (3 mentions)
U of Missouri, 1982 *Certification:* Anesthesiology
3009 N Ballas Rd #360-C, St Louis, 314-996-5287

De Board, James Warren (4 mentions)
U of Missouri, 1976 *Certification:* Anesthesiology
1465 S Grand Blvd, St Louis, 314-577-5622

Evers, Alex S. (3 mentions)
New York U, 1978 *Certification:* Anesthesiology, Critical Care Medicine, Internal Medicine
660 S Euclid Ave #2306, St Louis, 314-454-8701

Forand, Joseph Miskell (4 mentions)
St Louis U, 1981 *Certification:* Anesthesiology
10010 Kennerly Rd, St Louis, 314-525-1951
339 Consort Dr, Ballwin, 636-386-7222

Forstot, Robert Marc (3 mentions)
Washington U, 1987 *Certification:* Anesthesiology
615 S New Ballas Rd, St Louis, 636-386-9224

Gibson, William Patrick (6 mentions)
U of Arkansas, 1974
Certification: Anesthesiology, Internal Medicine
232 S Woods Mill Rd, Chesterfield, 314-205-6917

Krummenacher, Keith S. (17 mentions)
U of Missouri, 1983 *Certification:* Anesthesiology
615 S New Ballas Rd, St Louis, 636-386-9224

Leighton, Barbara Louise (4 mentions)
Johns Hopkins U, 1981 *Certification:* Anesthesiology
3015 N Ballas Rd, St Louis, 314-286-1045

Nielsen, Carl Helge (4 mentions)
FMS-Denmark, 1979 *Certification:* Anesthesiology
1 Barnes Jewish Hospital Plaza, St Louis, 314-362-6973

Niesen, George Hagen (3 mentions)
Ohio State U, 1986 *Certification:* Anesthesiology
232 S Woods Mill Rd, Chesterfield, 314-205-6917

Platin, Mitchell Ross (5 mentions)
Northeastern Ohio U, 1987 *Certification:* Anesthesiology
12634 Olive Blvd, St Louis, 314-996-8685

Ryan, Michael H. (3 mentions)
Certification: Anesthesiology
232 S Woods Mill Rd, Chesterfield, 314-434-1500

Schneider, Alan Richard (6 mentions)
SUNY-Downstate Med Coll, 1981 *Certification:* Anesthesiology
12303 De Paul Dr, Bridgeton, 314-344-7049

Slimack, Joseph Paul (3 mentions)
Rosalind Franklin U, 1984 *Certification:* Anesthesiology
3015 N Ballas Rd, St Louis, 314-996-5330

Tempelhoff, Rene (3 mentions)
FMS-France, 1974
660 S Euclid Ave, St Louis, 314-362-6973

Cardiac Surgery

Coordes, Cordie C. (13 mentions)
U of Nebraska, 1976 *Certification:* Surgery, Thoracic Surgery
222 S Woods Mill Rd #550, North Chesterfield, 314-434-3049
10004 Kennedy Rd #335, St Louis, 314-434-3049

Damiano, Ralph James, Jr. (17 mentions)
Duke U, 1980 *Certification:* Thoracic Surgery
4921 Parkview Pl, St Louis, 314-362-7327

Fiore, Andrew Charles (11 mentions)
St Louis U, 1977 *Certification:* Thoracic Surgery
1465 S Grand Blvd, St Louis, 314-268-4180

Huddleston, Charles Burford (12 mentions)
Vanderbilt U, 1978 *Certification:* Thoracic Surgery
1 Childrens Pl, St Louis, 314-454-6165
Barnes Hospital Plaza, St Louis, 314-454-6165

Kouchoukos, Nicholas Thomas (39 mentions)
Washington U, 1961 *Certification:* Surgery, Thoracic Surgery
3009 N Ballas Rd #266-C, St Louis, 314-996-5287

Leidenfrost, Ronald D. (20 mentions)
SUNY-Upstate Med U, 1973
Certification: Internal Medicine, Thoracic Surgery
222 S Woods Mill Rd #550-N, Chesterfield, 314-434-3049

Marbarger, John P. (14 mentions)
U of Illinois, 1972 *Certification:* Thoracic Surgery
625 S New Ballas Rd #R-7040, St Louis, 314-251-6970

Moon, Marc Richard (15 mentions)
Wayne State U, 1988 *Certification:* Surgery, Thoracic Surgery
4921 Parkview Pl, St Louis, 314-362-0993

Murphy, James Peter (24 mentions)
George Washington U, 1976 *Certification:* Thoracic Surgery
3009 N Ballas Rd #266-C, St Louis, 314-996-5287

Murphy, Michael C. (14 mentions)
U of Virginia, 1983 *Certification:* Thoracic Surgery
3009 N Ballas Rd #360-C, St Louis, 314-996-5287

Cardiology

Barzilai, Benico (4 mentions)
U of Illinois, 1978
Certification: Cardiovascular Disease, Internal Medicine
4921 Parkview Pl #8-A, St Louis, 314-362-1291

Beardslee, Michael A. (6 mentions)
St Louis U, 1991 *Certification:* Cardiovascular Disease
901 Patients First Dr, Washington, 636-239-2711

Bleyer, Frank Leahy (6 mentions)
Rush U, 1982
Certification: Cardiovascular Disease, Internal Medicine
3331 W DeYoung #100, Marion, IL, 618-998-7600
1245 S Mill St, Nashville, IL, 618-327-9333

Braverman, Alan C. (22 mentions)
U of Missouri-Kansas City, 1985
Certification: Cardiovascular Disease, Internal Medicine
4921 Parkview Pl #8-A, St Louis, 314-362-1291

Brodarick, Scott Allen (5 mentions)
U of Illinois, 1975
Certification: Cardiovascular Disease, Internal Medicine
222 S Woods Mill Rd #510N, Chesterfield, 314-205-6571

Cole, Patricia Lena (19 mentions)
Harvard U, 1981 *Certification:* Cardiovascular Disease,
Internal Medicine, Interventional Cardiology
450 N New Ballas Rd #170, St Louis, 314-993-6969

Das, Sundeep (5 mentions)
FMS-India, 1986 *Certification:* Cardiovascular Disease,
Internal Medicine, Interventional Cardiology
11155 Dunn Rd #304E, St Louis, 314-741-0911

Davison, Glenn Evan (4 mentions)
U of Rochester, 1989 *Certification:* Cardiovascular Disease
222 S Woods Mill Rd #510N, Chesterfield, 314-205-6568

Ferrara, Robert Paul (5 mentions)
U of Missouri-Kansas City, 1979
Certification: Cardiovascular Disease, Internal Medicine
621 S New Ballas Rd, St Louis, 314-251-5800
625 S New Ballas Rd #2015, St Louis, 314-251-5800

Goldmeier, Michael Gary (4 mentions)
Ohio State U, 1986 *Certification:* Cardiovascular Disease,
Internal Medicine, Interventional Cardiology
1001 S Kirkwood Rd #100, St Louis, 314-965-9980

Haikal, Majed Youssef (14 mentions)
FMS-Lebanon, 1975
Certification: Cardiovascular Disease, Internal Medicine
222 S Woods Mill Rd #500N, Chesterfield, 314-205-6699

Hess, John Philip, III (5 mentions)
Tulane U, 1974 *Certification:* Cardiovascular Disease,
Internal Medicine, Interventional Cardiology
1010 Old Des Peres Rd, St Louis, 314-432-2535
Hwy 72 N, Salem, 314-432-2535

Hubert, John William (15 mentions)
Washington U, 1975 *Certification:* Cardiovascular Disease,
Internal Medicine, Interventional Cardiology
625 S New Ballas Rd #2015, St Louis, 314-251-1700
755 Dunn Rd #160, Hazelwood, 314-251-1775
615 S New Ballas Rd, St Louis, 314-997-6789

Kardesch, David Jay (7 mentions)
U of Missouri-Kansas City, 1985 *Certification:* Cardiovascular
Disease, Internal Medicine, Interventional Cardiology
5401 Veterans Memorial Pkwy #101, St Peters, 636-939-4820

Kates, Andrew Marc (11 mentions)
Tufts U, 1994 *Certification:* Cardiovascular Disease
4921 Parkview Pl #8-A, St Louis, 314-362-1291

Kopitsky, Robert Gene (6 mentions)
Duke U, 1982 *Certification:* Cardiovascular Disease,
Internal Medicine, Interventional Cardiology
450 N New Ballas Rd #170, St Louis, 314-993-6969

Lite, Howard Steven (4 mentions)
U of Missouri, 1983
Certification: Cardiovascular Disease, Internal Medicine
1010 Old Des Peres Rd, St Louis, 314-432-2535

McKenzie, Clark Ryan (5 mentions)
U of Missouri-Kansas City, 1989
Certification: Cardiovascular Disease, Internal Medicine,
Interventional Cardiology, Nephrology
450 N New Ballas Rd #170, St Louis, 314-993-6969

Mezei, Leslie Eugene (5 mentions)
FMS-Hungary, 1982
Certification: Cardiovascular Disease, Internal Medicine
1176 Town And Country Commons, Chesterfield, 636-207-2233

Nordlicht, Scott Monroe (5 mentions)
SUNY-Downstate Med Coll, 1973
Certification: Cardiovascular Disease, Internal Medicine
1020 N Mason Rd #100, St Louis, 314-362-1291

Reiss, Craig K. (4 mentions)
U of Missouri-Kansas City, 1983
Certification: Cardiovascular Disease, Internal Medicine
1020 Mason Rd #100, St Louis, 314-362-1291
1 Barnes Hospital Plaza #16419, St Louis, 314-362-1291

Rinder, Morton Ronald (5 mentions)
U of Maryland, 1992 *Certification:* Cardiovascular Disease,
Internal Medicine, Interventional Cardiology
1176 Town And Country Commons, Chesterfield, 636-207-2233

Robiolio, Paul Arthur (10 mentions)
Washington U, 1989
Certification: Cardiovascular Disease, Internal Medicine
450 N New Ballas Rd #170, St Louis, 314-993-6969

Schwarze, Martin William (6 mentions)
A T Still U, 1973
2325 Dougherty Ferry Rd #205, St Louis, 314-966-9888
6 Jungermann Cir #108, St Peters, 636-928-4556

Sharkey, Angela Marie (9 mentions)
St Louis U, 1986 *Certification:* Pediatric Cardiology
1 Childrens Pl, St Louis, 314-454-6095

Soffer, Allen D. (8 mentions)
U of Missouri-Kansas City, 1983
Certification: Cardiovascular Disease, Internal Medicine
450 N New Ballas Rd #170, St Louis, 314-993-6969

Vournas, George Christopher (13 mentions)
St Louis U, 1976
Certification: Cardiovascular Disease, Internal Medicine
625 S New Ballas Rd #2015, St Louis, 314-251-1700
755 Dunn Rd #160, Hazelwood, 314-251-1775

Weiss, Alan Neal (6 mentions)
Ohio State U, 1966
Certification: Cardiovascular Disease, Internal Medicine
1020 Mason Rd, St Louis, 314-362-1291

Dermatology

Amato, Jason Bradley (7 mentions)
St Louis U, 1997 *Certification:* Dermatology
522 N New Ballas Rd #203, St Louis, 314-569-3323

Bayliss, Susan B. (12 mentions)
Certification: Dermatology, Pediatric Dermatology
1 Childrens Pl #2-D, St Louis, 314-454-2714
969 Mason Rd, St Louis, 314-996-8010

Bell, Richard Carl (7 mentions)
Washington U, 1988 *Certification:* Dermatology
222 S Woods Mill Rd #710N, Chesterfield, 314-576-1411

Cornelius, Lynn Anne (14 mentions)
U of Missouri, 1984 *Certification:* Dermatology
969 N Mason Rd #220, St Louis, 314-996-8010

Donnelly, James Warren (10 mentions)
Washington U, 1986 *Certification:* Dermatology
222 S Woods Mill Rd #710N, Chesterfield, 314-576-1411

Duvall, Joseph Michael (15 mentions)
U of Missouri, 1974 *Certification:* Dermatology
621 New Ballas Rd Bldg B #5002, St Louis, 314-432-3033

Forsman, Karen Edna (13 mentions)
Rush U, 1981 *Certification:* Dermatology, Internal
Medicine, Pulmonary Disease
969 N Mason Rd #220, St Louis, 314-996-8010

Fosko, Scott William (12 mentions)
U of Maryland, 1986
Certification: Dermatology, Internal Medicine
1755 S Grand Blvd, St Louis, 314-256-3400

Gibstine, Connie Francis (7 mentions)
U of Missouri, 1980 *Certification:* Dermatology
3009 N Ballas Rd #B-208, St Louis, 314-994-0200

Glaser, Dee A. (12 mentions)
U of Missouri-Kansas City, 1987 *Certification:* Dermatology
1755 S Grand Blvd, St Louis, 314-256-3400
2325 Dougherty Ferry Rd #102, St Louis, 314-256-3400

Miller, Charles William (8 mentions)
Washington U, 1972 *Certification:* Dermatology
10004 Kennerly Rd #395B, St Louis, 314-842-5660

Powell, John Adrian (7 mentions)
U of Michigan, 1971 *Certification:* Dermatology
1034 S Brentwood Blvd #1160, St Louis, 314-863-7080

Reese, Lester Thomas (11 mentions)
Tulane U, 1966 *Certification:* Dermatology
522 N New Ballas Rd #316, St Louis, 314-567-5873

Samuels, Lawrence Elliott (9 mentions)
Washington U, 1976 *Certification:* Dermatology
222 S Woods Mill Rd #480N, Chesterfield, 314-576-7336

Sheinbein, David Marc (6 mentions)
St Louis U, 1995 *Certification:* Dermatology
969 N Mason Rd #220, St Louis, 314-996-8010

Siegfried, Elaine Claire (13 mentions)
U of Missouri, 1985
Certification: Dermatology, Pediatric Dermatology
1465 S Grand Blvd, St Louis, 314-251-5551

Emergency Medicine

Brown, Lawrence Robert (6 mentions)
Washington U, 1990 *Certification:* Internal Medicine
660 S Euclid Ave, St Louis, 314-747-3000

Byrne, Laurie E. (4 mentions)
St Louis U, 1995 *Certification:* Emergency Medicine
3635 Vista Ave, St Louis, 314-577-8000

Chauhan, Vijai V. (3 mentions)
FMS-India, 1988 *Certification:* Emergency Medicine
525 Couch Ave, St Louis, 314-966-1500

Etzwiler, Lisa Susan (3 mentions)
Johns Hopkins U, 1985
Certification: Pediatric Emergency Medicine, Pediatrics
621 S New Ballas Rd #6006-B, St Louis, 314-251-6299

Fenton, Carter P., Jr. (3 mentions)
A T Still U, 1996
1001 Hwy K #6, O'Fallon, 636-978-9389

Ferguson, Edward W., Jr. (4 mentions)
U of Missouri-Kansas City, 1993
Certification: Emergency Medicine
10010 Kennerly Rd, St Louis, 314-525-1900

Fortney, John Paul (3 mentions)
FMS-St Maarten, 1983
Certification: Emergency Medicine, Internal Medicine
625 S New Ballas Rd, St Louis, 314-251-6000

Hartmann, Thomas Gerard (4 mentions)
Washington U, 1976
Certification: Emergency Medicine, Family Medicine
2345 Dougherty Ferry Rd, St Louis, 314-966-9666

Hill, Thomas Clark (3 mentions)
Washington U, 1972
Certification: Emergency Medicine, Family Medicine
12634 Olive Blvd, St Louis, 618-459-7134

Jaffe, David Michael (3 mentions)
U of Chicago, 1978 *Certification:* Emergency Medicine,
Pediatric Emergency Medicine, Pediatrics
660 S Euclid Ave #116, St Louis, 314-454-6299

Keithly, Dennis J. (15 mentions)
U of Missouri, 1972 *Certification:* Emergency Medicine
615 S New Ballas Rd, St Louis, 314-569-6090

Kella, Timothy Lee (7 mentions)
St Louis U, 1982 *Certification:* Internal Medicine
3015 N Ballas Rd, St Louis, 314-996-5227

Kennedy, Robert McMillan (7 mentions)
Med Coll of Georgia, 1980
Certification: Pediatric Emergency Medicine, Pediatrics
660 S Euclid Ave, St Louis, 314-454-2341

Larson, Stephen Fielding (3 mentions)
Emory U, 1988 *Certification:* Emergency Medicine
12303 De Paul Dr, Bridgeton, 314-344-6360

Lewis, Lawrence Martin (6 mentions)
U of Miami, 1976
Certification: Emergency Medicine, Internal Medicine
660 S Euclid Ave, St Louis, 314-747-3000

Meinzen, Michael John (4 mentions)
FMS-India, 1975
232 S Woods Mill Rd, Chesterfield, 314-205-6990

Milton, John Anthony (4 mentions)
Washington U, 1976
Certification: Emergency Medicine, Internal Medicine
6420 Clayton Rd, St Louis, 314-768-8360

Ockner, Samuel Aaron (9 mentions)
U of Cincinnati, 1984 *Certification:* Internal Medicine
3015 N Ballas Rd, St Louis, 314-996-5225

Ruoff, Brent Eric (4 mentions)
St Louis U, 1981
Certification: Emergency Medicine, Internal Medicine
660 S Euclid Ave, St Louis, 314-362-9202

Scalzo, Anthony James (10 mentions)
St Louis U, 1979 *Certification:* Medical Toxicology, Pediatric
Emergency Medicine, Pediatrics
1465 S Grand Blvd, St Louis, 314-577-5600

Wessely, James Richard (8 mentions)
U of Illinois, 1978 *Certification:* Emergency Medicine
232 S Woods Mill Rd, Chesterfield, 314-205-6990

Wheeler, Thomas F. (7 mentions)
U of Missouri, 1974 *Certification:* Emergency Medicine
615 S New Ballas Rd, St Louis, 314-569-6090

Wiele, Robert Dennis (3 mentions)
U of Missouri-Kansas City, 1978
Certification: Emergency Medicine, Internal Medicine
6420 Clayton Rd, St Louis, 314-768-8360

Endocrinology

Clutter, William Edward (8 mentions)
Ohio State U, 1975
Certification: Endocrinology and Metabolism, Internal Medicine
4921 Parkview Pl #5-C, St Louis, 314-362-7601

Etzkorn, James Robert (15 mentions)
St Louis U, 1973
Certification: Endocrinology and Metabolism, Internal Medicine
2821 N Ballas Rd #116, St Louis, 314-995-9718

Fishman, Norman (9 mentions)
Columbia U, 1974
Certification: Endocrinology and Metabolism, Internal Medicine
222 S Woods Mill Rd #410 N, Chesterfield, 314-469-6224

Gaitan, Daniel (9 mentions)
U of Mississippi, 1986 *Certification:* Endocrinology,
Diabetes, and Metabolism, Internal Medicine
969 N Mason Rd #145, St Louis, 314-878-6008

Oiknine, Ralph (6 mentions)
FMS-Grenada, 1999 *Certification:* Endocrinology, Diabetes,
and Metabolism, Internal Medicine
222 S Woods Mill Rd #410N, Chesterfield, 314-469-6224

Silverberg, Alan Bernard (6 mentions)
U of Kansas, 1972
Certification: Endocrinology and Metabolism, Internal Medicine
3660 Vista Ave, St Louis, 314-977-6157

Skor, Donald Alan (11 mentions)
Rush U, 1978
Certification: Endocrinology and Metabolism, Internal Medicine
4921 Parkview Pl, St Louis, 314-333-4100

Thampy, K. George (13 mentions)
St Louis U, 1997 *Certification:* Endocrinology, Diabetes,
and Metabolism, Internal Medicine
10004 Kennerly Rd #160-B, St Louis, 314-842-1588

Tobin, Garry Stuart (11 mentions)
Washington U, 1985 *Certification:* Endocrinology, Diabetes,
and Metabolism, Internal Medicine
4921 Parkview Pl #13-B, St Louis, 314-747-7300

Wadsworth, Harry Lee (22 mentions)
Texas Tech U, 1983 *Certification:* Internal Medicine
3009 N Ballas Rd #100, St Louis, 314-432-1111

Wiethop, Brian Vernon (6 mentions)
St Louis U, 1986 *Certification:* Endocrinology, Diabetes,
and Metabolism, Internal Medicine
11155 Dunn Rd #108-N, St Louis, 314-355-6779

Family Practice *(see note on page 9)*

Baker, Gregory Eden (3 mentions)
Meharry Med Coll, 1998 *Certification:* Family Medicine
8969 Watson Rd, St Louis, 314-918-9111

Burns, Lisa Cerneka (3 mentions)
U of Missouri, 1989 *Certification:* Family Medicine
16555 Manchester Rd #100, Grover, 314-977-5050

Cannon, Miguel Estephano (3 mentions)
St Louis U, 1987 *Certification:* Family Medicine, Sports Medicine
2325 Dougherty Ferry Rd #100, St Louis, 314-977-9600

Danis, Peter Godfrey, III (14 mentions)
St Louis U, 1981 *Certification:* Family Medicine
615 S New Ballas Rd, St Louis, 314-569-6010
12680 Olive Blvd #300, St Louis, 314-251-8888

Hargraves, Van E. (3 mentions)
U of California-Los Angeles, 1980 *Certification:* Family Medicine
5551 Winghaven Blvd #142, O'Fallon, 636-695-2510

Jennings, Timothy W. (3 mentions)
A T Still U, 1989
12255 De Paul Dr #200, Bridgeton, 314-344-7600

Lord, James Lawrence, Jr. (5 mentions)
U of Missouri, 1974
Certification: Family Medicine, Sports Medicine
12680 Olive Blvd #300, St Louis, 314-251-8888

Maestas, Daniel Joseph (3 mentions)
St Louis U, 1987 *Certification:* Family Medicine
9338 Olive Blvd #100, St Louis, 314-993-2400

Smith, Brian Michael (3 mentions)
Southern Illinois U, 1998 *Certification:* Family Medicine
300 Medical Plaza #310, Lake St Louis, 636-625-2662

Utech, Lori L. (5 mentions)
U of Wisconsin, 1983 *Certification:* Family Medicine
225 Clarkson Rd, Ballwin, 636-230-5050

Van Gundy, Jason Brett (4 mentions)
U of Iowa, 1998 *Certification:* Family Medicine
300 Medical Plaza #310, Lake St Louis, 636-625-2662

Gastroenterology

Aliperti, Giuseppe (9 mentions)
FMS-Italy, 1979
Certification: Gastroenterology, Internal Medicine
12855 N 40th Dr #175, St Louis, 314-628-9000

Bacon, Bruce Raymond (12 mentions)
Case Western Reserve U, 1975 *Certification:*
Gastroenterology, Internal Medicine, Transplant Hepatology
3660 Vista Ave, St Louis, 314-977-6150

Benage, David Donnelly (13 mentions)
U of Missouri, 1984
Certification: Gastroenterology, Internal Medicine
621 S New Ballas Rd #228-A, St Louis, 314-569-6973

Brady, Lynda Margaret (6 mentions)
Stony Brook U, 1989
Certification: Pediatric Gastroenterology, Pediatrics
621 S New Ballas Rd #140-A, St Louis, 314-996-0006

Burton, Frank R. (6 mentions)
U of Oklahoma, 1980
Certification: Gastroenterology, Internal Medicine
3660 Vista Ave, St Louis, 314-977-6150

Buse, Paul Edward (22 mentions)
Washington U, 1986
Certification: Gastroenterology, Internal Medicine
226 S Woods Mill Rd #52W, Chesterfield, 314-569-2620
3023 N Ballas Rd #520, St Louis, 314-569-2620
200 Brevco Plaza #208, Lake St Louis, 636-561-9020

Cort, David Howard Blaine (14 mentions)
U of Miami, 1980 *Certification:* Allergy & Immunology,
   Gastroenterology, Internal Medicine
226 S Woods Mill Rd #52-W, Chesterfield, 314-434-2399
3023 N Ballas Rd #520-D, St Louis, 314-569-2620

Edmundowicz, Steven A. (9 mentions)
Jefferson Med Coll, 1983
Certification: Gastroenterology, Internal Medicine
4921 Parkview Pl, St Louis, 314-747-3000

Farrell, John Sylvester (6 mentions)
St Louis U, 1973
Certification: Gastroenterology, Internal Medicine
621 S New Ballas Rd #4019-B, St Louis, 314-251-6966

Goran, David Alan (9 mentions)
Washington U, 1976
Certification: Gastroenterology, Internal Medicine
1040 N Mason Rd Bldg #206, St Louis, 314-878-1950

Presti, Michael Edward (16 mentions)
Washington U, 1986
Certification: Gastroenterology, Internal Medicine
621 S New Ballas Rd, St Louis, 314-251-5660

Rothbaum, Robert Jay (8 mentions)
U of Chicago, 1976
Certification: Pediatric Gastroenterology, Pediatrics
1 Childrens Pl, St Louis, 314-454-6173

Shuman, Robert B. (6 mentions)
U of Missouri, 1981
Certification: Gastroenterology, Internal Medicine
4652 Maryland Ave, St Louis, 314-367-3113

Walden, David Thomas (7 mentions)
U of Texas-Galveston, 1987
Certification: Gastroenterology, Internal Medicine
226 S Woods Mill Rd #52W, Chesterfield, 314-434-2399
3023 N Ballas Rd #520-D, St Louis, 314-569-2620

Weinstock, Leonard Biener (8 mentions)
U of Rochester, 1981
Certification: Gastroenterology, Internal Medicine
11525 Olde Cabin Rd, St Louis, 314-997-0554

Woodley, Michele C. (9 mentions)
Stony Brook U, 1986
Certification: Gastroenterology, Internal Medicine
3009 N Ballas Rd #350-C, St Louis, 314-432-5044

General Surgery

Altepeter, Henry M., III (6 mentions)
St Louis U, 1977 *Certification:* Surgery
621 S New Ballas Rd #7011B, St Louis, 314-251-6840

Beckman, Robert Fred (6 mentions)
U of Alabama, 1983 *Certification:* Surgery
12700 Southfork Rd #235, St Louis, 314-842-2226

Brunt, L. Michael (19 mentions)
Johns Hopkins U, 1980 *Certification:* Surgery
4921 Parkview Pl, St Louis, 314-454-7194

Cronin, Christopher Scott (14 mentions)
Georgetown U, 1989 *Certification:* Surgery
226 S Woods Mill Rd #49, Chesterfield, 314-434-1211

Guerra, Omar Martin (5 mentions)
U Central del Caribe, 1999 *Certification:* Surgery
555 N Ballas Rd #265, St Louis, 314-991-4644

Howard, Todd Kevin (6 mentions)
U of Cincinnati, 1981 *Certification:* Surgery
555 N Ballas Rd #265, St Louis, 314-991-4644

Hsueh, Eddy Chung-Chiang (5 mentions)
U of Chicago, 1991 *Certification:* Surgery
3635 Vista Ave, St Louis, 314-577-6027

Hurley, Joseph Jerome (10 mentions)
U of Missouri, 1971 *Certification:* Surgery
621 S New Ballas Rd #7011B, St Louis, 314-569-6840

Krajcovic, David Paul (6 mentions)
Washington U, 1969 *Certification:* Surgery
232 S Woods Mill Dr #200 E, Chesterfield, 314-434-1211

Limpert, Jonathan N. (6 mentions)
U of Missouri-Kansas City, 1999 *Certification:* Surgery
1035 Bellevue Ave #211, St Louis, 314-644-6300
533 Couch Ave #220, Kirkwood, 314-644-6300

Linehan, David Charles (5 mentions)
U of Massachusetts, 1990 *Certification:* Surgery
4921 Parkview Pl, St Louis, 314-747-3000

Ludwig, Mark A. (9 mentions)
Rosalind Franklin U, 1976 *Certification:* Surgery
555 N Ballas Rd #265, St Louis, 314-991-4644

Matthews, Brent Duane (4 mentions)
Indiana U, 1993 *Certification:* Surgery
4921 Parkview Pl, St Louis, 314-454-8877

Meiners, David Joseph (32 mentions)
St Louis U, 1977 *Certification:* Surgery
621 S New Ballas Rd #7011-B, St Louis, 314-251-6840

Meyer, Robert Charles (4 mentions)
St Louis U, 1976 *Certification:* Surgery
1035 Bellevue Ave #211, St Louis, 314-644-6300

Niesen, Thomas Edwin (20 mentions)
Tulane U, 1979 *Certification:* Surgery
226 S Woods Mill Rd #49, Chesterfield, 314-434-1211

Pitt, Darrell M. (4 mentions)
Kansas U Coll of Osteopathic Med, 1974
2325 Dougherty Ferry, St Louis, 314-965-8410

Pruett, Christopher S. (6 mentions)
St Louis U, 1996 *Certification:* Surgery
3009 N Ballas Rd #258, St Louis, 314-995-6999

Smith, Kenneth Gerald (4 mentions)
Southern Illinois U, 1993 *Certification:* Surgery
12348 Old Tesson Rd #180, St Louis, 314-842-6183

Zuke, Jeffrey Eric (11 mentions)
U of Missouri-Kansas City, 1979 *Certification:* Surgery
555 N Ballas Rd #265, St Louis, 314-991-4644

Geriatrics

Ban, David Joseph (5 mentions)
Oregon Health Sciences U, 1980
Certification: Geriatric Medicine, Internal Medicine
3009 N Ballas Rd #315, St Louis, 314-996-5900

Carr, David Brian (12 mentions)
U of Missouri, 1985
Certification: Geriatric Medicine, Internal Medicine
4488 Forest Park Ave, St Louis, 314-286-2700

Crecelius, Charles Adams (14 mentions)
St Louis U, 1984
Certification: Geriatric Medicine, Internal Medicine
675 Old Ballas Rd #101, St Louis, 314-567-7090

Flaherty, Joseph Henry (9 mentions)
St Louis U, 1990
Certification: Geriatric Medicine, Internal Medicine
1402 S Grand Blvd #M-238, St Louis, 314-977-8462

Gammack, Julie (5 mentions)
U of Minnesota, 1996
Certification: Geriatric Medicine, Internal Medicine
3660 Vista Ave, St Louis, 314-977-6055

Morley, John Edward (19 mentions)
FMS-South Africa, 1972 *Certification:* Endocrinology and
   Metabolism, Geriatric Medicine, Internal Medicine
3660 Vista Ave, St Louis, 314-977-6055

Raza, Hashim Syed (5 mentions)
U of Missouri-Kansas City, 1991
675 Old Ballas Rd #101, St Louis, 314-567-7090

Hematology/Oncology

Abbey, Elliot Efrem (6 mentions)
New York U, 1975
Certification: Internal Medicine, Medical Oncology
232 S Woods Mill Rd #330, Chesterfield, 314-205-6737

Blinder, Morey Alan (13 mentions)
St Louis U, 1981
Certification: Hematology, Internal Medicine, Medical Oncology
4921 Parkview Pl, St Louis, 314-747-3000

Borson, Rachel A. (5 mentions)
FMS-Canada, 1983
Certification: Hematology, Internal Medicine, Medical Oncology
450 N New Ballas Rd #270-W, St Louis, 314-989-1300

Busiek, Donald F. (15 mentions)
U of Missouri, 1983
Certification: Hematology, Internal Medicine, Medical Oncology
232 S Woods Mill Rd #330, Chesterfield, 314-205-6737

Cuevas, Juan D. (5 mentions)
FMS-Colombia, 1989 *Certification:* Medical Oncology
12255 De Paul Dr #260, Bridgeton, 314-291-3312

Glauber, James Girard (5 mentions)
U of Illinois, 1983
Certification: Internal Medicine, Medical Oncology
6400 Clayton Rd #302, St Louis, 314-645-3432

Greco, Alfred Orlando (8 mentions)
U of Missouri, 1975
Certification: Internal Medicine, Medical Oncology
12855 N 40 Dr #200, St Louis, 314-628-1210
12855 N Forty Dr, St Louis, 314-628-1210

Hanson, Robin Dale (6 mentions)
Washington U, 1993
Certification: Pediatric Hematology-Oncology, Pediatrics
607 S New Ballas Rd #2415, St Louis, 314-251-6986

Hayashi, Robert J. (5 mentions)
Washington U, 1986
Certification: Pediatric Hematology-Oncology, Pediatrics
1 Childrens Pl #9 S, St Louis, 314-454-6018

Kraetsch, Robert Elroy (6 mentions)
Washington U, 1969
Certification: Hematology, Internal Medicine, Medical Oncology
1475 Kisker Rd #180, St Charles, 636-442-7300

Luedke, Susan Liebowitz (5 mentions)
U of Rochester, 1972
Certification: Internal Medicine, Medical Oncology
6435 Chippewa St, St Louis, 314-989-1300

Lyss, Alan Philip (24 mentions)
Washington U, 1976
Certification: Internal Medicine, Medical Oncology
3015 N Ballas Rd, St Louis, 314-996-5514

Morris, Roy William (5 mentions)
St Louis U, 1972
Certification: Hematology, Internal Medicine, Medical Oncology
10012 Kennerly Rd #100, St Louis, 314-849-6066

Needles, Burton Morris (23 mentions)
Loyola U Chicago, 1974
Certification: Internal Medicine, Medical Oncology
607 S New Ballas Rd #3300, St Louis, 314-251-4400

Petruska, Paul Joseph (5 mentions)
St Louis U, 1967
Certification: Hematology, Internal Medicine, Medical Oncology
3660 Vista Ave #308, St Louis, 314-256-3850

Ratkin, Gary Alan (7 mentions)
Washington U, 1967 *Certification:* Hematology, Internal Medicine
3015 N Ballas Rd, St Louis, 314-996-5151

Schultz, Paul Kenneth (5 mentions)
U of Missouri, 1988 *Certification:* Medical Oncology
3015 N Ballas Rd, St Louis, 314-996-5151

Van Amburg, Albert L. (9 mentions)
Washington U, 1972
Certification: Internal Medicine, Medical Oncology
232 S Woods Mill Rd #330, Chesterfield, 314-205-6737

Weiss, Peter Douglas (10 mentions)
Case Western Reserve U, 1980
Certification: Internal Medicine, Medical Oncology
4921 Parkview Pl #14-B, St Louis, 314-454-5580
226 S Woods Mill Rd #35-W, Chesterfield, 314-275-9929

Wilkes, John David (5 mentions)
U of Missouri-Kansas City, 1988 *Certification:* Medical Oncology
1092 Wentzville Pkwy, Wentzville, 636-639-8600

Zenisek, Steven Charles (6 mentions)
St Louis U, 1976
Certification: Internal Medicine, Medical Oncology
12255 DePaul Dr, Bridgeton, 314-291-3312
533 Couch Ave #G-20, Kirkwood, 314-965-6411

Infectious Disease

Campbell, John William (24 mentions)
Washington U, 1977
Certification: Infectious Disease, Internal Medicine
222 S Woods Mill Rd #750-N, Chesterfield, 314-205-6600

Chambers, Guy William, III (12 mentions)
U of Massachusetts, 1979 *Certification:* Internal Medicine
6125 Clayton Ave #101, St Louis, 314-768-5616

Fraser, Victoria Jean (13 mentions)
U of Missouri, 1983 *Certification:* Internal Medicine
4570 Children's Pl, St Louis, 314-362-9098
1 Barnes Hospital Plaza, St Louis, 314-362-9098

Gardner, Morey (11 mentions)
U of Texas-Galveston, 1972
Certification: Infectious Disease, Internal Medicine
1035 Bellevue Ave #110, St Louis, 314-768-8778

German, Matthew Lawrence (8 mentions)
Robert W Johnson Med Sch, 1988
Certification: Infectious Disease, Internal Medicine
222 S Woods Mill Rd #750-N, Chesterfield, 314-434-1500

Gutwein, Michael B. (16 mentions)
Washington U, 1974
Certification: Infectious Disease, Internal Medicine
3009 N Ballas Rd #130, St Louis, 314-569-5540

Kennedy, Donald James (10 mentions)
U of Cincinnati, 1977
Certification: Infectious Disease, Internal Medicine
1100 S Grand Blvd, St Louis, 314-977-5500

Manian, Farrin Alan (42 mentions)
U of Missouri, 1981
Certification: Infectious Disease, Internal Medicine
621 S New Ballas Rd #7018, St Louis, 314-251-4949

Medoff, Gerald (10 mentions)
Washington U, 1962
Certification: Infectious Disease, Internal Medicine
4570 Childrens Pl, St Louis, 314-362-7601

Nellore, Suresh R. (11 mentions)
FMS-India, 1988 *Certification:* Infectious Disease
2325 Dougherty Ferry Rd #206, St Louis, 314-821-0900
10004 Kennerly Rd #368-B, St Louis, 314-577-5778

Robison, Leon Rice, III (9 mentions)
Case Western Reserve U, 1968
Certification: Infectious Disease, Internal Medicine
222 S Woods Mill Rd #750N, Chesterfield, 314-205-6600

Slom, Trevor Joel (8 mentions)
FMS-South Africa, 1989
Certification: Infectious Disease, Internal Medicine
2325 Dougherty Ferry Rd #206, St Louis, 314-821-0900
10004 Kennerly Rd #368-B, St Louis, 314-821-0900

Sosna, Jacob Phillip (14 mentions)
U of Missouri, 1973
Certification: Infectious Disease, Internal Medicine
621 S New Ballas Rd #598-A, St Louis, 314-251-5960

Storch, Gregory Alworth (14 mentions)
New York U, 1973
Certification: Infectious Disease, Internal Medicine
1 Childrens Pl, St Louis, 314-454-6079

Infertility

Odem, Randall Ray (14 mentions)
U of Iowa, 1981 *Certification:* Obstetrics & Gynecology,
Reproductive Endocrinology/Infertility
4444 Forest Park Ave #3100, St Louis, 314-286-2421

Silber, Sherman Jay (17 mentions)
U of Michigan, 1966 *Certification:* Urology
224 S Woods Mill Rd, Chesterfield, 314-576-1400

Witten, Berold Israel (13 mentions)
FMS-South Africa, 1975 *Certification:* Obstetrics &
Gynecology, Reproductive Endocrinology/Infertility
621 S New Ballas Rd #2002B, St Louis, 314-569-6753

Internal Medicine *(see note on page 9)*

Alvarez, Juan Manuel (3 mentions)
U of Michigan, 1987 *Certification:* Internal Medicine
1120 Shackelford Rd, Florissant, 314-921-4420

Avery, James Gardner (8 mentions)
U of Tennessee, 1990 *Certification:* Internal Medicine
114 N Taylor Ave, St Louis, 314-534-8600

Bakanas, Erin Lee (4 mentions)
U of Connecticut, 1987 *Certification:* Internal Medicine
3660 Vista Ave, St Louis, 314-977-6100

Balis, Fred Jeffrey (3 mentions)
Washington U, 1989 *Certification:* Internal Medicine
4652 Maryland Ave, St Louis, 314-367-3113

Ban, David Joseph (3 mentions)
Oregon Health Sciences U, 1980
Certification: Geriatric Medicine, Internal Medicine
3009 N Ballas Rd #315, St Louis, 314-996-5900

Bowe, Christopher Charles (3 mentions)
U of Missouri, 1981 *Certification:* Internal Medicine
12700 Southfork Rd #280, St Louis, 314-525-4990

Bowen, William Griffith (3 mentions)
U of North Carolina, 1974
Certification: Cardiovascular Disease, Internal Medicine
4652 Maryland Ave, St Louis, 314-367-3113

Brightfield, Ken R. (3 mentions)
U of Missouri, 1981 *Certification:* Internal Medicine
12855 N 40th Dr #280, St Louis, 314-432-4415

Brown, David Jasonvictor (3 mentions)
Washington U, 1995 *Certification:* Internal Medicine
969 Mason Rd, St Louis, 314-434-8828

Campbell, John William (3 mentions)
Washington U, 1977
Certification: Infectious Disease, Internal Medicine
222 S Woods Mill Rd #750-N, Chesterfield, 314-205-6600

Cohen, Shari Dobkin (4 mentions)
U of Missouri-Kansas City, 1987 *Certification:* Internal Medicine
605 Old Ballas Rd #200, St Louis, 314-872-8740

Daniels, John Stephen (4 mentions)
U of Arkansas, 1974
Certification: Endocrinology and Metabolism, Internal Medicine
4921 Parkview Pl, St Louis, 314-333-4100

Escher, Delbert Thomas, Jr. (3 mentions)
St Louis U, 1988 *Certification:* Internal Medicine
10511 Old Olive St Rd, St Louis, 314-993-2660

Esther, James Herbert (4 mentions)
Northwestern U, 1976
Certification: Internal Medicine, Rheumatology
226 S Woods Mill Rd #43W, Chesterfield, 314-205-6444

Fischbein, Lewis Conrad (7 mentions)
Washington U, 1974
Certification: Internal Medicine, Rheumatology
1 Barnes Hospital Plaza East Pavillion #16422, St Louis,
314-367-9595
1 Barnes Jewish Hospital Plaza, St Louis, 314-367-9595

Groesch, Scott David (4 mentions)
Washington U, 1994 *Certification:* Internal Medicine
4652 Maryland Ave, St Louis, 314-367-3113

Haskell, Darren Ray (4 mentions)
Wake Forest U, 1996 *Certification:* Internal Medicine
226 S Woods Mill Rd #43W, Chesterfield, 314-205-6444

Heaney, Robert Michael (3 mentions)
Creighton U, 1978 *Certification:* Internal Medicine
3660 Vista Ave #207, St Louis, 314-977-6100

Katzman, David Aron (3 mentions)
St Louis U, 1991 *Certification:* Internal Medicine
11709 Old Ballas Rd #101, St Louis, 314-993-1200

Ketchum, James Wallace (6 mentions)
Southern Illinois U, 1982 *Certification:* Internal Medicine
1585 Woodlake Dr #106, Chesterfield, 314-878-1905

Kunst, Edward John (3 mentions)
U of Missouri, 1980 *Certification:* Internal Medicine
2200 Barrett Station Rd, Manchester, 314-821-1313

Morris, Donald Gerard (7 mentions)
U of Missouri, 1993 *Certification:* Internal Medicine
3009 N Ballas Rd #315, St Louis, 314-996-5900

Oertli, Robert (3 mentions)
St Louis U, 1976 *Certification:* Internal Medicine
12345 W Bend Dr #300, St Louis, 314-849-6000

Olsen, Thomas Joseph (8 mentions)
St Louis U, 1979 *Certification:* Internal Medicine
1402 S Grand Blvd #12N, St Louis, 314-577-6100
3660 Vista Ave #207, St Louis, 314-577-6100

Page, Josey Mitchell, Jr. (3 mentions)
St Louis U, 1986 *Certification:* Internal Medicine
12255 De Paul Dr #550, Bridgeton, 314-291-9501

Raza, Hashim Syed (4 mentions)
U of Missouri-Kansas City, 1991
675 Old Ballas Rd #101, St Louis, 314-567-7090

Rehm, Charles H. (4 mentions)
St Louis U, 1975 *Certification:* Internal Medicine
621 S New Ballas Rd #142-A, St Louis, 314-251-5780

Saffa, James Dennis (6 mentions)
U of Missouri, 1975 *Certification:* Internal Medicine
12855 N 40th Dr #S-280, St Louis, 314-432-4415
621 S New Ballas Rd #142A, St Louis, 314-251-5780

Sanders, Stephen Gerard (3 mentions)
St Louis U, 1992 *Certification:* Internal Medicine
621 S New Ballas Rd #189-A, St Louis, 314-251-6335

Schneider, Paul Gerard (4 mentions)
St Louis U, 1976 *Certification:* Internal Medicine
8670 Big Bend Blvd #A, Webster Grove, 314-447-1900

Shore, Bernard L. (4 mentions)
Washington U, 1977
Certification: Internal Medicine, Pulmonary Disease
4652 Maryland Ave, St Louis, 314-367-3113

Skor, Donald Alan (3 mentions)
Rush U, 1978
Certification: Endocrinology and Metabolism, Internal Medicine
4921 Parkview Pl, St Louis, 314-333-4100

Soudah, Hani Charles (5 mentions)
FMS-Germany, 1983 *Certification:* Internal Medicine
12855 N 40 Dr #350, St Louis, 314-205-1926

Walden, Michael Jay (17 mentions)
U of Missouri, 1984 *Certification:* Internal Medicine
12855 N 40th Dr #S-280, St Louis, 314-432-4415

Weikart, Kevin David (3 mentions)
FMS-St Maarten, 1984 *Certification:* Internal Medicine
300 Medical Plaza #230, Lake St Louis, 636-625-1111

Nephrology

Antony, Karthikapalli A. (5 mentions)
FMS-India, 1989 *Certification:* Internal Medicine, Nephrology
10004 Kennerly Rd #315-A, St Louis, 314-843-3449

Bastani, Bahar (8 mentions)
FMS-Iran, 1977 *Certification:* Internal Medicine, Nephrology
3660 Vista Ave, St Louis, 314-977-6190

Buck, Stanley Wellington (5 mentions)
Washington U, 1977 *Certification:* Internal Medicine, Nephrology
11125 Dunn Rd #304, St Louis, 314-355-1166
3009 N Ballas Rd #142, St Louis, 314-993-4949

Cuddihee, Robert Emmet (5 mentions)
St Louis U, 1963
621 S New Ballas Rd #482-A, St Louis, 314-251-6856

Garcia, Juan C. (5 mentions)
U of Puerto Rico, 1982
Certification: Internal Medicine, Nephrology
3009 N Ballas Rd #356-C, St Louis, 314-991-0137

Hmiel, S. Paul (5 mentions)
Case Western Reserve U, 1989
Certification: Pediatric Nephrology, Pediatrics
1 Childrens Pl, St Louis, 314-454-6043

Martin, Kevin John (5 mentions)
FMS-Ireland, 1971 *Certification:* Internal Medicine, Nephrology
3660 Vista Ave, St Louis, 314-977-6190

Mellas, John G. (8 mentions)
U of Illinois, 1981 *Certification:* Internal Medicine, Nephrology
6400 Clayton St #216, St Louis, 314-842-9669
10004 Kennerly Rd #374-B, St Louis, 314-842-9669

Melo, Anibal Gonsalves (6 mentions)
Washington U, 1991 *Certification:* Nephrology
222 S Woods Mill Rd #750-N, Chesterfield, 314-205-6600

Pohlman, Thomas Ralph (15 mentions)
Washington U, 1976 *Certification:* Internal Medicine, Nephrology
222 S Woods Mill Rd #750N, Chesterfield, 314-205-6600

Purcell, Henry Edward (9 mentions)
St Louis U, 1984 *Certification:* Internal Medicine, Nephrology
6400 Clayton Rd #412, St Louis, 314-644-3535

Quadir, Humayun (7 mentions)
FMS-Bangladesh, 1962
Certification: Internal Medicine, Nephrology
10004 Kennerly Rd #315A, St Louis, 314-843-3449

Ravenscraft, Mark Douglas (18 mentions)
Washington U, 1983 *Certification:* Internal Medicine, Nephrology
621 S New Ballas Rd #3015-B, St Louis, 314-251-6344

Rothstein, Marcos (11 mentions)
FMS-Venezuela, 1974
Certification: Internal Medicine, Nephrology
324 De Baliviere Ave, St Louis, 314-367-9111
4921 Parkview Pl, St Louis, 314-286-0801

Seltzer, Jay Robert (18 mentions)
U of Missouri-Kansas City, 1987
Certification: Internal Medicine, Nephrology
3009 N Ballas Rd #142, St Louis, 314-993-4949
11125 Dunn Rd #304, St Louis, 314-355-1166

Singer, Gary G. (8 mentions)
FMS-Canada, 1987 *Certification:* Internal Medicine, Nephrology
70 Jungerman Cir #405, St Peters, 636-720-0310

Windus, David William (10 mentions)
Creighton U, 1978 *Certification:* Internal Medicine, Nephrology
660 S Euclid Ave, St Louis, 314-362-7206
4921 Parkview Pl, St Louis, 314-362-9096

Wood, Ellen Glenn (9 mentions)
U of Alabama, 1975
Certification: Pediatric Nephrology, Pediatrics
1465 S Grand Blvd, St Louis, 314-577-5600

Neurological Surgery

Abdulrauf, Saleem I. (10 mentions)
St Louis U, 1991 *Certification:* Neurological Surgery
3635 Vista Ave, St Louis, 314-577-8795

Backer, Robert Joseph (22 mentions)
St Louis U, 1981 *Certification:* Neurological Surgery
11605 Studt Ave #105, St Louis, 314-983-0344

Boland, Michael Francis (27 mentions)
U of Missouri, 1986 *Certification:* Neurological Surgery
232 S Woods Mill Rd, Chesterfield, 314-878-2888

Chicoine, Michael Robert (18 mentions)
U of California-Los Angeles, 1990
Certification: Neurological Surgery
660 S Euclid Ave, St Louis, 314-362-3570

Dacey, Ralph Gerard, Jr. (22 mentions)
U of Virginia, 1974
Certification: Internal Medicine, Neurological Surgery
517 S Euclid Ave, St Louis, 314-362-3571

Forget, Thomas Robert, Jr. (16 mentions)
Georgetown U, 1994 *Certification:* Neurological Surgery
621 S New Ballas Rd #297-A, St Louis, 314-251-6364

Leonard, Jeffrey Russell (9 mentions)
U of Washington, 1995 *Certification:* Neurological Surgery
1 Childrens Pl, St Louis, 314-454-2811

Picker, Selwyn (11 mentions)
FMS-South Africa, 1972 *Certification:* Neurological Surgery
621 S New Ballas Rd #310-A, St Louis, 314-251-6267

Polinsky, Michael Nathan (27 mentions)
Washington U, 1990 *Certification:* Neurological Surgery
232 S Woods Mill Rd, Chesterfield, 314-878-2888

Young, Paul H. (16 mentions)
St Louis U, 1975 *Certification:* Neurological Surgery
10012 Kennerly Rd #400, St Louis, 314-543-5999

Neurology

Awadalla, Sylvia (12 mentions)
Ohio State U, 1985 *Certification:* Neurology
1 Barnes Hospital Plaza #16304, St Louis, 314-747-4777

Benzaquen, Max Prely (5 mentions)
FMS-Peru, 1978 *Certification:* Neurology
224 S Woods Mill Rd #59, Chesterfield, 314-878-8744

Burris, Garret Charles (7 mentions)
Louisiana State U, 1968 *Certification:* Neurology with
Special Qualifications in Child Neurology, Pediatrics
226 S Woods Mill Rd #46W, Chesterfield, 314-275-7070

Cruz-Flores, Salvador (7 mentions)
FMS-Mexico, 1985 *Certification:* Neurology, Vascular Neurology
3660 Vista Ave, St Louis, 314-977-6082

Dobmeyer, Susan Matilda (5 mentions)
Ohio State U, 1984 *Certification:* Neurology
1034 S Brentwood Blvd #754, St Louis, 314-725-2010

Dooley, Joseph Michael (5 mentions)
St Louis U, 1958 *Certification:* Neurology
232 S Woods Mill Rd, Chesterfield, 314-878-2888

Goldring, James Michael (11 mentions)
Washington U, 1986 *Certification:* Neurology
3009 N Ballas Rd #209, St Louis, 314-567-3663
620 Maple Valley Dr, Farmington, 314-567-3663
509 Hammacher, Waterloo, IL, 314-567-3663

Green, Barbara Joan (12 mentions)
Rush U, 1982 *Certification:* Neurology
621 S New Ballas Rd #5018-B, St Louis, 314-569-6000

Hatlelid, John Michael (7 mentions)
Washington U, 1977 *Certification:* Neurology
1034 S Brentwood Blvd #754, St Louis, 314-725-2010

Head, Richard Anthony (9 mentions)
Indiana U, 1982 *Certification:* Neurology
10004 Kennerly Rd #391-B, St Louis, 314-843-8222

Jafri, Ahmed Hassan (5 mentions)
FMS-Pakistan, 1982 *Certification:* Clinical Neurophysiology,
Neurology, Vascular Neurology
12266 DePaul Dr #225, Bridgeton, 314-881-2700

Kinsella, Laurence Joseph (5 mentions)
St Louis U, 1985 *Certification:* Internal Medicine, Neurology
2325 Dougherty Ferry Rd #100, St Louis, 314-977-9600

Lemann, Walter, III (7 mentions)
Tulane U, 1979 *Certification:* Neurology
969 N Mason Rd #140, St Louis, 314-996-8830

Logan, William Richard (25 mentions)
U of Oklahoma, 1978 *Certification:* Internal Medicine, Neurology
621 S New Ballas Rd #5018-B, St Louis, 314-251-5910

Myers, Gary Harris (7 mentions)
U of Minnesota, 1968 *Certification:* Neurology
10004 Kennerly Rd #391-B, St Louis, 314-843-8222

Nemeth, Patti M. (12 mentions)
Washington U, 1993 *Certification:* Neurology
232 S Woods Mill Rd, Chesterfield, 314-878-2888

Perlmutter, Joel Synes (5 mentions)
U of Missouri, 1979 *Certification:* Neurology
660 S Euclid Ave, St Louis, 314-362-6908

Singer, Barry Alan (9 mentions)
Columbia U, 1992 *Certification:* Neurology
1 Barnes Jewish Hospital Plaza #16304, St Louis, 314-747-4777

Weiss, Stuart (11 mentions)
Washington U, 1954 *Certification:* Neurology, Neurology
with Special Qualifications in Child Neurology
1 Barnes Hospital Plaza #16304, St Louis, 314-747-4777

Obstetrics/Gynecology

Ahlering, George P. (3 mentions)
U of Missouri-Kansas City, 1982
Certification: Obstetrics & Gynecology
16216 Baxter Rd #100, Chesterfield, 636-449-4700

Anstey, John Thomas (3 mentions)
St Louis U, 1973 *Certification:* Obstetrics & Gynecology
3009 N Ballas Rd #356, St Louis, 314-432-2880

Appelbaum, John K. (3 mentions)
Certification: Obstetrics & Gynecology
3023 N Ballas Rd #120-D, St Louis, 314-432-3669

Biest, Scott Warren (4 mentions)
U of Missouri-Kansas City, 1989
Certification: Obstetrics & Gynecology
3023 N Ballas Rd #440, St Louis, 314-432-8181
1 Barnes Jewish Plaza #13606, St Louis, 314-367-7600

Boedeker, James Peter (3 mentions)
U of Missouri, 1975 *Certification:* Obstetrics & Gynecology
3555 Sunset Office Dr #107, St Louis, 314-238-9000

Bryan, Bruce Lohrmann (4 mentions)
Washington U, 1977 *Certification:* Obstetrics & Gynecology
1034 S Brentwood Blvd #946, St Louis, 314-725-9300

Derosa, Michael Joseph (3 mentions)
St Louis U, 1984 *Certification:* Obstetrics & Gynecology
621 S New Ballas Rd #695-A, St Louis, 314-872-7400
1120 Wolfrum Rd #103, St Charles, 314-872-7400

Dixon, Michael B. (4 mentions)
U of Missouri, 1981 *Certification:* Obstetrics & Gynecology
10004 Kennerly Rd #386-B, St Louis, 314-842-7910

Durel, Justin Henry (6 mentions)
U of Alabama, 1974 *Certification:* Obstetrics & Gynecology
621 S New Ballas Rd #695-A, St Louis, 314-872-7400
1120 Wolfrum Rd #103, St Charles, 314-872-7400

Jostes, Mark Joseph (3 mentions)
U of Missouri, 1981 *Certification:* Obstetrics & Gynecology
3009 N Ballas Rd #366C, St Louis, 314-569-2424

Klein, Jacob (8 mentions)
Jefferson Med Coll, 1968 *Certification:* Obstetrics & Gynecology
3009 N Ballas Rd #366C, St Louis, 314-569-2424

Levine, David Jay (3 mentions)
FMS-Mexico, 1976 *Certification:* Obstetrics & Gynecology
232 S Woods Mill Rd, Chesterfield, 314-205-6564

Matuszek, Janet (4 mentions)
A T Still U, 1992
209 First Executive Ave, St Peters, 636-936-8777

Maupin, Kathy Cartier (3 mentions)
U of Missouri, 1981 *Certification:* Obstetrics & Gynecology
10806 Olive Blvd, St Louis, 314-993-7009

McLaughlin, Carole (3 mentions)
St Louis U, 1993 *Certification:* Obstetrics & Gynecology
621 S New Ballas Rd #B-75, St Louis, 314-812-7564

Mormol, Jeffrey Stuart (4 mentions)
Washington U, 1991 *Certification:* Obstetrics & Gynecology
3844 S Lindbergh Blvd #200, St Louis, 314-842-0340

Mutch, David Gardner (5 mentions)
Washington U, 1980
Certification: Gynecologic Oncology, Obstetrics & Gynecology
4921 Parkview Pl, St Louis, 314-362-3181

Paul, Michael James (5 mentions)
Northwestern U, 1980
Certification: Maternal-Fetal Medicine, Obstetrics & Gynecology
3023 N Ballas Rd #450, St Louis, 314-747-1336

Pearse, Carlton Sherman (7 mentions)
Washington U, 1978 *Certification:* Obstetrics & Gynecology
226 S Woods Mill Rd #68-W, Chesterfield, 314-576-0930

Philpott, Timothy Charles (7 mentions)
Washington U, 1994 *Certification:* Obstetrics & Gynecology
3023 N Ballas Rd Bldg D #120, St Louis, 314-432-3669

Pignotti, Blase J. (3 mentions)
U of Illinois, 1982 *Certification:* Obstetrics & Gynecology
621 S New Ballas Rd #B-75, St Louis, 314-812-7564

Shaner, Thomas Patrick (14 mentions)
St Louis U, 1972 *Certification:* Obstetrics & Gynecology
621 S New Ballas Rd #695-A, St Louis, 314-872-7400
1120 Wolfrum Rd #103, St Charles, 314-872-7400

Shelton, Becky Rae (3 mentions)
St Louis U, 1984 *Certification:* Obstetrics & Gynecology
1715 Deer Tracks Trail #110, St Louis, 314-919-2600

Smith, Jennifer Helene (5 mentions)
Washington U, 1999 *Certification:* Obstetrics & Gynecology
3023 N Ballas Rd #440, St Louis, 314-432-8181

Stephens, Andrea Lee (3 mentions)
U of California-Los Angeles, 1987
Certification: Obstetrics & Gynecology
4921 Parkview Pl, St Louis, 314-362-7135

Turner, Jacqueline Sue (3 mentions)
Tulane U, 1983 *Certification:* Obstetrics & Gynecology
1 Barnes-Jewish Plaza #16312, St Louis, 314-361-9000

Wagner, Daniel G. (5 mentions)
St Louis U, 1989 *Certification:* Obstetrics & Gynecology
224 S Woods Mill Rd #750S, Chesterfield, 314-576-9797

Wasserman, Gary M. (7 mentions)
U of Missouri-Kansas City, 1980
Certification: Obstetrics & Gynecology
675 Old Ballas Rd #100, St Louis, 314-872-9206
621 S New Ballas Rd #105-B, St Louis, 314-872-9206

Weinstein, David L. (7 mentions)
St Louis U, 1985 *Certification:* Obstetrics & Gynecology
3023 N New Ballas Rd #440, St Louis, 314-432-8181

Ophthalmology

Berdy, Gregg Jonathan (7 mentions)
St Louis U, 1983 *Certification:* Ophthalmology
12990 Manchester Rd #200, St Louis, 314-966-5000

Bobrow, James Charles (4 mentions)
Johns Hopkins U, 1970 *Certification:* Ophthalmology
211 N Meramec Ave #304, St Louis, 314-721-1140

Bohigian, George M. (5 mentions)
St Louis U, 1965 *Certification:* Ophthalmology
1235 Water Tower Pl, Arnold, 636-296-8612
12990 Manchester Rd #202, Des Peres, 314-432-6137

Chu, Fred Chin (4 mentions)
Cornell U, 1971 *Certification:* Ophthalmology
224 S Woods Mill Rd #480S, Chesterfield, 314-542-0700

Chung, Sophia Mihe (7 mentions)
Duke U, 1985 *Certification:* Ophthalmology
1755 S Grand Blvd, St Louis, 314-256-3220

Cruz, Oscar Alfredo (7 mentions)
Louisiana State U, 1987 *Certification:* Ophthalmology
1465 S Grand Blvd, St Louis, 314-577-5660
13131 Tesson Ferry Rd, St Louis, 314-842-3535
1755 S Grand Blvd, St Louis, 314-256-3220

Donahoe, Michael Philip (8 mentions)
St Louis U, 1989 *Certification:* Ophthalmology
621 S New Ballas Rd #5006B, St Louis, 314-432-5478
12990 Manchester Rd #201, Des Peres, 314-909-0633

Feibel, Robert Marks (4 mentions)
Harvard U, 1969 *Certification:* Ophthalmology
1034 S Brentwood Blvd #UCT-410, St Louis, 314-727-6716

Gira, Joseph Pravoot (6 mentions)
U of Missouri-Kansas City, 1995 *Certification:* Ophthalmology
621 S New Ballas Rd #5006-B, St Louis, 314-432-5478
12990 Manchester Rd #201, Des Peres, 314-909-0633

Goodrich, Steven Donald (5 mentions)
U of Pennsylvania, 1979 *Certification:* Ophthalmology
621 S New Ballas Rd #585-A, Creve Coeur, 314-251-6478

Grand, Mark Gilbert (11 mentions)
Yale U, 1968 *Certification:* Ophthalmology
12990 Manchester Rd #103, St Louis, 314-367-1181
4921 Parkview Pl #12-B, St Louis, 314-367-1181

Lewis, Robert David (4 mentions)
St Louis U, 1975 *Certification:* Ophthalmology
12700 Southfork Rd #205, St Louis, 314-842-0582

Lueder, Gregg Thomas (8 mentions)
U of Iowa, 1985 *Certification:* Ophthalmology
1 Childrens Pl #2589, St Louis, 314-454-6026

Perlmutter, John Craig (4 mentions)
Cornell U, 1971 *Certification:* Ophthalmology
330 1st Capitol Dr #330, St Charles, 636-947-3937

Shepherd, James Banks, III (4 mentions)
Columbia U, 1997 *Certification:* Ophthalmology
4921 Parkview Pl, St Louis, 314-747-3000

Shields, Steven M. (17 mentions)
Certification: Ophthalmology
222 S Woods Mill Rd #660N, Chesterfield, 314-878-9902

Siegfried, Carla Jean (4 mentions)
U of Missouri-Kansas City, 1989 *Certification:* Ophthalmology
10 Barnswith Dr #201, St Louis, 314-996-3300

Slocum, Stephen G. (5 mentions)
St Louis U, 1975 *Certification:* Ophthalmology
222 S Woods Mill Rd #N-660, Chesterfield, 314-878-9902

Tychsen, Lawrence (5 mentions)
Georgetown U, 1979 *Certification:* Ophthalmology
1 Children's Pl #2S89, St Louis, 314-454-6026

Yoselevsky, Robert Steven (7 mentions)
St Louis U, 1974 *Certification:* Ophthalmology
621 S New Ballas Rd #5006-B, St Louis, 314-432-5478
9701 Landmark Pkwy Dr #110, St Louis, 314-432-5478
12990 Manchester Rd #201, Des Peres, 314-909-0633

Orthopedics

Andersen, David Allen (4 mentions)
Washington U, 1975 *Certification:* Orthopaedic Surgery
3009 N Ballas Rd #260-C, St Louis, 314-996-7190

Boyer, Martin I. (8 mentions)
FMS-Canada, 1988
Certification: Orthopaedic Surgery, Surgery of the Hand
4921 Parkview Pl, St Louis, 314-747-2510

Burns, Michael Francis (5 mentions)
St Louis U, 1979 *Certification:* Orthopaedic Surgery
1027 Bellevue Ave #25, St Louis, 314-983-4700
621 S New Ballas Rd #63-B, St Louis, 314-983-4700
845 N New Ballas Ct City Pl #5, St Louis, 314-983-4700
2 Progress Point Pkwy, O'Fallon, 314-983-4700

Emanuel, James Patrick (5 mentions)
Washington U, 1983 *Certification:* Orthopaedic Surgery
5 New Ballas Ct, St Louis, 314-997-1777

Fox, Thomas Joseph (6 mentions)
U of Missouri, 1979 *Certification:* Orthopaedic Surgery
1027 Bellevue Ave #25, St Louis, 314-983-4700
845 N New Ballas Ct City Place 5, St Louis, 314-983-4700

Galakatos, Gregory R. (5 mentions)
Washington U, 1991 *Certification:* Orthopaedic Surgery
621 S New Ballas Rd #5015-B, St Louis, 314-567-5850

Hulsey, Richard Eugene (5 mentions)
U of Missouri, 1983 *Certification:* Orthopaedic Surgery
1050 Old Des Peres Rd #100, St Louis, 314-569-0612
7245 VO Tech Rd, Bonne Terre, 314-569-0612

Jones, Bruce Neil (9 mentions)
Wayne State U, 1973 *Certification:* Orthopaedic Surgery
224 S Woods Mill Rd #255 South Bldg, Chesterfield,
  314-434-3240

Kramer, Robert Scott (5 mentions)
Washington U, 1983 *Certification:* Orthopaedic Surgery
3844 S Lindbergh St, St Louis, 314-432-2323
3009 N Ballas Rd #105-B, St Louis, 314-432-2323

Kriegshauser, Lawrence A. (7 mentions)
U of Missouri, 1978 *Certification:* Orthopaedic Surgery
12639 Old Tesson Rd #115, St Louis, 314-849-0311

Lux, Paul Sherman (5 mentions)
Tulane U, 1983 *Certification:* Orthopaedic Surgery
14825 N Outer 40 #200, Chesterfield, 314-336-2555

Martin, Daniel Joseph, Jr. (10 mentions)
St Louis U, 1986 *Certification:* Orthopaedic Surgery
621 S New Ballas Rd #5015, St Louis, 314-567-5850

Martin, Jeffrey Wackher (6 mentions)
Case Western Reserve U, 1981 *Certification:* Orthopaedic Surgery
1040 N Mason Rd #G03, St Louis, 314-434-0030

Matava, Matthew Joseph (5 mentions)
U of Missouri-Kansas City, 1987
Certification: Orthopaedic Sports Medicine, Orthopaedic Surgery
1 Barnes Hospital Plaza, St Louis, 314-747-2511

Moed, Berton Roy (4 mentions)
St Louis U, 1976 *Certification:* Orthopaedic Surgery
3635 Vista Ave, St Louis, 314-577-8850

Otis, Stephanie Anne (8 mentions)
Vanderbilt U, 1988 *Certification:* Orthopaedic Surgery
1027 Bellevue Ave #25, St Louis, 314-983-4700
845 N New Ballas Ct City Place 5, St Louis, 314-983-4700
621 S New Ballas Rd #3017-B, St Louis, 314-983-4700

Piontek, Jerome Gregory (6 mentions)
St Louis U, 1979 *Certification:* Orthopaedic Surgery
222 S Woods Mill Rd, Chesterfield, 314-576-7076

Place, Howard Michael (7 mentions)
St Louis U, 1983 *Certification:* Orthopaedic Surgery
3635 Vista Ave, St Louis, 314-256-3850

Riew, K. Daniel (7 mentions)
Case Western Reserve U, 1984
Certification: Internal Medicine, Orthopaedic Surgery
4921 Parkview Pl, St Louis, 314-747-2534

Rouse, Andrew McCown (4 mentions)
Washington U, 1986 *Certification:* Orthopaedic Surgery
224 S Woods Mill Rd #330, Chesterfield, 314-576-7013

Schlafly, Edward F., Jr. (5 mentions)
Washington U, 1980 *Certification:* Orthopaedic Surgery
224 S Woods Mill Rd #330, Chesterfield, 314-576-7013

Schoenecker, Perry Lee (4 mentions)
U of Wisconsin, 1968 *Certification:* Orthopaedic Surgery
1 Children's Pl #4-S-60, St Louis, 314-872-7824
2001 S Lindbergh Blvd, St Louis, 314-872-7824

Schroer, William Carlton (5 mentions)
Washington U, 1989 *Certification:* Orthopaedic Surgery
12266 De Paul Dr #220, Bridgeton, 314-291-3399

Susi, Jesse George (8 mentions)
St Louis U, 1979 *Certification:* Orthopaedic Surgery
845 N New Ballas Ct, St Louis, 314-983-4700

Tessier, John Evan (6 mentions)
Creighton U, 1980 *Certification:* Orthopaedic Surgery
845 N New Ballas Ct City Place 5, St Louis, 314-983-4700
621 S New Ballas Rd #63-B, St Louis, 314-983-4700

Tull, Frank, IV (4 mentions)
Duke U, 1997 *Certification:* Orthopaedic Surgery
224 S Woods Mill Rd #255 South Bldg, Chesterfield,
   314-434-3240

Van Ryn, Jacques Simon (5 mentions)
Albany Med Coll, 1979 *Certification:* Orthopaedic Surgery
12266 De Paul Dr #220, Bridgeton, 314-291-3399

Wright, Rick Wayne (5 mentions)
U of Missouri, 1988
Certification: Orthopaedic Sports Medicine, Orthopaedic Surgery
1 Barnes Hospital Plaza #11300, St Louis, 314-747-2500
4921 Parkview Pl, St Louis, 314-747-2500

Yamaguchi, Ken (6 mentions)
George Washington U, 1989 *Certification:* Orthopaedic Surgery
4921 Parkview Pl 6th Fl, St Louis, 314-747-2500
1 Barnes Jewish Hospital Plaza, St Louis, 314-747-2534

Otorhinolaryngology

Bailey, Sean Brandon (7 mentions)
Tulane U, 1987 *Certification:* Otolaryngology
505 Couch Ave #330, St Louis, 314-965-9184

Bonacorsi, John Joseph (6 mentions)
St Louis U, 1973 *Certification:* Otolaryngology
12277 De Paul Dr #502, Bridgeton, 314-291-5307

Boyd, James Henry (9 mentions)
U of Missouri, 1985 *Certification:* Otolaryngology
607 S New Ballas Rd #2300, St Louis, 314-251-6394

Donovan, Thomas Joseph (11 mentions)
U of Cincinnati, 1971 *Certification:* Otolaryngology
1465 S Grand Blvd, St Louis, 314-577-5600

Druck, Norman Steven (13 mentions)
U of Illinois, 1970 *Certification:* Otolaryngology
226 S Woods Mill Dr #37-W, Chesterfield, 314-523-5310
5551 Winghaven Blvd, O'Fallon, 636-695-4244

Eisenbeis, John F. (9 mentions)
Washington U, 1988 *Certification:* Otolaryngology
3660 Vista Ave #312, St Louis, 314-977-5110
621 S New Ballas Rd #307, St Louis, 314-251-6362

Hardeman, Scott Howard (7 mentions)
U of Missouri-Kansas City, 1995 *Certification:* Otolaryngology
12399 Gravois Rd #102, St Louis, 314-843-3828

Haughey, Bruce Harwood (7 mentions)
FMS-New Zealand, 1977 *Certification:* Otolaryngology
605 Old Ballas Rd, St Louis, 314-362-7509
4921 Parkview Pl #11-A, St Louis, 314-362-7509
517 S Euclid Ave, St Louis, 314-362-7509

Lima, Jose Araujo (7 mentions)
FMS-Brazil, 1971 *Certification:* Otolaryngology
10004 Kennerly Rd #183-B, St Louis, 314-843-8400

Maack, Richard William (6 mentions)
U of Maryland, 1985 *Certification:* Otolaryngology
17000 Baxter #102, Chesterfield, 314-523-5330

Rosenblum, Barry N. (14 mentions)
U of Missouri-Kansas City, 1980 *Certification:* Otolaryngology
555 N Ballas Rd #265, St Louis, 314-991-4644

Varvares, Mark Alex (13 mentions)
St Louis U, 1986 *Certification:* Otolaryngology
3660 Vista Ave, St Louis, 314-977-5110

Wallace, Mark Steven (7 mentions)
Louisiana State U-Shreveport, 1987
Certification: Otolaryngology
607 S New Ballas Rd #2300, St Louis, 314-251-6394

West, Steven Eugene (7 mentions)
U of Pennsylvania, 1994 *Certification:* Otolaryngology
10004 Kennerly Rd #183-B, St Louis, 314-843-8400
9701 Landmark Pkwy #114, St Louis, 314-729-0077

Wild, Alan Paul Knight (11 mentions)
Tulane U, 1983 *Certification:* Otolaryngology
226 S Woods Mill Dr #37-W, Chesterfield, 314-523-5310
5551 Winghaven Blvd #230, O'Fallon, 636-695-4244

Pain Medicine

Dunteman, Edwin Dale (10 mentions)
U of Illinois, 1989 *Certification:* Anesthesiology, Pain Medicine
456 N New Ballas Rd #154, St Louis, 314-692-7246

Guarino, Anthony Herbert (7 mentions)
U of Maryland, 1992 *Certification:* Anesthesiology, Pain Medicine
1040 N Mason Rd #102, St Louis, 314-996-8631
969 N Mason Rd #240, St Louis, 314-996-8631

Johans, Thomas Gerard (12 mentions)
U of Missouri, 1977 *Certification:* Anesthesiology, Pain Medicine
1070 Old Des Peres Rd, St Louis, 314-821-8644

Smith, Brian Douglas (6 mentions)
U of Missouri, 1986 *Certification:* Anesthesiology, Pain Medicine
1070 Old Des Peres Rd, St Louis, 314-821-8644

Swarm, Robert Alexander (16 mentions)
Washington U, 1983 *Certification:* Anesthesiology, Pain Medicine
4921 Parkview Pl 10th Fl #A, St Louis, 314-362-8820

Pathology

Dehner, Louis Powell (8 mentions)
Washington U, 1966 *Certification:* Anatomic Pathology,
   Dermatopathology, Pediatric Pathology
1 Barnes Hospital Plaza, St Louis, 314-362-0150
660 S Euclid Ave, St Louis, 314-362-0101

Ferris, Charles Wesley (3 mentions)
Ohio State U, 1973
Certification: Anatomic Pathology & Clinical Pathology
3015 N Ballas Rd, St Louis, 314-996-5214

Fulling, Keith Harry (3 mentions)
Washington U, 1975
Certification: Anatomic Pathology, Cytopathology, Neuropathology
615 S New Ballas Rd, St Louis, 314-991-3556

Gardner, Laura Jane (4 mentions)
U of Illinois, 1989 *Certification:* Anatomic Pathology &
   Clinical Pathology, Cytopathology, Hematology
10010 Kennerly Rd, St Louis, 314-525-1144
417 Edgar Rd, St Louis, 314-525-1144

Gersell, Deborah Jo (3 mentions)
Washington U, 1975 *Certification:* Anatomic Pathology
615 S New Ballas Rd, St Louis, 314-251-4715

Humphrey, Peter Allen (5 mentions)
U of Kansas, 1984 *Certification:* Anatomic Pathology
1 Barnes Hospital Plaza, St Louis, 314-362-0112
660 S Euclid Ave, St Louis, 314-747-3000

Janney, Christine Gantner (5 mentions)
St Louis U, 1979 *Certification:* Anatomic Pathology
615 S New Ballas Rd, St Louis, 314-251-4715

Levy, Beth K. (3 mentions)
Certification: Anatomic Pathology & Clinical Pathology,
   Neuropathology
11155 Dunn Rd, St Louis, 314-741-9010

Lombardo, Joseph A. (3 mentions)
St Louis U, 1977
Certification: Anatomic Pathology & Clinical Pathology
300 1st Capitol Dr, St Charles, 636-947-5420

Maluf, Horacio Miguel (3 mentions)
FMS-Argentina, 1984 *Certification:* Anatomic Pathology
232 S Woods Mill Rd, Chesterfield, 314-205-6983

Martin, Scott Addington (8 mentions)
Duke U, 1973 *Certification:* Anatomic Pathology, Cytopathology
615 S New Ballas Rd, St Louis, 314-251-6243
200 Madison Ave, Washington, 636-239-8292

Merenda, Gloria Gallagher (3 mentions)
St Louis U, 1982
Certification: Anatomic Pathology & Clinical Pathology
6420 S Clayton Rd, St Louis, 314-768-8000

Perry, Arie (4 mentions)
U of Texas-Dallas, 1990 *Certification:* Anatomic Pathology
   & Clinical Pathology, Neuropathology
660 S Euclid Ave, St Louis, 314-362-0101

Ritter, Jon Herbert (5 mentions)
U of Minnesota, 1988 *Certification:* Anatomic Pathology
1 Barnes Jewish Hospital Plaza, St Louis, 314-362-0101
660 S Euclid Ave, St Louis, 314-362-0101

Santa Cruz, Daniel Jose (7 mentions)
FMS-Argentina, 1971
Certification: Anatomic Pathology, Dermatopathology
2326 Millpark Dr, St Louis, 314-991-4470

Schmidt, Robert Edward (3 mentions)
Washington U, 1976
Certification: Anatomic Pathology, Neuropathology
660 S Euclid Ave, St Louis, 314-362-7429

Pediatrics *(see note on page 9)*

Anderson, George C. (3 mentions)
St Louis U, 1993 *Certification:* Pediatrics
4116 Von Talge Rd #B, St Louis, 314-815-3331

Benoist, Walter Fischel (3 mentions)
Washington U, 1972 *Certification:* Pediatrics
12277 De Paul Dr #506, Bridgeton, 314-770-2300
224 S Woods Mill Rd #260-S, Chesterfield, 314-434-4010

Casey, Eliot Charles (4 mentions)
St Louis U, 1967 *Certification:* Pediatrics
1465 S Grand Blvd, St Louis, 314-577-5643
621 S New Ballas Rd, St Louis, 314-569-6150

Cole, Francis S. (4 mentions)
Yale U, 1973
Certification: Neonatal-Perinatal Medicine, Pediatrics
1 Childrens Pl, St Louis, 314-454-2244

Eaton, Adam Christopher (3 mentions)
Washington U, 1997 *Certification:* Pediatrics
2740 South Hwy 94 #A, St Peters, 636-441-5437

Epstein, Jay Stuart (3 mentions)
Emory U, 1983 *Certification:* Pediatrics
4488 Forest Park Ave #230, St Louis, 314-535-7855

Farberman, Elliott Henry (3 mentions)
St Louis U, 1973 *Certification:* Pediatrics
1224 Graham Rd #2005, Florissant, 314-921-7509
2630 Hwy K, O'Fallon, 636-240-1465

Fete, Timothy Joseph (6 mentions)
Washington U, 1977 *Certification:* Pediatrics
1465 S Grand Blvd, St Louis, 314-577-5600

Finn, Gregory Keith (3 mentions)
Washington U, 1992 *Certification:* Pediatrics
11940 Manchester Rd #E, Des Peres, 314-966-8500

Hartenbach, David Eugene (11 mentions)
U of Missouri, 1987 *Certification:* Pediatrics
11630 Studt Ave #200, St Louis, 314-567-7337

Heaney, Mary Susan (3 mentions)
Creighton U, 1978 *Certification:* Pediatrics
1465 S Grand Blvd, St Louis, 314-577-5643

Holmes, Nancy Elizabeth (3 mentions)
U of Missouri, 1976 *Certification:* Pediatrics
8888 Ladue Rd #130, St Louis, 314-862-4002

Irvine, Susan Marie (3 mentions)
St Louis U, 1993 *Certification:* Pediatrics
1035 Bellevue Ave #501, St Louis, 314-647-8045

Keating, James Peter (5 mentions)
Harvard U, 1963
Certification: Pediatric Gastroenterology, Pediatrics
1 Children's Pl #C, St Louis, 314-454-6006

Koenig, Joel Shelton (4 mentions)
Vanderbilt U, 1982
Certification: Neonatal-Perinatal Medicine, Pediatrics
3009 N Ballas Rd #141, St Louis, 314-994-0209

Kreusser, Katherine Lynn (3 mentions)
Indiana U, 1978 *Certification:* Pediatrics
8888 Ladue Rd #100, St Louis, 314-862-4050

Kung, Denise Huan-Hsuan (3 mentions)
Yale U, 1991 *Certification:* Pediatrics
226 S Woods Mill Rd #32W, Chesterfield, 314-576-1616

Levy, Kenneth Charles (4 mentions)
Rosalind Franklin U, 1988 *Certification:* Pediatrics
226 S Woods Mill Rd #36W, Chesterfield, 314-453-9666

Lindsey, Kelly J. (3 mentions)
U of Missouri-Kansas City, 1985 *Certification:* Pediatrics
1 Professional Dr #250, Alton, IL, 618-463-8636

Mathews, Patrice Faye (3 mentions)
U of Oklahoma, 1988 *Certification:* Pediatrics
621 S New Ballas Rd #2003-B, St Louis, 314-251-5811

McKinney, Thomas Casey (3 mentions)
Washington U, 1980 *Certification:* Pediatrics
226 S Woods Mill Rd #32W, Chesterfield, 314-576-1616

O'Neil, Jerome Hilary, Jr. (4 mentions)
St Louis U, 1981 *Certification:* Pediatrics
6526 Lansdowne Ave, St Louis, 314-353-8777

Plax, Daniel Sommers (13 mentions)
Washington U, 1993 *Certification:* Pediatrics
8888 Ladue Rd #100, St Louis, 314-862-4050

Polito-Colvin, Juanita C. (18 mentions)
U of Texas-Dallas, 1979 *Certification:* Pediatrics
226 S Woods Mill Rd 32W, Chesterfield, 314-576-1616

Quinn, Jennifer Stockton (3 mentions)
U of Kentucky, 1986 *Certification:* Pediatrics
456 N New Ballas Rd #304, St Louis, 314-567-6868

Sato, Richard William (5 mentions)
Washington U, 1977 *Certification:* Pediatrics
226 S Woods Mill Rd #32W, Chesterfield, 314-576-1616

Spewak, Robert David (3 mentions)
St Louis U, 1979 *Certification:* Pediatrics
6526 Lansdowne Ave, St Louis, 314-353-8777

Wolff, Patricia Barrett (6 mentions)
U of Minnesota, 1972 *Certification:* Pediatrics
4488 Forest Park Ave #230, St Louis, 314-535-7855

Plastic Surgery

Cabbabe, Edmond Bechir (8 mentions)
FMS-Syria, 1972 *Certification:* Plastic Surgery
10004 Kennerly Rd #165-B, St Louis, 314-842-5885

Caplin, David A. (16 mentions)
U of Cincinnati, 1975 *Certification:* Plastic Surgery
845 N New Ballas Ct #300, St Louis, 314-569-0130

Ettelson, Charles David (9 mentions)
Washington U, 1978 *Certification:* Plastic Surgery
222 S Woods Mill Rd #700N, Chesterfield, 314-878-7770

Francel, Thomas Joseph (11 mentions)
U of Cincinnati, 1982 *Certification:* Plastic Surgery, Surgery
621 S New Ballas Rd #1009-B, St Louis, 314-251-6845

German, David Scott (8 mentions)
St Louis U, 1985
Certification: Plastic Surgery, Surgery of the Hand
621 S New Ballas Rd #6003-B, St Louis, 314-991-2151

Mackinnon, Susan E. (13 mentions)
FMS-Canada, 1975
4921 Parkview Pl, St Louis, 314-747-3000

Maclin, Melvin Marlow, II (8 mentions)
Howard U, 1994 *Certification:* Plastic Surgery
845 N New Ballas Ct #300, St Louis, 314-569-0130

Marsh, Jeffrey Lowell (8 mentions)
Johns Hopkins U, 1970 *Certification:* Plastic Surgery
621 S New Ballas Rd #260-A, St Louis, 314-251-4772

O'Connell, Timothy Rogers (10 mentions)
St Louis U, 1971 *Certification:* Plastic Surgery
621 S New Ballas Rd #6003-B, St Louis, 314-991-2151

Paletta, Christian Edward (9 mentions)
U of North Carolina, 1978 *Certification:* Plastic Surgery
3635 Vista Ave, St Louis, 314-577-8793

Young, Vernon Le Roy (9 mentions)
U of Kentucky, 1970 *Certification:* Plastic Surgery
969 N Mason Rd #170, St Paul, 314-628-8200
1040 N Mason Rd #206, St Louis, 314-878-0520

Psychiatry

Bassett, Gregg Evan (4 mentions)
U of Miami, 1993 *Certification:* Psychiatry
3009 N Ballas Rd #227, St Louis, 314-567-5000

Chishti, Mohammad Imran (3 mentions)
FMS-Pakistan, 1990 *Certification:* Psychiatry
621 S New Ballas Rd #268-A, St Louis, 314-872-7792

Constantino, John N. (6 mentions)
Washington U, 1988
Certification: Child & Adolescent Psychiatry, Psychiatry
24 S Kingshighway Blvd, St Louis, 314-747-3000

Garcia-Ferrer, Eduardo L. (6 mentions)
FMS-Mexico, 1980
Certification: Addiction Psychiatry, Geriatric Psychiatry, Psychiatry
621 S New Ballas Rd #112-A, St Louis, 314-569-6545

Giuffra, Luis A. (5 mentions)
FMS-Peru, 1986
621 S Ballas Rd, St Louis, 314-251-7720

Grossberg, George T. (3 mentions)
St Louis U, 1975 *Certification:* Geriatric Psychiatry, Psychiatry
1438 S Grand Blvd, St Louis, 314-977-4829

Hicks, Frederick Gilbert (4 mentions)
U of Minnesota, 1981 *Certification:* Psychiatry
3009 N Ballas Rd #227, St Louis, 314-567-5000

Kreisman, Jerold Jay (3 mentions)
Cornell U, 1973 *Certification:* Psychiatry
11710 Old Ballas Rd #110, St Louis, 314-567-1958

Kuhn, Lawrence Fred (3 mentions)
Loyola U Chicago, 1972 *Certification:* Psychiatry
12255 DePaul Dr #500-N, Bridgeton, 314-344-7575

Mattingly, Gregory Warren (3 mentions)
Washington U, 1989 *Certification:* Psychiatry
330 1st Capitol Dr #390, St Charles, 636-946-8810

Nowotny, Thomas (3 mentions)
Washington U, 1985 *Certification:* Geriatric Psychiatry, Psychiatry
10805 Sunset Office Dr #401, St Louis, 314-909-8484

Packman, Paul Michael (4 mentions)
Washington U, 1963
8301 Maryland Ave #320, St Louis, 314-727-1666

Rifkin, Robert Howard (8 mentions)
U of Missouri, 1983 *Certification:* Psychiatry
3009 N Ballas Rd #227, St Louis, 314-567-5000

Robinson, Gordon Howard (5 mentions)
Washington U, 1986 *Certification:* Psychiatry
11710 Old Ballas Rd #110, St Louis, 314-567-1958

Ryall, Jo-Ellyn M. (3 mentions)
Washington U, 1975 *Certification:* Psychiatry
12166 Old Big Bend Rd #210, St Louis, 314-909-0121

Sky, Adam Jason (4 mentions)
U of Missouri-Kansas City, 1987 *Certification:* Psychiatry
1201 Bellevue Ave, St Louis, 314-647-4488

Smith, Stacey Lee (3 mentions)
Northwestern U, 1991 *Certification:* Psychiatry
4660 Maryland Ave #250, St Louis, 314-361-8566

Vickar, Garry Martin (3 mentions)
FMS-Canada, 1971 *Certification:* Psychiatry
11125 Dunn Rd #213, St Louis, 314-837-4900

Pulmonary Disease

Albers, Gary Michael (6 mentions)
St Louis U, 1985 *Certification:* Pediatric Pulmonology, Pediatrics
1465 S Grand Blvd, St Louis, 314-577-5600

Best, John Arthur (8 mentions)
FMS-Italy, 1977
Certification: Internal Medicine, Pulmonary Disease
222 S Woods Mill Rd #310N, Chesterfield, 314-576-6700

Botney, Mitchell David (20 mentions)
Ohio State U, 1984
Certification: Internal Medicine, Pulmonary Disease
3009 N Ballas Rd #256-C, St Louis, 314-692-2228

Brischetto, Michael J. (13 mentions)
St Louis U, 1977
Certification: Internal Medicine, Pulmonary Disease
621 S New Ballas Rd #483-A, St Louis, 314-251-4966

Ettinger, Neil Allan (9 mentions)
Washington U, 1983 *Certification:* Critical Care Medicine,
Internal Medicine, Pulmonary Disease
222 S Woods Mill Rd #310N, Chesterfield, 314-576-6700

Goldstein, Gary Robert (5 mentions)
U of Illinois, 1983 *Certification:* Critical Care Medicine,
Internal Medicine, Pulmonary Disease
11133 Dunn Rd, St Louis, 314-653-5007

Harris, Jeffrey Don (8 mentions)
FMS-St Maarten, 1983
Certification: Internal Medicine, Pulmonary Disease
2531 S Big Bend Blvd #1, St Louis, 314-647-7801

Lefrak, Stephen Simon (8 mentions)
SUNY-Downstate Med Coll, 1965
Certification: Internal Medicine, Pulmonary Disease
216 S Kings Hwy Blvd, St Louis, 314-454-7116

Marklin, Gary Francis (7 mentions)
U of Missouri, 1980 *Certification:* Critical Care Medicine,
Internal Medicine, Pulmonary Disease
4850 Lemay Ferry Rd #210, St Louis, 314-892-6565

Nayak, Ravi Parameshwar (6 mentions)
FMS-India, 1989 *Certification:* Critical Care Medicine,
Internal Medicine, Pulmonary Disease
3660 Vista Ave, St Louis, 314-977-4440

Nelson, Kirk Allen (7 mentions)
Kansas U Coll of Osteopathic Med, 1984 *Certification:* Critical
Care Medicine, Internal Medicine, Pulmonary Disease
11200 Tesson Fairy Rd #100, St Louis, 314-849-1500

Paranjothi, Subramanian (22 mentions)
Washington U, 1993 *Certification:* Critical Care Medicine,
Internal Medicine, Pulmonary Disease, Sleep Medicine
851 E 5th St #304, Washington, 314-251-4966

Potts, Daniel Eldon (15 mentions)
Washington U, 1972
Certification: Internal Medicine, Pulmonary Disease
222 S Woods Mill Rd #310N, Chesterfield, 314-576-6700

Shen, Anthony Shihin (11 mentions)
U of Missouri-Kansas City, 1980
Certification: Internal Medicine, Pulmonary Disease
3009 N Ballas Rd #251, St Louis, 314-569-2680

Spence, Thomas Henry, Jr. (6 mentions)
St Louis U, 1979
Certification: Internal Medicine, Pulmonary Disease
3009 N Ballas Rd #251, St Louis, 314-569-2680

Trulock, Elbert P., III (5 mentions)
Emory U, 1978
Certification: Internal Medicine, Pulmonary Disease
4921 Parkview Pl 8th Fl, St Louis, 314-454-8917

Wood, John A. (8 mentions)
Certification: Allergy & Immunology, Internal Medicine,
Pulmonary Disease
224 S Woods Mill Rd #500S, Chesterfield, 314-878-6260

Radiology—Diagnostic

Abuawad, Mazen Khalil (3 mentions)
FMS-Hungary, 1991 *Certification:* Diagnostic Radiology
10010 Kennerly Rd, St Louis, 314-525-1155

Applewhite, Thomas Arnold (10 mentions)
St Louis U, 1979
Certification: Diagnostic Radiology, Pediatric Radiology
615 S New Ballas Rd, St Louis, 314-251-6031

Balfe, Dennis Michael (4 mentions)
Med Coll of Wisconsin, 1975 *Certification:* Diagnostic Radiology
510 S Kingshighway Blvd, St Louis, 314-362-1053

Bhalla, Sanjeev (4 mentions)
Columbia U, 1994 *Certification:* Diagnostic Radiology
510 S Kingshighway Blvd #7, St Louis, 314-362-7092

Engels, John Thomas (3 mentions)
Rush U, 1984 *Certification:* Diagnostic Radiology
3015 N New Ballas Rd, St Louis, 314-996-5180
2 Progress Point Ct, O'Fallon, 636-344-2273
751 Sappington Bridge Rd, Sullivan, 573-468-4186
1225 Graham Rd, Florissant, 314-953-6000

Garvin, Charles F. (3 mentions)
U of Missouri-Kansas City, 1982
Certification: Diagnostic Radiology, Neuroradiology
232 S Woods Mill Rd, Chesterfield, 314-205-6100

Gresick, Robert Joseph, Jr. (4 mentions)
St Louis U, 1981 *Certification:* Diagnostic Radiology
12303 De Paul Dr, Bridgeton, 314-544-7143
525 Couch Ave, Kirkwood, 314-966-1524

Heiken, Jay Paul (3 mentions)
Columbia U, 1978 *Certification:* Diagnostic Radiology
510 S Kingshighway Blvd, St Louis, 314-362-1053

Levitt, Robert Gordon (4 mentions)
U of California-San Francisco, 1972
Certification: Diagnostic Radiology
12634 Olive Blvd, St Louis, 314-996-8511

Luisiri, Atchawee (4 mentions)
FMS-Thailand, 1974
Certification: Diagnostic Radiology, Pediatric Radiology
1465 S Grand Blvd, St Louis, 314-577-5652

McAlister, William Herbert (10 mentions)
Wayne State U, 1954 *Certification:* Pediatric Radiology, Radiology
1 Children's Pl, St Louis, 314-454-6229
510 S Kingshighway Blvd, St Louis, 314-454-6229

Mosher, Amy Ann (4 mentions)
U of Missouri, 1984 *Certification:* Diagnostic Radiology
3015 N New Ballas Rd, St Louis, 314-996-5180

Narra, Vamsidhar Rao (3 mentions)
FMS-India, 1990 *Certification:* Diagnostic Radiology
510 S Kingshighway Blvd, St Louis, 314-362-7092

Niemeyer, John Hart (5 mentions)
Washington U, 1982 *Certification:* Diagnostic Radiology,
Vascular & Interventional Radiology
3015 N Ballas Rd, St Louis, 314-996-5180

Reh, Thomas Edward (4 mentions)
St Louis U, 1969 *Certification:* Radiology
4 Sunnen Dr #120, St Louis, 314-768-8250
6420 Clayton Rd, St Louis, 314-768-8250

Root, Jonathan Daniel (4 mentions)
Temple U, 1983
Certification: Diagnostic Radiology, Internal Medicine
300 1st Capitol Dr, St Charles, 636-947-5444

Thomasson, Jeffrey Lee (8 mentions)
Washington U, 1982
Certification: Diagnostic Radiology, Neuroradiology
615 S New Ballas Rd, St Louis, 314-251-6031

Thornton, Christopher O. (4 mentions)
U of Missouri-Kansas City, 1994
Certification: Diagnostic Radiology
3015 N New Ballas Rd, St Louis, 314-996-5180

Totty, William Gene (3 mentions)
U of Tennessee, 1975 *Certification:* Diagnostic Radiology
510 S Kingshighway Blvd, St Louis, 314-362-2916

Vollmar, Theodore Martin (4 mentions)
St Louis U, 1984 *Certification:* Diagnostic Radiology
10010 Kennerly Rd, St Louis, 314-525-4492

Radiology—Therapeutic

Bradley, Jeffrey Dee (4 mentions)
U of Arkansas, 1993 *Certification:* Radiation Oncology
4921 Parkview Pl, St Louis, 314-747-7236

Butler, David Ferrell (9 mentions)
U of Virginia, 1989 *Certification:* Radiation Oncology
232 S Woods Mill Rd #110 E, Chesterfield, 314-542-4998

Fagundes, Humberto M. (7 mentions)
FMS-Brazil, 1987 *Certification:* Radiation Oncology
3015 N Ballas Rd, St Louis, 314-996-5157

Frazier, Robert Christian (7 mentions)
Virginia Commonwealth U, 1996
Certification: Radiation Oncology
607 S New Ballas Rd, St Louis, 314-251-6844

Haddad, Labib F. (10 mentions)
St Louis U, 1993 *Certification:* Diagnostic Radiology,
Vascular & Interventional Radiology
615 S New Ballas Rd, St Louis, 314-251-6031

Halverson, Karen Johnson (4 mentions)
Washington U, 1985 *Certification:* Radiation Oncology
232 S Woods Mill Rd #110 E, Chesterfield, 314-542-4998

Michalski, Jeff Michael (5 mentions)
Med Coll of Wisconsin, 1986 *Certification:* Radiation Oncology
4921 Parkview Pl, St Louis, 314-747-9600

Picus, Daniel (4 mentions)
U of Chicago, 1981 *Certification:* Diagnostic Radiology,
Vascular & Interventional Radiology
510 S Kingshighway Blvd, St Louis, 314-362-7130

Sutphen, Eric John (4 mentions)
St Louis U, 1987 *Certification:* Radiation Oncology
10010 Kennerly Rd, St Louis, 314-525-1688

Rehabilitation

Fischer, Ronald Louis (6 mentions)
U of Missouri, 1985
Certification: Physical Medicine & Rehabilitation
226 S Woods Mill Rd #59-W, Chesterfield, 314-878-7630

Metzler, John Paul (5 mentions)
U of Texas-Galveston, 1995 *Certification:* Pain Medicine,
Physical Medicine & Rehabilitation, Sports Medicine
4921 Parkview Pl, St Louis, 314-747-2823

Ogle, Abna Althea (4 mentions)
Howard U, 1986 *Certification:* Physical Medicine &
Rehabilitation, Spinal Cord Injury Medicine
300 First Capitol St, St Charles, 636-947-5373
12303 De Paul Dr, Bridgeton, 314-344-6460
6420 Clayton Rd, St Louis, 314-768-5205

Page, Jennifer Lynn (10 mentions)
U of Missouri-Kansas City, 1992
Certification: Pain Medicine, Physical Medicine & Rehabilitation
10016 Kennerly Rd, St Louis, 314-525-4545

Prather, Heidi (6 mentions)
Kansas U Coll of Osteopathic Med, 1991 *Certification:* Pain
Medicine, Physical Medicine & Rehabilitation, Sports Medicine
1 Barnes Jewish Hospital Plaza #11300, St Louis, 314-747-2500

Sohn, Daniel Gregory (3 mentions)
U of Missouri, 1985
Certification: Pain Medicine, Physical Medicine & Rehabilitation
845 N New Ballas Ct #5, St Louis, 314-983-4700

Tate, Sandra Lee (3 mentions)
Southern Illinois U, 1987
Certification: Physical Medicine & Rehabilitation
505 Couch Ave #25, St Louis, 314-966-0111
12855 N 40 Dr #125, St Louis, 314-966-0111

Wice, Martin B. (15 mentions)
Northwestern U, 1977 *Certification:* Internal Medicine,
    Physical Medicine & Rehabilitation
14561 N Outer Fprty #201, St Louis, 314-881-4290
621 S New Ballas Rd #6017B, St Louis, 314-569-6945

Rheumatology

Atkinson, John Patterson (8 mentions)
U of Kansas, 1969 *Certification:* Allergy & Immunology,
    Internal Medicine, Rheumatology
4921 Parkview Pl 5th Fl #C, St Louis, 314-286-2635
660 S Euclid Ave, St Louis, 314-454-7279

Baldassare, Andrew Robert (9 mentions)
St Louis U, 1971 *Certification:* Internal Medicine, Rheumatology
522 N New Ballas Rd #240, St Louis, 314-567-5100
330 1st Capitol Dr #310, St Charles, 636-946-4006

Brasington, Richard D., Jr. (14 mentions)
Duke U, 1980 *Certification:* Internal Medicine, Rheumatology
4921 Parkview Pl, St Louis, 314-362-7601

Divalerio, Richard M., Jr. (6 mentions)
Washington U, 1988
Certification: Internal Medicine, Rheumatology
3009 N Ballas Rd #100, St Louis, 314-432-1111

Esther, James Herbert (9 mentions)
Northwestern U, 1976
Certification: Internal Medicine, Rheumatology
226 S Woods Mill Rd #43W, Chesterfield, 314-205-6444

Kiehl, Mary Miller (6 mentions)
U of California-San Diego, 1990
Certification: Internal Medicine, Rheumatology
1 Barnes Hospital Plaza East Pavillion #16422, St Louis,
    314-367-9595
1 Barnes Jewish Hospital Plaza, St Louis, 314-367-9595

Moore, Terry Lynn (19 mentions)
St Louis U, 1972 *Certification:* Internal Medicine, Rheumatology
3660 Vista Ave, St Louis, 314-977-6070

Ross, Stephen Craig (6 mentions)
St Louis U, 1977 *Certification:* Internal Medicine, Rheumatology
522 N New Ballas Rd #240, St Louis, 314-567-5100
330 1st Capitol Dr #310, St Charles, 636-946-4006

Schneider, Robert Jay (10 mentions)
Johns Hopkins U, 1976
Certification: Internal Medicine, Rheumatology
3023 N Ballas Rd #500-D, St Louis, 314-567-4541

Weiss, Terry Drew (11 mentions)
St Louis U, 1972 *Certification:* Internal Medicine, Rheumatology
522 N New Ballas Rd #240, St Louis, 314-567-5100
330 1st Capitol Dr #310, St Charles, 636-946-4006

White, Andrew James (8 mentions)
U of Texas-Dallas, 1994
Certification: Pediatric Rheumatology, Pediatrics
1 Childrens Pl, St Louis, 314-454-6124

Thoracic Surgery

Blucher, Mark Lawrence (8 mentions)
New York U, 1994 *Certification:* Surgery, Thoracic Surgery
625 S New Ballas Rd #7040, St Louis, 314-251-6970

Coordes, Cordie C. (7 mentions)
U of Nebraska, 1976 *Certification:* Surgery, Thoracic Surgery
222 S Woods Mill Rd #550-N, Chesterfield, 314-434-3049

Mauney, Michael Clark (8 mentions)
Duke U, 1991 *Certification:* Surgery, Thoracic Surgery
3009 N Ballas Rd #266-C, St Louis, 314-996-5287

Meyers, Bryan Fitch (21 mentions)
U of Chicago, 1986 *Certification:* Thoracic Surgery
4921 Parkview Pl, St Louis, 314-362-8598
1040 N Mason Rd #201, St Louis, 314-996-3179

Murphy, Michael C. (11 mentions)
U of Virginia, 1983 *Certification:* Thoracic Surgery
3009 N Ballas Rd #360-C, St Louis, 314-569-5287

Naunheim, Keith Shelby (22 mentions)
U of Chicago, 1978 *Certification:* Thoracic Surgery
3655 Vista Ave, St Louis, 314-577-6131

Patterson, George A. (45 mentions)
FMS-Canada, 1974
4921 Parkview Pl 8th Fl, St Louis, 314-362-6025

Suen, Hon Chi (14 mentions)
FMS-China, 1982 *Certification:* Surgery, Thoracic Surgery
70 Jungermann Cir #201, St Peters, 636-916-9525
1004 Kennerly Rd #110-A, St Louis, 636-916-9525

Urology

Adkins, Kent Lewis (7 mentions)
U of Virginia, 1999 *Certification:* Urology
11125 Dunn Rd #208, St Louis, 314-355-3733
12255 DePaul Dr, St Louis, 314-315-9916
607 S New Ballas Rd #3100, St Louis, 314-315-9914

Andriole, Gerald Louis (21 mentions)
Jefferson Med Coll, 1978 *Certification:* Urology
1 Barnes Hospital Plaza, St Louis, 314-362-8200
2 Progress Point Pkwy #101-G, O'Fallon, 636-344-3970

Anglo, Luis Joseph (12 mentions)
U of Missouri, 1989 *Certification:* Urology
607 S New Ballas Rd #3100, St Louis, 314-315-9914

Austin, Paul Farmer (7 mentions)
U of Kentucky, 1991 *Certification:* Pediatric Urology, Urology
1 Childrens Pl, St Louis, 314-454-2298

Chehval, Micheal John (13 mentions)
St Louis U, 1967 *Certification:* Urology
621 S New Ballas Rd #6002-B, St Louis, 314-251-2626

Coplen, Douglas Edward (11 mentions)
Indiana U, 1985 *Certification:* Pediatric Urology, Urology
1 Childrens Pl, St Louis, 314-454-6034

De Guerre, Ronald Keith (9 mentions)
Washington U, 1974 *Certification:* Urology
12277 De Paul Dr #501, Bridgeton, 314-739-8844
11155 Dunn Rd #309-E, St Louis, 314-741-9010
112 Piper Hill Dr #12, St Peters, 636-939-9202

Feit, Robert Michael (12 mentions)
Indiana U, 1973 *Certification:* Urology
10296 Big Bend Blvd #205, St Louis, 314-315-9911

Figenshau, Robert S. (7 mentions)
U of Minnesota, 1987 *Certification:* Urology
4921 Parkview Pl, St Louis, 314-362-8200

Gaum, Leonard David (15 mentions)
FMS-Canada, 1973 *Certification:* Urology
621 S New Ballas Rd #6011B, St Louis, 314-569-1750

Keetch, David William (18 mentions)
U of Utah, 1987 *Certification:* Urology
12855 N 40 Dr #375, St Louis, 314-567-6071

Marcus, Michael David (9 mentions)
U of Cincinnati, 1985 *Certification:* Urology
1029 Big Bend Blvd, St Louis, 314-645-6454

Scully, Thomas Francis (10 mentions)
Indiana U, 1978 *Certification:* Urology
1029 Big Bend Blvd, St Louis, 314-645-6454

Shands, Courtney, III (10 mentions)
Vanderbilt U, 1982 *Certification:* Urology
12855 N 40 Dr #375, St Louis, 314-432-4575

Spellman, Matthew Joseph (8 mentions)
U of Iowa, 1997 *Certification:* Urology
12855 N 40th Dr #375, St Louis, 314-432-4575

White, Brad Christopher (8 mentions)
Loyola U Chicago, 1993 *Certification:* Urology
12855 N 40 Dr #375, St Louis, 314-567-6071

Vascular Surgery

Allen, Brent Terry (35 mentions)
Washington U, 1979 *Certification:* Surgery, Vascular Surgery
555 N Ballas Rd #265, St Louis, 314-991-4644

Ludwig, Mark A. (16 mentions)
Rosalind Franklin U, 1976 *Certification:* Surgery
555 N Ballas Rd #265, St Louis, 314-991-4644

Mantese, Vito Anthony (17 mentions)
St Louis U, 1982 *Certification:* Surgery, Vascular Surgery
621 S New Ballas Rd #7063-R, St Louis, 314-251-6840

Niesen, Thomas Edwin (17 mentions)
Tulane U, 1979 *Certification:* Surgery
226 S Woods Mill Dr #49-W, Chesterfield, 314-434-1211

Pennell, Richard Carlton (13 mentions)
St Louis U, 1979 *Certification:* Surgery, Vascular Surgery
621 S New Ballas Rd #7063-R, St Louis, 314-251-6840

Sicard, Gregorio Arquel (30 mentions)
U of Puerto Rico, 1972 *Certification:* Vascular Surgery
4921 Parkview Pl, St Louis, 314-362-7841

Nevada

Las Vegas Area

Las Vegas Area
Including Clark County

Allergy/Immunology

Christensen, Jim (41 mentions)
U of Nevada, 1984
Certification: Allergy & Immunology, Internal Medicine
4 Sunset Way #A-3, Henderson, 702-434-9690
7200 Cathedral Rock Dr #220, Las Vegas, 702-307-7707

Mcknight, Andrew Sean (17 mentions)
FMS-Dominica, 1999
Certification: Allergy & Immunology, Pediatrics
2821 W Horizon Ridge Pkwy #101, Henderson, 702-212-5889

Tottori, David Hiroaki (17 mentions)
U of Hawaii, 1987 *Certification:* Allergy & Immunology, Pediatrics
4 Sunset Way #A3, Henderson, 702-436-7720
4000 E Charleston Blvd #100, Las Vegas, 702-432-9544
8413 W Lake Mead Blvd, Las Vegas, 702-242-5988

Anesthesiology

Detmer, Michael Dale (4 mentions)
U of Michigan, 1975 *Certification:* Anesthesiology
501 S Rancho Dr #A7, Las Vegas, 702-386-4700
2635 Box Canyon Dr, Las Vegas, 702-386-4700

Ho, Arthur C. (3 mentions)
FMS-Dominica, 1993 *Certification:* Anesthesiology
2450 W Charleston Blvd, Las Vegas, 702-877-8660

Hummel, Paul Steven (6 mentions)
Harvard U, 1982 *Certification:* Anesthesiology
3010 W Charleston Blvd #150, Las Vegas, 702-878-0070

Lee, Anthony Donald (4 mentions)
FMS-St Maarten, 1999 *Certification:* Anesthesiology
2320 Paseo Del Prado #203, Las Vegas, 702-808-8958

Scheller, Mark Stuart (3 mentions)
Med Coll of Wisconsin, 1980 *Certification:* Anesthesiology
3100 W Sahara Ave #209, Las Vegas, 702-362-8061

Smith, John Sheldon (3 mentions)
Northwestern U, 1981 *Certification:* Anesthesiology
3100 W Sahara Ave #209, Las Vegas, 702-362-8061
3131 La Canada St #216, Las Vegas, 702-734-6901

Stephens, Anthony Mark (3 mentions)
U of Oklahoma, 1988 *Certification:* Anesthesiology
2450 W Charleston Blvd, Las Vegas, 702-877-8660

Cardiac Surgery

Donahoe, Nancy Anne (10 mentions)
U of Florida, 1987 *Certification:* Thoracic Surgery
3131 La Canada St #217, Las Vegas, 702-737-3808

Feikes, Joseph Randall (21 mentions)
Loma Linda U, 1989 *Certification:* Thoracic Surgery
1090 E Desert Inn Rd #202, Las Vegas, 702-735-1454
1701 N Green Valley Pkwy #5-C, Henderson, 702-735-1454

Smith, Vernon Curtiss, Jr. (8 mentions)
Wake Forest U, 1979 *Certification:* Thoracic Surgery
3131 LaCanada St #217, Las Vegas, 702-737-3808
3131 La Canada St #217, Las Vegas, 702-737-3808

Wiencek, Robert G., Jr. (28 mentions)
St Louis U, 1983 *Certification:* Surgery, Thoracic Surgery
1701 N Green Valley Pkwy #5C, Henderson, 702-614-6550
3150 N Tenaya Way #340, Las Vegas, 702-360-3330
1090 E Desert Inn Rd #200, Las Vegas, 702-735-1454
3059 S Maryland Pkwy #202, Las Vegas, 702-735-1454

Cardiology

Dadourian, Berge Jack (5 mentions)
U of California-Los Angeles, 1982 *Certification:* Cardiovascular
Disease, Internal Medicine, Interventional Cardiology
3121 S Maryland Pkwy #512, Las Vegas, 702-796-7150
3150 N Tenaya Way #460, Las Vegas, 702-233-1000

Green, Samuel E. (4 mentions)
Albany Med Coll, 1987
Certification: Cardiovascular Disease, Internal Medicine
3121 S Maryland Pkwy #512, Las Vegas, 702-796-7150
3150 N Tenaya Way #460, Las Vegas, 702-233-1000

Heeren, Paul V. (5 mentions)
Wayne State U, 1974
Certification: Cardiovascular Disease, Internal Medicine
3150 N Tenaya Way #320, Henderson, 702-731-8224

Kamboj, Ejaz U. (4 mentions)
FMS-Pakistan, 1986
Certification: Cardiovascular Disease, Interventional Cardiology
1700 N Buffalo Dr #100, Las Vegas, 702-650-0009
1707 W Charleston Blvd #230, Las Vegas, 609-426-1601

Lambert, Thomas Lloyd (5 mentions)
Duke U, 1986
Certification: Cardiovascular Disease, Internal Medicine
2010 Goldring Ave #308, Las Vegas, 702-598-3999
3150 N Tenaya Way #135, Las Vegas, 702-598-3999

Miranda, Cres P., Jr. (7 mentions)
U of California-San Francisco, 1985 *Certification:* Cardiovascular
Disease, Internal Medicine, Interventional Cardiology
7455 W Washington Ave #300, Las Vegas, 702-240-6482

Mock, James Edward, Jr. (5 mentions)
U of Minnesota, 1989 *Certification:* Cardiovascular Disease
2800 N Tenaya #202, Las Vegas, 702-255-8877

Nee, Jeannette (4 mentions)
Mount Sinai Sch of Med, 1986 *Certification:* Cardiovascular
Disease, Internal Medicine, Interventional Cardiology
2300 Corporate Cir #100, Henderson, 702-731-8224

Patel, Janmejay J. (7 mentions)
FMS-United Kingdom, 1987 *Certification:* Cardiovascular
Disease, Internal Medicine, Interventional Cardiology
4275 S Burnhaven Ave #335, Las Vegas, 702-731-5510

Portz, Stephen Jerome (8 mentions)
U of Kansas, 1982 *Certification:* Cardiovascular Disease,
Internal Medicine, Interventional Cardiology
10001 S Eastern Ave #203, Henderson, 702-733-8600
3201 S Maryland Pkwy #502, Las Vegas, 702-733-8600

Spaccavento, Leo J. (4 mentions)
Hahnemann U, 1978 *Certification:* Cardiovascular Disease,
Internal Medicine, Interventional Cardiology
2470 E Flamingo Rd #A, Las Vegas, 702-566-4278
108 E Lake Mead Dr #302, Henderson, 702-566-4278

Dermatology

Blanchard, Lucius (8 mentions)
U of North Carolina, 1968
Certification: Dermatology, Internal Medicine
4488 S Pecos Rd, Las Vegas, 702-436-1001
630 S Rancho Dr #E, Las Vegas, 702-258-0708
2851 Business Park Ct #120, Las Vegas, 702-360-2100

Strimling, Robert Bernard (6 mentions)
U of Miami, 1990 *Certification:* Dermatology
3150 N Tenaya Way #350, Las Vegas, 702-243-6400

Thomas, Douglas Arthur (22 mentions)
U of Southern California, 1985 *Certification:* Dermatology
9097 W Post Rd #100, Las Vegas, 702-430-5333

Woodson, Johnnie Maurice (8 mentions)
Wayne State U, 1990
229 N Pecos Rd #100, Henderson, 702-367-6370
2800 N Tenaya Way #203, Las Vegas, 702-367-6370

Emergency Medicine

Berkeley, Ross Philip (3 mentions)
U of California-San Francisco, 1997
Certification: Emergency Medicine
1800 W Charleston Blvd, Las Vegas, 702-385-0890
3001 St Rose Pkwy, Henderson, 702-616-5000

Davidson, Jeff Alan (5 mentions)
U of Arizona, 1990 *Certification:* Emergency Medicine
620 Shadow Ln, Las Vegas, 702-259-1228
500 N Rainbow Blvd #203, Las Vegas, 702-259-1228

Homansky, Edwin Phillip (4 mentions)
Med Coll of Georgia, 1976 *Certification:* Internal Medicine
500 N Rainbow Blvd #203, Las Vegas, 702-259-1228

Lemon, Dennis Charles (3 mentions)
Des Moines U, 1978 *Certification:* Emergency Medicine
3100 N Tenaya Way, Las Vegas, 702-255-5025

Miller, Randall S. (3 mentions)
U of Texas-Houston, 1990
Certification: Pediatric Emergency Medicine
620 Shadow Ln, Las Vegas, 702-388-4000

O'Connor, Marc Keeffe (3 mentions)
FMS-Grenada, 1988
3186 S Maryland Pkwy, Las Vegas, 702-731-8741

Pape, Frank Gerard, III (4 mentions)
Kansas U Coll of Osteopathic Med, 1988
620 Shadow Ln, Las Vegas, 702-259-1228

Slattery, David Edward (3 mentions)
U of Nevada, 1993 *Certification:* Emergency Medicine
901 Rancho Ln #135, Las Vegas, 702-383-1958

Slaughter, Kevin Teal (3 mentions)
Western U, 1996 *Certification:* Emergency Medicine
620 Shadow Ln, Las Vegas, 702-259-1228

Endocrinology

Berelowitz, Brian Alfred (19 mentions)
FMS-South Africa, 1973
Certification: Endocrinology and Metabolism, Internal Medicine
653 N Town Center Dr #315, Las Vegas, 702-804-9486

Dewan, Asheesh K. (7 mentions)
FMS-Grenada, 1996
5235 S Durango Dr, Las Vegas, 702-851-7287

Ismail, Firhaad (9 mentions)
FMS-South Africa, 1974
Certification: Endocrinology and Metabolism, Internal Medicine
4275 Burnham Ave #325, Las Vegas, 702-792-4500
2470 E Flamingo Rd #C, Las Vegas, 702-792-4500

Litchfield, William Reid (18 mentions)
FMS-Canada, 1990
Certification: Endocrinology, Diabetes, and Metabolism
2510 Wigwam Pkwy #102, Henderson, 702-434-8400
2415 W Horizon Ridge Pkwy, Henderson, 702-434-8400

Toffel, Freddie Gary (8 mentions)
Med Coll of Pennsylvania, 1979
Certification: Endocrinology and Metabolism, Internal Medicine
2700 E Sunset Rd #D34, Las Vegas, 702-736-2021

Wong, Milton Kwaileong (10 mentions)
U of Hawaii, 1986
8925 W Sahara Ave, Las Vegas, 702-387-8868

Family Practice *(see note on page 9)*

Forte, Dana Marie (5 mentions)
Western U, 1992 *Certification:* Family Medicine
7730 W Cheyenne Ave #107, Las Vegas, 702-240-8646
4845 S Rainbow Blvd #402, Las Vegas, 702-362-9800

Gumina, Antonio (3 mentions)
U of Nevada, 1998
2510 Wigwam Pkwy #104, Henderson, 702-947-1000

Haworth, Lisa (5 mentions)
U of Nevada, 1996 *Certification:* Family Medicine
10001 S Eastern Ave #305, Henderson, 702-719-6003

Hunt, Thomas James (4 mentions)
New York Med Coll, 1992 *Certification:* Family Medicine
2410 Fire Mesa St #180, Las Vegas, 702-992-6888

Lampinen, Steven Douglas (4 mentions)
U of Nevada, 1995 *Certification:* Family Medicine
517 Rose St, Las Vegas, 702-366-1206

Nardell, Ronald Dominic (3 mentions)
Drexel U, 1999 *Certification:* Family Medicine
3150 N Tenaya Way #370, Las Vegas, 702-558-2111

Ng, Jeffrey Patrick (3 mentions)
Rosalind Franklin U, 1995 *Certification:* Family Medicine
4845 S Rainbow Blvd #402, Las Vegas, 702-362-9800
7730 W Cheyenne Ave #107, Las Vegas, 702-240-8646

Sparks, Amy Renee (5 mentions)
U of Kansas, 1997 *Certification:* Family Medicine
653 N Town Center Dr #514, Las Vegas, 702-243-2689
10155 W Twain Ave #110, Las Vegas, 702-243-2689

Welborn, Dara Joan (3 mentions)
U of Nevada, 1999 *Certification:* Family Medicine
10001 S Eastern Ave #309, Henderson, 702-269-6345

White, Sanford Franklin (4 mentions)
U of Kansas, 1999 *Certification:* Family Medicine
7751 W Flamingo Rd #A, Las Vegas, 702-951-3400
5771 S Fort Apache Rd #100, Las Vegas, 702-951-3400

Gastroenterology

Baron, Howard Ian (10 mentions)
U of Minnesota, 1986
Certification: Pediatric Gastroenterology, Pediatrics
3196 S Maryland Pkwy #309, Las Vegas, 702-791-0477

Frankel, Desha A. (10 mentions)
Northeastern Ohio U, 1982
Certification: Gastroenterology, Internal Medicine
2121 E Flamingo Rd #206, Las Vegas, 702-791-5900
10001 S Eastern Ave #400, Henderson, 702-791-5900
2625 Wigwam Pkwy #112, Henderson, 702-791-5900
1040 Wigwam Pkwy #110, Henderson, 702-791-5900

Haikal, Osama Omar (6 mentions)
FMS-Egypt, 1978
Certification: Gastroenterology, Internal Medicine
2136 E Desert Inn Rd #A, Las Vegas, 702-386-0580
10001 S Eastern Ave #400, Henderson, 702-734-0505

Kwok, Donald L. (9 mentions)
U of Texas-Dallas, 1987 *Certification:* Gastroenterology
2615 Box Canyon Dr, Las Vegas, 702-228-0781

Kwok, Gregory M. (8 mentions)
U of Texas-Dallas, 1990 *Certification:* Gastroenterology
2615 Box Canyon Dr, Las Vegas, 702-228-2663

Nemec, Frank John, Jr. (15 mentions)
U of California-Los Angeles, 1979
Certification: Gastroenterology, Internal Medicine
9280 W Sunset Rd #414, Las Vegas, 702-796-0231

General Surgery

Dort, Sean David (6 mentions)
U of South Florida, 1989 *Certification:* Surgery
10001 S Eastern Ave #200, Henderson, 702-914-2420
999 Adams Blvd #104, Boulder City, 702-293-0602
98 E Lake Mead Pkwy #202, Henderson, 702-565-0050

Fusco, Arthur Arnaldo (5 mentions)
George Washington U, 1986 *Certification:* Surgery
700 Shadow Ln, Las Vegas, 702-382-8222
653 N Town Center Dr #606, Las Vegas, 702-382-8222

Gardner, Lawrence David (5 mentions)
FMS-Canada, 1970
3006 S Maryland Pkwy #630, Las Vegas, 702-733-0222

Hanna, Bernadine Alaric (4 mentions)
Howard U, 1995 *Certification:* Surgery
6140 S Fort Apache Rd #100, Las Vegas, 702-384-1160

Hofflander, Ronald S. (7 mentions)
U of Minnesota, 1994 *Certification:* Surgery
3201 S Maryland Pkwy #601, Las Vegas, 702-894-4440

Horsley, Stephen Brent (4 mentions)
8530 W Sunset Rd #240, Las Vegas, 702-796-0022

Iwamoto, Craig Lewis (5 mentions)
St Louis U, 1996 *Certification:* Surgery
1111 Shadow Ln, Las Vegas, 702-383-4040
7200 Cathedral Rock Dr #250, Las Vegas, 702-383-4040

Maranon, William Robert (4 mentions)
U of California-San Diego, 1984
2911 N Tenaya Way #104, Las Vegas, 702-889-9129

Mcbride, Stephen Daniel (7 mentions)
Tufts U, 1980 *Certification:* Surgery
700 Shadow Ln #370, Las Vegas, 702-382-8222
5380 S Rainbow Blvd, Las Vegas, 702-362-5059

Reyna, Troy Michael (4 mentions)
Georgetown U, 1977 *Certification:* Pediatric Surgery, Surgery
3121 S Maryland Pkwy #400, Las Vegas, 702-650-2500

Ripplinger, Gregg Mills (4 mentions)
U of Nevada, 1981 *Certification:* Surgery
10001 S Eastern Ave #200, Henderson, 702-914-2420
999 Adams Blvd #104, Boulder City, 702-293-0602
98 E Lake Mead Pkwy #202, Henderson, 702-565-0050

Teng, Francis Waibun (14 mentions)
U of Nevada, 1991 *Certification:* Surgery
3150 N Tenaya Way #680, Las Vegas, 702-838-5888

Geriatrics

Hartlieb, Donald Carson (7 mentions)
FMS-Grenada, 1981
4275 S Burnham Ave #130, Las Vegas, 702-733-8871

Hematology/Oncology

Allen, Heather Jeanne (9 mentions)
U of California-San Francisco, 1976
3730 S Eastern Ave, Las Vegas, 702-952-3400

Bernstein, Jonathan (10 mentions)
U of Rochester, 1991
Certification: Pediatric Hematology-Oncology, Pediatrics
1090 E Desert Inn Rd #200, Las Vegas, 702-732-0971

Kingsley, Edwin Charles (16 mentions)
U of Utah, 1980
Certification: Internal Medicine, Medical Oncology
3730 S Eastern Ave, Las Vegas, 702-952-3400

Michael, Paul Edward (8 mentions)
U of Texas-Galveston, 1980
Certification: Internal Medicine, Medical Oncology
9280 W Sunset Rd #100, Las Vegas, 702-952-1251

Wierman, Ann Maura (10 mentions)
Baylor U, 1989
Certification: Internal Medicine, Medical Oncology
1950 E Desert Inn Rd #A, Las Vegas, 702-735-7154
2851 N Tenaya Way #101, Las Vegas, 702-735-7154
8285 W Arby Ave #100-B, Las Vegas, 702-735-7154

Infectious Disease

Hruska, Jerome Frank (19 mentions)
U of Chicago, 1970
Certification: Infectious Disease, Internal Medicine
3006 S Maryland Pkwy #780, Las Vegas, 702-737-0740

Lipman, Brian Jonathan (14 mentions)
U of Buffalo, 1983
Certification: Infectious Disease, Internal Medicine
901 Rancho Ln #265, Las Vegas, 702-380-4242
3100 W Charleston Blvd #204, Las Vegas, 702-380-4242
6088 S Durango Dr #100, Las Vegas, 702-380-4242

Shockley, Ronald Ashley (8 mentions)
Ohio State U, 1995 *Certification:* Infectious Disease
3006 S Maryland Pkwy #780, Las Vegas, 702-369-5582

Speck, Eugene Lewis (13 mentions)
George Washington U, 1969
Certification: Infectious Disease, Internal Medicine
3006 S Maryland Pkwy #780, Las Vegas, 702-737-0740

Infertility

Daneshmand, Said Taghi (13 mentions)
New York Med Coll, 1993 *Certification:* Obstetrics &
  Gynecology, Reproductive Endocrinology/Infertility
8851 W Sahara Ave #100, Las Vegas, 702-254-1777

McConnell, Rachel (7 mentions)
Louisiana State U-Shreveport, 1986 *Certification:* Obstetrics
  & Gynecology, Reproductive Endocrinology/Infertility
653 N Town Center Dr #206, Las Vegas, 702-341-6616

Shapiro, Bruce Steven (12 mentions)
U of Nevada, 1982 *Certification:* Obstetrics & Gynecology,
  Reproductive Endocrinology/Infertility
8851 W Sahara Ave #100, Las Vegas, 702-254-1777
11251 S Eastern Ave #150, Las Vegas, 702-254-1777

Internal Medicine *(see note on page 9)*

Adjovu, Seth Kabutey (3 mentions)
FMS-Ghana, 1985 *Certification:* Pediatrics
1815 E Lake Mead Blvd #204, North Las Vegas, 702-798-1233

Cruvant, Ethan Milton (3 mentions)
Washington U, 1984 *Certification:* Internal Medicine
3006 S Maryland Pkwy #750, Las Vegas, 702-735-8734

Gong, Robert Charles (5 mentions)
U of Southern California, 1987 *Certification:* Internal Medicine
10001 S Eastern Ave #101, Henderson, 702-614-0850

Handelman, Mark Charles (4 mentions)
U of Nevada, 1990
3150 N Tenaya Way #565, Las Vegas, 702-796-3847

Miller, Stephen Harlan (6 mentions)
Northwestern U, 1982 *Certification:* Internal Medicine
53 Town Center Dr #306, Las Vegas, 702-243-7483

Neibaur, Russell Newel (3 mentions)
U of Nevada, 1984 *Certification:* Internal Medicine
861 Coronado Center Dr #103, Henderson, 702-990-0622

Petruso, Michael John (22 mentions)
U of Nevada, 1988 *Certification:* Internal Medicine
2020 Goldring Ave #206, Las Vegas, 702-382-0900
3006 S Maryland Pkwy #400, Las Vegas, 702-369-5582
850 S Rancho Dr, Las Vegas, 702-369-5582

Shoemaker, William Richard (3 mentions)
U of California-San Francisco, 1986
Certification: Internal Medicine
2870 S Maryland Pkwy #300, Las Vegas, 702-735-0258

Steckler, Theresa Lynne (9 mentions)
U of Texas-Houston, 1981 *Certification:* Internal Medicine
653 N Town Center Dr #306, Las Vegas, 702-243-7483

Thompson, Bradley Jay (3 mentions)
Johns Hopkins U, 1979 *Certification:* Internal Medicine
3650 S Eastern Ave #300, Las Vegas, 702-796-8036

Nephrology

Aigbe, Michael O. (8 mentions)
FMS-Nigeria, 1984 *Certification:* Pediatric Nephrology, Pediatrics
7271 W Sahara #110, Las Vegas, 702-639-1700

Gross, Michael Lester (11 mentions)
New York U, 1975 *Certification:* Internal Medicine, Nephrology
1750 E Desert Inn Rd #200, Las Vegas, 702-732-2438

Lehrner, Lawrence M. (6 mentions)
Indiana U, 1976 *Certification:* Internal Medicine, Nephrology
500 S Rancho Dr #12, Las Vegas, 702-877-1887

Leiserowitz, Marc (8 mentions)
FMS-South Africa, 1978
Certification: Internal Medicine, Nephrology
500 S Rancho Dr #12, Las Vegas, 702-877-1887

Sela, Zvi (6 mentions)
FMS-Israel, 1985
653 N Town Center Dr #315, Las Vegas, 702-877-1887

Takiyyuddin, Marwan Adib (7 mentions)
FMS-Lebanon, 1982 *Certification:* Internal Medicine, Nephrology
1750 E Desert Inn Rd, Las Vegas, 702-732-2438

Neurological Surgery

Anson, John Arthur (21 mentions)
U of Illinois, 1984 *Certification:* Neurological Surgery
3061 S Maryland Pkwy #200, Las Vegas, 702-737-1948

Duke, Derek A. (32 mentions)
U of Missouri-Kansas City, 1993
Certification: Neurological Surgery
861 Coronado Center Dr #200, Henderson, 702-737-1948

Neurology

Cabahug, Omar Baring (5 mentions)
FMS-Philippines, 1986 *Certification:* Neurology
2500 Wigwam Pkwy #112, Henderson, 702-914-6994

Diaz, Luis Leon (6 mentions)
FMS-Mexico, 1982 *Certification:* Neurology
653 N Town Center Dr #312, Las Vegas, 702-233-0755

Glyman, Steven Alan (8 mentions)
U of California-Los Angeles, 1981 *Certification:* Neurology
1707 W Charleston Rd #220, Las Vegas, 702-731-9110

Halthore, Srinivas N. (6 mentions)
FMS-India, 1980 *Certification:* Neurology with Special
  Qualifications in Child Neurology
2020 E Desert Inn Rd, Las Vegas, 702-796-5505

Johns, Donald William (6 mentions)
U of New Mexico, 1986
2020 E Desert Inn Rd, Las Vegas, 702-796-5505

Selco, Scott (5 mentions)
U of Illinois, 1999 *Certification:* Neurology, Vascular Neurology
3186 S Maryland Pkwy, Las Vegas, 702-731-8115

Obstetrics/Gynecology

Gondy, Anita (3 mentions)
FMS-India, 1986 *Certification:* Obstetrics & Gynecology
7160 Smoke Ranch Rd, Las Vegas, 702-254-8900

Goodhead, Marsha (4 mentions)
FMS-Canada, 1975 *Certification:* Obstetrics & Gynecology
3201 S Maryland Pkwy #205, Las Vegas, 702-731-4215

Iriye, Brian Keith (5 mentions)
U of California-San Diego, 1989
Certification: Maternal-Fetal Medicine, Obstetrics & Gynecology
2011 Pinto Ln, Las Vegas, 702-382-3200
2040 W Charleston Blvd #601, Las Vegas, 702-382-3200

Jameson, Florence Neal (10 mentions)
U of California-Los Angeles, 1981
Certification: Obstetrics & Gynecology
5281 S Eastern Ave, Las Vegas, 702-262-9676

Kartzinel, David Evan (3 mentions)
SUNY-Downstate Med Coll, 1992
Certification: Obstetrics & Gynecology
3196 S Maryland Pkwy #410, Las Vegas, 702-731-6000

Lewis, Michelle M. (7 mentions)
Des Moines U, 1989 *Certification:* Obstetrics & Gynecology
1701 N Green Valley Pkwy #3A, Henderson, 702-566-3040
1409 E Lake Mead Blvd, North Las Vegas, 702-657-5551
715 Mall Ring Cir #100, Henderson, 702-597-1145

Martin, John Vianney (5 mentions)
U of Nevada, 1992 *Certification:* Obstetrics & Gynecology
2851 N Tenaya Way #103, Las Vegas, 702-255-2022
2050 Mariner Dr #120, Las Vegas, 702-255-2022

Miller, Donna Major (7 mentions)
U of Texas-Houston, 1990 *Certification:* Obstetrics & Gynecology
2821 W Horizon Ridge Pkwy #130, Henderson, 702-862-8862
4275 Burnham Ave #260, Las Vegas, 702-260-0600

Sauter, Timothy Thomas (3 mentions)
U of Nevada, 1994 *Certification:* Obstetrics & Gynecology
8480 S Eastern Ave #F, Las Vegas, 702-914-6900

Swainston, Darin (3 mentions)
U of Nevada, 1991 *Certification:* Obstetrics & Gynecology
1950 Pinto Ln, Las Vegas, 702-385-3000
2050 Mariner Dr #120, Las Vegas, 702-255-2022
2851 N Tenaya Way #103, Las Vegas, 702-255-2022

Turner, Carla Ann (3 mentions)
U of Nevada, 1996 *Certification:* Obstetrics & Gynecology
2821 W Horizon Ridge Pkwy #130, Henderson, 702-862-8862

Volker, K. Warren (7 mentions)
U of North Dakota, 1997 *Certification:* Obstetrics & Gynecology
653 N Town Center Dr #602, Las Vegas, 702-255-3547
1800 W Charleston Blvd, Las Vegas, 702-383-2000

Ophthalmology

Doubrava, Mark William (6 mentions)
U of Nevada, 1989 *Certification:* Ophthalmology
9011 W Sahara Ave #101, Las Vegas, 702-794-2020
4324 S Eastern Ave #A, Las Vegas, 702-794-2020

Hsu, Gregory S. R. (9 mentions)
Western U, 1990
299 N Pecos Rd, Henderson, 702-450-6000
3663 E Sunset Rd #201, Las Vegas, 702-456-8389

McMickle, George Raymond (5 mentions)
Georgetown U, 1995
653 N Town Center Dr #318, Las Vegas, 702-215-6950

Nelson, Marietta (16 mentions)
Med Coll of Georgia, 1979
Certification: Ophthalmology, Pediatrics
2020 Goldring Ave #401, Las Vegas, 702-384-2020
2800 N Tenaya Way #102, Las Vegas, 702-384-2020

Reddy, Ravindranath K. (6 mentions)
U of Michigan, 1993 *Certification:* Ophthalmology
3575 Pecos McLeod, Las Vegas, 702-731-2088
2475 W Horizon Ridge, Henderson, 702-731-2088
2100 N Rampart Blvd, Las Vegas, 702-731-2088

Shin, Grace S. (5 mentions)
Tulane U, 1990 *Certification:* Ophthalmology
3802 Meadows Ln #B, Las Vegas, 702-870-2020
3016 W Charleston Blvd #100, Las Vegas, 702-870-2020

Stein, Emil Alexander (5 mentions)
U of California-Los Angeles, 1985 *Certification:* Ophthalmology
2090 E Flamingo Rd #200, Las Vegas, 702-733-9271
7730 W Sheyenne Ave #103, Las Vegas, 702-869-6326

Orthopedics

Barry, Mark A. (7 mentions)
FMS-Canada, 1984 *Certification:* Orthopaedic Surgery
105 N Pecos Rd #112, Henderson, 702-263-9082
3150 N Tenaya Way #100, Las Vegas, 702-869-3486
2800 E Desert Inn Rd #100, Las Vegas, 702-731-1616
2930 W Horizon Ridge Pkwy #100, Henderson, 702-263-9082

Bradford, Michael Stephen (5 mentions)
FMS-Canada, 1986 *Certification:* Orthopaedic Surgery
2650 N Tenaya Way #301, Las Vegas, 702-878-0393

Briggs, Richard Rasmussen (5 mentions)
George Washington U, 1976 *Certification:* Orthopaedic Surgery
7200 Cathedral Rock Dr #170, Las Vegas, 702-256-8500

Camp, Jonathan Franz (6 mentions)
U of Utah, 1981 *Certification:* Orthopaedic Surgery
10001 S Eastern Ave #407, Henderson, 702-434-6920
1525 E Windmill Ln #201, Las Vegas, 702-434-6920

Cichon, Jeffrey Peter (4 mentions)
Washington U, 1979
Certification: Orthopaedic Sports Medicine, Orthopaedic Surgery
3570 E Flamingo Rd, Las Vegas, 702-454-3400

Hoer, Steven Russell (5 mentions)
Med Coll of Wisconsin, 1988 *Certification:* Orthopaedic Surgery
100 N Green Valley Pkwy #310, Henderson, 702-565-6565
10001 S Eastern Ave #102, Henderson, 702-565-6565

Nielson, Jason Howard (4 mentions)
Albert Einstein Coll of Med, 1999
Certification: Orthopaedic Surgery
1525 E Windmill Ln #201, Las Vegas, 702-434-6920

Sylvain, Gerald Mark (4 mentions)
U of Nevada, 1991 *Certification:* Orthopaedic Surgery
701 S Tonopah Dr, Las Vegas, 702-388-1008
3100 W Charleston Blvd #200, Las Vegas, 702-258-2020

Thomas, Steven Clark (6 mentions)
Johns Hopkins U, 1984 *Certification:* Orthopaedic Surgery
9499 W Charleston Blvd #200, Las Vegas, 702-933-9393

Yee, Randall E. (7 mentions)
Kansas U Coll of Osteopathic Med, 1996
9280 W Sunset Rd #422, Las Vegas, 702-740-5327

Otorhinolaryngology

Foggia, David Anthony (7 mentions)
U of Iowa, 1986 *Certification:* Otolaryngology
3131 LaCanada St #241, Las Vegas, 702-792-6700
10001 S Eastern Ave #209, Henderson, 702-792-6700
7040 Smoke Ranch Rd, Las Vegas, 702-792-6700

Goll, Frederick, III (9 mentions)
U of Iowa, 1991 *Certification:* Otolaryngology
10001 S Eastern Ave #209, Henderson, 702-792-6700
3131 La Canada St #241, Las Vegas, 702-792-6700
7040 Smoke Ranch Rd, Las Vegas, 702-792-6700

Nasri-Chenijani, Sina (7 mentions)
Yale U, 1989 *Certification:* Otolaryngology
3150 N Tenaya Way #575, Las Vegas, 702-804-4729
3101 S Maryland Pkwy #102, Las Vegas, 702-732-4491

Schroeder, Walter William (23 mentions)
U of South Florida, 1982 *Certification:* Otolaryngology
10001 S Eastern Ave #209, Las Vegas, 702-792-6700
3131 La Canada St #241, Las Vegas, 702-792-6700
7040 Smoke Ranch Rd, Las Vegas, 702-792-6700

Tolan, Timothy Matthew (10 mentions)
St Louis U, 1987 *Certification:* Otolaryngology
5785 S Fort Apache Rd, Las Vegas, 702-735-1400

Yu, Larry Mengpo (7 mentions)
St Louis U, 1990 *Certification:* Otolaryngology
3131 LaCanada St #241, Las Vegas, 702-792-6700
10001 S Eastern Ave #209, Henderson, 702-792-6700
7040 Smoke Ranch Rd, Las Vegas, 702-792-6700

Pain Medicine

Bien, Robert (7 mentions)
FMS-Philippines, 1983
Certification: Emergency Medicine, Pain Medicine
7050 Smoke Ranch Rd #130, Las Vegas, 702-233-9911

Fishell, Michael L. (4 mentions)
U of Utah, 1990 *Certification:* Anesthesiology, Pain Medicine
129 W Lake Mead Dr #B18, Henderson, 702-564-4440
866 Seven Hills Dr #203, Henderson, 702-932-0606

Kim, Daniel Kunil (5 mentions)
Rush U, 1983 *Certification:* Anesthesiology, Pain Medicine
5701 W Charleston Blvd #202, Las Vegas, 702-259-5550
6950 W Desert Inn Rd #110, Las Vegas, 702-259-5550

Marx, James Gelsin (3 mentions)
U of Nebraska, 1973 *Certification:* Anesthesiology
608 S Jones Blvd, Las Vegas, 702-878-4568

McKenna, Michael John (4 mentions)
Harvard U, 1984 *Certification:* Anesthesiology, Pain Medicine
901 Rancho Ln #135, Las Vegas, 702-307-7700
6070 S Fort Apache Rd #100, Las Vegas, 702-307-7700

Vogel, Rainer Silvan (4 mentions)
FMS-Switzerland, 1997
Certification: Anesthesiology, Pain Medicine
100 N Green Valley Pkwy #340, Henderson, 702-990-4530

Pathology

Bilodeau, Laura Lynn (4 mentions)
Indiana U, 1988
Certification: Anatomic Pathology & Clinical Pathology
4230 Burnham Ave, Las Vegas, 702-733-7866

Erling, Marcus Anthony (4 mentions)
U of Alabama, 1978
Certification: Anatomic Pathology & Clinical Pathology
3059 S Maryland Pkwy #100, Las Vegas, 702-732-3441

Scully, Peter Aylward (8 mentions)
Cornell U, 1983
Certification: Anatomic Pathology & Clinical Pathology
4230 Burnham Ave, Las Vegas, 702-733-7866

Voss, Craig Alan (3 mentions)
Tulane U, 1969
Certification: Anatomic Pathology & Clinical Pathology
4230 Burnham Ave, Las Vegas, 702-733-7866

Pediatrics *(see note on page 9)*

Conti, Ralph Mark (9 mentions)
Robert W Johnson Med Sch, 1986 *Certification:* Pediatrics
6301 Mountain Vista St #205, Henderson, 702-614-5437
6850 N Durango Dr #202, Las Vegas, 702-614-5437
10001 S Eastern Ave #103, Henderson, 702-614-5437

Downey, William L., Jr. (4 mentions)
U of California-Davis, 1982 *Certification:* Pediatrics
653 N Town Center Dr #406, Las Vegas, 702-260-4525

Duddy, Blair Kaichen (3 mentions)
U of California-Los Angeles, 1990 *Certification:* Pediatrics
3150 N Tenaya Way #260, Las Vegas, 702-870-2099

Glasser, Lisa Ilona (5 mentions)
U of Maryland, 1992 *Certification:* Pediatrics
8352 W Warm Springs Rd #210, Las Vegas, 702-944-4028

Hodapp, Heath H. (3 mentions)
U of Nevada, 1997 *Certification:* Pediatrics
10911 S Eastern Ave #100, Henderson, 702-564-8556

Hyun, Rosemary Y. (10 mentions)
U Central del Caribe, 1987
10911 S Eastern Ave, Henderson, 702-564-8556

Lepore, John (3 mentions)
New York Coll of Osteopathic Med, 2001 *Certification:* Pediatrics
653 N Town Center Dr #80, Las Vegas, 702-765-5437

Neyland, Beverly Ann (3 mentions)
Meharry Med Coll, 1971 *Certification:* Pediatrics
2040 W Charleston Blvd #402, Las Vegas, 702-671-2231
3006 S Maryland Pkwy #315, Las Vegas, 702-992-6868
1524 Pinto Ln, Las Vegas, 702-383-3642

Nishihara, Ryan Masatoshi (3 mentions)
U of Hawaii, 1993 *Certification:* Pediatrics
653 N Town Center Dr #200, Las Vegas, 702-436-7337

Weidenfeld, Laura L. (4 mentions)
Tufts U, 1993 *Certification:* Pediatrics
653 N Town Center Dr #106, Las Vegas, 702-363-3000

Wijesinghe, Carrie Ghegan (4 mentions)
Med Coll of Pennsylvania, 1997 *Certification:* Pediatrics
2779 Sunridge Heights Pkwy, Henderson, 702-248-7337

Plastic Surgery

Anson, Goesel (12 mentions)
U of Illinois, 1983 *Certification:* Plastic Surgery, Surgery
8530 W Sunset Rd #130, Las Vegas, 702-822-2100

Garcia, Julio Luis (12 mentions)
U of Illinois, 1983 *Certification:* Plastic Surgery
3017 W Charleston Blvd #80, Las Vegas, 702-870-0058
6020 S Rainbow Blvd #C2, Las Vegas, 702-870-0058

Zamboni, William Arnold (8 mentions)
U of Nevada, 1984
Certification: Plastic Surgery, Surgery of the Hand
1707 W Charleston Blvd #190, Las Vegas, 702-671-5110

Psychiatry

Duffy, Sean Reid (3 mentions)
U of California-Irvine, 1990 *Certification:* Psychiatry
1885 Village Center Cir #150, Las Vegas, 702-360-2800

Durette, Lisa Ann (3 mentions)
U of South Carolina, 1999
Certification: Child & Adolescent Psychiatry, Psychiatry
2580 Montessouri St #101, Las Vegas, 702-873-2400
7000 W Mountain Dr, Las Vegas, 702-873-2400

Manjooran, Jacob (4 mentions)
FMS-India, 1993 *Certification:* Psychiatry
1650 Community College Dr, Las Vegas, 702-486-4400

Ngo, Renee Lim (4 mentions)
FMS-Philippines, 1986
3680 E Sunset Rd, Las Vegas, 702-855-0748

Rubin, Scott Alvin (3 mentions)
U of California-San Francisco, 1980 *Certification:* Psychiatry
1800 Industrial Rd #110, Las Vegas, 702-380-8200

Slagle, Dodge Alan (7 mentions)
Ohio U Coll of Osteopathic Med, 1985 *Certification:* Psychiatry
100 N Green Valley Pkwy #325, Henderson, 702-454-0201
1090 Wigwam Pkwy #100, Henderson, 702-454-0201

Pulmonary Disease

Brandes, William Charles (5 mentions)
Louisiana State U, 1988
Certification: Critical Care Medicine, Internal Medicine
2000 Goldring Ave, Las Vegas, 702-384-5101
2110 E Flamingo Rd #100, Las Vegas, 702-731-9559
7200 Cathedral Rock Ave #140, Las Vegas, 702-255-7245

Chemplavil, Thomson K. (5 mentions)
FMS-India, 1992
Certification: Critical Care Medicine, Pulmonary Disease
8965 S Pecos Rd #11A, Henderson, 702-735-4094

Collier, John Blakely (7 mentions)
New York Med Coll, 1988
Certification: Critical Care Medicine, Pulmonary Disease
3101 S Maryland Pkwy #100, Las Vegas, 702-869-0855
3150 N Tenaya Way #125, Las Vegas, 702-869-0855
9280 W Sunset Rd #312, Las Vegas, 702-737-5864
3121 S Maryland Pkwy #502, Las Vegas, 702-737-5864

McPherson, Charles Donald (11 mentions)
Mayo Med Sch, 1983
Certification: Internal Medicine, Pulmonary Disease
3121 S Maryland Pkwy #502, Las Vegas, 702-851-0200

Nakamura, Craig Tadashi (8 mentions)
U of Hawaii, 1993
Certification: Pediatric Pulmonology, Pediatrics
3838 Meadows Ln, Las Vegas, 702-598-4411
3820 Meadows Ln, Las Vegas, 702-598-4411
1524 Pinto Ln, Las Vegas, 702-383-3642

Pinto, John Francis (10 mentions)
St Louis U, 1972
Certification: Internal Medicine, Pulmonary Disease
2225 E Flamingo Rd #103, Las Vegas, 702-734-2292
2510 Wigwam Pkwy #103, Henderson, 702-734-2292
6787 W Tropicana Ave #100, Las Vegas, 702-893-0020

Stewart, Paul Alan (6 mentions)
U of California-Davis, 1973
Certification: Internal Medicine, Pulmonary Disease
2000 Goldring Ave, Las Vegas, 702-384-5101
2031 McDaniel St #150, North Las Vegas, 702-657-5180
2211 E Flamingo Rd #100, Las Vegas, 702-731-9559
901 Rancho Ln #230, Las Vegas, 702-382-2919
2110 E Flamingo Rd #100, Las Vegas, 702-382-2919

Tu, George Shih (7 mentions)
Eastern Virginia Med Sch, 1994
Certification: Critical Care Medicine, Pulmonary Disease
3150 N Tenaya Way #125, Las Vegas, 702-869-0855
3121 S Maryland Pkwy #502, Las Vegas, 702-737-5864
9280 W Sunset Rd #312, Las Vegas, 702-737-5864

Wojcik, John J. (8 mentions)
Albert Einstein Coll of Med, 1989
Certification: Pulmonary Disease
9280 W Sunset Rd #312, Las Vegas, 702-737-5864

Radiology—Diagnostic

Agrawal, Rajneesh (5 mentions)
Northwestern U, 1992
Certification: Diagnostic Radiology, Neuroradiology
2020 Palomino Ln #100, Las Vegas, 702-384-5210

Bandt, Paul Douglas (5 mentions)
U of Minnesota, 1966
Certification: Diagnostic Radiology, Nuclear Medicine
2020 Palomino Ln #100, Las Vegas, 702-384-5210

Berthoty, Dean Philip (3 mentions)
FMS-Canada, 1982 *Certification:* Diagnostic Radiology
3186 S Maryland Pkwy, Las Vegas, 702-731-8060

Blake, Lindsey Carlton (3 mentions)
Med U of South Carolina, 1988
Certification: Diagnostic Radiology
7130 Smoke Ranch Rd, Las Vegas, 702-304-8135

Johnson, Jeffrey Loren (4 mentions)
Med Coll of Georgia, 1989 *Certification:* Diagnostic Radiology
3186 S Maryland Pkwy, Las Vegas, 702-731-8060

Laussade, Mark Rice (3 mentions)
U of Texas-Dallas, 1978 *Certification:* Diagnostic Radiology
3186 S Maryland Pkwy, Las Vegas, 702-255-5080
3061 S Maryland Pkwy #102, Las Vegas, 702-731-2888
3100 N Tenaya Way, Las Vegas, 702-731-2888

Mazzu, Dianne (4 mentions)
U of Nevada, 1991 *Certification:* Diagnostic Radiology
2020 Palomino Ln, Las Vegas, 702-384-5210
7205 Cathedral Rock Dr #230, Las Vegas, 702-759-4300

Montes, Arthur Andrew (3 mentions)
U of Illinois, 1992 *Certification:* Diagnostic Radiology
3186 S Maryland Pkwy, Las Vegas, 702-731-8060

Murakami, Dana Makoto (4 mentions)
U of California-Los Angeles, 1987
Certification: Diagnostic Radiology
800 Shadow Ln, Las Vegas, 702-388-4640
2555 Montessouri St #C, Las Vegas, 702-477-0772

Pomerantz, Marc Jay (3 mentions)
St Louis U, 1981 *Certification:* Diagnostic Radiology
620 Shadow Ln, Las Vegas, 702-388-4640
2555 Montessouri St #C, Las Vegas, 702-477-0772

Radiology—Therapeutic

Agrawal, Rajneesh (6 mentions)
Northwestern U, 1992
Certification: Diagnostic Radiology, Neuroradiology
2020 Palomino Ln #100, Las Vegas, 702-384-5210
3920 S Eastern Ave #100, Las Vegas, 702-256-6545

Curtis, Danny Lee (4 mentions)
Wayne State U, 1981
Certification: Internal Medicine, Diagnostic Radiology
624 S Tonopah Dr, Las Vegas, 702-386-6863
10001 S Eastern Ave, Henderson, 702-952-3339
655 N Town Center Dr, Las Vegas, 702-233-2200
3730 S Eastern Ave, Las Vegas, 702-369-6762

Rehabilitation

Chue, Bevins Kinwood (3 mentions)
U of California-Los Angeles, 1987
Certification: Physical Medicine & Rehabilitation
10870 S Eastern Ave #103, Henderson, 702-386-1041

Gao, Robert Rong (6 mentions)
FMS-China, 1985
Certification: Physical Medicine & Rehabilitation
229 N Pecos Rd #120, Henderson, 702-269-0781

Gnoyski, Joseph Michael (5 mentions)
U of Kansas, 1991
Certification: Physical Medicine & Rehabilitation
653 N Town Center Dr #410, Las Vegas, 702-869-5270

Wise, Samuel Arthur (9 mentions)
U of Nevada, 1982
Certification: Physical Medicine & Rehabilitation
3201 S Maryland Pkwy #514, Las Vegas, 702-893-0800

Rheumatology

Clifford, Michael Eugene (9 mentions)
U of Illinois, 1973
Certification: Internal Medicine, Rheumatology
7151 Cascade Valley Ct #103, Las Vegas, 702-944-5444

Yung, Christianne Meeyun (8 mentions)
U of California-San Diego, 1988 *Certification:* Rheumatology
10001 S Eastern Ave #306, Henderson, 702-614-6868

Thoracic Surgery

Feikes, Joseph Randall (6 mentions)
Loma Linda U, 1989 *Certification:* Thoracic Surgery
3059 S Maryland Pkwy #202, Las Vegas, 702-735-1454
1701 N Green Valley Pkwy #5-C, Henderson, 702-735-1454

Pockey, Maurice (9 mentions)
FMS-South Africa, 1964
1701 N Green Valley Pkwy #5-C, Las Vegas, 702-735-1454
3059 S Maryland Pkwy #202, Las Vegas, 702-735-1454

Wiencek, Robert G., Jr. (6 mentions)
St Louis U, 1983 *Certification:* Surgery, Thoracic Surgery
1701 N Green Valley Pkwy #5C, Henderson, 702-614-6550
3150 N Tenaya Way #340, Las Vegas, 702-360-3330
1090 E Desert Inn Rd #200, Las Vegas, 702-735-1454
3059 S Maryland Pkwy #202, Las Vegas, 702-735-1454

Urology

Ganesan, George S. (7 mentions)
Certification: Pediatric Urology, Urology
653 Town Center Dr #114, Las Vegas, 702-369-4999
1701 Green Valley Pkwy Bldg 8 #D, Henderson, 702-369-4999
3121 S Maryland Pkwy #400, Las Vegas, 702-369-4999

Grigoryev, Victor E. (6 mentions)
U of Missouri, 1988
2901 N Tenaya Way #100, Las Vegas, 702-385-1980
10001 S Eastern Ave #408, Henderson, 702-233-0727
3121 S Maryland Pkwy #220, Las Vegas, 702-233-0727
700 Shadow Ln #400, Las Vegas, 702-233-0727
7500 Smoke Ranch Rd #200, Las Vegas, 702-233-0727

Housley, Helen Tamiko (7 mentions)
U of California-San Diego, 1993 *Certification:* Urology
5701 W Charleston Blvd #201, Las Vegas, 702-877-0814
56 N Pecos Rd #B, Henderson, 702-877-0814

McBeath, Robert Byron (6 mentions)
U of Nevada, 1988 *Certification:* Urology
5701 W Charleston Blvd #201, Las Vegas, 702-877-0814

Slavis, Scott Avery (12 mentions)
U of Miami, 1982 *Certification:* Urology
3121 S Maryland Pkwy #420, Las Vegas, 702-796-8669

Verni, Michael Peter (6 mentions)
George Washington U, 1995 *Certification:* Urology
653 N Town Center Dr #302, Las Vegas, 702-212-3428

Zommick, Jason Noel (8 mentions)
Brown U, 1995 *Certification:* Urology
5701 W Charleston Blvd #201, Las Vegas, 702-877-0814

Vascular Surgery

Chino, Eric Strom (8 mentions)
Oregon Health Sciences U, 1978
Certification: Surgery, Vascular Surgery
3150 N Tenaya Way #560, Las Vegas, 702-228-8600

New Jersey

New York Metropolitan Area—page 309

Northern and Central New Jersey—page 283

Delaware Valley Area—page 401

Northern and Central New Jersey

Including Bergen, Essex, Hudson, Hunterdon, Middlesex, Monmouth, Morris, Passaic, Somerset, Sussex, Union, and Warren Counties

Allergy/Immunology

Bielory, Leonard (7 mentions)
New Jersey Med Sch, 1980 *Certification:* Allergy & Immunology, Diagnostic Laboratory Immunology, Internal Medicine
90 Bergen St #4700, Newark, 973-972-2762
400 Mountain Ave, Springfield, 973-912-9817

Brown, David Kenneth (15 mentions)
U of Toledo, 1981
Certification: Allergy & Immunology, Internal Medicine
33 Overlook Rd #307, Summit, 908-522-9696

Chernack, William Jay (11 mentions)
New York Med Coll, 1970
Certification: Allergy & Immunology, Pediatrics
28 Franklin Pl, Morristown, 973-538-7271

Falk, Theodore (6 mentions)
FMS-Belgium, 1977 *Certification:* Pediatrics
63 Grand Ave, River Edge, 201-487-2900

Fost, Arthur Franklin (10 mentions)
Jefferson Med Coll, 1963
Certification: Allergy & Immunology, Pediatrics
197 Bloomfield Ave, Verona, 973-857-0330

Fost, David Appell (9 mentions)
Jefferson Med Coll, 1992 *Certification:* Allergy & Immunology
197 Bloomfield Ave, Verona, 973-857-0330

Fox, James Allen (8 mentions)
Yale U, 1977 *Certification:* Allergy & Immunology, Pediatrics
3461 US Hwy 22, Branchburg, 908-725-4788

From, Stuart Bruce (6 mentions)
New York Med Coll, 1987 *Certification:* Allergy & Immunology
309 Engle St #2, Englewood, 201-568-1480

Harish, Ziv (9 mentions)
FMS-Israel, 1983 *Certification:* Allergy & Immunology
200 Engle St #18, Englewood, 201-871-7475

Hicks, Patricia (9 mentions)
Pennsylvania State U, 1973
Certification: Allergy & Immunology, Pediatrics
119 1st St #5, Ho-Ho-Kus, 201-444-5277

Kashkin, Jay M. (6 mentions)
FMS-Dominican Republic, 1983 *Certification:* Pediatrics
23-00 State Rt 208, Fair Lawn, 201-794-7400

Kesarwala, Hemant Hansraj (14 mentions)
FMS-India, 1971 *Certification:* Allergy & Immunology, Pediatrics
3084 State Rt 27 #6, Kendall Park, 732-821-0595

Klein, Robert Michael (8 mentions)
New York Med Coll, 1976 *Certification:* Pediatrics
1005 Clifton Ave, Clifton, 973-773-7400

Le Benger, Kerry (11 mentions)
New York Med Coll, 1980
Certification: Allergy & Immunology, Internal Medicine
1 Diamond Hill Rd, Berkeley Heights, 908-273-4300

Michelis, Mary Ann (27 mentions)
U of Pittsburgh, 1975 *Certification:* Allergy & Immunology, Diagnostic Laboratory Immunology, Internal Medicine
30 Prospect Ave, Hackensack, 201-996-2065

Oppenheimer, John Jacob (14 mentions)
Temple U, 1986
Certification: Allergy & Immunology, Internal Medicine
1 Springfield Ave, Summit, 908-934-0555
8 Saddle Rd #101, Cedar Knolls, 973-267-9393

Perlman, Donald Bret (13 mentions)
Mount Sinai Sch of Med, 1973
Certification: Allergy & Immunology, Pediatrics
101 Old Short Hills Rd #407, West Orange, 973-736-7722
25 Kensington Ave, Jersey City, 973-736-7722

Sher, Ellen Ruth (10 mentions)
Georgetown U, 1986
Certification: Allergy & Immunology, Internal Medicine
8 Tindall Rd, Middletown, 732-671-7676
802 W Park Ave #213, Ocean, 732-695-2555

Silverstein, Leonard (9 mentions)
Duke U, 1987 *Certification:* Allergy & Immunology
82 E Allendale Rd #7-B, Saddle River, 201-236-8282
51 Rt 23 S, Riverdale, 973-831-5799

Weiss, Steven Jay (7 mentions)
Rosalind Franklin U, 1982
Certification: Allergy & Immunology, Internal Medicine
209 S Livingston Ave, Livingston, 973-992-4171
381 Chestnut St, Union, 908-688-6200

Anesthesiology

Cizmar, Stephan (6 mentions)
FMS-Italy, 1974
1 Clara Maass Dr, Belleville, 973-450-2703
42 Avon Dr, Essex Fells, 973-450-2703

Cohen, Dale Leonard (3 mentions)
Temple U, 1987
Certification: Anesthesiology, Critical Care Medicine
100 Madison Ave, Morristown, 973-971-6824

De Angelis, Lawrence J. (4 mentions)
U of Buffalo, 1971 *Certification:* Anesthesiology, Internal Medicine, Pulmonary Disease
33 Overlook Rd #311, Summit, 908-598-1500

Dent, Dean Anthony (4 mentions)
George Washington U, 1978 *Certification:* Anesthesiology
100 Madison Ave, Morristown, 973-631-8119

Dorian, Robert Setrag (5 mentions)
Robert W Johnson Med Sch, 1981
Certification: Anesthesiology, Pain Medicine
94 Old Short Hills Rd, Livingston, 973-322-5512

Goldzweig, Peter A. (3 mentions)
New York Coll of Osteopathic Med, 1993
Certification: Anesthesiology
350 Engle St, Englewood, 201-871-6073

Gourishankar, Ruplanaik (4 mentions)
FMS-India, 1970 *Certification:* Anesthesiology
94 Old Short Hills Rd, Livingston, 973-322-5512

Gwertzman, Alan Randall (3 mentions)
New Jersey Med Sch, 1989 *Certification:* Anesthesiology
718 Teaneck Rd, Teaneck, 201-833-3000

Hummel, Andrew E. (5 mentions)
Philadelphia Coll of Osteopathic Med, 1986
Certification: Anesthesiology
30 Prospect Ave, Hackensack, 201-996-2419

Hunter, Christine W. (3 mentions)
Certification: Anesthesiology
1 Robert Wood Johnson Pl, New Brunswick, 732-937-8841

Ietta, Michael Angelo (7 mentions)
Stony Brook U, 1985 *Certification:* Anesthesiology
223 N Van Dien Ave, Ridgewood, 201-847-9320

Klele, Christo Selim (3 mentions)
Robert W Johnson Med Sch, 1989 *Certification:* Anesthesiology
1176 Hamburg Tpke, Wayne, 973-365-4583

Labove, Phillip Stuart (3 mentions)
Columbia U, 1978
Certification: Anesthesiology, Internal Medicine
100 Madison Ave, Morristown, 800-991-9133

Levy, Stuart Jay (5 mentions)
U of Pennsylvania, 1979 *Certification:* Anesthesiology
100 Madison Ave, Morristown, 973-971-6824

Lewis, Walter Michael (4 mentions)
New York Med Coll, 1991 *Certification:* Anesthesiology
100 Madison Ave, Morristown, 973-971-6824

Lutz, Philip Edward (3 mentions)
FMS-Grenada, 1984 *Certification:* Anesthesiology
185 Fairfield Ave #2-A, West Caldwell, 973-226-1230

Mizrahi, Marc Eliott (3 mentions)
SUNY-Downstate Med Coll, 1988 *Certification:* Anesthesiology
350 Engle St, Englewood, 201-871-6073

Naturman, Roy Edward (4 mentions)
Tufts U, 1983 *Certification:* Anesthesiology, Internal Medicine
33 Overlook Rd #311, Summit, 908-598-1500

Nolasco, Cesar Villanueva (3 mentions)
FMS-Philippines, 1978 *Certification:* Anesthesiology
30 Prospect Ave, Hackensack, 201-996-2419

Pacific, Scott (5 mentions)
SUNY-Downstate Med Coll, 1991 *Certification:* Anesthesiology
33 Overlook Rd #311, Summit, 908-598-1500
1 Diamond Hill Rd, Berkeley Heights, 908-273-4300

Patankar, Srikanth S. (3 mentions)
FMS-India, 1984 *Certification:* Anesthesiology
94 Old Short Hills Rd #B-1, Livingston, 973-322-5512

Perelman, Seth Ilan (3 mentions)
New York U, 1989 *Certification:* Anesthesiology
350 Engle St, Englewood, 201-894-3238

Pirak, Leon (3 mentions)
FMS-Mexico, 1981 *Certification:* Anesthesiology
225 Williamson St, Elizabeth, 908-994-5204

Ragukonis, Thomas P. (3 mentions)
New Jersey Med Sch, 1991 *Certification:* Anesthesiology
30 W Century Rd #310, Paramus, 201-634-9000
5600 JFK Blvd #106, West New York, 201-969-9500
950 W Chestnut St, Union, 908-688-1100
799 Bloomfield Ave #301, Verona, 973-857-7600

Ramundo, Giovanni B. (4 mentions)
Pennsylvania State U, 1990
Certification: Anesthesiology, Pain Medicine
187 Millburn Ave #101, Millburn, 973-322-8223

Reddy, Matt M. (3 mentions)
FMS-India, 1972
30 Prospect Ave, Hackensack, 201-996-2419

Ruda, William Alexander (6 mentions)
New York U, 1980
Certification: Anesthesiology, Internal Medicine
110 Rehill Ave, Somerville, 908-685-2940

Sahota, Manpreet S. (3 mentions)
FMS-India, 1983 *Certification:* Anesthesiology
201 Lyons Ave, Newark, 973-926-7143

Secoy, John Walton (4 mentions)
FMS-Grenada, 1988 *Certification:* Anesthesiology
1 Bay Ave, Newark, 800-720-1664

Shander, Aryeh (4 mentions)
U of Vermont, 1977 *Certification:* Anesthesiology, Critical Care
Medicine, Internal Medicine, Undersea & Hyperbaric Medicine
350 Engle St, Englewood, 201-894-3238

Siegel, Scott Stephen (4 mentions)
Med Coll of Pennsylvania, 1986 *Certification:* Anesthesiology
285 Davidson Ave #301, Somerset, 732-271-1400

Solina, Alann Richard (3 mentions)
FMS-Grenada, 1986 *Certification:* Anesthesiology
1 Robert Wood Johnson Pl, New Brunswick, 732-937-8841

Sperrazza, James C. (3 mentions)
Jefferson Med Coll, 1994 *Certification:* Anesthesiology
254 Easton Ave, New Brunswick, 732-745-8600

Stennett, Richard Ainsley (5 mentions)
Columbia U, 1990
Certification: Anesthesiology, Critical Care Medicine
100 Madison Ave, Morristown, 973-631-8119

Walker, John Stewart (5 mentions)
New York Coll of Osteopathic Med, 1990
Certification: Anesthesia
110 Rehill Ave, Summerville, 908-685-2940

Winikoff, Stephen Paul (4 mentions)
Rosalind Franklin U, 1982
Certification: Anesthesiology, Pediatrics
703 Main St, Paterson, 973-754-2323

Xagoraris, Andreas Ector (3 mentions)
Robert W Johnson Med Sch, 1993 *Certification:* Anesthesiology
30 Prospect Ave, Hackensack, 201-996-2419

Cardiac Surgery

Anderson, Mark Berger (14 mentions)
New York Med Coll, 1988 *Certification:* Surgery, Thoracic Surgery
125 Paterson St, New Brunswick, 732-235-7800

Asgarian, Kourosh (8 mentions)
New York Coll of Osteopathic Med, 1993
Certification: Surgery, Thoracic Surgery
20 Prospect Ave #900, Hackensack, 201-996-2261

Bronstein, Eric Hunter (8 mentions)
Stony Brook U, 1987 *Certification:* Surgery, Thoracic Surgery
703 Main St, Paterson, 793-754-2486

Brown, John Muir, III (38 mentions)
Cornell U, 1986 *Certification:* Surgery, Thoracic Surgery
100 Madison Ave, Morristown, 973-971-7300
95 Madison Ave, Morristown, 973-971-7300

Burns, Paul Gerard (9 mentions)
Columbia U, 1989 *Certification:* Surgery, Thoracic Surgery
94 Old Short Hills Rd, Livingston, 973-322-2200

Elmann, Elie (12 mentions)
New York Med Coll, 1987 *Certification:* Surgery, Thoracic Surgery
20 Prospect Ave #900, Hackensack, 201-996-2261

Ergin, Mehmet Arisan (11 mentions)
Certification: Thoracic Surgery
350 Engle St, Englewood, 201-894-3636

Greeley, Drew Peter (8 mentions)
New Jersey Med Sch, 1992
Certification: Surgery, Thoracic Surgery
1944 State Route 33 #201, Neptune, 732-776-4622

Kaushik, Raj R. (8 mentions)
FMS-India, 1978 *Certification:* Thoracic Surgery
350 Boulevard #130, Passaic, 973-365-4567

Klein, James J. (8 mentions)
Stony Brook U, 1990 *Certification:* Surgery, Thoracic Surgery
350 Engle St, Englewood, 201-894-3636

McCullough, Jock Nash (6 mentions)
New Jersey Med Sch, 1987
Certification: Surgery, Thoracic Surgery
350 Engle St #1000, Hackensack, 201-894-3636

Mindich, Bruce Paul (6 mentions)
SUNY-Downstate Med Coll, 1972 *Certification:* Thoracic Surgery
223 N Van Dien Ave, Ridgewood, 201-447-8377

Rodriguez, Alejandro L. (7 mentions)
U of Connecticut, 1988 *Certification:* Surgery, Thoracic Surgery
95 Madison Ave #201, Morristown, 973-971-7300

Saunders, Craig Raymond (15 mentions)
U of Iowa, 1970 *Certification:* Thoracic Surgery
201 Lyons Ave #G-5, Newark, 973-926-6938

Scholz, Peter M. (10 mentions)
FMS-Switzerland, 1970 *Certification:* Thoracic Surgery
125 Paterson St, New Brunswick, 732-235-7800

Zapolanski, Alex J. (7 mentions)
FMS-Argentina, 1973 *Certification:* Thoracic Surgery
223 N Van Dien Ave, Ridgewood, 201-447-8377

Cardiology

Altmann, Dory Bert (6 mentions)
Yale U, 1986 *Certification:* Cardiovascular Disease, Internal
Medicine, Interventional Cardiology
593 Cranbury Rd, East Brunswick, 732-390-3333

Altszuler, Henry Mark (7 mentions)
New York U, 1982 *Certification:* Cardiovascular Disease,
Internal Medicine, Interventional Cardiology
1511 Park Ave #2, South Plainfield, 908-756-4438

Andrews, Paul Matthew (4 mentions)
SUNY-Downstate Med Coll, 1994 *Certification:* Cardiovascular
Disease, Internal Medicine, Interventional Cardiology
222 Cedar Ln #208, Teaneck, 201-907-0442

Angeli, Stephen John (4 mentions)
SUNY-Downstate Med Coll, 1981 *Certification:* Cardiovascular
Disease, Internal Medicine, Interventional Cardiology
222 Cedar Ln #309, Teaneck, 201-836-1788

Antonucci, Lawrence C. (4 mentions)
FMS-Italy, 1984 *Certification:* Internal Medicine
95 Madison Ave #B-1, Morristown, 908-879-1500
415 State Route 24, Chester, 908-879-1500

Bannerman, Kenneth Scott (3 mentions)
New York Med Coll, 1975
Certification: Cardiovascular Disease, Internal Medicine
1310 Broad St, Bloomfield, 973-338-0800
62 S Fullerton Ave, Montclair, 973-746-8585

Baruchin, Mitchell Alan (3 mentions)
Mount Sinai Sch of Med, 1984
Certification: Cardiovascular Disease, Internal Medicine
120 Franklin St, Jersey City, 201-601-3999

Beamer, Andrew Douglas (3 mentions)
Johns Hopkins U, 1982
Certification: Cardiovascular Disease, Internal Medicine
1 Diamond Hill Rd, Berkeley Heights, 908-273-4300

Blitz, Lawrence Robert (4 mentions)
New York U, 1990
Certification: Cardiovascular Disease, Interventional Cardiology
1777 Hamburg Tpke #102, Wayne, 973-831-7455

Blum, Mark Alan (6 mentions)
Mount Sinai Sch of Med, 1983 *Certification:* Cardiovascular
Disease, Internal Medicine, Interventional Cardiology
95 Madison Ave #A-10, Morristown, 973-889-9001

Blumberg, Edwin Douglas (3 mentions)
Columbia U, 1968
Certification: Cardiovascular Disease, Internal Medicine
1511 Park Ave #2, South Plainfield, 908-756-4438

Brown, Elliot Mitchell (4 mentions)
New York Med Coll, 1988
Certification: Cardiovascular Disease, Internal Medicine
1030 Clifton Ave, Clifton, 973-778-3777
61 Beaverbrook Rd, Lincoln Park, 973-778-3777

Catania, Raymond (3 mentions)
Des Moines U, 1989
Certification: Cardiovascular Disease, Internal Medicine
8 Tempe Wick Rd, Mendham, 973-543-2288

Chaaban, Fadi Nemer (4 mentions)
FMS-Lebanon, 1990
Certification: Cardiovascular Disease, Internal Medicine
769 Northfield Ave #220, West Orange, 973-731-9442
5 Franklin Ave #502, Belleville, 973-429-8333

Checton, John Burt (7 mentions)
New Jersey Med Sch, 1978
Certification: Cardiovascular Disease, Internal Medicine
215 Brighton Ave, Long Branch, 732-222-5143
222 Schanck Rd #4, Freehold, 732-431-1332
301 Bingham Ave #C, Ocean, 732-663-0300

Ciccone, John Michael (3 mentions)
New Jersey Med Sch, 1979
Certification: Cardiovascular Disease, Internal Medicine
741 Northfield Ave #205, West Orange, 973-467-1544

Cohen, Barry Mark (3 mentions)
FMS-Canada, 1980 *Certification:* Cardiovascular Disease,
Internal Medicine, Interventional Cardiology
211 Mountain Ave, Springfield, 973-467-0005

Daniels, Jeffrey Samuel (6 mentions)
Albany Med Coll, 1980
Certification: Cardiovascular Disease, Internal Medicine
215 Brighton Ave, Long Branch, 732-222-5143
222 Schanck Rd #44, Freehold, 732-431-1332
301 Bingham Ave #C, Ocean, 732-663-0300

Di Filippo, John A. (5 mentions)
FMS-Italy, 1977 *Certification:* Internal Medicine
230 Sherman Ave #H, Glen Ridge, 973-743-4114

Edlin, Dale E. (3 mentions)
U of Cincinnati, 1979
Certification: Cardiovascular Disease, Internal Medicine
179 Ave at the Commons, Shrewsbury, 732-741-7400
21 N Gilbert St #100, Tinton Falls, 732-741-7400

Eichman, Gerard T. (3 mentions)
FMS-Dominica, 1988
Certification: Cardiovascular Disease, Internal Medicine
222 Cedar Ln #309, Teaneck, 201-836-1788

Erlebacher, Jay Allen (4 mentions)
SUNY-Upstate Med U, 1975
Certification: Cardiovascular Disease, Internal Medicine
177 N Dean St, Englewood, 201-569-4901

Freilich, David (5 mentions)
299 Madison Ave #205, Morristown, 973-292-1020

Gabelman, Mark Scott (3 mentions)
Mount Sinai Sch of Med, 1980 *Certification:* Cardiovascular
Disease, Critical Care Medicine, Internal Medicine
7704 Marine Rd, North Bergen, 201-869-1313

Gantz, Kenneth Barry (7 mentions)
Cornell U, 1976 *Certification:* Cardiovascular Disease,
Internal Medicine, Interventional Cardiology
161 Millburn Ave, Millburn, 973-467-4220
654 Broadway, Bayonne, 201-243-9999

Goldberg, Mark C. (4 mentions)
New Jersey Med Sch, 1986
Certification: Cardiovascular Disease, Internal Medicine
741 Northfield Ave #205, West Orange, 973-467-1544

Goldweit, Richard Scott (6 mentions)
Cornell U, 1982 *Certification:* Cardiovascular Disease,
Internal Medicine, Interventional Cardiology
177 N Dean St, Englewood, 201-569-4901

Grossman, Steven H. (5 mentions)
FMS-Italy, 1979
Certification: Cardiovascular Disease, Internal Medicine
16-01 Broadway, Fair Lawn, 201-475-5050
1114 Clifton Ave, Clifton, 973-471-5250

Guss, Stephen Bernard (4 mentions)
Harvard U, 1968 *Certification:* Cardiovascular Disease,
Internal Medicine, Interventional Cardiology
182 South St #5, Morristown, 973-267-3944

Hamdan, Aiman M. (3 mentions)
FMS-Jordan, 1991 *Certification:* Cardiovascular Disease,
Internal Medicine, Interventional Cardiology
16-01 Broadway, Fair Lawn, 201-475-5050
1011 Main Ave, Clifton, 973-777-9595

Hawthorne, Keith Allen (3 mentions)
FMS-Dominican Republic, 1984 *Certification:* Cardiovascular
Disease, Internal Medicine, Interventional Cardiology
769 Northfield Ave #220, West Orange, 973-731-9442
5 Franklin Ave #502, Belleville, 973-429-8333

Hupart, Preston (3 mentions)
New York Coll of Osteopathic Med, 1987
Certification: Cardiovascular Disease, Interventional Cardiology
120 Franklin St, Jersey City, 201-601-3999

Julie, Edward (5 mentions)
Albert Einstein Coll of Med, 1980
Certification: Cardiovascular Disease, Internal Medicine
1030 Clifton Ave, Clifton, 973-778-3777
61 Beaverbrook Rd, Lincoln Park, 973-694-8001

Klapholz, Marc (6 mentions)
Certification: Cardiovascular Disease, Internal Medicine,
Interventional Cardiology
90 Bergen St #3500, Newark, 973-972-2573

Kothavale, Avinash Annash (3 mentions)
Case Western Reserve U, 1999
Certification: Cardiovascular Disease, Internal Medicine
1 Diamond Hill Rd, Berkeley Heights, 908-277-8721

Krell, Mark Jeffrey (3 mentions)
New York U, 1979 *Certification:* Cardiovascular Disease,
Internal Medicine, Interventional Cardiology
1 Springfield Ave #2-A, Summit, 908-273-1999

Kukafka, Sheldon Jay (3 mentions)
SUNY-Downstate Med Coll, 1992
Certification: Cardiovascular Disease
75 Veronica Ave #101, Somerset, 732-613-9313
15-H Briar Hill Ct, East Brunswick, 732-613-9313
111 E Union Valley Rd #201, Monroe Township, 609-409-6856

Landers, David Benjamin (3 mentions)
Georgetown U, 1979 *Certification:* Cardiovascular Disease,
Internal Medicine, Interventional Cardiology
222 Cedar Ln #208, Teaneck, 201-907-0442

Landzberg, Joel Serg (4 mentions)
Columbia U, 1983 *Certification:* Cardiovascular Disease,
Internal Medicine, Interventional Cardiology
333 Old Hook Rd #200, Westwood, 201-664-0201

Lapa, Alan Scott (3 mentions)
FMS-Grenada, 1987
Certification: Cardiovascular Disease, Interventional Cardiology
329 Belleville Ave, Bloomfield, 973-748-3800

Lebowitz, Nate E. (3 mentions)
Cornell U, 1991 *Certification:* Cardiovascular Disease
2200 Fletcher Ave, Fort Lee, 201-461-6200

Lee, William K. (3 mentions)
FMS-South Korea, 1969 *Certification:* Cardiovascular
Disease, Internal Medicine, Interventional Cardiology
43 Yawpo Ave #2, Oakland, 201-337-0066

Leeds, Richard Steven (3 mentions)
New York Med Coll, 1981
Certification: Cardiovascular Disease, Internal Medicine
225 Jackson St, Bridgewater, 908-526-8668
331 US Hwy 206 #1-A, Hillsborough, 908-431-0600

Lux, Michael S. (3 mentions)
New York U, 1977 *Certification:* Cardiovascular Disease,
Internal Medicine, Interventional Cardiology
211 Mountain Ave, Springfield, 973-467-0005
10 Mountain Blvd, Warren, 973-467-0005

Mahal, Sharan Singh (3 mentions)
FMS-India, 1984 *Certification:* Cardiovascular Disease,
Internal Medicine, Interventional Cardiology
225 Jackson St, Bridgewater, 908-526-8668
331 US Hwy 206 #1-A, Hillsborough, 908-431-0600

Mahdi, Lawrence Farid (7 mentions)
FMS-St Maarten, 1982 *Certification:* Cardiovascular
Disease, Internal Medicine, Interventional Cardiology
329 Belleville Ave, Bloomfield, 973-748-3800

Marans, Zvi S. (7 mentions)
U of Pennsylvania, 1984 *Certification:* Pediatric Cardiology
205 Robin Rd #100, Paramus, 201-599-0026
3959 Broadway, New York, NY, 212-305-4432

Mariano, Domenic L. (4 mentions)
Nova Southeastern Coll of Osteopathic Med, 1990
Certification: Interventional Cardiology
946 Bloomfield Ave, Glen Ridge, 973-743-1121

Matican, Jeffrey Steven (4 mentions)
New York Med Coll, 1982 *Certification:* Cardiovascular
Disease, Internal Medicine, Interventional Cardiology
309 Engle St #5, Englewood, 201-503-1920

Mattina, Charles J. (3 mentions)
New York U, 1981
Certification: Cardiovascular Disease, Internal Medicine
215 Brighton Ave, Long Branch, 732-222-5143
301 Bingham Ave #C, Ocean, 732-663-0300
222 Schanck Rd #4, Freehold, 732-431-1332

Moreyra, Abel Ennio (3 mentions)
FMS-Argentina, 1967 *Certification:* Cardiovascular Disease,
Internal Medicine, Interventional Cardiology
125 Paterson St #5200, New Brunswick, 732-235-7208

Noveck, Howard Daniel (3 mentions)
FMS-Israel, 1983 *Certification:* Cardiovascular Disease,
Internal Medicine, Interventional Cardiology
225 May St #F, Edison, 732-738-8855
3 Hospital Plaza #305, Old Bridge, 732-679-0108
7 Centre Dr #13, Monroe Township, 609-655-8860

Patel, Sanjeev Naran (4 mentions)
New Jersey Med Sch, 1993 *Certification:* Cardiovascular Disease
38 Mayhill St, Saddle Brook, 201-843-1019

Randazzo, Domenick Neal (10 mentions)
Tufts U, 1990 *Certification:* Cardiovascular Disease,
Internal Medicine, Interventional Cardiology
8 Tempe Wick Rd, Mendham, 973-543-2288
95 Madison Ave #A-10, Morristown, 973-898-0400
440 Route 22 E, Bridgewater, 908-218-5533

Raska, Karel (3 mentions)
Harvard U, 1989 *Certification:* Cardiovascular Disease
182 South St #5, Morristown, 973-267-3944

Ricculli, Nicholas P. (5 mentions)
New Jersey Sch of Osteopathic Med, 1985
Certification: Cardiovascular Disease, Internal Medicine
8 Tempe Wick Rd, Mendham, 973-543-2288
95 Madison Ave #A-10, Morristown, 973-898-0400
440 Route 22E, Bridgewater, 908-218-5533

Roelke, Marc (3 mentions)
Columbia U, 1987 *Certification:* Cardiovascular Disease,
Clinical Cardiac Electrophysiology, Internal Medicine
101 Old Short Hills Rd #120, West Orange, 973-731-9598
769 Northfield Ave #220, West Orange, 973-731-9442
5 Franklin Ave #502, Belleville, 973-429-8333

Rogal, Gary J. (5 mentions)
George Washington U, 1978
Certification: Cardiovascular Disease, Internal Medicine
769 Northfield Ave #220, West Orange, 973-731-9442
94 Old Short Hills Rd, Livingston, 973-731-9442

Rosen, Craig Michael (3 mentions)
New York U, 1993
Certification: Cardiovascular Disease, Interventional Cardiology
182 South St #5, Morristown, 973-267-3944

Rothman, Howard Charles (4 mentions)
U of Cincinnati, 1970
Certification: Cardiovascular Disease, Internal Medicine
2200 Fletcher Ave, Fort Lee, 201-461-6200

Santana, Jose (3 mentions)
U Central del Caribe, 1985
Certification: Cardiovascular Disease, Internal Medicine
425 70th St, Guttenberg, 201-854-0055

Saroff, Alan Lester (5 mentions)
SUNY-Upstate Med U, 1965
Certification: Cardiovascular Disease, Internal Medicine
123 Highland Ave #302, Glen Ridge, 973-748-9555

Saulino, Patrick F. (4 mentions)
Georgetown U, 1981
Certification: Cardiovascular Disease, Internal Medicine
225 Jackson St, Bridgewater, 908-526-8668
331 US Hwy 206 #1-A, Hillsborough, 908-431-0600

Schaer, David Harold (4 mentions)
U of California-San Diego, 1981 *Certification:* Cardiovascular
Disease, Internal Medicine, Interventional Cardiology
593 Cranbury Rd, East Brunswick, 732-390-3333

Schwartz, Jeffrey Glenn (3 mentions)
Cornell U, 1994 *Certification:* Cardiovascular Disease
182 South St #5, Morristown, 973-267-3944

Shamoon, Fayez E. (3 mentions)
FMS-Jordan, 1981 *Certification:* Cardiovascular Disease,
Internal Medicine, Interventional Cardiology
111 Central Ave, Newark, 973-877-5160

Shell, Roger Alan (3 mentions)
Robert W Johnson Med Sch, 1977
Certification: Cardiovascular Disease, Internal Medicine
593 Cranbury Rd, East Brunswick, 732-390-3333

Sheris, Steven Jay (3 mentions)
Robert W Johnson Med Sch, 1988
Certification: Cardiovascular Disease, Internal Medicine
29 South St, New Providence, 908-464-4200
7 Mount Bethel Rd, Warren, 908-464-4200

Singal, Dinesh Kumar (3 mentions)
FMS-India, 1983 *Certification:* Cardiovascular Disease,
Internal Medicine, Interventional Cardiology
1543 Route 27 #14, Somerset, 732-846-7000
18 Center Dr #203, Monroe Township, 732-846-7000

Sotsky, Gerald (11 mentions)
Mount Sinai Sch of Med, 1981
Certification: Cardiovascular Disease, Internal Medicine
1200 E Ridgewood Ave #2, Ridgewood, 201-670-8660

Sotsky, Mark Ira (3 mentions)
Certification: Cardiovascular Disease, Internal Medicine
1200 E Ridgewood Ave, Ridgewood, 201-670-8660

Stein, Aaron Abraham (3 mentions)
SUNY-Downstate Med Coll, 1979 *Certification:* Cardiovascular
Disease, Critical Care Medicine, Internal Medicine
7704 Marine Rd, North Bergen, 201-869-1313

Stein, Elliott Mark (3 mentions)
Jefferson Med Coll, 1964
Certification: Cardiovascular Disease, Internal Medicine
211 Mountain Ave, Springfield, 973-467-0005

Strain, Janet Elizabeth (3 mentions)
Certification: Cardiovascular Disease, Internal Medicine,
Interventional Cardiology
297 Lafayette Ave, Hawthorne, 973-423-9388

Stroh, Jack Abraham (3 mentions)
Albert Einstein Coll of Med, 1984 *Certification:* Cardiovascular
Disease, Internal Medicine, Interventional Cardiology
75 Veronica Ave #101, Somerset, 732-247-7444
15-H Briar Hill Ct, East Brunswick, 732-613-9313
111 E Union Valley Rd #201, Monroe Township, 609-409-6856

Suede, Samuel (7 mentions)
SUNY-Downstate Med Coll, 1986
Certification: Cardiovascular Disease, Internal Medicine
285 Grand Ave #5, Englewood, 201-568-3690

Von Poelnitz, Audrey (3 mentions)
U of Pennsylvania, 1979 *Certification:* Cardiovascular
Disease, Internal Medicine, Interventional Cardiology
182 South St #5, Morristown, 973-267-3944

Wang, Robert Lehsueh (5 mentions)
Mount Sinai Sch of Med, 1983 *Certification:* Cardiovascular
Disease, Internal Medicine, Interventional Cardiology
356 US Hwy 46 2nd Fl, Mountain Lakes, 973-586-3400

Wangenheim, Paul Michael (3 mentions)
New Jersey Med Sch, 1982
Certification: Cardiovascular Disease, Internal Medicine
741 Northfield Ave #205, West Orange, 973-467-1544

Watson, Rita Marie (3 mentions)
Harvard U, 1976 *Certification:* Cardiovascular Disease,
Internal Medicine, Interventional Cardiology
215 Brighton Ave, Long Branch, 732-222-5143

White, Thomas M. (4 mentions)
459 Jack Martin Blvd #4, Brick, 732-458-6200

Zales, Vincent R. (3 mentions)
FMS-Dominican Republic, 1981
Certification: Pediatric Cardiology, Pediatrics
2 Apple Farm Rd, Middletown, 732-671-5659
1623 Route 88 #A, Brick, 732-458-9666

Zucker, Mark Jay (4 mentions)
Northwestern U, 1981
Certification: Cardiovascular Disease, Internal Medicine
201 Lyons Ave #G-5, Newark, 973-926-7205

Dermatology

Applebaum-Farkas, Paige S. (4 mentions)
Albert Einstein Coll of Med, 1989 *Certification:* Dermatology
1200 E Ridgewood Ave, Ridgewood, 201-493-1717

Bisaccia, Emil P., Jr. (4 mentions)
U of Toledo, 1979 *Certification:* Dermatology
66 Sunset Strip #301, Succasunna, 973-927-3636
182 South St #1, Morristown, 973-267-0300

Blackwell, Martin (4 mentions)
New Jersey Sch of Osteopathic Med, 1988
136 Woodside Ave, Newton, 973-300-0555
653 Willow Grove St #2700, Hackettstown, 908-852-9600

Brauner, Gary Jules (4 mentions)
Harvard U, 1967 *Certification:* Dermatology, Dermatopathology
1625 Anderson Ave, Fort Lee, 201-461-5522
125 E 61st St, New York, NY, 212-421-5080

Cassetty, Christopher T. (5 mentions)
U of Oklahoma, 2000 *Certification:* Dermatology
8 Main St #20, Flemington, 908-782-1647

Connolly, Adrian Lawrence (5 mentions)
New Jersey Med Sch, 1975 *Certification:* Dermatology
101 Old Short Hills Rd #503, West Orange, 973-731-9131

Corey, Timothy James (4 mentions)
Columbia U, 1975 *Certification:* Dermatology
180 Ramapo Valley Rd, Oakland, 201-337-5100
400 State Route 17 #1, Ridgewood, 201-652-4536

Eisenberg, Richard Randy (4 mentions)
Cornell U, 1982 *Certification:* Dermatology, Internal Medicine
40 Stirling Rd #203, Watchung, 908-753-4144

Fernandez-Obregon, A. C. (6 mentions)
New York Med Coll, 1978 *Certification:* Dermatology
10 Church Twrs, Hoboken, 201-795-3376

Fialkoff, Cheryl N. (10 mentions)
Albert Einstein Coll of Med, 1986 *Certification:* Dermatology
182 South St #1, Morristown, 973-267-0300
66 Sunset Strip #301, Succasunna, 973-927-3636
80 N Gaston Ave, Somerville, 908-429-9900
14 Church St, Basking Ridge, 973-267-0300
80 W End Ave, Somerville, 908-429-9900

Fishman, Miriam (10 mentions)
New York U, 1978 *Certification:* Dermatology
216 Engle St, Englewood, 201-569-5678

Fox, Alissa Benimoff (6 mentions)
New York U, 1980 *Certification:* Dermatology
3461 US Hwy 22, Branchburg, 908-725-4788

Gilson, Cynthia Tutnauer (7 mentions)
SUNY-Downstate Med Coll, 1983 *Certification:* Dermatology
223 Monmouth Rd, West Long Branch, 732-870-2992

Groisser, Daniel Stuart (5 mentions)
Cornell U, 1986 *Certification:* Dermatology, Internal Medicine
347 Mt Pleasant Ave, West Orange, 973-571-2121

Grossman, Kenneth Alan (7 mentions)
SUNY-Downstate Med Coll, 1977
Certification: Dermatology, Internal Medicine
180 White Rd #103, Little Silver, 732-842-5222

Gruber, Gabriel George (7 mentions)
Harvard U, 1972 *Certification:* Dermatology, Internal Medicine
1 Diamond Hill Rd, Berkeley Heights, 908-273-4300

Hametz, Irwin (6 mentions)
New York Med Coll, 1973 *Certification:* Dermatology
77-55 Schanck Rd #B-3, Freehold, 732-572-1751

Lee, Jane Mengchuan (4 mentions)
U of California-San Francisco, 1994 *Certification:* Dermatology
18 Bridge St Bldg B, Metuchen, 732-635-1200

Ligresti, Dominick J. (5 mentions)
Mount Sinai Sch of Med, 1978 *Certification:* Dermatology
36 Newark Ave #120, Belleville, 973-759-6569

Machler, Brian C. (23 mentions)
New Jersey Med Sch, 1991 *Certification:* Dermatology
101 Old Short Hills Rd, West Orange, 973-736-9535

Marinaro, Robert Edward (6 mentions)
U of Rochester, 1981 *Certification:* Dermatology
20 Community Pl, Morristown, 973-538-4544

Maso, Martha Jane (4 mentions)
New Jersey Med Sch, 1986
Certification: Dermatology, Occupational Medicine
390 Old Hook Rd, Westwood, 201-666-9550

Milgraum, Sandy Saul (4 mentions)
FMS-Australia, 1979
Certification: Dermatology, Pediatric Dermatology
81 Brunswick Woods Dr, East Brunswick, 732-613-0300

Nossa, Robert (5 mentions)
Stony Brook U, 1997 *Certification:* Dermatology
60 Pompton Ave, Verona, 973-571-2121

Notari, Teresa V. (6 mentions)
SUNY-Downstate Med Coll, 1991 *Certification:* Dermatology
33 Overlook Rd #209, Summit, 908-598-7200

Orsini, William John (7 mentions)
New Jersey Med Sch, 1972
Certification: Dermatology, Internal Medicine
223 Monmouth Rd, West Long Branch, 732-870-2992

Pappert, Amy S. (6 mentions)
Robert W Johnson Med Sch, 1989 *Certification:* Dermatology
1 Worlds Fair Dr, Somerset, 732-743-5437

Rabner, Deborah Wiener (7 mentions)
Northwestern U, 1984 *Certification:* Dermatology
1140 Bloomfield Ave, West Caldwell, 973-575-6880

Rapaport, Jeffrey Alan (4 mentions)
Emory U, 1978 *Certification:* Dermatology
333 Sylvan Ave #207, Englewood Cliffs, 201-227-1555

Ravits, Margaret Sue (5 mentions)
U of Miami, 1975 *Certification:* Dermatology
130 Kinderkamack Rd, River Edge, 201-692-0800

Reilly, George D. (5 mentions)
New Jersey Med Sch, 1977
Certification: Dermatology, Internal Medicine
31 Mountain Blvd #Q, Warren, 908-753-7773

Resnikoff, Forrest Peter (6 mentions)
Rosalind Franklin U, 1981
Certification: Dermatology, Internal Medicine
170 Ave at The Commons, Shrewsbury, 732-542-6300

Sapadin, Allen Nathan (4 mentions)
Mount Sinai Sch of Med, 1988 *Certification:* Dermatology
370 Summit Ave, Hackensack, 201-525-0057
156 Hewes St, Brooklyn, NY, 718-797-3677

Satra, Karin Helene (4 mentions)
Columbia U, 1985 *Certification:* Dermatology, Internal Medicine
180 Ramapo Valley Rd, Oakland, 201-337-5100
400 State Route 17 #1, Ridgewood, 201-652-4536

Scherl, Sharon (8 mentions)
New York Med Coll, 1988 *Certification:* Dermatology
45 Central Ave, Tenafly, 201-568-8400

Shin, Helen Theresa (7 mentions)
Cornell U, 1995
Certification: Dermatology, Pediatric Dermatology
360 Essex St #201, Hackensack, 201-336-8697

Szylit, Jo-Ann (5 mentions)
Stony Brook U, 1978
Certification: Dermatology, Internal Medicine
135 Kinnelon Rd #103, Kinnelon, 973-838-1771

Tanzer, Floyd Richard (4 mentions)
SUNY-Downstate Med Coll, 1973 *Certification:* Dermatology
992 Clifton Ave 1st Fl, Clifton, 973-365-1800

Weinberg, Harvey I. (5 mentions)
U of Buffalo, 1969 *Certification:* Dermatology
199 Baldwin Rd #230, Parsippany, 973-335-2560

Weinstein, Rita (9 mentions)
New York U, 1969 *Certification:* Dermatology
603 Cranbury Rd, East Brunswick, 732-545-5366

Emergency Medicine

Amato, Christopher Scott (3 mentions)
U of Maryland, 1994
Certification: Pediatric Emergency Medicine, Pediatrics
100 Madison Ave, Morristown, 973-971-5007

Baddoura, Rachid (5 mentions)
FMS-Lebanon, 1974 *Certification:* Emergency Medicine,
Internal Medicine, Pulmonary Disease
223 N Van Dien Ave, Ridgewood, 201-447-8000

Becker, George L., III (8 mentions)
Jefferson Med Coll, 1994 *Certification:* Emergency Medicine
223 N Van Dien Ave, Ridgewood, 201-447-8000

Borgen, Ruth E. (4 mentions)
Mount Sinai Sch of Med, 1986
Certification: Pediatric Emergency Medicine, Pediatrics
30 Prospect Ave, Hackensack, 201-996-5430

Dellapi, Andrew (5 mentions)
New Jersey Med Sch, 1994 *Certification:* Emergency Medicine
97 West Pkwy, Pompton Plains, 973-831-5000

Devadan, Phillip Sunil (3 mentions)
FMS-Grenada, 1997 *Certification:* Pediatrics
97 W Parkway, Pompton Plains, 973-831-5484

Freer, Christopher F. (5 mentions)
New Jersey Sch of Osteopathic Med, 1995
Certification: Emergency Medicine
651 W Mount Pleasant Ave, Livingston, 973-740-0607
100 Madison Ave, Morristown, 973-740-0607

Gerardi, Michael Joseph (5 mentions)
Georgetown U, 1985 *Certification:* Emergency Medicine,
Internal Medicine, Pediatric Emergency Medicine
100 Madison Ave, Morristown, 973-740-0607

Goldfarb, Stephen Allen (3 mentions)
FMS-Mexico, 1972
651 Willow Grove St, Hackettstown, 908-852-5100

Hanlon, Catherine Ann (4 mentions)
Hahnemann U, 1983
Certification: Emergency Medicine, Internal Medicine
300 2nd Ave, Long Branch, 732-870-5014

Hartmann, Anthony William (4 mentions)
SUNY-Upstate Med U, 1984 *Certification:* Emergency Medicine
110 Rehill Ave, Somerville, 973-740-0607
100 Madison Ave, Morristown, 973-740-0607

Hewitt, Kevin (5 mentions)
Certification: Emergency Medicine
30 Prospect Ave, Hackensack, 201-996-4614

Indruk, William Lorion (3 mentions)
Georgetown U, 1974 *Certification:* Emergency Medicine
651 W Mount Pleasant Ave, Livingston, 973-740-0607
100 Madison Ave, Morristown, 973-740-0607

Kintzel, Timothy (3 mentions)
Certification: Emergency Medicine
350 Engle St, Englewood, 201-894-3000

Lee, Peter Haesuk (3 mentions)
SUNY-Downstate Med Coll, 1994
Certification: Pediatric Emergency Medicine, Pediatrics
223 N Van Dien Ave, Ridgewood, 201-447-8000

McEnrue, James A. (4 mentions)
Georgetown U, 1975
Certification: Emergency Medicine, Internal Medicine
94 Old Short Hills Rd, Livingston, 973-322-5180

Melrose, Mark A. (7 mentions)
1 Bay Ave, Montclair, 973-429-6000

Pirigyi, Paul Robert (6 mentions)
Jefferson Med Coll, 1975 *Certification:* Emergency Medicine
254 Easton Ave, New Brunswick, 732-745-8600

Pruden, James N. (7 mentions)
Howard U, 1979 *Certification:* Emergency Medicine
703 Main St, Paterson, 973-754-2240
668 Grant Terr, Teaneck, 973-754-2059

Reyman, Lynn Deborah (3 mentions)
New York U, 1982
Certification: Emergency Medicine, Internal Medicine
94 Old Short Hills Rd, Livingston, 973-322-5180

Roma, Kevin P. (3 mentions)
Certification: Emergency Medicine
1 Riverview Plaza, Red Bank, 732-530-2204

Rubinstein, Howard Arthur (3 mentions)
New Jersey Med Sch, 1992
Certification: Emergency Medicine, Internal Medicine
1 Riverview Plaza, Red Bank, 732-530-2204

Schwab, Richard Michael (7 mentions)
U of Southern California, 1977
Certification: Emergency Medicine
718 Teaneck Rd, Teaneck, 201-833-3229

Sendyk, Henry P. (3 mentions)
FMS-Dominica, 1981 *Certification:* Emergency Medicine
99 Beauvoire Ave, Summit, 908-522-2232

Shih, Richard Dee (4 mentions)
Jefferson Med Coll, 1988
Certification: Emergency Medicine, Medical Toxicology
651 Mount Pleasant Ave, Livingston, 973-740-0607

Silverman, Brian S. (3 mentions)
718 Teaneck Rd, Teaneck, 201-833-3913

Skiba, Chester John, Jr. (3 mentions)
FMS-St Maarten, 1983 *Certification:* Internal Medicine
651 Willow Grove St, Hackettstown, 908-852-5100

Sweeney, Robert Louis (8 mentions)
New Jersey Sch of Osteopathic Med, 1981 *Certification:*
Emergency Medicine, Pediatric Emergency Medicine, Pediatrics
1945 State Route 33, Neptune, 732-776-4510
425 Jack Martin Blvd, Brick, 732-840-3380

Tapnio, Cezar Benjamin O. (3 mentions)
FMS-Philippines, 1981 *Certification:* Emergency Medicine
1945 State Route #33, Neptune, 732-776-4203

Tartacoff, Randy Steven (3 mentions)
Mount Sinai Sch of Med, 1980
Certification: Emergency Medicine
718 Teaneck Rd, Teaneck, 201-833-3000

Vogel, Mark F. X. (4 mentions)
Georgetown U, 1981 *Certification:* Emergency Medicine
223 N Van Dien Ave, Ridgewood, 201-447-8000

Yamin, Edward (5 mentions)
FMS-Dominican Republic, 1992
Certification: Emergency Medicine
30 Prospect Ave, Hackensack, 201-996-4614

Endocrinology

Agrin, Richard Joel (5 mentions)
U of Pennsylvania, 1971
Certification: Endocrinology and Metabolism, Internal Medicine
137 Louis St, New Brunswick, 732-545-1065

Amorosa, Louis Francis (13 mentions)
New Jersey Med Sch, 1969
Certification: Endocrinology and Metabolism, Internal Medicine
125 Paterson St #5100, New Brunswick, 732-235-7219

Apelian, Ara Zouseph (5 mentions)
FMS-Lebanon, 1981
Certification: Endocrinology and Metabolism, Internal Medicine
1056 Stelton Rd, Piscataway, 732-463-0303

Baranetsky, Nicholas G. (10 mentions)
New York Med Coll, 1974
Certification: Endocrinology and Metabolism, Internal Medicine
268 King Blvd, Newark, 973-877-5185
312 Belleville Tpke #3-A, North Arlington, 201-997-5522

Bucholtz, Harvey Kenneth (5 mentions)
SUNY-Upstate Med U, 1968
Certification: Endocrinology and Metabolism, Internal Medicine
2 Route 27 #501, Edison, 732-549-7470

Cobin, Rhoda H. (12 mentions)
U of Puerto Rico, 1969
Certification: Endocrinology and Metabolism, Internal Medicine
75 N Maple Ave #202, Ridgewood, 201-444-5552

Covello, Lucy F. (5 mentions)
FMS-Dominica, 1984
1524 State Rt 23, Butler, 973-838-3112

Davis, Maris Readling (10 mentions)
Columbia U, 1983
Certification: Endocrinology and Metabolism, Internal Medicine
119 Grove St, Montclair, 973-744-3733

Dower, Samuel M. (8 mentions)
New York U, 1981
Certification: Endocrinology and Metabolism, Internal Medicine
200 S Orange Ave #219, Livingston, 973-322-7200

Fuhrman, Robert Alan (8 mentions)
Rosalind Franklin U, 1966
Certification: Endocrinology and Metabolism, Internal Medicine
552 Westfield Ave, Westfield, 908-654-3377

Gewirtz, George Paul (6 mentions)
Harvard U, 1965
Certification: Endocrinology and Metabolism, Internal Medicine
200 S Orange Ave #219, Livingston, 973-322-7200

Giangola, Joseph (5 mentions)
FMS-Italy, 1978 *Certification:* Internal Medicine
810 Main St, Hackensack, 201-488-5922

Hannoush, Peter Yousef (8 mentions)
Robert W Johnson Med Sch, 1992 *Certification:*
Endocrinology, Diabetes, and Metabolism, Internal Medicine
380 Sutton Ave, Hackensack, 201-488-8766

Hrymoc, Zofia (8 mentions)
FMS-Poland, 1975 *Certification:* Endocrinology, Diabetes, and Metabolism, Internal Medicine
9 Auer Ct #A, East Brunswick, 732-390-6666

Kelman, Adam Scott (7 mentions)
Rush U, 1993
Certification: Endocrinology, Diabetes, and Metabolism
75 N Maple Ave #202, Ridgewood, 201-444-5552

Levy, Ian Harold (5 mentions)
New York Coll of Osteopathic Med, 1987
245 E Main St, Ramsey, 201-327-5551
261 Old Hook Rd, Westwood, 201-358-0047

Maman, Arie (11 mentions)
FMS-France, 1974
Certification: Endocrinology and Metabolism, Internal Medicine
D3 Brier Hill Ct, East Brunswick, 732-613-0707

Nambi, Sridhar S. (8 mentions)
FMS-India, 1984
22 Old Short Hills Rd #201, Livingston, 973-535-8870

Nassberg, Barton Manuel (7 mentions)
FMS-Belgium, 1979
Certification: Endocrinology and Metabolism, Internal Medicine
723 N Beers St #2G, Holmdel, 732-739-0200
515 Iron Bridge Rd, Freehold, 732-780-5885

Nevin, Marie Eithne (19 mentions)
New Jersey Med Sch, 1986 *Certification:* Endocrinology, Diabetes, and Metabolism, Internal Medicine
25 Lindsley Dr #203, Morristown, 973-267-9099

Novogroder, Michael (5 mentions)
SUNY-Upstate Med U, 1969
Certification: Pediatric Endocrinology, Pediatrics
704 Palisade Ave, Teaneck, 201-836-4301

Rosenbaum, Robert Leon (6 mentions)
Columbia U, 1975
Certification: Endocrinology and Metabolism, Internal Medicine
1 Diamond Hill Rd, Berkeley Heights, 908-273-4300

Selinger, Sharon Eve (5 mentions)
Cornell U, 1981
Certification: Endocrinology and Metabolism, Internal Medicine
1 Springfield Ave #1-A, Summit, 908-273-8300

Sherry, Stephen Howard (16 mentions)
U of Connecticut, 1976
Certification: Endocrinology and Metabolism, Internal Medicine
119 Grove St, Montclair, 973-744-3733

Spiler, Ira Jonah (8 mentions)
Albert Einstein Coll of Med, 1971
Certification: Endocrinology and Metabolism, Internal Medicine
3 Hospital Plaza #307, Old Bridge, 732-360-1122
530 New Brunswick Ave, Perth Amboy, 732-324-5015

Starkman, Harold S. (5 mentions)
Albert Einstein Coll of Med, 1976
Certification: Pediatric Endocrinology, Pediatrics
100 Madison Ave, Morristown, 973-971-4340

Stock, Jerrold Michael (9 mentions)
U of Chicago, 1968
Certification: Endocrinology and Metabolism, Internal Medicine
25 Lindsley Dr #203, Morristown, 973-267-9099

Tohme, Jack Fuad (18 mentions)
FMS-Lebanon, 1974
Certification: Endocrinology and Metabolism, Internal Medicine
265 Ackerman Ave #101, Ridgewood, 201-444-4363

Torrens Del Toro, Javier (5 mentions)
Boston U, 1991 *Certification:* Endocrinology, Diabetes, and Metabolism, Internal Medicine
9100 Wescott Dr #101, Flemington, 908-237-6990

Wiesen, Mark (15 mentions)
Columbia U, 1975
Certification: Endocrinology and Metabolism, Internal Medicine
1118 Clifton Ave, Clifton, 973-471-2692
870 Palisade Ave #203, Teaneck, 201-836-5655

Family Practice *(see note on page 9)*

Boorujy, Dean P. (4 mentions)
Philadelphia Coll of Osteopathic Med, 1993
Certification: Family Medicine
65 E Northfield Rd #H, Livingston, 973-422-9595

Bucek, John Ladislav (4 mentions)
Mount Sinai Sch of Med, 1993 *Certification:* Family Medicine
110 Rehill Ave, Somerville, 908-685-2900

Delisi, Michael D. (4 mentions)
FMS-Mexico, 1980
Certification: Family Medicine, Geriatric Medicine
1135 Broad St #201, Clifton, 973-754-4100

Eskow, Raymond Paul (3 mentions)
New Jersey Med Sch, 1991 *Certification:* Family Medicine
44 Godwin Ave, Midland Park, 201-444-5992

Flores, Jose C. (8 mentions)
New Jersey Sch of Osteopathic Med, 1988
Certification: Family Medicine
230 Sherman Ave #A, Glen Ridge, 973-743-2321

Glatter, Frederic G. (3 mentions)
Pennsylvania State U, 1984 *Certification:* Family Medicine
27 S 5th Ave, Highland Park, 732-819-9696

Gorman, Robert Thomas (4 mentions)
New Jersey Med Sch, 1982 *Certification:* Family Medicine
271 Grove Ave #A, Verona, 973-239-2600

Grobstein, Naomi Sarah (3 mentions)
New Jersey Med Sch, 1980 *Certification:* Family Medicine
48 Fairfield St, Montclair, 973-744-8511

Gross, Harvey Robert (10 mentions)
Boston U, 1970
Certification: Family Medicine, Geriatric Medicine
370 Grand Ave #102, Englewood, 201-567-3370

Haddad, A. John (3 mentions)
Certification: Family Medicine
370 State Route 35 #101, Red Bank, 732-758-0048

Kaufman, Irving Henry (3 mentions)
FMS-Italy, 1983 *Certification:* Adolescent Medicine, Family Medicine, Geriatric Medicine
1303 Route 27, Somerset, 732-249-1500

Kaye, Susan T. (3 mentions)
New York U, 1979 *Certification:* Family Medicine
33 Overlook Rd #L-01, Summit, 908-522-5700

Kripsak, John Phillip (3 mentions)
A T Still U, 1987
766 US Hwy 202/206, Bridgewater, 908-722-0808

Leipsner, George (3 mentions)
FMS-Italy, 1966
57 W Pleasant Ave, Maywood, 201-488-2111

Mazzoccoli, Vito (3 mentions)
FMS-Italy, 1987
110 Bloomfield Ave, Caldwell, 973-403-3200

McCampbell, Edwin Lee (4 mentions)
Howard U, 1968 *Certification:* Family Medicine
85 S Harrison St #201, East Orange, 973-672-3829

McCarrick, Thomas Patrick (4 mentions)
New York U, 1982 *Certification:* Family Medicine
271 Grove Ave, Verona, 973-239-2600

Miller, Arthur Hal (3 mentions)
FMS-Mexico, 1980 *Certification:* Family Medicine
505 Raritan Ave, Highland Park, 732-393-1331

Murray, Richard Stanley (3 mentions)
FMS-Mexico, 1975 *Certification:* Family Medicine
271 Grove Ave, Verona, 973-239-2600

Nitti, Michele (8 mentions)
New Jersey Sch of Osteopathic Med, 1988
Certification: Family Medicine
230 Sherman Ave #A, Glen Ridge, 973-743-2321

Qualter, John J., Jr. (3 mentions)
Philadelphia Coll of Osteopathic Med, 1961
264 Boyden Ave, Maplewood, 973-761-5200

Schlam, Everett Wax (3 mentions)
Robert W Johnson Med Sch, 1986 *Certification:* Adolescent Medicine, Family Medicine, Sports Medicine
799 Bloomfield Ave, Verona, 973-746-7050

Tabachnick, John F. (11 mentions)
Mount Sinai Sch of Med, 1979 *Certification:* Family Medicine
563 Westfield Ave, Westfield, 908-232-5858

Witt, Virginia Marie (3 mentions)
Duke U, 1997
150 Warren St #118, Jersey City, 201-309-3000
789 Ave C, Bayonne, 201-339-2620

Zacharias, Daniel (4 mentions)
Rosalind Franklin U, 1978 *Certification:* Emergency Medicine
7 Short Hills Ave, Short Hills, 973-912-0006

Gastroenterology

Accurso, Charles Anthony (7 mentions)
New Jersey Med Sch, 1984
Certification: Gastroenterology, Internal Medicine
511 Courtyard Dr, Hillsborough, 908-218-9222

Askin, Matthew Peter (4 mentions)
Mount Sinai Sch of Med, 1996
Certification: Gastroenterology, Internal Medicine
101 Old Short Hills Rd #217, West Orange, 973-731-4600

Bae, Samuel Y. (4 mentions)
Certification: Gastroenterology
1100 Wescott Dr, Flemington, 908-788-6448

Barrison, Adam F. (8 mentions)
New York U, 1995 *Certification:* Gastroenterology
1 Hiamond Hill Rd, Berkeley Heights, 908-277-8940

Belladonna, Joseph A., Jr. (5 mentions)
Cornell U, 1969
Certification: Gastroenterology, Internal Medicine
1 Diamond Hill Rd, Berkeley Heights, 908-273-4300

Ben-Menachem, Tamir (9 mentions)
FMS-Israel, 1988
Certification: Gastroenterology, Internal Medicine
125 Paterson St, New Brunswick, 732-235-6513

Binns, Joseph Francis, III (5 mentions)
Robert W Johnson Med Sch, 1987
Certification: Gastroenterology, Internal Medicine
365 Broad St #1E, Red Bank, 732-842-4294

Bleicher, Robert Howard (8 mentions)
Columbia U, 1978
Certification: Gastroenterology, Internal Medicine
1825 State Rt 23, Wayne, 973-633-1484

Blumberg, Darren Reich (11 mentions)
FMS-Grenada, 1996
Certification: Gastroenterology, Internal Medicine
65 Ridgedale Ave, Cedar Knolls, 973-401-0500

Dalena, John Michael (13 mentions)
New Jersey Med Sch, 1985
Certification: Gastroenterology, Internal Medicine
65 Ridgedale Ave, Cedar Knolls, 973-401-0500

David, Steven (4 mentions)
Mount Sinai Sch of Med, 1986
Certification: Gastroenterology, Internal Medicine
1825 State Route 23, Wayne, 973-633-1484

De Maio, Ralph Ames (4 mentions)
FMS-Italy, 1976 *Certification:* Internal Medicine
205 Browertown Rd #206, West Paterson, 973-837-0230

De Pasquale, Joseph R. (4 mentions)
FMS-Italy, 1983
Certification: Gastroenterology, Internal Medicine
111 Central Ave, Newark, 973-877-5351
5 Franklin Ave #109, Belleville, 973-759-7240

De Vito, Fiore John, Jr. (4 mentions)
FMS-Mexico, 1981
Certification: Gastroenterology, Internal Medicine
946 Bloomfield Ave, Glen Ridge, 973-743-6447

Feit, David Louis (9 mentions)
Columbia U, 1981
Certification: Gastroenterology, Internal Medicine
385 Prospect Ave, Hackensack, 201-488-3003
20 Prospect Ave #613, Hackensack, 201-336-8111

Fiest, Thomas Carl (8 mentions)
Philadelphia Coll of Osteopathic Med, 1985
Certification: Gastroenterology, Internal Medicine
142 Hwy 355, Eatontown, 732-389-5004

Finkelstein, Warren (10 mentions)
Virginia Commonwealth U, 1972
Certification: Gastroenterology, Internal Medicine
123 Highland Ave #103, Glen Ridge, 973-429-8800

Franzese, John N. (9 mentions)
FMS-Grenada, 1988 *Certification:* Gastroenterology
396 Main St, Chatham, 973-701-8277

Goldberg, Charles Stephen (5 mentions)
U of Rochester, 1978
Certification: Gastroenterology, Internal Medicine
127 Pine St, Montclair, 973-233-9559

Goldenberg, David Alan (4 mentions)
New York Med Coll, 1974
Certification: Gastroenterology, Internal Medicine
1165 Park Ave, Plainfield, 908-754-2992

Goldfarb, Michael (5 mentions)
Georgetown U, 1978
Certification: Gastroenterology, Internal Medicine
2130 Millburn Ave #C-6, Maplewood, 973-762-8200

Imbesi, John (6 mentions)
Certification: Gastroenterology, Internal Medicine
123 Highland Ave #103, Glen Ridge, 973-429-8800

Irakam, Surya Prakash (4 mentions)
FMS-India, 1991
Certification: Gastroenterology, Internal Medicine
286 E Main St, Somerville, 908-231-1999
515 Church St #2, Bound Brook, 908-231-1999

Kastuar, Satya Prakash (4 mentions)
FMS-India, 1978
Certification: Gastroenterology, Internal Medicine
2480 State Route 27, North Brunswick, 732-821-0011

Kenny, Raymond Patrick (5 mentions)
Stony Brook U, 1981
Certification: Gastroenterology, Internal Medicine
123 Highland Ave #103, Glen Ridge, 973-429-8800

Kerner, Michael Bernard (8 mentions)
Wake Forest U, 1971
Certification: Gastroenterology, Internal Medicine
25 Morris Ave, Springfield, 973-467-1313

Krawet, Steven Howard (10 mentions)
Robert W Johnson Med Sch, 1989 *Certification:* Gastroenterology
557 Cranbury Rd #1, East Brunswick, 732-390-5534

Luppescu, Neal Edwin (5 mentions)
Columbia U, 1983
Certification: Gastroenterology, Internal Medicine
10 N Gaston Ave #101, Somerville, 908-595-0601

Mogan, Glen Raymond (7 mentions)
SUNY-Upstate Med U, 1975
Certification: Gastroenterology, Internal Medicine
741 Northfield Ave #204, West Orange, 973-731-8686

Oh, Sangbaek Charles (6 mentions)
Mount Sinai Sch of Med, 1991 *Certification:* Gastroenterology
200 Highland Ave #110, Glen Ridge, 973-748-9166

Panella, Vincent Stephen (5 mentions)
New York Med Coll, 1982
Certification: Gastroenterology, Internal Medicine
420 Grand Ave #101, Englewood, 201-569-7044

Rahmin, Michael Gabriel (12 mentions)
New York U, 1989
Certification: Gastroenterology, Internal Medicine
140 Chestnut St #300, Ridgewood, 201-444-2600

Ramamoorthy, Ravishankar (6 mentions)
New Jersey Med Sch, 1995 *Certification:* Gastroenterology
159 Summit Ave, Hackensack, 201-343-7272

Rizvi, Masood Ahmed (4 mentions)
FMS-India, 1968
Certification: Gastroenterology, Internal Medicine
900 Pompton Ave #B1, Cedar Grove, 973-239-5656

Rosenheck, David Mark (7 mentions)
New Jersey Med Sch, 1983
Certification: Gastroenterology, Internal Medicine
205 May St, Edison, 732-661-9225
3 Hospital Plaza, Old Bridge, 732-360-2282

Rosh, Joel R. (10 mentions)
Certification: Pediatric Gastroenterology
100 Madison Ave, Morristown, 973-971-5676

Roth, Joseph Meyer (4 mentions)
U of Pittsburgh, 1981
Certification: Gastroenterology, Internal Medicine
71 Union Ave, Rutherford, 201-842-0020
925 Clifton Ave, Clifton, 973-458-0408

Rubinoff, Mitchell Jay (9 mentions)
Mount Sinai Sch of Med, 1979
Certification: Gastroenterology, Internal Medicine
140 Chestnut St #300, Ridgewood, 201-444-2600

Sampson, Ruby Jean (4 mentions)
New Jersey Med Sch, 1983
Certification: Gastroenterology, Internal Medicine
106 Valley St, South Orange, 973-313-9300

Schmidt, Michael Henry (4 mentions)
Rosalind Franklin U, 1985
Certification: Gastroenterology, Internal Medicine
1600 Parker Ave, Fort Lee, 201-461-2507
1086 Teaneck Rd #3-B, Teaneck, 201-837-9636

Schrader, Zalman Reuben (13 mentions)
Albert Einstein Coll of Med, 1961
Certification: Gastroenterology, Internal Medicine
101 Old Short Hills Rd #217, West Orange, 973-731-4600

Schuman, Robert William (9 mentions)
Duke U, 1989 *Certification:* Gastroenterology
101 Old Short Hills Rd #217, West Orange, 973-731-4600

Sedarat, Ali (4 mentions)
FMS-Iran, 1980
Certification: Gastroenterology, Internal Medicine
159 Summit Ave, Hackensack, 201-343-7272

Sloan, William Charles (9 mentions)
U of Pennsylvania, 1965
Certification: Gastroenterology, Internal Medicine
101 Old Short Hills Rd, West Orange, 973-731-4600

Soriano, John Gennaro (7 mentions)
FMS-Mexico, 1981
Certification: Gastroenterology, Internal Medicine
16 Pocono Rd #201, Denville, 973-627-4430

Spinnell, Mitchell Kyle (7 mentions)
U of Buffalo, 1991 *Certification:* Gastroenterology
1555 Center Ave, Fort Lee, 201-945-6564

Spira, Robert Sidney (4 mentions)
New York U, 1975
Certification: Gastroenterology, Internal Medicine
111 Central Ave, Newark, 973-877-5351
5 Franklin Ave #109, Belleville, 973-759-7240

Sunaryo, Francis Pudji (4 mentions)
FMS-Indonesia, 1971
Certification: Pediatric Gastroenterology, Pediatrics
201 Lyons Ave, Newark, 973-926-7280
400 Osborne Terr, Newark, 973-926-7328
200 S Orange Ave, Livingston, 973-322-7600

Tanchel, Mark E. (10 mentions)
Tufts U, 1994 *Certification:* Gastroenterology
385 Prospect Ave, Hackensack, 201-488-3003

Wallach, Carl Brett (6 mentions)
U of Miami, 1985
Certification: Gastroenterology, Internal Medicine
195 Columbia Tpke, Florham Park, 973-410-0959

Zingler, Barry Martin (10 mentions)
Robert W Johnson Med Sch, 1985
Certification: Gastroenterology, Internal Medicine
1555 Center Ave, Fort Lee, 201-945-6564

General Surgery

Abkin, Alexander D. (3 mentions)
FMS-Russia, 1986 *Certification:* Surgery
147 Columbia Tpke #308, Florham Park, 973-410-9700

Ahlborn, Thomas Nesbitt (17 mentions)
Columbia U, 1980 *Certification:* Surgery
385 S Maple Ave, Glen Rock, 201-444-5757

Amirata, Edwin A. (6 mentions)
Tufts U, 1990 *Certification:* Surgery
5 Franklin Ave #406, Belleville, 973-759-4499

Ballem, Ramamohana V. (18 mentions)
Certification: Surgery
230 Sherman Ave #C, Glen Ridge, 973-744-8585

Barbalinardo, Joseph Peter (4 mentions)
FMS-Mexico, 1978 *Certification:* Surgery
123 Highland Ave #202, Glen Ridge, 973-429-7600

Barbalinardo, Robert J. (5 mentions)
New Jersey Med Sch, 1982 *Certification:* Surgery
123 Highland Ave #202, Glen Ridge, 973-429-7600

Bello, John Joseph Mario (5 mentions)
FMS-Dominica, 1984 *Certification:* Surgery
1100 Wescott Dr #302, Flemington, 908-788-6464

Bello, Joseph Mario (3 mentions)
George Washington U, 1986 *Certification:* Surgery
1100 Wescott Dr #300, Flemington, 908-788-6464

Benson, Douglas Noding (5 mentions)
New Jersey Med Sch, 1971 *Certification:* Surgery
83 Summit Ave, Hackensack, 201-646-0010

Borao, Frank Joseph (3 mentions)
New Jersey Med Sch, 1994 *Certification:* Surgery
1131 Broad St #105, Shrewsbury, 732-389-1331

Boyarsky, Andrew Harold (10 mentions)
Robert W Johnson Med Sch, 1980
Certification: Surgery, Surgical Critical Care
125 Paterson St, New Brunswick, 732-235-7920

Brautigan, Robert Anthony (3 mentions)
New Jersey Med Sch, 1997 *Certification:* Surgery
5 Franklin Ave #406, Belleville, 973-759-4499

Bufalini, Bruno (4 mentions)
FMS-Italy, 1970
200 Grand Ave #203, Englewood, 201-871-0303

Campion, Thomas W. (6 mentions)
New Jersey Med Sch, 1980 *Certification:* Surgery
1 Doctors Park, Hackettstown, 908-850-9548

Carter, Mitchel Scott (10 mentions)
Rosalind Franklin U, 1979 *Certification:* Surgery
261 James St #2-G, Morristown, 973-267-6400
100 Madison Ave #4201, Morristown, 973-267-6400

Cauda, Joseph Elmo (4 mentions)
FMS-Mexico, 1980 *Certification:* Surgery
1131 Broad St #101, Shrewsbury, 732-542-8118

Chagares, Stephen Arthur (10 mentions)
Robert W Johnson Med Sch, 1990 *Certification:* Surgery
180 Ave of The Commons, Shrewsbury, 732-460-1300

Chamberlain, Ronald Scott (4 mentions)
George Washington U, 1991 *Certification:* Surgery
94 Old Short Hills Rd, Livingston, 973-322-5195

Chang, Patrick Kung Sun (10 mentions)
FMS-Australia, 1970 *Certification:* Surgery
101 Old Short Hills Rd #206, West Orange, 973-731-5005

Chevinsky, Aaron Harry (10 mentions)
Stony Brook U, 1983 *Certification:* Surgery, Surgical Critical Care
261 James St #2-G, Morristown, 973-539-5115

Colaco, Rodolfo (3 mentions)
FMS-India, 1974 *Certification:* Surgery
431 Elmora Ave, Elizabeth, 908-353-4177

Cuppari, Anthony Lawrence (5 mentions)
FMS-Dominica, 1985 *Certification:* Surgery
29 Columbia Tpke #202, Florham Park, 973-966-8900
76 Prospect St, Newark, 973-966-8900
85 S Jefferson St, Orange, 973-966-8900
25 E Willow St, Willburn, 973-966-8900

Curtiss, Steven I. (5 mentions)
Albany Med Coll, 1986 *Certification:* Surgery, Vascular Surgery
31 River Rd, Highland Park, 732-846-9500
J-2 Brier Hill Ct, East Brunswick, 732-238-2227

Dasmahapatra, Kumar S. (4 mentions)
FMS-India, 1974 *Certification:* Surgery
225 May St #A, Edison, 732-346-5400

Diehl, William L. (12 mentions)
FMS-Mexico, 1981 *Certification:* Surgery
261 James St #2-G, Morristown, 973-267-6400
100 Madison Ave #4201, Morristown, 973-267-6400

Drascher, Gary A. (5 mentions)
Mount Sinai Sch of Med, 1981 *Certification:* Surgery
515 Church St #1, Bound Brook, 732-356-0770

Feteiha, Muhammad Saleh (3 mentions)
Tufts U, 1995 *Certification:* Surgery
155 Morris Ave 2nd Fl, Springfield, 908-232-2300

Franco, Charles D. (4 mentions)
New Jersey Med Sch, 1982
Certification: Surgery, Vascular Surgery
81 Veronica Ave #205, Somerset, 732-246-8266

Fresco, Silvia (8 mentions)
New Jersey Med Sch, 1992 *Certification:* Surgery
123 Highland Ave #202, Glen Ridge, 973-429-7600

Fried, Kenneth S. (6 mentions)
New York U, 1978 *Certification:* Surgery
180 N Dean St #2, Englewood, 201-568-8666

Gandhi, Rajinder Pal (7 mentions)
Certification: Pediatric Surgery, Surgery
30 W Century Rd #235, Paramus, 201-225-9440

Geffner, Stuart Roy (6 mentions)
New Jersey Med Sch, 1988 *Certification:* Surgery
94 Old Short Hills Rd, Livingston, 973-322-5000

Goldenkranz, Robert Jay (5 mentions)
Cornell U, 1972 *Certification:* Surgery
225 Millburn Ave #104B, Millburn, 973-379-5888

Goldfarb, Michael Allen (4 mentions)
New York U, 1967 *Certification:* Surgery
279 3rd Ave #103, Long Branch, 732-870-6060

Gross, Eric L. (4 mentions)
Mount Sinai Sch of Med, 1988 *Certification:* Surgery
657 Willow Grove St #302, Hackettstown, 908-852-7482

Harrison, Lawrence Evan (3 mentions)
Temple U, 1988 *Certification:* Surgery
185 S Orange Ave, Newark, 973-972-2400
90 Bergen St, Newark, 973-972-1110

Hayne, Walter Charles (4 mentions)
Temple U, 1991 *Certification:* Surgery
241 Mamouth Rd, West Long Branch, 732-403-2075

Ibrahim, Ibrahim (6 mentions)
New York U, 1966 *Certification:* Surgery
375 Engle St, Englewood, 201-227-5533

Kagan, Peter Evan (3 mentions)
FMS-Grenada, 1997 *Certification:* Surgery, Vascular Surgery
23 Summit Ave, Hackensack, 201-342-7979

Kane, Edwin P. (5 mentions)
FMS-Italy, 1978 *Certification:* Surgery
1100 Clifton Ave, Clifton, 973-778-0100

Konigsberg, Stephen F. (3 mentions)
Harvard U, 1962 *Certification:* Surgery, Vascular Surgery
31 River Rd, Highland Park, 732-846-9500
22 Brier Hill Ct, East Brunswick, 732-238-2227

Licata, Joseph John, Jr. (17 mentions)
FMS-Mexico, 1984 *Certification:* Surgery
245 E Main St, Ramsey, 201-327-0220

Mandel, Marc Steven (8 mentions)
Albert Einstein Coll of Med, 1985 *Certification:* Surgery
25 E Willow St, Millburn, 908-598-0966
1030 ST Georges Ave #201, Avenel, 732-855-7989

Mandel, Mark Steven (3 mentions)
Stony Brook U, 1986 *Certification:* Surgery
595 Chestnut Ridge Rd, Woodcliff Lake, 201-391-2020

McCain, Donald Andrew (3 mentions)
Albert Einstein Coll of Med, 1991 *Certification:* Surgery
20 Prospect Ave #603, Hackensack, 201-541-5986

Parker, Glenn Scot (3 mentions)
Robert W Johnson Med Sch, 1988
Certification: Colon & Rectal Surgery, Surgery
255 Monmouth Rd, Oakhurst, 732-531-5445
459 Jack Martin Blvd, Brick, 732-836-1500

Pereira, Stephen Gomes (5 mentions)
Robert W Johnson Med Sch, 1991 *Certification:* Surgery
90 Prospect Ave, Hackensack, 201-343-3433

Poole, John William (7 mentions)
U of Virginia, 1982 *Certification:* Surgery
83 Summit Ave, Hackensack, 201-646-0010

Potter, Steven Darren (3 mentions)
New Jersey Med Sch, 1990 *Certification:* Surgery
287 Boulevard #1, Pompton Plains, 973-839-7400

Rolandelli, Rolando H. (3 mentions)
Certification: Surgery
95 Madison Ave #304-C, Morristown, 973-971-7200

Rosen, Scott Farrell (3 mentions)
New York U, 1993 *Certification:* Surgery, Vascular Surgery
31 River Rd, Highland Park, 732-846-9500
22 Brier Hill Ct, East Brunswick, 732-238-2227

Sacco, Margaret Mary (3 mentions)
Hahnemann U, 1986 *Certification:* Surgery
22 Jackson Ave, Pompton Plains, 973-835-0564

Seenivasan, Thangamani (5 mentions)
FMS-India, 1985 *Certification:* Surgery
611 Courtyard Dr, Hillsborough, 908-722-0030

Sherman, Mark David (3 mentions)
U of Miami, 1974 *Certification:* Surgery
1200 E Ridgewood Ave 2nd Fl, Ridgewood, 201-444-1775

Silvestri, Fred (4 mentions)
SUNY-Downstate Med Coll, 1983
Certification: Surgery, Surgical Critical Care
375 Engle St, Englewood, 201-894-0400

Starker, Paul Matthew (24 mentions)
Columbia U, 1980 *Certification:* Surgery
11 Overlook Rd #160, Summit, 908-608-9001

Strom, Karl William (4 mentions)
FMS-Grenada, 1998 *Certification:* Surgery
123 Highland Ave #202, Glen Ridge, 973-429-7600

Sugarmann, William Meyer (7 mentions)
U of Connecticut, 1992 *Certification:* Surgery
515 Church St #1, Bound Brook, 732-356-0770

Sultan, Ronald Harry (3 mentions)
New York U, 1973 *Certification:* Surgery
2255 John F Kennedy Blvd, Jersey City, 201-434-3305

Sussman, Barry Clark (4 mentions)
New York U, 1973 *Certification:* Surgery
375 Engle St, Englewood, 201-894-0400

Swaminathan, Anangur P. (5 mentions)
FMS-India, 1966 *Certification:* Surgery
225 May St #A, Edison, 732-346-5400

Trooskin, Stanley Zachary (5 mentions)
U of Pittsburgh, 1975 *Certification:* Surgery
125 Paterson St, New Brunswick, 732-235-7920

Ward, David Scott (3 mentions)
Robert W Johnson Med Sch, 1994 *Certification:* Surgery
261 James St #2-G, Morristown, 973-267-6400
100 Madison Ave #4201, Morristown, 973-267-6400

Wolodiger, Fred Ashley (3 mentions)
SUNY-Downstate Med Coll, 1980
Certification: Surgery, Vascular Surgery
375 Engle St, Englewood, 201-894-0400

Geriatrics

Bahler, Emily S. (3 mentions)
New York Coll of Osteopathic Med, 2000
Certification: Geriatric Medicine, Internal Medicine
701 S Livingston Ave #2-F, Livingston, 973-535-9294

Diano, Rowen Gumapas (6 mentions)
FMS-Philippines, 1983
Certification: Geriatric Medicine, Internal Medicine
48 N Fullerton Ave, Montclair, 973-744-5049

Graber, David Jacob (3 mentions)
New York U, 1975 *Certification:* Gastroenterology, Geriatric
    Medicine, Internal Medicine
925 Allwood Rd, Clifton, 973-777-7911

Gross, Harvey Robert (6 mentions)
Boston U, 1970
Certification: Family Medicine, Geriatric Medicine
370 Grand Ave #102, Englewood, 201-567-3370

Katz, Terri Feldman (4 mentions)
George Washington U, 1986
Certification: Geriatric Medicine, Internal Medicine
655 Pomander Walk #239, Teaneck, 201-836-2990

Kim, John (3 mentions)
FMS-South Korea, 1989
2 Sears Dr, Paramus, 201-262-2333

Leifer, Bennett Philip (11 mentions)
SUNY-Upstate Med U, 1986
Certification: Geriatric Medicine, Internal Medicine
301 Godwin Ave, Midland Park, 201-444-4526

Leventhal, Elaine Annette (5 mentions)
U of Wisconsin, 1974
Certification: Geriatric Medicine, Internal Medicine
125 Paterson St, New Brunswick, 732-235-6500

Redling, Theresa M. (3 mentions)
New Jersey Sch of Osteopathic Med, 1987
Certification: Geriatric Medicine, Internal Medicine
201 Lyons Ave, Newark, 973-926-8491

Ross, Joel Steven (4 mentions)
SUNY-Downstate Med Coll, 1981 *Certification:* Internal Medicine
4 Industrial Way W, Eatontown, 732-571-1535

Ryan, Joseph John (6 mentions)
SUNY-Downstate Med Coll, 1970 *Certification:*
   Gastroenterology, Geriatric Medicine, Internal Medicine
95 Madison Ave, Morristown, 973-971-7165

Schaer, Teresa McKinley (13 mentions)
U of California-San Diego, 1981 *Certification:* Internal Medicine
35 Clyde Rd #104, Somerset, 732-873-1999

Schor, Joshua David (9 mentions)
Yale U, 1985 *Certification:* Geriatric Medicine, Internal Medicine
65 Circle Dr, Hastings-on-Hudson, NY, 877-209-2041

Shah, Pradip (3 mentions)
FMS-India, 1982
459 Passaic Ave, West Caldwell, 973-276-3026

Steel, R. Knight (7 mentions)
Columbia U, 1965 *Certification:* Internal Medicine
5 Summit Ave, Hackensack, 201-336-8760
30 Prospect Ave, Hackensack, 201-996-2503

Suri, Ritu (3 mentions)
FMS-India, 1992
Certification: Family Medicine, Geriatric Medicine
245 Engle St, Englewood, 201-569-5330

Wolf, James Henry (3 mentions)
New York U, 1974
Certification: Geriatric Medicine, Internal Medicine
19 E Main St #1, Mendham, 973-543-6505

Hematology/Oncology

Adler, Kenneth R. (16 mentions)
Albany Med Coll, 1973
Certification: Hematology, Internal Medicine
100 Madison Ave, Morristown, 973-538-5210

Alter, Robert S. (7 mentions)
Rosalind Franklin U, 1988
20 Prospect Ave #400, Hackensack, 201-996-5900

Attas, Lewis Michael (9 mentions)
Mount Sinai Sch of Med, 1982
Certification: Hematology, Internal Medicine, Medical Oncology
350 Engle St, Englewood, 201-568-5250
718 Teaneck Rd, Teaneck, 201-227-6008

Blankstein, Kenneth (4 mentions)
New York Med Coll, 1984
Certification: Hematology, Internal Medicine, Medical Oncology
2100 Wescott Dr, Flemington, 908-788-6461

Botti, Anthony Charles (9 mentions)
FMS-Spain, 1982
Certification: Hematology, Internal Medicine, Medical Oncology
349 E Northfield Rd #200, Livingston, 973-597-0900

Celo, Jovenia Soriano (4 mentions)
FMS-Philippines, 1978 *Certification:* Anatomic Pathology &
   Clinical Pathology, Internal Medicine, Medical Oncology
1314 Park Ave, Plainfield, 908-754-0400

Cohen, Alice Joy (5 mentions)
Rosalind Franklin U, 1981
Certification: Hematology, Internal Medicine, Medical Oncology
201 Lyons Ave, Newark, 973-926-7230

Cohen, Seth Daniel (6 mentions)
U of Buffalo, 1998
Certification: Internal Medicine, Medical Oncology
100 State Hwy 36 #1-B, West Long Branch, 732-222-1711

Conde, Miguel A. (4 mentions)
Columbia U, 1986
Certification: Hematology, Internal Medicine, Medical Oncology
94 Old Short Hills Rd, Livingston, 973-322-5200

Condemi, Giuseppe (6 mentions)
FMS-Dominica, 1998
Certification: Internal Medicine, Medical Oncology
350 Engle St, Englewood, 201-568-5250

Conti, John August (16 mentions)
New Jersey Med Sch, 1986 *Certification:* Hospice and
   Palliative Medicine, Internal Medicine, Medical Oncology
1 Bay Ave #2, Montclair, 973-744-8000
36 Newark Ave #304, Belleville, 973-751-8880

De Rosa, William (5 mentions)
A T Still U, 1980
Certification: Hematology, Internal Medicine, Medical Oncology
100 Madison Ave, Morristown, 973-538-5210

Di Paolo, Patrick J. (4 mentions)
FMS-Italy, 1983
Certification: Internal Medicine, Medical Oncology
781 Bloomfield Ave, Montclair, 973-744-7979

Druck, Mark (6 mentions)
SUNY-Downstate Med Coll, 1977
Certification: Hematology, Internal Medicine, Medical Oncology
210 Palisade Ave, Jersey City, 201-963-2213

Early, Ellen Marie (4 mentions)
Georgetown U, 1991
100 Madison Ave 2nd Fl, Morristown, 973-538-5210

Fang, Bruno S. (9 mentions)
FMS-Brazil, 1991
Certification: Hematology, Internal Medicine, Medical Oncology
205 Easton Ave, New Brunswick, 732-828-9570
J-2 Brier Hill Ct, East Brunswick, 732-390-7750

Fein, Robert P. (7 mentions)
New York U, 1979
Certification: Internal Medicine, Medical Oncology
75 Veronica Ave #201, Somerset, 732-246-4882
111 Union Valley Rd #205, Monroe Township, 609-395-5577

Fernbach, Barry Richard (10 mentions)
Harvard U, 1971
Certification: Hematology, Internal Medicine, Medical Oncology
1 Valley Health Plaza, Paramus, 201-634-5353

Fitzgerald, Denis B. (8 mentions)
SUNY-Downstate Med Coll, 1978
Certification: Hematology, Internal Medicine, Medical Oncology
180 White Rd #101, Little Silver, 732-530-8666

Forte, Francis Americus (8 mentions)
Albert Einstein Coll of Med, 1964
Certification: Hematology, Internal Medicine, Medical Oncology
350 Engle St, Englewood, 201-568-5250

Frank, Martin J. (7 mentions)
George Washington U, 1982
Certification: Internal Medicine, Medical Oncology
97 West Pkwy Collins Pavillion, Pompton Plains, 973-831-5451

Gerstein, Gary (5 mentions)
Jefferson Med Coll, 1973
Certification: Hematology, Internal Medicine
100 Madison Ave 2nd Fl, Morristown, 973-538-5210

Halpern, Steven Lon (4 mentions)
Rosalind Franklin U, 1976
Certification: Pediatric Hematology-Oncology, Pediatrics
30 Prospect Ave, Hackensack, 201-996-5437

Harper, Harry David (7 mentions)
Baylor U, 1977
Certification: Hematology, Internal Medicine, Medical Oncology
20 Prospect Ave #400, Hackensack, 201-996-5900

Jennis, Andrew Abraham (6 mentions)
Columbia U, 1985
Certification: Hematology, Internal Medicine, Medical Oncology
20 Prospect Ave #400, Hackensack, 201-996-5900

Kamalakar, Peri (6 mentions)
FMS-India, 1967
Certification: Pediatric Hematology-Oncology, Pediatrics
201 Lyons Ave, Newark, 973-926-7161
300 2nd Ave, Long Branch, 732-923-7455

Karp, George Isaac (6 mentions)
Columbia U, 1976
Certification: Hematology, Internal Medicine, Medical Oncology
205 Easton Ave, New Brunswick, 732-828-9570
J-2 Brier Hill Ct, East Brunswick, 732-390-7750

Leff, Charles Allen (4 mentions)
SUNY-Upstate Med U, 1968
Certification: Hematology, Internal Medicine, Medical Oncology
1314 Park Ave, Plainfield, 908-754-0400
30 Rehill Ave #2400, Somerville, 908-927-8722

Leitner, Stuart Philip (5 mentions)
Mount Sinai Sch of Med, 1979
Certification: Internal Medicine, Medical Oncology
94 Old Short Hills Rd, Livingston, 973-322-5852

Levitz, Jason Sanford (4 mentions)
FMS-Israel, 1999
Certification: Hematology, Internal Medicine, Medical Oncology
23 Pocono Rd, Denville, 973-316-1701
100 Madison Ave, Morristown, 973-267-9543

Ligresti, Louise Grace (10 mentions)
SUNY-Upstate Med U, 1991
Certification: Hematology, Medical Oncology
1 Valley Health Plaza, Paramus, 201-634-5353

Lowenthal, Dennis Alan (7 mentions)
Boston U, 1979
Certification: Hematology, Internal Medicine, Medical Oncology
99 Beauvoir Ave, Summit, 908-608-0078

Maroules, Michael (6 mentions)
FMS-Greece, 1979 *Certification:* Anatomic Pathology,
   Hematology, Internal Medicine, Medical Oncology
1135 Broad St #3, Clifton, 862-591-2002

Mencel, Peter Jan (6 mentions)
FMS-Poland, 1982
Certification: Internal Medicine, Medical Oncology
1707 Atlantic Ave, Manasquan, 732-528-0760

Moriarty, Daniel Joseph (8 mentions)
U of Vermont, 1976
Certification: Internal Medicine, Medical Oncology
99 Beauvoir Ave, Summit, 908-608-0078

Nissenblatt, Michael J. (14 mentions)
Columbia U, 1973
Certification: Internal Medicine, Medical Oncology
205 Easton Ave, New Brunswick, 732-828-9570
J-2 Brier Hill Ct, East Brunswick, 732-390-7750

Papish, Steven William (12 mentions)
U of Pennsylvania, 1974
Certification: Hematology, Internal Medicine, Medical Oncology
100 Madison Ave 2nd Fl, Morristown, 973-538-5210

Pascal, Mark Stanley (4 mentions)
Jefferson Med Coll, 1973
Certification: Internal Medicine, Medical Oncology
20 Prospect Ave #400, Hackensack, 201-996-5900

Pliner, Lillian Francine (5 mentions)
Stony Brook U, 1980
Certification: Internal Medicine, Medical Oncology
90 Bergen St #4500, Newark, 973-972-6257
150 Bergen St #UHD-106, Newark, 973-972-5110

Porcelli, Marcus Peter (5 mentions)
FMS-Italy, 1983
Certification: Hematology, Internal Medicine, Medical Oncology
75 Veronica Ave #201, Somerset, 732-246-4882
111 Union Valley Rd #205, Monroe Township, 732-246-4882

Rakowski, Thomas John (8 mentions)
SUNY-Upstate Med U, 1976
Certification: Internal Medicine, Medical Oncology
301 Godwin Ave, Midland Park, 201-444-4526

Rivera, Yadyra (4 mentions)
U Central del Caribe, 1992
Certification: Hematology, Internal Medicine, Medical Oncology
718 Teaneck Rd, Teaneck, 201-227-6008

Sagorin, Charles Elliot (4 mentions)
SUNY-Downstate Med Coll, 1971
Certification: Hematology, Internal Medicine, Medical Oncology
127 Pine St #6, Montclair, 973-783-3300

Salwitz, James Cogill (4 mentions)
Robert W Johnson Med Sch, 1981
Certification: Internal Medicine, Medical Oncology
205 Easton Ave, New Brunswick, 732-828-9570
J-2 Brier Hill Ct, East Brunswick, 732-390-7750

Savopoulos, Andreas A. (4 mentions)
FMS-Greece, 1974
Certification: Hematology, Internal Medicine, Medical Oncology
401 Pleasant Valley Way, West Orange, 973-669-5931

Schleider, Michael Allan (9 mentions)
U of Pennsylvania, 1969
Certification: Hematology, Internal Medicine, Medical Oncology
350 Engle St, Englewood, 201-568-5250

Schuman, Richard Michael (5 mentions)
Hahnemann U, 1980
Certification: Hematology, Internal Medicine, Medical Oncology
34-36 Progress St #B2, Edison, 908-757-9696

Scoppetuolo, Michael (5 mentions)
Rosalind Franklin U, 1979
Certification: Internal Medicine, Medical Oncology
94 Old Short Hills Rd, Livingston, 973-322-5200

Sharon, David Julius (7 mentions)
New York Med Coll, 1977
Certification: Internal Medicine, Medical Oncology
100 State Route 36 #1-B, West Long Branch, 732-222-1711

Toomey, Kathleen Clare (11 mentions)
FMS-Italy, 1978
Certification: Hematology, Internal Medicine, Medical Oncology
30 Rehill Ave #2500, Somerville, 908-927-8700

Uhm, Kyudong (4 mentions)
FMS-South Korea, 1969
Certification: Hematology, Internal Medicine, Medical Oncology
1117 US Hwy 46 #205, Clifton, 973-471-0981

Waintraub, Stanley Eli (7 mentions)
New York Med Coll, 1977
Certification: Hematology, Internal Medicine, Medical Oncology
20 Prospect Ave #400, Hackensack, 201-996-5900

Wax, Michael Barry (11 mentions)
Med Coll of Pennsylvania, 1977
Certification: Internal Medicine, Medical Oncology
1 Diamond Hill Rd, Berkeley Heights, 908-273-4300
99 Beauvoir Ave, Summit, 908-522-8326

Wu, Hen Vai (4 mentions)
FMS-Taiwan, 1972
Certification: Hematology, Internal Medicine, Medical Oncology
30 Rehill Ave, Somerville, 908-927-8700

Zager, Robert F. (7 mentions)
Cornell U, 1968
Certification: Hematology, Internal Medicine, Medical Oncology
1 Bay Ave, Montclair, 973-259-3555

Zauber, Neil Peter (6 mentions)
Johns Hopkins U, 1971
Certification: Hematology, Internal Medicine
22 Old Short Hills Rd, Livingston, 973-533-9299

Infectious Disease

Allegra, Donald Thomas (17 mentions)
Harvard U, 1974
Certification: Infectious Disease, Internal Medicine
765 State Rt 10, Randolph, 973-989-0068
8 Saddle Rd #203, Cedar Knolls, 973-993-5950

Baez Bernal, Juan Carlos (6 mentions)
FMS-Colombia, 1991
Certification: Infectious Disease, Internal Medicine
525 Central Ave, Westfield, 908-233-0895

Birch, Thomas Merrill (17 mentions)
U of Wisconsin, 1983
Certification: Infectious Disease, Internal Medicine
718 Teaneck Rd, Teaneck, 201-833-7274

Bishburg, Eliahou (5 mentions)
FMS-Israel, 1980
Certification: Infectious Disease, Internal Medicine
201 Lyons Ave, Newark, 973-926-5212

Casey, Kathleen King (8 mentions)
Robert W Johnson Med Sch, 1982
Certification: Infectious Disease, Internal Medicine
71 Davis Ave, Neptune, 732-776-4700
2240 Route 33 2nd Fl #A, Neptune City, 732-897-3995
1945 Route 33, Neptune, 732-776-4302

Deshaw, Max G. (20 mentions)
U of Minnesota, 1988
Certification: Infectious Disease, Internal Medicine
11 Hill St, Morristown, 973-538-5844

Diamond, Gigi Randy (17 mentions)
FMS-Spain, 1982
Certification: Infectious Disease, Internal Medicine
349 E Northfield Rd #200, Livingston, 973-597-0900

Frank, Elliot (6 mentions)
Yale U, 1978 *Certification:* Infectious Disease, Internal Medicine
71 Davis Ave, Neptune, 732-776-4700
1945 Route 33, Neptune, 732-776-4302
2240 Route 33 2nd Fl #A, Neptune City, 732-897-3995

French, Eugene C. (8 mentions)
FMS-Dominica, 1988 *Certification:* Internal Medicine
75 Summit Ave, Hackensack, 201-343-2778

Gaffin, Neil (5 mentions)
Hahnemann U, 1993 *Certification:* Infectious Disease
141 Dayton St #201, Ridgewood, 201-447-6468

Greenman, James Lawrence (14 mentions)
Albert Einstein Coll of Med, 1982
Certification: Infectious Disease, Internal Medicine
475 Springfield Ave #220, Summit, 908-233-0895
525 Central Ave #C, Westfield, 908-233-0895

Gugliotta, Joseph Louis (10 mentions)
Albert Einstein Coll of Med, 1974
Certification: Infectious Disease, Internal Medicine
1100 Wescott Dr, Flemington, 908-788-6474

Gupta, Punit Kumar (6 mentions)
New Jersey Med Sch, 1999
Certification: Infectious Disease, Internal Medicine
285 Lexington Ave, Passaic, 973-495-5994

Herman, David Jeffrey (8 mentions)
U of Missouri, 1985
Certification: Infectious Disease, Internal Medicine
105 Raider Blvd #101, Hillsborough, 908-281-0221

Kapila, Rajendra (8 mentions)
FMS-India, 1964
Certification: Infectious Disease, Internal Medicine
90 Bergen St #4500, Newark, 973-972-2502

Knackmuhs, Gary Glenn (7 mentions)
New York Med Coll, 1976
Certification: Infectious Disease, Internal Medicine
141 Dayton St #201, Ridgewood, 201-447-6468

Kocher, Jeffrey (11 mentions)
Cornell U, 1980
Certification: Infectious Disease, Internal Medicine
25 Rockwood Pl, Englewood, 201-568-3335

Levine, Jerome Fredric (13 mentions)
New York U, 1976
Certification: Infectious Disease, Internal Medicine
20 Prospect Ave #507, Hackensack, 201-487-4088

Lintz, David Irwin (5 mentions)
Jefferson Med Coll, 1970
Certification: Infectious Disease, Internal Medicine
525 Central Ave, Westfield, 908-233-0895

Louie, Ted (10 mentions)
Stony Brook U, 1990
Certification: Infectious Disease, Internal Medicine
579A Cranbury Rd #102, East Brunswick, 732-613-0711
579-A Cranbury Rd #102, East Brunswick, 732-613-0711

Macapinlac, Eric Victor A. (8 mentions)
FMS-Philippines, 1993
Certification: Infectious Disease, Internal Medicine
199 Broad St #2A, Bloomfield, 973-748-4583

McManus, Edward John (6 mentions)
New Jersey Med Sch, 1982
Certification: Infectious Disease, Internal Medicine
765 State Rt 10, Randolph, 973-989-0068
8 Saddle Rd #203, Cedar Knolls, 973-993-5950

Middleton, John Richard (5 mentions)
New Jersey Med Sch, 1970
Certification: Infectious Disease, Internal Medicine
3 Hospital Plaza #208, Old Bridge, 732-360-2700
530 New Brunswick Ave, Perth Amboy, 732-360-2700

Miller, Lincoln Paul (8 mentions)
FMS-Israel, 1985
Certification: Infectious Disease, Internal Medicine
1500 Pleasant Valley Way #201, West Orange, 973-966-6400

Nahass, Ronald George (19 mentions)
Robert W Johnson Med Sch, 1982
Certification: Infectious Disease, Internal Medicine
105 Raider Blvd #101, Hillsborough, 908-491-1068

Najjar, Sessine (6 mentions)
FMS-Lebanon, 1974
Certification: Infectious Disease, Internal Medicine
975 Clifton Ave, Clifton, 973-778-8666

Nastro, Lawrence Joseph (5 mentions)
SUNY-Downstate Med Coll, 1965 *Certification:* Infectious
  Disease, Internal Medicine, Pulmonary Disease
1 Diamond Hill Rd, Berkeley Heights, 908-273-4300

O'Grady, John Patrick (12 mentions)
Robert W Johnson Med Sch, 1990
Certification: Infectious Disease, Internal Medicine
11 Hill St, Morristown, 973-538-5844

Piwoz, Julia Ann (6 mentions)
Hahnemann U, 1991
Certification: Pediatric Infectious Diseases, Pediatrics
30 Prospect Ave, Hackensack, 201-996-5308

Salaki, John Stephen (5 mentions)
New Jersey Med Sch, 1971
95 Madison Ave #411, Morristown, 973-971-7165

Sensakovic, John W. (5 mentions)
New Jersey Med Sch, 1977
Certification: Infectious Disease, Internal Medicine
113 James St, Edison, 732-549-3449

Shariati, Nasseredin (6 mentions)
FMS-Iran, 1972
2345 Lamington Rd #103, Bedminster, 908-234-2295

Slavin, Kevin Alan (5 mentions)
U of California-Los Angeles, 1993
Certification: Pediatric Infectious Diseases, Pediatrics
30 Prospect Ave, Hackensack, 201-996-5308

Smith, Leon George (15 mentions)
Georgetown U, 1956
Certification: Infectious Disease, Internal Medicine
189 Eagle Rock Ave, Roseland, 973-226-3359
268 Martin Luther King Blvd, Newark, 973-877-5481

Snepar, Richard Alan (11 mentions)
Cornell U, 1976
Certification: Infectious Disease, Internal Medicine
579A Cranbury Rd #102, East Brunswick, 732-613-0711
579-A Cranbury Rd #102, East Brunswick, 732-613-0711

Soroko, Theresa Ann (21 mentions)
FMS-Grenada, 1984
Certification: Infectious Disease, Internal Medicine
199 Broad St #2A, Bloomfield, 973-748-4583

Sotsky, Carol (18 mentions)
New York Med Coll, 1982
141 Dayton St #201, Ridgewood, 201-447-6468

Weiner, Peter Robert (5 mentions)
Georgetown U, 1981
Certification: Infectious Disease, Internal Medicine
96 Millburn Ave #200A, Millburn, 908-686-7542

Weisholtz, Steven Jay (16 mentions)
U of Pennsylvania, 1978
Certification: Infectious Disease, Internal Medicine
25 Rockwood Pl, Englewood, 201-568-3335

Williams, Stephen Joseph (8 mentions)
U of Missouri, 1998
Certification: Infectious Disease, Internal Medicine
105 Raider Blvd, Hillsborough, 908-725-2522

Infertility

Bergh, Paul Akos (8 mentions)
Robert W Johnson Med Sch, 1983 *Certification:* Obstetrics
& Gynecology, Reproductive Endocrinology/Infertility
111 Madison Ave #100, Morristown, 973-971-4600
769 Northfield Ave #288, West Orange, 973-325-2229

Chen, Serena Homei (5 mentions)
Duke U, 1988 *Certification:* Obstetrics & Gynecology,
Reproductive Endocrinology/Infertility
94 Old Short Hills Rd #403, Livingston, 973-322-8286

Damien, Miguel (10 mentions)
Dartmouth Coll, 1982 *Certification:* Obstetrics &
Gynecology, Reproductive Endocrinology/Infertility
200 White Rd #214, Little Silver, 732-758-6511

Drews, Michael Robert (7 mentions)
Cornell U, 1986 *Certification:* Obstetrics & Gynecology,
Reproductive Endocrinology/Infertility
111 Madison Ave, Morristown, 973-971-4600

Lesorgen, Philip R. (8 mentions)
Boston U, 1977 *Certification:* Obstetrics & Gynecology
106 Grand Ave, Englewood, 201-569-6979

McGovern, Peter Gerard (6 mentions)
New York U, 1986 *Certification:* Obstetrics & Gynecology,
Reproductive Endocrinology/Infertility
214 Terrace Ave, Hasbrouck Heights, 201-288-6330

Nasseri, Ali (4 mentions)
Certification: Obstetrics & Gynecology, Reproductive
Endocrinology/Infertility
1 Valley Health Plaza 1st Fl, Paramus, 201-634-5400

Ransom, Mark Xavier (5 mentions)
Robert W Johnson Med Sch, 1987 *Certification:* Obstetrics
& Gynecology, Reproductive Endocrinology/Infertility
57 Willowbrook Blvd, Wayne, 973-754-4055

Scott, Richard Thomas, Jr. (8 mentions)
U of Virginia, 1983 *Certification:* Obstetrics & Gynecology,
Reproductive Endocrinology/Infertility
111 Madison Ave #100, Morristown, 973-971-4600

Seaman, Eric Keith (4 mentions)
New York U, 1989 *Certification:* Urology
741 Northfield Ave #206, West Orange, 973-325-6100

Slowey, Michael John (5 mentions)
U of Tennessee, 1987 *Certification:* Obstetrics &
Gynecology, Reproductive Endocrinology/Infertility
111 Madison Ave #100, Morristown, 973-971-4600
25 Rockwood Pl #126, Englewood, 201-569-7773

Ziegler, William Francis (5 mentions)
Des Moines U, 1990 *Certification:* Obstetrics & Gynecology,
Reproductive Endocrinology/Infertility
4000 State Route 66 #125, Tinton Falls, 732-918-2500

Internal Medicine *(see note on page 9)*

Bell, Kevin Edmund (12 mentions)
Columbia U, 1975 *Certification:* Internal Medicine
10 Mountain Blvd, Warren, 908-226-9000

Beresford, Dianne W. (3 mentions)
FMS-Grenada, 1983
50 Newark Ave #108, Belleville, 973-751-4818

Bonaventura, Lisa Marie (3 mentions)
U of Cincinnati, 1986 *Certification:* Internal Medicine
2345 Lamington Rd #104, Bedminster, 908-781-9661

Boorujy, Dean P. (3 mentions)
Philadelphia Coll of Osteopathic Med, 1993
Certification: Family Medicine
65 E Northfield Rd #H, Livingston, 973-422-9595

Brodman, Richard Rory (3 mentions)
SUNY-Downstate Med Coll, 1973
Certification: Internal Medicine, Rheumatology
345 Somerset St, North Plainfield, 908-561-7440

Brunnquell, Stephen Boyle (4 mentions)
New Jersey Med Sch, 1989 *Certification:* Internal Medicine
24 Elm St, Harrington Park, 201-784-0123
274 County Rd #A, Tenafly, 201-568-0493

Carson, Jeffrey Lee (6 mentions)
Hahnemann U, 1977 *Certification:* Internal Medicine
125 Paterson St, New Brunswick, 732-235-6500

Catanese, Betty (4 mentions)
New York Med Coll, 1983
315 E Main St, Somerville, 908-722-3442

Davidoff, Bernard Mark (4 mentions)
Columbia U, 1973 *Certification:* Internal Medicine
101 Madison Ave, Morristown, 973-267-7770
144 Speedwell Ave, Morristown, 973-267-7770

Davis, Lawrence J. (4 mentions)
Johns Hopkins U, 1991 *Certification:* Internal Medicine
177 N Dean St #207, Englewood, 201-567-0446

Ferreira, Gabriela Simoes (3 mentions)
Dartmouth Coll, 1992 *Certification:* Internal Medicine
125 Paterson Sr #5100-A, New Brunswick, 732-235-6968

Fine, Alan Ira (3 mentions)
New York Med Coll, 1962 *Certification:* Internal Medicine
8 Mountain Blvd, Warren, 908-561-8600

Fortunato, F. Dana (3 mentions)
New Jersey Med Sch, 1975
Certification: Internal Medicine, Pulmonary Disease
127 Pine St, Montclair, 973-744-4075

Gold, Jeffrey Lawrence (6 mentions)
FMS-Mexico, 1977 *Certification:* Internal Medicine
1135 Broad St #205, Clifton, 973-471-8850

Granet, Kenneth Mark (11 mentions)
SUNY-Downstate Med Coll, 1984 *Certification:* Internal Medicine
615 Hope Rd Bldg #3, Eatontown, 732-542-3030

Gribbon, John J. (6 mentions)
New Jersey Med Sch, 1977 *Certification:* Internal Medicine
62 S Fullerton Ave, Montclair, 973-744-3382

Haggerty, Mary Ann (4 mentions)
New Jersey Med Sch, 1979
Certification: Geriatric Medicine, Internal Medicine
90 Bergen St, Newark, 973-972-1880

Hart, Karen (3 mentions)
Washington U, 1997 *Certification:* Internal Medicine
301 Godwin Ave #1, Midland Park, 201-444-4526

Holtz, Howard Alan (6 mentions)
New Jersey Med Sch, 1981
Certification: Geriatric Medicine, Internal Medicine
1500 Pleasant Valley Way #205, West Orange, 973-669-9797

Hope, Lisa Dawn (3 mentions)
New Jersey Med Sch, 2002 *Certification:* Internal Medicine
301 Godwin Ave #1, Midland Park, 201-444-4526

Jain, Deepak Kumar (3 mentions)
FMS-Grenada, 1998 *Certification:* Internal Medicine
75 Veronica Ave #204, Somerset, 732-828-0550
111 Union Valley Rd #203, Monroe Township, 609-655-2255

Katz, Manny David (4 mentions)
Albert Einstein Coll of Med, 1997 *Certification:* Internal Medicine
25 Rockwood Pl, Englewood, 201-568-3335

Kloos, Thomas Hans (4 mentions)
U of Louisville, 1979 *Certification:* Internal Medicine
8 Mountain Blvd, Warren, 908-561-8600

Krupp, Edward (5 mentions)
New Jersey Sch of Osteopathic Med, 1999
Certification: Internal Medicine
29 The Crescent, Montclair, 973-783-0800

Marella, Gregg Gerard (3 mentions)
Pennsylvania State U, 1993 *Certification:* Internal Medicine
19 E Main St #1, Mendham, 973-543-6505

Maron, Scott Michael (3 mentions)
Baylor U, 1992 *Certification:* Internal Medicine
10 James St #150, Florham Park, 973-539-1155

Neiman, Deborah Lynn (3 mentions)
New York Med Coll, 1984 *Certification:* Internal Medicine
311 Omni Dr, Hillsborough, 908-281-0632
1 Robertson Dr, Bedminster, 908-470-9377

Pontecorvo, Martin Joseph (3 mentions)
New York Coll of Osteopathic Med, 1988
Certification: Internal Medicine
1072 Valley Rd, Stirling, 908-604-8464
256 Columbia Tpke #109, Florham Park, 973-514-1767

Postighone, Carl Joseph (8 mentions)
New York Coll of Osteopathic Med, 1988
Certification: Internal Medicine
1072 Valley Rd, Stirling, 908-604-8464
256 Columbia Tpke #109, Florham Park, 973-514-1767

Ramos, Maria (4 mentions)
FMS-Dominica, 1988 *Certification:* Internal Medicine
147 Main St #6, Lodi, 973-777-2888

Renna, Carmen Mary (3 mentions)
Albert Einstein Coll of Med, 1981 *Certification:* Internal Medicine
95 Madison Ave #405, Morristown, 973-829-9998

Rommer, James Andrew (7 mentions)
Cornell U, 1978 *Certification:* Internal Medicine
349 E Northfield Rd #110, Livingston, 973-992-2227

Russo, John Anthony (5 mentions)
FMS-Mexico, 1981 *Certification:* Internal Medicine
1500 Pleasant Valley Way #201, West Orange, 973-736-8119

Schiffner, Craig Alan (3 mentions)
George Washington U, 1977 *Certification:* Internal Medicine
95 Madison Ave #A00, Morristown, 973-538-1388

Schmidt, Alvin Manuel (5 mentions)
FMS-Spain, 1978
741 Northfield Ave #100-B, West Orange, 973-325-0006

Schwartzer, Thomas A. (6 mentions)
Robert W Johnson Med Sch, 1993
Certification: Internal Medicine
75 Veronica Ave #204, Somerset, 732-828-0550
111 Union Valley Rd #203, Monroe Township, 609-655-2255

Shapiro, Jonathan Allan (5 mentions)
New York U, 1973
25 Rockwood Pl, Englewood, 201-568-3335

Simon, Susan Marie (3 mentions)
Boston U, 1996 *Certification:* Internal Medicine
225 May St #E, Edison, 732-661-2020

Sutter, David Brand (3 mentions)
Georgetown U, 1973 *Certification:* Internal Medicine
6 Prospect St, Midland Park, 201-670-0002

Tamres, David Michael (4 mentions)
Mount Sinai Sch of Med, 1996 *Certification:* Internal Medicine
95 Madison Ave #405, Morristown, 973-829-9998

Weine, Gary Robert (3 mentions)
Cornell U, 1976 *Certification:* Internal Medicine
95 Madison Ave #405, Morristown, 973-829-9998

Nephrology

Abramovici, Mirel (5 mentions)
FMS-Belgium, 1985 *Certification:* Internal Medicine, Nephrology
140 Grand Ave #201, Englewood, 201-567-5787

Ackad, Alexandre-Samir V. (7 mentions)
FMS-Egypt, 1964 *Certification:* Internal Medicine, Nephrology
44 Godwin Ave #301, Midland Park, 201-447-0013

Arbes, Spiros Michael (5 mentions)
FMS-Philippines, 1982
Certification: Internal Medicine, Nephrology
6 Industrial Way W #B, Eatontown, 732-460-1200

Aronoff, Benjamin William (6 mentions)
Albert Einstein Coll of Med, 1999
Certification: Internal Medicine, Nephrology
870 Palisade Ave #202, Teaneck, 201-836-0897

Bell, Alvin (5 mentions)
Temple U, 1978 *Certification:* Internal Medicine, Nephrology
129 Grove St, Montclair, 973-783-6110

Byrd, Lawrence H. (8 mentions)
Med Coll of Pennsylvania, 1973
Certification: Internal Medicine, Nephrology
22 Old Short Hills Rd #212, Livingston, 973-994-4550

Chandran, Chandra B. (6 mentions)
FMS-India, 1971 *Certification:* Internal Medicine, Nephrology
246 Hamburg Pike, Wayne, 973-653-3366

Covit, Andrew B. (10 mentions)
SUNY-Downstate Med Coll, 1979
Certification: Internal Medicine, Nephrology
8 Old Bridge Tpke, South River, 732-390-4888
901 W Main St, Freehold, 732-625-0707

Fine, Paul Leonard (14 mentions)
Yale U, 1979 *Certification:* Internal Medicine, Nephrology
2 Franklin Pl, Morristown, 973-267-7673

Flis, Raymond S. (8 mentions)
A T Still U, 1971 *Certification:* Internal Medicine, Nephrology
6 Industrial Way W #B, Eatontown, 732-460-1200

Goldstein, Carl S. (9 mentions)
Washington U, 1978 *Certification:* Internal Medicine, Nephrology
215 North Ave W, Westfield, 908-232-4321

Grodstein, Gerald (7 mentions)
SUNY-Downstate Med Coll, 1974
Certification: Internal Medicine, Nephrology
177 N Dean St, Englewood, 201-567-0446
6701 Bergenline Ave, West New York, 201-567-0446

Gudis, Steven Mark (6 mentions)
Mount Sinai Sch of Med, 1977
Certification: Internal Medicine, Nephrology
121 Center Grove Rd, Randolph, 973-361-3737

Haratz, Alan Bert (5 mentions)
Hahnemann U, 1979
Certification: Internal Medicine, Nephrology
6 Industrial Way W #B, Eatontown, 732-460-1200

Joseph, Rosy E. (7 mentions)
Columbia U, 1990 *Certification:* Internal Medicine, Nephrology
160 Overlook Ave, Hackensack, 201-646-0110

Kabis, Suzanne Mechanic (14 mentions)
Robert W Johnson Med Sch, 1979
Certification: Internal Medicine, Nephrology
1350 Hamilton St, Somerset, 732-246-2626

Kozlowski, Jeffrey P. (16 mentions)
New York U, 1978 *Certification:* Internal Medicine, Nephrology
44 Godwin Ave #301, Midland Park, 201-447-0013

Liss, Kenneth A. (5 mentions)
Philadelphia Coll of Osteopathic Med, 1990
6 Industrial Way W #B, Eatontown, 732-460-1200

Lyman, Neil Warren (14 mentions)
Albert Einstein Coll of Med, 1973
Certification: Internal Medicine, Nephrology
769 Northfield Ave #200, West Orange, 973-736-2212

Manning, Eric Carlyle (6 mentions)
U of California-Davis, 1985
Certification: Internal Medicine, Nephrology
719 US Hwy 206, Hillsborough, 908-904-9055

Mehta, Sudhir Harkisandas (5 mentions)
FMS-India, 1972 *Certification:* Internal Medicine, Nephrology
201 Union Ave #B, Bridgewater, 908-722-0106

Miele, Bevon David (10 mentions)
FMS-Israel, 1983 *Certification:* Internal Medicine, Nephrology
2 Kings Ct #207, Flemington, 908-806-4466

Notkin, Joel (11 mentions)
New York U, 1959
526 Bloomfield Ave, Caldwell, 973-226-0500

Price, Barbara Ellen (8 mentions)
Tufts U, 1989 *Certification:* Internal Medicine, Nephrology
2 Franklin Pl, Morristown, 973-267-7673

Stack, Jay Irving (8 mentions)
U of Pennsylvania, 1976
Certification: Internal Medicine, Nephrology
2 Franklin Pl, Morristown, 973-267-7673

Thomsen, Stephen (5 mentions)
FMS-Italy, 1977 *Certification:* Internal Medicine, Nephrology
123 Highland Ave #G3, Glen Ridge, 973-429-1881
510 31st St, Union City, 201-866-3322

Weiss, Lynne Shari (5 mentions)
Hahnemann U, 1974
Certification: Pediatric Nephrology, Pediatrics
89 French St, New Brunswick, 732-235-6230

Weizman, Howard Barry (12 mentions)
Albert Einstein Coll of Med, 1982
Certification: Internal Medicine, Nephrology
44 Godwin Ave, Midland Park, 201-447-0013

Neurological Surgery

Arginteanu, Marc Shaun (8 mentions)
Certification: Neurological Surgery
309 Engle St #6, Englewood, 201-569-7737
1158 5th Ave, New York, NY, 212-410-6990

Beyerl, Brian David (14 mentions)
Johns Hopkins U, 1980 *Certification:* Neurological Surgery
310 Madison Ave, Morristown, 973-285-7800

Clemente, Roderick J. (15 mentions)
FMS-Italy, 1978 *Certification:* Neurological Surgery
96 Gates Ave, Montclair, 973-744-7111

Hodosh, Richard Michael (12 mentions)
U of Cincinnati, 1972 *Certification:* Neurological Surgery
99 Beauvoir Ave, Summit, 908-522-4979

Hubschmann, Otakar R. (10 mentions)
FMS-Czech Republic, 1967 *Certification:* Neurological Surgery
101 Old Short Hills Rd #409, West Orange, 973-322-6732

Kaptain, George John (10 mentions)
U of Virginia, 1993 *Certification:* Neurological Surgery
20 Prospect Ave #907, Hackensack, 201-342-2550
680 Kinderkamaek Rd #300, Oradell, 201-342-2550

Knightly, John Joseph (26 mentions)
New Jersey Med Sch, 1985 *Certification:* Neurological Surgery
310 Madison Ave, Morristown, 973-285-7800

Koziol, Joseph M. (11 mentions)
Robert W Johnson Med Sch, 1983
Certification: Neurological Surgery
101 Old Short Hills Rd #409, West Orange, 888-724-7123

More, Jay (9 mentions)
New York Med Coll, 1987 *Certification:* Neurological Surgery
1952 US Hwy 22, Bound Brook, 732-302-1720

Nosko, Michael Gerrik (9 mentions)
FMS-Canada, 1982 *Certification:* Neurological Surgery
125 Paterson St #2100, New Brunswick, 732-235-7756

Raab, Rajnik Weerackody (8 mentions)
SUNY-Downstate Med Coll, 1997
1 W Ridgewood Ave #208, Paramus, 201-445-8666
1680 Route 23 N, Wayne, 973-633-1122

Vingan, Roy David (9 mentions)
SUNY-Downstate Med Coll, 1985
Certification: Neurological Surgery
20 Prospect Ave #907, Hackensack, 201-342-2550
680 Kinderkamack Rd #300, Oradell, 201-342-2550

Zampella, Edward Joseph (11 mentions)
U of Alabama, 1982 *Certification:* Neurological Surgery
310 Madison Ave, Morristown, 973-285-7800

Neurology

Alweiss, Gary Steven (9 mentions)
Mount Sinai Sch of Med, 1988 *Certification:* Neurology
25 Rockwood Pl #110, Englewood, 201-894-5805

Angels, Robert Raymond (4 mentions)
Albert Einstein Coll of Med, 1983 *Certification:* Neurology
211 Essex St #401, Hackensack, 201-646-1200

Behar, Roger (7 mentions)
New York Med Coll, 1980
Certification: Internal Medicine, Neurology
9 Center Dr #130, Monroe, 609-395-7615
51 Veronica Ave, Somerset, 732-246-1311
601 Ewing St #B-5, Princeton, 609-497-0300

Blady, David (20 mentions)
SUNY-Downstate Med Coll, 1983 *Certification:* Neurology
230 Sherman Ave #K, Glen Ridge, 973-743-9555
1100 Clifton Ave, Clifton, 973-743-9555

Cerny, Kenneth Rudolph (5 mentions)
Columbia U, 1976 *Certification:* Neurology
310 Madison Ave #120, Morristown, 973-285-1446

Charles, James A. (4 mentions)
New Jersey Med Sch, 1978
Certification: Clinical Neurophysiology, Neurology
956 Kennedy Blvd #1, Bayonne, 201-858-2457
8841 Kennedy Blvd, North Bergen, 201-854-6614

Chodosh, Eliot Howard (4 mentions)
FMS-Mexico, 1981 *Certification:* Neurology
220 Hamburg Tpke #16, Wayne, 973-942-4778

Citak, Kenneth Anton (7 mentions)
New York U, 1986 *Certification:* Neurology
1200 E Ridgewood Ave, Ridgewood, 201-444-0868

Clark-Brown, Ruth L. (4 mentions)
New Jersey Med Sch, 1986 *Certification:* Neurology
185 Central Ave #611, East Orange, 973-678-5607

Cook, Stuart Donald (4 mentions)
U of Vermont, 1962 *Certification:* Neurology
90 Bergen St #8100, Newark, 973-972-2550

Deutsch, Alan David (4 mentions)
New Jersey Sch of Osteopathic Med, 1987 *Certification:* Neurology
1944 State Route 33 #206, Neptune, 732-774-8282
190 Jack Martin Blvd Bldg B-3, Brick, 732-785-1500

Diamond, Mark Steven (10 mentions)
Jefferson Med Coll, 1977 *Certification:* Neurology
310 Madison Ave #120, Morristown, 973-285-1446

Englestein, Eric Steven (8 mentions)
New Jersey Med Sch, 1978 *Certification:* Neurology
369 W Blackwell St, Dover, 973-361-7606
350 Sparta Ave Bldg A, Sparta, 973-729-1111
254 Mountain Ave #105, Hackettstown, 908-850-5505

Fellman, Damon Maurice (11 mentions)
U of Cincinnati, 1970
Certification: Neurology, Vascular Neurology
211 Essex St #202, Hackensack, 201-488-1515

Fox, Stuart Warren (11 mentions)
Cornell U, 1975 *Certification:* Internal Medicine, Neurology
310 Madison Ave #120, Morristown, 973-285-1446

Friedlander, Devin (16 mentions)
Certification: Neurology
51 Veronica Ave, Somerset, 732-246-1311

Gainey, Patrick Joseph (12 mentions)
Robert W Johnson Med Sch, 1988 *Certification:* Neurology
51 Veronicas Ave #202, Somerset, 732-246-1311
9 Centre Dr #130, Monroe Township, 609-395-7615

Gilson, Noah Robert (7 mentions)
Loyola U Chicago, 1982 *Certification:* Neurology
107 Monmouth Rd #110, West Long Branch, 732-935-1850

Herman, Martin Neal (4 mentions)
Northwestern U, 1964 *Certification:* Neurology
107 Monmouth Rd #110, West Long Branch, 732-935-1850

Holland, Neil Robert (12 mentions)
FMS-United Kingdom, 1991 *Certification:* Clinical
   Neurophysiology, Neurology, Neuromuscular Medicine
107 Monmouth Rd #110, West Long Branch, 732-935-1850

Kailas, Michael George (4 mentions)
FMS-Italy, 1980
699 Teaneck Rd, Teaneck, 201-287-0300

Knep, Stanley J. (9 mentions)
FMS-South Africa, 1965 *Certification:* Neurology
905 Alwood Rd #105, Clifton, 973-471-3680

Lequerica, Steve Anthony (4 mentions)
Boston U, 1981 *Certification:* Neurology
905 Alwood Rd #105, Clifton, 973-471-3680

Levin, Kenneth A. (6 mentions)
Indiana U, 1982 *Certification:* Neurology
1200 E Ridgewood Ave, Ridgewood, 201-444-0868

Levy, Kirk Jay (6 mentions)
Stony Brook U, 1993
Certification: Clinical Neurophysiology, Neurology
25 Rockwood Pl #110, Englewood, 201-894-5805

Lijtmaer, Hugo N. (5 mentions)
FMS-Argentina, 1968 *Certification:* Neurology
1200 E Ridgewood Ave, Ridgewood, 201-444-0868

Morse, Brian J. (4 mentions)
Midwestern U Chicago Coll of Osteopathic Med, 2000
Certification: Neurology
95 Madison Ave #103, Morristown, 973-455-7444

Motiwala, Rajeev S. (6 mentions)
FMS-India, 1979 *Certification:* Neurology
211 Essex St #402, Hackensack, 201-343-6604
710 W 168th St #246, New York, NY, 212-305-6876

Patel, Poorvi K. (4 mentions)
FMS-India, 1972 *Certification:* Neurology with Special
   Qualifications in Child Neurology, Pediatrics
81 Two Bridges Rd, Fairfield, 973-569-6370
186 Rochelle Ave, Rochelle, 201-843-9713

Perron, Reed C. (7 mentions)
U of Rochester, 1966 *Certification:* Neurology
1200 E Ridgewood Ave, Ridgewood, 201-444-0868

Potluri, Srinivasa Rao (10 mentions)
FMS-India, 1994
Certification: Clinical Neurophysiology, Neurology
676 Route 202 - 206 N, Bridgewater, 908-218-1180

Raab, Vicki Ellen (4 mentions)
U of Texas-San Antonio, 1984 *Certification:* Neurology
1405 Hwy 35 N #103, Ocean, 732-663-1161
1640 Hwy 88 W, Brick, 732-202-1411

Robinton, John Edward (6 mentions)
Cornell U, 1978
Certification: Clinical Neurophysiology, Neurology
33 N Fullerton Ave, Montclair, 973-783-6303

Rosenberg, Richard Seth (5 mentions)
FMS-Israel, 1981 *Certification:* Internal Medicine, Neurology
310 Madison Ave #120, Morristown, 973-285-1446

Ruderman, Marvin Ira (9 mentions)
Columbia U, 1976 *Certification:* Neurology
1099 Bloomfield Ave, West Caldwell, 973-439-7000

Schanzer, Bernard (6 mentions)
FMS-Belgium, 1962 *Certification:* Neurology
700 N Broad St, Elizabeth, 908-354-3994

Sobelman, Joseph S. (5 mentions)
FMS-Mexico, 1982
22 Old Short Hills Rd #106, Livingston, 973-994-1123

Vaccaro, John J. (10 mentions)
Eastern Virginia Med Sch, 1992 *Certification:* Neurology
230 Sherman Ave #K, Glen Ridge, 973-743-9555
1100 Clifton Ave, Clifton, 973-743-9555

Van Engel, Daniel R. (6 mentions)
SUNY-Upstate Med U, 1973 *Certification:* Neurology
1200 E Ridgewood Ave East Wing 2nd Fl, Ridgewood,
   201-444-0868

Vigman, Melvin Paul (5 mentions)
Hahnemann U, 1964 *Certification:* Neurology
47 Maple St #104, Summit, 908-277-2722

Willner, Joseph Harrison (5 mentions)
New York U, 1970 *Certification:* Neurology
25 Rockwood Pl #110, Englewood, 201-894-5805

Obstetrics/Gynecology

Aguilar, Raul (3 mentions)
Ponce Sch of Med, 1983 *Certification:* Obstetrics & Gynecology
129 Washington St #200, Hoboken, 201-798-4044

Alam, Abu Sajjadul (4 mentions)
FMS-Bangladesh, 1972 *Certification:* Obstetrics & Gynecology
779 Springfield Ave, Summit, 908-273-5907

Bissinger, Craig Lawrence (5 mentions)
Ohio State U, 1982 *Certification:* Obstetrics & Gynecology
50 Cherry Hill Rd #303, Parsippany, 973-335-8500

Bochner, Ronnie Z. (7 mentions)
Mount Sinai Sch of Med, 1981
Certification: Obstetrics & Gynecology
3270 State Rt 27 #2200, Kendall Park, 732-422-8989
761 River Ave #D, Lakewood, 732-905-6466
224 Taylors Mills Rd, Manalapan, 732-431-4041

Bowers, Mamie Sue (3 mentions)
Robert W Johnson Med Sch, 1985
Certification: Obstetrics & Gynecology
1100 Wescott Dr #105, Flemington, 908-788-6469

Butler, David George (5 mentions)
SUNY-Downstate Med Coll, 1965
Certification: Obstetrics & Gynecology
420 Grand Ave, Englewood, 201-871-4040

Cernadas, Maureen (3 mentions)
Robert W Johnson Med Sch, 1991
Certification: Obstetrics & Gynecology
561 Cranbury Rd, East Brunswick, 732-257-0081
812 Courtyard Dr, Hillsborough, 908-725-2510

Chervenak, Donald Michael (4 mentions)
Boston U, 1980 *Certification:* Obstetrics & Gynecology
15 James St, Florham Park, 973-822-8181
102 Ferry St, Newark, 973-344-9104

Cooperman, Alan Stewart (4 mentions)
FMS-Italy, 1968 *Certification:* Obstetrics & Gynecology
235 Millburn Ave, Millburn, 973-467-9440

Crane, Stephen Edward (4 mentions)
New Jersey Med Sch, 1986 *Certification:* Obstetrics & Gynecology
776 Northfield Ave #201, West Orange, 973-731-7707
825 Bloomfield Ave #103, Verona, 973-239-5010

Daly, Mary Veronica (4 mentions)
Wake Forest U, 1979 *Certification:* Obstetrics & Gynecology
101 Madison Ave #405, Morristown, 973-267-7272
20 Commerce Blvd #1-C, Succasunna, 973-927-1188

David, Gwen Lynita (3 mentions)
U of North Carolina, 1989 *Certification:* Obstetrics & Gynecology
95 Northfield Ave, West Orange, 973-736-4505

De Graaff, Doreen E. (4 mentions)
New Jersey Med Sch, 1988 *Certification:* Obstetrics & Gynecology
22 Old Short Hills Rd #112, Livingston, 973-740-1330

De Grande, Gary C. (6 mentions)
FMS-Mexico, 1977 *Certification:* Obstetrics & Gynecology
33 N Fullerton Ave, Montclair, 973-744-2226

De Marsico, Richard (4 mentions)
Georgetown U, 1974 *Certification:* Obstetrics & Gynecology
33 N Fullerton Ave, Montclair, 973-744-2226

Dias-Martin, Karen (3 mentions)
U of Cincinnati, 1984 *Certification:* Obstetrics & Gynecology
200 Highland Ave #230, Glen Ridge, 973-743-8585

Englert, Christopher A. (5 mentions)
Certification: Obstetrics & Gynecology
420 Grand Ave, Englewood, 201-871-4040

Forster, Judith Karen (3 mentions)
New Jersey Med Sch, 1993 *Certification:* Obstetrics & Gynecology
4575 Route 27, Kingston, 609-683-7979

Friedman, Harvey Y. (3 mentions)
New York U, 1981 *Certification:* Obstetrics & Gynecology
401 S Van Brunt St #405, Englewood, 201-871-4346

Gliksman, Michele I. (3 mentions)
New York U, 1990 *Certification:* Obstetrics & Gynecology
155 N Washington Ave, Bergenfield, 201-384-8310

Goldberg, Michael Ira (5 mentions)
FMS-Italy, 1970
Certification: Gynecologic Oncology, Obstetrics & Gynecology
205 May St #201, Edison, 732-661-9225
3 Hospital Plaza #415, Old Bridge, 732-760-2282

Graebe, Robert Alan (4 mentions)
FMS-Mexico, 1977 *Certification:* Obstetrics & Gynecology
1131 Broad St #104, Shrewsbury, 732-542-8118

Gross, Arthur H. (6 mentions)
Brown U, 1992 *Certification:* Obstetrics & Gynecology
370 Grand Ave #202, Englewood, 201-894-9599

Hammond, Kelly Condon (3 mentions)
Brown U, 1991 *Certification:* Obstetrics & Gynecology
180 White Rd #209, Little Silver, 732-842-0673
1 Bethany Rd #31, Hazlet, 732-264-7687

Iammatteo, Matthew Daniel (15 mentions)
FMS-Dominica, 1985 *Certification:* Obstetrics & Gynecology
111 Madison Ave #311, Morristown, 973-971-9950

Ivan, Joseph Robert (3 mentions)
New Jersey Med Sch, 1989 *Certification:* Obstetrics & Gynecology
784 Chimney Rock Rd #G, Martinsville, 732-271-1771

Jacoby, Dana Brian (3 mentions)
Hahnemann U, 1993 *Certification:* Obstetrics & Gynecology
766 Shrewsbury Ave, Tinton Falls, 732-530-4545

Kaye, Alissa Ellen (4 mentions)
Jefferson Med Coll, 2000 *Certification:* Obstetrics & Gynecology
31 S Union Ave, Cranford, 908-272-8676

Kaye, Gary Lenard (3 mentions)
Rosalind Franklin U, 1974 *Certification:* Obstetrics & Gynecology
31 S Union Ave, Cranford, 908-272-8676

Klachko, Daria Anna (6 mentions)
New Jersey Med Sch, 1993 *Certification:* Obstetrics & Gynecology
769 Northfield Ave #236, West Orange, 973-325-5670

Ladocsi, Lewis Thomas (3 mentions)
New Jersey Med Sch, 1970 *Certification:* Obstetrics & Gynecology
776 Northfield Ave #201, West Orange, 973-731-7707

Lambert-Woolley, Margaret (3 mentions)
New Jersey Med Sch, 1986 *Certification:* Obstetrics & Gynecology
240 Wall St #300, West Long Branch, 732-229-1288

Lobraico, Dominick (3 mentions)
Philadelphia Coll of Osteopathic Med, 1990
Certification: Obstetrics & Gynecology
1019 Broadway, West Long Branch, 732-229-6797
911 E COunty Line Rd, Lakewood, 732-367-9299

Lundberg, John Lawrence (3 mentions)
SUNY-Downstate Med Coll, 1988
Certification: Obstetrics & Gynecology
3270 Route 27 #2200, Kendall Park, 732-422-8989
761 River Ave #D, Lakewood, 732-905-6466
224 Taylors Mills Rd, Manalapan, 732-431-4041

Myers, Mary Kay (4 mentions)
Certification: Obstetrics & Gynecology
80 Eisenhower Dr 3200 #200, Paramus, 201-843-2800

Patrusky, Karen L. (5 mentions)
Certification: Obstetrics & Gynecology
401 S Van Brunt St, Englewood, 201-871-4346

Pregenzer, Gerard Joseph (3 mentions)
New Jersey Med Sch, 1983 *Certification:* Obstetrics & Gynecology
65 Mountain Blvd Ext #201, Warren, 732-469-9400

Rathauser, Robert Hans (4 mentions)
New York U, 1979 *Certification:* Obstetrics & Gynecology
3270 State Rt 27 #2200, Kendall Park, 732-422-8989
761 River Ave #D, Lakewood, 732-905-6466
224 Taylors Mills Rd, Manalapan, 732-431-4041

Rezvani, Fred F. (5 mentions)
FMS-Grenada, 1983 *Certification:* Obstetrics & Gynecology
119 Prospect St, Ridgewood, 201-444-1600

Rubenstein, Andrew Frank (4 mentions)
Hahnemann U, 1990 *Certification:* Obstetrics & Gynecology
82 E Allendale Rd #1A, Saddle River, 201-934-5050

Russo, Thomas Orlando (3 mentions)
New York Med Coll, 1987 *Certification:* Obstetrics & Gynecology
80 Eisenhower Dr, Paramus, 201-843-2800

Thani, Suresh Radhakishin (3 mentions)
FMS-Jamaica, 1977 *Certification:* Obstetrics & Gynecology
566 Nye Ave, Irvington, 973-399-9155

Van Horn, Lawrence Gordon (3 mentions)
New Jersey Med Sch, 1997 *Certification:* Obstetrics & Gynecology
1924 State Route 35 #122, Wall Township, 732-280-8088

Weiss, Nofit (3 mentions)
Albert Einstein Coll of Med, 1995
286 Engle St, Englewood, 201-569-6190

Ophthalmology

Angioletti, Lee Mitchell (3 mentions)
New York Med Coll, 1989 *Certification:* Ophthalmology
1617 Palisade Ave, Fort Lee, 201-947-1900

Benedetto, Dominick A. (3 mentions)
U of Florida, 1975 *Certification:* Ophthalmology
124 Ave B, Bayonne, 201-436-1150
111 Madison Ave #301, Morristown, 973-984-9798

Bontempo, Carl Peter (3 mentions)
Hahnemann U, 1979 *Certification:* Ophthalmology
279 3rd Ave #204, Long Branch, 732-222-7373
100 Commons Way #230, Holmdel, 732-796-7140

Boozan, John Matthew (4 mentions)
U of Cincinnati, 1983 *Certification:* Ophthalmology
33 Overlook Rd #407, Summit, 908-277-1166
776 E 3rd Ave #3, Roselle, 908-298-8558

Brown, Robert Stephen (4 mentions)
Boston U, 1994 *Certification:* Ophthalmology
751 Teaneck Rd #B, Teaneck, 201-833-0006

Caputo, Anthony R. (4 mentions)
FMS-Italy, 1969 *Certification:* Ophthalmology
556 Eagle Rock Ave, Roseland, 973-228-3111
1 Clara Maass Dr, Belleville, 973-450-2000

Chen, Lucy (5 mentions)
Boston U, 1985 *Certification:* Internal Medicine, Ophthalmology
95 Madison Ave #301, Morristown, 973-540-8814

Cohen, Steven B. (3 mentions)
New York U, 1978 *Certification:* Ophthalmology
349 E Northfield Rd #100, Livingston, 973-716-0123
95 Madison Ave #A-03, Morristown, 973-716-0123

Confino, Joel (3 mentions)
Albert Einstein Coll of Med, 1980 *Certification:* Ophthalmology
592 Springfield Ave, Westfield, 908-789-8999

Davidson, Lawrence Marc (4 mentions)
SUNY-Downstate Med Coll, 1969 *Certification:* Ophthalmology
825 Bloomfield Ave, Verona, 973-239-4000

Del Negro, Ralph Gerard (5 mentions)
New Jersey Sch of Osteopathic Med, 1986
1809 Corlies Ave, Neptune, 732-774-5566

Ditkoff, Jonathan W. (7 mentions)
SUNY-Upstate Med U, 1989 *Certification:* Ophthalmology
108 Broughton Ave, Bloomfield, 973-743-1331

Edison, Barry J. (5 mentions)
New York Coll of Osteopathic Med, 1996
142 Hwy #107, Eatontown, 732-542-0300
100 Drumpoint Rd, Brick, 732-477-7190

Eichler, Joel David (3 mentions)
George Washington U, 1988 *Certification:* Ophthalmology
5 Franklin Ave #209, Belleville, 973-751-6060
66 Sunset Strip #107, Succasunna, 973-584-4451
124 Ave B #1, Bayonne, 201-436-1150
46 Eagle Rock Ave, East Hanover, 973-560-1500
108-112 Broughton Ave, Bloomfield, 973-743-1331

Engel, Mark Leslie (4 mentions)
SUNY-Downstate Med Coll, 1971 *Certification:* Ophthalmology
733 N Beers St #U4, Holmdel, 732-739-0707

Fechtner, Robert D. (3 mentions)
U of Michigan, 1982 *Certification:* Ophthalmology
90 Bergen St #6100, Newark, 973-972-2030

Friedberg, Mark Alan (3 mentions)
U of Pennsylvania, 1986 *Certification:* Ophthalmology
70 E Front St, Red Bank, 732-741-0858
7 State Route 27 #101, Edison, 732-494-6720

Frohman, Larry Philip (3 mentions)
U of Pennsylvania, 1980 *Certification:* Ophthalmology
556 Eagle Rock Ave #206, Roseland, 973-972-2108
90 Bergen St #6100, Newark, 973-972-2026

Glatt, Herbert Leonard (4 mentions)
FMS-Mexico, 1979 *Certification:* Ophthalmology
1025 Broad St, Bloomfield, 973-338-1001

Gordon, Stephen Jay (3 mentions)
New York Med Coll, 1977 *Certification:* Ophthalmology
317 Cleveland Ave, Highland Park, 732-545-0362
579-A Cranbury Rd #101, East Brunswick, 732-254-0097

Greenfield, Donald Alan (3 mentions)
Temple U, 1968 *Certification:* Ophthalmology
288 Millburn Ave, Millburn, 973-912-9100

Han, Stella I. (3 mentions)
Certification: Ophthalmology
4 Cornwall Ct, East Brunswick, 732-613-9191
678 US Hwy 202/206 #2, Bridgewater, 908-203-9009

Henick, Arlene Michele (3 mentions)
Albert Einstein Coll of Med, 1990 *Certification:* Ophthalmology
301 Bridge Plaza N, Fort Lee, 208-947-1786

Hersh, Peter Stephen (3 mentions)
Johns Hopkins U, 1982 *Certification:* Ophthalmology
90 Bergen St #6100, Newark, 973-972-2034
300 Frank W Burr Blvd #71, Teaneck, 201-692-9434

Hoffman, David Sandor (3 mentions)
Med Coll of Pennsylvania, 1983 *Certification:* Ophthalmology
803 Springfield Ave, Summit, 908-273-9500

Holtz, S. Jerome (7 mentions)
SUNY-Upstate Med U, 1968 *Certification:* Ophthalmology
108 Broughton Ave, Bloomfield, 973-743-1331

Kahn, Walter J. (7 mentions)
U of Chicago, 1959 *Certification:* Ophthalmology
70 E Front St, Red Bank, 732-741-0858

Kazam, Ezra Samir (4 mentions)
SUNY-Downstate Med Coll, 1973 *Certification:* Ophthalmology
2 Washington Pl, Morristown, 973-267-8755

Krawitz, Mark Jeffrey (4 mentions)
Jefferson Med Coll, 1980 *Certification:* Ophthalmology
65 Mountain Blvd Ext #105, Warren, 732-356-6200
213 Stelton Rd, Piscataway, 732-752-9090

Kristan, Ronald W. (9 mentions)
New York U, 1980 *Certification:* Ophthalmology
279 3rd Ave #204, Long Branch, 732-222-7373
100 Commons Way #230, Holmdel, 732-796-7140

Lappin, Harold Stephen (4 mentions)
New York U, 1966 *Certification:* Ophthalmology
500 Willow Grove St, Hackettstown, 908-852-2220

Lilley, Eileen Robin (4 mentions)
Duke U, 1990 *Certification:* Ophthalmology
201 Union Ave Bldg 2 #F, Bridgewater, 908-231-1110

Liva, Douglas Francis (3 mentions)
U of Miami, 1981 *Certification:* Ophthalmology
1 W Ridgewood Ave, Paramus, 201-444-7770

Lopatynsky, Marta Oksana (7 mentions)
Albany Med Coll, 1986 *Certification:* Ophthalmology
261 James St #2D, Morristown, 973-984-3937

Mang, Justin (3 mentions)
Jefferson Med Coll, 1969 *Certification:* Ophthalmology
240 Williamson St #505, Elizabeth, 908-289-0250

Marano, Matthew Joseph, Jr. (6 mentions)
George Washington U, 1978 *Certification:* Ophthalmology
556 Eagle Rock Ave #104, Roseland, 973-226-4211
120 Millburn Ave #204, Millburn, 973-467-1810
306 Martin Luther King Jr Blvd, Newark, 973-877-5000

Medford, David Joel (3 mentions)
New Jersey Med Sch, 1984 *Certification:* Ophthalmology
95 Madison Ave #400, Morristown, 973-984-5005
81 Northfield Ave 1st Fl, West Orange, 973-736-3322

Mickey, Kevin John (5 mentions)
New Jersey Med Sch, 1986 *Certification:* Ophthalmology
57 Willowbrook Blvd, Wayne, 973-256-4111

Mirsky, Robert Gary (4 mentions)
Virginia Commonwealth U, 1975 *Certification:* Ophthalmology
745 Northfield Ave, West Orange, 973-736-1016

Mund, Michael Leonard (3 mentions)
SUNY-Downstate Med Coll, 1963 *Certification:* Ophthalmology
1187 Main Ave #1-F, Clifton, 973-546-6161

Nussbaum, Peter (3 mentions)
New York Med Coll, 1969 *Certification:* Ophthalmology
22 Old Short Hills Rd #104, Livingston, 973-992-5200

Pomerantz, Scott Barry (6 mentions)
Emory U, 1986 *Certification:* Ophthalmology
523 Forest Ave, Paramus, 201-262-5070

Rosenberg, Michael Eric (5 mentions)
New York U, 1992 *Certification:* Ophthalmology
301 Bridge Plaza N, Fort Lee, 201-947-1786

Salz, Alan Gilbert (9 mentions)
Boston U, 1981 *Certification:* Ophthalmology
201 Union Ave Bldg 2 #F, Bridgewater, 908-231-1110

Santamaria, Jaime, II (3 mentions)
Columbia U, 1973 *Certification:* Ophthalmology
104 Market St, Perth Amboy, 732-826-5159
100 Menlo Park, Edison, 732-826-5159

Schanzer, Barry Mark (3 mentions)
New York U, 1991 *Certification:* Ophthalmology
1812 Oak Tree Rd, Edison, 732-548-0700

Seery, Christopher Martin (3 mentions)
New Jersey Med Sch, 1984 *Certification:* Ophthalmology
90 Millburn Ave, Millburn, 973-762-2300
5 Franklin Ave, Belleville, 973-450-5100

Stabile, John Rene (14 mentions)
New York Med Coll, 1976 *Certification:* Ophthalmology
111 Dean Dr, Tenafly, 201-567-5995

Turtel, Lawrence Steven (3 mentions)
Columbia U, 1986 *Certification:* Ophthalmology
3333 Fairmont Ave, Ocean, 732-988-4000

Wagner, Rudolph Stephen (3 mentions)
New Jersey Med Sch, 1978 *Certification:* Ophthalmology
556 Eagle Rock Ave, Roseland, 973-228-3111
1 Clara Maass Dr, Belleville, 973-751-1702

Orthopedics

Archer, Jonathan M. (6 mentions)
Certification: Orthopaedic Surgery
730 Palisade Ave, Teaneck, 201-353-9000
106 Grand Ave, Englewood, 201-608-0100
15 Vervalen St, Closter, 201-784-6800

Avella, Douglas G. (5 mentions)
FMS-Mexico, 1979 *Certification:* Orthopaedic Surgery
140 Chestnut St, Ridgewood, 201-612-9988

Benevenia, Joseph (4 mentions)
New Jersey Med Sch, 1984 *Certification:* Orthopaedic Surgery
90 Bergen St #1200, Newark, 973-972-2153

Berman, Mark (8 mentions)
Mount Sinai Sch of Med, 1981 *Certification:* Orthopaedic Surgery
211 Essex St #402, Hackensack, 201-489-8250

Chase, Mark David (8 mentions)
Boston U, 1983 *Certification:* Orthopaedic Surgery
200 Highland Ave, Glen Ridge, 973-746-2200

D'Agostini, Robert J., Jr. (6 mentions)
Certification: Orthopaedic Surgery
1590 US Hwy 206 N, Bedminster, 908-234-2002

Decter, Edward M. (4 mentions)
Creighton U, 1975 *Certification:* Orthopaedic Surgery
1500 Pleasant Valley Way #101, West Orange, 973-669-5600

Distefano, Michael Charles (4 mentions)
Albert Einstein Coll of Med, 1977
Certification: Orthopaedic Sports Medicine, Orthopaedic Surgery
140 N State Route 17N #255, Paramus, 201-261-5501

Femino, Frank Placido (12 mentions)
New Jersey Med Sch, 1990 *Certification:* Orthopaedic Surgery
5 Franklin Ave #202, Belleville, 973-751-0111

Fietti, Vincent G., Jr. (4 mentions)
Certification: Orthopaedic Surgery
1011 Clifton Ave #1, Clifton, 973-777-3400

Gatt, Charles John, Jr. (7 mentions)
Robert W Johnson Med Sch, 1989
Certification: Orthopaedic Sports Medicine, Orthopaedic Surgery
215 Easton Ave, New Brunswick, 732-545-0400
562 Easton Ave, Somerset, 732-565-5450
211 N Harrison St, Princeton, 609-683-7800

Hartzband, Mark A. (5 mentions)
FMS-Canada, 1978 *Certification:* Orthopaedic Surgery
10 Forest Ave, Paramus, 201-291-4040

Hiramoto, Harlan Edward (6 mentions)
U of South Alabama, 1980 *Certification:* Orthopaedic Surgery
762 US Hwy 202/206, Bridgewater, 908-429-7600

Hurley, John Aloysius (13 mentions)
New York U, 1980
Certification: Orthopaedic Sports Medicine, Orthopaedic Surgery
111 Madison Ave #400, Morristown, 973-971-6898

Implicito, Dante Anthony (4 mentions)
New Jersey Med Sch, 1990 *Certification:* Orthopaedic Surgery
1 W Ridgewood Ave #307, Paramus, 201-251-7725

Kovatis, Paul Evan (4 mentions)
New Jersey Med Sch, 1989
2 Forest Ave, Paramus, 201-587-1111

Lee, Jen Fei (4 mentions)
Mount Sinai Sch of Med, 1992
Certification: Orthopaedic Surgery, Surgery of the Hand
730 Palisade Ave, Teaneck, 201-692-8900
15 Vervalen St, Closter, 201-784-6800
106 Grand Ave, Englewood, 201-608-0100

Lombardi, Paul (10 mentions)
Albert Einstein Coll of Med, 1993
Certification: Orthopaedic Surgery
160 E Hanover Ave, Cedar Knolls, 973-538-2334

Matarese, William Andrew (4 mentions)
U of Connecticut, 1983 *Certification:* Orthopaedic Surgery
342 Hamburg Tpke #205, Wayne, 973-595-7779

McBride, Mark J. (5 mentions)
Georgetown U, 1980
Certification: Orthopaedic Surgery, Surgery of the Hand
160 E Hanover Ave, Cedar Knolls, 973-538-2334

McInerney, Vincent K. (8 mentions)
New Jersey Med Sch, 1977 *Certification:* Orthopaedic Surgery
504 Valley Rd #200, Wayne, 973-694-2690

Mendes, John Francis (9 mentions)
Cornell U, 1976 *Certification:* Orthopaedic Surgery
200 Highland Ave, Glen Ridge, 973-746-2200

Oppenheim, William Ciler (6 mentions)
Rush U, 1977 *Certification:* Orthopaedic Surgery
609 Morris Ave, Springfield, 973-379-1991

Owens, John (4 mentions)
Columbia U, 1989 *Certification:* Orthopaedic Surgery
15 Vervalen St, Closter, 201-784-6800
730 Palisades Ave, Teaneck, 201-353-9000
106 Grand Ave, Englewood, 201-608-0100

Pizzurro, Joseph Patrick (4 mentions)
St Louis U, 1963 *Certification:* Orthopaedic Surgery
85 S Maple Ave, Ridgewood, 201-445-2830

Polakoff, Donald Richard (5 mentions)
Cornell U, 1979 *Certification:* Orthopaedic Surgery
18 Centre Dr, Monroe, 609-655-1818

Reich, Steven Mark (6 mentions)
Albert Einstein Coll of Med, 1986
Certification: Orthopaedic Surgery
2186 State Rt 27 #1-A, North Brunswick, 732-422-1222
21 Kilmer Dr #2, Morganville, 732-617-9500

Reicher, Oscar A. (4 mentions)
U of Pittsburgh, 1979 *Certification:* Orthopaedic Surgery
2035 Hamburg Tpke #D, Wayne, 973-616-0200
61 Beaverbrook Rd #201, Lincoln Park, 973-686-9292

Rieger, Mark Alan (7 mentions)
U of Connecticut, 1983 *Certification:* Orthopaedic Surgery
218 Ridgedale Ave #104, Cedar Knolls, 973-538-7700

Robbins, Steven Gary (5 mentions)
FMS-Mexico, 1980 *Certification:* Orthopaedic Surgery
1500 Pleasant Valley Way #101, West Orange, 973-669-5600

Rombough, Gary Robert (6 mentions)
Albany Med Coll, 1976 *Certification:* Orthopaedic Surgery
141 Central Ave, Montclair, 973-746-6844

Rosa, Richard Angelo (4 mentions)
New Jersey Med Sch, 1978 *Certification:* Orthopaedic Surgery
741 Northfield Ave #200, West Orange, 973-736-9980

Rubman, Marc (5 mentions)
Stony Brook U, 1987 *Certification:* Orthopaedic Surgery
121 Center Grove Rd, Randolph, 973-366-4411
261 James St #3-F, Morristown, 973-538-0029
50 Cherry Hill Rd #203, Parsippany, 973-263-2828

Salzer, Richard Louis, Jr. (4 mentions)
Tufts U, 1973 *Certification:* Orthopaedic Surgery
401 S Van Brunt St, Englewood, 201-569-2770

Sarokhan, Alan Joseph (11 mentions)
Harvard U, 1977 *Certification:* Orthopaedic Surgery
33 Overlook Rd #201, Summit, 908-522-4555
10 Mountain Blvd, Warren, 908-757-4444

Schneider, Stephen (5 mentions)
FMS-Mexico, 1972 *Certification:* Orthopaedic Surgery
515 Church St #3-A, Bound Brook, 732-469-6160

Sieler, Shawn Douglas (4 mentions)
Robert W Johnson Med Sch, 1991
Certification: Orthopaedic Surgery
2186 State Hwy 27 #1A, North Brunswick, 732-422-1222

Tozzi, John Michael (6 mentions)
Rosalind Franklin U, 1983 *Certification:* Orthopaedic Surgery
2164 Hwy 35, Sea Girt, 732-240-6060
365 Broad St #2-W, Red Bank, 732-933-4300

Tria, Alfred Jacques, Jr. (4 mentions)
Harvard U, 1972 *Certification:* Orthopaedic Surgery
1527 Route 27 #1300, Somerset, 732-249-4444

Otorhinolaryngology

Baredes, Soly (10 mentions)
Columbia U, 1976 *Certification:* Otolaryngology
90 Bergen St #7200, Newark, 973-226-3444
556 Eagle Rock Ave, Roseland, 973-226-3444
40 Bergen St, Newark, 973-972-9000

Bortniker, David Leonard (8 mentions)
Albert Einstein Coll of Med, 1980 *Certification:* Otolaryngology
242 E Main St, Somerville, 908-704-9696
324 Sputh Ave E, Westfield, 908-704-9696

Cece, John Anthony (6 mentions)
Robert W Johnson Med Sch, 1981 *Certification:* Otolaryngology
1001 Clifton Ave, Clifton, 973-777-5151
1211 Hamburg Tpke #205, Wayne, 973-633-0808

Davis, Orrin (5 mentions)
Northwestern U, 1981 *Certification:* Otolaryngology
315 Cedar Ln, Teaneck, 201-837-2174
44 Godwin Ave 3rd Fl, Midland Park, 201-445-2900

Drake, William, III (11 mentions)
New Jersey Med Sch, 1989 *Certification:* Otolaryngology
189 Elm St, Westfield, 908-233-5500

Edelman, Bruce Allen (7 mentions)
New York U, 1984 *Certification:* Otolaryngology
B-3 Cornwall Dr, East Brunswick, 732-238-0300
37 Clyde Rd #103, Somerset, 732-873-6863

Eisenberg, Lee David (13 mentions)
SUNY-Downstate Med Coll, 1971 *Certification:* Otolaryngology
177 N Dean St, Englewood, 201-567-2771
385 Prospect Ave #2, Hackensack, 201-883-1062

Giacchi, Renato John (8 mentions)
New York U, 1993 *Certification:* Otolaryngology
95 Madison Ave #105, Morristown, 973-644-0808

Goldrich, Michael Seth (6 mentions)
George Washington U, 1989 *Certification:* Otolaryngology
181 Somerset St, New Brunswick, 732-247-2401

Highstein, Charles Ivan (7 mentions)
U of Maryland, 1979 *Certification:* Otolaryngology
577 Cranbury Rd #3-LL, East Brunswick, 732-613-0600
280 Main St, Metuchen, 732-494-7777
87 Route 520, Morganville, 732-617-0300

Ho, Bryan Tao (10 mentions)
Mount Sinai Sch of Med, 1989 *Certification:* Otolaryngology
216 Eagle St #101, Englewood, 201-816-9800

Inouye, Masayuki (8 mentions)
Stony Brook U, 1996 *Certification:* Otolaryngology
20 Prospect Ave #909, Hackensack, 201-489-6520

Lazar, Amy D. (6 mentions)
Rosalind Franklin U, 1992 *Certification:* Otolaryngology
56 Union Ave, Somerville, 908-722-1022

Lebenger, Jeffrey Drew (8 mentions)
New York Med Coll, 1984 *Certification:* Otolaryngology
1 Diamond Hill Rd, Berkeley Heights, 908-273-4300

Lee, Derek Saiwah (5 mentions)
U of Arizona, 1992 *Certification:* Otolaryngology
201 S Livingston Ave #2G, Livingston, 973-716-9716

Liu, Edmund Shyh-Cheng (9 mentions)
Tufts U, 1996 *Certification:* Otolaryngology
799 Bloomfield Ave #111, Verona, 973-571-1933

Low, Ronald Brian (6 mentions)
Rosalind Franklin U, 1969 *Certification:* Otolaryngology
20 Prospect Ave #909, Hackensack, 201-489-6520

Mitskavich, Mary Teresa (6 mentions)
U of Pittsburgh, 1991 *Certification:* Otolaryngology
3700 Route 133, Neptune, 732-280-7855

Morrow, Todd Andrew (5 mentions)
Jefferson Med Coll, 1986 *Certification:* Otolaryngology
741 Northfield Ave #104, West Orange, 973-243-0600

Peron, Didier Louis (6 mentions)
FMS-France, 1970 *Certification:* Otolaryngology
26 Madison Ave, Morristown, 973-267-1850

Prabhat, Arvind (5 mentions)
Cornell U, 1992 *Certification:* Otolaryngology
1131 Broad St #103, Shrewsbury, 732-389-3388

Rosenbaum, Jeffrey Mark (7 mentions)
Albany Med Coll, 1973 *Certification:* Otolaryngology
B-3 Cornwall Dr, East Brunswick, 732-238-0300
37 Clyde Rd #103, Somerset, 732-873-6863

Scherl, Michael P. (6 mentions)
Albany Med Coll, 1982 *Certification:* Otolaryngology
219 Old Hook Rd, Westwood, 201-666-8787
163 Engle St #1-B, Englewood, 201-569-6189

Shaari, Christopher M. (8 mentions)
Albany Med Coll, 1991 *Certification:* Otolaryngology
20 Prospect Ave #712, Hackensack, 201-342-8060

Shah, Darsit Kanaiyalal (6 mentions)
Med Coll of Pennsylvania, 1991 *Certification:* Otolaryngology
1131 Broad St #103, Shrewsbury, 732-389-3388

Surow, Jason Barry (9 mentions)
U of Pennsylvania, 1982 *Certification:* Otolaryngology
44 Godwin Ave, Midland Park, 201-445-2900
315 Cedar Ln, Teaneck, 201-837-2174

Zbar, Lloyd Irwin Stanley (7 mentions)
FMS-Canada, 1964 *Certification:* Otolaryngology
200 Highland Ave, Glen Ridge, 973-744-2424

Pain Medicine

Conyack, David G. (4 mentions)
New York Coll of Osteopathic Med, 1992
Certification: Anesthesiology
200 S Orange Ave #201, Livingston, 973-322-7246

Das, Vivek T. (7 mentions)
Robert W Johnson Med Sch, 1991
Certification: Anesthesiology, Pain Medicine
80 W End Ave, Somerville, 908-704-8088

Datta, Samyadev (5 mentions)
FMS-India, 1979 *Certification:* Anesthesiology, Pain Medicine
200 Passaic St, Hackensack, 201-488-7246

Demesmin, Didier (8 mentions)
Certification: Anesthesiology, Pain Medicine
65 James St, Edison, 732-321-7070
78 Easton Ave #1-A, New Brunswick, 732-828-1003

Gudin, Jeffery (7 mentions)
Certification: Anesthesiology, Pain Medicine
350 Engle St, Englewood, 201-894-3595

Kaufman, Andrew Greg (9 mentions)
U of Virginia, 1988 *Certification:* Anesthesiology, Pain Medicine
33 Overlook Rd #311, Summit, 908-598-0196

Marini, Robert A. (4 mentions)
Certification: Pain Medicine, Physical Medicine & Rehabilitation
234 Mount Prospect Ave, Newark, 973-482-5303
77 Newark Ave, Belleville, 973-482-5303

Metzger, Scott Eric (8 mentions)
Boston U, 1992 *Certification:* Anesthesiology, Pain Medicine
160 Ave At The Common #1, Shrewsbury, 732-380-0200

Oza, Rohit (5 mentions)
Robert W Johnson Med Sch, 1999
Certification: Pain Medicine, Physical Medicine & Rehabilitation
1 Diamond Hill Rd, Berkeley Heights, 908-273-4300

Pak, H. Rae (5 mentions)
New Jersey Sch of Osteopathic Med, 1988
Certification: Anesthesiology, Pain Medicine
200 S Orange Ave #201, Livingston, 973-322-7246

Parikh, Sanjiv R. (4 mentions)
FMS-India, 1986 *Certification:* Anesthesiology, Pain Medicine
85 Orient Way, Rutherford, 973-720-8600
1680 Route 23 N #160, Wayne, 973-815-0003

Ragukonis, Thomas P. (4 mentions)
New Jersey Med Sch, 1991 *Certification:* Anesthesiology
30 W Century Rd #310, Paramus, 201-634-9000
799 Bloomfield Ave #301, Verona, 973-857-7600
5600 JFK Blvd #106, West New York, 201-969-9500
950 W Chestnut St, Union, 908-688-1100

Ramundo, Giovanni B. (12 mentions)
Pennsylvania State U, 1990
Certification: Anesthesiology, Pain Medicine
187 Millburn Ave #101, Millburn, 973-322-8223

Rudman, Michael Evan (10 mentions)
Pennsylvania State U, 1988
Certification: Anesthesiology, Pain Medicine
100 Madison Ave, Morristown, 973-971-6824

Secoy, John Walton (5 mentions)
FMS-Grenada, 1988 *Certification:* Anesthesiology
1 Bay Ave, Newark, 800-720-1664

Silverman, Robert (9 mentions)
Northeastern Ohio U, 1993
Certification: Anesthesiology, Pain Medicine
1 Valley Health Plaza, Paramus, 201-634-5555

Staats, Peter Sean (8 mentions)
U of Michigan, 1989 *Certification:* Anesthesiology, Pain Medicine
160 Ave of The Common #1, Shrewsbury, 732-380-0200

Umanoff, Michael David (5 mentions)
FMS-Mexico, 1981 *Certification:* Anesthesiology, Pain Medicine
703 Main St, Paterson, 973-754-2323

Valenza, Joseph P. (4 mentions)
SUNY-Downstate Med Coll, 1992
Certification: Pain Medicine, Physical Medicine & Rehabilitation
1199 Pleasant Valley Way, West Orange, 973-731-3600
300 Market St, Saddle Brook, 201-368-6000
201 Pleasant Hill Rd, Chester, 973-584-7500

Winne, Richard Paul, Jr. (18 mentions)
New Jersey Med Sch, 1987 *Certification:* Anesthesiology
100 Madison Ave, Morristown, 973-971-6824

Pathology

Benisch, Barry (4 mentions)
U of Buffalo, 1967
Certification: Anatomic Pathology & Clinical Pathology
865 Stone St, Rahway, 732-499-6139

D'Aguillo, Anthony F. (5 mentions)
Creighton U, 1972 *Certification:* Anatomic Pathology &
Clinical Pathology, Cytopathology
110 Rehill Ave, Somerville, 908-685-2935

Dardik, Michael (3 mentions)
Certification: Anatomic Pathology & Clinical Pathology
94 Old Short Hills Rd, Livingston, 973-322-5000

Dise, Craig Allen (4 mentions)
U of Pennsylvania, 1975 *Certification:* Anatomic Pathology
100 Madison Ave #26, Morristown, 973-971-5600

Harawi, Sami Joseph (7 mentions)
FMS-Lebanon, 1974 *Certification:* Anatomic Pathology,
Clinical Pathology, Cytopathology
30 Prospect Ave, Hackensack, 201-996-4817

Katz, Robert Samuel (4 mentions)
Albert Einstein Coll of Med, 1975 *Certification:* Anatomic
Pathology & Clinical Pathology, Hematology
100 Madison Ave, Morristown, 973-971-5600

Kimler, Stephen Charles (14 mentions)
SUNY-Downstate Med Coll, 1970
Certification: Anatomic Pathology & Clinical Pathology
1 Bay Ave, Montclair, 973-429-6164

Krumerman, Martin S. (5 mentions)
New York U, 1965
Certification: Anatomic Pathology & Clinical Pathology
525 Route 70, Brick, 732-920-1772

Lara, Jonathan F. (5 mentions)
FMS-Philippines, 1984 *Certification:* Anatomic Pathology &
Clinical Pathology, Cytopathology
94 Old Short Hills Rd, Livingston, 973-322-5762

Magidson, Jory Glen (9 mentions)
Columbia U, 1978
Certification: Anatomic Pathology & Clinical Pathology
100 Madison Ave, Morristown, 973-971-5600

Peters, Stephen Roger (6 mentions)
Boston U, 1979
Certification: Anatomic Pathology & Clinical Pathology
30 Prospect Ave, Hackensack, 201-996-2000

Sanchez, Miguel (17 mentions)
FMS-Spain, 1969 *Certification:* Anatomic Pathology,
Clinical Pathology, Cytopathology
350 Engle St, Englewood, 201-894-3423

Stahl, Rosalyn Esther (5 mentions)
Albert Einstein Coll of Med, 1976 *Certification:* Anatomic
Pathology & Clinical Pathology, Cytopathology
350 Engle St, Englewood, 201-894-3422

Stanford, Brian J. (3 mentions)
Nova Southeastern Coll of Osteopathic Med, 1990
Certification: Anatomic Pathology & Clinical Pathology,
Hematology
110 Rehill Ave, Somerville, 908-685-2935

Pediatrics *(see note on page 9)*

Ashton, Julie A. (3 mentions)
New Jersey Med Sch, 1987 *Certification:* Pediatrics
91 S Jefferson Rd #200, Whippany, 973-538-6116

Asnes, Russell Samuel (7 mentions)
Tufts U, 1963 *Certification:* Pediatrics
32 Franklin St, Tenafly, 201-569-2400
26 Park Pl, Paramus, 201-262-1140
301 Bridge Plaza N #15, Fort Lee, 201-592-8787

Banschick, Harry (3 mentions)
FMS-Mexico, 1977 *Certification:* Pediatrics
2500 Lemoine Ave #200, Fort Lee, 201-592-9210

Bienstock, Jeffrey Marc (3 mentions)
FMS-Mexico, 1983 *Certification:* Pediatrics
20-20 Fair Lawn Ave, Fair Lawn, 201-791-4545
400 Franklin Tpke #108, Mahwah, 201-529-4545
901 Route 23, Pompton Plains, 973-831-4545

Brown, Melissa M. (4 mentions)
U of Toledo, 1981 *Certification:* Pediatrics
241 Millburn Ave #241-B, Millburn, 973-376-9000

Butensky, Arthur (3 mentions)
New Jersey Med Sch, 1980 *Certification:* Pediatrics
3155 Route 10 #104, Denville, 973-361-4900
1129 Bloomfield Ave #100, West Caldwell, 973-575-8585

Chazen, Kenneth Aaron (4 mentions)
FMS-France, 1973 *Certification:* Pediatrics
272 Broad St, Red Bank, 732-741-0456
3350 Hwy 138 Bldg 1 #116, Wall Township, 732-681-0300

Chefitz, Dalya (3 mentions)
Robert W Johnson Med Sch, 1990 *Certification:* Pediatrics
427-429 S Main St, Phillipsburg, 908-454-4600

Cohen, Martin Lewis (4 mentions)
SUNY-Upstate Med U, 1967 *Certification:* Pediatrics
261 James St #1-G, Morristown, 973-540-9393

Cuddihy, Kathleen Marie (3 mentions)
New Jersey Med Sch, 1996 *Certification:* Pediatrics
180 South St, New Providence, 908-771-9824

De Bruin, William John (3 mentions)
New Jersey Med Sch, 1984
Certification: Pediatric Critical Care Medicine
703 Main St, Paterson, 973-754-2544

Fisher, Margaret C. (3 mentions)
U of California-Los Angeles, 1975
Certification: Pediatric Infectious Diseases, Pediatrics
300 2nd Ave, Long Branch, 732-923-7250

Fortin, Robert Glenn (3 mentions)
U of Pennsylvania, 1989 *Certification:* Pediatrics
281 Summerhill Rd, East Brunswick, 732-390-8400

Fried, Ruth Ellen (3 mentions)
New York Med Coll, 1976
180 N Dean St, Englewood, 201-568-1120

Gruenwald, Laurence D. (5 mentions)
New Jersey Med Sch, 1975 *Certification:* Pediatrics
90 Millburn Ave, Millburn, 973-378-7990

Handler, Robert William (3 mentions)
New Jersey Med Sch, 1975 *Certification:* Pediatrics
1140 Parsippany Blvd #102, Parsippany, 973-263-0066

Harlow, Paul Joseph (8 mentions)
SUNY-Downstate Med Coll, 1974
Certification: Pediatric Hematology-Oncology, Pediatrics
90 Prospect Ave #1A, Hackensack, 201-342-4001
50 S Franklin Tpke, Ramsey, 201-934-2949

Harvey, Karanja Danielle (3 mentions)
Yale U, 1996 *Certification:* Pediatrics
1-C new Amwell Rd, Hillsborough, 908-874-5038
155 Union Ave, Bridgewater, 908-725-1802

Iglesias-Rodriguez, H. (3 mentions)
FMS-Dominican Republic, 1984
776 Shrewsbury Ave, Tinton Falls, 732-758-1223

Kerensky, Kirk Mark (4 mentions)
U of Pennsylvania, 1978
Certification: Pediatric Endocrinology, Pediatrics
804 W Park Ave #B, Ocean, 732-531-0010
300 2nd Ave #021, Long Branch, 732-923-6085

Kintiroglou, Constantinos (4 mentions)
FMS-Greece, 1969
Certification: Neonatal-Perinatal Medicine, Pediatrics
1500 Pleasant Valley Way #306, West Orange, 973-243-0002

Lubin, Alan Barry (4 mentions)
New York U, 1971 *Certification:* Pediatrics
173 S Orange Ave, South Orange, 973-762-0400

Mulgaonkar, Ujwala S. (3 mentions)
FMS-India, 1978 *Certification:* Pediatrics
65 E Northfield Rd, Livingston, 973-992-0810

Namerow, David Mark (6 mentions)
U of Louisville, 1972 *Certification:* Pediatrics
20-20 Fair Lawn Ave, Fair Lawn, 201-791-4545
400 Franklin Tpke #108, Mahwah, 201-529-4545
901 Rt 23 S, Pompton Plains, 973-831-4545

Peng, Patricia E. (5 mentions)
Midwestern U Chicago Coll of Osteopathic Med, 1993
Certification: Pediatrics
169 Mine Brook Rd, Bernardsville, 908-766-0034

Polisin, Michael John (3 mentions)
FMS-Italy, 1985 *Certification:* Pediatrics
47 Maple St #107, Summit, 908-273-5866

Rabinowitz, Arnold Henry (3 mentions)
FMS-Mexico, 1979 *Certification:* Pediatrics
22 Madison Ave #31, Paramus, 201-291-9797

Rabinowitz, Robert Charles (6 mentions)
U of Pittsburgh, 1974 *Certification:* Pediatrics
395 Pleasant Valley Way, West Orange, 973-731-6100

Riegelhaupt, Rona (3 mentions)
Mount Sinai Sch of Med, 1984 *Certification:* Pediatrics
17-10 Fair Lawn Ave, Fair Lawn, 201-794-8585
1011 Clifton Ave, Clifton, 973-249-1231
940 Main St, Hackensack, 201-487-1521

Rigtrup, Edward David (3 mentions)
New York Med Coll, 1975 *Certification:* Pediatrics
73 Park St, Montclair, 973-746-7375

Rosenblatt, Joshua Seth (3 mentions)
New Jersey Med Sch, 1984 *Certification:* Pediatrics
201 Lyons Ave, Newark, 973-926-4446

Sasson, Elias (3 mentions)
SUNY-Downstate Med Coll, 1974 *Certification:* Pediatrics
804 W Park Ave, Ocean, 732-531-0010
219 Taylor Mill Rd, Manalapan, 732-577-0088
820 E Punch City Line Rd, Lakewood, 732-370-8500

Sugarman, Lynn Michele (5 mentions)
Harvard U, 1977 *Certification:* Pediatrics
32 Franklin St, Tenafly, 201-569-2400
26 Park Ave, Paramus, 201-262-1140

Thomas, Alan Ewart (3 mentions)
U Central del Caribe, 1992 *Certification:* Pediatrics
1 Diamond Hill Rd, Berkeley Heights, 908-277-8601

Tiefenbrunn, Larry Jay (3 mentions)
Albert Einstein Coll of Med, 1982 *Certification:* Pediatrics
281 Summerhill Rd, East Brunswick, 732-390-8400

Vigorita, John Floyd (5 mentions)
FMS-Mexico, 1974
33 Overlook Rd #101, Summit, 908-273-1112

Yankus, Wayne Arthur (5 mentions)
FMS-Mexico, 1975 *Certification:* Pediatrics
44 Godwin Ave #200, Midland Park, 201-444-8389

Yegen, Lonna Uta Kane (3 mentions)
New York U, 1972 *Certification:* Pediatrics
500 Piermont Rd, Closter, 201-784-3200

Yorke, Eric Robert (3 mentions)
Columbia U, 1982 *Certification:* Pediatrics
155 Union Ave, Bridgewater, 908-725-1802
1-C New Amwell Rd, Hillsborough, 908-874-5035
2345 Lamington Rd #101, Bedminster, 908-470-1124

Plastic Surgery

Berlet, Anthony Clayton (7 mentions)
New Jersey Med Sch, 1986 *Certification:* Plastic Surgery
908 Pompton Ave #A-1, Cedar Grove, 973-857-7757

Boss, William Kilian (6 mentions)
New Jersey Med Sch, 1975 *Certification:* Plastic Surgery
385 Prospect Ave, Hackensack, 201-488-1035

Colon, Francisco Gerardo (6 mentions)
Columbia U, 1987 *Certification:* Plastic Surgery
124 Columbia Tpke, Florham Park, 973-822-3000

Conn, Michael Joseph (5 mentions)
Georgetown U, 1986 *Certification:* Plastic Surgery
870 Palisade Ave #203, Teaneck, 201-836-9296
1 Lethbridge Plaza, Mahwah, 201-529-3232
191 Hamburg Tpke #3, Pompton Lakes, 973-839-3900

D'Amico, Richard Anthony (10 mentions)
New York U, 1976 *Certification:* Plastic Surgery
180 N Dean St #3NE, Englewood, 201-567-9595

Elkwood, Andrew I. (10 mentions)
Albany Med Coll, 1988 *Certification:* Plastic Surgery, Surgery
535 Sycamore Ave, Shrewsbury, 732-741-0970

Loverme, Paul J. (8 mentions)
Certification: Plastic Surgery
825 Bloomfield Ave S #205, Verona, 973-857-9499

Momeni, Reza (7 mentions)
Med Coll of Pennsylvania, 1998 *Certification:* Plastic Surgery
1 Diamond Hill Rd, Berkeley Heights, 908-273-4300

Najmi, Jamsheed Khodadad (5 mentions)
FMS-India, 1969 *Certification:* Plastic Surgery
201 Union Ave #B, Bridgewater, 908-722-6450

Nini, Kevin Todd (6 mentions)
Robert W Johnson Med Sch, 1984 *Certification:* Plastic Surgery
78 Easton Ave, New Brunswick, 609-921-2922

Olson, Robert Martin (5 mentions)
U of Pennsylvania, 1974 *Certification:* Plastic Surgery
78 Easton Ave, New Brunswick, 609-921-2922

Pyo, Daniel (10 mentions)
Mount Sinai Sch of Med, 1990
Certification: Plastic Surgery, Surgery
131 Madison Ave #120, Morristown, 973-540-1169

Rafizadeh, Farhad (6 mentions)
FMS-Switzerland, 1975 *Certification:* Plastic Surgery
101 Madison Ave #105, Morristown, 973-267-0928

Rauscher, Gregory Edwin (6 mentions)
SUNY-Downstate Med Coll, 1972 *Certification:* Plastic Surgery
20 Prospect Ave #600, Hackensack, 201-488-1036

Rothenberg, Bennett C. (8 mentions)
Howard U, 1986 *Certification:* Plastic Surgery
22 Old Short Hills Rd #101, Livingston, 973-994-3311

Salas, Arya Peter (5 mentions)
New York Med Coll, 1991 *Certification:* Plastic Surgery
101 Old Short Hills Rd #501, West Orange, 973-731-2000

Shafaie, Farrokh (5 mentions)
Certification: Plastic Surgery
33 Overlook Rd #302, Summit, 908-522-1777

Spiro, Scott Alan (8 mentions)
New Jersey Med Sch, 1988 *Certification:* Plastic Surgery
101 Old Short Hills Rd #510, West Orange, 973-736-5907

Starker, Isaac (22 mentions)
New York U, 1981 *Certification:* Plastic Surgery
124 Columbia Tpke, Florham Park, 973-822-3000

Sterman, Harris Robert (8 mentions)
SUNY-Downstate Med Coll, 1985 *Certification:* Plastic Surgery
870 Palisade Ave #203, Teaneck, 201-836-4111

Tepper, Howard Norman (5 mentions)
Albert Einstein Coll of Med, 1975 *Certification:* Plastic Surgery
522 E Broad St, Westfield, 908-654-6540
33 Overlook Rd #411, Summit, 908-522-0880
27 Mountain Blvd #9, Warren, 908-561-0080

Tutela, Rocco Robert (6 mentions)
FMS-Italy, 1969 *Certification:* Plastic Surgery
347 Mount Pleasant Ave #101, West Orange, 973-669-1240

Winters, Richard Mark (6 mentions)
U of Connecticut, 1990 *Certification:* Plastic Surgery
20 Prospect Ave #501, Hackensack, 201-487-3400

Zbar, Ross Ian Seth (10 mentions)
Yale U, 1992 *Certification:* Otolaryngology, Plastic Surgery
200 Highland Ave #240, Glen Ridge, 973-743-4800

Zubowski, Robert (8 mentions)
FMS-Mexico, 1983 *Certification:* Plastic Surgery
1 Sears Dr, Paramus, 201-261-7550

Psychiatry

Bolo, Peter (8 mentions)
Columbia U, 1985 *Certification:* Psychiatry
99 Beauvoir Ave, Summit, 908-522-2226

Cancellieri, Francis L. (3 mentions)
FMS-St Maarten, 1986 *Certification:* Psychiatry
300 2nd Ave, Long Branch, 732-728-9001
279 3rd Ave #51, Long Branch, 732-728-9001

Donnellan, Joseph A. (3 mentions)
New Jersey Med Sch, 1986 *Certification:* Psychiatry
422 Courtyard Dr, Hillsborough, 908-725-5595

Fitzsimmons, Adriana M. (4 mentions)
Robert W Johnson Med Sch, 1998 *Certification:* Psychiatry
3535 State Route 66 Bldg 5 #3003, Neptune, 732-643-4350

Flood, Mark James (3 mentions)
Texas Tech U, 1987 *Certification:* Psychiatry
140 Prospect Ave #4, Hackensack, 201-488-6543

Jones, Frank Allen (3 mentions)
Case Western Reserve U, 1972 *Certification:* Psychiatry
2186 Route 27 #2A, North Brunswick, 732-422-0800

Latimer, Edward Alexander (7 mentions)
New Jersey Med Sch, 1988 *Certification:* Psychiatry
24 Portland Pl, Montclair, 973-744-1880

Lichtman, Kenneth J. (3 mentions)
FMS-Belgium, 1971 *Certification:* Psychiatry
251 Main St, Metuchen, 732-549-2220

Liebhauser, Catherine Ann (4 mentions)
FMS-Mexico, 1983 *Certification:* Forensic Psychiatry, Psychiatry
85 Park St, Montclair, 973-746-7712

Mishra, Arunesh Kumar (3 mentions)
FMS-India, 1983 *Certification:* Geriatric Psychiatry, Psychiatry
500 Lawrie St, Perth Amboy, 732-324-5033

Rosenfeld, David Neil (3 mentions)
Robert W Johnson Med Sch, 1988 *Certification:* Psychiatry
265 Ackerman Ave, Ridgewood, 201-447-5630

Schumeister, Robert (4 mentions)
Albert Einstein Coll of Med, 1990 *Certification:* Psychiatry
285 Engle St, Englewood, 201-569-1133

Taylor, Clifford Aubrey (4 mentions)
Harvard U, 1978 *Certification:* Psychiatry
261 James St #2E, Morristown, 973-540-1656

Wagle, Sharad (4 mentions)
FMS-India, 1972 *Certification:* Psychiatry
718 Teaneck Rd, Teaneck, 201-833-3291

Zeman, David (5 mentions)
SUNY-Downstate Med Coll, 1989
Certification: Geriatric Psychiatry, Psychiatry
29 N Livingston Ave, Livingston, 973-953-8580

Zornitzer, Michael Robert (4 mentions)
SUNY-Downstate Med Coll, 1971 *Certification:* Psychiatry
2 W Northfield Rd, Livingston, 973-992-6090

Zykorie, David (3 mentions)
New York U, 1969 *Certification:* Psychiatry
25 Brunswick Woods Dr, East Brunswick, 732-257-9599
1937 Route 35, Wall Township, 732-974-9641

Pulmonary Disease

Ash, Carol E. (4 mentions)
New Jersey Sch of Osteopathic Med, 1989
331 US Hwy 206, Hillsborough, 908-231-6180

Benton, Marc Lawrence (8 mentions)
Mount Sinai Sch of Med, 1982 *Certification:* Critical Care Medicine, Internal Medicine, Pulmonary Disease
101 Madison Ave #205, Morristown, 973-267-9393
8 Saddle Rd #101, Cedar Knolls, 973-267-9393
95 Mount Kemble Ave, Morristown, 973-971-4567

Brauntuch, Glenn Ralph (4 mentions)
Columbia U, 1978
Certification: Internal Medicine, Pulmonary Disease
180 Engle St, Englewood, 201-567-2050

Capone, Robert Anthony (16 mentions)
Columbia U, 1978 *Certification:* Critical Care Medicine, Internal Medicine, Pulmonary Disease
101 Madison Ave #205, Morristown, 973-267-9393
8 Saddle Rd #101, Cedar Knolls, 973-267-9393
95 Mount Kemble Ave, Morristown, 973-971-4567

Cerrone, Federico (5 mentions)
Georgetown U, 1986 *Certification:* Critical Care Medicine, Internal Medicine, Pulmonary Disease, Sleep Medicine
1 Springfield Ave, Summit, 973-267-9393

Dadaian, Jack Hagop (9 mentions)
New Jersey Med Sch, 1962
Certification: Internal Medicine, Pulmonary Disease
123 Highland Ave #301, Glen Ridge, 973-746-7474

Daniskas, Efthymios I. (10 mentions)
Robert W Johnson Med Sch, 1977 *Certification:* Internal Medicine, Pulmonary Disease, Sleep Medicine
123 Highland Ave #301, Glen Ridge, 973-680-8822

Das, Arvind Kumar (4 mentions)
FMS-India, 1982 *Certification:* Critical Care Medicine, Internal Medicine, Pulmonary Disease
81 Veronica Ave #201, Somerset, 732-246-1441

Davis, George Charles (6 mentions)
Hahnemann U, 1973 *Certification:* Critical Care Medicine, Internal Medicine, Pulmonary Disease
279 3rd Ave #510, Long Branch, 732-870-0650
300 2nd Ave, Long Branch, 732-870-0650

De Fusco, Kenneth T. (6 mentions)
FMS-Italy, 1968
Certification: Internal Medicine, Pulmonary Disease
2 W Northfield Rd, Livingston, 973-994-1544

Dimitry, Edward A., Jr. (9 mentions)
Hahnemann U, 1988 *Certification:* Critical Care Medicine, Internal Medicine, Pulmonary Disease
101 Madison Ave #205, Morristown, 973-267-9393
8 Saddle Rd #101, Cedar Knolls, 973-267-9393

Fein, Edward Dennis (6 mentions)
Mount Sinai Sch of Med, 1989 *Certification:* Critical Care Medicine, Internal Medicine, Pulmonary Disease
333 Forsgate Dr #201, Jamesburg, 732-658-5307
172 Summerhill Rd #5, East Brunswick, 732-658-5307

Fortunato, F. Dana (4 mentions)
New Jersey Med Sch, 1975
Certification: Internal Medicine, Pulmonary Disease
127 Pine St, Montclair, 973-744-4075

Goldstein, Keith Ty (6 mentions)
U of Buffalo, 1983 *Certification:* Critical Care Medicine, Internal Medicine, Pulmonary Disease
1 Wescott Dr #102, Flemington, 908-237-1148

Greenberg, Martin Jay (4 mentions)
FMS-Dominica, 1983 *Certification:* Internal Medicine
124 E Mount Pleasant Ave, Livingston, 973-994-4130

Grizzanti, Joseph N. (6 mentions)
Philadelphia Coll of Osteopathic Med, 1976 *Certification:* Allergy & Immunology, Internal Medicine, Pulmonary Disease
297 Lafayette Ave, Hawthorne, 973-790-4111

Harangozo, Andrea Maria (7 mentions)
New York U, 1984 *Certification:* Critical Care Medicine, Internal Medicine, Pulmonary Disease
593 Cranbury Rd #1-A, East Brunswick, 732-613-8880

Hoffman, Frank Anthony (7 mentions)
Rush U, 1978 *Certification:* Internal Medicine
160 Walnut St, Montclair, 973-783-5276

Hutt, Douglas Allen (5 mentions)
Columbia U, 1982 *Certification:* Critical Care Medicine, Internal Medicine, Pulmonary Disease
593 Cranbury Rd #1-A, East Brunswick, 732-613-8880

Hutter, Deborah A. Marie (4 mentions)
Creighton U, 1997 *Certification:* Critical Care Medicine, Internal Medicine, Pulmonary Disease, Sleep Medicine
170 Prospect Ave #20, Hackensack, 201-996-0232

Jacoby, Steven Clifford (4 mentions)
Yale U, 1999 *Certification:* Critical Care Medicine, Internal Medicine, Pulmonary Disease
44 Godwin Ave, Midland Park, 201-689-7755

Kanengiser, Steven Jay (4 mentions)
U of California-San Francisco, 1984
Certification: Pediatric Pulmonology, Pediatrics
505 Goffle Rd, Ridgewood, 201-447-8026

Klukowicz, Alan John (4 mentions)
FMS-Mexico, 1980
Certification: Internal Medicine, Pulmonary Disease
62 S Fullerton Ave, Montclair, 973-744-9125

Levine, Selwyn Eric (5 mentions)
New York U, 1982
Certification: Internal Medicine, Pulmonary Disease
200 Grand Ave, Englewood, 201-871-3636
8305 Bergenline Ave #A, North Bergen, 201-854-7200

Lucas, Robin (7 mentions)
FMS-St Maarten, 1983 *Certification:* Critical Care Medicine, Internal Medicine, Pulmonary Disease
35 Clyde Rd #105, Somerset, 732-873-9682

Mekkawy, Ahmed Abdel H. M. (4 mentions)
FMS-Egypt, 1976 *Certification:* Internal Medicine
925 Clifton Ave #101, Clifton, 973-778-5070

Melamed, Marc S. (9 mentions)
New York U, 1977
Certification: Critical Care Medicine, Internal Medicine
44 Godwin Ave, Midland Park, 201-689-7755
297 Lafayette Ave, Hawthorne, 201-689-7755

Mickey, Aileen Ann (6 mentions)
Robert W Johnson Med Sch, 1991 *Certification:* Critical
Care Medicine, Internal Medicine, Pulmonary Disease
35 Clyde Rd #105, Somerset, 732-873-9682

Oei, Erwin John (9 mentions)
Robert W Johnson Med Sch, 1992 *Certification:* Critical
Care Medicine, Internal Medicine, Pulmonary Disease
8 Saddle Rd #101, Cedar Knolls, 973-267-9393

Polkow, Melvin S. (12 mentions)
SUNY-Downstate Med Coll, 1977 *Certification:* Critical Care
Medicine, Internal Medicine, Pulmonary Disease
211 Essex St #302, Hackensack, 201-498-1311

Pristas, Adrian Michael (4 mentions)
FMS-Mexico, 1988 *Certification:* Pulmonary Disease
108 Ave of Two Rivers, Rumson, 732-747-3666

Rose, Henry John (4 mentions)
New Jersey Med Sch, 1979 *Certification:* Critical Care
Medicine, Internal Medicine, Pulmonary Disease
639 Ridge Rd, Lyndhurst, 201-939-8741

Royall, John Douglas (4 mentions)
U of Virginia, 1970
Certification: Internal Medicine, Pulmonary Disease
108 Ave of Two Rivers, Rumson, 732-747-0591

Santomauro, Emanuele A. (5 mentions)
FMS-Dominica, 1988
Certification: Critical Care Medicine, Internal Medicine,
Pulmonary Disease, Undersea & Hyperbaric Medicine
211 Essex St #302, Hackensack, 201-498-1311

Schiffman, Philip L. (4 mentions)
SUNY-Downstate Med Coll, 1972 *Certification:* Critical Care
Medicine, Internal Medicine, Pulmonary Disease
593 Cranbury Rd #1-A, East Brunswick, 732-613-8880

Scoopo, Frederic John (19 mentions)
U of Connecticut, 1988 *Certification:* Critical Care Medicine,
Internal Medicine, Pediatrics, Pulmonary Disease
8 Saddle Rd, Cedar Knolls, 973-267-9393

Shah, Smita Shamji (10 mentions)
FMS-India, 1980 *Certification:* Critical Care Medicine,
Internal Medicine, Pulmonary Disease
96 Millburn Ave #200-A, Millburn, 973-763-6800

Silberstein, Stuart Lee (6 mentions)
Mount Sinai Sch of Med, 1972
Certification: Internal Medicine, Pulmonary Disease
180 N Dean St 2nd Fl, Englewood, 201-871-8366

Solis, Robert Agustin (6 mentions)
FMS-Grenada, 1988
Certification: Internal Medicine, Pulmonary Disease
205 Browertown Rd #202, West Paterson, 973-785-7515

Sussman, Robert (11 mentions)
Albert Einstein Coll of Med, 1981 *Certification:* Critical Care
Medicine, Internal Medicine, Pulmonary Disease
1 Springfield Ave, Summit, 973-267-9393

Villa, John J. (5 mentions)
New Jersey Sch of Osteopathic Med, 1989 *Certification:* Critical
Care Medicine, Internal Medicine, Pulmonary Disease
211 Essex St #302, Hackensack, 201-498-1311

Weitzman, Robert Harris (4 mentions)
New Jersey Med Sch, 1966
Certification: Internal Medicine, Pulmonary Disease
547 E Broad St, Westfield, 908-232-1554

Wolf, Barry Z. (4 mentions)
New York U, 1982 *Certification:* Critical Care Medicine,
Internal Medicine, Pulmonary Disease
2 Lincoln Hwy #301, Edison, 732-549-7380
3 Hospital Plaza #315, Old Bridge, 732-360-2255

Radiology—Diagnostic

Agress, Harry, Jr. (5 mentions)
Tufts U, 1972
Certification: Diagnostic Radiology, Nuclear Medicine
30 Prospect Ave, Hackensack, 201-996-2200
130 Kinderkamack Rd #201, River Edge, 201-488-2660
555 Kinderkamack Rd #1, Oradell, 201-599-1311
30 S Newman St, Hackensack, 201-488-1188

Aluri, Bhanu S. (3 mentions)
FMS-India, 1988
Certification: Diagnostic Radiology, Neuroradiology
703- Main St, Paterson, 973-754-2624

Amorosa, Judith E. Korek (5 mentions)
New Jersey Med Sch, 1970 *Certification:* Diagnostic Radiology
579 Cranbury Rd, East Brunswick, 732-390-0011

Brunetti, Jacqueline (7 mentions)
Certification: Diagnostic Radiology, Nuclear Medicine,
Nuclear Radiology
718 Teaneck Rd, Teaneck, 201-833-3000

Budin, Joel Aryeh (7 mentions)
Columbia U, 1969 *Certification:* Diagnostic Radiology
30 S Newman St, Hackensack, 201-488-1188
30 Prospect Ave, Hackensack, 201-996-2200
130 Kinderkamack Rd #200, River Edge, 201-488-2660

Dembner, Alan (5 mentions)
Tufts U, 1973 *Certification:* Diagnostic Radiology
94 Old Short Hills Rd, Livingston, 973-322-5800

Donnelly, Brian (4 mentions)
Jefferson Med Coll, 1971 *Certification:* Diagnostic Radiology
2100 Westcott Dr, Flemington, 908-788-6388

Ginsberg, Ferris (3 mentions)
New Jersey Sch of Osteopathic Med, 1981
Certification: Diagnostic Radiology, Nuclear Radiology
2128 Kings Hwy, Oakhurst, 732-493-8444

Goldfischer, Mindy (4 mentions)
Certification: Diagnostic Radiology
350 Engle St, Englewood, 201-894-3530

Honickman, Steven P. (3 mentions)
Duke U, 1976 *Certification:* Diagnostic Radiology
201 Union Ave #G, Bridgewater, 908-725-1291

Horn, Eva M. (3 mentions)
New York U, 1978 *Certification:* Diagnostic Radiology
718 Teaneck Rd, Teaneck, 201-833-3000

Horner, Neil Brian (3 mentions)
Robert W Johnson Med Sch, 1983 *Certification:* Diagnostic
Radiology, Neuroradiology, Nuclear Radiology
151 Summit Ave, Summit, 908-277-3314
118 Elm St, Westfield, 908-277-3314

Jewel, Kenneth Lee (7 mentions)
U of Buffalo, 1968 *Certification:* Diagnostic Radiology
20 High St, Nutley, 973-284-0038
1140 Bloomfield Ave #101, West Caldwell, 973-228-5330
116 Park St, Montclair, 973-746-2525

Keller, Irwin Aaron (6 mentions)
New York Med Coll, 1980
Certification: Diagnostic Radiology, Neuroradiology
579 Cranbury Rd, East Brunswick, 732-390-0011

Kessler, Howard (3 mentions)
FMS-Belgium, 1969 *Certification:* Nuclear Medicine, Radiology
445 Chestnut St, Union, 908-687-6054

Kronfeld, Gary (4 mentions)
FMS-Mexico, 1981
Certification: Diagnostic Radiology, Pediatric Radiology
3830 Park Ave, Edison, 732-494-9061

Lazar, Eric Bruce (3 mentions)
Northwestern U, 1992
Certification: Diagnostic Radiology, Neuroradiology
201 Union Ave #G, Bridgewater, 908-725-1291

Lerner, Elliot J. (3 mentions)
Brown U, 1985
Certification: Diagnostic Radiology, Neuroradiology
20 Franklin Tpke, Waldwick, 201-445-8822
223 N Van Dien Ave, Ridgewood, 201-447-8822

Lubat, Edward (6 mentions)
Jefferson Med Coll, 1982
Certification: Diagnostic Radiology, Nuclear Medicine
20 Franklin Tpke, Waldwick, 201-445-8822
223 N Van Dien Ave, Ridgewood, 201-447-8822

Matuozzi, William David (4 mentions)
SUNY-Downstate Med Coll, 1984
Certification: Diagnostic Radiology
151 Summit Ave #1, Summit, 908-277-3313
118 Elm St, Westfield, 908-277-3313

McCarthy, Denise M. (5 mentions)
Columbia U, 1989 *Certification:* Diagnostic Radiology
66 Maple Ave, Morristown, 973-267-5700

Panush, David (4 mentions)
Certification: Diagnostic Radiology
30 Prospect Ave, Hackensack, 201-996-2200
130 Kinderkamack Rd, River Edge, 201-489-0874
30 S Newman St, Hackensack, 201-488-1188

Pollack, Michael (3 mentions)
New York U
116 Park St, Montclair, 973-661-4674
20 High St, Nutley, 973-661-4674
1140 Bloomfield Ave, West Caldwell, 973-661-4674

Rakow, Joel Ivan (4 mentions)
Albert Einstein Coll of Med, 1982
Certification: Diagnostic Radiology
30 Prospect Ave, Hackensack, 201-996-2254
130 Kinderkamack Rd #201, River Edge, 201-488-2660
555 Kinderkamack Rd #1, Oradell, 201-599-1311
30 S Newman St, Hackensack, 201-488-1188

Rosenfeld, David Leonard (4 mentions)
U of Pittsburgh, 1967 *Certification:* Radiology
579 Cranbury Rd, East Brunswick, 732-390-0011

Ruchman, Richard Bruce (3 mentions)
U of Michigan, 1980
Certification: Diagnostic Radiology, Nuclear Medicine
1131 Broad St #110, Shrewsbury, 732-578-9640
300 2nd Ave, Long Branch, 732-923-6806

Schonfeld, Steven Mark (3 mentions)
Mount Sinai Sch of Med, 1978
Certification: Diagnostic Radiology, Neuroradiology
579 Cranbury Rd, East Brunswick, 732-390-0011

Shapiro, Mark Linden (12 mentions)
SUNY-Downstate Med Coll, 1988
Certification: Diagnostic Radiology
350 Engle St, Englewood, 201-894-3415

Singletary, Linda A. (3 mentions)
New Jersey Med Sch, 1990 *Certification:* Diagnostic Radiology
20 High St, Nutley, 973-284-0038
116 Park St, Montclair, 973-284-0038
1140 Bloomfield Ave #101, West Caldwell, 973-284-0038

Smith, Peter Lloyd (3 mentions)
Washington U, 1987 *Certification:* Diagnostic Radiology,
Vascular & Interventional Radiology
65 Fernwood Rd, Summit, 201-858-4590

Snieckus, Peter John (8 mentions)
New Jersey Med Sch, 1982 *Certification:* Diagnostic Radiology
118 Elm St, Westfield, 908-277-3314

Yuppa, Frank Raymond (13 mentions)
New Jersey Med Sch, 1981
Certification: Diagnostic Radiology, Neuroradiology
703 Main St, Paterson, 973-754-2646

Radiology—Therapeutic

Blank, Kenneth Robert (3 mentions)
Albert Einstein Coll of Med, 1992
Certification: Radiation Oncology
1 Clara Maass Dr, Belleville, 973-450-2270

Calhoun, Sean K. (7 mentions)
New Jersey Sch of Osteopathic Med, 1996 *Certification:*
    Diagnostic Radiology, Vascular & Interventional Radiology
100 Madison Ave, Morristown, 973-971-5370

Desai, Gopal Rao (4 mentions)
FMS-India, 1979 *Certification:* Radiation Oncology
70 Parker Ave, Passaic, 732-745-8590
254 Eaton Ave, New Brunswick, 732-745-8590

Ferrone, George J. (4 mentions)
Certification: Diagnostic Radiology, Vascular &
    Interventional Radiology
30 Prospect Ave, Hackensack, 201-996-2200

Garten, Alan J. (6 mentions)
Tufts U, 1986 *Certification:* Diagnostic Radiology, Vascular
    & Interventional Radiology
94 Old Short Hills Rd, Livingston, 973-322-5000

Goodman, Robert Leon (5 mentions)
Columbia U, 1966 *Certification:* Internal Medicine, Medical
    Oncology, Therapeutic Radiology
94 Old Short Hills Rd, Livingston, 973-322-5630

Haas, Alexander Z. (3 mentions)
FMS-Croatia, 1962 *Certification:* Therapeutic Radiology
254 Easton Ave, New Brunswick, 732-745-8590

Heimann, James Arthur (4 mentions)
U of Rochester, 1982 *Certification:* Diagnostic Radiology,
    Vascular & Interventional Radiology
5 Franklin Ave #510, Belleville, 973-450-2038

Karp, Eric Andrew (3 mentions)
Mount Sinai Sch of Med, 1986 *Certification:* Radiation Oncology
892 Trussler Pl, Rahway, 732-382-5550

Knee, Robert (3 mentions)
SUNY-Downstate Med Coll, 1978
Certification: Therapeutic Radiology
254 Easton Ave, New Brunswick, 732-745-8590

McCarthy, Cornelius S. (3 mentions)
U of Pennsylvania, 1989 *Certification:* Diagnostic Radiology,
    Vascular & Interventional Radiology
94 Old Short Hills Rd, Livingston, 973-322-5800

Nosher, John Louis (4 mentions)
Jefferson Med Coll, 1971 *Certification:* Diagnostic
    Radiology, Vascular & Interventional Radiology
579 Cranbury Rd #A, East Brunswick, 732-390-0040
800 Ryders Ln, East Brunswick, 732-390-0040

Novick, Andrew Simon (6 mentions)
Mount Sinai Sch of Med, 1982 *Certification:* Diagnostic Radiology
201 Lyons Ave, Newark, 973-926-7035
741 Lordfeld Ave #105, West Orange, 973-243-9729
2130 Millburn Ave #A8, Maplewood, 973-912-0404

Rosenbluth, Benjamin Dov (4 mentions)
Harvard U, 2001 *Certification:* Radiation Oncology
718 Teaneck Rd, Teaneck, 201-541-5900

Schwartz, Jeanne R. (3 mentions)
SUNY-Downstate Med Coll, 1979 *Certification:* Diagnostic
    Radiology, Vascular & Interventional Radiology
100 Madison Ave, Morristown, 973-971-5370

Schwartz, Louis E. (7 mentions)
SUNY-Downstate Med Coll, 1974
Certification: Pediatrics, Therapeutic Radiology
33 Overlook Rd #L05, Summit, 908-522-2051

Siegel, Randall Louis (6 mentions)
U of Pennsylvania, 1986 *Certification:* Diagnostic Radiology,
    Vascular & Interventional Radiology
579 Cranbury Rd, East Brunswick, 732-390-0011

Smith, Peter Lloyd (4 mentions)
Washington U, 1987 *Certification:* Diagnostic Radiology,
    Vascular & Interventional Radiology
65 Fernwood Rd, Summit, 201-858-4590

Snieckus, Peter John (3 mentions)
New Jersey Med Sch, 1982 *Certification:* Diagnostic Radiology
151 Summit Ave #1, Summit, 908-277-3314
118 Elm St, Westfield, 908-277-3314

Stabile, Richard John (4 mentions)
New York Med Coll, 1971 *Certification:* Therapeutic Radiology
99 Beauvoir St, Summit, 908-522-2000

Tomkovich, Kenneth R. (3 mentions)
New Jersey Med Sch, 1993 *Certification:* Diagnostic
    Radiology, Vascular & Interventional Radiology
1001 W Main St, Freehold, 732-462-3302

Vialotti, Charles Pilgrim (8 mentions)
New York Med Coll, 1971 *Certification:* Therapeutic Radiology
718 Teaneck Rd, Teaneck, 201-541-5900

Wesson, Michael Forbes (3 mentions)
U of Virginia, 1983 *Certification:* Radiation Oncology
1 Valley Health Plaza, Paramus, 201-634-5403

Wong, James R. (3 mentions)
Harvard U, 1986 *Certification:* Radiation Oncology
100 Madison Ave, Morristown, 973-971-5329

Yablonsky, Thaddeus Mark (8 mentions)
Robert W Johnson Med Sch, 1990 *Certification:* Diagnostic
    Radiology, Vascular & Interventional Radiology
100 Madison Ave, Morristown, 973-971-5370

Zablow, Andrew I. (3 mentions)
FMS-Mexico, 1981 *Certification:* Radiation Oncology
94 Old Short Hills Rd, Livingston, 973-322-5630

Rehabilitation

Abend, Paul Isaac (3 mentions)
New Jersey Sch of Osteopathic Med, 1987
Certification: Physical Medicine & Rehabilitation
243 Bridge St, Metuchen, 732-516-1042

Baker, Elizabeth Anne (7 mentions)
Columbia U, 1989
Certification: Pain Medicine, Physical Medicine & Rehabilitation
106 Grand Ave, Englewood, 201-503-1900

Buddle, Patrick Michael (6 mentions)
FMS-Grenada, 1982
Certification: Physical Medicine & Rehabilitation
700 Hwy 71, Sea Girt, 908-974-8100

Cava, Thomas J. (4 mentions)
U of Miami, 1987
Certification: Physical Medicine & Rehabilitation
960 Pleasant Valley Way, West Orange, 973-243-1177

Cooperman, Todd J. (4 mentions)
Stony Brook U, 1993
Certification: Physical Medicine & Rehabilitation
2 Center Plaza, Tinton Falls, 732-460-5360

Diamond, Martin (3 mentions)
U of Pittsburgh, 1975 *Certification:* Pediatric Rehabilitation
    Medicine, Pediatrics, Physical Medicine & Rehabilitation
116 S Euclid Ave, Westfield, 908-233-4801

Gangemi, Edwin M. (6 mentions)
FMS-Mexico, 1986
Certification: Physical Medicine & Rehabilitation
234 Mount Prospect Ave, Newark, 973-482-5303
319 60th St #1, West New York, 201-319-1339
77 Newark Ave #1, Belleville, 973-844-9220
711 32nd St, Union City, 973-482-5303
57 Route 46, Hackettstown, 973-482-5303

Gombas, George F. (3 mentions)
New Jersey Med Sch, 1990 *Certification:* Internal Medicine,
    Physical Medicine & Rehabilitation, Spinal Cord Injury Medicine
42 Chuckanutt Dr, Oakland, 201-337-1331

Kirshblum, Steven C. (4 mentions)
Certification: Physical Medicine & Rehabilitation, Spinal
    Cord Injury Medicine
1199 Pleasant Valley Way, West Orange, 973-731-3600

Liss, Donald (3 mentions)
Wayne State U, 1979
Certification: Physical Medicine & Rehabilitation
500 Grand Ave #1, Englewood, 201-567-2277
3736 Henry Hudson Pkwy, Bronx, NY, 718-548-1800

Liss, Howard (8 mentions)
Wayne State U, 1977
Certification: Physical Medicine & Rehabilitation
500 Grand Ave, Englewood, 201-567-2277

Malone, Richard J. (3 mentions)
New Jersey Sch of Osteopathic Med, 1990
Certification: Physical Medicine & Rehabilitation
65 James St, Edison, 732-321-7000

Mulford, Gregory John (7 mentions)
Robert W Johnson Med Sch, 1985
Certification: Physical Medicine & Rehabilitation
95 Mt Kemble Ave, Morristown, 973-267-2293

Novick, Ellen Soberman (4 mentions)
Mount Sinai Sch of Med, 1982
Certification: Physical Medicine & Rehabilitation
1 Bay Ave, Montclair, 973-429-6050
1 Greenwood Ave, Montclair, 973-746-2424

Rempson, Joseph Hunter (5 mentions)
SUNY-Downstate Med Coll, 1990 *Certification:* Internal
    Medicine, Physical Medicine & Rehabilitation
99 Beauvoir Ave, Summit, 973-267-2293

Shumko, John Zachary (6 mentions)
New Jersey Med Sch, 1992
Certification: Physical Medicine & Rehabilitation
200 S Orange Ave #118, Livingston, 973-322-7909

Skerker, Robert Scott (4 mentions)
U of Massachusetts, 1986
Certification: Physical Medicine & Rehabilitation
95 Mount Kemble Ave, Morristown, 973-267-2293

Rheumatology

Arbit, David Lewis (7 mentions)
New Jersey Med Sch, 1987
Certification: Internal Medicine, Rheumatology
31-00 Broadway, Fair Lawn, 201-796-2255

Cannarozzi, Nicholas A. (12 mentions)
Hahnemann U, 1965
Certification: Internal Medicine, Rheumatology
127 Pine St, Montclair, 973-783-6000

Gonter, Neil J. (8 mentions)
SUNY-Upstate Med U, 1998
Certification: Internal Medicine, Rheumatology
1415 Queen Anne Rd, Teaneck, 201-837-7788

Kepecs, Gilbert (8 mentions)
Albert Einstein Coll of Med, 1986
Certification: Internal Medicine, Rheumatology
385 Prospect Ave, Hackensack, 201-498-9060

Kimura, Yukiko (10 mentions)
Albert Einstein Coll of Med, 1982
Certification: Pediatric Rheumatology, Pediatrics
30 Prospect Ave, Hackensack, 201-996-5306

Kopelman, Rima Gail (8 mentions)
Columbia U, 1977
Certification: Internal Medicine, Rheumatology
301 Godwin Ave, Midland Park, 201-444-4526

Kramer, Neil (11 mentions)
U of Pennsylvania, 1974
Certification: Internal Medicine, Rheumatology
200 S Orange Ave #107, Livingston, 973-322-7400

Leibowitz, Evan Howard (7 mentions)
New Jersey Med Sch, 1996
Certification: Internal Medicine, Rheumatology
301 Godwin Ave, Midland Park, 201-444-4526

McWhorter, John E., IV (7 mentions)
New Jersey Med Sch, 1968
Certification: Internal Medicine, Rheumatology
201 Union Ave #D, Bridgewater, 908-722-5380

Miguel, Eduardo E. P. (6 mentions)
FMS-Paraguay, 1966 *Certification:* Internal Medicine
12 E Palisade Ave, Englewood, 201-816-9266

Nucatola, Thomas Robert (6 mentions)
SUNY-Downstate Med Coll, 1985
Certification: Internal Medicine, Rheumatology
316 E Broad St, Westfield, 908-301-9800

Pasik, Deborah (10 mentions)
Certification: Internal Medicine, Rheumatology
8 Saddle Rd #102, Cedar Knolls, 973-984-9796

Rosenstein, Elliot David (20 mentions)
Mount Sinai Sch of Med, 1978
Certification: Internal Medicine, Rheumatology
200 S Orange Ave #107, Livingston, 973-322-7400

Storch, Marc Ira (8 mentions)
FMS-Israel, 1987 *Certification:* Rheumatology
103 Omni Dr, Hillsborough, 908-281-0010
1100 Wescott Dr, Flemington, 908-284-9221

Widman, David (13 mentions)
Harvard U, 1975 *Certification:* Internal Medicine, Rheumatology
95 Madison Ave #A-04, Morristown, 973-540-9198

Worth, David Allen (9 mentions)
U of Rochester, 1971
Certification: Internal Medicine, Rheumatology
2376 Morris Ave, Union, 908-686-6616

Thoracic Surgery

Bocage, Jean Philippe (15 mentions)
Robert W Johnson Med Sch, 1984 *Certification:* Thoracic Surgery
35 Clyde Rd #104, Somerset, 732-247-3002

Bolanowski, Paul Joseph P. (7 mentions)
New Jersey Med Sch, 1965
Certification: Surgery, Thoracic Surgery
219 S Broad St #1, Elizabeth, 908-352-8110

Bronstein, Eric Hunter (6 mentions)
Stony Brook U, 1987 *Certification:* Surgery, Thoracic Surgery
703 Main St, Paterson, 973-754-2486

Caccavale, Robert J. (17 mentions)
U of Buffalo, 1981 *Certification:* Thoracic Surgery
35 Clyde Rd #104, Somerset, 732-247-3002

Christakos, Manny E. (6 mentions)
U of Buffalo, 1971 *Certification:* Thoracic Surgery
871 Allwood Rd 2nd Fl, Clifton, 973-779-2270

Ciocon, Hermogenes L. (7 mentions)
FMS-Philippines, 1962 *Certification:* Surgery, Thoracic Surgery
871 Allwood Rd 2nd Fl, Clifton, 973-779-2270

Elmann, Elie (6 mentions)
New York Med Coll, 1987 *Certification:* Surgery, Thoracic Surgery
20 Prospect Ave #900, Hackensack, 201-996-2261

Forman, Mark Howard (11 mentions)
Tulane U, 1976 *Certification:* Thoracic Surgery
1500 Pleasant Valley Way #302, West Orange, 973-324-0988

Langenfeld, John Eugene (8 mentions)
Rush U, 1987 *Certification:* Thoracic Surgery
125 Paterson St, New Brunswick, 732-235-7800

Syracuse, Donald C. (8 mentions)
Columbia U, 1973 *Certification:* Thoracic Surgery
5 Franklin Ave #302, Belleville, 973-759-9000

Thompson, Robert Michael (11 mentions)
FMS-Italy, 1979 *Certification:* Thoracic Surgery
301 Bingham Ave #A, Ocean, 732-775-9077

Widmann, Mark Dennis (30 mentions)
Yale U, 1987 *Certification:* Thoracic Surgery
100 Madison Ave #4401, Morristown, 973-644-4844

Zairis, Ignatios S. (10 mentions)
FMS-Greece, 1973 *Certification:* Surgery
741 Teaneck Rd, Teaneck, 201-837-8282
354 Old Hook Rd #105, Westwood, 201-664-2400

Urology

Atlas, Ian (23 mentions)
Mount Sinai Sch of Med, 1984 *Certification:* Urology
261 James St #3A, Morristown, 973-539-0333
385 State Hwy 24, Chester, 973-539-0333
100 Madison Ave, Morristown, 973-539-0333

Boorjian, Peter Charles (16 mentions)
SUNY-Downstate Med Coll, 1971 *Certification:* Urology
777 Bloomfield Ave, Glen Ridge, 973-429-0462

Catanese, Anthony Joseph (12 mentions)
New York Med Coll, 1983 *Certification:* Urology
315 E Main St, Somerville, 908-722-6900

Chang, David Tsuwei (5 mentions)
Columbia U, 1994 *Certification:* Urology
205 Browertown Rd, West Paterson, 973-890-9168
975 Clifton Ave #1, Clifton, 973-778-0170

Curlik, Martin Richard (5 mentions)
FMS-Mexico, 1980 *Certification:* Urology
138 S Euclid Ave, Westfield, 908-654-6366

Detorres, Wayne Raymond (5 mentions)
Tufts U, 1988 *Certification:* Urology
4 Godwin Ave, Midland Park, 201-444-7070

Esposito, Michael (5 mentions)
New Jersey Med Sch, 1994 *Certification:* Urology
255 W Spring Valley Ave, Maywood, 201-487-8866

Garden, Richard Joseph (6 mentions)
Mount Sinai Sch of Med, 1987 *Certification:* Urology
555 Kinder Karmack Rd, Oradell, 201-664-0677

Geltzeiler, Jules Mark (5 mentions)
Hahnemann U, 1979 *Certification:* Urology
279 3rd Ave #101, Long Branch, 732-222-2111
10 Neptune Blvd #103, Neptune, 732-775-4886
25 Kilmer Dr #214, Morganville, 732-536-8880

Hajjar, John H. (9 mentions)
Georgetown U, 1981 *Certification:* Urology
15-01 Broadway, Fair Lawn, 201-791-4544
630 E Palisade Ave #3, Englewood Cliffs, 201-503-1503

Ioffreda, Richard Edward (6 mentions)
Jefferson Med Coll, 1987 *Certification:* Urology
1250 Marigold St, New Brunswick, 732-545-8259

Katz, Jeffrey Ivan (5 mentions)
FMS-Italy, 1970 *Certification:* Urology
741 Northfield Ave #206, West Orange, 973-325-6100

Katz, Steven A. (7 mentions)
U of Buffalo, 1969 *Certification:* Urology
75 S Dean St, Englewood, 201-816-1900
663 Palisade Ave #304, Cliffside Park, 201-313-1933

Kaynan, Ayal Menashe (5 mentions)
Duke U, 1994 *Certification:* Urology
261 James St #3A, Morristown, 973-539-0333
100 Madison St, Morristown, 973-539-0333

Keselman, Ira G. (5 mentions)
Boston U, 1989 *Certification:* Urology
279 3rd Ave #101, Long Branch, 732-222-2111
25 Kilmer Dr #214, Morganville, 732-536-8880
10 Neptune Blvd #103, Neptune, 732-775-4886

Krieger, Alan Philip (5 mentions)
FMS-Mexico, 1984 *Certification:* Urology
700 N Broad St #302, Elizabeth, 908-355-3077
1600 St Georges Ave #111, Rahway, 732-499-0111

Margolis, Eric Judd (8 mentions)
SUNY-Upstate Med U, 1990 *Certification:* Urology
75 S Dean St, Englewood, 201-816-1900

Patel, Rupa T. (5 mentions)
Certification: Urology
10 Parsonage Rd #118, Edison, 732-494-9400
3 Hospital Plaza #200, Old Bridge, 732-679-2010

Pressler, Lee Brian (5 mentions)
New York Med Coll, 1990 *Certification:* Urology
95 Madison Ave #302, Morristown, 973-656-0600

Rilli, Charles Francis (5 mentions)
New Jersey Med Sch, 1984 *Certification:* Urology
256 Broad St, Bloomfield, 973-743-4450
243 Chestnut St #2, Newark, 973-344-9133
213 S Frank Rogers Blvd, Harrison, 973-482-7070

Ring, Kenneth Scott (7 mentions)
Mount Sinai Sch of Med, 1985 *Certification:* Urology
275 Orchard St, Westfield, 908-654-5100
776 E 3rd Ave, Roselle, 908-654-5100

Rotolo, James Ernest (5 mentions)
Georgetown U, 1984 *Certification:* Urology
2401 Hwy 35, Manasquan, 732-223-7877

Saidi, James (10 mentions)
U of Texas-Dallas, 1994 *Certification:* Urology
777 Bloomfield Ave, Glen Ridge, 973-746-3322

Sanzone, John Joseph (6 mentions)
Wake Forest U, 1992 *Certification:* Urology
2025 Hamburg Tpke #F, Wayne, 973-831-0011
1031 McBride Ave #D-108, West Paterson, 973-256-4038
1033 Clifton Ave #1, Clifton, 973-473-5700

Sawczuk, Ihor Steven (8 mentions)
Med Coll of Pennsylvania, 1979 *Certification:* Urology
360 Essex St #403, Hackensack, 201-336-8090

Shoengold, Stuart David (5 mentions)
New Jersey Med Sch, 1976 *Certification:* Urology
225 Millburn Ave, Millburn, 973-373-3001

Shulman, Yale (5 mentions)
Albert Einstein Coll of Med, 1976 *Certification:* Urology
2255 John F Kennedy Blvd, Jersey City, 201-433-1057

Siegal, John Dale (6 mentions)
U of Pennsylvania, 1982 *Certification:* Urology
1 Diamond Hill Rd, Berkeley Heights, 908-273-4300

Siegel, Andrew L. (5 mentions)
Rosalind Franklin U, 1981 *Certification:* Urology
20 Prospect Ave #715, Hackensack, 201-342-6600

Solomon, Michael Ira (9 mentions)
Albert Einstein Coll of Med, 1978 *Certification:* Internal Medicine
123 Millburn Ave, Millburn, 973-376-1244

Stock, Jeffrey Allen (7 mentions)
Mount Sinai Sch of Med, 1988 *Certification:* Urology
101 Old Short Hills Rd #203, West Orange, 973-325-7188
282 US Hwy 46, Denville, 973-627-4055

Sutaria, Perry Maganlal (6 mentions)
Cornell U, 1992 *Certification:* Urology
261 James St #1A, Morristown, 973-539-1050

Taylor, David Lewis (26 mentions)
U of Michigan, 1979 *Certification:* Urology
261 James St #3A, Morristown, 973-539-0333

Walmsley, Konstantin (7 mentions)
Vanderbilt U, 1997 *Certification:* Urology
777 Bloomfield Ave, Glen Ridge, 973-746-3322

Weiss, Robert Edward (7 mentions)
New York U, 1985 *Certification:* Urology
195 Little Albany St, New Brunswick, 732-235-8515
125 Patterson St, New Brunswick, 732-235-8853
1 World Fair Dr, Somerset, 732-235-8853

Vascular Surgery

Brener, Bruce Jeffrey (18 mentions)
Harvard U, 1966 *Certification:* Surgery, Vascular Surgery
200 S Orange Ave, Livingston, 973-322-7233

Char, Daniel Jay (10 mentions)
Stony Brook U, 1995 *Certification:* Surgery, Vascular Surgery
1124 E Ridgewood Ave #104, Ridgewood, 201-444-5353
419 E Main St, Middletown, NY, 201-444-5353

Holmes, Raymond Joseph (11 mentions)
FMS-Grenada, 1997 *Certification:* Surgery, Vascular Surgery
5 Franklin Ave #302, Belleville, 973-759-9000

Napolitano, Massimo Mark (12 mentions)
FMS-Italy, 1984 *Certification:* Surgery, Vascular Surgery
20 Prospect Ave #707, Hackensack, 201-343-0040

Resnikoff, Michael (17 mentions)
New York Med Coll, 1990 *Certification:* Surgery, Vascular Surgery
131 Madison Ave #140, Morristown, 973-540-9700
16 Pocono Rd #208, Denville, 973-540-9700

New York

Rochester Area—page 339
Buffalo Area—page 305

New York
Metropolitan
Area—
page 309

Buffalo Area
Including Erie and Niagara Counties

Allergy/Immunology

Ambrus, Julian L., Jr. (12 mentions)
Jefferson Med Coll, 1979
Certification: Allergy & Immunology, Internal Medicine
100 High St, Buffalo, 716-859-2524

Donovan, Kathleen Marie (15 mentions)
New York Coll of Osteopathic Med, 1985
Certification: Allergy & Immunology, Internal Medicine
6245D Sheridan Dr #116, Buffalo, 716-631-0380
3800 Delaware Ave #102, Kenmore, 716-875-3800

Lillie, Madeline Ambrus (15 mentions)
Wayne State U, 1976
Certification: Allergy & Immunology, Pediatrics
6245 Sheridan Dr #116, Williamsville, 716-631-0380
3800 Delaware Ave, Kenmore, 716-875-3800

Rockoff, Jeffrey Bruce (11 mentions)
FMS-Philippines, 1984 *Certification:* Allergy & Immunology
3839 Delaware Ave, Kenmore, 716-876-8980
2540 Sheridan Dr, Tonawanda, 716-874-8980

Anesthesiology

Karas, Paul Bernard (3 mentions)
U of Buffalo, 1987 *Certification:* Anesthesiology
2157 Main St, Buffalo, 716-836-7510
2121 Main St #111, Buffalo, 716-836-7510

Lema, Mark J. (6 mentions)
SUNY-Downstate Med Coll, 1982
Certification: Anesthesiology, Pain Medicine
666 Elm & Carlton St, Buffalo, 716-845-4851

Wang, Alan (6 mentions)
SUNY-Upstate Med U, 1994 *Certification:* Anesthesiology
2121 Main St #111, Buffalo, 716-836-7510

Cardiac Surgery

Aldridge, Janerio (9 mentions)
U of Buffalo, 1975 *Certification:* Thoracic Surgery
3 Gates Cir, Buffalo, 716-885-0602

Ashraf, Mohammad Hashmat (12 mentions)
FMS-Bangladesh, 1969
3 Gates Cir, Buffalo, 716-885-0602

Bell-Thomson, John (7 mentions)
Certification: Thoracic Surgery
462 Grider St, Buffalo, 716-898-5111

Grosner, Gary (15 mentions)
U of Connecticut, 1982 *Certification:* Surgery, Thoracic Surgery
100 High St, Buffalo, 716-859-2243

Cardiology

Bhayana, Ranjan (4 mentions)
U of Buffalo, 1990 *Certification:* Cardiovascular Disease
6333 Main St, Williamsville, 716-630-1000

Boersma, Ronald Bartlett (4 mentions)
Creighton U, 1968
Certification: Cardiovascular Disease, Internal Medicine
825 Wehrle Dr, Buffalo, 716-634-3243

Chaskes, Michael Jay (3 mentions)
U of Buffalo, 1983
825 Wehrle Dr, Buffalo, 716-634-3243

Conley, James George (3 mentions)
SUNY-Downstate Med Coll, 1975 *Certification:* Cardiovascular
Disease, Internal Medicine, Interventional Cardiology
100 High St, Buffalo, 716-859-2981

Corbelli, Richard James (4 mentions)
U of Buffalo, 1982 *Certification:* Cardiovascular Disease
6460 Main St, Williamsville, 716-634-5100

Dashkoff, Neil (3 mentions)
New York U, 1969 *Certification:* Cardiovascular Disease,
Internal Medicine, Interventional Cardiology
462 Grider St, Buffalo, 716-894-1255

Farhi, Eli Ralph (5 mentions)
Harvard U, 1982 *Certification:* Cardiovascular Disease,
Internal Medicine, Interventional Cardiology
85 High St, Buffalo, 716-857-8611
295 Essjay Rd, Williamsville, 716-857-8611

Gatewood, Robert Payne (12 mentions)
Georgetown U, 1974
Certification: Cardiovascular Disease, Internal Medicine
6460 Main St, Williamsville, 716-634-5100

Graham, Susan P. (4 mentions)
U of Texas-Houston, 1982
Certification: Cardiovascular Disease, Internal Medicine
100 High St, Buffalo, 716-859-7280

Hong, Michael Joseph (3 mentions)
U of Hawaii, 1983
3091 William St, Cheektowaga, 716-822-3098
3435 Bailey Ave, Buffalo, 716-835-2966

Matthews, George Edmead (3 mentions)
Cornell U, 1979 *Certification:* Cardiovascular Disease,
Critical Care Medicine, Internal Medicine
6460 Main St, Williamsville, 716-634-5100

Morris, William Maxwell (3 mentions)
FMS-Canada, 1977
Certification: Cardiovascular Disease, Internal Medicine
85 High St, Buffalo, 716-857-8659

Orie, Joseph Daniel (9 mentions)
Georgetown U, 1988 *Certification:* Pediatric Cardiology
936 Delaware Ave #100, Buffalo, 716-885-5437

Pieroni, Daniel R. (3 mentions)
Georgetown U, 1964 *Certification:* Pediatric Cardiology, Pediatrics
936 Delaware Ave #100, Buffalo, 716-885-5437

Roland, Jean-Michel Alain (4 mentions)
FMS-France, 1971
936 Delaware Ave #100, Buffalo, 716-885-5437

Sekovski, Blaze (3 mentions)
Stanford U, 1981
Certification: Cardiovascular Disease, Internal Medicine
85 High St, Buffalo, 716-630-1022
295 Essjay Rd, Williamsville, 716-630-1022
3345 Southwestern Blvd, Orchard Park, 716-630-1022

Switzer, Donald Frank (4 mentions)
U of Buffalo, 1980
Certification: Cardiovascular Disease, Internal Medicine
6333 Main St, Buffalo, 716-630-1000

Dermatology

Altman, David Joel (9 mentions)
U of Buffalo, 1992 *Certification:* Dermatology
5225 Sheridan Dr, Buffalo, 716-810-0610

Kalb, Robert E. (11 mentions)
SUNY-Downstate Med Coll, 1982 *Certification:* Dermatology
295 Essjay Rd, Williamsville, 716-630-1102

Kulick, Kevin B. (6 mentions)
U of Buffalo, 1976 *Certification:* Dermatology
3839 Delaware Ave, Kenmore, 716-874-2134

Ramchand, Subash Chander (7 mentions)
FMS-India, 1961 *Certification:* Anatomic Pathology, Clinical
    Pathology, Dermatology, Dermatopathology
6934 Williams Rd #650, Niagara Falls, 716-298-8130

Rothman, Ilene Leslie (6 mentions)
Temple U, 1980
Certification: Dermatology, Pediatric Dermatology, Pediatrics
219 Bryant St, Buffalo, 716-878-8172

Wirth, Paul Bernard (8 mentions)
U of Buffalo, 1988
295 Essjay Rd, Buffalo, 716-630-1000

Emergency Medicine

Cosgrove, Edward Joseph (3 mentions)
U of Buffalo, 1994 *Certification:* Internal Medicine
7616 Transient Rd, Williamsville, 716-204-4500

Elman, Richard Steven (5 mentions)
U of Buffalo, 1978 *Certification:* Emergency Medicine
565 Abbott Rd, Buffalo, 716-826-7000

Lillis, Kathleen A. (5 mentions)
Certification: Pediatric Emergency Medicine
219 Bryant St, Buffalo, 716-878-7406

Podlas, Mark Robert (6 mentions)
FMS-Mexico, 1985 *Certification:* Internal Medicine
1595 Bailey Ave, Buffalo, 716-893-8550

Pundt, Mark Richard (3 mentions)
U of Buffalo, 1989 *Certification:* Emergency Medicine
3980 Sheridan Dr, Amherst, 716-929-2800
3 Gate Cir, Buffalo, 716-887-4007
1540 Maple Rd, Williamsville, 716-568-6551

Teuscher, Josette Anna (4 mentions)
U of Buffalo, 1987 *Certification:* Emergency Medicine
100 High St, Buffalo, 716-859-7100

Endocrinology

Giardino, Karen Frances (11 mentions)
U of Buffalo, 1985
1000 Youngs Rd #207, Williamsville, 716-636-1947

Lippes, Howard Alvin (21 mentions)
U of Buffalo, 1977
Certification: Endocrinology and Metabolism, Internal Medicine
297 Spindrift Dr #200, Williamsville, 716-635-0688

Quattrin, Teresa (7 mentions)
FMS-Italy, 1982 *Certification:* Pediatric Endocrinology, Pediatrics
219 Bryant St, Buffalo, 716-878-7588

Ryan, Augustine John, Jr. (7 mentions)
Cornell U, 1978
Certification: Endocrinology and Metabolism, Internal Medicine
3980 Sheridan Dr #601, Amherst, 716-882-6544

Spinaris, Toni M. (7 mentions)
New York Coll of Osteopathic Med, 1989
600 Harlem Rd, West Seneca, 716-332-2121

Torre, Joseph John (8 mentions)
Boston U, 1972
Certification: Endocrinology and Metabolism, Internal Medicine
85 High St, Buffalo, 716-857-8620

Family Practice *(see note on page 9)*

Harbison, Andrew James (5 mentions)
Midwestern U Chicago Coll of Osteopathic Med, 1994
30 N Union Rd, Williamsville, 716-839-8000

Johnson, David Norman (3 mentions)
New York Med Coll, 1976 *Certification:* Family Medicine
2914 Elmwood Ave, Buffalo, 716-875-6700

Martinke, David John (4 mentions)
New York Coll of Osteopathic Med, 1986
30 N Union Rd, Williamsville, 716-839-8000

Meaney-Elman, Nora E. (3 mentions)
U of Buffalo, 1984 *Certification:* Family Medicine
1829 Maple Rd #201, Buffalo, 716-839-7107

Gastroenterology

Bartolone, Christopher J. (7 mentions)
U of Buffalo, 1989 *Certification:* Gastroenterology
60 Maple Rd, Buffalo, 716-626-5250

Corasanti, James Gerard (17 mentions)
U of Buffalo, 1983
Certification: Gastroenterology, Internal Medicine
9 Limestone Dr, Buffalo, 716-631-2517
3345 Southwestern Blvd, Orchard Park, 716-631-2517

Kaplan, Richard Dana (6 mentions)
FMS-Italy, 1983
60 Maple Rd, Williamsville, 716-626-5250

Kozower, Michael (8 mentions)
SUNY-Upstate Med U, 1967
Certification: Gastroenterology, Internal Medicine
60 Maple Rd, Buffalo, 716-626-5250

Piscatelli, James Joseph (6 mentions)
U of Connecticut, 1988 *Certification:* Gastroenterology
9 Limestone Dr, Williamsville, 716-631-2517
1491 Sheridan Dr, Tonawanda, 716-631-2517

Weinrieb, Ilja J. (6 mentions)
U of Buffalo, 1971
Certification: Gastroenterology, Internal Medicine
1150 Youngs Rd #205, Buffalo, 716-636-9056

General Surgery

Alvarez-Perez, Julio A. (7 mentions)
FMS-Dominican Republic, 1981 *Certification:* Surgery
310 Sterling Dr #105, Orchard Park, 716-675-7730

Caty, Michael Gerard (5 mentions)
U of Massachusetts, 1985 *Certification:* Pediatric Surgery, Surgery
219 Bryant St, Buffalo, 716-878-7802

Dawli, Naim A. (5 mentions)
FMS-Syria, 1974 *Certification:* Surgery
2121 Main St #207, Buffalo, 716-834-2400
12845 Broadway St, Alden, 716-937-4540

Dayton, Merril Taylor (5 mentions)
U of Utah, 1976 *Certification:* Surgery
100 High St, Buffalo, 716-859-3556

Eckhert, Kenneth H., Jr. (3 mentions)
U of Buffalo, 1968 *Certification:* Surgery
295 Essjay Rd, Williamsville, 716-631-3707

Evans, Evan John (6 mentions)
U of Nebraska, 1974 *Certification:* Surgery
1150 Youngs Rd #110, Buffalo, 716-636-9004

Hickey, Donald Douglas (5 mentions)
U of Buffalo, 1978 *Certification:* Surgery, Surgical Critical Care
4476 Main St #104, Amherst, 716-204-5933
1829 Maple Rd #202, Williamsville, 716-204-5933

Kulaylat, Mahmoud M. N. (3 mentions)
FMS-Egypt, 1978 *Certification:* Colon & Rectal Surgery, Surgery
100 High St, Buffalo, 716-898-3556

O'Donnell, Katherine Anne (3 mentions)
U of Buffalo, 1993 *Certification:* Surgery
130 Empire Dr, Buffalo, 716-834-4350
6000 N Bailey Ave, Buffalo, 716-834-4350
1026 Union Rd, West Seneca, 716-712-0858

Patterson, Daniel J. (3 mentions)
U of New England Coll of Osteopathic Med, 1999
310 Sterling Dr #105, Orchard Park, 716-675-7730

Rade, Michael P. (3 mentions)
U of Buffalo, 1975 *Certification:* Surgery
550 Center Rd, Buffalo, 716-675-1414

Rainstein, Miguel Alberto (5 mentions)
FMS-Argentina, 1973 *Certification:* Surgery
3495 Bailey Ave, Buffalo, 716-834-9200

Ralabate, Joseph Angelo (10 mentions)
Creighton U, 1970 *Certification:* Surgery
2450 Elmwood Ave, Buffalo, 716-873-7335

Reynhout, Jonathan Carl (8 mentions)
U of Buffalo, 1968 *Certification:* Surgery
6333 Main St, Buffalo, 716-631-8400

Steinig, Jeffrey Paul (4 mentions)
U of Buffalo, 1988 *Certification:* Surgery
310 Sterling Dr #105, Orchard Park, 716-675-7730

Talhouk, Akram Shakib (3 mentions)
FMS-Lebanon, 1982 *Certification:* Surgery, Surgical Critical Care
85 High St, Buffalo, 716-857-8648
295 Essjay Rd, Williamsville, 716-857-8648

Geriatrics

Garbarino, Kenneth A. (6 mentions)
FMS-Grenada, 1984 *Certification:* Internal Medicine
3 Gates Cir, Buffalo, 716-887-5880

Naughton, Bruce James (6 mentions)
U of Buffalo, 1979
Certification: Hospice and Palliative Medicine, Internal Medicine
3 Gates Cir, Buffalo, 716-887-5880

Ramadan, Fadi (3 mentions)
FMS-Lebanon, 1992
Certification: Geriatric Medicine, Internal Medicine
3 Gates Cir, Buffalo, 716-887-4690

Stall, Robert Scott (4 mentions)
U of Buffalo, 1983 *Certification:* Internal Medicine
350 Greenhaven Terr, Tonawanda, 716-213-4345

Hematology/Oncology

Brecher, Martin (12 mentions)
U of Buffalo, 1972
Certification: Pediatric Hematology-Oncology, Pediatrics
Elm & Carlton St, Buffalo, 716-845-2333
219 Bryant St, Buffalo, 716-878-7349

Chary, Kandala K. (7 mentions)
FMS-India, 1970
Certification: Internal Medicine, Medical Oncology
45 Spindrift Dr #100, Buffalo, 716-565-0355

Conway, James Thomas (12 mentions)
U of Buffalo, 1980
Certification: Hematology, Internal Medicine, Medical Oncology
295 Essjay Rd, Buffalo, 716-630-1000

Early, Amy Papalia (4 mentions)
Hahnemann U, 1976
Certification: Internal Medicine, Medical Oncology
295 Essjay Rd, Buffalo, 716-630-1000

Garbes, Isosceles Dizon (10 mentions)
FMS-Philippines, 1978
Certification: Hematology, Internal Medicine, Medical Oncology
3612 Seneca St, Buffalo, 716-674-3104

Hong, Frederick (7 mentions)
U of Vermont, 1983
Certification: Hematology, Internal Medicine, Medical Oncology
45 Spindrift Dr #100, Buffalo, 716-565-0355

Lawrence, William Douglas (4 mentions)
Jefferson Med Coll, 1974
Certification: Hematology, Internal Medicine
45 Spindrift Dr #100, Williamsville, 716-565-0355

Soniwala, Saifuddin (5 mentions)
FMS-Pakistan, 1987
180 Park Club Ln #250, Buffalo, 716-833-1444

Infectious Disease

Antalek, Matthew David (19 mentions)
New York Coll of Osteopathic Med, 1985
Certification: Infectious Disease, Internal Medicine
1829 Maple Rd #202, Williamsville, 716-204-5933

Brass, Corstiaan (31 mentions)
FMS-Canada, 1973
Certification: Infectious Disease, Internal Medicine
2355 Union Rd, Cheektowaga, 716-857-8603

Cumbo, Thomas Anthony (12 mentions)
U of Buffalo, 1999
Certification: Infectious Disease, Internal Medicine
1150 Youngs Rd #207, Williamsville, 716-688-1480

Faden, Howard Syd (8 mentions)
U of Maryland, 1969
Certification: Pediatric Infectious Diseases, Pediatrics
219 Bryant St, Buffalo, 716-878-7290

Hocko, Michael (7 mentions)
U of Buffalo, 1983
Certification: Infectious Disease, Internal Medicine
2475 Harlem Rd, Buffalo, 716-893-3835

Welliver, Robert Charles (7 mentions)
U of Florida, 1972
Certification: Pediatric Infectious Diseases, Pediatrics
219 Bryant St, Buffalo, 716-878-7312

Infertility

Crickard, Kent (12 mentions)
U of Rochester, 1972 *Certification:* Obstetrics &
 Gynecology, Reproductive Endocrinology/Infertility
4510 Main St, Buffalo, 716-839-3057

Sperrazza, Ralph Charles (14 mentions)
U of Rochester, 1972 *Certification:* Obstetrics & Gynecology
4510 Main St 2nd Fl, Buffalo, 716-839-3057

Internal Medicine *(see note on page 9)*

Charles, Richard Edward (4 mentions)
U of Buffalo, 1996 *Certification:* Internal Medicine
85 High St, Buffalo, 716-857-8641

Gabryel, Timothy Francis (3 mentions)
U of Buffalo, 1976 *Certification:* Internal Medicine
290 Center Rd, Buffalo, 716-675-0707

Kawinski, Bohdan Jerzy (3 mentions)
FMS-Poland, 1978
2605 Harlem Rd, Cheektowaga, 716-891-2400

Kuritzky, Paul M. (5 mentions)
U of Buffalo, 1973 *Certification:* Internal Medicine
54 Alcona Ave, Amherst, 716-832-6207

Notaro, John C. (3 mentions)
Albany Med Coll, 1988 *Certification:* Internal Medicine
3345 Southwestern Blvd, Orchard Park, 716-656-4806

Perna, Anthony F. (4 mentions)
FMS-Mexico, 1980 *Certification:* Internal Medicine
1430 Colvin Blvd, Buffalo, 716-874-4060

Shafik, Ihab Mahmoud (3 mentions)
FMS-Egypt, 1976
18 Limestone Dr #5, Buffalo, 716-632-1400

Snow, Irene Sharon (5 mentions)
U of Buffalo, 1980 *Certification:* Internal Medicine
295 Essjay Rd, Williamsville, 716-630-1000

Stehlik, Edward Anthony (3 mentions)
Tufts U, 1977 *Certification:* Internal Medicine
1783 Colvin Blvd, Buffalo, 716-874-2150

Zakrzewski, Les (3 mentions)
FMS-Poland, 1980 *Certification:* Internal Medicine
721 Center Rd, Buffalo, 716-677-4070

Nephrology

Kohli, Romesh Kumar (7 mentions)
FMS-India, 1965 *Certification:* Internal Medicine
621 10th St, Niagara Falls, 716-285-0103
85 High St, Williamsville, 716-857-8613

Ryan, James Evirs, III (14 mentions)
FMS-Mexico, 1983 *Certification:* Nephrology
220 Red Tail #1, Orchard Park, 716-712-0864

Springate, James Edward (7 mentions)
Johns Hopkins U, 1981 *Certification:* Pediatric Nephrology
219 Bryant St, Buffalo, 716-878-7275

Sridhar, Nagaraja Rao (6 mentions)
FMS-India, 1982 *Certification:* Internal Medicine, Nephrology
85 High St, Buffalo, 716-857-8607
295 Essjay Rd, Williamsville, 716-857-8607
518 Abbott Rd, Buffalo, 716-857-8607

Venuto, Rocco Charles (8 mentions)
U of Buffalo, 1967 *Certification:* Internal Medicine, Nephrology
462 Grider St, Buffalo, 716-898-4803

Waz, Wayne Richard (7 mentions)
U of Buffalo, 1988 *Certification:* Pediatric Nephrology
219 Bryant St, Buffalo, 716-878-7275

Neurological Surgery

Egnatchik, James Gregory (13 mentions)
U of Buffalo, 1979 *Certification:* Neurological Surgery
550 Orchard Park Rd #B-103, West Seneca, 716-677-5005

Gibbons, Kevin John (9 mentions)
Albany Med Coll, 1986 *Certification:* Neurological Surgery
3 Gates Cir, Buffalo, 716-887-5200

Guterman, Lee Rand (8 mentions)
U of Buffalo, 1989 *Certification:* Neurological Surgery
1000 Youngs Rd #204, Buffalo, 716-803-1504

Hopkins, Leo Nelson, III (12 mentions)
Albany Med Coll, 1969 *Certification:* Neurological Surgery
3 Gates Cir, Buffalo, 716-887-5200

Levy, Elad Israel (11 mentions)
George Washington U, 1997 *Certification:* Neurological Surgery
3 Gates Cir, Buffalo, 716-887-5200

Moreland, Douglas Brian (8 mentions)
U of Buffalo, 1984 *Certification:* Neurological Surgery
180 Park Club Ln #100, Buffalo, 716-839-9402

Neurology

Battaglia, Michael Joseph (9 mentions)
U of New England Coll of Osteopathic Med, 1986
Certification: Neurology
85 High St, Buffalo, 716-857-8624
3345 Southwestern Blvd, Orchard Park, 716-857-8624

Duffner, Patricia D. K. (5 mentions)
U of Buffalo, 1972 *Certification:* Neurology with Special
 Qualifications in Child Neurology, Pediatrics
219 Bryant St, Buffalo, 716-878-7840

Holmlund, Tomas Henry (6 mentions)
FMS-Sweden, 1985 *Certification:* Neurology
3980 Sheridan Dr #600, Buffalo, 716-250-2000

Kalonaros, George C. (4 mentions)
FMS-Greece, 1979
2950 Elmwood Ave, Buffalo, 716-447-7260

Mechtler, Laszlo L. (12 mentions)
FMS-Hungary, 1984 *Certification:* Neurology
Elm & Carlton St, Buffalo, 716-845-3154
3980 Sheridan Dr, Buffalo, 716-250-2000

Munschauer, Frederick E. (8 mentions)
FMS-Canada, 1979 *Certification:* Internal Medicine, Neurology
100 High St, Buffalo, 716-859-7540

Obstetrics/Gynecology

Bartels, Edward Kelly (4 mentions)
U of Buffalo, 1980 *Certification:* Obstetrics & Gynecology
6440 Transit Rd, Depew, 716-684-5454
3834 Delaware Ave, Buffalo, 716-877-1221

Bruno, August Andrew, Jr. (4 mentions)
U of Buffalo, 1991 *Certification:* Obstetrics & Gynecology
410 Abbott Rd, Buffalo, 716-656-4811

Lele, Amol (6 mentions)
FMS-India, 1966
Certification: Maternal-Fetal Medicine, Obstetrics & Gynecology
239 Bryant St, Buffalo, 716-878-7509
11 Summer St #2, Buffalo, 716-881-0400

Powalski, Robert John, Jr. (8 mentions)
FMS-Dominican Republic, 1982
Certification: Obstetrics & Gynecology
3834 Delaware Ave, Buffalo, 716-877-1221
6440 Transit Rd, Depew, 716-684-5454

Todoro, Carmen Michael (3 mentions)
U of Buffalo, 1986 *Certification:* Obstetrics & Gynecology
4845 Transit Rd, Depew, 716-656-2200
3050 Orchard Park Rd, Buffalo, 716-675-5222

Trevett, Millicent Hope (3 mentions)
U of Buffalo, 1996 *Certification:* Obstetrics & Gynecology
4041 Delaware Ave, Tonawanda, 716-876-5512

Weissman, Mark A. (6 mentions)
FMS-Philippines, 1984 *Certification:* Obstetrics & Gynecology
6440 Transit Rd, Depew, 716-684-5454
3834 Delaware Ave, Buffalo, 716-877-1221

Ophthalmology

Awner, Steven (4 mentions)
Baylor U, 1989 *Certification:* Ophthalmology
3980 Sheridan Dr #402, Buffalo, 716-204-4516

Gulati, Ashvani Kumar (5 mentions)
U of Buffalo, 1987 *Certification:* Ophthalmology
3750 Delaware Ave, Buffalo, 716-874-2455

Lincoff-Cohen, Norah S. (5 mentions)
U of Buffalo, 1988 *Certification:* Ophthalmology
100 High St, Buffalo, 716-859-7596

Niles, Charles Ross (4 mentions)
U of Buffalo, 1983 *Certification:* Ophthalmology
5851 Main St, Williamsville, 716-632-3545

Patel, Dilipkumar J. (4 mentions)
FMS-India, 1965 *Certification:* Ophthalmology
65 Wehrle Dr, Buffalo, 716-837-1090

Reidy, James Joseph (7 mentions)
Loyola U Chicago, 1983 *Certification:* Ophthalmology
1176 Main St, Buffalo, 716-881-7900

Reynolds, James Dennis (6 mentions)
U of Buffalo, 1978 *Certification:* Ophthalmology
1176 Main St, Buffalo, 716-881-7916

Schaefer, Daniel Paul (5 mentions)
U of Buffalo, 1981 *Certification:* Ophthalmology
4590 Main St, Buffalo, 716-839-3535

Orthopedics

Falcone, Joseph Philip (4 mentions)
Des Moines U, 1992
36 N Union Rd, Williamsville, 716-204-1101

Ferrick, Michael Reed (4 mentions)
U of Michigan, 1992 *Certification:* Orthopaedic Surgery
219 Bryant St, Buffalo, 716-878-7171
4949 Harlem Rd, Amherst, 716-204-3251
100 High St, Buffalo, 716-859-1256

Lapoint, Paul Justin (4 mentions)
Philadelphia Coll of Osteopathic Med, 1990
36 N Union Rd, Williamsville, 716-204-1101

O'Donnell, John Leonard (5 mentions)
U of Michigan, 1987 *Certification:* Orthopaedic Surgery
3673 Southwestern Blvd, Orchard Park, 716-662-8083

Phillips, Matthew John (4 mentions)
U of Buffalo, 1991 *Certification:* Orthopaedic Surgery
4949 Harlem Rd, Amherst, 716-204-3280

Romanowski, Marcus R. (5 mentions)
U of Buffalo, 1993 *Certification:* Orthopaedic Surgery
4510 Main St, Buffalo, 716-839-0632

Slough, James Alan (4 mentions)
U of Michigan, 1984 *Certification:* Orthopaedic Surgery
3925 Sheridan Dr, Amherst, 716-250-9999

Stube, Keith Charles (8 mentions)
SUNY-Upstate Med U, 1988 *Certification:* Orthopaedic Surgery
100 Corporate Pkwy #112, Buffalo, 716-839-5858

Otorhinolaryngology

Campione, Peter Anthony (5 mentions)
FMS-Belgium, 1977 *Certification:* Otolaryngology
518 Abbott Rd, Buffalo, 716-823-4962

Chmiel, James (5 mentions)
U of Buffalo, 1994 *Certification:* Otolaryngology
3950 E Robinson Rd #106, Buffalo, 716-691-3500

Diaz-Ordaz, Ernesto A. (10 mentions)
FMS-Mexico, 1979 *Certification:* Otolaryngology
180 Park Club Ln #200, Buffalo, 716-634-7350
12845 Broadway St, Alden, 716-634-7350

Parikh, Parag Parmanand (7 mentions)
U of Buffalo, 1999 *Certification:* Otolaryngology
6941 Elaine Dr, Niagara Falls, 716-282-2041

Pizzuto, Michael Paul (12 mentions)
SUNY-Upstate Med U, 1985 *Certification:* Otolaryngology
8207 Main St #5, Williamsville, 716-632-2000

Pain Medicine

Gosy, Eugene J. (12 mentions)
FMS-Hungary, 1984 *Certification:* Neurology
100 College Pkwy #220, Buffalo, 716-626-9900

Lema, Mark J. (6 mentions)
SUNY-Downstate Med Coll, 1982
Certification: Anesthesiology, Pain Medicine
666 Elm & Carlton St, Buffalo, 716-845-4851

Peer, Gerald L. (6 mentions)
U of Buffalo, 1981 *Certification:* Anesthesiology, Pain Medicine
1230 Eggert Rd, Amherst, 716-838-0640

Waghmarae, Romanth (5 mentions)
FMS-South Africa, 1981
Certification: Anesthesiology, Pain Medicine
1515 Kensington Ave, Buffalo, 716-446-5900

Pathology

Asirwathan, John Edwin (3 mentions)
FMS-India, 1969
2157 Main St, Buffalo, 716-862-1559

Cheney, Richard T. (3 mentions)
U of New Mexico, 1980 *Certification:* Anatomic Pathology &
   Clinical Pathology, Cytopathology, Dermatopathology
Elm & Carlton St, Buffalo, 716-845-3511

Helm, Thomas N. (3 mentions)
Albany Med Coll, 1987
Certification: Dermatology, Dermatopathology
6255 Sheridan Dr #B-208, Williamsville, 716-630-2582

Sands, Amy M. Skarin (5 mentions)
U of Rochester, 1980
Certification: Anatomic Pathology, Cytopathology, Hematology
100 High St, Buffalo, 716-859-2140

Pediatrics *(see note on page 9)*

Cozza, Thomas F. (4 mentions)
U of Illinois, 1978 *Certification:* Pediatrics
25 Hopkins Rd, Buffalo, 716-632-8050

Lana, Steven Joseph (4 mentions)
U of Rochester, 1982 *Certification:* Pediatrics
2550 Delaware Ave, Buffalo, 716-884-0230

Mattimore, Colleen Anne (3 mentions)
U of Buffalo, 1991
5800 Big Tree Rd, Orchard Park, 716-662-7337

McNally, G. Lawrence (5 mentions)
Stony Brook U, 1985 *Certification:* Pediatrics
8643 Sheridan Dr, Buffalo, 716-565-9030

Sasankan, Krishna (3 mentions)
FMS-India, 1979 *Certification:* Pediatrics
6000 N Bailey Ave #1-C, Buffalo, 716-834-4522

Plastic Surgery

Anain, Shirley Ann (18 mentions)
U of Buffalo, 1985 *Certification:* Plastic Surgery
4949 Harlem Rd, Amherst, 716-838-1333

Giacobbe, Andrew Philip (7 mentions)
U of Buffalo, 1986 *Certification:* Otolaryngology, Plastic Surgery
7 Hopkins Rd, Buffalo, 716-634-5555
3040 Amsdell Rd, Hamburg, 716-634-5555

Graff, Jonathan Aaron (12 mentions)
U of Buffalo, 1983
5611 Main St, Buffalo, 716-631-8500

Meilman, Jeffrey Gregory (7 mentions)
U of Rochester, 1969
Certification: Otolaryngology, Plastic Surgery
811 Maple Rd, Williamsville, 716-626-5300

Perry, Robert Johnson, Jr. (10 mentions)
U of Texas-Dallas, 1975
Certification: Otolaryngology, Plastic Surgery
6932 Williams Rd #1700, Niagara Falls, 716-297-7040

Psychiatry

Ashton, Adam Keller (4 mentions)
U of Buffalo, 1987 *Certification:* Psychiatry
85 Bryant Woods S, Amherst, 716-689-3333

Kang, Balvinder Singh (3 mentions)
FMS-India, 1972 *Certification:* Psychiatry
3802 Seneca St, West Seneca, 716-677-5418

Martin, Christopher G. (3 mentions)
U of Buffalo, 1991
Certification: Child & Adolescent Psychiatry, Psychiatry
85 Bryant Woods S, Amherst, 716-689-3333

Wilinsky, Howard Charles (6 mentions)
U of Buffalo, 1961 *Certification:* Psychiatry
765 Wehrle Dr, Buffalo, 716-633-1240

Wolin, Richard Elliot (5 mentions)
U of Buffalo, 1964 *Certification:* Psychiatry
6245 Sheridan Dr #316, Williamsville, 716-630-1204

Pulmonary Disease

Durante, David J. (9 mentions)
Wayne State U, 1981 *Certification:* Critical Care Medicine,
   Internal Medicine, Pulmonary Disease
290 Center Rd, Buffalo, 716-677-0850

Gelfer, Alexander Boris (5 mentions)
FMS-Russia, 1972
Certification: Internal Medicine, Pulmonary Disease
297 Spindrift Dr #100, Buffalo, 716-631-8863

Gibbons, William J. (6 mentions)
Certification: Critical Care Medicine, Internal Medicine,
   Pulmonary Disease
100 High St #B-6, Buffalo, 716-859-2271

Neu, Jeffery Robert (5 mentions)
U of Illinois, 1983
Certification: Internal Medicine, Pulmonary Disease
6460 Main St, Buffalo, 716-634-5100

Rabadi, Nashat Hanna (21 mentions)
FMS-Grenada, 1988
295 Essjay Rd, Williamsville, 716-630-1100
85 High St, Buffalo, 716-630-1100

Sfeir, Norman John (6 mentions)
U of Kentucky, 1980
Certification: Internal Medicine, Pulmonary Disease
297 Spindrift Dr #100, Buffalo, 716-631-8863

Sherif, Sherif (5 mentions)
FMS-Egypt, 1977
85 High St, Buffalo, 716-857-8646
295 Essjay Rd, Williamsville, 716-857-8646

Radiology—Diagnostic

Christensen, Steven Lynn (4 mentions)
U of Colorado, 1979 *Certification:* Diagnostic Radiology
100 College Pkwy #180, Buffalo, 716-836-1902

Ferin, Peter (4 mentions)
Mount Sinai Sch of Med, 1981 *Certification:* Diagnostic Radiology
5300 Military Rd, Lewiston, 716-298-2278

Licata, Michael (4 mentions)
U of Buffalo, 1989 *Certification:* Diagnostic Radiology
3040 Amsdell Rd, Hamburg, 716-649-9000
3050 Orchard Park Rd, West Seneca, 716-649-9000
550 Orchard Park Rd, West Seneca, 716-649-9000

Montgomery, Paul (8 mentions)
Georgetown U, 1978 *Certification:* Diagnostic Radiology
100 College Pkwy #180, Buffalo, 716-636-1902

Serghany, Joseph Emile (3 mentions)
FMS-Lebanon, 1988 *Certification:* Diagnostic Radiology
425 Michigan Ave, Buffalo, 716-848-2160
222 Genesee St, Buffalo, 716-689-1901

Sung, Janet Hyunsook (9 mentions)
FMS-South Korea, 1971 *Certification:* Radiology
4711 Transit Rd, Depew, 716-631-2500
55 Spindrift Dr #101, Williamsville, 716-631-2500
4855 Camp Rd #500, Hamburg, 716-631-2500

Radiology—Therapeutic

Cromwell, Brian Gordon (7 mentions)
U of Buffalo, 1985 *Certification:* Diagnostic Radiology
565 Abbott Rd, Buffalo, 716-826-7000

Shah, Dhiren K. (6 mentions)
Robert W Johnson Med Sch, 1990
Certification: Radiation Oncology
3085 Harlem Rd, Cheektowaga, 716-844-5500

Shin, Kyu H. (4 mentions)
FMS-South Korea, 1968 *Certification:* Therapeutic Radiology
2950 Elmwood Ave, Kenmore, 716-871-0181
810 Davison Rd, Lockport, 716-438-5486

Rehabilitation

Czyrny, James J. (5 mentions)
U of Buffalo, 1981
Certification: Physical Medicine & Rehabilitation
462 Grider St, Buffalo, 716-898-3106
4949 Harlem Rd, Amherst, 716-898-3106

Geraci, Michael Charles, Jr. (6 mentions)
FMS-Mexico, 1983
Certification: Physical Medicine & Rehabilitation
200 Sterling Dr, Orchard Park, 716-677-4484
100 College Pkwy #100, Buffalo, 716-626-0093
4949 Harlem Rd #300, Amherst, 716-626-0093

McAdam, Frederick B. (4 mentions)
U of Buffalo, 1983
Certification: Physical Medicine & Rehabilitation
200 Sterling Dr, Orchard Park, 716-677-4487
4949 Harlem Rd #300, Amherst, 716-626-0093

Rheumatology

Ambrus, Julian L., Jr. (7 mentions)
Jefferson Med Coll, 1979
Certification: Allergy & Immunology, Internal Medicine
100 High St, Buffalo, 716-859-1333

Grisanti, Joseph Michael (10 mentions)
U of Rochester, 1984
Certification: Internal Medicine, Rheumatology
3055 Southwestern Blvd, Orchard Park, 716-675-2500

Grisanti, Michael Wayne (14 mentions)
FMS-Italy, 1983 *Certification:* Internal Medicine, Rheumatology
3055 Southwestern Blvd, Orchard Park, 716-675-2500

Martinez, Carlos Luis (7 mentions)
FMS-Mexico, 1979
2291 Union Rd, West Seneca, 716-668-6146

Thoracic Surgery

Jajkowski, Mark Robert (5 mentions)
U of Buffalo, 1996 *Certification:* Surgery, Thoracic Surgery
2695 Harlem Rd, Buffalo, 716-332-3505

Takita, Hiroshi (8 mentions)
FMS-Japan, 1954 *Certification:* Surgery, Thoracic Surgery
3 Gates Cir, Buffalo, 716-885-0602

Urology

Aliotta, Philip Joseph (9 mentions)
FMS-Mexico, 1981 *Certification:* Urology
6645 Main St, Buffalo, 716-631-0932
3085 Harlem Rd, Cheektowaga, 716-844-5350

Barlog, Kevin John (10 mentions)
U of Buffalo, 1982 *Certification:* Urology
3085 Harlem Rd, West Seneca, 716-844-5000

Gilbert, Richard Norman (7 mentions)
U of Buffalo, 1988 *Certification:* Urology
3085 Harlem Rd, West Seneca, 716-844-5000

Griswold, John Joseph (7 mentions)
U of Buffalo, 1987 *Certification:* Urology
295 Essjay Rd, Williamsville, 716-630-1050
85 High St, Buffalo, 716-857-8800

Skomra, Christopher Jude (6 mentions)
U of Buffalo, 1989 *Certification:* Urology
3085 Harlem Rd, West Seneca, 716-844-5000

Williot, Pierre Emile (7 mentions)
FMS-Canada, 1981 *Certification:* Pediatric Urology, Urology
219 Bryant St, Buffalo, 716-878-7393

Vascular Surgery

Anain, Joseph Marcelo, Sr. (10 mentions)
FMS-Argentina, 1959 *Certification:* Surgery, Vascular Surgery
2121 Main St #316, Buffalo, 716-837-2400

Anain, Paul Michael (19 mentions)
U of Buffalo, 1992 *Certification:* Surgery, Vascular Surgery
2121 Main St #316, Buffalo, 716-837-2400

New York Metropolitan Area

Including New York City, Long Island, and Westchester County

Allergy/Immunology

Adimoolam, Seetharaman (4 mentions)
FMS-India, 1969 *Certification:* Allergy & Immunology, Pediatrics
1756 Richmond Ave, Staten Island, 718-238-0700
461 100th St, Brooklyn, 718-238-0700

Bassett, Clifford (5 mentions)
FMS-Mexico, 1984 *Certification:* Allergy & Immunology
150 Broadway #616, New York, 212-964-1295
635 Madison Ave 19th Fl, New York, 212-260-6078
381 Park Ave S #1020, New York, 212-260-6078
77 Mercer St #2, New York, 212-274-1999

Boxer, Mitchell Barry (4 mentions)
New York Med Coll, 1981
Certification: Allergy & Immunology, Internal Medicine
560 Northern Blvd #209, Great Neck, 516-482-0910
811 Walt Whitman Rd, Melville, 631-423-8488

Buchbinder, Ellen Maud (13 mentions)
Tulane U, 1978
Certification: Allergy & Immunology, Internal Medicine
111 E 88th St #1B, New York, 212-410-3246

Chandler, Michael J. (10 mentions)
Wayne State U, 1981
Certification: Allergy & Immunology, Internal Medicine
115 E 61st St, New York, 212-486-6715

Corn, Beth Eve (6 mentions)
Albert Einstein Coll of Med, 1989
Certification: Allergy & Immunology
5 E 98th St, New York, 212-241-0764

Corriel, Robert Neil (5 mentions)
Wake Forest U, 1976
Certification: Allergy & Immunology, Pediatrics
1129 Northern Blvd #300, Manhasset, 516-365-6077

Cunningham-Rundles, Charlotte (5 mentions)
Columbia U, 1969 *Certification:* Internal Medicine
240 E 68th St, New York, 212-737-8973

Dattwyler, Raymond J. (6 mentions)
U of Buffalo, 1973 *Certification:* Allergy & Immunology, Diagnostic Laboratory Immunology, Internal Medicine
241 E Main St, Huntington, 631-367-5391

Davis-Lorton, Mark Alan (7 mentions)
Med Coll of Pennsylvania, 1992
Certification: Allergy & Immunology, Internal Medicine
120 Mineola Blvd #410, Mineola, 516-663-2097

Ehrlich, Paul Mordecai (9 mentions)
New York U, 1970
Certification: Allergy & Immunology, Pediatrics
35 E 35th St, New York, 212-685-4225

Fonacier, Luz Sison (6 mentions)
FMS-Philippines, 1978
Certification: Allergy & Immunology, Internal Medicine
120 Mineola Blvd #410, Mineola, 516-663-2097

Frieri, Marianne (4 mentions)
Loyola U Chicago, 1978 *Certification:* Allergy & Immunology,
   Diagnostic Laboratory Immunology, Internal Medicine
2201 Hempstead Tpke, East Meadow, 516-572-6501

Fusillo, Christine A. (6 mentions)
New York U, 1980
Certification: Allergy & Immunology, Pediatrics
55 S Broadway #1, Tarrytown, 914-631-3283
Stony Brook University Cedarwood Hall, Valhalla, 914-493-1342

Geraci-Ciardullo, Kira A. (16 mentions)
Columbia U, 1980
Certification: Allergy & Immunology, Pediatrics
1600 Harrison Ave #304, Mamaroneck, 914-777-1179

Gerardi, Eugene Nicholas (4 mentions)
FMS-Mexico, 1975
1171 Old Country Rd #5, Plainview, 516-938-7676
500 W Main St #216, Babylon, 631-669-6350

Goldstein, Stanley (7 mentions)
New York Med Coll, 1975 *Certification:* Allergy &
   Immunology, Pediatric Pulmonology, Pediatrics
242 Merrick Rd #401, Rockville Centre, 516-536-7336

Grubman, Samuel D. (4 mentions)
Mount Sinai Sch of Med, 1983
Certification: Allergy & Immunology, Pediatrics
154 W 14 St 4th Fl, New York, 212-616-4122

Guida, Louis Edward, Jr. (7 mentions)
FMS-Grenada, 1984
Certification: Allergy & Immunology, Pediatrics
649 W Montauk Hwy, Bay Shore, 631-665-2700

Jerome, Cynthia (4 mentions)
Albert Einstein Coll of Med, 1992
Certification: Allergy & Immunology
75 S Broadway, White Plains, 914-949-3888

Lang, Paul Bruce (12 mentions)
Cornell U, 1973 *Certification:* Allergy & Immunology, Pediatrics
1 Hollow Ln #110, New Hyde Park, 516-365-6666
32 Village Sq, Glen Cove, 516-676-1111
775 Park Ave #125, Huntington, 631-271-2222
145 Manetto Hill Rd #110, Plainview, 516-933-3333

Maitland, Anne Lydia (4 mentions)
U of Pennsylvania, 1997
Certification: Allergy & Immunology, Internal Medicine
5 E 98th St, New York, 212-241-9767

Markovics, Sharon B. (11 mentions)
Albert Einstein Coll of Med, 1975
Certification: Allergy & Immunology, Pediatrics
1129 Northern Blvd #300, Manhasset, 516-365-6077

Mayer, Daniel Lawrence (9 mentions)
FMS-Italy, 1978 *Certification:* Allergy & Immunology, Pediatrics
263 E Main St, Smithtown, 631-366-5252

Novick, Brian E. (8 mentions)
FMS-Mexico, 1978
Certification: Allergy & Immunology, Pediatrics
30 Newbridge Rd, East Meadow, 516-731-5740
11821 Queens Blvd #601, Forest Hills, 718-261-3663

Osleeb, Craig S. (7 mentions)
Certification: Allergy & Immunology, Pediatrics
90 S Bedford Rd, Mount Kisco, 914-241-1050

Pollowitz, James Allen (7 mentions)
New York U, 1973
Certification: Allergy & Immunology, Pediatrics
281 Garth Rd #A, Scarsdale, 914-472-3833

Rosenstreich, David Leon (6 mentions)
New York U, 1967 *Certification:* Allergy & Immunology,
   Diagnostic Laboratory Immunology, Internal Medicine
40 Hillside Rd, Larchmont, 718-405-8323
1515 Blondell Ave, Bronx, 718-405-8300
1300 Morris Park Ave, Bronx, 718-430-2120
3514 Bainbridge St, Bronx, 718-231-2997

Rubin, James Milton (4 mentions)
New York Med Coll, 1960
Certification: Allergy & Immunology, Internal Medicine
35 E 35th St #202, New York, 212-685-4225

Sampson, Hugh A. (9 mentions)
U of Buffalo, 1975
Certification: Allergy & Immunology, Pediatrics
1 Gustave L Levy Pl, New York, 212-241-5548

Shepherd, Gillian Mary (8 mentions)
New York Med Coll, 1976
Certification: Allergy & Immunology, Internal Medicine
235 E 67th St #203, New York, 212-288-9300

Sicherer, Scott Howard (9 mentions)
Johns Hopkins U, 1990
Certification: Allergy & Immunology, Pediatrics
5 E 98th St, New York, 212-241-5548
1 Gustave L Levy Pl, New York, 212-731-7990

Sicklick, Marc Joseph (8 mentions)
Albert Einstein Coll of Med, 1974
Certification: Allergy & Immunology, Pediatrics
123 Grove Ave #110, Cedarhurst, 516-569-5550

Weinstock, Gary Alan (4 mentions)
Albany Med Coll, 1979 *Certification:* Allergy & Immunology,
   Internal Medicine, Pulmonary Disease
310 E Shore Rd #207, Great Neck, 516-487-1073

Weiss, Steven Jay (4 mentions)
Stony Brook U, 1991 *Certification:* Allergy & Immunology
175 Jericho Tpke #121, Syosset, 516-921-2267

Wertheim, David Lewis (5 mentions)
Med Coll of Pennsylvania, 1988
Certification: Allergy & Immunology
2800 Marcus Ave, Lake Success, 516-608-2898

Anesthesiology

Abel, Mark (3 mentions)
New York U, 1986 *Certification:* Anesthesiology
240 Central Park S, New York, 212-241-6426
111 E 210th St, Bronx, 718-920-4321

Berger, David Benjamin (3 mentions)
New York Med Coll, 1980 *Certification:* Anesthesiology
101 St Andrews Ln, Glen Cove, 516-674-7591

Caruana, Dennis Salvatore (3 mentions)
Georgetown U, 1979
Certification: Anesthesiology, Internal Medicine
301 E Main St, Bay Shore, 631-968-3000

Cohen, Leonard Irwin (3 mentions)
Mount Sinai Sch of Med, 1981
Certification: Anesthesiology, Internal Medicine
Davis Ave & E Post Rd, White Plains, 914-681-0600

Cowan, Douglas Edward (3 mentions)
U of Nebraska, 1986 *Certification:* Anesthesiology
34 S Bedford Rd, Mount Kisco, 914-242-5621

Gallagher, Richard F. (4 mentions)
New York U, 1973
Certification: Anesthesiology, Internal Medicine
Davis Ave & E Post Rd, White Plains, 914-681-0600

George, Derick T. (3 mentions)
New York U, 1986 *Certification:* Anesthesiology
333 Route 25-A #225, Rocky Point, 631-744-3671

Glassman, Kevin Michael (3 mentions)
SUNY-Downstate Med Coll, 1986 *Certification:* Anesthesiology
58 School St #102, Glen Cove, 516-674-0404

Hausman, Laurence M. (5 mentions)
U of Southern California, 1989 *Certification:* Anesthesiology
1 Gustave L Levy Pl, New York, 212-241-7475

Heyer, Eric John (4 mentions)
Albert Einstein Coll of Med, 1975
Certification: Anesthesiology, Neurology
622 W 168th St, New York, 212-305-2179

Jackson, Mark Anthony (3 mentions)
Albert Einstein Coll of Med, 1994 *Certification:* Anesthesiology
1825 E Chester Rd, Bronx, 718-904-2872

La Porta, Robert F. (3 mentions)
Stony Brook U, 1986 *Certification:* Anesthesiology
101 St Andrews Ln, Glen Cove, 516-674-7591

Lehman, Frederick Richard (4 mentions)
SUNY-Downstate Med Coll, 1999 *Certification:* Anesthesiology
333 Route 25a #225, Rocky Point, 631-744-3671

Leibowitz, Andrew Barry (3 mentions)
Mount Sinai Sch of Med, 1983 *Certification:* Anesthesiology,
   Critical Care Medicine, Internal Medicine
1 Gustave L Levy Pl #1016, New York, 212-241-6500

Lesser, Jonathan Baird (6 mentions)
Certification: Anesthesiology
1000 10th Ave, New York, 212-523-2500

Levin, Serle Kevin (3 mentions)
Cornell U, 1989 *Certification:* Anesthesiology
800 Westchester Ave, Rye Brook, 914-681-0600

Malhotra, Vinod (4 mentions)
FMS-India, 1974
525 E 68th St, New York, 212-746-2777

Meyers, Michael Bruce (4 mentions)
Jefferson Med Coll, 1973 *Certification:* Anesthesiology
300 Community Dr, Manhasset, 516-562-4887

Nardi, Dominic Jerry (4 mentions)
Johns Hopkins U, 1975 *Certification:* Anesthesiology
333 E Shore Rd, Manhasset, 516-562-4887

Nataloni, Robert C. (4 mentions)
FMS-Italy, 1981
333 Route 25-A #225, Rocky Point, 631-744-3671

Opperman, Sheldon B. (3 mentions)
Certification: Anesthesiology
100 E 77th St, New York, 212-434-2890
210 E 64th St, New York, 212-838-9200

Pesso, Raymond Mitchell (3 mentions)
Morehouse Coll, 1990 *Certification:* Anesthesiology
5 Arista Dr, Dix Hills, 516-659-2771

Reich, David Louis (7 mentions)
Jefferson Med Coll, 1982 *Certification:* Anesthesiology
1 Gustave L Levy Pl #1010, New York, 212-241-6500

Samson, Gil Melchor (3 mentions)
FMS-Philippines, 1977 *Certification:* Anesthesiology
216 1st St, Mineola, 516-741-0570

Sherman, Scott Charles (9 mentions)
U of Buffalo, 1984 *Certification:* Anesthesiology
333 Route 25-A #225, Rocky Point, 631-744-3671
2 Shen Ct, Setauket, 631-331-0103

Shoum, Steven Mark (3 mentions)
Yale U, 1978 *Certification:* Anesthesiology, Pain Medicine
77 N Centre Ave #202, Rockville Centre, 516-764-7246

Slepian, Ralph Lee (3 mentions)
Med Coll of Wisconsin, 1984 *Certification:* Anesthesiology
345 E 73rd St, New York, 212-746-2846
525 E 68th St, New York, 212-746-2894

Starr, Don M. (3 mentions)
U of Rochester, 1989 *Certification:* Anesthesiology, Pediatrics
800 West Chester Rd, Rye Brook, 914-428-5454

Strobel, Alan F. (4 mentions)
SUNY-Downstate Med Coll, 1987 *Certification:* Anesthesiology
300 Community Dr, Manhasset, 516-562-4887

Walker, Peter F. (3 mentions)
Boston U, 1969 *Certification:* Anesthesiology
300 Community Dr, Manhasset, 516-562-4887

Cardiac Surgery

Adams, David Harold (18 mentions)
Duke U, 1983 *Certification:* Thoracic Surgery
1190 5th Ave, New York, 212-659-6800

Colangelo, Roberto G. (6 mentions)
New York U, 1990 *Certification:* Thoracic Surgery
100 Port Washington Blvd, Roslyn, 516-365-8372

Galloway, Aubrey C. (14 mentions)
Tulane U, 1978 *Certification:* Thoracic Surgery
530 1st Ave, New York, 800-557-7185

Girardi, Leonard Nick, Jr. (18 mentions)
Cornell U, 1989 *Certification:* Surgery, Thoracic Surgery
525 E 68th St #404, New York, 212-746-5194

Graver, L. Michael (6 mentions)
Albany Med Coll, 1977 *Certification:* Surgery, Thoracic Surgery
27005 76th Ave, New Hyde Park, 718-470-7460

Hall, Michael Howard (6 mentions)
U of Kentucky, 1972 *Certification:* Surgery, Thoracic Surgery
300 Community Dr, Manhasset, 516-562-4970

Hartman, Alan Roy (34 mentions)
Mount Sinai Sch of Med, 1979
Certification: Surgery, Surgical Critical Care, Thoracic Surgery
300 Community Dr, Manhasset, 516-562-0100

Isom, Ottis Wayne (22 mentions)
U of Texas-Dallas, 1965 *Certification:* Surgery, Thoracic Surgery
525 E 68th St #M404, New York, 212-746-5151

Krieger, Karl Hemingway (20 mentions)
Johns Hopkins U, 1975 *Certification:* Thoracic Surgery
525 E 68th St #404, New York, 212-746-5152

Michler, Robert E. (7 mentions)
Dartmouth Coll, 1981 *Certification:* Thoracic Surgery
3400 Bainbridge Ave, Bronx, 718-920-7000
200 S Broadway, Tarrytown, 914-631-2895

Oz, Mehmet Cengiz (25 mentions)
U of Pennsylvania, 1986 *Certification:* Thoracic Surgery
177 Fort Washington Ave, New York, 212-305-4434

Robinson, Newell Bruce (7 mentions)
U of Mississippi, 1977 *Certification:* Surgery, Thoracic Surgery
100 Port Washington Blvd #G-01, Roslyn, 516-627-2173

Schubach, Scott Leslie (20 mentions)
Baylor U, 1983
Certification: Surgery, Surgical Critical Care, Thoracic Surgery
120 Mineola Blvd #300, Mineola, 516-663-4400

Smith, Craig Richey (20 mentions)
Case Western Reserve U, 1977 *Certification:* Thoracic Surgery
177 Fort Washington Ave #435, New York, 212-305-8312

Spielvogel, David (9 mentions)
SUNY-Downstate Med Coll, 1990 *Certification:* Thoracic Surgery
95 Grasslands Rd, Valhalla, 914-493-8793

Stelzer, Paul Edward (8 mentions)
Columbia U, 1972 *Certification:* Thoracic Surgery
5 E 98th Sr, New York, 212-659-6871

Subramanian, Valavanur A. (9 mentions)
FMS-India, 1962 *Certification:* Surgery, Thoracic Surgery
130 E 77th St 4th Fl, New York, 212-434-3000

Taylor, James R., Jr. (10 mentions)
Med U of South Carolina, 1984
Certification: Surgery, Thoracic Surgery
100 Port Washington Blvd #G-01, Roslyn, 516-627-2173

Tranbaugh, Robert F. (9 mentions)
U of Pennsylvania, 1976 *Certification:* Thoracic Surgery
317 E 17th St, New York, 212-420-2584
10 Nathan D Perlman Pl Dept Psych, New York, 212-420-2584

Cardiology

Applebaum, Robert M. (3 mentions)
New York U, 1989
Certification: Cardiovascular Disease, Internal Medicine
530 1st Ave #4-G, New York, 212-263-7229

Arkonac, Burak Mehmet (3 mentions)
FMS-Turkey, 1986
Certification: Cardiovascular Disease, Interventional Cardiology
100 Port Washington Blvd #105, Roslyn, 516-390-9640

Berdoff, Russell Lindsay (3 mentions)
New York Med Coll, 1975
Certification: Cardiovascular Disease, Internal Medicine
67 Irving Pl #7, New York, 212-979-9224

Berger, William Jay (4 mentions)
New York Med Coll, 1979
Certification: Cardiovascular Disease, Internal Medicine
2001 Marcus Ave #S250, New Hyde Park, 516-488-4428

Biancaniello, Thomas M. (5 mentions)
New York Med Coll, 1975
Certification: Pediatric Cardiology, Pediatrics
450 Waverly Ave #8, Patchogue, 631-444-5437
100 Nicolls Rd 5th Fl, Stony Brook, 631-444-5437

Bierman, Fredrick Zachary (5 mentions)
SUNY-Downstate Med Coll, 1973
Certification: Pediatric Cardiology, Pediatrics
269-01 76th Ave #CH-139, New Hyde Park, 516-470-7350

Blau, William Louis (4 mentions)
SUNY-Upstate Med U, 1986
Certification: Cardiovascular Disease, Internal Medicine
310 E Shore Rd #104, Great Neck, 516-829-9550

Blaufarb, Ira Stephen (5 mentions)
Jefferson Med Coll, 1991 *Certification:* Cardiovascular Disease
158 E 84th St, New York, 212-535-6340

Breen, William John (7 mentions)
New York Med Coll, 1977
Certification: Cardiovascular Disease, Internal Medicine
43 Crossways Park Dr, Woodbury, 516-938-3000

Brief, George (6 mentions)
FMS-Romania, 1961
Certification: Cardiovascular Disease, Internal Medicine
176 E 77th St #1A, New York, 212-744-1852

Bruno, Peter Frank (4 mentions)
FMS-Italy, 1969
Certification: Cardiovascular Disease, Internal Medicine
45 Research Way #108, East Setauket, 631-941-2704

Campagna, Robert Don (3 mentions)
Cornell U, 1989
Certification: Cardiovascular Disease, Internal Medicine
425 E 61st St #6, New York, 212-752-2000

Caracta, Antonio Reyes (4 mentions)
FMS-Philippines, 1963
Certification: Cardiovascular Disease, Internal Medicine
491 Bard Ave, Staten Island, 718-727-1590

Catanese, James Walter (3 mentions)
Albany Med Coll, 1988 *Certification:* Cardiovascular Disease
1888 Commerce St, Yorktown Heights, 914-242-9400
105 S Bedford Rd #320, Mount Kisco, 914-242-9400

Chikvashvili, Daniel I. (3 mentions)
FMS-Russia, 1981
Certification: Cardiovascular Disease, Internal Medicine
119-60 Metropolitan Ave, Staten Island, 718-916-9757

Chinitz, Larry A. (3 mentions)
New York U, 1979
Certification: Cardiovascular Disease, Internal Medicine
560 1st Ave, New York, 212-263-5656
530 1st Ave, New York, 212-263-7149
403 E 34th St, New York, 212-263-7149

Cooper, Jerome Abraham (3 mentions)
SUNY-Downstate Med Coll, 1961
Certification: Cardiovascular Disease, Internal Medicine
150 Lockwood Ave #28, New Rochelle, 914-633-7870

Coppola, John T. (5 mentions)
Certification: Cardiovascular Disease, Internal Medicine,
Interventional Cardiology
275 7th Ave 3rd Fl, New York, 646-660-9999

Covey, Stephen Hugh (3 mentions)
Albert Einstein Coll of Med, 1989
Certification: Cardiovascular Disease, Internal Medicine
242 Merrick Rd #402, Rockville Centre, 516-763-2800

Cramer, Marvin Edward (3 mentions)
Jefferson Med Coll, 1969
Certification: Cardiovascular Disease, Internal Medicine
225 Community Dr #130, Great Neck, 516-504-0474

Cunningham, Thomas F. (4 mentions)
Cornell U, 1983
Certification: Cardiovascular Disease, Internal Medicine
1000 Northern Blvd #120, Great Neck, 516-466-8900

D'Agate, David J. (3 mentions)
New York Coll of Osteopathic Med, 1999
Certification: Cardiovascular Disease, Internal Medicine
260 Middle Country Rd #214, Smithtown, 631-265-5050

Darrow, Bruce Jonathan (3 mentions)
Washington U, 1997
Certification: Cardiovascular Disease, Internal Medicine
1 Gustave L Levy Pl, New York, 212-241-8544
5 E 98th St 3rd, New York, 2112-241-854

Davison, Edward Terry (4 mentions)
Wake Forest U, 1959
Certification: Cardiovascular Disease, Internal Medicine
300 Franklin Ave, Valley Stream, 516-599-8280
520 Franklin Ave, Garden City, 516-746-6220

Del Guzzo, Luciano (5 mentions)
New York Med Coll, 1977
Certification: Cardiovascular Disease, Internal Medicine
425 W 59th St #8-B, New York, 212-376-3187

Deutsch, Ezra (3 mentions)
Harvard U, 1982 *Certification:* Cardiovascular Disease,
Internal Medicine, Interventional Cardiology
260 E Main St #214, Smithtown, 631-265-5050

Dresdale, Robert Jay (3 mentions)
Columbia U, 1972
Certification: Cardiovascular Disease, Internal Medicine
225 Community Dr #130, Great Neck, 516-504-0474

Drusin, Ronald Edmond (4 mentions)
Columbia U, 1966
Certification: Cardiovascular Disease, Internal Medicine
161 Fort Washington Ave, New York, 212-305-5371

Fass, Arthur Eugene (4 mentions)
New York Med Coll, 1976
Certification: Cardiovascular Disease, Internal Medicine
465 N State Rd, Briarcliff, 914-762-5810

Feld, Michael (7 mentions)
Pennsylvania State U, 1977
Certification: Cardiovascular Disease, Internal Medicine
777 N Broadway, Tarrytown, 914-366-3752

Forman, Robert (3 mentions)
1825 Eastchester Rd, Bronx, 718-904-2927

Fox, Arthur Charles (3 mentions)
New York U, 1948
Certification: Cardiovascular Disease, Internal Medicine
530 1st Ave, New York, 212-263-7229

Fox, Martin Leon (3 mentions)
New York U, 1961
Certification: Cardiovascular Disease, Internal Medicine
109 E 38th St, New York, 212-686-3410

Franko, David M. (3 mentions)
Albany Med Coll, 1992
45 Research Way #108, East Setauket, 631-941-2704

Fuster, Valentin De C. (12 mentions)
FMS-Spain, 1968
Certification: Cardiovascular Disease, Internal Medicine
1190 5th Ave, New York, 212-241-7911

Gitler, Bernard (3 mentions)
Cornell U, 1976 *Certification:* Cardiovascular Disease,
   Critical Care Medicine, Internal Medicine
150 Lockwood Ave, New Rochelle, 914-633-7870

Gliklich, Jerry I. (8 mentions)
Columbia U, 1975
Certification: Cardiovascular Disease, Internal Medicine
161 Fort Washington Ave #535, New York, 212-305-5588

Goldberg, Barry Edward (4 mentions)
Loyola U Chicago, 1988
Certification: Pediatric Cardiology, Pediatrics
655 Deer Park Dr, Babylon, 631-321-2100

Goldberg, Douglas Alan (3 mentions)
SUNY-Downstate Med Coll, 1983
Certification: Cardiovascular Disease, Internal Medicine
1 Expressway Plaza #220, Roslyn Heights, 516-626-0700

Goldberg, Harvey Lee (4 mentions)
Cornell U, 1976
Certification: Cardiovascular Disease, Internal Medicine
425 E 61st St, New York, 212-752-2000

Goldberg, Joel (7 mentions)
Pennsylvania State U, 1978
Certification: Cardiovascular Disease, Internal Medicine
310 E Shore Rd #104, Great Neck, 516-829-9550

Goldberg, Steven Mark (4 mentions)
U of Pennsylvania, 1979
Certification: Cardiovascular Disease, Internal Medicine
1010 Northern Blvd, Great Neck, 516-390-2430

Green, Stephen Joseph (4 mentions)
Tufts U, 1980 *Certification:* Cardiovascular Disease,
   Internal Medicine, Interventional Cardiology
300 Community Dr, Manhasset, 516-562-4100

Greenberg, Mark Arnold (4 mentions)
U of Illinois, 1973 *Certification:* Cardiovascular Disease,
   Internal Medicine, Interventional Cardiology
111 E 210th St, Bronx, 718-920-5573

Greif, Richard Hanan (3 mentions)
New York Med Coll, 1975
Certification: Cardiovascular Disease, Internal Medicine
127 S Broadway, Yonkers, 914-965-6060

Grossman, David Seth (7 mentions)
U of Pennsylvania, 1988
43 Crossways Park Dr, Woodbury, 516-938-3000

Harnick, Paul Eliot (3 mentions)
SUNY-Downstate Med Coll, 1977
Certification: Cardiovascular Disease, Internal Medicine
975 Stewart Ave, Garden City, 516-222-6490

Hecht, Alan Jay (3 mentions)
Northwestern U, 1981
Certification: Cardiovascular Disease, Internal Medicine
1075 Park Ave, New York, 212-876-0845

Infantino, Michael N. (3 mentions)
SUNY-Downstate Med Coll, 1981
Certification: Cardiovascular Disease, Internal Medicine
275 7th Ave, New York, 646-660-9999

Inra, Lawrence Albert (3 mentions)
Johns Hopkins U, 1976
Certification: Cardiovascular Disease, Internal Medicine
407 E 70th St, New York, 212-249-1019

Kahn, Martin Laurence (7 mentions)
New York U, 1963
Certification: Cardiovascular Disease, Internal Medicine
530 1st Ave, New York, 212-263-7228
40 E 84th St, New York, 212-263-7228

Katz, Edward Steven (4 mentions)
New York U, 1985
Certification: Cardiovascular Disease, Internal Medicine
530 1st Ave #9-U, New York, 212-263-7463

Katz, Stanley (8 mentions)
Certification: Cardiovascular Disease, Internal Medicine,
   Interventional Cardiology
300 Community Dr, Manhasset, 516-562-4281

Kay, Richard Harlan (4 mentions)
Johns Hopkins U, 1976
Certification: Cardiovascular Disease, Internal Medicine
19 Bradhurst Ave #700, Hawthorne, 914-593-7800

Keltz, Theodore N. (6 mentions)
Albany Med Coll, 1980
Certification: Cardiovascular Disease, Internal Medicine
150 Lockwood Ave #LL2, New Rochelle, 914-633-7870

Kiewe, Randy Paul (3 mentions)
U of Pittsburgh, 1994 *Certification:* Cardiovascular Disease
2001 Marcus Ave #W285, Lake Success, 516-775-0055

Koss, Jerome Harvey (6 mentions)
Albert Einstein Coll of Med, 1974 *Certification:* Cardiovascular
   Disease, Internal Medicine, Interventional Cardiology
3003 New Hyde Park Rd #406, New Hyde Park, 516-358-5401

Lawson, William Eric (3 mentions)
Robert W Johnson Med Sch, 1977 *Certification:* Cardiovascular
   Disease, Internal Medicine, Interventional Cardiology
Stony Brook Health Sciences Center #T16-080, Stony Brook,
   631-444-1060

Lee, Johnny (4 mentions)
Mount Sinai Sch of Med, 1995
Certification: Cardiovascular Disease, Interventional Cardiology
35 E 35th St, New York, 212-532-0888

Lefkowitz, David (3 mentions)
SUNY-Downstate Med Coll, 1987
Certification: Cardiovascular Disease
407 E 70th St, New York, 212-288-4200

Leonard, Daniel Andrew (5 mentions)
U of Cincinnati, 1981
Certification: Cardiovascular Disease, Internal Medicine
110 S Bedford Rd, Mount Kisco, 914-241-1050

Levy, Daniel Kenneth (6 mentions)
Mount Sinai Sch of Med, 1990
Certification: Cardiovascular Disease, Internal Medicine
3201 Grand Concourse, Bronx, 718-933-2244

Lieb, Mark Edward (8 mentions)
Boston U, 1988 *Certification:* Cardiovascular Disease
90 S Bedford Rd #110, Mount Kisco, 845-278-7000
185 Route 312, Brewster, 845-278-7000

Lipton, Mark S. (3 mentions)
New York U, 1978
Certification: Cardiovascular Disease, Internal Medicine
635 Madison Ave, New York, 212-439-6690

Marzo, Kevin Phillip (5 mentions)
Northwestern U, 1985 *Certification:* Cardiovascular
   Disease, Internal Medicine, Interventional Cardiology
120 Mineola Blvd #500, Mineola, 516-663-4480

Masciello, Michael A. (3 mentions)
U of Miami, 1980 *Certification:* Cardiovascular Disease,
   Critical Care Medicine, Internal Medicine
540 Union Blvd, West Islip, 631-669-2555

Mattes, Leonard Michael (3 mentions)
Tulane U, 1962
Certification: Cardiovascular Disease, Internal Medicine
1199 Park Ave Apt 1-F, New York, 212-876-7045

Meller, Jennifer Aileen (9 mentions)
New York U, 1996 *Certification:* Internal Medicine
2600 Netherland Ave #125, Bronx, 718-548-7036
1020 Park Ave, New York, 646-403-9685

Menegus, Mark A. (3 mentions)
Certification: Cardiovascular Disease, Internal Medicine,
   Interventional Cardiology
111 E 210th St, Bronx, 718-920-5573

Moses, Jeffrey Warren (5 mentions)
U of Pennsylvania, 1974 *Certification:* Cardiovascular
   Disease, Internal Medicine, Interventional Cardiology
161 Ft Washington Ave, New York, 212-305-7060

Nash, Ira Steven (4 mentions)
Harvard U, 1984
Certification: Cardiovascular Disease, Internal Medicine
1 Gustave L Levy Pl, New York, 212-241-3282
5 E 98th St, New York, 212-241-3282
1190 5th Ave, New York, 212-241-3282

Ng, Kaman (4 mentions)
Mount Sinai Sch of Med, 1996
Certification: Cardiovascular Disease, Internal Medicine
2318 31st St #4, Astoria, 718-777-7742
4401 Francis Lewis Blvd, Bayside, 718-423-3355

Novack, Henry Frederick (5 mentions)
Mount Sinai Sch of Med, 1980
Certification: Cardiovascular Disease, Internal Medicine
425 W 59th St #8-B, New York, 212-376-3187

O'Brien, Francis J., Jr. (4 mentions)
Harvard U, 1982
Certification: Cardiovascular Disease, Internal Medicine
317 E 34th St #7, New York, 212-726-7400

Ong, Lawrence (3 mentions)
U of California-San Francisco, 1976 *Certification:* Cardiovascular
   Disease, Internal Medicine, Interventional Cardiology
300 Community Dr, Manhasset, 516-562-4100

Oruci, Edward H. (3 mentions)
George Washington U, 1989
Certification: Cardiovascular Disease, Interventional Cardiology
100 Port Washington Blvd #603, Roslyn, 516-365-6444

Papapietro, Nicholas V. (3 mentions)
SUNY-Downstate Med Coll, 1991
Certification: Cardiovascular Disease, Internal Medicine
851 Manhattan Ave, Brooklyn, 718-752-7280
1555 3rd Ave, New York, 212-870-9497
207 E 16th St, New York, 212-870-9497

Pappas, Thomas William (6 mentions)
Cornell U, 1983 *Certification:* Cardiovascular Disease,
   Internal Medicine, Interventional Cardiology
100 Port Washington Blvd #105, Roslyn, 516-390-9640

Parness, Ira Allen (4 mentions)
SUNY-Downstate Med Coll, 1979
Certification: Pediatric Cardiology, Pediatrics
1468 Madison Ave #350, New York, 212-241-6637

Pearson, John W. (5 mentions)
U of Missouri, 1976
Certification: Cardiovascular Disease, Internal Medicine
1279 E Main St, Riverhead, 631-727-2100
201 Manor Pl, Greenport, 631-477-2701

Pepe, Anthony John (3 mentions)
Columbia U, 1970
Certification: Cardiovascular Disease, Internal Medicine
425 W 59th St #8-B, New York, 212-376-3187

Petrossian, George Armen (4 mentions)
Mount Sinai Sch of Med, 1983 *Certification:* Cardiovascular
   Disease, Internal Medicine, Interventional Cardiology
1405 Old Northern Blvd, Roslyn, 516-484-6777

Post, Martin Roger (5 mentions)
SUNY-Upstate Med U, 1967
Certification: Cardiovascular Disease, Internal Medicine
425 E 61st St, New York, 212-752-2000

Rastegar, Raymonda (4 mentions)
Mount Sinai Sch of Med, 1990
Certification: Cardiovascular Disease
148 E 38th St, New York, 212-679-4488

Reitano, John M. (7 mentions)
New York U, 1978
Certification: Cardiovascular Disease, Internal Medicine
220 N Belle Mead Rd, East Setauket, 631-941-2273
2500 Nesconset Hwy 1, Stony Brook, 631-689-7700
75 N Country Rd, Port Jefferson, 631-473-1320

Reitman, Milton Jesse (4 mentions)
New York Med Coll, 1969
Certification: Pediatric Cardiology, Pediatrics
100 Port Washington Blvd, Roslyn, 516-365-3340
5505 Nesconset Hwy #207, Mount Sinai, 631-331-5014
631 Montauk Hwy #4, West Islip, 631-669-9624
70-31 108th St, Forest Hills, 718-520-5464

Ribaudo, Thomas Philip (6 mentions)
Georgetown U, 1978
Certification: Cardiovascular Disease, Internal Medicine
45 Research Way #108, East Setauket, 631-941-2704

Robbins, Mitchell Andrew (4 mentions)
SUNY-Downstate Med Coll, 1975
Certification: Cardiovascular Disease, Internal Medicine
1000 Northern Blvd #120, Great Neck, 516-466-8900

Romanello, Paul Peter (9 mentions)
SUNY-Upstate Med U, 1983
Certification: Cardiovascular Disease, Internal Medicine
158 E 84th St, New York, 212-535-6340

Rutkovsky, Edward Victor (4 mentions)
New York U, 1984
Certification: Cardiovascular Disease, Internal Medicine
2035 Lakeville Rd #101, New Hyde Park, 516-328-9797

Saporita, Mark (3 mentions)
SUNY-Upstate Med U, 1992
Certification: Cardiovascular Disease, Internal Medicine
1279 E Main St, Riverhead, 631-727-2100

Schick, David (3 mentions)
Albert Einstein Coll of Med, 1966
Certification: Cardiovascular Disease, Internal Medicine
3201 Grand Concourse, Bronx, 718-933-2244
2711 Henry Hudson Pkwy, Bronx, 718-933-2244

Schiff, Russell J. (3 mentions)
Stony Brook U, 1981
Certification: Pediatric Cardiology, Pediatrics
120 Mineola Blvd #210, Mineola, 516-663-4600

Schiffer, Mark Benjamin (4 mentions)
Northwestern U, 1977
Certification: Cardiovascular Disease, Internal Medicine
158 E 84th St, New York, 212-535-6340

Schifter, David Ross (5 mentions)
FMS-Grenada, 1985
Certification: Cardiovascular Disease, Internal Medicine
108 Prospect Park W, Brooklyn, 718-499-5300

Schwartz, Allan (9 mentions)
Columbia U, 1974
Certification: Cardiovascular Disease, Internal Medicine
161 Fort Washington Ave #304, New York, 212-305-3308

Seinfeld, David (4 mentions)
Albert Einstein Coll of Med, 1973
Certification: Cardiovascular Disease, Internal Medicine
20 E 68th St #214, New York, 212-288-1538

Shani, Jacob (3 mentions)
FMS-Israel, 1975 *Certification:* Cardiovascular Disease,
   Internal Medicine, Interventional Cardiology
4802 10th Ave, Brooklyn, 718-283-7489

Shimony, Rony Y. (3 mentions)
U of Buffalo, 1984
Certification: Cardiovascular Disease, Internal Medicine
425 E 61st St 4th Fl, New York, 212-752-2700

Shlofmitz, Richard Alan (17 mentions)
New York U, 1980
Certification: Cardiovascular Disease, Internal Medicine
100 Port Washington Blvd #105, Roslyn, 516-390-9640

Silver, Michael M. (3 mentions)
SUNY-Downstate Med Coll, 1977
Certification: Cardiovascular Disease, Internal Medicine
33 Davis Ave, White Plains, 914-948-3630

Singer, Marc A. (3 mentions)
Albert Einstein Coll of Med, 1985 *Certification:* Internal Medicine
2800 Marcus Ave #203, Lake Success, 516-775-6666

Slater, William Roy (7 mentions)
Harvard U, 1978 *Certification:* Cardiovascular Disease,
   Clinical Cardiac Electrophysiology, Internal Medicine
530 1st Ave #9-U, New York, 212-263-7463

Squire, Anthony (7 mentions)
Mount Sinai Sch of Med, 1978
Certification: Cardiovascular Disease, Internal Medicine
1120 Park Ave, New York, 212-410-4800

Stein, Neil H. (3 mentions)
Columbia U, 1981
Certification: Cardiovascular Disease, Internal Medicine
225 Community Dr #130, Great Neck, 516-504-0474

Steinberg, Eric (3 mentions)
Nova Southeastern Coll of Osteopathic Med, 1988
Certification: Cardiovascular Disease
480 E Bay Dr, Long Beach, 516-670-9355
300 Franklin Ave, Valley Stream, 516-887-7000

Tartaglia, Joseph John (5 mentions)
FMS-Italy, 1983 *Certification:* Cardiovascular Disease,
   Geriatric Medicine, Internal Medicine
311 North St #402, White Plains, 914-946-3388

Tenenbaum, Joseph (4 mentions)
Harvard U, 1974
Certification: Cardiovascular Disease, Internal Medicine
161 Fort Washington Ave, New York, 212-305-5288

Tenet, William John (3 mentions)
FMS-Italy, 1980
Certification: Cardiovascular Disease, Internal Medicine
2318 31st St #4, Astoria, 718-777-7742

Unger, Allen Harvey (5 mentions)
SUNY-Upstate Med U, 1960
Certification: Cardiovascular Disease, Internal Medicine
12 E 86th St, New York, 212-734-6000

Vorchheimer, David Allen (3 mentions)
Albert Einstein Coll of Med, 1987
Certification: Cardiovascular Disease, Internal Medicine
1 Gustave L Levy Pl #1030, New York, 212-241-4258
5 E 98th St, New York, 212-241-4258

Wallach, Ronald (4 mentions)
Columbia U, 1970
Certification: Cardiovascular Disease, Internal Medicine
110 S Bedford Rd, Mount Kisco, 914-241-1050

Weintraub, Howard Seth (3 mentions)
New York U, 1976
Certification: Cardiovascular Disease, Internal Medicine
345 E 37th St Rm 308, New York, 212-599-5030

Weiss, Melvin Barry (5 mentions)
SUNY-Downstate Med Coll, 1967 *Certification:* Cardiovascular
   Disease, Internal Medicine, Interventional Cardiology
95 Grasslands Rd, Valhalla, 914-493-7199
19 Bradhurst Ave #700, Hawthorne, 914-593-7800

Dermatology

Basuk, Pamela Jeri (5 mentions)
New York U, 1984 *Certification:* Dermatology
2011 Union Blvd #1, Bay Shore, 631-666-2900

Brazin, Stewart A. (4 mentions)
SUNY-Downstate Med Coll, 1973 *Certification:* Dermatology
210 E Sunrise Hwy #202, Valley Stream, 516-825-8910

Bruder, Philip (4 mentions)
New York U, 1987 *Certification:* Dermatology
245 E 63rd St #107, New York, 212-980-9292

Cohen, Russell Wayne (4 mentions)
Albert Einstein Coll of Med, 1985 *Certification:* Dermatology
258 Merrick Rd, Oceanside, 516-766-0345
303 E Park Ave #E, Long Beach, 516-432-7124
2900 Hempstead Tpke #104, Levittown, 516-520-5280

Cohen, Steven Robert (5 mentions)
U of Pennsylvania, 1971 *Certification:* Dermatology
3514 Bainbridge Ave, Bronx, 866-633-8255

Contard, Paul Christopher (4 mentions)
Mount Sinai Sch of Med, 1988 *Certification:* Dermatology
1372 Clove Rd, Staten Island, 718-447-7110
1368 Clove Rd, Staten Island, 718-447-7110

De Leo, Vincent Anthony (5 mentions)
Louisiana State U, 1969 *Certification:* Dermatology
425 W 59th St #5C, New York, 212-523-6003
10 Union Sq E #2, New York, 212-844-8800
1090 Amsterdam Ave, New York, 212-523-5898

Demar, Leon Kenneth (5 mentions)
New York U, 1973 *Certification:* Dermatology
985 5th Ave, New York, 212-988-9010

Ellis, Jeffrey Ira (5 mentions)
SUNY-Downstate Med Coll, 2002 *Certification:* Dermatology
2 Patton Pl, Plainview, 516-488-7546

Falcon, Ronald Harlan (5 mentions)
SUNY-Downstate Med Coll, 1985 *Certification:* Dermatology
604 E Park Ave, Long Beach, 516-432-0011

Franks, Andrew George, Jr. (5 mentions)
New York Med Coll, 1971
Certification: Dermatology, Internal Medicine, Rheumatology
530 1st Ave #7-R, New York, 212-263-5889

Garofalo, John Anthony (11 mentions)
Cornell U, 1976 *Certification:* Dermatology, Internal Medicine
233 E Shore Rd #102, Great Neck, 516-773-4500

Goldberg, Neil S. (7 mentions)
Northwestern U, 1982 *Certification:* Dermatology
222 Westchester Ave #203, White Plains, 914-761-8140
77 Pondfield Rd, Bronxville, 914-337-4499

Gordon, Marsha Lynn (4 mentions)
U of Pennsylvania, 1984 *Certification:* Dermatology
5 E 98th St #1048, New York, 212-241-9773

Grossman, Marc Eliot (12 mentions)
U of Pennsylvania, 1974
Certification: Dermatology, Internal Medicine
12 Greenridge Ave, White Plains, 914-946-1101

Hale, Elizabeth K. (4 mentions)
New York U, 1998 *Certification:* Dermatology
317 E 34th St, New York, 212-686-7306

Hochman, Herbert Allen (11 mentions)
Tulane U, 1970 *Certification:* Dermatology
1020 Park Ave, New York, 212-861-1656

Howanitz, Nancy Carolyn (4 mentions)
Temple U, 1975 *Certification:* Dermatology
700 Post Rd #24, Scarsdale, 914-725-5150

Kaplan, Sherri Kapel (6 mentions)
Certification: Dermatology
1055 Saw Mill River Rd #208, Ardsley, 914-693-7191

Kristal, Leonard (27 mentions)
Rosalind Franklin U, 1986
Certification: Dermatology, Pediatric Dermatology, Pediatrics
2001 Marcus Ave #540, Lake Success, 516-352-6151

Lashinsky, Alvin M. (6 mentions)
New York U, 1956 *Certification:* Dermatology
8037 Broadway, Flushing, 718-898-8600
1955 Merrick Rd #100, Merrick, 516-223-1223

Lebwohl, Mark Gabriel (21 mentions)
Harvard U, 1978 *Certification:* Dermatology, Internal Medicine
5 E 98th St, New York, 212-241-9728

Lefkovits, Albert Meyer (8 mentions)
New York Med Coll, 1962
1040 Park Ave, New York, 212-861-9600

Leichter, Carl M. (8 mentions)
Cornell U, 1974 *Certification:* Dermatology
258 Merrick Rd, Oceanside, 516-766-0345
2900 Hempstead Tpke #104, Levittown, 516-520-5280
303 E Park Ave #E, Long Beach, 516-432-7124

Levy, Ross Stuart (7 mentions)
Albert Einstein Coll of Med, 1976 *Certification:* Dermatology
110 S Bedford Rd, Mount Kisco, 914-242-1355

Mattison, Timothy D. (7 mentions)
Dartmouth Coll, 1976 *Certification:* Dermatology
90 S Bedford Rd, Mount Kisco, 914-241-1050
110 S Bedford Rd, Mount Kisco, 914-241-1050

Moynihan, Gavan David (6 mentions)
Howard U, 1973 *Certification:* Dermatology
332 E Main St, Bay Shore, 631-666-0500

Newburger, Amy E. (11 mentions)
New York U, 1974 *Certification:* Dermatology
2 Overhill Rd #330, Scarsdale, 914-725-1800

Notaro, Antoinette P. (4 mentions)
SUNY-Downstate Med Coll, 1978 *Certification:* Dermatology
13405 Main Rd, Mattituck, 631-298-1122

Onorato, Joseph (5 mentions)
SUNY-Downstate Med Coll, 1989 *Certification:* Dermatology
54 New Hyde Park Rd, Garden City, 516-488-1313
29 Village Sq, Glen Cove, 516-676-3554

Orbuch, Philip (4 mentions)
FMS-Israel, 1981 *Certification:* Dermatology
345 E 37th St #307, New York, 212-532-5355
4277 Hempstead Tpke #206, Bethpage, 516-731-6505

Orlow, Seth Jay (10 mentions)
Albert Einstein Coll of Med, 1986
Certification: Dermatology, Pediatric Dermatology
530 1st Ave #7R, New York, 212-263-5889

Ostad, Ariel (4 mentions)
New York U, 1991 *Certification:* Dermatology
897 Lexington Ave, New York, 212-517-7900

Pereira, Frederick Andrew (7 mentions)
New Jersey Med Sch, 1968 *Certification:* Dermatology
5114 Kissena Blvd, Flushing, 718-359-4425

Rigel, Darrell Spencer (4 mentions)
George Washington U, 1978 *Certification:* Dermatology
35 E 35th St #208, New York, 212-684-5964

Schneiderman, Paul Ira (4 mentions)
SUNY-Upstate Med U, 1971 *Certification:* Dermatology
175 Jericho Tpke #224, Syosset, 516-921-8688

Schulman, David Baldinger (4 mentions)
New York U, 1992 *Certification:* Dermatology
130 Pondville Rd #2, Bronxville, 914-337-3253

Shelton, Ronald Morris (4 mentions)
SUNY-Upstate Med U, 1984 *Certification:* Dermatology
260 E 66th St, New York, 212-593-1818

Shupack, Jerome Leonard (6 mentions)
Columbia U, 1963 *Certification:* Dermatology
530 1st Ave #7-F, New York, 212-263-7344

Slear, Amy Elizabeth (5 mentions)
SUNY-Downstate Med Coll, 2002 *Certification:* Dermatology
2 Patton Pl, Plainview, 516-488-7546

Stillman, Michael Allen (4 mentions)
SUNY-Downstate Med Coll, 1967 *Certification:* Dermatology
111 Bedford Rd, Katonah, 914-232-3135

Walther, Robert Raymond (4 mentions)
U of North Carolina, 1973
Certification: Dermatology, Internal Medicine
161 Fort Washington Ave 12th Fl, New York, 212-305-5293
16 E 60th St 3rd Fl, New York, 212-326-8465

Warner, Robert Leslie (4 mentions)
SUNY-Downstate Med Coll, 1977 *Certification:* Dermatology
580 Park Ave, New York, 212-752-3692

Wolfin, Nancy Sue (7 mentions)
Albert Einstein Coll of Med, 1980
Certification: Dermatology, Internal Medicine
310 E Shore Rd, Great Neck, 516-829-4464

Zweibel, Stuart M. (4 mentions)
Mount Sinai Sch of Med, 1985 *Certification:* Dermatology
185 Kisco Ave #3, Mount Kisco, 914-472-7023

Emergency Medicine

Carlisi, Anthony M. (3 mentions)
FMS-United Kingdom, 1985
4295 Hempstead Tpke, Bethpage, 516 520 2201

Davidson, Steven J. (3 mentions)
Temple U, 1975 *Certification:* Emergency Medicine
4802 10th Ave, Brooklyn, 718-283-6030

Flomenbaum, Neal Edward (4 mentions)
Albert Einstein Coll of Med, 1973
Certification: Emergency Medicine, Internal Medicine
525 E 68th St 11th Fl, New York, 212-746-0780

Gewirtz, Michael F. (3 mentions)
FMS-Dominican Republic, 1982 *Certification:* Internal Medicine
5645 Main St, Flushing, 718-670-1021

Goldfrank, Lewis R. (5 mentions)
FMS-Belgium, 1970 *Certification:* Emergency Medicine,
Internal Medicine, Medical Toxicology
462 1st Ave #345-E, New York, 212-562-3346

Haydock, Timothy Gerrish (4 mentions)
Case Western Reserve U, 1979 *Certification:* Emergency Medicine
41 E Post Rd, White Plains, 914-681-0600

Hunt, John Edward, III (3 mentions)
Georgetown U, 1997 *Certification:* Emergency Medicine
240 Meeting House Ln, Southampton, 631-726-8420
595 Hampton Rd, Southampton, 631-283-0918

Husk, Gregg Armin (4 mentions)
U of Chicago, 1975
Certification: Emergency Medicine, Internal Medicine
1st Ave & 16th St, New York, 212-420-2847

Jacobson, Sheldon (3 mentions)
Albert Einstein Coll of Med
Certification: Emergency Medicine, Internal Medicine
One Gustave L Levy Pl, New York, 212-241-6500

Jagoda, Andrew Sam (3 mentions)
Georgetown U, 1982 *Certification:* Emergency Medicine
100th St And Madison Ave, New York, 212-241-0101
1 Gustave L Levy Pl, New York, 212-241-0002

Khan, Faiz Ahmed (4 mentions)
Albany Med Coll, 1995
Certification: Emergency Medicine, Internal Medicine
2201 Hempstead Tpk, East Meadow, 516-572-6175

Korn, Robert S. (3 mentions)
Northwestern U, 1979 *Certification:* Emergency Medicine,
Pediatric Emergency Medicine, Pediatrics
301 E Main St, Bay Shore, 631-968-3000

Lahn, Michael Ian (3 mentions)
Rosalind Franklin U, 1990 *Certification:* Emergency Medicine
16 Guion Pl, New Rochelle, 914-632-5000

Larsen, Erik Andrew (4 mentions)
Certification: Emergency Medicine
41 E Post Rd, White Plains, 914-681-0600

Marin, Michael Mac (6 mentions)
Rosalind Franklin U, 1981
Certification: Emergency Medicine, Internal Medicine
5 E 98th St, New York, 212-241-7646

McMahon, Brian (3 mentions)
New York U *Certification:* Emergency Medicine
1300 Roanoke Ave, Riverhead, 631-548-6000

Murphy, Daniel G. (4 mentions)
Rosalind Franklin U, 1988 *Certification:* Emergency Medicine
1000 N Village Ave, Rockville Centre, 516-705-2380

Nigro, Emil J. (3 mentions)
FMS-Mexico, 1975 *Certification:* Emergency Medicine
701 N Broadway, Sleepy Hollow, 914-366-1554

Pastula, Leonard T., II (5 mentions)
Midwestern U Chicago Coll of Osteopathic Med, 1997
Certification: Emergency Medicine
200 Belle Terre Rd, Port Jefferson, 631-474-6000

Richardson, Barbara K. (6 mentions)
Cornell U, 1978
Certification: Emergency Medicine, Internal Medicine
1 Gustave L Levy Pl #1149, New York, 212-241-5856
100th St And Madison Ave, New York, 212-241-6794

Roit, Zhanna (3 mentions)
FMS-Ukraine, 1972
Certification: Emergency Medicine, Internal Medicine
300 Community Dr, Manhasset, 516-562-3090

Rudolph, Gary Steven (6 mentions)
Cornell U, 1981
Certification: Emergency Medicine, Internal Medicine
300 Community Dr, Manhasset, 516-562-3090

Sama, Andrew Eric (12 mentions)
Cornell U, 1981 *Certification:* Emergency Medicine,
Internal Medicine, Pediatric Emergency Medicine
300 Community Dr, Manhasset, 516-562-4125
270 Park Ave, Huntington, 631-351-2000

Savasta, Joseph Neil (5 mentions)
FMS-Belgium, 1979
Certification: Emergency Medicine, Internal Medicine
Stony Brook Health Sciences Center #4, Stony Brook,
631-444-2465

Stillman, Mark Corey (4 mentions)
Columbia U, 1999 *Certification:* Emergency Medicine
1000 10th Ave, New York, 212-523-4000

Viccellio, Peter (3 mentions)
Harvard U
101 Nicolls Rd 4th Fl #080, Stony Brook, 631-444-2499

Williamson, Dawn Ellen (3 mentions)
SUNY-Downstate Med Coll, 1991
Certification: Emergency Medicine, Internal Medicine
455 E Bay Dr, Long Beach, 516-897-1100

Endocrinology

Albin, Joan (4 mentions)
New York Med Coll, 1967
Certification: Endocrinology and Metabolism, Internal Medicine
140 Lockwood Ave #212, New Rochelle, 914-235-8503

Bergman, Donald Arthur (8 mentions)
Jefferson Med Coll, 1971
Certification: Endocrinology and Metabolism, Internal Medicine
1199 Park Ave #1-F, New York, 212-876-7333

Bloomgarden, David K. (5 mentions)
New York U, 1977
Certification: Endocrinology and Metabolism, Internal Medicine
600 Mamaroneck Ave #101, Harrison, 914-722-7980

Bloomgarden, Zachary T. (4 mentions)
Albert Einstein Coll of Med, 1974
Certification: Endocrinology and Metabolism, Internal Medicine
35 E 85th St, New York, 212-879-5933

Blum, Manfred (5 mentions)
New York U, 1957
Certification: Endocrinology and Metabolism, Internal Medicine
530 1st Ave, New York, 212-263-7444

Brand, Howard A. (5 mentions)
Robert W Johnson Med Sch, 1984 *Certification:*
    Endocrinology, Diabetes, and Metabolism, Internal Medicine
2500 Nesconset Hwy, Stony Brook, 631-751-7772

Breen, Tracy Lynn (5 mentions)
New York U, 1997 *Certification:* Endocrinology, Diabetes,
    and Metabolism, Internal Medicine
5 E 98th St, New York, 212-241-7975

Breidbart, Rory Steven (4 mentions)
FMS-Israel, 1987 *Certification:* Endocrinology, Diabetes,
    and Metabolism, Internal Medicine
29 Barstow Rd #305, Great Neck, 516-482-0347

Brett, Elise Michelle (6 mentions)
Mount Sinai Sch of Med, 1994 *Certification:* Endocrinology,
    Diabetes, and Metabolism, Internal Medicine
1192 Park Ave Ground Fl, New York, 212-831-2100

Buckberg, Phillip Roger (4 mentions)
SUNY-Downstate Med Coll, 1973
36 7th Ave, New York, 212-807-8129

Davies, Terry F. (5 mentions)
FMS-United Kingdom
One Gustave L Levy Pl, New York, 212-241-6500

Felig, Philip (15 mentions)
Yale U, 1961 *Certification:* Internal Medicine
1056 5th Ave, New York, 212-534-5900

Fiedler, Robert Philip (6 mentions)
Albert Einstein Coll of Med, 1964
Certification: Endocrinology and Metabolism, Internal Medicine
1175 Park Ave, New York, 212-289-6500

Friedman, Seth Gerald (7 mentions)
Mount Sinai Sch of Med, 1988 *Certification:* Endocrinology,
    Diabetes, and Metabolism, Internal Medicine
560 Northern Blvd #101, Great Neck, 516-466-6165

Gelato, Marie Catherine (5 mentions)
Michigan State U, 1979
Certification: Endocrinology and Metabolism, Internal Medicine
26 Research Way, East Setauket, 631-444-0580

Goldstein, Howard Mark (4 mentions)
FMS-Mexico, 1978
Certification: Endocrinology and Metabolism, Internal Medicine
105 Hillside Ave #A, Williston Park, 516-746-4080

Greene, Loren Wissner (10 mentions)
New York U, 1975
Certification: Endocrinology and Metabolism, Internal Medicine
530 1st Ave, New York, 212-263-7449

Jacobs, Thomas Price (8 mentions)
Johns Hopkins U, 1968
Certification: Endocrinology and Metabolism, Internal Medicine
161 Fort Washington Ave #210, New York, 212-305-5578

Kantor, Alan Bernard (4 mentions)
FMS-South Africa, 1975
Certification: Endocrinology and Metabolism, Internal Medicine
1940 Commerce St #310, Yorktown Heights, 914-245-1111

Khan, Farida (6 mentions)
FMS-India, 1962
Certification: Endocrinology and Metabolism, Internal Medicine
506 6th St, Brooklyn, 718-246-8600
263 7th Ave, Brooklyn, 718-246-8600

Klein, Irwin Lester (10 mentions)
New York U, 1973
Certification: Endocrinology and Metabolism, Internal Medicine
2800 Marcus Ave #200, Lake Success, 516-708-2540

Liebowitz, Jonas (5 mentions)
SUNY-Downstate Med Coll, 1990
770B McLean Ave, Yonkers, 914-237-3636

Lomasky, Steven Jay (12 mentions)
FMS-Israel, 1982
Certification: Endocrinology and Metabolism, Internal Medicine
242 Merrick Rd #403, Rockville Centre, 516-536-3700

Lorber, Daniel Louis (4 mentions)
Albert Einstein Coll of Med, 1972
Certification: Endocrinology and Metabolism, Internal Medicine
5945 161st St, Flushing, 718-762-3111

Margulies, Paul Laurence (14 mentions)
U of Chicago, 1970
Certification: Endocrinology and Metabolism, Internal Medicine
444 Community Dr #312, Manhasset, 516-627-1366

McConnell, Robert John (6 mentions)
Columbia U, 1973
Certification: Endocrinology and Metabolism, Internal Medicine
161 Fort Washington Ave #210, New York, 212-305-5579

Mechanick, Jeffrey Ian (7 mentions)
Mount Sinai Sch of Med, 1985 *Certification:* Endocrinology,
    Diabetes, and Metabolism, Internal Medicine
1192 Park Ave, New York, 212-831-2100

Merker, Edward (4 mentions)
New York U, 1965 *Certification:* Endocrinology and
    Metabolism, Geriatric Medicine, Internal Medicine
35 E 85th St, New York, 212-288-1110
237 E 20th St Apt 1-A, New York, 212-777-3280
215 E 95th St, New York, 212-996-8000

Morduchowitz, Stuart M. (4 mentions)
Albert Einstein Coll of Med, 1992
Certification: Endocrinology, Diabetes, and Metabolism
2201 Hempstead Tpke, East Meadow, 516-572-6504

Powell, Jeffrey Scott (7 mentions)
Albert Einstein Coll of Med, 1995 *Certification:*
    Endocrinology, Diabetes, and Metabolism, Internal Medicine
90 S Bedford Rd, Mount Kisco, 914-241-1050

Rayfield, Elliot James (6 mentions)
Jefferson Med Coll, 1967
Certification: Endocrinology and Metabolism, Internal Medicine
1150 Park Ave #90, New York, 212-427-9191

Richardson, Stephen B. (5 mentions)
FMS-United Kingdom, 1971
Certification: Endocrinology and Metabolism, Internal Medicine
530 1st Ave #4-K, New York, 212-263-2666

Silverberg, Arnold I. (6 mentions)
Albert Einstein Coll of Med, 1961
Certification: Endocrinology and Metabolism, Internal Medicine
908 48th St, Brooklyn, 718-283-6200

Sirota, David King (5 mentions)
Washington U, 1960
Certification: Endocrinology and Metabolism, Internal Medicine
1175 Park Ave, New York, 212-427-5600

Surks, Martin I. (8 mentions)
New York U, 1960
Certification: Endocrinology and Metabolism, Internal Medicine
3411 Lane Ave, Bronx, 718-920-4331

Tibaldi, Joseph Michael (7 mentions)
Mount Sinai Sch of Med, 1979
Certification: Endocrinology and Metabolism, Internal Medicine
5945 161st St, Flushing, 718-762-3111

Tulpan, Maria Olga V. (4 mentions)
FMS-Romania, 1994
Certification: Endocrinology, Diabetes, and Metabolism
40 Park Ave, New York, 212-679-7363

Vaswani, Ashok Nanikram (4 mentions)
FMS-India, 1970
Certification: Endocrinology and Metabolism, Internal Medicine
901 Stewart Ave #204, Garden City, 516-739-0414

Weinerman, Stuart Alan (4 mentions)
Albert Einstein Coll of Med, 1984
Certification: Endocrinology and Metabolism, Internal Medicine
2800 Marcus Ave #200, Lake Success, 516-708-2540

Wilson, Thomas Allen (6 mentions)
U of Pennsylvania, 1973
Certification: Pediatric Endocrinology, Pediatrics
Stony Brook Health Sciences Center, Stony Brook, 631-444-3429

Family Practice *(see note on page 9)*

Edelstein, Martin Peter (11 mentions)
FMS-Canada, 1971 *Certification:* Family Medicine
11 Beverly Rd, Great Neck, 516-487-1614

Finamore, Carmen (3 mentions)
FMS-Italy, 1983 *Certification:* Family Medicine
536 Mineola Ave, Carle Place, 516-333-5054

Fisher, George Costa (3 mentions)
FMS-United Kingdom, 1979 *Certification:* Family Medicine
799 Park Ave, New York, 212-439-9800
2233 33rd St, Astoria, 718-726-1000

Fishkin, Michael Mark (4 mentions)
Des Moines U, 1973 *Certification:* Family Medicine
2500 Nesconset Hwy Bldg 70, Stony Brook, 631-751-3322

Kelly, Gerald J. (3 mentions)
New York Coll of Osteopathic Med, 1993
Certification: Family Medicine
181 N Belle Mead Rd, East Setauket, 631-444-4620

Levy, Albert (4 mentions)
FMS-Brazil, 1973 *Certification:* Family Medicine
911 Park Ave, New York, 212-288-7193

Mattimoe, Derek Noel (5 mentions)
Columbia U, 1997 *Certification:* Family Medicine
2500 Nesconset Hwy Bldg 70, Stony Brook, 631-751-3322

Merker, Edward L. (4 mentions)
Albert Einstein Coll of Med, 1981 *Certification:* Family Medicine
180 Marble Ave, Pleasantville, 914-769-7300

Morrow, Robert Warren (3 mentions)
Mount Sinai Sch of Med, 1974 *Certification:* Family Medicine
5997 Riverdale Ave, Bronx, 718-884-9803

Nussbaum, Monte Jay (5 mentions)
Columbia U, 1982 *Certification:* Family Medicine
185 Merrick Rd, Lynbrook, 516-593-3535

Rechter, Lesley (4 mentions)
New York Med Coll, 1976 *Certification:* Family Medicine
54 Birchwood Park Dr, Jericho, 516-933-6850

Roth, Alan R. (3 mentions)
New York Coll of Osteopathic Med, 1986
Certification: Family Medicine, Hospice and Palliative Medicine
11940 Metropolitan Ave, Kew Gardens, 718-849-0624

Schechter, Marc (3 mentions)
New York Coll of Osteopathic Med, 1996
1181 Old Country Rd #3, Plainview, 516-931-2320

Schiller, Robert Mark (3 mentions)
New York U, 1982 *Certification:* Family Medicine
16 E 16th St, New York, 212-924-7744

Sharpe, Arleen Suzette (3 mentions)
Stony Brook U, 1988 *Certification:* Family Medicine
18 Ashford Ave, Dobbs Ferry, 914-693-1660

Strongwater, Richard (3 mentions)
SUNY-Upstate Med U, 1981 *Certification:* Family Medicine
180 Marble Ave, Pleasantville, 914-769-7300

Sussman, Howard Robert (3 mentions)
Stony Brook U, 1996 *Certification:* Family Medicine
181 N Belle Mead Ave #2, East Setauket, 631-444-4620

Sutton, Ira Jonathon (3 mentions)
Albert Einstein Coll of Med, 1980 *Certification:* Family Medicine
77 Quaker Ridge Rd #101, New Rochelle, 914-636-0077

Gastroenterology

Abittan, Chaim Simon (3 mentions)
FMS-Israel, 1994 *Certification:* Gastroenterology
233 E Shore Rd #101, Great Neck, 516-487-2444

Ackert, John Joseph (5 mentions)
New York U, 1972
Certification: Gastroenterology, Internal Medicine
232 E 30th St, New York, 212-889-5544

Agus, Saul Gerald (4 mentions)
New York U, 1968
Certification: Gastroenterology, Internal Medicine
1080 5th Ave, New York, 212-860-0841

Aisenberg, James (3 mentions)
Harvard U, 1987
Certification: Gastroenterology, Internal Medicine
3111 E 79th St #2-A, New York, 212-996-6633

Attia, Alan Lawrence (3 mentions)
Columbia U, 1990
350 W 58th St, New York, 212-262-7873

Baranowski, Robert John (3 mentions)
Temple U, 1988 *Certification:* Gastroenterology
3400 Nesconset Hwy #101, East Setauket, 631-751-8700

Basu, Prithwijit (3 mentions)
FMS-India, 1980
Certification: Gastroenterology, Internal Medicine
5 Station Sq, Forest Hills, 718-897-0584

Basuk, Paul Manes (3 mentions)
Northwestern U, 1980
Certification: Gastroenterology, Internal Medicine
210 E 86th St #201, New York, 212-861-9715

Benkov, Keith Jeffrey (6 mentions)
Mount Sinai Sch of Med, 1979
Certification: Pediatric Gastroenterology, Pediatrics
5 E 98th St, New York, 212-241-5415

Bermanski, Paul (5 mentions)
Mount Sinai Sch of Med, 1983
Certification: Gastroenterology, Internal Medicine
195 E Main St, Huntington, 631-549-8181

Bernstein, David Eric (4 mentions)
Stony Brook U, 1988
Certification: Gastroenterology, Internal Medicine
300 Community Dr, Manhasset, 516-562-4281

Bernstein, Gary Richard (8 mentions)
U of Miami, 1981
Certification: Gastroenterology, Internal Medicine
3400 Nesconset Hwy #101, East Setauket, 631-751-8700

Bienstock, Bernard (3 mentions)
SUNY-Downstate Med Coll, 1987
Certification: Gastroenterology, Internal Medicine
509 W Merrick Rd, Valley Stream, 516-561-8188

Brenner, Stephen Michael (4 mentions)
New York Med Coll, 1962
Certification: Gastroenterology, Internal Medicine
2711 Henry Hudson Pkwy, Bronx, 718-548-2481

Breslaw, Jerome Samuel (4 mentions)
Rosalind Franklin U, 1966
Certification: Gastroenterology, Internal Medicine
235 E 67th St, New York, 212-628-5700

Caccese, William John (3 mentions)
SUNY-Downstate Med Coll, 1978
Certification: Gastroenterology, Internal Medicine
700 Old Country Rd #206, Plainview, 516-681-1200

Celifarco, Anthony John (5 mentions)
FMS-Mexico, 1983
Certification: Gastroenterology, Internal Medicine
1991 Marcus Ave #101, Lake Success, 516-365-4949

Chang, Peter Kyle (8 mentions)
Mount Sinai Sch of Med, 1996
Certification: Gastroenterology, Internal Medicine
1049 Park Ave #1-C, New York, 212-427-9888

Chapman, Mark Lawrence (3 mentions)
SUNY-Downstate Med Coll, 1961
Certification: Gastroenterology, Internal Medicine
12 E 86th St, New York, 212-861-2000

Chinitz, Marvin Aaron (11 mentions)
Boston U, 1978
Certification: Gastroenterology, Internal Medicine
90 S Bedford Rd, Mount Kisco, 914-241-1050

Chun, Alexander (3 mentions)
FMS-Philippines, 1985
132 E 76th St #2-A, New York, 212-988-2900

Cohen, Lawrence Bruce (10 mentions)
Hahnemann U, 1978
Certification: Gastroenterology, Internal Medicine
311 E 79th St #2-A, New York, 212-996-6633

Cohn, William Jay (6 mentions)
Virginia Commonwealth U, 1972
Certification: Gastroenterology, Internal Medicine
3400 Nesconset Hwy #101, East Setauket, 631-751-8700

Coman, Eugene Anthony (6 mentions)
Columbia U, 1985
Certification: Gastroenterology, Internal Medicine
3400 Nesconset Hwy #101, East Setauket, 631-751-8700

Duva, Joseph Michael (4 mentions)
Mount Sinai Sch of Med, 1978
Certification: Gastroenterology, Internal Medicine
887 Old Country Rd #A, Riverhead, 631-727-6122

Dworkin, Brad Mitchell (4 mentions)
Jefferson Med Coll, 1976
Certification: Gastroenterology, Internal Medicine
95 Grasslands Rd, Valhalla, 914-493-7337

Eskreis, David Samuel (6 mentions)
George Washington U, 1982
Certification: Gastroenterology, Internal Medicine
2001 Marcus Ave #W-85, Lake Success, 516-326-2700

Fath, Robert Bernard, Jr. (7 mentions)
U of Mississippi, 1978
Certification: Gastroenterology, Internal Medicine
470 Mamaroneck Ave #206, White Plains, 914-946-6800

Faust, Michael J. (3 mentions)
New York U, 1978
Certification: Gastroenterology, Internal Medicine
345 E 37th St, New York, 212-986-3330

Felder, Joseph (3 mentions)
U of Texas-San Antonio, 1987
115 E 57th St #510, New York, 212-472-8039

Fenster, Jay Samuel (5 mentions)
SUNY-Downstate Med Coll, 1986
Certification: Gastroenterology, Internal Medicine
657 Central Ave, Cedarhurst, 516-374-0670

Field, Barry Elliot (7 mentions)
Albert Einstein Coll of Med, 1972
Certification: Gastroenterology, Internal Medicine
777 N Broadway #305, Sleepy Hollow, 914-366-6120

Field, Steven Phillip (3 mentions)
Certification: Gastroenterology, Internal Medicine
245 E 35th St, New York, 212-686-9477
560 1st Ave, New York, 212-686-9677

Frank, Michael Simon (3 mentions)
Albert Einstein Coll of Med, 1974
Certification: Gastroenterology, Internal Medicine
9 E 63rd St, New York, 212-593-7170
1600 Hering Ave, Bronx, 718-931-4700

Freiman, Hal Jeffrey (3 mentions)
Albany Med Coll, 1978
Certification: Gastroenterology, Internal Medicine
59 W 12th St, New York, 212-206-0074

Friedlander, Charles Norman (5 mentions)
SUNY-Downstate Med Coll, 1968
Certification: Gastroenterology, Internal Medicine
232 E 30th St, New York, 212-889-5544

Gendler, Seth Lorin (7 mentions)
Rush U, 1983 *Certification:* Gastroenterology, Internal Medicine
16 Guion Pl, New Rochelle, 914-632-5000
140 Lockwood Ave, New Rochelle, 914-235-9333

George, James (3 mentions)
Albert Einstein Coll of Med, 1988 *Certification:* Gastroenterology
1751 York Ave, New York, 212-369-2490

Gerson, Charles David (3 mentions)
SUNY-Downstate Med Coll, 1962
Certification: Gastroenterology, Internal Medicine
80 Central Park W, New York, 212-496-6161

Gold, David Mitchell (5 mentions)
Albert Einstein Coll of Med, 1987
Certification: Pediatric Gastroenterology
655 Deer Parks Ave, Babylon, 631-321-2100

Goldberg, Myron D. (4 mentions)
Albert Einstein Coll of Med, 1971
Certification: Gastroenterology, Internal Medicine
110 E 59th St, New York, 212-583-2900

Goldman, Ira S. (4 mentions)
Columbia U, 1977
Certification: Gastroenterology, Internal Medicine
310 E Shore Rd #206, Great Neck, 516-487-7677

Gould, Perry Craig (3 mentions)
New York Med Coll, 1977
Certification: Gastroenterology, Internal Medicine
1103 Stewart Ave, Garden City, 516-248-3737

Green, Peter Henry Rae (5 mentions)
FMS-Australia, 1970
180 Fort Washington Ave #956, New York, 212-305-5590

Gutwein, Isadore Philip (3 mentions)
Albert Einstein Coll of Med, 1973
Certification: Gastroenterology, Internal Medicine
3765 Riverdale Ave #8, Bronx, 718-549-4267

Haber, Gregory B. (3 mentions)
FMS-Canada, 1970
100 E 77th St 2nd Fl, New York, 212-434-6279

Harrison, Aaron Richard (4 mentions)
Albert Einstein Coll of Med, 1974
Certification: Gastroenterology, Internal Medicine
375 E Main St #21, Bay Shore, 631-968-8288

Heier, Stephen K. (4 mentions)
Albany Med Coll, 1976
Certification: Gastroenterology, Internal Medicine
755 N Broadway, Sleepy Hollow, 914-594-9494

Huh, Chihee C. (3 mentions)
Certification: Gastroenterology, Internal Medicine
8701-A Shore Rd, Brooklyn, 718-759-0400

Ingber, Scott (3 mentions)
Brown U, 1985 *Certification:* Gastroenterology, Internal Medicine
325 Park Ave #115, Huntington, 631-351-3817

Jacobson, Ira M. (4 mentions)
Columbia U, 1979 *Certification:* Gastroenterology, Internal
Medicine, Transplant Hepatology
1305 York Ave 4th Fl, New York, 212-746-2115

Jaffin, Barry Wayne (6 mentions)
Mount Sinai Sch of Med, 1981
Certification: Gastroenterology, Internal Medicine
620 Columbus Ave, New York, 212-721-2600

Kahn, Oren (4 mentions)
Albert Einstein Coll of Med, 1990
Certification: Gastroenterology, Internal Medicine
90 S Bedford Rd, Mount Kisco, 914-241-1050

Katz, Henry Joseph (4 mentions)
Albany Med Coll, 1980
Certification: Gastroenterology, Internal Medicine
1234 Central Park Ave #3-A, Yonkers, 914-793-1600
18 Ashford Ave #2-E, Dobbs Ferry, 914-591-4360

Katz, Seymour (10 mentions)
New York U, 1964
Certification: Gastroenterology, Internal Medicine
1000 Northern Blvd, Great Neck, 516-466-2340

Kavaler, Leon (3 mentions)
SUNY-Upstate Med U, 1989 *Certification:* Gastroenterology
68 E 86th St, New York, 212-535-1845

Klein, Robert Anthony (4 mentions)
New York Med Coll, 1978
Certification: Gastroenterology, Internal Medicine
300 Old Country Rd #31, Mineola, 516-294-9380
202 W Park Ave, Long Beach, 516-431-1101

Knapp, Albert Bruce (6 mentions)
Columbia U, 1979
Certification: Gastroenterology, Internal Medicine
21 E 79th St, New York, 212-737-3446

Kongara, Kavita Rani (3 mentions)
U of Missouri-Kansas City, 1993 *Certification:* Gastroenterology
222 Station Plaza N #428, Mineola, 516-663-2066

Kornbluth, Asher 'Arthur' (5 mentions)
Certification: Gastroenterology, Internal Medicine
1751 York Ave, New York, 212-369-2490

Krumholz, Michael P. (4 mentions)
Certification: Gastroenterology, Internal Medicine
111 E 80th St #1C, New York, 212-734-5533

Lambroza, Arnon (4 mentions)
Albert Einstein Coll of Med, 1984
Certification: Gastroenterology, Internal Medicine
950 Park Ave, New York, 212-517-7570

Landau, Steven R. (4 mentions)
New York U, 1981
Certification: Gastroenterology, Internal Medicine
30 Greenridge Ave, White Plains, 914-328-8555

Lazar, Robert Michael (6 mentions)
FMS-Mexico, 1981
Certification: Gastroenterology, Internal Medicine
48 Route 25-A #107, Smithtown, 631-862-3680

Lebovics, Edward (6 mentions)
New York U, 1980
Certification: Gastroenterology, Internal Medicine
95 Grasslands Rd, Valhalla, 914-493-7337

Legnani, Peter E. (3 mentions)
U of Connecticut, 1995 *Certification:* Gastroenterology
1751 York Ave, New York, 212-369-2490

Levy, Joseph S. (5 mentions)
FMS-Israel, 1973
Certification: Pediatric Gastroenterology, Pediatrics
160 E 32nd St 2nd Fl, New York, 212-263-5407

Lewis, Blair Seth (5 mentions)
Albert Einstein Coll of Med, 1982
Certification: Gastroenterology, Internal Medicine
1067 5th Ave, New York, 212-369-6600

Lichtiger, Simon (3 mentions)
New York U, 1979 *Certification:* Internal Medicine
1755 York Ave, New York, 212-831-4900

Lowenstein, Joel (4 mentions)
630 E Park Ave, Long Beach, 516-432-2900

Magun, Arthur Marc (4 mentions)
Mount Sinai Sch of Med, 1977
Certification: Gastroenterology, Internal Medicine
161 Fort Washington Ave #338, New York, 212-305-5287
16 E 60th St #321, New York, 212-305-5287

Markowitz, David Daniel (10 mentions)
Columbia U, 1985
Certification: Gastroenterology, Internal Medicine
161 Fort Washington Ave #853, New York, 212-305-1024

Mayer, Lloyd Frederick (3 mentions)
Mount Sinai Sch of Med, 1976
Certification: Gastroenterology, Internal Medicine
5 E 98th St, New York, 212-241-0764

McKinley, Matthew John (12 mentions)
Creighton U, 1975
Certification: Gastroenterology, Internal Medicine
2800 Marcus Ave #201, Lake Success, 516-622-6076

Mehta, Dhiren C. (4 mentions)
FMS-India, 1990
Certification: Gastroenterology, Internal Medicine
41 Bay Ave, East Moriches, 631-878-1543
36 Osprey Ave, Riverhead, 631-727-4171

Milano, Andrew M. (3 mentions)
New York U, 1964
Certification: Gastroenterology, Internal Medicine
530 1st Ave #4-K, New York, 212-263-7483

Miller, Kenneth Marc (4 mentions)
New York U, 1995 *Certification:* Gastroenterology
311 E 79th St #2-A, New York, 212-996-6633

Miskovitz, Paul Frederick (3 mentions)
Cornell U, 1975
Certification: Gastroenterology, Internal Medicine
635 Madison Ave, New York, 212-717-4966

Mustacchia, Paul James (3 mentions)
U of Buffalo, 1994
Certification: Gastroenterology, Internal Medicine
2201 Hempstead Tpke, East Meadow, 516-572-6504

Naso, Kristin Patrick (4 mentions)
New York Coll of Osteopathic Med, 1985
Certification: Gastroenterology, Internal Medicine
223 Hampton Rd, Southampton, 631-287-7100

Noyer, Charles McLoughlin (5 mentions)
SUNY-Downstate Med Coll, 1988 *Certification:* Gastroenterology
2 Gannett Dr, White Plains, 914-683-1555

Pacheco, Paulo Alexandre (4 mentions)
Brown U, 1993 *Certification:* Gastroenterology
38 E 57th St, New York, 212-326-8999

Pais, Shireen Andrade (4 mentions)
FMS-India, 1996
95 Grasslands Rd #206, Valhalla, 914-493-7337

Pearlman, Kenneth I. (4 mentions)
Albany Med Coll, 1983
Certification: Gastroenterology, Internal Medicine
317 E 34th St, New York, 212-726-7444

Pervil, Paul Roy (7 mentions)
FMS-Mexico, 1976
Certification: Gastroenterology, Internal Medicine
146A Manetto Hill Rd #205, Plainview, 516-822-4404

Pfeffer, Robert Douglas (7 mentions)
New York U, 1984
Certification: Gastroenterology, Internal Medicine
317 E 34th St, New York, 212-726-7447

Pochapin, Mark Bennett (3 mentions)
Cornell U, 1988 *Certification:* Gastroenterology
525 E 68th St, New York, 212-746-4014
1315 York Ave, New York, 212-746-4014

Present, Daniel Herbert (3 mentions)
SUNY-Downstate Med Coll, 1959
Certification: Gastroenterology, Internal Medicine
12 E 86th St, New York, 212-861-2000

Rosemarin, Jack Ira (5 mentions)
New York Med Coll, 1978
Certification: Gastroenterology, Internal Medicine
2 Gannett Dr, White Plains, 914-683-1555

Roston, Alfred David (4 mentions)
New York U, 1989 *Certification:* Gastroenterology
2 Gannett Dr, White Plains, 914-683-1555

Rubin, Peter Henry (5 mentions)
U of Rochester, 1970
Certification: Gastroenterology, Internal Medicine
920 Park Ave, New York, 212-535-3400

Sable, Robert Allen (4 mentions)
Albert Einstein Coll of Med, 1973 *Certification:*
Gastroenterology, Geriatric Medicine, Internal Medicine
3765 Riverdale Ave #7, Bronx, 718-549-4267
2371 Arthur Ave, Bronx, 718-364-6199

Schmerin, Michael Joel (4 mentions)
Jefferson Med Coll, 1973
Certification: Gastroenterology, Internal Medicine
1060 Park Ave, New York, 212-348-3166

Schnall, H. Alan (4 mentions)
New York U, 1980
Certification: Gastroenterology, Internal Medicine
11045 Queens Blvd #103, Forest Hills, 718-520-0600

Schulman, Nathan David (9 mentions)
U of Kentucky, 1980 *Certification:* Internal Medicine
192 E Shore Rd, Great Neck, 516-487-4500

Singh, Charnjit (5 mentions)
Boston U, 1991 *Certification:* Gastroenterology
30 Hempstead Ave #154, Rockville Centre, 516-763-0556

Sloyer, Alan F. (4 mentions)
SUNY-Downstate Med Coll, 1982
Certification: Gastroenterology, Internal Medicine
233 E Shore Rd #101, Great Neck, 516-487-2444

Tack, Kevin Lloyd (6 mentions)
U of Buffalo, 1988
Certification: Gastroenterology, Internal Medicine
1615 Northern Blvd #G-1, Manhasset, 516-627-9355

Tepper, Robert Eric (4 mentions)
Med Coll of Pennsylvania, 1987
Certification: Gastroenterology, Internal Medicine
1000 Northern Blvd #140, Great Neck, 516-466-2340

Tripodi, Joseph (3 mentions)
New York Coll of Osteopathic Med, 1989
Certification: Gastroenterology
1991 Marcus Ave #101, Lake Success, 516-365-4949

Waye, Jerome Donar (4 mentions)
Boston U, 1958
Certification: Gastroenterology, Internal Medicine
650 Park Ave, New York, 212-439-7779

Wayne, Peter Kim (6 mentions)
Albert Einstein Coll of Med, 1976
Certification: Gastroenterology, Internal Medicine
469 N Broadway, Yonkers, 914-969-1115

General Surgery

Aldoroty, Robert A. (3 mentions)
Columbia U, 1984 *Certification:* Surgery
1060 5th Ave, New York, 212-426-9614

Amory, Spencer Eugene (6 mentions)
Johns Hopkins U, 1983 *Certification:* Surgery
5141 Broadway #3-178, New York, 212-932-5221

Attiyeh, Fadi (5 mentions)
FMS-Lebanon, 1969
Certification: Colon & Rectal Surgery, Surgery
425 W 59th St #8-BI, New York, 212-307-1144

Bauer, Joel Jay (4 mentions)
New York U, 1967 *Certification:* Surgery
25 E 69th St, New York, 212-517-8600

Becker, Kenneth John (3 mentions)
SUNY-Downstate Med Coll, 1986
2201 Hempstead Tpke, East Meadow, 516-546-2448
155 W Merrick Rd #202, Freeport, 516-546-2448

Benowitz, Joel (3 mentions)
FMS-Mexico, 1975 *Certification:* Surgery
206 W Park Ave, Long Beach, 516-889-9100

Capizzi, Anthony Joseph (3 mentions)
New York Med Coll, 1983 *Certification:* Surgery
786 Montauk Hwy, West Islip, 631-669-3700

Cehelsky, Ihor John (4 mentions)
Ohio State U, 1977 *Certification:* Surgery
110 S Bedford Rd, Mount Kisco, 914-241-1050

Chabot, John Anthony (3 mentions)
Dartmouth Coll, 1983 *Certification:* Surgery
161 Fort Washington Ave #F-18, New York, 212-305-9468

Chernobelsky, Leonid (3 mentions)
FMS-Latvia, 1986 *Certification:* Surgery
150 brighton 11th St, Brooklyn, 718-616-1622

Clarke, James Lincoln (6 mentions)
Cornell U, 1981 *Certification:* Surgery
30 Central Park S #13-A, New York, 212-737-2050

Cohen, Bradley David (4 mentions)
Mount Sinai Sch of Med, 1983 *Certification:* Surgery
111 Carleton Ave #2-A, Islip Terrace, 631-581-4400

Cohen, Franklin Stanley (4 mentions)
U of Florida, 1989 *Certification:* Surgery
212 E 70th St, New York, 212-472-2772

Conte, Charles Carmine (3 mentions)
Dartmouth Coll, 1981 *Certification:* Surgery
600 Northern Blvd #111, Great Neck, 516-487-9454

Dawson, M. Shane (4 mentions)
Louisiana State U, 1998 *Certification:* Surgery
132 E 76th St #2-A, New York, 212-396-9860

De Noto, George, III (8 mentions)
Stony Brook U, 1988 *Certification:* Surgery
1999 Marcus Ave, Lake Success, 516-233-3600

Divino, Celia Marie (5 mentions)
SUNY-Downstate Med Coll, 1992 *Certification:* Surgery
1 Gustave L Levy Pl #1259, New York, 212-241-0460
5 E 98th St, New York, 212-241-3348

Fahey, Thomas Joseph, III (6 mentions)
Cornell U, 1986 *Certification:* Surgery
525 E 68th St, New York, 212-746-5130

Ferzli, George S. (4 mentions)
FMS-Lebanon, 1979 *Certification:* Surgery, Surgical Critical Care
65 Cromwell Ave, Staten Island, 718-667-8100

Fitterman, Glen (12 mentions)
SUNY-Downstate Med Coll, 1985 *Certification:* Surgery
700 Old Country Rd #204, Plainview, 516-931-5800

Francfort, John Wall (7 mentions)
New Jersey Med Sch, 1980
Certification: Surgery, Vascular Surgery
580 Union Blvd, West Islip, 631-321-6801

Gardezi, Syed Q. (5 mentions)
FMS-Pakistan, 1983 *Certification:* Surgery
1435 86th St #3, Brooklyn, 718-680-4000

Geller, Evan Richard (8 mentions)
U of Michigan, 1982 *Certification:* Surgery, Surgical Critical Care
625 Belle Terre Rd #201, Port Jefferson, 631-474-0707

Gordon, Mark Stephen (13 mentions)
Northwestern U, 1982 *Certification:* Surgery
2 Longview Ave #302, White Plains, 914-684-5884

Gouge, Thomas Hamilton (3 mentions)
Yale U, 1970 *Certification:* Surgery
423 E 23rd St, New York, 212-686-7500

Gudavalli, R. M. Prasad (4 mentions)
FMS-India, 1965 *Certification:* Surgery
2323 60th St, Brooklyn, 718-645-2929
7702 16th Ave, Brooklyn, 718-645-2929

Halpern, David Keith (6 mentions)
Northwestern U, 1990 *Certification:* Surgery
300 Old Country Rd #101, Mineola, 516-741-4138

Harris, Fred (4 mentions)
FMS-France, 1976 *Certification:* Surgery
1160 5th Ave #105, New York, 212-861-2217
222 Westchester Ave #403, White Plains, 914-287-0110

Harris, Michael T. (10 mentions)
Columbia U, 1988 *Certification:* Surgery
5-E 98th St #1259, New York, 212-241-1763

Held, Douglas Keith (11 mentions)
SUNY-Downstate Med Coll, 1980
Certification: Colon & Rectal Surgery, Surgery
1300 Union Tpke #108, New Hyde Park, 516-488-2743

Heymann, A. Douglas (7 mentions)
Albert Einstein Coll of Med, 1965 *Certification:* Surgery
122 E 76th St #1-B, New York, 212-628-4192

Hofstetter, Steven Roy (3 mentions)
SUNY-Upstate Med U, 1971 *Certification:* Surgery
530 1st Ave #6-C, New York, 212-263-7302

Iraci, Joseph Cirino (5 mentions)
New York Med Coll, 1977
Certification: Surgery, Surgical Critical Care
122 E 76th St #1B, New York, 212-249-0469

Josephson, Lynn Gerleman (3 mentions)
Mount Sinai Sch of Med, 1977 *Certification:* Surgery
170 Maple Ave #502, White Plains, 914-949-4609

Kaleya, Ronald Nathaniel (8 mentions)
Cornell U, 1980 *Certification:* Surgery
111 E 210th St, Bronx, 718-920-4800

Kassel, Barry Andrew (5 mentions)
U of Buffalo, 1973 *Certification:* Surgery
110 S Bedford Rd, Mount Kisco, 914-241-1050
90 S Bedford Rd, Mount Kisco, 914-241-1050

Katz, Lester Brian (9 mentions)
Certification: Surgery
1010 5th Ave, New York, 212-879-6677

Katz, Paul (4 mentions)
Hahnemann U, 1966 *Certification:* Surgery
310 E Shore Rd #203, Great Neck, 516-482-8657

Kaul, Ashutosh (4 mentions)
FMS-India, 1988 *Certification:* Surgery
19 Bradhurst Ave #1700, Hawthorne, 914-347-0162

Khalife, Michael Elia (14 mentions)
FMS-Lebanon, 1978 *Certification:* Surgery
300 Old Country Rd #101, Mineola, 516-741-4138

Kimmelstiel, Fred Michael (5 mentions)
New York Med Coll, 1980 *Certification:* Surgery
225 W 71st St, New York, 212-362-6060

Kumar, Sampath R. (4 mentions)
Certification: Surgery
7517 6th Ave, Brooklyn, 718-630-5777
150 55th St #1, Brooklyn, 718-630-7000

Kurtz, Lewis Myles (5 mentions)
FMS-Italy, 1971 *Certification:* Surgery
310 E Shore Rd #203, Great Neck, 516-482-8657

Kwauk, Sam Tsung-Ming (4 mentions)
FMS-Canada, 1984 *Certification:* Surgery
41-47 Elizabeth St #507, New York, 212-966-8890

Lau, Har Chi (3 mentions)
Med Coll of Pennsylvania, 1992 *Certification:* Surgery
777 N Broadway #204, Sleepy Hollow, 914-631-3660

Liang, Howard Grant (4 mentions)
Washington U, 1974
530 1st Ave #6C, New York, 212-263-7302

Licalzi, Luke King (4 mentions)
Albany Med Coll, 1975 *Certification:* Surgery
77 N Centre Ave #208, Rockville Centre, 516-764-5455

Lieberman, Michael D. (5 mentions)
New Jersey Med Sch, 1985 *Certification:* Surgery
525 E 68th St, New York, 212-746-5434
1315 York Ave, New York, 212-746-5434

Lieffrig, Alfred G. (3 mentions)
FMS-Belgium, 1959 *Certification:* Surgery
48 Route 25a #308, Smithtown, 631-979-6858

Litvak, Stephen (4 mentions)
FMS-Mexico, 1973 *Certification:* Surgery
2500 Marcus Ave, New Hyde Park, 516-365-9748

Maffucci, Leonard (3 mentions)
New York Med Coll, 1985 *Certification:* Surgery
140 Lockwood Ave #103, New Rochelle, 914-632-9650

Manolas, Panagiotis A. (3 mentions)
FMS-Greece, 1982 *Certification:* Surgery
3016 30th Dr, Astoria, 718-626-0707

Merriam, Louis Thayer, III (4 mentions)
Columbia U, 1991 *Certification:* Surgery
37 Research Way, East Setauket, 631-444-4545

Midulla, Peter Steven (4 mentions)
Albert Einstein Coll of Med, 1990
Certification: Pediatric Surgery, Surgery
5 E 98th St, New York, 212-241-7646

Moore, Eric Davidson (8 mentions)
Columbia U, 1975 *Certification:* Surgery
30 W 60th St #1H, New York, 212-247-6575

Morrissey, Kevin Peter (3 mentions)
Cornell U, 1965 *Certification:* Surgery
50 E 69th St, New York, 212-249-8000

Newman, Elliot (12 mentions)
New York U, 1986 *Certification:* Surgery
530 1st Ave #6C, New York, 212-263-7302
550 1st Ave, New York, 212-263-7302

Nowak, Eugene John (8 mentions)
New Jersey Med Sch, 1975 *Certification:* Surgery
325 E 79th St, New York, 212-517-6693
2365 Boston Post Rd, Larchmont, 914-834-6600

Nussbaum, Jeffrey K. (3 mentions)
Northwestern U, 1979 *Certification:* Surgery
157 Broadway, Amityville, 631-598-7757

Pacholka-Moran, James R. (4 mentions)
FMS-Canada, 1986 *Certification:* Surgery
314 W 14th St, New York, 212-620-0144

Pachter, Hersch Leon (16 mentions)
New York U, 1971 *Certification:* Surgery
530 1st Ave #6C, New York, 212-263-7302

Pence, Maria (3 mentions)
SUNY-Downstate Med Coll, 1995 *Certification:* Surgery
110 S Bedford Rd, Mount Kisco, 914-241-1050
185 Route 312, Brewster, 845-471-2287

Pertsemlidis, David S. (3 mentions)
New York U, 1996 *Certification:* Surgery
1199 Park Ave #1A, New York, 212-860-1056

Plummer, Robert Leonard (3 mentions)
Robert W Johnson Med Sch, 1983 *Certification:* Surgery
176 E Mosholu Pkwy S, Bronx, 718-367-6100

Pomeranz, Lee Alexander (4 mentions)
SUNY-Downstate Med Coll, 1979 *Certification:* Surgery
700 Old Country Rd #205, Plainview, 516-822-1433

Procaccino, Angelo John (14 mentions)
New York Med Coll, 1979 *Certification:* Surgery
310 E Shore Rd #203, Great Neck, 516-482-8657

Procaccino, John A. (4 mentions)
New York Med Coll, 1984
Certification: Colon & Rectal Surgery, Surgery
900 Northern Blvd #100, Great Neck, 516-730-2100

Puente, Anibal Oscar (3 mentions)
FMS-Argentina, 1991 *Certification:* Surgery
1578 Williamsbridge Rd, Bronx, 718-904-1400
111 E 210th St, Bronx, 718-904-1400
227 E 19th St, New York, 718-904-1400
600 E 233rd St, Bronx, 718-904-1400
2475 Saint Raymonds Ave, Bronx, 718-904-1400

Raniolo, Robert John (8 mentions)
FMS-Mexico, 1981 *Certification:* Surgery
777 N Broadway #204, Sleepy Hollow, 914-631-3660

Reich, Michael (3 mentions)
SUNY-Downstate Med Coll, 1965 *Certification:* Surgery
6960 108th St, Forest Hills, 718-544-0442

Reiner, Mark Allen (4 mentions)
SUNY-Downstate Med Coll, 1974 *Certification:* Surgery
1010 5th Ave, New York, 212-879-6677

Romero, Carlos Augusto (4 mentions)
FMS-Argentina, 1969 *Certification:* Surgery
173 Mineola Blvd #401, Mineola, 516-741-6464

Roth, Aaron Edward (4 mentions)
Rosalind Franklin U, 1989
Certification: Surgery, Surgical Critical Care
311 North St #203, White Plains, 914-949-3988

Salky, Barry A. (8 mentions)
U of Tennessee, 1970 *Certification:* Surgery
5 E 98th Sr, New York, 212-241-6156

Sas, Norman Shaw (5 mentions)
New York Med Coll, 1974 *Certification:* Surgery
3220 Fairfield Ave, Bronx, 718-549-0700

Savino, John Anthony (10 mentions)
FMS-Italy, 1968 *Certification:* Surgery
19 Bradhurst Ave, Hawthorne, 914-594-4352

Schrager, Randall Evan (4 mentions)
Jefferson Med Coll, 1988 *Certification:* Surgery
226 N Belle Mead Rd #C, East Setauket, 631-706-0018

Shamamian, Peter (7 mentions)
Certification: Surgery
530 1st Ave, New York, 212-263-7301

Shapiro, Nella Irene (5 mentions)
Albert Einstein Coll of Med, 1972 *Certification:* Surgery
2425 Eastchester Rd, Bronx, 718-405-0400

Shapiro, Richard Lawrence (3 mentions)
New York U, 1988 *Certification:* Surgery
160 E 34th St, New York, 212-731-5347

Silva, Miguel Ruben (5 mentions)
Mount Sinai Sch of Med, 1991 *Certification:* Surgery
1554 Astor Ave, Bronx, 718-881-7800

Smith, McCarthy George (3 mentions)
FMS-St Maarten, 1981 *Certification:* Surgery
26 Pondfield Rd W, Bronxville, 914-961-1212

Sussman, Howard Lawrence (3 mentions)
New York Med Coll, 1984 *Certification:* Surgery
123 Maple Ave, Cedarhurst, 516-612-7390
51-15 Beach Channel Dr, Far Rockaway, 718-734-2252

Tannenbaum, Gary Alan (3 mentions)
Columbia U, 1983 *Certification:* Surgery, Vascular Surgery
984 N Broadway #501, Yonkers, 914-965-2606

Vine, Anthony James (13 mentions)
Vanderbilt U, 1989
1010 5th Ave, New York, 212-879-6677

Vitolo, Joseph Robert (7 mentions)
Cornell U, 1985 *Certification:* Surgery
48 Route 25-A #308, Smithtown, 631-265-7744

Walsh, C. Bruce (4 mentions)
FMS-Mexico, 1980 *Certification:* Surgery, Surgical Critical Care
140 Lockwood Ave #103, New Rochelle, 914-636-3373

Ward, Robert Jude (10 mentions)
Columbia U, 1978 *Certification:* Surgery
2800 Marcus Ave #201, New Hyde Park, 631-622-6120

Weber, Carl Paul (4 mentions)
Albert Einstein Coll of Med, 1962 *Certification:* Surgery
170 Maple Ave, White Plains, 914-948-1000

Weber, Philip A. (8 mentions)
Brown U, 1993 *Certification:* Surgery
170 Maple Ave #502, White Plains, 914-948-1000

Zeitlin, Alan P. (3 mentions)
U of Miami, 1974 *Certification:* Surgery
6960 108th St, Forest Hills, 718-544-0442

Zingale, Robert Gerard (3 mentions)
SUNY-Downstate Med Coll, 1983
Certification: Surgery, Surgical Critical Care
158 E Main St, Huntington, 631-271-1822

Geriatrics

Berger, Jeffrey Todd (6 mentions)
Stony Brook U, 1988
Certification: Hospice and Palliative Medicine, Internal Medicine
222 Station Plaza N #518, Mineola, 516-663-2588

Bloom, Patricia Ann S. (9 mentions)
U of Minnesota, 1975 *Certification:* Internal Medicine
1440 Madison Ave, New York, 212-659-8552

Callahan, Eileen H. (3 mentions)
Certification: Geriatric Medicine, Internal Medicine
1440 Madison Ave, New York, 212-659-8552

Cammer Paris, Barbara E. (6 mentions)
SUNY-Downstate Med Coll, 1977
Certification: Geriatric Medicine, Internal Medicine
4802 10th Ave, Brooklyn, 718-283-6150

Ehrlich, Amy Rebecca (3 mentions)
Harvard U, 1985
Certification: Geriatric Medicine, Internal Medicine
3400 Bainbridge Ave, Bronx, 718-920-6723

Freedman, Michael Leonard (9 mentions)
Tufts U, 1963 *Certification:* Hematology, Internal Medicine
530 1st Ave, New York, 212-263-7043
550 1st Ave, New York, 212-263-7043

Guzik, Howard Jay (14 mentions)
Albert Einstein Coll of Med, 1981
Certification: Geriatric Medicine, Internal Medicine
2800 Marcus Ave #200, New Hyde Park, 516-708-2520
865 Northern Blvd #201, Great Neck, 516-622-5046

Jacobs, Laurie Gail (4 mentions)
Columbia U, 1985
Certification: Geriatric Medicine, Internal Medicine
3400 Bainbridge Ave, Bronx, 718-920-6723

Jhamb, Sashi Bala (3 mentions)
FMS-India, 1967 *Certification:* Internal Medicine
375 Main St, Islip, 631-277-0591

Lanman, Geraldine May (6 mentions)
FMS-Canada, 1980 *Certification:* Internal Medicine
1 Delaware Dr #48, Lake Success, 516-876-4100
972 Brush Hollow Rd, Westbury, 516-876-4100

Lofaso, Veronica Marie (3 mentions)
Albert Einstein Coll of Med, 1994 *Certification:* Internal Medicine
1484 1st Ave, New York, 212-746-7000

Macina, Lucy Ann O. (5 mentions)
Loyola U Chicago, 1978
Certification: Geriatric Medicine, Internal Medicine
222 Station Plaza N #518, Mineola, 516-663-2588

Meier, Diane Eve (9 mentions)
Northwestern U, 1977 *Certification:* Geriatric Medicine,
Hospice and Palliative Medicine, Internal Medicine
1440 Madison Ave 99th St 1st Fl, New York, 212-659-8552

Perskin, Michael H. (4 mentions)
Brown U, 1986
Certification: Geriatric Medicine, Internal Medicine
530 1st Ave #3-D, New York, 212-679-1410

Hematology/Oncology

Ahmed, Tauseef (4 mentions)
FMS-Pakistan, 1976
Certification: Hematology, Internal Medicine, Medical Oncology
19 Bradhurst Ave #2100, Hawthorne, 914-493-8374

Akhund, Birgis (4 mentions)
FMS-Lebanon, 1986
Certification: Hematology, Internal Medicine, Medical Oncology
180 E Pulaski Rd, Huntington Station, 631-425-2121

Allen, Steven Lee (11 mentions)
Johns Hopkins U, 1977
Certification: Hematology, Internal Medicine, Medical Oncology
450 Lakeville Rd, Lake Success, 516-734-8900

Amorosi, Edward Lawrence (5 mentions)
New York U, 1959
Certification: Hematology, Internal Medicine, Medical Oncology
530 1st Ave #9N, New York, 212-263-7080
160 E 34th St, New York, 212-731-5187

Atkins, Carl David (6 mentions)
Tufts U, 1979 *Certification:* Internal Medicine, Medical Oncology
242 Merrick Rd #301, Rockville Centre, 516-536-1455

Atlas, Mark (3 mentions)
Albert Einstein Coll of Med, 1989
Certification: Pediatric Hematology-Oncology, Pediatrics
26901 76th Ave, New Hyde Park, 718-470-3470

Atweh, George Fuad (3 mentions)
FMS-Lebanon, 1978 *Certification:* Internal Medicine
1468 Madison Ave, New York, 212-241-0337

Avvento, Louis J. (5 mentions)
FMS-Italy, 1981
Certification: Hematology, Internal Medicine, Medical Oncology
1333 E Main St, Riverhead, 631-727-8500
325 Meeting House Ln #405, Southampton, 631-283-5555

Bader, Paul Bruce (6 mentions)
Wayne State U, 1979
Certification: Internal Medicine, Medical Oncology
11247 Queens Blvd #209, Forest Hills, 718-263-7766

Balopole, Wendy L. (3 mentions)
Certification: Internal Medicine, Medical Oncology
520 Franklin Ave #253, Garden City, 516-742-5353

Barbasch, Avi (3 mentions)
FMS-Mexico, 1975 *Certification:* Medical Oncology
1050 Park Ave, New York, 212-860-3292

Bashevkin, Michael L. (4 mentions)
SUNY-Downstate Med Coll, 1973
Certification: Hematology, Internal Medicine, Medical Oncology
1660 E 14th St #501, Brooklyn, 718-382-8500

Bernhardt, Bernard (4 mentions)
Northwestern U, 1961
Certification: Hematology, Internal Medicine, Medical Oncology
50 Guion Pl, New Rochelle, 914-632-5397

Brower, Mark Steven (4 mentions)
Johns Hopkins U, 1974
Certification: Hematology, Internal Medicine, Medical Oncology
310 E 72nd St, New York, 212-717-2995

Buchholz, Michael Seth (3 mentions)
270 Pulaski Rd #D, Greenlawn, 631-427-6060

Caruso, Rocco Francesco (17 mentions)
U of Pennsylvania, 1979
Certification: Hematology, Internal Medicine, Medical Oncology
2500 Nesconset Hwy Bldg 26-B, Stony Brook, 631-751-8305

Chachoua, Abraham (6 mentions)
FMS-Australia, 1978
160 E 34th St, New York, 212-652-1910

Citron, Marc Laurence (3 mentions)
Wayne State U, 1974
Certification: Internal Medicine, Medical Oncology
2800 Marcus Ave, Lake Success, 516-622-6150

Coleman, Morton (4 mentions)
Virginia Commonwealth U, 1963
Certification: Hematology, Internal Medicine, Medical Oncology
407 E 70th St 3rd Fl, New York, 212-517-5900

Costin, Dan (7 mentions)
U of California-San Francisco, 1987
Certification: Hematology, Internal Medicine, Medical Oncology
2 Longview Ave #201, White Plains, 914-684-2779

Daya, Rami K. (5 mentions)
FMS-Syria, 1981 *Certification:* Internal Medicine
9920 4th Ave #311, Brooklyn, 718-921-1672

Diaz, Michael (3 mentions)
Certification: Internal Medicine, Hematology
1112 Park Ave, New York, 212-876-4500

Donnelly, Gerard Brian (10 mentions)
Georgetown U, 1993 *Certification:* Hematology, Medical Oncology
1201 Northern Blvd, Manhasset, 516-627-1221

Dosik, David Charles (3 mentions)
SUNY-Downstate Med Coll, 1990
Certification: Hematology, Medical Oncology
506 6th St, Brooklyn, 718-780-5240

Dosik, Harvey (5 mentions)
New York U, 1963 *Certification:* Hematology, Internal Medicine
506 6th St, Brooklyn, 718-780-5246

Dutcher, Janice Jean P. (3 mentions)
U of California-Davis, 1975
Certification: Internal Medicine, Medical Oncology
600 E 233rd St, Bronx, 718-920-9900

Forlenza, Thomas J. (4 mentions)
Boston U, 1977
Certification: Blood Banking, Hematology, Hospice and
   Palliative Medicine, Internal Medicine, Medical Oncology
102 Hart Blvd, Staten Island, 718-816-4949

Frankel, Etta B. (3 mentions)
Certification: Hematology, Internal Medicine, Medical Oncology
425 W 59th St, New York, 212-492-5500
1000 10th Ave, New York, 212-523-4000

Gelfand, Robert Matthew (4 mentions)
SUNY-Downstate Med Coll, 1990
Certification: Hematology, Medical Oncology
142 E 81st St, New York, 212-879-3496

Ginsberg, Ari Leonard (6 mentions)
Albert Einstein Coll of Med, 1997
Certification: Hematology, Internal Medicine, Medical Oncology
44 S Bayles Ave #218, Port Washington, 516-883-0122

Gold, Kenneth David (5 mentions)
Baylor U, 1977
Certification: Hematology, Internal Medicine, Medical Oncology
24 E Main St, Bay Shore, 631-666-6752

Goldberg, Arthur I. (4 mentions)
SUNY-Downstate Med Coll, 1969
Certification: Internal Medicine, Medical Oncology
121 E 79th St, New York, 212-249-0030

Goldberg, Jonathan Serle (4 mentions)
Mount Sinai Sch of Med, 1994
Certification: Hematology, Internal Medicine, Medical Oncology
90 S Bedford Rd, Mount Kisco, 914-241-1050

Grossbard, Michael L. (5 mentions)
Yale U, 1986 *Certification:* Internal Medicine, Medical Oncology
1000 10th Ave, New York, 212-523-5419

Gruenstein, Steven (9 mentions)
FMS-Italy, 1983
Certification: Internal Medicine, Medical Oncology
12 E 86th St, New York, 212-861-6660

Hindenburg, Alexander A. (6 mentions)
Robert W Johnson Med Sch, 1978
Certification: Hematology, Internal Medicine, Medical Oncology
200 Old Country Rd #450, Mineola, 516-663-9500

Hirschman, Richard James (3 mentions)
Johns Hopkins U, 1965
Certification: Hematology, Internal Medicine, Medical Oncology
247 3rd Ave #401, New York, 212-228-0471

Hymes, Kenneth Barry (4 mentions)
SUNY-Upstate Med U, 1975
Certification: Hematology, Internal Medicine, Medical Oncology
160 E 34th St, New York, 212-731-5189

Kalra, Jagmohan K. (3 mentions)
FMS-India, 1970
Certification: Hematology, Internal Medicine, Medical Oncology
2500 Marcus Ave #110, New Hyde Park, 516-358-7700

Kaplan, Barry H. (6 mentions)
Johns Hopkins U, 1962
Certification: Hematology, Internal Medicine, Medical Oncology
176-60 Union Tpke #360, Fresh Meadows, 718-460-2300

Kappel, Bruce Ira (3 mentions)
Emory U, 1982
Certification: Hematology, Internal Medicine, Medical Oncology
40 Crossways Park Dr, Syosset, 516-921-5533

Kessler, Leonard (3 mentions)
Albert Einstein Coll of Med, 1975
Certification: Hematology, Internal Medicine, Medical Oncology
242 Merrick Rd #301, Rockville Centre, 516-536-1455

Klafter, Robert Justin (3 mentions)
New York U, 1994 *Certification:* Hematology, Medical Oncology
12 E 86th St, New York, 212-861-6660

Kolitz, Jonathan Eliahu (3 mentions)
Yale U, 1979
Certification: Hematology, Internal Medicine, Medical Oncology
450 Lakeville Rd, New Hyde Park, 516-734-8900

Kreditor, Maxim (3 mentions)
FMS-Israel, 1998
Certification: Hematology, Internal Medicine, Medical Oncology
380 2nd St, New York, 212-448-9555

Landau, Leon Charles (6 mentions)
Albert Einstein Coll of Med, 1971
Certification: Hematology, Internal Medicine, Medical Oncology
75 E Gun Hill Rd, Bronx, 718-655-3932
18 Ashford Ave #2W, Dobbs Ferry, 914-693-1322

Lester, Thomas John (4 mentions)
Robert W Johnson Med Sch, 1979
Certification: Hematology, Internal Medicine, Medical Oncology
111 Bedford Rd, Katonah, 914-232-3135

Levendoglu-Tugal, Oya (3 mentions)
FMS-Turkey, 1974
Certification: Pediatric Hematology-Oncology, Pediatrics
19 Bradhurst Ave #1400, Hawthorne, 914-493-7997

Lipera, William J. (7 mentions)
Certification: Hematology, Internal Medicine, Medical Oncology
235 N Belle Mead Rd, East Setauket, 631-751-3000

Marino, John Steven (5 mentions)
New York Med Coll, 1979
Certification: Internal Medicine, Medical Oncology
44 S Bayles Ave #218, Port Washington, 516-883-0122

Marsh, Jonathan Harris (6 mentions)
Stony Brook U, 1986
Certification: Hematology, Internal Medicine, Medical Oncology
410 Lakeville Rd #311, Lake Success, 516-358-2400

McNelis, Brian Thomas (5 mentions)
Georgetown U, 1988 *Certification:* Hematology, Medical Oncology
44 S Bayles Ave #218, Port Washington, 516-883-0122

Mears, John Gregory (4 mentions)
Columbia U, 1973 *Certification:* Hematology, Internal Medicine
161 Fort Washington Ave #923, New York, 212-305-3506

Meyer, Richard Jay (5 mentions)
Mount Sinai Sch of Med, 1972
Certification: Hematology, Internal Medicine, Medical Oncology
1111 Park Ave, New York, 212-427-7700

Milano, Eileen Sheehy (3 mentions)
Jefferson Med Coll, 1987
101 Saint Andrews Lane, Glen Cove, 516-674-7430

Mittelman, Abraham (9 mentions)
FMS-Mexico, 1977
311 North St, White Plains, 914-681-0025

Moore, Anne (8 mentions)
Columbia U, 1969
Certification: Hematology, Internal Medicine, Medical Oncology
425 E 61st St 8th Fl, New York, 212-746-7336

Moskovits, Tibor (3 mentions)
Certification: Hematology, Internal Medicine, Medical Oncology
160 E 34th St, New York, 212-731-5191

Parker, Robert Ingalls (10 mentions)
Brown U, 1976
Certification: Pediatric Hematology-Oncology, Pediatrics
101 Nicolls Rd 5th Fl, Stony Brook, 631-444-7720

Pasmantier, Mark Weisler (4 mentions)
New York U, 1966
Certification: Hematology, Internal Medicine, Medical Oncology
407 E 70th St, New York, 212-517-5900

Pavlick, Anna Catherine (3 mentions)
New Jersey Sch of Osteopathic Med, 1990
Certification: Medical Oncology
160 E 34th St, New York, 212-731-5431

Phillips, Elizabeth A. (3 mentions)
U of Washington, 1969
Certification: Hematology, Internal Medicine, Medical Oncology
50 Guion Pl, New Rochelle, 914-632-5397

Rai, Kanti Roop (4 mentions)
FMS-India, 1955 *Certification:* Pediatrics
27005 76th Ave, New Hyde Park, 718-470-8930
410 Lakeview Rd #212, New Hyde Park, 516-470-4050

Ramirez, Mark Anthony (5 mentions)
Cornell U, 1982
Certification: Hematology, Internal Medicine, Medical Oncology
60 E 208th St, Bronx, 718-405-1700

Raphael, Bruce Gordon (14 mentions)
FMS-Canada, 1975
Certification: Hematology, Internal Medicine, Medical Oncology
530 1st Ave #9N, New York, 212-263-7085
160 E 34th St, New York, 212-731-5185

Rizvi, Hasan A. (3 mentions)
FMS-Pakistan, 1975 *Certification:* Hematology, Medical Oncology
180 E Main St #5, Bay Shore, 631-666-0262

Rothman, Ivan K. (4 mentions)
New York U, 1971
Certification: Hematology, Internal Medicine, Medical Oncology
242 Merrick Rd #301, Rockville Centre, 516-536-1455

New York 321

Ruggiero, Joseph T. (3 mentions)
New York U, 1977
Certification: Hematology, Internal Medicine, Medical Oncology
428 E 72nd St #300, New York, 212-746-2083

Sadan, Sara (10 mentions)
FMS-Israel, 1984
Certification: Internal Medicine, Medical Oncology
400 E Main St, Mount Kisco, 914-684-8100
244 Westchester Ave #411, West Harrison, 914-684-8100

Samuel, Edward T. (3 mentions)
Duke U, 1973
Certification: Hematology, Internal Medicine, Medical Oncology
235 N Belle Mead Rd, East Setauket, 631-751-3000

Sara, Gabriel (7 mentions)
FMS-Lebanon, 1980
Certification: Hematology, Internal Medicine, Medical Oncology
1000 10th Ave, New York, 212-523-7580

Schneider, Jeffrey Gary (3 mentions)
Yale U, 1986
Certification: Hematology, Internal Medicine, Medical Oncology
200 Old Country Rd #450, Mineola, 516-663-9500

Schwartz, Paula Ruth (7 mentions)
SUNY-Downstate Med Coll, 1980
Certification: Hematology, Internal Medicine
3003 New Hyde Park Rd #401, New Hyde Park, 516-354-5700
100 Manetto Hill Rd #104, Plainview, 516-935-9111

Spaccavento, Colette M. (3 mentions)
Robert W Johnson Med Sch, 1979
Certification: Hematology, Internal Medicine, Medical Oncology
110 E 59th St #9-C, New York, 212-583-2969

Staszewski, Harry (4 mentions)
Yale U, 1978
Certification: Hematology, Internal Medicine, Medical Oncology
200 Old Country Rd #450, Mineola, 516-663-9500

Sun, Nancy (5 mentions)
U of Pittsburgh, 1989
Certification: Hematology, Medical Oncology
40 Crossways Park Dr, Woodbury, 516-921-5533

Theodorakis, Michael E. (3 mentions)
SUNY-Upstate Med U, 1977
Certification: Hematology, Internal Medicine, Medical Oncology
235 N Belle Mead Rd, East Setauket, 631-751-3000

Vinciguerra, Vincent Paul (9 mentions)
Georgetown U, 1966
Certification: Hematology, Internal Medicine, Medical Oncology
450 Lakeville Rd, Lake Success, 516-734-8900

Vogel, James M. (3 mentions)
Columbia U, 1962
Certification: Hematology, Internal Medicine, Medical Oncology
1125 Park Ave, New York, 212-369-4250

Wang, Jen C. (3 mentions)
Certification: Hematology, Internal Medicine, Medical Oncology
5 E Walnut St, Long Beach, 516-889-7447
4128 Haight St, Flushing, 718-762-6059
6323 7th Ave, Brooklyn, 718-283-6900

Weinblatt, Mark E. (8 mentions)
Albert Einstein Coll of Med, 1976
Certification: Pediatric Hematology-Oncology, Pediatrics
200 Old Country Rd #440, Mineola, 516-663-9400

Weiner, Doron (4 mentions)
FMS-Mexico, 1985
Certification: Hematology, Internal Medicine, Medical Oncology
2209 Merrick Rd, Merrick, 516-546-5000

Weiselberg, Lora Rose (9 mentions)
New York Med Coll, 1975
Certification: Hematology, Internal Medicine, Medical Oncology
300 Community Dr, Manhasset, 516-734-8900
450 Lakeville Rd, Lake Success, 516-734-8900

Wiener, Leo (6 mentions)
Georgetown U, 1975
Certification: Internal Medicine, Medical Oncology
520 Franklin Ave #253, Garden City, 516-742-5353

Wisch, Nathaniel (12 mentions)
Northwestern U, 1958
Certification: Hematology, Internal Medicine, Medical Oncology
12 E 86th St, New York, 212-861-6660

Yoe, Joseph P. (3 mentions)
Certification: Hematology, Internal Medicine, Medical Oncology
1919 Madison Ave, New York, 212-987-1777
535 W 110th St #1-D, New York, 212-864-8888

Zervos, George Alexandru (3 mentions)
FMS-Romania, 1980
Certification: Internal Medicine, Medical Oncology
333 Glen Head Rd, Glen Head, 516-609-3010

Infectious Disease

Berkey, Peter Ben (5 mentions)
U Central del Caribe, 1980
Certification: Infectious Disease, Internal Medicine
970 N Broadway #212, Yonkers, 914-376-1543

Berman, Daniel S. (4 mentions)
New York U, 1982
Certification: Infectious Disease, Internal Medicine
56 Doyer Ave, White Plains, 914-948-0500

Brause, Barry David (4 mentions)
U of Pittsburgh, 1970
Certification: Infectious Disease, Internal Medicine
535 E 70th St, New York, 212-774-7151

Brieff, David Ben (6 mentions)
Columbia U, 1984
Certification: Infectious Disease, Internal Medicine
44 S Bayles Ave #216, Port Washington, 516-767-7771

Bulbin, Alan Marshall (4 mentions)
U of South Florida, 1988 *Certification:* Infectious Disease
44 S Bayles Ave #216, Port Washington, 516-767-7771

Chapnick, Edward Kurt (7 mentions)
SUNY-Downstate Med Coll, 1985
Certification: Infectious Disease, Internal Medicine
4802 10th Ave, Brooklyn, 718-283-7492

Croen, Kenneth Daniel (8 mentions)
Albert Einstein Coll of Med, 1980
Certification: Infectious Disease, Internal Medicine
259 Heathcote Rd, Scarsdale, 914-723-8100

Cunha, Burke Anthony (11 mentions)
Pennsylvania State U, 1972
Certification: Infectious Disease, Internal Medicine
222 Station Plaza N #432, Mineola, 516-663-2507

Epstein, Marcia Ellen S. (12 mentions)
Harvard U, 1983
Certification: Infectious Disease, Internal Medicine
300 Community Dr, Manhasset, 516-562-4280

Farber, Bruce Frederick (17 mentions)
Northwestern U, 1976
Certification: Infectious Disease, Internal Medicine
300 Community Dr, Manhasset, 516-562-4280

Flood, Mary Theresa (4 mentions)
Columbia U, 1987
Certification: Infectious Disease, Internal Medicine
161 Fort Washington Ave #2221, New York, 212-305-8039

Forni, Arthur Louis (5 mentions)
Certification: Infectious Disease, Internal Medicine
210 Westchester Ave, West Harrison, 914-682-6511

Gray, Michael Timothy (4 mentions)
Albert Einstein Coll of Med, 1991 *Certification:* Infectious Disease
786 Montauk Hwy, West Islip, 631-376-6075

Greene, Jeffrey Bruce (8 mentions)
New York U, 1976
Certification: Infectious Disease, Internal Medicine
104 E 40th St #603, New York, 212-375-2940

Greenspan, Joel (7 mentions)
SUNY-Upstate Med U, 1969
Certification: Infectious Disease, Internal Medicine
44 S Bayles Ave #216, Port Washington, 516-767-7771

Gumprecht, Jeffrey Paul (34 mentions)
Albany Med Coll, 1983
Certification: Infectious Disease, Internal Medicine
1100 Park Ave #1-C, New York, 212-427-9550

Hammer, Glenn Steven (24 mentions)
New York U, 1969
Certification: Infectious Disease, Internal Medicine
1100 Park Ave, New York, 212-427-9550

Hartman, Barry Jay (13 mentions)
Certification: Infectious Disease, Internal Medicine
407 E 70th St #409, New York, 212-744-4882

Ingwer, Irwin (4 mentions)
Jefferson Med Coll, 1970
Certification: Infectious Disease, Internal Medicine
789 Old Country Rd, Plainview, 516-433-3600

Karter, Dennis Lee (4 mentions)
U of California-San Francisco, 1984
Certification: Infectious Disease, Internal Medicine
31 Washington Sq W, New York, 212-475-8833

Klein, Arthur Stuart (15 mentions)
SUNY-Downstate Med Coll, 1983
Certification: Infectious Disease, Internal Medicine
14 Technology Dr #10, East Setauket, 631-689-5400

Krilov, Leonard Roy (13 mentions)
Columbia U, 1978
Certification: Pediatric Infectious Diseases, Pediatrics
120 Mineola Blvd #210, Mineola, 516-663-9570

Lederman, Jeffrey Alan (4 mentions)
Jefferson Med Coll, 1988
Certification: Infectious Disease, Internal Medicine
16 Guion Pl, New Rochelle, 914-632-5000

Lewin, Sharon (5 mentions)
FMS-Canada, 1975
Certification: Infectious Disease, Internal Medicine
139 W 82nd St, New York, 212-496-7200

Lipsky, William Michael (6 mentions)
FMS-Dominican Republic, 1980
Certification: Infectious Disease, Internal Medicine
724 E Park Ave, Long Beach, 516-608-2006

Louie, Eddie (13 mentions)
New York U, 1979
Certification: Infectious Disease, Internal Medicine
345 E 37th St #207, New York, 212-682-9202

Mandell, William Fredrick (7 mentions)
New York Med Coll, 1981
Certification: Infectious Disease, Internal Medicine
31 Washington Sq W, New York, 212-475-8833

McMeeking, Alexander A. (6 mentions)
New Jersey Med Sch, 1982
Certification: Infectious Disease, Internal Medicine
104 E 40th St #507, New York, 212-375-2560

Miller, Dennis Keith (13 mentions)
Rush U, 1982 *Certification:* Infectious Disease, Internal Medicine
4 E 76th St, New York, 212-472-1237

Miller, Michael Harrison (5 mentions)
George Washington U, 1968
Certification: Infectious Disease, Internal Medicine
540 N State Rd, Briarcliff Manor, 914-762-2276

Mobarakai, Neville K. (6 mentions)
Certification: Infectious Disease, Internal Medicine
1408 Richmond Rd, Staten Island, 718-816-3362

Neibart, Eric Paul (14 mentions)
New Jersey Med Sch, 1980
Certification: Infectious Disease, Internal Medicine
1100 Park Ave #1-C, New York, 212-427-9550

Nizza, Philip (5 mentions)
New York Coll of Osteopathic Med, 1997
Certification: Infectious Disease, Internal Medicine
14 Technology Dr #10, East Setauket, 631-689-5400

Perlman, David Charles (5 mentions)
Albert Einstein Coll of Med, 1983
Certification: Infectious Disease, Internal Medicine
10 Union Sq E #3-F, New York, 212-420-4470

Pollock, Alan Albert (5 mentions)
New York Med Coll, 1972
Certification: Infectious Disease, Internal Medicine
184 E 70th St, New York, 212-988-2702

Press, Robert Arthur (9 mentions)
New York U, 1973
Certification: Infectious Disease, Internal Medicine
530 1st Ave #4G, New York, 212-263-7229

Raffalli, John Thomas (8 mentions)
SUNY-Downstate Med Coll, 1989
Certification: Infectious Disease, Internal Medicine
90 S Bedford Rd, Mount Kisco, 914-241-1050

Rubin, Lorry Glen (9 mentions)
Rush U, 1978
Certification: Pediatric Infectious Diseases, Pediatrics
26901 76th Ave, New Hyde Park, 718-470-3480

Scafuri, Frank (6 mentions)
New York Coll of Osteopathic Med, 1999
Certification: Infectious Disease, Internal Medicine
2435 Victory Blvd, Staten Island, 718-370-3730

Scoma, Salvatore (7 mentions)
FMS-Italy, 1970
173 Mineola Blvd #401-A, Mineola, 516-746-2212

Scully, Brian Edward (10 mentions)
FMS-Ireland, 1971
Certification: Infectious Disease, Internal Medicine
630 W 168th St, New York, 212-305-8039

Shah, Vijay Ratilal (5 mentions)
FMS-India, 1984
Certification: Infectious Disease, Internal Medicine
129 Broadway, Amityville, 516-626-5330
2485 Cedar Swamp Rd, Glen Head, 516-626-5330

Singer, Carol Frances (4 mentions)
Cornell U, 1970
Certification: Infectious Disease, Internal Medicine
27005 76th Ave #226, New Hyde Park, 718-470-7291

Smith, Miriam Ann (4 mentions)
U of Cincinnati, 1979
Certification: Infectious Disease, Internal Medicine
27005 76th Ave #226, New Hyde Park, 718-470-7290

Stavropoulos, Christine F. (4 mentions)
Med Coll of Pennsylvania, 1985
Certification: Infectious Disease, Internal Medicine
30 W 60th St, New York, 212-582-5006

Tenenbaum, Marvin Julius (15 mentions)
Virginia Commonwealth U, 1971
Certification: Infectious Disease, Internal Medicine
44 S Bayles Ave #916, Port Washington, 516-767-7771

Tompkins, David Charles (7 mentions)
Stony Brook U, 1982
Certification: Infectious Disease, Internal Medicine
100 Nicolls Rd, Stony Brook, 631-444-1660
205 N Belle Mead Rd, Stony Brook, 631-444-1660

Welch, Peter Charles (7 mentions)
U of Buffalo, 1974
Certification: Infectious Disease, Internal Medicine
16 Orchard Dr, Armonk, 914-273-3404

Wenglin, Barry David (9 mentions)
Columbia U, 1967
Certification: Infectious Disease, Internal Medicine
56 Doyer Ave, White Plains, 914-948-0500

Wolff, John L. E. (4 mentions)
Temple U, 1952
Certification: Infectious Disease, Internal Medicine
1160 5th Ave #105, New York, 212-772-1700

Wormser, Gary Paul (14 mentions)
Johns Hopkins U, 1972
Certification: Infectious Disease, Internal Medicine
Munger Pavillion #245, Valhalla, 914-493-8865
301 E 79th St #7S, New York, 212-861-8939

Yancovitz, Stanley Roy (5 mentions)
SUNY-Downstate Med Coll, 1967
Certification: Infectious Disease, Internal Medicine
10 Union Sq E #3, New York, 212-420-2600

Zelenetz, Paul Daniel (5 mentions)
New York Med Coll, 1995 *Certification:* Infectious Disease
268 Sea Cliff Ave, Sea Cliff, 516-656-6500

Infertility

Brenner, Steven Hal (5 mentions)
SUNY-Downstate Med Coll, 1978 *Certification:* Obstetrics & Gynecology, Reproductive Endocrinology/Infertility
2001 Marcus Ave #N213, New Hyde Park, 516-358-6363
510 Broadhollow Rd #112, Melville, 631-752-0606

Copperman, Alan Barry (7 mentions)
New York Med Coll, 1989 *Certification:* Obstetrics & Gynecology, Reproductive Endocrinology/Infertility
635 Madison Ave 10th Fl, New York, 212-756-5777

David, Sami Salim (6 mentions)
Columbia U, 1971 *Certification:* Obstetrics & Gynecology
1047 Park Ave, New York, 212-831-0430

Davis, Owen Kidder (7 mentions)
Wake Forest U, 1982 *Certification:* Obstetrics & Gynecology, Reproductive Endocrinology/Infertility
1305 York Ave, New York, 212-746-1765

Grazi, Richard V. (7 mentions)
U of Buffalo, 1981 *Certification:* Obstetrics & Gynecology, Reproductive Endocrinology/Infertility
1355 84th St, Brooklyn, 718-283-8600

Grifo, James Anthony (16 mentions)
Case Western Reserve U, 1984 *Certification:* Obstetrics & Gynecology, Reproductive Endocrinology/Infertility
660 1st Ave 5th Fl, New York, 212-263-7978

Hershlag, Avner (7 mentions)
FMS-Israel, 1977 *Certification:* Obstetrics & Gynecology, Reproductive Endocrinology/Infertility
300 Community Dr, Manhasset, 516-562-2229

Keltz, Martin David (4 mentions)
New York U, 1989 *Certification:* Obstetrics & Gynecology, Reproductive Endocrinology/Infertility
425 W 59th St, New York, 212-523-7751

Kenigsberg, Daniel Joseph (8 mentions)
New York Med Coll, 1978 *Certification:* Obstetrics & Gynecology, Reproductive Endocrinology/Infertility
8 Corporate Center Dr #101, Melville, 631-752-0606
2001 Marcus Ave #N-213, New Hyde Park, 516-358-6363

Kreiner, David (6 mentions)
SUNY-Downstate Med Coll, 1981
Certification: Obstetrics & Gynecology
1074 Old Country Rd, Plainview, 516-939-2229
701 Route 25-A, Mount Sinai, 631-331-8088

Lieman, Harry Jay (5 mentions)
SUNY-Downstate Med Coll, 1990 *Certification:* Obstetrics & Gynecology, Reproductive Endocrinology/Infertility
141 S Central Ave, Hartsdale, 914-997-1060

Palter, Steven Frederic (4 mentions)
Boston U, 1990 *Certification:* Obstetrics & Gynecology, Reproductive Endocrinology/Infertility
243 Jericho Tpke, Syosset, 516-682-8900

Rosenfeld, David Louis (12 mentions)
U of Pennsylvania, 1970 *Certification:* Obstetrics & Gynecology, Reproductive Endocrinology/Infertility
300 Community Dr, Manhasset, 516-562-2229

Rosenwaks, Zev (23 mentions)
SUNY-Downstate Med Coll, 1972 *Certification:* Obstetrics & Gynecology, Reproductive Endocrinology/Infertility
505 E 70th St, New York, 646-962-3246
1305 York Ave, New York, 212-746-1743

Scholl, Gerald Martin (7 mentions)
New York U, 1973 *Certification:* Obstetrics & Gynecology, Reproductive Endocrinology/Infertility
300 Community Dr, Manhasset, 516-562-2229

Spandorfer, Steven David (4 mentions)
Emory U, 1988 *Certification:* Obstetrics & Gynecology, Reproductive Endocrinology/Infertility
505 E 70th St, New York, 212-746-1638

Stangel, John Jeffery (9 mentions)
New York Med Coll, 1969 *Certification:* Obstetrics & Gynecology, Reproductive Endocrinology/Infertility
70 Maple Ave, Rye, 914-967-6800

Internal Medicine *(see note on page 9)*

Adler, Bradley Keith (3 mentions)
SUNY-Downstate Med Coll, 1999 *Certification:* Internal Medicine
50 Popham Rd, Scarsdale, 914-723-5566

Adler, Marc Steven (3 mentions)
SUNY-Upstate Med U, 1992 *Certification:* Internal Medicine
230 Hilton Ave #20, Hempstead, 516-538-0300

Alter, Sheldon (5 mentions)
Rosalind Franklin U, 1961
Certification: Internal Medicine, Nephrology
33 Davis Ave, White Plains, 914-948-3630

Ammazzalorso, Michael D. (4 mentions)
SUNY-Downstate Med Coll, 1987
Certification: Geriatric Medicine, Internal Medicine
222 Station Plaza N #310, Mineola, 516-663-2051

Balter, Richard A. (5 mentions)
New York U, 1978 *Certification:* Internal Medicine
5225 Nesconset Hwy #15, Port Jefferson Station, 631-331-1000

Bardes, Charles L. (4 mentions)
U of Pennsylvania, 1986 *Certification:* Internal Medicine
505 E 70th St #460, New York, 212-746-1333

Bendit, Ezra Jacob (5 mentions)
New Jersey Med Sch, 1984 *Certification:* Internal Medicine
1181 Old Country Rd #3, Plainview, 516-931-2320

Berland, Doris G. (3 mentions)
SUNY-Upstate Med U, 1996
1615 Northern Blvd #GR-3, Manhasset, 516-627-3717

Bush, Michael Neal (3 mentions)
SUNY-Downstate Med Coll, 1978 *Certification:* Internal Medicine
115 E 57th St #630, New York, 212-583-2990

Charap, Mitchell H. (5 mentions)
New York U, 1977 *Certification:* Internal Medicine
530 1st Ave #7B, New York, 212-263-7442

Cohen, Richard Peter (4 mentions)
Cornell U, 1975 *Certification:* Internal Medicine
235 E 67th St #205, New York, 212-734-6464

Cohn, Symra Ann (3 mentions)
New York Med Coll, 1991 *Certification:* Internal Medicine
3 E 71st st 1st Fl, New York, 212-288-1302

Colangelo, Daniel Anthony (3 mentions)
New York U, 1980 *Certification:* Internal Medicine
1600 Harrison Ave #G-105, Mamaroneck, 914-698-4466

Cordaro, Anthony Francis (3 mentions)
FMS-Italy, 1970 *Certification:* Internal Medicine
271 Jericho Tpke, Floral Park, 516-352-1414

Della Ratta, Ralph K. (3 mentions)
SUNY-Upstate Med U, 1985 *Certification:* Internal Medicine
222 Station Plaza N #310, Mineola, 516-663-2051

Federbush, Richard Bart (5 mentions)
FMS-Mexico, 1985 *Certification:* Internal Medicine
175 Jericho Tpke #216, Syosset, 516-364-9800

Feltheimer, Seth David (3 mentions)
FMS-Spain, 1981 *Certification:* Internal Medicine
161 Fort Washington Ave #336, New York, 212-305-8669

Friedling, Steven Paul (4 mentions)
SUNY-Downstate Med Coll, 1968
Certification: Infectious Disease, Internal Medicine
267 E Main St Bldg A, Smithtown, 631-724-2000

Goldberger, Erica Dale (3 mentions)
Cornell U, 1996 *Certification:* Internal Medicine
50 Popham Rd, Scarsdale, 914-723-5566

Gottridge, Jo Anne (3 mentions)
Case Western Reserve U, 1980 *Certification:* Internal Medicine
865 Northern Blvd #102, Great Neck, 516-622-5000

Greaney, Edward J. (3 mentions)
317 E 34th St #7, New York, 212-726-7400

Grieco, Anthony John (4 mentions)
New York U, 1963 *Certification:* Internal Medicine
530 1st Ave #7-B, New York, 212-263-7272

Hallal, Edward John, Jr. (5 mentions)
FMS-Grenada, 1984 *Certification:* Internal Medicine
180 E Main St, Bay Shore, 631-665-0027

Hauptman, Allen S. (4 mentions)
New York U, 1978 *Certification:* Internal Medicine
317 E 34th St, New York, 212-726-7494

Horbar, Gary Michael (7 mentions)
New York Med Coll, 1976 *Certification:* Internal Medicine
6 E 85th St, New York, 212-570-9119

Kendler, Jason Scott (5 mentions)
U of Pennsylvania, 1992
Certification: Infectious Disease, Internal Medicine
310 E 72nd St, New York, 212-249-3440

Knoepflmacher, Paul (7 mentions)
New Jersey Med Sch, 1996 *Certification:* Internal Medicine
108 E 96th St, New York, 212-410-6610

Krieger, Sharon Marie (6 mentions)
Louisiana State U, 1991 *Certification:* Internal Medicine
90 S Bedford Rd, Mount Kisco, 914-241-1050

Leonard, Michael Richard (3 mentions)
Mount Sinai Sch of Med, 1992 *Certification:* Internal Medicine
1550 York Ave, New York, 212-249-8056

Lewin, Neal Andrew (4 mentions)
SUNY-Downstate Med Coll, 1974
Certification: Emergency Medicine, Internal Medicine
120 E 36th St #1B, New York, 212-889-2813

Lisio, Arnold Louis (3 mentions)
U of Rochester, 1961 *Certification:* Internal Medicine
903 Park Ave, New York, 212-249-8535

Margulis, Steven Michael (4 mentions)
Albert Einstein Coll of Med, 1997 *Certification:* Internal Medicine
90 S Bedford Rd, Mount Kisco, 914-241-1050

Matta, Raymond Joseph (4 mentions)
U of Pittsburgh, 1969
Certification: Cardiovascular Disease, Internal Medicine
1120 Park Ave, New York, 212-410-5800

Meixler, Steven Martin (3 mentions)
Boston U, 1984 *Certification:* Critical Care Medicine,
Internal Medicine, Pulmonary Disease
210 Westchester Ave, West Harrison, 914-682-0700

Nash, Thomas W. (3 mentions)
New York U, 1978 *Certification:* Infectious Disease, Internal
Medicine, Pulmonary Disease
310 E 72nd St, New York, 212-734-6612

Nyer, Kenneth Lloyd (3 mentions)
Albert Einstein Coll of Med, 1984
Certification: Geriatric Medicine, Internal Medicine
1610 Williamsbridge Rd, Bronx, 718-409-6400

Ostuni, John Anthony (4 mentions)
SUNY-Downstate Med Coll, 1971 *Certification:*
Endocrinology and Metabolism, Internal Medicine
155 W Merrick Rd, Freeport, 516-379-3139

Outon, Andre (3 mentions)
FMS-Dominican Republic, 1986
128 Ashford Ave, Dobbs Ferry, 914-674-1141

Peterson, Stephen J. (9 mentions)
FMS-Philippines, 1982 *Certification:* Internal Medicine
Munger Pavillion #149, Valhalla, 914-493-8370
311 North St #207, White Plains, 914-681-0926

Sarnataro, Robert Edmund (3 mentions)
SUNY-Downstate Med Coll, 1982 *Certification:* Internal Medicine
287 Northern Blvd #106, Great Neck, 516-773-3030
3229 162nd St, Flushing, 718-358-6389

Scavron, Jeffrey Neil (4 mentions)
FMS-Italy, 1979 *Certification:* Internal Medicine
1181 Old Country Rd, Plainview, 516-931-2320

Silverman, David A. (5 mentions)
Columbia U, 1976 *Certification:* Internal Medicine
239 Central Park W, New York, 212-496-1929

Sklaroff, Herschel Joseph (3 mentions)
U of Pennsylvania, 1961
Certification: Cardiovascular Disease, Internal Medicine
1175 Park Ave, New York, 212-289-6500

Strauss, Michael Leopold (3 mentions)
FMS-Belgium, 1980 *Certification:* Internal Medicine
310 E 14th St, New York, 212-979-4204

Taibi, William Louis (9 mentions)
SUNY-Upstate Med U, 1985 *Certification:* Internal Medicine
710 Main St, Port Jefferson, 631-474-4000

Turro, James Joseph (7 mentions)
Cornell U, 1982 *Certification:* Internal Medicine
90 S Bedford Rd, Mount Kisco, 914-241-1050

Nephrology

Adler, Stephen (7 mentions)
19 Bradhurst Ave #100, Hawthorne, 914-493-7701

Alpert, Bertram Edward (4 mentions)
New York Med Coll, 1972
Certification: Internal Medicine, Nephrology
1366 Victory Blvd, Staten Island, 718-273-3400

Appel, Gerald Bernard (8 mentions)
Albert Einstein Coll of Med, 1972
Certification: Internal Medicine, Nephrology
622 W 168th St #4-124, New York, 212-305-3273

Barbato, Ralph T. (6 mentions)
New York Coll of Osteopathic Med, 1994
Certification: Internal Medicine, Nephrology
340 Howells Rd #A, Bay Shore, 631-666-2808

Bellucci, Alessandro (8 mentions)
FMS-Italy, 1975 *Certification:* Internal Medicine, Nephrology
100 Community Dr, Great Neck, 516-465-8200

Buzzeo, Louis Anthony (9 mentions)
Tufts U, 1972 *Certification:* Internal Medicine, Nephrology
777 N Broadway #203, Sleepy Hollow, 914-332-9100

Charytan, Chaim (3 mentions)
Albert Einstein Coll of Med, 1964
Certification: Internal Medicine, Nephrology
1874 Pelham Pkwy S, Bronx, 718-931-5800
5645 Main St, Flushing, 718-931-5800

Constantiner, Arturo (3 mentions)
FMS-Mexico, 1974 *Certification:* Internal Medicine, Nephrology
19 Beekman St #6, New York, 212-349-8455

Criss, Adam N. (4 mentions)
New York Coll of Osteopathic Med, 1997
Certification: Internal Medicine, Nephrology
488 Great Neck Rd #225, Great Neck, 516-775-4545
1999 Marcus Ave #216, Lake Success, 516-775-4545

Dasgupta, Manash Kamal (7 mentions)
FMS-India, 1966 *Certification:* Internal Medicine, Nephrology
9 Central Park Ave #A, Yonkers, 914-376-3330

De Fabritus, Albert M. (3 mentions)
New York Med Coll, 1973
Certification: Internal Medicine, Nephrology
36 7th Ave #418, New York, 212-807-8817

Devita, Maria Virginia (5 mentions)
Georgetown U, 1984 *Certification:* Internal Medicine, Nephrology
130 E 77th St, New York, 212-439-9251

Dreznin, Stephen Ross (5 mentions)
FMS-Dominican Republic, 1983
Certification: Internal Medicine, Nephrology
77 N Centre Ave #300, Rockville Centre, 516-764-5807

Faitell, David Adam (4 mentions)
U of Rochester, 1982
Certification: Internal Medicine, Nephrology
2 Prohealth Plaza, Lake Success, 516-622-6116

Frank, William Martin (6 mentions)
U of Iowa, 1972 *Certification:* Internal Medicine, Nephrology
340 Howells Rd #A, Bay Shore, 631-666-2808

Friedmann, Paul (3 mentions)
Certification: Internal Medicine, Nephrology
77 N Centre Ave #300, Rockville Centre, 516-764-5807

Frumkin, Gail Nurit (3 mentions)
FMS-Mexico, 1984
10025 Queens Blvd, Forest Hills, 718-830-3333
6620 Queens Blvd, Woodside, 718-457-3000

Gardenswartz, Mark Howard (8 mentions)
U of Colorado, 1975 *Certification:* Critical Care Medicine,
Internal Medicine, Nephrology
110 E 59th St, New York, 212-583-2930

Garrick, Renee E. (11 mentions)
Rush U, 1978 *Certification:* Internal Medicine, Nephrology
19 Bradhurst Ave #206-N, Hawthorne, 914-493-7701

Gilbert, Richard Michael (7 mentions)
New York U, 1968 *Certification:* Internal Medicine, Nephrology
530 1st Ave #4A, New York, 212-263-7131

Golden, Ronald Aaron (3 mentions)
New York U, 1967 *Certification:* Internal Medicine, Nephrology
1874 Pelham Pkwy S, Bronx, 718-931-5800
5645 Main St, Flushing, 718-931-5800

Goldstein, Marvin Hirsh (3 mentions)
Virginia Commonwealth U, 1957
Certification: Internal Medicine, Nephrology
1225 Park Ave #1E, New York, 212-410-7100

Greenberg, Sheldon (3 mentions)
Albert Einstein Coll of Med, 1987
Certification: Internal Medicine, Nephrology
4719 Fort Hamilton, Brooklyn, 718-283-1625
1401 Newkirk Ave, Brooklyn, 718-283-1625

Haller, Jeffrey Ezra (4 mentions)
Albert Einstein Coll of Med, 1995
Certification: Internal Medicine, Nephrology
1999 Marcus Ave, Lake Success, 516-775-4545

Hauser, A. Daniel (3 mentions)
Yale U, 1953 *Certification:* Internal Medicine, Nephrology
55 E 87th St #1C, New York, 212-348-4300

Ilamathi, Ekambaram (8 mentions)
FMS-India, 1973 *Certification:* Internal Medicine, Nephrology
1725 N Ocean Ave, Medford, 631-289-8000
2500 Nesconset Hwy Bldg 14A, Stony Brook, 631-689-7800

Imbriano, Louis Joseph (6 mentions)
FMS-Italy, 1972 *Certification:* Internal Medicine, Nephrology
200 Old Country Rd #135, Mineola, 516-663-2169

Kaufman, Allen Mark (3 mentions)
U of Rochester, 1975
Certification: Internal Medicine, Nephrology
1555 3rd Ave, New York, 212-870-9400

Kirsch, Mitchell Gary (4 mentions)
New York Med Coll, 1981
Certification: Internal Medicine, Nephrology
2500 Nesconset Hwy, Stony Brook, 631-689-7800

Korrapati, Madhusudanarao (3 mentions)
FMS-India, 1981 *Certification:* Nephrology
877 Stewart Ave #1, Garden City, 516-745-0500
4169 Iris Pl, Bethpage, 516-745-0500

Langs, Charles Elliot (5 mentions)
Albert Einstein Coll of Med, 1980
Certification: Internal Medicine, Nephrology
530 1st Ave, New York, 212-263-0705

Lax, Douglas S. (3 mentions)
New York Coll of Osteopathic Med, 1983
Certification: Internal Medicine, Nephrology
242 Merrick Rd #304, Rockville Centre, 516-764-7070

Lipner, Henry Irwin (5 mentions)
New York U, 1968 *Certification:* Internal Medicine, Nephrology
1435 86th St, Brooklyn, 718-648-0101

Lowenstein, Jerome (3 mentions)
New York U, 1957 *Certification:* Internal Medicine, Nephrology
530 1st Ave, New York, 212-263-7439

Lynn, Robert Isaac (5 mentions)
Columbia U, 1974
1200 Waters Pl #M-104, Bronx, 718-794-1200

Mailloux, Lionel U. (15 mentions)
Hahnemann U, 1962
Certification: Internal Medicine, Nephrology
50 Seaview Blvd, Port Washington, 516-484-6093

Masani, Naveed N. (3 mentions)
Stony Brook U, 1999 *Certification:* Internal Medicine, Nephrology
200 Old Country Rd #135, Mineola, 516-663-2169

Meisels, Ira Steven (7 mentions)
Yale U, 1990 *Certification:* Internal Medicine, Nephrology
425 W 59th St, New York, 212-492-5500

Michelis, Michael Frank (3 mentions)
George Washington U, 1963 *Certification:* Internal Medicine
130 E 77th St, New York, 212-988-3506

Orin, Gary Bruce (3 mentions)
SUNY-Downstate Med Coll, 1981
Certification: Internal Medicine, Nephrology
311 E 79th St #C, New York, 212-288-4300

Prince, Simon E. (3 mentions)
New York Coll of Osteopathic Med, 1997
Certification: Internal Medicine, Nephrology
1165 Northern Blvd #304, Manhasset, 516-365-5570

Raciti, Alfred (6 mentions)
FMS-Belgium, 1981 *Certification:* Internal Medicine, Nephrology
701 Route 25A #B-1, Mount Sinai, 631-331-4403

Rodman, John Stephen (4 mentions)
Columbia U, 1970 *Certification:* Internal Medicine, Nephrology
435 E 57th St, New York, 212-752-3043

Rucker, Steve Wolf (3 mentions)
U of Pittsburgh, 1983
Certification: Internal Medicine, Nephrology
1999 Marcus Ave, Lake Success, 516-775-4545

Saboor, Sadia (3 mentions)
FMS-Pakistan, 1993 *Certification:* Internal Medicine, Nephrology
1730 Central Park Ave #3-P, Yonkers, 914-779-0141

Sagar, Sushil (5 mentions)
FMS-India, 1977 *Certification:* Internal Medicine, Nephrology
4250 Hempstead Tpke #19, Bethpage, 516-735-5522

Saltzman, Martin Jay (8 mentions)
SUNY-Downstate Med Coll, 1972
Certification: Internal Medicine, Nephrology
41 S Bedford Rd, Mount Kisco, 914-666-5588

Schwarz, Richard B. (3 mentions)
New York U, 1979
Certification: Geriatric Medicine, Internal Medicine, Nephrology
325 Park Ave, Huntington, 631-351-3784

Serur, David (3 mentions)
SUNY-Downstate Med Coll, 1988
Certification: Internal Medicine, Nephrology
505 E 70th St, New York, 212-746-1583

Sherman, Raymond Lionel (8 mentions)
SUNY-Downstate Med Coll, 1961
Certification: Internal Medicine, Nephrology
407 E 70th St, New York, 212-879-8245

Stein, Richard Marshall (5 mentions)
SUNY-Downstate Med Coll, 1958
Certification: Internal Medicine, Nephrology
1 Gustave L Levy Pl, New York, 212-241-4060
5 E 98th St, New York, 212-241-4060

Tan, Reynaldo G. (3 mentions)
FMS-Philippines, 1988
Certification: Internal Medicine, Nephrology
7101 Narrows Ave, Brooklyn, 718-836-0225

Tepedino, Gerard J. (3 mentions)
New York U, 2000 *Certification:* Internal Medicine, Nephrology
1165 Northern Blvd #304, Manhasset, 516-365-5570

Trachtman, Howard (5 mentions)
U of Pennsylvania, 1978
Certification: Pediatric Nephrology, Pediatrics
26901 76th Ave #365, New Hyde Park, 718-470-3491

Vassalotti, Joseph Alfred (3 mentions)
Stony Brook U, 1989 *Certification:* Internal Medicine, Nephrology
5 E 98th St, New York, 212-241-4060

Weisstuch, Joseph Marc (6 mentions)
New York U, 1985 *Certification:* Internal Medicine, Nephrology
530 1st Ave #4B, New York, 212-263-0705

Wenger, Norma Lee (6 mentions)
Med Coll of Pennsylvania, 1973
Certification: Internal Medicine, Nephrology
242 Merrick Rd #304, Rockville Centre, 516-764-7070

Williams, Brent Allan (3 mentions)
U of Rochester, 1997
Certification: Internal Medicine, Nephrology
36 7th Ave #517, New York, 212-620-3097
510 526 Ave Of The Americas, New York, 212-675-6880
153 W 11th St, New York, 212-604-7000
336 342 W 13th St, New York, 212-675-6880

Williams, Gail Duff Shute (5 mentions)
Columbia U, 1968 *Certification:* Internal Medicine, Nephrology
161 Fort Washington Ave #351, New York, 212-305-5376

Winchester, James Frank (3 mentions)
FMS-United Kingdom, 1969 *Certification:* Internal Medicine
10 Union Sq E, New York, 212-420-4070

Winston, Jonathan Allan (18 mentions)
George Washington U, 1977
Certification: Internal Medicine, Nephrology
5 E 98th St 11th Fl, New York, 212-241-4060
1 Gustave L Levy Pl, New York, 212-241-4060

Neurological Surgery

Brisman, Michael H. (8 mentions)
Columbia U, 1992 *Certification:* Neurological Surgery
100 Merrick Rd #128-W, Rockville Centre, 516-255-9031

Camins, Martin Bruce (9 mentions)
Rosalind Franklin U, 1969 *Certification:* Neurological Surgery
205 E 68th St #T1C, New York, 212-570-0100

Chalif, David Jeffrey (6 mentions)
U of Chicago, 1979 *Certification:* Neurological Surgery
300 Community Dr, Manhasset, 516-562-3070

Chiles, Bennie W., III (8 mentions)
U of California-San Francisco, 1991
Certification: Neurological Surgery
280 N Central Ave #235, Hartsdale, 914-332-0396

Davis, Raphael Paul (23 mentions)
Mount Sinai Sch of Med, 1981 *Certification:* Neurological Surgery
2500 Rt 347 Bldg 16 #63, Stony Brook, 631 444 1213
225 W Montauk Hwy, Hampton Bays, 631-444-1213
2500 Nesconset Hwy #63, Stony Brook, 631-444-1213

Elowitz, Eric Howard (6 mentions)
SUNY-Downstate Med Coll, 1986
Certification: Neurological Surgery
425 W 59th St, New York, 212-523-8500
1000 10th Ave, New York, 212-636-3660
110 E 59th St #10-A, New York, 212-523-8500

Epstein, Nancy Ellen (12 mentions)
Columbia U, 1976 *Certification:* Neurological Surgery
410 Lakeville Rd #204, New Hyde Park, 516-354-3401

Jafar, Jafar Jewad (8 mentions)
FMS-Iran, 1976 *Certification:* Neurological Surgery
530 1st Ave #8R, New York, 212-263-6312

Kelly, Patrick J. (8 mentions)
U of Buffalo, 1966 *Certification:* Neurological Surgery
530 1st Ave #8-R, New York, 212-263-8002
380 2nd Ave, New York, 212-477-8180

Lansen, Thomas Allen (7 mentions)
Med Coll of Wisconsin, 1973 *Certification:* Neurological Surgery
222 Westchester Ave #310, White Plains, 914-948-2288

Mittler, Mark A. (7 mentions)
U of Rochester, 1991 *Certification:* Neurological Surgery
410 Lakeville Rd #204, New Hyde Park, 516-354-3401

Mullins, Kevin James (10 mentions)
U of Rochester, 1991 *Certification:* Neurological Surgery
1175 Montauk Hwy #6, West Islip, 631-422-5371

Murali, Raj (6 mentions)
FMS-India, 1968 *Certification:* Neurological Surgery
170 W 12th St, New York, 212-604-7767
19 Bradhurst Ave #2800, Hawthorne, 914-493-8392

Perin, Noel (9 mentions)
FMS-Sri Lanka, 1973 *Certification:* Neurological Surgery
425 W 59th St, New York, 212-523-6720

Post, Kalmon Dolgin (23 mentions)
New York U, 1967 *Certification:* Neurological Surgery
5 E 98th St, New York, 212-241-0933
1 Gustave L Levy Pl, New York, 212-241-9638

Sen, Chandra Nath (9 mentions)
FMS-India, 1977 *Certification:* Neurological Surgery
425 W 59th St, New York, 212-523-6720

Solomon, Robert Alan (10 mentions)
Johns Hopkins U, 1980 *Certification:* Neurological Surgery
710 W 168th St, New York, 212-305-4118

Souweidane, Mark Musa (6 mentions)
Wayne State U, 1988 *Certification:* Neurological Surgery
520 E 70th St #651, New York, 212-746-2363
1275 York Ave, New York, 212-639-2000

Stern, Jack (7 mentions)
Albert Einstein Coll of Med, 1974
Certification: Neurological Surgery
244 Westchester Ave #310, West Harrison, 914-948-6688

Tabaddor, Kamran (7 mentions)
FMS-Iran, 1967 *Certification:* Neurological Surgery
3328 Bainbridge Ave, Bronx, 718-655-9111

Wisoff, Jeffrey Howard (10 mentions)
George Washington U, 1978 *Certification:* Neurological Surgery
317 E 34th St #1002, New York, 212-263-6419

Neurology

Appelbaum, J. C. (3 mentions)
Philadelphia Coll of Osteopathic Med, 1977
5907 175th Pl, Flushing, 718-939-0800

April, Robert Samuel (5 mentions)
U of California-San Francisco, 1960 *Certification:* Neurology
4 E 88th St, New York, 212-722-7800

Blanck, Richard Howard (9 mentions)
New Jersey Med Sch, 1973
Certification: Internal Medicine, Neurology
1000 Northern Blvd #150, Great Neck, 516-466-4700

Bronster, David J. (6 mentions)
Mount Sinai Sch of Med, 1979 *Certification:* Neurology
3 E 83rd St, New York, 212-772-0008

Carniciu, Sanda (7 mentions)
FMS-Romania, 1987
Certification: Clinical Neurophysiology, Neurology
245 N Broadway #102, Sleepy Hollow, 914-631-6888

Caronna, John Joseph (3 mentions)
Cornell U, 1965 *Certification:* Neurology
520 E 70th St #607, New York, 212-746-2304

Carver, Alan Charles (3 mentions)
Boston U, 1995 *Certification:* Neurology
5 E 98th St, New York, 212-241-7076

Charney, Jonathan Z. (4 mentions)
New York Med Coll, 1969 *Certification:* Neurology
1111 Park Ave #1H, New York, 212-831-2886

Cohen, Anthony S. (9 mentions)
FMS-South Africa, 1968 *Certification:* Neurology
1000 Northern Blvd #150, Great Neck, 516-466-4700

Cohen, Daniel Hirsh (4 mentions)
U of Miami, 1980 *Certification:* Neurology
370 E Main St #1, Bay Shore, 631-666-4767

Delfiner, Joel Steven (7 mentions)
U of Pennsylvania, 1979
Certification: Clinical Neurophysiology, Neurology
1000 10th Ave, New York, 212-523-6521

Devinsky, Orrin (6 mentions)
Certification: Neurology
403 E 34th St, New York, 212-263-8871

Einberg, Kenneth Richard (3 mentions)
Rosalind Franklin U, 1983
27005 76th Ave #222, New Hyde Park, 718-470-7321

Favate, Albert Samuel (3 mentions)
FMS-Mexico, 1983 *Certification:* Neurology
80 5th Ave #1605, New York, 212-675-3878

Fink, Matthew E. (6 mentions)
U of Pittsburgh, 1976
Certification: Internal Medicine, Neurology, Vascular Neurology
1305 York Ave, New York, 212-746-4564

Gatewood, Caroline V. (3 mentions)
Med Coll of Pennsylvania, 1992 *Certification:* Neurology
7555 Main Rd, Mattituck, 631-734-2450

Gendelman, Seymour (14 mentions)
George Washington U, 1964 *Certification:* Neurology
5 E 98th St, New York, 212-241-7076

Geraci, Anthony Paul (3 mentions)
Mount Sinai Sch of Med, 1995 *Certification:* Neurology
445 77th St, Brooklyn, 718-238-6250
350 Broadway #205, New York, 718-238-6250

Gerber, Oded (8 mentions)
SUNY-Downstate Med Coll, 1972 *Certification:* Neurology
Stony Brook Health SciencesS Ctr #12-020, Stony Brook, 631-444-2599
179 N Belle Mead Rd, East Setauket, 631-444-2599

Goodgold, Albert L. (3 mentions)
FMS-Switzerland, 1955
530 1st Ave #5A, New York, 212-263-7205

Gottesman, Malcolm Howard (4 mentions)
Albany Med Coll, 1978 *Certification:* Neurology, Psychiatry
200 Old Country Rd #125, Mineola, 516-663-4525

Greenwood, Jack Michael (9 mentions)
New York U, 1974 *Certification:* Neurology with Special
   Qualifications in Child Neurology
120 N Country Rd, Port Jefferson, 631-474-0444

Gudesblatt, Mark (4 mentions)
Cornell U, 1980 *Certification:* Neurology
280 E Main St, Bay Shore, 631-666-3939
77 Medford Ave #C, Patchogue, 631-758-1910

Haimovic, Itzhak C. (17 mentions)
New York Med Coll, 1975 *Certification:* Neurology
170 Great Neck Rd, Great Neck, 516-487-4464

Herbstein, Diego J. (3 mentions)
FMS-Argentina, 1968 *Certification:* Neurology
170 E 77th St #1-D, New York, 212-794-2281
59-16 174th St, Fresh Meadows, 718-460-6765

Hughes, John Boland (3 mentions)
Harvard U, 1971 *Certification:* Internal Medicine
4170 Bronx Blvd, Bronx, 718-920-9074
600 East 233rd St, Bronx, 718-920-9843
95 Grasslands Rd, Valhalla, 914-594-4296
14 Elm St, Cornwall, 845-534-2144

Hussain, Mohammad Sajid (3 mentions)
FMS-India, 1995 *Certification:* Internal Medicine
221 Broadway #204, Amityville, 631-598-4897

Kazmi, Mahmood M. (3 mentions)
FMS-Egypt, 1984 *Certification:* Psychiatry
3328 Bainbridge Ave, Bronx, 718-515-4347

Kefalos, John Louis (3 mentions)
FMS-Greece, 1978 *Certification:* Neurology
777 Sunrise Hwy #200, Lynbrook, 516-887-3516

Keilson, Marshall Jay (4 mentions)
Albert Einstein Coll of Med, 1977 *Certification:* Neurology
4802 10th Ave, Brooklyn, 718-283-7470

Kessler, Jeffrey Theodore (11 mentions)
Cornell U, 1969 *Certification:* Internal Medicine, Neurology
1000 Northern Blvd #150, Great Neck, 516-466-4700

Klebanoff, Louise M. (3 mentions)
Georgetown U, 1984 *Certification:* Neurology
10 Union Sq E #2, New York, 212-844-8486

Kranzler, Leon Stephan (3 mentions)
U of Pennsylvania, 1985 *Certification:* Neurology
244 Westchester Ave S #315, White Plains, 914-946-9444
30 Davis Ave, White Plains, 914-946-9444

Le Brun, Yves A. (6 mentions)
FMS-Argentina, 1969 *Certification:* Neurology
244 Westchester Ave #315, White Plains, 914-946-9444
30 Davis Ave, White Plains, 914-946-9444

Levy, Lewis Alan (3 mentions)
SUNY-Downstate Med Coll, 1973 *Certification:* Neurology
227 Franklin Ave, Hewlett, 516-887-3516
777 Sunrise Hwy #200, Lynbrook, 516-887-3516

Lewis, Linda Donelle (10 mentions)
West Virginia U, 1965 *Certification:* Neurology
710 W 168th St #236, New York, 212-305-5246

Libman, Richard Benjamin (3 mentions)
FMS-Canada, 1986 *Certification:* Neurology, Vascular Neurology
27005 76th Ave #222, New Hyde Park, 718-470-7260

Lublin, Fred David (3 mentions)
Jefferson Med Coll, 1972 *Certification:* Neurology
5 E 98th St, New York, 212-241-6854

Macaluso, Claude (4 mentions)
FMS-Italy, 1982
80 5th Ave #1605, New York, 212-675-3878

Macgowan, Daniel James L. (3 mentions)
FMS-Ireland, 1989
Certification: Clinical Neurophysiology, Neurology
10 Union Sq E #2, New York, 212-844-8497

Mallin, Jeffrey Elliott (3 mentions)
FMS-Mexico, 1982 *Certification:* Neurology
3003 New Hyde Park Rd #200, New Hyde Park, 516-488-1888

Marks, Stephen Jeffrey (5 mentions)
New York Med Coll, 1980
Certification: Neurology, Vascular Neurology
19 Bradhurst Ave, Hawthorne, 914-345-1313

Misra, Ajay Kumar (6 mentions)
FMS-India, 1979
Certification: Clinical Neurophysiology, Neurology
880 N Broadway, Massapequa, 516-541-0300
80 E Jericho Tpke #202, Mineola, 516-747-0000

Muste, Maria (5 mentions)
FMS-Romania, 1992 *Certification:* Internal Medicine, Neurology
244 Westchester Ave #315, West Harrison, 914-946-9444

Neophytides, Andreas N. (3 mentions)
FMS-Greece, 1970 *Certification:* Neurology
650 1st Ave, New York, 212-213-9580

Olarte, Marcelo Ramon (8 mentions)
FMS-Argentina, 1970 *Certification:* Neurology
710 W 168th St #246, New York, 212-305-1832

Ostrovskiy, Denis Alekseyevich (3 mentions)
Certification: Clinical Neurophysiology, Neurology
1000 Northern Blvd, Great Neck, 516-466-4700

Pedley, Timothy A. (3 mentions)
Yale U, 1969 *Certification:* Neurology
710 W 168th St, New York, 212-305-6489

Perel, Allan Brian (4 mentions)
SUNY-Downstate Med Coll, 1985 *Certification:* Neurology
27 New Dorp Ln, Staten Island, 718-667-3800

Petito, Frank Alfred, Jr. (8 mentions)
Columbia U, 1967 *Certification:* Neurology
525 E 68th St #607, New York, 212-746-2309

Pflaster, Norman Lee (5 mentions)
Rosalind Franklin U, 1987 *Certification:* Neurology
877 E Main St, Riverhead, 631-727-0660
365 County Rd 39-A #7, Southampton, 631-287-2500
280 E Main St, Bay Shore, 631-666-3939

Podwall, David (4 mentions)
Albert Einstein Coll of Med, 1999 *Certification:* Neurology
1000 Northern Blvd #150, Great Neck, 516-466-4700

Ragone, Philip Salvatore (13 mentions)
New York Med Coll, 1982
Certification: Internal Medicine, Neurology
1010 Northern Blvd #136, Great Neck, 516-482-4100

Rapoport, Samuel (4 mentions)
Cornell U, 1976 *Certification:* Neurology
354 E 76th St, New York, 212-570-0642

Reich, Edward J. (5 mentions)
U of Buffalo, 1966 *Certification:* Neurology
55 E 72nd St, New York, 212-794-2777

Robinson, Lawrence Jay (6 mentions)
Hahnemann U, 1975 *Certification:* Neurology
333 Glen Head Rd #140, Glen Head, 516-759-4014

Rosenkilde, Carl Emil (7 mentions)
Albert Einstein Coll of Med, 1985 *Certification:* Neurology
91 Smith Ave, Mount Kisco, 914-241-1717

Rudansky, Max Charchat (4 mentions)
Jefferson Med Coll, 1979 *Certification:* Neurology
755 New York Ave #309, Huntington, 631-351-1250

Salgado, Miran W. (7 mentions)
FMS-Sri Lanka, 1985
Certification: Neurology, Vascular Neurology
506 6th St, Brooklyn, 718-246-8614

Sauter, Michael Ottmar (6 mentions)
Loyola U Chicago, 1971
Certification: Internal Medicine, Neurology
120 N Country Rd, Port Jefferson, 631-331-6667

Schaefer, John Andrew (14 mentions)
FMS-Australia, 1968 *Certification:* Neurology
523 E 72nd St 8th Fl, New York, 212-570-5685

Schneider, Adam Jason (3 mentions)
Albert Einstein Coll of Med, 1992 *Certification:* Neurology
8243 Jericho Tpke #280, Woodbury, 516-367-8040

Schwartz, Kenny Alan (4 mentions)
New Jersey Med Sch, 1979 *Certification:* Neurology
310 N Highland Ave #4, Ossining, 914-941-4415
245 N Broadway #202, Tarrytown, 914-366-0588
52 Main St, Bedford Hills, 914-234-7600

Selman, Jay Edward (7 mentions)
U of Texas-Dallas, 1973 *Certification:* Neurodevelopmental
   Disabilities, Neurology with Special Qualifications in Child
   Neurology, Pediatrics, Sleep Medicine
95 Bradhurst Ave, Valhalla, 914-666-8080

Silverman, Ronald Myron (4 mentions)
Albert Einstein Coll of Med, 1972 *Certification:* Neurology
4 Studio Arc, Bronxville, 914-337-2022
280 Mamaroneck Ave, White Plains, 914-997-1141

Smallberg, Gerald Jay (5 mentions)
Yale U, 1969 *Certification:* Neurology
1010 5th Ave, New York, 212-535-5348

Smith, Robin Errol (3 mentions)
FMS-South Africa, 1985 *Certification:* Neurology with
   Special Qualifications in Child Neurology, Pediatrics
410 Lakeville Rd #105, New Hyde Park, 516-465-5255

Snyder, David Howard (3 mentions)
U of Maryland, 1969 *Certification:* Neurology
170 E 77th St #1-D, New York, 212-794-2281
59-16 174th St, Fresh Meadows, 718-460-6765

Sobol, Norman Jacob (3 mentions)
U of Chicago, 1974 *Certification:* Internal Medicine, Neurology
3131 Kings Hwy #C-7, Brooklyn, 718-677-0009

Stacy, Charles Brecknock, Jr. (10 mentions)
Cornell U, 1977 *Certification:* Neurology
1107 5th Ave, New York, 212-876-8614

Sternman, David (4 mentions)
New York Med Coll, 1982
Certification: Internal Medicine, Neurology
1886 Broadway, New York, 212-586-1111
234 E 149th St, Bronx, 212-586-1111

Stubgen, Joerg Patrick (3 mentions)
FMS-South Africa, 1983
Certification: Clinical Neurophysiology, Neurology
525 E 68th St #607, New York, 212-746-2334

Sweet, Richard David (7 mentions)
Washington U, 1963 *Certification:* Neurology
244 Westchester Ave #315, West Harrison, 914-946-9444

Swerdlow, Michael Lewis (11 mentions)
U of Pennsylvania, 1967 *Certification:* Neurology
111 E 210th St, Bronx, 718-920-4178

Szabo, Albert Z. (8 mentions)
FMS-Hungary, 1988 *Certification:* Neurology
90 S Bedford Rd, Mount Kisco, 914-241-1050

Turner, Ira Michael (3 mentions)
SUNY-Downstate Med Coll, 1972 *Certification:* Neurology
824 Old Country Rd, Plainview, 516-822-2230

Weinberg, Harold Jay (16 mentions)
Albert Einstein Coll of Med, 1978 *Certification:* Neurology
650 1st Ave, New York, 212-213-9339

Wirkowski, Elzbieta (5 mentions)
FMS-Poland, 1984
Certification: Neurology, Psychiatry, Vascular Neurology
200 Old Country Rd #125, Mineola, 516-663-4525

Wolf, Steven M. (4 mentions)
Albany Med Coll, 1989
Certification: Clinical Neurophysiology, Neurology with
   Special Qualifications in Child Neurology, Pediatrics
141 S Central Park Ave #102, Hartsdale, 212-844-6944
170 E End Ave, New York, 212-870-8506
10 Union Sq E, New York, 212-870-8506

Wolintz, Robyn Joy (6 mentions)
SUNY-Downstate Med Coll, 1992 *Certification:* Neurology
883 65th St, Brooklyn, 718-283-7470
4802 10th Ave, Brooklyn, 718-283-7470

Wright, Paul (7 mentions)
FMS-Israel, 1996 *Certification:* Neurology
1000 Northern Blvd #150, Great Neck, 516-466-4700

Yin, June (3 mentions)
FMS-China, 1987 *Certification:* Neurology
136-20 38th Ave #6-G, Flushing, 718-888-0968

Younger, David Steven (3 mentions)
Columbia U, 1981 *Certification:* Internal Medicine, Neurology
715 Park Ave, New York, 212-535-4314
36 7th Ave #507, New York, 212-255-7544

Zalzal, Pierre Georges M. (4 mentions)
FMS-Lebanon, 1967 *Certification:* Neurology, Vascular Neurology
450 Bay Ridge Pkwy, Brooklyn, 718-630-5622
5616 6th Ave, Brooklyn, 718-439-5440

Zuckerman, Mark Julian (3 mentions)
FMS-Belgium, 1983
Certification: Clinical Neurophysiology, Neurology
363 Route 111 #102, Smithtown, 631-360-3366

Obstetrics/Gynecology

Agnant, Guirlaine Leonore (3 mentions)
FMS-Mexico, 1981 *Certification:* Obstetrics & Gynecology
100 Stevens Ave, Mount Vernon, 914-668-6366

Bachman, Ira Neil (4 mentions)
Stony Brook U, 1991 *Certification:* Obstetrics & Gynecology
660 Central Ave, Cedarhurst, 516-569-1131

Baxi, Laxmi Vibhakar (4 mentions)
FMS-India, 1963 *Certification:* Obstetrics & Gynecology
161 Fort Washington Ave, New York, 212-305-5899
16 E 60th St, New York, 212-305-5899

Berlin, Scott (3 mentions)
Rosalind Franklin U, 1990 *Certification:* Obstetrics & Gynecology
2330 Union Blvd, Islip, 631-224-4200

Bernstein, Robert Mark (5 mentions)
FMS-Mexico, 1979 *Certification:* Obstetrics & Gynecology
3111 New Hyde Park Rd, North Hills, 516-365-6100

Brasner, Shari Eileen (5 mentions)
New York U, 1991 *Certification:* Obstetrics & Gynecology
1123 Park Ave, New York, 917-492-9200

Brightman, Rebecca Cecile (5 mentions)
Mount Sinai Sch of Med, 1986
Certification: Obstetrics & Gynecology
134 E 93rd St, New York, 212-348-7800

Brodman, Michael Lewis (8 mentions)
Mount Sinai Sch of Med, 1982
Certification: Obstetrics & Gynecology
5 E 98th St, New York, 212-241-7575

Brownstein, Ilana Lyn (3 mentions)
Tufts U, 1997 *Certification:* Obstetrics & Gynecology
408 E 76th St, New York, 212-535-7400

Burns, Elisa Eve (6 mentions)
Columbia U, 1982 *Certification:* Obstetrics & Gynecology
90 S Bedford Rd, Mount Kisco, 914-241-1050

Buterman, Irving (7 mentions)
FMS-Netherlands, 1971 *Certification:* Obstetrics & Gynecology
950 Park Ave, New York, 212-472-8200

Chalas, Eva (4 mentions)
Stony Brook U, 1981
Certification: Gynecologic Oncology, Obstetrics & Gynecology
1077 W Jericho Tpke, Smithtown, 631-864-5440

Chervenak, Francis A. (5 mentions)
Jefferson Med Coll, 1976
Certification: Maternal-Fetal Medicine, Obstetrics & Gynecology
525 E 68th St, New York, 212-746-3184

D'Alton, Mary Elizabeth (3 mentions)
FMS-Ireland, 1976
Certification: Maternal-Fetal Medicine, Obstetrics & Gynecology
161 Fort Washington Ave #401, New York, 212-305-7334

Davenport, Deborah Morgan (7 mentions)
U of Pennsylvania, 1975 *Certification:* Obstetrics & Gynecology
100 S Jersey Ave #16, East Setauket, 631-689-6400

Dobrenis, Andrea Horris (3 mentions)
Cornell U, 1988 *Certification:* Obstetrics & Gynecology
525 E 68th St, New York, 212-746-3000

Dor, Nathan (5 mentions)
FMS-Israel, 1972
Certification: Maternal-Fetal Medicine, Obstetrics & Gynecology
943 48th St, Brooklyn, 718-853-1535

Droesch, James Norbert (3 mentions)
SUNY-Downstate Med Coll, 1982
Certification: Obstetrics & Gynecology
100 S Jersey Ave #16, East Setauket, 631-689-6400

Dunetz, Carol Lynn (3 mentions)
SUNY-Upstate Med U, 1979 *Certification:* Obstetrics & Gynecology
2001 Marcus Ave #W-75, New Hyde Park, 516-488-2757

Economos, Kathy (3 mentions)
SUNY-Downstate Med Coll, 1986
Certification: Gynecologic Oncology, Obstetrics & Gynecology
506 6th St, Brooklyn, 718-780-3272

Edersheim, Terri Gallen (4 mentions)
Albert Einstein Coll of Med, 1980
Certification: Maternal-Fetal Medicine, Obstetrics & Gynecology
523 E 72nd St #917, New York, 212-472-5340

Fried-Oginski, Wendy (6 mentions)
Albert Einstein Coll of Med, 1991
Certification: Obstetrics & Gynecology
3111 New Hyde Park Rd, North Hills, 516-365-6100

Friedman, Frederick, Jr. (3 mentions)
SUNY-Downstate Med Coll, 1985
Certification: Obstetrics & Gynecology
1729 E 12th St, Brooklyn, 718-998-7751
5 E 98th St, New York, 212-241-9393
47 E 88th St, New York, 212-534-0200
1648 E 14th St, Brooklyn, 718-375-6370

Friedman, Lynn (9 mentions)
New York U, 1984 *Certification:* Obstetrics & Gynecology
885 Park Ave, New York, 212-737-3282

Gentilesco, Michael (4 mentions)
Albert Einstein Coll of Med, 1980
Certification: Obstetrics & Gynecology
48 Route 25-A #207, Smithtown, 631-862-3800
2500 Nesconset Hwy Bldg 10-A, Stony Brook, 631-862-3800

Giuffrida, Regina Marie (8 mentions)
New York Med Coll, 1980 *Certification:* Obstetrics & Gynecology
90 S Bedford Rd, Mount Kisco, 914-241-1050

Goldstein, Laurie Ruth (3 mentions)
Stony Brook U, 1980 *Certification:* Obstetrics & Gynecology
134 E 93rd St, New York, 212-348-7800

Goldstein, Martin S. (3 mentions)
SUNY-Upstate Med U, 1966 *Certification:* Obstetrics & Gynecology
40 E 84th St, New York, 212-472-6500

Griffin, Todd Russell (4 mentions)
Stony Brook U, 1993 *Certification:* Obstetrics & Gynecology
6 Technology Dr, East Setauket, 631-444-4686

Jacob, Jessica Ruth (5 mentions)
New York U, 1983 *Certification:* Obstetrics & Gynecology
3003 New Hyde Park Rd #407, New Hyde Park, 516-488-8145

Judge, Peter Adam (5 mentions)
Georgetown U, 1985 *Certification:* Obstetrics & Gynecology
320 Montauk Hwy, West Islip, 631-587-2500

Khoury, Nabil (5 mentions)
FMS-France, 1988 *Certification:* Internal Medicine
141 S Central Ave #101, Hartsdale, 914-285-0530
15 N Broadway, White Plains, 914-328-8444

Kim, Joyce Myonghee (3 mentions)
Mount Sinai Sch of Med, 1986
Certification: Obstetrics & Gynecology
885 Park Ave, New York, 212-737-3282

Kirshenbaum, Nancy W. (3 mentions)
Mount Sinai Sch of Med, 1980
Certification: Maternal-Fetal Medicine, Obstetrics & Gynecology
700 White Plains #207, Scarsdale, 914-472-0512

Klein, Victor Robert (6 mentions)
SUNY-Downstate Med Coll, 1980 *Certification:* Clinical
  Genetics, Maternal-Fetal Medicine, Obstetrics & Gynecology
825 Northern Blvd #301, Great Neck, 516-472-5700

Kraft, Howard J. (4 mentions)
SUNY-Downstate Med Coll, 1975
Certification: Obstetrics & Gynecology
2 Pro Health Plaza, New Hyde Park, 516-608-6800

Legatt, Elizabeth Jane (3 mentions)
SUNY-Downstate Med Coll, 1976
Certification: Obstetrics & Gynecology
1 Theall Rd, Rye, 914-253-4912

Levin, Samuel (3 mentions)
Brown U, 1992 *Certification:* Obstetrics & Gynecology
103 E 86th St, New York, 212-369-5422

Lupin, Jay Stephen (6 mentions)
Tulane U, 1978 *Certification:* Obstetrics & Gynecology
170 Maple Ave #309, White Plains, 914-949-8338

Marchbein, Harvey Steven (3 mentions)
Med Coll of Wisconsin, 1975
Certification: Obstetrics & Gynecology
560 Northern Blvd #103, Great Neck, 516-482-8741
79 Froehlich Blvd, Woodbury, 516-496-3900

Marin, Morisa Jenny (4 mentions)
Boston U, 1986 *Certification:* Obstetrics & Gynecology
48 Route 25-A #207, Smithtown, 631-862-3800
2500 Nesconset Hwy Bldg 10-A, Stony Brook, 631-862-3800

Marks, Janice Kleinick (4 mentions)
New York U, 1985
215 E 79th St, New York, 212-794-0200

McKenna, Brian Patrick (3 mentions)
Stony Brook U, 1988 *Certification:* Obstetrics & Gynecology
48 Route 25-A #301, Smithtown, 631-862-3770

Mendelowitz, Lawrence G. (5 mentions)
New York U, 1976 *Certification:* Obstetrics & Gynecology
755 N Broadway #560, Sleepy Hollow, 914-631-0337

Mikhail, Magdy Girgis S. (3 mentions)
FMS-Egypt, 1977 *Certification:* Obstetrics & Gynecology
1276 Fulton Ave, Bronx, 718-901-8486

Miller, Jeffrey Neil (3 mentions)
SUNY-Upstate Med U, 1988 *Certification:* Obstetrics & Gynecology
877 Stewart Ave #7, Garden City, 516-222-0722

Moritz, Jacques Leonard (4 mentions)
U of Miami, 1988 *Certification:* Obstetrics & Gynecology
315 W 57th St #204, New York, 212-603-4160

Moss, Douglas Glen (3 mentions)
Mount Sinai Sch of Med, 1988
Certification: Obstetrics & Gynecology
1160 Park Ave, New York, 212-860-2600

Nimaroff, Michael Leslie (6 mentions)
New Jersey Med Sch, 1987 *Certification:* Obstetrics & Gynecology
825 Northern Blvd #301, Great Neck, 516-472-5700

Ostroff, Marci (3 mentions)
Mount Sinai Sch of Med, 1987
Certification: Obstetrics & Gynecology
410 Lakeville Rd #305, Lake Success, 516-437-4300

Pollak, Lorey H. (3 mentions)
New York Med Coll, 1972
2000 N Village Ave #104, Rockville Centre, 516-678-4222

Porges, Robert F. (4 mentions)
SUNY-Downstate Med Coll, 1955
Certification: Obstetrics & Gynecology
530 1st Ave, New York, 212-263-6362

Poynor, Elizabeth Ann (3 mentions)
Columbia U, 1988
Certification: Gynecologic Oncology, Obstetrics & Gynecology
1050 5th Ave, New York, 212-426-2700

Randolph, Paula Ann (4 mentions)
Columbia U, 1983 *Certification:* Obstetrics & Gynecology
635 Madison Ave, New York, 212-317-4544
161 Fort Washington Ave, New York, 212-317-4544
622 W 168th St, New York, 212-305-5487

Rebarber, Andrei (5 mentions)
SUNY-Upstate Med U, 1991
Certification: Maternal-Fetal Medicine, Obstetrics & Gynecology
1245 Madison Ave, New York, 212-677-6591
70 E 90th St, New York, 212-722-7409
530 1st Ave #7-V, New York, 212-263-7021

Saad, Andre Hani (3 mentions)
New York U, 1990 *Certification:* Obstetrics & Gynecology
372 Post Ave, Westbury, 516-333-1444
86-43 195th St, Richmond Hill, 718-849-8674
82-12 155th Ave, Howard Beach, 718-843-6300

Sadaty, Anita Fatima (3 mentions)
Cornell U, 1994 *Certification:* Obstetrics & Gynecology
900 Northern Blvd #220, Great Neck, 516-466-0778

Shapiro, Evan Bruce (6 mentions)
U of Buffalo, 1981 *Certification:* Obstetrics & Gynecology
5515 Little Neck Pkwy, Little Neck, 718-281-1800

Shaw, F. Michael (3 mentions)
Certification: Obstetrics & Gynecology
90 S Bedford Rd, Bedford, 914-242-1380

Silverman, Frank (4 mentions)
Tulane U, 1975 *Certification:* Obstetrics & Gynecology
530 1st Ave #10-N, New York, 212-263-5858

Silverstein, Michael L. (4 mentions)
Case Western Reserve U, 1991
Certification: Obstetrics & Gynecology
70 E 90th St, New York, 212-722-7409

Silverstein, Michele K. (3 mentions)
Albert Einstein Coll of Med, 1992
Certification: Obstetrics & Gynecology
134 E 93rd St, New York, 212-348-7800

Simone, Adrienne Laurette (3 mentions)
Robert W Johnson Med Sch, 1993
Certification: Obstetrics & Gynecology
161 6th Ave 13th Fl, New York, 212-627-1222
266 E 78th St, New York, 212-452-2800

Trongone, Richard James (6 mentions)
Mount Sinai Sch of Med, 1981
Certification: Obstetrics & Gynecology
1615 Northern Blvd, Manhasset, 516-365-2500

Valderrama, Lydia (3 mentions)
Stony Brook U, 1979 *Certification:* Obstetrics & Gynecology
135 Mineola Blvd, Mineola, 516-741-4321

Vetere, Patrick Frank (4 mentions)
Creighton U, 1974 *Certification:* Obstetrics & Gynecology
520 Franklin Ave #L21, Garden City, 516-746-0010

Waldman, Joshua Lee (3 mentions)
Albany Med Coll, 1993 *Certification:* Obstetrics & Gynecology
700 Post Rd #270, Scarsdale, 914-423-4111
333 Henry Hudson Pkwy #1-C, Riverdale, 718-543-5624

Wright, Mia Miika (3 mentions)
Columbia U, 1992 *Certification:* Obstetrics & Gynecology
210 Westchester Ave, White Plains, 914-682-0732

Wysoki, Randee Sue (4 mentions)
Georgetown U, 1982 *Certification:* Obstetrics & Gynecology
170 Maple Ave #309, White Plains, 914-949-8338

Yale, Suzanne Iva (3 mentions)
Robert W Johnson Med Sch, 1977
Certification: Obstetrics & Gynecology
768 Park Ave, New York, 212-744-9300

Young, Bruce Kenneth (3 mentions)
New York U, 1963
Certification: Maternal-Fetal Medicine, Obstetrics & Gynecology
530 1st Ave S #5-G, New York, 212-263-6359

Ophthalmology

Abramson, David Harold (4 mentions)
Albert Einstein Coll of Med, 1969 *Certification:* Ophthalmology
70 E 66th St, New York, 212-744-1700
1275 York Ave, New York, 212-639-2000

Aharon, Raphael (3 mentions)
Albert Einstein Coll of Med, 1980 *Certification:* Ophthalmology
10837 71st Ave, Forest Hills, 718-268-6120

Asbell, Penny Abigail (3 mentions)
U of Buffalo, 1975 *Certification:* Ophthalmology
17 E 102nd St, New York, 212-241-7977
1 Gustave L Levy Pl, New York, 212-241-7977

Blanco, Joseph Anthony (3 mentions)
New Jersey Med Sch, 1978 *Certification:* Ophthalmology
133 Plandome Rd, Manhasset, 516-627-0033

Bocian, Franklin Leslie (3 mentions)
SUNY-Downstate Med Coll, 1964 *Certification:* Ophthalmology
140 Lockwood Ave #220, New Rochelle, 914-235-9500

Campolattaro, Brian N. (3 mentions)
New Jersey Med Sch, 1990 *Certification:* Ophthalmology
30 E 40th St #405, New York, 212-684-3980
1075 Central Park Ave #403, Scarsdale, 914-713-3390

Chang, Stanley (9 mentions)
Columbia U, 1974 *Certification:* Ophthalmology
635 W 165th St, New York, 212-305-9535
1 E 71st St, New York, 646-422-0200

Coad, Christopher Thomas (5 mentions)
Baylor U, 1983 *Certification:* Ophthalmology
157 W 19th St, New York, 212-727-3717

Cotliar, Arthur M. (3 mentions)
Albert Einstein Coll of Med, 1978 *Certification:* Ophthalmology
635 W 165th St, New York, 212-305-2241

Cykiert, Robert C. (5 mentions)
New York Med Coll, 1976 *Certification:* Ophthalmology
345 E 37th St #210, New York, 212-922-1430

Deramo, Vincent Anthony (5 mentions)
Georgetown U, 1995 *Certification:* Ophthalmology
600 Northern Blvd #216, Great Neck, 516-466-0390

Dieck, William Brian (3 mentions)
New York Med Coll, 1983 *Certification:* Ophthalmology
185 Kisco Ave, Mount Kisco, 914-666-4939

Dodick, Jack Murray (4 mentions)
FMS-Canada, 1963 *Certification:* Ophthalmology
535 Parks Ave, New York, 212-288-7638

Dolphin, Kip W. (4 mentions)
Certification: Ophthalmology
155 E 72nd St, New York, 212-744-9480

Donnenfeld, Eric David (6 mentions)
Dartmouth Coll, 1980 *Certification:* Ophthalmology
2000 N Village Ave #402, Rockville Centre, 516-766-2519
865 Merrick Ave #80-N, Westbury, 516-872-8309

Eichenbaum, Joseph Walter (4 mentions)
Yale U, 1973 *Certification:* Ophthalmology
1050 Park Ave, New York, 212-289-7200

Ellis, Rachel Fremder (5 mentions)
SUNY-Downstate Med Coll, 2003
161-10 Union Tpke, Flushing Meadows, 718-380-5070

Ferrone, Philip Joseph (3 mentions)
Harvard U, 1989 *Certification:* Ophthalmology
600 Northern Blvd #216, Great Neck, 516-466-0390

Flugman, Mark Stephen (3 mentions)
FMS-Mexico, 1978 *Certification:* Ophthalmology
176 N Village Ave #2A, Rockville Centre, 516-766-6400

Fracassa, Mario Joseph (5 mentions)
New York Med Coll, 1967 *Certification:* Ophthalmology
732 Old Country Rd, Plainview, 516-822-3911

Fuchs, Wayne S. (4 mentions)
Mount Sinai Sch of Med, 1979 *Certification:* Ophthalmology
121 E 60th St, New York, 212-319-8205

Gibralter, Richard Paul (4 mentions)
Mount Sinai Sch of Med, 1976 *Certification:* Ophthalmology
154 E 71st St, New York, 212-628-2202

Girardi, Anthony (4 mentions)
Stony Brook U, 1980 *Certification:* Ophthalmology
8 Medical Plaza, Glen Cove, 516-676-4596

Greenbaum, Allen Solomon (3 mentions)
Mount Sinai Sch of Med, 1979 *Certification:* Ophthalmology
170 Maple Ave #508, White Plains, 914-949-9200
984 N Broadway #L-02, Yonkers, 914-476-0650

Guillory, Samuel Lester (16 mentions)
Certification: Ophthalmology
1103 Park Ave, New York, 212-860-5400

Hatsis, Alexander Philip (3 mentions)
FMS-Italy, 1978 *Certification:* Ophthalmology
2 Lincoln Ave #401, Rockville Centre, 516-763-4106

Kaplan, Idida Abramovsky (3 mentions)
Mount Sinai Sch of Med, 1979 *Certification:* Ophthalmology
935 Northern Blvd #204, Great Neck, 516-466-1168

Kaufmann, Cheryl Sue Katz (3 mentions)
New York U, 1972 *Certification:* Ophthalmology
4370 Kissena Blvd, Flushing, 718-353-5970

Kesden, Dennis Mark (3 mentions)
Cornell U, 1976 *Certification:* Ophthalmology
649 Broadway, Massapequa, 516-798-1411

Kuhns, Thomas Robert (3 mentions)
Harvard U, 1959 *Certification:* Ophthalmology
120 E 36th St #1-C, New York, 212-685-9320

Kupersmith, Mark Jeffrey (5 mentions)
Northwestern U, 1974 *Certification:* Neurology, Ophthalmology
1000 10th Ave 10th Fl, New York, 212-636-3200

Ky, Willy (3 mentions)
Mount Sinai Sch of Med, 1994 *Certification:* Ophthalmology
2110 Northern Blvd #208, Manhasset, 516-627-5113

Levitzky, Munro Joseph (5 mentions)
Columbia U, 1961 *Certification:* Ophthalmology
161 Madison Ave, New York, 212-725-5225

Lichtenstein, Eric Adam (3 mentions)
Albany Med Coll, 1994 *Certification:* Ophthalmology
19213 Union Tpke, Fresh Meadows, 718-468-9800
218 2nd Ave, New York, 212-979-4253

Lieberman, Theodore William (5 mentions)
Yale U, 1958 *Certification:* Ophthalmology
70 E 96th St #1-B, New York, 212-722-5477

Mandelbaum, Sidney (4 mentions)
Yale U, 1976 *Certification:* Ophthalmology
178 E 71st St, New York, 212-650-0400

Marks, Alan Bruce (7 mentions)
New York Med Coll, 1978 *Certification:* Ophthalmology
2110 Northern Blvd #208, Manhasset, 516-627-5113

Martin, Jeffrey Lawrence (3 mentions)
Stony Brook U, 1994 *Certification:* Ophthalmology
260 E Main St #201, Smithtown, 631-265-8780

Michalos, Peter (6 mentions)
SUNY-Downstate Med Coll, 1986 *Certification:* Ophthalmology
365 County Rd #39-A, Southampton, 212-628-0500
16 E 60th St, New York, 212-628-0500

Moadel, Ken (3 mentions)
U of Miami, 1989 *Certification:* Ophthalmology
317 Madison Ave #1215, New York, 212-490-3937

Newton, Michael Joseph (3 mentions)
Tufts U, 1971 *Certification:* Ophthalmology
799 Park Ave, New York, 212-861-0146

Oats, Jack Kenneth (3 mentions)
Loyola U Chicago, 1984 *Certification:* Ophthalmology
2500 Nesconset Hwy, Stony Brook, 631-941-1400

Obstbaum, Stephen Allan (5 mentions)
New York Med Coll, 1967 *Certification:* Ophthalmology
121 E 60th St, New York, 212-477-7540

Odell, Peter Michael (3 mentions)
Tufts U, 1968 *Certification:* Ophthalmology
53 E 70th St, New York, 212-288-8025
720 Park Ave, New York, 212-288-8025

Packer, Samuel (9 mentions)
SUNY-Downstate Med Coll, 1966 *Certification:* Ophthalmology
600 Northern Blvd #214, Great Neck, 510-465-8400

Phillips, Howard P. (5 mentions)
New York U, 1977 *Certification:* Ophthalmology
24 Saw Mill River Rd, Hawthorne, 914-345-3937

Plotycia, Steven M. (5 mentions)
Columbia U, 1982 *Certification:* Ophthalmology
205 W End Ave #1P, New York, 212-724-4430

Potash, Seth David (3 mentions)
Stony Brook U, 1988 *Certification:* Ophthalmology
170 Maple Ave #402, White Plains, 914-949-9200

Ritterband, David Carl (3 mentions)
New York Med Coll, 1990 *Certification:* Ophthalmology
310 E 14th St, New York, 212-505-6550

Rubin, Laurence (3 mentions)
New York Med Coll, 1980 *Certification:* Ophthalmology
4277 Hempstead Tpke #109, Bethpage, 516-796-4030

Saffra, Norman A. (9 mentions)
Albert Einstein Coll of Med, 1988 *Certification:* Ophthalmology
902 49th St, Brooklyn, 718-283-8000

Schneck, Gideon Lloyd (5 mentions)
Boston U, 1986 *Certification:* Ophthalmology
33 Research Way, East Setauket, 631-246-9140
800 Woodbury Rd #K, Woodbury, 516-682-9140
2500 Nesconset Hwy Bldg 17-B, Stony Brook, 631-246-9140

Shakin, Jeffrey Lynn (3 mentions)
New York Med Coll, 1975 *Certification:* Ophthalmology
600 Northern Blvd #216, Great Neck, 516-466-0390

Sheren, Scott Bryan (4 mentions)
SUNY-Upstate Med U, 1986 *Certification:* Ophthalmology
669 Whiskey Rd, Ridge, 631-744-8020

Shulman, Julius (4 mentions)
SUNY-Downstate Med Coll, 1969 *Certification:* Ophthalmology
229 E 79th St, New York, 212-861-6200

Sibony, Patrick A. (3 mentions)
Boston U, 1977 *Certification:* Ophthalmology
33 Research Way, East Setauket, 631-444-4090

Steele, Mark Alan (6 mentions)
New York U, 1986 *Certification:* Ophthalmology
1552 49th St, Brooklyn, 718-435-2020
40 W 72nd St, New York, 718-435-2020

Stein, Mark (5 mentions)
Albert Einstein Coll of Med, 1971 *Certification:* Ophthalmology
2185 Wantagh Ave, Wantagh, 516-785-3900
689 Broadway, Massapequa, 516-541-4141

Storm, Richard (3 mentions)
SUNY-Downstate Med Coll, 1975
Certification: Ophthalmology, Pediatrics
303 E Park Ave, Long Beach, 516-431-2020

Tung, George (3 mentions)
Cornell U, 1983 *Certification:* Ophthalmology
560 Northern Blvd #101, Great Neck, 516-504-2020
2450 Merrick Rd, Bellmore, 516-783-0300

Udell, Ira Jeffrey (3 mentions)
Tulane U, 1974 *Certification:* Ophthalmology
600 Northern Blvd #214, Great Neck, 631-470-2020

Wang, Frederick Mark (3 mentions)
Albert Einstein Coll of Med, 1972
Certification: Ophthalmology, Pediatrics
30 E 40th St #405, New York, 212-684-3980
1075 Central Park Ave #403, Scarsdale, 914-713-3390

Whitmore, Wayne Graham (3 mentions)
Dartmouth Coll, 1977 *Certification:* Ophthalmology
116 E 68th St, New York, 212-249-3030

Wisnicki, H. Jay (3 mentions)
SUNY-Upstate Med U, 1981 *Certification:* Ophthalmology
10 Union Sq E, New York, 212-844-8181
218 2nd Ave, New York, 212-979-4253

Zaidman, Gerald Walter (3 mentions)
Albert Einstein Coll of Med, 1975 *Certification:* Ophthalmology
95 Grasslands Rd #1100, Valhalla, 914-493-1599

Orthopedics

Allen, Answorth Anthony (3 mentions)
Cornell U, 1988 *Certification:* Orthopaedic Surgery
535 E 70th St, New York, 212-606-1447

Alpert, Scott Wayne (4 mentions)
Harvard U, 1989 *Certification:* Orthopaedic Surgery
33 Walt Whitman Rd #200B, Huntington Station, 631-423-4090

Altchek, David Wilson (4 mentions)
Cornell U, 1982 *Certification:* Orthopaedic Surgery
525 E 71st St, New York, 212-606-1909
535 E 70th St, New York, 212-606-1000

Asnis, Stanley Edwin (13 mentions)
Washington U, 1968 *Certification:* Orthopaedic Surgery
600 Northern Blvd #300, Great Neck, 516-627-8717

Asprinio, David Edward (8 mentions)
U of Vermont, 1986 *Certification:* Orthopaedic Surgery
19 Bradhurst Ave, Hawthorne, 914-789-2700

Barron, Otis Alton, Jr. (3 mentions)
Tulane U, 1989
Certification: Orthopaedic Surgery, Surgery of the Hand
1000 10th Ave, New York, 212-523-7590

Besser, Walter (3 mentions)
FMS-Spain, 1968 *Certification:* Orthopaedic Surgery
3071 29th St, Astoria, 718-204-7752
8201 37th Ave, Jackson Heights, 718-335-5800

Bhupathi, C. Srinivasa (3 mentions)
FMS-India, 1966 *Certification:* Orthopaedic Surgery
11 Ralph Pl, Staten Island, 718-447-6545
9920 4th Ave #309, Brooklyn, 718-921-0014

Bigliani, Louis Urban (5 mentions)
Loyola U Chicago, 1972 *Certification:* Orthopaedic Surgery
622 W 168th St, New York, 212-305-5564

Bitan, Fabien David (4 mentions)
FMS-France, 1985
130 E 77th St 7th floor, New York, 212-717-7463

Bleifeld, Charles Jerome (4 mentions)
George Washington U, 1968 *Certification:* Orthopaedic Surgery
48 Route 25-A #106, Smithtown, 631-863-1007

Bosco, Joseph Anthony (5 mentions)
U of Vermont, 1986 *Certification:* Orthopaedic Surgery
530 1st Ave, New York, 718-206-6923

Bostrom, Mathias P. (4 mentions)
Johns Hopkins U, 1989 *Certification:* Orthopaedic Surgery
535 E 70th St, New York, 212-606-1674

Burak, Corey (3 mentions)
SUNY-Upstate Med U, 1999 *Certification:* Orthopaedic Surgery
24 Saw Mill River Rd #206, Hawthorne, 914-631-7777
819 Yonkers Ave, Yonkers, 914-375-7777

Capozzi, James Dean (8 mentions)
Mount Sinai Sch of Med, 1981 *Certification:* Orthopaedic Surgery
1065 Park Ave, New York, 212-289-0700

Cappellino, Anthony (4 mentions)
Stony Brook U, 1992 *Certification:* Orthopaedic Surgery
400 W Main St #304, Babylon, 631-321-0033

Cobelli, Neil John (4 mentions)
Dartmouth Coll, 1976 *Certification:* Orthopaedic Surgery
1695 Eastchester Rd, Bronx, 718-920-2060

Corso, Salvatore John (3 mentions)
SUNY-Downstate Med Coll, 1987
Certification: Orthopaedic Surgery
205 Froehlich Farm Blvd, Woodbury, 516-364-0070

D'Agostino, Richard Joseph (5 mentions)
Mount Sinai Sch of Med, 1982 *Certification:* Orthopaedic Surgery
600 Northern Blvd #300, Great Neck, 516-627-8717
800 Community Dr, Manhasset, 631-466-3351

Dines, David Michael (5 mentions)
New Jersey Med Sch, 1974 *Certification:* Orthopaedic Surgery
935 Northern Blvd #303, Great Neck, 516-482-1037

Drucker, David A. (4 mentions)
Rosalind Franklin U, 1983 *Certification:* Orthopaedic Surgery
1460 Victory Blvd, Staten Island, 718-448-3210
1099 Targee St, Staten Island, 718-448-3210

Dubrow, Eric Neil (5 mentions)
FMS-Belgium, 1979 *Certification:* Orthopaedic Surgery
6 Technology Dr #100, East Setauket, 631-689-6698

Fabian, Dennis F. (4 mentions)
Philadelphia Coll of Osteopathic Med, 1972
Certification: Orthopaedic Surgery
95 University Pl, New York, 212-604-1350

Feliccia, Joseph (8 mentions)
Hahnemann U, 1974 *Certification:* Orthopaedic Surgery
6900 4th Ave, Brooklyn, 718-238-6400

Flatow, Evan Lloyd (7 mentions)
Columbia U, 1981 *Certification:* Orthopaedic Surgery
5 E 98th St, New York, 212-241-8892

Gidumal, Ramesh Hira (5 mentions)
Mount Sinai Sch of Med, 1980 *Certification:* Orthopaedic Surgery
530 1st Ave #5D, New York, 212-263-6137
530 5th Ave, New York, 212-263-6137

Gilbert, Marvin Stanley (7 mentions)
Columbia U, 1964 *Certification:* Orthopaedic Surgery
1065 Park Ave, New York, 212-289-0700

Green, Daniel William (3 mentions)
U of Texas-Galveston, 1991 *Certification:* Orthopaedic Surgery
535 E 70th St, New York, 212-606-1000

Grossman, Mark Geoffrey (3 mentions)
SUNY-Downstate Med Coll, 1996
Certification: Orthopaedic Sports Medicine, Orthopaedic Surgery
1300 Franklin Ave, Garden City, 516-747-8900

Haig, Scott Vanderwink (4 mentions)
Yale U, 1984 *Certification:* Orthopaedic Surgery
700 White Plains Post Rd, Scarsdale, 914-723-4244

Harwin, Steven F. (3 mentions)
SUNY-Upstate Med U, 1971 *Certification:* Orthopaedic Surgery
910 Park Ave, New York, 212-861-9800
3555 Bainbridge Ave, Bronx, 718-655-2400

Hecht, Andrew Craig (3 mentions)
Harvard U, 1994 *Certification:* Orthopaedic Surgery
5 E 98th St, New York, 212-241-8892

Hershman, Elliott Bruce (12 mentions)
U of Rochester, 1979 *Certification:* Orthopaedic Surgery
130 E 77th St, New York, 212-744-8114
2800 Marcus Ave #102, Lake Success, 516-622-6040

Hershon, Stuart Joel (3 mentions)
New York Med Coll, 1963 *Certification:* Orthopaedic Surgery
333 E Shore Rd #101, Manhasset, 516-466-3351
16 E 60th St, New York, 212-935-0464

Hubbell, John D. (3 mentions)
Georgetown U, 1994 *Certification:* Orthopaedic Surgery
635 Belle Terre Rd, Port Jefferson, 631-474-0008
315 Meeting House Ln, Southampton, 631-283-0355

Kiernan, Howard A., Jr. (7 mentions)
New York U, 1966 *Certification:* Orthopaedic Surgery
161 Fort Washington Ave, New York, 212-305-5241

Klion, Mark J. (5 mentions)
Mount Sinai Sch of Med, 1989 *Certification:* Orthopaedic Surgery
1065 Park Ave, New York, 212-289-0700

Krauss, Eugene Steven (5 mentions)
Columbia U, 1982 *Certification:* Orthopaedic Surgery
833 Northern Blvd #220, Great Neck, 516-622-7910
301 E Main St, Bay Shore, 631-675-4900
31 Main Rd, Riverhead, 631-369-5000

Labiak, John J. (5 mentions)
SUNY-Upstate Med U, 1986 *Certification:* Orthopaedic Surgery
290 E Main St #200, Smithtown, 631-265-1855

Lajam, Claudette Malvina (4 mentions)
Cornell U, 1999
25 35 31st Ave, Long Island City, 718-274-2600
76 55 Austin St, Forest Hills, 718-987-2228
1408 Ocean Ave, Brooklyn, 718-338-0909
101 24 Queens Blvd5, Forest Hills, 718-275-2788
2535 31st Ave, Astoria, 718-274-2600

Legouri, Richard Anthony (3 mentions)
FMS-Mexico, 1972
635 Belle Terre Rd #101, Port Jefferson, 631-474-0008

Levine, William Noah (3 mentions)
Case Western Reserve U, 1990 *Certification:* Orthopaedic Surgery
622 W 168th St, New York, 212-305-5974

Levy, I. Martin (3 mentions)
New York Med Coll, 1976 *Certification:* Orthopaedic Surgery
1695 Eastchester Rd, Bronx, 718-405-8132

Luks, Howard Jay (5 mentions)
New York Med Coll, 1991 *Certification:* Orthopaedic Surgery
19 Bradhurst Ave, Hawthorne, 914-789-2700

Macaulay, William Bernard (3 mentions)
Columbia U, 1992 *Certification:* Orthopaedic Surgery
622 W 168th St, New York, 212-305-5974

Mani, Vijay John (3 mentions)
Certification: Orthopaedic Surgery
161 Atlantic Ave, Brooklyn, 718-855-0088

Marwin, Scott Eliot (4 mentions)
U of Buffalo, 1987 *Certification:* Orthopaedic Surgery
410 Lakeville Rd #303, New Hyde Park, 516-216-5782

Mauri, Thomas Michael (7 mentions)
Albany Med Coll, 1980 *Certification:* Orthopaedic Surgery
865 Northern Blvd, Great Neck, 516-918-6300

McCann, Peter Damian (4 mentions)
Columbia U, 1980 *Certification:* Orthopaedic Surgery
10 Union Sq E #3, New York, 212-870-9764

McGinley, Brian Joseph (6 mentions)
Columbia U, 1992 *Certification:* Orthopaedic Surgery
635 Belle Terre Rd, Port Jefferson, 631-474-0008

Menezes, Placido Antonio (3 mentions)
FMS-India, 1969 *Certification:* Orthopaedic Surgery
543 2nd St, Brooklyn, 718-788-7600

Montgomery, Kenneth Dale (4 mentions)
U of California-San Francisco, 1990
Certification: Orthopaedic Sports Medicine, Orthopaedic Surgery
2800 Marcus Ave, New Hyde Park, 516-622-6040
130 E 77th St, New York, 212-744-8114

Moskovich, Ronald (4 mentions)
FMS-South Africa, 1978 *Certification:* Orthopaedic Surgery
301 E 17th St, New York, 212-598-6622

Parisi, Ralph Felix (3 mentions)
FMS-Italy, 1963 *Certification:* Orthopaedic Surgery
651 Old Country Rd #200, Plainview, 516-681-8822

Pellicci, Paul Mario (5 mentions)
Cornell U, 1975 *Certification:* Orthopaedic Surgery
535 E 70th St #354, New York, 212-606-1010

Penna, James (3 mentions)
SUNY-Downstate Med Coll, 1996
Certification: Orthopaedic Surgery
14 Technology Dr #11, East Setauket, 631-444-4230

Peris, Marshal David (3 mentions)
U of Pittsburgh, 1996 *Certification:* Orthopaedic Surgery
90 S Bedford Rd, Mount Kisco, 914-241-1050

Petraco, Douglas Matthew (5 mentions)
Cornell U, 1992 *Certification:* Orthopaedic Surgery
6 Technology Dr #100, East Setauket, 631-689-6698
74 Commerce Dr #4 Bldg C, Wading River, 631-689-6698
6144 Route 25-A, Wading River, 631-689-6698

Putterman, Eric Arthur (6 mentions)
Mount Sinai Sch of Med, 1980 *Certification:* Orthopaedic Surgery
651 Old Country Rd #200, Plainview, 516-681-8822

Richmond, Jeffrey Howard (4 mentions)
Cornell U, 1996 *Certification:* Orthopaedic Surgery
600 Northern Blvd #300, Great Neck, 516-627-8717

Rodriguez, Jose Antonio (3 mentions)
Columbia U, 1989
535 E 70th St 6th Fl, New York, 646-797-8700

Rose, Louis Charles (3 mentions)
Robert W Johnson Med Sch, 1981
Certification: Orthopaedic Surgery
3058 E Tremont Ave, Bronx, 718-409-0500

Roye, David Price, Jr. (3 mentions)
Columbia U, 1975 *Certification:* Orthopaedic Surgery
3959 Broadway #8N, New York, 212-305-5475
161 Fort Washington Ave, New York, 212-305-5475

Ruotolo, Charles James (3 mentions)
New York Med Coll, 1995 *Certification:* Orthopaedic Surgery
5500 Merrick Rd, Massapequa, 516-795-3033
2201 Hempstead Tpke #668, East Meadow, 516-572-6702

Schefer, Alan Jay (4 mentions)
Hahnemann U, 1990
Certification: Orthopaedic Surgery, Surgery of the Hand
90 S Bedford Rd, Mount Kisco, 914-241-1050

Schlesinger, Iris Elaine (3 mentions)
Albany Med Coll, 1983 *Certification:* Orthopaedic Surgery
19 Bradhurst Ave, Hawthorne, 914-789-2700

Scott, W. Norman (3 mentions)
Cornell U, 1972 *Certification:* Orthopaedic Surgery
1001 Franklin Ave, Garden City, 516-536-6888
210 E 64 St 4th Fl, New York, 212-434-4301

Sculco, Thomas Peter (5 mentions)
Columbia U, 1969 *Certification:* Orthopaedic Surgery
535 E 70th St, New York, 212-606-1475

Seebacher, Jay R. (3 mentions)
Georgetown U, 1976 *Certification:* Orthopaedic Surgery
24 Saw Mill River Rd #206, Hawthorne, 914-631-7777

Sgaglione, Nicholas A. (4 mentions)
Mount Sinai Sch of Med, 1983 *Certification:* Orthopaedic Surgery
600 Northern Blvd #300, Great Neck, 516-627-8717

Sherman, Mark Frederick (3 mentions)
New York U, 1975 *Certification:* Orthopaedic Surgery
1551 Richmond Rd, Staten Island, 718-351-6500

Sherman, Orrin Howard (3 mentions)
George Washington U, 1978 *Certification:* Orthopaedic Surgery
530 1st Ave #8U, New York, 212-263-8961

Simonson, Barry Glen (3 mentions)
Mount Sinai Sch of Med, 1984 *Certification:* Orthopaedic Surgery
825 Northern Blvd, Great Neck, 516-773-7500
10 Medical Plaza, Glen Cove, 516-609-9494

Small, Robert David (11 mentions)
New York Med Coll, 1977 *Certification:* Orthopaedic Surgery
7 Reservoir Rd, White Plains, 914-684-0300

Teplitz, Glenn Alan (4 mentions)
Tulane U, 1987 *Certification:* Orthopaedic Surgery
1300 Franklin Ave #UL3A, Garden City, 516-747-8900
2339 Hempstead Tpke, East Meadow, 516-747-8900

Tischler, Henry Mark (5 mentions)
SUNY-Downstate Med Coll, 1985
Certification: Orthopaedic Surgery
263 7th Ave, Brooklyn, 718-246-8704

Tuckman, David Victor (3 mentions)
Albert Einstein Coll of Med, 1998
Certification: Orthopaedic Surgery
600 Northern Blvd #300, Great Neck, 516-627-8717

Ulin, Richard Irwin (3 mentions)
Columbia U, 1962 *Certification:* Orthopaedic Surgery
1095 Park Ave, New York, 212-860-0905

Unis, William Anthony (3 mentions)
FMS-Canada, 1968 *Certification:* Orthopaedic Surgery
77 Pondfield Rd, Bronxville, 914-793-0999

Vesey, Kevin Gallagher (4 mentions)
SUNY-Downstate Med Coll, 1980
Certification: Orthopaedic Surgery
48 Route 25-A #106, Smithtown, 631-862-3660

Walsh, Raymond Barry (3 mentions)
FMS-United Kingdom, 1974 *Certification:* Orthopaedic Surgery
355 Ovington Ave, Brooklyn, 718-238-6400
6900 4th Ave, Brooklyn, 718-238-6400

Weinfeld, Steven Bennett (3 mentions)
Albany Med Coll, 1990 *Certification:* Orthopaedic Surgery
5 E 98th St, New York, 212-241-8892

Weinstein, Richard Neil (4 mentions)
New York U, 1991
Certification: Orthopaedic Sports Medicine, Orthopaedic Surgery
210 Westchester Ave, White Plains, 914-684-0202

Zambetti, George J., Jr. (3 mentions)
Albany Med Coll, 1976 *Certification:* Orthopaedic Surgery
343 W 58th St, New York, 212-765-2260

Zelicof, Steven (4 mentions)
U of Pennsylvania, 1983 *Certification:* Orthopaedic Surgery
600 Mamaroneck Rd #101, Harrison, 914-686-0111

Zitner, David Thomas (5 mentions)
Mount Sinai Sch of Med, 1976 *Certification:* Orthopaedic Surgery
651 Old Country Rd #200, Plainview, 516-681-8822

Zuckerman, Joseph D. (8 mentions)
Med Coll of Wisconsin, 1978 *Certification:* Orthopaedic Surgery
301 E 17th St, New York, 212-598-6674

Otorhinolaryngology

April, Max Michael (7 mentions)
Boston U, 1985 *Certification:* Otolaryngology
1305 York Ave 5th Floor, New York, 646-962-2225
173 Froehlich Farm Blvd, Woodbury, 516-682-8288

Beckhardt, Russell Neil (5 mentions)
Mount Sinai Sch of Med, 1988 *Certification:* Otolaryngology
738 Franklin Ave, Franklin Square, 516-355-0505

Bergstein, Michael (6 mentions)
Mount Sinai Sch of Med, 1985 *Certification:* Otolaryngology
2649 Strang Blvd, Yorktown Heights, 914-245-2681
358 N Broadway, Sleepy Hollow, 914-631-3053

Bernard, Peter Jay (5 mentions)
Mount Sinai Sch of Med, 1982 *Certification:* Otolaryngology
55 E 87th St #1-K, New York, 212-289-1731

Bernstein, Joseph Michael (4 mentions)
New York U, 1991 *Certification:* Otolaryngology
244 Westchester Ave #215, White Plains, 212-263-8237

Costantino, Peter David (4 mentions)
Northwestern U, 1984 *Certification:* Otolaryngology
425 W 59th St, New York, 212-262-4444

Ditkoff, Michael Kenneth (9 mentions)
SUNY-Upstate Med U, 1994 *Certification:* Otolaryngology
333 E Shore Rd, Manhasset, 516-482-8778

Edelstein, David R. (5 mentions)
Boston U, 1980 *Certification:* Otolaryngology
1421 3rd Ave, New York, 212-452-1500
210 E 64th St 3rd Fl, New York, 212-605-3789

Eisman, Wayne Brook (5 mentions)
Baylor U, 1975 *Certification:* Otolaryngology
75 S Broadway #300, White Plains, 914-949-3888

Genden, Eric Michael (12 mentions)
Mount Sinai Sch of Med, 1992 *Certification:* Otolaryngology
5 E 98th St, New York, 212-241-9410

Gold, Scott David (8 mentions)
Mount Sinai Sch of Med, 1979 *Certification:* Otolaryngology
36A E 36th St #200, New York, 212-889-8575
9 W 67th St, New York, 212-501-0500

Goldofsky, Elliot (8 mentions)
Mount Sinai Sch of Med, 1984 *Certification:* Otolaryngology
600 Northern Blvd #100, Great Neck, 516-482-3223

Grosso, John Joseph (6 mentions)
SUNY-Upstate Med U, 1986 *Certification:* Otolaryngology
875 Old Country Rd, Plainview, 516-931-5552
150 Sunrise Hwy #109, Lindenhurst, 631-226-1800

Huo, Jerry (4 mentions)
Mount Sinai Sch of Med, 1991 *Certification:* Otolaryngology
525 E 68th St, New York, 718-670-0006

Kacker, Ashutosh (5 mentions)
FMS-India, 1990 *Certification:* Otolaryngology
1305 York Ave, New York, 212-746-5097

Kates, Matthew Jonathan (4 mentions)
Cornell U, 1986 *Certification:* Otolaryngology
26 Burling Ln, New Rochelle, 914-636-0104

Keller, Jeffrey Lewis (4 mentions)
Stanford U, 1990 *Certification:* Otolaryngology
90 S Bedford Rd, Mount Kisco, 914-242-2735

Kuhel, William Isadore (4 mentions)
U of Michigan, 1983 *Certification:* Otolaryngology
1305 York Ave, New York, 212-746-2230

Kuriloff, Daniel Benjamin (4 mentions)
Mount Sinai Sch of Med, 1982 *Certification:* Otolaryngology
425 W 59th St, New York, 212-262-4444

Lawson, William (4 mentions)
New York U, 1965 *Certification:* Otolaryngology
5 E 98th St 8th Fl, New York, 212-241-9410

Litman, Richard Steven (8 mentions)
Wake Forest U, 1971 *Certification:* Otolaryngology
251 E Oakland Ave, Port Jefferson, 631-654-3833

Matar, Salim Antoine (8 mentions)
FMS-Lebanon, 1984 *Certification:* Otolaryngology
640 Belle Terre Rd #C, Port Jefferson, 631-928-7750

Merer, David Mitchell (4 mentions)
Albert Einstein Coll of Med, 1990 *Certification:* Otolaryngology
1055 Saw Mill River Rd #101, Ardsley, 914-693-7636

Mittleman, Myles (5 mentions)
Med Coll of Wisconsin, 1975
5847 Francis Lewis Blvd, Oakland Gardens, 718-225-5400
10740 Queens Blvd #204, Forest Hills, 718-268-8845

Modlin, Saul Michael (7 mentions)
U of Maryland, 1988 *Certification:* Otolaryngology
300 Garden City Plaza #248, Garden City, 516-739-0333

Moisa, Idel I. (4 mentions)
Albert Einstein Coll of Med, 1983 *Certification:* Otolaryngology
3 School St, Glen Cove, 516-671-0085

Moscatello, Augustine L. (8 mentions)
Mount Sinai Sch of Med, 1982 *Certification:* Otolaryngology
1055 Saw Mill River Rd #101, Ardsley, 914-693-7637
14 Rye Ridge Plaza, Rye Brook, 914-693-7637

Nass, Richard Laurence (5 mentions)
New York U, 1975 *Certification:* Otolaryngology
1430 2nd Ave #108, New York, 212-734-4515

Perlman, Philip Warren (11 mentions)
SUNY-Downstate Med Coll, 1983 *Certification:* Otolaryngology
333 E Shore Rd, Manhasset, 516-482-8778

Persky, Mark Stephen (9 mentions)
SUNY-Upstate Med U, 1972 *Certification:* Otolaryngology
10 Union Sq E #4-J, New York, 212-844-8648

Pincus, Robert Lawrence (4 mentions)
U of Michigan, 1978 *Certification:* Otolaryngology
36 E 36th St #A, New York, 212-889-8575
9 W 67th St, New York, 212-501-0500

Roland, J. Thomas, Jr. (5 mentions)
Temple U, 1983 *Certification:* Neurotology, Otolaryngology
530 1st Ave #85, New York, 212-263-5565

Rosner, Louis Martin (4 mentions)
Rosalind Franklin U, 1978 *Certification:* Otolaryngology
176 N Village Ave #1A, Rockville Centre, 516-678-0303

Rothschild, Michael Alan (8 mentions)
Yale U, 1988 *Certification:* Otolaryngology
1175 Park Ave, New York, 212-996-2559
5 E 98th St, New York, 212-241-9410

Rothstein, Stephen Grant (6 mentions)
Rosalind Franklin U, 1982 *Certification:* Otolaryngology
530 1st Ave #3C, New York, 212-263-7505

Sacks, Steven H. (5 mentions)
Washington U, 1977 *Certification:* Otolaryngology
210 E 86th St, New York, 212-722-5570

Scott, John Charles (4 mentions)
U of Michigan, 1988 *Certification:* Otolaryngology
110 S Bedford Rd, Mount Kisco, 914-241-1050

Setzen, Michael (6 mentions)
FMS-South Africa, 1974 *Certification:* Otolaryngology
333 E Shore Rd, Manhasset, 516-482-8778

Shemen, Larry J. (5 mentions)
Certification: Otolaryngology
233 E 69th St #1D, New York, 212-472-8882
10721 Queens Blvd #3-A, Flushing, 718-520-1594

Shugar, Joel Murray Allan (4 mentions)
FMS-Canada, 1972 *Certification:* Otolaryngology
55 E 87th St #1K, New York, 212-289-1731

Smith, Jonathan Cope (4 mentions)
Vanderbilt U, 1998 *Certification:* Otolaryngology
1200 Waters Pl, Bronx, 718-863-4366

Smith, Richard Vance (8 mentions)
U of Vermont, 1990 *Certification:* Otolaryngology
111 E 210th St, Bronx, 718-920-4646
3400 Bainbridge Ave, Bronx, 718-920-4646

Soletic, Raymond Luke (4 mentions)
FMS-Mexico, 1982 *Certification:* Otolaryngology
1615 Northern Blvd #201, Manhasset, 516-365-7952

Urken, Mark Lawrence (4 mentions)
U of Virginia, 1981 *Certification:* Otolaryngology
10 Union Sq E #5-B, New York, 212-844-8775

Ward, Robert F. (8 mentions)
Cornell U, 1981 *Certification:* Otolaryngology
525 E 68th St, New York, 212-746-2224
2800 Marcus Ave, New Hyde Park, 516-622-6000
173 Froehlich Farm Blvd, Woodbury, 516-682-8288

Werber, Josh Leonard (4 mentions)
New York Med Coll, 1985 *Certification:* Otolaryngology
833 Northern Blvd, Great Neck, 516-829-3466

Woo, Peak (7 mentions)
Boston U, 1978 *Certification:* Otolaryngology
300 Central Park W, New York, 212-580-1004

Yung, Richard Tsun Tak (4 mentions)
Columbia U, 1993 *Certification:* Otolaryngology
75 S Broadway, White Plains, 914-949-3888

Zelman, Warren Henry (6 mentions)
Rosalind Franklin U, 1982 *Certification:* Otolaryngology
975 Franklin Ave #203B, Garden City, 516-739-3999

Pain Medicine

Adipietro, Frank Joseph (4 mentions)
SUNY-Downstate Med Coll, 1983 *Certification:* Anesthesiology
201 Manor Pl, Greenport, 631-477-1000

Agin, Carole W. (7 mentions)
Rosalind Franklin U, 1986
Certification: Anesthesiology, Pain Medicine
2 Edmund D Pellegrino Rd, Stony Brook, 631-638-0800

Brietstein, Daniel (3 mentions)
FMS-Mexico, 1987 *Certification:* Anesthesiology
3 Delaware Dr, Lake Success, 516-622-6105

Chapman, Kenneth Bradley (3 mentions)
FMS-Grenada, 2001 *Certification:* Anesthesiology, Pain Medicine
1 W 85th St #1C, New York, 646-290-7532

Duarte, Robert Alfonso (3 mentions)
Ponce Sch of Med, 1986 *Certification:* Neurology
1554 Northern Blvd, Manhasset, 516-719-7246

Freedman, Gordon Matthew (7 mentions)
FMS-Israel, 1985 *Certification:* Anesthesiology, Pain Medicine
1540 York Rd, New York, 212-288-2180

Fuss, Richard Jay (3 mentions)
FMS-Mexico, 1978 *Certification:* Anesthesiology
222 Station Plaza N #438, Mineola, 516-663-2216

Fyman, Phillip N. (6 mentions)
Cornell U, 1976
Certification: Anesthesiology, Internal Medicine, Pain Medicine
2001 Marcus Ave #S-20, New Hyde Park, 516-358-4673
121 Eileen Way, Syosset, 516-496-4964

Handszer, Jacob (5 mentions)
Certification: Anesthesiology, Pain Medicine
43 Kensico Dr 2nd Fl, Mount Kisco, 914-666-8866

Hertz, Ronny (4 mentions)
Certification: Anesthesiology, Pain Medicine
1000 10th Ave, New York, 212-523-2500

Kirschen, Neil B. (4 mentions)
FMS-Mexico, 1981 *Certification:* Anesthesiology
77 N Centre Ave #202, Rockville Centre, 516-764-7246

Kreitzer, Joel Michael (21 mentions)
Albert Einstein Coll of Med, 1985
Certification: Anesthesiology, Pain Medicine
2731 Crescent St, Astoria, 718-204-2683
1540 York Rd, New York, 212-288-2180

Kushnerik, Vadim (3 mentions)
Stony Brook U, 1996
360 Court St, Brooklyn, 718-422-5023
170 William St #294, New York, 212-312-5247

Litman, Steven Jeffrey (3 mentions)
New York Med Coll, 1987
Certification: Anesthesiology, Pain Medicine
387 E Main St #104, Bay Shore, 631-665-0075
75 N Country Rd, Port Jefferson, 631-665-0075

Malits, Bella (4 mentions)
New York Med Coll, 1990
Certification: Anesthesiology, Pain Medicine
34 S Bedford Rd, Mount Kisco, 914-242-4400

Modugu, Sathish R. (5 mentions)
FMS-India, 1989
Certification: Pain Medicine, Physical Medicine & Rehabilitation
220 N Central Park Ave, Hartsdale, 914-681-9750
755 N Broadway, Sleepy Hollow, 914-681-9750

Pinsky, Steven Harris (7 mentions)
Albert Einstein Coll of Med, 1989
Certification: Anesthesiology, Pain Medicine
176 N Village Ave #2D, Rockville Centre, 516-764-4875

Portenoy, Russell Keith (9 mentions)
U of Maryland, 1980
Certification: Hospice and Palliative Medicine, Neurology
10 Union Sq E #4-K, New York, 212-844-1403

Stamatos, John M. (10 mentions)
Uniformed Services U of Health Sciences, 1987
Certification: Anesthesiology, Pain Medicine
221 Jericho Tpke, Syosset, 516-496-6447

Weingarten, Alexander E. (4 mentions)
SUNY-Upstate Med U, 1980
Certification: Anesthesiology, Pain Medicine
2001 Marcus Ave #W-8, New Hyde Park, 516-358-4673

Pathology

Bleiweiss, Ira Jay (5 mentions)
FMS-Grenada, 1984
Certification: Anatomic Pathology & Clinical Pathology
1468 Madison Ave, New York, 212-241-9159

Chu, Paul (3 mentions)
New York U, 1987 *Certification:* Dermatology, Dermatopathology
100 Midland Ave, Port Chester, 914-636-0136

Chumas, John Charles (5 mentions)
St Louis U, 1976
Certification: Anatomic Pathology & Clinical Pathology
200 Belle Terre Rd, Port Jefferson, 631-474-6183

Cohen, Jean-Marc (3 mentions)
FMS-France, 1983
Certification: Anatomic Pathology, Cytopathology
10 Union Sq E, New York, 212-420-2124

Donovan, Virginia Marilyn (3 mentions)
Johns Hopkins U, 1981
Certification: Anatomic Pathology & Clinical Pathology
222 Station Plaza N, Mineola, 516-663-2468

Engellenner, William (3 mentions)
Certification: Anatomic Pathology & Clinical Pathology,
Cytopathology, Hematology
1000 Montauk Hwy, West Islip, 631-376-3990

Gottlieb, Geoffrey Jon (4 mentions)
Cornell U, 1976
Certification: Anatomic Pathology, Dermatopathology
145 E 32nd St #10, New York, 212-889-6225

Harpaz, Noam (3 mentions)
Certification: Anatomic Pathology & Clinical Pathology
1 Gustave L Levy Pl, New York, 212-241-9115

Knowles, Daniel Marshall (3 mentions)
U of Chicago, 1973
Certification: Anatomic Pathology, Immunopathology
1300 York Ave, New York, 212-746-6464
525 E 68th St, New York, 212-746-6464

Miller, Frederick (3 mentions)
New York U, 1961
Certification: Anatomic Pathology & Clinical Pathology
101 Nicolls Rd #766, Stony Brook, 631-444-2222

Mizrachi, Howard Hayim (3 mentions)
U of Vermont, 1983
Certification: Anatomic Pathology & Clinical Pathology
560 1st Ave, New York, 914-681-1244

Nochomovitz, Lucien E. (3 mentions)
FMS-South Africa, 1970 *Certification:* Anatomic Pathology
300 Community Dr, Manhasset, 516-562-3249

Phelps, Robert George (5 mentions)
U of Pennsylvania, 1979
5 E 98th St, New York, 212-241-9728
1 Gustave L Levy Pl, New York, 212-241-8014

Rosenblum, Marc K. (3 mentions)
U of Miami, 1979
Certification: Anatomic Pathology, Neuropathology
1275 York Ave, New York, 212-639-5905

Strauchen, James Arthur (4 mentions)
New York U, 1972 *Certification:* Anatomic Pathology,
Hematology, Internal Medicine, Medical Oncology
1 Gustave L Levy Pl, New York, 212-241-9142

Pediatrics *(see note on page 9)*

Amer, Jeffrey A. (3 mentions)
Jefferson Med Coll, 1981 *Certification:* Pediatrics
38 S Oyster Bay Rd, Syosset, 516-682-0555

Barash, Fred S. (3 mentions)
SUNY-Downstate Med Coll, 1976 *Certification:* Pediatrics
333 E Shore Rd #201, Manhasset, 516-829-3044

Barsh, Elliot Bruce (3 mentions)
New York U, 1984 *Certification:* Pediatrics
110 S Bedford Rd, Mount Kisco, 914-241-1050

Berman, Morton Henry (5 mentions)
New York U, 1966 *Certification:* Pediatrics
244 Westchester Ave #210, West Harrison, 914-948-6855

Bernstein, Harvey Eric (6 mentions)
U of Pennsylvania, 1973 *Certification:* Pediatrics
260 E Main St #107, Smithtown, 631-979-8780

Bialik, Ilya (3 mentions)
FMS-Ukraine, 1984 *Certification:* Pediatrics
502 8th Ave, Brooklyn, 718-780-5780

Bomback, Fredric Michael (11 mentions)
New York U, 1969 *Certification:* Pediatrics
99 Fieldstone Dr, Hartsdale, 914-428-2120

Brovender, Bruce Jay (4 mentions)
FMS-Italy, 1984 *Certification:* Pediatrics
1559 York Ave, New York, 212-585-3329

Burstin, Harris E. (3 mentions)
FMS-Mexico, 1977 *Certification:* Pediatrics
317 E 34th St, New York, 212-725-6300
20 Plaza St E, Brooklyn, 212-725-6300

Caravella, Salvatore J. (3 mentions)
FMS-Dominican Republic, 1981 *Certification:* Pediatrics
124 Main St #1, Huntington, 631-423-0044

Chianese, Maurice Joseph (3 mentions)
New York Med Coll, 1986 *Certification:* Pediatrics
2 Pro Health Plaza, Lake Success, 516-622-7337

Childs, Marc Evan (3 mentions)
Case Western Reserve U, 1991 *Certification:* Pediatrics
185 Route 312, Brewster, 845-278-6626
90 S Bedford Rd, Mount Kisco, 914-241-1050

Conway, Edward E., Jr. (4 mentions)
SUNY-Downstate Med Coll, 1984
Certification: Pediatric Critical Care Medicine, Pediatrics
1st Ave & 16th St, New York, 212-855-1333

Edelstein, Gary Stuart (9 mentions)
New York U, 1990 *Certification:* Pediatrics
16 E 60th St #410, New York, 212-326-3351

Gerba, William Michael (3 mentions)
Albert Einstein Coll of Med, 1974
Certification: Pediatric Hematology-Oncology, Pediatrics
935 Northern Blvd #300, Great Neck, 516-466-5437

Goldstein, Judith G. (4 mentions)
SUNY-Downstate Med Coll, 1972 *Certification:* Pediatrics
1559 York Ave, New York, 212-585-3329

Gould, Eric Franklin (4 mentions)
New York Med Coll, 1970 *Certification:* Pediatrics
15 Barstow Rd, Great Neck, 516-829-9409

Grunfeld, Paul (7 mentions)
FMS-Romania, 1960 *Certification:* Pediatrics
1111 Park Ave, New York, 212-534-3000

Hyman, Susan Soslau (3 mentions)
SUNY-Downstate Med Coll, 1968 *Certification:* Pediatrics
15 Barstow Rd, Great Neck, 516-829-9409

Katz, Kenneth H. (3 mentions)
New York Med Coll, 1973 *Certification:* Pediatrics
99 Fieldstone Dr, Hartsdale, 914-428-2120

Kotin, Neal M. (3 mentions)
Albany Med Coll, 1982
Certification: Pediatric Pulmonology, Pediatrics
1125 Park Ave, New York, 212-289-1400

La Sala, Stephen Ralph (5 mentions)
FMS-France, 1973 *Certification:* Pediatrics
450 Plandome Rd, Manhasset, 516-627-6555

Lazarus, George Mitchell (6 mentions)
Columbia U, 1971 *Certification:* Pediatrics
106 E 78th St, New York, 212-744-0840

Lazarus, Herbert M. (3 mentions)
New Jersey Med Sch, 1983
Certification: Pediatric Rheumatology, Pediatrics
390 W End Ave, New York, 212-787-1444
495 Central Park Ave #305, Scarsdale, 914-725-7555

Licata, Joseph Carl (3 mentions)
FMS-Italy, 1978 *Certification:* Pediatrics
1559 York Ave, New York, 212-585-3329

Melman, Yelena (4 mentions)
FMS-Azerbaijan, 1976
88 E Main St, East Islip, 631-581-3232
800 Broadway Ave, Holbrook, 631-563-2294

Mercier, Thomas Robert (3 mentions)
Pennsylvania State U, 1977 *Certification:* Pediatrics
1045 Love Ln, Mattituck, 631-298-5454

Milman, Marina (3 mentions)
FMS-Russia, 1985 *Certification:* Pediatrics
107 Northern Blvd #201, Great Neck, 516-487-6565

Mirante, Rosanna (4 mentions)
New York U, 1990 *Certification:* Pediatrics
55 E 87th St #1-G, New York, 212-722-0707

Monti, Louis Gerard (3 mentions)
Mount Sinai Sch of Med, 1980 *Certification:* Pediatrics
55 E 87th St #1G, New York, 212-722-0707

Murphy, Ramon Jeremiah C. (9 mentions)
Northwestern U, 1969 *Certification:* Pediatrics
1245 Park Ave, New York, 212-427-0540

Pasquariello, Palmo Joseph (5 mentions)
New York Med Coll, 1985 *Certification:* Pediatrics
1559 York Ave, New York, 212-585-3329

Popper, Laura (3 mentions)
Columbia U, 1974 *Certification:* Pediatrics
116 E 66th St #1C, New York, 212-794-2136

Prezioso, Paula J. (4 mentions)
SUNY-Downstate Med Coll, 1987 *Certification:* Pediatrics
317 E 34th St, New York, 212-725-6300
20 Plaza St E, Brooklyn, 212-725-6300

Rabinowicz, Morris (4 mentions)
SUNY-Downstate Med Coll, 1978 *Certification:* Pediatrics
995 Old Country Rd, Plainview, 516-935-7333

Raucher, Harold Seth (4 mentions)
Mount Sinai Sch of Med, 1978
Certification: Pediatric Infectious Diseases, Pediatrics
1125 Park Ave #1B, New York, 212-289-1400

Resmovits, Marvin (4 mentions)
U of Buffalo, 1979 *Certification:* Pediatrics
107 Northern Blvd #201, Great Neck, 516-487-6565

Richel, Peter Laurence (4 mentions)
FMS-Dominican Republic, 1983 *Certification:* Pediatrics
36 Smith Ave #1, Mount Kisco, 914-666-6655

Rosen, Stephanie W. (3 mentions)
New York Med Coll, 1993
173 E Shore Rd, Great Neck, 516-487-4020

Sheehy, John Paul (3 mentions)
New York Med Coll, 1975 *Certification:* Pediatrics
10 Medical Plaza #301, Glen Cove, 516-676-7116

Shelov, Steven Patrick (3 mentions)
Med Coll of Wisconsin, 1971 *Certification:* Pediatrics
4802 10th Ave, Brooklyn, 718-283-6150

Stein, Barry Bialer (3 mentions)
FMS-South Africa, 1980 *Certification:* Pediatrics
1125 Parks Ave, New York, 212-289-1400

Turow, Victor Daniel (3 mentions)
SUNY-Downstate Med Coll, 1978 *Certification:* Pediatrics
833 Northern Blvd #140, Great Neck, 516-504-0606

Vayner, Senya (3 mentions)
FMS-Russia, 1970 *Certification:* Pediatrics
1761 E 12th St, Brooklyn, 718-336-1111

Versfelt, Mary Garber (3 mentions)
Columbia U, 1978 *Certification:* Pediatrics
26 Rye Ridge Plaza, Rye Brook, 914-251-1100

Wager, Marc Douglas (4 mentions)
Albert Einstein Coll of Med, 1981 *Certification:* Pediatrics
140 Lockwood Ave #115, New Rochelle, 914-235-3800
77 Quaker Ridge Rd, New Rochelle, 914-235-3800

Woletsky, Ira Paul (3 mentions)
FMS-Grenada, 1981 *Certification:* Pediatrics
1111 Montauk Hwy, West Islip, 631-661-2510

Yaker, Michael Neal (3 mentions)
Mount Sinai Sch of Med, 1992 *Certification:* Pediatrics
620 Columbus Ave, New York, 212-874-4500

Zimmerman, Sol Shea (11 mentions)
New York U, 1972 *Certification:* Pediatrics
317 E 34th St, New York, 212-725-6300
20 Plaza St E, Brooklyn, 718-857-5500

Zoltan, Irving (5 mentions)
Albert Einstein Coll of Med, 1974 *Certification:* Pediatrics
1613 Tenbroeck Ave, Bronx, 718-828-9060

Plastic Surgery

Adler, Hilton C. (4 mentions)
FMS-Mexico, 1978 *Certification:* Plastic Surgery
179 N Belle Mead Rd #1, East Setauket, 631-751-4400

Anton, John Roque (4 mentions)
U of Vermont, 1981 *Certification:* Plastic Surgery
138 Old Town Rd, Southampton, 631-283-9100

Baker, Daniel C. (5 mentions)
Columbia U, 1968 *Certification:* Plastic Surgery
65 E 66th St, New York, 212-734-9695

Beran, Samuel J. (8 mentions)
Albany Med Coll, 1990 *Certification:* Plastic Surgery
10 Chester Ave, White Plains, 914-761-8667
91 Smith Ave, Mount Kisco, 914-241-1911

Brewer, Bruce William (5 mentions)
SUNY-Downstate Med Coll, 1975 *Certification:* Plastic Surgery
999 Franklin Ave, Garden City, 516-742-3404

Broumand, Stafford R. (4 mentions)
Yale U, 1985 *Certification:* Plastic Surgery
740 Park Ave, New York, 212-879-7900
309 Engle St, Englewood, NJ, 212-879-7900

Ciardullo, Robert Carl (7 mentions)
Johns Hopkins U, 1976 *Certification:* Plastic Surgery
170 Maple Ave #305, White Plains, 914-948-4636

Dagum, Alexander B. (4 mentions)
Certification: Plastic Surgery, Surgery of the Hand
24 Research Way #100, East Setauket, 631-444-4666
14 Technology Dr, East Setauket, 631-444-4666

De Vita, Gregory Anthony (4 mentions)
SUNY-Downstate Med Coll, 1980 *Certification:* Plastic Surgery
242 Merrick Rd #302, Rockville Centre, 516-536-5858
650 Northern Blvd, Great Neck, 516-466-7000

Duboys, Elliot B. (6 mentions)
FMS-Belgium, 1977 *Certification:* Plastic Surgery
864 W Jericho Tpke, Woodbury, 516-921-2244

Feinberg, Joseph (6 mentions)
Certification: Plastic Surgery
1201 Northern Blvd, Manhasset, 516-869-6200

Feingold, Randall Scott (4 mentions)
Albany Med Coll, 1987 *Certification:* Plastic Surgery
833 Northern Blvd #160, Great Neck, 516-498-8400

Freedman, Alan Marc (4 mentions)
U of Massachusetts, 1981 *Certification:* Plastic Surgery
885 Northern Blvd, Great Neck, 516-487-6700

Gayle, Lloyd B. (4 mentions)
New York U, 1983 *Certification:* Plastic Surgery
50 E 69th St, New York, 212-452-5121
6645 Main St, Flushing, 718-670-2675

Goldberg, Neal David (4 mentions)
New York U, 1999 *Certification:* Plastic Surgery
128 Ashford ave, Dobbs Ferry, 914-559-1107
2 Longview Ave #301, White Plains, 914-559-1107

Grant, Robert T. (4 mentions)
Albany Med Coll, 1983 *Certification:* Plastic Surgery, Surgery
161 Fort Washington Ave #601, New York, 212-305-3103

Greenberg, Burt Mel (4 mentions)
SUNY-Upstate Med U, 1979 *Certification:* Plastic Surgery
833 Northern Blvd #230, Great Neck, 516-466-6600

Groeger, William Edward (4 mentions)
SUNY-Downstate Med Coll, 1972 *Certification:* Plastic Surgery
1490 Broadway #201, Hewlett, 516-887-5502

Hoffman, Lloyd Alan (6 mentions)
Northwestern U, 1978 *Certification:* Plastic Surgery
12 E 68th St, New York, 212-861-1640

Israeli, Ron (6 mentions)
Boston U, 1990 *Certification:* Plastic Surgery
1800 Clove Rd, Staten Island, 718-720-6040

Jetter, Robert Bruce (4 mentions)
Albert Einstein Coll of Med, 1979 *Certification:* Plastic Surgery
875 Park Ave, New York, 212-517-5200
50 E 69th St, New York, 212-517-5200

Karp, Nolan S. (5 mentions)
Northwestern U, 1983 *Certification:* Plastic Surgery
305 E 47th St #1-A, New York, 212-263-6004

Karpinski, Richard H. S. (4 mentions)
Harvard U, 1971 *Certification:* Plastic Surgery
200 Central Park S, New York, 212-977-9797

Keegan, Leo Martin, Jr. (4 mentions)
Mount Sinai Sch of Med, 1986 *Certification:* Plastic Surgery
1125 5th Ave, New York, 212-288-9800

Kessler, Martin Elliot (6 mentions)
Cornell U, 1980 *Certification:* Plastic Surgery
650 Northern Blvd, Great Neck, 516-536-5858
242 Merrick Rd #302, Rockville Centre, 516-536-5858

Kiridly, Nabil Khorshid (4 mentions)
FMS-Egypt, 1980
267 E Main St, Smithtown, 631-366-2220
240 Patchogue-Yaphawk Rd #102, East Patchogue,
   631-447-9840

Labruna, Anthony Nunzio (5 mentions)
Cornell U, 1990 *Certification:* Otolaryngology, Plastic Surgery
1305 York Ave, New York, 212-746-3142

McCarthy, Joseph Gerald (11 mentions)
Columbia U, 1964 *Certification:* Plastic Surgery, Surgery
722 Park Ave, New York, 212-628-4420
560 1st Ave, New York, 212-263-5834

Petro, Jane E. Arbuckle (9 mentions)
Pennsylvania State U, 1972 *Certification:* Plastic Surgery
3010 West Chester Ave, Purchase, 914-428-8881
400 E Main St, Mount Kisco, 914-242-7610

Reiffel, Robert Siskind (6 mentions)
Columbia U, 1972 *Certification:* Plastic Surgery
12 Greenridge Ave #203, White Plains, 914-683-1400

Roth, Douglas Albert (8 mentions)
New York U, 1990 *Certification:* Plastic Surgery, Surgery
110 S Bedford Rd, Mount Kisco, 914-241-1050

Roth, Malcolm Zachary (5 mentions)
New York Med Coll, 1982
Certification: Plastic Surgery, Surgery of the Hand
925 49th St, Brooklyn, 718-283-7022
325 E 72nd St, New York, 212-879-5600

Sasson, Homayoun Nazarian (6 mentions)
U of Massachusetts, 1988
1000 Northern Blvd #370, Great Neck, 516-487-5017

Sherman, John Eric (4 mentions)
New York Med Coll, 1975 *Certification:* Plastic Surgery
1016 5th Ave, New York, 212-535-2300

Simpson, Roger Lawrence (5 mentions)
FMS-Belgium, 1974 *Certification:* Plastic Surgery
999 Franklin Ave, Garden City, 516-742-3404

Skolnik, Richard Alan (5 mentions)
Cornell U, 1976 *Certification:* Plastic Surgery
21 E 87th St #1-A, New York, 212-722-1977

Sterry, Thomas P. (5 mentions)
Certification: Plastic Surgery
895 Park Ave, New York, 212-249-4020

Sultan, Mark Raymond (16 mentions)
Certification: Plastic Surgery
1100 Park Ave, New York, 212-360-0700

Tabbal, Nicolas G. (6 mentions)
FMS-Lebanon, 1972 *Certification:* Plastic Surgery
521 Parks Ave, New York, 212-644-5800

Taub, Peter James (11 mentions)
Albert Einstein Coll of Med, 1993
Certification: Plastic Surgery, Surgery
155 White Plains Rd, Tarrytown, 914-366-6139
5 E 98th St #14, New York, 212-241-7646

Thorne, Charles H. (4 mentions)
U of California-Los Angeles, 1981 *Certification:* Plastic Surgery
812 Park Ave, New York, 212-794-0044
550 1st Ave #8-V, New York, 212-794-0044

Ting, Jess (9 mentions)
Columbia U, 1995
Certification: Plastic Surgery, Surgery of the Hand
1 Gustave L Levy Pl, New York, 212-241-5873
5 E 98th St, New York, 212-241-3336

Uria, Antonio Luis (5 mentions)
Boston U, 1992 *Certification:* Plastic Surgery, Surgery
650 Northern Blvd, Great Neck, 516-466-7000
242 Merrick Rd #302, Rockville Centre, 516-466-7000

Weiss, Paul Richard (4 mentions)
Tulane U, 1969 *Certification:* Plastic Surgery, Surgery
1049 5th Ave #2-D, New York, 212-861-8000

Zimbler, Marc Samuel (4 mentions)
Mount Sinai Sch of Med, 1993 *Certification:* Otolaryngology
10 Union Sq E, New York, 212-844-6712

Psychiatry

Alexopoulos, George S. (3 mentions)
FMS-Greece, 1970 *Certification:* Geriatric Psychiatry, Psychiatry
21 Bloomingdale Rd, White Plains, 914-997-5767

Badikian, Arthur Victoire (4 mentions)
U of Florida, 1976 *Certification:* Psychiatry
600 Mamaroneck Ave #106, Harrison, 914-948-4277

Carone, Patrick Francis (4 mentions)
Johns Hopkins U, 1970 *Certification:* Psychiatry
2000 N Village Ave #305, Rockville Centre, 516-766-2871

Cole, Steven A. (3 mentions)
Duke U, 1974 *Certification:* Geriatric Psychiatry, Psychiatry,
   Psychosomatic Medicine
Stony Brook Health Sciences Center, Stony Brook, 631-444-2571

Fabian, Christopher Andrew (3 mentions)
Certification: Psychiatry
33 5th Ave, New York, 212-673-5230

Fornari, Victor Masliah (4 mentions)
SUNY-Downstate Med Coll, 1979
Certification: Child Psychiatry, Psychiatry
17 N Circle Dr, Great Neck, 718-470-3510

Heisman, Alexander (3 mentions)
FMS-Russia, 1976 *Certification:* Forensic Psychiatry,
   Psychiatry, Psychosomatic Medicine
2520 Kings Hwy, Brooklyn, 718-449-1705

Iyer, Mala Sridhar (4 mentions)
FMS-India, 1980 *Certification:* Psychiatry
2780 Middle Country Rd #306, Lake Grove, 631-981-8300

Klein, Donald F. (3 mentions)
SUNY-Downstate Med Coll, 1952 *Certification:* Psychiatry
182 E 79th St #E, New York, 212-543-6249

Mandelstam, Arnold (3 mentions)
U of Massachusetts, 1979 *Certification:* Psychiatry
2391 Bell Blvd #202, Bayside, 718-479-6699

McDowell, David M. (3 mentions)
Columbia U, 1989 *Certification:* Psychiatry
37 W 57th St 6th Fl, New York, 212-750-7801

Najarian, Louis Marshall (3 mentions)
St Louis U, 1968 *Certification:* Child Psychiatry, Psychiatry
324 Park Ave, Manhasset, 516-627-3980

Perry, Bradford (5 mentions)
U of Miami, 1984 *Certification:* Psychiatry
455 Central Park Ave #214, Scarsdale, 914-472-2167

Perry, Paul G. (4 mentions)
Georgetown U, 1968 *Certification:* Psychiatry
30 E 76th St #3A, New York, 212-772-3788

Reddy, Stanley Prabhakar (3 mentions)
FMS-India, 1972
871 E Park Ave, Long Beach, 516-889-8844

Rosen, Bruce Ira (3 mentions)
Loyola U Chicago, 1971 *Certification:* Psychiatry
222 Middle Country Rd, Smithtown, 631-265-6868

Schrage, Howell Evan (3 mentions)
SUNY-Downstate Med Coll, 1981
Certification: Geriatric Psychiatry, Psychiatry
83 S Bedford Rd, Mount Kisco, 914-666-4814

Strauss, Gordon Jay (3 mentions)
Washington U, 1997
Certification: Psychiatry, Psychosomatic Medicine
1141 Parks Ave W #1, New York, 212-831-4140

Zenn, Richard David (4 mentions)
Boston U, 1987 *Certification:* Addiction Psychiatry, Psychiatry
101 Saint Andrews Ln, Glen Cove, 516-674-7814

Zolkind, Neil Arther (3 mentions)
George Washington U, 1976 *Certification:* Psychiatry
95 Grasslands Rd, Valhalla, 914-493-1818
280 Dobbs Ferry Rd, White Plains, 914-332-5162

Pulmonary Disease

Baram, Daniel (6 mentions)
Jefferson Med Coll, 1990 *Certification:* Critical Care
   Medicine, Internal Medicine, Pulmonary Disease
26 Research Way, East Setauket, 631-444-0580

Berland, Jay Steven (5 mentions)
SUNY-Upstate Med U, 1995 *Certification:* Critical Care
   Medicine, Internal Medicine, Pulmonary Disease
6 Ohio Dr #201, Lake Success, 516-328-8700

Berman, Andrew Russell (3 mentions)
Stony Brook U, 1988 *Certification:* Critical Care Medicine,
   Internal Medicine, Pulmonary Disease
1515 Blondell Ave #220, Bronx, 866-633-8255
111 E 210th St, Bronx, 866-633-8255

Breidbart, David Martin (11 mentions)
SUNY-Downstate Med Coll, 1979
Certification: Internal Medicine, Pulmonary Disease
6 Ohio Dr #201, Lake Success, 516-328-8700

Casper, Theodore (3 mentions)
Columbia U, 1980 *Certification:* Critical Care Medicine,
   Internal Medicine, Pulmonary Disease
1250 Waters Pl #506, Bronx, 718-892-1200

Ciccarelli, Ciro Anthony (6 mentions)
FMS-Italy, 1985 *Certification:* Internal Medicine
444 Merrick Rd, Lynbrook, 516-593-9500

Deluca, Richard Vincent (3 mentions)
SUNY-Downstate Med Coll, 1990 *Certification:* Critical Care
  Medicine, Internal Medicine, Pulmonary Disease
3322 Bainbridge Ave, Bronx, 718-884-2000

Depalo, Louis Ralph (8 mentions)
New York Med Coll, 1982 *Certification:* Critical Care
  Medicine, Internal Medicine, Pulmonary Disease
1130 Park Ave, New York, 212-289-3627

Di Fabrizio, Larry (3 mentions)
Washington U, 1984 *Certification:* Critical Care Medicine,
  Internal Medicine, Pulmonary Disease
111 E 80th St, New York, 212-517-8488
100 E 77th St, New York, 212-434-2900

Dicosmo, Bruno Francesco (3 mentions)
U of Connecticut, 1988 *Certification:* Critical Care
  Medicine, Internal Medicine, Pulmonary Disease
1 Theall Rd, Rye, 914-848-8777

Dipalo, Francis J. (3 mentions)
New York Coll of Osteopathic Med, 1993
Certification: Internal Medicine, Pulmonary Disease
222 E Main St, Smithtown, 631-265-0266

Dobkin, Jay Barry (3 mentions)
Albert Einstein Coll of Med, 1979 *Certification:* Critical Care
  Medicine, Internal Medicine, Pulmonary Disease
1575 Blondell Ave #200, Bronx, 866-633-8255

Dozor, Allen Jay (4 mentions)
Pennsylvania State U, 1977
Certification: Pediatric Pulmonology, Pediatrics
19 Bradhurst Ave #1400, Hawthorne, 914-493-7585

Fishman, Donald Roy (4 mentions)
U of Pennsylvania, 1973
Certification: Internal Medicine, Pulmonary Disease
200 W 57th St #1201, New York, 212-765-5151

Frimer, Richard Bruce (5 mentions)
U of Buffalo, 1980 *Certification:* Critical Care Medicine,
  Internal Medicine, Pulmonary Disease
170 Maple Ave, White Plains, 914-328-0932

Garay, Stuart Martin (5 mentions)
Harvard U, 1974
Certification: Internal Medicine, Pulmonary Disease
436 3rd Ave, New York, 212-685-6660

Garofano, Suzette Ann (3 mentions)
Stony Brook U, 1986 *Certification:* Critical Care Medicine,
  Internal Medicine, Pulmonary Disease
530 1st Ave #5-E, New York, 212-263-8865

Hurewitz, Adam (5 mentions)
New York Med Coll, 1973
Certification: Internal Medicine, Pulmonary Disease
222 Station Plaza N #400, Mineola, 516-663-2834

Janus, Denise (4 mentions)
New York U, 1991
6 Ohio Dr #201, Lake Success, 516-328-8700

Kamelhar, David Lawrence (7 mentions)
New York U, 1974
Certification: Internal Medicine, Pulmonary Disease
436 3rd Ave, New York, 212-685-6660

Karbowitz, Stephen Robert (5 mentions)
Albert Einstein Coll of Med, 1971
Certification: Internal Medicine, Pulmonary Disease
5645 Main St, Flushing, 718-670-1405

Karnik, Ashok (3 mentions)
FMS-India, 1967
Certification: Internal Medicine, Pulmonary Disease
2201 Hempstead Tpke, East Meadow, 516-572-8714

Karp, Jason Bruce (14 mentions)
SUNY-Downstate Med Coll, 1988 *Certification:* Critical Care
  Medicine, Internal Medicine, Pulmonary Disease
6 Ohio Dr, Lake Success, 516-328-8700

Kattan, Meyer (3 mentions)
FMS-Canada, 1973
Certification: Pediatric Pulmonology, Pediatrics
3959 Broadway, New York, 212-305-2406

Kazachkov, Mikhail (3 mentions)
FMS-Russia, 1984
Certification: Pediatric Pulmonology, Pediatrics
4802 10th Ave, Brooklyn, 718-283-7500
511 Bay Ridge Pkwy, Brooklyn, 718-836-6330

Keller, Raymond Stanley (3 mentions)
New York Med Coll, 1966
Certification: Internal Medicine, Pulmonary Disease
55 E 34th St, New York, 212-252-6158

Klapholz, Ari (3 mentions)
New York Med Coll, 1984 *Certification:* Critical Care Medicine,
  Internal Medicine, Pulmonary Disease, Sleep Medicine
275 7th Ave, New York, 646-660-9999

Klapper, Philip Jacob (5 mentions)
Certification: Critical Care Medicine, Internal Medicine,
  Pulmonary Disease
3322 Bainbridge Ave, Bronx, 718-884-2000

Klares, Scott (9 mentions)
New York Med Coll, 1992 *Certification:* Critical Care
  Medicine, Internal Medicine, Pulmonary Disease
90 S Bedford Rd, Mount Kisco, 914-241-1050
185 Route 312, Brewster, 845-278-4300

Kolodny, Erwin (3 mentions)
New York U, 1973
Certification: Internal Medicine, Pulmonary Disease
650 1st Ave, New York, 212-213-0090

Kutnick, Robert Alan (4 mentions)
Albert Einstein Coll of Med, 1974
Certification: Internal Medicine, Pulmonary Disease
14 E 90th St #1-D, New York, 212-427-4700

Lehrman, Stuart G. (6 mentions)
SUNY-Downstate Med Coll, 1978
Certification: Critical Care Medicine, Internal Medicine,
  Pulmonary Disease, Sleep Medicine
Macy Pavillion 1st Fl, Valhalla, 914-493-7517
95 Grasslands Rd, Valhalla, 914-285-7518

Libby, Daniel Miles (7 mentions)
Baylor U, 1974
Certification: Internal Medicine, Pulmonary Disease
635 Madison Ave #1101, New York, 212-628-6611

Maguire, George Paul (3 mentions)
SUNY-Downstate Med Coll, 1972 *Certification:* Critical Care
  Medicine, Internal Medicine, Pulmonary Disease
Macy Pavillion, Valhalla, 914-493-7518

Malasky, Charlotte Rose (3 mentions)
New York Med Coll, 1977 *Certification:* Critical Care
  Medicine, Internal Medicine, Pulmonary Disease
1250 Waters Pl #506, Bronx, 718-892-1200

Maniatis, Theodore (5 mentions)
SUNY-Upstate Med U, 1980 *Certification:* Critical Care
  Medicine, Internal Medicine, Pulmonary Disease
501 Seaview Ave #301, Staten Island, 718-980-5700

Mann, Jack Michael (3 mentions)
FMS-Italy, 1980
Certification: Internal Medicine, Pulmonary Disease
4223 Francis Lewis Blvd, Bayside, 718-225-5106

Marcus, Philip (9 mentions)
SUNY-Downstate Med Coll, 1973 *Certification:* Critical Care
  Medicine, Internal Medicine, Pulmonary Disease
233 E Shore Rd #112, Great Neck, 516-482-7810
643 Broadway, Massapequa, 516-798-1066

McGregor, Carlton C. (3 mentions)
Certification: Internal Medicine
161 Fort Washington Ave #318, New York, 212-305-8175

Meixler, Steven Martin (3 mentions)
Boston U, 1984 *Certification:* Critical Care Medicine,
  Internal Medicine, Pulmonary Disease
210 Westchester Ave, West Harrison, 914-682-0700

Mensch, Alan R. (8 mentions)
Rosalind Franklin U, 1973
Certification: Internal Medicine, Pulmonary Disease
453 S Oyster Bay Rd, Plainview, 516-433-2922

Mermelstein, Steve A. (3 mentions)
Albert Einstein Coll of Med, 1977
Certification: Internal Medicine, Pulmonary Disease
444 Merrick Rd, Lynbrook, 516-593-9500

Mina, Bushra A. (6 mentions)
Certification: Critical Care Medicine, Internal Medicine,
  Pulmonary Disease
155 E 76th St #1-C, New York, 212-794-2800

Multz, Alan Scott (3 mentions)
Boston U, 1985 *Certification:* Critical Care Medicine,
  Internal Medicine, Pulmonary Disease
410 Lakeville Rd #107, New Hyde Park, 516-465-5400

Nash, Thomas W. (3 mentions)
New York U, 1978 *Certification:* Infectious Disease, Internal
  Medicine, Pulmonary Disease
310 E 72nd St, New York, 212-734-6612

Newmark, Ian H. (3 mentions)
SUNY-Downstate Med Coll, 1979 *Certification:* Critical Care
  Medicine, Internal Medicine, Pulmonary Disease
8 Greenfield Rd, Syosset, 516-496-7900

Niederman, Michael Steven (5 mentions)
Boston U, 1977 *Certification:* Critical Care Medicine,
  Internal Medicine, Pulmonary Disease
222 Station Plaza N #400, Mineola, 516-663-2834

Padilla, Maria Luisa (7 mentions)
Mount Sinai Sch of Med, 1975
Certification: Internal Medicine, Pulmonary Disease
5 E 98th St, New York, 212-241-5656
1 Gustave L Levy Pl, New York, 212-241-5656

Pechman, Paul (4 mentions)
Boston U, 1977 *Certification:* Critical Care Medicine,
  Geriatric Medicine, Internal Medicine, Pulmonary Disease
259 Heathcote Rd, Scarsdale, 914-723-8100

Prager, Kenneth Michael (6 mentions)
Harvard U, 1968 *Certification:* Internal Medicine
161 Fort Washington Ave #310, New York, 212-305-5535

Rosen, Mark Jeffrey (3 mentions)
Brown U, 1975 *Certification:* Critical Care Medicine,
  Internal Medicine, Pulmonary Disease
410 Lakeview Rd #107, New Hyde Park, 516-465-5400

Rossoff, Leonard Jacob (3 mentions)
FMS-Canada, 1972
Certification: Internal Medicine, Pulmonary Disease
410 Lakeville Rd #107, New Hyde Park, 516-465-5400
27005 76th Ave, New Hyde Park, 516-470-7230

Saleh, Anthony George (5 mentions)
FMS-Grenada, 1985
Certification: Internal Medicine, Pulmonary Disease
7206 7th Ave, Brooklyn, 718-745-1200

Sanders, Abraham (5 mentions)
SUNY-Downstate Med Coll, 1976 *Certification:* Critical Care
  Medicine, Internal Medicine, Pulmonary Disease
520 E 70th #505, New York, 212-746-2250

Schneyer, Barton Lewis (4 mentions)
Jefferson Med Coll, 1972 *Certification:* Critical Care
  Medicine, Internal Medicine, Pulmonary Disease
222 E Main St #200, Smithtown, 631-780-9992

Schulster, Paul Leonard (3 mentions)
U of Kentucky, 1972
442 E Waukena Ave, Oceanside, 516-599-8234

Schultz, Barbara Lynne (14 mentions)
Mount Sinai Sch of Med, 1983
Certification: Internal Medicine, Pulmonary Disease
927 Park Ave, New York, 212-517-8680

Sha, Kenneth K. (3 mentions)
FMS-Myanmar, 1986 *Certification:* Critical Care Medicine,
Internal Medicine, Pulmonary Disease
142-20 Franklin Ave, Flushing, 718-358-8889

Sherman, William (6 mentions)
SUNY-Downstate Med Coll, 1981
Certification: Internal Medicine, Pulmonary Disease
100 Manetto Rd, Plainview, 516-933-1088

Silverman, Joel Richard (5 mentions)
U of Oklahoma, 1974 *Certification:* Critical Care Medicine,
Internal Medicine, Pulmonary Disease
11120 Queens Blvd, Forest Hills, 718-544-4224

Sklarek, Howard Michael (3 mentions)
U of Buffalo, 1981 *Certification:* Critical Care Medicine,
Internal Medicine, Pulmonary Disease
325 Meeting House Ln Bldg 1 #K, Southampton, 631-283-8008

Sourour, Magdi Sadek (3 mentions)
FMS-Egypt, 1976 *Certification:* Critical Care Medicine,
Internal Medicine, Pulmonary Disease
2000 N Village Ave #208, Rockville Centre, 516-766-1466

Steiger, David Joseph (4 mentions)
FMS-United Kingdom, 1981 *Certification:* Critical Care
Medicine, Internal Medicine, Pulmonary Disease
305 2nd Ave #16, New York, 212-598-6516

Stein, Sidney Kaufman (3 mentions)
SUNY-Downstate Med Coll, 1979
Certification: Internal Medicine, Pulmonary Disease
55 E 34th St, New York, 212-879-7776

Steinberg, Harry Norman (5 mentions)
Temple U, 1966
410 Lakeville Rd #107, New Hyde Park, 516-465-5400
27005 76th Ave, New Hyde Park, 718-470-7231

Teirstein, Alvin S. (14 mentions)
SUNY-Downstate Med Coll, 1953
Certification: Internal Medicine, Pulmonary Disease
5 E 98th St, New York, 212-241-5656
1 Gustave L Levy Pl, New York, 212-241-5656

Thomashow, Byron Martin (13 mentions)
Columbia U, 1974
Certification: Internal Medicine, Pulmonary Disease
161 Fort Washington Ave #311, New York, 212-305-5261

Thurm, Craig Alan (3 mentions)
Albert Einstein Coll of Med, 1987 *Certification:* Critical Care
Medicine, Internal Medicine, Pulmonary Disease
13420 Jamaica Ave, Richmond Hill, 718-206-6742

Turken, Arthur N. (5 mentions)
Albert Einstein Coll of Med, 1990 *Certification:* Critical Care
Medicine, Internal Medicine, Pulmonary Disease
100 S Highland Ave, Ossining, 914-762-0243

Walser, Lawrence Albert (3 mentions)
SUNY-Downstate Med Coll, 1979 *Certification:* Critical Care
Medicine, Internal Medicine, Pulmonary Disease
185 Old Country Rd #3, Riverhead, 631-727-2523

Weinberg, Barry Jay (5 mentions)
SUNY-Downstate Med Coll, 1989
Certification: Pulmonary Disease
210 E 86th St #603, New York, 212-744-5555

Weinberg, Harlan Richard (4 mentions)
U of Connecticut, 1981 *Certification:* Critical Care
Medicine, Internal Medicine, Pulmonary Disease
83 S Bedford Rd, Mount Kisco, 914-241-8356

Weinstein, Paul David (4 mentions)
Mount Sinai Sch of Med, 1984 *Certification:* Critical Care
Medicine, Internal Medicine, Pulmonary Disease
1075 Central Park Ave #101, Scarsdale, 914-725-6688

Yip, Chun Keung (4 mentions)
Albert Einstein Coll of Med, 1976
Certification: Internal Medicine, Pulmonary Disease
67 Hudson St #1-A, New York, 212-732-6756
161 Fort Washington Ave #311, New York, 212-305-8548

Radiology—Diagnostic

Austin, John Holcombe M. (4 mentions)
Yale U, 1965 *Certification:* Diagnostic Radiology
622 W 168th St, New York, 212-305-2986

Bello, Jacqueline Anne (3 mentions)
Columbia U, 1980 *Certification:* Diagnostic Radiology
111 E 210th St, Bronx, 718-920-4030

Cohen, Burton Asher (11 mentions)
New York Med Coll, 1975 *Certification:* Diagnostic Radiology
1 E 82nd St, New York, 212-535-9770

Edelstein, Barbara Ann (3 mentions)
New York Med Coll, 1977 *Certification:* Diagnostic Radiology
1045 Park Ave, New York, 212-860-7700

Fagelman, Donald (4 mentions)
SUNY-Upstate Med U, 1975
Certification: Diagnostic Radiology, Nuclear Radiology
935 Northern Blvd, Great Neck, 516-829-4414

Grappell, Paul M. (7 mentions)
SUNY-Downstate Med Coll, 1967 *Certification:* Radiology
146 Manetto Hill Rd, Plainview, 516-822-3666

Heimowitz, Howard (3 mentions)
FMS-Mexico, 1976 *Certification:* Diagnostic Radiology
175 Jericho Tpke #120, Syosset, 516-867-1164

Hertz, Marc A. (6 mentions)
Howard U, 1979 *Certification:* Diagnostic Radiology
90 S Bedford Rd, Mount Kisco, 914-241-1050

Hibbard, Claire Alexandra (3 mentions)
Columbia U, 1984 *Certification:* Diagnostic Radiology
185 Route 312, Brewster, 845-278-4300

Katz, David L. (4 mentions)
Emory U, 1983 *Certification:* Diagnostic Radiology
560 Northern Blvd #111, Great Neck, 516-504-1600

Katz, Douglas Scott (5 mentions)
Stony Brook U, 1990 *Certification:* Diagnostic Radiology
120 Mineola Blvd #LL10, Mineola, 516-663-4510

Kazam, Elias (4 mentions)
Certification: Diagnostic Radiology, Nuclear Medicine
400 E 66th St, New York, 212-838-4243

Khoury, Paul Thomas (9 mentions)
FMS-Lebanon, 1973
Certification: Diagnostic Radiology, Nuclear Radiology
Davis Ave & E Post Rd, White Plains, 914-681-1260
122 Maple Ave, White Plains, 914-285-9808

Lerman, Jay Edward (5 mentions)
Albert Einstein Coll of Med, 1986
Certification: Diagnostic Radiology
6511 Fort Hamilton Pkwy, Brooklyn, 718-491-4545

Levenbrown, Jack (3 mentions)
George Washington U, 1968 *Certification:* Diagnostic
Radiology, Pediatric Radiology, Pediatrics
300 Community Dr, Manhasset, 516-562-4795

Macari, Michael (4 mentions)
Boston U, 1991 *Certification:* Diagnostic Radiology
560 1st Ave, New York, 212-263-0232

Maklansky, Daniel M. (7 mentions)
SUNY-Downstate Med Coll, 1956 *Certification:* Radiology
165 E 84th St, New York, 212-535-9770

Maklansky, Joseph John (4 mentions)
Mount Sinai Sch of Med, 1997 *Certification:* Diagnostic Radiology
1 E 82nd St, New York, 212-535-9770

Megibow, Alec Jeffrey (8 mentions)
SUNY-Upstate Med U, 1974 *Certification:* Diagnostic Radiology
530 1st Ave, New York, 212-263-5222
560 1st Ave, New York, 212-263-5222
403 E 34th St, New York, 212-263-5222

Minken, Todd Jeffrey (3 mentions)
U of Rochester, 1989 *Certification:* Diagnostic Radiology,
Vascular & Interventional Radiology
967 N Broadway, Yonkers, 914-964-4321

Mitnick, Julia Sharon (4 mentions)
New York U, 1972 *Certification:* Diagnostic Radiology
650 1st Ave 2nd Fl, New York, 212-213-3208

Okon, Stephen A. (3 mentions)
Yale U, 1994 *Certification:* Diagnostic Radiology
310 E 14th St, New York, 212-979-4000
424 E 89th St, New York, 212-410-5100

Parnell, John Vincent (3 mentions)
SUNY-Downstate Med Coll, 1998
Certification: Diagnostic Radiology
375 E Main St #12, Bay Shore, 631-666-5620

Pek, Henry (4 mentions)
FMS-Belgium, 1975 *Certification:* Diagnostic Radiology
935 Northern Blvd, Great Neck, 516-829-3557

Pfaff, H. Charles (3 mentions)
U of North Carolina, 1987 *Certification:* Diagnostic Radiology
144 4th Ave, New York, 212-473-2300

Potter, Hollis J. (3 mentions)
New York Med Coll, 1985 *Certification:* Diagnostic Radiology
535 E 70th St, New York, 212-606-1023

Schonholz, Lyris Ann (5 mentions)
Mount Sinai Sch of Med, 1983 *Certification:* Diagnostic Radiology
488 Madison Ave #1220, New York, 212-755-7656

Sherman, Craig Harvey (3 mentions)
Jefferson Med Coll, 1982 *Certification:* Diagnostic
Radiology, Neuroradiology, Nuclear Medicine
400 E 66th St Ground Fl, New York, 212-486-5510

Sherman, Scott Jeffrey (4 mentions)
Northwestern U, 1979
Certification: Diagnostic Radiology, Nuclear Medicine
100 Port Washington Blvd, Roslyn, 516-562-6500

Walker, James Thaddeus (6 mentions)
New York Med Coll, 1978 *Certification:* Diagnostic Radiology
146 Manetto Hill Rd, Plainview, 516-822-3666

Weck, Steven Duncan (3 mentions)
New York U, 1973 *Certification:* Diagnostic Radiology
101 Saint Andrews Ln, Glen Cove, 516-674-7540

Zito, Joseph Louis (8 mentions)
Georgetown U, 1974 *Certification:* Diagnostic Radiology
765 Stewart Ave, Garden City, 516-222-2323
6 Ohio Dr #104, Lake Success, 516-773-6611

Radiology—Therapeutic

Berenstein, Alejandro (5 mentions)
FMS-Mexico, 1970 *Certification:* Diagnostic Radiology
1000 10th Ave, New York, 212-636-3400

Bosworth, Jay Leonard (7 mentions)
Albert Einstein Coll of Med, 1970
Certification: Therapeutic Radiology
1129 Northern Blvd #101, Manhasset, 516-365-6544
990 Stewart Ave, Garden City, 516-222-2022
700 Stewart Ave, Garden City, 516-222-2020
230 Hilton Ave #117, Hempstead, 516-481-9255

Dalton, Jack Frederick (7 mentions)
U of Pittsburgh, 1970 *Certification:* Hematology, Internal Medicine, Medical Oncology, Therapeutic Radiology
106-14 70th Ave, Forest Hills, 718-520-6620
1421 3rd Ave, New York, 212-535-8931
10614 70th Ave, Forest Hills, 718-520-6620

Formenti, Sylvia Chiara (3 mentions)
FMS-Italy, 1980
160 E 34th St, New York, 212-731-5003

Greben, Craig Robert (3 mentions)
New York Med Coll, 1991 *Certification:* Diagnostic Radiology, Vascular & Interventional Radiology
300 Community Dr, Manhasset, 516-562-4795

Harrison, Louis Benjamin (8 mentions)
SUNY-Downstate Med Coll, 1982
Certification: Therapeutic Radiology
10 Union Sq E, New York, 212-844-8087

Katz, Alan J. (3 mentions)
New York U, 1977 *Certification:* Therapeutic Radiology
259 1st St, Mineola, 516-663-2501

Lee, Henry Jay (3 mentions)
U of Chicago, 1993 *Certification:* Radiation Oncology
2 Longview Ave, White Plains, 914-681-2727
Davis Ave & E Post Rd, White Plains, 914-681-2728

Lookstein, Robert Andrew (6 mentions)
SUNY-Downstate Med Coll, 1995 *Certification:* Diagnostic Radiology, Vascular & Interventional Radiology
1176 5th Ave & 99th St, New York, 212-241-6381
1184 5th Ave & 100th St, New York, 212-241-7409

Pollack, Jed Michael (5 mentions)
U of New Mexico, 1981 *Certification:* Therapeutic Radiology
6 Ohio Dr, New Hyde Park, 516-222-2022
990 Stewart Ave, Garden City, 516-222-2022

Potters, Louis (3 mentions)
New Jersey Med Sch, 1985
Certification: Internal Medicine, Radiation Oncology
270-05 76th Ave, New Hyde Park, 718-470-7190

Siegel, David Neal (4 mentions)
New Jersey Med Sch, 1986 *Certification:* Diagnostic Radiology, Vascular & Interventional Radiology
270-05 76th Ave, New Hyde Park, 718-470-7178

Stevens, Randy Ellen (3 mentions)
New York U, 1986
Certification: Internal Medicine, Radiation Oncology
2 Longview Ave, White Plains, 914-681-2727
Davis Ave & E Post Rd, White Plains, 914-681-2729

Tinger, Alfred (6 mentions)
SUNY-Downstate Med Coll, 1992
Certification: Radiation Oncology
970 N Broadway #101, Yonkers, 914-969-1600

Train, John Samuel (7 mentions)
New York Med Coll, 1967 *Certification:* Radiology
Davis Ave & E Post Rd, White Plains, 914-681-1260

Weintraub, Joshua Lorin (4 mentions)
Wayne State U, 1991 *Certification:* Diagnostic Radiology, Vascular & Interventional Radiology
1 Gustave L Levy Pl, New York, 212-241-8333

Rehabilitation

Ahn, Jung Hwan (3 mentions)
FMS-South Korea, 1970 *Certification:* Physical Medicine & Rehabilitation, Spinal Cord Injury Medicine
400 E 34th St #421, New York, 212-263-6122

Flanagan, Steven Robert (3 mentions)
Certification: Physical Medicine & Rehabilitation
400 E 34th St #223-B, New York, 212-263-6105

Frieden, Richard Ashley (4 mentions)
New York Med Coll, 1984
Certification: Physical Medicine & Rehabilitation
5 E 98th St, New York, 212-241-6335

Hadjiyane, Pericles S. (3 mentions)
SUNY-Downstate Med Coll, 1992
Certification: Physical Medicine & Rehabilitation
455 E Bay Dr, Long Beach, 516-897-1065

Lipetz, Jason Scott (3 mentions)
Columbia U, 1994 *Certification:* Pain Medicine, Physical Medicine & Rehabilitation
801 Merrick Ave, East Meadow, 516-393-8941

Marin, Edgar L. (3 mentions)
FMS-Paraguay, 1972
Certification: Physical Medicine & Rehabilitation
8 Saxon Ave #A, Bay Shore, 631-665-6717

O'Dell, Michael Wayne (4 mentions)
Indiana U, 1985 *Certification:* Physical Medicine & Rehabilitation
525 E 68th St 18th Fl, New York, 212-746-1500

Pechman, Karen (4 mentions)
Boston U, 1980 *Certification:* Physical Medicine & Rehabilitation
170 Maple Ave #510, White Plains, 914-683-0020

Pici, Ralph Angelo (3 mentions)
FMS-Italy, 1964 *Certification:* Physical Medicine & Rehabilitation
55 Palmer Ave, Bronxville, 914-787-3370

Ragnarsson, Kristjan T. (16 mentions)
FMS-Iceland, 1969
Certification: Physical Medicine & Rehabilitation
5 E 98th St #1240, New York, 212-659-9370

Randolph, Audrey Louise (4 mentions)
Med Coll of Pennsylvania, 1964
Certification: Physical Medicine & Rehabilitation
19 Bradhurst Ave #2450-N, Hawthorne, 914-909-4168

Rashbaum, Ira Glenn (3 mentions)
SUNY-Upstate Med U, 1989
Certification: Physical Medicine & Rehabilitation
400 E 34th St #RR-119, New York, 212-263-6477

Root, Barry Clifford (9 mentions)
Ohio State U, 1984 *Certification:* Physical Medicine & Rehabilitation, Spinal Cord Injury Medicine
101 St Andrews Ln, Glen Cove, 516-674-7501
4 Expressway Plaza #110, Roslyn Heights, 516-621-4062

Semel-Concepcion, J. (5 mentions)
Albert Einstein Coll of Med, 1992
Certification: Pediatrics, Physical Medicine & Rehabilitation
200 Belle Terre Rd #E-140, Port Jefferson, 631-474-6879

Shapiro, Eric Dale (3 mentions)
FMS-Mexico, 1980
Certification: Physical Medicine & Rehabilitation
380 Montauk Hwy, West Islip, 631-422-6600

Stein, Adam Benjamin (5 mentions)
New York U, 1987 *Certification:* Physical Medicine & Rehabilitation, Spinal Cord Injury Medicine
825 Northern Blvd, Great Neck, 516-465-8609

Stein, Perry Joseph (4 mentions)
FMS-Mexico, 1985
Certification: Physical Medicine & Rehabilitation
383 Ocean Pkwy, Brooklyn, 718-941-6000

Varlotta, Gerard Philip (3 mentions)
New York Coll of Osteopathic Med, 1983
Certification: Physical Medicine & Rehabilitation
317 E 34th St, New York, 212-686-9383

Rheumatology

Abramson, Steven Barry (5 mentions)
Harvard U, 1974 *Certification:* Internal Medicine, Rheumatology
305 2nd Ave, New York, 212-598-6516

Argyros, Thomas George (4 mentions)
New York U, 1954 *Certification:* Internal Medicine
122 E 76th St, New York, 212-988-7680

Berger, Jack Jicchak (6 mentions)
Albert Einstein Coll of Med, 1976
Certification: Internal Medicine, Rheumatology
210 Westchester Ave, West Harrison, 914-682-0700

Blume, Ralph Stuart (7 mentions)
Columbia U, 1964
Certification: Internal Medicine, Rheumatology
161 Fort Washington Ave #537, New York, 212-305-5512

Brancato, Lenore (4 mentions)
Boston U, 1984 *Certification:* Rheumatology
1044 Northern Blvd #104, Roslyn, 212-252-6000

Carsons, Steven Eric (11 mentions)
New York Med Coll, 1975 *Certification:* Diagnostic Laboratory Immunology, Internal Medicine, Rheumatology
120 Mineola Blvd #410, Mineola, 576-663-2097

Cohen, Daniel H. (6 mentions)
New York U, 1978
Certification: Internal Medicine, Rheumatology
1157 Broadway, Hewlett, 516-295-4481

Eichenfield, Andrew H. (7 mentions)
Rosalind Franklin U, 1978
Certification: Pediatric Rheumatology, Pediatrics
5 E 98th St 8th Fl, New York, 212-241-1865
3959 Broadway #CHN-106, New York, 212-305-9304

Faller, Jason (6 mentions)
U of Pennsylvania, 1977
Certification: Internal Medicine, Rheumatology
333 W 57th St #104, New York, 212-307-6880

Fischer, Harry David (6 mentions)
Mount Sinai Sch of Med, 1979
Certification: Internal Medicine, Rheumatology
10 Union Sq E #3-D, New York, 212-844-8101

Furie, Richard Alan (5 mentions)
Cornell U, 1979 *Certification:* Internal Medicine, Rheumatology
2800 Marcus Ave, Lake Success, 516-708-2500

Given, William Price, Jr. (10 mentions)
Cornell U, 1978 *Certification:* Internal Medicine, Rheumatology
287 Northern Blvd, Great Neck, 516-487-0757

Gottlieb, Beth S. (5 mentions)
FMS-Israel, 1992
Certification: Pediatric Rheumatology, Pediatrics
26901 76th Ave, New Hyde Park, 718-470-3530

Greisman, Stewart G. (7 mentions)
Yale U, 1981 *Certification:* Internal Medicine, Rheumatology
457 W 57th St, New York, 212-265-1471

Hamburger, Max I. (7 mentions)
Albert Einstein Coll of Med, 1973
Certification: Internal Medicine, Rheumatology
1895 Walt Whitman Rd, Melville, 631-249-9525
7 Medical Dr #D, Port Jefferson Station, 631-928-4885

Horowitz, Mark David (8 mentions)
Northeastern Ohio U, 1983
Certification: Internal Medicine, Rheumatology
21 E 90th St, New York, 212-860-3077

Jarrett, Mark Paul (4 mentions)
New York U, 1975 *Certification:* Geriatric Medicine, Internal Medicine, Rheumatology
1534 Victory Blvd, Staten Island, 718-447-0055

Kaell, Alan Todd (15 mentions)
Brown U, 1978 *Certification:* Geriatric Medicine, Internal Medicine, Rheumatology
7 Medical Dr, Port Jefferson Station, 631-928-4885
315 Middle Country Rd, Smithtown, 631-360-7778

Kerr, Leslie Dubin (4 mentions)
Columbia U, 1980
Certification: Internal Medicine, Rheumatology
1 Gustave L Levy Pl, New York, 212-659-9210

Kleiner, Myron Isaiah (4 mentions)
Mount Sinai Sch of Med, 1977
Certification: Internal Medicine, Rheumatology
180 E Main St #4, Bay Shore, 631-654-3363

Lans, David Mitchell (4 mentions)
Des Moines U, 1981 *Certification:* Allergy & Immunology,
    Internal Medicine, Rheumatology
838 Pelhamdale Ave, New Rochelle, 914-235-5577

Lehman, Thomas J. A. (6 mentions)
Jefferson Med Coll, 1974
Certification: Pediatric Rheumatology, Pediatrics
535 E 70th St, New York, 212-606-1000

Lenci, Margaret Mary (5 mentions)
SUNY-Downstate Med Coll, 1980
Certification: Internal Medicine, Rheumatology
90 S Bedford Rd, Mount Kisco, 914-241-1050

Lipstein-Kresch, Esther (6 mentions)
Certification: Internal Medicine, Rheumatology
2 Pro Health Plaza, Lake Success, 516-622-6090

Magid, Steven Kay (5 mentions)
Cornell U, 1976 *Certification:* Internal Medicine, Rheumatology
535 E 70th St #778, New York, 212-606-1060

Marchetta, Paula A. (4 mentions)
New York U, 1983
Certification: Internal Medicine, Rheumatology
40 Park Ave, New York, 212-696-5415

Marmur, Ronen (5 mentions)
Albert Einstein Coll of Med, 1998
Certification: Internal Medicine, Rheumatology
90 S Bedford Rd, Mount Kisco, 914-241-1050
185 Route 312, Brewster, 845-278-4300

Mascarenhas, Bento S. (4 mentions)
FMS-India, 1962 *Certification:* Internal Medicine, Rheumatology
785 Mamaroneck Ave, White Plains, 914-597-2272
77 Pondfield Rd, Bronxville, 914-337-5879

Meredith, Gary S. (4 mentions)
New York U, 1981
Certification: Internal Medicine, Rheumatology
242 Merrick Rd #303, Rockville Centre, 516-536-9424

Mitnick, Hal Jeffrey (10 mentions)
New York U, 1972
Certification: Internal Medicine, Rheumatology
333 E 34th St #1C, New York, 212-889-7217

Mund, Douglas Jay (4 mentions)
SUNY-Downstate Med Coll, 1975
Certification: Internal Medicine, Rheumatology
1575 Hillside Ave #102, New Hyde Park, 516-354-3400
350 S broadway, Hicksville, 516-938-0100

Paget, Stephen A. (8 mentions)
SUNY-Downstate Med Coll, 1971
Certification: Internal Medicine, Rheumatology
535 E 70th St #721, New York, 212-606-1845

Porges, Andrew Jay (4 mentions)
Cornell U, 1986 *Certification:* Internal Medicine, Rheumatology
1044 Northern Blvd #104, Roslyn, 516-484-6880

Reinitz, Elizabeth (5 mentions)
Albert Einstein Coll of Med, 1976
Certification: Internal Medicine, Rheumatology
259 Heathcote Rd, Scarsdale, 914-723-8100

Rosenblum, Gary (4 mentions)
New York Coll of Osteopathic Med, 1987
Certification: Internal Medicine, Rheumatology
120 Mineola Blvd #410, Mineola, 516-663-2097

Russell, Linda Alice (5 mentions)
Tufts U, 1989 *Certification:* Internal Medicine, Rheumatology
535 E 70th St, New York, 212-606-1305

Schiff, Carl Frank (9 mentions)
Yale U, 1980 *Certification:* Internal Medicine, Rheumatology
4802 10th Ave Bldg 3, Brooklyn, 718-283-8519

Schorn, Karen Hermoine (9 mentions)
FMS-Mexico, 1982
Certification: Internal Medicine, Rheumatology
4277 Hempstead Tpke #209, Bethpage, 516-731-7770
124 Main St #10, Huntington, 631-385-5030

Schwartzman, Sergio (4 mentions)
Mount Sinai Sch of Med, 1982
Certification: Internal Medicine, Rheumatology
535 E 70th St #715-W, New York, 212-606-1557

Spiera, Harry (33 mentions)
New York U, 1958
Certification: Internal Medicine, Rheumatology
1088 Park Ave, New York, 212-860-4000

Spiera, Robert Forman (10 mentions)
Yale U, 1989 *Certification:* Internal Medicine, Rheumatology
1088 Park Ave, New York, 212-860-2100

Sullivan, James Michael (6 mentions)
SUNY-Upstate Med U, 1974
Certification: Internal Medicine, Rheumatology
566 Broadway, Massapequa, 516-541-6262
181 E Jericho Tpke, Mineola, 516-248-6262

Tseng, Chunge (6 mentions)
SUNY-Downstate Med Coll, 1990 *Certification:* Rheumatology
305 2nd Ave #16, New York, 718-539-5555

Thoracic Surgery

Altorki, Nasser Khaled A. (8 mentions)
FMS-Egypt, 1977 *Certification:* Surgery, Thoracic Surgery
525 E 68th St #M-404, New York, 212-746-5156

Bilfinger, Thomas Victor (5 mentions)
FMS-Switzerland, 1978
Certification: Surgery, Surgical Critical Care, Thoracic Surgery
24 Research Way #200, East Patchogue, 631-444-1213
31 Main Rd, Riverhead, 631-444-1213

Connery, Cliff Patrick (9 mentions)
Eastern Virginia Med Sch, 1984
Certification: Surgery, Surgical Critical Care, Thoracic Surgery
1000 10th Ave 2nd Fl, New York, 212-523-7475

Crawford, Bernard K., Jr. (8 mentions)
George Washington U, 1980 *Certification:* Thoracic Surgery
530 1st Ave #9-V, New York, 212-263-7365

Durban, Lawrence Howard (4 mentions)
Cornell U, 1982 *Certification:* Surgery, Thoracic Surgery
100 Port Washington Blvd #G-01, Roslyn, 516-627-2173

Fox, Stewart (7 mentions)
Virginia Commonwealth U, 1972 *Certification:* Thoracic Surgery
444 Merrick Rd #380, Lynbrook, 516-255-5010

Glassman, Lawrence R. (6 mentions)
New York U, 1981 *Certification:* Thoracic Surgery
530 1st Ave #6D, New York, 212-263-7102
550 1st Ave, New York, 212-263-7102

Keller, Steven Matthew (5 mentions)
Albany Med Coll, 1977 *Certification:* Thoracic Surgery
3400 Bainbridge Ave, Bronx, 718-920-7580
1695 E Chester Rd, Bronx, 718-920-7580

Kline, Gary Michael (4 mentions)
Wayne State U, 1986 *Certification:* Surgery, Thoracic Surgery
410 Lakeview Rd #310, New Hyde Park, 516-233-1952

Krellenstein, Daniel J. (5 mentions)
U of Buffalo, 1964 *Certification:* Surgery, Thoracic Surgery
16 E 98th St #1F, New York, 212-423-9311

Palatt, Terry (8 mentions)
FMS-Grenada, 1981 *Certification:* Thoracic Surgery
111 Carleton Ave #2-A, Islip Terrace, 631-581-4400

Pass, Harvey Ira (4 mentions)
Duke U, 1973 *Certification:* Thoracic Surgery
160 E 34th St, New York, 212-731-5414
530 1st Ave, New York, 212-263-6384

Port, Jeffrey Lloyd (4 mentions)
New York U, 1991 *Certification:* Surgery, Thoracic Surgery
525 E 68th St #110, New York, 212-746-5197
525 East 68th St #110, New York, 212-746-5190

Rusch, Valerie Williams (4 mentions)
Columbia U, 1975 *Certification:* Surgery, Thoracic Surgery
1275 York Ave, New York, 212-639-5873

Saha, Chanchal Kumar (5 mentions)
FMS-India, 1965 *Certification:* Thoracic Surgery
754 Old Country Rd, Plainview, 516-931-0182

Schubach, Scott Leslie (5 mentions)
Baylor U, 1983
Certification: Surgery, Surgical Critical Care, Thoracic Surgery
120 Mineola Blvd #300, Mineola, 516-663-4400

Sonett, Joshua Robert (4 mentions)
Certification: Surgery, Thoracic Surgery
161 Fort Washington Ave #301, New York, 212-305-3408

Spier, Laurence Nelson (15 mentions)
SUNY-Downstate Med Coll, 1990 *Certification:* Thoracic Surgery
1000 Northern Blvd #380, Great Neck, 516-773-0096

Streisand, Robert Lewis (7 mentions)
SUNY-Downstate Med Coll, 1966
Certification: Surgery, Thoracic Surgery
4 Lyon Pl, White Plains, 914-948-6633

Zelen, Jonathan (4 mentions)
U of Colorado, 1986 *Certification:* Surgery, Thoracic Surgery
775 Park Ave #355, Huntington, 631-928-4225

Zervos, Michael (8 mentions)
FMS-Greece, 1991 *Certification:* Surgery
530 1st Ave, New York, 212-263-7300

Urology

Armenakas, Noel Anthony (6 mentions)
FMS-Greece, 1985 *Certification:* Urology
880 5th Ave, New York, 212-535-1950

Ashley, Richard Noel (6 mentions)
New York Med Coll, 1972 *Certification:* Urology
233 7th St #203, Garden City, 516-294-7666

Badillo, Felix Luis (12 mentions)
Cornell U, 1978 *Certification:* Urology
535 Plandome Rd, Manhasset, 516-627-6188

Bar-Chama, Nathan Chaim (6 mentions)
Albert Einstein Coll of Med, 1987 *Certification:* Urology
5 E 98th St, New York, 212-241-4812

Benson, Mitchell C. (4 mentions)
Columbia U, 1977 *Certification:* Urology
161 Fort Washington Ave #1153, New York, 212-305-5201
16 E 60th St, New York, 212-305-5201

Birkhoff, John David (4 mentions)
Columbia U, 1969 *Certification:* Urology
161 Fort Washington Ave #347, New York, 212-305-5421

Boczko, Stanley Howard (4 mentions)
Albert Einstein Coll of Med, 1973 *Certification:* Urology
23 E 79th St, New York, 212-628-1800
1695 E Chester Rd, Bronx, 718-863-7777
1234 Central Park Ave #3-A, Yonkers, 914-961-7212

Brodherson, Michael S. (4 mentions)
SUNY-Downstate Med Coll, 1973 *Certification:* Urology
4 E 76th St, New York, 212-794-2749

Bromberg, Warren Douglas (7 mentions)
Johns Hopkins U, 1985 *Certification:* Urology
110 S Bedford Rd, Mount Kisco, 914-241-1050
90 S Bedford Rd, Mount Kisco, 914-241-1050

Choudhury, Muhammad S. (5 mentions)
FMS-Bangladesh, 1972 *Certification:* Urology
19 Bradhurst Ave #1900, Hawthorne, 914-493-7617

D'Esposito, Robert Francis (4 mentions)
FMS-Italy, 1971 *Certification:* Urology
601 Franklin Ave #300, Garden City, 516-742-3200

Dillon, Robert W. (11 mentions)
New York Med Coll, 1973 *Certification:* Urology
58 E 79th St, New York, 212-794-9000

Fracchia, John Alfred (5 mentions)
New Jersey Med Sch, 1973 *Certification:* Urology
245 E 54th St, New York, 212-772-3686

Glassman, Charles Norman (11 mentions)
Tufts U, 1973 *Certification:* Urology
170 Maple Ave #104, White Plains, 914-949-7556

Gluck, Robert William (4 mentions)
SUNY-Downstate Med Coll, 1982 *Certification:* Urology
120 E 34th St, New York, 212-686-1140

Gribetz, Michael Elliot (11 mentions)
Albert Einstein Coll of Med, 1973 *Certification:* Urology
1155 Park Ave, New York, 212-831-1300

Hall, Simon J. (6 mentions)
Columbia U, 1988 *Certification:* Urology
5 E 98th St, New York, 212-241-4812

Hershman, Jack Ira (4 mentions)
Mount Sinai Sch of Med, 1981 *Certification:* Urology
777 N Broadway #309, North Tarrytown, 914-631-3331
132 Maple St, Croton-on-Hudson, 914-271-9331
101 S Bedford Rd #413, Mount Kisco, 914-242-1666

Housman, Arno D. (4 mentions)
SUNY-Downstate Med Coll, 1980 *Certification:* Urology
325 S Highland Ave, Briarcliff, 914-941-0617

Kavoussi, Louis Raphael (4 mentions)
U of Buffalo, 1983 *Certification:* Urology
450 Lakeville Rd, New Hyde Park, 516-734-8500

Kim, Albert Nelson (5 mentions)
Columbia U, 1985 *Certification:* Urology
2500 Nesconset Hwy Bldg 21 #76, Stony Brook, 631-751-4000

Kirschenbaum, Alexander (9 mentions)
Mount Sinai Sch of Med, 1980 *Certification:* Urology
58 E 79th St #A, New York, 646-422-0926

Layne, Jeffrey Todd (5 mentions)
Stony Brook U, 1989 *Certification:* Urology
1181 Old Country Rd #1, Plainview, 516-933-6060

Lepor, Herbert (5 mentions)
Johns Hopkins U, 1979 *Certification:* Urology
150 E 32nd St, New York, 646-825-6300

Lerner, Seth Edward (8 mentions)
SUNY-Downstate Med Coll, 1988 *Certification:* Urology
170 Maple Ave #104, White Plains, 914-949-7556

Lieberman, Elliott Rafael (5 mentions)
SUNY-Downstate Med Coll, 1976 *Certification:* Urology
875 Old Country Rd #301, Plainview, 516-931-1710

Lowe, Franklin Charles (5 mentions)
Columbia U, 1979 *Certification:* Urology
425 W 59th St, New York, 212-523-7790
1090 Amsterdam Ave #7-G, New York, 212-523-2326

Lumerman, Jeffrey Howard (4 mentions)
Albert Einstein Coll of Med, 1993 *Certification:* Urology
601 Franklin Ave, Garden City, 516-742-3200
2 Prohealth Plaza 1st Fl, Lake Success, 516-622-6110

Luntz, Robert Kevin (5 mentions)
Cornell U, 1992 *Certification:* Urology
875 Old Country Rd #301, Plainview, 516-931-1710

Lynn, Howard S. (6 mentions)
Albany Med Coll, 1984 *Certification:* Urology
373 Route 111 #7, Smithtown, 631-360-7450

Mashioff, Robert Harold (5 mentions)
Kansas U Coll of Osteopathic Med, 1970
4100 Duff Pl, Seaford, 516-520-8080

McGovern, Thomas Patrick (6 mentions)
Cornell U, 1974 *Certification:* Urology
927 5th Ave, New York, 212-772-7411

McKiernan, James Michael (4 mentions)
Columbia U, 1993 *Certification:* Urology
161 Fort Washington Ave, New York, 212-305-5201

Mills, Carl (7 mentions)
George Washington U, 1975 *Certification:* Urology
250 Patchogue Yaphank Rd, East Patchogue, 631-475-5051
635 Belle Terre Rd #202, Port Jefferson, 631-473-1058

Muecke, Edward Carl (4 mentions)
Cornell U, 1957 *Certification:* Urology
880 5th Ave, New York, 212-570-6800

Munkelwitz, Robert A. (5 mentions)
Stony Brook U, 1991 *Certification:* Urology
117 Hampton Rd, Southampton, 631-287-8600

Nagler, Harris Mark (4 mentions)
Temple U, 1975 *Certification:* Urology
10 Union Sq E #3A, New York, 212-844-8900

Owens, George Francis (4 mentions)
New York Med Coll, 1979 *Certification:* Urology
311 North St #201, White Plains, 914-946-1406

Palese, Michael Alexander (5 mentions)
Mount Sinai Sch of Med, 1997 *Certification:* Urology
5 E 98th St, New York, 212-241-7437

Palmer, Lane Stuart (4 mentions)
Albert Einstein Coll of Med, 1989
Certification: Pediatric Urology, Urology
1999 Marcus Ave #M-18, Lake Success, 516-466-6953

Reda, Edward F. (5 mentions)
FMS-Mexico, 1976 *Certification:* Urology
150 White Plains Rd #306, Tarrytown, 914-493-8628

Riechers, Roger Neil (6 mentions)
New York U, 1968 *Certification:* Urology
110 S Bedford Rd, Mount Kisco, 914-242-1520

Samadi, David Babak (4 mentions)
Stony Brook U, 1994 *Certification:* Urology
625 Madison Ave, New York, 212-241-8779
1 Gustave L Levy Pl, New York, 212-241-8779

Schiff, Jonathan David (4 mentions)
Mount Sinai Sch of Med, 1999 *Certification:* Urology
1120 Park Ave, New York, 212-996-6660

Schlussel, Richard N. (4 mentions)
Certification: Urology
3959 Broadway, New York, 212-305-1114

Sigler, Lawrence Jeffrey (4 mentions)
New York Med Coll, 1980 *Certification:* Urology
26 Pondfield Rd W, Bronxville, 914-793-1200

Sosa, R. Ernest (6 mentions)
Cornell U, 1978 *Certification:* Urology
880 5th Ave, New York, 212-535-1950

Steckel, Joph (20 mentions)
Cornell U, 1986 *Certification:* Urology
450 Lakeville Rd, New Hyde Park, 516-734-8500

Taneja, Samir Sagar (7 mentions)
Northwestern U, 1990 *Certification:* Urology
150 E 32nd St, New York, 646-825-6300

Trauzzi, Stephen John (5 mentions)
Georgetown U, 1988 *Certification:* Urology
120 Warren St, New Rochelle, 914-636-2121

Usher, Sol Martin (6 mentions)
New York U, 1972 *Certification:* Urology
12 Greenridge Ave, White Plains, 914-682-7477
3333 Henry Hudson Pkwy Apt 1-H, Bronx, 718-543-0990

Vapnek, Jonathan Mark (8 mentions)
U of California-San Diego, 1986 *Certification:* Urology
229 E 79th St #1-A, New York, 212-717-9500

Vaughan, Edwin D., Jr. (5 mentions)
U of Virginia, 1965 *Certification:* Urology
525 E 68th St #900, New York, 212-746-5480

Vascular Surgery

Adelman, Mark Alan (15 mentions)
New York U, 1985 *Certification:* Surgery, Vascular Surgery
530 1st Ave #6F, New York, 212-263-7311

Babu, Sateesh C. (16 mentions)
FMS-India, 1969 *Certification:* Vascular Surgery
19 Bradhurst Ave #700, Hawthorne, 914-593-1200

Benvenisty, Alan I. (7 mentions)
Certification: Surgery, Vascular Surgery
1090 Amsterdam Ave 12th Fl, New York, 212-523-4700

Giangola, Gary (11 mentions)
New York U, 1980 *Certification:* Vascular Surgery
530 1st Ave #6-A, New York, 718-226-6800
425 W 59th St Fl 7B, New York, 718-226-6800
130 E 77th St, New York, 718-226-6800
256 Mason Ave, New York, 718-226-6800

Green, Richard Michael (8 mentions)
U of Rochester, 1970 *Certification:* Vascular Surgery
130 E 77th St, New York, 212-434-3420

Harrington, Elizabeth R. B. (14 mentions)
New York Med Coll, 1975 *Certification:* Surgery, Vascular Surgery
1225 Park Ave #1D, New York, 212-876-7400

Hines, George L. (18 mentions)
Boston U, 1969 *Certification:* Thoracic Surgery, Vascular Surgery
120 Mineola Blvd #300, Mineola, 516-663-4400

Kent, Kenneth Craig (8 mentions)
U of California-San Francisco, 1981
Certification: Surgery, Vascular Surgery
525 E 68th St #M014, New York, 212-746-5192

Licalzi, Luke King (7 mentions)
Albany Med Coll, 1975 *Certification:* Surgery
77 N Centre Ave #208, Rockville Centre, 516-764-5455

Marin, Michael L. (11 mentions)
Mount Sinai Sch of Med, 1984 *Certification:* Surgery
5 E 98th St, New York, 212-241-7646

Nowygrod, Roman (8 mentions)
Columbia U, 1970 *Certification:* Surgery, Vascular Surgery
161 Fort Washington Ave, New York, 212-305-1165

Pollina, Robert Michael (7 mentions)
SUNY-Downstate Med Coll, 1988 *Certification:* Vascular Surgery
1110 Hallock Ave, Port Jefferson Station, 631-476-9100
152 N Ocean Ave, Patchogue, 631-207-0400

Riles, Thomas Stewart (7 mentions)
Baylor U, 1969 *Certification:* Vascular Surgery
530 1st Ave #6F, New York, 212-263-7311

Rosalsky Rockman, Caron (7 mentions)
New York U, 1990 *Certification:* Surgery, Vascular Surgery
530 1st Ave #6F, New York, 212-263-7311

Schanzer, Harry (7 mentions)
FMS-Chile, 1968 *Certification:* Vascular Surgery
993 Park Ave, New York, 212-396-1254

Schwartz, Kenneth Stuart (8 mentions)
Albert Einstein Coll of Med, 1977 *Certification:* Surgery
1 Theall Rd, Rye, 914-723-7737

Todd, George Joseph (9 mentions)
Pennsylvania State U, 1974
Certification: Surgery, Vascular Surgery
1000 10th Ave, New York, 212-523-7481

Rochester Area
Including Monroe County

Allergy/Immunology

Condemi, John Joseph (20 mentions)
Albany Med Coll, 1957
Certification: Allergy & Immunology, Internal Medicine
300 Meridian Ctr #305, Rochester, 716-442-0150

Looney, Richard John (9 mentions)
U of Rochester, 1976 *Certification:* Allergy & Immunology,
Infectious Disease, Internal Medicine, Rheumatology
4901 Lac De Ville Blvd #240, Rochester, 585-341-7900

Anesthesiology

Cortese, Dominick Anthony (3 mentions)
Mount Sinai Sch of Med, 1985 *Certification:* Anesthesiology
1425 Portland Ave, Rochester, 585-922-4159

McCrumb, Fred Rodgers (4 mentions)
U of Rochester, 1992 *Certification:* Anesthesiology
601 Elmwood Ave, Rochester, 585-341-6269

Papadakos, Peter John (3 mentions)
Mount Sinai Sch of Med, 1983
Certification: Anesthesiology, Critical Care Medicine
601 Elmwood Ave, Rochester, 585-275-2141

Potenza, Vito John (3 mentions)
U of Rochester, 1984 *Certification:* Anesthesiology
1555 Long Pond Rd, Rochester, 585-723-7000

Robotham, James Lawrence (3 mentions)
Boston U, 1970 *Certification:* Anesthesiology, Pediatrics
601 Elmwood Ave, Rochester, 585-275-2141

Sabnis, Lata Ulhas (5 mentions)
FMS-India, 1974 *Certification:* Anesthesiology
601 Elmwood Ave, Rochester, 585-275-2141

Zigarowicz, Georgianne (4 mentions)
U of Buffalo, 1981 *Certification:* Anesthesiology
1425 Portland Ave, Rochester, 585-922-4159

Cardiac Surgery

Kirshner, Ronald Lee (13 mentions)
Temple U, 1978 *Certification:* Thoracic Surgery
1415 Portland Ave #240, Rochester, 585-544-6550

Knight, Peter Arnold (13 mentions)
New York Med Coll, 1980 *Certification:* Thoracic Surgery
601 Elmwood Ave, Rochester, 585-275-5384

Cardiology

Gacioch, Gerald Matthew (5 mentions)
Johns Hopkins U, 1984 *Certification:* Cardiovascular
Disease, Internal Medicine, Interventional Cardiology
1445 Portland Ave #104, Rochester, 585-338-2700

Hsi, David Hao (5 mentions)
FMS-China, 1983
Certification: Cardiovascular Disease, Internal Medicine
1561 Long Pond Rd #401, Rochester, 585-723-7872

Pancio, George, II (6 mentions)
U of Buffalo, 1992 *Certification:* Cardiovascular Disease
2365 S Clinton Ave #100, Rochester, 585-442-5320

Rao, Krishna M. D. (5 mentions)
FMS-India, 1981 *Certification:* Cardiovascular Disease
1445 Portland Ave #104, Rochester, 585-338-2700

Varon, Maurice Edward (14 mentions)
Mount Sinai Sch of Med, 1987
Certification: Cardiovascular Disease, Internal Medicine
2365 Clinton Ave S #100, Rochester, 585-442-5320

Williford, Daniel James (4 mentions)
Georgetown U, 1983
Certification: Cardiovascular Disease, Internal Medicine
2365 Clinton Ave S #100, Rochester, 585-442-5320
38 E South St, Geneseo, 585-243-5790

Dermatology

Brooks, Walter S. (6 mentions)
U of Rochester, 1982 *Certification:* Dermatology
730 Weiland Rd, Rochester, 585-719-9600

Brown, Marc David (8 mentions)
Georgetown U, 1979 *Certification:* Dermatology
601 Elmwood Ave #697, Rochester, 585-275-9208

Holm, Allison Leslie (8 mentions)
U of Rochester, 1987
Certification: Dermatology, Pediatric Dermatology
30 N Union St #105, Rochester, 585-232-8940

Xenias, Stephen John (8 mentions)
U of Rochester, 1977 *Certification:* Dermatology
1716 Ridge Rd E, Rochester, 585-544-7320
1716 E Ridge Rd, Rochester, 585-544-7320

Emergency Medicine

Bazarian, Jeffrey John (3 mentions)
U of Rochester, 1987 *Certification:* Internal Medicine
601 Elmwood Ave, Rochester, 585-341-3015

Conners, Gregory Paul (5 mentions)
Stony Brook U, 1989
Certification: Pediatric Emergency Medicine, Pediatrics
601 Elmwood Ave #655, Rochester, 585-463-2942

Dailey, Brian Dennison (6 mentions)
Certification: Emergency Medicine
1425 Portland Ave, Rochester, 585-922-4000

Pasternack, Joel (3 mentions)
U of Rochester, 1980 *Certification:* Emergency Medicine
601 Elmwood Ave #655, Rochester, 585-463-2902

Sullivan, Pamela Cori (3 mentions)
Med Coll of Pennsylvania, 1990
1425 Portland Ave, Rochester, 585-922-4000

Wolfe, Steven Marc (5 mentions)
New York Coll of Osteopathic Med, 1986
Certification: Internal Medicine
156 West Ave, Brockport, 585-395-6095

Endocrinology

Bingham, Robert James (9 mentions)
Johns Hopkins U, 1993 *Certification:* Endocrinology,
Diabetes, and Metabolism, Internal Medicine
224 Alexander St #200, Rochester, 585-922-8400

Freedman, Zachary Roy (12 mentions)
U of Rochester, 1974
Certification: Endocrinology and Metabolism, Internal Medicine
224 Alexander St #200, Rochester, 585-922-8400

Heinig, Robert Eugene (21 mentions)
Oregon Health Sciences U, 1969 *Certification:* Endocrinology
and Metabolism, Internal Medicine, Nephrology
1425 Portland Ave, Rochester, 716-922-4344

Jospe, Nicholas (6 mentions)
FMS-Belgium, 1981
Certification: Pediatric Endocrinology, Pediatrics
601 Elmwood Ave, Rochester, 585-274-7744

Wittlin, Steven David (7 mentions)
FMS-Israel, 1975
Certification: Endocrinology and Metabolism, Internal Medicine
601 Elmwood Ave, Rochester, 585-275-2901

Family Practice *(see note on page 9)*

Campbell, Thomas Lothrop (4 mentions)
Harvard U, 1979 *Certification:* Family Medicine
777 Clinton Ave S, Rochester, 585-279-4800

Newman, David Michael (3 mentions)
Case Western Reserve U, 1980 *Certification:* Family Medicine
4079 Lake Rd N, Brockport, 585-637-0151

Zoghlin, Benson Louis (3 mentions)
U of Buffalo, 1984 *Certification:* Family Medicine
279 East Ave, Hilton, 585-392-9100

Gastroenterology

Baratta, Anthony Vincent (5 mentions)
U of Rochester, 1987 *Certification:* Gastroenterology
1065 Senator Keating Blvd #220, Rochester, 585-467-0650

Casey, Kevin John (8 mentions)
Case Western Reserve U, 1987
Certification: Gastroenterology, Internal Medicine
1425 Portland Ave, Rochester, 585-922-4136

Dunnigan, Karin Joan (5 mentions)
U of Rochester, 1976
Certification: Gastroenterology, Internal Medicine
1425 Portland Ave, Rochester, 585-922-4136

Hsu, Joseph Jue-Teng (6 mentions)
U of Maryland, 1986
Certification: Gastroenterology, Internal Medicine
1065 Senator Keating Blvd #220, Rochester, 585-271-8860

General Surgery

Caldwell, Christopher B. (11 mentions)
U of Vermont, 1982 *Certification:* Surgery
10 Hagen Dr #240, Rochester, 585-383-8830

Chang, Vincent Dawshuih (20 mentions)
U of Chicago, 1983 *Certification:* Surgery
1299 Portland Ave #3, Rochester, 585-922-5520

Doerr, Ralph Joseph (3 mentions)
SUNY-Downstate Med Coll, 1981 *Certification:* Surgery
1415 Portland Ave #245, Rochester, 585-922-4715

George, Robert William (3 mentions)
U of Rochester, 1969 *Certification:* Surgery
1415 Portland Ave #155, Rochester, 585-342-0140

Hirokawa, Theodore Irino (4 mentions)
U of Rochester, 1974 *Certification:* Surgery
990 South Ave #201, Rochester, 585-473-1580

Johnson, Joseph Andrew (7 mentions)
New York Med Coll, 1988 *Certification:* Surgery
1000 South Ave, Rochester, 585-341-0366

Nadaraja, Nagendra (7 mentions)
FMS-Sri Lanka, 1963 *Certification:* Surgery
1561 Long Pond Rd #107, Rochester, 585-723-8686

O'Malley, William E. (4 mentions)
Certification: Surgery
1000 South Ave, Rochester, 585-341-6543

Oates, Theodore Kensell (4 mentions)
Duke U, 1971 *Certification:* Surgery
1415 Portland Ave #155, Rochester, 585-342-0140

Risolo, John Philip (4 mentions)
SUNY-Upstate Med U, 1994 *Certification:* Surgery
1770 Long Pond Rd, Rochester, 585-247-4770

Schoeniger, Luke Otto (5 mentions)
New York U, 1988 *Certification:* Surgery
601 Elmwood Ave, Rochester, 585-273-4713
2400 S Clinton Ave, Rochester, 585-273-4713

Geriatrics

Golden, Reynold Stephen (5 mentions)
SUNY-Upstate Med U, 1962
Certification: Family Medicine, Internal Medicine
105 Canal Landing Blvd #1, Rochester, 585-368-4050

Hall, William John (4 mentions)
U of Michigan, 1965
Certification: Internal Medicine, Pulmonary Disease
1000 South Ave, Rochester, 585-341-6202

Katz, Paul Richard (4 mentions)
U of Michigan, 1977
Certification: Geriatric Medicine, Internal Medicine
435 E Henrietta Rd, Rochester, 585-760-6350

McCann, Robert Michael (6 mentions)
SUNY-Upstate Med U, 1982
Certification: Geriatric Medicine, Internal Medicine
1000 South Ave, Rochester, 585-341-6770

Mittereder, Richard F. (5 mentions)
U of Pittsburgh, 1979
Certification: Family Medicine, Geriatric Medicine
105 Canal Landing Blvd #1, Rochester, 585-581-6000

Rich, Steven Albert (3 mentions)
U of Rochester, 1984
Certification: Geriatric Medicine, Internal Medicine
1415 Portland Ave, Rochester, 585-922-0390

Hematology/Oncology

Friedberg, Jonathan W. (4 mentions)
Harvard U, 1994 *Certification:* Hematology, Medical Oncology
601 Elmwood Ave, Rochester, 585-275-5823

Korones, David Nathan (4 mentions)
Vanderbilt U, 1983
Certification: Pediatric Hematology-Oncology, Pediatrics
601 Elmwood Ave #777, Rochester, 585-275-7787

Kouides, Peter Andrew (13 mentions)
SUNY-Upstate Med U, 1986
Certification: Hematology, Internal Medicine, Medical Oncology
1425 Portland Ave, Rochester, 585-922-4020

Phatak, Pradyumna D. (7 mentions)
FMS-India, 1981
Certification: Hematology, Internal Medicine, Medical Oncology
1425 Portland Ave, Rochester, 585-922-4020

Sham, Ronald Lewis (4 mentions)
Pennsylvania State U, 1984
Certification: Hematology, Internal Medicine
1425 Portland Ave, Rochester, 585-922-4020

Smith, Brian Drew (4 mentions)
U of Rochester, 1978
Certification: Hematology, Internal Medicine
1000 South Ave, Rochester, 585-341-8238

Woodlock, Timothy James (7 mentions)
U of Rochester, 1980
Certification: Hematology, Internal Medicine, Medical Oncology
89 Genesee St 1st Fl, Rochester, 585-368-3381
1561 Long Pond Rd #110, Rochester, 585-368-3381

Infectious Disease

Betts, Robert Frank (15 mentions)
U of Rochester, 1964 *Certification:* Internal Medicine
601 Elmwood Ave #689, Rochester, 585-275-5871

Chessin, Lawrence Norman (6 mentions)
New York U, 1963
222 Alexander St #3000, Rochester, 585-922-8700

El-Daher, Nayef Torki M. (7 mentions)
FMS-Egypt, 1977
Certification: Infectious Disease, Internal Medicine
89 Genesse St #3-K, Rochester, 585-368-3506

Mock, David Jay (4 mentions)
U of Michigan, 1978
Certification: Infectious Disease, Internal Medicine
2 Coulter Rd, Clifton Springs, 315-462-9561

Walsh, Edward E. (6 mentions)
SUNY-Downstate Med Coll, 1974
Certification: Infectious Disease, Internal Medicine
1425 Portland Ave, Rochester, 585-922-4003

Infertility

Hoeger, Kathleen M. (8 mentions)
Jefferson Med Coll, 1988 *Certification:* Obstetrics &
 Gynecology, Reproductive Endocrinology/Infertility
601 Elmwood Ave #AC5, Rochester, 585-275-7891
500 Red Creek Dr #220, Rochester, 585-487-3378

Lewis, Vivian (4 mentions)
Columbia U, 1977 *Certification:* Obstetrics & Gynecology,
 Reproductive Endocrinology/Infertility
601 Elmwood Ave #668, Rochester, 585-275-7891
500 Red Creek Dr #220, Rochester, 585-487-3378

Phipps, William Revelle (4 mentions)
Johns Hopkins U, 1980 *Certification:* Obstetrics &
 Gynecology, Reproductive Endocrinology/Infertility
601 Elmwood Ave #668, Rochester, 585-275-7891
500 Red Creek Dr #220, Rochester, 585-487-3378

Queenan, John Thomas, Jr. (4 mentions)
U of Pennsylvania, 1988 *Certification:* Obstetrics &
 Gynecology, Reproductive Endocrinology/Infertility
601 Elmwood Ave #661, Rochester, 585-275-7891
500 Redcreek Dr #220, Rochester, 585-487-3378

Internal Medicine *(see note on page 9)*

Berliant, Marc Norman (5 mentions)
U of Illinois, 1977 *Certification:* Internal Medicine
400 White Spruce Blvd #A, Rochester, 585-427-9950

Constantino, Richard Samuel (3 mentions)
U of Rochester, 1978 *Certification:* Internal Medicine
1445 Portland Ave #302, Rochester, 585-544-0830

Genier, John Leo (4 mentions)
U of Rochester, 1989 *Certification:* Internal Medicine
420 Cross Keys Office Park, Fairport, 585-223-4620

Iacobucci, James Joseph (3 mentions)
Robert W Johnson Med Sch, 1996
Certification: Internal Medicine
2030 Monroe Ave, Rochester, 585-241-9910

Kerper, Robert Michael (6 mentions)
Temple U, 1984 *Certification:* Internal Medicine
26 S Goodman St, Rochester, 585-244-0674

Kurnath, Joseph F. (3 mentions)
New Jersey Med Sch, 1979
Certification: Geriatric Medicine, Internal Medicine
1655 Elmwood Ave #125, Rochester, 585-641-0400
30 Hagen Dr #310, Rochester, 585-641-0400

Magglo, Russell Philip (4 mentions)
U of Rochester, 1984
125 Lattimore Rd #256, Rochester, 585-271-5250

Mayewski, Raymond John (3 mentions)
Temple U, 1972
Certification: Internal Medicine, Pulmonary Disease
601 Elmwood Ave #612, Rochester, 585-275-4786

Papa, Louis John, Jr. (4 mentions)
Stony Brook U, 1989 *Certification:* Internal Medicine
2400 Clinton Ave S #230, Rochester, 585-341-7210

Rolls, William Paul (3 mentions)
U of Rochester, 1980 *Certification:* Internal Medicine
1850 E Ridge Rd #11, Rochester, 585-336-9370

Suozzi, Anthony Joseph (3 mentions)
U of Rochester, 1983 *Certification:* Internal Medicine
2400 Clinton Ave S #110, Rochester, 585-341-7139

Wilmot, Patrick William (3 mentions)
U of Rochester, 1991 *Certification:* Internal Medicine
2400 Clinton Ave S #110, Rochester, 585-271-0671

Nephrology

Bernstein, Paul Levitan (5 mentions)
Albert Einstein Coll of Med, 1988
Certification: Internal Medicine, Nephrology
1425 Portland Ave, Rochester, 585-922-4798
370 Ridge Rd E #20, Rochester, 585-922-0400

Choudhry, Wajid Mahmood (4 mentions)
FMS-Pakistan, 1985 *Certification:* Internal Medicine, Nephrology
1561 Long Pond Rd #302, Rochester, 585-723-1120

Hix, John Kevin (4 mentions)
Ohio State U, 1999 *Certification:* Internal Medicine, Nephrology
370 Ridge Rd E #20, Rochester, 585-922-0400

Jain, Vijay K. (5 mentions)
FMS-India, 1971 *Certification:* Nephrology
1561 Long Pond Rd #302, Rochester, 585-723-1120

Monk, Rebeca Denise (5 mentions)
Columbia U, 1988 *Certification:* Internal Medicine, Nephrology
601 Elmwood Ave, Rochester, 585-275-4517

Schiff, Melissa Jeanne (4 mentions)
Boston U, 1978 *Certification:* Internal Medicine, Nephrology
1000 South Ave, Rochester, 585-341-6895
335 Mount Vernon Ave, Rochester, 585-341-6896

Silver, Stephen Mark (11 mentions)
SUNY-Upstate Med U, 1980
Certification: Internal Medicine, Nephrology
1425 Portland Ave, Rochester, 585-922-4707

Neurological Surgery

Maurer, Paul Kurt (21 mentions)
U of Rochester, 1980 *Certification:* Neurological Surgery
1401 Stone Rd #303, Rochester, 585-581-6790

Maxwell, James Thomas (20 mentions)
Columbia U, 1975 *Certification:* Neurological Surgery
1445 Portland Ave #304, Rochester, 585-342-7170

Pilcher, Webster H. (11 mentions)
U of Rochester, 1983 *Certification:* Neurological Surgery
601 Elmwood Ave #670, Rochester, 585-275-7944

Neurology

Barbano, Richard L. (4 mentions)
Albert Einstein Coll of Med, 1989 *Certification:* Neurology
601 Elmwood Ave, Rochester, 585-341-7500
919 Westfall Rd #220, Rochester, 585-341-7500

Griggs, Robert Charles (3 mentions)
U of Pennsylvania, 1964
Certification: Internal Medicine, Neurology, Vascular Neurology
601 Elmwood Ave, Rochester, 585-275-2559

Lesser, Harold (5 mentions)
U of Rochester, 1989 *Certification:* Neurology
1415 Portland Ave #480, Rochester, 585-544-7979

Marzulo, David Charles (4 mentions)
Midwestern U Chicago Coll of Osteopathic Med, 1980
Certification: Neurology
30 Erie Canal Dr #G, Rochester, 585-227-3950

O'Sullivan, John Alfred (4 mentions)
FMS-Ireland, 1962 *Certification:* Neurology
103 Canal Landing Blvd, Rochester, 585-723-7972

Pettee, Allen D., II (4 mentions)
SUNY-Upstate Med U, 1991
Certification: Clinical Neurophysiology, Neurology
2101 Lac De Ville Blvd #1, Rochester, 585-546-3265

Samkoff, Lawrence Mark (3 mentions)
New York Med Coll, 1984 *Certification:* Neurology
1425 Portland Ave, Rochester, 585-922-4371
601 Elmwood Ave #605, Rochester, 585-275-7854

Obstetrics/Gynecology

Eigg, Marc Howard (4 mentions)
SUNY-Upstate Med U, 1992 *Certification:* Obstetrics & Gynecology
3101 Ridge Rd W #D, Rochester, 585-225-1580
1682 Empire Blvd #200, Webster, 585-671-6790

Jones, Albert Pierce, Jr. (4 mentions)
Med U of South Carolina, 1975
Certification: Obstetrics & Gynecology
995 Senator Keating Blvd #340, Rochester, 585-368-4455

Scibetta, Joseph James (5 mentions)
U of Rochester, 1964 *Certification:* Obstetrics & Gynecology
125 Lattimore Rd #200, Rochester, 585-461-5940

Surgeon, Coral L. (4 mentions)
U of Buffalo, 1980 *Certification:* Obstetrics & Gynecology
1815 S Clinton Ave #610, Rochester, 585-244-3430
1630 Empire Blvd #2, Webster, 585-787-8480

Ophthalmology

Asselin, Dennis Arthur (6 mentions)
U of Rochester, 1981
Certification: Internal Medicine, Ophthalmology
2301 Lac De Ville Blvd, Rochester, 585-244-0332
1016 Elmgrove Rd, Rochester, 585-429-5330

Feldon, Steven Elliott (6 mentions)
Albert Einstein Coll of Med, 1973 *Certification:* Ophthalmology
210 Crittenden Blvd, Rochester, 585-273-3937

Gruber, Alan Howard (3 mentions)
U of Rochester, 1980 *Certification:* Ophthalmology
2100 Clinton Ave S, Rochester, 585-244-6011
2300 W Ridge Rd, Rochester, 585-225-1890

Markowitz, Gary David (3 mentions)
Columbia U, 1989 *Certification:* Ophthalmology
2301 Lac De Ville Blvd, Rochester, 585-244-0332
1016 Elmgrove Rd, Rochester, 585-429-5330

Sterns, Gwen Kunken (5 mentions)
Med Coll of Pennsylvania, 1970 *Certification:* Ophthalmology
1425 Portland Ave, Rochester, 585-922-4794

Tingley, Donald Howard (4 mentions)
U of Buffalo, 1985 *Certification:* Ophthalmology
1015 Ridge Rd, Webster, 585-872-1300

Orthopedics

Baumhauer, Judith Ford (4 mentions)
U of Vermont, 1989 *Certification:* Orthopaedic Surgery
601 Elmwood Ave #665, Rochester, 585-275-5933
4901 Lac De Ville Blvd, Rochester, 585-275-5169

Kates, Stephen Lloyd (4 mentions)
Northwestern U, 1984 *Certification:* Orthopaedic Surgery
4901 Lac Deville Blvd Bldg D, Rochester, 585-275-5321
1000 South Ave, Rochester, 585-275-5321

Klotz, Michael James (5 mentions)
Columbia U, 1990 *Certification:* Orthopaedic Surgery
125 Red Creek Dr #205, Rochester, 585-321-0340

Lewish, Gregory Daniel (7 mentions)
U of Virginia, 1977 *Certification:* Orthopaedic Surgery
2211 Lyell Ave #7, Rochester, 585-429-6440

Maloney, Michael Dennis (6 mentions)
Georgetown U, 1992 *Certification:* Orthopaedic Surgery
601 Elmwood Ave #665, Rochester, 585-275-7379

Rashid, Rola Husayn (5 mentions)
SUNY-Upstate Med U, 1997 *Certification:* Orthopaedic Surgery
20 Hagen Dr, Rochester, 585-218-9651

Tanner, Edward Clein, III (7 mentions)
U of Rochester, 1976 *Certification:* Orthopaedic Surgery
1445 Portland Ave #210, Rochester, 585-266-2010

Otorhinolaryngology

Coniglio, John Urban (14 mentions)
U of Rochester, 1985 *Certification:* Otolaryngology
1065 Senator Keating Blvd #240, Rochester, 585-256-3550

Hengerer, Arthur Stewart (8 mentions)
Albany Med Coll, 1968 *Certification:* Otolaryngology
2365 Clinton Ave S #200, Rochester, 585-758-5700

Mulbury, Peter Edwin (11 mentions)
U of Rochester, 1970 *Certification:* Otolaryngology
2561 Lac De Ville Blvd #100, Rochester, 585-442-4200
1415 Portland Ave #200, Rochester, 585-442-4200

Pain Medicine

Dotson, Eric David (4 mentions)
U of Vermont, 1992 *Certification:* Anesthesiology, Pain Medicine
1425 Portland Ave, Rochester, 585-922-4159

Nemani, Ajai K. (4 mentions)
Certification: Anesthesiology, Pain Medicine
30 Hagen Dr #230, Rochester, 585-899-3450
2619 Culver Rd #2, Rochester, 585-899-3450

Thanik, Jaimala (7 mentions)
FMS-India, 1970 *Certification:* Anesthesiology
990 South Ave #205, Rochester, 585-244-7748

Pathology

Powers, James (3 mentions)
Certification: Anatomic Pathology, Neuropathology
601 Elmwood Ave, Rochester, 585-275-3191

Riedy, Dawn Kathleen (4 mentions)
Certification: Anatomic Pathology, Cytopathology
1425 Portland Ave, Rochester, 585-922-4121

Ryan, Charlotte K. (3 mentions)
Certification: Anatomic Pathology
601 Elmwood Ave, Rochester, 585-275-3191

Ryan, Daniel (5 mentions)
Certification: Anatomic Pathology & Clinical Pathology
601 Elmwood Ave, Rochester, 585-275-3191

Pediatrics *(see note on page 9)*

Francis, Anne B. (4 mentions)
U of Pittsburgh, 1973 *Certification:* Pediatrics
125 Lattimore Rd, Rochester, 585-244-9720
1000 Pittsford Victor Rd, Pittsford, 585-381-3780

Lewis, Edward David (5 mentions)
U of Rochester, 1978 *Certification:* Pediatrics
880 Westfall Rd #E, Rochester, 585-442-1421

Schor, Nina F. (4 mentions)
Certification: Neurology with Special Qualifications in Child Neurology, Pediatrics
601 Elmwood Ave #777, Rochester, 585-275-4673

Plastic Surgery

Girotto, John Alan (7 mentions)
Washington U, 1994 *Certification:* Plastic Surgery
601 Elmwood Ave, Rochester, 585-275-1000
995 Senator Keating Blvd #205, Rochester, 585-275-1000

Pennino, Ralph Paul (7 mentions)
Georgetown U, 1979
Certification: Plastic Surgery, Surgery of the Hand
1445 Portland Ave #G01, Rochester, 585-922-5840
10 Hagen Dr #310, Rochester, 585-922-5840

Vega, Stephen J. (7 mentions)
U of Pennsylvania, 1999 *Certification:* Plastic Surgery
601 Elmwood Ave #661, Rochester, 585-275-1000
995 Senator Keating Blvd #205, Rochester, 585-275-1000

Pulmonary Disease

Finigan, Michael Moran (4 mentions)
U of Rochester, 1959
Certification: Internal Medicine, Pulmonary Disease
400 Red Creek Dr #110, Rochester, 585-486-0147

Lee, David Kuo-Ping (4 mentions)
Columbia U, 1979 *Certification:* Critical Care Medicine, Internal Medicine, Pulmonary Disease
1425 Portland Ave, Rochester, 585-922-4409

Levy, Paul Christopher (4 mentions)
Ohio State U, 1981 *Certification:* Critical Care Medicine, Internal Medicine, Pulmonary Disease
601 Elmwood Ave #692, Rochester, 585-275-4861

Swinburne, Andrew James (7 mentions)
SUNY-Upstate Med U, 1969
Certification: Internal Medicine, Pulmonary Disease
1425 Portland Ave, Rochester, 585-922-4409

Radiology—Diagnostic

Broder, Jonathan David (3 mentions)
U of Pittsburgh, 1995 *Certification:* Diagnostic Radiology, Vascular & Interventional Radiology
1415 Portland Ave, Rochester, 585-922-4000

Segal, Arthur Jay (4 mentions)
SUNY-Upstate Med U, 1968 *Certification:* Diagnostic Radiology
1415 Portland Ave #480, Rochester, 585-336-5000

Zinkin, Edward Bernard (7 mentions)
Albert Einstein Coll of Med, 1969
Certification: Diagnostic Radiology
1425 Portland Ave, Rochester, 585-336-5000

Radiology—Therapeutic

Atanas, Meri (5 mentions)
Tufts U, 1987 *Certification:* Radiation Oncology
1425 Portland Ave, Rochester, 585-922-4031

Broder, Jonathan David (3 mentions)
U of Pittsburgh, 1995 *Certification:* Diagnostic Radiology, Vascular & Interventional Radiology
1415 Portland Ave, Rochester, 585-922-4000

Okunieff, Paul Gershom (3 mentions)
Harvard U, 1982 *Certification:* Therapeutic Radiology
601 Elmwood Ave, Rochester, 585-275-2171

Schroeder, Keith Gerald (3 mentions)
U of Rochester, 1990 *Certification:* Diagnostic Radiology
2263 Clinton Ave S, Rochester, 585-241-6400
995 Senator Keating Blvd #100, Rochester, 585-241-6600

Rehabilitation

Dombovy, Mary Lynne (5 mentions)
Mayo Med Sch, 1981 *Certification:* Neurology, Physical Medicine & Rehabilitation, Vascular Neurology
89 Genesee St, Rochester, 585-368-3120
1555 Longpond Rd, Rochester, 585-723-7000

Poduri, Kanakadurga Rao (3 mentions)
FMS-India, 1970 *Certification:* Physical Medicine & Rehabilitation, Spinal Cord Injury Medicine
601 Elmwood Ave #664-urmc, Rochester, 585-275-3271

Rheumatology

Looney, Richard John (5 mentions)
U of Rochester, 1976 *Certification:* Allergy & Immunology, Infectious Disease, Internal Medicine, Rheumatology
4901 Lac De Ville Blvd #240, Rochester, 585-341-7900

Shlotzhauer, Tammi Louise (13 mentions)
U of Rochester, 1985
Certification: Internal Medicine, Rheumatology
500 Helendale Rd #90, Rochester, 585-288-0530

Thoracic Surgery

Watson, Thomas J. (16 mentions)
Certification: Surgery, Thoracic Surgery
601 Elmwood Ave, Rochester, 585-275-1509

Urology

Eichel, Louis (7 mentions)
U of Rochester, 1996 *Certification:* Urology
2615 Culver Rd #100, Rochester, 585-336-5320
2420 Ridgeway Ave, Rochester, 585-227-4000

Erturk, Erdal (6 mentions)
FMS-Turkey, 1979 *Certification:* Urology
601 Elmwood Ave, Rochester, 585-275-3690
2400 Clinton Ave S Bldg H #150, Rochester, 585-275-3690

Oleyourryk, Gregory John (8 mentions)
Cornell U, 1995 *Certification:* Urology
2615 Culver Rd #100, Rochester, 585-336-5320
80 West Ave, Brockport, 585-637-7200
2420 Ridgeway Ave, Rochester, 585-227-4000

Valvo, John Russell (6 mentions)
U of Buffalo, 1978 *Certification:* Urology
2615 Culver Rd #100, Rochester, 585-336-5320
80 West Ave, Brockport, 585-637-7200
2420 Ridgeway Ave, Rochester, 585-227-4000

Vascular Surgery

Illig, Karl Armistead (12 mentions)
Cornell U, 1988 *Certification:* Vascular Surgery
200 White Spruce Blvd, Rochester, 585-279-5100

Riggs, Patrick Nelson (9 mentions)
Wake Forest U, 1988 *Certification:* Vascular Surgery
1445 Portland Ave #108, Rochester, 585-922-5550

Svoboda, Jerry Joseph (10 mentions)
Hahnemann U, 1977 *Certification:* Surgery, Vascular Surgery
3525 Buffalo Rd, Rochester, 585-594-2000

North Carolina

Forsyth and Guilford Counties—page 343
Triangle Area—page 356
Mecklenburg County—page 349

Forsyth and Guilford Counties

Allergy/Immunology

Kozlow, Eric Jon (19 mentions)
Certification: Allergy & Immunology, Internal Medicine
120 Davis St, Asheboro, 336-629-5770
104 E Northwood St, Greensboro, 336-373-0936

Sane, Aneysa Christine (10 mentions)
Duke U, 1986
Certification: Allergy & Immunology, Pulmonary Disease
Wake Forest University Baptist Med Ctr, Winston-Salem,
   336-716-4649

Sharma, Ranjan (11 mentions)
East Carolina U, 1986 *Certification:* Allergy & Immunology
3201 Brassfield Rd #400, Greensboro, 336-282-2300
2280 S Church St #202, Burlington, 336-227-1901

Anesthesiology

Bertrand, Scott Alan (4 mentions)
Baylor U, 1973 *Certification:* Anesthesiology
1211 Virginia St, Greensboro, 336-272-0012

Calicott, Randy Wayne (3 mentions)
U of Tennessee, 1992 *Certification:* Anesthesiology
Wake Forest University Baptist Med Ctr, Winston-Salem,
   336-716-3988

Crews, David Allen (6 mentions)
U of North Carolina, 1981 *Certification:* Anesthesiology
3625 N Elm St #110A, Greensboro, 336-282-4840

Eisenach, James Conrad (3 mentions)
U of California-San Francisco, 1982 *Certification:* Anesthesiology
3333 Silas Creek Pkwy, Winston-Salem, 336-716-4498

Floyd, Herbert Mynatt (3 mentions)
Wake Forest U, 1971 *Certification:* Anesthesiology
Wake Forest University Baptist Med Ctr, Winston-Salem,
   336-716-2255

Frederick, Charles Eugene (3 mentions)
U of Iowa, 1981 *Certification:* Anesthesiology
3625 N Elm St #110A, Greensboro, 336-282-4840

Hatchett, John Franklin (4 mentions)
U of North Carolina, 1987 *Certification:* Anesthesiology
3625 N Elm St #110A, Greensboro, 336-282-4840

Jackson, Kyle Edward (3 mentions)
St Louis U, 1986 *Certification:* Anesthesiology
3625 N Elm St #110A, Greensboro, 336-282-4840

Joslin, David Coker (5 mentions)
U of North Carolina, 1985
Certification: Anesthesiology, Internal Medicine
3625 N Elm St #110A, Greensboro, 336-282-4840

Kennedy, Daniel Joseph (3 mentions)
U of Louisville, 1987 *Certification:* Anesthesiology, Critical
   Care Medicine, Internal Medicine
145 Kimel Park Dr #300, Winston-Salem, 336-768-3212

Olympio, Michael Allen (6 mentions)
U of Florida, 1982 *Certification:* Anesthesiology
Wake Forest University Baptist Med Ctr, Winston-Salem,
   336-716-2255

Potter, Patricia Lynn (3 mentions)
Wake Forest U, 1976 *Certification:* Anesthesiology
1211 Virginia St, Greensboro, 336-272-0012

Ririe, Douglas Gordon (3 mentions)
U of North Carolina, 1990 *Certification:* Anesthesiology
Wake Forest University Baptist Med Ctr, Winston-Salem,
   336-716-2255

Roy, Raymond Clyde (3 mentions)
Tulane U, 1974 *Certification:* Anesthesiology
Wake Forest University Baptist Med Ctr, Winston-Salem,
   336-716-4497

Royster, Roger Lee (3 mentions)
Wake Forest U, 1975
Certification: Anesthesiology, Cardiovascular Disease,
   Critical Care Medicine, Internal Medicine
300 S Hawthorne Rd, Winston-Salem, 336-716-2255

Singer, James Daniel (3 mentions)
U of North Carolina, 1989 *Certification:* Anesthesiology
3625 N Elm St #110-A, Greensboro, 336-282-4840

Smith, Timothy Earl (4 mentions)
Wake Forest U, 1994 *Certification:* Anesthesiology
Wake Forest University Baptist Med Ctr, Winston-Salem,
   336-716-2255

Speight, Kevin Lewis (4 mentions)
Med U of South Carolina, 1985
Certification: Anesthesiology, Pain Medicine
401 Ferndale Blvd, High Point, 336-882-2567

Tobin, Joseph R. (9 mentions)
SUNY-Upstate Med U, 1983 *Certification:* Anesthesiology,
   Pediatric Critical Care Medicine, Pediatrics
Wake Forest University Baptist Med Ctr, Winston-Salem,
   336-716-4498

Vance, John Hale (6 mentions)
Wake Forest U, 1982 *Certification:* Anesthesiology
401 Ferndale Blvd, High Point, 336-882-2567

Williams, Elliott Fennell (9 mentions)
U of North Carolina, 1988 *Certification:* Anesthesiology
401 Ferndale Blvd, High Point, 336-882-2567

Cardiac Surgery

Bartle, Bryan Kurt (11 mentions)
U of Maryland, 1986 *Certification:* Surgery, Thoracic Surgery
301 E Wendover Ave #411, Greensboro, 336-832-3200

Gerhardt, Edward Burton (14 mentions)
U of Virginia, 1981 *Certification:* Surgery, Thoracic Surgery
301 E Wendover Ave #411, Greensboro, 336-832-3200

Hines, Michael Herbert (11 mentions)
Wake Forest U, 1986 *Certification:* Thoracic Surgery
Wake Forest University Baptist Med Ctr, Winston-Salem,
   336-716-2281

Kon, Neal David (29 mentions)
U of Florida, 1979 *Certification:* Thoracic Surgery
Wake Forest University Baptist Med Ctr, Winston-Salem,
   336-716-4338

Cardiology

Applegate, Robert Joseph (7 mentions)
U of Virginia, 1980 *Certification:* Cardiovascular Disease,
   Internal Medicine, Interventional Cardiology
Wake Forest University Baptist Med Ctr, Winston-Salem,
   336-716-6674

Bohle, David J. (12 mentions)
U of Texas-San Antonio, 1989 *Certification:* Cardiovascular
   Disease, Interventional Cardiology
186 Kimel Park Dr, Winston-Salem, 336-277-2000

Brodie, Bruce Rogers (12 mentions)
Washington U, 1970 *Certification:* Cardiovascular Disease,
   Internal Medicine, Interventional Cardiology
1126 N Church St #300, Greensboro, 336-547-1752

Cheek, Herman Barrett (6 mentions)
Wake Forest U, 1983 *Certification:* Cardiovascular Disease,
   Internal Medicine, Interventional Cardiology
306 Westwood Ave #401, High Point, 336-885-6168

Givens, Davidson Howard (6 mentions)
Wake Forest U, 1976
Certification: Cardiovascular Disease, Internal Medicine
186 Kimel Park Dr, Winston-Salem, 336-277-2000

Little, William Campbell (8 mentions)
Ohio State U, 1975 *Certification:* Cardiovascular Disease,
  Internal Medicine, Interventional Cardiology
300 S Hawthorne Rd Clinical Sciences Bldg 7th Fl,
  Winston-Salem, 336-716-2746

Oskarsson, Helgi Julius (6 mentions)
FMS-Iceland, 1983 *Certification:* Cardiovascular Disease,
  Internal Medicine, Interventional Cardiology
300 Gatewood Ave, High Point, 336-802-2125

Smith, Henry W. B. (14 mentions)
Harvard U, 1978 *Certification:* Cardiovascular Disease,
  Internal Medicine, Interventional Cardiology
301 E Wendover Ave #310, Greensboro, 336-275-4096

Stuckey, Thomas David (10 mentions)
Ohio State U, 1979 *Certification:* Cardiovascular Disease,
  Internal Medicine, Interventional Cardiology
1126 N Church St #300, Greensboro, 336-547-1752

Tennant, Stanley Neal (5 mentions)
Wake Forest U, 1978 *Certification:* Cardiovascular Disease,
  Internal Medicine, Interventional Cardiology
1002 N Church St #103, Greensboro, 336-272-6133

Dermatology

Feldman, Steven Richard (6 mentions)
Duke U, 1985 *Certification:* Dermatology, Dermatopathology
Wake Forest University Baptist Med Ctr, Winston-Salem,
  336-716-3926

Fleischer, Alan B., Jr. (7 mentions)
U of Missouri, 1987 *Certification:* Dermatology
Wake Forest University Baptist Med Ctr, Winston-Salem,
  336-716-3926

Gruber, Hope M. (10 mentions)
Temple U, 1982 *Certification:* Dermatology
510 N Elam Ave #303, Greensboro, 336-632-9272

Hall, John Howland, Jr. (7 mentions)
Wake Forest U, 1988 *Certification:* Dermatology
1305 W Wendover Ave #D, Greensboro, 336-333-9111

Houston, Frank Matt (6 mentions)
Louisiana State U, 1964 *Certification:* Dermatology
2704 Saint Jude St, Greensboro, 336-954-7546
2704 St Jude St, Greensboro, 336-954-7546

Jorizzo, Joseph L. (8 mentions)
Boston U, 1975 *Certification:* Dermatology
Wake Forest University Baptist Med Ctr, Winston-Salem,
  336-716-3926

Migliardi, Robert Tad (6 mentions)
Med U of South Carolina, 1992
Certification: Dermatology, Dermatopathology
404 Westwood Ave #107, High Point, 336-887-3195
231 Harmon Ln, Kernersville, 336-996-1173
6 Medical Park Dr, Lexington, 336-249-2404

Turner, W. Harrison, III (8 mentions)
Virginia Commonwealth U, 1968 *Certification:* Dermatology
2704 Saint Jude St, Greensboro, 336-954-7546

Williford, Phillip Mabon (7 mentions)
U of North Carolina, 1981
Certification: Dermatology, Internal Medicine
Wake Forest University Baptist Med Ctr, Winston-Salem,
  336-716-3119

Emergency Medicine

Allen, Anthony Terrance (5 mentions)
Ohio State U, 1995 *Certification:* Emergency Medicine
1200 N Elm St, Greensboro, 336-832-2945

Alson, Roy Lee (4 mentions)
Wake Forest U, 1985 *Certification:* Emergency Medicine
Wake Forest University Baptist Med Ctr, Winston-Salem,
  336-716-2193

Fisher, David Michael (4 mentions)
Wake Forest U, 1996 *Certification:* Emergency Medicine
601 N Elm St, High Point, 336-878-6115

Hoekstra, James William (9 mentions)
U of Michigan, 1984 *Certification:* Emergency Medicine
5711 Shamrock Glen Ln, Lewisville, 336-716-2255

Horton, Paul Edward (5 mentions)
U of Texas-Galveston, 1976 *Certification:* Emergency Medicine
3333 Silas Creek Pkwy, Winston-Salem, 336-765-9328

Jacubowitz, Sam (7 mentions)
Temple U, 1987 *Certification:* Emergency Medicine
1200 N Elm St, Greensboro, 336-832-2945

Lowdermilk, Tad Williams (4 mentions)
U of Miami, 1974
3333 Silas Creek Pkwy, Winston-Salem, 336-765-9328

Manthey, David Edwin (4 mentions)
U of Virginia, 1991 *Certification:* Emergency Medicine
Wake Forest University Baptist Med Ctr, Winston-Salem,
  336-713-9100

Mayer, Norman Michael (7 mentions)
Wake Forest U, 1975 *Certification:* Emergency Medicine
1200 N Elm St, Greensboro, 336-832-2945

Molpus, John Lane (5 mentions)
U of South Florida, 1998 *Certification:* Emergency Medicine
1200 N Elm St, Greensboro, 336-832-7000

Nadkarni, Milan D. (4 mentions)
FMS-India, 1982
Certification: Pediatric Emergency Medicine, Pediatrics
Wake Forest University Baptist Med Ctr, Winston-Salem,
  336-713-9100

Endocrinology

Altheimer, Michael David (8 mentions)
U of Iowa, 1981
Certification: Endocrinology and Metabolism, Internal Medicine
1002 N Church St #400, Greensboro, 336-378-1074

Balan, Bindubal K. (10 mentions)
FMS-India, 1993 *Certification:* Endocrinology, Diabetes,
  and Metabolism, Internal Medicine
3824 N Elm St, Greensboro, 336-482-2300

Doerr, Monica Elizabeth (9 mentions)
U of Miami, 1988
Certification: Endocrinology, Diabetes, and Metabolism
604 W Main St, Jamestown, 336-802-2015

Ober, Karl Patrick (17 mentions)
U of Florida, 1974
Certification: Endocrinology and Metabolism, Internal Medicine
Wake Forest University Baptist Med Ctr, Winston-Salem,
  336-716-2076

South, Stephen Alan (9 mentions)
Wake Forest U, 1987 *Certification:* Endocrinology,
  Diabetes, and Metabolism, Internal Medicine
2703 Henry St, Greensboro, 336-621-8911

Trujillo, Jaime E. (8 mentions)
FMS-Colombia, 1972 *Certification:* Internal Medicine
3080 Trenwest Dr, Winston-Salem, 336-768-0496

Family Practice *(see note on page 9)*

Blomgren, Peter Frederick (4 mentions)
Indiana U, 1974 *Certification:* Family Medicine
317 W Wendover Ave, Greensboro, 336-373-1794

Cassiano, Coley James (3 mentions)
U of Buffalo, 1975 *Certification:* Family Medicine
301 E Wendover Ave #215, Greensboro, 336-379-1156

Celestino, Frank Samuel, Jr. (5 mentions)
U of Rochester, 1978
Certification: Family Medicine, Geriatric Medicine
Wake Forest University Baptist Med Ctr, Winston-Salem,
  336-716-4479

Coates, Michael Lee (8 mentions)
Virginia Commonwealth U, 1974 *Certification:* Adolescent
  Medicine, Emergency Medicine, Family Medicine
Wake Forest University Baptist Med Ctr, Winston-Salem,
  336-716-2255

Ehinger, Robert Richard (3 mentions)
U of North Carolina, 1990 *Certification:* Family Medicine
301 E Wendover Ave #215, Greensboro, 336-379-1156

Fried, Robert Leslie (3 mentions)
Albany Med Coll, 1980 *Certification:* Family Medicine
1510 NC Hwy 68 N, Oak Ridge, 336-644-0111

Haimes, David Michael (4 mentions)
U of Florida, 1979 *Certification:* Family Medicine
905 Phillips Ave, High Point, 336-802-2040

Hawks, Al N. (3 mentions)
Wake Forest U, 1979 *Certification:* Family Medicine
4510 Premier Dr, High Point, 336-802-2210
905 Phillips Ave, High Point, 336-802-2040

Jackson, David Stone, Jr. (3 mentions)
Wake Forest U, 1973 *Certification:* Family Medicine
1920 W First St Piedmont Plaza 1 3rd Fl, Winston-Salem,
  336-716-4479

Keller, David Charles (3 mentions)
Washington U, 1974 *Certification:* Family Medicine
317 W Wendover Ave, Greensboro, 336-373-1794

Kelly, Robert George (3 mentions)
Med U of South Carolina, 1974 *Certification:* Family Medicine
100 Robinhood Medical Plaza, Winston-Salem, 336-718-0800

Latham-Sadler, Brenda A. (3 mentions)
Wake Forest U, 1982 *Certification:* Family Medicine
8519 Brook Meadow Ln, Lewisville, 336-716-2255

Mazzocchi, Annmarie (6 mentions)
Columbia U, 1982 *Certification:* Family Medicine
1591 Yanceyville St #200, Greensboro, 336-232-0180

Roach, John Grover, III (3 mentions)
Wake Forest U, 1977 *Certification:* Family Medicine
105 Vest Mill Cir, Winston-Salem, 336-718-7800

Gastroenterology

Brodie, Dora M. (6 mentions)
Duke U, 1975
520 N Elam Ave, Greensboro, 336-273-4200

Bruggen, Joel Thomas (12 mentions)
U of Kansas, 1983
Certification: Gastroenterology, Internal Medicine
Wake Forest University Baptist Med Ctr, Winston-Salem,
  336-716-4621

Buccini, Robert Vincent (16 mentions)
U of Chicago, 1981
Certification: Gastroenterology, Internal Medicine
1002 N Church St #201, Greensboro, 336-378-0713

Gilliam, John Hugh, III (12 mentions)
Virginia Commonwealth U, 1970
Certification: Gastroenterology, Internal Medicine
Wake Forest University Baptist Med Ctr, Winston-Salem,
336-716-4621

Koch, Kenneth Louis, Jr. (6 mentions)
U of Iowa, 1975
Certification: Gastroenterology, Internal Medicine
Wake Forest University Baptist Med Ctr, Winston-Salem,
336-716-2255

Mann, Jyothi Nat (7 mentions)
FMS-India, 1985 *Certification:* Gastroenterology
1593 Yanceyville St #100, Greensboro, 336-275-1306

Medoff, Jeffrey Roy (6 mentions)
New York Med Coll, 1977
Certification: Gastroenterology, Internal Medicine
7 Corporate Center Ct #C, Greensboro, 336-286-0033

Mishra, Girish (8 mentions)
U of Missouri, 1992 *Certification:* Gastroenterology
Wake Forest University Baptist Med Ctr, Winston-Salem,
336-716-2255

Murphy, Daniel William (7 mentions)
U of Cincinnati, 1981
Certification: Gastroenterology, Internal Medicine
1901 S Hawthorne Rd #310, Winston-Salem, 336-760-4340

General Surgery

Albertson, David Allen (16 mentions)
U of Virginia, 1972 *Certification:* Surgery
Wake Forest University Baptist Med Ctr, Winston-Salem,
336-716-4442

Gerkin, Todd Michael (13 mentions)
U of Virginia, 1987 *Certification:* Surgery
1002 N Church St #302, Greensboro, 336-387-8100

Howerton, Russell Mars (13 mentions)
Vanderbilt U, 1983 *Certification:* Surgery
Wake Forest University Baptist Med Ctr, Winston-Salem,
336-716-9262

Hoxworth, Benjamin Tappan (6 mentions)
U of Cincinnati, 1980 *Certification:* Surgery
1002 N Church St #302, Greensboro, 336-387-8100

Ingram, Haywood Melton (5 mentions)
Wake Forest U, 1978 *Certification:* Surgery
1002 N Church St #302, Greensboro, 336-274-8444

Mann, John W. F. (7 mentions)
Wake Forest U, 1993 *Certification:* Surgery
2915 Lyndhurst Ave, Winston-Salem, 336-765-5221

Martin, Matthew Brunson (8 mentions)
U of Texas-Dallas, 1979 *Certification:* Surgery
1002 N Church St #302, Greensboro, 336-387-8100

Newman, David Harold (5 mentions)
Wake Forest U, 1980 *Certification:* Surgery
1002 N Church St #302, Greensboro, 336-387-8100

Rosenbower, Todd James (10 mentions)
Indiana U, 1991 *Certification:* Surgery
1002 N Church St #302, Greensboro, 336-275-8415

Streck, Christian John (6 mentions)
U of Florida, 1971 *Certification:* Surgery
1002 N Church St #302, Greensboro, 336-387-8100

Stuart, Samuel Patrick, Jr. (6 mentions)
U of North Carolina, 1985 *Certification:* Surgery
2933 Maplewood Ave #4, Winston-Salem, 336-765-0155

Waters, Gregory Stiegler (8 mentions)
East Carolina U, 1990
Certification: Colon & Rectal Surgery, Surgery
300 S Hawthorne Rd, Winston-Salem, 336-716-2255

Geriatrics

Green, Arthur Gerrish, III (6 mentions)
Tulane U, 1973
Certification: Geriatric Medicine, Internal Medicine
1309 N Elm St, Greensboro, 336-544-5400

Lyles, Mary Fennell (9 mentions)
U of Mississippi, 1975
Certification: Geriatric Medicine, Internal Medicine
Wake Forest University Baptist Med Ctr, Winston-Salem,
336-713-8548

Stoneking, Hal Thomas (16 mentions)
U of Kentucky, 1983
Certification: Geriatric Medicine, Internal Medicine
301 E Wendover Ave #200, Greensboro, 336-274-3241
5 Roswell Ct, Greensboro, 336-274-3241

Williamson, Jeff Douglas (11 mentions)
Certification: Internal Medicine
Wake Forest University Baptist Med Ctr, Winston-Salem,
336-713-8583

Hematology/Oncology

Chinnasami, Bernard Ravi (6 mentions)
FMS-India, 1988
302 Westwood Ave, High Point, 336-802-2500

Granfortuna, James M. (14 mentions)
Mount Sinai Sch of Med, 1980
Certification: Hematology, Internal Medicine, Medical Oncology
501 N Elam Ave, Greensboro, 336-832-1100
516 Van Buren Rd, Eden, 336-623-6862

Grote, Thomas Howard (6 mentions)
Duke U, 1981 *Certification:* Internal Medicine, Medical Oncology
1010 Bethesda Ct, Winston-Salem, 336-277-8800

Hopkins, Judith Owen (6 mentions)
U of Virginia, 1977
Certification: Internal Medicine, Medical Oncology
1010 Bethesda Ct, Winston-Salem, 336-277-8800

Hurd, David Duane (6 mentions)
U of Illinois, 1974
Certification: Internal Medicine, Medical Oncology
300 S Hawthorne Ln, Winston-Salem, 336-716-2088

Magrinat, Gustav Charles (22 mentions)
U of North Carolina, 1987
Certification: Hematology, Internal Medicine, Medical Oncology
501 N Elam Ave, Greensboro, 336-832-1100

McLean, Thomas Williams (7 mentions)
Med U of South Carolina, 1990
Certification: Pediatric Hematology-Oncology, Pediatrics
Wake Forest University Baptist Med Ctr, Winston-Salem,
336-713-4500

Powell, Bayard Lowery (19 mentions)
U of North Carolina, 1980
Certification: Internal Medicine, Medical Oncology
Wake Forest University Baptist Med Ctr, Winston-Salem,
336-713-5440

Sanders, George Herbert S. (6 mentions)
U of North Carolina, 1988
Certification: Hematology, Internal Medicine, Medical Oncology
302 Westwood Ave, High Point, 336-802-2500

Sherrill, Gary Bradley (16 mentions)
U of North Carolina, 1989
Certification: Hematology, Medical Oncology
501 N Elam Ave, Greensboro, 336-832-1100

Infectious Disease

Campbell, John Franklin (17 mentions)
Emory U, 1981
Certification: Infectious Disease, Internal Medicine
1200 N Elm St, Greensboro, 336-832-8560

High, Kevin Paul (17 mentions)
U of Virginia, 1986
Certification: Infectious Disease, Internal Medicine
300 S Hawthorne Rd, Winston-Salem, 336-716-2700

Lane, Timothy Walter (25 mentions)
Cornell U, 1971
Certification: Infectious Disease, Internal Medicine
1200 N Elm St, Greensboro, 336-832-8062

Link, Arthur Stanley (15 mentions)
Columbia U, 1972
Certification: Infectious Disease, Internal Medicine
1381 Westgate Center Dr, Winston-Salem, 336-718-0480

Peacock, James Edward, Jr. (25 mentions)
U of North Carolina, 1975
Certification: Infectious Disease, Internal Medicine
Wake Forest University Baptist Med Ctr, Winston-Salem,
336-716-2700

Pegram, Paul Samuel, Jr. (11 mentions)
Wake Forest U, 1970
Certification: Infectious Disease, Internal Medicine
Wake Forest University Baptist Med Ctr, Winston-Salem,
336-716-4262

Robinson, Edward N., Jr. (12 mentions)
Wake Forest U, 1979
Certification: Infectious Disease, Internal Medicine
1200 N Elm St, Greensboro, 336-832-8560

Infertility

Mezer, Howard Cabitt (13 mentions)
Tufts U, 1977 *Certification:* Obstetrics & Gynecology
1103 N Elm St, Greensboro, 336-272-0911

Yalcinkaya, Tamer M. (5 mentions)
FMS-Turkey, 1983 *Certification:* Obstetrics & Gynecology,
Reproductive Endocrinology/Infertility
Wake Forest University Baptist Med Ctr, Winston-Salem,
336-716-6476

Internal Medicine *(see note on page 9)*

Aronson, Richard Adler (4 mentions)
Wake Forest U, 1986 *Certification:* Internal Medicine
2703 Henry St, Greensboro, 336-621-8911

Eberle, Robert Adam (4 mentions)
Wake Forest U, 1982 *Certification:* Internal Medicine
1381 Westgate Center Dr, Winston-Salem, 336-718-0100

Gates, Robert Nevill (7 mentions)
U of North Carolina, 1983 *Certification:* Internal Medicine
301 E Wendover Ave #200, Greensboro, 336-274-3241

Griffin, John Joseph, Jr. (4 mentions)
Baylor U, 1989 *Certification:* Internal Medicine
301 E Wendover Ave #200, Greensboro, 336-274-3241

Jobe, Daniel Brian (3 mentions)
Wake Forest U, 1993 *Certification:* Internal Medicine
604 W Main St, Jamestown, 336-802-2015

Millman, Franklyn Milton (3 mentions)
U of California-San Francisco, 1967
Certification: Allergy & Immunology, Internal Medicine
Wake Forest University Baptist Med Ctr, Winston-Salem,
336-716-3787

Morrow, Phillip Ray, Jr. (3 mentions)
Certification: Internal Medicine
Wake Forest University Baptist Med Ctr, Winston-Salem, 336-716-2255

O'Brien, Francis X., Jr. (6 mentions)
Temple U, 1985 *Certification:* Internal Medicine
Wake Forest University Baptist Med Ctr, Winston-Salem, 336-716-3787

Osborne, James Charles (5 mentions)
U of North Carolina, 1983 *Certification:* Internal Medicine
301 E Wendover Ave #200, Greensboro, 336-274-3241

Perini, Mark Andrew (7 mentions)
Wake Forest U, 1998 *Certification:* Internal Medicine
2703 Henry St, Greensboro, 336-621-8911

Ramachandran, Ajith (3 mentions)
FMS-India, 1991 *Certification:* Internal Medicine
1511 Westover Ter #201, Greensboro, 336-373-0611

Rice, William Yates, III (23 mentions)
Wake Forest U, 1989 *Certification:* Internal Medicine
Wake Forest University Baptist Med Ctr, Winston-Salem, 336-716-3787

Russo, John M. (3 mentions)
SUNY-Upstate Med U, 1998 *Certification:* Internal Medicine
2703 Henry St, Greensboro, 336-621-8911

Tonuzi, Racquel Marie (3 mentions)
U of Buffalo, 1999 *Certification:* Internal Medicine
624 Quaker Ln, High Point, 336-802-2025

Nephrology

Adams, Patricia Lee (7 mentions)
Wake Forest U, 1974 *Certification:* Internal Medicine, Nephrology
Wake Forest University Baptist Med Ctr, Winston-Salem, 336-716-4650

Burkart, John Mark (7 mentions)
Rush U, 1979 *Certification:* Internal Medicine, Nephrology
300 S Hawthorne Rd, Winston-Salem, 336-716-3963

Deterding, James Le Roy (14 mentions)
U of Nebraska, 1979 *Certification:* Internal Medicine, Nephrology
309 New St, Greensboro, 336-379-9708

Dilley, James Richard (13 mentions)
West Virginia U, 1974 *Certification:* Critical Care Medicine, Internal Medicine, Nephrology
730 Highland Oaks Dr #201, Winston-Salem, 336-768-2425

Fox, Richard Franklin (9 mentions)
U of North Carolina, 1975
Certification: Internal Medicine, Nephrology
309 New St, Greensboro, 336-379-9708

Freedman, Barry Ira (12 mentions)
SUNY-Downstate Med Coll, 1984
Certification: Internal Medicine, Nephrology
300 S Hawthorne Ln, Winston-Salem, 336-716-4650

Powell, Alvin Caldwell (10 mentions)
Tufts U, 1982 *Certification:* Internal Medicine, Nephrology
309 New St, Greensboro, 336-379-9708

Zekan, Jeanne Marie (7 mentions)
Marshall U, 1987 *Certification:* Internal Medicine, Nephrology
404 Westwood Ave #105, High Point, 336-882-6500

Neurological Surgery

Bell, William O. (8 mentions)
Hahnemann U, 1977 *Certification:* Neurological Surgery
2810 Maplewood Ave, Winston-Salem, 336-768-1811

Branch, Charles Leon, Jr. (9 mentions)
U of Texas-Dallas, 1981 *Certification:* Neurological Surgery
Wake Forest University Baptist Med Ctr, Winston-Salem, 336-716-4083

Brown, William Ray, Jr. (16 mentions)
Wake Forest U, 1970 *Certification:* Neurological Surgery
160 Kimel Forest Dr #250, Winston-Salem, 336-765-7655

Elsner, Henry Joseph (13 mentions)
Robert W Johnson Med Sch, 1983
Certification: Neurological Surgery
301 E Wendover Ave #211, Greensboro, 336-272-4578
1130 N Church St #200, Greensboro, 336-272-4578

Nudelman, Robert Wayne (8 mentions)
Boston U, 1982 *Certification:* Neurological Surgery
1130 N Church St #200, Greensboro, 336-272-4578

Roy, Mark William (10 mentions)
U of Kentucky, 1987 *Certification:* Neurological Surgery
1130 N Church St #200, Greensboro, 336-272-4578

Stern, Joseph David (12 mentions)
U of Michigan, 1989 *Certification:* Neurological Surgery
1130 N Church St #200, Greensboro, 336-272-4578

Tatter, Stephen Bradley (17 mentions)
Cornell U, 1990 *Certification:* Neurological Surgery
300 S Hawthorne Rd, Winston-Salem, 336-716-4081

Wilson, John Allen, Jr. (9 mentions)
Jefferson Med Coll, 1982 *Certification:* Neurological Surgery
Wake Forest University Baptist Med Ctr, Winston-Salem, 336-716-4081

Neurology

Bell, William Lynn (5 mentions)
Wake Forest U, 1977 *Certification:* Clinical Neurophysiology, Internal Medicine, Neurology
Wake Forest University Baptist Med Ctr, Winston-Salem, 336-716-4101
2810 Maplewood Ave, Winston-Salem, 336-768-1811

Bey, Richard Doud (5 mentions)
Yale U, 1979 *Certification:* Neurology
2933 Maplewood Ave #1, Winston-Salem, 336-765-5553
1492 Rymco Dr, Winston-Salem, 336-765-5553

Hickling, William Henry (12 mentions)
Cornell U, 1978 *Certification:* Neurology with Special Qualifications in Child Neurology, Pediatrics
1126 N Church St #200, Greensboro, 336-273-2511
1046 E Wendover Ave, Greensboro, 336-272-1050

Jackson, Travis Harold (6 mentions)
Baylor U, 1975 *Certification:* Neurology
175 Kimel Park Dr #125, Winston-Salem, 336-768-6347

Lefkowitz, David Solomon (5 mentions)
Wake Forest U, 1978 *Certification:* Neurology
Wake Forest University Baptist Med Ctr, Winston-Salem, 336-716-2333

Love, James McLean (28 mentions)
Duke U, 1972 *Certification:* Neurology
1126 N Church St #200, Greensboro, 336-273-2511

Sater, Richard Arnold (6 mentions)
Duke U, 1991 *Certification:* Clinical Neurophysiology, Neurology, Pain Medicine, Sleep Medicine
624 Quaker Ln #C206, High Point, 336-802-2080

Sethi, Pramodkumar (7 mentions)
FMS-India, 1989 *Certification:* Neurology, Vascular Neurology
1126 N Church St #200, Greensboro, 336-273-2511

Willis, Charles Keith (9 mentions)
U of Virginia, 1984 *Certification:* Neurology
1126 N Church St #200, Greensboro, 336-273-2511

Obstetrics/Gynecology

Cousins, Sheronette Ann (3 mentions)
Brown U, 1987 *Certification:* Obstetrics & Gynecology
1908 Lendew St, Greensboro, 336-273-2835

Davis, Wesley Boyd (3 mentions)
U of North Carolina, 1997 *Certification:* Obstetrics & Gynecology
1908 Lendew St, Greensboro, 336-273-2835

Dickstein, Sherry Anne (4 mentions)
U of Vermont, 1978 *Certification:* Obstetrics & Gynecology
1908 Lendew St, Greensboro, 336-273-2835

Evans, Charles B. (3 mentions)
U of South Florida, 1984 *Certification:* Obstetrics & Gynecology
2830 Maplewood Ave #B, Winston-Salem, 336-794-1444

Fernandez, Andrea S. (6 mentions)
Virginia Commonwealth U, 1999
Certification: Obstetrics & Gynecology
Wake Forest University Baptist Med Ctr, Winston-Salem, 336-716-4039

Fletcher, Richard Van, Jr. (3 mentions)
Vanderbilt U, 1974 *Certification:* Obstetrics & Gynecology
721 N Elm St #102, High Point, 336-802-2010

Grewal, Michelle Lynette (6 mentions)
U of North Carolina, 1995 *Certification:* Obstetrics & Gynecology
1507 Westover Ter #C, Greensboro, 336-273-3661

Haygood, Vanessa Pearline (3 mentions)
Harvard U, 1978 *Certification:* Obstetrics & Gynecology
301 W Wendover #400, Greensboro, 336-286-6565

Hedrick, Richard E., Jr. (4 mentions)
Wake Forest U, 1979 *Certification:* Obstetrics & Gynecology
1806 S Hawthorne Rd #102, Winston-Salem, 336-768-3632

Holland, Richard Mark (3 mentions)
U of Kentucky, 1980 *Certification:* Obstetrics & Gynecology
1507 Westover Ter, Greensboro, 336-273-3661

Jacobs, Bradley Edgar (3 mentions)
U of Alabama, 1997 *Certification:* Obstetrics & Gynecology
2927 Lyndhurst Ave, Winston-Salem, 336-765-9350
445 Pineview Dr #110, Kernersville, 336-993-4532

Jacobs, James Curtis (3 mentions)
U of North Carolina, 1986 *Certification:* Obstetrics & Gynecology
306 Westwood Ave #501, High Point, 336-885-0149
601 N Elm St, High Point, 336-885-0149

Lentz, Samuel Smith (5 mentions)
Wake Forest U, 1978
Certification: Gynecologic Oncology, Obstetrics & Gynecology
Wake Forest University Baptist Med Ctr, Winston-Salem, 336-716-2255

Lewis, Andrew Jon (3 mentions)
Wake Forest U, 1998 *Certification:* Obstetrics & Gynecology
245 Charlois Blvd, Winston-Salem, 336-659-4777

Lomax, Charles Weston (3 mentions)
Wake Forest U, 1968 *Certification:* Obstetrics & Gynecology
311 W Wendover Ave, Greensboro, 336-274-1200

Louk, Douglas Keith (6 mentions)
Eastern Virginia Med Sch, 1984
Certification: Obstetrics & Gynecology
400 N Elm St, High Point, 336-802-2120

Lowe, David C. (3 mentions)
U of Missouri, 1991 *Certification:* Obstetrics & Gynecology
1507 Westover Ter, Greensboro, 336-273-3661

McComb, John Sanford (3 mentions)
Wake Forest U, 1980 *Certification:* Obstetrics & Gynecology
1507 Westover Ter, Greensboro, 336-273-3661

Merrill, David Caswell (4 mentions)
Med Coll of Wisconsin, 1987
Certification: Maternal-Fetal Medicine, Obstetrics & Gynecology
Wake Forest University Baptist Med Ctr, Winston-Salem, 336-716-4039

Miller, Brigitte Eva (4 mentions)
FMS-Germany, 1977
Certification: Gynecologic Oncology, Obstetrics & Gynecology
Wake Forest University Baptist Med Ctr, Winston-Salem, 336-716-6673

Patel, Kalpen N. (4 mentions)
U of Texas-Galveston, 1994 *Certification:* Obstetrics & Gynecology
400 N Elm St, High Point, 336-889-4353

Pippitt, Charles H., Jr. (3 mentions)
Wake Forest U, 1979
Certification: Gynecologic Oncology, Obstetrics & Gynecology
1010 Bethesda Ct, Winston-Salem, 336-277-8800
276 Old Mocksville Rd #800, Statesville, 704-873-5150

Pollard, Harold C., III (3 mentions)
U of North Carolina, 1973 *Certification:* Obstetrics & Gynecology
2927 Lyndhurst Ave, Winston-Salem, 336-765-9350
445 Pineview Dr #110, Kernersville, 336-993-4532

Sansing, Mary Tinsley (4 mentions)
Louisiana State U, 1981 *Certification:* Obstetrics & Gynecology
400 N Elm St, High Point, 336-802-2120

Taavon, Richard Joseph (4 mentions)
U of Maryland, 1988 *Certification:* Obstetrics & Gynecology
1908 Lendew St, Greensboro, 336-273-2835

Ophthalmology

Davanzo, Robert John (8 mentions)
U of North Carolina, 1981
307 Lindsay St, High Point, 336-802-2020

Gould, Sigmund S. (5 mentions)
U of Buffalo, 1971 *Certification:* Ophthalmology
405 Pkwy #B, Greensboro, 336-274-2441

Greven, Craig Michael (20 mentions)
Wake Forest U, 1983 *Certification:* Ophthalmology
Wake Forest University Baptist Med Ctr, Winston-Salem,
336-716-4091

Groat, Robert Lanier (6 mentions)
Harvard U, 1970 *Certification:* Ophthalmology
1317 N Elm St #4, Greensboro, 336-378-1442

Martin, Timothy John (6 mentions)
Virginia Commonwealth U, 1986 *Certification:* Ophthalmology
Wake Forest University Baptist Med Ctr, Winston-Salem,
336-716-4091

Rankin, Gary A. (6 mentions)
Baylor U, 1986 *Certification:* Ophthalmology
1204 Maple St, Greensboro, 336-294-8258

Stoneburner, Sara Ellen (6 mentions)
Duke U, 1983 *Certification:* Ophthalmology
8 N Pointe Ct, Greensboro, 336-274-4626

Yeatts, Robert Patrick (6 mentions)
Wake Forest U, 1978 *Certification:* Ophthalmology
Wake Forest University Baptist Med Ctr, Winston-Salem,
336-716-4091

Young, William Oliver (8 mentions)
Med U of South Carolina, 1989 *Certification:* Ophthalmology
1305C W Wendover Ave #C, Greensboro, 336-271-2007

Orthopedics

Aluisio, Frank Victor (8 mentions)
Emory U, 1991 *Certification:* Orthopaedic Surgery
1401 Benjamin Pkwy, Greensboro, 336-545-5000
3200 Northline Ave #200, Greensboro, 336-544-3900

Dalldorf, Peter Gilbert (7 mentions)
U of North Carolina, 1988 *Certification:* Orthopaedic Surgery
1915 Lendew St, Greensboro, 336-275-3325

Gramig, William M., III (5 mentions)
U of Tennessee, 1993
Certification: Orthopaedic Surgery, Surgery of the Hand
1401 Benjamin Pkwy, Greensboro, 336-545-5000

Koman, L. Andrew (12 mentions)
Duke U, 1974
Certification: Orthopaedic Surgery, Surgery of the Hand
Wake Forest University Baptist Med Ctr, Winston-Salem,
336-716-2255

Martin, David Franklin (5 mentions)
Johns Hopkins U, 1982
Certification: Orthopaedic Sports Medicine, Orthopaedic Surgery
Wake Forest University Baptist Med Ctr, Winston-Salem,
336-716-2255
131 Miller St, Winston-Salem, 336-716-4207

Olin, Matthew David (5 mentions)
Wake Forest U, 1998 *Certification:* Orthopaedic Surgery
1401 Benjamin Pkwy, Greensboro, 336-545-5000
3200 Northline Ave #200, Greensboro, 336-544-3900

Teasdall, Robert Douglas (6 mentions)
Wayne State U, 1986 *Certification:* Orthopaedic Surgery
Wake Forest University Baptist Med Ctr, Winston-Salem,
336-716-2255

Wainer, Robert Alan (7 mentions)
U of North Carolina, 1984 *Certification:* Orthopaedic Surgery
1130 N Church St #100, Greensboro, 336-375-2300

Ward, William Goode (5 mentions)
Duke U, 1978 *Certification:* Orthopaedic Surgery
Wake Forest University Baptist Med Ctr, Winston-Salem,
336-716-3952
131 Miller St, Winston-Salem, 336-716-8200

Webb, Lawrence Xavier (7 mentions)
Temple U, 1978 *Certification:* Orthopaedic Surgery
131 Miller St, Winston-Salem, 336-716-8095

Weller, Edward Brooks (5 mentions)
U of Louisville, 1979 *Certification:* Orthopaedic Surgery
611 N Lindsay St #200, High Point, 336-841-6262

Whitfield, Peter White (7 mentions)
George Washington U, 1974 *Certification:* Orthopaedic Surgery
201 E Wendover Ave, Greensboro, 336-275-6318
209 Lindsay St #204, High Point, 336-887-8400

Otorhinolaryngology

Browne, James Dale (15 mentions)
Med Coll of Georgia, 1982 *Certification:* Otolaryngology
300 S Hawthorne Ln, Winston-Salem, 336-716-4161

Jacob, Sera Leigh (11 mentions)
U of Kansas, 1994 *Certification:* Otolaryngology
321 W Wendover Ave, Greensboro, 336-379-9445
1107 S Main St, Reedsville, 336-348-6664

May, John Scott (11 mentions)
Wake Forest U, 1982 *Certification:* Otolaryngology
Wake Forest University Baptist Med Ctr, Winston-Salem,
336-716-4161

Moore, David Ferguson, Jr. (13 mentions)
U of Tennessee, 1988 *Certification:* Otolaryngology
624 Quaker Ln #208-C, High Point, 336-802-2085

Phipps, Carl David (8 mentions)
Wake Forest U, 1993 *Certification:* Otolaryngology
624 Quaker Ln #C-208, High Point, 336-802-2085

Rosen, Jefry H. (8 mentions)
Mount Sinai Sch of Med, 1992 *Certification:* Otolaryngology
321 W Wendover Ave, Greensboro, 336-379-9445
1107 S Main St, Reedsville, 336-348-6664

Shoemaker, David Link (9 mentions)
Duke U, 1990 *Certification:* Otolaryngology
321 W Wendover Ave, Greensboro, 336-379-9445
1107 S Main St, Reedsville, 336-348-6664

Wolicki, Karol Thaddeus (11 mentions)
U of Virginia, 1981 *Certification:* Otolaryngology
321 W Wendover Ave, Greensboro, 336-379-9445
1107 S Main St, Reedsville, 336-348-6664

Pain Medicine

Phillips, Mark Lucas (6 mentions)
Wake Forest U, 1980
Certification: Anesthesiology, Internal Medicine, Rheumatology
522 N Elam Ave #203, Greensboro, 336-852-8444

Rauck, Richard Lee (13 mentions)
Wake Forest U, 1982 *Certification:* Anesthesiology, Pain Medicine
1950 S Hawthorne Rd, Winston-Salem, 336-718-4002
145 Kimel Park Dr #330, Winston-Salem, 336-765-6181

Pathology

Andree, Ernest Ashmore (8 mentions)
FMS-Sri Lanka, 1979
Certification: Anatomic Pathology & Clinical Pathology
1200 N Elm St, Greensboro, 336-832-8074

Cappellari, James Oliver (5 mentions)
Virginia Commonwealth U, 1985 *Certification:* Anatomic
Pathology & Clinical Pathology, Cytopathology
Wake Forest University Baptist Med Ctr, Winston-Salem,
336-716-4311

Eggers, Gerald Wood (9 mentions)
U of South Alabama, 1978
Certification: Anatomic Pathology & Clinical Pathology
3333 Silas Creek Pkwy, Winston-Salem, 336-718-3736

Garvin, Abbott Julian (7 mentions)
Med U of South Carolina, 1972 *Certification:* Anatomic Pathology
Wake Forest University Baptist Med Ctr, Winston-Salem,
336-716-4311

Geisinger, Kim R. (7 mentions)
Med Coll of Pennsylvania, 1976 *Certification:* Anatomic
Pathology, Clinical Pathology, Cytopathology
Wake Forest University Baptist Med Ctr, Winston-Salem,
336-716-4312

Hopkins, Marbry Benjamin, III (5 mentions)
U of Virginia, 1977 *Certification:* Anatomic Pathology &
Clinical Pathology, Blood Banking
601 N Elm St, High Point, 336-878-6064

Patrick, John David (5 mentions)
U of South Carolina, 1987 *Certification:* Anatomic
Pathology & Clinical Pathology, Cytopathology
501 N Elam Ave, Greensboro, 336-832-0452

Shaw, Jo Ann (8 mentions)
West Virginia U, 1986
1200 N Elm St, Greensboro, 336-832-8074

Stahr, Benjamin Joseph (5 mentions)
U of Kentucky, 1981 *Certification:* Anatomic Pathology &
Clinical Pathology, Dermatopathology
706 Green Valley Rd #104, Greensboro, 336-387-2500

Pediatrics *(see note on page 9)*

Akintemi, Olakunle B. (3 mentions)
FMS-Nigeria, 1977 *Certification:* Pediatrics
1200 N Elm St, Greensboro, 336-832-7000

Alexander, Mary B. (4 mentions)
New Jersey Med Sch, 1979 *Certification:* Pediatrics
510 N Elam Ave #202, Greensboro, 336-299-3183

Anderson, James C., IV (11 mentions)
Baylor U, 1993 *Certification:* Pediatrics
611 Lindsay St #102, High Point, 336-882-4171
624 Quaker Ln #200A, High Point, 336-802-2100

Bell, Alfred Dudley (3 mentions)
Wake Forest U, 1993 *Certification:* Pediatrics
200 Robinhood Medical Plaza, Winston-Salem, 336-718-8000

Brassfield, Mark Mossman (4 mentions)
Northwestern U, 1982 *Certification:* Pediatrics
2707 Henry St, Greensboro, 336-574-4280

Ford, Robert Virgil, Jr. (4 mentions)
Wake Forest U, 1971 *Certification:* Pediatrics
2909 Maplewood Ave, Winston-Salem, 336-794-3380

Gable, Elizabeth Kaye (4 mentions)
Wake Forest U, 1983 *Certification:* Pediatrics
1200 N Elm St, Greensboro, 336-832-8064

Givner, Laurence Bruce (3 mentions)
U of Maryland, 1978
Certification: Pediatric Infectious Diseases, Pediatrics
Wake Forest University Baptist Med Ctr, Winston-Salem, 336-713-4500

Hunsinger, Susan (3 mentions)
Certification: Pediatrics
114 Kinderton Blvd, Advance, 336-998-9742

Lowe, Melissa Vaughn (3 mentions)
Med U of South Carolina, 1991 *Certification:* Pediatrics
2707 Henry St, Greensboro, 336-574-4280

Lucas, Kathleen Ellen (4 mentions)
Marshall U, 1984 *Certification:* Pediatrics
1416 Yanceyville St, Greensboro, 336-510-5510

Rierson-Smith, Leslie (3 mentions)
East Carolina U, 1993 *Certification:* Pediatrics
861 Old Winston Rd #103, Kernersville, 336-802-2300

Rubin, David Martin (3 mentions)
U of North Carolina, 1968 *Certification:* Pediatrics
1124 N Church St, Greensboro, 336-373-1245

Satterwhite, William M., III (5 mentions)
Wake Forest U, 1997 *Certification:* Pediatrics
2821 Maplewood Ave, Winston-Salem, 336-718-3960

Sinal, Sara A. Hendricks (4 mentions)
U of North Carolina, 1971 *Certification:* Pediatrics
Wake Forest University Baptist Med Ctr, Winston-Salem, 336-716-2588

Wofford, Marcia McKee (4 mentions)
Certification: Pediatric Hematology-Oncology, Pediatrics
Wake Forest University Baptist Med Ctr, Winston-Salem, 336-716-4085

Plastic Surgery

Argenta, Louis Charles (13 mentions)
U of Michigan, 1969 *Certification:* Plastic Surgery
Wake Forest University Baptist Med Ctr, Winston-Salem, 336-716-4171

Barber, William Byron, II (16 mentions)
Med U of South Carolina, 1979 *Certification:* Plastic Surgery
1591 Yanceyville St #100, Greensboro, 336-275-3430

Bowers, David (12 mentions)
Wake Forest U, 1980 *Certification:* Plastic Surgery
1126 N Church St #101, Greensboro, 336-275-0919

David, Lisa Renee (9 mentions)
Indiana U, 1991 *Certification:* Plastic Surgery, Surgery
300 S Hawthorne Ln, Winston-Salem, 336-716-4171

De Franzo, Anthony John (9 mentions)
George Washington U, 1973 *Certification:* Plastic Surgery
Wake Forest University Baptist Med Ctr, Winston-Salem, 336-716-4150

Holderness, Howard, Jr. (9 mentions)
U of North Carolina, 1965 *Certification:* Plastic Surgery, Surgery
1126 N Church St #101, Greensboro, 336-275-0919

Marks, Malcolm Wernick (11 mentions)
Louisiana State U, 1975 *Certification:* Plastic Surgery
Wake Forest University Baptist Med Ctr, Winston-Salem, 336-716-4171

Schneider, Andrew Mark (12 mentions)
Virginia Commonwealth U, 1991
Certification: Plastic Surgery, Surgery
2901 Maplewood Ave, Winston-Salem, 336-765-8620

Psychiatry

Andrew, Raymond Hall (3 mentions)
U of Illinois, 1970 *Certification:* Psychiatry
1066 W 4th St #102, Winston-Salem, 336-723-2303

Farah, Brian Andrew (7 mentions)
Med U of South Carolina, 1990 *Certification:* Psychiatry
320 Boulevard St, High Point, 336-878-6098

Kaur, Rupinder (3 mentions)
FMS-India, 1982 *Certification:* Psychiatry
706 Green Valley Rd #100, Greensboro, 336-854-6100

McCall, William Vaughn (9 mentions)
Duke U, 1984
Certification: Geriatric Psychiatry, Psychiatry, Sleep Medicine
Wake Forest University Baptist Med Ctr, Winston-Salem, 336-716-4551

McKinney, Parish Ann (5 mentions)
East Carolina U, 1993 *Certification:* Psychiatry
3817 Lawndale Dr #D, Greensboro, 336-282-1251

Peters, Donald Walter (4 mentions)
U of North Carolina, 1982 *Certification:* Psychiatry
Wake Forest University Baptist Med Ctr, Winston-Salem, 336-716-4551

Stephens, Wayland Chad (3 mentions)
Duke U, 1980 *Certification:* Family Medicine, Psychiatry
2990 Bethesda Pl #602-A, Winston-Salem, 336-768-8281

Williford, James Scott (7 mentions)
U of North Carolina, 1989 *Certification:* Psychiatry
700 Walter Reed Dr, Greensboro, 336-832-9700

Pulmonary Disease

Chin, Robert, Jr. (7 mentions)
George Washington U, 1978 *Certification:* Critical Care Medicine, Internal Medicine, Pulmonary Disease
Wake Forest University Baptist Med Ctr, Winston-Salem, 336-716-4649

Clance, Keith Montgomery (12 mentions)
U of South Florida, 1986
Certification: Internal Medicine, Pulmonary Disease
520 N Elam Ave, Greensboro, 336-547-1700

Fussell, Kevin Michael (7 mentions)
Med Coll of Georgia, 1997 *Certification:* Critical Care Medicine, Internal Medicine, Pulmonary Disease
3001 Lyndhurst Ave, Winston-Salem, 336-765-0383

Hinson, Thomas Riley (9 mentions)
U of North Carolina, 1979 *Certification:* Critical Care Medicine, Internal Medicine, Pulmonary Disease
3001 Lyndhurst Ave, Winston-Salem, 336-765-0383

Hite, Robert Duncan, Jr. (10 mentions)
U of Texas-Houston, 1986 *Certification:* Critical Care Medicine, Internal Medicine, Pulmonary Disease
Wake Forest University Baptist Med Ctr, Winston-Salem, 336-716-4649

Sigal, Barry William (9 mentions)
Med Coll of Georgia, 1982
Certification: Internal Medicine, Pulmonary Disease
3001 Lyndhurst Ave, Winston-Salem, 336-765-0383

Wert, Michael Bruce (11 mentions)
Vanderbilt U, 1982 *Certification:* Critical Care Medicine, Internal Medicine, Pulmonary Disease
520 N Elam Ave, Greensboro, 336-547-1700

Wright, Patrick E., Jr. (10 mentions)
Vanderbilt U, 1982 *Certification:* Critical Care Medicine, Internal Medicine, Pulmonary Disease
520 N Elam Ave, Greensboro, 336-547-1801

Young, Clinton Driver (8 mentions)
U of Virginia, 1974
Certification: Internal Medicine, Pulmonary Disease
520 N Elam Ave, Greensboro, 336-547-1801

Radiology—Diagnostic

Basile, Vito (3 mentions)
U of North Carolina, 1991 *Certification:* Diagnostic Radiology
3155 Maplewood Ave, Winston-Salem, 336-794-4372
3105 St Regis Rd, Greensboro, 336-765-6312

Bechtold, Robert Edmond (3 mentions)
Washington U, 1979 *Certification:* Diagnostic Radiology
Wake Forest University Baptist Med Ctr, Winston-Salem, 336-716-4316

Chiles, Caroline (3 mentions)
Certification: Diagnostic Radiology
Wake Forest University Baptist Med Ctr, Winston-Salem, 336-716-2471

Clark, D. Charles, Jr. (5 mentions)
U of Kansas, 1986
Certification: Diagnostic Radiology, Neuroradiology
315 W Wendover Ave, Greensboro, 336-433-5000
301 E Wendover Ave, Greensboro, 336-433-5000
1002 N Church St, Greensboro, 336-271-4999

Deveshwar, Sanjeev (3 mentions)
FMS-United Kingdom, 1979
Certification: Diagnostic Radiology, Neurology
1317 N Elm St #1B, Greensboro, 336-274-4285

Elster, Allen De Vaney (3 mentions)
Baylor U, 1980
Certification: Diagnostic Radiology, Neuroradiology
Wake Forest University Baptist Med Ctr, Winston-Salem, 336-716-4316

Fischer, Gary Jay (3 mentions)
U of Missouri, 1972 *Certification:* Diagnostic Radiology
1317 N Elm St #1B, Greensboro, 336-274-4285

Freimanis, Rita Irene (4 mentions)
Wake Forest U, 1985 *Certification:* Diagnostic Radiology
Wake Forest University Baptist Med Ctr, Winston-Salem, 336-716-4316

Shogry, Mark Edward (4 mentions)
Vanderbilt U, 1985
Certification: Diagnostic Radiology, Neuroradiology
1317 N Elm St #1B, Greensboro, 336-274-4285

Wiggins, Thomas Barnes (3 mentions)
Wake Forest U, 1983 *Certification:* Diagnostic Radiology
3155 Maplewood Ave, Winston-Salem, 336-794-4372
280 Broad St #F, Kernersville, 336-765-6312

Williams, Daniel Walter (3 mentions)
U of North Carolina, 1984
Certification: Diagnostic Radiology, Neuroradiology
Wake Forest University Baptist Med Ctr, Winston-Salem, 336-716-7235

Zagoria, Ronald Jay (4 mentions)
U of Maryland, 1983 *Certification:* Diagnostic Radiology, Vascular & Interventional Radiology
Wake Forest University Baptist Med Ctr, Winston-Salem, 336-716-4316

Radiology—Therapeutic

Blackstock, Arthur W., Jr. (5 mentions)
East Carolina U, 1989 *Certification:* Radiation Oncology
Wake Forest University Baptist Med Ctr, Winston-Salem,
336-713-3600

Shaw, Edward Gus (6 mentions)
Rush U, 1983 *Certification:* Radiation Oncology
Wake Forest University Baptist Med Ctr, Winston-Salem,
336-716-4647

Yamagata, Glenn Takeshi (10 mentions)
U of Rochester, 1993 *Certification:* Diagnostic Radiology,
Vascular & Interventional Radiology
1317 N Elm St #1B, Greensboro, 336-274-4285
1200 N Elm St, Greensboro, 336-832-7360

Rehabilitation

McLean, James Martin (5 mentions)
U of North Carolina, 1989
Certification: Physical Medicine & Rehabilitation
3333 Silas Creek Pkwy, Winston-Salem, 336-718-5763

Pelligra, Salvatore John (3 mentions)
Albany Med Coll, 1981
Certification: Physical Medicine & Rehabilitation
2718 Henry St, Greensboro, 336-375-1007

Rheumatology

Levitin, Peter Mark (11 mentions)
U of Pennsylvania, 1969
Certification: Internal Medicine, Rheumatology
301 E Wendover Ave #200, Greensboro, 336-274-3241

O'Rourke, Kenneth Stuart (12 mentions)
George Washington U, 1983
Certification: Internal Medicine, Rheumatology
Wake Forest University Baptist Med Ctr, Winston-Salem,
336-716-4209

Thoracic Surgery

Burney, Donald Patrick (21 mentions)
Washington U, 1970 *Certification:* Surgery, Thoracic Surgery
301 E Wendover Ave #411, Greensboro, 336-832-3200

Duncan, David Allen (8 mentions)
U of Florida, 1984 *Certification:* Surgery, Thoracic Surgery
2827 Lyndhurst Ave #205, Winston-Salem, 336-768-9535

Oaks, Timothy Eugene (13 mentions)
Pennsylvania State U, 1984 *Certification:* Thoracic Surgery
Wake Forest University Baptist Med Ctr, Winston-Salem,
336-716-2255

Urology

Assimos, Dean George (16 mentions)
Loyola U Chicago, 1977 *Certification:* Urology
Wake Forest University Baptist Med Ctr, Winston-Salem,
336-716-4131

Atala, Anthony (11 mentions)
U of Louisville, 1985 *Certification:* Pediatric Urology, Urology
Wake Forest University Baptist Med Ctr, Winston-Salem,
336-716-4131

Coughlin, Paul William F. (7 mentions)
U of North Carolina, 1978 *Certification:* Urology
218 Gatewood Ave, High Point, 336-802-2030

Davis, Ronald Lee, III (19 mentions)
Louisiana State U, 1981 *Certification:* Urology
509 N Elam Ave #2, Greensboro, 336-275-6115

Griffin, Andrew Steven (12 mentions)
Wake Forest U, 1983 *Certification:* Urology
180 Kimel Park Dr #110, Winston-Salem, 336-277-1717

Humphries, Raleigh Green (7 mentions)
U of Virginia, 1983 *Certification:* Urology
509 N Elam Ave #2, Greensboro, 336-275-6115

Smith, John Joseph, III (10 mentions)
Georgetown U, 1983 *Certification:* Urology
140 Charlois Blvd, Winston-Salem, 336-716-4131

Vascular Surgery

Early, Todd Franklin (12 mentions)
Eastern Virginia Med Sch, 1985
Certification: Surgery, Vascular Surgery
2704 Henry St, Greensboro, 336-621-3777

Edwards, Matthew Stevens (13 mentions)
U of Virginia, 1995 *Certification:* Surgery, Vascular Surgery
Wake Forest University Baptist Med Ctr, Winston-Salem,
336-716-2255

Hansen, Kimberley J. (20 mentions)
U of Alabama, 1980
Certification: Surgery, Surgical Critical Care, Vascular Surgery
Wake Forest University Baptist Med Ctr, Winston-Salem,
336-716-4151

Hayes, Paul Gregory (14 mentions)
FMS-Canada, 1982
Certification: Surgery, Surgical Critical Care, Vascular Surgery
2704 Henry St, Greensboro, 336-621-3777

Thompson, Burke E. (12 mentions)
U of South Florida, 1996
Certification: Surgery, Surgical Critical Care
1002 N Church St #302, Greensboro, 336-274-8444

Mecklenburg County

Allergy/Immunology

Klimas, John T. (21 mentions)
U of Buffalo, 1973
Certification: Allergy & Immunology, Pediatrics
2630 E 7th St #100, Charlotte, 704-372-7900

Norris, John Gray (10 mentions)
Med Coll of Georgia, 1993 *Certification:* Allergy & Immunology
2630 E 7th St #100, Charlotte, 704-372-7900

O'Connor, Maeve Edel (24 mentions)
U of South Carolina, 1997
Certification: Allergy & Immunology, Internal Medicine
2630 E 7th St #100, Charlotte, 704-372-7900
14135 Ballantyne Corporate Pl #225, Charlotte, 704-542-8521
900 Branchview Dr #100, Concord, 704-792-1131
1315 E Sunset Dr #203, Monroe, 704-289-3900

Anesthesiology

Buchanan, Dale Conway (3 mentions)
Med U of South Carolina, 1982
Certification: Anesthesiology, Pediatrics
200 Hawthorne Ln, Charlotte, 704-384-4274

Cameron, Calvin Brian (4 mentions)
FMS-Canada, 1977 *Certification:* Anesthesiology
200 Hawthorne Ln, Charlotte, 704-377-9410

Coyle, Joseph Paul (6 mentions)
Hahnemann U, 1978
Certification: Anesthesiology, Critical Care Medicine
1000 Blythe Blvd, Charlotte, 704-377-5772

Doolittle, Thomas P. (3 mentions)
Med Coll of Wisconsin, 1990 *Certification:* Anesthesiology
1000 Blythe Blvd, Charlotte, 704-377-5772
927 East Blvd, Charlotte, 704-377-5772

Ducey, Joseph Paul (10 mentions)
U of California-Irvine, 1981
Certification: Anesthesiology, Internal Medicine
200 Hawthorne Ln, Charlotte, 704-384-4274

Ebert, John Peter (3 mentions)
Midwestern U Chicago Coll of Osteopathic Med, 1973
Certification: Anesthesiology
200 Hawthorne Ln, Charlotte, 704-384-4274

Geller, Harley Steven (5 mentions)
U of Minnesota, 1983 *Certification:* Anesthesiology
1000 Blythe Blvd, Charlotte, 704-377-5772

Gray, Brian Thomas (3 mentions)
U of Texas-Houston, 1986 *Certification:* Anesthesiology
200 Hawthorne Ln, Charlotte, 704-384-4274

Hershey, Charles Dana, Jr. (4 mentions)
U of Pennsylvania, 1970 *Certification:* Anesthesiology
1000 Blythe Blvd, Charlotte, 704-377-5772

Holway, Brent Patrick (5 mentions)
Duke U, 1988
Certification: Anesthesiology, Critical Care Medicine
927 East Blvd, Charlotte, 704-377-5772

McCulloch, Harlan Arthur (5 mentions)
U of Toledo, 1984 *Certification:* Anesthesiology
927 East Blvd, Charlotte, 704-377-5772

Miller, Joshua Seth (3 mentions)
Med U of South Carolina, 1986
Certification: Anesthesiology, Pain Medicine
1000 Blythe Blvd, Charlotte, 704-377-5772

Morales, Richard (3 mentions)
Yale U, 1983 *Certification:* Anesthesiology
200 Hawthorne Ln, Charlotte, 704-384-4274

Romanoff, Mark Elliott (3 mentions)
U of Connecticut, 1983
Certification: Anesthesiology, Pain Medicine
8220 University Exec Park Dr #128, Charlotte, 704-549-1888
927 East Blvd, Charlotte, 704-377-5772

Scharf, Carl James (3 mentions)
Creighton U, 1978 *Certification:* Anesthesiology
200 Hawthorne Ln, Charlotte, 704-384-4274

Velardo, Bernard (10 mentions)
Wayne State U, 1984
Certification: Anesthesiology, Critical Care Medicine
1000 Blythe Blvd, Charlotte, 704-377-5772
927 East Blvd, Charlotte, 704-377-5772

Williford, John K., Jr. (9 mentions)
Wake Forest U, 1979 *Certification:* Anesthesiology
200 Hawthorne Ln, Charlotte, 704-384-4274

Cardiac Surgery

Andrews, David Scott (13 mentions)
Ohio State U, 1975 *Certification:* Thoracic Surgery
301 Hawthorne Ln #200, Charlotte, 704-316-5100

Edwards, Charles Hillman (25 mentions)
U of North Carolina, 1973 *Certification:* Thoracic Surgery
301 Hawthorne Ln #200, Charlotte, 704-316-5100
156 Centre Church Rd #207, Mooresville, 704-799-3939

Reames, Mark Kevin (21 mentions)
Med U of South Carolina, 1985
Certification: Surgery, Thoracic Surgery
1001 Blythe Blvd #300, Charlotte, 704-373-0212

Skipper, Eric R. (21 mentions)
Wake Forest U, 1985 *Certification:* Surgery, Thoracic Surgery
1001 Blythe Blvd #300, Charlotte, 704-373-1500

Stiegel, Robert Mark (16 mentions)
U of North Carolina, 1979 *Certification:* Thoracic Surgery
1001 Blythe Blvd #300, Charlotte, 704-373-0212

Cardiology

Clinard, George Craig (4 mentions)
Wake Forest U, 1990
Certification: Cardiovascular Disease, Internal Medicine
101 E WT Harris Blvd #1213, Charlotte, 704-549-8997

Framm, David Jonathan (7 mentions)
George Washington U, 1986
Certification: Cardiovascular Disease, Internal Medicine
1900 Brunswick Ave, Charlotte, 704-358-4400

Frank, Theodore Alan (7 mentions)
U of Pennsylvania, 1992 *Certification:* Cardiovascular Disease
1001 Blythe Blvd #300, Charlotte, 704-373-0212

Greene, Craig Alan (14 mentions)
Med U of South Carolina, 1986 *Certification:* Pediatric Cardiology
1718 E 4th St #304, Charlotte, 704-316-1220

Gulati, Sanjeev Kumar (5 mentions)
U of Pennsylvania, 1994 *Certification:* Cardiovascular Disease
1001 Blythe Blvd #300, Charlotte, 704-373-0212
10344 Park Rd #100, Charlotte, 704-543-0546

Holshouser, John Warren (4 mentions)
U of North Carolina, 1996 *Certification:* Cardiovascular
Disease, Clinical Cardiac Electrophysiology, Internal Medicine
1001 Blythe Blvd #300, Charlotte, 704-373-0212

Iwaoka, Robert Steven (10 mentions)
U of Illinois, 1981 *Certification:* Cardiovascular Disease,
Internal Medicine, Interventional Cardiology
1718 E 4th St #501, Charlotte, 704-343-9800

Jacoby, Richard Michael (4 mentions)
Temple U, 1986 *Certification:* Cardiovascular Disease,
Internal Medicine, Interventional Cardiology
309 S Sharon Amity Rd #200, Charlotte, 704-944-1135
19620 W Catawba Ave #204, Cornelius, 704-896-8547

McMillan, Edward Beman (7 mentions)
Duke U, 1990
Certification: Cardiovascular Disease, Internal Medicine
1718 E 4th St #501, Charlotte, 704-343-9800

Miller, Richard F. (4 mentions)
Certification: Cardiovascular Disease, Internal Medicine
15110 John J Delaney Dr, Charlotte, 704-302-8100
332 Sam Newwell Rd 2nd Fl, Matthews, 704-302-8500

Ohmstede, David Picman (5 mentions)
Wake Forest U, 1996 *Certification:* Pediatric Cardiology
1718 E 4th St #304, Charlotte, 704-316-1220

Owen, Dale, Jr. (4 mentions)
Wake Forest U, 1986
Certification: Cardiovascular Disease, Internal Medicine
1900 Brunswick Ave, Charlotte, 704-358-4400

Pasquini, John Aldo (16 mentions)
U of Connecticut, 1980 *Certification:* Cardiovascular
Disease, Internal Medicine, Interventional Cardiology
1718 E 4th St #501, Charlotte, 704-343-9800
911 W Henderson St #230, Salisbury, 704-633-9620

Roberts, William Stanley (8 mentions)
U of Virginia, 1975
Certification: Cardiovascular Disease, Internal Medicine
2630 E 7th St #210, Charlotte, 704-334-0600

Rose, Geoffrey Andrew (21 mentions)
U of Pennsylvania, 1988
Certification: Cardiovascular Disease, Internal Medicine
1001 Blythe Blvd #300, Charlotte, 704-373-0212

Uszenski, Ronald T. (7 mentions)
FMS-Grenada, 1986
Certification: Cardiovascular Disease, Internal Medicine
10030 Gilead Rd, Huntersville, 704-887-4530

Weeks, Kenneth Durham (10 mentions)
Duke U, 1974
Certification: Cardiovascular Disease, Internal Medicine
16525 Holly Crest Ln #230, Huntersville, 704-887-4530

Wilson, Bryan Hadley (6 mentions)
Duke U, 1980 *Certification:* Cardiovascular Disease,
Internal Medicine, Interventional Cardiology
1001 Blythe Blvd #300, Charlotte, 704-373-0212

Dermatology

Brown, Charles Jacob (5 mentions)
U of North Carolina, 1987 *Certification:* Dermatology
2310 Randolph Rd, Charlotte, 704-376-9849

Edwards, Irene Elizabeth (9 mentions)
Wake Forest U, 1976
Certification: Dermatology, Internal Medicine, Pediatrics
4335 Colwick Rd #B, Charlotte, 704-367-9777

Fraser, Donald Doyle (5 mentions)
New Jersey Med Sch, 1980 *Certification:* Dermatology
1901 Brunswick Ave #240, Charlotte, 704-377-3299

Reid, John Heyward (5 mentions)
Med U of South Carolina, 1973 *Certification:* Dermatology
1401 Matthews Township Pkwy #220, Matthews, 704-384-6025

Roddey, Patricia K. (11 mentions)
U of North Carolina, 1990 *Certification:* Dermatology
3030 Randolph Rd, Charlotte, 704-302-8200

Smith, Rebecca L. (7 mentions)
Baylor U, 1990 *Certification:* Dermatology, Pediatric Dermatology
1700 1st Baxter Crossing #101, Fort Mill, SC, 803-802-3376

Snyder, Christopher Alan (7 mentions)
East Tennessee State U, 1988 *Certification:* Dermatology
1928 Randolph Rd #316, Charlotte, 704-344-8846

Thompson, John Albert, Jr. (8 mentions)
Wake Forest U, 1967 *Certification:* Dermatology
2310 Randolph Rd, Charlotte, 704-376-9849

Wernikoff, Stuart Yale (14 mentions)
U of Buffalo, 1983 *Certification:* Dermatology
2015 Randolph Rd #210, Charlotte, 704-333-8811

Emergency Medicine

Clark, John Blue, Jr. (5 mentions)
Vanderbilt U, 1973
Certification: Emergency Medicine, Internal Medicine
200 Hawthorne Ln, Charlotte, 704-377-2424

Fletcher, Sidney Marc (12 mentions)
U of Texas-Dallas, 1994 *Certification:* Emergency Medicine
200 Hawthorne Ln, Charlotte, 704-377-2424

Garvey, Joseph L., Jr. (4 mentions)
U of Cincinnati, 1988 *Certification:* Emergency Medicine
1000 Blythe Blvd, Charlotte, 704-355-3181

Hall, Timothy James (3 mentions)
U of North Carolina, 1983 *Certification:* Emergency Medicine
3101 Latrobe Dr, Charlotte, 704-376-7362

Kline, Jeffrey Allen (3 mentions)
Virginia Commonwealth U, 1990
Certification: Emergency Medicine
1000 Blythe Blvd, Charlotte, 704-355-3181

Lietz, Timothy Edward (3 mentions)
Ohio State U, 1990 *Certification:* Emergency Medicine
200 Hawthorne Ln, Charlotte, 704-377-2424

Marx, John Andrew (10 mentions)
Stanford U, 1977 *Certification:* Emergency Medicine
1000 Blythe Blvd, Charlotte, 704-355-3181

McBryde, John Peter (11 mentions)
Med U of South Carolina, 1992
Certification: Emergency Medicine, Sports Medicine
1000 Blythe Blvd, Charlotte, 704-355-3181

Ringwood, John William (4 mentions)
Wake Forest U, 1977
Certification: Pediatric Emergency Medicine, Pediatrics
200 Hawthorne Ln, Charlotte, 704-377-2424

Sullivan, David Matthew (3 mentions)
Hahnemann U, 1996 *Certification:* Emergency Medicine
1000 Blythe Blvd, Charlotte, 704-355-3181

Zban, William Matthew (6 mentions)
Marshall U, 1989 *Certification:* Emergency Medicine
1900 Randolph Rd #900, Charlotte, 704-377-2424

Endocrinology

Bracken, Roberta Samelson (12 mentions)
Temple U, 1983 *Certification:* Endocrinology, Diabetes, and
Metabolism, Internal Medicine
335 N Caswell Rd, Charlotte, 704-338-6300
1918 Randolph Rd #220, Charlotte, 704-316-1125

Kleinmann, Richard Eckert (23 mentions)
U of Pennsylvania, 1973
Certification: Endocrinology and Metabolism, Internal Medicine
1918 Randolph Rd #220, Charlotte, 704-316-1125

Miller, Edith Hamilton (8 mentions)
Med U of South Carolina, 1975
Certification: Endocrinology and Metabolism, Internal Medicine
1025 Morehead Medical Dr #500, Charlotte, 704-446-2320
1000 Blythe Blvd, Charlotte, 704-355-3165
1350 S Kings Dr, Charlotte, 704-446-1242

Parker, Mark William (15 mentions)
Ohio State U, 1978
Certification: Pediatric Endocrinology, Pediatrics
130 Providence Rd, Charlotte, 704-334-7950

Robinson, Douglas Baird (16 mentions)
U of Pittsburgh, 1985 *Certification:* Endocrinology,
Diabetes, and Metabolism, Internal Medicine
1001 Blythe Blvd #500, Charlotte, 704-355-5100

Rolband, Gary Charles (12 mentions)
U of Vermont, 1986 *Certification:* Endocrinology, Diabetes, and Metabolism, Internal Medicine
4525 Cameron Valley Pkwy #4100, Charlotte, 704-302-8310

Spitz, Adam Frederick (12 mentions)
SUNY-Downstate Med Coll, 1988 *Certification:* Endocrinology, Diabetes, and Metabolism, Internal Medicine
1918 Randolph Rd #220, Charlotte, 704-316-1125

Family Practice *(see note on page 9)*

Almquist, Robert Earl (4 mentions)
Columbia U, 1982 *Certification:* Family Medicine
10000 Park Cedar Dr, Charlotte, 704-542-6577

Barringer, Loveleen (3 mentions)
Wayne State U, 1997 *Certification:* Family Medicine
16525 Holly Crest Ln #150, Huntersville, 704-384-1725

Barringer, Thomas Avery, III (3 mentions)
U of North Carolina, 1979 *Certification:* Family Medicine
5516 Central Ave, Charlotte, 704-446-1000

Cook, David Martin (4 mentions)
U of North Carolina, 1990 *Certification:* Family Medicine
19485 Old Jeton Rd #100, Cornelius, 704-384-1775

Crawford, John Thomas (6 mentions)
Wake Forest U, 1987 *Certification:* Family Medicine
9101 Monroe Rd #155, Charlotte, 704-384-1260

Devine, Brian David (4 mentions)
Jefferson Med Coll, 1997 *Certification:* Family Medicine
10220 Prosperity Park Dr #300, Charlotte, 704-384-1425

Hall, Mary Nolan (5 mentions)
Cornell U, 1983 *Certification:* Family Medicine
5516 Central Ave, Charlotte, 704-446-1000

Hoben, Michael Skow (8 mentions)
U of North Carolina, 1998 *Certification:* Family Medicine
200 Greenwich Rd, Charlotte, 704-384-8680

McMillan, Marshall P. (4 mentions)
Med U of South Carolina, 1984 *Certification:* Family Medicine
9101 Monroe Rd #155, Charlotte, 704-384-1260

Menscer, Darlyne (4 mentions)
U of North Carolina, 1979
Certification: Family Medicine, Geriatric Medicine
1350 S Kings Dr, Charlotte, 704-446-1000

Mueller, Andrew T. (3 mentions)
U of North Carolina, 1996 *Certification:* Family Medicine
5818 Blakeney Dr #200-B, Charlotte, 704-316-5080

Saxe, Jessica Schorr (3 mentions)
Tufts U, 1977 *Certification:* Family Medicine
1801 Rozzelles Ferry Rd, Charlotte, 704-446-9987

Teigland, Lillian M. (4 mentions)
Duke U, 1980 *Certification:* Family Medicine
6324 Fairview Rd #201, Charlotte, 704-384-0588

Wolff, Christian George (4 mentions)
U of Alabama, 1994 *Certification:* Family Medicine
19485 Old Jetton Rd, Cornelius, 704-384-1775

Wrinkle, Geoffrey Thomas (3 mentions)
U of Virginia, 1993 *Certification:* Family Medicine
10000 Park Cedar Dr, Charlotte, 704-542-6577

Zink, Irene Marie (3 mentions)
U of Cincinnati, 1996 *Certification:* Family Medicine
1801 Rozzelles Ferry Rd, Charlotte, 704-446-9987

Gastroenterology

Brann, Oscar Sven (6 mentions)
Baylor U, 1984 *Certification:* Gastroenterology, Internal Medicine, Transplant Hepatology
3030 Randolph Rd #200, Charlotte, 704-302-8200

Deal, Stephen Edgar (10 mentions)
U of North Carolina, 1986
Certification: Gastroenterology, Internal Medicine
1450 Matthews Township Pkwy, Matthews, 704-372-7974
300 Billingsley Rd, Charlotte, 704-372-7974

Gaspari, Michael Marion (7 mentions)
Hahnemann U, 1981
Certification: Gastroenterology, Internal Medicine
300 Billingsley Rd, Charlotte, 704-372-7974

Gavigan, Thomas Joseph (10 mentions)
Georgetown U, 1974
Certification: Gastroenterology, Internal Medicine
1450 Matthews Township Pkwy #400, Matthews, 704-377-4009
2015 Randolph Rd #208, Charlotte, 704-377-4009

Hanson, John Stephen (14 mentions)
Washington U, 1979 *Certification:* Gastroenterology, Internal Medicine, Transplant Hepatology
2015 Randolph Rd #208, Charlotte, 704-377-4009

Houck, William Stokes, III (9 mentions)
Med U of South Carolina, 1991
Certification: Pediatric Gastroenterology
1718 4th St #208, Charlotte, 704-316-5060
527 S New Hope Rd, Gastonia, 704-316-5060

Pacicco, Thomas John (16 mentions)
New York Med Coll, 1985
Certification: Gastroenterology, Internal Medicine
1001 Blythe Blvd #500, Charlotte, 704-355-5100
3025 Springbank Ln #100, Charlotte, 704-542-2543

Roberts, Thomas Adams, Jr. (7 mentions)
U of North Carolina, 1970
Certification: Gastroenterology, Internal Medicine
2015 Randolph Rd #208, Charlotte, 704-377-4009

Roddey, John Gardiner, Jr. (8 mentions)
U of North Carolina, 1990
Certification: Gastroenterology, Internal Medicine
2015 Randolph Rd #208, Charlotte, 704-377-4009

Sandberg, James William (14 mentions)
Med Coll of Wisconsin, 1987
Certification: Pediatric Gastroenterology
1718 E 4th St #208, Charlotte, 704-316-5060

Scobey, Martin William (6 mentions)
U of Tennessee, 1980
Certification: Gastroenterology, Internal Medicine
1001 Blythe Blvd, Charlotte, 704-355-1451

Sigmon, Richard Lee, Jr. (11 mentions)
U of North Carolina, 1979
Certification: Gastroenterology, Internal Medicine, Pediatrics
1001 Blythe Blvd #403, Charlotte, 704-355-5100
3025 Springbank Ln #100, Charlotte, 704-446-2620

Smith, David Scott (8 mentions)
U of South Alabama, 1998
Certification: Gastroenterology, Internal Medicine
3035 Randolph Rd, Charlotte, 704-302-8200

Werth, Thomas Edward (6 mentions)
U of Kansas, 1985 *Certification:* Gastroenterology, Internal Medicine, Transplant Hepatology
6324 Fsirview Rd #204, Charlotte, 704-377-4009

Yavorski, Robert Thomas (23 mentions)
Tulane U, 1987 *Certification:* Gastroenterology, Internal Medicine
1001 Blythe Blvd #500, Charlotte, 704-355-5100

General Surgery

Attorri, Robert Joseph (4 mentions)
U of Pennsylvania, 1984 *Certification:* Pediatric Surgery
1900 Randolph Rd #210, Charlotte, 704-370-0223

Bohn, Jeffrey Andrew (6 mentions)
U of Cincinnati, 1980 *Certification:* Surgery
1918 Randolph Rd #500, Charlotte, 704-342-8105
1450 Matthews Township Pkwy, Matthews, 704-342-8105

Collin, Charles Frederick (5 mentions)
Tulane U, 1975 *Certification:* Surgery
1918 Randolph Rd #500, Charlotte, 704-342-8105

Evans, Ernest Craig (12 mentions)
Med U of South Carolina, 1973 *Certification:* Surgery
1918 Randolph Rd #130, Charlotte, 704-364-8100

Flippo, Teresa Skidmore (6 mentions)
West Virginia U, 1986 *Certification:* Surgery
1000 Blythe Blvd, Charlotte, 704-355-7176

Fowler, Wyatt Charles (11 mentions)
Wake Forest U, 1985 *Certification:* Surgery
2104 Randolph Rd, Charlotte, 704-377-3900

Godwin, Winston Y., Jr. (6 mentions)
Med U of South Carolina, 1978 *Certification:* Surgery
1450 Matthews Township Pkwy #360, Matthews, 704-841-1444
101 E WT Harris Blvd #2221, Charlotte, 704-547-9196
1918 Randolph Rd #130, Matthews, 704-364-8100

Heniford, Brant Todd (8 mentions)
Med U of South Carolina, 1989 *Certification:* Surgery
1001 Blythe Blvd #602, Charlotte, 704-355-1813

Kercher, Kent Williams (13 mentions)
U of North Carolina, 1994 *Certification:* Surgery
1025 Morehead Medical Dr #200, Charlotte, 704-355-1813

Lowe, Carl Jarrett, Jr. (7 mentions)
Emory U, 1997 *Certification:* Surgery
2104 Randolph Rd, Charlotte, 704-377-3900
1450 Matthews Township Pkwy #320, Matthews, 704-377-3900

Morton, Duncan (6 mentions)
U of North Carolina, 1966 *Certification:* Pediatric Surgery
1900 Randolph Rd #210, Charlotte, 704-370-0223

Novick, Thomas Leonard (14 mentions)
Duke U, 1978 *Certification:* Surgery
1918 Randolph Rd #500, Charlotte, 704-342-8105

Orland, Paul Jay (4 mentions)
U of Rochester, 1988 *Certification:* Surgery, Vascular Surgery
1918 Randolph Rd #780, Charlotte, 704-342-8105

Parsons, Marshal Ray (6 mentions)
U of New Mexico, 1977 *Certification:* Surgery
2104 Randolph Rd, Charlotte, 704-377-3900
1450 Matthews Township Pkwy #320, Matthews, 704-377-3900

Pederson, Lee Carl (6 mentions)
U of Oklahoma, 1994 *Certification:* Surgery
1918 Randolph Rd #130, Charlotte, 704-364-8100

Turk, Peter Smith (17 mentions)
Indiana U, 1985 *Certification:* Surgery
2104 Randolph Rd, Charlotte, 704-377-3900

Webster, Leslie Tillotson (4 mentions)
Case Western Reserve U, 1994 *Certification:* Surgery
1918 Randolph Rd #130, Charlotte, 704-364-8100
10512 Park Rd #111, Charlotte, 704-542-3631

White, Richard L., Jr. (5 mentions)
Columbia U, 1986 *Certification:* Surgery
1000 Blythe Blvd #600, Charlotte, 704-355-2884

Zbinden, Louis H., III (5 mentions)
U of Texas-Dallas, 1990 *Certification:* Surgery
1416 E Morehead St #201, Charlotte, 704-333-0741
10344 Park Rd, Charlotte, 704-541-3104

Geriatrics

Honeycutt, Danny Morris (10 mentions)
Wake Forest U, 1979
Certification: Family Medicine, Geriatric Medicine
332 Sam Newell Rd #2000, Matthews, 704-302-8375

Menscer, Darlyne (4 mentions)
U of North Carolina, 1979
Certification: Family Medicine, Geriatric Medicine
5516 Central Ave, Charlotte, 704-446-1000

Hematology/Oncology

Boyd, James Francis (30 mentions)
Duke U, 1974
2711 Randolph Rd #100, Charlotte, 704-342-1900

Brick, Wendy Gram (8 mentions)
Med Coll of Georgia, 1995
Certification: Internal Medicine, Medical Oncology
1025 Morehead Medical Dr #200, Charlotte, 704-302-8000

Chapman, Geoffrey Sewall (12 mentions)
U of California-San Francisco, 1975
Certification: Hematology, Internal Medicine, Medical Oncology
2711 Randolph Rd #100, Charlotte, 704-342-1900

Frenette, Gary Patrick (27 mentions)
U of Michigan, 1990
Certification: Internal Medicine, Medical Oncology
1100 S Tryon St #400, Charlotte, 704-446-9046

Hauch, Thomas Wray (7 mentions)
Northwestern U, 1972
Certification: Hematology, Internal Medicine, Medical Oncology
411 Billingsley Rd #103, Charlotte, 704-344-1995

Limentani, Steven A. (12 mentions)
Tufts U, 1986
Certification: Hematology, Internal Medicine, Medical Oncology
1100 S Tryon St #400, Charlotte, 704-446-9046

Mahoney, John Francis (13 mentions)
U of Pittsburgh, 1984
Certification: Internal Medicine, Medical Oncology
1001 Blythe Blvd #500, Charlotte, 704-355-5100
1100 S Tryon St #400, Charlotte, 704-446-9046

Miller, David Weldon (9 mentions)
Med Coll of Georgia, 1990
Certification: Hematology, Internal Medicine, Medical Oncology
1025 Morehead Medical Dr #200, Charlotte, 704-302-8000

Mogul, Mark Jeffrey (13 mentions)
SUNY-Upstate Med U, 1987
301 Hawthorne #100, Charlotte, 704-384-1900

Taylor, Harvey Grant (7 mentions)
Duke U, 1972
Certification: Hematology, Internal Medicine, Medical Oncology
2711 Randolph Rd #100, Charlotte, 704-342-1900

Infectious Disease

Ahmed, Amina (16 mentions)
U of North Carolina, 1990
Certification: Pediatric Infectious Diseases
100 Blythe Blvd #200-C, Charlotte, 704-381-8840

Lackey, Philip Carlyle (10 mentions)
U of North Carolina, 1990
Certification: Infectious Disease, Internal Medicine
4539 Hedgemore Dr #100, Charlotte, 704-331-9669

McCurdy, Lewis Hall, III (16 mentions)
U of Alabama, 1996
Certification: Infectious Disease, Internal Medicine
4539 Hedgemore Dr #100, Charlotte, 704-331-9669

Rupar, David Gerard (10 mentions)
Georgetown U, 1979
Certification: Pediatric Infectious Diseases, Pediatrics
100 Blythe Blvd #200, Charlotte, 704-381-8840

Tanner, David Cleon (32 mentions)
Med Coll of Georgia, 1986 *Certification:* Infectious Disease, Internal Medicine, Medical Microbiology
4539 Hedgemore Dr #100, Charlotte, 704-331-9669

Verville, Thomas David (18 mentions)
U of Oklahoma, 1988
Certification: Infectious Disease, Internal Medicine
4539 Hedgemore Dr #100, Charlotte, 704-331-9669

Infertility

Teaff, Nancy Lee (9 mentions)
U of North Carolina, 1978 *Certification:* Obstetrics & Gynecology, Reproductive Endocrinology/Infertility
1524 E Morehead St, Charlotte, 704-343-3400

Wing, Richard Lee (26 mentions)
U of North Carolina, 1976 *Certification:* Obstetrics & Gynecology
1524 E Morehead St, Charlotte, 704-343-3400

Internal Medicine *(see note on page 9)*

Adcock, Jimmie Warren (12 mentions)
U of North Carolina, 1982 *Certification:* Internal Medicine
1918 Randolph Rd #420, Charlotte, 704-384-7085

Ayers, Lorri A. (3 mentions)
Ohio State U, 1990 *Certification:* Internal Medicine
4525 Cameron Valley Pkwy, Charlotte, 704-770-3200

Batchelor, Thomas Allen (4 mentions)
U of Virginia, 1994 *Certification:* Internal Medicine
16455 Statesville Rd #360, Huntersville, 704-801-3300

Benedum, John Loyle (3 mentions)
West Virginia U, 1973 *Certification:* Internal Medicine
3030 Randolph Rd #200, Charlotte, 704-302-8200

Bowen, Robert Calvin, III (8 mentions)
U of North Carolina, 1999 *Certification:* Internal Medicine
3030 Randolph Rd #200, Charlotte, 704-302-8200

Ferree, Charles Elliot (4 mentions)
U of North Carolina, 1980 *Certification:* Internal Medicine
10512 Park Rd Ext, Charlotte, 704-302-8900

Friedland, Michael Brian (8 mentions)
Mount Sinai Sch of Med, 1992 *Certification:* Internal Medicine
1001 Blythe Blvd, Charlotte, 704-355-5100

Furney, Scott Leo (3 mentions)
U of Michigan, 1992 *Certification:* Internal Medicine
1350 S Kings Dr, Charlotte, 704-446-1242

Gibson, John McNeill (3 mentions)
U of North Carolina, 1972 *Certification:* Internal Medicine
16455 Statesville Rd #200, Huntersville, 704-302-8600

Harrell, Jane Stubbs (4 mentions)
Wake Forest U, 2000 *Certification:* Internal Medicine
1025 Morehead Medical Dr #200, Charlotte, 704-302-8000

Heyer, Robert Allan (4 mentions)
U of Texas-Dallas, 1973
Certification: Internal Medicine, Pulmonary Disease
1000 Blythe Blvd, Charlotte, 704-355-5100
1350 S Kings Dr, Charlotte, 704-446-1242

Hudson, Albert Denning (7 mentions)
U of North Carolina, 1986 *Certification:* Internal Medicine
1001 Blythe Blvd #500, Charlotte, 704-355-5100
1000 Blythe Blvd, Charlotte, 704-355-5100

Justis, Peter Stinnett (7 mentions)
East Carolina U, 1990 *Certification:* Internal Medicine
1001 Blythe Blvd #500, Charlotte, 704-355-5100
1000 Blythe Blvd, Charlotte, 704-355-5100

Kane, Loren Scott (3 mentions)
U of Buffalo, 1997 *Certification:* Internal Medicine
2700 Coltsgate Rd #101, Charlotte, 704-367-4373

Kirk, Benjamin Alan (3 mentions)
West Virginia U, 1996 *Certification:* Internal Medicine
1001 Blythe Blvd #500, Charlotte, 704-355-5100

Landis, Eric Tyler (5 mentions)
U of North Carolina, 1997 *Certification:* Internal Medicine
10512 Park Rd #201, Charlotte, 704-302-8700
1000 Blythe Blvd, Charlotte, 704-355-2000

Malone, David Paul (5 mentions)
West Virginia U, 1990 *Certification:* Internal Medicine
1401 Matthews Township Pkwy #200, Matthews, 704-384-6901

Parker, Thomas Eugene (8 mentions)
Ohio State U, 1974 *Certification:* Internal Medicine
330 Billingsley Rd #101, Charlotte, 704-384-1605

Rich, Charles B., Jr. (4 mentions)
Wake Forest U, 1982 *Certification:* Internal Medicine
200 S College St #500, Charlotte, 704-302-8800

Russ, Donald James (6 mentions)
U of Maryland, 1973 *Certification:* Internal Medicine
4525 Cameron Valley Pkwy, Charlotte, 704-770-3200

Sensenbrenner, John W. (4 mentions)
East Carolina U, 1984
8821 Blakeney Professional Dr, Charlotte, 704-887-1101

Shapiro, Marvin B. (3 mentions)
U of Alabama, 1966
Certification: Gastroenterology, Internal Medicine
1001 Blythe Blvd #500, Charlotte, 704-355-5100
1000 Blythe Blvd, Charlotte, 704-355-5100

Shoaf, Edwin Huss, Jr. (14 mentions)
Wake Forest U, 1975 *Certification:* Internal Medicine
1918 Randolph Rd #350, Charlotte, 704-384-1750

Weidner, Gregory Robert (5 mentions)
U of Rochester, 1991 *Certification:* Internal Medicine
15110 John Delaney Dr #200, Charlotte, 704-302-8100

Nephrology

Blake, Paul S. (11 mentions)
Ohio U Coll of Osteopathic Med, 1990
Certification: Internal Medicine, Nephrology
2301 W Morehead St, Charlotte, 704-333-4217

Cremisi, Henry David (12 mentions)
Tufts U, 1988 *Certification:* Internal Medicine, Nephrology
2301 W Morehead St, Charlotte, 704-333-4217

Griffith, Todd Frederick (8 mentions)
U of North Carolina, 1997
Certification: Internal Medicine, Nephrology
2711 Randolph Rd #400, Charlotte, 704-348-2992

Gritter, Nancy Jo (23 mentions)
Indiana U, 1992 *Certification:* Internal Medicine, Nephrology
2711 Randolph Rd #400, Charlotte, 704-348-2992

Hart, George Milburn (14 mentions)
Wake Forest U, 1986 *Certification:* Internal Medicine, Nephrology
2711 Randolph Rd #400, Charlotte, 704-348-2992

Massengill, Susan Foster (6 mentions)
East Carolina U, 1987 *Certification:* Pediatric Nephrology
100 Blythe Blvd #200-C, Charlotte, 704-381-8840

Tierney, Daniel Joseph (6 mentions)
Case Western Reserve U, 1995 *Certification:* Nephrology
2711 Randolph Rd #400, Charlotte, 704-348-2992

Turner, Murray Wells (9 mentions)
Wake Forest U, 1980 *Certification:* Internal Medicine, Nephrology
2711 Randolph Rd #400, Charlotte, 704-348-2992

Neurological Surgery

Adamson, Tim Eugene (30 mentions)
Vanderbilt U, 1985 *Certification:* Neurological Surgery
225 Baldwin Ave, Charlotte, 704-376-1605

Asher, Anthony Lawrence (12 mentions)
Wayne State U, 1987 *Certification:* Neurological Surgery
225 Baldwin Ave, Charlotte, 704-376-1605

Dyer, Emmet Hunter (18 mentions)
U of Mississippi, 1988 *Certification:* Neurological Surgery
1010 Edgehill Rd N, Charlotte, 704-376-1605
225 Baldwin Ave, Charlotte, 704-376-1605

Heafner, Michael Daniel (13 mentions)
Wake Forest U, 1979 *Certification:* Neurological Surgery
225 Baldwin Ave, Charlotte, 704-376-1605

Van Der Veer, Craig A. (17 mentions)
Rosalind Franklin U, 1979 *Certification:* Neurological Surgery
225 Baldwin Ave, Charlotte, 704-376-1605

Neurology

Borresen, Thor Erik (5 mentions)
New Jersey Med Sch, 1979 *Certification:* Neurology
1900 Randolph Rd #1010, Charlotte, 704-334-7311

Chaconas, Aris Evan (20 mentions)
Georgetown U, 1988 *Certification:* Neurology
1718 E 4th #404, Charlotte, 704-384-9437
1900 Randolph Rd #1010, Charlotte, 704-334-7311

Diedrich, Andrea Lynn (27 mentions)
Emory U, 1992
3541 Randolph Rd, Charlotte, 704-377-9323

Hart, Carolyn Elizabeth (7 mentions)
Emory U, 1987 *Certification:* Neurology with Special
Qualifications in Child Neurology
1900 Randolph Rd #1010, Charlotte, 704-334-7311

Nelson, Teresita Y. (9 mentions)
U of Texas-Galveston, 1989 *Certification:* Neurology with
Special Qualifications in Child Neurology
2311 Copper Way #200, Charlotte, 704-541-8788

Pfeiffer, Frederick E., II (13 mentions)
Vanderbilt U, 1976 *Certification:* Internal Medicine, Neurology
1900 Randolph Rd #1010, Charlotte, 704-334-7311

Pugh, James Edwin, Jr. (8 mentions)
U of Pennsylvania, 1967 *Certification:* Neurology
1900 Randolph Rd #1010, Charlotte, 704-334-7311

Putman, Steven Frederick (24 mentions)
Northwestern U, 1978 *Certification:* Neurology
12311 Copper Way #200, Charlotte, 704-541-8788

Schmidt, Jeffrey J. (6 mentions)
Certification: Neurology
1918 Randolph Rd #400, Charlotte, 704-384-9437

Shauger, Kenneth Leslie (5 mentions)
U of North Carolina, 1993 *Certification:* Neurology
1010 Edgehill Rd N, Charlotte, 704-446-1900

Obstetrics/Gynecology

Beurskens, Maureen Leonie (6 mentions)
U of Massachusetts, 1981 *Certification:* Obstetrics & Gynecology
1025 Morehead Medical Dr #400, Charlotte, 704-446-1700
7810 Providence Rd #101, Charlotte, 704-543-0093
16455 Statesville Rd #480, Huntersville, 704-446-1700

Bohmer, James Thomas (4 mentions)
U of Kansas, 1995 *Certification:* Obstetrics & Gynecology
1718 E 4th St #307, Charlotte, 704-384-1620
15825 John J Delaney Dr #200, Charlotte, 704-384-1620

De Hoff, Philip W. (3 mentions)
U of South Florida, 1980 *Certification:* Obstetrics & Gynecology
1718 E 4th St #907, Charlotte, 704-372-4000

Fishburne, Cary N., Jr. (3 mentions)
U of Virginia, 1994 *Certification:* Obstetrics & Gynecology
150 Providence Rd, Charlotte, 704-973-2106
1450 Matthews Township Pkwy #200, Matthews, 704-246-1846

Fletcher, Amy Marie (3 mentions)
Wake Forest U, 1996 *Certification:* Obstetrics & Gynecology
1718 E 4th St #307, Charlotte, 704-384-1620

Freeman-Kwaku, Mala A. (3 mentions)
U of Virginia, 1998 *Certification:* Obstetrics & Gynecology
3125 Springbank Ln #B, Charlotte, 704-341-1103

Gourley, Blanton Craig (4 mentions)
U of North Carolina, 1981 *Certification:* Obstetrics & Gynecology
16455 Statesville Rd #480, Huntersville, 704-373-1541
1025 Morehead Medical Dr #400, Charlotte, 704-373-1541

Hall, James Bryan (3 mentions)
Med U of South Carolina, 1974
Certification: Gynecologic Oncology, Obstetrics & Gynecology
1025 Morehead Medical Dr #600, Charlotte, 704-355-3149

Harouny, Victor R. (4 mentions)
Certification: Obstetrics & Gynecology
1450 Matthews Township Pkwy #200, Matthews, 704-246-1846

Harston, Phillip Reed (4 mentions)
U of Louisville, 1979 *Certification:* Obstetrics & Gynecology
2711 Randolph Rd #512, Charlotte, 704-333-4104

Lindner, Leslie Hansen (6 mentions)
U of Pennsylvania, 1992
1025 Morehead Medical Dr #400, Charlotte, 704-373-1541
7810 Providence Rd, Charlotte, 704-446-1700

Lucas, Jack Alan (4 mentions)
U of North Carolina, 1982 *Certification:* Obstetrics & Gynecology
1025 Morehead Medical Dr #450, Charlotte, 704-541-8287
1350 S Kings Dr, Charlotte, 704-342-4323

Palermo, Nancy Anne (5 mentions)
U of South Florida, 1990
1718 E 4th St #307, Charlotte, 704-384-1620

Parker, Gregory Dean (3 mentions)
U of North Carolina, 1984 *Certification:* Obstetrics & Gynecology
1718 E 4th St #707, Charlotte, 704-344-1000

Pixley, Roland Laurens (4 mentions)
Wake Forest U, 1983 *Certification:* Obstetrics & Gynecology
1023 Edgehill Rd S, Charlotte, 704-373-1541
1025 Morehead Medical Dr #400, Charlotte, 704-373-1541
7810 Providence Rd, Charlotte, 704-373-0209

Schneider, Scott Matthew (3 mentions)
George Washington U, 1990
Certification: Obstetrics & Gynecology
150 Providence Rd, Charlotte, 704-973-2106
10340 Park Rd, Charlotte, 704-384-1344

Sharawy, Ehab Mohamed (3 mentions)
Med Coll of Georgia, 1994 *Certification:* Obstetrics & Gynecology
10030 Gilead Rd #350, Huntersville, 704-316-4830

Svendsen, Thor Owen (3 mentions)
U of North Carolina, 1992 *Certification:* Obstetrics & Gynecology
1718 E 4th St #307, Charlotte, 704-384-1620

Taylor, John Bruce (11 mentions)
Virginia Commonwealth U, 1978
Certification: Obstetrics & Gynecology
7810 Providence Rd, Charlotte, 704-446-7800
1025 Morehead Medical Dr, Charlotte, 704-446-7800

Ward, Simon Vivian, III (7 mentions)
Louisiana State U, 1981 *Certification:* Obstetrics & Gynecology
1718 E 4th St #307, Charlotte, 704-384-1620
15825 John J Delaney Dr #200, Charlotte, 704-384-1620

Whitten, Mary Kathryn (9 mentions)
Med Coll of Georgia, 1993 *Certification:* Obstetrics & Gynecology
7810 Providence Rd #105, Charlotte, 704-342-4323
1025 Morehead Medical Dr #400, Charlotte, 704-446-7800

Yavorski, Sarah Schlater (5 mentions)
Tulane U, 1983 *Certification:* Obstetrics & Gynecology
1718 E 4th St #307, Charlotte, 704-384-1620

Ophthalmology

Blotnick, Charles Adam (4 mentions)
U of Vermont, 1992 *Certification:* Ophthalmology
2015 Randolph Rd #108, Charlotte, 704-334-2020

Branner, William Arthur (8 mentions)
U of North Carolina, 1986 *Certification:* Ophthalmology
4335 Colwick Rd, Charlotte, 704-364-7400
16600 Birkdale Commons Pkwy #E, Huntersville, 704-895-8200

Browning, David Judson (5 mentions)
Duke U, 1981 *Certification:* Ophthalmology
900 branchview Dr, Concord, 704-295-3255

Flores, Robert Andrew (4 mentions)
Harvard U, 1986 *Certification:* Ophthalmology
6035 Fairview Rd, Charlotte, 704-295-3000

Gaskin, Lewis Reed (4 mentions)
Emory U, 1980 *Certification:* Ophthalmology
135 S Sharon Amity Rd #100, Charlotte, 704-365-0555

Jaben, Scott Leonard (6 mentions)
U of Miami, 1977 *Certification:* Ophthalmology
6035 Fairview Rd, Charlotte, 704-295-3000
1632 E Roosevelt Blvd, Monroe, 704-295-3725

Krug, Joseph H., Jr. (6 mentions)
Columbia U, 1982 *Certification:* Ophthalmology
135 S Sharon Amity Rd #100, Charlotte, 704-365-0555

Malton, Mark Leland (4 mentions)
U of Michigan, 1982 *Certification:* Ophthalmology
135 S Sharon Amity Rd #100, Charlotte, 704-365-0555

Marshall, Charles Foster, Jr. (5 mentions)
Med U of South Carolina, 1969 *Certification:* Ophthalmology
135 S Sharon Amity Rd #100, Charlotte, 704-365-0555
19900 W Catawba Ave, Cornelius, 704-892-1000
7903 Providence Rd #150, Charlotte, 704-341-3220

Rotberg, Michael Howard (6 mentions)
Duke U, 1979 *Certification:* Ophthalmology
6035 Fairview Rd, Charlotte, 704-295-3000
1401 Matthews Township Pkwy #101, Matthews, 704-295-3550

Saunders, Timothy Gray (21 mentions)
U of North Carolina, 1981 *Certification:* Ophthalmology
1401 Matthews Township Pkwy #101, Matthews, 704-295-3550
6035 Fairview Rd, Charlotte, 704-295-3170

Stewart, Donald Houston (4 mentions)
SUNY-Upstate Med U, 1990 *Certification:* Ophthalmology
6035 Fairview Rd, Charlotte, 704-295-3000
1401 Matthews Township Pkwy #101, Matthews, 704-295-3550

Ugland, David Nels (13 mentions)
Baylor U, 1980 *Certification:* Ophthalmology
135 S Sharon Amity Rd #100, Charlotte, 704-365-0555

Weidman, Frederick H., III (8 mentions)
West Virginia U, 1984 *Certification:* Ophthalmology
10520 Park Rd #100, Charlotte, 704-541-6127
135 S Sharon Amity Rd #100, Charlotte, 704-365-0555

Orthopedics

Anderson, Robert Bentley (11 mentions)
Med Coll of Wisconsin, 1983 *Certification:* Orthopaedic Surgery
1001 Blythe Blvd #200, Charlotte, 704-373-0544
1025 Morehead Medical Dr #300, Charlotte, 704-373-0544

Barron, Jerry Lynn (5 mentions)
U of Texas-Galveston, 1984 *Certification:* Orthopaedic Surgery
449 Wendover Rd, Charlotte, 704-365-6730

Beaver, Walter B., Jr. (5 mentions)
U of North Carolina, 1984 *Certification:* Orthopaedic Surgery
1915 Randolph Rd, Charlotte, 704-339-1000
1025 Morehead Medical Dr #300, Charlotte, 704-547-7319

Connor, Patrick Michael (5 mentions)
U of Oklahoma, 1990
Certification: Orthopaedic Sports Medicine, Orthopaedic Surgery
1025 Morehead Medical Dr #300, Charlotte, 704-323-2000
1915 Randolph Rd, Charlotte, 704-339-1000

D'Alessandro, Donald F. (11 mentions)
Georgetown U, 1983
Certification: Orthopaedic Sports Medicine, Orthopaedic Surgery
1001 Blythe Blvd #200, Charlotte, 704-347-5448
1025 Morehead Medical Dr #300, Charlotte, 704-323-2000

Dunaway, Howard Yates, III (5 mentions)
Wake Forest U, 1977 *Certification:* Orthopaedic Surgery
1915 Randolph Rd, Charlotte, 704-339-1000

Fehring, Thomas Keith (6 mentions)
U of Texas-Galveston, 1980 *Certification:* Orthopaedic Surgery
1915 Randolph Rd, Charlotte, 704-339-1000

Frick, Steven Lee (15 mentions)
Med U of South Carolina, 1991
Certification: Orthopaedic Surgery
1001 Blythe Blvd #200-B, Charlotte, 704-381-8870

Griffin, William Lewis (5 mentions)
U of Louisville, 1982 *Certification:* Orthopaedic Surgery
1915 Randolph Rd, Charlotte, 704-339-1000

Kneisl, Jeffrey S. (5 mentions)
Northwestern U, 1980 *Certification:* Orthopaedic Surgery
1000 Blythe Blvd, Charlotte, 704-446-1340

Mason, J. Bohannon (6 mentions)
Med U of South Carolina, 1989
Certification: Orthopaedic Surgery
10512 Park Rd #101, Charlotte, 704-339-1000

McCoy, Thomas Hatton (8 mentions)
U of North Carolina, 1981 *Certification:* Orthopaedic Surgery
1915 Randolph Rd, Charlotte, 704-339-1036

Mokris, Jeffrey George (7 mentions)
U of Cincinnati, 1979 *Certification:* Orthopaedic Surgery
1025 Morehead Medical Dr #300, Charlotte, 704-323-2000
1915 Randolph Rd, Charlotte, 704-339-1000

Perlik, Paul Christopher (4 mentions)
Eastern Virginia Med Sch, 1978
Certification: Orthopaedic Surgery, Surgery of the Hand
1915 Randolph Rd, Charlotte, 704-339-1000

Wattenbarger, John M. (7 mentions)
U of Texas-Dallas, 1988 *Certification:* Orthopaedic Surgery
1025 Morehead Medical Dr #300, Charlotte, 704-373-0544

Otorhinolaryngology

Blumer, John Redmond (14 mentions)
U of Minnesota, 1987 *Certification:* Otolaryngology
6035 Fairview Rd, Charlotte, 704-295-3000

Caldwell, William McKamie (17 mentions)
East Carolina U, 1998 *Certification:* Otolaryngology
1918 Randolph Rd #310, Charlotte, 704-376-1220

Goldberg, Trevor Ian (9 mentions)
FMS-South Africa, 1975 *Certification:* Otolaryngology
5933 Blakeney Parks Dr #200, Charlotte, 704-295-3000

Hoover, Hunter Ashley (14 mentions)
U of North Carolina, 1988 *Certification:* Otolaryngology
6035 Fairview Rd, Charlotte, 704-295-3000

Kamerer, Donald B., Jr. (18 mentions)
Harvard U, 1982 *Certification:* Otolaryngology
6035 Fairview Rd, Charlotte, 704-295-3000

Levine, Joshua David (6 mentions)
Boston U, 1997 *Certification:* Otolaryngology
1918 Randolph Rd #310, Charlotte, 704-376-1220

Sicard, Michael William (7 mentions)
Duke U, 1993 *Certification:* Otolaryngology
1401 Matthews Township Pkwy #101, Charlotte, 704-295-3550

Silver, John Robert (11 mentions)
U of North Carolina, 1988 *Certification:* Otolaryngology
1401 Matthews Township Pkwy #101, Matthews, 803-328-1864
6035 Fairview Rd, Charlotte, 704-295-3000

Weigel, Mark Turner (6 mentions)
Northeastern Ohio U, 1983 *Certification:* Otolaryngology
16455 Statesville Rd #280, Huntersville, 704-295-3600

Pain Medicine

Boortz-Marx, Richard Levi (11 mentions)
Wayne State U, 1991 *Certification:* Anesthesiology, Pain Medicine
1718 E 4th St #300, Charlotte, 704-316-1570

Miller, Joshua Seth (11 mentions)
Med U of South Carolina, 1986
Certification: Anesthesiology, Pain Medicine
1000 Blythe Blvd, Charlotte, 704-377-5772

Pathology

Ballinger, William Edwards, Jr. (5 mentions)
U of Florida, 1974
Certification: Anatomic Pathology, Neuropathology
1000 Blythe Blvd, Charlotte, 704-355-2251

Banks, Peter M. (12 mentions)
Harvard U, 1971 *Certification:* Anatomic Pathology
101 E Wt Harris Blvd #1212, Charlotte, 704-549-8444

Benjamin, Sanford Philip (4 mentions)
Wayne State U, 1968
Certification: Anatomic Pathology & Clinical Pathology
101 E WT Harris Blvd #1212, Charlotte, 704-549-8444

Cohen, Arthur Robert (23 mentions)
Baylor U, 1977 *Certification:* Anatomic Pathology & Clinical Pathology, Cytopathology
200 Hawthorne Ln, Charlotte, 704-384-4814

Lipford, Edward Holdman (7 mentions)
Vanderbilt U, 1977
Certification: Anatomic Pathology & Clinical Pathology
1000 Blythe Blvd #506, Charlotte, 704-355-3467
101 E Wt Harris Blvd #1212, Charlotte, 704-549-8444

Poston, William Karnes, Jr. (7 mentions)
West Virginia U, 1979 *Certification:* Anatomic Pathology & Clinical Pathology, Hematology
200 Hawthorne Ln, Charlotte, 704-384-4814

Schwartz, Jared Naphtali (6 mentions)
Duke U, 1973 *Certification:* Anatomic Pathology & Clinical Pathology, Cytopathology, Medical Microbiology
200 Hawthorne Ln, Charlotte, 704-384-4814

Pediatrics *(see note on page 9)*

Alderman, James Francis (3 mentions)
Med U of South Carolina, 1982 *Certification:* Pediatrics
10348 Park Rd #300, Charlotte, 704-367-7400

Almquist, Perry Futral (3 mentions)
U of Virginia, 1982 *Certification:* Pediatrics
4501 Cameron Valley Pkwy #100, Charlotte, 704-367-7400

Clegg, Herbert William, II (5 mentions)
Duke U, 1975
Certification: Pediatric Infectious Diseases, Pediatrics
2600 E 7th St #100, Charlotte, 704-384-8800

Eichenbrenner, Timothy J. (6 mentions)
Eastern Virginia Med Sch, 1979 *Certification:* Pediatrics
2630 E 7th St #101, Charlotte, 704-384-1000

Ezzo, Stephen James (3 mentions)
St Louis U, 1985 *Certification:* Pediatrics
1401 Matthews Township #100, Matthews, 704-384-1080

Giftos, Peter Michael (3 mentions)
U of Florida, 1999 *Certification:* Pediatrics
2600 E 7th St #100, Charlotte, 704-384-8800

Golembe, Barry L. (4 mentions)
Virginia Commonwealth U, 1974 *Certification:* Pediatrics
4105 Matthews Mint Hill Rd, Charlotte, 704-365-0760

Holladay, Glenn Clyde (6 mentions)
Med U of South Carolina, 1980 *Certification:* Pediatrics
2630 E 7th St #101, Charlotte, 704-384-1000

Kocmond, Jonathan Howard (3 mentions)
U of Illinois, 1997 *Certification:* Pediatrics
1315 East Blvd #280, Charlotte, 704-384-1866

Neale, Wirt Thomas (3 mentions)
U of Tennessee, 1969 *Certification:* Pediatrics
1315 East Blvd #280, Charlotte, 704-384-1866

Plonk, John Butler, Jr. (4 mentions)
U of North Carolina, 1981 *Certification:* Pediatrics
427 N Wendover Rd, Charlotte, 704-364-3740

Ryan, Amy Garrett (4 mentions)
U of Virginia, 1995 *Certification:* Pediatrics
2600 E 7th St #100, Charlotte, 704-384-8800

Samarel, Matthew David (3 mentions)
Tufts U, 1988 *Certification:* Pediatrics
8169 Ardykell Rd, Charlotte, 704-542-5540

Satterfield, Jamison J. (6 mentions)
Med Coll of Georgia, 1986 *Certification:* Pediatrics
7800 Providence Rd #203, Charlotte, 704-543-6662

Shaffner, Susan Casper (3 mentions)
Wake Forest U, 1984 *Certification:* Pediatrics
4501 Cameron Valley Pkwy #100, Charlotte, 704-367-7400

Shulstad, Andrew Robert (6 mentions)
Med Coll of Georgia, 1996 *Certification:* Pediatrics
4501 Cameron Valley Pkwy #100, Charlotte, 704-367-7400

Smolen, Paul Mathieu (4 mentions)
Robert W Johnson Med Sch, 1978 *Certification:* Pediatrics
14214 Ballantyne Lake Rd #300, Charlotte, 704-540-4460

Swetenburg, Raymond Lee (11 mentions)
Duke U, 1976 *Certification:* Pediatrics
2600 E 7th St #100, Charlotte, 704-384-8800

Williams, Laramie Ann (4 mentions)
U of Florida, 1987 *Certification:* Pediatrics
7800 Providence Rd #203, Charlotte, 704-543-6662

Plastic Surgery

Bicket, William John, II (5 mentions)
U of North Carolina, 1983 *Certification:* Plastic Surgery, Surgery
1450 Matthews Township Pkwy #270, Matthews, 704-845-9800

Capizzi, Peter Joseph (8 mentions)
Eastern Virginia Med Sch, 1990
Certification: Plastic Surgery, Surgery
2215 Randolph Rd, Charlotte, 704-655-8988
8712 Lindholm Dr #308, Huntersville, 704-655-8988

Ferrari, Victor Steven (5 mentions)
U of North Carolina, 1987 *Certification:* Plastic Surgery
1635 Matthews Township Pkwy, Matthews, 704-844-8344

Graper, Robert Gordon (7 mentions)
U of Cincinnati, 1982 *Certification:* Plastic Surgery
2915 Coltsgate Rd #103, Charlotte, 704-375-7111

Matthews, David Cary (24 mentions)
U of Cincinnati, 1974 *Certification:* Plastic Surgery
1719 South Blvd #B, Charlotte, 704-375-2955

Smith, Kevin Lindsay (6 mentions)
Eastern Virginia Med Sch, 1979 *Certification:* Plastic Surgery
2215 Randolph Rd, Charlotte, 704-372-6846

Watterson, Paul A. (9 mentions)
George Washington U, 1982 *Certification:* Plastic Surgery
2215 Randolph Rd, Charlotte, 704-372-6846

Psychiatry

Humphrey, John Edward, Jr. (12 mentions)
Duke U, 1975 *Certification:* Psychiatry
3303 Latrobe Dr, Charlotte, 704-945-2200

Lurie, Scott N. (8 mentions)
Duke U, 1987 *Certification:* Psychiatry
1132 Greenwood Cliffs, Charlotte, 704-376-6577

Melvin, Jean Allen (3 mentions)
U of North Carolina, 1986 *Certification:* Psychiatry
3303 Latrobe Dr, Charlotte, 704-362-2663

Reddick, Bradley Harris (6 mentions)
U of Tennessee, 1996
Certification: Child & Adolescent Psychiatry, Psychiatry
3303 Latrobe Dr, Charlotte, 704-362-2663

Reger, Lance Boyd (3 mentions)
Med U of South Carolina, 1999 *Certification:* Psychiatry
6845 Fairview Rd, Charlotte, 704-969-1147

Roberts, Eugene L., Jr. (7 mentions)
U of Mississippi, 1978
Certification: Psychiatry, Psychosomatic Medicine
501 Billingsley Rd, Charlotte, 704-358-2820

Sunderland, Brent (7 mentions)
U of Texas-Houston, 1990
Certification: Child & Adolescent Psychiatry, Psychiatry
1718 E 4th St #601, Charlotte, 704-384-1246

Sutherland, Steven M. (8 mentions)
East Tennessee State U, 1986 *Certification:* Psychiatry
3303 Latrobe Dr, Charlotte, 704-362-2663

Pulmonary Disease

Black, Hugh Ratchford, II (6 mentions)
U of Virginia, 1990 *Certification:* Pediatric Pulmonology
8045 Providence Rd #300, Charlotte, 704-341-9600

Dalto, Carmine (13 mentions)
New York U, 1976 *Certification:* Critical Care Medicine,
Internal Medicine, Pulmonary Disease
1900 Randolph Rd #216, Charlotte, 704-384-9900
1450 Matthews Township Pkwy #230, Matthews, 704-384-9900

Garner, Stuart Joseph (22 mentions)
Emory U, 1980 *Certification:* Critical Care Medicine,
Internal Medicine, Pulmonary Disease
1900 Randolph Rd #216, Charlotte, 704-384-9900

Hendler, Jay Mark (11 mentions)
New York U, 1985 *Certification:* Critical Care Medicine,
Internal Medicine, Pulmonary Disease
1900 Randolph Rd #216, Charlotte, 704-384-9900
1450 Mathews Township Pkwy #2310, Matthews, 704-384-9900

Howard, Daniel Karl (16 mentions)
U of Wisconsin, 1987 *Certification:* Critical Care Medicine,
Internal Medicine, Pulmonary Disease
1001 Blythe Blvd #500, Charlotte, 704-355-5100
1000 Blythe Blvd, Charlotte, 704-355-5100

Jones, James Buckner (11 mentions)
Vanderbilt U, 1979
Certification: Internal Medicine, Pulmonary Disease
4525 Cameron Valley Pkwy, Charlotte, 704-302-8340

Kremers, Scott Alex (9 mentions)
Indiana U, 1974
Certification: Internal Medicine, Pulmonary Disease
1918 Randolph Rd #450, Charlotte, 704-342-8140

Lindblom, Scott Shannon (19 mentions)
Med Coll of Wisconsin, 1989 *Certification:* Critical Care
Medicine, Internal Medicine, Pulmonary Disease
1001 Blythe Blvd #500, Charlotte, 704-355-5100
1000 Blythe Blvd, Charlotte, 704-355-5100

Roe, David Wilson (8 mentions)
Southern Illinois U, 1996 *Certification:* Critical Care
Medicine, Internal Medicine, Pulmonary Disease
1900 Randolph Rd #216, Charlotte, 704-384-9900
10030 Gilead Rd #220, Huntersville, 704-384-9900

Radiology—Diagnostic

Burns, M. Alan (4 mentions)
Vanderbilt U, 1986 *Certification:* Diagnostic Radiology,
Vascular & Interventional Radiology
200 Hawthorne Ln, Charlotte, 704-384-4057

Guilford, William Bonner (4 mentions)
U of North Carolina, 1973 *Certification:* Diagnostic Radiology
1001 Blythe Blvd #103, Charlotte, 704-355-6200

Hartley, William Stuart (8 mentions)
U of North Carolina, 1987 *Certification:* Diagnostic Radiology
3030 Latrobe Dr, Charlotte, 704-362-1945
1025 Morehead Medical Dr #200, Charlotte, 704-302-8000

Hollenberg, Bennett Roy (6 mentions)
Indiana U, 1981 *Certification:* Diagnostic Radiology
200 Hawthorne Ln, Charlotte, 704-384-4056

Howard, John Dale (3 mentions)
Indiana U, 1985
Certification: Diagnostic Radiology, Neuroradiology
3030 Latrobe Dr, Charlotte, 704-362-1945
1001 Blythe Blvd #103, Charlotte, 704-355-2270

Insko, Erik Kenton (3 mentions)
U of Pennsylvania, 1996 *Certification:* Diagnostic Radiology
3623 Latrobe Dr #216, Charlotte, 704-384-4056

Mittl, Robert Louis, Jr. (3 mentions)
Washington U, 1985 *Certification:* Diagnostic Radiology,
Internal Medicine, Neuroradiology
1001 Blythe Blvd #103, Charlotte, 704-355-6200

Nixon, John Randall (3 mentions)
U of Texas-Dallas, 1978
Certification: Diagnostic Radiology, Neurology
200 Hawthorne Ln, Charlotte, 704-384-4057

Oliver, James Henry, III (7 mentions)
Med Coll of Georgia, 1985 *Certification:* Diagnostic Radiology
1701 East Blvd, Charlotte, 704-362-1945
3030 Latrobe Dr, Charlotte, 704-362-1945

Quillin, Shawn Paul (9 mentions)
Washington U, 1990 *Certification:* Diagnostic Radiology
200 Hawthorne Ln, Charlotte, 704-384-4056

Talarico, Carmen L. (7 mentions)
Ohio State U, 1979
Certification: Diagnostic Radiology, Pediatric Radiology
1001 Blythe Blvd #103, Charlotte, 704-355-6200

Tobben, Paul John (6 mentions)
Vanderbilt U, 1984
Certification: Diagnostic Radiology, Neuroradiology
200 Hawthorne Ln, Charlotte, 704-384-4056

Radiology—Therapeutic

Burns, Martin Alan (4 mentions)
Vanderbilt U, 1986 *Certification:* Diagnostic Radiology,
Vascular & Interventional Radiology
3623 Latrobe Dr #216, Charlotte, 704-332-1291

Fraser, Robert W., III (6 mentions)
U of Pennsylvania, 1975 *Certification:* Therapeutic Radiology
1000 Blythe Blvd #3809, Charlotte, 704-355-2272

Haake, Michael Robert (4 mentions)
Indiana U, 1980
Certification: Internal Medicine, Radiation Oncology
1000 Blythe Blvd, Charlotte, 704-333-7376
200 Queens Rd #400, Charlotte, 704-333-7376

McGinnis, L. Scott, III (4 mentions)
Med Coll of Georgia, 1989 *Certification:* Radiation Oncology
200 Hawthorne Ln, Charlotte, 704-384-4188
200 Queens Rd #400, Charlotte, 704-333-7376

Plunkett, Steven Rockwell (5 mentions)
Med Coll of Georgia, 1978 *Certification:* Therapeutic Radiology
1400 Matthews Township Pkwy, Matthews, 704-845-8800
200 Queens Rd #400, Charlotte, 704-333-7376

Warlick, William Byrd, Jr. (4 mentions)
Med Coll of Georgia, 1994 *Certification:* Radiation Oncology
200 Hawthorne Ln, Charlotte, 704-384-4188

Rehabilitation

Bockenek, William Louis (10 mentions)
U of South Florida, 1986 *Certification:* Physical Medicine &
Rehabilitation, Spinal Cord Injury Medicine
1100 Blythe Blvd, Charlotte, 704-355-4330

Hammond, Flora McConnell (4 mentions)
Tulane U, 1990 *Certification:* Physical Medicine & Rehabilitation
1100 Blythe Blvd, Charlotte, 704-355-9047

Nelson, Maureen Rose (4 mentions)
U of Illinois, 1985 *Certification:* Pediatric Rehabilitation
Medicine, Physical Medicine & Rehabilitation
1100 Blythe Blvd, Charlotte, 704-355-4330

Rissmiller, Sonya Gorski (8 mentions)
Virginia Commonwealth U, 1995
Certification: Physical Medicine & Rehabilitation
3030 Randolph Rd #105, Charlotte, 704-512-4400

Taub, Neal Stephen (5 mentions)
Baylor U, 1987
Certification: Pain Medicine, Physical Medicine & Rehabilitation
3535 Randolph Rd #208, Charlotte, 704-442-9805

Rheumatology

Kipnis, Robert Joel (19 mentions)
Duke U, 1985 *Certification:* Internal Medicine, Rheumatology
1918 Randolph Rd #600, Charlotte, 704-342-0252

Laster, Andrew Jay (18 mentions)
Johns Hopkins U, 1979
Certification: Internal Medicine, Rheumatology
1918 Randolph Rd #600, Charlotte, 704-342-0252

Maniloff, Gary Bruce (8 mentions)
FMS-Israel, 1981 *Certification:* Internal Medicine, Rheumatology
1918 Randolph Rd #600, Charlotte, 704-342-0252

Robertson, Cheryl Reis (9 mentions)
U of Kentucky, 1985
Certification: Internal Medicine, Rheumatology
4525 Cameron Valley Pkwy #4100, Charlotte, 704-302-8320

Sundberg, Thomas C. (11 mentions)
FMS-Germany, 1976
Certification: Internal Medicine, Rheumatology
4525 Cameron Valley Pkwy #4100, Charlotte, 704-302-8320

Thoracic Surgery

Edwards, Charles Hillman (9 mentions)
U of North Carolina, 1973 *Certification:* Thoracic Surgery
156 Centre Church Rd #207, Mooresville, 704-799-3939
301 Hawthorne Ln #200, Charlotte, 704-316-5100

Harr, Charles Dulaney (17 mentions)
Wake Forest U, 1983 *Certification:* Surgery, Thoracic Surgery
301 Hawthorne Ln #200, Charlotte, 704-316-5100

Howe, Harold Ragan, Jr. (19 mentions)
Wake Forest U, 1980 *Certification:* Thoracic Surgery
301 Hawthorne Ln #200, Charlotte, 704-316-5100

Reames, Mark Kevin (23 mentions)
Med U of South Carolina, 1985
Certification: Surgery, Thoracic Surgery
1001 Blythe Blvd #300, Charlotte, 704-373-0212

Urology

Gajewski, Timothy Andrew (6 mentions)
U of Tennessee, 1985 *Certification:* Urology
101 E WT Harris Blvd #5202, Charlotte, 704-547-1495

Ganem, Jacques Paul (9 mentions)
SUNY-Downstate Med Coll, 1993 *Certification:* Urology
1718 E 4th St #807, Charlotte, 704-375-5755

Gazak, John Michael (8 mentions)
U of Pennsylvania, 1974
Certification: Pediatric Urology, Urology
16525 Holly Crest Ln #230, Huntersville, 704-334-3033

Kennelly, Michael Joseph (10 mentions)
U of Cincinnati, 1989 *Certification:* Urology
1023 Edgehill Rd S, Charlotte, 704-355-8686

Kirkland, John Alvin, Jr. (21 mentions)
U of North Carolina, 1985 *Certification:* Urology
201 Queens Rd, Charlotte, 704-372-5180

Peretsman, Samuel Jay (18 mentions)
Boston U, 1983 *Certification:* Urology
201 Queens Rd, Charlotte, 704-372-5180

Perez, Luis Manuel (16 mentions)
Albert Einstein Coll of Med, 1988
Certification: Pediatric Urology, Urology
1718 E 4th St #805, Charlotte, 704-376-5636

Phillips, Thomas Hogeman (8 mentions)
George Washington U, 1984 *Certification:* Urology
1415 Matthews Township Pkwy, Matthews, 704-841-8877

Teigland, Chris Michael (24 mentions)
Duke U, 1980 *Certification:* Urology
1023 Edgehill Rd S, Charlotte, 704-355-8686

Vick, Ralph Nelson (8 mentions)
U of North Carolina, 1997 *Certification:* Urology
16455 Statesville Rd #420, Huntersville, 704-892-2949

Watson, Daniel Lee (13 mentions)
Johns Hopkins U, 1990 *Certification:* Urology
201 Queens Rd, Charlotte, 704-372-5180

Vascular Surgery

Holleman, Jeremiah H., Jr. (20 mentions)
Tulane U, 1971 *Certification:* Surgery
1001 Blythe Blvd #300, Charlotte, 704-373-0212

Roush, Timothy Starling (18 mentions)
Uniformed Services U of Health Sciences, 1984
Certification: Surgery, Vascular Surgery
1001 Blythe Blvd #300, Charlotte, 704-373-0212

Triangle Area
Including Durham, Orange, and Wake Counties

Allergy/Immunology

Aarons, Alan Lawrence (13 mentions)
U of Maryland, 1988
Certification: Allergy & Immunology, Internal Medicine
2615 Lake Dr #301, Raleigh, 919-787-5995
300 Asheville Ave #300, Cary, 919-859-8144

Bressler, Peter Bartlett (8 mentions)
Duke U, 1981
Certification: Allergy & Immunology, Internal Medicine
5915 Farrington Rd #106, Chapel Hill, 919-401-6000

Dunn, Karen Diane (13 mentions)
New York Med Coll, 1976
Certification: Allergy & Immunology, Pediatrics
6340 Quadrangle Dr #70, Chapel Hill, 919-493-6580
2615 Lake Dr #301, Raleigh, 919-787-5995
300 Asheville Ave #300, Cary, 919-859-8144

La Force, Craig Fred (25 mentions)
Jefferson Med Coll, 1975
Certification: Allergy & Immunology, Pediatrics
2615 E Lake Dr #301, Raleigh, 919-787-5995
6340 Quadrangle Dr #320, Chapel Hill, 919-493-6580
300 Asheville Ave #300, Cary, 919-859-8144

Anesthesiology

Bailey, Ann Geryl (3 mentions)
Southern Illinois U, 1980 *Certification:* Anesthesiology, Pediatrics
101 Manning Dr, Chapel Hill, 919-966-5136

Daniel, Walter Eugene, III (3 mentions)
U of North Carolina, 1979 *Certification:* Anesthesiology
3100 Spring Forest Rd #130, Raleigh, 919-873-9533

Georges, Linda Swinson (3 mentions)
Med Coll of Georgia, 1976 *Certification:* Anesthesiology
101 Manning Dr, Chapel Hill, 919-966-5136

Hoellerich, Vincent L. (9 mentions)
U of Nebraska, 1983
Certification: Anesthesiology, Critical Care Medicine
4420 Lake Boone Trail, Raleigh, 919-784-3034

Maccioli, Gerald Anthony (4 mentions)
U of Nevada, 1984
Certification: Anesthesiology, Critical Care Medicine
4420 Lake Boone Trail, Raleigh, 919-784-3034

Mason, Eric W. (10 mentions)
U of Miami, 1980
Certification: Anesthesiology, Critical Care Medicine
4420 Lake Boone Trail, Raleigh, 919-784-3034

Mayer, David T. (4 mentions)
Certification: Anesthesiology
101 Manning Dr, Chapel Hill, 919-966-7890

Newman, Mark Franklin (3 mentions)
U of Louisville, 1985 *Certification:* Anesthesiology
Duke University Med Ctr #3094, Durham, 919-681-6646

Nicholson, Charles H., III (4 mentions)
U of Buffalo, 1982 *Certification:* Anesthesiology
3100 Spring Forest Rd #130, Raleigh, 919-873-9533

Norfleet, Edward Alvin (8 mentions)
U of North Carolina, 1970 *Certification:* Anesthesiology
101 Manning Dr #2201-N, Chapel Hill, 919-966-5136

Passannante, Anthony N. (4 mentions)
SUNY-Upstate Med U, 1985
Certification: Anesthesiology, Internal Medicine
101 Manning Dr #2201-N, Chapel Hill, 919-966-5136

Stolp, Bryant Walter (3 mentions)
U of North Carolina, 1988
Certification: Anesthesiology, Undersea & Hyperbaric Medicine
Duke University Med Ctr #3094, Durham, 919-681-6069

Valley, Robert David (6 mentions)
U of Virginia, 1980 *Certification:* Anesthesiology, Pediatrics
101 Manning Dr #2201-N, Chapel Hill, 919-966-5136

Woodard, Paul Richard (3 mentions)
U of North Carolina, 1979 *Certification:* Anesthesiology
3000 New Bern Ave, Raleigh, 919-350-5645

Cardiac Surgery

Atkinson, Alvan William (7 mentions)
Jefferson Med Coll, 1971 *Certification:* Thoracic Surgery
3000 New Bern Ave #1100, Raleigh, 919-231-6333

Glower, Donald Duane, Jr. (10 mentions)
Johns Hopkins U, 1980 *Certification:* Thoracic Surgery
Duke South Clinic - Trent Dr, Durham, 919-681-5789
43 Westridge Dr, Durham, 919-684-8111

Landvater, Lance Eric (24 mentions)
Wake Forest U, 1977 *Certification:* Thoracic Surgery
3000 New Bern Ave #1100, Raleigh, 919-231-6333

Peyton, Robert B. (8 mentions)
New York U, 1977 *Certification:* Thoracic Surgery
3000 New Bern Ave #1100, Raleigh, 919-231-6333

Cardiology

Bashore, Thomas Michael (3 mentions)
Ohio State U, 1972
Certification: Cardiovascular Disease, Internal Medicine
3116 N Duke St #7412, Durham, 919-681-2990
Duke University Med Ctr, Durham, 919-684-2407

Blazing, Michael August (5 mentions)
U of California-San Francisco, 1987
Certification: Cardiovascular Disease, Internal Medicine
3116 N Duke St, Durham, 919-681-5816
6301 Herndon Rd, Durham, 919-681-5816

Buchanan, Robert A., Jr. (3 mentions)
Wake Forest U, 1969
Certification: Cardiovascular Disease, Internal Medicine
2609 N Duke St #700, Durham, 919-220-5510

Cheely, George Rayburn (5 mentions)
U of Pennsylvania, 1974
Certification: Cardiovascular Disease, Internal Medicine
3000 New Bern Ave #G1200, Raleigh, 919-231-6132

Daw, Jeffrey Richard (4 mentions)
U of North Carolina, 1990
300 Ashville Ave #301, Cary, 919-851-6901

Frantz, Elman Grady (3 mentions)
Pennsylvania State U, 1981
Certification: Pediatric Cardiology, Pediatrics
101 Manning Dr, Chapel Hill, 919-966-4131

Garimella, Rama Goli (4 mentions)
FMS-India, 1988
Certification: Cardiovascular Disease, Internal Medicine
300 Keisler Dr #204, Cary, 919-233-0059

Go, Brian Mingtao (3 mentions)
Hahnemann U, 1992
Certification: Cardiovascular Disease, Interventional Cardiology
3000 New Bern Ave #G1200, Raleigh, 919-231-6132

Harrison, John Kevin (3 mentions)
New York U, 1984 *Certification:* Cardiovascular Disease,
Internal Medicine, Interventional Cardiology
3116 N Duke St, Durham, 919-681-3763

Henke, Elizabeth (6 mentions)
FMS-United Kingdom, 1974 *Certification:* Cardiovascular
Disease, Clinical Genetics, Internal Medicine
2609 N Duke St #700, Durham, 919-220-5510

Kelly, James Reginald (4 mentions)
Duke U, 1970 *Certification:* Internal Medicine
3475 Erwin Rd, Durham, 919-660-6746

Mangano, Charles Angelo, Jr. (11 mentions)
U of Rochester, 1974
Certification: Cardiovascular Disease, Internal Medicine
3000 New Bern Ave #1200, Raleigh, 919-231-6132

Mann, James Tift, III (3 mentions)
U of North Carolina, 1969
Certification: Cardiovascular Disease, Internal Medicine
3000 New Bern Ave #G-100, Raleigh, 919-231-8253

Miller, Paula Freeman (4 mentions)
U of North Carolina, 1983 *Certification:* Internal Medicine
300 Meadowmont Village Cir #313, Chapel Hill, 919-966-7244

Mobarek, Sameh Khamis A. H. (3 mentions)
FMS-Egypt, 1982
300 Ashville Ave #301, Cary, 919-851-6901
4325 Lake Boone Trail #315, Raleigh, 919-420-1347
3000 New Bern Ave #G-100, Raleigh, 919-231-8253

Noneman, Jack W., Jr. (3 mentions)
U of North Carolina, 1977
Certification: Cardiovascular Disease, Internal Medicine
3324 Six Forks Rd, Raleigh, 919-781-7772
868 Timber Dr, Garner, 919-662-5001
8300 Health Park Dr #327, Raleigh, 919-861-5950

O'Connor, Christopher M. (3 mentions)
U of Maryland, 1983
Certification: Cardiovascular Disease, Internal Medicine
6301 Herndon Rd, Durham, 919-572-6095

Ohman, Erik Magnus (3 mentions)
FMS-Ireland, 1981
6301 Herndon Rd, Durham, 919-681-5816

Peterson, Eric David (3 mentions)
U of Pittsburgh, 1988 *Certification:* Cardiovascular Disease
2400 Pratt St, Durham, 919-668-8830

Rose, Gregory Charles (4 mentions)
St Louis U, 1980
Certification: Cardiovascular Disease, Internal Medicine
4325 Lake Boone Trail #315, Raleigh, 919-420-1347
3000 New Bern Ave #G-100, Raleigh, 919-231-8253

Sinden, John Rankin (4 mentions)
Wake Forest U, 1985 *Certification:* Cardiovascular Disease,
Internal Medicine, Interventional Cardiology
3000 New Bern Ave #1200, Raleigh, 919-231-6132

Tate, David Andrew (5 mentions)
U of North Carolina, 1982 *Certification:* Cardiovascular
Disease, Internal Medicine, Interventional Cardiology
101 Manning Dr, Chapel Hill, 919-966-5141

Usher, Bruce Warren, Jr. (3 mentions)
Med U of South Carolina, 1993
Certification: Cardiovascular Disease
300 Ashville Ave #301, Cary, 919-851-6901

Dermatology

Andrus, Thomas Ross, Jr. (5 mentions)
U of North Carolina, 1978 *Certification:* Dermatology
3809 Computer Dr #200, Raleigh, 919-782-3782

Challgren, Eric Daniel (7 mentions)
U of Toledo, 1998 *Certification:* Dermatology
4201 Lake Boone Trail #200, Raleigh, 919-782-2152

Echt, Audrey Faye (7 mentions)
Indiana U, 1990 *Certification:* Dermatology
10931 Raven Ridge Rd #101, Raleigh, 919-870-6600

Murray, John Carroll (8 mentions)
Duke U, 1977 *Certification:* Dermatology
Duke South Clinic - Trent Dr, Durham, 919-684-2393

Nasir, Adnan M. (10 mentions)
U of Rochester, 1995 *Certification:* Dermatology
4414 Lake Boone Trail, Raleigh, 919-781-1001

Queen, Laurinda Lee (9 mentions)
U of Arizona, 1981
3921 Sunset Ridge Rd #202, Raleigh, 919-783-7877

Thomas, Nancy Ellen (5 mentions)
Cornell U, 1987 *Certification:* Dermatology
101 Manning Dr, Chapel Hill, 919-966-2485

Emergency Medicine

Brownstein, Robert Andrew (3 mentions)
U of California-Los Angeles, 1991
Certification: Emergency Medicine
4420 Lake Boone Trail, Raleigh, 919-787-9097

Di Lorenzo, Robert Alan (4 mentions)
U of Illinois, 1983 *Certification:* Emergency Medicine
2500 Blue Ridge Rd #417, Raleigh, 919-787-9097

Frush, Karen S. (3 mentions)
Duke U, 1986
Certification: Pediatric Emergency Medicine, Pediatrics
2424 Erwin Rd Bldg 1, Durham, 919-668-3749

Haugan, Charul G. (5 mentions)
U of Minnesota, 1998 *Certification:* Emergency Medicine
4420 Lakeboone Trail, Raleigh, 919-784-3100

Kelsch, John Martin, Sr. (5 mentions)
U of Louisville, 1976 *Certification:* Emergency Medicine
1638 Owen Dr, Fayetteville, 910-609-6350

Manning, James Elbert (3 mentions)
U of North Carolina, 1985 *Certification:* Emergency Medicine
101 Manning Dr, Chapel Hill, 919-966-4131

McHugh, Damian Francis (4 mentions)
FMS-United Kingdom, 1990 *Certification:* Emergency Medicine
4420 Lake Boone Trail, Raleigh, 919-784-3038

Weiss, Brian D. (3 mentions)
Virginia Commonwealth U, 1984
Certification: Emergency Medicine
4420 Lake Boone Trail, Raleigh, 919-787-9097

Endocrinology

Azzi, Anthony Francesco (8 mentions)
Med Coll of Georgia, 1984
Certification: Endocrinology and Metabolism, Internal Medicine
10224 Durant Rd #109, Raleigh, 919-329-2711

Becker, Denis I. (13 mentions)
U of Kentucky, 1972
Certification: Endocrinology and Metabolism, Internal Medicine
3410 Executive Dr #205, Raleigh, 919-876-7692

Berlin, Corey (7 mentions)
Hahnemann U, 1992
3410 Executive Dr #205, Raleigh, 919-876-7692

Buse, John Bernard (8 mentions)
Duke U, 1986 *Certification:* Endocrinology, Diabetes, and
Metabolism, Internal Medicine
5316 Highgate Dr #125, Durham, 919-966-0134
5039 Old Clinic School of Medicine UNC, Chapel Hill,
919-966-0134

Coxe, James Sherwood, III (17 mentions)
U of North Carolina, 1971
Certification: Endocrinology and Metabolism, Internal Medicine
2704 Toxey Dr, Raleigh, 919-878-1819

Gamblin, George Thomas (9 mentions)
U of Mississippi, 1977
Certification: Endocrinology and Metabolism, Internal Medicine
8341 Bamford Way #103, Raleigh, 919-845-3332

McNeill, Diana Bures (7 mentions)
Duke U, 1982
Certification: Endocrinology and Metabolism, Internal Medicine
200 Trent Dr, Durham, 919-668-7630

Spratt, Susan Elizabeth (8 mentions)
Harvard U, 1995 *Certification:* Endocrinology, Diabetes,
and Metabolism, Internal Medicine
Duke University Med Ctr #3311, Durham, 919-684-4490
2301 Erwin Rd, Durham, 919-684-4490

Family Practice (see note on page 9)

Crumpler, Randall Scott (3 mentions)
Wake Forest U, 1980 *Certification:* Family Medicine
801 Poole Dr, Garner, 919-779-1440

Guiteras, George Patrick (4 mentions)
U of North Carolina, 1969 *Certification:* Family Medicine
120 Conner Dr #200, Chapel Hill, 919-967-8291

Gwyther, Robert Edwin, Jr. (3 mentions)
U of Toledo, 1975 *Certification:* Family Medicine
101 Manning Dr, Chapel Hill, 919-966-4131

Hammer, Douglas Ira (5 mentions)
Tufts U, 1962
Certification: Family Medicine, General Preventive Medicine
2605 Blue Ridge Rd #300, Raleigh, 919-787-3448

Hamrick, Alger Vason (3 mentions)
U of North Carolina, 1972 *Certification:* Family Medicine
4414 Lake Boone Trail #502, Raleigh, 919-875-0539

Lee, William David, Jr. (5 mentions)
U of North Carolina, 1974 *Certification:* Family Medicine
2605 Blue Ridge Rd #300, Raleigh, 919-787-3448

Pennington, Robert Clay (3 mentions)
U of North Carolina, 1986 *Certification:* Internal Medicine
4309 Medical Park Dr #200, Durham, 919-471-4484

Gastroenterology

Barish, Charles Franklin (9 mentions)
U of Florida, 1980
Certification: Gastroenterology, Internal Medicine
3100 Blue Ridge Rd #300, Raleigh, 919-781-7500
2417 Atrium Dr #101, Raleigh, 919-791-2060

Branch, Malcolm Stanley (4 mentions)
Med Coll of Georgia, 1984
Certification: Gastroenterology, Internal Medicine
107 Duke S #3, Durham, 919-684-3787

Brazer, Scott Robert (5 mentions)
Case Western Reserve U, 1981
Certification: Gastroenterology, Internal Medicine
249 E NC Hwy 54 #200, Durham, 919-806-8322

De Lissio, Michael Gerard (5 mentions)
U of Buffalo, 1980
Certification: Gastroenterology, Internal Medicine
1000 Crescent Green Dr #102, Cary, 919-816-4948

McKay, Michael Dixon (6 mentions)
Med Coll of Georgia, 1982
Certification: Gastroenterology, Internal Medicine
2417 Atrium Dr #150, Raleigh, 919-791-2040
8300 Health Park #209, Raleigh, 919-645-4230

Newell, Lanny Richard (4 mentions)
U of North Carolina, 1975
Certification: Gastroenterology, Internal Medicine
2600 Atlantic Ave #100, Raleigh, 919-881-9999

Patel, Rig S. (10 mentions)
FMS-United Kingdom, 1989
Certification: Gastroenterology, Internal Medicine
8300 Health Park #209, Raleigh, 919-645-4230
2417 Atrium Dr #150, Raleigh, 919-791-2040

Pollock, Morris Arthur (6 mentions)
Jefferson Med Coll, 1969
Certification: Gastroenterology, Internal Medicine
2417 Atrium Dr #150, Raleigh, 919-791-2040
8300 Health Park #209, Raleigh, 919-645-4230

Scarlett, Yolanda Valjene (4 mentions)
U of North Carolina, 1989 *Certification:* Gastroenterology
101 Manning Dr, Chapel Hill, 919-966-4131

Schwarz, Ronald Paul (12 mentions)
Cornell U, 1977
Certification: Gastroenterology, Internal Medicine
2601 Lake Dr #201, Raleigh, 919-783-4888
4420 Lake Boone Trail, Raleigh, 919-783-4888

Spanarkel, Marybeth (6 mentions)
Duke U, 1979 *Certification:* Gastroenterology, Internal Medicine
2609 N Duke St #503, Durham, 919-479-0860

Tendler, David Andrew (7 mentions)
Yale U, 1993 *Certification:* Gastroenterology, Internal Medicine
249 E NC Hwy 54 #200, Durham, 919-806-8322

Tumbapura, Anil Prakash (4 mentions)
FMS-India, 1991 *Certification:* Gastroenterology
2600 Atlantic Ave #100, Raleigh, 919-881-9999

General Surgery

Cannon, Woodward (5 mentions)
Harvard U, 1970 *Certification:* Surgery
2800 Blue Ridge Rd #503, Raleigh, 919-782-8210

Chiulli, Richard Allen (12 mentions)
Boston U, 1977 *Certification:* Surgery
2800 Blue Ridge Rd #503, Raleigh, 919-782-8210

Cline, William Tucker (4 mentions)
Duke U, 1978 *Certification:* Surgery
2800 Blue Ridge Rd #201, Raleigh, 919-420-5000

Duberman, Eric David (4 mentions)
Columbia U, 1985 *Certification:* Colon & Rectal Surgery, Surgery
216 Ashville Ave #30, Cary, 919-859-4747

Eddleman, David Beauchamp (3 mentions)
Emory U, 2000 *Certification:* Surgery
2800 Blue Ridge Rd #503, Raleigh, 919-782-8210

Faust, Kirk Berry (4 mentions)
U of Alabama, 1982 *Certification:* Surgery
1101 Dresser Ct, Raleigh, 919-876-2010

Maddox, Thomas Wilbur (12 mentions)
U of Alabama, 1979 *Certification:* Surgery
2800 Blue Ridge Rd #503, Raleigh, 919-782-8210

Meyer, Anthony Andrew (7 mentions)
U of Chicago, 1977 *Certification:* Surgery, Surgical Critical Care
101 Manning Dr, Chapel Hill, 919-966-4321

Meyers, Michael Owen (4 mentions)
Wake Forest U, 1995 *Certification:* Surgery
101 Manning Dr, Chapel Hill, 919-966-4131

Ng, Peter Conrad (3 mentions)
East Carolina U, 1996 *Certification:* Surgery
1101 Dresser Ct, Raleigh, 919-876-2010

Pappas, Theodore Nick (6 mentions)
Ohio State U, 1981 *Certification:* Surgery
508 Fulton St, Durham, 919-286-0411

Paschal, George W. (14 mentions)
Wake Forest U, 1973 *Certification:* Surgery
2800 Blue Ridge Rd #503, Raleigh, 919-782-8210

Stirman, Jerry Archibald (3 mentions)
U of Texas-Galveston, 1974 *Certification:* Surgery
1101 Dresser Ct, Raleigh, 919-876-2010

Udekwu, Pascal Osita (3 mentions)
FMS-Nigeria, 1980
Certification: Pediatrics, Surgery, Surgical Critical Care
3024 New Bern Ave #200, Raleigh, 919-350-2800

Vig, Daniel Robert (6 mentions)
U of Wisconsin, 1992 *Certification.* Surgery
2800 Blue Ridge Rd #503, Raleigh, 919-782-8210

Watters, Christopher Roy (4 mentions)
U of Michigan, 1983 *Certification:* Surgery
1212 Cedarhurst Dr #102, Raleigh, 919-431-9911

Weinreb, Seth Marshall (4 mentions)
Harvard U, 1996 *Certification:* Surgery
2800 Blue Ridge Rd #503, Raleigh, 919-782-8210

Wilke, Lee Gravatt (3 mentions)
Duke U, 1993 *Certification:* Surgery
3116 N Duke St, Durham, 919-660-2244

Wilson, James S., Jr. (8 mentions)
U of North Carolina, 1975 *Certification:* Surgery
3116 N Duke St, Durham, 919-660-2324

Geriatrics

Cohen, Harvey Jay (5 mentions)
SUNY-Downstate Med Coll, 1965
Certification: Hematology, Internal Medicine
Duke University Busse Bldg #3502, Durham, 919-660-7502

Colon-Emeric, Cathleen S. (3 mentions)
Johns Hopkins U, 1994
Certification: Geriatric Medicine, Internal Medicine
508 Fulton St, Durham, 919-286-0411

Greganti, Mac Andrew (5 mentions)
U of Mississippi, 1972 *Certification:* Internal Medicine
101 Manning Dr, Chapel Hill, 919-966-7244

Hanson, Laura Catherine (3 mentions)
Harvard U, 1986 *Certification:* Geriatric Medicine, Hospice
and Palliative Medicine, Internal Medicine
101 Manning Dr, Chapel Hill, 919-966-7244

Kizer, J. Stephen (3 mentions)
Duke U, 1970 *Certification:* Internal Medicine
147 Macnider Hall, Chapel Hill, 919-966-1456

Lyles, Kenneth Ward (3 mentions)
Virginia Commonwealth U, 1974 *Certification:* Endocrinology
and Metabolism, Geriatric Medicine, Internal Medicine
508 Fulton St, Durham, 919-660-7520

Parsons, James Sheridan (7 mentions)
U of North Carolina, 1976
Certification: Geriatric Medicine, Internal Medicine
704 W Jones St, Raleigh, 919-832-5125

Schmader, Kenneth Edwin (3 mentions)
Wake Forest U, 1980
Certification: Geriatric Medicine, Internal Medicine
4020 N Roxboro Ave, Durham, 919-660-7572

Hematology/Oncology

Bernard, Stephen Alan (3 mentions)
U of North Carolina, 1973 *Certification:* Hospice and
Palliative Medicine, Internal Medicine, Medical Oncology
101 Manning Dr, Chapel Hill, 919-966-3311

Berry, William R. (3 mentions)
Duke U, 1974
Certification: Hematology, Internal Medicine, Medical Oncology
4101 Macon Pond Rd, Raleigh, 919-781-7070

Blatt, Julie (3 mentions)
Johns Hopkins U, 1976
Certification: Pediatric Hematology-Oncology, Pediatrics
101 Manning Dr, Chapel Hill, 919-966-6669

Campbell, Elizabeth E. (6 mentions)
Duke U, 1982 *Certification:* Internal Medicine, Medical Oncology
4101 Macon Pond Rd, Raleigh, 919-781-7070

Crane, Jeffrey Major (12 mentions)
U of Florida, 1977
Certification: Hematology, Internal Medicine, Medical Oncology
4420 Lake Boone Trail #200, Raleigh, 919-784-6818

Dees, Elizabeth Claire (3 mentions)
Duke U, 1993 *Certification:* Medical Oncology
101 Manning Dr, Chapel Hill, 919-966-3311

Deutsch, Margaret Ann (3 mentions)
Med Coll of Wisconsin, 1984
Certification: Internal Medicine, Medical Oncology
10010 Falls of Neuse Rd #203, Raleigh, 919-431-9201

Dunlap, William Marshall (3 mentions)
Duke U, 1965
3521 Haworth Dr, Raleigh, 919-782-1806

Elkordy, Maha Abdul (6 mentions)
U of North Carolina, 1988
Certification: Internal Medicine, Medical Oncology
216 Ashville Ave #20, Cary, 919-852-1994
4101 Mason Pond Rd, Raleigh, 919-781-7070

Gockerman, Jon Paul (4 mentions)
U of Chicago, 1967
Certification: Hematology, Internal Medicine, Medical Oncology
Duke South Clinic - Trent Dr, Durham, 919-684-8964

Gold, Stuart Harrison (7 mentions)
Vanderbilt U, 1981
Certification: Pediatric Hematology-Oncology, Pediatrics
101 Manning Dr, Chapel Hill, 919-966-3311

Graham, Mark L., II (11 mentions)
Mayo Med Sch, 1982 *Certification:* Internal Medicine
300 Ashville Ave #310, Cary, 919-233-8585

Hathorn, James Walker (6 mentions)
Duke U, 1979 *Certification:* Internal Medicine
4411 Ben Franklin Blvd, Durham, 919-477-0047

Kritz, Alan Daniel (10 mentions)
Washington U, 1985
Certification: Hematology, Internal Medicine, Medical Oncology
4101 Macon Pond Rd, Raleigh, 919-781-7070

Marcom, Paul K. (3 mentions)
Baylor U, 1989
Certification: Internal Medicine, Medical Oncology
Duke University Med Ctr, Durham, 919-684-3877

Moore, Joseph Odell (4 mentions)
Johns Hopkins U, 1970
Certification: Internal Medicine, Medical Oncology
Duke South Clinic - Trent Dr, Durham, 919-684-8964

O'Neil, Bert Howard (4 mentions)
U of California-Los Angeles, 1994 *Certification:* Medical Oncology
101 Manning Dr, Chapel Hill, 919-966-7648

Ortel, Thomas L. (4 mentions)
Indiana U, 1985 *Certification:* Hematology, Internal Medicine
Duke University Med Ctr, Durham, 919-684-5350

Spiritos, Michael David (4 mentions)
Cornell U, 1983
Certification: Hematology, Internal Medicine, Medical Oncology
3404 Wake Forest Rd #202, Raleigh, 919-954-3050

Voorhees, Peter Michael (4 mentions)
U of Michigan, 1997 *Certification:* Hematology, Internal Medicine
101 Manning Dr, Chapel Hill, 919-966-3311

Yoffe, Mark (10 mentions)
U of Florida, 1977
Certification: Internal Medicine, Medical Oncology
4101 Macon Pond Rd, Raleigh, 919-781-7070

Zeitler, Kenneth Dale (15 mentions)
Columbia U, 1975
Certification: Hematology, Internal Medicine, Medical Oncology
4420 Lake Boone Trail #200, Raleigh, 919-784-6818

Infectious Disease

Becherer, Paul Robert (7 mentions)
U of Illinois, 1983
Certification: Infectious Disease, Internal Medicine
2304 Wesvill Ct #240, Raleigh, 919-571-1567

Brown, Edwin Alan (4 mentions)
U of Alabama, 1983
Certification: Infectious Disease, Internal Medicine
2304 Wesvill Ct #240, Raleigh, 919-571-1567

Cohen, Myron Scott (4 mentions)
Rush U, 1974 *Certification:* Infectious Disease, Internal Medicine
101 Manning Dr, Chapel Hill, 919-966-2536

Corey, G. Ralph (4 mentions)
Baylor U, 1973
Certification: Infectious Disease, Internal Medicine
Duke South Clinic - Trent Dr, Durham, 919-668-7630

Engemann, John Joseph (5 mentions)
Wayne State U, 1996
Certification: Infectious Disease, Internal Medicine
2304 Wesvill Ct, Raleigh, 919-571-1567

Haywood, Hubert B. (21 mentions)
U of North Carolina, 1972
Certification: Infectious Disease, Internal Medicine
2304 Wesvill Ct #240, Raleigh, 919-571-1567

Ingram, Christopher William (15 mentions)
Wake Forest U, 1983
Certification: Infectious Disease, Internal Medicine
2304 Wesvill Ct #240, Raleigh, 919-571-1567

Morris, Vicki Morgan (15 mentions)
U of Virginia, 1987
Certification: Infectious Disease, Internal Medicine
2304 Wesvill Ct #240, Raleigh, 919-571-1567

Sexton, Daniel John (7 mentions)
Northwestern U, 1971
Certification: Infectious Disease, Internal Medicine
200 Trent Dr, Durham, 919-684-4596

Weber, David Jay (4 mentions)
U of California-San Diego, 1977 *Certification:* Infectious Disease, Internal Medicine, Public Health & General Preventive Medicine
101 Manning Dr, Chapel Hill, 919-966-4131

Infertility

Couchman, Grace Marie (7 mentions)
U of Colorado, 1985 *Certification:* Obstetrics & Gynecology, Reproductive Endocrinology/Infertility
2601 Lake Dr #301, Raleigh, 919-782-5911

Walmer, David Keith (5 mentions)
U of North Carolina, 1983 *Certification:* Obstetrics & Gynecology, Reproductive Endocrinology/Infertility
5704 Fayetteville Rd, Durham, 919-572-4673

Internal Medicine *(see note on page 9)*

Adams, Martha B. (3 mentions)
U of Virginia, 1976 *Certification:* Internal Medicine
3475 Irwin Rd, Durham, 919-660-6746

Atree, Susheel Vaidya (3 mentions)
Hahnemann U, 1996 *Certification:* Internal Medicine
10000 Falls of Neuse Rd #201, Raleigh, 919-848-6946

Brown, Teresa Grace (3 mentions)
U of North Carolina, 1982
3643 N Roxboro St, Durham, 919-471-4840

Greganti, Mac Andrew (5 mentions)
U of Mississippi, 1972 *Certification:* Internal Medicine
101 Manning Dr, Chapel Hill, 919-966-7244

Hardison, Mitchell Dale (4 mentions)
U of North Carolina, 1980 *Certification:* Internal Medicine
3900 Browning Pl #101, Raleigh, 919-781-9650

Harper, Wayne Lee (6 mentions)
Duke U, 1978 *Certification:* Internal Medicine
3100 Blue Ridge Rd #300, Raleigh, 919-781-7500

Helton, Todd Edward (3 mentions)
East Carolina U, 1998 *Certification:* Internal Medicine
3900 Browning Pl #101, Raleigh, 919-781-9650

Liebowitz, Steven Marc (8 mentions)
New York U, 1982 *Certification:* Internal Medicine
3850 Ed Dr #100, Raleigh, 919-788-9588

Marucheck, John Thomas (3 mentions)
U of Oklahoma, 1978 *Certification:* Internal Medicine
3320 Wake Forest Rd #310, Raleigh, 919-855-8911

O'Connell, Patrick Austin (3 mentions)
U of North Carolina, 2000 *Certification:* Internal Medicine
2304 Wesvill Ct #210, Raleigh, 919-571-9247

Rees, Michael Stevens (3 mentions)
Vanderbilt U, 1976 *Certification:* Internal Medicine
3200 Blue Ridge Rd #210, Raleigh, 919-781-9979

Winslow, Bristol R. (3 mentions)
U of North Carolina, 1994 *Certification:* Internal Medicine
4205 Ben Franklin Blvd, Durham, 919-477-6900

Nephrology

Casey, Michael Joseph (7 mentions)
U of North Carolina, 1996
Certification: Internal Medicine, Nephrology
3604 Bush St, Raleigh, 919-876-7807

Falk, Ronald J. (4 mentions)
U of North Carolina, 1977
Certification: Internal Medicine, Nephrology
101 Manning Dr, Chapel Hill, 919-966-4131

Godwin, James Edward (9 mentions)
U of Kansas, 1991 *Certification:* Nephrology
23 Sunnybrook Rd #145, Raleigh, 919-231-3966
580 New Waverly Pl #210, Cary, 919-231-3966

Gutman, Robert Allan (4 mentions)
U of Florida, 1962 *Certification:* Internal Medicine, Nephrology
4419 Ben Franklin Blvd, Durham, 919-477-3005

Kovalik, Eugene C. (5 mentions)
FMS-Canada, 1987 *Certification:* Internal Medicine, Nephrology
Duke South Clinic - Trent Dr, Durham, 919-684-8111

Monahan, Michael (6 mentions)
Emory U, 1984 *Certification:* Internal Medicine, Nephrology
3604 Bush St, Raleigh, 919-876-7807
545 E Market St, Smithfield, 919-876-7807
605 Tilgman Dr, Dunn, 919-876-7807

Rothman, Mark David (9 mentions)
FMS-Mexico, 1980 *Certification:* Internal Medicine, Nephrology
3604 Bush St, Raleigh, 919-876-7807
545 E Market St, Smithfield, 919-876-7807
605 Tilgman Dr, Dunn, 919-876-7807

Schmidt, Robert Scott (7 mentions)
Med Coll of Wisconsin, 1989
23 Sunnybrook Rd #145, Raleigh, 919-231-3966
580 New Waverly Pl #210, Cary, 919-231-3966

Smith, Stephen Richard (4 mentions)
Duke U, 1985 *Certification:* Internal Medicine, Nephrology
Duke University Med Ctr #3014, Durham, 919-660-6858

Vaidya, Prabhakar Narhari (10 mentions)
FMS-India, 1969 *Certification:* Internal Medicine, Nephrology
23 Sunnybrook Rd #145, Raleigh, 919-231-3966

Neurological Surgery

Allen, Robert Lee (10 mentions)
Wake Forest U, 1979 *Certification:* Neurological Surgery
5838 Six Forks Rd #100, Raleigh, 919-785-3400

Ewend, Matthew Glaize (11 mentions)
Johns Hopkins U, 1990 *Certification:* Neurological Surgery
101 Manning Dr, Chapel Hill, 919-966-7890

Friedman, Allan Howard (15 mentions)
U of Illinois, 1974 *Certification:* Neurological Surgery
Duke South Clinic - Trent Dr, Durham, 919-681-6421

Koeleveld, Robin F. (32 mentions)
Columbia U, 1985 *Certification:* Neurological Surgery
5838 Six Forks Rd #100, Raleigh, 919-785-3400

Lacin, Robert (9 mentions)
FMS-Switzerland, 1986 *Certification:* Neurological Surgery
4414 Lake Boone Trail #402, Raleigh, 919-781-8313

Margraf, Russell Reid (7 mentions)
Albany Med Coll, 1996 *Certification:* Neurological Surgery
5838 Six Forks Rd #100, Raleigh, 919-785-3400

Rich, Kenneth John (7 mentions)
U of Buffalo, 1978 *Certification:* Neurological Surgery
1100 Dresser Ct #100, Raleigh, 919-850-9911

Neurology

Bowman, Michael Higgins (7 mentions)
Ohio State U, 1976 *Certification:* Neurology
1540 Sunday Dr, Raleigh, 919-782-3456

Carnes, Kenneth Michael (5 mentions)
Washington U, 1992 *Certification:* Neurology
1540 Sunday Dr, Raleigh, 919-782-3456

Finkel, Alan Glen (3 mentions)
U of Buffalo, 1985 *Certification:* Neurology, Pain Medicine
101 Manning Dr, Chapel Hill, 919-966-2527

Freedman, Steven Mitchell (27 mentions)
U of Pennsylvania, 1972 *Certification:* Neurology
1540 Sunday Dr, Raleigh, 919-782-3456

Gabr, Rhonda Winstead (4 mentions)
West Virginia U, 1998 *Certification:* Neurology
1540 Sunday Dr, Raleigh, 919-782-3456

Glenn, Susan Annette (12 mentions)
U of Oklahoma, 1993
Certification: Clinical Neurophysiology, Neurology
1540 Sunday Dr, Raleigh, 919-782-3456

Goetzl, Ugo (3 mentions)
New York Med Coll, 1968 *Certification:* Neurology, Psychiatry
3901 N Roxboro Rd #501, Durham, 919-719-8834

Hull, Keith Lowell, Jr. (8 mentions)
Duke U, 1975 *Certification:* Neurology
1540 Sunday Dr, Raleigh, 919-782-3456

Kahn, Kevin Alexander (3 mentions)
Med U of South Carolina, 1992
Certification: Neurology, Pain Medicine
101 Manning Dr, Chapel Hill, 919-966-2527

Massey, Edward Wayne (3 mentions)
U of Texas-Galveston, 1970
200 Trent Dr, Durham, 919-668-7600

Morgenlander, Joel C. (9 mentions)
U of Pittsburgh, 1986 *Certification:* Neurology
1 Trent Dr #L, Durham, 919-668-7600

Peterson, Paul C. (3 mentions)
U of Texas-Galveston, 1995 *Certification:* Emergency
   Medicine, Neurology, Vascular Neurology
3480 Wake Forrest Rd, Raleigh, 919-862-5620

Wooten, John D., III (7 mentions)
Wake Forest U, 1984 *Certification:* Neurology with Special
   Qualifications in Child Neurology
1520 Sunday Dr, Raleigh, 919-719-8825

Obstetrics/Gynecology

Carter, Jean Whitmore (3 mentions)
U of North Carolina, 1978 *Certification:* Obstetrics & Gynecology
4414 Lake Boone Trail #210, Raleigh, 919-571-1040

Clifford, Susann Levy (3 mentions)
U of Florida, 1993 *Certification:* Obstetrics & Gynecology
1512 E Franklin St #100, Chapel Hill, 919-687-4688

Connolly, Anna Marie (3 mentions)
Tufts U, 1991 *Certification:* Obstetrics & Gynecology
101 Manning Dr, Chapel Hill, 919-966-2131

Ford, Anne C. (9 mentions)
U of North Carolina, 1988 *Certification:* Obstetrics & Gynecology
1512 E Franklin St #100, Chapel Hill, 919-687-4688

Haakenson, Gary A. (4 mentions)
Baylor U, 1972 *Certification:* Obstetrics & Gynecology
2417 Atrium Dr #200, Raleigh, 919-781-9555

Harden, Paul, Jr. (3 mentions)
Temple U, 1979 *Certification:* Obstetrics & Gynecology
3805 Computer Dr, Raleigh, 919-781-6200
2011 Falls Valley Dr #104, Raleigh, 919-781-6200

Henderson, David Yeardley (6 mentions)
Virginia Commonwealth U, 1981
Certification: Obstetrics & Gynecology
2417 Atrium Dr #200, Raleigh, 919-781-9555

McKenzie, Sheppard A., III (5 mentions)
U of North Carolina, 1974
Certification: Internal Medicine, Obstetrics & Gynecology
3805 Computer Dr, Raleigh, 919-781-6200
2011 Falls Valley Dr #104, Raleigh, 919-781-6200

Smith, Michael David (3 mentions)
Wake Forest U, 1986 *Certification:* Obstetrics & Gynecology
3805 Computer Dr, Raleigh, 919-781-6200
2011 Falls Valley Dr #104, Raleigh, 919-781-6200

Teasley, Myra Lynn (4 mentions)
U of Tennessee, 1985 *Certification:* Obstetrics & Gynecology
4414 Lake Boone Trail #300, Raleigh, 919-781-5510

Thorp, John Mercer, Jr. (3 mentions)
East Carolina U, 1983
Certification: Maternal-Fetal Medicine, Obstetrics & Gynecology
101 Manning Dr, Chapel Hill, 919-966-2131

Tosky, George Michael (5 mentions)
Wake Forest U, 1981 *Certification:* Obstetrics & Gynecology
4414 Lake Boone Trail #308, Raleigh, 919-781-7450
1505 SW Cary {kwy, Cary, 919-467-2249

Woodruff, Leon Festus, Jr. (6 mentions)
Wake Forest U, 1972 *Certification:* Obstetrics & Gynecology
4414 Lake Boone Trail #300, Raleigh, 919-781-5510

Ophthalmology

Bell, Dorothy McFarland (3 mentions)
U of Chicago, 1975 *Certification:* Ophthalmology
4102 N Roxboro St, Durham, 919-595-2000

Board, Robert Jeffrey (6 mentions)
Duke U, 1974 *Certification:* Ophthalmology
3320 Executive Dr #111, Raleigh, 919-876-2427

Friedland, Beth Rena (4 mentions)
U of Florida, 1979 *Certification:* Ophthalmology
5306 NC Hwy 55 #102, Durham, 919-544-5375

Gulledge, Sidney Loy, III (3 mentions)
Wake Forest U, 1976 *Certification:* Ophthalmology
4301 Lake Boone Trail #200, Raleigh, 919-782-5210

Kelly, Michael Walker (3 mentions)
U of Texas-Dallas, 1983 *Certification:* Ophthalmology
10321 Lumley Rd, Raleigh, 919-781-3937

Kim, Terry (3 mentions)
Duke U, 1992 *Certification:* Ophthalmology
2100 Erwin Rd, Durham, 919-684-8111

Perry, Dwight Dean (3 mentions)
U of North Carolina, 1980 *Certification:* Ophthalmology
4102 N Roxboro St, Durham, 919-595-2000

Robinson, Charles Hall, Jr. (5 mentions)
Duke U, 1975 *Certification:* Ophthalmology
2709 Blue Ridge Rd #100, Raleigh, 919-782-5400

Smith, Patricia Walsh (8 mentions)
Tulane U, 1981 *Certification:* Ophthalmology
2406 Blue Ridge Rd #280, Raleigh, 919-256-2500

Stone, Robert Thomas, Jr. (3 mentions)
U of North Carolina, 1994 *Certification:* Ophthalmology
105 SW Cary Pkwy #200, Cary, 919-467-4500

Ward, John Thomas (5 mentions)
U of Oklahoma, 1981 *Certification:* Ophthalmology
105 SW Cary Pkwy #200, Cary, 919-467-4500

Orthopedics

Almekinders, Louis C. (3 mentions)
FMS-Netherlands, 1980
Certification: Orthopaedic Sports Medicine, Orthopaedic Surgery
3609 SW Durham Dr, Durham, 919-471-9622

Andrew, Wallace F., Jr. (3 mentions)
U of Virginia, 1975 *Certification:* Orthopaedic Surgery
3515 Glenwood Ave, Raleigh, 919-781-5600

Boone, David Warner (3 mentions)
U of North Carolina, 1987 *Certification:* Orthopaedic Surgery
3515 Glenwood Ave, Raleigh, 919-781-5600

Campion, Edmund Ronan (3 mentions)
Dartmouth Coll, 1981 *Certification:* Orthopaedic Surgery
101 Manning Dr, Chapel Hill, 919-962-6637

Caudle, Robert Joseph (7 mentions)
Wake Forest U, 1981 *Certification:* Orthopaedic Surgery
3633 Harden Rd #102, Raleigh, 919-788-8797

Dirschl, Douglas Ray (4 mentions)
Oregon Health Sciences U, 1988
Certification: Orthopaedic Surgery
101 Manning Dr, Chapel Hill, 919-962-6637

Fajgenbaum, David Moniek (5 mentions)
Tulane U, 1975 *Certification:* Orthopaedic Surgery
3410 Executive Dr #103, Raleigh, 919-872-5296

Fajgenbaum, Michael C. (6 mentions)
Tulane U, 1982 *Certification:* Orthopaedic Surgery
3410 Executive Dr #103, Raleigh, 919-872-5296

Goldner, Richard Douglas (3 mentions)
Duke U, 1974
Certification: Orthopaedic Surgery, Surgery of the Hand
Duke University Med Ctr, Durham, 919-684-6461

Martini, Douglas John (4 mentions)
U of Virginia, 1987 *Certification:* Orthopaedic Surgery
1120 SE Cary Pkwy #100, Cary, 919-467-4992
1005 Vandora Springs Rd, Garner, 919-779-3861

Olcott, Christopher W. (6 mentions)
U of Rochester, 1991 *Certification:* Orthopaedic Surgery
101 Manning Dr, Chapel Hill, 919-962-6637

Smith, Lyman S. W. (3 mentions)
Duke U, 1984 *Certification:* Orthopaedic Surgery
3515 Glenwood Ave, Raleigh, 919-781-5600

Speer, Kevin Paul (3 mentions)
Johns Hopkins U, 1985 *Certification:* Orthopaedic Surgery
3404 Wake Forest Rd #201, Raleigh, 919-256-1511

Vaughn, Bradley Kent (9 mentions)
U of Illinois, 1979 *Certification:* Orthopaedic Surgery
3515 Glenwood Ave, Raleigh, 919-781-5600

Wood, Mark Lyndon (5 mentions)
U of North Carolina, 1999 *Certification:* Orthopaedic Surgery
3009 New Bern Ave, Raleigh, 919-232-5020

Wyker, Robert Terlinck (8 mentions)
U of Virginia, 1982 *Certification:* Orthopaedic Surgery
3515 Glenwood Ave, Raleigh, 919-781-5600

Otorhinolaryngology

Boyce, Stephen Eugene (8 mentions)
U of Florida, 1982 *Certification:* Otolaryngology
3010 Anderson Dr, Raleigh, 919-787-7171
1505 SW Cary Pkwy, Cary, 919-367-9774

Dennis, Steven Henry (8 mentions)
U of North Carolina, 1981 *Certification:* Otolaryngology
3100 Blue Ridge Rd #201, Raleigh, 919-787-1374
835 Wake Forest Business Park #B, Wake Forest, 919-556-8454
800 Benson Rd #10, Garner, 919-662-8181

Garside, John Arthur (5 mentions)
U of North Carolina, 1993 *Certification:* Otolaryngology
1110 SE Cary Pkwy #100, Cary, 919-859-6771

Meredith, Scott Davis (8 mentions)
U of Virginia, 1987 *Certification:* Otolaryngology
4101 Macon Pond Rd, Raleigh, 919-781-7070
110 Falls of Neuse Rd #203, Raleigh, 919-431-9201

Pillsbury, Harold C., III (5 mentions)
George Washington U, 1972
Certification: Neurotology, Otolaryngology
101 Manning Dr, Chapel Hill, 919-966-6483

Price, Harvey Craig (13 mentions)
U of North Carolina, 1978 *Certification:* Otolaryngology
3100 Blue Ridge Rd #201, Raleigh, 919-787-1374
800 Benson Rd #10, Garner, 919-662-8181

Pugh, Magda El-Raheb (7 mentions)
FMS-Egypt, 1978 *Certification:* Otolaryngology
10010 Falls of Neuse Rd #12, Raleigh, 919-790-2255

Shockley, William Wilson (5 mentions)
Indiana U, 1976 *Certification:* Otolaryngology
101 Manning Dr, Chapel Hill, 919-966-6483

Wilkins, Stanley A., Jr. (6 mentions)
U of North Carolina, 1982 *Certification:* Otolaryngology
3100 Blue Ridge Rd #201, Raleigh, 919-787-1374
835 Wake Forest Business Park #B, Wake Forest, 919-556-8454
800 Benson Rd #10, Garner, 919-662-8181

Pain Medicine

Huh, Billy Keon (5 mentions)
U of Alabama, 1993 *Certification:* Anesthesiology, Pain Medicine
932 Morreene Rd, Durham, 919-684-7246

Kittelberger, Keith Paul (4 mentions)
Meharry Med Coll, 1988
Certification: Anesthesiology, Pain Medicine
4420 Lake Boone Trail, Raleigh, 919-784-3034

Pathology

Benson, John Dewitt (7 mentions)
U of North Carolina, 1978
Certification: Anatomic Pathology & Clinical Pathology
4420 Lake Boone Trail, Raleigh, 919-784-3063

Carter, Timothy Robert (6 mentions)
U of Virginia, 1984
Certification: Anatomic Pathology & Clinical Pathology
4420 Lake Boone Trail, Raleigh, 919-784-3063

Chiavetta, Stephen V. (7 mentions)
Med Coll of Wisconsin, 1969 *Certification:* Anatomic
Pathology & Clinical Pathology, Hematology
4420 Lake Boone Trail, Raleigh, 919-784-3040

Maygarden, Susan Jane B. (4 mentions)
Virginia Commonwealth U, 1983 *Certification:* Anatomic
Pathology & Clinical Pathology, Cytopathology
101 Manning Dr, Chapel Hill, 919-966-4131

Smith, Vincent Charles (3 mentions)
U of North Carolina, 1997
Certification: Anatomic Pathology & Clinical Pathology
4420 Lake Boone Trail, Raleigh, 919-784-3072

Sorge, John Phillip (11 mentions)
U of Rochester, 1982
Certification: Anatomic Pathology & Clinical Pathology
4420 Lake Boone Trail, Raleigh, 919-784-3063

Pediatrics *(see note on page 9)*

Auman, George Louis (3 mentions)
Wake Forest U, 1968 *Certification:* Pediatrics
4414 Lake Boone Trail #103, Raleigh, 919-787-0266

Byerley, Julie Story (3 mentions)
Duke U, 1998 *Certification:* Pediatrics
101 Manning Dr, Chapel Hill, 919-966-7244

Foster, Sharon M. (3 mentions)
U of North Carolina, 1979
Certification: Internal Medicine, Pediatrics
1921 Falls Valley Dr, Raleigh, 919-872-0250

Franklin, Earl Ruffin (3 mentions)
U of North Carolina, 1973 *Certification:* Pediatrics
3801 Computer Dr #200, Raleigh, 919-782-5273

Jeffers, Robert Gordon (5 mentions)
Tulane U, 1974 *Certification:* Pediatrics
2406 Blue Ridge Rd #100, Raleigh, 919-786-5001

Kubicki, Steven Paul (3 mentions)
George Washington U, 1984 *Certification:* Pediatrics
742 McKnight Dr #110, Knightdale, 919-782-5273

Mann, Larry Douglas (4 mentions)
Marshall U, 1983 *Certification:* Pediatrics
2406 Blue Ridge Rd #100, Raleigh, 919-786-5001

Merritt, Kathy Ann (3 mentions)
Duke U, 1985
Certification: Developmental-Behavioral Pediatrics, Pediatrics
205 Sage Rd #100, Chapel Hill, 919-942-4173

Plastic Surgery

Carlino, Richard Edward (14 mentions)
Robert W Johnson Med Sch, 1984 *Certification:* Plastic Surgery
3633 Harden Rd #200, Raleigh, 919-785-0505

Davis, Glenn Miller (7 mentions)
Med U of South Carolina, 1974 *Certification:* Plastic Surgery
2304 Wesvill Ct #360, Raleigh, 919-785-1220

High, Rhett Charles (8 mentions)
Johns Hopkins U, 1989 *Certification:* Plastic Surgery
1112 Dresser Ct, Raleigh, 919-872-2616

Hultman, Charles Scott (8 mentions)
U of Pittsburgh, 1990
Certification: Plastic Surgery, Surgery, Surgical Critical Care
101 Manning Dr, Chapel Hill, 919-966-4446

Levin, L. Scott (8 mentions)
Temple U, 1982 *Certification:* Orthopaedic Surgery, Plastic
Surgery, Surgery of the Hand
Duke South Clinic - Trent Dr, Durham, 919-668-0132

Lyle, William Glenn (7 mentions)
Wayne State U, 1986 *Certification:* Plastic Surgery
1112 Dresser Ct, Raleigh, 919-872-2616

Oschwald, Donald L. A., Jr. (14 mentions)
U of New Mexico, 1978 *Certification:* Plastic Surgery
3633 Harden Rd #200, Raleigh, 919-785-0505

Van Aalst, John Ananda (6 mentions)
Vanderbilt U, 1993 *Certification:* Plastic Surgery, Surgery
101 Manning Dr, Chapel Hill, 919-966-4446

Psychiatry

Barringer, Thaddeus J., Jr. (4 mentions)
Tulane U, 1978 *Certification:* Psychiatry
3900 Browning Pl #201, Raleigh, 919-787-7125

Bashford, Robert Alonzo (3 mentions)
U of North Carolina, 1971
Certification: Obstetrics & Gynecology, Psychiatry
101 Manning Dr, Chapel Hill, 919-966-4131

Comer, Wilson Sidney, Jr. (3 mentions)
U of North Carolina, 1977 *Certification:* Psychiatry
867 Washington St, Raleigh, 919-833-5867

Gittelman, David Kalman (3 mentions)
Philadelphia Coll of Osteopathic Med, 1983
Certification: Psychiatry
3024 New Bern Ave #200, Raleigh, 919-350-2800

Ostrow, Barry Seymour (3 mentions)
U of Michigan, 1966 *Certification:* Geriatric Psychiatry, Psychiatry
3900 Browning Pl #201, Raleigh, 919-787-7125

Weisler, Richard Harry (3 mentions)
U of North Carolina, 1976 *Certification:* Psychiatry
700 Spring Forest Rd #125, Raleigh, 919-872-5900

Zarzar, Michael Nakhleh (3 mentions)
U of North Carolina, 1984 *Certification:* Psychiatry
4301 Lake Boone Trail #210, Raleigh, 919-278-2041

Pulmonary Disease

Donohue, James Francis (5 mentions)
New Jersey Med Sch, 1969
Certification: Internal Medicine, Pulmonary Disease
103 Mason Farm Rd, Chapel Hill, 919-966-6838

Flescher, Jonathan (12 mentions)
Albert Einstein Coll of Med, 1983 *Certification:* Internal
Medicine, Pulmonary Disease, Sleep Medicine
3100 Blue Ridge Rd #100, Raleigh, 919-781-7500

Govert, Joseph Alan (5 mentions)
U of California-Irvine, 1989
Certification: Internal Medicine, Pulmonary Disease
Duke University Med Ctr, Durham, 919-681-5919

Hart, Timothy Bertrand (11 mentions)
Virginia Commonwealth U, 1979
Certification: Internal Medicine, Pulmonary Disease
23 Sunnybrook Rd #113, Raleigh, 919-250-0580

Hayes, D. Allen (26 mentions)
U of Virginia, 1972
Certification: Internal Medicine, Pulmonary Disease
3480 Wake Forest Rd #414, Raleigh, 919-862-5520

Henry, Marianna Matthews (3 mentions)
U of North Carolina, 1977
Certification: Pediatric Pulmonology, Pediatrics
101 Manning Dr, Chapel Hill, 919-966-4131

Kunstling, Ted Richard (4 mentions)
Duke U, 1968
Certification: Internal Medicine, Pulmonary Disease
3480 Wake Forest Rd #414, Raleigh, 919-862-5520

Kussin, Peter Samuel (4 mentions)
Mount Sinai Sch of Med, 1985
Certification: Internal Medicine, Pulmonary Disease
3116 N Duke St, Durham, 919-660-2372

Powers, Mark Anthony (3 mentions)
Dartmouth Coll, 1977 *Certification:* Critical Care Medicine,
Internal Medicine, Pulmonary Disease
4309 Medical Park Dr #100, Durham, 919-620-7300

Rabil, Donald M. (6 mentions)
Certification: Internal Medicine, Pulmonary Disease
3480 Wake Forest Rd #414, Raleigh, 919-862-5520

Rivera, M. Patricia (3 mentions)
Stony Brook U, 1985 *Certification:* Internal Medicine
101 Manning Dr, Chapel Hill, 919-966-7933

Radiology—Diagnostic

Burge, Holly Jean (3 mentions)
Ohio State U, 1985 *Certification:* Diagnostic Radiology
3949 Browning Pl, Raleigh, 919-787-7411

Coates, George Glenn (3 mentions)
U of California-Irvine, 1990 *Certification:* Diagnostic Radiology
3614 Haworth Dr, Raleigh, 919-787-7411
3949 Browning Pl, Raleigh, 919-787-7411

Detweiler, Donald Gene (6 mentions)
Emory U, 1978 *Certification:* Diagnostic Radiology
4420 Lake Boone Trail, Raleigh, 919-784-3023

Payne, Cynthia Susan (4 mentions)
U of Toledo, 1980 *Certification:* Diagnostic Radiology, Neurology
4420 Lake Boone Trail, Raleigh, 919-784-3023

Pope, Charles Vance (3 mentions)
U of North Carolina, 1976 *Certification:* Diagnostic Radiology
4301 Lake Boone Trail #103, Raleigh, 919-781-6707
3821 Merton Dr, Raleigh, 919-787-7411

Rosen, Alan Lee (4 mentions)
U of Rochester, 1979 *Certification:* Diagnostic Radiology
114 Wind Chime Ct, Raleigh, 919-847-6431

Weber, Andrew Bernard (4 mentions)
Temple U, 1987 *Certification:* Diagnostic Radiology
4420 Lake Boone Trail, Raleigh, 919-784-3023

Radiology—Therapeutic

Ornitz, Robert David (4 mentions)
U of Oklahoma, 1971 *Certification:* Therapeutic Radiology
4420 Lake Boone Trail, Raleigh, 919-784-3018
7 Berkshire Rd, Smithfield, 919-938-0008

Scarantino, Charles Walter (8 mentions)
Wake Forest U, 1973 *Certification:* Therapeutic Radiology
4420 Lake Boone Trail, Raleigh, 919-784-3018
7 Berkshire Rd, Smithfield, 919-938-0008

Sidhu, Kulbir Kolby (4 mentions)
FMS-Canada, 1995 *Certification:* Radiation Oncology
4101 Macon Pond Rd, Raleigh, 919-781-7070

Rehabilitation

O'Brien, Patrick James (13 mentions)
New York Med Coll, 1981
Certification: Physical Medicine & Rehabilitation
3000 New Bern Ave, Raleigh, 919-350-8779

Sanitate, Scott Steven (3 mentions)
Wayne State U, 1988
Certification: Pain Medicine, Physical Medicine & Rehabilitation
2309 Sparger Rd, Durham, 919-309-0911
1110 SE Cary Pkwy #103, Cary, 919-467-4992

Rheumatology

Brothers, George B., Jr. (5 mentions)
Tufts U, 1976 *Certification:* Internal Medicine, Rheumatology
940 Martin Luther King Jr Blvd, Chapel Hill, 919-942-5123

Chmelewski, Walter L. (8 mentions)
U of Pittsburgh, 1986
Certification: Internal Medicine, Rheumatology
2418 Blue Ridge Rd #105, Raleigh, 919-881-8272

Jonas, Beth Laurie (5 mentions)
SUNY-Upstate Med U, 1989 *Certification:* Rheumatology
3100 Mason Farm Rd, Chapel Hill, 919-966-4131

Ross, Ana Silvia (11 mentions)
FMS-Brazil, 1985 *Certification:* Internal Medicine, Rheumatology
2418 Blue Ridge Rd #105, Raleigh, 919-881-8272

Sinclair, Sherry Lynn (7 mentions)
East Carolina U, 1993 *Certification:* Internal Medicine, Rheumatology
2418 Blue Ridge Rd #105, Raleigh, 919-881-8272

Thoracic Surgery

D'Amico, Thomas A. (11 mentions)
Columbia U, 1987 *Certification:* Surgery, Thoracic Surgery
Duke University Med Ctr, Durham, 919-684-4891

Peyton, Robert B. (5 mentions)
New York U, 1977 *Certification:* Thoracic Surgery
3000 New Bern Ave #1100, Raleigh, 919-231-6333

White, David Cloid (16 mentions)
U of Virginia, 1996 *Certification:* Surgery, Thoracic Surgery
3480 Wake Forest Rd, Raleigh, 919-862-5520

Urology

Benevides, Marc David (5 mentions)
U of North Carolina, 1995 *Certification:* Urology
3320 Wake Forest Rd #320, Raleigh, 919-790-5500
226 Asheville Ave #40, Cary, 919-851-5482

Bennett, Brian Charles (6 mentions)
Vanderbilt U, 1989 *Certification:* Urology
2800 Blue Ridge Rd #405, Raleigh, 919-881-0287

Carson, Culley Clyde (5 mentions)
George Washington U, 1971 *Certification:* Urology
101 Manning Dr #BW-427, Chapel Hill, 919-966-2571

Chawla, Sameer Naren (9 mentions)
Temple U, 1999 *Certification:* Urology
23 Sunnybrook Rd #197, Raleigh, 919-350-7330
10000 Falls of Neuse Rd, Raleigh, 919-350-1570

Kane, Richard Douglas (9 mentions)
Northwestern U, 1971 *Certification:* Urology
4301 Lake Boone Trail, Raleigh, 919-782-1255

Leatherman, Hugh K., Jr. (10 mentions)
Med U of South Carolina, 1981 *Certification:* Urology
3320 Wake Forest Rd #320, Raleigh, 919-790-0036
226 Ashville Ave #40, Cary, 919-851-5482

Leet, Douglas Charles (12 mentions)
U of Chicago, 1975 *Certification:* Urology
3320 Wake Forest Rd #320, Raleigh, 919-790-0036
226 Ashville Ave #40, Cary, 919-851-5482
2800 Blueridge Rd #405, Raleigh, 919-881-0287

Pruthi, Raj Som (5 mentions)
Duke U, 1992 *Certification:* Urology
101 Manning Dr, Chapel Hill, 919-966-1315

Robertson, Cary Nobles (5 mentions)
Tulane U, 1977 *Certification:* Urology
Duke University Med Ctr #1108, Durham, 919-681-6768

Weiner, John S. (5 mentions)
Tulane U, 1988
Duke University Med Ctr #3831, Durham, 919-684-6994

Vascular Surgery

Clark, George T., III (11 mentions)
U of North Carolina, 1985 *Certification:* Vascular Surgery
2800 Blue Ridge Rd #500, Raleigh, 919-235-3400

Fogartie, James E., Jr. (15 mentions)
Med U of South Carolina, 1982
Certification: Surgery, Vascular Surgery
2800 Blue Ridge Rd #500, Raleigh, 919-235-3400

McCann, Richard Lucas (8 mentions)
Cornell U, 1974 *Certification:* Surgery, Vascular Surgery
200 Trent Dr #2-B, Durham, 919-684-2620
105 Wisteria Dr, Chapel Hill, 919-684-8111

Ohio

Cleveland Area—page 371

Columbus Area—page 382

Cincinnati Area—page 363

Cincinnati Area
Including Hamilton County

Allergy/Immunology

Bernstein, David Isaac (9 mentions)
U of Cincinnati, 1977 *Certification:* Allergy & Immunology,
Diagnostic Laboratory Immunology, Internal Medicine
8444 Winton Rd, Cincinnati, 513-931-0775

Bernstein, Jonathan Abram (16 mentions)
U of Cincinnati, 1985
Certification: Allergy & Immunology, Internal Medicine
8444 Winton Rd, Cincinnati, 513-931-0770
9275 Montgomery Rd #300, Cincinnati, 513-931-0775

Bobbitt, Ralph Carter, Jr. (10 mentions)
Certification: Allergy & Immunology, Pediatrics
7629 Kenwood Rd, Cincinnati, 513-984-5666

Fischer, Thomas Joseph (11 mentions)
U of Cincinnati, 1971
Certification: Allergy & Immunology, Pediatrics
8245 Northcreek Dr, Cincinnati, 513-745-4706

Ghory, Ann Clark (8 mentions)
Ohio State U, 1976
Certification: Allergy & Immunology, Pediatrics
7495 State Rd #350, Cincinnati, 513-624-1901
9600 Children Dr #500, Mason, 513-573-7050
2727 Madison Rd #300, Cincinnati, 513-861-0222
6350 Glenway Ave #200, Cincinnati, 513-861-0222

Ghory, Patricia K. (11 mentions)
U of Cincinnati, 1980
Certification: Allergy & Immunology, Pediatrics
2727 Madison Rd #300, Cincinnati, 513-861-0222
9600 Children Dr #500, Mason, 513-573-7050
7495 State Rd #350, Cincinnati, 513-624-1901
6350 Glenway Ave #200, Cincinnati, 513-861-0222

Newman, Lawrence Jay (10 mentions)
U of Michigan, 1976
Certification: Allergy & Immunology, Pediatrics
10597 Montgomery Rd #200, Cincinnati, 513-793-6861

Anesthesiology

Beckmeyer, William Peter (3 mentions)
U of Cincinnati, 1987 *Certification:* Anesthesiology
2446 Kipling Ave, Cincinnati, 513-853-5612

Bridenbaugh, Diann Hurd (3 mentions)
U of Cincinnati, 1990
2368 Victory Pkwy #501, Cincinnati, 513-872-7100
231 Albert Sabin Way, Cincinnati, 513-558-4701

Bromley, Joel Jay (3 mentions)
Indiana U, 1981 *Certification:* Anesthesiology
10500 Montgomery Rd, Cincinnati, 513-745-1111

Cionni, Anthony Steven (8 mentions)
U of Cincinnati, 1982 *Certification:* Anesthesiology
375 Dixmyth Ave, Cincinnati, 513-872-2432

Friedrich, Andrew D. (4 mentions)
U of Rochester, 1995
Certification: Anesthesiology, Critical Care Medicine
234 Goodman St, Cincinnati, 513-872-7388

Gregg, Richard Van (3 mentions)
U of Louisville, 1981 *Certification:* Anesthesiology
2139 Auburn Ave, Cincinnati, 513-585-2422

Harris, William Edward (5 mentions)
Ohio State U, 1992 *Certification:* Anesthesiology
8261 Cornell Rd, Cincinnati, 513-891-0022

Kurth, Charles Dean (3 mentions)
U of Wisconsin, 1982 *Certification:* Anesthesiology, Pediatrics
3333 Burnet Ave, Cincinnati, 513-636-4408

Loon, Martin Harvey (5 mentions)
FMS-South Africa, 1969 *Certification:* Anesthesiology
3217 Clifton Ave, Cincinnati, 513-861-2490

Megois, Lee Stephen (4 mentions)
U of Cincinnati, 1978 *Certification:* Anesthesiology
7500 State Rd, Cincinnati, 859-341-7356

Molnar, James Martin (3 mentions)
Ohio State U, 1982
Certification: Anesthesiology, Internal Medicine, Pain Medicine
8261 Cornell Rd #630, Cincinnati, 513-891-0022

Raithel, Donald James (3 mentions)
Northwestern U, 1985 *Certification:* Anesthesiology
2139 Auburn Ave, Cincinnati, 513-585-2422

Roth, Jeffrey Louis (5 mentions)
U of Miami, 1978 *Certification:* Anesthesiology
7800 Concord Hills Pl, Cincinnati, 513-686-5093

Sobolewski, Thomas Paul (3 mentions)
U of Wisconsin, 1993 *Certification:* Anesthesiology
375 Dixmyth Ave, Cincinnati, 513-872-2432

Tobias, Brian (5 mentions)
FMS-South Africa, 1966 *Certification:* Anesthesiology
3407 Clifton Ave, Cincinnati, 513-861-2490

Vaughan, Brian Newell (3 mentions)
Georgetown U, 2001 *Certification:* Anesthesiology
2139 Auburn Ave, Cincinnati, 513-585-2422
3145 Hamilton-Mason Rd, Hamilton, 513-894-8888
4850 Red Bank Expy, Cincinnati, 513-272-3448

Cardiac Surgery

Hiratzka, Loren Forrest (16 mentions)
U of Iowa, 1970 *Certification:* Thoracic Surgery
4030 Smith Rd #300, Cincinnati, 513-421-3494

Ivey, Tom Dexter (12 mentions)
U of Wisconsin, 1970 *Certification:* Thoracic Surgery
2123 Auburn Ave #238, Cincinnati, 513-651-1180

Mitts, Donald Louis (16 mentions)
U of Kentucky, 1971 *Certification:* Thoracic Surgery
2123 Auburn Ave #238, Cincinnati, 513-651-1180

Park, Steven Earl (10 mentions)
U of Chicago, 1985 *Certification:* Surgery, Thoracic Surgery
4030 Smith Rd #300, Cincinnati, 513-421-3494

Smith, John Michael (38 mentions)
U of Louisville, 1989 *Certification:* Surgery, Thoracic Surgery
4030 Smith Rd #300, Cincinnati, 513-421-3494

Vester, Samuel Russell (24 mentions)
U of Cincinnati, 1983 *Certification:* Surgery, Thoracic Surgery
4030 Smith Rd #300, Cincinnati, 513-421-3494

Cardiology

Abbottsmith, Charles Wisdom (4 mentions)
FMS-Canada, 1963 *Certification:* Cardiovascular Disease,
Internal Medicine, Interventional Cardiology
2123 Auburn Ave #136, Cincinnati, 513-721-8881

Babbitt, David Gerard (4 mentions)
Wright State U, 1983
Certification: Cardiovascular Disease, Internal Medicine
2123 Auburn Ave #624, Cincinnati, 513-751-8100

Broderick, Thomas Michael (10 mentions)
U of Cincinnati, 1983 *Certification:* Cardiovascular Disease,
   Internal Medicine, Interventional Cardiology
2123 Auburn Ave #136, Cincinnati, 513-721-8881

Caples, Pete Ledley (5 mentions)
U of Virginia, 1971
Certification: Cardiovascular Disease, Internal Medicine
10506 Montgomery Rd #504, Cincinnati, 513-792-7800

Gerson, Myron Craig (5 mentions)
Indiana U, 1972
Certification: Cardiovascular Disease, Internal Medicine
222 Piedmont Ave #4000, Cincinnati, 513-558-3074
7770 University Ct #2000, West Chester, 513-475-7465

Ghazi, Freidoon (5 mentions)
FMS-Iran, 1977
Certification: Cardiovascular Disease, Internal Medicine
3219 Clifton Ave #400, Cincinnati, 513-861-1260

Glassman, Alan Daniel (4 mentions)
U of Cincinnati, 1976
Certification: Cardiovascular Disease, Internal Medicine
2841 Boudinot Ave #200, Cincinnati, 513-661-5222
2454 Kipling Ave #G20, Cincinnati, 513-541-0700
4750 E Galbraith Rd #103, Cincinnati, 513-985-0022

Hackworth, Joe Nathan (7 mentions)
U of Alabama, 1975
Certification: Cardiovascular Disease, Internal Medicine
10496 Montgomery Rd #104, Cincinnati, 513-861-5555

Hattemer, Charles Ryan (24 mentions)
Case Western Reserve U, 1985
Certification: Cardiovascular Disease, Internal Medicine
2123 Auburn Ave #624, Cincinnati, 513-751-8100

Hutchins, Matthew George (5 mentions)
U of Cincinnati, 1994
Certification: Cardiovascular Disease, Interventional Cardiology
2123 Auburn Ave #624, Cincinnati, 513-751-8100

Kereiakes, Dean James (19 mentions)
U of Cincinnati, 1978
Certification: Cardiovascular Disease, Internal Medicine
2123 Auburn Ave #136, Cincinnati, 513-721-8881

Reed, David Craig (8 mentions)
U of Cincinnati, 1981
Certification: Cardiovascular Disease, Internal Medicine
3219 Clifton Ave #400, Cincinnati, 513-861-1260
1060 Nimitzview, Cincinnati, 513-861-1260
3020 Hospital Dr, Batavia, 513-861-1260

Reginelli, Joel Peter (8 mentions)
Ohio State U, 1995
Certification: Cardiovascular Disease, Interventional Cardiology
10525 Montgomery Rd, Cincinnati, 513-745-9800

Shea, Patrick John (4 mentions)
U of Michigan, 1980
Certification: Cardiovascular Disease, Internal Medicine
10506 Montgomery Rd #504, Cincinnati, 513-792-7800

Thoresen, Christopher Jon (8 mentions)
U of Wisconsin, 1986
Certification: Cardiovascular Disease, Internal Medicine
10506 Montgomery Rd #504, Cincinnati, 513-792-7800

Toltzis, Robert Joshua (4 mentions)
Hahnemann U, 1974
Certification: Cardiovascular Disease, Internal Medicine
625 Eden Park Dr #340, Cincinnati, 513-651-0222

Tondow, David, Jr. (4 mentions)
Georgetown U, 1970
Certification: Cardiovascular Disease, Internal Medicine
3219 Clifton Ave #400, Cincinnati, 513-861-1260

Wayne, Donald Louis (22 mentions)
Rosalind Franklin U, 1983
Certification: Cardiovascular Disease, Internal Medicine
4760 E Galbraith Rd #205, Cincinnati, 513-985-0741

Weintraub, Neal Lee (4 mentions)
Tulane U, 1984
Certification: Cardiovascular Disease, Internal Medicine
222 Piedmont Ave #1200, Cincinnati, 513-475-8521

Dermatology

Adams, Brian Burke (11 mentions)
Yale U, 1995 *Certification:* Dermatology
222 Piedmont Ave #5300, Cincinnati, 513-475-7630

Anderson, Debra Sue (8 mentions)
U of Cincinnati, 1983 *Certification:* Dermatology
10506 Montgomery Rd #402, Cincinnati, 513-791-6161

Cardone, John Scott (6 mentions)
U of Cincinnati, 1988 *Certification:* Dermatology
2859 Boudinot Ave #307, Cincinnati, 513-662-2500

Eisen, Drore (14 mentions)
Virginia Commonwealth U, 1986 *Certification:* Dermatology
7691 5 Mile Rd, Cincinnati, 513-791-6161
10506 Montgomery Rd #402, Cincinnati, 513-791-6161

Fu, Juian-Juian Liu (7 mentions)
U of Cincinnati, 1986 *Certification:* Dermatology
4834 Socialville Foster Rd #20, Mason, 513-459-1988

Lucky, Anne Weissman (12 mentions)
Yale U, 1970 *Certification:* Dermatology, Pediatric
   Dermatology, Pediatric Endocrinology, Pediatrics
2123 Auburn Ave, Cincinnati, 513-579-9191
7691 5 Mile Rd #312, Cincinnati, 513-232-3332
10506 Montgomery Rd #402, Cincinnati, 513-791-6161

Lucky, Paul Andrew (17 mentions)
Yale U, 1972 *Certification:* Dermatology, Internal Medicine
2123 Auburn Ave, Cincinnati, 513-579-9191
10506 Montgomery Rd #402, Cincinnati, 513-791-6161
7691 5 Mile Rd, Cincinnati, 513-232-3332

Morgan, Michael Andrew (12 mentions)
U of North Carolina, 1995 *Certification:* Dermatology
10506 Montgomery Rd #402, Cincinnati, 513-791-6161
2123 Auburn Ave, Cincinnati, 513-579-9191
7691 5 Mile Rd #312, Cincinnati, 513-232-3332

Mutasim, Diya F. (6 mentions)
FMS-Lebanon, 1979
Certification: Dermatological Immunology/Diagnostic and
   Laboratory Immunology, Dermatology, Dermatopathology
222 Piedmont Ave #5300, Cincinnati, 513-475-7630
3200 Vine St, Cincinnati, 513-861-3100

Nordlund, James J. (7 mentions)
U of Minnesota, 1965
Certification: Dermatology, Internal Medicine
8245 Northcreek Dr, Cincinnati, 513-745-4706

Emergency Medicine

Collins, Sean Patrick (3 mentions)
U of Wisconsin, 1997 *Certification:* Emergency Medicine
234 Goodman St, Cincinnati, 513-558-8079

Craven, Jeffrey Alan (4 mentions)
U of Cincinnati, 1976
Certification: Emergency Medicine, Internal Medicine
311 Straight St, Cincinnati, 513-559-2236

Drury, Timothy William (3 mentions)
U of Louisville, 1984 *Certification:* Emergency Medicine
415 Greenwell Ave, Cincinnati, 513-557-3333
3131 Queen City Ave, Cincinnati, 513-557-3333
10450 New Haven Rd, Harrison, 513-557-3333

Fermann, Gregory Joseph (9 mentions)
U of Cincinnati, 1992 *Certification:* Emergency Medicine
2139 Auburn Ave, Cincinnati, 513-558-5281

Fitzpatrick, Timothy J. (3 mentions)
U of Cincinnati, 1985 *Certification:* Emergency Medicine
3131 Queen City Ave, Cincinnati, 513-557-3200

Gibler, Walter Brian (5 mentions)
Vanderbilt U, 1981 *Certification:* Emergency Medicine
231 Albert Sanin Way, Cincinnati, 513-558-5281
234 Goodman St #769, Cincinnati, 513-558-5281

Gries, Gary Edward (6 mentions)
U of Toledo, 1979 *Certification:* Emergency Medicine
6211 Salem Rd, Cincinnati, 513-624-4644
7500 State Rd, Cincinnati, 513-624-4644

Leenellett, Elizabeth E. (3 mentions)
U of Michigan, 1995 *Certification:* Emergency Medicine
2139 Auburn Ave, Cincinnati, 513-585-2235

McKimm, Douglas James (3 mentions)
Stanford U, 1980
Certification: Emergency Medicine, Occupational Medicine
415 Greenwell Ave, Cincinnati, 513-557-3333

Moellman, Joseph John (5 mentions)
U of Cincinnati, 1992 *Certification:* Emergency Medicine
231 Albert Sabin Way #0769, Cincinnati, 513-558-8991

Oblinger, Phillip F. (3 mentions)
U of Virginia, 1982 *Certification:* Emergency Medicine
10500 Montgomery Rd, Cincinnati, 513-745-1200
415 Greenwell Ave, Cincinnati, 513-557-3333
3131 Queen City Ave, Cincinnati, 513-557-3333

Osterlund, Mary Elizabeth (5 mentions)
Georgetown U, 1996 *Certification:* Emergency Medicine
2139 Auburn Ave, Cincinnati, 513-585-2235

Pancioli, Arthur Martin (3 mentions)
U of Michigan, 1991 *Certification:* Emergency Medicine
234 Goodman Ave, Cincinnati, 513-584-5700
4777 E Galbraith Rd, Cincinnati, 513-686-3204
231 Albert Sabin Way, Cincinnati, 513-281-4400

Ruddy, Richard M. (3 mentions)
Georgetown U, 1976
Certification: Pediatric Emergency Medicine, Pediatrics
3333 Burnet Ave, Cincinnati, 513-636-7966

Ryan, Richard Joseph (8 mentions)
New York Med Coll, 1990 *Certification:* Emergency Medicine
2139 Auburn Ave, Cincinnati, 513-558-8104
231 Bethesda Ave, Cincinnati, 513-558-5281

Stadnik, John Clifton (3 mentions)
Wayne State U, 1992 *Certification:* Emergency Medicine
415 Greenwell Ave, Cincinnati, 513-557-3333
3131 Queen City Ave, Cincinnati, 513-557-3333
10450 New Haven Rd, Harrison, 513-557-3333

Van Zile, Jonathan William (3 mentions)
Med U of South Carolina, 1982
Certification: Emergency Medicine, Internal Medicine
4777 E Galbraith Rd, Cincinnati, 513-686-3204

Yamaguchi, Steven Phillip (3 mentions)
U of Cincinnati, 1995 *Certification:* Emergency Medicine
3000 Mack Rd, Fairfield, 513-870-7001

Endocrinology

Collins, Francis Martin (9 mentions)
U of Chicago, 1975
Certification: Endocrinology and Metabolism, Internal Medicine
463 Ohio Pike #300, Cincinnati, 513-528-5600

D'Alessio, David Andrew (8 mentions)
U of Wisconsin, 1983
Certification: Endocrinology and Metabolism, Internal Medicine
222 Piedmont Ave SW #6300, Cincinnati, 513-475-7400
3200 Vine St, Cincinnati, 513-487-6062

Maeder, Michael Charles (26 mentions)
Ohio State U, 1971
Certification: Endocrinology and Metabolism, Internal Medicine
2727 Madison Rd #208, Cincinnati, 513-321-0833

Mangu, Padma (6 mentions)
FMS-India, 1991
Certification: Endocrinology, Diabetes, and Metabolism
55 Progress Pl, Cincinnati, 513-346-5000
2915 Clifton Ave, Cincinnati, 513-872-2031
8245 Northcreek Dr, Cincinnati, 513-745-4706
7423 Mason Montgomery Rd, Mason, 513-229-6000

Miller, Sharon Christine (15 mentions)
U of Cincinnati, 1997 *Certification:* Endocrinology,
    Diabetes, and Metabolism, Internal Medicine
4360 Cooper Rd #201, Cincinnati, 513-861-0012

Williams, Timothy C. (21 mentions)
U of Cincinnati, 1978
Certification: Endocrinology and Metabolism, Internal Medicine
4360 Cooper Rd #201, Cincinnati, 513-861-0012

Family Practice *(see note on page 9)*

Caldemeyer, Robert Durward (3 mentions)
Virginia Commonwealth U, 1982 *Certification:* Family Medicine
24 Compton Rd, Cincinnati, 513-761-2776

Dumont, Francis Emile (5 mentions)
U of Cincinnati, 1990 *Certification:* Family Medicine
1060 Nimitzview Dr #210, Cincinnati, 513-232-8400

Lehenbauer, Martin Paul (3 mentions)
U of Cincinnati, 1981 *Certification:* Family Medicine
608 Reading Rd #C, Mason, 513-398-3445

McCarren, Timothy John (5 mentions)
U of Cincinnati, 1977 *Certification:* Family Medicine
6331 Glenway Ave, Cincinnati, 513-389-1400

Moody, Douglas Clay (5 mentions)
U of Cincinnati, 1985 *Certification:* Family Medicine
9030 Montgomery Rd, Cincinnati, 513-891-2211

Nunlist-Young, Donald G. (3 mentions)
U of Rochester, 1972 *Certification:* Family Medicine
2567 Erie Ave, Cincinnati, 513-871-7848

Pflum, Joseph John (4 mentions)
Wright State U, 1986 *Certification:* Family Medicine
4750 E Galbraith Rd #210, Cincinnati, 513-686-4830

Pritts, Sarah Dahlgren (3 mentions)
Northwestern U, 1996 *Certification:* Family Medicine
305 Crescent Ave, Cincinnati, 513-821-0275

Reilly, Eugene William (3 mentions)
U of Cincinnati, 1991 *Certification:* Family Medicine
7631 Cheviot Rd, Cincinnati, 513-741-5845

Rubin, Barry Alec (3 mentions)
Des Moines U, 1973
910 Loveland-Maderia Rd, Loveland, 513-683-5700

Sweeney, Christopher D. (6 mentions)
Wayne State U, 1978 *Certification:* Family Medicine
10475 Reading Rd #405, Cincinnati, 513-585-9600

Tobias, Barbara Bowman (3 mentions)
U of Cincinnati, 1987 *Certification:* Family Medicine
175 W Galbraith Rd, Cincinnati, 513-585-5700

Webb, Barry Warren (4 mentions)
U of Cincinnati, 1974 *Certification:* Family Medicine
212 W Sharon Rd, Cincinnati, 513-771-7213

Gastroenterology

Bekal, Pradeepkumar (7 mentions)
FMS-India, 1984 *Certification:* Gastroenterology
2925 Vernon Pl #100, Cincinnati, 513-751-6667
2859 Boudinot Ave #307, Cincinnati, 513-389-7300
8271 Cornell Rd #730, Cincinnati, 513-936-0700
2990 Mack Rd #107, Cincinnati, 513-860-4801

Bongiovanni, Gail Lucile (10 mentions)
Case Western Reserve U, 1977
Certification: Gastroenterology, Internal Medicine
2123 Auburn Ave #720, Cincinnati, 513-721-5300
8260 N Creek Dr #110, Cincinnati, 513-721-5300
8260 Northcreek Dr #310, Cincinnati, 513-936-8700

Chun, Andrew Byungsuk (5 mentions)
Jefferson Med Coll, 1991
Certification: Gastroenterology, Internal Medicine
2915 Clifton Ave, Cincinnati, 513-872-2063
55 Progress Pl, Cincinnati, 513-346-5000
2001 Anderson Ferry Rd, Cincinnati, 513-922-1200
8245 Northcreek Dr, Cincinnati, 513-745-4706

Cranley, James Peter (16 mentions)
U of Cincinnati, 1980
Certification: Gastroenterology, Internal Medicine
317 Howell Ave, Cincinnati, 513-751-2255
3652 Werk Rd, Cincinnati, 513-451-6001

Gilinsky, Norman Harris (9 mentions)
FMS-South Africa, 1973
Certification: Gastroenterology, Internal Medicine
222 Piedmont Ave #6000, Cincinnati, 513-475-7505
305 Crescent Ave, Cincinnati, 513-821-0275
9275 Montgomery Rd #200, Cincinnati, 513-475-8520

Ionna, Stephen Lawrence (12 mentions)
U of Cincinnati, 1985
Certification: Gastroenterology, Internal Medicine
6620 Clough Pike, Cincinnati, 513-231-9010
2123 Auburn Ave #722, Cincinnati, 513-231-9010

Jonas, Mark Edward (5 mentions)
SUNY-Downstate Med Coll, 1990 *Certification:*
    Gastroenterology, Internal Medicine, Transplant Hepatology
8271 Connell Rd #730, Cincinnati, 513-936-0700
2925 Vernon Pl #100, Cincinnati, 513-751-6667

Kindel, Robert Matthew (8 mentions)
U of Cincinnati, 1993
Certification: Gastroenterology, Internal Medicine
317 Howell Ave, Cincinnati, 513-751-2255
2450 Kipling Ave #104, Cincinnati, 513-751-2255
3652 Werk Rd, Cincinnati, 513-451-6001

Kreines, Michael David (15 mentions)
U of Cincinnati, 1983
Certification: Gastroenterology, Internal Medicine
2925 Vernon Pl #100, Cincinnati, 513-751-6667
8271 Cornell Rd #730, Cincinnati, 513-936-0700
2990 Mack Rd #107, Cincinnati, 513-860-4801
2841 Boudinot Ave #304, Cincinnati, 513-389-7300

Krone, Robert Emil, Jr. (5 mentions)
U of Cincinnati, 1979
Certification: Gastroenterology, Internal Medicine
6620 Clough Pike, Cincinnati, 513-231-9010
2123 Auburn Ave #722, Cincinnati, 513-231-9010

Manegold, Mark Andrew (10 mentions)
Ohio State U, 1982
Certification: Gastroenterology, Internal Medicine
317 Howell Ave, Cincinnati, 513-751-2255
2450 Kipling Ave #104, Cincinnati, 513-751-2255
3652 Werk Rd, Cincinnati, 513-451-6001

Martin, Stephen Paul (5 mentions)
U of Cincinnati, 1988 *Certification:* Gastroenterology
2925 Vernon Pl #100, Cincinnati, 513-751-6667
8271 Cornell Rd #730, Cincinnati, 513-936-0700
2990 Mack Rd #107, Cincinnati, 513-860-4801
2841 Boudinot Ave #304, Cincinnati, 513-389-7300

Peck, Allan Lawrence (7 mentions)
U of Cincinnati, 1988 *Certification:* Gastroenterology
10600 Montgomery Rd #200, Cincinnati, 513-794-5600

Ramprasad, Krishnamurthy (9 mentions)
FMS-India, 1975
Certification: Gastroenterology, Internal Medicine
2925 Vernon Pl #100, Cincinnati, 513-751-6667
2841 Boudinot Ave #304, Cincinnati, 513-389-7300
8271 Cornell Rd #730, Cincinnati, 513-936-0700
2990 Mack Rd #107, Cincinnati, 513-860-4801

Safdi, Alan Victor (6 mentions)
U of Cincinnati, 1978
Certification: Gastroenterology, Internal Medicine
2925 Vernon Pl #100, Cincinnati, 513-751-6667
8271 Cornell Rd #730, Cincinnati, 513-936-0700
2990 Mack Rd #107, Cincinnati, 513-860-4801
2841 Boudinot Ave #304, Cincinnati, 513-389-7300

Safdi, Michael Andrew (12 mentions)
U of Cincinnati, 1975
Certification: Gastroenterology, Internal Medicine
2925 Vernon Pl #100, Cincinnati, 513-751-6667
8271 Cornell Rd #730, Cincinnati, 513-936-0700
2990 Mack Rd #107, Cincinnati, 513-860-4801
2841 Boudinot Ave #304, Cincinnati, 513-389-7300

Shakoor, Tariq (10 mentions)
FMS-Pakistan, 1978
Certification: Gastroenterology, Internal Medicine
10600 Montgomery Rd #200, Cincinnati, 513-794-5600

General Surgery

Bradley, Robert Graydon (6 mentions)
U of Cincinnati, 1998 *Certification:* Surgery
4760 E Galbraith Rd #108, Cincinnati, 513-791-0707

Crafton, William Boyd (20 mentions)
Virginia Commonwealth U, 1982 *Certification:* Surgery
2123 Auburn Ave, Cincinnati, 513-723-9000

Donovan, Stuart Lee (8 mentions)
Wright State U, 1986 *Certification:* Surgery
7502 State Rd #1180, Cincinnati, 513-232-8181
10506 Montgomery Rd #209, Cincinnati, 513-221-3760

Ellis, Bryan J. (4 mentions)
Ohio U Coll of Osteopathic Med, 1993 *Certification:* Surgery
100 Aarow Spring Blvd #2000, Lebanon, 713-791-6099
4260 Glendale Milford Rd #102, Blue Ash, 513-791-6099

Fischer, David Richard (27 mentions)
U of Cincinnati, 1996 *Certification:* Surgery
2123 Auburn Ave #368, Cincinnati, 513-475-8787
231 Albert Sabin Way, Cincinnati, 513-558-4787

Grannan, Kevin Joseph (8 mentions)
Ohio State U, 1982 *Certification:* Surgery
2915 Clifton Ave, Cincinnati, 513-346-5000
2001 Anderson Ferry Rd, Cincinnati, 513-922-1200
55 Progress Pl, Springdale, 513-346-5000

Guenther, Joseph Michael (4 mentions)
U of Michigan, 1987 *Certification:* Surgery
3747 W Fork Rd, Cincinnati, 513-961-4335
20 Medical Village Dr #394, Edgewood, KY, 859-578-0442

Jennings, Mark Richard (4 mentions)
Case Western Reserve U, 2000
3747 W Fork Rd, Cincinnati, 513-961-4335

Johannigman, Jay Albert (4 mentions)
Case Western Reserve U, 1983
Certification: Surgery, Surgical Critical Care
222 Piedmont Ave #7000, Cincinnati, 513-475-8787

Kerlakian, George M. (7 mentions)
FMS-Lebanon, 1981 *Certification:* Surgery
8245 Northcreek Dr, Cincinnati, 513-745-4706
2915 Clifton Ave, Cincinnati, 513-872-2000
7810 5 Mile Rd, Cincinnati, 513-232-1253

Kirkpatrick, David D., III (12 mentions)
Case Western Reserve U, 1981 *Certification:* Surgery
7502 State Rd #1180, Cincinnati, 513-232-8181
10506 Montgomery Rd #209, Cincinnati, 513-232-8181

Logeman, Jay Paul (4 mentions)
Case Western Reserve U, 1984 *Certification:* Surgery
11147 Montgomery Rd #200, Cincinnati, 513-984-4150

Maynard, Thomas Curry (16 mentions)
U of Arkansas, 1979 *Certification:* Surgery
10506 Montgomery Rd #209, Cincinnati, 513-232-8181
7502 State Rd #1180, Cincinnati, 513-232-8181

Miller, George Edward (4 mentions)
FMS-Canada, 1965 *Certification:* Surgery
20 Medical Village Dr #338, Edgewood, KY, 859-341-8202

Morin, Richard P. (5 mentions)
Med Coll of Wisconsin, 1978 *Certification:* Surgery
4260 Glendale Milford Rd #102, Blue Ash, 513-791-6099

Ogg, Cari Ann (4 mentions)
Wright State U, 2001 *Certification:* Surgery
4760 E Galbraith Rd #108, Cincinnati, 513-791-0707

Popp, Martin Blaine (4 mentions)
U of Pennsylvania, 1968 *Certification:* Surgery
2123 Auburn Ave #420, Cincinnati, 513-421-4504

Saba, Alexander Khamis (11 mentions)
U of Cincinnati, 1988 *Certification:* Surgery
3219 Clifton Ave #215, Cincinnati, 513-872-3595
2852 Boudinot Rd #203, Cincinnati, 513-542-4200
2450 Kipling Ave #G3, Cincinnati, 513-542-4200

Van Gilse, William Victor (7 mentions)
Ohio State U, 1975 *Certification:* Surgery
10506 Montgomery Rd, Cincinnati, 513-232-8181

Geriatrics

Davis, Susan S. (4 mentions)
305 Crescent Ave, Cincinnatti, 513-821-0275
141 Health Profesional Bldg, Cincinnati, 513-584-0650

Mueller, Stephen David (19 mentions)
U of Cincinnati, 1979
Certification: Geriatric Medicine, Internal Medicine
3200 Burnet Ave, Cincinnati, 513-585-9384

Warshaw, Gregg Alan (5 mentions)
U of Michigan, 1976
Certification: Family Medicine, Geriatric Medicine
141 Health Professional Bldg, Cincinnati, 513-723-5373

Hematology/Oncology

Barreau, Jose Gerardo (5 mentions)
FMS-Dominican Republic, 1999
Certification: Hematology, Internal Medicine, Medical Oncology
5520 Cheviot Rd, Cincinnati, 513-451-4033

Bhaskaran, Jayapandian (10 mentions)
FMS-India, 1968
Certification: Hematology, Internal Medicine, Medical Oncology
2452 Kipling Ave, Cincinnati, 513-451-4033
3219 Clifton Ave, Cincinnati, 513-451-4033
5520 Cheviot Rd, Cincinnati, 513-451-4033

Broun, E. Randolph (5 mentions)
Certification: Internal Medicine, Medical Oncology
4725 E Galbraith Rd #320, Cincinnati, 513-891-4800
4350 Malsbary Rd #100, Cincinnati, 513-891-4800
8000 5 Mile Rd #105, Cincinnati, 513-624-1920

Cody, Robert L. (10 mentions)
U of Louisville, 1980
Certification: Hematology, Internal Medicine, Medical Oncology
2727 Madison Rd #400, Cincinnati, 513-321-4333
2139 Auburn Ave Lvl D, Cincinnati, 513-585-2323

Drosick, David Randolph (5 mentions)
West Virginia U, 1985
Certification: Internal Medicine, Medical Oncology
199 William Howard Taft Rd, Cincinnati, 513-751-4448

Essell, James Herbert (8 mentions)
U of Cincinnati, 1985
Certification: Hematology, Internal Medicine, Medical Oncology
4725 E Galbraith Rd #320, Cincinnati, 513-793-6052

Kirlin, David Lee (5 mentions)
U of Cincinnati, 1971
Certification: Internal Medicine, Medical Oncology
4350 Malsbary Rd #100, Cincinnati, 812-934-3707
606 Wilson Creek Rd, Lawrenceburg, IN, 812-537-1911
630 W Main St #304, Wilmington, 937-383-2537

Leming, Philip Deering (23 mentions)
U of Louisville, 1975
Certification: Hematology, Internal Medicine, Medical Oncology
2727 Madison Rd #400, Cincinnati, 513-321-4333
3000 Mack Rd, Fairfield, 513-321-4333

Lower, Elyse Ellen (5 mentions)
U of Cincinnati, 1981
Certification: Internal Medicine, Medical Oncology
199 William Howard Taft Rd, Cincinnati, 513-751-4448

Maher, James Frederick (8 mentions)
U of Oklahoma, 1997
Certification: Internal Medicine, Medical Oncology
5520 Cheviot Rd, Cincinnati, 513-451-4033

Neuss, Michael Norbert (11 mentions)
Duke U, 1979 *Certification:* Internal Medicine, Medical Oncology
4350 Malsbary Rd #200, Cincinnati, 513-751-2273

Palascak, Joseph Edward (14 mentions)
Jefferson Med Coll, 1968
Certification: Hematology, Internal Medicine
234 Goodman St, Cincinnati, 513-558-4233

Ruehlman, Peter George (9 mentions)
U of Cincinnati, 1978
Certification: Internal Medicine, Medical Oncology
199 William Howard Taft Rd, Cincinnati, 513-624-1920
8000 Five Mile Rd #213, Cincinnati, 513-624-1920
4350 Malsbary Rd #100, Cincinnati, 513-891-4800
4760 E Galbraith Rd #208, Cincinnati, 513-891-1200
4725 E Galbraith Rd, Cincinnati, 513-793-6052

Ward, Patrick John (5 mentions)
Ohio State U, 1997
Certification: Internal Medicine, Medical Oncology
4350 Malsbary Rd #100, Cincinnati, 513-891-4800

Waterhouse, David Michael (9 mentions)
U of Massachusetts, 1985
Certification: Internal Medicine, Medical Oncology
4350 Malsbary Rd #200, Cincinnati, 513-751-2273

Infectious Disease

Blatt, Stephen Patrick (22 mentions)
U of Cincinnati, 1985
Certification: Infectious Disease, Internal Medicine
330 Straight St #400, Cincinnati, 513-624-0999

Dunn, Corwin R. (14 mentions)
U of Illinois, 1964
Certification: Infectious Disease, Internal Medicine
2123 Auburn Ave #242, Cincinnati, 513-721-2024

Goodman, Richard Paul (22 mentions)
Case Western Reserve U, 1990
Certification: Infectious Disease, Internal Medicine
330 Straight St #400, Cincinnati, 513-624-0999

Hamilton, Bruce Abbott (16 mentions)
U of Cincinnati, 1978
Certification: Infectious Disease, Internal Medicine
330 Straight St #400, Cincinnati, 513-624-0999

Kuby, Mark Benjamin (9 mentions)
U of Cincinnati, 1974
Certification: Infectious Disease, Internal Medicine
4750 E Galbraith Rd #207, Cincinnati, 513-686-4800

La Marre, Thomas David, Jr. (17 mentions)
Ohio State U, 1996
Certification: Infectious Disease, Internal Medicine
330 Straight St #400, Cincinnati, 513-624-0999

Ng, Silvania Cristina (15 mentions)
FMS-Brazil, 1981
10495 Montgomery Rd #17, Cincinnati, 513-984-2775

Infertility

Awadalla, Sherif George (15 mentions)
U of Cincinnati, 1981 *Certification:* Obstetrics &
Gynecology, Reproductive Endocrinology/Infertility
3805 Edwards Rd #450, Cincinnati, 513-924-5550

Scheiber, Michael David (12 mentions)
U of California-San Francisco, 1990 *Certification:* Obstetrics
& Gynecology, Reproductive Endocrinology/Infertility
3805 Edwards Rd #450, Cincinnati, 513-924-5550

Thomas, Michael Anthony (10 mentions)
U of Illinois, 1984 *Certification:* Obstetrics & Gynecology,
Reproductive Endocrinology/Infertility
2123 Auburn Ave #A-44, Cincinnati, 513-585-2355

Internal Medicine *(see note on page 9)*

Alexander, Marc Albert (7 mentions)
U of Cincinnati, 1981 *Certification:* Internal Medicine
6350 Glenway Ave #400, Cincinnati, 513-481-3400

Bibler, Mark Richard (9 mentions)
Northwestern U, 1980
Certification: Infectious Disease, Internal Medicine
222 Piedmont Ave #6000, Cincinnati, 513-475-7880

Brook, Barry Allen (8 mentions)
U of Cincinnati, 1983 *Certification:* Internal Medicine
4750 E Galbraith Rd #207, Cincinnati, 513-686-4840

Cleves, G. Stephen (4 mentions)
U of Cincinnati, 1988 *Certification:* Internal Medicine
2753 Erie Ave, Cincinnati, 513-871-2340

Craig, Jeffrey Lee (4 mentions)
U of Louisville, 1991 *Certification:* Internal Medicine
3805 Edwards Rd #300, Cincinnati, 513-585-9700

Dammel, Richard Milton (3 mentions)
U of Cincinnati, 1975 *Certification:* Internal Medicine
2475 W Galbraith Rd #C, Cincinnati, 513-931-2400

Hochwalt, James Michael (4 mentions)
U of Cincinnati, 1988 *Certification:* Internal Medicine
2135 Dana Ave #210, Cincinnati, 513-351-1200

Jennings, Michael Robert (15 mentions)
U of Cincinnati, 1982 *Certification:* Internal Medicine
2123 Auburn Ave #334, Cincinnati, 513-585-1500

Kaminski, Nancy Karen (4 mentions)
U of Cincinnati, 1986 *Certification:* Internal Medicine
2135 Dana Ave #210, Cincinnati, 513-351-1200

Kortekamp, Gerard Edward (3 mentions)
U of Cincinnati, 1982 *Certification:* Internal Medicine
2123 Auburn Ave #520, Cincinnati, 513-585-1300

La Franconi, Paula J. (3 mentions)
FMS-Germany, 1985 *Certification:* Internal Medicine
55 Progress Pl, Cincinnati, 513-346-5000

Lang, James Edward (3 mentions)
U of Cincinnati, 1985
4260 Glendale Milford Rd #202, Cincinnati, 513-563-6883

Larkin, Lisa Conrad (9 mentions)
Yale U, 1988 *Certification:* Internal Medicine
4460 Red Bank Expy #100, Cincinnati, 513-272-7080

Lundberg, Thomas George (5 mentions)
U of Cincinnati, 1989 *Certification:* Internal Medicine
11340 Montgomery Rd #208, Cincinnati, 513-489-7457

Martin, Vincent Thomas (4 mentions)
U of Cincinnati, 1984 *Certification:* Internal Medicine
222 Piedmont Ave #6000, Cincinnati, 513-475-7880

Mathis, Bradley Randall (7 mentions)
U of Cincinnati, 1995 *Certification:* Internal Medicine
222 Piedmont Ave #6000, Cincinnati, 513-475-7880

Mowery, Clifford Scott (4 mentions)
U of Cincinnati, 1984 *Certification:* Internal Medicine
4750 E Galbraith Rd #210, Cincinnati, 513-686-4820

Rouan, Gregory Wayne (10 mentions)
U of Cincinnati, 1980 *Certification:* Internal Medicine
222 Piedmont Ave #6000, Cincinnati, 513-475-7880

Webster, Warren Richmond (10 mentions)
U of Cincinnati, 1970 *Certification:* Internal Medicine
2727 Madison Rd #208, Cincinnati, 513-321-0833

Weinberg, Nolan Louis (5 mentions)
U of Minnesota, 1974 *Certification:* Internal Medicine
7825 Laurel Ave, Madeira, 513-561-4811

Wilson, David Gene (4 mentions)
U of Toledo, 1976 *Certification:* Internal Medicine
8000 5 Mile Rd #305, Cincinnati, 513-232-3500

Nephrology

Albers, Frank John (5 mentions)
U of Cincinnati, 1984
Certification: Internal Medicine, Nephrology
3219 Clifton Ave #325, Cincinnati, 513-861-0800
7631 Cheviot Rd Unit 2, Cincinnati, 513-542-3400
2123 Auburn Ave, Cincinnati, 513-241-5630
2450 Kipling Ave #G5, Cincinnati, 919-684-3389
11322 Springfield Pike, Cincinnati, 919-684-3389
10496 Montgomery Rd #110, Cincinnati, 513-791-7572

Cardi, Michael Anthony (21 mentions)
Harvard U, 1977 *Certification:* Internal Medicine, Nephrology
2123 Auburn Ave #404, Cincinnati, 513-241-5630
3219 Clifton Ave #320, Cincinnati, 513-861-0800

Dumbauld, Steven La Mar (19 mentions)
U of Toledo, 1975 *Certification:* Internal Medicine, Nephrology
3219 Clifton Ave #325, Cincinnati, 513-861-0800

Estes, Robin (5 mentions)
U of Illinois, 1978 *Certification:* Internal Medicine, Nephrology
1210 Hicks Blvd, Fairfield, 513-939-3975
10496 Montgomery Rd, Cincinnati, 513-791-7572

Kant, Kotagel Shashi (5 mentions)
FMS-India, 1970 *Certification:* Internal Medicine, Nephrology
231 Albert Sabin Way Rm G259, Cincinnati, 513-558-5471
222 Piedmont Ave #6000, Cincinnati, 513-475-8524

Stephens, Gregory William (8 mentions)
U of Kentucky, 1979 *Certification:* Internal Medicine, Nephrology
3219 Clifton Ave #325, Cincinnati, 513-861-0800
2123 Auburn Ave, Cincinnati, 513-241-5630

Neurological Surgery

Bohinski, Robert John (19 mentions)
U of Cincinnati, 1996 *Certification:* Neurological Surgery
2123 Auburn Ave #441, Cincinnati, 513-221-1100

Kuntz, Charles David (10 mentions)
Case Western Reserve U, 1991 *Certification:* Neurological Surgery
222 Piedmont Ave #3100, Cincinnati, 513-475-8667

Shahbabian, Set (13 mentions)
FMS-Iran, 1969 *Certification:* Neurological Surgery
3285 Westbourne Dr, Cincinnati, 513-922-4810

Tew, John McLellan, Jr. (17 mentions)
Wake Forest U, 1961 *Certification:* Neurological Surgery
506 Oak St, Cincinnati, 513-475-8641
222 Piedmont Ave #3100, Cincinnati, 513-569-5341

Tobler, William Donn (26 mentions)
U of Cincinnati, 1978 *Certification:* Neurological Surgery
2123 Auburn Ave #441, Cincinnati, 513-221-1100

Neurology

Broderick, Joseph Paul (15 mentions)
U of Cincinnati, 1982
Certification: Neurology, Vascular Neurology
222 Piedmont Ave #3200, Cincinnati, 513-475-8730

Hughes, Arthur Lee (5 mentions)
U of Maryland, 1967 *Certification:* Neurology
3285 Westbourne Dr, Cincinnati, 513-451-6200

Kanter, Daniel Stuart (9 mentions)
Case Western Reserve U, 1987 *Certification:* Neurology
222 Piedmont Ave #3200, Cincinnati, 513-475-8730

Neel, Robert Walton, IV (17 mentions)
U of Cincinnati, 2000 *Certification:* Neurology
222 Piedmont Ave #3200, Cincinnati, 513-475-8730

Privitera, Michael D., Jr. (5 mentions)
SUNY-Upstate Med U, 1980 *Certification:* Neurology
222 Piedmont Ave #3200, Cincinnati, 513-475-8730

Reed, Robert Lewis (34 mentions)
U of Cincinnati, 1966 *Certification:* Neurology
111 Wellington Pl, Cincinnati, 513-241-2370

Rorick, Marvin H., III (8 mentions)
U of Cincinnati, 1984 *Certification:* Neurology
111 Wellington Pl, Cincinnati, 513-241-2370
10550 Montgomery Rd #33, Cincinnati, 513-939-5360

Schmerler, Michael (11 mentions)
Northwestern U, 1973 *Certification:* Internal Medicine, Neurology
111 Wellington Pl, Cincinnati, 513-936-5360

Zadikoff, Colin M. (15 mentions)
FMS-South Africa, 1968 *Certification:* Neurology with Special Qualifications in Child Neurology
111 Wellington Pl, Cincinnati, 513-241-2370
2450 Kipling #103, Cincinnati, 513-241-2370

Obstetrics/Gynecology

Allen, Bruce Howard (3 mentions)
U of Louisville, 1975 *Certification:* Obstetrics & Gynecology
2752 Erie Ave #3, Cincinnati, 513-871-0290

Bhati, Anant Ram (3 mentions)
FMS-India, 1965 *Certification:* Obstetrics & Gynecology
10190 Springfield Pike, Cincinnati, 513-772-7600

Busacco, Bradley (3 mentions)
U of Florida, 1979 *Certification:* Obstetrics & Gynecology
7495 State Rd #325, Cincinnati, 513-233-2000

Clark, Elizabeth Ann (4 mentions)
U of Cincinnati, 1982 *Certification:* Obstetrics & Gynecology
10475 Reading Rd #307, Cincinnati, 513-563-2202
3219 Clifton Ave #125, Cincinnati, 513-751-1919

Dehoop, Thomas Art (3 mentions)
Med Coll of Wisconsin, 1990
Certification: Obstetrics & Gynecology
222 Piedmont Ave #5100, Cincinnati, 513-475-8588

Draznik, Michael Robert (3 mentions)
U of Cincinnati, 1978 *Certification:* Obstetrics & Gynecology
2055 Reading Rd #480, Cincinnati, 513-579-0707
7450 Mason Montgomery Rd #202, Mason, 513-579-0707

Egner, Carol Lynn (4 mentions)
U of Toledo, 1981 *Certification:* Obstetrics & Gynecology
6480 Harrison Ave #300, Cincinnati, 513-662-8222

Froehlich, Kurt William (3 mentions)
U of Cincinnati, 1992 *Certification:* Obstetrics & Gynecology
9030 Montgomery Rd, Cincinnati, 513-791-5950

Gass, Margery L. S. (3 mentions)
U of Cincinnati, 1980 *Certification:* Obstetrics & Gynecology
222 Piedmont Ave #5100, Cincinnati, 513-475-8588

Green, Jennifer Ach (4 mentions)
U of Cincinnati, 1997 *Certification:* Obstetrics & Gynecology
2123 Auburn Ave #528, Cincinnati, 513-792-5800
10506 Montgomery Rd #204, Cincinnati, 513-792-5810

Hoopes, Terri Wallace (5 mentions)
U of Cincinnati, 1988 *Certification:* Obstetrics & Gynecology
3219 Clifton Ave #230, Cincinnati, 513-559-9411
1149 Stone Dr #100, Harrison, 513-559-9411

Katz, Molly Ann (3 mentions)
U of Toledo, 1977 *Certification:* Obstetrics & Gynecology
71 E Hollister St, Cincinnati, 513-723-0909

Le Masters, Margaret Mary (4 mentions)
U of Cincinnati, 1982 *Certification:* Obstetrics & Gynecology
10475 Reading Rd #307, Evandale, 513-563-2202

Lippert, Wayne Arthur (4 mentions)
U of Cincinnati, 1969 *Certification:* Obstetrics & Gynecology
2123 Auburn Ave #122, Cincinnati, 513-381-1400
7730 Montgomery Rd, Cincinnati, 513-381-1400

Lum, Ted Michael (3 mentions)
U of Toledo, 1980 *Certification:* Obstetrics & Gynecology
2825 Burnet Ave #208, Cincinnati, 513-221-6300

Nelson, Elbert John Thomas (3 mentions)
Meharry Med Coll, 1967 *Certification:* Obstetrics & Gynecology
222 Piedmont Ave #5100, Cincinnati, 513-475-8588

Ollendorff, Arthur T. (3 mentions)
Northwestern U, 1993 *Certification:* Obstetrics & Gynecology
222 Piedmont Ave #5100, Cincinnati, 513-475-8588
231 Albert Sabin Way, Cincinnati, 513-475-8588
4027 Eastern Ave, Cincinnati, 513-321-2202

Polzin, William James (3 mentions)
Med Coll of Wisconsin, 1983
Certification: Maternal-Fetal Medicine, Obstetrics & Gynecology
375 Dixmyth Ave, Cincinnati, 513-872-4300

Puttmann, Ambrose Anthony (5 mentions)
U of Cincinnati, 1983 *Certification:* Obstetrics & Gynecology
2859 Boudinot Ave #101, Cincinnati, 513-481-5100

Roberts, Mable Moy (3 mentions)
Case Western Reserve U, 1994
Certification: Obstetrics & Gynecology
91212 Montgomery Rd #100, Cincinnati, 513-791-4088
608 Reading Rd #A, Mason, 513-791-4088

Schwartz, David Bruce (3 mentions)
U of Michigan, 1978 *Certification:* Obstetrics & Gynecology
2123 Auburn Ave #320, Cincinnati, 513-241-4223

Smith, Graig William (4 mentions)
U of Toledo, 1981 *Certification:* Obstetrics & Gynecology
3219 Clifton Ave #230, Cincinnati, 513-559-9411

Stamler, Eric Franklin (8 mentions)
U of Cincinnati, 1985 *Certification:* Obstetrics & Gynecology
6350 Glenway Ave #205, Cincinnati, 513-922-6666
7777 University Dr #C, West Chester, 513-922-6666
2123 Auburn Ave, Cincinnati, 513-922-6666

Stephens, Robert Joseph, Jr. (3 mentions)
U of Cincinnati, 1979 *Certification:* Obstetrics & Gynecology
6350 Glenway Ave #205, Cincinnati, 513-922-6666
2123 Auburn Ave, Cincinnati, 513-922-6666
7777 University Dr #C, West Chester, 513-922-6666

Vardaka, Marianna C. (3 mentions)
FMS-Greece, 1981 *Certification:* Obstetrics & Gynecology
4760 E Galbraith Rd #200, Cincinnati, 513-985-9017

Wendel, James Schoelles (6 mentions)
U of Cincinnati, 1982 *Certification:* Obstetrics & Gynecology
608 Reading Rd #A, Cincinnati, 513-791-4080
9122 Montgomery Rd #100, Cincinnati, 513-791-4088

Yang, Lisa (3 mentions)
Indiana U, 1988 *Certification:* Obstetrics & Gynecology
4420 Aicholtz Rd, Cincinnati, 513-752-9122
440 Ray Norrsh Dr, Cincinnati, 513-671-7700

Zabrecky, Anna (3 mentions)
U of Cincinnati, 1985 *Certification:* Obstetrics & Gynecology
7495 State Rd #300, Cincinnati, 513-231-3447

Ophthalmology

Bell, Howard Lee (6 mentions)
Ohio State U, 1981 *Certification:* Ophthalmology
7527A State Rd, Anderson Township, 513-232-5550
3050 Hospital Dr #100, Batavia, 513-732-1718

Benza, Robert (8 mentions)
U of Cincinnati, 1990 *Certification:* Ophthalmology
7850 Camargo Rd, Cincinnati, 513-561-5655

Bibler, Lindsay Wilson (7 mentions)
Northwestern U, 1980 *Certification:* Ophthalmology
8040 Hosbrook Rd #100, Cincinnati, 513-891-0473

Golnik, Karl Clifford (4 mentions)
Johns Hopkins U, 1986 *Certification:* Ophthalmology
222 Piedmont Ave #1700, Cincinnati, 513-475-7758
1945 Cei Dr, Cincinnati, 513-984-5133

Klugo, Karen (4 mentions)
Certification: Ophthalmology
4750 E Galbraith Rd #105, Cincinnati, 513-745-9787

Kondash, Stephen Thomas (4 mentions)
U of Cincinnati, 1987 *Certification:* Ophthalmology
2841 Boudinot Ave #300, Cincinnati, 513-389-9911

Kulwin, Dwight Robert (4 mentions)
U of Chicago, 1973 *Certification:* Ophthalmology
3219 Clifton Ave #110, Cincinnati, 513-618-3300
222 Piedmont Ave #1600, Cincinnati, 513-475-7642
1945 Cei Dr, Cincinnati, 513-984-5133

Osher, Robert Henry (5 mentions)
U of Rochester, 1976 *Certification:* Ophthalmology
1945 Cei Dr, Cincinnati, 513-984-5133

Petersen, Michael Richard (4 mentions)
U of Miami, 1986 *Certification:* Ophthalmology
1945 Cei Dr, Cincinnati, 513-984-5133

Robbins, Andrew F., Jr. (6 mentions)
U of Cincinnati, 1973 *Certification:* Ophthalmology
4760 Red Bank Rd #108, Cincinnati, 513-531-2020

Sands, Joshua Jonathan (9 mentions)
Creighton U, 1982 *Certification:* Ophthalmology
222 Piedmont Ave #1700, Cincinnati, 513-475-7292

Wander, Arden Hale (4 mentions)
U of Cincinnati, 1967 *Certification:* Ophthalmology
222 Piedmont Ave #1700, Cincinnati, 513-475-7294

Werner, Robert Blair (4 mentions)
U of Cincinnati, 1979 *Certification:* Ophthalmology
330 Straight St #201, Cincinnati, 513-221-7788

West, Constance Elizabeth (6 mentions)
U of Massachusetts, 1986 *Certification:* Ophthalmology
3333 Burnet Ave, Cincinnati, 513-636-4751

Orthopedics

Andrews, Michelle (4 mentions)
Hahnemann U, 1985 *Certification:* Orthopaedic Surgery
12115 Sheraton Ln, Cincinnati, 513-891-3200
10663 Montgomery Rd, Cincinnati, 513-891-3200
311 Straight St, Cincinnati, 513-559-2810

Archdeacon, Michael T. (5 mentions)
Ohio State U, 1993 *Certification:* Orthopaedic Surgery
222 Piedmont Ave #2200, Cincinnati, 513-475-8690
9275 Montgomery Rd #300, Cincinnati, 513-475-8690

Burger, Robert Richard (7 mentions)
U of Cincinnati, 1985
Certification: Orthopaedic Sports Medicine, Orthopaedic Surgery
6480 Harrison Ave #100, Cincinnati, 513-354-3700

Favorito, Paul Joseph (4 mentions)
U of Buffalo, 1993 *Certification:* Orthopaedic Surgery
7575 5 Mile Rd, Cincinnati, 513-232-6677
6350 Glenway Ave #415, Cincinnati, 513-721-1111
4701 Creek Rd #110, Cincinnati, 513-733-8894

Funk, Daniel Allen (12 mentions)
U of Cincinnati, 1981 *Certification:* Orthopaedic Surgery
3950 Red Bank Rd, Cincinnati, 513-333-2580

Heidt, Robert S. (4 mentions)
Certification: Orthopaedic Surgery
7575 5 Mile Rd, Cincinnati, 513-721-1111
4701 Creek Rd #110, Cincinnati, 513-733-8894

Henderson, Clyde Edward (5 mentions)
U of Cincinnati, 1977 *Certification:* Orthopaedic Surgery
4600 Smith Rd #B, Cincinnati, 513-221-4848

Kirk, Patrick Gerard (21 mentions)
Rush U, 1985 *Certification:* Orthopaedic Surgery
4760 E Galbraith Rd #109, Cincinnati, 513-791-5200

Lim, Edward V. A. (6 mentions)
FMS-Philippines, 1977 *Certification:* Orthopaedic Surgery
2123 Auburn Ave #231, Cincinnati, 513-791-5200
4760 S Galbraith #109, Cincinnati, 513-791-5200

Noyes, Frank (4 mentions)
George Washington U, 1966 *Certification:* Orthopaedic Surgery
10663 Montgomery Rd, Cincinnati, 513-346-7292

Pruis, Dirk Thomas (10 mentions)
Indiana U, 1980 *Certification:* Orthopaedic Surgery
8044 Montgomery Rd #100, Cincinnati, 513-985-3700
3050 Mack Rd #310, Fairfield, 513-985-3700
7450 Mason Montgomery Rd #104, Mason, 513-985-3700
8311 Montgomery Rd, Cincinatti, 513-985-3700
4900 Wunnenbeng Way, West Chester, 513-985-3700

Reilly, Kevin Eugene (4 mentions)
U of Cincinnati, 1990 *Certification:* Orthopaedic Surgery
5589 Cheviot Rd, Cincinnati, 513-733-8894
6350 Glenway Ave #415, Cincinnati, 513-618-2096

Shockley, Thomas Edward (4 mentions)
Meharry Med Coll, 1986 *Certification:* Orthopaedic Surgery
4600 Smith Rd #B, Norwood, 513-221-4848
7450 Mason Montgomery Rd #208, Mason, 513-221-4848

Stanfield, Denver Thomas (5 mentions)
U of Cincinnati, 1985 *Certification:* Orthopaedic Surgery
7575 5 Mile Rd, Cincinnati, 513-232-6677
4701 Creek Rd #110, Cincinnati, 513-733-8894

Stern, Peter Joseph (5 mentions)
Washington U, 1970
Certification: Orthopaedic Surgery, Surgery of the Hand
538 Oak St #200, Cincinnati, 513-961-4263
222 Piedmont Ave #2200, Cincinnati, 513-475-8690

Swank, Michael Lawson (13 mentions)
Northwestern U, 1987 *Certification:* Orthopaedic Surgery
8250 Kenwood Crossing Way #101, Cincinnati, 513-221-5500
2841 Boudinot Ave #202, Cincinnati, 513-221-5500

Thomas, Joseph David (13 mentions)
U of Cincinnati, 1985 *Certification:* Orthopaedic Surgery
8044 Montgomery Rd #100, Cincinnati, 513-985-3700
3050 Mack Rd #310, Fairfield, 513-985-3700
7450 Mason Montgomery Rd #104, Mason, 513-985-3700
4900 Wunnenberg Way, West Chester, 513-985-3700
8311 Montgomery Rd, Cincinnati, 513-985-3700

Wyrick, John Dwight (4 mentions)
Wright State U, 1984
Certification: Orthopaedic Surgery, Surgery of the Hand
222 Piedmont Ave #2200, Cincinnati, 513-475-8690
9275 Montgomery Rd #300, Cincinnati, 513-475-8690

Otorhinolaryngology

Baluyot, Sabino T., Jr. (9 mentions)
FMS-Philippines, 1963 *Certification:* Otolaryngology
7763 Montgomery Rd, Cincinnati, 513-891-6634

Ca Jacob, Daniel Emerson (8 mentions)
U of Cincinnati, 1981 *Certification:* Otolaryngology
55 Progress Pl, Cincinnati, 513-346-5000
2001 Anderson Ferry Rd, Cincinnati, 513-872-2095
2915 Clifton Ave, Cincinnati, 513-872-2055

Coors, Raymond R., Jr (9 mentions)
U of Cincinnati, 1976 *Certification:* Otolaryngology
8250 Winton Rd #200, Cincinnati, 513-931-8216

Deutsch, Mark David (11 mentions)
U of Cincinnati, 1991 *Certification:* Otolaryngology
11135 Montgomery Rd, Cincinnati, 513-793-9600
630 W Main St #105, Wilmington, 937-382-7798
100 Arrow Spring Blvd #G-108, Lebanon, 513-282-7425

Hellmann, Joseph Richard (9 mentions)
U of Cincinnati, 1987 *Certification:* Otolaryngology
2123 Auburn Ave #209, Cincinnati, 513-421-5558
7691 5 Mile Rd #214, Cincinnati, 513-232-3277
4760 E Galb Rd #118, Cincinnati, 513-421-5558

Kereiakes, Thomas James (21 mentions)
U of Cincinnati, 1980 *Certification:* Otolaryngology
2123 Auburn Ave #209, Cincinnati, 513-421-5558
7691 5 Mile Rd #214, Cincinnati, 513-232-3277

Nurre, John William, II (8 mentions)
U of Cincinnati, 1983 *Certification:* Otolaryngology
6040 Harrison Ave, Cincinnati, 513-451-1544

Peerless, Alter Gerson (8 mentions)
U of Cincinnati, 1973 *Certification:* Otolaryngology
9403 Kenwood Rd #C204, Cincinnati, 513-936-0500

Steward, David L., Jr. (10 mentions)
U of Cincinnati, 1994 *Certification:* Otolaryngology
222 Piedmont Ave #5200, Cincinnati, 513-475-8427
7700 University Ct #3900, West Chester, 513-475-8400

Tami, Thomas Allen (6 mentions)
St Louis U, 1979 *Certification:* Otolaryngology
55 Progress Pl, Cincinnati, 513-346-5000
375 Dixmyth Ave, Cincinnati, 513-872-1400

Wilson, Keith Michael (8 mentions)
Cornell U, 1986 *Certification:* Otolaryngology
222 Piedmont Ave #5200, Cincinnati, 513-475-8400
7700 University Ct #3900, West Chester, 513-475-8400

Wood, Michael David (26 mentions)
U of Cincinnati, 1979 *Certification:* Otolaryngology
2123 Auburn Ave #209, Cincinnati, 513-421-5558
7691 5 Mile Rd #214, Cincinnati, 513-232-3277

Pain Medicine

Akbik, Hammam Hadi (4 mentions)
FMS-Syria, 1988 *Certification:* Anesthesiology
234 Goodman St, Cincinnati, 513-475-8282

Atluri, Sairam Lakshmi (6 mentions)
FMS-India, 1991 *Certification:* Anesthesiology, Pain Medicine
7655 5 Mile Rd #117, Cincinnati, 513-624-7525

Gregg, Richard Van (6 mentions)
U of Louisville, 1981 *Certification:* Anesthesiology
2139 Auburn Ave, Cincinnati, 513-585-2422

Gunzenhaeuser, Leslie F. (6 mentions)
Ohio State U, 1977
Certification: Anesthesiology, Internal Medicine
2139 Auburn Ave, Cincinnati, 513-585-2482

Minhas, Rajbir S. (4 mentions)
9825 Kenwood Rd #200, Cincinnati, 513-221-5500
2841 Boudinot Ave #202, Cincinnati, 513-221-5500

Molnar, James Martin (13 mentions)
Ohio State U, 1982
Certification: Anesthesiology, Internal Medicine, Pain Medicine
8261 Cornell Rd #630, Cincinnati, 513-891-0022

Pathology

Cabanas, Victor Yambing (3 mentions)
FMS-Philippines, 1966 *Certification:* Anatomic Pathology &
   Clinical Pathology, Hematology, Immunopathology
2446 Kipling Ave, Cincinnati, 513-853-5816

Lucas, Frederick Vance, Jr. (4 mentions)
U of Missouri, 1975 *Certification:* Anatomic Pathology &
   Clinical Pathology, Hematology
2139 Auburn Ave, Cincinnati, 513-585-1111

Monroe, Kevin Dale (4 mentions)
Louisiana State U, 1978
Certification: Anatomic Pathology & Clinical Pathology
4777 E Galbraith Rd, Cincinnati, 513-686-3288

Nazek, Mohammad Khoder (3 mentions)
FMS-Jordan, 1982 *Certification:* Anatomic Pathology,
   Cytopathology, Neuropathology
2139 Auburn Ave, Cincinnati, 513-585-1266

Panke, Thomas Walter (14 mentions)
U of Rochester, 1970 *Certification:* Anatomic Pathology &
   Clinical Pathology, Hematology
375 Dixmyth Ave, Cincinnati, 513-872-2639

Vago, John Francis (3 mentions)
Ohio State U, 1982 *Certification:* Anatomic Pathology &
   Clinical Pathology, Hematology
2139 Auburn Ave, Cincinnati, 513-585-1111

Westermann, Cindy Denese (4 mentions)
U of Cincinnati, 1985 *Certification:* Anatomic Pathology &
   Clinical Pathology, Cytopathology
7500 State Rd, Cincinnati, 513-624-4500

Pediatrics *(see note on page 9)*

Bagamery, Nancy Sue (5 mentions)
U of Cincinnati, 1983 *Certification:* Pediatrics
3006 Portsmouth Ave, Cincinnati, 513-871-0684

Brown, Elizabeth Halcyon (6 mentions)
U of Virginia, 1980 *Certification:* Pediatrics
3006 Portsmouth Ave, Cincinnati, 513-871-0684

De Witt, Thomas Gebhard (4 mentions)
U of Rochester, 1976 *Certification:* Pediatrics
3333 Burnet Ave, Cincinnati, 513-636-4506

Deblasis, Nancy MacLeod (3 mentions)
U of Cincinnati, 1981 *Certification:* Pediatrics
8245 Northcreek Dr, Cincinnati, 513-745-4706

Fernandez, Otilia (3 mentions)
U of Cincinnati, 1984 *Certification:* Pediatrics
11258 Lebanon Rd, Cincinnati, 513-563-0044

Herman, Roger William (3 mentions)
U of Illinois, 1973 *Certification:* Pediatrics
7400 Jager Ct, Cincinnati, 513-232-8100

Joseph, Evelyn Claire (3 mentions)
U of Cincinnati, 1982 *Certification:* Pediatrics
3006 Portsmouth Ave, Cincinnati, 513-871-0684

Mueller, Caroline V. (5 mentions)
U of Cincinnati, 1990 *Certification:* Internal Medicine, Pediatrics
3333 Burnet Ave, Cincinnati, 513-636-4200
234 Goodman St 2nd Fl, Cincinnati, 513-584-7425

Reidy, Kevin Michael (3 mentions)
Baylor U, 1991 *Certification:* Pediatrics
2865 Chancellor Dr #225, Crestview Hills, KY, 859-341-5400

Saluke, Ann Marie (4 mentions)
U of Cincinnati, 1980 *Certification:* Pediatrics
7400 Jager Ct, Cincinnati, 513-232-8100
1126 W Ohio Pike, Amelia, 513-232-8100

Spiess, Libbey Mary (5 mentions)
U of Cincinnati, 1992 *Certification:* Pediatrics
6350 Glenway Ave #300, Cincinnati, 513-481-9700
10450 New Haven Rd #3, Harrison, 513-202-1113

Thind, Rosy K. (3 mentions)
Certification: Pediatrics
9070 Winton Rd, Cincinnati, 513-522-7600

Wetzler, Karin Margaret (3 mentions)
Ohio State U, 1988 *Certification:* Pediatrics
8245 Northcreek Dr, Cincinnati, 513-745-4706

Plastic Surgery

Butterfield, Jennifer L. (8 mentions)
U of Toledo, 1996 *Certification:* Plastic Surgery
4750 E Galbraith Rd #215, Cincinnati, 513-891-5610

Columbus, Michael Joseph (11 mentions)
Jefferson Med Coll, 1985 *Certification:* Plastic Surgery
4850 Red Bank Rd #2, Cincinnati, 513-791-4440

Kitzmiller, William John (11 mentions)
Duke U, 1983
Certification: Plastic Surgery, Surgery, Surgery of the Hand
7700 University Ct #1700, West Chester, 513-475-8888

Leadbetter, Michael G. (12 mentions)
Ohio State U, 1974 *Certification:* Plastic Surgery
4850 Red Bank Rd #2, Cincinnati, 513-791-4440
340 Thomas More Pkwy #100, Covington, KY, 859-331-8777
3723 Hauck Rd, Cincinnati, 513-791-4440

Mangat, Devinder Singh (9 mentions)
U of Kentucky, 1973 *Certification:* Otolaryngology
8044 Montgomery Rd #230, Cincinnati, 513-984-3223
133 Barnwood Dr, Edgewood, KY, 859-331-9600

McKenna, Peter James (10 mentions)
U of Cincinnati, 1985 *Certification:* Plastic Surgery
10577 Montgomery Rd, Cincinnati, 513-793-5772
8000 5 Mile Rd, Cincinnati, 513-793-5712
3219 Clifton Ave #300, Cincinnati, 513-872-4134

Psychiatry

Auvil, Dallas Gregory (5 mentions)
Case Western Reserve U, 1986 *Certification:* Psychiatry
4075 Old Western Row Rd, Mason, 513-536-4673

Gale, Melvin S. (3 mentions)
SUNY-Downstate Med Coll, 1969
Certification: Geriatric Psychiatry, Psychiatry
2123 Auburn Ave #428, Cincinnati, 513-241-1811

Gureasko, Michael Allan (3 mentions)
Rosalind Franklin U, 1969
Certification: Addiction Psychiatry, Psychiatry
2123 Auburn Ave #415, Cincinnati, 513-281-8840

Hawkins, James Robert (5 mentions)
U of Cincinnati, 1971 *Certification:* Psychiatry
415 Straight St #300, Cincinnati, 513-721-0990

Kaplan, Marcia Joan (3 mentions)
U of Texas-Dallas, 1982 *Certification:* Psychiatry
3001 Highland Ave, Cincinnati, 513-961-7799

Keck, Paul E., Jr. (4 mentions)
Mount Sinai Sch of Med, 1983 *Certification:* Psychiatry
4075 Old Western Row Rd, Mason, 888-536-4673

Keys, Michael Arnold (6 mentions)
U of Cincinnati, 1983
Certification: Geriatric Psychiatry, Psychiatry
4075 Old Western Row Rd, Mason, 513-536-0605

Knox, Sarah Margaret (3 mentions)
U of Cincinnati, 1980
4090 Rose Hill Ave, Cincinnati, 513-221-8457
3001 Highland Ave, Cincinnati, 513-221-8457

Kuykendal, Robert Lee (3 mentions)
U of North Carolina, 1971 *Certification:* Psychiatry
820 Delta Ave, Cincinnati, 513-321-9902

Vivian, Rodney Elgar (3 mentions)
U of Cincinnati, 1975
Certification: Child & Adolescent Psychiatry, Psychiatry
8000 5 Mile Rd #240, Cincinnati, 513-232-3070

Pulmonary Disease

Baughman, Robert Phillip (8 mentions)
Case Western Reserve U, 1977
Certification: Internal Medicine, Pulmonary Disease
Eden Ave & Albert Sabin Way #1001, Cincinnati, 513-584-5225
222 Piedmont Ave, Cincinnati, 513-475-8520
9275 Montgomery Rd #200, Cincinnati, 513-475-8520
2139 Auburn Ave, Cincinnati, 513-585-2000
151 W Galbraith Rd, Cincinnati, 513-948-2500

Dama, Sunil Kumar (9 mentions)
FMS-India, 1993 *Certification:* Critical Care Medicine,
   Internal Medicine, Pulmonary Disease
2123 Auburn Ave #401, Cincinnati, 513-241-5489

Dortin, David J., Jr. (7 mentions)
Kansas U Coll of Osteopathic Med, 1968
Certification: Internal Medicine, Pulmonary Disease
4760 E Galbraith Rd #203, Cincinnati, 513-985-9800

Eisentrout, Craig Alan (12 mentions)
U of Cincinnati, 1982 *Certification:* Critical Care Medicine,
   Internal Medicine, Pulmonary Disease
10496 Montgomery Rd, Cincinnati, 513-793-2654
7502 State Rd #2260, Cincinnati, 513-793-2654

Hayner, Christopher E. (7 mentions)
Marshall U, 1987 *Certification:* Critical Care Medicine,
   Internal Medicine, Pulmonary Disease
8245 Northcreek Dr, Cincinnati, 513-745-4706
2915 Clifton Ave, Cincinnati, 513-872-2031

Kennealy, James Andrew (6 mentions)
U of Cincinnati, 1971 *Certification:* Critical Care Medicine,
   Internal Medicine, Pulmonary Disease
3248 Westbourne Dr #1, Cincinnati, 513-451-1974

Mallick, Shahla (6 mentions)
FMS-Pakistan, 1989 *Certification:* Critical Care Medicine,
   Internal Medicine, Pulmonary Disease
3248 Westbourne Dr, Cincinnati, 513-872-5292

McCormack, Frank X. (6 mentions)
U of Texas-Galveston, 1982 *Certification:* Critical Care
   Medicine, Internal Medicine, Pulmonary Disease
222 Piedmont Ave #4000, Cincinnati, 513-475-8523

Orabella, Christopher M. (11 mentions)
Ohio State U, 1991 *Certification:* Critical Care Medicine,
   Internal Medicine, Pulmonary Disease
2123 Auburn Ave #401, Cincinnati, 513-241-5489

Parker, Thomas John (14 mentions)
U of Cincinnati, 1978 *Certification:* Critical Care Medicine,
Internal Medicine, Pulmonary Disease
2001 Anderson Ferry Rd, Cincinnati, 513-922-1200
2915 Clifton Ave, Cincinnati, 513-872-2055

Pina, Elsira (5 mentions)
Philadelphia Coll of Osteopathic Med, 1989 *Certification:*
Critical Care Medicine, Internal Medicine, Pulmonary Disease
222 Piedmont Ave #4000, Cincinnati, 513-475-8523

Scott, Mark Joseph (15 mentions)
Ohio State U, 1986 *Certification:* Critical Care Medicine,
Internal Medicine, Pulmonary Disease
2123 Auburn Ave #401, Cincinnati, 513-241-5489

Thorpe, Joseph Edward (22 mentions)
Ohio State U, 1978 *Certification:* Critical Care Medicine,
Internal Medicine, Pulmonary Disease
10496 Montgomery Rd, Cincinnati, 513-793-2654
7502 State Rd #2260, Cincinnati, 513-793-2654

Wiltse, David William (19 mentions)
Yale U, 1975 *Certification:* Internal Medicine, Pulmonary Disease
3248 Westbourne Dr #1, Cincinnati, 513-451-1930

Radiology—Diagnostic

Asher, Anthony John (3 mentions)
U of Cincinnati, 1986 *Certification:* Diagnostic Radiology
7500 State Rd, Cincinnati, 513-231-8885

Bernstein, Joseph E. (3 mentions)
Rosalind Franklin U, 1983 *Certification:* Diagnostic Radiology
4170 Rosslyn Dr #B, Cincinnati, 513-872-4500
4777 E Galbraith Rd, Cincinnati, 513-686-3263

Botsford, John Alan (6 mentions)
U of Cincinnati, 1978 *Certification:* Diagnostic Radiology
311 Straight St, Cincinnati, 513-559-2260
600 Wilson Creek Rd, Lawrenceburg, IN, 812-537-8105

Budde, Richard B., Jr. (4 mentions)
U of Cincinnati, 1984 *Certification:* Diagnostic Radiology,
Vascular & Interventional Radiology
2139 Auburn Ave, Cincinnati, 513-872-4500

Bulas, Robert Victor (4 mentions)
Ohio State U, 1989 *Certification:* Diagnostic Radiology
4170 Rosslyn Dr #B, Cincinnati, 513-872-4500
2139 Auburn Ave, Cincinnati, 513-585-2421

Choe, Kyuran Ann (4 mentions)
U of Massachusetts, 1987
Certification: Diagnostic Radiology, Nuclear Radiology
234 Goodman St, Cincinnati, 513-584-2146

Drew, William Rogers (3 mentions)
U of Cincinnati, 1986 *Certification:* Diagnostic Radiology
311 Straight St, Cincinnati, 513-559-2260

Ernst, Robert James (6 mentions)
U of Cincinnati, 1987 *Certification:* Diagnostic Radiology
2139 Auburn Ave, Cincinnati, 513-585-2665
477 E Galbraith Rd, Cincinnati, 513-686-3261
630 Eaton Ave, Hamilton, 513-867-2311

Kleimeyer, Ted Allen (4 mentions)
U of Cincinnati, 1978 *Certification:* Diagnostic Radiology
3131 Queen City Ave, Cincinnati, 513-389-5000

Kuntz, Charles Henne (5 mentions)
U of Cincinnati, 1963 *Certification:* Radiology
10550 Montgomery Rd #15, Cincinnati, 513-984-1443

Lukin, Robert Roy (5 mentions)
U of Cincinnati, 1965
Certification: Diagnostic Radiology, Neuroradiology
234 Goodman St, Cincinnati, 513-584-6095

Meranus, James Moss (3 mentions)
Case Western Reserve U, 1986 *Certification:* Diagnostic Radiology
375 Dixmyth Ave, Cincinnati, 513-872-2611

Miller, Timothy John (5 mentions)
U of Cincinnati, 1987
Certification: Diagnostic Radiology, Neuroradiology
375 Dixmyth Ave, Cincinnati, 513-872-2611
2915 Clifton Ave, Cincinnati, 513-872-2061

Moulton, Jonathan S. (3 mentions)
Hahnemann U, 1982 *Certification:* Diagnostic Radiology
234 Goodman St #M-1-2146, Cincinnati, 513-584-2146

Perlman, Steven Jay (3 mentions)
U of Toledo, 1980 *Certification:* Diagnostic Radiology
4170 Rosslyn Dr #B, Cincinnati, 513-872-4500
4777 E Galbraith Rd, Cincinnati, 513-686-3263

Pomeranz, Stephen Jory (4 mentions)
U of Cincinnati, 1981 *Certification:* Diagnostic Radiology with
Special Competence in Nuclear Radiology, Neuroradiology
5400 Kennedy Ave, Cincinnati, 513-351-3100
6 Paul Brown Stadium, Cincinnati, 513-455-4999

Powers, Gerald Tyrone (3 mentions)
U of Michigan, 1978 *Certification:* Diagnostic Radiology
5400 Kennedy Ave, Cincinnati, 513-281-3400

Rost, Raymond Cliffor, Jr. (8 mentions)
U of Cincinnati, 1979 *Certification:* Diagnostic Radiology
2139 Auburn Ave, Cincinnati, 513-585-2421
4170 Rosslyn Dr #B, Cincinnati, 513-872-4500

Strife, Janet R. Lang (3 mentions)
New Jersey Med Sch, 1968
Certification: Diagnostic Radiology, Pediatric Radiology
3333 Burnet Ave, Cincinnati, 513-636-8058

Weber, James Lawrence (5 mentions)
U of Cincinnati, 1980 *Certification:* Diagnostic Radiology
7500 State Rd, Cincinnati, 513-624-4580

Weinberg, Susan G. (6 mentions)
Case Western Reserve U, 1976 *Certification:* Diagnostic Radiology
10500 Montgomery Rd #15, Cincinnati, 513-745-1114

Radiology—Therapeutic

Barrett, William Lannon (12 mentions)
U of Cincinnati, 1987 *Certification:* Radiation Oncology
234 Goodman, Cincinnati, 513-584-3494

Budde, Richard B., Jr. (5 mentions)
U of Cincinnati, 1984 *Certification:* Diagnostic Radiology,
Vascular & Interventional Radiology
2139 Auburn Ave, Cincinnati, 513-872-4500

Geier, Rodney Phelps (5 mentions)
U of Cincinnati, 1984 *Certification:* Radiation Oncology
8000 5 Mile Rd #105, Cincinnati, 513-624-4025
100 William Howard Taft Rd, Cincinnati, 513-751-4448

Haggerty, Michael Francis (5 mentions)
U of Cincinnati, 1986 *Certification:* Diagnostic Radiology,
Vascular & Interventional Radiology
10500 Montgomery Rd #15, Cincinnati, 513-745-1114

Morand, Thomas Michael (4 mentions)
U of Cincinnati, 1978 *Certification:* Therapeutic Radiology
2452 Kipling Ave, Cincinnati, 513-681-7800
375 Dixmyth Ave, Cincinnati, 513-872-2611

Schlueter, Francis J. (5 mentions)
U of Cincinnati, 1990 *Certification:* Diagnostic Radiology,
Vascular & Interventional Radiology
375 Dixmyth Ave, Cincinnati, 513-872-2611

Traiforos, James Terry (4 mentions)
U of Cincinnati, 1999 *Certification:* Diagnostic Radiology
4170 Rosslyn Dr #B, Cincinnati, 513-872-4500
4777 E Galbraith Rd, Cincinnati, 513-686-3263

White, Daniel Robert (5 mentions)
U of Cincinnati, 1985 *Certification:* Radiation Oncology
2452 Kiplong Ave, Cincinnati, 513-681-7800

Rehabilitation

Goddard, Mark Joseph (9 mentions)
U of Cincinnati, 1983
Certification: Physical Medicine & Rehabilitation
151 W Galbraith Rd, Cincinnati, 513-418-2707

Heis, Stephen Dale (4 mentions)
U of Cincinnati, 1980
Certification: Physical Medicine & Rehabilitation
8000 5 Mile Rd #340, Cincinnati, 513-232-8800
2450 Kipling Ave #203, Cincinnati, 513-853-5036

Kissel, David Joseph (4 mentions)
U of Cincinnati, 1981
Certification: Physical Medicine & Rehabilitation
6200 Pfeiffer Rd #390, Cincinnati, 513-891-3373

McDonough, Nancy K. (6 mentions)
U of Cincinnati, 1987
Certification: Physical Medicine & Rehabilitation
7810 5 Mile Rd, Cincinnati, 513-232-1253

Orlando, Marc Patrick (6 mentions)
U of Cincinnati, 1993
Certification: Physical Medicine & Rehabilitation
7423 Mason Montgomery Rd, Mason, 513-229-6000
2915 Clifton Ave, Cincinnati, 513-872-2000
2001 Anderson Ferry Rd, Cincinnati, 513-872-4222

Pruitt, David William (3 mentions)
Loyola U Chicago, 1998 *Certification:* Pediatric
Rehabilitation Medicine, Physical Medicine & Rehabilitation
3333 Burnet Ave, Cincinnati, 513-636-4200

Rissover, Janalee Krick (3 mentions)
U of Toledo, 1985
Certification: Physical Medicine & Rehabilitation
8000 5 Mile Rd #340, Cincinnati, 513-232-8800
2450 Kipling Ave #203, Cincinnati, 513-853-5036

Walsh, William E., Jr. (4 mentions)
Ohio State U, 1982
Certification: Physical Medicine & Rehabilitation
6200 Pfeiffer Rd #390, Cincinnati, 513-891-3373

Wunder, Steve Scott (14 mentions)
U of Cincinnati, 1980
Certification: Physical Medicine & Rehabilitation
2915 Clifton Ave, Cincinnati, 513-559-3355

Rheumatology

De Buys, Paige Ann (6 mentions)
U of Cincinnati, 2000
Certification: Internal Medicine, Rheumatology
2123 Auburn Ave #322, Cincinnati, 513-351-0800

Delorenzo, Gregory Joseph (10 mentions)
Ohio State U, 1987 *Certification:* Rheumatology
55 Progress Pl, Cincinnati, 513-346-5000
2001 Anderson Ferry Rd, Cincinnati, 513-922-1200
7810 5 Mile Rd, Cincinnati, 513-232-1253

Flaspohler, Louis Edward (16 mentions)
U of Cincinnati, 1997
Certification: Internal Medicine, Rheumatology
2100 Sherman Ave #110, Cincinnati, 513-351-0800

Fritz, Deborah Ann (10 mentions)
U of Louisville, 1982
Certification: Internal Medicine, Rheumatology
10550 Montgomery Rd #23, Cincinnati, 513-984-3313

Hiltz, Robert Emmett (11 mentions)
U of Louisville, 1989
Certification: Internal Medicine, Rheumatology
7794 5 Mile Rd #280, Cincinnati, 513-624-4937

Houk, John Lawrence (6 mentions)
U of Cincinnati, 1965 *Certification:* Internal Medicine
2123 Auburn Ave #630, Cincinnati, 513-585-1970
3652 Werk Rd, Cincinnati, 513-585-1970

Luggen, Michael Edmund (12 mentions)
Columbia U, 1974
Certification: Internal Medicine, Rheumatology
311 Straight St, Cincinnati, 513-559-2787
2123 Auburn Ave, Cincinnati, 513-585-1970

Petrovic, Olga Maria (6 mentions)
Ohio State U, 1974
Certification: Internal Medicine, Rheumatology
8952 Winton Rd, Cincinnati, 513-357-5254

Pordy, Michael Gregory (7 mentions)
St Louis U, 1976
Certification: Internal Medicine, Rheumatology
4760 E Galbraith Rd #114, Cincinnati, 513-281-7600

Thoracic Surgery

Glaser, Richard Stephen (13 mentions)
Wayne State U, 1971 *Certification:* Thoracic Surgery
10496 Montgomery Rd #101, Cincinnati, 513-794-9500
3219 Clifton Ave #335, Cincinnati, 513-794-9500

Park, Steven Earl (14 mentions)
U of Chicago, 1985 *Certification:* Surgery, Thoracic Surgery
4030 Smith Rd #300, Cincinnati, 513-421-3494

Reed, Michael Floren (12 mentions)
Harvard U, 1991 *Certification:* Surgery, Thoracic Surgery
222 Piedmont Ave #7000, Cincinnati, 513-475-8780
231 Albert B Sabin Way, Cincinnati, 513-584-1387

Smith, John Michael (13 mentions)
U of Louisville, 1989 *Certification:* Surgery, Thoracic Surgery
4030 Smith Rd #300, Cincinnati, 513-421-3494

Vester, Samuel Russell (12 mentions)
U of Cincinnati, 1983 *Certification:* Surgery, Thoracic Surgery
4030 Smith Rd #300, Cincinnati, 513-421-3494

Urology

Bennett, Stephen Garrett (16 mentions)
Ohio State U, 1996 *Certification:* Urology
2123 Auburn Ave #108, Cincinnati, 513-721-7373

Bracken, Robert Bruce (14 mentions)
FMS-Canada, 1966 *Certification:* Urology
222 Piedmont Ave #7000, Cincinnati, 513-475-8787
305 Crescent Ave, Wyoming, 513-821-0275

Braun, Karl Bruce (9 mentions)
U of Cincinnati, 1981 *Certification:* Urology
4700 Smith Rd #L, Cincinnati, 513-366-4000
10700 Montgomery Rd #319, Cincinnati, 513-793-2835
7794 5 Mile Rd #200, Cincinnati, 513-232-6360

Buffington, Philip Jay (13 mentions)
U of Cincinnati, 1984 *Certification:* Urology
4700 Smith Rd #L, Cincinnati, 513-366-4000
10700 Montgomery Rd #319, Cincinnati, 513-793-2835
7794 5 Mile Rd #200, Cincinnati, 513-232-6360

Cordell, Alan Spencer (7 mentions)
U of Louisville, 1973 *Certification:* Urology
4700 Smith Rd #L, Cincinnati, 513-366-4000
2450 Kipling Ave #112-A, Cincinnati, 513-662-0222
2859 Boudinot Ave #206, Cincinnati, 513-662-0222

Delworth, Mark Gerard (19 mentions)
U of Kansas, 1988 *Certification:* Urology
4700 Smith Rd #L, Cincinnati, 513-366-4000
10700 Montgomery Rd #300, Cincinnati, 513-793-2835

Kuhn, Eric Joseph (19 mentions)
Loyola U Chicago, 1985 *Certification:* Urology
2859 Boudinot #206, Cincinnati, 513-662-0222
2450 Kipling Ave #205, Cincinnati, 513-681-2700

Pliskin, Marc J. (8 mentions)
Philadelphia Coll of Osteopathic Med, 1983 *Certification:* Urology
4700 Smith Rd #L, Cincinnati, 513-366-4000
2450 Kipling Ave #111, Cincinnati, 513-681-2700
2859 Boudinot Ave #206, Cincinnati, 513-662-0222

Shank, Reed Albert, III (23 mentions)
U of Cincinnati, 1984 *Certification:* Urology
2123 Auburn Ave #108, Cincinnati, 513-721-7373

Zipkin, Jeffrey Warren (10 mentions)
Ohio State U, 1977 *Certification:* Urology
10475 Reading Rd #206, Cincinnati, 513-563-7222

Vascular Surgery

Annenberg, Alan Jon (17 mentions)
Ohio State U, 1982 *Certification:* Vascular Surgery
4030 Smith Rd #300, Norwood, 513-421-3494

Giglia, Joseph Samuel (12 mentions)
U of Buffalo, 1989
Certification: Surgery, Surgical Critical Care, Vascular Surgery
2123 Auburn Ave, Cincinnati, 513-241-9929
231 Albert Sabin Way, Cincinnati, 513-558-1050
222 Piedmont Ave #7000, Cincinnati, 513-475-8787

Muck, Patrick Edward (12 mentions)
U of Kentucky, 1996 *Certification:* Surgery, Vascular Surgery
3219 Clifton Ave #215, Cincinnati, 513-872-3595
7502 State Rd #1180, Cincinnati, 513-232-8181
10506 Montgomery Rd #209, Cincinnati, 513-794-1601

Roedersheimer, Louis R. (14 mentions)
U of Cincinnati, 1975 *Certification:* Surgery, Vascular Surgery
3747 W Fork Rd, Cincinnati, 513-961-4335

Cleveland Area

Including Cuyahoga, Lake, and Lorain Counties

Allergy/Immunology

Berger, Melvin (6 mentions)
Case Western Reserve U, 1976
Certification: Allergy & Immunology, Pediatrics
11100 Euclid Ave, Cleveland, 216-844-3237

Hostoffer, Robert W. (12 mentions)
Philadelphia Coll of Osteopathic Med, 1985
1611 S Green Rd #231, Cleveland, 216-381-3333

Hsieh, Fred (6 mentions)
Brown U, 1995
Certification: Allergy & Immunology, Internal Medicine
9500 Euclid Ave #A-90, Cleveland, 216-444-3504

Knauer, Kent Alan (12 mentions)
U of Kentucky, 1975
Certification: Allergy & Immunology, Internal Medicine
3909 Orange Pl #2300, Orange Village, 216-896-1850
9000 Mentor Ave #103, Mentor, 440-974-4114

Melton, Alton L., Jr. (7 mentions)
U of North Carolina, 1982
Certification: Allergy & Immunology, Pediatrics
9500 Euclid Ave #A-120, Cleveland, 216-444-6817

Panuto, John A., Jr. (9 mentions)
Wright State U, 1988 *Certification:* Allergy & Immunology
25761 Lorain Rd #3, North Olmsted, 440-779-1112
252 E Broad St, Elyria, 440-329-7760
5500 Ridge Rd #226, Cleveland, 440-329-7760

Sher, Theodore H. (24 mentions)
SUNY-Downstate Med Coll, 1974
Certification: Allergy & Immunology, Pediatrics
1611 S Green Rd #231, South Euclid, 216-381-3333

Anesthesiology

Ayad, Sabry Salama (4 mentions)
FMS-Egypt, 1990 *Certification:* Anesthesiology
18101 Lorain Ave, Cleveland, 216-476-7052

D'Amico, Joseph A. (3 mentions)
Case Western Reserve U, 1982
Certification: Anesthesiology, Internal Medicine
7007 Powers Blvd, Parma, 440-743-3000

Ebrahim, Zeyd Yusuf (5 mentions)
FMS-India, 1975 *Certification:* Anesthesiology
9500 Euclid Ave #E-31, Cleveland, 216-444-4632

Graber, Raymond Gregory (4 mentions)
U of Buffalo, 1984 *Certification:* Anesthesiology
11100 Euclid Ave, Cleveland, 216-844-3777

Mandel, Morris Meyer (3 mentions)
Ohio State U, 1981 *Certification:* Anesthesiology
6803 Mayfield Rd, Cleveland, 440-449-4500

Mayers, Douglas B. (5 mentions)
Washington U, 1977 *Certification:* Anesthesiology
26900 Cedar Rd, Beachwood, 216-839-3537

Nearman, Howard Sloman (13 mentions)
Case Western Reserve U, 1976
Certification: Anesthesiology, Critical Care Medicine
11100 Euclid Ave, Cleveland, 216-844-7330

Niezgoda, Julie Jan (9 mentions)
Ohio State U, 1985 *Certification:* Anesthesiology
9500 Euclid Ave #P-21, Cleveland, 216-444-0278

Norcia, Matthew Patrick (4 mentions)
Case Western Reserve U, 1991
Certification: Anesthesiology, Critical Care Medicine
11100 Euclid Ave, Cleveland, 216-844-3777

O'Hara, Jerome F., Jr. (3 mentions)
U of Toledo, 1987 *Certification:* Anesthesiology
9500 Euclid Ave, Cleveland, 216-444-8278

Rowbottom, James Richard (7 mentions)
U of Cincinnati, 1987
Certification: Anesthesiology, Critical Care Medicine
11100 Euclid Ave, Cleveland, 216-844-7334

Scerbo, John Joseph (4 mentions)
U of Toledo, 1988 *Certification:* Anesthesiology
36000 Euclid Ave, Willoughby, 440-350-0832

Stork, John Ernest (4 mentions)
U of Maryland, 1978 *Certification:* Anesthesiology, Internal
   Medicine, Nephrology, Pediatrics
11100 Euclid Ave, Cleveland, 216-844-3777

Sung, Wai W. (3 mentions)
FMS-China, 1989 *Certification:* Anesthesiology
9500 Euclid Ave, Cleveland, 206-444-4208

Cardiac Surgery

Akhrass, Rami (10 mentions)
FMS-Syria, 1987 *Certification:* Surgery, Thoracic Surgery
9500 Euclid Ave, Cleveland, 216-444-2200
36100 Euclid Ave #280, Willoughby, 440-918-4640

Botham, Mark Judson (18 mentions)
Cornell U, 1979 *Certification:* Thoracic Surgery
6770 Mayfield Rd, Mayfield Heights, 216-445-6860

Lahorra, Joseph Anthony (9 mentions)
Johns Hopkins U, 1988 *Certification:* Thoracic Surgery
6707 Powers Blvd #303, Cleveland, 440-887-9816

Lytle, Bruce W. (25 mentions)
Harvard U, 1971 *Certification:* Thoracic Surgery
9500 Euclid Ave #F-25, Cleveland, 216-444-6962

Markowitz, Alan Harvey (31 mentions)
Albany Med Coll, 1970 *Certification:* Thoracic Surgery
11100 Euclid Ave, Cleveland, 216-844-3992

Pettersson, Gosta Bengt (5 mentions)
FMS-Sweden, 1971
9500 Euclid Ave, Cleveland, 216-444-2035

Sabik, Joseph Frank (13 mentions)
Harvard U, 1987 *Certification:* Thoracic Surgery
9500 Euclid Ave #F-24, Cleveland, 216-444-6788

Smedira, Nicholas G. (13 mentions)
U of Rochester, 1984 *Certification:* Thoracic Surgery
9500 Euclid Ave #F-25, Cleveland, 216-445-7052

Cardiology

Al-Mubarak, Nadim A. (3 mentions)
FMS-Austria, 1987 *Certification:* Interventional Cardiology
2500 Center Ridge Rd #1100, Westlake, 440-835-8922
14601 Detroit Ave #730, Lakewood, 440-835-8922

Burma, Gerald Melvin (3 mentions)
Case Western Reserve U, 1978 *Certification:* Cardiovascular
   Disease, Internal Medicine, Interventional Cardiology
6525 Powers Blvd, Cleveland, 440-882-0075

Cunningham, Michael John (3 mentions)
U of Utah, 1982 *Certification:* Cardiovascular Disease,
   Internal Medicine, Interventional Cardiology
11100 Euclid Ave #108, Cleveland, 216-383-6060
18599 Lakeshore Blvd, Euclid, 216-383-6060
44 Blaine Ave #100, Bedford, 440-735-3702

Deucher, Michael Francis (4 mentions)
Ohio State U, 1994
Certification: Cardiovascular Disease, Internal Medicine
7255 Old Oak Blvd #C-208, Middleburg Heights, 440-816-2708
6707 Powers Blvd #308, Cleveland, 440-887-9645

Doyle, Timothy P. (8 mentions)
Loyola U Chicago, 1979
Certification: Cardiovascular Disease, Internal Medicine
36100 Euclid Ave #120, Willoughby, 440-951-8360
9500 Mentor Ave #360, Mentor, 440-352-9554

Effron, Barry Allan (19 mentions)
Ohio State U, 1978
Certification: Cardiovascular Disease, Internal Medicine
11100 Euclid Ave, Cleveland, 216-844-3800
3909 Orange Pl, Orange Village, 216-844-3800

Espinosa, Roger G. (4 mentions)
FMS-Philippines, 1979
Certification: Cardiovascular Disease, Internal Medicine
124 Liberty St #B, Painesville, 440-352-4956
35717 Euclid Ave, Willoughby, 440-942-4890

Fang, Jim Chentson (8 mentions)
Duke U, 1988 *Certification:* Cardiovascular Disease
11100 Euclid Ave, Cleveland, 216-844-3800
3909 Orange Pl, Beachwood, 216-844-3800
960 Clague Rd, Westlake, 216-844-3800

Farhat, Naim Zreik (4 mentions)
FMS-Syria, 1980 *Certification:* Cardiovascular Disease,
   Internal Medicine, Interventional Cardiology
125 E Broad St #305, Elyria, 440-414-9100

Griffin, Brian P. (3 mentions)
FMS-Ireland, 1979
Certification: Cardiovascular Disease, Internal Medicine
9500 Euclid Ave #J-1, Cleveland, 216-444-6697

Grimm, Richard Allen (3 mentions)
Ohio U Coll of Osteopathic Med, 1986
Certification: Cardiovascular Disease
9500 Euclid Ave, Cleveland, 216-444-6697

Hammer, Donald Frank (3 mentions)
Ohio State U, 1978
Certification: Cardiovascular Disease, Internal Medicine
9500 Euclid Ave J2-4, Cleveland, 216-444-6697

Hanna, Michael A. (3 mentions)
FMS-Syria, 1964
Certification: Cardiovascular Disease, Internal Medicine
6770 Mayfield Rd, Cleveland, 440-461-0038

Hobbs, Robert Edward (4 mentions)
Jefferson Med Coll, 1974
Certification: Cardiovascular Disease, Internal Medicine
9500 Euclid Ave #J-34, Cleveland, 216-444-6697

Joyce, David Blaine (5 mentions)
U of Cincinnati, 1982
Certification: Cardiovascular Disease, Internal Medicine
3600 Kolbe Rd #127, Lorain, 440-414-9200

Koch, James Michael (3 mentions)
U of Cincinnati, 1985
Certification: Cardiovascular Disease, Internal Medicine
99 N Line Cir #235, Euclid, 216-692-7875
6701 Rockside Rd Concord Point Bldg #100, Independence,
   216-328-0418
27155 Chardon Rd #201, Richmond Heights, 440-516-4800

Mackall, Judith Anne (3 mentions)
Wright State U, 1987 *Certification:* Cardiovascular Disease,
   Clinical Cardiac Electrophysiology, Internal Medicine
11100 Euclid Ave, Cleveland, 216-844-3800
3903 Orange Pl, Orange Village, 216-844-3800
900 Mentor Ave, Mentor, 216-844-3800

Maroo, Prafulchandra V. (3 mentions)
FMS-India, 1968 *Certification:* Cardiovascular Disease,
   Interventional Cardiology, Internal Medicine
18099 Lorain Ave, Cleveland, 216-252-2770

Nair, Ravi Narayan (5 mentions)
FMS-India, 1978 *Certification:* Cardiovascular Disease,
   Internal Medicine, Interventional Cardiology
9500 Euclid Ave, Cleveland, 216-444-2000

Nukta, Emad M. (5 mentions)
FMS-Syria, 1981 *Certification:* Cardiovascular Disease,
   Internal Medicine, Interventional Cardiology
20455 Lorain Rd 2nd Fl, Fairview, 216-333-8600

Raymond, Russell E. (4 mentions)
Midwestern U Chicago Coll of Osteopathic Med, 1979
Certification: Cardiovascular Disease, Internal Medicine,
   Interventional Cardiology
9500 Euclid Ave #J-23, Cleveland, 216-444-6697

Samsa, John A. (5 mentions)
Ohio U Coll of Osteopathic Med, 1988
Certification: Cardiovascular Disease, Interventional Cardiology
36100 Euclid Ave #120, Willoughby, 440-951-8360
9500 Mentor Ave #360, Mentor, 440-352-9554

Schaeffer, John William (7 mentions)
Ohio State U, 1971
Certification: Cardiovascular Disease, Internal Medicine
3600 Kolbe Rd #127, Lorain, 440-204-4000
125 E Broad St #305, Elyria, 440-414-9100

Scharfstein, Jonathan S. (3 mentions)
U of Pennsylvania, 1987 *Certification:* Cardiovascular
   Disease, Internal Medicine, Interventional Cardiology
6801 Mayfield Rd #444, Mayfield Heights, 440-449-8890

Simon, Daniel Ira (7 mentions)
11100 Euclid Ave, Cleveland, 216-844-8151

Siwik, Ernest S. (3 mentions)
Wayne State U, 1989 *Certification:* Pediatric Cardiology
11100 Euclid Ave, Cleveland, 216-844-3528

Sterba, Richard (4 mentions)
Ohio State U, 1974 *Certification:* Pediatric Cardiology, Pediatrics
9500 Euclid Ave, Cleveland, 216-444-6386

Tchou, Patrick Joseph (4 mentions)
Case Western Reserve U, 1979 *Certification:* Cardiovascular
   Disease, Clinical Cardiac Electrophysiology, Internal Medicine
9500 Euclid Ave #F15, Cleveland, 216-444-6697
26900 Cedar Rd #18-N, Beachwood, 216-839-3300

Underwood, Donald Arthur (6 mentions)
Case Western Reserve U, 1975
Certification: Cardiovascular Disease, Internal Medicine
9500 Euclid Ave #F-15, Cleveland, 216-444-6697

Vekstein, Vladimir I. (5 mentions)
New York U, 1984 *Certification:* Cardiovascular Disease,
   Internal Medicine, Interventional Cardiology
6801 Mayfield Rd #444, Mayfield Heights, 440-449-8890

Vlastaris, Anthony George (3 mentions)
Case Western Reserve U, 1991
Certification: Cardiovascular Disease
29099 Health Campus Dr #270, Westlake, 440-333-8600
20455 Lorain Rd 2nd Fl, Cleveland, 440-333-8600

Young, James Benard (4 mentions)
Baylor U, 1974
Certification: Cardiovascular Disease, Internal Medicine
9500 Euclid Ave #F-25, Cleveland, 216-444-2270

Dermatology

Bailin, Philip Lawrence (5 mentions)
Northwestern U, 1968 *Certification:* Dermatology
9500 Euclid Ave #A-61, Cleveland, 216-444-2115
26900 Cedar Rd #27-N, Beachwood, 216-839-3000

Baud, Eric Bret (4 mentions)
Case Western Reserve U, 1992 *Certification:* Dermatology
1611 S Green Rd #146, South Euclid, 216-382-3806
5 Severance Cir #410, Cleveland Heights, 216-382-8244
2001 Crocker Rd #500, Westlake, 440-617-1522

Benjamin, Jaye E. (8 mentions)
U of Cincinnati, 1978 *Certification:* Dermatology
36060 Euclid Ave #202, Willoughby, 440-942-4226

Bergfeld, Wilma L. Fowler (4 mentions)
Temple U, 1964 *Certification:* Dermatology, Dermatopathology
9500 Euclid Ave #A-61, Cleveland, 216-444-5722
26900 Cedar Rd #27-N, Beachwood, 216-839-3000

Cooper, Kevin D. (14 mentions)
U of Florida, 1977 *Certification:* Dermatological Immunology/
   Diagnostic and Laboratory Immunology, Dermatology
11100 Euclid Ave #3516, Cleveland, 216-844-8200

Davis, Pamela Harris (5 mentions)
Wright State U, 1984
Certification: Dermatology, Internal Medicine
2500 Metrohealth Dr, Cleveland, 216-778-3030

Diwan, Renuka (5 mentions)
FMS-India, 1982 *Certification:* Dermatology
29101 Health Campus Dr #300, Westlake, 440-871-9832

Hirsh, Fred Stanley (5 mentions)
Ohio State U, 1972 *Certification:* Dermatology
6551 Wilson Mills Rd #101, Cleveland, 440-460-2884

Lynch, William Stafford (5 mentions)
George Washington U, 1970 *Certification:* Dermatology
1611 S Green Rd #146, South Euclid, 216-382-3806
5850 Landerbrook Dr #304, Cleveland, 440-442-1200
6820 Ridge Rd #201, Cleveland, 440-845-1146

Mancuso, Michael Gregory (5 mentions)
FMS-Mexico, 1975 *Certification:* Dermatology
33001 Solon Rd #211, Solon, 440-248-2955

McDonnell, Jonelle S. (5 mentions)
U of Toledo, 1987 *Certification:* Dermatology
9500 Euclid Ave #A-61, Cleveland, 216-444-5729

Mulligan, Kathleen Anne (4 mentions)
Case Western Reserve U, 1992 *Certification:* Dermatology
1991 Crocker Rd #310, Westlake, 440-617-9114

Polster, Amy Melissa (4 mentions)
Case Western Reserve U, 1999 *Certification:* Dermatology
551 E Washington St, Chagrin Falls, 440-893-9393

Taub, Steven Jeffrey (7 mentions)
SUNY-Downstate Med Coll, 1976 *Certification:* Dermatology
6803 Mayfield Rd #510, Cleveland, 440-461-7001

Tomecki, Kenneth Joseph (6 mentions)
Columbia U, 1972 *Certification:* Dermatology
9500 Euclid Ave #A-61, Cleveland, 216-444-2651

Vidimos, Allison Therese (15 mentions)
Indiana U, 1985 *Certification:* Dermatology
9500 Euclid Ave #A-61, Cleveland, 216-444-3345

Emergency Medicine

Anderson, Eric (3 mentions)
Case Western Reserve U *Certification:* Emergency Medicine
9500 Euclid Ave, Cleveland, 216-445-4556

Cooper, Joseph Donald (3 mentions)
Ohio U Coll of Osteopathic Med, 1995
Certification: Emergency Medicine
18101 Lorain Ave, Cleveland, 216-476-7000

Cunningham, Carol Anita (5 mentions)
U of Cincinnati, 1986 *Certification:* Emergency Medicine
36000 Euclid Ave, Willoughby, 440-953-6203

Cydulka, Rita Kay (6 mentions)
Northwestern U, 1980
Certification: Emergency Medicine, Internal Medicine
2500 Metrohealth Dr, Cleveland, 216-778-7800

Emerman, Charles Louis (4 mentions)
U of Toledo, 1979 *Certification:* Emergency Medicine
2500 Metrohealth Dr, Cleveland, 216-778-7800

Glauser, Jonathan Mark (5 mentions)
Temple U, 1976 *Certification:* Emergency Medicine,
   Pediatric Emergency Medicine
9500 Euclid Ave #E-19, Cleveland, 216-445-4550

Michelson, Edward Allen (5 mentions)
Washington U, 1982
Certification: Emergency Medicine, Internal Medicine
11100 Euclid Ave, Cleveland, 216-844-3836

Moffa, Donald Anthony, Jr. (4 mentions)
Ohio State U, 1990 *Certification:* Emergency Medicine
9500 Euclid Ave #E-19, Cleveland, 216-445-1904

Pennington, Jeffrey E. (3 mentions)
Indiana U, 1991 *Certification:* Emergency Medicine
2500 Metrohealth Dr, Cleveland, 216-778-7800

Seitz, Roy Edward (5 mentions)
U of Cincinnati, 1978
Certification: Emergency Medicine, Family Medicine
29000 Center Ridge Rd, Westlake, 440-835-8000

Endocrinology

Arafah, Bahauddin Mahmdud (17 mentions)
FMS-Lebanon, 1976
Certification: Endocrinology and Metabolism, Internal Medicine
11100 Euclid Ave, Cleveland, 216-844-3142

Brenner, Robert Scott (10 mentions)
Ohio State U, 1969
Certification: Endocrinology and Metabolism, Internal Medicine
3733 Park East Dr #105, Beachwood, 216-504-0001

Hoogwerf, Byron James (9 mentions)
U of Minnesota, 1971
Certification: Endocrinology and Metabolism, Internal Medicine
9500 Euclid Ave #A-53, Cleveland, 216-444-8347

Madhun, Zuhayr T. (8 mentions)
FMS-Lebanon, 1987 *Certification:* Endocrinology, Diabetes,
   and Metabolism, Internal Medicine
23250 Chagrin Blvd #201, Beachwood, 216-504-8888

Mandel, Martin Lee (6 mentions)
Ohio State U, 1972
Certification: Endocrinology and Metabolism, Internal Medicine
36100 Euclid Ave #320, Willoughby, 440-951-1073

Mehta, Adi E. (10 mentions)
FMS-Canada, 1974 *Certification:* Internal Medicine
9500 Euclid Ave #A-53, Cleveland, 216-444-6568

Morrow, Jay Stuart (14 mentions)
Pennsylvania State U, 1976
Certification: Endocrinology and Metabolism, Internal Medicine
3733 Park East Dr #105, Beachwood, 216-504-0001

Murphy, Thomas Aquinas (12 mentions)
Washington U, 1978
Certification: Endocrinology and Metabolism, Internal Medicine
2500 Metrohealth Dr, Cleveland, 216-778-5371

Nasr, Christian Elias (5 mentions)
FMS-Lebanon, 1988
Certification: Endocrinology, Diabetes, and Metabolism
9500 Euclid Ave, Cleveland, 440-204-7400
5700 Cooper Foster Park Rd W, Lorain, 440-204-7400

Rogers, Douglas George (6 mentions)
Rosalind Franklin U, 1978
Certification: Pediatric Endocrinology, Pediatrics
9500 Euclid Ave, Cleveland, 216-444-5437

Schnall, Adrian Michael (9 mentions)
Yale U, 1969 *Certification:* Endocrinology, Diabetes, and
   Metabolism, Internal Medicine
1611 S Green Rd #065, Cleveland, 216-291-4300

Weiss, Daniel (7 mentions)
U of Texas-Dallas, 1979
Certification: Endocrinology and Metabolism, Internal Medicine
8300 Tyler Blvd, Mentor, 440-266-5000

Family Practice *(see note on page 9)*

Cadesky, Alan S. (8 mentions)
FMS-Canada, 1978 *Certification:* Family Medicine
11100 Euclid Ave #1200, Cleveland, 216-844-3944

Kikano, George E. (12 mentions)
FMS-Lebanon, 1986 *Certification:* Family Medicine
11100 Euclid Ave, Cleveland, 216-844-3791
1611 S Green Rd, South Euclid, 216-297-2081

Znidarsic, Robert Mark (6 mentions)
U of Toledo, 1995 *Certification:* Family Medicine
510 5th Ave, Chardon, 440-279-1500

Gastroenterology

Achkar, Edgar (8 mentions)
FMS-Lebanon, 1963
Certification: Gastroenterology, Internal Medicine
9500 Euclid Ave, Cleveland, 216-444-6536

Brinberg, Don Edward (6 mentions)
Harvard U, 1982
Certification: Gastroenterology, Internal Medicine
5900 Landerbrook Dr #195, Cleveland, 440-461-2550
36100 Euclid Ave #270, Willoughby, 440-461-2793

Brzezinski, Aaron (7 mentions)
FMS-Mexico, 1981
Certification: Gastroenterology, Internal Medicine
9500 Euclid Ave, Cleveland, 216-444-6536

Cameron, R. Bruce (5 mentions)
Case Western Reserve U, 1979
Certification: Gastroenterology, Internal Medicine
1611 S Green Rd, South Euclid, 216-767-8198

Chak, Amitabh (14 mentions)
Columbia U, 1984
Certification: Gastroenterology, Internal Medicine
11100 Euclid Ave, Cleveland, 216-844-5386

Dumot, John Adam (7 mentions)
Ohio U Coll of Osteopathic Med, 1990
9500 Euclid Ave #A-30, Cleveland, 216-444-6536

Falk, Gary Warren (8 mentions)
U of Rochester, 1980
Certification: Gastroenterology, Internal Medicine
9500 Euclid Ave #A-30, Cleveland, 216-444-1762

Friedenberg, Keith Alan (6 mentions)
U of California-Los Angeles, 1988 *Certification:* Gastroenterology
9485 Mentor Ave #105, Mentor, 440-205-1225

Geraci, Kevin Thomas (4 mentions)
Ohio State U, 1967
Certification: Gastroenterology, Internal Medicine
1611 S Green Rd #160, Cleveland, 216-381-8109
8185 E Washington St #2, Chagrin Falls, 440-708-1555

Gottesman, David Lawrence (5 mentions)
New York U, 1975
Certification: Gastroenterology, Internal Medicine
6770 Mayfield Rd, Cleveland, 440-461-2550
5900 Landerbrook Dr, Mayfield Heights, 440-461-2550

Hupertz, Vera Frantsov (4 mentions)
U of Rochester, 1982 *Certification:* Pediatric Gastroenterology,
   Pediatric Transplant Hepatology, Pediatrics
9500 Euclid Ave #A-111, Cleveland, 216-444-0964
6770 Mayfield Rd #220, Mayfield Heights, 216-444-9000

Issa, Khaled (6 mentions)
FMS-Syria, 1983
Certification: Gastroenterology, Internal Medicine
850 Columbia Rd #200, Westlake, 440-808-1212

Kaplan, Barbara Sue (4 mentions)
U of Cincinnati, 1978
Certification: Pediatric Gastroenterology, Pediatrics
9500 Euclid Ave, Cleveland, 216-444-9000

Katz, Jeffry Adam (7 mentions)
Case Western Reserve U, 1987
Certification: Gastroenterology, Internal Medicine
11100 Euclid Ave, Cleveland, 216-844-5386

Kessler, Fred Bruce (4 mentions)
George Washington U, 1975
Certification: Gastroenterology, Internal Medicine
6770 Mayfield Rd, Cleveland, 440-461-2550

Kirsch, Michael (4 mentions)
New York U, 1985
Certification: Gastroenterology, Internal Medicine
34940 Ridge Rd #B, Willoughby, 440-953-1899

Lisi, James Edward (4 mentions)
Wright State U, 1989 *Certification:* Gastroenterology
125 E Broad St #114, Elyria, 440-329-5943

Post, Anthony Benjamin (7 mentions)
Case Western Reserve U, 1986 *Certification:*
  Gastroenterology, Internal Medicine, Transplant Hepatology
11100 Euclid Ave, Cleveland, 216-844-5386

Rood, Richard Paul (5 mentions)
Wright State U, 1982
Certification: Gastroenterology, Internal Medicine
34940 Ridge Rd #B, Willoughby, 440-953-1899
9485 Mentor Ave #203, Mentor, 440-205-5740
99 Northline Cir #215, Cleveland, 216-692-0802

Rozman, Raymond William (4 mentions)
Case Western Reserve U, 1984
Certification: Gastroenterology, Internal Medicine
8185 E Washington St #2, Chagrin Falls, 440-708-1555

Springer, Michael Don (5 mentions)
U of Iowa, 1976
Certification: Gastroenterology, Internal Medicine
850 Columbia Rd #200, Westlake, 440-808-1212

Tabbaa, Mousab (10 mentions)
FMS-Syria, 1981
Certification: Gastroenterology, Internal Medicine
850 Columbia Rd #200, Westlake, 440-808-1212

Vargo, John Joseph, II (5 mentions)
U of Rochester, 1985
Certification: Gastroenterology, Internal Medicine
9500 Euclid Ave 3rd Fl, Cleveland, 216-444-6536

Wolf, Jason M. (4 mentions)
U of Texas-Dallas, 1997
Certification: Gastroenterology, Internal Medicine
6770 Mayfield Rd #424, Cleveland, 440-461-2550
5900 Lander-brook Dr #195, Cleveland, 440-461-2550

Wyllie, Robert (6 mentions)
Indiana U, 1976
Certification: Pediatric Gastroenterology, Pediatrics
9500 Euclid Ave #A-111, Cleveland, 216-444-2237

Yang, Peter (4 mentions)
Johns Hopkins U, 1977
Certification: Gastroenterology, Internal Medicine
5900 Landerbrook Dr #190, Mayfield Heights, 440-461-2550

Zuccaro, Gregory Donald (4 mentions)
U of Buffalo, 1983
Certification: Gastroenterology, Internal Medicine
9500 Euclid Ave #A-30, Cleveland, 216-444-0784

General Surgery

Baringer, David Charles (3 mentions)
Ohio State U, 1978
30033 Clemens Rd, Westlake, 440-899-5555
16761 Southpark Ctr, Strongsville, 440-878-2500

Bogard, Brent M. (4 mentions)
U of Texas-San Antonio, 1987 *Certification:* Surgery
20455 Lorain Rd #353, Fairview Park, 440-673-0100
30033 Clemens Rd, Westlake, 440-808-7888

Borison, Daniel I. (4 mentions)
New York U, 1987 *Certification:* Surgery
6770 Mayfield Rd, Cleveland, 440-684-0000

Brandt, Christopher P. (4 mentions)
Case Western Reserve U, 1984 *Certification:* Surgery
2500 Metrohealth Dr, Cleveland, 216-778-4797

Chand, Bipan (4 mentions)
U of Missouri-Kansas City, 1996 *Certification:* Surgery
9500 Euclid Ave #M-61, Cleveland, 216-444-6668

Difiore, John William (4 mentions)
Columbia U, 1988 *Certification:* Pediatric Surgery, Surgery
9500 Euclid Ave #1714, Cleveland, 216-444-5522
6780 Mayfield Rd, Cleveland, 440-449-4550

Dorsky, John (4 mentions)
Cornell U, 1981 *Certification:* Surgery
9500 Euclid Ave, Cleveland, 440-449-1101
6770 Mayfield Rd, Cleveland, 440-449-1101
2570 SOM Center Rd, Willoughby, 440-943-2500

Ferron, John Patrick (3 mentions)
Rosalind Franklin U, 1979 *Certification:* Surgery
9500 Mentor Ave #300, Mentor, 440-354-0377

Hardacre, Jeffrey Max (3 mentions)
Duke U, 1996 *Certification:* Surgery
11100 Euclid Ave, Cleveland, 216-844-7874

Lee, Kenneth (7 mentions)
Case Western Reserve U, 1991 *Certification:* Surgery
20455 Lorain Rd #353, Fairview Park, 440-673-0100

Magnuson, David Kurt (3 mentions)
U of Minnesota, 1984 *Certification:* Pediatric Surgery, Surgery
9500 Euclid Ave, Cleveland, 216-445-4051

Malangoni, Mark Alan (4 mentions)
Indiana U, 1975 *Certification:* Surgery, Surgical Critical Care
2500 Metrohealth Dr, Cleveland, 216-778-4558

Malgieri, James Anthony (15 mentions)
Georgetown U, 1979 *Certification:* Surgery
6770 Mayfield Rd #348, Mayfield Heights, 440-449-1101
9500 Euclid Ave, Cleveland, 440-449-1101

McHenry, Christopher R. (6 mentions)
Northeastern Ohio U, 1984 *Certification:* Surgery
2500 Metrohealth Dr, Cleveland, 216-778-4753

Merlino, James I. (4 mentions)
Case Western Reserve U, 1997
Certification: Colon & Rectal Surgery, Surgery
2500 Metrohealth Dr, Cleveland, 216-778-4391

Onders, Raymond Peter (11 mentions)
Northeastern Ohio U, 1988 *Certification:* Surgery
11100 Euclid Ave, Cleveland, 216-844-7874

Petraiuolo, William James (8 mentions)
U of Vermont, 1986 *Certification:* Surgery
36060 Euclid Ave #204, Willoughby, 440-602-6553

Ponsky, Jeffrey L. (17 mentions)
Case Western Reserve U, 1971 *Certification:* Surgery
11100 Euclid Ave, Cleveland, 216-844-7874

Pritchard, Timothy James (7 mentions)
Harvard U, 1981 *Certification:* Colon & Rectal Surgery, Surgery
9500 Mentor Ave #300, Mentor, 440-354-0377

Renner, Patrick A. (3 mentions)
U of Cincinnati, 1988 *Certification:* Surgery
6707 Powers Blvd #100, Cleveland, 440-886-1247

Reynolds, Harry Lewis, Jr. (4 mentions)
Case Western Reserve U, 1986
Certification: Colon & Rectal Surgery, Surgery
11100 Euclid Ave, Cleveland, 216-844-7874

Rosenblatt, Steven M. (13 mentions)
Case Western Reserve U, 1994 *Certification:* Surgery
26900 Cedar Rd #27-N, Beachwood, 216-839-3000
9500 Euclid Ave #A-80, Cleveland, 216-444-2000

Shenk, Robert Ritchie (3 mentions)
Case Western Reserve U, 1978 *Certification:* Surgery
11100 Euclid Ave, Cleveland, 216-844-7874

Stallion, Anthony (3 mentions)
U of Michigan, 1987 *Certification:* Pediatric Surgery, Surgery
9500 Euclid Ave, Cleveland, 216-444-5437

Stellato, Thomas A. (13 mentions)
Georgetown U, 1975 *Certification:* Surgery
1611 S Green Rd #07, South Euclid, 216-382-7146
11100 Euclid Ave #2100, Cleveland, 216-844-3021

Vogt, David Paul (5 mentions)
Northwestern U, 1975 *Certification:* Surgery
9500 Euclid Ave #A-110, Cleveland, 216-444-6968

Walsh, R. Matthew (17 mentions)
Med Coll of Wisconsin, 1985 *Certification:* Surgery
9500 Euclid Ave, Cleveland, 216-445-7576

Warner, Keith M. (3 mentions)
U of Kentucky, 1979 *Certification:* Surgery
125 E Broad St #219, Elyria, 440-326-5250
6100 Rockside Woods Blvd N #351, Independence,
  216-643-2780

Geriatrics

Baum, Stephen Alexander (5 mentions)
Pennsylvania State U, 1979 *Certification:* Internal Medicine
9485 Mentor Ave #210-A, Mentor, 440-205-5833

Boxer, Rebecca Sue (3 mentions)
U of Pennsylvania, 1997
Certification: Geriatric Medicine, Internal Medicine
11100 Euclid Ave, Cleveland, 214-844-2500

Campbell, James Wiley (8 mentions)
U of Cincinnati, 1984
Certification: Family Medicine, Geriatric Medicine
2500 Metrohealth Dr, Cleveland, 216-778-5737

Chrismer, Lynn C., Jr. (3 mentions)
Ohio State U, 1975
Certification: Geriatric Medicine, Internal Medicine
5700 Cooper Foster Park Rd W, Lorain, 440-204-7400

Degolia, Peter Alexander (3 mentions)
Rush U, 1990 *Certification:* Family Medicine, Geriatric
  Medicine, Hospice and Palliative Medicine
12200 Fairhill RD, Cleveland, 216-844-6338
1100 Euclid Ave, Cleveland, 216-844-6338

Messinger-Rapport, B. (4 mentions)
Case Western Reserve U, 1989
Certification: Geriatric Medicine, Internal Medicine
9500 Euclid Ave #A-91, Cleveland, 216-444-6801

Suh, Theodore Tongun (3 mentions)
U of Cincinnati, 1998
Certification: Geriatric Medicine, Internal Medicine
9500 Euclid Ave #A-91, Cleveland, 216-444-0319

Hematology/Oncology

Adelstein, David Joseph (5 mentions)
New York U, 1975
Certification: Hematology, Internal Medicine, Medical Oncology
9500 Euclid Ave #R-35, Cleveland, 216-444-6833

Berman, Brian William (10 mentions)
Temple U, 1975
Certification: Pediatric Hematology-Oncology, Pediatrics
11100 Euclid Ave, Cleveland, 216-844-8260

Bolwell, Brian James (6 mentions)
Case Western Reserve U, 1981
Certification: Internal Medicine, Medical Oncology
9500 Euclid Ave #R-32, Cleveland, 216-444-6922

Daw, Hamed (5 mentions)
FMS-Belgium, 1988 *Certification:* Hematology, Medical Oncology
18200 Lorain Ave, Cleveland, 216-476-7606
30033 Clemens Rd, Cleveland, 440-899-5555

Dickman, Elliott Roy (8 mentions)
Albert Einstein Coll of Med, 1976
Certification: Hematology, Internal Medicine, Medical Oncology
5885 Landerbrook Dr, Mayfield Heights, 440-460-1616

Dowlati, Afshin (4 mentions)
FMS-Belgium, 1992
Certification: Internal Medicine, Medical Oncology
11100 Euclid Ave, Cleveland, 216-844-3951

Escuro, Ruben Sales (5 mentions)
FMS-Philippines, 1981
Certification: Hematology, Internal Medicine, Medical Oncology
41201 Schadden Rd #2, Elyria, 440-324-0401

Gerson, Stanton L. (6 mentions)
Harvard U, 1977
Certification: Hematology, Internal Medicine, Medical Oncology
11100 Euclid Ave, Cleveland, 216-368-1176

Greenfield, Aric William (4 mentions)
U of Toledo, 1981
Certification: Internal Medicine, Medical Oncology
2550 SOM Center Rd, Willoughby, 440-943-2500

Kalaycioglu, Matt Etem (4 mentions)
West Virginia U, 1988
9500 Euclid Ave #R-35, Cleveland, 216-444-3705

Krishamurthi, Smitha S. (4 mentions)
11100 Euclid Ave, Cleveland, 216-844-1006
3909 Orange Pl #1100, Chagrin, 216-844-1006

Lichtin, Alan Eli (11 mentions)
U of Cincinnati, 1980
Certification: Hematology, Internal Medicine, Medical Oncology
9500 Euclid Ave #R-35, Cleveland, 216-444-6823

Lubin, Alan (4 mentions)
Ohio State U, 1963
Certification: Hematology, Internal Medicine, Medical Oncology
730 SOM Center Rd #305, Cleveland, 440-442-4260

Makkar, Vinit Kumar (5 mentions)
Northeastern Ohio U, 1989
Certification: Internal Medicine, Medical Oncology
26900 Cedar Rd #330-S, Beachwood, 216-839-2990

O'Brien, Timothy Edwin (6 mentions)
U of Rochester, 1989
Certification: Hematology, Medical Oncology
2500 Metrohealth Dr, Cleveland, 216-778-5802

Pelley, Robert James (5 mentions)
U of Cincinnati, 1980
Certification: Hematology, Internal Medicine, Medical Oncology
9500 Euclid Ave #R-35, Cleveland, 216-444-6833

Saltzman, Joel Nathan (5 mentions)
Ohio State U, 1997
Certification: Internal Medicine, Medical Oncology
9485 Mentor Ave #3, Mentor, 440-205-5755

Schnur, Gary Arnold (4 mentions)
Albany Med Coll, 1979
Certification: Internal Medicine, Medical Oncology
26900 Cedar Rd #330-S, Beachwood, 216-839-2990

Sidloski, Jay E. (4 mentions)
Des Moines U, 1997
Certification: Hematology, Internal Medicine, Medical Oncology
41201 Schadden Rd #2, Elyria, 440-324-0401

Silverman, Paula (14 mentions)
Case Western Reserve U, 1981
Certification: Internal Medicine, Medical Oncology
11100 Euclid Ave, Cleveland, 216-844-8510
1611 S Green Rd, South Euclid, 216-844-8510

Spiro, Timothy Peter (5 mentions)
FMS-Australia, 1974
Certification: Internal Medicine, Medical Oncology
18200 Lorain Ave, Cleveland, 216-476-7606

Teston, Lois Jane (7 mentions)
Case Western Reserve U, 1996
Certification: Internal Medicine, Medical Oncology
3909 Orange Pl #1100, Orange Village, 216-896-1750

Van Heeckeren, Willem Jan (5 mentions)
Case Western Reserve U, 2002
Certification: Hematology, Internal Medicine, Medical Oncology
9485 Mentor Ave #200, Mentor, 440-205-5755
1100 Euclid Ave, Cleveland, 440-205-5755

Infectious Disease

Abbud, Rita (5 mentions)
FMS-Lebanon, 1988
Certification: Infectious Disease, Internal Medicine
1800 Livingston Ave #101, Lorain, 440-233-1093

Armitage, Keith Barclay (24 mentions)
U of Colorado, 1986
Certification: Infectious Disease, Internal Medicine
11100 Euclid Ave #LB-3575, Cleveland, 216-844-1709

Avery, Robin K. (10 mentions)
Harvard U, 1985
Certification: Infectious Disease, Internal Medicine
9500 Euclid Ave #S-32, Cleveland, 216-444-8977

Cox, Diethra Diane (6 mentions)
Meharry Med Coll, 1982 *Certification:* Internal Medicine
9485 Mentor Ave #103, Cleveland, 440-205-0242
2816 E 116th St, Cleveland, 216-957-4000

Goldfarb, Johanna (11 mentions)
Johns Hopkins U, 1974
Certification: Pediatric Infectious Diseases, Pediatrics
9500 Euclid Ave #525, Cleveland, 216-444-3608

Gopalakrishna, K. V. (8 mentions)
FMS-India, 1965
Certification: Infectious Disease, Internal Medicine
18101 Lorain Ave, Cleveland, 216-476-7106

Gordon, Steven Mark (13 mentions)
Cornell U, 1984
Certification: Infectious Disease, Internal Medicine
9500 Euclid Ave, Cleveland, 216-444-8845

Gustaferro, Cynthia A. (8 mentions)
U of South Dakota, 1987
Certification: Infectious Disease, Internal Medicine
6770 Mayfield Rd #443, Cleveland, 440-460-2842

Hutt, David Mark (13 mentions)
Case Western Reserve U, 1979
Certification: Infectious Disease, Internal Medicine
6770 Mayfield Rd #443, Cleveland, 440-460-2842

Isada, Carlos M. (6 mentions)
U of Buffalo, 1986 *Certification:* Infectious Disease
9500 Euclid Ave #S-32, Cleveland, 216-444-8845

Kalayjian, Robert Charles (6 mentions)
Tufts U, 1982 *Certification:* Infectious Disease, Internal Medicine
2500 Metrohealth Dr, Cleveland, 216-778-2053

Marino, John A., III (8 mentions)
Certification: Infectious Disease, Internal Medicine
6770 Mayfield Rd #443, Cleveland, 440-460-2842

Persaud, Roberta Bender (6 mentions)
Wright State U, 1984 *Certification:* Internal Medicine
29099 Health Campus Dr #110, Westlake, 440-835-6169

Rehm, Susan J. (10 mentions)
U of Nebraska, 1978
Certification: Infectious Disease, Internal Medicine
9500 Euclid Ave #S-32, Cleveland, 216-444-6847

Sabella, Camille (6 mentions)
Northeastern Ohio U, 1987
Certification: Pediatric Infectious Diseases, Pediatrics
9500 Euclid Ave #525, Cleveland, 216-444-3608

Salata, Robert Andrew (21 mentions)
Case Western Reserve U, 1979
Certification: Infectious Disease, Internal Medicine
11100 Euclid Ave, Cleveland, 216-844-2085

Shekar, Raja (6 mentions)
FMS-India, 1969
Certification: Infectious Disease, Internal Medicine
3609 Park East Dr, Beachwood, 440-460-2842

Szathmary, Eva Ann (5 mentions)
FMS-Hungary, 1991 *Certification:* Infectious Disease
3609 E Parks Dr, Beachwood, 216-360-9480
6681 Ridge Rd #204, Parma, 440-884-2909

Tomford, J. Walton (16 mentions)
Johns Hopkins U, 1975
Certification: Infectious Disease, Internal Medicine
9500 Euclid Ave #S-32, Cleveland, 216-444-6847

Infertility

Falcone, Tammaso (11 mentions)
FMS-Canada, 1981 *Certification:* Obstetrics & Gynecology,
Reproductive Endocrinology/Infertility
9500 Euclid Ave #A-81, Cleveland, 216-444-6601

Goldfarb, James Morris (19 mentions)
Ohio State U, 1973 *Certification:* Obstetrics & Gynecology,
Reproductive Endocrinology/Infertility
26900 Cedar Rd #200, Cleveland, 216-839-3100

Hurd, William Ward (7 mentions)
U of Alabama, 1979 *Certification:* Obstetrics & Gynecology,
Reproductive Endocrinology/Infertility
11100 Euclid Ave, Cleveland, 216-844-1514
5850 Landerbrook Dr, Mayfield Heights, 216-844-1514
960 Clague Rd, Westlake, 216-844-1514

Liu, James H. (6 mentions)
Ohio State U, 1977 *Certification:* Obstetrics & Gynecology,
Reproductive Endocrinology/Infertility
11100 Euclid Ave, Cleveland, 216-844-3941

Internal Medicine *(see note on page 9)*

Anderson, Philip Alden (3 mentions)
Case Western Reserve U, 1978 *Certification:* Internal Medicine
1611 S Green Rd #260, Cleveland, 216-291-1650

Bal, Baljit Singh (3 mentions)
SUNY-Upstate Med U, 1990 *Certification:* Internal Medicine
26900 Cedar Rd #26N, Beachwood, 216-839-3000

Baniewicz, John Joseph (6 mentions)
Northeastern Ohio U, 1988 *Certification:* Internal Medicine
9485 Mentor Ave #210-A, Mentor, 440-205-5835

Bronson, David Leigh (4 mentions)
U of Vermont, 1973
Certification: Geriatric Medicine, Internal Medicine
9500 Euclid Ave #A-91, Cleveland, 216-444-0325

Buchinsky, Roy Marc (3 mentions)
FMS-South Africa, 1989 *Certification:* Internal Medicine
5850 Landerbrook Dr #100, Cleveland, 440-646-2200

Campbell, John P. (3 mentions)
Pennsylvania State U, 1972
Certification: Endocrinology and Metabolism, Internal Medicine
9500 Euclid Ave #A-11, Cleveland, 216-444-5707

Cirino, Robert Allan (4 mentions)
Case Western Reserve U, 1990 *Certification:* Internal Medicine
1611 S Green Rd #260, Cleveland, 216-381-9383

Debs, Michael E. (3 mentions)
FMS-Bulgaria, 1987 *Certification:* Internal Medicine
14320 Ridge Rd, North Royalton, 440-230-2400

Eiswerth, Thomas F., Jr. (9 mentions)
U of Cincinnati, 1992 *Certification:* Internal Medicine
9485 Mentor Ave #210-A, Mentor, 440-205-5808

Faiman, Matthew (3 mentions)
FMS-Canada, 1999 *Certification:* Internal Medicine
5001 Rockside Rd, Independence, 216-986-4000

Gliner, Boris (3 mentions)
FMS-Russia, 1977 *Certification:* Internal Medicine
4200 Warrensville Center Rd #430, Beachwood, 216-751-9770

Gutierrez, James Francis (5 mentions)
Case Western Reserve U, 1990 *Certification:* Internal Medicine
30033 Clemens Rd, Westlake, 440-899-5555

Isaacson, J. Harry (11 mentions)
U of Michigan, 1984 *Certification:* Internal Medicine
9500 Euclid Ave #A-91, Cleveland, 216-444-0730

Klarfeld, Jonathan Eric (3 mentions)
Cornell U, 1978 *Certification:* Internal Medicine
23250 Mercantile Rd, Beachwood, 216-464-7878

Lang, Richard S. (8 mentions)
U of Cincinnati, 1979
Certification: Internal Medicine, Occupational Medicine
9500 Euclid Ave #A-11, Cleveland, 216-444-5707

Leizman, Debra Sue (3 mentions)
U of Cincinnati, 1987 *Certification:* Internal Medicine
11100 Euclid Ave, Cleveland, 216-844-8500
3909 Orange Pl #3100, Orange Village, 216-896-1774

Mayer, Mark Edward (3 mentions)
U of Illinois, 1982
Certification: Geriatric Medicine, Internal Medicine
9500 Euclid Ave #A-91, Cleveland, 216-445-5310

Rudolph, Stephen A. (6 mentions)
Case Western Reserve U, 1988 *Certification:* Internal Medicine
1611 S Green Rd #260, Cleveland, 216-381-1367

Schnall, Adrian Michael (3 mentions)
Yale U, 1969 *Certification:* Endocrinology, Diabetes, and
   Metabolism, Internal Medicine
1611 S Green Rd #065, Cleveland, 216-291-4300

Nephrology

Anton, Hany (5 mentions)
FMS-Egypt, 1992 *Certification:* Internal Medicine, Nephrology
19133 Hilliard Blvd, Rocky River, 216-228-5500

Azem, Jamal Mouayad (10 mentions)
FMS-Syria, 1981 *Certification:* Internal Medicine, Nephrology
36100 Euclid Ave #330-A, Willoughby, 440-269-8020

Berger, Bruce Edward (11 mentions)
SUNY-Upstate Med U, 1978
Certification: Internal Medicine, Nephrology
11100 Euclid Ave, Cleveland, 216-844-8500

De Oreo, Peter Butler (4 mentions)
Case Western Reserve U, 1972
Certification: Internal Medicine, Nephrology
1611 S Green Rd #160, Cleveland, 216-297-2073

Fatica, Richard Anthony (4 mentions)
Virginia Commonwealth U, 1993 *Certification:* Nephrology
9500 Euclid Ave, Cleveland, 216-445-9953

Flauto, Ronald Patrick (9 mentions)
Midwestern U Chicago Coll of Osteopathic Med, 1996
Certification: Internal Medicine, Nephrology
6681 Ridge Rd #302, Cleveland, 440-743-4884
7725 Old Oak Blvd #B-301, Cleveland, 440-743-4884

Hall, Phillip Marvin (5 mentions)
Ohio State U, 1965 *Certification:* Internal Medicine, Nephrology
9500 Euclid Ave, Cleveland, 216-444-6771

Hanna, Haifa (5 mentions)
FMS-Syria, 1964
6770 Mayfield Rd #333, Cleveland, 440-461-0038
20050 Harvard Ave #103, Warrensville Heights, 216-491-0600

Hricik, Donald Edward (5 mentions)
Georgetown U, 1977 *Certification:* Internal Medicine, Nephrology
11100 Euclid Ave, Cleveland, 216-844-3133

Lautman, Jeffrey Howard (5 mentions)
Ohio State U, 1986 *Certification:* Internal Medicine, Nephrology
25301 Euclid Ave 2nd Fl, Cleveland, 216-261-6263

Lazar, Andrew Evan (4 mentions)
Wayne State U, 1998 *Certification:* Internal Medicine, Nephrology
3619 Park E, Beachwood, 216-896-0639

Miclat, Romeo Sapuriada (4 mentions)
FMS-Philippines, 1970 *Certification:* Internal Medicine
1060 Abbe Rd N, Elyria, 440-365-9371

Miller, Sanford A. (5 mentions)
U of Cincinnati, 1969
Certification: Internal Medicine, Nephrology
5 Severance Cir #510, Cleveland Heights, 216-291-4891

Nally, Joseph Vahey, Jr. (9 mentions)
Ohio State U, 1975 *Certification:* Internal Medicine, Nephrology
9500 Euclid Ave, Cleveland, 216-444-8897

Poggio, Emilio D. (4 mentions)
FMS-Argentina, 1993
Certification: Internal Medicine, Nephrology
9500 Euclid Ave, Cleveland, 216-444-5383

Pohl, Marc Alfred (5 mentions)
Case Western Reserve U, 1966
Certification: Internal Medicine, Nephrology
9500 Euclid Ave, Cleveland, 216-444-6776

Schreiber, Martin Joseph (14 mentions)
Wake Forest U, 1976 *Certification:* Internal Medicine, Nephrology
9500 Euclid Ave, Cleveland, 216-444-6365

Sedor, John Reid (5 mentions)
U of Virginia, 1978 *Certification:* Internal Medicine, Nephrology
2500 Metrohealth Dr, Cleveland, 216-778-4993

Smith, Michael Charles (8 mentions)
Ohio State U, 1971 *Certification:* Internal Medicine, Nephrology
11100 Euclid Ave, Cleveland, 216-844-3683

Wish, Jay Barry (7 mentions)
Tufts U, 1974 *Certification:* Internal Medicine, Nephrology
11100 Euclid Ave, Cleveland, 216-844-8272

Neurological Surgery

Anderson, James Stephen (7 mentions)
U of California-Irvine, 1986 *Certification:* Neurological Surgery
2500 Metrohealth Dr, Cleveland, 216-778-4391

Barnett, Gene Henry (11 mentions)
Case Western Reserve U, 1980 *Certification:* Neurological Surgery
9500 Euclid Ave #R-20, Cleveland, 216-444-5381

Benzel, Edward Charles (7 mentions)
Med Coll of Wisconsin, 1975 *Certification:* Neurological Surgery
9500 Euclid Ave #S-80, Cleveland, 216-444-2225

Bingaman, William Emanuel (8 mentions)
Temple U, 1990 *Certification:* Neurological Surgery
9500 Euclid Ave #S-80, Cleveland, 216-444-5670

Cohen, Alan R. (16 mentions)
Cornell U, 1978 *Certification:* Neurological Surgery
11100 Euclid Ave #B-501, Cleveland, 216-844-5741

Itani, Abdul Latif (9 mentions)
FMS-Lebanon, 1968 *Certification:* Neurological Surgery
2785 SOM Center Rd, Willoughby, 440-975-5575

Kalfas, Iain H. (6 mentions)
Northeastern Ohio U, 1982 *Certification:* Neurological Surgery
9500 Euclid Ave #S-80, Cleveland, 216-444-9064

Luciano, Mark Gregory (10 mentions)
U of Chicago, 1985 *Certification:* Neurological Surgery
9500 Euclid Ave #S-80, Cleveland, 216-444-5747

Rezai, Ali Reza (6 mentions)
U of Southern California, 1990 *Certification:* Neurological Surgery
9500 Euclid Ave #S-31, Cleveland, 216-444-2210

Ruch, Theresa O'Connor D. (16 mentions)
Case Western Reserve U, 1979 *Certification:* Neurological Surgery
2785 SOM Center Rd, Willoughby, 440-975-5575

Selman, Warren Richard (25 mentions)
Case Western Reserve U, 1977 *Certification:* Neurological Surgery
11100 Euclid Ave, Cleveland, 216-844-5745

Neurology

Bambakidis, Peter (5 mentions)
Case Western Reserve U, 1984 *Certification:* Clinical
   Neurophysiology, Neurology, Vascular Neurology
25200 Center Ridge Rd #2100, Westlake, 440-331-4053

Bass, Nancy Ellyn (4 mentions)
Southern Illinois U, 1990 *Certification:* Neurology with
   Special Qualifications in Child Neurology
11100 Euclid Ave, Cleveland, 216-844-3691

Chelimsky, Thomas Charles (5 mentions)
Washington U, 1983
Certification: Internal Medicine, Neurology, Pain Medicine
11100 Euclid Ave, Cleveland, 216-844-3495

Daroff, Robert Barry (5 mentions)
U of Pennsylvania, 1961 *Certification:* Neurology
11100 Euclid Ave, Cleveland, 216-844-3192

Dashefsky, Larry Howard (4 mentions)
FMS-Canada, 1981
Certification: Clinical Neurophysiology, Neurology
6803 Mayfield Rd #409, Cleveland, 440-449-2000

Devereaux, Michael William (14 mentions)
Baylor U, 1968 *Certification:* Neurology
11100 Euclid Ave, Cleveland, 216-844-3591

Friedman, Neil Roy (7 mentions)
FMS-South Africa, 1987 *Certification:* Neurology with
   Special Qualifications in Child Neurology, Pediatrics
9500 Euclid Ave #S-71, Cleveland, 216-444-5559

Furlan, Anthony John (8 mentions)
Loyola U Chicago, 1973
Certification: Neurology, Vascular Neurology
11100 Euclid Ave 5th Fl, Cleveland, 216-844-3193

Hanna, Joseph Patrick (5 mentions)
U of Cincinnati, 1988
Certification: Neurology, Vascular Neurology
2500 Metrohealth Dr, Cleveland, 216-778-3958

Katirji, Bashar (4 mentions)
FMS-Syria, 1977 *Certification:* Clinical Neurophysiology,
   Neurology, Neuromuscular Medicine
11100 Euclid Ave, Cleveland, 216-844-4854
1611 Green Rd, South Euclid, 216-844-4854

Lederman, Richard J. (4 mentions)
U of Buffalo, 1966 *Certification:* Neurology
9500 Euclid Ave #S-91, Cleveland, 216-444-5545

Levin, Kerry Hartley (8 mentions)
Johns Hopkins U, 1977 *Certification:* Clinical
   Neurophysiology, Neurology, Neuromuscular Medicine
9500 Euclid Ave #S-9, Cleveland, 216-444-5559

Mahajan, Darshan (4 mentions)
FMS-India, 1973 *Certification:* Neurology
673 E River St, Elyria, 440-323-6422
3600 Kolbe Rd #109, Lorain, 440-323-6422

Miller, Daniel William (4 mentions)
Ohio State U, 1998 *Certification:* Clinical Neurophysiology,
Neurology, Neuromuscular Medicine
11100 Euclid Ave, Cleveland, 216-844-3192
1611 Green Rd, South Euclid, 216-844-3192

Nayak, Sagarika (4 mentions)
Wright State U, 1986 *Certification:* Neurology
24723 Detroit Rd, Westlake, 440-250-0325
29099 Health Campus Dr #390, Westlake, 440-250-0325

Rorick, Mark Benjamin (5 mentions)
Case Western Reserve U, 1985 *Certification:* Neurology
35040 Chardon Rd #110, Willoughby, 440-946-1200

Rothner, A. David (4 mentions)
U of Illinois, 1965 *Certification:* Neurology with Special
Qualifications in Child Neurology, Pediatrics
9500 Euclid Ave #S-71, Cleveland, 216-444-5514

Scher, Mark Steven (4 mentions)
SUNY-Downstate Med Coll, 1976 *Certification:* Neurology
with Special Qualifications in Child Neurology, Pediatrics
11100 Euclid Ave, Cleveland, 216-844-3691

Sunshine, Joshua Jay (8 mentions)
Albert Einstein Coll of Med, 1991 *Certification:* Neurology
35040 Chardon Rd #110, Willoughby, 440-946-1200

Sweeney, Patrick J. (5 mentions)
U of Buffalo, 1964 *Certification:* Neurology
9500 Euclid Ave #S-91, Cleveland, 216-444-5563

Westbrook, Edward Lloyd (13 mentions)
Cornell U, 1965 *Certification:* Neurology
11100 Euclid Ave, Cleveland, 216-844-3191
1611 Green Rd, South Euclid, 216-844-3192

Zayat, Joseph (5 mentions)
Certification: Clinical Neurophysiology, Internal Medicine,
Neurology
26900 Cedar Rd, Beachwood, 216-839-3000

Obstetrics/Gynecology

Alton, John Anthony (3 mentions)
Ohio State U, 1992 *Certification:* Obstetrics & Gynecology
7255 Old Oak Blvd #C-202, Cleveland, 440-816-5390
18181 Pearl Rd #B-206, Strongsville, 440-816-4930

Alvarez, Benito A. (3 mentions)
FMS-Costa Rica, 1988 *Certification:* Obstetrics & Gynecology
6770 Mayfield Rd, Cleveland, 440-312-7775

Ashby-Vincent, Karen L. (4 mentions)
Case Western Reserve U, 1988
Certification: Obstetrics & Gynecology
11100 Euclid Ave #1200, Cleveland, 216-844-3941

Bashour, Fadi S. (4 mentions)
FMS-Syria, 1989 *Certification:* Obstetrics & Gynecology
7575 Northcliff Ave #302, Cleveland, 216-398-5988

Bradley, Linda Darlene (3 mentions)
U of Cincinnati, 1981 *Certification:* Obstetrics & Gynecology
9500 Euclid Ave #A-81, Cleveland, 216-444-3435

Brzozowski, Philip Chris (3 mentions)
Pennsylvania State U, 1980 *Certification:* Obstetrics & Gynecology
36001 Euclid Ave #C-7, Willoughby, 440-602-6710

Cameron, John Jeffery (3 mentions)
Case Western Reserve U, 1984
13170 Ravenna Rd #116, Chardon, 440-285-0828

David, Laura Jean (9 mentions)
Washington U, 1978 *Certification:* Obstetrics & Gynecology
1611 S Green Rd #216, South Euclid, 216-381-2223

Dierker, LeRoy Joseph, Jr. (3 mentions)
U of Iowa, 1968
Certification: Maternal-Fetal Medicine, Obstetrics & Gynecology
2500 Metrohealth Dr #G-240, Cleveland, 216-778-3550

Falcone, Tommaso (7 mentions)
FMS-Canada, 1981 *Certification:* Obstetrics & Gynecology,
Reproductive Endocrinology/Infertility
9500 Euclid Ave, Cleveland, 216-444-1758

Fisher, Gretchen Lynne (3 mentions)
Harvard U, 1993 *Certification:* Obstetrics & Gynecology
5001 Rockside Rd, Independence, 216-986-4000

Greenfield, Marjorie Lisa (4 mentions)
Case Western Reserve U, 1983
Certification: Obstetrics & Gynecology
11100 Euclid Ave #1200, Cleveland, 216-844-3941

Grosel, Gary Michael (3 mentions)
Wright State U, 1990 *Certification:* Obstetrics & Gynecology
36901 American Way, Avon, 440-930-6200
20800 Westgate Blvd, Cleveland, 440-930-6200
2900 Center Ridge Rd, Westlake, 440-930-6200

Guerrieri, James Paul, Jr. (3 mentions)
U of Toledo, 1987 *Certification:* Obstetrics & Gynecology
6770 Mayfield Rd, Cleveland, 440-312-8383

Gyves, Michael Thomas (5 mentions)
Cornell U, 1968
Certification: Maternal-Fetal Medicine, Obstetrics & Gynecology
5850 Landerbrook Dr #3, Cleveland, 440-720-3250
11100 Euclid Ave #1200, Cleveland, 216-844-3941

Hendryx, Paula Victoria (3 mentions)
Northeastern Ohio U, 1987 *Certification:* Obstetrics & Gynecology
2500 Metrohealth Dr #G-231-F, Cleveland, 216-778-7758

Jaffe, Karen Marie (4 mentions)
Wright State U, 1986 *Certification:* Obstetrics & Gynecology
1611 S Green Rd #216, South Euclid, 216-381-2223

Janicki, Thomas I. (3 mentions)
FMS-Poland, 1974 *Certification:* Obstetrics & Gynecology
1611 S Green Rd #216, South Euclid, 216-381-2223

Judge, Nancy Elizabeth (10 mentions)
U of Massachusetts, 1977
Certification: Maternal-Fetal Medicine, Obstetrics & Gynecology
11100 Euclid Ave #1200, Cleveland, 216-844-3941

McKenzie, Margaret L. (5 mentions)
Washington U, 1988 *Certification:* Obstetrics & Gynecology
9500 Euclid Ave, Cleveland, 216-444-6601
18099 Lorain Rd #437, Cleveland, 216-444-6601
26900 Cedar Rd #2220-S, Beachwood, 216-836-3150
16761 Southpark Ctr, Strongsville, 440-878-2500
29800 Bainbridge Rd, Solon, 440-519-6800
6674 Tippecanoe Rd #3, Canfield, 330-702-1950

Pasqualone, Sarah Norment (4 mentions)
Case Western Reserve U, 1992
Certification: Obstetrics & Gynecology
35040 Chardon Rd Bldg 7 #205, Willoughby Hills, 440-918-4630

Peskin, Barry David (5 mentions)
FMS-South Africa, 1984 *Certification:* Obstetrics & Gynecology
26900 Cedar Rd #200-S, Beachwood, 216-839-3100

Peskin, Julian Leon (4 mentions)
FMS-South Africa, 1984 *Certification:* Obstetrics & Gynecology
26900 Cedar Rd #200S, Beachwood, 216-839-3100

Rao, Dinkar V. (3 mentions)
FMS-India, 1971 *Certification:* Obstetrics & Gynecology
6770 Mayfield Rd #223, Cleveland, 440-461-9060

Sutherland, Sharon Ann (3 mentions)
Ohio State U, 1992 *Certification:* Obstetrics & Gynecology
16761 Southpark Ctr, Strongsville, 440-878-2500

Vito, Liese Kasparek (6 mentions)
U of Pennsylvania, 1991 *Certification:* Obstetrics & Gynecology
35040 Chardon Rd #205, Willoughby, 440-918-4630
9485 Mentor Ave #202, Mentor, 440-918-4630

Walters, Mark Douglas (4 mentions)
Ohio State U, 1980 *Certification:* Obstetrics & Gynecology
9500 Euclid Ave #A-81, Cleveland, 216-444-6601

Young, Diane E. (3 mentions)
2550 SOM Center Rd, Willoughby, 440-943-2500

Ophthalmology

Annable, William Lawrence (9 mentions)
U of Pennsylvania, 1971 *Certification:* Ophthalmology
1611 S Green Rd #306-C, Cleveland, 216-382-8022

Bardenstein, David Sander (4 mentions)
U of Michigan, 1979 *Certification:* Ophthalmology
11100 Euclid Ave, Cleveland, 216-844-3601
5850 Landerbrook Dr #306, Cleveland, 440-449-9990

Bruner, William Evans, II (3 mentions)
Case Western Reserve U, 1975 *Certification:* Ophthalmology
1611 S Green Rd #306-C, Cleveland, 216-382-8022

Costin, John August (6 mentions)
Case Western Reserve U, 1975 *Certification:* Ophthalmology
5700 Cooper Foster Park Rd W, Lorain, 440-988-4040

Craven, Paul William (3 mentions)
Ohio State U, 1980 *Certification:* Ophthalmology
4859 Dover Center Rd #7, North Olmsted, 440-734-4090

Eippert, Gregory Alan (3 mentions)
U of Toledo, 1992 *Certification:* Ophthalmology
9485 Mentor Ave #110, Mentor, 440-255-1115

Huang, Suber S. (6 mentions)
Albert Einstein Coll of Med, 1985 *Certification:* Ophthalmology
11100 Euclid Ave, Cleveland, 216-844-7640
5850 Landerbrook Dr #306, Cleveland, 440-449-9990
4121 State Rd 306, Willoughby, 440-946-1119

Kaiser, Peter Kazuo (3 mentions)
Harvard U, 1992 *Certification:* Ophthalmology
9500 Euclid Ave #I-30, Cleveland, 216-444-2030
6761 Southpark Ctr, Strongsville, 440-878-2500

Kosmorsky, Gregory S. (4 mentions)
Philadelphia Coll of Osteopathic Med, 1979
Certification: Neurology, Ophthalmology
9500 Euclid Ave #I-20, Cleveland, 216-444-2030
16761 Southpark Ctr #ST-20, Strongsville, 440-878-2500

Lamping, Kathleen Anne (3 mentions)
U of Cincinnati, 1978 *Certification:* Ophthalmology
1611 S Green Rd #306-A, Cleveland, 216-291-9770

Langston, Roger H. S. (4 mentions)
FMS-Canada, 1965 *Certification:* Ophthalmology
9500 Euclid Ave #I-30, Cleveland, 216-444-2030

Lass, Jonathan Hershel (7 mentions)
Boston U, 1973 *Certification:* Ophthalmology
11100 Euclid Ave, Cleveland, 216-844-3601
5850 Landerbrook Dr #306, Cleveland, 440-449-9990
4212 State Rt 306, Willoughby, 440-946-1119
950 Clague Rd, Westlake, 440-250-2020

Lowder, Careen (4 mentions)
Case Western Reserve U, 1978 *Certification:* Ophthalmology
9500 Euclid Ave #I-30, Cleveland, 216-444-2030

Lynk, Rodney Hamilton (3 mentions)
Howard U, 1971 *Certification:* Ophthalmology
1180 E Broad St, Elyria, 440-365-5965

Marcotty, Andreas (5 mentions)
Wayne State U, 1978 *Certification:* Ophthalmology
9500 Euclid Ave, Cleveland, 216-444-2200
16761 Southpark Ctr, Strongsville, 440-878-2500

Markowitz, Martin Alan (3 mentions)
Rosalind Franklin U, 1965 *Certification:* Ophthalmology
6770 Mayfield Rd, Cleveland, 440-461-4733

Meisler, David Mark (5 mentions)
Ohio State U, 1976 *Certification:* Ophthalmology
9500 Euclid Ave #I-32, Cleveland, 216-444-2030

Perla, Bernard David (3 mentions)
U of Cincinnati, 1990 *Certification:* Ophthalmology
36100 Euclid Ave #450, Willoughby, 440-946-9555

Prokopius, Michael J. (4 mentions)
Northeastern Ohio U, 1991 *Certification:* Ophthalmology
2500 Metrohealth Dr, Cleveland, 216-778-4253

Pugh, David Bentley (4 mentions)
Wayne State U, 1977 *Certification:* Ophthalmology
18599 Lake Shore Blvd #301, Cleveland, 216-383-5900
9000 Mentor Ave #102, Mentor, 440-974-4141

Sears, Jonathan Eliot (3 mentions)
Yale U, 1992 *Certification:* Ophthalmology
9500 Euclid Ave #I-30, Cleveland, 216-444-2030

Shaughnessy, Michael Paul (3 mentions)
U of Toledo, 1997 *Certification:* Ophthalmology
1611 S Green Rd #306-C, Cleveland, 216-382-8022
2500 Metrohealth Dr, Cleveland, 216-382-8022

Shin, Carl Kwaangsik (3 mentions)
Ohio State U, 1978 *Certification:* Ophthalmology
126 S Saint Clair St, Painesville, 440-354-6900

Singerman, Lawrence Jay (3 mentions)
Wayne State U, 1969 *Certification:* Ophthalmology
3401 Enterprise Pkwy #300, Beachwood, 216-831-5700
9485 Mentor Ave #205, Mentor, 440-205-4444
7225 Old Oak Blvd #B303, Cleveland, 440-243-7400

Stern, Robert Martin (5 mentions)
U of Buffalo, 1982 *Certification:* Ophthalmology
29101 Health Campus Dr #340, Westlake, 440-835-6255

Traboulsi, Elias (5 mentions)
FMS-Lebanon, 1982
Certification: Clinical Genetics, Ophthalmology
9500 Euclid Ave #A31, Cleveland, 216-444-2030

Orthopedics

Bell, Gordon R. (5 mentions)
FMS-Canada, 1977 *Certification:* Orthopaedic Surgery
9500 Euclid Ave #A-41, Cleveland, 216-444-8126

Bergfeld, John Albert (3 mentions)
Temple U, 1964 *Certification:* Orthopaedic Surgery
9500 Euclid Ave, Cleveland, 216-445-4836
16761 Southpark Ctr, Strongsville, 440-878-2500

Brems, John Joseph (7 mentions)
Georgetown U, 1978 *Certification:* Orthopaedic Surgery
9500 Euclid Ave, Cleveland, 216-692-7774

Bucchieri, John Stephen (3 mentions)
Columbia U, 1993
Certification: Orthopaedic Surgery, Surgery of the Hand
9500 Mentor Ave #210, Mentor, 440-352-1711
36060 Euclid Ave #104, Willoughby, 440-942-1050

Cooperman, Daniel Roy (3 mentions)
U of Chicago, 1974 *Certification:* Orthopaedic Surgery
11100 Euclid Ave, Cleveland, 216-844-7200

Froimson, Mark Ian (5 mentions)
Tulane U, 1985 *Certification:* Orthopaedic Surgery
9500 Euclid Ave, Cleveland, 216-444-2663
26900 Cedar Rd #305-S, Beachwood, 216-839-3700

Furey, Christopher George (4 mentions)
Case Western Reserve U, 1991 *Certification:* Orthopaedic Surgery
11100 Euclid Ave, Cleveland, 216-844-7200

Getty, Patrick John (3 mentions)
U of Chicago, 1991 *Certification:* Orthopaedic Surgery
11100 Euclid Ave, Cleveland, 216-844-7200

Gilmore, Allison (3 mentions)
Case Western Reserve U, 1994 *Certification:* Orthopaedic Surgery
11100 Euclid Ave, Cleveland, 216-844-7200

Goldberg, Victor (3 mentions)
SUNY-Downstate Med Coll, 1964
Certification: Orthopaedic Surgery
11100 Euclid Ave, Cleveland, 216-844-3044

Goodfellow, Donald Bruce (13 mentions)
Case Western Reserve U, 1977 *Certification:* Orthopaedic Surgery
1611 S Green Rd #27, South Euclid, 216-291-9955
11100 Euclid Ave, Cleveland, 216-291-2495

Goodwin, Ryan Carey (3 mentions)
Case Western Reserve U, 1998 *Certification:* Orthopaedic Surgery
9500 Euclid Ave #A-41, Cleveland, 216-444-4024

Grant, Richard Edward (3 mentions)
Howard U, 1976 *Certification:* Orthopaedic Surgery
11100 Euclid Ave, Cleveland, 216-844-7200

Helper, Stephen Dunn (4 mentions)
Case Western Reserve U, 1983 *Certification:* Orthopaedic Surgery
29001 Cedar Rd #519, Lyndhurst, 440-449-6291

Iannotti, Joseph Patrick (4 mentions)
Northwestern U, 1979 *Certification:* Orthopaedic Surgery
9500 Euclid Ave, Cleveland, 216-445-5151

Kraay, Matthew Joseph (12 mentions)
Wayne State U, 1983 *Certification:* Orthopaedic Surgery
11100 Euclid Ave, Cleveland, 216-844-7200

Krebs, Viktor Erik (4 mentions)
Ohio State U, 1992 *Certification:* Orthopaedic Surgery
9500 Euclid Ave #A-41, Cleveland, 216-444-2606
30033 Clemens Rd, Westlake, 440-899-5600

Kuivila, Thomas E. (4 mentions)
Oregon Health Sciences U, 1983
Certification: Orthopaedic Surgery
9500 Euclid Ave #A-41, Cleveland, 216-444-2741

Lacey, Stephen Henderson (4 mentions)
Ohio State U, 1969
Certification: Orthopaedic Surgery, Surgery of the Hand
1611 S Green Rd #027, South Cleveland, 216-291-5778
11100 Euclid Ave, Cleveland, 216-291-5778

Levy, Matthew Eric (4 mentions)
Case Western Reserve U, 1990 *Certification:* Orthopaedic Surgery
50 Blaine Ave #2300, Bedford, 440-232-8719

Marcus, Randall Evan (3 mentions)
Louisiana State U, 1975 *Certification:* Orthopaedic Surgery
11100 Euclid Ave, Cleveland, 216-844-7200

McCoy, Blane William (6 mentions)
St Louis U, 1977 *Certification:* Orthopaedic Surgery
6115 Powers Blvd #100, Cleveland, 440-842-1570
18660 Bagley Rd #102, Cleveland, 440-243-2100

Moore, Timothy Alan (4 mentions)
Wright State U, 1998 *Certification:* Orthopaedic Surgery
2500 Metrohealth Dr, Cleveland, 216-778-4393

Myers, Frank Jay (12 mentions)
A T Still U, 1981
7551 Fredle Dr, Concord, 440-350-9595
6550 N Ridge Rd #201, Madison, 440-428-1944

Panigutti, Mark Anthony (3 mentions)
Case Western Reserve U, 1993 *Certification:* Orthopaedic Surgery
7255 Old Oak Blvd #C-405, Middleburg Heights, 440-816-5380

Parker, Richard Dean (9 mentions)
Ohio State U, 1981
Certification: Orthopaedic Sports Medicine, Orthopaedic Surgery
5555 Transportation Blvd, Garfield Heights, 216-518-3471
5001 Rockside Rd, Independence, 216-986-4000

Patterson, Brendan M. (3 mentions)
Case Western Reserve U, 1986 *Certification:* Orthopaedic Surgery
2500 Metrohealth Dr, Cleveland, 216-778-3677

Saluan, Paul Maron (3 mentions)
Case Western Reserve U, 1993 *Certification:* Orthopaedic Surgery
16761 Southpark Ctr, Strongsville, 440-878-2500
555 Transportation Blvd, Cleveland, 216-518-3473

Seitz, William Henry, Jr. (3 mentions)
Columbia U, 1979
Certification: Orthopaedic Surgery, Surgery of the Hand
26900 Cedar Rd #305-S, Cleveland, 216-839-3700

Sontich, John Kurt (3 mentions)
U of Cincinnati, 1987 *Certification:* Orthopaedic Surgery
2500 Metrohealth Dr, Cleveland, 216-778-4040
1044 Belmont Ave, Youngstown, 330-480-3990

Thompson, George Harman (5 mentions)
U of Oklahoma, 1970 *Certification:* Orthopaedic Surgery
11100 Euclid Ave, Cleveland, 216-844-7200

Victoroff, Brian Nicholas (3 mentions)
Case Western Reserve U, 1986 *Certification:* Orthopaedic Surgery
11100 Euclid Ave, Cleveland, 216-844-7200

Wilber, John Howard (5 mentions)
Case Western Reserve U, 1978 *Certification:* Orthopaedic Surgery
11100 Euclid Ave, Cleveland, 216-844-7200

Zanotti, Robert Michael (4 mentions)
U of Pennsylvania, 1991 *Certification:* Orthopaedic Surgery
5275 N Abbe Rd, Sheffield Village, 440-284-5650
409 East Ave, Elyria, 440-988-6060
224 W Lorain St #B, Oberlin, 440-988-6950
254 Cleveland Ave, Amherst, 440-988-6237
5001 Transportation Dr, Sheffield Village, 440-329-2800

Otorhinolaryngology

Abelson, Tom Isaac (14 mentions)
Case Western Reserve U, 1976 *Certification:* Otolaryngology
29800 Bainbridge Rd, Solon, 440-519-6950
26900 Cedar Rd #27-N, Beachwood, 216-839-3000

Arnold, James Edward (16 mentions)
U of Texas-San Antonio, 1977 *Certification:* Otolaryngology
11100 Euclid Ave, Cleveland, 216-844-6000

Brown, Bert Matt (8 mentions)
U of Cincinnati, 1983 *Certification:* Otolaryngology
5400 Transportation Blvd, Garfield Heights, 216-662-3373
6770 Mayfield Rd #210, Mayfield Heights, 440-461-0150

Carter, Joseph Benjamin (7 mentions)
U of Minnesota, 1974 *Certification:* Otolaryngology
2500 Metrohealth Dr, Cleveland, 216-778-5791

Gaugler, Michael David (6 mentions)
U of Cincinnati, 1996 *Certification:* Otolaryngology
9500 Mentor Ave #200, Mentor, 440-352-1474
36060 Euclid Ave #201, Willoughby, 440-975-1422

Katz, Robert Lawrence (5 mentions)
Case Western Reserve U, 1963 *Certification:* Otolaryngology
29800 Bainbridge Rd, Solon, 440-519-6950

Krakovitz, Paul Rabin (10 mentions)
Indiana U, 1997 *Certification:* Otolaryngology
9500 Euclid Ave #A-71, Cleveland, 216-444-3061
26900 Cedar Rd #27-N, Beachwood, 216-839-3000

Lavertu, Pierre (13 mentions)
FMS-Canada, 1976 *Certification:* Otolaryngology
11100 Euclid Ave 4th Fl, Cleveland, 216-844-4773

Megerian, Cliff Andrew (13 mentions)
U of Michigan, 1988 *Certification:* Neurotology, Otolaryngology
11100 Euclid Ave, Cleveland, 216-844-6000

Mehle, Mark Emil (5 mentions)
Northeastern Ohio U, 1987 *Certification:* Otolaryngology
25761 Lorain Rd #3, North Olmsted, 440-779-1112
252 E Broad St, Elyria, 440-329-7760
5500 Ridge Rd #226, Cleveland, 440-329-7760

Reisman, Allen Tony (9 mentions)
Rosalind Franklin U, 1993 *Certification:* Otolaryngology
11100 Euclid Ave, Cleveland, 216-844-7190

Vito, Kenneth Joseph (6 mentions)
U of Pennsylvania, 1991 *Certification:* Otolaryngology
9500 Mentor Ave #200, Mentor, 440-352-1474
36060 Euclid Ave #201, Willoughby, 440-975-1422

Wood, Benjamin Gray (5 mentions)
FMS-Canada, 1968 *Certification:* Otolaryngology
9500 Euclid Ave #A-71, Cleveland, 216-444-5700

Pain Medicine

Covington, Edward C., Jr. (7 mentions)
U of Tennessee, 1970 *Certification:* Pain Medicine, Psychiatry
9500 Euclid Ave #C-21, Cleveland, 216-444-5964

Dews, Teresa Elaine (6 mentions)
Case Western Reserve U, 1988
Certification: Anesthesiology, Pain Medicine
6803 Mayfield Rd Bldg 1 #200, Cleveland, 444-312-7146

Hayek, Selim Michel (7 mentions)
FMS-Lebanon, 1991 *Certification:* Anesthesiology, Pain Medicine
11100 Euclid Ave #B-270, Cleveland, 216-844-3771

Rosenberg, Samuel (4 mentions)
FMS-Mexico, 1984
Certification: Anesthesiology, Internal Medicine, Pain Medicine
13207 Ravenna Rd, Chardon, 440-285-6975
5885 Lander Brook Dr, Mayfield Heights, 440-285-6975

Salama, Sherif Aziz (4 mentions)
FMS-Egypt, 1985 *Certification:* Anesthesiology, Pain Medicine
9500 Euclid Ave, Cleveland, 800-223-2273
26900 Cedar Rd, Beachwood, 216-839-3333

Pathology

Abdul-Karim, Fadi William (8 mentions)
FMS-Lebanon, 1979
Certification: Anatomic Pathology, Cytopathology
11100 Euclid Ave, Cleveland, 216-844-1817

Barcelo, Mark Jeffrey (7 mentions)
Case Western Reserve U, 1987 *Certification:* Anatomic Pathology & Clinical Pathology, Cytopathology
89 E High St #9, Painesville, 440-354-4208

Biscotti, Charles Vincent (4 mentions)
Case Western Reserve U, 1983 *Certification:* Anatomic Pathology & Clinical Pathology, Cytopathology
9500 Euclid Ave #L-25, Cleveland, 216-444-5777

Farver, Carol Frances (4 mentions)
Yale U, 1985 *Certification:* Anatomic Pathology
9500 Euclid Ave #L-25, Cleveland, 216-444-5777

Goldblum, John Reid (10 mentions)
U of Michigan, 1989 *Certification:* Anatomic Pathology
9500 Euclid Ave #L-25, Cleveland, 216-444-6781
2490 Blossom Ln, Beachwood, 216-444-6781

Jacobs, Gretta Hazel (3 mentions)
FMS-South Africa, 1972 *Certification:* Anatomic Pathology
11100 Euclid Ave, Cleveland, 216-844-1817

Keep, David James (3 mentions)
Case Western Reserve U, 1992
Certification: Anatomic Pathology & Clinical Pathology
36000 Euclid Ave, Willoughby, 440-953-9600
89 E High St #9, Painesville, 440-354-4208

Nunez, Carlos (3 mentions)
FMS-Spain, 1972
Certification: Anatomic Pathology, Cytopathology
6780 Mayfield Rd, Cleveland, 440-312-4525

Redline, Raymond Wayne (4 mentions)
Boston U, 1979 *Certification:* Anatomic Pathology & Clinical Pathology, Pediatric Pathology
11100 Euclid Ave, Cleveland, 216-844-1817

Setrakian, Sebouh (3 mentions)
FMS-Belgium, 1983 *Certification:* Anatomic Pathology & Clinical Pathology, Cytopathology
18101 Lorain Ave, Cleveland, 216-476-7108

Tomashefski, Joseph F., Jr. (6 mentions)
Case Western Reserve U, 1976
Certification: Anatomic Pathology & Clinical Pathology
2500 Metrohealth Dr, Cleveland, 216-778-5181

Willis, Joseph Edward, Jr. (3 mentions)
FMS-Ireland, 1982 *Certification:* Anatomic Pathology & Clinical Pathology, Cytopathology
11100 Euclid Ave, Cleveland, 216-844-7494

Pediatrics *(see note on page 9)*

Dell, Michael S. (7 mentions)
Harvard U, 1992 *Certification:* Pediatrics
11100 Euclid Ave, Cleveland, 216-844-3971

Francy, Scott Alan (3 mentions)
Ohio State U, 1996 *Certification:* Pediatrics
5700 Cooper Foster Park Rd, Lorain, 440-204-7400

Golonka, Gregory Gerard (3 mentions)
Ohio State U, 1993 *Certification:* Pediatrics
6909 Royalton Rd #304, Brecksville, 440-526-8222
18181 Pearl Rd #A-200, Strongsville, 440-816-4950

Hellerstein, Elizabeth L. (4 mentions)
Case Western Reserve U, 1991 *Certification:* Pediatrics
1611 S Green Rd, Cleveland, 216-382-3800

Imrie, Elizabeth Ruth (8 mentions)
FMS-Ireland, 1964
29800 Bainbridge Rd, Solon, 440-519-6900

Kriwinsky, Jan (3 mentions)
Ohio State U, 1984 *Certification:* Pediatrics
3690 Orange Pl #100, Beachwood, 216-831-7337

Lampe, John Bernard (10 mentions)
Case Western Reserve U, 1977 *Certification:* Pediatrics
29800 Bainbridge Rd, Solon, 440-519-6800

Leslie, James Thomas (4 mentions)
U of Cincinnati, 1987 *Certification:* Pediatrics
1611 S Green Rd, Cleveland, 216-382-3800

Lock, Joseph Charles (4 mentions)
U of Toledo, 1975 *Certification:* Pediatrics
26900 Cedar Rd #27-N, Beachwood, 216-839-3600

Lucker, John Donald (3 mentions)
U of Rochester, 1957 *Certification:* Pediatrics
9485 Mentor Ave #101, Mentor, 440-205-5800
36001 Euclid Ave #B16, Willoughby, 440-942-4844

Macknin, Michael Larry (10 mentions)
Harvard U, 1975 *Certification:* Pediatrics
9500 Euclid Ave #A-120, Cleveland, 216-444-5512
13951 Terr Rd, Cleveland, 216-761-3300

Rome, Ellen Sue (4 mentions)
Case Western Reserve U, 1988
Certification: Adolescent Medicine, Pediatrics
9500 Euclid Ave #A-120, Cleveland, 216-444-3566

Rosenthal, Alan Howard (4 mentions)
Case Western Reserve U, 1983
3690 Orange Pl #100, Beachwood, 216-831-7337

Santos, Susan Kovacs (5 mentions)
U of Cincinnati, 1996 *Certification:* Pediatrics
2500 Metrohealth Dr, Cleveland, 216-778-2222

Senders, Shelly David (7 mentions)
Albert Einstein Coll of Med, 1983 *Certification:* Pediatrics
2054 S Green Rd, South Euclid, 216-291-9210
2226 Warrensville Center Rd, Cleveland, 216-291-9210

Van Keuls, Nancy D. (3 mentions)
Ohio State U, 1988 *Certification:* Pediatrics
30033 Clemens Rd, Westlake, 440-899-5555

Wyllie, Robert (3 mentions)
Indiana U, 1976
Certification: Pediatric Gastroenterology, Pediatrics
9500 Euclid Ave #A-111, Cleveland, 216-444-2237

Plastic Surgery

Goldman, Steven Andrew (6 mentions)
U of Pittsburgh, 1993
Certification: Otolaryngology, Plastic Surgery
3609 Park East Dr #206, Cleveland, 216-514-8899

Guyuron, Bahman (14 mentions)
FMS-Iran, 1971 *Certification:* Plastic Surgery
29017 Cedar Rd, Lyndhurst, 440-461-7999

Michelow, Bryan Joseph (9 mentions)
FMS-South Africa, 1979 *Certification:* Plastic Surgery
3733 Park East Dr #107, Beachwood, 216-595-6800

Pandrangi, Vasu (5 mentions)
FMS-India, 1971 *Certification:* Plastic Surgery
29103 Center Ridge Rd, Westlake, 440-835-6196
6681 Ridge Rd #303, Cleveland, 440-888-5858
7255 Old Oak Blvd #C-212, Cleveland, 440-816-2725

Papay, Francis Anthony (16 mentions)
Northeastern Ohio U, 1984
Certification: Otolaryngology, Plastic Surgery
9500 Euclid Ave #A-60, Cleveland, 216-444-6905

Vanek, Paul Frank, Jr. (5 mentions)
U of Rochester, 1989 *Certification:* Plastic Surgery, Surgery
9485 Mentor Ave #100, Mentor, 440-205-5750

Zins, James Edward (12 mentions)
U of Pennsylvania, 1974 *Certification:* Plastic Surgery
9500 Euclid Ave #A60, Cleveland, 216-444-6900

Psychiatry

Calabrese, Joseph Richard (7 mentions)
Ohio State U, 1980 *Certification:* Psychiatry
10524 Euclid Ave, Cleveland, 216-844-2865

Covington, Edward C., Jr. (3 mentions)
U of Tennessee, 1970 *Certification:* Pain Medicine, Psychiatry
9500 Euclid Ave #C-21, Cleveland, 216-444-5964

Fox, David Laurence (3 mentions)
Case Western Reserve U, 1987 *Certification:* Psychiatry
6115 Powers Blvd #204, Parma, 440-743-2121

Franco, Kathleen Susan N. (7 mentions)
U of Toledo, 1975
Certification: Psychiatry, Psychosomatic Medicine
9500 Euclid Ave #P-57, Cleveland, 216-444-2671

Glazer, John Prescott (6 mentions)
U of California-San Diego, 1972 *Certification:* Child & Adolescent Psychiatry, Pediatrics, Psychiatry
9500 Euclid Ave #P-57, Cleveland, 216-444-5812

Gonsalves-Ebrahim, Lilian V. (8 mentions)
Certification: Psychiatry
9500 Euclid Ave, Cleveland, 216-444-5812

Hertzer, John Leslie (4 mentions)
U of Toledo, 1994
Certification: Child & Adolescent Psychiatry, Psychiatry
10524 Euclid Ave, Cleveland, 216-844-3881

Pozuelo, Leopoldo Jose (4 mentions)
FMS-Spain, 1988
Certification: Psychiatry, Psychosomatic Medicine
9500 Euclid Ave, Cleveland, 216-444-5812

Quinn, Kathleen May (5 mentions)
Harvard U, 1975 *Certification:* Child & Adolescent Psychiatry, Forensic Psychiatry, Psychiatry
9500 Euclid Ave #P-57, Cleveland, 216-444-5812

Ronis, Robert Jeremy (5 mentions)
Case Western Reserve U, 1982
Certification: Addiction Psychiatry, Psychiatry
10524 Euclid Ave, Cleveland, 216-844-3883

Tesar, George E. (5 mentions)
Mayo Med Sch, 1977 *Certification:* Internal Medicine, Psychiatry
9500 Euclid Ave, Cleveland, 216-445-6224

Weiss, Robert Stanley (3 mentions)
U of Cincinnati, 1968 *Certification:* Psychiatry
2500 Metrohealth Dr, Cleveland, 216-778-4631

Yamini Sharif, Bahman (3 mentions)
FMS-Iran, 1975 *Certification:* Psychiatry
8334 Mentor Ave #103, Mentor, 440-266-0770

Pulmonary Disease

Birnkrant, David Jonathan (4 mentions)
Yale U, 1985 *Certification:* Pediatric Pulmonology, Pediatrics
2500 Metrohealth Dr, Cleveland, 216-778-2222

Dinga, Marc James (8 mentions)
U of Minnesota, 1978 *Certification:* Critical Care Medicine, Internal Medicine, Pulmonary Disease
4212 Route 306 #110, Willoughby, 440-953-9135

Gerblich, Adi A. (4 mentions)
FMS-Israel, 1972 *Certification:* Critical Care Medicine, Internal Medicine, Pulmonary Disease
6770 Mayfield Rd #305, Cleveland, 440-442-2554

Hejal, Rana Bashir (4 mentions)
FMS-Lebanon, 1988 *Certification:* Critical Care Medicine, Internal Medicine, Pulmonary Disease
11100 Euclid Ave, Cleveland, 216-844-3201

Kaplan, Gary Brian (9 mentions)
SUNY-Upstate Med U, 1982 *Certification:* Critical Care Medicine, Internal Medicine, Pulmonary Disease
36001 Euclid Ave #C6, Willoughby, 440-946-0053

Kern, Jeffrey Alan (6 mentions)
U of Wisconsin, 1979
Certification: Internal Medicine, Pulmonary Disease
11100 Euclid Ave, Cleveland, 216-844-3201

Kilroy, Terence Edward (4 mentions)
U of Cincinnati, 1979 *Certification:* Critical Care Medicine, Internal Medicine, Pulmonary Disease
14701 Detroit Ave #650, Lakewood, 216-228-1700

Mazzone, Peter J. (4 mentions)
FMS-Canada, 1994 *Certification:* Critical Care Medicine, Internal Medicine, Pulmonary Disease
9500 Euclid Ave #A-90, Cleveland, 216-444-6500

Meden, Glenn Joseph (7 mentions)
Ohio State U, 1979 *Certification:* Critical Care Medicine, Internal Medicine, Pulmonary Disease
6770 Mayfield Rd #305, Cleveland, 440-442-2554

Mehta, Atul Chandrakant (12 mentions)
FMS-India, 1974
Certification: Internal Medicine, Pulmonary Disease
9500 Euclid Ave #A-90, Cleveland, 216-444-2911

Montenegro, Hugo D. (5 mentions)
FMS-Peru, 1966 *Certification:* Critical Care Medicine, Internal Medicine, Pulmonary Disease
11100 Euclid Ave, Cleveland, 216-844-3875

O'Neill, Beverly V. (6 mentions)
Ohio State U, 1987 *Certification:* Critical Care Medicine, Internal Medicine, Pulmonary Disease
99 N Line Cir #235, Euclid, 216-692-7848

Ramadugu, Ashok (5 mentions)
FMS-India, 1982 *Certification:* Critical Care Medicine, Internal Medicine, Pulmonary Disease
661 E River St #B, Elyria, 440-323-0082

Schilz, Robert John (6 mentions)
Michigan State U Coll of Osteopathic Med, 1988
11100 Euclid Ave, Cleveland, 216-844-3201

Sopko, Joseph Anthony (4 mentions)
Tufts U, 1974 *Certification:* Critical Care Medicine, Internal Medicine, Pulmonary Disease
6701 Rockside Rd #100, Independence, 216-328-0418
2322 E 22nd St #202, Cleveland, 216-566-0302

Stoller, James Kevin (7 mentions)
Yale U, 1979 *Certification:* Critical Care Medicine, Internal Medicine, Pulmonary Disease
9500 Euclid Ave #A-90, Cleveland, 216-444-1960

Weiner, David M. (6 mentions)
Tufts U, 1976
Certification: Internal Medicine, Pulmonary Disease
12000 McCracken Rd #201, Garfield Heights, 216-662-5600
6820 Ridge Rd #104, Parma, 440-888-5691

Wiedemann, Herbert P. (8 mentions)
Cornell U, 1977
Certification: Internal Medicine, Pulmonary Disease
9500 Euclid Ave, Cleveland, 216-444-8335

Radiology—Diagnostic

Baker, Mark Early (5 mentions)
Loyola U Chicago, 1978 *Certification:* Diagnostic Radiology
9500 Euclid Ave #HB-6, Cleveland, 216-444-6638

Borkowski, Gregory Peter (3 mentions)
Jefferson Med Coll, 1971 *Certification:* Diagnostic Radiology
9500 Euclid Ave #P-34, Cleveland, 216-444-6625

Dengel, Fredrich Harold (4 mentions)
Loma Linda U, 1978 *Certification:* Diagnostic Radiology
1720 Cooper Foster Park Rd W #B, Lorain, 440-989-4480

Greicius, Francis A. (9 mentions)
Case Western Reserve U, 1972 *Certification:* Diagnostic Radiology
25001 Emery Rd #100, Cleveland, 216-831-1733
36000 Euclid Ave, Willoughby, 440-953-6042
7007 Powers Blvd, Parma, 440-743-2020

Haaga, John Robert (8 mentions)
Ohio State U, 1970 *Certification:* Diagnostic Radiology
11100 Euclid Ave #B-004, Cleveland, 216-844-3858

Konstan, Robert Michael (3 mentions)
Ohio State U, 1987 *Certification:* Diagnostic Radiology
29000 Center Ridge Rd, Westlake, 440-414-6046

Modic, Michael Terrence (5 mentions)
Case Western Reserve U, 1975
Certification: Diagnostic Radiology, Neuroradiology
9500 Euclid Ave #T-13, Cleveland, 216-444-9308

Morrison, Stuart C. (4 mentions)
FMS-United Kingdom, 1970
Certification: Diagnostic Radiology, Pediatric Radiology
9500 Euclid Ave #HB-6, Cleveland, 216-444-6621

Nakamoto, Dean Akira (4 mentions)
Case Western Reserve U, 1987 *Certification:* Diagnostic Radiology
11100 Euclid Ave, Cleveland, 216-844-3182

Reid, Janet Russell (7 mentions)
FMS-Canada, 1987 *Certification:* Diagnostic Radiology
9500 Euclid Ave #HB-6, Cleveland, 216-444-6621

Remer, Erick Marc (4 mentions)
U of Michigan, 1988 *Certification:* Diagnostic Radiology
9500 Euclid Ave #A-21, Cleveland, 216-445-5005

Ruggieri, Paul Michael (3 mentions)
Robert W Johnson Med Sch, 1984
Certification: Diagnostic Radiology, Neuroradiology
9500 Euclid Ave #4-L-102, Cleveland, 216-445-7035

Steiger, David Alan (4 mentions)
Case Western Reserve U, 1981 *Certification:* Diagnostic Radiology
36000 Euclid Ave, Willoughby, 440-953-6043
25001 Emery Rd #100, Cleveland, 216-831-1733
7007 Powers Blvd, Parma, 440-743-2020

Weinert, Dayna May (3 mentions)
Case Western Reserve U, 1982
Certification: Diagnostic Radiology, Pediatric Radiology
11100 Euclid Ave #2600, Cleveland, 216-844-3858

Radiology—Therapeutic

Blair, Henry Frank (5 mentions)
U of Cincinnati, 1986 *Certification:* Radiation Oncology
6780 Mayfield Rd, Mayfield Heights, 440-312-4700
9500 Euclid Ave, Cleveland, 440-312-4700

Einstein, Douglas Bennett (3 mentions)
Albert Einstein Coll of Med, 1996
Certification: Radiation Oncology
11100 Euclid Ave, Cleveland, 216-844-3103

Geisinger, Michael Adam (3 mentions)
Loyola U Chicago, 1977 *Certification:* Diagnostic Radiology, Vascular & Interventional Radiology
9500 Euclid Ave #HB-6, Cleveland, 216-444-6621

Owens, Douglas Blair (4 mentions)
Case Western Reserve U, 1983 *Certification:* Diagnostic Radiology, Vascular & Interventional Radiology
7007 Powers Blvd, Parma, 440-743-2020
25001 Emery Rd #100, Cleveland, 216-831-1733
36000 Euclid Ave, Willoughby, 440-953-6042

Sands, Mark Jason (3 mentions)
Northwestern U, 1990 *Certification:* Diagnostic Radiology, Vascular & Interventional Radiology
9500 Euclid Ave #HB-6, Cleveland, 216-444-2000

Suh, John H. (4 mentions)
U of Miami, 1990 *Certification:* Radiation Oncology
9500 Euclid Ave #T-28, Cleveland, 216-444-5574

Sunshine, Jeffrey L. (3 mentions)
Case Western Reserve U, 1990
Certification: Diagnostic Radiology, Neuroradiology
11100 Euclid Ave, Cleveland, 216-844-3112

Rehabilitation

Chae, John (4 mentions)
New Jersey Med Sch, 1990
Certification: Physical Medicine & Rehabilitation
2500 Metrohealth Dr, Cleveland, 216-778-4414

Frost, Frederick Sheehan (8 mentions)
Northwestern U, 1983 *Certification:* Physical Medicine & Rehabilitation, Spinal Cord Injury Medicine
2500 Metrohealth Dr, Cleveland, 216-778-4414
9500 Euclid Ave #C-21, Cleveland, 216-444-2225
30033 Clemens Rd, Westlake, 440-899-5641

Sahgal, Vinod (3 mentions)
FMS-India, 1960
Certification: Physical Medicine & Rehabilitation
11100 Euclid Ave #LKS-5007, Cleveland, 216-983-5263

Venesy, Deborah Ann (3 mentions)
Wright State U, 1986
Certification: Physical Medicine & Rehabilitation
29800 Bainbridge Rd, Solon, 440-519-6800
9500 Euclid Ave #C-21, Cleveland, 216-444-2225

Rheumatology

Askari, Ali (11 mentions)
Case Western Reserve U, 1997
Certification: Internal Medicine, Rheumatology
3909 Orange Pl, Orange Village, 216-844-6001
11100 Euclid Ave, Cleveland, 216-844-6001

Deal, Chad Logan (7 mentions)
U of Arkansas, 1977
Certification: Internal Medicine, Rheumatology
9500 Euclid Ave #A-50, Cleveland, 216-444-6575

Foley, Terrence George (6 mentions)
Case Western Reserve U, 1986
Certification: Internal Medicine, Rheumatology
36100 Euclid Ave #170, Willoughby, 440-953-8700

Goulder Abelson, Abby M. (11 mentions)
Case Western Reserve U, 1979
Certification: Internal Medicine, Rheumatology
9500 Euclid Ave #A-50, Cleveland, 216-444-2200

Granieri, Janice Angela (4 mentions)
Case Western Reserve U, 1987
Certification: Internal Medicine, Rheumatology
2550 SOM Center Rd, Willoughby, 440-943-2500

Hashkes, Philip Joseph (4 mentions)
FMS-Israel, 1988 *Certification:* Pediatrics
9500 Euclid Ave #A-50, Cleveland, 216-444-5632

Hoffman, Gary Stuart (8 mentions)
Virginia Commonwealth U, 1971
Certification: Internal Medicine, Rheumatology
9500 Euclid Ave #A-50, Cleveland, 216-445-6996

Mandell, Brian Franklin (11 mentions)
New York U, 1980
Certification: Internal Medicine, Rheumatology
9500 Euclid Ave #A-50, Cleveland, 216-445-6580

Moskowitz, Roland Wallace (5 mentions)
Temple U, 1953 *Certification:* Internal Medicine, Rheumatology
11100 Euclid Ave, Cleveland, 216-591-1443

Sexton-Cicero, Donna Jean (4 mentions)
Ohio State U, 1987
Certification: Internal Medicine, Rheumatology
960 Clague Rd #3201, Westlake, 440-250-2070

Spalding, Steven James (4 mentions)
Wright State U, 2001 *Certification:* Pediatrics
9500 Euclid Ave, Cleveland, 216-445-1099

Stein, Richard Lawrence (10 mentions)
Case Western Reserve U, 1982
Certification: Internal Medicine, Rheumatology
33001 Solon Rd #202, Solon, 440-349-1100

Thoracic Surgery

Botham, Mark Judson (5 mentions)
Cornell U, 1979 *Certification:* Thoracic Surgery
5770 Mayfild Rd, Mayfield Heights, 216-445-6860

Linden, Philip Aaron (5 mentions)
U of Pennsylvania, 1992 *Certification:* Surgery, Thoracic Surgery
11100 Euclid Ave, Cleveland, 216-844-7142

Mason, David Park (8 mentions)
Columbia U, 1994 *Certification:* Surgery, Thoracic Surgery
9500 Euclid Ave #F-24, Cleveland, 216-445-6860

Murthy, Sudish (7 mentions)
Columbia U, 1992 *Certification:* Surgery, Thoracic Surgery
9500 Euclid Ave #F-24, Cleveland, 216-444-5640

Rice, Thomas William (24 mentions)
FMS-Canada, 1978 *Certification:* Surgery, Thoracic Surgery
9500 Euclid Ave #F-24, Cleveland, 216-444-1921

Robke, Jason Michael (6 mentions)
U of Toledo, 1997 *Certification:* Surgery, Thoracic Surgery
11100 Euclid Ave, Cleveland, 216-844-5770

Urology

Barkoukis, Michael Thomas (5 mentions)
Case Western Reserve U, 1977 *Certification:* Urology
6900 Pearl Rd #200, Middleburg Heights, 440-845-0900

Bodner, Donald Roger (6 mentions)
Indiana U, 1979 *Certification:* Urology
11100 Euclid Ave, Cleveland, 216-844-5661
1611 S Green Rd #106, Cleveland, 216-844-7667

Elder, Jack S. (4 mentions)
U of Oklahoma, 1976 *Certification:* Urology
11100 Euclid Ave, Cleveland, 216-844-8455
2500 Metrohealth Dr, Cleveland, 216-844-1016

Gill, Inderbir S. (10 mentions)
FMS-India, 1979 *Certification:* Urology
9500 Euclid Ave #A-100, Cleveland, 216-444-5600

Goldfarb, David (5 mentions)
Temple U, 1985 *Certification:* Urology
9500 Euclid Ave #A-100, Cleveland, 216-444-5600

Jevnikar, Frank William (7 mentions)
U of Toledo, 1997 *Certification:* Urology
9500 Mentor Ave #370, Mentor, 440-946-4555

Jones, J. Stephen (6 mentions)
U of Arkansas, 1996 *Certification:* Urology
9500 Euclid Ave, Cleveland, 216-839-3666

Klein, Eric (14 mentions)
U of Pittsburgh, 1981 *Certification:* Urology
9500 Euclid Ave #A-100, Cleveland, 216-444-5600

Lamb, Steven Alan (7 mentions)
U of Illinois, 1979 *Certification:* Urology
18099 Lorain Ave #141, Cleveland, 216-941-0333
29101 Health Campus Dr #310, Westlake, 440-892-6600

Levine, Frederic Jay (7 mentions)
Case Western Reserve U, 1983 *Certification:* Urology
6803 Mayfield Rd #418, Mayfield Heights, 440-753-0018
36001 Euclid Ave #C-14, Willoughby, 440-753-0018

Ponsky, Lee Evan (13 mentions)
Case Western Reserve U, 1997 *Certification:* Urology
11100 Euclid Ave, Cleveland, 216-844-3009
3909 Orange Rd #4300, Orange Village, 216-844-7761

Reese, Christopher Simon (6 mentions)
U of Toledo, 1989 *Certification:* Urology
18099 Lorain Ave #141, Cleveland, 216-941-0333
29101 Health Campus Dr #310, Westlake, 440-892-6600

Reigle, Melissa D. (4 mentions)
Case Western Reserve U, 1992 *Certification:* Urology
6803 Mayfield Rd #418, Mayfield Heights, 440-753-0018
36001 Euclid Ave #C-14, Willoughby, 440-753-0018

Ross, Jonathan Harry (7 mentions)
U of Michigan, 1986 *Certification:* Pediatric Urology, Urology
9500 Euclid Ave #A-100, Cleveland, 216-444-5437
125 E Broad St #208-A, Elyria, 440-329-7315

Seftel, Allen Donald (5 mentions)
SUNY-Downstate Med Coll, 1984 *Certification:* Urology
1611 S Green Rd, Cleveland, 216-844-3009
11100 Euclid Ave, Cleveland, 216-844-3009
2500 Bolwell, Cleveland, 216-844-3009

Siminovitch, Jeffrey M. P. (5 mentions)
FMS-Canada, 1974 *Certification:* Urology
9500 Mentor Ave #370, Mentor, 440-946-4555

Spirnak, J. Patrick (6 mentions)
Emory U, 1977 *Certification:* Urology
5319 Hoag Dr, Elyria, 440-930-6060
3600 Kolbe Rd #220, Lorain, 440-282-5522

Vasavada, Sandip Prasan (4 mentions)
Northeastern Ohio U, 1991 *Certification:* Urology
9500 Euclid Ave, Cleveland, 216-444-5600

Vascular Surgery

Alexander, J. Jeffrey (8 mentions)
Certification: Surgery, Vascular Surgery
2500 Metrohealth Dr, Cleveland, 216-778-4811

Anton, George E. (6 mentions)
Howard U, 1978 *Certification:* Surgery, Vascular Surgery
9500 Euclid Ave, Cleveland, 440-461-1150

Baele, Henry R. (8 mentions)
Indiana U, 1980 *Certification:* Vascular Surgery
11100 Euclid Ave, Cleveland, 216-844-3013

Clair, Daniel Gerard (10 mentions)
U of Virginia, 1986 *Certification:* Surgery, Vascular Surgery
9500 Euclid Ave #S-40, Cleveland, 216-444-4508

Krajewski, Leonard Paul (6 mentions)
Hahnemann U, 1973 *Certification:* Surgery, Vascular Surgery
9500 Euclid Ave #S-40, Cleveland, 216-444-4508

Rizzo, Anthony (7 mentions)
Temple U, 1990 *Certification:* Surgery, Vascular Surgery
6801 Mayfield Rd #146, Cleveland, 440-461-1150

Rollins, David L. (7 mentions)
Rosalind Franklin U, 1976
Certification: Surgery, Vascular Surgery
36060 Euclid Ave #107, Willoughby, 440-269-8346

Wong, Virginia Louise (7 mentions)
SUNY-Downstate Med Coll, 1995
Certification: Surgery, Vascular Surgery
11100 Euclid Ave, Cleveland, 216-844-3013

Columbus Area
Including Franklin County

Allergy/Immunology

Friedman, Roger Alan (28 mentions)
Ohio State U, 1977
Certification: Allergy & Immunology, Pediatrics
5877 Cleveland Ave, Columbus, 614-891-0550
6350 Frantz Rd #C, Dublin, 614-766-4903

Rupp, Germain H. (10 mentions)
St Louis U, 1968 *Certification:* Allergy & Immunology, Pediatrics
5877 Cleveland Ave, Columbus, 614-891-0550
6350 Frantz Rd #C, Dublin, 614-766-4903

Anesthesiology

Berliner, Scott Robert (3 mentions)
Ohio State U, 1990 *Certification:* Anesthesiology, Pain Medicine
6001 E Broad St, Columbus, 614-552-0061

Blair, John Goldsberry (3 mentions)
Ohio State U, 1992 *Certification:* Anesthesiology
111 S Grant Ave, Columbus, 614-566-9983

Caldwell, David McKean (3 mentions)
Ohio State U, 1997 *Certification:* Anesthesiology
3535 Olentangy River Rd, Columbus, 614-457-2306

Donovan, Joseph William (6 mentions)
U of Rochester, 1986
Certification: Allergy & Immunology, Pediatrics
5151 Reed Rd #105-B, Columbus, 614-566-4919

Dowling, Todd Michael (3 mentions)
Ohio State U, 1991 *Certification:* Anesthesiology
262 Neil Ave #500, Columbus, 614-827-6600

Rauck, Charles Riley (3 mentions)
Ohio State U, 1984 *Certification:* Anesthesiology, Pain Medicine
793 W State St, Columbus, 614-234-5000

Sawyer, David Matthew (3 mentions)
Virginia Commonwealth U, 1986 *Certification:* Anesthesiology
793 W State St, Columbus, 614-552-0061

Smyke, Norman Alan, Jr. (5 mentions)
Ohio State U, 1989 *Certification:* Anesthesiology
111 S Grant Ave, Columbus, 614-566-9983

Tingley, David Alan (4 mentions)
U of Texas-Dallas, 1986 *Certification:* Anesthesiology
700 Childrens Dr, Columbus, 614-722-4200

Yunker, Douglas Eugene (3 mentions)
Ohio State U, 1982 *Certification:* Anesthesiology
3535 Olentangy River Rd, Columbus, 614-457-2306

Cardiac Surgery

Blossom, Geoffrey Barton (15 mentions)
U of Toledo, 1988 *Certification:* Surgery, Thoracic Surgery
3555 Olentangy River Rd #2070, Columbus, 614-261-8377

Duff, Steven Barron (25 mentions)
U of Cincinnati, 1981 *Certification:* Thoracic Surgery
3555 Olentangy River Rd #2070, Columbus, 614-261-8377

Esterline, William J. (12 mentions)
Certification: Thoracic Surgery
85 McNaughten Rd #110, Columbus, 614-856-9100

Fanning, William James, IV (18 mentions)
Ohio State U, 1979
Certification: Internal Medicine, Thoracic Surgery
85 McNaughten Rd #110, Columbus, 614-856-9100

Watson, Daniel R. (13 mentions)
Northeastern Ohio U, 1983
Certification: Surgery, Thoracic Surgery
3555 Olentangy River Rd #2070, Columbus, 614-261-8377

Cardiology

Chapekis, Anthony T. (6 mentions)
U of Michigan, 1983 *Certification:* Cardiovascular Disease,
   Internal Medicine, Interventional Cardiology
3705 Olentangy River Rd #100, Columbus, 614-262-6772

Costa, John Joseph (5 mentions)
Ohio State U, 1994 *Certification:* Cardiovascular Disease
3525 Olentangy River Rd #6300, Columbus, 614-459-7676

Davakis, Nicholas James (4 mentions)
Ohio State U, 1981
Certification: Cardiovascular Disease, Internal Medicine
765 N Hamilton Rd #120, Gahanna, 614-337-9800
6905 Hospital Dr #240, Dublin, 614-324-9090

Fisher, John Allen (7 mentions)
Ohio State U, 1981
Certification: Cardiovascular Disease, Internal Medicine
745 W State St #750, Columbus, 614-224-2281
85 McNaughten Rd #300, Columbus, 614-864-6644

Fleishman, Bruce Lawrence (13 mentions)
Rosalind Franklin U, 1980
Certification: Cardiovascular Disease, Internal Medicine
6905 Hospital Dr #240, Dublin, 614-324-9090
765 N Hamilton Rd #120, Gahanna, 614-337-9800

Good, Arnold Paul (4 mentions)
New York Med Coll, 1985
Certification: Cardiovascular Disease, Internal Medicine
765 N Hamilton Rd #120, Gahanna, 614-337-9800
6905 Hospital Dr #240, Dublin, 614-324-9090

Hackett, Francis Kevin (8 mentions)
Ohio State U, 1986 *Certification:* Cardiovascular Disease,
   Clinical Cardiac Electrophysiology, Internal Medicine
745 W State St #750, Columbus, 614-224-2281
85 McNaughten Rd #300, Columbus, 614-224-2281

Millhon, Judson Severn (8 mentions)
Ohio State U, 1990
Certification: Cardiovascular Disease, Interventional Cardiology
500 Thomas Ln #3A, Columbus, 614-459-7676
3525 Olentangy River Rd #6300, Columbus, 614-459-7676

Murnane, Michael Robert (10 mentions)
Ohio State U, 1981 *Certification:* Cardiovascular Disease,
   Internal Medicine, Interventional Cardiology
745 W State St #750, Columbus, 614-224-2281
85 McNaughten Rd #300, Columbus, 614-224-2281

Noble, Charles W., II (4 mentions)
U of Toledo, 1985
Certification: Cardiovascular Disease, Internal Medicine
423 E Town St, Columbus, 614-464-0884

Teske, Douglas William (4 mentions)
U of Iowa, 1971 *Certification:* Pediatric Cardiology, Pediatrics
700 Childrens Dr, Columbus, 614-722-2000

Timko, Timothy Lee (8 mentions)
Northeastern Ohio U, 1986 *Certification:* Cardiovascular
   Disease, Internal Medicine, Interventional Cardiology
3525 Olentangy River Rd #6300, Columbus, 614-459-7676

Yakubov, Steven Joseph (11 mentions)
Northeastern Ohio U, 1985 *Certification:* Cardiovascular
   Disease, Internal Medicine, Interventional Cardiology
3705 Olentangy River Rd #100, Columbus, 614-262-6772

Dermatology

Bechtel, Mark Allen (35 mentions)
Indiana U, 1977 *Certification:* Dermatology
5965 E Broad St #290, Columbus, 614-864-8302
4068 Gantz Rd, Grove City, 614-864-8302

Londeree, Gwyn Renee (6 mentions)
Ohio State U, 1994 *Certification:* Dermatology
4900 Gettysburg Rd, Columbus, 614-442-0100

Mosser, Joy Lynn (10 mentions)
Northeastern Ohio U, 1993
Certification: Dermatology, Pediatric Dermatology
660 Cooper Rd #400, Westerville, 614-898-7546

Rau, Robert Carson (20 mentions)
U of Cincinnati, 1967 *Certification:* Dermatology
3545 Olentangy River Rd #124, Columbus, 614-268-2748

Scarborough, Dwight Allen (5 mentions)
Loma Linda U, 1979 *Certification:* Dermatology
650 Shawan Falls Dr, Dublin, 614-764-1711

Schuen, Wendy Diane (5 mentions)
Ohio State U, 1988 *Certification:* Dermatology
955 Proprietors Rd, Worthington, 614-847-0039

Siegle, Ronald Jay (10 mentions)
SUNY-Upstate Med U, 1979 *Certification:* Dermatology
428 County Line Rd, Westerville, 614-847-4100

Zyniewicz, Kelley Joann (6 mentions)
Michigan State U, 1985 *Certification:* Dermatology
660 Cooper Rd #400, Westerville, 614-898-7546

Emergency Medicine

Bell, Peter Alan (3 mentions)
U of New England Coll of Osteopathic Med, 1984
50 Old Village Rd #210, Columbus, 614-566-8983
51 W Broad St, Columbus, 614-566-4357

Bullock, Thomas Robert (4 mentions)
George Washington U, 1979 *Certification:* Emergency Medicine
6001 E Broad St, Columbus, 614-234-6000
793 W State St, Columbus, 614-234-5000

Decker, Gregory Harry (5 mentions)
Ohio State U, 1982 *Certification:* Emergency Medicine
3535 Olentangy River Rd, Columbus, 614-566-5321

Drstvensek, John Andrew (8 mentions)
Ohio State U, 1976 *Certification:* Emergency Medicine
111 S Grant Ave, Columbus, 614-566-9270

Eskin, Steven James (4 mentions)
Albany Med Coll, 1985 *Certification:* Emergency Medicine
3535 Olentangy River Rd, Columbus, 614-566-5000

Gabriel, Paul W. (8 mentions)
Emory U, 1980 *Certification:* Emergency Medicine
111 S Grant Ave, Columbus, 614-566-9270

Gora, Alan Gerard (6 mentions)
Loyola U Chicago, 1992 *Certification:* Emergency Medicine
750 Mount Carmel Mall #300, Columbus, 614-224-6420

Hiestand, Brian Charles (3 mentions)
Ohio State U, 1998 *Certification:* Emergency Medicine
1492 E Broad St, Columbus, 614-293-8305
376 W 10th Ave, Columbus, 614-293-8305

Jones, Bruce G. (5 mentions)
Philadelphia Coll of Osteopathic Med, 1994
5100 W Broad St, Columbus, 614-544-1810

Lutmerding, Medard R., Jr. (7 mentions)
Ohio State U, 1975 *Certification:* Emergency Medicine
750 Mount Carmel Mall #300, Columbus, 614-224-6420

Mihalov, Leslie Kay (8 mentions)
U of Toledo, 1984
Certification: Pediatric Emergency Medicine, Pediatrics
700 Childrens Dr, Columbus, 614-722-4384

Moseley, Mark Glenn (4 mentions)
Ohio State U, 2002 *Certification:* Emergency Medicine
410 W 10th Ave, Columbus, 614-293-8305

Smith, David Michael (3 mentions)
Ohio State U, 1974 *Certification:* Emergency Medicine
1496 Old Henderson Rd, Columbus, 614-326-7742
6200 Cleveland Ave, Columbus, 614-566-0590
765 N Hamilton Rd, Columbus, 614-566-0520

Yamarick, Warren Kyle (13 mentions)
Ohio State U, 1984 *Certification:* Emergency Medicine
3535 Olentangy River Rd, Columbus, 614-566-5000

Endocrinology

Anderson, Samuel Ray (14 mentions)
U of Cincinnati, 1997 *Certification:* Endocrinology,
Diabetes, and Metabolism, Internal Medicine
500 Thomas Ln #3G, Columbus, 614-457-7732

Blackman, John David (11 mentions)
Robert W Johnson Med Sch, 1984
Certification: Endocrinology and Metabolism, Internal Medicine
500 E Main St #100, Columbus, 614-566-9922

Bucci, Angela C. (7 mentions)
Des Moines U, 1995
4825 Knightsbridge Blvd #B, Columbus, 614-451-9612

Jackson, Rebecca Dorothy (8 mentions)
Ohio State U, 1978 *Certification:* Internal Medicine
1581 Dodd Dr, Columbus, 614-292-3800
456 W 10th Ave, Columbus, 614-292-3800

Katz, Charles Meyer (11 mentions)
U of Pittsburgh, 1968
Certification: Endocrinology and Metabolism, Internal Medicine
941 Chatham Ln #206, Columbus, 614-457-7746

Larrimer, John Navin (10 mentions)
Ohio State U, 1972
Certification: Endocrinology and Metabolism, Internal Medicine
6100 E Main St #102, Columbus, 614-367-0675

Reddy, Pallavy Gopal (6 mentions)
U of Miami, 1998 *Certification:* Endocrinology, Diabetes,
and Metabolism, Internal Medicine
7281 Sawmill Rd, Dublin, 614-764-0707

Schuster, Dara P. (8 mentions)
Certification: Endocrinology, Diabetes, and Metabolism,
Internal Medicine
456 W 10th Ave, Columbus, 614-293-6989

Tallo, Diane (21 mentions)
Ohio State U, 1974
Certification: Endocrinology and Metabolism, Internal Medicine
500 Thomas Ln #3G, Columbus, 614-457-7732

Zipf, William Byron (8 mentions)
Ohio State U, 1972
Certification: Pediatric Endocrinology, Pediatrics
55 Dillmont Dr #100, Columbus, 614-839-3040

Family Practice *(see note on page 9)*

Barr, James J. (7 mentions)
FMS-Guatemala, 1980 *Certification:* Family Medicine
250 W Bridge St #101, Dublin, 614-761-2244

Blosser, Thomas Laurence (4 mentions)
Ohio State U, 1981 *Certification:* Family Medicine
3311 Tremont Rd #101, Columbus, 614-457-4806

Bope, Edward Tharp (10 mentions)
Ohio State U, 1976 *Certification:* Adolescent Medicine,
Family Medicine, Hospice and Palliative Medicine
697 Thomas Ln, Columbus, 614-566-5414

Burke, William James (3 mentions)
Ohio U Coll of Osteopathic Med, 1988
2030 Stringtown Rd, Grove City, 614-544-0101

Dusseau, Paul David (12 mentions)
Ohio State U, 1974
3311 Tremont Rd #101, Columbus, 614-457-4806

Fahey, Patrick Joseph (4 mentions)
U of Illinois, 1975 *Certification:* Family Medicine
2231 N High St #103, Columbus, 614-293-2700

Hollingsworth, Patricia F. (3 mentions)
U of Iowa, 1985 *Certification:* Family Medicine
3900 E Livingston Ave, Columbus, 614-237-0904

Long, Ricky Lee (4 mentions)
Ohio State U, 1973
3311 Tremont Rd #101, Columbus, 614-457-4806

Skully, Robert James (3 mentions)
Ohio State U, 1979
Certification: Family Medicine, Geriatric Medicine
111 S Grant Ave, Columbus, 614-566-9108

Williams, Glenn Robert, Jr. (3 mentions)
Ohio State U, 1998 *Certification:* Family Medicine
874 Proprietors Rd, Worthington, 614-885-9405

Winzenread, John Warren (6 mentions)
Ohio State U, 1982 *Certification:* Family Medicine
3311 Tremont Rd #101, Columbus, 614-457-4806

Zaino, Robert Paul (5 mentions)
Ohio State U, 1987 *Certification:* Family Medicine
765 N Hamilton Rd #255, Gahanna, 614-337-9100

Gastroenterology

Edgin, Richard Alan (10 mentions)
Texas Tech U, 1976
Certification: Gastroenterology, Internal Medicine
3820 Olentangy River Rd, Columbus, 614-864-1087
85 McNaughten Rd #320, Columbus, 614-864-1087
777 W State St #402, Columbus, 614-864-1087
6620 Perimeter Dr #200, Dublin, 614-864-1087

Gibbons, Gregory David (11 mentions)
West Virginia U, 1979
Certification: Gastroenterology, Internal Medicine
3820 Olentangy River Rd, Columbus, 614-457-1213
777 W State St #402, Columbus, 614-221-8355
85 McNaughten Rd, Columbus, 614-457-1213
6670 Perimeter Dr, Dublin, 614-457-1213

Levin, Douglas Michael (9 mentions)
New York U, 1969
Certification: Gastroenterology, Internal Medicine
410 W 10th Ave 2nd Fl, Columbus, 614-293-6255

Miller, Scott Michael (9 mentions)
Ohio State U, 1985
Certification: Gastroenterology, Internal Medicine
85 McNaughten Rd #320, Columbus, 614-221-8355
777 W State St #400, Columbus, 614-221-8355

Pfeil, Sheryl Ann (6 mentions)
Ohio State U, 1984
Certification: Gastroenterology, Internal Medicine
395 W 12th Ave #292, Columbus, 614-293-4262
3900 Stoneridge Ln, Dublin, 614-798-7905

Ransbottom, Thomas Craig (12 mentions)
Ohio State U, 1979
Certification: Gastroenterology, Internal Medicine
3820 Olentangy River Rd, Columbus, 614-457-1213
777 W State St #402, Columbus, 614-221-8355
85 McNaughten Rd, Columbus, 614-457-1213
6670 Perimeter Dr, Dublin, 614-457-1213

Salt, William Bradley, II (15 mentions)
Ohio State U, 1972
Certification: Gastroenterology, Internal Medicine
777 W State St #400, Columbus, 614-221-8355
5969 E Broad St #307, Columbus, 614-864-1087
3820 Olentangy River Rd, Columbus, 614-457-1213

Taxier, Michael (9 mentions)
U of Buffalo, 1975
Certification: Gastroenterology, Internal Medicine
3820 Olentangy River Rd, Columbus, 614-457-1213
777 W State St #402, Columbus, 614-221-8355
6670 Perimeter Dr, Dublin, 614-457-1213
85 McNaughten Rd, Columbus, 614-457-1213

General Surgery

Arnold, Mark William (4 mentions)
New York U, 1983 *Certification:* Colon & Rectal Surgery, Surgery
4830 Knightsbridge Blvd #J, Columbus, 614-293-8562
300 W 10th Ave, Columbus, 614-293-8133

Campbell, Albert James (5 mentions)
U of Missouri, 1983 *Certification:* Surgery
285 E State St #620, Columbus, 614-469-7621

Chambers, Lowell W. (5 mentions)
U of Kentucky, 1996 *Certification:* Surgery
777 W State St #501, Columbus, 614-222-8000

Ellison, Edwin C. (9 mentions)
Med Coll of Wisconsin, 1976 *Certification:* Surgery
300 W 10th Ave, Columbus, 614-293-9722

Fisher, Stephen T. (5 mentions)
Philadelphia Coll of Osteopathic Med, 1985
5539 Hilliard Rome Office Park, Hilliard, 614-771-2444

Innes, Jeffrey Thomas (15 mentions)
U of California-Davis, 1981 *Certification:* Surgery
285 E State St #620, Columbus, 614-469-7621

Keith, Jason Christopher (8 mentions)
Ohio State U, 1995 *Certification:* Surgery
777 W State St #501, Columbus, 614-222-8000

Kennedy, George Mitchell (5 mentions)
West Virginia U, 1988 *Certification:* Surgery
3545 Olentangy River Rd #226, Columbus, 614-261-1900

King, Denis Renz (6 mentions)
Hahnemann U, 1969 *Certification:* Pediatric Surgery, Surgery
555 S 18th St #6-C, Columbus, 614-722-3900

Leff, John David (7 mentions)
Ohio State U, 1996 *Certification:* Surgery
3545 Olentangy River Rd #226, Columbus, 614-261-1900

Lilly, Larry Joe (5 mentions)
Ohio State U, 1975 *Certification:* Surgery
3555 Olentangy River Rd #2020, Columbus, 614-262-9922

Matyas, John Andrew (12 mentions)
Ohio State U, 1975 *Certification:* Surgery
3555 Olentangy River Rd #2000, Columbus, 614-263-1865

Melvin, W. Scott (7 mentions)
U of Toledo, 1987 *Certification:* Surgery
4830 Knightsbridge Blvd #J, Columbus, 614-293-3230

Nichols, Keith E. (4 mentions)
Northeastern Ohio U, 1984 *Certification:* Surgery
3555 Olentangy River Rd #2000, Columbus, 614-263-1865

Sivard, James Gordon, Jr. (7 mentions)
Ohio State U, 1978 *Certification:* Surgery
3555 Olentangy River Rd #2000, Columbus, 614-263-1865

Taylor, Philip H., Jr. (10 mentions)
Certification: Surgery
3545 Olentangy River Rd #525, Columbus, 614-261-1900

Toscano, Robert Louis (10 mentions)
Indiana U, 1991 *Certification:* Surgery
3545 Olentangy River Rd #226, Columbus, 614-261-1900

Turner, Jeffrey Layne (5 mentions)
Wright State U, 1992 *Certification:* Surgery
777 W State St #501, Columbus, 614-222-8000

Geriatrics

Lamb, James F. (5 mentions)
Certification: Internal Medicine
2050 Kimmy Rd #2400, Columbus, 614-293-8054

Schuda, Marian (5 mentions)
Ohio State U, 1979
Certification: Geriatric Medicine, Internal Medicine
3724 Olentangy River Rd #A, Columbus, 614-566-4660

Hematology/Oncology

George, Christopher S. (15 mentions)
U of Cincinnati, 1991 *Certification:* Hematology, Hospice and Palliative Medicine, Internal Medicine, Medical Oncology
810 Jasonway Ave #A, Columbus, 614-442-3130

Grainger, Andrew Vincent (4 mentions)
Creighton U, 1997
Certification: Hematology, Internal Medicine, Medical Oncology
810 Jasonway Ave #A, Columbus, 614-442-3130

Hofmeister, Joseph Konrad (4 mentions)
U of Pittsburgh, 1994
Certification: Hematology, Internal Medicine, Medical Oncology
810 Jasonway Ave #A, Columbus, 614-442-3130

Kourlas, Peter James (12 mentions)
Ohio State U, 1995 *Certification:* Hematology, Medical Oncology
810 Jasonway Ave #A, Columbus, 614-442-3130

Moore, Timothy David (9 mentions)
U of Pittsburgh, 1981
Certification: Hematology, Internal Medicine, Medical Oncology
3100 Plaza Properties Blvd, Columbus, 614-388-6000

Porcu, Pierluigi (4 mentions)
FMS-Italy, 1987 *Certification:* Hematology, Medical Oncology
320 W 10th Ave, Columbus, 614-293-9424

Segal, Mark Louis (13 mentions)
Ohio State U, 1976
Certification: Hematology, Internal Medicine, Medical Oncology
3100 Plaza Properties Blvd, Columbus, 614-464-9292

Sweeney, Thomas J. (9 mentions)
Certification: Internal Medicine, Medical Oncology
810 Jasonway Ave #A, Columbus, 614-442-3130

Zangmeister, Jeffrey (11 mentions)
Ohio State U, 1981
Certification: Internal Medicine, Medical Oncology
3100 Plaza Properties Blvd, Columbus, 614-464-9292

Infectious Disease

Baird, Ian McNicoll (34 mentions)
FMS-United Kingdom, 1969
Certification: Infectious Disease, Internal Medicine
3545 Olentangy River Rd #430, Columbus, 614-268-9487
3555 Olentangy River Rd #3020, Columbus, 614-268-9487

Gianakopoulos, George J. (12 mentions)
Ohio State U, 1985
Certification: Infectious Disease, Internal Medicine
3545 Olentangy River Rd #430, Columbus, 614-268-9487
3555 Olentangy River Rd #3020, Columbus, 614-268-9487

Kusumi, Rodney Kent (29 mentions)
U of Cincinnati, 1975
Certification: Infectious Disease, Internal Medicine
685 Bryden Rd, Columbus, 614-461-3214

Para, Michael Francis (16 mentions)
Ohio State U, 1974
Certification: Infectious Disease, Internal Medicine
456 W 10th Ave #4801, Columbus, 614-293-5666

Parsons, James Norman (16 mentions)
Ohio State U, 1974
Certification: Infectious Disease, Internal Medicine
2970 W Broad St, Columbus, 614-279-0808

Smith, James Hansen (9 mentions)
Indiana U, 1990 *Certification:* Infectious Disease
685 Bryden Rd, Columbus, 614-461-3214

Infertility

Schmidt, Grant (10 mentions)
U of Missouri, 1976 *Certification:* Obstetrics & Gynecology, Reproductive Endocrinology/Infertility
4830 Knightsbridge Blvd #E, Columbus, 614-451-2280

Williams, Steven Ross (14 mentions)
Ohio State U, 1981 *Certification:* Obstetrics & Gynecology, Reproductive Endocrinology/Infertility
4830 Knightsbridge Blvd #E, Columbus, 614-451-2280

Internal Medicine *(see note on page 9)*

Brennan, John Kelley (3 mentions)
Ohio State U, 1971 *Certification:* Internal Medicine
5969 E Broad St, Columbus, 614-864-6010

Burgin, Michael Alan (3 mentions)
Ohio State U, 1978 *Certification:* Internal Medicine
4053 W Dublin Granville Rd, Dublin, 614-293-0080

Cooney, Michael John (5 mentions)
Ohio State U, 1970 *Certification:* Internal Medicine
719 W Town St, Columbus, 614-228-3036

Fosselman, Douglas Dale (3 mentions)
Ohio State U, 1982 *Certification:* Internal Medicine
555 W Schrock Rd #110, Westerville, 614-882-0708

Hackman, Mark Allen (3 mentions)
U of Toledo, 1982 *Certification:* Internal Medicine
5969 E Broad St, Columbus, 614-864-6010

Kelley, Amy Rickly (4 mentions)
U of Toledo, 1989 *Certification:* Internal Medicine
770 Jasonway Ave, Columbus, 614-459-2950

Kreger, Cynthia Gail (4 mentions)
Ohio State U, 1985 *Certification:* Internal Medicine
3900 Stoneridge Ln, Dublin, 614-293-0080

La Hue, David Scott (5 mentions)
Northeastern Ohio U, 1981 *Certification:* Internal Medicine
4825 Knightsbridge Blvd, Columbus, 614-451-9612

Melaragno, Daniel Philip (10 mentions)
Ohio State U, 1984 *Certification:* Internal Medicine
3400 Olentangy River Rd #150, Columbus, 614-267-8371

Neiger, David Robert (3 mentions)
Ohio State U, 1981 *Certification:* Internal Medicine
770 Jasonway Ave #G-2, Columbus, 614-459-3687

Palma, Robert Anthony (3 mentions)
Des Moines U, 1973
104 N Murray Hill Rd, Columbus, 614-878-6413

Prenger, Scott Alan (3 mentions)
U of Cincinnati, 1997 *Certification:* Internal Medicine
631 Copeland Mill Rd #A, Westerville, 614-508-2672

Ricaurte, Mark Douglas (3 mentions)
Northeastern Ohio U, 1986 *Certification:* Internal Medicine
719 W Town St, Columbus, 614-228-3036

Sleesman, Henry Craig (3 mentions)
Ohio State U, 1974 *Certification:* Internal Medicine
3400 Olentangy River Rd #150, Columbus, 614-267-8371

Steginsky, Alan David (4 mentions)
Ohio State U, 1983 *Certification:* Internal Medicine
4030 W Henderson Rd, Columbus, 614-442-7550

Varveris, Maria Yiannaki (4 mentions)
Northeastern Ohio U, 1998 *Certification:* Internal Medicine
4030 W Henderson Rd, Columbus, 614-442-7550

Weed, Harrison Goodale (3 mentions)
Boston U, 1987
Certification: Infectious Disease, Internal Medicine
2050 Kinny Rd #2400, Columbus, 614-293-8054

Wilson, Ian James (5 mentions)
FMS-United Kingdom, 1977 *Certification:* Internal Medicine
484 County Line Rd W #200, Westerville, 614-891-8080

Wulf, John William (8 mentions)
U of Toledo, 1985 *Certification:* Internal Medicine
4030 W Henderson Rd, Columbus, 614-442-7550

Nephrology

Agra, Anthony Dean (7 mentions)
Wright State U, 1995 *Certification:* Nephrology
51 S Souder Ave 1st Fl, Columbus, 614-223-0043

Lewis, James William (17 mentions)
Loyola U Chicago, 1967
Certification: Internal Medicine, Nephrology
500 Thomas Ln #4-A, Columbus, 614-538-2250

MacLaurin, John Peter (5 mentions)
A T Still U, 1972
285 E State St #150, Columbus, 614-460-6100

Mentser, Mark Irwin (5 mentions)
Ohio State U, 1973 *Certification:* Pediatric Nephrology, Pediatrics
555 S 18th St, Columbus, 614-722-4554

Saunders, Christopher S. (12 mentions)
Case Western Reserve U, 1982
Certification: Internal Medicine, Nephrology
500 Thomas Ln #4-A, Columbus, 614-538-2250

Schroeder, Kevin Lee (7 mentions)
Ohio State U, 1997 *Certification:* Internal Medicine, Nephrology
500 Thomas Ln #4-A, Columbus, 614-538-2250

Singri, Naveen (5 mentions)
U of Cincinnati, 1997
Certification: Internal Medicine, Nephrology
500 Thomas Ln #4-A, Columbus, 614-538-2250

Wehrum, Henry L. (7 mentions)
Ohio U Coll of Osteopathic Med, 1985
985 W 3rd Ave, Columbus, 614-291-0022

Wilmer, William Arnold (5 mentions)
U of Toledo, 1988 *Certification:* Internal Medicine, Nephrology
495 Cooper Rd #425, Westerville, 614-823-8500
1550 Sheridan Dr, Lincolnshire, 740-475-0058

Neurological Surgery

Bay, Janet Winifred (33 mentions)
Ohio State U, 1973 *Certification:* Neurological Surgery
931 Chatham Ln #200, Columbus, 614-457-4880

Brightman, Rebecca Paige (7 mentions)
Boston U, 1984 *Certification:* Neurological Surgery
3555 Olentangy River Rd #3050, Columbus, 614-268-3094
931 Chatham Ln #200, Columbus, 614-457-4880

Chiocca, Ennio Antonio (7 mentions)
U of Texas-Houston, 1988 *Certification:* Neurological Surgery
410 W 10th Ave, Columbus, 614-293-9312

Kosnik, Edward James (9 mentions)
U of Maryland, 1969 *Certification:* Neurological Surgery
700 Childrens Dr, Columbus, 614-722-2000

Neurology

Arce, Erick (10 mentions)
FMS-Germany, 1990 *Certification:* Neurology
931 Chatham Ln #200, Columbus, 614-457-4880

Berarducci, Albert L., Jr. (5 mentions)
New York U, 1975 *Certification:* Neurology
931 Chatham Ln #200, Columbus, 614-457-4880
3535 Olentangy River Rd, Columbus, 614-324-6692

Eubank, Geoffrey (10 mentions)
Ohio State U, 1991 *Certification:* Neurology, Vascular Neurology
931 Chatham Ln #200, Columbus, 614-324-1445

Fahey, Brian (5 mentions)
Ohio U Coll of Osteopathic Med, 1986
165 N Murray Hill Rd, Columbus, 614-870-3669
4995 Bradenton Ave, Dublin, 614-760-5972
7811 Flint Rd, Columbus, 614-433-2000

Freidenberg, Donald L. (4 mentions)
Kansas U Coll of Osteopathic Med, 1980 *Certification:* Neurology
2121 Bethel Rd #F, Columbus, 614-547-3100

Kissel, John Thomas (6 mentions)
Northwestern U, 1978
Certification: Neurology, Neuromuscular Medicine
1654 Upham Dr, Columbus, 614-293-4981
456 W 10th Ave, Columbus, 614-293-4981

Lo, Warren David (5 mentions)
Certification: Neurology with Special Qualifications in Child
 Neurology, Pediatrics
700 Childrens Dr, Columbus, 614-722-4554

O'Donnell, Francis Joseph (5 mentions)
A T Still U, 1985
70 S Cleveland Ave #A, Westerville, 614-890-6555
1313 Olentangy River Rd, Columbus, 614-294-3708

Walz, Elizabeth Terese (6 mentions)
Ohio State U, 1989 *Certification:* Neurology
750 Mt Carmel Mall #250, Columbus, 614-228-4616

Obstetrics/Gynecology

Ananth, Uma (3 mentions)
FMS-India, 1975 *Certification:* Obstetrics & Gynecology
4845 Knightsbridge Blvd #220, Columbus, 614-583-5552

Beattie, James F., Jr. (3 mentions)
Ohio State U, 1981 *Certification:* Obstetrics & Gynecology
750 Mount Carmel Mall #100, Columbus, 614-434-2400

Bell, David Clarence (6 mentions)
Ohio State U, 1981 *Certification:* Obstetrics & Gynecology
1315 W Lane Ave, Columbus, 614-457-4827
10244 Sawmill Pkwy, Powell, 614-457-4827

Blumenfeld, Michael L. (3 mentions)
Ohio State U, 1985 *Certification:* Obstetrics & Gynecology
456 W 10th Ave #2-B, Columbus, 614-293-3069

Boyles, Melissa Lee (3 mentions)
Indiana U, 1988 *Certification:* Obstetrics & Gynecology
3525 Olentangy River Rd #6350, Columbus, 614-734-3347

Copeland, Christopher M. (8 mentions)
Ohio State U, 1978 *Certification:* Obstetrics & Gynecology
1315 W Lane Ave, Columbus, 614-457-4827

Doyle, Susan Kugel (3 mentions)
Ohio State U, 1984 *Certification:* Obstetrics & Gynecology
1375 Cherry Way Dr #110, Gahanna, 614-475-0811

Greco, Carol Jean (11 mentions)
Ohio State U, 1987 *Certification:* Obstetrics & Gynecology
1315 W Lane Ave, Columbus, 614-457-4827

Harmon, Thomas Louis (3 mentions)
Ohio State U, 1988 *Certification:* Obstetrics & Gynecology
6565 Worthington Galena Rd #A-102, Worthington,
 614-885-8167
7450 Hospital Dr #200, Dublin, 614-885-8167

Jenkins, Carol S. (3 mentions)
Ohio State U, 1992 *Certification:* Obstetrics & Gynecology
55 Dillmont Dr, Columbus, 614-431-1634

Keder, Lisa Margret (3 mentions)
Ohio State U, 1989 *Certification:* Obstetrics & Gynecology
4053 W Dublin Granville Rd, Dublin, 614-764-2262

Krantz, Carl Arnold (7 mentions)
Ohio State U, 1972 *Certification:* Obstetrics & Gynecology
7450 Hospital Dr #200, Dublin, 614-885-8167
6565 Worthington Galena #A-102, Columbus, 614-885-8167

Lutter, Kathleen Quinn (4 mentions)
Northeastern Ohio U, 1984 *Certification:* Obstetrics & Gynecology
3545 Olentangy River Rd #401, Columbus, 614-261-0101

Melillo, Jason Victor (5 mentions)
Ohio State U, 1997 *Certification:* Obstetrics & Gynecology
1315 W Lane Ave, Columbus, 614-457-4827

Parnes, Marc Louis (5 mentions)
Northeastern Ohio U, 1981 *Certification:* Obstetrics & Gynecology
904 Eastwind Dr, Westerville, 614-890-1914

Roncone, Jennifer A. (4 mentions)
5131 Beacon Hill Rd #220, Columbus, 614-544-2430
5131 Beacon Hill Rd #340, Columbus, 614-544-1006

Russ, John Steve (3 mentions)
Ohio State U, 1977 *Certification:* Obstetrics & Gynecology
1080 Beecher Xing N, Columbus, 614-476-4101

Samuels, Philip (3 mentions)
Texas Tech U, 1980
Certification: Maternal-Fetal Medicine, Obstetrics & Gynecology
2050 Kenny Rd, Columbus, 614-293-2222

Sprague, Michael Steven (3 mentions)
St Louis U, 1978 *Certification:* Obstetrics & Gynecology
1080 Beecher Crossing N, Columbus, 614-476-4101

Turner, Leslie Paige (6 mentions)
Ohio State U, 1993 *Certification:* Obstetrics & Gynecology
3535 Fishinger Blvd #280, Hilliard, 614-777-1440

Underwood, Richard N. (4 mentions)
Ohio U Coll of Osteopathic Med, 1985
495 Cooper Rd #218, Westerville, 614-865-9502

Ophthalmology

Allen, John Geoffrey (4 mentions)
Ohio State U, 1986 *Certification:* Ophthalmology
3525 Olentangy River Rd #5310, Columbus, 614-267-4122

Boyle, Kenneth Andrew, Jr. (4 mentions)
Ohio State U, 1993 *Certification:* Ophthalmology
3525 Olentangy River Rd #5310, Columbus, 614-267-4122

Cahill, Kenneth Vern (9 mentions)
Ohio State U, 1979 *Certification:* Ophthalmology
262 Neil Ave #430, Columbus, 614-221-7464

Doyle, Louise A. (8 mentions)
A T Still U, 1982
2020 Kenny Rd, Columbus, 614-488-8000

Epitropoulos, Alice T. (4 mentions)
Ohio State U, 1989 *Certification:* Ophthalmology
340 E Town St #8-200, Columbus, 614-221-7464
262 Neil Ave #430, Columbus, 614-221-7464

Hickey, Charles Joseph (5 mentions)
Ohio State U, 1979 *Certification:* Ophthalmology
3814 Broadway, Grove City, 614-766-2006
5155 Bradenton Ave 2nd Fl, Dublin, 614-766-2006
5965 E Broad St, Columbus, 614-751-4070
1430 Columbus Ave, Washington Courthouse, 740-333-2743

Katz, Steven Edward (6 mentions)
Ohio State U, 1990 *Certification:* Ophthalmology
456 W 10th Ave, Columbus, 614-293-6892

McGregor, Mary Lou (8 mentions)
Northeastern Ohio U, 1985
555 S 18th St #4-C, Columbus, 614-224-6222

Moses, James Lloyd (9 mentions)
Case Western Reserve U, 1973 *Certification:* Ophthalmology
6441 Winchester Blvd #1, Canal Winchester, 614-834-1263
2680 W Broad St, Columbus, 614-274-2020

Rogers, Gary Leigh (5 mentions)
Ohio State U, 1968 *Certification:* Ophthalmology
555 S 18th St #4-C, Columbus, 614-224-6222

Rogers, Nicholas Alan (4 mentions)
Ohio State U, 2002 *Certification:* Ophthalmology
2250 N Bank Dr, Columbus, 614-451-7550
85 E Main St, New Albany, 614-304-2050

Stechschulte, John Robert (5 mentions)
Ohio State U, 1980 *Certification:* Ophthalmology
262 Neil Ave #320, Columbus, 614-228-4500

Weber, Paul August (4 mentions)
Northwestern U, 1974 *Certification:* Ophthalmology
456 W 10th Ave #5-A, Columbus, 614-293-8116

Whitaker, Todd Edwin (5 mentions)
Ohio State U, 1996 *Certification:* Ophthalmology
2250 N Bank Dr, Columbus, 614-451-7550
85 E Main St, New Albany, 614-305-2050

Orthopedics

Beebe, Allan Carlisle (6 mentions)
Northwestern U, 1983 *Certification:* Orthopaedic Surgery
479 Parsons Ave, Columbus, 614-461-7972

Berasi, Carl C. (5 mentions)
Midwestern U Chicago Coll of Osteopathic Med, 1979
70 S Cleveland Ave #A, Westerville, 614-890-6555

Duffey, Timothy Patrick (5 mentions)
Midwestern U Chicago Coll of Osteopathic Med, 1982
1313 Olentangy River Rd, Columbus, 614-890-6555
70 S Cleveland Ave #A, Westerville, 614-890-6555

Edwards, Peter H., Jr. (4 mentions)
Ohio State U, 1988 *Certification:* Orthopaedic Surgery
4605 Sawmill Rd, Columbus, 614-459-4600

Jones, Grant Lloyd (5 mentions)
Ohio State U, 1992
Certification: Orthopaedic Sports Medicine, Orthopaedic Surgery
2050 Kenny Rd #3100, Columbus, 614-293-3600

Kaeding, Christopher C. (4 mentions)
Northwestern U, 1983
Certification: Orthopaedic Sports Medicine, Orthopaedic Surgery
2050 Kenny Rd #3100, Columbus, 614-293-3600

McShane, Michael (12 mentions)
Northeastern Ohio U, 1983 *Certification:* Orthopaedic Surgery
4605 Sawmill Rd, Columbus, 614-827-8700

Melaragno, Paul (8 mentions)
Ohio State U, 1992 *Certification:* Orthopaedic Surgery
4605 Sawmill Rd, Columbus, 614-827-8700

Mileti, Joseph (4 mentions)
Ohio State U, 1996 *Certification:* Orthopaedic Surgery
4605 Sawmill Rd, Columbus, 614-827-8700

Rosenberg, Gerald M. (5 mentions)
Ohio State U, 1979 *Certification:* Orthopaedic Surgery
7277 Smiths Mill Rd #200, New Albany, 614-220-0398

Vansteyn, Scott Jeffrey (7 mentions)
Duke U, 1990 *Certification:* Orthopaedic Surgery
4605 Sawmill Rd, Columbus, 614-827-8700

Watson, Larry William (12 mentions)
Marshall U, 1986 *Certification:* Orthopaedic Surgery
4605 Sawmill Rd, Columbus, 614-459-4600

Otorhinolaryngology

Forrest, Lowell Arick (10 mentions)
Ohio State U, 1988 *Certification:* Otolaryngology
456 W 10th Ave, Columbus, 617-293-8150

Grant, Iain Lachlan (6 mentions)
FMS-New Zealand, 1984 *Certification:* Otolaryngology
1830 Bethel Rd, Columbus, 614-583-3687

Hiltbrand, Jeffery Bruce (7 mentions)
Ohio State U, 1984 *Certification:* Otolaryngology
4300 Clime Rd #100, Columbus, 614-275-4300

Lowery, James Douglas (6 mentions)
Ohio State U, 1986 *Certification:* Otolaryngology
974 Bethel Rd, Columbus, 614-538-2424

O'Brien, Blaize Andrew (9 mentions)
Ohio State U, 1996 *Certification:* Otolaryngology
974 Bethel Rd, Columbus, 614-538-2424

Schuller, David Edward (6 mentions)
Ohio State U, 1970 *Certification:* Otolaryngology
456 W 10th Ave, Columbus, 614-293-8074

Tobin, Evan Joseph (8 mentions)
U of Texas-Dallas, 1992 *Certification:* Otolaryngology
6499 E Broad St #A, Columbus, 614-755-5151

Welling, D. Bradley (7 mentions)
U of Utah, 1983 *Certification:* Neurotology, Otolaryngology
456 W 10th Ave, Columbus, 614-293-8150

Willett, Darryl Neal (22 mentions)
Ohio State U, 1991 *Certification:* Otolaryngology
974 Bethel Rd, Columbus, 614-538-2424

Pain Medicine

Deshpande, Kedar Krishna (4 mentions)
FMS-St Maarten, 1998
Certification: Physical Medicine & Rehabilitation
1080 Polaris Pkwy #200, Columbus, 614-468-0300
1120 Polaris Pkwy #202, Columbus, 614-433-0264

McDowell, Gladstone, II (10 mentions)
U of Texas-San Antonio, 1982
3100 Plaza Properties, Westerville, 614-383-6450

Pathology

Accetta, Peter Anthony (8 mentions)
U of Cincinnati, 1979
Certification: Anatomic Pathology & Clinical Pathology
3535 Olentangy River Rd, Columbus, 614-566-5526
111 S Grant Ave, Columbus, 614-566-9143

Anker, Ruth Lynn (5 mentions)
Michigan State U Coll of Osteopathic Med, 1976
Certification: Anatomic Pathology & Clinical Pathology
5100 W Broad St, Columbus, 614-544-1000

Brownell, Mark David (6 mentions)
SUNY-Upstate Med U, 1980
Certification: Anatomic Pathology, Hematology
3535 Olentangy River Rd, Columbus, 614-566-5526

Forsthoefel, Kevin F. (7 mentions)
U of Cincinnati, 1987
Certification: Anatomic Pathology & Clinical Pathology
3535 Olentangy River Rd, Columbus, 614-566-5526

Kelsten, Martin Lee (3 mentions)
U of Iowa, 1982 *Certification:* Anatomic Pathology &
  Clinical Pathology, Cytopathology
3535 Olentangy River Rd, Columbus, 614-566-5526

Nicely, Charles Jon (4 mentions)
Ohio State U, 1988 *Certification:* Anatomic Pathology &
  Clinical Pathology, Hematology
3535 Olentangy River Rd, Columbus, 614-566-5526

Sedmak, Daniel D. (4 mentions)
Certification: Anatomic Pathology & Clinical Pathology,
  Immunopathology
370 W (th Ave, Columbus, 614-292-3684

Wakely, Paul E. (3 mentions)
Certification: Anatomic Pathology & Clinical Pathology,
  Cytopathology, Pediatric Pathology
410 W 10th Ave, Columbus, 614-293-4880

Pediatrics *(see note on page 9)*

Barrett, Gregory Alan (18 mentions)
Ohio State U, 1978 *Certification:* Pediatrics
4885 Olentangy River Rd #210, Columbus, 614-267-7878

Budin, Lee Eric (3 mentions)
Ohio State U, 1990 *Certification:* Pediatrics
6096 E Main St #112, Columbus, 614-434-5437

Kelch, Lisa Brandstaetter (3 mentions)
Ohio State U, 1990 *Certification:* Pediatrics
3931 Berry Leaf Ln, Hilliard, 614-777-1800

Mastruserio, Jennifer J. (3 mentions)
U of Cincinnati, 1991 *Certification:* Pediatrics
5072 Reed Rd, Columbus, 614-326-1600

Morrison, Matthew Joseph (3 mentions)
St Louis U, 1997 *Certification:* Pediatrics
5072 Reed Rd, Columbus, 614-326-1600

Petrella, Richard Anthony (5 mentions)
Ohio State U, 1977 *Certification:* Pediatrics
595 Copeland Mill Rd #2A, Westerville, 614-899-0000

Robbins, Darryl Andrew (6 mentions)
Philadelphia Coll of Osteopathic Med, 1971
Certification: Pediatrics
453 Waterbury Ct #100, Gahanna, 614-471-0652

Rogers, Ann (3 mentions)
Ohio State U, 1970
Certification: Neonatal-Perinatal Medicine, Pediatrics
6905 Hospital Dr #100, Dublin, 614-791-2000

Rothermel, Kim Gage (7 mentions)
Rush U, 1975
Certification: Pediatric Hematology-Oncology, Pediatrics
5040 Bradenton Ave, Dublin, 614-766-3344

White, Jennifer Lynn (4 mentions)
Ohio State U, 1986
4885 Olentangy River Rd #210, Columbus, 614-267-7878

Williams, Gwynette M. (3 mentions)
Ohio State U, 1982 *Certification:* Pediatrics
4885 Olentangy River Rd #210, Columbus, 614-267-7878

Plastic Surgery

Holland, Gregory Carl (7 mentions)
Ohio State U, 1987 *Certification:* Plastic Surgery
750 Mt Carmel Mall #390, Columbus, 614-224-2828
5965 E Broad St, Columbus, 614-224-2828

Ruberg, Robert Lionel (17 mentions)
Harvard U, 1967 *Certification:* Plastic Surgery, Surgery
4830 Knightsbridge Blvd #G, Columbus, 614-293-8566
555 S 18th St #6-G, Columbus, 614-293-8580
410 W 10th Ave, Columbus, 614-293-8560

Sullivan, Christine Roth (7 mentions)
Ohio State U, 1982 *Certification:* Plastic Surgery
7706 Olentangy River Rd, Columbus, 614-436-8888

Vasko, Susan Dietrich (11 mentions)
Ohio State U, 1986 *Certification:* Plastic Surgery
4971 Arlington Center Blvd, Columbus, 614-246-6900

Wakelin, John Keene, III (7 mentions)
Ohio State U, 2000 *Certification:* Plastic Surgery
4971 Arlington Centre Blvd, Columbus, 614-246-6900

Psychiatry

Campo, John Vincent (3 mentions)
U of Pennsylvania, 1982 *Certification:* Child & Adolescent
  Psychiatry, Pediatrics, Psychiatry
Harding Hospital, Columbus, 614-722-2291

Chan, Michael Alan (18 mentions)
Wayne State U, 1982 *Certification:* Psychiatry
750 Mt Carmel Mall #220, Columbus, 614-234-2970

Opremcak, Colleen (7 mentions)
Ohio State U, 1982
Certification: Psychiatry, Psychosomatic Medicine
3535 Olentangy River Rd, Columbus, 614-566-4924

Romeo, Freddie P. (3 mentions)
Ohio State U, 1990 *Certification:* Psychiatry
750 Mount Carmel Mall #220, Columbus, 614-234-2970

Ware, Kevin Vaughn (4 mentions)
U of Toledo, 1991 *Certification:* Psychiatry
750 Mount Carmel Mall #220, Columbus, 614-234-2970

Pulmonary Disease

Allen, James N., Jr. (19 mentions)
Ohio State U, 1984 *Certification:* Critical Care Medicine,
  Internal Medicine, Pulmonary Disease
456 W 10th Ave, Columbus, 614-247-7707
1492 E Broad St, Columbus, 614-257-3000
2050 Kenny Rd, Columbus, 614-293-4925

Boes, Thomas Joseph (24 mentions)
Ohio State U, 1981 *Certification:* Critical Care Medicine,
  Internal Medicine, Pulmonary Disease
3545 Olentangy River Rd #201, Columbus, 614-267-8585

Borchers, Susan Denise (7 mentions)
Ohio State U, 1990 *Certification:* Pulmonary Disease
7630 Rivers Edge Dr, Columbus, 614-540-3944

Chinn, William Michael (5 mentions)
Ohio State U, 1969
Certification: Internal Medicine, Pulmonary Disease
745 W State St #510, Columbus, 614-464-0788

Corriveau, Michael L. (9 mentions)
Certification: Critical Care Medicine, Internal Medicine, Pulmonary Disease
745 W State St #510, Columbus, 614-464-0788

Hawley, Philip Caldwell (19 mentions)
Duke U, 1975 *Certification:* Critical Care Medicine, Internal Medicine, Pulmonary Disease
111 S Grant Ave, Columbus, 614-566-9143

Klein, James A. (5 mentions)
U of Kentucky, 1981 *Certification:* Critical Care Medicine, Internal Medicine, Pulmonary Disease
85 McNaughten Rd #130, Columbus, 614-577-8322

Marsh, Clay B. (5 mentions)
West Virginia U, 1985 *Certification:* Critical Care Medicine, Internal Medicine, Pulmonary Disease
473 W 12th Ave, Columbus, 614-292-4270

St. John, Roy Carl (6 mentions)
Ohio State U, 1985 *Certification:* Critical Care Medicine, Internal Medicine, Pulmonary Disease
745 W State St #610, Columbus, 614-224-0093

Radiology—Diagnostic

Adler, Brent Hale (3 mentions)
U of Michigan, 1989
Certification: Diagnostic Radiology, Pediatric Radiology
700 Childrens Dr, Columbus, 614-722-2359

Borgess, Mary Pat (3 mentions)
Ohio State U, 1976 *Certification:* Diagnostic Radiology
3525 Olentangy River Rd #5360, Columbus, 614-340-7741

Buse, Thomas Marce (6 mentions)
U of Cincinnati, 1992 *Certification:* Diagnostic Radiology
3525 Olentangy River Rd #5360, Columbus, 614-340-7741

Kemp, Susan M. (3 mentions)
Temple U, 1981
Certification: Diagnostic Radiology, Neuroradiology
3525 Olentangy River Rd #5360, Columbus, 614-340-7747

Levey, Michael Steven (5 mentions)
Ohio State U, 1986 *Certification:* Diagnostic Radiology
111 S Grant Ave, Columbus, 614-566-9231

Lombardi, Thomas James (3 mentions)
Wayne State U, 1989 *Certification:* Diagnostic Radiology
3525 Olentangy River Rd #5360, Columbus, 614-340-7741

McFarland, Dan Ross (4 mentions)
Ohio State U, 1963 *Certification:* Nuclear Medicine, Radiology
3525 Olentangy River Rd #5360, Columbus, 614-340-7747

Pema, Peter James (3 mentions)
Ohio State U, 1987
Certification: Diagnostic Radiology, Neuroradiology
3525 Olentangy River Rd #5360, Columbus, 614-340-7741

White, Daniel Jo (4 mentions)
Ohio State U, 1986 *Certification:* Diagnostic Radiology
793 W State St, Columbus, 614-234-5100

Wiot, Jerome Geoffrey (7 mentions)
U of Cincinnati, 1982
Certification: Diagnostic Radiology, Neuroradiology
3525 Olentangy River Rd #5360, Columbus, 614-340-7741

Radiology—Therapeutic

Hogan, Mark Joseph (4 mentions)
U of Cincinnati, 1989
Certification: Diagnostic Radiology, Pediatric Radiology
700 Childrens Dr, Columbus, 614-722-2359

La Rosa, Joseph Lawrence (5 mentions)
Ohio State U, 1982 *Certification:* Diagnostic Radiology, Vascular & Interventional Radiology
111 S Grant Ave, Columbus, 614-566-9231

Lippert, John Allan (10 mentions)
U of Maryland, 1994 *Certification:* Diagnostic Radiology, Vascular & Interventional Radiology
3535 Olentangy River Rd #5362, Columbus, 614-340-7741

Pedrick, Thomas J. (5 mentions)
U of Cincinnati, 1981 *Certification:* Therapeutic Radiology
3535 Olentangy River Rd, Columbus, 614-566-5560

Pema, Peter James (5 mentions)
Ohio State U, 1987
Certification: Diagnostic Radiology, Neuroradiology
3525 Olentangy River Rd #5360, Columbus, 614-340-7741

Shiels, William Eugene, II (6 mentions)
Philadelphia Coll of Osteopathic Med, 1983
Certification: Diagnostic Radiology, Pediatric Radiology
700 Childrens Dr, Columbus, 614-722-2363

Van Aman, Michael Elwin (4 mentions)
Ohio State U, 1971 *Certification:* Diagnostic Radiology
793 W State St, Columbus, 614-234-5100

Verrill, Andrew David (4 mentions)
Ohio State U, 1977 *Certification:* Diagnostic Radiology, Vascular & Interventional Radiology
550 Thrush Rill Ct, Powell, 614-234-5100

Rehabilitation

Cannell, Christopher D. (3 mentions)
Wright State U, 1984
Certification: Physical Medicine & Rehabilitation
70 S Cleveland Ave, Westerville, 740-368-5039

Clairmont, Albert Clement (3 mentions)
FMS-Jamaica, 1974
Certification: Pediatrics, Physical Medicine & Rehabilitation
480 W 9th Ave, Columbus, 614-293-3801

Everhart-McDonald, M. A. (4 mentions)
Ohio State U, 1984
Certification: Physical Medicine & Rehabilitation
1010 Bethel Rd, Columbus, 614-459-4825

Otis, Scott Michael (3 mentions)
Ohio State U, 1996
Certification: Physical Medicine & Rehabilitation
70 S Cleveland Ave #A, Westerville, 614-890-6555
1313 Olentangy River Rd, Columbus, 614-294-3708

Perkins, Robert Harrison (4 mentions)
Ohio State U, 1995
Certification: Physical Medicine & Rehabilitation
3555 Olentangy River Rd #1010, Columbus, 614-566-4191

Piero, David Lee (3 mentions)
Ohio State U, 1971
Certification: Physical Medicine & Rehabilitation
5975 E Broad St #302, Columbus, 614-234-6464

Powers, James Joseph (7 mentions)
Ohio State U, 1965
Certification: Physical Medicine & Rehabilitation
340 E Town St #8-700, Columbus, 614-566-9397

Rindler, Julie Pauline (3 mentions)
Ohio State U, 1987
Certification: Physical Medicine & Rehabilitation
3555 Olentangy River Rd #1010, Columbus, 614-267-3300

Skeels, Thomas D. (3 mentions)
Ohio U Coll of Osteopathic Med, 1982
Certification: Physical Medicine & Rehabilitation
1313 Olentangy River Rd, Columbus, 614-890-6555

Strakowski, Jeffrey Allen (5 mentions)
Indiana U, 1990 *Certification:* Pain Medicine, Physical Medicine & Rehabilitation, Spinal Cord Injury Medicine, Sports Medicine
3555 Olentangy River Rd #1010, Columbus, 614-566-4191

Vaughan, Nancy Morgan (6 mentions)
Wright State U, 1994
Certification: Pain Medicine, Physical Medicine & Rehabilitation
4605 Sawmill Rd, Columbus, 614-459-4600

Wolfe, Claire V. Rendar (3 mentions)
Ohio State U, 1968
Certification: Physical Medicine & Rehabilitation
4605 Sawmill Rd, Columbus, 614-827-8700

Rheumatology

Flood, Joseph (17 mentions)
Georgetown U, 1979
Certification: Internal Medicine, Rheumatology
500 E Main St #230, Columbus, 614-464-4667

Hashmi, Shereen (9 mentions)
FMS-Pakistan, 1984 *Certification:* Geriatric Medicine, Internal Medicine, Rheumatology
439 E Wilson Bridge Rd, Worthington, 614-781-1749
8000 Ravines Edge Ct #202, Columbus, 614-781-1749

Whisler, Ronald Lloyd (12 mentions)
Ohio State U, 1968
Certification: Internal Medicine, Rheumatology
480 Medical Center Dr #2056, Columbus, 614-293-8093

Thoracic Surgery

Duff, Steven Barron (21 mentions)
U of Cincinnati, 1981 *Certification:* Thoracic Surgery
3555 Olentangy River Rd #2070, Columbus, 614-261-8377

Esterline, William J. (10 mentions)
Certification: Thoracic Surgery
85 McNaughten Rd #110, Columbus, 614-856-9100

Ross, Patrick, Jr. (8 mentions)
St Louis, 1983 *Certification:* Surgery, Thoracic Surgery
410 W 10th Ave #N-839, Columbus, 614-293-4509

Tishko, D. J. (7 mentions)
U of Cincinnati, 1983 *Certification:* Thoracic Surgery
5965 E Broad St #340, Columbus, 614-234-7505

Urology

Burgers, John Kevin (15 mentions)
Johns Hopkins U, 1984 *Certification:* Urology
3555 Olentangy River Rd #4020, Columbus, 614-268-2323

Gianakopoulos, William P. (10 mentions)
Wright State U, 1987 *Certification:* Urology
340 E Town St #7-200, Columbus, 614-221-2888

Ho, George Tseng (14 mentions)
Northwestern U, 1988 *Certification:* Urology
500 E Main St #220, Columbus, 614-222-3369

Koff, Stephen Andrew (10 mentions)
Duke U, 1969 *Certification:* Urology
700 Childrens Dr, Columbus, 614-722-2000

Vascular Surgery

Smead, William Lewis (11 mentions)
Vanderbilt U, 1972 *Certification:* Surgery, Vascular Surgery
456 W 10th Ave, Columbus, 614-293-8536
1654 Upham Dr, Columbus, 614-293-8536

Vaccaro, Patrick Samuel (19 mentions)
U of Cincinnati, 1975 *Certification:* Surgery, Vascular Surgery
1654 Upham Dr, Columbus, 614-293-8536
452 W 10th Ave, Columbus, 614-293-8536
1492 E Broad St #1100, Columbus, 614-234-0444
5969 E Broad St #303, Columbus, 614-234-0444

Oklahoma

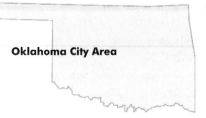

Oklahoma City Area

Oklahoma City Area
Including Canadian, Cleveland, and Oklahoma Counties

Allergy/Immunology

Bozalis, John Russell (9 mentions)
U of Oklahoma, 1965
Certification: Allergy & Immunology, Internal Medicine
750 NE 13th St #300, Oklahoma City, 405-235-0040

Filley, Warren Vernon (8 mentions)
U of Kansas, 1976
Certification: Allergy & Immunology, Internal Medicine
750 NE 13th St #300, Oklahoma City, 405-235-0040

Tarpay, Martha M. (14 mentions)
FMS-Hungary, 1965
Certification: Allergy & Immunology, Pediatrics
4200 W Memorial Rd #206, Oklahoma City, 405-752-0393

Anesthesiology

Bicket, Paul Charles (3 mentions)
U of Oklahoma, 1977 *Certification:* Anesthesiology
4200 W Memorial Rd #703, Oklahoma City, 405-755-1080

Borsky, Bart Jonathan (3 mentions)
Virginia Commonwealth U, 1987 *Certification:* Anesthesiology
3300 NW Expressway St, Oklahoma City, 405-951-2815

Cunningham, Jay D. (3 mentions)
Oklahoma State U Coll of Osteopathic Med, 1987
Certification: Anesthesiology
4200 W Memorial Rd #703, Oklahoma City, 405-755-1080

Fuller, Bennett E. (7 mentions)
U of Oklahoma, 1986 *Certification:* Anesthesiology
4200 W Memorial Rd #703, Oklahoma City, 405-755-1080

Fuller, Falon Dee (3 mentions)
U of Oklahoma, 1984 *Certification:* Anesthesiology
6232 Cypress Grove, Oklahoma City, 405-749-2733

Gawey, Bradley Joseph (3 mentions)
Louisiana State U, 1989 *Certification:* Anesthesiology
3300 NW Expressway St, Oklahoma City, 405-951-2815

Hill, A. Dodge, Jr. (3 mentions)
U of Oklahoma, 1966 *Certification:* Anesthesiology
4400 Will Rogers Pkwy #105, Oklahoma City, 405-947-5557

Maxwell, Scott Winn (5 mentions)
U of Oklahoma, 1987 *Certification:* Anesthesiology
4200 W Memorial Rd #703, Oklahoma City, 405-755-1080

Mueller, Steven Alfred (5 mentions)
U of Oklahoma, 1980 *Certification:* Anesthesiology
1111 N Lee Ave #236, Oklahoma City, 405-272-9641

Smith, George Keith (3 mentions)
U of Oklahoma, 1986 *Certification:* Anesthesiology
9500 Broadway Ext, Oklahoma City, 405-475-0680

Yasuda, Paul Steven (4 mentions)
U of New Mexico, 1989 *Certification:* Anesthesiology
920 Stanton L Young Blvd, Oklahoma City, 405-848-2217

Cardiac Surgery

Bodenhamer, Robert Mark (11 mentions)
U of Oklahoma, 1979 *Certification:* Thoracic Surgery
4050 W Memorial Rd, Oklahoma City, 405-608-3927

Kanaly, Paul Joseph (20 mentions)
U of Oklahoma, 1974 *Certification:* Thoracic Surgery
3433 NW 56th St #700, Oklahoma City, 405-945-3148
3433 NW 56th St #670, Oklahoma City, 405-951-4345

Randolph, John (15 mentions)
U of Oklahoma, 1981 *Certification:* Thoracic Surgery
4050 W Memorial Rd, Oklahoma City, 405-608-3800

Cardiology

Adamson, Philip Bentley (5 mentions)
U of Oklahoma, 1991
4050 W Memorial Rd #3, Oklahoma City, 405-608-3800

Clark, Robert Mel (4 mentions)
U of Oklahoma, 1978
Certification: Cardiovascular Disease, Internal Medicine
3433 NW 56th St #400, Oklahoma City, 405-947-3341

Harvey, John R. (8 mentions)
U of Oklahoma, 1981 *Certification:* Cardiovascular Disease,
   Internal Medicine, Interventional Cardiology
4050 W Memorial Rd, Oklahoma City, 405-608-3800

Lane, Richard Thomas (5 mentions)
Texas Tech U, 1984
Certification: Cardiovascular Disease, Internal Medicine
3433 NW 56th St #400, Oklahoma City, 405-947-3341

Schmidt, Dwayne Allen (6 mentions)
U of Oklahoma, 1983 *Certification:* Cardiovascular Disease,
   Internal Medicine, Interventional Cardiology
4050 W Memorial Rd, Oklahoma City, 405-608-3800

Scott, Brooke D. (4 mentions)
U of Oklahoma, 1985 *Certification:* Cardiovascular Disease,
   Internal Medicine, Interventional Cardiology
105 S Bryant Ave #401, Edmond, 405-340-2121
4050 W Memorial Rd 3rd Fl, Oklahoma City, 405-608-3800

Tahirkheli, Naeem Khan (4 mentions)
FMS-Pakistan, 1988 *Certification:* Interventional Cardiology
4221 S Western Ave #4000, Oklahoma City, 405-631-0588
4050 W Memorial Rd 3rd Fl, Oklahoma City, 405-608-3800

Valuck, Jonathan Eric (4 mentions)
U of Missouri, 1988
Certification: Cardiovascular Disease, Interventional Cardiology
4050 W Memorial Rd, Oklahoma City, 405-608-3800

Williams, John Michael (4 mentions)
U of Oklahoma, 1992 *Certification:* Cardiovascular Disease
4050 W Memorial Rd #3-A, Oklahoma City, 405-608-3800

Wong, Kenneth M. (7 mentions)
Texas Tech U, 1988 *Certification:* Cardiovascular Disease
3433 NW 56th St, Oklahoma City, 405-947-3341

Dermatology

Abbott, Craig Leon (10 mentions)
U of Oklahoma, 1990
Certification: Dermatology, Dermatopathology
3500 S Western Ave, Oklahoma City, 405-632-5565

Dawkins, Mark Alan (9 mentions)
U of Oklahoma, 1994 *Certification:* Dermatology
13174 N MacArthur Blvd, Oklahoma City, 405-721-5555

Gawey, Elizabeth Parro (9 mentions)
Louisiana State U, 1989 *Certification:* Dermatology
3435 NW 56th St #500, Oklahoma City, 405-951-8711

Lehr, Robert Blaine (9 mentions)
U of Oklahoma, 1990 *Certification:* Dermatology
5701 N Portland Ave #310, Oklahoma City, 405-951-4949

Emergency Medicine

Askins, Dale C. (4 mentions)
A T Still U, 1979
4401 W Memorial Rd, Oklahoma City, 405-271-2240

Bair, Jack Martin (3 mentions)
U of Kansas, 1982 *Certification:* Emergency Medicine
1000 N Lee Ave, Oklahoma City, 405-272-6152

Brindley, Jerry Dean (4 mentions)
U of Oklahoma, 1978 *Certification:* Emergency Medicine
5501 N Portland Ave, Oklahoma City, 405-604-6145

Crook, Richard Harold (3 mentions)
U of Oklahoma, 1973 *Certification:* Emergency Medicine
3233 NW 63rd St, Oklahoma City, 405-767-0534

Donnell, Dan Duffy (4 mentions)
U of Oklahoma, 1978 *Certification:* Emergency Medicine
2804 Cactus Dr, Edmond, 405-610-8843

Frantz, Robert Ray, Jr. (5 mentions)
U of Oklahoma, 1996 *Certification:* Emergency Medicine
901 N Porter Ave, Norman, 405-307-1000

Heigle, Richard Bruce (6 mentions)
U of Oklahoma, 1990 *Certification:* Emergency Medicine
3300 NW Expressway St, Oklahoma City, 405-949-3155

Lipe, Mark Gregory (4 mentions)
U of Oklahoma, 1987 *Certification:* Family Medicine
4401 W Memorial Rd #121, Oklahoma City, 405-752-3733

McBee, Marty Dale (7 mentions)
Oklahoma State U Coll of Osteopathic Med, 1991
4401 W Memorial Rd, Oklahoma City, 405-307-1000

Myers, Richard L. (3 mentions)
Oklahoma State U Coll of Osteopathic Med, 1981
Certification: Emergency Medicine
3300 NW Expressway St, Oklahoma City, 405-949-4029

Orcutt, Paul D. (5 mentions)
U of Oklahoma, 1976 *Certification:* Emergency Medicine
4300 W Memorial Rd, Oklahoma City, 405-752-3715
4401 S Western Ave, Oklahoma City, 405-752-3715

Wilson, Brent Curtiss (3 mentions)
Loma Linda U, 1989 *Certification:* Emergency Medicine
3300 NW Expressway St, Oklahoma City, 405-949-4029

Endocrinology

Draelos, Matthew Theodore (13 mentions)
U of New Mexico, 1985 *Certification:* Endocrinology,
Diabetes, and Metabolism, Internal Medicine
200 N bryant Ave #100, Edmond, 405-330-2362

Muchmore, John Stephen (16 mentions)
U of Oklahoma, 1975
Certification: Endocrinology and Metabolism, Internal Medicine
3366 NW Expressway St #500, Oklahoma City, 405-945-4700

Painton, Ronald Phillip (16 mentions)
U of Oklahoma, 1972
Certification: Endocrinology and Metabolism, Internal Medicine
5401 N Portland Ave #310, Oklahoma City, 405-951-4160

Family Practice *(see note on page 9)*

Barrett, James Richard (5 mentions)
Johns Hopkins U, 1987
Certification: Family Medicine, Sports Medicine
900 NE 10th St, Oklahoma City, 405-271-4311

Corley, Stanley Dean (3 mentions)
U of Oklahoma, 1978 *Certification:* Family Medicine
5201 W Memorial Rd, Oklahoma City, 405-755-4050

Dimski, Robert Conrad (3 mentions)
U of Texas-San Antonio, 1983 *Certification:* Family Medicine
1212 S Douglas Blvd, Midwest City, 405-736-6811

Hirsch, Jeffrey Gene (5 mentions)
U of Oklahoma, 1975
120 N Robinson Ave #153-W, Oklahoma City, 405-232-3111

O'Connor, Helen Diana (3 mentions)
Oklahoma State U Coll of Osteopathic Med, 1987
9809 S Pennsylvania Ave, Oklahoma City, 405-692-1557

Thayer, James Frank (3 mentions)
U of Oklahoma, 1978
5720 W Memorial Rd, Oklahoma City, 405-470-7100

Zubialde, John Pierre (3 mentions)
U of New Mexico, 1984 *Certification:* Family Medicine
900 NE 10th St, Oklahoma City, 405-271-4224

Gastroenterology

Bookman, Larry A. (5 mentions)
U of Oklahoma, 1977 *Certification:* Internal Medicine
8121 National Ave #303, Oklahoma City, 405-737-4464

Kindley, Karen A. (5 mentions)
U of Texas-Galveston, 1988
4200 W Memorial Rd #901, Oklahoma City, 405-749-4247

Raczkowski, Carl Andrew (6 mentions)
U of Oklahoma, 1990
3366 NW Expressway St #400, Oklahoma City, 405-702-1300

Rankin, Robert Allyn (7 mentions)
U of Iowa, 1973
Certification: Gastroenterology, Internal Medicine
3366 NW Expressway St #400, Oklahoma City, 405-702-1300

Serbousek, Leann C. (5 mentions)
U of Nebraska, 1985 *Certification:* Gastroenterology
4200 W Memorial Rd #901, Oklahoma City, 405-749-4247

Wilson, Robert Lyon (5 mentions)
U of Oklahoma, 1980
4201 S Western Ave, Oklahoma City, 405-632-4000

Zuerker, Joe Carroll (9 mentions)
Texas Tech U, 1981
Certification: Gastroenterology, Internal Medicine
4200 W Memorial Rd #901, Oklahoma City, 405-749-4247

General Surgery

Boggs, Brian Robert (13 mentions)
U of Oklahoma, 1981 *Certification:* Surgery, Thoracic Surgery
4140 W Memorial Rd #615, Oklahoma City, 405-749-4255

Cannon, Jay Paul (5 mentions)
U of Oklahoma, 1970 *Certification:* Surgery
3435 NW 56th St #210, Oklahoma City, 405-945-4240

Carey, John Christopher (6 mentions)
U of Oklahoma, 1980 *Certification:* Surgery
4221 S Western Ave #5045, Oklahoma City, 405-631-7676

Connally, Tom Shi (4 mentions)
U of Texas-Dallas, 1998 *Certification:* Surgery
500 E Robinson St #2300, Norman, 405-329-4102

Cooke, Robert Northington (10 mentions)
U of Oklahoma, 1980 *Certification:* Surgery
3435 NW 56th St #410, Oklahoma City, 405-945-4414

Hemric, Ned D., Jr. (4 mentions)
Eastern Virginia Med Sch, 1984 *Certification:* Surgery
3435 NW 56th St #707, Oklahoma City, 405-601-0300

Jackson, Jimmie Keith (9 mentions)
U of Oklahoma, 1965
1211 N Shartel Ave #200, Oklahoma City, 405-232-4211
3330 NW 56th St #616, Oklahoma City, 405-232-4211

McNeely, Dennis Reed (5 mentions)
U of Oklahoma, 1979 *Certification:* Surgery
3433 NW 56th St #820, Oklahoma City, 405-945-4771

Postier, Russell Glen (5 mentions)
U of Oklahoma, 1975 *Certification:* Surgery
825 NE 10th St, Oklahoma City, 405-271-7912
920 Stanton L Young Blvd, Oklahoma City, 405-271-7912

Shavney, Teresa Marie (7 mentions)
U of Oklahoma, 1979 *Certification:* Surgery
5701 N Portland Ave #225A, Oklahoma City, 405-949-6494
3435 NW 56th St #211, Oklahoma City, 405-949-6494

Thomas, Ralph Cullen (5 mentions)
U of Kansas, 1972 *Certification:* Surgery
4140 W Memorial Rd #615, Oklahoma City, 405-749-4255

Totoro, James Amedio (15 mentions)
U of Oklahoma, 1975 *Certification:* Surgery
4205 McAuley Blvd #305, Oklahoma City, 405-749-7060

Webb, Kent Harris (5 mentions)
U of Oklahoma, 1983 *Certification:* Surgery
1000 SW 44th St #100, Oklahoma City, 405-632-4616

Geriatrics

Cranmer, Kerry Wayne (4 mentions)
U of Oklahoma, 1975
3545 NW 58th St #750, Oklahoma City, 405-949-2005

Shadid, Ralph Oscar (4 mentions)
U of Oklahoma, 1980 *Certification:* Internal Medicine
5300 N Independence #280, Oklahoma City, 405-949-6880

Winn, Peter Arkell-Scott (4 mentions)
FMS-Canada, 1978 *Certification:* Family Medicine, Geriatric
Medicine, Hospice and Palliative Medicine
900 NE 10th St, Oklahoma City, 405-271-3537

Hematology/Oncology

Ganick, Ralph G. (8 mentions)
Boston U, 1967
Certification: Hematology, Internal Medicine, Medical Oncology
1011 N Dewey Ave, Oklahoma City, 405-228-7100

Geister, Brian Vincent (9 mentions)
U of Oklahoma, 1982
Certification: Internal Medicine, Medical Oncology
3366 NW Expressway St #200, Oklahoma City, 405-943-9988
11100 Hefner Pointe Dr, Oklahoma City, 405-749-0415

Hamilton, Stephen Anthony (5 mentions)
U of Oklahoma, 1991 *Certification:* Medical Oncology
230 N Midwest Blvd, Oklahoma City, 405-737-8455

Hollen, Charles Warren (5 mentions)
U of Oklahoma, 1985 *Certification:* Medical Oncology
3525 NW 56th St, Oklahoma City, 405-942-9200

Hussein, Khader Khalid (7 mentions)
FMS-Lebanon, 1967
Certification: Hematology, Internal Medicine, Medical Oncology
4301 S Western Ave, Oklahoma City, 405-631-0919

Keefer, Mike J. (10 mentions)
U of Oklahoma, 1981
Certification: Internal Medicine, Medical Oncology
4205 McAuley Blvd #375, Oklahoma City, 405-751-4343
11100 Hefner Pointe Dr, Oklahoma City, 405-751-4343

McMinn, Johnny Russell, Jr. (5 mentions)
U of Oklahoma, 1997
Certification: Hematology, Internal Medicine, Medical Oncology
3366 NW Expressway St #200, Oklahoma City, 405-943-9988

Reitz, Craig Lee (6 mentions)
U of Oklahoma, 1979
Certification: Internal Medicine, Medical Oncology
4205 McAuley Blvd #375, Oklahoma City, 405-751-4343

Selby, George Basil (5 mentions)
U of Oklahoma, 1980
Certification: Hematology, Internal Medicine, Medical Oncology
825 NE 10th St, Oklahoma City, 405-271-8299

Toma, Aleda Ann (5 mentions)
U of Oklahoma, 1984
Certification: Internal Medicine, Medical Oncology
3525 NW 56th St #100-D, Oklahoma City, 405-942-9200

Infectious Disease

Brown, Aline C. (11 mentions)
U of Oklahoma, 1981
Certification: Infectious Disease, Internal Medicine
3400 NW Expressway St #410, Oklahoma City, 405-945-4811

Chansolme, David Henri (13 mentions)
U of Oklahoma, 1997
Certification: Infectious Disease, Internal Medicine
4221 S Western Ave #5050, Oklahoma City, 405-644-6464

Harkess, John Rudman (21 mentions)
Med Coll of Georgia, 1982
Certification: Infectious Disease, Internal Medicine
729 S Boulevard St, Edmond, 405-844-2922

Kirk, James L., Jr. (20 mentions)
U of Oklahoma, 1982
Certification: Infectious Disease, Internal Medicine
729 S Boulevard St, Edmond, 405-844-2922

Ramgopal, Vadakepat (21 mentions)
FMS-India, 1969
Certification: Infectious Disease, Internal Medicine
3400 NW Expressway St #410, Oklahoma City, 405-945-4811

Wlodaver, Clifford Grover (12 mentions)
Cornell U, 1976
Certification: Infectious Disease, Internal Medicine
3400 NW Expressway St #410, Oklahoma City, 405-945-4274

Infertility

Kallenberger, David Alan (22 mentions)
U of Oklahoma, 1975 *Certification:* Obstetrics & Gynecology
3433 NW 56th St #210-B, Oklahoma City, 405-945-4701

Reshef, Eli (26 mentions)
Baylor U, 1984 *Certification:* Obstetrics & Gynecology,
   Reproductive Endocrinology/Infertility
3433 NW 56th St #210-B, Oklahoma City, 405-945-4701

Internal Medicine *(see note on page 9)*

Beckerley, Robert James (3 mentions)
Med Coll of Wisconsin, 1976 *Certification:* Internal Medicine
3433 NW 56th St #560, Oklahoma City, 405-917-3518

Buckley, Dustan Pierce (3 mentions)
U of Oklahoma, 1992 *Certification:* Internal Medicine
4140 W Memorial Dr #303, Oklahoma City, 405-749-7030

Dimick, Susan Miller (5 mentions)
U of Oklahoma, 1984 *Certification:* Internal Medicine
3317 E Memorial Rd #103, Edmond, 405-475-0100

Drooby, S. A. Dean (3 mentions)
FMS-Australia, 1980 *Certification:* Internal Medicine
4140 W Memorial Rd #602, Oklahoma City, 405-749-4223

Saadah, Hanna Abdallah (3 mentions)
FMS-Lebanon, 1971
Certification: Infectious Disease, Internal Medicine
4205 McAuley Blvd #400, Oklahoma City, 405-749-4260

Shadid, Ralph Oscar (3 mentions)
U of Oklahoma, 1980 *Certification:* Internal Medicine
425 NW 42nd St, Oklahoma City, 405-949-6880

Vannatta, Jerry Burr (3 mentions)
U of Oklahoma, 1975 *Certification:* Internal Medicine
825 NE 10th St, Oklahoma City, 405-271-3445

Nephrology

Allen, Henry Muriel (6 mentions)
Kansas U Coll of Osteopathic Med, 1986
2149 SW 59th St #104, Oklahoma City, 405-682-0721

Carter, Bradley Dean (6 mentions)
U of Oklahoma, 1995
Certification: Internal Medicine, Nephrology
3366 NW Expressway St #550, Oklahoma City, 405-942-5442

Czerwinski, Anthony William (6 mentions)
St Louis U, 1959 *Certification:* Internal Medicine, Nephrology
4221 S Western Ave #2040, Oklahoma City, 405-644-5151

Rankin, Laura Ann Isaacs (9 mentions)
U of Iowa, 1973 *Certification:* Internal Medicine, Nephrology
3366 NW Expressway St #550, Oklahoma City, 405-942-5442

Wilson, Lorraine Theresa (9 mentions)
U of Oklahoma, 1978
Certification: Internal Medicine, Nephrology
13901 McCally Blvd #100, Oklahoma City, 405-748-5800

Neurological Surgery

Barry, Christopher John (7 mentions)
Loyola U Chicago, 1998
535 NW 9th St #205, Oklahoma City, 405-733-9400

Pelofsky, Stanley (9 mentions)
U of Oklahoma, 1966 *Certification:* Neurological Surgery
4120 W Memorial Rd #30, Oklahoma City, 405-748-3300

Remondino, Robert Louis (9 mentions)
U of Oklahoma, 1980 *Certification:* Neurological Surgery
4120 W Memorial Rd #300, Oklahoma City, 405-748-3300

Reynolds, William Emery (7 mentions)
U of Oklahoma, 1981 *Certification:* Neurological Surgery
4120 W Memorial Rd #208, Oklahoma City, 405-755-3540

Neurology

Banowetz, John Mike (7 mentions)
U of Oklahoma, 1973 *Certification:* Neurology
4120 W Memorial Rd #218, Oklahoma City, 405-302-2661

Beson, Brent Allen (8 mentions)
U of Oklahoma, 1999 *Certification:* Neurology
4221 S Western Ave #5000, Oklahoma City, 405-644-5160

Davis, Lawrence William (12 mentions)
U of Oklahoma, 1975 *Certification:* Neurology
3433 NW 56th St #600, Oklahoma City, 405-942-8586

Morgan, Charles Henry (9 mentions)
U of Oklahoma, 1972 *Certification:* Neurology
4221 S Western Ave #5000, Oklahoma City, 405-644-5160

Shipley, Winston D., II (7 mentions)
U of Oklahoma, 1984 *Certification:* Neurology
4120 W Memorial Rd #218, Oklahoma City, 405-302-2661

Wasemiller, Wayne Lee (10 mentions)
U of Oklahoma, 1975 *Certification:* Neurology
4120 W Memorial Rd #218, Oklahoma City, 405-302-2661

Obstetrics/Gynecology

Barki, May Li (4 mentions)
U of Oklahoma, 1977 *Certification:* Obstetrics & Gynecology
4140 W Memorial Rd #500, Oklahoma City, 405-755-7430

Chambers, Susan Louise (7 mentions)
U of Oklahoma, 1982 *Certification:* Obstetrics & Gynecology
11200 N Portland Ave, Oklahoma City, 405-936-1000

Doeden, Andrea (4 mentions)
U of Minnesota, 1993 *Certification:* Obstetrics & Gynecology
10900 Heffner Pointe Dr #505, Oklahoma City, 405-936-1000

Goff, Darren Walter (4 mentions)
U of Utah, 1996 *Certification:* Obstetrics & Gynecology
4140 W Memorial Rd #215, Oklahoma City, 405-242-4030

Gold, Karen Pearce (4 mentions)
U of Oklahoma, 1994 *Certification:* Obstetrics & Gynecology
3435 NW 56th St #404, Oklahoma City, 405-946-4735

Mackie, Laura L. (5 mentions)
U of Oklahoma, 1978 *Certification:* Obstetrics & Gynecology
11200 N Portland Ave, Oklahoma City, 405-936-1000

Ophthalmology

Bogie, Charles Paul, III (4 mentions)
U of Oklahoma, 1997 *Certification:* Ophthalmology
1005 Medical Park Blvd, Edmond, 405-348-0913
608 Stanton L Young Blvd, Oklahoma City, 405-271-6060

Bradford, Cynthia A. (7 mentions)
U of Texas-Galveston, 1983 *Certification:* Ophthalmology
608 Stanton L Young Blvd, Oklahoma City, 405-271-6060

Crain, Russell Dean (4 mentions)
U of Oklahoma, 1982 *Certification:* Ophthalmology
11011 Hefner Pointe Dr #B, Oklahoma City, 405-971-9393

Hummel, J. Chris (4 mentions)
U of Oklahoma, 1993 *Certification:* Ophthalmology
4205 McAuley Blvd #401, Oklahoma City, 405-755-6111

Johnston, Jay Carter (10 mentions)
U of Oklahoma, 1966 *Certification:* Ophthalmology
4200 W Memorial Rd #101, Oklahoma City, 405-749-4280

Korber, David Eugene (4 mentions)
U of Kansas, 1993 *Certification:* Ophthalmology
5320 N Portland Ave, Oklahoma City, 405-947-3330

Richard, James Marshall (6 mentions)
U of Oklahoma, 1974 *Certification:* Ophthalmology
11013 Hefner Pointe Dr, Oklahoma City, 405-751-2020

Walters, Roland A., III (4 mentions)
U of Oklahoma, 1968 *Certification:* Ophthalmology
5701 N Portland Ave #101, Oklahoma City, 405-949-6177

Wolf, Thomas Charles, Jr. (9 mentions)
U of Oklahoma, 1980 *Certification:* Ophthalmology
3431 S Blvd St #106, Edmond, 405-562-2036
2150 S Douglas Blvd #C, Oklahoma City, 405-632-6913

Orthopedics

Anderson, John Willis (5 mentions)
U of Oklahoma, 1989 *Certification:* Orthopaedic Surgery
3301 NW 50th St, Oklahoma City, 405-947-0911

Hale, William (5 mentions)
U of Oklahoma, 1993 *Certification:* Orthopaedic Surgery
14100 Parkway Commons Dr #202, Oklahoma City,
   405-749-9820

Janssen, Thomas P. (4 mentions)
U of Oklahoma, 1979 *Certification:* Orthopaedic Surgery
1110 N Lee Ave, Oklahoma City, 405-230-9000

Johnson, James Calvin (4 mentions)
U of Oklahoma, 1984 *Certification:* Orthopaedic Surgery
6205 N Santa Fe Ave #200, Oklahoma City, 405-427-6776

Langerman, Richard J., Jr. (5 mentions)
Oklahoma State U Coll of Osteopathic Med, 1987
8100 S Walker Ave #A, Oklahoma City, 405-632-4468

O'Brien, M. Sean (6 mentions)
Oklahoma State U Coll of Osteopathic Med, 1996
1230 SW 89th St #A, Oklahoma City, 405-759-2663

Schnebel, Brock Emil (5 mentions)
U of Oklahoma, 1981 *Certification:* Orthopaedic Surgery
1110 N Lee Ave, Oklahoma City, 405-552-9410
3700 36th Ave NW, Norman, 405-230-9600

Yates, Carlan Kent (5 mentions)
U of Oklahoma, 1981
Certification: Orthopaedic Sports Medicine, Orthopaedic Surgery
1110 N Lee Ave, Oklahoma City, 405-230-9000
3700 36th Ave NW, Norman, 405-230-9600

Otorhinolaryngology

Medina, Jesus Edilberto (10 mentions)
FMS-Peru, 1974 *Certification:* Otolaryngology
825 NE 10th St, Oklahoma City, 405-271-7559

Richards, Steven Vance (9 mentions)
U of Oklahoma, 1998 *Certification:* Otolaryngology
4200 W Memorial Rd #606, Oklahoma City, 405-755-1930

Sigmon, Jason Brandt (8 mentions)
U of Oklahoma, 1997 *Certification:* Otolaryngology
3435 NW 56th St #303, Oklahoma City, 405-945-4819

Pain Medicine

Mitchell, Scott Anthony (8 mentions)
Oklahoma State U Coll of Osteopathic Med, 1988
Certification: Anesthesiology, Pain Medicine
3601 NW 138th St #202, Oklahoma City, 405-775-9355
6510 South Western Ave, Oklahoma City, 405-775-9355

Yates, Gaylan Dean (6 mentions)
U of Oklahoma, 1984
Certification: Anesthesiology, Pain Medicine
14101 Parkway Commons Dr, Oklahoma City, 405-749-2766

Pathology

Brinkworth, James Michael (5 mentions)
U of Oklahoma, 1978
Certification: Anatomic Pathology & Clinical Pathology
1000 N Lee Ave, Oklahoma City, 405-272-7065

Oneson, Ruth Hannon (4 mentions)
U of Maryland, 1983 *Certification:* Anatomic Pathology &
Clinical Pathology, Cytopathology
3509 French Park Dr #D, Edmond, 405-715-4500

Pediatrics *(see note on page 9)*

Aston, Patrice Adele (3 mentions)
Oklahoma State U Coll of Osteopathic Med, 1979
Certification: Pediatrics
3400 NW Expressway St #815, Oklahoma City, 405-945-4990

Bowen, Dina M. (3 mentions)
U of Oklahoma, 1994 *Certification:* Pediatrics
1445 Health Center Pkwy, Yukon, 405-577-6700

Crittenden, Mickey Eugene (4 mentions)
U of Oklahoma, 1973 *Certification:* Pediatrics
1919 E Memorial Rd, Oklahoma City, 405-341-7009

Krause, Steven Gregory (3 mentions)
U of Oklahoma, 1977 *Certification:* Pediatrics
4140 W Memorial Rd #413, Oklahoma City, 405-755-2230

Morrow, Julie M. (5 mentions)
Oklahoma State U Coll of Osteopathic Med, 1994
Certification: Pediatrics
608 NW 9th St #3000, Oklahoma City, 405-272-7337

Stanford, Richard Emil (14 mentions)
FMS-St Lucia, 1985 *Certification:* Pediatrics
3435 NW 56th St #800, Oklahoma City, 405-945-4795

Stephens, George Kellogg (4 mentions)
U of Oklahoma, 1984 *Certification:* Pediatrics
1919 E Memorial Rd, Oklahoma City, 405-341-7009

Thompson, Roger Allen (3 mentions)
U of Oklahoma, 1988
608 NW 9th St #3000, Oklahoma City, 405-272-7337
940 NE 13th St, Oklahoma City, 405-271-4412

Wilber, Don Lane (4 mentions)
U of Oklahoma, 1978 *Certification:* Pediatrics
600 National Ave, Oklahoma City, 405-869-7700

Plastic Surgery

Hein, Robert Alan (11 mentions)
U of Oklahoma, 1983 *Certification:* Plastic Surgery, Surgery
4140 W Memorial Rd #621, Oklahoma City, 405-749-4224

Love, Tim Rodney (12 mentions)
U of Oklahoma, 1983 *Certification:* Plastic Surgery
11101 Hefner Pointe Dr #104, Oklahoma City, 405-751-5683

Psychiatry

Ardis, Janita M. (4 mentions)
FMS-United Kingdom, 1974 *Certification:* Psychiatry
3817 NW Expressway St #710, Oklahoma City, 405-943-8924

Chesler, Donald Bruce (4 mentions)
U of Oklahoma, 1984 *Certification:* Psychiatry
801 N Air Depot Blvd, Midwest City, 405-733-9516

Gutierrez, Ana M. (3 mentions)
7530 NW 23rd St #B, Bethany, 405-495-6340

Krishna, Ravu Murali (8 mentions)
FMS-India, 1971 *Certification:* Psychiatry
5100 N Brookline Ave #900, Oklahoma City, 405-604-3170

Rousseau, Arthur William (5 mentions)
U of Oklahoma, 1978 *Certification:* Psychiatry
4205 McAuley Blvd #480, Oklahoma City, 405-755-4700

Vinekar, Shreekumar S. (3 mentions)
FMS-India, 1966
Certification: Child Psychiatry, Geriatric Psychiatry, Psychiatry
920 Stanton L Young Blvd, Oklahoma City, 405-271-4219

Pulmonary Disease

Britt, Matthew Joseph (8 mentions)
U of Oklahoma, 1985
Certification: Critical Care Medicine, Pulmonary Disease
3400 NW Expressway St #105, Oklahoma City, 405-947-3335

Cook, William Wesley (6 mentions)
U of Oklahoma, 1972
Certification: Internal Medicine, Pulmonary Disease
3366 NW Expressway St #660, Oklahoma City, 405-947-3345

Fixley, Mark Steven (7 mentions)
U of Kansas, 1972 *Certification:* Critical Care Medicine,
Internal Medicine, Pulmonary Disease
4050 W Memorial Rd, Oklahoma City, 405-608-3800

Gasbarra, Dianne B. (5 mentions)
U of Oklahoma, 1981 *Certification:* Critical Care Medicine,
Internal Medicine, Pulmonary Disease, Sleep Medicine
4200 W Memorial Rd #708, Oklahoma City, 405-749-0210

Huff, John E. (7 mentions)
U of Oklahoma, 1981 *Certification:* Critical Care Medicine,
Internal Medicine, Pulmonary Disease
3400 NW Expressway St #105, Oklahoma City, 405-947-3335

Imes, Norman Kerr, Jr. (6 mentions)
U of Oklahoma, 1970 *Certification:* Internal Medicine,
Pulmonary Disease, Sleep Medicine
3555 NW 58th St #800, Oklahoma City, 405-942-6620

McKinnis, Gregory Hunt (6 mentions)
Uniformed Services U of Health Sciences, 1992
Certification: Critical Care Medicine, Pulmonary Disease
2801 Parklawn Dr #201, Midwest City, 405-736-9100

Williams, Elwood F. (8 mentions)
U of Oklahoma, 1984
4140 W Memorial Rd #421, Oklahoma City, 405-749-4210

Wood, Richard G. (8 mentions)
Oklahoma State U Coll of Osteopathic Med, 1979
Certification: Critical Care Medicine, Internal Medicine
4200 W Memorial Rd, Oklahoma City, 405-752-5864

Radiology—Diagnostic

Andrezik, Joseph Albert (3 mentions)
U of Oklahoma, 1987 *Certification:* Diagnostic Radiology
4625 S Western Ave, Oklahoma City, 405-632-2323

Beam, Chester Wray (3 mentions)
U of Oklahoma, 1975 *Certification:* Diagnostic Radiology
601 NW 11th St, Oklahoma City, 405-236-4564

Crooks, James D. (3 mentions)
U of Oklahoma, 1976 *Certification:* Diagnostic Radiology
902 S Bryant Ave, Edmond, 405-348-1900

Falcon, Oscar, Jr. (3 mentions)
U of Oklahoma, 1992 *Certification:* Diagnostic Radiology
2300 S Douglas Blvd, Midwest City, 405-736-9222

Hendrix, James Lawrence (3 mentions)
U of Oklahoma, 1986 *Certification:* Diagnostic Radiology
4625 S Western Ave, Oklahoma City, 405-632-2323

McCollom, Vance Edmond (3 mentions)
Certification: Diagnostic Radiology, Vascular &
Interventional Radiology
4625 S Western Ave, Oklahoma City, 405-632-2323

Mitchell, Debra Sue (3 mentions)
U of Oklahoma, 1982 *Certification:* Diagnostic Radiology
2601 Kelley Pointe Pkwy #101, Edmond, 405-844-2601

Owen, John Albert (3 mentions)
U of Oklahoma, 1985 *Certification:* Diagnostic Radiology
3330 NW 56th St #206, Oklahoma City, 405-945-4740

Stratemeier, Phillip Hans (3 mentions)
U of Kansas, 1972 *Certification:* Diagnostic Radiology
601 NW 11th St, Oklahoma City, 405-236-4564

Radiology—Therapeutic

Cassidy, Francis P., Jr. (8 mentions)
U of Pittsburgh, 1979 *Certification:* Diagnostic Radiology,
Vascular & Interventional Radiology
3330 NW 56th St #206, Oklahoma City, 405-945-4740
3433 NW 56th St #C10, Oklahoma City, 405-945-4232

McCollom, Vance Edmond (4 mentions)
Certification: Diagnostic Radiology, Vascular &
Interventional Radiology
4625 S Western Ave, Oklahoma City, 405-632-2323

Medbery, Clinton Amos, III (4 mentions)
Med U of South Carolina, 1976 *Certification:* Internal
Medicine, Medical Oncology, Radiation Oncology
1000 N Lee Ave, Oklahoma City, 405-272-7311

Morrison, Astrid E. (6 mentions)
U of Oklahoma, 1991 *Certification:* Radiation Oncology
1000 N Lee Ave, Oklahoma City, 405-272-7311

Rehabilitation

Bisson, Albert Joseph (7 mentions)
U of Oklahoma, 1989
Certification: Physical Medicine & Rehabilitation
4120 W Memorial Rd #118, Oklahoma City, 405-748-4700

Bouvette, Christopher M. (5 mentions)
U of Louisville, 1991
Certification: Pain Medicine, Physical Medicine & Rehabilitation
4120 W Memorial Rd #118, Oklahoma City, 405-748-4700

Moorad, Amal E. (4 mentions)
U of Oklahoma, 1975 *Certification:* Internal Medicine
4221 S Western Ave #3010, Oklahoma City, 405-636-7450

Schick, Gary Don (5 mentions)
U of Oklahoma, 1995 *Certification:* Internal Medicine,
   Physical Medicine & Rehabilitation
1110 N Lee Ave, Oklahoma City, 405-230-9000

Self, Kristi Goodwin (6 mentions)
U of Oklahoma, 1988
Certification: Physical Medicine & Rehabilitation
721 NW 6th St, Oklahoma City, 405-235-5135

Smith, Shawn M. (4 mentions)
5100 N Brookline Ave, Oklahoma City, 405-605-8780

Tipton, David Brent (5 mentions)
U of Oklahoma, 1988
Certification: Pain Medicine, Physical Medicine & Rehabilitation
5100 N Brookline Ave #530, Oklahoma City, 405-604-6652

Washburn, Tonya Cress (5 mentions)
U of Oklahoma, 1988
Certification: Physical Medicine & Rehabilitation
721 NW 6th St, Oklahoma City, 405-235-5135

Rheumatology

Carson, Craig Weldon (9 mentions)
U of Utah, 1985 *Certification:* Internal Medicine, Rheumatology
1701 Renaissance Blvd #110, Edmond, 405-844-4978

Codding, Christine Ellen (7 mentions)
U of Oklahoma, 1986 *Certification:* Rheumatology
1221 N Shartel Ave #700, Oklahoma City, 405-702-6700

Delafield, Frederick (6 mentions)
U of South Florida, 1980
Certification: Internal Medicine, Rheumatology
4200 W Memorial Rd #313, Oklahoma City, 405-749-4290

Schnitz, William Martin (6 mentions)
U of Oklahoma, 1987
Certification: Internal Medicine, Rheumatology
5701 N Portland Ave #210, Oklahoma City, 405-949-6481

Taylor-Albert, Elizabeth (9 mentions)
Duke U, 1987
4200 W Memorial Rd #812, Oklahoma City, 405-749-7025

Thoracic Surgery

Bodenhamer, Robert Mark (8 mentions)
U of Oklahoma, 1979 *Certification:* Thoracic Surgery
4050 W Memorial Rd, Oklahoma City, 405-608-3927

Kanaly, Paul Joseph (17 mentions)
U of Oklahoma, 1974 *Certification:* Thoracic Surgery
3433 NW 56th St #700, Oklahoma City, 405-945-3148
3433 NW 56th St #670, Oklahoma City, 405-951-4345

Peyton, Marvin Dale (9 mentions)
U of Oklahoma, 1971 *Certification:* Thoracic Surgery
825 NE 10th St, Oklahoma City, 405-271-7001
920 Stanton L Young Blvd, Oklahoma City, 405-271-5789

Randolph, John Douglas (8 mentions)
U of Oklahoma, 1981 *Certification:* Thoracic Surgery
4050 W Memorial Rd, Oklahoma City, 405-608-3800

Urology

Archer, James Stephen (12 mentions)
U of Oklahoma, 1980 *Certification:* Urology
1211 N Shartel Ave #300, Oklahoma City, 405-235-8008

Barnes, Daniel P. (7 mentions)
U of Oklahoma, 1983 *Certification:* Urology
11000 Hefner Pointe Dr, Oklahoma City, 405-749-9644

Herlihy, Richard E. (7 mentions)
U of Oklahoma, 1979 *Certification:* Urology
4140 W Memorial Rd #611, Oklahoma City, 405-749-4288

Little, J. Samuel, Jr. (10 mentions)
Washington U, 1987 *Certification:* Urology
11000 Hefner Pointe Dr, Oklahoma City, 405-749-9655

Miller, William Jess (10 mentions)
U of Oklahoma, 1980 *Certification:* Urology
3433 NW 56th St #920, Oklahoma City, 405-949-2322

Samara, Esber Nabeeh S. (6 mentions)
U of Oklahoma, 1968 *Certification:* Urology
3433 NW 56th St #920, Oklahoma City, 405-943-1137

Vascular Surgery

Melton, Jimmy G. (10 mentions)
Oklahoma State U Coll of Osteopathic Med, 1988
4050 W Memorial Rd, Oklahoma City, 405-608-3800

Oregon

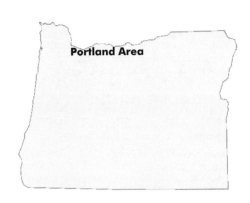

Portland Area

Portland Area

Including Clackamas, Clark, Multnomah, and Washington Counties

Allergy/Immunology

Baker, James William (7 mentions)
U of Wisconsin, 1970
Certification: Allergy & Immunology, Pediatrics
3975 SW Mercantile Dr #158, Lake Oswego, 503-636-9011

Lawrence, Robert (10 mentions)
Med Coll of Wisconsin, 1976
Certification: Allergy & Immunology, Pediatrics
3550 N Interstate Ave, Portland, 503-285-9321

Montanaro, Anthony (16 mentions)
U of Washington, 1978 *Certification:* Allergy &
    Immunology, Internal Medicine, Rheumatology
3181 SW Sam Jackson Park Rd, Portland, 503-494-8531
511 SW 10th Ave #1301, Portland, 503-228-0155
1130 NW 22nd Ave #220, Portland, 503-227-5935

O'Hollaren, Mark Thomas (11 mentions)
Oregon Health Sciences U, 1980
Certification: Allergy & Immunology, Internal Medicine
511 SW 10th Ave #1301, Portland, 503-228-0155

Anesthesiology

Bolton, Bruce Kirk (4 mentions)
Oregon Health Sciences U, 1988 *Certification:* Anesthesiology
120 NW 14th Ave #300, Portland, 503-299-9906

Carr, Richard Dale (3 mentions)
U of Hawaii, 1984 *Certification:* Anesthesiology, Pediatrics
3181 SW Sam Jackson Park Rd, Portland, 503-494-5370

Casey, Janice Eileen (5 mentions)
U of Missouri, 1978
120 NW 14th Ave #300, Portland, 503-299-9906

Farris, R. David (6 mentions)
U of California-San Diego, 1981 *Certification:* Anesthesiology
120 NW 14th Ave #300, Portland, 503-299-9906

Hiroshige, Stephen Nobuo (3 mentions)
U of Toledo, 1989 *Certification:* Anesthesiology
120 NW 14th Ave #300, Portland, 503-299-9906

Keeler, Donald Kerry (3 mentions)
U of California-San Diego, 1981
Certification: Anesthesiology, Internal Medicine
120 NW 14th Ave #300, Portland, 503-299-9906

Kirsch, Jeffrey Robert (6 mentions)
U of Michigan, 1983 *Certification:* Anesthesiology
3181 SW Sam Jackson Park Rd, Portland, 503-494-5370

Lei, Stan Sizheng (3 mentions)
FMS-China, 1983 *Certification:* Anesthesiology
120 NW 14th Ave #300, Portland, 503-299-9906

Provost, Pierre Eusebe (3 mentions)
Boston U, 1987 *Certification:* Anesthesiology
400 NE Mother Joseph Pl, Vancouver, WA, 360-567-3281

Schiller, Nicholas K. (4 mentions)
Oregon Health Sciences U, 1991 *Certification:* Anesthesiology
400 NE Mother Joseph Pl, Vancouver, WA, 360-567-3281

Stoler, Eric Michael (4 mentions)
U of California-San Francisco, 1985 *Certification:* Anesthesiology
400 NE Mother Joseph Pl, Vancouver, WA, 360-567-3281

Wright, Gregory Lyle (4 mentions)
U of Illinois, 1973 *Certification:* Anesthesiology
120 NW 14th Ave #300, Portland, 503-299-9906

Cardiac Surgery

Douville, Emery C. (21 mentions)
U of California-Los Angeles, 1982
Certification: Surgery, Thoracic Surgery
507 NE 47th Ave, Portland, 503-963-3030
1111 NE 99th Ave #201, Portland, 503-963-3030

Furnary, Anthony Paul (8 mentions)
Jefferson Med Coll, 1984 *Certification:* Surgery, Thoracic Surgery
9155 SW Barnes Rd #240, Portland, 503-297-1419

Hill, Jonathan Grant (11 mentions)
U of Southern California, 1975 *Certification:* Thoracic Surgery
2222 NW Lovejoy St #315, Portland, 503-226-6321

Ott, Gary Yee (18 mentions)
Jefferson Med Coll, 1983
Certification: Surgery, Surgical Critical Care, Thoracic Surgery
1111 NE 99th Ave #201, Portland, 503-963-3030

Slater, Matthew Simon (9 mentions)
Eastern Virginia Med Sch, 1993
Certification: Surgery, Thoracic Surgery
3181 SW Sam Jackson Park Rd, Portland, 503-494-7820

Tsen, Andrew Cho (14 mentions)
U of Kansas, 1988 *Certification:* Surgery, Thoracic Surgery
2222 NW Lovejoy St #315, Portland, 503-963-3030
10202 SE 32nd Ave #702, Portland, 503-963-3030

Cardiology

Angel, Aaron L. (4 mentions)
U of Texas-San Antonio, 1985
Certification: Cardiovascular Disease, Internal Medicine
2211 E Mill Plain Blvd, Vancouver, WA, 360-418-6001

Crispell, Kathy Ann (8 mentions)
Tulane U, 1990 *Certification:* Cardiovascular Disease
10180 SE Sunnyside Rd, Clackamas, 503-652-2880

Dawley, Douglas Lee (6 mentions)
Stanford U, 1980
Certification: Cardiovascular Disease, Internal Medicine
1111 NE 99th Ave #201, Portland, 503-963-3030

Fulmer, Alison (6 mentions)
U of California-Irvine, 1983
Certification: Cardiovascular Disease, Internal Medicine
9205 SW Barnes Rd #200, Portland, 503-216-1880

Goldring, Maureen Burke (5 mentions)
U of Connecticut, 1976
Certification: Cardiovascular Disease, Internal Medicine
2222 NW Lovejoy St #606, Portland, 503-229-7554

Greves, John Hans, III (5 mentions)
Indiana U, 1972 *Certification:* Cardiovascular Disease,
    Internal Medicine, Interventional Cardiology
700 NE 87th Ave, Vancouver, WA, 360-254-1240

Grewe, Kathy (9 mentions)
Oregon Health Sciences U, 1983
Certification: Cardiovascular Disease
300 N Graham St #320, Portland, 503-281-0448

Hodson, Robert Walter (4 mentions)
Oregon Health Sciences U, 1981 *Certification:* Cardiovascular
    Disease, Internal Medicine, Interventional Cardiology
1111 NE 99th Ave #201, Portland, 503-963-3030

King, Douglas Hoff (6 mentions)
U of Washington, 1979
Certification: Pediatric Cardiology, Pediatrics
501 N Graham St #330, Portland, 503-280-3418

Lewis, Sandra Jean (6 mentions)
Stanford U, 1977
Certification: Cardiovascular Disease, Internal Medicine
2222 NW Lovejoy St #606, Portland, 503-229-7554

McAnulty, John H., Jr. (15 mentions)
Tufts U, 1969 *Certification:* Cardiovascular Disease, Clinical Cardiac Electrophysiology, Internal Medicine
3181 SW Sam Jackson Park Rd, Portland, 503-494-8750
1130 NW 22nd Ave #220, Portland, 503-413-7970

Ratkovec, Ranae Marie (4 mentions)
U of Nebraska, 1984
Certification: Cardiovascular Disease, Internal Medicine
1111 NE 99th Ave #201, Portland, 503-963-3030

Reinhart, Steven Earl (12 mentions)
Oregon Health Sciences U, 1978
Certification: Cardiovascular Disease, Internal Medicine
1111 NE 99th Ave #201, Portland, 503-963-3030

Reller, Mark Douglas (4 mentions)
U of Cincinnati, 1977
Certification: Pediatric Cardiology, Pediatrics
707 SW Gaines St, Portland, 503-494-2192
2241 Lloyd Ctr, Portland, 503-494-8417
3181 SW Sam Jackson Park Rd, Portland, 503-494-8311

Simkoff, William Louis (4 mentions)
U of Cincinnati, 1975 *Certification:* Cardiovascular Disease, Internal Medicine, Interventional Cardiology
9427 SW Barnes Rd #498, Portland, 503-297-6234

Strauss, Richard (9 mentions)
U of Southern California, 1977
Certification: Cardiovascular Disease, Internal Medicine
10180 SE Sunnyside Rd, Clackamas, 503-571-3658

Wilson, Michael Allen (4 mentions)
U of Michigan, 1981 *Certification:* Cardiovascular Disease, Internal Medicine, Interventional Cardiology
9472 SW Barnes Rd #498, Portland, 503-297-6234

Dermatology

Collins, Scott Andrew (5 mentions)
Baylor U, 1987 *Certification:* Dermatology
10215 SW Hall Blvd, Portland, 503-245-2415

Gass, Susan Danielle (4 mentions)
Rosalind Franklin U, 1988 *Certification:* Dermatology
4855 Sw Western Ave, Beaverton, 503-350-2411

Krol, Alfons L. (7 mentions)
Certification: Dermatology, Pediatric Dermatology
3181 SW Sam Jackson Park Rd, Portland, 503-494-8311

Lyons, Mary Lorraine (4 mentions)
Rosalind Franklin U, 1978 *Certification:* Dermatology
4855 SW Western Ave, Beaverton, 503-350-2415

Miller, Debbie Lee (9 mentions)
U of Washington, 1983
Certification: Dermatology, Internal Medicine
2565 NW Lovejoy St #100, Portland, 503-279-9700

Norris, Patricia Lynn (5 mentions)
Oregon Health Sciences U, 1994 *Certification:* Dermatology
2222 NW Lovejoy St #412, Portland, 503-227-7117

Pitt, Andrew Edward (4 mentions)
Oregon Health Sciences U, 1986 *Certification:* Dermatology
17704 Jean Way #102, Lake Oswego, 503-635-9221

Rich, Phoebe (7 mentions)
Oregon Health Sciences U, 1984 *Certification:* Dermatology
2565 NW Lovejoy St #200, Portland, 503-226-3376

Sisk, Clark Edmund (8 mentions)
Washington U, 1978 *Certification:* Dermatology
3600 N Interstate Ave, Portland, 503-331-3033

Storrs, Frances Judy (4 mentions)
Cornell U, 1964 *Certification:* Dermatology
3303 SW Bond Ave #CH-16-D, Portland, 503-494-4713

Swanson, Neil Axel (4 mentions)
U of Rochester, 1976 *Certification:* Dermatology
3303 SW Bond Ave #CH-16-D, Portland, 503-494-4713

Tavelli, Bert Gregory (10 mentions)
U of Colorado, 1982 *Certification:* Dermatology
1130 NW 22nd Ave #330, Portland, 503-295-2366

Emergency Medicine

Andrews, Christopher Ray (7 mentions)
Med Coll of Georgia, 1992 *Certification:* Emergency Medicine
9205 SW Barnes Rd, Portland, 503-216-2567

Bell, Marty Craig (5 mentions)
Georgetown U, 1984 *Certification:* Emergency Medicine
400 NE Mother Joseph Pl, Vancouver, WA, 360-514-2142

Carnevale, Tony John (6 mentions)
Loyola U Chicago, 1992 *Certification:* Emergency Medicine
10180 SE Sunnyside Rd, Clackamas, 503-652-2880

Lewis, Timothy Wade (5 mentions)
U of Washington, 1991 *Certification:* Emergency Medicine
4805 NE Glisan St, Portland, 503-215-6000

Lorts, Gregory Byron (3 mentions)
Oregon Health Sciences U, 1974
Certification: Emergency Medicine
4805 NE Glisan St, Portland, 503-215-6000

Vissers, Robert John (3 mentions)
FMS-Canada, 1990 *Certification:* Emergency Medicine
2801 N Gantenbein Ave, Portland, 503-413-4121

Endocrinology

Bergstrom, Richard Walter (6 mentions)
U of Washington, 1983
Certification: Endocrinology and Metabolism, Internal Medicine
1130 NW 22nd Ave #400, Portland, 503-274-4884

Bookin, Stephen Oscar (11 mentions)
U of Iowa, 1969
Certification: Endocrinology and Metabolism, Internal Medicine
9155 SW Barnes Rd #317, Portland, 503-297-3336
1130 NW 22nd Ave #400, Portland, 503-274-4884

Boston, Bruce Alan (6 mentions)
Oregon Health Sciences U, 1988
Certification: Pediatric Endocrinology, Pediatrics
3181 SW Sam Jackson Park Rd, Portland, 503-494-1926

Burford, Patricia Anne (11 mentions)
FMS-United Kingdom, 1987
5050 NE Hoyt St #157, Portland, 503-445-8080

Curosh, Nancy Ann (5 mentions)
U of Arizona, 1986 *Certification:* Internal Medicine
5050 NE Hoyt St #234, Portland, 503-238-2941

Glauber, Harry Steven (10 mentions)
FMS-South Africa, 1978
Certification: Endocrinology and Metabolism, Internal Medicine
10180 SE Sunnyside Rd, Clackamas, 503-652-2880

Greenberg, Craig Phillip (5 mentions)
Loyola U Chicago, 1980
Certification: Endocrinology and Metabolism, Internal Medicine
10101 SE Main St #3010, Portland, 503-255-3404
6475 SW Borland Rd #M, Tualatin, 503-255-3404

Herson, Michael Kevin (10 mentions)
Rosalind Franklin U, 1981
Certification: Endocrinology and Metabolism, Internal Medicine
10180 SE Sunnyside Rd, Clackamas, 503-571-8484

Neifing, James Lester (10 mentions)
U of Illinois, 1986
Certification: Endocrinology, Diabetes, and Metabolism
1130 NW 22nd Ave #400, Portland, 503-274-4884
9155 SW Barnes Rd #302, Portland, 503-297-3336

Prihoda, James Sheldon (7 mentions)
U of Illinois, 1985 *Certification:* Endocrinology, Diabetes, and Metabolism, Internal Medicine
3325 N Interstate Ave, Portland, 503-280-5060

Family Practice *(see note on page 9)*

Bulger, Arthur R. (4 mentions)
11510 SE Stark St, Portland, 503-256-0636

Chesnutt, James Clive (3 mentions)
Oregon Health Sciences U, 1989
Certification: Family Medicine, Sports Medicine
3181 SW Sam Jackson Park Rd, Portland, 503-494-6400

Fagnan, Lyle James (3 mentions)
Oregon Health Sciences U, 1971 *Certification:* Family Medicine
4411 SW Vermont St, Portland, 503-494-9992

Fields, Scott Allen (3 mentions)
U of Washington, 1986 *Certification:* Family Medicine
3181 SW Sam Jackson Park Rd, Portland, 503-494-8573
3303 SW Bond Ave, Portland, 503-494-8573
3930 SE Division St, Portland, 503-418-3900

Geddes, Gary Ross (3 mentions)
FMS-Canada, 1974
12400 NW Cornell Rd #100, Portland, 503-626-0939

Reagan, Bonnie (8 mentions)
Oregon Health Sciences U, 1984 *Certification:* Family Medicine
541 NE 20th Ave #210, Portland, 503-233-6940

Reagan, Joshua David (5 mentions)
U of California-San Francisco, 2000
Certification: Family Medicine
541 NE 20th Ave #210, Portland, 503-233-6940

Sullivan, Joseph William (5 mentions)
U of California-San Francisco, 1985
Certification: Family Medicine
5050 NE Hoyt St #240, Portland, 503-215-6480

Villegas, Lydia Antonieta (3 mentions)
U of Nevada, 1992 *Certification:* Family Medicine
5050 NE Hoyt St #240, Portland, 503-215-6480

Williams, Terry Randall (4 mentions)
Oregon Health Sciences U, 1982 *Certification:* Family Medicine
7101 NE 137th Ave, Vancouver, WA, 360-418-6001

Gastroenterology

Baumeister, Frank J., Jr. (9 mentions)
U of Miami, 1961
Certification: Gastroenterology, Internal Medicine
1130 NW 22nd Ave #410, Portland, 503-229-7137

Bennetts, Roland William (6 mentions)
Stanford U, 1973
Certification: Gastroenterology, Internal Medicine
1130 NW 22nd Ave #410, Portland, 503-229-7137

Casimo, Matthew Anthony (6 mentions)
U of Vermont, 1984
Certification: Gastroenterology, Internal Medicine
700 NE 87th Ave, Vancouver, WA, 360-254-1240

Fausel, Craig Stephen (8 mentions)
SUNY-Upstate Med U, 1976
Certification: Gastroenterology, Internal Medicine
1111 NE 99th Ave #301, Portland, 503-258-1755

Fennerty, Michael Brian (6 mentions)
Creighton U, 1980
Certification: Gastroenterology, Internal Medicine
3181 SW Sam Jackson Park Rd, Portland, 503-494-8577

Phillips, Michael Gregory (14 mentions)
Oregon Health Sciences U, 1986
Certification: Gastroenterology, Internal Medicine
5050 NE Hoyt St #611, Portland, 503-215-6844
1111 NE 99th Ave #301, Portland, 503-258-1755

Poorman, Jay Clifford (5 mentions)
Washington U, 1988
Certification: Gastroenterology, Internal Medicine
501 N Graham St #465, Portland, 503-282-5559

Schlippert, William Charles (6 mentions)
Temple U, 1971
Certification: Gastroenterology, Internal Medicine
10000 SE Main St, Portland, 503-255-3054

Shneidman, Robert James (13 mentions)
U of Texas-Houston, 1982
Certification: Gastroenterology, Internal Medicine
3500 N Interstate Ave, Portland, 503-285-9321

Sleven, Rodger Alan (11 mentions)
U of California-San Francisco, 1976
Certification: Gastroenterology, Internal Medicine
9701 SW Barnes Rd #300, Portland, 503-297-8081

Terry, Annie B. (12 mentions)
U of Buffalo, 1971
Certification: Pediatric Gastroenterology, Pediatrics
3181 SW Sam Jackson Park Rd, Portland, 503-494-1078

Wang, Anne H. (10 mentions)
Oregon Health Sciences U, 1987
Certification: Gastroenterology, Internal Medicine
1111 NE 99th Ave #301, Portland, 503-258-1755

General Surgery

Aliabadi-Wahle, S. (7 mentions)
Tulane U, 1995 *Certification:* Surgery
5050 NE Hoyt St #411, Portland, 503-281-0561

Cook, David W. (5 mentions)
Oregon Health Sciences U, 1984 *Certification:* Surgery
9155 SW Barnes Rd #940, Portland, 503-297-1351
19250 SW 65th Ave #240, Tualatin, 503-691-9895

Cramer, Andrew Benjamin (8 mentions)
Oregon Health Sciences U, 1986 *Certification:* Surgery
19250 SW 65th Ave #220, Tualatin, 503-692-5650

Gilbert, Wayne Francis (5 mentions)
St Louis U, 1987 *Certification:* Surgery
9427 SW Barnes Rd, Portland, 503-203-2120

Giswold, Mary Elizabeth (4 mentions)
U of Wisconsin, 1998 *Certification:* Surgery
10100 SE Sunnyside Rd, Clackamas, 503-240-6225

Hunter, John Greenleaf (4 mentions)
U of Pennsylvania, 1981 *Certification:* Surgery
3181 SW Sam Jackson Park Rd, Portland, 503-494-8372

Imatani, James, Jr. (4 mentions)
U of Colorado, 1980 *Certification:* Surgery
5050 NE Hoyt St #610, Portland, 503-231-0377

Irish, C. Edwin (7 mentions)
U of Vermont, 1974 *Certification:* Surgery
1130 NW 22nd Ave #500, Portland, 503-229-7339

Johnson, Nathalie Mcdowell (6 mentions)
Virginia Commonwealth U, 1986 *Certification:* Surgery
1130 NW 22nd Ave #500, Portland, 503-229-7339

Lehti, Patrick Michael (6 mentions)
U of California-San Diego, 1978 *Certification:* Surgery
24900 SE Stark St #208, Gresham, 503-661-4526
5050 NE Hoyt St #411, Portland, 503-239-4324

Lester, Steven Edward (5 mentions)
U of Washington, 1986 *Certification:* Surgery
9427 SW Barnes Rd, Portland, 503-203-2120

Oh, George Richard (4 mentions)
Stanford U, 1980 *Certification:* Surgery
9427 SW Barnes Rd, Portland, 503-203-2120

Pulito, Joseph F. (4 mentions)
Georgetown U, 1973 *Certification:* Surgery
501 N Graham St #555, Portland, 503-288-7535
6485 SW Borland Rd #E, Tualatin, 503-692-0444

Rippey, Wesley Edward (8 mentions)
Loma Linda U, 1976 *Certification:* Surgery
10000 SE Main St #408, Portland, 503-255-9303

Sheppard, Brett C. (5 mentions)
Rosalind Franklin U, 1984 *Certification:* Surgery
3181 SW Sam Jackson Park Rd, Portland, 503-494-8372

Slovic, Steven Brent (4 mentions)
Yale U, 1988 *Certification:* Surgery
700 NE 87th Ave, Vancouver, WA, 360-254-1240
200 NE Mother Joseph Pl #330, Vancouver, WA, 360-397-3119

Soot, Laurel C. (4 mentions)
U of Washington, 1994 *Certification:* Surgery
9155 SW Barnes Rd #940, Portland, 503-297-1351

Wolf, Ronald Frank (8 mentions)
Oregon Health Sciences U, 1987 *Certification:* Surgery
9155 SW Barnes Rd #940, Portland, 503-297-1351

Yu, Kelvin Chiu (9 mentions)
U of California-San Francisco, 1990 *Certification:* Surgery
5050 NE Hoyt St #610, Portland, 503-231-0377

Zelko, John Robert (14 mentions)
U of Hawaii, 1978 *Certification:* Surgery
1040 NW 22nd Ave #560, Portland, 503-281-0561

Geriatrics

Hayward, Arthur D. Alanson (4 mentions)
Columbia U, 1972 *Certification:* Internal Medicine
2701 NW Vaughn St #140, Portland, 503-499-5200

Hodges, Marian Osborne (7 mentions)
Columbia U, 1985
Certification: Geriatric Medicine, Internal Medicine
5050 NE Hoyt St #540, Portland, 503-215-6600

Miura, Lisa Noelle (5 mentions)
U of Pennsylvania, 1997
Certification: Geriatric Medicine, Internal Medicine
2800 N Vancouver Ave #230, Portland, 503-413-2901

Newton, Patricia Anne (9 mentions)
Virginia Commonwealth U, 1976
Certification: Geriatric Medicine, Internal Medicine
1200 NW 23rd Ave, Portland, 503-413-7074

Shepard, Mary Alice (4 mentions)
U of California-San Francisco, 1978
Certification: Geriatric Medicine, Internal Medicine
2211 E Mill Plain Blvd, Vancouver, WA, 360-418-6001
7101 NE 137th Ave, Vancouver, WA, 360-418-6001

Hematology/Oncology

Andersen, Jay Christopher (5 mentions)
U of Kansas, 1996
Certification: Hematology, Internal Medicine, Medical Oncology
9555 SW Barnes Rd #150, Portland, 503-297-7403
265 N Broadway St, Portland, 503-297-7403

Braun, Marcus Paul (4 mentions)
U of Washington, 1986
Certification: Internal Medicine, Medical Oncology
210 SE 136th Ave, Vancouver, WA, 360-944-9889

Deloughery, Thomas Grier (5 mentions)
Indiana U, 1985 *Certification:* Blood Banking/Transfusion
Medicine, Hematology, Internal Medicine, Medical Oncology
3181 SW Sam Jackson Park Rd #L-586, Portland, 503-494-6594

Ey, Frederick S. (8 mentions)
Oregon Health Sciences U, 1984
Certification: Internal Medicine, Medical Oncology
15700 SW Greystone Ct, Beaverton, 503-203-1000
19875 SW 65th Ave #220, Tualatin, 503-885-9789

Hansen, Keith Sherman (4 mentions)
Wake Forest U, 1971
Certification: Hematology, Internal Medicine
265 N Broadway St, Portland, 503-280-1223

Kujovich, Jody Lynn (4 mentions)
Harvard U, 1989
265 N Broadway St, Portland, 503-280-1223

Lewis, Stacy Kay (4 mentions)
Washington U, 1988 *Certification:* Hematology, Medical Oncology
9155 SW Barnes Rd #533, Portland, 503-216-6300

Lycette, Jennifer Lynn (4 mentions)
U of Washington, 2000
Certification: Hematology, Internal Medicine, Medical Oncology
3600 N Interstate Ave, Portland, 503-331-6500

Menashe, Jeffrey Irving (6 mentions)
Oregon Health Sciences U, 1981
Certification: Hematology, Internal Medicine, Medical Oncology
5050 NE Hoyt St #256, Portland, 503-239-7767

Nichols, Craig Randal (4 mentions)
Oregon Health Sciences U, 1978
Certification: Internal Medicine, Medical Oncology
4805 NE Glisan St, Portland, 503-215-5696

Orwoll, Rebecca Lynn (6 mentions)
Oregon Health Sciences U, 1979
Certification: Hematology, Internal Medicine
5050 NE Hoyt St #256, Portland, 503-239-7767

Smith, John Washburn, II (4 mentions)
Jefferson Med Coll, 1981
Certification: Internal Medicine, Medical Oncology
5050 NE Hoyt St #256, Portland, 503-239-7767

Takahasi, Gary Wayne (5 mentions)
U of Hawaii, 1984
15700 SW Graystone Ct, Beaverton, 503-203-1000

Tirumali, Nagendra R. (8 mentions)
FMS-India, 1974
Certification: Hematology, Internal Medicine, Medical Oncology
3600 N Interstate Ave, Portland, 503-331-6500

Urba, Walter John (5 mentions)
U of Miami, 1981
Certification: Internal Medicine, Medical Oncology
4805 NE Glisan St, Portland, 503-215-5696

Weinstein, Ralph Elliott (9 mentions)
SUNY-Upstate Med U, 1982
Certification: Hematology, Internal Medicine, Medical Oncology
265 N Broadway St, Portland, 503-280-1223

Infectious Disease

Crislip, Mark Alden (28 mentions)
Oregon Health Sciences U, 1983
Certification: Infectious Disease, Internal Medicine
1015 NW 22nd Ave, Portland, 503-413-8407

Dworkin, Ronald Jeffrey (12 mentions)
Mount Sinai Sch of Med, 1984
Certification: Infectious Disease, Internal Medicine
5050 NE Hoyt St #540, Portland, 503-215-6600

Gilbert, David Norman (10 mentions)
Oregon Health Sciences U, 1964
Certification: Infectious Disease, Internal Medicine
5050 NE Hoyt St #540, Portland, 503-215-6600

Kane, Joseph Alan (18 mentions)
Harvard U, 1974 *Certification:* Internal Medicine
9900 SE Sunnyside Rd, Clackamas, 503-571-3165

Leggett, James E., Jr. (9 mentions)
U of Kentucky, 1980
Certification: Infectious Disease, Internal Medicine
5050 NE Hoyt St #540, Portland, 503-215-6600

Paisley, John William (10 mentions)
Harvard U, 1973 *Certification:* Medical Microbiology, Pediatrics
2801 N Gantenbein Ave, Portland, 503-413-2042

Riley, Keith Bernard (11 mentions)
U of Southern California, 1983
Certification: Infectious Disease, Internal Medicine
9900 SE Sunnyside Rd, Clackamas, 503-571-3165

Sehdev, Paul Singh (10 mentions)
U of Kansas, 1993 *Certification:* Infectious Disease
9155 SW Barnes Rd #304, Portland, 503-216-7000

Slaughter, Sarah Ellen (9 mentions)
Indiana U, 1990 *Certification:* Infectious Disease
5050 NE Hoyt St #540, Portland, 503-215-6600

Infertility

Hesla, John S. (13 mentions)
Oregon Health Sciences U, 1982 *Certification:* Obstetrics &
  Gynecology, Reproductive Endocrinology/Infertility
2222 NW Lovejoy St #304, Portland, 503-274-4994

Matteri, Robert Keith (11 mentions)
Emory U, 1978 *Certification:* Internal Medicine, Obstetrics
  & Gynecology, Reproductive Endocrinology/Infertility
2222 NW Lovejoy St #304, Portland, 503-274-4994

Internal Medicine *(see note on page 9)*

Amato, Daniel Frank (4 mentions)
Oregon Health Sciences U, 1971 *Certification:* Internal Medicine
5050 NE Hoyt St #454, Portland, 503-215-6405

Beeson, Steven Carter (3 mentions)
Oregon Health Sciences U, 1986 *Certification:* Internal Medicine
9155 SW Barnes Rd #340, Portland, 503-605-9200

Choo, Christine E. (5 mentions)
Albert Einstein Coll of Med, 1996 *Certification:* Internal Medicine
10180 SE Sunnyside Rd, Clackamas, 503-571-3414

Coodley, Gregg (3 mentions)
U of California-San Diego, 1985 *Certification:* Internal Medicine
2400 SW Vermont St, Portland, 503-452-0915

Dodge, Cyril Sheldon (3 mentions)
U of North Carolina, 1975 *Certification:* Internal Medicine
700 NE 87th Ave, Vancouver, WA, 360-253-1285

Gilden, Daniel Joseph (3 mentions)
U of Missouri, 1985 *Certification:* Internal Medicine
2801 N Gantenbein Ave, Portland, 503-413-2200

Gross, Bennett Raymond (3 mentions)
Case Western Reserve U, 1995 *Certification:* Internal Medicine
9800 SE Sunnyside Rd, Clackamas, 503-652-2880

Hassell, Miles (4 mentions)
FMS-Australia, 1988 *Certification:* Internal Medicine
9155 SW Barnes Rd #302, Portland, 503-291-1777

Jones, Sean Eric (3 mentions)
Yale U, 1986 *Certification:* Internal Medicine
3550 N Interstate Ave, Portland, 503-285-9321

Kurz, Frank Joseph (3 mentions)
Baylor U, 1977 *Certification:* Internal Medicine
2222 NW Lovejoy St #505, Portland, 503-226-4091

Marr, Curtis (3 mentions)
Oregon Health Sciences U, 1988 *Certification:* Internal Medicine
1130 NW 22nd Ave, Portland, 503-413-8988

Mirka, Alar (3 mentions)
Oregon Health Sciences U, 1982 *Certification:* Internal Medicine
1130 NW 22nd Ave #220, Portland, 503-413-8988

Pena, Porfirio (3 mentions)
Oregon Health Sciences U, 1986 *Certification:* Internal Medicine
5050 NE Hoyt St #203, Portland, 503-230-9224

Reis, Thomas Charles (3 mentions)
Creighton U, 1969 *Certification:* Internal Medicine
700 NE 87th Ave, Vancouver, WA, 360-254-1240

Reuler, James Bruce (6 mentions)
U of Chicago, 1973 *Certification:* Internal Medicine
3710 SW Us Veterans Hospital Rd, Portland, 503-273-5014

Root, Leslie L. (3 mentions)
Oregon Health Sciences U, 1994 *Certification:* Internal Medicine
501 N Graham St #100, Portland, 503-249-5780

Nephrology

Hilbelink, Todd Ronald (6 mentions)
Ohio State U, 1996 *Certification:* Internal Medicine, Nephrology
5314 NE Irving St, Portland, 503-284-1937

Kauffman, Susan M. (10 mentions)
Oregon Health Sciences U, 1981
Certification: Internal Medicine, Nephrology
6902 SE Lake Rd #100, Milwaukie, 503-786-1167

Kuehnel, Edward George (9 mentions)
SUNY-Downstate Med Coll, 1970
Certification: Internal Medicine, Nephrology
10201 SE Main St #27, Portland, 503-256-0877

Raguram, Parthasarathy (6 mentions)
FMS-India, 1989 *Certification:* Internal Medicine, Nephrology
5314 NE Irving St, Portland, 503-284-1937

Steed, Leslie Marie (6 mentions)
U of Washington, 1987
Certification: Internal Medicine, Nephrology
1130 NW 22nd Ave #640, Portland, 503-229-7976

Thorp, Micah L. (6 mentions)
Des Moines U, 1995 *Certification:* Internal Medicine, Nephrology
6902 SE Lake Rd #100, Milwaukie, 503-786-1167

Walczyk, Michael Hanley (15 mentions)
Hahnemann U, 1981
Certification: Internal Medicine, Nephrology
1130 NW 22nd Ave #640, Portland, 503-229-7976

Neurological Surgery

Abtin, Keyvan (6 mentions)
U of Minnesota, 1994 *Certification:* Neurological Surgery
333 SE 7th Ave #4050, Hillsboro, 503-924-2444

Delashaw, Johnny B., Jr. (9 mentions)
U of Washington, 1983 *Certification:* Neurological Surgery
3181 SW Sam Jackson Park Rd #L-472, Portland, 503-494-7737
3303 SW Bond Ave #CH-8N, Portland, 503-494-7737

Grewe, Kent Michael (7 mentions)
Oregon Health Sciences U, 1983
Certification: Neurological Surgery
501 N Graham St #545, Portland, 503-288-5151

Kuether, Todd Allen (6 mentions)
U of Kansas, 1993 *Certification:* Neurological Surgery
9155 SW Barnes Rd #440, Portland, 503-297-3766

O'Neill, Oisin R. (11 mentions)
FMS-Ireland, 1985 *Certification:* Neurological Surgery
9155 SW Barnes Rd #440, Portland, 503-297-3766

Polin, Richard Sanders (7 mentions)
Certification: Neurological Surgery
9800 SE Sunnyside Rd, Clackamas, 503-571-5780
10100 SE Sunnyside Rd, Clackamas, 503-571-5780

Rohrer, Daniel C. (9 mentions)
New York Med Coll, 1987 *Certification:* Neurological Surgery
9155 SW Barnes Rd #210, Portland, 503-546-3503

Rosenbaum, Thomas Jay (12 mentions)
Oregon Health Sciences U, 1973
Certification: Neurological Surgery
2222 NW Lovejoy St #516, Portland, 503-229-8470

Selden, Nathan R. (8 mentions)
Harvard U, 1993 *Certification:* Neurological Surgery
3181 SW Sam Jackson Park Rd, Portland, 503-494-4314

Wehby, Monica (8 mentions)
Baylor U, 1988 *Certification:* Neurological Surgery
5050 NE Hoyt St #347, Portland, 503-232-2130
9155 SW Barnes Rd #440, Portland, 503-297-3766
501 N Graham St #330-B, Portland, 503-443-3690

Neurology

Brown, Jeffrey Josiah (4 mentions)
George Washington U, 1982 *Certification:* Neurology
501 N Graham St #515, Portland, 503-282-0943

Clark, Gregory Lynn (8 mentions)
U of Maryland, 1983 *Certification:* Neurology
10180 SE Sunnyside Rd, Clackamas, 503-652-2880

Cohan, Stanley Lawrence (4 mentions)
SUNY-Downstate Med Coll, 1968 *Certification:* Neurology
9427 SW Barnes Rd #595, Portland, 503-216-1060

Ellison, Catherine Marie (7 mentions)
Oregon Health Sciences U, 1982 *Certification:* Neurology
5050 NE Hoyt St #315, Portland, 503-963-3100

Gancher, Stephen Theo (4 mentions)
Wake Forest U, 1980 *Certification:* Neurology
3550 N Interstate Ave, Portland, 503-285-9321

Kao, Amy (4 mentions)
Northwestern U, 1997 *Certification:* Neurology with Special
  Qualifications in Child Neurology, Pediatrics
707 SW Gaines St, Portland, 503-494-0188

Leonard, Hubert Arnold (4 mentions)
Oregon Health Sciences U, 1973 *Certification:* Neurology
1040 NW 22nd Ave #420, Portland, 503-229-7606

Lowenkopf, Theodore John (4 mentions)
Jefferson Med Coll, 1993
Certification: Neurology, Vascular Neurology
9427 SW Barnes Rd #595, Portland, 503-216-2346

Rosenbaum, Richard Barry (12 mentions)
Harvard U, 1971 *Certification:* Internal Medicine, Neurology
5050 NE Hoyt St #315, Portland, 503-963-3100

Rosenbaum, Robert Alan (7 mentions)
Johns Hopkins U, 1968 *Certification:* Neurology
5050 NE Hoyt St #315, Portland, 503-963-3100

Stigler, Jack Reece (7 mentions)
A T Still U, 1985 *Certification:* Neurology
10180 SE Sunnyside Rd, Clackamas, 503-652-2880

Taylor, Howard Scott (4 mentions)
Med Coll of Georgia, 1988 *Certification:* Neurology
10000 SE Main St #307, Portland, 503-256-3034

Zarelli, Greg R. (9 mentions)
Baylor U, 1996 *Certification:* Neurology
10180 SE Sunnyside Rd, Clackamas, 503-571-3664

Obstetrics/Gynecology

Barrett, Robin Wachunas (4 mentions)
Ohio State U, 1997 *Certification:* Obstetrics & Gynecology
2222 NW Lovejoy St #619, Portland, 503-229-7720
12442 SW Scholls Ferry Rd #206, Tigard, 503-579-6061

Bauer, Maxine Elaine (4 mentions)
Emory U, 1995 *Certification:* Obstetrics & Gynecology
5050 NE Hoyt St #421, Portland, 503-239-6800

Collins, Michael Sean (5 mentions)
Med U of South Carolina, 1977
Certification: Obstetrics & Gynecology
1130 NW 22nd Ave #120, Portland, 503-229-7353
9555 SW Barnes Rd #260, Portland, 503-624-2044

Corbin, Christine Marie (3 mentions)
Northeastern Ohio U, 1990 *Certification:* Obstetrics & Gynecology
4660 NE Belknap Ct #109, Hillsboro, 503-693-1944

Curtis, Audrey Ellen (3 mentions)
U of California-San Francisco, 1995
Certification: Obstetrics & Gynecology
10100 SE Sunnyside Rd, Clackamas, 503-571-2946

De Castro, Enrique C. M. (3 mentions)
FMS-Mexico, 1957 *Certification:* Obstetrics & Gynecology
2222 NW Lovejoy St #619, Portland, 503-229-7720

Drake, Brian Eugene (3 mentions)
Texas Tech U, 1997 *Certification:* Obstetrics & Gynecology
10000 SE Main St #309, Portland, 503-257-7757

Dyson, Robert Duane (3 mentions)
Oregon Health Sciences U, 1977
Certification: Obstetrics & Gynecology
177 NE 102nd Ave, Portland, 503-254-1399

Flath, Thomas Oakley (3 mentions)
U of Iowa, 1973 *Certification:* Obstetrics & Gynecology
501 N Graham St #525, Portland, 503-249-5454

Gibbens, Janet Lee (3 mentions)
Oregon Health Sciences U, 1983
Certification: Obstetrics & Gynecology
5050 NE Hoyt St #421, Portland, 503-239-6800

Grant, Nancy Marie (6 mentions)
Med Coll of Wisconsin, 1993
Certification: Obstetrics & Gynecology
5050 NE Hoyt St #421, Portland, 503-239-6800

Hulton, Leslie Gail (4 mentions)
U of California-Irvine, 1980 *Certification:* Obstetrics & Gynecology
1130 NW 22nd Ave #520, Portland, 503-274-4800

Leclair, Catherine Marie (3 mentions)
U of Vermont, 1995 *Certification:* Obstetrics & Gynecology
3181 SW Sam Jackson Park Rd, Portland, 503-494-9000
2241 Lloyd Ctr, Portland, 503-494-8417

Merrill, Patrick Andrew (3 mentions)
Baylor U, 1980 *Certification:* Obstetrics & Gynecology
300 N Graham St #100, Portland, 503-413-1122

Newhall, Elizabeth P. (5 mentions)
U of California-Davis, 1979 *Certification:* Obstetrics & Gynecology
2801 N Gantenbein Ave #1100, Portland, 503-284-5220
511 SW 10th Ave #905, Portland, 503-224-3435

Nichols, Mark (4 mentions)
U of California-Davis *Certification:* Obstetrics & Gynecology
808 SW Campus Dr 7th Fl, Portland, 503-418-4500

Olmstead, Drea (6 mentions)
U of Washington, 1990 *Certification:* Obstetrics & Gynecology
19250 SW 65th Ave #300, Tualatin, 503-692-1242

Polo, Oscar Raphael (4 mentions)
U of Oklahoma, 1987 *Certification:* Obstetrics & Gynecology
5050 NE Hoyt St #421, Portland, 503-239-6800

Reindl, Elizabeth Ann (3 mentions)
St Louis U, 1996 *Certification:* Obstetrics & Gynecology
9427 SW Barnes Rd #395, Portland, 503-216-2602

Sang, Nora Michelle (3 mentions)
Oregon Health Sciences U, 1994
Certification: Obstetrics & Gynecology
1130 NW 22nd Ave #120, Portland, 503-229-7353
9555 SW Barnes Rd #260, Portland, 503-624-2044

Stempel, James Ernest (3 mentions)
Oregon Health Sciences U, 1978
Certification: Obstetrics & Gynecology
501 N Graham St #525, Portland, 503-249-5454
5050 NE Hoyt St #359, Portland, 503-249-5454

Vick, Harold Gregory (3 mentions)
Oregon Health Sciences U, 1970
Certification: Obstetrics & Gynecology
19250 SW 65th Ave #300, Tualatin, 503-692-1242

Ophthalmology

Bentley, Robert Wells (6 mentions)
Oregon Health Sciences U, 1983 *Certification:* Ophthalmology
1955 NW Northrup St, Portland, 503-227-2020
15405 SW 116th Ave #204, King City, 503-227-2020
9555 SW Barnes Rd #201, Portland, 503-227-2020

Chung, Kelly Denise (4 mentions)
Loma Linda U, 1989 *Certification:* Ophthalmology
3375 SW Terwilliger Blvd, Portland, 503-494-4029

Crawford, Thomas Irving, II (6 mentions)
U of Texas-Dallas, 1980 *Certification:* Ophthalmology
5050 NE Hoyt St #445, Portland, 503-231-0166

Goodman, Shawn (3 mentions)
Med Coll of Pennsylvania, 1981 *Certification:* Ophthalmology
4035 SW Mercantile Dr #201, Lake Oswego, 503-635-4436

Holland, Daniel Ray (4 mentions)
U of Texas-Dallas, 1993 *Certification:* Ophthalmology
10819 SE Stark St #200, Portland, 503-255-2291
5050 NE Hoyt St #245, Portland, 503-255-2291
24601 SE Stark St, Gresham, 503-255-2291

Lindquist, Grant Richard (4 mentions)
Oregon Health Sciences U, 1981
Certification: Internal Medicine, Ophthalmology
19250 SW 65th Ave #215, Tualatin, 503-692-3630
5050 NE Hoyt St #445, Portland, 503-231-0166
434 Villa Rd, Newberg, 503-538-1341

Marsh, Peter Bradley (4 mentions)
Oregon Health Sciences U, 1993 *Certification:* Ophthalmology
12100 SE Stevens Ct #106, Happy Valley, 503-331-6330

Saulson, Roger Moss (4 mentions)
U of Texas-San Antonio, 1985 *Certification:* Ophthalmology
5050 NE Hoyt St #245, Portland, 503-255-2291
10819 SE Stark St #200, Portland, 503-255-2291
24601 SE Stark St, Troutdale, 503-255-2291
12050 SE Stevens Rd #400, Portland, 503-255-2291

Terry, Mark Andrew (3 mentions)
St Louis U, 1979 *Certification:* Ophthalmology
1040 NW 22nd Ave #200, Portland, 503-413-8202

Waldman, James Roger (3 mentions)
U of California-San Francisco, 1970 *Certification:* Ophthalmology
10819 SE Stark St #200, Portland, 503-255-2291
5050 NE Hoyt St #245, Portland, 503-255-2291
24601 SE Stark St, Troutdale, 503-255-2291

Weleber, Richard Gordon (3 mentions)
Oregon Health Sciences U, 1967
Certification: Clinical Genetics, Ophthalmology
3375 SW Terwilliger Blvd, Portland, 503-494-3000

Wentzien, James Bond (10 mentions)
U of Iowa, 1990 *Certification:* Ophthalmology
12100 SE Stevens Ct #106, Happy Valley, 503-653-1442

Orthopedics

Achterman, Christopher A. (4 mentions)
Washington U, 1972 *Certification:* Orthopaedic Surgery
501 N Graham St #200, Portland, 503-413-4488
2222 NW Lovejoy St #419, Portland, 503-413-4488

Barmada, Adam (3 mentions)
U of Illinois, 1996 *Certification:* Orthopaedic Surgery
501 N Graham St #200, Portland, 503-413-4488

Baum, Geoffrey Emerson (3 mentions)
Michigan State U Coll of Osteopathic Med, 1979
6564 Laked Rd #104, Milwaukie, 503-231-1086

Boardman, David Laurence (10 mentions)
U of California-Davis, 1992 *Certification:* Orthopaedic Surgery
9900 SE Sunnyside Rd, Clackamas, 503-571-3864

Buuck, David Alan (4 mentions)
U of Wisconsin, 1988 *Certification:* Orthopaedic Surgery
862 SE Oak St #3B, Hillsboro, 503-844-6599

Colorito, Anthony Ivar (3 mentions)
Columbia U, 1994 *Certification:* Orthopaedic Surgery
1515 NW 18th Ave #300, Portland, 503-224-8399

Duwelius, Paul Jude (5 mentions)
Creighton U, 1982 *Certification:* Orthopaedic Surgery
11782 SW Barnes Rd #300, Portland, 503-297-5551

Grewe, Scott Roberts (6 mentions)
Oregon Health Sciences U, 1983
Certification: Orthopaedic Surgery
15755 SW Sequoia Pkwy #200, Tigard, 503-639-6002

Hanley, Patrick L. (3 mentions)
Wayne State U, 1981 *Certification:* Orthopaedic Surgery
10000 SE Main St #402, Portland, 503-256-5866

Hikes, David Christopher (3 mentions)
Wayne State U, 1977 *Certification:* Orthopaedic Surgery
5050 NE Hoyt St #668, Portland, 503-239-7099

Hoff, Steven Frederick (5 mentions)
Creighton U, 1973 *Certification:* Orthopaedic Surgery
5050 NE Hoyt St #660, Portland, 503-231-4914

Irvine, Gregory William (9 mentions)
U of Michigan, 1978 *Certification:* Orthopaedic Surgery
15755 SW Sequoia Pkwy #200, Tigard, 503-639-6002

Jenkins, Loren Edward (4 mentions)
Baylor U, 1985 *Certification:* Orthopaedic Surgery
9900 SE Sunnyside Rd, Clackamas, 503-652-2880
3325 N Interstate Ave, Portland, 503-652-2880

Pelmas, Carol Jean (5 mentions)
Dartmouth Coll, 1985
Certification: Orthopaedic Sports Medicine, Orthopaedic Surgery
9427 SW Barnes Rd, Portland, 503-203-2086

Renwick, Stephen Einar (6 mentions)
U of Southern California, 1989 *Certification:* Orthopaedic Surgery
9427 SW Barnes Rd, Portland, 503-203-2110

Roberts, Donald William (4 mentions)
Stanford U, 1980 *Certification:* Orthopaedic Surgery
200 NE Mother Joseph Pl #210, Vancouver, WA, 360-254-6161

Rubinstein, Richard Allan (3 mentions)
Oregon Health Sciences U, 1986
Certification: Orthopaedic Surgery
5050 NE Hoyt St #138, Portland, 503-238-1061

Ruesch, Paul David (3 mentions)
Wayne State U, 1990 *Certification:* Orthopaedic Surgery
10202 SE 32nd Ave #101, Portland, 503-659-1769

Sedgewick, Terrence A. (3 mentions)
Wayne State U, 1987 *Certification:* Orthopaedic Surgery
1508 Division St #105, Oregon City, 503-656-0836
19250 SW 65th Ave #100, Tualatin, 503-692-0366

Switlyk, Paul Anthony (3 mentions)
New Jersey Med Sch, 1979 *Certification:* Orthopaedic Surgery
1515 NW 18th Ave #300, Portland, 503-224-8399

Turker, Ronald Jeff (3 mentions)
SUNY-Upstate Med U, 1987 *Certification:* Orthopaedic Surgery
9427 South West Barnes Rd, Portland, 503-203-2140

Weintraub, Ira Michael (9 mentions)
Indiana U, 1976 *Certification:* Orthopaedic Surgery
1515 NW 18th Ave #300, Portland, 503-224-8399

Weston, Mark Cecil (3 mentions)
U of Nebraska, 1990 *Certification:* Orthopaedic Surgery
9155 SW Barnes Rd #210, Portland, 503-546-3503
11782 SW Barnes Rd #300, Portland, 503-214-5200

Wilson, Robert Joseph (6 mentions)
U of Arizona, 1977 *Certification:* Orthopaedic Surgery
15755 SW Sequoia Pkwy #200, Tigard, 503-639-6002

Wyman, Michael B. (7 mentions)
Oregon Health Sciences U, 1983
Certification: Orthopaedic Surgery
5050 NE Hoyt St #340, Portland, 503-234-9861

Yoo, Jung Uck (4 mentions)
U of Chicago, 1984 *Certification:* Orthopaedic Surgery
3181 SW Sam Jackson Park Rd, Portland, 503-494-8311
3303 SW Bond Ave, Portland, 503-494-6400

Otorhinolaryngology

Barlow, Darryk Wayne (5 mentions)
U of Washington, 1990 *Certification:* Otolaryngology
10101 SE Main St #2004, Portland, 503-257-3204

Cave, Colin Robert (9 mentions)
U of California-San Francisco, 1989 *Certification:* Otolaryngology
4855 SW Western Ave, Beaverton, 503-350-2427
9205 SW Barnes Rd, Portland, 503-350-2427

Cleland-Zamudio, Suzanne (5 mentions)
Oregon Health Sciences U, 1993 *Certification:* Otolaryngology
10535 NE Glisan St #350, Portland, 503-408-1323
501 N Graham St #455, Portland, 503-408-1323
2850 SE Powell Baly Rd #207, Gresham, 503-408-1323

Cohen, James Isaac (7 mentions)
FMS-Canada, 1978 *Certification:* Otolaryngology
3710 SW US Veterans Hosp Rd, Portland, 503-220-8262

Cuyler, James Paul (5 mentions)
FMS-Canada, 1976 *Certification:* Otolaryngology
1849 NW Kearney St #300, Portland, 503-553-3664
9427 SW Barnes Rd #598, Portland, 503-553-3664

Flaming, Michael Boyd (12 mentions)
Oregon Health Sciences U, 1982 *Certification:* Otolaryngology
5050 NE Hoyt St #655, Portland, 503-239-6673

Hoffmann, Dieter F., Jr. (9 mentions)
U of Illinois, 1983 *Certification:* Otolaryngology
9900 SE Sunnyside Rd, Clackamas, 503-652-2880

Kim, Edsel U. (6 mentions)
New York U, 1996 *Certification:* Otolaryngology
2222 NW Lovejoy St #607, Portland, 503-222-3638
9155 Barnes Rd #208, Portland, 503-222-3638

Lundeberg, Duane Allen (6 mentions)
Oregon Health Sciences U, 1977 *Certification:* Otolaryngology
2222 NW Lovejoy St #622, Portland, 503-229-8455

Milczuk, Henry Alexander (8 mentions)
U of California-Davis, 1985 *Certification:* Otolaryngology
3181 SW Sam Jackson Park Rd, Portland, 503-494-8510

Pedersen, Andrew Dale (9 mentions)
Oregon Health Sciences U, 1991 *Certification:* Otolaryngology
5050 NE Hoyt St #655, Portland, 503-239-6673

Thomas, Larry Richard (11 mentions)
Ohio State U, 1972 *Certification:* Otolaryngology
2222 NW Lovejoy St #622, Portland, 503-229-8455

Wobig, Roger John (6 mentions)
Oregon Health Sciences U, 1994 *Certification:* Otolaryngology
24076 SE Stark St #230, Portland, 503-256-0038

Pain Medicine

Blatt, Jonathan Matthew (4 mentions)
Rosalind Franklin U, 1983 *Certification:* Anesthesiology
120 NW 14th Ave #300, Portland, 503-299-9906

Kallgren, Mark Andrew (5 mentions)
U of Arizona, 1989 *Certification:* Anesthesiology, Pain Medicine
1849 NW Kearny St #201, Portland, 503-517-3785
120 NW 14th Ave #300, Portland, 503-299-9906
2800 N Vancouver Ave #230, Portland, 503-413-2213

Kaur-Jayaram, Navnit (4 mentions)
FMS-India, 1976 *Certification:* Anesthesiology
9155 SW Barnes Rd #934, Portland, 503-292-7005
310 Villa Rd, Newberg, 503-292-7005
725 S Wahanna Rd, Seaside, 503-292-7005

Rosenblum, Stuart Michael (5 mentions)
Oregon Health Sciences U, 1980
Certification: Anesthesiology, Pain Medicine
1849 NW Kearney Rd #201, Portland, 503-517-3785

Stacey, Brett Russell (6 mentions)
U of Michigan, 1986 *Certification:* Anesthesiology, Pain Medicine
3181 SW Sam Jackson Park Rd, Portland, 503-494-5370

Pathology

Corless, Christopher Lee (4 mentions)
Washington U, 1988 *Certification:* Anatomic Pathology
3181 SW Sam Jackson Park Rd, Portland, 503-494-8276

Durham, James B. (4 mentions)
U of Missouri, 1974 *Certification:* Anatomic Pathology &
  Clinical Pathology, Dermatopathology
4805 NE Glisan St, Portland, 503-215-6096

Dworkin, Lawrence Alan (5 mentions)
U of Cincinnati, 1975
Certification: Anatomic Pathology & Clinical Pathology
13705 NE Airport Way, Portland, 503-258-6852

Lee, Randall G. (4 mentions)
U of Utah, 1976
Certification: Anatomic Pathology & Clinical Pathology
10340 SW Nimbus Ave, Portland, 503-274-2486

Sauer, David Austin (3 mentions)
Oregon Health Sciences U, 1996 *Certification:* Anatomic
  Pathology & Clinical Pathology, Cytopathology
3181 SW Sam Jackson Park Rd, Portland, 503-494-8276

Thompson, John Jones (4 mentions)
Yale U, 1974
Certification: Anatomic Pathology & Clinical Pathology
13705 NE Airport Way, Portland, 503-258-6858

Weeks, Douglas A. (4 mentions)
Loma Linda U, 1974
Certification: Anatomic Pathology & Clinical Pathology
3181 SW Sam Jackson Park Rd, Portland, 503-494-8276

White, Clifton Robert, Jr. (3 mentions)
U of California-Los Angeles, 1971
Certification: Dermatology, Dermatopathology
3303 SW Bond Ave, Portland, 503-494-5245

Pediatrics *(see note on page 9)*

Bradeen, Resa Lynn (3 mentions)
U of Louisville, 1990 *Certification:* Pediatrics
10535 NE Glisan St #300, Portland, 503-261-1171

Burns, Beryl Margaret (4 mentions)
FMS-South Africa, 1976 *Certification:* Pediatrics
9800 SE Sunnyside Rd, Clackamas, 503-652-2880

Davis, J. Steven (5 mentions)
Loma Linda U, 1973 *Certification:* Pediatrics
10000 SE Main St #105, Portland, 503-255-3544

Ferre, Barbara K. (7 mentions)
U of Illinois, 1980 *Certification:* Pediatrics
1130 NW 22nd Ave #320, Portland, 503-295-2546

Ferrell, Cynthia Lynn (4 mentions)
U of Nevada, 1992 *Certification:* Pediatrics
3181 SW Sam Jackson Park Rd, Portland, 503-494-8311

Hargunani, Dana Elizabeth (5 mentions)
Georgetown U, 2001 *Certification:* Pediatrics
3181 SW Sam Jackson Park Rd, Portland, 503-494-8311

Liebo, Jeffrey Stephen (3 mentions)
U of Minnesota, 1970 *Certification:* Pediatrics
9800 SE Sunnyside Rd, Clackamas, 503-652-2880

Moshofsky, Dean Arthur (3 mentions)
Oregon Health Sciences U, 1983 *Certification:* Pediatrics
1960 NW 167th Pl, Beaverton, 503-531-3434

Rosenbloom, Jay Stanton (3 mentions)
Oregon Health Sciences U, 1996 *Certification:* Pediatrics
2525 NW Lovejoy St #200, Portland, 503-227-0671
4103 SW Mercantile Dr, Lake Oswego, 503-636-4508

Schunk, Jack Phillip (6 mentions)
Oregon Health Sciences U, 1983 *Certification:* Pediatrics
2525 NW Lovejoy St #200, Portland, 503-227-0671
4103 Mercantile Dr, Lake Oswego, 503-636-4508

Plastic Surgery

Burgess, Elisa Anneli (8 mentions)
Oregon Health Sciences U, 1993
Certification: Plastic Surgery, Surgery
15865 Coones Ferry Rd #101, Lake Oswego, 503-699-6464

Busby, Richard Colin (6 mentions)
U of Colorado, 1981 *Certification:* Plastic Surgery
9155 SW Barnes Rd #930, Portland, 503-297-1515

Canepa, Clifford Steven (12 mentions)
Albany Med Coll, 1983
Certification: Plastic Surgery, Surgery of the Hand
9155 SW Barnes Rd #532, Portland, 503-292-9737
5050 NE Hoyt St #221, Portland, 503-234-7006

Hansen, Juliana Ehrman (8 mentions)
U of Washington, 1988 *Certification:* Plastic Surgery
3181 SW Sam Jackson Park Rd #L-352-A, Portland,
  503-494-7824

Ladizinsky, Daniel Alan (7 mentions)
U of Michigan, 1984 *Certification:* Plastic Surgery
9900 SE Sunnyside Rd, Clackamas, 503-571-3162

Waldorf, Kathleen Anne (8 mentions)
Georgetown U, 1986 *Certification:* Plastic Surgery
12400 NW Cornell Rd #200, Portland, 503-646-0101
501 N Graham St #320, Portland, 503-280-8870

Webber, Bruce R. (9 mentions)
FMS-Mexico, 1977 *Certification:* Plastic Surgery
9155 SW Barnes Rd #532, Portland, 503-292-9737
3439 NE Sandy Blvd, Portland, 503-284-8841

Zegzula, Henry Daniel, Jr. (10 mentions)
St Louis U, 1991 *Certification:* Plastic Surgery
3439 NE Sandy Blvd, Portland, 503-284-8841
1040 NW 22nd Ave #610, Portland, 503-288-9646

Psychiatry

Cafferky, Ronald Edwin (3 mentions)
Loma Linda U, 1976 *Certification:* Psychiatry
2700 NE Anderson St #D-4, Vancouver, WA, 503-699-5260

Keepers, George Alan (3 mentions)
Baylor U, 1977 *Certification:* Psychiatry
3181 SW Sam Jackson Park Rd, Portland, 503-494-8311

Oken, Stuart Lee (4 mentions)
U of Kentucky, 1966 *Certification:* Psychiatry
4855 SW Western Ave, Beaverton, 503-249-3434

Weinstein, M. Howard (3 mentions)
Tufts U, 1967 *Certification:* Psychiatry
1220 SW Morrison St #525, Portland, 503-223-6360

Pulmonary Disease

Flick, Gregory Robert (5 mentions)
U of Pennsylvania, 1977
Certification: Internal Medicine, Pulmonary Disease
9155 SW Barnes Rd #830, Portland, 503-297-3778

Fowler, John Christian (6 mentions)
FMS-South Africa, 1976 *Certification:* Critical Care
   Medicine, Internal Medicine, Pulmonary Disease
700 NE 87th Ave, Vancouver, WA, 360-254-1240

Lazarus, Howard M. (5 mentions)
FMS-Canada, 1991
Certification: Critical Care Medicine, Pulmonary Disease
9155 SW Barnes Rd #840, Portland, 503-297-3778

Lewis, Michael Scott (6 mentions)
Med Coll of Georgia, 1980
Certification: Internal Medicine, Pulmonary Disease
1130 NW 22nd Ave #220, Portland, 503-413-8988

Libby, Louis Samuels (11 mentions)
George Washington U, 1977 *Certification:* Critical Care
   Medicine, Internal Medicine, Pulmonary Disease
1111 NE 99th Ave, Portland, 503-963-3030

Morganroth, Melvin Lee (5 mentions)
U of Michigan, 1978 *Certification:* Critical Care Medicine,
   Internal Medicine, Pulmonary Disease
1111 NE 99th Ave, Portland, 503-963-3030

Rettmann, Jonathan Allyn (9 mentions)
Oregon Health Sciences U, 1997 *Certification:* Critical Care
   Medicine, Internal Medicine, Pulmonary Disease
10180 SE Sunnyside Rd, Clackamas, 503-652-2880

Riddick, Carl Anthony (7 mentions)
Johns Hopkins U, 1984 *Certification:* Critical Care
   Medicine, Internal Medicine, Pulmonary Disease
9155 SW Barnes Rd #840, Portland, 503-297-3778

Schaumberg, Thomas Hyland (10 mentions)
U of Colorado, 1986 *Certification:* Critical Care Medicine,
   Internal Medicine, Pulmonary Disease
1111 NE 99th Ave, Portland, 503-963-3030

Schmidt, David Martin (5 mentions)
Certification: Pulmonary Disease
10180 SE Sunnyside Rd, Clackamas, 503-652-2880

Sherbin, Vandy Lee (6 mentions)
Case Western Reserve U, 1990
Certification: Critical Care Medicine
3181 SW Sam Jackson Park Rd, Portland, 503-494-8311

Radiology—Diagnostic

Dobos, Nora (3 mentions)
Oregon Health Sciences U, 1998
Certification: Diagnostic Radiology
3181 SW Sam Jackson Park Rd, Portland, 503-494-4498

Gosselin, Marc V. (4 mentions)
FMS-Canada, 1991 *Certification:* Diagnostic Radiology
3181 SW Sam Jackson Park Rd, Portland, 503-494-4498

Heller, Lloyd Emerson, Jr. (4 mentions)
Hahnemann U, 1993 *Certification:* Diagnostic Radiology
9205 SW Barnes Rd, Portland, 503-216-2181

Israel, Robert Scott (3 mentions)
U of Pennsylvania, 1984 *Certification:* Diagnostic Radiology
10123 SE Market St, Portland, 503-251-6132

Neuman, Michael Jay (3 mentions)
U of Wisconsin, 1986
4805 NE Gleason St, Portland, 503-215-6079

Qaisi, Waleed Ghazi (3 mentions)
U of Kentucky, 1994 *Certification:* Diagnostic Radiology
2801 N Gantenbein Ave, Portland, 503-413-4032

Sheley, Robert Curtis (3 mentions)
Oregon Health Sciences U, 1988 *Certification:* Diagnostic
   Radiology, Vascular & Interventional Radiology
2701 NW Vaughn St #425, Portland, 503-413-7127

Speirs, Robert Thomas, III (3 mentions)
Certification: Diagnostic Radiology
3500 N Interstate Ave, Portland, 503-285-9321

Thurmond, Amy Suzanne (4 mentions)
U of California-Los Angeles, 1982
Certification: Diagnostic Radiology
8950 SW Nimbus Ave, Beaverton, 503-643-7226

Urman, Steven Maxwell (3 mentions)
Oregon Health Sciences U, 1985
Certification: Diagnostic Radiology
735 NW 19th Ave, Portland, 503-220-0066
221-G NE 104th Ave #106, Vancouver, WA, 360-253-2525

Warfel, Thomas Edward (3 mentions)
U of Pittsburgh, 1997 *Certification:* Diagnostic Radiology
4805 NE Glisan St, Portland, 503-215-1111
400 NE Mother Joseph Pl, Vancouver, WA, 509-922-1661

Warnock, Gerald Lloyd (3 mentions)
Oregon Health Sciences U, 1958 *Certification:* Radiology
233 NE 102nd Ave, Portland, 503-253-1105
4212 NE Broadway St #3, Portland, 503-249-8787

Radiology—Therapeutic

Bader, Stephen Blake (5 mentions)
U of Washington, 1984
Certification: Internal Medicine, Radiation Oncology
5050 NE Hoyt St, Portland, 503-215-6029
9205 SW Barnes Rd, Portland, 503-216-2195

Cox, Andrew Gordon (5 mentions)
Oregon Health Sciences U, 1993 *Certification:* Diagnostic
   Radiology, Vascular & Interventional Radiology
2701 NW Vaughn St #425, Portland, 503-413-7127

Kaufman, John Andrew (4 mentions)
Boston U, 1982 *Certification:* Diagnostic Radiology,
   Vascular & Interventional Radiology
3181 SW Sam Jackson Park Rd, Portland, 503-494-9000

Keller, Frederick Saul (6 mentions)
U of Pennsylvania, 1968 *Certification:* Diagnostic Radiology,
   Vascular & Interventional Radiology
3181 SW Sam Jackson Park Rd #L605, Portland, 503-494-7660

Prasad, Atanu (4 mentions)
New York U, 1993 *Certification:* Diagnostic Radiology
10180 SE Sunnyside Rd, Clackamas, 503-571-8388

Rehabilitation

Andersen, Steven Scott (4 mentions)
Wayne State U, 1986
Certification: Physical Medicine & Rehabilitation
5050 NE Hoyt St #353, Portland, 503-230-2833

Cockrell, Janice Louise (5 mentions)
Northwestern U, 1972
Certification: Pediatrics, Physical Medicine & Rehabilitation
2801 N Gantenbein Ave, Portland, 503-413-4505
3181 SW Sam Jackson Park Rd, Portland, 503-494-8311

Djergaian, Robert Steven (4 mentions)
Jefferson Med Coll, 1979
Certification: Physical Medicine & Rehabilitation
200 NE Mother Joseph Pl #100, Vancouver, WA, 360-514-3142

Erb, Danielle Laure (3 mentions)
Oregon Health Sciences U, 1986
Certification: Physical Medicine & Rehabilitation
1815 SW Marlow #110, Portland, 503-296-0918

Hoeflich, Molly Lynn (9 mentions)
Oregon Health Sciences U, 1981
Certification: Physical Medicine & Rehabilitation
5050 NE Hoyt St #353, Portland, 503-230-2833

Niles, Sally Lindsay (3 mentions)
Oregon Health Sciences U, 1986
Certification: Physical Medicine & Rehabilitation
3710 SW US Veterans Hospital Rd, Portland, 503-220-8262

Shih, Mark M. (3 mentions)
U of Minnesota, 1994 *Certification:* Pediatric Rehabilitation
   Medicine, Pediatrics, Physical Medicine & Rehabilitation
2801 N Gantenbein Ave, Portland, 503-413-4505

Valleroy, Marie Lucetta (3 mentions)
U of Texas-San Antonio, 1979
Certification: Physical Medicine & Rehabilitation
1040 NW 22nd Ave, Portland, 503-413-6294

Ward, Gary Allen (6 mentions)
U of Minnesota, 1972
Certification: Physical Medicine & Rehabilitation
1040 NW 22nd Ave #320, Portland, 503-413-6294

Rheumatology

Bonafede, Rosario Peter (8 mentions)
FMS-South Africa, 1974 *Certification:* Rheumatology
5050 NE Hoyt St #155, Portland, 503-215-6819

Kingsbury, Daniel Joseph (6 mentions)
U of Tennessee, 1988
Certification: Pediatric Rheumatology, Pediatrics
2801 N Gantenbein Ave, Portland, 503-413-4505

Wernick, Richard (7 mentions)
Georgetown U, 1973
Certification: Internal Medicine, Rheumatology
5050 NE Hoyt St #155, Portland, 503-215-6819

Thoracic Surgery

Bisio, James Michael (6 mentions)
Oregon Health Sciences U, 1977 *Certification:* Surgery
9900 SE Sunnyside Rd, Clackamas, 503-240-6225

Furnary, Anthony Paul (7 mentions)
Jefferson Med Coll, 1984 *Certification:* Surgery, Thoracic Surgery
9155 SW Barnes Rd #240, Portland, 503-297-1419

Handy, John Rutherford (10 mentions)
Duke U, 1983 *Certification:* Surgery, Thoracic Surgery
1111 NE 99th Ave #201, Portland, 503-963-3030

Schipper, Paul Henry (7 mentions)
U of Iowa, 1996 *Certification:* Surgery, Thoracic Surgery
3181 SW Sam Jackson Park Rd, Portland, 503-494-7820

Sukumar, Mithran S. (6 mentions)
FMS-India, 1990 *Certification:* Surgery, Thoracic Surgery
3181 SW Sam Jackson Park Rd, Portland, 503-494-7820

Urology

Kaempf, Michael Jerome (15 mentions)
Oregon Health Sciences U, 1972 *Certification:* Urology
1130 NW 22nd Ave #535, Portland, 503-274-4999
500 N COlumbia River Hwy, St Helens, 503-274-4999

Lashley, David Brian (8 mentions)
Oregon Health Sciences U, 1993
Certification: Pediatric Urology, Urology
2230 NW Pettygrove St #210, Portland, 503-223-6223

Lowe, Bruce Alan (9 mentions)
U of Kansas, 1976 *Certification:* Urology
2230 NW Pettygrove St #210, Portland, 503-223-6223

McEvoy, Kevin Michael (6 mentions)
Loyola U Chicago, 1985 *Certification:* Urology
501 N Graham St #420, Portland, 503-288-7303
1130 NW 22nd Ave #535, Portland, 503-274-4999

Menashe, David Scott (11 mentions)
Oregon Health Sciences U, 1983 *Certification:* Urology
5050 NE Hoyt St #514, Portland, 503-215-2399

O'Hollaren, Patrick Sean (12 mentions)
Oregon Health Sciences U, 1987 *Certification:* Urology
501 N Graham St #420, Portland, 503-288-7303

Wicklund, Roger Allen (6 mentions)
U of Wisconsin, 1974 *Certification:* Urology
9427 SW Barnes Rd, Portland, 503-203-2120

Vascular Surgery

Wiest, John Walter (13 mentions)
U of California-Los Angeles, 1979 *Certification:* Vascular Surgery
9155 SW Barnes Rd #321, Portland, 503-292-0070

Williamson, Weldon Kent (11 mentions)
Wake Forest U, 1993 *Certification:* Surgery, Vascular Surgery
9155 SW Barnes Rd #321, Portland, 503-292-0070

Pennsylvania

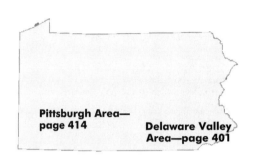

Pittsburgh Area—
page 414

Delaware Valley
Area—page 401

Delaware Valley Area

Including Bucks, Chester, Delaware, Montgomery, and
Philadelphia Counties in Pennsylvania; Burlington, Camden, and
Gloucester Counties in New Jersey; and New Castle County, Delaware

Allergy/Immunology

Bantz, Eric Walter (5 mentions)
SUNY-Buffalo, 1977
Certification: Allergy & Immunology, Pediatrics
103 Old Marlton Pike #211, Medford, NJ, 609-953-7500

Becker, Jack Michael (5 mentions)
Temple U, 1986 *Certification:* Allergy & Immunology
233 E Lancaster Ave #118, Ardmore, PA, 610-642-1643
2300 Computer Ave, Willow Grove, PA, 610-642-1643

Cohn, John Robert (14 mentions)
Jefferson Med Coll, 1976 *Certification:* Allergy &
   Immunology, Internal Medicine, Pulmonary Disease
1015 Chestnut St #1300, Philadelphia, PA, 215-923-7685

Dunsky, Eliot Harold (5 mentions)
FMS-Israel, 1971 *Certification:* Allergy & Immunology, Pediatrics
205 N Broad St #300, Philadelphia, PA, 215-569-1111
301 E Cityline Ave #140, Bala Cynwyd, PA, 610-660-0777

Fleekop, Philip Donald (8 mentions)
Emory U, 1981
Certification: Allergy & Immunology, Internal Medicine
2300 Computer Ave #3M-66, Willow Grove, PA, 215-659-5480

Gatti, Eugene A. (10 mentions)
Georgetown U, 1982
Certification: Allergy & Immunology, Pediatrics
54 E Main St, Marlton, NJ, 856-988-0570
409 Kings Hwy S, Cherry Hill, NJ, 856-988-0570
485 Williamstown-New Freedom Rd, Sicklerville, NJ,
   856-988-0570

Gawchik, Sandra Mary (6 mentions)
U of Kansas, 1970
Certification: Allergy & Immunology, Pediatrics
300 Evergreen Dr #180, Glen Mills, PA, 610-876-5570

Glasofer, Eric David (8 mentions)
Jefferson Med Coll, 1978
Certification: Allergy & Immunology, Pediatrics
1000 White Horse Rd #904, Voorhees, NJ, 856-772-1200
1533 Haddon Ave #104, Camden, NJ, 856-757-3848

Goldstein, Marc Fred (5 mentions)
U of Pennsylvania, 1979 *Certification:* Allergy & Immunology,
   Diagnostic Laboratory Immunology, Internal Medicine
608 N Broad St #310, Woodbury, NJ, 856-251-9951
210 Ark Rd #109, Mount Laurel, NJ, 856-235-8282
404 Middletown Blvd #305, Langhorne, PA, 215-750-7040
2137 Welsh Rd #2-B, Philadelphia, PA, 215-677-4433
205 N Broad St #300, Philadelphia, PA, 215-569-1111

Lania-Howarth, Maria (4 mentions)
New Jersey Med Sch, 1984 *Certification:* Allergy & Immunology
6400 Main St, Voorhees, NJ, 856-751-9339
4 Plaza Dr #401, Fewell, NJ, 856-270-4050

Litz, Steven Andrew (4 mentions)
FMS-Mexico, 1979
Certification: Allergy & Immunology, Internal Medicine
2301 E Evesham Rd #605, Voorhees, NJ, 856-772-0043
600 Jessup Rd #102, West Deptford, NJ, 856-845-3100
2505 Chestnut Ave, Vineland, NJ, 856-696-9596

Marcotte, Gregory Vincent (7 mentions)
New York U, 1992 *Certification:* Allergy & Immunology
1700 Shallcross Ave #1, Wilmington, DE, 302-655-4471

Martin, George L. (6 mentions)
Rosalind Franklin U, 1975
Certification: Allergy & Immunology, Internal Medicine
100 E Lancaster Ave Lankenau Bldg #237, Wynnewood, PA,
   610-649-9300
841 Garrett Rd, Upper Darby, PA, 610-352-3323

Rohr, Albert Schumm (8 mentions)
U of Texas-Galveston, 1977
Certification: Allergy & Immunology, Internal Medicine
875 County Line Rd #107, Bryn Mawr, PA, 610-527-2000
209 W Lancaster Ave, Paoli, PA, 610-527-2000

Rooklin, Anthony Robert (8 mentions)
Jefferson Med Coll, 1972
Certification: Allergy & Immunology, Pediatrics
1 Presidents Dr Presidents House, Upland, PA, 610-876-1249
300 Evergreen Dr, Glen Mills, PA, 610-579-3670

Shelanski, Sharon Lillian (4 mentions)
Med Coll of Pennsylvania, 1983 *Certification:* Internal Medicine
841 Garett Rd, Upper Darby, PA, 610-352-3323
100 E Lancaster Ave #237, Wynnewood, PA, 610-649-9300

Spitzer, Ira Edward (8 mentions)
Philadelphia Coll of Osteopathic Med, 1976
370 Middletown Blvd #504, Langhorne, PA, 215-750-0315

Wodell, Ruthven Adriance (7 mentions)
Oregon Health Sciences U, 1980
Certification: Allergy & Immunology, Pediatrics
491 Allendale Rd #111, King of Prussia, PA, 610-768-9323
233 E Lancaster Ave 2nd Fl, Ardmore, PA, 610-642-1643

Anesthesiology

Barnette, Rodger Edward (5 mentions)
Temple U, 1979 *Certification:* Anesthesiology, Critical Care
   Medicine, Internal Medicine
3401 N Broad St, Philadelphia, PA, 215-707-3326

Cwik, Jason Charles (3 mentions)
Jefferson Med Coll, 1988 *Certification:* Anesthesiology
800 Spruce St Shac Bldg 9th Fl, Philadelphia, PA, 215-829-3868

Dorsey, Alfred Thomas, Jr. (3 mentions)
Hahnemann U, 1981
Certification: Anesthesiology, Critical Care Medicine, Pediatrics
1600 Rockland Rd, Wilmington, DE, 302-651-5321

Etter, Mark Stewart (6 mentions)
Jefferson Med Coll, 1975
Certification: Anesthesiology, Critical Care Medicine
1200 Old York Rd, Abington, PA, 215-481-2336

Everts, Erich A. (5 mentions)
Jefferson Med Coll, 1979 *Certification:* Anesthesiology, Pediatrics
1201 Langhorne-Newtown Rd, Langhorne, PA, 215-710-2196

Fine, Richard Howard (4 mentions)
New York Med Coll, 1984 *Certification:* Anesthesiology
5501 Old York Rd, Philadelphia, PA, 215-456-9661

Garber, Scott Jeffery (3 mentions)
Temple U, 1989 *Certification:* Anesthesiology, Pain Medicine
701 E Marshall St, West Chester, PA, 610-431-5387

Gargiulo, Richard Francis (3 mentions)
Robert W Johnson Med Sch, 1983 *Certification:* Anesthesiology
160 Madison Ave, Mount Holly, NJ, 609-265-7800

Goldstein, William Mark (3 mentions)
Virginia Commonwealth U, 1981
Certification: Anesthesiology, Internal Medicine
175 E Chester Pike, Ridley Park, PA, 610-595-6410

Grunwald, Zvi (8 mentions)
FMS-Israel, 1982 *Certification:* Anesthesiology
111 S 11th St, Philadelphia, PA, 215-955-1147

Heyman, David M. (4 mentions)
Philadelphia Coll of Osteopathic Med, 1985
Certification: Anesthesiology
2701 Dekalb Pike, Norristown, PA, 215-748-9000

Horrow, Jay Charles (4 mentions)
U of Pennsylvania, 1977 *Certification:* Anesthesiology
1800 Concord Pike, Wilmington, DE, 302-886-3000

Isaacson, William Scott (5 mentions)
Med Coll of Pennsylvania, 1982 *Certification:* Anesthesiology
2010 West Chester Pike, Havertown, PA, 610-853-7780
175 E Chester Pike, Ridley Park, PA, 610-595-6410

Nicolson, Susan Craig (3 mentions)
U of Pennsylvania, 1976 *Certification:* Anesthesiology
34th & Civic Center Blvd #1, Philadelphia, PA, 215-590-1874

Noone, James Francis (4 mentions)
St Louis U, 1973 *Certification:* Anesthesiology, Pain Medicine
1650 Huntingdon Pike #313, Meadowbrook, PA, 215-938-3413

Sasso, Philip John (3 mentions)
Jefferson Med Coll, 1988 *Certification:* Anesthesiology
1200 Old York Rd, Abington, PA, 215-481-2336

Silverstein, Kenneth Lee (3 mentions)
New York U, 1985 *Certification:* Anesthesiology
4755 Ogletown-Stanton Rd #2603, Newark, DE, 302-733-2670

Cardiac Surgery

Acker, Michael A. (11 mentions)
Brown U, 1981 *Certification:* Surgery, Thoracic Surgery
3400 Spruce St, Philadelphia, PA, 215-349-8305

Addonizio, V. Paul (14 mentions)
Cornell U, 1974 *Certification:* Thoracic Surgery
1200 Old York Rd 5th Fl, Abington, PA, 215-481-4200

Bavaria, Joseph Edward (12 mentions)
Tulane U, 1983 *Certification:* Thoracic Surgery
34th & Spruce Sts, Philadelphia, PA, 215-662-2017

Boova, Robert S. (8 mentions)
Jefferson Med Coll, 1977 *Certification:* Thoracic Surgery
830 Old Lancaster Rd #203, Bryn Mawr, PA, 610-527-1600

Deshpande, Anil Shriram (8 mentions)
FMS-India, 1974 *Certification:* Thoracic Surgery
1203 Langhorne-Newtown Rd #308, Langhorne, PA,
   215-752-3330

Goldman, Scott Michael (20 mentions)
Jefferson Med Coll, 1976 *Certification:* Surgery, Thoracic Surgery
100 Lancaster Ave Lankenau Bldg #280, Wynnewood, PA,
   610-896-9255

McClurken, James B. (17 mentions)
Temple U, 1976 *Certification:* Surgery, Thoracic Surgery
3401 N Broad St #300, Philadelphia, PA, 215-707-8303
595 W State St, Doylestown, PA, 215-345-2906

Sutter, Francis Paul (10 mentions)
Philadelphia Coll of Osteopathic Med, 1976
Certification: Thoracic Surgery
100 Lancaster Ave Lankenau Bldg #280, Wynnewood, PA,
   610-896-9255

Cardiology

Baffa, Jeanne Marie (4 mentions)
U of Pennsylvania, 1985 *Certification:* Pediatric Cardiology
1600 Rockland Rd, Wilmington, DE, 302-651-6600
599 Arcola Rd, Collegeville, PA, 302-651-6600

Belasco, Robert (4 mentions)
Temple U, 1973
Certification: Cardiovascular Disease, Internal Medicine
342 W Germantown Pike, East Norriton, PA, 610-272-3253
555 2nd Ave, Collegeville, PA, 610-831-0300

Blaber, Reginald (5 mentions)
Hahnemann U, 1989
Certification: Cardiovascular Disease, Internal Medicine
63 Kresson Rd #101, Cherry Hill, NJ, 856-428-4100
730 N Broad St #200, Woodbury, NJ, 856-251-2340

Coady, Paul M. (3 mentions)
Temple U, 1984 *Certification:* Cardiovascular Disease,
   Internal Medicine, Interventional Cardiology
100 Lancaster Ave #380, Wynnewood, PA, 610-649-8599

De Pace, Nicholas Louis (3 mentions)
Mount Sinai Sch of Med, 1978
Certification: Cardiovascular Disease, Internal Medicine
438 Gaintown Rd #8, Sewell, NJ, 856-589-6034
2070 Springdale Rd #100, Cherry Hill, NJ, 856-751-0058

Eisen, Howard Joel (3 mentions)
U of Pennsylvania, 1981
Certification: Cardiovascular Disease, Internal Medicine
230 N Broad St, Philadelphia, PA, 215-762-4200

Fields, Ronald Harris (5 mentions)
Pennsylvania State U, 1982 *Certification:* Cardiovascular
   Disease, Internal Medicine, Interventional Cardiology
1205 Langhorne-Newtown Rd #204, Langhorne, PA,
   215-750-7818
7 Upper Holland Rd, Richboro, PA, 215-750-7818

Finch, Mark Thomas (6 mentions)
Cornell U, 1984
Certification: Cardiovascular Disease, Internal Medicine
128 Route 70, Medford, NJ, 609-714-2421
2051 Briggs Rd, Mount Laurel, NJ, 856-234-3332
103 Old Marlton Pike #212, Medford, NJ, 609-953-7106
700 Route 130 N #107, Cinnaminson, NJ, 856-786-7144
1 Sheffield Dr #102, Columbus, NJ, 609-920-9941

Fish, Frank Henry (6 mentions)
New Jersey Med Sch, 1970
Certification: Cardiovascular Disease, Internal Medicine
128 Route 70, Medford, NJ, 609-714-2421
2051 Briggs Rd, Mount Laurel, NJ, 856-234-3332
103 Old Marlton Pike #212, Medford, NJ, 609-953-7106
700 Route 130 N #107, Cinnaminson, NJ, 856-303-0781
1 Sheffield Dr #102, Columbus, NJ, 609-920-9941

Garden, Jack (4 mentions)
Mount Sinai Sch of Med, 1983
Certification: Cardiovascular Disease, Internal Medicine
834 Chestnut St #202-M, Philadelphia, PA, 215-923-0690
1339 Porter St, Philadelphia, PA, 215-389-0600

Ginsberg, Fredric Lee (3 mentions)
Jefferson Med Coll, 1977
Certification: Cardiovascular Disease, Internal Medicine
1210 Brace Rd #103, Cherry Hill, NJ, 856-342-2034

Goldenberg, Edward Mark (3 mentions)
Creighton U, 1972
Certification: Cardiovascular Disease, Internal Medicine
3521 Silverside Rd #1-C, Wilmington, DE, 302-477-6510
86 Omega Dr Bldg B #86, Newark, DE, 302-368-7762

Haaz, William Stephen (5 mentions)
Temple U, 1975
Certification: Cardiovascular Disease, Internal Medicine
1650 Huntingdon Pike #352, Meadowbrook, PA, 215-947-9218

Harper, Glenn Robert (3 mentions)
Med Coll of Pennsylvania, 1985 *Certification:* Cardiovascular
   Disease, Clinical Cardiac Electrophysiology, Internal Medicine
830 Old Lancaster Rd #105, Bryn Mawr, PA, 610-527-1165
100 E Lancaster Ave #556, Wynnewood, PA, 610-649-6980

Herlich, Michael Bruce (3 mentions)
Hahnemann U, 1982
Certification: Cardiovascular Disease, Internal Medicine
210 W Atlantic Ave, Haddon Heights, NJ, 856-546-3003

Herling, Irving Marc (5 mentions)
U of Pennsylvania, 1974
Certification: Cardiovascular Disease, Internal Medicine
3400 Spruce St Penn Tower #800, Philadelphia, PA,
   215-662-6020
250 King of Prussia Rd, Radnor, PA, 610-902-2273

Hodess, Arthur Bart (3 mentions)
Columbia U, 1974 *Certification:* Cardiovascular Disease,
   Critical Care Medicine, Internal Medicine
3025 Zinn Rd, Thorndale, PA, 610-384-2211

Joffe, Ian (3 mentions)
FMS-South Africa, 1987
Certification: Cardiovascular Disease, Internal Medicine
2309 E Evesham Rd #201, Voorhees, NJ, 856-424-3600

Kolansky, Daniel M. (4 mentions)
Yale U, 1984 *Certification:* Cardiovascular Disease, Internal
   Medicine, Interventional Cardiology
3400 Spruce St, Philadelphia, PA, 215-662-2178
250 King of Prussia, Radnor, PA, 610-902-2273

Kowey, Peter Russell (3 mentions)
U of Pennsylvania, 1975
Certification: Cardiovascular Disease, Internal Medicine
100 E Lancaster Ave Lankenau Bldg E #556, Wynnewood, PA,
   610-649-6980

Leidig, Gilbert A., Jr. (3 mentions)
U of Pennsylvania, 1984 *Certification:* Cardiovascular
   Disease, Internal Medicine, Interventional Cardiology
1 Centurian Dr #200, Newark, DE, 302-366-8600
1401 Foulk Rd, Wilmington, DE, 302-478-5055

McGeehin, Frank C., III (6 mentions)
Temple U, 1980 *Certification:* Cardiovascular Disease,
   Internal Medicine, Interventional Cardiology
100 Lancaster Ave Medical Bldg E #356, Wynnewood, PA,
   610-649-7625

Norris, Robert Bruce (3 mentions)
New York U, 1984
Certification: Cardiovascular Disease, Internal Medicine
230 W Washington Sq 3rd Fl, Philadelphia, PA, 215-829-5064

Orth, Donald William (3 mentions)
U of Pennsylvania, 1971
Certification: Cardiovascular Disease, Internal Medicine
2309 E Evesham Rd #201, Voorhees, NJ, 856-424-3600

Rader, Daniel James (3 mentions)
Med Coll of Pennsylvania, 1984 *Certification:* Internal Medicine
51 N 39th St #2A, Philadelphia, PA, 215-662-9994

Segal, Bernard Louis (8 mentions)
FMS-Canada, 1955
Certification: Cardiovascular Disease, Internal Medicine
401 E City Line Ave #525, Bala Cynwyd, PA, 610-667-5555
925 Chestnut St, Philadelphia, PA, 215-955-5050

Shapiro, Timothy Alan (6 mentions)
Yale U, 1985 *Certification:* Cardiovascular Disease, Internal
   Medicine, Interventional Cardiology
100 Lancaster Ave Med Science Bldg #380, Wynnewood, PA,
   610-649-8599

Stever, Samuel Williams (4 mentions)
Philadelphia Coll of Osteopathic Med, 1978
301 Oxford Valley Rd #901, Yardley, PA, 215-321-7400
100 Green Ln #3, Bristol, PA, 215-321-7400

Stillabower, Michael E. (4 mentions)
Jefferson Med Coll, 1976 *Certification:* Cardiovascular Disease, Internal Medicine, Interventional Cardiology
3521 Silverside Rd #1-C, Wilmington, DE, 302-477-6510
86 Omega Dr Blgd B #86, Newark, DE, 302-368-7762

Walsh, Deirdre Victor (4 mentions)
Hahnemann U, 1987
Certification: Cardiovascular Disease, Internal Medicine
1205 Langhorne-Newtown Rd #204, Langhorne, PA, 215-750-7818
7 Upper Holland Rd, Richboro, PA, 215-750-7818

Warnick, William Clay (7 mentions)
Hahnemann U, 1989 *Certification:* Cardiovascular Disease
915 Old Fern Hill Rd Bldg A5, West Chester, PA, 610-696-2850
404 McFarlan Rd #102, Kennett Square, PA, 610-444-9362

Watson, Robert A., III (7 mentions)
U of Louisville, 1982 *Certification:* Cardiovascular Disease, Internal Medicine, Interventional Cardiology
1010 Horsham Rd #201, North Wales, PA, 215-517-1000
790 Penlyn Bluebell Pike, Bluebell, PA, 215-517-1000
225 Newtown Rd #216, Warminster, PA, 215-517-1000
1235 Old York Rd #22, Abington, PA, 215-517-1000

Waxman, Harvey Louis (5 mentions)
Mount Sinai Sch of Med, 1974 *Certification:* Cardiovascular Disease, Clinical Cardiac Electrophysiology, Internal Medicine
51 N 39th St, Philadelphia, PA, 856-216-0300
1400 E Route 70, Cherry Hill, NJ, 856-216-0300

Weinstock, Perry Jay (16 mentions)
New Jersey Med Sch, 1985
Certification: Cardiovascular Disease, Internal Medicine
1210 Brace Rd #103, Cherry Hill, NJ, 856-427-9316
900 Centennial Blvd #H, Voorhees, NJ, 856-325-6700
3 Cooper Plaza #311, Camden, NJ, 856-342-3044

Weitz, Howard Hy (10 mentions)
Jefferson Med Coll, 1978
Certification: Cardiovascular Disease, Internal Medicine
925 Chestnut St Fl Mezzanine, Philadelphia, PA, 215-955-6672

Wolf, Nelson Marc (3 mentions)
Temple U, 1968 *Certification:* Cardiovascular Disease, Internal Medicine, Interventional Cardiology
3401 N Broad St #945, Philadelphia, PA, 215-707-3347

Zimmer, Ross Randall (3 mentions)
Temple U, 1989 *Certification:* Cardiovascular Disease
51 N 39th St, Philadelphia, PA, 215-662-9189
1400 Route 70 E, Cherry Hill, NJ, 856-216-0300

Dermatology

Benedetto, Anthony V. (3 mentions)
Philadelphia Coll of Osteopathic Med, 1974
Certification: Dermatology
2221 Garrett Rd, Drexel Hill, PA, 610-623-5885
1200 Locust St #1, Philadelphia, PA, 215-546-3666

Binnick, Steven Arthur (3 mentions)
Hahnemann U, 1973
Certification: Dermatology, Dermatopathology
531 W Germantown Pike #200, Plymouth Meeting, PA, 610-828-0400

Brown, Diana (3 mentions)
Jefferson Med Coll, 1979 *Certification:* Dermatology
8200 Flourtown Ave #13, Wyndmoor, PA, 215-233-0506

Camishion, Germaine Mary (4 mentions)
Jefferson Med Coll, 1985 *Certification:* Dermatology
702 E Main St, Moorestown, NJ, 856-235-6565

Chung, Grace Unsil (6 mentions)
SUNY-Upstate Med U, 1985 *Certification:* Dermatology
17 W Red Bank Ave #205, Woodbury, NJ, 856-384-1964

Deasey, Karen Kulik (5 mentions)
Med Coll of Pennsylvania, 1976 *Certification:* Dermatology
875 County Line Rd #207, Bryn Mawr, PA, 610-525-1920

Egan, Christine Lynn (4 mentions)
U of Pennsylvania, 1992 *Certification:* Dermatology
101 Chesley Dr #100, Media, PA, 610-566-7111
1790 Route 202, Glen Mills, PA, 610-459-1900

Friter, Barry Steven (3 mentions)
Temple U, 1984 *Certification:* Dermatology
2301 Huntingdon Pike, Huntingdon Valley, PA, 215-947-7500

Gottlieb, Scott Lawrence (4 mentions)
Cornell U, 1990 *Certification:* Dermatology
201 Reeceville Rd #35, Coatesville, PA, 610-594-6660
501 Gordon Dr, Exton, PA, 610-594-6660
701 E Baltimore Pike, Kennett Square, PA, 610-444-0070

Green, Justin Jacob (3 mentions)
Robert W Johnson Med Sch, 1998 *Certification:* Dermatology
100 Brick Rd #306, Marlton, NJ, 856-596-0111
3 Cooper Plaza #215, Camden, NJ, 856-342-2439

Greenbaum, Steven Samuel (5 mentions)
Tulane U, 1983 *Certification:* Dermatology
1528 Walnut St #1101, Philadelphia, PA, 215-735-4994

Gross, Paul Robert (8 mentions)
U of Pennsylvania, 1962
Certification: Dermatology, Dermatopathology
220 S 8th St, Philadelphia, PA, 215-829-3576

Heymann, Warren Richard (16 mentions)
Albert Einstein Coll of Med, 1979 *Certification:* Dermatology, Dermatopathology, Pediatric Dermatology
100 Brick Rd #306, Marlton, NJ, 856-596-0111
3 Cooper Plaza #215, Camden, NJ, 856-342-2439

Ho, Magdalene Yuen Yee (3 mentions)
U of Pennsylvania, 1977 *Certification:* Dermatology
7500 Central Ave #109, Philadelphia, PA, 215-342-1144

Hyde, Patrice Marie (7 mentions)
Jefferson Med Coll, 1980 *Certification:* Dermatology, Pediatrics
1600 Rockland Rd, Wilmington, DE, 302-651-5145
833 Chestnut St #740, Philadelphia, PA, 215-955-6680

James, William Danl (3 mentions)
Indiana U, 1977 *Certification:* Dermatological Immunology/Diagnostic and Laboratory Immunology, Dermatology
250 King of Prussia Rd, Radnor, PA, 610-902-2400
3400 Spruce St, Philadelphia, PA, 215-662-2737

Koblenzer, Peter Johann (3 mentions)
FMS-United Kingdom, 1951
Certification: Dermatology, Pediatrics
303 Chester Ave, Moorestown, NJ, 856-235-1178
1812 Delancey Pl, Philadelphia, PA, 215-545-4674

Lawrence, Naomi (4 mentions)
Tulane U, 1987 *Certification:* Dermatology, Dermatopathology
10000 Sagemore Dr #10103, Marlton, NJ, 856-596-3040

Lessin, Stuart Robert (8 mentions)
Temple U, 1982 *Certification:* Dermatology
8 Huntingdon Pike, Rockledge, PA, 215-728-2570

Lopresti, Nicholas Philip (3 mentions)
Jefferson Med Coll, 1996 *Certification:* Dermatology
112 White Horse Pike, Haddon Heights, NJ, 856-546-5353

Manders, Steven Marc (6 mentions)
Robert W Johnson Med Sch, 1988
Certification: Dermatology, Pediatric Dermatology
100 Brick Rd #306, Marlton, NJ, 856-596-0111
3 Cooper Plaza, Camden, NJ, 856-342-2439

Miller, Emily S. (3 mentions)
U of Pittsburgh, 1978 *Certification:* Dermatology
112 White Horse Pike, Haddon Heights, NJ, 856-546-5353

Panzer, Peter B. (3 mentions)
Temple U, 1974 *Certification:* Dermatology
537 Stanton Christiana Rd #207, Newark, DE, 302-633-7550

Roling, Daniel B. (6 mentions)
U of Pennsylvania, 1997 *Certification:* Dermatology
933 E Haverford Rd, Bryn Mawr, PA, 610-642-1090
259 E Lancaster Ave, Wynnewood, PA, 610-642-1090

Scheiner, Robin Beth (3 mentions)
Temple U, 1986 *Certification:* Dermatology
100 W Sproul Rd #120, Springfield, PA, 610-544-8100
1011 W Baltimore Pike #205, West Grove, PA, 610-869-1251

Toporcer, Mary Barbara (4 mentions)
Hahnemann U, 1984
Certification: Dermatology, Internal Medicine
800 W State St #303, Doylestown, PA, 215-230-9988

Uberti-Benz, Marie O. (5 mentions)
Jefferson Med Coll, 1978 *Certification:* Dermatology
3910 Powelton Ave 2nd Fl, Philadelphia, PA, 215-662-8229

Weiss, Rochelle Rudolph (3 mentions)
U of Pennsylvania, 1993 *Certification:* Dermatology
259 E Lancaster Ave, Wynnewood, PA, 610-642-1090
933 Haverford Rd, Bryn Mawr, PA, 610-642-1090

Werth, Victoria Patricia (5 mentions)
Johns Hopkins U, 1980
Certification: Dermatological Immunology/Diagnostic and Laboratory Immunology, Dermatology, Internal Medicine
3400 Spruce St Rhoads Pavillion 2nd Fl, Philadelphia, PA, 215-662-2737

Winter, Jonathan M. (4 mentions)
Albert Einstein Coll of Med, 1984 *Certification:* Dermatology
100 Kings Way E #A1, Sewell, NJ, 856-589-3331

Yan, Albert C. (3 mentions)
U of Pennsylvania, 1993
Certification: Dermatology, Pediatric Dermatology, Pediatrics
3550 Market St, Philadelphia, PA, 215-590-2169
481 John Young Way, Exton, PA, 215-590-6200

Ziskind, Michele J. (5 mentions)
Virginia Commonwealth U, 1979 *Certification:* Dermatology
100 E Lancaster Ave Lankenau Bldg E #456, Wynnewood, PA, 610-649-8541

Emergency Medicine

Christopher, Theodore A. (3 mentions)
Mount Sinai Sch of Med, 1981
Certification: Emergency Medicine, Internal Medicine
1020 Sansom St #239, Philadelphia, PA, 215-955-6844

Cronan, Kathleen Marie (4 mentions)
Temple U, 1984
Certification: Pediatric Emergency Medicine, Pediatrics
1600 Rockland Rd, Wilmington, DE, 302-651-4296

Dipasquale, Anthony (3 mentions)
2301 E Allegheny Ave, Philadelphia, PA, 215-291-3600

Flamma, John C. (3 mentions)
FMS-Grenada, 1988 *Certification:* Internal Medicine
51 N 39th St, Philadelphia, PA, 215-662-8215

Harris, Russell Howard (3 mentions)
Temple U, 1981 *Certification:* Emergency Medicine
1600 Haddon Ave, Camden, NJ, 856-757-3803

Kidwell, Kendel Grant (6 mentions)
Ohio State U, 1980 *Certification:* Emergency Medicine
1200 Old York Rd, Abington, PA, 215-481-4335

Levine, Brian Jay (3 mentions)
U of Vermont, 1995 *Certification:* Emergency Medicine
4755 Ogletown-Stanton Rd, Newark, DE, 302-733-1840

Madden, John Francis (5 mentions)
FMS-Grenada, 1981 *Certification:* Emergency Medicine
4755 Ogletown-Stanton Rd, Newark, DE, 302-733-1840

McCabe, James Leo, III (3 mentions)
Jefferson Med Coll, 1988 *Certification:* Emergency Medicine
435 Hurffville Cross Key, Turnersville, NJ, 856-582-2816

Morris, Jeffrey Bruce (4 mentions)
Hahnemann U, 1977
Certification: Emergency Medicine, Internal Medicine
175 Madison Ave, Mount Holly, NJ, 609-267-0700

Sacchetti, Alfred D., Jr. (7 mentions)
Med Coll of Pennsylvania, 1979
Certification: Emergency Medicine
1600 Haddon Ave, Camden, NJ, 856-757-3803

Shaw, Kathy Nunn (3 mentions)
Mount Sinai Sch of Med, 1982
Certification: Pediatric Emergency Medicine, Pediatrics
34th & Civic Center Blvd, Philadelphia, PA, 215-590-1000

Wald, David Alan (4 mentions)
Philadelphia Coll of Osteopathic Med, 1992
1316 W Ontario St, Philadelphia, PA, 215-707-5879

Endocrinology

Anolik, Jonathan Robert (7 mentions)
Loyola U Chicago, 1977
Certification: Endocrinology and Metabolism, Internal Medicine
703 E Main St, Moorestown, NJ, 856-727-0900

Fallon, Joseph James (15 mentions)
Rosalind Franklin U, 1979
Certification: Endocrinology and Metabolism, Internal Medicine
2301 Evesham Rd #210, Voorhees, NJ, 856-853-1111
603 N Broad St #200, Woodbury, NJ, 856-853-1111

Fitzpatrick, Ruth Ann P. (5 mentions)
Med Coll of Pennsylvania, 1967
Certification: Endocrinology and Metabolism, Internal Medicine
1 Medical Center Blvd #424, Chester, PA, 610-872-8200

Goren, Elihu Norman (8 mentions)
Albert Einstein Coll of Med, 1973
Certification: Endocrinology and Metabolism, Internal Medicine
2303 N Broad St, Colmar, PA, 215-997-9441
633 W Germantown Pike #105, Plymouth Meeting, PA, 610-941-6799

Haddad, Ghada (7 mentions)
FMS-Lebanon, 1987
Certification: Endocrinology, Diabetes, and Metabolism
1210 Brace Rd #107, Cherry Hill, NJ, 856-795-3597
3 Cooper Plaza #215, Camden, NJ, 856-342-2439

Kane, Matthew Stephen (5 mentions)
FMS-Canada, 1984
Certification: Endocrinology and Metabolism, Internal Medicine
795 E Marshall St #102C, West Chester, PA, 610-431-7929

Koch, Cheryl Ann (6 mentions)
Pennsylvania State U, 1989 *Certification:* Endocrinology, Diabetes, and Metabolism, Internal Medicine
933 E Haverford Rd, Bryn Mawr, PA, 610-527-1604

Lenhard, M. James (6 mentions)
Albany Med Coll, 1987
Certification: Endocrinology, Diabetes, and Metabolism
3506 Kennett Pike, Wilmington, DE, 302-661-3070

Mandel, Susan Jennifer (7 mentions)
Columbia U, 1986 *Certification:* Endocrinology, Diabetes, and Metabolism, Internal Medicine
3400 Spruce St 1 Maloney, Philadelphia, PA, 215-662-2300

McGrath, Glenn Alan (10 mentions)
Pennsylvania State U, 1987
Certification: Endocrinology, Diabetes, and Metabolism
2300 Computer Ave #H-39, Willow Grove, PA, 215-657-5200
101 Progress Dr #B, Doylestown, PA, 215-657-5200

Mihailovic, Vesna (5 mentions)
FMS-Croatia, 1971
Certification: Endocrinology and Metabolism, Internal Medicine
1210 Brace Rd #107, Cherry Hill, NJ, 856-795-3597

Miller, Jeffrey Lynn (5 mentions)
FMS-South Africa, 1974
Certification: Endocrinology and Metabolism, Internal Medicine
211 S 9th St #600, Philadelphia, PA, 215-955-1925

Nagelberg, Steven Brooks (5 mentions)
Columbia U, 1978
Certification: Endocrinology and Metabolism, Internal Medicine
555 E City Line Ave #930, Bala Cynwyd, PA, 610-667-7525
9501 Roosevelt Blvd #314, Philadelphia, PA, 215-969-9511

Ruby, Edward Bernard (7 mentions)
Jefferson Med Coll, 1971
Certification: Endocrinology and Metabolism, Internal Medicine
1015 Chestnut St #910, Philadelphia, PA, 215-955-7285
1501 Lansdowne Ave #203, Darby, PA, 610-534-6260

Schorr, Alan Bruce (6 mentions)
Kirksville Coll of Osteopathic Med, 1981
380 Middletown Blvd #710, Langhorne, PA, 215-750-1691

Tavani, Deebeanne M. (8 mentions)
Philadelphia Coll of Osteopathic Med, 1986
Certification: Endocrinology, Diabetes, and Metabolism
100 E Lancaster Ave #463, Wynnewood, PA, 610-896-5170

West, Valerie Anne (10 mentions)
Jefferson Med Coll, 1976 *Certification:* Endocrinology and Metabolism, Internal Medicine
4745 Ogletown-Stanton Rd #208, Newark, DE, 302-731-0606

Family Practice *(see note on page 9)*

Demedio, William Joseph (3 mentions)
Temple U, 1987 *Certification:* Family Medicine
701 N Duke St, Lancaster, PA, 717-299-4644

Lytton, Margaret Steane (4 mentions)
Med Coll of Pennsylvania, 1979 *Certification:* Family Medicine
145 N Narberth Ave, Narberth, PA, 610-667-0650

Mambu, Joseph Fred (3 mentions)
Jefferson Med Coll, 1973
Certification: Family Medicine, Geriatric Medicine
714 N Bethlehem Pike #101, Lower Gwynedd, PA, 215-540-4411

Matthews, Warren Bruce (3 mentions)
Jefferson Med Coll, 1977 *Certification:* Family Medicine
8101 Washington Ln #101, Wyncote, PA, 215-886-0440

Pedicino, Alexander Robert (5 mentions)
Jefferson Med Coll, 1975 *Certification:* Family Medicine
1650 Huntingdon Pike #301, Meadowbrook, PA, 215-947-8170

Perkel, Robert Louis (5 mentions)
Albert Einstein Coll of Med, 1978 *Certification:* Family Medicine
833 Chestnut St E #301, Philadelphia, PA, 215-955-7190

Permut, Stephen Robert (3 mentions)
Temple U, 1972
Certification: Family Medicine, Internal Medicine
3322 N Broad St, Philadelphia, PA, 215-707-4600

Renzi, Michael A. (4 mentions)
Philadelphia Coll of Osteopathic Med, 1991
Certification: Internal Medicine
318 White Horse Pike, Haddon Heights, NJ, 856-547-6000

Russell, John Joseph (3 mentions)
Pennsylvania State U, 1990 *Certification:* Family Medicine
500 Old York Rd, Jenkintown, PA, 215-481-2725

Sacharok, Cynthia Anne (3 mentions)
Jefferson Med Coll, 1988 *Certification:* Family Medicine
500 W MacDade Blvd, Folsom, PA, 610-619-7300

Sandler, Susan Meredith (3 mentions)
Med Coll of Pennsylvania, 1989 *Certification:* Family Medicine
121 Coulter Ave #102, Ardmore, PA, 610-649-5033

Spiro, Paul David (3 mentions)
U of Pennsylvania, 1984 *Certification:* Family Medicine
4897 York Rd, Buckingham, PA, 215-862-4766
Logan Sq #9, New Hope, PA, 215-862-4766

Studdiford, James S., III (3 mentions)
Georgetown U, 1969 *Certification:* Internal Medicine
833 Chestnut St E #301, Philadelphia, PA, 215-955-7190

Wender, Richard Charles (7 mentions)
U of Pennsylvania, 1979 *Certification:* Family Medicine
833 Chestnut St E #301, Philadelphia, PA, 215-955-7190

Zalut, David Scott (3 mentions)
Med Coll of Pennsylvania, 1982 *Certification:* Family Medicine
1000 White Horse Rd #806, Voorhees, NJ, 856-770-0022

Gastroenterology

Battle, William Michael (4 mentions)
U of Pennsylvania, 1972
Certification: Gastroenterology, Internal Medicine
1403 Rhawn St, Philadelphia, PA, 215-332-8100

Deitch, Christopher W. (4 mentions)
Hahnemann U, 1993
Certification: Gastroenterology, Internal Medicine
501 Fellowship Rd #101, Mount Laurel, NJ, 856-642-2133
3 Cooper Plaza #215, Camden, NJ, 856-342-2439

DiMarino, Anthony J., Jr. (11 mentions)
Hahnemann U, 1968
Certification: Gastroenterology, Internal Medicine
17 W Red Bank Ave #302, Woodbury, NJ, 856-848-4464

Elfant, Adam Ben (10 mentions)
Robert W Johnson Med Sch, 1989 *Certification:* Gastroenterology
501 Fellowship Rd #101, Mount Laurel, NJ, 856-642-2133
1 Plaza Dr #215, Sewell, NJ, 856-270-4080
1 Cooper Plaza, Camden, NJ, 856-757-7732

Friehling, Jane Susan (5 mentions)
Kirksville Coll of Osteopathic Med, 1978
406 Lippincott Dr #E, Marlton, NJ, 856-983-1900
807 Haddon Ave #201, Haddonfield, NJ, 856-428-2112

Guttmann, Harvey (10 mentions)
Cornell U, 1979
Certification: Gastroenterology, Internal Medicine
1095 Rydal Rd #100, Rydal, PA, 267-620-1100

Haimowitz, Bernard (4 mentions)
Jefferson Med Coll, 1985
Certification: Gastroenterology, Internal Medicine
4745 Ogletown-Stanton Rd #134, Newark, DE, 302-738-5300

Katzka, David A. (10 mentions)
Mount Sinai Sch of Med, 1980
Certification: Gastroenterology, Internal Medicine
3400 Spruce St Dulles Bldg 3rd Fl, Philadelphia, PA, 215-349-8222
250 King of Prussia Rd, Radnor, PA, 610-902-1500

Kelly, Kevin John (4 mentions)
Georgetown U, 1980
Certification: Pediatric Gastroenterology, Pediatrics
2701 Blair Mill Rd, Willow Grove, PA, 215-293-8800
Erie Ave & Front St, Philadelphia, PA, 215-427-5000

Kutscher, Jeffrey Joseph (4 mentions)
Case Western Reserve U, 1977
Certification: Gastroenterology, Internal Medicine
693 Main St #A-2, Lumberton, NJ, 609-265-1700

Leonard, Maurice David (7 mentions)
Albert Einstein Coll of Med, 1982
Certification: Gastroenterology, Internal Medicine
693 Main St #A-2, Lumberton, NJ, 609-265-1700

Libster, Boris (5 mentions)
New York Coll of Osteopathic Med, 1982
Certification: Gastroenterology, Internal Medicine
217 White Horse Pike, Haddon Heights, NJ, 856-547-9595

Lipshutz, William Herman (5 mentions)
U of Pennsylvania, 1967
Certification: Gastroenterology, Internal Medicine
230 W Washington Sq 4th Fl, Philadelphia, PA, 215-829-3561

Mercogliano, Giancarlo (5 mentions)
Hahnemann U, 1983
Certification: Gastroenterology, Internal Medicine
100 E Lancaster Ave #252, Wynnewood, PA, 610-896-7360
2050 West Chester Pike #200, Havertown, PA, 610-449-1525

Nussbaum, Steven Joel (4 mentions)
SUNY-Downstate Med Coll, 1974
Certification: Gastroenterology, Internal Medicine
1010 W Chester Pike #202, Havertown, PA, 610-789-3510

Thornton, James Joseph, III (8 mentions)
Temple U, 1964
Certification: Gastroenterology, Internal Medicine
100 E Lancaster Ave #252, Wynnewood, PA, 610-896-7360
2050 West Chester Pike #200, Havertown, PA, 610-449-1525

Turnier, Auguste Philippe (5 mentions)
Med Coll of Pennsylvania, 1986
Certification: Gastroenterology, Internal Medicine
501 Haddon Ave #9, Haddonfield, NJ, 856-428-6024

Volpe, John A. (4 mentions)
Des Moines U, 1983
333 N Oxford Valley Rd #402, Fairless Hills, PA, 215-949-2650

Zitin, Marc Allen (5 mentions)
Hahnemann U, 1985 *Certification:* Internal Medicine
100 E Lancaster Ave #252, Wynnewood, PA, 610-896-8335
2050 West Chester Pike #200, Havertown, PA, 610-449-1525

General Surgery

Abdel-Misih, Raafat Z. (3 mentions)
FMS-Egypt, 1971 *Certification:* Surgery
1021 Gilpin Ave #203, Wilmington, DE, 302-658-7533

Atabek, Umur Mehmet (8 mentions)
U of Maryland, 1980 *Certification:* Surgery
3 Cooper Plaza #403, Camden, NJ, 856-342-2270
900 Centennial Blvd #G, Voorhees, NJ, 856-325-6565

Bar, Allen Herbert (5 mentions)
Tufts U, 1967 *Certification:* Surgery
301 S 8th St #4A, Philadelphia, PA, 215-829-8455

Boynton, Christopher Jay (5 mentions)
New Jersey Med Sch, 1982 *Certification:* Surgery
131 Madison Ave, Mount Holly, NJ, 609-267-7050

Carp, Ned Zachary (4 mentions)
Temple U, 1984 *Certification:* Surgery
100 Lancaster Ave Lankenau Bldg #275, Wynnewood, PA, 610-642-1908

Cody, William (3 mentions)
Columbia U, 1982 *Certification:* Colon & Rectal Surgery, Surgery
1935 Route 70 E, Cherry Hill, NJ, 856-428-7700

Cohen, Murray Jay (3 mentions)
Temple U, 1981 *Certification:* Surgery, Surgical Critical Care
1100 Walnut St #500, Philadelphia, PA, 215-955-8813

Coletta, Anthony Vincent (12 mentions)
Jefferson Med Coll, 1979 *Certification:* Surgery
830 Old Lancaster Rd #306, Bryn Mawr, PA, 610-527-1185

De Leon, Miguel L. (3 mentions)
FMS-Philippines, 1975
Certification: Colon & Rectal Surgery, Surgery
1935 Route 70 E, Cherry Hill, NJ, 856-428-7700

Derrick, Bruce Melvin (3 mentions)
Temple U, 1975 *Certification:* Surgery
599 W State St #301, Doylestown, PA, 215-348-7195

Doolin, Edward John (3 mentions)
Northwestern U, 1979
Certification: Pediatric Surgery, Surgery, Surgical Critical Care
34th St & Civic Center Blvd 5th Fl, Philadelphia, PA, 215-590-2730
1012 Laurel Oak Rd, Voorhees, NJ, 856-435-1300

Drebin, Jeffrey Adam (4 mentions)
Harvard U, 1987 *Certification:* Surgery
3400 Spruce St 4th Fl, Philadelphia, PA, 215-662-2050

Dunn, Stephen Philip (4 mentions)
Indiana U, 1978
Certification: Pediatric Surgery, Surgery, Surgical Critical Care
1600 Rockland Rd, Wilmington, DE, 302-651-4888

Finkelstein, Gary Stan (3 mentions)
Temple U, 1974 *Certification:* Surgery
670 Lawn Ave #1-A, Sellersville, PA, 215-257-3697

Fox, Timothy Trudeau (8 mentions)
New Jersey Med Sch, 1982 *Certification:* Surgery
11 Industrial Blvd #102, Paoli, PA, 610-640-4650

Frankel, Arthur Mark (4 mentions)
Temple U, 1978 *Certification:* Surgery
1245 Highland Ave #600, Abington, PA, 215-886-1020

Frazier, Thomas Gibson (4 mentions)
U of Pennsylvania, 1968 *Certification:* Surgery
101 S Bryn Mawr Ave #201, Bryn Mawr, PA, 610-520-0700

Grabiak, Thomas Anthony (3 mentions)
Jefferson Med Coll, 1980 *Certification:* Surgery
502 Centennial Blvd #7, Voorhees, NJ, 856-596-7440

Haith, Linwood Ross (3 mentions)
Harvard U, 1976 *Certification:* Surgery, Surgical Critical Care
1 Medical Center Blvd #241, Upland, PA, 610-619-7400

Harbison, Sean Patrick (3 mentions)
Temple U, 1986 *Certification:* Surgery
3401 N Broad St, Philadelphia, PA, 215-707-2072
2346 E Allegheny Ave, Philadelphia, PA, 215-423-4356

Jacobelli, Michael Charles (5 mentions)
Pennsylvania State U, 1979 *Certification:* Surgery
1205 Langhorne-Newtown Rd #106, Langhorne, PA, 215-757-5131

Josloff, Robert Kevin (3 mentions)
Jefferson Med Coll, 1989 *Certification:* Surgery
1245 Highland Ave #600, Abington, PA, 215-887-3990

Kairys, John Charles (3 mentions)
Jefferson Med Coll, 1988 *Certification:* Surgery
1100 Walnut St, Philadelphia, PA, 215-955-5528

Kirkland, Matt Lockwood (3 mentions)
Jefferson Med Coll, 1983 *Certification:* Surgery
700 Spruce St #507, Philadelphia, PA, 215-829-3697

Kliefoth, William L. (3 mentions)
Philadelphia Coll of Osteopathic Med, 1981
402 Middletown Blvd #212, Langhorne, PA, 215-750-6010

Marchildon, Michael Bert (3 mentions)
Stanford U, 1968 *Certification:* Pediatric Surgery, Surgery
1000 White Horse Rd #204, Voorhees, NJ, 856-309-8508
2500 English Creek Rd #1000, Atlantic City, NJ, 609-641-3700

Marcucci, Michael Charles (4 mentions)
Hahnemann U, 1982 *Certification:* Surgery
219 N Broad St 8th Fl, Philadelphia, PA, 215-762-3430
1726 S Broad St #103, Philadelphia, PA, 215-762-3430
5735 Ridge Ave #202, Philadelphia, PA, 215-762-3430

Nance, Michael Lewis (4 mentions)
Louisiana State U, 1988
Certification: Pediatric Surgery, Surgery, Surgical Critical Care
324 S 34th St, Philadelphia, PA, 215-590-2468
500 W Butler Ave, Chalfont, PA, 215-997-5730

Nussbaum, Michael Lynn (4 mentions)
Indiana U, 1982 *Certification:* Surgery
1208 Highland Ave, Abington, PA, 215-887-3565

Patton, Mary Lou (3 mentions)
Med Coll of Ohio, 1979
Certification: Surgery, Surgical Critical Care
1 Medical Center Blvd #241, Chester, PA, 610-619-7400
300 Evergreen Dr #130, Glen Mills, PA, 610-619-7400

Pello, Mark Joel (8 mentions)
Jefferson Med Coll, 1975
Certification: Colon & Rectal Surgery, Surgery
6017 Main St, Voorhees, NJ, 856-342-2270
2 Cooper Plaza #403, Camden, NJ, 856-342-2270

Rose, David (8 mentions)
Columbia U, 1977 *Certification:* Surgery
830 Old Lancaster Rd Medical Bldg N #306, Bryn Mawr, PA, 610-527-1185

Santos, Rodrigo R. (4 mentions)
FMS-Philippines, 1967
17 White Horse Pike #6, Haddon Heights, NJ, 856-547-5522

Smink, Robert Danl, Jr. (3 mentions)
Case Western Reserve U, 1966 *Certification:* Surgery
100 Lancaster Ave #275, Wynnewood, PA, 610-642-1908

Trajtenberg, Jorge A. (4 mentions)
FMS-Argentina, 1974 *Certification:* Surgery
915 Old Fern Hill Rd #B201, West Chester, PA, 610-436-6696
402 McFarlan Rd, Kennett Square, PA, 610-436-6696

Winter, Howard Jeffrey (5 mentions)
Albert Einstein Coll of Med, 1974 *Certification:* Surgery
502 Centennial Blvd #7, Voorhees, NJ, 856-596-7440

Zern, Jeffry (3 mentions)
Temple U, 1991 *Certification:* Surgery
4735 Ogletown-Stanton Rd #1211, Newark, DE, 302-623-3850

Geriatrics

Cavalieri, Thomas A. (9 mentions)
Des Moines U, 1976
Certification: Geriatric Medicine, Internal Medicine
42 E Laurel Rd #1800, Stratford, NJ, 856-566-6843

Chopra, Anita (4 mentions)
FMS-India, 1973
Certification: Geriatric Medicine, Internal Medicine
42 E Laurel Rd #1800, Stratford, NJ, 856-566-6000
1417 Brace Rd, Cherry Hill, NJ, 856-795-3131

Curtin, Patricia Mary (4 mentions)
Jefferson Med Coll, 1988
Certification: Geriatric Medicine, Internal Medicine
501 W 14th St #5236, Wilmington, DE, 302-428-4646

Galinsky, David Elliot (4 mentions)
Temple U, 1971
Certification: Geriatric Medicine, Internal Medicine
100 Lancaster Ave #467E, Wynnewood, PA, 610-896-7424
10000 Shannondell Dr, Eagleville, PA, 610-728-5241
2101 Belmont Ave, Philadelphia, PA, 215-871-5258

Goldis, Michael Edward (3 mentions)
Des Moines U, 1988
119 E Laurel Rd, Stratford, NJ, 856-346-3469

Hofmann, Mary McLoone (7 mentions)
Temple U, 1988
Certification: Geriatric Medicine, Internal Medicine
1245 Highland Ave #302, Abington, PA, 215-481-4350

Johnson, Jerry Calvin (3 mentions)
Case Western Reserve U, 1974
Certification: Geriatric Medicine, Internal Medicine
3615 Chestnut St, Philadelphia, PA, 215-898-1548

Reichard, Rita A. (4 mentions)
Temple U, 1991
Certification: Geriatric Medicine, Internal Medicine
1245 Highland Ave #302, Abington, PA, 800-934-0404

Simpson, David Albert (3 mentions)
FMS-Mexico, 1987 *Certification:* Family Medicine
1401 Foulk Rd, Wilmington, DE, 302-477-3300

Sitkoff, Andrew D. (3 mentions)
Philadelphia Coll of Osteopathic Med, 1985
Certification: Geriatric Medicine, Internal Medicine
400 E Marshall St, West Chester, PA, 610-241-3050

Hematology/Oncology

Alley, Evan Wayne (3 mentions)
U of Kansas, 1996
Certification: Hematology, Internal Medicine, Medical Oncology
240 Middletown Blvd #205, Langhorne, PA, 215-752-2424
1201 Langhorne Newtown Rd, Langhorne, PA, 215-710-2000

Bapat, Ashok Ramchandra (4 mentions)
FMS-India, 1973
Certification: Hematology, Internal Medicine, Medical Oncology
705 White Horse Rd #D105, Voorhees, NJ, 856-435-1777
900 Medical Center Dr #200, Sewell, NJ, 856-582-0550
17 W Red Bank Ave #202, Woodbury, NJ, 856-848-5560

Blatt, Philip Mark (3 mentions)
Washington U, 1969 *Certification:* Hematology, Internal Medicine
4735 Ogletown-Stanton Rd #2225, Newark, DE, 302-737-7700

Cairoli, Maurice James (3 mentions)
New York Med Coll, 1984
Certification: Internal Medicine, Medical Oncology
175 Madison Ave #4, Mount Holly, NJ, 609-702-1900

Callahan, Kevin J. (3 mentions)
U of New England, 1987
608 N Broad St #300, Woodbury, NJ, 856-686-1002
1930 Marlton Pike E #V107, Cherry Hill, NJ, 856-424-3311

Chernoff, Marc J. (4 mentions)
Philadelphia Coll of Osteopathic Med, 1991
Certification: Hematology, Medical Oncology
2510 Maryland Rd #175, Willow Grove, PA, 215-706-2034
1648 Huntingdon Pike #1000, Meadowbrook, PA, 215-947-5460

Crilley, Pamela A. (3 mentions)
Philadelphia Coll of Osteopathic Med, 1979
Certification: Hematology, Internal Medicine, Medical Oncology
230 N Broad St, Philadelphia, PA, 215-762-7735
205 Newtown Rd, Warminster, PA, 215-441-7417

Entmacher, Michael Saml (3 mentions)
Duke U, 1969
Certification: Hematology, Internal Medicine, Medical Oncology
175 Madison Ave #4, Mount Holly, NJ, 609-702-1900

Feeney, Kendra J. (3 mentions)
Hahnemann U, 1994
Certification: Hematology, Internal Medicine, Medical Oncology
111 S 11th St #4240, Philadelphia, PA, 215-955-8874
925 Chestnut St #220-A, Philadelphia, PA, 215-955-8874

Fellin, Frederick Michael (5 mentions)
Jefferson Med Coll, 1979
Certification: Hematology, Internal Medicine, Medical Oncology
834 Walnut St, Philadelphia, PA, 215-955-6039
8815 Germantown Ave #16, Philadelphia, PA, 215-955-6039
1330 Powell St #308, Morristown, PA, 215-955-6039
1541 Powell St, Morristown, PA, 215-955-6039

Flomenberg, Neal (4 mentions)
Jefferson Med Coll, 1976
Certification: Hematology, Internal Medicine, Medical Oncology
125 S 9th St #801, Philadelphia, PA, 215-955-9642
925 Chestnut St #220-A, Philadelphia, PA, 215-955-8874

Fox, Kevin Reitnour (4 mentions)
Johns Hopkins U, 1981
Certification: Internal Medicine, Medical Oncology
3400 Spruce St Penn Tower 14th Fl, Philadelphia, PA,
215-662-7469

Fox, Stephen C. (3 mentions)
Boston U, 1974
Certification: Internal Medicine, Medical Oncology
21 Industrial Blvd #204, Paoli, PA, 610-647-2747

Gilman, Paul Barth (4 mentions)
Jefferson Med Coll, 1976
Certification: Hematology, Internal Medicine, Medical Oncology
100 E Lancaster Ave #13-20, Wynnewood, PA, 610-645-2494

Goldberg, Jack (7 mentions)
SUNY-Upstate Med U, 1973
Certification: Hematology, Internal Medicine, Medical Oncology
409 Route 70 E, Cherry Hill, NJ, 856-429-1519
51 N 39th St #220, Philadelphia, PA, 215-662-9801

Grana, Generosa (9 mentions)
Northwestern U, 1985
Certification: Internal Medicine, Medical Oncology
900 Centennial Blvd #M-2, Voorhees, NJ, 856-325-6750

Hageboutros, Alexandre (12 mentions)
FMS-Lebanon, 1987
Certification: Hematology, Internal Medicine, Medical Oncology
900 Centennial Blvd #M2, Voorhees, NJ, 856-325-6750

Henry, David Holden (3 mentions)
U of Pennsylvania, 1975
Certification: Hematology, Internal Medicine, Medical Oncology
230 W Washington Sq 2nd Fl, Philadelphia, PA, 215-829-6088
250 King of Prussia Rd #1B, Radnor, PA, 610-902-5950

Hoessly, Michel (3 mentions)
FMS-Switzerland, 1980
Certification: Hematology, Internal Medicine, Medical Oncology
209 W Lancaster Ave #100, Paoli, PA, 610-725-0650

Leighton, John Charles, Jr. (6 mentions)
Temple U, 1989
Certification: Hematology, Internal Medicine, Medical Oncology
5501 Old York Rd 1st Fl, Philadelphia, PA, 215-456-3880
9880 Bustleton Ave #208, Philadelphia, PA, 215-969-6960

Mann, Michael Patrick (3 mentions)
Philadelphia Coll of Osteopathic Med, 1976
240 Middletown Blvd #205, Langhorne, PA, 215-752-2424
1201 Langhorne Newtown Rd, Langhorne, PA, 215-710-2000

Mason, Bernard Arthur (3 mentions)
U of Pennsylvania, 1972
Certification: Hematology, Internal Medicine, Medical Oncology
230 W Washington Sq 2nd Fl, Philadelphia, PA, 215-829-6088
250 King of Prussia Rd #1B, Radnor, PA, 610-902-5950

Mastrangelo, Michael Joseph (3 mentions)
Johns Hopkins U, 1964
Certification: Internal Medicine, Medical Oncology
111 S 11th St #G4240, Philadelphia, PA, 215-955-8874
925 Chestnut St #220-A, Philadelphia, PA, 215-955-8874

McLaughlin, Carlin (4 mentions)
Philadelphia Coll of Osteopathic Med, 1984
240 Middletown Blvd #205, Langhorne, PA, 215-752-2424
1201 Langhorne Newtown Rd, Langhorne, PA, 215-710-2000

Mintzer, David Michael (6 mentions)
Jefferson Med Coll, 1977
Certification: Hematology, Internal Medicine, Medical Oncology
230 W Washington Sq 2nd Fl, Philadelphia, PA, 215-829-6088
250 King of Prussia Rd #1B, Radnor, PA, 610-902-5950

Pemberton, Clifford H. (3 mentions)
Jefferson Med Coll, 1978 *Certification:* Hematology,
Hospice and Palliative Medicine, Internal Medicine
100 Lancaster Ave #B-20, Wynnewood, PA, 610-645-2494

Pickens, Peter Vincent (5 mentions)
Mount Sinai Sch of Med, 1978
Certification: Internal Medicine, Medical Oncology
1648 Huntingdon Pike #1000, Meadowbrook, PA, 215-947-5460
2510 Maryland Rd Willow Wood Bldg, Willow Grove, PA,
215-706-2034

Poretta, Trina Ann (5 mentions)
New Jersey Sch of Osteopathic Med, 1996
705 White Horse Rd #D105, Voorhees, NJ, 856-435-1777

Rao, Angara Koneti (4 mentions)
FMS-India, 1974 *Certification:* Hematology, Internal Medicine
3400 N Broad St OMS #300, Philadelphia, PA, 215-707-4684

Redmond, John, III (4 mentions)
Emory U, 1974
Certification: Hematology, Internal Medicine, Medical Oncology
1200 Old York Rd, Abington, PA, 215-481-2400

Reilly, Robert E. (4 mentions)
New York Coll of Osteopathic Med, 1981
1205 Langhorne-Yardley Rd #407, Langhorne, PA, 215-750-8079
3300 Tilman Dr #201, Bensalem, PA, 215-633-3473

Rose, Lewis Jay (4 mentions)
Harvard U, 1978
Certification: Hematology, Internal Medicine, Medical Oncology
1015 Chestnut St #1321, Philadelphia, PA, 215-923-5676
1328 Ritner St, Philadelphia, PA, 215-334-5315
2701 Holme Ave #302, Philadelphia, PA, 215-624-8138

Ross, David Howard (4 mentions)
Temple U, 1968
Certification: Hematology, Internal Medicine, Medical Oncology
900 Medical Center Dr #200, Sewell, NJ, 856-582-0550
705 White Horse Rd #D105, Voorhees, NJ, 856-435-1777
17 W Red Bank Ave #202, Woodbury, NJ, 856-435-1777

Rubin, Rene (4 mentions)
FMS-Mexico, 1981
207 N Broad St, Philadelphia, PA, 215-561-0809

Rubin, Ronald Neal (4 mentions)
Temple U, 1972 *Certification:* Hematology, Internal Medicine
3401 N Broad St, Philadelphia, PA, 215-707-4675

Siegel, Norman Henry (4 mentions)
U of Pittsburgh, 1965
Certification: Hematology, Internal Medicine, Medical Oncology
1930 Route 70 E #V107, Cherry Hill, NJ, 856-424-3311

Slease, Robert Bradley (4 mentions)
U of Kansas, 1972 *Certification:* Hematology, Internal Medicine
4735 Ogletown-Stanton Rd #2225, Newark, DE, 302-737-7700

Vivacqua, Raymond John (3 mentions)
Jefferson Med Coll, 1960
Certification: Hematology, Internal Medicine
1 Medical Center Blvd #341, Upland, PA, 610-619-7420
196 W Sproul Rd #106, Springfield, PA, 610-328-1258
1 Bartol Ave #103, Ridley Park, PA, 610-521-6885

Weinstein, Alan Stanley (6 mentions)
U of Pennsylvania, 1971
175 Madison Ave #4, Mount Holly, NJ, 609-702-1900

Infectious Disease

Braffman, Michael Neil (6 mentions)
U of Pennsylvania, 1980
Certification: Infectious Disease, Internal Medicine
301 S 8th St #1B, Philadelphia, PA, 215-829-5354

Braun, Todd Ian (9 mentions)
Hahnemann U, 1981
Certification: Infectious Disease, Internal Medicine
1235 Old York Rd Levy Plaza #220, Abington, PA, 215-481-6350

Buckley, R. Michael, Jr. (6 mentions)
Yale U, 1972 *Certification:* Infectious Disease, Internal Medicine
1 Pine St W, Philadelphia, PA, 214-829-3000

Condoluci, David Vincent (9 mentions)
Philadelphia Coll of Osteopathic Med, 1976
709 Haddonfield-Berlin Rd, Voorhees, NJ, 856-566-3190

De Simone, Joseph Andrew (6 mentions)
Hahnemann U, 1994
Certification: Infectious Disease, Internal Medicine
834 Walnut St #650, Philadelphia, PA, 215-955-5161

Goren, Ronald Claude (15 mentions)
Temple U, 1973
Certification: Infectious Disease, Internal Medicine
9501 Roosevelt Blvd #208, Philadelphia, PA, 215-464-9634

Ingerman, Mark (16 mentions)
Jefferson Med Coll, 1981
Certification: Infectious Disease, Internal Medicine
100 Lancaster Ave Lankenau Bldg E #164, Wynnewood, PA,
610-896-0210

Kim, Young Shik (6 mentions)
Yale U, 1986 *Certification:* Infectious Disease, Internal Medicine
255 W Lancaster Ave #121, Paoli, PA, 610-560-0014
933 Haverford Rd, Bryn Mawr, PA, 610-527-8118

Liu, Hans Hamilton (7 mentions)
Harvard U, 1978
Certification: Infectious Disease, Internal Medicine
933 E Haverford Rd, Bryn Mawr, PA, 610-527-8118

Livornese, Lawrence L., Jr. (9 mentions)
New Jersey Med Sch, 1986
Certification: Infectious Disease, Internal Medicine
100 E Lancaster Ave #164, Wynnewood, PA, 610-896-0210

Long, Sarah Sundborg (9 mentions)
Jefferson Med Coll, 1970
Certification: Pediatric Infectious Diseases, Pediatrics
E Erie Ave & N Front St, Philadelphia, PA, 215-427-5201

Lorber, Bennett (18 mentions)
U of Pennsylvania, 1968
Certification: Infectious Disease, Internal Medicine
3401 N Broad St #500, Philadelphia, PA, 215-707-3807

Marcus, Donald Keith (7 mentions)
Boston U, 1983
Certification: Infectious Disease, Internal Medicine
9501 Roosevelt Blvd #208, Philadelphia, PA, 215-464-9634

Nieman, Roger Elsworth (7 mentions)
Johns Hopkins U, 1973
Certification: Infectious Disease, Internal Medicine
1235 Old York Rd #220, Abington, PA, 215-481-6350

Peterson, John W. (6 mentions)
Robert W Johnson Med Sch, 1985
Certification: Infectious Disease, Internal Medicine
1001 Briggs Rd #250, Mount Laurel, NJ, 856-866-7466

Reboli, Annette C. (9 mentions)
Georgetown U, 1981
Certification: Infectious Disease, Internal Medicine
3 Cooper Plaza #215, Camden, NJ, 856-757-7760

Santoro, Jerome (9 mentions)
Temple U, 1972
Certification: Infectious Disease, Internal Medicine
100 Lancaster Ave Bldg E #164, Wynnewood, PA, 610-896-0210

Spitzer, Peter Gordon (9 mentions)
Louisiana State U, 1981
Certification: Infectious Disease, Internal Medicine
933 E Haverford Rd, Bryn Mawr, PA, 610-527-8118

Stern, John J. (11 mentions)
New York U, 1979
Certification: Infectious Disease, Internal Medicine
301 S 8th St #1B, Philadelphia, PA, 215-829-5354

Infertility

Barmat, Larry Ian (4 mentions)
Temple U, 1991 *Certification:* Obstetrics & Gynecology,
Reproductive Endocrinology/Infertility
1245 Highland Ave #404, Abington, PA, 215-887-2010
1690 Sumneytown Pike, Lansdale, PA, 215-855-7511

Castelbaum, Arthur Jay (4 mentions)
Washington U, 1988 *Certification:* Obstetrics & Gynecology,
Reproductive Endocrinology/Infertility
1650 Huntingdon Pike #154, Meadowbrook, PA, 215-938-1515

Check, Jerome Harvey (8 mentions)
Hahnemann U, 1971
Certification: Endocrinology and Metabolism, Internal Medicine
7447 Old York Rd, Melrose Park, PA, 215-635-4400
8002 Greentree Commons #E, Marlton, NJ, 856-751-5575

Freedman, Martin Frederic (6 mentions)
Wayne State U, 1977 *Certification:* Obstetrics & Gynecology,
Reproductive Endocrinology/Infertility
1650 Huntingdon Pike #154, Meadowbrook, PA, 215-938-1515

Glassner, Michael J. (6 mentions)
Albany Med Coll, 1984 *Certification:* Obstetrics & Gynecology
130 S Bryn Mawr Ave Wing D #1000, Bryn Mawr, PA,
610-527-0800
11 Industrial Blvd #100, Paoli, PA, 610-993-8200

Schinfeld, Jay Scott (5 mentions)
Jefferson Med Coll, 1974 *Certification:* Obstetrics &
Gynecology, Reproductive Endocrinology/Infertility
1245 Highland Ave #404, Abington, PA, 215-887-2010
1690 Sumneytown Pike, Lansdale, PA, 215-855-7511

Skaf, Robert A. (5 mentions)
FMS-Syria, 1973 *Certification:* Obstetrics & Gynecology,
Reproductive Endocrinology/Infertility
2500 English Creek Ave #225, Egg Harbor Township, NJ,
609-813-2192
400 Lippincott Dr #130, Marlton, NJ, 856-596-2233

Somkuti, Stephen George (4 mentions)
U of North Carolina, 1989 *Certification:* Obstetrics &
Gynecology, Reproductive Endocrinology/Infertility
1245 Highland Ave #404, Abington, PA, 215-887-2010
1690 Sumneytown Pike, Lansdale, PA, 215-855-7511

Internal Medicine *(see note on page 9)*

Agard, Reynold Steve (3 mentions)
Pennsylvania State U, 1996 *Certification:* Internal Medicine
410 Foulk Rd #200-B, Wilmington, DE, 302-762-6675

Beggs, Nancy Hsueh (3 mentions)
Temple U, 1986 *Certification:* Internal Medicine
900 Centennial Blvd #L, Voorhees, NJ, 856-325-6770

Berna, Ronald Anthony (3 mentions)
Jefferson Med Coll, 1989 *Certification:* Internal Medicine
509 S Lenola Rd #3, Moorestown, NJ, 856-234-2722

Berna, William (3 mentions)
New Jersey Med Sch, 1985 *Certification:* Internal Medicine
509 S Lenola Rd #3, Moorestown, NJ, 856-234-2722

Boselli, Joseph Mark (5 mentions)
Hahnemann U, 1982 *Certification:* Internal Medicine
205 N Broad St #100, Philadelphia, PA, 215-587-8008

Cato, Robert Keith (3 mentions)
Cornell U, 1993 *Certification:* Internal Medicine
39th & Market Sts #102, Philadelphia, PA, 215-662-9990

Ciccarelli, Stephanie Lee (3 mentions)
Wake Forest U, 1993 *Certification:* Emergency Medicine
701 E Marshall St #380, West Chester, PA, 610-738-2762

Daniels, Roger Bruce (7 mentions)
U of Pennsylvania, 1960 *Certification:* Internal Medicine
1100 Walnut St #601, Philadelphia, PA, 215-955-3523

Dorshimer, Gary William (4 mentions)
U of Pennsylvania, 1981
Certification: Internal Medicine, Sports Medicine
727 Delancey St, Philadelphia, PA, 215-829-3523

Fenton, Bradley Wayne (5 mentions)
Harvard U, 1976
Certification: Infectious Disease, Internal Medicine
1100 Walnut St #601, Philadelphia, PA, 215-955-9330
401 City Ave #525, Bala Cynwyd, PA, 215-955-9330

Gerber, Steven L. (5 mentions)
Temple U, 1984 *Certification:* Internal Medicine
1025 Marlton Pike W, Cherry Hill, NJ, 856-429-6858

Greer, William Robson (3 mentions)
U of Pennsylvania, 1993 *Certification:* Internal Medicine
21 Industrial Blvd #200, Paoli, PA, 610-651-0370

Hockfield, Hal Scott (4 mentions)
Temple U, 1985 *Certification:* Internal Medicine
1235 Old York Rd #113, Abington, PA, 215-481-6180
1380 Easton Rd, Warrington, PA, 215-491-1000

Killion, Matthew Joseph (3 mentions)
Jefferson Med Coll, 1993 *Certification:* Internal Medicine
1015 Chestnut St #1506, Philadelphia, PA, 215-503-2700

Kolander, Scott A. (3 mentions)
Hahnemann U, 1982
Certification: Geriatric Medicine, Internal Medicine
1230 Parkway Ave #303, West Trenton, NJ, 609-883-5454

Laskin, David Allen (3 mentions)
Hahnemann U, 1978
Certification: Geriatric Medicine, Internal Medicine
400 Grove Rd #102, Thorofare, NJ, 856-845-8010

Leuzzi, Rosemarie Anne (3 mentions)
U of Pittsburgh, 1989 *Certification:* Internal Medicine
900 Centennial Blvd #L, Voorhees, NJ, 856-325-6770

Ling, Henry Tsewei (10 mentions)
Jefferson Med Coll, 1986 *Certification:* Internal Medicine
100 E Lancaster Ave #140, Wynnewood, PA, 610-642-6990

Merli, Geno Joseph (9 mentions)
Jefferson Med Coll, 1975 *Certification:* Internal Medicine
833 Chestnut St #702, Philadelphia, PA, 215-955-6540

Miller, Howard Alan (3 mentions)
Hahnemann U, 1974 *Certification:* Internal Medicine
205 N Broad St #100, Philadelphia, PA, 215-587-8008

Newell, Glenn Casey (3 mentions)
FMS-Dominican Republic, 1981
Certification: Internal Medicine, Nephrology
1 Cooper Plaza #222, Camden, NJ, 856-342-3150
3 Cooper Plaza #215, Camden, NJ, 856-342-2439

Peet, Alisa (3 mentions)
Temple U, 2000 *Certification:* Internal Medicine
1316 W Ontario St 1st Fl, Philadelphia, PA, 215-707-1800

Rigotti, Joseph A. (4 mentions)
Philadelphia Coll of Osteopathic Med, 1984
Certification: Internal Medicine
500 Old York Rd, Jenkintown, PA, 215-886-0174

Rusk, Matthew Harrison (4 mentions)
U of Pennsylvania, 1992 *Certification:* Internal Medicine
39th & Market Sts, Philadelphia, PA, 215-662-9990

Shonberg, Barbara Hollis (6 mentions)
U of Pennsylvania, 1979 *Certification:* Internal Medicine
970 Town Center Dr #C-15, Langhorne, PA, 215-752-8866

Viner, Edward D. (5 mentions)
U of Pennsylvania, 1960
Certification: Hematology, Internal Medicine, Medical Oncology
3 Cooper Plaza #215, Camden, NJ, 856-342-2017

Nephrology

Benz, Robert Lawrence (5 mentions)
Jefferson Med Coll, 1978
Certification: Internal Medicine, Nephrology
100 E Lancaster Ave #130, Wynnewood, PA, 610-649-1175

Berns, Jeffrey Scott (6 mentions)
Case Western Reserve U, 1981
Certification: Internal Medicine, Nephrology
3400 Spruce St #210, Philadelphia, PA, 215-662-2638

Brown, Anthony (4 mentions)
Philadelphia Coll of Osteopathic Med, 1984
Certification: Internal Medicine, Nephrology
201 Laurel Oak Rd, Voorhees, NJ, 856-237-8060

Burke, James Francis (11 mentions)
Jefferson Med Coll, 1966
Certification: Internal Medicine, Nephrology
111 S 11th St Gibbon Bldg #G4290, Philadelphia, PA,
215-955-6550

Cohen, Raphael Mayer (4 mentions)
Harvard U, 1977 *Certification:* Internal Medicine, Nephrology
51 N 39th St Bldg 240, Philadelphia, PA, 215-662-8730

Conrad, Michael James (5 mentions)
U of Massachusetts, 1981
Certification: Internal Medicine, Nephrology
1025 Briggs Rd #148, Mount Laurel, NJ, 856-222-1975

Cox, Robert Walter (4 mentions)
Jefferson Med Coll, 1970
Certification: Internal Medicine, Nephrology
4923 Ogletown-Stanton Rd #200, Newark, DE, 302-225-0451
111 W High St, Elkton, MD, 410-620-9200
29 Gooden Ave, Dover, DE, 302-734-3227

Dressler, Robert Mark (5 mentions)
FMS-Israel, 1983 *Certification:* Internal Medicine, Nephrology
4923 Ogletown-Stanton Rd #200, Newark, DE, 302-292-0811

Goldman, Jesse Mark (4 mentions)
New York Med Coll, 1987
Certification: Internal Medicine, Nephrology
3401 N Broad St 4th Fl, Philadelphia, PA, 215-707-3416

Hovick, Edward Thomas (5 mentions)
Med Coll of Pennsylvania, 1988 *Certification:* Nephrology
750 Main St #305, Phoenixville, PA, 610-933-8006
420 W Linfield Rd Bldg B #100, Limerick, PA, 610-495-1992

Kelepouris, Ellie (4 mentions)
FMS-Greece, 1975 *Certification:* Nephrology
3322 N Broad St 2nd Fl, Philadelphia, PA, 215-707-4600

Kurnik, Brenda Chinn (4 mentions)
Washington U, 1978 *Certification:* Internal Medicine, Nephrology
769 Route 70 E #C-125, Marlton, NJ, 856-988-8064

Pitone, Joseph Michael (5 mentions)
Philadelphia Coll of Osteopathic Med, 1972
300 Medical Center Dr #A, Sewell, NJ, 856-218-4991
201 Laurel Oak Rd #B, Voorhees, NJ, 856-566-5488

Polnerow, Michael K. (4 mentions)
Philadelphia Coll of Osteopathic Med, 1978
701 N Clayton St #401, Wilmington, DE, 302-421-9411
700 W Lea Blvd #G2, Wilmington, DE, 302-762-8585

Silva, Patricio (4 mentions)
FMS-Chile, 1964
33-22 N Broad St, Philadelphia, PA, 215-707-4600

Sirota, Robert Alan (4 mentions)
Yale U, 1973 *Certification:* Internal Medicine, Nephrology
735 Fitzwatertown Rd, Willow Grove, PA, 215-657-2012
8001 Roosevelt Blvd #502, Philadelphia, PA, 215-624-6610

Smith, Matthew T. (4 mentions)
U of Texas-Galveston, 1998
Certification: Internal Medicine, Nephrology
860 Springdale Dr #100, Exton, PA, 610-524-3703

Stein, Harold (4 mentions)
SUNY-Downstate Med Coll, 1976
Certification: Internal Medicine, Nephrology
735 Fitzwatertown Rd, Willow Grove, PA, 215-657-2012

Superdock, Keith Robert (6 mentions)
Jefferson Med Coll, 1986
Certification: Internal Medicine, Nephrology
100 E Lancaster Ave #130, Wynnewood, PA, 610-649-1175

Weisberg, Lawrence S. (9 mentions)
Temple U, 1981 *Certification:* Internal Medicine, Nephrology
401 Haddon Ave, Camden, NJ, 856-342-2439
1030 Kings Hwy N #310, Cherry Hill, NJ, 856-342-2439
3 Cooper Plaza, Camden, NJ, 856-342-2439

Yudis, Melvin (9 mentions)
Jefferson Med Coll, 1963
Certification: Internal Medicine, Nephrology
735 Fitzwatertown Rd, Willow Grove, PA, 215-657-2012

Zappacosta, Anthony R. (4 mentions)
Hahnemann U, 1969
Certification: Internal Medicine, Nephrology
130 S Bryn Mawr Ave, Bryn Mawr, PA, 610-525-8110

Zollner, Gregory Paul (5 mentions)
Robert W Johnson Med Sch, 1988
Certification: Internal Medicine, Nephrology
240 Middletown Blvd #200, Langhorne, PA, 215-757-5772

Neurological Surgery

Andrews, David Wallace (13 mentions)
U of Colorado, 1983 *Certification:* Neurological Surgery
909 Walnut St 2nd Fl, Philadelphia, PA, 215-955-7000

Barrer, Steven Jon (12 mentions)
Hahnemann U, 1976 *Certification:* Neurological Surgery
2510 Maryland Rd Willow Wood Bldg #185, Willow Grove, PA, 215-657-5886
1010 Horsham Rd #201, North Wales, PA, 215-657-5886

Dante, Stephen Joseph (8 mentions)
U of Connecticut, 1983 *Certification:* Neurological Surgery
909 Walnut St 2nd Fl, Philadelphia, PA, 215-955-7000
443 Laurel Oak Rd 2nd Fl, Voorhees, NJ, 215-955-7000
2500 English Creek Ave, Egg Harbor Township, NJ, 609-677-6060

Goldman, H. Warren (7 mentions)
New York Med Coll, 1973 *Certification:* Neurological Surgery
3 Cooper Plaza #411, Camden, NJ, 856-342-3400

Grady, M. Sean (7 mentions)
Georgetown U, 1981 *Certification:* Neurological Surgery
3400 Spruce St, Philadelphia, PA, 215-662-3483

Kenning, James Alan (18 mentions)
Jefferson Med Coll, 1974 *Certification:* Neurological Surgery
958 County Line Rd, Bryn Mawr, PA, 610-527-2443

Marcotte, Paul John (10 mentions)
FMS-Canada, 1984 *Certification:* Neurological Surgery
3400 Spruce St Silverstein Bldg 3rd Fl, Philadelphia, PA, 215-349-8327
330 S 9th St 4th Fl, Philadelphia, PA, 215-829-7144

Rosenwasser, Robert Hillel (16 mentions)
Louisiana State U, 1979 *Certification:* Neurological Surgery
909 Walnut St 2nd Fl, Philadelphia, PA, 215-503-7004

Turtz, Alan Richard (12 mentions)
Med Coll of Pennsylvania, 1986
Certification: Neurological Surgery
3 Cooper Plaza #411, Camden, NJ, 856-342-2701

Neurology

Abidi, S. Manzoor (8 mentions)
FMS-India, 1964 *Certification:* Neurology
504 Route 38 E, Maple Shade, NJ, 856-866-0466
44 Nautilus Dr, Manahawkin, NJ, 609-597-0427

Azizi, Sayed Ausim (6 mentions)
U of Texas-Southwestern, 1990 *Certification:* Neurology
3401 N Broad St #C525, Philadelphia, PA, 215-707-3040

Bell, Rodney Donald (5 mentions)
Oregon Health Sciences U, 1972
Certification: Internal Medicine, Neurology, Vascular Neurology
900 Walnut St #200, Philadelphia, PA, 215-955-6692

Brock, David Geoffrey (3 mentions)
SUNY-Buffalo, 1988 *Certification:* Neurology, Vascular Neurology
900 Walnut St #200, Philadelphia, PA, 215-955-7951

Burke, James Murray, Jr. (4 mentions)
U of Rochester, 1978 *Certification:* Internal Medicine, Neurology
2701 Blair Mill Rd #8, Willow Grove, PA, 215-957-9250
1245 Highland Ave #301, Abington, PA, 215-886-7000

Cooper, Gregory William (3 mentions)
Albany Med Coll, 1983 *Certification:* Neurology
1650 Huntingdon Pike #258, Meadowbrook, PA, 215-938-7730

Desouza, Bryan Xavier (5 mentions)
Yale U, 1985 *Certification:* Clinical Neurophysiology, Neurology
100 E Lancaster Ave #312, Wynnewood, PA, 610-649-6090

Diamond, B. Franklin (6 mentions)
U of Pittsburgh, 1967 *Certification:* Neurology
2701 Blair Mill Rd #8, Willow Grove, PA, 215-886-7000
1245 Highland Ave #301, Abington, PA, 215-886-7000

Dinsmore, Steven Thomas (4 mentions)
Philadelphia Coll of Osteopathic Med, 1982
Certification: Neurology
42 E Laurel Rd #1800, Stratford, NJ, 856-566-6843

Dresser, Lee Potter (3 mentions)
Wake Forest U, 1987 *Certification:* Neurology
620 Stanton Christiana Rd #302, Newark, DE, 302-892-9400

Edelsohn, Lanny (5 mentions)
Hahnemann U, 1967 *Certification:* Neurology
774 Christiana Rd #201, Newark, DE, 302-731-3017

Eisner, Richard A. (7 mentions)
New Jersey Med Sch, 1977 *Certification:* Neurology
830 Old Lancaster Rd Bldg #206, Bryn Mawr, PA, 610-527-8140

Fink, Alan Jay (5 mentions)
SUNY-Buffalo, 1970 *Certification:* Neurology
774 Christiana Rd #201, Newark, DE, 302-731-3017

Galetta, Steven Louis (3 mentions)
Cornell U, 1983 *Certification:* Neurology
3400 Spruce St 3 W Gates, Philadelphia, PA, 215-662-3381

Gollomp, Stephen Michael (5 mentions)
Albany Med Coll, 1976
Certification: Clinical Neurophysiology, Neurology
100 E Lancaster Ave Lankenau Bldg #161, Wynnewood, PA, 610-642-5371

Goodman, Michael H. (4 mentions)
FMS-Dominica, 1986
1000 White Horse Rd Bldg 800 #802, Voorhees, NJ, 856-435-0400

Graham, Thomas Hild (9 mentions)
Pennsylvania State U, 1978 *Certification:* Neurology
11 Industrial Blvd Paoli Pointe #204, Paoli, PA, 610-644-6251

Grayum, Bradley Patrick (4 mentions)
Hahnemann U, 1983
Certification: Neurology, Vascular Neurology
1 Medical Center Blvd #533, Chester, PA, 610-874-1184

Horowitz, Gary R. (3 mentions)
Midwestern U, 1971 *Certification:* Neurology
5401 Old York Rd Klein Bldg #300, Philadelphia, PA, 215-456-7190
9880 Bustleton Ave Einstein Ctr 1 #220, Philadelphia, PA, 215-456-7190
60 E Township Line Rd PM&R Bldg Main Fl, Elkins Park, PA, 215-456-7190

Hurtig, Howard Irving (7 mentions)
Tulane U, 1966 *Certification:* Neurology
330 S 9th St, Philadelphia, PA, 215-829-6500

Jackel, Roy Allen (3 mentions)
U of Pittsburgh, 1981 *Certification:* Neurology
124 Dekalb Pike, North Wales, PA, 215-699-3727
800 W State St #101, Doylestown, PA, 215-230-9998
3 Life Mark Dr #3, Sellersville, PA, 215-257-0182

Jacobson, Mercedes Paula (5 mentions)
Columbia U, 1987
Certification: Clinical Neurophysiology, Neurology
3401 N Broad St #525C, Philadelphia, PA, 215-707-8910
3401 N Broad St #D-101, Philadelphia, PA, 215-707-8910

Kerson, Lawrence Alan (8 mentions)
U of Pennsylvania, 1968 *Certification:* Neurology
1340 Dekalb St #1, Norristown, PA, 610-279-7443
1811 Bethlehem Pike #A104, Flourtown, PA, 215-836-3462
430 Park Ave, Collegeville, PA, 610-831-2182

Legido, Agustin (3 mentions)
FMS-Spain, 1980 *Certification:* Neurology with Special Qualifications in Child Neurology, Pediatrics
E Erie Ave & N Front St, Philadelphia, PA, 215-427-5470

Mandel, Steven (6 mentions)
Albert Einstein Coll of Med, 1975 *Certification:* Neurology
1015 Chestnut St #810, Philadelphia, PA, 215-574-0075
151 Fries Mill Rd #506, Turnersville, NJ, 856-228-0006

Matarese, Emil Lawrence (8 mentions)
New Jersey Med Sch, 1982 *Certification:* Neurology
1205 Langhorne-Newtown Rd #201, Langhorne, PA,
 215-741-9555

Mazlin, Steven Eric (5 mentions)
New York U, 1984 *Certification:* Neurology
940 Town Center Dr #F-50, Langhorne, PA, 215-710-8644

Melnick, Paul (3 mentions)
Certification: Neurology
111 W High St #107, Elkton, MD, 410-392-7044

Mirsen, Thomas (8 mentions)
SUNY-Downstate Med Coll, 1982
Certification: Neurology, Vascular Neurology
3 Cooper Plaza #320, Camden, NJ, 856-342-2445
1210 Brace Rd #107, Cherry Hill, NJ, 856-342-2445
1 Plaza Dr Bunker Hill Plaza #103, Sewell, NJ, 856-342-2445

Pearlstein, Louis (3 mentions)
Philadelphia Coll of Osteopathic Med, 1978
Certification: Neurology
3070 Bristol Pike Bldg 2 #124, Bensalem, PA, 215-245-0272

Rubin, Mitchell Jay (3 mentions)
U of Pennsylvania, 1981 *Certification:* Neurology
693 Main St #D, Lumberton, NJ, 609-261-7600

Schwartzman, Robert Jay (3 mentions)
U of Pennsylvania, 1965
Certification: Internal Medicine, Neurology
219 N Broad St 7th Fl, Philadelphia, PA, 215-762-7090

Stern, Matthew Bruce (3 mentions)
Duke U, 1978 *Certification:* Neurology
330 S 9th St, Philadelphia, PA, 215-829-6500

Tabby, David Stuart (3 mentions)
Philadelphia Coll of Osteopathic Med, 1984
Certification: Neurology
1331 E Wyoming Ave, Philadelphia, PA, 215-762-6915
219 N Broad St, Philadelphia, PA, 215-762-6915

Zechowy, Allen Charles (4 mentions)
U of Maryland, 1974 *Certification:* Neurology
570 Egg Harbor Rd, Sewell, NJ, 856-218-1770
1415 Marlton Pike E #204, Cherry Hill, NJ, 856-795-2000

Obstetrics/Gynecology

Askinas, Alan Michael (3 mentions)
U of Illinois, 1980 *Certification:* Obstetrics & Gynecology
404 McFarlan Rd #301, Kennett Square, PA, 610-692-3434
600 E Marshall St #305, West Chester, PA, 610-692-3434
915 Old Fern Hill Rd #600, West Chester, PA, 610-692-3434

Ayres, Ronald E. (4 mentions)
Philadelphia Coll of Osteopathic Med, 1968
100 Kings Way E #B5, Sewell, NJ, 856-589-1414
42 E Laurel Rd #2500, Stratford, NJ, 856-566-7090
570 Egg Harbor Rd #C-2, Sewell, NJ, 856-589-1414

Chatwani, Ashwin Jamnadas (4 mentions)
FMS-India, 1973
3401 N Broad St Outpatient Bldg 7th Fl, Philadelphia, PA,
 215-707-1373

Craparo, Jocelyn Lopez (3 mentions)
FMS-Dominican Republic, 1983
Certification: Obstetrics & Gynecology
919 Conestoga Rd Bldg 1 #104, Rosemont, PA, 610-525-6400
3855 W Chester Pl #305, Newtown Square, PA, 610-525-6400

Dein, Robert Allen (3 mentions)
U of Pennsylvania, 1983 *Certification:* Obstetrics & Gynecology
1030 E Lancaster Ave, Bryn Mawr, PA, 610-525-3225
100 Deerfield Ln #225, Malvern, PA, 610-525-3225
140 W Germantown Pike, Plymouth Meeting, PA, 610-525-3225

Fossum, Gregory Thomas (3 mentions)
U of Wisconsin, 1982 *Certification:* Obstetrics &
 Gynecology, Reproductive Endocrinology/Infertility
834 Chestnut St #300, Philadelphia, PA, 215-955-5000

Frankel, Leslie Berman (3 mentions)
Temple U, 1978 *Certification:* Obstetrics & Gynecology
2300 Computer Rd #E-25, Willow Grove, PA, 215-366-1160

Franzblau, Natali Robin (4 mentions)
Albert Einstein Coll of Med, 1989
Certification: Obstetrics & Gynecology
1103 Kings Hwy N #201, Cherry Hill, NJ, 856-321-1800
3 Cooper Plaza #301, Camden, NJ, 856-321-1800

Hernandez, Enrique (4 mentions)
U of Puerto Rico, 1977
Certification: Gynecologic Oncology, Obstetrics & Gynecology
3401 N Broad St, Philadelphia, PA, 215-707-3015
1648 Huntingdon Pike, Meadowbrook, PA, 215-707-3015
7602 Central Ave, Philadelphia, PA, 215-707-3015

Jacobson, Barry Jay (3 mentions)
Jefferson Med Coll, 1980 *Certification:* Obstetrics & Gynecology
2100 Keystone Ave #707, Drexel Hill, PA, 610-626-7070
723 Saxer Ave, Springfield, PA, 610-543-9343
100 N Church Rd 3rd Fl, Ardmore, PA, 610-649-3575

Jaffe, Ronald Morton (3 mentions)
Temple U, 1959 *Certification:* Obstetrics & Gynecology
1103 Kings Hwy N #201, Cherry Hill, NJ, 856-321-1800

Kaufman, Susan I. (4 mentions)
Philadelphia Coll of Osteopathic Med, 1981
Certification: Obstetrics & Gynecology
1930 Hwy 70 E #S93, Cherry Hill, NJ, 856-424-8091

Maynard, Christine W. (3 mentions)
George Washington U, 1981
Certification: Obstetrics & Gynecology
4600 New Linden Hill Rd #202, Wilmington, DE, 302-995-7073

McBride, Molly Ann (3 mentions)
Med Coll of Pennsylvania, 1994
Certification: Obstetrics & Gynecology
1100 N Grant Ave, Wilmington, DE, 302-421-4670

Mellen, Arthur William, IV (5 mentions)
Jefferson Med Coll, 1980 *Certification:* Obstetrics & Gynecology
301 S 8th St #3-D, Philadelphia, PA, 215-829-5300

Michaelson, Robert I. (3 mentions)
Jefferson Med Coll, 1976 *Certification:* Obstetrics & Gynecology
1245 Highland Ave #G-01, Abington, PA, 215-672-2229
1811 Bethlehem Pike A-110, Flourtown, PA, 215-672-2229
2300 Computer Ave, Willow Grove, PA, 215-366-1160

Montgomery, Owen C. (5 mentions)
Hahnemann U, 1981 *Certification:* Obstetrics & Gynecology
255 S 17th St, Philadelphia, PA, 215-546-9330
400 E Church St, Blackwood, NJ, 856-228-8066

Moranz, Joel Gross (3 mentions)
U of Pennsylvania, 1972 *Certification:* Obstetrics & Gynecology
100 E Chester Pike, Ridley Park, PA, 610-521-4311
196 W Sproul Rd #208, Springfield, PA, 610-521-4311
300 Evergreen Dr, Glen Mills, PA, 610-521-4311

Noumoff, Joel S. (3 mentions)
New York U, 1973
Certification: Gynecologic Oncology, Obstetrics & Gynecology
1 Medical Center Blvd #441, Chester, PA, 610-876-9640

Porcelan, Jane B. (3 mentions)
Med Coll of Pennsylvania, 1983
Certification: Obstetrics & Gynecology
100 E Lancaster Ave Lankenau Bldg W #433, Wynnewood, PA,
 610-896-8840
325 W Central Ave #100, Malvern, PA, 610-251-9433

Roberts, Nancy S. (6 mentions)
Jefferson Med Coll, 1976
Certification: Maternal-Fetal Medicine, Obstetrics & Gynecology
100 Lancaster Ave Lankenau Bldg E #353, Wynnewood, PA,
 610-649-9021

Wolf, Abigail (4 mentions)
Temple U, 1995 *Certification:* Obstetrics & Gynecology
834 Chestnut St #300, Philadelphia, PA, 215-955-5000

Wu, Christine (4 mentions)
Med Coll of Pennsylvania, 1987
Certification: Obstetrics & Gynecology
834 Chestnut St #T171, Philadelphia, PA, 215-955-1804

Zeidman, Joan Helene (3 mentions)
Temple U, 1987 *Certification:* Obstetrics & Gynecology
919 Conestoga Rd Bldg 1 #104, Rosemont, PA, 610-525-6400
3855 W Chester Pl #305, Newtown Square, PA, 610-525-6400

Ophthalmology

Armstrong, Thomas A. (5 mentions)
Temple U, 1978 *Certification:* Ophthalmology
345 N York Rd, Hatboro, PA, 215-672-9030
1550 Old York Rd, Abington, PA, 215-784-0220

Bannett, Gregg Allen (4 mentions)
New Jersey Sch of Osteopathic Med, 1985
Certification: Ophthalmology
2201 Chapel Ave W #105, Cherry Hill, NJ, 856-488-6550
620 N Broad St, Woodbury, NJ, 856-853-5554

Bresalier, Saul (3 mentions)
Des Moines U, 1964
1401 Marlton Pike E #18, Cherry Hill, NJ, 856-428-5797

Brucker, Alexander Jay (4 mentions)
New York Med Coll, 1972 *Certification:* Ophthalmology
51 N 39th St, Philadelphia, PA, 215-662-8100
250 King of Prussia Rd, Radnor, PA, 215-902-1609

Cohen, Sander Mzeskind (4 mentions)
Johns Hopkins U, 1983 *Certification:* Ophthalmology
25 Homestead Dr #A, Columbus, NJ, 609-298-0888
509 S Lenola Rd #11A, Moorestown, NJ, 856-234-0222

Dugan, John Donald, Jr. (3 mentions)
Johns Hopkins U, 1990 *Certification:* Ophthalmology
1140 White Horse Rd, Voorhees, NJ, 856-784-3366

Ehrlich, Dion Ralph (4 mentions)
George Washington U, 1973 *Certification:* Ophthalmology
7500 Central Ave #103, Philadelphia, PA, 215-342-5452
1245 Highland Ave #G04, Abington, PA, 215-576-1677

Fisher, Joanna Maria (3 mentions)
Med Coll of Pennsylvania, 1982 *Certification:* Ophthalmology
2643 Huntingdon Pike, Huntingdon Valley, PA, 215-938-7878

Goldman, Stephen Marc (3 mentions)
Med Coll of Pennsylvania, 1985 *Certification:* Ophthalmology
700 Spruce St #100, Philadelphia, PA, 215-829-5311

Greenbaum, Marvin Henry (5 mentions)
George Washington U, 1979 *Certification:* Ophthalmology
501 Belmont Ave, Bala Cynwyd, PA, 610-667-4066

Grossman, Harry David (3 mentions)
Jefferson Med Coll, 1993 *Certification:* Ophthalmology
100 Brick Rd #115, Marlton, NJ, 856-983-1400

Hirsch, Stuart Ellis (3 mentions)
Ohio State U, 1968 *Certification:* Ophthalmology
360 Middletown Blvd #402, Langhorne, PA, 215-757-6200

Kindermann, Wilfred Reed (5 mentions)
U of Rochester, 1975 *Certification:* Ophthalmology
3001 Chapel Ave W #200, Cherry Hill, NJ, 856-667-3937

Koller, Harold Paul (3 mentions)
Tulane U, 1964 *Certification:* Ophthalmology
1650 Huntingdon Pike #150, Meadowbrook, PA, 215-947-6660
2301 E Evesham Rd #503, Voorhees, NJ, 856-770-0030
840 Walnut St, Philadelphia, PA, 215-947-6660

Lehman, Sharon (3 mentions)
Jefferson Med Coll, 1985 *Certification:* Ophthalmology
1600 Rockland Rd, Wilmington, DE, 302-651-5040

Lichtenstein, Stephen B. (3 mentions)
Jefferson Med Coll, 1974 *Certification:* Ophthalmology
40 Monument Rd 5th Fl, Bala Cynwyd, PA, 610-664-8880
840 Walnut St #1240, Philadelphia, PA, 610-664-8880

Liss, Robert Phillip (3 mentions)
SUNY-Downstate Med Coll, 1985 *Certification:* Ophthalmology
915 Old Fern Hill Rd Bldg #B, West Chester, PA, 610-696-1230
740 W Lincoln Hwy, Exton, PA, 610-696-1230

Mills, Monte Dean (3 mentions)
Baylor U, 1988 *Certification:* Ophthalmology
500 W Butler Ave, Chalfont, PA, 215-997-5730
34th & Civic Center Blvd, Philadelphia, PA, 215-590-2791

Nachbar, James George (3 mentions)
U of Michigan, 1980 *Certification:* Ophthalmology
25 Homestead Dr #A, Columbus, NJ, 856-234-0222
103 Old Marlton Pike, Medford, NJ, 609-714-8761
509 S Lenola Rd #11, Moorestown, NJ, 856-234-0222

Naids, Richard Eric (3 mentions)
Temple U, 1984 *Certification:* Ophthalmology
2818 Cottman Ave, Philadelphia, PA, 215-331-4141
9501 Roosevelt Blvd #101, Philadelphia, PA, 215-673-1500

Olurin, Temidayo A. (4 mentions)
FMS-Nigeria, 1989 *Certification:* Ophthalmology
1403 N Rodney St, Wilmington, DE, 302-654-4800

Prince, Richard Blair (3 mentions)
U of Pennsylvania, 1983 *Certification:* Ophthalmology
319 2nd St Pike, Southampton, PA, 215-355-4428
352 E Butler Ave, New Britain, PA, 215-230-4700

Santore, Louis Xavier (5 mentions)
Temple U, 1980
100 E Lancaster Ave #36, Wynnewood, PA, 610-642-4392

Sergott, Robert Charles (3 mentions)
Johns Hopkins U, 1975 *Certification:* Ophthalmology
840 Walnut St #930, Philadelphia, PA, 215-928-3130
100 W Lancaster Ave #256, Wynnewood, PA, 610-649-1970

Shields, Jerry Allen (3 mentions)
U of Michigan, 1964 *Certification:* Ophthalmology
840 Walnut St, Philadelphia, PA, 215-928-3105

Spechler, Floyd Fabien (4 mentions)
Jefferson Med Coll, 1971 *Certification:* Ophthalmology
1802 Berlin Rd, Cherry Hill, NJ, 856-354-1717

Stein, Harmon Charles (3 mentions)
New York Med Coll, 1979 *Certification:* Ophthalmology
451 S State St, Newtown, PA, 215-968-5000
1568 Woodbourne Rd #2, Levittown, PA, 215-943-7800
2495 Brunswick Pike, Lawrenceville, NJ, 609-882-8828

Volpe, Nicholas Joseph (3 mentions)
SUNY-Downstate Med Coll, 1987 *Certification:* Ophthalmology
51 N 39th St #501, Philadelphia, PA, 215-662-8100
3400 Spruce St, Philadelphia, PA, 215-662-8100

Williams, Christopher A. (5 mentions)
U of Iowa, 1988 *Certification:* Ophthalmology
30 Medical Center Blvd #104, Chester, PA, 610-874-5261
2 W Baltimore Ave, Media, PA, 610-874-5261
300 Evergreen Dr #100, Glen Mills, PA, 610-874-5261

Wilson, Martin Conway (3 mentions)
Temple U, 1990 *Certification:* Ophthalmology
155 W Lancaster Ave, Paoli, PA, 610-993-8083

Wong, Stephen Willis (3 mentions)
Jefferson Med Coll, 1972 *Certification:* Ophthalmology
3401 N Broad St, Philadelphia, PA, 215-707-3185

Orthopedics

Abboudi, Jack (3 mentions)
Robert W Johnson Med Sch, 1994
Certification: Orthopaedic Surgery, Surgery of the Hand
830 Old Lancaster Rd #300, Bryn Mawr, PA, 610-527-9000
235 W Lancaster Ave, Devon, PA, 610-688-6767

Bartolozzi, Arthur R., III (4 mentions)
U of California-San Diego, 1981
Certification: Orthopaedic Surgery
1400 Marlton Pike E, Cherry Hill, NJ, 856-857-9020
800 Spruce St, Philadelphia, PA, 215-829-2222

Benner, John Henry (4 mentions)
Jefferson Med Coll, 1973 *Certification:* Orthopaedic Surgery
915 Old Fern Hill Rd #A-1, West Chester, PA, 610-692-6280
402 McFarlan Rd #101, Kennett Square, PA, 610-692-6280

Booth, Robert Emrey, Jr. (12 mentions)
U of Pennsylvania, 1971 *Certification:* Orthopaedic Surgery
800 Spruce St, Philadelphia, PA, 215-829-2222

Cairone, Stephen S. (3 mentions)
Philadelphia Coll of Osteopathic Med, 1999
111 Floral Vale Blvd #B, Yardley, PA, 267-757-0560

Craft, David Victor (3 mentions)
Jefferson Med Coll, 1988 *Certification:* Orthopaedic Surgery
2400 Maryland Rd #20, Willow Grove, PA, 215-830-8700
599 W State St, Doylestown, PA, 215-830-8700

De Long, William George, Jr. (9 mentions)
Temple U, 1978 *Certification:* Orthopaedic Surgery
801 Ostrum St, Bethlehem, PA, 610-954-1735

Dellose, Steven Michael (3 mentions)
Jefferson Med Coll, 1996 *Certification:* Orthopaedic Surgery
1941 Limestone Rd #101, Wilmington, DE, 302-633-3555
3519 Silverside Rd #200, Wilmington, DE, 302-633-3555

Farrell, Joseph (4 mentions)
Philadelphia Coll of Osteopathic Med, 1978 *Certification:* Surgery
737 Main St #6-B, Lumberton, NJ, 609-267-9400

Flynn, John Matthew (3 mentions)
U of Pittsburgh, 1989 *Certification:* Orthopaedic Surgery
34th St & Civic Center Blvd, Philadelphia, PA, 215-590-1527
210 Mall Blvd, King of Prussia, PA, 610-768-9470

Fras, Christian Ivan (3 mentions)
Columbia U, 1994 *Certification:* Orthopaedic Surgery
1991 Sproul Rd #300-A, Broomall, PA, 610-353-5079
100 Lancaster Ave 2nd Fl, Wynnewood, PA, 610-353-5079

Fuller, David Alden (3 mentions)
U of Pennsylvania, 1991
Certification: Orthopaedic Surgery, Surgery of the Hand
6117 Main St, Voorhees, NJ, 856-325-6677
401 Kings Hwy S #3-A, Cherry Hill, NJ, 856-547-0201

Giammattei, Frank Presby (5 mentions)
U of Cincinnati, 1980 *Certification:* Orthopaedic Surgery
1 Medical Center Blvd #324, Upland, PA, 610-876-0347
300 Evergreen Dr #200, Glen Mills, PA, 610-579-3450
200 E State St #108, Media, PA, 610-566-4236

Good, Robert Paul (12 mentions)
Jefferson Med Coll, 1973 *Certification:* Orthopaedic Surgery
27 S Bryn Mawr Ave, Bryn Mawr, PA, 610-688-6767
235 Lancaster Ave, Devon, PA, 610-688-6767

Gratch, Michael James (3 mentions)
Temple U, 1976 *Certification:* Orthopaedic Surgery
2400 Maryland Rd #20, Willow Grove, PA, 215-830-8700

Handal, John A. (5 mentions)
Med Coll of Pennsylvania, 1979
Certification: Orthopaedic Surgery
201 Old York Rd #202, Jenkintown, PA, 215-885-6979
5501 Old York Rd Willow Crest Bldg 4th Fl, Philadelphia, PA, 215-456-7900

Harrer, Michael Francis (4 mentions)
Jefferson Med Coll, 1993 *Certification:* Orthopaedic Surgery
600 Somerdale Rd #113, Voorhees, NJ, 856-795-1945

Hume, Eric Lynn (12 mentions)
SUNY-Upstate Med U, 1978 *Certification:* Orthopaedic Surgery
401 S Kings Hwy #3-A, Cherry Hill, NJ, 856-547-0201

Israelite, Craig Lane (3 mentions)
Hahnemann U, 1987 *Certification:* Orthopaedic Surgery
51 N 39th St, Philadelphia, PA, 215-662-3340
409 Route 70 E, Cherry Hill, NJ, 856-429-0505

Lackman, Richard Danl (3 mentions)
U of Pennsylvania, 1977 *Certification:* Orthopaedic Surgery
301 S 8th St, Philadelphia, PA, 215-829-5022

Lazarus, Mark David (3 mentions)
New Jersey Med Sch, 1988 *Certification:* Orthopaedic Surgery
925 Chestnut St 5th Fl, Philadelphia, PA, 215-955-3458
443 Laurel Oak Rd #130, Voorhees, NJ, 215-955-3458

MacKenzie, William George (4 mentions)
FMS-Canada, 1980 *Certification:* Orthopaedic Surgery
1600 Rockland Rd, Wilmington, DE, 302-651-5890

Mooar, Pekka Antero (6 mentions)
U of Cincinnati, 1979 *Certification:* Orthopaedic Surgery
3401 N Broad St 5th Fl, Philadelphia, PA, 215-707-2111
44 Commerce Dr, Fort Washington, PA, 215-641-0700
7601 Central Ave Friends Hall, Philadelphia, PA, 215-214-6655

O'Dowd, Thomas James (3 mentions)
Cornell U, 1979 *Certification:* Orthopaedic Surgery
901 Route 168 #307, Turnersville, NJ, 856-227-7566
120 Carnie Blvd #4, Voorhees, NJ, 856-424-8866
502 Centennial Blvd, Voorhees, NJ, 856-424-8866

Schmidt, Richard George (3 mentions)
Pennsylvania State U, 1980 *Certification:* Orthopaedic Surgery
15 Presidential Blvd #300, Bala Cynwyd, PA, 610-667-2663
1991 Sproul Rd, Broomall, PA, 610-667-2663

Schoifet, Scott David (4 mentions)
Columbia U, 1983 *Certification:* Orthopaedic Surgery
737 Main St #6, Lumberton, NJ, 609-267-9400

Sharkey, Peter Francis (4 mentions)
SUNY-Upstate Med U, 1984 *Certification:* Orthopaedic Surgery
1068 W Baltimore Pike #3109, Media, PA, 610-744-2600
925 Chestnut St #5, Philadelphia, PA, 215-955-3458
170 N Henderson Rd, King of Prussia, PA, 215-955-3458

Simmons, Cheston (3 mentions)
Jefferson Med Coll, 1987 *Certification:* Orthopaedic Surgery
915 Old Fern Hill Rd Bldg A #1, West Chester, PA, 610-692-6280
402 McFarlan Rd #101, Kennett Square, PA, 610-444-1344

Sobel, Mark (3 mentions)
New York U, 1980 *Certification:* Orthopaedic Surgery
525 Route 73 S #303, Marlton, NJ, 856-596-0555

Star, Andrew Michael (8 mentions)
Northwestern U, 1982 *Certification:* Orthopaedic Surgery
2400 Maryland Rd #20, Willow Grove, PA, 215-830-8700
1327 Old York Rd, Abington, PA, 215-830-8700

Stollsteimer, George T. (6 mentions)
Temple U, 1991
Certification: Orthopaedic Sports Medicine, Orthopaedic Surgery
111-B Floral Vale Blvd, Yardley, PA, 267-757-0560

Thoder, Joseph J., Jr. (5 mentions)
Temple U, 1982
Certification: Orthopaedic Surgery, Surgery of the Hand
7604 Central Ave #100, Philadelphia, PA, 215-214-6655
2301 E Allegheny Ave, Philadelphia, PA, 215-291-3777
3401 N Broad St, Philadelphia, PA, 215-707-2111

Trevlyn, Dean William (4 mentions)
U of Pennsylvania, 1987 *Certification:* Orthopaedic Surgery
2004 Sproul Rd #102, Broomall, PA, 610-353-0800

Vaccaro, Alexander R., III (3 mentions)
Georgetown U, 1987 *Certification:* Orthopaedic Surgery
925 Chestnut St 5th Fl, Philadelphia, PA, 215-955-3458

Vernace, Joseph Victor (5 mentions)
Jefferson Med Coll, 1982 *Certification:* Orthopaedic Surgery
101 S Bryn Mawr Ave #200, Bryn Mawr, PA, 610-527-9500

Zurbach, James Michael (3 mentions)
Pennsylvania State U, 1980 *Certification:* Orthopaedic Surgery
1 Medical Center Blvd #324, Upland, PA, 610-876-0347
300 Evergreen Dr #200, Glen Mills, PA, 610-579-3450
200 E State St #108, Media, PA, 610-566-4236

Otorhinolaryngology

Cantrell, Harry (7 mentions)
Pennsylvania State U, 1982 *Certification:* Otolaryngology
1307 Whitehorse Rd Bldg A, Voorhees, NJ, 856-346-0200

Drezner, Dean (13 mentions)
Temple U, 1984 *Certification:* Otolaryngology
3 Cooper Plaza #411, Camden, NJ, 856-342-3275

Gadomski, Stephen Peter (7 mentions)
Jefferson Med Coll, 1981 *Certification:* Otolaryngology
130 N Haddon Ave, Haddonfield, NJ, 856-429-5055
1307 White Horse Rd #A-100, Voorhees, NJ, 856-346-0200
485 Williamstown-New Freedom Rd, Sicklerville, NJ, 856-237-8020
204 Ark Rd #102, Mount Laurel, NJ, 856-778-0559

Gallagher, John Timothy (7 mentions)
Hahnemann U, 1982 *Certification:* Otolaryngology
670 Woodbourne Rd, Langhorne, PA, 267-689-1000

Isaacson, Glenn Charles (7 mentions)
U of Pennsylvania, 1982 *Certification:* Otolaryngology
3509 N Broad St Fl 6W, Philadelphia, PA, 215-707-7300
1077 Rydal Rd #201, Rydal, PA, 215-707-7300

Keane, William Martin (11 mentions)
Harvard U, 1970 *Certification:* Otolaryngology
925 Chestnut St 6th Fl, Philadelphia, PA, 215-955-6760

Marchant, Frances E. (7 mentions)
Jefferson Med Coll, 1988 *Certification:* Otolaryngology
830 Old Lancaster Rd #209, Bryn Mawr, PA, 610-527-1436
3855 W Chester Pike #2455, Newtown Square, PA, 610-527-1430

Ramzy, Joseph I. (8 mentions)
Baylor U, 1985 *Certification:* Otolaryngology
774 Christiana Rd #107, Newark, DE, 302-709-0860

Sataloff, Robert T. (7 mentions)
Jefferson Med Coll, 1975 *Certification:* Otolaryngology
1721 Pine St, Philadelphia, PA, 215-545-3322

Schwartz, David Neal (6 mentions)
Boston U, 1982 *Certification:* Otolaryngology
620 N Broad St #1, Woodbury, NJ, 856-848-0700
1910 Route 70 E #3, Cherry Hill, NJ, 856-424-5010
103 Old Marlton Pike #219, Medford, NJ, 609-953-7145
1113 Hospital Dr #103, Willingboro, NJ, 609-871-3366
539 Egg Harbor Rd #6, Sewell, NJ, 856-589-8600

Sheppard, William Macon (5 mentions)
Med U of South Carolina, 1997 *Certification:* Otolaryngology
2700 Silverside Rd #3-A, Wilmington, DE, 302-478-9878
2600 Glasgow Ave #212, Newark, DE, 302-478-9878

Smith, Bradford Davison (5 mentions)
U of Pittsburgh, 1982 *Certification:* Otolaryngology
100 Lancaster Ave 33 Lankenau Bldg W, Wynnewood, PA, 610-896-6800

Surkin, Marc Ivan (5 mentions)
Jefferson Med Coll, 1978 *Certification:* Otolaryngology
301 W Chester Pike #101, Havertown, PA, 610-446-6900
1201 County Line Rd, Bryn Mawr, PA, 610-446-6900

Teixido, Michael Thomas (7 mentions)
Wake Forest U, 1985 *Certification:* Otolaryngology
1941 Limestone Rd #210, Wilmington, DE, 302-998-0300

Ward, Michael Joseph (6 mentions)
Georgetown U, 1989 *Certification:* Otolaryngology
689 Unionville Rd #2, Kennett Square, PA, 610-925-5551
1 Commerce Blvd #201, West Grove, PA, 610-345-0977

Pain Medicine

Carr, Alan D. (3 mentions)
Des Moines U, 1984
1804 Berlin Rd, Cherry Hill, NJ, 856-489-3300

Frank, Evan David (3 mentions)
U of Pennsylvania, 1982
Certification: Anesthesiology, Pain Medicine
1840 South St Tuttleman Bldg 2nd Fl, Philadelphia, PA, 215-893-7246

Galapo, Simon (4 mentions)
SUNY-Downstate Med Coll, 1998
Certification: Anesthesiology, Pain Medicine
1650 Huntingdon Pike #357, Meadowbrook, PA, 215-938-1999

Jermyn, Richard T. (4 mentions)
Philadelphia Coll of Osteopathic Med, 1992
Certification: Physical Medicine & Rehabilitation
42 E Laurel Rd #1700, Stratford, NJ, 856-566-7010

Kim, Philip Sunghan (3 mentions)
Loyola U Chicago, 1992
Certification: Anesthesiology, Pain Medicine
7th & Clayton Sts 5th Fl, Wilmington, DE, 302-575-8205
101 Bryn Mawr Ave #200, Bryn Mawr, PA, 610-527-9500

Lee, David Charles (3 mentions)
U of Virginia, 1983
520 Stokes Rd #A4, Medford, NJ, 609-714-7774

Ratner, Eric Rolf (3 mentions)
Pennsylvania State U, 1989
Certification: Anesthesiology, Pain Medicine
6200 Frankford Ave #1, Philadelphia, PA, 215-535-3980

Rogers, Kenneth Herman (6 mentions)
New York Coll of Osteopathic Med, 1985
Certification: Anesthesiology, Pain Medicine
805 Copper Rd #2, Voorhees, NJ, 856-489-9822
302 Hurffville Cross Keys Rd, Sewell, NJ, 856-218-7647

Rosenthal, Scott E. (3 mentions)
Philadelphia Coll of Osteopathic Med, 1994
Certification: Anesthesiology, Pain Medicine
1200 Old York Rd, Abington, PA, 215-481-2336
2701 Blair Mill Rd #35, Willow Grove, PA, 215-957-1108
820 Town Center Dr, Langhorne, PA, 267-212-5000

Sasso, Philip John (3 mentions)
Jefferson Med Coll, 1988 *Certification:* Anesthesiology
1200 Old York Rd, Abington, PA, 215-481-2336
2701 Blair Mill Rd #35, Willow Grove, PA, 215-957-1108
820 Town Center Dr, Langhorne, PA, 267-212-5000

Slipman, Curtis W. (3 mentions)
Baylor U, 1983
Certification: Physical Medicine & Rehabilitation
3400 Spruce St, Philadelphia, PA, 215-662-3259

Zavitsanos, Thomas Peter (4 mentions)
Temple U, 1986 *Certification:* Anesthesiology
Knight & Red Lion Rds, Philadelphia, PA, 215-612-4060

Pathology

Auerbach, Herbert Edward (6 mentions)
Philadelphia Coll of Osteopathic Med, 1981
Certification: Anatomic Pathology & Clinical Pathology
1200 Old York Rd, Abington, PA, 215-481-2352

Catalano, Edison (6 mentions)
FMS-Uruguay, 1967
Certification: Anatomic Pathology & Clinical Pathology
1 Cooper Plaza, Camden, NJ, 856-342-2506

Farber, John (4 mentions)
U of California-San Francisco, 1966
Certification: Anatomic Pathology
285 E Main Bldg, Philadelphia, PA, 215-503-5028

Patchefsky, Arthur (10 mentions)
Hahnemann U, 1963 *Certification:* Anatomic Pathology
333 Cottman Ave, Philadelphia, PA, 215-728-5390

Saul, Scott Howard (6 mentions)
U of Pittsburgh, 1979
Certification: Anatomic Pathology & Clinical Pathology
701 E Marshall St, West Chester, PA, 610-431-5182

Wright, David Manfred (4 mentions)
U of Pennsylvania, 1973 *Certification:* Anatomic Pathology & Clinical Pathology, Medical Microbiology
100 Medical Campus Dr, Lansdale, PA, 215-368-2100

Pediatrics *(see note on page 9)*

Barbera, Lawrence Stewart (3 mentions)
Hahnemann U, 1960 *Certification:* Pediatrics
866 W Bristol Rd, Warminster, PA, 215-293-6010

Di Santo, Joseph (4 mentions)
SUNY-Buffalo, 1975 *Certification:* Pediatrics
3521 Silverside Rd, Wilmington, DE, 302-478-7805

Emmett, Gary Allen (3 mentions)
Jefferson Med Coll, 1976 *Certification:* Pediatrics
833 Chestnut St #300, Philadelphia, PA, 215-955-6755

Frumin, Vera Lynne (3 mentions)
Temple U, 1981 *Certification:* Pediatrics
1650 Huntingdon Pike #320-21, Meadowbrook, PA, 215-947-1447

Klinow, Linda Faye (3 mentions)
Rosalind Franklin U, 1981 *Certification:* Pediatrics
950 Haverford Rd #107, Bryn Mawr, PA, 610-527-4715
418 E Lancaster Ave, Wayne, PA, 610-687-3600

Langer, Burton Harris (3 mentions)
U of Pennsylvania, 1986 *Certification:* Pediatrics
11 Industrial Blvd #2, Paoli, PA, 610-642-9200
100 E Lancaster Ave #400, Wynnewood, PA, 610-642-9200

McCoy, Andrea (3 mentions)
Pennsylvania State U, 1986 *Certification:* Pediatrics
3509 W Broad St, Philadelphia, PA, 215-707-6000

McSorley, Maryann Bidi (3 mentions)
U of Pennsylvania, 1983 *Certification:* Pediatrics
1233 Locust St #400, Philadelphia, PA, 215-545-8188

Olivieri, Robert Mark (3 mentions)
Uniformed Services U of Health Sciences, 1987
Certification: Pediatrics
722 Yorklyn Rd #100, Hockessin, DE, 302-235-1188

Rosof, Edward (3 mentions)
Jefferson Med Coll, 1971 *Certification:* Pediatrics
525 S Route 73 #102, Marlton, NJ, 856-596-3434
856 S White Horse Pike #2, Hammonton, NJ, 609-704-8848

Sharrar, William G. (9 mentions)
U of Pennsylvania, 1966 *Certification:* Pediatrics
3 Cooper Plaza #520, Camden, NJ, 856-342-2298
6400 Main St, Voorhees, NJ, 856-751-9339

Plastic Surgery

Bucky, Louis Philip (6 mentions)
Harvard U, 1986 *Certification:* Plastic Surgery
230 W Washington Sq #101, Philadelphia, PA, 215-829-6320
200 W Montgomery Ave, Ardmore, PA, 610-649-2433

Buinewicz, Brian Robert (8 mentions)
Jefferson Med Coll, 1985
Certification: Plastic Surgery, Undersea & Hyperbaric Medicine
3655 Route 202 #225, Doylestown, PA, 215-230-4013

Fahey, Ann Leilani (4 mentions)
Cornell U, 1988 *Certification:* Plastic Surgery
6017 Main St, Voorhees, NJ, 856-325-6767
3 Cooper Plaza #403, Camden, NJ, 856-342-3114
2 Plaza Dr, Sewell, NJ, 856-270-4150

Fox, James W., IV (11 mentions)
Jefferson Med Coll, 1970 *Certification:* Plastic Surgery
840 Walnut St 15th Fl, Philadelphia, PA, 215-625-6630

Gabay, Raphael (4 mentions)
Philadelphia Coll of Osteopathic Med, 1987
9500 Roosevelt Blvd, Philadelphia, PA, 215-969-5650

Gatti, John E. (4 mentions)
Georgetown U, 1978 *Certification:* Plastic Surgery
409 Kings Hwy S, Cherry Hill, NJ, 856-354-6100

Lohner, Ronald Adolf (6 mentions)
New Jersey Med Sch, 1986 *Certification:* Plastic Surgery
919 Conestoga Rd Bldg 1 #200, Rosemont, PA, 610-519-0600

Low, David Wei-Wen (5 mentions)
Harvard U, 1980 *Certification:* Plastic Surgery
3400 Spruce St Penn Tower 10th Fl, Philadelphia, PA, 215-662-2040
3400 Civic Center Blvd 1st Fl, Philadelphia, PA, 215-590-2208

Matthews, Martha S. (8 mentions)
Jefferson Med Coll, 1981 *Certification:* Plastic Surgery
6017 Main St, Voorhees, NJ, 856-325-6767

Mitra, Amitabha (6 mentions)
FMS-India, 1968
Certification: Plastic Surgery, Surgery of the Hand
205 N broad St #200, Philadelphia, PA, 215-557-7227

Nardella, Guy Michael, Jr. (6 mentions)
Jefferson Med Coll, 1974
Certification: Plastic Surgery, Surgery of the Hand
1088 W Baltimore Pike #2405, Media, PA, 610-566-6744
2004 Foulk Rd #3, Wilmington, DE, 302-478-5800

Noone, R. Barrett (8 mentions)
U of Pennsylvania, 1965 *Certification:* Plastic Surgery, Surgery
888 Glenbrook Ave, Bryn Mawr, PA, 610-527-4833

Sorokin, Evan Scott (7 mentions)
Hahnemann U, 1998 *Certification:* Plastic Surgery
100 Brick Rd #215, Marlton, NJ, 856-797-0202

Whitaker, Linton Andin (4 mentions)
Tulane U, 1962 *Certification:* Plastic Surgery, Surgery
3400 Spruce St Penn Tower 10th Fl, Philadelphia, PA, 215-662-2040
3400 Civic Center Blvd 1st Fl, Philadelphia, PA, 215-590-2208

Wingate, Gary F. (4 mentions)
Northwestern U, 1984 *Certification:* Plastic Surgery
460 Creamery Way #110, Exton, PA, 610-524-8244
30 Darby Rd, Paoli, PA, 610-524-8244

Zavitsanos, George Peter (4 mentions)
Temple U, 1988 *Certification:* Plastic Surgery, Surgery
467 Pennsylvania Ave #203, Fort Washington, PA, 215-641-2300
3998 Red Lion Rd, Philadelphia, PA, 215-641-2300

Psychiatry

Baron, David A. (4 mentions)
Philadelphia Coll of Osteopathic Med, 1978
Certification: Psychiatry
100 E Lehigh Ave #305, Philadelphia, PA, 215-707-8483

Dunn, Jeffrey B. (5 mentions)
New Jersey Med Sch *Certification:* Child & Adolescent Psychiatry, Forensic Psychiatry, Psychiatry
3 Cooper Plaza #307, Camden, NJ, 856-342-2328

Leonard, Doug (5 mentions)
New Jersey Sch of Osteopathic Med, 1988
2250 Chapel Ave W #100, Cherry Hill, NJ, 856-482-9000

Nemerof, Victor Jay (3 mentions)
U of Kansas, 1980
Certification: Physical Medicine & Rehabilitation, Psychiatry
970 Town Center Dr #C12, Langhorne, PA, 215-757-1915
727 Welsh Rd #202, Huntingdon Valley, PA, 215-914-2119

Newmark, Thomas Stefan (8 mentions)
Hahnemann U, 1970 *Certification:* Geriatric Psychiatry, Psychiatry, Psychosomatic Medicine
3 Cooper Plaza #307, Camden, NJ, 856-342-2328

Smith, Timothy Craig (4 mentions)
Jefferson Med Coll, 1989
Certification: Geriatric Psychiatry, Psychiatry
4641 Roosevelt Blvd, Philadelphia, PA, 215-831-7853

Tavani, Carol A. (4 mentions)
Jefferson Med Coll, 1979 *Certification:* Psychiatry
4745 Ogletown-Stanton Rd #124, Newark, DE, 302-454-9900

Vergare, Michael John (3 mentions)
Hahnemann U, 1971
Certification: Geriatric Psychiatry, Psychiatry
833 Chestnut St #210, Philadelphia, PA, 215-955-1628

Pulmonary Disease

Aaronson, Gary Alan (6 mentions)
Philadelphia Coll of Osteopathic Med, 1983
Red Lion & Knights Rds, Philadelphia, PA, 215-612-8500
240 Middletown Blvd, Langhorne, PA, 215-612-8500

Berkowitz, Leonard B. (5 mentions)
SUNY-Downstate Med Coll, 1972
Certification: Internal Medicine, Pulmonary Disease
1 Medical Center Blvd, Chester, PA, 610-619-7460
300 Evergreen Dr #140, Glen Mills, PA, 610-619-7460

Bermingham, John (4 mentions)
New Jersey Sch of Osteopathic Med, 1985
100 Carnie Blvd #A-5, Voorhees, NJ, 856-751-8777

Casey, Michael Paul (4 mentions)
SUNY-Downstate Med Coll, 1971
Certification: Internal Medicine, Pulmonary Disease
700 Spruce St #500, Philadelphia, PA, 215-829-5027

Cohn, John Robert (4 mentions)
Jefferson Med Coll, 1976 *Certification:* Allergy & Immunology, Internal Medicine, Pulmonary Disease
1015 Chestnut St #1300, Philadelphia, PA, 215-923-7685

D'Alonzo, Gilbert Edward (7 mentions)
Philadelphia Coll of Osteopathic Med, 1977
3401 N Broad St Zone D, Philadelphia, PA, 215-707-3336
2301 E Allegheny Ave, Philadelphia, PA, 215-291-3881

Dhand, Sandeep (4 mentions)
FMS-India, 1972 *Certification:* Critical Care Medicine, Internal Medicine, Pulmonary Disease
1650 Huntingdon Pike #305, Meadowbrook, PA, 215-947-6404

Hansen-Flaschen, John H. (5 mentions)
New York U, 1976
Certification: Internal Medicine, Pulmonary Disease
3400 Spruce St Radvin Bldg 3rd Fl #F, Philadelphia, PA, 215-662-3202

Horowitz, Ira (4 mentions)
Hahnemann U, 1985 *Certification:* Critical Care Medicine, Internal Medicine, Pulmonary Disease
1930 E Marlton Pike #77, Cherry Hill, NJ, 856-424-4525

Kane, Gregory Charles (5 mentions)
Jefferson Med Coll, 1987 *Certification:* Critical Care Medicine, Internal Medicine, Pulmonary Disease
834 Walnut St #650, Philadelphia, PA, 215-955-5161

King, Earl (4 mentions)
Pennsylvania State U, 1986 *Certification:* Critical Care Medicine, Internal Medicine, Pulmonary Disease
333 Cottman Ave, Philadelphia, PA, 215-728-5703

Kotloff, Robert Mark (4 mentions)
Yale U, 1983 *Certification:* Critical Care Medicine, Internal Medicine, Pulmonary Disease
3400 Spruce St, Philadelphia, PA, 215-349-5488

Lugano, Eugene Michael (4 mentions)
U of Pennsylvania, 1975
Certification: Internal Medicine, Pulmonary Disease
700 Spruce St #500, Philadelphia, PA, 215-829-5027

Meyer, Thomas James (5 mentions)
Jefferson Med Coll, 1986 *Certification:* Critical Care Medicine, Internal Medicine, Pulmonary Disease
100 Lancaster Ave Lankenau Bldg W #230, Wynnewood, PA, 610-642-3796

Morowitz, William Allen (5 mentions)
U of Illinois, 1970 *Certification:* Internal Medicine
100 Carnie Blvd #A5, Voorhees, NJ, 856-751-8777

Panitch, Howard Barry (4 mentions)
U of Pittsburgh, 1982
Certification: Pediatric Pulmonology, Pediatrics
S 34th St & Civic Center Blvd, Philadelphia, PA, 215-590-1000

Peterson, Donald Duane (6 mentions)
Harvard U, 1975 *Certification:* Critical Care Medicine, Internal Medicine, Pulmonary Disease
100 Lancaster Ave #230, Wynnewood, PA, 610-642-3796

Pitman, Andrew Paul (12 mentions)
SUNY-Downstate Med Coll, 1979 *Certification:* Critical Care Medicine, Internal Medicine, Pulmonary Disease
830 Old Lancaster Rd Bldg N #101, Bryn Mawr, PA, 610-527-4896

Pope, Alan Raymond (5 mentions)
U of Connecticut, 1980 *Certification:* Critical Care Medicine, Internal Medicine, Pulmonary Disease
108 Kings Hwy S, Cherry Hill, NJ, 856-429-1800

Pratter, Melvin R. (9 mentions)
SUNY-Buffalo, 1973 *Certification:* Critical Care Medicine, Internal Medicine, Pulmonary Disease
900 Centennial Blvd, Voorhees, NJ, 856-325-6543
3 Cooper Plaza #312, Camden, NJ, 856-342-2406

Prince, David Saml (7 mentions)
U of Maryland, 1979 *Certification:* Critical Care Medicine, Internal Medicine, Pulmonary Disease
830 Old Lancaster Rd Bldg N #101, Bryn Mawr, PA, 610-527-4896

Promisloff, Robert A. (6 mentions)
Philadelphia Coll of Osteopathic Med, 1973 *Certification:* Critical Care Medicine, Internal Medicine, Pulmonary Disease
1001 City Line Ave #W-113, Wynnewood, PA, 610-896-0280
227 N Broad St 2nd Fl, Philadelphia, PA, 610-896-0280

Shusterman, Richard David (4 mentions)
Med Coll of Pennsylvania, 1983 *Certification:* Critical Care Medicine, Internal Medicine, Pulmonary Disease
1205 Langhorne-Newtown Rd #301, Langhorne, PA, 215-757-1414
2630 Holme Ave #104, Philadelphia, PA, 215-332-9095
501 Bath Rd #217, Bristol, PA, 215-785-9500

Swartz, Morris Alan (4 mentions)
U of Rochester, 1975 *Certification:* Critical Care Medicine, Internal Medicine, Pulmonary Disease
51 N 39th St #Phi-1, Philadelphia, PA, 215-662-8717

Szekely, Les Attila (5 mentions)
Med Coll of Ohio, 1990 *Certification:* Critical Care Medicine, Internal Medicine, Pulmonary Disease
1980 S Easton Rd, Doylestown, PA, 215-348-1310

Wendell, Gary David (4 mentions)
U of Vermont, 1982 *Certification:* Critical Care Medicine, Internal Medicine, Pulmonary Disease
1 Medical Center Blvd #422, Chester, PA, 610-619-7460

Radiology—Diagnostic

Baraldi, Raymond L., Jr. (7 mentions)
Jefferson Med Coll, 1976
Certification: Diagnostic Radiology, Internal Medicine
1 Cooper Plaza, Camden, NJ, 856-342-2383

Breckenridge, John William (3 mentions)
Jefferson Med Coll, 1970 *Certification:* Diagnostic Radiology
1200 Old York Rd, Abington, PA, 215-481-2087

Curtin, Andrew Joseph (5 mentions)
Jefferson Med Coll, 1983
Certification: Diagnostic Radiology, Neuroradiology
100 Lancaster Ave, Wynnewood, PA, 610-645-2804

Curtis, John Ashton (3 mentions)
Columbia U, 1972 *Certification:* Diagnostic Radiology
6650 Browning Rd #M14, Pennsauken, NJ, 856-665-3330

Faerber, Eric Norman (4 mentions)
FMS-South Africa, 1966 *Certification:* Diagnostic Radiology
Erie Ave & Front St #133-1, Philadelphia, PA, 215-427-5230

Forsted, David Henry (3 mentions)
Rosalind Franklin U, 1970 *Certification:* Diagnostic Radiology
255 W Lancaster Ave, Paoli, PA, 610-648-1070

Jungreis, Charles Andrew (3 mentions)
SUNY-Downstate Med Coll, 1980
Certification: Diagnostic Radiology, Neuroradiology
3401 N Broad St #702, Philadelphia, PA, 215-707-7237

Keller, Marc Sheldon (3 mentions)
George Washington U, 1977
Certification: Diagnostic Radiology, Pediatric Radiology
324 S 34th St, Philadelphia, PA, 267-425-7145

Levy, David Welsh (3 mentions)
Temple U, 1982 *Certification:* Diagnostic Radiology
1004 Haddonfield Rd, Cherry Hill, NJ, 856-662-7733

Milestone, Barton Neil (3 mentions)
Yale U, 1981 *Certification:* Diagnostic Radiology
333 Cottman Ave, Philadelphia, PA, 215-728-2570

Skalina, Stefan Michael (4 mentions)
Case Western Reserve U, 1979
Certification: Diagnostic Radiology, Pediatrics
1 Medical Center Blvd, Upland, PA, 610-447-2595
200 E State St #200, Media, PA, 610-627-5804
190 W Sproul Rd, Springfield, PA, 610-328-8785

Radiology—Therapeutic

Bonn, Joseph (5 mentions)
U of Virginia, 1979 *Certification:* Diagnostic Radiology,
   Vascular & Interventional Radiology
100 Lancaster Ave, Wynnewood, PA, 610-645-2826

Curtis, Paul Ashton (4 mentions)
Hahnemann U, 1979 *Certification:* Diagnostic Radiology
101 Carnie Blvd, Voorhees, NJ, 856-325-3782

Fisher, Scot Adam (4 mentions)
Philadelphia Coll of Osteopathic Med, 1982
Certification: Radiation Oncology
3998 Red Lion Rd, Philadelphia, PA, 215-612-4300

Garcia, Mark Joseph (3 mentions)
Jefferson Med Coll, 1989 *Certification:* Diagnostic Radiology
4755 Ogletown-Stanton Rd, Newark, DE, 302-733-5625

O'Moore, Paul Vincent (4 mentions)
U of Pennsylvania, 1983 *Certification:* Diagnostic Radiology,
   Vascular & Interventional Radiology
1200 Old York Rd, Abington, PA, 215-481-2071

Stein, Eric Joel (3 mentions)
U of Pennsylvania, 1979 *Certification:* Diagnostic Radiology
130 S Bryn Mawr Ave, Bryn Mawr, PA, 610-526-3453

Rehabilitation

Bernal, Guillermo Jose (3 mentions)
U of Puerto Rico, 1986
Certification: Physical Medicine & Rehabilitation
805 Floral Vale Blvd #6, Yardley, PA, 215-968-4901

Bernstein, Larry Norman (3 mentions)
SUNY-Upstate Med U, 1983
Certification: Physical Medicine & Rehabilitation
100 E Lancaster Ave, Wynnewood, PA, 610-645-2210

Bodofsky, Elliot Bruce (8 mentions)
Temple U, 1984 *Certification:* Physical Medicine & Rehabilitation
390 N Broadway #100, Pennsville, NJ, 856-678-6411
1 Cooper Plaza #550, Camden, NJ, 856-342-2040
1101 Kings Hwy N #100, Cherry Hill, NJ, 856-414-6112

Eschbach, Kelly Sue (4 mentions)
Hahnemann U, 1991
Certification: Physical Medicine & Rehabilitation
501 W 14th St 6th Fl, Wilmington, DE, 302-428-2717

Gallagher, Edward Joseph, Jr. (3 mentions)
West Virginia U, 1978
Certification: Physical Medicine & Rehabilitation
1600 Haddon Ave, Camden, NJ, 856-757-3879
636 Kings Hwy, Woodbury, NJ, 856-757-3879

Jermyn, Richard T. (4 mentions)
Philadelphia Coll of Osteopathic Med, 1992
Certification: Physical Medicine & Rehabilitation
42 E Laurel Rd #1700, Stratford, NJ, 856-566-7010

Kamen, Leonard B. (4 mentions)
West Virginia Sch of Osteopathic Med, 1983
Certification: Pain Medicine, Physical Medicine & Rehabilitation
9892 Bustleton Ave, Philadelphia, PA, 215-673-6552

Maitin, Ian Bruce (4 mentions)
Jefferson Med Coll, 1989
Certification: Physical Medicine & Rehabilitation
3401 N Broad St, Philadelphia, PA, 215-707-7021

Ragone, Daniel Joseph, Jr. (4 mentions)
FMS-Grenada, 1983
Certification: Physical Medicine & Rehabilitation
3829 Church Rd #A, Mount Laurel, NJ, 856-222-9713

Siegfried, Jay Worth (9 mentions)
U of Cincinnati, 1978
Certification: Physical Medicine & Rehabilitation
100 E Lancaster Ave, Wynnewood, PA, 610-645-3391

Weinik, Michael M. (4 mentions)
Philadelphia Coll of Osteopathic Med, 1985
Certification: Physical Medicine & Rehabilitation
3401 N Broad St, Philadelphia, PA, 215-707-3646
255 S 17th St #2101, Philadelphia, PA, 215-707-9663

Rheumatology

Getzoff, Barry L. (10 mentions)
Philadelphia Coll of Osteopathic Med, 1960
300 Middletown Blvd #103, Langhorne, PA, 215-752-8680

Goldsmith, Donald Peter (6 mentions)
U of Vermont, 1967 *Certification:* Allergy & Immunology,
   Pediatric Rheumatology, Pediatrics
Erie Ave & Front St, Philadelphia, PA, 215-427-5051
153 Brodhead Rd, Bethlehem, PA, 610-954-4975

Grimmett, Brian Lee (5 mentions)
New Jersey Med Sch, 1970
Certification: Internal Medicine, Rheumatology
3201 Route 38 W, Mount Laurel, NJ, 856-235-0001
2309 E Evesham Rd #101, Voorhees, NJ, 856-424-5005

Hoffman, Bruce Ira (9 mentions)
Temple U, 1974 *Certification:* Internal Medicine, Rheumatology
301 City Ave #100, Bala Cynwyd, PA, 215-725-7400
7908 Bustleton Ave #B, Philadelphia, PA, 215-725-7400

Leventhal, Lawrence Jay (5 mentions)
Hahnemann U, 1984
Certification: Internal Medicine, Rheumatology
219 N Broad St, Philadelphia, PA, 215-762-7300

Norden, Daniel Kanof (5 mentions)
Temple U, 1986 *Certification:* Internal Medicine, Rheumatology
170 W Germantown Pike C2, East Norristown, PA, 610-277-2750
262A Bethlehem Pike #100, Colmar, PA, 215-997-8530

Pullman-Moar, Sally W. (6 mentions)
U of Cincinnati, 1980
Certification: Internal Medicine, Rheumatology
100 Lancaster Ave #418, Wynnewood, PA, 610-823-5979
3900 Woodland Ave, Philadelphia, PA, 215-823-5800

Rose, Carlos Daniel (6 mentions)
FMS-Argentina, 1978
Certification: Pediatric Rheumatology, Pediatrics
1600 Rockland Rd, Wilmington, DE, 302-651-5970

Solomon, Sheldon Dubrow (6 mentions)
Temple U, 1964 *Certification:* Internal Medicine, Rheumatology
2309 E Evesham Rd #101, Voorhees, NJ, 856-424-4626

Thoracic Surgery

Bavaria, Joseph Edward (5 mentions)
Tulane U, 1983 *Certification:* Thoracic Surgery
34th & Spruce Sts, Philadelphia, PA, 215-662-2017

Cooper, Joel (5 mentions)
3400 Spruce St 4th Fl, Philadelphia, PA, 215-662-2022

Friedberg, Joseph Stewart (5 mentions)
Harvard U, 1986 *Certification:* Surgery, Thoracic Surgery
51 N 39th St #266, Philadelphia, PA, 215-662-9195

Heim, John August (6 mentions)
New Jersey Med Sch, 1985
Certification: Surgery, Thoracic Surgery
3998 Red Lion Rd #214, Philadelphia, PA, 215-612-5050
240 Middletown Blvd #101-C, Langhorne, PA, 215-612-5050

Lotano, Vincent Ercole (6 mentions)
Robert W Johnson Med Sch, 1993
Certification: Surgery, Thoracic Surgery
700 Spruce St #305, Philadelphia, PA, 215-829-2092

Pechet, Taine Tayardvale (5 mentions)
Harvard U, 1992 *Certification:* Surgery, Thoracic Surgery
51 N 39th St #250, Philadelphia, PA, 215-662-9195
1 E New York Ave, Somers Point, NJ, 215-662-9195

Urology

Amster, Melanie Ina (4 mentions)
Hahnemann U, 1991 *Certification:* Urology
1216 Arch St, Philadelphia, PA, 215-563-1199
51 N 39th St, Philadelphia, PA, 215-563-1199

Bergmann, Leigh Scott (4 mentions)
U of Pennsylvania, 1986 *Certification:* Urology
919 Conestoga Rd Bldg 1 #300, Bryn Mawr, PA, 610-525-6580

Bernstein, Guy Thomas (6 mentions)
Columbia U, 1982 *Certification:* Urology
245 S Bryn Mawr Ave, Bryn Mawr, PA, 610-525-2515

Blatstein, Lee M. (6 mentions)
Philadelphia Coll of Osteopathic Med, 1984
1313 Dekalb St, Norristown, PA, 610-277-5025
125 Medical Campus Dr #305, Lansdale, PA, 215-361-2301

Charles, Robert Seth (14 mentions)
Temple U, 1980 *Certification:* Urology
1235 Old York Rd #210, Abington, PA, 215-517-1100

Coll, Milton Emanuel (9 mentions)
Med Coll of Pennsylvania, 1981 *Certification:* Urology
3998 Red Lion Rd #305, Philadelphia, PA, 215-632-8882

Ellis, David J. (5 mentions)
Jefferson Med Coll, 1981 *Certification:* Urology
919 Conestoga Rd Bldg 1 #300, Rosemont, PA, 610-525-6580

Fallick, Mark Lawrence (4 mentions)
Tufts U, 1991 *Certification:* Urology
502 Centennial Blvd #2, Voorhees, NJ, 856-751-7772
301 White Horse Pike, Haddon Heights, NJ, 856-547-1115

Figueroa, T. Ernesto (7 mentions)
Tulane U, 1983 *Certification:* Pediatric Urology, Urology
1600 Rockland Rd, Wilmington, DE, 302-651-5980
833 E Chestnut St #300, Philadelphia, PA, 215-955-6892

Gabale, Devon R. (5 mentions)
FMS-India, 1979 *Certification:* Urology
1205 Langhorne-Newtown Rd #304-A, Langhorne, PA,
  215-750-0100

Goldstein, Larry Edwin (4 mentions)
Jefferson Med Coll, 1973 *Certification:* Urology
833 Chestnut St #703, Philadelphia, PA, 215-955-1000

Gomella, Leonard Gabriel (10 mentions)
U of Kentucky, 1980 *Certification:* Urology
833 Chestnut St #703, Philadelphia, PA, 215-955-6961

Handler, Jay Joel (4 mentions)
U of Pittsburgh, 1968 *Certification:* Urology
2137 Welsh Rd #2D, Philadelphia, PA, 215-698-7333

Harryhill, Joseph Francis (5 mentions)
Ohio State U, 1986 *Certification:* Urology
299 S 8th St, Philadelphia, PA, 215-829-3409
700 Spruce St #304, Philadelphia, PA, 215-829-3521

Kapp, Anton, Jr. (4 mentions)
Temple U, 1981 *Certification:* Urology
2301 Huntingdon Pike #201, Huntingdon Valley, PA,
  215-947-4105
2701 Holme Ave #101, Philadelphia, PA, 215-335-3535

Kotler, Mitchell Neal (5 mentions)
George Washington U, 1984 *Certification:* Urology
17 W Red Bank Ave #303, Woodbury, NJ, 856-853-0955
406 Lippincott Dr #F, Marlton, NJ, 856-985-6800
63 Kresson Rd #103, Cherry Hill, NJ, 856-985-6800

Krisch, Evan Barry (8 mentions)
Jefferson Med Coll, 1983 *Certification:* Urology
502 Centennial Blvd #2, Voorhees, NJ, 856-751-7772

Lee, David Inkoo (4 mentions)
Loma Linda U, 1995 *Certification:* Urology
51 N 39th St, Philadelphia, PA, 215-662-8699

Lobis, Michael (4 mentions)
Temple U, 1990 *Certification:* Urology
1801 Rockland Rd #300, Wilmington, DE, 302-652-8990
2600 Glasgow Ave #2-222, Newark, DE, 302-838-5210

Malloy, Terrence Reed (5 mentions)
U of Pennsylvania, 1963 *Certification:* Urology
299 S 8th St, Philadelphia, PA, 215-925-1846

Marmar, Joel L. (4 mentions)
U of Pennsylvania, 1964 *Certification:* Urology
3 Cooper Plaza #411, Camden, NJ, 856-963-3577
127 Church Rd, Marlton, NJ, 856-817-3000
900 Centennial Blvd, Voorhees, NJ, 856-325-6565

McGinnis, David Earl (4 mentions)
U of Texas-San Antonio, 1987
919 Conestoga Rd Bldg 1 #300, Bryn Mawr, PA, 610-525-6580

Pontari, Michael Arthur (5 mentions)
Pennsylvania State U, 1986 *Certification:* Urology
3401 N Broad St #330-C, Philadelphia, PA, 215-707-3375
255 S 17th St #2101, Philadelphia, PA, 215-707-9663

Ruenes, Albert, Jr. (4 mentions)
Columbia U, 1988 *Certification:* Urology
303 W State St, Doylestown, PA, 215-672-0500
205 Newtown Rd #102, Warminster, PA, 215-672-0500

Schnall, Robert Ira (7 mentions)
Temple U, 1982 *Certification:* Urology
100 Lancaster Ave Bldg E #361, Wynnewood, PA, 610-649-8590

Wein, Alan Jerome (11 mentions)
U of Pennsylvania, 1966 *Certification:* Urology
Penn Tower Hotel Bldg 9th Fl, Philadelphia, PA, 215-662-2891

Vascular Surgery

Alexander, James B. (13 mentions)
U of Pennsylvania, 1980 *Certification:* Surgery, Vascular Surgery
3 Cooper Plaza #411, Camden, NJ, 856-342-2151
900 Central Blvd, Voorhees, NJ, 856-325-6565
127 Church Rd, Marlton, NJ, 856-817-3000

Calligaro, Keith Don (9 mentions)
New Jersey Med Sch, 1982
Certification: Surgery, Vascular Surgery
700 Spruce St #101, Philadelphia, PA, 215-829-5000
8 S Dennis Rd, Cape May Courthouse, NJ, 215-829-5000

Carabasi, Ralph Anthony (12 mentions)
Jefferson Med Coll, 1977 *Certification:* Vascular Surgery
744 W Lancaster Ave #225, Wayne, PA, 610-687-5347

Carpenter, Jeffrey Palmer (5 mentions)
Yale U, 1986 *Certification:* Surgery, Vascular Surgery
6017 Main St, Voorhees, NJ, 856-325-6516
3 Cooper Plaza #403, Camden, NJ, 856-342-2272

Dimuzio, Paul Joseph (5 mentions)
U of Pennsylvania, 1989 *Certification:* Vascular Surgery
111 S 11th St #6350, Philadelphia, PA, 215-955-8304

Fairman, Ronald Marc (9 mentions)
Jefferson Med Coll, 1977 *Certification:* Vascular Surgery
3400 Spruce St Silverstein Bldg 4th Fl, Philadelphia, PA,
  215-614-0308

Ierardi, Ralph Peter (7 mentions)
Emory U, 1988 *Certification:* Surgery, Vascular Surgery
187 East Ave, Woodstown, NJ, 302-733-5700
4765 Ogletown-Stanton Rd #1-E-20, Newark, DE, 302-733-5700

Mattson, Ronald Joseph (7 mentions)
Temple U, 1971 *Certification:* Surgery
830 Old Lancaster Rd #306, Bryn Mawr, PA, 610-527-1185
11 Industrial Blvd, Paoli, PA, 610-647-3077
215 Old Fern Hill Rd Bldg B #201, West Chester, PA,
  610-436-6696

Patton, Gerald Morgan (5 mentions)
U of Miami, 1987 *Certification:* Surgery, Vascular Surgery
830 Old Lancaster Rd Medical Bldg N #306, Bryn Mawr, PA,
  610-527-1185
11 Industrial Blvd, Paoli, PA, 610-647-3077
215 Old Fern Hill Rd Bldg B #201, West Chester, PA,
  610-436-6696

Roberts, Andrew Bayard (15 mentions)
U of Minnesota, 1975 *Certification:* Surgery, Vascular Surgery
7500 Central Ave #200, Philadelphia, PA, 215-728-3240
3401 N Broad St, Philadelphia, PA, 215-707-3622

Schickler, William John, III (6 mentions)
Cornell U, 1979 *Certification:* Surgery, Vascular Surgery
620 Stanton Christiana Rd #305, Newark, DE, 302-999-0144

Sullivan, Theodore Robert (5 mentions)
Temple U, 1988 *Certification:* Surgery, Vascular Surgery
1245 Highland Ave #600, Abington, PA, 215-887-5934

Uribe, Alexander (6 mentions)
FMS-Colombia, 1978 *Certification:* Surgery, Vascular Surgery
100 E Lancaster Ave Lankenau Bldg #275, Wynnewood, PA,
  610-642-1908

Pittsburgh Area

Including Allegheny County

Allergy/Immunology

Green, Richard Lee (14 mentions)
Duke U, 1968
Certification: Allergy & Immunology, Internal Medicine
320 Fort Duquesne Blvd #380, Pittsburgh, 412-471-3818
2585 Freeport Rd #210, Pittsburgh, 412-828-3800

Landay, Ronald Allan (7 mentions)
U of Pittsburgh, 1973
Certification: Allergy & Immunology, Pediatrics
180 Fort Couch Rd #375, Pittsburgh, 412-833-8811
1385 Washington Rd #101, Washington, 724-228-7710

Anesthesiology

Boretsky, Robert H. (3 mentions)
Jefferson Med Coll, 1982 *Certification:* Anesthesiology
200 Lothrop St #C-200, Pittsburgh, 412-647-3262

Caldwell, John Christian (6 mentions)
U of Pittsburgh, 1990 *Certification:* Anesthesiology
200 Lothrop St #C-200, Pittsburgh, 412-647-3262

Davis, Peter Jonathan (5 mentions)
Albert Einstein Coll of Med, 1977
Certification: Anesthesiology, Pediatrics
3705 5th Ave, Pittsburgh, 412-692-5325

Murray, Andrew Walter (3 mentions)
FMS-South Africa, 1994 *Certification:* Anesthesiology
200 Lothrop St #C, Pittsburgh, 412-647-3260

Shay, Paul Larew (7 mentions)
U of Pittsburgh, 1976 *Certification:* Anesthesiology
815 Freeport Rd, Pittsburgh, 412-784-4396

Sonbolian, Nasser Jacob (4 mentions)
FMS-Iran, 1968 *Certification:* Anesthesiology
200 Lothrop St #200, Pittsburgh, 412-647-3262

Sullivan, Erin Ann (3 mentions)
Louisiana State U, 1986 *Certification:* Anesthesiology
200 Lothrop St #C-200, Pittsburgh, 412-647-3262

Waters, Jonathan Hale (5 mentions)
George Washington U, 1986 *Certification:* Anesthesiology
300 Halket St, Pittsburgh, 412-641-4260

Williams, John Phillip (3 mentions)
Baylor U, 1979
Certification: Anesthesiology, Critical Care Medicine
3550 Terrace St, Pittsburgh, 412-647-2907

Cardiac Surgery

Benckart, Daniel Harrington (10 mentions)
Georgetown U, 1977
Certification: Surgery, Thoracic Surgery, Vascular Surgery
301 1st Ave #B, Tarentum, 724-226-0773
304 Evans Dr #401, Ellwood City, 724-226-0773
320 E North Ave, Pittsburgh, 412-359-8820

Culig, Michael Herman (6 mentions)
Harvard U, 1982 *Certification:* Surgery, Thoracic Surgery
4815 Liberty Ave #156, Pittsburgh, 412-688-9810
2566 Haymaker Rd #203, Monroeville, 412-688-9810

Dimarco, Ross F., Jr. (8 mentions)
Jefferson Med Coll, 1973 *Certification:* Surgery, Thoracic Surgery
400 Holiday Dr #101, Pittsburgh, 412-444-0098

Machiraju, V. R. (10 mentions)
FMS-India, 1969 *Certification:* Thoracic Surgery
5200 Centre Ave #715, Pittsburgh, 412-623-3140

Magovern, George Jerome, Jr. (12 mentions)
Certification: Surgery, Thoracic Surgery
320 E North Ave, Pittsburgh, 412-359-8820

Morell, Victor Onofre (6 mentions)
Ponce Sch of Med, 1988 *Certification:* Thoracic Surgery
3705 5th Ave, Pittsburgh, 412-692-5218

Navid, Forozan (6 mentions)
U of Virginia, 1988 *Certification:* Surgery, Thoracic Surgery
5200 Centre Ave #715, Pittsburgh, 412-623-2994

Park, Kyung S. (6 mentions)
Certification: Surgery, Thoracic Surgery
575 Coal Valley Rd #504, Clairton, 412-469-7900

Pellegrini, Ronald Virgil (23 mentions)
Jefferson Med Coll, 1963 *Certification:* Surgery, Thoracic Surgery
9104 Babcock Blvd #5105, Pittsburgh, 412-369-4603

Wei, Lawrence Ming (18 mentions)
U of Pittsburgh, 1982 *Certification:* Surgery, Thoracic Surgery
200 Lothrop St #C-700, Pittsburgh, 412-648-6351

Woelfel, George Frederick (9 mentions)
Med Coll of Wisconsin, 1978 *Certification:* Thoracic Surgery
400 Holiday Dr #101, Pittsburgh, 412-444-0098

Cardiology

Anderson, William Deaton (5 mentions)
Duke U, 1988
Certification: Cardiovascular Disease, Interventional Cardiology
200 Lothrop St, Pittsburgh, 412-647-6000
9104 Babcock Blvd #4106, Pittsburgh, 412-366-2010
9380 McKnight Rd #201, Pittsburgh, 412-367-8202
2100 Jane St #603, Pittsburgh, 412-488-6420
120 Lytton Ave #100-B, Pittsburgh, 412-802-3000

Aziz, Abdul Rab (3 mentions)
FMS-Afghanistan, 1977 *Certification:* Cardiovascular
Disease, Internal Medicine, Interventional Cardiology
125 Daugherty Dr #301, Monroeville, 412-856-4666

Beerman, Lee Bankin (9 mentions)
U of Pittsburgh, 1974
Certification: Pediatric Cardiology, Pediatrics
3705 5th Ave, Pittsburgh, 412-692-5540

Buffer, Sam A., Jr. (3 mentions)
U of Pittsburgh, 1988 *Certification:* Cardiovascular Disease
9365 McKnight Rd #700, Pittsburgh, 412-367-8202

Counihan, Peter James (9 mentions)
FMS-Ireland, 1983
200 Lothrop St, Pittsburgh, 412-781-4860

Crock, Frederick William (3 mentions)
Temple U, 1978
Certification: Cardiovascular Disease, Internal Medicine
200 Lothrop St #5-B, Pittsburgh, 412-802-3000

Edmundowicz, Daniel (11 mentions)
Hahnemann U, 1990 *Certification:* Internal Medicine
120 Lytton Ave #302, Pittsburgh, 412-802-3000
339 6th Ave #530-A, Pittsburgh, 412-560-8762

Farah, Tony George (4 mentions)
FMS-Lebanon, 1984 *Certification:* Cardiovascular Disease,
Internal Medicine, Interventional Cardiology
490 E North Ave #307, Pittsburgh, 412-321-0680
202 Jacob Murphy Ln, Uniontown, 724-430-0890

Follansbee, William Phillips (14 mentions)
U of Pennsylvania, 1974
Certification: Cardiovascular Disease, Internal Medicine
200 Lothrop St #A-429, Pittsburgh, 412-647-3437

Friedman, Abe W. (7 mentions)
Rosalind Franklin U, 1974 *Certification:* Cardiovascular
Disease, Critical Care Medicine, Internal Medicine
5845 Centre Ave, Pittsburgh, 412-363-7474

Grandis, Donald Jay (6 mentions)
Virginia Commonwealth U, 1985
Certification: Cardiovascular Disease, Internal Medicine
575 Coal Valley Rd #574, Jefferson Hills, 412-469-7660

Gulati, Vijay Kumar (4 mentions)
Tufts U, 1991
Certification: Internal Medicine, Interventional Cardiology
200 Delafield Rd #3010, Pittsburgh, 412-781-4860

Katz, William Edward (5 mentions)
Ohio State U, 1986
Certification: Cardiovascular Disease, Internal Medicine
200 Lothrop St, Pittsburgh, 412-647-7718

Lally, Francis Leonard (4 mentions)
Hahnemann U, 1976
Certification: Cardiovascular Disease, Internal Medicine
12 Quaker Village Shopping Ctr, Leetsdale, 412-741-2700

Landfair, Roy Joseph (5 mentions)
U of Pittsburgh, 1972
Certification: Cardiovascular Disease, Internal Medicine
1300 Oxford Dr #1-A, Bethel Park, 412-347-3240
1501 Locust St #1070, Pittsburgh, 412-325-3090

Lasorda, David M. (5 mentions)
Philadelphia Coll of Osteopathic Med, 1983
Certification: Cardiovascular Disease, Internal Medicine,
Interventional Cardiology
490 E North Ave #307, Pittsburgh, 412-359-5822

Lee, Jenifer Elizabeth (6 mentions)
Boston U, 1987
Certification: Cardiovascular Disease, Internal Medicine
200 Lothrop St #5-B, Pittsburgh, 412-647-6000

Lee, Joon Sup (4 mentions)
Duke U, 1988 *Certification:* Cardiovascular Disease,
Internal Medicine, Interventional Cardiology
200 Lothrop St, Pittsburgh, 412-781-4860

O'Toole, James Dennis (7 mentions)
St Louis U, 1966 *Certification:* Cardiovascular Disease,
Internal Medicine, Interventional Cardiology
5200 Centre Ave #703, Pittsburgh, 412-687-8300

Reis, Steven Eric (6 mentions)
Harvard U, 1987
Certification: Cardiovascular Disease, Internal Medicine
120 Lytton Ave #100-B, Pittsburgh, 412-802-3014

Rubin, Daniel Albert (5 mentions)
U of Buffalo, 1986 *Certification:* Anatomic Pathology &
Clinical Pathology, Cardiovascular Disease, Cytopathology,
Internal Medicine, Interventional Cardiology
575 Coal Valley Rd #574, Jefferson Hills, 412-469-7660

Sherman, Frederick Scott (3 mentions)
Yale U, 1975 *Certification:* Pediatric Cardiology, Pediatrics
300 Halket St, Pittsburgh, 412-641-4107

Smitherman, Thomas Cecil (7 mentions)
U of Alabama, 1967
Certification: Cardiovascular Disease, Internal Medicine
200 Lothrop St #5-B, Pittsburgh, 412-647-6000

Ward, John R. (6 mentions)
Philadelphia Coll of Osteopathic Med, 1989
Certification: Cardiovascular Disease, Interventional Cardiology
5200 Centre Ave #206, Pittsburgh, 412-621-1500
969 Greentree Rd, Pittsburgh, 412-621-1500

Warde, Donal (9 mentions)
FMS-Ireland, 1972
Certification: Cardiovascular Disease, Internal Medicine
320 E North Ave, Pittsburgh, 412-359-3550

Webber, Steven Alan (3 mentions)
FMS-United Kingdom, 1983
Certification: Pediatric Cardiology, Pediatrics
3705 5th Ave, Pittsburgh, 412-692-5544

Dermatology

Caserio, Rebecca Joann (6 mentions)
U of Pittsburgh, 1975
Certification: Dermatology, Internal Medicine
241 Freeport Rd #7, Pittsburgh, 412-784-1606

Costa, Melanie Elizabeth (6 mentions)
U of Pittsburgh, 1990 *Certification:* Dermatology
4727 Friendship Ave, Pittsburgh, 412-683-5211
1000 Stonewood Dr #200, Wexford, 724-778-3020

English, Joseph C., III (7 mentions)
Pennsylvania State U, 1991 *Certification:* Dermatology
3601 5th Ave, Pittsburgh, 412-647-4200

Gehris, Robin Paige (6 mentions)
U of Pittsburgh, 1997
Certification: Dermatology, Pediatric Dermatology, Pediatrics
11279 Perry Hwy #108, Wexford, 724-933-9190

Lally, Margaret Sue (20 mentions)
U of Pittsburgh, 1985 *Certification:* Dermatology
1382 Old Freeport Rd, Pittsburgh, 412-967-1192

Pawelski, Lisa Alexandra (6 mentions)
U of Pittsburgh, 1986
Certification: Dermatology, Internal Medicine
3424 William Penn Hwy, Pittsburgh, 412-824-9600

Small, Judith Ann (13 mentions)
U of Rochester, 1978 *Certification:* Dermatology
420 E North Ave #406, Pittsburgh, 412-359-3376

Zitelli, John Albert (14 mentions)
U of Pittsburgh, 1976 *Certification:* Dermatology
5200 Centre Ave #303, Pittsburgh, 412-681-9400
575 Coal Valley Rd #360, Clairton, 412-466-9400

Emergency Medicine

Dunmire, Susan Mitchell (11 mentions)
U of Pittsburgh, 1985 *Certification:* Emergency Medicine
200 Lothrop St, Pittsburgh, 412-647-3336

Harchelroad, Fred P., Jr. (5 mentions)
Pennsylvania State U, 1982
Certification: Emergency Medicine, Medical Toxicology
320 E North Ave, Pittsburgh, 412-359-3252

Karasic, Raymond Bennett (3 mentions)
Johns Hopkins U, 1977
Certification: Emergency Medicine, Pediatric Emergency
Medicine, Pediatric Infectious Diseases, Pediatrics
3705 5th Ave, Pittsburgh, 412-692-7692

Kristan, William Gerard (3 mentions)
U of Pittsburgh, 1980 *Certification:* Emergency Medicine
9100 Babcock Blvd, Pittsburgh, 412-367-6310
2 Hot Metal St, Pittsburgh, 412-432-7424

MacLeod, Bruce Alan (3 mentions)
U of Cincinnati, 1987 *Certification:* Emergency Medicine
1400 Locust St, Pittsburgh, 412-232-5625

Natali, David George (5 mentions)
U of Pittsburgh, 1980 *Certification:* Emergency Medicine
2580 Haymaker Rd, Monroeville, 412-858-2323

Nicholas, James Elbert (6 mentions)
U of Pittsburgh, 1975
Certification: Emergency Medicine, Internal Medicine
2 Hot Metal St, Pittsburgh, 412-432-7424

Pangburn, Thomas L. M. (4 mentions)
U of Pittsburgh, 1993 *Certification:* Emergency Medicine
720 Blackburn Rd, Sewickley, 412-749-7076

Paris, Paul Marc (5 mentions)
U of Pittsburgh, 1976
Certification: Emergency Medicine, Internal Medicine
230 McKee Pl, Pittsburgh, 412-647-8285

Roth, Ronald Neal (4 mentions)
U of Pittsburgh, 1982 *Certification:* Emergency Medicine
200 Lothrop St, Pittsburgh, 412-647-1101

Rottinghaus, David M. (3 mentions)
U of Toledo, 1998 *Certification:* Emergency Medicine
320 E North Ave, Pittsburgh, 412-359-3252

Saladino, Richard Anthony (5 mentions)
U of Missouri, 1985 *Certification:* Pediatric Emergency Medicine
3705 5th Ave, Pittsburgh, 412-692-7692

Solot, Jerald A. (3 mentions)
A T Still U, 1971 *Certification:* Emergency Medicine
5230 Center Ave, Pittsburgh, 412-623-2121

Van Fleet, Timothy A. (5 mentions)
Wright State U, 1983 *Certification:* Family Medicine
2 Hot Metal St, Pittsburgh, 412-432-7424

Wadas, Richard (3 mentions)
Certification: Emergency Medicine
2 Hot Metal St, Pittsburgh, 412-432-7424

Yealy, Donald Matthew (14 mentions)
Med Coll of Pennsylvania, 1985
Certification: Emergency Medicine
200 Lothrop St, Pittsburgh, 412-221-5399

Endocrinology

Amico, Janet Ann (5 mentions)
Med Coll of Pennsylvania, 1975
Certification: Endocrinology and Metabolism, Internal Medicine
3601 5th Ave #3-B, Pittsburgh, 412-586-9700

Bahl, Sachin (7 mentions)
FMS-Grenada, 1997 *Certification:* Endocrinology, Diabetes,
  and Metabolism, Internal Medicine
10922 Frankstown Rd, Pittsburgh, 412-241-6111

Bahl, Vijay Kumar (9 mentions)
FMS-Uganda, 1971
Certification: Endocrinology and Metabolism, Internal Medicine
10922 Frankstown Rd, Pittsburgh, 412-241-6111
5230 Centre Ave, Pittsburgh, 412-623-2456

Buonocore, Camille Marie (7 mentions)
U of Buffalo, 1987 *Certification:* Endocrinology, Diabetes,
  and Metabolism, Internal Medicine
2000 Oxford Dr #130, Bethel Park, 412-942-2140

Evron, Wayne A. (7 mentions)
U of Pennsylvania, 1980
Certification: Endocrinology and Metabolism, Internal Medicine
2566 Haymaker Rd #201, Monroeville, 412-373-9250
5140 Liberty Ave, Pittsburgh, 412-683-4550
1029 Country Club Rd #204, Monongahela, 724-258-4048

Gordon, Murray Bruce (14 mentions)
Albany Med Coll, 1977
Certification: Endocrinology and Metabolism, Internal Medicine
420 E North Ave #E-205, Pittsburgh, 412-359-3426

Hodak, Steven Paul (5 mentions)
Georgetown U, 1999 *Certification:* Endocrinology, Diabetes,
  and Metabolism, Internal Medicine
3601 5th Ave #3-B, Pittsburgh, 412-586-9700

Johnston, Jann M. (9 mentions)
Pennsylvania State U, 1979
Certification: Endocrinology and Metabolism, Internal Medicine
1350 Locust St #5120, Pittsburgh, 412-469-3300

Korytkowski, Mary Teresa (11 mentions)
U of North Carolina, 1982
Certification: Endocrinology and Metabolism, Internal Medicine
3601 5th Ave #3-B, Pittsburgh, 412-586-9700

Lebeau, Shane O. (5 mentions)
Certification: Endocrinology, Diabetes, and Metabolism,
  Internal Medicine
3601 5th Ave, Pittsburgh, 412-648-8630

Rao, Rayasam Harsha (8 mentions)
FMS-India, 1974
Certification: Endocrinology and Metabolism, Internal Medicine
3601 5th Ave #3-B, Pittsburgh, 412-586-9700

Family Practice *(see note on page 9)*

Blandino, David A. (3 mentions)
U of Pittsburgh, 1978 *Certification:* Family Medicine
5215 Centre Ave, Pittsburgh, 412-623-2287

Boyd, Anne Susan (3 mentions)
Case Western Reserve U, 1994
Certification: Family Medicine, Sports Medicine
3937 Butler St, Pittsburgh, 412-622-7343
301 11th St #C, New Kensington, 724-334-3640

Chopra, Monica I. (3 mentions)
Wright State U, 2003 *Certification:* Family Medicine
1000 Higbee Dr #104, Bethel Park, 412-833-6176

Dishart, Paul Warren (4 mentions)
Med Coll of Wisconsin, 1959 *Certification:* Family Medicine
100 Delafield Rd #108, Pittsburgh, 412-784-4234

Essig, Michael J. (3 mentions)
U of Pittsburgh, 1978 *Certification:* Family Medicine
309 Smithfield St, Pittsburgh, 412-471-2111

Fuge, La Donna Helaine (4 mentions)
Hahnemann U, 1985 *Certification:* Family Medicine
300 Penn Center Blvd #702, Pittsburgh, 412-816-2273

Furlong, Natalie Vaccari (5 mentions)
U of New England Coll of Osteopathic Med, 1994
Certification: Family Medicine
1000 Higbee Dr #104, Bethel Park, 412-833-6176
495 E Waterfront Dr #250, Homestead, 412-462-0527

John, Lawrence Richard (4 mentions)
Case Western Reserve U, 1977 *Certification:* Family Medicine
100 Delafield Rd #313, Pittsburgh, 412-781-0400

Karp, Michael A. (4 mentions)
Temple U, 1988 *Certification:* Family Medicine
72 1st St, Ambridge, 724-266-3239

Lagnese, John Michael (4 mentions)
Dartmouth Coll, 1978 *Certification:* Family Medicine
103 Gamma Dr #120, Pittsburgh, 412-781-1917

McGonigal, Michael P. (3 mentions)
U of Virginia, 1980
Certification: Family Medicine, Geriatric Medicine
1000 Higbee Dr #104, Bethel Park, 412-833-6176
495 E Waterfront Dr #250, Homestead, 412-462-0527

Middleton, Donald Bell (12 mentions)
U of Rochester, 1972 *Certification:* Internal Medicine, Pediatrics
100 Delafield Rd #213, Pittsburgh, 412-782-2101
600 Watercrest Way, Cheswick, 724-274-9420

Rabinowitz, Jerry Paul (3 mentions)
U of Pennsylvania, 1977 *Certification:* Family Medicine
5173 Liberty Ave, Pittsburgh, 412-682-3411

Gastroenterology

Abo, Steven Robert (5 mentions)
Albert Einstein Coll of Med, 1990 *Certification:* Gastroenterology
300 Halket St #5600, Pittsburgh, 412-641-2135

Dubner, Howard Murray (5 mentions)
New York U, 1987
Certification: Gastroenterology, Internal Medicine
5200 Centre Ave #409, Pittsburgh, 412-623-3105

Kelly, Thomas James (7 mentions)
Tufts U, 1972 *Certification:* Gastroenterology, Internal Medicine
100 Delafield Rd #307, Pittsburgh, 412-784-1110
356 Freeport St #205, New Kensington, 412-784-1110
1600 Wildlife Lodge Rd, Lowerburrell, 412-784-1110

Lebovitz, Paul Jay (11 mentions)
Albert Einstein Coll of Med, 1987
Certification: Gastroenterology, Internal Medicine
1307 Federal St #301, Pittsburgh, 412-359-8900
5140 Liberty Ave, Bloomfield, 412-359-8900

McGrath, Kevin Michael (6 mentions)
Certification: Gastroenterology
200 Lothrop St, Pittsburgh, 412-648-9325

Mitre, Ricardo Javier (9 mentions)
FMS-Bolivia, 1967
Certification: Gastroenterology, Internal Medicine
925 Brighton Rd Gateway Twrs #370, Pittsburgh, 412-321-1648

Schoen, Robert E. (8 mentions)
Columbia U, 1984
Certification: Gastroenterology, Internal Medicine
200 Lothrop St, Pittsburgh, 412-647-8666

Slivka, Adam (18 mentions)
Mount Sinai Sch of Med, 1988
Certification: Gastroenterology, Internal Medicine
200 Lothrop St Fl M, Pittsburgh, 412-647-8666

Weinberg, Lee Martin (5 mentions)
U of Pittsburgh, 1976
Certification: Gastroenterology, Internal Medicine
5200 Centre Ave #409, Pittsburgh, 412-623-3105

Wood, John Michael (15 mentions)
Case Western Reserve U, 1972
Certification: Gastroenterology, Internal Medicine
100 Delafield Rd #307, Pittsburgh, 412-784-1110
356 Freeport St #205, New Kensington, 412-784-1110
1600 Wildlife Lodge Rd, Lowerburrell, 412-784-1110

General Surgery

Atkinson, Donald Paul (6 mentions)
Certification: Surgery
420 E North Ave #304, Pittsburgh, 412-359-4068

Bartels, Christopher J. (6 mentions)
U of Virginia, 1990 *Certification:* Surgery
100 Delafield Rd #313, Pittsburgh, 412-782-2400

Bartlett, David Lawrence (3 mentions)
U of Texas-Houston, 1987 *Certification:* Surgery
5150 Centre Ave, Pittsburgh, 412-692-2852

Cobb, Charles Franklin (7 mentions)
U of Chicago, 1974 *Certification:* Surgery
320 E North Ave, Pittsburgh, 412-359-3131

Evans, Leonard Elliot (6 mentions)
U of Pittsburgh, 1976 *Certification:* Surgery
5200 Centre Ave #604, Pittsburgh, 412-623-2894

Evans, Steven (6 mentions)
George Washington U, 1985 *Certification:* Surgery
5200 Centre Ave #604, Pittsburgh, 412-623-2894

Fingeret, Arnold E. (3 mentions)
U of Buffalo, 1970 *Certification:* Surgery
1200 Brooks Ln #150, Jefferson Hills, 412-469-7110

Gaines, Barbara Anne (4 mentions)
U of Virginia, 1990
Certification: Pediatric Surgery, Surgery, Surgical Critical Care
3705 5th Ave, Pittsburgh, 412-692-7280

Gannon, Mark Patrick (4 mentions)
U of Pittsburgh, 1986 *Certification:* Surgery
1200 Brooks Ln #150, Clairton, 412-469-7110

Garrett, Kevin Owen (12 mentions)
U of Pittsburgh, 1987 *Certification:* Surgery
100 Delafield Rd #113, Pittsburgh, 412-782-2400

Goldstein, Sharon Lynne (3 mentions)
Albert Einstein Coll of Med, 1995 *Certification:* Surgery
100 Delafield Rd #113, Pittsburgh, 412-782-2400

Hughes, Steven John (4 mentions)
Mayo Med Sch, 1993 *Certification:* Surgery, Surgical Critical Care
3550 Terrace St #497, Pittsburgh, 412-647-0132

Jacob, Timothy Douglas (3 mentions)
Temple U, 1988 *Certification:* Surgery
9104 Babcock Blvd #3111, Pittsburgh, 412-364-5490

Kane, Timothy Dennis (4 mentions)
SUNY-Upstate Med U, 1992
Certification: Pediatric Surgery, Surgery
3705 5th Ave, Pittsburgh, 412-692-6110

Kummant, Peter Karl (3 mentions)
U of Pittsburgh, 1984 *Certification:* Surgery
1200 Brooks Ln #150, Clairton, 412-469-7110

Lee, Kenneth Kwockwah (17 mentions)
U of Chicago, 1981 *Certification:* Surgery
3550 Terrace St #497-S, Pittsburgh, 412-647-0457

Lewis, Richard Peter (7 mentions)
U of Pittsburgh, 1973 *Certification:* Surgery
5750 Centre Ave #430, Pittsburgh, 412-363-8811

Maratta, Jan William (4 mentions)
FMS-Italy, 1970
986 Brodhead Rd, Coraopolis, 412-262-2121
2591 Wexford Bayne Rd, Sewickley, 412-262-2121

McKeating, John Anthony (6 mentions)
U of Pittsburgh, 1985 *Certification:* Surgery
1350 Locust St #407, Pittsburgh, 412-281-2255
3104 Unionville Rd #180, Cranberry Township, 412-281-2255

Ochoa, Juan B. (3 mentions)
FMS-Colombia, 1982
Certification: Surgery, Surgical Critical Care
200 Lothrop St #F-1264, Pittsburgh, 412-647-0421

Peitzman, Andrew Bertram (14 mentions)
U of Pittsburgh, 1976
Certification: Surgery, Surgical Critical Care
200 Lothrop St, Pittsburgh, 412-647-0635

Ripepi, Antonio John (4 mentions)
Jefferson Med Coll, 1993 *Certification:* Surgery
500 N Lewis Run Rd #101, West Mifflin, 412-466-4121

Rubin, Joshua Tarbut (3 mentions)
George Washington U, 1979 *Certification:* Surgery
5115 Centre Ave, Pittsburgh, 412-692-2862

Schraut, Wolfgang Hans (6 mentions)
FMS-Germany, 1970 *Certification:* Surgery
3550 Terrace St #SH-497, Pittsburgh, 412-647-0311

Semins, Howard (3 mentions)
U of Maryland, 1968 *Certification:* Surgery
4815 Liberty Ave, Pittsburgh, 412-578-0282

Young, Joseph Charles (5 mentions)
St Louis U, 1971 *Certification:* Surgery
320 E North Ave, Pittsburgh, 412-359-3131

Geriatrics

Prendergast, John Michael (5 mentions)
FMS-Ireland, 1972
Certification: Geriatric Medicine, Internal Medicine
1350 Locust St #G-102, Pittsburgh, 412-232-8494
393 Vanadium Rd #307, Pittsburgh, 412-232-8494

Resnick, Neil Martin (5 mentions)
Stanford U, 1977 *Certification:* Internal Medicine
3471 5th Ave, Pittsburgh, 412-692-2360

Rodriguez, Eric Gibson (7 mentions)
George Washington U, 1979
Certification: Geriatric Medicine, Internal Medicine
3459 5th Ave 4th Fl, Pittsburgh, 412-692-4200

Rubin, Fred Howard (14 mentions)
Pennsylvania State U, 1975
Certification: Geriatric Medicine, Internal Medicine
5200 Centre Ave #405, Pittsburgh, 412-623-2700

Towers, Adele E. (9 mentions)
U of Connecticut, 1986
Certification: Geriatric Medicine, Internal Medicine
3459 5th Ave 4th Fl, Pittsburgh, 412-692-4200

Hematology/Oncology

Bontempo, Franklin A. (4 mentions)
Hahnemann U, 1976 *Certification:* Internal Medicine
5115 Centre Ave, Pittsburgh, 412-692-4724
3636 Blvd of the Allies, Pittsburgh, 412-209-7406

Brufsky, Adam Matthew (5 mentions)
U of Connecticut, 1990
Certification: Internal Medicine, Medical Oncology
300 Halket St #4628, Pittsburgh, 412-641-4530

Doyle, Alfred Pirnie (5 mentions)
U of Pennsylvania, 1954
Certification: Hematology, Internal Medicine, Medical Oncology
1600 Coraopolis Heights Rd, Coraopolis, 412-329-2500

Ellis, Peter Gerard (11 mentions)
U of Pittsburgh, 1985
Certification: Internal Medicine, Medical Oncology
200 Delafield Rd #3050, Pittsburgh, 412-781-3744

Fierro, Ronald Francis (6 mentions)
Temple U, 1983
Certification: Internal Medicine, Medical Oncology
101 Drake Rd #P, Pittsburgh, 412-831-1320

Friedland, David Michael (7 mentions)
U of Maryland, 1989 *Certification:* Medical Oncology
5115 Centre Ave, Pittsburgh, 412-235-1020

Georgiadis, Mark Sarris (9 mentions)
U of Pennsylvania, 1987
Certification: Hematology, Medical Oncology
200 Delafield Rd #3050, Pittsburgh, 412-781-3744

Greenberg, Larisa (7 mentions)
FMS-Ukraine, 1975 *Certification:* Medical Oncology
320 E North Ave, Pittsburgh, 412-359-6147

Jacobs, Samuel Angel (7 mentions)
U of Rochester, 1971
Certification: Internal Medicine, Medical Oncology
5115 Centre Ave, Pittsburgh, 412-235-1020

Marks, Stanley M. (15 mentions)
U of Pittsburgh, 1973
Certification: Hematology, Internal Medicine
5115 Centre Ave, Pittsburgh, 412-235-1020

Pietragallo, Louis Daniel (4 mentions)
Jefferson Med Coll, 1972
Certification: Hematology, Internal Medicine
101 Drake Rd #B, Pittsburgh, 412-831-1320

Raymond, Jane Molnar (4 mentions)
Brown U, 1986
Certification: Hematology, Internal Medicine, Medical Oncology
320 E North Ave, Pittsburgh, 412-359-6147

Safyan, Eric Lee (8 mentions)
U of Pittsburgh, 1981
Certification: Internal Medicine, Medical Oncology
1400 Locust St #G-104, Pittsburgh, 412-232-7328

Sherry, Michael McClain (7 mentions)
U of Pittsburgh, 1980
Certification: Hematology, Internal Medicine, Medical Oncology
1600 Coraopolis Heights Rd, Coraopolis, 412-329-2500

Spero, Joel A. (4 mentions)
Georgetown U, 1970 *Certification:* Internal Medicine
320 E North Ave, Pittsburgh, 412-359-6147

Wollman, Michael R. (7 mentions)
SUNY-Downstate Med Coll, 1968
Certification: Pediatric Hematology-Oncology, Pediatrics
3705 5th Ave, Pittsburgh, 412-692-5055

Infectious Disease

Byers, Karin Elizabeth (11 mentions)
Temple U, 1991
Certification: Infectious Disease, Internal Medicine
320 E North Ave, Pittsburgh, 412-359-3683
3601 5th Ave, Pittsburgh, 412-648-6401

Colodny, Stephen Michael (10 mentions)
New York Med Coll, 1981
Certification: Infectious Disease, Internal Medicine
101 Drake Rd #C, Pittsburgh, 412-347-0057

Michaels, Marian Gail (7 mentions)
U of Pennsylvania, 1985
Certification: Pediatric Infectious Diseases, Pediatrics
3705 5th Ave, Pittsburgh, 412-692-7438

Pontzer, Raymond Edward (17 mentions)
Med Coll of Pennsylvania, 1979
Certification: Infectious Disease, Internal Medicine
137 Freeport Rd, Aspinwall, 412-784-9440

Rao, Nalini G. (14 mentions)
FMS-India, 1970
Certification: Infectious Disease, Internal Medicine
5750 Centre Ave #510, Pittsburgh, 412-661-1633

Volosky, Robert Louis (14 mentions)
Georgetown U, 1985
Certification: Infectious Disease, Internal Medicine
4778 Liberty Ave, Pittsburgh, 412-681-0966

Weber, David Robert (15 mentions)
U of Maryland, 1981
Certification: Infectious Disease, Internal Medicine
5200 Centre Ave #203, Pittsburgh, 412-578-9747

Infertility

Sanfilippo, Joseph S. (7 mentions)
Rosalind Franklin U, 1973 *Certification:* Obstetrics &
Gynecology, Reproductive Endocrinology/Infertility
300 Halket St, Pittsburgh, 412-641-1204

Wakim, Najib G. (11 mentions)
FMS-Lebanon, 1978 *Certification:* Obstetrics & Gynecology,
Reproductive Endocrinology/Infertility
300 Halket St, Pittsburgh, 412-641-1600

Internal Medicine *(see note on page 9)*

Bigi, Lori M. (4 mentions)
Certification: Internal Medicine
3459 5th Ave #9-S, Pittsburgh, 412-647-1987

Buranosky, Raquel A. (3 mentions)
Duke U, 1994 *Certification:* Internal Medicine
3459 5th Ave, Pittsburgh, 412-692-4888

Campbell, Timothy Michael (6 mentions)
West Virginia U, 1986 *Certification:* Internal Medicine
1400 Locust St #5109, Pittsburgh, 412-281-2575

Donnelly, Edward Joseph (10 mentions)
U of Kansas, 1974 *Certification:* Internal Medicine
3471 5th Ave #101, Pittsburgh, 412-621-3662
241-251 Freeport Rd #3, Pittsburgh, 412-781-8566

Finikiotis, Michael W. (11 mentions)
U of Pittsburgh, 1989 *Certification:* Internal Medicine
6301 Forbes Ave #301, Pittsburgh, 412-422-5970

Gleason, James Andrew (4 mentions)
U of Pittsburgh, 1976 *Certification:* Internal Medicine
1789 S Braddock Ave, Pittsburgh, 412-244-8760
580 S Aiken Ave #400, Pittsburgh, 412-687-8760

Grumet, Bernard Alan (3 mentions)
Jefferson Med Coll, 1972 *Certification:* Internal Medicine
6301 Forbes Ave #301, Pittsburgh, 412-422-5970

Hasley, Peggy Braasch (5 mentions)
U of Pittsburgh, 1985 *Certification:* Internal Medicine
3459 5th Ave, Pittsburgh, 412-692-4888

Itskowitz, Marc Samuel (3 mentions)
Med Coll of Pennsylvania, 1998 *Certification:* Internal Medicine
1307 Federal St #304, Pittsburgh, 412-359-3682
490 E North Ave #107, Pittsburgh, 412-359-3682

Jarvis, James Robert (3 mentions)
U of Pittsburgh, 1996 *Certification:* Internal Medicine
5215 Centre Ave #100, Pittsburgh, 412-623-6200

Kapoor, Wishwa Nath (3 mentions)
Washington U, 1975 *Certification:* Internal Medicine
3459 5th Ave, Pittsburgh, 412-692-4888

Kokales, John George (5 mentions)
U of Pittsburgh, 1973 *Certification:* Internal Medicine
120 Lytton Ave, Pittsburgh, 412-647-4545

Kroboth, Frank James (9 mentions)
SUNY-Upstate Med U, 1976 *Certification:* Internal Medicine
3459 5th Ave, Pittsburgh, 412-692-4888

Kushner, Donald Allen (3 mentions)
U of Pittsburgh, 1989 *Certification:* Internal Medicine
1050 Bower Hill Rd #202, Pittsburgh, 412-572-6122
533 Washington Ave #205, Bridgeville, 412-257-4484

McNeil, Melissa Ann (4 mentions)
U of Pittsburgh, 1980 *Certification:* Internal Medicine
3459 5th Ave, Pittsburgh, 412-692-4888

Philbin, Terence J. (4 mentions)
Loyola U Chicago, 1983 *Certification:* Internal Medicine
92 Bradford Ave, Pittsburgh, 412-922-2111
1400 Locust St, Pittsburgh, 412-922-2111

Rossman, Gerald George (4 mentions)
Hahnemann U, 1984 *Certification:* Internal Medicine
490 E North Ave #200, Pittsburgh, 412-321-8882

Solano, Francis X., Jr. (11 mentions)
Hahnemann U, 1980 *Certification:* Internal Medicine
120 Lytton Ave #1A, Pittsburgh, 412-647-4545

Spinola, Anthony (3 mentions)
U of Pittsburgh, 1995 *Certification:* Internal Medicine
5215 Centre St #100, Pittsburgh, 412-623-6200

Vargo, Scott Michael (4 mentions)
Hahnemann U, 1996 *Certification:* Internal Medicine
1307 Federal St #304, Pittsburgh, 412-359-3682

Wisneski, John Thomas, Jr. (5 mentions)
Washington U, 1981 *Certification:* Internal Medicine
241-251 Freeport Rd #3, Pittsburgh, 412-781-8566
3471 5th Ave #1111, Pittsburgh, 412-621-3662

Nephrology

Ellis, Demetrius (6 mentions)
U of Buffalo, 1973 *Certification:* Pediatric Nephrology, Pediatrics
3705 5th Ave, Pittsburgh, 412-692-5325

Johnston, James Ray (21 mentions)
U of Pittsburgh, 1979
Certification: Internal Medicine, Nephrology
3550 Terrace St #A-915, Pittsburgh, 412-647-8394

Lawlor, Maureen (6 mentions)
Temple U, 1981 *Certification:* Internal Medicine, Nephrology
1401 Forbes Ave #350, Pittsburgh, 412-232-8688

Levenson, David J. (10 mentions)
Harvard U, 1976 *Certification:* Internal Medicine, Nephrology
5140 Liberty Ave, Pittsburgh, 412-683-4550

Mikhael, Nabil Harby (6 mentions)
FMS-Egypt, 1985 *Certification:* Internal Medicine, Nephrology
1200 Brooks Ln #G10, Clairton, 412-469-6956

Mitro, Robert Nicholas (7 mentions)
Philadelphia Coll of Osteopathic Med, 1980
Certification: Internal Medicine, Nephrology
1200 Brooks Ln #G-10, Clairton, 412-469-6956

Moritz, Michael Larcdo (6 mentions)
U of Chicago, 1991 *Certification:* Pediatric Nephrology, Pediatrics
3705 5th Ave, Pittsburgh, 412-692-5325

Piraino, Beth Holley (18 mentions)
Med Coll of Pennsylvania, 1977
Certification: Internal Medicine, Nephrology
3504 5th Ave #200, Pittsburgh, 412-383-4899

Selvaggio, Adriana M. (13 mentions)
Temple U, 1981 *Certification:* Internal Medicine, Nephrology
100 Delafield Rd #215, Pittsburgh, 412-784-5144
5200 Centre Ave #205, Pittsburgh, 412-687-5190
1200 Brooks Ln #G-10, Clairton, 412-469-6956

Neurological Surgery

Baghai, Parviz (8 mentions)
FMS-Iran, 1974 *Certification:* Neurological Surgery
420 E North Ave E Wing #302, Pittsburgh, 412-321-3033

Bejjani, Ghassan K. (10 mentions)
FMS-Lebanon, 1991 *Certification:* Neurological Surgery
532 S Aiken Ave #400, Pittsburgh, 412-623-6910

Bellotte, Jonathan B. (8 mentions)
West Virginia U, 1999
420 E North Ave #302, Pittsburgh, 412-359-6200

Bookwalter, John William (8 mentions)
Loyola U Chicago, 1976 *Certification:* Neurological Surgery
5000 McKnight Rd #202, Pittsburgh, 412-369-4517

Kassam, Amin B. (12 mentions)
FMS-Canada, 1991
200 Lothrop St, Pittsburgh, 412-647-3685

Lunsford, Lawrence Dade (11 mentions)
Columbia U, 1974
200 Lothrop St #F-158, Pittsburgh, 412-647-0953

Maroon, Joseph C. (13 mentions)
Indiana U, 1965 *Certification:* Neurological Surgery
200 Lothrop St, Pittsburgh, 412-647-3604

Pollack, Ian Fredric (7 mentions)
Johns Hopkins U, 1984 *Certification:* Neurological Surgery
3705 5th Ave, Pittsburgh, 412-692-5090

Wecht, Daniel Alan (9 mentions)
U of Pennsylvania, 1989 *Certification:* Neurological Surgery
5200 Centre Ave #616, Pittsburgh, 412-682-4400
500 Hospital Way, McKeesport, 412-647-9341
100 Delafield Rd, Pittsburgh, 412-647-9341
200 Lothrop St, Pittsburgh, 412-647-9341

Neurology

Bergman, Ira (8 mentions)
U of Chicago, 1974 *Certification:* Neurology with Special Qualifications in Child Neurology, Pediatrics
3705 5th Ave, Pittsburgh, 412-692-5520

Berk, H. Ronald (4 mentions)
Ohio State U, 1977 *Certification:* Clinical Neurophysiology, Internal Medicine, Neurology
4815 Liberty Ave #426, Pittsburgh, 412-682-2536

Brillman, Jon (9 mentions)
U of Pittsburgh, 1967 *Certification:* Neurology
420 E North Ave #206, Pittsburgh, 412-359-8850

Busis, Neil Amdur (9 mentions)
U of Pennsylvania, 1977 *Certification:* Neurology
532 S Aiken Ave #507, Pittsburgh, 412-681-2000

Heyman, Rock Alan (4 mentions)
Ohio State U, 1985 *Certification:* Neurology
3471 5th Ave #811, Pittsburgh, 412-692-4920

Kasdan, Richard Bruce (5 mentions)
U of Pittsburgh, 1972 *Certification:* Neurology
5750 Centre Ave #100, Pittsburgh, 412-361-4576
575 Coal Valley Rd #104, Clairton, 412-469-1701
655 Rodi Rd, Pittsburgh, 412-241-7380

Kunschner, Lara Jeanne (6 mentions)
U of Pittsburgh, 1994 *Certification:* Neurology
420 E North Ave #206, Pittsburgh, 412-359-8850

Lacomis, David (7 mentions)
Pennsylvania State U, 1987
Certification: Clinical Neurophysiology, Neurology
3459 5th Ave, Pittsburgh, 412-692-4888

Rice, Eileen Marie R. (4 mentions)
U of Pittsburgh, 1974 *Certification:* Internal Medicine, Neurology
200 Delafield Rd #2000, Pittsburgh, 412-782-4211

Shymansky, J. Stephen (9 mentions)
West Virginia U, 1986 *Certification:* Neurology
2566 Haymaker Rd #101, Monroeville, 412-856-5335

Valeriano, James Philip (4 mentions)
U of Pittsburgh, 1980 *Certification:* Neurology
420 E North Ave #206, Pittsburgh, 412-359-8850

Wechsler, Lawrence R. (13 mentions)
U of Pennsylvania, 1978
Certification: Internal Medicine, Neurology, Vascular Neurology
3471 5th Ave #810, Pittsburgh, 412-692-4924

Weisman, Richard Alan (6 mentions)
U of Pennsylvania, 1969 *Certification:* Neurology
5750 Centre Ave #100, Pittsburgh, 412-361-4576
575 Coal Valley Rd #104, Clairton, 412-361-4576

Zaretskaya, Marina (7 mentions)
Certification: Neurology
1350 Locust St #402, Pittsburgh, 412-232-8683

Obstetrics/Gynecology

Andrew-Jaja, Carey (3 mentions)
Certification: Obstetrics & Gynecology
2599 Wexford Bayne Rd #1000-D, Sewickley, 412-641-8833

Dietrick, David J. (3 mentions)
1350 Locust St #301, Pittsburgh, 412-471-4488
180 Fort Couch Rd #450, Pittsburgh, 412-471-4488

Edwards, Robert Page (3 mentions)
U of Pittsburgh, 1984
Certification: Gynecologic Oncology, Obstetrics & Gynecology
300 Halket St #0610, Pittsburgh, 412-641-5411

Guido, Richard Scott (3 mentions)
U of Rochester, 1987 *Certification:* Obstetrics & Gynecology
300 Halket St, Pittsburgh, 412-641-1440

Hugo, Maryanne (7 mentions)
U of Pittsburgh, 1988 *Certification:* Obstetrics & Gynecology
4075 Monroeville Blvd #222, Monroeville, 412-856-6674
3380 Blvd of the Allies #1, Pittsburgh, 412-621-7575
1330 Old Freeport Rd #1-A, Pittsburgh, 412-784-8844

Kaminski, Robert John (3 mentions)
U of Pittsburgh, 1974 *Certification:* Obstetrics & Gynecology
300 Halkett St #0610, Pittsburgh, 412-641-6412

Krupski, Carol Ann (6 mentions)
U of Pittsburgh, 1982 *Certification:* Obstetrics & Gynecology
850 Clairton Blvd #3100, Pittsburgh, 412-466-2115
300 Halket St, Pittsburgh, 412-641-6223

Moraca, John Idolo (3 mentions)
U of Pittsburgh, 1959 *Certification:* Obstetrics & Gynecology
301 Ohio River Blvd, Sewickley, 412-741-6530
1009 Beaver Grade Rd #200, New Township, 412-264-2450

Morrison, Bruce William (3 mentions)
U of Pennsylvania, 1984 *Certification:* Obstetrics & Gynecology
200 Delafield Rd #2010, Pittsburgh, 412-782-0500

Pollack, Dean Nelson (3 mentions)
New York Med Coll, 1982 *Certification:* Obstetrics & Gynecology
5200 Centre Ave #316, Pittsburgh, 412-621-1660

Portman, Mary Ann (3 mentions)
Temple U, 1975 *Certification:* Obstetrics & Gynecology
300 Halket St, Pittsburgh, 412-641-8889

Rehder, Karen Viestenz (3 mentions)
St Louis U, 1982 *Certification:* Obstetrics & Gynecology
580 S Aiken Ave #500, Pittsburgh, 412-688-3653

Scioscia, Eugene A., Jr. (6 mentions)
U of Pittsburgh, 1985 *Certification:* Obstetrics & Gynecology
490 E North Ave, Pittsburgh, 412-322-4545
320 E North Ave, Pittsburgh, 412-359-3355

Thomas, Robert Drexel (4 mentions)
U of Pittsburgh, 1980 *Certification:* Obstetrics & Gynecology
3380 Blvd of the Allies #1, Pittsburgh, 412-621-7575
1330 Old Freeport Rd #1-A, Pittsburgh, 412-647-1000

Thomas, Ronald Lee (3 mentions)
U of Pittsburgh, 1981
Certification: Maternal-Fetal Medicine, Obstetrics & Gynecology
320 E North Ave, Pittsburgh, 412-359-4186
1307 Federal St #B-100, Pittsburgh, 412-359-3437

Wiesenfeld, Harold C. (8 mentions)
FMS-Canada, 1987 *Certification:* Obstetrics & Gynecology
300 Halket St #0610, Pittsburgh, 412-641-6412

Ophthalmology

Balouris, Chris Anthony (4 mentions)
U of Pittsburgh, 1984 *Certification:* Ophthalmology
200 Delafield Rd #2020, Pittsburgh, 412-784-9060
7000 Stonewood Dr #200, Wexford, 724-940-4001

Charley, John Andrew (4 mentions)
U of Pittsburgh, 1983 *Certification:* Ophthalmology
1340 Old Freeport Rd #1A, Pittsburgh, 412-967-9505

Cheng, Kenneth Paul (5 mentions)
U of Pittsburgh, 1984 *Certification:* Ophthalmology
1000 Stonewood Dr #310, Wexford, 724-934-3333
713 Washington Rd, Pittsburgh, 724-934-3333

Cibik, Lisa Marie (4 mentions)
U of Pittsburgh, 1983 *Certification:* Ophthalmology
125 Daugherty Dr #320, Monroeville, 412-373-3344
9970 Mountain View Dr #200, West Mifflin, 412-653-3080

Condon, Garry Pascal (4 mentions)
FMS-Canada, 1981 *Certification:* Ophthalmology
420 E North Ave #116, Pittsburgh, 412-359-6300

Dhaliwal, Deepinder K. (5 mentions)
Northwestern U, 1990 *Certification:* Ophthalmology
203 Lothrop St 7th Fl, Pittsburgh, 412-647-2200

Olsen, Karl Raymond (4 mentions)
Northwestern U, 1980 *Certification:* Ophthalmology
3501 Forbes Ave #500, Pittsburgh, 412-683-5300
969 Eisenhower Blvd, Johnstown, 412-683-5300

Roba, Laurie Ann (4 mentions)
U of Buffalo, 1988 *Certification:* Ophthalmology
1326 Freeport Rd #200, Pittsburgh, 412-963-0414

Schuman, Joel Steven (4 mentions)
Mount Sinai Sch of Med, 1984 *Certification:* Ophthalmology
203 Lothrop St, Pittsburgh, 412-647-2200

Stafford, Marshall W. (4 mentions)
Jefferson Med Coll, 1990 *Certification:* Ophthalmology
100 Delafield Rd, Pittsburgh, 412-782-5900

Verstraeten, Thierry C. (5 mentions)
FMS-Belgium, 1984 *Certification:* Ophthalmology
420 E North Ave #116, Pittsburgh, 412-359-6300

Watters, Edmond Clair (6 mentions)
George Washington U, 1968 *Certification:* Ophthalmology
100 Delafield Rd #201, Pittsburgh, 412-782-5900

Waxman, Evan Lewis (7 mentions)
Mount Sinai Sch of Med, 1994 *Certification:* Ophthalmology
203 Lothrop St, Pittsburgh, 412-647-2200

Orthopedics

Altman, Daniel T. (6 mentions)
Temple U, 1990 *Certification:* Orthopaedic Surgery
1307 Federal St, Pittsburgh, 412-359-3895

Baratz, Mark Everett (4 mentions)
U of Pittsburgh, 1984
Certification: Orthopaedic Surgery, Surgery of the Hand
1307 Federal St #2, Pittsburgh, 412-359-3895

Bradley, James Philip (13 mentions)
Georgetown U, 1982 *Certification:* Orthopaedic Surgery
200 Delafield Rd #4010, Pittsburgh, 412-784-5770
3400 S Water St, Pittsburgh, 412-784-5770

Burke, Charles Joseph, III (4 mentions)
U of Cincinnati, 1981 *Certification:* Orthopaedic Surgery
200 Delafield Rd #4010, Pittsburgh, 412-784-5770
6001 Stonewood Dr, Wexford, 412-784-5770
1300 Oxford Blvd #1C, Bethel Park, 412-784-5770

Crossett, Lawrence Scott (6 mentions)
Temple U, 1981 *Certification:* Orthopaedic Surgery
5200 Centre Ave #415, Pittsburgh, 412-687-3900
3471 5th Ave #1010, Pittsburgh, 412-687-3900

D'Antonio, James A. (4 mentions)
U of Pittsburgh, 1968 *Certification:* Orthopaedic Surgery
725 Cherrington Pkwy #200, Moon Township, 412-262-7800

De Meo, Patrick Joseph (8 mentions)
Wayne State U, 1986 *Certification:* Orthopaedic Surgery
1307 Federal St #2, Pittsburgh, 412-359-3895

Digioia, Anthony M., III (6 mentions)
Harvard U, 1986 *Certification:* Orthopaedic Surgery
300 Halket St #1601, Pittsburgh, 412-683-7272

Fu, Ho-Keung Fred (10 mentions)
U of Pittsburgh, 1977 *Certification:* Orthopaedic Surgery
5200 Centre Ave #415, Pittsburgh, 412-687-3900

Goitz, Robert Joseph (5 mentions)
Johns Hopkins U, 1992
Certification: Orthopaedic Surgery, Surgery of the Hand
1500 Oxford Dr, Bethel Park, 412-687-3900

Goodman, Mark Alvin (10 mentions)
SUNY-Downstate Med Coll, 1974
Certification: Orthopaedic Surgery
5200 Centre Ave #506, Pittsburgh, 412-687-3900

Groff, Yram Jan (7 mentions)
U of Pittsburgh, 1995 *Certification:* Orthopaedic Surgery
4815 Liberty Ave, Pittsburgh, 412-683-1717

Gruen, Gary Scott (4 mentions)
Temple U, 1983 *Certification:* Orthopaedic Surgery
5200 Centre Ave #415, Pittsburgh, 412-687-3900

Harner, Christopher D. (5 mentions)
U of Michigan, 1981
Certification: Orthopaedic Sports Medicine, Orthopaedic Surgery
3200 S Water St, Pittsburgh, 412-432-3600

Miller, Michael David (5 mentions)
Wayne State U, 1975 *Certification:* Orthopaedic Surgery
5820 Centre Ave, Pittsburgh, 412-661-5500
1030 Broadview Blvd, Brackenridge, 724-224-8700

Papas, Spiro Nicholas (4 mentions)
U of Pittsburgh, 1980 *Certification:* Orthopaedic Surgery
200 Delafield Rd #1040, Pittsburgh, 412-782-3990

Richman, Jory Donald (4 mentions)
Case Western Reserve U, 1986 *Certification:* Orthopaedic Surgery
1350 Locust St #220, Pittsburgh, 412-232-5800

Sangimino, Mark J. (4 mentions)
Certification: Orthopaedic Surgery
1307 Federal St #2, Pittsburgh, 412-359-3895

Silvaggio, Vincent Joseph (4 mentions)
U of Pittsburgh, 1987 *Certification:* Orthopaedic Surgery
200 Delafield Rd #1040, Pittsburgh, 412-782-3990

Sotereanos, Nicholas G. (5 mentions)
Hahnemann U, 1986 *Certification:* Orthopaedic Surgery
1307 Federal St, Pittsburgh, 412-359-3895

Otorhinolaryngology

Arriaga, Moises A. (7 mentions)
Brown U, 1985 *Certification:* Neurotology, Otolaryngology
420 E North Ave #402, Pittsburgh, 412-321-2480

Blaugrund, James Ean (9 mentions)
Yale U, 1992 *Certification:* Otolaryngology
9104 Babcock Blvd #3112, Pittsburgh, 412-321-1810
490 E North Ave #207, Pittsburgh, 412-321-1810

Carrau, Ricardo Luis (7 mentions)
U of Puerto Rico, 1981 *Certification:* Otolaryngology
200 Lothrop St #300, Pittsburgh, 412-647-2100
5200 Centre Ave #211, Pittsburgh, 412-621-0123

De Marino, David Philip (9 mentions)
Pennsylvania State U, 1981 *Certification:* Otolaryngology
1300 Oxford Dr #LLC, Bethel Park, 412-831-7570
575 Coal Valley Rd #511, Clairton, 412-466-0101

Golla, Suman (8 mentions)
U of Maryland, 1995
203 Lothrop St #500, Pittsburgh, 412-647-2100

Gottlieb, Michael Alan (6 mentions)
Temple U, 1986 *Certification:* Otolaryngology
3447 Forbes Ave, Pittsburgh, 412-681-2300
500 Hospital Way, McKeesport, 412-664-2795
2580 Haymaker Rd #105, Monroeville, 412-372-3336

Hirsch, Barry Eliot (6 mentions)
U of Pennsylvania, 1977
Certification: Neurotology, Otolaryngology
203 Lothrop St #300, Pittsburgh, 412-647-2100
5200 Centre Ave #211, Pittsburgh, 412-621-0123

Johnson, Jonas Talmadge (14 mentions)
SUNY-Upstate Med U, 1972 *Certification:* Otolaryngology
200 Lothrop St #300, Pittsburgh, 412-647-2100
5200 Centre Ave #211, Pittsburgh, 412-621-0123

Pollice, Philip Adelmo (6 mentions)
U of Pennsylvania, 1991 *Certification:* Otolaryngology
9104 Babcock Blvd #3112, Pittsburgh, 412-366-3889
501 Smith Dr #1, Cranberry Township, 724-772-2711
1400 Locust St #D-5122, Pittsburgh, 412-281-0322

Schaitkin, Barry Michael (10 mentions)
Pennsylvania State U, 1984 *Certification:* Otolaryngology
5200 Centre Ave, Pittsburgh, 412-621-0123

Snyderman, Carl Henry (6 mentions)
U of Chicago, 1982 *Certification:* Otolaryngology
200 Lothrop St #300, Pittsburgh, 412-647-2100
5200 Centre Ave #211, Pittsburgh, 412-621-0123

Turner, Joseph (11 mentions)
Ohio State U, 1975 *Certification:* Otolaryngology
3447 Forbes Ave, Pittsburgh, 412-681-2300
2580 Haymaker Rd #105, Monroeville, 412-372-3336

Pain Medicine

Bernstein, Cheryl Denise (5 mentions)
U of Rochester, 1994 *Certification:* Neurology, Pain Medicine
5750 Centre Ave #400, Pittsburgh, 412-665-8030

Chelly, Jacques Elie (5 mentions)
FMS-France, 1976
5230 Centre Ave #M-104, Pittsburgh, 412-623-4135
200 Lothrop St, Pittsburgh, 412-647-3260

Cope, Doris Kathleen (9 mentions)
Med Coll of Georgia, 1982
Certification: Anesthesiology, Pain Medicine
200 Delafield Rd, Pittsburgh, 412-784-5119

Kabazie, Abraham John, Jr. (9 mentions)
Med Coll of Pennsylvania, 1992
Certification: Anesthesiology, Pain Medicine
5124 Liberty Ave, Pittsburgh, 412-578-5635

Pathology

Jaffe, Ronald (3 mentions)
FMS-South Africa, 1969
Certification: Anatomic Pathology, Pediatric Pathology
3705 5th Ave, Pittsburgh, 412-692-5650

MacPherson, Trevor A. (5 mentions)
FMS-South Africa, 1970 *Certification:* Anatomic Pathology
300 Halket St #4420, Pittsburgh, 412-641-4641

Mostoufizadeh, Mahpareh (3 mentions)
FMS-Iran, 1973
Certification: Anatomic Pathology, Clinical Pathology
5499 William Flynn Hwy, Gibsonia, 412-247-4500

Silverman, Jan Franklin (6 mentions)
Virginia Commonwealth U, 1970 *Certification:* Anatomic
   Pathology & Clinical Pathology, Cytopathology
320 E North Ave, Pittsburgh, 412-359-3526

Singh, Jagjit (3 mentions)
FMS-India, 1982 *Certification:* Anatomic Pathology &
   Clinical Pathology, Cytopathology
815 Freeport Rd, Pittsburgh, 412-784-4130

Swerdlow, Steven Howard (3 mentions)
Harvard U, 1975
Certification: Anatomic Pathology & Clinical Pathology
200 Lothrop St, Pittsburgh, 412-647-5191

Teot, Lisa Anne (3 mentions)
George Washington U, 1986 *Certification:* Anatomic
   Pathology & Clinical Pathology, Cytopathology
5150 Center Ave, Pittsburgh, 412-623-3765

Yousem, Samuel Alan (4 mentions)
U of Maryland, 1981
Certification: Anatomic Pathology, Cytopathology
200 Lothrop St #A610, Pittsburgh, 412-647-6193

Pediatrics *(see note on page 9)*

Agustin, Amelia V. (3 mentions)
FMS-Philippines, 1965 *Certification:* Pediatrics
20397 Route 19 #220, Cranberry Township, 724-772-5430

Butler, Lawrence James (4 mentions)
U of Pittsburgh, 1990 *Certification:* Pediatrics
4923 Centre Ave, Pittsburgh, 412-681-1050

Cowden, Sharon Norrine (3 mentions)
U of Pittsburgh, 1990 *Certification:* Pediatrics
4923 Centre Ave, Pittsburgh, 412-681-1050

Giga, Judith Sue (3 mentions)
Ohio State U, 1975 *Certification:* Pediatrics
1370 Washington Pike #107, Bridgeville, 412-221-0160

Hofkosh, Dena (3 mentions)
New York U, 1979
Certification: Neurodevelopmental Disabilities, Pediatrics
3705 5th Ave, Pittsburgh, 412-692-6530

McIntire, Sara Charlotte (3 mentions)
U of California-Davis, 1984 *Certification:* Pediatrics
3705 5th Ave, Pittsburgh, 412-692-5325

Rowland, Paul Leslie, III (8 mentions)
U of Pittsburgh, 1990 *Certification:* Pediatrics
4923 Centre Ave, Pittsburgh, 412-681-1050

Serbin, Scott Ronald (3 mentions)
U of Pittsburgh, 1982 *Certification:* Pediatrics
1606 Twin Oaks Dr, Sewickley, 412-366-1266

Tucker, James Newman (3 mentions)
Columbia U, 1978 *Certification:* Pediatrics
105 Gamma Dr #300, Pittsburgh, 724-224-3900

Urbach, Andrew Harley (3 mentions)
U of Buffalo, 1979 *Certification:* Pediatrics
3705 5th Ave, Pittsburgh, 412-692-5325

Wolynn, Todd Howard (3 mentions)
U of Pittsburgh, 1992 *Certification:* Pediatrics
850 Clairton Blvd #3300, Pittsburgh, 412-466-5004
4070 Beechwood Blvd, Pittsburgh, 412-521-6511

Zitelli, Basil John (8 mentions)
U of Pittsburgh, 1971 *Certification:* Pediatrics
3705 5th Ave, Pittsburgh, 412-692-5325

Plastic Surgery

Edington, Howard David J. (10 mentions)
Temple U, 1981 *Certification:* Plastic Surgery, Surgery
300 Halket St, Pittsburgh, 412-641-4274
5150 Centre Ave, Pittsburgh, 412-692-2852

Heckler, Frederick Roger (11 mentions)
Tufts U, 1966
Certification: Plastic Surgery, Surgery, Surgery of the Hand
320 E North Ave #401, Pittsburgh, 412-359-4352

Liang, Marc Daniel (16 mentions)
U of Cincinnati, 1978 *Certification:* Plastic Surgery
580 S Aiken Ave #203, Pittsburgh, 412-687-3950

Russavage, James Michael (9 mentions)
U of Pittsburgh, 1987 *Certification:* Plastic Surgery
3601 5th Ave, Pittsburgh, 724-832-3892
3471 5th Ave #1103, Pittsburgh, 412-647-6485

Shestak, Kenneth C. (8 mentions)
Tufts U, 1976 *Certification:* Plastic Surgery
3380 Blvd of the Allies #158, Pittsburgh, 412-641-4828

Stofman, Guy Marc (7 mentions)
Jefferson Med Coll, 1984
Certification: Otolaryngology, Plastic Surgery
1350 Locust St #G-103, Pittsburgh, 412-232-5616

Swartz, William Michael (11 mentions)
U of Colorado, 1972
Certification: Plastic Surgery, Surgery of the Hand
5750 Centre Ave #180, Pittsburgh, 412-661-5380

White, Michael John (15 mentions)
U of Wisconsin, 1980
Certification: Plastic Surgery, Surgery of the Hand
320 E North Ave, Pittsburgh, 412-359-4352
9365 McKnight Rd #200, Pittsburgh, 412-367-8998

Psychiatry

Birmaher, Boris (3 mentions)
FMS-Colombia, 1977
Certification: Child & Adolescent Psychiatry, Psychiatry
3811 Ohara St, Pittsburgh, 412-624-2100
300 Halket St, Pittsburgh, 412-624-1000

Borrero, Guillermo (5 mentions)
FMS-Colombia, 1967 *Certification:* Psychiatry
575 Coal Valley Rd #303, Clairton, 412-469-8933

Haskett, Roger (4 mentions)
FMS-Australia, 1968 *Certification:* Psychiatry
3811 O'Hara St, Pittsburgh, 412-624-2100

Kupfer, David Jerome (4 mentions)
Yale U, 1965 *Certification:* Psychiatry
3811 O'Hara St, Pittsburgh, 412-624-2100

Meyer, Viveca Ann (3 mentions)
Eastern Virginia Med Sch, 1980
Certification: Child & Adolescent Psychiatry, Psychiatry
300 Halket St, Pittsburgh, 412-624-1000

Nathan, Swami (7 mentions)
FMS-India, 1969 *Certification:* Psychiatry
4 Allegheny Ctr, Pittsburgh, 412-330-4363

Spina, Horacio A. (3 mentions)
FMS-Argentina, 1968 *Certification:* Psychiatry
1050 Bower Hill Rd #303, Pittsburgh, 412-561-5775

Pulmonary Disease

Carlin, Brian Wintrode (5 mentions)
Pennsylvania State U, 1981 *Certification:* Critical Care
   Medicine, Internal Medicine, Pulmonary Disease
490 E North Ave #300, Pittsburgh, 412-321-3344

Celko, David Al (4 mentions)
Hahnemann U, 1975 *Certification:* Internal Medicine
1050 Bower Hill Rd #306, Pittsburgh, 412-572-6168
40 E Pike St, Canonsburg, 724-746-0744

Donahoe, Michael Patrick (4 mentions)
Hahnemann U, 1983 *Certification:* Critical Care Medicine,
   Internal Medicine, Pulmonary Disease
3459 5th Ave, Pittsburgh, 412-648-6161

Faber, Christopher Neal (7 mentions)
U of Pittsburgh, 1984 *Certification:* Critical Care Medicine,
   Internal Medicine, Pulmonary Disease
3459 5th Ave, Pittsburgh, 412-648-6161

Fiehler, Paul Cecil (4 mentions)
U of Pittsburgh, 1976 *Certification:* Geriatric Medicine,
   Internal Medicine, Pulmonary Disease, Sleep Medicine
5131 Liberty Ave, Pittsburgh, 412-687-5573
1601 Union Ave #E, Natrona Heights, 724-226-8217

Hammerman, Samuel I. (6 mentions)
Certification: Critical Care Medicine, Internal Medicine,
   Pulmonary Disease
5200 Centre Ave #610, Pittsburgh, 412-304-8804

Harris, Steven Phillip (4 mentions)
U of Buffalo, 1991 *Certification:* Critical Care Medicine,
   Internal Medicine, Pulmonary Disease
9104 Babcock Blvd #2103, Pittsburgh, 412-367-5020

Kaplan, Peter Donald (6 mentions)
U of Illinois, 1967
Certification: Internal Medicine, Pulmonary Disease
490 E North Ave #300, Pittsburgh, 412-321-3344

Kreit, John William, Jr. (5 mentions)
Duke U, 1981 *Certification:* Critical Care Medicine, Internal
  Medicine, Pulmonary Disease
3601 5th Ave, Pittsburgh, 412-648-6161

Kurland, Geoffrey (4 mentions)
Stanford U, 1973 *Certification:* Allergy & Immunology,
  Pediatric Pulmonology, Pediatrics
3705 5th Ave, Pittsburgh, 412-692-5630

Laufe, Marc David (4 mentions)
U of Pennsylvania, 1981 *Certification:* Critical Care
  Medicine, Internal Medicine, Pulmonary Disease
5200 Centre Ave #304, Pittsburgh, 412-687-6400

Patti, Mitchell James (13 mentions)
SUNY-Downstate Med Coll, 1986 *Certification:* Critical Care
  Medicine, Internal Medicine, Pulmonary Disease
200 Delafield Rd #2040, Pittsburgh, 412-784-5888

Raffensperger, John A. (5 mentions)
U of Pittsburgh, 1985 *Certification:* Critical Care Medicine,
  Internal Medicine, Pulmonary Disease
200 Delafield Rd #2040, Pittsburgh, 412-784-5888

Reilly, Patrick Gerard (4 mentions)
FMS-Ireland, 1987 *Certification:* Critical Care Medicine,
  Internal Medicine, Pulmonary Disease
1350 Locust St #308, Pittsburgh, 412-232-5549

Schauble, Thomas Lee (4 mentions)
Temple U, 1983 *Certification:* Critical Care Medicine,
  Internal Medicine, Pulmonary Disease
9104 Babcock Blvd #2103, Pittsburgh, 412-367-5020

Sotos, Steven N. (4 mentions)
FMS-Greece, 1971
Certification: Internal Medicine, Pulmonary Disease
2580 Haymaker Rd #301, Monroeville, 412-373-7247

Stiller, Ronald A. (4 mentions)
George Washington U, 1982 *Certification:* Critical Care
  Medicine, Internal Medicine, Pulmonary Disease
5200 Centre Ave, Pittsburgh, 412-621-1200
580 S Aiken Ave #400, Pittsburgh, 412-687-3355

Strollo, Patrick J., Jr. (9 mentions)
Uniformed Services U of Health Sciences, 1981
Certification: Internal Medicine, Pulmonary Disease, Sleep
  Medicine
3459 5th Ave, Pittsburgh, 412-692-2880

Weinberg, Joel Howard (6 mentions)
U of Pittsburgh, 1976 *Certification:* Critical Care Medicine,
  Internal Medicine, Pulmonary Disease
5200 Centre Ave, Pittsburgh, 412-621-1200

Wilson, David Oscar (7 mentions)
U of Pittsburgh, 1980 *Certification:* Critical Care Medicine,
  Internal Medicine, Occupational Medicine, Pulmonary Disease
580 S Aiken Ave #400, Pittsburgh, 412-687-3355
5115 Centre Ave, Pittsburgh, 412-687-3355

Zikos, Antonios (10 mentions)
Philadelphia Coll of Osteopathic Med, 1983 *Certification:*
  Critical Care Medicine, Internal Medicine, Pulmonary Disease
490 E North Ave #301, Pittsburgh, 412-322-7202

Radiology—Diagnostic

Beasley, Harley Scott (3 mentions)
Indiana U, 1993 *Certification:* Diagnostic Radiology
370 S 5th Ave #3950, Pittsburgh, 412-647-3550

Branstetter, Barton F., IV (5 mentions)
U of California-San Diego, 1995
Certification: Diagnostic Radiology, Neuroradiology
200 Lothrop St, Pittsburgh, 412-647-3530

Carlin, Beatrice A. (5 mentions)
U of Pittsburgh, 1979 *Certification:* Diagnostic Radiology
1400 Locust St, Pittsburgh, 412-232-7909

Drnovsek, Valerie (3 mentions)
FMS-Croatia, 1987 *Certification:* Diagnostic Radiology
565 Coal Valley Rd, Pittsburgh, 412-469-5715

Federle, Michael Peter (9 mentions)
Georgetown U, 1974 *Certification:* Diagnostic Radiology
200 Lothrop St, Pittsburgh, 412-647-3550

Fuhrman, Carl Robert (11 mentions)
U of Pittsburgh, 1979 *Certification:* Diagnostic Radiology
200 Lothrop St #E-177, Pittsburgh, 412-647-7288

Fukui, Melanie B. (6 mentions)
U of Pittsburgh, 1987
Certification: Diagnostic Radiology, Neuroradiology
320 E North Ave, Pittsburgh, 412-359-3131

Lupetin, Anthony Robert (5 mentions)
SUNY-Downstate Med Coll, 1976
Certification: Diagnostic Radiology
320 E North Ave, Pittsburgh, 412-359-3131

Sumkin, Jules (4 mentions)
Ohio U Coll of Osteopathic Med, 1980
Certification: Diagnostic Radiology
300 Halket St, Pittsburgh, 412-641-1976

Towers, Jeffrey Dalton (3 mentions)
U of Connecticut, 1986 *Certification:* Diagnostic Radiology
200 Lothrop St, Pittsburgh, 412-647-3553

Tublin, Mitchell Evan (5 mentions)
U of Buffalo, 1988 *Certification:* Diagnostic Radiology
200 Lothrop St, Pittsburgh, 412-647-3550
3601 5th Ave, Pittsburgh, 412-647-4900

Radiology—Therapeutic

Beriwal, Sushil (4 mentions)
FMS-India, 1994 *Certification:* Radiation Oncology
300 Halket St, Pittsburgh, 412-641-4600

Deutsch, Melvin (7 mentions)
New York U, 1964 *Certification:* Therapeutic Radiology
200 Lothrop St 3rd Fl, Pittsburgh, 412-647-3600

Flickinger, John Charles (4 mentions)
U of Chicago, 1981 *Certification:* Therapeutic Radiology
200 Lothrop St, Pittsburgh, 412-647-3600

Gabriele, Michael W. (3 mentions)
Certification: Diagnostic Radiology, Vascular &
  Interventional Radiology
720 Blackburn Rd, Sewickley, 412-749-7230

Kiproff, Paul Michael (6 mentions)
Jefferson Med Coll, 1984 *Certification:* Diagnostic
  Radiology, Vascular & Interventional Radiology
320 E North Ave, Pittsburgh, 412-359-4163

Ku, Andrew (3 mentions)
Columbia U, 1984
Certification: Diagnostic Radiology, Neuroradiology
320 E North Ave, Pittsburgh, 412-359-4163

McLean, Gordon Kennedy (3 mentions)
Dartmouth Coll, 1975 *Certification:* Diagnostic Radiology,
  Vascular & Interventional Radiology
4800 Friendship Ave, Pittsburgh, 412-578-1790

Wholey, Mark H. (8 mentions)
Hahnemann U, 1953 *Certification:* Radiology
5230 Centre Ave #EG-01, Pittsburgh, 412-623-2083

Rehabilitation

Goldberg, Gary (5 mentions)
FMS-Canada, 1977
Certification: Physical Medicine & Rehabilitation
1350 Locust St #409, Pittsburgh, 412-232-7608

Ketzan, Tibor (5 mentions)
FMS-Hungary, 1972
Certification: Physical Medicine & Rehabilitation
720 Blackburn Rd, Sewickley, 412-749-7127

Lieber, Paul Spencer (4 mentions)
Rosalind Franklin U, 1986
Certification: Pain Medicine, Physical Medicine & Rehabilitation
107 Gamma Dr #220, Pittsburgh, 412-963-6480

Munin, Michael Craig (6 mentions)
Jefferson Med Coll, 1988
Certification: Physical Medicine & Rehabilitation
200 Lothrop St, Pittsburgh, 412-692-4400
3471 5th Ave #1010, Pittsburgh, 412-692-4400

Reidy, Edward Donahue (4 mentions)
U of Buffalo, 1994
Certification: Physical Medicine & Rehabilitation
9401 McKnight Rd #202, Pittsburgh, 412-367-0600
142 Clearview Cir, Butler, 412-367-0600

Swan, Barbara Ellen (6 mentions)
Jefferson Med Coll, 1981
Certification: Physical Medicine & Rehabilitation
1307 Federal St #2, Pittsburgh, 877-660-6777

Rheumatology

Achkar, Antonio Amin (7 mentions)
Case Western Reserve U, 1988
Certification: Internal Medicine, Rheumatology
3500 5th Ave, Pittsburgh, 412-682-2434

Helfrich, David John (15 mentions)
U of Pittsburgh, 1983
Certification: Internal Medicine, Rheumatology
2000 Oxford Dr #113, Bethel Park, 412-831-1929
1000 Locust St #G-102, Pittsburgh, 412-232-5539

Medsger, Thomas Arnold, Jr. (11 mentions)
U of Pennsylvania, 1962
Certification: Internal Medicine, Rheumatology
3601 5th Ave #2-B, Pittsburgh, 412-647-6700

Oddis, Chester Vincent (9 mentions)
Pennsylvania State U, 1980
Certification: Internal Medicine, Rheumatology
3601 5th Ave #2-B, Pittsburgh, 412-647-6700

Osial, Thaddeus A., Jr. (9 mentions)
U of Pittsburgh, 1976
Certification: Internal Medicine, Rheumatology
200 Delafield Rd #4040, Pittsburgh, 412-784-1466
339 6th Ave 4th Fl, Pittsburgh, 412-281-1594

Starz, Terence Weaver (13 mentions)
Jefferson Med Coll, 1971
Certification: Internal Medicine, Rheumatology
3500 5th Ave 4th Fl, Pittsburgh, 412-682-2434

Wasko, Mary C. Morgan (6 mentions)
U of North Carolina, 1983
Certification: Internal Medicine, Rheumatology
3601 5th Ave #5-B, Pittsburgh, 412-647-6700

Thoracic Surgery

Christie, Neil Alexander (15 mentions)
FMS-Canada, 1987 *Certification:* Thoracic Surgery
5200 Centre Ave #715, Pittsburgh, 412-623-2025
200 Lothrop St, Pittsburgh, 412-647-4700

Ferson, Peter Fleming (9 mentions)
U of Pittsburgh, 1973 *Certification:* Thoracic Surgery
200 Lothrop St #C-800, Pittsburgh, 412-647-7555

Keenan, Robert James (17 mentions)
FMS-Canada, 1984 *Certification:* Surgery
320 E North Ave #363, Pittsburgh, 412-359-6137

Maley, Richard Hardy (10 mentions)
Hahnemann U, 1988 *Certification:* Surgery, Thoracic Surgery
320 E North Ave #363, Pittsburgh, 412-359-8820

Pettiford, Brian Lamar (9 mentions)
U of Pittsburgh, 1996 *Certification:* Surgery, Thoracic Surgery
200 Lothrop St, Pittsburgh, 412-647-7371

Urology

Benoit, Ronald Martin, Jr. (8 mentions)
U of Pittsburgh, 1990 *Certification:* Urology
5200 Centre Ave #209, Pittsburgh, 412-605-3021

Cohen, Jeffrey Kirk (12 mentions)
SUNY-Upstate Med U, 1979 *Certification:* Urology
2360 Hospital Dr, Aliquippa, 724-857-0530
1307 Federal St #300, Pittsburgh, 412-281-1757
4141 Washington Rd, McMurray, 724-225-0990

Franz, John (6 mentions)
Georgetown U, 1968 *Certification:* Urology
200 Delafield Rd #3060, Pittsburgh, 412-781-6448
1050 Bower Hill Rd #101, Pittsburgh, 412-572-6194

Gup, Daniel Irvin (7 mentions)
U of Pennsylvania, 1984 *Certification:* Urology
200 Delafield Rd, Pittsburgh, 412-781-6448

Hrebinko, Ronald Lee, Jr. (7 mentions)
U of Pittsburgh, 1986 *Certification:* Urology
5200 Centre Ave Med Ctr Bldg #209, Pittsburgh, 412-605-3022

Miller, Ralph J., Jr. (10 mentions)
U of Pittsburgh, 1984 *Certification:* Urology
1307 Federal St #300, Pittsburgh, 412-281-1757
105 Bradford Rd #100, Wexford, 724-934-1488
Heatherbre Sq, Indiana, 724-465-2056
320 E North Ave, Pittsburgh, 412-281-1757

Nelson, Joel Byron (20 mentions)
Northwestern U, 1988 *Certification:* Urology
5200 Centre Ave #209, Pittsburgh, 412-605-3013

Sagan, Elizabeth Rose (10 mentions)
U of Pittsburgh, 1979 *Certification:* Urology
300 Halket St #2541, Pittsburgh, 412-641-1818

Sholder, Arnold Jay (7 mentions)
U of Illinois, 1979 *Certification:* Urology
1050 Bower Hill Rd #105, Pittsburgh, 412-572-6194
200 Delafield Rd #3060, Pittsburgh, 412-781-6448

Vascular Surgery

Leers, Steven A. (11 mentions)
U of Massachusetts, 1978 *Certification:* Vascular Surgery
5200 Centre Ave #307, Pittsburgh, 412-623-3333
815 Freeport Ave #113, Pittsburgh, 412-623-3333
329 S Pleasant Ave, Somerset, 412-623-3333

Makaroun, Michel S. (20 mentions)
FMS-Lebanon, 1978 *Certification:* Surgery, Vascular Surgery
200 Lothrop St #A-1011, Pittsburgh, 412-623-3333

Steed, David Luther (17 mentions)
U of Pittsburgh, 1973 *Certification:* Surgery, Vascular Surgery
200 Lothrop St #A-1011, Pittsburgh, 412-623-3333

Rhode Island

Allergy/Immunology

Katzen, David Robert (14 mentions)
Albert Einstein Coll of Med, 1979
Certification: Allergy & Immunology, Pediatrics
400 Bald Hill Rd #527, Warwick, 401-739-5901

Ricci, Anthony Raymond (23 mentions)
Brown U, 1984
63 Cedar Ave #7, East Greenwich, 401-885-5757

Zwetchkenbaum, John F. (18 mentions)
Boston U, 1985
Certification: Allergy & Immunology, Internal Medicine
1065 Hope St, Providence, 401-751-1235
2 Wake Robin Rd #201, Lincoln, 401-334-0410

Anesthesiology

Barakat, Abdul R. (6 mentions)
Certification: Anesthesiology, Critical Care Medicine, Pain Medicine
219 Cass Ave #13, Woonsocket, 401-766-7700

Baziotis, Peter E. (7 mentions)
Brown U, 1990 *Certification:* Anesthesiology
111 Brewster St, Pawtucket, 401-729-2849
200 Main St #350, Pawtucket, 401-365-6300

Bert, Arthur Anthony (7 mentions)
Mount Sinai Sch of Med, 1981 *Certification:* Anesthesiology
593 Eddy St, Providence, 401-444-5142

Browning, Richard Amblard (5 mentions)
Brown U, 1978 *Certification:* Anesthesiology, Pediatrics
593 Eddy St, Providence, 401-444-5142

Chang, Su-Pen B. (3 mentions)
Brown U, 1988
Certification: Anesthesiology, Critical Care Medicine
164 Summit Ave, Providence, 401-793-4575

Connelly, Timothy G. (6 mentions)
U of New England Coll of Osteopathic Med, 1986
Certification: Anesthesiology
825 Chalkstone Ave, Providence, 401-456-2125

Migliori, Julius C. (3 mentions)
FMS-Italy, 1957 *Certification:* Anesthesiology
200 High Service Ave, North Providence, 401-456-3139
18 Applewood Rd, Cranston, 401-456-3139

Minn, Mary Christine (5 mentions)
New York U, 1991 *Certification:* Anesthesiology, Pain Medicine
25 Wells St, Westerly, 401-596-7477

Cardiac Surgery

Fingleton, James Gerard (32 mentions)
Temple U, 1985 *Certification:* Thoracic Surgery
208 Collyer St, Providence, 401-421-4200

Singh, Arun Kumar (59 mentions)
FMS-India, 1967 *Certification:* Surgery, Thoracic Surgery
2 Dudley St #470, Providence, 401-274-7546

Cardiology

Bourganos, George (4 mentions)
Certification: Cardiovascular Disease
35 Wells St, Westerly, 401-596-7880

Drew, Thomas Martin (5 mentions)
Columbia U, 1971 *Certification:* Cardiovascular Disease, Internal Medicine, Interventional Cardiology
2 Dudley St #360, Providence, 401-444-4501
450 Veterans Memorial Pkwy Bldg 15-1, East Providence, 401-228-2020

Feit, Lloyd Robert (8 mentions)
SUNY-Downstate Med Coll, 1984
Certification: Pediatric Cardiology, Pediatrics
593 Eddy St, Providence, 401-444-5984
1 Hoppin St, Providence, 401-444-4612

Fera, Steven Raymond (7 mentions)
Georgetown U, 1981
Certification: Cardiovascular Disease, Internal Medicine
70 Kenyon Ave #103, Wakefield, 401-789-5770
320 Phillips St #204, North Kingstown, 401-294-5831
426 Scrabbletown Rd #F, North Kingstown, 401-294-5831

Gilson, Michael Frederick (4 mentions)
Columbia U, 1986
Certification: Cardiovascular Disease, Internal Medicine
450 Veterans Memorial Pkwy Bldg 15, East Providence, 401-435-3220

Gutman, Ned Henry (5 mentions)
U of Maryland, 1989 *Certification:* Cardiovascular Disease
19 Friendship St, Newport, 401-849-0844
407 East Ave #130, Pawtucket, 401-726-7776

Korr, Kenneth Spencer (5 mentions)
FMS-Spain, 1975 *Certification:* Cardiovascular Disease, Internal Medicine, Interventional Cardiology
208 Collyer St #101, Providence, 401-793-7191

Lanna, Thomas V. (5 mentions)
Brown U, 1992 *Certification:* Cardiovascular Disease
68 Cumberland St #103, Woonsocket, 401-762-3838

Levin, William Allan (8 mentions)
U of Vermont, 1975
Certification: Cardiovascular Disease, Internal Medicine
41 Sardenson Rd #205, Smithfield, 401-349-0366

Levine, Daniel Jonathan (17 mentions)
Columbia U, 1987
Certification: Cardiovascular Disease, Internal Medicine
450 Veterans Mem Pkwy Bldg 15, East Providence, 401-228-2020

Luttmann, Christopher J. (9 mentions)
Albany Med Coll, 1982
Certification: Cardiovascular Disease, Internal Medicine
407 East Ave #130, Pawtucket, 401-849-0844
19 Friendship St, Newport, 401-849-0844

Mazza, Joseph P. (14 mentions)
George Washington U, 1989 *Certification:* Cardiovascular Disease
68 Cumberland St, Woonsocket, 401-762-3838

Noonan, Thomas Edward (4 mentions)
Tufts U, 1991 *Certification:* Cardiovascular Disease
333 School St #206, Pawtucket, 401-723-1210
1 Randall Sq #401, Providence, 401-223-0223

Sadaniantz, Ara (5 mentions)
SUNY-Downstate Med Coll, 1981
Certification: Cardiovascular Disease, Internal Medicine
1 Randall Sq #305, Providence, 401-223-0223

Spinale, Joseph W. (4 mentions)
Ohio U Coll of Osteopathic Med, 1989
1076 N Main St #3, Providence, 401-273-2552

Williams, David Owen (7 mentions)
Hahnemann U, 1969 *Certification:* Cardiovascular Disease, Internal Medicine, Interventional Cardiology
593 Eddy St, Providence, 401-444-4581
2 Dudley St #360, Providence, 401-444-4581

Ziegler, James William (4 mentions)
U of Florida, 1984 *Certification:* Pediatric Cardiology, Pediatrics
593 Eddy St, Providence, 401-444-4612

Dermatology

Farrell, David Sears (7 mentions)
U of Cincinnati, 1976 *Certification:* Dermatology
450 Veterans Memorial Pkwy Bldg 11-2, East Providence, 401-438-9150

Frankel, Ellen Henrie (10 mentions)
New York Med Coll, 1979
750 Reservoir Ave, Cranston, 401-943-0761

Iler, Lynn Elizabeth (9 mentions)
Brown U, 1995 *Certification:* Dermatology
400 Bald Hill Rd, Warwick, 401-738-4323

McDonald, Charles J. (10 mentions)
Howard U, 1960 *Certification:* Dermatology
593 Eddy St #APC-10, Providence, 401-444-7959

Pedvis-Leftick, Anita (6 mentions)
FMS-Canada, 1974 *Certification:* Dermatology
50 Maude St, Providence, 401-456-2590
1351 S County Trail #302, East Greenwich, 401-886-5663

Solis, Jon Stephen (9 mentions)
Uniformed Services U of Health Sciences, 1985
Certification: Dermatology
17 Wells St #203, Westerly, 401-348-0660

Vittimberga, Gwenn M. (8 mentions)
Brown U, 1985 *Certification:* Dermatology
1180 Hope St, Bristol, 401-253-8900
286 Maple Ave, Barrington, 401-247-0610

Wilkel, Caroline Susan (7 mentions)
U of Connecticut, 1985
Certification: Dermatology, Dermatopathology
2850 S County Trail #2, East Greenwich, 401-885-4100

Emergency Medicine

Anderson, Angela Clyneta (10 mentions)
Case Western Reserve U, 1985
Certification: Pediatric Emergency Medicine, Pediatrics
593 Eddy St, Providence, 401-444-4900

Bubly, Gary (7 mentions)
U of Massachusetts, 1987
Certification: Emergency Medicine, Internal Medicine
164 Summit Ave, Providence, 401-793-3100

Callahan, Charles Michael (3 mentions)
Temple U, 1979
164 Summit Ave, Providence, 401-793-3100

Conlin, William Michael (4 mentions)
New Jersey Med Sch, 1978
Certification: Emergency Medicine, Internal Medicine
25 Wells St, Westerly, 401-596-6000

Dinwoodie, Robert G. (8 mentions)
U of New England Coll of Osteopathic Med, 1986
30 Hill Dr, East Greenwich, 401-737-7010

Drury, Timothy Robert (7 mentions)
Pennsylvania State U, 1974
Certification: Emergency Medicine, Sports Medicine
100 Kenyon Ave, Wakefield, 401-782-8000

Germano, Thomas Gary (3 mentions)
Georgetown U, 1989 *Certification:* Emergency Medicine
455 Toll Gate Rd, Warwick, 401-736-4288
164 Summit Ave, Providence, 401-793-3100

Graves, Peter Frederick (3 mentions)
U of Massachusetts, 1999 *Certification:* Emergency Medicine
11 Friendship St, Newport, 401-845-1593

Hebel, Glenn Arnold (6 mentions)
U of California-San Diego, 1991
Certification: Emergency Medicine
11 Friendship St, Newport, 401-845-1594

Lewander, William Jeffrey (5 mentions)
Albert Einstein Coll of Med, 1979
Certification: Pediatric Emergency Medicine, Pediatrics
593 Eddy St, Providence, 401-444-4900

Nestor, Elizabeth M. (3 mentions)
Northwestern U, 1991 *Certification:* Emergency Medicine
593 Eddy St, Providence, 401-444-4000

Pinkes, Victor Alexis (3 mentions)
Rosalind Franklin U, 1993 *Certification:* Emergency Medicine
164 Summit Ave, Providence, 401-793-3100

Renzi, Richard Michael (8 mentions)
FMS-Italy, 1984 *Certification:* Emergency Medicine
164 Summit Ave, Providence, 401-793-3100

Robitaille, Marcia Berry (4 mentions)
Baylor U, 1998 *Certification:* Emergency Medicine
111 Brewster St, Pawtucket, 401-729-2000
310 Maple Ave, Barrington, 401-247-2870

Sabina, William Henry (4 mentions)
Boston U, 1995 *Certification:* Emergency Medicine
100 Kenyon Ave, Wakefield, 401-782-8000

Savitt, Daniel Lawrence (4 mentions)
U of Massachusetts, 1983 *Certification:* Emergency Medicine
164 Summit Ave, Providence, 401-444-5120
111 Brewster St, Pawtucket, 401-444-4247

Stengel, Charles Leigh (4 mentions)
U of Pennsylvania, 1991 *Certification:* Emergency Medicine
11 Friendship St, Newport, 401-846-6400

Zink, Brian Jeffrey (3 mentions)
U of Rochester, 1984 *Certification:* Emergency Medicine
593 Eddy St, Providence, 401-444-5141

Endocrinology

Campbell, Nathalie A. (8 mentions)
FMS-Canada, 1994
Certification: Endocrinology, Diabetes, and Metabolism
470 Tollgate Rd #202, Warwick, 401-737-1485

Kahn, Charles Bernard (16 mentions)
U of Colorado, 1963
Certification: Endocrinology and Metabolism, Internal Medicine
49 Seekonk St, Providence, 401-351-7100

Krauss, Dennis Sherwin (9 mentions)
U of Vermont, 1974
Certification: Endocrinology and Metabolism, Internal Medicine
49 Seekonk St, Providence, 401-351-7100

Ortiz, Roberto (7 mentions)
FMS-Mexico, 1985
Certification: Endocrinology, Diabetes, and Metabolism
49 Seekonk St, Providence, 401-351-7100

Thomas, Valerie Ann (28 mentions)
Tufts U, 1986 *Certification:* Endocrinology, Diabetes, and
  Metabolism, Internal Medicine
49 Seekonk St, Providence, 401-351-7100
1180 Hope St, Bristol, 401-351-7100

Tucci, Joseph Ralph (12 mentions)
Boston U, 1959
Certification: Endocrinology and Metabolism, Internal Medicine
50 Maude St, Providence, 401-456-5716

Family Practice *(see note on page 9)*

Arcand, Denise M. (3 mentions)
FMS-Canada, 1998 *Certification:* Family Medicine
1079 Main St #A, West Warwick, 401-828-2663

Bossian, John L. (3 mentions)
Des Moines U, 1983 *Certification:* Family Medicine
66 Main St, Wakefield, 401-789-1600

Campagnari, Chris A. (5 mentions)
U of Massachusetts, 1991 *Certification:* Family Medicine
823 Main St, Hope Valley, 401-539-2461

Carter, David Paull (8 mentions)
FMS-Belgium, 1977 *Certification:* Family Medicine
174 Armistice Blvd #1A, Pawtucket, 401-723-7578

Cleary, Colleen Anne (3 mentions)
Stony Brook U, 1986
174 Armistice Blvd, Pawtucket, 401-723-7578

Felder, Michael Frederick (3 mentions)
Des Moines U, 1981 *Certification:* Family Medicine
1035 Post Rd, Warwick, 401-941-2830

Fine, Michael David (16 mentions)
Case Western Reserve U, 1983 *Certification:* Family Medicine
727 East Ave #2, Pawtucket, 401-725-6160
33 Banielson Pike #B, North Scituate, 401-934-3545

Golomb, Duane Thomas (3 mentions)
Brown U, 1983 *Certification:* Family Medicine
766 Washington St, Coventry, 401-822-2772

Gonzalez, Michael Joseph Beatty (4 mentions)
FMS-Philippines, 1991 *Certification:* Family Medicine
7260 Post Rd, North Kingstown, 401-294-9184

Green, Thomas L. (4 mentions)
Philadelphia Coll of Osteopathic Med, 1978
Certification: Family Medicine
688 Frenchtown Rd #1, East Greenwich, 401-885-5193

Klein, Michael D. (3 mentions)
Brown U, 2000 *Certification:* Family Medicine
727 East Ave #2, Pawtucket, 401-725-6160
33 Danielson Pike #B, North Scituate, 401-934-3545

Leibowitz, David E. (4 mentions)
U of New England Coll of Osteopathic Med, 1986
851 Main St, Warren, 401-247-1000

Leonard, Polly (3 mentions)
U of New England Coll of Osteopathic Med, 1996
455 Tollgate Rd, Warwick, 401-737-7000
390 Toll Gate Rd #203, Warwick, 401-732-2031

Levin, William D. (3 mentions)
U of Buffalo, 1972 *Certification:* Family Medicine
19 Friendship St #130, Newport, 401-845-2113

Maguire, Stephen (3 mentions)
Des Moines U, 1981
360 Kingstown Rd #200, Narragansett, 401-783-6940

Puerini, Albert J. (4 mentions)
FMS-Mexico, 1978 *Certification:* Family Medicine
725 Reservoir Ave #102, Cranston, 401-943-6910

Thomas, Budio J. (4 mentions)
A T Still U, 1975
15 Bay Spring Ave, Barrington, 401-246-1010

Warcup, Thomas K. (3 mentions)
U of New England Coll of Osteopathic Med, 1998
4533 S County Trail, Charlestown, 401-364-1268

Gastroenterology

Califano, Nicholas Alan (10 mentions)
FMS-Italy, 1971
Certification: Gastroenterology, Internal Medicine
33 Staniford St, Providence, 401-421-8800

Connors, Pamela Jo (6 mentions)
Boston U, 1986
Certification: Gastroenterology, Internal Medicine
45 Wells St #103, Westerly, 401-596-6330
23 Clara Dr, Mystic, CT, 401-596-6330

De Nucci, Thomas Dominic (6 mentions)
Brown U, 1980 *Certification:* Gastroenterology, Internal Medicine
33 Staniford St, Providence, 401-421-8800

Elevado, Morris Paul (9 mentions)
U of Buffalo, 1997
Certification: Gastroenterology, Internal Medicine
1150 Reservoir Ave #201, Cranston, 401-943-1300

Greenspan, Neil Robert (9 mentions)
Mount Sinai Sch of Med, 1984
Certification: Gastroenterology, Internal Medicine
1 Randall Sq #305, Providence, 401-274-4800
333 School St #303, Pawtucket, 401-726-3450
44 W River St, Providence, 401-274-4800

Lidofsky, Sheldon (6 mentions)
SUNY-Downstate Med Coll, 1975
Certification: Gastroenterology, Internal Medicine
33 Staniford St, Providence, 401-421-8800

Quirk, Daniel Mark (7 mentions)
Brown U, 1991 *Certification:* Gastroenterology
33 Staniford St, Providence, 401-421-8800

Shah, Samir Ashok (13 mentions)
Harvard U, 1992
Certification: Gastroenterology, Internal Medicine
1 Randall Sq #305, Providence, 401-274-4800
333 School St #303, Pawtucket, 401-726-3450
44 W River St, Providence, 401-274-4800

Spellun, Joel Steven (6 mentions)
Cornell U, 1982
Certification: Gastroenterology, Internal Medicine
100 Highland Ave #103, Providence, 401-421-6306
1524 Atwood Ave #245, Johnston, 401-421-6306
148 W River St #3, Providence, 401-421-6306

General Surgery

Capuano, Umberto (10 mentions)
Brown U, 1982 *Certification:* Surgery
70 Kenyon Ave #325, Wakefield, 401-792-7001
320 Phillips St #201, North Kingstown, 401-792-7001
100 Kenyon Ave, Wakefield, 401-782-8000

Cloutier, David Robert (7 mentions)
Dartmouth Coll, 1998 *Certification:* Surgery
195 Collyer St #302, Providence, 401-793-5702

Cutitar, Marlene (7 mentions)
Brown U, 1986 *Certification:* Surgery
1 Randall Sq #402, Providence, 401-273-5441

Dowd, Andrew Joseph (4 mentions)
Loyola U Chicago, 1992 *Certification:* Surgery
70 Kenyon Ave #325, South Kingstown, 401-782-4640

Dyer, Candace Lesley (5 mentions)
Brown U, 1980 *Certification:* Surgery
390 Toll Gate Rd, Warwick, 401-739-8010

Emmick, Christine Marie (6 mentions)
Albany Med Coll, 1993 *Certification:* Surgery
333 School St, Pawtucket, 401-728-1300
100 Highland Ave #307, Providence, 401-421-7706

Latina, Joseph Anthony (5 mentions)
Med Coll of Wisconsin, 1968 *Certification:* Surgery
1145 Reservoir Ave #302, Cranston, 401-946-2370

Luke, Michael Arthur (4 mentions)
U of Buffalo, 1979
501 Great Rd #205, North Smithfield, 401-766-4304

McAteer, Allison Louise (5 mentions)
Tufts U, 1995 *Certification:* Surgery
70 Kenyon Ave #325, Wakefield, 401-766-4302

Migliori, Stephen Julius (8 mentions)
Hahnemann U, 1987 *Certification:* Surgery
2 Dudley St #470, Providence, 401-553-8353

Pohl, Dieter (11 mentions)
FMS-Germany, 1988 *Certification:* Surgery
1539 Atwood Ave #201, Johnston, 401-521-6310

Pricolo, Victor (19 mentions)
FMS-Italy, 1981 *Certification:* Surgery
2 Dudley St #370, Providence, 401-553-8306

Roye, Gary Dean (5 mentions)
U of Miami, 1992 *Certification:* Surgery
2 Dudley St #470, Providence, 401-553-8310

Ryder, Beth Ann (6 mentions)
Tufts U, 1999 *Certification:* Surgery
2 Dudley St #470, Providence, 401-553-8303
285 Governor St, Providence, 401-553-8303

Shahinian, Thomas Karekin (12 mentions)
FMS-Italy, 1968 *Certification:* Surgery
2 Dudley St #470, Providence, 401-553-8308

Vakharia, Jamsheed B. (19 mentions)
FMS-Pakistan, 1990 *Certification:* Surgery
195 Collyer St #302, Providence, 401-793-5702

Zaklynsky, Orest Vsevolod (4 mentions)
SUNY-Downstate Med Coll, 1969 *Certification:* Surgery
220 Bellevue Ave, Newport, 401-849-1113

Geriatrics

Besdine, Richard W. (4 mentions)
U of Pennsylvania, 1965 *Certification:* Geriatric Medicine,
Infectious Disease, Internal Medicine
593 Eddy St, Providence, 703-444-5248

McNicoll, Lynn (7 mentions)
FMS-Canada, 1996
Certification: Geriatric Medicine, Internal Medicine
407 East Ave #110, Pawtucket, 401-444-5248

Murphy, John Brian (8 mentions)
SUNY-Downstate Med Coll, 1980
Certification: Family Medicine, Geriatric Medicine
407 East Ave #110, Pawtucket, 401-728-7270

Stoukides, John Aristotle (13 mentions)
Tufts U, 1989 *Certification:* Hospice and Palliative
Medicine, Internal Medicine
2 Atlantic Blvd, North Providence, 401-231-0450

Hematology/Oncology

Butera, James Nicholas (7 mentions)
U of Massachusetts, 1994
Certification: Hematology, Medical Oncology
593 Eddy St, Providence, 401-444-5395

Forman, Edwin Noel (12 mentions)
U of Pennsylvania, 1960
Certification: Pediatric Hematology-Oncology, Pediatrics
593 Eddy St, Providence, 401-444-5171

Legare, Robert Duffy (13 mentions)
Tufts U, 1990
Certification: Hematology, Internal Medicine, Medical Oncology
101 Dudley St, Providence, 401-453-7520
11 Wells St, Westerly, 401-596-1630

Mega, Anthony Emmanuel (8 mentions)
Dartmouth Coll, 1988
Certification: Hematology, Medical Oncology
164 Summit Ave #3, Providence, 401-793-2920

Nadeem, Ahmed (8 mentions)
FMS-Pakistan, 1981
Certification: Hematology, Internal Medicine, Medical Oncology
115 Cass Ave #2, Woonsocket, 401-767-1541

Papa, Alessandro (6 mentions)
Brown U, 1984
Certification: Hematology, Internal Medicine, Medical Oncology
19 Friendship St #360, Newport, 401-849-8787

Safran, Howard (10 mentions)
Certification: Hematology, Internal Medicine, Medical Oncology
164 Summit Ave, Providence, 401-793-2920

Sambandam, S. Thirugnana (17 mentions)
FMS-India, 1970
Certification: Hematology, Internal Medicine, Medical Oncology
1220 Pontiac Ave #101, Cranston, 401-245-7393
639 Medicon Ave, Warren, 401-245-7393
1180 Hope St, Bristol, 401-245-7393

Schiffman, Fred Jay (11 mentions)
New York U, 1973
Certification: Hematology, Internal Medicine, Medical Oncology
164 Summit Ave #3, Providence, 401-793-2920

Smythe, James Leighton (9 mentions)
Baylor U, 1977
Certification: Internal Medicine, Medical Oncology
24 Salt Pond Rd #G2, Wakefield, 401-783-6670

Testa, Anthony Frank (6 mentions)
U of Cincinnati, 1973
Certification: Internal Medicine, Medical Oncology
1524 Atwood Ave #340, Johnston, 401-273-0220

Wittels, Edward Gerard (10 mentions)
SUNY-Downstate Med Coll, 1972
Certification: Hematology, Internal Medicine, Medical Oncology
164 Summit Ave #3, Providence, 401-793-2920

Infectious Disease

Dennehy, Penelope Hill (12 mentions)
Tufts U, 1976
Certification: Pediatric Infectious Diseases, Pediatrics
593 Eddy St, Providence, 401-444-4298

Fischer, Staci (16 mentions)
Louisiana State U, 1990
Certification: Infectious Disease, Internal Medicine
593 Eddy St, Providence, 401-444-8130

Flanigan, Timothy Palen (8 mentions)
Cornell U, 1983
Certification: Infectious Disease, Internal Medicine
164 Summit Ave #E, Providence, 401-793-2928

Fort, Glenn G. (10 mentions)
FMS-Spain, 1983
Certification: Infectious Disease, Internal Medicine
200 High Service Ave, North Providence, 401-456-3164
115 Cass Ave, Woonsocket, 401-766-3428

Lonks, John Richard (12 mentions)
New Jersey Med Sch, 1986
Certification: Infectious Disease, Internal Medicine
164 Summit Ave, Providence, 401-793-4620

Lowe, David A. (10 mentions)
Harvard U, 1971
Certification: Infectious Disease, Internal Medicine
455 Toll Gate Rd, Warwick, 401-738-6865
615 Jefferson Blvd, Warwick, 401-738-6865

Mermel, Leonard Alan (10 mentions)
Des Moines U, 1984
Certification: Infectious Disease, Internal Medicine
593 Eddy St, Providence, 401-444-8130

Mikolich, Dennis John (9 mentions)
FMS-Dominican Republic, 1980
1150 Reservoir Ave #103, Cranston, 401-943-8685

Silverblatt, Fred Joel (8 mentions)
New York U, 1962
Certification: Infectious Disease, Internal Medicine
50 Maude St, Providence, 401-456-2437
1351 S County Trail, East Greenwich, 401-886-5663

Infertility

Frishman, Gary Nathan (12 mentions)
Columbia U, 1985 *Certification:* Obstetrics & Gynecology,
Reproductive Endocrinology/Infertility
101 Dudley St, Providence, 401-274-1122
1 Blackstone Pl 1st Fl, Providence, 401-453-7500

Wheeler, Carol Anne (8 mentions)
Jefferson Med Coll, 1980 *Certification:* Obstetrics &
Gynecology, Reproductive Endocrinology/Infertility
101 Dudley St, Providence, 401-274-1122

Internal Medicine *(see note on page 9)*

Amin, Kim Samir (6 mentions)
U of Michigan, 1980 *Certification:* Internal Medicine
333 School St #215, Pawtucket, 401-724-6070

Balon, Stanley Richard (3 mentions)
Boston U, 1979 *Certification:* Internal Medicine
175 Nate Whipple Hwy #204, Cumberland, 401-658-1744

Basile, Francis X., Jr. (5 mentions)
Cornell U, 1992 *Certification:* Internal Medicine
285 Governor St, Providence, 401-228-3490

Bledsoe, Thomas Arthur (3 mentions)
Brown U, 1988 *Certification:* Internal Medicine
285 Governor St #200, Providence, 401-228-3480

Brex, Charles John, III (3 mentions)
New York Med Coll, 1975 *Certification:* Internal Medicine
450 Veterans Memorial Pkwy #404, East Providence,
  401-435-3400

Corcoran, J. Russell (3 mentions)
Georgetown U, 1982
Certification: Geriatric Medicine, Internal Medicine
70 Kenyon Ave #321, Wakefield, 401-783-0084

Dennison, Allen M. (3 mentions)
Columbia U, 1980 *Certification:* Internal Medicine
286 Maple Ave, Barrington, 401-247-0610
1180 Hope St, Bristol, 401-253-8900

Herbert, Christine V. (4 mentions)
Brown U, 1987 *Certification:* Internal Medicine
407 East Ave #110, Pawtucket, 401-728-7270

Jacobs, Mark Dennis (3 mentions)
Albert Einstein Coll of Med, 1975 *Certification:* Internal Medicine
41 Anderson Rd #201, Smithfield, 401-949-0300

Jeremiah, Jennifer (3 mentions)
Brown U, 1989 *Certification:* Internal Medicine
111 Plain St, Providence, 401-444-1770

Marcoux, David Alfred (13 mentions)
Med Coll of Wisconsin, 1988 *Certification:* Internal Medicine
407 East Ave #120, Pawtucket, 401-725-4700

McNiece, Donald M. (4 mentions)
SUNY-Downstate Med Coll, 1976 *Certification:* Internal Medicine
24 Salt Pond Rd, Wakefield, 401-789-2424

O'Leary, John Louis (3 mentions)
U of New England Coll of Osteopathic Med, 1984
Certification: Internal Medicine
24 Salt Pond Rd #H1, Wakefield, 401-789-2424

Schoenfeld, Larry Jay (8 mentions)
Jefferson Med Coll, 1977 *Certification:* Internal Medicine
900 Warren Ave #400, East Providence, 401-331-1221

Wu, Tony Chaui (4 mentions)
Robert W Johnson Med Sch, 1993
Certification: Internal Medicine
285 Governor St, Providence, 401-228-3490

Nephrology

Cottiero, Richard Anthony (14 mentions)
Tufts U, 1985 *Certification:* Internal Medicine, Nephrology
1076 N Main St, Providence, 401-861-7711

Endreny, Raymond Guy (16 mentions)
Hahnemann U, 1973
Certification: Internal Medicine, Nephrology
318 Waterman Ave #328, East Providence, 401-438-5950
1526 Atwood Ave, Johnston, 401-438-5950
2100 Diamond Hill Rd, Woonsocket, 401-438-5950

Lee, George (7 mentions)
Boston U, 1992 *Certification:* Internal Medicine, Nephrology
318 Waterman Ave, East Providence, 401-438-5950
50 Memorial Blvd, Newport, 401-438-5950

Mancini, Mark Joseph (10 mentions)
U of Connecticut, 1992
Certification: Internal Medicine, Nephrology
17 Wells St #202, Westerly, 401-596-3313

Serra, Robert Michael (7 mentions)
U of Virginia, 1974 *Certification:* Internal Medicine, Nephrology
17 Wells St, Westerly, 401-596-3313
70 Kenyon Ave, Wakefield, 401-782-0090

Yoburn, David Crocker (10 mentions)
U of Nebraska, 1975 *Certification:* Internal Medicine, Nephrology
1076 N Main St, Providence, 401-861-7711
125 Corliss St, Providence, 401-521-9300

Zipin, Steven Bertram (14 mentions)
SUNY-Downstate Med Coll, 1970
Certification: Internal Medicine, Nephrology
318 Waterman Ave, East Providence, 401-438-5950
2100 Diamond Hill Rd, Woonsocket, 401-438-5950

Neurological Surgery

Doberstein, Curtis E. (26 mentions)
FMS-Canada, 1988 *Certification:* Neurological Surgery
1 Davol Sq #302, Providence, 401-455-1749
100 Butler Dr, Providence, 401-444-8040

Guglielmo, Maria Ann (12 mentions)
Brown U, 1992 *Certification:* Neurological Surgery
300 Toll Gate Rd #101D, Warwick, 401-739-4988

Saris, Stephen Clayton (12 mentions)
Boston U, 1979 *Certification:* Neurological Surgery
3 Davol Sq #B200, Providence, 401-453-3545

Neurology

Bellafiore, Peter Joseph (8 mentions)
U of Vermont, 1991 *Certification:* Neurology
70 Kenyon Ave, Wakefield, 401-789-4885
81 Beach St, Westerly, 401-596-9039

Friedman, Joseph Harold (5 mentions)
Columbia U, 1978 *Certification:* Neurology
227 Centerville Rd, Warwick, 401-729-2483

Gaitanis, John Nicholas (5 mentions)
Brown U, 1996 *Certification:* Clinical Neurophysiology,
  Neurology with Special Qualifications in Child Neurology
593 Eddy St, Providence, 401-444-4345

Gordon, Norman Mervyn (16 mentions)
FMS-South Africa, 1979
Certification: Internal Medicine, Neurology
450 Veterans Memorial Pkwy Bldg 11, Riverside, 401-431-1860

Iqbal, S. M. Arshad (5 mentions)
FMS-Pakistan, 1988 *Certification:* Neurology
4519 Post Rd, Warwick, 401-886-7866

Jones, Elaine Celeste (6 mentions)
Med U of South Carolina, 1994 *Certification:* Neurology
814 Metacom Ave, Bristol, 401-396-5200

Karanasias, Petro (7 mentions)
FMS-Turkey, 1971
100 Highland Ave #303, Providence, 401-272-1883

L'Europa, Gary Anthony (6 mentions)
Brown U, 1983 *Certification:* Clinical Neurophysiology, Neurology
227 Centerville Rd, Warwick, 401-732-3332

Obstetrics/Gynecology

Bowling, Kathleen Cote (17 mentions)
Dartmouth Coll, 1982 *Certification:* Obstetrics & Gynecology
235 Plain St, Providence, 401-421-1710

Cassin, Kathleen A. (3 mentions)
Brown U, 1982 *Certification:* Obstetrics & Gynecology
70 Kenyon Ave #323, Wakefield, 401-284-1370

Fitzgerald, Kathleen (3 mentions)
Georgetown U, 1974 *Certification:* Obstetrics & Gynecology
120 Dudley St #305, Providence, 401-453-7555

Gedney, James Christopher (3 mentions)
Oregon Health Sciences U, 1977
Certification: Obstetrics & Gynecology
50 Memorial Blvd, Newport, 401-847-2290

Hanna, Cynthia M. (4 mentions)
Jefferson Med Coll, 1985
333 School St #205, Pawtucket, 401-724-0600

Joseph, Jeffrey Francis (4 mentions)
New York Med Coll, 1989 *Certification:* Obstetrics & Gynecology
70 Kenyon Ave, Wakefield, 401-782-9900

Neuhauser, Andrew P. (4 mentions)
George Washington U, 1983
Certification: Obstetrics & Gynecology
45 East Ave, Westerly, 401-596-1905

Nisbet, John Douglas (6 mentions)
New York Med Coll, 1983 *Certification:* Obstetrics & Gynecology
390 Toll Gate Rd #201, Warwick, 401-738-8800

O'Brien, James Anthony (4 mentions)
FMS-Ireland, 1979 *Certification:* Obstetrics & Gynecology
235 Plain St #401, Providence, 401-421-1710

Penkala, Jan Joseph (3 mentions)
FMS-Mexico, 1978 *Certification:* Obstetrics & Gynecology
6 Blackstone Valley Pl #501, Lincoln, 401-334-2229

Rameaka, Lisa Marie (8 mentions)
U of Vermont, 1998 *Certification:* Obstetrics & Gynecology
85 Kenyon Ave, Wakefield, 401-789-0661

Shah-Hosseini, Bahram (3 mentions)
FMS-Iran, 1967 *Certification:* Obstetrics & Gynecology
2 Dudley St #510, Providence, 401-453-3433

Spurrell, Timothy Patrick (3 mentions)
U of Connecticut, 1996 *Certification:* Obstetrics & Gynecology
166 Toll Gate Rd, Warwick, 401-739-2000

Walker, William Scott (3 mentions)
U of Texas-Dallas, 1984 *Certification:* Obstetrics & Gynecology
1 Randall Sq #205, Providence, 401-331-6980

Wiggins, Doreen L. (4 mentions)
Certification: Obstetrics & Gynecology
297 Promenade St, Providence, 401-490-6464
1050 Main St, East Greenwich, 401-886-4200

Ophthalmology

Asher, Ira Henry (4 mentions)
Albert Einstein Coll of Med, 1971 *Certification:* Ophthalmology
65 Boston Neck Rd, North Kingstown, 401-294-4506
24 Salt Pond Rd #D1, Wakefield, 401-789-3444

Bahr, Robert Lawrence (8 mentions)
Harvard U, 1971 *Certification:* Ophthalmology
150 E Manning St, Providence, 508-679-0150
386 High St, Fall River, MA, 508-679-0150
1524 Atwood Ave #240, Johnston, 401-272-2110

Collins, Charles M. (4 mentions)
Uniformed Services U of Health Sciences, 1986
Certification: Ophthalmology
42 Valley Rd, Middletown, 401-847-1383

Donahue, John Peter (4 mentions)
U of Colorado, 1994 *Certification:* Ophthalmology
150 E Manning St, Providence, 401-272-2020

Figueroa, Francis Xavier (8 mentions)
Tufts U, 1991 *Certification:* Ophthalmology
1220 Pontiac Ave #304, Cranston, 401-942-2626
975 Pontiac Ave, Cranston, 401-942-2626

Koch, Paul S. (11 mentions)
Tufts U, 1977 *Certification:* Ophthalmology
566 Toll Gate Rd, Warwick, 401-738-4800
255 Cass Ave, Woonsocket, 401-738-4800
1404 Atwood Ave #1, Johnston, 401-943-6000
7805 Post Rd, North Kingstown, 401-294-1010

Larkin, Durga Strohl (4 mentions)
Duke U, 1987 *Certification:* Ophthalmology
65 Boston Neck Rd, North Kingstown, 401-294-2671
24 Salt Pond Rd #D1, Wakefield, 401-789-3444

Loporchio, Salvatore J. (5 mentions)
Brown U, 1985 *Certification:* Ophthalmology
35 Sockanosset Cross Rd #4, Cranston, 401-946-8011

Rivera, David Rafael (4 mentions)
Georgetown U, 1987 *Certification:* Ophthalmology
45 Wells St, Westerly, 401-596-4959

Tien, D. Robbins (8 mentions)
U of Michigan, 1983 *Certification:* Ophthalmology
2 Dudley St #505, Providence, 401-444-7008
400 Bald Hill Rd, Warwick, 401-737-5206

Tsiaras, William George (9 mentions)
U of Cincinnati, 1974
Certification: Internal Medicine, Ophthalmology
100 Dudley St 3rd Fl, Providence, 401-831-4592
1 Hoppin St, Providence, 401-831-4592

Wepman, Barry Michael (4 mentions)
Wayne State U, 1972 *Certification:* Ophthalmology
70 Kenyon Ave #211, Wakefield, 401-783-7009

Woodcome, Harold A., Jr. (4 mentions)
Boston U, 1972 *Certification:* Ophthalmology
690 Eddy St, Providence, 401-274-5844

Orthopedics

Aaron, Roy Kenneth (4 mentions)
SUNY-Downstate Med Coll, 1969
Certification: Orthopaedic Surgery
100 Butler Dr, Providence, 401-274-9660
2 Dudley St, Providence, 401-274-9660
353 Blackstone Blvd, Providence, 401-274-9660

Belanger, Michael James (7 mentions)
U of Vermont, 1993 *Certification:* Orthopaedic Surgery
1524 Atwood Ave #140, Johnston, 401-729-3851
111 Brewster St, Pawtucket, 401-729-3851

Burns, David B. (6 mentions)
U of New England Coll of Osteopathic Med, 1984
1 High St, Wakefield, 401-789-1422

Cote, Phillippe Sylvestre (8 mentions)
U of Vermont, 1979 *Certification:* Orthopaedic Surgery
285 Promenade St, Providence, 401-459-4001

Di Robbio, Carl C., Jr. (5 mentions)
Georgetown U, 1971 *Certification:* Orthopaedic Surgery
2345 Mendon Rd, Woonsocket, 401-765-0700

Eberson, Craig Politt (7 mentions)
Robert W Johnson Med Sch, 1995
Certification: Orthopaedic Surgery
2 Dudley St #200, Providence, 401-457-1500

Ehrlich, Michael G. (7 mentions)
Columbia U, 1963 *Certification:* Orthopaedic Surgery
2 Dudley St #200, Providence, 401-457-1540

Fadale, Paul D. (8 mentions)
U of Buffalo, 1981 *Certification:* Orthopaedic Surgery
2 Dudley St #200, Providence, 401-457-1535

Froehlich, John Alan (5 mentions)
U of Rochester, 1983 *Certification:* Orthopaedic Surgery
2 Dudley St #200, Providence, 401-457-1525

Graff, Steven Neal (5 mentions)
Columbia U, 1987
Certification: Orthopaedic Surgery, Surgery of the Hand
588 Pawtucket Ave, Pawtucket, 401-722-2400
6 Blackstone Valley Pl #530, Lincoln, 401-334-3700

Gross, Stephen Barrett (6 mentions)
Dartmouth Coll, 1985 *Certification:* Orthopaedic Surgery
81 Beach St, Westerly, 401-596-9039

Hulstyn, Michael Jan (4 mentions)
Brown U, 1986 *Certification:* Orthopaedic Surgery
2 Dudley St #200, Providence, 401-457-1530

Lucas, Phillip Richard (6 mentions)
Med Coll of Wisconsin, 1973 *Certification:* Orthopaedic Surgery
2 Dudley St #370, Providence, 401-457-1565

Marchand, Robert Cary (6 mentions)
Cornell U, 1983 *Certification:* Orthopaedic Surgery
1 High St, Wakefield, 401-789-1422
6 Quarry Rd, Kingston, 401-874-2246

Mariorenzi, Louis John (7 mentions)
Brown U, 1980 *Certification:* Orthopaedic Surgery
725 Reservoir Ave #101, Cranston, 401-944-3800

Shalvoy, Robert Michael (7 mentions)
New Jersey Med Sch, 1984 *Certification:* Orthopaedic Surgery
100 Butler Dr, Providence, 401-277-0790

Otorhinolaryngology

Andreozzi, Mark Peter (7 mentions)
U of New England Coll of Osteopathic Med, 1987
3520 Post Rd, Warwick, 401-785-0976
900 Warren Ave #305, East Providence, 401-785-0976

Gibson, Sharon Elizabeth (13 mentions)
U of Michigan, 1987 *Certification:* Otolaryngology
118 Dudley St, Providence, 401-274-2300
1351 S County Trail #303, East Greenwich, 401-885-8484
130 Waterman St, Providence, 401-274-3277

McRae, Robert G. (12 mentions)
Tufts U, 1976 *Certification:* Otolaryngology
1351 S County Trail #303, East Greenwich, 401-885-8484
118 Dudley St, Providence, 401-274-2300

Tarro, John Matthew (13 mentions)
Tulane U, 1992 *Certification:* Otolaryngology
333 School St, Pawtucket, 401-728-0140
132 Old River Rd #B2, Lincoln, 401-333-8664
1524 Atwood Ave, Johnston, 401-272-2457
2138 Mendon Rd #204, Cumberland, 401-333-8664

Tipirneni, Prabhakar Rao (9 mentions)
FMS-India, 1974
24 Salt Pond Rd #H2, Wakefield, 401-789-0227
215 Toll Gate Rd #303, Warwick, 401-732-5522

Pain Medicine

Chopra, Pradeep (8 mentions)
FMS-India, 1988 *Certification:* Anesthesiology, Pain Medicine
102 Smithfield Ave, Pawtucket, 401-729-4985
3 Davol Sq #B200, Providence, 401-453-3545

Pathology

De Lellis, Ronald Albert (7 mentions)
Tufts U, 1966 *Certification:* Anatomic Pathology
593 Eddy St, Providence, 401-444-5151

Giampaolo, Casimiro M. (4 mentions)
U of Chicago, 1970
Certification: Anatomic Pathology, Clinical Pathology
100 Kenyon Ave, Wakefield, 401-782-8020

Goldstein, Lisa Joyce (3 mentions)
Brown U, 1982
Certification: Anatomic Pathology & Clinical Pathology
164 Summit Ave, Providence, 401-793-4245

Kessimian, Noubar (3 mentions)
FMS-Argentina, 1973
Certification: Anatomic Pathology & Clinical Pathology
111 Brewster St, Pawtucket, 401-729-2393

Khorsand, Jila (6 mentions)
FMS-Iran, 1976
Certification: Anatomic Pathology & Clinical Pathology
825 Chalkstone Ave, Providence, 401-456-2162
25 Well St, Westerly, 401-348-3320

Qi, Jiafan (3 mentions)
FMS-China, 1982 *Certification:* Anatomic Pathology &
Clinical Pathology, Cytopathology
115 Cass Ave, Woonsocket, 401-769-4100

Stancu, Mirela (3 mentions)
FMS-Romania, 1991 *Certification:* Anatomic Pathology &
Clinical Pathology, Hematology
825 Chalkstone Ave, Providence, 401-456-2662
50 Maude St, Providence, 401-456-2662

Wang, Scott E. (4 mentions)
Boston U, 1980 *Certification:* Anatomic Pathology &
Clinical Pathology, Cytopathology
11 Friendship St, Newport, 401-845-1280

Pediatrics *(see note on page 9)*

Corcoran, Celeste C. (6 mentions)
Georgetown U, 1982 *Certification:* Pediatrics
70 Kenyon Ave #101, Wakefield, 401-789-5924

Dennison, Jane Mackenzie (3 mentions)
Columbia U, 1980 *Certification:* Pediatrics
234 Maple Ave, Barrington, 401-247-1644

Ettefagh, Keivan (3 mentions)
U of Texas-Dallas, 1984 *Certification:* Pediatrics
50 Memorial Blvd, Newport, 401-847-2290

Greco, Richard Germano (5 mentions)
Tufts U, 1967 *Certification:* Pediatrics
50 Amaral St, Riverside, 401-434-8009

Griffith, Robert Thomas (7 mentions)
U of Rochester, 1983 *Certification:* Pediatrics
450 Veterans Mem Pkwy Bldg 10, East Providence, 401-438-6888

McGookin, Edward Dobson (6 mentions)
SUNY-Upstate Med U, 1993 *Certification:* Pediatrics
900 Warren Ave, East Providence, 401-421-6481

Murray, Mary E. (3 mentions)
Stony Brook U, 1987
70 Kenyon Ave #101, Wakefield, 401-789-5924

Salm, Jennifer M. (3 mentions)
SUNY-Upstate Med U, 1998 *Certification:* Pediatrics
50 Memorial Blvd, Newport, 401-847-2290

Shaw, Judith Gibbs (3 mentions)
Brown U, 1978 *Certification:* Pediatrics
900 Warren Ave, East Providence, 401-421-6481

Silversmith, Howard Gregg (5 mentions)
Stony Brook U, 1997 *Certification:* Pediatrics
1351 S County Trail #205, East Greenwich, 401-886-7881

Plastic Surgery

Barrall, David Timothy (20 mentions)
Brown U, 1981 *Certification:* Plastic Surgery, Surgery of the Hand
151 Waterman St, Providence, 401-274-0700
696 Newport Ave, Attleboro, MA, 508-226-4191

Roettinger, Walter F. (11 mentions)
U of Virginia, 1972 *Certification:* Plastic Surgery
222 Bellevue Ave, Newport, 401-849-2826

Sullivan, Patrick Kevin (20 mentions)
Mayo Med Sch, 1979
Certification: Otolaryngology, Plastic Surgery
235 Plain St #502, Providence, 401-831-8300

Psychiatry

Burock, Jeffrey Michael (3 mentions)
Creighton U, 1999 *Certification:* Geriatric Psychiatry,
   Psychiatry, Psychosomatic Medicine
164 Summit Ave, Providence, 401-793-4300

Daamen, Maximilian J. (3 mentions)
Tufts U, 1974
355 Angell St #11, Providence, 401-831-5423

Goldberg, Richard J. (6 mentions)
U of Buffalo, 1974 *Certification:* Geriatric Psychiatry, Psychiatry
593 Eddy St APC Bldg #971, Providence, 401-444-5291

Harrington, Colin James (10 mentions)
Tufts U, 1988 *Certification:* Psychiatry, Psychosomatic Medicine
593 Eddy St APC Bldg #970, Providence, 401-444-3418

Kazim, Ali (3 mentions)
FMS-Pakistan, 1984 *Certification:* Forensic Psychiatry, Psychiatry
593 Eddy St, Providence, 401-444-4000

Parmentier, A. Hilton (4 mentions)
FMS-Dominica, 1984
360 Kingstown Rd, Narragansett, 401-515-0007

Scaramella, Thomas Jerry (5 mentions)
U of Pennsylvania, 1969 *Certification:* Psychiatry
480 Hope St, Providence, 401-274-3343

Stiener, Gregory Paul (3 mentions)
Indiana U, 1992
Certification: Child & Adolescent Psychiatry, Psychiatry
339 Angell St, Providence, 401-273-5605

Pulmonary Disease

Braman, Sidney Stuart (6 mentions)
Temple U, 1967
Certification: Internal Medicine, Pulmonary Disease
593 Eddy St APC Bldg #475, Providence, 401-444-3570

Corrao, William Michael (13 mentions)
U of Rochester, 1972
Certification: Internal Medicine, Pulmonary Disease
593 Eddy St APC Bldg #475, Providence, 401-444-3570

Donat, Walter Edward (19 mentions)
Brown U, 1977 *Certification:* Cardiovascular Disease, Critical
   Care Medicine, Internal Medicine, Pulmonary Disease
593 Eddy St APC Bldg #475, Providence, 401-444-3570

Hebert, Anne Marie (11 mentions)
Dartmouth Coll, 1982
Certification: Internal Medicine, Pulmonary Disease
360 Kingston Rd #207, Narragansett, 401-789-0774

Myers, James Robert (13 mentions)
U of Wisconsin, 1972
Certification: Internal Medicine, Pulmonary Disease
450 Veterans Mem Pkwy, East Providence, 401-435-5522

Passero, Michael Anthony (7 mentions)
Harvard U, 1969
Certification: Internal Medicine, Pulmonary Disease
50 Maude St 3rd Fl, Providence, 401-456-5714

Puppi, Leon Denis (7 mentions)
FMS-Romania, 1984 *Certification:* Critical Care Medicine,
   Internal Medicine, Pulmonary Disease, Sleep Medicine
360 Kingstown Rd #207, Narragansett, 401-789-0774

Raimondo, Thomas J. (11 mentions)
U of New England Coll of Osteopathic Med, 1985
Certification: Internal Medicine
1050 Warwick Ave, Warwick, 401-467-6210

Sherman, Charles Bruce (12 mentions)
Hahnemann U, 1981
Certification: Internal Medicine, Pulmonary Disease
450 Veterans Mem Pkwy Bldg 6, East Providence, 401-435-5533

Radiology—Diagnostic

Black, Richard Alan (4 mentions)
SUNY-Downstate Med Coll, 1980
Certification: Diagnostic Radiology
65 Sockanosset Crossroads, Cranston, 401-943-1454

Cronan, John Joseph (4 mentions)
Albany Med Coll, 1976 *Certification:* Diagnostic Radiology
593 Eddy St, Providence, 401-444-5184

Gold, Richard Lawrence (9 mentions)
U of Massachusetts, 1982 *Certification:* Diagnostic
   Radiology, Internal Medicine, Neuroradiology
164 Summit Ave, Providence, 401-793-4480

Hillstrom, Mary Martha (3 mentions)
Brown U, 1988 *Certification:* Diagnostic Radiology
164 Summit Ave, Providence, 401-793-4480

Iannuccilli, Nicholas D. (3 mentions)
FMS-Italy, 1969 *Certification:* Diagnostic Radiology
1515 Smith St, North Providence, 401-353-1600
115 Cass Ave #2, Woonsocket, 401-769-4100

Kutcher, Theodore John (3 mentions)
U of Vermont, 1988 *Certification:* Diagnostic Radiology
11 Friendship St, Newport, 401-845-4253

Mainiero, Martha Beretta (4 mentions)
Tufts U, 1989 *Certification:* Diagnostic Radiology
1525 Wampanoag Trail, Riverside, 401-432-2400
20 Catamore Blvd, East Providence, 401-432-2520

Mayo-Smith, William W. (3 mentions)
Cornell U, 1984 *Certification:* Diagnostic Radiology
20 Catamore Blvd, East Providence, 401-432-2520

McCarten, Kathleen Mary (3 mentions)
Med Coll of Pennsylvania, 1970
Certification: Diagnostic Radiology, Pediatric Radiology
593 Eddy St, Providence, 401-444-6883
1525 Wampanoag Trail, Riverside, 401-432-2400
20 Catamore Blvd, East Providence, 401-432-2520

Movson, Jonathan S. (9 mentions)
FMS-South Africa, 1982
Certification: Diagnostic Radiology, Nuclear Radiology
164 Summit Ave, Providence, 401-793-4400
1525 Wampanoag Trail, Riverside, 401-432-2400
20 Catamore Blvd, East Providence, 401-432-2520

Rogg, Jeffrey Michael (5 mentions)
New York U, 1982
Certification: Diagnostic Radiology, Neuroradiology
593 Eddy St, Providence, 401-444-5184

Rosenthal, Charles Mark (3 mentions)
Cornell U, 1981 *Certification:* Diagnostic Radiology
115 Cass Ave, Woonsocket, 401-769-4100

Schepps, Barbara (3 mentions)
Hahnemann U, 1968 *Certification:* Radiology
1525 Wampanoag Trail #101, East Providence, 401-433-1166
101 Dudley St, Providence, 401-274-2553
20 Catamore Blvd, East Providence, 401-432-2520

Shapiro, Bradley A. (3 mentions)
U of Massachusetts, 1980 *Certification:* Diagnostic Radiology
111 Brewster St, Pawtucket, 401-729-2359
1000 Broad St, Central Falls, 401-726-1800

Wallach, Michael Tide (12 mentions)
Case Western Reserve U, 1981
Certification: Diagnostic Radiology, Pediatric Radiology
101 Dudley St, Providence, 401-274-2553

Radiology—Therapeutic

Binek, Robert Edward (6 mentions)
U of Michigan, 1984 *Certification:* Diagnostic Radiology
   with Special Competence in Nuclear Radiology
455 Toll Gate Rd, Warwick, 401-737-7010
1130 Ten Rod Rd #D201, North Kingstown, 401-295-8655

Maddock, Philip G. (4 mentions)
FMS-Ireland, 1967
450 Toll Gate Rd, Warwick, 401-732-2300

Paolella, Landy Peter (10 mentions)
FMS-Mexico, 1980 *Certification:* Diagnostic Radiology
455 Toll Gate Rd, Warwick, 401-737-7010
1130 Ten Rod Rd #D-201, North Kingstown, 401-295-8655

Triedman, Scott A. (7 mentions)
Brown U, 1985 *Certification:* Radiation Oncology
825 N Main St, Providence, 401-521-9700

Rehabilitation

Lazarus, Bruce A. (6 mentions)
Brown U, 1981 *Certification:* Physical Medicine & Rehabilitation
111 Brewster St, Pawtucket, 401-729-2326

Parziale, John Robert (8 mentions)
U of Connecticut, 1983
Certification: Physical Medicine & Rehabilitation
450 Veterans Memorial Pkwy, East Providence, 401-435-2288

Rheumatology

Conte, John Michael (10 mentions)
U of Connecticut, 1978
Certification: Internal Medicine, Rheumatology
49 Seekonk St #1, Providence, 401-351-2280

Horwitz, Harold Milton (14 mentions)
Tufts U, 1968 *Certification:* Internal Medicine, Rheumatology
49 Seekonk St #1, Providence, 401-351-2280

Lally, Edward Vincent (17 mentions)
Boston U, 1975 *Certification:* Internal Medicine, Rheumatology
2 Dudley St #370, Providence, 401-444-6120

Parker, Virginia Schmidt (9 mentions)
Brown U, 1976 *Certification:* Internal Medicine
300 Toll Gate Rd #104, Warwick, 401-738-2607

Silversmith, Wendy R. (12 mentions)
Certification: Internal Medicine, Rheumatology
45 Wells St #203-B, Westerly, 401-348-2180

Zimmermann, Bernard, III (9 mentions)
West Virginia U, 1979
Certification: Internal Medicine, Rheumatology
825 Chalkstone Ave, Providence, 401-456-2200

Thoracic Surgery

Cooper, George Norman, Jr. (9 mentions)
New Jersey Med Sch, 1961
Certification: Surgery, Thoracic Surgery
840 Greenwich Ave, Warwick, 401-739-0011

Ng, Thomas (31 mentions)
FMS-Canada, 1993 *Certification:* Surgery
2 Dudley St #470, Providence, 401-553-8320

Urology

Caldamone, Anthony Angelo (19 mentions)
Brown U, 1975 *Certification:* Pediatric Urology, Urology
2 Dudley St #185, Providence, 401-421-0710

Colagiovanni, Steven Marc (7 mentions)
Tufts U, 1989 *Certification:* Urology
1524 Atwood Ave #322, Johnston, 401-331-7400
2 Wake Robin Rd Unit 205, Lincoln, 401-331-7400

Heffernan, John Philip (9 mentions)
Georgetown U, 1986 *Certification:* Urology
70 Kenyon Ave, Wakefield, 401-783-1896
38 Powell Ave, Newport, 401-847-2418
38 Powel Ave, Newport, 401-783-1896

Iannotti, Harry Michael (8 mentions)
Boston U, 1966 *Certification:* Urology
105 Keene St, Providence, 401-521-4333
1165 N Main St, Providence, 401-521-4333

Miller, E. Bradley (7 mentions)
U of Massachusetts, 1987 *Certification:* Urology
450 Veterans Mem Pkwy, East Providence, 401-435-8488
2 Wake Robin Rd #104, Lincoln, 401-435-5533

Moule, Bernard A. (9 mentions)
Tufts U, 1972 *Certification:* Urology
450 Veterans Memorial Pkwy, East Providence, 401-435-8484

Sarazen, Arnold A., Jr. (9 mentions)
Brown U, 1987 *Certification:* Urology
38 Powel Ave, Newport, 401-847-2418
70 Kenyon Ave #322, Wakefield, 401-783-1896

Vascular Surgery

Marcaccio, Edward J., Jr. (20 mentions)
U of Rochester, 1986 *Certification:* Surgery, Vascular Surgery
2 Dudley St #470, Providence, 401-553-8318

Slaiby, Jeffrey Michael (20 mentions)
U of Vermont, 1988 *Certification:* Surgery, Vascular Surgery
2 Dudley St #470, Providence, 401-553-8333
1351 S County Trail #215, East Greenwich, 401-553-8333
1524 Atwood Ave, Johnston, 401-553-8333

Tennessee

Nashville Area—page 435

Memphis Area—page 430

Memphis Area

Including Crittendon, DeSoto, and Shelby Counties

Allergy/Immunology

Blaiss, Michael Steven (15 mentions)
U of Tennessee, 1976
Certification: Allergy & Immunology, Pediatrics
7205 Wolf River Blvd #200, Germantown, 901-757-6100

Lieberman, Phillip Louis (39 mentions)
U of Tennessee, 1965
Certification: Allergy & Immunology, Internal Medicine
7205 Wolf River Blvd #200, Germantown, 901-757-6100

Anesthesiology

Bridgewater, Jovie N. (4 mentions)
Meharry Med Coll, 1982 *Certification:* Anesthesiology
391 S Crest Cir #209, Southaven, MS, 662-349-2659

Higdon, Dennis Alan (7 mentions)
U of Tennessee, 1970 *Certification:* Anesthesiology
1755 Kirby Pkwy #330, Memphis, 901-725-5846

Lazarov, Stuart J. (6 mentions)
U of Tennessee, 1987 *Certification:* Anesthesiology
1900 Exeter Rd #210, Germantown, 901-818-2160

Leppert, William Michael (6 mentions)
U of Tennessee, 1981 *Certification:* Anesthesiology
1755 Kirby Pkwy #330, Memphis, 901-725-5846

Thompson, Gregory Lamar (3 mentions)
U of Tennessee, 1989 *Certification:* Anesthesiology
1755 Kirby Pkwy #330, Memphis, 901-725-5846

Wu, Bo (3 mentions)
FMS-China, 1985 *Certification:* Anesthesiology
6005 Park Ave, Memphis, 901-682-2872

Cardiac Surgery

Carter, Russell Allan (13 mentions)
U of Tennessee, 1988
Certification: Surgery, Thoracic Surgery, Vascular Surgery
6029 Walnut Grove Rd #401, Memphis, 901-747-3066

Garrett, Harvey E., Jr. (30 mentions)
Vanderbilt U, 1979
Certification: Surgery, Thoracic Surgery, Vascular Surgery
6029 Walnut Grove Rd #401, Memphis, 901-747-3066

Schoettle, Glenn P., Jr. (13 mentions)
U of Tennessee, 1972 *Certification:* Surgery
1325 Eastmoreland Ave #220, Memphis, 901-725-9450

Wolf, Rodney Yale (13 mentions)
U of Tennessee, 1961 *Certification:* Surgery, Thoracic Surgery
6029 Walnut Grove Rd #401, Memphis, 901-747-3066

Cardiology

Allen, Ray M., Jr. (5 mentions)
U of Tennessee, 1982
Certification: Cardiovascular Disease, Internal Medicine
80 Humphreys Ctr #202, Memphis, 901-747-3330

Anderson, Keith G. (8 mentions)
U of Tennessee, 1984 *Certification:* Cardiovascular Disease,
Internal Medicine, Interventional Cardiology
7460 Wolf River Blvd, Germantown, 901-725-6708

Douglas, Dane Edward (4 mentions)
East Tennessee State U, 1989
6401 Poplar Ave #402, Memphis, 901-682-7774

Gubin, Steven Sydney (10 mentions)
U of Tennessee, 1985
Certification: Cardiovascular Disease, Internal Medicine
8060 Wolf River Blvd, Germantown, 901-271-1000

Hess, Paul George (5 mentions)
Cornell U, 1972 *Certification:* Cardiovascular Disease,
Clinical Cardiac Electrophysiology, Internal Medicine
6025 Walnut Grove Rd #111, Memphis, 901-818-0300

McDonald, Michael Baird (14 mentions)
U of Tennessee, 1982 *Certification:* Cardiovascular Disease,
Internal Medicine, Interventional Cardiology
7460 Wolf River Blvd, Germantown, 901-725-6708

Samaha, Joseph K. (6 mentions)
U of Tennessee, 1976
Certification: Cardiovascular Disease, Internal Medicine
6025 Walnut Grove Rd #111, Memphis, 901-818-0300

Smith, Stacy (7 mentions)
U of Southern California, 1986 *Certification:* Cardiovascular
Disease, Internal Medicine, Interventional Cardiology
6025 Walnut Grove Rd #111, Memphis, 901-818-0300

Waller, Benjamin Rush, III (5 mentions)
U of Tennessee, 1987 *Certification:* Pediatric Cardiology
777 Washington Ave #350, Memphis, 901-287-4571

Wolford, David Charles (4 mentions)
U of Tennessee, 1989
Certification: Cardiovascular Disease, Interventional Cardiology
80 Humphreys Ctr #200, Memphis, 901-271-1000
8060 Wolf River Blvd, Germantown, 901-271-1000

Dermatology

Amonette, Rex A. (10 mentions)
U of Arkansas, 1966 *Certification:* Dermatology
1455 Union Ave, Memphis, 901-726-6655

Schneider, Michael A. (12 mentions)
U of Tennessee, 1988 *Certification:* Dermatology
1335 Cordova Cv, Germantown, 901-753-2794

Tanenbaum, Mark Harris (7 mentions)
U of Miami, 1960 *Certification:* Dermatology
760 E Brookhaven Cir, Memphis, 901-761-0500

Emergency Medicine

Dargie, Tripp A. (4 mentions)
U of Tennessee, 1997 *Certification:* Internal Medicine, Pediatrics
7691 Poplar Ave, Germantown, 901-516-6970

Holley, Joseph Eugene, Jr. (4 mentions)
U of Mississippi, 1985 *Certification:* Emergency Medicine
1500 W Poplar Ave, Collierville, 901-861-9114

Musicante, Sergio A. (4 mentions)
U of Tennessee, 1995
5725 N Angela Rd, Memphis, 901-227-7640

Thompson, Stanley Craig (4 mentions)
U of Tennessee, 1996 *Certification:* Emergency Medicine
7601 Southcrest Pkwy, Southaven, MS, 662-772-4000

Walther, Ray (6 mentions)
U of Alabama, 1980 *Certification:* Emergency Medicine
1265 Union Ave, Memphis, 901-516-7000

Witherington, John M. (4 mentions)
U of Tennessee, 1982 *Certification:* Internal Medicine
5959 Park Ave, Memphis, 901-765-2182

Endocrinology

Cohen, Alan Jay (35 mentions)
Howard U, 1979 *Certification:* Pediatric Endocrinology, Pediatrics
5659 S Rex Rd, Memphis, 901-763-3636

Goodman, Ralph Conrad (15 mentions)
U of Tennessee, 1974
Certification: Endocrinology and Metabolism, Internal Medicine
6027 Walnut Grove Rd #307, Memphis, 901-681-0346

Sacks, Harold S. (15 mentions)
FMS-South Africa, 1967
Certification: Endocrinology and Metabolism, Internal Medicine
6027 Walnut Grove Rd #307, Memphis, 901-681-0346

Family Practice *(see note on page 9)*

Crawford, John Daniel (4 mentions)
U of Tennessee, 1978 *Certification:* Family Medicine
790 W Poplar Ave, Collierville, 901-853-9700

Warren, Jeffery Steven (6 mentions)
Duke U, 1982
Certification: Emergency Medicine, Family Medicine
3109 Walnut Grove Rd, Memphis, 901-458-0162

Gastroenterology

Cattau, Edward L., Jr. (10 mentions)
U of North Carolina, 1976
Certification: Gastroenterology, Internal Medicine
8000 Wolf River Blvd #200, Germantown, 901-747-3630

Dragutsky, Michael S. (8 mentions)
Texas A&M U, 1982
Certification: Gastroenterology, Internal Medicine
1310 Wolf Park Dr, Germantown, 901-624-5151
1324 Wolf Park Dr, Germantown, 901-755-9110

Frederick, Randall Carl (6 mentions)
U of Tennessee, 1979
Certification: Gastroenterology, Internal Medicine
8000 Wolf River Blvd #200, Germantown, 901-747-3630

Lewis, Myron (9 mentions)
Columbia U, 1963
Certification: Gastroenterology, Internal Medicine
8000 Wolf River Blvd #200, Germantown, 901-747-3630

Sloas, David Dale (8 mentions)
U of Tennessee, 1981
Certification: Gastroenterology, Internal Medicine
1407 Union Ave #1400, Memphis, 901-272-9296

Towne, Thomas Carter (7 mentions)
U of Tennessee, 1977
Certification: Gastroenterology, Internal Medicine
8000 Wolf River Blvd #200, Germantown, 901-747-3630

Wooten, Robert Strode (6 mentions)
Tulane U, 1981 *Certification:* Internal Medicine
1310 Wolf Park Dr, Germantown, 901-624-5151
1324 Wolf Park Dr, Germantown, 901-755-9110

General Surgery

Andrews, Charles R. (10 mentions)
U of Tennessee, 1976 *Certification:* Surgery
6027 Walnut Grove Rd #212, Memphis, 901-761-5031

Behrman, Stephen Wheeler (6 mentions)
Boston U, 1987 *Certification:* Surgery
7945 Wolf River Blvd, Germantown, 901-347-8270

Ellis, Richard A. (4 mentions)
U of Tennessee, 1984 *Certification:* Surgery
7655 Poplar Ave #230, Germantown, 901-753-6163

Francis, Hugh, III (10 mentions)
Vanderbilt U, 1984 *Certification:* Surgery, Vascular Surgery
6005 Park Ave #821B, Memphis, 901-726-1056
6029 Walnut Grove Rd #404, Memphis, 901-726-1056

King, W. Scott, Jr. (15 mentions)
U of Tennessee, 1973 *Certification:* Surgery
1325 Eastmoreland Ave #580, Memphis, 901-726-1056

Miller, Mark Page (10 mentions)
U of Mississippi, 1983 *Certification:* Surgery
7655 Poplar Ave #230, Germantown, 901-753-6163

Morisy, Lee Richard (5 mentions)
Rosalind Franklin U, 1980 *Certification:* Surgery
6025 Walnut Grove Rd #201, Memphis, 901-685-6066

Pritchard, Frances E. (5 mentions)
U of Tennessee, 1984
Certification: Surgery, Surgical Critical Care
7945 Wolf River Blvd, Germantown, 901-347-8270

Smith, Stanley Leon (12 mentions)
U of Tennessee, 1974 *Certification:* Surgery
6027 Walnut Grove Rd #116, Memphis, 901-761-1155

Voeller, Guy Russell (11 mentions)
Tulane U, 1982 *Certification:* Surgery, Vascular Surgery
50 Humphreys Ctr #30, Memphis, 901-747-2312

Geriatrics

Akins, Derene Ellen (5 mentions)
Med Coll of Georgia, 1978 *Certification:* Internal Medicine
6027 Walnut Grove Rd #201, Memphis, 901-683-0417

Burns, Robert (10 mentions)
U of Buffalo, 1983
Certification: Geriatric Medicine, Internal Medicine
2714 Union Ave #150, Memphis, 901-725-0872

Hematology/Oncology

Baskin, Reed Carl (7 mentions)
U of Tennessee, 1966
Certification: Hematology, Internal Medicine, Medical Oncology
1331 Union Ave #800, Memphis, 901-725-1785
2996 Kate Bond Rd #100, Memphis, 901-767-4520

Blakely, Laura Johnetta (4 mentions)
U of Tennessee, 1998
Certification: Internal Medicine, Medical Oncology
100 N Humphreys Blvd #100, Memphis, 901-683-0055

Dugdale, Marion (6 mentions)
Harvard U, 1954 *Certification:* Hematology, Internal Medicine
842 Jefferson Ave, Memphis, 901-545-8248
880 Madison Ave, Memphis, 901-545-8535

Gore, Margaret (4 mentions)
Duke U, 1986
Certification: Hematology, Internal Medicine, Medical Oncology
6005 Park Ave #1000B, Memphis, 901-685-5655

Gravenor, Donald S. (5 mentions)
FMS-Canada, 1981
Certification: Hematology, Internal Medicine, Medical Oncology
6005 Park Ave #1000B, Memphis, 901-685-5655

Jones, Clyde Michael (4 mentions)
U of Alabama, 1974
Certification: Hematology, Internal Medicine, Medical Oncology
7710 Wolf River Cir, Germantown, 901-685-5969

Lawson, Ronald David (6 mentions)
U of Tennessee, 1973
Certification: Internal Medicine, Medical Oncology
1588 Union Ave, Memphis, 901-322-0251

Pallera, Arnel Molina (10 mentions)
U of Tennessee, 1995 *Certification:* Hematology, Internal
Medicine, Medical Oncology, Pediatrics
100 N Humphreys Blvd, Memphis, 901-683-0055

Reed, Jarvis Dewayne (5 mentions)
U of Tennessee, 1986
100 N Humphreys Blvd, Memphis, 901-683-0055
1588 Union Ave, Memphis, 901-322-0251
7668 Airways Blvd, Southaven, MS, 662-349-9556

Richey, Sylvia Sellers (4 mentions)
U of Alabama, 1997
Certification: Internal Medicine, Medical Oncology
100 N Humphreys Blvd, Memphis, 901-683-0055

Schwartzberg, Lee Steven (12 mentions)
New York Med Coll, 1980
Certification: Hematology, Internal Medicine, Medical Oncology
100 N Humphreys Blvd, Memphis, 901-683-0055

Tauer, Kurt Walter (9 mentions)
St Louis U, 1980
Certification: Internal Medicine, Medical Oncology
100 N Humphreys Blvd, Memphis, 901-683-0055

Weeks, Albert Earle (8 mentions)
U of Texas-Houston, 1983
Certification: Hematology, Internal Medicine, Medical Oncology
6005 Park Ave #1000B, Memphis, 901-685-5655

Infectious Disease

Gelfand, Michael (8 mentions)
U of Texas-Dallas, 1977
Certification: Infectious Disease, Internal Medicine
1325 Eastmoreland Ave #365, Memphis, 901-448-7000

Land, Mack Alan (13 mentions)
U of Tennessee, 1973
Certification: Infectious Disease, Internal Medicine
880 Madison Ave, Memphis, 901-545-7446

Simmons, Bryan Paul (8 mentions)
Vanderbilt U, 1976
Certification: Infectious Disease, Internal Medicine
188 S Bellevue Blvd #408, Memphis, 901-516-8231

Threlkeld, Michael Gavin (29 mentions)
U of Tennessee, 1983
Certification: Infectious Disease, Internal Medicine
5210 Poplar Ave #200, Memphis, 901-685-3490

Threlkeld, Stephen Colin (26 mentions)
U of Alabama, 1990
5210 Poplar Ave #200, Memphis, 901-685-3490

Infertility

Ke, Raymond Weehan (17 mentions)
FMS-Canada, 1986 *Certification:* Obstetrics & Gynecology,
Reproductive Endocrinology/Infertility
80 Humphreys Ctr #307, Memphis, 901-747-2229

Kutteh, William Hanna (8 mentions)
Wake Forest U, 1985 *Certification:* Obstetrics & Gynecology,
    Reproductive Endocrinology/Infertility
80 Humphreys Ctr #307, Memphis, 901-747-2229

Internal Medicine *(see note on page 9)*

Buttross, John Boustany (5 mentions)
U of Mississippi, 1981 *Certification:* Internal Medicine
6799 Great Oaks Rd #250, Germantown, 901-821-8300

Finn, Cary Martin (3 mentions)
East Tennessee State U, 1986
6025 Walnut Grove Rd #301, Memphis, 901-767-3321

Franklin, Edward Arthur (4 mentions)
U of Tennessee, 1991 *Certification:* Internal Medicine
2215 West St, Germantown, 901-756-4338

Freeland, Lynda Jo (4 mentions)
U of Tennessee, 1981 *Certification:* Internal Medicine
7690 Wolf River Cir, Germantown, 901-756-1231

Light, William Harry (5 mentions)
U of Tennessee, 1979 *Certification:* Internal Medicine
7715 Wolf River Blvd, Germantown, 901-328-6031
6025 Walnut Grove Rd #206, Memphis, 901-328-6031

Miller, Stephen Thomas (3 mentions)
Johns Hopkins U, 1970
Certification: Geriatric Medicine, Internal Medicine
1325 Eastmoreland Ave #101, Memphis, 901-516-8785

Overby, Steven Todd (3 mentions)
U of Mississippi, 1996 *Certification:* Internal Medicine
8040 Wolf River Blvd #200, Germantown, 901-726-0200

Taylor, Martha Neumann (3 mentions)
U of Tennessee, 1982 *Certification:* Internal Medicine
7690 Wolf River Cir, Germantown, 901-756-1231

Weiss, William Todd (6 mentions)
East Tennessee State U, 1990 *Certification:* Internal Medicine
6027 Walnut Grove Rd #103, Memphis, 901-763-1695

Wright, David Bruce (4 mentions)
U of South Florida, 1979 *Certification:* Internal Medicine
8066 Walnut Run Rd #200, Cordova, 901-751-9794

Young, Mark Scott (4 mentions)
U of Arkansas, 1982
6005 Park Ave #728-B, Memphis, 901-761-9097

Nephrology

Ebaugh, Lynn (10 mentions)
U of South Alabama, 1988 *Certification:* Nephrology
7640 Wolf River Cir, Germantown, 901-755-0208

Hernandez, Jacinto Angel (6 mentions)
FMS-Spain, 1974 *Certification:* Internal Medicine, Nephrology
310 S Rhodes St, West Memphis, AR, 901-565-0244
6490 Mount Moriah Rd Ext, Memphis, 901-565-0244

Jones, Deborah Price (6 mentions)
U of Tennessee, 1983
Certification: Pediatric Nephrology, Pediatrics
777 Washington Ave #P-110, Memphis, 901-287-5342

Kelley, Bobby J. (10 mentions)
U of Tennessee, 1963
Certification: Internal Medicine, Nephrology
50 Humphreys Blvd #28-A, Memphis, 901-747-3501

Morris, John Thomas, III (6 mentions)
U of Tennessee, 1995 *Certification:* Nephrology
7640 Wolf River Cir, Germantown, 901-755-0208

Ruiz, Julio Pablo (6 mentions)
FMS-Dominican Republic, 1985 *Certification:* Nephrology
6490 Mt Moriah Rd #200, Memphis, 901-528-9565

Stegman, Marc Hadley (6 mentions)
U of Tennessee, 1982 *Certification:* Critical Care Medicine,
    Internal Medicine, Nephrology
2225 Union Ave #100, Memphis, 901-726-1161

Neurological Surgery

Crosby, Glenn Allen, II (7 mentions)
U of Tennessee, 1989 *Certification:* Neurological Surgery
6027 Walnut Grove Rd #409, Memphis, 901-683-4594

Robertson, Jon Hobson (8 mentions)
U of Tennessee, 1971 *Certification:* Neurological Surgery
6325 Humphreys Blvd, Memphis, 901-522-7700

Sanford, Robert Alexander (7 mentions)
U of Arkansas, 1967 *Certification:* Neurological Surgery
6325 Humphreys Blvd, Memphis, 901-522-7700

Sills, Allen Kent, Jr. (8 mentions)
Johns Hopkins U, 1990 *Certification:* Neurological Surgery
6325 Humphreys Blvd, Memphis, 901-522-2548

Smith, Maurice Mell (10 mentions)
U of Southern California, 1988
6325 Humphreys Blvd, Memphis, 901-522-7700

Watridge, Clarence Boyett (30 mentions)
U of Tennessee, 1975 *Certification:* Neurological Surgery
6325 Humphreys Blvd, Memphis, 901-522-7700

Neurology

Arnold, Thomas Winn (11 mentions)
U of Tennessee, 1983 *Certification:* Neurology
8000 Centerview Pkwy #300, Cordova, 901-747-1111

Bertorini, Tulio E. (11 mentions)
Certification: Neurology
1211 Union Ave #400, Memphis, 901-725-8920

Natarajan, Shiva S. (8 mentions)
FMS-India, 1991 *Certification:* Neurology
7645 Wolf River Cir, Germantown, 901-405-0275

Segal, Robert Henry (5 mentions)
U of Tennessee, 1983 *Certification:* Neurology
8000 Centerview Pkwy #300, Cordova, 901-747-1111

Stein, Lee (19 mentions)
Med Coll of Georgia, 1981 *Certification:* Neurology
8000 Centerview Pkwy #300, Cordova, 901-747-1111

Vasu, Renga I. (15 mentions)
FMS-India, 1973 *Certification:* Neurology
8000 Centerview Pkwy #300, Cordova, 901-747-1111

Wright, Lance Jefferson (9 mentions)
U of Texas-Houston, 1986 *Certification:* Neurology
6325 Humphreys Blvd, Memphis, 901-522-7700

Obstetrics/Gynecology

Chauhan, Heather Pearson (3 mentions)
U of Tennessee, 2000 *Certification:* Obstetrics & Gynecology
6215 Humphreys Blvd #500, Memphis, 901-682-0630

Joe, Penn Quork (4 mentions)
U of Tennessee, 1980 *Certification:* Obstetrics & Gynecology
6215 Humphreys Blvd #401, Memphis, 901-767-8442
7705 Poplar Ave #340, Germantown, 901-767-8442

Kennedy, Albert Franklin (3 mentions)
U of Tennessee, 1986 *Certification:* Obstetrics & Gynecology
6215 Humphreys Blvd #500, Memphis, 901-682-0630

Ling, Frank Wen-Yung (7 mentions)
U of Texas-Dallas, 1974 *Certification:* Obstetrics & Gynecology
7800 Wolf Trail Cove, Germantown, 901-682-9222

Long, Diane M. (3 mentions)
U of Tennessee, 1982 *Certification:* Obstetrics & Gynecology
6215 Humphreys Blvd #500, Memphis, 901-682-0630

Lynn, Carol I. (3 mentions)
Certification: Obstetrics & Gynecology
2136 Exeter Dr #103, Germantown, 901-755-2900

McDonald, Mary Neumann (6 mentions)
U of Tennessee, 1983 *Certification:* Obstetrics & Gynecology
625 Humphreys Blvd #200, Memphis, 901-752-4500

Murrmann, Susan Ann (3 mentions)
Rosalind Franklin U, 1987 *Certification:* Obstetrics & Gynecology
6215 Humphreys Blvd #200, Memphis, 901-752-4500
7705 Poplar Ave #110, Germantown, 901-752-4500

Sullivant, Henry Paul (9 mentions)
U of Mississippi, 1979 *Certification:* Obstetrics & Gynecology
6215 Humphreys Blvd #500, Memphis, 901-682-0630

Tejwani, Indurani (4 mentions)
FMS-India, 1966 *Certification:* Obstetrics & Gynecology
6005 Park Ave #508, Memphis, 901-682-2469

Wortham, George F., III (3 mentions)
U of Tennessee, 1983 *Certification:* Obstetrics & Gynecology
6215 Humphreys Blvd #401, Memphis, 901-767-8442
7900 Hwy 64, Bartlett, 901-373-9221

Ophthalmology

Byrd, Kathryn Woods (6 mentions)
U of Tennessee, 1988 *Certification:* Ophthalmology
6515 Poplar Ave #112, Memphis, 901-681-9600

Charles, Steven Thomas (5 mentions)
U of Miami, 1969 *Certification:* Ophthalmology
6401 Poplar Ave #190, Memphis, 901-767-4499

Fleming, James Christian (12 mentions)
U of Tennessee, 1974 *Certification:* Ophthalmology
930 Madison Ave #200, Memphis, 901-448-6650
7945 Wolf River Blvd #240, Germantown, 901-347-8240

Furr, Philip Marvin (4 mentions)
U of Mississippi, 1980
920 Madison Ave #605, Memphis, 901-522-1700

Gettelfinger, Thomas C. (4 mentions)
Harvard U, 1966 *Certification:* Ophthalmology
6485 Poplar Ave, Memphis, 901-767-3937

Hamilton, Ralph F. (6 mentions)
Certification: Ophthalmology
6238 Poplar Ave, Memphis, 901-761-4292

Hidaji, Faramarz Fred (5 mentions)
U of Tennessee, 1992 *Certification:* Ophthalmology
6252 Poplar Ave, Memphis, 901-754-3937

Passons, Gary Allen (10 mentions)
U of Tennessee, 1980 *Certification:* Ophthalmology
909 Ridgeway Loop Rd, Memphis, 901-683-1112

Schaeffer, Alan Randall (4 mentions)
U of Missouri-Kansas City, 1987 *Certification:* Ophthalmology
775 Goodman Rd E, Southaven, MS, 662-349-1827
9075 E Sandidge Cv, Olive Branch, MS, 662-895-4949

Orthopedics

Austin, Susan Marguerite (5 mentions)
U of Tennessee, 1989 *Certification:* Orthopaedic Surgery
6286 Briarcrest Ave, Memphis, 901-259-1600

Beaty, James Harold (10 mentions)
U of Tennessee, 1976 *Certification:* Orthopaedic Surgery
1400 S Germantown Rd, Germantown, 901-759-3125

Ennis, Richard Lyn (5 mentions)
U of Tennessee, 1971 *Certification:* Orthopaedic Surgery
6005 Park Ave #430B, Memphis, 901-682-9161

Guyton, James Lawrence (7 mentions)
Harvard U, 1985 *Certification:* Orthopaedic Surgery
1400 S Germantown Rd, Germantown, 901-759-3100

Harkess, James Wilson (8 mentions)
Med Coll of Georgia, 1982 *Certification:* Orthopaedic Surgery
1400 S Germantown Rd, Germantown, 901-759-3100

Holcomb, Randall Lawrence (8 mentions)
U of Tennessee, 1978 *Certification:* Orthopaedic Surgery
6286 Briarcrest Ave, Memphis, 901-259-1600

Lavelle, David Glen (7 mentions)
U of Tennessee, 1979 *Certification:* Orthopaedic Surgery
1400 S Germantown Rd, Germantown, 901-759-3131

Lindy, Peter Barnes (4 mentions)
Tulane U, 1989
6005 Park Ave #309, Memphis, 901-682-5642

Manugian, Arsen H. (6 mentions)
FMS-United Kingdom, 1972 *Certification:* Orthopaedic Surgery
4816 Riverdale Rd, Memphis, 901-624-8251
3980 New Covington Pike #200, Memphis, 901-624-8251
1325 Eastmoreland Ave #260, Memphis, 901-725-5136
8040 Wolf River Blvd #100, Germantown, 901-756-0068

Miller, Robert Horace, III (5 mentions)
Vanderbilt U, 1980
Certification: Orthopaedic Sports Medicine, Orthopaedic Surgery
1400 S Germantown Rd, Germantown, 901-759-3100

Neel, Michael Daniel (5 mentions)
U of Tennessee, 1989 *Certification:* Orthopaedic Surgery
1068 Cresthaven Rd #400, Memphis, 901-259-1600

Warner, William C., Jr. (6 mentions)
Tulane U, 1983 *Certification:* Orthopaedic Surgery
1400 S Germantown Rd, Germantown, 901-759-3142

Otorhinolaryngology

Beckford, Neal S. (16 mentions)
Howard U, 1980 *Certification:* Otolaryngology
7675 Wolf River Cir #202, Germantown, 901-737-3021
975 Swinnea Rdg #1, Southaven, MS, 662-349-0448

Duncan, Thane Edward (11 mentions)
Wake Forest U, 1987 *Certification:* Otolaryngology
8090 Walnut Run Rd, Cordova, 901-755-5300

Klug, Dean Anthony (16 mentions)
U of Arkansas, 1988 *Certification:* Otolaryngology
6286 Briar Crest Ave #300, Memphis, 901-755-5300

Long, Thomas Edward (9 mentions)
U of Tennessee, 1973 *Certification:* Otolaryngology
7675 Wolf River Cir #202, Germantown, 901-737-3021
975 Swinnea Ridge #1, Southaven, MS, 662-349-0448

Touliatos, John Spero (7 mentions)
U of Tennessee, 1995 *Certification:* Otolaryngology
6286 Briarcrest Ave #300, Memphis, 901-767-7750

Pain Medicine

Green, Phillip Edward (8 mentions)
U of Arkansas, 1984 *Certification:* Anesthesiology
6005 Park Ave #502, Memphis, 901-761-0800

Mays, Kit Sanford (22 mentions)
U of Tennessee, 1972
55 Humphreys Ctr #200, Memphis, 901-747-0040

Parker, Autry James, Jr. (10 mentions)
Yale U, 1988 *Certification:* Anesthesiology
6005 Park Ave #802, Memphis, 901-763-0037

Schnapp, Moacir (9 mentions)
FMS-Brazil, 1976
55 Humphreys Ctr #200, Memphis, 901-747-0040

Pathology

Bugg, Michael Frederick (4 mentions)
Louisiana State U, 1988
Certification: Anatomic Pathology & Clinical Pathology
7550 Wolf River Blvd #200, Germantown, 901-542-6800

Callihan, Thomas Ralph (3 mentions)
George Washington U, 1973
Certification: Anatomic Pathology & Clinical Pathology
7550 Wolf River Blvd #200, Germantown, 901-542-6800

Groshart, Kenneth Dean (4 mentions)
U of Tennessee, 1972 *Certification:* Anatomic Pathology &
Clinical Pathology, Internal Medicine
7550 Wolf River Blvd #200, Germantown, 901-542-6800

Handorf, Charles Russell (5 mentions)
U of Tennessee, 1977
Certification: Anatomic Pathology & Clinical Pathology
1211 Union Ave #300, Memphis, 901-725-7551

Joyner, Royce Etienne (3 mentions)
Vanderbilt U, 1979
Certification: Anatomic Pathology & Clinical Pathology
1211 Union Ave #300, Memphis, 901-725-7551

O'Brien, Thomas Francis, Jr. (5 mentions)
U of Tennessee, 1986
Certification: Anatomic Pathology & Clinical Pathology
1211 Union Ave #200, Memphis, 901-725-7551

Spencer, Gene David, Jr. (5 mentions)
U of Mississippi, 1987
Certification: Anatomic Pathology & Clinical Pathology
7550 Wolf River Blvd #200, Germantown, 901-542-6800

White, Frank Louis (3 mentions)
U of Tennessee, 1969 *Certification:* Anatomic Pathology &
Clinical Pathology, Hematology
1211 Union Ave #300, Memphis, 901-516-7182

Pediatrics *(see note on page 9)*

Edwards, Lelon (6 mentions)
U of Tennessee, 1981 *Certification:* Pediatrics
2004 Exeter Rd, Germantown, 901-757-3530

Fesmire, William Murray (6 mentions)
U of Tennessee, 1984
120 Crescent Dr, Collierville, 901-757-3560

Frizzell, Noel K. (7 mentions)
U of Tennessee, 1977 *Certification:* Pediatrics
777 Washington Ave #410, Memphis, 901-523-2945

Saino, James D. (3 mentions)
U of Tennessee, 1977 *Certification:* Pediatrics
1172 Vickery Ln, Cordova, 901-757-0095

Senter, Anthony M. (3 mentions)
U of Tennessee, 1984
2002 Exeter Rd, Germantown, 901-757-3570

Threlkeld, William Cleage (3 mentions)
U of Tennessee, 1954 *Certification:* Pediatrics
8110 Walnut Run Rd, Cordova, 901-754-9600

Plastic Surgery

Adams, Robert Louis (14 mentions)
U of Tennessee, 1977
80 Humphreys Center Dr #100, Memphis, 901-761-9030

Burruss, George Lewis (18 mentions)
U of Tennessee, 1977 *Certification:* Plastic Surgery
80 Humphreys Center Dr #100, Memphis, 901-761-9030

Efird, Walter G., III (9 mentions)
Tulane U, 1983 *Certification:* Plastic Surgery, Surgery
1329 Cordova Cv, Germantown, 901-737-2345

Goshorn, Neumon Taylor (9 mentions)
U of Mississippi, 1980 *Certification:* Plastic Surgery
80 Humphreys Ctr #100, Memphis, 901-756-3838

Koleyni, Asghar (7 mentions)
FMS-Iran, 1962
6005 Park Ave #1007B, Memphis, 901-761-2400

Psychiatry

Bannister, Thomas Glenn (5 mentions)
U of Tennessee, 1989
5384 Poplar Ave #106, Memphis, 901-255-3030

Berry, Karen (6 mentions)
U of Tennessee, 1984 *Certification:* Psychiatry
1715 Aaron Brenner Dr #326, Memphis, 901-405-6474

Black, Audria K. (3 mentions)
Certification: Psychiatry
8000 Centerview Pkwy #104, Cordova, 901-755-6280

Bomar, John Cornelios, Jr. (3 mentions)
U of Tennessee, 1993
6750 Poplar Ave #620, Memphis, 901-755-9908

Boyd, Daniel Street (5 mentions)
U of Tennessee, 1990 *Certification:* Psychiatry
2911 Bruswick Rd, Memphis, 901-377-4700

Buchalter, Robert (6 mentions)
U of Tennessee, 1964 *Certification:* Psychiatry
6005 Park Ave #524-B, Memphis, 901-767-0500

Clein, Paul David (3 mentions)
Med Coll of Georgia, 1990
Certification: Child & Adolescent Psychiatry
2911 Brunswick Rd, Memphis, 901-377-4700

Digaetano, Dolores Maria (5 mentions)
Certification: Psychiatry
8316 Macon Terr #103, Cordova, 901-757-0568

Heston, Jerry Dale (5 mentions)
U of South Florida, 1981
Certification: Child & Adolescent Psychiatry, Pediatrics, Psychiatry
1135 Cully Rd #100, Cordova, 901-752-1980

Hill, Paul Bryan (9 mentions)
U of Tennessee, 1985 *Certification:* Geriatric Psychiatry,
Psychiatry, Psychosomatic Medicine
1715 Aaron Brenner Dr #326, Memphis, 901-405-6440

Hoehn, Robert Gardell (3 mentions)
U of Tennessee, 1989 *Certification:* Child & Adolescent Psychiatry
1384 Cordova Rd #1, Germantown, 901-753-7700

Rice, Steven Nicholas (5 mentions)
Tulane U, 1976 *Certification:* Psychiatry
6005 Park Ave #630-B, Memphis, 901-767-3241

Pulmonary Disease

Aguillard, Robert Neal (8 mentions)
Louisiana State U-Shreveport, 1984 *Certification:* Critical
Care Medicine, Internal Medicine, Pulmonary Disease
5050 Poplar Ave #800, Memphis, 901-276-2662

Deaton, Paul Rumble (6 mentions)
U of Tennessee, 1987 *Certification:* Critical Care Medicine,
Internal Medicine, Pulmonary Disease
5050 Poplar Ave #800, Memphis, 901-276-2662

Fox, Roy Cecil (8 mentions)
U of Mississippi, 1985 *Certification:* Critical Care Medicine,
Internal Medicine, Pulmonary Disease
5050 Poplar Ave #800, Memphis, 901-276-2662

Golden, Emmel B., Jr. (23 mentions)
U of Tennessee, 1975
Certification: Internal Medicine, Pulmonary Disease
6025 Walnut Grove Rd #508, Memphis, 901-767-5864

Mariencheck, William Irvin (8 mentions)
U of Tennessee, 1965
Certification: Internal Medicine, Pulmonary Disease
5050 Poplar Ave #800, Memphis, 901-276-2662

Wilons, Michael David (6 mentions)
U of Tennessee, 1972
6025 Walnut Grove Rd #508, Memphis, 901-767-5864

Radiology—Diagnostic

Carruth, Paul Clay (3 mentions)
U of Tennessee, 1992 *Certification:* Diagnostic Radiology
7691 Poplar Ave, Germantown, 907-685-2696

Flinn, George Shea, Jr. (5 mentions)
U of Tennessee, 1969 *Certification:* Nuclear Medicine, Radiology
188 S Bellevue Blvd #222, Memphis, 901-726-1178
2120 S Germantown Rd, Germantown, 901-755-5562

Krisle, Joe Richard, Jr. (4 mentions)
U of Tennessee, 1973 *Certification:* Diagnostic Radiology
6019 Walnut Grove Rd, Memphis, 901-747-1000

Laster, Robert Eugene, Jr. (3 mentions)
U of Tennessee, 1970 *Certification:* Radiology
1661 International Place Dr #350, Memphis, 901-685-2696

Machin, James Elliott (4 mentions)
Indiana U, 1978 *Certification:* Diagnostic Radiology
6305 Humphreys Blvd #205, Memphis, 901-747-1000

Optican, Robert Joseph (11 mentions)
Washington U, 1988 *Certification:* Diagnostic Radiology
6019 Walnut Grove Rd, Memphis, 901-747-1000

Parvey, Louis Swig (7 mentions)
U of Tennessee, 1968 *Certification:* Diagnostic Radiology
6401 Poplar Ave #100, Memphis, 901-387-2340

Pinstein, Martin Lee (3 mentions)
U of Mississippi, 1973 *Certification:* Diagnostic Radiology
5959 Park Ave, Memphis, 901-765-2191
6005 Park Ave #101-B, Memphis, 901-685-3114

Routt, William Edward, Jr. (5 mentions)
U of Tennessee, 1977 *Certification:* Diagnostic Radiology
1661 International Dr #400, Memphis, 901-291-2400

Witte, Dexter H., III (10 mentions)
U of Tennessee, 1985 *Certification:* Diagnostic Radiology
6019 Walnut Grove Rd, Memphis, 901-747-1000

Radiology—Therapeutic

Roberts, Jon Alan (4 mentions)
East Tennessee State U, 1990 *Certification:* Diagnostic Radiology
7691 Poplar Ave, Germantown, 901-683-1890

Zeni, Phillip T., Jr. (5 mentions)
U of Arkansas, 1994 *Certification:* Diagnostic Radiology,
Vascular & Interventional Radiology
6019 Walnut Grove Rd, Memphis, 901-747-1000
6305 Humphreys Blvd #205, Memphis, 901-747-1000

Rehabilitation

Cunningham, Dale Preston (6 mentions)
U of Tennessee, 1986
Certification: Physical Medicine & Rehabilitation
3265 W Sarazen's Cir #101, Memphis, 901-737-9787

Cunningham, Mark Lane (4 mentions)
U of Tennessee, 1983
Certification: Physical Medicine & Rehabilitation
7601 Southcrest Pkwy, Southaven, MS, 662-772-4000

Greene, Robert W., Jr. (4 mentions)
U of Tennessee, 1985
Certification: Physical Medicine & Rehabilitation
220 S Claybrook St #500, Memphis, 901-722-5833

Rheumatology

Adams, Robert Franklin (11 mentions)
U of Tennessee, 1963 *Certification:* Internal Medicine
388 S Pauline St, Memphis, 901-525-0278
6263 Poplar Ave #503, Memphis, 901-685-2481

Arkin, Charles Richard (12 mentions)
U of Tennessee, 1964
Certification: Internal Medicine, Rheumatology
540 Trinity Creek Cv, Cordova, 901-309-5000

Ash, Judy Duxbury (9 mentions)
U of Tennessee, 1986
Certification: Internal Medicine, Rheumatology
540 Trinity Creek Cv, Cordova, 901-309-5000

Boatright, Michael David (10 mentions)
U of Tennessee, 2000
Certification: Internal Medicine, Rheumatology
540 Trinity Creek Cv, Cordova, 901-309-5000

Holt, Huey Thomas, Jr. (11 mentions)
U of Tennessee, 1987 *Certification:* Rheumatology
388 S Pauline St, Memphis, 901-525-0278

Thoracic Surgery

Garrett, Harvey E., Jr. (13 mentions)
Vanderbilt U, 1979
Certification: Surgery, Thoracic Surgery, Vascular Surgery
6029 Walnut Grove Rd #401, Memphis, 901-747-3066

Robbins, Samuel Gwin, Jr. (9 mentions)
U of Tennessee, 1971 *Certification:* Thoracic Surgery
6005 Park Ave #329B, Memphis, 901-761-2470

Wolf, Rodney Yale (7 mentions)
U of Tennessee, 1961 *Certification:* Surgery, Thoracic Surgery
6029 Walnut Grove Rd #401, Memphis, 901-747-3066

Urology

Chauhan, Ravi Dinesh (8 mentions)
U of Tennessee, 1999 *Certification:* Urology
1325 Wolf Park Dr #102, Germantown, 901-252-3400

Conrad, Lynn Wilson (9 mentions)
U of Tennessee, 1969 *Certification:* Urology
1325 Wolf Park Dr #102, Germantown, 901-252-3400

Greenberger, Mark David (6 mentions)
Emory U, 1994 *Certification:* Urology
6029 Walnut Grove Rd #300, Memphis, 901-767-8158
7420 Guthrie Dr N #111, Southaven, MS, 662-349-2220

Gubin, David Alvin (6 mentions)
U of Tennessee, 1993 *Certification:* Urology
6029 Walnut Grove Rd #300, Memphis, 901-767-8158

McSwain, Harold Michael (7 mentions)
U of Tennessee, 1977 *Certification:* Urology
1325 Wolf Park Dr #102, Germantown, 901-252-3400

Pearson, Richard M. (20 mentions)
U of Tennessee, 1971 *Certification:* Urology
1325 Wolf Park Dr #102, Germantown, 901-252-3400

Shelton, Thomas Berkeley (6 mentions)
U of Tennessee, 1981 *Certification:* Urology
1325 Wolf Park Dr #102, Germantown, 901-252-3400

Walzer, Yair (9 mentions)
FMS-Canada, 1976 *Certification:* Urology
640 N Germantown Pkwy #200, Cordova, 901-753-9821

Vascular Surgery

Burke, Larry Dale (14 mentions)
Washington U, 1972 *Certification:* Surgery
6025 Walnut Grove Rd #311, Memphis, 901-683-6166

Garrett, Harvey E., Jr. (8 mentions)
Vanderbilt U, 1979
Certification: Surgery, Thoracic Surgery, Vascular Surgery
6029 Walnut Grove Rd #401, Memphis, 901-747-3066

Nashville Area
Including Davidson County

Allergy/Immunology

Marney, Samuel Rowe, Jr. (9 mentions)
U of Virginia, 1960 *Certification:* Allergy & Immunology, Diagnostic Laboratory Immunology, Internal Medicine
2611 W End Ave #210, Nashville, 615-322-2727

Sanders, Dan Sumner, III (10 mentions)
Vanderbilt U, 1978
Certification: Allergy & Immunology, Pediatrics
300 20th Ave N #100, Nashville, 615-340-4731

Tanner, S. Bobo (6 mentions)
Wake Forest U, 1983 *Certification:* Allergy & Immunology, Internal Medicine, Rheumatology
2611 W End Ave #210, Nashville, 615-322-2727

Wolf, Bruce Lee (13 mentions)
U of Louisville, 1982
Certification: Allergy & Immunology, Internal Medicine
4230 Harding Pike #307, Nashville, 615-292-8299

Anesthesiology

Crawford, Walter M., Jr. (3 mentions)
U of Tennessee, 1983
Certification: Anesthesiology, Internal Medicine
110 29th Ave N #201, Nashville, 615-327-4304

Dalton, John Charles (5 mentions)
Loma Linda U, 1983 *Certification:* Anesthesiology
110 29th Ave N #202, Nashville, 615-327-4304
2000 Church St, Nashville, 615-284-5555

Siegel, Marc Neal (4 mentions)
U of Texas-San Antonio, 1985 *Certification:* Anesthesiology
110 29th Ave N #202, Nashville, 615-327-4304
345 23rd Ave N #201, Nashville, 615-327-1123

Cardiac Surgery

Austin, John Clayton (7 mentions)
U of Oklahoma, 1982 *Certification:* Thoracic Surgery
2010 Church St #736, Nashville, 615-329-7878

Drinkwater, Davis Clapp (6 mentions)
U of Vermont, 1976 *Certification:* Thoracic Surgery
2400 Patterson St #400, Nashville, 615-342-5812

Petracek, Michael Ray (13 mentions)
Johns Hopkins U, 1971 *Certification:* Thoracic Surgery
1215 21st Ave S, Nashville, 615-343-9195

Shuman, Todd Alan (6 mentions)
Vanderbilt U, 1983
Certification: Surgery, Surgical Critical Care, Thoracic Surgery
4230 Harding Rd #501, Nashville, 615-385-4781

Wilcox, Allen Brian, Jr. (6 mentions)
U of Tennessee, 1986 *Certification:* Thoracic Surgery
2010 Church St #303, Nashville, 615-329-7878

Cardiology

Baker, Michael Thomas (5 mentions)
U of Tennessee, 1990 *Certification:* Cardiovascular Disease
1215 21st Ave S #5209, Nashville, 615-322-2318
1420 W Baddour Pkwy, Lebanon, 615-547-7778

Cage, John Bright (4 mentions)
Texas Tech U, 1987 *Certification:* Cardiovascular Disease
222 22nd Ave N #400, Nashville, 615-329-5144

Christenberry, Robert H. (5 mentions)
U of Alabama, 1979
Certification: Cardiovascular Disease, Internal Medicine
222 22nd Ave N #400, Nashville, 615-329-5144

Churchwell, Andre Lemont (7 mentions)
Harvard U, 1979
Certification: Cardiovascular Disease, Internal Medicine
1215 21st Ave S #5209, Nashville, 615-322-3000

Crumbo, Donald Slider (3 mentions)
Vanderbilt U, 1971
Certification: Cardiovascular Disease, Internal Medicine
5651 Frist Blvd #603, Hermitage, 615-889-1968

Fleet, William Floyd, III (3 mentions)
U of North Carolina, 1986 *Certification:* Cardiovascular Disease, Internal Medicine, Interventional Cardiology
222 22nd Ave N #400, Nashville, 615-329-5144

Fredi, Joseph Lawrence (3 mentions)
U of Tennessee, 1983 *Certification:* Cardiovascular Disease, Internal Medicine, Interventional Cardiology
1215 Medical Center E, Nashville, 615-322-2318

Hood, Rob Reid (4 mentions)
Tulane U, 1980
Certification: Cardiovascular Disease, Internal Medicine
1215 21st Ave S #5209, Nashville, 615-322-3000

Jones, R. Christopher (3 mentions)
Vanderbilt U, 1998 *Certification:* Cardiovascular Disease, Clinical Cardiac Electrophysiology, Internal Medicine
2400 Patterson St #502, Nashville, 615-515-1900

Kreth, Timothy Kerwin (4 mentions)
U of Arkansas, 1980 *Certification:* Cardiovascular Disease, Internal Medicine, Interventional Cardiology
5651 Frist Blvd #603, Hermitage, 615-889-1968

McPherson, John Addison (4 mentions)
U of California-Los Angeles, 1993
Certification: Cardiovascular Disease, Interventional Cardiology
1215 21st Ave S #5209, Nashville, 615-322-2318

McRae, Andrew T., III (3 mentions)
Mercer U, 1996
Certification: Cardiovascular Disease, Internal Medicine
2400 Patterson St #502, Nashville, 615-515-1900

Waldo, Douglas Anthony (5 mentions)
U of Buffalo, 1979
Certification: Cardiovascular Disease, Internal Medicine
2400 Patterson St #215, Nashville, 615-515-2929

Dermatology

Horowitz, David Harvey (4 mentions)
Meharry Med Coll, 1970 *Certification:* Dermatology
1900 Patterson St #205, Nashville, 615-329-0341

Langley, Melissa (4 mentions)
Emory U, 1986 *Certification:* Dermatology, Internal Medicine
250 25th Ave N #307, Nashville, 615-321-1020

Loven, Keith H. (4 mentions)
Vanderbilt U, 1983 *Certification:* Dermatology
201 Bluebird Dr, Goodlettsville, 615-859-7546

Moody, Brent Robert (4 mentions)
Emory U, 1996 *Certification:* Dermatology, Internal Medicine
3098 Campbell Station Pkwy #A-201, Springhill, 615-322-1221
1900 Patterson St #201, Nashville, 615-322-1221

Rand, Heidi Katherine (4 mentions)
Southern Illinois U, 1997 *Certification:* Dermatology
222 22nd Ave N #100, Nashville, 615-324-1205

Sitton, Barbara Cameron (4 mentions)
U of Virginia, 1988 *Certification:* Dermatology
1900 Patterson St #202, Nashville, 615-327-2075

Smith, Michael Lee (5 mentions)
East Carolina U, 1983
Certification: Dermatology, Pediatric Dermatology, Pediatrics
1301 22nd Ave S #3903, Nashville, 615-322-6485

Zanolli, Michael Dominic (7 mentions)
U of Tennessee, 1981 *Certification:* Dermatology
4230 Harding Rd #609-E, Nashville, 615-222-3442

Zic, John Alan (6 mentions)
Vanderbilt U, 1991 *Certification:* Dermatology
3601 Vanderbilt Clinic, Nashville, 615-322-6485

Emergency Medicine

Bonner, Kevin J., Jr. (3 mentions)
FMS-Canada, 1978 *Certification:* Emergency Medicine
1 Vantage Way, Nashville, 615-329-4020
400 N Highland Ave, Murfreesboro, 615-396-6900

Hoover, Bradley Whitt (3 mentions)
U of Tennessee, 1989 *Certification:* Emergency Medicine
5655 Frist Blvd, Hermitage, 615-316-3150

Hutton, Robert Meredith (7 mentions)
West Virginia U, 1976 *Certification:* Emergency Medicine
1 Vantage Way #B-240, Nashville, 615-329-4020

Marsden, Mark Edward (4 mentions)
Louisiana State U-Shreveport, 1990
Certification: Emergency Medicine
4220 Harding Pike, Nashville, 615-222-6733

Pasto-Crosby, Douglas J. (3 mentions)
SUNY-Upstate Med U, 1980
Certification: Emergency Medicine, Family Medicine
4220 Harding Pike, Nashville, 615-222-6733

Singer, Gary D. (3 mentions)
2300 Patterson St, Nashville, 615-342-1000

Slovis, Corey Mitchell (5 mentions)
New Jersey Med Sch, 1975
Certification: Emergency Medicine, Internal Medicine
2312 Valley Brook Rd, Nashville, 615-936-1315
703 Oxford House, Nashville, 615-936-1315

Walker, Andy, III (5 mentions)
U of Tennessee, 1985
5655 Frist Blvd, Hermitage, 615-316-3000

Endocrinology

Carlson, Michael Glenn (7 mentions)
Vanderbilt U, 1985 *Certification:* Endocrinology, Diabetes,
   and Metabolism, Internal Medicine
2400 Patterson St #418, Nashville, 615-342-5909

Fassler, Cheryl Ann (5 mentions)
Ohio State U, 1982
Certification: Endocrinology and Metabolism, Internal Medicine
2000 Church St, Nashville, 615-284-5167

Gaume, James Alan (5 mentions)
U of Southern California, 1976
Certification: Endocrinology and Metabolism, Internal Medicine
4230 Harding Pike #527, Nashville, 615-386-3067

Interlandi, John William (5 mentions)
Vanderbilt U, 1976
Certification: Endocrinology and Metabolism, Internal Medicine
5651 Frist Blvd #208, Hermitage, 615-871-7258

McRae, John Radford (5 mentions)
Duke U, 1972
Certification: Endocrinology and Metabolism, Internal Medicine
4230 Harding Rd #527, Nashville, 615-386-3067

Najjar, Jennifer Lee (5 mentions)
Tufts U, 1977 *Certification:* Pediatric Endocrinology, Pediatrics
2200 Childrens Way, Nashville, 615-322-7427

Sullivan, James Nelson (4 mentions)
Vanderbilt U, 1974
Certification: Endocrinology and Metabolism, Internal Medicine
1919 Charlotte Ave #100, Nashville, 615-340-1342

Wierum, Craig (7 mentions)
U of North Carolina, 1990 *Certification:* Endocrinology,
   Diabetes, and Metabolism, Internal Medicine
222 22nd Ave N #100, Nashville, 615-284-2222

Family Practice *(see note on page 9)*

Mertens, Michael John (3 mentions)
U of Tennessee, 1997 *Certification:* Family Medicine
5045 Old Hickory Dr #200, Hermitage, 615-883-6545

Sanders, Burton Parker (6 mentions)
FMS-Mexico, 1981 *Certification:* Family Medicine
2400 Patterson St #500, Nashville, 615-327-7400

Gastroenterology

Bailey, Allan Harold (4 mentions)
Indiana U, 1980
Certification: Gastroenterology, Internal Medicine
2010 Church St #420, Nashville, 615-329-2141
397 Wallace Rd #407, Nashville, 615-832-5530
3443 Dickerson Pike #430, Nashville, 615-868-1064

James, G. Whit (5 mentions)
Wake Forest U, 1987 *Certification:* Gastroenterology
5651 Frist Blvd #309, Hermitage, 615-885-1093

Lewis, Thomas Jackson, Jr. (6 mentions)
Med Coll of Georgia, 1989 *Certification:* Gastroenterology
2400 Patterson St #101, Nashville, 615-342-5909

Lind, Christopher D. (8 mentions)
Vanderbilt U, 1981
Certification: Gastroenterology, Internal Medicine
1301 Medical Center Dr #1660, Nashville, 615-322-0128

Mertz, Howard Randall (5 mentions)
Baylor U, 1986 *Certification:* Gastroenterology, Internal Medicine
4320 Harding Rd #309-W, Nashville, 615-383-0165

Mitchell, Douglas Park (5 mentions)
Vanderbilt U, 1969
Certification: Gastroenterology, Internal Medicine
222 22nd Ave N #100, Nashville, 615-284-2222

Price, Neil Morgan (4 mentions)
U of Texas-San Antonio, 1981
Certification: Gastroenterology, Internal Medicine
300 20th Ave N, Nashville, 615-284-1400

Pruitt, Ronald Edward (5 mentions)
U of North Carolina, 1984
Certification: Gastroenterology, Internal Medicine
4230 Harding Pike #309-W, Nashville, 615-383-0165

Stein, Ira Edward (6 mentions)
U of Tennessee, 1990 *Certification:* Gastroenterology
2400 Patterson St #515, Nashville, 615-327-2111

Wright, George Dewey (5 mentions)
Vanderbilt U, 1981
Certification: Gastroenterology, Internal Medicine
222 22nd Ave N #100, Nashville, 615-284-2222

General Surgery

Ballinger, Jeanne Field (9 mentions)
Harvard U, 1977 *Certification:* Surgery
4230 Harding Pike #302, Nashville, 615-292-7708

Boskind, John Andrew (5 mentions)
Loma Linda U, 1997 *Certification:* Surgery
5651 Frist Blvd #709, Hermitage, 615-883-5646

Bradham, William Glenn (3 mentions)
Med U of South Carolina, 1987 *Certification:* Surgery
2400 Patterson St #220, Nashville, 615-333-6996

Cooper, Mark Elbert (4 mentions)
U of Alabama, 1988 *Certification:* Surgery
356 24th Ave N #400, Nashville, 615-329-7887

Garrard, Clifford Louis (4 mentions)
Vanderbilt U, 1990 *Certification:* Surgery, Vascular Surgery
356 24th Ave N #400, Nashville, 615-329-7887

McDowell, James G. (3 mentions)
U of Texas-San Antonio, 1998 *Certification:* Surgery
2021 Church St #104, Nashville, 618-284-2400
356 24th Ave N #400, Nashville, 615-329-7887

Mulherin, Joseph Louis, Jr. (3 mentions)
Med Coll of Georgia, 1971 *Certification:* Surgery, Vascular Surgery
4230 Harding Pike #525, Nashville, 615-385-1547

Polk, William Howard, Jr. (7 mentions)
Vanderbilt U, 1985 *Certification:* Surgery
356 24th Ave N #400, Nashville, 615-329-7887

Sharp, Kenneth Warren (4 mentions)
Johns Hopkins U, 1977 *Certification:* Surgery
21st & Garland Aves Med Ctr N #5203, Nashville, 615-322-0259
1211 22nd Ave S, Nashville, 615-322-3000

Geriatrics

Garman, Richard William, Jr. (4 mentions)
U of Louisville, 1980 *Certification:* Internal Medicine
300 20th Ave N #9, Nashville, 615-284-1400

Powers, James Stephen (12 mentions)
U of Rochester, 1977
Certification: Geriatric Medicine, Internal Medicine
1215 21st Ave S, Nashville, 615-936-3274

Hematology/Oncology

Cooper, Robert Seth (5 mentions)
Louisiana State U, 1971
Certification: Hematology, Internal Medicine
4230 Harding Rd #707, Nashville, 615-385-3751

Dickson, Natalie R. (3 mentions)
FMS-Jamaica, 1991
Certification: Hematology, Internal Medicine, Medical Oncology
4230 Harding Pike #707, Nashville, 615-385-3751

Greco, Frank Anthony (4 mentions)
West Virginia U, 1972
Certification: Internal Medicine, Medical Oncology
250 25th Ave N #100, Nashville, 615-320-5090

Greer, John Pettry (5 mentions)
Vanderbilt U, 1976 *Certification:* Hematology, Internal
   Medicine, Medical Oncology, Pediatrics
2311 Pierce Ave #227, Nashville, 615-936-1803

Magee, Michael Joseph (4 mentions)
U of Tennessee, 1977
Certification: Hematology, Internal Medicine, Medical Oncology
222 20th Ave N #506, Nashville, 615-329-7870

Penley, William Charles (3 mentions)
Wake Forest U, 1982
Certification: Internal Medicine, Medical Oncology
300 20th Ave N #301, Nashville, 615-329-0570

Raefsky, Eric Lee (13 mentions)
Temple U, 1980
Certification: Hematology, Internal Medicine, Medical Oncology
5653 Frist Blvd #434, Hermitage, 615-871-9996

Rogers, Karl Malone (5 mentions)
Rush U, 1987 *Certification:* Internal Medicine, Medical Oncology
2011 Church St #701, Nashville, 615-284-2310

Toomey, Mitchell Alan (3 mentions)
U of Tennessee, 1984
Certification: Internal Medicine, Medical Oncology
5653 Frist Blvd #434, Hermitage, 615-871-9996

Whitlock, James Alan (3 mentions)
Vanderbilt U, 1984 *Certification:* Pediatric Hematology-Oncology
2220 Pierce Ave, Nashville, 615-936-1762

Willis, Carl Rogaston (3 mentions)
U of Alabama, 1993
Certification: Hematology, Internal Medicine, Medical Oncology
2011 Church St #701, Nashville, 615-284-2310

Infectious Disease

Carr, Mark Barham (7 mentions)
U of Kentucky, 1985
Certification: Infectious Disease, Internal Medicine
2000 Church St, Nashville, 615-284-5167

Edwards, Kathryn M. C. (6 mentions)
U of Iowa, 1973
Certification: Pediatric Infectious Diseases, Pediatrics
2200 Childrens Way #2510, Nashville, 615-322-2250

Felts, Stephen Karey (4 mentions)
U of Mississippi, 1968 *Certification:* Internal Medicine
5653 Frist Blvd #531, Hermitage, 615-846-4500

Horton, Juli G. (9 mentions)
Certification: Infectious Disease
2400 Patterson St #400, Nashville, 615-342-5900

Latham, Robert Harry (8 mentions)
Vanderbilt U, 1977
Certification: Infectious Disease, Internal Medicine
4220 Harding Rd, Nashville, 615-222-6611

McNabb, Paul Carter (12 mentions)
U of Tennessee, 1974
Certification: Infectious Disease, Internal Medicine
2000 Church St, Nashville, 615-284-5167

Patel, Jayesh Ambubhai (5 mentions)
FMS-Nigeria, 1984 *Certification:* Infectious Disease
3443 Dickerson Pike #210, Nashville, 615-234-6411

Raffanti, Stephen P. (5 mentions)
FMS-Italy, 1985
Certification: Infectious Disease, Internal Medicine
345 24th Ave N #103, Nashville, 615-321-9556

Infertility

Hill, George Alan (13 mentions)
U of Tennessee, 1980 *Certification:* Obstetrics &
   Gynecology, Reproductive Endocrinology/Infertility
345 23rd Ave N #401, Nashville, 615-321-4740

Weitzman, Glenn Allen (7 mentions)
Johns Hopkins U, 1982 *Certification:* Obstetrics &
   Gynecology, Reproductive Endocrinology/Infertility
345 23rd Ave N #401, Nashville, 615-321-4740

Internal Medicine *(see note on page 9)*

Allen, David Wayne (7 mentions)
East Tennessee State U, 1989 *Certification:* Internal Medicine
2400 Patterson St #400, Nashville, 615-342-5900

Gibson, John Ragan (4 mentions)
Washington U, 1979 *Certification:* Internal Medicine
300 20th Ave N, Nashville, 615-284-1400

Heusinkveld, David C. (3 mentions)
Vanderbilt U, 1991 *Certification:* Internal Medicine
2400 Patterson St #119, Nashville, 615-329-9508

Hock, Richard Lloyd (4 mentions)
Vanderbilt U, 1987 *Certification:* Internal Medicine
1211 22nd Ave S, Nashville, 615-936-1016

Lancaster, James Alan (3 mentions)
U of Mississippi, 1993 *Certification:* Internal Medicine
4230 Harding Rd #400, Nashville, 615-297-2700

Richards, Bruce Earle (3 mentions)
Vanderbilt U, 1982 *Certification:* Internal Medicine
300 20th Ave N #7, Nashville, 615-284-1400

Sutton, Hyatt Dibrell (3 mentions)
U of Alabama, 1994 *Certification:* Internal Medicine
2400 Patterson St #400, Nashville, 615-342-5900

Nephrology

Anand, Vinita (6 mentions)
FMS-India, 1978 *Certification:* Internal Medicine, Nephrology
2021 Church St #305, Nashville, 615-329-5072
100 Academy St, Dixon, 615-329-5072

Atkinson, Ralph Creyton (6 mentions)
U of Mississippi, 1985
Certification: Internal Medicine, Nephrology
28 White Bridge Rd #300, Nashville, 615-356-4111

Hunley, Tracy Earl (4 mentions)
U of Tennessee, 1991
Certification: Pediatric Nephrology, Pediatrics
2200 Children's Way 11205 Doctors Off Tower 11th Fl, Nashville,
   615-322-7416

Hymes, Jeffrey L. (3 mentions)
Albert Einstein Coll of Med, 1977 *Certification:* Critical Care
   Medicine, Internal Medicine, Nephrology
28 White Bridge Rd #300, Nashville, 615-356-4111

Kaplan, Mark Randall (4 mentions)
Vanderbilt U, 1988 *Certification:* Internal Medicine, Nephrology
28 White Bridge Rd #300, Nashville, 615-356-4111

Lee, Stanley Michael (8 mentions)
FMS-Ireland, 1970 *Certification:* Internal Medicine, Nephrology
28 White Bridge Rd #300, Nashville, 615-356-4111

Lewis, Julia Breyer (3 mentions)
U of Illinois, 1980
3601 The Vandervilt Clinic, Nashville, 615-343-7592

Pettus, William Harold (7 mentions)
U of Tennessee, 1980
Certification: Internal Medicine, Nephrology
2021 Church St #305, Nashville, 615-329-5072
100 Academy St, Dixon, 615-329-5072

Rocco, Vito K. (8 mentions)
U of Southern California, 1981 *Certification:* Critical Care
   Medicine, Internal Medicine, Nephrology
28 White Bridge Rd #300, Nashville, 615-356-4111

Taylor, Robert Kevin (4 mentions)
U of Colorado, 1989 *Certification:* Internal Medicine, Nephrology
28 White Bridge Rd #300, Nashville, 615-356-4111

Neurological Surgery

Abram, Steven Ronald (5 mentions)
Loyola U Chicago, 1985 *Certification:* Neurological Surgery
4230 Harding Rd #605, Nashville, 615-327-9543
2011 Murphy Ave #401, Nashville, 615-327-9543

Hampf, Carl Richard (8 mentions)
Vanderbilt U, 1982 *Certification:* Neurological Surgery
4230 Harding Rd #605, Nashville, 615-327-9543
2011 Murphy Ave #401, Nashville, 615-327-9543

Howell, Everette Irl, Jr. (9 mentions)
Vanderbilt U, 1969 *Certification:* Neurological Surgery
2011 Murphy Ave #401, Nashville, 615-327-9543
4230 Harding Rd #605, Nashville, 615-327-9543

Neurology

Brandes, Jan Lewis (4 mentions)
Vanderbilt U, 1989 *Certification:* Neurology
300 20th Ave N #603, Nashville, 615-284-4680

Fallis, Robert John (4 mentions)
U of Kentucky, 1979 *Certification:* Neurology
4230 Harding Pike #501, Nashville, 615-383-8575

Graham, Steven Donald (4 mentions)
U of Alabama, 1987 *Certification:* Neurology
2410 Patterson St #204, Nashville, 615-329-0100

Hagenau, Curtis James (7 mentions)
Vanderbilt U, 1982 *Certification:* Neurology
222 22nd Ave N #100, Nashville, 615-284-2222

Hoos, Richard Tipton (3 mentions)
Vanderbilt U, 1973 *Certification:* Neurology
300 20th Ave N #7, Nashville, 615-284-1400

Kaminski, Michael James (12 mentions)
U of Illinois, 1976
Certification: Internal Medicine, Neurology, Vascular Neurology
4230 Harding Rd #501, Nashville, 615-383-8575

Kirshner, Howard Stephen (3 mentions)
Harvard U, 1972 *Certification:* Neurology, Vascular Neurology
2100 Pierce Ave #362, Nashville, 615-936-0060

Lim, Noel Pung (3 mentions)
FMS-Philippines, 1993
5651 Frist Blvd #308, Hermitage, 615-391-8160

Uskavitch, David Robert (3 mentions)
U of Virginia, 1987 *Certification:* Neurology
1301 Medical Center Dr #3930, Nashville, 615-936-0060

Wagner, Martin Henry (3 mentions)
Baylor U, 1978 *Certification:* Neurology
5651 Frist Blvd #413, Hermitage, 615-885-0110

Woodard, Craig S. (3 mentions)
U of Texas-San Antonio, 1987 *Certification:* Neurology
222 22nd Ave N #100, Nashville, 615-284-2222

Obstetrics/Gynecology

Adkins, Royce Terrell (3 mentions)
Baylor U, 1983 *Certification:* Obstetrics & Gynecology
2011 Murphy Ave #200, Nashville, 615-301-1000

Blake, Mary Ann (4 mentions)
U of Alabama, 1982 *Certification:* Obstetrics & Gynecology
2011 Murphy Ave #601, Nashville, 615-329-9586
2201 Murphy Ave #102, Nashville, 615-329-9586

Bressman, Phillip L. (3 mentions)
Vanderbilt U, 1979 *Certification:* Obstetrics & Gynecology
2011 Murphy Ave #200, Nashville, 615-301-1000

Brown, Douglas Harrison (5 mentions)
U of Alabama, 1976 *Certification:* Obstetrics & Gynecology
222 22nd Ave N #100, Nashville, 615-284-2222

Lipsitz, Nancy B. (5 mentions)
U of Rochester, 1993 *Certification:* Obstetrics & Gynecology
222 22nd Ave N #100, Nashville, 615-284-2222
220 Village At Vanderbilt, Nashville, 615-936-1103

Oldfield, Elizabeth Lynn (4 mentions)
U of Tennessee, 1983 *Certification:* Obstetrics & Gynecology
2011 Murphy Ave #200, Nashville, 615-301-1000

Rush, Charles Bennett (3 mentions)
U of Cincinnati, 1984 *Certification:* Obstetrics & Gynecology
1211 21st Ave S, Nashville, 615-936-1103

Schlechter, Nicole L. (5 mentions)
Vanderbilt U, 1990 *Certification:* Obstetrics & Gynecology
300 20th Ave N #302, Nashville, 615-340-4655

Woods, Grayson Noel (3 mentions)
East Tennessee State U, 1998
Certification: Obstetrics & Gynecology
4230 Harding Pike #603, Nashville, 615-222-3737

Ophthalmology

Bond, John Benjamin (3 mentions)
Vanderbilt U, 1955 *Certification:* Ophthalmology
2201 Murphy Ave #210, Nashville, 615-327-3443

Bounds, Inez Boyd (3 mentions)
U of Tennessee, 1986 *Certification:* Ophthalmology
1919 Charlotte Ave #220, Nashville, 615-327-1519

Conrad, James Francis (4 mentions)
U of Michigan, 1980 *Certification:* Ophthalmology
4306 Harding Rd #308, Nashville, 615-269-3401

Ezell, Meredith Ann (3 mentions)
U of Tennessee, 1982 *Certification:* Ophthalmology
5410 Old Hickory Blvd, Hermitage, 615-883-2356

Gates, William Gene (5 mentions)
Louisiana State U-Shreveport, 1989 *Certification:* Ophthalmology
5410 Old Hickory Blvd, Hermitage, 615-883-2356

Groos, Erich Bryan, Jr. (3 mentions)
Vanderbilt U, 1987 *Certification:* Ophthalmology
2011 Murphy Ave, Nashville, 615-320-7200
310 25th Ave N #105, Nashville, 615-329-9023

Johns, Karla J. (6 mentions)
Vanderbilt U, 1980 *Certification:* Ophthalmology
1919 Charlotte Ave #220, Nashville, 615-327-1711

Shivitz, Ira Alan (3 mentions)
Vanderbilt U, 1978 *Certification:* Ophthalmology
310 25th Ave N #105, Nashville, 615-329-9023
2400 Patterson St #201, Nashville, 615-320-7200

Sternberg, Paul, Jr. (3 mentions)
U of Chicago, 1979 *Certification:* Ophthalmology
2311 Pierce Ave, Nashville, 615-936-1453

Orthopedics

Anderson, Allen F. (3 mentions)
U of Tennessee, 1976
Certification: Orthopaedic Sports Medicine, Orthopaedic Surgery
4230 Harding Pike #1000, Nashville, 615-383-2693

Chenger, Joseph D. (3 mentions)
FMS-Canada, 1977 *Certification:* Orthopaedic Surgery
2400 Patterson St #300, Nashville, 615-342-6300

Dube, Walter William (3 mentions)
East Tennessee State U, 1997 *Certification:* Orthopaedic Surgery
5651 Frist Blvd #400, Hermitage, 615-391-4545

Elrod, Burton Folk (6 mentions)
U of Tennessee, 1975 *Certification:* Orthopaedic Surgery
2021 Church St #200, Nashville, 615-284-2000

Garside, William B., Jr. (3 mentions)
U of North Carolina, 1990 *Certification:* Orthopaedic Surgery
301 21st Ave N, Nashville, 615-329-6600

Herring, Jeffrey Lance (4 mentions)
U of Oklahoma, 1986 *Certification:* Orthopaedic Surgery
301 21st Ave N, Nashville, 615-329-6600

Lawrence, Jeffrey Pettus (3 mentions)
U of Tennessee, 1983
Certification: Orthopaedic Sports Medicine, Orthopaedic Surgery
2400 Patterson St #300, Nashville, 615-342-6300

Moore, David Ryan (3 mentions)
Vanderbilt U, 1998 *Certification:* Orthopaedic Surgery
2021 Church St #200, Nashville, 615-284-2000

Reid, Michael Lynn (3 mentions)
U of Arkansas, 1975 *Certification:* Orthopaedic Surgery
5651 Frist Blvd #500, Hermitage, 615-889-3340

Shell, William Alfred, Jr. (3 mentions)
U of Tennessee, 1981 *Certification:* Orthopaedic Surgery
4230 Harding Pike #1000, Nashville, 615-383-2693

Otorhinolaryngology

Bryant, Grady Lee, Jr. (9 mentions)
Vanderbilt U, 1992 *Certification:* Otolaryngology
3901 Central Pike #351, Hermitage, 615-889-8802

Cate, Ronald Cooke (5 mentions)
U of Tennessee, 1973 *Certification:* Otolaryngology
2410 Patterson St #210, Nashville, 615-329-1681

Crook, Jerrall P., Jr. (7 mentions)
U of Tennessee, 1984 *Certification:* Otolaryngology
2011 Church St #683, Nashville, 615-340-4000
4323 Carothers Pkwy #408, Franklin, 615-340-4000

Fortune, David Scott (6 mentions)
Vanderbilt U, 1993 *Certification:* Otolaryngology
3901 Central Pike #351, Hermitage, 615-889-8802

Mitchell, Stephen A. (5 mentions)
U of Michigan, 1973 *Certification:* Otolaryngology
4230 Harding Rd #803, Nashville, 615-386-9089

Netterville, James Lee (4 mentions)
U of Tennessee, 1980 *Certification:* Otolaryngology
1215 21st Ave S #7209, Nashville, 615-322-6180

Ries, William Russell (6 mentions)
U of Tennessee, 1978 *Certification:* Otolaryngology
1215 Medical Center Dr #7209, Nashville, 615-322-3000

Pain Medicine

Johnson, Benjamin Wilbur, Jr. (4 mentions)
U of Illinois, 1980 *Certification:* Anesthesiology, Pain Medicine
2011 Murphy Ave #301, Nashville, 615-936-1206

Kroll, Peter Brian (3 mentions)
Loma Linda U, 1997 *Certification:* Anesthesiology, Pain Medicine
353 New Shackle Island Rd #219-B, Hendersonville,
615-824-2014

Pathology

Bluth, Raymond F., Jr. (3 mentions)
Vanderbilt U, 1988 *Certification:* Anatomic Pathology &
Clinical Pathology, Cytopathology
2000 Church St, Nashville, 615-284-5229
2010 Church St #615, Nashville, 615-284-7950

Canale, Daniel Doyle, Jr. (5 mentions)
Vanderbilt U, 1971
Certification: Anatomic Pathology & Clinical Pathology
2000 Church St, Nashville, 615-284-5229
2010 Church St #615, Nashville, 615-284-7950

Erickson, Douglas Joseph (3 mentions)
Duke U, 1978
Certification: Anatomic Pathology & Clinical Pathology
2300 Patterson St, Nashville, 615-221-4400

Page, David Lee (5 mentions)
Johns Hopkins U, 1966
Certification: Anatomic Pathology, Dermatopathology
1161 21st Ave S, Nashville, 615-322-3759

Pediatrics *(see note on page 9)*

Hamilton, Eddie Dewayne (3 mentions)
Vanderbilt U, 1985 *Certification:* Pediatrics
343 Franklin Rd #210, Brentwood, 615-373-2248

Keown, Mary Elizabeth (6 mentions)
U of Alabama, 1983 *Certification:* Pediatrics
2201 Murphy Ave #201, Nashville, 615-327-0536

Long, William R. (6 mentions)
U of Kentucky, 1973 *Certification:* Pediatrics
5819 Old Harding Rd, Nashville, 615-352-2990

Mallard, Robert Elwood (6 mentions)
Vanderbilt U, 1974 *Certification:* Pediatrics
2325 Crestmoor Rd 1st Fl, Nashville, 615-284-2260

Patton, Christopher M. (5 mentions)
U of Tennessee, 1994 *Certification:* Pediatrics
5819 Old Harding Rd, Nashville, 615-352-2990

Plastic Surgery

Buckspan, Glenn Scott (5 mentions)
U of Texas-Galveston, 1974 *Certification:* Plastic Surgery
2204 Crestmoor Rd, Nashville, 615-385-3309

Chester, Caroline Hudson (5 mentions)
U of Tennessee, 1983 *Certification:* Plastic Surgery
2201 Murphy Ave #403, Nashville, 615-320-3773

Delozier, Joseph Benjamin (8 mentions)
U of Tennessee, 1982 *Certification:* Plastic Surgery
209 23rd Ave N, Nashville, 615-565-9000

Orcutt, Thomas William (6 mentions)
Vanderbilt U, 1968 *Certification:* Plastic Surgery, Surgery
310 23rd Ave N #100, Nashville, 615-321-1010

Oslin, Bryan Dewey (10 mentions)
Vanderbilt U, 1988 *Certification:* Plastic Surgery
4230 Harding Rd #101, Nashville, 615-234-3223

Shack, Robert Bruce (6 mentions)
U of Texas-Galveston, 1973
Certification: Plastic Surgery, Surgery of the Hand
1301 22nd Ave S, Nashville, 615-322-2350

Psychiatry

Jack, Robert Allen (3 mentions)
Oregon Health Sciences U, 1979 *Certification:* Psychiatry
310 25th Ave N #307, Nashville, 615-250-6700

Petrie, William Marshall (4 mentions)
Vanderbilt U, 1972 *Certification:* Geriatric Psychiatry, Psychiatry
310 25th Ave N #307, Nashville, 615-250-6725

West, William Scott (3 mentions)
U of Tennessee, 1982 *Certification:* Psychiatry
30 Burton Hills Blvd #375, Nashville, 615-327-4877

Pulmonary Disease

Canonico, Angelo Edward (3 mentions)
U of Tennessee, 1984
Certification: Internal Medicine, Pulmonary Disease
4230 Harding Pike #400, Nashville, 615-297-2700

Esbenshade, Aaron M., Jr. (7 mentions)
U of Florida, 1976 *Certification:* Internal Medicine
5651 Frist Blvd #408, Hermitage, 615-883-9781
4733 Andrew Jackson Pkwy, Hermitage, 615-883-3044

Heyman, Stephen Joel (4 mentions)
U of Rochester, 1984 *Certification:* Critical Care Medicine,
Internal Medicine, Pulmonary Disease
300 20th Ave N #9, Nashville, 615-284-1400

Jarvis, David Alan (5 mentions)
U of Louisville, 1973
Certification: Internal Medicine, Pulmonary Disease
2400 Patterson St, Nashville, 615-342-5900

Lancaster, Lisa Hood (3 mentions)
Med Coll of Georgia, 1993 *Certification:* Critical Care
Medicine, Internal Medicine, Pulmonary Disease
1301 Medical Center Dr #B-817, Nashville, 615-322-2386

Mangialardi, Robert J. (6 mentions)
Vanderbilt U, 1991
Certification: Critical Care Medicine, Pulmonary Disease
2400 Patterson St #400, Nashville, 615-342-5900

Niedermeyer, Michael E. (6 mentions)
Georgetown U, 1978 *Certification:* Critical Care Medicine,
Internal Medicine, Pulmonary Disease
300 20th Ave N #503, Nashville, 615-284-5098

Peters, Mark Thomas (5 mentions)
Ohio State U, 1987 *Certification:* Critical Care Medicine,
Internal Medicine, Pediatric Pulmonology, Pulmonary Disease
4230 Harding Pike #400, Nashville, 615-297-2700

Wright, Jeffrey Glen (4 mentions)
Vanderbilt U, 1997 *Certification:* Critical Care Medicine,
Internal Medicine, Pulmonary Disease
4230 Harding Pike #400, Nashville, 615-297-2700

Radiology—Diagnostic

Arildsen, Ronald Curtis (3 mentions)
Columbia U, 1981 *Certification:* Diagnostic Radiology
1161 21st Ave S, Nashville, 615-343-8516

Awh, Mark Hunchul (3 mentions)
U of Mississippi, 1988 *Certification:* Diagnostic Radiology
8 Cadillac Dr #200, Brentwood, 865-694-0062

Baker, Jack Richard (3 mentions)
U of Kentucky, 1985 *Certification:* Diagnostic Radiology
210 25th Ave N #602, Nashville, 615-312-0600

Earthman, Webb Johnston (4 mentions)
Vanderbilt U, 1982 *Certification:* Diagnostic Radiology
210 25th Ave N #602, Nashville, 615-312-0600

Gray, Scott David (3 mentions)
U of Pittsburgh, 1991 *Certification:* Diagnostic Radiology
210 25th Ave N #602, Nashville, 615-312-0600

Weaver, Gregory Rynn (3 mentions)
U of Kentucky, 1981
Certification: Diagnostic Radiology, Nuclear Radiology
210 25th Ave N #602, Nashville, 615-312-0600

Wunder, Daniel Jay (3 mentions)
U of South Dakota, 1990 *Certification:* Diagnostic
Radiology, Vascular & Interventional Radiology
28 White Bridge Rd #111, Nashville, 615-356-3999

Radiology—Therapeutic

Earthman, Webb Johnston (3 mentions)
Vanderbilt U, 1982 *Certification:* Diagnostic Radiology
210 25th Ave N #602, Nashville, 615-312-0600

Priest, Edward McCall (4 mentions)
U of Tennessee, 1974 *Certification:* Diagnostic Radiology,
Internal Medicine, Vascular & Interventional Radiology
2018 Murphy Ave #200, Nashville, 615-312-0600

Rehabilitation

McHugh, Daniel Joseph (3 mentions)
U of Louisville, 1991
Certification: Pain Medicine, Physical Medicine & Rehabilitation
2400 Patterson St #300, Nashville, 615-342-6300
394 Harding Pl #200, Nashville, 615-834-4482

Rheumatology

Byrd, Victor Morris (6 mentions)
U of Louisville, 1991
Certification: Internal Medicine, Rheumatology
222 22nd Ave N #100, Nashville, 615-284-2222

Lagrone, Robert Paul (7 mentions)
Vanderbilt U, 1987
Certification: Internal Medicine, Rheumatology
2001 Charlotte Ave #102, Nashville, 615-321-3277
4230 Harding Rd #E-801, Nashville, 615-321-3277

Meadors, Marvin Porter (5 mentions)
U of Mississippi, 1984
Certification: Internal Medicine, Rheumatology
2410 Patterson St #106, Nashville, 615-340-4611

Sergent, John Stanley (6 mentions)
Vanderbilt U, 1966
Certification: Internal Medicine, Rheumatology
1301 22nd Ave S, Nashville, 615-343-9324

Steigelfest, Eli (5 mentions)
Albert Einstein Coll of Med, 1995
Certification: Internal Medicine, Rheumatology
2001 Mallory Ln #100, Franklin, 615-764-4450

Thoracic Surgery

Nesbitt, Jonathan Carl (10 mentions)
Georgetown U, 1981 *Certification:* Surgery, Thoracic Surgery
1301 Medical Center Dr #2971, Nashville, 615-322-0064

Polk, William Howard, Jr. (4 mentions)
Vanderbilt U, 1985 *Certification:* Surgery
356 24th Ave N #400, Nashville, 615-329-7887

Roberts, John Robert (4 mentions)
Yale U, 1985 *Certification:* Surgery, Thoracic Surgery
356 24th Ave N #400, Nashville, 615-329-7887

Walton, Kenneth Brian (4 mentions)
Texas Tech U, 1998 *Certification:* Surgery
5653 Frist Blvd #730, Hermitage, 615-872-1092

Wilcox, Allen Brian, Jr. (4 mentions)
U of Tennessee, 1986 *Certification:* Thoracic Surgery
2010 Church St #303, Nashville, 615-329-7878

Urology

Concepcion, Raoul Sioco (5 mentions)
U of Toledo, 1984 *Certification:* Urology
2801 Charlotte Ave, Nashville, 615-250-9200

Cookson, Michael Shawn (5 mentions)
U of Oklahoma, 1988 *Certification:* Urology
1211 Medical Center Dr, Nashville, 615-322-2880

Eckstein, Charles William (5 mentions)
Vanderbilt U, 1976 *Certification:* Urology
2801 Charlotte Ave, Nashville, 615-250-9200
3443 Dickerson Pike #160, Nashville, 615-860-1702

Ezell, Gilbert D. (4 mentions)
U of Tennessee, 1983 *Certification:* Urology
2801 Charlotte Ave, Nashville, 615-250-9200
5651 Frist Blvd #616, Hermitage, 615-391-4394

Flora, Mark Dudley (8 mentions)
Indiana U, 1985 *Certification:* Urology
2801 Charlotte Ave, Nashville, 615-250-9200

Hagan, Keith W. (5 mentions)
Vanderbilt U, 1969 *Certification:* Urology
2801 Charlotte Ave, Nashville, 615-250-9200

Knoll, L. Dean (4 mentions)
Rosalind Franklin U, 1982 *Certification:* Urology
345 23rd Ave N #212, Nashville, 615-327-2055

Warner, John Jeffrey (9 mentions)
Northwestern U, 1976 *Certification:* Urology
4230 Harding Rd #521, Nashville, 615-269-2655

Vascular Surgery

Garrard, Clifford Louis (5 mentions)
Vanderbilt U, 1990 *Certification:* Surgery, Vascular Surgery
356 24th Ave N #400, Nashville, 615-329-7887

Meacham, Patrick Wallace (5 mentions)
Vanderbilt U, 1976
353 New Shackle Island Rd, Hendersonville, 615-826-2127

Texas

Dallas-Fort Worth Area—page 440

Travis County—page 467
Houston Area—page 450
San Antonio Area—page 460

Dallas-Fort Worth Area

Including Dallas and Tarrant Counties

Allergy/Immunology

Ginchansky, Elliot Joel (5 mentions)
SUNY-Downstate Med Coll, 1971
Certification: Allergy & Immunology, Pediatrics
7777 Forest Ln #C-530, Dallas, 972-566-7576

Gross, Gary Neil (26 mentions)
U of Texas-Dallas, 1969
Certification: Allergy & Immunology, Internal Medicine
5499 Glen Lakes Dr #100, Dallas, 214-691-1330

Lanier, Bobby Quentin (10 mentions)
U of Texas-Galveston, 1970
Certification: Allergy & Immunology, Pediatrics
6407 Southwest Blvd, Fort Worth, 817-731-9198

Lee, Jane Joo (6 mentions)
U of California-Los Angeles, 1994
Certification: Allergy & Immunology
411 N Washington Ave #2400, Dallas, 214-370-5700

Lumry, William Raymond (20 mentions)
U of Texas-Galveston, 1977
Certification: Allergy & Immunology, Internal Medicine
9900 N Central Expy #525, Dallas, 214-373-7374

Rogers, Robert Jean (13 mentions)
U of Texas-Dallas, 1979
Certification: Allergy & Immunology, Pediatrics
5929 Lovell Ave, Fort Worth, 817-315-2550

Ruff, Michael Edward (6 mentions)
U of Texas-Galveston, 1978
Certification: Allergy & Immunology, Pediatrics
5499 Glen Lakes Dr #100, Dallas, 214-691-1330

Tanna, Rajendra Khetsi (14 mentions)
FMS-India, 1973 *Certification:* Allergy & Immunology, Pediatrics
1000 College Ave, Fort Worth, 817-336-8855

Tremblay, Normand Francis (5 mentions)
U of Vermont, 1970
Certification: Allergy & Immunology, Pediatrics
5929 Lovell Ave, Fort Worth, 817-315-2550

Wasserman, Richard L. (7 mentions)
U of Texas-Dallas, 1977
Certification: Allergy & Immunology, Pediatrics
7777 Forest Ln #B332, Dallas, 972-566-7788

Anesthesiology

Daughety, Michael Jewel (5 mentions)
U of Texas-Galveston, 1966 *Certification:* Anesthesiology
1901 N MacArthur Blvd, Irving, 972-715-5000

Fraga, Mark Joseph (3 mentions)
U of Texas-Dallas, 1989 *Certification:* Anesthesiology
221 W Colorado Blvd #845, Dallas, 214-946-1133

Frankfurt, Alan Irwin (5 mentions)
U of Texas-Dallas, 1981 *Certification:* Anesthesiology
13601 Preston Rd #900W, Dallas, 972-714-2810

Gunning, Thomas C., III (4 mentions)
U of Texas-Dallas, 1986 *Certification:* Anesthesiology
6301 Gaston Ave #400W, Dallas, 214-827-3610

Harper, James David (8 mentions)
Oregon Health Sciences U, 1971 *Certification:* Anesthesiology
1301 Pennsylvania Ave, Fort Worth, 817-731-2875
13601 Preston Rd #900-W, Dallas, 972-233-1999

Ivy, Roy, III (3 mentions)
U of Texas-Dallas, 1995 *Certification:* Anesthesiology
4131 N Central Expy #435, Dallas, 214-252-3501

Kleinman, Samuel Eleazar (5 mentions)
Texas Tech U, 1988 *Certification:* Anesthesiology
801 7th Ave, Fort Worth, 682-885-4054

Marcel, Randy Joseph (4 mentions)
Mercer U, 1991 *Certification:* Anesthesiology
8220 Walnut Hill Ln #505, Dallas, 972-233-9139

Minton, Gordon H. (4 mentions)
Texas Tech U, 1989 *Certification:* Anesthesiology
1500 S Main St, Fort Worth, 817-927-1417

Monk, Joe Edwin (3 mentions)
U of Texas-Galveston, 1985 *Certification:* Anesthesiology
6301 Gaston Ave #400, Dallas, 214-217-8001
3600 Gaston Ave, Dallas, 214-824-2851

Parks, Robert Irvin (3 mentions)
U of Texas-Dallas, 1972 *Certification:* Anesthesiology
6301 Gaston Ave #400, Dallas, 214-824-2851

Pickett, Creighton A., III (4 mentions)
Texas Tech U, 1998 *Certification:* Anesthesiology
2630 West Frwy, Fort Worth, 817-529-1143

Ramsay, Michael Anthony E. (13 mentions)
FMS-United Kingdom, 1968 *Certification:* Anesthesiology
3600 Gaston Ave #400, Dallas, 214-824-2851

Sears, Kristin N. (3 mentions)
Des Moines U, 1981
13601 Preston Rd #900-W, Dallas, 972-233-1999
4401 Booth Calloway Rd, North Richland Hills, 817-255-1195

Valek, Timothy Ray (4 mentions)
U of Texas-San Antonio, 1983 *Certification:* Anesthesiology
6301 Gaston Ave #400, Dallas, 214-824-2851

Cardiac Surgery

Dewey, Todd M. (11 mentions)
Texas Tech U, 1990 *Certification:* Thoracic Surgery
7777 Forest Ln #A323, Dallas, 972-566-4866

Hebeler, Robert F., Jr. (18 mentions)
Tulane U, 1977 *Certification:* Thoracic Surgery
3409 Worth St #720, Dallas, 214-821-3603

Henry, Albert Carl, III (9 mentions)
U of Texas-Houston, 1974 *Certification:* Thoracic Surgery
3409 Worth St #720, Dallas, 214-821-3603

Jay, John Laurence (8 mentions)
Baylor U, 1984 *Certification:* Surgery, Thoracic Surgery
221 W Colorado Blvd #825, Dallas, 214-942-5222

Lin, Jeffrey Chaipui (9 mentions)
Baylor U, 1992 *Certification:* Surgery, Thoracic Surgery
909 9th Ave #210, Fort Worth, 817-335-1131

Mack, Michael Joseph (10 mentions)
St Louis U, 1973
Certification: Internal Medicine, Thoracic Surgery
7777 Forest Ln #A323, Dallas, 972-566-4866

Matter, Gregory John (12 mentions)
Baylor U, 1985 *Certification:* Thoracic Surgery
621 N Hall St #500, Dallas, 214-841-2000

Nazarian, Manouchehr (9 mentions)
FMS-Iran, 1962 *Certification:* Surgery, Thoracic Surgery
757 8th Ave #A, Fort Worth, 817-336-4454

Platt, Melvin Ray (10 mentions)
Baylor U, 1965 *Certification:* Surgery, Thoracic Surgery
8230 Walnut Hill Ln #208, Dallas, 214-692-6135

Ryan, William H., III (15 mentions)
U of North Carolina, 1977 *Certification:* Thoracic Surgery
8230 Walnut Hill Ln #208, Dallas, 214-692-6135

Vigness, Richard Martell (11 mentions)
U of Texas-Houston, 1981 *Certification:* Thoracic Surgery
1307 8th Ave #601, Fort Worth, 817-926-3320

Cardiology

Afridi, Imran (3 mentions)
FMS-Pakistan, 1988 *Certification:* Cardiovascular Disease
221 W Colorado Blvd #205, Dallas, 214-942-5511
820 S Carrier Pkwy, Granbury, 214-942-5511

Anderson, Allan Lynn (4 mentions)
Baylor U, 1976
Certification: Cardiovascular Disease, Internal Medicine
7777 Forest Ln #A-341, Dallas, 972-566-5700

Boehrer, James D. (6 mentions)
U of Chicago, 1987
Certification: Cardiovascular Disease, Interventional Cardiology
5939 Harry Hines Blvd #630, Dallas, 214-688-0228

Carry, Melissa Moore (6 mentions)
U of Arkansas, 1983
Certification: Cardiovascular Disease, Internal Medicine
621 N Hall St #400, Dallas, 214-824-8721

Das, Tony S. (5 mentions)
Baylor U, 1990 *Certification:* Interventional Cardiology
7150 Greenville Ave #500, Dallas, 214-369-3613
9301 N Central Expy #410, Dallas, 244-265-6350

Durand, John Lars (5 mentions)
U of Arizona, 1977 *Certification:* Cardiovascular Disease,
   Internal Medicine, Interventional Cardiology
1300 W Terrell Ave #500, Fort Worth, 817-252-5000
6100 Harris Pkwy #1200, Fort Worth, 817-263-3724

Eichhorn, Eric Joel (3 mentions)
Baylor U, 1979 *Certification:* Cardiovascular Disease,
   Internal Medicine, Interventional Cardiology
7777 Forest Ln #A202, Dallas, 972-566-7733

Gottlich, Charles Morton (8 mentions)
U of Texas-Dallas, 1970
Certification: Cardiovascular Disease, Internal Medicine
621 N Hall St #500, Dallas, 972-841-2000

Grodin, Jerrold Michael (5 mentions)
FMS-Mexico, 1977
Certification: Cardiovascular Disease, Internal Medicine
621 N Hall St #400, Dallas, 214-826-5000

Harper, John Frank (8 mentions)
U of Texas-Dallas, 1972
Certification: Cardiovascular Disease, Internal Medicine
8230 Walnut Hill Ln #7204, Dallas, 214-345-6000

Hess, Susan Lynn (3 mentions)
Baylor U, 1985 *Certification:* Pediatric Cardiology
1600 Lancaster Dr #101, Grapevine, 817-310-3683

Jenkins, George Mark (3 mentions)
Johns Hopkins U, 1988
Certification: Cardiovascular Disease, Internal Medicine
221 W Colorado Blvd #730, Dallas, 214-946-9898

Levine, David (4 mentions)
Washington U, 1981 *Certification:* Cardiovascular Disease,
   Clinical Cardiac Electrophysiology, Internal Medicine
221 W Colorado Blvd #831, Dallas, 214-946-8856

Liao, Robert (3 mentions)
U of Texas-Dallas, 1993 *Certification:* Cardiovascular
   Disease, Internal Medicine, Interventional Cardiology
7777 Forest Ln #C-860, Dallas, 214-688-0228

McNamara, Brian Thompson (3 mentions)
FMS-Canada, 1986 *Certification:* Cardiovascular Disease,
   Internal Medicine, Interventional Cardiology
1300 W Rosedale St, Fort Worth, 817-338-1300

Pugh, Billie Raymond (4 mentions)
U of Texas-Galveston, 1972
Certification: Cardiovascular Disease, Internal Medicine
1300 W Terrell Ave #500, Fort Worth, 817-252-5097
6100 Harris Pkwy #1200, Fort Worth, 817-263-3724

Redish, Gregory Alan (3 mentions)
Indiana U, 1978
Certification: Cardiovascular Disease, Internal Medicine
9330 Poppy Dr #405, Dallas, 214-361-9535

Rosenthal, J. Edward (4 mentions)
U of Texas-Dallas, 1967
Certification: Cardiovascular Disease, Internal Medicine
7777 Forest Ln #A202, Dallas, 972-566-7733

Saland, Kenneth Edward (3 mentions)
U of New Mexico, 1993
Certification: Cardiovascular Disease, Interventional Cardiology
7150 Greenville Ave #500, Dallas, 214-369-3613
9301 N Central Expy #410, Dallas, 244-265-6350

Schwade, Jack Lester (3 mentions)
U of Texas-Dallas, 1966
Certification: Cardiovascular Disease, Internal Medicine
7777 Forest Ln #A-202, Dallas, 792-566-7733

Steelman, Rush Barrett (4 mentions)
Hahnemann U, 1963
Certification: Cardiovascular Disease, Internal Medicine
8440 Walnut Hill Ln #700, Dallas, 214-361-3300

Stoler, Robert Craig (6 mentions)
Duke U, 1990
Certification: Cardiovascular Disease, Interventional Cardiology
621 N Hall St #400, Dallas, 214-824-8721

Tan, John Lionghan (4 mentions)
Stanford U, 1992 *Certification:* Cardiovascular Disease
8440 Walnut Hill Ln #700, Dallas, 214-361-3300
4510 Dr #313, McKinney, 214-361-3300

Vallabhan, Ravi C. (5 mentions)
U of Texas-San Antonio, 1988
Certification: Cardiovascular Disease, Interventional Cardiology
621 N Hall St #500, Dallas, 214-841-2000

Warner, John Jay (4 mentions)
Vanderbilt U, 1992
Certification: Cardiovascular Disease, Interventional Cardiology
5323 Harry Hines Blvd, Dallas, 214-645-7500

Dermatology

Bateman, Cathleen Pekor (4 mentions)
U of Texas-Galveston, 1978 *Certification:* Dermatology
130 W Belt Line Rd #2, Cedar Hill, 972-293-3720

Cather, Jennifer Ann (10 mentions)
U of Texas-Dallas, 1994 *Certification:* Dermatology
9101 N Central Expy #150, Dallas, 214-265-1818

Clegg, Cynthia O. (4 mentions)
U of Texas-Dallas, 1997 *Certification:* Dermatology
9301 N Central Expy #180, Dallas, 214-420-7070

Cook, Lucius P., III (4 mentions)
U of Tennessee, 1970 *Certification:* Dermatology
7777 Forest Ln #B-218, Dallas, 972-566-7655

Costner, Melissa Irene (5 mentions)
U of Texas-Houston, 1993
Certification: Dermatology, Dermatopathology
9301 N Central Expy #180, Dallas, 214-420-7070

Ghali, Fred E. (12 mentions)
U of Texas-Dallas, 1993
Certification: Dermatology, Pediatric Dermatology, Pediatrics
1325 W Northwest Hwy, Grapevine, 817-421-3376

Herndon, James Henry, Jr. (8 mentions)
U of Texas-Dallas, 1963 *Certification:* Dermatology
8230 Walnut Hill Ln #500, Dallas, 214-739-5821

Hurley, Mary Elizabeth (4 mentions)
Tulane U, 1996 *Certification:* Dermatology
9301 N Central Expy #180, Dallas, 214-420-7070

Malouf, Peter J. (4 mentions)
U of North Texas, 1995 *Certification:* Dermatology
2801 S Hulen St #400, Fort Worth, 817-921-2838

Menter, Martin Alan (17 mentions)
FMS-South Africa, 1966 *Certification:* Dermatology
3900 Junius St #145, Dallas, 972-386-7546

Michaelson, Jerold Dennis (9 mentions)
U of Texas-Dallas, 1967 *Certification:* Dermatology
8220 Walnut Hill Ln #512, Dallas, 214-369-8130

Miller, Douglas Scott (6 mentions)
U of Texas-Galveston, 1981 *Certification:* Dermatology
1622 8th Ave #100, Fort Worth, 817-927-2332
912 Foster Ln, Weatherford, 817-927-2332

Park, Betty Lee (4 mentions)
Northwestern U, 2001 *Certification:* Dermatology
7777 Forest Ln #C-755, Dallas, 972-566-2600

Roberts, Robin A. (17 mentions)
U of Texas-Dallas, 1982 *Certification:* Dermatology
6100 SW Blvd #100, Fort Worth, 817-989-1221

Sears, Laura Lea (4 mentions)
Texas Tech U, 1984 *Certification:* Dermatology
3900 Junius #710, Dallas, 214-987-3376
5924 Royal Ln #104, Dallas, 214-987-3376
1333 Corporate Dr #121, Irving, 214-987-3376

Sklar, Jerald Louis (10 mentions)
U of Texas-Galveston, 1987 *Certification:* Dermatology
1333 Corporate Dr #121, Irving, 972-580-8440
5924 Royal Ln #104-B, Dallas, 214-692-6566
3900 Junius #710, Dallas, 214-987-3376

Stetler, Lori Donohue (6 mentions)
U of Texas-Dallas, 1989 *Certification:* Dermatology
8201 Preston Rd #350, Dallas, 214-631-7546

Taylor, Robert S., III (4 mentions)
U of Texas-Galveston, 1985
5323 Harry Hines Blvd, Dallas, 214-645-2400

Thomas, Danny Ray (7 mentions)
U of Texas-Galveston, 1979 *Certification:* Dermatology
6100 SW Blvd #100, Fort Worth, 817-989-1595

Emergency Medicine

Aaron, Kimberly D. (8 mentions)
Baylor U, 1991
Certification: Pediatric Emergency Medicine, Pediatrics
801 7th Ave, Fort Worth, 682-885-4095

Black, C. Sean (5 mentions)
U of Texas-Houston, 1993 *Certification:* Emergency Medicine
8160 Walnut Hill Ln, Dallas, 214-345-5930

Bower, Kevin Rudy (3 mentions)
Northwestern U, 1981 *Certification:* Emergency Medicine
1901 N Macarthur Blvd, Irving, 972-579-8110

Broders, Albert C., III (7 mentions)
Duke U, 1974
Certification: Emergency Medicine, Internal Medicine
8160 Walnut Hill Ln #200, Dallas, 214-345-6789

Bush, Matthew D. (7 mentions)
U of Texas-Dallas, 1996 *Certification:* Emergency Medicine
7777 Forest Lane, Dallas, 972-566-8888

Dixon, Richard P. (4 mentions)
U of Texas-San Antonio, 1987 *Certification:* Family Medicine
1301 Pennsylvania Ave, Fort Worth, 817-882-2000

Frenzel, Hoyt W. (3 mentions)
U of Texas-San Antonio, 1998 *Certification:* Emergency Medicine
800 W Randol Mill Rd, Arlington, 817-548-6200

Myers, John H. (3 mentions)
Texas Tech U, 1991 *Certification:* Emergency Medicine,
  Pediatric Emergency Medicine
7777 Forest Ln, Dallas, 972-566-7000

Nelson, Darren L. (3 mentions)
Texas A&M U, 1996 *Certification:* Emergency Medicine
3301 Matlock Rd, Arlington, 817-467-7486

Noah, Terrence D., Jr. (4 mentions)
U of Tennessee, 1979 *Certification:* Emergency Medicine
3500 Gaston Ave, Dallas, 214-820-2505

Norcross, William Harold (5 mentions)
U of Texas-San Antonio, 1981
Certification: Emergency Medicine, Internal Medicine
8200 Walnut Hill Ln, Dallas, 214-345-6789

Packard, Dighton Carl (11 mentions)
U of Texas-San Antonio, 1974 *Certification:* Emergency Medicine
3500 Gaston Ave, Dallas, 214-820-2501
1717 mAIN sT #5200, Dallas, 214-712-2036

Pepe, Paul Ernest (3 mentions)
U of California-San Francisco, 1976 *Certification:* Emergency
  Medicine, Internal Medicine, Pulmonary Disease
5323 Harry Hines Blvd, Dallas, 214-648-4812

Portera, Louis Anthony (5 mentions)
U of Mississippi, 1973
Certification: Emergency Medicine, Internal Medicine
3500 Gaston Ave, Dallas, 214-820-2501
1717 Main St #5200, Dallas, 214-712-2036

Till, Mark Andrew (4 mentions)
Baylor U, 1983 *Certification:* Internal Medicine
8200 Walnut Hill Lane, Dallas, 214-345-6789

Trotter, Elliott R. (7 mentions)
U of Texas-San Antonio, 1987 *Certification:* Family Medicine
1301 Pennsylvania Ave, Fort Worth, 817-882-2000

Endocrinology

Aronoff, Stephen Louis (11 mentions)
U of Texas-Dallas, 1972
Certification: Endocrinology and Metabolism, Internal Medicine
10260 N Central Expy #100, Dallas, 214-363-5535

Bajaj, Chris P. (7 mentions)
U of North Texas, 2000 *Certification:* Endocrinology,
  Diabetes, and Metabolism, Internal Medicine
7241 Hawkinsview Dr, Fort Worth, 817-263-0007

Chakmakjian, Zaven Hagop (9 mentions)
FMS-Lebanon, 1963
Certification: Endocrinology and Metabolism, Internal Medicine
910 N Central Expy, Dallas, 214-823-6435

Dorfman, Steven George (5 mentions)
Loyola U Chicago, 1970
Certification: Endocrinology and Metabolism, Internal Medicine
10260 N Central Expy #100, Dallas, 214-363-5535

Leffert, Jonathan David (9 mentions)
U of Minnesota, 1983 *Certification:* Endocrinology,
  Diabetes, and Metabolism, Internal Medicine
9301 N Central Expy #570, Dallas, 214-369-5992

Leshin, Mark (7 mentions)
Washington U, 1974
Certification: Endocrinology and Metabolism, Internal Medicine
3600 Gaston Ave #1160, Dallas, 214-828-1276

Mair, Kenneth A. (7 mentions)
Baylor U, 1991 *Certification:* Endocrinology, Diabetes, and
  Metabolism, Internal Medicine
1325 Pennsylvania Ave #560, Fort Worth, 817-820-2897

Marynick, Samuel Philip (10 mentions)
U of Texas-Dallas, 1972
Certification: Endocrinology and Metabolism, Internal Medicine
3600 Gaston Ave #502, Dallas, 214-828-2444

Milburn, Joseph L., Jr. (6 mentions)
U of Texas-Dallas, 1984 *Certification:* Endocrinology,
  Diabetes, and Metabolism, Internal Medicine
2021 N Macarthur Blvd #515, Irving, 972-259-3282

Sachson, Richard A. (16 mentions)
SUNY-Downstate Med Coll, 1968
Certification: Endocrinology and Metabolism, Internal Medicine
10260 N Central Expy #100, Dallas, 214-363-5535

Sher, Ellen Susan (5 mentions)
George Washington U, 1990
Certification: Pediatric Endocrinology
7777 Forest Ln #B-303, Dallas, 972-566-8833

Thornton, Paul S. (6 mentions)
FMS-Ireland, 1984 *Certification:* Pediatric Endocrinology
901 7th Ave #410, Fort Worth, 682-885-7960
750 Mid Cities Blvd #100, Hurst, 817-605-4500

Welch, Brian J. (5 mentions)
U of Texas-Dallas, 2000 *Certification:* Endocrinology,
  Diabetes, and Metabolism, Internal Medicine
910 N Central Expy, Dallas, 214-823-6435

Wilson, David Brooks (8 mentions)
U of Kentucky, 1972
Certification: Endocrinology and Metabolism, Internal Medicine
1325 Pennsylvania Ave #560, Fort Worth, 817-820-2890

Family Practice *(see note on page 9)*

Behr, Leonard Michael (6 mentions)
FMS-South Africa, 1967
8230 Walnut Hill Ln #600, Dallas, 214-363-5660

Berlando, Richard Allan (5 mentions)
FMS-Canada, 1979 *Certification:* Family Medicine
2540 N Galloway Ave #203, Mesquite, 972-682-0700

Bleakney, Dana Allison (5 mentions)
U of Texas-Dallas, 1999 *Certification:* Family Medicine
3600 Gaston Ave #454, Dallas, 214-820-8300

Culpepper, Guy Lee (3 mentions)
U of Texas-Houston, 1984 *Certification:* Family Medicine
17110 Dallas Pkwy #100, Dallas, 972-380-7000

Gross, Perry Edward (4 mentions)
Rosalind Franklin U, 1952 *Certification:* Family Medicine
3600 Gaston Ave #454, Dallas, 214-820-8300

Murphy, James A., Jr. (3 mentions)
U of Texas-Houston, 1976 *Certification:* Family Medicine
1533 Merrimac Cir #100, Fort Worth, 817-336-4040

Roaten, Shelley Poe, Jr. (3 mentions)
U of Texas-San Antonio, 1974 *Certification:* Family Medicine
6263 Harry Hines Blvd, Dallas, 214-648-1399

Tranchina, Sara Eileen (5 mentions)
U of Texas-Dallas, 1990 *Certification:* Family Medicine
8230 Walnut Hill Ln #800, Dallas, 214-239-4990

Turner, David L. (3 mentions)
U of Texas-Dallas, 1982
7777 Forest Ln #C420, Dallas, 972-566-7706

Gastroenterology

Anderson, Paul Kenneth (9 mentions)
Tulane U, 1976 *Certification:* Gastroenterology, Internal Medicine
4708 Alliance Blvd #200, Plano, 972-758-6000

De Marco, Daniel C. (8 mentions)
U of Texas-Dallas, 1981
Certification: Gastroenterology, Internal Medicine
3434 Swiss Ave #206, Dallas, 214-545-3990

Deas, Thomas Malcolm, Jr. (4 mentions)
Louisiana State U-Shreveport, 1978
Certification: Gastroenterology, Internal Medicine
1201 Summit Ave #500, Fort Worth, 817-336-0379
6445 Harris Pkwy #100, Fort Worth, 817-361-6900

Dewar, Thomas Norman (7 mentions)
U of Texas-Dallas, 1986
Certification: Gastroenterology, Internal Medicine
6445 Harris Pkwy #100, Fort Worth, 817-361-6900

Elwazir, Esmail Mohamed (4 mentions)
Columbia U, 1992
Certification: Gastroenterology, Internal Medicine
3409 Worth St #700, Dallas, 214-820-2266

Gottesman, Andrew Rodney (4 mentions)
U of Texas-Galveston, 1986 *Certification:* Gastroenterology
7515 Greenville Ave #706, Dallas, 214-360-9877

Hamilton, Kenneth W. (5 mentions)
Texas A&M U, 1992 *Certification:* Internal Medicine
909 Southeast Pkwy #105, Azle, 817-238-0735

Hodges, William Gregory (4 mentions)
U of Texas-Dallas, 1988 *Certification:* Gastroenterology
3409 Worth St #700, Dallas, 214-820-2266

Hunt, Lyn Irene (4 mentions)
U of Texas-Galveston, 1976
Certification: Pediatric Gastroenterology, Pediatrics
750 8th Ave #200, Fort Worth, 682-885-1605

Jain, Rajeev (5 mentions)
Baylor U, 1993 *Certification:* Gastroenterology
8230 Walnut Hill Ln #610, Dallas, 214-345-7398

Katzman, Steven M. (6 mentions)
FMS-Mexico, 1980
Certification: Gastroenterology, Internal Medicine
701 Tuscan #110, Irving, 214-496-1100

Miller, Mark Raymond (4 mentions)
U of Oklahoma, 1989
Certification: Gastroenterology, Internal Medicine
777 Walter Reed Blvd #301, Garland, 972-487-8855

Ogunmola, Nicholas A. (6 mentions)
FMS-Nigeria, 1990
Certification: Pediatric Gastroenterology, Pediatrics
750 8th Ave #200, Fort Worth, 682-885-1990

Polter, Daniel Earl (4 mentions)
U of Texas-Dallas, 1959
Certification: Gastroenterology, Internal Medicine
712 N Washington Ave #200, Dallas, 214-545-3990

Richardson, Charles Talmadge (8 mentions)
U of Texas-Dallas, 1966 *Certification:* Internal Medicine
3409 Worth St #700, Dallas, 214-820-2266

Rogoff, Thomas Michael (8 mentions)
Case Western Reserve U, 1972
Certification: Gastroenterology, Internal Medicine
7777 Forest Ln #C-675, Dallas, 972-566-6667

Rubin, Allen W. (9 mentions)
Jefferson Med Coll, 1967
Certification: Gastroenterology, Internal Medicine
701 Tuscan #110, Irving, 214-879-6900

Sandoval, Ruben Ernesto (4 mentions)
Creighton U, 1990 *Certification:* Gastroenterology
9330 Poppy Dr #501, Dallas, 214-327-2727

Schwartz, Armond Gluck, Jr. (5 mentions)
U of Texas-Dallas, 1976
Certification: Gastroenterology, Internal Medicine
221 W Colorado Blvd #630, Dallas, 214-941-6891

Stevens, William E. (5 mentions)
U of Texas-Dallas, 1987
Certification: Gastroenterology, Internal Medicine
8230 Walnut Hill Ln #610, Dallas, 214-345-7398

Tarnasky, Paul Randall (9 mentions)
U of Washington, 1989
Certification: Gastroenterology, Internal Medicine
221 W Colorado Blvd #630, Dallas, 214-941-6891

General Surgery

Allen, Scott Eugene (4 mentions)
U of Texas-Galveston, 1978 *Certification:* Surgery
1001 N Waldrop Dr #802, Arlington, 817-275-3309

Arnold, David Thomas (4 mentions)
U of Arkansas, 1996 *Certification:* Surgery
3808 Swiss Ave, Dallas, 214-823-2650

Aronoff, Ronald Joseph (4 mentions)
U of Texas-Dallas, 1977 *Certification:* Surgery
7777 Forest Ln #B-111, Dallas, 972-566-4444

Bell, Christopher L. (3 mentions)
Texas Tech U, 2000 *Certification:* Surgery
7777 Forest Ln #A214, Dallas, 972-566-7860

Black, Timothy Lee (5 mentions)
U of Tennessee, 1979 *Certification:* Surgery
1433 W Humboldt St, Fort Worth, 682-885-7080

Brancel, Dale H. (3 mentions)
U of North Texas, 1980
809 W Harwood Rd #201, Hurst, 817-267-8222

Castaneda, Antonio A. (4 mentions)
U of Texas-Dallas, 1995 *Certification:* Surgery
1325 Pennsylvania Ave #777, Fort Worth, 817-698-9700

Clifford, Edward James (4 mentions)
U of Texas-Dallas, 1986 *Certification:* Surgery
2001 N Macarthur Blvd #255, Irving, 972-254-9399

Collins, Mark Francis (3 mentions)
U of Texas-Houston, 1983 *Certification:* Surgery
1821 8th Ave, Fort Worth, 817-927-2329

Crawford, John Lloyd, Jr. (11 mentions)
Harvard U, 1977 *Certification:* Surgery
1325 Pennsylvania Ave, Fort Worth, 817-332-2998

Derrick, Howard C., III (3 mentions)
Med Coll of Georgia, 1972 *Certification:* Surgery
3600 Gaston Ave #958, Dallas, 214-826-6276

Dickerman, Richard M. (5 mentions)
Albany Med Coll, 1971 *Certification:* Surgery
221 W Colorado Blvd #100, Dallas, 214-943-8605

Dresel, Alexandra (4 mentions)
U of Wisconsin, 1998 *Certification:* Surgery
8210 Walnut Hill Ln #609, Dallas, 214-369-4571

Dyslin, David Cole (3 mentions)
Tulane U, 1990 *Certification:* Surgery
1001 N Waldrop Dr #802, Arlington, 817-275-3309

Eaton, Jerome Patrick (3 mentions)
Certification: Surgery
1604 Hospital Pkwy #505, Bedford, 817-267-2678

Henry, R. Stanley (10 mentions)
U of Texas-Dallas, 1973 *Certification:* Surgery
5939 Harry Hines Blvd #827, Dallas, 214-648-3067

Iglesias, Jose Luis (3 mentions)
U of Texas-Dallas, 1992 *Certification:* Pediatric Surgery, Surgery
901 7th Ave #210, Fort Worth, 817-336-7881

Jeyarajah, Dhiresh Rohan (3 mentions)
Brown U, 1989 *Certification:* Surgery
221 W Colorado Blvd #100, Dallas, 214-943-8605

Jones, Ronald Coy (3 mentions)
U of Tennessee, 1957 *Certification:* Surgery
3500 Gaston Ave, Dallas, 214-820-2468

Katz, Andres Ungar (5 mentions)
FMS-Spain, 1972 *Certification:* Surgery
8230 Walnut Hill Ln #408, Dallas, 214-369-5432

Kuhn, Joseph Allen (3 mentions)
U of Texas-Galveston, 1984
Certification: Surgery, Surgical Critical Care
3409 Worth St #420, Dallas, 214-824-9963

Lamont, Jeffrey Paul (3 mentions)
U of Michigan, 1996 *Certification:* Surgery
3409 Worth St #420, Dallas, 214-824-9963

Lieberman, Zelig H. (5 mentions)
Tulane U, 1950 *Certification:* Surgery
3600 Gaston Ave #958, Dallas, 214-826-6276

Lorimer, Douglas David (5 mentions)
U of Texas-Galveston, 1976 *Certification:* Surgery
1000 9th Ave, Fort Worth, 817-336-4200

Matin, Sina (4 mentions)
Virginia Commonwealth U, 1993 *Certification:* Surgery
2001 N Macarthur Blvd #255, Irving, 972-254-9399

Miller, James Paul (5 mentions)
Hahnemann U, 1981 *Certification:* Pediatric Surgery, Surgery
1433 W Humboldt St, Fort Worth, 682-885-7080

Newsome, Thomas Willingham (3 mentions)
Johns Hopkins U, 1967
3600 Gaston Ave #904, Dallas, 214-821-5410

Norman, James Lee (3 mentions)
U of Texas-Galveston, 1971 *Certification:* Surgery
1650 W Magnolia Ave #100, Fort Worth, 817-924-4464

Parker, Ralph R. (3 mentions)
U of Texas-Dallas, 1990 *Certification:* Surgery
701 Tuscan #225, Irving, 214-637-1999

Preskitt, John Thomas (16 mentions)
U of Texas-Dallas, 1975 *Certification:* Surgery
3600 Gaston Ave #958, Dallas, 214-826-6276

Sewell, Robert Walter (4 mentions)
U of Texas-Galveston, 1974 *Certification:* Surgery
1545 E Southlake Blvd #140, South Lake, 817-267-4555
1604 Hospital Pkwy #505, Bedford, 817-267-4555

Shires, George Thomas, III (6 mentions)
Duke U, 1978 *Certification:* Surgery
8230 Walnut Hill Ln #408, Dallas, 214-369-5432

Smith, Bruce Allen (6 mentions)
U of Texas-Dallas, 1978 *Certification:* Surgery
3600 Gaston Ave #710, Dallas, 214-827-5820

Vaughan, William Glaze (4 mentions)
Med Coll of Georgia, 1987
Certification: Pediatric Surgery, Surgery
901 7th Ave #210, Fort Worth, 817-336-7881
2020 W Hwy 114 #110, Grapevine, 817-336-7881
7100 Oakmont Blvd #201, Fort Worth, 817-336-7881

Westmoreland, Matthew V. (4 mentions)
U of Texas-Dallas, 1984 *Certification:* Surgery
3808 Swiss Ave, Dallas, 214-823-2650

Winter, John William, IV (3 mentions)
Tulane U, 1973 *Certification:* Surgery
7777 Forest Ln #A214, Dallas, 972-566-7860

Wootan, Richard Charles (3 mentions)
U of Texas-Dallas, 1977 *Certification:* Surgery
9335 Garland Rd, Dallas, 214-324-2824

Geriatrics

Belfi, Kendra Lee Jensen (5 mentions)
U of Texas-Dallas, 1972
Certification: Geriatric Medicine, Internal Medicine
909 9th Ave #300, Fort Worth, 817-336-7191

Carroll, Michael Lindsey (4 mentions)
Texas Tech U, 1979
9208 Elam Rd #220, Dallas, 214-398-3251

Knebl, Janice Ann (12 mentions)
Philadelphia Coll of Osteopathic Med, 1982
Certification: Internal Medicine
855 Montgomery St 3rd Fl, Fort Worth, 817-735-2200

Rubin, Craig Douglas (5 mentions)
New Jersey Med Sch, 1982
Certification: Geriatric Medicine, Internal Medicine
5323 Harry Hines Blvd, Dallas, 214-648-2992

Sherwood, Dorothy (5 mentions)
U of Cincinnati, 1979
Certification: Geriatric Medicine, Internal Medicine
8210 Walnut Hill Ln #230, Dallas, 972-284-7000

Hematology/Oncology

Bordelon, James Harold (6 mentions)
Louisiana State U, 1968
Certification: Hematology, Internal Medicine, Medical Oncology
1001 12th Ave #200, Fort Worth, 817-338-4333

Brooks, Barry Don (6 mentions)
U of Texas-Dallas, 1976
Certification: Internal Medicine, Medical Oncology
7777 Forest Ln #D-400, Dallas, 972-566-7790

Cooper, Barry (14 mentions)
Johns Hopkins U, 1971
Certification: Hematology, Internal Medicine, Medical Oncology
3535 Worth St, Dallas, 214-370-1000

Cox, John V. (4 mentions)
U of North Texas, 1978
Certification: Hematology, Internal Medicine, Medical Oncology
3555 W Wheatland Rd, Dallas, 972-709-2580

Haley, Barbara Jean (4 mentions)
U of Texas-Dallas, 1976
Certification: Hematology, Internal Medicine
2201 Inwood Rd, Dallas, 214-645-4673

Holmes, Houston E., III (8 mentions)
U of Texas-Dallas, 1990
Certification: Hematology, Internal Medicine, Medical Oncology
3535 Worth St, Dallas, 214-370-1000

Juturi, Jaya Vanisri (4 mentions)
FMS-India, 1993 *Certification:* Hematology, Medical Oncology
8440 Walnut Hill Ln #600, Dallas, 214-739-1706

Kerr, Ronald Neal (4 mentions)
U of Texas-Dallas, 1979
Certification: Internal Medicine, Medical Oncology
7777 Forest Ln #D-300, Dallas, 972-566-7790

Mandell, H. Lance (5 mentions)
Baylor U, 1990
800 W Magnolia Ave, Fort Worth, 817-333-0125

Mennel, Robert Gary (13 mentions)
U of Pennsylvania, 1970
Certification: Internal Medicine, Medical Oncology
3535 Worth St #270, Dallas, 214-370-1000

Milam, Mary (9 mentions)
U of Texas-Dallas, 1975
Certification: Internal Medicine, Medical Oncology
1307 8th Ave #205, Fort Worth, 817-924-4300

Negron, Angel G. (6 mentions)
U of Puerto Rico, 1970
Certification: Hematology, Internal Medicine, Medical Oncology
1001 12th Ave #200, Fort Worth, 817-332-7394

Nugent, John Lawrence E. (4 mentions)
U of Texas-Dallas, 1973
Certification: Internal Medicine, Medical Oncology
1001 12th Ave #200, Fort Worth, 817-850-2000

Perkins, Steve (7 mentions)
FMS-South Africa, 1978
Certification: Hematology, Internal Medicine, Medical Oncology
5939 Harry Hines Blvd #800, Dallas, 214-879-6250
2001 N Macarthur Blvd #750, Irving, 469-417-0406

Sanders, Joann Marie (4 mentions)
St Louis U, 1982
Certification: Pediatric Hematology-Oncology, Pediatrics
901 7th Ave #220, Fort Worth, 682-885-4020

Savin, Michael Alan (9 mentions)
U of Pittsburgh, 1969
Certification: Hematology, Internal Medicine, Medical Oncology
7777 Forest Ln #D-400, Dallas, 972-566-7790

Strauss, James Fredric (5 mentions)
New York U, 1972
Certification: Hematology, Internal Medicine, Medical Oncology
8220 Walnut Hill Ln #700, Dallas, 214-739-4175

Sunderland, Margaret C. (4 mentions)
Oregon Health Sciences U, 1982 *Certification:* Internal Medicine
2001 N macArthur Blvd #630, Irving, 972-256-3537

Turner, James Malcolm (5 mentions)
U of Michigan, 1982
Certification: Hematology, Internal Medicine, Medical Oncology
1615 Hospital Pkwy #300, Bedford, 817-267-4201

Wilfong, Lalan S. (4 mentions)
U of Texas-Dallas, 1997
Certification: Hematology, Internal Medicine, Medical Oncology
8220 Walnut Hill Ln #700, Dallas, 214-739-4175

Infectious Disease

Allen, David Michael (11 mentions)
U of Texas-Dallas, 1983
Certification: Infectious Disease, Internal Medicine
7777 Forest Ln #B-412, Dallas, 972-661-5550

Barbaro, Daniel John (19 mentions)
New York Med Coll, 1981
Certification: Infectious Disease, Internal Medicine
1125 College Ave, Fort Worth, 817-810-9810

Davis, Steven Gabe (11 mentions)
Indiana U, 1986
Certification: Infectious Disease, Internal Medicine
5939 Harry Hines Blvd #845, Dallas, 214-689-7806

Goodman, Edward Leo (17 mentions)
Cornell U, 1968
Certification: Infectious Disease, Internal Medicine
8230 Walnut Hill Ln #414, Dallas, 214-691-8306

Liddell, Allison (8 mentions)
U of Texas-Dallas, 1994 *Certification:* Infectious Disease
8230 Walnut Hill Ln #414, Dallas, 214-691-8306

Luby, James Phillip (6 mentions)
Northwestern U, 1961
Certification: Infectious Disease, Internal Medicine
5323 Harry Hines Blvd #E3608, Dallas, 214-648-3480

McDonald, Cheryl K. (7 mentions)
U of Texas-Dallas, 1989
Certification: Infectious Disease, Internal Medicine
1125 College Ave, Fort Worth, 817-810-9810

Murphey, Donald K. (7 mentions)
U of Texas-San Antonio, 1986
Certification: Pediatric Infectious Diseases, Pediatrics
801 7th Ave, Fort Worth, 682-885-1485

Seidenfeld, Steven M. (7 mentions)
New York U, 1977
Certification: Infectious Disease, Internal Medicine
7777 Forest Ln #B412, Dallas, 972-661-5550

Shelton, Mark McGregor (9 mentions)
Texas A&M U, 1983
Certification: Pediatric Infectious Diseases, Pediatrics
800 7th Ave, Fort Worth, 682-885-3920
801 7th Ave, Fort Worth, 682-885-1485

Sloan, Louis Marshall (25 mentions)
U of Texas-San Antonio, 1989
Certification: Infectious Disease, Internal Medicine
3409 Worth St #710, Dallas, 214-823-2533

Sutker, William Levin (17 mentions)
Rosalind Franklin U, 1974
Certification: Infectious Disease, Internal Medicine
3409 Worth St #710, Dallas, 214-823-2533

Whitworth, Mary Suzanne (8 mentions)
U of Texas-Galveston, 1990
Certification: Pediatric Infectious Diseases, Pediatrics
801 7th Ave, Fort Worth, 682-885-1485

Infertility

Chantilis, Samuel J. (8 mentions)
U of Texas-Dallas, 1987 *Certification:* Obstetrics &
Gynecology, Reproductive Endocrinology/Infertility
8160 Walnut Hill Ln #328, Dallas, 214-363-5965

Doody, Kevin J. (8 mentions)
Baylor U, 1982 *Certification:* Obstetrics & Gynecology,
Reproductive Endocrinology/Infertility
1701 Park Place Ave, Bedford, 817-540-1157
4461 Colt Rd #307, Frisco, 817-540-1157

Kaufmann, Robert Alan (6 mentions)
FMS-Israel, 1984 *Certification:* Obstetrics & Gynecology,
Reproductive Endocrinology/Infertility
800 5th Ave #210, Fort Worth, 817-348-8145

Marynick, Samuel Philip (6 mentions)
U of Texas-Dallas, 1972
Certification: Endocrinology and Metabolism, Internal Medicine
3600 Gaston Ave #506, Dallas, 214-828-2244

Putman, John Michael (13 mentions)
Med Coll of Georgia, 1973 *Certification:* Obstetrics & Gynecology
3600 Gaston Ave #504, Dallas, 214-821-2274

Internal Medicine *(see note on page 9)*

Adamo, Michael Paul (5 mentions)
U of North Texas, 1980 *Certification:* Internal Medicine
1650 W Magnolia Ave #207, Fort Worth, 817-923-2677

Anderson, Amy Stevens (3 mentions)
U of Texas-Galveston, 1992 *Certification:* Internal Medicine
3434 Swiss Ave #320, Dallas, 214-828-5060

Ashai, Daud Hussain (3 mentions)
FMS-Pakistan, 1985
Certification: Critical Care Medicine, Internal Medicine
1001 College Ave, Fort Worth, 817-336-6000

Chung, Andrew Dongwook (3 mentions)
Tufts U, 1992 *Certification:* Internal Medicine
3600 Gaston Ave #1001 Barnett Tower, Dallas, 214-824-4585

Click, Robert Reed, Jr. (3 mentions)
U of Texas-Dallas, 1975 *Certification:* Internal Medicine
5323 Harry Hines Blvd, Dallas, 214-645-8620

Davenport, Norman Alan (4 mentions)
U of Texas-Galveston, 1977 *Certification:* Internal Medicine
1622 8th Ave #110, Fort Worth, 817-926-2571

Dearden, Craig Lee (4 mentions)
Texas Tech U, 1979 *Certification:* Internal Medicine
1000 9th Ave #C, Fort Worth, 817-332-3039

Demartini, Robert Vincent (3 mentions)
New York Med Coll, 1987 *Certification:* Internal Medicine
1600 W College St #490, Grapevine, 817-481-1511

Eldridge, James K. (3 mentions)
U of Texas-Galveston, 1999 *Certification:* Internal Medicine
800 5th Ave #300, Fort Worth, 817-334-1400

Fine, Robert Lee (3 mentions)
U of Texas-Dallas, 1978
Certification: Hospice and Palliative Medicine, Internal Medicine
3434 Swiss Ave #205, Dallas, 214-828-5090

Fleschler, Mark Joe (6 mentions)
U of Texas-Dallas, 1984
Certification: Geriatric Medicine, Internal Medicine
8210 Walnut Hill Ln #604, Dallas, 214-368-7787

Frater, Dirk Anthony (4 mentions)
Albert Einstein Coll of Med, 1984 *Certification:* Internal Medicine
8230 Walnut Hill Ln #818, Dallas, 214-373-3475

Haddox, Robert J. (3 mentions)
U of Texas-Dallas, 1983 *Certification:* Internal Medicine
1130 Beachview St #100, Dallas, 214-321-6485

Johnson, Steven E. (4 mentions)
Certification: Internal Medicine
800 5th Ave #300, Fort Worth, 817-334-1400

Jones, R. Ellwood, III (3 mentions)
Certification: Internal Medicine
5303 Harry Hines Blvd, Dallas, 214-645-8610

Koster, Robert Louis (3 mentions)
U of Miami, 1971 *Certification:* Internal Medicine
3600 Gaston Ave #1001, Dallas, 214-824-4585

Leach, Steven Lamar (4 mentions)
U of Chicago, 1993 *Certification:* Internal Medicine
5323 Harry Hines Blvd, Dallas, 214-645-8610

Neubach, Paul Arnold (8 mentions)
U of Texas-Galveston, 1975 *Certification:* Internal Medicine
3434 Swiss Ave #410, Dallas, 214-828-5010

Owen, Stuart Frederick (5 mentions)
U of Michigan, 1977 *Certification:* Internal Medicine
3600 Gaston Ave #1004, Dallas, 214-827-7600

Penny, Richard Edward (4 mentions)
U of Texas-Galveston, 1972 *Certification:* Internal Medicine
6100 Harris Pkwy #345, Fort Worth, 817-346-5960

Phillips, Gregory Joseph (5 mentions)
U of Texas-Dallas, 1974 *Certification:* Internal Medicine
1050 5th Ave #J, Fort Worth, 817-336-1200
1201 Summit Ave, Fort Worth, 817-332-2020

Phillips, Jeffrey Harris (4 mentions)
Temple U, 1983 *Certification:* Internal Medicine
8210 Walnut Hill Ln #604, Dallas, 214-368-7787

Reed, William Gary (5 mentions)
U of Texas-Dallas, 1977 *Certification:* Internal Medicine
5303 Harry Hines Blvd 8th Fl #200, Dallas, 214-645-8600

Rothstein, Joseph Martin (3 mentions)
U of Texas-Dallas, 1981 *Certification:* Internal Medicine
3600 Gaston Ave #1004, Dallas, 214-827-7600

Salam, Ambareen (3 mentions)
U of Texas-San Antonio, 1994
7777 Forest Ln #C-420, Dallas, 972-566-5568

Smith, Weldon Lloyd, Jr. (5 mentions)
U of Texas-Dallas, 1976 *Certification:* Internal Medicine
3434 Swiss Ave #430, Dallas, 214-820-0111

Winter, Fred David, Jr. (4 mentions)
U of Texas-Galveston, 1975 *Certification:* Internal Medicine
3434 Swiss Ave #105, Dallas, 214-828-0010

Young, John David, Jr. (3 mentions)
U of Virginia, 1980 *Certification:* Internal Medicine
2001 N Macarthur Blvd #500A, Irving, 972-251-4050

Nephrology

Aragon, Michael A. (5 mentions)
U of Texas-Houston, 2000
Certification: Internal Medicine, Nephrology
3030 Matlock Rd #205, Arlington, 817-375-0610

Cano, Adriana (4 mentions)
U of Texas-Dallas, 1986
Certification: Internal Medicine, Nephrology
5939 Harry Hines Blvd #500, Dallas, 214-638-6600

Emmett, Michael (5 mentions)
Temple U, 1971 *Certification:* Internal Medicine, Nephrology
3500 Gaston Ave, Dallas, 214-820-6277

Fenves, Andrew Zoltan (18 mentions)
U of Texas-Dallas, 1979
Certification: Internal Medicine, Nephrology
3601 Swiss Ave #200, Dallas, 214-358-2300

Gratch, Jack Orrin (4 mentions)
Philadelphia Coll of Osteopathic Med, 1974
1700 Mistletoe Blvd, Fort Worth, 817-927-2612
1032 Sandy Ln, Fort Worth, 817-429-1944

Hays, Steven R. (4 mentions)
U of Illinois, 1979 *Certification:* Internal Medicine, Nephrology
3601 Swiss Ave, Dallas, 214-358-2300

Hirt, Darrell Lee (4 mentions)
U of Texas-Dallas, 1981
Certification: Internal Medicine, Nephrology
1000 W Cannon St, Fort Worth, 817-877-5858

Levy, Freda Lynne (4 mentions)
U of Texas-Dallas, 1985
Certification: Internal Medicine, Nephrology
1150 N Bishop Ave #100, Dallas, 214-358-2300

Mauk, Richard Harold (5 mentions)
Ohio State U, 1972 *Certification:* Internal Medicine, Nephrology
950 W Magnolia Ave, Fort Worth, 817-336-5060

Rinner, Steven Eric (18 mentions)
U of Buffalo, 1967 *Certification:* Internal Medicine, Nephrology
13154 Coit Rd #100, Dallas, 214-358-2300

Silverstein, Alanna M. (4 mentions)
U of Texas-Galveston, 1978 *Certification:* Internal Medicine
820 W Arapaho Rd #200, Richardson, 972-498-4500

Thompson, Jeffrey Reed (8 mentions)
U of Illinois, 1982 *Certification:* Internal Medicine, Nephrology
5939 Harry Hines Blvd #500, Dallas, 214-638-6600

Wall, Bruce Raleigh (11 mentions)
Tulane U, 1981 *Certification:* Internal Medicine, Nephrology
13154 Coit Rd #100, Dallas, 214-358-2300

Neurological Surgery

Barnett, David Wesley (28 mentions)
U of Texas-Dallas, 1989 *Certification:* Neurological Surgery
3600 Gaston Ave Barnett Tower #907, Dallas, 214-823-2052
1601 Lancaster Dr, Grapevine, 817-310-0521

Desaloms, John Michael (12 mentions)
Baylor U, 1992 *Certification:* Neurological Surgery
8230 Walnut Hill Ln #220, Dallas, 214-750-3646
4708 Alliance Blvd #620, Plano, 972-665-4810
1105 Central Expy, Allen, 972-747-6393

Donahue, David Jerome (10 mentions)
U of Tennessee, 1978 *Certification:* Neurological Surgery
901 7th Ave #120, Fort Worth, 682-885-2500

Jackson, Richard H. (12 mentions)
U of Oklahoma, 1976 *Certification:* Neurological Surgery
8230 Walnut Hill Ln #220, Dallas, 214-750-3646
4708 Alliance Blvd #620, Plano, 972-665-4810

Mickey, Bruce Edward (18 mentions)
U of Texas-Dallas, 1978 *Certification:* Neurological Surgery
5161 Harry Hines Blvd 5th Fl, Dallas, 214-645-2300

Moody, James Aubrey (7 mentions)
U of Texas-Galveston, 1972 *Certification:* Neurological Surgery
221 W Colorado Blvd #155, Dallas, 214-941-7724

Samson, Duke Staples (11 mentions)
Washington U, 1969 *Certification:* Neurological Surgery
5323 Harry Hines Blvd, Dallas, 214-648-3529

Smith, Gregory Heath (8 mentions)
A T Still U, 1984
1319 Summit Ave #200, Fort Worth, 817-336-0551

Neurology

Adams, Quentin Mark (4 mentions)
U of Texas-San Antonio, 1985 *Certification:* Neurology
1207 Hall Johnson Rd, Collegeville, 817-849-8490

Chen, Connie Lynn (5 mentions)
Johns Hopkins U, 1998
Certification: Neurology, Vascular Neurology
7515 Greenville Ave #400, Dallas, 214-750-9977

Chin, Lincoln Fitzalbert (6 mentions)
FMS-Jamaica, 1972 *Certification:* Neurology
1650 W Rosedale St, Fort Worth, 817-336-1181

El-Feky, Waleed Hamed (5 mentions)
FMS-Egypt, 1990
Certification: Clinical Neurophysiology, Neurology, Sleep Medicine
6301 Gaston Ave #400-W, Dallas, 214-827-3610

Frohman, Elliott Mark (5 mentions)
U of California-Irvine, 1990 *Certification:* Neurology
5323 Harry Hines Blvd, Dallas, 214-648-9574

Herzog, Steven Paul (7 mentions)
U of Arizona, 1985 *Certification:* Neurology
6301 Gaston Ave #400W, Dallas, 214-827-3610

Hinton, Richard Charles (8 mentions)
Baylor U, 1972 *Certification:* Internal Medicine, Neurology
7515 Greenville Ave #400, Dallas, 214-750-9977

Kelfer, Howard Michael (7 mentions)
Tufts U, 1976 *Certification:* Neurology with Special
Qualifications in Child Neurology, Pediatrics
901 7th Ave #120, Fort Worth, 682-885-2500

Khalid, Mohammad (4 mentions)
FMS-Pakistan, 1975 *Certification:* Neurology
5939 Harry Hines Blvd #745, Dallas, 214-879-6373

Marks, Warren Alan (4 mentions)
Texas Tech U, 1983 *Certification:* Neurology with Special
Qualifications in Child Neurology
901 7th Ave #120, Fort Worth, 682-885-2500

Martin, Alan William (6 mentions)
Texas A&M U, 1984 *Certification:* Clinical Neurophysiology,
Neurology, Neuromuscular Medicine
6301 Gaston Ave #400W, Dallas, 214-827-3610

Melamed, Norma Bernice (9 mentions)
FMS-South Africa, 1978 *Certification:* Neurology
12810 Hillcrest Rd #220, Dallas, 972-991-8466

Ryals, Brian Douglas (4 mentions)
U of Oklahoma, 1985 *Certification:* Neurology with Special
Qualifications in Child Neurology, Pediatrics
901 7th Ave #120, Fort Worth, 682-885-2500

Shalan, Gregg Andrew (4 mentions)
New Jersey Med Sch, 1990
Certification: Neurology, Vascular Neurology
1441 N Beckley Ave, Dallas, 214-947-1837

Tran, Duc (5 mentions)
Georgetown U, 1995
Certification: Clinical Neurophysiology, Neurology
7515 Greenville Ave #400, Dallas, 214-750-9977

Tunell, Gary Lee (13 mentions)
U of Missouri, 1975 *Certification:* Neurology
6301 Gaston Ave #400W, Dallas, 214-827-3610

Obstetrics/Gynecology

Abbott, Philip Don (3 mentions)
U of Texas-Dallas, 1961 *Certification:* Obstetrics & Gynecology
3700 Rufe Snow Dr, North Richland Hills, 817-590-2395

Bakos, Sharon Mae (6 mentions)
Baylor U, 1982 *Certification:* Obstetrics & Gynecology
1311 N Washington Ave, Dallas, 214-824-2563

Bertrand, John David (3 mentions)
U of Texas-Dallas, 1975 *Certification:* Obstetrics & Gynecology
8305 Walnut Hill Ln #100, Dallas, 214-363-7801

Bradford, Laura Anne (3 mentions)
Texas Tech U, 1992 *Certification:* Obstetrics & Gynecology
851 W Terrell Ave, Fort Worth, 817-926-4118

Carlos, Joseph J. (3 mentions)
Michigan State U, 1977 *Certification:* Obstetrics & Gynecology
7777 Forest Ln #D560, Dallas, 972-566-4862

Carrington, Frederick L. (3 mentions)
U of Texas-Galveston, 1973 *Certification:* Obstetrics & Gynecology
6100 Harris Pkwy #140, Fort Worth, 817-346-5336

Carter, Julian Gayden (4 mentions)
U of Texas-Galveston, 1978 *Certification:* Obstetrics & Gynecology
1311 N Washington Ave, Dallas, 214-824-2563

England, Michael John (3 mentions)
FMS-South Africa, 1979 *Certification:* Obstetrics & Gynecology
1250 8th Ave #330, Fort Worth, 817-923-5559

Goss, Jan Jensen (3 mentions)
U of Washington, 1975 *Certification:* Obstetrics & Gynecology
7777 Forest Lane Bldg B #433, Dallas, 972-566-8878

Gunby, Robert Tau, Jr. (10 mentions)
Med Coll of Georgia, 1971 *Certification:* Obstetrics & Gynecology
4224 Swiss Ave, Dallas, 214-821-9938

Herd, James P. (8 mentions)
Certification: Obstetrics & Gynecology
1250 8th Ave, Fort Worth, 817-923-0023

Howell, Robert Michael (3 mentions)
U of Texas-Houston, 1986 *Certification:* Obstetrics & Gynecology
6100 Harris Pkwy #140, Fort Worth, 817-346-5336

Joseph, Richard Joseph (6 mentions)
U of Mississippi, 1970 *Certification:* Obstetrics & Gynecology
3600 Gaston Ave #300, Dallas, 214-824-3200
1600 Republic Pkwy #160, Mesquite, 972-613-6336

Kinney, Cheryl Cox (3 mentions)
Indiana U, 1981 *Certification:* Obstetrics & Gynecology
7777 Forest Ln Bldg B #433, Dallas, 972-566-8878

Neal, Kerry Doyle (3 mentions)
U of Tennessee, 1982 *Certification:* Obstetrics & Gynecology
1600 W College St #1101, Grapevine, 817-424-3112

Nokleberg, Jane Ellen (3 mentions)
Rosalind Franklin U, 1995 *Certification:* Obstetrics & Gynecology
8305 Walnut Hill Ln #100, Dallas, 214-363-7801

Payne, Paul Bradley (3 mentions)
Texas Tech U, 1980 *Certification:* Obstetrics & Gynecology
4224 Swiss Ave, Dallas, 214-821-9938

Robbins, Cynthia R. (3 mentions)
Certification: Obstetrics & Gynecology
851 W Terrell Ave, Fort Worth, 817-926-4118

Sakovich, Stephen Peter (3 mentions)
Texas Tech U, 1982 *Certification:* Obstetrics & Gynecology
3501 N Macarthur Blvd #500, Irving, 972-256-3700

Schermerhorn, James E. (3 mentions)
U of Texas-Dallas, 1980 *Certification:* Obstetrics & Gynecology
1151 N Buckner Blvd #206, Dallas, 214-320-8447

Vernon, Kim (3 mentions)
U of Texas-San Antonio, 1979
Certification: Obstetrics & Gynecology
7777 Forest Ln #D-570, Dallas, 972-566-4660

Watson, Robert Kent (5 mentions)
U of Texas-San Antonio, 1979
Certification: Obstetrics & Gynecology
1300 W Terrell Ave #300, Fort Worth, 817-923-5558
1250 8th Ave #440, Fort Worth, 817-923-5558

Ophthalmology

Berry, William Larkin (4 mentions)
U of Texas-Dallas, 1967 *Certification:* Ophthalmology
3600 Gaston Ave #609, Dallas, 214-826-8201

Cichocki, Jonathan J. (3 mentions)
Wayne State U, 1976
818 W Terrell Ave, Fort Worth, 817-335-1875

Fagadau, Warren Robert (5 mentions)
U of Texas-Dallas, 1978 *Certification:* Ophthalmology
6131 Luther Ln #216, Dallas, 214-987-2020

Gilliland, Grant Donald (7 mentions)
U of Texas-Dallas, 1988 *Certification:* Ophthalmology
9301 N Central Expy #595, Dallas, 214-522-7733

Hendricks, George David, Jr. (3 mentions)
U of Texas-Dallas, 1980 *Certification:* Ophthalmology
1201 Summit Ave, Fort Worth, 817-332-2020
804 Santa Fe Rd, Weatherford, 817-594-9500

Itani, Kamel M. (3 mentions)
FMS-Lebanon, 1983 *Certification:* Ophthalmology
5303 Harry Hines Blvd, Dallas, 214-645-2020

Merritt, James Hansel (4 mentions)
U of Texas-Houston, 1978 *Certification:* Ophthalmology
8230 Walnut Hill Ln #508, Dallas, 214-369-0555

Milner, Michael Spencer (10 mentions)
Louisiana State U-Shreveport, 1990 *Certification:* Ophthalmology
3600 Gaston Ave #609, Dallas, 214-826-8201

Mong, Michael A. (3 mentions)
U of Texas-Dallas, 1984 *Certification:* Ophthalmology
1600 W College St #390, Grapevine, 817-481-8955

Moninger, George A. (4 mentions)
U of Texas-Houston, 1991 *Certification:* Ophthalmology
10 Medical Pkwy #102, Dallas, 972-241-2564

Newman, Gordon Harry (3 mentions)
New York Med Coll, 1963 *Certification:* Ophthalmology
5744 Lyndon B Johnson Frwy #150, Dallas, 972-392-2020
1708 Coit Rd #240, Plano, 972-312-9312

Norman, Alan A. (7 mentions)
Baylor U, 1996 *Certification:* Ophthalmology
1325 Pennsylvania Ave #110, Fort Worth, 817-878-5454
2201 E Lama Blvd #290, Arlington, 817-878-5454

Packwood, Eric Alan (10 mentions)
Baylor U, 1995 *Certification:* Ophthalmology
1325 Pennsylvania Ave #110, Fort Worth, 817-878-5454
2201 E Lamar Blvd #290, Arlington, 817-640-1211

Ranelle, Brian D. (12 mentions)
Kansas U Coll of Osteopathic Med, 1972
Certification: Ophthalmology
1350 S Main St #1200, Fort Worth, 817-731-8080

Rosenthal, Harry, Jr. (3 mentions)
U of Texas-Houston, 1983 *Certification:* Ophthalmology
4974 Overton Ridge Blvd, Fort Worth, 817-423-3937
1643 Lancaster #305, Grapevine, 817-423-3937
1100 SE 1st St #4, Mineral Wells, 817-423-3937

Saland, Karen Bassichis (4 mentions)
U of Texas-Dallas, 1999
8210 Walnut Hill Ln, Dallas, 214-691-8000

Slusher, Norman (6 mentions)
U of Missouri, 1974 *Certification:* Ophthalmology
3600 Gaston Ave #964, Dallas, 214-826-7470

Smith, Craig Douglas (3 mentions)
Baylor U, 1976 *Certification:* Ophthalmology
12222 Merit Dr #1420, Dallas, 972-233-6237

Smith, Judson Paul (3 mentions)
U of Texas-Galveston, 1972 *Certification:* Ophthalmology
1350 S Main St #3100, Fort Worth, 817-338-4081

Tenery, Robert Mayo, Jr. (3 mentions)
U of Texas-Galveston, 1968 *Certification:* Ophthalmology
7777 Forest Ln #-B424, Dallas, 972-566-8200

Uhr, Barry Wayne (8 mentions)
U of Texas-Dallas, 1965 *Certification:* Ophthalmology
3600 Gaston Ave #609, Dallas, 214-826-8201

Orthopedics

Brown, David S. (3 mentions)
U of Texas-Dallas, 1995 *Certification:* Orthopaedic Surgery
2020 W State Hwy 114 #110, Grapevine, 817-310-0810

Burke, Ronald G. (5 mentions)
U of Texas-Houston, 1989 *Certification:* Orthopaedic Surgery
901 7th Ave #110, Fort Worth, 682-885-4405

Burkhead, Wayne, Jr. (5 mentions)
U of Texas-Galveston, 1978 *Certification:* Orthopaedic Surgery
9301 N Central Expy #400, Dallas, 214-220-2468

Champine, Michael J. (5 mentions)
U of Texas-San Antonio, 1988 *Certification:* Orthopaedic Surgery
8210 Walnut Hill Ln #130, Dallas, 214-750-1207
6020 W Parker Rd, Plano, 214-378-1438

Conway, John Evert (6 mentions)
U of Texas-Houston, 1983 *Certification:* Orthopaedic Surgery
800 5th Ave #500, Fort Worth, 817-878-5300

Cooper, Daniel E. (5 mentions)
U of Texas-Dallas, 1984 *Certification:* Orthopaedic Surgery
9301 N Central Expy #400, Dallas, 214-220-2468

Dossett, Andrew Bienvenu (5 mentions)
U of Texas-Dallas, 1988 *Certification:* Orthopaedic Surgery
9301 N Central Expy #400, Dallas, 214-220-2468

Frederick, Hugh Allen (3 mentions)
U of Texas-Galveston, 1985
Certification: Orthopaedic Surgery, Surgery of the Hand
9301 N Central Expy #350, Dallas, 214-528-4185

Gill, Kevin (4 mentions)
Baylor U, 1980 *Certification:* Orthopaedic Surgery
1801 Inwood Rd, Dallas, 214-645-8270

Hamilton, Hinton H., III (4 mentions)
U of Texas-Galveston, 1970 *Certification:* Orthopaedic Surgery
901 7th Ave #110, Fort Worth, 682-885-4405

Hopkins, Shelton George (3 mentions)
U of Texas-Dallas, 1971 *Certification:* Orthopaedic Surgery
7777 Forest Ln #C-106, Dallas, 972-566-7874
411 N Washington Ave #7000, Dallas, 214-823-7090

Hull, Christopher K. (3 mentions)
U of North Texas, 1979
3625 Camp Bowie Blvd, Fort Worth, 817-737-8880
1308 Paluxy Rd #C, Granbury, 817-579-9300

Jones, Alan L. (3 mentions)
Baylor U, 1987 *Certification:* Orthopaedic Surgery
3409 Worth Ave #320, Dallas, 214-820-8350

Kelly, Patrick F. (3 mentions)
A T Still U, 1993
4375 Booth Calloway Rd #410, North Richland Hills,
817-595-5890

Krishnan, Sumant G. (3 mentions)
Baylor U, 1995 *Certification:* Orthopaedic Surgery
9301 N Central Expy #400, Dallas, 214-220-2468

Lichtman, David Michael (3 mentions)
SUNY-Downstate Med Coll, 1966
Certification: Orthopaedic Surgery, Surgery of the Hand
1500 S Main St, Fort Worth, 817-222-2377

Medlock, Virgil B., III (3 mentions)
U of Texas-Dallas, 1995 *Certification:* Orthopaedic Surgery
7777 Forest Ln #C106, Dallas, 972-566-7874
411 N Washington Ave #7000, Dallas, 214-823-7090

Messer, Larry Durward (3 mentions)
U of Texas-Galveston, 1972 *Certification:* Orthopaedic Surgery
901 7th Ave #110, Fort Worth, 682-885-4405
801 7th Ave, Fort Worth, 682-885-2140

Milne, Joseph C. (3 mentions)
Baylor U, 1987 *Certification:* Orthopaedic Surgery
1651 W Rosedale St #100, Fort Worth, 817-335-4316

Montgomery, James Bertram (11 mentions)
U of Texas-Dallas, 1977 *Certification:* Orthopaedic Surgery
7115 Greenville Ave #310, Dallas, 214-265-3200

Park, Andrew Eunkoo (4 mentions)
Northwestern U, 1997 *Certification:* Orthopaedic Surgery
3900 Junius St #705, Dallas, 214-370-3006

Paschal, Scott Owen (3 mentions)
U of Texas-Dallas, 1982 *Certification:* Orthopaedic Surgery
7115 Greenville Ave #310, Dallas, 214-265-3200

Peters, Pat Andrew (3 mentions)
U of Texas-San Antonio, 1983 *Certification:* Orthopaedic Surgery
2535 Ira E Woods Ave, Grapevine, 817-589-0393

Peters, Paul C., Jr. (3 mentions)
U of Texas-Dallas, 1984 *Certification:* Orthopaedic Surgery
9301 N Central Expy #400, Dallas, 214-220-2468

Pollifrone, James J. (3 mentions)
Ohio U Coll of Osteopathic Med, 1984
800 Orthopedic Way, Arlington, 817-375-5200

Rathjen, Kurt Walter (8 mentions)
U of Texas-Dallas, 1983 *Certification:* Orthopaedic Surgery
411 N Washington Ave #7500, Dallas, 214-824-4866

Richards, John Andrew (4 mentions)
U of Texas-Dallas, 1971 *Certification:* Orthopaedic Surgery
556 8th Ave, Fort Worth, 817-336-6222

Rutherford, Charles Storey (4 mentions)
U of Texas-Dallas, 1980 *Certification:* Orthopaedic Surgery
7777 Forest Ln #C-106, Dallas, 972-566-7874
411 N Washington Ave #7000, Dallas, 214-823-7090

Scheinberg, Robert Russell (5 mentions)
U of Tennessee, 1985 *Certification:* Orthopaedic Surgery
8210 Walnut Hill Ln #130, Dallas, 214-750-1207

Schmidt, Robert Herman (3 mentions)
U of Virginia, 1978 *Certification:* Orthopaedic Surgery
750 8th Ave #400, Fort Worth, 817-877-3432

Schubert, Richard Darryl (3 mentions)
U of Texas-Dallas, 1979
2909 Lemmon Ave, Dallas, 214-220-2468

Snoots, Wynne McCallie (4 mentions)
U of Texas-Dallas, 1964 *Certification:* Orthopaedic Surgery
3434 Swiss Ave #104, Dallas, 214-824-5544

Todd, Joe Mack (4 mentions)
U of Texas-Galveston, 1975 *Certification:* Orthopaedic Surgery
1300 W Rosedale St #B, Fort Worth, 817-921-3461

Wagner, Russell A. (3 mentions)
U of Texas-Dallas, 1987 *Certification:* Orthopaedic Surgery
855 Montgomery St 5th Fl, Fort Worth, 817-735-2900

Wheeless, Glenn Stephen (3 mentions)
U of Texas-Dallas, 1981 *Certification:* Orthopaedic Surgery
4780 N Josey Lane, Carrollton, 972-492-1334

Zoys, George N. (3 mentions)
U of Texas-San Antonio, 1995 *Certification:* Orthopaedic Surgery
2241 Peggy Ln #A, Garland, 972-276-0536

Otorhinolaryngology

Burkett, Robert Judson (6 mentions)
U of Texas-Galveston, 1962 *Certification:* Otolaryngology
800 8th Ave #618, Fort Worth, 817-335-6336

Ducic, Yadranko (6 mentions)
FMS-Canada, 1991 *Certification:* Otolaryngology
1420 8th Ave #101, Fort Worth, 817-927-1171
923 Pennsylvania Ave #100, Fort Worth, 817-920-0484

Gamble, Bradford Allen (5 mentions)
U of Texas-Dallas, 1993 *Certification:* Otolaryngology
8230 Walnut Hill Ln #420, Dallas, 214-265-0800

Hardin, Mark Alan (6 mentions)
Baylor U, 1982 *Certification:* Otolaryngology
3434 Swiss Ave #204, Dallas, 214-821-1809

Janicki, Peter Thomas (4 mentions)
Baylor U, 1986 *Certification:* Otolaryngology
1615 Hospital Pkwy #210, Bedford, 817-589-2072

Jordan, Jennifer Ann (5 mentions)
Indiana U, 1993 *Certification:* Otolaryngology
1130 Beachview St #240, Dallas, 214-324-0418

Kapadia, Lav Anupam (4 mentions)
U of Missouri-Kansas City, 1994 *Certification:* Otolaryngology
400 W Lyndon B Johnson Frwy #360, Irving, 972-402-8404

Kronenberger, Michael B. (5 mentions)
Baylor U, 1991 *Certification:* Otolaryngology
411 N Washington Ave #2800, Dallas, 214-826-3681

Landers, Stephen Alan (7 mentions)
Wake Forest U, 1983 *Certification:* Otolaryngology
1004 N Washington Ave, Dallas, 214-826-8600
7515 Greenville Ave #806, Dallas, 214-691-0800

Marple, Bradley Franklin (8 mentions)
U of Oklahoma, 1988 *Certification:* Otolaryngology
5303 Harry Hines Blvd #106, Dallas, 214-645-8898

Mock, Presley M. (6 mentions)
U of Texas-San Antonio, 1986 *Certification:* Otolaryngology
8440 Walnut Hill Ln #500, Dallas, 972-345-1494

Oxford, Lance Edward (8 mentions)
U of Texas-Dallas, 1999 *Certification:* Otolaryngology
411 N Washington Ave #2800, Dallas, 214-826-3681

Palmer, J. Mark (9 mentions)
Baylor U, 1982 *Certification:* Otolaryngology
800 8th Ave #426, Fort Worth, 817-334-0686

Roland, Peter Sargent (6 mentions)
U of Texas-Galveston, 1976
Certification: Neurotology, Otolaryngology
5303 Harry Hines Blvd #106, Dallas, 214-645-8898

Schultz, Barbara Ann (4 mentions)
U of Texas-Dallas, 1980 *Certification:* Otolaryngology
5303 Harry Hines Blvd #106, Dallas, 214-645-8898

Strange, Leslie C., III (4 mentions)
U of Texas-Dallas, 1970 *Certification:* Otolaryngology
800 8th Ave 3rd Fl #326, Fort Worth, 817-870-2611

Theilen, Frank W. (7 mentions)
U of Texas-Galveston, 1982 *Certification:* Otolaryngology
400 W Lyndon B Johnson Frwy #360, Irving, 972-402-8404

Trone, Timothy Howard (4 mentions)
U of Texas-Dallas, 1974 *Certification:* Otolaryngology
7777 Forest Ln #B-107, Dallas, 972-566-8300

Weprin, Lawrence Scott (11 mentions)
U of Illinois, 1966 *Certification:* Otolaryngology
7150 N President George Bush Hwy #202, Garland,
972-414-0408
3600 Gaston Ave #911, Dallas, 214-745-1090

Pain Medicine

Bulger, Robert Raymond (4 mentions)
Mayo Med Sch, 1980 *Certification:* Anesthesiology, Pain Medicine
8320 Walnut Hill Ln #320, Dallas, 214-265-9991

Grant, Paul Anthony (7 mentions)
FMS-Jamaica, 1966
800 5th Ave #410, Fort Worth, 817-332-6092

Haynsworth, Robert F., Jr. (4 mentions)
U of Texas-Houston, 1981
Certification: Anesthesiology, Pain Medicine
2520 N Central Expy #400, Richardson, 972-231-1591

Hilliard, Duane Ashley (3 mentions)
Loma Linda U, 1998 *Certification:* Anesthesiology
221 W Colorado Blvd #845, Dallas, 214-946-1133

Konen, Andrew Albert (4 mentions)
Texas A&M U, 1995 *Certification:* Anesthesiology, Pain Medicine
9301 N Central Expy #585, Dallas, 214-252-9432
13601 Preston Rd #900-W, Dallas, 972-233-1999

Lloyd, Aaron Thomas (7 mentions)
Pennsylvania State U, 1990 *Certification:* Anesthesiology
7988 W Virginia Dr #100, Dallas, 972-572-6101

Mathe, Alvin J. (3 mentions)
U of North Texas, 1989 *Certification:* Internal Medicine
3500 Camp Bowie Blvd, Fort Worth, 817-735-2660

Noe, Carl Edward (11 mentions)
U of Texas-San Antonio, 1984 *Certification:* Anesthesiology,
Critical Care Medicine, Pain Medicine
3600 Gaston Ave #360, Dallas, 214-820-7246
5323 Harry Hines Blvd, Dallas, 214-648-2774
9301 N Central Expy #320, Dallas, 214-373-7246

Racz, Tibor A. (3 mentions)
U of Texas-Galveston, 1992
Certification: Anesthesiology, Pain Medicine
6435 S Farm 549 #102, Heath, 214-461-0026
3500 Gaston Ave, Dallas, 214-820-2139
6901 Snider Plaza #300, Dallas, 214-461-0026

Stepteau, Torrence James (3 mentions)
Meharry Med Coll, 1993
Certification: Anesthesiology, Pain Medicine
809 W Harwood Rd #205, Hurst, 817-479-1500

Will, Kelly R. (3 mentions)
U of Texas-Galveston, 1984
Certification: Anesthesiology, Pain Medicine
8220 Walnut Hill Ln #202, Dallas, 214-345-5656

Zoys, Timothy N. (5 mentions)
Texas Tech U, 1990
7777 Forest Ln #C-204, Dallas, 972-566-8999

Pathology

Benjamin, Denis R. (5 mentions)
FMS-South Africa, 1968 *Certification:* Anatomic Pathology
& Clinical Pathology, Pediatric Pathology
801 7th Ave, Fort Worth, 682-885-4289

Burns, Dennis Kendall (3 mentions)
U of Texas-Dallas, 1978 *Certification:* Anatomic Pathology
& Clinical Pathology, Neuropathology
5323 Harry Hines Blvd #H-2130, Dallas, 214-648-2148

Cockerell, Clay Jefferies (4 mentions)
Baylor U, 1981 *Certification:* Dermatology, Dermatopathology
2330 Butler St #115, Dallas, 214-638-2222

Dickey, William Thomas (5 mentions)
U of Texas-Dallas, 1970
Certification: Anatomic Pathology & Clinical Pathology
1901 N Macarthur Blvd, Irving, 972-840-2804

Dickson, Beverly Ann (5 mentions)
U of Texas-San Antonio, 1984
Certification: Anatomic Pathology & Clinical Pathology
8200 Walnut Hill Ln, Dallas, 214-345-7280

Dysert, Peter Allen, II (6 mentions)
U of Oklahoma, 1979
Certification: Anatomic Pathology & Clinical Pathology
3600 Gaston Ave #261, Dallas, 214-818-9100

Embrey, Jeffrey R. (3 mentions)
U of Texas-Dallas, 1982
Certification: Anatomic Pathology & Clinical Pathology
1901 N Macarthur Blvd, Irving, 972-840-2804

Gregg, Susan (3 mentions)
Vanderbilt U, 1979 *Certification:* Anatomic Pathology &
Clinical Pathology, Cytopathology
1401 Pennsylvania Ave, Fort Worth, 817-250-5659

Herlihy, William G. (3 mentions)
Certification: Anatomic Pathology & Clinical Pathology
3600 Gaston Ave #261, Dallas, 214-818-9100

McDonald, John Edward (3 mentions)
U of Texas-Houston, 1982
Certification: Anatomic Pathology & Clinical Pathology,
Blood Banking/Transfusion Medicine, Cytopathology
4401 Booth Calloway, North Richland Hills, 817-255-1926

Meyer, Richard Lutz (5 mentions)
Baylor U, 1983 *Certification:* Anatomic Pathology & Clinical
Pathology, Medical Microbiology
3600 Gaston Ave #261, Dallas, 214-820-2251

Savino, Daniel Angel (7 mentions)
FMS-Argentina, 1972
Certification: Anatomic Pathology & Clinical Pathology
3600 Gaston Ave #261, Dallas, 214-818-9100

Voet, Richard Leo (3 mentions)
U of Cincinnati, 1975
Certification: Anatomic Pathology & Clinical Pathology
8200 Walnut Hill Ln, Dallas, 214-345-7280

Weathers, Seaborn Beck (4 mentions)
U of Texas-Dallas, 1972
Certification: Anatomic Pathology & Clinical Pathology
7777 Forest Ln, Dallas, 972-566-7285

Pediatrics *(see note on page 9)*

Blair, Ronald M., Jr. (3 mentions)
U of Texas-San Antonio, 1985 *Certification:* Pediatrics
7777 Forest Ln #B-445, Dallas, 972-284-7770

Brown, Michael Edwin (4 mentions)
Vanderbilt U, 1978 *Certification:* Pediatrics
8355 Walnut Hill Ln #200, Dallas, 214-369-7634

Burns, Debra Lou (3 mentions)
Wake Forest U, 1983 *Certification:* Pediatrics
8355 Walnut Hill Ln #105, Dallas, 214-368-3659

Cavazos, Ramiro David (4 mentions)
U of Texas-Galveston, 1972 *Certification:* Pediatrics
1108 S Henderson St, Fort Worth, 817-335-3255

Finkelman, Ross Leland (3 mentions)
Ohio State U, 1965 *Certification:* Pediatrics
8355 Walnut Hill Ln #200, Dallas, 214-369-7634

Hanig, Joseph Arthur (3 mentions)
U of Tennessee, 1980 *Certification:* Pediatrics
8355 Walnut Hill Ln #105, Dallas, 214-368-3659

Jones, Mark Stinson (4 mentions)
U of Texas-Houston, 1995 *Certification:* Pediatrics
1108 S Henderson St, Fort Worth, 817-335-3255

Karam, Albert Gerard (6 mentions)
Louisiana State U-Shreveport, 1981 *Certification:* Pediatrics
12200 Park Central Dr #405-B, Dallas, 972-341-9696

Mercer, Bradley S. (3 mentions)
U of Texas-Houston, 1992 *Certification:* Pediatrics
3200 Riverfront Dr #103, Fort Worth, 817-336-3800

Murphy, James Nolan, III (3 mentions)
U of Texas-Dallas, 1966 *Certification:* Pediatrics
1533 Merrimac Cir #100, Fort Worth, 817-336-4040

Neely, Joe B. (3 mentions)
U of Texas-Dallas, 1990 *Certification:* Pediatrics
8325 Walnut Hill Ln #225, Dallas, 214-691-3535

Peterman, Joseph P. (4 mentions)
U of Texas-Dallas, 1987 *Certification:* Pediatrics
8222 Douglas Ave #500, Dallas, 972-982-0777

Prestidge, Claude B. (3 mentions)
U of Texas-Dallas, 1968 *Certification:* Pediatrics
8355 Walnut Hill Ln #200, Dallas, 214-369-7634

Rhodes, Ray Norwood, Jr. (5 mentions)
Baylor U, 1974 *Certification:* Pediatrics
6401 Harris Pkwy #100, Fort Worth, 817-346-2525

Rogers, Jeffrey B. (3 mentions)
U of Texas-Dallas, 1986 *Certification:* Pediatrics
3200 Riverfront Dr #103, Fort Worth, 817-336-3800

Schorlemer, Roger O'Lee (3 mentions)
U of Texas-Dallas, 1964 *Certification:* Pediatrics
8355 Walnut Hill Ln #105, Dallas, 214-368-3659

Seidel, Jack D. (4 mentions)
U of Texas-Dallas, 1987 *Certification:* Pediatrics
1 Medical Pkwy #253, Dallas, 972-243-5437

Worsley, Jon Ben (3 mentions)
U of Texas-Dallas, 1995 *Certification:* Pediatrics
6401 Harris Pkwy #100, Fort Worth, 817-346-2525

Yaeger, Matthew Melville (3 mentions)
U of Texas-Houston, 1992 *Certification:* Pediatrics
8325 Walnut Hill Ln #225, Dallas, 214-691-3535

Plastic Surgery

Anderson, Brady Edward (4 mentions)
Texas Tech U, 2003 *Certification:* Surgery
4447 N Central Expy #110, Dallas, 214-226-9534

Brown, Byron Lindsay (7 mentions)
U of Texas-Dallas, 1962 *Certification:* Plastic Surgery
3600 Gaston Ave #751, Dallas, 214-823-9652

Burns, John L. (6 mentions)
U of Texas-Galveston, 1998 *Certification:* Plastic Surgery
9101 N Central Expy, Dallas, 214-823-5023

Carpenter, William M. (6 mentions)
Texas Tech U, 1986 *Certification:* Plastic Surgery
3409 Worth St #630, Dallas, 214-827-8407

Faires, Raymond Alan (7 mentions)
Baylor U, 1976 *Certification:* Plastic Surgery
1325 Pennsylvania Ave #325, Fort Worth, 817-878-5325

Ghazali, Basith Mohammed (5 mentions)
FMS-Pakistan, 1988 *Certification:* Plastic Surgery
909 9th Ave #300, Fort Worth, 817-870-9074

Gunter, Jack Pershing (4 mentions)
U of Oklahoma, 1963
Certification: Otolaryngology, Plastic Surgery
8144 Walnut Hill Ln #170, Dallas, 214-369-8123

Ha, Richard Youngmin (5 mentions)
Indiana U, 1997 *Certification:* Plastic Surgery
2350 N Stemmons Frwy, Dallas, 214-456-8888
9101 N Central Expy #600, Dallas, 214-818-0935

Heistein, Jonathan Barry (4 mentions)
Robert W Johnson Med Sch, 1996 *Certification:* Plastic Surgery
800 8th Ave #240, Fort Worth, 817-820-0000

Hodges, Patrick Lynn (9 mentions)
U of Texas-Dallas, 1975 *Certification:* Plastic Surgery
8220 Walnut Hill Ln #206, Dallas, 214-739-5760

Kenkel, Jeffrey Miller (8 mentions)
Georgetown U, 1989 *Certification:* Plastic Surgery
1801 Inwood Rd, Dallas, 214-645-3119

Kunkel, Kelly Raymond (6 mentions)
U of Texas-Galveston, 1986 *Certification:* Plastic Surgery
800 8th Ave, Fort Worth, 817-335-5200

Le Blanc, Danielle Marie (7 mentions)
U of Texas-Dallas, 1999 *Certification:* Plastic Surgery
800 8th Ave #416, Fort Worth, 817-698-9990

Newsom, Hamlet Tatum (5 mentions)
U of Alabama, 1967 *Certification:* Plastic Surgery, Surgery
8220 Walnut Hill Ln #314, Dallas, 214-750-5510

Pruitt, Bryan H. (4 mentions)
U of Texas-Galveston, 1985 *Certification:* Plastic Surgery
8315 Walnut Hill Ln #125, Dallas, 214-363-6000

Reaves, Larry Earl (17 mentions)
U of Texas-Dallas, 1978 *Certification:* Plastic Surgery
800 8th Ave #606, Fort Worth, 817-335-4755

Rohrich, Rodney James (5 mentions)
Baylor U, 1979 *Certification:* Plastic Surgery, Surgery of the Hand
9101 N Central Expy, Dallas, 214-821-9114
1801 Inwood Rd, Dallas, 214-645-3119

Saretsky, Neil Howard (4 mentions)
U of Michigan, 1974 *Certification:* Plastic Surgery
5468 La Sierra Dr #100, Dallas, 214-368-4970

Psychiatry

Banner, Mary Christine (3 mentions)
U of Nebraska, 1988
1522 Cooper St, Fort Worth, 682-885-1050

Holiner, Joel Alan (4 mentions)
U of Texas-Dallas, 1979
Certification: Addiction Psychiatry, Psychiatry
7777 Forest Ln #C833, Dallas, 972-566-4591
120 S Central #107, McKinney, 469-742-0199

Kowalski, Debra Atkisson (4 mentions)
Texas Tech U, 1986
Certification: Child & Adolescent Psychiatry, Psychiatry
6410 Southwest Blvd #205, Benbrook, 817-735-4430

Murphy, Thomas Mead (5 mentions)
U of Oklahoma, 1968
Certification: Child & Adolescent Psychiatry, Psychiatry
1522 Cooper St, Fort Worth, 682-885-1050

Secrest, Leslie Harold (3 mentions)
U of Texas-Dallas, 1968 *Certification:* Psychiatry
8200 Walnut Hill Ln, Dallas, 214-987-9456

Tyler, David Lendon (3 mentions)
U of Texas-San Antonio, 1976 *Certification:* Psychiatry
5323 Harry Hines Blvd, Dallas, 214-645-3768

Vobach, Stephen F. (5 mentions)
U of Texas-Houston, 1989 *Certification:* Psychiatry
3600 Gaston Ave #1155, Dallas, 214-824-2273

Pulmonary Disease

Agoro, Adesubomi B. (4 mentions)
FMS-Nigeria, 1986 *Certification:* Critical Care Medicine,
Internal Medicine, Pulmonary Disease
508 S Adams St #100, Fort Worth, 817-882-9901

Ausloos, Ken Allen (11 mentions)
Med Coll of Wisconsin, 1986 *Certification:* Critical Care
Medicine, Internal Medicine, Pulmonary Disease
3600 Gaston Ave #806, Dallas, 214-824-8521

Aviles, Arturo Emilio (4 mentions)
FMS-El Salvador, 1965 *Certification:* Critical Care Medicine,
Internal Medicine, Pulmonary Disease
221 W Colorado Blvd #424, Dallas, 214-941-1366

Black, Robert Dan (6 mentions)
U of Texas-Dallas, 1980 *Certification:* Critical Care
Medicine, Internal Medicine, Pulmonary Disease
3600 Gaston Ave #806, Dallas, 214-824-8521

Burk, John Robert (6 mentions)
U of Virginia, 1970 *Certification:* Internal Medicine
1521 Cooper St, Fort Worth, 817-336-5864

Carew, Julye Nesbitt (5 mentions)
Certification: Critical Care Medicine, Internal Medicine,
Pulmonary Disease
8210 Walnut Hill Ln #314, Dallas, 214-363-8447

Connelly, Kevin G. (5 mentions)
U of Texas-Dallas, 1989 *Certification:* Critical Care
Medicine, Internal Medicine, Pulmonary Disease
6100 Harris Pkwy #285, Fort Worth, 817-263-5864

Cunningham, James Calvin (9 mentions)
U of Texas-Galveston, 1981
Certification: Pediatric Pulmonology, Pediatrics
901 7th Ave #420, Fort Worth, 682-885-6299

Dambro, Nancy N. (4 mentions)
Tufts U, 1979 *Certification:* Pediatric Pulmonology, Pediatrics
901 7th Ave #420, Fort Worth, 682-885-6299

Ferris, Mark Charles (5 mentions)
U of Oklahoma, 1988 *Certification:* Critical Care Medicine,
Internal Medicine, Pulmonary Disease
9330 Poppy Dr #407, Dallas, 214-328-5487

Hadeed, Sami K. W. (4 mentions)
FMS-Syria, 1980 *Certification:* Pediatric Pulmonology
901 7th Ave #420, Fort Worth, 682-885-6299

Heidbrink, Peter Jay (6 mentions)
Baylor U, 1973
Certification: Internal Medicine, Pulmonary Disease
2001 N Macarthur Blvd #450, Irving, 972-259-3221

Hughes, John David (5 mentions)
U of Texas-Dallas, 1978 *Certification:* Critical Care
Medicine, Internal Medicine, Pulmonary Disease
6124 W Parker Rd #131, Plano, 214-778-1075

Jones, Gary Lewis (6 mentions)
Baylor U, 1977 *Certification:* Critical Care Medicine,
Internal Medicine, Pulmonary Disease
1604 Hospital Pkwy #403, Bedford, 817-354-9545

Luterman, David Lynn (6 mentions)
U of Texas-Dallas, 1970 *Certification:* Internal Medicine,
Pulmonary Disease, Sleep Medicine
3600 Gaston Ave #806, Dallas, 214-824-8521

McDonald, Stuart D. (11 mentions)
U of Texas-Dallas, 1987 *Certification:* Critical Care
Medicine, Internal Medicine, Pulmonary Disease
1521 Cooper St, Fort Worth, 817-336-5864

Millard, Mark Warren (5 mentions)
U of Texas-Dallas, 1976
Certification: Internal Medicine, Pulmonary Disease
4004 Worth St #300, Dallas, 214-820-3500

Pender, John Teal (5 mentions)
U of Texas-Dallas, 1974 *Certification:* Critical Care
Medicine, Internal Medicine, Pulmonary Disease
1201 Fairmount Ave, Fort Worth, 817-335-5288

Rosenblatt, Randall Lee (6 mentions)
Indiana U, 1973
Certification: Internal Medicine, Pulmonary Disease
5939 Harry Hines Blvd #600, Dallas, 214-645-6491

Rousseau, Wyatt E. (4 mentions)
Vanderbilt U, 1969
Certification: Internal Medicine, Pulmonary Disease
8220 Walnut Hill Ln #408, Dallas, 214-361-9777

Shulkin, Allan Neil (12 mentions)
U of Texas-San Antonio, 1975
Certification: Internal Medicine, Pulmonary Disease
7777 Forest Ln #B202, Dallas, 972-566-8900

Viroslav, Joseph (5 mentions)
FMS-Mexico, 1962
Certification: Internal Medicine, Pulmonary Disease
5939 Harry Hines Blvd #711, Dallas, 214-879-6555

Wait, Juliette Louise (5 mentions)
U of Kansas, 1974 *Certification:* Critical Care Medicine,
Internal Medicine, Pulmonary Disease
7777 Forest Ln #B-222, Dallas, 972-566-7007

Weinmeister, Kenney Don (5 mentions)
U of Oklahoma, 1987 *Certification:* Critical Care Medicine,
Internal Medicine, Pulmonary Disease
8220 Walnut Hill Ln #408, Dallas, 214-361-9777

Weinstein, Gary Lewis (13 mentions)
U of Kansas, 1986 *Certification:* Critical Care Medicine,
Internal Medicine, Pulmonary Disease
8220 Walnut Hill Ln #408, Dallas, 214-361-9777

Radiology—Diagnostic

Altshuler, Steven Lane (3 mentions)
Columbia U, 1981 *Certification:* Diagnostic Radiology
850 Hwy 243 W, Kaufman, 972-932-7390
102 E Moore Ave #214, Terrel, 972-551-1530

Aronson, Stuart Allan (5 mentions)
Case Western Reserve U, 1984 *Certification:* Diagnostic Radiology
816 W Cannon St, Fort Worth, 817-321-0300

Ellenbogen, Paul Harris (3 mentions)
SUNY-Downstate Med Coll, 1973
Certification: Diagnostic Radiology
8230 Walnut Hill Ln #100, Dallas, 214-345-6905
7515 Greenville Ave #710, Dallas, 214-363-8378

Ford, Kenneth L., III (3 mentions)
Baylor U, 1991 *Certification:* Diagnostic Radiology
3500 Gaston Ave, Dallas, 214-820-3216

Gordon, Murray Jacob (3 mentions)
U of Texas-Dallas, 1974 *Certification:* Diagnostic Radiology
12700 Park Central Dr #430, Dallas, 972-566-7866

Livingston, Thomas S. (4 mentions)
U of Texas-Galveston, 1982 *Certification:* Diagnostic
Radiology, Vascular & Interventional Radiology
1400 8th Ave, Fort Worth, 817-927-6151

Oshman, Daniel Gregory (13 mentions)
U of Texas-Dallas, 1977
Certification: Diagnostic Radiology, Pediatric Radiology
316 W Cannon St, Fort Worth, 817-321-0313
801 7th Ave, Fort Worth, 817-885-4082

Postma, Tom Wedekind (4 mentions)
U of Florida, 1976
Certification: Diagnostic Radiology, Nuclear Radiology
12700 Park Central Dr #430, Dallas, 972-239-8902

Schultz, Steven M. (4 mentions)
U of Texas-Dallas, 1984 *Certification:* Diagnostic Radiology
816 W Cannon St, Fort Worth, 817-331-0300

Sherry, Cynthia Stark (5 mentions)
U of Texas-Dallas, 1983 *Certification:* Diagnostic Radiology
8230 Walnut Hill Ln #100, Dallas, 214-345-6905
7515 Greenville Ave #710, Dallas, 214-363-8378

Smerud, Michael John (5 mentions)
Mayo Med Sch, 1980 *Certification:* Diagnostic Radiology
3500 Gaston Ave, Dallas, 214-820-3216

Toppins, Anthony Charles (3 mentions)
U of Oklahoma, 1996 *Certification:* Diagnostic Radiology
3500 Gaston Ave, Dallas, 214-820-3216

Zibilich, Mark Walter (4 mentions)
U of Texas-Dallas, 1978 *Certification:* Diagnostic Radiology
3500 Gaston Ave, Dallas, 214-820-3216

Radiology—Therapeutic

Appel, Noah Bennett (5 mentions)
Washington U, 1997 *Certification:* Diagnostic Radiology,
Vascular & Interventional Radiology
8200 Walnut Hill Rd, Dallas, 214-345-7770

Barker, Jerry Lee, Jr. (3 mentions)
Certification: Hospice and Palliative Medicine, Radiation Oncology
1450 8th Ave, Fort Worth, 817-923-4423

Cheek, Brennen S. (3 mentions)
Texas Tech U, 1994 *Certification:* Radiation Oncology
3535 Worth St, Dallas, 214-370-1400

Diamond, Norman George (4 mentions)
Columbia U, 1974 *Certification:* Diagnostic Radiology,
Vascular & Interventional Radiology
3500 Gaston Ave, Dallas, 214-820-3216

Dittman, William Ira (7 mentions)
U of Texas-San Antonio, 1972 *Certification:* Diagnostic
Radiology, Vascular & Interventional Radiology
8200 Walnut Hill Ln, Dallas, 214-345-7770
8230 Walnut Hill Ln #100, Dallas, 214-345-6905
7515 Greenville Ave #710, Dallas, 972-759-5140

Dolmatch, Bart Lewis (3 mentions)
Duke U, 1982 *Certification:* Diagnostic Radiology
5323 Harry Hines Blvd, Dallas, 214-645-8990

Hise, Joseph Henry (6 mentions)
Texas A&M U, 1984
Certification: Diagnostic Radiology, Neuroradiology
3500 Gaston Ave, Dallas, 214-820-3216

Livingston, Thomas S. (3 mentions)
U of Texas-Galveston, 1982 *Certification:* Diagnostic
Radiology, Vascular & Interventional Radiology
1400 8th Ave, Fort Worth, 817-927-6151

Senzer, Neil N. (3 mentions)
U of Buffalo, 1971 *Certification:* Pediatric
Hematology-Oncology, Pediatrics, Therapeutic Radiology
3535 Worth St, Dallas, 214-370-1400

Slonim, Suzanne M. (4 mentions)
George Washington U, 1989 *Certification:* Diagnostic
Radiology, Vascular & Interventional Radiology
1441 N Beckley, Dallas, 214-946-4397

Van Meter, Travis Allen (4 mentions)
U of Texas-Houston, 1992 *Certification:* Diagnostic
Radiology, Vascular & Interventional Radiology
1750 N Hampton Rd, Desoto, 214-946-4397

Wilcox, Barry N. (5 mentions)
U of Texas-San Antonio, 1992 *Certification:* Radiation Oncology
3535 Worth St, Dallas, 214-370-1400

Rehabilitation

Bixler, Glenn George (4 mentions)
U of Texas-San Antonio, 1985
Certification: Physical Medicine & Rehabilitation
1325 Pennsylvania Ave #290, Fort Worth, 817-878-5690

Carlile, Mary Culver (7 mentions)
U of Oklahoma, 1988
Certification: Physical Medicine & Rehabilitation
909 N Washington Ave, Dallas, 214-820-9593

Flores, Victor H. (3 mentions)
FMS-Dominican Republic, 1982
Certification: Physical Medicine & Rehabilitation
901 College Ave, Fort Worth, 817-336-7422
901 Medical Centre Dr #A, Arlington, 817-461-8343

Kowalske, Karen Jean (5 mentions)
U of Florida, 1986
Certification: Physical Medicine & Rehabilitation
5323 Harry Hines Blvd #104, Dallas, 214-645-2080

Porter, Leslie D. (7 mentions)
U of Texas-Houston, 1983
Certification: Physical Medicine & Rehabilitation
909 N Washington Ave, Dallas, 214-820-9593

Scott, James Alan (4 mentions)
U of California-Davis, 1981
Certification: Physical Medicine & Rehabilitation
1325 Pennsylvania Ave #290, Fort Worth, 817-878-5690

Wilson, Amy J. (11 mentions)
U of Texas-Houston, 1992
Certification: Physical Medicine & Rehabilitation
909 N Washington Ave, Dallas, 214-820-9593

Rheumatology

Barbosa, Leyka M. (5 mentions)
Ponce Sch of Med, 1989 *Certification:* Rheumatology
7777 Forest Ln #C-610, Dallas, 972-566-6599

Brodsky, Alan Lawrence (5 mentions)
Washington U, 1967
Certification: Internal Medicine, Rheumatology
8440 Walnut Hill Ln #340, Dallas, 214-696-1600

Cheatum, Don Elwood (6 mentions)
Washington U, 1964
Certification: Internal Medicine, Rheumatology
8440 Walnut Hill Ln #400, Dallas, 214-345-1407

Chubick, Andrew, Jr. (5 mentions)
Case Western Reserve U, 1970
Certification: Internal Medicine, Rheumatology
712 N Washington Ave #300, Dallas, 214-823-6503

Cohen, Stanley Bruce (15 mentions)
U of Alabama, 1975
Certification: Internal Medicine, Rheumatology
5939 Harry Hines Blvd #400, Dallas, 214-540-0700

Cush, John Joseph (9 mentions)
FMS-Grenada, 1981
Certification: Internal Medicine, Rheumatology
9900 N Central Expy #550, Dallas, 214-373-4321

Isaacs, Emily Merrell (11 mentions)
U of Connecticut, 1980
Certification: Internal Medicine, Rheumatology
909 9th Ave #400, Fort Worth, 817-336-7191

Lehmann, Claudio Straus (10 mentions)
FMS-Chile, 1963
1325 Pennsylvania Ave #680, Fort Worth, 817-336-1011

Merriman, Richard Charles (9 mentions)
U of Michigan, 1970
Certification: Internal Medicine, Rheumatology
712 N Washington Ave #300, Dallas, 214-823-6503

Rubin, Bernard Ross (7 mentions)
Midwestern U Chicago Coll of Osteopathic Med, 1976
Certification: Internal Medicine, Rheumatology
855 Montgomery St, Fort Worth, 817-735-2660

Thoracic Surgery

Hebeler, Robert F., Jr. (8 mentions)
Tulane U, 1977 *Certification:* Thoracic Surgery
3409 Worth St #720, Dallas, 214-821-3603

Henry, Albert Carl, III (6 mentions)
U of Texas-Houston, 1974 *Certification:* Thoracic Surgery
3409 Worth St #720, Dallas, 214-821-3603

Schorn, Larry Wayne (6 mentions)
U of Texas-Dallas, 1973 *Certification:* Thoracic Surgery
1110 Cottonwood Ln #210, Irving, 972-259-4781

Urology

Cadeddu, Jeffrey Anthony (4 mentions)
Johns Hopkins U, 1993 *Certification:* Urology
5303 Harry Hines Blvd, Dallas, 214-645-8765

Feagins, Brian A. (5 mentions)
U of Texas-Dallas, 1987 *Certification:* Urology
8210 Walnut Hill Ln #208, Dallas, 214-691-1902
8160 Walnut Hill Ln #001, Dallas, 214-360-1535
7424 Greenville Ave #211, Dallas, 214-691-1902
8230 Walnut Hill Ln #700, Dallas, 214-691-1902

Fine, Joshua K. (11 mentions)
Texas Tech U, 1988 *Certification:* Urology
3600 Gaston Ave Barnett Tower #1002, Dallas, 214-826-6235

Frost, Steve Marshall (11 mentions)
U of Texas-Dallas, 1975 *Certification:* Urology
3600 Gaston Ave #1205, Dallas, 214-826-6021

Gruber, Michael B. (5 mentions)
U of Texas-Galveston, 1977 *Certification:* Urology
7777 Forest Ln #C-618, Dallas, 972-566-7771

Hollander, Ira Neil (5 mentions)
U of Texas-Dallas, 1977 *Certification:* Urology
1300 W Terrell Ave #405, Fort Worth, 817-336-5711

Kadesky, Keith T. (5 mentions)
U of Texas-Dallas, 1988 *Certification:* Urology
8210 Walnut Hill Ln #208, Dallas, 214-691-1902
6124 W Parker Rd #434, Plano, 214-691-1902
8230 Walnut Hill Ln #700, Dallas, 214-691-1902

Mason, Roy Carrington (5 mentions)
U of North Texas, 1990
1411 N Beckly Ave #3, Dallas, 214-948-3101

Pinto, Kirk J. (6 mentions)
Texas Tech U, 1990 *Certification:* Pediatric Urology, Urology
1325 Pennsylvania Ave #550, Fort Worth, 817-336-5429

Roehrborn, Claus Georg (5 mentions)
FMS-Germany, 1980 *Certification:* Urology
5303 Harry Hines Blvd, Dallas, 214-645-8765

Schnitzer, Ben (4 mentions)
U of Texas-Dallas, 1957 *Certification:* Urology
3600 Gaston Ave #508, Dallas, 214-824-0171

Schoenvogel, Robert Clifton (9 mentions)
U of Texas-Dallas, 1974 *Certification:* Urology
3409 Worth St Sammons Tower #540, Dallas, 214-827-1602

Smith, Eric Bryan (4 mentions)
U of Texas-Dallas, 2000 *Certification:* Urology
3600 Gaston Ave #1002, Dallas, 214-826-6235

Wilner, Matthew Leonard (4 mentions)
New York U, 1984 *Certification:* Urology
8210 Walnut Hill Ln #404, Dallas, 214-691-1902

Worsham, Sidney Almon, III (7 mentions)
U of Texas-Galveston, 1971 *Certification:* Urology
800 8th Ave #626, Fort Worth, 817-877-1288

Young, Todd Everett (4 mentions)
U of North Texas, 1995
7100 Oakmont Blvd #201, Fort Worth, 817-871-9069
1001 12th Ave #140, Fort Worth, 817-871-9069
2006 Fall Creek Hwy, Granbury, 817-871-9069

Vascular Surgery

Clagett, George Patrick (9 mentions)
U of Virginia, 1969 *Certification:* Vascular Surgery
5939 Harry Hines Blvd, Dallas, 214-645-0548

Pearl, Gregory John (21 mentions)
Tulane U, 1980 *Certification:* Vascular Surgery
621 N Hall St #100, Dallas, 214-821-9600

Houston Area

Including Harris County

Allergy/Immunology

Abramson, Stuart Lee (3 mentions)
Baylor U, 1984 *Certification:* Allergy & Immunology,
  Diagnostic Laboratory Immunology, Pediatrics
6701 Fannin St, Houston, 832-824-1319
1504 Taub Loop, Houston, 713-873-5437

Bethea, Louise Huffman (7 mentions)
U of Mississippi, 1972
Certification: Allergy & Immunology, Pediatrics
17070 Red Oak Dr #107, Houston, 281-580-6494

Brown, Lewis Alan (3 mentions)
Vanderbilt U, 1976
Certification: Allergy & Immunology, Pediatrics
2900 Smith St #215, Houston, 713-759-1086
15400 SW Frwy #125, Sugar Land, 281-242-0131
12606 W Houston Center Blvd #260, Houston, 281-531-4901

Engler, David B. (5 mentions)
Baylor U, 1985
Certification: Allergy & Immunology, Internal Medicine
4600 Fairmont Pkwy #107, Pasadena, 281-991-6750
7707 Fannin St #100, Houston, 713-797-0993

Harrison, Lyndall F. (5 mentions)
U of Texas-Houston, 1986 *Certification:* Allergy & Immunology
2727 W Holcombe Blvd, Houston, 713-442-0000

Hoffman, Leonard Seymour (3 mentions)
U of Texas-Galveston, 1965
Certification: Allergy & Immunology, Pediatrics
909 Frostwood Dr #155, Houston, 713-973-0051

Huston, David Paul (7 mentions)
Wake Forest U, 1973
Certification: Allergy & Immunology, Diagnostic Laboratory
  Immunology, Internal Medicine, Rheumatology
6550 Fannin St #1101, Houston, 713-798-2500

Kline, Glenn Brown (4 mentions)
U of Texas-Galveston, 1983
Certification: Allergy & Immunology, Pediatrics
909 Frostwood Dr #155, Houston, 713-973-0051
8955 Hwy 6 N #100, Houston, 281-858-5708

Moore, Kristin Ann (11 mentions)
U of Texas-Galveston, 1980
Certification: Allergy & Immunology, Internal Medicine
7707 Fannin St #195, Houston, 713-797-0045
561 Medical Center Blvd #G, Webster, 281-332-2348

Shearer, William Thomas (5 mentions)
Washington U, 1970 *Certification:* Allergy & Immunology,
  Diagnostic Laboratory Immunology, Pediatrics
6701 Fannin St, Houston, 832-824-1319

Zambrano, Juan Carlos (3 mentions)
FMS-Ecuador, 1991 *Certification:* Allergy & Immunology
909 Frostwood Dr #155, Houston, 713-973-0051
8955 Hwy 6 N #100, Houston, 281-858-5708

Anesthesiology

Baker, Byron Wycke (4 mentions)
Baylor U, 1981 *Certification:* Anesthesiology
2411 Fountain View Dr #200, Houston, 713-620-4000

Boozalis, Steve Theodore (3 mentions)
U of Texas-Galveston, 1984 *Certification:* Anesthesiology
2411 Fountain View Dr #200, Houston, 713-620-4000

Calder, Cynthia T. (3 mentions)
Emory U, 1985 *Certification:* Anesthesiology
2411 Fountain View Dr #200, Houston, 713-620-4000
7401 S Main St, Houston, 713-620-4000
6460 Fannin St, Houston, 713-620-4000

Comeaux, Guy Louis (3 mentions)
Louisiana State U, 1971 *Certification:* Anesthesiology
2411 Fountain View Dr #200, Houston, 713-620-4000

Cooper, John Robert, Jr. (4 mentions)
Tulane U, 1972
Certification: Anesthesiology, Critical Care Medicine
6720 Bertner St, Houston, 832-355-2666

Falbey, Francis B., Jr. (3 mentions)
Texas Tech U, 1988 *Certification:* Anesthesiology
2411 Fountain View Dr #200, Houston, 713-620-4020

Giam, Patrick Yean-Yong (3 mentions)
Baylor U, 1984 *Certification:* Anesthesiology
2411 Fountain View, Houston, 713-620-4000

Kavanagh, Robert James, Jr. (3 mentions)
U of Texas-Houston, 1977 *Certification:* Anesthesiology
4747 Bellaire Blvd #580, Bellaire, 713-659-3284

Lauzon, John Parry, Jr. (3 mentions)
U of Texas-Galveston, 1966 *Certification:* Anesthesiology
2411 Fountain View Dr #200, Houston, 713-620-4000

Rosas, Alejandro E. (3 mentions)
FMS-Mexico, 1979 *Certification:* Anesthesiology
2411 Fountain View Dr #200, Houston, 713-620-4000

Tobon-Randall, Beatriz L. (3 mentions)
U of Texas-Dallas, 1986 *Certification:* Anesthesiology
333 N Texas Ave, Webster, 281-335-1700

Wong, Timothy S. (3 mentions)
U of Texas-Dallas, 1986 *Certification:* Anesthesiology
2525 North Loop W #210, Houston, 713-426-1669

Cardiac Surgery

Frazier, Oscar Howard (8 mentions)
Baylor U, 1967 *Certification:* Surgery, Thoracic Surgery
1101 Bates Ave #C-355, Houston, 713-791-3000

Gibson, Donald M. (6 mentions)
Certification: Surgery, Thoracic Surgery
902 Frostwood Dr #144, Houston, 713-973-7222

Howell, Jimmy Frank (8 mentions)
Baylor U, 1957 *Certification:* Surgery, Thoracic Surgery
6560 Fannin St #1824, Houston, 713-790-4573

Lawrie, Gerald Murray (12 mentions)
FMS-Australia, 1969
6560 Fannin St #1842, Houston, 713-790-2089

Noon, George Paul (13 mentions)
Baylor U, 1960 *Certification:* Surgery, Thoracic Surgery
6560 Fannin St #1860, Houston, 713-790-3155

Ott, David Alan (19 mentions)
Baylor U, 1972 *Certification:* Thoracic Surgery
1101 Bates Ave #P514, Houston, 713-791-4900
6720 Bertner St, Houston, 713-791-4900

Ramchandani, Mahesh K. (7 mentions)
FMS-United Kingdom, 1982
Certification: Surgery, Thoracic Surgery
6560 Fannin St #1836, Houston, 713-790-2822

Reardon, Michael Joseph (18 mentions)
Baylor U, 1978 *Certification:* Thoracic Surgery
6560 Fannin St #1006, Houston, 713-441-5200

Reul, Ross M. (6 mentions)
Baylor U, 1993 *Certification:* Surgery, Thoracic Surgery
1101 Bates Ave #P-514, Houston, 832-355-4900

Safi, Hazim Jawad (6 mentions)
FMS-Iraq, 1970 *Certification:* Thoracic Surgery, Vascular Surgery
6410 Fannin St #450, Houston, 713-500-5304

Cardiology

Ali, Mir Nadir (4 mentions)
FMS-India, 1984
250 Blossom St #130, Webster, 281-557-1215

Aquino, Vincent (3 mentions)
U of Florida, 1980 *Certification:* Cardiovascular Disease,
Internal Medicine, Interventional Cardiology
411 Lantern Bend Dr #100, Houston, 281-444-3278
17350 St Lukes Way #400, The Woodlands, 281-444-3278

Avendano, Amilcar (3 mentions)
FMS-Guatemala, 1986 *Certification:* Cardiovascular
Disease, Internal Medicine, Interventional Cardiology
17400 Red Oak Dr, Houston, 281-893-8640

Berman, Philip Leonard (3 mentions)
New York Med Coll, 1982
Certification: Cardiovascular Disease, Internal Medicine
1631 North Loop W #520, Houston, 713-861-2424
915 Gessner Rd #900, Houston, 713-464-6006

Bhalla, Rajk (3 mentions)
FMS-India, 1970
Certification: Cardiovascular Disease, Internal Medicine
2060 Space Park Dr #108, Houston, 281-333-4848
300 Edgewood Dr, Friendswood, 281-333-4848

Farmer, John Alan (4 mentions)
U of Texas-Dallas, 1974
6620 Main St #1225, Houston, 713-798-2545

Garcia, Jonas (3 mentions)
U of Texas-Houston, 1978 *Certification:* Internal Medicine
1213 Hermann Dr #830, Houston, 713-522-9934

Gordon, Michael James (3 mentions)
Ohio State U, 1971
Certification: Cardiovascular Disease, Internal Medicine
6400 Fannin St #3000, Houston, 713-790-0841

Hauksnecht, Mark John (4 mentions)
Baylor U, 1980 *Certification:* Cardiovascular Disease,
Internal Medicine, Interventional Cardiology
6400 Fannin St #3000, Houston, 713-790-0841

Hogan, Patrick J. (4 mentions)
Georgetown U, 1970 *Certification:* Cardiovascular Disease,
Internal Medicine, Interventional Cardiology
6624 Fannin St #2220, Houston, 713-791-9400

Jeroudi, Mohamed Oussama (3 mentions)
FMS-Syria, 1980 *Certification:* Cardiovascular Disease,
Internal Medicine, Interventional Cardiology
4102 Woodlawn Ave #220, Pasadena, 713-475-5940

Lisman, Kevin A. (6 mentions)
U of Texas-Dallas, 1995
Certification: Cardiovascular Disease, Interventional Cardiology
6400 Fannin St #3000, Houston, 713-790-0841

Lubetkin, Sanford Jay (4 mentions)
Georgetown U, 1977
Certification: Cardiovascular Disease, Internal Medicine
7737 Southwest Frwy #780, Houston, 713-988-9512

Mann, Douglas Lowell (3 mentions)
Temple U, 1979
Certification: Cardiovascular Disease, Internal Medicine
6620 Main St #1225, Houston, 713-798-2545

Massin, Edward Krauss (4 mentions)
Washington U, 1965
Certification: Cardiovascular Disease, Internal Medicine
6624 Fannin St #2310, Houston, 713-796-2668

Massum-Khani, Gholam Ali (3 mentions)
FMS-Iran, 1971 *Certification:* Cardiovascular Disease,
Clinical Cardiac Electrophysiology, Internal Medicine
6624 Fannin St #2480, Houston, 713-529-5530

Mortazavi, Ali (3 mentions)
FMS-Iran, 1979
Certification: Cardiovascular Disease, Interventional Cardiology
6624 Fannin St 20th Fl, Houston, 713-442-0000

Mullins, Jackie Allen (4 mentions)
U of Oklahoma, 1982 *Certification:* Cardiovascular Disease,
Internal Medicine, Interventional Cardiology
3337 Plainview St #8, Pasadena, 713-941-6083

Nishikawa, Akira (3 mentions)
FMS-Japan, 1977 *Certification:* Cardiovascular Disease,
Internal Medicine, Interventional Cardiology
12121 Richmond Ave #204, Houston, 281-558-0400

Raizner, Albert Edwin (14 mentions)
SUNY-Downstate Med Coll, 1967 *Certification:* Cardiovascular
Disease, Internal Medicine, Interventional Cardiology
6550 Fannin St #2021, Houston, 713-790-9125

Rosales, Oscar Rafael (4 mentions)
FMS-Colombia, 1983 *Certification:* Cardiovascular Disease,
Internal Medicine, Interventional Cardiology
6400 Fannin St #2220, Houston, 713-796-2220

Rubin, Howard Stanton (3 mentions)
U of Texas-Galveston, 1974 *Certification:* Cardiovascular
Disease, Internal Medicine, Interventional Cardiology
6400 Fannin St #3000, Houston, 713-790-0841

Smalling, Richard Warren (6 mentions)
U of Texas-Houston, 1975 *Certification:* Cardiovascular
Disease, Internal Medicine, Interventional Cardiology
6410 Fannin St #600, Houston, 832-325-7211

Solomon, Stuart Lowell (10 mentions)
U of Texas-San Antonio, 1978 *Certification:* Cardiovascular
Disease, Internal Medicine, Interventional Cardiology
6400 Fannin St #3000, Houston, 713-790-0841

Springer, Arthur Jonathan (3 mentions)
New York Med Coll, 1975 *Certification:* Cardiovascular
Disease, Internal Medicine, Interventional Cardiology
1707 Sunset Blvd, Houston, 713-526-5511

Suneja, Randeep (3 mentions)
FMS-India, 1983
Certification: Cardiovascular Disease, Internal Medicine
20710 Westheimer Pkwy, Katy, 281-646-9000
1601 Main St #108, Richmond, 281-342-3900

Walton, Brian Leroy (3 mentions)
U of Kansas, 1997 *Certification:* Cardiovascular Disease,
Internal Medicine, Interventional Cardiology
6550 Fannin St #2021, Houston, 713-790-9125

Willerson, James Thornton (6 mentions)
Baylor U, 1965
Certification: Cardiovascular Disease, Internal Medicine
6410 Fannin St #600, Houston, 832-325-7211

Woodruff, Amy L. (5 mentions)
Baylor U, 1995
Certification: Cardiovascular Disease, Internal Medicine
6624 Fannin St #2720, Houston, 713-795-5014

Younis, Antoine G. (6 mentions)
Certification: Cardiovascular Disease, Internal Medicine,
Interventional Cardiology
6624 Fannin St #2420, Houston, 713-790-0400

Dermatology

Basler, Elizabeth A. (4 mentions)
Baylor U, 1985 *Certification:* Dermatology
7505 S Main St #530, Houston, 713-799-1129

Bean, Samuel Franklin (3 mentions)
U of Texas-Galveston, 1962
Certification: Dermatology, Dermatopathology
1200 Binz St #1110, Houston, 713-523-8200

Beckman, Bradley Irwin (3 mentions)
U of Texas-Galveston, 1978 *Certification:* Dermatology
909 Frostwood Dr #105, Houston, 713-984-2222

Bruce, Suzanne (4 mentions)
Baylor U, 1981 *Certification:* Dermatology
1900 Saint James Pl #600, Houston, 713-796-9199

Chernosky, Debra Lynn (5 mentions)
U of Texas-Houston, 1985 *Certification:* Dermatology
4646 Wild Indigo St #100, Houston, 713-790-9270

Duffy, Jennie Ann Ozog (3 mentions)
Baylor U, 1978 *Certification:* Dermatology
6560 Fannin St #724, Houston, 713-790-0058

Fuerst, Jan Fredric (3 mentions)
U of Texas-Dallas, 1971 *Certification:* Dermatology
909 Frostwood Dr #311, Houston, 713-468-7033

Goldberg, Leonard Harry (4 mentions)
FMS-South Africa, 1967 *Certification:* Dermatology
7515 Main St #240, Houston, 713-791-9966

Greenberg, Cindy Alicia (3 mentions)
U of Miami, 1986 *Certification:* Dermatology, Dermatopathology
7515 Main St #770, Houston, 713-797-6171

Guzick, Norman David (3 mentions)
U of Texas-Galveston, 1972
Certification: Dermatology, Dermatopathology
7777 Southwest Frwy #956, Houston, 713-772-7202

Hebert, Adelaide Ann (4 mentions)
Tulane U, 1980
Certification: Dermatology, Pediatric Dermatology
6655 Travis St #600, Houston, 713-500-8260
1515 Holcomb Blvd, Houston, 713-792-6161

Hsu-Wong, Sylvia (6 mentions)
Baylor U, 1989 *Certification:* Dermatology
6620 Main St, Houston, 713-798-6131

Mahoney, Stephen E. (3 mentions)
U of Texas-Dallas, 1988 *Certification:* Dermatology
12606 W Houston Center Blvd #110, Houston, 281-558-3376

Metry, Denise Walker (5 mentions)
U of Texas-Houston, 1995
Certification: Dermatology, Pediatric Dermatology
6701 Fannin St 8th Fl, Houston, 832-822-3463

Nelson, Bruce R. (3 mentions)
U of Texas-Houston, 1985 *Certification:* Dermatology
6655 Travis St #840, Houston, 713-745-6647
920 Medical Plaza Dr #490, The Woodlands, 713-745-6647

Orengo, Ida F. (9 mentions)
Baylor U, 1987 *Certification:* Dermatology
6620 Main St #1425, Houston, 713-798-6131
2002 Holcombe Blvd #1A509, Houston, 713-791-1414

Parsons, Jessica L. (3 mentions)
U of Southern California, 1990 *Certification:* Dermatology
915 Gessner Rd #860, Houston, 713-468-2200

Price, Mark A. (3 mentions)
Baylor U, 1991 *Certification:* Dermatology
1200 Binz St #1040, Houston, 713-528-8882

Rapini, Ronald Peter (5 mentions)
Ohio State U, 1978
Certification: Dermatology, Dermatopathology
6655 Travis St #600, Houston, 713-500-8260
1515 Holcombe Blvd, Houston, 713-500-8334

Rosen, Theodore (5 mentions)
U of Michigan, 1974 *Certification:* Dermatology
6620 Main St #1425, Houston, 713-798-6131
2002 Holcombe Blvd #129, Houston, 713-794-7129

Schmidt, Jimmy D. (5 mentions)
Certification: Dermatology, Dermatopathology
701 FM1960 Rd W, Houston, 281-440-1288

Shah, Farah (4 mentions)
U of Texas-Houston, 1989 *Certification:* Dermatology
6560 Fannin St #724, Houston, 713-790-0058

Tschen, Jaime Antonio (3 mentions)
FMS-Guatemala, 1975 *Certification:* Anatomic Pathology,
  Dermatology, Dermatopathology
4747 Bellaire Blvd #575, Bellaire, 713-660-9444

Wolf, John Eaton, Jr. (10 mentions)
U of Texas-Galveston, 1965 *Certification:* Dermatology
6620 Main St #1425, Houston, 713-798-6131

Emergency Medicine

Finkelstein, Jeremy Paul (3 mentions)
U of Maryland, 1994 *Certification:* Emergency Medicine
6565 Fannin St, Houston, 713-441-4467

Kalina, Jeffrey Earl (6 mentions)
St Louis U, 1994 *Certification:* Emergency Medicine
6565 Fannin St, Houston, 713-441-4467

King, Brent Russell (3 mentions)
U of Texas-Houston, 1983 *Certification:* Emergency
  Medicine, Pediatric Emergency Medicine, Pediatrics
6411 Fannin St, Houston, 713-500-7863

Shook, Joan Elizabeth (3 mentions)
U of Cincinnati, 1981
Certification: Pediatric Emergency Medicine, Pediatrics
6621 Fannin St, Houston, 832-824-5497

Endocrinology

Brown, Jeffrey Stuart (5 mentions)
Rosalind Franklin U, 1976
Certification: Endocrinology and Metabolism, Internal Medicine
909 Dairy Ashford St #205, Houston, 281-589-2681

Cunningham, Glenn Ross (5 mentions)
U of Oklahoma, 1966
Certification: Endocrinology and Metabolism, Internal Medicine
6624 Fannin St #1180, Houston, 713-798-2500
6620 Main St #1250, Houston, 713-798-2500

Garber, Alan Joel (4 mentions)
Temple U, 1968
6620 Main St 12th Fl, Houston, 713-798-0153

Hamilton, Dale James (7 mentions)
St Louis U, 1978
Certification: Endocrinology and Metabolism, Internal Medicine
6550 Fannin St #1101, Houston, 713-441-0006

Kormeier, Lucy Caudill (4 mentions)
U of Texas-Houston, 1989
Certification: Endocrinology, Diabetes, and Metabolism
2500 Fondrea #120, Houston, 713-781-4600
1429 Hwy 6 S, Houston, 713-781-4600

Mallette, Lawrence Edward (4 mentions)
Vanderbilt U, 1970
Certification: Endocrinology and Metabolism, Internal Medicine
8200 Wednesbury Ln #380, Houston, 713-271-2030

Nader-Eftekhari, Shahla (5 mentions)
FMS-United Kingdom, 1970
6410 Fannin St #600, Houston, 832-325-7161

Robbins, Richard James (4 mentions)
Creighton U, 1975
Certification: Endocrinology and Metabolism, Internal Medicine
6550 Fannin St #1661A, Houston, 713-441-6640

Rochen, Jeffrey (4 mentions)
Baylor U, 1987 *Certification:* Endocrinology, Diabetes, and
  Metabolism, Internal Medicine
2727 W Holcombe Blvd, Houston, 713-442-0338

Rodriguez Gonzalez, V. (8 mentions)
U of Puerto Rico, 1989
2201 W Holcombe Blvd #245, Houston, 713-796-1188

Roy, Bhaskar Kumar (5 mentions)
FMS-India, 1974
Certification: Endocrinology and Metabolism, Internal Medicine
915 Gessner Rd #680, Houston, 713-461-8850

Rubenfeld, Sheldon (8 mentions)
Georgetown U, 1971
Certification: Endocrinology and Metabolism, Internal Medicine
7515 Main St #690, Houston, 713-795-5750

Shapiro, Lorie M. (6 mentions)
U of Texas-Houston, 1983
Certification: Endocrinology and Metabolism, Internal Medicine
909 Dairy Ashford St #205, Houston, 281-589-2681

Shiver, Tiana M. (6 mentions)
U of Texas-San Antonio, 1986
Certification: Endocrinology, Diabetes, and Metabolism
6655 Travis St #960, Houston, 713-523-0414

Steiner, Alton Louis (5 mentions)
Columbia U, 1962
1315 St Joseph Pkwy #1705, Houston, 713-756-8530

Wilson, Howard King (5 mentions)
U of Cincinnati, 1975 *Certification:* Internal Medicine
1200 Binz St #1410, Houston, 713-523-9508

Zimmerman, Stanley Jay (7 mentions)
U of Texas-Dallas, 1955
Certification: Geriatric Medicine, Internal Medicine
7707 Fannin St #250, Houston, 713-797-9999

Family Practice *(see note on page 9)*

Boone, Hal Browning (3 mentions)
U of Texas-Dallas, 1972
6243 Fairmont Pkwy #100, Pasadena, 281-487-1000

De Broeck, Julius Anthony (3 mentions)
Baylor U, 1981 *Certification:* Family Medicine
5870 Hwy 6 N #106, Houston, 281-550-2547

Fowler, Grant C. (4 mentions)
U of Texas-Houston, 1984 *Certification:* Family Medicine,
  Geriatric Medicine, Sports Medicine
6410 Fannin St #250, Houston, 713-500-7604
1776 Yorktown #150, Houston, 713-572-8122

Solomos, Nicholas J. (6 mentions)
U of Texas-Houston, 1989 *Certification:* Family Medicine
2727 W Holcombe St 1st Fl, Houston, 713-442-0000

Spann, Stephen Jimmie (4 mentions)
Baylor U, 1975 *Certification:* Family Medicine
6620 Main St #1250, Houston, 713-798-7700
3701 Kirby Dr #100, Houston, 713-798-7700

Vanzant, Robert Courtenay (3 mentions)
Baylor U, 1974 *Certification:* Family Medicine
10497 Town And Country Way #360, Houston, 713-341-2100

Wolf, Cyril (3 mentions)
FMS-South Africa, 1968 *Certification:* Family Medicine
902 Frostwood Dr #290, Houston, 713-467-7400

Zenner, George O., III (3 mentions)
U of Texas-Houston, 1986 *Certification:* Family Medicine
5757 Woodway Dr #260, Houston, 713-977-0971

Gastroenterology

Abrol, Rajeshwar P. (3 mentions)
FMS-India, 1982
Certification: Gastroenterology, Internal Medicine
425 Holderrieth Blvd #113, Tomball, 281-351-6464

Barroso, Alberto Oswaldo (6 mentions)
FMS-Brazil, 1966
Certification: Gastroenterology, Internal Medicine
6560 Fannin St #1660, Houston, 713-797-9595

Bridges, Margaret E. (4 mentions)
Med U of South Carolina, 1973
Certification: Gastroenterology, Internal Medicine
6560 Fannin St #1404, Houston, 713-715-5840

Clemmons, John Benjamin (3 mentions)
Howard U, 1975
Certification: Gastroenterology, Internal Medicine
1213 Hermann Dr #420, Houston, 713-528-6562

Davis, Robert Errol (4 mentions)
Med U of South Carolina, 1969
Certification: Gastroenterology, Internal Medicine
7777 Southwest Frwy #708, Houston, 713-977-9095
1111 Hwy 6 #105, Sugar Land, 281-491-9779

Dobbs, Stuart Myron (11 mentions)
Med Coll of Georgia, 1975
Certification: Gastroenterology, Internal Medicine
6560 Fannin St #1708, Houston, 713-795-5447

Ergun, Gulchin Ayshe (3 mentions)
Case Western Reserve U, 1984
Certification: Gastroenterology, Internal Medicine
6560 Fannin St #1160, Houston, 713-933-2650

Fein, Steven Alan (3 mentions)
U of Florida, 1976
Certification: Gastroenterology, Internal Medicine
3315 Burke Rd #202, Pasadena, 713-946-9513

Flax, Ira Lynwood (5 mentions)
Virginia Commonwealth U, 1974
Certification: Gastroenterology, Internal Medicine
915 Gessner Rd #850, Houston, 713-461-1026

Frankel, Norman Bruce (5 mentions)
Albert Einstein Coll of Med, 1965
Certification: Gastroenterology, Internal Medicine
6624 Fannin St #1700, Houston, 713-526-5511

Galati, Joseph S. (3 mentions)
FMS-Grenada, 1987 *Certification:* Gastroenterology
6624 Fannin St #1990, Houston, 713-794-0700

Gossett, Garland William (3 mentions)
Howard U, 1985
Certification: Gastroenterology, Internal Medicine
2000 Crawford St #1325, Houston, 713-659-2666

Hochman, Fredric Lyone (9 mentions)
FMS-Canada, 1974
Certification: Gastroenterology, Internal Medicine
6624 Fannin St #2580, Houston, 713-797-0808

Hughes, John Irison (5 mentions)
U of South Florida, 1975
Certification: Gastroenterology, Internal Medicine
2727 W Holcombe Blvd, Houston, 713-442-0000
6624 Fannin St #1700, Houston, 713-442-0000

Johnson, Craig David (3 mentions)
Indiana U, 1971
Certification: Gastroenterology, Internal Medicine
6560 Fannin St #1625, Houston, 713-791-1800

Kaplan, Brian H. (4 mentions)
Baylor U, 1984 *Certification:* Gastroenterology, Internal Medicine
6624 Fannin St #1920, Houston, 713-796-9711

Karpen, Saul Joseph (3 mentions)
Mount Sinai Sch of Med, 1989 *Certification:* Pediatric
   Gastroenterology, Pediatric Transplant Hepatology
6701 Fannin St, Houston, 832-822-3131

Mauk, Paul Martin (3 mentions)
Baylor U, 1980 *Certification:* Gastroenterology, Internal Medicine
915 Gessner Rd #850, Houston, 713-461-1026

Rachal, Lindy Thaddeus (6 mentions)
U of Texas-Houston, 1983
Certification: Gastroenterology, Internal Medicine
7580 Fannin St #210, Houston, 713-521-0039

Raijman, Isaac Langsam (5 mentions)
FMS-Mexico, 1984
Certification: Gastroenterology, Internal Medicine
6620 Main St #1510, Houston, 713-795-4444

Rao, Jyoti (3 mentions)
FMS-India, 1987
444 Fm 1959 Rd, Houston, 281-481-9400

Reddy, Gurunath Thota (4 mentions)
FMS-India, 1981
Certification: Gastroenterology, Internal Medicine
18955 Memorial Dr N #500, Humble, 281-446-2224
275 Lantern Bend #200, Houston, 281-440-0101
920 Medical Plaza Dr #480, The Woodlands, 281-296-8200

Reid, Barbara S. (3 mentions)
Duke U *Certification:* Pediatric Gastroenterology, Pediatrics
6621 Fannin St, Houston, 832-822-3131

Sachs, Ian Lee (4 mentions)
Northwestern U, 1972
Certification: Gastroenterology, Internal Medicine
6550 Fannin St #2101, Houston, 713-795-4357

Schmulen, Arthur Carl (3 mentions)
Louisiana State U, 1973
Certification: Gastroenterology, Internal Medicine
6560 Fannin St #1625, Houston, 713-791-1800

Schneider, Franz Emil (3 mentions)
FMS-Guatemala, 1985
Certification: Gastroenterology, Internal Medicine
444 Fm 1959 Rd, Houston, 281-481-9400

Schwarz, Peter Joseph (3 mentions)
U of Illinois, 1987 *Certification:* Gastroenterology
6560 Fannin St #1008, Houston, 713-795-8282

Stavinoha, Michael Wayne (4 mentions)
U of Texas-Galveston, 1984
Certification: Gastroenterology, Internal Medicine
1631 North Loop W #655, Houston, 713-869-8200

Trabanino, Jose Guillermo (4 mentions)
FMS-El Salvador, 1971
Certification: Gastroenterology, Internal Medicine
7777 Southwest Frwy #708, Houston, 713-776-1074

Urrutia, Fernando M. (3 mentions)
Certification: Gastroenterology, Internal Medicine
6624 Fannin St #2280, Houston, 713-796-0035

Verm, Ray Alan (7 mentions)
Baylor U, 1971 *Certification:* Gastroenterology, Internal Medicine
6560 Fannin St #1625, Houston, 713-791-1800

Whalen, George Edward (3 mentions)
Med Coll of Wisconsin, 1959
7737 Southwest Frwy #860, Houston, 713-988-7188

Woods, Karen L. (4 mentions)
U of Missouri-Kansas City, 1983
Certification: Gastroenterology, Internal Medicine
6560 Fannin St #2000, Houston, 713-383-7800

General Surgery

Ahmad, Ataurrabb (3 mentions)
Louisiana State U, 1995 *Certification:* Surgery
11301 Fallbrook Dr #204, Houston, 281-970-8484

Appel, Michael Frederick (14 mentions)
Baylor U, 1961 *Certification:* Surgery
6624 Fannin St #2500, Houston, 713-795-5600

Ayyar, Subramanyam M. (4 mentions)
U of Texas-Houston, 1994 *Certification:* Surgery
1631 North Loop W #220, Houston, 713-426-2400
21216 Northwest Ctr #250, Houston, 713-426-2400

Baker, Treneth (4 mentions)
U of Missouri-Kansas City, 1995 *Certification:* Surgery
2727 W Holcombe Blvd, Houston, 713-442-0000
15655 Cypresswood Medical Dr #410, Houston, 713-442-1700

Bloss, Robert Scott (5 mentions)
U of Texas-Dallas, 1974 *Certification:* Pediatric Surgery
6624 Fannin St #1590, Houston, 713-796-2327

Brunicardi, Francis Charles (4 mentions)
Robert W Johnson Med Sch, 1980 *Certification:* Surgery
6620 Main St #1425, Houston, 713-798-5700

Burbridge, Gail Everett (3 mentions)
U of Nebraska, 1972 *Certification:* Surgery
1200 Binz St #1362, Houston, 713-523-2411

Caplan, Richard Edward (3 mentions)
U of Texas-Dallas, 1980 *Certification:* Surgery
6560 Fannin St #1008, Houston, 713-795-8585

Coselli, Michael Pool (4 mentions)
U of Texas-Galveston, 1983 *Certification:* Surgery
6560 Fannin St #1608, Houston, 713-796-1608

Davis, Garth Philip (5 mentions)
Baylor U, 1996 *Certification:* Surgery
6560 Fannin St #738, Houston, 713-528-0597

Davis, Robert (5 mentions)
FMS-South Africa, 1963 *Certification:* Surgery
6560 Fannin St #738, Houston, 713-528-0597

Duke, James Henry, Jr. (5 mentions)
U of Texas-Dallas, 1960 *Certification:* Surgery
6410 Fannin St #1400, Houston, 832-325-7125

Kleinman, Michael H. (12 mentions)
U of Texas-Dallas, 1983 *Certification:* Surgery
7500 Beechnut St #240, Houston, 713-981-7777

Leiva, Jorge Ignacio (4 mentions)
FMS-Mexico, 1991 *Certification:* Surgery
21216 Northwest Center #250, Cypress, 713-426-2400
1631 North Loop W #220, Houston, 713-426-2400

Oggero, Kelly Steven (6 mentions)
U of Texas-Houston, 1985 *Certification:* Surgery
2060 Space Park Dr #100, Houston, 281-333-1703

Ponce De Leon, Guillermo (3 mentions)
Certification: Surgery
7737 Southwest Frwy #520, Houston, 713-772-1200

Quast, Don Carlfred (6 mentions)
Baylor U, 1958 *Certification:* Surgery, Thoracic Surgery
1213 Hermann Dr #560, Houston, 713-521-0017

Reardon, Patrick Ray (7 mentions)
Baylor U, 1983 *Certification:* Surgery
6550 Fannin St #2435, Houston, 713-790-3140

Redwine, William Allen (14 mentions)
U of Texas-Dallas, 1969 *Certification:* Surgery
6624 Fannin St #2400, Houston, 713-790-9151

Rosenberg, Wade Ronald (6 mentions)
U of Texas-Houston, 1981 *Certification:* Surgery
6560 Fannin St #1402, Houston, 713-790-4830

Sehorn, Timothy Jamison (6 mentions)
U of Texas-Houston, 1996 *Certification:* Surgery
7515 S Main St #350, Houston, 713-797-9500

Tomm, Karl Elmer (3 mentions)
Northwestern U, 1965 *Certification:* Surgery, Thoracic Surgery
6560 Fannin St #1846, Houston, 713-797-1303

Turnquest, Dexter Godfrey (4 mentions)
U of South Florida, 1989 *Certification:* Surgery
17070 Red Oak Dr #507, Houston, 281-444-8090

Wallace, James Oran (5 mentions)
U of Kentucky, 1973 *Certification:* Surgery
6624 Fannin St #2400, Houston, 713-790-9151

Wallace, Patrick Joseph (3 mentions)
U of Chicago, 1989 *Certification:* Surgery
1315 St Joseph Pkwy #1800, Houston, 713-652-3161

Watson, Larry Cordell (5 mentions)
U of Texas-Galveston, 1972 *Certification:* Surgery
2060 Space Park Dr #100, Houston, 281-333-1703

Wesson, David E. (3 mentions)
FMS-Canada, 1973 *Certification:* Pediatric Surgery, Surgery
6701 Fannin St, Houston, 832-822-3135

Wheeler, Kevin D. (6 mentions)
Baylor U, 1986 *Certification:* Surgery
1140 Business Center Dr #400, Houston, 713-464-1981

Geriatrics

Levy, Steven Jay (3 mentions)
Philadelphia Coll of Osteopathic Med, 1970
Certification: Internal Medicine
1140 Westmont Dr #300, Houston, 713-451-4100

Moquist, Dale C. (3 mentions)
Certification: Family Medicine, Geriatric Medicine
7737 Southwest Frwy #400, Houston, 713-456-5320

Salmeron, Geraldine (4 mentions)
Baylor U, 1975 *Certification:* Internal Medicine, Rheumatology
6620 Main St #1225, Houston, 713-798-2500

Hematology/Oncology

Abramowitz, Joel (6 mentions)
SUNY-Downstate Med Coll, 1976
Certification: Hematology, Internal Medicine, Medical Oncology
925 Gessner Rd #310, Houston, 713-467-1630

Baker, Kelty R. (3 mentions)
Baylor U, 1993 *Certification:* Hematology, Internal Medicine
6560 Fannin St #1260, Houston, 713-795-0933

Bernicker, Eric H. (5 mentions)
Baylor U, 1990
Certification: Internal Medicine, Medical Oncology
1707 Sunset Blvd, Houston, 713-526-5511

Campos, Luis Talavera (3 mentions)
FMS-Peru, 1969
Certification: Internal Medicine, Medical Oncology
920 Frostwood Dr #780, Houston, 713-827-9525

Conlon, Charles Lee (10 mentions)
U of Texas-Galveston, 1975 *Certification:* Blood Banking,
Hematology, Internal Medicine, Medical Oncology
7777 Southwest Frwy #744, Houston, 713-484-7050
16675 SW Frwy #200, Sugar Land, 281-165-5454

Crow, Mary Kurtz (4 mentions)
Baylor U, 1989
Certification: Hematology, Internal Medicine, Medical Oncology
17323 Red Oak Dr, Houston, 281-440-5006

Escudier, Susan M. (5 mentions)
Baylor U, 1985
Certification: Hematology, Internal Medicine, Medical Oncology
7515 S Main St #740, Houston, 713-795-0202

Haq, Mohamed Maqbool-Ul (6 mentions)
FMS-India, 1974
Certification: Internal Medicine, Medical Oncology
3301 Plainview St #D-1, Pasadena, 713-947-2142

Heyne, Kirk Edward (7 mentions)
Baylor U, 1981
Certification: Internal Medicine, Medical Oncology
1707 Sunset Blvd, Houston, 713-526-5511

Holmes, Frankie Ann (3 mentions)
Virginia Commonwealth U, 1976
Certification: Internal Medicine, Medical Oncology
909 Frostwood Dr #221, Houston, 713-467-1722

Hoots, William Keith (5 mentions)
U of North Carolina, 1975
Certification: Pediatric Hematology-Oncology, Pediatrics
6410 Fannin St #500, Houston, 832-325-7111

Lynch, Garrett Rushing (8 mentions)
Baylor U, 1974
Certification: Internal Medicine, Medical Oncology
6550 Fannin St #1053, Houston, 713-798-3750
6620 Main St #1375, Houston, 713-798-2500

Macheledt, Janet Elaine (3 mentions)
U of Texas-Houston, 1986
Certification: Hematology, Internal Medicine, Medical Oncology
909 Frostwood Dr #221, Houston, 713-467-1722
1331 W Grand Pkwy N #3040, Katy, 713-467-1722

Manner, Charles Elmer (6 mentions)
U of Maryland, 1975
Certification: Hematology, Internal Medicine
1213 Hermann Dr #855, Houston, 713-529-3619

McCarthy, John Joseph (3 mentions)
Baylor U, 1976 *Certification:* Hematology, Internal Medicine
6411 Fannin St, Houston, 713-704-4060

Natelson, Ethan Allen (4 mentions)
Baylor U, 1966 *Certification:* Hematology, Internal Medicine
6550 Fannin St #1101, Houston, 713-441-0006

Quraishi, Mohammed Ali (3 mentions)
FMS-India, 1972
Certification: Internal Medicine, Medical Oncology
3326 Watters Rd #A, Pasadena, 713-941-3400

Rice, Lawrence (8 mentions)
Emory U, 1974 *Certification:* Hematology, Internal Medicine
6550 Fannin St #1101, Houston, 713-441-0006

Infectious Disease

Bradshaw, Major W. (4 mentions)
Baylor U, 1967
Certification: Infectious Disease, Internal Medicine
One Baylor Plaza, Houston, 713-798-8918

Burnazian, George Ghazaros (5 mentions)
FMS-Romania, 1966 *Certification:* Internal Medicine
1200 Binz St #530, Houston, 713-527-5626

Castillo, Luis Enrique G. (6 mentions)
FMS-Peru, 1975
Certification: Infectious Disease, Internal Medicine
607 Timberdale Ln #200, Houston, 281-444-9590

Dupont, Herbert L. (5 mentions)
Emory U, 1965 *Certification:* Internal Medicine
6720 Bertner St, Houston, 832-355-4122

Fainstein, Victor (12 mentions)
FMS-Mexico, 1973 *Certification:* Infectious Disease
6560 Fannin St #1540, Houston, 713-799-9997
6624 Fannin St, Houston, 713-442-1023

Gathe, Joseph Clayton, Jr. (4 mentions)
Baylor U, 1981
Certification: Infectious Disease, Internal Medicine
4900 Fannin St, Houston, 713-526-9821

Gentry, Layne Oral (6 mentions)
Oregon Health Sciences U, 1965
Certification: Infectious Disease, Internal Medicine
6624 Fannin St #1410, Houston, 713-791-4882
6720 Bertner St, Houston, 713-791-4888

Harris, Richard Lowell (10 mentions)
Baylor U, 1978
Certification: Infectious Disease, Internal Medicine
6560 Fannin St #2204, Houston, 713-793-7550

Kaplan, Sheldon Lee (5 mentions)
U of Missouri, 1973
Certification: Pediatric Infectious Diseases, Pediatrics
6701 Fannin St, Houston, 832-824-4330
1504 Taub Loop, Houston, 713-873-5437

Kielhofner, Marcia Ann (4 mentions)
U of Missouri-Kansas City, 1984
Certification: Infectious Disease, Internal Medicine
6624 Fannin St #1410, Houston, 713-791-4882

Lo, Carson Tan (5 mentions)
FMS-Philippines, 1985
Certification: Infectious Disease, Internal Medicine
1331 W Grand Pkwy N #310, Katy, 281-599-3222

Portnoy, Benjamin Lee (6 mentions)
Case Western Reserve U, 1970 *Certification:* Internal Medicine
1200 Binz St #1020, Houston, 713-524-8700

Price, Todd Marshall (4 mentions)
Oral Roberts U, 1983
915 Gessner Rd #620, Houston, 713-935-9057

Samo, Tobias Charles (13 mentions)
Rosalind Franklin U, 1978
Certification: Infectious Disease, Internal Medicine
6560 Fannin St #1540, Houston, 713-799-9997
6624 Fannin St, Houston, 713-442-1023

Septimus, Edward Joel (5 mentions)
Baylor U, 1972
Certification: Infectious Disease, Internal Medicine
4257 Albans Rd, Houston, 281-714-5689
6550 Fannin St #981, Houston, 713-441-7715

Shah, Seema (4 mentions)
U of Puerto Rico, 1983
Certification: Infectious Disease, Internal Medicine
6560 Fannin St #2204, Houston, 713-793-7550

Siebert, William Terry (4 mentions)
Baylor U, 1972
Certification: Infectious Disease, Internal Medicine
1315 St Joseph Pkwy #1710, Houston, 713-757-7475

Zeluff, Barry James (12 mentions)
Baylor U, 1978
Certification: Infectious Disease, Internal Medicine
6624 Fannin St #1410, Houston, 713-791-4882

Infertility

Allon, Michael A. (5 mentions)
Texas Tech U, 1990 *Certification:* Obstetrics & Gynecology,
Reproductive Endocrinology/Infertility
10901 Katy Frwy, Houston, 713-467-4488
17198 St Lukes Way #410, The Woodlands, 713-467-4488

Dunn, Randall Clifford (6 mentions)
Baylor U, 1980 *Certification:* Obstetrics & Gynecology,
Reproductive Endocrinology/Infertility
7900 Fannin St #4000, Houston, 713-512-7000
4724 Sweetwater Blvd #105, Sugar Land, 832-553-5483

Grunert, George M. (4 mentions)
Baylor U, 1973 *Certification:* Obstetrics & Gynecology
7900 Fannin St #4000, Houston, 713-512-7000

Hickman, Timothy N. (11 mentions)
St Louis U, 1990 *Certification:* Obstetrics & Gynecology,
Reproductive Endocrinology/Infertility
920 Frostwood Dr #720, Houston, 713-465-1211
1120 Medical Center Dr #335, The Woodlands, 713-465-1211

Lipshultz, Larry I. (5 mentions)
U of Pennsylvania, 1968 *Certification:* Urology
6560 Fannin St #2100, Houston, 713-798-4001
6560 Fannin St #1402, Houston, 713-798-6163

McKenzie, Laurie Evenson (6 mentions)
U of Florida, 1997 *Certification:* Obstetrics & Gynecology,
Reproductive Endocrinology/Infertility
920 Frostwood Dr #720, Houston, 713-465-1211
1120 Medical Plaza Dr #335, The Woodlands, 713-465-1211

Schnell, Vicki Lynn (4 mentions)
Baylor U, 1983 *Certification:* Obstetrics & Gynecology,
Reproductive Endocrinology/Infertility
3701 Kirby Dr #840, Houston, 713-807-0234
1015 Medeical Center Blvd #2100, Webster, 281-332-0073
3560 Delaware Ave, Beaumont, 281-332-0073

Internal Medicine *(see note on page 9)*

Baxter, Thomas Leroy, III (5 mentions)
Jefferson Med Coll, 1970 *Certification:* Internal Medicine
6560 Fannin St #1408, Houston, 713-790-2651

Ehrlich, Lisa L. (3 mentions)
U of Texas-Galveston, 1993 *Certification:* Internal Medicine
6624 Fannin St #1210, Houston, 713-790-9806

Eichelberger, John F. (5 mentions)
U of Texas-Galveston, 1982 *Certification:* Internal Medicine
1707 Sunset Blvd, Houston, 713-526-5511

Hoffman, Alan S. (3 mentions)
Baylor U, 1985 *Certification:* Internal Medicine
6624 Fannin St #2380, Houston, 713-790-1790

Jackson, Robert Evan (4 mentions)
U of Texas-Galveston, 1981 *Certification:* Internal Medicine
6560 Fannin St #1130, Houston, 713-797-1087

Lent, William Allen (3 mentions)
U of Texas-Houston, 1979 *Certification:* Internal Medicine
1200 Binz St Medical Center Plz #1410, Houston, 713-526-5606

Lenz, Matthew L. (4 mentions)
Baylor U, 1984 *Certification:* Internal Medicine
1707 Sunset Blvd, Houston, 713-526-5511

Lin, Tony Jiann (3 mentions)
Baylor U, 1990 *Certification:* Internal Medicine
6624 Fannin St, Houston, 713-442-0120

Lisse, Scott A. (4 mentions)
Baylor U, 1989 *Certification:* Internal Medicine
6560 Fannin St #1130, Houston, 713-797-1087

Muntz, James Edwin (4 mentions)
Baylor U, 1975 *Certification:* Internal Medicine
6550 Fannin St #2339, Houston, 713-795-4847

Niefield, Stewart Lee (5 mentions)
Baylor U, 1980 *Certification:* Internal Medicine
6560 Fannin St #1130, Houston, 713-797-1087

Robben, Christopher Paul (3 mentions)
New York U, 1982 *Certification:* Internal Medicine
6560 Fannin St, Houston, 713-441-4280

Rubin, Robert Jay (6 mentions)
Baylor U, 1977 *Certification:* Internal Medicine
6560 Fannin St #1130, Houston, 713-797-1087

Vicroy, Theresa Gay (3 mentions)
Washington U, 1984 *Certification:* Internal Medicine
6560 Fannin St #1012, Houston, 281-657-0770

White, Martin Ray (5 mentions)
Baylor U, 1977 *Certification:* Hematology, Internal Medicine
1707 Sunset Blvd, Houston, 713-526-5511

Nephrology

Brennan, Thomas S. (4 mentions)
Loyola U Chicago, 1979
Certification: Internal Medicine, Nephrology
1415 La Concha Ln, Houston, 713-790-9080

Brewer, Eileen Doyle (4 mentions)
Washington U, 1971
Certification: Pediatric Nephrology, Pediatrics
6701 Fannin St, Houston, 832-824-3800

Crumb, Charles Kenneth (4 mentions)
U of Missouri, 1968 *Certification:* Internal Medicine, Nephrology
7777 Southwest Frwy #304, Houston, 713-270-4545

Dinerstein, Stevan L. (8 mentions)
U of Texas-Dallas, 1973 *Certification:* Internal Medicine
6560 Fannin St #2204, Houston, 713-793-7550

Etheridge, Whitson B., II (5 mentions)
Baylor U, 1971 *Certification:* Internal Medicine, Nephrology
8876 Gulf Frwy #215, Houston, 713-947-9509
6720 Bertner St, Houston, 713-791-2648

Foley, Richard James (4 mentions)
U of Illinois, 1977 *Certification:* Internal Medicine, Nephrology
607 Timberdale Ln #201, Houston, 281-440-3005

Kupor, Lary Richard (5 mentions)
Harvard U, 1967 *Certification:* Internal Medicine, Nephrology
1315 St Joseph Pkwy #1106, Houston, 713-951-0421

Muniz, Henry (4 mentions)
U of Miami, 1974 *Certification:* Internal Medicine, Nephrology
3337 Plainview St #B-6, Pasadena, 713-947-9507
250 Blossom St #275, Clearlake, 281-332-2059

Olivero, Juan J., Sr. (15 mentions)
Certification: Internal Medicine, Nephrology
6560 Fannin St #2206, Houston, 713-790-4615

Porter, Robert Hale (4 mentions)
Virginia Commonwealth U, 1972
Certification: Internal Medicine, Nephrology
7777 Southwest Frwy #304, Houston, 713-270-4545

Ralph, Ronald Bert (3 mentions)
U of Texas-Galveston, 2000
Certification: Internal Medicine, Nephrology
1200 Binz St #1180, Houston, 713-520-6790

Sheth, Anil Uttamchand (7 mentions)
FMS-India, 1974 *Certification:* Internal Medicine, Nephrology
915 Gessner Rd #360, Houston, 713-468-5440
1331 Grand Pkwy #320, Katy, 713-468-5440
21216 NW Frwy #410, Cypress, 281-571-8090

Suki, Wadi Nagib (11 mentions)
FMS-Lebanon, 1959 *Certification:* Internal Medicine, Nephrology
2256 Holcombe Blvd, Houston, 713-790-9080
1415 La Concha Ln, Houston, 713-790-9080

Neurological Surgery

Aldama-Luebbert, Alfonso (5 mentions)
Baylor U, 1974 *Certification:* Neurological Surgery
6560 Fannin St #1200, Houston, 713-790-1211

Blacklock, Jerry Bob (7 mentions)
U of Mississippi, 1979 *Certification:* Neurological Surgery
6560 Fannin St #900, Houston, 713-441-3807

Cech, David Allen (5 mentions)
SUNY-Downstate Med Coll, 1978
Certification: Neurological Surgery
6560 Fannin St #1200, Houston, 713-790-1211

Grossman, Robert George (8 mentions)
Columbia U, 1957 *Certification:* Neurological Surgery
6560 Fannin #944, Houston, 713-798-4696
6560 Fannin St #800, Houston, 713-798-6929

Harper, Richard Louis (23 mentions)
Baylor U, 1971 *Certification:* Neurological Surgery
6560 Fannin St #1200, Houston, 713-790-1211

Mims, Thomas Jefferson, Jr. (8 mentions)
Louisiana State U-Shreveport, 1976
Certification: Neurological Surgery
6624 Fannin St #SLT-2340, Houston, 713-799-8993

Pakzaban, Peyman (6 mentions)
Baylor U, 1989 *Certification:* Neurological Surgery
3801 Vista Rd #440, Pasadena, 713-941-0008

Rose, James Ellington (6 mentions)
U of Texas-Galveston, 1968 *Certification:* Neurological Surgery
6560 Fannin St #944, Houston, 713-798-4696

Weil, Stuart M. (17 mentions)
U of Texas-Houston, 1984 *Certification:* Neurological Surgery
6624 Fannin St #2140, Houston, 713-794-0500

Neurology

Alpert, Jack Nathaniel (14 mentions)
Tufts U, 1964 *Certification:* Neurology
6624 Fannin St #1550, Houston, 713-795-4785

Appel, Stanley Hersh (6 mentions)
Columbia U, 1960 *Certification:* Neurology
6560 Fannin St #802, Houston, 713-441-3760

Cherches, Igor M. (10 mentions)
Baylor U, 1990 *Certification:* Neurology
7505 Main St #290, Houston, 713-795-0074

Derman, Howard S. (3 mentions)
Rush U, 1974 *Certification:* Neurology
6560 Fannin St #802, Houston, 713-441-5077

Evans, Randolph Warren (4 mentions)
Baylor U, 1978 *Certification:* Neurology
1200 Binz St #1370, Houston, 713-528-0725

Fayle, Robert W. (3 mentions)
U of Texas-Houston, 1976
Certification: Neurology, Sleep Medicine
403 Ogletree Dr, Livingston, 713-529-1914

Grotta, James Charles (5 mentions)
U of Virginia, 1971 *Certification:* Neurology, Vascular Neurology
6410 Fannin St #1014, Houston, 832-325-7080

Hershkowitz, Leonard (4 mentions)
Wayne State U, 1970 *Certification:* Neurology
7500 Beechnut Ln #135, Houston, 713-777-4122

Irr, William George (6 mentions)
West Virginia U, 1991 *Certification:* Neurology
6624 Fannin St #1550, Houston, 713-795-4785

Jones, Julia Leigh (12 mentions)
Tulane U, 1987 *Certification:* Neurology
7505 Main St #290, Houston, 713-795-0074

Killian, James Mahony (3 mentions)
Med Coll of Wisconsin, 1958 *Certification:* Neurology
6501 Fannin St #NB-336, Houston, 713-798-5989

Lai, Eugene C. (6 mentions)
Baylor U, 1986 *Certification:* Neurology
6550 Fannin St #1801, Houston, 713-798-7290

Lorente-Dinnbier, Lorenzo (3 mentions)
FMS-Spain, 1968 *Certification:* Neurology
800 Peakwood Dr #4D, Houston, 281-440-6066

Mancias, Pedro (3 mentions)
U of Texas-Houston, 1988 *Certification:* Clinical Neurophysiology,
Neurology with Special Qualifications in Child Neurology
6410 Fannin St #1010, Houston, 832-325-7151

Martin, Raymond A. (4 mentions)
U of Buffalo, 1968 *Certification:* Neurology
6410 Fannin St #1014, Houston, 832-325-7080

Monday, Kimberly E. (4 mentions)
Baylor U, 1992 *Certification:* Clinical Neurophysiology, Neurology
4141 Vista Rd, Pasadena, 713-947-3100
8633 Broadway St #109, Pearland, 281-922-7222

Newmark, Michael Ede (5 mentions)
Columbia U, 1972 *Certification:* Neurology
2727 W Holcombe Blvd, Houston, 713-442-0000

Ohanian, Sevak T. (4 mentions)
U of Texas-Houston, 1995 *Certification:* Neurology
10575 Katy Frwy #425, Houston, 713-461-7878

Sermas, Angelo (8 mentions)
Baylor U, 1978 *Certification:* Neurology
6624 Fannin St #1550, Houston, 713-795-4785

Simpson, Ericka Portley (3 mentions)
U of Texas-Houston, 1995
Certification: Neurology, Neuromuscular Medicine
6560 Fannin St #802, Houston, 713-441-3336

Singh, Balbir (4 mentions)
FMS-India, 1977 *Certification:* Neurology with Special
Qualifications in Child Neurology
455 School St #20, Tomball, 281-357-5678

Obstetrics/Gynecology

Adam, Karolina (5 mentions)
Med Coll of Pennsylvania, 1983
Certification: Maternal-Fetal Medicine, Obstetrics & Gynecology
7400 Fannin St 700, Houston, 713-791-9700

Brown, Dale, Jr. (7 mentions)
U of Texas-Galveston, 1964 *Certification:* Obstetrics & Gynecology
6620 Main St #1450, Houston, 713-798-7500

Carpenter, Robert J., Jr. (7 mentions)
Baylor U, 1973
Certification: Maternal-Fetal Medicine, Obstetrics & Gynecology
6624 Fannin St St Lukem Med Tower #2720, Houston,
713-795-4600

Cook, Paul Issa (5 mentions)
U of Texas-Houston, 1988 *Certification:* Obstetrics & Gynecology
6400 Fannin St #1900, Houston, 713-796-2200

Dinh, Tri A. (3 mentions)
Baylor U, 1992
Certification: Gynecologic Oncology, Obstetrics & Gynecology
6550 Fannin St #901, Houston, 713-441-1026
16655 Southwest Frwy, Sugar Land, 281-274-7000

Dryden, Damla K. (4 mentions)
Washington U, 1997 *Certification:* Obstetrics & Gynecology
6624 Fannin St #1800, Houston, 713-797-1144

Gogola, Jon Ramon (6 mentions)
U of Alabama, 1993 *Certification:* Obstetrics & Gynecology
920 Frostwood Dr #610, Houston, 713-935-9791

Haufrect, Eric Jay (10 mentions)
Baylor U, 1973 *Certification:* Obstetrics & Gynecology
6550 Fannin St #2221, Houston, 713-797-9666

Hoffman, Lynn Preston (4 mentions)
Baylor U, 1975 *Certification:* Obstetrics & Gynecology
6500 Fannin #1980, Houston, 713-335-0335

Nanda, Roz (3 mentions)
Rosalind Franklin U, 1991 *Certification:* Obstetrics & Gynecology
6400 Fannin St #1900, Houston, 713-796-2200

Nebgen, Denise (3 mentions)
Northwestern U, 1997 *Certification:* Obstetrics & Gynecology
6550 Fannin St #2201, Houston, 713-797-9498

Pinell, Phillip M. (4 mentions)
Baylor U, 1987 *Certification:* Obstetrics & Gynecology
7400 Fannin St #700, Houston, 713-791-9700

Reiss, Anh (4 mentions)
SUNY-Downstate Med Coll, 1995
Certification: Obstetrics & Gynecology
7879 Southwest Frwy #510, Houston, 713-541-3376

Simon, Terry Lee (3 mentions)
Baylor U, 1977 *Certification:* Obstetrics & Gynecology
7515 Main St #340, Houston, 713-797-9209

Smith, Frances A. (3 mentions)
Baylor U, 1981 *Certification:* Obstetrics & Gynecology
1221 McKinney St #300, Houston, 713-442-4700
7900 Fannin St #2100, Houston, 713-442-7300

Van Sickle, Mary Lou (4 mentions)
U of Texas-San Antonio, 1985
Certification: Obstetrics & Gynecology
7777 Southwest Frwy #616, Houston, 713-773-3983

Young, Amy Elise (4 mentions)
U of Mississippi, 1990 *Certification:* Obstetrics & Gynecology
6620 Main St #1450, Houston, 713-798-7500

Zepeda, David Edward (6 mentions)
U of Texas-San Antonio, 1974
Certification: Obstetrics & Gynecology
6624 Fannin St #1800, Houston, 713-798-8956

Ophthalmology

Brown, David Mark (4 mentions)
Baylor U, 1987 *Certification:* Ophthalmology
6560 Fannin St, Houston, 713-524-3434

Coburn, Amy Grossman (11 mentions)
Baylor U, 1985 *Certification:* Ophthalmology
6624 Fannin St #2100, Houston, 713-791-1431
6560 Fannin St #1840, Houston, 713-791-1431

Cohen, Joel Steven (4 mentions)
Tulane U, 1973 *Certification:* Ophthalmology
13300 Hargrave Rd #300, Houston, 281-890-1784

Dawson, Peter Sutherland (3 mentions)
FMS-Canada, 1964 *Certification:* Ophthalmology
1631 North Loop W #500, Houston, 713-869-6400
1229 Campbell Rd, Houston, 713-467-6600
829 Peckwood Dr, Houston, 281-537-0100

Goldman, Daniel Isser (4 mentions)
Washington U, 1976 *Certification:* Ophthalmology
3333 Bayshore Blvd #280, Pasadena, 713-943-8671

Green, Mary Trotter (7 mentions)
Baylor U, 1982 *Certification:* Ophthalmology
6624 Fannin St #2105, Houston, 713-791-9494
4 Chelsea Blvd, Houston, 713-521-4442

Hamburg, Sol (5 mentions)
Yale U, 1981 *Certification:* Ophthalmology
12121 Richmond Ave #115, Houston, 281-493-1733

Hamill, Marshall Bowes (5 mentions)
Baylor U, 1979 *Certification:* Ophthalmology
6550 Fannin St #1501, Houston, 713-798-6100

Holz, Eric Robert (3 mentions)
Baylor U, 1989 *Certification:* Ophthalmology
6560 Fannin St #2200, Houston, 713-798-3880

Jarrett, Alan (4 mentions)
U of Tennessee, 1969 *Certification:* Ophthalmology
909 Frostwood Dr #226, Houston, 713-461-1169

Jones, Danny Brigman (4 mentions)
Duke U, 1962 *Certification:* Ophthalmology
6550 Fannin St #1501, Houston, 713-798-6100

Koch, Douglas Donald (6 mentions)
Harvard U, 1977 *Certification:* Ophthalmology
6550 Fannin St #1501, Houston, 713-798-6100

Lewis, Richard Alan (4 mentions)
U of Michigan, 1969 *Certification:* Ophthalmology
6550 Fannin St #1501, Houston, 713-798-6100

Pflugfelder, Stephen Carl (3 mentions)
SUNY-Upstate Med U, 1981 *Certification:* Ophthalmology
6550 Fannin St #1501, Houston, 713-798-6100

Quayle, William Henry (3 mentions)
U of Missouri, 1973 *Certification:* Ophthalmology
2855 Gramercy St, Houston, 713-668-6828
1220 Augusta Dr #100, Houston, 713-668-6828

Sanders, Marc R. (4 mentions)
Baylor U, 1989 *Certification:* Ophthalmology
3405 Edloe St #300, Houston, 713-797-1500
1213 Hermann Dr #110, Houston, 713-795-4500

Webb, Nancy E. R. (3 mentions)
Baylor U, 1974 *Certification:* Ophthalmology
2727 W Holcombe Blvd, Houston, 713-442-0000

Orthopedics

Bennett, James B. (3 mentions)
Certification: Orthopaedic Surgery, Surgery of the Hand
7401 Main St, Houston, 713-799-2300

Bryan, William Jay (7 mentions)
Baylor U, 1975 *Certification:* Orthopaedic Surgery
6560 Fannin St #400, Houston, 713-986-6100

Clanton, Thomas Oscar (4 mentions)
Baylor U, 1976 *Certification:* Orthopaedic Surgery
6410 Fannin St #950, Houston, 832-325-7141

Clyburn, Terry Alan (3 mentions)
U of Texas-Galveston, 1979 *Certification:* Orthopaedic Surgery
5420 West Loop S #2400, Bellaire, 713-357-4752

Criswell, Allen Ross (3 mentions)
Temple U, 1971 *Certification:* Orthopaedic Surgery
707 S Fry Rd #255, Katy, 281-829-2000
1315 St Joseph Pkwy #800, Houston, 713-650-6900

Cuellar, Alberto (3 mentions)
U of Texas-Galveston, 1984 *Certification:* Orthopaedic Surgery
17270 Red Oak Dr #200, Houston, 281-440-6960

Davino, Nelson Anthony (3 mentions)
U of Texas-San Antonio, 1984 *Certification:* Orthopaedic Surgery
21220 Kingsland Blvd, Katy, 281-492-9532
1517 Thompson Hwy, Richmond, 281-344-1715

Epps, Howard Robert (4 mentions)
Johns Hopkins U, 1989 *Certification:* Orthopaedic Surgery
7401 Main St, Houston, 713-799-2300

First, Kenneth Robert (3 mentions)
Harvard U, 1983
Certification: Orthopaedic Sports Medicine, Orthopaedic Surgery
1100 Hercules Ave #100, Houston, 281-335-1111

Gerow, Frank T. (3 mentions)
Baylor U, 1990 *Certification:* Orthopaedic Surgery
6624 Fannin St, Houston, 713-790-1818

Granberry, William M. (4 mentions)
Baylor U, 1986 *Certification:* Orthopaedic Surgery
6624 Fannin St #2600, Houston, 713-790-1818

Kearns, Richard Joseph (7 mentions)
Georgetown U, 1975 *Certification:* Orthopaedic Surgery
7401 Main St, Houston, 713-799-2300

Kreuzer, Stefan Werner (3 mentions)
U of Texas-San Antonio, 1995 *Certification:* Orthopaedic Surgery
909 Frostwood Dr #251, Houston, 713-827-9316

Landon, Glenn Carey (9 mentions)
Loyola U Chicago, 1975 *Certification:* Orthopaedic Surgery
2727 W Holcombe Blvd, Houston, 713-442-0000
830 Gemini St, Houston, 713-442-4500

Marco, Rex Alexander (5 mentions)
U of California-Los Angeles, 1992
Certification: Orthopaedic Surgery
6700 West Loop S #110, Bellaire, 713-838-8300

Mathis, Kenneth Bradford (6 mentions)
U of Texas-Dallas, 1985 *Certification:* Orthopaedic Surgery
6550 Fannin St #2500, Houston, 713-441-3740

Monmouth, Michael Anthony (3 mentions)
Harvard U, 1983 *Certification:* Orthopaedic Surgery
2020 Nasa Pkwy #200, Houston, 281-333-5114

Parr, Thomas Jackson (5 mentions)
U of Texas-Dallas, 1975 *Certification:* Orthopaedic Surgery
14090 South West Frwy #130, Sugar Land, 281-491-7111

Parsley, Brian Strake (3 mentions)
U of Texas-Houston, 1983 *Certification:* Orthopaedic Surgery
15200 SW Frwy #175, Sugar Land, 713-986-6000
6620 Main St, Houston, 713-986-6016

Siff, Sherwin Jay (6 mentions)
U of Pittsburgh, 1964 *Certification:* Orthopaedic Surgery
6624 Fannin St #2600, Houston, 713-790-1818

Sitter, Timothy Christian (3 mentions)
U of Texas-Houston, 1987 *Certification:* Orthopaedic Surgery
1201 Brooks St, Sugar Land, 281-690-4678
7500 Beechnut St #175, Houston, 713-772-5000

Valdez, Ray R. (3 mentions)
U of Texas-Galveston, 1983 *Certification:* Orthopaedic Surgery
7500 Beechnut St #175, Houston, 713-772-5000
1201 Brooks St, Sugar Land, 281-690-4678

Watters, William Charles, II (3 mentions)
Harvard U, 1974 *Certification:* Orthopaedic Surgery
6624 Fannin St #2600, Houston, 713-790-1818

Winston, Leland Alfred (3 mentions)
U of Texas-Galveston, 1973 *Certification:* Orthopaedic Surgery
6500 Fannin St #400, Houston, 713-441-3460
2802 Garth Rd #109, Baytown, 832-556-0880

Otorhinolaryngology

Alford, Bobby Ray (5 mentions)
Baylor U, 1956 *Certification:* Otolaryngology
6501 Fannin St #NA102, Houston, 713-798-3200

Alford, Eugene Landon (6 mentions)
U of Texas-San Antonio, 1986 *Certification:* Otolaryngology
6550 Fannin St #2001, Houston, 713-796-2001
16651 Southwest Frwy #320, Sugar Land, 281-340-3200

Ashe, Herbert John, Jr. (5 mentions)
Louisiana State U, 1980 *Certification:* Otolaryngology
2727 W Holcombe Blvd, Houston, 713-442-0000

Conrad, Larry Paul (5 mentions)
Wake Forest U, 1969 *Certification:* Otolaryngology
1200 Binz St #1230, Houston, 713-524-9209

Donovan, Donald Thomas (10 mentions)
Baylor U, 1976 *Certification:* Otolaryngology
6550 Fannin St #1701, Houston, 713-798-5464

Edmonds, Joseph Lindsay (4 mentions)
U of Kansas, 1993 *Certification:* Otolaryngology
6550 Fannin St #2001, Houston, 713-796-2001
16651 Southwest Frwy #320, Sugar Land, 281-340-3200

Grant, James (4 mentions)
U of Texas-Galveston, 1994 *Certification:* Otolaryngology
561 Medical Center Blvd #A, Webster, 281-338-1423

Moorhead, John Cary (10 mentions)
Baylor U, 1989 *Certification:* Otolaryngology
915 Gessner Rd #225, Houston, 713-467-5787

Moses, Ron Lee (10 mentions)
Johns Hopkins U, 1993 *Certification:* Otolaryngology
6624 Fannin St #1480, Houston, 713-795-5343

Parke, Robert Barton, Jr. (6 mentions)
Baylor U, 1973 *Certification:* Otolaryngology
6550 Fannin St, Houston, 713-798-5900

Patt, Bradford Stewart (4 mentions)
Louisiana State U, 1986 *Certification:* Otolaryngology
7777 Southwest Frwy #820, Houston, 281-649-7000
915 Gessner Rd #280, Houston, 713-461-2626

Powitzky, Eric S. (4 mentions)
Baylor U, 1996 *Certification:* Otolaryngology
6624 Fannin St #1480, Houston, 713-795-5343

Weber, Samuel Coleman (11 mentions)
U of Tennessee, 1965 *Certification:* Otolaryngology
6624 Fannin St #1480, Houston, 713-795-5343

Pain Medicine

Benny, Benoy Varkey (3 mentions)
FMS-Trinidad, 1999
Certification: Pain Medicine, Physical Medicine & Rehabilitation
6620 Main St #1375, Houston, 713-798-7246

Charnov, Jeffrey Hal (4 mentions)
U of California-Irvine, 1988
Certification: Anesthesiology, Pain Medicine
909 Frostwood Dr #310, Houston, 713-932-0770

Doctor, Uday V. (10 mentions)
U of Texas-San Antonio, 1983
Certification: Anesthesiology, Pain Medicine
7505 S Main #150, Houston, 713-790-1500

Edmondson, Everton A. (3 mentions)
New York U, 1980 *Certification:* Neurology, Pain Medicine
6560 Fannin St #2202, Houston, 713-797-1180

McCann, Michael T. (3 mentions)
U of Texas-Dallas, 1987
Certification: Anesthesiology, Pain Medicine
7505 Main St #150, Houston, 713-790-1500

Thomas, Abraham G. (4 mentions)
U of Texas-Houston, 1991
Certification: Anesthesiology, Pain Medicine
5420 W West, Bellaire, 713-797-0876

Pathology

Ayala, Alberto Gabriel (4 mentions)
FMS-Mexico, 1962 *Certification:* Anatomic Pathology
6565 Fannin St #227, Houston, 713-441-1339
6411 Fannin St, Houston, 713-500-5301

Balsaver, Ashok Mukund (4 mentions)
FMS-India, 1960
Certification: Anatomic Pathology & Clinical Pathology
6565 Fannin St #M-227, Houston, 713-441-1922

Kemp, Bonnie Lucas (3 mentions)
Baylor U, 1987 *Certification:* Anatomic Pathology & Clinical Pathology, Dermatopathology
921 Gessner Rd, Houston, 713-932-3776

Mody, Dina (4 mentions)
FMS-India, 1979 *Certification:* Anatomic Pathology & Clinical Pathology, Cytopathology
6565 Fannin St, Houston, 713-441-6420

Moore, Jeffrey G. (3 mentions)
Loyola U Chicago, 1990 *Certification:* Anatomic Pathology & Clinical Pathology, Cytopathology
10700 Richmond Ave #320, Houston, 713-432-1100

Salter, James Edward, Jr. (5 mentions)
U of Mississippi, 1986 *Certification:* Anatomic Pathology & Clinical Pathology, Cytopathology
921 Gessner Rd, Houston, 713-242-3776

Schwartz, Mary Rebecca (12 mentions)
Washington U, 1978 *Certification:* Anatomic Pathology & Clinical Pathology, Cytopathology
6565 Fannin St #237-A, Houston, 713-394-6482

Shannon, Rhonda L. (6 mentions)
U of Texas-Houston, 1984
Certification: Anatomic Pathology & Clinical Pathology
6720 Bertner St, Houston, 713-791-2942

Stavinoha, John Lamar, Jr. (4 mentions)
U of Texas-San Antonio, 1983 *Certification:* Anatomic Pathology & Clinical Pathology, Cytopathology
7600 Beechnut St, Houston, 713-456-5271

Wheeler, Thomas Michael (9 mentions)
Baylor U, 1977 *Certification:* Anatomic Pathology & Clinical Pathology, Cytopathology
7501 Fannin St, Houston, 713-375-7000
504 Medical Center Blvd, Conrad, 713-432-1100

Pediatrics *(see note on page 9)*

Bootin, Debra Mucasey (3 mentions)
Baylor U, 1986 *Certification:* Pediatrics
7400 Fannin St #900, Houston, 713-795-9500

Dreessen, Philip Ray (3 mentions)
Baylor U, 1967 *Certification:* Pediatrics
4101 Greenbriar St #100, Houston, 713-526-6443

Finnila, Lara Baranov (3 mentions)
U of Texas-Houston, 1999 *Certification:* Pediatrics
4101 Greenbriar St #100, Houston, 713-526-6443

Ho, Hubert Yute (4 mentions)
Baylor U, 1993 *Certification:* Pediatrics
15400 Southwest Frwy #300, Sugar Land, 281-491-3636

Pocsik, Stephanie (3 mentions)
Virginia Commonwealth U, 1988 *Certification:* Pediatrics
16 Professional Park Dr, Webster, 281-332-3503

Schaffer, Don Minchen (3 mentions)
Baylor U, 1976 *Certification:* Pediatrics
7900 Fannin St #3300, Houston, 713-630-0660
1330 Kingwood Dr, Kingwood, 281-359-5711

Thaller, Richard Michael (3 mentions)
U of Missouri, 1969 *Certification:* Pediatrics
9055 Katy Frwy #420, Houston, 713-464-0560

Plastic Surgery

Agris, Joseph (6 mentions)
Albany Med Coll, 1968 *Certification:* Plastic Surgery
6560 Fannin St #1730, Houston, 713-797-1700

Casso, Daniel (3 mentions)
U of Texas-Dallas, 1984 *Certification:* Plastic Surgery
2020 Nasa Pkwy #260, Houston, 281-333-3500

Collins, Donald R. (5 mentions)
U of Texas-Houston, 1987 *Certification:* Plastic Surgery
1315 St Joseph Pkwy #900, Houston, 713-650-0800

Friedman, Jeffrey David (13 mentions)
Baylor U, 1985 *Certification:* Plastic Surgery
6560 Fannin St #800, Houston, 713-798-8070

Garcia, Jan (3 mentions)
U of Puerto Rico, 1975 *Certification:* Plastic Surgery
333 N Texas Ave #2200, Webster, 281-338-2766

Hamilton, Steven M. (3 mentions)
U of Texas-Houston, 1982 *Certification:* Plastic Surgery
6624 Fannin St #1650, Houston, 713-797-1007

Klebuc, Michael John A. (4 mentions)
FMS-Canada, 1993 *Certification:* Plastic Surgery
6560 Fannin St #800, Houston, 713-441-6108

Kridel, Russell William Hayes (4 mentions)
U of Cincinnati, 1975 *Certification:* Otolaryngology
6655 Travis St #900, Houston, 713-526-5665

Lee, David Aubrey (7 mentions)
Louisiana State U, 1970
Certification: Otolaryngology, Plastic Surgery
6560 Fannin St #1760, Houston, 713-795-5584

Melissinos, Emmanuel G. (3 mentions)
FMS-Greece, 1969 *Certification:* Plastic Surgery
6410 Fannin St #1220, Houston, 713-790-0723

Patronella, Christopher K. (3 mentions)
U of Texas-Galveston, 1982 *Certification:* Plastic Surgery
12727 Kimberley Ln #300, Houston, 713-799-9999

Rappaport, Norman Harvey (3 mentions)
Hahnemann U, 1975 *Certification:* Plastic Surgery
6560 Fannin St #1812, Houston, 713-790-4500

Reisman, Neal Robert (4 mentions)
Temple U, 1973 *Certification:* Plastic Surgery
6624 Fannin St #1600, Houston, 713-795-5353

Stal, Samuel (5 mentions)
Loyola U Chicago, 1974
Certification: Otolaryngology, Plastic Surgery
6550 Fannin St #1625, Houston, 713-798-6141
6701 Fannin St #620, Houston, 832-822-3189

Vanik, Richard Kenneth (4 mentions)
U of Illinois, 1977
Certification: Plastic Surgery, Surgery of the Hand
7777 Southwest Frwy #500, Houston, 713-981-7900

Withers, Edward Hodges (6 mentions)
U of Texas-Galveston, 1971 *Certification:* Plastic Surgery
6550 Fannin St #2427, Houston, 713-799-2525

Yosowitz, Philip (3 mentions)
U of California-Los Angeles, 1968
Certification: Plastic Surgery, Surgery
7515 Main St #730, Houston, 713-797-1488

Psychiatry

Chacko, Ranjit Cherian (8 mentions)
FMS-Sri Lanka, 1971
Certification: Geriatric Psychiatry, Psychiatry
6655 Travis St #590, Houston, 713-798-4880

Fink, Aaron Harlan (3 mentions)
Baylor U, 1982
Certification: Child & Adolescent Psychiatry, Psychiatry
4550 Post Oak Place Dr #320, Houston, 713-622-5480

Gutierrez, Jose Asuncion (3 mentions)
FMS-Colombia, 1967 *Certification:* Psychiatry
7500 Beechnut St #214, Houston, 713-772-6519

Hauser, Harris Milton (3 mentions)
Baylor U, 1955 *Certification:* Neurology, Psychiatry
5959 West Loop S #400, Bellaire, 713-838-0052

Noel, Richard L. (3 mentions)
U of Texas-Galveston, 1988 *Certification:* Addiction Psychiatry, Geriatric Psychiatry, Psychiatry
530 Wells Fargo Dr #110, Houston, 281-440-6899

Ray, Priscilla (7 mentions)
Baylor U, 1974 *Certification:* Psychiatry
6624 Fannin St #2120, Houston, 713-797-0112

Spector, Ivan Charles (3 mentions)
U of Texas-Houston, 1983 *Certification:* Addiction Psychiatry, Geriatric Psychiatry, Psychiatry
3100 Weslayan St #350, Houston, 713-963-0769

Yudofsky, Stuart Charles (8 mentions)
Baylor U, 1970 *Certification:* Psychiatry
6655 Travis St #700, Houston, 713-798-4945

Pulmonary Disease

Bajwa, Mohsin Kalim (3 mentions)
FMS-Pakistan, 1982 *Certification:* Critical Care Medicine, Internal Medicine, Pulmonary Disease
411 Lantern Bend Dr #235, Houston, 281-537-6300

Bloom, Kim (11 mentions)
Stanford U, 1974
Certification: Internal Medicine, Pulmonary Disease
6550 Fannin St #2403, Houston, 713-790-6250

Bradley, Bernard Leo (3 mentions)
FMS-Ireland, 1969 *Certification:* Internal Medicine, Occupational Medicine, Pulmonary Disease
4003 Woodlawn Ave, Pasadena, 713-941-0088

Colasurdo, Giuseppe N. (3 mentions)
FMS-Italy, 1985 *Certification:* Pediatric Pulmonology
6410 Fannin St #500, Houston, 832-325-6516

Dahlberg, Carl G. Wolfe (5 mentions)
Baylor U, 1986 *Certification:* Critical Care Medicine, Internal Medicine, Pulmonary Disease
6624 Fannin St #1730, Houston, 713-255-4000

Doerr, Clinton Harold (3 mentions)
Baylor U, 1995
Certification: Critical Care Medicine, Pulmonary Disease
6624 Fannin St #1730, Houston, 713-255-4000

Gonzalez, Jorge Mario (7 mentions)
FMS-Guatemala, 1977 *Certification:* Critical Care Medicine, Internal Medicine, Pulmonary Disease
6550 Fannin St #2317, Houston, 713-790-9400

Herlihy, James Patrick (5 mentions)
Georgetown U, 1984 *Certification:* Critical Care Medicine, Internal Medicine, Pulmonary Disease
6624 Fannin St #1730, Houston, 713-255-4000

Kawley, F. Adam (3 mentions)
Certification: Critical Care Medicine, Internal Medicine, Pulmonary Disease
920 Frostwood Dr #620, Houston, 713-461-4333

Kochar, Harmohinder Singh (3 mentions)
FMS-India, 1978 *Certification:* Critical Care Medicine, Internal Medicine, Pulmonary Disease
1631 North Loop W #600, Houston, 713-863-0902

Lunn, William Wilburn, II (3 mentions)
U of Texas-Dallas, 1990 *Certification:* Critical Care Medicine, Internal Medicine, Pulmonary Disease
6620 Main St, Houston, 713-798-2500

Manian, Prasad (6 mentions)
FMS-India, 1986 *Certification:* Critical Care Medicine, Internal Medicine, Pulmonary Disease, Sleep Medicine
6624 Fannin St #1730, Houston, 713-255-4000

Pirtle, Philip L. (3 mentions)
U of Texas-Galveston, 1990 *Certification:* Critical Care Medicine, Internal Medicine, Pulmonary Disease
909 Graham Dr #B, Tomball, 281-357-0111

Reinoso, Mauricio A. (3 mentions)
FMS-Ecuador, 1984 *Certification:* Critical Care Medicine, Internal Medicine, Pulmonary Disease, Sleep Medicine
3521 Pown Center Blvd S, Sugar Land, 281-980-1330

Roman, Ana Estela (3 mentions)
FMS-Uruguay, 1977
6560 Fannin St #1406, Houston, 713-796-7200

Salcedo, Victor (4 mentions)
FMS-Mexico, 1978 *Certification:* Critical Care Medicine, Internal Medicine, Pulmonary Disease
7737 Southwest Frwy #570, Houston, 713-777-4217

Solis, Robert Thomas (8 mentions)
Yale U, 1965 *Certification:* Internal Medicine, Pulmonary Disease
6720 Bertner St, Houston, 713-791-2660

Stadnyk, Alexander Nestor (3 mentions)
FMS-Canada, 1981
Certification: Internal Medicine, Pulmonary Disease
6624 Fannin St #1450, Houston, 713-799-9916

Stein, David Alan (4 mentions)
New York Med Coll, 1975
Certification: Internal Medicine, Pulmonary Disease
4003 Woodlawn Ave, Pasadena, 713-941-0088

Toppell, Kenneth Lawrence (3 mentions)
Emory U, 1968
Certification: Internal Medicine, Pulmonary Disease
1213 Hermann Dr #570, Houston, 713-524-3900

Venkatesh, S. R. (5 mentions)
FMS-India, 1975 *Certification:* Critical Care Medicine, Internal Medicine, Pulmonary Disease
11307 W FM 1960 #100, Houston, 281-955-0338

Vodnala, Srinivas (5 mentions)
FMS-India, 1994 *Certification:* Critical Care Medicine, Internal Medicine, Pulmonary Disease
11307 W FM 1960 #100, Houston, 281-955-0338

Walker, Brian D. (3 mentions)
FMS-United Kingdom, 1971 *Certification:* Internal Medicine, Pulmonary Disease, Medical Oncology
6624 Fannin St #1730, Houston, 713-255-4000

Radiology—Diagnostic

Abdo, George Joe (4 mentions)
U of Texas-Galveston, 1967 *Certification:* Diagnostic Radiology
800 Peakwood Dr #5-E, Houston, 281-440-5158

Brady, Jett R. (3 mentions)
U of Texas-Houston, 1991 *Certification:* Diagnostic Radiology
12951 South Frwy, Houston, 713-526-5771

De Santos, Luis Alonso (3 mentions)
FMS-Spain, 1969 *Certification:* Diagnostic Radiology
1415 S Loop W, Houston, 713-861-8200

Gillespie, John Charles (3 mentions)
U of Louisville, 1979 *Certification:* Diagnostic Radiology
3120 Southwest Frwy #530, Houston, 713-627-9729

Nisbet, John J. (3 mentions)
Baylor U, 1995
Certification: Diagnostic Radiology, Neuroradiology
12951 South Frwy, Houston, 713-526-5771

Sax, Steven Lawrence (3 mentions)
Baylor U, 1981 *Certification:* Diagnostic Radiology
6565 Fannin St, Houston, 713-394-6795

Shah, Yogesh P. (3 mentions)
FMS-India, 1977 *Certification:* Diagnostic Radiology
7600 Fannin St, Houston, 713-779-1387
2800 S Macgregor Way, Houston, 713-791-7115
5304 Pocahontas St, Bellaire, 713-791-7115

Venta, Luz A. (3 mentions)
U of Chicago, 1983 *Certification:* Diagnostic Radiology
6550 Fannin St #SM-749, Houston, 713-441-5097

Willis, James Patrick (3 mentions)
U of Wisconsin, 1993 *Certification:* Diagnostic Radiology
12951 South Frwy, Houston, 713-526-5771

Radiology—Therapeutic

Behar, Robert Alexander (3 mentions)
U of Chicago, 1987 *Certification:* Radiation Oncology
1216 NW Frwy, Cypress, 281-517-9544

Brady, Jett R. (3 mentions)
U of Texas-Houston, 1991 *Certification:* Diagnostic Radiology
12951 South Frwy, Houston, 713-526-5771

Buchholz, Thomas Arthur (3 mentions)
Tufts U, 1988 *Certification:* Radiation Oncology
1515 Holcombe Blvd #97, Houston, 713-792-6161

Katz, Philip Bernard (3 mentions)
New York Med Coll, 1977 *Certification:* Diagnostic Radiology, Vascular & Interventional Radiology
800 Peakwood Dr #5-E, Houston, 281-440-5158

King, Karl (3 mentions)
Washington U, 1985
Certification: Internal Medicine, Radiation Oncology
15500 South West Frwy, Sugar Land, 281-274-8200

Mawad, Michel Elie (6 mentions)
FMS-Lebanon, 1976
Certification: Diagnostic Radiology, Neuroradiology
6720 bertner #MC-4-267, Houston, 832-355-7788
6565 Fannin St, Houston, 713-790-2001

Shkedy, Clive I. (3 mentions)
FMS-South Africa, 1987 *Certification:* Radiation Oncology
909 Frostwood Dr #152, Houston, 713-932-3500

Teh, Bin Sing (4 mentions)
Certification: Radiation Oncology
6565 Fannin St, Houston, 713-441-4800

Woo, Shiao Yuo (3 mentions)
FMS-Malaysia, 1972 *Certification:* Pediatric Hematology-Oncology, Pediatrics, Radiation Oncology
1515 Holcombe Blvd, Houston, 713-563-2300

Rehabilitation

Chan, Andy Sungkin (3 mentions)
Boston U, 1998 *Certification:* Physical Medicine & Rehabilitation
8325 Broadway #202-93, Pairland, 713-535-3999

Cianca, John Christopher (3 mentions)
Albany Med Coll, 1988
Certification: Physical Medicine & Rehabilitation, Sports Medicine
3440 Richmond Ave, Houston, 713-627-3156

Donovan, William Henry (3 mentions)
Albany Med Coll, 1966
Certification: Physical Medicine & Rehabilitation
1333 Moursund St, Houston, 713-799-5000

Garden, Fae Greenberg (4 mentions)
Cornell U, 1985 *Certification:* Physical Medicine & Rehabilitation
6624 Fannin St #2330, Houston, 713-798-4061

Kaldis, Teresa P. (5 mentions)
U of Texas-Houston, 1995 *Certification:* Internal Medicine,
Physical Medicine & Rehabilitation
6550 Fannin St #2500, Houston, 713-441-6391

Kevorkian, Charles George (11 mentions)
FMS-Australia, 1973
Certification: Physical Medicine & Rehabilitation
6624 Fannin St #2330, Houston, 713-798-4061

Rosenblatt, Michael Jay (3 mentions)
Rosalind Franklin U, 1989
Certification: Physical Medicine & Rehabilitation
655 E Medical Center Blvd, Webster, 281-218-8797

Rheumatology

Arnett, Frank C., Jr. (11 mentions)
U of Cincinnati, 1968 *Certification:* Diagnostic Laboratory
Immunology, Internal Medicine, Rheumatology
6410 Fannin St #600, Houston, 832-325-7191

Jones, Holly June (6 mentions)
U of Toledo, 1992
7515 S Main St #670, Houston, 713-795-0500

McCain, Angela (7 mentions)
U of Texas-Houston, 1984
Certification: Internal Medicine, Rheumatology
16659 South West Frwy #235, Sugar Land, 281-980-2717

Pegram, Samuel Bruce (6 mentions)
Ohio State U, 1980 *Certification:* Internal Medicine
4825 Almeda Rd, Houston, 713-521-7865

Rubin, Richard Alan (17 mentions)
Baylor U, 1984 *Certification:* Internal Medicine
7515 S Main St #670, Houston, 713-795-0500

Sessoms, Sandra Lee (28 mentions)
Baylor U, 1978 *Certification:* Internal Medicine, Rheumatology
6550 Fannin St #2500, Houston, 713-441-3980

Waller, Philip Alan (5 mentions)
Loyola U Chicago, 1988
Certification: Internal Medicine, Rheumatology
12553 Gulf Frwy, Houston, 281-481-8557

Thoracic Surgery

Blackmon, Shanda Jo (5 mentions)
Morehouse Coll, 1998 *Certification:* Surgery, Thoracic Surgery
6550 Fannin St #1661, Houston, 713-441-5155

Khalil, Kamal Ghaleb (6 mentions)
FMS-Egypt, 1961
Certification: Surgery, Thoracic Surgery, Vascular Surgery
6410 Fannin St #480, Houston, 832-325-7600

Noon, George Paul (6 mentions)
Baylor U, 1960 *Certification:* Surgery, Thoracic Surgery
6560 Fannin St #1860, Houston, 713-790-3155

Reardon, Michael Joseph (7 mentions)
Baylor U, 1978 *Certification:* Thoracic Surgery
6560 Fannin St #1006, Houston, 713-441-5200

Reardon, Patrick Ray (7 mentions)
Baylor U, 1983 *Certification:* Surgery
6550 Fannin St #2435, Houston, 713-790-3140

Urology

Anhalt, Melvyn Alan (4 mentions)
U of Alabama, 1964 *Certification:* Urology
915 Gessner Rd #720, Houston, 713-830-9100

Axelrad, Samuel Donald (4 mentions)
U of Texas-Galveston, 1964 *Certification:* Urology
7777 Southwest Frwy #1032, Houston, 713-771-9224

Boone, Timothy B. (5 mentions)
U of Texas-Houston, 1985 *Certification:* Urology
6560 Fannin St #2100, Houston, 713-798-4001

Coburn, Michael (5 mentions)
New York U, 1982 *Certification:* Urology
6560 Fannin St #2100, Houston, 713-798-3498
6620 Main St #1325, Houston, 713-798-4001

Delhey, Karen Ann (5 mentions)
U of Michigan, 1986 *Certification:* Urology
6560 Fannin St #1900, Houston, 713-791-9900

Fishman, Irving Joshua (5 mentions)
FMS-Canada, 1971 *Certification:* Urology
6624 Fannin St #1980, Houston, 713-790-1800

Flores-Sandoval, Felipe N. (4 mentions)
FMS-Guatemala, 1973 *Certification:* Urology
6624 Fannin St #2280, Houston, 713-799-8896

Goldfarb, Richard Alan (9 mentions)
Baylor U, 1977 *Certification:* Urology
6560 Fannin St #1440, Houston, 713-790-9700

Gonzales, Edmond T., Jr. (4 mentions)
Tulane U, 1965 *Certification:* Pediatric Urology, Urology
6701 Fannin St #660, Houston, 832-822-3160

Hurwitz, Gary Stephen (4 mentions)
U of Texas-Dallas, 1984 *Certification:* Urology
3333 Bayshore Blvd #340, Pasadena, 713-910-9428

Lapin, Stephen L. (12 mentions)
Baylor U, 1986 *Certification:* Urology
6560 Fannin St #1440, Houston, 713-790-9700

Lewitton, Michael (4 mentions)
Columbia U, 1994 *Certification:* Urology
6560 Fannin St #1440, Houston, 713-790-9700

Lipshultz, Larry I. (5 mentions)
U of Pennsylvania, 1968 *Certification:* Urology
6560 Fannin St #2100, Houston, 713-798-4001
6560 Fannin St #1402, Houston, 713-798-6163

McDonald, Robert Emmett (5 mentions)
U of Texas-Dallas, 1978 *Certification:* Urology
1740 W 27th St #315, Houston, 713-864-0533
2724 Yale St, Houston, 713-861-9990

Miles, Brian John (12 mentions)
U of Michigan, 1974 *Certification:* Urology
6560 Fannin St #2100, Houston, 713-798-4001
6624 Fannin St #2280, Houston, 713-798-5137
7026 Old Katy Rd #276, Houston, 713-621-7436

Nickell, Kevin G. (6 mentions)
U of Texas-Houston, 1989 *Certification:* Urology
7777 Southwest Frwy #1032, Houston, 713-771-9224

Powers, Brian Coyne (6 mentions)
Baylor U, 1977 *Certification:* Urology
6560 Fannin St #1270, Houston, 713-790-9779

Roth, David Robert (4 mentions)
U of Southern California, 1978
Certification: Pediatric Urology, Urology
6701 Fannin St, Houston, 832-822-3160

Schiffman, Zvi Jacob (4 mentions)
FMS-Israel, 1974 *Certification:* Urology
7777 Southwest Frwy #1032, Houston, 713-771-9224

Selzman, Andrew A. (4 mentions)
U of Texas-San Antonio, 1989 *Certification:* Urology
915 Gessner Rd #720, Houston, 713-830-9100

Sutton, Mark Allen (4 mentions)
U of Washington, 1992 *Certification:* Urology
6560 Fannin St #1270, Houston, 713-790-9779

Vascular Surgery

Khalil, Kamal Ghaleb (6 mentions)
FMS-Egypt, 1961
Certification: Surgery, Thoracic Surgery, Vascular Surgery
6410 Fannin St #480, Houston, 832-325-7600

Ott, David Alan (8 mentions)
Baylor U, 1972 *Certification:* Thoracic Surgery
1101 Bates Ave #P-514, Houston, 832-355-4917
6720 Bertner St, Houston, 832-355-4917

Rosenberg, Wade Ronald (7 mentions)
U of Texas-Houston, 1981 *Certification:* Surgery
6560 Fannin St #1402, Houston, 713-790-4830

San Antonio Area
Including Bexar County

Allergy/Immunology

Diaz, Joseph David (17 mentions)
U of Texas-Galveston, 1983
Certification: Allergy & Immunology, Internal Medicine
2414 Babcock Rd #109, San Antonio, 210-616-0882
525 Oak Centre Dr #400, San Antonio, 210-490-1400

Dilley, Dennis E. (6 mentions)
U of Texas-San Antonio, 1995
Certification: Allergy & Immunology, Pediatrics
7711 Louis Pasteur Dr #407, San Antonio, 210-614-4405

Gupta, Priyanka (6 mentions)
Michigan State U, 1999
Certification: Allergy & Immunology, Internal Medicine
705 Landa St #F, New Braunfels, 830-609-0998
12501 Judson Rd #202, San Antonio, 830-609-0998

Jacobs, Robert Lee (9 mentions)
U of Alabama, 1968
Certification: Allergy & Immunology, Internal Medicine
999 E Basse Rd #103, San Antonio, 210-821-6697
8285 Fredericksburg Rd, San Antonio, 210-614-3923

Laham, Michel Nicolas (6 mentions)
U of Florida, 1971
Certification: Allergy & Immunology, Internal Medicine
1303 McCullough Ave #161, San Antonio, 210-226-3500

Ramirez, Daniel Alberto (6 mentions)
U of Puerto Rico, 1973
Certification: Allergy & Immunology, Internal Medicine
8287 Fredericksburg Rd, San Antonio, 210-692-0634
999 E Basse Rd #112, San Antonio, 210-821-6697
8285 Fredericksburg Rd, San Antonio, 210-614-3923

Vaughn, Adrianne Dewalt (6 mentions)
104 Gallery Cir #126, San Antonio, 210-499-0033

Wood, Dale Allen (12 mentions)
U of Texas-Dallas, 1969 *Certification:* Pediatrics
341 E Hildebrand Ave, San Antonio, 210-826-6141

Anesthesiology

Day, Randall Wayne (4 mentions)
U of New Mexico, 1990 *Certification:* Anesthesiology
4242 Medical Dr #3100, San Antonio, 210-615-1197

Ellis, Jay S., Jr. (3 mentions)
Uniformed Services U of Health Sciences, 1982
Certification: Anesthesiology, Pain Medicine
4499 Medical Dr #393, San Antonio, 210-615-1187
4242 Medical Dr #3100, San Antonio, 210-615-1187

Harle, Mark Allan (4 mentions)
Texas Tech U, 1986 *Certification:* Anesthesiology
4242 Medical Dr #3100, San Antonio, 210-615-1187

Kercheville, Scott Eugene (5 mentions)
U of Texas-Galveston, 1983 *Certification:* Anesthesiology
7703 FLoyd Curl Dr #7838, San Antonio, 210-567-4500

Limon, David Thomas (4 mentions)
U of Minnesota, 1984 *Certification:* Anesthesiology
4242 Medical Dr #3100, San Antonio, 210-615-1197

Pollard, Trevor Gordon (3 mentions)
U of Texas-Galveston, 1980
Certification: Anesthesiology, Pediatrics
4242 Medical Dr #3100, San Antonio, 210-615-1187

Rasch, Deborah Kay (5 mentions)
U of Texas-Galveston, 1978
Certification: Anesthesiology, Pediatrics
7703 Floyd Curl Dr, San Antonio, 210-615-1197

Richardson, John S. (3 mentions)
U of Texas-Galveston, 1975 *Certification:* Anesthesiology
7703 Floyd Curl Dr #7838, San Antonio, 210-567-4503

Sharp, William T. (3 mentions)
U of Texas-Galveston, 1986 *Certification:* Anesthesiology
4242 Medical Dr #3100, San Antonio, 210-615-1187

Cardiac Surgery

Calhoon, John H. (17 mentions)
Baylor U, 1981 *Certification:* Surgery, Thoracic Surgery
7703 Floyd Curl Dr, San Antonio, 210-567-7000

Davis, William Michael (18 mentions)
Baylor U, 1984 *Certification:* Surgery, Thoracic Surgery
4330 Medical Dr #325, San Antonio, 210-615-7700

Garrison, James R., Jr. (13 mentions)
Texas Tech U, 1990 *Certification:* Surgery, Thoracic Surgery
4330 Medical Dr #325, San Antonio, 210-615-7700

Hamner, Lawrence R., III (18 mentions)
U of Texas-Dallas, 1981 *Certification:* Thoracic Surgery
4330 Medical Dr #325, San Antonio, 210-615-7700

Otero, Carmelo (8 mentions)
U of Puerto Rico, 1981 *Certification:* Thoracic Surgery
4330 Medical Dr #275, San Antonio, 210-615-6626

Smith, J. Marvin, III (14 mentions)
Tulane U, 1972 *Certification:* Surgery, Thoracic Surgery
6800 IH10 W #300, San Antonio, 210-616-0008

Zorrilla-Rios, Leopoldo (10 mentions)
FMS-Mexico, 1965 *Certification:* Surgery, Thoracic Surgery
4330 Medical Dr #325, San Antonio, 210-615-7700

Cardiology

Alvarez, Jorge A. (4 mentions)
U of Texas-San Antonio, 2000 *Certification:* Cardiovascular
Disease, Internal Medicine, Interventional Cardiology
4411 Medical Dr #300, San Antonio, 210-614-5400

Bailey, Steven Roderick (7 mentions)
Oregon Health Sciences U, 1978 *Certification:* Cardiovascular
Disease, Internal Medicine, Interventional Cardiology
7703 Floyd Curl Dr, San Antonio, 210-567-4601
4647 Medical Dr, San Antonio, 210-592-0400

Eades, Thomas William (4 mentions)
U of Tennessee, 1969 *Certification:* Cardiovascular Disease,
Internal Medicine, Interventional Cardiology
1200 Brooklyn Ave #200, San Antonio, 210-225-4566

Garza, Ricardo A. (4 mentions)
U of Texas-Dallas, 1984
Certification: Cardiovascular Disease, Internal Medicine
7711 Louis Pasteur Dr, San Antonio, 210-614-6391

Glasow, Patrick Francis (5 mentions)
Med U of South Carolina, 1978
Certification: Pediatric Cardiology, Pediatrics
1901 Babcock Rd #301, San Antonio, 210-341-7722

James, Kevin Frank (5 mentions)
Baylor U, 1978
Certification: Cardiovascular Disease, Internal Medicine
1933 NE Loop #410, San Antonio, 210-804-6000
12709 Toepperwein Rd #308, San Antonio, 210-599-2020

Koppes, Gerald Max (7 mentions)
U of Kansas, 1972 *Certification:* Cardiovascular Disease,
Internal Medicine, Interventional Cardiology
1303 McCullough Ave #300, San Antonio, 210-270-2992
19276 Stone Oak Pkwy, San Antonio, 210-270-2992

Lopez, Fernando (5 mentions)
Stanford U, 1992
Certification: Cardiovascular Disease, Internal Medicine
7711 Louis Pasteur Dr, San Antonio, 210-614-6391

Mulrow, John Patrick (7 mentions)
New York Med Coll, 1978 *Certification:* Cardiovascular
Disease, Internal Medicine, Interventional Cardiology
4411 Medical Dr #300, San Antonio, 210-614-5400

Rabinowitz, Abram Charles (5 mentions)
U of Texas-San Antonio, 1975 *Certification:* Cardiovascular
Disease, Internal Medicine, Interventional Cardiology
4330 Medical Dr #500, San Antonio, 210-692-1414
701 Water St #402, Kerrville, 830-896-3730
409 Madrid St, Castroville, 830-937-2575

Rogers, James Henry, Jr. (5 mentions)
Med Coll of Georgia, 1971
Certification: Pediatric Cardiology, Pediatrics
1901 Babcock Rd #301, San Antonio, 210-341-7722

Schnitzler, Robert N. (15 mentions)
U of Buffalo, 1965
Certification: Cardiovascular Disease, Internal Medicine
4330 Medical Dr #400, San Antonio, 210-615-0600

Seaworth, John Fortune (5 mentions)
Washington U, 1976
Certification: Cardiovascular Disease, Internal Medicine
1933 NE Loop 410, San Antonio, 210-804-6000

Triana, Jose Fernando (5 mentions)
FMS-Colombia, 1983 *Certification:* Cardiovascular Disease,
Internal Medicine, Interventional Cardiology
4411 Medical Dr #300, San Antonio, 210-614-5400

White, David Hopkins (5 mentions)
U of Texas-San Antonio, 1972
Certification: Cardiovascular Disease, Internal Medicine
4330 Medical Dr #200, San Antonio, 210-616-0801
109 Falls Ct #300, Boerne, 830-249-1700

Wilks, Richard Frederick (4 mentions)
U of Buffalo, 1986
Certification: Cardiovascular Disease, Internal Medicine
1933 NE Loop 410, San Antonio, 210-804-6000

Wu, William Chien Lin (7 mentions)
FMS-Taiwan, 1982 *Certification:* Cardiovascular Disease,
Internal Medicine, Interventional Cardiology
6800 IH 10 W #200, San Antonio, 210-271-3203

Zinn, Philip D. (8 mentions)
U of Texas-Dallas, 1982
Certification: Cardiovascular Disease, Internal Medicine
4411 Medical Dr #300, San Antonio, 210-614-5400

Dermatology

Beightler, Eloise Lizzie (4 mentions)
U of Texas-Galveston, 1986 *Certification:* Dermatology
18540 Sigma Rd, San Antonio, 210-490-4661

Duncan, Scott Cullers (10 mentions)
U of Texas-San Antonio, 1972 *Certification:* Dermatology
999 E Basse Rd #105, San Antonio, 210-824-7001

Furner, Bonnie J. Baird (9 mentions)
U of Texas-San Antonio, 1983 *Certification:* Dermatology
8122 Datapoint Dr #1110, San Antonio, 210-616-0448

Gonzalez, John J. (5 mentions)
U of Texas-San Antonio, 1976 *Certification:* Dermatology
2829 Babcock #629, San Antonio, 210-615-8460

Henslee, Scott M. (9 mentions)
U of Texas-San Antonio, 1998 *Certification:* Dermatology
7950 Floyd Curl Dr #909, San Antonio, 210-614-3575

Hughes, Philip Stuart H. (5 mentions)
U of Iowa, 1969 *Certification:* Dermatology
7940 Floyd Curl Dr #1010, San Antonio, 210-614-7411

Magnon, Robert Jay (10 mentions)
U of Texas-Galveston, 1976 *Certification:* Dermatology
1303 McCullough Ave #525, San Antonio, 210-225-2769
1255 Ashby St #B, Seguin, 830-372-1648

Ochs, Robert L. (4 mentions)
Certification: Dermatology
14855 Blanco Rd #214, San Antonio, 210-493-1568

Thompson, Gregory Wilkins (4 mentions)
U of Texas-Galveston, 1971 *Certification:* Dermatology
14615 San Pedro Ave #200, San Antonio, 210-494-5192
4242 E Southcross Blvd #17, San Antonio, 210-333-8902

Tichy, Elizabeth Hughes (4 mentions)
U of Texas-San Antonio, 2001 *Certification:* Dermatology
7940 Floyd Curl Dr #1010, San Antonio, 210-617-5585

Vela, Raul, III (4 mentions)
Baylor U, 1984 *Certification:* Dermatology
7950 Floyd Curl Dr #909, San Antonio, 210-614-3575

Weinstein, Mark Berton (12 mentions)
U of Texas-San Antonio, 1973 *Certification:* Dermatology
7950 Floyd Curl #909, San Antonio, 210-614-3575
999 E Basse Rd #127, San Antonio, 210-614-3575

Emergency Medicine

Bates, Brian A. (3 mentions)
U of Texas-San Antonio, 1987
Certification: Pediatric Emergency Medicine, Pediatrics
7700 Floyd Curl Dr, San Antonio, 210-575-4444

Baynton, Barr L. (3 mentions)
U of Oklahoma, 1978 *Certification:* Emergency Medicine
7700 Floyd Curl Dr, San Antonio, 210-575-4444

Gerstenkorn, Craig Bruce (3 mentions)
U of Minnesota, 1987 *Certification:* Emergency Medicine
7700 Floyd Curl Dr, San Antonio, 210-575-4444

Guerrero, Martin G. (3 mentions)
FMS-Mexico, 1981
33 N Santa Rosa St, San Antonio, 210-704-2880

Guz, Evan Craig (3 mentions)
U of Michigan, 1991 *Certification:* Emergency Medicine
16414 San Pedro Ave #355, San Antonio, 210-495-9860

Hartsell, Floyd Wright (6 mentions)
Certification: Emergency Medicine
8401 Datapoint Dr #130, San Antonio, 210-614-0180

Row, James Michael (3 mentions)
U of Alabama, 1978 *Certification:* Emergency Medicine
7700 Floyd Curl Dr, San Antonio, 210-575-4444

Scribbick, Arie T. (3 mentions)
Certification: Emergency Medicine
8401 Datapoint Dr #500, San Antonio, 210-614-0180

Taylor, Tim (3 mentions)
Texas Tech U, 1998 *Certification:* Emergency Medicine
16414 San Pedro Ave #355, San Antonio, 210-495-9860

Endocrinology

Akright, Laura Elizabeth (9 mentions)
Washington U, 1980
Certification: Endocrinology and Metabolism, Internal Medicine
8715 Village Dr #508, San Antonio, 210-650-3360

Becker, Richard Arthur (10 mentions)
U of Texas-San Antonio, 1971
Certification: Endocrinology and Metabolism, Internal Medicine
1303 McCullough Ave #374, San Antonio, 210-223-5483

Cruz, Jaime Oscar (7 mentions)
Tufts U, 1985 *Certification:* Endocrinology, Diabetes, and
Metabolism, Internal Medicine
215 E Quincy St #319, San Antonio, 210-946-2520
155 E Sonterra Blvd #105, San Antonio, 210-946-2520

Fetchick, Dianne Marie (7 mentions)
U of Miami, 1980
Certification: Endocrinology and Metabolism, Internal Medicine
8715 Village Dr #508, San Antonio, 210-650-3360

Fischer, Jerome S. (11 mentions)
Jefferson Med Coll, 1977
Certification: Endocrinology and Metabolism, Internal Medicine
5107 Medical Dr, San Antonio, 210-614-8612

Garza, Ramon (5 mentions)
FMS-Dominican Republic, 1986 *Certification:* Endocrinology,
Diabetes, and Metabolism, Internal Medicine
155 E Sonterra Blvd #105, San Antonio, 210-946-2520

Kipnes, Mark Steven (6 mentions)
Hahnemann U, 1979
Certification: Endocrinology and Metabolism, Internal Medicine
5107 Medical Dr, San Antonio, 210-614-8612

Menendez, Carlos Eugenio (10 mentions)
Columbia U, 1969
Certification: Endocrinology and Metabolism, Internal Medicine
4499 Medical Dr #226, San Antonio, 210-692-7684
711 Lehman Dr, Kerrville, 830-257-5733

Schwartz, Sherwyn Leon (8 mentions)
U of Illinois, 1972
Certification: Endocrinology and Metabolism, Internal Medicine
5107 Medical Dr, San Antonio, 210-614-8612

Uy, Harry Lim (8 mentions)
FMS-Philippines, 1986 *Certification:* Endocrinology,
Diabetes, and Metabolism, Internal Medicine
1303 McCullough Ave #374, San Antonio, 210-223-5483

Vadakekalam, Jacob (5 mentions)
FMS-India, 1981 *Certification:* Endocrinology, Diabetes,
and Metabolism, Internal Medicine
5107 Medical Dr, San Antonio, 210-614-8612

Welch, Michelle Dawn (6 mentions)
Albany Med Coll, 1997 *Certification:* Endocrinology,
Diabetes, and Metabolism, Internal Medicine
540 Madison Oak Dr #400, San Antonio, 210-494-3739

Family Practice *(see note on page 9)*

Baros, James Albert, Jr. (3 mentions)
Texas Tech U, 1983
19276 Stone Oak Pkwy #102, San Antonio, 210-494-7172

Bocanegra, Javier C. (3 mentions)
U of Texas-San Antonio, 1986 *Certification:* Family Medicine
1616 Callaghan Rd, San Antonio, 210-435-1218

Comfort, Kevin Patrick (3 mentions)
U of Washington, 1980 *Certification:* Family Medicine
8715 Village Dr #510, San Antonio, 210-637-0000

Heller, Kimberly Koester (5 mentions)
U of Texas-San Antonio, 1985 *Certification:* Family Medicine
4318 Woodcock Dr #120, San Antonio, 210-735-5225

Horn, Curtis Scott (5 mentions)
U of Texas-San Antonio, 1979 *Certification:* Family Medicine
303 W Sunset Rd #101, San Antonio, 210-824-5201

Kuebker, Craig William (3 mentions)
U of Texas-San Antonio, 1981 *Certification:* Family Medicine
9480 Huebner Rd #100, San Antonio, 210-614-8831

Mueller, Francis William (4 mentions)
Texas Tech U, 1983 *Certification:* Family Medicine
9480 Huebner Rd #100, San Antonio, 210-614-8090

Ramirez, Stephen F. (3 mentions)
U of Texas-Houston, 1995
109 Gallery Cir #131, San Antonio, 210-490-5100

Richmond, George M., Jr. (8 mentions)
U of Texas-San Antonio, 1984 *Certification:* Family Medicine
1303 McCullough Ave #135, San Antonio, 210-227-9214

Shimotsu, Karen S. (5 mentions)
U of Texas-Dallas, 1986 *Certification:* Family Medicine
14855 Blanco Rd #204, San Antonio, 210-493-5330

Gastroenterology

Chumley, Delbert Lee (14 mentions)
U of Texas-Galveston, 1971
Certification: Gastroenterology, Internal Medicine
8214 Wurzbach Rd, San Antonio, 210-614-1234

Dar, Seema A. (5 mentions)
FMS-India, 1986 *Certification:* Gastroenterology
3338 Oakwell Ct #205, San Antonio, 210-656-3715

Flores, Eddie (5 mentions)
U of Texas-Dallas, 1989 *Certification:* Gastroenterology
520 E Euclid Ave, San Antonio, 210-271-0606

Garza, Homero Remedios (6 mentions)
Harvard U, 1976
Certification: Gastroenterology, Internal Medicine
7950 Floyd Curl Dr #805, San Antonio, 210-692-0707

Guerra, Ernesto, Jr. (5 mentions)
U of California-San Diego, 1976
Certification: Gastroenterology, Internal Medicine
520 E Euclid Ave, San Antonio, 210-271-0606

Havranek, Russell Dean (8 mentions)
U of Nebraska, 1998
Certification: Gastroenterology, Internal Medicine
8550 Datapoint Dr #LL100, San Antonio, 210-615-8308
1009 S Miliam #100, Fredericksburg, 210-615-8308
5307 Broadway #110, San Antonio, 210-615-8308

Hearne, Steven Eric (9 mentions)
Baylor U, 1984 *Certification:* Gastroenterology, Internal Medicine
112709 Toepperwein Rd #301, San Antonio, 210-828-8400

Kadakia, Shailesh C. (8 mentions)
FMS-India, 1973
Certification: Gastroenterology, Internal Medicine
225 E Sonterra Blvd #215, San Antonio, 210-481-7477

Otero, Richard Luis (10 mentions)
U of Texas-Dallas, 1978
Certification: Gastroenterology, Internal Medicine
520 E Euclid Ave, San Antonio, 210-271-0606
4212 E Southcross Blvd #120, San Antonio, 210-923-6238

Pruitt, Alejandro (6 mentions)
Uniformed Services U of Health Sciences, 1993
Certification: Gastroenterology
8214 Wurzbach Rd, San Antonio, 210-614-1234

Ramos, Steven Ray (5 mentions)
Baylor U, 1980 *Certification:* Gastroenterology, Internal Medicine
520 E Euclid Ave, San Antonio, 210-271-0606
7333 Barlite Blvd #320, San Antonio, 210-271-0606

Stump, David Lee (7 mentions)
Indiana U, 1980
Certification: Gastroenterology, Internal Medicine
8550 Datapoint Dr #LL-100, San Antonio, 210-615-8308
1009 S Miliam Dr #100, Fredericksburg, 210-615-8308
5307 Broadway #110, San Antonio, 210-615-8308

Swan, John Thomas (6 mentions)
U of Texas-Galveston, 1980
Certification: Gastroenterology, Internal Medicine
8214 Wurzbach Rd, San Antonio, 210-614-1234

Theard, Joycelyn Marie (10 mentions)
Harvard U, 1977
Certification: Gastroenterology, Internal Medicine
8527 Village Dr #207, San Antonio, 210-656-3070
3338 Oakwell Ct #205, San Antonio, 210-656-3070

General Surgery

Abbate, Steven Michael (5 mentions)
Mayo Med Sch, 1996 *Certification:* Surgery
8038 Wurzbach Rd #210, San Antonio, 210-949-0650

Boone Valdez, Heliodoro (3 mentions)
FMS-Mexico, 1966
343 W Houston St #512, San Antonio, 210-225-4316

Bradshaw, William Hollis (3 mentions)
U of Texas-Houston, 1985 *Certification:* Surgery
8534 Village Dr #B, San Antonio, 210-654-6340

Cardenas, Michael Anthony (3 mentions)
U of Texas-Dallas, 1983 *Certification:* Surgery
8042 Wurzbach Rd #310, San Antonio, 210-614-5113

Dilworth, Donald David (7 mentions)
Certification: Surgery
8715 Village Dr #608, San Antonio, 210-657-2100

Etlinger, John E. (7 mentions)
Texas Tech U, 1975 *Certification:* Surgery
1303 McCullough Ave #235, San Antonio, 210-229-9290

Fischer, Richard Emil (9 mentions)
U of Texas-San Antonio, 1980 *Certification:* Surgery
12709 Toepperwein Rd #203, San Antonio, 210-653-9307
19016 Stone Oak Pkwy #210, San Antonio, 210-404-9950

Franklin, Morris E., Jr. (5 mentions)
U of Texas-Dallas, 1967 *Certification:* Surgery
4242 E Southcross Blvd #1, San Antonio, 210-333-7510

Glass, Jeffrey L. (3 mentions)
U of Texas-San Antonio, 1990 *Certification:* Surgery
4242 E Southcross Blvd #1, San Antonio, 210-333-7510
540 Madison Oak Dr #330, San Antonio, 210-333-7510

Hall, Gary Marvin (6 mentions)
U of Texas-Dallas, 1981 *Certification:* Surgery
12709 Toepperwein Rd #203, Live Oak, 210-653-9307
19016 Stone Oak Pkwy #210, San Antonio, 210-404-9958

Hollimon, Peter Wilson (6 mentions)
U of Texas-San Antonio, 1976 *Certification:* Surgery
8534 Village Dr #E, San Antonio, 210-654-4583

Jaso, Rene Gilbert (3 mentions)
Michigan State U, 1973 *Certification:* Internal Medicine, Surgery
1303 McCullough Ave #538, San Antonio, 210-226-5350

Johnston, Joe Eric (5 mentions)
U of Texas-San Antonio, 1997
Certification: Surgery, Surgical Critical Care
8042 Wurzbach Rd #310, San Antonio, 210-614-5113

Metersky, John B. (7 mentions)
U of Texas-San Antonio, 1996 *Certification:* Surgery
7950 Floyd Curl Dr #810, San Antonio, 210-614-7300

Mimari, George Edward (14 mentions)
U of Texas-Galveston, 1973 *Certification:* Surgery
8042 Wurzbach Rd #630, San Antonio, 210-614-5067

Mullins, David C. (6 mentions)
U of Texas-Dallas, 1988 *Certification:* Surgery
7950 Floyd Curl Dr #700, San Antonio, 210-614-3388

Oliver, Boyce Boyd, Jr. (10 mentions)
U of Texas-Galveston, 1970 *Certification:* Surgery
1303 McCullough Ave #235, San Antonio, 210-225-1916

Pilcher, John Alsop, Jr. (3 mentions)
U of Virginia, 1990 *Certification:* Surgery
9150 Huebrer Rd #250, San Antonio, 210-614-3370

Rittenhouse, Mark Charles (3 mentions)
U of Oklahoma, 1970 *Certification:* Surgery
7940 Floyd Curl Dr #840, San Antonio, 210-614-3349

Robinson, Douglas W. (10 mentions)
U of Texas-Galveston, 1973 *Certification:* Surgery
8042 Wurzbach Rd #310, San Antonio, 210-614-5113

Rosenthal, Arthur (15 mentions)
Hahnemann U, 1969 *Certification:* Surgery
8042 Wurzbach Rd #480, San Antonio, 210-616-0657

Stewart, Ronald Mack (5 mentions)
U of Texas-San Antonio, 1985
Certification: Surgery, Surgical Critical Care
7703 Floyd Curl Dr, San Antonio, 210-567-3623

Tramer, Jonathan O. (6 mentions)
Case Western Reserve U, 1969 *Certification:* Surgery
8042 Wurzbach Rd #310, San Antonio, 210-614-5113

Woodard, Russell Lynn (12 mentions)
U of Tennessee, 1988 *Certification:* Surgery
8042 Wurzbach Rd #310, San Antonio, 210-614-5113

Geriatrics

Garcia, Paul D. (3 mentions)
U of Texas-Houston, 1987
Certification: Geriatric Medicine, Internal Medicine
6218 NW Loop 410, San Antonio, 210-523-1411

Lichtenstein, Michael Joseph (5 mentions)
Baylor U, 1978
Certification: Geriatric Medicine, Internal Medicine
4647 Medical Dr, San Antonio, 210-592-0150

Moszkowicz, Marvin Rene (3 mentions)
FMS-Mexico, 1975
5282 Medical Dr #312, San Antonio, 210-699-3815

Hematology/Oncology

Dice, Y. Gia (11 mentions)
Hahnemann U, 1994
Certification: Hematology, Internal Medicine, Medical Oncology
4411 Medical Dr #100, San Antonio, 210-595-5300

Drengler, Ronald L. (6 mentions)
FMS-Paraguay, 1988 *Certification:* Medical Oncology
7979 Wurzbach Rd #Z-325, San Antonio, 210-593-5700

Fichtel, Lisa Meyer (5 mentions)
U of Texas-Dallas, 1991 *Certification:* Medical Oncology
155 E Sonterra Blvd #200, San Antonio, 210-404-0606

Gordon, David Hugh (5 mentions)
Case Western Reserve U, 1971
Certification: Hematology, Internal Medicine, Medical Oncology
540 Madison Oak Dr #200, San Antonio, 210-545-6972
2130 NE Loop 410 #100, San Antonio, 210-656-7177

Guzley, Gregory Joseph (12 mentions)
Baylor U, 1978
Certification: Hematology, Internal Medicine, Medical Oncology
4411 Medical Dr #100, San Antonio, 210-595-5300

Holahan, Joseph Richard (5 mentions)
U of Florida, 1973 *Certification:* Hematology, Internal Medicine
7979 Wurzbach Rd, San Antonio, 210-616-5700

Kalter, Steven Paul (12 mentions)
Baylor U, 1978
Certification: Hematology, Internal Medicine, Medical Oncology
7979 Wurzbach Rd, San Antonio, 210-616-5700

Kapoor, Rohit (5 mentions)
FMS-India, 1982
Certification: Internal Medicine, Medical Oncology
12602 Toepperwein Rd #202, San Antonio, 210-655-0075

Lang, Amy Solomon (4 mentions)
U of Texas-San Antonio, 1991 *Certification:* Medical Oncology
7979 Wurzbach Rd, San Antonio, 210-616-5700

Lyons, Roger Michael (14 mentions)
FMS-Canada, 1967 *Certification:* Hematology, Internal Medicine
4411 Medical Dr #100, San Antonio, 210-595-5300

Medellin, Jesse Earl (5 mentions)
U of Texas-Galveston, 1989 *Certification:* Medical Oncology
1200 Brooklyn Ave #115, San Antonio, 210-224-6531

Patel, Mahendra C. (8 mentions)
FMS-Zambia, 1981 *Certification:* Pediatrics
7711 Louis Pasteur Dr #502, San Antonio, 210-614-9973

Santiago, Manuel Antonio (7 mentions)
U of Puerto Rico, 1986
Certification: Hematology, Internal Medicine
4411 Medical Dr #100, San Antonio, 210-595-5300

Smith, Lon Shelby (8 mentions)
Louisiana State U-Shreveport, 1979
Certification: Internal Medicine, Medical Oncology
7979 Wurzbach Rd #Z325, San Antonio, 210-616-5700
155 E Sonterra Blvd #200, San Antonio, 210-616-5700

Ulmer, Scott Christopher (4 mentions)
Oregon Health Sciences U, 1996
Certification: Hematology, Internal Medicine, Medical Oncology
8715 Village Dr, San Antonio, 210-593-5600
155 E Sonterra Blvd #200, San Antonio, 210-404-0606

Wilks, Sharon Thomas (7 mentions)
Uniformed Services U of Health Sciences, 1986
Certification: Hematology, Internal Medicine, Medical Oncology
2130 NE Loop 410 #100, San Antonio, 210-637-0641

Infectious Disease

Cisneros, Luis A. (17 mentions)
FMS-Peru, 1975
Certification: Infectious Disease, Internal Medicine
343 W Houston St #808, San Antonio, 210-224-9616

De Witt, Caroline (13 mentions)
U of Texas-San Antonio, 1994
Certification: Infectious Disease, Internal Medicine
8042 Wurzbach Rd #280, San Antonio, 210-614-8100

Fetchick, Richard Joseph (40 mentions)
U of Miami, 1980
Certification: Infectious Disease, Internal Medicine
8042 Wurzbach Rd Physician's Plaza II #280, San Antonio,
  210-614-8100

Lerner, Charles Jay (10 mentions)
St Louis U, 1966 *Certification:* Internal Medicine
8042 Wurzbach Rd #280, San Antonio, 210-614-8100

Thorner, Richard Eric (21 mentions)
Harvard U, 1971
Certification: Infectious Disease, Internal Medicine
8042 Wurzbach Rd #280, San Antonio, 210-614-8100

Wood, Bruce Andrew (16 mentions)
Baylor U, 1979
Certification: Infectious Disease, Internal Medicine
8800 Village Dr #201, San Antonio, 210-656-3079

Zajac, Robert Alan (11 mentions)
Louisiana State U, 1981
Certification: Infectious Disease, Internal Medicine
150 E Sonterra #170, San Antonio, 210-481-2800
343-W Houston St #306, San Antonio, 210-212-4595

Infertility

Martin, Joseph Edward (10 mentions)
U of Texas-Galveston, 1963 *Certification:* Obstetrics & Gynecology
4499 Medical Dr #200, San Antonio, 210-692-0577

Neal, Gregory S. (6 mentions)
Texas A&M U, 1988 *Certification:* Obstetrics & Gynecology,
Reproductive Endocrinology/Infertility
4499 Medical Dr #200, San Antonio, 210-692-0577

Internal Medicine *(see note on page 9)*

Benson, Vernon Roger (3 mentions)
U of Minnesota, 1962 *Certification:* Internal Medicine
255 E Sonterra Blvd #100, San Antonio, 210-404-0000

Bergman, Randy Norman (3 mentions)
U of Miami, 1979 *Certification:* Internal Medicine
12602 Toepperwein Rd #100, San Antonio, 210-650-9669

Cawley, Carmen (3 mentions)
U of Texas-San Antonio, 1990 *Certification:* Internal Medicine
701 S Zarzamona St, San Antonio, 210-358-7575

Curry, Mitchell (3 mentions)
Ponce Sch of Med, 1993 *Certification:* Internal Medicine
21 Spurs Ln #230, San Antonio, 210-690-0202

Dickson, John E. (3 mentions)
U of Texas-Galveston, 1988 *Certification:* Internal Medicine
325 E Sonterra Blvd #200, San Antonio, 210-402-3069

Ford, George Almond, III (6 mentions)
U of Virginia, 1976 *Certification:* Internal Medicine
225 E Sonterra Blvd #100, San Antonio, 210-404-0000

Galan, John P. (6 mentions)
U of Texas-San Antonio, 1995 *Certification:* Internal Medicine
7210 Louis Pasteur Dr #100, San Antonio, 210-614-4000

Goff, Robert Burnside, Jr. (3 mentions)
FMS-Mexico, 1980
7210 Louis Pasteur Dr #100, San Antonio, 210-614-4000

Hernandez, Timothy A. (4 mentions)
U of Texas-San Antonio, 1995 *Certification:* Internal Medicine
7940 Floyd Curl Dr #520, San Antonio, 210-616-0709

Isaeff, Mark Andrew (3 mentions)
George Washington U, 1998 *Certification:* Internal Medicine
1303 McCullough Ave #600, San Antonio, 210-225-2551

Juarez, Daniel (4 mentions)
Creighton U, 1978 *Certification:* Internal Medicine
1303 N McCullough #248, San Antonio, 210-220-3737

Kayser, Bradley Basch (7 mentions)
Tulane U, 1981 *Certification:* Internal Medicine
7210 Louis Pasteur Dr #100, San Antonio, 210-614-4000

Lozano, Michael E. (3 mentions)
U of Texas-San Antonio, 1994 *Certification:* Internal Medicine
21 Spurs Ln #230, San Antonio, 210-690-0202

Matlock, John Sidney (4 mentions)
Baylor U, 1979
Certification: Geriatric Medicine, Internal Medicine
8401 Datapoint Dr #401, San Antonio, 210-949-2202

Riddoch, Mark David (4 mentions)
U of Texas-Houston, 1985 *Certification:* Internal Medicine
8401 Datapoint Dr #401, San Antonio, 210-949-2200

Vanover, Randall Mark (4 mentions)
Wayne State U, 1981 *Certification:* Internal Medicine
12602 Toepperwein Rd #100, Live Oak, 210-650-9669

Wiesenthal, Martin Jerome (5 mentions)
U of Texas-San Antonio, 1975 *Certification:* Internal Medicine
8038 Wurzbach Rd #320, San Antonio, 210-614-3365

Yoo, Harrison Wonhee (6 mentions)
U of Texas-Dallas, 1990 *Certification:* Internal Medicine
225 E Sonterra Blvd #100, San Antonio, 210-404-0000

Nephrology

Alvarez, Flavio H. (7 mentions)
FMS-Colombia, 1989
Certification: Internal Medicine, Nephrology
11481 Toepperwein Rd #1202, San Antonio, 210-655-8470

Blond, Carl Joseph (4 mentions)
U of Texas-San Antonio, 1976
Certification: Internal Medicine, Nephrology
2391 NE Loop 410 #405, San Antonio, 210-654-7326
7142 San Pedro Ave #120, San Antonio, 210-228-0743

Dukes, Carl E. (6 mentions)
U of Rochester, 1976
Certification: Internal Medicine, Nephrology
2011 E Houston St #101-A, San Antonio, 210-226-1717

Fried, Terrance A. (5 mentions)
Virginia Commonwealth U, 1977
Certification: Internal Medicine, Nephrology
1008 Brooklyn Ave, San Antonio, 210-228-0743

Garza, Rodolfo O. (5 mentions)
U of Texas-San Antonio, 1997
Certification: Internal Medicine, Nephrology
116 Gallery Cir #101, San Antonio, 210-495-8280

Hart, Polly Denise (6 mentions)
U of Missouri, 1981
714 E Quincy St, San Antonio, 210-270-7760

Hura, Claudia (16 mentions)
Ohio State U, 1979 *Certification:* Internal Medicine, Nephrology
8042 Wurzbach Rd #500, San Antonio, 210-692-7228

Isbell, K. Melissa Ray (7 mentions)
U of Texas-Galveston, 1990
Certification: Internal Medicine, Nephrology
7434 Louis Pasteur Dr #109, San Antonio, 210-614-1515

Mulgrew, Paraic Joseph (4 mentions)
FMS-Ireland, 1969 *Certification:* Internal Medicine, Nephrology
2829 Babcock Rd #300, San Antonio, 210-705-6700
7434 Louis Pasteur Dr #109, San Antonio, 210-614-1515

Reineck, Henry John (5 mentions)
Ohio State U, 1970 *Certification:* Internal Medicine, Nephrology
8042 Wurzbach Rd #500, San Antonio, 210-692-7228

Rosenblatt, Steven Gerald (4 mentions)
Cornell U, 1971 *Certification:* Internal Medicine, Nephrology
8042 Wurzbach Rd #500, San Antonio, 210-692-7228

Sharaf, Rashid (6 mentions)
FMS-Pakistan, 1991 *Certification:* Internal Medicine, Nephrology
8038 Wurzbach Rd #480, San Antonio, 210-615-7057

Smolens, Peter (7 mentions)
Temple U, 1975 *Certification:* Internal Medicine, Nephrology
2391 NE Loop 410 #405, San Antonio, 210-654-7326

Neurological Surgery

Bogaev, Christopher A. (24 mentions)
U of Virginia, 1992 *Certification:* Neurological Surgery
4410 Medical Dr #610, San Antonio, 210-614-2453

Fichtel, Frank Manuel (7 mentions)
U of Texas-Dallas, 1993 *Certification:* Neurological Surgery
4410 Medical Dr #600, San Antonio, 210-615-5200

Hilton, Donald L., Jr. (15 mentions)
U of Texas-Galveston, 1988 *Certification:* Neurological Surgery
4410 Medical Dr #610, San Antonio, 210-614-2453

Kingman, Thomas A. (12 mentions)
U of Texas-Dallas, 1980 *Certification:* Neurological Surgery
4410 Medical Dr #600, San Antonio, 210-615-5200

Neely, Warren F. (7 mentions)
U of Louisville, 1972 *Certification:* Neurological Surgery
4410 Medical Dr #600, San Antonio, 210-615-5200

Swann, Karl Winston (8 mentions)
U of Michigan, 1979 *Certification:* Neurological Surgery
4410 Medical Dr #610, San Antonio, 210-614-2453

Vardiman, Arnold B. (18 mentions)
U of Texas-Dallas, 1989 *Certification:* Neurological Surgery
4410 Medical Dr #610, San Antonio, 210-614-2453

Neurology

Altman, David Joseph (5 mentions)
U of Connecticut, 1996 *Certification:* Neurology
1314 E Sonterra Blvd #601, San Antonio, 210-490-0016

Bass, Ann Doan-Do (9 mentions)
U of Texas-San Antonio, 1993 *Certification:* Neurology
1314 E Sonterra Blvd #601, San Antonio, 210-490-0016

Delaney, B. Peyton (18 mentions)
U of Texas-Galveston, 1973 *Certification:* Neurology
4499 Medical Dr #122, San Antonio, 210-616-0665

Gross, Sheldon G. (8 mentions)
U of Texas-San Antonio, 1977 *Certification:* Neurology with
Special Qualifications in Child Neurology, Pediatrics
4499 Medical Dr #396, San Antonio, 210-614-3737

Merren, Michael David (7 mentions)
Med Coll of Georgia, 1967 *Certification:* Neurology
9119 Cinnamon Hl, San Antonio, 210-690-1901

Neeley, Samuel Robert (4 mentions)
U of Nebraska, 1976 *Certification:* Internal Medicine, Neurology
4410 Medical Dr #520, San Antonio, 210-615-2320

Tomasovic, Jerry Jack (5 mentions)
U of Chicago, 1965 *Certification:* Neurology with Special
Qualifications in Child Neurology, Pediatrics
525 Oak Centre Dr #400, San Antonio, 210-615-2333

Zuflacht, Michael (4 mentions)
FMS-Switzerland, 1964
2833 Babcock Rd #435, San Antonio, 210-614-5855

Obstetrics/Gynecology

Akright, Bruce Donald (5 mentions)
Washington U, 1980 *Certification:* Obstetrics & Gynecology
8715 Village Dr #410, San Antonio, 210-653-5501
502 Madison Oak Dr #240, San Antonio, 210-495-1900
12602 Toepperwein Rd #201, Live Oak, 210-650-9978

Cox, Bryan Matthew (3 mentions)
U of Texas-Dallas, 1983 *Certification:* Obstetrics & Gynecology
7711 Louis Pasteur Dr #200, San Antonio, 210-692-9500

Farhart, Scott Allen (4 mentions)
U of Texas-San Antonio, 1985
Certification: Obstetrics & Gynecology
12602 Toepperwein Rd #201, San Antonio, 210-650-9978
502 Madison Oak Dr #240, San Antonio, 210-495-1900

Farina, Jose Manuel (5 mentions)
FMS-Mexico, 1983 *Certification:* Obstetrics & Gynecology
1200 Brooklyn Ave #220, San Antonio, 210-228-0705

Harle, Brian Waid (3 mentions)
Texas Tech U, 1988 *Certification:* Obstetrics & Gynecology
7711 Louis Pasteur Dr #200, San Antonio, 210-692-9500

Heck, Heidi R. (4 mentions)
U of Texas-Dallas, 1985 *Certification:* Obstetrics & Gynecology
7711 Louis Pasteur Dr #200, San Antonio, 210-692-9500

Honore, Charles Rudolph (5 mentions)
U of Texas-San Antonio, 1975
Certification: Obstetrics & Gynecology
7711 Louis Pasteur Dr #902, San Antonio, 210-692-9500

Jacobs, Jennifer D'Ann (3 mentions)
U of Texas-San Antonio, 1994
Certification: Obstetrics & Gynecology
7950 Floyd Curl Dr #300, San Antonio, 210-615-6505

King, Elizabeth A. (4 mentions)
Texas A&M U, 2001 *Certification:* Obstetrics & Gynecology
502 Madison Oak Dr #240, San Antonio, 210-495-1900

Lopez, Marco Antonio, Jr. (3 mentions)
U of Texas-San Antonio, 1971
Certification: Obstetrics & Gynecology
4499 Medical Dr #306, San Antonio, 210-614-4963
920 San Pedro Ave #100, San Antonio, 210-475-9020

Ruiz, Jose Manuel, III (3 mentions)
Louisiana State U, 1986 *Certification:* Obstetrics & Gynecology
367 E Ramsey Rd, San Antonio, 210-520-8484
7940 Floyd Curl Dr #900, San Antonio, 210-520-8484

Schorlemer, Robert (4 mentions)
U of Texas-Dallas, 1964 *Certification:* Obstetrics & Gynecology
4499 Medical Dr #119, San Antonio, 210-614-9400

Skop, Ingrid Ruth (3 mentions)
Washington U, 1992 *Certification:* Obstetrics & Gynecology
8715 Village Dr #410, San Antonio, 210-653-5501
12602 Toepperwein Rd #201, Live Oak, 210-650-9978

Vanover, Marilyn Jean (4 mentions)
Wayne State U, 1981 *Certification:* Obstetrics & Gynecology
8715 Village Dr #300, San Antonio, 210-946-1300

Ophthalmology

Adams, Donald Fayron (3 mentions)
U of Texas-San Antonio, 1981 *Certification:* Ophthalmology
1919 Oakwell Farms Pkwy #120, San Antonio, 210-824-2800

Arno, Mary Hannah H. (6 mentions)
U of Texas-San Antonio, 1974 *Certification:* Ophthalmology
224 W Evergreen St, San Antonio, 210-225-3377

Berry, Jon Mark (3 mentions)
U of Texas-Dallas, 1990 *Certification:* Ophthalmology
11601 Toepperwein Rd, Live Oak, 210-946-2020

Braverman, Sheldon Philip (3 mentions)
SUNY-Upstate Med U, 1959 *Certification:* Ophthalmology
1100 N Main Ave, San Antonio, 210-222-2154

Campagna, John Anthony (3 mentions)
U of Pittsburgh, 1988 *Certification:* Ophthalmology
414 Navarro St #400, San Antonio, 800-322-5056
1804 NE Loop 410 #270, San Antonio, 210-223-5561
1514 W Oaklawn Rd, Pleasanton, 210-223-5561

Evans, Richard Milner (3 mentions)
U of Texas-Galveston, 1971 *Certification:* Ophthalmology
9157 Huebner Rd, San Antonio, 210-697-2020
11900 Crownpoint Dr #140, San Antonio, 210-697-2020
315 N San Saba #970, San Antonio, 210-697-2020
98 Briggs St #980, San Antonio, 210-928-2015
109 Gallery Cir #139, San Antonio, 210-491-1920

Held, Kristin Story (9 mentions)
U of Texas-San Antonio, 1985 *Certification:* Ophthalmology
325 E Sonterra Blvd #100, San Antonio, 210-490-6759

Hughes, Jane Lindell (8 mentions)
U of Texas-San Antonio, 1980 *Certification:* Ophthalmology
21 Spurs Ln #220, San Antonio, 210-614-5566

Kozlovsky, John F. (3 mentions)
Baylor U, 1990 *Certification:* Ophthalmology
2929 Mossrock #104, San Antonio, 210-377-0350

Lindhorst, Grace C. (3 mentions)
U of Texas-San Antonio, 2003 *Certification:* Ophthalmology
21 Spurs Lane #220, San Antonio, 210-614-5566

Mein, Calvin Einar (4 mentions)
U of Illinois, 1975 *Certification:* Ophthalmology
9480 Huebner Rd #310, San Antonio, 210-615-1311

Miramontes, Loretta May (3 mentions)
U of California-San Francisco, 1979 *Certification:* Ophthalmology
215 E Quincy St #505, San Antonio, 210-222-9172

Nevarez, Hector L. (4 mentions)
FMS-Dominican Republic, 1977 *Certification:* Ophthalmology
730 N Main Ave #418, San Antonio, 210-224-6633

San Martin, Roberto (3 mentions)
U of California-Los Angeles, 1974 *Certification:* Ophthalmology
315 N San Saba #100, San Antonio, 210-225-3937

Scales, David Kenneth (3 mentions)
Uniformed Services U of Health Sciences, 1982
Certification: Ophthalmology
9623 Huebner Rd #100, San Antonio, 210-615-6565

Shulman, David George (3 mentions)
Creighton U, 1973 *Certification:* Ophthalmology
999 E Basse Rd #127, San Antonio, 210-821-6901

Speights, James William (3 mentions)
Baylor U, 1968 *Certification:* Ophthalmology
7940 Floyd Curl Dr #820, San Antonio, 210-615-8413
315 N San Saba #1070, San Antonio, 210-615-8413

Taylor, Joel Z. (4 mentions)
U of Texas-San Antonio, 1975 *Certification:* Ophthalmology
7434 Louis Pasteur Dr, San Antonio, 210-615-8451

Trujillo, Fernando (3 mentions)
FMS-Colombia, 1992 *Certification:* Ophthalmology
999 E Basse Rd #127, San Antonio, 210-821-6901

Zwaan, Johan T. (3 mentions)
FMS-Netherlands, 1963 *Certification:* Ophthalmology
8038 Wurzbach Rd #520, San Antonio, 210-615-8474

Orthopedics

Burkhart, Stephen Shelby (8 mentions)
U of Texas-Galveston, 1976 *Certification:* Orthopaedic Surgery
400 Concord Plaza Dr #300, San Antonio, 210-489-7220
150 E Sonterra Blvd #300, San Antonio, 210-489-7220

Casillas, Mark (6 mentions)
U of Texas-San Antonio, 1991 *Certification:* Orthopaedic Surgery
150 E Sonterra Blvd #300, San Antonio, 210-225-5741

Curtis, Ralph John, Jr. (5 mentions)
U of Texas-San Antonio, 1980 *Certification:* Orthopaedic Surgery
21 Spurs Ln #300, San Antonio, 210-699-8326
5921 Broadway St, San Antonio, 210-699-8326

De Lee, Jesse Clyde (14 mentions)
U of Texas-Galveston, 1970 *Certification:* Orthopaedic Surgery
2829 Babcock Rd #700, San Antonio, 210-593-1475

Evans, John Allan (5 mentions)
FMS-Canada, 1970 *Certification:* Orthopaedic Surgery
2829 Babcock Rd #700, San Antonio, 210-593-1480

Fox, David Lester (8 mentions)
U of Oklahoma, 1984 *Certification:* Orthopaedic Surgery
12709 Toepperwein Rd #101, Live Oak, 210-477-5151
8800 Village Dr #101, San Antonio, 210-477-5151

Goletz, Ty Henry (5 mentions)
U of Wisconsin, 1977 *Certification:* Orthopaedic Surgery
7940 Floyd Curl Dr #560, San Antonio, 210-692-7400

Greenfield, Gerald Q., Jr. (4 mentions)
Johns Hopkins U, 1978 *Certification:* Orthopaedic Surgery
2829 Babcock Rd #700, San Antonio, 210-615-1616

Lunke, Roger James (5 mentions)
U of Wisconsin, 1974 *Certification:* Orthopaedic Surgery
540 Madison Oak Dr #350, San Antonio, 210-490-7470
1303 McCullough Ave #264, San Antonio, 210-225-0156

Pontius, Uwe Rainer (9 mentions)
Tulane U, 1976 *Certification:* Orthopaedic Surgery
7940 Floyd Curl Dr #560, San Antonio, 210-692-7400

Schmidt, David Richard (8 mentions)
U of Texas-San Antonio, 1980
Certification: Orthopaedic Surgery, Surgery of the Hand
21 Spurs Ln #300, San Antonio, 210-699-8326
5921 Broadway St, San Antonio, 210-699-8326

Schulze, Brian E. (7 mentions)
U of Texas-Houston, 1994 *Certification:* Orthopaedic Surgery
12709 Topperwein Dr #101, San Antonio, 210-477-5151
8800 Village Dr #101, San Antonio, 210-477-5151

Sledge, Scott L. (4 mentions)
U of Texas-Dallas, 1985 *Certification:* Orthopaedic Surgery
12709 Toepperwein Rd #101, San Antonio, 210-477-5151
8800 Village Dr #101, San Antonio, 210-477-5151

Tolin, Brad Steven (7 mentions)
U of Toledo, 1986 *Certification:* Orthopaedic Surgery
400 Concord Plaza #300, San Antonio, 210-225-5741
1200 Brooklyn Ave #320, San Antonio, 210-225-5741
150 E Sonterra Blvd #300, San Antonio, 210-225-5741

Warman, Jeffrey Robert (4 mentions)
SUNY-Downstate Med Coll, 1986
Certification: Orthopaedic Surgery
18626 Hardy Oak Blvd #320, San Antonio, 210-497-4186

Otorhinolaryngology

Bain, Walter Mathis (7 mentions)
U of Texas-San Antonio, 1975 *Certification:* Otolaryngology
1303 McCullough Ave #242, San Antonio, 210-226-8982

Biediger, Charles P. (5 mentions)
U of Texas-San Antonio, 1992 *Certification:* Otolaryngology
19026 Stone Oak Pkwy #110, San Antonio, 210-545-0404
7940 Floyd Curl Dr #400, San Antonio, 210-545-0404

Bonilla, Juan Alfredo (7 mentions)
U of Texas-San Antonio, 1983 *Certification:* Otolaryngology
16723 Huebner Rd, San Antonio, 210-733-4368

Brown, Patrick Nelson (14 mentions)
U of Texas-Galveston, 1991 *Certification:* Otolaryngology
4775 Hamilton Wolfe Rd #1, San Antonio, 210-615-8332
4025 E Southcross Blvd #8, San Antonio, 210-337-1050

Browne, Kevin Brian (7 mentions)
Texas Tech U, 1983 *Certification:* Otolaryngology
4499 Medical Dr 2nd Fl, San Antonio, 210-615-8177

Gordon, William Wade (5 mentions)
Baylor U, 1970 *Certification:* Otolaryngology
7940 Floyd Curl Dr #400, San Antonio, 210-616-0096

Nau, Thomas William (8 mentions)
U of Texas-San Antonio, 1982 *Certification:* Otolaryngology
7940 Floyd Curl Dr #400, San Antonio, 210-616-0096

Newman, Richard Kurt (10 mentions)
U of Texas-San Antonio, 1972 *Certification:* Otolaryngology
4775 Hamilton Wolfe Rd #1, San Antonio, 210-616-0283

Rosenbloom, Jeffrey S. (5 mentions)
U of Texas-Dallas, 1992 *Certification:* Otolaryngology
7940 Floyd Curl Dr #400, San Antonio, 210-545-0404
19026 Stone Oak Pkwy #110, San Antonio, 210-545-0404

Ruiz, Gilbert Manuel (10 mentions)
U of Texas-San Antonio, 1979 *Certification:* Otolaryngology
315 N San Saba #1195, San Antonio, 210-225-3136
4775 Hamilton Wolfe Rd #1, San Antonio, 210-614-1326

Pain Medicine

Bacon, Donald David (4 mentions)
Certification: Anesthesiology, Pain Medicine
403 Treeline Park #200, San Antonio, 210-805-9994
7434 Louis Pasteur Dr #205, San Antonio, 210-805-9800
9150 Huebner Rd #100, San Antonio, 210-654-1000

Carrasco, Arnulfo T. (5 mentions)
Texas Tech U, 1987
4763 Hamilton Wolfe Rd #200, San Antonio, 210-614-4825

Dar, Urfan (4 mentions)
FMS-India, 1988 *Certification:* Anesthesiology
19284 Stone Oak Pkwy #101, San Antonio, 210-268-0129

Duncan, Ellen B. (5 mentions)
U of Texas-San Antonio, 1991 *Certification:* Anesthesiology
1303 McCullough Ave #229, San Antonio, 210-477-2411

Jones, Stephanie S. (6 mentions)
U of Texas-San Antonio, 1992
Certification: Anesthesiology, Pain Medicine
403 Treeline Park #200, San Antonio, 210-805-9800

Singh, Prafulla Chandra (5 mentions)
FMS-India, 1987 *Certification:* Anesthesiology, Pain Medicine
1200 Brooklyn Ave #140, San Antonio, 210-527-1166

Pathology

Bannayan, George Abcar (5 mentions)
FMS-Lebanon, 1957
Certification: Anatomic Pathology & Clinical Pathology
8026 Floyd Curl Dr, San Antonio, 210-575-8150

Hinchey, William Woolford (4 mentions)
U of Texas-San Antonio, 1978
Certification: Anatomic Pathology & Clinical Pathology
601 Canterbury Hill St, San Antonio, 210-826-4701

Joyce, Roby P. (5 mentions)
Certification: Anatomic Pathology & Clinical Pathology, Neurology
12412 Judson Rd, San Antonio, 210-757-5113

Kardos, Thomas Frank (8 mentions)
New York Med Coll, 1978
Certification: Anatomic Pathology, Cytopathology
301 N Frio St, San Antonio, 210-477-5800

Larson, Paula R. (6 mentions)
U of Wisconsin, 1978 *Certification:* Anatomic Pathology &
Clinical Pathology, Cytopathology
7700 Floyd Curl Dr, San Antonio, 210-575-4845

Richmond, Cliff Morgan (3 mentions)
U of Texas-San Antonio, 1982
Certification: Anatomic Pathology & Clinical Pathology
2827 Babcock Rd, San Antonio, 210-892-3700

Rone, Valerie Rene (7 mentions)
U of Missouri, 1978 *Certification:* Anatomic Pathology &
Clinical Pathology, Cytopathology
1310 McCullough Ave, San Antonio, 210-271-9293
301 N Frio St, San Antonio, 210-271-9293

Pediatrics *(see note on page 9)*

Benbow, Marshall James (6 mentions)
U of Texas-Galveston, 1978 *Certification:* Pediatrics
5282 Medical Dr #310, San Antonio, 210-614-8687

Hall, Graham T. (5 mentions)
U of Texas-San Antonio, 1987
7959 Broadway St #600, San Antonio, 210-826-7033

Littlefield, Christine A. (6 mentions)
U of Texas-San Antonio, 1978 *Certification:* Pediatrics
7007 Bandera Rd #19, San Antonio, 210-680-6000

Mayes, Thomas Cullee (4 mentions)
Georgetown U, 1984
Certification: Pediatric Critical Care Medicine, Pediatrics
7703 Floyd Curl Dr, San Antonio, 210-567-5200

Ornes, Rene Michael (3 mentions)
U of Texas-Dallas, 1976 *Certification:* Pediatrics
8606 Village Dr #A, San Antonio, 210-657-0220

Ostrower, Valerie Ger (7 mentions)
New York Med Coll, 1968 *Certification:* Pediatrics
4499 Medical Dr #280, San Antonio, 210-614-4499
502 Madison Oak #340, San Antonio, 210-495-5552

Purnell, Lewis M. (3 mentions)
U of Texas-Dallas, 1982 *Certification:* Pediatrics
5282 Medical Dr #310, San Antonio, 210-614-8687

Sheikh, Shahzad A. (3 mentions)
FMS-Pakistan, 1982 *Certification:* Pediatrics
14351 Blanco Rd, San Antonio, 210-492-0900

Trevino, Daniel Gerard (3 mentions)
FMS-Mexico, 1990
123 Stone Oak Loop, San Antonio, 210-495-7334

Plastic Surgery

Garza, Jaime Ruperto (12 mentions)
Louisiana State U, 1987
Certification: Otolaryngology, Plastic Surgery
21 Spurs Ln #120, San Antonio, 210-616-0301

Ledoux, Peter Robert (9 mentions)
Wayne State U, 1987 *Certification:* Plastic Surgery
9635 Huebner Rd, San Antonio, 210-692-1181

Levine, Richard Allen (12 mentions)
U of Buffalo, 1975 *Certification:* Plastic Surgery
4499 Medical Dr #316, San Antonio, 210-614-2747

Schaffer, Eric S. (5 mentions)
New York U, 1978 *Certification:* Plastic Surgery, Surgery
1303 McCullough Ave #363, San Antonio, 210-227-3223

Psychiatry

Bowden, Charles Lee (3 mentions)
Baylor U, 1964 *Certification:* Psychiatry
7703 Floyd Curl Dr, San Antonio, 210-567-5405

Elliott, Boyce, III (3 mentions)
U of Texas-Galveston, 1966 *Certification:* Psychiatry
4242 Medical Dr, San Antonio, 210-308-5533

Flatley, Mary Ann (5 mentions)
U of Texas-San Antonio, 1979 *Certification:* Psychiatry
7744 Broadway St #103, San Antonio, 210-824-7171

Gelfond, Stephen D. (3 mentions)
Jefferson Med Coll, 1968 *Certification:* Psychiatry
2727 Babcock Rd #B, San Antonio, 210-614-9334

Pliszka, Steven Ray (4 mentions)
U of Texas-San Antonio, 1981
Certification: Child & Adolescent Psychiatry, Psychiatry
7703 Floyd Curl Dr, San Antonio, 210-567-5475

Ticknor, Christopher B. (11 mentions)
U of Texas-San Antonio, 1982 *Certification:* Psychiatry
1202 E Sonterra Blvd #202, San Antonio, 210-692-7775

Tierney, John Gregory, II (3 mentions)
U of Texas-San Antonio, 1988
Certification: Geriatric Psychiatry, Psychiatry
1202 E Sonterra Blvd #202, San Antonio, 210-615-8458

Weiss, Thomas Roderick (3 mentions)
U of Texas-San Antonio, 1981 *Certification:* Addiction Psychiatry,
Geriatric Psychiatry, Psychiatry, Psychosomatic Medicine
8122 Datapoint Dr #1010, San Antonio, 210-614-5561

Pulmonary Disease

Andrews, Charles Porter (12 mentions)
U of Texas-Dallas, 1975
Certification: Internal Medicine, Pulmonary Disease
4410 Medical Dr #440, San Antonio, 210-692-9400

Bell, Randall Clarence (14 mentions)
U of Kansas, 1978
Certification: Internal Medicine, Pulmonary Disease
4410 Medical Dr #440, San Antonio, 210-692-9400

Burch, Charles J. (9 mentions)
U of Texas-San Antonio, 1996 *Certification:* Critical Care
Medicine, Internal Medicine, Pulmonary Disease
4410 Medical Dr #440, San Antonio, 210-692-9400

Deal, Leonard E., Jr. (5 mentions)
U of New Mexico, 1992 *Certification:* Critical Care Medicine,
Internal Medicine, Pulmonary Disease
8715 Village Dr #520, San Antonio, 210-656-3600
8800 VIllage Dr #209, San Antonio, 210-656-3600

Homma, Arturo (4 mentions)
FMS-Mexico, 1991
Certification: Critical Care Medicine, Pulmonary Disease
7950 Floyd Curl Dr #620, San Antonio, 210-692-0361

Marks, David Alan (4 mentions)
U of Texas-San Antonio, 2001 *Certification:* Critical Care
Medicine, Internal Medicine, Pulmonary Disease
540 Madison Oak Dr #560, San Antonio, 210-494-4220

Melo, Jairo A. (11 mentions)
FMS-Colombia, 1991
Certification: Critical Care Medicine, Pulmonary Disease
4410 Medical Dr #440, San Antonio, 210-692-9400

Orozco, Carlos Raul (4 mentions)
U of Texas-Galveston, 1974
Certification: Internal Medicine, Pulmonary Disease
343 W Houston St #706, San Antonio, 210-227-0193
221 Lexington Ave Apt 319, San Antonio, 210-227-0193

Patel, Tarak J. (4 mentions)
Texas Tech U, 1997
Certification: Pediatric Pulmonology, Pediatrics
525 Oak Center Dr #400, San Antonio, 210-494-3397

Schenk, David Anthony (6 mentions)
Tulane U, 1977 *Certification:* Critical Care Medicine,
Internal Medicine, Pulmonary Disease, Sleep Medicine
7950 Floyd Curl Dr #620, San Antonio, 210-692-0361

Songco, Gary Max (6 mentions)
Rosalind Franklin U, 1982
Certification: Internal Medicine, Pulmonary Disease
1200 Brooklyn Ave #250, San Antonio, 210-226-5933

Walsh, Andrew L., III (4 mentions)
U of Texas-San Antonio, 1987 *Certification:* Critical Care
Medicine, Internal Medicine, Pulmonary Disease
1200 Brooklyn Ave #250, San Antonio, 210-226-5933

Wooley, Michael Wayne (7 mentions)
U of Texas-Dallas, 1974 *Certification:* Internal Medicine,
Pulmonary Disease, Sleep Medicine
7950 Floyd Curl Dr #620, San Antonio, 210-692-0361

Zamora, Cynthia A. (4 mentions)
U of Texas-Dallas, 1983 *Certification:* Critical Care
Medicine, Internal Medicine, Pulmonary Disease
1603 Babcock Rd #101, San Antonio, 210-340-7700

Radiology—Diagnostic

Andersen, Garrett Karl (4 mentions)
U of Texas-Dallas, 1997 *Certification:* Diagnostic Radiology
8401 Datapoint Dr #600, San Antonio, 210-616-7796

Cone, Robert O., III (4 mentions)
U of Texas-San Antonio, 1978 *Certification:* Diagnostic Radiology
8401 Datapoint Dr #600, San Antonio, 210-616-7796
9150 Huebner Rd #195, San Antonio, 210-561-7170

Dunlap, Joel Adrian (4 mentions)
Med U of South Carolina, 1987
Certification: Diagnostic Radiology
8401 Datapoint Dr #600, San Antonio, 210-616-7796

Gilley, James Stanley (6 mentions)
U of Virginia, 1977 *Certification:* Diagnostic Radiology
8401 Datapoint Dr #600, San Antonio, 210-616-7796

Goldstein, Harvey Martin (9 mentions)
Northwestern U, 1966 *Certification:* Diagnostic Radiology
8401 Datapoint Dr #600, San Antonio, 210-616-7796

Hendrick, Eric P. (3 mentions)
U of Texas-Galveston, 1994
Certification: Diagnostic Radiology, Pediatric Radiology
8401 Datapoint Dr #600, San Antonio, 210-616-7796

Hibri, Nadi Salah (3 mentions)
FMS-Lebanon, 1973 *Certification:* Diagnostic Radiology
2829 Babcock Rd #215, San Antonio, 210-733-4400
1310 Mccullough Ave, San Antonio, 210-733-4400

Kapila, Ashwani (3 mentions)
FMS-India, 1975
Certification: Diagnostic Radiology, Neuroradiology
440 Piedras Dr #200, San Antonio, 210-733-4400

Napier, Dacia Janel (3 mentions)
U of Texas-Houston, 1997 *Certification:* Diagnostic Radiology
900 Isom Rd #210, San Antonio, 210-455-0167

Ratner, Adam V. (4 mentions)
U of Texas-Dallas, 1985 *Certification:* Diagnostic Radiology
2829 Babcock Rd, San Antonio, 210-617-6300
4400 S Piedras Dr #200-A, San Antonio, 210-224-1888

Vasquez, Robert Eloy (8 mentions)
U of Texas-Galveston, 1983 *Certification:* Diagnostic Radiology
8401 Datapoint Dr #600, San Antonio, 210-616-7796

Wiersig, Jeremy N. (4 mentions)
U of Texas-Dallas, 1987 *Certification:* Diagnostic Radiology
18802 Meisner Dr, San Antonio, 210-572-2222

Radiology—Therapeutic

Lutz, James Douglas (7 mentions)
U of Texas-Dallas, 1987 *Certification:* Diagnostic Radiology,
   Vascular & Interventional Radiology
4400 S Piedras Dr #200A, San Antonio, 210-737-1155

Thomas, John W. (5 mentions)
U of Texas-Houston, 1988 *Certification:* Diagnostic Radiology
9150 Huebner Rd #130, San Antonio, 210-616-7780

Wegert, Steven John (8 mentions)
U of Toledo, 1987 *Certification:* Diagnostic Radiology,
   Vascular & Interventional Radiology
8401 Datapoint Dr #600, San Antonio, 210-616-7796

Rehabilitation

Barker, Michael Paul (4 mentions)
U of Texas-Galveston, 1989
Certification: Physical Medicine & Rehabilitation
9643 Huebner Rd #103, San Antonio, 210-615-3892

Goldstein, Alasdair M. (9 mentions)
U of Texas-San Antonio, 1993
Certification: Physical Medicine & Rehabilitation
9643 Huebner Rd #103, San Antonio, 210-614-8222

Pecha, Marc Daniel (4 mentions)
U of Tennessee, 1995
Certification: Physical Medicine & Rehabilitation
2701 Babcock Rd #A, San Antonio, 210-614-3225

Rana-Manocha, Jahnavi (4 mentions)
Rosalind Franklin U, 1999
Certification: Physical Medicine & Rehabilitation
2701 Babcock Rd #A, San Antonio, 210-614-3225

Roman, Angel Manuel, Jr. (3 mentions)
U of Texas-San Antonio, 1978 *Certification:* Physical
   Medicine & Rehabilitation, Undersea & Hyperbaric Medicine
2833 Babcock Rd #110, San Antonio, 210-692-2000

Santos, Jose A. (5 mentions)
Baylor U, 1983 *Certification:* Physical Medicine & Rehabilitation
2701 Babcock Rd #A, San Antonio, 210-614-3225

Rheumatology

Ballester-Fiallo, Ana (4 mentions)
U of Puerto Rico, 1982
Certification: Internal Medicine, Rheumatology
730 N Main, San Antonio, 210-225-1575

Kempf, Kevin James (7 mentions)
Baylor U, 1991 *Certification:* Rheumatology
19272 Stone Oak Pkwy #101, San Antonio, 210-265-8851
8527 Village Dr #207, San Antonio, 210-656-3926

Molina, Rodolfo (11 mentions)
Baylor U, 1976 *Certification:* Internal Medicine, Rheumatology
4511 Horizon Hill Blvd #150, San Antonio, 210-477-2626

Nelson, Mark William (5 mentions)
Med Coll of Georgia, 1976
Certification: Internal Medicine, Rheumatology
3338 Oakwell Ct #114, San Antonio, 210-656-5000

Pineda, Emily R. (5 mentions)
5414 Fredericksburg Rd #150, San Antonio, 210-615-9800

Rosenberg, Gerald T. (5 mentions)
St Louis U, 1978 *Certification:* Internal Medicine, Rheumatology
4511 Horizon Hill Blvd #150, San Antonio, 210-477-2626

Suarez, Laura A. (4 mentions)
U of Texas-Galveston, 1986
Certification: Internal Medicine, Rheumatology
155 E Sonterra Blvd #211, San Antonio, 210-490-1111

Thoracic Surgery

Hamner, Lawrence R., III (5 mentions)
U of Texas-Dallas, 1981 *Certification:* Thoracic Surgery
4330 Medical Dr #325, San Antonio, 210-615-7700

Johnson, Scott Bostow (12 mentions)
U of New Mexico, 1987
Certification: Surgery, Surgical Critical Care, Thoracic Surgery
7703 Floyd Curl Dr, San Antonio, 210-567-5615

Lyda, Timothy Stuart (9 mentions)
U of Texas-San Antonio, 1986
Certification: Surgery, Thoracic Surgery
4330 Medical Dr #325, San Antonio, 210-615-7700

Smith, J. Marvin, III (6 mentions)
Tulane U, 1972 *Certification:* Surgery, Thoracic Surgery
6800 IH10 W #300, San Antonio, 210-616-0008

Urology

Case, John Robert (9 mentions)
Tulane U, 1998 *Certification:* Urology
8711 Village Dr #312, San Antonio, 210-655-2411
502 Madison Oaks Dr #250, San Antonio, 210-545-1000

Fitch, William Pilcher, III (7 mentions)
Tulane U, 1968 *Certification:* Urology
7909 fredericksburg Rd #110, San Antonio, 210-614-4544

Harmon, William James (5 mentions)
U of Chicago, 1991 *Certification:* Urology
7909 Fredericksburg Rd #110, San Antonio, 210-614-4544

Hlavinka, Timothy Charles (6 mentions)
U of Texas-Galveston, 1984 *Certification:* Urology
7909 Fredericksburg Rd #110, San Antonio, 210-614-4544

Kella, Naveen (5 mentions)
U of Texas-Dallas, 1998 *Certification:* Urology
7909 Fredericksburg Rd #110, San Antonio, 210-614-4544

O'Neill, Thomas Kevin (7 mentions)
Indiana U, 1979 *Certification:* Urology
7909 Fredericksburg Rd, San Antonio, 210-614-4544
255 E Sonterra Blvd #203, San Antonio, 210-499-5158

Sarosdy, Michael Francis (8 mentions)
U of Texas-San Antonio, 1977 *Certification:* Urology
4499 Medical Dr #218, San Antonio, 210-615-3899

Sepulveda, Rene (5 mentions)
U of Puerto Rico, 1974 *Certification:* Urology
7909 Fredericksburg Rd #110, San Antonio, 210-731-2050
12709 Toepperwein Rd #110, San Antonio, 210-564-8000

Singleton, Randall Parris (9 mentions)
U of Oklahoma, 1968 *Certification:* Urology
7909 Fredericksburg Rd #110, San Antonio, 210-614-4544

Thompson, Ian Murchie, Jr. (8 mentions)
Tulane U, 1980 *Certification:* Urology
7703 Floyd Curl Dr, San Antonio, 210-567-5640

Vassar, George John (7 mentions)
U of Texas-San Antonio, 1994 *Certification:* Urology
8711 Village Dr #312, San Antonio, 210-655-2411
502 Madison Oak #250, San Antonio, 210-545-1000

Vick, Sammy C. (6 mentions)
U of Texas-San Antonio, 1989 *Certification:* Urology
8038 Wurzbach Rd #430, San Antonio, 210-616-0410

Vascular Surgery

Kirk, William O. (10 mentions)
U of Texas-Dallas, 1987 *Certification:* Surgery, Vascular Surgery
8715 Village Dr #518, San Antonio, 210-656-5098

Ortega, Gerardo (12 mentions)
FMS-Mexico, 1974 *Certification:* Vascular Surgery
111 Dallas St #200-A, San Antonio, 210-225-6508

Sykes, Mellick Tweedy (10 mentions)
U of Texas-Galveston, 1976 *Certification:* Vascular Surgery
7950 Floyd Curl Dr #109, San Antonio, 210-692-9700

Tamez, Daniel David (9 mentions)
U of Texas-San Antonio, 1976 *Certification:* Surgery
111 Dallas St #200-A, San Antonio, 210-225-6508

Thompson, Robert Knox (9 mentions)
U of Tennessee, 1983 *Certification:* Surgery, Vascular Surgery
8715 Village Dr #518, San Antonio, 210-656-5098
19141 Stone Oak Pkwy #401, San Antonio, 210-483-8822

Wolf, Edward Anthony, Jr. (18 mentions)
Creighton U, 1967 *Certification:* Surgery, Vascular Surgery
4330 Medical Dr #225, San Antonio, 210-614-7414

Travis County

Allergy/Immunology

Cook, Robert David (11 mentions)
U of Texas-Dallas, 1977
Certification: Allergy & Immunology, Internal Medicine
4150 N Lamar Blvd, Austin, 512-467-0978

Peters, Edward John (8 mentions)
U of Texas-Galveston, 1980 *Certification:* Allergy &
Immunology, Internal Medicine, Pulmonary Disease
800 W 34th St #201, Austin, 512-454-5821

Villacis, John Francisco (7 mentions)
Texas Tech U, 1999
Certification: Allergy & Immunology, Internal Medicine
12221 N Mo Pac Expy, Austin, 512-901-4002

Anesthesiology

Allen, Erick Seth (4 mentions)
U of Texas-Galveston, 1991 *Certification:* Anesthesiology
8140 N Mo Pac Expy #3-210, Austin, 512-343-2292

Brand, Jeffrey D. (3 mentions)
Baylor U, 1991 *Certification:* Anesthesiology
3705 Medical Pkwy #570, Austin, 512-454-2554

Chapin, James Carlson (4 mentions)
U of Michigan, 1974 *Certification:* Anesthesiology
8140 N Mo Pac Expy #3-210, Austin, 512-343-2292

Flusche, Gary Allen (3 mentions)
U of Texas-Dallas, 1982 *Certification:* Anesthesiology
3705 Medical Pkwy #570, Austin, 512-454-2554

Furst, Edward Dunton (7 mentions)
Texas Tech U, 1986 *Certification:* Anesthesiology, Pediatrics
3705 Medical Pkwy #570, Austin, 512-454-2454

Gunn, Holly C. (3 mentions)
U of Pennsylvania, 1990 *Certification:* Anesthesiology
3705 Medical Pkwy #570, Austin, 512-454-2554

Jones, Stacy L. (5 mentions)
U of Texas-San Antonio, 1989 *Certification:* Anesthesiology
3705 Medical Pkwy #570, Austin, 512-454-2554

McMichael, James Patrick (3 mentions)
U of Texas-San Antonio, 1970 *Certification:* Anesthesiology
3705 Medical Pkwy #570, Austin, 512-454-2554

Metcalf, Steven (3 mentions)
U of Colorado, 1987 *Certification:* Anesthesiology, Pediatrics
3705 Medical Pkwy #570, Austin, 512-454-2554

Rockwell, Jeffrey John (3 mentions)
U of Arizona, 1992 *Certification:* Anesthesiology
8140 N Mo Pac Expy #3-210, Austin, 512-343-2292

Rutman, Steven M. (5 mentions)
U of Texas-Dallas, 1993 *Certification:* Anesthesiology
3705 Medical Pkwy #570, Austin, 512-454-2554

Scholl, Catherine Lee (7 mentions)
U of Texas-Galveston, 1981 *Certification:* Anesthesiology
8140 N Mo Pac Expy Bldg 3 #210, Austin, 512-343-2292

Cardiac Surgery

Dewan, Stephen James (26 mentions)
Baylor U, 1979 *Certification:* Surgery, Thoracic Surgery
1010 W 40th St, Austin, 512-459-8753

Hume, Andrew Tucker (13 mentions)
U of Mississippi, 1989 *Certification:* Surgery, Thoracic Surgery
1010 W 40th St, Austin, 512-459-8753

Cardiology

Chafizadeh, Edward Robert (10 mentions)
Baylor U, 1989
Certification: Cardiovascular Disease, Interventional Cardiology
1015 E 32nd St #508, Austin, 512-480-3145

Cishek, Mary Beth (5 mentions)
St Louis U, 1988 *Certification:* Cardiovascular Disease
1301 W 38th St #705, Austin, 512-441-1633

Damore, Stuart (7 mentions)
St Louis U, 1974 *Certification:* Cardiovascular Disease,
Internal Medicine, Interventional Cardiology
12221 N Mo Pac Expy, Austin, 512-901-4051

Hayes, David Wayne (5 mentions)
U of Kansas, 1984
Certification: Cardiovascular Disease, Internal Medicine
900 E 30th St #315, Austin, 512-474-5551

Morris, David Lyonel (13 mentions)
U of Texas-Galveston, 1974
Certification: Cardiovascular Disease, Internal Medicine
3801 N Lamar Blvd #300, Austin, 512-206-3600
1301 W 38th St #500, Austin, 512-206-3600
11149 Research Blvd #125, Austin, 512-206-3600

Otero, Javier (4 mentions)
FMS-Spain, 1990
Certification: Cardiovascular Disease, Interventional Cardiology
1015 E 32nd St #508, Austin, 512-441-1633

Roach, Paul Jeffrey (5 mentions)
Northwestern U, 1984
Certification: Cardiovascular Disease, Internal Medicine
1015 E 32nd St #508, Austin, 800-555-5595

Robinson, William Archie, Jr. (5 mentions)
Baylor U, 1965
Certification: Cardiovascular Disease, Internal Medicine
3801 N Lamar Blvd #300, Austin, 512-206-3600
11149 Research Blvd #125, Austin, 512-206-3600

Rowe, Stuart Allen (4 mentions)
Johns Hopkins U, 1981
Certification: Pediatric Cardiology, Pediatrics
4314 Medical Pkwy #200, Austin, 512-454-1110

Shapiro, Ronald Bruce (4 mentions)
U of North Carolina, 1987 *Certification:* Pediatric Cardiology
900 E 30th St #311, Austin, 512-320-8388

Tucker, Paul A., II (6 mentions)
Baylor U, 1987
Certification: Cardiovascular Disease, Interventional Cardiology
4316 James Casey St, Austin, 512-441-1633

Watkins, Michael George (8 mentions)
U of Texas-Houston, 1981
Certification: Cardiovascular Disease, Internal Medicine
1301 W 38th St #500, Austin, 512-617-6000

Wright, Karen L. (4 mentions)
Northwestern U, 1986 *Certification:* Pediatric Cardiology
4314 Medical Pkwy #200, Austin, 512-454-1110

Dermatology

Dozier, Susan Elizabeth (7 mentions)
U of Texas-Galveston, 1989 *Certification:* Dermatology
8240 N Mo Pac Expy #355, Austin, 512-527-9020

Dubois, Janet C. (9 mentions)
U of Texas-San Antonio, 1987 *Certification:* Dermatology
11671 Jollyville Rd #104, Austin, 512-345-3599

Funicella, Toni (8 mentions)
U of Texas-Galveston, 1972
Certification: Dermatology, Internal Medicine
13740 Research Blvd #P-4, Austin, 512-250-5521

Jarratt, Michael Taylor (6 mentions)
U of Texas-Dallas, 1966 *Certification:* Dermatology
8140 N Mo Pac Expy #3-116, Austin, 512-345-1350

Ramsdell, William Marshall (9 mentions)
Baylor U, 1979 *Certification:* Dermatology
102 Westlake Dr #100, West Lake Hills, 512-448-2777

Schaefer, Dale Glenn (12 mentions)
Baylor U, 1983 *Certification:* Dermatology
3807 Spicewood Springs Rd #200, Austin, 512-476-9195

Emergency Medicine

Adams, Joanne Gordon (5 mentions)
Certification: Pediatric Emergency Medicine
601 E 15th St, Austin, 512-324-7024

Blewett, John Henry (3 mentions)
Albany Med Coll, 1971 *Certification:* Emergency Medicine
919 E 32nd St, Austin, 512-397-4240

Burr, Mark Christopher (3 mentions)
U of Oklahoma, 1982 *Certification:* Emergency Medicine
12221 N Mo Pac Expy, Austin, 512-901-1000

Chilton, Raymond L., III (3 mentions)
Baylor U, 1990 *Certification:* Emergency Medicine
3801 N Lamar Blvd, Austin, 512-407-7700

Crocker, Patrick James (12 mentions)
Des Moines U, 1980 *Certification:* Emergency Medicine
4900 Mueller Blvd, Austin, 512-324-4000

Mendelson, Neil A. (3 mentions)
U of Texas-Dallas, 1994 *Certification:* Emergency Medicine
901 W Ben White Blvd, Austin, 512-448-7160

Mills, Robert Douglas (3 mentions)
Texas Tech U, 1983 *Certification:* Internal Medicine
12221 N Mo Pac Expy, Austin, 512-901-1100

Mitchell, Gary Ralph (3 mentions)
Certification: Emergency Medicine
901 W Ben White Blvd, Austin, 512-448-7160

Roberts, Sam S., III (6 mentions)
Certification: Emergency Medicine
720 W 34th St #101, Austin, 512-452-8533

Ziebell, Christopher M. (4 mentions)
U of Minnesota, 1990 *Certification:* Emergency Medicine
720 W 34th St #101, Austin, 512-452-8533

Endocrinology

Blevins, Thomas Craig (48 mentions)
Baylor U, 1981
Certification: Endocrinology and Metabolism, Internal Medicine
6500 N Mo Pac Expy #3-200, Austin, 512-458-8400

Fehrenkamp, Steven Harry (9 mentions)
U of Texas-Dallas, 1977
Certification: Endocrinology and Metabolism, Internal Medicine
4310 James Casey St #1-A, Austin, 512-445-2833

Scumpia, Simona M. (9 mentions)
FMS-Romania, 1980 *Certification:* Endocrinology, Diabetes, and Metabolism, Internal Medicine
2200 Park Bend Dr #3-300, Austin, 512-467-2727

Family Practice *(see note on page 9)*

Brooke, William F. (4 mentions)
Baylor U, 1986 *Certification:* Family Medicine
2400 Cedar Blvd, Austin, 512-901-4026

Byrd, Charles Ronald, Jr. (3 mentions)
Louisiana State U-Shreveport, 1992
Certification: Family Medicine
2712 Bee Cave Rd #122, Austin, 512-328-2752

Hausman-Cohen, Sharon R. (3 mentions)
Harvard U, 1993 *Certification:* Family Medicine
11149 Research Blvd #210, Austin, 512-231-1901

Joseph, David G. (5 mentions)
U of Texas-San Antonio, 1987 *Certification:* Family Medicine
2400 Cedar Blvd, Austin, 512-901-4026

Keinarth, Paul D. (4 mentions)
U of Texas-San Antonio, 1987 *Certification:* Family Medicine
5222 Burnet Rd #200, Austin, 512-459-9889

Ligon, Laurence A. (3 mentions)
U of Texas-Galveston, 1986 *Certification:* Family Medicine
912 S Capital of Texas Hwy #100, West Lake Hills, 512-306-8360

Margolin, Steven Philip (3 mentions)
Ohio State U, 1976
5222 Burnet Rd, Austin, 512-459-9889

Markley, Michelle Le (4 mentions)
U of Texas-Galveston, 1997 *Certification:* Family Medicine
3708 Jefferson St, Austin, 512-452-2244

Pampe, Eugene David (3 mentions)
U of Texas-Houston, 1981 *Certification:* Family Medicine
6012 W William Cannon Dr #D101, Austin, 512-892-6441

Rhodes, Kerry Don (3 mentions)
U of Texas-San Antonio, 1990 *Certification:* Family Medicine
631 W 38th St #2, Austin, 512-459-3177

Gastroenterology

Dabaghi, Rashad Eugene (11 mentions)
U of Texas-Dallas, 1975
Certification: Gastroenterology, Internal Medicine
1111 W 34th St #200, Austin, 512-454-4588

Frachtman, Robert Lee (9 mentions)
U of Texas-Dallas, 1978
Certification: Gastroenterology, Internal Medicine
1111 W 34th St #200, Austin, 512-454-4588

Gagneja, Harish Kumar (7 mentions)
FMS-India, 1991 *Certification:* Gastroenterology
1015 E 32nd St #408, Austin, 512-469-9966

Lubin, Craig Howard (20 mentions)
U of Oklahoma, 1977
Certification: Gastroenterology, Internal Medicine
1111 W 34th St #200, Austin, 512-454-4588

Ridgeway, Mona Chiai Lin (7 mentions)
Harvard U, 1997
Certification: Gastroenterology, Internal Medicine
1111 W 34th St #200, Austin, 512-454-4588

Sperling, Richard Michael (9 mentions)
Baylor U, 1988 *Certification:* Gastroenterology
1111 W 34th St #200, Austin, 512-454-4588

Willeford, George, III (7 mentions)
U of Texas-Dallas, 1975
Certification: Gastroenterology, Internal Medicine
1111 W 34th St #200, Austin, 512-454-4588

Ziebert, John J. (8 mentions)
Certification: Gastroenterology
11111 Research Blvd #390, Austin, 512-244-2273

Zwiener, Robert Jeffrey (7 mentions)
U of Texas-San Antonio, 1983
Certification: Pediatric Gastroenterology, Pediatrics
1301 Barbara Jordan Blvd #200, Austin, 512-628-1800
1 Chisholm Trail #200, Round Rock, 512-628-1800

General Surgery

Abikhaled, John A. (8 mentions)
Baylor U, 1992 *Certification:* Surgery
3901 Medical Pkwy #301, Austin, 512-467-7151

Ashworth, Rodney Brian (6 mentions)
U of Texas-Dallas, 1989 *Certification:* Surgery
1015 E 32nd St #308, Austin, 512-472-1381
12201 Renfert Way #335, Austin, 512-472-1381
4007 James Casey Blvd #A-230, Austin, 512-472-1381

Askew, Robert E., Jr. (16 mentions)
U of Texas-Galveston, 1986 *Certification:* Surgery
3901 Medical Pkwy #200, Austin, 512-467-7151

Jones, H. Lamar (12 mentions)
U of Texas-Galveston, 1972 *Certification:* Surgery
3901 Medical Pkwy #200, Austin, 512-467-7151

Markus, Robert M., Jr. (15 mentions)
U of Texas-Dallas, 1990 *Certification:* Surgery
1015 E 32nd St #308, Austin, 512-472-1381
4007 James Casey Blvd Bldg A #230, Austin, 512-472-1381
12201 Renfert Way #335, Austin, 512-472-1381

Sankar, Aravind B. (5 mentions)
U of Texas-Galveston, 1995 *Certification:* Surgery
12201 Renfert Way #335, Austin, 512-836-3210

Victor, Brant Edward (13 mentions)
U of Texas-Houston, 1984 *Certification:* Surgery
3901 Medical Pkwy #200, Austin, 512-467-7151

Geriatrics

Guerrero, Laura J. (4 mentions)
U of Texas-San Antonio, 1977 *Certification:* Internal Medicine
12222 N Mo Pac Expy, Austin, 514-901-4009

Russell, Peggy Martin (18 mentions)
U of North Texas, 1979 *Certification:* Internal Medicine
320 W 13th St #1-A, Austin, 512-477-4088
2122 Park Bend Dr, Austin, 512-836-9777
11127 Circle Dr, Austin, 512-288-8844
11110 Tom Adams Dr, Austin, 512-836-1515

Hematology/Oncology

Fain, Jerry D. (6 mentions)
U of Texas-Galveston, 1987
Certification: Hematology, Internal Medicine, Medical Oncology
901 W 38th St #200, Austin, 512-421-4100
2000 Scenic Dr, Georgetown, 512-421-4100

Hellerstedt, Beth A. (11 mentions)
U of Pittsburgh, 1997
Certification: Hematology, Internal Medicine, Medical Oncology
6204 Balcones Dr, Austin, 512-302-1771

Kasper, Michael Lawrence (19 mentions)
Johns Hopkins U, 1979
Certification: Hematology, Internal Medicine, Medical Oncology
6204 Balcones Dr, Austin, 512-302-1771

Lockhart, Sharon K. (6 mentions)
U of Texas-Houston, 1982 *Certification:* Pediatrics
1301 Barbara Jordan Blvd #401, Austin, 512-628-1900

Sandbach, John Franklin (9 mentions)
U of Kentucky, 1971
Certification: Hematology, Internal Medicine, Medical Oncology
6204 Balcones Dr, Austin, 512-302-1771

Tokaz, Laurence Kevin (11 mentions)
U of Texas-Dallas, 1979
Certification: Internal Medicine, Medical Oncology
4101 James Casey St #100, Austin, 512-447-2202

Tucker, Thomas Boynton (9 mentions)
U of Texas-Dallas, 1984
Certification: Internal Medicine, Medical Oncology
901 W 38th St #200, Austin, 512-421-4100
4101 James Casey #250, Austin, 612-440-7888

Infectious Disease

Bagwell, John Todd (37 mentions)
U of Texas-Galveston, 1980
Certification: Infectious Disease, Internal Medicine
1301 W 38th St #403, Austin, 512-459-0301

Bissett, Jack Daulton (38 mentions)
U of Texas-Galveston, 1981
1301 W 38th St #403, Austin, 512-459-0301

Infertility

Silverberg, Kaylen Mark (16 mentions)
Baylor U, 1984 *Certification:* Obstetrics & Gynecology, Reproductive Endocrinology/Infertility
6500 N Mo Pac Expy, Austin, 512-451-0149

Vaughn, Thomas Claude (23 mentions)
U of Texas-Galveston, 1974 *Certification:* Obstetrics & Gynecology, Reproductive Endocrinology/Infertility
6500 N Mo Pac Expy, Austin, 512-451-0149

Internal Medicine *(see note on page 9)*

Alexander, Anne Lynn (3 mentions)
U of Texas-Dallas, 1990 *Certification:* Internal Medicine
2911 Medical Arts St #18-A, Austin, 512-476-0190

Alsup, Ace Hill, III (21 mentions)
U of Texas-Galveston, 1972 *Certification:* Internal Medicine
3407 Glenview Ave, Austin, 512-459-3149

Booton, Steve Kirkwood (3 mentions)
U of Texas-Houston, 1983
Certification: Geriatric Medicine, Internal Medicine
900 E 30th St #100, Austin, 512-477-1405

Foster, Nancy Elizabeth (4 mentions)
U of Texas-Galveston, 1983 *Certification:* Internal Medicine
1301 W 38th St #402, Austin, 512-459-6503

Fung, Frederick H. (3 mentions)
Certification: Internal Medicine
12221 N Mo Pac Expy, Austin, 512-901-4009

Haydon, Hans Peter (3 mentions)
U of Texas-Galveston, 1980 *Certification:* Internal Medicine
6835 Austin Center Blvd, Austin, 512-346-6611

Hoverman, Isabel Vreeland (4 mentions)
Duke U, 1972 *Certification:* Internal Medicine
3407 Glenview Ave, Austin, 512-459-3149

Kroll, Kenneth C. (3 mentions)
U of Texas-Houston, 1985 *Certification:* Internal Medicine
1301 W 38th St #601, Austin, 512-454-5171

Lockett, William Cleveland (3 mentions)
Baylor U, 1977 *Certification:* Internal Medicine
4315 James Casey St, Austin, 512-460-3403

Marcus, Howard Richard (4 mentions)
Tufts U, 1971 *Certification:* Internal Medicine
6835 Austin Center Blvd, Austin, 512-346-6611

Miller, Lysbeth Wheelus (3 mentions)
U of Texas-San Antonio, 1979 *Certification:* Internal Medicine
313 E 12th St, Austin, 512-324-8880

Nutson, Peter Alan (4 mentions)
U of California-Davis, 1994 *Certification:* Internal Medicine
1301 W 38th St #402, Austin, 512-459-6503

Ream, Roy Scott (3 mentions)
Ohio State U, 1973 *Certification:* Internal Medicine
3407 Glenview Ave, Austin, 512-459-3149

Robinson, Frank E. (5 mentions)
Baylor U, 1980 *Certification:* Internal Medicine
3407 Glenview Ave, Austin, 512-459-3149

Romain, Michael Anthony (3 mentions)
Stony Brook U, 1993
12221 N Mo Pac Expy, Austin, 512-901-1111

Schneider, Adam J. (10 mentions)
U of Texas-Dallas, 1993 *Certification:* Internal Medicine
1301 W 38th St #601, Austin, 512-454-5171

Sonstein, Allen (4 mentions)
Jefferson Med Coll, 1972 *Certification:* Internal Medicine
7201 Manchaca Rd #B, Austin, 512-443-3577

Nephrology

Berry, Phillip Lee (7 mentions)
Baylor U, 1974 *Certification:* Pediatric Nephrology, Pediatrics
1301 Barbara Jordan Blvd #200, Austin, 512-628-1800

Betts, Judith Ann (13 mentions)
U of Texas-Dallas, 1985
Certification: Internal Medicine, Nephrology
408 W 45th St, Austin, 512-451-5800

Hines, Timothy Reed (12 mentions)
Baylor U, 1986 *Certification:* Internal Medicine, Nephrology
408 W 45th St, Austin, 512-451-5800

Welch, Byron Russell (8 mentions)
U of Texas-Dallas, 1985
Certification: Internal Medicine, Nephrology
4100 Duval Rd #4-102, Austin, 512-832-0999

Neurological Surgery

Hummell, Matthew Kimberly (8 mentions)
U of Texas-San Antonio, 1986 *Certification:* Neurological Surgery
400 W 15th St #800, Austin, 512-306-1323

Kemper, Craig Martin (9 mentions)
U of Texas-Galveston, 1988 *Certification:* Neurological Surgery
400 W 15th St #800, Austin, 512-306-1323

Peterson, Daniel Lee (11 mentions)
U of Colorado, 1988 *Certification:* Neurological Surgery
400 W 15th St #800, Austin, 512-306-1323

Tumu, Hari (11 mentions)
U of Mississippi, 1996
400 W 15th St #800, Austin, 512-306-1323

Neurology

Aldredge, Horatio Ransome (5 mentions)
Harvard U, 1964 *Certification:* Neurology
313 E 12th St #100, Austin, 512-324-3096

Camp, Darryl (10 mentions)
Certification: Neurology, Vascular Neurology
313 E 12th St #100, Austin, 512-324-9660

Hill, Thomas Andrew (7 mentions)
U of Texas-Galveston, 1972 *Certification:* Neurology
1015 E 32nd St #406, Austin, 512-495-1850

Kane, Jeffrey S. (6 mentions)
U of Texas-Dallas, 1995 *Certification:* Clinical Neurophysiology, Neurology with Special Qualifications in Child Neurology
1301 Barbara Jordan Blvd #200, Austin, 512-628-1800

Morledge, David Walker (9 mentions)
Texas Tech U, 1986 *Certification:* Neurology
711 W 38th St Bldg F1, Austin, 512-458-6121

Reading, Patience H. (8 mentions)
Certification: Neurology
12221 N Mo Pac Expy, Austin, 512-901-4011

Tallman, Richard Dean (6 mentions)
Mayo Med Sch, 1977 *Certification:* Internal Medicine, Neurology
12221 N Mo Pac Expy, Austin, 512-901-4011

York, Jennifer A. (6 mentions)
Baylor U, 1993
Certification: Clinical Neurophysiology, Neurology, Sleep Medicine
5750 Balcones Dr #110, Austin, 512-458-2600

Obstetrics/Gynecology

Binford, Nancy E. (3 mentions)
U of Texas-Dallas, 1994 *Certification:* Obstetrics & Gynecology
3705 Medical Pkwy #540, Austin, 512-452-8888

Breen, Michael Timothy (5 mentions)
U of Texas-Galveston, 1981
Certification: Family Medicine, Obstetrics & Gynecology
313 E 12th St, Austin, 512-324-8670

Cowan, Robert Kyle, Jr. (6 mentions)
U of Texas-Galveston, 1991 *Certification:* Obstetrics & Gynecology
1301 W 38th St #109, Austin, 512-451-8211

Cutler, Wendy (4 mentions)
U of Colorado, 1999 *Certification:* Obstetrics & Gynecology
12221 N Mo Pac Expy, Austin, 512-901-4013

Doss, Noble Webster (3 mentions)
U of Texas-Dallas, 1973 *Certification:* Obstetrics & Gynecology
4201 Marathon Blvd #301, Austin, 512-451-7991

Neyman, Sherry Lamar (6 mentions)
U of Texas-Dallas, 1992 *Certification:* Obstetrics & Gynecology
12201 Renfert Way #215, Austin, 512-425-3875

Nunnelly, Patrick Dale (3 mentions)
U of Texas-Galveston, 1977 *Certification:* Obstetrics & Gynecology
1301 W 38th St #300, Austin, 512-454-5721

Pevoto, Patrick S. (3 mentions)
U of Texas-Galveston, 1983 *Certification:* Obstetrics & Gynecology
11111 Research Blvd #450, Austin, 512-241-7200

Phillips, Michael F. (6 mentions)
U of Texas-Houston, 1988 *Certification:* Obstetrics & Gynecology
1301 W 38th St #109, Austin, 512-451-8211

Schmitz, Martha E. (3 mentions)
U of Texas-Galveston, 1989 *Certification:* Obstetrics & Gynecology
4007 James Casey #A-240, Austin, 512-394-0054

Seeker, Christopher Glenn (5 mentions)
U of Texas-San Antonio, 1984
Certification: Obstetrics & Gynecology
1301 W 38th St #109, Austin, 512-451-8211

Swenson, Karen Grace (11 mentions)
Baylor U, 1981 *Certification:* Obstetrics & Gynecology
1305 W 34th St #308, Austin, 512-494-8082

Uribe, Marco Arturo (3 mentions)
Baylor U, 1983 *Certification:* Obstetrics & Gynecology
1301 W 38th St #109, Austin, 512-451-8211

Weihs, Diana Gay (10 mentions)
Baylor U, 1981 *Certification:* Obstetrics & Gynecology
1305 W 34th St #308, Austin, 512-459-8082

Ophthalmology

Berger, Michelle A. (5 mentions)
Med Coll of Wisconsin, 1981 *Certification:* Ophthalmology
4100 Duval Rd, Austin, 512-997-7750

Broberg, Peter Harlan (7 mentions)
Baylor U, 1978 *Certification:* Ophthalmology
4207 James Casey St #305, Austin, 512-447-6096

Buckingham, Dawn Carlisle (4 mentions)
U of Texas-Galveston, 1997 *Certification:* Ophthalmology
5011 Burnet Rd, Austin, 512-583-2020
1101 W 40th St, Austin, 512-583-2020

Busse, Franklin K., Jr. (7 mentions)
Baylor U, 1988 *Certification:* Ophthalmology
4700 Seton Center Pkwy #150, Austin, 512-345-3595

Chandler, Thomas Yoder (7 mentions)
U of Texas-Houston, 1981
Certification: Internal Medicine, Ophthalmology
12221 N Mo Pac Expy, Austin, 512-901-4014

Harper, Clio A., III (5 mentions)
U of Oklahoma, 1988 *Certification:* Ophthalmology
801 W 38th St #200, Austin, 512-451-0103

Shepler, Maria Cristina (5 mentions)
U of Oklahoma, 1998 *Certification:* Ophthalmology
12221 N Mo Pac Expy, Austin, 512-901-4014

Smith, Randolph T. (5 mentions)
U of Texas-Galveston, 2001 *Certification:* Ophthalmology
3300 W Anderson Ln #308, Austin, 512-335-4300

Walters, Thomas R. (4 mentions)
U of Texas-Dallas, 1982 *Certification:* Ophthalmology
1700 S Mo Pac Expy, Austin, 512-327-7000
5717 Balcones Dr, Austin, 512-327-7000

Orthopedics

Bergin-Nader, Barbara Lee (5 mentions)
Texas Tech U, 1981 *Certification:* Orthopaedic Surgery
4700 Seton Center Pkwy #200, Austin, 512-476-7150

Carter, Shelby Henry, III (18 mentions)
New York U, 1980 *Certification:* Orthopaedic Surgery
1301 W 38th St #102, Austin, 512-454-4561

Davis, Donald Robert (7 mentions)
U of Texas-San Antonio, 1972 *Certification:* Orthopaedic Surgery
630 W 34th St #302, Austin, 512-459-3228
1401 Medical Pkwy #B-120, Cedar Park, 512-459-3228

Elenz, Douglas Reed (4 mentions)
U of Texas-Houston, 1990 *Certification:* Orthopaedic Surgery
900 W 38th St #300, Austin, 512-450-1300

Kahn, Anthony (5 mentions)
FMS-South Africa, 1983 *Certification:* Orthopaedic Surgery
1301 Barbara Jordan Blvd #300, Austin, 512-478-8116

Malone, Charles Bruce, III (5 mentions)
Duke U, 1969 *Certification:* Orthopaedic Surgery
1015 E 32nd St #101, Austin, 512-477-6341

Pearce, Stephen Moe (5 mentions)
U of Texas-Dallas, 1979 *Certification:* Orthopaedic Surgery
1015 E 32nd St #101, Austin, 512-477-6341

Savage, David Clyde (7 mentions)
Baylor U, 1988 *Certification:* Orthopaedic Surgery
4534 W Gate Blvd #110, Austin, 512-892-1220

Seaquist, Jack Linden (4 mentions)
Baylor U, 1972 *Certification:* Orthopaedic Surgery
1301 W 38th St #102, Austin, 512-454-4561

Shapiro, Jay (5 mentions)
U of Texas-Galveston, 1984 *Certification:* Orthopaedic Surgery
1301 Barbara Jordan Blvd #300, Austin, 512-478-8116

Windler, Edwin Carey (6 mentions)
Baylor U, 1973 *Certification:* Orthopaedic Surgery
900 W 38th St #300, Austin, 512-450-1300

Otorhinolaryngology

Huang, Patti Chiasue (11 mentions)
Duke U, 1994 *Certification:* Otolaryngology
12221 N Mo Pac Expy, Austin, 512-901-4006

Morgan, Arthur Boyd (11 mentions)
Baylor U, 1975 *Certification:* Otolaryngology
3705 Medical Pkwy #205, Austin, 512-459-8783

Scholl, Peter Dennis (22 mentions)
U of Texas-Houston, 1981 *Certification:* Otolaryngology
3705 Medical Pkwy #310, Austin, 512-458-6391
7200 Wyoming Springs Rd, Round Rock, 512-388-2217

Zapalac, Jeffrey Scott, Jr. (10 mentions)
U of Texas-Dallas, 1996 *Certification:* Otolaryngology
3705 Medical Pkwy #310, Austin, 512-458-6391
7200 Wyoming Springs Rd, Round Rock, 512-388-2217

Pain Medicine

Haro, Julian Lowell (8 mentions)
Louisiana State U, 1974
Certification: Anesthesiology, Pain Medicine
15808 FM 620 N #215, Austin, 512-454-9426
900 W 38th St #400, Austin, 512-454-9426

Wills, Robert P. (7 mentions)
U of Texas-Dallas, 1989 *Certification:* Anesthesiology
2501 W William Cannon Dr #401, Austin, 512-416-7246

Pathology

Collins, Phillip Clyde (10 mentions)
U of Texas-Dallas, 1977
Certification: Anatomic Pathology & Clinical Pathology
12221 N Mo Pac Expy, Austin, 512-901-1216

Eckert, Edward Randolph (4 mentions)
Texas A&M U, 1984
Certification: Anatomic Pathology & Clinical Pathology
12221 N Mo Pac Expy, Austin, 512-901-1215

Listrom, Margaret Barron (10 mentions)
U of Virginia, 1980 *Certification:* Anatomic Pathology &
    Clinical Pathology, Cytopathology
9200 Wall St, Austin, 512-339-1275

Riopel, Maureen Ann (6 mentions)
U of South Carolina, 1991
Certification: Anatomic Pathology & Clinical Pathology
9200 Wall St, Austin, 512-339-1275

Pediatrics *(see note on page 9)*

Aiello, Leslie Franklin (4 mentions)
Ohio State U, 1972 *Certification:* Pediatrics
1500 W 38th St #20, Austin, 512-458-5323

Brown, Ari Zamutt (3 mentions)
Baylor U, 1992 *Certification:* Pediatrics
2400 Cedar Bend Rd, Austin, 512-901-4016

Caldwell, William David (7 mentions)
Tulane U, 1973 *Certification:* Pediatrics
1305 W 34th St #210, Austin, 512-454-0406

Ellis, Leighton Elizabeth (3 mentions)
U of South Florida, 1988 *Certification:* Pediatrics
12201 Renfert Way #110, Austin, 512-491-5125

Glazener, Wesley S. (4 mentions)
U of Texas-Houston, 1988 *Certification:* Pediatrics
1305 W 34th St #206, Austin, 512-454-8691

Guerrero, Juan Manuel (4 mentions)
U of Texas-Dallas, 1981 *Certification:* Pediatrics
2400 Cedar Bend Rd, Austin, 512-901-4016

Johnson, Mary Marvin (3 mentions)
Wake Forest U, 1977 *Certification:* Pediatrics
4700 Seton Center Pkwy #125, Austin, 512-338-8500

Louis, Jack Allan (4 mentions)
U of Texas-San Antonio, 1977 *Certification:* Pediatrics
711 W 38th St #C2, Austin, 512-458-6717

Lowrey, Robert Warren (3 mentions)
Louisiana State U, 1981 *Certification:* Pediatrics
6835 Austin Center Blvd, Austin, 512-346-6611

Mirrop, Samuel A. (4 mentions)
U of Texas-Dallas, 1989 *Certification:* Pediatrics
1500 W 38th St #20, Austin, 512-458-5323

Nauert, Beth Webb (3 mentions)
Texas A&M U, 1981 *Certification:* Pediatrics
4315 James Casey St, Austin, 512-460-3404

Ramirez, Jaime Eduardo (5 mentions)
U of Texas-Galveston, 1983 *Certification:* Pediatrics
1111 W 34th St #102, Austin, 512-467-1600

Terwelp, Daniel Rome (3 mentions)
U of Texas-Houston, 1975 *Certification:* Pediatrics
3410 Far West Blvd, Austin, 512-345-6758

Worrel, John Richard (3 mentions)
U of Texas-Dallas, 1979 *Certification:* Pediatrics
2400 Cedar Bend Dr, Austin, 512-901-4016

Plastic Surgery

Cullington, James Richard (6 mentions)
U of Texas-Galveston, 1972 *Certification:* Plastic Surgery
1010 W 9th St, Austin, 512-472-5382

Haydon, M. Scott (5 mentions)
U of Texas-Galveston, 1994 *Certification:* Plastic Surgery
3003 Bee Cave Rd #203, Austin, 512-300-2600

Mosier, David M. (5 mentions)
FMS-Mexico, 1984 *Certification:* Plastic Surgery
6818 Austin Center Blvd #206, Austin, 512-338-4404

Tjelmeland, Kelly Eugene (7 mentions)
Baylor U, 1993 *Certification:* Plastic Surgery
4220 Bull Creek Rd, Austin, 512-617-7500

Turner, David Michael (6 mentions)
Texas Tech U, 1980 *Certification:* Plastic Surgery
711 W 38th St #C-8, Austin, 512-458-9133

Wilder, Alfred Christian (8 mentions)
Baylor U, 1977 *Certification:* Plastic Surgery
3003 Bee Cave Rd #203, Austin, 512-459-1234

Psychiatry

Hauser, Lawrence Allan (4 mentions)
U of Texas-San Antonio, 1981
Certification: Psychiatry, Psychosomatic Medicine
1600 W 38th St #404, Austin, 512-454-7741

Kreisle, James Edwin, Jr. (5 mentions)
Emory U, 1975 *Certification:* Psychiatry
1600 W 38th St #321, Austin, 512-454-5716

Streusand, William Charles (5 mentions)
Baylor U, 1980 *Certification:* Child & Adolescent Psychiatry,
    Psychiatry, Psychosomatic Medicine
1600 W 38th St #212, Austin, 512-452-2929

Tullis, William Hershey (4 mentions)
U of Texas-San Antonio, 1978 *Certification:* Psychiatry
1600 W 38th St #321, Austin, 512-454-5716

Pulmonary Disease

Deaton, William Joel (19 mentions)
Baylor U, 1969 *Certification:* Critical Care Medicine,
    Internal Medicine, Pulmonary Disease
1305 W 34th St #400, Austin, 512-459-6599

Gilbey, Laura Kathryn (7 mentions)
Baylor U, 1995
Certification: Critical Care Medicine, Pulmonary Disease
12201 Renfert Way #260, Austin, 512-977-0123

Shapiro, Michael (22 mentions)
U of Texas-Galveston, 1978 *Certification:* Critical Care
    Medicine, Internal Medicine, Pulmonary Disease
1305 W 34th St #400, Austin, 512-459-6599

Weingarten, Jordan S. (7 mentions)
Baylor U, 1980 *Certification:* Critical Care Medicine,
    Internal Medicine, Pulmonary Disease
1305 W 34th St #400, Austin, 512-459-6599

Radiology—Diagnostic

Barr, Lori Lee (3 mentions)
Louisiana State U-Shreveport, 1984
Certification: Diagnostic Radiology, Pediatric Radiology
10900 Stonelake Blvd #250, Austin, 512-795-5100

Bell, Gregory Kittredge (3 mentions)
Marshall U, 1991 *Certification:* Diagnostic Radiology
8038 Mesa Dr, Austin, 512-901-8729
12221 N MoMac Expy, Austin, 512-901-1300

Butschek, Chris Matthew (5 mentions)
U of Texas-Dallas, 1978 *Certification:* Diagnostic Radiology
11113 Research Blvd, Austin, 512-324-6000

Chen, Dillon (3 mentions)
U of California-San Francisco, 1995
Certification: Diagnostic Radiology
8038 Mesa Dr, Austin, 512-901-8729
12221 MoPac Expy N, Austin, 512-901-1300

Fletcher, Thomas Boudol (5 mentions)
U of Texas-Dallas, 1983 *Certification:* Diagnostic Radiology
10900 Stonelake Blvd #250, Austin, 512-795-5100

Goldblatt, David (3 mentions)
U of Cincinnati, 1980
Certification: Diagnostic Radiology, Neuroradiology
10900 Stonelake Blvd #250, Austin, 512-795-5100

Harper, Michael T. (4 mentions)
U of Texas-San Antonio, 1990 *Certification:* Diagnostic Radiology
4706 Balcones Dr, Austin, 512-619-5130

Leake, David Ray (4 mentions)
U of Texas-Galveston, 1978
Certification: Diagnostic Radiology, Neuroradiology
10900 Stone Lake Blvd #250, Austin, 512-328-4984

Manning, John Edward, Jr. (4 mentions)
Columbia U, 1993 *Certification:* Diagnostic Radiology,
Vascular & Interventional Radiology
10900 Stonelake Blvd #250, Austin, 512-795-5100

Martin, Michael Beckett (6 mentions)
U of Arkansas, 1975 *Certification:* Diagnostic Radiology,
Vascular & Interventional Radiology
10900 Stonelake Blvd #250, Austin, 512-795-5100

Trevino, Anthony K. (4 mentions)
Baylor U, 1989 *Certification:* Diagnostic Radiology
10900 Stonelake Blvd #250, Austin, 512-795-5100

Truong, Binh Cu (3 mentions)
Louisiana State U-Shreveport, 1993
Certification: Diagnostic Radiology, Pediatric Radiology
10900 Stonelake Blvd #250, Austin, 512-795-5100

Radiology—Therapeutic

Manning, John Edward, Jr. (7 mentions)
Columbia U, 1993 *Certification:* Diagnostic Radiology,
Vascular & Interventional Radiology
10900 Stonelake Blvd #250, Austin, 512-795-5100

Martin, Michael Beckett (6 mentions)
U of Arkansas, 1975 *Certification:* Diagnostic Radiology,
Vascular & Interventional Radiology
10900 Stonelake Blvd #250, Austin, 512-795-5100

Rutledge, John Neal (5 mentions)
U of Oklahoma, 1980
Certification: Diagnostic Radiology, Neuroradiology
10900 Stonelake Blvd #250, Austin, 512-795-5100

Rehabilitation

Queralt, Mark V. (4 mentions)
U of Texas-Dallas, 1992
Certification: Pain Medicine, Physical Medicine & Rehabilitation
3724 Executive Center Dr #G10, Austin, 512-345-5925

Smith, Charlotte Hoehne (10 mentions)
Baylor U, 1986 *Certification:* Physical Medicine &
Rehabilitation, Spinal Cord Injury Medicine
1215 Red River #427, Austin, 512-479-3554
601 E 15th St, Austin, 512-479-3559

Volpe, Joseph Andrew (4 mentions)
U of Texas-Galveston, 1994
Certification: Physical Medicine & Rehabilitation
12221 N Mo Pac Expy, Austin, 512-901-4011

Rheumatology

Sayers, Brian Sam (22 mentions)
U of Texas-Dallas, 1981
Certification: Internal Medicine, Rheumatology
1301 W 38th St #110, Austin, 512-454-3631

Tew, Monty B. (16 mentions)
Certification: Internal Medicine, Rheumatology
12221 N Mo Pac Expy, Austin, 512-901-4018

Thoracic Surgery

Dewan, Stephen James (8 mentions)
Baylor U, 1979 *Certification:* Surgery, Thoracic Surgery
1010 W 40th St, Austin, 512-459-8753

Hume, Andrew Tucker (10 mentions)
U of Mississippi, 1989 *Certification:* Surgery, Thoracic Surgery
1010 W 40th St, Austin, 512-459-8753

King, Lewis G. (9 mentions)
U of Texas-Galveston, 1984
Certification: Surgery, Thoracic Surgery
6500 N Mo Pac Expy #2207, Austin, 512-494-9985

Urology

Cortez, Jose Carlos (9 mentions)
Baylor U, 1985 *Certification:* Pediatric Urology, Urology
1301 Barbara Jordan Blvd #302, Austin, 512-472-6134

Hardeman, Stephen Walter (14 mentions)
U of Texas-Dallas, 1980 *Certification:* Urology
11410 Jollyville Rd #1101, Austin, 512-231-1444

Kocurek, Jeffrey Neal (13 mentions)
U of Texas-Galveston, 1991 *Certification:* Urology
3100 Red River St #2, Austin, 512-477-5905

Phillips, David L. (12 mentions)
U of Texas-San Antonio, 1988 *Certification:* Urology
4007 James Casey St #C-150, Austin, 512-443-5988

Vascular Surgery

Church, Phillip John (17 mentions)
U of Texas-Dallas, 1975 *Certification:* Vascular Surgery
1010 W 40th St, Austin, 512-459-8753

Jobe, Jeffrey Scott (14 mentions)
Texas Tech U, 1979 *Certification:* Vascular Surgery
1010 W 40th St, Austin, 512-459-8753

Settle, Stephen Michael (18 mentions)
U of Texas-Dallas, 1986 *Certification:* Surgery, Vascular Surgery
1010 W 40th St, Austin, 512-459-8753

Utah

Salt Lake City Area

Including Salt Lake County

Allergy/Immunology

Bernhisel-Broadbent, Jan (14 mentions)
U of Utah, 1983 *Certification:* Allergy & Immunology, Pediatrics
2000 S 900, Salt Lake City, 801-464-7660

Gourley, David Scott (7 mentions)
Temple U, 1981 *Certification:* Allergy & Immunology, Pediatrics
6065 Fashion Blvd #255, Salt Lake City, 801-266-4115

Henry, Anthony Robert (7 mentions)
Baylor U, 1977 *Certification:* Allergy & Immunology, Internal Medicine, Nephrology
6065 Fashion Blvd #255, Salt Lake City, 801-266-4115

Anesthesiology

Cahalan, Michael Kermit (4 mentions)
Temple U, 1975 *Certification:* Anesthesiology
30 N 1900 E #3C444-50M, Salt Lake City, 801-581-6393

Cowley, Cris G. (3 mentions)
U of Utah, 1977 *Certification:* Anesthesiology
400 C St, Salt Lake City, 801-993-9582

Enslin, Kyle Richard (4 mentions)
U of California-Los Angeles, 1978
Certification: Anesthesiology, Internal Medicine
1954 Fort Union Blvd #104, Salt Lake City, 801-993-9530

Hurst, Scott (6 mentions)
Certification: Anesthesiology
400 C St, Salt Lake City, 801-993-9582
1954 Fort Union Blvd, Salt Lake City, 801-408-3200

Mulroy, John Joseph, Jr. (3 mentions)
Washington U, 1979 *Certification:* Anesthesiology, Pediatrics
100 N Medical Dr, Salt Lake City, 801-993-9551

Peters, Jeffrey Leigh (3 mentions)
U of Utah, 1974 *Certification:* Anesthesiology
1954 Fort Union Blvd #104, Salt Lake City, 801-993-9530

Petersen, Peggy Brinkmann (3 mentions)
U of Utah, 1985 *Certification:* Anesthesiology
1200 E 3900 S #30, Salt Lake City, 801-268-7415
1954 E Fort Union Blvd #104, Salt Lake City, 801-993-9530

Smith, Homer Redd (3 mentions)
U of Utah, 1979 *Certification:* Anesthesiology
1954 Fort Union Blvd #104, Salt Lake City, 801-993-9530

Cardiac Surgery

Karwande, Shreekanth V. (14 mentions)
FMS-India, 1974 *Certification:* Thoracic Surgery
1160 E 3900 S #2000, Salt Lake City, 801-743-4750

Thorne, J. Kent (15 mentions)
U of Utah, 1978 *Certification:* Thoracic Surgery
1160 E 3900 S #2000, Salt Lake City, 801-266-3418

Cardiology

Anderson, Jeffrey Lance (5 mentions)
Harvard U, 1972 *Certification:* Cardiovascular Disease, Clinical Cardiac Electrophysiology, Internal Medicine
5121 S Cottonwood Dr, Murray, 801-507-4000

Borchardt, Roger Lee (3 mentions)
FMS-Mexico, 1988 *Certification:* Interventional Cardiology
3725 W 4100 S, Salt Lake City, 801-968-1818
3584 W 9000 S #209, West Jordan, 801-676-3776

Brown, Ronald Earl (7 mentions)
U of Utah, 1988 *Certification:* Interventional Cardiology
1160 E 3900 S #2000, Salt Lake City, 801-266-3418

Burke, James Lee (3 mentions)
U of Texas-Galveston, 1973 *Certification:* Cardiovascular Disease, Internal Medicine, Interventional Cardiology
324 10th Ave #206, Salt Lake City, 801-408-3900
5169 S Cottonwood St #510, Salt Lake City, 801-408-3900

Calame, Thomas Robert (6 mentions)
U of Maryland, 1973 *Certification:* Cardiovascular Disease, Internal Medicine, Interventional Cardiology
82 S 1100 E #103, Salt Lake City, 801-746-4440
3590 W 90th St #240, West Jordan, 801-532-0204

Fowles, Robert Earl (6 mentions)
Harvard U, 1973
Certification: Cardiovascular Disease, Internal Medicine
333 S 900 E, Salt Lake City, 801-535-8399

Freedman, Roger A. (3 mentions)
Harvard U, 1978 *Certification:* Cardiovascular Disease, Clinical Cardiac Electrophysiology, Internal Medicine
100 N Medical Dr, Salt Lake City, 801-581-7715

Horton, Steven Curtis (3 mentions)
Baylor U, 1980
Certification: Cardiovascular Disease, Internal Medicine
324 10th Ave, Salt Lake City, 801-408-3900
5169 S Cottonwood St #510, Salt Lake City, 801-408-3900

Nielson, Kenneth George (3 mentions)
U of Utah, 1988 *Certification:* Cardiovascular Disease
1160 E 3900 S #2000, Salt Lake City, 801-266-3418

Revenaugh, James Robert (3 mentions)
Northwestern U, 1987
Certification: Cardiovascular Disease, Interventional Cardiology
324 10th Ave #206, Salt Lake City, 801-408-3900
5169 S Cottonwodd St #510, Salt Lake City, 801-408-3900

Rokeach, Steven Alan (3 mentions)
U of Miami, 1975
Certification: Cardiovascular Disease, Internal Medicine
5169 S Cottonwood St #B-620, Murray, 801-507-8600
9660 S 1300 E, Sandy, 801-507-8600

Sharma, Pawan K. (3 mentions)
FMS-India, 1980
Certification: Cardiovascular Disease, Interventional Cardiology
1160 East 3900 South #2000, Salt Lake City, 801-266-3418
3725 West 4100 S, West Valley City, 801-968-1818

Zubair, Imran (5 mentions)
U of Alabama, 1985 *Certification:* Cardiovascular Disease, Internal Medicine, Interventional Cardiology
82 S 1100 E #103, Salt Lake City, 801-764-4440

Dermatology

Bradley, Rulon Ralph (5 mentions)
U of Utah, 1974 *Certification:* Dermatology
166 E 5900 S #B-111, Salt Lake City, 801-268-9672

Hansen, C. David (6 mentions)
U of Utah, 1973 *Certification:* Dermatology
50 N Medical Dr, Salt Lake City, 801-581-7837

Jensen, Joseph Dean (5 mentions)
U of Utah, 1990 *Certification:* Dermatology
7396 S Union Park Ave #201, Midvale, 801-567-1400

Reese, Don Loren (5 mentions)
U of Utah, 1977 *Certification:* Dermatology
3725 W 4100 S, West Valley City, 801-965-3736

Swinyer, Leonard James (13 mentions)
U of Vermont, 1966
Certification: Dermatology, Dermatopathology
3920 S 1100 E #310, Salt Lake City, 801-266-8841

Vanderhooft, Sheryll Land (8 mentions)
U of Utah, 1988 *Certification:* Dermatology
100 N Medical Dr, Salt Lake City, 801-581-6465

Zone, John Joseph (12 mentions)
SUNY-Upstate Med U, 1971
Certification: Dermatological Immunology/Diagnostic and Laboratory Immunology, Dermatology, Internal Medicine
50 N Medical Dr, Salt Lake City, 801-551-2955

Emergency Medicine

Bolte, Robert Glenn (4 mentions)
U of Kentucky, 1977
Certification: Pediatric Emergency Medicine, Pediatrics
100 N Mario Capecchi Dr, Salt Lake City, 801-587-7450

Duffy, Owen H. (3 mentions)
U of Utah, 1976
Certification: Emergency Medicine, Internal Medicine
8th Ave & C St, Salt Lake City, 801-408-1181
5121 S Cottonwood St, Murray, 801-507-6600

Hartsell, Stephen Carl (3 mentions)
U of North Carolina, 1982 *Certification:* Emergency Medicine
50 N Medical Dr, Salt Lake City, 801-581-2292

Hildebrand, William E., III (3 mentions)
U of Utah, 1982 *Certification:* Internal Medicine
8th Ave & C St, Salt Lake City, 801-408-1181
5121 S Cottonwood St, Murray, 801-507-6600

Schunk, Jeffrey Edward (3 mentions)
Oregon Health Sciences U, 1983
Certification: Pediatric Emergency Medicine, Pediatrics
100 N Mario Capecchi Dr, Salt Lake City, 801-587-7450

Shiozawa, Brian Elwood (5 mentions)
U of Washington, 1981 *Certification:* Emergency Medicine
1200 E 3900 S, Salt Lake City, 801-268-7975

Swanson, Eric R. (3 mentions)
U of Utah, 1992 *Certification:* Emergency Medicine
50 N Medical Dr, Salt Lake City, 801-581-2292

Endocrinology

Clarke, Dana H. (6 mentions)
U of Maryland, 1966
Certification: Endocrinology and Metabolism, Internal Medicine
615 Arapeen Dr #100, Salt Lake City, 801-581-7761

Falahati-Nini, Alireza (5 mentions)
FMS-Austria, 1994
Certification: Endocrinology, Diabetes, and Metabolism
1250 E 3900 S #420, Salt Lake City, 801-269-9939

Grua, James Russell (13 mentions)
U of Utah, 1986 *Certification:* Endocrinology, Diabetes, and Metabolism, Internal Medicine
333 S 900 E, Salt Lake City, 801-535-8398

Family Practice *(see note on page 9)*

Sanyer, Osman Necmi (4 mentions)
U of Wisconsin, 1983 *Certification:* Family Medicine
555 S Foothill Dr, Salt Lake City, 801-581-8000

Gastroenterology

Box, Terry Dean (6 mentions)
U of Texas-Dallas, 1977 *Certification:* Gastroenterology, Internal Medicine, Transplant Hepatology
6360 S 3000 E #310, Salt Lake City, 801-944-3144

Clark, Holly B. (5 mentions)
U of Arizona, 1997
Certification: Gastroenterology, Internal Medicine
1250 E 3900 S #360, Salt Lake City, 801-263-3041

Harnsberger, Janet Kuska (8 mentions)
U of California-Los Angeles, 1978
Certification: Pediatric Gastroenterology, Pediatrics
5770 S 250 E #330, Salt Lake City, 801-314-4444

Heiner, Andrew Martin (5 mentions)
U of Texas-Galveston, 1987 *Certification:* Gastroenterology
9829 S 300 E #200, Sandy, 801-619-9000

Pedersen, Peder Jens (9 mentions)
U of Minnesota, 1993 *Certification:* Gastroenterology
1250 E 3900 S #360, Salt Lake City, 801-263-3041

General Surgery

Belnap, Le Grand Petty (3 mentions)
U of Utah, 1973 *Certification:* Surgery
1250 E 3900 S #220, Salt Lake City, 801-262-9782
5169 S Cottonwood St #320, Murray, 801-507-3380

Christensen, Brent James (13 mentions)
U of Utah, 1984 *Certification:* Surgery
324 Kent Ave #224, Salt Lake City, 801-408-7660

Fine, Stephanie Grace (4 mentions)
U of New Mexico, 1989 *Certification:* Surgery
3584 W 9000 S #304, West Jordan, 801-562-3150

Hashimoto, Edward George (3 mentions)
U of Utah, 1981
9690 S 1300 E #220, Sandy, 801-571-2027

Leckman, Scott Albert (4 mentions)
U of Utah, 1983 *Certification:* Surgery
1220 E 3900 S #3-G, Salt Lake City, 801-268-4924

Lloyd, Erika Christine (3 mentions)
Tufts U, 1993 *Certification:* Surgery
1220 E 3900 S #4A, Salt Lake City, 801-263-8511

Mintz, Steven Jay (7 mentions)
U of Texas-Dallas, 1976 *Certification:* Surgery
24 S 1100 E #201, Salt Lake City, 801-478-0010

Mulvihill, Sean Jordan (3 mentions)
U of Southern California, 1981 *Certification:* Surgery
30 N 1900 E #3B110, Salt Lake City, 801-581-7167
2000 Circle of Hope Dr, Salt Lake City, 801-581-7167

Naylor, Robert G. (4 mentions)
U of Utah, 1969
1220 E 3900 S #4A, Salt Lake City, 801-263-8511

Nelson, Edward Waller (3 mentions)
U of Utah, 1974 *Certification:* Surgery
30 N 1900 E, Salt Lake City, 801-581-7738
2000 Circle of Hope Dr, Salt Lake City, 801-581-7738

Price, Raymond Richard (4 mentions)
Harvard U, 1987 *Certification:* Surgery
5169 S Cottonwood St #410, Murray, 801-535-8189

Price, Robert Sheldon (3 mentions)
U of Utah, 1989 *Certification:* Surgery
5169 S Cottonwood St #410, Murray, 801-507-1600

Rasmussen, Clark J. (5 mentions)
U of Utah, 1992 *Certification:* Surgery
5169 S Cottonwood St #410, Murray, 801-507-1600

Rees, William Vincent (3 mentions)
Cornell U, 1974 *Certification:* Surgery
333 S 900 E, Salt Lake City, 801-535-8163

Stevens, Mark Howard (4 mentions)
U of Utah, 1981 *Certification:* Surgery
5169 S Cottonwood St, Murray, 501-507-3460

Voorhees, Hugh David (5 mentions)
U of Utah, 1972
4000 S 700 E #9, Salt Lake City, 801-262-3564

Geriatrics

Brunker, Cherie Pratt (10 mentions)
U of Utah, 1987
Certification: Geriatric Medicine, Internal Medicine
8th Ave & C St, Salt Lake City, 801-408-8600

Lane, Keith Joseph (4 mentions)
FMS-Mexico, 1981
Certification: Geriatric Medicine, Internal Medicine
82 S 1100 E #204, Salt Lake City, 801-350-4602

Wood, James S. (4 mentions)
Certification: Internal Medicine
1414 E 4500 S #1, Salt Lake City, 801-272-0255

Hematology/Oncology

Buys, Saundra S. (6 mentions)
Tufts U, 1979
Certification: Hematology, Internal Medicine, Medical Oncology
1950 Circle of Hope Dr, Salt Lake City, 801-585-0303

Di Fiore, Kent C. (6 mentions)
George Washington U, 1975
3838 S 700 E #100, Salt Lake City, 801-269-0231

Ford, Clyde De Jong (4 mentions)
U of Utah, 1971
Certification: Internal Medicine, Medical Oncology
8th Ave & C St, Salt Lake City, 801-408-2229

Harker, William Graydon (7 mentions)
U of Utah, 1975
Certification: Internal Medicine, Medical Oncology
3838 S 700 E #100, Salt Lake City, 801-262-9494

Legant, Patricia (5 mentions)
Columbia U, 1977
Certification: Internal Medicine, Medical Oncology
164 E 5900 S #A106, Salt Lake City, 801-263-3003

Lemmons, Richard Scott (8 mentions)
George Washington U, 1980
100 N Mario Capecchi Dr, Salt Lake City, 801-662-1000

Ward, John Harris (6 mentions)
U of Utah, 1976
Certification: Hematology, Internal Medicine, Medical Oncology
2000 Circle of Hope Dr #2100, Salt Lake City, 801-585-0255

Infectious Disease

Amber, Ina Judith (6 mentions)
Wayne State U, 1979
Certification: Infectious Disease, Internal Medicine
1151 E 3900 S #B-299, Salt Lake City, 801-268-6830

Byington, Carrie Lynn (5 mentions)
Baylor U, 1989
Certification: Pediatric Infectious Diseases, Pediatrics
50 N Medical Dr, Salt Lake City, 801-581-3501

Oliver, Marquam Riddell (11 mentions)
George Washington U, 1989
Certification: Infectious Disease, Internal Medicine
1160 E 3900 S #1200, Salt Lake City, 801-261-9651

Pavia, Andrew T. (6 mentions)
Brown U, 1981 *Certification:* Internal Medicine
50 N Medical Dr, Salt Lake City, 801-585-2031

Updike, Wanda Susanne (8 mentions)
Virginia Commonwealth U, 1982
Certification: Infectious Disease, Internal Medicine
1060 E 100 S #L10, Salt Lake City, 801-328-1260

Infertility

Heiner, James Spencer (6 mentions)
U of Texas-Galveston, 1985 *Certification:* Obstetrics &
   Gynecology, Reproductive Endocrinology/Infertility
10150 Petunia Way, Sandy, 801-878-8888

Peterson, C. Matthew (5 mentions)
U of California-San Diego, 2000 *Certification:* Obstetrics &
   Gynecology, Reproductive Endocrinology/Infertility
50 N Medical Dr #2B200, Salt Lake City, 801-581-3834
675 Arapeen Dr #209, Salt Lake City, 801-581-3834

Internal Medicine *(see note on page 9)*

Ahn, Yong Hui (3 mentions)
U of Kentucky, 1988 *Certification:* Internal Medicine
1060 E 100 S #L-10, Salt Lake City, 801-328-1260

Aslami, Stephen Shane (6 mentions)
U of Utah, 1993 *Certification:* Internal Medicine
1160 E 3900 S #1200, Salt Lake City, 801-261-9651

Caine, Thomas Hugh (6 mentions)
U of Utah, 1963
50 N Medical Dr, Salt Lake City, 801-581-7818

Hanlon, Beth Chapman (5 mentions)
U of Texas-Houston, 1987 *Certification:* Internal Medicine
1060 E 100 S #L-10, Salt Lake City, 801-328-1260

Lunt, Margaret Sydnie (3 mentions)
U of New Mexico, 1995
1160 E 3900 S #1200, Salt Lake City, 801-261-9651

Miller, Thomas Lee (3 mentions)
George Washington U, 1988 *Certification:* Internal Medicine
555 Foothill Blvd, Salt Lake City, 801-581-7790

Roberts, Philip Leonard (4 mentions)
Baylor U, 1976 *Certification:* Internal Medicine
10965 State St #100, Sandy, 801-572-0311
10965 S State St #100, Sandy, 801-572-0311

Nephrology

Cline, Richard Clark (10 mentions)
U of Texas-Dallas, 1984 *Certification:* Internal Medicine
650 E 4500 S, Salt Lake City, 801-288-2634

Gregory, Martin C. (4 mentions)
Certification: Internal Medicine, Nephrology
30 N 1900 E, Salt Lake City, 801-581-6709

Lambert, Richard Gary (4 mentions)
U of Utah, 1972 *Certification:* Internal Medicine, Nephrology
650 E 4500 S #300, Salt Lake City, 801-288-2634

Sherbotie, Joseph R. (5 mentions)
Pennsylvania State U, 1982 *Certification:* Pediatric Nephrology
100 N Medical Dr, Salt Lake City, 801-588-2000

Stinson, James Battey (4 mentions)
U of Texas-Galveston, 1974
Certification: Internal Medicine, Nephrology
650 E 4500 S #210, Salt Lake City, 801-288-2634

Tien, Dave Thang (5 mentions)
U of Texas-Dallas, 1996
Certification: Internal Medicine, Nephrology
650 E 4500 S #210, Salt Lake City, 801-288-2634

Neurological Surgery

Couldwell, William Tupper (7 mentions)
FMS-Canada, 1984 *Certification:* Neurological Surgery
50 N Medical Dr, Salt Lake City, 801-585-6040

Hood, Robert Sidney (12 mentions)
U of Oklahoma, 1970 *Certification:* Neurological Surgery
24 S 1100 E #302, Salt Lake City, 801-531-7806

Margetts, Jeffrey C. (6 mentions)
U of Utah, 1981 *Certification:* Neurological Surgery
1250 E 3900 S #200, Salt Lake City, 801-264-9521

Reichman, Mark Vernon (10 mentions)
Loyola U Chicago, 1984 *Certification:* Neurological Surgery
5169 S Cottonwood St #500, Murray, 801-507-9555

Neurology

Banks, Diana Darr (5 mentions)
U of Tennessee, 1988 *Certification:* Neurology
5323 Woodrow St #201, Salt Lake City, 801-261-4711

Black, Evan G. (5 mentions)
U of Utah, 1991 *Certification:* Neurology
5323 Woodrow St #201, Salt Lake City, 801-261-4711

Digre, Kathleen Bernice (3 mentions)
U of Iowa, 1981 *Certification:* Neurology
65 N Mario Capecchi Dr, Salt Lake City, 801-581-2352

Duvernay, Patrice Ann (3 mentions)
Dartmouth Coll, 1989 *Certification:* Neurology
333 S 900 E, Salt Lake City, 801-535-8163

Filloux, Francis Maurice (6 mentions)
U of California-Los Angeles, 1981 *Certification:* Neurology
   with Special Qualifications in Child Neurology, Pediatrics
100 N Medical Dr, Salt Lake City, 801-587-7575

Foley, John F. (5 mentions)
Med Coll of Wisconsin, 1983 *Certification:* Neurology
370 E 9th Ave #106, Salt Lake City, 801-408-5700

James, Mary Elena (3 mentions)
U of Texas-Galveston, 1991 *Certification:* Neurology
1002 E South Temple #207, Salt Lake City, 801-364-1110

Renner, David Roman (4 mentions)
U of Nebraska, 1997 *Certification:* Neurology
175 N Medical Dr 4th Fl, Salt Lake City, 801-585-7575

Thompson, Joel Adrian (4 mentions)
U of Colorado, 1969 *Certification:* Neurology with Special
   Qualifications in Child Neurology, Pediatrics
100 N Medical Dr, Salt Lake City, 801-587-7575
50 N Medical Dr, Salt Lake City, 801-587-7478

Williams, Dorothy Louise (3 mentions)
Indiana U, 1996
2295 Foothill Dr, Salt Lake City, 801-486-3021

Zimmerman, Susan Michelle (3 mentions)
Indiana U, 2001 *Certification:* Neurology
3725 W 4100 S, Salt Lake City, 801-965-3600

Obstetrics/Gynecology

Branch, David Ware, Jr. (3 mentions)
Virginia Commonwealth U, 1979
Certification: Obstetrics & Gynecology
5121 S Cottonwood St #102, Murray, 801-507-7400

Dodson, Mark Kane (3 mentions)
East Tennessee State U, 1988
Certification: Gynecologic Oncology, Obstetrics & Gynecology
1950 Circle of Hope Dr, Salt Lake City, 801-585-0100

Hansen, Scott Eugene (3 mentions)
U of California-San Diego, 1989
Certification: Obstetrics & Gynecology
3570 W 9000 S #210, West Jordan, 801-569-2626

Hurst, Barbara (3 mentions)
U of Utah, 1986 *Certification:* Obstetrics & Gynecology
348 E 4500 S 3200, Salt Lake City, 801-262-9800

Johnson, Jason Lynn (3 mentions)
U of Minnesota, 1994 *Certification:* Obstetrics & Gynecology
850 E 300 S #1, Salt Lake City, 801-322-1214

Kinghorn, Jennifer Carter (4 mentions)
U of Utah, 2000 *Certification:* Obstetrics & Gynecology
1140 E 3900 S #410, Salt Lake City, 801-262-8666

Larkin, Ronald Max (6 mentions)
U of Utah, 1975 *Certification:* Obstetrics & Gynecology
5063 S Cottonwood St #400, Murray, 801-507-1950

Sharp, Howard Cannon (8 mentions)
U of Utah, 1947 *Certification:* Obstetrics & Gynecology
50 N Medical Dr #2B200, Salt Lake City, 801-581-7640
555 Foothill Dr, Salt Lake City, 801-581-7640
30 N 1900 East #2B 200, Salt Lake City, 801-581-7092

Yamashiro, Vernon Koyu (3 mentions)
Loma Linda U, 1984
1151 E 3900 S #B-299, Salt Lake City, 801-268-6811

Ophthalmology

Alder, John Bryant (4 mentions)
Oregon Health Sciences U, 1991 *Certification:* Ophthalmology
164 E 5900 S #A101, Salt Lake City, 801-262-3344

Benator, Rachel Sharon (3 mentions)
U of Texas-Dallas, 1986 *Certification:* Ophthalmology
1025 E 3300 S #B, Salt Lake City, 801-281-2020

Christiansen, Robert M. (3 mentions)
U of Utah, 1978 *Certification:* Ophthalmology
324 10th Ave #260, Salt Lake City, 801-408-3937

Crandall, Alan Slade (3 mentions)
U of Utah, 1973 *Certification:* Ophthalmology
4400 S 700 E #240, Salt Lake City, 801-264-4464
65 N Mario Capecchio Dr, Salt Lake City, 801-581-2352

Digre, Kathleen Bernice (3 mentions)
U of Iowa, 1981 *Certification:* Neurology
65 N Mario Capecchi Dr, Salt Lake City, 801-581-2352

Faber, David Wayne (4 mentions)
U of California-San Diego, 1991 *Certification:* Ophthalmology
4400 S 700 E, Salt Lake City, 801-264-4444

Hoffman, Robert Orin (10 mentions)
U of Utah, 1981 *Certification:* Ophthalmology
100 N Mario Capecchi Dr, Salt Lake City, 801-581-2352

Olson, Randall J. (6 mentions)
U of Utah, 1973 *Certification:* Ophthalmology
65 Mario Capecchi Dr, Salt Lake City, 801-585-6622

Stanford, Gary Brewster (3 mentions)
FMS-Canada, 1961 *Certification:* Ophthalmology
1250 E 3900 S #310, Salt Lake City, 801-263-2020

Orthopedics

Bourne, Michael Hal (10 mentions)
U of Utah, 1984 *Certification:* Orthopaedic Surgery
1160 E 3900 S #5000, Salt Lake City, 801-262-8486

Cooper, Andrew D. (4 mentions)
Med U of South Carolina, 1999
Certification: Orthopaedic Surgery
82 S 1100 E #303, Salt Lake City, 801-533-2002

Mariani, Ernest Marc (11 mentions)
U of Utah, 1981 *Certification:* Orthopaedic Surgery
1160 E 3900 S #5000, Salt Lake City, 801-262-8486

Novak, Peter Jerry (4 mentions)
U of Utah, 1988 *Certification:* Orthopaedic Surgery
1160 E 3900 S #5000, Salt Lake City, 801-262-8486

Peters, Christopher (4 mentions)
Certification: Orthopaedic Surgery
590 Wakara Way, Salt Lake City, 801-587-7109

Samuelson, Kent Mitchell (6 mentions)
U of Utah, 1971 *Certification:* Orthopaedic Surgery
370 9th Ave #205, Salt Lake City, 801-408-8700

Otorhinolaryngology

Hunter, Robert Gail (10 mentions)
U of Utah, 1987 *Certification:* Otolaryngology
5169 S Cottonwood St #310, Murray, 801-507-3444
5770 S 250 E #475, Salt Lake City, 801-268-6900

Sharma, Pramod Kumar (6 mentions)
U of Buffalo, 1991 *Certification:* Otolaryngology
22 S 900 E, Salt Lake City, 801-328-2522

Pain Medicine

Brogan, Shane Edward (3 mentions)
FMS-Ireland, 1997 *Certification:* Anesthesiology, Pain Medicine
546 Chipeta Way #220, Salt Lake City, 801-581-7246

Hare, Bradford D. (3 mentions)
U of Utah, 1975 *Certification:* Anesthesiology, Pain Medicine
546 Chipeta Way #220, Salt Lake City, 801-581-7246
50 N Medical Dr, Salt Lake City, 801-213-3800

Matsumura, Kyle Shigeru (3 mentions)
U of Utah, 1993 *Certification:* Anesthesiology, Pain Medicine
6321 S Redwood Rd #102, Salt Lake City, 801-685-7246

Webster, Lynn Roy (13 mentions)
U of Nebraska, 1976 *Certification:* Anesthesiology, Pain Medicine
3838 S 700 E, Salt Lake City, 801-261-4988

Pathology

Abbott, Thomas M. (6 mentions)
Certification: Anatomic Pathology & Clinical Pathology
1200 E 3900 S, Salt Lake City, 801-268-7177

Hammond, M. Elizabeth H. (4 mentions)
U of Utah, 1967
8th Ave & C St, Salt Lake City, 801-507-7970

Smith, Gregory Phillip (3 mentions)
Emory U, 1986 *Certification:* Anatomic Pathology & Clinical
Pathology, Hematology
1200 E 3900 S, Salt Lake City, 801-268-7177

Pediatrics *(see note on page 9)*

Borgenicht, Louis (4 mentions)
Case Western Reserve U, 1970 *Certification:* Pediatrics
850 E 300 S #5, Salt Lake City, 801-531-8689

Havlik, Kevin Loras (3 mentions)
U of Iowa, 1980 *Certification:* Pediatrics
2000 S 900 E, Salt Lake City, 801-464-7660

Lam, Toan Hoang (3 mentions)
U of Hawaii, 1980 *Certification:* Pediatrics
1060 E 100 S #400, Salt Lake City, 801-521-2640

Metcalf, Thomas James (6 mentions)
Stanford U, 1970 *Certification:* Pediatrics
1140 E 3900 S #360, Salt Lake City, 801-264-8686

Ralston, Charles William, III (4 mentions)
U of North Carolina, 1975
Certification: Developmental-Behavioral Pediatrics, Pediatrics
5770 S 250 E #290, Salt Lake City, 801-747-8700

Strong, Richard Kline (3 mentions)
U of Utah, 1978 *Certification:* Pediatrics
9720 S 1300 E, Sandy, 801-571-8550

Plastic Surgery

Allred, Bryce Dee (4 mentions)
FMS-Mexico, 1977 *Certification:* Plastic Surgery
3584 W 9000 S #400, West Jordan, 801-596-2456

Chick, Leland R. (13 mentions)
U of Kentucky, 1981 *Certification:* Plastic Surgery
24 S 1100 E #201, Salt Lake City, 801-322-1188

Florence, Lauren O. (4 mentions)
U of Utah, 1981 *Certification:* Plastic Surgery
1250 E 3900 S #330, Salt Lake City, 801-264-9111

Leonard, Larry Givens (4 mentions)
Johns Hopkins U, 1971 *Certification:* Plastic Surgery
1820 Sidewinder Dr, Park City, 435-647-0074
440 D St #202, Salt Lake City, 801-408-2508

Rockwell, William Bradford (7 mentions)
Washington U, 1984
Certification: Plastic Surgery, Surgery of the Hand
555 S Foothill Blvd, Salt Lake City, 801-585-7762
50 N Medical Dr #5, Salt Lake City, 801-585-7762

Self, John Michael (4 mentions)
U of Alabama, 1978
11762 S State Rd #260, Draper, 801-266-3671

Thomas, David Snow (6 mentions)
U of Utah, 1978 *Certification:* Plastic Surgery
370 9th Ave #200, Salt Lake City, 801-355-0731

Psychiatry

Foote, Mark Charles (3 mentions)
George Washington U, 1989 *Certification:* Psychiatry
8th Ave & C St, Salt Lake City, 801-408-1038
333 S 900 E, Salt Lake City, 801-535-8163

Gray, Douglas (3 mentions)
U of Colorado, 1985
Certification: Child & Adolescent Psychiatry, Psychiatry
50 N Medical Dr #9, Salt Lake City, 801-581-8915

Moench, Louis Alan (5 mentions)
U of Utah, 1970 *Certification:* Forensic Psychiatry, Psychiatry
8th Ave & C St, Salt Lake City, 801-408-1038
333 S 900 E, Salt Lake City, 801-535-8163

Mohr, Michaela Siemes (4 mentions)
FMS-Germany, 1966 *Certification:* Psychiatry
1514 Emerson Ave, Salt Lake City, 801-466-1822

Pulmonary Disease

Elstad, Mark Richard (5 mentions)
U of Minnesota, 1980
Certification: Internal Medicine, Pulmonary Disease
50 N Medical Dr, Salt Lake City, 801-581-7806
500 Foothill Dr, Salt Lake City, 801-584-5603

Francis, Kurt Fribley (8 mentions)
U of Oklahoma, 1981 *Certification:* Critical Care Medicine,
Internal Medicine, Pulmonary Disease
1220 E 3900 S #2C, Salt Lake City, 801-263-2482

Kurrus, Jeffrey Anton (10 mentions)
U of Utah, 1991
Certification: Critical Care Medicine, Pulmonary Disease
1220 E 3900 S #2C, Salt Lake City, 801-263-2482

Pearl, James Everett (10 mentions)
U of Miami, 1975 *Certification:* Internal Medicine
324 10th Ave #170, Salt Lake City, 801-322-1000

Thomsen, George (4 mentions)
Loma Linda U, 1984 *Certification:* Critical Care Medicine,
Internal Medicine, Pulmonary Disease
5121 Cottonwood St, Murray, 801-507-4829

Uchida, Derek Akio (4 mentions)
Stanford U, 1982 *Certification:* Pediatric Pulmonology
100 N Medical Dr, Salt Lake City, 801-588-2000

Radiology—Diagnostic

Boyer, Richard Stuart (3 mentions)
U of Utah, 1973 *Certification:* Diagnostic Radiology, Internal
Medicine, Neuroradiology, Pediatric Radiology, Rheumatology
50 N Medical Dr, Salt Lake City, 801-662-1900

Kennedy, Anne Maria (4 mentions)
FMS-Ireland, 1982 *Certification:* Diagnostic Radiology
50 N Medical Dr, Salt Lake City, 801-581-7553

Mann, Howard (3 mentions)
FMS-South Africa, 1978 *Certification:* Diagnostic Radiology
50 N Medical Dr, Salt Lake City, 801-581-7553

Osborn, Anne Gregory (4 mentions)
Stanford U, 1970
Certification: Diagnostic Radiology, Neuroradiology
50 N Medical Dr, Salt Lake City, 801-581-7553

Woodward, Paula Jean (3 mentions)
U of Colorado, 1984 *Certification:* Diagnostic Radiology
50 N Medical Dr #1A71, Salt Lake City, 801-581-7553
30 N 1900 East #1A71, Salt Lake City, 801-581-8699

Radiology—Therapeutic

Hathaway, Peter Blaine (5 mentions)
U of Utah, 1993 *Certification:* Diagnostic Radiology,
Vascular & Interventional Radiology
1200 E 3900 S, Salt Lake City, 801-298-1300
650 E 4500 S #100, Salt Lake City, 801-298-1300

Jacobs, John M. (3 mentions)
U of Missouri-Kansas City, 1981 *Certification:* Diagnostic
Radiology with Special Competence in Nuclear Radiology
8th Ave & C St, Salt Lake City, 801-408-5201
5121 Cottonwood St, Murray, 501-507-5303

Rehabilitation

Davis, Alan Munter (3 mentions)
FMS-Grenada, 1987
Certification: Physical Medicine & Rehabilitation
50 N Medical Dr, Salt Lake City, 801-581-2311
30 N 900 E, Salt Lake City, 801-581-2267

Dodds, Thomas Andrew (3 mentions)
Dartmouth Coll, 1986
Certification: Physical Medicine & Rehabilitation
5171 S Cottonwood St #810, Murray, 801-507-9800

Rheumatology

Bohnsack, John F. (5 mentions)
U of Virginia, 1978
Certification: Pediatric Rheumatology, Pediatrics
100 N Medical Dr, Salt Lake City, 801-588-2000

Clegg, Daniel Orme (8 mentions)
U of Utah, 1977 *Certification:* Internal Medicine, Rheumatology
50 N Medical Dr #Q, Salt Lake City, 801-581-7724

Stromquist, Don Leonard (5 mentions)
Yale U, 1982 *Certification:* Internal Medicine, Rheumatology
324 10th Ave #250, Salt Lake City, 801-408-2600

Thoracic Surgery

Collins, Michael Patrick (13 mentions)
U of New Mexico, 1974 *Certification:* Thoracic Surgery
370 9th Ave #208, Salt Lake City, 801-408-2260

Karwande, Shreekanth V. (9 mentions)
FMS-India, 1974 *Certification:* Thoracic Surgery
1160 E 3900 S #3500, Salt Lake City, 801-743-4750

Urology

Cartwright, Patrick Carol (12 mentions)
U of Texas-Dallas, 1984 *Certification:* Urology
100 N Medical Dr #2200, Salt Lake City, 861-662-5555

Childs, Lane Clifford (8 mentions)
U of Texas-San Antonio, 1987 *Certification:* Urology
4252 Highland Dr #200, Salt Lake City, 801-993-1714

Gange, Steven Norris (6 mentions)
U of California-Los Angeles, 1986 *Certification:* Urology
4252 S Highland Dr #200, Salt Lake City, 801-993-1800

Hamilton, Blake Douglas (7 mentions)
U of California-San Francisco, 1991 *Certification:* Urology
50 N Medical Dr #3A-100, Salt Lake City, 801-581-7674

Hopkins, Scott Alan (8 mentions)
U of Utah, 1994 *Certification:* Urology
4252 Highland Dr #200, Salt Lake City, 801-993-1800

Snow, Brent Walter (9 mentions)
U of Utah, 1978 *Certification:* Urology
100 N Medical Dr, Salt Lake City, 801-662-5555
50 N Medical Dr #2, Salt Lake City, 801-581-7674

Stout, Lisa (7 mentions)
George Washington U, 1990 *Certification:* Urology
1060 E 100 S #110, Salt Lake City, 801-531-9453
181 E 5600 S #130, Murray, 801-266-8664

Vascular Surgery

Goodman, Greg Robert (9 mentions)
U of Texas-Dallas, 1987 *Certification:* Surgery, Vascular Surgery
370 9th Ave #208, Salt Lake City, 801-408-1000

Merrell, Steven William (10 mentions)
Vanderbilt U, 1983 *Certification:* Vascular Surgery
370 9th Ave #208, Salt Lake City, 801-408-1000
5325 S Woodrow St, Murray, 801-713-1010

Virginia

Washington, DC, Area—page 117

Richmond-Petersburg Area—page 481

Norfolk Area—page 477

Norfolk Area

Including City of Norfolk

Allergy/Immunology

Kelly, Cynthia Szelc (8 mentions)
Wayne State U, 1985
Certification: Allergy & Immunology, Pediatrics
601 Childrens Ln, Norfolk, 757-668-8255

Radin, Robert Charles (14 mentions)
U of Cincinnati, 1977
Certification: Allergy & Immunology, Internal Medicine
3386 Holland Rd #202, Virginia Beach, 757-468-6058

Anesthesiology

Polak, Mark Richard (4 mentions)
A T Still U, 1991 *Certification:* Anesthesiology
601 Childrens Ln, Norfolk, 757-668-7007

Stiner, Allan Ewing, Jr. (3 mentions)
Jefferson Med Coll, 1981 *Certification:* Anesthesiology
134 Business Parks Dr, Virginia Beach, 757-473-0044

Cardiac Surgery

Fleischer, Kirk Joachim (8 mentions)
U of Virginia, 1991 *Certification:* Surgery, Thoracic Surgery
600 Gresham Dr #8600, Norfolk, 757-388-6005

Gilbert, Christian L. (6 mentions)
Certification: Thoracic Surgery
3828 Old Shell Rd, Virginia Beach, 757-705-0492

Newton, Joseph R., Jr. (7 mentions)
Duke U, 1984 *Certification:* Surgery, Thoracic Surgery
600 Gresham Dr #8600, Norfolk, 757-388-6005

Cardiology

Brush, John Elliott, Jr. (5 mentions)
U of Virginia, 1980 *Certification:* Cardiovascular Disease,
Internal Medicine, Interventional Cardiology
844 Kempsville Rd #204, Norfolk, 757-261-0700

Herre, John Milton (3 mentions)
Vanderbilt U, 1977 *Certification:* Cardiovascular Disease,
Clinical Cardiac Electrophysiology, Internal Medicine
100 Kingsley Ln #200, Norfolk, 757-889-5351

Klevan, Thomas (3 mentions)
Yale U, 1981 *Certification:* Cardiovascular Disease, Internal
Medicine, Interventional Cardiology
100 Kingsley Ln #200, Norfolk, 757-889-5351

Lipskis, Donald Joseph (8 mentions)
Loyola U Chicago, 1977 *Certification:* Cardiovascular
Disease, Internal Medicine, Interventional Cardiology
100 Kingsley Ln #200, Norfolk, 757-889-5351

Parker, John Patrick (10 mentions)
Ohio State U, 1973 *Certification:* Cardiovascular Disease,
Internal Medicine, Interventional Cardiology
844 Kempsville Rd #204, Norfolk, 757-261-0700

Stine, Ronald Arthur (3 mentions)
Indiana U, 1978 *Certification:* Cardiovascular Disease,
Internal Medicine, Interventional Cardiology
844 Kempsville Rd #204, Norfolk, 757-261-0700

Dermatology

Edmonds, Beatrix (4 mentions)
Louisiana State U, 1991 *Certification:* Dermatology
5249 Providence Rd, Virginia Beach, 757-467-3900
1157 First Colonial Dr, Virginia Beach, 757-333-8001

Henry, Reginald B., III (7 mentions)
U of Virginia, 1982 *Certification:* Dermatology
850 Kempsville Rd, Norfolk, 757-261-0020

Hood, Antoinette B. Foote (5 mentions)
Vanderbilt U, 1967
Certification: Dermatology, Dermatopathology
825 Fairfax Ave, Norfolk, 757-261-6000
400 Gresham Dr #100, Norfolk, 757-624-2273

Pariser, David Michael (3 mentions)
Virginia Commonwealth U, 1972
Certification: Dermatology, Dermatopathology
1120 First Colonial Rd #200, Virginia Beach, 757-496-5085
400 Gresham Dr, Norfolk, 757-622-6315
6161 Kempsville Cir #345, Norfolk, 757-461-5656

Pariser, Robert Jay (5 mentions)
Virginia Commonwealth U, 1974
Certification: Dermatological Immunology/Diagnostic and
Laboratory Immunology, Dermatology
400 Gresham Dr #601, Norfolk, 757-622-6315
6161 Kempsville Cir #345, Norfolk, 757-461-5656

Scott, Margery B. Atkins (3 mentions)
Meharry Med Coll, 1971 *Certification:* Dermatology
825 Fairfax Ave, Norfolk, 757-622-6315

Sharpe, Larry Odell (5 mentions)
Virginia Commonwealth U, 1965 *Certification:* Dermatology
504 Depaul Ave Atrium Bldg, Chesapeake, 757-489-2273

Williams, Judith Virginia (6 mentions)
Pennsylvania State U, 1984
Certification: Dermatology, Pediatric Dermatology
612 Kingsborough Sq #301, Chesapeake, 757-668-7546
601 Childrens Ln, Norfolk, 757-668-7546
11783 Rock Landing Dr, Newport News, 757-668-8781

Emergency Medicine

Counselman, Francis Lee (16 mentions)
Eastern Virginia Med Sch, 1983
Certification: Emergency Medicine
4092 Foxwood Dr #101, Virginia Beach, 757-467-4200

Qureshi, Faiqa Aftab (4 mentions)
FMS-Pakistan, 1973
Certification: Pediatric Emergency Medicine, Pediatrics
601 Childrens Ln, Norfolk, 757-668-9222

Endocrinology

Harrison, Howard Courtenay (5 mentions)
Certification: Endocrinology and Metabolism, Internal Medicine
1101 First Colonial Rd #101, Virginia Beach, 757-496-9020

Mason, M. Elizabeth (5 mentions)
U of Cincinnati, 1984 *Certification:* Endocrinology,
Diabetes, and Metabolism, Internal Medicine
855 W Brambleton Ave, Norfolk, 757-446-5600

Richardson, Donald W. (12 mentions)
Virginia Commonwealth U, 1976 *Certification:*
  Endocrinology and Metabolism, Endocrinology, Diabetes,
  and Metabolism, Geriatric Medicine, Internal Medicine
855 W Brambleton Ave, Norfolk, 757-446-5600

Saadeh, Ghandi M. (8 mentions)
FMS-Lebanon, 1983 *Certification:* Endocrinology, Diabetes,
  and Metabolism, Internal Medicine
850 Kempsville Rd, Norfolk, 757-261-5976

Satin-Smith, Marta S. (6 mentions)
SUNY-Downstate Med Coll, 1989
Certification: Pediatric Endocrinology
601 Childrens Ln, Virginia Beach, 757-668-7237
733 Volvo Pkwy #400, Chesapeake, 757-668-7237

Family Practice *(see note on page 9)*

Eng, Benjamin Peter (4 mentions)
Eastern Virginia Med Sch, 1977 *Certification:* Family Medicine
825 Fairfax Ave, Norfolk, 757-446-5955

Grant, Thomas R., Jr. (5 mentions)
Wake Forest U, 1982
Certification: Family Medicine, Geriatric Medicine
825 Fairfax Ave, Norfolk, 757-446-5955

Skees, Mark Evan (3 mentions)
Eastern Virginia Med Sch, 1983 *Certification:* Family Medicine
425 W 20th St #1, Norfolk, 757-623-8642

Gastroenterology

Caplan, Stephen Robert (3 mentions)
U of Virginia, 1966
Certification: Gastroenterology, Internal Medicine
400 Gresham Dr 3205, Norfolk, 757-622-6601

Gamsey, Alan Jay (4 mentions)
Virginia Commonwealth U, 1975
Certification: Gastroenterology, Internal Medicine
160 Kingsley Ln #200, Norfolk, 757-889-6800
112 Gainsborough Sq #200, Chesapeake, 757-547-0798

Johnson, David Allan (11 mentions)
Virginia Commonwealth U, 1980
Certification: Gastroenterology, Internal Medicine
885 Kempsville Rd #114, Norfolk, 757-466-0165

Kobak, Gregory Evan (3 mentions)
Hahnemann U, 1997 *Certification:* Pediatric Gastroenterology
601 Childrens Ln, Norfolk, 757-668-7240

Ryan, Michael James (14 mentions)
Johns Hopkins U, 1979 *Certification:* Gastroenterology,
  Internal Medicine, Transplant Hepatology
885 Kempsville Rd #114, Norfolk, 757-460-4101
844 Kempsville Rd #106, Norfolk, 804-466-0165

Tsou, Victor Marc (4 mentions)
Wayne State U, 1984
Certification: Pediatric Gastroenterology, Pediatrics
601 Childrens Ln, Norfolk, 757-668-7240

Wootton, Frank Taylor, III (3 mentions)
Eastern Virginia Med Sch, 1985
Certification: Gastroenterology, Internal Medicine
885 Kempsville Rd #114, Norfolk, 757-466-0165

General Surgery

Fontana, Mark Ambrose (3 mentions)
Uniformed Services U of Health Sciences, 1992
Certification: Surgery
880 Kempsville Rd #1000, Norfolk, 757-461-2515
250 W Brambleton Ave #101, Norfolk, 757-622-2649

Gould, Randolph J. (6 mentions)
Eastern Virginia Med Sch, 1978 *Certification:* Surgery
250 W Brambleton Ave #101, Norfolk, 757-622-2649
880 Kempsville Rd #1000, Norfolk, 757-461-2515

Hubbard, George Wilkins (3 mentions)
U of Virginia, 1976 *Certification:* Surgery
880 Kempsville Rd #1000, Norfolk, 757-461-2515

Ives, Charles Everett (4 mentions)
Northwestern U, 1974 *Certification:* Surgery
160 Kingsley Ln #400, Norfolk, 757-889-6500

Kelly, Robert Edward, Jr. (3 mentions)
Johns Hopkins U, 1985 *Certification:* Pediatric Surgery, Surgery
601 Childrens Ln, Norfolk, 757-668-7703

Knowles, Robert C. (3 mentions)
Certification: Surgery
160 Kingsley Ln #400, Norfolk, 757-889-6500

Perry, Roger Hobart (5 mentions)
U of Virginia, 1955 *Certification:* Surgery
825 Fairfax Ave #610, Norfolk, 757-446-8950

Weireter, Leonard J. (5 mentions)
U of Buffalo, 1980 *Certification:* Surgery, Surgical Critical Care
825 Fairfax Ave, Norfolk, 757-446-8950

Wohlgemuth, Stephen David (12 mentions)
Tufts U, 1983 *Certification:* Surgery
600 Gresham Dr #8630, Norfolk, 757-388-6120

Geriatrics

Hovland, William Neal (4 mentions)
Virginia Commonwealth U, 1974
Certification: Geriatric Medicine, Internal Medicine
110 Kingsley Ln #309, Norfolk, 757-889-2006

Newman, Rosanne (7 mentions)
FMS-Israel, 1983
Certification: Geriatric Medicine, Internal Medicine
825 Fairfax Ave, Norfolk, 757-446-7040

Hematology/Oncology

Alberico, Thomas A. (7 mentions)
West Virginia U, 1979
Certification: Hematology, Internal Medicine, Medical Oncology
1950 Glen Mitchell Dr, Virginia Beach, 757-368-0437
5900 Lake Wright Dr #300, Norfolk, 757-466-8683

Alexander, Burton F. (4 mentions)
U of Virginia, 1992
Certification: Hematology, Internal Medicine, Medical Oncology
5900 Lake Wright Dr, Norfolk, 757-466-8683

Bevan, Herbert E., III (3 mentions)
Washington U, 1980
Certification: Pediatric Hematology-Oncology, Pediatrics
601 Childrens Ln, Norfolk, 757-668-7007

Conkling, Paul Robert (5 mentions)
Ohio State U, 1982
Certification: Hematology, Internal Medicine, Medical Oncology
5900 Lake Wright Dr, Norfolk, 757-466-8683

Cross, Scott James (6 mentions)
Ohio State U, 1997
Certification: Hematology, Internal Medicine, Medical Oncology
1950 Clen Mitchell Dr #102, Virginia Beach, 757-368-0437
6160 Kempsville Cir #300-B, Norfolk, 757-466-8683

George, Edward Richard (5 mentions)
U of Miami, 1971
Certification: Hematology, Internal Medicine, Medical Oncology
5900 Lake Wright Dr, Norfolk, 757-466-8683

Lee, Michael Edward (5 mentions)
U of North Carolina, 1988 *Certification:* Medical Oncology
5900 Lake Wright Dr, Norfolk, 757-466-8683
1950 Glenn Mitchell Dr #102, Virginia Beach, 757-368-0437

McGaughey, Dean S., III (6 mentions)
U of Chicago, 1994 *Certification:* Medical Oncology
5900 Lake Wright Dr, Norfolk, 757-466-8683

Owen, William Conally (5 mentions)
Wake Forest U, 1986
Certification: Pediatric Hematology-Oncology, Pediatrics
601 Childrens Ln, Norfolk, 757-668-7007

Werner, Eric James (5 mentions)
Jefferson Med Coll, 1978
Certification: Pediatric Hematology-Oncology, Pediatrics
601 Childrens Ln, Norfolk, 757-668-7007

Infectious Disease

Buescher, Edward Stephen (5 mentions)
Johns Hopkins U, 1975
Certification: Pediatric Infectious Diseases, Pediatrics
855 W Brambleton Ave, Norfolk, 757-668-6464

Fisher, Randall Garth (6 mentions)
Tulane U, 1988
Certification: Pediatric Infectious Diseases, Pediatrics
601 Childrens Ln, Norfolk, 757-668-7238

Miller, Scott Arnold (7 mentions)
U of Virginia, 1977
Certification: Infectious Disease, Internal Medicine
850 Kempsville Rd, Norfolk, 757-261-5946

Oldfield, Edward Charles (11 mentions)
U of Virginia, 1975
Certification: Infectious Disease, Internal Medicine
825 Fairfax Ave #545, Norfolk, 757-446-8999

Schaefer, John Charles (5 mentions)
New Jersey Med Sch, 1970
Certification: Infectious Disease, Internal Medicine
6161 Kempsville Cir #220, Norfolk, 757-455-9036

Warner, John Francis (11 mentions)
U of North Carolina, 1962
Certification: Infectious Disease, Internal Medicine
850 Kempsville Rd, Norfolk, 757-261-0020

Infertility

Poe-Zeigler, Robin (4 mentions)
Eastern Virginia Med Sch, 1989
Certification: Obstetrics & Gynecology
1181 First Colonial Rd #100, Virginia Beach, 757-496-5370

Internal Medicine *(see note on page 9)*

Becher, John David (3 mentions)
Eastern Virginia Med Sch, 1976 *Certification:* Internal Medicine
850 Kempsville Rd, Norfolk, 757-261-5910

Cohen, Alan Mathew (3 mentions)
Washington U, 1982 *Certification:* Internal Medicine
400 W Brambleton Ave #104, Norfolk, 757-627-7700

Flemmer, Mark C. (3 mentions)
FMS-South Africa, 1978
Certification: Geriatric Medicine, Internal Medicine
825 Fairfax Ave #410, Norfolk, 757-446-8910

Grulke, David C. (3 mentions)
Duke U, 1975 *Certification:* Internal Medicine
400 W Brambleton Ave #202, Norfolk, 757-623-6624

Lisner, Charles Alan (3 mentions)
U of Virginia, 1993 *Certification:* Internal Medicine
229 W Bute St #910, Norfolk, 757-388-1844

Manser, Thomas Joseph (5 mentions)
Michigan State U, 1981 *Certification:* Internal Medicine
825 Fairfax Ave #445, Norfolk, 757-446-8920

Nephrology

McCune, Thomas Robert (9 mentions)
Eastern Virginia Med Sch, 1985
Certification: Internal Medicine, Nephrology
400 gresham Dr #907, Norfolk, 757-627-7301

Raafat, Reem H. (4 mentions)
FMS-Jordan, 1989 *Certification:* Pediatric Nephrology, Pediatrics
601 Childrens Ln, Norfolk, 757-668-7244

Restaino, Irene G. (6 mentions)
St Louis U, 1984 *Certification:* Pediatric Nephrology, Pediatrics
601 Childrens Ln, Norfolk, 757-668-7244

Whelan, Thomas V. (10 mentions)
Certification: Internal Medicine, Nephrology
400 Gresham Dr #900, Norfolk, 757-623-0005

Neurological Surgery

Di Lustro, Joseph Frank (6 mentions)
Eastern Virginia Med Sch, 1983
Certification: Neurological Surgery
601 Childrens Ln, Norfolk, 757-668-7990

Partington, Jonathan P. (8 mentions)
Case Western Reserve U, 1980 *Certification:* Neurological Surgery
580 E Main St #200, Norfolk, 757-625-4455

Waters, David Carl (14 mentions)
U of Michigan, 1980 *Certification:* Neurological Surgery
580 E Main St #200, Norfolk, 757-625-4455

Neurology

Bowles, Mary Allison (3 mentions)
U of Nebraska, 1995 *Certification:* Neurology
6161 Kempsville Cir #315, Norfolk, 757-461-5400
160 Kingsley Ln #203, Norfolk, 757-423-6917

Frank, L. Matthew (3 mentions)
U of Connecticut, 1973 *Certification:* Neurology with
    Special Qualifications in Child Neurology, Pediatrics
850 Southampton Ave, Norfolk, 757-668-9920
733 Volvo Pkwy, Chesapeake, 757-668-9920

Lewis, Donald Wray (3 mentions)
Virginia Commonwealth U, 1979 *Certification:* Neurology
    with Special Qualifications in Child Neurology, Pediatrics
850 Southampton Ave 3rd Fl, Norfolk, 757-668-9920

Northam, Ralph Shearer (3 mentions)
Eastern Virginia Med Sch, 1984 *Certification:* Neurology
    with Special Qualifications in Child Neurology, Pediatrics
850 Southampton Ave, Norfolk, 757-668-9920

Rice, Marcus Charles (12 mentions)
U of Rochester, 1976 *Certification:* Neurology
6161 Kempsville Cir #315, Norfolk, 757-461-5400
160 Kingsley Ln #203, Norfolk, 757-423-6917

Williams, Armistead D. (17 mentions)
U of Virginia, 1972 *Certification:* Neurology
6161 Kempsville Cir #315, Norfolk, 757-461-5400
160 Kingsley Ln #203, Norfolk, 757-423-6917

Obstetrics/Gynecology

Crockford, Jon Lee (3 mentions)
U of Virginia, 1975 *Certification:* Obstetrics & Gynecology
880 Kempsville Rd #2200, Norfolk, 757-466-6350
250 W Brambleton Ave #202, Norfolk, 757-466-6350
300 Medical Pkwy #308, Chesapeake, 757-466-6350

Hughes, Gilbert Theodore (3 mentions)
Eastern Virginia Med Sch, 1981
Certification: Obstetrics & Gynecology
100 Kingsley Ln 3400, Norfolk, 757-451-0929

Muhlendorf, Ivan Kenneth (4 mentions)
U of Virginia, 1973 *Certification:* Obstetrics & Gynecology
844 Kempsville Rd #208, Norfolk, 757-461-3890
828 Healthy Way #330, Virginia Beach, 757-461-3890

Puritz, Holly Suzanne (5 mentions)
Tufts U, 1983 *Certification:* Obstetrics & Gynecology
880 Kempsville Rd #2200, Norfolk, 757-466-6350
300 Medical Pkwy #308, Chesapeake, 757-466-6350
250 W Brambleton Ave #201, Norfolk, 757-466-6350

Whibley, Theresa Waters (6 mentions)
Eastern Virginia Med Sch, 1982
Certification: Obstetrics & Gynecology
400 Gresham Dr #811, Norfolk, 757-623-3845

Ophthalmology

Crouch, Earl R., Jr. (4 mentions)
Virginia Commonwealth U, 1969 *Certification:* Ophthalmology
880 Kempsville Rd #2500, Norfolk, 757-461-0050

Lall-Trail, Joel K. (3 mentions)
SUNY-Upstate Med U, 1995 *Certification:* Ophthalmology
885 Kempsville Rd #101, Norfolk, 757-461-1444

Reda, Annette Williams (10 mentions)
U of Illinois, 1972 *Certification:* Ophthalmology
885 Kempsville Rd #101, Norfolk, 757-461-1444

Scoper, Stephen Vincent (6 mentions)
U of Mississippi, 1984 *Certification:* Ophthalmology
241 Corporate Blvd, Norfolk, 757-622-2200

Orthopedics

Bonner, Kevin Francis (6 mentions)
Georgetown U, 1993
Certification: Orthopaedic Sports Medicine, Orthopaedic Surgery
5716 Cleveland St #200, Virginia Beach, 757-490-4802

Distasio, Anthony J., II (3 mentions)
Georgetown U, 1986 *Certification:* Orthopaedic Surgery
600 Gresham Dr, Norfolk, 757-388-5680
150 Burnetts Way, Suffolk, 757-539-9333

Gibson, Wilford Keith (3 mentions)
Virginia Commonwealth U, 1985
Certification: Orthopaedic Sports Medicine, Orthopaedic Surgery
160 Kingsley Ln #405, Norfolk, 757-321-3300
844 Kempsville Rd #101, Norfolk, 757-321-3300
1800 Camelot Dr #300, Virginia Beach, 757-321-3300
1975 Glen Mitchell Dr #200, Virginia Beach, 757-321-3300

Molligan, Harry Joseph (4 mentions)
Louisiana State U, 1983 *Certification:* Orthopaedic Surgery
600 Gresham Dr, Norfolk, 757-388-5680

Schaffer, John Joseph (6 mentions)
St Louis U, 1982 *Certification:* Orthopaedic Surgery
844 Kempsville Rd, Norfolk, 757-321-3300
1800 Camelot Dr #300, Virginia Beach, 757-321-3300

Shall, Lawrence M. (4 mentions)
U of Toledo, 1980
Certification: Orthopaedic Sports Medicine, Orthopaedic Surgery
6275 E Virginia Beach Blvd #300, Norfolk, 757-461-1688

St. Remy, Carl R. (3 mentions)
Certification: Orthopaedic Surgery
171 Kempsville Rd #201, Norfolk, 757-668-6550

Wagner, John Stanley (3 mentions)
U of Rochester, 1973 *Certification:* Orthopaedic Surgery
6275 E Virginia Beach Blvd #300, Norfolk, 757-461-1688

Otorhinolaryngology

Darrow, David H. (4 mentions)
Duke U, 1987 *Certification:* Otolaryngology
601 Childrens Ln 2nd Fl, Norfolk, 757-668-9327
733 Volvo Pkwy #300, Chesapeake, 757-547-0027
825 Fairfax Ave #510, Norfolk, 757-446-5934

Derkay, Craig Steven (5 mentions)
Virginia Commonwealth U, 1983 *Certification:* Otolaryngology
601 Childrens Ln 2nd Fl, Norfolk, 757-668-9327
825 Fairfax Ave #510, Norfolk, 757-446-5934
733 Volvo Pkwy #300, Chesapeake, 757-547-0027

Deutsch, Brian Douglas (3 mentions)
U of Virginia, 1988 *Certification:* Otolaryngology
901 Hampton Blvd, Norfolk, 757-623-0526
885 Kempsville Rd #304, Norfolk, 757-623-0526
680 Kingsborough Sq #A, Chesapeake, 757-623-0526

Kalafsky, John Thomas (8 mentions)
Temple U, 1983 *Certification:* Otolaryngology
901 Hampton Blvd, Norfolk, 757-623-0526
885 Kempsville Rd #304, Norfolk, 757-623-0526
680 Kingsborough Sq #A, Chesapeake, 757-623-0526

Karakla, Daniel William (13 mentions)
Uniformed Services U of Health Sciences, 1986
Certification: Otolaryngology
825 Fairfax Ave, Norfolk, 757-446-5934

Roche, John P. (3 mentions)
Hahnemann U, 1993 *Certification:* Otolaryngology
901 Hampton Blvd, Norfolk, 757-623-0526
680 Kingsborough Sq #A, Chesapeake, 727-623-0526
885 Kempsville Rd #304, Norfolk, 727-623-0526

Strasnick, Barry (4 mentions)
Baylor U, 1985 *Certification:* Otolaryngology
150 Kingsley Ln, Norfolk, 757-889-6670

Wadsworth, Jeffery T. (4 mentions)
U of South Florida, 1993 *Certification:* Otolaryngology
825 Fairfax Ave, Norfolk, 757-446-5934

Pain Medicine

Barr, Lisa Binder (5 mentions)
Eastern Virginia Med Sch, 1983
Certification: Physical Medicine & Rehabilitation
1788 Republic Rd #200, Virginia Beach, 757-422-2966
637 Kingsborough Sq #G, Chesapeake, 757-548-5102
665 Lowry Rd #100, Norfolk, 757-422-2966

Quidgley Nevarres, Antonio (5 mentions)
U of Puerto Rico, 1999
Certification: Pain Medicine, Physical Medicine & Rehabilitation
825 Fairfax Ave, Norfolk, 757-446-5915

Ton, Martin Vuthat (4 mentions)
Columbia U, 1989 *Certification:* Anesthesiology, Pain Medicine
1080 1st Colonial Rd, Virginia Beach, 757-395-6455
134 Business Parks Dr, Virginia Beach, 757-473-0044

Pathology

Stanley, Scott J. (3 mentions)
Loyola U Chicago, 1981
Certification: Anatomic Pathology & Clinical Pathology
600 Gresham Dr, Norfolk, 757-388-3221

Werner, Alice Sheri (4 mentions)
Eastern Virginia Med Sch, 1980 *Certification:* Anatomic Pathology
  & Clinical Pathology, Blood Banking, Pediatric Pathology
601 Childrens Ln, Norfolk, 757-668-7000

Pediatrics *(see note on page 9)*

Fink, Fredric Neil (5 mentions)
U of Virginia, 1982 *Certification:* Pediatrics
160 Kingsley Ln #305, Norfolk, 757-489-3551
300 Medical Pkwy #222, Chesapeake, 757-436-1770
449 Dominion Blvd S #3, Chesapeake, 757-312-9220
885 Kempsville Rd #200, Norfolk, 757-461-6342

Fink, Robert Alan (5 mentions)
U of Virginia, 1980 *Certification:* Pediatrics
160 Kingsley Ln #305, Norfolk, 757-489-3551
300 Medical Pkwy #222, Chesapeake, 757-436-1770
885 Kempsville Rd #200, Norfolk, 757-461-6342
449 Dominion Blvd S #3, Chesapeake, 757-312-9220

Karp, Glenda Steinberg (4 mentions)
FMS-Canada, 1980 *Certification:* Pediatrics
171 Kempsville Rd #B, Norfolk, 757-668-6500

Livingood, Jennifer C. (3 mentions)
Virginia Commonwealth U, 1999 *Certification:* Pediatrics
1909 Granby St #A, Norfolk, 757-640-0022
880 Kempsville Rd #2600, Norfolk, 757-466-6582

Plastic Surgery

Carraway, James Howard (4 mentions)
U of Virginia, 1962 *Certification:* Plastic Surgery, Surgery
5589 Greenwich Rd #100, Virginia Beach, 757-557-0300

Colen, Lawrence Bruce (9 mentions)
Dartmouth Coll, 1975 *Certification:* Plastic Surgery
6161 Kempsville Cir #300, Norfolk, 757-466-1000

Jones, Guy Trengove (4 mentions)
FMS-South Africa, 1971
100 Kingsley Ln #302, Norfolk, 757-423-2166

Uroskie, Theodore W., Jr. (8 mentions)
Hahnemann U, 1995 *Certification:* Plastic Surgery, Surgery
6161 Kempsville Cir #300, Norfolk, 757-466-1000

Psychiatry

Light, Robert Thomas (3 mentions)
FMS-St Maarten, 1999 *Certification:* Psychiatry
1500 E Little Creek Rd #205, Norfolk, 757-587-4744

Pulmonary Disease

Bowers, John Thomas (12 mentions)
U of Vermont, 1976 *Certification:* Critical Care Medicine,
  Internal Medicine, Pulmonary Disease
850 Kempsville Rd #10, Norfolk, 757-261-5977

Callender, Charles Wynter (4 mentions)
Virginia Commonwealth U, 1995 *Certification:* Critical Care
  Medicine, Internal Medicine, Pulmonary Disease
400 greshaw Dr #301, Norfolk, 757-446-5758

Epstein, Cynthia Esther (3 mentions)
U of Buffalo, 1995
Certification: Pediatric Pulmonology, Pediatrics
601 Childrens Ln, Norfolk, 757-668-7426

Garnett, Alfred R., Jr. (10 mentions)
Virginia Commonwealth U, 1979 *Certification:* Critical Care
  Medicine, Internal Medicine, Pulmonary Disease
850 Kempsville Rd, Norfolk, 757-466-5988
600 Gresham Dr, Norfolk, 757-388-6115

Gowen, Marilyn Alley (6 mentions)
Virginia Commonwealth U, 1979
Certification: Pediatric Pulmonology, Pediatrics
601 Childrens Ln, Norfolk, 757-668-7426

Silva, Carlos Adolfo (5 mentions)
FMS-Nicaragua, 1982
Certification: Critical Care Medicine, Geriatric Medicine, Internal
  Medicine, Pulmonary Disease, Undersea & Hyperbaric Medicine
160 Kingsley Ln #103, Norfolk, 757-889-6677

Tomlinson, James R., Jr. (3 mentions)
U of Virginia, 1980 *Certification:* Critical Care Medicine,
  Internal Medicine, Pulmonary Disease
850 Kempsville Rd, Norfolk, 757-261-5977

Radiology—Diagnostic

Donnal, John Fitzpatrick (5 mentions)
U of Virginia, 1983
Certification: Diagnostic Radiology, Neuroradiology
6330 N Center Dr #220, Norfolk, 757-466-0089

Grasso, Susanne Ng (3 mentions)
Eastern Virginia Med Sch, 1991
Certification: Diagnostic Radiology, Pediatric Radiology
6330 N Center Dr #220, Norfolk, 757-466-0089

Kushner, David M. (3 mentions)
Case Western Reserve U, 1986
Certification: Diagnostic Radiology, Nuclear Radiology
6330 N Center Dr #220, Norfolk, 757-466-0089

Weissberger, Marshall A. (3 mentions)
George Washington U, 1983 *Certification:* Diagnostic Radiology
6330 N Center Dr #220, Norfolk, 757-466-0089

Radiology—Therapeutic

Agola, John Christopher (8 mentions)
SUNY-Downstate Med Coll, 1987
Certification: Diagnostic Radiology
6330 N Center Dr #220, Norfolk, 757-466-0089

Vingan, Harlan Lawrence (9 mentions)
SUNY-Downstate Med Coll, 1983 *Certification:* Diagnostic
  Radiology, Vascular & Interventional Radiology
6330 N Center Dr #220, Norfolk, 757-466-0089

Rehabilitation

Barr, Lisa Binder (3 mentions)
Eastern Virginia Med Sch, 1983
Certification: Physical Medicine & Rehabilitation
1788 Republic Rd #200, Virginia Beach, 757-422-2966
637 Kingsborough Sq #G, Chesapeake, 757-548-5102
665 Lowry Rd #100, Norfolk, 757-422-2966

Shelton, Jean Elizabeth (3 mentions)
U of Tennessee, 1972
Certification: Pediatrics, Physical Medicine & Rehabilitation
850 Southampton Blvd, Norfolk, 757-668-9915

Walker, Robert (4 mentions)
Certification: Physical Medicine & Rehabilitation
721 Fairfax Ave, Norfolk, 757-446-5915

Rheumatology

Clarkson, Sarah Bull (6 mentions)
Med U of South Carolina, 1979
Certification: Internal Medicine, Rheumatology
6275 E Virginia Beach Blvd #200, Norfolk, 757-461-3400
300 Medical Pkwy, Chesapeake, 757-547-1822

Denio, Alfred Elon, III (7 mentions)
U of Pittsburgh, 1981
Certification: Internal Medicine, Rheumatology
6275 E Virginia Beach Blvd #200, Norfolk, 757-461-3400
300 Medical Pkwy, Chesapeake, 757-547-1822

Lidman, Roger William (8 mentions)
Johns Hopkins U, 1975
Certification: Internal Medicine, Rheumatology
6275 E Virginia Beach Blvd #200, Norfolk, 757-461-3400
300 Medical Pkwy #112, Chesapeake, 757-547-1822

Reed, William Washington (5 mentions)
Virginia Commonwealth U, 1978
Certification: Internal Medicine, Rheumatology
160 Kingsley Ln #505, Norfolk, 757-889-6633

Thoracic Surgery

Hubbard, George Wilkins (7 mentions)
U of Virginia, 1976 *Certification:* Surgery
880 Kempsville Rd #1000, Norfolk, 757-561-2515

Newton, Joseph R., Jr. (13 mentions)
Duke U, 1984 *Certification:* Surgery, Thoracic Surgery
600 Gresham Dr #8600, Norfolk, 757-388-6005

Urology

Drucker, Jacob Ralph (5 mentions)
Virginia Commonwealth U, 1972 *Certification:* Urology
885 Kempsville Rd #304, Chesapeake, 757-461-7200

Eure, Gregg Rountree (3 mentions)
Virginia Commonwealth U, 1985 *Certification:* Urology
1200 First Colonial Rd #100-D, Virginia Beach, 757-481-3556

Fabrizio, Michael Dean (6 mentions)
Virginia Commonwealth U, 1992 *Certification:* Urology
400 W Brambleton Ave #100, Norfolk, 757-457-5170

Rawls, William Holland (7 mentions)
Eastern Virginia Med Sch, 1985 *Certification:* Urology
100 Kingsley Ln #404, Norfolk, 757-489-4111
113 Gainsborough Sq #202, Chesapeake, 757-547-0121

Robey, Edwin Lee (13 mentions)
Wake Forest U, 1980 *Certification:* Urology
6333 Center Dr, Norfolk, 757-457-5100

Vascular Surgery

Gayle, Robert Gordon (6 mentions)
U of Pittsburgh, 1973 *Certification:* Vascular Surgery
250 W Brambleton Ave #101, Norfolk, 757-470-5570
171 N Main St, Suffolk, 757-539-4470

Stokes, Gordon Kavanaugh (11 mentions)
Jefferson Med Coll, 1988 *Certification:* Surgery, Vascular Surgery
397 Littneck Rd #100, Virginia Beach, 757-470-5570
600 Gresham Dr #8260, Norfolk, 757-622-2649

Richmond-Petersburg Area

Including Cities of Richmond, Colonial Heights, Dinwiddie, Hopewell, Petersburg; and Chesterfield, Hanover, Henrico, and Prince George Counties

Allergy/Immunology

Call, Robert Somerville (14 mentions)
U of Virginia, 1987 *Certification:* Allergy & Immunology
9920 Independence Park Dr #100, Richmond, 804-285-7420

Feinstein, Barry Keith (7 mentions)
FMS-Mexico, 1979
Certification: Allergy & Immunology, Internal Medicine
7605 Forest Ave #103, Richmond, 804-288-0055
14351 Sommerville Ct, Midlothian, 804-320-2419

Anesthesiology

Bennett, Joel Alan (3 mentions)
Hahnemann U, 1987 *Certification:* Anesthesiology
1401 Johnston Willis Dr, Richmond, 804-330-2000

Estes, Michael Dugan (3 mentions)
Virginia Commonwealth U, 1980
Certification: Anesthesiology, Pediatrics
5855 Bremo Rd #100, Richmond, 804-288-6258

Janes, John Raymond, Jr. (3 mentions)
U of Illinois, 1978 *Certification:* Anesthesiology
5855 Bremo Rd #100, Richmond, 804-288-6258

Meadows, James Charles, Jr. (6 mentions)
U of Miami, 1976 *Certification:* Anesthesiology, Internal Medicine
5855 Bremo Rd #100, Richmond, 804-288-6258

Montgomery, Margaret T. (3 mentions)
Virginia Commonwealth U, 1986 *Certification:* Anesthesiology
1902 Grove Ave, Richmond, 804-353-6813

Stone, James Walter, Jr. (7 mentions)
U of Virginia, 1981 *Certification:* Anesthesiology
10800 Midlothian Tpk #265, Richmond, 804-594-2622
1401 Johnston Willis Dr, Richmond, 804-330-2000

Cardiac Surgery

Bladergroen, Mark R. (11 mentions)
Certification: Thoracic Surgery
5875 Bremo Rd #G-5, Richmond, 804-287-7840

Katz, Marc R. (13 mentions)
Tulane U, 1981 *Certification:* Thoracic Surgery
5875 Bremo Rd #G-5, Richmond, 804-287-7840

Zocco, Joseph James (27 mentions)
New Jersey Med Sch, 1973 *Certification:* Thoracic Surgery
7101 Jahnke Rd, Richmond, 804-320-2751

Cardiology

Burns, Carolyn A. (4 mentions)
U of Pittsburgh, 1986
Certification: Cardiovascular Disease, Internal Medicine
5875 Bremo Rd #501, Richmond, 804-282-2685
7605 Forest Ave #303, Richmond, 804-288-0061

Cross, Steven Wayne (5 mentions)
Virginia Commonwealth U, 1979 *Certification:* Cardiovascular Disease, Internal Medicine, Interventional Cardiology
7605 Forest Ave #303, Richmond, 804-288-0061

Dunnington, Gansevoort H. (4 mentions)
Virginia Commonwealth U, 1972
Certification: Cardiovascular Disease, Internal Medicine
5875 Bremo Rd #501, Richmond, 804-282-2685

Ellenbogen, Kenneth Alan (6 mentions)
Johns Hopkins U, 1980 *Certification:* Cardiovascular Disease, Clinical Cardiac Electrophysiology, Internal Medicine
1250 E Marshall St, Richmond, 804-828-7565

Evans, Charles Garland, Jr. (5 mentions)
Virginia Commonwealth U, 1981 *Certification:* Cardiovascular Disease, Internal Medicine, Interventional Cardiology
7401 Beaufont Springs Dr #100, Richmond, 804-323-5011

Han, Jiho Joseph (4 mentions)
U of Buffalo, 1987
Certification: Cardiovascular Disease, Interventional Cardiology
201 W Poythress St, Hopewell, 804-458-1740

Jennings, C. Foster, Jr. (9 mentions)
U of Virginia, 1982
Certification: Cardiovascular Disease, Internal Medicine
7401 Beaufont Springs Dr #100, Richmond, 804-323-5011

Johns, Mark Edward (7 mentions)
Virginia Commonwealth U, 1987
Certification: Cardiovascular Disease, Internal Medicine
13572 Waterford Pl, Midlothian, 804-560-8782

Kapadia, Shaival Jayesh (7 mentions)
U of Virginia, 1989 *Certification:* Cardiovascular Disease
681 Hioaks Rd #H, Richmond, 804-323-1804

Nelson, Charles Wellman (4 mentions)
U of Virginia, 1985
Certification: Internal Medicine, Interventional Cardiology
5224 Monument Ave, Richmond, 804-288-4137

Newton, Calvin Mark (4 mentions)
Med U of South Carolina, 1981 *Certification:* Cardiovascular Disease, Internal Medicine, Interventional Cardiology
7401 Beaufont Springs Dr #100, Richmond, 804-323-5011

Nicholson, Christopher S. (4 mentions)
Indiana U, 1990
Certification: Cardiovascular Disease, Internal Medicine
7702 E Parham Rd #106, Richmond, 804-346-2070
7603 Forest Ave #202, Richmond, 804-288-0134

Thomas, Shelton Wayne (4 mentions)
U of Virginia, 1979 *Certification:* Cardiovascular Disease, Internal Medicine, Interventional Cardiology
7605 Forest Ave #303, Richmond, 804-288-0061

Vetrovec, George Wayne (8 mentions)
U of Virginia, 1970 *Certification:* Cardiovascular Disease, Internal Medicine, Interventional Cardiology
417 N 11th St, Richmond, 804-828-7700

Dermatology

Blanchard, Lawrence E., III (7 mentions)
Washington U, 1976 *Certification:* Dermatology
5421 Patterson Ave, Richmond, 804-285-2006
10710 Midlothian Tpke #401, Richmond, 804-794-2307

Garrett, Algin Baylor (7 mentions)
Pennsylvania State U, 1978 *Certification:* Dermatology
8700 Stony Point Pkwy, Richmond, 804-775-4500
9000 Stony Point Pkwy, Richmond, 804-560-8919

Hoover, Shelley Kae (5 mentions)
Virginia Commonwealth U, 1994 *Certification:* Dermatology
8600 Staples Mill Rd, Richmond, 804-264-4545

Konerding, Hazel S. (6 mentions)
U of Miami, 1973 *Certification:* Dermatology
7001 Forest Ave #300, Richmond, 804-282-0831

Nunley, Julia Annriley (8 mentions)
Case Western Reserve U, 1983
Certification: Dermatology, Internal Medicine, Nephrology
9000 Stony Point Pkwy, Richmond, 804-560-8919

Royal, Pamela Jofrances (6 mentions)
Eastern Virginia Med Sch, 1986 *Certification:* Dermatology
505 W Leigh St 3306, Richmond, 804-775-0957

Seely, Georgia Ann (11 mentions)
East Carolina U, 1989
Certification: Dermatology, Internal Medicine
5421 Patterson Ave, Richmond, 804-285-2006

Vernon, Hazel Jane (6 mentions)
Washington U, 1983
Certification: Dermatology, Pediatric Dermatology
7001 Forest Ave #300, Richmond, 804-282-0831

Emergency Medicine

Barnes, Tamera Counts (3 mentions)
Virginia Commonwealth U, 1989
Certification: Emergency Medicine
1401 Johnston Willis Dr, Richmond, 804-330-2000

English, Eric Martin (11 mentions)
Virginia Commonwealth U, 1990 *Certification:* Family Medicine
1401 Johnston Willis Dr, Richmond, 804-330-2000

Ernst, Arthur Clifford (4 mentions)
Virginia Commonwealth U, 1982 *Certification:* Family Medicine
7700 E Parham Rd, Richmond, 804-747-5600

Ervin, William Sherman, III (4 mentions)
Certification: Emergency Medicine
7101 Jahnke Rd, Richmond, 804-330-2000

Kramer, Marc Stephen (3 mentions)
Virginia Commonwealth U, 1978 *Certification:* Family Medicine
8260 Atlee Rd, Mechanicsville, 804-764-6334

Ornato, Joseph P. (4 mentions)
Boston U, 1971 *Certification:* Cardiovascular Disease, Emergency Medicine, Internal Medicine
1201 E Marshall St, Richmond, 804-828-5250

Powell, Robert Gilliam (9 mentions)
Virginia Commonwealth U, 1974
Certification: Emergency Medicine
5801 Bremo Rd, Richmond, 804-281-8184

Shields, Charles P., III (3 mentions)
Ohio State U, 1982 *Certification:* Internal Medicine
1602 Skipwith Rd, Richmond, 804-289-4500

Endocrinology

Berger, Meredith M. (7 mentions)
Marshall U, 1994
Certification: Endocrinology, Diabetes, and Metabolism
1401 Johnston Willis Dr #1200, Richmond, 804-272-2702

Burris, Allen Stuart (16 mentions)
New York Med Coll, 1981
Certification: Endocrinology and Metabolism, Internal Medicine
1401 Johnston Willis Dr #1200, Richmond, 804-272-2702

Castellucci, Robert Peter (11 mentions)
FMS-Grenada, 1982
Certification: Endocrinology and Metabolism, Internal Medicine
5875 Bremo Rd #500, Richmond, 804-282-9899

Downs, Robert W., Jr. (7 mentions)
Duke U, 1974
Certification: Endocrinology and Metabolism, Internal Medicine
417 N 11th St 4th Fl, Richmond, 804-828-9695

Gardner, David Franklin (12 mentions)
New York U, 1971
Certification: Endocrinology and Metabolism, Internal Medicine
474 N 11th St, Richmond, 804-828-2161

Phillips, Ben Dixon (8 mentions)
Med U of South Carolina, 1999 *Certification:* Endocrinology,
Diabetes, and Metabolism, Internal Medicine
2384 Colony Crossing Pl, Midlothian, 804-423-3636

Sicat, Jeffrey Mariano (8 mentions)
Virginia Commonwealth U, 1999 *Certification:*
Endocrinology, Diabetes, and Metabolism, Internal Medicine
2384 Colony Crossing Pl, Midlothian, 804-423-3636

Wigand, James Peter (9 mentions)
Virginia Commonwealth U, 1973
Certification: Endocrinology and Metabolism, Internal Medicine
7153 Jahnke Rd, Richmond, 804-272-7564

Family Practice *(see note on page 9)*

Dageforde, James Russell (3 mentions)
Baylor U, 1975 *Certification:* Family Medicine
2200 Pump Rd #100, Richmond, 804-741-7141

Gergoudis, Richard Lewis (4 mentions)
U of Virginia, 1986 *Certification:* Family Medicine
1800 Glenside Dr #110, Richmond, 804-288-1800

Hoffman, Richard Henry (3 mentions)
Virginia Commonwealth U, 1982 *Certification:* Family Medicine
2500 Pocoshock Pl #104, Richmond, 804-276-9305

Kuzel, Anton John (5 mentions)
U of Illinois, 1981 *Certification:* Family Medicine
40109 11th St, Richmond, 804-828-5883

Morrissette, W. Philip, III (4 mentions)
U of Virginia, 1976 *Certification:* Family Medicine
13332 Midlothian Tpke, Midlothian, 804-794-5598

Solan, Stuart M. (3 mentions)
Virginia Commonwealth U, 1977 *Certification:* Family Medicine
7229 Forest Ave #112, Richmond, 804-282-2655

Verheul, John Willem (4 mentions)
FMS-Netherlands, 1984 *Certification:* Family Medicine
1471 Johnston Willis Dr, Richmond, 804-320-3999
13911 St Francis Blvd #101, Midlothian, 804-320-3999

Whitehurst-Cook, Michelle (3 mentions)
Virginia Commonwealth U, 1979 *Certification:* Family Medicine
401 N 11th St, Richmond, 804-828-5883

Gastroenterology

Brand, William Thomas, Jr. (12 mentions)
Virginia Commonwealth U, 1980
Certification: Gastroenterology, Internal Medicine
7603 Forest Ave #306, Richmond, 804-285-4465
2369 Staples Mill Rd #200, Richmond, 804-285-8206

Haverty, Howard Onno, Jr. (13 mentions)
Eastern Virginia Med Sch, 1985
Certification: Gastroenterology, Internal Medicine
223 Wadsworth Dr, Richmond, 804-560-9852

Monroe, Paul Sheldon (6 mentions)
U of Chicago, 1975
Certification: Gastroenterology, Internal Medicine
2369 Staples Mill Rd #200, Richmond, 804-285-8206
5855 Bremo Rd #706, Richmond, 804-285-4465

Ramsey, Edward J. (5 mentions)
Virginia Commonwealth U, 1973
Certification: Gastroenterology, Internal Medicine
223 Wadsworth Dr, Richmond, 804-330-4021

Woogen, Scott D. (7 mentions)
New York U, 1981
Certification: Gastroenterology, Internal Medicine
4000-A Glenside Dr, Richmond, 804-560-9856
223 Wadsworth Dr, Richmond, 804-560-9856

Zfass, Alvin Martin (5 mentions)
Virginia Commonwealth U, 1957
Certification: Gastroenterology, Internal Medicine
417 N 11th St, Richmond, 804-828-4060

General Surgery

Bettinger, David Alan (10 mentions)
Virginia Commonwealth U, 1989 *Certification:* Surgery
1051 Johnston Willis Dr #200, Richmond, 804-320-2705

Binns, Richard Lawrence (14 mentions)
U of Virginia, 1982 *Certification:* Surgery, Vascular Surgery
1051 Johnston Willis Dr, Richmond, 804-560-5972

Deitrick, John C. (6 mentions)
U of Michigan, 1982 *Certification:* Surgery, Vascular Surgery
1051 Johnston Willis Dr, Richmond, 804-320-1325

Felsen, Ruth Brenda (3 mentions)
Harvard U, 1990 *Certification:* Surgery
1401 Johnston Willis Dr, Richmond, 804-560-5960

Hyslop, John Wesley (3 mentions)
Tulane U, 1977 *Certification:* Surgery
1051 Johnston WIllis Dr #200, Richmond, 804-560-5974

Kelley, William Edwin (7 mentions)
Boston U, 1973 *Certification:* Surgery
8921 Three Chopt Rd #300, Richmond, 804-285-9416

Knaysi, George Albert (5 mentions)
SUNY-Upstate Med U, 1965 *Certification:* Surgery
8921 Three Chopt Rd #300, Richmond, 804-285-9416

Makhoul, Raymond George (3 mentions)
U of Chicago, 1982 *Certification:* Surgery, Vascular Surgery
8700 Stony Point Pkwy #140, Richmond, 804-330-8024
1051 Johnston Willis Dr #200, Richmond, 804-320-2705

Melzig, Eric Perry (5 mentions)
Tufts U, 1972 *Certification:* Surgery
8921 Three Chopt Rd #300, Richmond, 804-285-9416

Parker, George A. (5 mentions)
Boston U, 1972 *Certification:* Surgery
5855 Bremo Rd #506, Richmond, 804-285-3225

Rose, Amy Kathleen (5 mentions)
Vanderbilt U, 1994 *Certification:* Surgery
1401 Johnston Willis Dr, Richmond, 804-320-2705

Schroder, Gregory Louis (4 mentions)
Virginia Commonwealth U, 1987 *Certification:* Surgery
8921 Three Chopt Rd #300, Richmond, 804-285-9416
5855 Bremo Rd #402, Richmond, 804-285-4133

Swartz, Steven Eugene (4 mentions)
Baylor U, 1983 *Certification:* Surgery
1401 Johnston Willis Dr, Richmond, 804-320-2705

Geriatrics

Boling, Peter Avery (9 mentions)
U of Rochester, 1981
Certification: Geriatric Medicine, Internal Medicine
417 N 11th St, Richmond, 804-828-9357

Furman, Stanley Nelson (9 mentions)
FMS-St Maarten, 1981
Certification: Geriatric Medicine, Internal Medicine
5855 Bremo Rd #207, Richmond, 804-237-1665

James, Joseph Alexander (4 mentions)
Albert Einstein Coll of Med, 1988
Certification: Geriatric Medicine, Internal Medicine
1441 Johnston Willis Dr, Richmond, 804-320-1333

Stanley, Holly Lyn (4 mentions)
U of Florida, 1981 *Certification:* Internal Medicine
206 Twinridge Ln, Richmond, 877-329-5900

Hematology/Oncology

Gonzalez, Pablo Miguel (12 mentions)
FMS-Argentina, 1987
Certification: Hematology, Internal Medicine, Medical Oncology
1401 Johnston Willis Dr #400, Richmond, 804-330-7990

Hackney, Mary Helen (6 mentions)
East Carolina U, 1988 *Certification:* Hematology, Hospice and
Palliative Medicine, Internal Medicine, Medical Oncology
401 College St, Richmond, 804-828-0450

Lewkow, Lawrence Michael (17 mentions)
New York Med Coll, 1975
1401 Johnston Willis Dr, Richmond, 804-330-7990

May, James Terrell (5 mentions)
Virginia Commonwealth U, 1973
Certification: Internal Medicine, Medical Oncology
1401 Johnston Willis Dr #400, Richmond, 804-330-7990

Mitchell, R. Brian (5 mentions)
Duke U, 1985
6605 W Broad St #A, Richmond, 804-287-3000

Smith, Thomas Joseph (12 mentions)
Yale U, 1979 *Certification:* Hospice and Palliative Medicine,
Internal Medicine, Medical Oncology
9000 Stony Point Pkwy, Richmond, 804-327-3055

Infectious Disease

Brooks, James Webster, Jr. (28 mentions)
Virginia Commonwealth U, 1980
Certification: Infectious Disease, Internal Medicine
7605 Forest Ave #410, Richmond, 804-353-4000

James, George Watson, IV (8 mentions)
U of Virginia, 1973
Certification: Infectious Disease, Internal Medicine
7117 Jahnke Rd, Richmond, 804-228-6880

Rowles, David M. (10 mentions)
Certification: Infectious Disease, Internal Medicine
7605 Forest Ave #410, Richmond, 804-285-1833

Infertility

Edelstein, Michael C. (6 mentions)
Washington U, 1984 *Certification:* Obstetrics & Gynecology, Reproductive Endocrinology/Infertility
10710 Midlothian Tpke #331, Richmond, 804-379-9000
9030 Stony Point Pkwy #390, Richmond, 804-379-9000

Steingold, Kenneth Alan (18 mentions)
Virginia Commonwealth U, 1979 *Certification:* Obstetrics & Gynecology, Reproductive Endocrinology/Infertility
10710 Midlothian Tpke #331, Richmond, 804-379-9000

Internal Medicine *(see note on page 9)*

Du, Beth Shioching (3 mentions)
Virginia Commonwealth U, 1997 *Certification:* Internal Medicine
5855 Bremo Rd #403, Richmond, 804-288-3079

Johnson, Betty Anne (4 mentions)
Harvard U, 1982 *Certification:* Internal Medicine
417 N 11th St ACC Bldg, Richmond, 804-828-9357

Jones, Sidney Rivers, III (4 mentions)
Virginia Commonwealth U, 1989 *Certification:* Internal Medicine
7001 Forest Ave #2500, Richmond, 804-282-7857

Lothe, Anand Prakash (4 mentions)
Wake Forest U, 1995 *Certification:* Internal Medicine
5855 Bremo Rd #403, Richmond, 804-288-3079

Mehfoud, G. Joseph (3 mentions)
Eastern Virginia Med Sch, 1989 *Certification:* Internal Medicine
8923 Three Chopt Rd #101, Richmond, 804-288-0057
1807 Huguenot Rd, Midlothian, 804-378-7373

Ray, Brenda Julia (3 mentions)
Virginia Commonwealth U, 1981 *Certification:* Internal Medicine
7660 E Parham Rd #205, Richmond, 804-747-1176

Smallwood, Katherine L. (6 mentions)
U of Virginia, 1980 *Certification:* Internal Medicine
7702 E Parham Rd #205, Richmond, 804-346-1630

Wasserman, Brian Mark (4 mentions)
Virginia Commonwealth U, 1974 *Certification:* Internal Medicine
7153 Jahnke Rd, Richmond, 804-272-7564

Young, Stephen Charles (7 mentions)
Virginia Commonwealth U, 1987 *Certification:* Internal Medicine
1401 Johnston Willis Dr #1200, Richmond, 804-272-2702

Nephrology

Condro, Peter, Jr. (18 mentions)
U of Buffalo, 1979 *Certification:* Internal Medicine, Nephrology
671 Hioaks Rd #B, Richmond, 804-272-5814

Gehr, Todd (8 mentions)
Certification: Internal Medicine, Nephrology
417 N 11th St, Richmond, 804-828-9683

Peppiatt, Harry Brian (18 mentions)
Virginia Commonwealth U, 1983
Certification: Internal Medicine, Nephrology
671 Hioaks Rd #B, Richmond, 804-272-5814

Starkman, Martin Tobias (22 mentions)
Med Coll of Wisconsin, 1974
Certification: Internal Medicine, Nephrology
7603 Forest Ave #303, Richmond, 804-282-8005

Neurological Surgery

Sahni, K. Singh (16 mentions)
FMS-Iran, 1977
1651 N Parham Rd, Richmond, 804-288-8204

Salvant, Jackson Boland (11 mentions)
Virginia Commonwealth U, 1988
Certification: Neurological Surgery
1651 N Parham Rd, Richmond, 804-288-8204

White, William Richard (21 mentions)
Cornell U, 1968 *Certification:* Neurological Surgery
1651 N Parham Rd, Richmond, 804-288-8204

Neurology

Brush, John Joseph (8 mentions)
Med Coll of Wisconsin, 1970 *Certification:* Neurology
165 Wadsworth Dr, Richmond, 804-272-9146

Cohen, Robert Jay (11 mentions)
Virginia Commonwealth U, 1976 *Certification:* Neurology
7301 Forest Ave #300, Richmond, 804-282-1100

Epps, Stacey Lawrence (4 mentions)
Georgetown U, 1997 *Certification:* Neurology
165 Wadsworth Dr, Richmond, 804-272-9146

Harris, Joseph Kim (6 mentions)
Indiana U, 1981 *Certification:* Internal Medicine
7301 Forest Ave #300, Richmond, 804-288-2742

Katchinoff, Barry Lester (4 mentions)
FMS-Belgium, 1977 *Certification:* Neurology
7131 Jahnke Rd, Richmond, 804-272-6828
7305 Boulders View, Richmond, 804-272-6828

Leaton, Edward Montgomery (8 mentions)
Northwestern U, 1979 *Certification:* Neurology
14355 Sommerville Ct, Midlothian, 804-379-7721

O'Bannon, John Maurice (9 mentions)
Virginia Commonwealth U, 1973 *Certification:* Neurology
7301 Forest Ave #300, Richmond, 804-288-2742

Thurston, Stephen Ellyson (6 mentions)
Virginia Commonwealth U, 1979 *Certification:* Neurology
7301 Forest Ave #300, Richmond, 804-282-1100

White, Robert Jerome (12 mentions)
Virginia Commonwealth U, 1985 *Certification:* Neurology
165 Wadsworth Dr, Richmond, 804-560-0772

Obstetrics/Gynecology

Broocker, Warren Alan (3 mentions)
Temple U, 1973 *Certification:* Obstetrics & Gynecology
10710 Midlothian Tpke #200, Richmond, 804-897-2100

Hirata, Alice Jean (12 mentions)
Virginia Commonwealth U, 1987
Certification: Obstetrics & Gynecology
5875 Bremo Rd #400, Richmond, 804-288-4084

Knapp, Karen Elizabeth (5 mentions)
U of Arizona, 1985 *Certification:* Obstetrics & Gynecology
5855 Bremo Rd #605, Richmond, 804-285-8806

Reutinger, David Charles (4 mentions)
U of Texas-Houston, 1982 *Certification:* Obstetrics & Gynecology
10710 Midlothian Tpke #200, Richmond, 804-897-2100

Tuckey-Larus, Corinne N. (4 mentions)
Jefferson Med Coll, 1987 *Certification:* Obstetrics & Gynecology
10710 Midlothian Tpke, Richmond, 804-897-2100

Wilbanks, Peter Thornton (3 mentions)
Virginia Commonwealth U, 1989
Certification: Obstetrics & Gynecology
5875 Bremo Rd #400, Richmond, 804-288-4084

Ophthalmology

Benson, William H. (4 mentions)
West Virginia U, 1986 *Certification:* Ophthalmology
8700 Stony Point Pkwy, Richmond, 804-323-0830

Brown, Donna Dodson (6 mentions)
East Tennessee State U, 1984 *Certification:* Ophthalmology
400 Westhampton Sta, Richmond, 804-287-4200

Bullock, John Paul, Jr. (11 mentions)
Med U of South Carolina, 1974 *Certification:* Ophthalmology
400 Westhampton Sta, Richmond, 804-287-4248

Jones, Ethnie Small (4 mentions)
Johns Hopkins U, 1987 *Certification:* Ophthalmology
101 Cowardin Ave #101, Richmond, 804-233-0292

Leslie, Evan Joel (3 mentions)
U of Miami, 1978 *Certification:* Ophthalmology
1475 Johnston Willis Dr, Richmond, 804-287-4930
400 Westhampton Station, Richmond, 804-642-4200

McElroy, Anne Howell (3 mentions)
Case Western Reserve U, 1987
7229 Forest Ave #104, Richmond, 804-285-7307

Sakowski, Anthony D., Jr. (4 mentions)
Virginia Commonwealth U, 1969 *Certification:* Ophthalmology
400 Westhampton Station, Richmond, 804-287-4200

Trice, Edmund Winston (3 mentions)
Virginia Commonwealth U, 1981 *Certification:* Ophthalmology
400 Westhampton Sta, Richmond, 804-287-4200

Wortham, Edwin, V (3 mentions)
Northwestern U, 1983 *Certification:* Ophthalmology
8700 Stony Point Pkwy #210, Richmond, 804-272-8040

Orthopedics

Burkhardt, Barry Webster (4 mentions)
Tufts U, 1972 *Certification:* Orthopaedic Surgery
1400 Johnston Willis Dr #A, Richmond, 804-379-8088

Caldwell, Paul Estil, III (5 mentions)
Virginia Commonwealth U, 1999
Certification: Orthopaedic Surgery
1501 Maple Ave #200, Richmond, 804-285-2300

De Blois, Mark Edwin (6 mentions)
Wayne State U, 1980 *Certification:* Orthopaedic Surgery
500 Hioaks Rd #B, Richmond, 804-320-1339

Garnett, Lockett Wooton (5 mentions)
Virginia Commonwealth U, 1979
Certification: Orthopaedic Surgery
5899 Bremo Rd #100, Richmond, 804-288-8512

Jiranek, William A. (4 mentions)
Certification: Orthopaedic Surgery
9000 Strong Point Pkwy, Richmond, 804-228-4155

Jones, Mark McClellan (13 mentions)
Virginia Commonwealth U, 1987
Certification: Orthopaedic Surgery
1400 Johnston Willis Dr #A, Richmond, 804-379-8088

Loughran, Thomas P. (4 mentions)
Virginia Commonwealth U, 1977
Certification: Orthopaedic Surgery
1300 W Broad St, Richmond, 804-828-0713

Nordt, William E., III (5 mentions)
Robert W Johnson Med Sch, 1983
Certification: Orthopaedic Surgery
7601 Forest Ave #228, Richmond, 804-288-3136

Smith, Julious P., III (5 mentions)
U of Virginia, 1994 *Certification:* Orthopaedic Surgery
5899 Bremo Rd #100, Richmond, 804-288-8512

Wilson, Jeffrey Kent (4 mentions)
U of California-Davis, 1978
Certification: Orthopaedic Surgery
8266 Atlee Rd #133, Mechanicsville, 804-730-2121

Young, D. Christopher (6 mentions)
Duke U, 1978 *Certification:* Orthopaedic Surgery
500 Hioaks Rd #B, Richmond, 804-320-1339

Zuelzer, Wilhelm A. (4 mentions)
U of Texas-San Antonio, 1975 *Certification:* Orthopaedic Surgery
9000 Stony Point Pkwy, Richmond, 804-560-8945

Otorhinolaryngology

Burke, Alan J. (6 mentions)
FMS-United Kingdom, 1991 *Certification:* Otolaryngology
5875 Bremo Rd #303, Richmond, 804-484-3734

Hickman, Clifton Claude (7 mentions)
U of Illinois, 1976 *Certification:* Otolaryngology
5875 Bremo Rd #303, Richmond, 804-282-7614

Perlman, Michael Romney (7 mentions)
U of Kansas, 1979 *Certification:* Otolaryngology
5875 Bremo Rd #303, Richmond, 804-282-7614

Reiter, Evan Ralph (6 mentions)
Harvard U, 1993 *Certification:* Otolaryngology
8700 Stony Point Pkwy, Richmond, 804-323-0830

Tarasidis, Nicholas G. (6 mentions)
Virginia Commonwealth U, 1985 *Certification:* Otolaryngology
5875 Bremo Rd #303, Richmond, 804-282-7614

Pain Medicine

Barsanti, John Michael (9 mentions)
Virginia Commonwealth U, 1988
Certification: Anesthesiology, Pain Medicine
1501 Maple Ave #301, Richmond, 804-288-7246

Long, Stephen Paul (18 mentions)
Virginia Commonwealth U, 1986
Certification: Anesthesiology, Pain Medicine
1501 Maple Ave #301, Richmond, 850-228-7246

Pathology

De Blois, Georgean Graham (10 mentions)
Wayne State U, 1980
Certification: Anatomic Pathology & Clinical Pathology
7101 Jahnke Rd, Richmond, 804-323-8824

Gates, Beverly Diane (3 mentions)
Louisiana State U, 1980
Certification: Anatomic Pathology & Clinical Pathology
7700 E Parham Rd, Richmond, 804-747-5675

Grimes, Margaret Mary (3 mentions)
New York Med Coll, 1975
Certification: Anatomic Pathology & Clinical Pathology
1200 E Marshall St, Richmond, 804-828-9738

Johnson, Danna Elizabeth (4 mentions)
SUNY-Upstate Med U, 1980 *Certification:* Anatomic
Pathology, Cytopathology, Internal Medicine
1401 Johnston Willis Dr, Richmond, 800-468-6620

Nichols, Guy Eddy (6 mentions)
U of Virginia, 1988 *Certification:* Anatomic Pathology &
Clinical Pathology, Cytopathology, Hematology
5801 Bremo Rd 2nd Fl, Richmond, 804-285-2011

Pierce, Catherine V. (3 mentions)
Virginia Commonwealth U, 1990
Certification: Anatomic Pathology & Clinical Pathology
7101 Jahnke Rd, Richmond, 804-323-8824

Thomas, George Walter (4 mentions)
Virginia Commonwealth U, 1972
Certification: Anatomic Pathology & Clinical Pathology
1401 Johnston Willis Dr, Richmond, 804-323-8824

Pediatrics *(see note on page 9)*

Andrako, John David (6 mentions)
Virginia Commonwealth U, 1975
7113 Three Chopt Rd #101, Richmond, 804-282-4205

Rowe, George Thomas (4 mentions)
Virginia Commonwealth U, 1988 *Certification:* Pediatrics
10410 Ridgefield Pkwy, Richmond, 804-754-3776

Shreve, Mark J. (4 mentions)
Certification: Pediatrics
7113 3 Chopt Rd #101, Richmond, 804-282-4205

Terry, Charles Vaden (6 mentions)
Eastern Virginia Med Sch, 1983 *Certification:* Pediatrics
10410 Ridgefield Pkwy, Richmond, 804-754-7422

Plastic Surgery

Blanchet, Nadia P. (19 mentions)
New York U, 1981 *Certification:* Plastic Surgery
9210 Forest Hill Ave #B1, Richmond, 804-320-8545

Ladocsi, Lewis Thomas, IV (8 mentions)
Virginia Commonwealth U, 1992
Certification: Plastic Surgery, Surgery
5899 Bremo Rd #205, Richmond, 804-285-4115
1451 Johnston Willis Dr, Richmond, 804-560-7311

Olshansky, Kenneth (8 mentions)
Virginia Commonwealth U, 1968 *Certification:* Plastic Surgery
5875 Bremo Rd #212, Richmond, 804-282-7965

Pozez, Andrea L. (7 mentions)
FMS-Mexico, 1980 *Certification:* Plastic Surgery
401 N 11th St, Richmond, 804-828-3035
7301 Forest Ave, Richmond, 804-828-3035

Williams, Mason Miller (8 mentions)
Virginia Commonwealth U, 1973
Certification: Otolaryngology, Plastic Surgery
5899 Bremo Rd #205, Richmond, 804-285-4115

Wornom, Issac Leake, III (7 mentions)
U of Virginia, 1981 *Certification:* Plastic Surgery
5899 Bremo Rd #205, Richmond, 804-285-4115
1451 Johnston Willis Dr, Richmond, 804-560-7311

Psychiatry

Buxton, Martin N. (6 mentions)
FMS-Mexico, 1971 *Certification:* Child Psychiatry, Psychiatry
7101 Jahnke Rd, Richmond, 804-323-8282

Levenson, James Lloyd (7 mentions)
U of Michigan, 1977 *Certification:* Geriatric Psychiatry,
Psychiatry, Psychosomatic Medicine
1200 E Broad St, Richmond, 804-828-0762

Shield, James Asa (8 mentions)
U of Virginia, 1964 *Certification:* Psychiatry
1000 Boulders Pkwy #202, Richmond, 804-320-7881

Silverman, Joel J. (3 mentions)
U of Kansas, 1969 *Certification:* Psychiatry
1250 E Marshall St, Richmond, 804-828-9157

Pulmonary Disease

Apostle, James Andrew (6 mentions)
Virginia Commonwealth U, 1995
Certification: Critical Care Medicine, Pulmonary Disease
2354 Colony Crossing Pl, Midlothian, 804-639-9910

Fairman, Paiul Ralph (5 mentions)
U of Missouri, 1972
Certification: Internal Medicine, Pulmonary Disease
1200 E Broad St, Richmond, 828-907-1804

Fowler, Alpha Alsbury, III (6 mentions)
Med Coll of Georgia, 1975 *Certification:* Critical Care
Medicine, Internal Medicine, Pulmonary Disease
417 N 11th St 4th Fl, Richmond, 804-828-2161

Giessel, Glenn Matthew (7 mentions)
Baylor U, 1978
Certification: Internal Medicine, Pulmonary Disease
1000 Boulders Pkwy, Richmond, 804-320-4243

Hey, Jamie Cooper (10 mentions)
Jefferson Med Coll, 1993 *Certification:* Critical Care
Medicine, Internal Medicine, Pulmonary Disease
1000 Boulders Pkwy, Richmond, 804-320-4243

Miksa, Andrea Kay (7 mentions)
U of Mississippi, 1984 *Certification:* Critical Care Medicine,
Internal Medicine, Pulmonary Disease
1603 Santa Rosa Rd, Richmond, 804-288-2711

Puryear, Douglas Wayne (5 mentions)
Virginia Commonwealth U, 1989
Certification: Critical Care Medicine, Pulmonary Disease
2354 Colony Crossing Pl, Midlothian, 804-639-9910

Radow, Scott K. (7 mentions)
West Virginia U, 1977 *Certification:* Critical Care Medicine,
Internal Medicine, Pulmonary Disease
1603 Santa Rosa Rd #101, Richmond, 804-741-7025

Smith, Rodney Hall (5 mentions)
Virginia Commonwealth U, 1970
Certification: Internal Medicine, Pulmonary Disease
1000 Boulders Pkwy, Richmond, 804-320-4243

Torrisi, Peter Francis (5 mentions)
New York Med Coll, 1980 *Certification:* Critical Care
Medicine, Internal Medicine, Pulmonary Disease
1000 Boulders Pkwy, Richmond, 804-320-4243

Radiology—Diagnostic

Fulcher, Ann Simpson (4 mentions)
Virginia Commonwealth U, 1987
Certification: Diagnostic Radiology
1101 E Marshall St, Richmond, 804-828-5426

Girevendulis, Alexander K. (3 mentions)
FMS-Greece, 1972
Certification: Diagnostic Radiology, Neuroradiology
2602 Buford Rd, Richmond, 804-272-8806

Kuta, Arnold John (7 mentions)
U of Iowa, 1979 *Certification:* Diagnostic Radiology,
Internal Medicine, Neuroradiology
2602 Buford Rd, Richmond, 804-272-8806

Laine, Fred Julius (3 mentions)
FMS-Mexico, 1980
Certification: Diagnostic Radiology, Neuroradiology
2602 Buford Rd, Richmond, 804-272-8806

May, David Alan (3 mentions)
U of North Carolina, 1988 *Certification:* Diagnostic Radiology
2602 Buford Rd, Richmond, 804-272-8806

Reece, Gerry Lee (3 mentions)
Duke U, 1993
Certification: Diagnostic Radiology, Pediatric Radiology
2602 Buford Rd, Richmond, 804-272-8806

THESE DOCTORS ARE AMONG
THE BEST PLASTIC SURGEONS IN AMERICA

Each doctor has been peer-nominated and selected by the nation's leading providers of information on top doctors.

All doctors are board certified by the American Board of Plastic Surgery (ABPS).

Dr. Daniel Mills
Laguna Beach, CA

LOS ANGELES
Daniel Mills, MD
31852 Pacific Coast Highway
Laguna Beach, CA
949-499-2800
www.DanMillsMD.com
Castle Connolly – America's Top Doctors

SALT LAKE CITY
Renato Saltz, MD
Salt Lake City, UT Location:
5445 South Highland Drive

Park City, UT Location:
1820 Sidewinder Drive
888-744-9502
www.SaltzPlasticSurgery.com
Best Doctors, Inc. – Best Doctors in America®

ATLANTA
Foad Nahai, MD
3200 Downwood Circle, Atlanta, GA
404-351-0051
www.PacesPlasticSurgery.com
Castle Connolly – America's Top Doctors

T. Roderick Hester, Jr., MD
3200 Downwood Circle, Atlanta, GA
404-351-0051
www.PacesPlasticSurgery.com
Castle Connolly – America's Top Doctors

PHILADELPHIA
Paul M. Glat, MD
191 Presidential Boulevard
Bala Cynwyd, PA
610-980-4000
www.DrGlat.com
Castle Connolly – America's Top Doctors

LAS VEGAS
Michael C. Edwards, MD
653 North Town Center Drive
Las Vegas, NV
702-248-8989
www.MEdwardsMD.com
Castle Connolly – America's Top Doctors

WASHINGTON, DC
George J. Bitar, MD
3023 Hamaker Court
Fairfax, VA
703-206-0506
www.DrBitar.com
Washingtonian Magazine – Top Doctors Issue

THESE DOCTORS ARE AMONG
THE BEST DOCTORS IN NEW YORK

Each doctor has been included in a "Best Doctors" issue of

www.nymag.com

All Doctors are Board Certified

Dr. Paul M. Brisson
Spine Surgery

SPINE SURGERY
Paul M. Brisson, MD
51 East 25th Street
New York, NY
212-813-3632
www.NYSpineCare.com

CARDIOLOGY
Jeffrey S. Borer, MD
Cardiovascular Medicine and The Howard
Gilman Institute for Heart Valve Disease
SUNY Downstate Medical Center, Brooklyn & NY, NY
212-289-7777   www.GilmanHeartValve.us
Heart Valve Society of America
www.HeartValveSocietyOfAmerica.org

HAIR TRANSPLANTATION
Robert M. Bernstein, MD
Center for Hair Restoration
110 East 55th Street, New York, NY
212-826-2400
www.BernsteinMedical.com

SPORTS MEDICINE
Jonathan L. Glashow, MD
Shoulder, Knee, Arthroscopic Surgery
737 Park Avenue, New York, NY
212-794-5096
www.GlashowMD.com

PLASTIC SURGERY
John E. Sherman, MD
1016 Fifth Avenue, New York, NY
212-535-2300
www.NYPlasticSurg.com

HAND SURGERY
Mark E. Pruzansky, MD
*Hand, Wrist & Elbow Surgery,
Sports Injuries*
975 Park Ave., New York, NY
212-249-8700
www.HandSport.us

ORTHOPAEDIC TUMOR SURGERY
James C. Wittig, MD
Bone, Muscle and Joint Tumors
NYC office: Mount Sinai Medical Center
Long Island office: Lake Success
NJ offices: Hackensack / Morristown
212-241-1807   www.TumorSurgery.org

THESE DOCTORS ARE AMONG
THE BEST LASIK SURGEONS IN AMERICA

Each doctor has been peer-nominated and/or selected by the nation's leading providers of information on top doctors, including:
Castle Connolly - America's Top Doctors
Orlando magazine - Best Doctors Issue
Trusted LASIK Surgeons Directory

LASIK surgeons specialize in vision correction procedures for nearsightedness, farsightedness, astigmatism and presbyopia to reduce dependency on contact lenses and eye glasses.

All doctors are board certified by the American Board of Ophthalmology.

Dr. Phillip C. Hoopes
Sandy, UT

SALT LAKE CITY
Phillip C. Hoopes, MD
10011 S. Centennial Parkway
Sandy, UT
877-30-LASIK (877-305-2745)
www.HoopesVision.com

ORLANDO
Jeffrey B. Robin, MD
Orlando, FL location:
155 Cranes Roost Boulevard
Altamonte Springs, FL
Jacksonville, FL location:
8705 Perimeter Park Boulevard
866-973-EYES (3937)
www.LasikPlus.com/OrlandoTopDoc

CHICAGO
Dimitri T. Azar, MD
UIC Department of Ophthalmology
30 N. Michigan Avenue
Chicago, IL
312-996-2020
www.MillenniumParkEyeCenter.com

CINCINNATI
David M. Schneider, MD
8760 Union Centre Boulevard
West Chester, OH
800-385-EYES (3937)
www.MidwestEyeCenter.com

KANSAS CITY
Daniel S. Durrie, MD
5520 College Boulevard
Overland Park, KS
913-491-3330
www.DurrieVision.com

TAMPA
Lewis R. Groden, MD
2202 North Westshore Blvd.
Tampa, FL
866-983-EYES (3937)
www.LasikPlus.com/TampaTopDoc

DALLAS
R. Wayne Bowman, MD
UT Southwestern Medical Center
Laser Center for Vision Care
1801 Inwood Road, Dallas, TX
888-663-2020 www.utswLasik.com

www.TheTopPhysicians.com

Szucs, Richard Alexander (3 mentions)
Jefferson Med Coll, 1982 *Certification:* Diagnostic Radiology
1508 Willow Lawn Dr #117, Richmond, 804-281-8237

Thompson, Jeffrey Keith (7 mentions)
U of Alabama, 1990 *Certification:* Diagnostic Radiology
2602 Buford Rd, Richmond, 804-272-8806

Radiology—Therapeutic

Arthur, Douglas William (5 mentions)
Wake Forest U, 1989 *Certification:* Radiation Oncology
401 N 11th St, Richmond, 804-828-7232

Chin, Judy Ling (4 mentions)
Virginia Commonwealth U, 1982
Certification: Internal Medicine, Radiation Oncology
5711 Staples Mill Rd #100, Richmond, 804-266-7762

Hull, Jeffrey Eaton (9 mentions)
Duke U, 1984 *Certification:* Diagnostic Radiology, Vascular
& Interventional Radiology
2602 Buford Rd, Richmond, 804-272-8806

Spinos, Efstathios (4 mentions)
U of South Florida, 1980 *Certification:* Diagnostic
Radiology, Vascular & Interventional Radiology
2602 Buford Rd, Richmond, 804-272-8806

Rehabilitation

Hawkins, Hillary (5 mentions)
Virginia Commonwealth U, 1989
Certification: Physical Medicine & Rehabilitation
8254 Atlee Rd, Mechanicsville, 804-342-4300

Jones, Albert M., Jr. (4 mentions)
U of Tennessee, 1983
Certification: Physical Medicine & Rehabilitation
8254 Atlee Rd, Mechanicsville, 804-342-4300

Khokhar, Manmohan Singh (3 mentions)
FMS-India, 1981
Certification: Physical Medicine & Rehabilitation
1427 Johnston Willis Dr, Richmond, 804-330-2324

McKinley, William Oscar (3 mentions)
Albany Med Coll, 1985 *Certification:* Physical Medicine &
Rehabilitation, Spinal Cord Injury Medicine
417 N 11th St, Richmond, 804-828-4097

Silver, Timothy Milton (3 mentions)
East Carolina U, 1997
Certification: Physical Medicine & Rehabilitation
13700 St Francis Blvd #300, Midlothian, 804-764-1001

Rheumatology

Brodeur, James Philip (6 mentions)
U of Virginia, 1985
Certification: Internal Medicine, Rheumatology
8201 Atlee Rd #B, Mechanicsville, 804-730-5222

Buckley, Lenore Margaret (8 mentions)
U of Rochester, 1977 *Certification:* Internal Medicine,
Pediatric Rheumatology, Pediatrics, Rheumatology
1250 E Marshall St, Richmond, 804-828-9690
9000 Stony Point Pkwy, Richmond, 804-560-8920

Coutlakis, Peter James (9 mentions)
Virginia Commonwealth U, 1994 *Certification:* Rheumatology
1401 Johnston Willis Dr #4100, Richmond, 804-323-1401

Jessee, Edgar Forrest, Jr. (9 mentions)
Virginia Commonwealth U, 1975
Certification: Internal Medicine, Rheumatology
1401 Johnston Willis Dr #4100, Richmond, 804-323-1401

Maestrello, Steven Joseph (7 mentions)
Virginia Commonwealth U, 1990 *Certification:* Rheumatology
7702 E Parham Rd #304, Richmond, 804-346-1551

Strachan, Michael Joel (7 mentions)
Virginia Commonwealth U, 1974 *Certification:* Internal Medicine
7702 E Parham Rd #101, Richmond, 804-288-7901

Thoracic Surgery

Buckman, Peter Daniel (9 mentions)
U of Connecticut, 1986 *Certification:* Surgery, Thoracic Surgery
2004 Bremo Rd #103, Richmond, 804-565-0383

Lockhart, Charles Gregory (19 mentions)
U of Missouri, 1977 *Certification:* Thoracic Surgery
7109 Jahnke Rd, Richmond, 804-864-5300

Urology

Glazier, David Brendan (7 mentions)
FMS-Ireland, 1990 *Certification:* Urology
9105 Stony Point Dr, Richmond, 804-560-4483
5224 Monument Ave, Richmond, 804-288-4137
436 Claremont Ct #108, Colonial Heights, 804-524-8959

Graham, Sam D. (5 mentions)
U of Virginia, 1946 *Certification:* Urology
7135 Jahnke Rd, Richmond, 804-323-0226

Koo, Harry Pontahk (5 mentions)
U of Rochester, 1987 *Certification:* Urology
401 N 11th St, Richmond, 804-828-9331

Rollins, Kent Lawton (7 mentions)
U of South Carolina, 1981 *Certification:* Urology
9105 Stony Point Dr, Richmond, 804-560-4483
436 Claremont Ct #108, Colonial Heights, 804-524-8959

Sliwinski, Anthony M. (5 mentions)
Georgetown U, 1986 *Certification:* Urology
9105 Stony Point Dr, Richmond, 804-330-5105
8228 Meadowbridge Rd, Mechanicsville, 804-730-5023

Winslow, Boyd Holden (6 mentions)
Harvard U, 1974 *Certification:* Urology
8700 Stony Point Pkwy #250, Richmond, 804-272-2411

Vascular Surgery

Deitrick, John C. (7 mentions)
U of Michigan, 1982 *Certification:* Surgery, Vascular Surgery
1051 Johnston Willis Dr, Richmond, 804-320-1325

Makhoul, Raymond George (7 mentions)
U of Chicago, 1982 *Certification:* Surgery, Vascular Surgery
8700 Stony Point Pkwy, Richmond, 804-775-4500

Mendez Picon, Gerardo P. (7 mentions)
FMS-Spain, 1966 *Certification:* Surgery
8921 Three Chopt Rd #300, Richmond, 804-285-9416

Zimmerman, Barklie Waters (7 mentions)
Virginia Commonwealth U, 1980
Certification: Surgery, Vascular Surgery
8921 Three Chopt Rd #300, Richmond, 804-285-9416

Washington

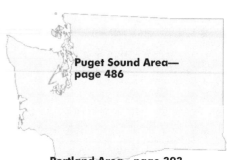

**Puget Sound Area—
page 486**

Portland Area—page 393

Puget Sound Area

Including King, Kitsap, Mason, Pierce, Skagit, Snohomish, and Thurston Counties

Allergy/Immunology

Altman, Leonard Charles (6 mentions)
Harvard U, 1969
Certification: Allergy & Immunology, Internal Medicine
4540 Sand Point Way NE #200, Seattle, 206-527-1200

Farrington, Mary Lisa (6 mentions)
Indiana U, 1987 *Certification:* Allergy & Immunology
1100 9th Ave, Seattle, 206-341-0404

Krouse, Howard Alan (7 mentions)
U of Washington, 1970
Certification: Allergy & Immunology, Internal Medicine
11511 NE 10th St, Bellevue, 425-883-5459
20200 54th Ave W, Lynnwood, 425-883-5459
275 Bronson Way NE, Renton, 425-883-5459

Lammert, Joyce Kathleen (10 mentions)
U of North Carolina, 1985
Certification: Allergy & Immunology, Internal Medicine
1100 9th Ave, Seattle, 206-223-6173

Mokha, Arvinder Singh (7 mentions)
U of Maryland, 1995
Certification: Allergy & Immunology, Internal Medicine
1145 Broadway, Seattle, 206-860-4487
509 Olive Way #900, Seattle, 206-860-4700

Robinson, David McKinney (7 mentions)
St Louis U, 1983
Certification: Allergy & Immunology, Internal Medicine
1100 9th Ave, Seattle, 206-223-6173
33501 1st Way S, Federal Way, 253-874-1610

Weiss, Michael Elliot (10 mentions)
Stony Brook U, 1981
Certification: Allergy & Immunology, Internal Medicine
8301 161st Ave NE #208, Redmond, 425-885-0261

Anesthesiology

Artru, Alan Arthur (3 mentions)
Med Coll of Wisconsin, 1975 *Certification:* Anesthesiology
1959 NE Pacific St #EE-201, Seattle, 206-598-4260

Bailey, Desiray C. (3 mentions)
U of Nebraska, 1975 *Certification:* Anesthesiology
2700 152nd Ave NE, Redmond, 425-883-5130

Baker, Ray Merville, Jr. (4 mentions)
U of California-Irvine, 1985 *Certification:* Anesthesiology
12301 NE 10th Pl #101, Bellevue, 425-454-1111

Baldini, Daniel J. (5 mentions)
Virginia Commonwealth U, 1977 *Certification:* Anesthesiology
11511 NE 10th St, Bellevue, 425-502-3000

Batra, Manbir S. (3 mentions)
FMS-India, 1963
1100 9th Ave #B2-AN, Seattle, 206-223-6980

Beppu, William James (5 mentions)
Stanford U, 1972 *Certification:* Anesthesiology
3624 Ensign Rd NE #B, Olympia, 360-438-6400

Gertler, Robert Andrew (4 mentions)
Case Western Reserve U, 1978 *Certification:* Anesthesiology
201 16th Ave E, Seattle, 206-326-3895

Hammen, Michael J. (3 mentions)
U of California-San Diego, 1991 *Certification:* Anesthesiology
407 14th Ave SE, Puyallup, 253-697-4000

Helman, James Diller (5 mentions)
U of Miami, 1983 *Certification:* Anesthesiology, Pain Medicine
1100 9th Ave, Seattle, 206-223-6600

Lam, Arthur M. (7 mentions)
FMS-Canada, 1974 *Certification:* Anesthesiology
325 9th Ave, Seattle, 206-731-3000

Lynn, Anne Marie (3 mentions)
Stanford U, 1975 *Certification:* Anesthesiology, Pediatrics
4800 Sand Point Way NE #W9824, Seattle, 206-987-2518

Markowitz, Stephen (5 mentions)
FMS-South Africa, 1983 *Certification:* Anesthesiology
900 Terry Ave 3rd Fl, Seattle, 206-382-1021

Ross, Brian Kent (4 mentions)
U of Washington, 1983 *Certification:* Anesthesiology
1959 NE Pacific St #1124, Seattle, 206-543-6814

Rupp, Stephen Mitchell (5 mentions)
U of Michigan, 1978 *Certification:* Anesthesiology
1100 9th Ave #B2-AN, Seattle, 206-223-6980

Snee, Karen Lynne (4 mentions)
U of Virginia, 1989 *Certification:* Anesthesiology
201 16th Ave E, Seattle, 206-326-3606

Tupper, Bradley James (3 mentions)
U of Pennsylvania, 1982 *Certification:* Anesthesiology
747 Broadway, Seattle, 206-215-3656

Wright, Ian Howard (7 mentions)
FMS-United Kingdom, 1980 *Certification:* Anesthesiology
747 Broadway, Seattle, 206-215-3656

Cardiac Surgery

Aldea, Gabriel (9 mentions)
Columbia U, 1981 *Certification:* Thoracic Surgery
1959 NE Pacific St, Seattle, 206-543-3093

Gartman, David Miner (9 mentions)
Louisiana State U, 1980 *Certification:* Thoracic Surgery
1600 E Jefferson St #110, Seattle, 206-320-7300

Hill, Mark E. (11 mentions)
U of Utah, 1989 *Certification:* Surgery, Thoracic Surgery
1100 9th Ave, Seattle, 206-223-6198

Paull, Daniel Leonard (14 mentions)
Tufts U, 1978 *Certification:* Surgery, Thoracic Surgery
1100 9th Ave, Seattle, 203-223-6600

Verrier, Edward Donald (15 mentions)
Tufts U, 1974 *Certification:* Thoracic Surgery
1959 NE Pacific St, Seattle, 206-685-3370

Cardiology

Albro, Peter Carey (6 mentions)
Columbia U, 1970
Certification: Cardiovascular Disease, Internal Medicine
550 17th Ave #400, Seattle, 206-860-2302

Amidon, Thomas Morton (6 mentions)
Duke U, 1986
Certification: Cardiovascular Disease, Internal Medicine
1407 116th Ave NE #200, Bellevue, 425-454-2656

Dash, Harold (5 mentions)
Harvard U, 1974 *Certification:* Cardiovascular Disease,
  Internal Medicine, Interventional Cardiology
3901 Hoyt Ave, Everett, 425-339-5411

Demopulos, Peter (10 mentions)
Stanford U, 1981 *Certification:* Cardiovascular Disease,
  Internal Medicine, Interventional Cardiology
1730 Minor Ave #1010, Seattle, 206-215-4545
1560 N 115th St #205, Seattle, 206-361-9416

Dewhurst, Timothy Andrew (4 mentions)
FMS-Canada, 1986 *Certification:* Cardiovascular Disease,
  Internal Medicine, Interventional Cardiology
550 17th Ave #400, Seattle, 206-860-2302
2208 NW Market St #410, Seattle, 206-320-3202

Doucette, Joseph W. (9 mentions)
Harvard U, 1984 *Certification:* Cardiovascular Disease,
  Internal Medicine, Interventional Cardiology
1135 116th Ave NE #600, Bellevue, 425-454-2656

English, Milton Tate, III (4 mentions)
U of Missouri, 1969 *Certification:* Cardiovascular Disease,
  Internal Medicine, Interventional Cardiology
550 17th Ave #580, Seattle, 206-215-4545

Fahmy, Raed Nicola (4 mentions)
George Washington U, 1985
Certification: Cardiovascular Disease, Internal Medicine
1802 Yakima Ave #307, Tacoma, 253-627-1244
4700 Point Fosdick Dr NW #320, Gig Harbor, 253-853-6092

Fellows, Christopher Lee (7 mentions)
Oregon Health Sciences U, 1980 *Certification:* Cardiovascular
  Disease, Clinical Cardiac Electrophysiology, Internal Medicine
1201 Terry Ave, Seattle, 206-223-6661

Gibbons, Edward Francis (5 mentions)
U of Chicago, 1978
Certification: Cardiovascular Disease, Internal Medicine
1100 9th Ave, Seattle, 206-223-6989

Haynes, Robert Earl (6 mentions)
U of Cincinnati, 1972
Certification: Cardiovascular Disease, Internal Medicine
12333 NE 130th Ln #320, Kirkland, 425-899-0555

Holmes, John Richard (5 mentions)
U of Washington, 1978
Certification: Cardiovascular Disease, Internal Medicine
1201 Terry Ave 3rd Fl, Seattle, 206-223-6666

Kudenchuk, Peter James (4 mentions)
U of Washington, 1979 *Certification:* Cardiovascular Disease,
  Clinical Cardiac Electrophysiology, Internal Medicine
1959 NE Pacific St, Seattle, 206-685-4176

Kures, Peter Rodney (4 mentions)
U of Chicago, 1987 *Certification:* Cardiovascular Disease,
  Internal Medicine, Interventional Cardiology
6520 226th Pl SE #150, Issaquah, 425-454-1560
13033 Bel-Red Rd #230, Bellevue, 425-454-1560

Lewis, Howard Stites (7 mentions)
U of Washington, 1983 *Certification:* Cardiovascular
  Disease, Internal Medicine, Interventional Cardiology
550 17th Ave #630, Seattle, 206-861-8550

Longo, Michael Joseph (5 mentions)
SUNY-Buffalo, 1992 *Certification:* Cardiovascular Disease
1100 9th Ave, Seattle, 206-341-1111
13014 120th Ave NE, Kirkland, 425-814-5100

McCloskey, John Patrick (4 mentions)
U of California-San Francisco, 1983
Certification: Pediatric Cardiology
314 MLK Jr Way #303, Tacoma, 253-396-4868
4033 Talbot Rd S #540, Renton, 253-396-4868
1911 Cooks Hill Rd, Centralia, 253-396-4868
11102 Sunrise Blvd E #106, Puyallup, 253-396-4868
615 Lilly Rd NE #175, Olympia, 253-396-4868

Olsen, John Vester (8 mentions)
New York U, 1980
Certification: Cardiovascular Disease, Internal Medicine
550 17th Ave #630, Seattle, 206-861-8550
1104 Basich Blvd, Aberdeen, 360-532-2633

Page, Richard L. (5 mentions)
Duke U, 1984 *Certification:* Cardiovascular Disease,
  Clinical Cardiac Electrophysiology, Internal Medicine
1959 NE Pacific St, Seattle, 206-543-8584

Resnick, Arthur D. (16 mentions)
Harvard U, 1979
Certification: Cardiovascular Disease, Internal Medicine
125 16th Ave E 2nd Fl, Seattle, 206-326-3020

Schneider, James Stephen (4 mentions)
Dartmouth Coll, 1975
Certification: Cardiovascular Disease, Internal Medicine
12333 NE 130th Ln #320, Kirkland, 425-899-0555

Speck, Sarah Marshall (7 mentions)
U of Illinois, 1977
Certification: Cardiovascular Disease, Internal Medicine
500 17th Ave #100, Seattle, 206-320-4500

Stefanelli, Christopher B. (6 mentions)
Creighton U, 1997 *Certification:* Pediatric Cardiology
314 MLK Jr Way #303, Tacoma, 253-396-4868
4033 Talbot Rd S #540, Renton, 253-396-4868
1911 Cooks Hill Rd, Centralia, 253-396-4868
11102 Sunrise Blvd E #106, Puyallup, 253-396-4868
615 Lilly Rd NE #175, Olympia, 253-396-4868

Sytman, Alexander Ludwik (9 mentions)
U of Washington, 1963 *Certification:* Cardiovascular
  Disease, Internal Medicine, Interventional Cardiology
515 Minor Ave #300, Seattle, 206-386-9500

Weeks, Gary Lawrence (6 mentions)
Northwestern U, 1980 *Certification:* Cardiovascular
  Disease, Internal Medicine, Interventional Cardiology
1536 N 115th St #200, Seattle, 206-363-1004
7315 212th St SW #205, Edmonds, 425-776-6999

Wilkinson, Daniel V., Jr. (5 mentions)
Hahnemann U, 1980 *Certification:* Cardiovascular Disease,
  Clinical Cardiac Electrophysiology, Internal Medicine
1536 N 115th St #200, Seattle, 206-363-1004

Dermatology

Abson, Kim Gittere (10 mentions)
U of Washington, 1986 *Certification:* Dermatology
1145 Broadway, Seattle, 206-329-1760

Antezana, Marcos A. (5 mentions)
U of Washington, 1999 *Certification:* Dermatology
1145 Broadway, Seattle, 206-860-2387

Colven, Roy Mitchell (7 mentions)
U of Washington, 1987
Certification: Dermatology, Internal Medicine
325 9th Ave, Seattle, 206-744-3241

Francis, Julie Sleder (7 mentions)
U of Washington, 1984 *Certification:* Dermatology
14030 NE 24th St #202, Bellevue, 425-454-1104

Goffe, Bernard Saul (6 mentions)
U of Washington, 1962
Certification: Dermatology, Dermatopathology
1730 Minor Ave #1000, Seattle, 206-267-2100

Johnson, Sylvia Christine (7 mentions)
Case Western Reserve U, 1970
Certification: Dermatology, Internal Medicine
125 16th Ave E, Seattle, 206-326-2635

Komorous, James Michael (7 mentions)
U of Washington, 1973
Certification: Dermatology, Dermatopathology
1901 S Union Ave #B2003, Tacoma, 253-752-7705
1006 N H St, Aberdeen, 360-537-6391

Lawlor, Kean Brendan (8 mentions)
U of Missouri-Kansas City, 1989 *Certification:* Dermatology
3216 NE 45th Pl #203, Seattle, 206-525-1168

Leaf, Frederick Arvid (8 mentions)
U of Washington, 1982 *Certification:* Dermatology
11011 Meridian Ave N #200, Seattle, 206-860-4748
1145 Broadway #2L, Seattle, 206-329-1760

Ochs, Ulrike Isabel (11 mentions)
Northwestern U, 1988 *Certification:* Dermatology
1201 Terry Ave 9th Fl, Seattle, 206-223-6781

Olerud, John Everett (16 mentions)
U of Washington, 1971
Certification: Dermatology, Internal Medicine
4225 Roosevelt Way NE 4th Fl, Seattle, 206-598-4067

Sybert, Virginia Phyllis (6 mentions)
SUNY-Buffalo, 1974 *Certification:* Clinical Genetics, Pediatrics
125 16th Ave E Central South Bldg 3rd Fl, Seattle, 206-326-2111

Valentine, Mark Conrad (7 mentions)
Johns Hopkins U, 1974 *Certification:* Dermatology
3327 Colby Ave, Everett, 425-258-6767

Emergency Medicine

Copass, Michael Keys, II (9 mentions)
Northwestern U, 1964
325 9th Ave, Seattle, 206-744-3263

Grundy, Robert Duncan (5 mentions)
FMS-United Kingdom, 1970
Certification: Emergency Medicine, Internal Medicine
50 16th Ave, Seattle, 206-320-2000

Jobe, Kathleen Ann (6 mentions)
U of Colorado, 1986 *Certification:* Emergency Medicine
1959 NE Pacific St, Seattle, 206-598-4000

Marshall, Stephen Watt (5 mentions)
Oregon Health Sciences U, 1982
Certification: Emergency Medicine, Internal Medicine
1035 116th Ave NE, Bellevue, 425-688-5100

Endocrinology

Broyles, Frances E. (18 mentions)
U of Florida, 1984 *Certification:* Internal Medicine
515 Minor Ave #300, Seattle, 206-386-9500

Davies, Matthew Donald (7 mentions)
U of Illinois, 1994 *Certification:* Endocrinology, Diabetes,
  and Metabolism, Internal Medicine
1229 Madison St #1500, Seattle, 206-386-9500

Enzmann, Gary David (7 mentions)
U of Michigan, 1976
Certification: Endocrinology and Metabolism, Internal Medicine
1229 Madison St #1500, Seattle, 206-386-9500

Graf, Ronald Jonathan (5 mentions)
Albany Med Coll, 1971
Certification: Endocrinology and Metabolism, Internal Medicine
1901 S Cedar St #205, Tacoma, 253-627-9122

Gross, Kenneth M. (13 mentions)
Stony Brook U, 1976
Certification: Endocrinology and Metabolism, Internal Medicine
1145 Broadway, Seattle, 206-860-2389

Heitritter, Shannon Marie (5 mentions)
Harvard U, 2000 *Certification:* Endocrinology, Diabetes,
  and Metabolism, Internal Medicine
1145 Broadway, Seattle, 206-860-2385

McCowen, Karl David (10 mentions)
Baylor U, 1971
Certification: Endocrinology and Metabolism, Internal Medicine
1628 S Mildred St #104, Tacoma, 253-565-6777

Moore, George Walter (6 mentions)
U of Oklahoma, 1972
Certification: Endocrinology and Metabolism, Internal Medicine
1330 Rockefeller Ave #330, Everett, 425-259-4413

Murray, Robert William (5 mentions)
Med Coll of Wisconsin, 1975
Certification: Endocrinology and Metabolism, Internal Medicine
1145 Broadway #1J, Seattle, 206-860-2316

Skoglund, Rodney Dan (6 mentions)
Johns Hopkins U, 1966
Certification: Endocrinology and Metabolism, Internal Medicine
16259 Sylvester Rd SW #504, Burien, 206-242-7900

Family Practice *(see note on page 9)*

Brown, Katherine Olivia (3 mentions)
U of Pennsylvania, 1990 *Certification:* Family Medicine
509 Olive Way #900, Seattle, 206-860-4700

Caittden, Robert Andrew (6 mentions)
U of Washington, 1976
325 9th Ave, Seattle, 206-744-6928

Egnal, Antony Saul (3 mentions)
FMS-South Africa, 1985 *Certification:* Family Medicine
1200 112th Ave NE #C-160, Bellevue, 425-453-1039

Gayman, John Parker (3 mentions)
Stanford U, 1979 *Certification:* Family Medicine, Sports Medicine
125 16th Ave E, Seattle, 206-326-3530

Heidrich, Fred Edmund, III (4 mentions)
Stanford U, 1976
Certification: Family Medicine, Geriatric Medicine
125 16th Ave E, Seattle, 206-326-3530

McDonald, Pamela H. (4 mentions)
U of Washington, 1977 *Certification:* Family Medicine
3216 NE 45th Pl #200, Seattle, 206-525-4000

McIntyre, Scott Talley (3 mentions)
U of Washington, 1982 *Certification:* Family Medicine
3216 NE 45th Pl #200, Seattle, 206-525-4000

Morrison, Laurel E. (3 mentions)
U of Washington, 1995 *Certification:* Family Medicine
13014 120th Ave NE, Kirkland, 425-814-5100

Pittenger, Kim Richard (6 mentions)
U of Cincinnati, 1979 *Certification:* Family Medicine
13014 120th Ave NE, Kirkland, 425-814-5100

Raymer, Patricia Annelle (4 mentions)
U of Washington, 1989 *Certification:* Family Medicine
509 Olive Way #900, Seattle, 206-860-4700

Rohrenbach, Michael L. (4 mentions)
Western U, 1989 *Certification:* Family Medicine
4410 106th St SW, Mukilteo, 425-493-6014

Thomas, John Bradley (3 mentions)
U of Washington, 1977 *Certification:* Family Medicine
4413 38th Ave NE, Seattle, 206-523-1545

Wanderer, Michael Joseph (3 mentions)
U of Washington, 1972 *Certification:* Family Medicine
125 16th Ave E, Seattle, 206-326-3530

White, Kelly Ross (3 mentions)
U of Colorado, 1987 *Certification:* Family Medicine
509 Olive Way #900, Seattle, 206-860-4700

Gastroenterology

Bohorfoush, Anthony G., III (7 mentions)
Creighton U, 1981
Certification: Gastroenterology, Internal Medicine
501 N 34th St #101, Seattle, 206-215-3355
801 Broadway #725, Seattle, 206-215-3355

Brandabur, John Joseph (8 mentions)
U of Cincinnati, 1984
Certification: Gastroenterology, Internal Medicine
1100 9th Ave, Seattle, 206-223-6600
100 NE Gilman Blvd, Issaquah, 425-557-8000

Christie, Dennis Lee (6 mentions)
Northwestern U, 1968
Certification: Pediatric Gastroenterology, Pediatrics
4800 Sand Point Way NE Whale 6, Seattle, 206-987-2521

Cox, George John, Jr. (6 mentions)
U of Washington, 1985
Certification: Gastroenterology, Internal Medicine
3927 Rucker Ave, Everett, 425-259-0966

Driscoll, Richard H., Jr. (8 mentions)
U of Pennsylvania, 1972
Certification: Gastroenterology, Internal Medicine
515 Minor Ave #200, Seattle, 206-386-9500

Feld, Andrew Dean (7 mentions)
Emory U, 1976 *Certification:* Gastroenterology, Internal Medicine
125 16th Ave E #2, Seattle, 206-326-3050

Gilbert, David Anthony (12 mentions)
U of Chicago, 1973
Certification: Gastroenterology, Internal Medicine
1145 Broadway, Seattle, 206-860-4543

Kimmey, Michael Bryant (7 mentions)
Washington U, 1979
Certification: Gastroenterology, Internal Medicine
1112 6th Ave Health Sciences Bldg #AA103K, Tacoma,
253-272-8664

Kozarek, Richard Anthony (18 mentions)
U of Wisconsin, 1973
Certification: Gastroenterology, Internal Medicine
1100 9th Ave, Seattle, 206-223-6934

Sanford, Robert Leslie (7 mentions)
U of Chicago, 1975
Certification: Gastroenterology, Internal Medicine
515 Minor Ave #200, Seattle, 206-386-9500

Schembre, Drew Blackham (5 mentions)
New Jersey Med Sch, 1988
Certification: Gastroenterology, Internal Medicine
1100 9th Ave, Seattle, 206-223-2319

Sloane, T. Robin (7 mentions)
Tulane U, 1986 *Certification:* Gastroenterology, Internal Medicine
11800 NE 128th St #100, Kirkland, 425-899-4500

Wohlman, Robert A. (9 mentions)
St Louis U, 1981
Certification: Gastroenterology, Internal Medicine
1135 116th Ave NE #560, Bellevue, 425-454-4768

Ylvisaker, J. Thomas (14 mentions)
U of Minnesota, 1970
Certification: Gastroenterology, Internal Medicine
11511 NE 10th St, Bellevue, 425-502-3000

General Surgery

Barr, Darlene (4 mentions)
U of Alabama, 1985 *Certification:* Surgery
801 Broadway #300, Seattle, 206-215-3508

Biehl, Thomas Robert (6 mentions)
U of California-San Diego, 1987 *Certification:* Surgery
1100 9th Ave 6th Fl, Seattle, 206-223-6638

Brakstad, Mark Thomas (7 mentions)
U of Washington, 1983 *Certification:* Pediatrics, Surgery
1560 N 115th St #102, Seattle, 206-363-2882

Byrd, David Roland (7 mentions)
Tulane U, 1982 *Certification:* Surgery
1959 NE Pacific St #356410, Seattle, 206-598-9458

Chao, C. Tien-Bao (8 mentions)
Columbia U, 1989 *Certification:* Surgery
201 16th Ave E, Seattle, 206-326-3222

Clinch, Kelly Andrew (4 mentions)
U of Washington, 1994 *Certification:* Surgery
12333 NE 130th Ln #420, Kirkland, 425-899-5500

Counter, Steven Frank (4 mentions)
Med Coll of Wisconsin, 1994 *Certification:* Surgery
1145 Broadway 2nd Fl, Seattle, 206-860-2301
11011 Meridian Ave #200, Seattle, 206-860-2301

Dellinger, Evan Patchen (5 mentions)
Harvard U, 1970 *Certification:* Surgery
1700 116th Ave NE, Bellevue, 425-646-7777
1959 NE Pacific St, Seattle, 206-598-4477

Florence, Michael Glenn (13 mentions)
Emory U, 1975 *Certification:* Surgery
1221 Madison St #1411, Seattle, 206-386-6700

Hart, Michael Jude (13 mentions)
Yale U, 1971 *Certification:* Surgery
1221 Madison St #1411, Seattle, 206-386-6700

Horton, Marc Douglas (7 mentions)
U of Washington, 1987 *Certification:* Surgery
1221 Madison St #1411, Seattle, 206-386-6700

Johnson, Marlon Cooper (7 mentions)
U of North Carolina, 1990 *Certification:* Surgery
12333 NE 130th Ln #420, Kirkland, 425-899-5500

Johnson, Morris Glenn (4 mentions)
U of Virginia, 1979 *Certification:* Internal Medicine, Surgery
1400 E Kincaid St, Mount Vernon, 360-428-2586

Lau, Wayne Ming (4 mentions)
Tufts U, 1991 *Certification:* Surgery
4011 Talbot Rd S #420, Renton, 425-251-1322

Minami, Eiji (11 mentions)
Loma Linda U, 1975 *Certification:* Internal Medicine, Surgery
1135 116th Ave NE #550, Bellevue, 425-688-1916

Moonka, Ravi (4 mentions)
U of Pennsylvania, 1990 *Certification:* Surgery
1100 9th Ave, Seattle, 206-341-0060

Reagan, Thomas Richard (4 mentions)
U of Minnesota, 1965 *Certification:* Surgery
11511 NE 10th St, Bellevue, 425-502-3000

Ryan, John Austin, Jr. (6 mentions)
U of Michigan, 1969 *Certification:* Surgery
1100 9th Ave Buck Pavillion 6th Fl, Seattle, 206-223-6629

Sawin, Robert Stanford (4 mentions)
U of Pittsburgh, 1982
Certification: Pediatric Surgery, Surgery, Surgical Critical Care
4800 Sand Point Way NE #W7729, Seattle, 206-987-2794

Sinanan, Mika Narad (19 mentions)
Johns Hopkins U, 1980 *Certification:* Surgery
1959 NE Pacific St, Seattle, 206-543-5511

St. Pierre, Joseph Raoul, Jr. (4 mentions)
Boston U, 1969 *Certification:* Surgery
201 16th Ave E, Seattle, 206-326-3222

Stowell, Virginia Anne (5 mentions)
Rush U, 1987 *Certification:* Surgery
3124 S 19th St #220, Tacoma, 253-301-5050

Thirlby, Richard Coller (8 mentions)
U of Michigan, 1978 *Certification:* Surgery
1100 9th Ave 6th Fl, Seattle, 206-223-6636

Ting, Andrew (4 mentions)
FMS-Canada, 1990 *Certification:* Surgery
801 Broadway #300, Seattle, 206-215-3500

Towbin, Michael Anthony (5 mentions)
U of California-San Francisco, 1983 *Certification:* Surgery
12333 NE 130th Ln #420, Kirkland, 425-899-5500

Traverso, L. William (6 mentions)
U of California-Los Angeles, 1973 *Certification:* Surgery
1100 9th Ave 6th Fl, Seattle, 206-223-8855

Waldhausen, John H. (5 mentions)
Pennsylvania State U, 1986
Certification: Pediatric Surgery, Surgery
4800 Sand Point Way NE #W7729, Seattle, 206-987-2794

Wechter, Debra Gerry (4 mentions)
U of California-Davis, 1980 *Certification:* Surgery
1100 9th Ave, Seattle, 206-341-0060

Geriatrics

Abrass, Itamar B. (6 mentions)
U of California-San Francisco, 1966
Certification: Endocrinology and Metabolism, Internal Medicine
325 9th Ave, Seattle, 206-744-4191

Addison, John Hamilton (6 mentions)
U of Washington, 1979 *Certification:* Internal Medicine
7707 SE 27th St #110, Mercer Island, 206-275-3588

Kaner, Richard Alan (6 mentions)
U of Washington, 1984 *Certification:* Internal Medicine
1750 112th Ave NE #A102, Bellevue, 425-637-1022

Levine, Martin Daniel (7 mentions)
Case Western Reserve U, 1997
Certification: Family Medicine, Geriatric Medicine
140 SW 146th St, Burien, 206-901-2400

McCormick, Wayne C. (8 mentions)
Washington U, 1983 *Certification:* Geriatric Medicine, Internal
Medicine, Public Health & General Preventive Medicine
325 9th Ave, Seattle, 206-744-4191

Sauvage, Lester Rosaire (7 mentions)
St Louis U, 1983
Certification: Geriatric Medicine, Internal Medicine
7707 SE 27th St #104-111, Mercer Island, 206-275-3588

Smith, Connie Jo (6 mentions)
U of Washington, 1984
Certification: Geriatric Medicine, Internal Medicine
11521 NE 128th St #100, Kirkland, 425-899-6800

Williams, Henry Joseph (9 mentions)
U of Arizona, 1975
Certification: Geriatric Medicine, Internal Medicine
1750 112th Ave NE #A101, Bellevue, 425-688-5234

Hematology/Oncology

Aboulafia, David Michael (15 mentions)
U of Michigan, 1983
Certification: Hematology, Internal Medicine, Medical Oncology
1100 9th Ave #C2, Seattle, 206-223-6193

Back, Anthony Lee (3 mentions)
Harvard U, 1984 *Certification:* Hospice and Palliative
Medicine, Internal Medicine, Medical Oncology
825 Eastlake Ave E, Seattle, 206-288-7222

Batson, Oliver Andrew (4 mentions)
Johns Hopkins U, 1984
Certification: Hematology, Internal Medicine, Medical Oncology
1717 13th St, Everett, 425-297-5500

Birchfield, George R. (4 mentions)
U of Washington, 1985
Certification: Hematology, Internal Medicine, Medical Oncology
1560 N 115th St #G16, Seattle, 206-365-8252

Broudy, Virginia C. (9 mentions)
U of California-San Francisco, 1980
Certification: Hematology, Internal Medicine, Medical Oncology
325 9th Ave, Seattle, 206-744-3241

Callahan, Steven Kent (4 mentions)
U of Vermont, 1976
Certification: Internal Medicine, Medical Oncology
125 16th Ave E, Seattle, 206-326-3000

Colman, Lauren Kenneth (3 mentions)
U of Washington, 1975
Certification: Hematology, Internal Medicine, Medical Oncology
4545 Point Fosdick Dr NW #215, Gig Harbor, 253-530-8060

Congdon, James Edward, Jr. (6 mentions)
Midwestern U, 1972
Certification: Hematology, Internal Medicine, Medical Oncology
1717 13th St #300, Everett, 425-297-5500

Crossland, Kathryn D. (6 mentions)
Harvard U, 1984
Certification: Hematology, Internal Medicine, Medical Oncology
1135 116th Ave NE #230, Bellevue, 425-454-2148

Geyer, Jeffrey Russell (4 mentions)
Wayne State U, 1977
Certification: Pediatric Hematology-Oncology, Pediatrics
4800 Sand Point Way NE, Seattle, 206-987-6664

Ginsberg, Steven (5 mentions)
SUNY-Downstate Med Coll, 1984
Certification: Hematology, Internal Medicine, Medical Oncology
201 16th Ave E, Seattle, 206-326-3119
2930 Maple St, Everett, 206-326-3119

Goldberg, Sheldon Zackery (6 mentions)
New York U, 1978
Certification: Hematology, Internal Medicine, Medical Oncology
515 Minor Ave #170, Seattle, 206-386-9500

Golden, Jane Borkowski (3 mentions)
Johns Hopkins U, 1994 *Certification:* Medical Oncology
12303 NE 130th La #120, Kirkland, 425-899-3181

Hammond, William P. (8 mentions)
Tufts U, 1972
Certification: Hematology, Internal Medicine, Medical Oncology
515 Minor Ave #170, Seattle, 206-386-9500
1200 112th Ave NE #B-250, Bellevue, 425-462-1132

Harlan, John Marshall (4 mentions)
U of Chicago, 1973
Certification: Hematology, Internal Medicine, Medical Oncology
325 9th Ave, Seattle, 206-744-5314

Hawkins, Douglas Scott (3 mentions)
Harvard U, 1990 *Certification:* Pediatric Hematology-Oncology
4800 Sand Point Way NE #B-6553, Seattle, 206-987-2106

Jacobs, Andrew David (5 mentions)
FMS-United Kingdom, 1977
Certification: Hematology, Internal Medicine, Medical Oncology
1100 9th Ave #C2, Seattle, 206-223-6193

Johnson, Joseph Lowell (3 mentions)
Tulane U, 1983
Certification: Internal Medicine, Medical Oncology
2720 Clare Ave #A, Bremerton, 360-479-6154

Kovach, Nicholas Lee (4 mentions)
Oregon Health Sciences U, 1984
Certification: Hematology, Internal Medicine
1135 116th Ave NE #230, Bellevue, 425-454-2148

Lechner, James John (4 mentions)
U of California-Los Angeles, 1982
Certification: Internal Medicine, Medical Oncology
4525 3rd Ave SE #200, Lacey, 360-413-1471
954 Anderson Dr #102, Aberdeen, 360-533-6906

Lee, Douglas Jonathan (7 mentions)
Yale U, 1981 *Certification:* Internal Medicine, Medical Oncology
1560 N 115th St #G16, Seattle, 206-365-8252

Li, Henry Yeh (6 mentions)
Stanford U, 1996
Certification: Hematology, Internal Medicine, Medical Oncology
1145 Broadway, Seattle, 206-860-2371

Louie, Ronald Richard (4 mentions)
Med Coll of Ohio, 1980
Certification: Pediatric Hematology-Oncology, Pediatrics
311 S L St, Tacoma, 253-403-3131

McCroskey, Robert Donald (3 mentions)
U of Washington, 1983
Certification: Hematology, Internal Medicine, Medical Oncology
400 15th Ave SE #D, Puyallup, 253-697-4800

Milder, Michael Stuart (6 mentions)
Washington U, 1970 *Certification:* Internal Medicine,
Medical Oncology, Nuclear Medicine
1221 Madison St 2nd Fl, Seattle, 206-386-2242
5410 Barnes Ave NW, Seattle, 206-781-6010

Petersdorf, Stephen H. (6 mentions)
Brown U, 1983
Certification: Hematology, Internal Medicine, Medical Oncology
825 Eastlake Ave E, Seattle, 206-288-7400

Picozzi, Vincent Joseph, Jr. (5 mentions)
Stanford U, 1978
Certification: Hematology, Internal Medicine, Medical Oncology
1100 9th Ave #C2, Seattle, 206-223-6193

Press, Oliver William (3 mentions)
U of Washington, 1979
Certification: Internal Medicine, Medical Oncology
825 Eastlake Ave E, Seattle, 206-288-7222

Reimer, Ronald Robert (3 mentions)
Michigan State U, 1973
Certification: Internal Medicine, Medical Oncology
2720 Clare Ave #A, Bremerton, 360-479-6154

Rinn, Kristine Josephine (3 mentions)
U of Washington, 1992 *Certification:* Medical Oncology
1221 Madison St #200, Seattle, 206-386-3900

Rivkin, Saul Eugene (4 mentions)
U of Washington, 1964
1221 Madison St 2nd Fl, Seattle, 206-386-2323

Saikaly, Elie Phillip (4 mentions)
U of Iowa, 1979
Certification: Internal Medicine, Medical Oncology
1717 13th St, Everett, 425-297-5500

Senecal, Francis Mark (12 mentions)
Indiana U, 1977
Certification: Hematology, Internal Medicine, Medical Oncology
1624 S I St #102, Tacoma, 253-383-3366
34509 9th Ave S #107, Federal Way, 253-952-8349

Smith, J. Walter (6 mentions)
U of Chicago, 1976
Certification: Hematology, Internal Medicine, Medical Oncology
1135 116th Ave NE #230, Bellevue, 425-454-2148

Takasugi, Bonnie Jean (4 mentions)
U of Washington, 1978
Certification: Internal Medicine, Medical Oncology
16233 Sylvester Rd SW #110, Burien, 206-439-5578

Thompson, John Ainslie (3 mentions)
U of Alabama, 1979
Certification: Internal Medicine, Medical Oncology
825 Eastlake Ave E, Seattle, 206-288-7222

Van Haelst, Carol (4 mentions)
FMS-Belgium, 1982
Certification: Hematology, Internal Medicine, Medical Oncology
12303 NE 130th Ln #120, Kirkland, 425-899-3181

White, David Abbott (5 mentions)
Yale U, 1982
Certification: Hematology, Internal Medicine, Medical Oncology
1145 Broadway, Seattle, 206-860-2341

Infectious Disease

Cairns, Michael Raymond (11 mentions)
Jefferson Med Coll, 1981
Certification: Infectious Disease, Internal Medicine
1200 112th Ave NE #B-250, Bellevue, 425-462-1132

Ehni, William Frederick (12 mentions)
U of Washington, 1982
Certification: Infectious Disease, Internal Medicine
21701 76th Ave W #200, Edmonds, 425-744-1740

Hashisaki, Peter Alan (17 mentions)
U of Washington, 1975
Certification: Infectious Disease, Internal Medicine
1200 116th Ave NE #D, Bellevue, 425-455-8248

Marsh, Peter K. (8 mentions)
Jefferson Med Coll, 1976
Certification: Infectious Disease, Internal Medicine
1624 S I St #405, Tacoma, 253-627-4123

Matlock, Michael Lee (8 mentions)
U of Washington, 1975 *Certification:* Infectious Disease,
Internal Medicine, Medical Microbiology
3525 Ensign Rd NE #2, Olympia, 360-459-1213

Pauk, John S. (9 mentions)
Duke U, 1993 *Certification:* Infectious Disease
1145 Broadway #3D, Seattle, 206-860-4533

Riedo, Francis X. (15 mentions)
Johns Hopkins U, 1981
Certification: Infectious Disease, Internal Medicine
11911 NE 132nd St #100, Kirkland, 425-899-5100

Siegel, Martin Stuart (35 mentions)
Case Western Reserve U, 1972
Certification: Infectious Disease, Internal Medicine
1145 Broadway, Seattle, 206-860-4531

Spach, David Henry (8 mentions)
Duke U, 1986 *Certification:* Infectious Disease, Internal Medicine
325 9th Ave, Seattle, 206-744-5100

Infertility

Hickok, Lee Richard (10 mentions)
U of Washington, 1984 *Certification:* Obstetrics & Gynecology
1101 Madison St #1050, Seattle, 206-515-0000

Johnson, Kevin M. (4 mentions)
U of Texas-Southwestern, 1985 *Certification:* Obstetrics &
Gynecology, Reproductive Endocrinology/Infertility
13125 121st Way NE, Kirkland, 425-646-4700
1135 116th Ave NE #640, Bellevue, 425-646-4700

Klein, Nancy Allen (5 mentions)
Vanderbilt U, 1985 *Certification:* Obstetrics & Gynecology,
Reproductive Endocrinology/Infertility
1545 116 Ave NE #102, Bellevue, 206-301-5000
1505 Westlake Ave N #400, Seattle, 206-301-5000

Letterie, Gerard S. (4 mentions)
Philadelphia Coll of Osteopathic Med, 1978 *Certification:*
Obstetrics & Gynecology, Reproductive Endocrinology/Infertility
12333 NE 130th Ln #220, Kirkland, 425-284-4400

Marshall, Lorna A. (8 mentions)
Northwestern U, 1979 *Certification:* Obstetrics &
Gynecology, Reproductive Endocrinology/Infertility
1101 Madison St #1050, Seattle, 206-515-0000

Internal Medicine *(see note on page 9)*

Abdallah, Paul Sam (5 mentions)
U of California-San Francisco, 1969
Certification: Internal Medicine
515 Minor Ave #200, Seattle, 206-386-9522

Cotton, Elisabeth M. (3 mentions)
FMS-Canada, 1984 *Certification:* Internal Medicine
1135 116th Ave NE #110, Bellevue, 425-455-8222

Efird, Alex Christopher (3 mentions)
U of Southern California, 1999 *Certification:* Internal Medicine
515 Minor Ave #300, Seattle, 206-386-9500

Franklin, Seth Bernard (3 mentions)
U of Washington, 1986 *Certification:* Internal Medicine
1221 Madison St #920, Seattle, 206-215-2550

Goldstein, Erika Ann (3 mentions)
U of Rochester, 1981 *Certification:* Internal Medicine
325 9th Ave, Seattle, 206-744-3098

Harris, Bradley Rennie (4 mentions)
U of Rochester, 1976 *Certification:* Internal Medicine
1145 Broadway #1E, Seattle, 206-860-2304

Hayashi, Steven Akira (6 mentions)
New York U, 1983 *Certification:* Internal Medicine
1100 9th Ave, Seattle, 206-583-2299

Hayden, Michael Norman (4 mentions)
Duke U, 1995 *Certification:* Internal Medicine
515 Minor Ave #300, Seattle, 206-386-9500

Hovsepian, Rafi (3 mentions)
Oral Roberts U, 1988 *Certification:* Internal Medicine
925 Seneca St, Seattle, 206-341-0736

Kober, Margo Marie (3 mentions)
U of Washington, 1992 *Certification:* Internal Medicine
515 Minor Ave #300, Seattle, 206-386-9500

Kojnok, Eva (3 mentions)
U of Rochester, 1994 *Certification:* Internal Medicine
515 Minor Ave #300, Seattle, 206-386-9500

Lamb, George Owen (4 mentions)
U of Washington, 1974 *Certification:* Internal Medicine
700 Lilly Rd NE, Olympia, 360-923-7000

Mihali, Alexander Karl (3 mentions)
Med Coll of Wisconsin, 1971 *Certification:* Internal Medicine
3124 S 19th St #C-140, Tacoma, 253-459-6510

Mora, Marc Walter (3 mentions)
U of California-San Francisco, 1990
Certification: Internal Medicine
201 16th Ave, Seattle, 206-326-2763

Paauw, Douglas Stephen (10 mentions)
U of Michigan, 1985 *Certification:* Internal Medicine
4245 Roosevelt Way NE 3rd Fl, Seattle, 206-598-8750

Rice, Sandra C. (4 mentions)
U of Washington, 1978 *Certification:* Internal Medicine
1407 116th Ave NE #200, Bellevue, 425-454-5046

Rossi, Ralph A. (4 mentions)
U of California-San Diego, 1991 *Certification:* Internal Medicine
1145 Broadway, Seattle, 206-860-4693

Sheffield, John Van Loon (3 mentions)
Harvard U, 1989 *Certification:* Internal Medicine
325 9th Ave 2nd Fl, Seattle, 206-744-5100

Smyth, Cynthia Marie (3 mentions)
Jefferson Med Coll, 1993 *Certification:* Internal Medicine
515 Minor Ave #300, Seattle, 206-386-9500

Stimson, John Boyd (3 mentions)
U of Washington, 1981 *Certification:* Internal Medicine
1145 Broadway #1-L, Seattle, 206-860-2319

Sutton, Paul Randolph (3 mentions)
U of Chicago, 1994 *Certification:* Internal Medicine
4245 Roosevelt Way NE, Seattle, 206-598-8750

Vassall, John Henry (3 mentions)
U of Washington, 1978 *Certification:* Internal Medicine
515 Minor Ave #300, Seattle, 206-386-9500

Williams, Henry Joseph (3 mentions)
U of Arizona, 1975
Certification: Geriatric Medicine, Internal Medicine
1750 112th Ave NE #A101, Bellevue, 425-637-1022

Nephrology

Cryst, Cyrus (9 mentions)
U of Chicago, 1984 *Certification:* Internal Medicine, Nephrology
1100 9th Ave 7th Fl, Seattle, 206-223-6673

Keech, Pamila R. (11 mentions)
Loyola U Chicago, 1987
Certification: Internal Medicine, Nephrology
11711 NE 12th St #2B, Bellevue, 425-990-8866

Ochi, Rex Ford (14 mentions)
U of Washington, 1980
Certification: Internal Medicine, Nephrology
1145 Broadway, Seattle, 206-329-1760

Perkinson, Diana T. (16 mentions)
U of Alabama, 1979 *Certification:* Internal Medicine, Nephrology
515 Minor Ave #300, Seattle, 206-386-9500
1560 N 115th St #110, Seattle, 206-367-0660

Neurological Surgery

Ellenbogen, Richard G. (12 mentions)
Brown U, 1983 *Certification:* Neurological Surgery
4800 Sand Point Way NE, Seattle, 206-987-2544
325 9th Ave, Seattle, 206-731-3000

Laohaprasit, Varun (10 mentions)
FMS-Thailand, 1978 *Certification:* Neurological Surgery
1600 116th Ave NE #302, Bellevue, 425-455-5440
13107 121st Way NE, Kirkland, 425-899-6200

Nussbaum, Charles Enzer (8 mentions)
U of Rochester, 1984 *Certification:* Neurological Surgery
1100 9th Ave 7th Fl, Seattle, 206-223-7525

Pearce, Jeffrey Erle (9 mentions)
U of Minnesota, 1978 *Certification:* Neurological Surgery
1600 116th Ave NE #302, Bellevue, 425-455-5440
13107 121st Way NE, Kirkland, 425-899-6200

Raisis, James Emanuel (8 mentions)
U of Colorado, 1970 *Certification:* Neurological Surgery
801 Broadway #617, Seattle, 206-623-0922

Rapport, Richard L., II (7 mentions)
U of Michigan, 1969 *Certification:* Neurological Surgery
125 16th Ave E, Seattle, 206-326-3080

Young, Jacob Nathan (7 mentions)
Duke U, 1986 *Certification:* Neurological Surgery
1515 116th Ave NE #302, Bellevue, 425-456-0922

Neurology

Berg, William Ellis (4 mentions)
U of California-San Diego, 1995 *Certification:* Neurology
515 Minor Ave #210, Seattle, 206-386-9500
1801 NW Market St #403, Ballard, 206-386-9500

Elliott, Michael Alan (7 mentions)
George Washington U, 1990 *Certification:* Neurology
1201 Terry Ave, Seattle, 206-341-0420

Fosmire, Daniel Perry (8 mentions)
Rosalind Franklin U, 1987 *Certification:* Neurology
1231 116th Ave NE #203, Bellevue, 425-709-7055

Gierke, Eric Paul (5 mentions)
U of Washington, 1990
Certification: Clinical Neurophysiology, Neurology
3901 Hoyt Ave, Everett, 425-339-5408

Glass, Stephen Tolman (6 mentions)
U of Vermont, 1974 *Certification:* Neurology with Special
  Qualifications in Child Neurology, Pediatrics
17924 140th Ave NE #200, Woodinville, 425-424-9200

Huddlestone, John Robert (8 mentions)
U of Michigan, 1971 *Certification:* Neurology
915 6th Ave #200, Tacoma, 253-403-7299

Johnson, Rodney James (4 mentions)
Pennsylvania State U, 1982 *Certification:* Neurology
1600 116th Ave NE #302, Bellevue, 425-455-5440
450 NW Gilman Blvd #305, Issaquah, 425-391-8619

Kraus, Eric Edward (9 mentions)
U of Minnesota, 1991
Certification: Clinical Neurophysiology, Neurology
1959 NE Pacific St #B356169, Seattle, 206-543-2340

Likosky, William Harris (5 mentions)
U of Vermont, 1966 *Certification:* Neurology
515 Minor Ave #210, Seattle, 206-386-9500

Longstreth, William Thacher, Jr. (6 mentions)
U of Pennsylvania, 1975
325 9th Ave, Seattle, 206-744-3422

Mesher, Richard Alan (18 mentions)
U of Washington, 1979 *Certification:* Neurology
125 16th Ave E, Seattle, 206-326-3080

Murphy, Lawrence Cullum (9 mentions)
U of Washington, 1983 *Certification:* Neurology
550 17th Ave #540, Seattle, 206-386-2800

Ravits, John Meyer (6 mentions)
Mayo Med Sch, 1979 *Certification:* Clinical
  Neurophysiology, Neurology, Neuromuscular Medicine
1201 Terry Ave 7th Fl, Seattle, 206-341-0420

Reif, Mary Ellen (7 mentions)
U of Iowa, 1978 *Certification:* Neurology
515 Minor Ave #210, Seattle, 206-386-9500

Scearce, Timothy Andrew (15 mentions)
Georgetown U, 1988 *Certification:* Neurology
125 16th Ave E, Seattle, 206-326-2702

Taylor, Lynne Patricia (5 mentions)
Washington U, 1982 *Certification:* Neurology
1201 Terry Ave, Seattle, 206-341-0420

Obstetrics/Gynecology

Bohmke, Karen Lynn (8 mentions)
U of California-Davis, 1980 *Certification:* Obstetrics & Gynecology
1101 Madison St #1150, Seattle, 206-386-3400

Bridges, Ann Marjorie (4 mentions)
Northwestern U, 1986 *Certification:* Obstetrics & Gynecology
1101 Madison St #900, Seattle, 206-860-4541

Cheng, Edith Yeetak (6 mentions)
U of Washington, 1987 *Certification:* Clinical Genetics,
  Maternal-Fetal Medicine, Obstetrics & Gynecology
1959 NE Pacific St, Seattle, 206-598-3300

Cole, Robin Elizabeth (4 mentions)
U of Washington, 1983 *Certification:* Obstetrics & Gynecology
1229 Madison St #1500, Seattle, 206-292-2200

Conner, Raymond Mize (3 mentions)
U of Mississippi, 1976 *Certification:* Obstetrics & Gynecology
1535 116th Ave NE #100, Bellevue, 425-455-0244

Daniel, Anna Gustanna (4 mentions)
Harvard U, 1981 *Certification:* Obstetrics & Gynecology
1101 Madison St #950, Seattle, 206-682-5800

Davenport, Cricket Hewitt (3 mentions)
U of Michigan, 1974 *Certification:* Obstetrics & Gynecology
310 15th Ave E #NB-2, Seattle, 206-326-3500

Dimer, Jane Ann (9 mentions)
Northwestern U, 1988 *Certification:* Obstetrics & Gynecology
310 15th Ave E #NB-2, Seattle, 206-326-3500

Easterling, Thomas R., III (3 mentions)
U of North Carolina, 1981
Certification: Maternal-Fetal Medicine, Obstetrics & Gynecology
1959 NE Pacific St, Seattle, 206-598-4070

Evans, Elisabeth Lorna (3 mentions)
U of Washington, 1975 *Certification:* Obstetrics & Gynecology
6520 226th Pl SE #120, Issaquah, 425-391-8886

Faulkner, Noreen C. (3 mentions)
U of Michigan, 1988 *Certification:* Obstetrics & Gynecology
1200 112th Ave NE Bldg B, Bellevue, 425-462-1132
1229 Madison St #1500, Seattle, 206-292-2200

Frankwick, Dawn Marie (3 mentions)
Med Coll of Wisconsin, 1983
Certification: Obstetrics & Gynecology
10330 Meridian Ave N #200, Seattle, 206-368-6644

Grice, Jeffrey L. (4 mentions)
Texas Tech U, 1993 *Certification:* Obstetrics & Gynecology
310 15th Ave E #NB-2, Seattle, 206-326-3500

Harding, James Alfred (3 mentions)
U of Vermont, 1983
Certification: Maternal-Fetal Medicine, Obstetrics & Gynecology
4033 Talbert Rd S #450, Renton, 425-656-5520

Hasselquist, Mary Beth (7 mentions)
Mayo Med Sch, 1980 *Certification:* Obstetrics & Gynecology
310 15th Ave E #NB-2, Seattle, 206-326-3500

Hutchison, Margaret L. (5 mentions)
U of Washington, 1989 *Certification:* Obstetrics & Gynecology
801 Broadway #623, Seattle, 206-682-5800

Johannsen, Tracy Ann (3 mentions)
U of Washington, 1982 *Certification:* Obstetrics & Gynecology
1101 Madison St #1150, Seattle, 206-386-3400

Lieppman, Robert Eric (4 mentions)
U of Texas-Galveston, 1974 *Certification:* Obstetrics & Gynecology
1101 Madison St, Seattle, 206-965-1700

Luthy, David Adair (6 mentions)
Northwestern U, 1973
Certification: Maternal-Fetal Medicine, Obstetrics & Gynecology
1229 Madison St #750, Seattle, 206-386-2101

McDermott, Tiffany Marie (3 mentions)
New Jersey Med Sch, 1993 *Certification:* Obstetrics & Gynecology
1101 Madison St #900, Seattle, 206-860-4541

Mihalov, Linda S. (3 mentions)
U of Illinois, 1980 *Certification:* Obstetrics & Gynecology
1201 Terry Ave, Seattle, 206-223-6191

Morell, Patrick William (3 mentions)
U of Nebraska, 1975 *Certification:* Obstetrics & Gynecology
12303 NE 130th Ln #420, Kirkland, 425-899-6400

Nelson, Karen Marie (3 mentions)
Northwestern U, 1988 *Certification:* Obstetrics & Gynecology
314 MLK Jr Way #400, Tacoma, 253-627-0666

Nickel, Gary Wayne (3 mentions)
Wake Forest U, 1977 *Certification:* Obstetrics & Gynecology
222 N J St #A, Tacoma, 253-572-4664

O'Neil, Nancy Anne (6 mentions)
Northwestern U, 1978 *Certification:* Obstetrics & Gynecology
1101 Madison St #1150, Seattle, 206-386-3400

Sorenson, Laurie Thomas (4 mentions)
U of North Dakota, 1986 *Certification:* Obstetrics & Gynecology
615 Lilly Rd NE #200, Olympia, 360-413-8413

Ophthalmology

Barr, David Holbrook (5 mentions)
U of California-San Francisco, 1974 *Certification:* Ophthalmology
10564 5th Ave NE #402, Seattle, 206-363-8855

Barrall, Janet Louise (4 mentions)
U of Washington, 1989 *Certification:* Ophthalmology
100 NE Gilman Blvd, Issaquah, 425-557-8000

Bassett, Kent La Mar (3 mentions)
U of Washington, 1979 *Certification:* Ophthalmology
1300 116th Ave NE, Bellevue, 425-454-7912

Birnbach, Charles David (3 mentions)
New York U, 1992 *Certification:* Ophthalmology
2821 Northup Way #200, Bellevue, 425-576-0225

Carroll, Brant Franklin (3 mentions)
U of Southern California, 1991 *Certification:* Ophthalmology
5300 17th Ave NW, Seattle, 206-784-3350

Chen, Philip Peihai (3 mentions)
Yale U, 1991 *Certification:* Ophthalmology
1959 NE Pacific St #356460, Seattle, 206-598-4011

Choy, Elizabeth Suenghae (5 mentions)
U of Washington, 1984 *Certification:* Ophthalmology
1101 Madison St #900, Seattle, 206-860-4550

Cowen, Sheldon Jay (3 mentions)
U of Michigan, 1982 *Certification:* Ophthalmology
515 Minor Ave #160, Seattle, 206-624-5288

Deem, Clark W. (6 mentions)
Washington U, 1968 *Certification:* Ophthalmology
4717 S 19th St #101, Tacoma, 253-272-4600

Epley, K. David (4 mentions)
Oregon Health Sciences U, 1993 *Certification:* Ophthalmology
1101 Madison St #600, Seattle, 206-215-2020
2100 Little Mountain Ln, Mount Vernon, 360-416-6735

Francis, Robert Rankin (8 mentions)
U of Washington, 1984 *Certification:* Ophthalmology
1221 Madison St #1002, Seattle, 206-215-3850

Hughes, Grady Maxson (3 mentions)
U of Washington, 1982 *Certification:* Ophthalmology
1600 E Jefferson St #202, Seattle, 206-320-5686

Kinyoun, James Lovgren (5 mentions)
U of Nebraska, 1971 *Certification:* Ophthalmology
1959 NE Pacific St #356460, Seattle, 206-598-4011

Lee, Michael Edward (3 mentions)
U of California-San Francisco, 1986 *Certification:* Ophthalmology
11511 NE 10th St, Bellevue, 425-502-3000

Mensher, John Howard (3 mentions)
New York Med Coll, 1967 *Certification:* Ophthalmology
1101 Madison St, Seattle, 206-860-4550

Rotkis, Walter Molden (3 mentions)
U of Illinois, 1972
Certification: Internal Medicine, Ophthalmology
1221 Madison St #1420, Seattle, 206-386-2516
1901 S Union Ave #8224, Tacoma, 206-386-2516

Shelley, Peter Bennett (4 mentions)
U of Pennsylvania, 1970 *Certification:* Ophthalmology
32123 1st Ave S #A3, Federal Way, 253-838-6272
311 S L St, Tacoma, 253-403-3131

Shields, Jerry Richard (3 mentions)
Med Coll of Georgia, 1997 *Certification:* Ophthalmology
1703 S Meridian St #101, Puyallup, 253-848-3000

Weiss, Avery Harold (4 mentions)
U of Miami, 1974 *Certification:* Ophthalmology
4800 Sand Point Way NE, Seattle, 206-987-2039

Orthopedics

Barronian, Alan Dirk (3 mentions)
U of Washington, 1985 *Certification:* Orthopaedic Surgery
16259 Sylvester Rd SW #501, Burien, 206-243-1100

Brandes, Clayton B. (3 mentions)
U of Southern California, 1991 *Certification:* Orthopaedic Surgery
1231 116th Ave NE #100, Bellevue, 425-454-5344

Bruckner, James David (6 mentions)
Creighton U, 1984 *Certification:* Orthopaedic Surgery
1231 116th Ave NE #100, Bellevue, 425-454-5344

Chansky, Howard Alan (3 mentions)
U of Pennsylvania, 1987 *Certification:* Orthopaedic Surgery
1660 S Columbian Way #112, Seattle, 206-764-2215
4245 Roosevelt Way NE, Seattle, 206-598-4288

Chapman, Jens Robert (5 mentions)
FMS-Germany, 1983 *Certification:* Orthopaedic Surgery
325 9th Ave, Seattle, 206-744-3462
4245 Roosevelt Way NE, Seattle, 206-598-4288

Chi, Thomas Daehun (3 mentions)
Harvard U, 1994 *Certification:* Orthopaedic Surgery
1135 116th Ave NE #510, Bellevue, 425-455-3600
600 NW Gilman Blvd #E, Issaquah, 425-392-3030

Clark, Herbert Royal (3 mentions)
U of North Carolina, 1982 *Certification:* Orthopaedic Surgery
10330 Meridian Ave N #270, Seattle, 206-526-8444

Conrad, Ernest Upshur, III (5 mentions)
U of Virginia, 1979 *Certification:* Orthopaedic Surgery
4800 Sand Point Way NE, Seattle, 206-987-2109
4245 Roosevelt Way NE, Seattle, 206-598-4288

Cross, Thomas L. (3 mentions)
Kirksville Coll of Osteopathic Med, 1981
34709 9th Ave S #B500, Federal Way, 253-838-8552

Crutcher, James Page, Jr. (6 mentions)
U of Washington, 1984 *Certification:* Orthopaedic Surgery
601 Broadway 6th Fl, Seattle, 206-386-2600

Falicov, Alexis (4 mentions)
Harvard U, 1999 *Certification:* Orthopaedic Surgery
601 Broadway #6, Seattle, 206-386-2600

Flugstad, Daniel Lloyd (8 mentions)
U of Washington, 1980 *Certification:* Orthopaedic Surgery
1145 Broadway, Seattle, 206-329-1760

Franklin, Jonathan Louis (3 mentions)
U of Washington, 1983 *Certification:* Orthopaedic Surgery
2409 N 45th St, Seattle, 206-633-8100
1801 NW Market St #403, Seattle, 206-784-8833

Green, Thomas Morrison (3 mentions)
U of Washington, 1969 *Certification:* Orthopaedic Surgery
1100 9th Ave, Seattle, 206-223-7530
222 12th Ave NE, Bellevue, 425-637-1855

Hansen, Sigvard T., Jr. (3 mentions)
U of Washington, 1961 *Certification:* Orthopaedic Surgery
325 9th Ave, Seattle, 206-744-4830

Holland, Lawrence E. (4 mentions)
U of California-Los Angeles, 1981
601 Broadway, Seattle, 206-386-2600

Hormel, Scott Edward (4 mentions)
U of Washington, 1990 *Certification:* Orthopaedic Surgery
1600 E Jefferson St #600, Seattle, 206-325-4464

Jackson, Allen Willis (4 mentions)
George Washington U, 1969 *Certification:* Orthopaedic Surgery
10330 Meridian Ave N #270, Seattle, 206-526-8444

Kirby, Richard Murray (3 mentions)
U of Washington, 1977 *Certification:* Orthopaedic Surgery
1600 E Jefferson St #600, Seattle, 206-325-4464

Leopold, Seth Samuel (5 mentions)
Cornell U, 1993 *Certification:* Orthopaedic Surgery
1700 116th Ave NE, Bellevue, 425-646-7777
4245 Roosevelt Way NE, Seattle, 206-598-4288

Matsen, Frederick A., III (9 mentions)
Baylor U, 1968 *Certification:* Orthopaedic Surgery
4245 Roosevelt Way NE, Seattle, 206-598-4288

McAllister, Craig M. (6 mentions)
U of Washington, 1985 *Certification:* Orthopaedic Surgery
12911 120th Ave NE #H210, Kirkland, 425-823-4000

Mirza, Sohail Kassim (3 mentions)
U of Colorado, 1989 *Certification:* Orthopaedic Surgery
401 Broadway E #2075, Seattle, 206-744-9351
325 9th St, Seattle, 206-744-9351

Morris, Joseph Newton (6 mentions)
U of Virginia, 1972 *Certification:* Orthopaedic Surgery
125 16th Ave E, Seattle, 206-326-3150

Morris, Michael Edward (5 mentions)
U of California-Irvine, 1981 *Certification:* Orthopaedic Surgery
1100 9th Ave, Seattle, 206-223-7530

Rajacich, Nicholas (5 mentions)
Johns Hopkins U, 1982 *Certification:* Orthopaedic Surgery
311 S L St, Tacoma, 253-403-1507

Ratcliffe, Steven Severns (3 mentions)
Indiana U, 1977 *Certification:* Orthopaedic Surgery
1135 116th Ave NE #510, Bellevue, 425-455-3600
600 NW Gilman Blvd #E, Issaquah, 425-392-3030

Robinson, Raymond Paul (4 mentions)
Columbia U, 1975 *Certification:* Orthopaedic Surgery
1100 9th Ave, Seattle, 206-223-7530

Sailer, Michael Joachim (4 mentions)
U of Washington, 1987 *Certification:* Orthopaedic Surgery
1135 116th Ave NE #510, Bellevue, 425-455-3600
600 NW Gilman Blvd #E, Issaquah, 425-392-3030

Saliman, Laurel Hanck (3 mentions)
U of Colorado, 1997 *Certification:* Orthopaedic Surgery
1101 Madison St #800, Seattle, 206-215-2700
15419 NE 20th St #104, Bellevue, 206-215-2700

Sangeorzan, Bruce Joseph (3 mentions)
Wayne State U, 1981 *Certification:* Orthopaedic Surgery
1660 S Columbian Way #112, Seattle, 206-764-2215
325 9th Ave, Seattle, 206-731-3462

Smith, Kevin Leon (5 mentions)
Southern Illinois U, 1990 *Certification:* Orthopaedic Surgery
125 16th Ave E, Seattle, 206-326-3150

Sorensen, Lyle (9 mentions)
U of Washington, 1988 *Certification:* Orthopaedic Surgery
1201 Terry Ave, Seattle, 206-223-7530

Tanz, Henry Alan (3 mentions)
U of California-Los Angeles, 1974
Certification: Orthopaedic Surgery
209 MLK Jr Way, Tacoma, 800-858-9996

Thayer, John Lewis (4 mentions)
U of Washington, 1977 *Certification:* Orthopaedic Surgery
600 NW Gilman Blvd #E, Issaquah, 425-392-3030
1135 116th Ave NE #510, Bellevue, 425-455-3600

Thompson, W. Frederick (3 mentions)
Emory U, 1985 *Certification:* Orthopaedic Surgery
1550 S Union Ave #210, Tacoma, 253-752-0714

Trumble, Thomas Earl (3 mentions)
Yale U, 1979
Certification: Orthopaedic Surgery, Surgery of the Hand
1700 116th Ave NE, Bellevue, 425-646-7777
4245 Roosevelt Way NE, Seattle, 206-598-4288

Wagner, Theodore Anstey (3 mentions)
Temple U, 1968 *Certification:* Orthopaedic Surgery
4245 Roosevelt Way NE, Seattle, 206-598-4288

Watt, J. Michael (3 mentions)
Stanford U, 1985 *Certification:* Orthopaedic Surgery
1801 NW Market St #403, Seattle, 206-784-8833
2409 N 45th St, Seattle, 206-633-8100

Winquist, Robert Alan (5 mentions)
U of Washington, 1969 *Certification:* Orthopaedic Surgery
601 Broadway 7th Fl, Seattle, 206-386-2600

Wood, Alan Bridges (3 mentions)
Harvard U, 1975
Certification: Internal Medicine, Orthopaedic Surgery
209 MLK Jr Way, Tacoma, 253-596-3430

Yancey, Robert Allen (4 mentions)
Harvard U, 1983 *Certification:* Orthopaedic Surgery
4700 Point Fosdick Dr NW #111, Gig Harbor, 253-851-6075

Otorhinolaryngology

Adams, Jeffery Robert (4 mentions)
U of Washington, 1995 *Certification:* Otolaryngology
3927 Rucker Ave, Everett, 425-259-0966

Anonsen, Cynthia Kay (7 mentions)
U of Minnesota, 1979 *Certification:* Otolaryngology
1135 116th Ave NE #500, Bellevue, 425-454-3938

Bayles, Stephen Wesley (5 mentions)
Emory U, 1994 *Certification:* Otolaryngology
1201 Terry Ave, Seattle, 206-223-6374

Chu, Felix Way-Keon (5 mentions)
St Louis U, 1981 *Certification:* Otolaryngology
1145 Broadway, Seattle, 206-860-4769

Duckert, Larry Gene (6 mentions)
U of Minnesota, 1973 *Certification:* Otolaryngology
1959 NE Pacific St #NE-300, Seattle, 206-598-4022

Gilmer, Patricia A. (4 mentions)
Baylor U, 1984 *Certification:* Otolaryngology
128 Lilly Rd NE #202, Olympia, 360-357-6314

Glenn, Michael Gerard (6 mentions)
U of California-San Francisco, 1981 *Certification:* Otolaryngology
1100 9th Ave, Seattle, 206-223-6374
1201 Terry Ave, Seattle, 206-223-6374

Inglis, Andrew F., Jr. (6 mentions)
Med Coll of Pennsylvania, 1981 *Certification:* Otolaryngology
4800 Sand Point Way NE, Seattle, 206-987-2105

Langman, Alan Wayne (4 mentions)
Hahnemann U, 1982 *Certification:* Otolaryngology
9714 3rd Ave NE #100, Seattle, 206-523-5584

Lewis, Brent Ian (9 mentions)
U of Southern California, 1984 *Certification:* Otolaryngology
125 16th Ave E, Seattle, 206-326-3035

Manning, Scott Clark (4 mentions)
Tulane U, 1980 *Certification:* Otolaryngology
4800 Sand Point Way NE, Seattle, 206-987-2105

Moore, David Walter (8 mentions)
Indiana U, 1979 *Certification:* Otolaryngology
1221 Madison St #1523, Seattle, 206-292-6464

O'Leary-Stickney, K. M. (7 mentions)
U of Washington, 1986 *Certification:* Otolaryngology
1145 Broadway #1-A, Seattle, 206-329-1760

Pinczower, Eric F. (4 mentions)
U of California-Irvine, 1986 *Certification:* Otolaryngology
1800 116th Ave NE #102, Bellevue, 425-451-3710

Seely, Daniel Randolph (5 mentions)
Baylor U, 1987 *Certification:* Otolaryngology
1135 116th Ave NE #500, Bellevue, 425-454-3938
450 NW Gilman Blvd #203, Issaquah, 425-454-3938

Short, Steven Owen (5 mentions)
U of California-Los Angeles, 1980 *Certification:* Otolaryngology
11511 NE 10th St, Bellevue, 425-502-3000

Sie, Kathleen C. Y. (5 mentions)
U of Michigan, 1984 *Certification:* Otolaryngology
4800 Sand Point Way NE, Seattle, 206-987-2105

Souliere, Charles Robert, Jr. (4 mentions)
Yale U, 1981 *Certification:* Otolaryngology
1708 Yakima Ave #112, Tacoma, 253-627-6731

Weymuller, Ernest A., Jr. (7 mentions)
Harvard U, 1966 *Certification:* Otolaryngology
1959 NE Pacific St #BB1165, Seattle, 206-543-5230

Pain Medicine

Allen, Hugh Willison (4 mentions)
U of Southern California, 1988
Certification: Anesthesiology, Pain Medicine
1100 9th Ave #B2-AN, Seattle, 206-223-6980

Anderson, Corrie Thaddeus (5 mentions)
Stanford U, 1982 *Certification:* Anesthesiology, Pain Medicine
4800 Sand Point Way NE, Seattle, 206-987-2518

Baker, Ray Merville, Jr. (5 mentions)
U of California-Irvine, 1985 *Certification:* Anesthesiology
12301 NE 10th Pl #101, Bellevue, 425-454-1111

Fitzgibbon, Dermot R. (8 mentions)
FMS-Ireland, 1983 *Certification:* Anesthesiology, Pain Medicine
1959 NE Pacific St #EE201, Seattle, 206-598-4260

Hillyer, Jon Frederick (4 mentions)
U of Kansas, 1991 *Certification:* Anesthesiology
2601 Cherry Ave #304, Bremerton, 360-415-9110

Irving, Gordon A. (5 mentions)
FMS-United Kingdom, 1973
Certification: Anesthesiology, Pain Medicine
1101 Madison St #200, Seattle, 206-386-2013

Pathology

Bolen, John William (7 mentions)
U of Washington, 1975 *Certification:* Anatomic Pathology
1100 9th Ave #C-6-PTH, Seattle, 206-223-6861

Edmonson, Paul Frederick (3 mentions)
Mayo Med Sch, 1997
Certification: Anatomic Pathology & Clinical Pathology
1550 N 115th St, Seattle, 206-368-1779

Guinee, Donald G., Jr. (3 mentions)
Tulane U, 1986
Certification: Anatomic Pathology & Clinical Pathology
1100 9th Ave #C-6-PTH, Seattle, 206-223-6861

Kawamoto, Ernest Hiroshi (3 mentions)
U of Colorado, 1973
Certification: Anatomic Pathology & Clinical Pathology
21601 76th Ave W, Lynnwood, 425-640-4889

Kiviat, Nancy Carol (3 mentions)
U of Washington, 1975
Certification: Anatomic Pathology, Cytopathology
325 9th Ave, Seattle, 206-744-4277

Nordin, David Denton (5 mentions)
U of Minnesota, 1973
Certification: Anatomic Pathology & Clinical Pathology
1035 116th Ave NE, Bellevue, 425-688-5117

Rank, Joseph Paul (3 mentions)
U of Washington, 1990
Certification: Anatomic Pathology & Clinical Pathology
1229 Madison St #500, Seattle, 206-386-2822

Rhim, Jonathan Arch (3 mentions)
George Washington U, 1989
Certification: Anatomic Pathology, Dermatopathology
125 16th Ave E, Seattle, 206-326-3363

Roth, Rob Roy (4 mentions)
U of Colorado, 1974 *Certification:* Anatomic Pathology &
   Clinical Pathology, Chemical Pathology
315 MLK Jr Way, Tacoma, 253-403-1043

Rutledge, Joe Cathey (4 mentions)
Vanderbilt U, 1976 *Certification:* Anatomic Pathology &
   Clinical Pathology, Pediatric Pathology
4800 Sand Point Way NE, Seattle, 206-987-2103

Shenoy, Uma A. (3 mentions)
FMS-India, 1976
Certification: Anatomic Pathology & Clinical Pathology
125 16th Ave E, Seattle, 206-326-3363

Tickman, Ronald J. (3 mentions)
Emory U, 1984 *Certification:* Anatomic Pathology & Clinical
   Pathology, Cytopathology
1229 Madison St #500, Seattle, 206-386-2822

True, Lawrence Dashiell (3 mentions)
Tulane U, 1971 *Certification:* Anatomic Pathology
1959 NE Pacific St #356100, Seattle, 206-598-4027

Pediatrics *(see note on page 9)*

Allen, Jill Kay (6 mentions)
U of Washington, 1979 *Certification:* Pediatrics
201 16th Ave E, Seattle, 206-326-3000

Bloomer, Sarah Katherine (3 mentions)
Harvard U, 1979 *Certification:* Pediatrics
201 16th Ave E, Seattle, 206-326-3000

Braile, Margaret Edith (3 mentions)
U of Washington, 1988 *Certification:* Pediatrics
209 MLK Jr Way, Tacoma, 253-383-6120

Champoux, Ann N. (3 mentions)
U of Southern California, 1978 *Certification:* Pediatrics
4575 Sand Point Way NE #108, Seattle, 206-525-8000

Conn, Ruth Aileen (4 mentions)
U of Hawaii, 1984 *Certification:* Pediatrics
1201 Terry Ave, Seattle, 206-223-6188

Glassy, Danette Swanson (3 mentions)
U of Washington, 1986 *Certification:* Pediatrics
2553 76th Ave SE, Mercer Island, 206-275-2122

Klicpera, James Anton (4 mentions)
U of Chicago, 1975 *Certification:* Pediatrics
1818 121st St SE, Everett, 425-357-3305

Krober, Marvin Smith (3 mentions)
Case Western Reserve U, 1968
Certification: Pediatric Infectious Diseases, Pediatrics
125 16th Ave E, Seattle, 206-326-3530

Malliris, Ourania B. (3 mentions)
Harvard U, 1978 *Certification:* Pediatrics
7554 15th Ave NW, Seattle, 206-783-9300

Mason, Cole Vroman (3 mentions)
U of California-Los Angeles, 1972 *Certification:* Pediatrics
525 Lilly Rd NE #250, Olympia, 360-413-8470

Mauseth, Richard Scott (3 mentions)
U of Cincinnati, 1973
Certification: Pediatric Endocrinology, Pediatrics
17000 140th Ave NE #205, Woodinville, 425-483-5437

O'Neill, Tracie Markay (4 mentions)
U of Southern California, 1991
22717 SE 29th St, Sammamish, 425-391-7337

Smith, Donna Lee (8 mentions)
Oregon Health Sciences U, 1985 *Certification:* Pediatrics
4575 Sand Point Way NE #108, Seattle, 206-525-8000

Spector, Gary Brian (4 mentions)
U of Michigan, 1973 *Certification:* Pediatrics
1221 Madison St #910, Seattle, 206-292-2249

Plastic Surgery

Beshlian, Kevin Michael (5 mentions)
U of Virginia, 1982 *Certification:* Plastic Surgery
1201 Terry Ave, Seattle, 206-223-6831

Downey, Daniel Lee (12 mentions)
U of Washington, 1983 *Certification:* Plastic Surgery
1536 N 115th St #105, Seattle, 206-368-1160

Griffith, Thomas G. (4 mentions)
U of Washington, 1973 *Certification:* Orthopaedic Surgery,
   Plastic Surgery, Surgery of the Hand
3515 S 15th St #101, Tacoma, 253-756-0933

Gruss, Joseph (10 mentions)
FMS-South Africa, 1969
4800 Sand Point Way NE, Seattle, 206-987-2759

Kyllo, Jeffrey Eldon (7 mentions)
St Louis U, 1981 *Certification:* Plastic Surgery
1145 Broadway #1T, Seattle, 206-343-3118

Larrabee, Wayne Fox, Jr. (4 mentions)
Tulane U, 1971 *Certification:* Otolaryngology
600 Broadway #280, Seattle, 206-386-3550

Leff, Michael Alan (4 mentions)
U of Illinois, 1965 *Certification:* Plastic Surgery
1600 116th Ave NE #204, Bellevue, 425-454-5133

Murakami, Craig Stuart (4 mentions)
U of Washington, 1983 *Certification:* Otolaryngology
1201 Terry Ave 9th Fl, Seattle, 206-341-0693

Paige, Keith Thomas (7 mentions)
Harvard U, 1989 *Certification:* Plastic Surgery, Surgery
1201 Terry Ave, Seattle, 206-223-6831
33501 First Way S, Federal Way, 253-838-2400

Vedder, Nicholas Blair (6 mentions)
Case Western Reserve U, 1981
Certification: Plastic Surgery, Surgery, Surgery of the Hand
325 9th Ave, Seattle, 206-744-5735
4245 Roosevelt Way NE, Seattle, 206-598-4288

Welk, Richard Andrew (8 mentions)
U of Michigan, 1981 *Certification:* Plastic Surgery
1145 Broadway, Seattle, 206-860-2317

Psychiatry

Juergens, Steven Manley (3 mentions)
Mayo Med Sch, 1979
Certification: Addiction Psychiatry, Psychiatry
11201 SE 8th St #105, Bellevue, 425-454-0255

Manos, Peter James (6 mentions)
U of Michigan, 1979 *Certification:* Psychiatry
1100 9th Ave, Seattle, 206-223-6600

Mitchell, Steven Randall (3 mentions)
U of Southern Alabama, 1981 *Certification:* Psychiatry
1801 NW Market St #311, Seattle, 206-783-2278

Sands, Robert Edward (4 mentions)
U of Washington, 1972 *Certification:* Child Psychiatry, Psychiatry
3609 S 19th St, Tacoma, 253-752-6056

Simon, Gregory Edward (5 mentions)
U of North Carolina, 1982
Certification: Internal Medicine, Psychiatry
1730 Minor Ave #1600, Seattle, 206-287-2578

Solan, William Joseph (4 mentions)
U of Washington, 1987 *Certification:* Psychiatry
1530 N 115th St #307, Seattle, 206-368-0966

Unutzer, Jurgen (3 mentions)
Vanderbilt U, 1990 *Certification:* Psychiatry
1959 NE Pacific St, Seattle, 206-685-5337

Wynn, John David (5 mentions)
U of Illinois, 1983 *Certification:* Internal Medicine, Psychiatry
1120 Cherry St #240, Seattle, 206-624-0296

Pulmonary Disease

Benditt, Joshua Oliver (7 mentions)
U of Washington, 1982
Certification: Internal Medicine, Pulmonary Disease
1959 NE Pacific St, Seattle, 206-543-3166

Bolin, Rex Warren (7 mentions)
U of Colorado, 1981
Certification: Internal Medicine, Pulmonary Disease
500 Lilly Rd NE #201, Olympia, 360-413-8272
1104 Basich Blvd, Aberdeen, 360-532-2633

Cary, Jeffrey Michael (7 mentions)
U of Colorado, 1972
Certification: Internal Medicine, Pulmonary Disease
1229 Madison St #300, Seattle, 206-386-9500
515 Minor Ave #300, Seattle, 206-386-9500

Finch, Derel (7 mentions)
U of Washington, 1995
Certification: Critical Care Medicine, Pulmonary Disease
515 Minor Ave #300, Seattle, 206-386-9500

Freudenberger, Todd Henry (8 mentions)
U of Washington, 1994
Certification: Critical Care Medicine, Pulmonary Disease
1135 116th Ave NE #600, Bellevue, 425-454-2671
6505 226th Pl SE #101, Issaquah, 425-454-2671

Gerbino, Anthony Joseph (8 mentions)
U of California-Los Angeles, 1992
Certification: Critical Care Medicine, Internal Medicine,
    Pulmonary Disease, Undersea & Hyperbaric Medicine
1100 9th Ave, Seattle, 206-223-6622

Hudson, Leonard D. (7 mentions)
U of Washington, 1964
Certification: Internal Medicine, Pulmonary Disease
325 9th Ave, Seattle, 206-744-3533

Huseby, Jon Sigurd (13 mentions)
George Washington U, 1970
Certification: Internal Medicine, Pulmonary Disease
1145 Broadway #1-L, Seattle, 206-860-2319

Keenan, Lynn Mary (8 mentions)
Jefferson Med Coll, 1987 *Certification:* Critical Care
    Medicine, Internal Medicine, Pulmonary Disease
125 16th Ave E, Seattle, 206-326-3200
209 Martin Luther King Way, Tacoma, 206-326-3200

Kirtland, Steven Howard (9 mentions)
U of California-San Diego, 1986 *Certification:* Critical Care
    Medicine, Internal Medicine, Pulmonary Disease,
    Undersea & Hyperbaric Medicine
1100 9th Ave, Seattle, 206-223-6622

Knodel, Arthur Raymond (7 mentions)
U of Washington, 1977 *Certification:* Critical Care Medicine,
    Internal Medicine, Pulmonary Disease
316 MLK Jr Way #401, Tacoma, 253-572-5140
35409 9th Ave S #104, Federal Way, 253-572-5140

Roper, Embra Arthur (10 mentions)
Med Coll of Georgia, 1981 *Certification:* Critical Care
    Medicine, Internal Medicine, Pulmonary Disease
1145 Broadway, Seattle, 206-329-1760

Rowlands, John Hamilton (8 mentions)
U of Washington, 1976
Certification: Internal Medicine, Pulmonary Disease
316 MLK Jr Way #401, Tacoma, 253-572-5140

Sandblom, Robert Edward (7 mentions)
U of Washington, 1976 *Certification:* Critical Care Medicine,
    Internal Medicine, Pulmonary Disease
11511 NE 10th St, Bellevue, 425-502-3000

Veal, Curtis Franklin (7 mentions)
Med Coll of Georgia, 1981 *Certification:* Critical Care
    Medicine, Internal Medicine, Pulmonary Disease
801 Broadway #814, Seattle, 206-386-6000

Radiology—Diagnostic

Bonifield, James Gee (3 mentions)
U of Texas-Southwestern, 1971
Certification: Diagnostic Radiology
3417 Ensign Rd NE, Olympia, 360-493-4600

Effmann, Eric Leonard (3 mentions)
Indiana U, 1967
Certification: Diagnostic Radiology, Pediatric Radiology
4800 Sand Point Way NE #R-5417, Seattle, 206-987-2134

Hillier, David Alfred (3 mentions)
Washington U, 1992 *Certification:* Diagnostic Radiology,
    Nuclear Medicine, Nuclear Radiology
201 16th Ave E, Seattle, 206-326-3260

Karl, Robert D., Jr. (6 mentions)
Med Coll of Wisconsin, 1972
Certification: Diagnostic Radiology, Nuclear Radiology
209 MLK Jr Way, Tacoma, 253-596-3470

Kinder, Eric Anthony (4 mentions)
U of California-San Francisco, 1997
Certification: Diagnostic Radiology, Neuroradiology
10700 Meridian Ave N #505, Seattle, 206-365-4100

Kramer, Dawna Jacobsen (4 mentions)
U of Washington, 1983 *Certification:* Diagnostic Radiology
1100 9th Ave #C5, Seattle, 206-223-6851

Porter, Bruce Arnold (3 mentions)
U of California-Davis, 1974 *Certification:* Diagnostic Radiology
1001 Boylston Ave, Seattle, 206-329-6767

Rohlfing, James Jeffrey (3 mentions)
U of Washington, 1986
Certification: Diagnostic Radiology, Neuroradiology
2700 Clare Ave, Bremerton, 360-479-6555

Rohrmann, Charles Albert, Jr. (4 mentions)
U of Washington, 1966 *Certification:* Diagnostic Radiology
1959 NE Pacific St #RR-215, Seattle, 206-543-3320

Romano, Allan Jack (3 mentions)
U of Washington, 1983 *Certification:* Diagnostic Radiology
728 134th St SW, Everett, 425-297-6200

Schmiedl, Udo Paul (8 mentions)
FMS-Germany, 1982 *Certification:* Diagnostic Radiology
1229 Madison St #900, Seattle, 206-292-6233

Shuman, William Phelps (6 mentions)
SUNY-Upstate Med U, 1973 *Certification:* Diagnostic Radiology
1959 NE Pacific St #RR215, Seattle, 206-543-3320

White, Donna Marie (3 mentions)
U of Washington, 1991 *Certification:* Diagnostic Radiology
209 MLK Jr Way, Tacoma, 253-596-3470

Witrak, Bonnie Jean (3 mentions)
Mayo Med Sch, 1979
Certification: Diagnostic Radiology, Neuroradiology
728 134th St SW #120, Everett, 425-297-6200

Radiology—Therapeutic

Herstein, Paul Robert (5 mentions)
Stanford U, 1974
Certification: Radiation Oncology, Therapeutic Radiology
201 16th Ave E, Seattle, 206-326-3490

Jensen, Ray S., Jr. (4 mentions)
Baylor U, 1990 *Certification:* Diagnostic Radiology, Vascular
    & Interventional Radiology
10700 Meridian Ave N #505, Seattle, 206-365-4100

Madsen, Berit L. (5 mentions)
Stanford U, 1989 *Certification:* Radiation Oncology
1100 9th Ave, Seattle, 206-223-6801

Robinson, David Hallock (6 mentions)
U of Washington, 1991 *Certification:* Diagnostic Radiology,
    Vascular & Interventional Radiology
1100 9th Ave, Seattle, 206-223-6901

Russell, Kenneth John (4 mentions)
Harvard U, 1979 *Certification:* Therapeutic Radiology
825 Eastlake Ave E, Seattle, 206-288-1024

Rehabilitation

Beck, Randi Marie (9 mentions)
Loyola U Chicago, 1987
Certification: Physical Medicine & Rehabilitation
125 16th Ave E, Seattle, 206-326-3097

Bell, Kathleen Reilly (4 mentions)
Temple U, 1981 *Certification:* Physical Medicine & Rehabilitation
1959 NE Pacific St 8th Fl, Seattle, 206-598-4590

Campbell, Cynthia Grant (5 mentions)
U of Cincinnati, 1982
Certification: Physical Medicine & Rehabilitation
1600 E Jefferson St #620, Seattle, 206-320-2675

Cantini, Evan Miller (5 mentions)
Wright State U, 1980
Certification: Physical Medicine & Rehabilitation
1530 N 115th St #305, Seattle, 206-362-2464

Cole, Andrew James (5 mentions)
U of Virginia, 1985
Certification: Physical Medicine & Rehabilitation
1750 112th Ave NE #D258, Bellevue, 425-451-2272
11800 NE 128th St #530, Kirkland, 425-823-7530

Esselman, Peter Carey (5 mentions)
U of Washington, 1986
Certification: Physical Medicine & Rehabilitation
325 9th Ave, Seattle, 206-744-5862

Forgette, Margaret Mary (4 mentions)
U of Washington, 1984
Certification: Physical Medicine & Rehabilitation
1600 E Jefferson St #620, Seattle, 206-320-2675

Herring, Stanley Alan (6 mentions)
U of Texas-Southwestern, 1979
Certification: Physical Medicine & Rehabilitation
325 9th Ave #3597, Seattle, 206-744-0401

Moore, Donna Elizabeth (4 mentions)
Rosalind Franklin U, 1985
Certification: Physical Medicine & Rehabilitation
2528 Wheaton Way #206, Bremerton, 360-373-8272

Odderson, Ib Rask (10 mentions)
Vanderbilt U, 1985
Certification: Physical Medicine & Rehabilitation
1700 116th Ave NE 1st Fl, Bellevue, 425-646-7777

Robinson, Lawrence R. (4 mentions)
Baylor U, 1982 *Certification:* Physical Medicine & Rehabilitation
325 9th Ave, Seattle, 206-744-5862
1959 NE Pacific St, Seattle, 206-598-5903

Tempest, David Peter (12 mentions)
Oregon Health Sciences U, 1979
Certification: Physical Medicine & Rehabilitation
1600 E Jefferson St #620, Seattle, 206-320-2675

Weinstein, Michael Simon (4 mentions)
U of Washington, 1983
Certification: Physical Medicine & Rehabilitation
1201 Terry Ave, Seattle, 206-223-6746

Rheumatology

Carlin, Jeffrey Steven (9 mentions)
New York U, 1975
Certification: Internal Medicine, Rheumatology
1201 Terry Ave, Seattle, 206-223-6824
19116 33rd Ave W, Lynnwood, 425-712-7900

Ettlinger, Robert Emil (6 mentions)
SUNY-Upstate Med U, 1972
Certification: Internal Medicine, Rheumatology
1901 S Cedar St #201, Tacoma, 253-272-2261

Gardner, Gregory Charles (12 mentions)
Baylor U, 1984 *Certification:* Internal Medicine, Rheumatology
1959 NE Pacific St #EA-300, Seattle, 206-598-4615

Mohai, Peter (7 mentions)
Emory U, 1975 *Certification:* Internal Medicine, Rheumatology
515 Minor Ave #300, Seattle, 206-386-9500
1200 112th Ave NE #B-250, Bellevue, 425-462-1132

Oppliger, Ina Rose (6 mentions)
U of Kansas, 1980
Certification: Internal Medicine, Rheumatology
209 MLK Jr Way, Tacoma, 253-596-3360

Overman, Steven Scott (9 mentions)
U of Alabama, 1975
Certification: Internal Medicine, Rheumatology
10330 Meridian Ave N #250, Seattle, 206-368-6123

Wener, Mark Howard (8 mentions)
Washington U, 1974 *Certification:* Diagnostic Laboratory
Immunology, Internal Medicine, Rheumatology
1959 NE Pacific St #EA 300, Seattle, 206-598-4615

Thoracic Surgery

Aye, Ralph Williams (24 mentions)
U of Pittsburgh, 1977 *Certification:* Surgery
1101 Madison St #850, Seattle, 206-215-6800

Froines, Eric John (6 mentions)
U of Washington, 1986 *Certification:* Surgery
201 16th Ave E, Seattle, 206-326-3222

Hill, Mark E. (6 mentions)
U of Utah, 1989 *Certification:* Surgery, Thoracic Surgery
1100 9th Ave, Seattle, 206-223-6198

Low, Donald Edward (13 mentions)
FMS-Canada, 1981
1100 9th Ave Buck Pavillion 6th Fl, Seattle, 206-223-6164

Vallieres, Eric (14 mentions)
FMS-Canada, 1982
1101 Madison St #850, Seattle, 206-215-6800

Wood, Douglas Earl (12 mentions)
Harvard U, 1983 *Certification:* Surgery, Thoracic Surgery
1959 NE Pacific St, Seattle, 206-598-1980

Urology

Chapman, Phillip Howe (9 mentions)
U of Washington, 1987 *Certification:* Urology
1101 Madison St #1400, Seattle, 206-386-6266

Corman, John Mayer (6 mentions)
Baylor U, 1992 *Certification:* Urology
1100 9th Ave 7th Fl, Seattle, 206-625-7373

Deck, Andrew J. (5 mentions)
U of California-Davis, 1995 *Certification:* Urology
11911 NE 132nd St #200, Kirkland, 425-899-5800

Ellis, William John (10 mentions)
Johns Hopkins U, 1985 *Certification:* Urology
1959 NE Pacific St #201, Seattle, 206-598-4294

Gandhi, Kevin Kishin (8 mentions)
Loyola U Chicago, 1986 *Certification:* Urology
618 S Meridian #B, Puyallup, 253-840-2161

Gasparich, James Peter (6 mentions)
U of Chicago, 1979 *Certification:* Urology
1221 Madison St #1210, Seattle, 206-292-6488

Harris, Christopher John (6 mentions)
U of New Mexico, 1976 *Certification:* Urology
209 MLK Jr Way, Tacoma, 253-596-3680

Kobashi, Kathleen Chizuko (8 mentions)
Hahnemann U, 1992 *Certification:* Urology
1100 9th Ave #C3, Seattle, 206-223-6176
222 112th Ave NE #101, Bellevue, 425-637-1855

Porter, James Roscoe, Jr. (5 mentions)
Med Coll of Ohio, 1990 *Certification:* Urology
1101 Madison St #1400, Seattle, 206-386-6266

Pritchett, T. Randy (5 mentions)
U of California-Los Angeles, 1980 *Certification:* Urology
1100 9th Ave, Seattle, 206-223-6772
19116 33rd Ave W, Lynnwood, 425-712-7900

Sood, Narender (5 mentions)
FMS-India, 1974 *Certification:* Urology
11911 NE 132nd St #200, Kirkland, 425-899-5800

Torgerson, Erik Lang (7 mentions)
Baylor U, 1994 *Certification:* Urology
1101 Madison St #1400, Seattle, 206-386-6266

Weissman, Robert Merrill (8 mentions)
U of Illinois, 1973 *Certification:* Urology
1135 116th Ave NE #620, Bellevue, 425-454-8016

Vascular Surgery

Johansen, Kaj Henry (20 mentions)
U of Washington, 1970 *Certification:* Surgery, Vascular Surgery
1600 E Jefferson St #101, Seattle, 206-320-3100

Lange, Brian Cole (6 mentions)
U of Washington, 1984 *Certification:* Surgery
801 Broadway #522, Seattle, 206-682-6087

McQuinn, William Charles, Jr. (6 mentions)
U of Mississippi, 1980 *Certification:* Surgery
201 16th Ave E, Seattle, 206-326-3222

Meissner, Mark Harmon (6 mentions)
U of Colorado, 1985 *Certification:* Surgery, Vascular Surgery
1959 NE Pacific St #356165, Seattle, 206-598-4477

Neuzil, Daniel Florian (9 mentions)
Johns Hopkins U, 1987 *Certification:* Surgery, Vascular Surgery
1100 9th Ave, Seattle, 206-341-0060

Pepper, Daniel (12 mentions)
Rush U, 1977 *Certification:* Surgery
12333 NE 130th Ln #425, Kirkland, 425-899-2678
1135 116th Ave NE #305, Bellevue, 425-453-1772

Raker, Edmond John (9 mentions)
Harvard U, 1974 *Certification:* Surgery, Vascular Surgery
1100 9th Ave #6, Seattle, 206-223-6950

Wong, Roman (13 mentions)
U of Maryland, 1978
801 Broadway #522, Seattle, 206-682-6087

Wisconsin

Milwaukee Area

Milwaukee Area

Including Milwaukee County

Allergy/Immunology

Chiu, Asriani Marisa (11 mentions)
Med Coll of Wisconsin, 1992
Certification: Allergy & Immunology, Internal Medicine
9000 W Wisconsin Ave #440, Milwaukee, 414-607-5280

Cohen, Steven Howard (7 mentions)
Ohio State U, 1972
Certification: Allergy & Immunology, Internal Medicine
11121 W Oklahoma Ave, Milwaukee, 414-545-1111

Fink, Jordan Norman (12 mentions)
U of Wisconsin, 1959
Certification: Allergy & Immunology, Internal Medicine
9000 W Wisconsin Ave #440, Milwaukee, 414-266-6450

Graves, Terry Spencer (5 mentions)
Med Coll of Wisconsin, 1973
Certification: Allergy & Immunology, Internal Medicine
2500 N Mayfair Rd #220, Wauwatosa, 414-475-9101
4811 S 76th St #400, Greenfield, 414-281-0404

Steven, Gary C. (6 mentions)
Med Coll of Wisconsin, 1991 *Certification:* Allergy & Immunology
8585 W Forest Home Ave #200, Greenfield, 414-529-8500
123 Wolf Run #5, Mukwonago, 262-363-6880

Zacharisen, Michael C. (11 mentions)
Med Coll of Wisconsin, 1988
Certification: Allergy & Immunology, Pediatrics
9000 W Wisconsin Ave #440, Milwaukee, 414-266-6450

Anesthesiology

Becker, Stephen Charles (8 mentions)
Med Coll of Wisconsin, 1982
Certification: Anesthesiology, Critical Care Medicine
2025 E Newport Ave, Milwaukee, 414-961-3300

Berens, Richard Joseph (8 mentions)
Med Coll of Wisconsin, 1984
Certification: Anesthesiology, Critical Care Medicine
9000 W Wisconsin Ave, Milwaukee, 414-266-2469

Guenther, Neil Roman (4 mentions)
Med Coll of Wisconsin, 1983
Certification: Anesthesiology, Internal Medicine
2900 W Oklahoma Ave, Milwaukee, 414-385-2380

Habibi, Saeed (4 mentions)
FMS-Iran, 1981 *Certification:* Anesthesiology, Critical Care
Medicine, Internal Medicine
2323 N Lake Dr, Milwaukee, 414-291-1000

Hoffman, George Milliard (8 mentions)
U of Pennsylvania, 1980 *Certification:* Anesthesiology,
Pediatric Critical Care Medicine, Pediatrics
9000 W Wisconsin Ave, Milwaukee, 414-266-3560

Kay, Jonathan (10 mentions)
Jefferson Med Coll, 1975 *Certification:* Anesthesiology,
Critical Care Medicine, Internal Medicine
2900 W Oklahoma Ave, Milwaukee, 414-385-2380

Lauer, Kathryn K. (10 mentions)
Med Coll of Wisconsin, 1984 *Certification:* Anesthesiology
9200 W Wisconsin Ave, Milwaukee, 414-805-3000

Cardiac Surgery

Downey, Francis Xavier (8 mentions)
U of Toledo, 1986 *Certification:* Surgery, Thoracic Surgery
2015 E Newport Ave #208, Milwaukee, 414-247-4500

McManus, Robert Patrick (13 mentions)
Boston U, 1979 *Certification:* Thoracic Surgery
10150 W National Ave #190, West Allis, 414-271-5119

Nicolosi, Alfred Carl (8 mentions)
Robert W Johnson Med Sch, 1984 *Certification:* Thoracic Surgery
9200 W Wisconsin Ave, Milwaukee, 414-805-6000

Tweddell, James Scott (13 mentions)
U of Cincinnati, 1985 *Certification:* Surgery, Thoracic Surgery
9000 W Wisconsin Ave, Milwaukee, 414-266-2638

Werner, Paul Herbert (13 mentions)
Rush U, 1975 *Certification:* Thoracic Surgery
2901 W Kinnikinnic River Pkwy #310, Milwaukee, 414-649-3990

Cardiology

Bajwa, Tanvir Khalid (6 mentions)
FMS-Pakistan, 1977 *Certification:* Cardiovascular Disease,
Internal Medicine, Interventional Cardiology
960 N 12th St #400, Milwaukee, 414-219-7653
2801 W Kinnickinnic River Pkwy #777, Milwaukee,
414-649-3370
2000 E Layton Ave #170, St Francis, 414-744-6589
6901 W Edgerton Ave, Milwaukee, 414-421-8400
1218 W Kilbourn Ave #124, Milwaukee, 414-219-7653

Berger, Stuart (9 mentions)
U of Wisconsin, 1979
Certification: Pediatric Cardiology, Pediatrics
9000 W Wisconsin Ave, Milwaukee, 414-266-2380

Bernstein, Paul Steven (3 mentions)
U of Chicago, 1976
Certification: Cardiovascular Disease, Internal Medicine
2801 W Kinnickinnic River Pkwy #840, Milwaukee,
414-649-3530

Biblo, Lee (3 mentions)
Case Western Reserve U, 1981 *Certification:* Cardiovascular
Disease, Clinical Cardiac Electrophysiology, Internal Medicine
9200 W Wisconsin Ave, Milwaukee, 414-805-3666

Cinquegrani, Michael P. (7 mentions)
Loyola U Chicago, 1978 *Certification:* Cardiovascular
Disease, Internal Medicine, Interventional Cardiology
9200 W Wisconsin Ave, Milwaukee, 414-805-6633

Frommelt, Peter Cyril (4 mentions)
U of Iowa, 1985 *Certification:* Pediatric Cardiology
9000 W Wisconsin Ave, Milwaukee, 414-266-2380

Keelan, Michael H., Jr. (5 mentions)
Med Coll of Wisconsin, 1960
Certification: Cardiovascular Disease, Internal Medicine
9200 W Wisconsin Ave, Milwaukee, 414-805-6633

Kleczka, James Fredrick (3 mentions)
Med Coll of Wisconsin, 1996
Certification: Cardiovascular Disease, Internal Medicine
9200 W Wisconsin Ave, Milwaukee, 414-805-3666

Leitschuh, Mark Linus (10 mentions)
Oregon Health Sciences U, 1982
Certification: Cardiovascular Disease, Internal Medicine
13133 N Port Washington Rd, Mequon, 262-243-3700

Mahn, Thomas Henning (7 mentions)
U of Wisconsin, 1980
Certification: Cardiovascular Disease, Internal Medicine
3070 N 51st St #106, Milwaukee, 414-442-9911
201 N Mayfair Rd, Wauwatosa, 414-442-9911

Marks, David Scott (5 mentions)
U of California-San Francisco, 1989 *Certification:* Cardiovascular Disease, Internal Medicine, Interventional Cardiology
9200 W Wisconsin Ave, Milwaukee, 414-805-3666

Port, Steven C. (6 mentions)
Mount Sinai Sch of Med, 1972
Certification: Cardiovascular Disease, Internal Medicine
2801 W Kinnickinnic River Pkwy #840, Milwaukee, 877-576-3530

Roth, Robert Barry (10 mentions)
Tulane U, 1982
Certification: Cardiovascular Disease, Internal Medicine
2350 N Lake Dr #400, Milwaukee, 414-271-1633
13133 N Port Washington Rd, Mequon, 414-243-5850

Schulgit, James Lawrence (5 mentions)
Med Coll of Wisconsin, 1981
Certification: Cardiovascular Disease, Internal Medicine
2901 W Kinnickinnic River Pkwy #105, Milwaukee, 414-649-3610

Siegel, Ronald (5 mentions)
Loyola U Chicago, 1971
9200 W Wisconsin Ave, Milwaukee, 414-805-3666

Thompson, Melish A. (3 mentions)
U of California-San Diego, 1972 *Certification:* Cardiovascular Disease, Internal Medicine, Interventional Cardiology
2015 E Newport Ave #M114, Milwaukee, 414-961-4100

Vellinga, Timothy (6 mentions)
U of Iowa, 1982 *Certification:* Cardiovascular Disease, Internal Medicine, Interventional Cardiology
601 N 99th St #201, Wauwatosa, 414-778-7790

Dermatology

Barnett, James H. (6 mentions)
Med Coll of Wisconsin, 1979 *Certification:* Dermatology
2600 N Mayfair Rd #810, Milwaukee, 414-771-1122

Drolet, Beth Ann (18 mentions)
Loyola U Chicago, 1991
Certification: Dermatology, Pediatric Dermatology
9000 W Wisconsin Ave, Milwaukee, 414-266-2000

Ethington, James Edward (9 mentions)
Loyola U Chicago, 1974 *Certification:* Dermatology
2923 W Layton Ave, Milwaukee, 414-281-0712

Neuburg, Marcelle (8 mentions)
Oregon Health Sciences U, 1982
Certification: Dermatology, Internal Medicine
9200 W Wisconsin Ave, Milwaukee, 414-805-5320

Russell, Thomas Joseph (18 mentions)
Med Coll of Wisconsin, 1962 *Certification:* Dermatology
14555 W National Ave #190, New Berlin, 262-754-4488
13800 W North Ave #100, Brookfield, 262-754-4488

Wilson, Barbara Dahl (14 mentions)
U of Minnesota, 1981 *Certification:* Dermatology
9200 W Wisconsin Ave, Milwaukee, 414-805-5320

Winston, Evonne Marie (6 mentions)
Rush U, 1975 *Certification:* Dermatology, Internal Medicine
2350 N Lake Dr #301, Milwaukee, 414-271-4211

Emergency Medicine

Croft, Howard Jeffrey (4 mentions)
U of Illinois, 1981 *Certification:* Emergency Medicine
111 E Wisconsin Ave #2000, Milwaukee, 414-290-6720

Gerschke, Gary Lee (6 mentions)
Northwestern U, 1974 *Certification:* Emergency Medicine
111 E Wisconsin Ave #2000, Milwaukee, 414-290-6720

Herson, Kathryn Julia (4 mentions)
Med Coll of Wisconsin, 1985 *Certification:* Emergency Medicine
111 E Wisconsin Ave #2000, Milwaukee, 414-290-6720

Whitcomb, John Elmer (3 mentions)
Yale U, 1977
Certification: Emergency Medicine, Internal Medicine
945 N 12th St, Milwaukee, 414-479-2371

Endocrinology

Drobny, Elaine Claire (6 mentions)
U of Arizona, 1977
Certification: Endocrinology and Metabolism, Internal Medicine
788 N Jefferson St #201, Milwaukee, 414-272-8950

Findling, James (25 mentions)
Northwestern U, 1975
Certification: Endocrinology and Metabolism, Internal Medicine
W 129 N 755 Westfield Dr Bldg A #203, Menomonee Falls, 414-649-6421

Jacobson, Mitchell Mayer (14 mentions)
Northwestern U, 1964 *Certification:* Internal Medicine
788 N Jefferson St, Milwaukee, 414-272-8950
13133 N Port Washington Rd, Mequon, 262-243-5000

Maas, Diana Lee (7 mentions)
Med Coll of Wisconsin, 1985 *Certification:* Endocrinology, Diabetes, and Metabolism, Internal Medicine
9200 W Wisconsin Ave, Milwaukee, 414-805-3666

Magill, Steven B. (8 mentions)
U of North Dakota, 1990
Certification: Endocrinology, Diabetes, and Metabolism
W 129 N 7055 Northfield Dr #201, Menomonee Falls, 262-253-7155

O'Shaughnessy, Irene (7 mentions)
U of Illinois, 1983 *Certification:* Endocrinology, Diabetes, and Metabolism, Internal Medicine
8700 W Wisconsin Ave 4th Fl, Milwaukee, 414-805-6550

Family Practice *(see note on page 9)*

Bower, Douglas John (3 mentions)
U of Wisconsin, 1979 *Certification:* Family Medicine
1155 N Mayfair Rd, Milwaukee, 414-456-5990

Fetherston, Michael P. (4 mentions)
Med Coll of Wisconsin, 1977 *Certification:* Family Medicine
9233 N Green Bay Rd, Milwaukee, 414-270-8150

Johnstone, Michael F. (3 mentions)
Med Coll of Wisconsin, 1982 *Certification:* Family Medicine
9233 N Green Bay Rd, Milwaukee, 414-270-8150

Meier, Mark Alan (4 mentions)
U of Chicago, 1984 *Certification:* Family Medicine
14555 W National Ave #160, New Berlin, 262-827-2977

Miller, John Joseph (5 mentions)
U of Wisconsin, 1979 *Certification:* Family Medicine
1901 E Capitol Dr, Shorewood, 414-962-7477

Papin, Kayleen Paige (3 mentions)
Med Coll of Wisconsin, 2001 *Certification:* Family Medicine
1155 N Mayfair Rd, Milwaukee, 414-456-5990

Gastroenterology

Bjork, John Theodore (5 mentions)
Med Coll of Wisconsin, 1971
Certification: Gastroenterology, Internal Medicine
2901 W Kinnickinnic River Pkwy #414, Milwaukee, 414-649-3750

Chung, Maurice W. (4 mentions)
Med Coll of Wisconsin, 1984
Certification: Gastroenterology, Internal Medicine
801 S 70th St, St Francis, 414-773-6600

Elgin, Drew Michael (10 mentions)
U of Iowa, 1980
Certification: Gastroenterology, Internal Medicine
13133 NPort Washington Rd #G-16, Mequon, 262-243-5000

Geenen, Joseph Edward (6 mentions)
Med Coll of Wisconsin, 1960
Certification: Gastroenterology, Internal Medicine
2801 W Kinnickinnic River Pkwy #1030, Milwaukee, 414-908-6500

Gerleman, Mary Catherine (4 mentions)
Med Coll of Wisconsin, 1985
Certification: Gastroenterology, Internal Medicine
2300 N Mayfair Rd #725, Milwaukee, 414-778-1911
2025 E Newport Ave, Milwaukee, 414-961-8110

Hanson, Jerome Thomas (4 mentions)
U of Wisconsin, 1974
Certification: Gastroenterology, Internal Medicine
2901 W Kinnickinnic River Pkwy #414, Milwaukee, 414-649-3750

Hogan, Walter Joseph (5 mentions)
Med Coll of Wisconsin, 1958 *Certification:* Internal Medicine
9200 W Wisconsin Ave, Milwaukee, 414-456-6836

Loo, Franklin David (4 mentions)
Med Coll of Wisconsin, 1975
Certification: Gastroenterology, Internal Medicine
2901 W Kinnickinnic River Pkwy #414, Milwaukee, 414-649-3750

Martinez, Alfonso M. (6 mentions)
FMS-Mexico, 1979 *Certification:* Pediatric Gastroenterology
9000 W Wisconsin Ave, Milwaukee, 414-805-3666
8701 W Watertown Plank Rd, Milwaukee, 414-266-3690

Regan, Patrick Thomas (8 mentions)
Northwestern U, 1972
Certification: Gastroenterology, Internal Medicine
788 N Jefferson St #401, Milwaukee, 414-272-8950
13133 N Port Washington Rd, Mequon, 262-243-5000

Rudolph, Colin D. (4 mentions)
Case Western Reserve U, 1982
Certification: Pediatric Gastroenterology, Pediatrics
9000 W Wisconsin Ave #710, Milwaukee, 414-607-5280

Saeian, Kia (8 mentions)
U of California-San Diego, 1992 *Certification:* Gastroenterology, Internal Medicine, Transplant Hepatology
9200 W Wisconsin Ave, Milwaukee, 414-805-3053

Schenck, Jeffrey Wayne (4 mentions)
Indiana U, 1980
Certification: Gastroenterology, Internal Medicine
13133 N Port Washington Rd #G-16, Mequon, 262-243-5000

Stepke, Chad Joseph (6 mentions)
Med Coll of Wisconsin, 1998
Certification: Gastroenterology, Internal Medicine
788 N Jefferson St #401, Milwaukee, 414-272-8950
2350 N Lake Dr #302, Milwaukee, 414-298-7100
801 S 70th St, Milwaukee, 414-773-6600

Stone, John Edward (6 mentions)
Case Western Reserve U, 1980
Certification: Gastroenterology, Internal Medicine
6200 W Bluemound Rd, Milwaukee, 414-771-5600
1033 N Mayfair Rd, Wauwatosa, 414-454-0600

General Surgery

Battista, Joseph C. (6 mentions)
Northwestern U, 1983 *Certification:* Surgery
3070 N 51st St #207, Milwaukee, 414-871-9500
6200 W Bluemound Rd, Milwaukee, 414-771-5600

Bowman, John Wilson (4 mentions)
U of Cincinnati, 1966 *Certification:* Surgery
2424 S 90th St #208, Milwaukee, 414-328-8080

Caballero, Gerardo Adan (3 mentions)
FMS-Mexico, 1983 *Certification:* Surgery
2000 E Layton Ave #260, St Francis, 414-649-3240
311 W Rawson Ave #225, Franklin, 414-649-3240

Carballo, Richard Ernest (3 mentions)
U of Illinois, 1988 *Certification:* Surgery, Vascular Surgery
2801 W Kinnickinnic River Pkwy #330, Milwaukee,
    414-649-3240

Cattey, Richard Paul (11 mentions)
Med Coll of Wisconsin, 1984 *Certification:* Surgery
2015 E Newport Ave #305, Milwaukee, 414-961-3254

Henry, Lyle Gene (12 mentions)
Indiana U, 1970 *Certification:* Surgery
2015 E Newport Ave, Milwaukee, 414-961-2120

Kappes, Steven Kenneth (3 mentions)
Indiana U, 1977 *Certification:* Surgery
3003 W Good Hope Rd, Milwaukee, 414-352-3100

Klinger, Dean Edward (5 mentions)
Med Coll of Wisconsin, 1980 *Certification:* Surgery
2801 W Kinnickinnic River Pkwy #330, Milwaukee,
    414-649-3240

Mahoney, James Leo (10 mentions)
Louisiana State U-Shreveport, 1983 *Certification:* Surgery
2801 W Kinnickinnic River Pkwy #330, Milwaukee,
    414-649-3240

Martinez, Francisco Jose (3 mentions)
FMS-Mexico, 1972 *Certification:* Surgery
3033 S 27th St #200, Milwaukee, 414-384-8388

Quebbeman, Edward John (5 mentions)
U of Illinois, 1972 *Certification:* Surgery
9200 W Wisconsin Ave, Milwaukee, 414-805-5800

Quinn, Theresa Marie (3 mentions)
Harvard U, 1992 *Certification:* Surgery
9200 W Wisconsin Ave, Milwaukee, 414-805-5800

Sato, Thomas Tad (4 mentions)
U of Southern California, 1988
Certification: Pediatric Surgery, Surgery
999 N 92nd St #320, Milwaukee, 414-266-6550

Schneider, Thomas Carl (3 mentions)
Med Coll of Wisconsin, 1974 *Certification:* Surgery
2311 N Prospect Ave, Milwaukee, 414-319-3000

Siverhus, Craig Alan (3 mentions)
Med Coll of Wisconsin, 1988 *Certification:* Surgery
2015 E Newport Ave #305, Milwaukee, 414-961-0531

Walker, Alonzo Patrick (3 mentions)
U of Florida, 1976 *Certification:* Surgery
9200 W Wisconsin Ave, Milwaukee, 414-805-5737

Wilson, Stuart Dickinson (5 mentions)
U of Illinois, 1960 *Certification:* Surgery
9200 W Wisconsin Ave, Milwaukee, 414-805-5723

Geriatrics

Burns, Edith Ann (4 mentions)
U of Wisconsin, 1981
Certification: Geriatric Medicine, Internal Medicine
5000 W National Ave, Milwaukee, 414-384-2775

Cohan, Mary Elizabeth (4 mentions)
St Louis U, 1984 *Certification:* Geriatric Medicine, Hospice
    and Palliative Medicine, Internal Medicine
9200 W Wisconsin Ave, Milwaukee, 414-805-3666

Duthie, Edmund H., Jr. (13 mentions)
Georgetown U, 1976
Certification: Geriatric Medicine, Internal Medicine
9200 W Wisconsin Ave, Milwaukee, 414-805-3666
5000 W National Ave, Milwaukee, 414-384-2775

Hematology/Oncology

Bomzer, Charles Alan (5 mentions)
Northwestern U, 1978
Certification: Hematology, Internal Medicine, Medical Oncology
4655 N Port Washington Rd #200, Milwaukee, 414-906-4400

Charlson, John Alan (8 mentions)
U of Iowa, 1999
Certification: Internal Medicine, Medical Oncology
9200 W Wisconsin Ave, Milwaukee, 414-805-3666

Chitambar, Christopher R. (4 mentions)
FMS-India, 1976
Certification: Hematology, Internal Medicine, Medical Oncology
9200 W Wisconsin Ave, Milwaukee, 414-805-6800

Divgi, Ajit B. (10 mentions)
FMS-India, 1969
Certification: Hematology, Internal Medicine, Medical Oncology
2801 W Kinnickinnic River Pkwy #930, Milwaukee,
    414-384-5111
4655 N Port Washington Rd #200, Milwaukee, 414-906-4400

Dubner, Howard Niles (8 mentions)
U of Illinois, 1969
Certification: Hematology, Internal Medicine, Medical Oncology
4655 N Port Washington Rd #200, Milwaukee, 414-906-4400

Hanson, John Pierrus (4 mentions)
Med Coll of Wisconsin, 1964
2901 W Kinnickinnic River Pkwy #415, Milwaukee,
    414-385-3086
1061 Commerce Blvd, Slinger, 262-644-2960

Margolis, David (7 mentions)
U of Wisconsin, 1989
Certification: Pediatric Hematology-Oncology
9000 W Wisconsin Ave, Milwaukee, 414-266-2420

Oesterling, Kurt F. (6 mentions)
Cornell U, 1977
Certification: Internal Medicine, Medical Oncology
1055 N Mayfair Rd #300, Wauwatosa, 414-476-8450

Ritch, Paul Steven (4 mentions)
Tufts U, 1973 *Certification:* Internal Medicine, Medical Oncology
9200 W Wisconsin Ave, Milwaukee, 414-805-6800

Taylor, Robert Fredrick (9 mentions)
Yale U, 1976
Certification: Hematology, Internal Medicine, Medical Oncology
4655 N Port Washington Rd #200, Milwaukee, 414-906-4400

Treisman, Jonathan Scott (7 mentions)
Wayne State U, 1984
Certification: Internal Medicine, Medical Oncology
2901 W Kinnickinnic River Pkwy #415, Milwaukee,
    414-385-3086
1061 Commerce Blvd, Slinger, 262-644-2960

Zukowski, Thomas Harry (8 mentions)
Rush U, 1994 *Certification:* Medical Oncology
4655 N Port Washington Rd #200, Milwaukee, 414-906-4400

Infectious Disease

Altmann, Claudia Lia (10 mentions)
Med Coll of Wisconsin, 1984
Certification: Infectious Disease, Internal Medicine
2025 E Newport Ave, Milwaukee, 414-326-1622

Brummitt, Charles Francis (18 mentions)
U of Wisconsin, 1982
Certification: Infectious Disease, Internal Medicine
2801 W Kinnickinnic River Pkwy #475, Milwaukee,
    414-649-3577
1032 S Cesar E Chavez Dr, Milwaukee, 414-672-1315

Buggy, Brian Patrick (32 mentions)
Med Coll of Wisconsin, 1977
Certification: Infectious Disease, Internal Medicine
2801 W Kinnickinnic River Pkwy #475, Milwaukee,
    414-649-3577

Chusid, Michael Joseph (7 mentions)
Yale U, 1970 *Certification:* Allergy & Immunology, Pediatric
    Infectious Diseases, Pediatrics
9000 W Wisconsin Ave, Milwaukee, 414-337-7070

Graham, Mary Beth (9 mentions)
Northwestern U, 1984
Certification: Infectious Disease, Internal Medicine
8701 W Watertown Plank Rd, Milwaukee, 414-805-6444

Havens, Peter Lucas (12 mentions)
U of Missouri-Kansas City, 1980 *Certification:* Pediatric Critical
    Care Medicine, Pediatric Infectious Diseases, Pediatrics
9000 W Wisconsin Ave #450, Milwaukee, 414-337-7070

Taft, Thomas Allan (8 mentions)
Med Coll of Wisconsin, 1981 *Certification:* Infectious Disease,
    Internal Medicine, Undersea & Hyperbaric Medicine
601 N 99th St #103, Wauwatosa, 414-453-5737

Infertility

Janik, Grace Marie (12 mentions)
Med Coll of Wisconsin, 1984
Certification: Obstetrics & Gynecology
2015 E Newport Ave #707, Milwaukee, 414-289-9668

Koh, Charles H. (9 mentions)
FMS-Singapore, 1967 *Certification:* Obstetrics & Gynecology
2015 E Newport Ave #707, Milwaukee, 414-289-9668

Strawn, Estil Young, Jr. (10 mentions)
U of Wisconsin, 1980 *Certification:* Obstetrics &
    Gynecology, Reproductive Endocrinology/Infertility
9200 W Wisconsin Ave, Milwaukee, 414-805-7370

Internal Medicine *(see note on page 9)*

Aldred, Jeffrey Allen (3 mentions)
U of Illinois, 1990 *Certification:* Internal Medicine
7400 W Rawson Ave #143, Franklin, 414-427-4080

Baugrud, Kathleen Ann (3 mentions)
Med Coll of Wisconsin, 1985 *Certification:* Internal Medicine
788 N Jefferson St #300, Milwaukee, 414-272-8950

Berry, Bruce Bart (8 mentions)
Med Coll of Wisconsin, 1983 *Certification:* Internal Medicine
2801 W Kinnickinnic River Pkwy #465, Milwaukee,
    414-649-3560

Chelmowski, Mark Kenneth (3 mentions)
U of Illinois, 1985
Certification: Geriatric Medicine, Internal Medicine
3003 W Good Hope Rd, Milwaukee, 414-352-3100

Golopol, Lawrence Allen (3 mentions)
Med Coll of Wisconsin, 1983 *Certification:* Internal Medicine
13850 W Capitol Dr, Brookfield, 262-790-1118

Jorgensen, Scott Alan (5 mentions)
Med Coll of Wisconsin, 1986 *Certification:* Internal Medicine
13133 N Port Washington #G-18, Mequon, 262-243-5000

Krippendorf, Robert L. (5 mentions)
Med Coll of Wisconsin, 1990 *Certification:* Internal Medicine
9200 W Wisconsin Ave 4th Fl, Milwaukee, 414-805-6850

Lamb, Geoffrey Campbell (3 mentions)
Dartmouth Coll, 1979 *Certification:* Internal Medicine
9200 W Wisconsin Ave, Milwaukee, 414-805-6850

Lodes, Mark William (3 mentions)
Med Coll of Wisconsin, 1997
Certification: Internal Medicine, Pediatrics
1155 N Mayfair Rd, Milwaukee, 414-456-5990

Mazzulla, James Patrick (3 mentions)
Northwestern U, 1975
Certification: Geriatric Medicine, Internal Medicine
2500 W Layton Ave #250, Milwaukee, 414-282-2006

Nordin, Daniel Jon (3 mentions)
U of Wisconsin, 1990 *Certification:* Internal Medicine
2801 W Kinnickinnic River Pkwy #135, Milwaukee,
    414-385-8600

Norton, Andrew John (3 mentions)
Jefferson Med Coll, 1982 *Certification:* Internal Medicine
9200 W Wisconsin Ave, Milwaukee, 414-805-3060

Parent, Gerard Thomas (3 mentions)
Johns Hopkins U, 1971
Certification: Cardiovascular Disease, Internal Medicine
2901 W Kinnickinnic River Pkwy, Milwaukee, 414-649-3790

Sanidas, John George (6 mentions)
Med Coll of Wisconsin, 1995 *Certification:* Internal Medicine
788 N Jefferson St #300, Milwaukee, 414-272-8950

Tobin, Benjamin, Jr. (3 mentions)
Med Coll of Wisconsin, 1996 *Certification:* Internal Medicine
840 N 87th St 2nd Fl, Milwaukee, 414-805-5540

Volberding, James Paul (8 mentions)
Southern Illinois U, 1982 *Certification:* Internal Medicine
788 N Jefferson St #300, Milwaukee, 414-272-8950

Nephrology

Brandes, James Carmen (5 mentions)
Med Coll of Wisconsin, 1985
Certification: Internal Medicine, Nephrology
3267 S 16th St #203, Milwaukee, 414-672-8282
2350 W Villard Ave #306, Milwaukee, 414-463-8680
3120 S 27th St, Milwaukee, 414-672-8282
7793 W Appleton Ave, Milwaukee, 414-873-3600

Elliott, William C., Jr. (5 mentions)
Indiana U, 1984 *Certification:* Internal Medicine, Nephrology
2901 W Kinnickinnic River Pkwy #405, Milwaukee,
    414-383-7744
12011 W North Ave, Milwaukee, 414-771-8228
9900 W Bluemound Rd, Wauwatosa, 414-777-5200

Fritsche, Claire (5 mentions)
Med Coll of Wisconsin, 1978
Certification: Internal Medicine, Nephrology
3267 S 16th St #203, Milwaukee, 414-672-8282
7793 W Appleton Ave, Milwaukee, 414-873-3600

Hanna, Matthew Harvey (22 mentions)
Southern Illinois U, 1979
Certification: Internal Medicine, Nephrology
2901 W Kinnickinnic River Pkwy #405, Milwaukee,
    414-383-7744
5650 N Greenbay Ave #100, Glendale, 414-431-5971
9900 W Bluemound Rd, Wauwatosa, 414-777-5200

Pan, Cynthia Gail (11 mentions)
Med Coll of Wisconsin, 1983
Certification: Pediatric Nephrology, Pediatrics
9000 W Wisconsin Ave, Milwaukee, 877-607-5280

Sievers, Stephen Glenn (11 mentions)
Med Coll of Wisconsin, 1984
Certification: Internal Medicine, Nephrology
5650 N Greenbay Ave #100, Glendale, 414-431-5971

Uy, Kathleen Wan (6 mentions)
FMS-Philippines, 1993 *Certification:* Nephrology
4021 N 52nd St, Milwaukee, 414-672-8282
7793 W Appleton Ave, Milwaukee, 414-873-3600
2801 W Kinnickinnic River Pkwy #435, Milwaukee,
    414-672-9200
3120 S 27th St, Milwaukee, 414-672-8282

Warren, Gregory V. (9 mentions)
FMS-India, 1977 *Certification:* Internal Medicine, Nephrology
3267 S 16th St #203, Milwaukee, 414-672-8282
7793 W Appleton Ave, Milwaukee, 414-873-3600
3120 S 27th St, Milwaukee, 414-672-8282
2000 E Layton Ave #200, St Francis, 414-672-8282

Neurological Surgery

Block, Spencer Jonathan (8 mentions)
Northwestern U, 1987 *Certification:* Neurological Surgery
960 N 12th St, Milwaukee, 414-438-6500
2000 E Layton Ave #100, St Francis, 414-438-6500

Deckard, Jack H. (15 mentions)
Indiana U, 1976 *Certification:* Neurological Surgery
2025 E Newport Ave #140, Milwaukee, 414-961-0089
13133 N Port Washington Rd #110, Mequon, 414-961-0089

Lee, Max (7 mentions)
U of Illinois, 1998
690 N 12th St, Milwaukee, 414-338-6500
2000 E Layton Ave #180, St Francis, 414-438-6500

Mueller, Wade Martin (16 mentions)
U of Wisconsin, 1983 *Certification:* Neurological Surgery
9200 W Wisconsin Ave, Milwaukee, 414-805-8710

Sinson, Grant Paul (8 mentions)
Northwestern U, 1989 *Certification:* Neurological Surgery
9200 W Wisconsin Ave, Milwaukee, 414-805-5408

White, Cully Richard (8 mentions)
Des Moines U, 1994
2901 W Kinnickinnic River Pkwy #201, Milwaukee,
    414-649-3232

Neurology

Book, Diane Sonia (4 mentions)
Med Coll of Wisconsin, 1991 *Certification:* Neurology
9200 W Wisconsin Ave, Milwaukee, 414-805-8710

Broderick, John Scott (3 mentions)
Med Coll of Wisconsin, 2002 *Certification:* Neurology
13133 N Port Washington Rd #G-06, Mequon, 262-243-8371

Jaradeh, Safwan Salim (6 mentions)
FMS-Syria, 1979
Certification: Clinical Neurophysiology, Neurology
9200 W Wisconsin Ave, Milwaukee, 414-805-8710

Khatri, Bhupendra Odhavji (5 mentions)
FMS-India, 1974 *Certification:* Neurology
2801 W Kinnickinnic River Pkwy #630, Milwaukee,
    414-385-1801

Kovnar, Edward Harry (4 mentions)
Washington U, 1977 *Certification:* Clinical Neurophysiology,
    Neurodevelopmental Disabilities, Neurology with Special
    Qualifications in Child Neurology, Pediatrics
3003 W Good Hope Rd, Milwaukee, 414-352-3100

Maas, Eric Francis (3 mentions)
Med Coll of Wisconsin, 1985 *Certification:* Neurology
3003 W Good Hope Rd, Milwaukee, 414-352-3100

Malkin, Mark Gordon (4 mentions)
FMS-Canada, 1979
9200 W Wisconsin Ave, Milwaukee, 414-805-5204

Mitchell, Michael James (9 mentions)
Med Coll of Wisconsin, 1997 *Certification:* Neurology
2511 N Prospect Ave #3-A, Milwaukee, 414-291-1285

Novom, Marc Jeffrey (3 mentions)
Med Coll of Wisconsin, 1972
Certification: Internal Medicine, Neurology
8989 N Port Washington Rd #122, Milwaukee, 414-351-6250

Saxena, Varun Kumar (5 mentions)
FMS-India, 1968 *Certification:* Neurology
2801 W Kinnickinnic River Pkwy #630, Milwaukee,
    414-385-1801

Spivack, Jonathan Wood (4 mentions)
Hahnemann U, 1987 *Certification:* Neurology
3003 W Good Hope Rd, Milwaukee, 414-352-3100
3289 N Mayfair Rd, Wauwatosa, 414-771-7900

Wooten, Marvin Ray (4 mentions)
Indiana U, 1979 *Certification:* Neurology
3003 W Good Hope Rd, Milwaukee, 414-352-3100

Zupanc, Mary Lynn (3 mentions)
U of California-Los Angeles, 1979
Certification: Clinical Neurophysiology, Neurology with
    Special Qualifications in Child Neurology, Pediatrics
9000 W Wisconsin Ave #CC-540, Milwaukee, 414-266-3464

Obstetrics/Gynecology

Barnabei, Vanessa Marie (8 mentions)
U of Virginia, 1985 *Certification:* Obstetrics & Gynecology
9200 W Wisconsin Ave, Milwaukee, 414-805-3666

Bear, Brian Jeffrey (6 mentions)
Med Coll of Wisconsin, 1984
Certification: Obstetrics & Gynecology
3289 N Mayfair Rd, Wauwatosa, 414-771-7900

Dolhun, Patricia Jean (8 mentions)
U of Wisconsin, 1981 *Certification:* Obstetrics & Gynecology
788 N Jefferson St #200, Milwaukee, 414-272-8950

King, Kathy Ann (3 mentions)
U of Wisconsin, 1997 *Certification:* Obstetrics & Gynecology
9200 W Wisconsin Ave, Milwaukee, 414-805-3666

Linn, James Gerard (4 mentions)
Med Coll of Wisconsin, 1980
Certification: Obstetrics & Gynecology
2311 N Prospect Ave, Milwaukee, 414-319-3000

Lund, Michael Robert (8 mentions)
U of Iowa, 1996 *Certification:* Obstetrics & Gynecology
9200 W Wisconsin Ave, Milwaukee, 414-805-3666

Newcomer, Julianne Ruth (5 mentions)
Med Coll of Wisconsin, 1987
Certification: Obstetrics & Gynecology
9200 W Wisconsin Ave, Milwaukee, 414-805-0331

Trebian, Kathleen (6 mentions)
Med Coll of Wisconsin, 1990
Certification: Obstetrics & Gynecology
2524 E Webster Pl #303, Milwaukee, 414-271-1116

Ophthalmology

Alpren, Thomas Victor P. (6 mentions)
Tufts U, 1971 *Certification:* Ophthalmology
6020 S Packard Ave, Cudahy, 414-769-6900
2500 W Layton Ave #110, Milwaukee, 414-281-0424

Foote, Peter Stedman (3 mentions)
U of Wisconsin, 1979 *Certification:* Ophthalmology
1684 N Prospect Ave, Milwaukee, 414-271-2020
17280 W North Ave #100, Brookfield, 262-786-0240
9200 W Loomis Rd #204, Franklin, 414-525-0525
500 W Brown Deer Rd, Milwaukee, 414-352-4883

Freedman, Mark Ian (7 mentions)
Med Coll of Wisconsin, 1983 *Certification:* Ophthalmology
10150 W National Ave #100, Milwaukee, 414-321-7520
3077 N Mayfair Rd #303, Milwaukee, 414-258-4550

Graves, Glenn Edward (3 mentions)
Stony Brook U, 1985 *Certification:* Ophthalmology
2500 W Layton Ave #110, Milwaukee, 414-281-0424
6080 S 108th St, Hales Corners, 414-425-9002

Han, Dennis Peter (3 mentions)
U of Michigan, 1981 *Certification:* Ophthalmology
925 N 87th St, Milwaukee, 414-456-2020

Harris, Gerald Jay (3 mentions)
Northwestern U, 1970 *Certification:* Ophthalmology
925 N 87th St, Milwaukee, 414-456-2020

Heuer, Dale Kennedy (3 mentions)
Northwestern U, 1978 *Certification:* Ophthalmology
925 N 87th St, Milwaukee, 414-456-2020

Koenig, Steven Brand (3 mentions)
Cornell U, 1977 *Certification:* Ophthalmology
925 N 87th St, Milwaukee, 414-456-2020

Reeser, Frederick H., Jr. (4 mentions)
U of Pennsylvania, 1965 *Certification:* Ophthalmology
2600 N Mayfair Rd #901, Milwaukee, 414-774-3484
2801 W Kinnickinnic River Pkwy #170, Milwaukee,
   414-649-4660

Rissell, Michael Tod (3 mentions)
Rush U, 1988 *Certification:* Ophthalmology
1249 W Liebau Rd #102, Mequon, 262-243-3001
2801 W Kinnickinnic River Pkwy #170, Milwaukee,
   414-385-8731
2000 E Layton Ave #110, St Francis, 414-481-8828

Ruttum, Mark Stuart (8 mentions)
Harvard U, 1976 *Certification:* Ophthalmology
925 N 87th St, Milwaukee, 414-456-7836
9000 W Wisconsin Ave, Milwaukee, 414-266-2020

Shafrin, Fred Max (3 mentions)
U of Wisconsin, 1978 *Certification:* Ophthalmology
5150 N Port Washington Rd #251, Milwaukee, 414-332-0606

Sheth, Bhavna Pravin (8 mentions)
Med Coll of Wisconsin, 1992 *Certification:* Ophthalmology
925 N 87th St, Milwaukee, 414-456-2020

Simons, Kenneth Bernard (3 mentions)
Boston U, 1980 *Certification:* Ophthalmology
925 N 87th St, Milwaukee, 414-456-2020

Sucher, Robert Alan (4 mentions)
Med Coll of Wisconsin, 1972 *Certification:* Ophthalmology
10150 W National Ave #100, West Allis, 414-321-7520

Young, Jeffrey Stephen (3 mentions)
Loyola U Chicago, 1988 *Certification:* Ophthalmology
N 89 W 16785 Appleton Ave, Menomonee Falls, 262-253-4000
908 W Washington St, West Bend, 262-306-3500

Orthopedics

Anderson, Michael John (4 mentions)
Med Coll of Wisconsin, 1988 *Certification:* Orthopaedic Surgery
W 180 N 7950 Townhall Rd, Menomonee Falls, 262-255-2500

Bauwens, Dale Edward (8 mentions)
U of Illinois, 1979 *Certification:* Orthopaedic Surgery
2500 N Mayfair Rd #500, Milwaukee, 414-257-2525
5000 W Chambers St, Milwaukee, 414-447-2000

Evanich, Christopher J. (6 mentions)
Med Coll of Wisconsin, 1990 *Certification:* Orthopaedic Surgery
2801 W Kinnickinnic River Pkwy #575, Milwaukee,
   414-643-8800

Flesch, James Richard (3 mentions)
U of Wisconsin, 1972 *Certification:* Orthopaedic Surgery
7545 N Port Washington Rd, Milwaukee, 414-351-3500
13133 N Port Washington Rd #116, Mequon, 262-243-3100

Guehlstorf, Daniel Wayne (4 mentions)
Med Coll of Wisconsin, 1993 *Certification:* Orthopaedic Surgery
2901 W Kinnickinnic River Pkwy #102, Milwaukee,
   414-384-6700
3111 W Rawson Ave #200, Franklin, 414-325-4320

Hackbarth, Donald A. (6 mentions)
Med Coll of Wisconsin, 1977 *Certification:* Orthopaedic Surgery
9200 W Wisconsin Ave, Milwaukee, 414-805-7424

Lyon, Roger Morton (3 mentions)
U of Chicago, 1985 *Certification:* Orthopaedic Surgery
9000 W Wisconsin Ave, Milwaukee, 414-266-2000

Middleton, Donald Kevin (4 mentions)
Northwestern U, 1988 *Certification:* Orthopaedic Surgery
3970 N Oakland Ave #300, Milwaukee, 414-961-0304

Rao, Raj D. (3 mentions)
FMS-India, 1984 *Certification:* Orthopaedic Surgery
9200 W Wisconsin Ave, Milwaukee, 414-805-7425

Rydlewicz, James Allen (3 mentions)
Med Coll of Wisconsin, 1967 *Certification:* Orthopaedic Surgery
5233 W Morgan Ave, Milwaukee, 414-321-8960

Schwab, Jeffrey Philip (8 mentions)
U of Minnesota, 1971 *Certification:* Orthopaedic Surgery
9200 W Wisconsin Ave, Milwaukee, 414-805-7458

Stiehl, James Bowen (4 mentions)
U of Illinois, 1975 *Certification:* Orthopaedic Surgery
575 W River Woods Pkwy #204, Milwaukee, 414-964-6789

Stone, James Wilkins (3 mentions)
Harvard U, 1982 *Certification:* Orthopaedic Surgery
2901 W Kinnickinnic River Pkwy #102, Milwaukee,
   414-384-6700
3111 W Rawson Ave #200, Franklin, 414-325-4320

Tassone, J. Channing (7 mentions)
U of Washington, 1996 *Certification:* Orthopaedic Surgery
9000 W Wisconsin Ave, Milwaukee, 414-266-2410

Thometz, John Gerard (5 mentions)
Northwestern U, 1978 *Certification:* Orthopaedic Surgery
9000 W Wisconsin Ave, Milwaukee, 414-266-2410

Trinkl, Steven Robert (3 mentions)
Med Coll of Wisconsin, 1989 *Certification:* Orthopaedic Surgery
2901 W Kinnickinnic River Pkwy #102, Milwaukee,
   414-384-6700
3111 W Rawson Ave #200, Franklin, 414-325-4320

Vetter, Carole S. (3 mentions)
Med Coll of Wisconsin, 1993
9200 W Wisconsin Ave, Milwaukee, 414-805-7464
8700 W Watertown Plank Rd, Milwaukee, 414-805-7100

Wright, Rory Ray (4 mentions)
Med Coll of Wisconsin, 1988 *Certification:* Orthopaedic Surgery
575 W River Woods Pkwy #100, Glendale, 414-332-6262

Otorhinolaryngology

Barton, James Robert (4 mentions)
West Virginia U, 1971 *Certification:* Otolaryngology
4600 W Loomis Rd #201, Milwaukee, 414-281-4466

Beste, David John (9 mentions)
Med Coll of Wisconsin, 1979 *Certification:* Otolaryngology
9000 W Wisconsin Ave #265, Milwaukee, 414-266-2761
3365 S 103rd St, Greenfield, 414-266-2761

Campbell, Bruce Hegstad (13 mentions)
Rush U, 1980 *Certification:* Otolaryngology
9200 W Wisconsin Ave, Milwaukee, 414-805-5580

Durkin, Gretchen (4 mentions)
Indiana U, 1981 *Certification:* Otolaryngology
2315 N Lake Dr #406, Milwaukee, 414-271-4141
13133 N Port Washington Rd #226, Mequon, 262-243-3660

Gogan, Robert Joseph (9 mentions)
Washington U, 1975 *Certification:* Otolaryngology
10520 N Port Washington Rd, Mequon, 262-241-8000
2000 E Layton Ave #100, Milwaukee, 414-744-6589
2727 W Cleveland Ave, Milwaukee, 262-241-8000

Harkins, Charles John (11 mentions)
U of Wisconsin, 1983 *Certification:* Otolaryngology
9200 W Wisconsin Ave, Milwaukee, 414-805-5580

Loehrl, Todd Alfred (5 mentions)
Med Coll of Wisconsin, 1991 *Certification:* Otolaryngology
9200 W Wisconsin Ave, Milwaukee, 414-805-5580

Nordstrom, Michael R. (4 mentions)
U of Illinois, 1987 *Certification:* Otolaryngology
4600 W Loomis Rd #201, Milwaukee, 414-281-4466

Robey, Thomas Charles (4 mentions)
Washington U, 1995 *Certification:* Otolaryngology
9000 W Wisconsin Ave #265, Milwaukee, 414-266-2761
3365 S 103rd St, Greenfield, 414-266-2761

Wermuth, Douglas John (5 mentions)
Med Coll of Wisconsin, 1984 *Certification:* Otolaryngology
6200 W Bluemound Rd, Milwaukee, 414-771-5600
2000 E Layton Ave #210, St Francis, 414-744-6589

Yale, Russell Steven (5 mentions)
Rosalind Franklin U, 1973 *Certification:* Otolaryngology
10520 N Port Washington Rd, Mequon, 262-241-8000
2000 E Layton Ave #100, St Francis, 414-744-6589
3611 S Chicago Rd, South Milwaukee, 414-762-7270

Pain Medicine

Abram, Stephen Edward (4 mentions)
Jefferson Med Coll, 1970
Certification: Anesthesiology, Pain Medicine
1155 N Mayfair Rd, Wauwatosa, 414-456-7601

Brusky, John Edward (7 mentions)
U of Wisconsin, 1984
Certification: Anesthesiology, Pain Medicine
4570 S 27th St, Milwaukee, 414-325-8720
3111 W Rawson Ave #210, Franklin, 414-325-4370

Donatello, Steven James (6 mentions)
U of Wisconsin, 1991 *Certification:* Anesthesiology
575 W Riverwood Pkwy, Glendale, 414-962-6700

Mortensen, Gordon Lee, Jr. (5 mentions)
Wayne State U, 1981 *Certification:* Anesthesiology
4570 S 27th St, Milwaukee, 414-325-8720
3111 W Rawson Ave #210, Franklin, 414-325-4370

Rusy, Lynn Marie (4 mentions)
U of Wisconsin, 1987 *Certification:* Anesthesiology
9000 W Wisconsin Ave, Milwaukee, 414-266-2775

Pathology

Jablonski, Chester William (4 mentions)
Indiana U, 1976
Certification: Anatomic Pathology & Clinical Pathology
2323 N Lake Dr, Milwaukee, 414-291-1130

Komorowski, Richard A. (4 mentions)
Med Coll of Wisconsin, 1967
Certification: Anatomic Pathology & Clinical Pathology
9200 W Wisconsin Ave, Milwaukee, 414-805-8443

Martinez-Torres, G. (5 mentions)
U of Illinois, 1988
sCertification: Anatomic Pathology & Clinical Pathology
2025 E Newport Ave, Milwaukee, 414-961-3930

Novak, Joseph Anthony (3 mentions)
FMS-Slovenia, 1990 *Certification:* Anatomic Pathology &
   Clinical Pathology, Cytopathology
2025 E Newport Ave, Milwaukee, 414-961-3300

Thakur, Anita (4 mentions)
FMS-India, 1977 *Certification:* Anatomic Pathology & Clinical Pathology, Cytopathology
2323 N Lake Dr, Milwaukee, 414-291-1989
1311 N Port Washington Rd, Mequon, 262-243-7402

Pediatrics *(see note on page 9)*

Donovan, Mary Wisniewski (3 mentions)
Med Coll of Wisconsin, 1985 *Certification:* Pediatrics
20611 Watertown Rd #C, Waukesha, 262-798-1810

Dorrington, Arthur Jordan (4 mentions)
Creighton U, 1972 *Certification:* Pediatrics
11035 W Forest Home Ave, Hales Corners, 414-425-5660

Fuller, Julie Ann (3 mentions)
Med Coll of Wisconsin, 1992 *Certification:* Pediatrics
2524 E Webster Pl #301, Milwaukee, 414-272-7009

Hambrook, M. Sarah (3 mentions)
Med Coll of Wisconsin, 1997 *Certification:* Pediatrics
2524 E Webster Pl #301, Milwaukee, 414-272-7009

Humphrey, John (3 mentions)
Med U of South Carolina, 1978
9000 W Wisconsin Ave, Milwaukee, 414-266-6469

Hunt, Sally Gluek (5 mentions)
FMS-Belgium, 1979 *Certification:* Pediatrics
10046 N Port Washington Rd, Mequon, 262-240-9744

Lautz, David Alan (3 mentions)
Indiana U, 1981 *Certification:* Pediatrics
11035 W Forest Home Ave, Hales Corners, 414-425-5660

Leach, William Craig (5 mentions)
Philadelphia Coll of Osteopathic Med, 1979
10909 W Bluemound Rd, Wauwatosa, 414-258-0606

Paley, Sharyl G. (5 mentions)
U of Wisconsin, 1993 *Certification:* Pediatrics
6373 N Jean Nicolet Rd #100, Glendale, 414-228-0099
5900 N Port Washington Rd, Milwaukee, 414-228-0099

Richter, Connie Lorraine (5 mentions)
Med Coll of Wisconsin, 1991 *Certification:* Pediatrics
3610 Michelle Witmer Memorial Dr #100, New Berlin, 262-789-6020
2035 N 25th St, Milwaukee, 262-789-6020

Rohloff, Robert Thomas (7 mentions)
Med Coll of Wisconsin, 1981 *Certification:* Pediatrics
3610 Michelle Witmer Memorial Dr #100, New Berlin, 262-789-6020
2035 N 25th St, Milwaukee, 414-266-6160

Sherman, David M. (3 mentions)
Albany Med Coll, 1985 *Certification:* Pediatrics
2000 E Layton Ave #100, St Francis, 414-744-6589

Plastic Surgery

Bock, Harvey Michael (9 mentions)
U of Wisconsin, 1971 *Certification:* Plastic Surgery
201 N Mayfair Rd, Milwaukee, 414-443-0033

Denny, Arlen Dwight (6 mentions)
U of Minnesota, 1976 *Certification:* Plastic Surgery
9000 W Wisconsin Ave, Milwaukee, 414-266-2825

Doermann, Andreas (6 mentions)
U of Wisconsin, 1981 *Certification:* Plastic Surgery
12203 N Corporate Pkwy, Mequon, 262-387-8200

Kinney, Thomas Edward (11 mentions)
Med Coll of Wisconsin, 1985 *Certification:* Plastic Surgery
13800 W North Ave #110, Brookfield, 262-717-4000

Loewenstein, Paul Willon (10 mentions)
Indiana U, 1976 *Certification:* Plastic Surgery
2300 N Mayfair Rd #795, Milwaukee, 262-717-4000
13800 W North Ave #110, Brookfield, 262-717-4000

Matloub, Hani Selman (6 mentions)
FMS-Iraq, 1970
Certification: Plastic Surgery, Surgery of the Hand
8700 W Watertown Plank Rd, Milwaukee, 414-805-5441

Sanger, James Robert (8 mentions)
U of Wisconsin, 1974
Certification: Plastic Surgery, Surgery of the Hand
9200 W Wisconsin Ave, Milwaukee, 414-805-5451
8700 W Watertown Plank Rd, Milwaukee, 414-805-5451

Psychiatry

Heinrich, Thomas William (4 mentions)
Med Coll of Wisconsin, 1996 *Certification:* Family Medicine, Psychiatry, Psychosomatic Medicine
1155 N Mayfair Rd, Milwaukee, 414-955-8950

Houghton, Mary Alice B. (3 mentions)
Yale U, 1966 *Certification:* Psychiatry
819 N Cass St, Milwaukee, 414-964-9201

Johnson, Kenneth Edward (6 mentions)
U of Illinois, 1985 *Certification:* Psychiatry
2015 E Newport Ave #411, Milwaukee, 414-962-3655

Keppel, Christina C. (3 mentions)
Loyola U Chicago, 1977 *Certification:* Psychiatry
1017 W Glen Oaks Ln #201, Mequon, 262-241-3698
2600 N Mayfair Rd #305, Wauwatosa, 262-241-3698

Lehrmann, Jon Arthur (5 mentions)
Med Coll of Wisconsin, 1990
Certification: Psychiatry, Psychosomatic Medicine
5000 W National Ave, Milwaukee, 414-384-2000

Rohr, John McLean, Jr. (5 mentions)
U of Wisconsin, 1972 *Certification:* Psychiatry
9401 W Beloit Rd #315, Milwaukee, 414-321-4908

Stevens, Bruce Robert (3 mentions)
Med Coll of Wisconsin, 1992 *Certification:* Psychiatry
1601 E Blackthorne Pl, Milwaukee, 414-967-4930

Taxman, Jeffrey Earle (3 mentions)
U of Wisconsin, 1982 *Certification:* Psychiatry
11501 N Port Washington Rd, Mequon, 262-241-8100

Pulmonary Disease

Biller, Julie Ann (4 mentions)
U of Chicago, 1983
Certification: Internal Medicine, Pulmonary Disease
9200 W Wisconsin Ave, Milwaukee, 414-266-6730

Botros, Emad S. (6 mentions)
FMS-Egypt, 1985 *Certification:* Pulmonary Disease
3070 N 51st St #402, Milwaukee, 414-871-2173

Gershan, William Mark (4 mentions)
Med Coll of Wisconsin, 1983 *Certification:* Pediatric Pulmonology
9000 W Wisconsin Ave, Milwaukee, 414-607-5280

Gronski, Theodore Joseph (5 mentions)
Med Coll of Wisconsin, 1985
2900 W Oklahoma Ave, Milwaukee, 414-649-6572

Harland, Russell William (6 mentions)
Med Coll of Wisconsin, 1987
Certification: Critical Care Medicine, Pulmonary Disease
N-14 W 23900 Stoneridge Dr, Waukesha, 262-574-7980

Katzoff, Michael Noah (8 mentions)
New York Med Coll, 1976
Certification: Internal Medicine, Pulmonary Disease
2801 W Kinnickinnic River Pkwy #445, Milwaukee, 414-649-5288
3237 S 16th St, Milwaukee, 414-389-3060

Lipchik, Randolph J. (8 mentions)
FMS-Canada, 1984 *Certification:* Critical Care Medicine, Internal Medicine, Pulmonary Disease
9200 W Wisconsin Ave, Milwaukee, 414-456-7040

Presberg, Kenneth William (6 mentions)
U of Illinois, 1984 *Certification:* Critical Care Medicine, Internal Medicine, Pulmonary Disease
9200 W Wisconsin Ave #2839, Milwaukee, 414-805-3666

Quintero, Diana Rebeca (5 mentions)
FMS-Colombia, 1993
Certification: Pediatric Pulmonology, Pediatrics
9000 W Wisconsin Ave, Milwaukee, 414-266-6730

Rasansky, Marc (13 mentions)
U of Wisconsin, 1975 *Certification:* Critical Care Medicine, Internal Medicine, Pulmonary Disease
960 N 12th St, Milwaukee, 414-219-7600
2015 E Newport Ave, Milwaukee, 414-219-7600

Rein, David Arnold (4 mentions)
U of Wisconsin, 1986 *Certification:* Critical Care Medicine, Internal Medicine, Pulmonary Disease
2900 W Oklahoma Ave, Milwaukee, 414-747-7723

Salud, Antonio De Villa, II (4 mentions)
Med Coll of Wisconsin, 1999
Certification: Internal Medicine, Pulmonary Disease
2025 E Newport Ave #765, Milwaukee, 414-961-5492

Radiology—Diagnostic

Beres, James Joseph (3 mentions)
U of Wisconsin, 1980 *Certification:* Diagnostic Radiology, Vascular & Interventional Radiology
2025 E Newport Ave, Milwaukee, 414-961-4149

Beres, Robert Allen (3 mentions)
U of Wisconsin, 1987 *Certification:* Diagnostic Radiology, Vascular & Interventional Radiology
2925 W Oklahoma Ave, Milwaukee, 414-649-6425

Berns, Thomas Francis (3 mentions)
Med Coll of Wisconsin, 1975 *Certification:* Diagnostic Radiology
2025 E Newport Ave, Milwaukee, 414-961-4149

Breger, Robert Karl (5 mentions)
Med Coll of Wisconsin, 1984
Certification: Diagnostic Radiology, Neuroradiology
2900 W Oklahoma Ave, Milwaukee, 414-649-6425
6150 W Layton Ave, Milwaukee, 414-282-4100

Carrera, Guillermo F. (7 mentions)
Harvard U, 1972 *Certification:* Diagnostic Radiology
9200 W Wisconsin Ave, Milwaukee, 414-805-3750

Dubin, Lawrence Mark (3 mentions)
Med Coll of Wisconsin, 1982 *Certification:* Diagnostic Radiology
945 N 12th St, Milwaukee, 414-219-7200
2000 E Layton Ave #130, St Francis, 414-766-9050

Glazer, Mark Steven (3 mentions)
FMS-Israel, 1988 *Certification:* Diagnostic Radiology
2000 E Layton Ave #130, St Francis, 414-744-6589

Goodman, Lawrence R. (4 mentions)
SUNY-Downstate Med Coll, 1968
Certification: Diagnostic Radiology
9200 W Wisconsin Ave #2803, Milwaukee, 414-805-3120

McWey, Patrick J. (9 mentions)
Med Coll of Wisconsin, 1978 *Certification:* Diagnostic Radiology
2323 N Lake Dr, Milwaukee, 414-291-1149

Olson, David Lewis (5 mentions)
Washington U, 1980 *Certification:* Diagnostic Radiology
2901 W Kinnickinnic River Pkwy #LL9, Milwaukee, 866-211-2578

Wells, Robert George (4 mentions)
Med Coll of Wisconsin, 1980 *Certification:* Diagnostic Radiology, Pediatric Radiology, Vascular & Interventional Radiology
9000 W Wisconsin Ave, Milwaukee, 414-266-3110

Radiology—Therapeutic

Bastin, Kenneth Tyrone (3 mentions)
Vanderbilt U, 1988 *Certification:* Radiation Oncology
2900 W Oklahoma Ave, Milwaukee, 414-649-6420
8901 W Lincoln Ave, West Allis, 414-328-6460

Beres, James Joseph (6 mentions)
U of Wisconsin, 1980 *Certification:* Diagnostic Radiology,
Vascular & Interventional Radiology
2025 E Newport Ave, Milwaukee, 414-961-3800

Braun, Michael Andrew (3 mentions)
U of Wisconsin, 1986 *Certification:* Diagnostic Radiology,
Vascular & Interventional Radiology
2323 N Lake Dr, Milwaukee, 414-291-1149
500 W Brown Deer Rd #202, Bayside, 414-434-0461

Erickson, Beth Ann (3 mentions)
Med Coll of Wisconsin, 1984 *Certification:* Radiation Oncology
9200 W Wisconsin Ave, Milwaukee, 414-805-4462

Lyon, Robert Douglas (5 mentions)
George Washington U, 1989 *Certification:* Diagnostic
Radiology, Vascular & Interventional Radiology
2323 N Lake Dr, Milwaukee, 414-291-1160

Olson, Carl Erling (3 mentions)
U of Wisconsin, 1969 *Certification:* Therapeutic Radiology
2350 N Lake Dr #G-01, Milwaukee, 414-961-3850

Rilling, William Scott (8 mentions)
U of Wisconsin, 1990 *Certification:* Diagnostic Radiology,
Vascular & Interventional Radiology
9200 W Wisconsin Ave, Milwaukee, 414-805-3700

Schultz, Christopher John (4 mentions)
Med Coll of Wisconsin, 1985 *Certification:* Radiation Oncology
9200 W Wisconsin Ave, Milwaukee, 414-805-4480

Wells, Robert George (3 mentions)
Med Coll of Wisconsin, 1980 *Certification:* Diagnostic Radiology,
Pediatric Radiology, Vascular & Interventional Radiology
9000 W Wisconsin Ave, Milwaukee, 414-266-3110

Rehabilitation

Braza, Diane Wolf (3 mentions)
Med Coll of Wisconsin, 1987
Certification: Pain Medicine, Physical Medicine & Rehabilitation
1155 N Mayfair Rd, Milwaukee, 414-456-7199

Cameron, Jeffrey Scott (5 mentions)
Northwestern U, 1979
Certification: Physical Medicine & Rehabilitation
2025 E Newport Ave, Milwaukee, 414-298-6735

Davidoff, Donna (3 mentions)
Med Coll of Wisconsin, 1978
Certification: Physical Medicine & Rehabilitation
2323 N Lake Dr, Milwaukee, 414-291-1066

Del Toro, David Ruben (5 mentions)
Indiana U, 1988 *Certification:* Physical Medicine & Rehabilitation
9200 W Wisconsin Ave, Milwaukee, 414-543-6388

Roffers, John Anthony (3 mentions)
Med Coll of Wisconsin, 1985
Certification: Physical Medicine & Rehabilitation
2025 E Newport Ave, Milwaukee, 414-961-4161

Rheumatology

Bergquist, Steven Robert (8 mentions)
Med Coll of Wisconsin, 1987 *Certification:* Rheumatology
2500 W Layton Ave #280, Milwaukee, 414-351-4009
7080 N Port Washington Rd, Milwaukee, 414-351-4009

Hanna, Miriam Naoum (10 mentions)
Wayne State U, 1980
Certification: Internal Medicine, Rheumatology
7080 N Port Washington Rd, Milwaukee, 414-351-4009

Hinkle, Stephen Currier (6 mentions)
Dartmouth Coll, 1973
Certification: Internal Medicine, Rheumatology
7080 N Port Washington Rd, Milwaukee, 414-351-4009

Nocton, James John, Jr. (9 mentions)
Johns Hopkins U, 1987
Certification: Pediatric Rheumatology, Pediatrics
9000 W Wisconsin Ave, Milwaukee, 414-266-2873

Oelke, Kurt Robert (5 mentions)
U of Wisconsin, 1997
Certification: Internal Medicine, Rheumatology
7080 N Port Washington Rd, Milwaukee, 414-351-4009

Ryan, Lawrence Matthew (7 mentions)
Loyola U Chicago, 1971
Certification: Internal Medicine, Rheumatology
9200 W Wisconsin Ave, Milwaukee, 414-805-7390

Thoracic Surgery

Gasparri, Mario Giacomo (7 mentions)
Med Coll of Wisconsin, 1993
Certification: Surgery, Thoracic Surgery
9200 W Wisconsin Ave, Milwaukee, 414-456-6904

Haasler, George Bruce (14 mentions)
Columbia U, 1977 *Certification:* Surgery, Thoracic Surgery
9200 W Wisconsin Ave, Milwaukee, 414-456-6902

Just, John Francis (12 mentions)
U of Illinois, 1961 *Certification:* Surgery, Thoracic Surgery
3333 N Mayfair Rd #209, Milwaukee, 414-258-0670

Krishnan, Santosh N. (8 mentions)
Yale U, 1997 *Certification:* Surgery, Thoracic Surgery
3333 N Mayfair Rd #209, Milwaukee, 414-258-0670

Urology

Balcom, Anthony H. (11 mentions)
Med Coll of Wisconsin, 1984
Certification: Pediatric Urology, Urology
9000 W Wisconsin Ave, Milwaukee, 414-266-3794

Derus, Jeffrey Arnold (10 mentions)
Med Coll of Wisconsin, 1985 *Certification:* Urology
3111 W Rayson Ave #235, Franklin, 414-672-6006
2801 W Kinnickinnic River Pkwy #370, Milwaukee,
414-672-6006

Dewire, Douglas Michael (7 mentions)
Indiana U, 1987 *Certification:* Urology
2015 E Newport Ave #707, Milwaukee, 414-289-9668

Kearns, Christopher M. (10 mentions)
Med Coll of Wisconsin, 1989 *Certification:* Urology
6135 Mill St, Cedarburg, 262-376-9488

Langenstroer, Peter (7 mentions)
Med Coll of Wisconsin, 1992 *Certification:* Urology
9200 W Wisconsin Ave, Milwaukee, 414-805-2120

Pope, John F. (8 mentions)
FMS-Grenada, 1981 *Certification:* Urology
17000 W North Ave #108-W, Brookfield, 262-782-4161
2424 S 90th St #304, West Allis, 414-328-8820

See, William Adelbert (8 mentions)
U of Chicago, 1982 *Certification:* Urology
9200 W Wisconsin Ave, Milwaukee, 414-805-2120

Slocum, Peter Albert (8 mentions)
U of Wisconsin, 1983 *Certification:* Urology
2015 E Newport Ave #500, Milwaukee, 414-961-7323

Waples, Mark James (15 mentions)
Case Western Reserve U, 1989 *Certification:* Urology
2801 W Kinnickinnic River Pkwy #370, Milwaukee,
414-672-6006
14555 W National Ave #150, New Berlin, 414-672-6006

Vascular Surgery

Carballo, Richard Ernest (8 mentions)
U of Illinois, 1988 *Certification:* Surgery, Vascular Surgery
2801 W Kinnickinnic River Pkwy #330, Milwaukee,
414-649-3240

Seabrook, Gary Robert (11 mentions)
Wayne State U, 1982 *Certification:* Surgery, Vascular Surgery
9200 W Wisconsin Ave, Milwaukee, 414-805-9160

Appendix A

Is Your Doctor Board Certified? Does It Matter?

In this book, in *CHECKBOOK* magazine, and in other publications and online materials, we try to give consumers as much information as possible to help you in selecting and working with the most important type of service provider in the health care field: physicians.

In this book, we tell you which physicians are most recommended by their peers. In other *CHECKBOOK* resources, we tell you how physicians are rated by patients. In addition, we advise that you check for hospital affiliations, medical school teaching responsibilities, use of electronic medical records, and other indicators of quality.

In addition, we consistently recommend that you select physicians who are "board certified," and we report on board certification status for physicians listed in this book. What does board certification mean, and why is it important?

In the U.S., there are 24 medical specialty boards, such as, the American Board of Thoracic Surgery and the American Board of Internal Medicine. These boards certify physicians in various specialties and subspecialties. For instance, the American Board of Internal Medicine certifies physicians in the specialty of internal medicine and in 18 subspecialties and areas of special qualifications—including cardiovascular disease, gastroenterology, geriatrics, and hematology.

To become certified, a physician must spend several years—in some cases, more than six years—*after medical school* getting supervised, in-practice training.

In addition, all specialty boards require passage of a written exam, completed without assistance, usually administered interactively by computer in a secure testing facility. Some specialties also require an oral exam. The exams are intended to assess medical knowledge and clinical judgment.

Until 1970, all specialty boards issued non-expiring certifications. At that time, the family practice board began issuing time-limited certifications. Over the following 30-plus years, other boards began issuing time-limited certifications, and now all boards issue only time-limited certifications. The certifications generally last for 10 years, but a few boards' certificates are for just six or seven years.

Doctors whose certificates are time-limited must successfully complete re-certification requirements or they can't call themselves board-certified. The requirements for re-certification, like the requirements for initial certification, include an unassisted written (computer-administered) exam, intended to measure clinical knowledge and judgment.

Since the individual specialty boards develop their own exams for certification and re-certification, the validity of the exams as measures of physician competence varies by board. On the exam for re-certification in general internal medicine, the largest specialty, the pass rate in a recent period of years ranged from 85 to 92 percent; the rates in other specialties may be higher or lower.

In the good exams, a test-taker is confronted with real-life situations where knowledge of current medical guidelines, along with good judgment, can be expected to lead to correct answers. Here is the type of case you might find on an exam: a 22-year-old male college student came to the doctor's office after fainting for less than a minute during wrestling practice; the patient had suffered previous episodes of lightheadedness and at age 10 was diagnosed with a heart murmur. The test-taker is given the results of several in-office examinations. Then the test-taker is expected to make a diagnosis.

In 1999, all of the specialty boards agreed to move beyond re-certification based on passing a test of knowledge and judgment to a program of "ABMS Maintenance of Certification®." The policy is that "maintenance of competence should be demonstrated throughout the physician's career by evidence of lifelong learning and ongoing improvement of practice." Each board is implementing this policy in its own way, but all are committed to a program that requires that the physician—

- *Maintain a license in good standing* with state licensing boards. If a physician has had his or her license revoked, the physician cannot participate in Maintenance of Certification, and having a license suspended, put on probation, or otherwise restricted might also disqualify a physician from participation.

- *Periodically do surveys of patients and of peers.* This requirement will take effect in 2010 for surveys of patients using a questionnaire that measures physician-patient communication, and will take effect in 2012 for surveys of peers, measuring communication skills and professionalism.
- *Periodically show evidence of knowledge and judgment,* typically by passing the same types of unassisted, written (computer-administered) exams that have been the basis for certification for many years.
- *Show evidence of a commitment to lifelong learning and involvement in a periodic self-assessment process,* targeted in particular on new developments in the physician's specialty field. Physicians can complete appropriate continuing education courses, and some boards have identified or created learning materials and computer-based interactive tools that a physician can use to learn about the newest developments in his or her field. The physician is expected to self-administer tests to identify knowledge gaps. One element of this requirement in coming years will be for the physician periodically to complete a patient safety self-assessment program.
- *Periodically show evidence of self-evaluation of performance in practice.* For example, with the American Board of Internal Medicine (ABIM), a physician might meet this requirement for a period by pulling data from case records for patients with a specific condition like diabetes or asthma, submitting the data to the board for evaluation, getting back from the board a report comparing the physician's practice patterns to national guidelines, developing a plan for improvements, and then measuring whether the improvements have worked. Through this process, a physician might discover, for instance, that he or she has information on LDL cholesterol results for too few diabetes patients and this awareness might prompt the physician to take steps to do better. Another example of a target for self-evaluation might be physician-patient communication; a physician might do surveys of patients, use the results to guide quality improvement, and then re-survey to assess the extent of improvement.

Except for the written tests of knowledge and judgment for time-limited certifications, Maintenance of Certification is not dependent on the results—the scores—from assessment activities. It is enough that the physician does the self-assessments, develops plans for improvements, and assesses the extent of improvement—regardless of how bad or good the physician looks in the assessments.

You can check whether any physician you are considering is board certified by checking the website of the American Board of Medical Specialties, the umbrella organization for the 24 individual specialty boards, at *www.abms.org* or by calling toll-free to 866-ASK-ABMS. If the physician you are considering is not board certified, he or she will not be listed. In the near future, you will also be able to check whether a physician you are considering is participating in ongoing Maintenance of Certification.

So, what useful information do the board certification system and ongoing Maintenance of Certification program provide you?

Unless you have a compelling reason to do otherwise, it is hard to see why you would choose a physician who is not board certified. But be aware that board certification is not a very discriminating measure. About 87 percent of physicians in the U.S. are certified.

Knowing how recently a physician has been certified or re-certified is important, since *there is substantial evidence that physician performance gets worse over time.* A 2005 article published in the *Annals of Internal Medicine* reviewed 62 studies that had examined the relationship between age or time in practice and various measures of quality—physician knowledge, adherence to recognized care guidelines, and medical outcomes. Of these studies, 45 reported decreasing performance on some or all quality measures over time, and only two reported improved performance.

Physicians who were certified for life can if they wish seek voluntary re-certification, but not many have done so. Those who don't point to the cost, the time required, the risk of failure, and other factors. For the relatively few physicians who have voluntarily become re-certified despite having a life-long certification, that diligence and self-scrutiny may be a meaningful indicator of quality.

It would be desirable for the specialty boards to create and advertise a concept like "recently certified" or "certification updated" so consumers could easily distinguish physicians whose certification status is based only on having been certified for life from those who are actively engaged in self-assessment and practice improvement. Unfortunately, on the *www.abms.org* website, the information that is available free to the public doesn't indicate when a physician was certified or tell whether a physician who had lifetime certification has voluntarily become re-certified. Some of the individual specialty boards do provide that information on their websites, but some provide virtually no consumer information. It would be desirable for the ABMS and all of the individual boards to have the information on their websites.

Participation in an ongoing Maintenance of Certification program is evidence that a physician is taking extra steps beyond getting initial certification to continue to keep up-to-date and improve. The planned reporting of participation information by the ABMS is an important step. This participation in Maintenance of Certification is especially important for physicians who got their initial certifications before certification became time-limited since these physicians do not have to take any self-improvement steps merely to remain board certified, but participation in Maintenance of Certification proves that they are in fact taking such steps and that they are passing exams and meeting other standards.

Are there additional types of comparative information specialty boards could provide consumers on individual physicians? Possibly.

First, it might be possible in the future for the boards to release to the public physicians' scores on the written exams of knowledge and judgment—at least information like "top 10 percent," "top 25 percent," or "top half." The boards can't unilaterally begin to report data that they have historically promised physicians would be kept confidential. But changes in confidentiality policies might be possible in the future. And even in the near term, the boards might consider releasing scores for physicians who give permission for such release. Disclosure of test scores would certainly put physicians out ahead of most professionals; it is not common to have one's personal test scores made public. But the advantage of releasing these scores is that they can be expected to reflect on aspects of quality that other measures of physician performance may miss.

Second, the boards might consider, for the future, working with physician leaders to change the self-assessment process into a process that has the combined purpose of self-assessment and public assessment. There are already various efforts underway— led by government agencies, health plans, employers, and consumer organizations—to increase public reporting of physician quality measures—for instance, measures from medical records showing whether a physician consistently gives all the appropriate tests and treatments to diabetes patients, or measures from patient surveys of how well the physician communicates. Some of the specialty boards are involved in these public measurement efforts, but more might be done to use the same data and analyses for public reporting and physician self-improvement purposes. The specialty boards have said that such public reporting is planned for the future at least for results of surveys of patients.

If measures are to be useful for public reporting, they will have to be standardized and independently collected. Currently a physician can self-select the diabetes cases he or she abstracts for the specialty board and can even cherry-pick to look good, or might decide to survey only patients who are likely to give good reports. There is not much harm in that when the data are being used only for self-assessment; worst case, when the physician gets a performance report back from the board, he or she might simply say, "Wow, I did that badly even though I was cheating."

For public reporting, the system has to be free of potential manipulation or bias. For clinical measures, the specialty boards would have to work with health plans, Medicare, and others to develop systems to collect data from medical records or claims records, for example. And for patient and peer survey measures, it will be important for the boards to use a nationwide standardized patient survey and standardized, audited process for selecting the persons to survey—so that the resulting measures can be used not only for physician practice improvement but also for public reporting. Having forward-thinking specialty boards involved in the development of measures might help to move the measurement process forward and to ensure that measures are well designed.

Public reporting of standardized measures would not only help you choose good physicians, but also would enable health plans to reward high-rated physicians and would facilitate public and peer recognition of top performers. All that might reinforce incentives for the kind of physician quality that is the mission of the specialty boards.

If the boards don't get actively involved in public reporting efforts, however, it is still important to remember that what is being done, and the progress that has been made toward continuing Maintenance of Certification, is important. Even without more public reporting, board certification provides tools for quality improvement, channels through which well-motivated physicians can fulfill a desire for professional improvement, and a way for each physician to demonstrate to patients and the public that he or she is committed to professional development.

It is important to realize that the commitment to professionalism and the desire to help others—not public scrutiny—have probably been the most important forces for quality in health care over the years. So fostering these motivations is a good thing.

Appendix B

Where to Complain and Get Information on Disciplinary Actions

Alabama

Alabama State Board of Medical Examiners
P.O. Box 946
Montgomery, AL 36101
334-242-4116
www.albme.org
Site allows consumers to check for disciplinary actions against specific doctors? **Yes**

Alaska

Alaska State Medical Board
Division of Occupational Licensing
550 West 7th Avenue, Suite 1500
Anchorage, AK 99501
907-269-8160
www.dced.state.ak.us/occ
Site allows consumers to check for disciplinary actions against specific doctors? **No,** but actions are summarized in monthly newsletters

Arizona

Arizona Medical Board
9545 East Doubletree Ranch Road
Scottsdale, AZ 85258
480-551-2700
www.azmd.gov
Site allows consumers to check for disciplinary actions against specific doctors? **Yes**

Arizona Board of Osteopathic Examiners in Medicine and Surgery
9535 East Doubletree Ranch Road
Scottsdale, AZ 85258
480-657-7703
www.azdo.gov
Site allows consumers to check for disciplinary actions against specific doctors? **Yes**

Arkansas

Arkansas State Medical Board
2100 Riverfront Drive
Little Rock, AR 72202
501-296-1802
www.armedicalboard.org
Site allows consumers to check for disciplinary actions against specific doctors? **Yes,** for only for actions taken since January 1, 2007

California

Medical Board of California
Central Complaint Unit
2005 Evergreen Street, Suite 1200
Sacramento, CA 95815
916-263-2382
www.medbd.ca.gov
Site allows consumers to check for disciplinary actions against specific doctors? **Yes**

Osteopathic Medical Board of California
1300 National Drive, Suite 150
Sacramento, CA 95834
916-928-8390
www.dca.ca.gov/osteopathic
Site allows consumers to check for disciplinary actions against specific doctors? **Yes**

Colorado

Colorado Board of Medical Examiners
1560 Broadway, Suite 1300
Denver, CO 80202
303-894-7690
www.dora.state.co.us/medical
Site allows consumers to check for disciplinary actions against specific doctors? **Yes**

Connecticut

Connecticut Medical Examining Board
Department of Public Health
Practitioner Investigations Unit
410 Capitol Avenue, MS#12HSR
P.O. Box 340308
Hartford, CT 06134
860-509-7603
www.ct.gov/dph
Site allows consumers to check for disciplinary actions against specific doctors? **Yes**

Delaware

Delaware Board of Medical Practice
Division of Professional Regulation
Attention: Investigative Administrator
861 Silver Lake Boulevard, Suite 203
Dover, DE 19904
302-739-4509
www.dpr.delaware.gov
Site allows consumers to check for disciplinary actions against specific doctors? **Yes**

District of Columbia

District of Columbia Board of Medicine
Health Professional Licensing Administration
717 14th Street, NW, Suite 600
Washington, DC 20005
202-724-4900
www.hpla.doh.dc.gov
Site allows consumers to check for disciplinary actions against specific doctors? **Yes**

Florida

Florida Board of Medicine
Department of Health
Consumer Services Unit
4052 Bald Cypress Way, Bin C-75
Tallahassee, FL 32399
850-245-4339
www.stateofflorida.com/florboarofme.html
Site allows consumers to check for
disciplinary actions against specific
doctors? **Yes**

Florida Board of Osteopathic Medicine
Department of Health
Consumer Services Unit
4052 Bald Cypress Way, Bin C-75
Tallahassee, FL 32399
850-245-4339
*www.doh.state.fl.us/mqa/osteopath/
os_home.html*
Site allows consumers to check for
disciplinary actions against specific
doctors? **Yes**

Georgia

Composite Board of Medical Examiners
2 Peachtree Street, NW, 36th Floor
Atlanta, GA 30303
404-657-6494
www.medicalboard.georgia.gov
Site allows consumers to check for
disciplinary actions against specific
doctors? **Yes**

Hawaii

Hawaii Board of Medical Examiners
Department of Commerce &
Consumer Affairs
P.O. Box 3469
Honolulu, HI 96801
808-587-3295
www.hawaii.gov/dcca/areas/pvl
Site allows consumers to check for
disciplinary actions against specific
doctors? **No**, but site publishes
summaries of actions for all doctors on a
month-to-month basis

Idaho

Idaho State Board of Medicine
1755 Westgate Drive, Suite 140
P.O. Box 83720
Boise, ID 83720
208-327-7000
www.bom.state.id.us
Site allows consumers to check for
disciplinary actions against specific
doctors? **Yes**

Illinois

Department of Professional Regulation
Complaint Intake Unit
100 West Randolph Street, Suite 9-300
Chicago, IL 60601
312-814-6910
www.idfpr.com/dpr
Site allows consumers to check for
disciplinary actions against specific
doctors? **Yes**

Indiana

Indiana Health Professions Bureau
Consumer Protection Division
Office of the Attorney General
302 West Washington Street, 5th Floor
Indianapolis, IN 46204
317-232-6330
www.in.gov/pla/medical.htm
Site allows consumers to check for
disciplinary actions against specific
doctors? **Yes**

Iowa

Iowa Board of Medicine
400 Southwest 8th Street, Suite C
Des Moines, IA 50309
515-281-5171
www.medicalboard.iowa.gov
Site allows consumers to check for
disciplinary actions against specific
doctors? **Yes**

Kansas

Kansas Board of Healing Arts
235 South Topeka Boulevard
Topeka, KS 66603
785-296-7413
www.ksbha.org
Site allows consumers to check for
disciplinary actions against specific
doctors? **Yes**

Kentucky

Kentucky Board of Medical Licensure
Hurstbourne Office Park
310 Whittington Parkway, Suite 1B
Louisville, KY 40222
502-429-7150
www.kbml.ky.gov
Site allows consumers to check for
disciplinary actions against specific
doctors? **No**, but actions are
summarized in monthly newsletters

Louisiana

State Board of Medical Examiners
P.O. Box 30250
New Orleans, LA 70190
504-524-6763
www.lsbme.louisiana.gov
Site allows consumers to check for
disciplinary actions against specific
doctors? **Yes**

Maine

Maine Board of Licensure in Medicine
137 State House Station
Augusta, ME 04333
207-287-3601
www.docboard.org/me/me_home.htm
Site allows consumers to check for
disciplinary actions against specific
doctors? **Yes**

Maine Board of Osteopathic Licensure
142 State House Station
Augusta, ME 04333
207-287-2480
www.maine.gov/osteo
Site allows consumers to check for
disciplinary actions against specific
doctors? **Yes**

Maryland

Maryland Board of Physicians
Intake Unit
4201 Patterson Avenue
Baltimore, MD 21215
410-764-4777
www.mbp.state.md.us
Site allows consumers to check for
disciplinary actions against specific
doctors? **Yes**

Massachusetts

Board of Registration in Medicine
200 Harvard Mill Square, Suite 330
Wakefield, MA 01880
781-876-8200
www.massmedboard.org
Site allows consumers to check for
disciplinary actions against specific
doctors? **Yes**

Michigan

Michigan Board of Medicine
Bureau of Health Professions
Health Regulatory Division
P.O. Box 30670
Lansing, MI 48909
517-373-9196
www.michigan.gov/mdch
Site allows consumers to check for
disciplinary actions against specific
doctors? **Yes**

Minnesota

Minnesota Board of Medical Practice
University Park Plaza
2829 University Avenue SE, Suite 500
Minneapolis, MN 55414
612-617-2130
www.bmp.state.mn.us
Site allows consumers to check for
disciplinary actions against specific
doctors? **Yes**

Mississippi

Mississippi State Board of Medical
Licensure
1867 Crain Ridge Drive, Suite 200-B
Jackson, MS 39216
601-987-3079
www.msbml.state.ms.us
Site allows consumers to check for
disciplinary actions against specific
doctors? **No**, license search shows
whether there is a "public record"
associated with the physician; obtaining
the actual record costs $25

Missouri

Board of Registration for the Healing Arts
3605 Missouri Blvd
P.O. Box 4
Jefferson City, MO 65102
573-751-0098
www.pr.mo.gov/healingarts.asp
Site allows consumers to check for
disciplinary actions against specific
doctors? **Yes**

Montana

Montana Board of Medical Examiners
Business Standards Division
301 South Park, 4th Floor
P.O. Box 200513
Helena, MT 59620
406-841-2362
www.mt.gov/dli/bsd/index.asp
Site allows consumers to check for
disciplinary actions against specific
doctors? **Yes**

Nebraska

Nebraska Division of Public Health
Office of Professional and Occupational
Investigations
1033 O Street, Suite 500
Lincoln, NE 68508
402-471-0175
www.dhhs.ne.gov
Site allows consumers to check for
disciplinary actions against specific
doctors? **Yes**

Nevada

State Board of Medical Examiners
Investigations Division
1105 Terminal Way, Suite 301
P.O. Box 7238
Reno, NV 89510
775-688-2559
www.medboard.nv.gov
Site allows consumers to check for
disciplinary actions against specific
doctors? **Yes**

State Board of Osteopathic Medicine
2860 East Flamingo Road, Suite D
Las Vegas, NV 89121
702-732-2147
www.bom.nv.gov
Site allows consumers to check for
disciplinary actions against specific
doctors? **Yes**

New Hampshire

New Hampshire Board of Medicine
2 Industrial Park Drive, Suite 8
Concord, NH 03301
603-271-1203
www.state.nh.us/medicine
Site allows consumers to check for
disciplinary actions against specific
doctors? **Yes**

New Jersey

State Board of Medical Examiners
140 East Front Street
P.O. Box 183
Trenton, NJ 08625
609-826-7100
www.njdoctorlist.com
Site allows consumers to check for
disciplinary actions against specific
doctors? **Yes**

New Mexico

State Board of Medical Examiners
Lamy Bldg, 2nd Floor
491 Old Santa Fe Trail
Santa Fe, NM 87501
505-827-5022
www.nmmb.state.nm.us
Site allows consumers to check for
disciplinary actions against specific
doctors? **Yes**

Board of Osteopathic Medical Examiners
2550 Cerrillos Road, 2nd Floor
Santa Fe, NM 87505
505-476-4950
www.rld.state.nm.us/osteopathy
Site allows consumers to check for
disciplinary actions against specific
doctors? **Yes**

New York

New York State Department of Health
Office of Professional Medical Conduct
433 River Street, Suite 303
Troy, NY 12180
518-402-0836
www.nydoctorprofile.com
Site allows consumers to check for
disciplinary actions against specific
doctors? **Yes**

North Carolina

North Carolina Medical Board
1203 Front Street
P.O. Box 20007
Raleigh, NC 27619
919-326-1100
www.ncmedboard.org
Site allows consumers to check for
disciplinary actions against specific
doctors? **Yes**

North Dakota

State Board of Medical Examiners
City Center Plaza
418 East Broadway Avenue, Suite 12
Bismarck, ND 58501
701-328-6500
www.ndbomex.com
Site allows consumers to check for
disciplinary actions against specific
doctors? **Yes**

Ohio

State Medical Board of Ohio
Public Inquiries
30 East Broad Street, 3rd Floor
Columbus, OH 43215
614-466-3934
www.med.ohio.gov
Site allows consumers to check for disciplinary actions against specific doctors? **Yes**

Oklahoma

Oklahoma State Board of Medical
Licensure and Supervision
Investigations Department
5104 North Francis Avenue, Suite C
P.O. Box 18256
Oklahoma City, OK 73154
405-848-6841
www.osbmls.state.ok.us
Site allows consumers to check for disciplinary actions against specific doctors? **Yes**

State Board of Osteopathic Examiners
4848 North Lincoln Boulevard, Suite 100
Oklahoma City, OK 73105
405-528-8625
www.ok.gov/osboe
Site allows consumers to check for disciplinary actions against specific doctors? **Yes**

Oregon

Oregon Medical Board
1500 Southwest First Avenue, Suite 620
Portland, OR 97201
971-673-2702
www.oregon.gov/omb
Site allows consumers to check for disciplinary actions against specific doctors? **Yes**

Pennsylvania

Pennsylvania Board of Medicine
Complaints Office
Department of State
2601 North Third Street
P.O. Box 2649
Harrisburg, PA 17105
717-783-1400
www.dos.state.pa.us/bpoa
Site allows consumers to check for disciplinary actions against specific doctors? **Yes**

Rhode Island

Board of Medical Licensure and Discipline
Department of Health
3 Capitol Hill, Room 205
Providence, RI 02908
401-222-5200
www.health.ri.gov/hsr/bmld
Site allows consumers to check for disciplinary actions against specific doctors? **Yes**

South Carolina

South Carolina Department of Labor,
Licensing, and Regulation
Office of Investigations and Enforcement
Board of Medical Examiners
P.O. Box 11329
Columbia, SC 29211
803-896-4470
www.llr.state.sc.us/pol/medical
Site allows consumers to check for disciplinary actions against specific doctors? **Yes**

South Dakota

South Dakota State Board of Medical
and Osteopathic Examiners
101 North Main Avenue, Suite 301
Sioux Falls, SD 57104
605-3367-7781
www.state.sd.us/dcr/medical
Site allows consumers to check for disciplinary actions against specific doctors? **Yes**

Tennessee

Tennessee Board of Medical Examiners
Office of Investigations
Heritage Place, Metro Center
227 French Landing, Suite 201
Nashville, TN 37243
615-741-8485
http://health.state.tn.us/Boards/ME/
Site allows consumers to check for disciplinary actions against specific doctors? **Yes**

Board of Osteopathic Examination
Office of Investigations
Heritage Place, Metro Center
227 French Landing, Suite 201
Nashville, TN 37243
615-532-3202
http://health.state.tn.us/boards/osteo
Site allows consumers to check for disciplinary actions against specific doctors? **Yes**

Texas

Texas Medical Board
Investigations Department, MC-263
P.O. Box 2018
Austin, TX 78768
512-305-7030
www.tmb.state.tx.us/
Site allows consumers to check for disciplinary actions against specific doctors? **Yes**

Utah

Division of Occupational &
Professional Licensing
P.O. Box 146741
Salt Lake City, UT 84114
801-530-6630
www.dopl.utah.gov
Site allows consumers to check for disciplinary actions against specific doctors? **Yes**

Vermont

Vermont Board of Medical Practice
Department of Health
108 Cherry Street
P.O. Box 70
Burlington, VT 05402
802-863-7200
www.healthvermont.gov
Site allows consumers to check for disciplinary actions against specific doctors? **Yes**

Vermont Board of Osteopathic
Physicians
Office of Professional Regulation
National Life Building, Floor 2
Montpelier, VT 05620
802-828-2875
www.vtprofessionals.org/oprl/osteopaths
Site allows consumers to check for disciplinary actions against specific doctors? **Yes**

Virginia

Virginia Board of Medicine
Department of Health Professions
Perimeter Center
9960 Mayland Drive, Suite 300
Richmond, VA 23233
804-367-4691
www.dhp.state.va.us/medicine
Site allows consumers to check for disciplinary actions against specific doctors? **Yes**

Washington

Washington State Department of Health
Health Systems Quality Assurance
P.O. Box 47857
Olympia, WA 98504
360-236-2620
www.doh.wa.gov/medical
Site allows consumers to check for
disciplinary actions against specific
doctors? **Yes**

Board of Osteopathic Medicine
1300 Quince St, SE
P.O. Box 47870
Olympia, WA 98504
360-236-4944
*www.doh.wa.gov/hsqa/professions/
Osteopath/default.htm*
Site allows consumers to check for
disciplinary actions against specific
doctors? **Yes**

West Virginia

West Virginia Board of Medicine
Complaint Committee
101 Dee Drive, Suite 103
Charleston, WV 25311
304-558-2921
www.wvdhhr.org/wvbom
Site allows consumers to check for
disciplinary actions against specific
doctors? **Yes**

West Virginia Board of Osteopathy
334 Penco Road
Weirton, WV 26062
304-723-4638
www.wvbdosteo.org
Site allows consumers to check for
disciplinary actions against specific
doctors? **No**

Wisconsin

Wisconsin Medical Examining Board
Department of Regulation & Licensing
P.O. Box 8935
Madison, WI 53708
608-266-7482
www.drl.state.wi.us
Site allows consumers to check for
disciplinary actions against specific
doctors? **Yes**

Wyoming

Wyoming Board of Medicine
320 West 25th Street, Suite 103
Cheyenne, WY 82002
307-778-7053
www.wyomedboard.state.wy.us
Site allows consumers to check for
disciplinary actions against specific
doctors? **Yes**